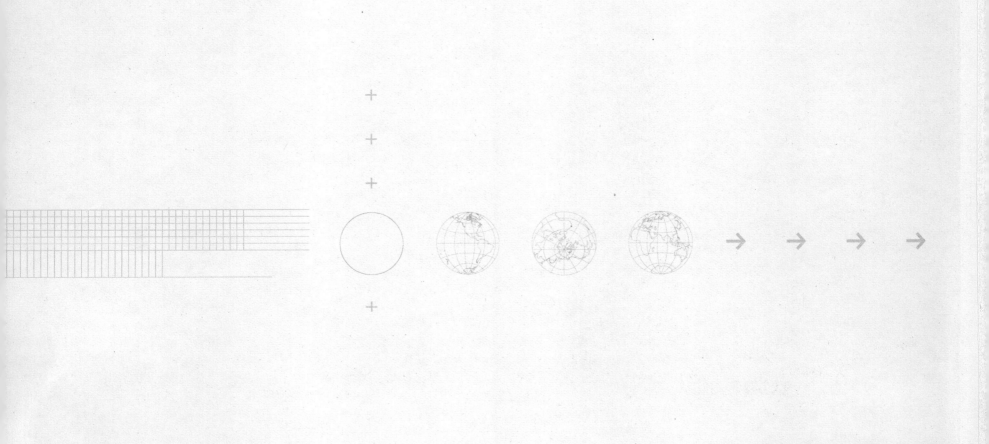

HarperCollins [NEW]
WORLD**ATLAS**

HARPERCOLLINS NEW WORLD ATLAS. Copyright © 2001 by HarperCollins*Publishers*.
All rights reserved. Printed in the United States of America. No part of this book
may be used or reproduced in any manner whatsoever without written permission
except in the case of brief quotations embodied in critical articles and reviews.
For information address Harpercollins Publishers Inc.,
10 East 53rd Street, New York, NY 10022.

HarperCollins books may be purchased for educational, business, or sales
promotional use. For information please write: Special Markets Department,
HarperCollins Publishers Inc., 10 East 53rd Street, New York, NY 10022.

First Published 2001 by HarperCollins*Publishers* Ltd

Maps © Bartholomew Ltd 2001

Collins® is a registered trademark of HarperCollins*Publishers* Ltd

Printed in Italy

Library of Congress Cataloging-in-Publication Data has been applied for.

ISBN 0 06 052120 1

The maps in this product are also available for purchase in digital format
from Bartholomew Mapping Solutions. For details and information visit
http://www.bartholomewmaps.com
or contact
Bartholomew Mapping Solutions
Tel: +44 (0) 141 306 3162
Fax: +44 (0) 141 306 3104
e-mail: bartholomew@harpercollins.co.uk

HarperCollins [NEW]
WORLDATLAS

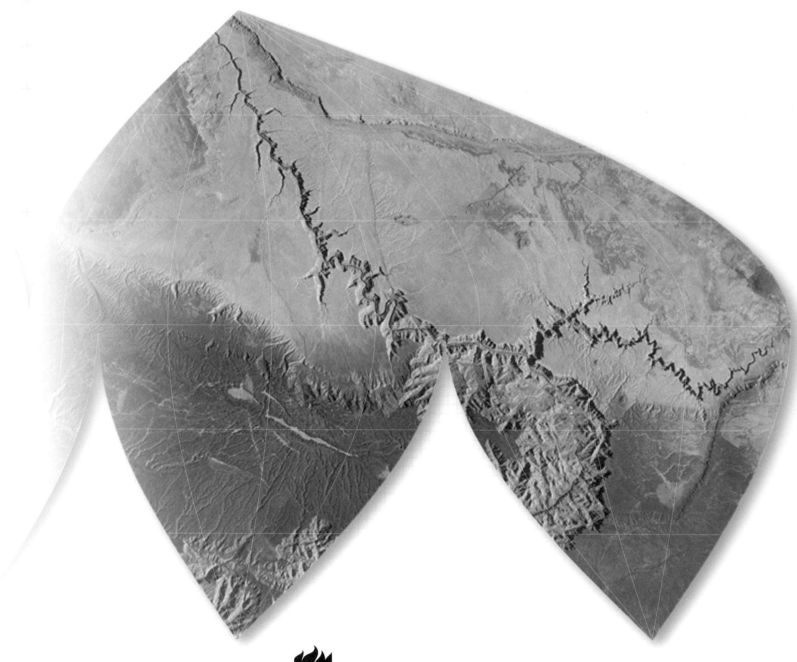

HarperResource
An Imprint of HarperCollinsPublishers

introduction

CONTENTS

The atlas is arranged into a world thematic section and continental sections as defined in the contents list below. Full details of the contents of each section can be found on the introductory spread within the section. As indicated on the contents list, each section is distinctively colour-coded to allow easy identification.

The continental sections contain detailed, comprehensive reference maps of the continent, which are preceded by introductory pages consisting of a mixture of statistical and thematic maps, geographical statistics, and photographs and images illustrating specific themes. Each map and thematic spread contains a 'connections' box, which indicates links to other pages in the atlas containing related information.

title	pages
world	6–7
[physical features]	8–9
[countries]	10–11
[land images]	12–13
[earthquakes and volcanoes]	14–15
[climate and weather]	16–17
[land cover]	18–19
[changes]	20–21
[population]	22–23
[cities]	24–25
[communications]	26–27
europe	28–29
[landscapes]	30–31
[countries]	32–33
[countries/issues]	34–35
[environments]	36–37
[reference maps]	38–59
asia	60–61
[landscapes]	62–63
[countries]	64–65
[countries/issues]	66–67
[changes]	68–69
[threats]	70–71
[reference maps]	72–109
africa	110–111
[landscapes]	112–113
[countries]	114–115
[countries/issues]	116–117
[locations]	118–119
[reference maps]	120–133

title	pages
oceania	134–135
[landscapes]	136–137
[countries]	138–139
[threats]	140–141
[features]	142–143
[reference maps]	144–153
northamerica	154–155
[landscapes]	156–157
[countries]	158–159
[threats]	160–161
[environments]	162–163
[reference maps]	164–187
southamerica	188–189
[landscapes]	190–191
[countries]	192–193
[contrasts]	194–195
[impacts]	196–197
[reference maps]	198–207
oceans and poles	208–209
oceans [features]	210–211
antarctica [features]	212–213
the arctic [features]	214–215
oceans and poles [reference maps]	216–224
index	225–335
acknowledgements	336

PROJECTIONS

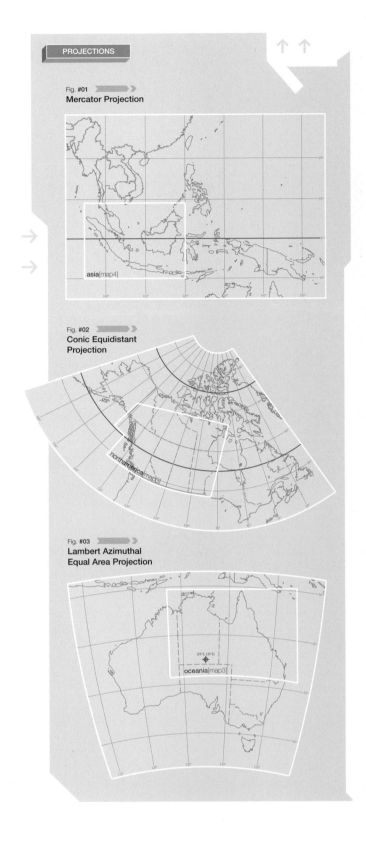

Fig. #01
Mercator Projection

Fig. #02
Conic Equidistant Projection

Fig. #03
Lambert Azimuthal Equal Area Projection

REFERENCE MAPS

Symbols and generalization

Maps show information by using signs, or symbols, which are designed to reflect the features on the Earth which they represent. Symbols can be in the form of points, lines, or areas and variations in the size, shape and colour of the symbols allow a great range of information to be shown. The symbols used on the reference maps are explained opposite.

Not all features on the ground can be shown, nor can all characteristics of a feature be depicted. Much detail has to be generalized to be clearly shown on the maps, the degree of generalization being determined largely by the scale of the map. As map scale decreases, fewer features can be shown, and their depiction becomes less detailed. The most common generalization techniques are selection and simplification. Selection is the inclusion of some features and the omission of others of less importance. Smaller scale maps can show fewer features than larger scales, and therefore only the more important features are selected. Simplification is the process of smoothing lines, combining areas, or slightly displacing symbols to add clarity. Smaller scale maps require more simplification. These techniques are carried out in such a way that the overall character of the area mapped is retained.

Scale

The amount of detail shown on a map is determined by its scale – the relationship between the size of an area shown on the map and the actual size of the area on the ground. Larger scales show more detail, smaller scales require more generalization and show less. The scale can be used to measure the distance between two points and to calculate comparative areas.

Scales used for the reference maps range from 1:3M (large scale) to 1:48M (small scale). Insets are used to show areas of the world of particular interest or which cannot be included in the page layouts in their true position. The scale used is indicated in the margin of each map.

Map projections

The 'projection' of the three-dimensional globe onto a two-dimensional map is always a problem for cartographers. All map projections introduce distortions to either shape, area or distances. Projections for the maps in this atlas have been specifically selected to minimize these distortions. The diagrams above illustrate three types of projection used. The red lines represent the 'centres' of the projections where there is no distortion and scale is correct.

Each reference map is cut to the shape of the graticule (the lines of latitude and longitude), which is determined by the projection used. This gives each map a unique shape, suggesting its position on the globe, as illustrated by the examples on the diagrams.

Geographical names

There is no single standard way of spelling names or of converting them from one alphabet, or symbol set, to another. Instead, conventional ways of spelling have evolved, and the results often differ significantly from the original name in the local language. Familiar examples in English include Munich (München in German), Florence (Firenze in Italian) and Moscow (Moskva from Russian). A further complication is that in many countries different languages are in use in different regions.

These factors, and any changes in official languages, have to be taken into account when creating maps. The policy in this atlas is generally to use local name forms which are officially recognized by the governments of the countries concerned. This is a basic principle laid down by the Permanent Committee on Geographical Names (PCGN) – the body responsible for determining official UK government policy on place names around the world. PCGN rules are also applied to the conversion of non-roman alphabet names, for example in the Russian Federation, into roman alphabet used in English.

However, English conventional name forms are used for the most well-known places for which such a form is in common use. In these cases, the local form is included in brackets on the map and appears as a cross-reference in the index. Other alternative names, such as well-known historical names or those in other languages, may also be included in brackets. All country names and those for international physical features appear in their English forms.

Boundaries

The status of nations and their boundaries, and the names associated with them, are shown in this atlas as they are in reality at the time of going to press, as far as can be ascertained. All recent changes of the status of nations and their boundaries have been taken into account. Where international boundaries are the subject of dispute, the aim is to take a strictly neutral viewpoint and every reasonable attempt is made to show where an active territorial dispute exists. Generally, prominence is given to the situation as it exists on the ground (the de facto situation). The depiction on the maps of boundaries and their current status varies accordingly.

International boundaries are shown on all the reference maps, and those of a large enough scale also include internal administrative boundaries of selected countries. The delineation of international boundaries in the sea is often a very contentious issue, and in many cases an official alignment is not defined. Boundaries in the sea are generally only shown where they are required to clarify the ownership of specific islands or island groups.

Indexing

All names appearing on the reference maps are included in the index and can be easily found from the information included in the index entry. Details of all alternative name forms are included in the index entries and as cross-references. Gazetteer entries, with important geographical information, are included for selected places and features. Full details of index policies and content can be found in the Introduction to the Index on page 225.

SETTLEMENTS

Population	National Capital	Administrative Capital	Other City or Town
over 5 million	BEIJING ✹	Tianjin ◉	New York ◉
1 million to 5 million	KĀBUL ✸	Sydney ◉	Kaohsiung ◉
500 000 to 1 million	BANGUI ✸	Trujillo ◎	Jeddah ◉
100 000 to 500 000	WELLINGTON ✸	Mansa ◎	Apucarana ◉
50 000 to 100 000	PORT OF SPAIN ✿	Potenza ◎	Arecibo ○
10 000 to 50 000	MALABO ✿	Chinhoyi ◦	Ceres ○
1 000 to 10 000	VALLETTA ✿	Ati ◦	Venta ○
under 1000		Chhukha ◦	Shapki ○

▭ Built-up area

BOUNDARIES

▭▭▭ International boundary

▪▪▪▪ Disputed international boundary or alignment unconfirmed

▭▭▭ Administrative boundary

•••• Ceasefire line

MISCELLANEOUS

‑‑‑‑‑ National park

‑‑‑‑‑ Reserve or Regional park

✿ Site of specific interest

▭▭▭ Wall

LAND AND SEA FEATURES

Desert

Oasis

Lava field

1234 Volcano
height in metres

Marsh

Ice cap / Glacier

Escarpment

Coral reef

1234 Pass
height in metres

LAKES AND RIVERS

Lake

Impermanent lake

Salt lake or lagoon

Impermanent salt lake

Dry salt lake or salt pan

123 Lake height
surface height above
sea level, in metres

—— River

‑‑‑‑ Impermanent river or watercourse

Waterfall

— Dam

Barrage

RELIEF

Contour intervals and layer colours

Continents

>6000m
5000-6000m
4000-5000m
3000-4000m
2000-3000m
1500-2000m
1000-1500m
500-1000m
200-500m
100-200m
0-100m
<0m

0-50m
50-100m
100-200m
200-500m
500-1000m
1000-2000m
2000-3000m
3000-4000m
4000-5000m
5000-6000m
>6000m

Oceans and Poles

>6000m
5000-6000m
4000-5000m
3000-4000m
2000-3000m
1000-2000m
500-1000m
200-500m
0-200m
<0m

0-200m
200-2000m
2000-3000m
3000-4000m
4000-5000m
5000-6000m
6000-7000m
>7000m

1234 Summit
height in metres

-123 Spot height
height in metres

123 Ocean deep
height in metres

TRANSPORT

Motorway (tunnel; under construction)

Main road (tunnel; under construction)

Secondary road (tunnel; under construction)

Track

Main railway (tunnel; under construction)

Secondary railway (tunnel; under construction)

Other railway (tunnel; under construction)

Canal

✈ Main airport

✈ Regional airport

SATELLITE IMAGERY

MAIN SATELLITES/SENSORS

satellite/sensor name	launch dates	owner	aims and applications	wavelengths	resolution of imagery	web address
Landsat 4, 5, 7	July 1972-April 1999	National Aeronautics and Space Administration (NASA), USA	The first satellite to be designed specifically for observing the Earth's surface. Originally set up to produce images of use for agriculture and geology. Today is of use for numerous environmental and scientific applications.	Visible, near-infrared, short-wave and thermal infrared wavelength bands.	15m in the panchromatic band (only on Landsat 7), 30m in the six visible, near and short-wave infrared bands and 60m in the thermal infrared band.	geo.arc.nasa.gov ls7pm3.gsfc.nasa.gov
SPOT 1, 2, 3, 4 (Satellite Pour l'Observation de la Terre)	February 1986-March 1998	Centre National d'Etudes Spatiales (CNES) and Spot Image, France	Particularly useful for monitoring land use, water resources research, coastal studies and cartography.	Visible and near infrared.	Panchromatic 10m. Multispectral 20m.	www.cnes.fr www.spotimage.fr
Space Shuttle	Regular launches from 1981	NASA, USA	Each shuttle mission has separate aims. Astronauts take photographs with high specification hand held cameras. The Shuttle Radar Topography Mission (SRTM) in 2000 obtained the most complete near-global high-resolution database of the earth's topography.	Visible with hand held cameras. Radar on SRTM Mission.	SRTM: 30m for US and 90m for rest of the world.	science.ksc.nasa.gov/shuttle/countdown www.jpl.nasa.gov/srtm
IKONOS	September 1999	Space Imaging	First commercial high-resolution satellite. Useful for a variety of applications mainly Cartography, Defence, Urban Planning, Agriculture, Forestry and Insurance.	Visible and near infrared.	Panchromatic 1m. Multispectral 4m.	www.spaceimaging.com

ADDITIONAL IMAGERY

satellite/sensor name	web address
ASTER	asterweb.jpl.nasa.gov www.nasda.go.jp
SeaWiFS	seawifs.gsfc.nasa.gov
Radarsat	www.rsi.ca
MODIS	modis.gsfc.nasa.gov
TOPEX/Poseidon	topex-www.jpl.nasa.gov
ERS-1 (European Space Agency) Earth Resources Satellite	earthnet.esrin.esa.it

PHOTOGRAPHS AND IMAGES

The thematic pages of the atlas contain a wide variety of photographs and images. These are a mixture of 3-D perspective views, terrestrial and aerial photographs and satellite imagery. All are used to illustrate specific themes and to give an indication of the variety of imagery, and different means of visualizing the Earth, available today. The main types of imagery used in the atlas are described in the table above.

Satellite imagery, and the related science of satellite remote sensing – the acquisition, processing and interpretation of images captured by satellites – is a particularly valuable tool in observing and monitoring the Earth. Satellite sensors can capture electromagnetic radiation in a variety of wavelengths, including those visible to the eye (colours), infrared wavelengths and microwave and radio radiation as detected by radar sensors. The data received by the sensors can be processed in different ways to allow detailed interpretation of the landscape and environmental conditions. Panchromatic images represent a single wavelength in values of grey (black and white) while multispectral sensors can combine several wavelengths in a single image. Imagery also varies in the amount of detail it can show. The ability to distinguish visual detail, and the size of the smallest feature which can be detected, is known as the image's resolution, and is usually expressed in metres.

SPOT

Landsat

Space Shuttle

IKONOS

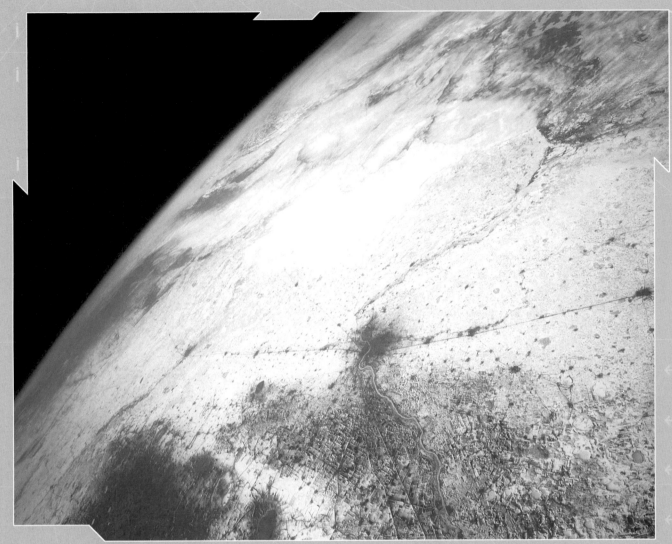

Omsk, *Russian Federation*

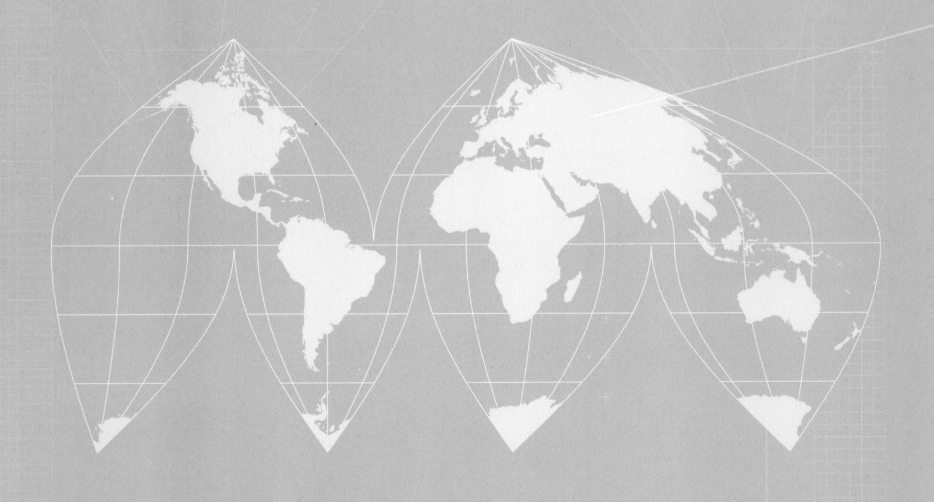

world

[contents]

1 Nile Delta and Sinai Peninsula, *Africa/Asia*

Several distinct physical features can be seen in this oblique Shuttle photograph which looks southeast from above the Mediterranean Sea over northeast Africa and southwest Asia. The dark, triangular area at the bottom of the photograph is the Nile delta. The Sinai peninsula in the centre of the image is flanked by the two elongated water bodies of the Gulf of Aqaba on the left, and the Gulf of Suez on the right. These gulfs merge to form the Red Sea. The Dead Sea is also visible on the left edge of the image.

Satellite/Sensor : Space Shuttle

2 Himalayas, *Asia*

The Himalayan mountain chain forms a major physical barrier across Jammu and Kashmir, northern India, Nepal and Bhutan and contains the world's highest mountains. This Space Shuttle photograph looks west along the mountains. The low plains on the left contain three major rivers, the Ganges, Indus and Brahmaputra. To the right of the permanently snow-capped mountains is the Plateau of Tibet, a vast barren area over 4 000 m above sea level.

Satellite/Sensor : Space Shuttle

Fig. #01
World physical features

>6000m	
5000-6000m	
4000-5000m	
3000-4000m	
2000-3000m	
1000-2000m	
500-1000m	
200-500m	
0-200m	
<0m	

0-200m	
200-2000m	
2000-3000m	
3000-4000m	
4000-5000m	
5000-6000m	
6000-7000m	
>7000m	

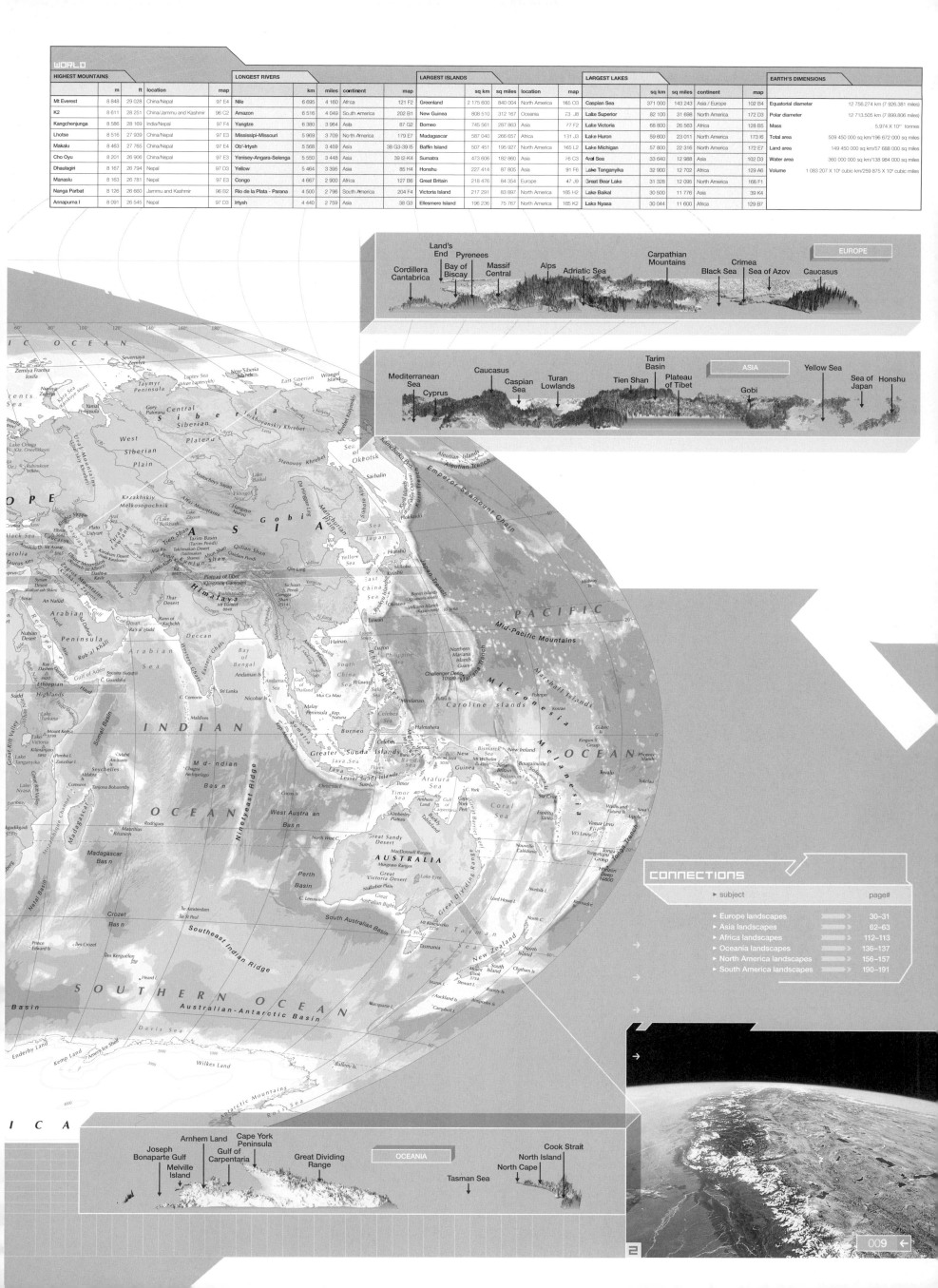

HIGHEST MOUNTAINS

	m	ft	location	map
Mt Everest	8 848	29 028	China/Nepal	97 E4
K2	8 611	28 251	China/Jammu and Kashmir	96 C2
Kangchenjunga	8 586	28 169	India/Nepal	97 F4
Lhotse	8 516	27 939	China/Nepal	97 E4
Makalu	8 463	27 765	China/Nepal	97 E3
Cho Oyu	8 201	26 906	China/Nepal	97 E3
Dhaulagiri	8 167	26 794	Nepal	97 D3
Manaslu	8 163	26 781	Nepal	97 E3
Nanga Parbat	8 126	26 660	Jammu and Kashmir	96 B2
Annapurna I	8 091	26 545	Nepal	97 D3

LONGEST RIVERS

	km	miles	continent	map
Nile	6 695	4 160	Africa	121 F2
Amazon	6 516	4 049	South America	202 B1
Yangtze	6 380	3 964	Asia	87 G2
Mississipi-Missouri	5 969	3 709	North America	179 E7
Ob'-Irtysh	5 568	3 459	Asia	38 G3-39 I5
Yenisey-Angara-Selenga	5 550	3 448	Asia	39 I2-K4
Yellow	5 464	3 395	Asia	85 H4
Congo	4 667	2 900	Africa	127 B6
Rio de la Plata - Parana	4 500	2 796	South America	204 F4
Irtysh	4 440	2 759	Asia	38 G3

LARGEST ISLANDS

	sq km	sq miles	location	map
Greenland	2 175 600	840 004	North America	165 O3
New Guinea	808 510	312 167	Oceania	73 J8
Borneo	745 561	287 863	Asia	77 F2
Madagascar	587 040	226 657	Africa	131 J3
Baffin Island	507 451	195 927	North America	165 L2
Sumatra	473 606	182 860	Asia	76 C3
Honshu	227 414	87 805	Asia	91 F6
Great Britain	218 476	84 354	Europe	47 J9
Victoria Island	217 291	83 897	North America	165 H2
Ellesmere Island	196 236	75 767	North America	165 K2

LARGEST LAKES

	sq km	sq miles	continent	map
Caspian Sea	371 000	143 243	Asia / Europe	102 B4
Lake Superior	82 100	31 698	North America	172 D3
Lake Victoria	68 800	26 563	Africa	128 B5
Lake Huron	59 600	23 011	North America	173 I6
Lake Michigan	57 800	22 316	North America	172 E7
Aral Sea	33 640	12 988	Asia	102 D4
Lake Tanganyika	32 900	12 702	Africa	129 A6
Great Bear Lake	31 328	12 095	North America	166 F1
Lake Baikal	30 500	11 776	Asia	39 K4
Lake Nyasa	30 044	11 600	Africa	129 B7

EARTH'S DIMENSIONS

Equatorial diameter	12 756.274 km (7 926.381 miles)
Polar diameter	12 713.505 km (7 899.806 miles)
Mass	5.974×10^{21} tonnes
Total area	509 450 000 sq km/196 672 000 sq miles
Land area	149 450 000 sq km/57 688 000 sq miles
Water area	360 000 000 sq km/138 984 000 sq miles
Volume	$1\ 083\ 207 \times 10^{6}$ cubic km/$259\ 875 \times 10^{6}$ cubic miles

EUROPE

Cordillera Cantabrica · Land's End · Bay of Biscay · Pyrenees · Massif Central · Alps · Adriatic Sea · Carpathian Mountains · Black Sea · Crimea · Sea of Azov · Caucasus

ASIA

Mediterranean Sea · Cyprus · Caucasus · Caspian Sea · Turan Lowlands · Tien Shan · Tarim Basin · Plateau of Tibet · Gobi · Yellow Sea · Sea of Japan · Honshu

OCEANIA

Joseph Bonaparte Gulf · Melville Island · Arnhem Land · Gulf of Carpentaria · Cape York Peninsula · Great Dividing Range · Tasman Sea · North Cape · North Island · Cook Strait

CONNECTIONS

► subject	page#
► Europe landscapes	30–31
► Asia landscapes	62–63
► Africa landscapes	112–113
► Oceania landscapes	136–137
► North America landscapes	156–157
► South America landscapes	190–191

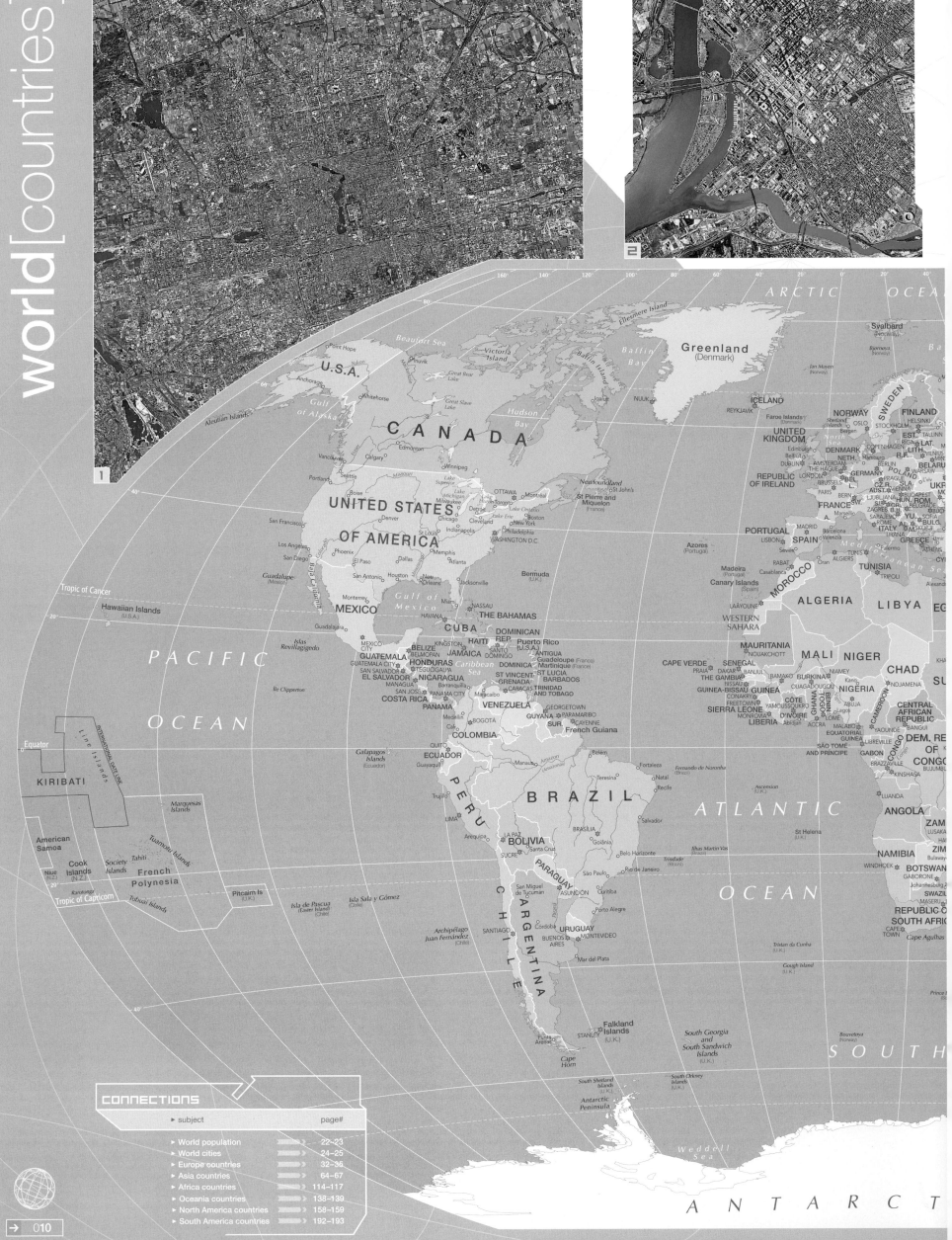

world[countries]

CONNECTIONS

1 Beijing, *China*

This infrared SPOT satellite image of Beijing shows the extent of the capital city of China spreading out from the Forbidden City and Tiananmen Square, just to the right of the lake in the centre. The central city has a very marked grid-iron street pattern, with very densely packed low-rise buildings. On the outskirts, areas of intensive cultivation are represented in shades of red.

Satellite/Sensor : SPOT

2 Washington, D.C., *United States of America*

The capital of the United States, Washington, D.C., is shown in this infrared aerial photograph. The city is situated on the confluence of the Potomac and Anacostia rivers, seen here to the left and bottom of the photograph respectively. It has become a leading political, educational and research centre. The Pentagon, home of the US Department of Defense is at the far left of the photograph and The Mall, the Capitol, the White House and Union Station can all be seen in the centre.

3 La Paz, *Bolivia*

This infrared satellite image shows the highest capital in the world, La Paz, which lies at a height of over 3 500 metres above sea level. It is located at the edge of the Altiplano between two mountain belts within the Andes mountains. The mountains seen at the top of the image have year-round snow cover. The grey-blue area to the right of centre is the urban area of La Paz, with the city's airport clearly visible to the west.

Satellite/Sensor : SPOT

4 Mauritania/Senegal, *Africa*

The Senegal river creates a natural border between the northeast African countries of Mauritania and Senegal. The top of this infrared satellite image shows the southern edge of the Sahara desert in Mauritania. The semi-desert southern fringe of the Sahara, the Sahel, stretches east from Mauritania to Chad. The orange-red colour in the bottom half of the image represents mixed scrub and bush savanna vegetation of Senegal.

Satellite/Sensor : SPOT

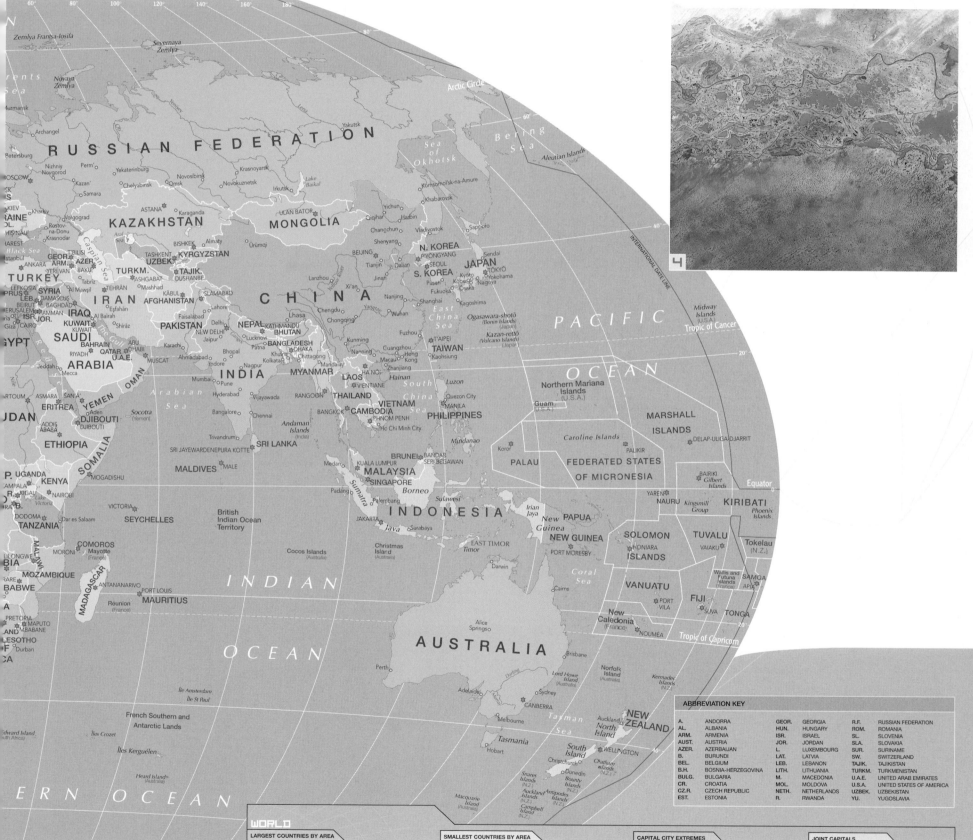

ABBREVIATION KEY

A.	ANDORRA	GEOR.	GEORGIA	R.F.	RUSSIAN FEDERATION
AL.	ALBANIA	HUN.	HUNGARY	ROM.	ROMANIA
ARM.	ARMENIA	ISR.	ISRAEL	SL.	SLOVENIA
AUST.	AUSTRIA	JOR.	JORDAN	SLA.	SLOVAKIA
AZER.	AZERBAIJAN	L.	LUXEMBOURG	SUR.	SURINAME
B.	BURUNDI	LAT.	LATVIA	SW.	SWITZERLAND
BEL.	BELGIUM	LEB.	LEBANON	TAJIK.	TAJIKISTAN
B.H.	BOSNIA-HERZEGOVINA	LITH.	LITHUANIA	TURKM.	TURKMENISTAN
BULG.	BULGARIA	M.	MACEDONIA	U.A.E.	UNITED ARAB EMIRATES
CR.	CROATIA	MOL.	MOLDOVA	U.S.A.	UNITED STATES OF AMERICA
CZ.R.	CZECH REPUBLIC	NETH.	NETHERLANDS	UZBEK.	UZBEKISTAN
EST.	ESTONIA	R.	RWANDA	YU.	YUGOSLAVIA

WORLD

LARGEST COUNTRIES BY AREA

country	sq km	sq miles	map
1. Russian Federation	17 075 400	6 592 849	38–39
2. Canada	9 970 610	3 849 674	164–165
3. United States of America	9 809 378	3 787 422	170–171
4. China	9 584 492	3 700 593	80–81
5. Brazil	8 547 379	3 300 161	202–203
6. Australia	7 682 395	2 966 189	144–145
7. India	3 065 027	1 183 414	92–93
8. Argentina	2 766 889	1 068 302	204–205
9. Kazakhstan	2 717 300	1 049 155	102–103
10. Sudan	2 505 813	967 500	120–121

SMALLEST COUNTRIES BY AREA

country	sq km	sq miles	map
1. Vatican City	0.5	0.2	56
2. Monaco	2	1	51
3. Nauru	21	8	145
4. Tuvalu	25	10	145
5. San Marino	61	24	51
6. Liechtenstein	160	62	51
7. St Kitts and Nevis	261	101	187
8. Maldives	298	115	93
9. Grenada	378	145	187
10. St Vincent and the Grenadines	389	150	187

CAPITAL CITY EXTREMES

			map
Most populous	Tōkyō, Japan	26 444 000	91 F7
Least populous	Yaren, Nauru	600	145 F2
Highest	La Paz, Bolivia	3 636m / 11 910ft	200 C4
Lowest	Manama, Bahrain and Male, Maldives	100 B5 / 93 D10	
Furthest north	Nuuk, Greenland	64° 11'N	165 N3
Furthest south	Wellington, New Zealand	41° 18'S	152 I9
Furthest east	Funafuti, Tuvalu	179° 13'E	145 G2
Furthest west	Nuku'alofa, Tonga	175° 12'W	145 H4

JOINT CAPITALS

cities	country	map
Amsterdam/The Hague	Netherlands	48 C3 / 48 B3
La Paz/Sucre	Bolivia	200 C4 / 200 D4
Pretoria/Cape Town	South Africa	133 M2 / 132 C10

1 Orinoco River, *South America*

The Orinoco river flows from right to left in this Shuttle photograph which looks towards the southeast. The upper section of the image shows the dense forests of the western edge of the Guiana Highlands. The main tributary joining the Orinoco is the Meta river with the town of Puerto Páez at the confluence. The Orinoco and the Meta form part of the boundary between Colombia and Venezuela.

Satellite/Sensor : Space Shuttle

2 Zaskar Mountains, *Asia*

The brackish waters of Tso Morari lake, surrounded by the Zaskar Mountains, can be seen at the left hand edge of this Shuttle photograph. North is to the right of the image. The mountains form one of the ranges at the western end of the Himalayas in the disputed area of Jammu and Kashmir. The lake is more than 4 000 m above sea level, the surrounding mountains rise to over 6 000 m.

Satellite/Sensor : Space Shuttle

3 Altiplano, *South America*

The Altiplano is a high plateau which stretches from western Bolivia to southern Peru. It has an average height of over 3 600 m and is bordered to the west and east by two main ridges of the Andes mountains. This Shuttle photograph shows part of Lake Coipasa. Unusually, the water level is high. The lake is normally a dry lakebed for the majority of the year. The photograph shows individual volcanoes which are common in this region.

Satellite/Sensor : Space Shuttle

CONNECTIONS

▸ subject		page#
▸ Types of imagery		4-5
▸ World physical features		8-9
▸ Volcanoes		14-15
▸ Land cover types		18-19
▸ Coral reefs		140-141

4 French Polynesia, *Oceania*

This view of Bora-Bora, an island group within the Society Islands of French Polynesia in the southern Pacific Ocean, is typical of this area which consists of many scattered groups of islands. The main island, just visible at the top of the photograph, lies in a large lagoon surrounded by numerous coral reefs and small islands.

5 Greenland, *North America*

Icebergs are usually formed either by sections breaking off glaciers which flow into the sea or from the breaking up of ice-sheets as temperatures start to rise in spring. This one, off the northwest coast of Greenland in the Arctic Ocean, is surrounded by flat sections of broken up sea ice.

6 Namib Desert, *Africa*

This satellite image of the west coast of Africa clearly shows the natural barrier formed by the Kuiseb river at the northern edge of the Namib Desert in Namibia. To the north of the river are the Khomas Highlands which are rich in minerals, including uranium, to the south are the extensive dunes within the desert. The town of Walvis Bay is at the mouth of the river with the area's capital of Swakopmund just to the north.

Satellite/Sensor : Landsat

7 Canyonlands, *North America*

In this infrared satellite image of the Canyonlands region of the USA, vegetation shows as red, and forests as brown. The pale colours to the lower left of the image mark the area known as the Painted Desert. North is at the bottom. The image shows the upper reaches of the Grand Canyon, formed as a result of erosion by the Colorado River. The canyon ranges from six to twenty nine kilometres across.

Satellite/Sensor : SPOT

8 Taklimakan Desert, *Asia*

This image looks east over the Kunlun Shan mountains towards the Taklimakan Desert in the Tarim Pendi basin in China. The mountains mark the northern edge of the Plateau of Tibet. The southern edge of the plateau is the Himalayas. The dark areas in the desert at the top and on the left edge of the image are fertile areas, fed by intermittent rivers, around the towns of Hotan and Shache.

Satellite/Sensor : Space Shuttle

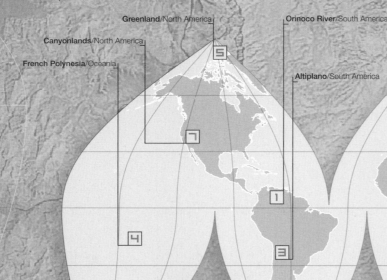

Greenland/North America
Orinoco River/South America
Taklimakan Desert/Asia
Canyonlands/North America
Zaskar Mountains/Asia
French Polynesia/Oceania
Altiplano/South America
Namib Desert/Africa

Sinusoidal Projection

Fig. #01
Earthquakes and volcanoes

world[earthquakes and volcanoes]

'Deadliest' earthquakes

Earthquakes of magnitude >=7.5

Earthquakes of magnitude 5.5–7.4

'Major' volcanoes

Other volcanoes

Hekla

Kocaeli (İzmit)

Erzincan

Spitak

EURASIAN PLATE

Dushanbe

Ashgabat

Kangra

Abruzzo

Manjil

Nepal/India

Khorāsan

Messina

Quetta

ARABIAN PLATE

NW Iran

Gujarat

Ech Chélif

AFRICAN PLATE

SOUTH AMERICAN PLATE

ANTARCTIC PLATE

Liaoning

Hebei

Ningxia

Gansu

EURASIAN

Dushanbe

Qinghai

Kangra

Quetta

Sichuan

Nepal/India

Gujarat

Yunnan/Sichuan

El Chichónal

Mt Pinatubo

Guatemala

Mayon

NORTH AMERICAN PLATE

Soufrière Hills

INDC

Gunung Galunggung

Kilauea

Bali

PACIFIC PLATE

COCOS PLATE

CARIBBEAN PLATE

Mt St Helens

Nevado del Ruiz

Volcán Galeras

SOUTH AMERICAN PLATE

Huánuco

NAZCA PLATE

Chillan

Volcán Llaima

SCOTIA PLATE

CONNECTIONS

▸ subject   page#

▸ World land images   12–13
▸ Asia threats   70–71
▸ Africa Rift Valley   118–119
▸ North America threats   160–161
▸ Ocean ridges and trenches   210–211

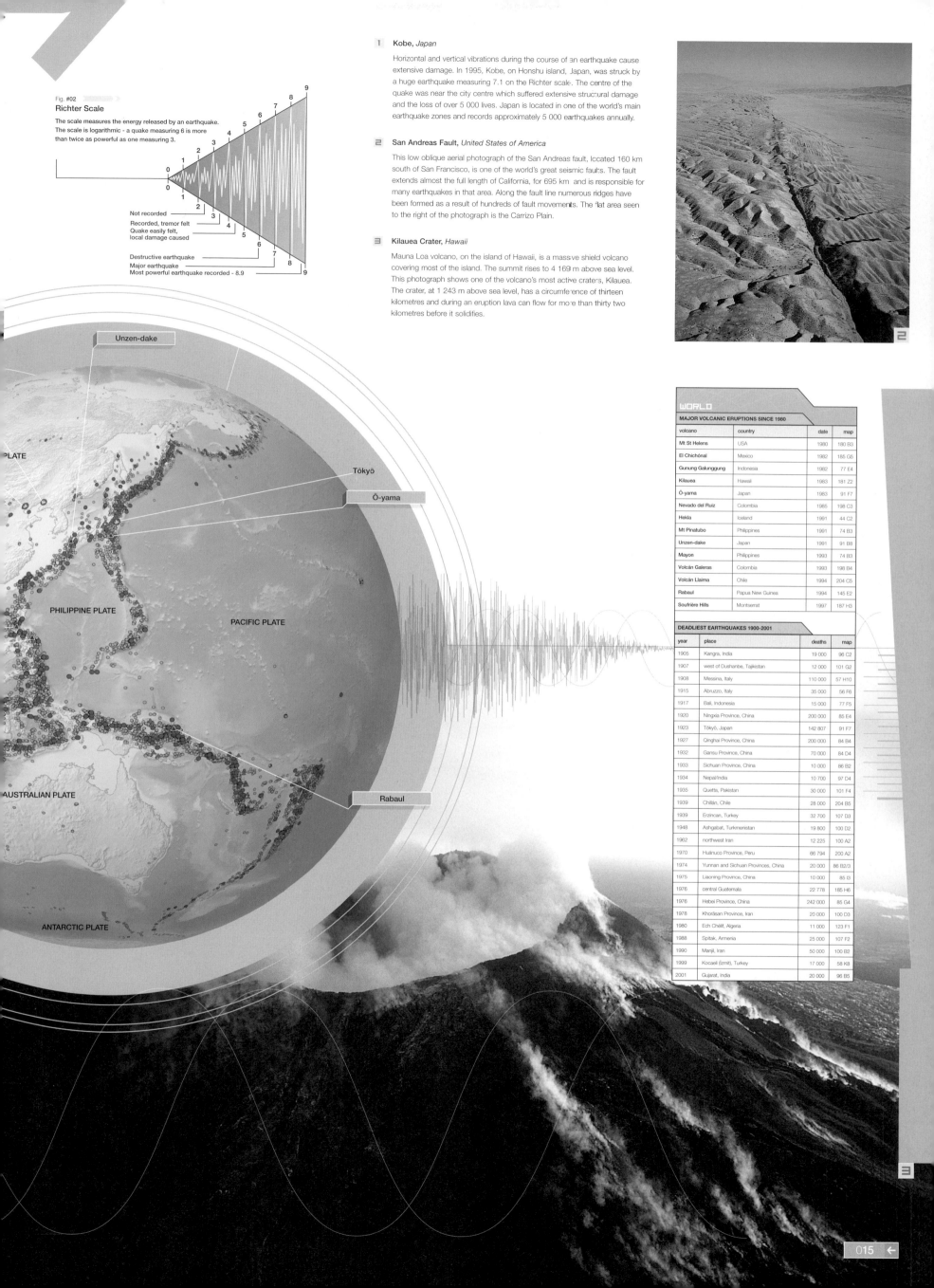

Fig. #02
Richter Scale

The scale measures the energy released by an earthquake.
The scale is logarithmic - a quake measuring 6 is more
than twice as powerful as one measuring 3.

Not recorded
Recorded, tremor felt
Quake easily felt,
local damage caused

Destructive earthquake
Major earthquake
Most powerful earthquake recorded - 8.9

1 Kobe, *Japan*

Horizontal and vertical vibrations during the course of an earthquake cause
extensive damage. In 1995, Kobe, on Honshu island, Japan, was struck by
a huge earthquake measuring 7.1 on the Richter scale. The centre of the
quake was near the city centre which suffered extensive structural damage
and the loss of over 5 000 lives. Japan is located in one of the world's main
earthquake zones and records approximately 5 000 earthquakes annually.

2 San Andreas Fault, *United States of America*

This low oblique aerial photograph of the San Andreas fault, located 160 km
south of San Francisco, is one of the world's great seismic faults. The fault
extends almost the full length of California, for 695 km and is responsible for
many earthquakes in that area. Along the fault line numerous ridges have
been formed as a result of hundreds of fault movements. The flat area seen
to the right of the photograph is the Carrizo Plain.

3 Kilauea Crater, *Hawaii*

Mauna Loa volcano, on the island of Hawaii, is a massive shield volcano
covering most of the island. The summit rises to 4 169 m above sea level.
This photograph shows one of the volcano's most active craters, Kilauea.
The crater, at 1 243 m above sea level, has a circumference of thirteen
kilometres and during an eruption lava can flow for more than thirty two
kilometres before it solidifies.

Unzen-dake

Tōkyō

Ō-yama

PLATE

PHILIPPINE PLATE

PACIFIC PLATE

AUSTRALIAN PLATE

Rabaul

ANTARCTIC PLATE

WORLD

MAJOR VOLCANIC ERUPTIONS SINCE 1980

volcano	country	date	map
Mt St Helens	USA	1980	180 B3
El Chichónal	Mexico	1982	185 G5
Gunung Galunggung	Indonesia	1982	77 E4
Kilauea	Hawaii	1983	181 Z2
Ō-yama	Japan	1983	91 F7
Nevado del Ruiz	Colombia	1985	198 C3
Hekla	Iceland	1991	44 C2
Mt Pinatubo	Philippines	1991	74 B3
Unzen-dake	Japan	1991	91 B8
Mayon	Philippines	1993	74 B3
Volcán Galeras	Colombia	1993	198 B4
Volcán Llaima	Chile	1994	204 C5
Rabaul	Papua New Guinea	1994	145 E2
Soufrière Hills	Montserrat	1997	187 H3

DEADLIEST EARTHQUAKES 1900-2001

year	place	deaths	map
1905	Kangra, India	19 000	96 C2
1907	west of Dushanbe, Tajikistan	12 000	101 G2
1908	Messina, Italy	110 000	57 H10
1915	Abruzzo, Italy	35 000	56 F6
1917	Bali, Indonesia	15 000	77 F5
1920	Ningxia Province, China	200 000	85 E4
1923	Tōkyō, Japan	142 807	91 F7
1927	Qinghai Province, China	200 000	84 B4
1932	Gansu Province, China	70 000	84 D4
1933	Sichuan Province, China	10 000	86 B2
1934	Nepal/India	10 700	97 D4
1935	Quetta, Pakistan	30 000	101 F4
1939	Chillán, Chile	28 000	204 B5
1939	Erzincan, Turkey	32 700	107 D3
1948	Ashgabat, Turkmenistan	19 800	100 D2
1962	northwest Iran	12 225	100 A2
1970	Huánuco Province, Peru	66 794	200 A2
1974	Yunnan and Sichuan Provinces, China	20 000	86 B2/3
1975	Liaoning Province, China	10 000	85 I3
1976	central Guatemala	22 778	185 H6
1976	Hebei Province, China	242 000	85 G4
1978	Khorāsān Province, Iran	20 000	100 D3
1980	Ech Chélif, Algeria	11 000	123 F1
1988	Spitak, Armenia	25 000	107 F2
1990	Manjil, Iran	50 000	100 B2
1999	Kocaeli (İzmit), Turkey	17 000	58 K8
2001	Gujarat, India	20 000	96 B5

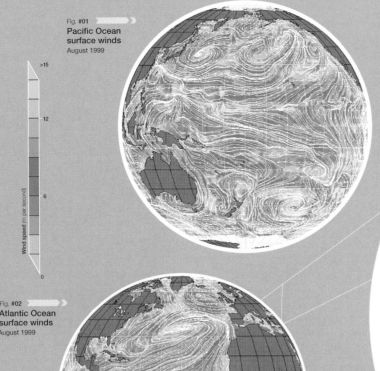

Fig. #01
Pacific Ocean surface winds
August 1999

Wind speed (m per second)
>15
12
6
0

Fig. #02
Atlantic Ocean surface winds
August 1999

Fig. #03
Indian Ocean surface winds
August 1999

Fig. #04
Satellite Image of Earth

Fig. #01-#03 Ocean surface winds

Winds play a major role in every aspect of weather on Earth. They affect the exchanges of heat, moisture and greenhouse gases between Earth's atmosphere and the oceans. These images were taken on 1 August 1999 from the QuikSCAT satellite carrying a radar instrument called a scatterometer which can record surface wind speeds in the oceans. In the image of the Pacific Ocean yellow spirals representing typhoon Olga can be seen moving around South Korea and the East China Sea. Intense winter storms can also be seen around Antarctica in all three images.

Satellite/Sensor : QuikSCAT/SeaWinds

Fig. #10-#11 Climate change in the future

Future climate change will depend to a large extent on the effect human activities have on the chemical composition of the atmosphere. As greenhouse gases and aerosol emissions increase the atmospheric temperatures rise. The map of predicted temperature in the 2050s shows that average annual temperatures may rise by as much as 5°C in some areas if current emission rates continue. The map of precipitation change shows some areas are likely to experience a significant increase in precipitation of over 3 mm per day, while others will experience a decrease. Such changes are likely to have significant impacts on sea level which could rise by as much as 50 cm in the next century. The changes would also have implications for water resources, food production and health.

Fig. #04 Satellite image of Earth

Images such as this from the Meteosat satellite provide valuable meteorological information on a global scale. Dense clouds appear white, thinner cloud cover as pink . A swirling frontal weather system is clearly seen in the Atlantic Ocean to the west of Europe.

Satellite/Sensor : Meteosat

Fig. #05
Major climatic regions and sub-types

Köppen classification system

A   Rainy climate with no winter: coolest month above 18°C (64.4°F).
B   Dry climates; limits are defined by formulae based on rainfall effectiveness: BS Steppe or semi-arid climate. BW Desert or arid climate.
*C Rainy climates with mild winters: coolest month above 0°C (32°F), but below 18°C (64.4°F); warmest month above 10°C (50°F).
*D Rainy climates with severe winters: coldest month below 0°C (32°F); warmest month above 10°C (50°F).
E   Polar climates with no warm season: warmest month below 10°C (50°F). ET Tundra climate: warmest month below 10°C (50°F) but above 0°C (32°F). EF Perpetual frost: all months below 0°C (32°F).
a   Warmest month above 22°C (71.6°F).
b   Warmest month below 22°C (71.6°F).
c   Less than four months over 10°C (50°F).
d   As 'c', but with severe cold: coldest month below -38°C (-36.4°F).
f   Constantly moist rainfall throughout the year.
*h Warmer dry: all months above 0°C (32°F).
*k Cooler dry: at least one month below 0°C (32°F).
m   Monsoon rain: short dry season, but is compensated by heavy rains during rest of the year.
n   Frequent fog.
s   Dry season in summer.
w   Dry season in winter.

* Modification of Köppen definition

Polar
EF   Ice cap
ET   Tundra

Cooler humid
Dc Dd   Subarctic
Db   Continental cool summer
Da   Continental warm summer

Warmer humid
Cb Cc   Temperate
Ca   Humid subtropical
Cs   Mediterranean

Dry
BS   Steppe
BW   Desert

Tropical humid
Aw As   Savanna
Af Am   Rain forest

CONNECTIONS

► subject	page#
► Asia threats	70–71
► Africa issues	116–117
► North America threats	160–161
► South America impacts	196–197
► Antarctica features	212–213
► Arctic features	214–215

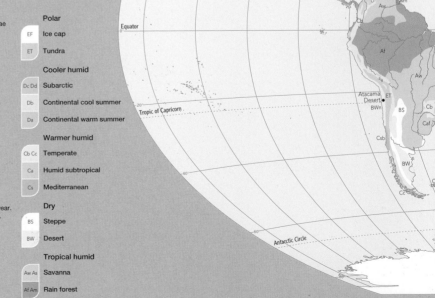

Fig. #06

Tracks of tropical storms

Wind speeds often over
160km per hour

⇨ Cyclone track   ⇨ Willy-willies   ▭ Source area of tropical storms
⇨ Typhoon track   ⇨ Hurricane track   ● Major tropical storm (1994–2000)

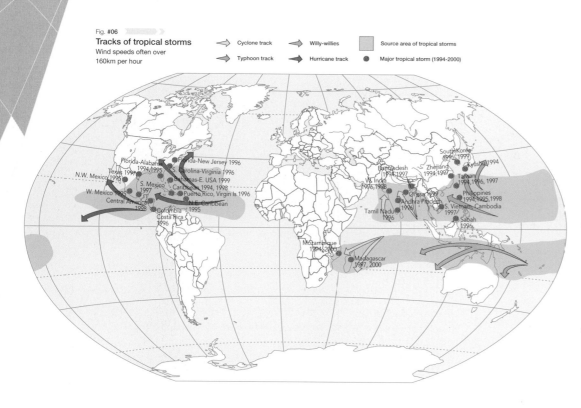

Fig. #07
Actual surface temperature
January

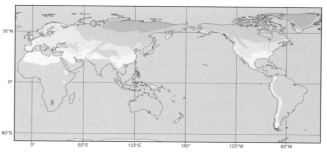

Fig. #08
Actual surface temperature
July

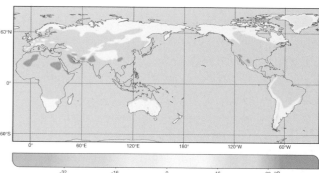

-32   -16   0   16   32 °C

Fig. #09
Average annual precipitation

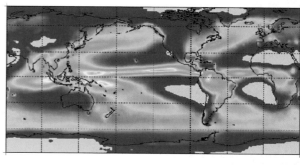

0   2.5   5   7.5   10
Precipitation (mm per day)

WORLD

WEATHER EXTREMES

Highest shade temperature	57.8°C/136°F Al 'Aziziyah, Libya (13th September 1922)
Hottest place — Annual mean	34.4°C/93.9°F Dalol, Ethiopia
Driest place — Annual mean	0.1 mm/0.004 inches Atacama Desert, Chile
Most sunshine — Annual mean	90% Yuma, Arizona, USA (over 4 000 hours)
Least sunshine	Nil for 182 days each year, South Pole
Lowest screen temperature	-89.2°C/-128.6°F Vostok Station, Antarctica (21st July 1983)
Coldest place — Annual mean	-56.6°C/-69.9°F Plateau Station, Antarctica
Wettest place — Annual mean	11 873 mm/467.4 inches Meghalaya, India
Most rainy days	Up to 350 per year Mount Waialeale, Hawaii, USA
Windiest place	322 km per hour/200 miles per hour in gales, Commonwealth Bay, Antarctica
Highest surface wind speed	
High altitude	372 km per hour/231 miles per hour Mount Washington, New Hampshire, USA (12th April 1934)
Low altitude	333 km per hour/207 miles per hour Qaanaaq (Thule), Greenland (8th March 1972)
Tornado	512 km per hour/318 miles per hour Oklahoma City, Oklahoma, USA (3rd May 1999)
Greatest snowfall	31 102 mm/1 224.5 inches Mount Rainier, Washington, USA (19th February 1971–18th February 1972)
Heaviest hailstones	1 kg/2.21 lb Gopalganj, Bangladesh (14th April 1986)
Thunder-days Average	251 days per year Tororo, Uganda
Highest barometric pressure	1 083.8 mb Agata, Siberia, Russian Federation (31st December 1968)
Lowest barometric pressure	870 mb 483 km/300 miles west of Guam, Pacific Ocean (12th October 1979)

Fig. #10-#11
Climate changes in the future

#10 **Precipitation in 2050s**
Predicted average precipitation change

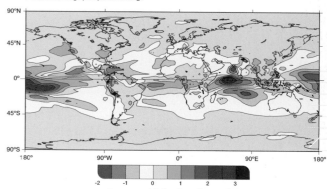

-2   -1   0   1   2   3
Average precipitation change (mm per day)

#11 **Temperature in 2050s**
Predicted annual mean temperature change

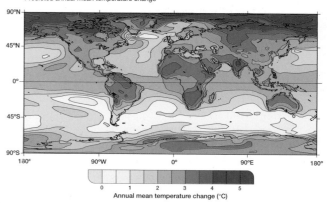

0   1   2   3   4   5
Annual mean temperature change (°C)

1

1 Wetland

Wetland areas make up less than 1 per cent of world land cover. This aerial photograph of the Okavango Delta in Botswana shows an unusual environment. Set in the centre of southern Africa, the Okavango river drains into this low lying area, not into the sea. The extent of the wetland varies with the amount of rainfall in the catchment area. The high water table allows for a wide diversity of vegetation to grow in an area surrounded by grassland.

2 Crops/Mosaic

Fertile land which is cultivated by man often produces geometric patterns. The infrared satellite image shows part of the Everglades swamp in Florida, USA, east of Lake Okeechobee. Bare fields appear as dark pink and planted fields as green. The pattern continues into the urban areas depicted in blue. Regular field systems such as these enable mechanized agriculture and crop diversification. The dark mottled area to the top right of the image is an undeveloped part of the Everglades.

Satellite/Sensor : Landsat

3 Urban

Representing approximately 0.2 per cent of total world land cover, the urban environment is probably the farthest removed from the Earth's original, natural land cover. This aerial view of Manhattan in New York, USA, shows the 'grid iron' street pattern typical of many modern cities. Major natural features, such as the Hudson River in this image, interrupt this regular plan. Parkland areas, such as that appearing at the top left of the image, are manufactured rather than natural.

4 Grass/Savanna

This view of Ngorongoro, Tanzania is typical of tropical savanna grasslands. Over 25 per cent of Africa's land cover falls within this category. Large areas of tropical grasslands also occur in South America and northern Australia, with temperate grasslands in North America (prairie) and Asia (steppe). Seasonal rainfall provides a regular cycle of lush, tall grass interspersed by scattered trees and shrubs. The savanna areas of east Africa support large numbers of wild animals.

5 Forest/Woodland

The type of woodland coverage in this photograph is tropical rainforest or jungle. This accounts for over 40 per cent of land cover in South America. Dense coverage includes tall hardwood trees which provide a high canopy over smaller trees and shrubs capable of surviving with little direct sunlight. Natural forest or woodland areas such as the Amazon are under continuous threat from the external pressures of agriculture, mineral exploration or urbanization.

6 Barren

The Hoggar region of Algeria is part of the 30 per cent of barren land in Africa, the most extensive land cover type on the continent. This area is a plateau of bare rock lying at a height of over 2 000 m above sea level. It is surrounded by the sandy desert of the Sahara. Rainfall is negligible and the extreme temperatures result in little, or no vegetation and wildlife.

7 Shrubland

Shrubland areas, shown here around Ayers Rock in central Australia, develop on the fringes of desert regions. Sporadic rainfall and less severe temperatures than in the deserts, are enough for hardy plants and shrubs to grow in the thin soil. Moving away from the desert areas, as conditions become less harsh, the vegetation changes and the range of plants increases.

8 Snow/Ice

The continent of Antarctica is almost completely covered by snow and ice. In the northern hemisphere, Spitsbergen, shown here, is one of a large group of islands within the Arctic Circle which is also permanently covered. There is no vegetation on land and any wildlife must survive on food caught in the sea. Although inhospitable areas at the polar extremes see little human interaction, they are affected by global increases in temperature. Resultant melting of glaciers and icecaps threatens a rise in sea level.

CONNECTIONS

► subject	page#
► Changes to land cover	20–21
► World cities	24–25
► North America environments	162–163
► South America contrasts	194–195
► Arctic regions	210–211

Fig. #01
Continental land cover composition

Land cover composition (per cent)

South America   North America   Eurasia   Australia   Antarctica   Africa

Legend:
- Urban
- Wetland
- Snow/Ice
- Barren
- Grass/Savanna
- Shrubland
- Crops/Mosaic
- Forest/Woodland

Fig. #02
Global land cover composition

0.2%   0.9%   11.4%   27.5%   12.6%   14.0%   14.2%   19.2%

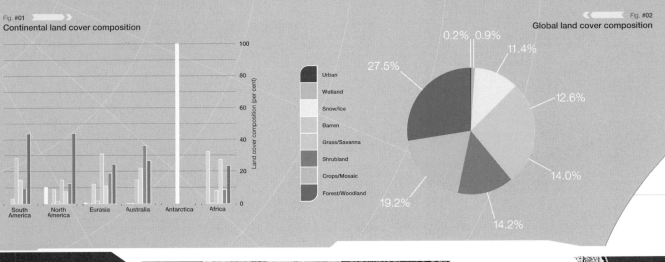

2

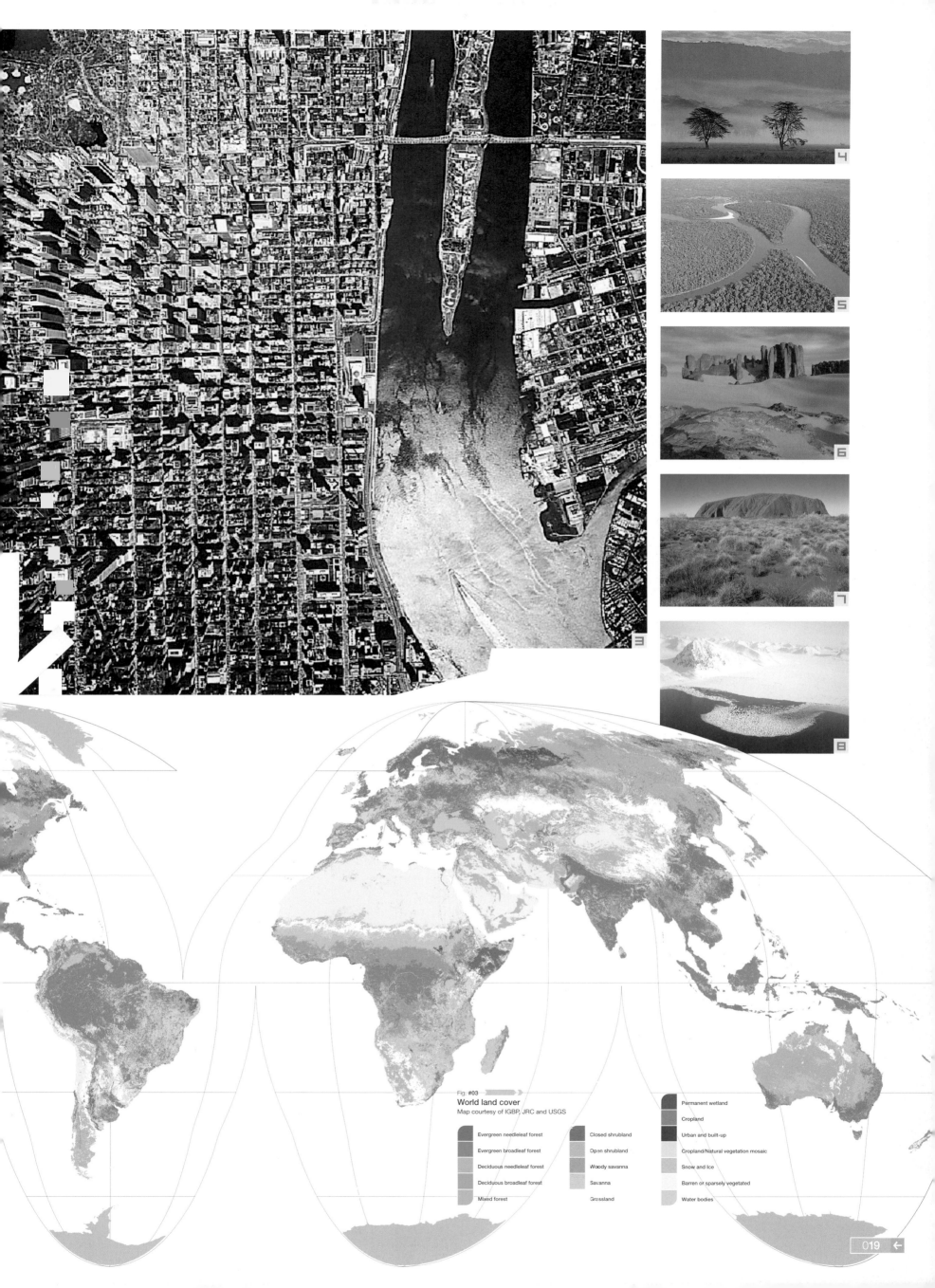

Fig. #03
World land cover
Map courtesy of IGBP, JRC and USGS

Evergreen needleleaf forest

Evergreen broadleaf forest

Deciduous needleleaf forest

Deciduous broadleaf forest

Mixed forest

Closed shrubland

Open shrubland

Woody savanna

Savanna

Grassland

Permanent wetland

Cropland

Urban and built-up

Cropland/Natural vegetation mosaic

Snow and Ice

Barren or sparsely vegetated

Water bodies

2 Changing Land Use

The changes in land use between Alberta, Canada (top) and Montana, USA (bottom) can be seen on this infrared satellite image. The straight international boundary runs diagonally from centre left to upper right. Intense cultivation on the US side has created regular field patterns, whereas on the Canadian side plantations of forest and thick mountain vegetation cover extensive areas.

Satellite/Sensor : Landsat

3 Deforestation

This aerial photograph shows the dramatic effect the clearcut logging method of deforestation can have on a landscape. The change in appearance and the effects on the immediate environment can be dramatic. It shows part of the northwest US state of Washington, which has large areas of thick forest, particularly on the western slopes of the Cascade mountain range. More than half of the state is forested and lumber and lumber-related products form the basis of much of the state's economic activity.

1 Changing River Courses

This aerial infrared photograph shows a small section of the Mississippi river near Lake Providence in Louisiana state. The pattern of old loops and bends identifies old courses of the river, showing changes which have occurred over many years. Some loops have become isolated 'oxbow' lakes as shown on the west bank of the river in the left of the image. At the bottom right one former loop of the river can be identified within the cultivated area.

4 Urban Growth

These Landsat images illustrate how such imagery can be used to monitor environmental change. They show the rapid urban growth which has taken place in and around Shenzhen, China, between 1988 (left) and 1996 (right). This city has benefited greatly from its location adjacent to Hong Kong. One of the most obvious changes is the development along the coastline, where huge off-shore structures and large areas of reclaimed land can be seen in the 1996 image. Much of the vegetation (red) in the left image has been cleared and replaced by urban development, leaving only scattered patches of the original vegetation.

Satellite/Sensor : Landsat

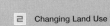

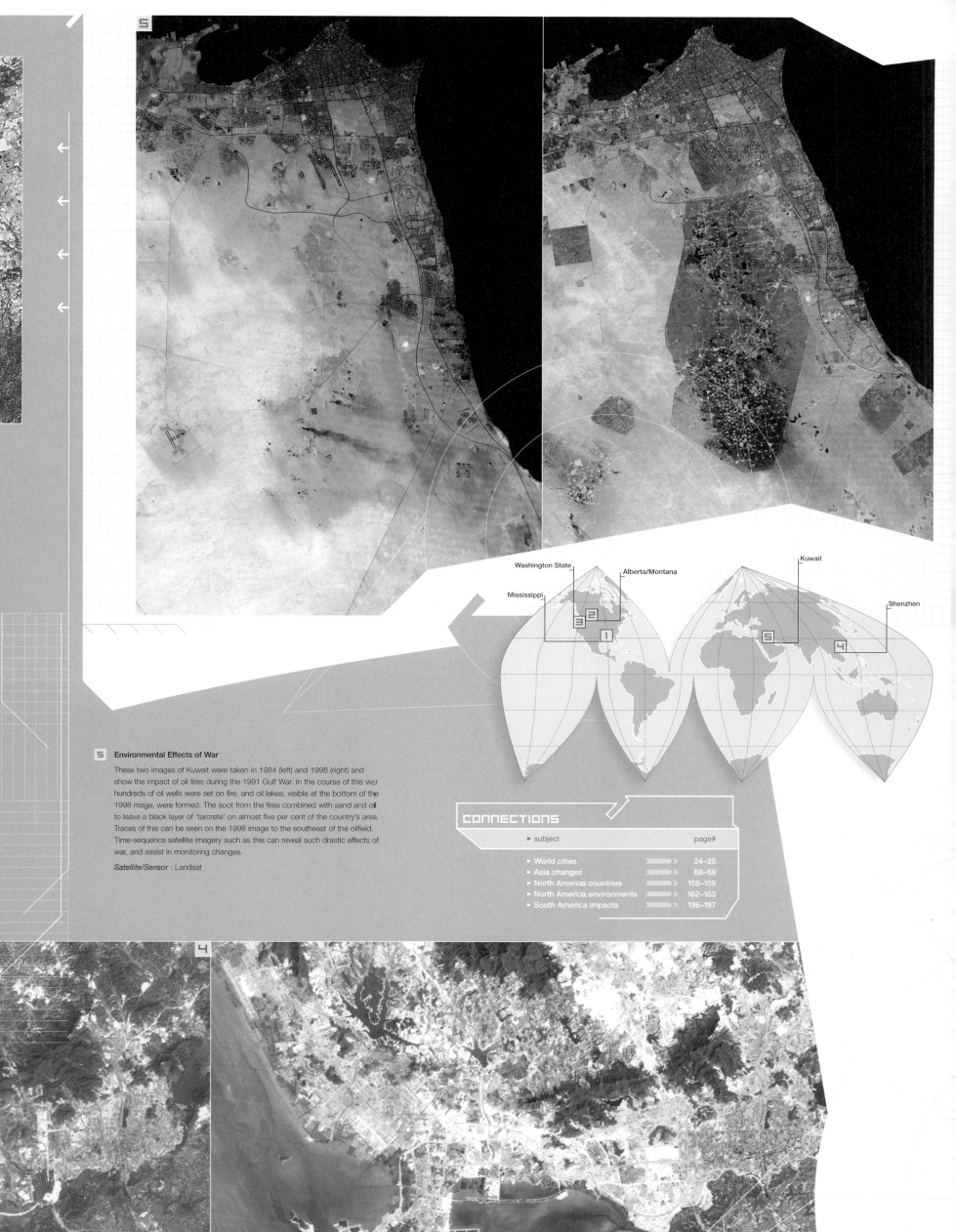

5 Environmental Effects of War

These two images of Kuwait were taken in 1984 (left) and 1998 (right) and show the impact of oil fires during the 1991 Gulf War. In the course of this war hundreds of oil wells were set on fire, and oil lakes, visible at the bottom of the 1998 image, were formed. The soot from the fires combined with sand and oil to leave a black layer of 'tarcrete' on almost five per cent of the country's area. Traces of this can be seen on the 1998 image to the southeast of the oilfield. Time-sequence satellite imagery such as this can reveal such drastic effects of war, and assist in monitoring changes.

Satellite/Sensor : Landsat

Washington State
Alberta/Montana
Mississippi
Kuwait
Shenzhen

CONNECTIONS

► subject	page#
► World cities	24–25
► Asia changes	68–69
► North America countries	158–159
► North America environments	162–163
► South America impacts	196–197

1

CONNECTIONS

► subject	page#
► World countries	10–11
► World cities	24–25
► Chinese migration	66–67
► Ethnic groups in the Balkans	34–35
► Arctic peoples	214–215

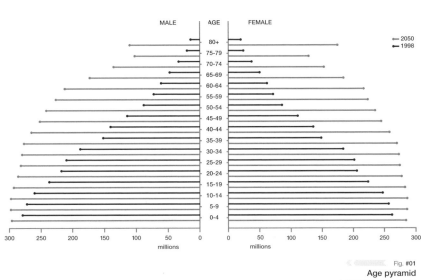

MALE	AGE	FEMALE

	80+	
	75-79	
	70-74	
	65-69	
	60-64	
	55-59	
	50-54	
	45-49	
	40-44	
	35-39	
	30-34	
	25-29	
	20-24	
	15-19	
	10-14	
	5-9	
	0-4	

300 250 200 150 100 50 0   0 50 100 150 200 250 300

millions   millions

— 2050
— 1998

Fig. #01
Age pyramid
Less developed countries

1   Village Settlement, *Botswana*

The Kalahari Desert stretches across the southwest and central part of Botswana and into Namibia and South Africa. This photograph shows a small village settlement in this very isolated and sparsely populated region. Such villages are usually temporary with the area's people living nomadic lives, moving on to new locations when food sources run low. Although surface water is practically non-existent in the desert, underlying groundwater supports deep-rooted shrubs and trees.

2   Tokyo, *Japan*

A small section of Tokyo, the world's largest city and the capital of Japan, is shown in this aerial photograph mosaic. The contrasting pattern of high-rise development and densely packed low-rise buildings is typical of many major Asian cities. While displaying all the characteristics of a modern city, it has retained much of its cultural and historical identity. It is renowned for its excellent transport systems and is the centre of government, industry, commerce and education in Japan.

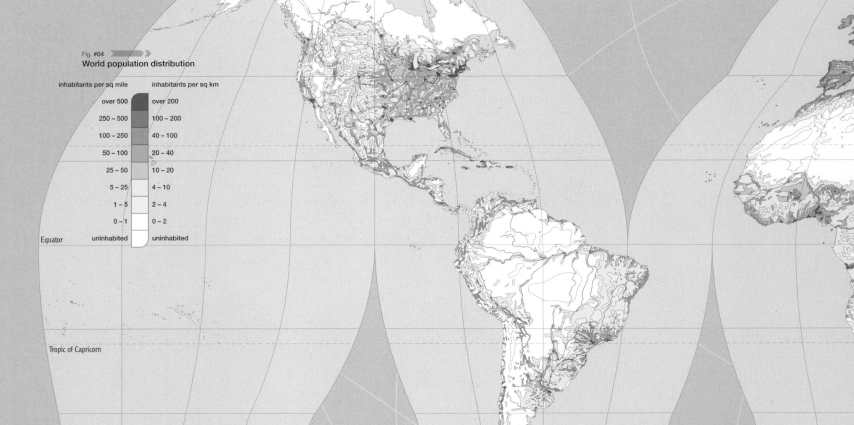

Fig. #03
World population growth by continent
1750-2050

Fig. #04
World population distribution

inhabitants per sq mile	inhabitants per sq km
over 500	over 200
250 – 500	100 – 200
100 – 250	40 – 100
50 – 100	20 – 40
25 – 50	10 – 20
5 – 25	4 – 10
1 – 5	2 – 4
0 – 1	0 – 2
uninhabited	uninhabited

Arctic circle

Equator

Tropic of Capricorn

Antarctic Circle

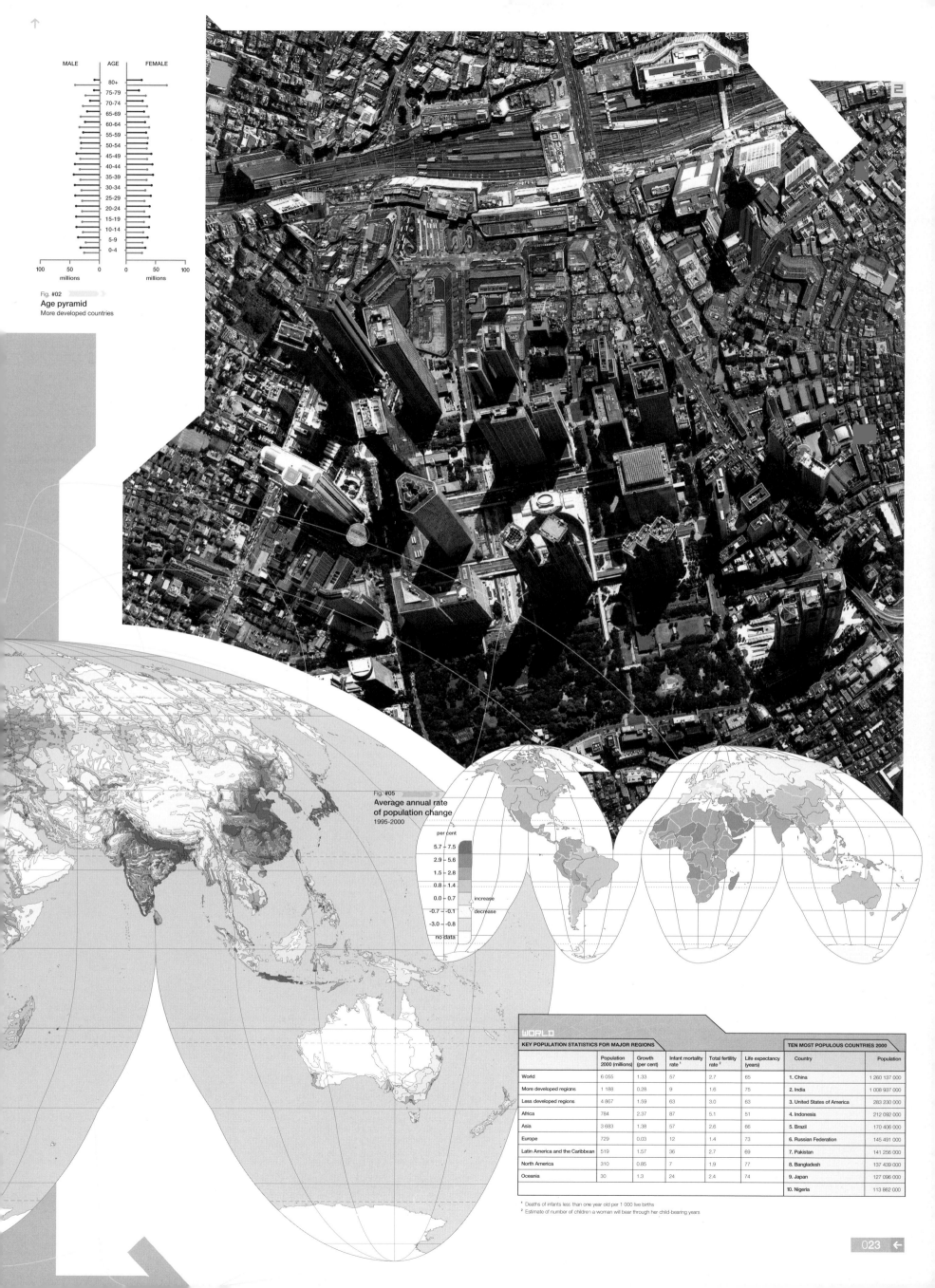

MALE   AGE   FEMALE

80+
75-79
70-74
65-69
60-64
55-59
50-54
45-49
40-44
35-39
30-34
25-29
20-24
15-19
10-14
5-9
0-4

100   50   0   0   50   100
   millions   millions

Fig. #02
Age pyramid
More developed countries

Fig. #05
**Average annual rate
of population change**
1995-2000

per cent
5.7 – 7.5
2.9 – 5.6
1.5 – 2.8
0.8 – 1.4
0.0 – 0.7   increase
-0.7 – -0.1   decrease
-3.0 – -0.8
no data

WORLD

KEY POPULATION STATISTICS FOR MAJOR REGIONS

	Population 2000 (millions)	Growth (per cent)	Infant mortality rate [1]	Total fertility rate [2]	Life expectancy (years)
World	6 055	1.33	57	2.7	65
More developed regions	1 188	0.28	9	1.6	75
Less developed regions	4 867	1.59	63	3.0	63
Africa	784	2.37	87	5.1	51
Asia	3 683	1.38	57	2.6	66
Europe	729	0.03	12	1.4	73
Latin America and the Caribbean	519	1.57	36	2.7	69
North America	310	0.85	7	1.9	77
Oceania	30	1.3	24	2.4	74

TEN MOST POPULOUS COUNTRIES 2000

Country	Population
1. China	1 260 137 000
2. India	1 008 937 000
3. United States of America	283 230 000
4. Indonesia	212 092 000
5. Brazil	170 406 000
6. Russian Federation	145 491 000
7. Pakistan	141 256 000
8. Bangladesh	137 439 000
9. Japan	127 096 000
10. Nigeria	113 862 000

[1] Deaths of infants less than one year old per 1 000 live births
[2] Estimate of number of children a woman will bear through her child-bearing years

world[cities]

1 San Francisco, *United States of America*

The city of San Francisco is situated on the peninsula which lies to the western side of San Francisco Bay. The Golden Gate, upper left, bridges the entrance to the bay and three other bridges are visible in the image. San Francisco has frequently suffered extensive damage from earthquakes and the two lakes south of the city mark the line of the San Andreas fault. The southern end of the bay is surrounded by a green patchwork of salt beds.

Satellite/Sensor : Landsat

2 Hong Kong, *China*

A British colony until 1997, Hong Kong is now a Special Administrative Region of China. This high resolution satellite image is centred on Hong Kong Harbour, with the Kowloon Peninsula to the north (top) and Hong Kong Island to the south. Much of the coastline shown is reclaimed land, including the old Kai Tak airport, seen in the top right of the image. This airport has been closed since the completion of the new Hong Kong International airport 25 kilometres west of the harbour.

Satellite/Sensor : IKONOS

3 Cairo, *Egypt*

This oblique aerial photograph looks north across the suburbs of southwest Cairo. There has been a major expansion of the city and its suburbs over the last fifty years and the city now has a population of over 10 million. The urban expansion brings the city up against the important historical site of the Giza Pyramids. The Pyramid of Khufu and the Great Sphinx can be seen at the left of the photograph.

4 Tokyo, *Japan*

This false-colour infrared image of Tokyo shows the northwest edge of Tokyo Bay. It shows just a small part of the vast expanse of Tokyo, the world's largest city with over 26 million inhabitants. The amount of land reclamation in the bay is obvious, and the reclaimed land includes Tokyo International (Haneda) Airport, at the bottom of the image. Vegetation shows as red, making the grounds of the Imperial Palace clearly visible in the top left.

Satellite/Sensor : Terra/ASTER

CONNECTIONS

► subject	page#
► World countries	10–11
► World land cover	18–19
► Urban growth	20–21
► World population	22–23
► Oceania capitals	138–139

Fig. #01
Urban Agglomerations
with over 1 million inhabitants

- over 20 million
- 10 million - 20 million
- 5 million - 10 million
- 2.5 million - 5 million
- 1 million - 2.5 million

Fig. #02

10 Million Cities

Dates at which cities attained 10 million population
1950-2015

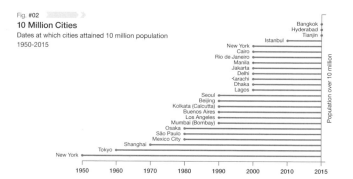

Bangkok
Hyderabad
Tianjin
Istanbul
New York
Cairo
Rio de Janeiro
Manila
Jakarta
Delhi
Karachi
Dhaka
Lagos
Seoul
Beijing
Kolkata (Calcutta)
Buenos Aires
Los Angeles
Mumbai (Bombay)
Osaka
São Paulo
Mexico City
Shanghai
Tokyo
New York

Population over 10 million

1950 1960 1970 1980 1990 2000 2010 2015

Fig. #03

World Top 10 Cities
1900-2015

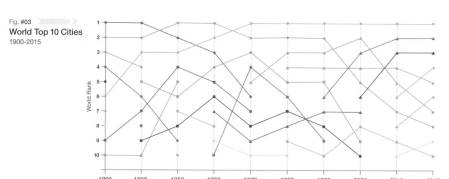

World Rank

1900 1930 1950 1960 1970 1980 1990 2000 2010 2015

- London
- New York
- Berlin
- Chigago
- Wuhan
- Tokyo
- Philadelphia
- St Petersburg
- Paris
- Moscow
- Shanghai
- Osaka
- Buenos Aires
- Essen
- Kolkata (Calcutta)
- Beijing
- Los Angeles
- Mexico City
- São Paulo
- Mumbai (Bombay)
- Lagos
- Dhaka
- Karachi
- Jakarta

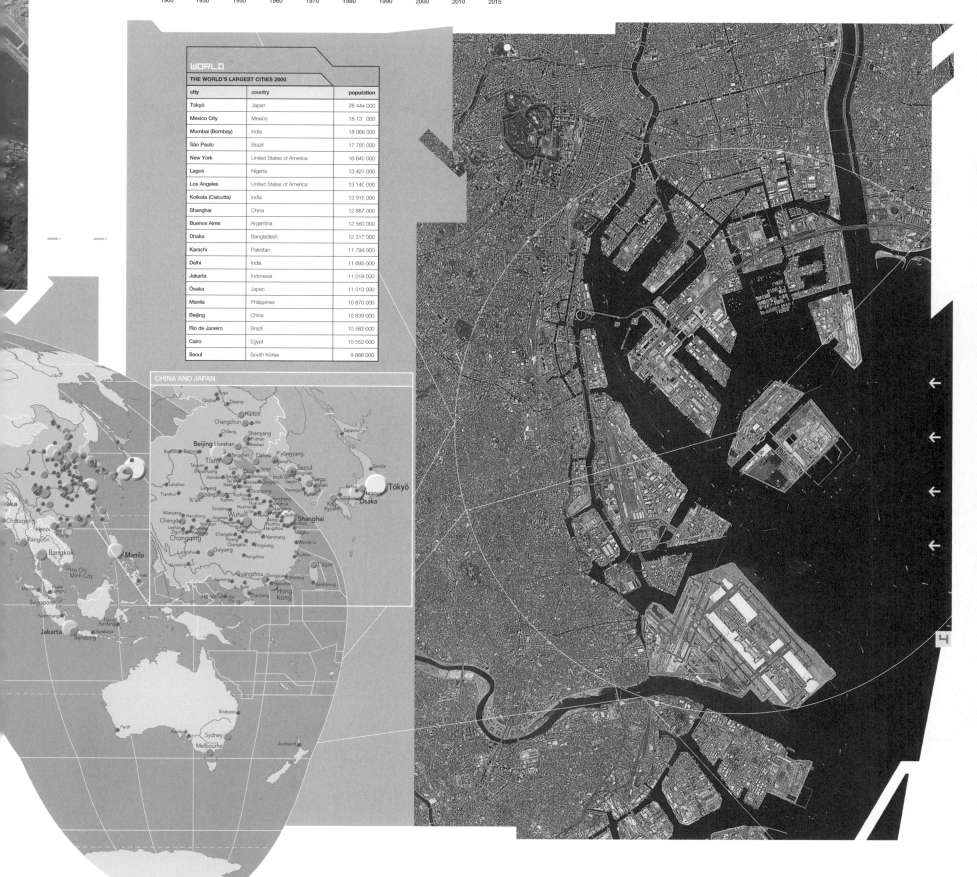

WORLD

THE WORLD'S LARGEST CITIES 2000		
city	country	population
Tōkyō	Japan	26 444 000
Mexico City	Mexico	18 13˙ 000
Mumbai (Bombay)	India	18 066 000
São Paulo	Brazil	17 755 000
New York	United States of America	16 640 000
Lagos	Nigeria	13 427 000
Los Angeles	United States of America	13 14C 000
Kolkata (Calcutta)	India	12 918 000
Shanghai	China	12 887 000
Buenos Aires	Argentina	12 560 000
Dhaka	Bangladesh	12 317 000
Karachi	Pakistan	11 794 000
Delhi	India	11 695 000
Jakarta	Indonesia	11 018 000
Ōsaka	Japan	11 013 000
Manila	Philippines	10 870 000
Beijing	China	10 839 000
Rio de Janeiro	Brazil	10 582 000
Cairo	Egypt	10 552 000
Seoul	South Korea	9 888 000

CHINA AND JAPAN

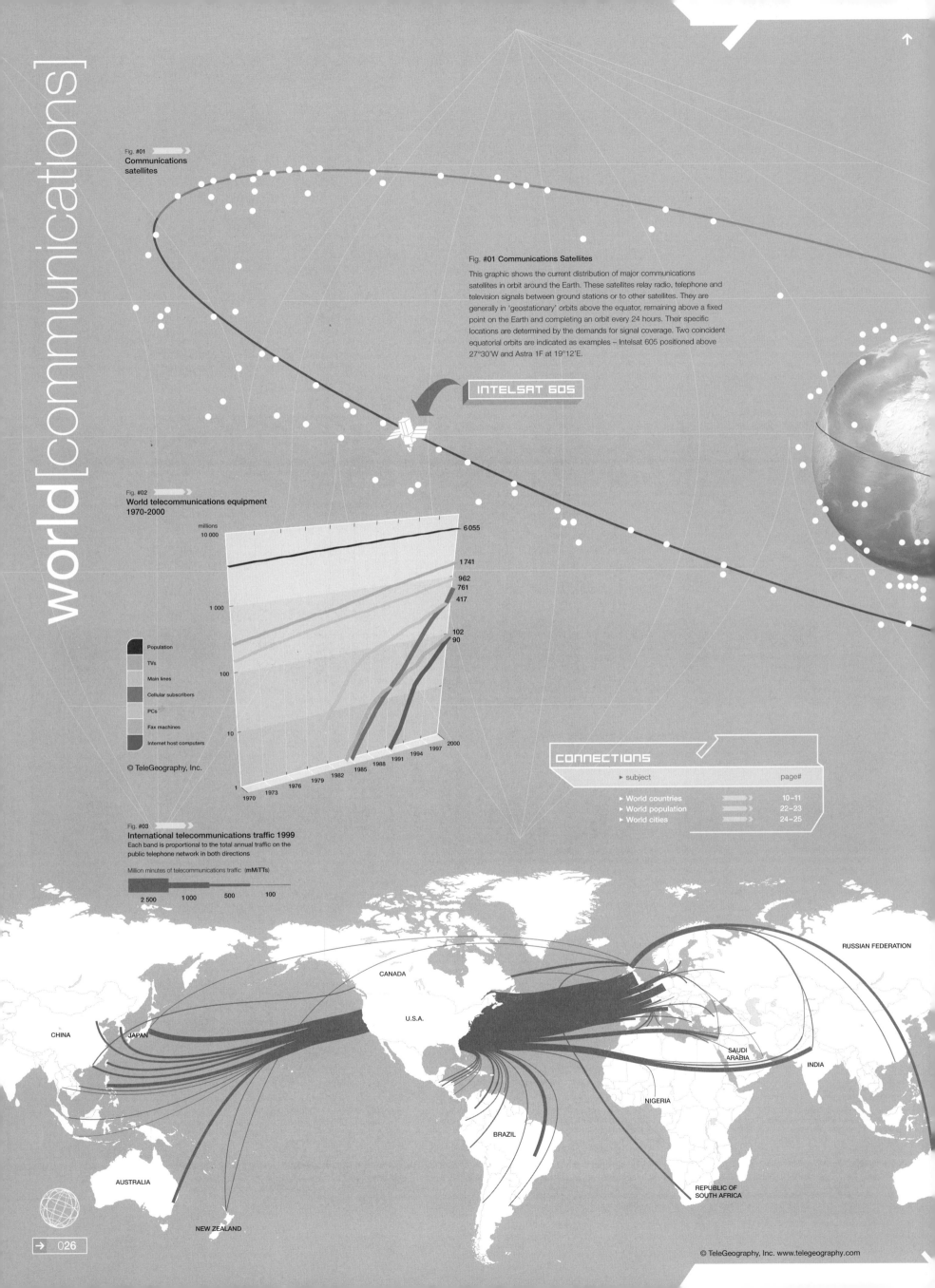

world[communications]

Fig. #01
Communications
satellites

Fig. #01 Communications Satellites

This graphic shows the current distribution of major communications satellites in orbit around the Earth. These satellites relay radio, telephone and television signals between ground stations or to other satellites. They are generally in 'geostationary' orbits above the equator, remaining above a fixed point on the Earth and completing an orbit every 24 hours. Their specific locations are determined by the demands for signal coverage. Two coincident equatorial orbits are indicated as examples – Intelsat 605 positioned above 27°30'W and Astra 1F at 19°12'E.

INTELSAT 605

Fig. #02
World telecommunications equipment
1970-2000

millions
10 000

6 055
1 741
962
761
417

102
90

1 000

100

10

1

Population
TVs
Main lines
Cellular subscribers
PCs
Fax machines
Internet host computers

© TeleGeography, Inc.

1970 1973 1976 1979 1982 1985 1988 1991 1994 1997 2000

CONNECTIONS

► subject	page#
► World countries	10–11
► World population	22–23
► World cities	24–25

Fig. #03
International telecommunications traffic 1999
Each band is proportional to the total annual traffic on the public telephone network in both directions

Million minutes of telecommunications traffic (mMiTTs)

2 500   1 000   500   100

RUSSIAN FEDERATION
CANADA
CHINA
JAPAN
U.S.A.
SAUDI ARABIA
INDIA
NIGERIA
BRAZIL
AUSTRALIA
REPUBLIC OF SOUTH AFRICA
NEW ZEALAND

© TeleGeography, Inc. www.telegeography.com

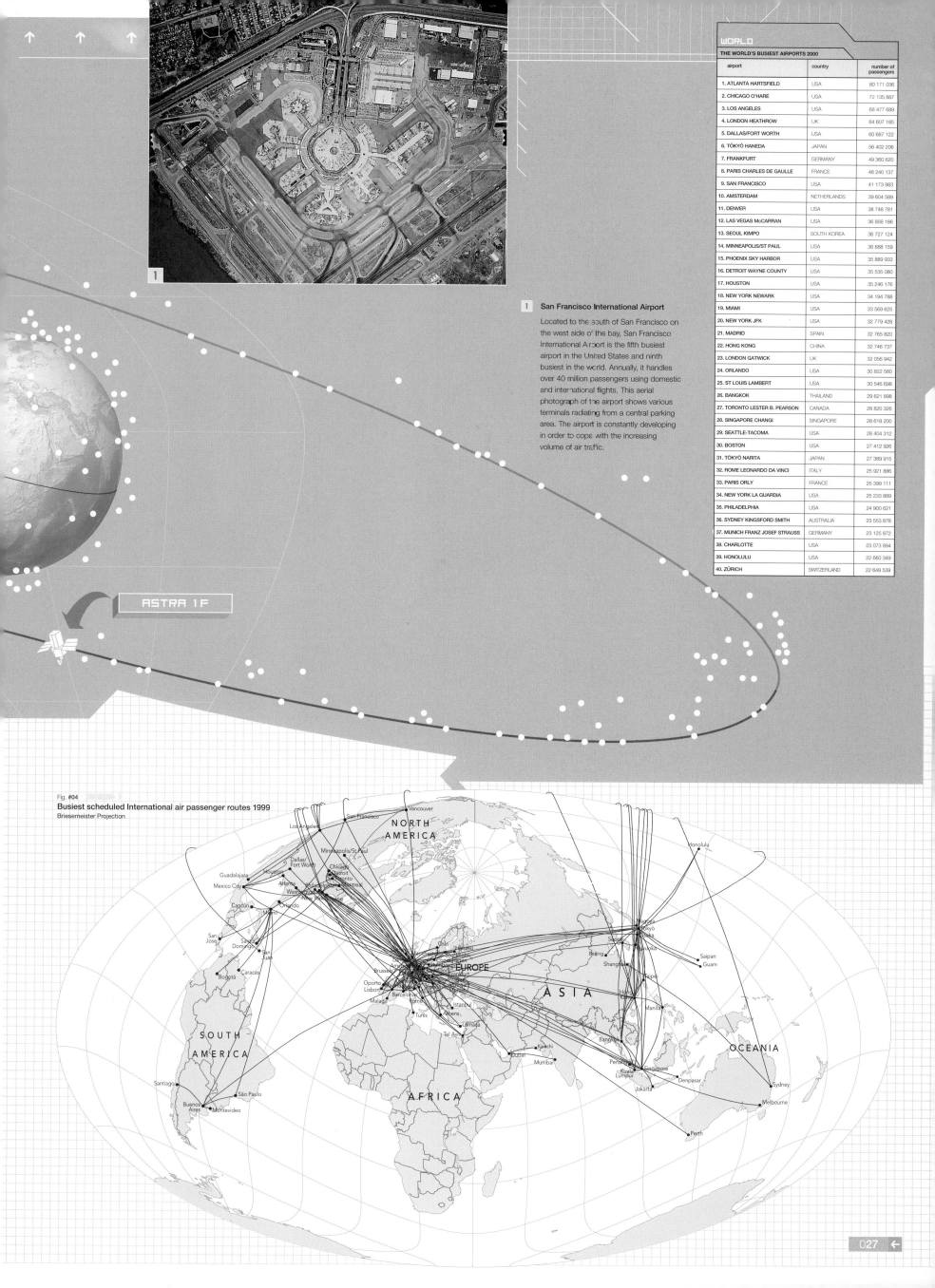

airport	country	number of passengers
1. ATLANTA HARTSFIELD	USA	80 171 036
2. CHICAGO O'HARE	USA	72 135 887
3. LOS ANGELES	USA	68 477 689
4. LONDON HEATHROW	UK	64 607 185
5. DALLAS/FORT WORTH	USA	60 687 122
6. TŌKYŌ HANEDA	JAPAN	56 402 206
7. FRANKFURT	GERMANY	49 360 620
8. PARIS CHARLES DE GAULLE	FRANCE	48 240 137
9. SAN FRANCISCO	USA	41 173 983
10. AMSTERDAM	NETHERLANDS	39 604 589
11. DENVER	USA	38 748 781
12. LAS VEGAS McCARRAN	USA	36 856 186
13. SEOUL KIMPO	SOUTH KOREA	36 727 124
14. MINNEAPOLIS/ST PAUL	USA	36 688 159
15. PHOENIX SKY HARBOR	USA	35 889 933
16. DETROIT WAYNE COUNTY	USA	35 535 080
17. HOUSTON	USA	35 246 176
18. NEW YORK NEWARK	USA	34 194 788
19. MIAMI	USA	33 569 625
20. NEW YORK JFK	USA	32 779 428
21. MADRID	SPAIN	32 765 820
22. HONG KONG	CHINA	32 746 737
23. LONDON GATWICK	UK	32 056 942
24. ORLANDO	USA	30 822 580
25. ST LOUIS LAMBERT	USA	30 546 698
26. BANGKOK	THAILAND	29 621 898
27. TORONTO LESTER B. PEARSON	CANADA	28 820 326
28. SINGAPORE CHANGI	SINGAPORE	28 618 200
29. SEATTLE-TACOMA	USA	28 404 312
30. BOSTON	USA	27 412 926
31. TŌKYŌ NARITA	JAPAN	27 389 915
32. ROME LEONARDO DA VINCI	ITALY	25 921 886
33. PARIS ORLY	FRANCE	25 399 111
34. NEW YORK LA GUARDIA	USA	25 233 889
35. PHILADELPHIA	USA	24 900 621
36. SYDNEY KINGSFORD SMITH	AUSTRALIA	23 553 878
37. MUNICH FRANZ JOSEF STRAUSS	GERMANY	23 125 872
38. CHARLOTTE	USA	23 073 894
39. HONOLULU	USA	22 660 349
40. ZÜRICH	SWITZERLAND	22 649 539

1 **San Francisco International Airport**

Located to the south of San Francisco on the west side of the bay, San Francisco International Airport is the fifth busiest airport in the United States and ninth busiest in the world. Annually, it handles over 40 million passengers using domestic and international flights. This aerial photograph of the airport shows various terminals radiating from a central parking area. The airport is constantly developing in order to cope with the increasing volume of air traffic.

ASTRA 1F

Fig. #04
Busiest scheduled International air passenger routes 1999
Briesemeister Projection

Alps, *France*

europe

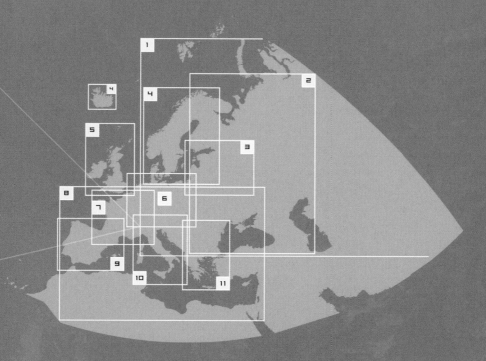

[contents]

		page#
europe [landscapes]		30–31
europe [countries]		32–33
europe [countries/issues]		34–35
europe [environments]		36–37

	map coverage	scale	page#
europe [map 1]	RUSSIAN FEDERATION	1:18 000 000	38-39
europe [map 2]	RUSSIAN FEDERATION West	1:7 500 000	40–41
europe [map 3]	ESTONIA, LATVIA, LITHUANIA and the MOSCOW REGION	1:3 000 000	42–43
europe [map 4]	ICELAND, NORWAY, SWEDEN, FINLAND and DENMARK	1:4 500 000	44–45
europe [map 5]	UNITED KINGDOM and REPUBLIC OF IRELAND	1:3 000 000	46–47
europe [map 6]	EUROPE North Central	1:3 000 000	48–49
europe [map 7]	FRANCE and SWITZERLAND	1:3 000 000	50–51
europe [map 8]	EUROPE South and the MEDITERRANEAN	1:9 000 000	52–53
europe [map 9]	SPAIN and PORTUGAL	1:3 000 000	54–55
europe [map 10]	ITALY, SLOVENIA, CROATIA and BOSNIA-HERZEGOVINA	1:3 000 000	56–57
europe [map 11]	EUROPE Southeast	1:3 000 000	58–59

europe[landscapes]

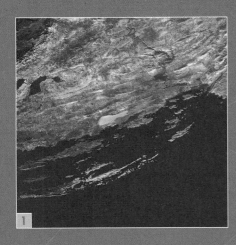
Europe, the world's second smallest continent, is located on the western tip of the vast Eurasian land-mass. The curve of mountain ranges, which includes the Alps, the Pyrenees and the Carpathians divides the north of the continent from the south. The highest peak in Europe, Mt Elbrus (5 642 m) lies in the Caucasus, the mountain range between the Black Sea and the Caspian Sea. North of these mountains, the rolling plains of Ukraine and European Russia extend to the Ural Mountains which, together with the Caucasus and the Bosporus in Turkey, form the physical boundary between Europe and Asia.

The Mediterranean Sea, in the south, is a large inland sea which is enclosed by mainland Europe to the north and west, Africa to the south, and Asia to the east. The Strait of Gibraltar connects the Mediterranean to the Atlantic Ocean on the west and in the southeast the Suez canal is the seaway to the Red Sea.

Largest island

Great Britain
218 476 sq km / 84 354 sq miles
Map reference 47 J7

CONNECTIONS

▶ subject		page#
▶ Types of imagery	⫸	4–5
▶ World physical features	⫸	8–9
▶ Arctic land cover	⫸	18–19
▶ European states and territories	⫸	32–33
▶ Reference maps of Europe	⫸	38–59

Spitsbergen

Norwegian Sea

Scandinavia

Gul
Both

Faroe Islands

North Sea

Elbe River

Rhine River

Great Britain

Ireland

Seine River

English Channel

Loire River

Massif Central

Bay of Biscay

Pyrenees

Balea

Atlantic Ocean

Iberian Peninsula

Tagus River

Strait of Gibraltar

Alps, *Europe*

The snow-capped crescent-shaped Alps, seen here in early spring, separate Italy from the rest of central Europe. The valley in the lower centre of the image is that of the Po river and also visible are Lake Garda, right of centre, and Lake Geneva left of the snow covered area. The Alps are the source of several major European rivers including the Danube, Rhine and Rhone. The highest peak in the mountain range, Mont Blanc 4 804 m, is located on the France/Italy border, centre left on the image.

Satellite/Sensor : MODIS

Volga Delta, *Russian Federation*

The Volga river flows south into the Caspian Sea, over 3 600 km from its source, making it Europe's longest river. In this high oblique shuttle photograph the river delta, viewed from the north, fans out into the landlocked Caspian Sea. The city of Astrakhan is situated at the head of the delta on the west bank of the river. The silt from the delta provides a rich environment for flora and fauna.

Satellite/Sensor : Space Shuttle

Novaya Zemlya

Barents Sea

Lappland

Ural Mountains

Lake Ladoga

Baltic Sea

North European Plain

Vistula River

Volga River

Don River

Dnieper River

Elbrus

Caspian Sea

Carpathian Mountains

Crimea

Caucasus

Danube River

Black Sea

Alps

Bosporus

Po River

Dalmatia

Adriatic Sea

Apennines

Corsica

Sardinia

Sicily

Crete

Islands

Mediterranean Sea

Highest point

Elbrus
Russian Federation
5 642 m / 18 510 feet
Map reference 107 E2

Longest river

Volga
3 688 km / 2 291 miles
Drainage basin
1 380 000 sq km / 533 000 sq miles
Map reference 41 I7

Largest lake

Caspian Sea
371 000 sq km / 143 243 sq miles
Map reference 102 B4

EUROPE

HIGHEST MOUNTAINS	m	ft	location	map
Elbrus	5 642	18 510	Russian Federation	107 E2
Gora Dykh-Tau	5 204	17 073	Russian Federation	41 G8
Shkhara	5 201	17 063	Georgia/Russian Federation	41 G8
Kazbek	5 047	16 558	Georgia/Russian Federation	107 F2
Mont Blanc	4 808	15 774	France/Italy	51 M7
Durfourspitze	4 634	15 203	Italy/Switzerland	51 N7

LARGEST ISLANDS	sq km	sq miles	map
Great Britain	218 476	84 354	47 J9
Iceland	102 820	39 699	44 inset
Novaya Zemlya	90 650	35 000	38 T2
Ireland	83 045	32 064	47 D11
Spitzbergen	37 814	14 600	38 B2
Sicily	25 426	9 817	57 F1

LONGEST RIVERS	km	miles	map
Volga	3 688	2 291	41 I7
Danube	2 850	1 770	58 K3
Dnieper	2 285	1 419	41 E7
Kama	2 028	1 260	40 J4
Don	1 931	1 199	41 F7
Pechora	1 802	1 119	38 F3

LAKES	sq km	sq miles	map
Caspian Sea	371 000	143 243	102 B4
Lake Ladoga	18 390	7 100	40 D3
Lake Onega	9 600	3 706	40 E3
Vänern	5 585	2 156	45 C4
Rybinskoye Vodokhranilishche	5 180	2 000	43 T3

LAND AREA		map
Most northerly point	Ostrov Rudol'fa, Russian Federation	38 F1
Most southerly point	Gavdos, Crete, Greece	59 F14
Most westerly point	Bjargtangar, Iceland	44 A2
Most easterly point	Mys Flissingskiy, Russian Federation	39 G2
Total land area: 9 908 599 sq km / 3 825 731 sq miles		

EUROPE
COUNTRIES

		area sq km	area sq miles	population	capital	languages	religions	currency	map
ALBANIA		28 748	11 100	3 134 000	Tirana (Tiranë)	Albanian, Greek	Sunni Muslim, Albanian Orthodox, Roman Catholic	Lek	58–59
ANDORRA		465	180	86 000	Andorra la Vella	Spanish, Catalan, French	Roman Catholic	French franc, Spanish peseta	55
AUSTRIA		83 855	32 377	8 080 000	Vienna (Wien)	German, Croatian, Turkish	Roman Catholic, Protestant	Schilling, Euro	48–49
BELARUS		207 600	80 155	10 187 000	Minsk	Belorussian, Russian	Belorussian Orthodox, Roman Catholic	Rouble	42–43
BELGIUM		30 520	11 784	10 249 000	Brussels (Bruxelles)	Dutch (Flemish), French (Walloon), German	Roman Catholic, Protestant	Franc, Euro	51
BOSNIA-HERZEGOVINA		51 130	19 741	3 977 000	Sarajevo	Bosnian, Serbian, Croatian	Sunni Muslim, Serbian Orthodox, Roman Catholic, Protestant	Marka	56
BULGARIA		110 994	42 855	7 949 000	Sofia (Sofiya)	Bulgarian, Turkish, Romany, Macedonian	Bulgarian Orthodox, Sunni Muslim	Lev	58
CROATIA		56 538	21 829	4 654 000	Zagreb	Croatian, Serbian	Roman Catholic, Serbian Orthodox, Sunni Muslim	Kuna	56
CZECH REPUBLIC		78 864	30 450	10 272 000	Prague (Praha)	Czech, Moravian, Slovak	Roman Catholic, Protestant	Koruna	49
DENMARK		43 075	16 631	5 320 000	Copenhagen (København)	Danish	Protestant	Krone	45
ESTONIA		45 200	17 452	1 393 000	Tallinn	Estonian, Russian	Protestant, Estonian and Russian Orthodox	Kroon	42
FINLAND		338 145	130 559	5 172 000	Helsinki (Helsingfors)	Finnish, Swedish	Protestant, Greek Orthodox	Markka, Euro	44–45
FRANCE		543 965	210 026	59 238 000	Paris	French, Arabic	Roman Catholic, Protestant, Sunni Muslim	Franc, Euro	50–51
GERMANY		357 028	137 849	82 017 000	Berlin	German, Turkish	Protestant, Roman Catholic	Mark, Euro	48–49
GREECE		131 957	50 949	10 610 000	Athens (Athina)	Greek	Greek Orthodox, Sunni Muslim	Drachma	58–59
HUNGARY		93 030	35 919	9 968 000	Budapest	Hungarian	Roman Catholic, Protestant	Forint	49
ICELAND		102 820	39 699	279 000	Reykjavik	Icelandic	Protestant	Króna	44
IRELAND, REPUBLIC OF		70 282	27 136	3 803 000	Dublin (Baile Átha Cliath)	English, Irish	Roman Catholic, Protestant	Punt, Euro	46–47
ITALY		301 245	116 311	57 530 000	Rome (Roma)	Italian	Roman Catholic	Lira, Euro	56–57
LATVIA		63 700	24 595	2 421 000	Riga	Latvian, Russian	Protestant, Roman Catholic, Russian Orthodox	Lat	42
LIECHTENSTEIN		160	62	33 000	Vaduz	German	Roman Catholic, Protestant	Swiss franc	51
LITHUANIA		65 200	25 174	3 696 000	Vilnius	Lithuanian, Russian, Polish	Roman Catholic, Protestant, Russian Orthodox	Litas	42
LUXEMBOURG		2 586	998	437 000	Luxembourg	Letzeburgish, German, French	Roman Catholic	Franc, Euro	51
MACEDONIA (F.Y.R.O.M.)		25 713	9 928	2 034 000	Skopje	Macedonian, Albanian, Turkish	Macedonian Orthodox, Sunni Muslim	Denar	58
MALTA		316	122	390 000	Valletta	Maltese, English	Roman Catholic	Lira	57
MOLDOVA		33 700	13 012	4 295 000	Chişinău (Kishinev)	Romanian, Ukrainian, Gagauz, Russian	Romanian Orthodox, Russian Orthodox	Leu	41
MONACO		2	1	33 000	Monaco-Ville	French, Monegasque, Italian	Roman Catholic	French franc	51
NETHERLANDS		41 526	16 033	15 864 000	Amsterdam/The Hague	Dutch, Frisian	Roman Catholic, Protestant, Sunni Muslim	Guilder, Euro	48
NORWAY		323 878	125 050	4 469 000	Oslo	Norwegian	Protestant, Roman Catholic	Krone	44–45

CONNECTIONS

▶ subject	page#
▶ World countries	10–11
▶ Europe landscapes	30–31
▶ Europe issues	34–35
▶ Reference maps of Europe	38–59
▶ Atlantic Ocean	216–217

1 Rock of Gibraltar, *Gibraltar, Europe*

The narrow passage of water, appearing as a horizontal band of blue across the centre of this photograph is the 13 km wide Strait of Gibraltar which connects the Atlantic Ocean to the Mediterranean Sea. The strait forms a physical boundary between the continents of Europe and Africa. The photograph shows the 426 m high Rock of Gibraltar, viewed from Ceuta, a small Spanish enclave in Morocco, on the northern coast of Africa.

2 Bosporus, *Turkey, Europe/Asia*

The continents of Europe and Asia are physically separated by a narrow strait of water, the Bosporus, in Turkey. The strait, which at its narrowest point is less than 1 km wide, is 31 km long and connects the Sea of Marmara in the north to the Black Sea in the south. It is straddled by the city of Istanbul. The strait and the city are clearly shown in this SPOT satellite image. Istanbul airport is located near the coast toward the lower left of the image.

Satellite/Sensor : SPOT

Berlin, *Germany*

Berlin, Germany's capital city until 1945, is now the national capital of the reunified Germany. In this near true-colour SPOT satellite image the path of the wall which formerly divided the city for over 25 years, can be seen on the northern outskirts of the city. In the top right, northeast of the river Spree which can be seen running across the centre of the image, is a large development of tower blocks built in the former Eastern sector.

Satellite/Sensor : SPOT

EUROPE

TOP 10 COUNTRIES BY AREA

	sq km	sq miles	map	world rank
1. RUSSIAN FEDERATION	17 075 400	6 592 849	38–39	1.
2. UKRAINE	603 700	233 090	41	44
3. FRANCE	543 965	210 026	50–51	48
4. SPAIN	504 782	194 897	54–55	51
5. SWEDEN	449 964	173 732	44–45	55
6. GERMANY	357 028	137 849	48–49	62
7. FINLAND	338 145	130 559	44–45	64
8. NORWAY	323 878	125 050	44–45	67
9. POLAND	312 683	120 728	49	69
10. ITALY	301 245	116 311	56–57	71

TOP 10 COUNTRIES BY POPULATION

	population	map	world rank
1. RUSSIAN FEDERATION	145 491 000	38–39	6
2. GERMANY	82 017 000	48–49	12
3. UNITED KINGDOM	59 634 000	46–47	20
4. FRANCE	59 238 000	50–51	21
5. ITALY	57 530 000	56–57	22
6. UKRAINE	49 568 000	41	24
7. SPAIN	39 910 000	54–55	29
8. POLAND	38 605 000	49	30
9. ROMANIA	22 438 000	58	44
10. NETHERLANDS	15 864 000	48	58

EUROPE

COUNTRIES

		area sq km	area sq miles	population	capital	languages	religions	currency	map
POLAND		312 683	120 728	38 605 000	Warsaw (Warszawa)	Polish, German	Roman Catholic, Polish Orthodox	Złoty	49
PORTUGAL		88 940	34 340	10 016 000	Lisbon (Lisboa)	Portuguese	Roman Catholic, Protestant	Escudo, Euro	54
ROMANIA		237 500	91 699	22 438 000	Bucharest (Bucureşti)	Romanian, Hungarian	Romanian Orthodox, Protestant, Roman Catholic	Leu	58
RUSSIAN FEDERATION		17 075 400	6 592 849	145 491 000	Moscow (Moskva)	Russian, Tatar, Ukrainian, local languages	Russian Orthodox, Sunni Muslim, Protestant	Rouble	38–39
SAN MARINO		61	24	27 000	San Marino	Italian	Roman Catholic	Italian lira	56
SLOVAKIA		49 035	18 933	5 399 000	Bratislava	Slovak, Hungarian, Czech	Roman Catholic, Protestant, Orthodox	Koruna	49
SLOVENIA		20 251	7 819	1 988 000	Ljubljana	Slovene, Croatian, Serbian	Roman Catholic, Protestant	Tólar	56
SPAIN		504 782	194 897	39 910 000	Madrid	Castilian, Catalan, Galician, Basque	Roman Catholic	Peseta, Euro	54–55
SWEDEN		449 964	173 732	8 842 000	Stockholm	Swedish	Protestant, Roman Catholic	Krona	44–45
SWITZERLAND		41 293	15 943	7 170 000	Bern (Berne)	German, French, Italian, Romansch	Roman Catholic, Protestant	Franc	51
UKRAINE		603 700	233 090	49 568 000	Kiev (Kyiv)	Ukrainian, Russian	Ukrainian Orthodox, Ukrainian Catholic, Roman Catholic	Hryvnia	41
UNITED KINGDOM		244 082	94 241	59 634 000	London	English, Welsh, Gaelic	Protestant, Roman Catholic, Muslim	Pound	46–47
VATICAN CITY		0.5	0.2	480	Vatican City	Italian	Roman Catholic	Italian lira	56
YUGOSLAVIA		102 173	39 449	10 552 000	Belgrade (Beograd)	Serbian, Albanian, Hungarian	Serbian Orthodox, Montenegrin Orthodox, Sunni Muslim	Dinar	58

DEPENDENT TERRITORIES

		territorial status	area sq km	area sq miles	population	capital	languages	religions	currency	map
Azores (Arquipélago dos Açores)		Autonomous Region of Portugal	2 300	888	243 600	Ponta Delgada	Portuguese	Roman Catholic, Protestant	Port. Escudo	216
Faroe Islands		Self-governing Danish Territory	1 399	540	46 000	Tórshavn (Thorshavn)	Faroese, Danish	Protestant	Danish krone	46
Gibraltar		United Kingdom Overseas Territory	7	3	27 000	Gibraltar	English, Spanish	Roman Catholic, Protestant, Sunni Muslim	Pound	54
Guernsey		United Kingdom Crown Dependency	78	30	64 555	St Peter Port	English, French	Protestant, Roman Catholic	Pound	50
Isle of Man		United Kingdom Crown Dependency	572	221	77 000	Douglas	English	Protestant, Roman Catholic	Pound	47
Jersey		United Kingdom Crown Dependency	116	45	89 136	St Helier	English, French	Protestant, Roman Catholic	Pound	50

1 The European Union

The European Union (EU) is a union of fifteen independent European states. It was founded as the European Economic Commission by the Treaty of Rome in 1957. Its purpose is to enhance political, economic and social cooperation. As shown on the map, the EU has grown from six to fifteen members and thirteen new applicants are currently negotiating for membership. The headquarters of the EU, in the Belgian capital Brussels, is the curved glass roofed building, known as the Hémicycle Européen, shown in the photograph.

Fig. #01
The European Union

- Founder members (1957)
- Joined in 1973
- Joined in 1981
- Joined in 1986
- Joined in 1995
- Current applicant
- Non-member

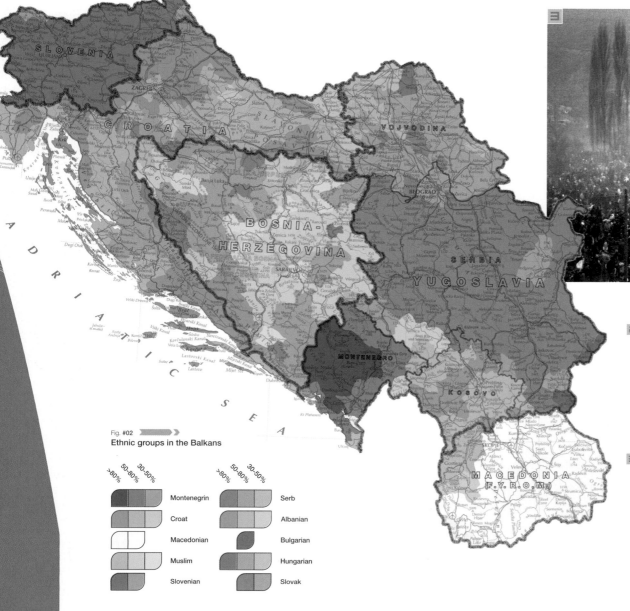

Fig. #02
Ethnic groups in the Balkans

	>80%	50-80%	30-50%			>80%	50-80%	30-50%
				Montenegrin					Serb
				Croat					Albanian
				Macedonian					Bulgarian
				Muslim					Hungarian
				Slovenian					Slovak

2 Caucasus, *Europe/Asia*

The Caucasus mountains extend from the eastern shores of the Black Sea to the southwest coast of the Caspian Sea and form an almost impenetrable barrier between Europe in the north, and Asia in the south. Europe's highest mountain, Elbrus, reaches 5 642 m in the western end of the range. The plains lying north of the Caucasus, seen in the lower half of this Shuttle photograph, are part of the Russian Federation and include the region of Chechnia. On the southern slopes of the mountains are the countries of Georgia and Azerbaijan.

Satellite/Sensor : Space Shuttle

3 The Balkans, *Europe*

The region of the Balkans has a long history of instability and ethnic conflict. The map shows the underlying complexity of the ethnic composition of the former country of Yugoslavia. The 1990 Yugoslav elections uncovered these divisions and over the next three years, four of the six Yugoslav republics – Croatia, Slovenia, Bosnia-Herzegovina and Macedonia – each declared their independence. The civil war continued until 1995 when the Dayton Peace Accord was established. In Kosovo, a sub-division of the Yugoslav republic of Serbia, the majority population of Muslim Albanians were forced to accept direct Serbian rule, and as a result support grew for the independence-seeking rebel Kosovo Liberation Army. In 1998 and 1999 the Serbs reacted through 'ethnic cleansing' of Kosovo, when many Kosovans were killed and, as shown in the photograph, thousands were forced to flee their homes. After NATO action, an agreement for Serb withdrawal was reached in June 1999.

CONNECTIONS

► subject		page#
► World physical features		8–9
► World countries		10–11
► Europe landscapes		30–31
► Europe countries		32–33
► Reference maps of Europe		38–59

europe[environments]

1 Lakelands, *Finland*

This aerial photograph, taken to the east of Kuopio, shows an environment typical of the lakeland areas of central Finland. The country is mostly lowland, with many lakes, marshes, and low hills. The vast forested interior plateau includes approximately 60 000 lakes, many of which are linked by short rivers, or canals to form commercial waterways.

2 Volcanic Environment, *Iceland*

The steam rising from the mountain side in this photograph is a result of volcanic activity. Iceland is a country with nearly 200 volcanoes, many of them still active. These create, and have created, great lava fields and rough mountainous terrain. Perhaps the most notable volcano is Hekla which rises to 1 491 m and had a major eruption in 1991. Hot springs and geysers are also common, and their geothermal energy is commonly used for domestic heating.

3 Mediterranean Island, *Europe*

This satellite image of the French island of Corsica in the Mediterranean Sea shows a mountainous island with some flat areas in the form of lagoons and marshes on the eastern coast. The highest point of the island is Monte Cinto, 2 706 m, which is towards the north of the pale, mountainous area.

Satellite/sensor : SPOT

4 Agricultural Region, *Italy*

The numerous rectangles in this satellite image are a patchwork of fields found in the Fucino plain, to the east of Avezzano, Italy. This area was formerly a lake which was drained in the mid-nineteenth century and now provides over 160 square kilometres of fertile farmland. Today the area is intensely cultivated with a variety of crops being grown, including cereals, potatoes, sugar beet, grapes and fruit.

Satellite/Sensor : Landsat

5 Planned Village, *The Netherlands*

This aerial photograph shows the village of Bourtange located in the extreme south-east of Groningen province in the Netherlands, less than 2 km from the German border. The star-shaped fortress dates back to the late sixteenth century. The old core of the village was restored in 1967 and has since been protected as a national monument.

6 Mountainous Coastline, *United Kingdom*

This satellite image of the west coast of Scotland clearly shows the effect of the last ice age on this landscape. Retreating glaciers left long, deep valleys, high mountains and a very rugged, indented coastline. The barren mountains are clearly identified as the white areas of bare rock. Water appears as darker areas with Loch Maree being the largest loch in the centre of the image.

Satellite/Sensor : Landsat

7 Urban Environment, *United Kingdom*

This aerial photograph shows part of the centre of London, the capital city of the United Kingdom. Westminster, the seat of the British government, is located on the left bank of the River Thames at the bottom of the photograph. Other notable features are Buckingham Palace (bottom left), St James's Park, Waterloo Station (bottom right) and the London Eye observation wheel in its flat construction position over the river, prior to its final erection and completion.

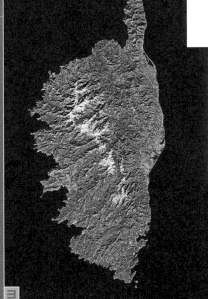

CONNECTIONS

► subject		page#
► World land cover types		18–19
► World cities		24–25
► Europe landscapes		30–31
► Reference maps of Europe		38–59
► North America environments		162–163

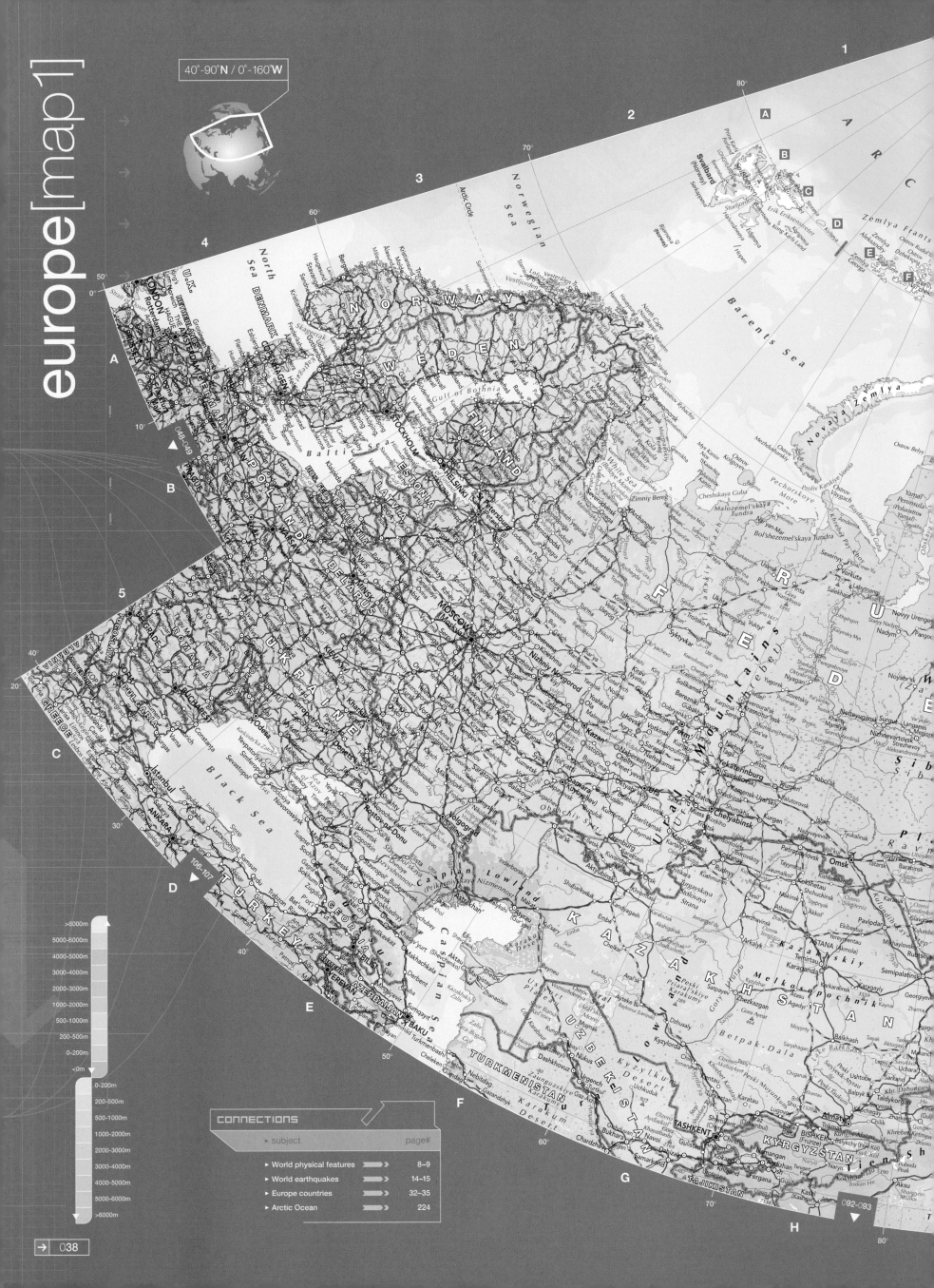

40°-90°N / 0°-160°W

>6000m
5000-6000m
4000-5000m
3000-4000m
2000-3000m
1000-2000m
500-1000m
200-500m
0-200m
<0m

0-200m
200-500m
500-1000m
1000-2000m
2000-3000m
3000-4000m
4000-5000m
5000-6000m
>6000m

CONNECTIONS

▶ subject	page#
▶ World physical features	8–9
▶ World earthquakes	14–15
▶ Europe countries	32–35
▶ Arctic Ocean	224

CONNECTIONS

▶ subject   page#

▲ World cities   24-25
▲ Europe landscapes   30-31
▲ Europe countries   32-35
▲ Europe environments   36-37

Ural Mountains
(Ural'skiy Khrebet)

Barents Sea

Pechorskoye More

Novaya Zemlya

NENETSKIY AVTONOMNYY OKRUG

RESPUBLIKA KOMI

Timanskiy Kryazh

White Sea
(Beloye More)

Kola Peninsula
(Kol'skiy Poluostrov)

MURMANSKAYA OBLAST'

ARKHANGEL'SKAYA OBLAST'

VOLOGODSKAYA OBLAST'

RESPUBLIKA KARELIYA

RUSSIAN

Murmansk

Archangel
Severodvinsk

Dvinskaya Guba

Onezhskaya Guba

Lake Onega

Lake Ladoga
(Ladozhskoye Ozero)

St Petersburg
(Sankt-Peterburg)

Moscow

TVERSKAYA OBLAST'

NOVGORODSKAYA OBLAST'

LENINGRADSKAYA OBLAST'

PSKOVSKAYA OBLAST'

KOSTROMSKAYA OBLAST'

KIROVSKAYA

RESPUBLIKA TATARSTAN

RESPUBLIKA BASHKORTOSTAN

Nizhniy Novgorod

NORWAY

SWEDEN

FINLAND

HELSINKI
(Helsingfors)

Gulf of Finland

TALLINN

ESTONIA

Gulf of Bothnia

Baltic Sea

Gulf of Riga

LATVIA

LITHUANIA

VILNIUS

048-040

41°-71°N / 20°-54°E

Conic Equidistant Projection

1:7 500 000

Administrative divisions in Russian
Federation numbered on the map:

1. RESPUBLIKA ADYGEYA (G7)
2. CHECHENSKAYA RESPUBLIKA (CHECHNIA) (H8)
3. RESPUBLIKA INGUSHETIYA (INGUSHETIA) (H8)
4. KABARDINO-BALKARSKAYA RESPUBLIKA (G8)
5. KARACHAYEVO-CHERKESSKAYA RESPUBLIKA (G8)
6. RESPUBLIKA SEVERNAYA OSETIYA-ALANIYA
   (NORTH OSSETIA) (H8)

europe[map3]

52°-61°N / 20°-40°E

CONNECTIONS

Elevation scale

>6000m
5000-6000m
4000-5000m
3000-4000m
2000-3000m
1500-2000m
1000-1500m
500-1000m
200-500m
100-200m
0-100m
<0m

0-50m
50-100m
100-200m
200-500m
500-1000m
1000-2000m
2000-3000m
3000-4000m
4000-5000m
5000-6000m
>6000m

1:3 000 000

miles
0   25   50   75   100   125
0 25 50 75 100 125 150 175 200
km

Conic Equidistant Projection

048-049

Map labels (selected):

Gulf of Bothnia · Åland Islands · Ålands Hav · Baltic Sea · Gulf of Finland · Gulf of Riga · Gulf of Gdańsk · Irbe Strait

FINLAND · VARSINAIS-SUOMI · LÄNSI-SUOMI · ETELÄ-SUOMI · HELSINKI (Helsingfors) · Turku (Åbo) · Espoo

ESTONIA · TALLINN · Hiiumaa · Saaremaa · Muhu · Pärnu · Viljandi · Lake Peipus

LATVIA · RĪGA · Ventspils · Liepāja · Jūrmala · Jelgava · Daugavpils · Vidzemes Centrālā Augstiene

LITHUANIA · VILNIUS · Klaipėda · Šiauliai · Panevėžys · Kaunas · Marijampolė · Alytus

RUSSIAN FEDERATION · KALININGRADSKAYA OBLAST · Kaliningrad · Chernyakhovsk

POLAND · WARSAW (Warszawa) · Mazowiecka · Mazurskie · Pojezierze · Płock · Białystok · Siedlce

BELARUS · MINSK · Hrodzyenskaya Voblasts · Brestskaya Voblasts · Minskaya Voblasts

ARCTIC OCEAN

Barents Sea

Norwegian Sea

RUSSIAN FEDERATION

FINLAND

CONNECTIONS

▶ subject   page#

▲ World countries   10–11
▲ World earthquakes and volcanoes 14–15
▲ Europe landscapes   30–31
▲ Europe countries   32–35
▲ Europe environments   36–37

1:4 500 000

miles 30
0   50
km

ICELAND

REYKJAVÍK

Faxaflói

Breiðafjörður

Arctic Circle

>6000m
5000–6000m
4000–5000m
3000–4000m
2000–3000m
1500–2000m
1000–1500m
500–1000m
200–500m
100–200m
0–100m
<0m

<0m
0–50m
50–100m
100–200m
200–500m
500–1000m
1000–2000m
2000–3000m
3000–4000m
4000–5000m
5000–6000m
>6000m

europe[map4]

54°–72°N / 4°–28°E

1:4 500 000

Conic Equidistant Projection

miles
km

048-049

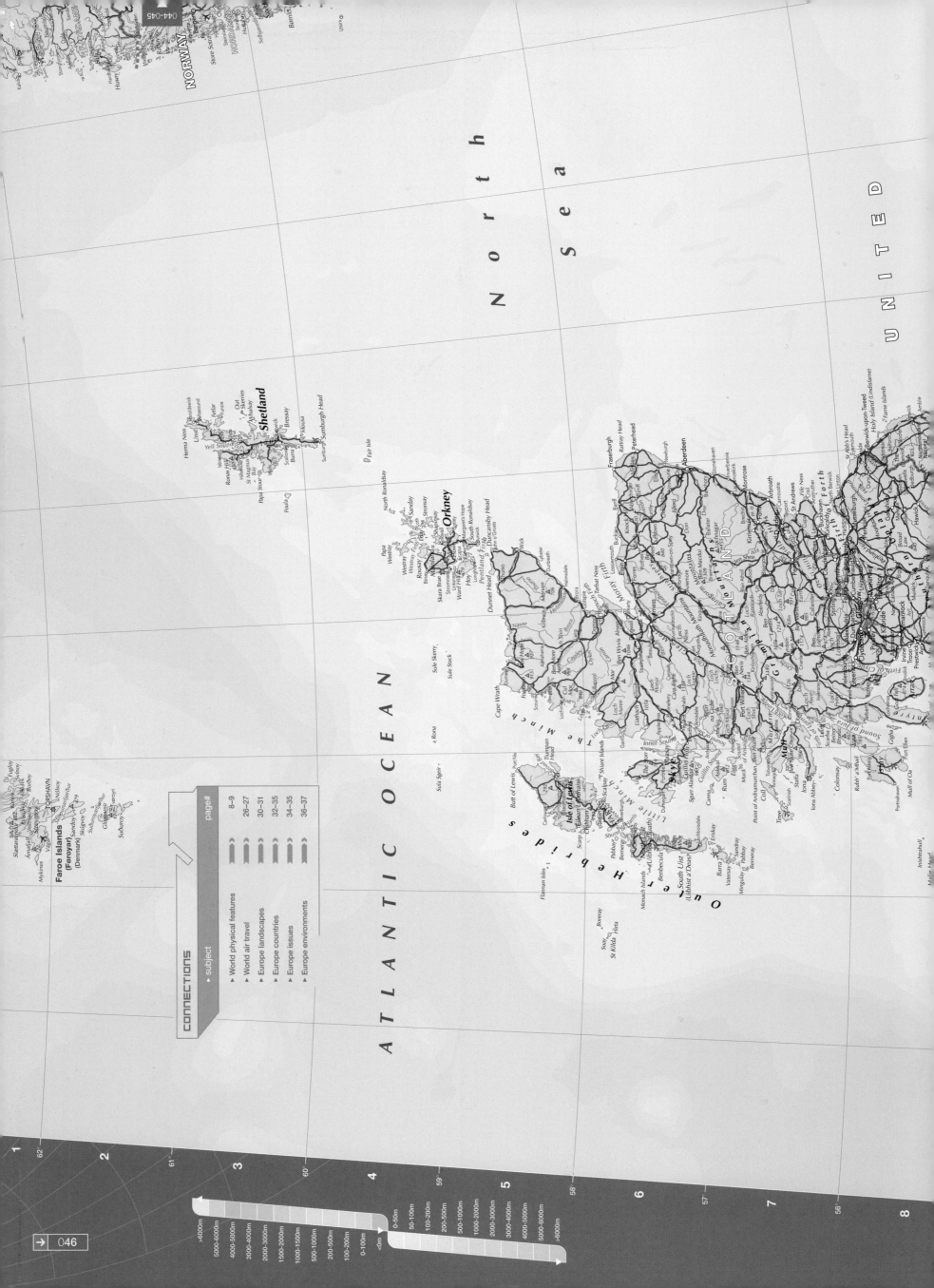

50°-62°N / 11°W-3°E

GREAT BRITAIN

UNITED KINGDOM

ENGLAND

WALES

Cambrian Mountains

REPUBLIC OF IRELAND

NORTHERN IRELAND

ULSTER

CONNAUGHT

LEINSTER

MUNSTER

FRANCE

BELGIUM

PICARDIE

HAUTE-NORMANDIE

Irish Sea

Celtic Sea

English Channel (La Manche)

St George's Channel

Bristol Channel

North Channel

Isle of Man (U.K.)

DOUGLAS

LONDON

DUBLIN (Baile Átha Cliath)

Cardiff (Caerdydd)

1:3 000 000

Conic Equidistant Projection

miles

km

050–051

europe[map6]

46°-55°N / 4°-22°E

North Sea

DENMARK

NETHERLANDS

BELGIUM

LUXEMBOURG

GERMANY

FRANCE

SWITZERLAND

ALPS

ITALIA

>6000m
5000-6000m
4000-5000m
3000-4000m
2000-3000m
1500-2000m
1000-1500m
500-1000m
200-500m
100-200m
0-100m
<0m

0-50m
50-100m
100-200m
200-500m
500-1000m
1000-2000m
2000-3000m
3000-4000m
4000-5000m
5000-6000m
>6000m

1 : 3 000 000

miles 0 25 50 75 100 125
km 0 25 50 75 100 125 150 175 200

Conic Equidistant Projection

050–051

056-057

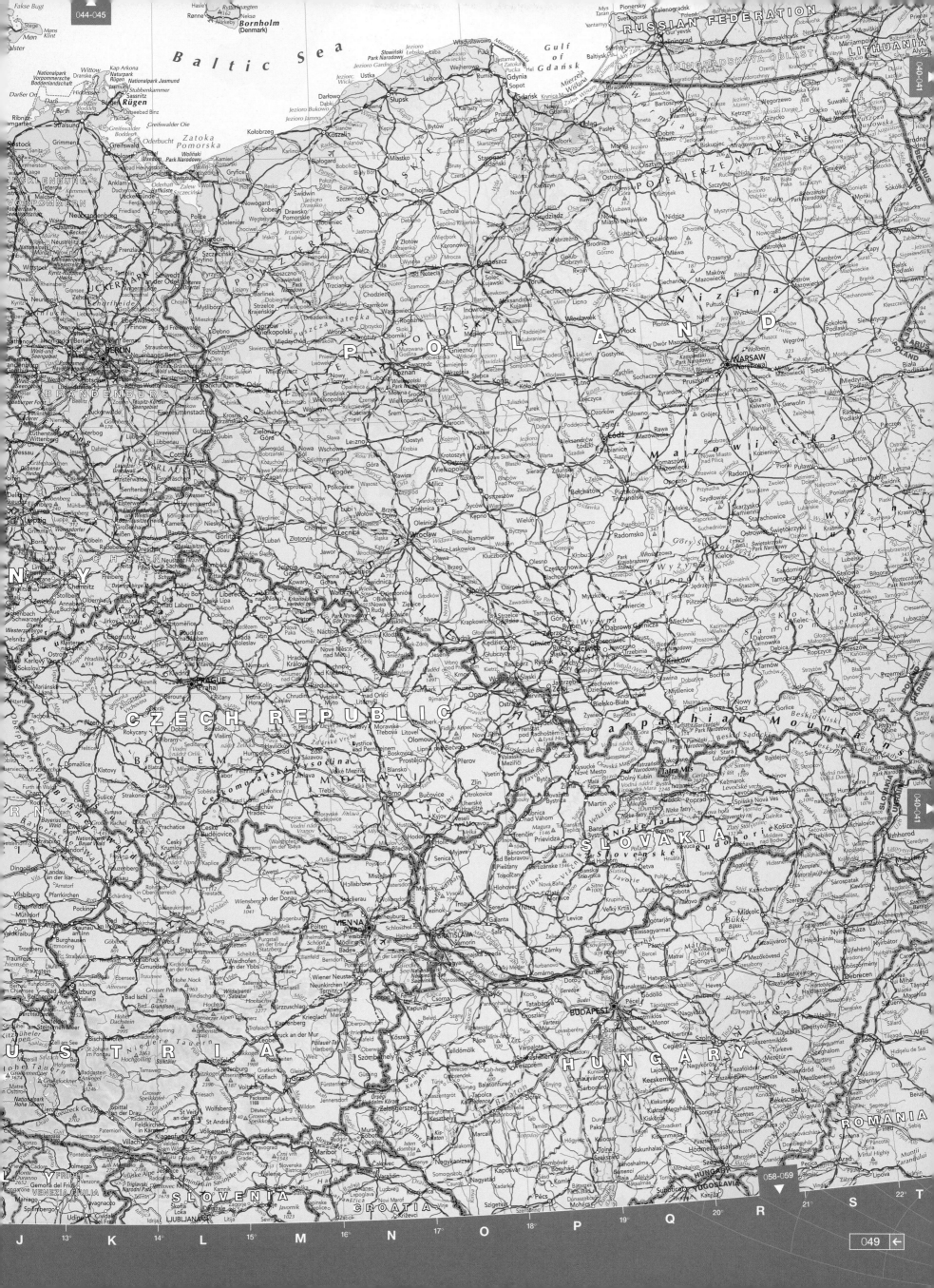

europe[map7]

43°-51°N / 6°W-11°E

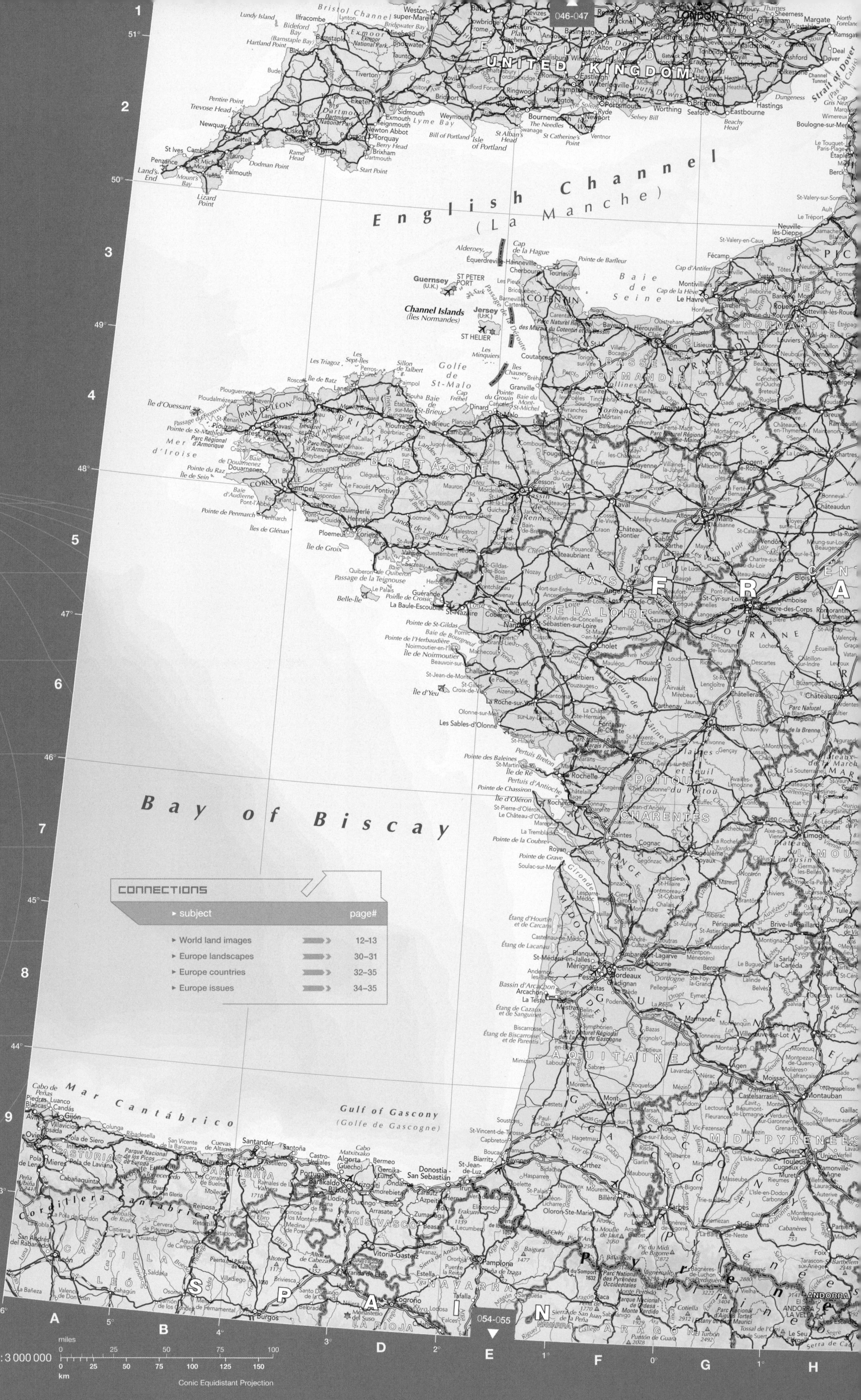

UNITED KINGDOM

English Channel
(La Manche)

Channel Islands
(Îles Normandes)

BRETAGNE

FRANCE

Bay of Biscay

Gulf of Gascony
(Golfe de Gascogne)

Mar Cantábrico

SPAIN

PYRÉNÉES

ANDORRA

CONNECTIONS

▶ subject   page#

▸ World land images   ⇒   12–13
▸ Europe landscapes   ⇒   30–31
▸ Europe countries   ⇒   32–35
▸ Europe issues   ⇒   34–35

>6000m
5000-6000m
4000-5000m
3000-4000m
2000-3000m
1500-2000m
1000-1500m
500-1000m
200-500m
100-200m
0-100m
<0m
0-50m
50-100m
100-200m
200-500m
500-1000m
1000-2000m
2000-3000m
3000-4000m
4000-5000m
5000-6000m
>6000m

→ 050

miles
0   25   50   75   100

1:3 000 000

km
0   25   50   75   100   125   150

Conic Equidistant Projection

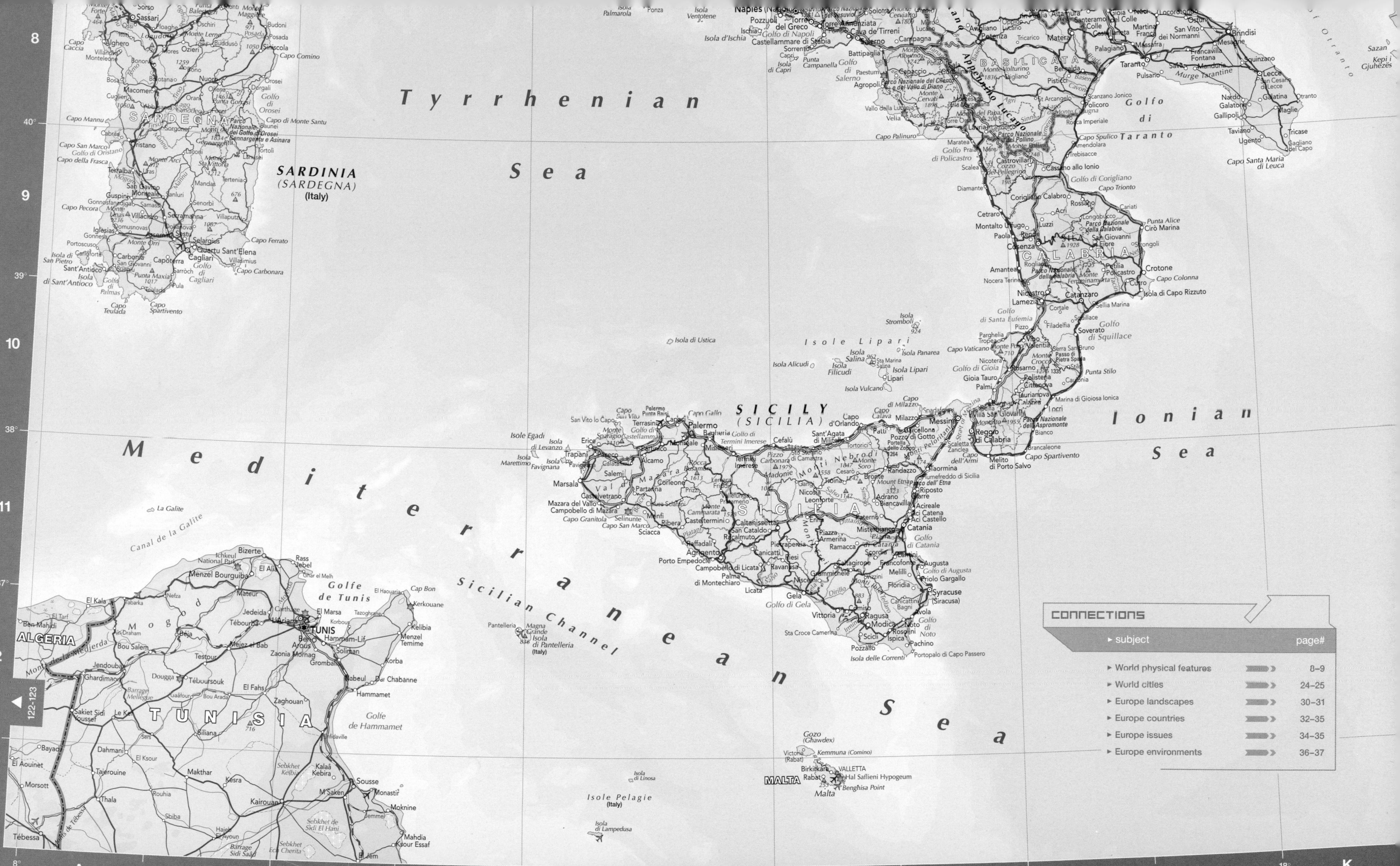
Tyrrhenian Sea
SARDINIA
(SARDEGNA)
(Italy)
Mediterranean Sea
Ionian Sea
Sicilian Channel
SICILY
(SICILIA)
Canal de la Galite
Golfo di Taranto
Golfo di Squillace
Golfe de Tunis
Golfe de Hammamet
Isole Lipari
Isole Pelagie
(Italy)
Isola di Pantelleria
(Italy)
TUNISIA
ALGERIA
MALTA
VALLETTA
TUNIS
Naples
Palermo
Messina
Reggio di Calabria
Catania
Syracuse
(Siracusa)
Cagliari
Sassari
Taranto
Brindisi
Lecce
Bizerte
Sousse
Kairouan
Gozo
(Ghawdex)
BASILICATA
CALABRIA
SARDEGNA
Appennino Lucano
8
9
10
11
12
13
A
B
C
D
E
F
G
H
I
J
K
8°
9°
10°
11°
12°
13°
14°
15°
16°
17°
18°
36°
37°
38°
39°
40°
122-123

CONNECTIONS

▸ subject	page#
▸ World physical features	8–9
▸ World cities	24–25
▸ Europe landscapes	30–31
▸ Europe countries	32–35
▸ Europe issues	34–35
▸ Europe environments	36–37

35°-48°N / 8°-19°E

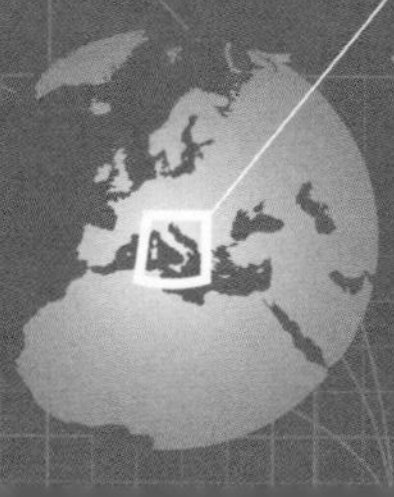

1:3 000 000

miles 0 25 50 75 100 125

km 0 25 50 75 100 125 150 175 200

Conic Equidistant Projection

europe[map10]

europe[map11]

35°-47°N / 19°-29°E

CONNECTIONS

▶ subject | page#
- ▲ Europe landscapes — 30–31
- ▲ Europe countries — 32–33
- ▲ Europe issues — 34–35
- ▲ Mediterranean Sea — 52–53

1:3 000 000
Conic Equidistant Projection

miles
km

Seas and regions:

Aegean Sea
Ionian Sea
Mediterranean Sea
Krytiko Pelagos
Mirtoö Pelagos
VOREIO AIGAIO
NOTIO AIGAIO

Countries and areas:

TURKEY
GREECE
MAKEDONIA
THESSALIA
STEREA ELLAS
DYTIKI ELLAS
PELOPONNISOS
ATTIKI
IPEIROS
Pindus Mountains

BALIKESIR
CANAKKALE
BURSA
KUTAHYA
MANISA
IZMIR
AYDIN
MUGLA
DENIZLI

Islands and places:

Corfu (Kérkyra)
Cephalonia (Kefallinía)
Zakynthos (Zante)
Ionian Islands
Lesbos (Lésvos)
Limnos
Chios
Ikaria
Samos
Patmos
Leros
Kos
Rhodes (Ródos)
Karpathos
Crete (Kríti)
Kárpathos
Cyclades (Kykládes)
Naxos
Paros
Mykonos
Tinos
Andros
Syros
Santorini (Thíra)
Ios
Amorgos
Astypalaia
Dodecanese (Dodekánisos)

ATHENS (Athína)
Piraeus
Patras
Ioannina
Gulf of Corinth
Voreioi Sporades
Evvoia
Chalkida
Thessaloniki

Gökçeada
Samothraki
Thrakikó

Osaka, *Japan*

asia

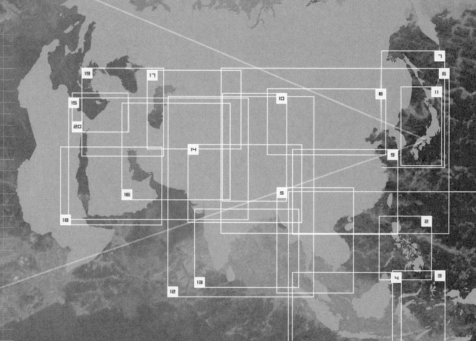

[contents]

		page#
asia [landscapes]		62–63
asia [countries]		64–65
asia [countries/issues]		66–67
asia [changes]		68–69
asia [threats]		70–71

	map coverage	scale	page#
asia [map 1]	ASIA Southeast	1:13 000 000	72–73
asia [map 2]	PHILIPPINES	1:6 000 000	74
asia [map 3]	INDONESIA Central	1:6 000 000	75
asia [map 4]	INDONESIA West, MALAYSIA and SINGAPORE	1:6 000 000	76–77
asia [map 5]	MYANMAR, THAILAND, LAOS and VIETNAM	1:6 000 000	78–79
asia [map 6]	ASIA East	1:13 000 000	80–81
asia [map 7]	ASIA Northeast	1:6 000 000	82–83
asia [map 8]	CHINA North and MONGOLIA	1:6 000 000	84–85
asia [map 9]	CHINA South	1:6 000 000	86–87
asia [map 10]	CHINA West	1:6 000 000	88–89
asia [map 11]	JAPAN	1:4 000 000	90–91
asia [map 12]	ASIA Central and South	1:12 000 000	92–93
asia [map 13]	INDIA South and SRI LANKA	1:6 000 000	94–95
asia [map 14]	INDIA North, BANGLADESH and NEPAL	1:6 000 000	96–97
asia [map 15]	ASIA Southwest	1:11 000 000	98–99
asia [map 16]	IRAN, AFGHANISTAN and PAKISTAN	1:6 000 000	100–101
asia [map 17]	KAZAKHSTAN, UZBEKISTAN and KYRGYZSTAN	1:6 000 000	102–103
asia [map 18]	SAUDI ARABIA and THE GULF STATES	1:6 000 000	104–105
asia [map 19]	TURKEY, IRAQ, and TRANS-CAUCASIAN REPUBLICS	1:6 000 000	106–107
asia [map 20]	MIDDLE EAST	1:3 000 000	108–109

asia[landscapes]

Largest drainage basin
Ob'-Irtysh
2 990 000 sq km / 1 154 000 sq miles
Map reference 38 G3-39 I5

Ob' River

Ural Mountains

Kirghiz
Steppe

Yenisey River

West Siberian
Plain

Siberia

Black Sea

Caucasus

Mediterranean
Sea

Irtysh River

Euphrates River

Elburz
Mountains

Caspian
Sea

Aral Sea

Lake Balkhash

Central Siberian
Plateau

Tigris River

Zagros
Mountains

Arabian
Peninsula

The Gulf

Hindu
Kush

Tien Shan

Altai Mountains

Lake Baikal

Tarim Pendi

Indus River

Kunlun Shan

Gobi

Himalaya

Plateau of Tibet

Yellow River

Largest lake
Caspian Sea
371 000 sq km / 143 243 sq miles
Map reference 102 B4

Mount Everest

Ganges River

Arabian Sea

Bay of
Bengal

Yangtze River

Sri Lanka

Highest point
Mt Everest
China/Nepal
8 848 m / 29 028 ft
Map reference 97 E4

Irrawaddy River

East
S

Indian Ocean

Gulf of
Thailand

Malay
Peninsula

South
China Sea

Ryuky

Longest river
Yangtze
6 380 km / 3 964 miles
Map reference 87 G2

Mekong River

Sumatra

Philippines

Borneo

Java

Java Sea

Celebes

Largest island
Borneo
745 561 sq km / 287 863 sq miles
Map reference 77 F2

Palau

Timor

New Guinea

Arctic Ocean

Lena River

Argun River

Heilong Jiang River

Sea of Okhotsk

Kamchatka Peninsula

Sea of Japan

China ...a

...slands

Honshu

Pacific Ocean

Northern Mariana Islands

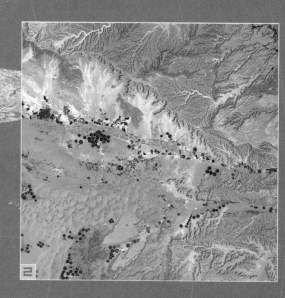

Asia is the world's largest continent and its huge range of physical features is evident in this perspective view from the southeast. These include in southwest Asia the Arabian Peninsula, in southern Asia the Indian subcontinent, in southeast Asia the vast Indonesian archipelago, in central Asia the Plateau of Tibet and the Gobi desert and in east Asia the volcanic islands of Japan and the Kamchatka Peninsula.

North to south, the continent extends over 76 degrees of latitude from the Arctic Ocean in the north to the southern tip of Indonesia in the south. The Ural Mountains and the Caucasus in the west form the boundary with Europe. Asia's most impressive mountain range is the Himalaya, which contains the world's highest peaks. The continent is drained by some of the world's longest rivers and the Caspian Sea is the world's largest lake or inland sea.

1 Himalayas, China/Nepal

This view of the Himalayas shows Mount Everest, at 8 848 m the world's highest mountain. The photograph looks south from the Plateau of Tibet, with its typical barren landscape in the foreground. The plateau lies at a height of over 4 000 m. The Himalayas mark the southern limit of the plateau and stretch for over 2 000 km, forming the northern limit of the Indian sub-continent.

2 Arabian Desert, Saudi Arabia

The arid desert areas to the southwest of Riyadh, Saudi Arabia are shown in this infrared satellite image. Sand shows as yellow and bare rock as grey. Extensive drainage patterns belie the fact that this area only receives 100 mm of rain each year. These are dry river beds for most of the year. The red dots are circular fields with centre-pivot irrigation systems. Water is fed through large revolving sprinklers.

Satellite/Sensor : SPOT

3 Ganges Delta, India

This infrared satellite image shows the Hugli river in the western part of the Ganges delta, flowing into the Bay of Bengal. Vegetation shows as red in the image and the pale blue areas depict water full of sediment. The strong red indicates areas of mangrove swamp. The delta is a huge area, over 300 km across. The fertile soil is intensively farmed but the area is often flooded, particularly as a result of tropical cyclones.

Satellite/Sensor : SPOT

ASIA

HIGHEST MOUNTAINS

	m	ft	location	map
Mt Everest	8 848	29 028	China/Nepal	97 E4
K2	8 611	28 251	China/Jammu and Kashmir	96 C2
Kangchenjunga	8 586	28 169	India/Nepal	97 F4
Lhotse	8 516	27 939	China/Nepal	97 E4
Makalu	8 463	27 765	China/Nepal	97 E4
Cho Oyu	8 201	26 906	China/Nepal	97 E3
Dhaulagiri	8 167	26 794	Nepal	97 D3
Manaslu	8 163	26 781	Nepal	97 E3
Nanga Parbat	8 126	26 660	Jammu and Kashmir	96 B2
Annapurna 1	8 091	26 545	Nepal	97 D3

LARGEST ISLANDS

	sq km	sq miles	map
Borneo	745 561	287 863	77 F2
Sumatra	473 606	182 860	76 C3
Honshu	227 414	87 805	91 F6
Celebes	189 216	73 057	75 B3
Java	132 188	51 038	77 E4
Luzon	104 690	40 421	76 B2
Mindanao	94 630	36 537	74 C5
Hokkaido	78 073	30 144	90 H3
Sakhalin	76 400	29 498	82 F2
Sri Lanka	65 610	25 332	94 D5
Kyushu	36 554	14 114	91 B8
Taiwan	35 873	13 851	87 G4

LONGEST RIVERS

	km	miles	map
Yangtze	6 380	3 964	87 G2
Ob'-Irtysh	5 568	3 459	38 G3 -39 I5
Yenisey-Angara -Selenga	5 550	3 448	39 I2-K4
Yellow	5 464	3 395	85 H4
Irtysh	4 440	2 759	38 G3
Mekong	4 425	2 749	79 D6
Heilong Jiang -Argun'	4 416	2 744	81 M3
Lena-Kirenga	4 400	2 734	39 M2 -K4
Yenisey	4 090	2 541	39 I2
Ob'	3 701	2 300	38 H3

LAKES

	sq km	sq miles	map
Caspian Sea	371 000	143 243	102 B4
Aral Sea	33 640	12 988	102 D3
Lake Baikal	30 500	11 776	39 K4
Lake Balkhash	17 400	6 718	103 H3
Ysyk-Köl	6 200	2 393	103 I4

LAND AREA

		map
Most northerly point	Mys Arkticheskiy, Russian Federation	39 J1
Most southerly point	Pamana, Indonesia	75 B5
Most westerly point	Bozcaada, Turkey	59 H9
Most easterly point	Mys Dezhneva, Russian Federation	39 T3

Total land area: 45 036 492 sq km / 17 388 686 sq miles

ASIA
COUNTRIES

		area sq km	area sq miles	population	capital	languages	religions	currency	map
AFGHANISTAN		652 225	251 825	21 765 000	Kābul	Dari, Pushtu, Uzbek, Turkmen	Sunni Muslim, Shi'a Muslim	Afghani	101
ARMENIA		29 800	11 506	3 787 000	Yerevan (Erevan)	Armenian, Azeri	Armenian Orthodox	Dram	107
AZERBAIJAN		86 600	33 436	8 041 000	Baku	Azeri, Armenian, Russian, Lezgian	Shi'a Muslim, Sunni Muslim, Russian and Armenian Orthodox	Manat	107
BAHRAIN		691	267	640 000	Manama (Al Manāmah)	Arabic, English	Shi'a Muslim, Sunni Muslim, Christian	Dinar	105
BANGLADESH		143 998	55 598	137 439 000	Dhaka (Dacca)	Bengali, English	Sunni Muslim, Hindu	Taka	97
BHUTAN		46 620	18 000	2 085 000	Thimphu	Dzongkha, Nepali, Assamese	Buddhist, Hindu	Ngultrum	97
BRUNEI		5 765	2 226	328 000	Bandar Seri Begawan	Malay, English, Chinese	Sunni Muslim, Buddhist, Christian	Dollar	77
CAMBODIA		181 000	69 884	13 104 000	Phnom Penh	Khmer, Vietnamese	Buddhist, Roman Catholic, Sunni Muslim	Riel	79
CHINA		9 584 492	3 700 593	1 260 137 000	Beijing (Peking)	Mandarin, Wu, Cantonese, Hsiang, regional languages	Confucian, Taoist, Buddhist, Christian, Sunni Muslim	Yuan	80–81
CYPRUS		9 251	3 572	784 000	Nicosia (Lefkosia)	Greek, Turkish, English	Greek Orthodox, Sunni Muslim	Pound	108
GEORGIA		69 700	26 911	5 262 000	T'bilisi	Georgian, Russian, Armenian, Azeri, Ossetian, Abkhaz	Georgian Orthodox, Russian Orthodox, Sunni Muslim	Lari	107
INDIA		3 065 027	1 183 414	1 008 937 000	New Delhi	Hindi, English, many regional languages	Hindu, Sunni Muslim, Shi'a Muslim, Sikh, Christian	Rupee	92–93
INDONESIA		1 919 445	741 102	212 092 000	Jakarta	Indonesian, local languages	Sunni Muslim, Protestant, Roman Catholic, Hindu, Buddhist	Rupiah	72–73
IRAN		1 648 000	636 296	70 330 000	Tehrān	Farsi, Azeri, Kurdish, regional languages	Shi'a Muslim, Sunni Muslim	Rial	100–101
IRAQ		438 317	169 235	22 946 000	Baghdād	Arabic, Kurdish, Turkmen	Shi'a Muslim, Sunni Muslim, Christian	Dinar	107
ISRAEL		20 770	8 019	6 040 000	Jerusalem (Yerushalayim) (El Quds)	Hebrew, Arabic	Jewish, Sunni Muslim, Christian, Druze	Shekel	108
JAPAN		377 727	145 841	127 096 000	Tōkyō	Japanese	Shintoist, Buddhist, Christian	Yen	90–91
JORDAN		89 206	34 443	4 913 000	'Ammān	Arabic	Sunni Muslim, Christian	Dinar	108–109
KAZAKHSTAN		2 717 300	1 049 155	16 172 000	Astana (Akmola)	Kazakh, Russian, Ukrainian, German, Uzbek, Tatar	Sunni Muslim, Russian Orthodox, Protestant	Tenge	102–103
KUWAIT		17 818	6 880	1 914 000	Kuwait (Al Kuwayt)	Arabic	Sunni Muslim, Shi'a Muslim, Christian, Hindu	Dinar	107
KYRGYZSTAN		198 500	76 641	4 921 000	Bishkek (Frunze)	Kyrgyz, Russian, Uzbek	Sunni Muslim, Russian Orthodox	Som	103
LAOS		236 800	91 429	5 279 000	Vientiane (Viangchan)	Lao, local languages	Buddhist, traditional beliefs	Kip	78–79
LEBANON		10 452	4 036	3 496 000	Beirut (Beyrouth)	Arabic, Armenian, French	Shi'a Muslim, Sunni Muslim, Christian	Pound	108–109
MALAYSIA		332 965	128 559	22 218 000	Kuala Lumpur	Malay, English, Chinese, Tamil, local languages	Sunni Muslim, Buddhist, Hindu, Christian, traditional beliefs	Ringgit	76–77
MALDIVES		298	115	291 000	Male	Divehi (Maldivian)	Sunni Muslim	Rufiyaa	93
MONGOLIA		1 565 000	604 250	2 533 000	Ulan Bator (Ulaanbaatar)	Khalka (Mongolian), Kazakh, local languages	Buddhist, Sunni Muslim	Tugrik	84–85
MYANMAR		676 577	261 228	47 749 000	Rangoon (Yangôn)	Burmese, Shan, Karen, local languages	Buddhist, Christian, Sunni Muslim	Kyat	78–79
NEPAL		147 181	56 827	23 043 000	Kathmandu	Nepali, Maithili, Bhojpuri, English, local languages	Hindu, Buddhist, Sunni Muslim	Rupee	96–97
NORTH KOREA		120 538	46 540	22 268 000	P'yŏngyang	Korean	Traditional beliefs, Chondoist, Buddhist	Won	82–83
OMAN		309 500	119 499	2 538 000	Muscat (Masqat)	Arabic, Baluchi, Indian languages	Ibadhi Muslim, Sunni Muslim	Rial	105

1 Middle East Boundaries

International boundaries are often visible from space because of differences in land use. In this Shuttle photograph the borders between Egypt, Gaza and Israel can be clearly identified. Grazing is the predominant agricultural activity in this part of Egypt, to the bottom of the image, and in Gaza in the centre, and has removed much of the vegetation. In contrast, Israel, to the east of the boundary, appears darker and more cultivated because of irrigation from the Jordan river.

Satellite/Sensor : Space Shuttle

2 Egypt/Gaza Border, *Middle East*

Borders between countries frequently follow the alignment of natural physical features, such as rivers, mountains or lake shores. Some borders, however, are demarcated only by man-made features, such as this fence at Rafah on the boundary between Egypt and Gaza. Gaza is a small semi-autonomous region on the southeast shore of the Mediterranean Sea. It is home to about 1 million Palestinian Arabs and was formerly under complete Israeli control.

3 The Great Wall, *China*

The Great Wall of China was built in various stages and forms over a period of 1 000 years from the third century BC. It is one of China's most distinctive and spectacular features. The wall is visible in this aerial photograph as a light coloured line running across the hills from lower right to upper left. Stretching a total length of over 2 400 km from the coast east of Beijing, to the Gobi desert in Gansu province, the wall was first built to protect China from the Mongols and nomadic peoples to the north of the country.

CONNECTIONS

▶ subject	page#
▶ World physical features	8–9
▶ World countries	10–11
▶ Asia landscapes	62–63
▶ Asia issues	66–67
▶ Reference maps of Asia	72–109

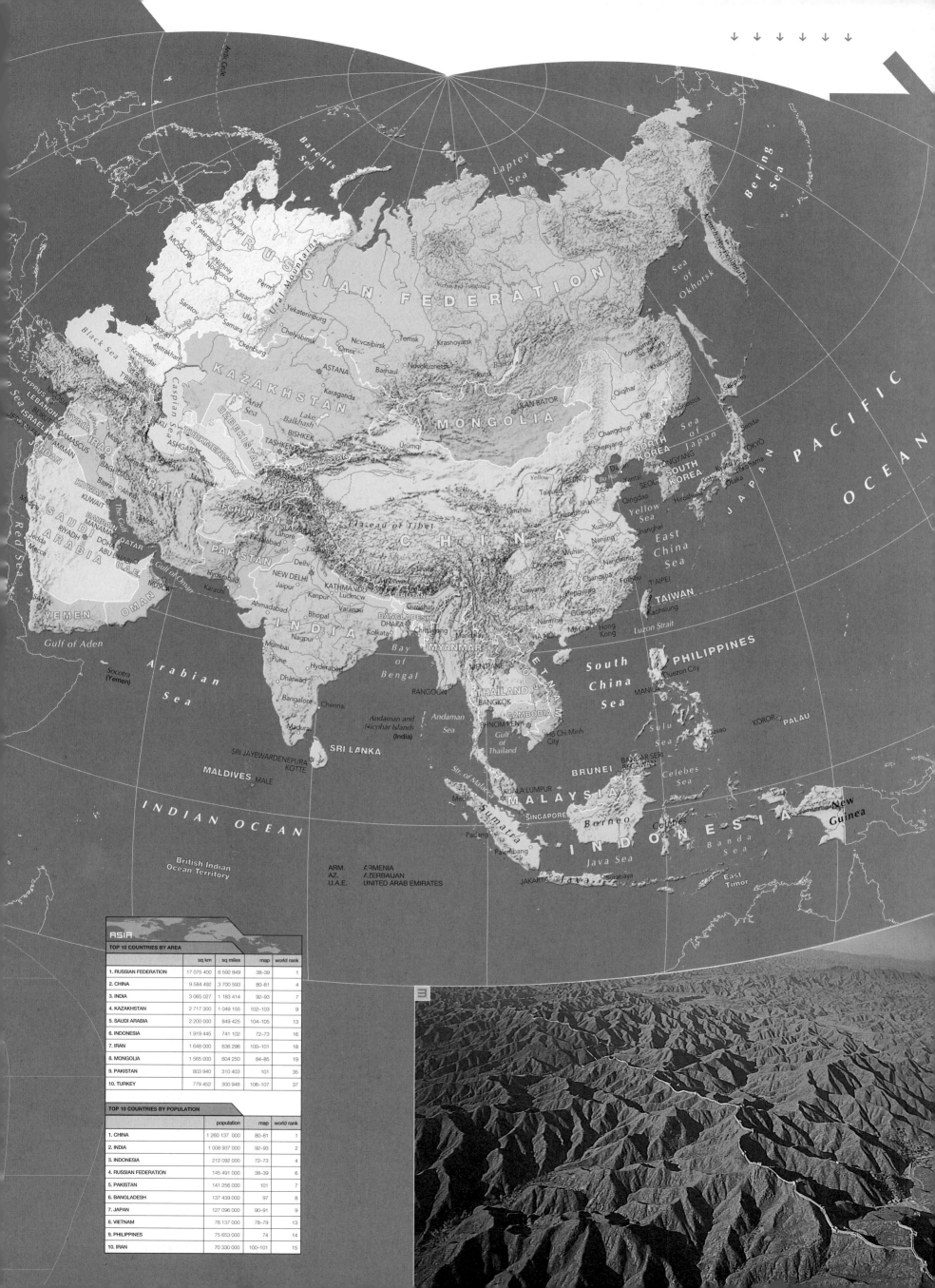

ASIA

TOP 10 COUNTRIES BY AREA

	sq km	sq miles	map	world rank
1. RUSSIAN FEDERATION	17 075 400	6 592 849	38–39	1
2. CHINA	9 584 492	3 700 593	80–81	4
3. INDIA	3 065 027	1 183 414	92–93	7
4. KAZAKHSTAN	2 717 300	1 049 155	102–103	9
5. SAUDI ARABIA	2 200 000	849 425	104–105	13
6. INDONESIA	1 919 445	741 102	72–73	16
7. IRAN	1 648 000	636 296	100–101	18
8. MONGOLIA	1 565 000	604 250	84–85	19
9. PAKISTAN	803 940	310 403	101	35
10. TURKEY	779 452	300 948	106–107	37

TOP 10 COUNTRIES BY POPULATION

	population	map	world rank
1. CHINA	1 260 137 000	80–81	1
2. INDIA	1 008 937 000	92–93	2
3. INDONESIA	212 092 000	72–73	4
4. RUSSIAN FEDERATION	145 491 000	38–39	6
5. PAKISTAN	141 256 000	101	7
6. BANGLADESH	137 439 000	97	8
7. JAPAN	127 096 000	90–91	9
8. VIETNAM	78 137 000	78–79	13
9. PHILIPPINES	75 653 000	74	14
10. IRAN	70 330 000	100–101	15

ARM. ARMENIA
AZ. AZERBAIJAN
U.A.E. UNITED ARAB EMIRATES

ASIA
COUNTRIES

		area sq km	area sq miles	population	capital	languages	religions	currency	map
PAKISTAN		803 940	310 403	141 256 000	Islamabad	Urdu, Punjabi, Sindhi, Pushtu, English	Sunni Muslim, Shi'a Muslim, Christian, Hindu	Rupee	101
PALAU		497	192	19 000	Koror	Palauan, English	Roman Catholic, Protestant, traditional beliefs	US dollar	73
PHILIPPINES		300 000	115 831	75 653 000	Manila	English, Pilipino, Cebuano, local languages	Roman Catholic, Protestant, Sunni Muslim, Aglipayan	Peso	74
QATAR		11 437	4 416	565 000	Doha (Ad Dawḩah)	Arabic	Sunni Muslim	Riyal	105
RUSSIAN FEDERATION		17 075 400	6 592 849	145 491 000	Moscow (Moskva)	Russian, Tatar, Ukrainian, local languages	Russian Orthodox, Sunni Muslim, Protestant	Rouble	38–39
SAUDI ARABIA		2 200 000	849 425	20 346 000	Riyadh (Ar Riyāḍ)	Arabic	Sunni Muslim, Shi'a Muslim	Riyal	104–105
SINGAPORE		639	247	4 018 000	Singapore	Chinese, English, Malay, Tamil	Buddhist, Taoist, Sunni Muslim, Christian, Hindu	Dollar	76
SOUTH KOREA		99 274	38 330	46 740 000	Seoul (Sŏul)	Korean	Buddhist, Protestant, Roman Catholic	Won	83
SRI LANKA		65 610	25 332	18 924 000	Sri Jayewardenepura Kotte	Sinhalese, Tamil, English	Buddhist, Hindu, Sunni Muslim, Roman Catholic	Rupee	94
SYRIA		185 180	71 498	16 189 000	Damascus (Dimashq)	Arabic, Kurdish, Armenian	Sunni Muslim, Shi'a Muslim, Christian	Pound	108–109
TAIWAN		36 179	13 969	22 300 000	T'aipei	Mandarin, Min, Hakka, local languages	Buddhist, Taoist, Confucian, Christian	Dollar	87
TAJIKISTAN		143 100	55 251	6 087 000	Dushanbe	Tajik, Uzbek, Russian	Sunni Muslim	Rouble	101
THAILAND		513 115	198 115	62 806 000	Bangkok (Krung Thep)	Thai, Lao, Chinese, Malay, Mon-Khmer languages	Buddhist, Sunni Muslim	Baht	78–79
TURKEY		779 452	300 948	66 668 000	Ankara	Turkish, Kurdish	Sunni Muslim, Shi'a Muslim	Lira	106–107
TURKMENISTAN		488 100	188 456	4 737 000	Ashgabat (Ashkhabad)	Turkmen, Uzbek, Russian	Sunni Muslim, Russian Orthodox	Manat	102–103
UNITED ARAB EMIRATES		83 600	32 278	2 606 000	Abu Dhabi (Abū Ẓaby)	Arabic, English	Sunni Muslim, Shi'a Muslim	Dirham	105
UZBEKISTAN		447 400	172 742	24 881 000	Tashkent	Uzbek, Russian, Tajik, Kazakh	Sunni Muslim, Russian Orthodox	Sum	102–103
VIETNAM		329 565	127 246	78 137 000	Ha Nôi	Vietnamese, Thai, Khmer, Chinese, local languages	Buddhist, Taoist, Roman Catholic, Cao Dai, Hoa Hao	Dong	78–79
YEMEN		527 968	203 850	18 349 000	Şan'ā'	Arabic	Sunni Muslim, Shi'a Muslim	Rial	104–105

DEPENDENT AND DISPUTED TERRITORIES

		territorial status	area sq km	area sq miles	population	capital	languages	religions	currency	map
British Indian Ocean Territory		United Kingdom Overseas Territory	60	23	uninhabited					219
Christmas Island		Australian External Territory	135	52	2 195	The Settlement	English	Buddhist, Sunni Muslim, Protestant, Roman Catholic	Australian dollar	72
Cocos Islands (Keeling Islands)		Australian External Territory	14	5	637	West Island	English	Sunni Muslim, Christian	Australian dollar	218
East Timor		under UN Transitional Administration	14 874	5 743	737 000	Dili	Portuguese, Tetun, English	Roman Catholic		75
French Southern and Antarctic Lands		French Overseas Territory	439 580	169 723	uninhabited					219
Gaza		semi-autonomous region	363	140	3 191 000*	Gaza	Arabic	Sunni Muslim, Shi'a Muslim	Israeli shekel	108
Heard and McDonald Islands		Australian External Territory	412	159	uninhabited					219
Jammu and Kashmir		Disputed territory (India/Pakistan)	222 236	85 806	13 000 000					96–97
West Bank		Disputed territory	5 860	2 263			Arabic, Hebrew	Sunni Muslim, Jewish, Shi'a Muslim, Christian		108

*includes occupied West Bank

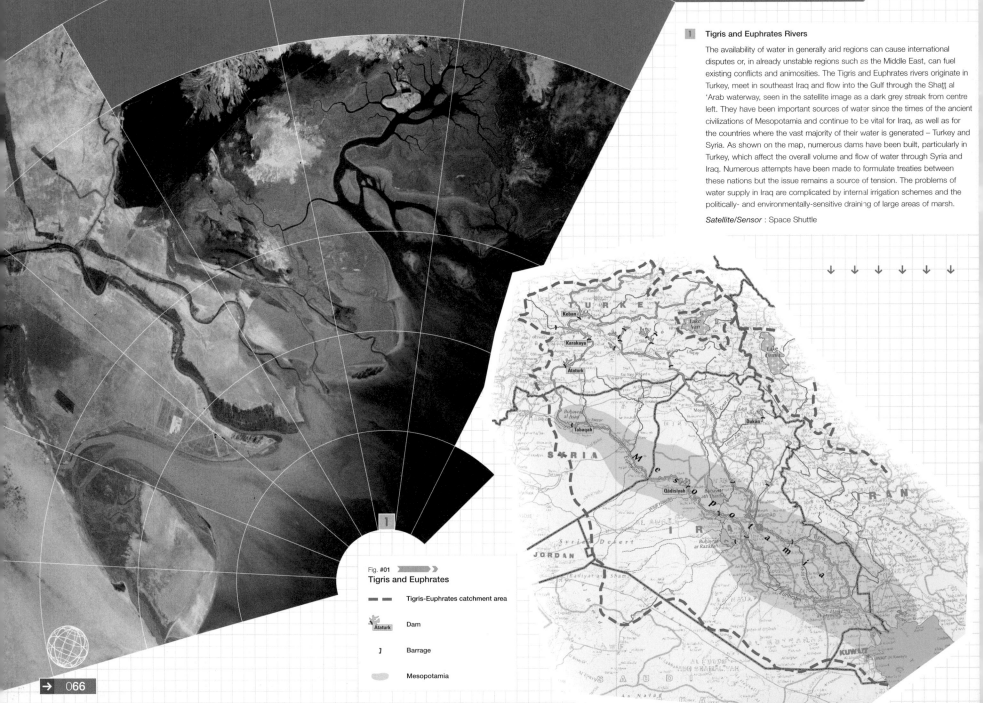

1   Tigris and Euphrates Rivers

The availability of water in generally arid regions can cause international disputes or, in already unstable regions such as the Middle East, can fuel existing conflicts and animosities. The Tigris and Euphrates rivers originate in Turkey, meet in southeast Iraq and flow into the Gulf through the Shaṭṭ al 'Arab waterway, seen in the satellite image as a dark grey streak from centre left. They have been important sources of water since the times of the ancient civilizations of Mesopotamia and continue to be vital for Iraq, as well as for the countries where the vast majority of their water is generated – Turkey and Syria. As shown on the map, numerous dams have been built, particularly in Turkey, which affect the overall volume and flow of water through Syria and Iraq. Numerous attempts have been made to formulate treaties between these nations but the issue remains a source of tension. The problems of water supply in Iraq are complicated by internal irrigation schemes and the politically- and environmentally-sensitive draining of large areas of marsh.

Satellite/Sensor : Space Shuttle

Fig. #01
Tigris and Euphrates

- – – Tigris-Euphrates catchment area
- Atatürk Dam
- Barrage
- Mesopotamia

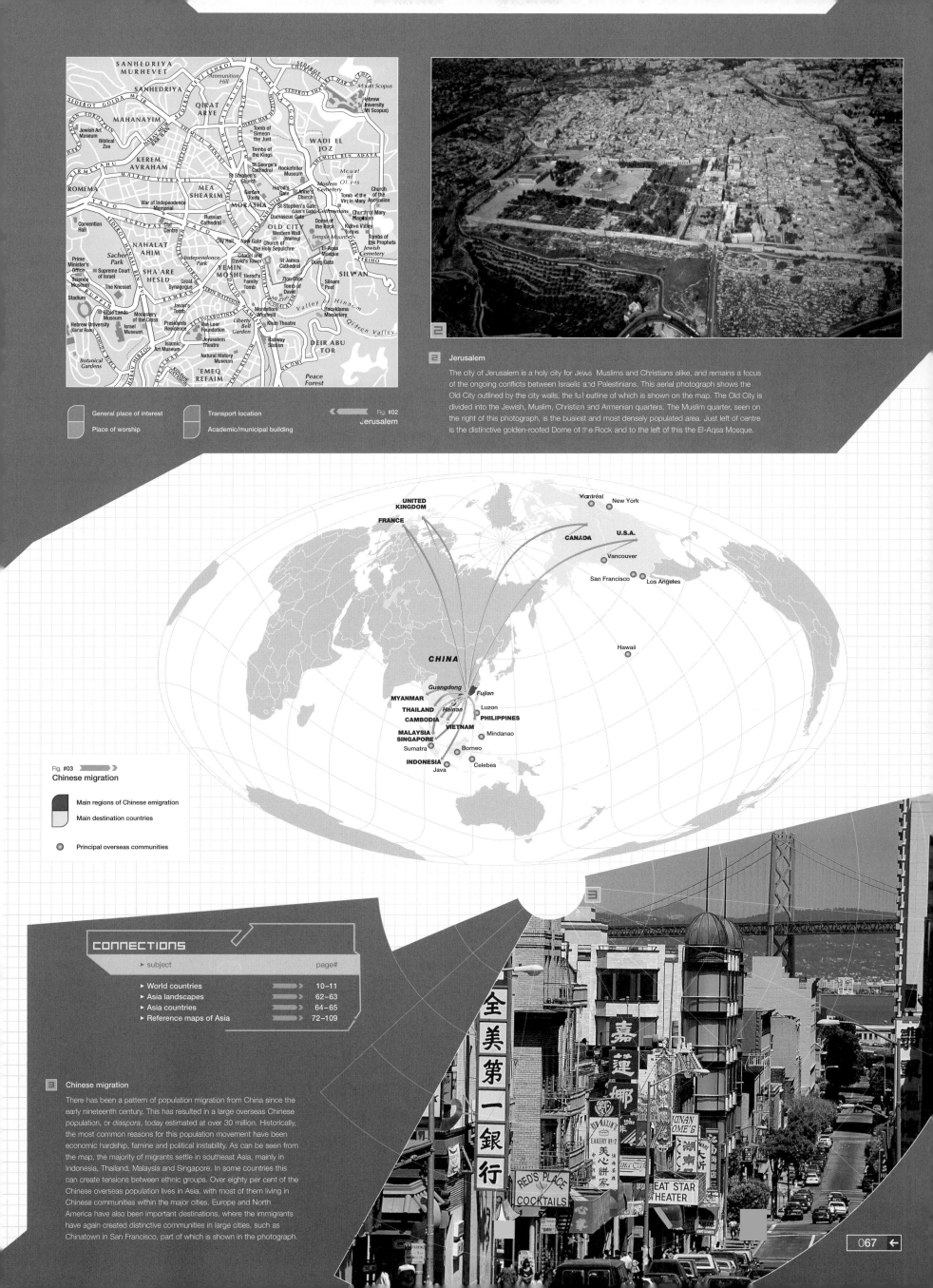

◄ Fig. #02
Jerusalem

General place of interest | **Transport location**
Place of worship | **Academic/municipal building**

2 Jerusalem

The city of Jerusalem is a holy city for Jews, Muslims and Christians alike, and remains a focus of the ongoing conflicts between Israelis and Palestinians. This aerial photograph shows the Old City outlined by the city walls, the full outline of which is shown on the map. The Old City is divided into the Jewish, Muslim, Christian and Armenian quarters. The Muslim quarter, seen on the right of this photograph, is the busiest and most densely populated area. Just left of centre is the distinctive golden-roofed Dome of the Rock and to the left of this the El-Aqsa Mosque.

Fig. #03
Chinese migration

■ Main regions of Chinese emigration
□ Main destination countries

● Principal overseas communities

CONNECTIONS

▸ subject | page#

▸ World countries — 10–11
▸ Asia landscapes — 62–63
▸ Asia countries — 64–65
▸ Reference maps of Asia — 72–109

3 Chinese migration

There has been a pattern of population migration from China since the early nineteenth century. This has resulted in a large overseas Chinese population, or *diaspora*, today estimated at over 30 million. Historically, the most common reasons for this population movement have been economic hardship, famine and political instability. As can be seen from the map, the majority of migrants settle in southeast Asia, mainly in Indonesia, Thailand, Malaysia and Singapore. In some countries this can create tensions between ethnic groups. Over eighty per cent of the Chinese overseas population lives in Asia, with most of them living in Chinese communities within the major cities. Europe and North America have also been important destinations, where the immigrants have again created distinctive communities in large cities, such as Chinatown in San Francisco, part of which is shown in the photograph.

CONNECTIONS

► subject	page#
► Types of imagery	4–5
► World changes	20–21
► Asia landscapes	62–63
► Asia issues	66–67
► Reference maps of Asia	72–109

1   Three Gorges Dam Project, *China*

The Three Gorges Dam Project on the Yangtze river is the world's largest hydroelectric project. The term refers to a 190 km stretch of the Yangtze river where it flows through the precipitous Quitang, Wu and Xiling gorges, as shown on the satellite image and map. The photograph at the top shows part of the project area before construction began in 1997. The centre photograph shows part of the construction work and gives some idea of the effect it will have on the landscape. When complete, the dam will be over two kilometres wide and will create a 620 km long reservoir which will engulf over 400 sq km of farmland, thirteen cities, hundreds of villages, and archaeological sites. While the project, due for completion in 2009, will improve flood management, generate electricity and transfer water to dry areas further north, it raises many social and environmental issues, including the resettlement of between 1–2 million people, the potential accumulation of pollutants and the destruction of precious natural habitats.

Satellite/Sensor : Landsat (bottom)

Fig. #01
Three Gorges Dam project

SHAANXI

HUBEI

0	miles	50	
0	kilometres		100

Area to be inundated

Area affected by Three Gorges Dam project

Three Gorges Dam

Gorge

Inundated town

Provincial boundary

Wuxi

Xiang Xi

Xingshan

Daning He

Wushan

Zigui

Kaixian

Fengjie

Badong

Xiling Gorge

Quitang Gorge

Wu Gorge

Gezhouba Dam

Yunyang

Sandouping

Yichang

Wanxian

Yangtze

SICHUAN

Zhongxian

Dong He

Fengdu

Shizhu

Changshou

Fuling

CHONGQING

Jiangbei

Mudong

Wu Jiang

Chongqing

Wulong

Jialing Jiang

Ba Xian

GUIZHOU

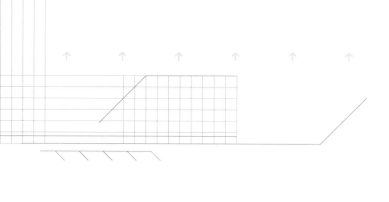

Lake Level Variations

A natural evaporation basin, the Kara-Bogaz-Gol is located in a semi-arid region of Turkmenistan on the eastern shore of the Caspian Sea. In these northwest-looking oblique Shuttle photographs the difference in water level, due to both evaporation and variation in the flow of water from the Caspian Sea into the basin, is striking. The 1985 image (top) shows water in only a small section near the western end. In contrast to this, the 1995 image (bottom) shows the water level to be high in the whole basin. The level of the Caspian Sea is normally approximately three metres above that of the basin, and water flows from one to the other through a dyke built in the late 1970s. However, low rainfall in the region can result in exceptionally low water levels in the Caspian Sea, which dramatically affect the amount of water flowing into the basin.

Satellite/Sensor : Space Shuttle

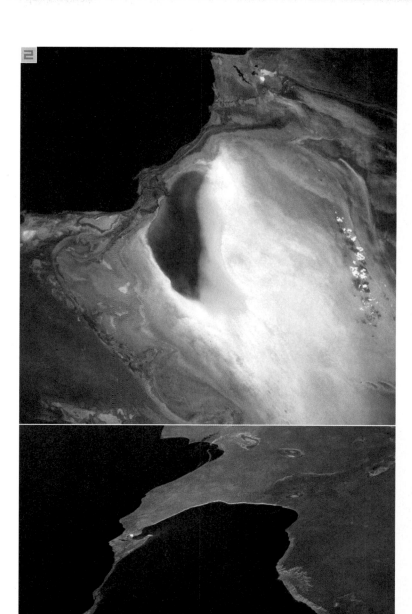

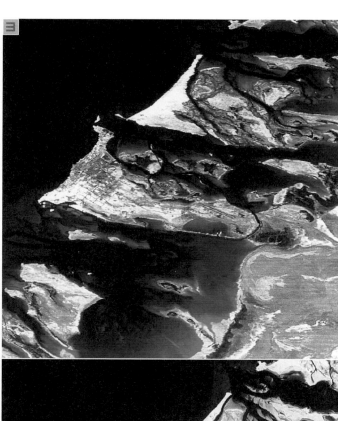

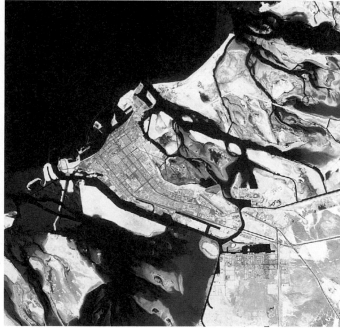

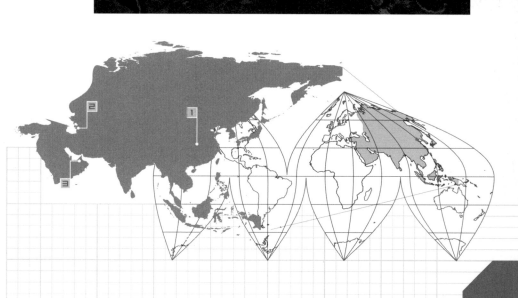

Urban Development and Land Reclamation

These satellite images show the development of the capital of the United Arab Emirates, Abu Dhabi. In the 1950s the town was little more than a small fishing village, but this changed after the discovery of offshore oil in the early 1960s. The changes, particularly to the extent of the city and to the coastline, in the period between the image at the top (1972) and the one below (1989), are dramatic. A national development program was implemented to help improve the city's harbour and to construct buildings, roads, and an international airport.

Satellite/Sensor : Landsat

1

CONNECTIONS

▶ subject	page#
▶ World earthquakes and volcanoes	14–15
▶ World tropical storms	16–17
▶ Mozambique floods	116–117
▶ North America threats	160–161

1 Tropical Storms

Tropical storms are among the most powerful and destructive weather systems on Earth. Worldwide between eighty and one hundred develop over tropical oceans each year. The northwest Pacific area experiences an average of thirty one typhoons annually and most of these occur between July and October. If they reach land they can cause extensive damage to property or loss of life as a result of high winds and heavy rain. This image gives an idea of the overall size of a typhoon as it moves westwards across the Pacific Ocean towards the island of Guam. Wind speeds in this typhoon reached over 370 km per hour.

Satellite/Sensor : GOES

2 Tropical Cyclone Hudah, *Southwest Indian Ocean*

Tropical cyclone Hudah was one of the most powerful storms ever seen in the Indian Ocean and was typical of the storms which frequently occur in the Pacific and Indian Oceans and which threaten the coasts of Asia and Africa. At the end of March 2000 the storm began a fairly straight westerly track across the entire south Indian Ocean, as shown on the map, struck Madagascar as an intense tropical cyclone, weakened, then regained intensity in the Mozambique Channel before making a final landfall in Mozambique on 9 April. This image was taken just before the cyclone hit the coast of Madagascar where wind gusts reached over 296 km per hour causing the destruction of 90% of the city of Antalaha.

Satellite/Sensor : MODIS

3 Bangladesh Cyclone Damage

Bangladesh, lying at the northern edge of the Bay of Bengal often experiences extreme climatic conditions which can wreak havoc. Cyclones regularly occur in the Bay of Bengal often having devastating effects on the flat coastal regions as shown in this photograph. In 1991 the country was hit by a massive cyclone which killed more than 140 000 people.

4 Klyuchevskaya Volcano, *Russian Federation*

Klyuchevskaya is the highest mountain in eastern Russian Federation and one of the most active volcanoes on the Kamchatka Peninsula. This view shows the major eruption of 1994 when the eruption cloud reached 18 300 m above sea level and the winds carried ash as far as 1 030 km to the southeast. The Kamchatka Peninsula is a sparsely populated area and the volcano's threat to human life is not serious. However, it lies on a major airline route and volcanic eruptions frequently cause aircraft to divert around the region.

Satellite/Sensor : Space Shuttle

Fig. #01

Tracks of tropical cyclones in the southwest Indian Ocean 2000

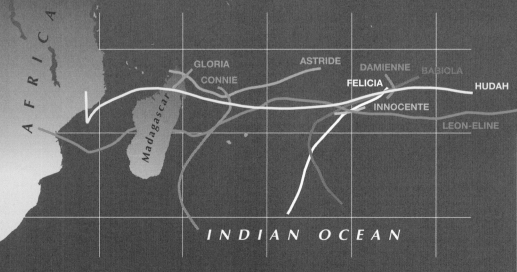

AFRICA

GLORIA
CONNIE
ASTRIDE
DAMIENNE
BABIOLA
FELICIA
HUDAH
INNOCENTE
LEON-ELINE

Madagascar

INDIAN OCEAN

3

2

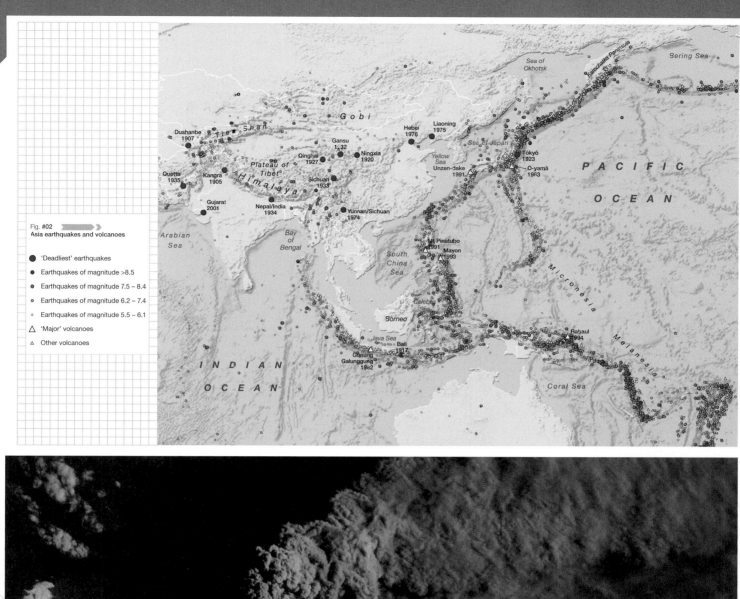

Fig. #02
Asia earthquakes and volcanoes

● 'Deadliest' earthquakes
● Earthquakes of magnitude >8.5
● Earthquakes of magnitude 7.5 – 8.4
○ Earthquakes of magnitude 6.2 – 7.4
○ Earthquakes of magnitude 5.5 – 6.1
△ 'Major' volcanoes
△ Other volcanoes

4

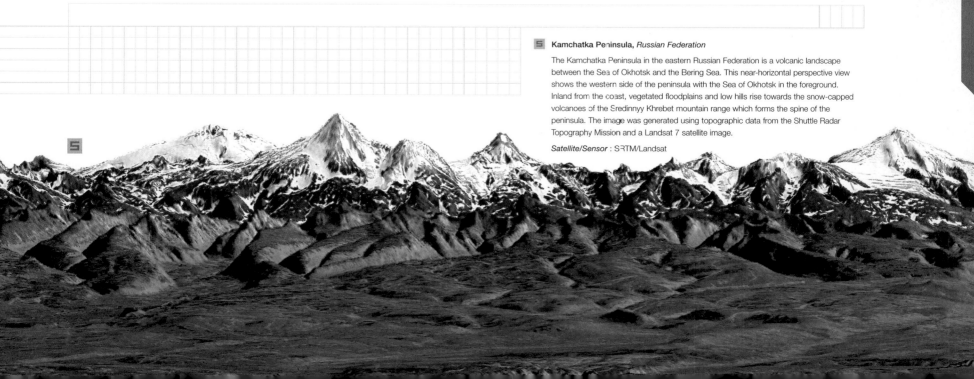

5   **Kamchatka Peninsula,** *Russian Federation*

The Kamchatka Peninsula in the eastern Russian Federation is a volcanic landscape
between the Sea of Okhotsk and the Bering Sea. This near-horizontal perspective view
shows the western side of the peninsula with the Sea of Okhotsk in the foreground.
Inland from the coast, vegetated floodplains and low hills rise towards the snow-capped
volcanoes of the Sredinnyy Khrebet mountain range which forms the spine of the
peninsula. The image was generated using topographic data from the Shuttle Radar
Topography Mission and a Landsat 7 satellite image.

Satellite/Sensor : SRTM/Landsat

5

11°S-26°N / 95°-147°E

080-081

092-093

PACIFIC OCEAN

East China Sea (Dong Hai)

Northern Mariana Islands (U.S.A.)

Philippine Sea

PHILIPPINES

Luzon

MANILA

Mindoro

Palawan

Samar

Panay

Negros

Leyte

Mindanao

Davao

Guam (U.S.A.)

HAGÅTÑA

FEDERATED STATES OF MICRONESIA

Caroline Islands

PALAU

KOROR

Palau Islands

Sulu Sea

Celebes Sea

Celebes (Sulawesi)

Ujung Pandang (Makassar)

Molucca Sea

Manado

Halmahera

Moluccas (Maluku)

Ceram Sea

Seram

Banda Sea

Flores Sea

Flores

DILI

EAST TIMOR

Timor

Sumba

Sumbawa

Arafura Sea

Sawu Sea

IRIAN JAYA

New Guinea

PAPUA NEW GUINEA

Jayapura

Bismarck Sea

Admiralty Islands

Bismarck Archipelago

PORT MORESBY

Gulf of Papua

AUSTRALIA

Cape York

CONNECTIONS

subject	page#
▸ World earthquakes and volcanoes	14–15
▸ World population growth	22–23
▸ Asia countries	64–67
▸ Asia threats	70–71
▸ Pacific Ocean	220–221

144-145

1:13 000 000

miles
0   100   200   300   400   500   600

km
0 100 200 300 400 500 600 700 800 900 1000

Mercator Projection

E   120°   F   125°   G   130°   H   135°   I   140°   J   145°   K

CONNECTIONS

5°-21°N / 117°-128°E

PHILIPPINES

Luzon

Philippine

Sea

South

China

Sea

Mindoro

Panay

Negros

Cebu

Bohol

Leyte

Samar

Sulu Sea

Celebes

Sea

Moro

Gulf

Mindanao

Palawan

SABAH

MALAYSIA

INDONESIA

Sulu Archipelago

Bohol Sea

MANILA

Quezon City

Davao

Luzon Strait

Batan Islands

Babuyan Islands

Balintang Channel

Babuyan Channel

Elevation scale:
>6000m
5000-6000m
4000-5000m
3000-4000m
2000-3000m
1000-2000m
500-1000m
200-500m
0-200m
<0m

0-200m
200-500m
500-1000m
1000-2000m
2000-3000m
3000-4000m
4000-5000m
5000-6000m
>6000m

076-077

075

miles
0   50   100   150   200   250

1:6 000 000

km
0   50   100   150   200   250   300   350   400

Mercator Projection

A   120°   B   124°   C   128°

1
20°
2
16°
3
12°
4
8°
5

12°S–5°N / 119°–130°E

076–077

072–073

1 : 6 000 000

Mercator Projection

asia[map4]

8°N-10°S / 95°-120°E

THAILAND

MALAYSIA

Peninsular Malaysia

KUALA LUMPUR

SINGAPORE

SUMATERA UTARA

SUMATERA BARAT

JAMBI

RIAU

BENGKULU

SUMATERA SELATAN

LAMPUNG

ACEH

INDONESIA

Medan

Padang

Palembang

Bengkulu

Banda Aceh

Simeuluë

Nias

Siberut

Kepulauan Mentawai

Kepulauan Riau

INDIAN

OCEAN

Equator

Strait of Malacca

Elevation legend:
>6000m
5000-6000m
4000-5000m
3000-4000m
2000-3000m
1000-2000m
500-1000m
200-500m
0-200m
<0m

0-200m
200-500m
500-1000m
1000-2000m
2000-3000m
3000-4000m
4000-5000m
5000-6000m
>6000m

Singapore inset

MALAYSIA

SINGAPORE

Johor Bahru

WOODLANDS

SEMBAWANG

YISHUN

CHANGI

JURONG

BUKIT TIMAH

TAMPINES

BEDOK

Strait of Singapore

Selat Johor

1 : 360 000

miles
km

103°40'   103°50'   104°00'

South China

Sea

PHILIPPINES

Sulu Sea

Celebes

Sea

BRUNEI

BANDAR SERI
BEGAWAN

MALAYSIA

SABAH

SARAWAK

KALIMANTAN
TIMUR

B o r n e o

KALIMANTAN BARAT

KALIMANTAN
TENGAH

KALIMANTAN
SELATAN

INDONESIA

Kuching

Pontianak

Bangka
Belitung

Celebes
(Sulawesi)

SULAWESI
SELATAN

Java Sea

Kepulauan Laut Kecil

JAKARTA

Bandung

Surabaya

Madura

JAWA BARAT

JAWA TENGAH

YOGYAKARTA

Java
(Jawa)

Bali

Denpasar

Lombok

Sumbawa

NUSA TENGGARA BARAT

Sumba

Bali Sea

Flores
Sea

Ujung
Pandang
(Makassar)

D   108°   E   112°   F   116°   G

1:6 000 000

miles
0   50   100   150   200   250

km
0   50   100 150 200 250 300 350 400

Mercator Projection

asia[map5]

5°29'N / 92°-110°E

1:6 000 000
Mercator Projection

CONNECTIONS

▶ subject	page#
▲ Asia landscapes	62–63
▲ Asia countries	64–67
▲ Chinese migration	66–67
▲ Asia threats	70–71
▶ Indian Ocean	218–219

076–077

asia[map6]

18°-55°N / 73°-140°E

0°92-093

Elevation scale:
>6000m
5000-6000m
4000-5000m
3000-4000m
2000-3000m
1000-2000m
500-1000m
200-500m
0-200m
<0m
0-200m
200-500m
500-1000m
1000-2000m
2000-3000m
3000-4000m
4000-5000m
5000-6000m
>6000m

Countries / Regions:
RUSSIAN
MONGOLIA
KAZAKHSTAN
KYRGYZSTAN
TAJIKISTAN
AFGHANISTAN
CHINA
XINJIANG UYGUR ZIZHIQU (SINKIANG)
QINGHAI
GANSU
SICHUAN
XIZANG ZIZHIQU (TIBET)
YUNNAN
INDIA
NEPAL
BHUTAN
BANGLADESH
MYANMAR
THAILAND
LAOS
VIETNAM
JAMMU AND KASHMIR
AKSAI CHIN
UTTAR PRADESH
MADHYA PRADESH
MAHARASHTRA
ORISSA
ANDHRA PRADESH
JHARKHAND
BIHAR
ASSAM
MEGHALAYA
NAGALAND
MIZORAM
ARUNACHAL PRADESH
KRASNOYARSKIY KRAY
IRKUTSKAYA OBLAST

Major cities / places:
Omsk, Novosibirsk, Tomsk, Kemerovo, Krasnoyarsk, Barnaul, Biysk, Semipalatinsk, Pavlodar, Karaganda, Balkhash, Almaty, Bishkek (Frunze), Ürümqi, Turpan (Turfan), Hami (Kumul), Kashi (Kashgar), Hotan, Golmud, Xining, Lanzhou (Lanchow), Chengdu, Mianyang, Irkutsk, Angarsk, Ulaangom, Hovd, Islamabad, Rawalpindi, Lahore, Srinagar, Faisalabad, Amritsar, Jalandhar, Meerut, Agra, Lucknow, Kanpur, Varanasi, Allahabad, Patna, Jabalpur, Nagpur, Raipur, Kolkata (Calcutta), Dhaka (Dacca), Chittagong, Kathmandu, Thimphu, Lhasa, Xigaze, Mount Everest, Mandalay, Vishakhapatnam, Bhubaneshwar, Cuttack, Kunming

Physical features:
Altay Mountains, Tien Shan, Tarim Basin (Tarim Pendi), Taklimakan Desert (Taklimakan Shamo), Kunlun Shan, Altun Shan, Qilian Shan, Plateau of Tibet (Qing Zang Gaoyuan), Tanggula Shan, Himalaya, Karakoram, Hindu Kush, Qaidam Pendi (Qaidam Basin), Junggar Pendi, Gobi, Bay of Bengal, Mouths of the Ganges, Lake Balkhash, Ysyk-Köl, Lop Nur, Nam Co, Brahmaputra, Yangtze, Yellow River

Administrative divisions numbered on the map:

RUSSIAN FEDERATION
1. AGINSKIY BURYATSKIY AVTONOMNYY OKRUG
2. UST'-ORDYNSKIY BURYATSKIY AVTONOMNYY OKRUG

CHINA
3. HEBEI
4. NINGXIA HUIZU ZIZHIQU

INDIA
5. TRIPURA

1:13 000 000

miles
0   100   200   300   400   500   600

km
0   100   200   300   400   500   600   700   800   900   1000

Albers Equal Area Conic Projection

PACIFIC

OCEAN

Sea
of
Japan
(East Sea)

Yellow
Sea
(Huang Hai)

East China
Sea
(Dong Hai)

NORTH KOREA

SOUTH KOREA

Korea Bay

Korea Strait

PYŌNGYANG

SEOUL (Sōul)

Pusan

Shikoku

Kyūshū

Kita-Kyūshū

Hiroshima

Ōsaka

Kyōto

Nagoya

Sendai

Cheju-do

Cheju

Liancourt Rocks

Izu-shotō

CONNECTIONS

▲ subject	page#
▲ World population	22–23
▲ World cities	24–25
▲ Asia landscapes	62–63
▲ Asia countries	64–67
▲ Pacific Ocean	220–221

1:6 000 000

Conic Equidistant Projection

miles
km

>6000m
5000–6000m
4000–5000m
3000–4000m
2000–3000m
1000–2000m
500–1000m
200–500m
0–200m
<0m

asia[map8]

34°-52°N / 92°-122°E

>6000m
5000-6000m
4000-5000m
3000-4000m
2000-3000m
1000-2000m
500-1000m
200-500m
0-200m
<0m

0-200m
200-500m
500-1000m
1000-2000m
2000-3000m
3000-4000m
4000-5000m
5000-6000m
>6000m

Yellow Sea
(Huang Hai)

miles
1:6 000 000

km

Conic Equidistant Projection

asia[map9]

18°-36°N / 96°-122°E

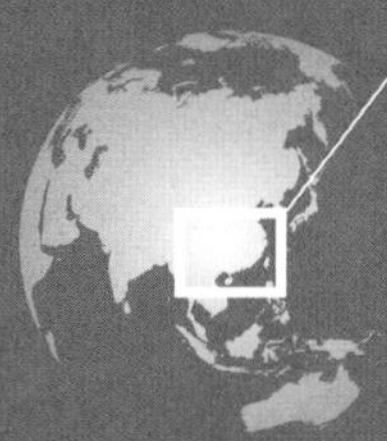

088-089

078-079

>6000m
5000-6000m
4000-5000m
3000-4000m
2000-3000m
1000-2000m
500-1000m
200-500m
0-200m
<0m

0-200m
200-500m
500-1000m
1000-2000m
2000-3000m
3000-4000m
4000-5000m
5000-6000m
>6000m

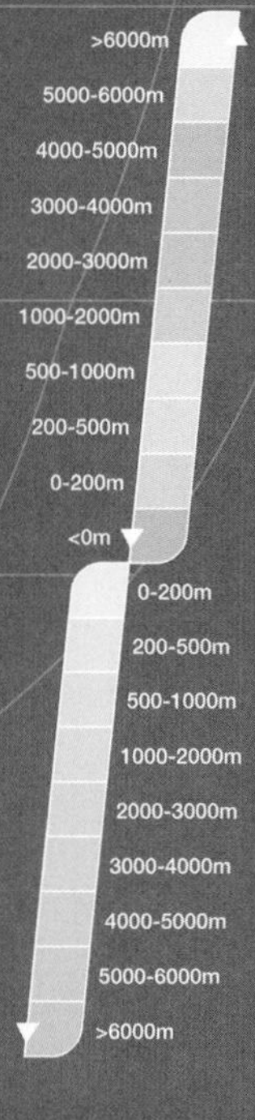

1 : 6 000 000

miles
0   50   100   150   200   250

km
0   50 100 150 200 250 300 350 400

Conic Equidistant Projection

084-085

078-079   THAILAND

QINGHAI
GANSU
NINGXIA
HUIZU ZIZHIQU
XIZANG ZIZHIQU (TIBET)
SICHUAN
GUIZHOU
YUNNAN
INDIA
MYANMAR
THAILAND
LAOS
VIETNAM
TONKIN
KACHIN
KAYAH
PEGU
SHAN PLATEAU

Lanzhou (Lanchow)
Chengdu
Chóngqìng
Mianyang
Nanchong
Zigong
Neijiang
Kunming
Guiyang
Zhaotong
Xichang
Panzhihua (Dukou)
Dali (Xiaguan)
Mandalay
Chiang Mai
HA NÔI
Hai Phong
Thanh Hoa
Vinh

Tropic of Cancer

32°
28°
24°
20°
18°

96°   100°   104°

A   B   C
1   2   3   4   5

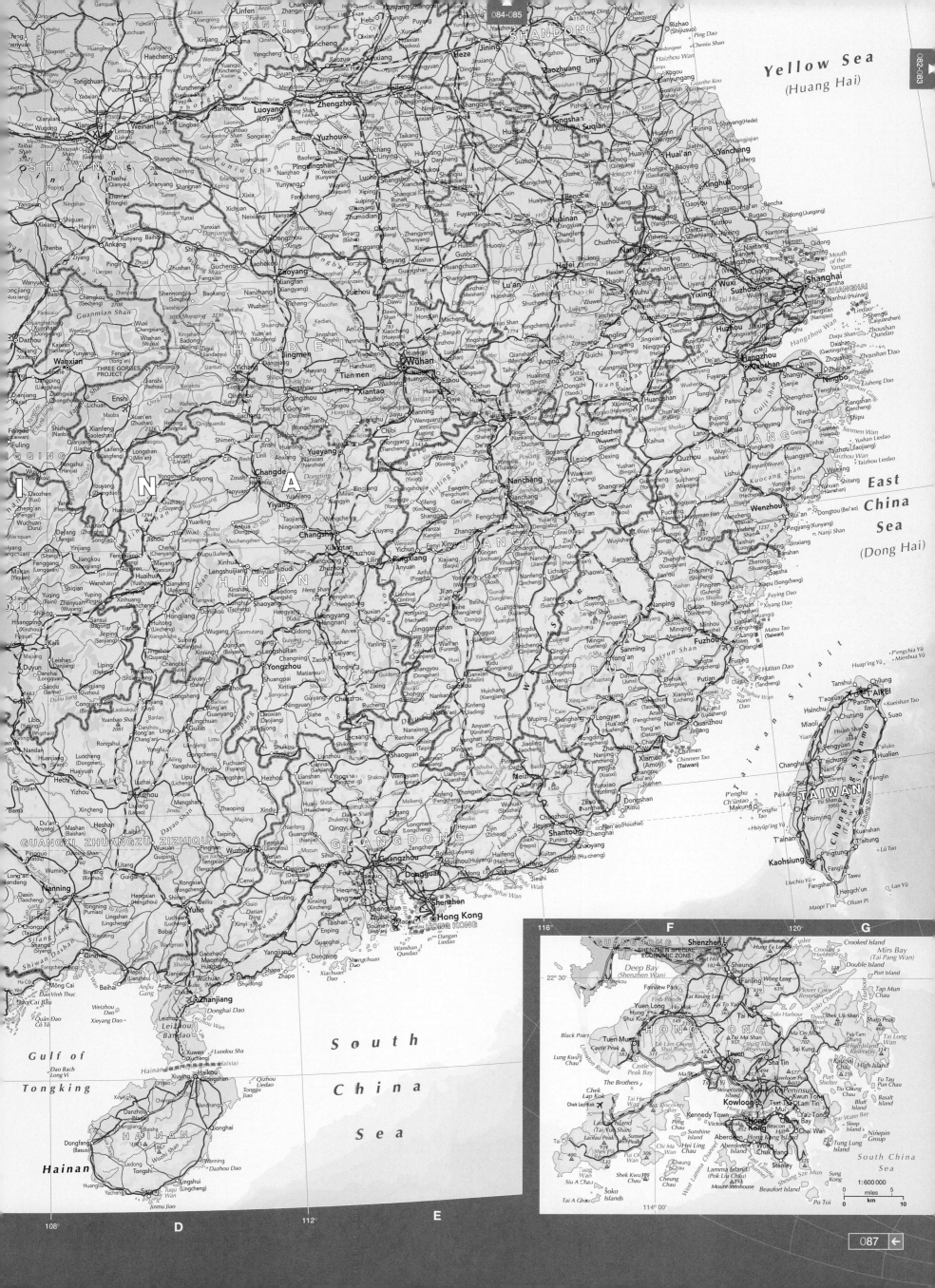

asia[map10]

26°-51'N / 74°-96'E

1:6 000 000

Conic Equidistant Projection

miles
0 50 100 150 200 250

km
0 50 100 150 200 250 300 350 400

CONNECTIONS

subject .... page#
▲ World physical features 8–9
▲ World land images 12–13
▲ Asia landscapes 62–63
▲ Asia countries 64–67

QINGHAI

Plateau of Tibet

Qing Zang Gaoyuan

XIZANG

Tangula Shan

BHUTAN

SIKKIM

ARUNACHAL PRADESH

ASSAM

NEPAL

KATHMANDU

Kunlun Shan

AKSAI CHIN
CLAIMED BY INDIA
UNDER CHINESE
ADMINISTRATION

JAMMU AND KASHMIR

LINE OF CONTROL

ZASKAR

Ladakh Range

Zaskar Range

HIMACHAL PRADESH

Srinagar

BALTISTAN

NORTHERN AREAS

HUNZA

HIMALAYA

PUNJAB

HARYANA

UTTARANCHAL

UTTAR PRADESH

RAJASTHAN

INDIA

Lahore

Ludhiana

Delhi

Meerut

Kanpur

Lucknow

Jaipur

Kathiawar

Himalaya

Ganges

096-097

100-101

Hotan

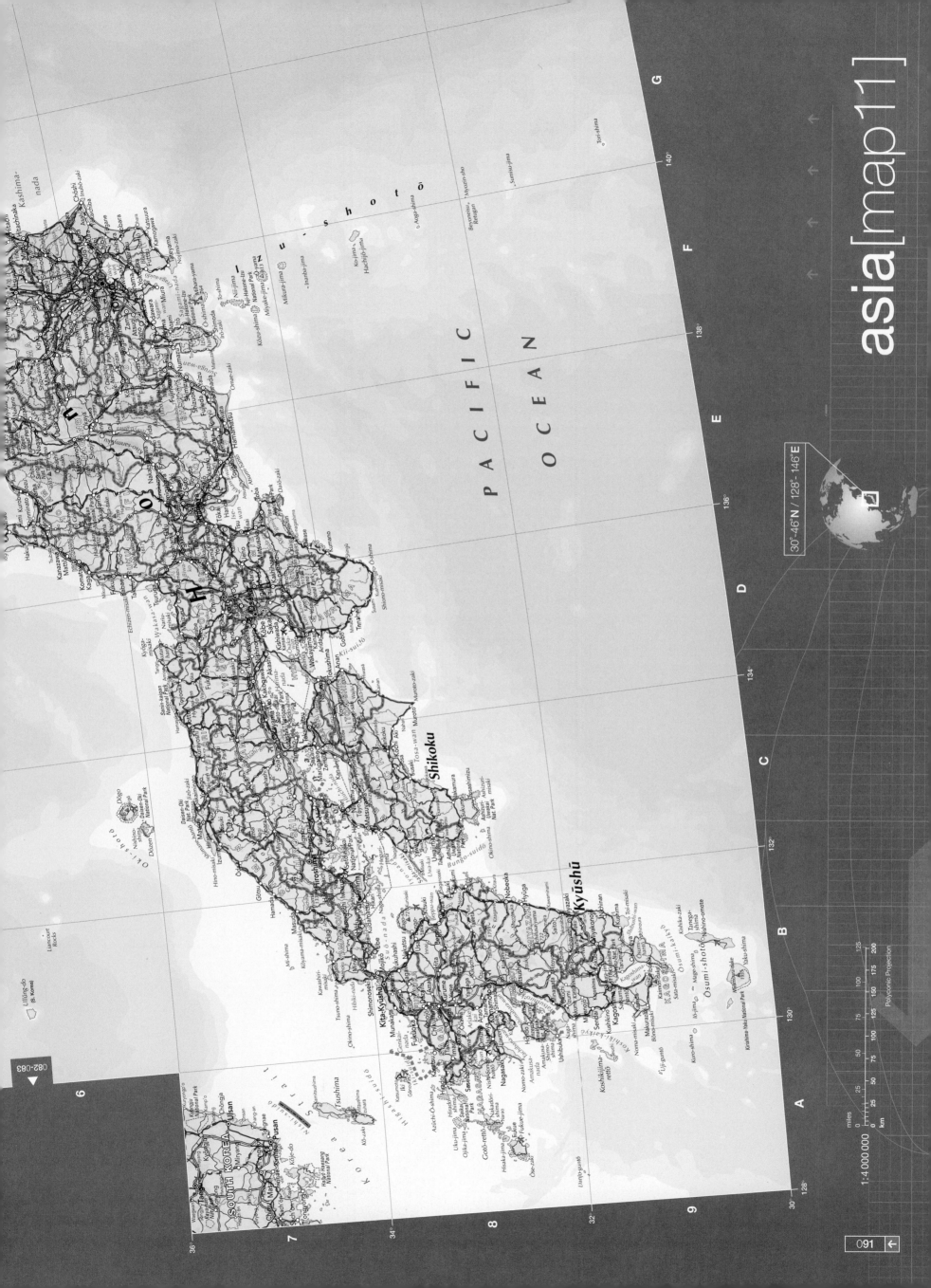

PACIFIC

OCEAN

Iu-shotō

Shikoku

Kyūshū

SOUTH KOREA

Korea Strait

Nishi-suidō

Higashi-suidō

Ōsumi-shotō

Oki-shotō

Ullŏng-do
(S. Korea)

Liancourt
Rocks

082–083

1 : 4 000 000

Polyconic Projection

miles

km

asia[map12]

1:12 000 000

1°S–50°N / 60°–97°E

CONNECTIONS

► subject	page#
▲ World physical features	8–9
▲ World land images	12–13
▲ World population	22–23
▲ World cities	24–25
▲ Asia landscapes	62–63
▲ Asia countries	64–67
▲ Asia threats	70–71

Albers Equal Area Conic Projection

Administrative divisions in India numbered on the map:

1. DADRA AND NAGAR HAVELI (D6)
2. DAMAN AND DIU (D6)
3. TRIPURA (H6)

miles
0 100 200 300 400 500

km
0 100 200 300 400 500 600 700 800

>6000m
5000–6000m
4000–5000m
3000–4000m
2000–3000m
1000–2000m
500–1000m
200–500m
0–200m
<0m

0–200m
200–500m
500–1000m
1000–2000m
2000–3000m
3000–4000m
4000–5000m
5000–6000m
>6000m

MYANMAR
THAILAND
INDIA
BANGLADESH
ORISSA
CHHATTISGARH
MAHARASHTRA
ANDHRA PRADESH
KARNATAKA
TAMIL NADU
KERALA
GOA
Deccan
MALDIVES
SRI LANKA
LAKSHADWEEP (India)
ANDAMAN AND NICOBAR ISLANDS (India)
INDONESIA

Arabian Sea
Bay of Bengal
Andaman Sea
INDIAN OCEAN
Laccadive Islands
Gulf of Mannar
Coromandel Coast
Malabar Coast

RANGOON (Yangon)
Kolkata (Calcutta)
Mumbai (Bombay)
Chennai (Madras)
Hyderabad
Bangalore
Pune (Poona)
Nagpur
Nashik
Aurangabad
Vadodara (Baroda)
Surat
Cochin (Kochi)
Calicut (Kozhikode)
Coimbatore
Madurai
Trivandrum (Thiruvananthapuram)
Vijayawada
Vishakhapatnam
Bhubaneshwar
Cuttack
Colombo
SRI JAYEWARDENEPURA KOTTE
MALE

asia[map13]

5°-22°N / 70°-96°E

Elevation legend:
- >6000m
- 5000-6000m
- 4000-5000m
- 3000-4000m
- 2000-3000m
- 1000-2000m
- 500-1000m
- 200-500m
- 0-200m
- <0m

- 0-200m
- 200-500m
- 500-1000m
- 1000-2000m
- 2000-3000m
- 3000-4000m
- 4000-5000m
- 5000-6000m
- >6000m

Seas and Waters

Arabian Sea

Gulf of Khambhat

Nine Degree Channel

Eight Degree Channel

Coromandel Coast

Gulf of Mannar

Laccadive Sea

States / Regions

GUJARAT

MADHYA PRADESH

CHHATTISGARH

MAHARASHTRA

ANDHRA PRADESH

KARNATAKA

KERALA

TAMIL NADU

GOA

Deccan

Islands

Laccadive Islands

Amindivi Islands

LAKSHADWEEP (India)

Cannanore Islands

MALDIVES

Major Cities

Mumbai (Bombay)

Thane

Pune (Poona)

Nashik

Aurangabad

Nagpur

Hyderabad

Secunderabad

Vijayawada

Bangalore

Chennai (Madras)

Mangalore

Calicut (Kozhikode)

Coimbatore

Cochin (Kochi)

Madurai

Trivandrum (Thiruvananthapuram)

Nagercoil

Cape Comorin

Sri Lanka

SRI LANKA

SRI JAYEWARDENEPURA KOTTE

Colombo

Moratuwa

Galle

Jaffna

Trincomalee

Kandy

Negombo

Bay

of

Bengal

INDIAN

OCEAN

Administrative divisions in India
numbered on the map:

1. DADRA AND NAGAR HAVELI (B1)
2. DAMAN AND DIU (A1,B1)
3. PONDICHERRY (D2,C4)

BANGLADESH

MYANMAR

Andaman
Islands

North
Andaman

Middle Andaman

South Andaman
Port Blair

ANDAMAN
AND
NICOBAR
ISLANDS
(India)

Andaman
Sea

Ten Degree Channel

Nicobar
Islands

Car Nicobar

Little Nicobar

Great
Nicobar

INDONESIA

CONNECTIONS

▶ subject   page#

▶ World tropical storms   16–17
▶ World population   22–23
▶ Asia landscapes   62–63
▶ Asia countries   64–67
▶ Indian Ocean   218–219

E   88°   F   92°   G

miles
1:6 000 000
0   50 100 150 200 250
km   0 50 100 150 200 250 300 350 400

Conic Equidistant Projection

asia[map14]

20°-38°N / 68°-96°E

100-101

>6000m
5000-6000m
4000-5000m
3000-4000m
2000-3000m
1000-2000m
500-1000m
200-500m
0-200m
<0m

0-200m
200-500m
500-1000m
1000-2000m
2000-3000m
3000-4000m
4000-5000m
5000-6000m
>6000m

Administrative divisions in India
numbered on the map:

1. DADRA AND NAGAR HAVELI (B5)
2. DAMAN AND DIU (A5,B5)

Arabian Sea

1:6 000 000

miles

km

Conic Equidistant Projection

13°-42°N / 30°-80°E

Administrative divisions in India
numbered on the map:

1. DADRA AND NAGAR HAVELI (I5)
2. DAMAN AND DIU (I5)

CONNECTIONS

▶ subject	page#
▶ World changes	20–21
▶ Asia landscapes	62–63
▶ Asia countries	64–67
▶ Asia issues	66–67
▶ Asia changes	68–69

1:11 000 000

miles

km

Albers Conic Equal Area Projection

asia[map]17

36°-54°N / 46°-79°E

040-041

>6000m
5000-6000m
4000-5000m
3000-4000m
2000-3000m
1000-2000m
500-1000m
200-500m
0-200m
<0m

0-200m
200-500m
500-1000m
1000-2000m
2000-3000m
3000-4000m
4000-5000m
5000-6000m
>6000m

Administrative regions in Uzbekistan numbered on the map:

1. ANDIZHANSKAYA OBLAST' (H4)
2. DZHIZAKSKAYA OBLAST' (F5)
3. FERGANSKAYA OBLAST' (G4)
4. KASHKADAR'INSKAYA OBLAST' (F5)
5. NAMANGANSKAYA OBLAST' (G4)
6. SAMARKANDSKAYA OBLAST' (F5)
7. SYRDAR'INSKAYA OBLAST' (G4)
8. TASHKENTSKAYA OBLAST' (G4)

12°-29°N / 33°-60°E

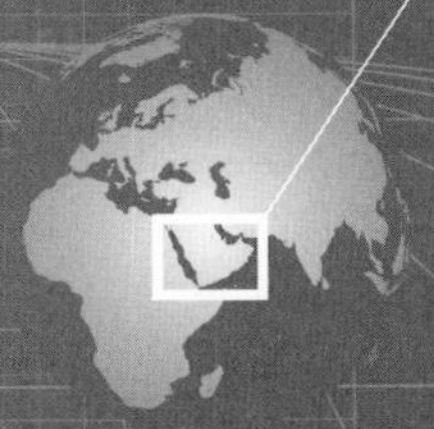

120-121

Elevation scale:
>6000m
5000-6000m
4000-5000m
3000-4000m
2000-3000m
1000-2000m
500-1000m
200-500m
0-200m
<0m

0-200m
200-500m
500-1000m
1000-2000m
2000-3000m
3000-4000m
4000-5000m
5000-6000m
>6000m

Grid references (left): 1, 2, 3, 4, 5

Latitude markings: 28°, 24°, Tropic of Cancer, 20°, 16°, 12°

Longitude markings: 33°, 36°, 40°, 44°

Major labels:

JORDAN

EGYPT
SINAI / JANÛB SÎNÂ
Mt Sinai 2285
El Tûr
Hurghada
Quseir
QENA
EL BAHR EL AHMAR
Gulf of Suez
Gulf of Aqaba

SAUDI ARABIA
TABÛK
An Nafûd
HÂ'IL
JABAL SHAMMAR
AL MADÎNAH
Medina (Al Madînah)
Yanbu' al Bahr
Rabigh
Jeddah (Jiddah)
Mecca (Makkah)
At Tâ'if
MAKKAH
'ASÎR
AL BÂHAH
Al Bâhah
BISHAH
ASMAR
AL QASÎM
Al Lith
Al Qunfidhah
TIHÂMAH
Khamis Mushayt
Abhā
JÎZÂN
Jîzân
Farasân Islands
SADAH
HAJJAH
SAN'Â'
San'â'
Hodeidah (Al Hudaydah)
AL MAHWÎT
IBB
LAHIJ
Ta'izz
Mocha (Al Mukhā)
DJIBOUTI

RED SEA
NUBIAN DESERT
Baiyuda Desert
SUDAN
NILE
Port Sudan (Bûr Sudan)
Suakin
Suakin Archipelago
Atbara
Berber
Shendi
KHARTOUM
KASSALA
Kassala
El Gezira
El Medani
GEDAREF
Gedaref
SENNAR
BLUE NILE

HALAIB TRIANGLE
UNDER SUDANESE ADMINISTRATION

ERITREA
ASMARA
Asmara
Keren
Massawa (Mitsiwa)
Dahlak Archipelago
Dahlak Marine National Park
BARKA
SENHIT
SAHEL
GASH AND SETIT
SERAE
AKELE GUZAI
DANKALIA
AFAR

ETHIOPIA
TIGRAY
AMHARA
Mek'ele
Gonder
Lake Tana
Aksum
Adwa
Adigrat
Simēn Mountains Nat. Park
Lalibela
Dese

Bottom grid references: A, B, C

asia[map19]

27°-44°N / 24°-52°E

>6000m
5000-6000m
4000-5000m
3000-4000m
2000-3000m
1000-2000m
500-1000m
200-500m
0-200m
<0m

0-200m
200-500m
500-1000m
1000-2000m
2000-3000m
3000-4000m
4000-5000m
5000-6000m
>6000m

Administrative divisions numbered on the map:

EGYPT
10. EL ISKANDARÎYA (C5)
11. BEHEIRA (C5)
12. EL QÂHIRA (C5)
13. DAQAHLÎYA (C5)
14. DUMYÂT (C5)
15. GHARBÎYA (C5)
16. ISMÂ'ÎLÎYA (D5)
17. KAFR EL SHEIKH (C5)
18. MINÛFÎYA (C5)
19. BÛR SAÎD (D5)
20. QALYÛBÎYA (C5)
21. SHARQÎYA (C5)
22. EL SUWEIS (D5)

IRAN
23. CHAHÂR MAHÂLL VA BAKHTÎARÎ (G4)
24. KOHKÎLÛYEH VA BÜYER AHMADÎ (G5)

28°-37°N / 30°-44°E

Administrative divisions in Egypt
numbered on the map

1. BŪR S'ĀID (D6)
2. DUMYĀT (C6)
3. KAFR EL SHEIKH (B6)
4. GHARBĪYA (C7)
5. MINŪFĪYA (C7)
6. QALYŪBĪYA (C7)

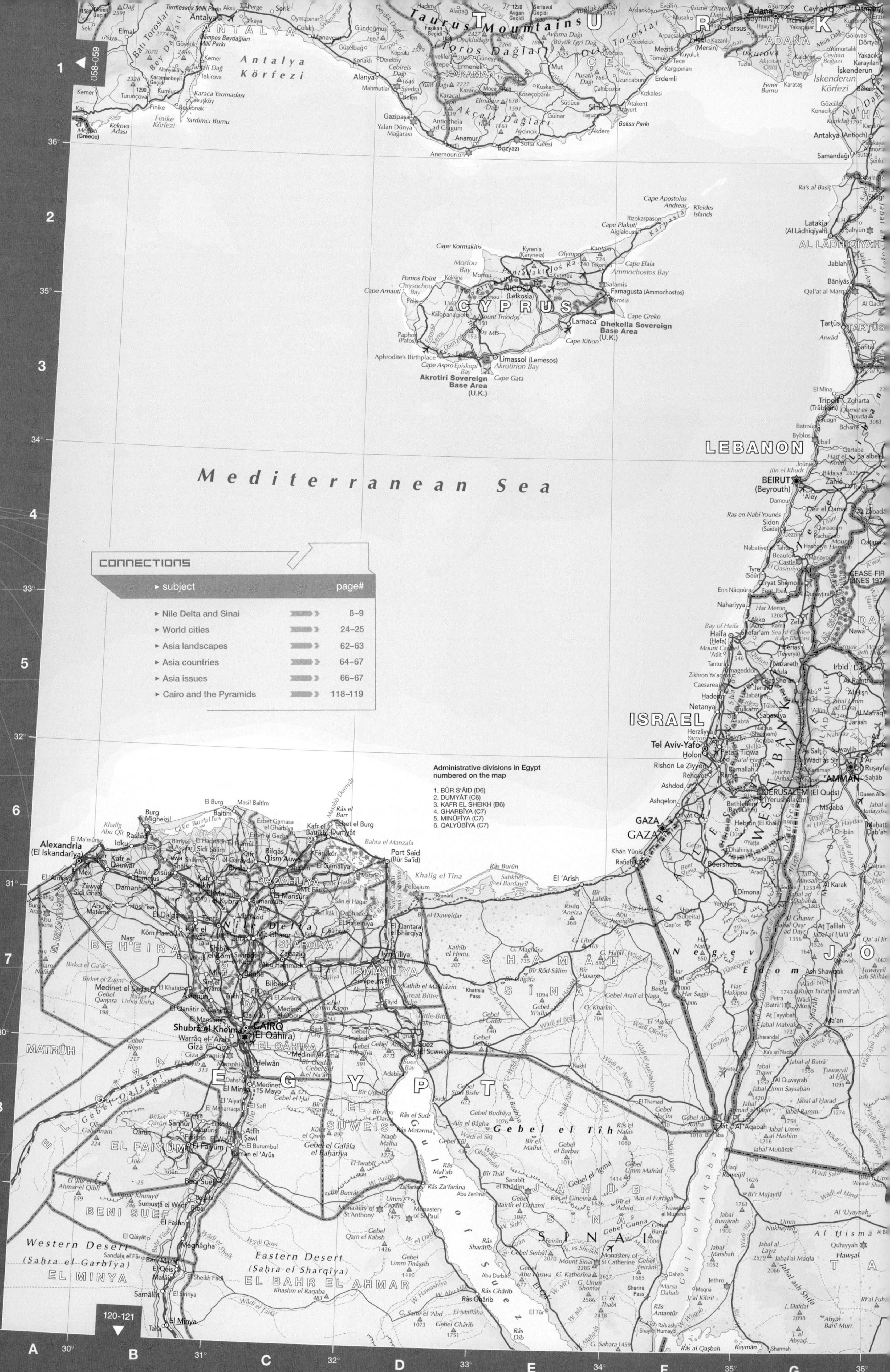

Mediterranean Sea

TURKEY

CYPRUS

LEBANON

BEIRUT
(Beyrouth)

ISRAEL

Tel Aviv-Yafo

JERUSALEM (El Quds)

GAZA

AMMAN

JORDAN

EGYPT

Alexandria
(El Iskandarîya)

CAIRO
(El Qâhira)

Giza (El Gîza)

Helwân

Western Desert
(Sahra el Gharbîya)

Eastern Desert
(Sahra el Sharqîya)

SINAI

Gebel el Tîh

BENI SUEF

EL FAIYÛM

EL MINYA

MATRÛH

BEH'EIRA

SHARQIYA

DAQAHLIYA

ISMAILIYA

Port Said
(Bûr Sa'îd)

Nile Delta

Elevation scale

| >6000m |
| 5000-6000m |
| 4000-5000m |
| 3000-4000m |
| 2000-3000m |
| 1500-2000m |
| 1000-1500m |
| 500-1000m |
| 200-500m |
| 100-200m |
| 0-100m |
| <0m |

Depth scale

| 0-200m |
| 200-500m |
| 500-1000m |
| 1000-2000m |
| 2000-3000m |
| 3000-4000m |
| 4000-5000m |
| 5000-6000m |
| >6000m |

Rift Valley, *Eritrea*

africa

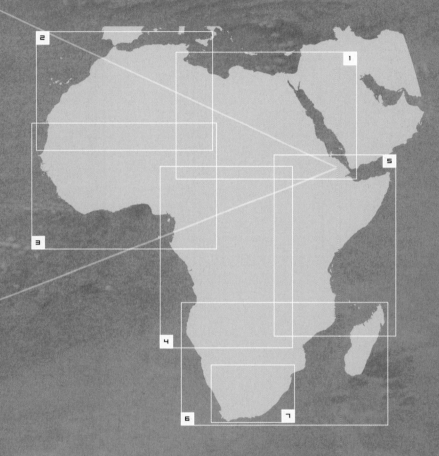

[contents]

			page#
africa [landscapes]			112–113
africa [countries]			114–115
africa [countries/issues]			116–117
africa [locations]			118–119

	map coverage	scale	page#
africa [map 1]	AFRICA Northeast	1:8 000 000	120–121
africa [map 2]	AFRICA Northwest	1:8 000 000	122–123
africa [map 3]	AFRICA West	1:8 000 000	124–125
africa [map 4]	AFRICA West Central	1:8 000 000	126–127
africa [map 5]	AFRICA East Central	1:8 000 000	128–129
africa [map 6]	AFRICA South	1:8 000 000	130–131
africa [map 7]	REPUBLIC OF SOUTH AFRICA	1:3 500 000	132–133

africa[landscapes]

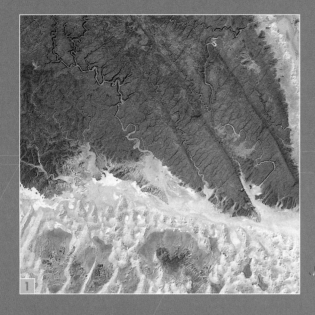

Africa, viewed here from above the southern Indian Ocean, is dominated by several striking physical features. The Sahara desert extends over most of the north and in the east the geological feature, known as the Great Rift Valley, extends from the valley of the river Jordan in Southwest Asia to Mozambique. The valley contains a string of major lakes including Lake Turkana, Lake Tanganyika and Lake Nyasa.

The river basin of the Congo, in central Africa draining into the Atlantic Ocean, is the second largest river basin in the world. The land south of the equator is higher than in the north and forms a massive plateau dissected by several large rivers which flow east to the Indian Ocean or west to the Atlantic. The most distinctive feature in the south is the Drakensberg, a range of mountains which run southwest to northeast through Lesotho and South Africa. The large island separated from Africa by the Mozambique Channel is Madagascar, the fourth largest island in the world.

1 Sahara Desert, *Algeria*

The Sahara desert crosses the continent of Africa from the Atlantic Ocean to the Red Sea. Within this vast area there is a great variety in topography with heights from 30 m below sea level to mountains over 3 300 m. This satellite image of east central Algeria shows the sand dunes stopping at the higher ground of the dark base rock. Although rain is scarce, dry river beds can be seen cutting through the rock.

Satellite/Sensor : SPOT

2 Congo River, *Democratic Republic of Congo*

This satellite image shows broken clouds above a heavily braided Congo river in Congo. The river is over 4 600 km long and has many long tributaries which result in a drainage basin of approximately 3 700 000 sq km. In this tropical area the river acts as a highway between communities where roads do not exist. The river flows into the Atlantic Ocean, forming the boundary between Angola and the Democratic Republic of Congo.

Satellite/Sensor : Space Shuttle

3 Atlas Mountains, *Morocco*

The Atlas Mountains of Morocco in northwest Africa form a major boundary between the Sahara desert and the fertile coastal plain. They are a composite of several ranges created from extensive fault movements and earthquakes, resulting in distinct rock layers and folds, as seen in this image. The dark areas are sandy beds of a seasonal river system.

Satellite/Sensor : SIR-C/X-SAR

Canary Islands

Atlas Mountains

Cape Verde Islands

Benue River

Niger River

Gulf of Guinea

Bioco

São Tome

Atlantic Ocean

Largest desert in the world
Sahara
9 065 000 sq km / 3 500 000 sq miles
Map reference 123 F4

Congo River

Largest drainage basin
Congo Basin
3 700 000 sq km / 1 429 000 sq miles
Map reference 126 C5

Bié Plateau

Victoria Falls

Namib Desert

Okavango Delta

Orange River

Kalahari Desert

Great Karoo

Drakensberg

Limpop

Cape of Good Hope

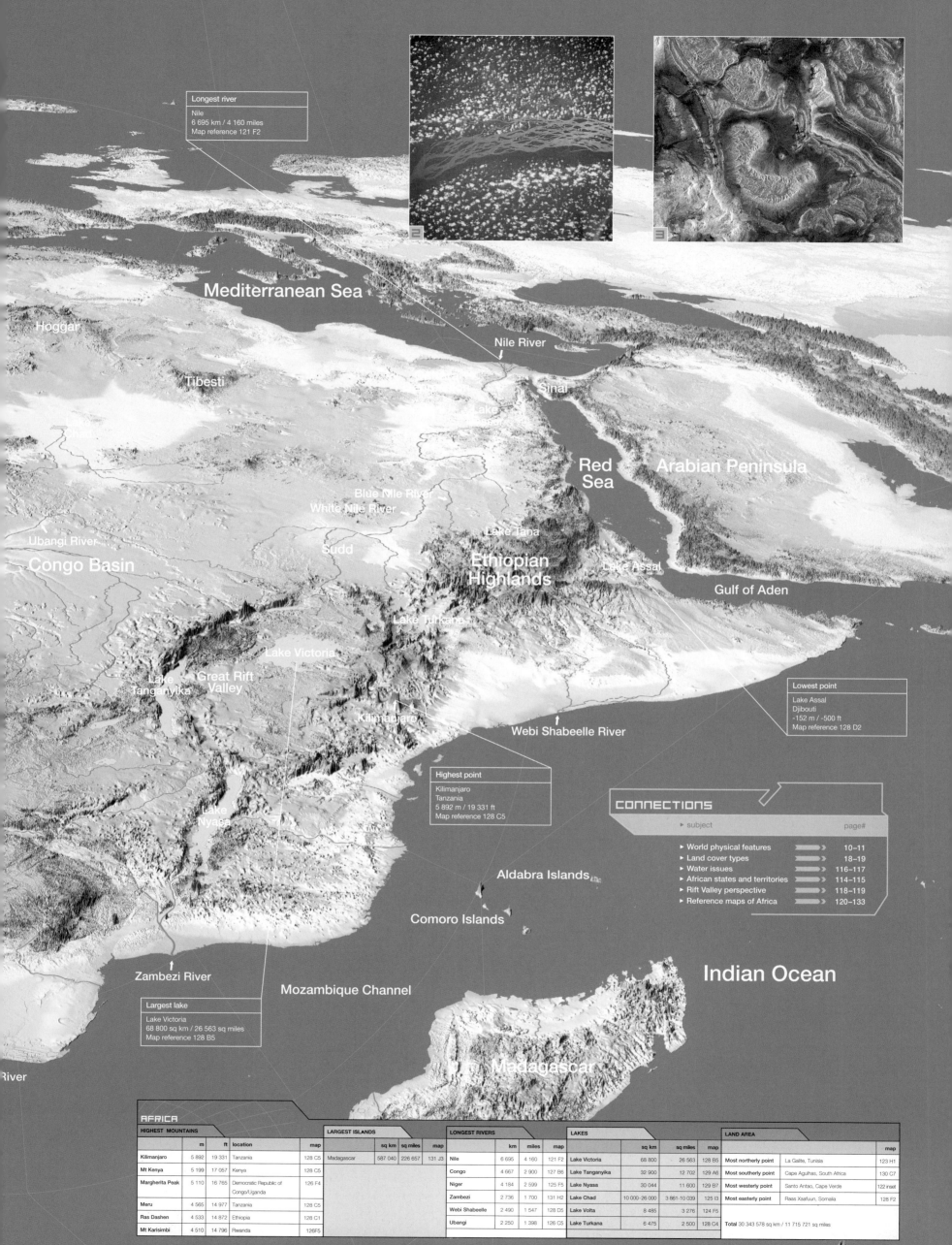

CONNECTIONS

► subject	page#
► World physical features	10–11
► Land cover types	18–19
► Water issues	116–117
► African states and territories	114–115
► Rift Valley perspective	118–119
► Reference maps of Africa	120–133

AFRICA

HIGHEST MOUNTAINS

	m	ft	location	map
Kilimanjaro	5 892	19 331	Tanzania	128 C5
Mt Kenya	5 199	17 057	Kenya	128 C5
Margherita Peak	5 110	16 765	Democratic Republic of Congo/Uganda	126 F4
Meru	4 565	14 977	Tanzania	128 C5
Ras Dashen	4 533	14 872	Ethiopia	128 C1
Mt Karisimbi	4 510	14 796	Rwanda	126 F5

LARGEST ISLANDS

	sq km	sq miles	map
Madagascar	587 040	226 657	131 J3

LONGEST RIVERS

	km	miles	map
Nile	6 695	4 160	121 F2
Congo	4 667	2 900	127 B6
Niger	4 184	2 599	125 F5
Zambezi	2 736	1 700	131 H2
Webi Shabeelle	2 490	1 547	128 D5
Ubangi	2 250	1 398	126 C5

LAKES

	sq km	sq miles	map
Lake Victoria	68 800	26 563	128 B5
Lake Tanganyika	32 900	12 702	129 A6
Lake Nyasa	30 044	11 600	125 F5
Lake Chad	10 000–26 000	3 861–10 039	125 I3
Lake Volta	8 485	3 276	124 F5
Lake Turkana	6 475	2 500	128 C4

LAND AREA

		map
Most northerly point	La Galite, Tunisia	123 H1
Most southerly point	Cape Agulhas, South Africa	130 C7
Most westerly point	Santo Antao, Cape Verde	122 inset
Most easterly point	Raas Xaafuun, Somalia	128 F2
Total 30 343 578 sq km / 11 715 721 sq miles		

africa[countries]

1 Border Post, *Algeria/Niger*

The border between Algeria and Niger lies in the centre of the Sahel region of Africa. Both countries have largely geometric borders in the relatively featureless landscape which offers no obvious physical boundaries. As a result simple indicators of the presence of a border, such as the marker shown in this photograph taken south of the actual boundary line, are the only features which advise of the passage from one country to the other.

2 Refugee Camp, *Tanzania*

Much internal migration in Africa has been instigated by war, ethnic conflict, economic disparities and famine. In 1994 over 2 million Rwandans fled to the neighbouring countries of Tanzania and the Democratic Republic of Congo to escape tribal war between Hutus and Tutsis. This photograph shows a refugee camp in Tanzania just across the border from Rwanda and gives an indication of the difficult conditions in such centres. Tanzania is currently one of East Africa's most important host countries with a refugee population of nearly half a million.

AFRICA
COUNTRIES

	area sq km	area sq miles	population	capital	languages	religions	currency	map
ALGERIA	2 381 741	919 595	30 291 000	Algiers (Alger)	Arabic, French, Berber	Sunni Muslim	Dinar	122–123
ANGOLA	1 246 700	481 354	13 134 000	Luanda	Portuguese, Bantu, local languages	Roman Catholic, Protestant, traditional beliefs	Kwanza	127
BENIN	112 620	43 483	6 272 000	Porto-Novo	French, Fon, Yoruba, Adja, local languages	Traditional beliefs, Roman Catholic, Sunni Muslim	CFA franc	125
BOTSWANA	581 370	224 468	1 541 000	Gaborone	English, Setswana, Shona, local languages	Traditional beliefs, Protestant, Roman Catholic	Pula	130–131
BURKINA	274 200	105 869	11 535 000	Ouagadougou	French, Moore (Mossi), Fulani, local languages	Sunni Muslim, traditional beliefs, Roman Catholic	CFA franc	124–125
BURUNDI	27 835	10 747	6 356 000	Bujumbura	Kirundi (Hutu, Tutsi), French	Roman Catholic, traditional beliefs, Protestant	Franc	126
CAMEROON	475 442	183 569	14 876 000	Yaoundé	French, English, Fang, Bamileke, local languages	Roman Catholic, traditional beliefs, Sunni Muslim, Protestant	CFA franc	126
CAPE VERDE	4 033	1 557	427 000	Praia	Portuguese, creole	Roman Catholic, Protestant	Escudo	124
CENTRAL AFRICAN REPUBLIC	622 436	240 324	3 717 000	Bangui	French, Sango, Banda, Baya, local languages	Protestant, Roman Catholic, traditional beliefs, Sunni Muslim	CFA franc	126
CHAD	1 284 000	495 755	7 885 000	Ndjamena	Arabic, French, Sara, local languages	Sunni Muslim, Roman Catholic, Protestant, traditional beliefs	CFA franc	120
COMOROS	1 862	719	706 000	Moroni	Comorian, French, Arabic	Sunni Muslim, Roman Catholic	Franc	129
CONGO	342 000	132 047	3 018 000	Brazzaville	French, Kongo, Monokutuba, local languages	Roman Catholic, Protestant, traditional beliefs, Sunni Muslim	CFA franc	126–127
CONGO, DEMOCRATIC REPUBLIC OF	2 345 410	905 568	50 948 000	Kinshasa	French, Lingala, Swahili, Kongo, local languages	Christian, Sunni Muslim	Franc	126–127
CÔTE D'IVOIRE	322 463	124 504	16 013 000	Yamoussoukro	French, creole, Akan, local languages	Sunni Muslim, Roman Catholic, traditional beliefs, Protestant	CFA franc	124
DJIBOUTI	23 200	8 958	632 000	Djibouti	Somali, Afar, French, Arabic	Sunni Muslim, Christian	Franc	128
EGYPT	1 000 250	386 199	67 884 000	Cairo (El Qâhira)	Arabic	Sunni Muslim, Coptic Christian	Pound	120–121
EQUATORIAL GUINEA	28 051	10 831	457 000	Malabo	Spanish, French, Fang	Roman Catholic, traditional beliefs	CFA franc	125
ERITREA	117 400	45 328	3 659 000	Asmara	Tigrinya, Tigre	Sunni Muslim, Coptic Christian	Nakfa	121
ETHIOPIA	1 133 880	437 794	62 908 000	Addis Ababa (Ādīs Ābeba)	Oromo, Amharic, Tigrinya, local languages	Ethiopian Orthodox, Sunni Muslim, traditional beliefs	Birr	128
GABON	267 667	103 347	1 230 000	Libreville	French, Fang, local languages	Roman Catholic, Protestant, traditional beliefs	CFA franc	126
THE GAMBIA	11 295	4 361	1 303 000	Banjul	English, Malinke, Fulani, Wolof	Sunni Muslim, Protestant	Dalasi	124
GHANA	238 537	92 100	19 306 000	Accra	English, Hausa, Akan, local languages	Christian, Sunni Muslim, traditional beliefs	Cedi	124–125
GUINEA	245 857	94 926	8 154 000	Conakry	French, Fulani, Malinke, local languages	Sunni Muslim, traditional beliefs, Christian	Franc	124
GUINEA-BISSAU	36 125	13 948	1 199 000	Bissau	Portuguese, crioulo, local languages	Traditional beliefs, Sunni Muslim, Christian	CFA franc	124
KENYA	582 646	224 961	30 669 000	Nairobi	Swahili, English, local languages	Christian, traditional beliefs	Shilling	128–129
LESOTHO	30 355	11 720	2 035 000	Maseru	Sesotho, English, Zulu	Christian, traditional beliefs	Loti	133
LIBERIA	111 369	43 000	2 913 000	Monrovia	English, creole, local languages	Traditional beliefs, Christian, Sunni Muslim	Dollar	124
LIBYA	1 759 540	679 362	5 290 000	Tripoli (Ṭarābulus)	Arabic, Berber	Sunni Muslim	Dinar	120
MADAGASCAR	587 041	226 658	15 970 000	Antananarivo	Malagasy, French	Traditional beliefs, Christian, Sunni Muslim	Franc	131
MALAWI	118 484	45 747	11 308 000	Lilongwe	Chichewa, English, local languages	Christian, traditional beliefs, Sunni Muslim	Kwacha	129
MALI	1 240 140	478 821	11 351 000	Bamako	French, Bambara, local languages	Sunni Muslim, traditional beliefs, Christian	CFA franc	124–125
MAURITANIA	1 030 700	397 955	2 665 000	Nouakchott	Arabic, French, local languages	Sunni Muslim	Ouguiya	122
MAURITIUS	2 040	788	1 161 000	Port Louis	English, creole, Hindi, Bhojpuri, French	Hindu, Roman Catholic, Sunni Muslim	Rupee	218
MOROCCO	446 550	172 414	29 878 000	Rabat	Arabic, Berber, French	Sunni Muslim	Dirham	122–123
MOZAMBIQUE	799 380	308 642	18 292 000	Maputo	Portuguese, Makua, Tsonga, local languages	Traditional beliefs, Roman Catholic, Sunni Muslim	Metical	131
NAMIBIA	824 292	318 261	1 757 000	Windhoek	English, Afrikaans, German, Ovambo, local languages	Protestant, Roman Catholic	Dollar	130
NIGER	1 267 000	489 191	10 832 000	Niamey	French, Hausa, Fulani, local languages	Sunni Muslim, traditional beliefs	CFA franc	125
NIGERIA	923 768	356 669	113 862 000	Abuja	English, Hausa, Yoruba, Ibo, Fulani, local languages	Sunni Muslim, Christian, traditional beliefs	Naira	125
RWANDA	26 338	10 169	7 609 000	Kigali	Kinyarwanda, French, English	Roman Catholic, traditional beliefs, Protestant	Franc	126
SÃO TOMÉ AND PRÍNCIPE	964	372	138 000	São Tomé	Portuguese, creole	Roman Catholic, Protestant	Dobra	125
SENEGAL	196 720	75 954	9 421 000	Dakar	French, Wolof, Fulani, local languages	Sunni Muslim, Roman Catholic, traditional beliefs	CFA franc	124
SEYCHELLES	455	176	80 000	Victoria	English, French, creole	Roman Catholic, Protestant	Rupee	218
SIERRA LEONE	71 740	27 699	4 405 000	Freetown	English, creole, Mende, Temne, local languages	Sunni Muslim, traditional beliefs	Leone	124
SOMALIA	637 657	246 201	8 778 000	Mogadishu (Muqdisho)	Somali, Arabic	Sunni Muslim	Shilling	128
SOUTH AFRICA, REPUBLIC OF	1 219 090	470 693	43 309 000	Pretoria/Cape Town	Afrikaans, English, nine official local languages	Protestant, Roman Catholic, Sunni Muslim, Hindu	Rand	130–131
SUDAN	2 505 813	967 500	31 095 000	Khartoum	Arabic, Dinka, Nubian, Beja, Nuer, local languages	Sunni Muslim, traditional beliefs, Christian	Dinar	120–121
SWAZILAND	17 364	6 704	925 000	Mbabane	Swazi, English	Christian, traditional beliefs	Lilangeni	133
TANZANIA	945 087	364 900	35 119 000	Dodoma	Swahili, English, Nyamwezi, local languages	Shi'a Muslim, Sunni Muslim, traditional beliefs, Christian	Shilling	128–129
TOGO	56 785	21 925	4 527 000	Lomé	French, Ewe, Kabre, local languages	Traditional beliefs, Christian, Sunni Muslim	CFA franc	125
TUNISIA	164 150	63 379	9 459 000	Tunis	Arabic, French	Sunni Muslim	Dinar	123
UGANDA	241 038	93 065	23 300 000	Kampala	English, Swahili, Luganda, local languages	Roman Catholic, Protestant, Sunni Muslim, traditional beliefs	Shilling	128
ZAMBIA	752 614	290 586	10 421 000	Lusaka	English, Bemba, Nyanja, Tonga, local languages	Christian, traditional beliefs	Kwacha	127
ZIMBABWE	390 759	150 873	12 627 000	Harare	English, Shona, Ndebele	Christian, traditional beliefs	Dollar	131

Equator

Tropic

AFRICA

TOP 10 COUNTRIES BY AREA

	sq km	sq miles	map	world rank
1. SUDAN	2 505 813	967 500	120–121	10
2. ALGERIA	2 381 741	919 595	122–123	11
3. CONGO, DEMOCRATIC REPUBLIC OF	2 345 410	905 568	126–127	12
4. LIBYA	1 759 540	679 362	120	17
5. CHAD	1 284 000	495 755	120	21
6. NIGER	1 267 000	489 191	125	22
7. ANGOLA	1 246 700	481 354	127	23
8. MALI	1 240 140	478 821	124–125	24
9. SOUTH AFRICA, REPUBLIC OF	1 219 090	470 693	130–131	25
10. ETHIOPIA	1 133 880	437 794	128	27

TOP 10 COUNTRIES BY POPULATION

	population	map	world rank
1. NIGERIA	113 862 000	125	10
2. EGYPT	67 884 000	120–121	16
3. ETHIOPIA	62 908 000	128	18
4. CONGO, DEMOCRATIC REPUBLIC OF	50 948 000	126–127	23
5. SOUTH AFRICA, REPUBLIC OF	43 309 000	130–131	27
6. TANZANIA	35 119 000	128–129	32
7. SUDAN	31 095 000	120–121	33
8. KENYA	30 669 000	128–129	35
9. ALGERIA	30 291 000	122–123	36
10. MOROCCO	29 878 000	122–123	37

CONNECTIONS

▸ subject	page#
▸ World physical features	8–9
▸ World countries	10–11
▸ Africa issues	116–117
▸ Reference maps of Africa	120–133

DEPENDENT AND DISPUTED TERRITORIES

		territorial status	area sq km	area sq miles	population	capital	languages	religions	currency	map
Canary Islands (Islas Canarias)		Autonomous Community of Spain	7 447	2 875	1 606 522	Santa Cruz de Tenerife, Las Palmas	Spanish	Roman Catholic	Peseta	122
Ceuta		Spanish Territory	19	7	68 796	Ceuta	Spanish, Arabic	Roman Catholic, Muslim	Peseta	122
Madeira		Autonomous Region of Portugal	779	301	259 000	Funchal	Portuguese	Roman Catholic, Protestant	Port. escudo	122
Mayotte		French Territorial Collectivity	373	144	144 944	Dzaoudzi	French, Mahorian	Sunni Muslim, Christian	French franc	129
Melilla		Spanish Territory	13	5	59 576	Melilla	Spanish, Arabic	Roman Catholic, Muslim	Peseta	123
Réunion		French Overseas Department	2 551	985	721 000	St-Denis	French, creole	Roman Catholic	French franc	218
St Helena and Dependencies		United Kingdom Overseas Territory	121	47	6 000	Jamestown	English	Protestant, Roman Catholic	Pound sterling	216
Western Sahara		Disputed territory (Morocco)	266 000	102 703	252 000	Laâyoune	Arabic	Sunni Muslim	Moroccan dirham	122

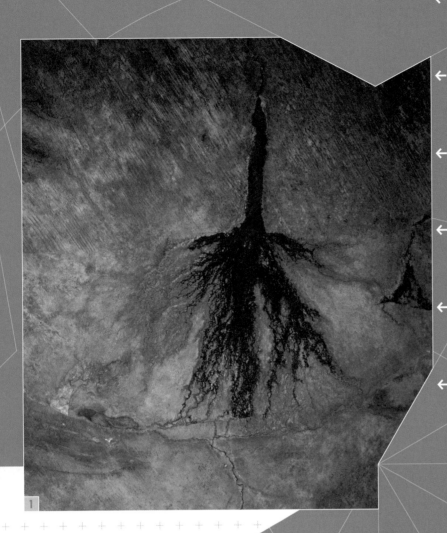

Okavango Delta, *Botswana*

This Shuttle photograph shows the world's largest inland delta, the Okavango Delta in Botswana. The Okavango river originates in southeast Angola and ends in this spectacular and unique alluvial plain covering 10 000 square kilometres. The river is fed by rains from October to March which produce rich seasonal vegetation and support great numbers of wildlife. Scientists have identified this to be one of the most ecologically sensitive areas on Earth.

Satellite/Sensor : Space Shuttle

CONNECTIONS

► subject		page#
► World physical features		8–9
► World countries		10–11
► World land cover types		18–19
► Africa countries		114–115
► Reference maps of Africa		120–133
► South America impacts		196–197

Nile Valley, *Egypt*

The Nile river winds through Egypt in this satellite image, ending in the distinctive triangular delta on the Mediterranean coast. The dark blue water and green vegetation of the irrigated valley and delta provide a striking contrast to the surrounding desert. Thick layers of silt carried downstream for thousands of years provide the delta with the most fertile soil in Africa. The Suez Canal is also visible on the image, providing a link between the Mediterranean Sea at the top of the image and the Gulf of Suez and the Red Sea to the right.

Satellite/Sensor : MODIS

Flooded Village, *Kenya*

This village near Garsen was flooded when the Tana river burst its banks. An increase in extreme weather patterns occurred throughout the world in 1998. Some cases were blamed on the periodic warming of Pacific Ocean waters known as El Niño. In east Africa the regular problems of drought were replaced by excessive rainfall which led to the destruction of crops and the threat of famine. This village felt the affect of Kenya's annual rainfall increasing by over 1000mm in 1998.

Fig. #01

Safe water
Percentage of total population using
improved drinking water sources 1999

per cent

91–100
66 – 90
52 – 65
31 – 51
0 – 30
no data

4 **Water Well,** *Burkina*

This scene in the Silmiougou Valley in Burkina is common across
much of Africa. Such basic wells and hand water pumps provide
an essential source of fresh water in large parts of the continent.
Finding sufficient water of good quality is a major challenge facing
much of Africa's population, particularly in sub-Saharan Africa
The map indicates the extent of this problem, with Africa having
some of the worst figures in the world for availability of improved
water. Impure water is a major contributory factor to disease, and
drought, with resultant food shortages, is a regular threat to the
lives of many people in the region.

5 **Mozambique Floods**

This pair of SPOT satellite images illustrates the large scale
flooding which hit Mozambique in early 2000. The course of
the Incomati river can clearly be seen in the 1998 image (left),
however the valley is flooded extensively in the 2000 image
(right) and is visible as a wide green feature down the centre of
the image. The flooding hit large areas of southern Africa and
left thousands homeless. Mozambique was the country worst
affected, particularly in the northern Maputo region shown in
the images.

Satellite/Sensor : SPOT

1 Cape Town, *Republic of South Africa*

Cape Town is the legislative capital of South Africa, the capital city of Western Cape Province and is located 40 km from the Cape of Good Hope. This view from Table Mountain shows the full extent of the city spreading out to the waterfront area on the shores of Table Bay.

2 Cairo, *Egypt*

The largest city in Africa and capital of Egypt, Cairo is situated on the right bank of the river Nile. The main built-up area appears grey in this image. The famous pyramids and the suburb of Giza are visible to the lower left where the city meets the desert. Cairo airport can be seen at the upper right. Agricultural areas, achieved by extensive irrigation, show as deep red around the city.

Satellite/Sensor : SPOT

3 The Great Rift Valley, *Africa*

The Great Rift Valley is a huge, linear depression which marks a series of geological faults resulting from tectonic activity. The section of the valley shown in this 3-D perspective view extends from Lake Nyasa in the south to the Red Sea coast in the north. The valley splits into two branches north of Lake Nyasa and then combines again through the Ethiopian Highlands. The western branch is very prominent in the image and contains several lakes, including Lake Tanganyika. The eastern branch passes to the west of Kilimanjaro, the highest mountain to the right of the image, and contains Lake Turkana on the northern border of Kenya.

4 Victoria Falls, *Zambia/Zimbabwe*

The Victoria Falls are located in the Zambezi river on the Zambia/Zimbabwe border near the town of Livingstone. The river is over 1.7 km wide at the point where the falls drop 108 m over a precipice into a narrow chasm. The volume of water in the falls varies with the seasons. Land on the Zimbabwe side of the falls is preserved as a national park.

5 Sahara Desert, *Africa*

This photograph was taken in the eastern Sahara in Libya and illustrates sharp contrasts in the landscape. At the top are huge sand dunes which have been shaped by the wind. The area in the middle view has been planted with trees, to prevent the movement of sand and soil, and the irrigated area in the near view is typical of a fertile oasis, where the land has been worked to produce crops and to support livestock.

6 The Pyramids, *Egypt*

The suburbs of Giza, shown on the left of this satellite image, spread out from the city of Cairo to an arid plateau on which stand the famous Great Pyramids. The largest, shown at the bottom centre of the image, is the Great Pyramid of Cheops. To the left of this are three small pyramids collectively known as the Pyramids of Queens. Above them is the Great Sphinx. The pyramid at the centre right of the image is Chephren and the small one at the top right is Mycerinus.

Satellite/Sensor : IKONOS

CONNECTIONS

► subject	page#
► Types of imagery	4–5
► World physical features	8–9
► World cities	24–25
► Africa landscapes	112–113
► Africa countries	114–117

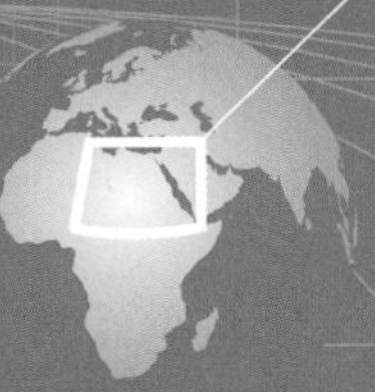

>6000m
5000-6000m
4000-5000m
3000-4000m
2000-3000m
1000-2000m
500-1000m
200-500m
0-200m
<0m

0-200m
200-500m
500-1000m
1000-2000m
2000-3000m
3000-4000m
4000-5000m
5000-6000m
>6000m

1
2
3
4
5
6
7

A B C D

Mediterranean Sea

Crete
(Kriti)
(Greece)

TUNISIA

TRIPOLI
(Tarābulus)

Gulf of Sirte
(Khalīj Surt)

Benghazi

CYRENAICA

Tubruq

TRIPOLITANIA

Al Hamādah al Hamrā'

Hammādat Tingharat

Idhān Awbārī

LIBYA

S a h a r a

Idhān Murzūq

Great Sand

Rebiana
Sand Sea
(Ramlat Rabyānah)

AS SARĪR

Sarīr
Tibesti

Jabal
Mountains of Tummo

ALGERIA

Tropic of Cancer

Plateau du Manguéni

Plateau
du Djado

Plateau
du Tchigai

Ténéré
du
Tafassâsset

A G A D E Z

Tibesti

Réserve Naturelle
Intégrale dite
Sanctuaire
des Addax

Réserve Naturelle
Nationale
de l'Aïr et du Ténéré

Erg du Ténéré

N I G E R

Erg de Bilma

BORKOU-ENNEDI-TIBESTI

Dépression du Mourdi

DIFFA

BODÉLÉ

Erg du Djourab

Ennedi

ZINDER

KANEM

C H A D

BILTINE

BATHA

Zinder

LAC

Lake Chad

OUADDAÏ

WESTERN
DARFUR

Marra
Plateau

BORNO

NIGERIA

Maiduguri

CAMEROON

NDJAMENA

CHARI-
BAGUIRMI

GUÉRA

SALAMAT

122-123

126-127

16°-40°N / 20°W-16°E

CONNECTIONS

A T L A N T I C

O C E A N

Arquipélago da Madeira
Ilha de Porto Santo
Machico **Madeira**
FUNCHAL (Portugal)
Ilhas Desertas

Ilhas Selvagens
(Portugal)

Canary Islands
(Spain)
Islas Canarias
La Palma   Santa Cruz   Lanzarote
2426 de la Palma
Tenerife   Arrecife
Pico del Teide Santa Cruz   Fuerteventura
La Gomera   de Tenerife   Puerto del Rosario
1500   Las Palmas
El Hierro   de Gran Canaria
Gran   Punta
Canaria   Pesebre

WESTERN

SAHARA

Tropic of Cancer

Ad Dakhla

M A U R I T A N I A

NOUAKCHOTT

SENEGAL

St-Louis

>6000m
5000-6000m
4000-5000m
3000-4000m
2000-3000m
1000-2000m
500-1000m
200-500m
0-200m
<0m

0-200m
200-500m
500-1000m
1000-2000m
2000-3000m
3000-4000m
4000-5000m
5000-6000m
>6000m

MADRID
PORTUGAL
LISBON
(Lisboa)
SPAIN
RABAT
Casablanca
MOROCCO
Marrakech

Agadir

Sidi Ifni

LAÂYOUNE

MAURITANIA

Nouâdhibou

Zouérat

TIRIS

ZEMMOUR

A D R A R

OUARÂNE

TOMBOUCT

1
2
3
4
5
6

A   B   C   D
20° 16° 12° 8° 4°

120-121

Administrative divisions
in Central African Republic
numbered on the map:

1. MAMBÉRÉ-KADÉÏ (I5)
2. NANA-MAMBÉRÉ (I5)
3. SANGHA MAMBÉRÉ (I6)

Gulf

of Guinea

CONNECTIONS

SÃO TOMÉ
AND
PRÍNCIPE

126-127

| E | F | G | H | I |

miles

1 : 8 000 000

km

Lambert Azimuthal Equal Area Projection

14°N-20°S / 8°-32°E

130-131

1:8 000 000

Lambert Azimuthal Equal Area Projection

miles

km

CONNECTIONS

▶ subject   page#

▲ World physical features   8-9
▲ Africa landscapes   112-113
▲ Africa countries   114-117
▶ Africa locations   118-119

>6000m
5000-6000m
4000-5000m
3000-4000m
2000-3000m
1000-2000m
500-1000m
200-500m
0-200m

0-200m
200-500m
500-1000m
1000-2000m
2000-3000m
3000-4000m
4000-5000m
5000-6000m
>6000m
<0m

ATLANTIC

OCEAN

TANZANIA

CONGO

ANGOLA

ZAMBIA

NAMIBIA

BOTSWANA

ZIMBABWE

MOZAMBIQUE

CONNECTIONS

► subject	page#
► World weather extremes	16–17
► Savanna land cover	18–19
► Africa countries	114–117
► Africa locations	118–119
► Indian Ocean map	218–219

Administrative regions in Tanzania
numbered on the map:

1. PEMBA NORTH (C6)
2. PEMBA SOUTH (C6)
3. ZANZIBAR NORTH (C6)
4. ZANZIBAR SOUTH (C6)
5. ZANZIBAR WEST (C6)

TANZANIA

MOZAMBIQUE

MADAGASCAR

MALAWI

ZAMBIA

ZIMBABWE

COMOROS

DEM. REP. CONGO

Great Rift Valley

Lake Malawi

Lake Tanganyika

Mozambique Channel

MORONI

Mayotte (France)

HARARE

LILONGWE

DODOMA

Dar es Salaam

Mombasa

Zanzibar Island

Pemba Island

Mafia Island

Aldabra Islands (Seychelles)

Farquhar Islands (Seychelles)

Providence Atoll

Îles Glorieuses

18°S-16°N / 29°-52°E

1:8 000 000

Lambert Azimuthal Equal Area Projection

km
miles

100 200 300 400 500

>6000m
5000-6000m
4000-5000m
3000-4000m
2000-3000m
1000-2000m
500-1000m
200-500m
0-200m
<0m
0-200m
200-500m
500-1000m
1000-2000m
2000-3000m
3000-4000m
4000-5000m
5000-6000m
>6000m

130-131

africa[map6]

14°-36°S / 8°-51°E

ATLANTIC

OCEAN

ANGOLA

NAMIBIA

WINDHOEK

Tropic of Capricorn

CAPE TOWN

Cape of Good Hope

miles
1 : 8 000 000

km

Lambert Azimuthal Equal Area Projection

ZAMBIA

MALAWI

NIASSA

CABO DELGADO

LUSAKA

TETE

NAMPULA

ZAMBEZIA

Nampula

Nacala

CENTRAL

HARARE

MANICALAND

ZIMBABWE

MATABELELAND
NORTH

MIDLANDS

MATABELELAND
SOUTH

MASVINGO

SOFALA

Beira

M
O
Z
A
M
B
I
Q
U
E

Mozambique Channel

Juan de Nova
(France)

Bassas da India
(France)

CENTRAL

BOTSWANA

INHAMBANE

GAZA

Tanjona Bobaomby

Antsiranana

ANTSIRAÑANA

Mahajanga

MAHAJANGA

INDIAN

OCEAN

NORTH
WEST

PRETORIA

Johannesburg

MPUMALANGA

MAPUTO

SWAZILAND

MBABANE

FREE
STATE

REPUBLIC OF

LESOTHO

MASERU

KWAZULU-NATAL

Durban

Juan de Nova
(France)

ANTANANARIVO

ANTANANARIVO

TOAMASINA

Toamasina

Antsirabe

Fianarantsoa

FIANARANTSOA

M
A
D
A
G
A
S
C
A
R

AFRICA

EASTERN
CAPE

Port Elizabeth

TOLIARA

Toliara

Tropic of Capricorn

Tanjona Vohimena

1 : 8 000 000

1 : 3 500 000

miles
0   25   50   75   100   125

km
0 25 50 75 100 125 150 175 200

Lambert Azimuthal Equal Area Projection

Great Barrier Reef, *Australia*

oceania

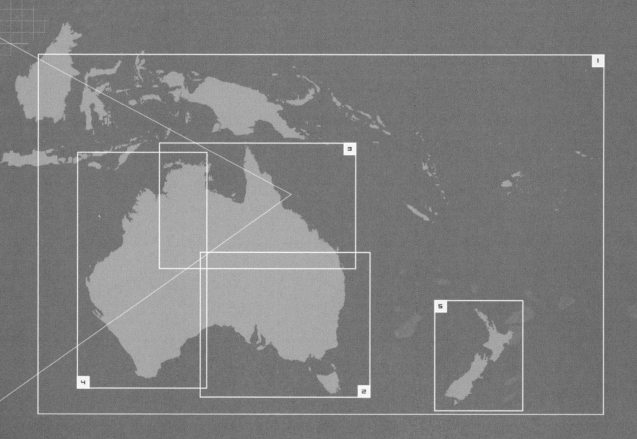

[contents]

		page#
oceania [landscapes]		136–137
oceania [countries]		138–139
oceania [threats]		140–141
oceania [features]		142–143

	map coverage	scale	page#
oceania [map 1]	AUSTRALIA and PACIFIC Southwest	1:18 000 000	144–145
oceania [map 2]	AUSTRALIA Southeast	1:6 000 000	146–147
oceania [map 3]	AUSTRALIA Northeast	1:6 000 000	148–149
oceania [map 4]	AUSTRALIA West	1:6 000 000	150–151
oceania [map 5]	NEW ZEALAND	1:3 250 000	152–153

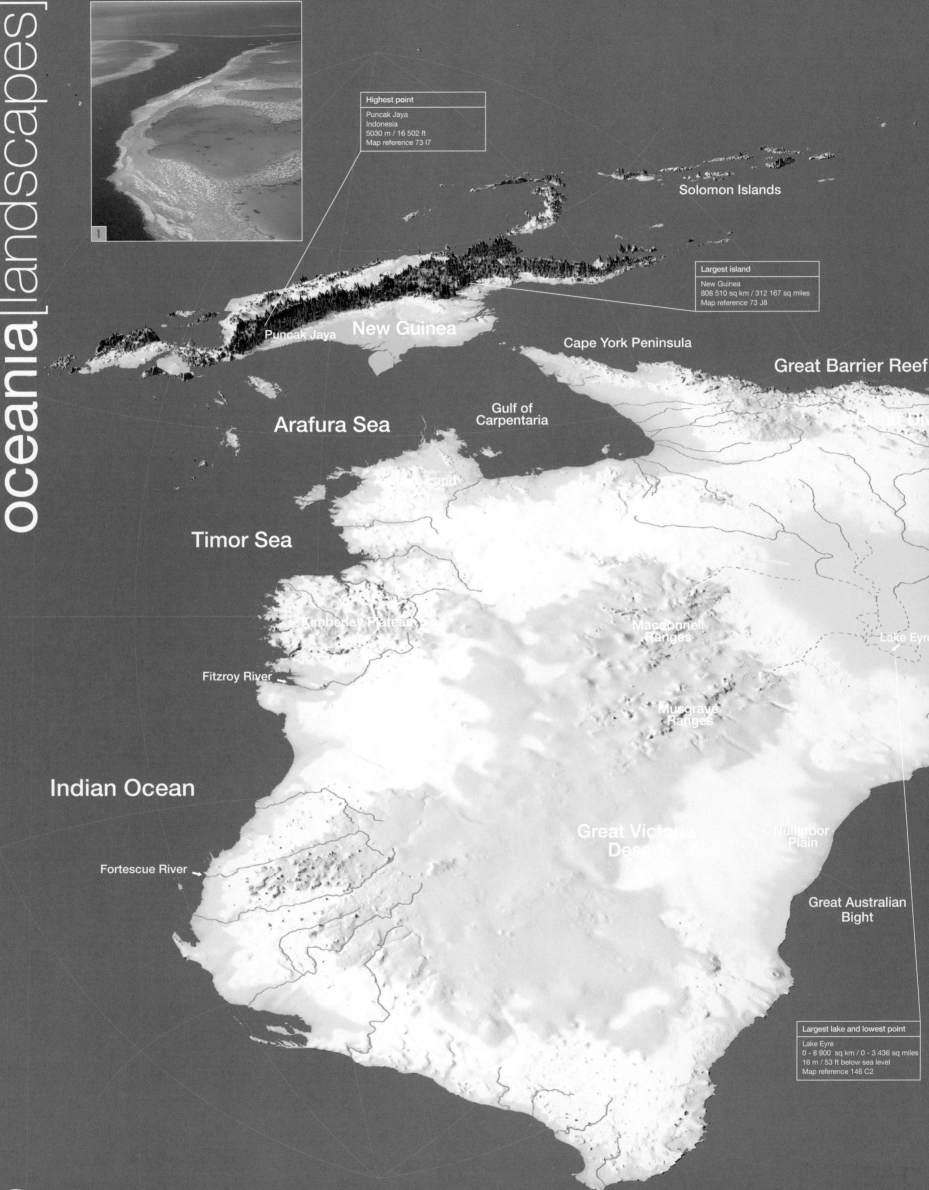

oceania[landscapes]

Highest point

Puncak Jaya
Indonesia
5030 m / 16 502 ft
Map reference 73 I7

Largest island

New Guinea
808 510 sq km / 312 167 sq miles
Map reference 73 J8

Solomon Islands

Puncak Jaya

New Guinea

Cape York Peninsula

Great Barrier Reef

Arafura Sea

Gulf of
Carpentaria

Great Div

Timor Sea

Kimberley Plateau

Macdonnell
Ranges

Lake Eyre

Indian Ocean

Fitzroy River

Musgrave
Ranges

Fortescue River

**Great Victoria
Desert**

Nullarbor
Plain

**Great Australian
Bight**

Largest lake and lowest point

Lake Eyre
0 - 8 900 sq km / 0 - 3 436 sq miles
16 m / 53 ft below sea level
Map reference 146 C2

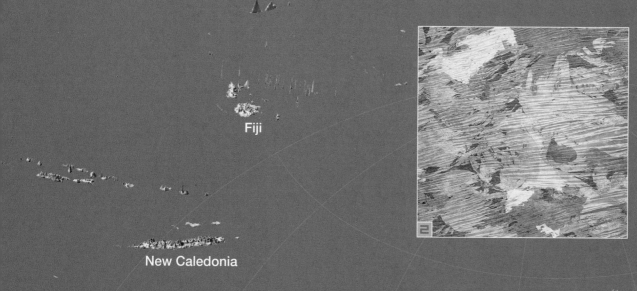

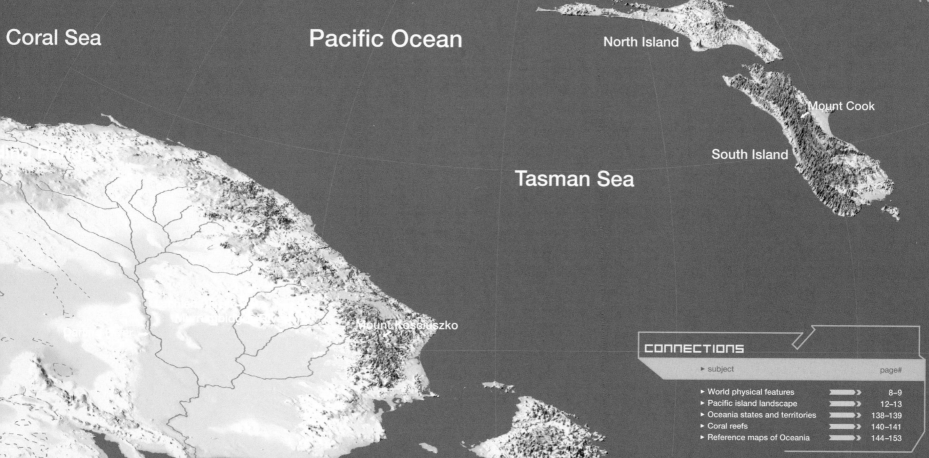

Fiji

New Caledonia

Coral Sea

Pacific Ocean

North Island

Mount Cook

South Island

Tasman Sea

Mount Kosciuszko

Murray River

Tasmania

Longest river
Murray-Darling
3 750 km / 2 330 miles
Map reference 146 C3

CONNECTIONS

▶ subject   page#

▶ World physical features ——————▶ 8–9
▶ Pacific island landscape ——————▶ 12–13
▶ Oceania states and territories ——————▶ 138–139
▶ Coral reefs ——————▶ 140–141
▶ Reference maps of Oceania ——————▶ 144–153

1   Great Barrier Reef, *Australia*

This photograph shows the Great Barrier Reef which stretches for over 2 000 km off the coast of Queensland, Australia. This is the largest area of coral reefs in the world, and consists of a mixture of small islands, reefs and atolls. Whitsunday Island, shown here, is typical of the landscape. Beyond the reef is the Coral Sea.

2   Gibson Desert, *Australia*

The Gibson Desert in Western Australia has distinctive long, thin dune-like ridges which are covered with resilient desert grasses. The different coloured patches are due to a combination of seasonal new growth and fire damage. The dark areas on this image indicate the most recent summer fire outbreaks. The darkness fades as new growth appears.

Satellite/Sensor : SPOT

3   Mount Cook, *New Zealand*

Mount Cook on South Island, New Zealand is the highest peak in the country at 3 754 m. This photograph looks southeast towards Lake Pukaki, close to the horizon on the left. The peak is part of the Southern Alps mountain range and the National Park surrounding Mount Cook is designated a World Heritage area. The bare rock face below the summit resulted from a major avalanche in 1991 which reduced the height of the mountain by 20 m.

The continent of Oceania comprises Australia, the islands of New Zealand, New Guinea and numerous small islands and island groups in the Pacific Ocean, including Micronesia, Melanesia and Polynesia. The main landmass of Australia is largely desert, with many salt lakes and a low artesian basin in the east central area. The mountains of the Great Dividing Range run parallel to the east coast and are the source of the main river system, the Murray-Darling. The Great Barrier Reef, which stretches off the coast of Queensland, Australia, is the world's largest deposit of coral.

New Guinea is a mountainous island, most of which is covered with tropical forest. New Zealand has a great variety of landscape types, from tropical environments in the north of North Island to sub-Antarctic conditions in the south of South Island. North Island has extensive volcanic areas and South Island s mountainous, being dominated by the Southern Alps range.

OCEANIA

HIGHEST MOUNTAINS

	m	ft	location	map
Puncak Jaya	5 030	16 502	Indonesia	73 I7
Puncak Trikora	4 730	15 518	Indonesia	73 I7
Puncak Mandala	4 700	15 420	Indonesia	73 I7
Puncak Yamin	4 595	15 075	Indonesia	73 I7
Mt Wilhelm	4 509	14 793	Papua New Guinea	73 J8
Mt Kubor	4 359	14 301	Papua New Guinea	73 J8

LARGEST ISLANDS

	sq km	sq miles	map
New Guinea	808 510	312 167	73 J8
South Island, New Zealand	151 215	58 384	153 F11
North Island, New Zealand	115 777	44 702	152 J6
Tasmania	67 800	26 178	147 E5

LONGEST RIVERS

	km	miles	map
Murray-Darling	3 750	2 330	146 C3
Darling	2 739	1 702	146 D3
Murray	2 589	1 608	146 C3
Murrumbidgee	1 690	1 050	147 E3
Lachlan	1 480	919	147 D3
Macquarie	950	590	147 E2

LAKES

	sq km	sq miles	map
Lake Eyre	0-8 900	0-3 436	146 C2
Lake Torrens	0-5 780	0-2 232	146 C2

LAND AREA

		map
Most northerly point	Eastern Island, North Pacific Ocean	220 H4
Most southerly point	Macquarie Island, South Pacific Ocean	220 F9
Most westerly point	Cape Inscription, Australia	151 A5
Most easterly point	Ile Clipperton, North Pacific Ocean	221 L5

Total land area: 8 844 516 sq km / 3 414 887 sq miles
(includes New Guinea and Pacific Island nations)

OCEANIA

COUNTRIES

		area sq km	area sq miles	population	capital	languages	religions	currency	map
AUSTRALIA		7 682 395	2 966 189	19 138 000	Canberra	English, Italian, Greek	Protestant, Roman Catholic, Orthodox	Dollar	144–145
FIJI		18 330	7 077	814 000	Suva	English, Fijian, Hindi	Christian, Hindu, Sunni Muslim	Dollar	145
KIRIBATI		717	277	83 000	Bairiki	Gilbertese, English	Roman Catholic, Protestant	Australian dollar	145
MARSHALL ISLANDS		181	70	51 000	Delap-Uliga-Djarrit	English, Marshallese	Protestant, Roman Catholic	US dollar	220
MICRONESIA, FEDERATED STATES OF		701	271	123 000	Palikir	English, Chuukese, Pohnpeian, local languages	Roman Catholic, Protestant	US dollar	220
NAURU		21	8	12 000	Yaren	Nauruan, English	Protestant, Roman Catholic	Australian dollar	145
NEW ZEALAND		270 534	104 454	3 778 000	Wellington	English, Maori	Protestant, Roman Catholic	Dollar	152–153
PAPUA NEW GUINEA		462 840	178 704	4 809 000	Port Moresby	English, Tok Pisin (creole), local languages	Protestant, Roman Catholic, traditional beliefs	Kina	144–145
SAMOA		2 831	1 093	159 000	Apia	Samoan, English	Protestant, Roman Catholic	Tala	145
SOLOMON ISLANDS		28 370	10 954	447 000	Honiara	English, creole, local languages	Protestant, Roman Catholic	Dollar	145
TONGA		748	289	99 000	Nuku'alofa	Tongan, English	Protestant, Roman Catholic	Pa'anga	145
TUVALU		25	10	11 000	Vaiaku	Tuvaluan, English	Protestant	Dollar	145
VANUATU		12 190	4 707	197 000	Port Vila	English, Bislama (creole), French	Protestant, Roman Catholic, traditional beliefs	Vatu	145

DEPENDENT TERRITORIES

		territorial status	area sq km	area sq miles	population	capital	languages	religions	currency	map
American Samoa		United States Unincorporated Territory	197	76	68 000	Fagatoga	Samoan, English	Protestant, Roman Catholic	US dollar	145
Ashmore and Cartier Islands		Australian External Territory	5	2	uninhabited					150
Baker Island		United States Unincorporated Territory	1	0.4	uninhabited					145
Cook Islands		Self-governing New Zealand Territory	293	113	20 000	Avarua	English, Maori	Protestant, Roman Catholic	Dollar	221
Coral Sea Islands Territory		Australian External Territory	22	8	uninhabited					145
French Polynesia		French Overseas Territory	3 265	1 261	233 000	Papeete	French, Tahitian, Polynesian languages	Protestant, Roman Catholic	Pacific franc	221
Guam		United States Unincorporated Territory	541	209	155 000	Agana	Chamorro, English, Tapalog	Roman Catholic	US dollar	73
Howland Island		United States Unincorporated Territory	2	1	uninhabited					145
Jarvis Island		United States Unincorporated Territory	5	2	uninhabited					221
Johnston Atoll		United States Unincorporated Territory	3	1	uninhabited					221
Kingman Reef		United States Unincorporated Territory	1	0.4	uninhabited					221
Midway Islands		United States Unincorporated Territory	6	2	uninhabited					220
New Caledonia		French Overseas Territory	19 058	7 358	215 000	Nouméa	French, local	Roman Catholic, Protestant, Sunni Muslim	Pacific franc	145
Niue		Self-governing New Zealand Overseas Territory	258	100	2 000	Alofi	English, Polynesian	Christian	NZ dollar	145
Norfolk Island		Australian External Territory	35	14	2 000	Kingston	English	Protestant, Roman Catholic	Australian Dollar	145
Northern Mariana Islands		United States Commonwealth	477	184	73 000	Capitol Hill	English, Chamorro, local languages	Roman Catholic	US dollar	73
Palmyra Atoll		United States Unincorporated Territory	12	5	uninhabited					221
Pitcairn Islands		United Kingdom Overseas Territory	45	17	68	Adamstown	English	Protestant	NZ dollar	221
Tokelau		New Zealand Overseas Territory	10	4	1 000		English, Tokelauan	Christian	NZ dollar	145
Wake Island		United States Unincorporated Territory	7	3	uninhabited					220
Wallis and Futuna Islands		French Overseas Territory	274	106	14 000	Mata\'utu	French, Wallisian, Futunian	Roman Catholic	Pacific franc	145

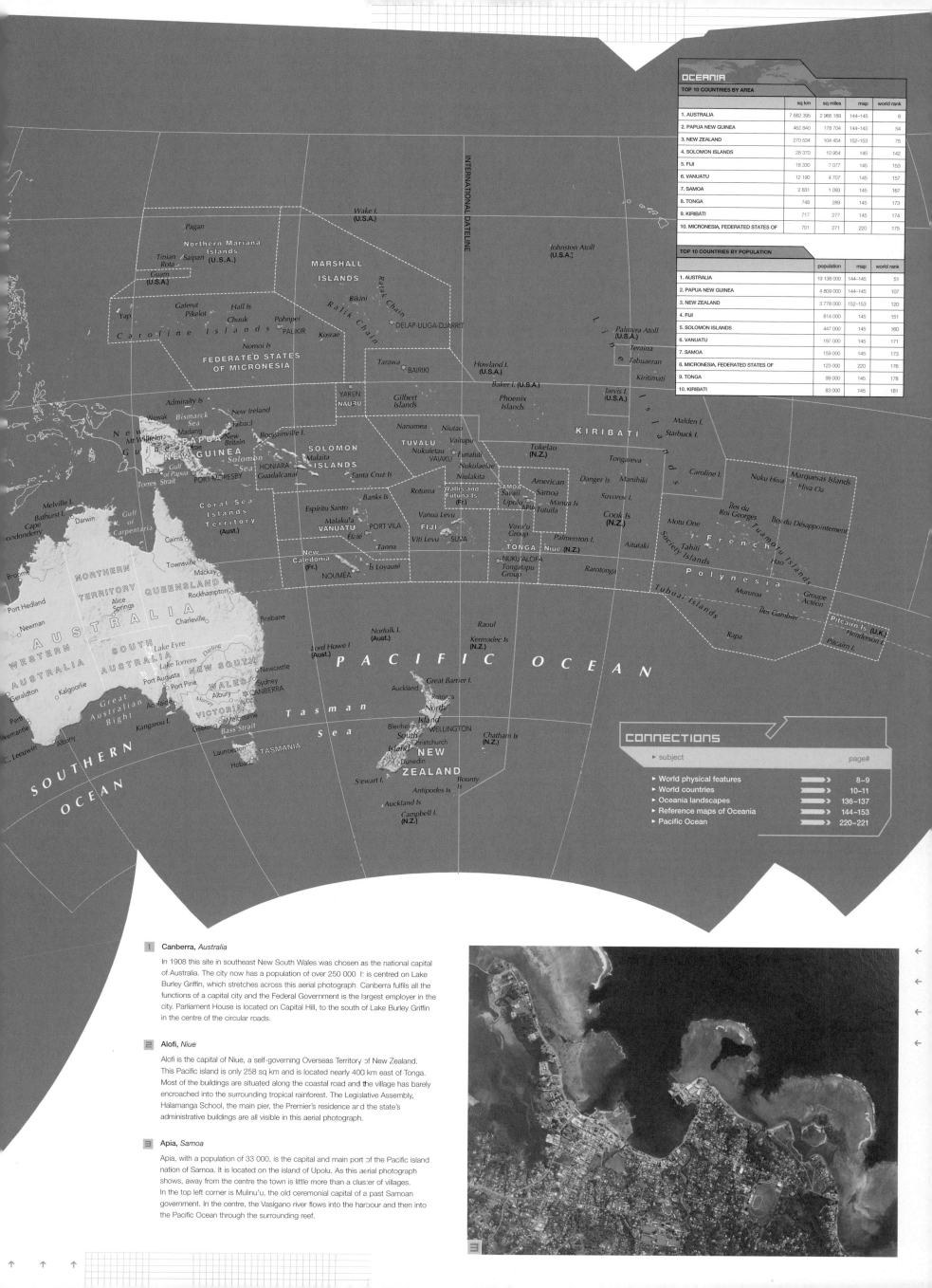

OCEANIA

TOP 10 COUNTRIES BY AREA

	sq km	sq miles	map	world rank
1. AUSTRALIA	7 682 395	2 966 189	144–145	6
2. PAPUA NEW GUINEA	462 840	178 704	144–145	54
3. NEW ZEALAND	270 534	104 454	152–153	75
4. SOLOMON ISLANDS	28 370	10 954	145	142
5. FIJI	18 330	7 077	153	153
6. VANUATU	12 190	4 707	145	157
7. SAMOA	2 831	1 093	145	167
8. TONGA	748	289	145	173
9. KIRIBATI	717	277	145	174
10. MICRONESIA, FEDERATED STATES OF	701	271	220	175

TOP 10 COUNTRIES BY POPULATION

	population	map	world rank
1. AUSTRALIA	19 138 000	144–145	51
2. PAPUA NEW GUINEA	4 809 000	144–145	107
3. NEW ZEALAND	3 778 000	152–153	120
4. FIJI	814 000	145	151
5. SOLOMON ISLANDS	447 000	145	160
6. VANUATU	197 000	145	171
7. SAMOA	159 000	145	173
8. MICRONESIA, FEDERATED STATES OF	123 000	220	176
9. TONGA	99 000	145	178
10. KIRIBATI	83 000	145	181

CONNECTIONS

subject	page#
▸ World physical features	8–9
▸ World countries	10–11
▸ Oceania landscapes	136–137
▸ Reference maps of Oceania	144–153
▸ Pacific Ocean	220–221

1 Canberra, *Australia*

In 1908 this site in southeast New South Wales was chosen as the national capital of Australia. The city now has a population of over 250 000. It is centred on Lake Burley Griffin, which stretches across this aerial photograph. Canberra fulfils all the functions of a capital city and the Federal Government is the largest employer in the city. Parliament House is located on Capital Hill, to the south of Lake Burley Griffin in the centre of the circular roads.

2 Alofi, *Niue*

Alofi is the capital of Niue, a self-governing Overseas Territory of New Zealand. This Pacific island is only 258 sq km and is located nearly 400 km east of Tonga. Most of the buildings are situated along the coastal road and the village has barely encroached into the surrounding tropical rainforest. The Legislative Assembly, Halamanga School, the main pier, the Premier's residence and the state's administrative buildings are all visible in this aerial photograph.

3 Apia, *Samoa*

Apia, with a population of 33 000, is the capital and main port of the Pacific island nation of Samoa. It is located on the island of Upolu. As this aerial photograph shows, away from the centre the town is little more than a cluster of villages. In the top left corner is Mulinu'u, the old ceremonial capital of a past Samoan government. In the centre, the Vasigano river flows into the harbour and then into the Pacific Ocean through the surrounding reef.

oceania[threats]

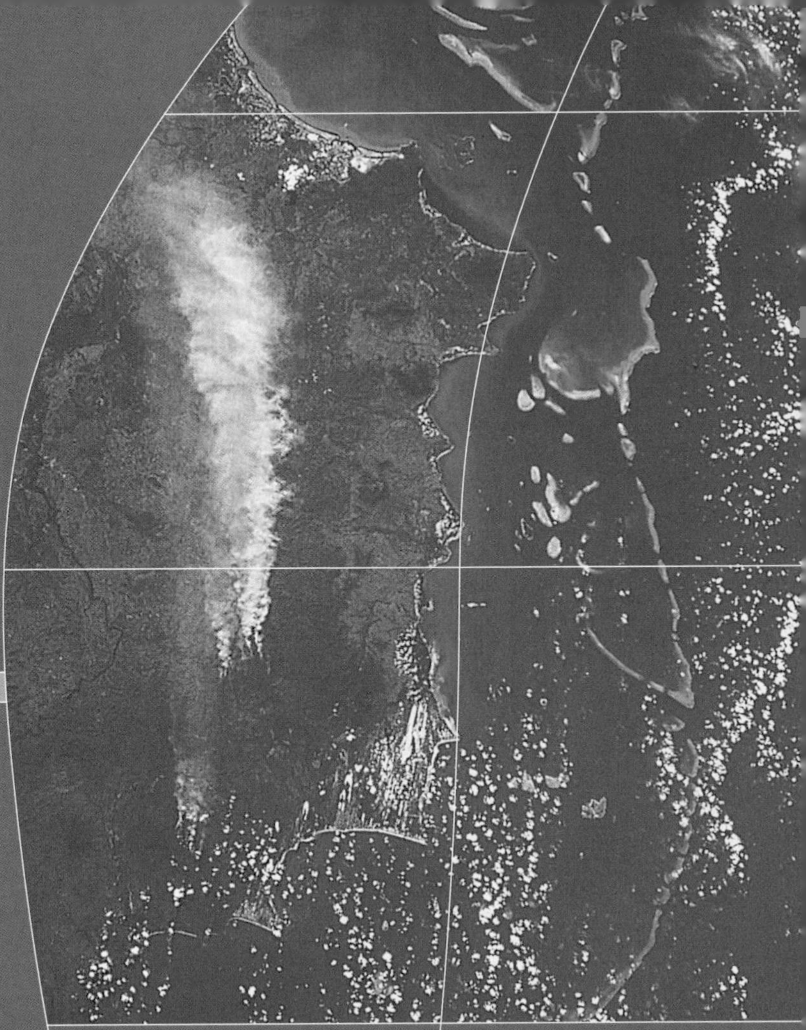

1 Australian Bushfires

Bushfires are an annual threat in the arid and savanna regions of Australia. Although fire can be of great benefit environmentally and ecologically, if it is not managed and controlled effectively it can have dramatic effects and can directly threaten settlements. In 1994 the suburbs of Sydney were affected by bushfires which destroyed 4 000 sq km of bush and grassland and in northern Australia over 300 000 sq km are affected each year. Satellite imagery, such as this image of a fire in northern Queensland, is an important tool in monitoring and managing bushfires. Imagery can be used to detect and map areas at risk, to map fire occurrences and to monitor post-fire recovery of the environment.

Satellite/Sensor : Apollo 7

CONNECTIONS

► subject		page#
► World land cover types		18–19
► World climate and weather		16–17
► Oceania landscapes		136–137
► Oceania features		142–143
► Pacific Ocean		220–221

Fig. #01
Australia salinity hazard

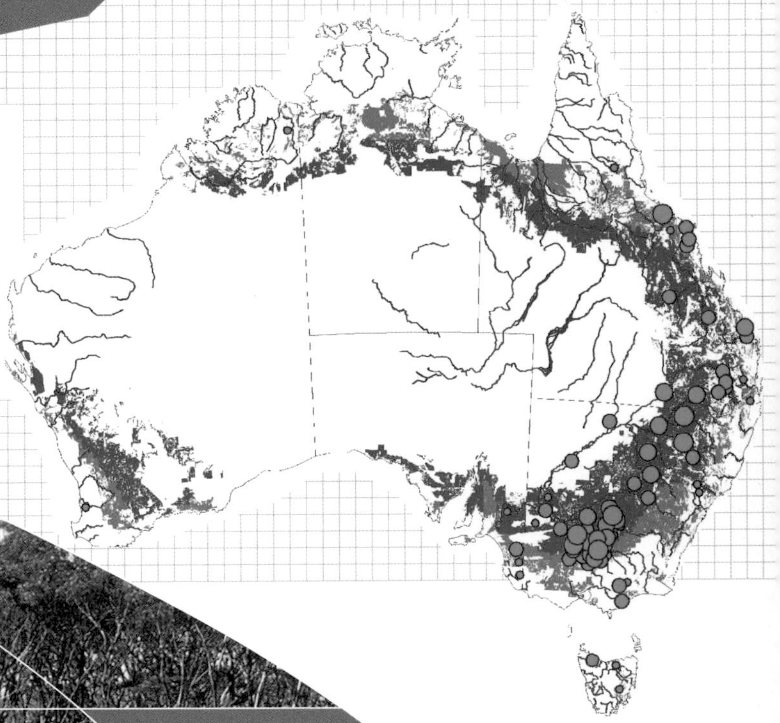

Cropland or pasture
Cropland

Irrigated areas
- >100 000ha
- 50 000 - 100 000ha
- 20 000 - 50 000ha
- 10 000 - 20 000ha

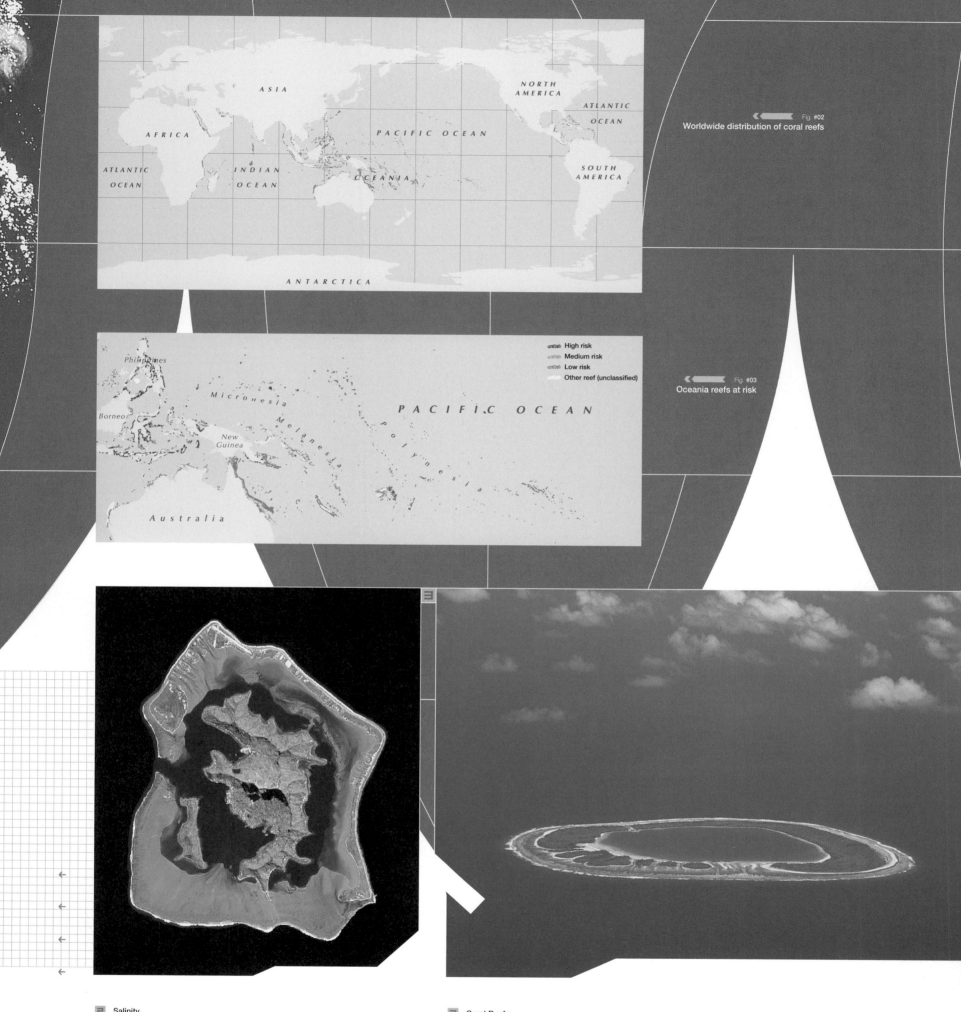

Fig. #02
Worldwide distribution of coral reefs

High risk
Medium risk
Low risk
Other reef (unclassified)

Fig. #03
Oceania reefs at risk

Salinity

Australia is a dry continent. Over millions of years, salt carried onshore from the sea by winds and deposited by rain has accumulated in the soils. This salt becomes a problem when native vegetation is cleared, allowing excess water to percolate through the soil. This raises groundwater levels, bringing the salt to the surface and leaching salt into streams and rivers. Irrigation schemes add more water, making the problem worse. Salt kills crops and pastureland, damages roads and buildings, impairs water quality for both irrigation and human consumption and reduces biodiversity. The photograph shows an area badly affected by salinity near Kellerberrin, Western Australia. Approximately 5.7 million hectares of Australia's farmland is currently affected by salinity and it is predicted that, unless effective solutions are implemented, 17 million hectares of land and 20 000 km of streams could be salinized by 2050. The map shows areas where salt stored in the landscape is being mobilised by surplus water, creating the risk of salinity.

Coral Reefs

Although coral reefs make up only less than a quarter of 1 per cent of the Earth's marine environment, they are vitally important habitats, being home to over 25 per cent of all known marine fish species. They are also important sources of food and tourist income, and they provide physical protection for vulnerable coastlines. Reefs are widely distributed around the world (Fig. #02) with major concentrations in the Caribbean Sea, the Indian Ocean, southeast Asia and the Pacific Ocean.

Reefs are fragile environments, and many are under threat from coastal development, pollution and overexploitation of marine resources. The degree of risk varies, with the reefs of southeast Asia under the greatest threat. Over 25 per cent of the world's reefs are judged to be at high risk. In the Pacific Ocean over 40 per cent of reefs are at risk (Fig. #03). The beauty and fragility of these environments are suggested in the images above. The aerial photograph (right) shows the coral island of Mataiva and the SPOT satellite image (left) shows the island and reefs of Bora-Bora. Both are in the Pacific territory of French Polynesia.

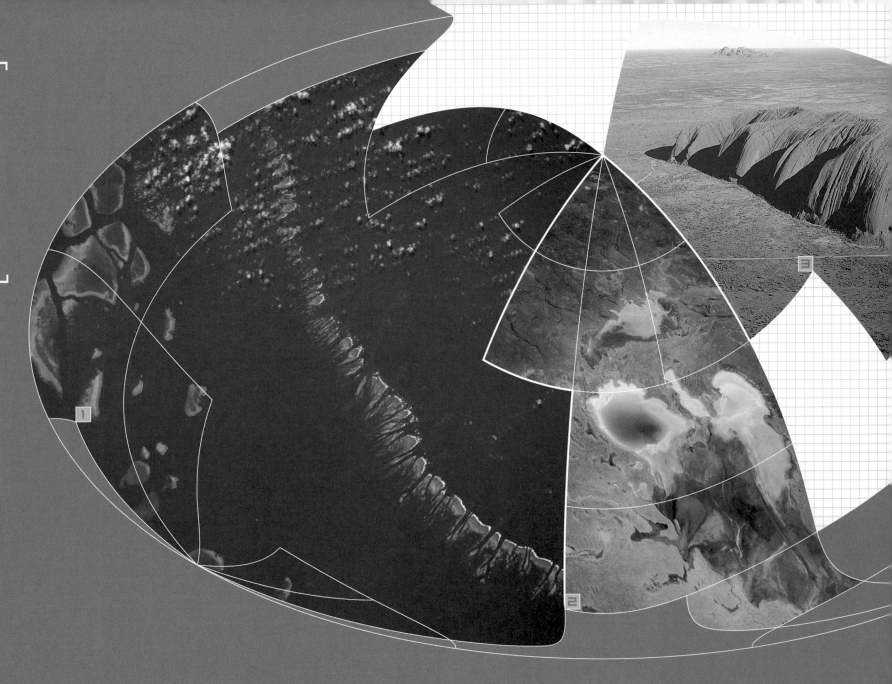

1 Great Barrier Reef, *Queensland, Australia*

This Shuttle photograph of the northern end of the Great Barrier Reef shows two separate reef zones. The line of unbroken coral reefs, at the bottom right of the image contrasts to the randomly spaced reefs in the shallow waters off the coast of the Cape York Peninsula, at the left hand edge. The image captures only a tiny fraction of the whole reef which extends over 2 000 km along the northeast coast of Queensland.

Satellite/Sensor : Space Shuttle

2 Lake Eyre, *South Australia, Australia*

Lake Eyre, situated in one of the driest regions in South Australia, is the largest salt lake in Australia. The lake actually comprises two lakes, Lake Eyre North and the much smaller Lake Eyre South. Salt has been washed into the lake from underlying marine sediments and when dry, which is its usual state, the lake bed is a glistening sheet of white salt. In this photograph, the lake, viewed from the north, is in the process of drying out after being at a higher level.

Satellite/Sensor : Space Shuttle

3 Uluru (Ayers Rock), *Northern Territory, Australia*

Uluru (Ayers Rock), is a large single rock outcrop which rises 350 m above the vast plain of central Australia. This aerial photograph, looking west, shows how the steep, almost vertical walls of the rock rise from the flat surrounding land. The rock is composed of a collection of vertically bedded strata. In the far distance of the photograph, a similar rock formation, the Olgas, can be seen.

4 Banks Peninsula, *New Zealand*

The only recognizable volcanic feature on South Island, New Zealand is Banks Peninsula. It has been extensively eroded over the years yet it still possess the circular shape and radial drainage pattern typical of many volcanoes. The peninsula has been formed by two overlapping volcanic centres which are separated by a large harbour, Akaroa Harbour. In this aerial photograph, the peninsula is viewed from the east and at the top the Canterbury Plains are just visible.

5 **Palm Valley,** *Northern Territory, Australia*

The dark brown and blue area of this radar image, is a broad valley located in the arid landscape of central Australia, approximately 50 km south west of Alice Springs. Palm Valley, the oval shaped feature at the top left of the image, contains many rare species of palms. The mountains of the Macdonnell Ranges are seen as curving bands of folded sedimentary outcrops. In the top right of the image, the river Finke cuts across the mountain ridge and continues in a deep canyon to the lower centre of the image.

Satellite/Sensor : Space Shuttle/SIR-C/X-SAR

6 **Sydney,** *Australia*

Sydney, the largest city in Australia and capital of New South Wales state, has one of the world's finest natural harbours. It is Australia's chief port, and its main cultural and industrial centre. This satellite image of the city, in which north is at the bottom, was captured by the IKONOS satellite in late 1999. The image highlights the renowned Sydney Opera house, located on Bennelong Point. Also clearly visible are the Royal Botanical Gardens and west of these the main urban area of the city centre.

Satellite/Sensor : IKONOS

7 **New Caledonia and Vanuatu,** *Pacific Ocean*

The long narrow island of New Caledonia lies in the southern Pacific Ocean approximately 1 500 km east of Queensland, Australia. The territory comprises one large island and several smaller ones. This SeaWiFS satellite image clearly shows the extensive reef formations which extend far out into the ocean. The island has a landscape of rugged mountains with little flat land. Almost obscured by clouds, at the top right of this image, is a group of islands which collectively make up the small republic of Vanuatu.

Satellite/Sensor : OrbView2/SeaWiFS

CONNECTIONS

► subject	page#
► Uluru (Ayers Rock)	18–19
► Oceania landscapes	136–137
► Oceania countries	138–139
► Coral reefs	140–141
► Southwest Pacific Ocean	144–145
► Pacific Ocean	220–221

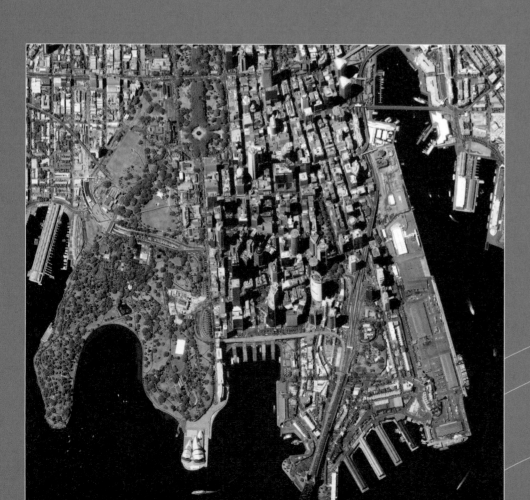

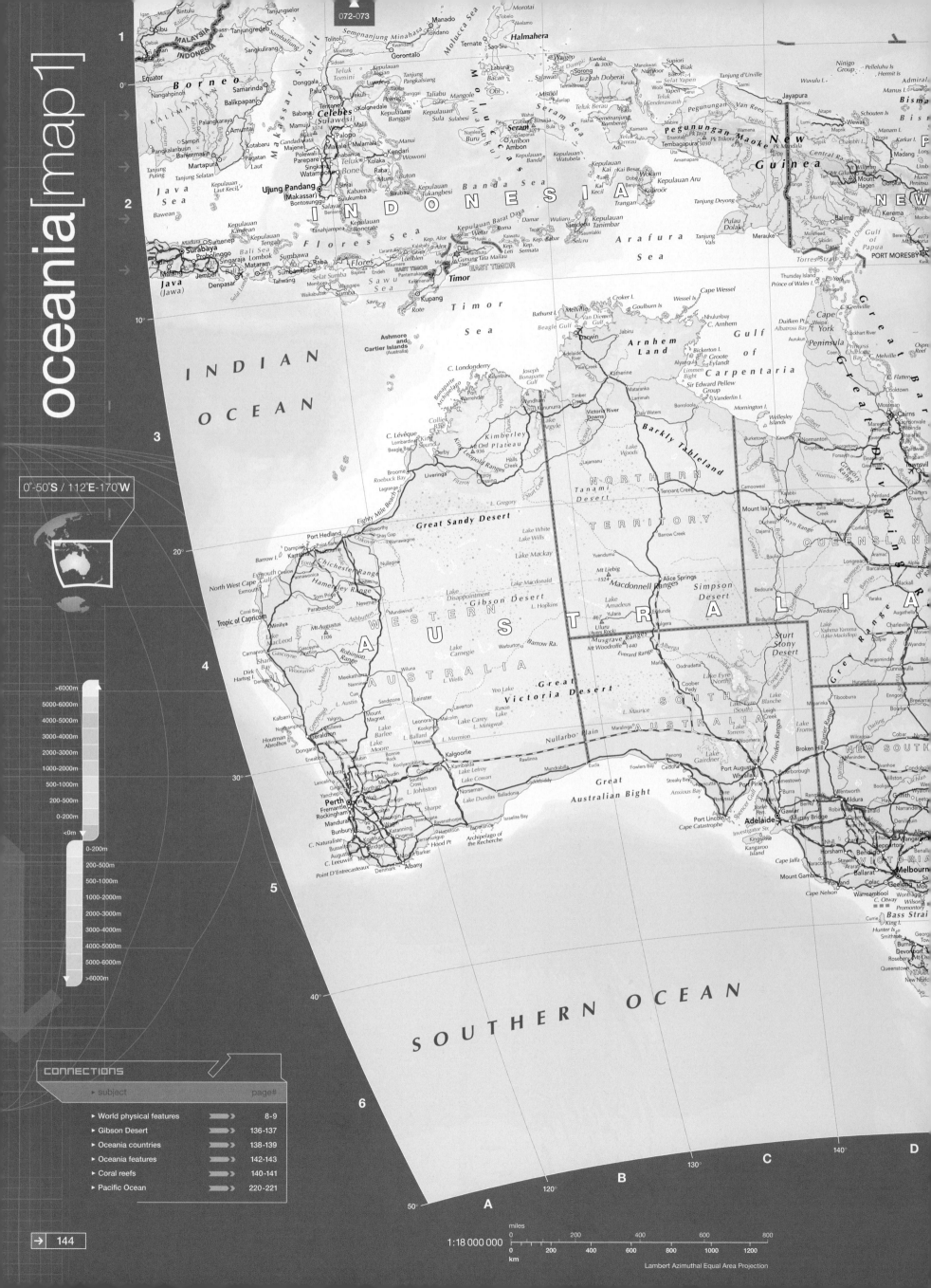

NAURU

KIRIBATI

Kapingamarangi
(Micronesia)

Abaiang
Tarakei
BAIRIKI
Maiana

Howland I.
(U.S.A.)
Baker I.
(U.S.A.)

Mussau I.
St Matthias
Group
New
Hanover
Kavieng
New
Ireland
Namatanai
Lihir Group
Tabar Is
Tanga Is
Feni Is
Green Is
Nuguria Is

Nauru
YAREN
Banaba
(Ocean I.)

Nonouti
Kuria
Abemama
Aranuka

Tabiteuea
Beru
Nikunau
Onotoa
Kingsmill Group
Tamana
Arorae

Phoenix
Islands
Kanton
Enderbury
McKean
Birnie
Ravaki
Manra

Nukumanu Is
Ontong Java
Atoll

Nanumea
Niutao

Nikumaroro
Orona

Rabaul
C. St George
Buka I.
Sohano
Bougainville
Island
Arawa
Buin
Korovou
Choiseul
Santa
Isabel
Buala

SOLOMON
ISLANDS

Roncador
Reef

Nanumanga
Nui
Niutao

Vaitupu
Nukufetau
Funafuti
VAIAKU

TUVALU

Nukulaelae

Tokelau
(New Zealand)
Atafu
Nukunonu
Fakaofo

GUINEA

Hoskins
New Britain
Kandrian
Hahnsdorf

Lae

Finschhafen
Morobe

Popondetta
Tufi

Goodenough I.
Fergusson I.
D'Entrecasteaux Is
Normanby I.

Abau
Samarai
Conflict Group

Louisiade Archipelago
Tagula I.

Shortland
Vella Lavella
Ranongga
New
Georgia
Sound
New
Georgia
Islands
Munda

Gizo
Kolombangara
Rendova

Russell
Is

Malu'u
Malaita
Maramasike

Kirakira

HONIARA
Guadalcanal
Aola
Avuavu

San Cristobal
(Makira)
Rennell

Stewart
Islands

Niulakita

Rotuma
(Fiji)

Wallis and
Futuna Islands
(France)

SAMOA

American
Samoa
(U.S.A.)

Duff Islands

Nupani
Lata
Ndeni
Swallow Islands
Santa Cruz Islands
Utupua

MATA'UTU
Îles Wallis

Mt Silisili
Falealupo
Savai'i

Apolima
Upolu
APIA
Maia

Manu'a
Tau

Coral
Sea

Coral Sea
Islands
Territory
(Australia)

Indispensable
Reefs

Vanikoro Is
Cherry I.
Mitre I.

Île Futuna Sigave
Îles de Hoorn
Île Alofi

Pouimau
Tutuila
FAGATOGO

Flinders
Reefs

Torres Is
Uréparapara
Vanua Lava
797
Banks Islands
Santa María I.

Niuafo'ou
210

Niuatoputapu
Tafahi

Hihifo

Marion Reef

Espíritu Santo
1829
Aoba
Maéwo
Luganville
Mt Marum
Pentecost I.
Malakula
Ambrym
Milip
Lamen
Shepherd Is

VANUATU

Cikobia
Vetauua
Great Sea Reef
Qelelevu
Labasa
Vanua Levu
Sosomo
Taveuni
Vanua Balavu

Northern
Lau Group

Fonualei
Toku

Vava'u Group
Vava'u

Îles Chesterfield

Récifs
d'Entrecasteaux
Grand Passage
Récif
de Cook
Grand Récif
de Belep
Récifs de
l'Astrolabe

PORT VILA
Éfaté

Erromango
Potnarin
Tanna
Lénakel
Futuna

Yasawa
Group
Tavua
Nadi
Ba
Rakiraki
Nairai
Koro

Sigatoka
SUVA
Viti Levu

Kadavu Passage
Vatulele
Moala
Kadavu
Matuku
Totoya

Southern
Lau Group

Niuafo'ou
(Falcon I.)

Fonuafo'ou
100
Late I.
150

Vava'u

Kao
Tofua
Ha'apai Group

TONGA

ALOFI
Niue
(New Zealand)

Nouvelle Calédonie

New Caledonia
(France)

Koumac
Houaïlou
Mont
Humboldt 1618
Bouloupari
NOUMÉA
Mont-Dore
Grand Récif
du Sud
Île des Pins
Île Walpole

Ouvéa
Fayaoué
Îles Loyauté
Lifou
Tadine
Maré

Anatom
(Aneityum)

Hunter I.
100

Ceva-i-Ra

FIJI

Vatoa

Tuvana-i-Colo
Ono-i-Lau

Ata

Fonuafo'ou
NUKU'ALOFA
Tongatapu
Group
'Eua
Tongatapu
Ohonua

Minerva
Reefs

PACIFIC OCEAN

Mackay
Sarina

Swain
Reefs

Saumarez
Reef

Bowen
Collinsville
Mt Dalrymple

Moranbah

Marlborough
Yeppoon
Rockhampton
Gladstone

Expedition
Range

Taroom

Middleton Reef

Elizabeth Reef

Norfolk Island
(Australia)

Theodore
Mundubbera
Biloela
Miriam Vale
Bundaberg
Childers
Maryborough
Fraser Island
Gayndah
Murgon
Gympie
Kingaroy
Nambour
Maroochydore
Caboolture
Toowoomba
Brisbane
Beenleigh
Gold Coast
Murwillumbah
Lismore
Casino
Ballina

Roma
Surat
Dalby
Oakey
Miles

St George

Goondiwindi
Warwick
Stanthorpe
Tenterfield

Darling
Lightning
Ridge

Moree
Narrabri
Inverell
Glen Innes
Grafton
Coffs Harbour

Lord Howe I.
(Australia)

Walgett

Wee Waa

Coonamble

Gilgandra

Warialda

Barradine

Tamworth
Gunnedah
Manilla
Macksville
Kempsey
Port Macquarie

WALES

Nyngan

Dubbo

Wellington
Orange
Bathurst

Mudgee

Armidale
Uralla
Walcha
Wauchope

Taree
Forster
Gloucester
Singleton
Maitland
Newcastle
The Entrance
Gosford

Three Kings
Islands
Cape Maria van Diemen
North Cape

Awanui

Kaitaia
Kaeo
Kerikeri
Kawakawa
Whangarei

Raoul I.
Kermadec Islands
(New Zealand)

Macauley I.
Curtis I.

Havre Rock

L'Espérance Rock

CANBERRA
JERVIS BAY TERRITORY
Nowra

Goulburn
Sydney
Wollongong

Dargaville
Takapuna
Auckland
Manukau

Great Barrier I.

Thames
Hamilton
Te Awamutu
Te Kuiti
Tokoroa
Taupo

Whakatane
East Cape

Gisborne

Tasman Sea

New Plymouth
Hawera
Wanganui

Mt Taranaki
(Mt Egmont)
1518
Ruapehu
2518
Fielding
Palmerston North

Napier
Hastings

Hawke Bay

Levin
Masterton

NEW
ZEALAND

Cape Farewell
Tasman
Bay
Riwaka
Richmond
Nelson

Lower Hutt
WELLINGTON
C. Palliser

Golden
Bay

Westport
Greymouth
Hokitika

Murchison
Blenheim
Kaikoura

South Island

Mt Cook
(Aoraki)
3754
Mt Aspiring
3030

Rangiora
Christchurch
Banks Peninsula

Chatham Islands
(New Zealand)

Chatham I.
Pitt I.
Waitangi

Cape Providence

Queenstown
Wanaka
Cromwell
Alexandra
Gore
Milton

Ashburton
Timaru
Waimate
Oamaru
Port Chalmers
Dunedin
Balclutha
Chaslands
Mistake

Invercargill

Stewart I.

South West
Cape

Snares
Islands

Bounty Islands
(New Zealand)

Antipodes Islands
(New Zealand)

148-149

150-151

Great Australian Bight

SOUTHERN OCEAN

WESTERN AUSTRALIA

Great Victoria Desert Conservation Park

Great Victoria Desert

Great Victoria Desert Nature Reserve

Anangu Pitjantjatjara Aboriginal Lands

Tomkinson Ranges

Mt Davies 1058
Mt Kintore 1071
Mt Woodroffe 1440
Mt Illbillee

Blyth Range
Birksgate Range
Sir Thomas

Warakurna-Wingellina-Irrunytju Aboriginal Reserve

Mt Aignes

Everard Range

Purndu Saltpan

L. Meramangye

Observatory Hill

Wyola Lake
Dey-Dey Lake
Leisler Hills
Lake Maurice
Wilkinson Lakes

Nurral Lakes
Halinor Lake

Serpentine Lakes

Wanna Lakes

Forrest Lakes

Maralinga-Tjarutja Aboriginal Lands

Ooldea Range

Woomera Prohibited Area

Mt Anthony

Nullarbor Plain

Nullarbor Regional Reserve

Nullarbor National Park

Cook
Fisher
Deakin
Hughes
Reid
Forrest

Eucla

Head of Bight

Well

Yalata Aboriginal Lands

Colona

Bookabie
Penong
Koonibba

Fowlers Bay

Yumbarra Conservation Park

Yellabina Regional Reserve

Ifould Lake

Lake Tallacootra

Mt Finke 361

SOUTH AUSTRALIA

AUSTRALIA

Coober Pedy

Cadney Park

Lake Cadibarrawirracanna

Mabel Creek

Tallaringa Conservation Park

Mt Eba

Roxby Downs

Andamooka

Lake Torrens

Lake Torrens National Park

Lake Eyre (North)

Lake Eyre National Park

Lake Eyre (South)

Simpson Desert Regional Reserve

Simpson Desert Conservation Park

Witjira National Park

Sturt Stony Desert

Innamincka Regional Reserve

Sturt National Park

Lake Howitt

Lake Hope

Lake Wakarinna

Cooper Creek

Strzelecki Regional Reserve

Lake Blanche

Lake Callabonna

Lake Frome

Lake Frome Regional Reserve

Gammon Ranges Nat. Park

Flinders Ranges

Flinders Ranges National Park

Marree

Finniss Springs Aboriginal Land

Oodnadatta

William Creek

Peake

Lake Gregory

Leigh Creek

Parachilna

Blinman

Wilpena

Cradock

Hawker

Orroroo

Carrieton

Quorn

Port Augusta

Whyalla

Iron Knob

Kimba

Cowell

Cleve

Cowell

Gawler Ranges

Lake Gairdner

Lake Gairdner National Park

Lake Everard

Lake Acraman

Yardea

Wudinna

Minnipa

Streaky Bay

Smoky Bay

Ceduna

Nuyts Archipelago

Nuyts Archipelago Conservation Park

St Francis Isles

Pt Bell
Pt Brown

Poochera

Cape Radstock

Anxious Bay

C. Finnis

Flinders Island

Investigator Group

Pearson Isles

Elliston

Mount Wedge

Eyre Peninsula

Lock

Cleve

Cummins

Coffin Bay

Coffin Bay Peninsula

Coffin Bay National Park

Greenly I.

Port Lincoln

Lincoln Nat. Park

C. Catastrophe

C. Carnot

Sleaford Bay

Gambier Is

C. Spencer

Thistle I.

Spencer Gulf

Hardwicke Bay

Wardang Island

Yorke Peninsula

Minlaton

Maitland

Wallaroo

Kadina

Moonta

Port Pirie

Crystal Brook

Gladstone

Jamestown

Peterborough

Orroroo

Mt Remarkable National Park

Melrose

Wilmington

Hawker

Gulf St Vincent

Adelaide

Port Wakefield

Balaklava

Clare

Burra

Morgan

Murray Bridge

Mount Barker

Strathalbyn

Victor Harbor

Goolwa

Encounter Bay

Investigator Strait

Kangaroo Island

Flinders Chase Nat. Park

Cape Borda

Kingscote

Penneshaw

Cape Gantheaume Conservation Park

C. de Couedic

Cape Jervis

Younghusband Peninsula

Coorong National Park

Meningie

Tailem Bend

Lake Albert

Lake Alexandrina

Tintinara

Keith

Bordertown

Naracoorte

Kingston S.E.

Lacepede Bay

Cape Jaffa

Robe

Beachport

Lake Bonney

Canunda Nat. Park

Millicent

Penola

Mount Gambier

Port MacDonnell

Mount Gambier Nat. Park

Discovery Bay Coastal Park

Discovery Bay

Portland

Cape Nelson

Portland Bay

Little Desert National Park

Big Desert Wilderness Park

Murray-Sunset National Park

Ngarkat Conservation Park

Billiat Conservation Park

Wyperfeld National Park

Lake Hindmarsh

Nhill

Bendigo

146

QUEENSLAND

Darling
Downs

NEW SOUTH WALES

Brisbane
Gold Coast
Tweed Heads

Moree

Tamworth

Port Macquarie

Sydney
Wollongong

CANBERRA
AUSTRALIAN
CAPITAL
TERRITORY
JERVIS BAY TERRITORY

VICTORIA

Melbourne
Geelong

Bass Strait

Furneaux
Group

Banks Strait

TASMANIA

Hobart

T a s m a n

S e a

144°   E   148°   F   152°   G   156°   H   160°

miles
0   50   100   150   200   250
1:6 000 000
0   50 100 150 200 250 300 350 400
km

Lambert Azimuthal Equal Area Projection

11°-28°S / 128°-154°E

150-151

146-147

Elevation legend:

>6000m
5000-6000m
4000-5000m
3000-4000m
2000-3000m
1000-2000m
500-1000m
200-500m
0-200m
<0m
0-200m
200-500m
500-1000m
1000-2000m
2000-3000m
3000-4000m
4000-5000m
5000-6000m
>6000m

Scale:

1:6 000 000

miles
0 50 100 150 200 250

km
0 50 100 150 200 250 300 350 400

Lambert Azimuthal Equal Area Projection

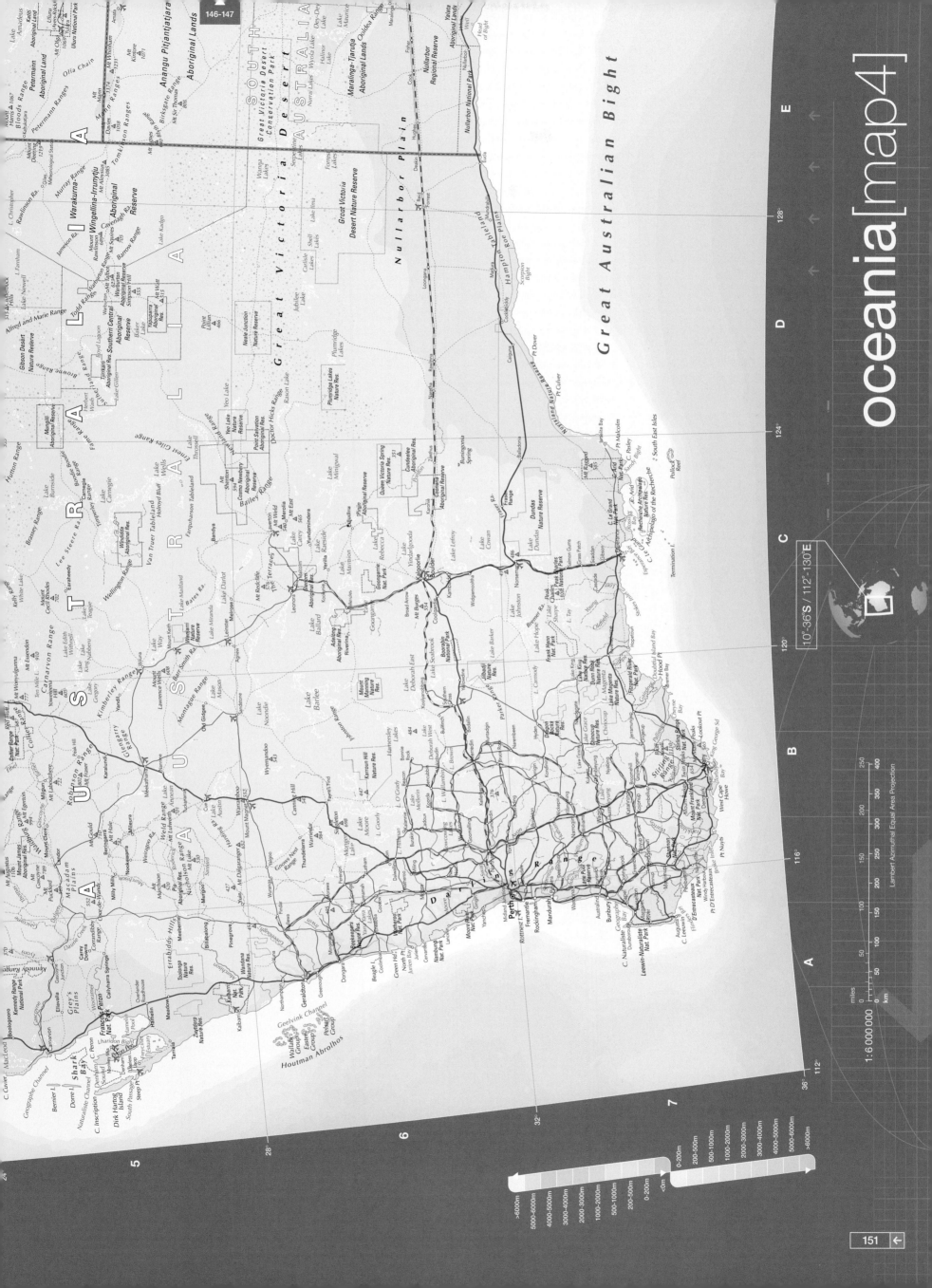

NORTH ISLAND

NEW ZEALAND

Tasman Sea

Bay of Plenty

Hawke Bay

Coromandel Peninsula

Auckland

WELLINGTON

Napier

>6000m
5000-6000m
4000-5000m
3000-4000m
2000-3000m
1500-2000m
1000-1500m
500-1000m
200-500m
100-200m
0-100m
<0m

0-200m
200-500m
500-1000m
1000-2000m
2000-3000m
3000-4000m
4000-5000m
5000-6000m
>6000m

oceania[map5]

34-47°S / 166-179°E

Conic Equidistant Projection

1:3 250 000

PACIFIC

OCEAN

SOUTH

ISLAND

Canterbury
Bight

Pegasus Bay

Banks
Peninsula

Christchurch

MARLBOROUGH

CANTERBURY

SOUTHERN ALPS

Dunedin

Otago Peninsula

Foveaux Strait

Stewart
Island

Fiordland
National
Park

Mount Aspiring
National Park

Westland National Park

SOUTHLAND

A B C D E F G H I J K L M

166° 167° 168° 169° 170° 171° 172° 173° 174° 175° 176° 177° 178° 179°

41° 42° 43° 44° 45° 46° 47°

9 10 11 12 13 14 15

Monument Valley, *Arizona, USA*

north**america**

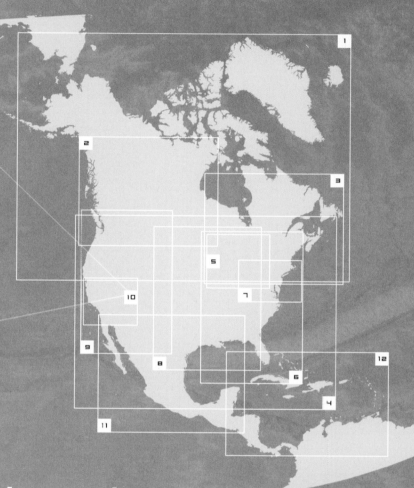

[contents]

	page#
northamerica [landscapes]	156–157
northamerica [countries]	158–159
northamerica [threats]	160–161
northamerica [environments]	162–163

	map coverage	scale	page#
northamerica [map 1]	CANADA	1:15 000 000	164–165
northamerica [map 2]	CANADA West	1:6 500 000	166–167
northamerica [map 3]	CANADA Central and East	1:6 500 000	168–169
northamerica [map 4]	UNITED STATES OF AMERICA	1:12 000 000	170–171
northamerica [map 5]	THE GREAT LAKES	1:3 000 000	172–173
northamerica [map 6]	UNITED STATES OF AMERICA East	1:6 500 000	174–175
northamerica [map 7]	UNITED STATES OF AMERICA Northeast	1:3 000 000	176–177
northamerica [map 8]	UNITED STATES OF AMERICA Central	1:6 500 000	178–179
northamerica [map 9]	UNITED STATES OF AMERICA West	1:6 500 000	180–181
northamerica [map 10]	UNITED STATES OF AMERICA Southwest	1:3 000 000	182–183
northamerica [map 11]	MEXICO	1:7 000 000	184–185
northamerica [map 12]	CENTRAL AMERICA and the CARIBBEAN	1:7 000 000	186–187

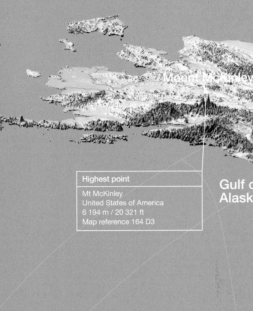

Arctic Ocean

Mount McKinley

Mackenzie River

Bear Lake

Island

Highest point
Mt McKinley
United States of America
6 194 m / 20 321 ft
Map reference 164 D3

Gulf of
Alaska

Coast
Mountains

Lake

Peace River

Pacific Ocean

Rocky
Mountains

Snake River

Winnip

Great Basin

Grand Canyon

Platte River

Lowest point
Death Valley
86 m / 282 ft below sea leval
Map reference 181 C5

Death
Valley

Great
Plains

Colorado River

Baja California

Gulf of
California

Sierra Madre
Occidental

North America is the largest continent in the western hemisphere. This view illustrates how the west coast is dominated by the Rocky Mountains which stretch from Alaska in the north through Canada, USA, Mexico and Central America. The Great Plains stretch gradually east of the Rockies, and extend from the Arctic Ocean to the Gulf of Mexico. The Appalachian Mountains dominate the east of the USA, with lowlands skirting the east coast of the continent and the Gulf of Mexico.

Major water bodies are the Great Lakes, and Great Slave Lake and Great Bear Lake in the Arctic regions of Canada. In the northeast, Hudson Bay is a huge inland sea connected to the Atlantic Ocean by the Hudson Strait. The large purple feature at the centre top of the image is the high, snow-covered plateau in Greenland. The Caribbean Sea contains numerous islands, stretching from the Bahamas to the north coast of South America. In the south the Isthmus of Panama forms the link between Central and South America.

1 Grand Canyon, Arizona, *USA*

The Grand Canyon in northern Arizona, USA, is the largest canyon in the world and one of the most famous World Heritage Sites. It has been established as a National Park since 1919. This aerial view shows how the canyon has been carved out by the Colorado river, exposing many layers of sedimentary rock. The canyon reaches depths of over 1.5 km and there are many peaks and smaller canyons within the main gorge.

2 Mackenzie River Delta, *Canada*

This photograph looks west across the delta of the Mackenzie river towards the Richardson Mountains in the Northwest Territories of Canada. The isolated village of Alavik is located inside the tight bend in the river. The severe climate means that the river is only navigable here between June and October. The Mackenzie, including the Peace and Finlay rivers to the east of the Great Slave Lake, is the second longest river system in North America.

3 Appalachian Mountains, *USA*

This photograph from the Space Shuttle shows the heavily wooded ridges of the Appalachian Mountains in southwest Virginia. This narrow range, which is only approximately 160 km wide, forms the principal mountains in the eastern United States and runs parallel to the Atlantic coast. In the area shown in this image, some peaks exceed 1 200 m in height. The valleys between the mountain ridges have rich agricultural soils

Satellite/Sensor: Space Shuttle

CONNECTIONS

► subject		page#
► World physical features		8–9
► World land images		12–13
► North American countries		158–159
► USA protected areas		162–163
► Reference maps of North America		164–187

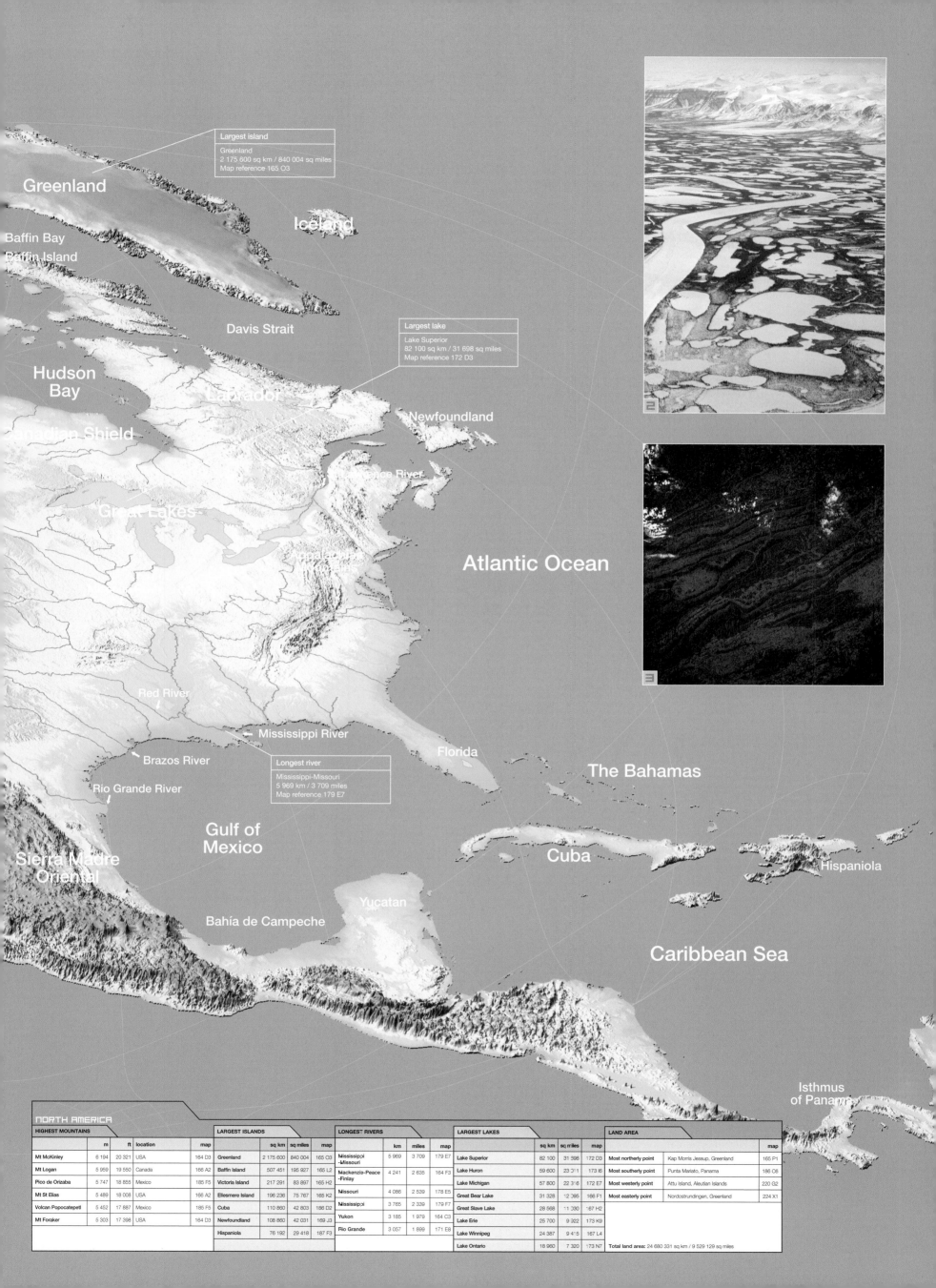

Greenland

Iceland

Baffin Bay

Baffin Island

Davis Strait

Hudson Bay

Labrador

Newfoundland

Canadian Shield

St Lawrence River

Great Lakes

Appalachian Mountains

Atlantic Ocean

Red River

Mississippi River

Brazos River

Florida

The Bahamas

Rio Grande River

Gulf of Mexico

Cuba

Hispaniola

Sierra Madre Oriental

Yucatan

Bahía de Campeche

Caribbean Sea

Isthmus of Panama

Largest island
Greenland
2 175 600 sq km / 840 004 sq miles
Map reference 165 O3

Largest lake
Lake Superior
82 100 sq km / 31 698 sq miles
Map reference 172 D3

Longest river
Mississippi-Missouri
5 969 km / 3 709 miles
Map reference 179 E7

NORTH AMERICA

HIGHEST MOUNTAINS					LARGEST ISLANDS				LONGEST RIVERS				LARGEST LAKES				LAND AREA		
	m	ft	location	map		sq km	sq miles	map		km	miles	map		sq km	sq miles	map			map
Mt McKinley	6 194	20 321	USA	164 D3	Greenland	2 175 600	840 004	165 O3	Mississippi-Missouri	5 969	3 709	179 E7	Lake Superior	82 100	31 698	172 D3	Most northerly point	Kap Morris Jessup, Greenland	165 P1
Mt Logan	5 959	19 550	Canada	166 A2	Baffin Island	507 451	195 927	165 L2	Mackenzie-Peace-Finlay	4 241	2 635	164 F3	Lake Huron	59 600	23 011	173 I6	Most southerly point	Punta Mariato, Panama	186 C6
Pico de Orizaba	5 747	18 855	Mexico	185 F5	Victoria Island	217 291	83 897	165 H2	Missouri	4 086	2 539	178 E5	Lake Michigan	57 800	22 316	172 E7	Most westerly point	Attu Island, Aleutian Islands	220 G2
Mt St Elias	5 489	18 008	USA	166 A2	Ellesmere Island	196 236	75 767	165 K2	Mississippi	3 765	2 339	179 F7	Great Bear Lake	31 328	12 095	166 F1	Most easterly point	Nordostrundingen, Greenland	224 X1
Volcan Popocatepetl	5 452	17 887	Mexico	185 F5	Cuba	110 860	42 803	186 D2	Mississippi	3 185	1 979	164 C3	Great Slave Lake	28 568	11 030	167 H2			
Mt Foraker	5 303	17 398	USA	164 D3	Newfoundland	108 860	42 031	169 J3	Yukon	3 057	1 899	171 E8	Lake Erie	25 700	9 322	173 K9			
					Hispaniola	76 192	29 418	187 F3	Rio Grande				Lake Winnipeg	24 387	9 415	167 L4			
													Lake Ontario	18 960	7 320	173 N7	Total land area: 24 680 331 sq km / 9 529 129 sq miles		

NORTH AMERICA
COUNTRIES

		area sq km	area sq miles	population	capital	languages	religions	currency	map
ANTIGUA AND BARBUDA		442	171	65 000	St John's	English, creole	Protestant, Roman Catholic	E. Carib. dollar	187
THE BAHAMAS		13 939	5 382	304 000	Nassau	English, creole	Protestant, Roman Catholic	Dollar	186–187
BARBADOS		430	166	267 000	Bridgetown	English, creole	Protestant, Roman Catholic	Dollar	187
BELIZE		22 965	8 867	226 000	Belmopan	English, Spanish, Mayan, creole	Roman Catholic, Protestant	Dollar	185
CANADA		9 970 610	3 849 674	30 757 000	Ottawa	English, French	Roman Catholic, Protestant, Eastern Orthodox, Jewish	Dollar	164–165
COSTA RICA		51 100	19 730	4 024 000	San José	Spanish	Roman Catholic, Protestant	Colón	186
CUBA		110 860	42 803	11 199 000	Havana (La Habana)	Spanish	Roman Catholic, Protestant	Peso	186–187
DOMINICA		750	290	71 000	Roseau	English, creole	Roman Catholic, Protestant	E. Carib. dollar	187
DOMINICAN REPUBLIC		48 442	18 704	8 373 000	Santo Domingo	Spanish, creole	Roman Catholic, Protestant	Peso	187
EL SALVADOR		21 041	8 124	6 278 000	San Salvador	Spanish	Roman Catholic, Protestant	Colón	185
GRENADA		378	146	94 000	St George's	English, creole	Roman Catholic, Protestant	E. Carib. dollar	187
GUATEMALA		108 890	42 043	11 385 000	Guatemala City	Spanish, Mayan languages	Roman Catholic, Protestant	Quetzal	185
HAITI		27 750	10 714	8 142 000	Port-au-Prince	French, creole	Roman Catholic, Protestant, Voodoo	Gourde	186
HONDURAS		112 088	43 277	6 417 000	Tegucigalpa	Spanish, Amerindian languages	Roman Catholic, Protestant	Lempira	186
JAMAICA		10 991	4 244	2 576 000	Kingston	English, creole	Protestant, Roman Catholic	Dollar	186
MEXICO		1 972 545	761 604	98 872 000	Mexico City	Spanish, Amerindian languages	Roman Catholic, Protestant	Peso	184–185
NICARAGUA		130 000	50 193	5 071 000	Managua	Spanish, Amerindian languages	Roman Catholic, Protestant	Córdoba	186
PANAMA		77 082	29 762	2 856 000	Panama City	Spanish, English, Amerindian languages	Roman Catholic, Protestant, Sunni Muslim	Balboa	186
ST KITTS AND NEVIS		261	101	38 000	Basseterre	English, creole	Protestant, Roman Catholic	E. Carib. dollar	187
ST LUCIA		616	238	148 000	Castries	English, creole	Roman Catholic, Protestant	E. Carib. dollar	187
ST VINCENT AND THE GRENADINES		389	150	112 000	Kingstown	English, creole	Protestant, Roman Catholic	E. Carib. dollar	187
TRINIDAD AND TOBAGO		5 130	1 981	1 294 000	Port of Spain	English, creole, Hindi	Roman Catholic, Hindu, Protestant, Sunni Muslim	Dollar	187
UNITED STATES OF AMERICA		9 809 378	3 787 422	283 230 000	Washington	English, Spanish	Protestant, Roman Catholic, Sunni Muslim, Jewish	Dollar	170–171

DEPENDENT TERRITORIES

		territorial status	area sq km	area sq miles	population	capital	languages	religions	currency	map
Anguilla		United Kingdom Overseas Territory	155	60	11 000	The Valley	English	Protestant, Roman Catholic	E. Carib. Dollar	187
Aruba		Self-governing Netherlands Territory	193	75	101 000	Oranjestad	Papiamento, Dutch, English	Roman Catholic, Protestant	Florin	187
Bermuda		United Kingdom Overseas Territory	54	21	63 000	Hamilton	English	Protestant, Roman Catholic	Dollar	171
Cayman Islands		United Kingdom Overseas Territory	259	100	38 000	George Town	English	Protestant, Roman Catholic	Dollar	186
Clipperton, Île		French Overseas Territory	7	3	uninhabited					221
Greenland		Self-governing Danish Territory	2 175 600	840 004	56 000	Nuuk (Godthåb)	Greenlandic, Danish	Protestant	Danish krone	165
Guadeloupe		French Overseas Department	1 780	687	428 000	Basse-Terre	French, creole	Roman Catholic	French franc	187
Martinique		French Overseas Department	1 079	417	383 000	Fort-de-France	French, creole	Roman Catholic, traditional beliefs	French franc	187
Montserrat		United Kingdom Overseas Territory	100	39	4 000	Plymouth	English	Protestant, Roman Catholic	E. Carib. Dollar	187
Navassa Island		United States Unincorporated Territory	5	2	uninhabited					186
Netherlands Antilles		Self-governing Netherlands Territory	800	309	215 000	Willemstad	Dutch, Papiamento, English	Roman Catholic, Protestant	NA guilder	187
Puerto Rico		United States Commonwealth	9 104	3 515	3 915 000	San Juan	Spanish, English	Roman Catholic, Protestant	US dollar	187
St Pierre and Miquelon		French Territorial Collectivity	242	93	7 000	St-Pierre	French	Roman Catholic	French franc	169
Turks and Caicos Islands		United Kingdom Overseas Territory	430	166	17 000	Grand Turk	English	Protestant	US dollar	187
Virgin Islands (U.K.)		United Kingdom Overseas Territory	153	59	24 000	Road Town	English	Protestant, Roman Catholic	US dollar	187
Virgin Islands (U.S.A.)		United States Unincorporated Territory	352	136	121 000	Charlotte Amalie	English, Spanish	Protestant, Roman Catholic	US dollar	187

1

Tropic of Cancer

Hawaiian Islands (U.S.A.)

Honolulu

HAWAII

2

3

CONNECTIONS

▶ subject	page#
▶ World physical features	8–9
▶ World countries	10–11
▶ North America landscapes	156–157
▶ North America environments	162–163
▶ Reference maps of North America	164–187

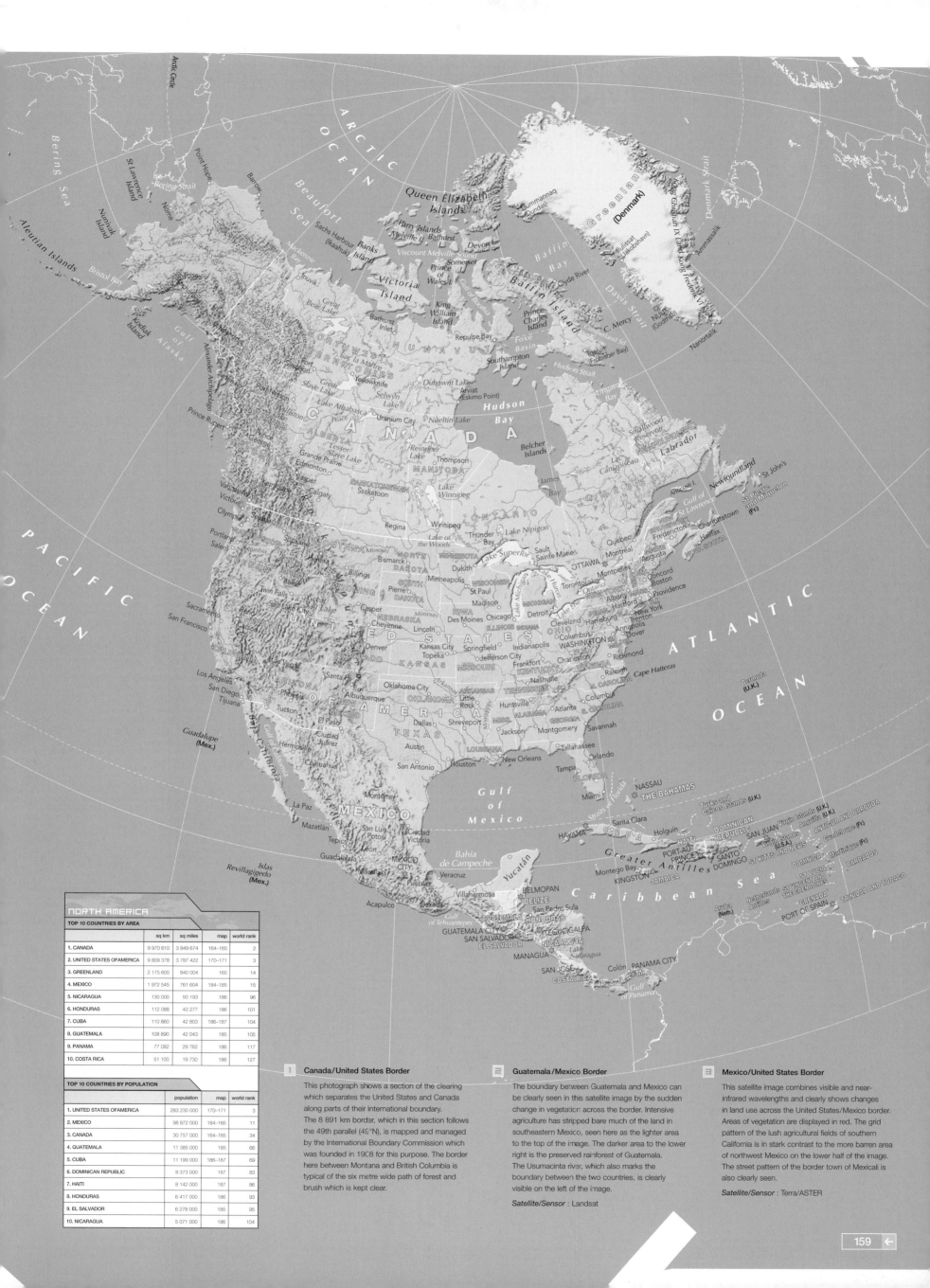

NORTH AMERICA

TOP 10 COUNTRIES BY AREA

	sq km	sq miles	map	world rank
1. CANADA	9 970 610	3 849 674	164–165	2
2. UNITED STATES OF AMERICA	9 809 378	3 787 422	170–171	3
3. GREENLAND	2 175 600	840 004	165	14
4. MEXICO	1 972 545	761 604	184–185	15
5. NICARAGUA	130 000	50 193	186	96
6. HONDURAS	112 088	43 277	186	101
7. CUBA	110 860	42 803	186–187	104
8. GUATEMALA	108 890	42 043	185	105
9. PANAMA	77 082	29 762	186	117
10. COSTA RICA	51 100	19 730	186	127

TOP 10 COUNTRIES BY POPULATION

	population	map	world rank
1. UNITED STATES OF AMERICA	283 230 000	170–171	3
2. MEXICO	98 872 000	184–185	11
3. CANADA	30 757 000	164–165	34
4. GUATEMALA	11 385 000	185	66
5. CUBA	11 199 000	186–187	69
6. DOMINICAN REPUBLIC	8 373 000	187	83
7. HAITI	8 142 000	187	86
8. HONDURAS	6 417 000	186	93
9. EL SALVADOR	6 278 000	185	95
10. NICARAGUA	5 071 000	186	104

1 Canada/United States Border

This photograph shows a section of the clearing which separates the United States and Canada along parts of their international boundary.
The 8 891 km border, which in this section follows the 49th parallel (49°N), is mapped and managed by the International Boundary Commission which was founded in 1908 for this purpose. The border here between Montana and British Columbia is typical of the six metre wide path of forest and brush which is kept clear.

2 Guatemala/Mexico Border

The boundary between Guatemala and Mexico can be clearly seen in this satellite image by the sudden change in vegetation across the border. Intensive agriculture has stripped bare much of the land in southeastern Mexico, seen here as the lighter area to the top of the image. The darker area to the lower right is the preserved rainforest of Guatemala. The Usumacinta river, which also marks the boundary between the two countries, is clearly visible on the left of the image.

Satellite/Sensor : Landsat

3 Mexico/United States Border

This satellite image combines visible and near-infrared wavelengths and clearly shows changes in land use across the United States/Mexico border. Areas of vegetation are displayed in red. The grid pattern of the lush agricultural fields of southern California is in stark contrast to the more barren area of northwest Mexico on the lower half of the image. The street pattern of the border town of Mexicali is also clearly seen.

Satellite/Sensor : Terra/ASTER

1 San Andreas Fault, *California, USA*

The San Andreas fault is a large break in the Earth's crust between the North American and Pacific plates. It runs for over 950 km from northwest California to the Gulf of California. Movement between the two plates causes earthquakes which present a serious threat to this part of the United States. The fault runs diagonally across this satellite image from left to right, with the supplementary Garlock fault stretching to the top of the image. The proximity of the faults to Los Angeles, the large grey area at the bottom of the image, is obvious.

Satellite/Sensor : Landsat

2 Mount St Helens, *Washington, USA*

After lying dormant since 1857, Mount St Helens in the Cascade mountain range in Washington state, USA erupted violently in May 1980. The eruption was one of the largest volcanic events in North American history and caused the loss of sixty lives. The explosion reduced the height of the mountain by 390 m and flattened trees and killed wildlife over an area of twenty five kilometres radius. The result was the new horseshoe-shaped crater seen in this aerial photograph.

3 Popocatépetl, *Mexico*

This false-colour satellite image shows the Mexican volcano Popocatépetl four days after its eruption in December 2000. The eruption sent molten rock high into the air and over 50 000 people were evacuated from the surrounding area. The bright green spot in the crater indicates that its temperature is still very high. The volcano lies only seventy kilometres southeast of Mexico City, and its name, which is the Aztec word for 'smoking mountain' is suggestive of the threat it presents.

Satellite/Sensor : SPOT

4 Atlantic Hurricanes

Tropical storms have different names in different parts of the world – typhoons in the northwest Pacific Ocean, cyclones in the Indian Ocean region and hurricanes in the Atlantic Ocean and east Pacific. The effects of their strong winds and heavy rain can be devastating.

The Atlantic hurricane season lasts from June to November, with the majority of storms occurring between August and October. The storms present a threat to the islands of the Caribbean and Bermuda and to the east coast of the United States of America. In both 1999 and 2000 there were eight tropical storms which reached hurricane force, as shown on the map Fig. #01. The most severe of these was Hurricane Floyd which developed during early September 1999. It achieved maximum sustained wind speeds of 249 km per hour and made landfall near Cape Fear, North Carolina, USA. Although wind speeds had dropped to around 166 km per hour, it had a devastating effect and fifty seven deaths were directly attributed to the hurricane, making it the deadliest US hurricane since 1972. The computer-generated images show Floyd just off the Florida coast and the inset image indicates wind directions and rainfall levels (yellow-orange over 10mm per hour) at the centre of the hurricane.

CONNECTIONS

► subject	page#
► World earthquakes and volcanoes	14–15
► World climate and weather	16–17
► Asia threats	70–71
► North America landscapes	156–157
► North America environments	162–163

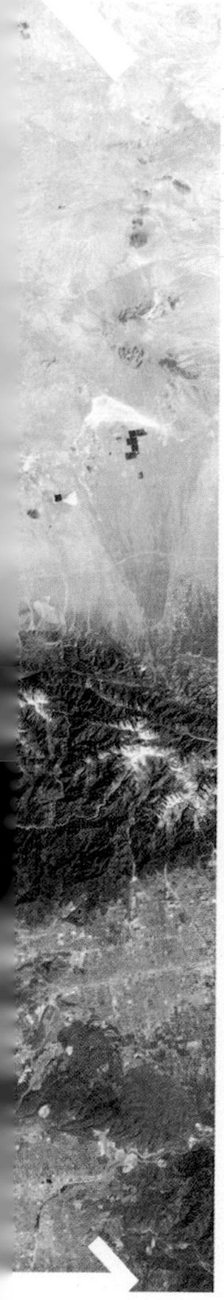

4
29.0 N
65.0 W
17.0 N
77.0 W

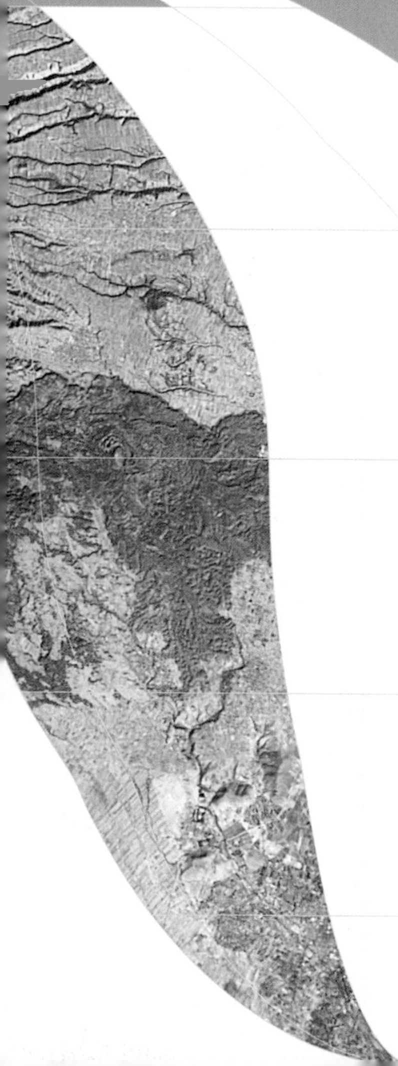

Fig. #01
Atlantic hurricane tracks
1999-2000

Hurricane Strength
1999
2000

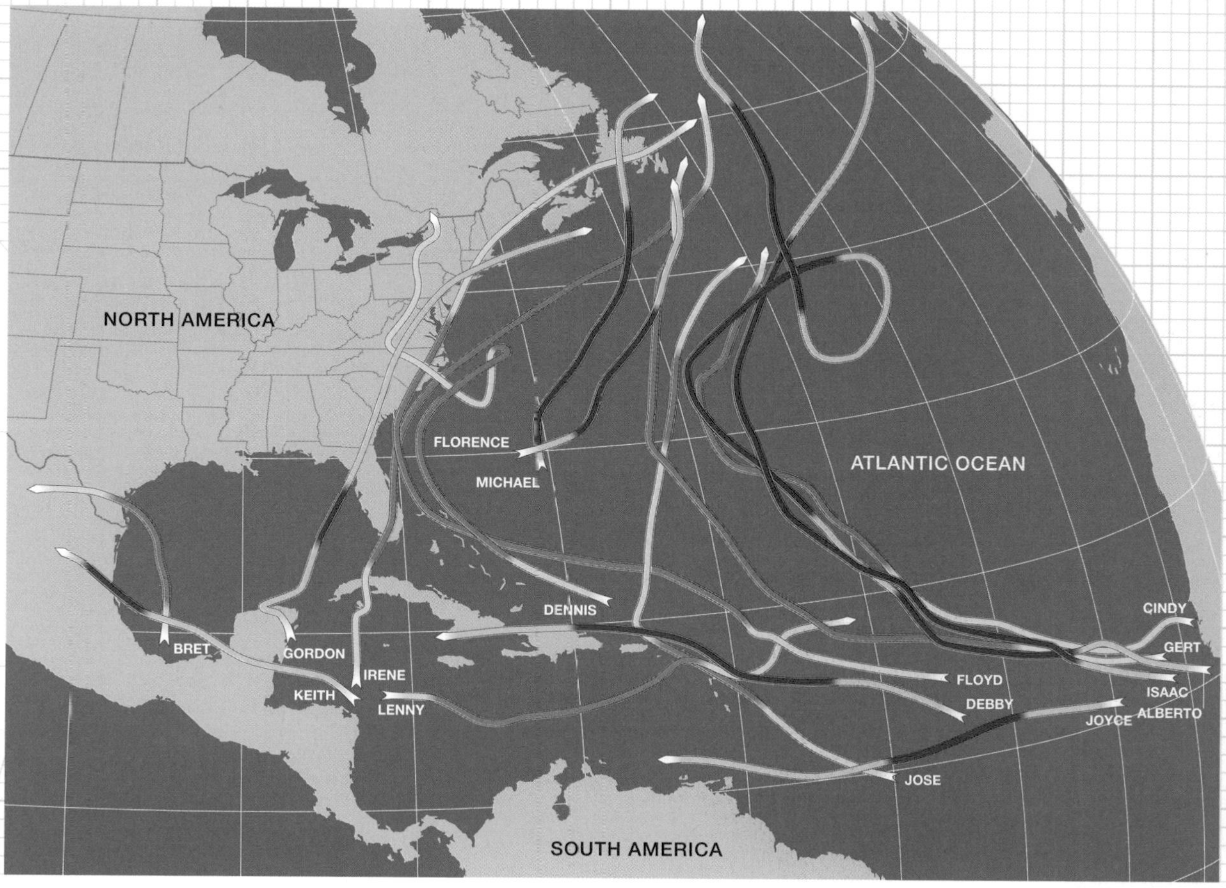
NORTH AMERICA
ATLANTIC OCEAN
SOUTH AMERICA
FLORENCE
MICHAEL
DENNIS
CINDY
GERT
ISAAC
ALBERTO
JOYCE
DEBBY
FLOYD
JOSE
BRET
GORDON
IRENE
KEITH
LENNY

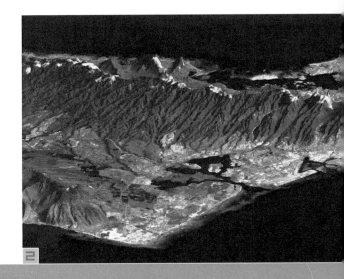

1 Suburbia, California, *USA*

A new housing development west of Stockton, California is shown in this vertical aerial photograph. Water-front properties are in great demand in this area and each house on the finger-like promontories has its own berth, with access via canals to the California Delta waterways of the Sacramento and San Joaquin rivers. Development is continuing on the empty plots at the lower right of the photograph.

2 Island Environment, Hawaii, *USA*

This image shows a perspective view of Honolulu and surrounding area on the Hawaiian island of Oahu. The three-dimensional effect is a result of using height data collected during the Shuttle Radar Topography Mission (SRTM) of the Space Shuttle Endeavour. This height data has been combined with a Landsat 7 satellite image which has been draped over the surface of the elevation model. Honolulu, Pearl Harbour, the Koolau mountain range and offshore reef patterns are all visible on the image.

Satellite/Sensor : Space Shuttle and Landsat

3 Great Plains, Montana, *USA*

A wheat farm on the Great Plains of Montana is shown in this aerial photograph. The high grasses of the Great Plains once sustained large herds of buffalo and the cattle and sheep of large ranches. Today the environment is dominated by large farms using modern extensive farming techniques.

4 Arctic Coastline, *Greenland*

This Space Shuttle photograph gives a northeast view of the south-southeast tip of Greenland. This is a typical scene of the glaciated coastline which surrounds the world's largest island. The dark elongated fingers are inlets, or fjords, which stretch from the North Atlantic Ocean towards the interior. Large white areas to the top of the image mark the start of the permanent ice cap which stretches north across the island to the Arctic Ocean.

Satellite/Sensor : Space Shuttle

5 Protected Environment, Yellowstone National Park, *USA*

The Lower Falls in the Grand Canyon of the Yellowstone River are one of many spectacular features in Yellowstone National Park, Wyoming. The park mainly lies within a volcanically active basin in the Rocky Mountains. It became the world's first national park in 1872 with the purpose of preserving this area of great natural beauty. As well as many geysers, hot springs, lakes and waterfalls the park has a rich variety of flora and fauna.

6 Irrigation, Wyoming, *USA*

This aerial photograph shows fields watered by centre-pivot irrigation next to the Bighorn river in northern Wyoming. This method of irrigation has created circular patterns in the landscape. Each circle is fed from a rotating structure of up to 300 m in length. The flow is carefully controlled so that the whole area is supplied with an equal amount of water. The system makes it possible to grow crops in otherwise infertile parts of the state.

CONNECTIONS

► subject	page#
► Land cover types	18–19
► World land use patterns	20–21
► Europe environments	36–37
► North America landscapes	156–157
► Reference maps of North America	164–187
► Arctic features	214–215

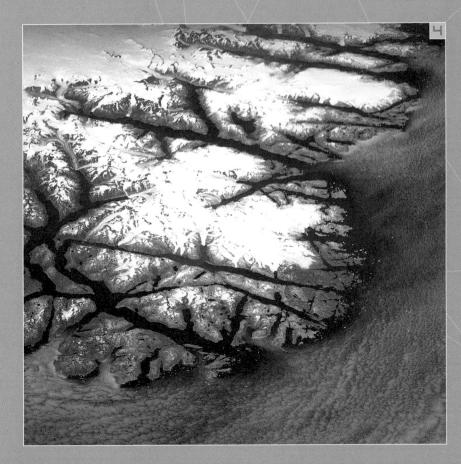

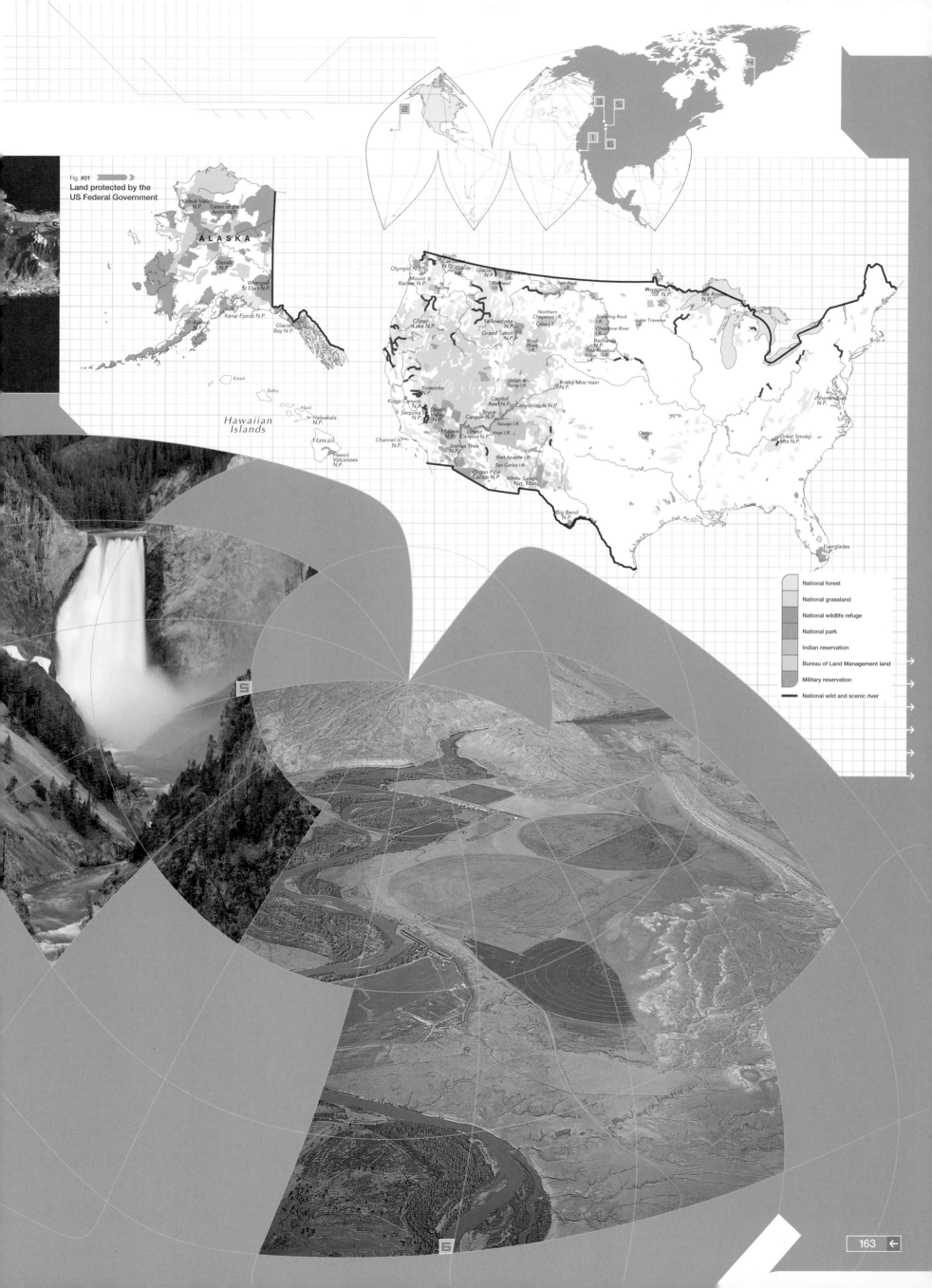

Fig. #01
Land protected by the
US Federal Government

ALASKA

Kobuk Valley
N.P.
Gates of the
Arctic N.P.

Denali
N.P.

Wrangell-
St Elias N.P.

Katmai
N.P.
Kenai Fjords N.P.

Glacier
Bay N.P.

Kauai

Oahu

Maui

Haleakala
N.P.

Hawaiian
Islands

Hawaii

Hawaii
Volcanoes
N.P.

Olympic N.P.
North
Cascades
N.P.
Colville
I.R.
Glacier
N.P.
Blackfeet
I.R.

Mount
Rainier N.P.
Yakima
I.R.
Flathead
I.R.
Fort Peck
I.R.
Voyageurs
N.P.
Isle Royale
N.P.

Crater
Lake N.P.
Yellowstone
Northern
Cheyenne I.R.
Crow I.R.
Standing Rock
I.R.
Lake Traverse

Grand Teton
N.P.
Wind
River
I.R.
Cheyenne River
I.R.
Badlands
N.P.
Pine Rosebud
Ridge I.R.

Yosemite
N.P.
Uintah &
Ouray I.R.
Rocky Mountain
N.P.

Kings Canyon
N.P.
Capitol
Reef N.P.
Canyonlands N.P.

Sequoia
N.P.
Death
Valley
N.P.
Bryce
Canyon N.P.
Navajo I.R.
Osage

Mojave
N.P.
Grand
Canyon N.P.
Hopi I.R.

Joshua Tree
N.P.

Channel Is.
N.P.

Organ Pipe
Cactus N.P.
Fort Apache I.R.
San Carlos I.R.
White Sands
Nat. Mon.

Great Smoky
Mts N.P.

Shenandoah
N.P.

Big Bend
N.P.

Everglades
N.P.

National forest

National grassland

National wildlife refuge

National park

Indian reservation

Bureau of Land Management land

Military reservation

National wild and scenic river

40°-85° N / 10°-180° W

CONNECTIONS

>6000m
5000-6000m
4000-5000m
3000-4000m
2000-3000m
1000-2000m
500-1000m
200-500m
0-200m
<0m

0-200m
200-500m
500-1000m
1000-2000m
2000-3000m
3000-4000m
4000-5000m
5000-6000m
>6000m

1:15 000 000

miles
0   200   400   600
0   200   400   600   800   1000
km

Lambert Conformal Conic Projection

RUSSIAN FEDERATION

ARCTIC OCEAN

Beaufort Sea

Chukchi Sea

Bering Strait

Aleutian Islands

Fox Islands

Gulf of Alaska

PACIFIC OCEAN

ALASKA

U.S.A.

Brooks Range

Alaska Range

Aleutian Range

Kuskokwim Mountains

Philip Smith Mountains

YUKON TERRITORY

NORTHWEST TERRITORIES

Great Bear Lake

Great Slave Lake

BRITISH COLUMBIA

ALBERTA

SASKATCHEWAN

Coast Mountains

Mackenzie Mountains

Cassiar Mountains

Rocky Mountains

Queen Charlotte Islands

Vancouver Island

WASHINGTON

OREGON

IDAHO

MONTANA

NEVADA

CALIFORNIA

WYOMING

UNITED STATES OF

COLORADO

170-171

130°   120°   110°

180°   170°   160°   150°   140°

Arctic Circle

48°-65°N / 92°-142°W

>6000m
5000-6000m
4000-5000m
3000-4000m
2000-3000m
1000-2000m
500-1000m
200-500m
0-200m
<0m

0-200m
200-500m
500-1000m
1000-2000m
2000-3000m
3000-4000m
4000-5000m
5000-6000m
>6000m

CONNECTIONS

▶ subject   page#

▶ World physical features   ➤ 8–9
▶ World changes   ➤ 20–21
▶ North America landscapes   ➤ 156–157
▶ North America countries   ➤ 158–159

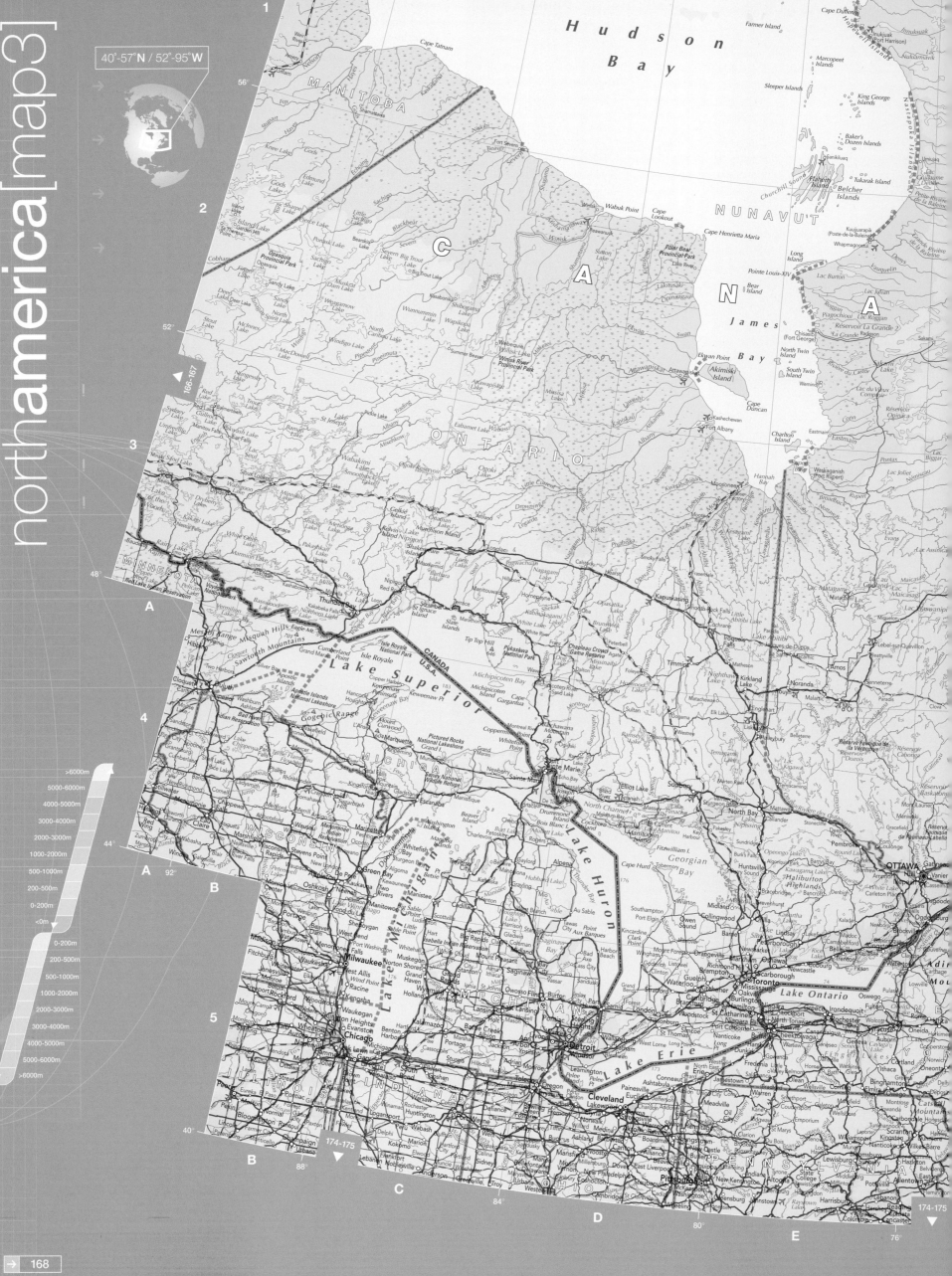

northamerica[map4]

17°-50°N / 67°-125°W

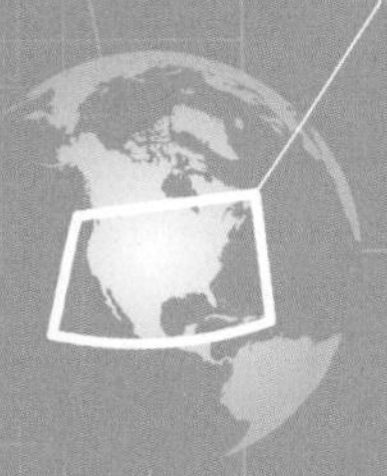

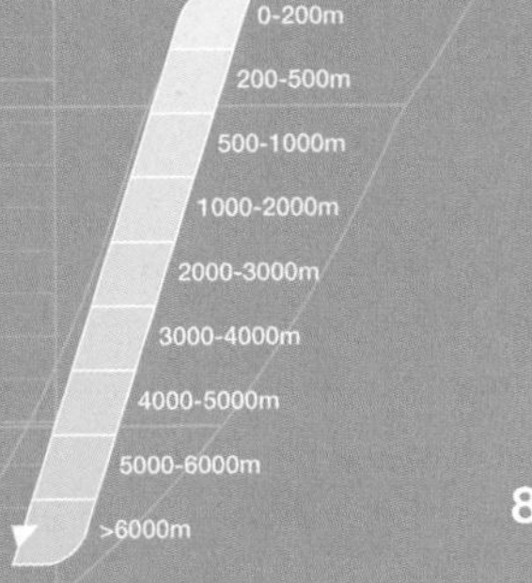

PACIFIC

OCEAN

UNITED OF AM

MEXICO

CALIFORNIA
NEVADA
OREGON
WASHINGTON
IDAHO
MONTANA
WYOMING
UTAH
COLORADO
ARIZONA
NEW MEXICO
BRITISH COLUMBIA
ALBERTA
SASKATCHEWAN
NORTH
NEBRASKA

Baja California
Gulf of California
Sierra Madre Occidental
Sierra Madre del Sur
Great Basin
Mojave Desert
High Desert
Channel Islands

Vancouver Island
Vancouver
Seattle
Portland
Sacramento
San Francisco
San Jose
Los Angeles
San Diego
Tijuana
Phoenix
Tucson
Denver
Albuquerque
El Paso
Ciudad Juárez
Chihuahua
Monterrey
Guadalajara
MEXICO CITY
Puebla
Mazatlán
Culiacán
Hermosillo
Calgary

Tropic of Cancer

>6000m
5000-6000m
4000-5000m
3000-4000m
2000-3000m
1000-2000m
500-1000m
200-500m
0-200m
<0m
0m
0-200m
200-500m
500-1000m
1000-2000m
2000-3000m
3000-4000m
4000-5000m
5000-6000m
>6000m

miles
0   100   200   300   400   500
0 100 200 300 400 500 600 700 800
km

1:12 000 000

Lambert Conformal Conic Projection

CANADA

ATLANTIC

OCEAN

Gulf of Mexico

Bermuda
(U.K.)
HAMILTON

THE
BAHAMAS

NASSAU

West Indies

Turks and
Caicos Islands
(U.K.)
GRAND TURK
(Cockburn Town)

HAVANA
(La Habana)

CUBA

Cayman Islands
(U.K.)

Caribbean Sea

JAMAICA
KINGSTON

HAITI
PORT-AU-PRINCE

DOMINICAN
REPUBLIC
SANTO
DOMINGO

Hispaniola

Yucatán

GUATEMALA

BELIZE
BELMOPAN

northamerica[map5]

41°-49° N / 76°-93° W

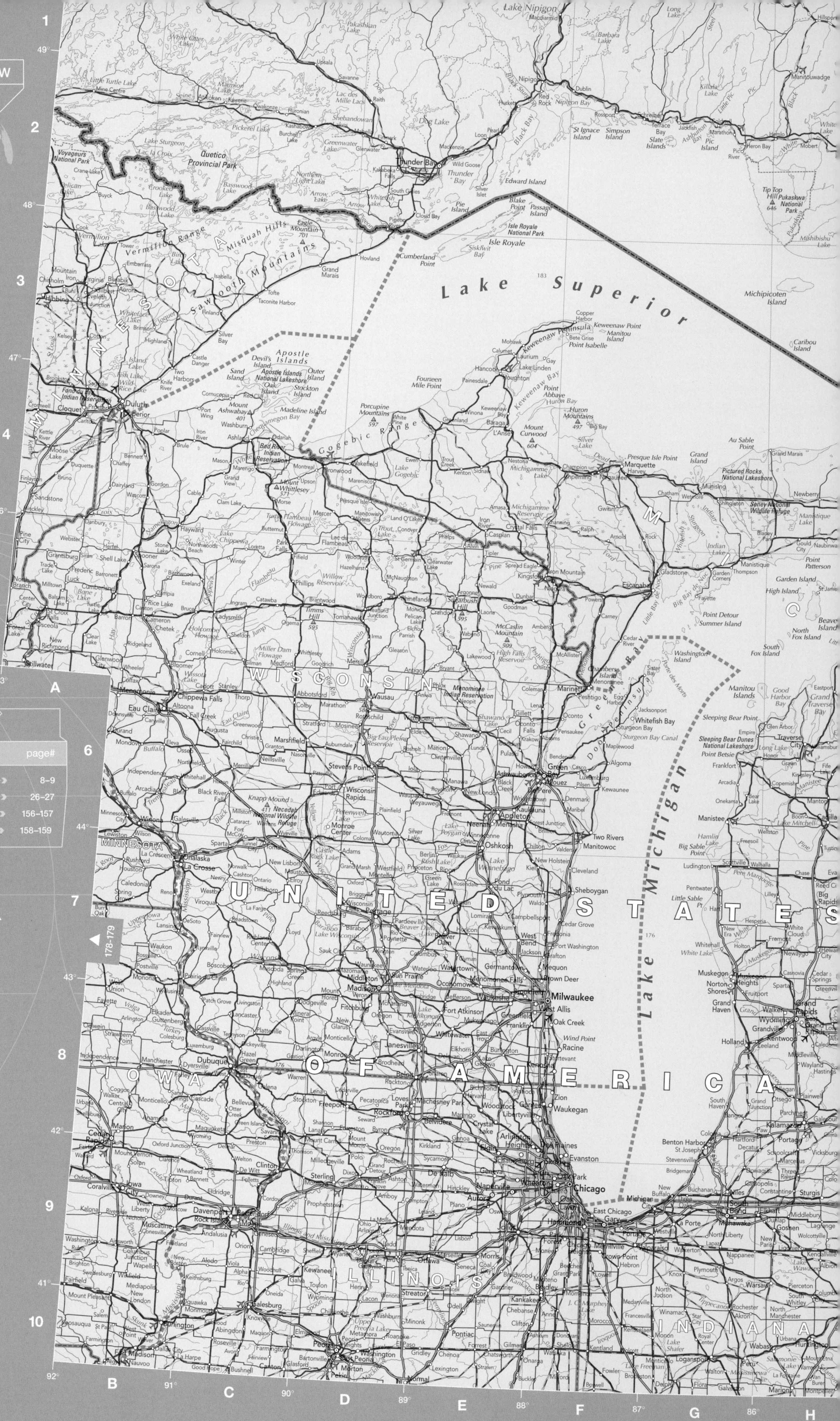

CONNECTIONS

▸ subject	page#
▸ World physical features	8–9
▸ World's busiest airports	26–27
▸ North America landscapes	156–157
▸ North America countries	158–159

>6000m
5000-6000m
4000-5000m
3000-4000m
2000-3000m
1500-2000m
1000-1500m
500-1000m
200-500m
100-200m
0-100m
<0m
0-50m
50-100m
100-200m
200-500m
500-1000m
1000-2000m
2000-3000m
3000-4000m
4000-5000m
5000-6000m
>6000m

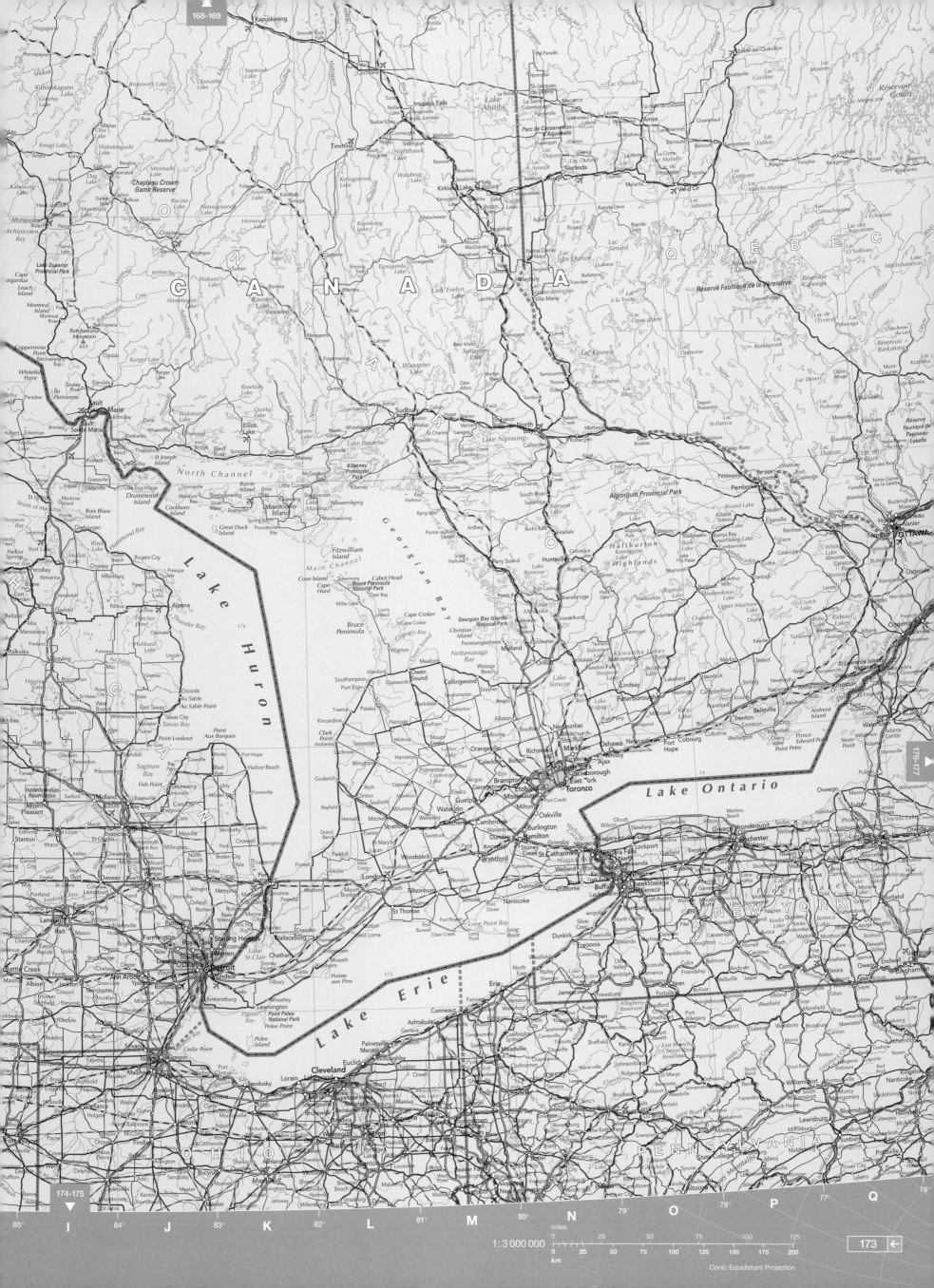

miles
0   25   50   75   100   125

1 : 3 000 000

0   25   50   75   100   125   150   175   200
km

Conic Equidistant Projection

Administrative divisions in the U.S.A.
numbered on map:

1. CONNECTICUT
2. MASSACHUSETTS
3. RHODE ISLAND
4. DELAWARE

ATLANTIC

OCEAN

THE
BAHAMAS

Little Abaco

Grand
Bahama

Great
Abaco

Little Bahama Bank

Great Bahama Bank

Eleuthera

NASSAU

Andros

Tongue of the Ocean

Exuma Cays

Cat Island

San Salvador

Long Island

Crooked Island

Acklins Island

Mayaguana

F l o r i d a

Miami
Fort
Lauderdale
West
Palm Beach

Key Largo National
Marine Sanctuary

Everglades National Park

Key West

Straits of Florida

CUBA

HAVANA
(La Habana)

Peninsula
de Zapata

Cienfuegos

Golfo
de Batabanó

Gulf

of

Mexico

SOUTH
CAROLINA

GEORGIA

FLORIDA

Jacksonville

Orlando

Tampa
St Petersburg

ALABAMA

LOUISIANA

MISSISSIPPI

New Orleans

Mississippi
Delta

Mobile

Montgomery

Tallahassee

Savannah

Charleston

Wilmington

Cape Fear

Myrtle Beach

7

8

Tropic of Cancer

22°–48′N / 92°–70°W

186–187

1:6 500 000

Lambert Conformal Conic Projection

miles
km

>6000m
5000–6000m
4000–5000m
3000–4000m
2000–3000m
1000–2000m
500–1000m
200–500m
0–200m

0–200m
200–500m
500–1000m
1000–2000m
2000–3000m
3000–4000m
4000–5000m
5000–6000m
>6000m

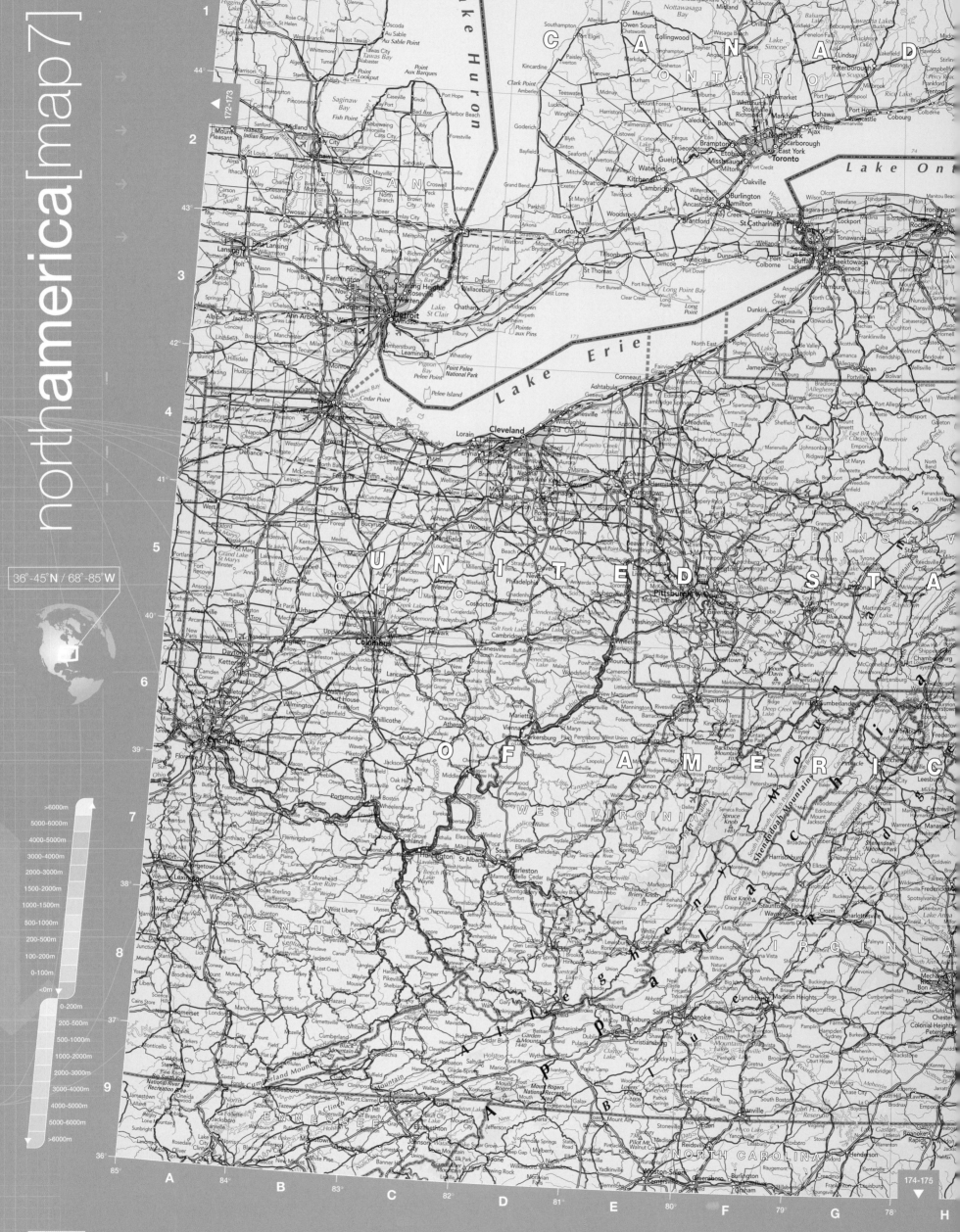

36°-45°N / 68°-85°W

>6000m
5000-6000m
4000-5000m
3000-4000m
2000-3000m
1500-2000m
1000-1500m
500-1000m
200-500m
100-200m
0-100m
<0m

0-200m
200-500m
500-1000m
1000-2000m
2000-3000m
3000-4000m
4000-5000m
5000-6000m
>6000m

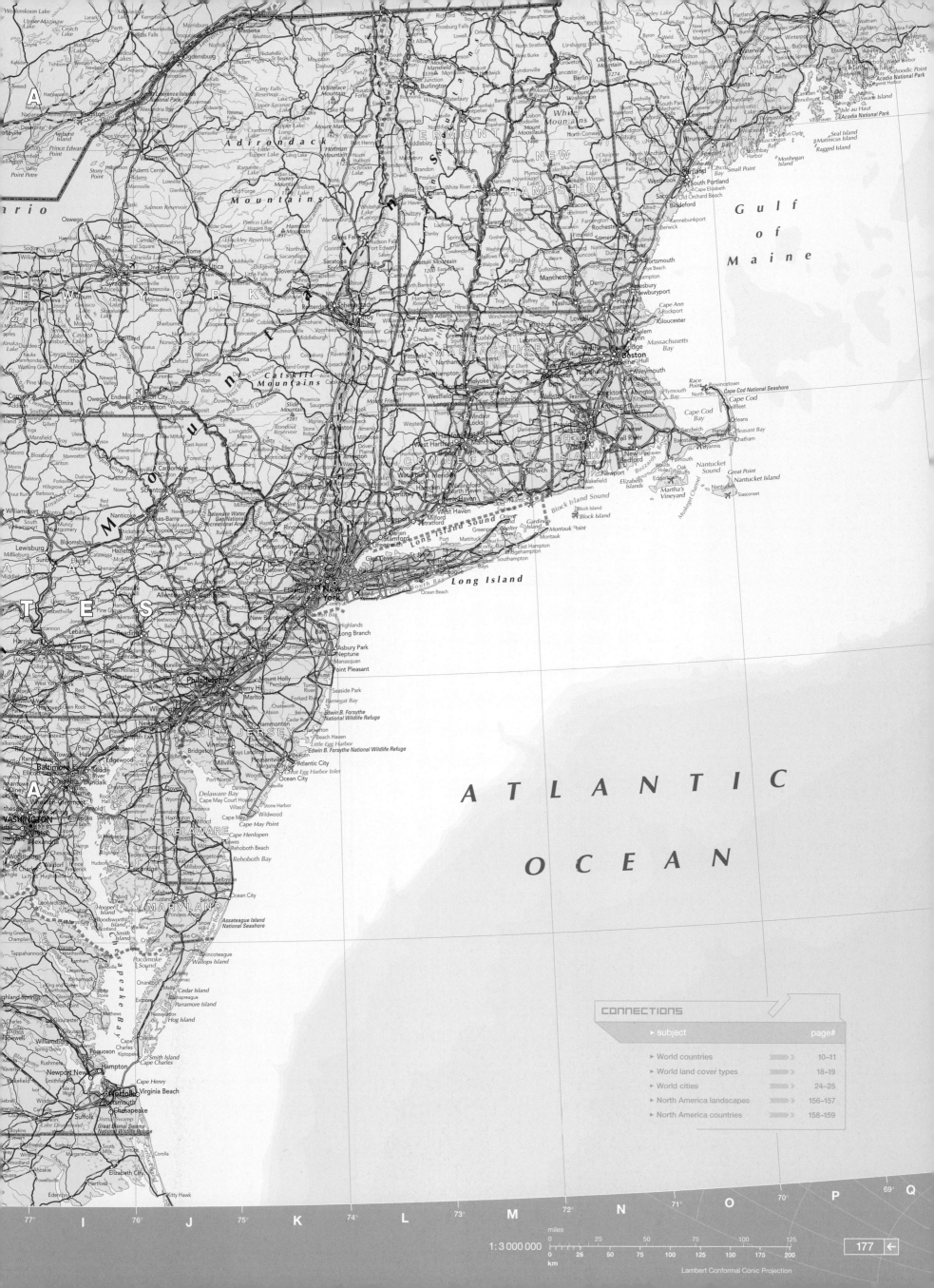

CONNECTIONS

▶ subject	page#
▶ World countries	10–11
▶ World land cover types	18–19
▶ World cities	24–25
▶ North America landscapes	156–157
▶ North America countries	158–159

1:3 000 000

miles
0   25   50   75   100   125

km
0   25   50   75   100   125   150   175   200

Lambert Conformal Conic Projection

25°·52'N / 82°·104'W

CONNECTIONS

subject	page#
▲ World physical features	8–9
▲ World changes	20–21
▲ North America countries	158–159
▲ North America environments	162–163

Gulf of Mexico

1 : 6 500 000

Lambert Conformal Conic Projection

1:6 500 000

27°·53'N / 103°·126°W

184-185 ▼

CONNECTIONS

▶ subject		page#
▲	World land images	12-13
▲	World earthquakes	14-15
▲	North America countries	158-159
▲	North America threats	160-161
▲	North America environments	162-163

Lambert Conformal Conic Projection

>6000m
5000-6000m
4000-5000m
3000-4000m
2000-3000m
1000-2000m
500-1000m
200-500m
0-200m
<0m
0-200m
200-500m
1000-2000m
2000-3000m
3000-4000m
4000-5000m
5000-6000m
>6000m

northamerica[map10]

32°-40°N / 109°-124°W

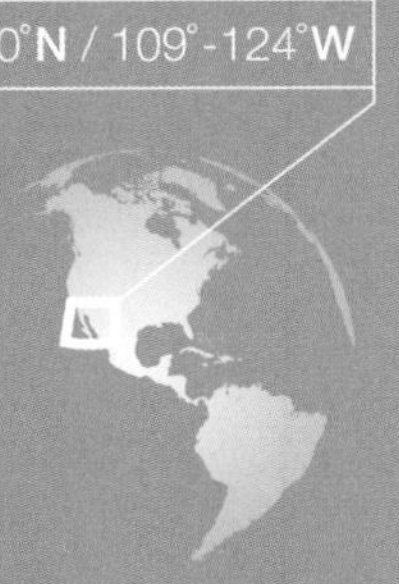

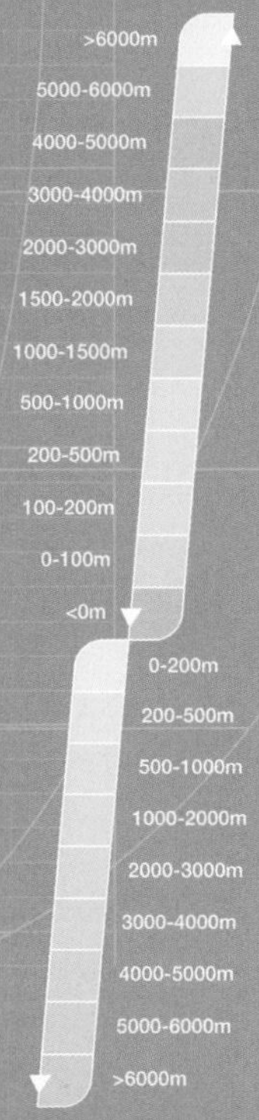

PACIFIC OCEAN

Legend (elevation):
>6000m
5000-6000m
4000-5000m
3000-4000m
2000-3000m
1500-2000m
1000-1500m
500-1000m
200-500m
100-200m
0-100m
<0m

0-200m
200-500m
500-1000m
1000-2000m
2000-3000m
3000-4000m
4000-5000m
5000-6000m
>6000m

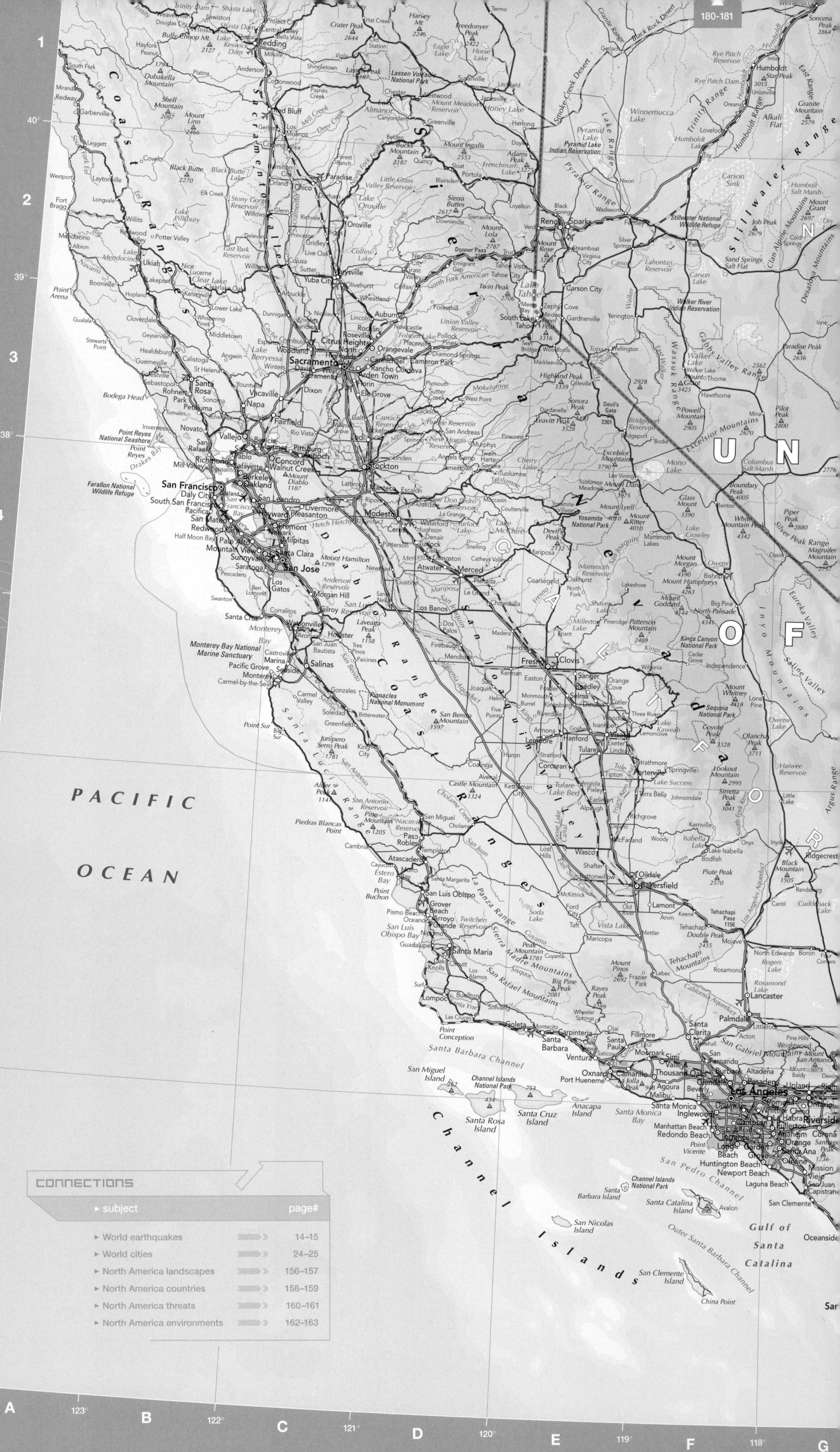

north america [map 11]

13°-32°N / 88°-116°W

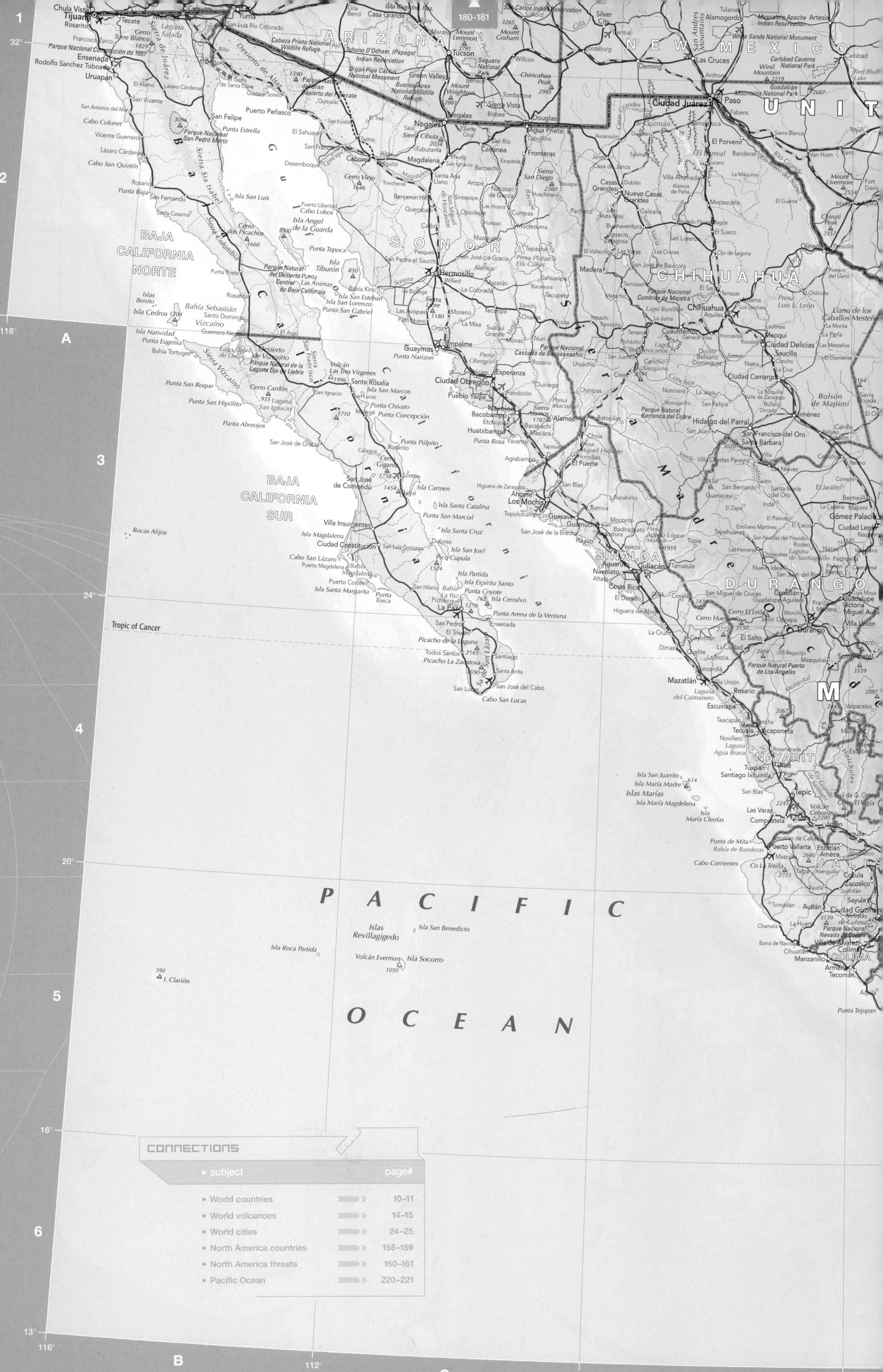

180-181
ARIZONA
NEW MEXICO
UNIT
BAJA CALIFORNIA NORTE
BAJA CALIFORNIA SUR
SONORA
CHIHUAHUA
SINALOA
DURANGO
NAYARIT
JALISCO
COLIMA
Gulf of California
Sierra Madre Occidental
PACIFIC OCEAN
Tropic of Cancer
Tijuana
Mexicali
Ensenada
Yuma
Tucson
Nogales
Hermosillo
Guaymas
Ciudad Obregón
Los Mochis
Culiacán
Mazatlán
La Paz
Cabo San Lucas
San José del Cabo
Ciudad Juárez
El Paso
Las Cruces
Chihuahua
Hidalgo del Parral
Durango
Tepic
Puerto Vallarta
Manzanillo
Colima
Ciudad Guzmán
Islas Revillagigedo
Isla Socorro
Isla San Benedicto
Isla Roca Partida
I. Clarión
Islas Marías
Isla Tiburón
Isla Cedros
Isla Angel de la Guarda
Bahía Sebastián Vizcaíno
Desierto de Vizcaíno
Santa Rosalía
Loreto
Ciudad Constitución
Rocas Alijos
A
B
C
D
1
2
3
4
5
6
32°
28°
24°
20°
16°
13°
118°
116°
112°
108°
104°

>6000m
5000-6000m
4000-5000m
3000-4000m
2000-3000m
1000-2000m
500-1000m
200-500m
0-200m
<0m
0-200m
200-500m
500-1000m
1000-2000m
2000-3000m
3000-4000m
4000-5000m
5000-6000m
>6000m

CONNECTIONS

subject	page#
World countries	10–11
World volcanoes	14–15
World cities	24–25
North America countries	158–159
North America threats	160–161
Pacific Ocean	220–221

178-179

UNITED STATES OF AMERICA
TEXAS
LOUISIANA
MISSISSIPPI
ALABAMA
FLORIDA
Gulf of Mexico
Bahía de Campeche
Gulf of Tehuantepec
MEXICO
COAHUILA
NUEVO LEÓN
TAMAULIPAS
SAN LUIS POTOSÍ
GUANAJUATO
QUERÉTARO
HIDALGO
VERACRUZ
MICHOACÁN
MÉXICO
PUEBLA
GUERRERO
OAXACA
TABASCO
CHIAPAS
CAMPECHE
YUCATÁN
QUINTANA ROO
BELIZE
GUATEMALA
HONDURAS
EL SALVADOR
MEXICO CITY
GUATEMALA CITY
SAN SALVADOR
BELMOPAN
Houston
San Antonio
Dallas
Fort Worth
Austin
New Orleans
Baton Rouge
Corpus Christi
Monterrey
Puebla
Veracruz
Mérida
Campeche
Villahermosa
Oaxaca
Acapulco
Guadalajara
Sierra Madre del Sur
Sierra Madre Oriental
Edwards Plateau
Yucatán
Istmo de Tehuantepec
Administrative divisions in Mexico numbered on the map:
1. AGUASCALIENTES
2. DISTRITO FEDERAL
3. MORELOS
4. TLAXCALA
E
F
G
H
I
100°
96°
92°
88°
1:7 000 000
miles
0
100
200
km
0
100
200
300
400
Lambert Conformal Conic Projection

186-187

6°-26°N / 60°-89°W

174-175

184-185

Gulf of Mexico

1

24°

Tropic of Cancer

2

MEXICO

YUCATÁN

QUINTANA ROO

Río Lagartos
Punta Yalkubul
Dzilam de Bravo
Tizimin
El Cuyo
Cabo Catoche
Isla Contoy
Isla Mujeres
Cancún
Valladolid
Chichén Itzá
Puerto Juárez
Leona Vicario
Puerto Morelos
Cozumel
Isla de Cozumel
Playa del Carmen
Tulum
Cedral
Felipe C. Puerto
Bahía de la Ascensión
Reserva de la Biósfera Sian Ka'an
Punta Herrero
Bahía del Espíritu Santo
Tekax
Peto
Santa Rosa
Chunhuhux
Xatil

20°

Bacalar
Chetumal
Calderitas
Boca Bacalar Chico
Banco Chinchorro
Orange Walk
Ambergris Cay
San Pedro
Altun Ha
Hicks Cays
George's Cay
Turneffe Islands
Lighthouse Reef
Glover Reef

3

BELIZE
BELMOPAN
San Ignacio
Belize
Dangriga
Maya Mountains 1120
1000
Jonathan Point
Punta Gorda

Yucatan Channel

16°

Gulf of Mexico

Yucatan Basin

HAVANA (La Habana)
Marianao
Guanabacoa
Artemisa
Güira
Consolación del Sur
Pinar del Río
San Juan y Martínez
Minas de Matahambre
Mantua
Península de Guanahacabibes
Cabo San Antonio
Cabo Corrientes
Bahía de Guadiana

Varadero
Cárdenas
Matanzas
Jovellanos
Colón
Los Arabos
Sagua la Grande
Santo Domingo
Remedios
Caibarién
Cayo Santa María
Archipiélago de Sabana
Madruga
Batabanó
Melena del Sur
Güines
Quivicán
Golfo de Batabanó
Isla de la Juventud
Nueva Gerona
Santa Fe
Cayos de San Felipe
La Fe
Punta Francés
Cayo Largo
Archipiélago de los Canarreos
Cayo del Rosario

CUBA

Antón Díaz
Cienfuegos
Trinidad
Sancti Spíritus
Ciego de Ávila
Morón
Esmeralda
Chambas
Jatibonico
Cabaiguán
Placetas
Santa Clara
Cayo Coco
Cayo Guillermo
Archipiélago de Camagüey
Nuevitas
Camagüey
Vertientes
Golfo de Ana María
Santa Cruz del Sur
Jardines de la Reina
Manzanillo
Campechuela
Niquero
Pilón
Cabo Cruz
Desembarco Del Granma National Park
Media Luna

Cayman Islands (U.K.)
GEORGE TOWN
Grand Cayman
Little Cayman
Cayman Brac
Spot Bay
Bodden Town
West Bay

Las Tunas
Holguín
Puerto Padre
Puerto Manatí
Gibara
Banes
Mayarí
Sierra Maestra
Palma Soriano
Bayamo
Jiguaní
Santiago de Cuba
Daiquirí
Guantánamo

FLORIDA
U.S.A.
North Port
Charlotte
Port Charlotte
Fort Myers
Cape Coral
Naples
Big Cypress National Preserve
Ten Thousand Islands
Everglades National Park
Cape Sable
Ponce de Leon Bay
Homestead
Hialeah
Miami
Miami Beach
Key Largo
Key West
Marathon
Key Largo National Marine Sanctuary
Islamorada
Marquesas Keys
Dry Tortugas
Pine Islands
Boca Chica Key

West Palm Beach
Palm Beach
Boca Raton
Delray Beach
Pompano Beach
Fort Lauderdale
Hollywood
Boynton Beach
Jupiter
Hobe Sound

Little Bahama Bank
Walker Cay
Grand Bahama
Freeport City
Great Abaco
Little Abaco
Cooper's Town
Marsh Harbour
Cherokee Sound
Hope Town

THE BAHAMAS
NASSAU
New Providence
Andros
Straits of Florida
Bimini Islands
Berry Islands
Eleuthera
Governor's Harbour
Rock Sound
Exuma Sound
Great Exuma
Little Exuma

Isla de la Bahía
Roatán
Utila
Guanaja
Parque Nacional Islas de Bahía
Cabo Camarón
Punta Sal

Gulf of Honduras
Puerto Cortés
Puerto Barrios
La Ceiba
Tela
Trujillo
Limón

HONDURAS
San Pedro Sula
Olanchito
Yoro
2347
Pico Bonito
El Progreso
Santa Bárbara
Comayagua
TEGUCIGALPA
Danlí
Juticalpa
Catacamas
Reserva Biósfera del Río Plátano
MOSQUITIA
Puerto Lempira
Cabo Gracias a Dios
Barra Kruta
Cabo Falso
Waspán

Yelucá 1128
Parque Nacional Patuca
Bonanza
Siuna
Rosita
Prinzapolka
Puerto Cabezas
Bocana de Paiwas

4

EL SALVADOR
SAN SALVADOR
San Vicente
San Miguel
Usulután
Santa Ana
Sonsonate
La Unión
San Francisco Gotera

NICARAGUA
Chinandega
Corinto
León
Poneloya
MANAGUA
Tipitapa
Masaya
Granada
Diriamba
Jinotepe
Masachapa
Estelí
Matagalpa
Boaco
Juigalpa
Santo Domingo
Rama
Bluefields
El Bluff
Laguna de Perlas
Punta de Perlas
Volcán Masaya
1994
1133
Lake Nicaragua
Isla de Ometepe
Rivas
San Carlos
Río San Juan
San Juan del Norte
Bahía de San Juan del Norte
Punta Gorda
Isla del Mono

COSTA DE MOSQUITO

Cayos Cajones
Cayos Becerro
Cayos Vivorillo
Banco Gorda
Arrecife de la Media Luna
Swan Islands (Honduras)

Serranilla Bank
Quita Sueño Bank (Colombia)
Serrana Bank (Colombia)
Isla de Providencia (Colombia)
Roncador Cay (Colombia)
Isla de San Andrés (Colombia)
Cayos del Este Sudeste (Colombia)
Cayos Albuquerque (Colombia)
Islas del Maíz (Corn Islands) (Nicaragua)

Montego Bay
Falmouth
Lucea
Savanna-la-Mar
Black River
May Pen
Spanish Town
JAMAICA
KINGSTON
Port Antonio
Morant Point
Portland Point
Morant Cays

Pedro Bank
Pedro Cays
Thunder Knoll
Rosalind Bank

C a r i b b e a n

5

COSTA RICA
SAN JOSÉ
Cartago
Liberia
Puntarenas
Alajuela
Heredia
Turrialba
Limón
Volcán Poás
Volcán Irazú
Volcán Arenal
1657
2708
Parque Nacional Tortuguero
Parque Nacional Braulio Carrillo
Península de Nicoya
Cabo Blanco
Golfo de Nicoya
Santa Cruz
Nicoya
Cabo Velas
Península de Osa
Golfo Dulce
Golfito
Quepos
Dominical
Bahía de Coronado
San Isidro
Parque Nacional Chirripó 3819
Parque Internacional La Amistad
Ciudad Neily
Paso Canoas

Cartagena
Isla de Barú

8°

PANAMA
PANAMA CITY
David
Santiago
Chitré
Las Tablas
Concepción
Volcán Barú
Parque Internacional La Amistad
Chiriquí
Puerto Armuelles
Golfo de Chiriquí
Isla de Coiba
Isla Cébaco
Península de Azuero
Cerro Hoya
Punta Mala
Golfo de Panamá
Archipiélago de las Perlas
Isla del Rey
Gulf of Panama
Colón
El Porvenir
Archipiélago de San Blas
Parque Nacional Portobelo
Lago Gatún
Cordillera de San Blas
La Chorrera
Golfo del Darién
Parque Nacional Los Corales del Rosario
Montería
Cabo Marzo
Parque Nacional Darién
Turbo
CHOCÓ
ANT
CO
CÓR
Medellín

6

6°

Lambert Conformal Conic Projection

1:7 000 000

miles
0 50 100 150 200 250 300
0 50 100 150 200 250 300 350 400 450 500
km

>6000m
5000-6000m
4000-5000m
3000-4000m
2000-3000m
1000-2000m
500-1000m
200-500m
0-200m
<0m

0-200m
200-500m
500-1000m
1000-2000m
2000-3000m
3000-4000m
4000-5000m
5000-6000m
>6000m

A 88° B 84° C 80° D 76°

West Indies

Turks and Caicos Islands (U.K.)

Puerto Rico (U.S.A.) SAN JUAN

HAITI
DOMINICAN REPUBLIC
PORT-AU-PRINCE
SANTO DOMINGO

Virgin Is (U.K.)
Virgin Is (U.S.A.)
CHARLOTTE AMALIE
Anguilla (U.K.)
THE VALLEY
St Martin (Fr.)
St-Barthélemy (Fr.)
Saba (Neth.)
St Eustatius (Neth.)
St Kitts
Nevis
BASSETERRE
ST KITTS AND NEVIS
Montserrat (U.K.)
PLYMOUTH

Barbuda
ANTIGUA AND BARBUDA
Antigua
ST JOHN'S

Guadeloupe (France)
BASSE-TERRE
Marie-Galante
Les Saintes

Aves (Venezuela)

DOMINICA
ROSEAU

Martinique (France)
FORT-DE-FRANCE

CASTRIES
ST LUCIA

St Vincent
KINGSTOWN
ST VINCENT AND THE GRENADINES
Bequia
Mustique
Canouan

BRIDGETOWN
BARBADOS

GRENADA
ST GEORGE'S
Grenville

Greater Antilles

Lesser Antilles

Leeward Islands

Windward Islands

CARIBBEAN SEA

Aruba (Neth.)
ORANJESTAD
Curaçao
WILLEMSTAD
Netherlands Antilles
Bonaire

Lesser Antilles

Golfo de Venezuela
Lake Maracaibo
Maracaibo

COLOMBIA

VENEZUELA
CARACAS
DISTRITO FEDERAL
Maracay
Valencia
Barcelona

Isla de Margarita
NUEVA ESPARTA
La Asunción

TRINIDAD AND TOBAGO
PORT OF SPAIN
Trinidad
Tobago

Ciudad Guayana
Ciudad Bolívar
BOLÍVAR

Orinoco
DELTA AMACURO

GUYANA

ZULIA
MÉRIDA
TÁCHIRA
BARINAS
APURE
ARAUCA
CASANARE
FALCÓN
LARA
PORTUGUESA
COJEDES
GUÁRICO
ANZOÁTEGUI
MONAGAS
SUCRE
MIRANDA
ARAGUA

Canaima National Park, *Venezuela*

southamerica

[contents]

	page#
southamerica [landscapes]	190–191
southamerica [countries]	192–193
southamerica [contrasts]	194–195
southamerica [impacts]	196–197

	map coverage	scale	page#
southamerica [map 1]	SOUTH AMERICA North	1:8 000 000	198–199
southamerica [map 2]	SOUTH AMERICA Central	1:8 000 000	200–201
southamerica [map 3]	SOUTH AMERICA East	1:8 000 000	202–203
southamerica [map 4]	SOUTH AMERICA South	1:8 000 000	204–205
southamerica [map 5]	BRAZIL Southeast	1:3 300 000	206–207

Gulf of
Mexico

Caribbean Sea

Lake
Maracaibo

Orinoco
River

Llanos

Guiana Highland

Largest drainage basin
Amazon
7 050 000 sq km / 2 722 000 sq miles
Map reference 199 F5

Negro River

Galapagos Islands

Japurá River

Amazon

Purus River

Selvas

Madeira River

Largest lake
Lake Titicaca
Bolivia / Peru
8 340 sq km / 3 220 sq miles
Map reference 200 C3

Lake
Titicaca

Altiplano

Atacama Desert

Pacific Ocean

Andes

Gran

Salado River

Parana River

Highest point
Cerro Aconcagua
Argentina
6 960 m / 22 834 ft
Map reference 204 C4

Cerro Aconcagua

Pampas

Colorado River

Negro River

Patagonia

Peninsula
Valdés

Lowest point
Peninsula Valdés
Argentina
40 m / 131 ft below sea level
Map reference 205 E6

Largest island
Isla Grande de Tierra del Fuego
Argentina/Chile
47 000 sq km / 18 147 sq miles
Map reference 205 C9

Falkland Islands

Tierra del Fuego

Cape Horn

CONNECTIONS

► subject	page#
► World physical features	8–9
► World land images	12–13
► South American states and territories	192–193
► Physical contrasts	194–195
► Reference maps of South America	198–207

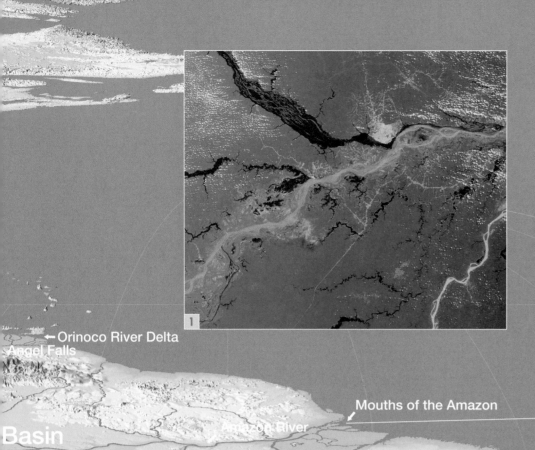

1

2

Longest river

Amazon
6 516 km / 4 049 miles
Map reference 202 B1

Orinoco River Delta
Angel Falls

Mouths of the Amazon

Amazon River

Basin

Sao Francisco River

Mato Grosso

Chaco

Brazilian Highlands

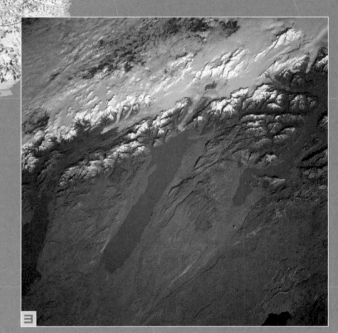

3

Uruguay River

Atlantic Ocean

Rio de la Plata

The spectacular Andes mountains dominate the western side of South America, bordering the Pacific for the entire length of the landmass. They stretch from Tierra del Fuego in the south, to Panama in the north. This huge mountain system has many volcanoes, is the source of many of the continent's large rivers, including the Amazon and Orinoco, and surrounds the Atacama Desert, the driest place on earth. The Altiplano is a high plateau within the Andes between the main west and east mountain ranges. Other upland areas include the Brazilian Highlands in the northeast and Patagonia, where the land rises steadily from the Atlantic coast to the Andes.

The Amazon Basin is a large lowland area, lying just south of the equator, through which the Amazon river and its many tributaries flow towards the huge delta on the Atlantic coast. The region contains vast areas of tropical rain forest. Huge, sparsely populated plains known as Llanos in the north and Pampas in the south provide further contrasts in the landscapes of the continent.

1 Amazon River, Brazil

The grey area on this satellite image is the isolated city of Manaus in northern Brazil. It sits at the confluence of the Amazon and Negro rivers. The Amazon, flowing from west to east, originates in the Andes mountains in Peru and carries a thick solution of silt and sand giving it a brown colour. The Negro river flows over hard base rock giving little sediment so the water is clearer, appearing dark in this image. The waters do not combine immediately but flow side by side for some distance before merging.

Satellite/Sensor : Terra, MISR

2 Pampas, Argentina

The Pampas grassland plains of Argentina stretch from the foothills of the Andes mountains to the east coast. This photograph shows the Pampas in Neuquen Province. Eastern areas tend to be better irrigated but the whole area supports a major livestock industry.

3 Lake Viedma, Argentina

Lake Viedma in the centre of this image, Lake Argentino to the left, and Lake San Martin to the right are situated in southern Argentina. This image looks southwest and shows the lakes being fed by meltwater from the glaciers of the Andes Mountains. Lake Viedma is over 300 m above sea level. Waters from it flow into Lake Argentino then into the Santa Cruz river, across the Patagonia plateau to the Atlantic Ocean. The snow-capped ridge behind the lakes forms the boundary between Argentina and Chile.

Satellite/Sensor : Space Shuttle

SOUTH AMERICA

HIGHEST MOUNTAINS

	m	ft	location	map
Cerro Aconcagua	6 960	22 834	Argentina	204 C4
Nevado Ojos del Salado	6 908	22 664	Argentina/Chile	204 C2
Cerro Bonete	6 872	22 546	Argentina	204 C2
Cerro Pissis	6 858	22 500	Argentina	204 C2
Cerro Tupungato	6 800	22 309	Argentina/Chile	204 C4
Cerro Meredario	6 770	22 211	Argentina	204 B3

LARGEST ISLANDS

	sq km	sq miles	map
Isla Grande de Tierra del Fuego	47 000	18 147	205 C9
Isla de Chiloe	8 394	3 240	205 B6
East Falkland	6 760	2 610	205 F8
West Falkland	5 413	2 090	205 E8

LONGEST RIVERS

	km	miles	map
Amazon	6 516	4 049	202 B1
Rio de la Plata-Parana	4 500	2 796	204 F4
Purus	3 218	1 999	199 F5
Madeira	3 200	1 988	199 G5
Sao Francisco	2 900	1 802	202 E4
Tocantins	2 750	1 708	202 B2

LAKES

	sq km	sq miles	map
Lake Titicaca	8 340	3 220	200 C3

LAND AREA

		map
Most northerly point	Punta Gallinas, Colombia	198 D1
Most southerly point	Cape Horn, Chile	205 D9
Most westerly point	Galapagos Islands, Ecuador	216 H6
Most easterly point	Ilhas Martin Vas, Atlantic Ocean	216 M7
Total land area: 17 815 420 sq km / 6 878 572 sq miles		

↓ ↓ ↓ ↓ ↓ ↓ ↓

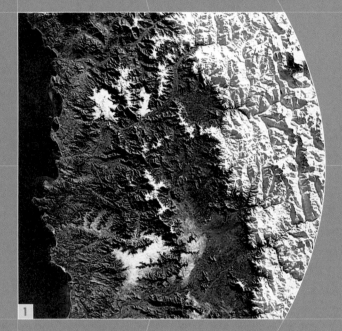

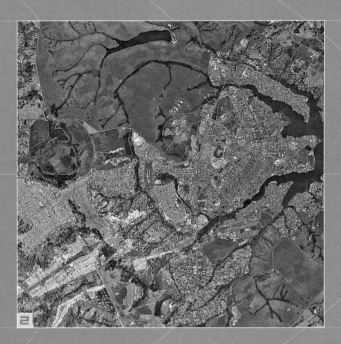

Equator

CONNECTIONS

► subject	page#
► World physical features	8–9
► World countries	10–11
► South America landscapes	190–191
► South America contrasts	194–195
► Reference maps of South America	198–207

SOUTH AMERICA

COUNTRIES

		area sq km	area sq miles	population	capital	languages	religions	currency	map
ARGENTINA		2 766 889	1 068 302	37 032 000	Buenos Aires	Spanish, Italian, Amerindian languages	Roman Catholic, Protestant	Peso	204–205
BOLIVIA		1 098 581	424 164	8 329 000	La Paz/Sucre	Spanish, Quechua, Aymara	Roman Catholic, Protestant, Baha'i	Boliviano	200–201
BRAZIL		8 547 379	3 300 161	170 406 000	Brasília	Portuguese	Roman Catholic, Protestant	Real	202–203
CHILE		756 945	292 258	15 211 000	Santiago	Spanish, Amerindian languages	Roman Catholic, Protestant	Peso	204–205
COLOMBIA		1 141 748	440 831	42 105 000	Bogotá	Spanish, Amerindian languages	Roman Catholic, Protestant	Peso	198
ECUADOR		272 045	105 037	12 646 000	Quito	Spanish, Quechua, other Amerindian languages	Roman Catholic	Sucre	198
GUYANA		214 969	83 000	761 000	Georgetown	English, creole, Amerindian languages	Protestant, Hindu, Roman Catholic, Sunni Muslim	Dollar	199
PARAGUAY		406 752	157 048	5 496 000	Asunción	Spanish, Guarani	Roman Catholic, Protestant	Guarani	201
PERU		1 285 216	496 225	25 662 000	Lima	Spanish, Quechua, Aymara	Roman Catholic, Protestant	Sol	200
SURINAME		163 820	63 251	417 000	Paramaribo	Dutch, Surinamese, English, Hindi	Hindu, Roman Catholic, Protestant, Sunni Muslim	Guilder	199
URUGUAY		176 215	68 037	3 337 000	Montevideo	Spanish	Roman Catholic, Protestant, Jewish	Peso	204
VENEZUELA		912 050	352 144	24 170 000	Caracas	Spanish, Amerindian languages	Roman Catholic, Protestant	Bolívar	198–199

DEPENDENT TERRITORIES

		territorial status	sq km	sq miles	population	capital	languages	religions	currency	map
Falkland Islands		United Kingdom Overseas Territory	12 170	4 699	2 000	Stanley	English	Protestant, Roman Catholic	Pound	205
French Guiana		French Overseas Department	90 000	34 749	165 000	Cayenne	French, creole	Roman Catholic	French franc	199
South Georgia and South Sandwich Islands		United Kingdom Overseas Territory	4 066	1 570	uninhabited					217

1 Santiago, Chile

In this Landsat satellite image, Santiago, capital city and main industrial centre of Chile, can be seen to the left of the snow-capped Andes mountains which form a natural boundary between Chile and its easterly neighbour, Argentina. The city, which has suffered many earthquakes and floods, was established as Chile's capital when the country became independent in 1818.

Satellite/Sensor : Landsat

2 Brasília, Brazil

Construction of Brasília as the administrative and political centre of Brazil began in 1956 and four years later it replaced Rio de Janeiro as the capital city of Brazil, South America's largest country. It is located on the Paraná, a headstream of the Tocantins river. In this infrared satellite image the city is in the centre, where buildings appear as light blue-grey. Lakes to the north and east of the city are blue-black, and vegetation along the small tributaries shows as red.

Satellite/Sensor : SPOT

3 Lake Titicaca, Bolivia/Peru

Lake Titicaca, located in a depression within the high plains (Altiplano) of South America, is the largest freshwater lake on the continent. The international boundary between Bolivia and Peru passes through the lake. In this oblique Shuttle photograph, the Andes mountains can be seen in the top right and bottom left. Persistent drought in the area has caused water levels to drop and expose the bottom of the lake, shown as white patches on the lake shore.

Satellite/Sensor : Space Shuttle

Caribbean Sea

ATLANTIC
OCEAN

PACIFIC

OCEAN

ATLANTIC

OCEAN

Barranquilla
Cartagena
Golfo del Darién
Gulf of Panama
Isla de Coco
Isla de Malpelo (Colombia)
Galapagos Islands (Ecuador)
CARACAS
Barquisimeto
Maracay
Cumaná
Maracaibo
Monteria
San Cristóbal
Orinoco
Ciudad Bolívar
VENEZUELA
Medellín
Tunja
Ibagué
BOGOTÁ
Puerto Ayacucho
Boa Vista
GEORGETOWN
PARAMARIBO
CAYENNE
GUYANA
SURINAME
French Guiana (Fr.)
COLOMBIA
Cali
Neiva
Pasto
QUITO
Manta
ECUADOR
Guayaquil
Cuenca
Golfo de Guayaquil
Iquitos
Putumayo
Japurá
Tonantins
Amazon
Santarém
Amazon
Belém
São Luís
Parnaíba
Manaus
Negro
Branco
PERU
Chiclayo
Trujillo
Pucallpa
Cruzeiro do Sul
Carauari
Yavari
Juruá
Purus
Madeira
Marañón
Rio Branco
Porto Velho
BRAZIL
Maraba
Tapajós
Iriri
Xingu
Tocantins
Fortaleza
Teresina
Natal
João Pessoa
Recife
Floresta
Juàzeiro
Maceió
LIMA
Huancayo
Cusco
Juliaca
Guaporé
Trinidad
Mamoré
Cuiabá
Araguaia
Tocantins
São Francisco
Teófilo Otôni
Aracaju
Salvador
LA PAZ
BOLIVIA
Arequipa
Cochabamba
Santa Cruz
SUCRE
Potosí
Tarija
Arica
Iquique
Antofagasta
Goiânia
BRASÍLIA
Patos de Minas
Uberaba
Belo Horizonte
Campo Grande
Araçatuba
Pedro Juan Caballero
Campinas
Vitória
Ilha da Trindade (Brazil)
Ilhas Martin Vas (Brazil)
Islas de los Desventurados (Chile)
Tropic of Capricorn
San Salvador de Jujuy
San Miguel de Tucumán
PARAGUAY
ASUNCIÓN
Maringá
São Paulo
Rio de Janeiro
Curitiba
Catamarca
La Rioja
Corrientes
Posadas
Iguaçu
Paraná
Santa Maria
Florianópolis
Archipiélago Juan Fernández (Chile)
San Juan
Aconcagua
Mendoza
Córdoba
Rosario
Paraná
Concordia
Porto Alegre
Rio Grande
Valparaíso
SANTIAGO
Salado
Santa Fé
URUGUAY
BUENOS AIRES
MONTEVIDEO
Rio de la Plata
ARGENTINA
CHILE
Concepción
Santa Rosa
Bahía Blanca
Mar del Plata
Neuquén
Negro
Viedma
Golfo San Matías
Isla de Chiloé
Trelew
Archipiélago de los Chonos
Golfo de San Jorge
Comodoro Rivadavia
Bahía Grande
STANLEY
Falkland Islands (U.K.)
Puerto Natales
Punta Arenas
Isla Grande de Tierra del Fuego
Ushuaia
Cape Horn
South Georgia and South Sandwich Islands (U.K.)
Antarctic Circle

SOUTH AMERICA

TOP 10 COUNTRIES BY AREA

	sq km	sq miles	map	world rank
1. BRAZIL	8 547 379	3 300 161	202–203	5
2. ARGENTINA	2 766 889	1 068 302	204–205	8
3. PERU	1 285 216	496 225	200	20
4. COLOMBIA	1 141 748	440 831	198	26
5. BOLIVIA	1 098 581	424 164	200–201	28
6. VENEZUELA	912 050	352 144	198–199	33
7. CHILE	756 945	292 258	204–205	38
8. PARAGUAY	406 752	157 048	201	59
9. ECUADOR	272 045	105 037	198	74
10. GUYANA	214 969	83 000	199	83

TOP 10 COUNTRIES BY POPULATION

	population	map	world rank
1. BRAZIL	170 406 000	202–203	5
2. COLOMBIA	42 105 000	198	28
3. ARGENTINA	37 032 000	204–205	31
4. PERU	25 662 000	200	38
5. VENEZUELA	24 170 000	198–199	40
6. CHILE	15 211 000	204–205	59
7. ECUADOR	12 646 000	198	63
8. BOLIVIA	8 329 000	200–201	84
9. PARAGUAY	5 496 000	201	97
10. URUGUAY	3 337 000	204	125

southamerica[contrasts]

1   La Paz, *Bolivia*

The Bolivian city of La Paz is the highest capital city in the world. It lies just southeast of Lake Titicaca, in a valley between the Cordillera Oriental and the Andes, sheltered from the severe winds and weather of the Altiplano. It has a population of over 1 million. The city was established by the Spanish conquistadors in the mid 1500's.

2   Farmland, *Ecuador*

On the western slopes of the Andes, erosion of the high volcanic peaks has created rich soils for farming, as seen here in Ecuador. The scattered farms are worked by indigenous Indian people who gather to sell, buy and barter at local weekly markets. Over 30 per cent of Ecuador's population is employed in agriculture and agricultural products account for almost half of the country's exports.

3   Glacier, *Patagonia*

Glaciers such as this, in the region of Patagonia, which straddles the Chile/Argentina border, are a great influence on the landscape. The surface of the glacier is deeply scarred by crevasses and patterns of debris within the ice indicate its current flow. Braided streams carry fine sediment away from the glacier.

Satellite/Sensor : Terra/ASTER

4   Galapagos Islands, *Ecuador*

This satellite image shows part of the Galapagos Islands, a group of islands created by volcanic activity. The craters of volcanoes on the main island of Isla Isabela and on Isla Fernandina to the west, can be clearly seen. Vegetation, which appears red, is limited as the landscape is dominated by lava flows. The Galapagos Islands are a group of isolated islands lying over 1 000 km west of the coast of Ecuador. They are renowned for their rich and unique wildlife.

Satellite/Sensor : SPOT

5   Andes Mountains

The Andes mountain range forms a formidable barrier down the whole length of the western side of the South American continent. This is clearly seen in this dramatic visualization created from digital terrain data. The western edge of the Andes descends steeply towards the Pacific Ocean with very little coastal lowland. Likewise to the east, the transition from high ground to low, flatter areas is also sudden, emphasizing the barrier of the mountains. To the south, the lowland areas form the grassy plains of the Pampas and to the north, the Amazon basin.

CONNECTIONS

► subject	page#
► La Paz	10–11
► World weather extremes	16–17
► Land cover types	18–19
► World's largest cities	24–25
► South America landscapes	190–191
► South America countries	192–193
► South America impacts	196–197

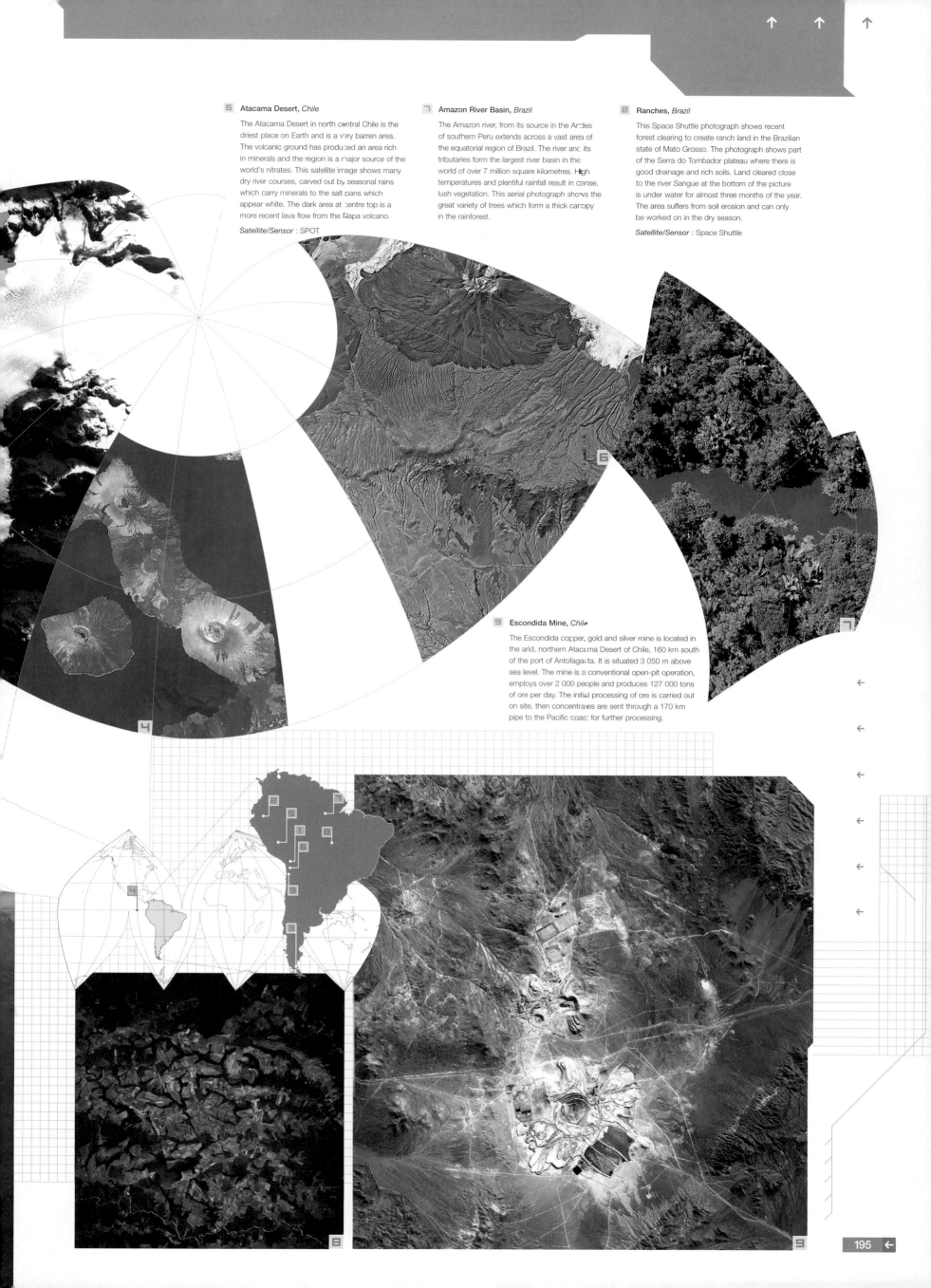

6 Atacama Desert, *Chile*

The Atacama Desert in north central Chile is the driest place on Earth and is a very barren area. The volcanic ground has produced an area rich in minerals and the region is a major source of the world's nitrates. This satellite image shows many dry river courses, carved out by seasonal rains which carry minerals to the salt pans which appear white. The dark area at centre top is a more recent lava flow from the Napa volcano.

Satellite/Sensor : SPOT

7 Amazon River Basin, *Brazil*

The Amazon river, from its source in the Andes of southern Peru extends across a vast area of the equatorial region of Brazil. The river and its tributaries form the largest river basin in the world of over 7 million square kilometres. High temperatures and plentiful rainfall result in dense, lush vegetation. This aerial photograph shows the great variety of trees which form a thick canopy in the rainforest.

8 Ranches, *Brazil*

This Space Shuttle photograph shows recent forest clearing to create ranch land in the Brazilian state of Mato Grosso. The photograph shows part of the Serra do Tombador plateau where there is good drainage and rich soils. Land cleared close to the river Sangue at the bottom of the picture is under water for almost three months of the year. The area suffers from soil erosion and can only be worked on in the dry season.

Satellite/Sensor : Space Shuttle

9 Escondida Mine, *Chile*

The Escondida copper, gold and silver mine is located in the arid, northern Atacama Desert of Chile, 160 km south of the port of Antofagasta. It is situated 3 050 m above sea level. The mine is a conventional open-pit operation, employs over 2 000 people and produces 127 000 tons of ore per day. The initial processing of ore is carried out on site, then concentrates are sent through a 170 km pipe to the Pacific coast for further processing.

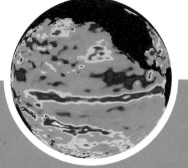
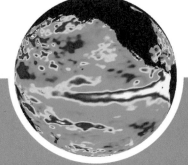

1

El Niño, *South America*

Periodically, atmospheric pressure becomes abnormally low in the middle of the Pacific Ocean and abnormally high over northern Australia. This results in the prevailing easterly winds weakening and changing direction. As a result, water off the west coast of South America becomes warmer by 4°–5°C. This phenomenon, known as El Niño, can have a dramatic effect on the world's climate, including higher rainfall in east Africa, and much lower rainfall and higher temperatures than normal in Australia.

The satellite images of the Earth show the development of El Niño during 1997. The red/white areas represent El Niño moving eastwards across the Pacific Ocean. The impacts of this on South America were drier conditions along the north coast, higher temperatures on the east and more rain in the northwest and southeast. The area most severely affected was the northwest coast. High river levels and flash floods were frequent and mudslides destroyed villages. Over 30 000 homes were lost in Peru during the course of the 1997–1998 El Niño event.

Satellite/Sensor : TOPEX/Poseidon

2

Mining, *South America*

The mineral distribution map of South America (Fig. #01) shows the great concentration of copper mining along the Andes mountain range. Large quantities of bauxite, the main ore for the production of aluminium, are mined in those areas with a tropical humid climate in the north of the continent. Symbol sizes on the map are proportional to mineral production as a percentage of world production, the largest representing over five per cent. While mining contributes enormously to the overall economy of South America, it also depletes natural resources and damages the environment. The photograph of the Bon Futuro tin mine in the Rondônia region of Brazil (number 7 on the map) shows how landscapes can be scarred by mining activities. Additional impacts can be the displacement of communities and the pollution of rivers and lakes.

Fig. #01
South America minerals

Metallic minerals

- Iron **Fe**
- Copper **Cu**
- Gold **Au**
- Aluminium **Al**
- Manganese **Mn**
- Lead **Pb**, Zinc **Zn**, Silver **Ag**
- Tin **Sn**, Antimony **Sb**
- Nickel **Ni**, Molybdenum **Mo**, Niobium **Nb**, Chromium **Cr**, Tungsten **W**

Industrial (non metallic) minerals

- Phosphate **P**, Borates **B**,
- Fluorspar **F**
- Diamonds **Diam.**

Symbol sizes reflect level of production from less than 1% to over 5% of world production.

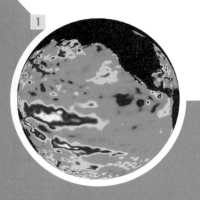

Argentina
1 Aguilar, **Pb, Zn, Ag**
2 Bajo de la Alumbrera, **Cu, Mo, Au**
3 El Pachon, **Cu, Mo, Au**
4 Northern Provinces, **B**

Bolivia
5 Potosí, Oruro, **Sn, Sb, Pb, Zn, Ag, W**

Brazil
6 Trombetas, **Al**
7 Rondônia, **Sn**
8 Carajás, **Fe**
9 Igarape Azul, Carajás, **Mn**
10 Caraiba, **Cu**
11 Campo Formoso, **Cr**
12 Cana Brava, **Cr**
13 Niquelândia, **Ni**
14 Morro do Niquel, **Ni**
15 Tocantins, **Ni**
16 Urucum, **Mn, Fe**
17 Vazante, **Pb, Zn**
18 Boquira, **Pb, Zn**
19 Jequitinhonha, **Diam.**
20 Araxá, **Nb, P**
21 Morro Velho, **Au**
22 Iron Quadrilateral, **Fe**
23 Morro da Fumaça, **F**
24 Roraima, **Diam.**

Chile
25 Chuquicamata, **Abra, Cu, Mo**
26 Escondida, El Salvador, **Cu, Mo, Au**
27 Disputada, Andina, Pelambres, **Cu, Mo**
28 El Teniente, **Cu, Mo**
29 Cerro Colorado, Quebrada Blanca, **Cu, Mo**
30 La Candelaria, **Cu, Mo, Au**
31 Atacama, **Fe**

Colombia
32 Titiribi, **Au**
33 Cerro Matoso, **Ni**

Ecuador
34 Portovelo, **Au**

Guyana
35 Guyana, **Al**
36 Omai, **Au**

Peru
37 Northern Peru, **Pb, Zn, Ag, Cu, Mo**
38 Cerro de Pasco, central Peru, **Pb, Zn, Ag, Cu, Mo**
39 Cuajone, Toquepala, **Cu, Mo**
40 Tintaya, **Cu, Mo**
41 Cerro Verde, **Cu, Mo**
42 Marcona, **Fe**
43 Yanacocha, **Au**

Suriname
44 Suriname, **Al**

Venezuela
45 Cedeno, **Al**
46 Cerro Bolivar, San Isidro, **Fe**
47 Cristinas, **Au, Cu**

≡ Deforestation, *Bolivia*

The two Landsat satellite images below were produced fifteen years apart.
The upper image shows an area of tropical rainforest near the Bolivian city of
Santa Cruz in 1984. The Piray river is the dark blue line in the bottom left of
the image. Forest and natural vegetation appears as green, bare ground as red.
The lower image, dated 1998, demonstrates the impact of deforestation in the
region. Huge areas of the forest east of the river have been completely cleared
for agriculture, in a similar way to that shown in the aerial photograph.
Destruction of the rainforest is a major environmental issue and interrupting
the forest canopy in this way causes humidity to drop rapidly and huge areas
of forest become vulnerable to fire.

Satellite/Sensor : Landsat

CONNECTICNS

► subject		page#
► World climate and weather	⟹	16–17
► World land cover types	⟹	18–19
► World changes	⟹	20–21
► South America landscapes	⟹	190–191
► South America countries	⟹	192–193
► South America contrasts	⟹	194–195

southamerica[map1]

8°S-14°N / 51°-82°W

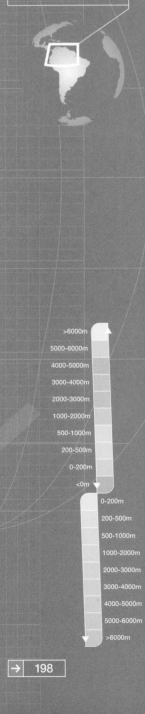

Administrative regions
numbered on the map:

COLOMBIA
1. QUINDÍO (C3)
2. RISARALDA (C3)
3. SANTAFÉ DE BOGOTÁ (C3)

ECUADOR
4. BOLÍVAR (B5)
5. CHIMBORAZO (B5)
6. TUNGURAHUA (B5)
7. ZAMORA-CHINCHIPE (B5)

>6000m
5000-6000m
4000-5000m
3000-4000m
2000-3000m
1000-2000m
500-1000m
200-500m
0-200m
<0m
0-200m
200-500m
500-1000m
1000-2000m
2000-3000m
3000-4000m
4000-5000m
5000-6000m
>6000m

southamerica[map2]

6°-28°S / 48°-80°W

PACIFIC OCEAN

Tropic of Capricorn

PERU

BOLIVIA

CHILE

LIMA
Callao
Arequipa
MOQUEGUA
TACNA
Arica
Iquique
Antofagasta
Calama
Tocopilla
LA PAZ
COCHABAMBA
SUCRE
POTOSI
ORURO
ANTOFAGASTA
TARAPACA
ATACAMA
CATAMARCA

LORETO
SAN MARTIN
AMAZONAS
CAJAMARCA
LA LIBERTAD
ANCASH
HUANUCO
PASCO
JUNIN
LIMA
HUANCAVELICA
AYACUCHO
APURIMAC
ICA
AREQUIPA
CUSCO
PUNO
MADRE DE DIOS
ACRE
PANDO
BENI
LA PAZ
ORURO
POTOSI

Chimbote
Trujillo
Chiclayo
Huancayo
Ayacucho
Cusco
Puno
Juliaca
Pucallpa
Rio Branco
Riberalta

>6000m
5000-6000m
4000-5000m
3000-4000m
2000-3000m
1000-2000m
500-1000m
200-500m
0-200m
<0m

→ 200

202-203

204-205

1 : 8 000 000

Lambert Azimuthal Equal Area Projection

southamerica[map3]

0°-31°S / 32°-56°W

1:8 000 000

Lambert Azimuthal Equal Area Projection

CONNECTIONS

► subject	page#
▲ World countries	10–11
▲ World population distribution	22–23
▲ World cities	24–25
▲ South America countries	192–193
▲ Atlantic Ocean	216–217

ATLANTIC

OCEAN

BRASIL

MINAS GERAIS

SÃO PAULO

Rio de Janeiro

São Paulo

PARANÁ

SANTA CATARINA

RIO GRANDE DO SUL

MATO GROSSO DO SUL

PARAGUAY

ARGENTINA

MISIONES

Porto Alegre

Curitiba

Santos

200-201

204-205

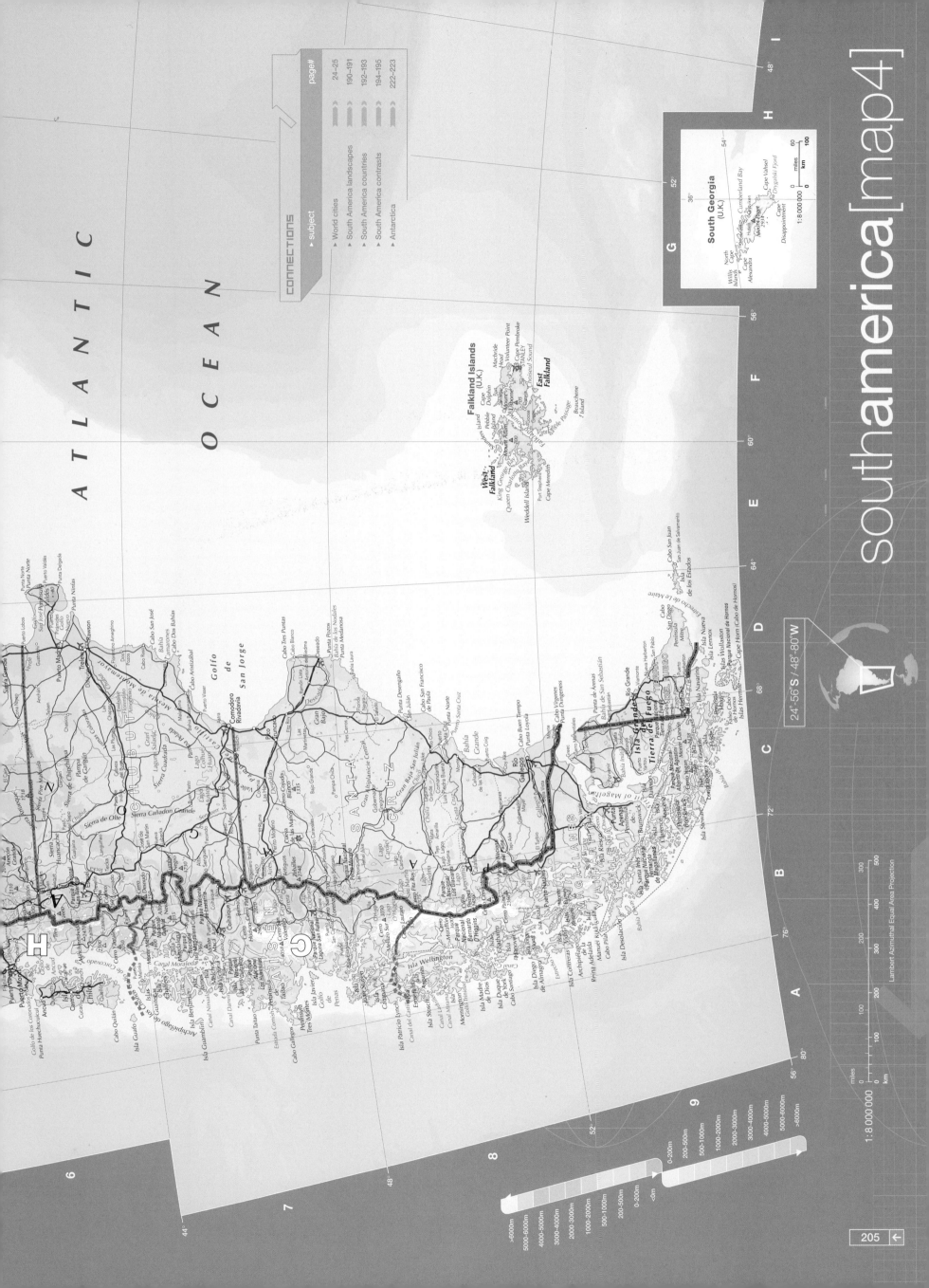

southamerica[map4]

15°-24°S / 38°-53°W

Elevation legend:
>6000m
5000-6000m
4000-5000m
3000-4000m
2000-3000m
1500-2000m
1000-1500m
500-1000m
200-500m
100-200m
0-100m
<0m

0-200m
200-500m
500-1000m
1000-2000m
2000-3000m
3000-4000m
4000-5000m
5000-6000m
>6000m

202-203
202-203

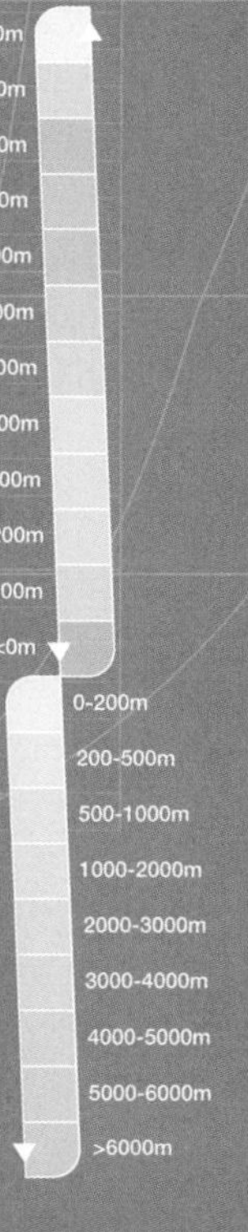

Paradise Bay, *Antarctica*

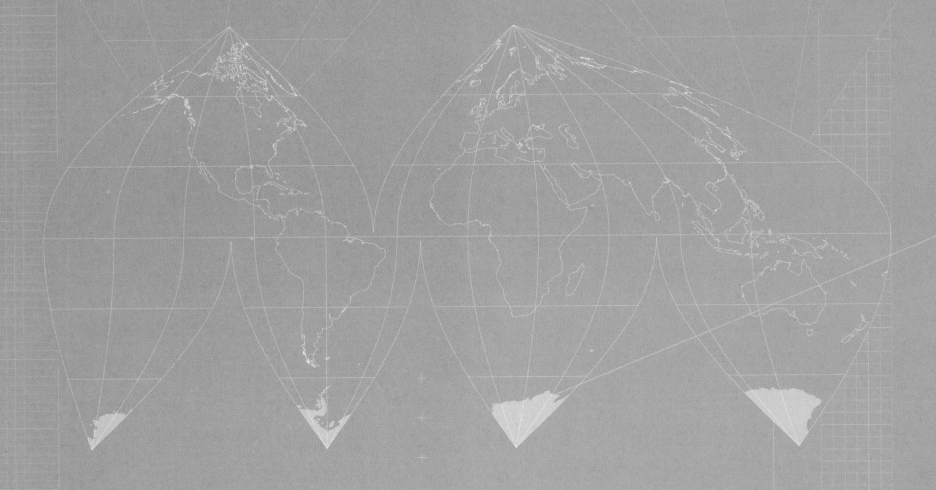

oceansandpoles

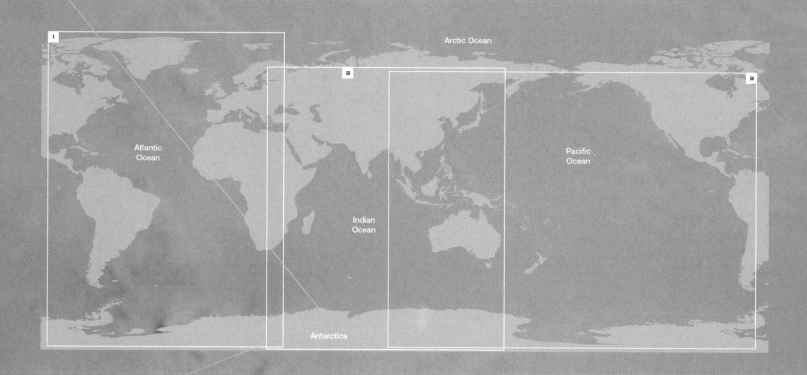

Arctic Ocean

Atlantic
Ocean

Pacific
Ocean

Indian
Ocean

Antarctica

[contents]

		page#
oceans [features]		210–211
antarctica [features]		212–213
thearctic [features]		214–215

	map coverage	scale	page#
oceans [map1]	ATLANTIC OCEAN	1:40 000 000	216–217
oceans [map 2]	INDIAN OCEAN	1:40 000 000	218–219
oceans [map 3]	PACIFIC OCEAN	1:45 000 000	220–221
antarctica [map 1]	ANTARCTICA	1:13 000 000	222–223
thearctic [map 1]	ARCTIC OCEAN	1:24 000 000	224

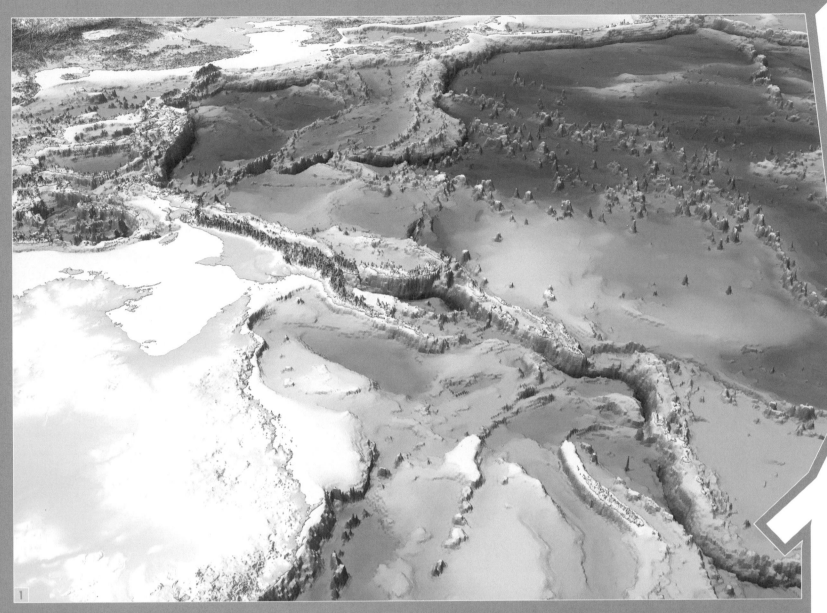

CONNECTIONS

▸ subject   page#

▸ World climate and weather   ▷▷▷   16–17
▸ South America impacts   ▷▷▷   196–197
▸ Atlantic Ocean   ▷▷▷   216–217
▸ Indian Ocean   ▷▷▷   218–219
▸ Pacific Ocean   ▷▷▷   220–221

Fig. #01 ▷▷▷▷▷
Ocean surface currents

→ Warm current
→ Cold current
→ Seasonal drift during northern winter

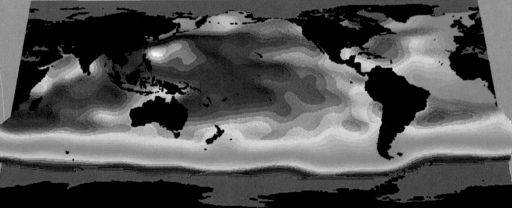

Fig. #02 ▷▷▷▷▷
Sea surface height

Fig. #01–#02 Sea surface currents and height

Most of the Earth's incoming solar radiation is
absorbed by the surface waters of the oceans.
The resultant warming is greatest around the
equator and ocean surface currents, as shown
on the map above (Fig. #01), redistribute the heat
around the globe. They are influenced by winds,
by density gradients caused by variations in
temperature and salinity, and by the Earth's
rotation which tends to deflect currents to the
right in the northern hemisphere and to the left in
the southern hemisphere. The circulation of ocean
currents is a major influence on the world's climate.
Sea surface circulation is reflected in variations
in sea surface height (Fig. #02) which can vary
greatly across currents. Currents flow along the
slopes and are strongest where the slopes
are steepest.

Satellite/Sensor : TOPEX/POSEIDON

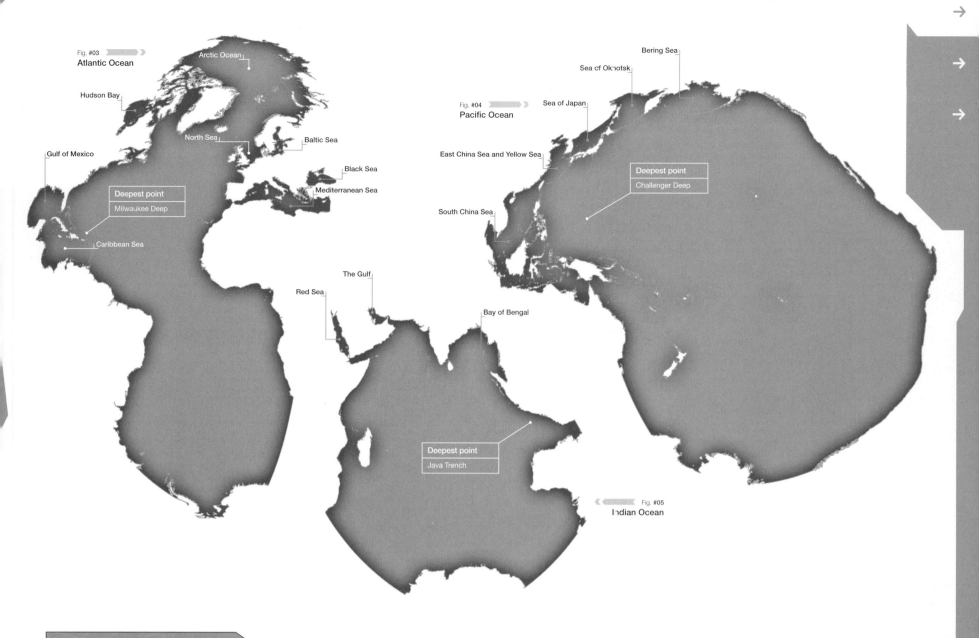

Fig. #03 Atlantic Ocean

Arctic Ocean

Hudson Bay

North Sea

Baltic Sea

Gulf of Mexico

Black Sea

Mediterranean Sea

Deepest point
Milwaukee Deep

Caribbean Sea

Bering Sea

Sea of Okhotsk

Fig. #04 Pacific Ocean

Sea of Japan

East China Sea and Yellow Sea

Deepest point
Challenger Deep

South China Sea

Red Sea

The Gulf

Bay of Bengal

Deepest point
Java Trench

Fig. #05 Indian Ocean

OCEANS

ATLANTIC OCEAN	area sq km	area sq miles	maximum depth metres	maximum depth feet	INDIAN OCEAN	area sq km	area sq miles	maximum depth metres	maximum depth feet	PACIFIC OCEAN	area sq km	area sq miles	maximum depth metres	maximum depth feet
Atlantic Ocean	86 557 000	33 420 000	8 605	28 231	Indian Ocean	73 427 000	28 350 000	7 125	23 376	Pacific Ocean	166 241 000	64 186 000	10 920	35 826
Arctic Ocean	9 485 000	3 662 000	5 450	17 880	Bay of Bengal	2 172 000	839 000	4 500	14 763	South China Sea	2 590 000	1 000 000	5 514	18 090
Caribbean Sea	2 512 000	970 000	7 680	25 196	Red Sea	453 000	175 000	3 040	9 973	Bering Sea	2 261 000	873 000	4 150	13 615
Mediterranean Sea	2 510 000	969 000	5 121	16 800	The Gulf	238 000	92 000	73	239	Sea of Okhotsk (Okhotskoye More)	1 392 000	537 000	3 363	11 033
Gulf of Mexico	1 544 000	596 000	3 504	11 495						East China Sea (Dong Hai) and Yellow Sea (Huang Hai)	1 202 000	464 000	2 717	8 913
Hudson Bay	1 233 000	476 000	259	849						Sea of Japan (East Sea)	1 013 000	391 000	3 743	12 280
North Sea	575 000	222 000	661	2 168										
Black Sea	508 000	196 000	2 245	7 365										
Baltic Sea	382 000	147 000	460	1 509										

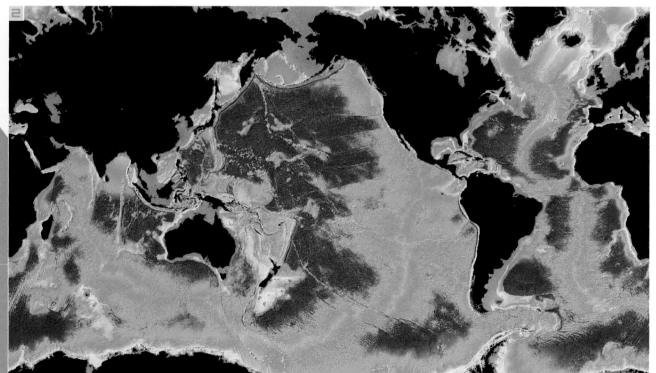

1 Perspective View, *Pacific Ocean*

This 3-D perspective view shows the sea trenches, ridges and basins of the western side of the Pacific Ocean. The image has been generated using sea depth values and extends from Australia and Melanesia at the bottom to Japan and the Kamchatka Peninsula at the top. Severe variations in depth of the sea bed are clearly seen. Deep trenches are shown by the darker areas. The New Hebrides, South Solomon and New Britain Trenches are visible at the bottom of the image and the Mariana Trench, the world's deepest, in the upper centre.

2 Global Seafloor Topography

This image has been produced from a combination of shipboard depth soundings and gravity data derived from satellite altimetry from the ERS-1 and Geosat satellites. The range of colours represents different depths of the ocean – from orange and yellow on the shallow continental shelves to dark blues in the deepest ocean trenches. The heavily fractured mid-ocean ridges (ranging from green to yellow) are particularly prominent.

ANTARCTICA		
HIGHEST MOUNTAINS		
	m	ft
Vinson Massif	4 897	16 066
Mt Tyree	4 852	15 918
Mt Kirkpatrick	4 528	14 855
Mt Markham	4 351	14 275
Mt Jackson	4 190	13 747
Mt Sidley	4 181	13 717
AREA		
	sq km	sq miles
Total land area (excluding ice shelves)	12 093 000	4 669 292
Ice shelves	1 559 000	601 954
Exposed rock	49 000	18 920
HEIGHTS		
	m	ft
Lowest bedrock elevation (Bentley Subglacial Trench)	-2 496	-8 189
Maximum ice thickness (Astrolabe Subglacial Basin)	4 776	15 669
Mean ice thickness (including ice shelves)	1 859	6 099
VOLUME		
	cubic km	cubic miles
Ice sheet (including ice shelves)	25 400 000	10 160 000
CLIMATE		
	°C	°F
Lowest screen temperature (Vostok Station, 21st July 1983)	-89.2	-128.6
Coldest place – Annual mean (Plateau Station)	-56.6	-69.9

1 Ozone Depletion

Since the 1970s, measurements have shown a thinning of the protective ozone layer in the Earth's atmosphere and the appearance of an ozone 'hole' over Antarctica. A major cause of this appears to be emissions of CFCs chlorofluorocarbons (CFCs) and halon gasses. This image from the Total Ozone Mapping Spectrometer (TOMS) sensor shows the ozone hole (blue) at its maximum extent of 11 million square miles in 2000. The unit of measurement for Ozone is the Dobson Unit (DU) with 300 being an average figure. In the image, yellow and orange represent high levels of 300–340DU, and dark blue low levels of 100–200 DU.

Satellite/Sensor : TOMS

2 Sea Ice Concentration

These images have been derived from data collected by the Special Sensor Microwave Imager (SSM/I) carried on US Department of Defense meteorological satellites. The colours represent ice concentration, ranging from the purple and red areas with a concentration of over 80 per cent, through to the green and yellow areas with concentrations between 20 and 40 per cent. The top image shows the ice at its lowest 2000 level in February, towards the end of the Antarctic summer. Ice builds up through the winter and by September (bottom), the ice is at its most extensive. In places the sea is frozen to a distance of over 1 000 km from the land.

Satellite/Sensor : SSM/I

3 Larsen Ice Shelf

This satellite image shows the edge of the Larsen Ice Shelf on the eastern side of the Antarctic Peninsula, and icebergs which have split, or 'calved' from the shelf. Ice shelves, which account for about 2 per cent of all Antarctic ice, typically undergo cycles of advance and retreat over many decades. Warmer surface temperatures over just a few months can cause an ice shelf to splinter and may prime it for a major collapse. This process can be expected to become more widespread if global, and particularly Antarctic summer, temperatures increase.

Satellite/Sensor : Landsat

4 Ice Sheet Thickness

Antarctica is covered by a permanent ice sheet that is in places more that 4 500 m thick. This map shows the thickness of ice, with the orange/red areas representing ice over 3 000 m thick. The thinnest ice is around the coast and on the high mountains, represented by the blue areas. The cross-section shows the ice cap (pale blue) in relation to the bedrock of Antarctica. This clearly shows that the thickest ice occurs above the deep glacial trenches, where the bedrock lies well below sea level.

5 Radar Image of Antarctica

This image of the whole of Antarctica is derived from data gathered by the Canadian RADARSAT satellite. In the image, light and dark areas represent relative measurements of radar reflectivity. Areas of finely powdered snow and smooth ice with few imperfections tend not to scatter radar waves projected against it, hence they appear dark. Irregular surfaces such as old, pitted ice, rock slides, and crevasses scatter the radar beam, giving a strong radar signal and thus appearing bright. Images such as this are valuable tools in the study of ice flow and stability on the continent.

Satellite/Sensor : RADARSAT

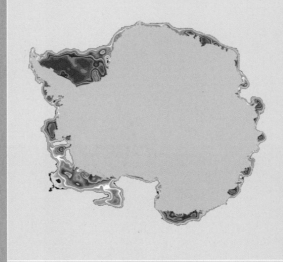

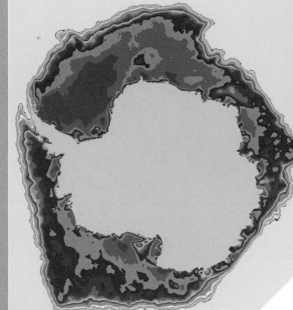

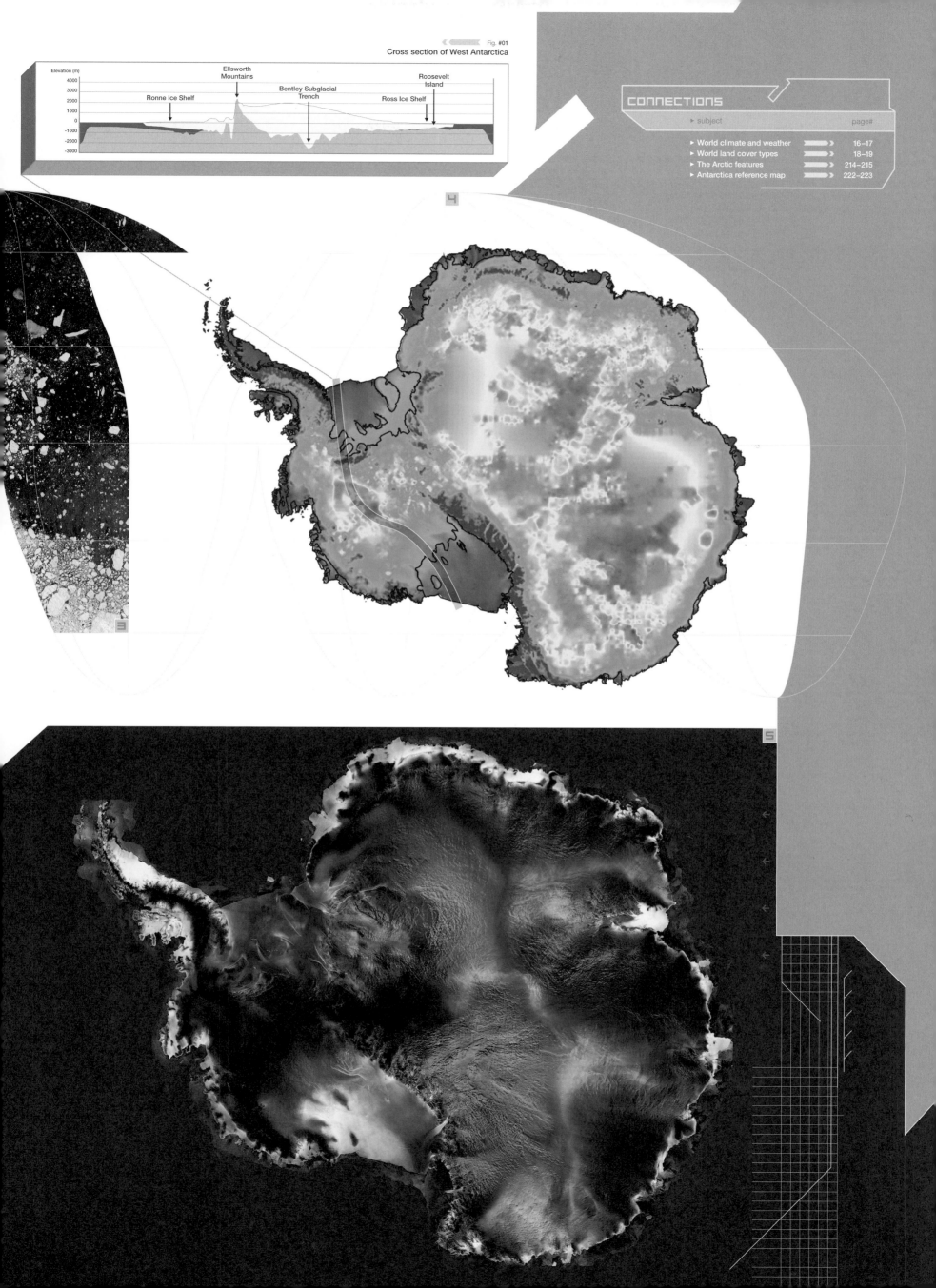

Fig. #01

Cross section of West Antarctica

Elevation (m)

4000
3000
2000
1000
0
-1000
-2000
-3000

Ellsworth
Mountains

Roosevelt
Island

Ronne Ice Shelf

Bentley Subglacial
Trench

Ross Ice Shelf

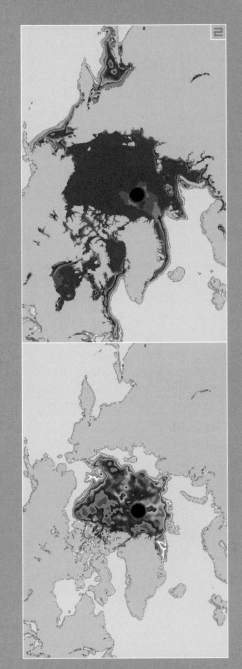

1 Tundra Landscape

Lakes and meandering rivers in a tundra landscape are shown in this photograph, taken in the short Arctic summer. Tundra is a cold-climate landscape type characterized by very low winter temperatures and short, cool summers. It is found in the region between 60°N and the Arctic ice cap and also at high altitudes beyond the climatic limits of tree growth. Tundra vegetation consists of dwarf shrubs, low herbaceous plants, lichens and mosses, on a permanently frozen subsoil.

2 Sea Ice Concentration

Although much of the Arctic Ocean is constantly frozen, there are wide variations in the amount of sea ice throughout the year, as shown by these images from the Special Sensor Microwave Imager (SSM/I). The purple areas show almost completely frozen sea (over ninety six per cent concentration) which extends as far south as Hudson Bay, Canada in February (top). By the end of the summer most of this ice has melted, as seen in the September image (bottom). The remaining sea ice at this time is thinner and more fragmented, even near the North Pole. Pink and brown areas represent concentrations of between sixty and eighty per cent.

Satellite/Sensor : SSM/I

Fig. #01 >>>>>
Peoples of the Arctic

The Arctic regions of Alaska, northern Canada, Greenland, and northern Scandinavia and Russian Federation contain the homelands of a diverse range of indigenous peoples. The main groups are shown on this map. These native peoples have subsisted for thousands of years on the resources of land and sea, as hunters, fishermen and reindeer herders. More recently, conflicts have arisen with governments eager to exploit the rich natural resources of the Arctic. There have also been moves towards greater autonomy for such groups. Most notably, in 1992 the Tungavik Federation of Nunavut and the government of Canada signed an agreement which addressed Inuit land claims and harvesting rights and established the new territory of Nunavut.

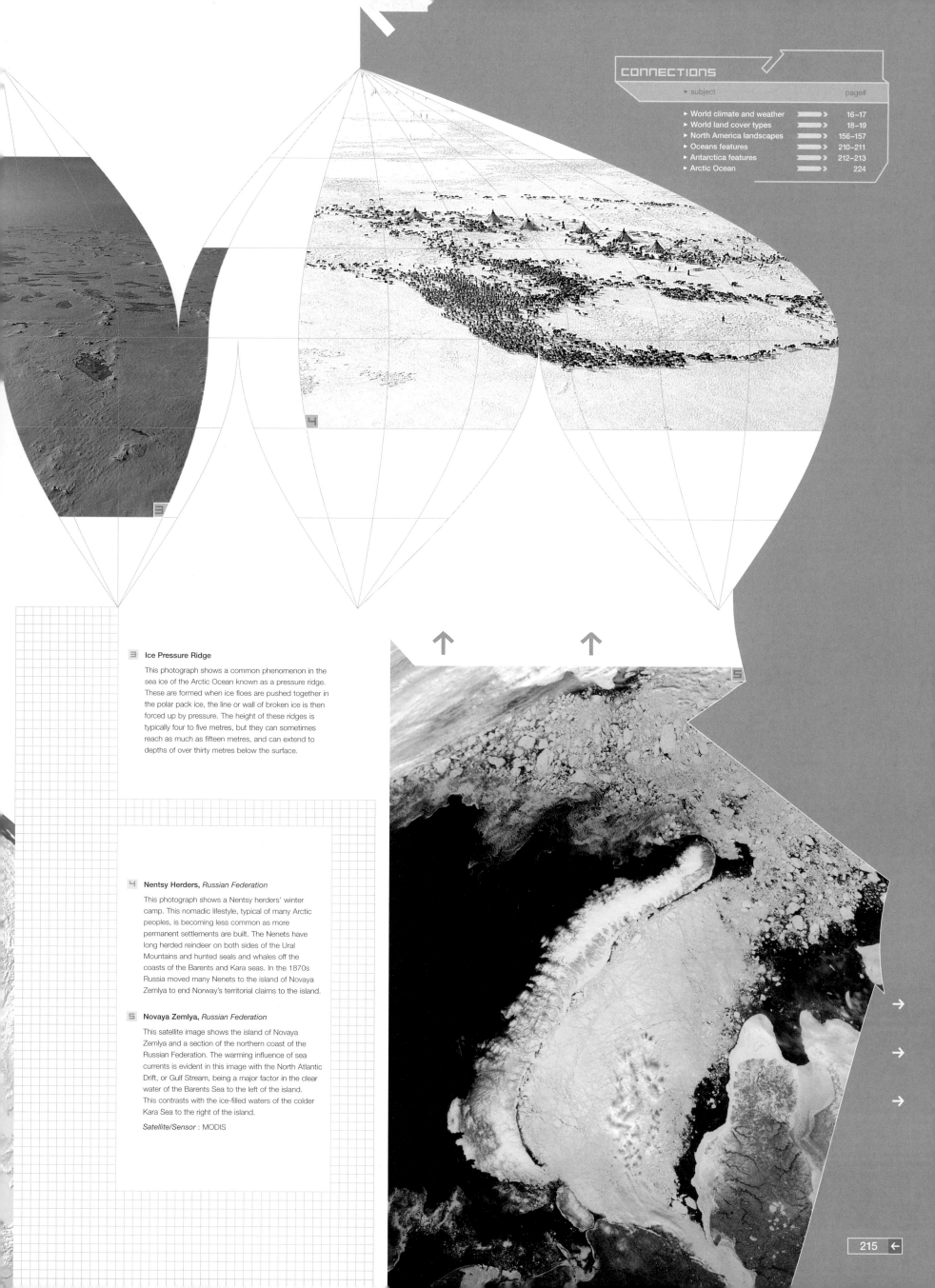

CONNECTIONS

▸ subject   page#

▸ World climate and weather   ▸   16–17
▸ World land cover types   ▸   18–19
▸ North America landscapes   ▸   156–157
▸ Oceans features   ▸   210–211
▸ Antarctica features   ▸   212–213
▸ Arctic Ocean   ▸   224

3 **Ice Pressure Ridge**

This photograph shows a common phenomenon in the
sea ice of the Arctic Ocean known as a pressure ridge.
These are formed when ice floes are pushed together in
the polar pack ice, the line or wall of broken ice is then
forced up by pressure. The height of these ridges is
typically four to five metres, but they can sometimes
reach as much as fifteen metres, and can extend to
depths of over thirty metres below the surface.

4 **Nentsy Herders,** *Russian Federation*

This photograph shows a Nentsy herders' winter
camp. This nomadic lifestyle, typical of many Arctic
peoples, is becoming less common as more
permanent settlements are built. The Nenets have
long herded reindeer on both sides of the Ural
Mountains and hunted seals and whales off the
coasts of the Barents and Kara seas. In the 1870s
Russia moved many Nenets to the island of Novaya
Zemlya to end Norway's territorial claims to the island.

5 **Novaya Zemlya,** *Russian Federation*

This satellite image shows the island of Novaya
Zemlya and a section of the northern coast of the
Russian Federation. The warming influence of sea
currents is evident in this image with the North Atlantic
Drift, or Gulf Stream, being a major factor in the clear
water of the Barents Sea to the left of the island.
This contrasts with the ice-filled waters of the colder
Kara Sea to the right of the island.

Satellite/Sensor : MODIS

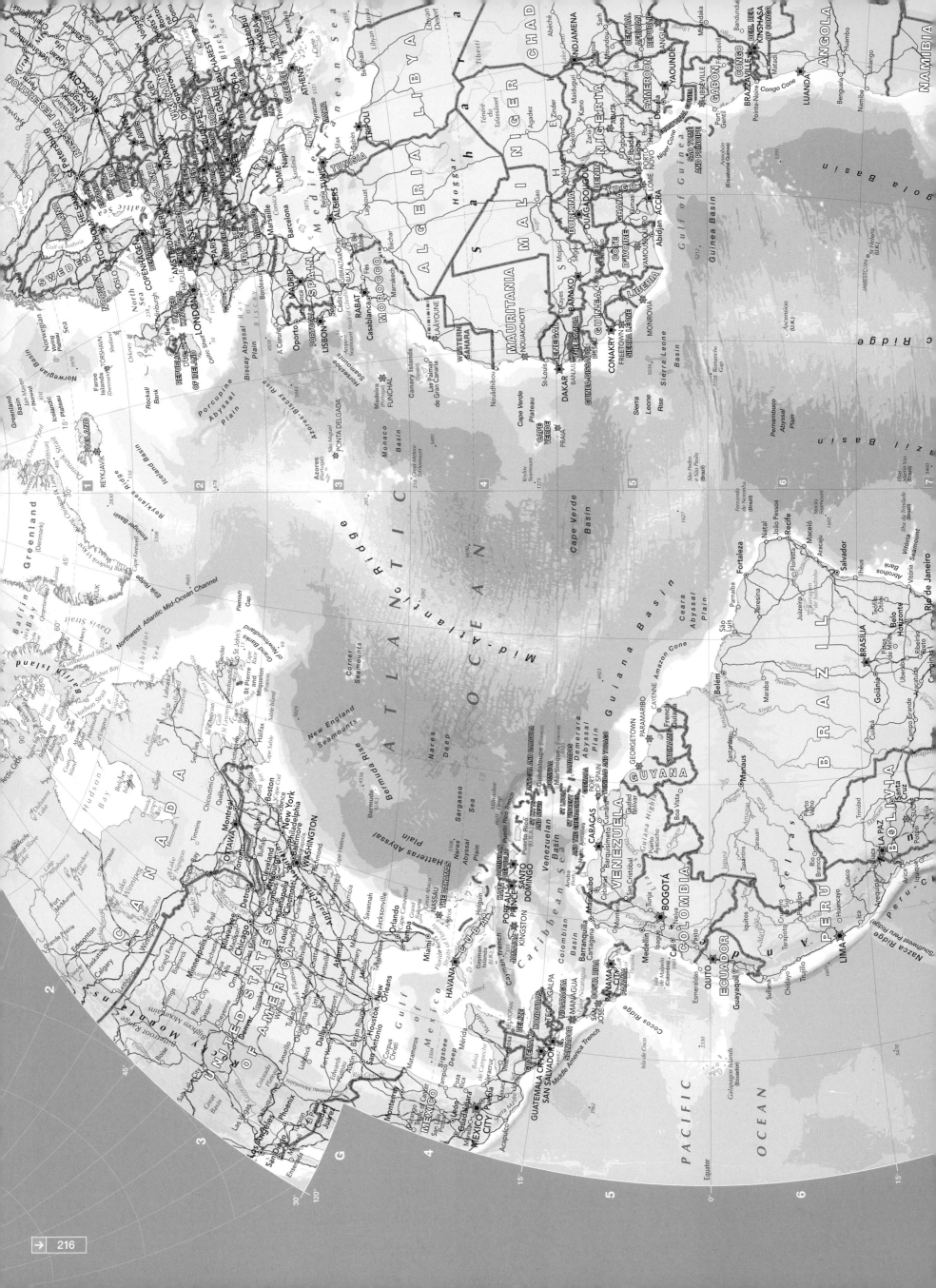

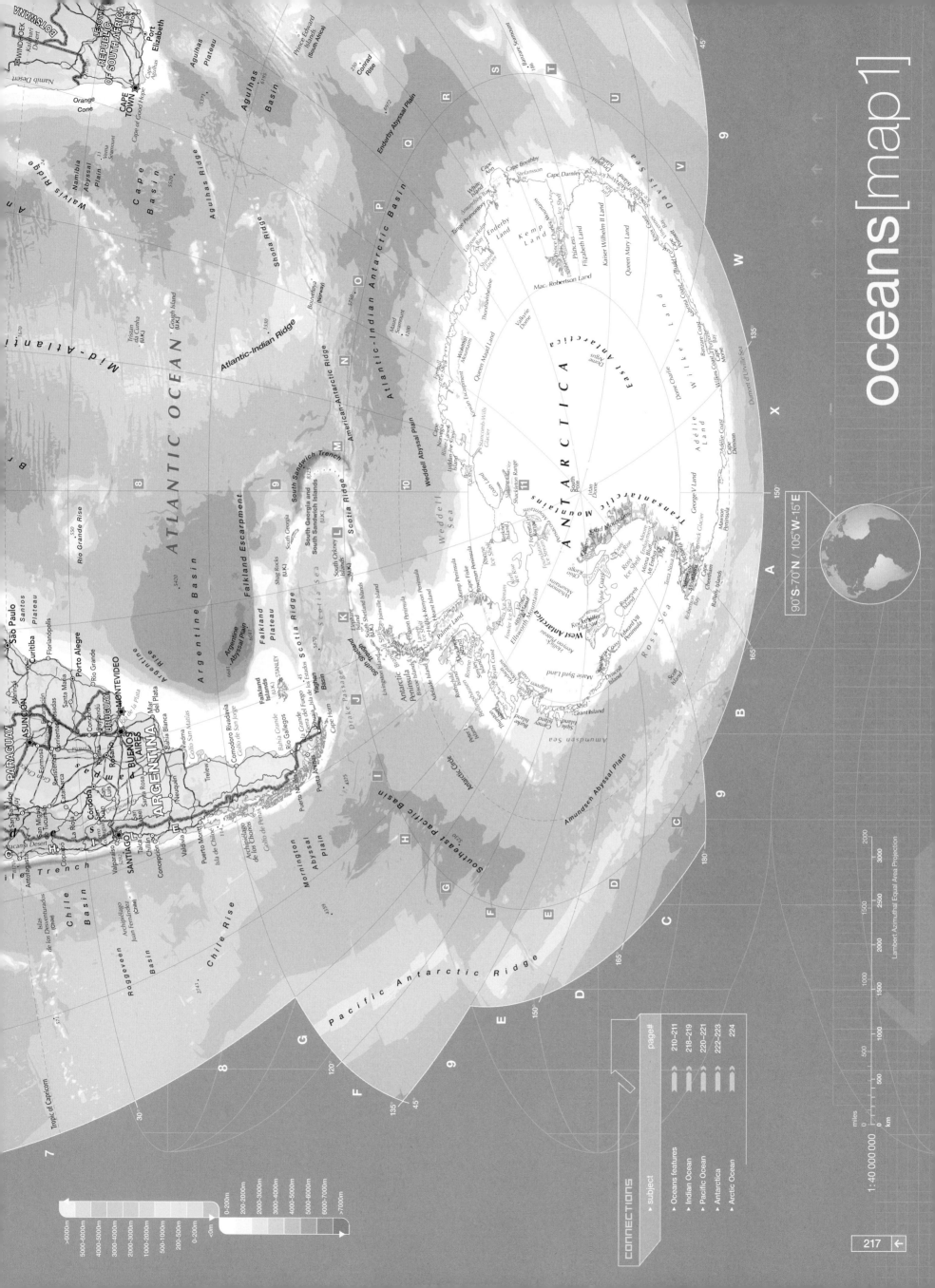

ATLANTIC OCEAN

ANTARCTICA

East Antarctica

West Antarctica

Weddell Sea

Ross Sea

Amundsen Sea

Mid-Atlantic Ridge

Atlantic-Indian Ridge

American-Antarctic Ridge

Atlantic-Indian Antarctic Basin

Pacific Antarctic Ridge

Southeast Pacific Basin

Mornington Abyssal Plain

Amundsen Abyssal Plain

Weddell Abyssal Plain

Endarby Abyssal Plain

Scotia Ridge

Scotia Sea

Drake Passage

Chile Rise

Chile Basin

Roggeveen Basin

Argentine Basin

Argentine Abyssal Plain

Falkland Plateau

Falkland Escarpment

Scotia Ridge

South Sandwich Trench

South Georgia and South Sandwich Islands (U.K.)

Falkland Islands (U.K.)

STANLEY

Cape Basin

Agulhas Basin

Agulhas Plateau

Agulhas Ridge

Shona Ridge

Conrad Rise

Prince Edward Islands (South Africa)

Walvis Ridge

Namibia Abyssal Plain

Rio Grande Rise

BUENOS AIRES

MONTEVIDEO

URUGUAY

ARGENTINA

PARAGUAY

ASUNCIÓN

São Paulo

Curitiba

Porto Alegre

Santos

SANTIAGO

Chile Trench

CAPE TOWN

REPUBLIC OF SOUTH AFRICA

Cape of Good Hope

Port Elizabeth

Namib Desert

Kalahari Desert

Tierra del Fuego

Cape Horn

Antarctic Peninsula

Transantarctic Mountains

South Pole

Tropic of Capricorn

90°S-70°N / 105°W-15°E

1:40 000 000

Lambert Azimuthal Equal Area Projection

miles

km

0-200m
200-2000m
2000-3000m
3000-4000m
4000-5000m
5000-6000m
6000-7000m
>7000m

<0m
0-200m
200-500m
500-1000m
1000-2000m
2000-3000m
3000-4000m
4000-5000m
5000-6000m
>6000m

CONNECTIONS

Subject   page#

Oceans features   210-211
Indian Ocean   218-219
Pacific Ocean   220-221
Antarctica   222-223
Arctic Ocean   224

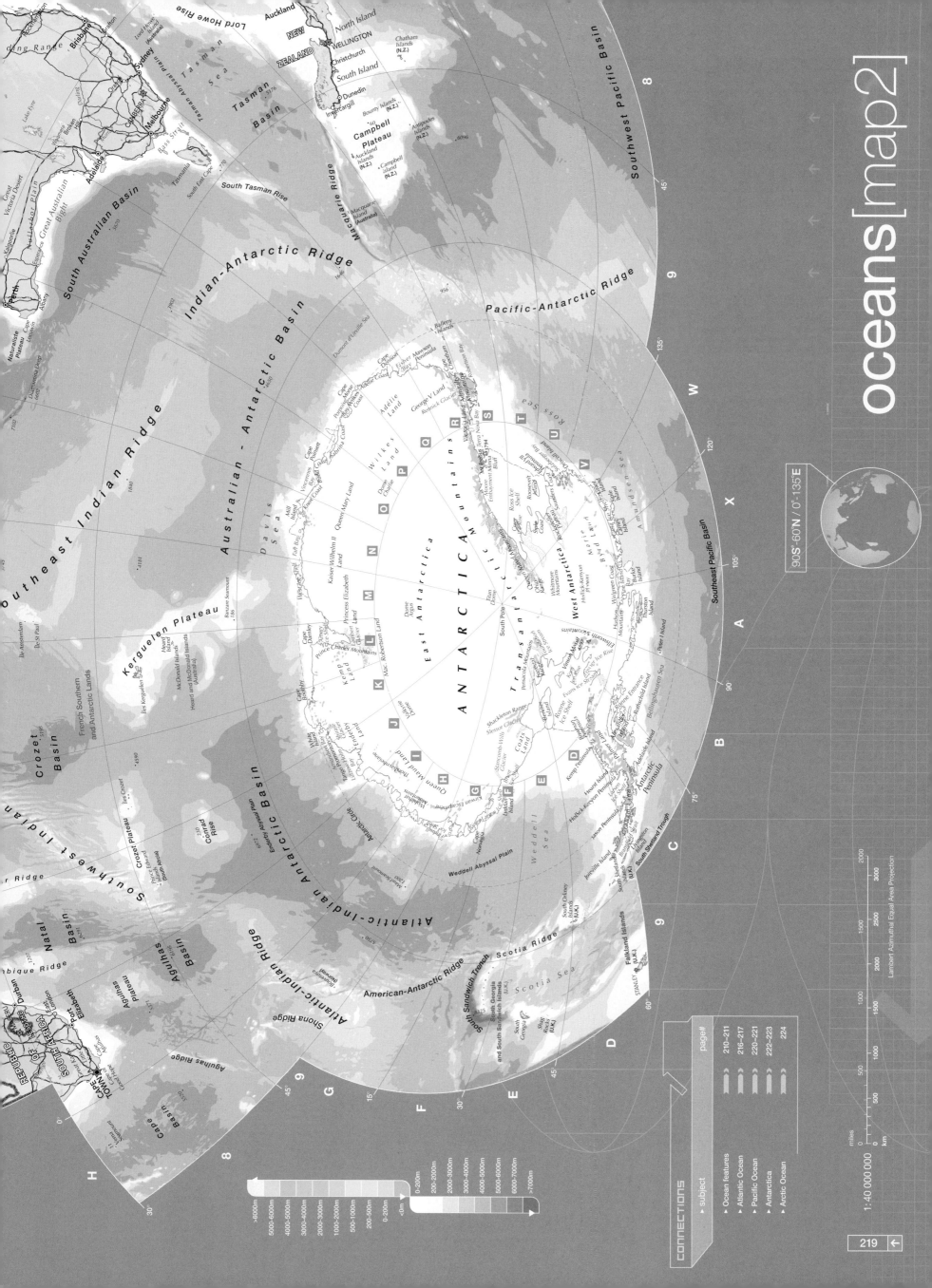

90°S·60°N / 0°·135°E

Lambert Azimuthal Equal Area Projection

1:40 000 000

miles
0   500   1000   1500   2000
km
0 500 1000   2000   2500   3000

90°S-60°N / 90°E-60°W

Depth scale:

>6000m
5000-6000m
4000-5000m
3000-4000m
2000-3000m
1000-2000m
500-1000m
200-500m
0-200m
<0m

0-200m
200-2000m
2000-3000m
3000-4000m
4000-5000m
5000-6000m
6000-7000m
>7000m

1:45 000 000

miles
0 500 1000 1500 2000

km
0 500 1000 1500 2000 2500 3000

Lambert Azimuthal Equal Area Projection

Selected map labels:

MONGOLIA · ULAN BATOR · Gobi · BEIJING · CHINA · Shenyang · Harbin · Changchun · NORTH KOREA · PYONGYANG · SOUTH KOREA · SEOUL · JAPAN · TOKYO · Osaka · Nagoya · Kyoto · Hiroshima · Sendai · Sapporo · Sea of Okhotsk · Kamchatka Peninsula · Kuril Trench · Kuril Islands · Sakhalin · Vladivostok · Aleutian

NEPAL · Kathmandu · Dhaka · Kolkata · Hyderabad · Visakhapatnam · Vijayawada · Bay of Bengal · MYANMAR · RANGOON · THAILAND · BANGKOK · LAOS · VIENTIANE · CAMBODIA · PHNOM PENH · VIETNAM · HANOI · Hô Chi Minh City · Đa Nang · Huê

PHILIPPINES · MANILA · Quezon City · Cebu · Davao · Mindanao · South China Sea · Hong Kong · Guangzhou · Haikou · Hainan · T'AIPEI · TAIWAN · Kaohsiung

MALAYSIA · KUALA LUMPUR · SINGAPORE · Medan · Sumatra · BRUNEI · BANDAR SERI BEGAWAN · Kuching · Borneo · Pontianak · INDONESIA · JAKARTA · Bandung · Surabaya · Semarang · Java · Bali Sea · Celebes · Makassar Strait · Banjarmasin · Palembang

PALAU · KOROR · FEDERATED STATES OF MICRONESIA · PALIKIR · MICRONESIA · MARSHALL ISLANDS · NAURU · MELANESIA · PAPUA NEW GUINEA · New Guinea · PORT MORESBY · SOLOMON ISLANDS · HONIARA · VANUATU · PORT VILA · FIJI · SUVA · TUVALU · TONGA · SAMOA · New Caledonia (France) · NOUMÉA · Wallis and Futuna Islands (France)

AUSTRALIA · CANBERRA · Sydney · Melbourne · Adelaide · Perth · Brisbane · Darwin · Townsville · Cairns · Alice Springs · Great Sandy Desert · Great Victoria Desert · Gulf of Carpentaria · Great Barrier Reef · Tasmania · Coral Sea · Tasman Sea

NEW ZEALAND · WELLINGTON · Auckland · Christchurch · Dunedin · North Island · South Island · Invercargill · Chatham Rise

INDIAN OCEAN · Northwest Pacific Basin · Mid-Pacific Mountains · Central Pacific Basin · West Mariana Basin · East Mariana Basin · Mariana Trench · Challenger Deep 10920 · Philippine Basin · Philippine Trench · Celebes Basin · West Australian Basin · North Australian Basin · South Australian Basin · Perth Basin · Java Trench (Sunda Trench) · Emperor Seamount Chain · Mapmakers Seamounts · Magellan Seamounts · Melanesian Basin · Coral Sea Basin · South Fiji Basin · Tasman Basin · Lord Howe Rise · New Caledonia Ridge · Norfolk Island Ridge · Kermadec Trench · Horizon Deep 10800 · Southeast Indian Ridge · Indian-Antarctic Ridge · Australian-Antarctic Basin · Ninetyeast Ridge

antarctica[map1]

50°-90°**S** / 0°-180°-0°

ARGENTINE CLAIM

BRITISH ANTARCTIC TERRITORY

Scale / Elevation legend:

- >6000m
- 5000-6000m
- 4000-5000m
- 3000-4000m
- 2000-3000m
- 1000-2000m
- 500-1000m
- 200-500m
- 0-200m
- <0m

- 0-200m
- 200-2000m
- 2000-3000m
- 3000-4000m
- 4000-5000m
- 5000-6000m
- 6000-7000m
- >7000m

Labels

Scotia Ridge
Scotia Sea
Scotia Ridge
Weddell Abyssal
Weddell Sea

Orcadas (Arg.)
Laurie Island
South Orkney Islands (U.K.)
Coronation Island

West Usborne
Mount Adam
Mount
STANLEY
East Falkland
Falkland Islands (U.K.)
West Falkland
Beauchene Island
Bougainville

Lyddan Island

Brunt Ice Shelf
Halley (U.K.)

ARGENTINA
Río Gallegos
Punta Dungeness
Bahía de San Sebastián
Río Grande
Estrecho de Le Maire
Isla de los Estados
Ushuaia
Isla Grande de Tierra del Fuego
Punta Arenas
CHILE
Cape Horn
Islas Wollaston
Isla Hermite
Isla Navarino
Isla Londonderry
Isla Desolación
Archipiélago de la Reina Adelaida
Isla Contreras

Yaghan Basin
Drake Passage
South Shetland Trough

CHILEAN CLAIM
Elephant Island
King George Island
South Shetland Islands
Bransfield Strait
Esperanza (Argentina)
Marambio (Argentina)
Robertson Island
Livingston Island
Smith Island
Brabant Island
Anvers Island
Palmer (U.S.A.)
Vernadsky (Ukraine)
Cape Disappointment
Cape Alexander
Antarctic Peninsula

San Martín (Argentina)
Rothera (U.K.)
Adelaide Island
Marguerite Bay
Alexander Island
GEORGE VI
Ronne Entrance
Charcot Island
Latady Island

Palmer Land
Cape Brooks
Cape Fiske
English Coast
Orville Coast

Belgrano II (Argentina)
Lassiter Coast
Berkner Island
Filchner Ice Shelf
Ronne Ice Shelf
Henry Ice Rise
Korff Ice Rise
Foundation Ice Stream

Evans Ice Stream
Fowler Peninsula
Carlson Inlet
Zumberge Coast
Fletcher Peninsula
Bryan Coast
Ellsworth Mountains
Sentinel Range
Mount Vinson
Heritage Range

ARGENTINE CLAIM
BRITISH ANTARCTIC TERRITORY
CHILEAN CLAIM

Bellingshausen Sea

Peter I Island

Thurston Island
Ellsworth Land

West Antarctica
Hollick-Kenyon Plateau
Mount Woollard 2637

Whitmore Mountains
Mount Seelig
Mount Radlinski 2749

Rockefeller Plateau

Amundsen Sea
Amundsen Ridges
Amundsen Abyssal Plain

Walgreen Coast
Bear Peninsula
Martin Peninsula
Getz Ice Shelf
Thwaites Glacier Tongue
Pine Island Glacier
Pine Island Bay

Marie Byrd Land
Kohler Range
Ford Range
Executive Committee Range
Rupert Coast
Shepard Island
Newman Island
Saunders Coast

SOUTHERN OCEAN

Southeast Pacific Basin

Pacific-Antarctic Ridge

ROSS

Antarctic Circle

Grid references

U   T   S   R   Q   P   O   N
V   W

1   2   3

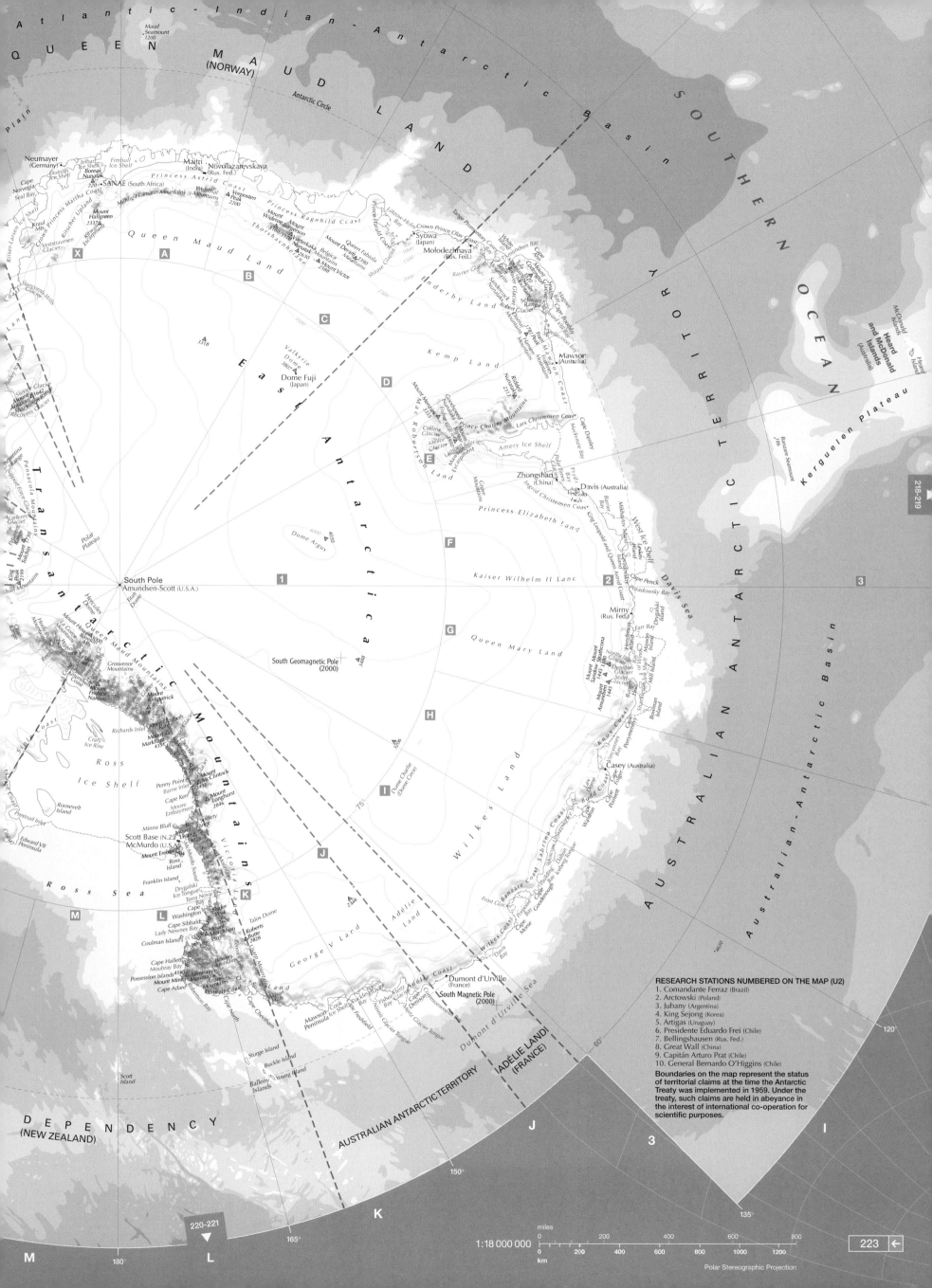

RESEARCH STATIONS NUMBERED ON THE MAP (U2)

1. Comandante Ferraz (Brazil)
2. Arctowski (Poland)
3. Jubany (Argentina)
4. King Sejong (Korea)
5. Artigas (Uruguay)
6. Presidente Eduardo Frei (Chile)
7. Bellingshausen (Rus. Fed.)
8. Great Wall (China)
9. Capitán Arturo Prat (Chile)
10. General Bernardo O'Higgins (Chile)

Boundaries on the map represent the status of territorial claims at the time the Antarctic Treaty was implemented in 1959. Under the treaty, such claims are held in abeyance in the interest of international co-operation for scientific purposes.

1:18 000 000

Polar Stereographic Projection

INTRODUCTION TO THE INDEX

The index includes all names shown on the reference maps in the atlas. Each entry includes the country or geographical area in which the feature is located, a page number and an alphanumeric reference. Additional entry details and aspects of the index are explained below.

Referencing

Names are referenced by page number and by grid reference. The grid reference relates to the alphanumeric values which appear in the margin of each map. These reflect the graticule on the map – the letter relates to longitude divisions, the number to latitude divisions.

Names are generally referenced to the largest scale map page on which they appear. For large geographical features, including countries, the reference is to the largest scale map on which the feature appears in its entirety, or on which the majority of it appears.

Rivers are referenced to their lowest downstream point – either their mouth or their confluence with another river. The river name will generally be positioned as close to this point as possible.

Alternative names

Alternative names appear as cross-references and refer the user to the index entry for the form of the name used on the map. Details of alternative names and their types also appear within the main entry. The different types of name form included are: alternative forms or spellings currently in common use; English conventional name forms normally used in English-language contexts; historical and former names; and long and short name forms.

For rivers with multiple names – for example those which flow through several countries – all alternative name forms are included within the main index entries, with details of the countries in which each form applies.

Administrative qualifiers

Administrative divisions are included in an entry to differentiate duplicate names – entries of exactly the same name and feature type within the one country – where these division names are shown on the maps. In such cases, duplicate names are alphabetized in the order of the administrative division names.

Additional qualifiers are included for names within selected geographical areas, to indicate more clearly their location.

Descriptors

Entries, other than those for towns and cities, include a descriptor indicating the type of geographical feature. Descriptors are not included where the type of feature is implicit in the name itself, unless there is a town or city of exactly the same name.

Insets

Where relevant, the index clearly indicates [inset] if a feature appears on an inset map.

Name forms and alphabetical order

Name forms are as they appear on the maps, with additional alternative forms included as cross-references. Names appear in full in the index, although they may appear in abbreviated form on the maps.

The Icelandic characters Þ and þ are transliterated and alphabetized as 'Th' and 'th'. The German character ß is alphabetized as 'ss'. Names beginning with Mac or Mc are alphabetized exactly as they appear. The terms Saint, Sainte, etc, are abbreviated to St, Ste, etc, but alphabetized as if in the full form.

Name form policies are explained in the Introduction to the Atlas (pp 4–5).

Numerical entries

Entries beginning with numerals appear at the beginning of the index, in numerical order. Elsewhere, numerals are alphabetized before 'a'.

Permuted terms

Names beginning with generic, geographical terms are permuted – the descriptive term is placed after, and the index alphabetized by, the main part of the name. For example, Mount Everest is indexed as Everest, Mount; Lake Superior as Superior, Lake. This policy is applied to all languages. Permuting has not been applied to names of towns, cities or administrative divisions beginning with such geographical terms. These remain in their full form, for example, Lake Isabella, USA.

Gazetteer entries and connections

Selected entries have been extended to include gazetteer-style information. Important geographical facts which relate specifically to the entry are included within the entry in coloured type.

Entries for features which also appear on, or which have a topical link to, the thematic pages of the atlas include a connection to those pages indicated by the symbol ➡➤.

Tables

Several tables, ranking geographical features by size, are included within the main index listing. Where possible these have been placed directly below the index entry for the feature ranked 1 in the table.

ABBREVIATIONS

admin. dist.	administrative district	imp. l.	impermanent lake	pref.	prefecture
admin. div.	administrative division	IN	Indiana	prov.	province
admin. reg.	administrative region	Indon.	Indonesia	pt	point
Afgh.	Afghanistan	Kazakh.	Kazakhstan	Qld	Queensland
AK	Alaska	KS	Kansas	Que.	Québec
AL	Alabama	KY	Kentucky	r.	river
Alg.	Algeria	Kyrg.	Kyrgyzstan	r. mouth	river mouth
AR	Arkansas	l.	lake	r. source	river source
Arg.	Argentina	LA	Louisiana	reg.	region
aut. comm.	autonomous community	lag.	lagoon	res.	reserve
aut. div.	autonomous division	Lith.	Lithuania	resr	reservoir
aut. reg.	autonomous region	Lux.	Luxembourg	RI	Rhode Island
aut. rep.	autonomous republic	MA	Massachusetts	Rus. Fed.	Russian Federation
AZ	Arizona	Madag.	Madagascar	S.	South
Azer.	Azerbaijan	Man.	Manitoba	S.A.	South Australia
b.	bay	MD	Maryland	salt l.	salt lake
B.C.	British Columbia	ME	Maine	Sask.	Saskatchewan
Bangl.	Bangladesh	Mex.	Mexico	SC	South Carolina
Bol.	Bolivia	MI	Michigan	SD	South Dakota
Bos.-Herz.	Bosnia-Herzegovina	MN	Minnesota	sea chan.	sea channel
Bulg.	Bulgaria	MO	Missouri	Sing.	Singapore
c.	cape	Moz.	Mozambique	Switz.	Switzerland
CA	California	MS	Mississippi	Tajik.	Tajikistan
Cent. Afr. Rep.	Central African Republic	MT	Montana	Tanz.	Tanzania
CO	Colorado	mt.	mountain	Tas.	Tasmania
Col.	Colombia	mts	mountains	ter.	territory
CT	Connecticut	N.	North	Thai.	Thailand
Czech Rep.	Czech Republic	N.B.	New Brunswick	TN	Tennessee
DC	District of Columbia	N.S.	Nova Scotia	Trin. and Tob.	Trinidad and Tobago
DE	Delaware	N.S.W.	New South Wales	Turkm.	Turkmenistan
Dem. Rep. Congo	Democratic Republic of Congo	N.T.	Northern Territory	TX	Texas
depr.	depression	N.W.T.	Northwest Territories	U.A.E.	United Arab Emirates
des.	desert	N.Z.	New Zealand	U.K.	United Kingdom
Dom. Rep.	Dominican Republic	nat. park	national park	U.S.A.	United States of America
E.	East, Eastern	nature res.	nature reserve	Ukr.	Ukraine
Equat. Guinea	Equatorial Guinea	NC	North Carolina	union terr.	union territory
esc.	escarpment	ND	North Dakota	UT	Utah
est.	estuary	NE	Nebraska	Uzbek.	Uzbekistan
Eth.	Ethiopia	Neth.	Netherlands	VA	Virginia
Fin.	Finland	NH	New Hampshire	Venez.	Venezuela
FL	Florida	NJ	New Jersey	Vic.	Victoria
for.	forest	NM	New Mexico	vol.	volcano
Fr. Guiana	French Guiana	NV	Nevada	vol. crater	volcanic crater
g.	gulf	NY	New York	VT	Vermont
GA	Georgia	OH	Ohio	W.	West, Western
Guat.	Guatemala	OK	Oklahoma	W.A.	Western Australia
H.K.	Hong Kong	OR	Oregon	WA	Washington
HI	Hawaii	P.E.I.	Prince Edward Island	WI	Wisconsin
Hond.	Honduras	P.N.G.	Papua New Guinea	WV	West Virginia
i.	island	PA	Pennsylvania	WY	Wyoming
IA	Iowa	pen.	peninsula	Y.T.	Yukon Territory
ID	Idaho	plat.	plateau	Yugo.	Yugoslavia
IL	Illinois	Port.	Portugal		

↓ 1

1st Cataract *rapids* Egypt **121** G3
2nd Cataract *rapids* Sudan **121** F4
3rd Cataract *rapids* Sudan **121** G5
4th Cataract *rapids* Sudan **121** G5
5th Cataract *rapids* Sudan **121** G5
9 de Julio Arg. **204** E4
long form Nueve de Julio
15th of May City Egypt *see*
Medinet 15 Mayo
25 de Mayo Buenos Aires Arg. **204** E4
long form Veinticinco de Mayo
25 de Mayo La Pampa Arg. **204** D5
long form Veinticinco de Mayo
25 de Mayo Mendoza Arg. **204** C4
long form Veinticinco de Mayo
26 Bakı Komissarı Azer. **107** Q3
also known as imeni 26 Bakinskikh
Komissarov; *formerly known as* Neftechala;
long form İyirmi Altı Bakı Komissarı
42nd Hill S. Africa **133** N5
70 Mile House Canada **166** F5
100 Mile House Canada **166** F5
150 Mile House Canada **166** F4

↓ A

Aabenraa Denmark *see* Åbenrå
Aachen Germany **48** D5
formerly known as Aix-la-Chapelle;
historically known as Aquae Grani or
Aquisgranum
Aadan Yabaal Somalia **128** E4
Aalborg Denmark *see* Ålborg
Aalen Germany **48** H7
Aalesund Norway *see* Ålesund
Aaley Lebanon *see* 'Aley
Aalst Belgium **51** K2
also spelt Alost
Aanaar Fin. *see* Inari
Äänekoski Fin. **44** N3
Aansluit S. Africa **132** G3
Aarau Switz. **51** O5
Aarberg Switz. **51** N5
Aareavaara Sweden **44** M2
Aarhus Denmark *see* Århus
Aarlen Belgium *see* Arlon
Aarschot Belgium **51** K2
Aasiaat Greenland **165** N3
also known as Egedesminde
Aath Belgium *see* Ath
Aavasaksa Fin. **44** M2
Aba China **86** B1
also known as Ngawa
Aba Dem. Rep. Congo **126** F4
Aba Nigeria **125** G5
Abā ad Dūd Saudi Arabia **104** D2
Abā al Afan *oasis* Saudi Arabia **105** E4
Abā al Qūr, Sha'īb *watercourse*
Saudi Arabia **109** N6
Abā ar Ruwāth, Wādi *watercourse*
Saudi Arabia **109** N7
Abacaxis *r.* Brazil **199** G6
Ābādān Iran **100** B4
English form Abadan
Abadan Iran *see* Ābādān
Abadan Iran **100** C4
Ābādān, Jazīreh *i.* Iran/Iraq **105** E1
Ābādeh Iran **100** C4
Ābādeh Ţashk Iran **100** C4
Abadia dos Dourados Brazil **206** F5
Abadiânia Brazil **206** E3
Abadla Alg. **123** F2
Abádszalók Hungary **49** R8
Abaeté Brazil **207** H6
Abaeté *r.* Brazil **207** H5
Abaetetuba Brazil **202** B2
Abagnar Qi China *see* Xilinhot
Abag Qi China *see* Xin Hot
Abai Para. **201** G6
Abaiang *atoll* Kiribati **145** G1
also known as Apaiang; *formerly known as* Apia
A Baiuca Spain **54** C1
Abaji Nigeria **125** G4
Abajo Peak U.S.A. **183** O4
Abakaliki Nigeria **125** H5
Abakan Rus. Fed. **80** E2
formerly known as Ust'-Abakanskoye
Abala Congo **126** B5
Abala Niger **125** F3
Abalak Niger **125** G3
Abalyanka *r.* Belarus **43** L7
Abana Turkey **106** C2
Abancay Peru **200** B3
Abanga *r.* Gabon **126** A5
Abapó Bol. **201** E4
Abariringa *i.* Kiribati *see* Kanton
Abarqū Iran **100** C4
A Barrela Spain **54** D2
Abarshahr Iran *see* Neyshābūr
Ābār 'Uwayrid Ţaḩtānī *well* Syria
109 K3
Abashiri Japan **90** I2
Abashiri-wan *b.* Japan **90** I2
Abasolo Mex. **185** F3
Abasula *waterhole* Kenya **128** C5
Abau P.N.G. **145** D3
Abava *r.* Latvia **42** C4
Abay Kazakh. **103** H3
also known as Churubay Nura; *formerly
known as* Abay Bazar
Abay Kazakh. *see* Karaul
Abaya, Lake Eth. **128** C3
also known as Ābaya Häyk'; *formerly known
as* Margherita, Lake
Ābaya Häyk' *l.* Eth. *see* Abaya, Lake
Abay Bazar Kazakh. *see* Abay
Abay Wenz *r.* Eth./Sudan **128** C2 *see*
Blue Nile
Abaza Rus. Fed. **80** E2
Abba Cent. Afr. Rep. **126** B3
Abbadia San Salvatore Italy **56** D6
Abbāsābād Iran **100** D3
Abbasanta *Sardegna* Italy **57** A8
Abbatis Villa France *see* Abbeville
Abbaye, Point U.S.A. **172** F3
Abbeville France **51** H2
historically known as Abbatis Villa
Abbeville GA U.S.A. **175** D6
Abbeville LA U.S.A. **179** D6
Abbeville SC U.S.A. **175** D5
Abbey Canada **167** I5
Abbeyfeale Rep. of Ireland **47** C11
Abbiategrasso Italy **56** A3
Abborrträsk Sweden **44** L2
Abbot, Mount Australia **149** E4
Abbot Bay Australia **149** E3
Abbotsford Canada **166** F5
Abbotsford U.S.A. **172** C6
Abbott NM U.S.A. **181** F5
Abbott VA U.S.A. **176** E8
Abbott WV U.S.A. **176** E7
Abbottabad Pak. **101** H3
Abchuha Belarus **43** K7
Abd, Oued el *watercourse* Alg. **55** L9
'Abd al 'Aziz, Jabal *hill* Syria **109** L1
'Abd al 'Aziz, Jabal *plat.* Syria **109** K1
'Abd al Kūrī *i.* Yemen **105** F5
'Abd Allah, Khawr *sea chan.* Iraq/Kuwait
107 G5
Abd al Ma'asīr *well* Saudi Arabia **104**
109 J7
Ābdānān Iran **100** A3
Abdollāhābād Iran **100** D2
Abdulino Rus. Fed. **41** J5

Abéché Chad **120** D6
also known as Abeshr
Abejukolo Nigeria **125** G5
Abelbod well Mali **125** E2
Abellinum Italy *see* Avellino
Abel Tasman National Park N.Z. **152** H8
Abemama *atoll* Kiribati **145** G1
also spelt Apamama
Abenab Namibia **130** C3
Abengourou Côte d'Ivoire **124** E5
Abenójar Spain **54** G6
Åbenrå Denmark **45** J5
also spelt Aabenraa
Abensberg Germany **48** I7
Abeokuta Nigeria **125** F5
Abera Eth. **128** B3
Abaeron U.K. **47** H11
Aberchirder U.K. **46** J6
Abercrombie *r.* Australia **147** F3
Abercorn Zambia *see* Mbala
Abercrombie *r.* Australia **147** F3
Aberdare U.K. **47** I12
Aberdare National Park Kenya **128** C5
Aberdaron U.K. **47** H11
Aberdaugleddau U.K. *see* Milford Haven
Aberdeen Australia **147** F3
Aberdeen Hong Kong China **87** [inset]
also known as Heung Kong Tsai
Aberdeen S. Africa **132** I9
Aberdeen U.K. **46** J6
historically known as Devana
Aberdeen MD U.S.A. **177** I6
Aberdeen MS U.S.A. **175** B5
Aberdeen OH U.S.A. **176** B7
Aberdeen SD U.S.A. **178** C2
Aberdeen WA U.S.A. **180** B3
Aberdeen Island Hong Kong China **87** [inset]
also known as Ap Lei Chau
Aberdeen Lake Canada **167** L1
Aberdeen Road S. Africa **133** I9
Aberfeldy U.K. **46** I7
Aberfoyle U.K. **46** I7
Abergavenny U.K. **47** I12
also known as Y Fenni; *historically known as*
Gobannium
Åbergelë Eth. **104** B5
Abergwaun U.K. *see* Fishguard
Aberhonddu U.K. *see* Brecon
Abermaw U.K. *see* Barmouth
Abernathy U.S.A. **179** B5
Abertawe U.K. *see* Swansea
Aberteifi U.K. *see* Cardigan
Aberystwyth U.K. **47** H11
Abeshr Chad *see* Abéché
Abez' Rus. Fed. **40** L2
Abhā Saudi Arabia **104** C4
Abhā, Jabal *hill* Saudi Arabia **104** C2
Abhanpur India **97** D5
Abhar Iran **100** B3
Abhar Rūd *r.* Iran **100** B3
Abia *state* Nigeria **125** G5
Abiad, Bahr el *r.* Sudan/Uganda **128** B2 *see*
White Nile
Ābiata Häyk' *l.* Eth. **128** C3
Abi-i Bazuft *r.* Iran **100** B4
Abibe, Serranía de *mts* Col. **198** C3

▶ **Abidjan** Côte d'Ivoire **124** D5
Former capital of Côte d'Ivoire.

Abiekwasputs *salt pan* S. Africa **132** E4
Ab-i-Istada *l.* Afgh. **101** G3
Abijatta-Shalla National Park Eth. **128** C3
also known as Rift Valley Lakes National
Park
Ab-i-Kavīr *salt flat* Iran **100** D3
Abiko Japan **91** G7
Abilene KS U.S.A. **178** C4
Abilene TX U.S.A. **179** C5
Abingdon U.K. **47** K12
Abingdon IL U.S.A. **172** C10
Abingdon VA U.S.A. **176** C9
Abington U.S.A. **177** O3
Abington Reef Australia **149** F3
Abinsk Rus. Fed. **41** F7
Abi-i-Panja *r.* Afgh./Tajik. *see* Pyandzh
Abi-i-Safed *r.* Afgh. **101** F2
Abiseo, Parque Nacional *nat. park* Peru
200 A1
Abisko *nationalpark* *nat. park* Sweden **44** L1
Abitibi *r.* Canada **168** D3
Abitibi, Lake Canada **168** D3
Āb Naft *r.* Iraq **107** F4
also known as Naft
Abnūb Egypt **121** F3
Åbo Fin. *see* Turku
Abohar India **96** B3
Aboisso Côte d'Ivoire **124** E5
Aboke Sudan **128** B2
Abomey Benin **125** F5
Abongabong, Gunung *mt.* Indon. **76** B1
Abong Mbang Cameroon **125** I6
Aboot Oman **105** F4
Aborlan Phil. **74** A4
Abou Déia Chad **126** C2
Abou Goulem Chad **120** D6
Aboumi Gabon **126** B5
Abqaiq Saudi Arabia **105** E2
also known as Buqayq
Abra, Lago del *l.* Arg. **204** E6
Abrad, Wādi *watercourse* Yemen **105** D5
Abraka Nigeria **125** F5
Abrams U.S.A. **172** E6
Abra Pampa Arg. **200** D5
Abre Campo Brazil **207** K7
Abreojos, Punta *pt* Mex. **184** B3
'Abrī Sudan **121** F4
Abrolhos, Arquipélago dos *is* Brazil **207** O5
Abrosovo Rus. Fed. **43** Q3
Abrud Romania **58** E2
Abruka *i.* Estonia **42** D3
Abruzzi Italy *see* Abruzzo
Abruzzi *admin. reg.* Italy **56** F6
also spelt Abruzzi
Abruzzo, Parco Nazionale d' *nat. park* Italy
56 F7
'Abs Yemen **104** C4
Absalom, Mount Antarctica **223** W1
Absaroka Range *mts* U.S.A. **180** E3
Absecon U.S.A. **177** K6
Abşeron Yarımadası *pen.* Azer. **107** G2
also known as Apsheronskiy Poluostrov
Absterna, Vozyera *l.* Belarus **42** I6
Abtar, Jabal *al hills* Syria **109** I3
Abū *ad* **Duhûr** Syria **109** I2
Abū al Husayn, Qā' *imp. l.* Jordan **109** J5
Abū'Alī *i.* Saudi Arabia **105** E2
Abu al Jirab *i.* U.A.E. **105** F3
Abū al Kūfah *waterhole* Iraq **109** N3
Abū 'Āmūd, Wādi *watercourse* Jordan
108 H7
Abū 'Arīsh Saudi Arabia **104** C4
Abu 'Aweigîla *well* Egypt **108** F7
Abū Ballūs *hill* Egypt **121** E3
Abū Da'ir *des.* Yemen **105** D4
Abu Deleiq Sudan **121** G6

▶ **Abu Dhabi** U.A.E. **105** F2
Capital of the United Arab Emirates. Also
spelt Abū Zabī.
asia [changes] ▶▶▶ 68–69

Abū Dībā' *waterhole* Saudi Arabia **104** B3
Abu Durba Egypt **108** E9
Abu el Matārīn Egypt **108** B7
Abufari Brazil **199** F6
Abū Farūkh, Wādi *watercourse* Iraq
109 O4
also spelt Ashqnsay
Abu Gabra Sudan **126** E2
Abu Gamel Sudan **104** B5
Abū Ghar, Wādi *watercourse* Iraq **109** M5
Abū Ghizlān *waterhole* Iraq **109** O3

Abū Ghurayb Iraq **109** P4
Abu Gubeiha Sudan **128** A2
Abu Hād, Wādi *watercourse* Egypt **108** E9
Abu Hafnah, Wādi *watercourse* Jordan
109 J5
Abu Haggag Egypt **121** E2
Abū Ḩallūfah, Jabal *hill* Jordan **109** H6
Abu Hamed Sudan **121** G5
Abu Hammād Egypt **108** C7
Abu Haraz Sudan **121** G5
Abu Hashim Sudan **121** G6
Abu Higar Sudan **121** G6
Abu Hummus Egypt **108** B6
Abu Huswa, Gebel *hill* Egypt **108** E9

▶ **Abuja** Nigeria **125** G4
Capital of Nigeria.

Abū Jaḩaf, Wādi *watercourse* Iraq **109** O5
Abū Kamāl Syria **109** L3
Abū Kammāsh Libya **120** A1
Abu Kebīr Egypt **108** C7
Abū Khamsāt, Sha'īb *watercourse* Iraq
109 O6
Abukuma-kōchi *plat.* Japan **90** G5
Abu La'ot *watercourse* Sudan **121** F6
Abū Latt Island Saudi Arabia **104** B3
Abu Matariq Sudan **126** E2
Abu Mena *tourist site* Egypt **121** F2
Abū Mīnā *tourist site* Egypt **108** A7
Abumombazi Dem. Rep. Congo **126** D4
Abu Musa *i.* The Gulf **105** F2
also known as Abū Mūsá, Jazireh-ye
Abū Mūsá, Jazireh-ye *i.* The Gulf *see*
Abu Musa
Abunã *r.* Bol. **200** D2
Abunã Brazil **200** D2
Abunai Brazil **199** E5
Abū Nā'im *well* Libya **120** C2
Åbune Yosëf *mt.* Eth. **128** C1
Abū Qīr, Khalīg *b.* Egypt **108** B6
Abū Qurīn Libya **120** B2
Abū Rāqah *well* Saudi Arabia **104** B2
Aburo *mt.* Dem. Rep. Congo **126** F4
Abu Road India **96** B4
Abū Rubayq Saudi Arabia **104** B3
Abū Rujmayn, Jabal *mts* Syria **109** J3
Abū Rūtha, Gebel *mt.* Egypt **108** F8
Abū Sallah *watercourse* Saudi Arabia **109** I9
Abū Sawādah *well* Saudi Arabia **105** D3
Abu Shagara, Ras *pt* Sudan **121** H4
Abu Simbel Egypt **121** F4
Abu Simbel Temple *tourist site* Egypt **121** F4
Abū Şukhayr Iraq **107** F5
Abū Sultān Egypt **108** D7
Abuta Japan **90** G3
Abu Tabaq *well* Sudan **121** G4
Abwong Sudan **128** B2
Åby Sweden **45** L4
Abyad Sudan **121** F6
Abyad, Jabal *al hill* Saudi Arabia **108** G9
Abyad, Jabal *al mts* Syria **109** I3
Abyān *governorate* Yemen **105** D5
Abyār al Hakīm *well* Libya **120** D2
Abyār an Nakhilan *well* Libya **120** D2
Abyār Banī Murr *well* Saudi Arabia **108** G9
Abydos Australia **150** B4
Abyei Sudan **126** E2
Åbyn Sweden **44** M2
Abyssinia *country* Africa *see* Ethiopia
Abzakovo Rus. Fed. **102** D1
Abzanovo Rus. Fed. **102** D1
Acacias Col. **198** C4
Academician Vernadskiy *research station*
Antarctica *see* Vernadsky
Academy Bay Rus. Fed. *see* Akademii, Zaliv
Academy Glacier Antarctica **223** T1
Acadia *prov.* Canada *see* Nova Scotia
Acadia National Park U.S.A. **177** Q1
Açailândia Brazil **202** C3
Acajutiba Brazil **202** E4
Acajutla El Salvador **185** H6
Acala Mex. **185** G5
Acamarachi *mt.* Chile *see* Pili, Cerro
Acámbaro Mex. **185** E4
Acampamento de Caça do Mucussso
Angola **127** D9
Acancéh Mex. **185** H4
Acandi Col. **198** B3
Acaponeta Mex. **184** D4
Acapulco Mex. **185** E5
long form Acapulco de Juárez
Acapulco de Juárez Mex. *see* Acapulco
Acará Brazil **202** B2
Acará *r.* Brazil **202** B2
Acaraú Brazil **202** D2
Acaraú *r.* Brazil **202** D2
Acaray, Represa de *resr* Para. **201** G6
Acari Brazil **202** E3
Acari *r.* Brazil **202** H2
Acarí Peru **200** B3
Acari *r.* Peru **200** B3
Acari, Serra *hills* Brazil/Guyana **199** G4
Acarigua Venez. **198** D2
Acatlan Mex. **185** F5
Acatzingo Mex. **185** F5
Acay, Nevado de *mt.* Arg. **200** D6
Acayucan Mex. **185** G5
Accho Israel *see* 'Akko
Accomac U.S.A. **177** J8
Accomack U.S.A. *see* Accomac

▶ **Accra** Ghana **125** E5
Capital of Ghana.

Aceguá Brazil **204** G3
Aceh *admin. dist.* Indon. **76** B1
formerly known as Acheh or Atjeh; *historically
known as* Achin
Aceuchal Spain **54** E6
Achacachi Bol. **200** C4
Achaguas Venez. **199** D3
Achalpur India **96** C5
formerly known as Dādra or Elichpur
Achampet India **94** C2
Achan Rus. Fed. **82** E2
formerly known as Bolon'
Achanta India **94** C2
Achayvayam Rus. Fed. **39** R3
also known as Aceh
Achel *admin. dist.* Indon. *see* Aceh
Achemmelmel *well* Mali **123** F3
Achemmim *well* Mauritania **124** D2
Acheng China **82** B3
Achern Germany **48** F7
Achhota India **94** D1
Achikulak Rus. Fed. **107** F1
Achill Island Rep. of Ireland **47** B10
Achim Germany **48** G2
Achin *admin. dist.* Indon. *see* Aceh
Achinsk Rus. Fed. **80** F1
Achisay Kazakh. **103** G4
Achit Rus. Fed. **40** K4
Achit Nuur *l.* Mongolia **84** A1
Achkhoy-Martan Rus. Fed. **107** F2
formerly known as Novoselskoye
Achlades, Akra *pt* Greece **59** G12

Achnasheen U.K. **46** G6
Achosa-Rudnya Belarus **43** M9
Aci Castello *Sicilia* Italy **57** H11
Aci Catena *Sicilia* Italy **57** H11
Acıgöl *l.* Turkey **106** B3
Acıpayam Turkey **106** B3
Acireale *Sicilia* Italy **57** H11
Ackerman U.S.A. **175** B5
Ackley U.S.A. **174** A3
Acklins Island Bahamas **187** E2
Acobamba Huancavelica Peru **200** B3
Acobamba Junín Peru **200** B3
Acomayo Cusco Peru **200** C3
Acomayo Huánuco Peru **200** A2

▶ **Aconcagua, Cerro** *mt.* Arg. **204** C4
Highest mountain in South America.
southamerica [landscapes] ▶▶▶ 190–191

Acopiara Brazil **202** E3
Acora Peru **200** C3
A Coruña Spain **54** C1
English form Corunna; *also spelt* La Coruña
Acostambo Peru **200** B3
Acoyapa Nicaragua **186** B5
Acquapendente Italy **56** D6
Acqui Terme Italy **56** A4
historically known as Aquae Statiellae
Acra U.S.A. **177** K3
Acragas *Sicilia* Italy *see* Agrigento
Acraman, Lake *salt flat* Australia **146** B3
Acre *r.* Brazil **200** D2
formerly known as Aquiry
Acre *state* Brazil **200** C2
Acre Israel *see* 'Akko
Acreúna Brazil **206** C3
Acri Italy **57** I9
Acton Canada **173** M7
Acton U.S.A. **177** N2
Actopán Mex. **185** F4
Açu *r.* Brazil **202** E3
Açuã *r.* Brazil **201** D1
Açucena Brazil **207** K6
Acunum Acusio France *see* Montélimar
Acureman Equat. Guinea **125** H6
Açurízal Brazil **201** F3
Ada Ghana **125** F5
Ada MN U.S.A. **178** C2
Ada OH U.S.A. **176** B5
Ada OK U.S.A. **179** C5
Ada *Vojvodina, Srbija* Yugo. **58** B3
also spelt Adaha
Ādaba Eth. **128** C3
Adabazar Turkey *see* Sakarya
Adabiya Egypt **108** D8
Adaf, Djebel *mts* Alg. **123** H5
Adaja *r.* Spain **54** G3
Adak Sweden **44** L2
Adalia Turkey *see* Antalya
Adam, Mount *hill* Falkland Is **205** F8
Adam, Mount *hill* Falkland Is **205** F8
Adamantina Brazil **206** B8
Adamaoua *prov.* Cameroon **125** I5
Adamas Greece **59** F12
also spelt Adhámas
Adamawa *state* Nigeria **125** H4
Adamclisi Romania **58** I4
Adamello *mt.* Italy **56** C2
Adamello-Brenta, Parco Naturale
nature res. Italy **56** C2
Adaminaby Australia **147** F3
Adamovka Rus. Fed. **102** D2
Adams KY U.S.A. **176** C7
Adams MA U.S.A. **177** L3
Adams NY U.S.A. **177** I2
Adams WI U.S.A. **172** D7
Adams, Cape Antarctica **222** T2
Adams, Mount N.Z. **153** E11
Adams Center U.S.A. **177** I2
Adams Lake Canada **166** G5
Adams McGill Reservoir U.S.A. **183** I3
Adams Mountain U.S.A. **166** D4
Adam's Peak Sri Lanka **94** D5
also known as Samanala or Sri Pada
Adams Peak U.S.A. **182** D2

▶ **Adamstown** Pitcairn Is **221** J7
Capital of the Pitcairn Islands.

Adamstown U.S.A. **177** I5
'Adan Yemen *see* Aden
Adana Turkey **106** C3
also known as Seyhan; *historically known as*
Ataniya
Adana *prov.* Turkey **108** G1
Adana Yemen *see* Aden
'Adan as Sughra Yemen **104** D5
English form Little Aden
Adang, Teluk *b.* Indon. **77** G3
Adani Nigeria **125** G5
Adapazarı Turkey *see* Sakarya
Adaran, Jabal *mt.* Yemen **105** D5
Adare, Rep. of Ireland **47 D11
Adare, Cape Antarctica **223** L2
Adatara-san *vol.* Japan **90** G5
Adavale Australia **149** E5
Ādaži Latvia **42** F4
Ad Dabbah Sudan *see* Ed Debba
Ad Dafinah Saudi Arabia **104** C3
Ad Daghghārah Iraq **107** F4
Ad Dahnā' *des.* Saudi Arabia **105** D3
also spelt Dahana
Ad Dakhīlyah *admin. reg.* Oman **105** Q3
Ad Dakhla W. Sahara **122** B5
also spelt Dakhla; *formerly known as* Villa
Cisneros
Ad Dālī Yemen **104** D5
Ad Damir Sudan *see* Ed Damer
Ad Dammām Saudi Arabia *see* Dammam
Addanki India **94** C3
Ad Dār al Ḩamrā' Saudi Arabia **104** B2
Ad Darb Saudi Arabia **104** C4
Adda Sud, Parco dell' Italy **56** B3
Ad Dawādimī Saudi Arabia **104** D2
Ad Dawḩah Qatar *see* Doha
Ad Dawr *plain* Syria **109** I3
Ad Dibīn Yemen **105** E4
Ad Dikākah *des.* Saudi Arabia **105** E4
Ad Dilam Saudi Arabia **105** D3
Ad Dīr'īyah Saudi Arabia **105** D3

▶ **Addis Ababa** Eth. **128** C2
Capital of Ethiopia. Also known as Ādīs Ābeba.

Addison U.S.A. **177** H3
Ad Diwānīyah Iraq **107** F5
also spelt Diwaniyah
Ad Diwānīyah *governorate* Iraq **107** F5
Al Qādisīyah
Addo S. Africa **133** J10
Addo Atoll Maldives *see* Addu Atoll
Addo Elephant National Park S. Africa
133 J10
Addu Atoll Maldives **93** D11
also known as Seenu Atoll; *also spelt* Addoo
Atoll
Ad Dulū'īyah Iraq **109** P3
Ad Duwaym Sudan *see* Ed Dueim

Ad Duwayris *well* Saudi Arabia **105** E3
Adel GA U.S.A. **175** D6
Adel IA U.S.A. **178** D3

▶ **Adelaide** Australia **146** C3
State capital of South Australia.

Adelaide Bahamas **175** E7
Adelaide S. Africa **133** K9
Adelaide Island Antarctica **222** T2
Adelaide River Australia **148** A2
Adelebsen Germany **48** G4
Adel Island Australia **150** C2
Adelfoi *i.* Greece **59** H12
Adélie Coast Antarctica *see* Adélie Land
Adélie Coast *reg.* Antarctica *see*
Adélie Land
Adélie Land *reg.* Antarctica **223** J2
also known as Adélie Coast or Terre Adélie
Adelong Aboriginal Reserve Australia
151 C5
Adelsheim Germany **48** G6
Adelunga Uzbek. **103** G4
Aden Yemen **104** D5
also spelt 'Adan; *historically known as* Adana
Aden, Gulf of Somalia/Yemen **128** E3
Adena U.S.A. **176** E5
Adenau Germany **48** D5
Aderbissinat Niger **125** G3
Adesar India **96** A5
Adhaman az Zaur, Wādi *watercourse* Iraq
109 N5
Adhámas Greece *see* Adamas
Adhan, Jabal *mt.* U.A.E. **105** G2
Adhanah, Wādi *watercourse* Yemen **104** C5
Adh Dhayd U.A.E. **105** F2
Adh Dhayūf *well* Saudi Arabia **107** E5
'Adhfā' *well* Saudi Arabia **107** E5
'Ādhiriyāt, Jibāl *al mts* Jordan **109** H7
Adhoi India **96** A5
Adi *i.* Indon. **73** H7
Ādī Ārk'ay Eth. **128** C1
Adicora Venez. **198** D2
Ādī Da'iro Eth. **104** B5
'Adid Umm Inderab *well* Sudan **121** F6
Adige *r.* Italy **56** E3
Adigey Autonomous Oblast *aut. rep.*
Rus. Fed. *see* Adygeya, Respublika
Ādigrat Eth. **128** C1
Adigüzel Baraji *resr* Turkey **106** B3
Adi Kwala Eritrea **121** H6
Adilabad India **94** C2
Adilanga Uganda **128** B4
Adilcevaz Turkey **107** E3
Adin U.S.A. **180** B4
Adiri Libya **120** B3
Adirondack Mountains U.S.A. **177** K1
Ādīs Ābeba Eth. *see* Addis Ababa
Ādīs Zemen Eth. **128** C1
Adi Ugri Eritrea *see* Mendefera
Adıyaman Turkey **107** D3
Adıyaman *prov.* Turkey **108** G1
Adjud Romania **58** I2
Adjumani Uganda **128** A4
Adlavik Islands Canada **169** J2
Admiralty Gulf Australia **150** D2
Admiralty Gulf Aboriginal Reserve
Australia **150** D2
Admiralty Inlet Canada **165** K2
Admiralty Island Canada **165** I3
Admiralty Island U.S.A. **164** F4
**Admiralty Island National Monument -
Kootznoowoo Wilderness** *nat. park*
U.S.A. **164** F4
Admiralty Islands P.N.G. **73** K7
Admiralty Mountains Antarctica **223** L2
Ādo Eth. **128** C3
Ado-Ekiti Nigeria **125** G5
Adok Sudan **128** A2
Adolfo Gonzáles Chaves Arg. **204** E5
Adolfsström Sweden **44** L2
Adolphus Island Australia **150** E2
Adonara *i.* Indon. **75** B5
also spelt Adunara
Adoni India **94** C3
Adour *r.* France **50** E9
Adra India **97** E5
Adra Spain **55** H8
Adra *r.* Spain **55** I8
Adramyttium Turkey *see* Edremit
Adramyttium, Gulf of Turkey *see*
Edremit Körfezi
Adrano *Sicilia* Italy **57** G11
also spelt Adremo; *historically known as*
Hadranum
Adrar Alg. **123** E4
Adrar *mts* Alg. **123** G4
Adrar *hills* Mali *see* Ifôghas, Adrar des
Adrar *admin. reg.* Mauritania **122** C5
Adraskand *r.* Afgh. **101** E3
Adrasmon Tajik. **101** G1
Adré Chad **120** D6
Adrian MI U.S.A. **173** I9
Adrian TX U.S.A. **179** B5
Adrianople Turkey *see* Edirne
Adrianopolis Turkey *see* Edirne
Adriatic Sea Europe **56** F4
Adua Eth. *see* Adwa
Adunara *i.* Indon. *see* Adonara
Adur India **94** C4
Adusa Dem. Rep. Congo **126** F4
Adutiškis Lith. **42** H6
Aduwa Eth. *see* Adwa
Adverse Well Australia **150** C4
Adwa Eth. **128** C1
also spelt Aduwa; *formerly spelt* Adua
Adwufia Ghana **124** E5
Adycha *r.* Rus. Fed. **39** N3
Adygeja India **94** D2
Adygea *aut. rep.* Rus. Fed. *see*
Adygeya, Respublika
Adygeya, Respublika *aut. rep.* Rus. Fed.
41 F7
formerly known as Adigey Autonomous
Oblast' or Adygeyskaya Avtonomnaya
Oblast'; *short form* Adygeya
Adygeysk Rus. Fed. **41** F7
formerly known as Teuchezhsk
Adygeyskaya Avtonomnaya Oblast'
aut. rep. Rus. Fed. *see* Adygeya, Respublika
Adyk Rus. Fed. **41** H7
formerly known as Yuzhnyy
Adzhiyan Turkm. **102** C3
Adzopé Côte d'Ivoire **124** E5
Adz'va *r.* Rus. Fed. **40** L2
Adz'vavom Rus. Fed. **40** L2
Aegean Sea Greece/Turkey **59** F10
Aegina *i.* Greece *see* Aigina
Aegna *i.* Estonia **42** F2
Aegviidu Estonia **42** G2
Aegyptus *country* Africa *see* Egypt
Aela Jordan *see* Al 'Aqabah
Aelana Jordan *see* Al 'Aqabah
Aelia Capitolina Israel/West Bank *see*
Jerusalem
Aelönlaplap *atoll* Marshall Is *see*
Ailinglapalap
Aenus Turkey *see* Enez
Ærø *i.* Denmark **45** H7
Aerzen Germany **48** G3
Aesernia Italy *see* Isernia
A Estrada Spain **54** C2
Āetsä Fin. **45** M3
Afabet Eritrea **121** H5
Afal *watercourse* Saudi Arabia *see*
'Ifāl, Wādī
Afanas'yevo Rus. Fed. **40** J4
Afándou Greece *see* Afantou
Afantou Greece **59** J12
also spelt Afándou

Afar admin. reg. Eth. 128 D1
Afar Oman 105 G3
Afar Depression Eritrea/Eth. 121 I6
Āfdem Eth. 128 D2
Afféri Côte d'Ivoire 124 E5
Affreville Alg. see Khemis Miliana
Afghānestān country Asia see Afghanistan
▶Afghanistan country Asia 101 E3
spelt Afghānestān in Dari and Pushtu
asia [countries] ➡ 64–67
Afgooye Somalia 128 E4
'Afīf Saudi Arabia 104 C3
Afikpo Nigeria 125 G5
Afim'ino Rus. Fed. 43 P4
Afiun Karahissar Turkey see Afyon
Åfjord Norway 44 J3
Aflou Alg. 123 F2
Afmadow Somalia 128 D4
Afognak Island U.S.A. 164 D4
Afojjar well Mauritania 124 B2
A Fonsagrada Spain 54 D1
also known as Fonsagrada
Afonso Cláudio Brazil 207 L7
Afragola Italy 56 G8
Afrânio Brazil 202 D4
Āfrēra Terara vol. Eth. 128 D1
Āfrēra YeChe'ew Hāyk' l. Eth. 128 D1
Africa Nova country Africa see Tunisia
'Afrīn Syria 109 H1
'Afrīn, Nahr r. Syria/Turkey 109 H1
Afşar Barajı resr Turkey 59 J10
Afşin Turkey 107 D3
also known as Efsus
Afsluitdijk barrage Neth. 48 C3
Aftol well Eth. 128 E3
Afton NY U.S.A. 177 J3
Afton WY U.S.A. 180 E4
Aftoût Faï depr. Mauritania 124 B2
Afuá Brazil 202 B2
'Afula Israel 108 G5
Afyon Turkey 106 B3
also known as Afyonkarahisar; historically known as Afiun Karahissar
Afyonkarahisar Turkey see Afyon
Aga Egypt 108 C7
Aga r. Rus. Fed. 85 G1
Aga-Buryat Autonomous Okrug admin. div. Rus. Fed. see Aginskiy Buryatskiy Avtonomnyy Okrug
Agadem well Niger 125 I2
Agadès Niger see Agadez
Agadez Niger 125 G2
also spelt Agadès
Agadez dept Niger 125 H2
Agadir Morocco 122 C3
Agadyr' Kazakh. 103 H2
also spelt Aqadyr
Agaie Nigeria 125 G4
Agalega Islands Mauritius 218 K6
Agalta nat. park Hond. 186 B4
Agana Guam see Hagåtña
Agapovka Rus. Fed. 102 D1
Agar India 96 C5
Agârak well Niger 125 G2
Agâraktem well Mali 122 D5
Agaro Eth. 128 C3
Agartala India 97 F5
Agashi India 94 B2
Agassiz National Wildlife Refuge nature res. U.S.A. 178 D1
Agate Canada 168 D3
Agathe France see Agde
Agathonisi i. Greece 59 H11
Agatti i. India 94 B4
Agawa r. Canada 173 I3
Agbor Bojiboji Nigeria 125 G5
Agboville Côte d'Ivoire 124 D5
Ağcabädi Azer. 107 F2
also spelt Agdzhabedi
Ağdam Azer. 107 F3
Ağdaş Azer. 107 F2
also spelt Agdash
Agdash Azer. see Ağdaş
Agde France 51 J9
historically known as Agathe
Agdzhabedi Azer. see Ağcabädi
Agedabia Libya see Ajdābiyā
Agen France 50 G8
historically known as Aginum
Agenebode Nigeria 125 G5
Āgere Maryam Eth. 128 C3
Ageyevo Rus. Fed. 43 R7
Aggeneys S. Africa 132 C6
Aggershus county Norway see Akershus
Aggteleki nat. park Hungary 49 R7
Agharri, Sha'īb al watercourse Iraq 109 L4
Aghezzaf well Mali 125 E2
also spelt Arezzaf
Aghil Pass China/Jammu and Kashmir 89 B4
Aghireşu Romania 58 E2
Aghouavil des. Mauritania 124 D2
Aghrijīt well Mauritania 124 C2
Aghzoumal, Sabkhat salt pan W. Sahara 122 B4
Agia Greece 59 D9
also spelt Ayiá
Agiabampo Mex. 184 C3
Agia Eirinis, Akra pt Greece 59 G9
Agia Marina Greece 59 H11
Agiasos Greece 59 H9
also spelt Ayiásos
Agia Vervara Greece 59 G13
Agigea Romania 58 J4
Agighiol Romania 58 J3
Agiguan i. N. Mariana Is see Aguijan
Ağın Turkey 107 D3
Aginskiy Buryatskiy Avtonomnyy Okrug admin. div. Rus. Fed. 85 G1
English form Aga-Buryat Autonomous Okrug
Aginskoye Rus. Fed. 85 G1
Aginum France see Agen
Agioi Apostoloi Greece 59 E10
Agioi Dimitrios Greece 59 E11
also spelt Áyios Dhimítrios
Agios Dimitrios, Akra pt Greece 59 F11
also spelt Áyios Dhimítris, Ákra
Agios Efstratios Greece 59 F9
Agios Efstratios i. Greece 59 G9
also spelt Áyios Evstrátios
Agios Fokas, Akra pt Greece 59 H9
Agios Georgios i. Greece 59 E11
also spelt Áyios Yeóryios
Agios Ioannis, Akra pt Greece 59 G13
Agios Kirykos Greece 59 H11
Agios Konstantinos Greece 59 D10
Agios Nikolaos Greece 59 G13
also spelt Áyios Nikólaos
Agios Paraskevi Greece 59 H9
Agios Petros Greece 59 D11
Agiou Orous, Kolpos b. Greece 59 E8
Agirwat Hills Sudan 121 G5
Agisanang S. Africa 133 J3
Agly r. France 51 J10
Agnantero Greece 59 C9
Agnes, Mount hill Australia 146 A1
Agnew Australia 151 C6
Agnew Lake Canada 173 L4
Agnibilékrou Côte d'Ivoire 124 E5
Agnita Romania 58 F3
Agniye-Afanas'yevsk Rus. Fed. 82 E2
Agno r. Italy 56 D3
Agnone Italy 56 G7
Ago-Are Nigeria 125 F4
Agogo Ghana 125 E5
Agona Junction Ghana 125 E5
Agong China 84 D4
Agounni Jefal well Mali 124 E2
Agoura U.S.A. 182 F7
Agous-n-Ehsel well Mali 125 F2
also known as Ehcel
Agout r. France 51 H9
Agra India 96 C4
Agrakhanskiy Poluostrov pen. Rus. Fed. 102 A4
Agram Croatia see Zagreb
Agreda Spain 55 J3
Agri r. Italy 57 I8
Ağrı Turkey 107 E3
also known as Karaköse
Agria Gramvousa i. Greece 59 E13
Ağrı Dağı mt. Turkey see Ararat, Mount
Agrigan i. N. Mariana Is see Agrihan
Agrigento Sicilia Italy 57 F11
formerly known as Girgenti; historically known as Acragas or Agrigentum
Agrigentum Sicilia Italy see Agrigento
Agrihan i. N. Mariana Is 73 K3
also spelt Agrigan; formerly spelt Grigan
Agrii r. Romania 58 E1
Agrinio Greece 59 C10
Agropoli Italy 57 G8
Agryz Rus. Fed. 40 J4
Ågskaret Norway 44 K2
Ağstafa Azer. 107 F2
Ağsu Azer. 107 G2
also spelt Akhsu
Agtertang S. Africa 133 J7
Agua Blanca Arg. 204 D5
Agua Boa Brazil 207 K4
Agua Brava, Laguna lag. Mex. 184 D4
Agua Clara Bol. 200 D3
Água Clara Brazil 206 A7
Aguaclara Col. 198 C3
Aguada Mex. 185 H5
Aguadilla Puerto Rico 187 G3
Aguado Cecilio Arg. 204 D6
Agua Doce do Norte Brazil 207 L5
Aguados, Serra dos mts Brazil 206 D9
Agua Dulce Bol. 200 D3
Aguadulce Panama 186 C5
Agua Escondida Arg. 204 C5
Agua Fria r. U.S.A. 183 L8
Aguanaval r. Mex. 185 E3
Aguanga U.S.A. 183 H8
Aguanqueterique Hond. 186 B4
Aguanus r. Canada 169 I3
Aguapeí Brazil 201 F4
Aguapeí r. Mato Grosso do Sul Brazil 206 B8
also known as Feio
Aguapeí r. Brazil 201 F3
Aguapeí, Serra hills Brazil 201 F4
Agua Prieta Mex. 184 C2
Aguaragüe, Cordillera de mts Bol. 201 E5
Aguaray Arg. 201 E5
A Guardia Spain 54 C3
also spelt La Guardia
Aguaro-Guariquito, Parque Nacional nat. park Venez. 199 E2
Aguaruto Mex. 184 D3
Aguas r. Spain 55 J7
Águas Belas Brazil 202 E4
Aguascalientes Mex. 185 E4
Aguascalientes state Mex. 185 E4
Águas Formosas Brazil 203 D6
Águas Vermelhas Brazil 207 L2
Aguasvivas r. Spain 55 K3
Agua Verde r. Brazil 201 F3
Agua Vermelha, Represa resr Brazil 206 C6
Aguaytía Peru 200 B2
Agudo Spain 54 G6
Agudos Brazil 206 E9
Águeda Port. 54 C4
Águeda r. Port./Spain 54 E3
Aguelal Niger 125 H2
Aguelhok Mali 125 F2
Aguemour, Oued watercourse Alg. 123 F4
Aguessis well Niger 123 H6
Aguié Niger 125 G3
Aguijan i. N. Mariana Is 73 K4
also spelt Agiguan
Aguila mt. Spain 55 J4
Aguila U.S.A. 183 K8
Aguilar de Campóo Spain 54 G2
Águilas Spain 55 J7
Aguililla Mex. 185 E5
Aguisan Phil. 74 B4
Agula'i Eth. 104 B5
Agulhas S. Africa 132 E11
▶Agulhas, Cape S. Africa 132 E11
Most southerly point of Africa.
Agulhas Negras mt. Brazil 203 C7
Agumtum Italy see San Candido
Agusan r. Phil. 74 C4
Agutaya i. Phil. 74 B4
Agva Turkey 106 B2
Agvali Rus. Fed. 102 A4
Agwarra Nigeria 125 G4
Agwei r. Sudan 128 B3
Ahaggar plat. Alg. see Hoggar
Ahakeye Aboriginal Land res. Australia 148 B4
Ahar Iran 100 A2
Ahaura N.Z. 153 F10
Ahaura r. N.Z. 153 F10
Ahaus Germany 48 E3
Ahigal Spain 54 E4
Ahillo mt. Spain 54 G7
Ahimanawa Range mts N.Z. 152 K6
Ahioma P.N.G. 149 F1
Ahipara N.Z. 152 H3
Ahipara Bay N.Z. 152 H3
Ahiri India 94 D2
Ahititi N.Z. 152 I6
Ahja r. Estonia 42 I3
Ahklun Mountains U.S.A. 164 C4
Ahlat Turkey 107 E3
Ahlen Germany 48 E4
Ahmadabad India 96 B5
formerly spelt Ahmedabad
Ahmadābād Iran 101 E3
Ahmad al Bāqir, Jabal mt. Jordan 108 G8
Ahmadnagar India 94 B2
formerly spelt Ahmednagar
Ahmadpur India 94 C2
also known as Rajura
Ahmadpur East Pak. 101 G4
Ahmadpur Sial Pak. 101 G4
Ahmar Mountains Eth. 128 D2
Ahmedabad India see Ahmadabad
Ahmednagar India see Ahmadnagar
Ahmetli Turkey 59 I10
Ahoada Nigeria 125 G5
Ahome Mex. 184 C3
Ahore India 96 B4
Ahoskie U.S.A. 177 I9
Ahram Iran 100 B4
Ahrāmāt el Jīzah tourist site Egypt see Giza Pyramids
Ahraura India 97 D4
Ahrensburg Germany 48 H2
Ähtäri Fin. 40 C3
Ahtme Estonia 42 I2
Āhū Iran 100 B4
Ahuacatlán Mex. 184 D4
Ahuachapán El Salvador 185 H6
Ahualulco Jalisco Mex. 184 E4
Ahualulco San Luis Potosí Mex. 185 E4
Ahun France 51 I6
Ahunapalu Estonia 42 I3
Ahuriri r. N.Z. 153 E12
Ahvāz Iran 100 B4
also spelt Ahwāz
Ahvenanmaa is Fin. see Åland Islands
Ahwa India 94 B1
Ahwar Yemen 105 D5
Ahwāz Iran see Ahvāz
Ai r. China 83 B3
Ai-Ais Namibia 130 C5
Ai-Ais Hot Springs and Fish River Canyon Park nature res. Namibia 130 C5
Aibag Gol r. China 85 F3
Aibetsu Japan 90 H3
Aichach Germany 48 I7
Aichi pref. Japan 91 E7
Aid U.S.A. 176 C7
Aida Japan 91 D7
Aidin Turkm. 102 C5
Aigiali Greece 59 G12
also spelt Aiyiáli
Aigialousa Cyprus 108 F2
also known as Yialousa
Aigina Greece 59 E11
Aigina i. Greece 59 E11
English form Aegina; also spelt Aíyina
Aiginio Greece 58 D8
also known as Aiyínion
Aigio Greece 59 D10
also known as Aíyion
Aigle Switz. 51 M6
Aigle de Chambeyron mt. France 51 M8
Aigoual, Mont mt. France 51 J8
Aiguá Uruguay 204 G4
Aiguebelle, Parc de Conservation d' nature res. Canada 173 O2
Aigües Tortes i Estany de St Maurici, Parque Nacional d' nat. park Spain 55 L2
Aiguille de Scolette mt. France/Italy 51 M7
Aiguilles d'Arves mts France 51 M7
Aiguille Verte mt. France 51 M7
Aigurande France 50 H6
Aihua China see Yunxian
Aihui China see Heihe
Aija Peru 200 A2
Aijal India see Aizawl
Aiken U.S.A. 175 D5
Ailao Shan mts China 86 B3
Aileron Australia 148 B4
Aileu East Timor 75 C5
Ailigandí Panama 186 D5
Ailing China 87 D3
Ailinglabelab atoll Marshall Is see Ailinglapalap
Ailinglapalap atoll Marshall Is 220 F6
also spelt Aelönlaplap or Ailinglabelab; formerly known as Lambert
Ailly-sur-Noye France 51 I3
Ailsa Craig Canada 173 L7
Ailsa Craig i. U.K. 47 G8
Aimogasta Arg. 204 D3
Aimorés, Serra dos hills Brazil 203 D6
Ain r. France 51 L7
'Aïn 'Amûr spring Egypt 121 F3
Ainaži Latvia 42 F4
Aïn Beïda Alg. 123 G2
formerly known as Daoud
Aïn Beni Mathar Morocco 123 E2
'Aïn Ben Tili Mauritania 122 C4
Aïn Bessem Alg. 55 O8
Aïn Biré well Mauritania 124 C2
Aïn Boucif Alg. 55 O9
'Aïn Dalla spring Egypt 121 E3
Aïn Defla Alg. 123 F1
formerly known as Duperré
Aïn Deheb Alg. 123 F2
Aïn Draham Tunisia 57 A12
Aïn el Bâgha well Egypt 108 E8
'Aïn el Furtâga well Egypt 108 F8
Aïn el Hadjadj well Alg. 123 F3
'Aïn el Hadjadj well Alg. 123 G4
Aïn el Hadjel Alg. 123 F2
Aïn el Maqfi spring Egypt 121 E3
Aïn Galakka spring Chad 120 C5
Aïn Mdila well Alg. 123 G2
Aïn-M'Lila Alg. 123 G1
Ainos nat. park Greece 59 B10
Aïn Oussera Alg. 123 F2
Aïn Salah Alg. see In Salah
Aïn Sefra Alg. 123 E2
Ainslie, Lake Canada 169 I4
Ainsworth IA U.S.A. 172 B9
Ainsworth NE U.S.A. 178 C3
Aintab Turkey see Gaziantep
Aïn Taya Alg. 55 O8
Aïn Tédélès Alg. 55 L9
Aïn Temouchent Alg. 123 E2
'Aïn Tibaghbagh spring Egypt 121 E2
'Aïn Timeira spring Egypt 121 E2
Aïn Ti-m Misaou well Alg. 123 F5
'Aïn Zeitûn Egypt 106 A5
Aipe Col. 198 C4
Aiquile Bol. 200 D4
Air i. Indon. 77 D2
also known as Raibu
Airão Brazil 199 F5
Airbangis Indon. 76 B2
Airdrie Canada 167 H5
Aire r. France 51 K3
Aire-sur-l'Adour France 50 F9
Air Force Island Canada 165 L3
Airgin Sum China 85 F3
Airhitam r. Indon. 77 E3
Airhitam, Teluk b. Indon. 77 E3
Airlie Beach Australia 149 F4
Airlie Island Australia 150 A4
Airolo Switz. 51 O6
Airpanas Indon. 75 C4
Air Ronge Canada 167 J4
Airvault France 50 F6
Aisatung Mountain Myanmar 78 A3
Aisch r. Germany 48 I6
Aisén admin. reg. Chile 205 B7
Aishalton Guyana 199 G4
Ai Shan hill China 85 I4
Aishihik Canada 166 B2
Aishihik Lake Canada 166 B2
Aisimi Greece see Aisymi
Aisne r. France 51 I3
Aïssa, Djebel mt. Alg. 123 E2
Aisymi Greece 58 G7
also spelt Aisími
Aitamännikkö Fin. 44 N2
Aitana mt. Spain 55 K6
Aitape P.N.G. 73 J7
also spelt Eitape
Aït Benhaddou tourist site Morocco 122 D3
Aitkin U.S.A. 174 A2
Aitoliko Greece 59 C10
Aitova Rus. Fed. 41 J5
Aiud Romania 58 E2
also known as Nagyenyed
Aivadzh Tajik. 101 G2
also spelt Ayvadzh
Aiviekste r. Latvia 42 G5
Aix France see Aix-en-Provence
Aix r. France 51 K7
Aix-en-Othe France 51 J4
Aix-en-Provence France 51 L9
historically known as Aquae Sextiae; short form Aix
Aixe-sur-Vienne France 50 H7
Aix-la-Chapelle Germany see Aachen
Aix-les-Bains France 51 L7
historically known as Aquae Gratianae
Āiy Ādī Eth. 128 C1
Aiyiáli Greece see Aigiali
Aíyina i. Greece see Aigina
Aiyínion Greece see Aiginio
Aíyion Greece see Aigio
Aizawl India 97 G5
formerly spelt Aijal
Aizenay France 50 E6
Aizkraukle Latvia 42 G5
formerly known as Stučka or Stuchka or imeni Petra Stuchki
Aizpute Latvia 42 C5
Aizu-wakamatsu Japan 90 F6
Ajā, Jibāl mts Saudi Arabia 104 C2
Ajaccio Corse France 52 D3
Ajaccio, Golfe d' b. Corse France 56 A7
Ajaigarh India 96 D4
Ajajú r. Col. 198 C4
Ajalpán Mex. 185 F5
Ajanta India 94 B1
Ajanta Range hills India see Sahyadriparvat Range
Ajasse Nigeria 125 G4
Ajax Canada 173 N7
Ajax, Mount N.Z. 153 G10
Ajayameru India see Ajmer
Ajban U.A.E. 105 F2
Aj Bogd Uul mts Mongolia 84 B2
Ajdābiyā Libya 120 D2
formerly spelt Agedabia
Ajdovščina Slovenia 56 F3
a-Jiddét des. Oman see Ḩarāsīs, Jiddat al
Ajigasawa Japan 90 G4
'Ajīj, Wādī al watercourse Iraq 109 M2
Ajimganj India 97 F4
Ajka Hungary 49 O8
'Ajlūn Jordan 108 G5
Ajman U.A.E. 105 F2
Ajmer India 96 B4
formerly known as Ajayameru or Ajmer-Merwara
Ajmer-Merwara India see Ajmer
Ajo U.S.A. 183 L9
Ajo, Mount U.S.A. 183 L9
Ajra India 94 B2
Ajuy Phil. 74 B4
Akāashat Iraq 107 D4
Akabira Japan 90 H3
Akabli Alg. 123 F4
Akaboun well Mali 125 F2
Akademii, Zaliv b. Rus. Fed. 82 E1
English form Academy Bay
Akademii Nauk, Khrebet mt. Tajik. see Akademiyai Fanho, Qatorkŭhi
Akademiyai Fanho, Qatorkŭhi mt. Tajik. 101 G2
also known as Akademii Nauk, Khrebet
Akagera National Park Rwanda 126 F5
also known as Kagera, Parc National de la or L'Akagera, Parc National de
Akagi Japan 91 C7
Akaishi-dake mt. Japan 91 F7
Āk'ak'ī Beseka Eth. 128 C2
Akalkot India 94 C2
Akama, Akra c. Cyprus see Arnauti, Cape
Akamagaseki Japan see Shimonoseki
Akamkpa Nigeria 125 H5
Akan Japan 90 I3
Akan-ko l. Japan 90 H3
Akan National Park Japan 90 I3
Akarkar well Niger 125 G3
Akarnanika mts Greece 59 B10
Akaroa N.Z. 153 G11
Akaroa Harbour N.Z. 153 G11
Akas reg. India 97 G4
'Akāsh, Wādī watercourse Iraq 109 L3
Akasha Sudan 121 F4
'Akāshāt Iraq 109 K4
Akashi Japan 91 D7
Äkäsjokisuu Fin. 44 M2
Akbakay Kazakh. 103 H3
Akbalyk Kazakh. 103 I3
also spelt Aqbalyq
Akbarābād Iran 100 C4
Akbarpur Uttar Pradesh India 96 D4
Akbarpur Uttar Pradesh India 97 D4
Akbasty Kazakh. 102 E3
Akbaytal Tajik. 101 H2
also known as Rabatakbaytal or Rabotoqbaytal
Akbaytal Pass Tajik. 101 H2
Akbeit Kazakh. 103 G2
also spelt Aqbeyit
Akbou Alg. 55 P8
Akbulak Rus. Fed. 102 C2
Akçadağ Turkey 107 D3
Akçakale Turkey 107 D3
Akçakertikbeli Geçidi pass Turkey 59 J9
Akçakoca Turkey 106 B2
Akçalı Dağları mt. Turkey 106 C3
Akçalı Dağları mts Turkey 108 D1
Akçaova Turkey 59 I11
Akçay r. Turkey 59 J11
Akchakaya, Vpadina depr. Turkm. 102 D4
Akchâr reg. Mauritania 124 B2
Akchatau Kazakh. 103 H3
also known as Aqshatau
Akchi Kazakh. see Akshiy
Akdağ mt. Turkey 59 J9
Akdağlar mts Turkey 106 B3
Akdağmadeni Turkey 106 C3
Akdepe Turkm. 102 D4
formerly known as Leninsk
Akdere Turkey 108 E1
Ak Dovurak Rus. Fed. 84 A1
Akelamo Indon. 75 D2
Akele Guzai prov. Eritrea 104 B5
Akelo Sudan 128 B3
Åkersberga Sweden 45 L4
Akershus county Norway 45 J3
also spelt Aggershus
Åkerstrømmen Norway 45 J3
Akespe Kazakh. 103 E3
Aketi Dem. Rep. Congo 126 D4
Akgyr Erezi hills Turkm. see Akkyr, Gory
Akhalgori Georgia 107 F2
formerly known as Leningori
Akhalk'alak'i Georgia 107 E2
Akhal Oblast admin. div. Turkm. see Akhal'skaya Oblast'
Akhal'skaya Oblast' admin. div. Turkm. 102 D5
English form Akhal Oblast; formerly known as Ashkhabadskaya Oblast'
Akhalts'ikhe Georgia 107 E2
Akhḑar, Al Jabal al mts Libya 120 D2
Akhḑar, Jabal mts Oman 105 G3
Akhḑar, Wādī al watercourse Saudi Arabia 109 H9
Akheloy Bulg. 58 I6
Akhisar Turkey 106 A3
historically known as Thyatira
Akhmīm Egypt 121 F3
also spelt Ekhmîm; historically known as Chemmis or Panoplis
Akhnoor Jammu and Kashmir 96 B2
Akhsu Azer. see Ağsu
Akhta Armenia see Hrazdan
Akhtarīn Syria 109 I1
Akhtubinsk Rus. Fed. 102 A2
Akhty Rus. Fed. 102 A4
Akhtyrka Ukr. see Okhtyrka
Aki Japan 91 C8
Akiéni Gabon 126 B5
Akimiski Island Canada 168 D2
Akıncılar Turkey see Selçuk
Akıncılar Turkey 107 D2
Åkirkeby Denmark 45 K5
Akishma r. Rus. Fed. 82 D1
Akita Japan 90 G5
Akita pref. Japan 90 G5
Akitio N.Z. 152 K8
Akjoujt Mauritania 124 B2
Akka Morocco 122 C3
Akkabak Kazakh. 103 G4
Akkajaure l. Sweden 44 L2
Akkala Uzbek. 102 D4
also spelt Oqqal"a
Akkem Rus. Fed. 88 D1
Akkerman Ukr. see Bilhorod-Dnistrovs'kyy
Akkermanovka Rus. Fed. 102 D2
Akkeshi Japan 90 I3
Akkeshi-wan b. Japan 90 I3
'Akko Israel 108 G5
historically known as Accho or Acre or St-Jean-d'Acre or Ptolemais
Akkol' Akmolinskaya Oblast' Kazakh. 103 G1
also spelt Aqköl; formerly known as Alekseyevka
Akkol' Almatinskaya Oblast' Kazakh. 103 H3
Akkol' Atyrauskaya Oblast' Kazakh. 41 [illegible]
also spelt Akkul' or Aqköl
Akkol' Zhambylskaya Oblast' Kazakh. 103 G4
Akköy Turkey 106 A3
Akkoy Turkey 59 K11
Akku Kazakh. 103 I2
formerly known as Lebyazh'ye
Akkul' Kazakh. see Akkol'
Akkum Kazakh. 103 F3
Akkuş Turkey 107 D2
Akkyr, Gory hills Turkm. 102 C4
also known as Akgyr Erezi
Akkystau Kazakh. 102 B3
also known as Aqqystaū
Aklavik Canada 164 F3
Aklera India 96 C4
Aklub reg. Saudi Arabia 104 D4
Ak-Mechet Kazakh. see Kyzylorda
Akmena r. Lith. 42 D6
Akmenė Lith. 42 D5
Akmenrags pt Latvia 42 C5
Akmeqit China 89 B4
Akmola Kazakh. see Astana
Akmola Oblast admin. div. Kazakh. see Akmolinskaya Oblast'
Akmolinsk Kazakh. see Astana
Akmolinskaya Oblast' admin. div. Kazakh. 103 G2
English form Aqmola Oblast; also known as Aqmola Oblysy; formerly known as Akmola or Tselinogradskaya Oblast'
Akniste Latvia 42 G5
Aknoul Morocco 122 E2
Akō Japan 91 D7
Akobo Sudan 128 B3
Akobo Wenz r. Eth./Sudan 128 B3
Akodia India 96 C5
Akola Maharashtra India 94 B2
Akola Maharashtra India 94 C1
Akom II Cameroon 125 H6
Akonolinga Cameroon 125 I6
Akop Sudan 126 F2
Akordat Eritrea 121 H6
Akören Turkey 106 C3
Akot India 96 C5
Akouménaye Fr. Guiana 199 H4
Akoupé Côte d'Ivoire 124 E5
Ak-Oyuk, Gora mt. Rus. Fed. 84 A1
Akpatok Island Canada 165 M3
Akqi China 88 B3
Akraifnio Greece 59 E10
Akranes Iceland 44 [inset] B2
Akrathos, Akra pt Greece 59 F8
Åkrē Iraq 109 O1
Akrérèb Niger 125 H2
Akritas, Akra pt Greece 59 C12
Akron CO U.S.A. 178 B3
Akron IN U.S.A. 172 G9
Akron OH U.S.A. 176 D4
Akrotiri Bay Cyprus 108 E3
also known as Akrotirion Bay or Akrotiriou, Kolpos
Akrotirion Bay Cyprus see Akrotiri Bay
Akrotiriou, Kolpos b. Cyprus see Akrotiri Bay
Akrotiri Sovereign Base Area military base Cyprus 108 D3
▶Aksai Chin terr. Asia 89 B5
Disputed territory (China/India). Also known as Aqsayqin Hit.
Aksakal Turkey 59 J8
Aksakovo Bulg. 58 I5
Aksakovo Rus. Fed. 40 J5
Aksaray Turkey 106 C3
Aksarka Rus. Fed. 38 G3
Aksay China 84 B4
also known as Hongliuwan
Aksay Kazakh. 102 C2
also spelt Aqsay; formerly known as Kazakhstan
Ak-Say r. Kyrg. 103 H4
Aksay Rus. Fed. 41 F7
Akşehir Turkey 106 B3
historically known as Philomelium
Akşehir Gölü l. Turkey 106 B3
Akseki Turkey 106 B3
Aksenovo Rus. Fed. 41 J5
Aks-e Rostam r. Iran 100 C4
Aksha Rus. Fed. 85 G1
Akshatau Kazakh. 102 C2
Akshiganak Kazakh. 103 E2
Akshiy Kazakh. 103 I4
also spelt Aqshi; formerly spelt Akchi
Akshukur Kazakh. 102 B4
also spelt Aqshuqyr
Aksu Xinjiang China 88 C3
Aksu Xinjiang China 88 C3
Aksu Almatinskaya Oblast' Kazakh. 103 I3
also spelt Aqsū
Aksu Pavlodarskaya Oblast' Kazakh. 103 I1
also spelt Aqsū; formerly known as Ermak or Yermak
Aksu Severnyy Kazakhstan Kazakh. 103 G1
also spelt Aqsū
Aksu Zapadnyy Kazakhstan Kazakh. 102 C2
Aksu r. Kazakh. 103 I3
Aksu r. Tajik. see Oksu
Aksu Turkey 108 B1
Aksu r. Turkey 107 B3
Aksuat Kustanayskaya Oblast' Kazakh. 103 F2
Aksuat Vostochnyy Kazakhstan Kazakh. 88 C2
also spelt Aqsūat
Aksuat, Ozero salt l. Kazakh. see Bol'shoy Aksuat, Ozero
Aksu-Ayuly Kazakh. 103 H2
also spelt Aqsū-Ayuly
Aksuek Kazakh. 103 H3
Aksu He r. China 88 C3
Āksum Eth. 128 C1
historically known as Axum
Aksume China 88 D2
Aksu-Zhabaglinskiy Zapovednik nature res. Kazakh. 103 G4
Aktag mt. China 89 D4
Ak-Tal Rus. Fed. 88 F1
Aktash Uzbek. 103 F5
also spelt Oqtosh
Aktau Karagandinskaya Oblast' Kazakh. 103 G3
Aktau Karagandinskaya Oblast' Kazakh. 103 H2
Aktau Mangistauskaya Oblast' Kazakh. 102 B4
also spelt Aqtaū; formerly known as Shevchenko
Aktepe Turkey 109 H1
Akto China 88 B4
Aktogay Karagandinskaya Oblast' Kazakh. 103 H2
also spelt Aqtoghay
Aktogay Pavlodarskaya Oblast' Kazakh. 103 H1
also spelt Aqtoghay; formerly known as Krasnokutsk or Krasnokutskoye
Aktogay Vostochnyy Kazakhstan Kazakh. 103 I3
Aktsyabrskaya Belarus 43 L6
also spelt Oktyabr'skaya
Aktsyabrski Belarus 43 J9
also spelt Oktyabr'skiy; formerly known as Karpilovka
Aktsyabrski Belarus 43 K7
also spelt Oktyabr'skiy
Aktumsyk Kazakh. 102 D3
Aktumsyk, Mys pt Uzbek. 102 D3
Ak-Tüz Kyrg. 103 H4
also spelt Aktyuz
Aktyubinsk Kazakh. 102 D2
also spelt Aqtöbe
Aktyubinskaya Oblast' admin. div. Kazakh. 102 D2
English form Aktyubinsk Oblast; also known as Aqtöbe Oblysy
Aktyubinsk Oblast admin. div. Kazakh. see Aktyubinskaya Oblast'
Aktyuz Kyrg. see Ak-Tüz
Akujärvi Fin. 44 N1
Akula Dem. Rep. Congo 126 D4
Akulichi Rus. Fed. 43 O8
Akulivik Canada 165 L3
Akumadan Ghana 125 E5
Akune Japan 91 B8
Akur mt. Uganda 128 B4
Akure Nigeria 125 G5
Akureyri Iceland 44 [inset] C2
Akuroa N.Z. 152 I4
Akwa Ibom state Nigeria 125 G5
Akwanga Nigeria 125 H4
Akyab Myanmar see Sittwe
Ak"yar Rus. Fed. 102 D2
Akyatan Gölü salt l. Turkey 108 G1
Akzhal Karagandinskaya Oblast' Kazakh. 103 H3
Akzhal Vostochnyy Kazakhstan Kazakh. 103 J2
also spelt Aqzhal
Akzhar Kzyl-Ordinskaya Oblast' Kazakh. 103 F3
Akzhar Vostochnyy Kazakhstan Kazakh. 88 C2
also spelt Aqzhar
Akzhar Zhambylskaya Oblast' Kazakh. 103 G4
Akzhaykyn, Ozero salt l. Kazakh. 103 F3
also known as Aqzhayqyn Köli
Ål Norway 45 J3
Ala r. Belarus 43 K9
Ala Italy 56 D3
'Alā, Jabal al hills Syria 109 H2
Alabama r. U.S.A. 175 C6
Alabama state U.S.A. 175 C5
Alabaster AL U.S.A. 175 C5
Alabaster MI U.S.A. 173 J6
Al 'Abṭīyah well Iraq 107 F5
Ala-Buka Kyrg. 103 G4
Al Abyaḑ Libya 120 B3
Al Abyār Libya 120 D1
Alaca Turkey 106 C2
also known as Huseyinabat
Alacahan Turkey 107 D3
Alaçam Turkey 106 C2
Alaçam Dağları mts Turkey 59 J9
Alacant Spain see Alicante
Alaçatı Turkey 59 H10
Alacrán, Arrecife reef Mex. 185 H4
Aladag mt. Bulg. 58 G7
Aladağ Turkey 106 C3
also known as Bademli
Ala Dag mt. Turkey 107 E3
Ala Dağlar mts Turkey 107 E3
Ala Dağları mts Turkey 106 C3
Al 'Adam Libya 120 D2
Alaejos Spain 54 F3
Al Aflāj reg. Saudi Arabia 105 D3
Alagadiço Brazil 199 F4
Alagapuram India 94 C4
Alag Hayrhan Uul mt. Mongolia 84 B2
Alagir Rus. Fed. 41 H8
Alagoas state Brazil 202 E4
Alagoinhas Brazil 202 E5
Alagón Spain 55 J3
Alagón r. Spain 54 E5
Alah r. Phil. 74 C5
Alahanpanjang Indon. 76 C3
Alahärmä Fin. 44 M3
Al Aḩmadī Kuwait 107 G5
Alaid, Ostrov i. Rus. Fed. see Atlasova, Ostrov
Alaior Spain 55 P5
Alai Range mts Asia 99 I2
also known as Alay Kyrka Toosu or Alayskiy Khrebet or Oloy, Qatorkŭhi
Ālaivān Iran 100 C3
Al Ajā'is hills Saudi Arabia 109 K8
Al 'Ajā'iz well Oman 105 G4
Al Ajām Saudi Arabia 105 E2
Alajärvi Fin. 44 M3
Alajaure naturreservat nature res. Sweden 44 M1
Al Ajfar Saudi Arabia 104 C2
Alajõgi r. Estonia 42 I2
Alajuela Costa Rica 186 B5
Alakanuk U.S.A. 164 C3
Alaknanda r. India 96 C3
Alakol', Ozero salt l. Kazakh. 88 C2
also known as Ala Kul
Ala Kul salt l. Kazakh. see Alakol', Ozero
Alakurtti Rus. Fed. 44 O2
Al 'Alamayn Egypt see El 'Alamein
Alalaú r. Brazil 199 F5
Al 'Alayyah Saudi Arabia 104 C4
Alama Somalia 128 D3
Al 'Amādīyah Iraq 107 E3
Alamagan i. N. Mariana Is 73 K3
also spelt Alamaguan
Alamaguan i. N. Mariana Is see Alamagan
Al 'Amār Saudi Arabia 104 D2
Al 'Amārah Iraq 107 F5
Ālamarvdasht watercourse Iran 100 C4
Ālamat'ā Eth. 104 B5
'Alam el Rûm, Râs pt Egypt 121 E2
Al Amghar waterhole Iraq 107 F5
Al Amghar waterhole Saudi Arabia 109 N7
Alamicamba Nicaragua 186 B4
Alaminos Phil. 74 A2
Alamito Creek r. U.S.A. 181 F7
Al Amlah Saudi Arabia 104 C3
'Alam Nafāza hill Egypt 108 A7
Alamo U.S.A. 174 B5
Alamo Dam U.S.A. 183 K7
Alamogordo U.S.A. 181 F6
Alamo Heights U.S.A. 179 C6
Alamos Sonora Mex. 184 C2
Alamos Sonora Mex. 184 C3
Alamos r. Mex. 185 E3
Alamos, Sierra mts Mex. 184 C3
Alamosa U.S.A. 181 F5
Alamosa Creek r. U.S.A. 181 F6
Alamos de Peña Mex. 184 D2
Alampur India 94 C3
Al 'Anād Yemen 104 D5
Alanäs Sweden 44 K2
Al Anbār governorate Iraq 107 E4
Åland is Fin. see Åland Islands
Aland r. Germany 48 I2
Aland India 94 C2
Aland r. Iran 107 F3
Åland Islands Fin. 45 L3
also known as Ahvenanmaa; short form Åland
Alands Hav sea chan. Fin./Sweden 45 L4
Alandur India 94 D3
Alangalang, Tanjung pt Indon. 77 G3
Alang Besar i. Indon. 76 C2
Alange, Embalse de resr Spain 54 E6
Alanggantang i. Indon. 76 D3
Alanson U.S.A. 173 I5
Alanya Turkey 106 C3
historically known as Coracesium
'Alā' od Dīn Iran 100 C4
Alapaha r. U.S.A. 175 D6
Alapakam India 94 C4
Alapli Turkey 41 D8
Alappuzha India see Alleppey
Alapur India 96 C4
Al 'Aqabah Jordan 108 G8
also spelt 'Aqaba; historically known as Aela or Aelana
Al 'Aqīq Saudi Arabia 104 C3
Al 'Aqūlah well Saudi Arabia 105 E3
Al 'Arabīyah i. Saudi Arabia 107 G6
Al 'Arabīyah as Sa'ūdīyah country Asia see Saudi Arabia
Alarcón, Embalse de resr Spain 55 I5
Al 'Arīḑah Saudi Arabia 104 C4
Al Arīn Saudi Arabia 104 C4
Al Arṭāwīyah Saudi Arabia 105 D2
Alas Indon. 77 G5
Alas, Selat sea chan. Indon. 77 G5

index

A

Alaşehir Turkey 106 B3
historically known as Philadelphia
Alash r. Rus. Fed. 88 E1
Alash, Plato plat. Rus. Fed. 88 E1
Alashiya ancient Asia see Cyprus
Al 'Āshūrīyah well Iraq 107 E5
Alaska state U.S.A. 164 E3
Alaska, Gulf of U.S.A. 164 E4
Alaska Highway Canada/U.S.A. 166 A2
Alaska Peninsula U.S.A. 164 C4
Alaska Range mts U.S.A. 164 E3
Al 'Assāfīyah Saudi Arabia 104 B1
Alassio Italy 56 A4
Alat Azer./Georgia 107 G3
Alat Uzbek. 103 E5
also spelt Olot
Alataw Shankou pass China/Kazakh. see Dzungarian Gate
Al 'Athāmīn hill Iraq 109 O7
Alatri Italy 56 F7
historically known as Aletrium
Al Atwā' well Saudi Arabia 104 C1
Alatyr' Rus. Fed. 40 H5
Alatyr' r. Rus. Fed. 40 H5
Alauksts l. Latvia 42 G4
Alausí Ecuador 198 B5
Alaverdi Armenia 107 F2
Alavieska Fin. 44 N2
Ala-Vuokki Fin. 44 O3
Alavus Fin. 44 M3
Alawa Aboriginal Land res. Australia 148 B2
Al Awābī Oman 105 G3
Al 'Awdah Saudi Arabia 105 D2
Alawoona Australia 146 D3
Al Awshazīyah Saudi Arabia 104 C2
Alaykel' Kyrg. see Alaykuu
Alaykuu Kyrg. 103 H4
also known as Këk-Art or Kögart or Kök-Art; formerly known as Alaykel'
Alay Kyrka Toosu mts Asia see Alai Range
Al 'Ayn Oman 105 G3
Al 'Ayn Saudi Arabia 104 B2
Al 'Ayn U.A.E. 105 F2
Alayskiy Khrebet mts Asia see Alai Range
Al A'zamīyah Iraq 109 P4
Alazani r. Azer./Georgia 107 F2
Alazeya r. Rus. Fed. 39 Q2
Al 'Azīzīyah Iraq 107 F4

▶Al 'Azīzīyah Libya 120 B1
Highest recorded shade temperature in the world.
world [climate and weather] ▶▶16–17

Alba Italy 51 O8
Alba U.S.A. 173 I6
Alba Adriatica Italy 56 F6
Al Ba'ā'ith Saudi Arabia 104 C2
Al Ba'ir Iraq 109 M1
Al Bāb Syria 109 I1
Albacete Spain 55 J5
Al Badā'i' Saudi Arabia 104 C2
Al Badī' Saudi Arabia 105 D3
Al Bādiyah al Janūbīyah hill Iraq 107 F5
Ålbæk Denmark 45 J1
Ålbæk Bugt b. Denmark 45 J1
Al'bagan, Gora mt. Rus. Fed. 88 D1
Al Bāḩah Saudi Arabia 104 C3
Al Bahrayn country Asia see Bahrain
Alba Iulia Romania 58 E2
also known as Gyulafehérvár; formerly known as Karlsburg; historically known as Apulum
Al Bajā' well U.A.E. 105 E2
Al Ba'jah Saudi Arabia 104 C2
Al Bakhrā well Saudi Arabia 104 C2
Al Bakkī Libya 120 B3
Albalate de Arzobispo Spain 55 K3
Albanel, Lac l. Canada 169 F3
▶Albania country Europe 58 B4
known as Republika e Shqipërisë in Albanian
europe [countries] ▶▶32–35
Albano Brazil 199 G5
Albany r. Canada 168 D2
Albany Jamaica 186 E2
Albany GA U.S.A. 175 C6
Albany MO U.S.A. 178 D4

▶Albany NY U.S.A. 177 L3
State capital of New York. Historically known as Fort Orange.

Albany OH U.S.A. 176 C6
Albany OR U.S.A. 180 B3
Albany TX U.S.A. 179 C5
Albany Downs Australia 147 F1
Albardão do Rio Maria coastal area Brazil 204 G4
Al Bardī depr. Saudi Arabia 109 K6
Al Bardī Libya 120 D2
Al Bāridah Saudi Arabia 109 K8
Al Barit waterhole Iraq 109 N6
Al Barrah Saudi Arabia 104 C3
Al Baṣrah Iraq see Basra
Al Baṣrah governorate Iraq 107 F5
Al Baṭḩā' marsh Iraq 107 F5
Al Bāṭinah admin. reg. Oman 105 G3
Al Bāṭinah i. Saudi Arabia 105 E2
Albatross Bay Australia 149 D2
Albatross Island Australia 147 E5
Albatross Point N.Z. 152 I6
Al Baydā' Libya 120 D1
also spelt Beida
Al Baydā' Yemen 105 D5
Al Baydā' governorate Yemen 105 D5
Albay Gulf Phil. 74 B3
Albemarle U.S.A. 174 D5
Albemarle Sea chan. U.S.A. 174 E4
Albenga Italy 56 A4
Alberche r. Spain 54 G4
Alberdi Para. 201 F6
Alberga watercourse Australia 146 B1

Albergaria-a-Velha Port. 54 C4
Albergian, Monte mt. Italy 51 M7
Albert Australia 147 E3
Albert r. Australia 148 C3
Albert France 51 I3
Albert, Lake Australia 146 C3
Albert, Lake Dem. Rep. Congo/Uganda 128 A4
formerly known as Mobutu, Lake or Mobutu Sese Seko, Lake
Albert, Parc National nat. park Dem. Rep. Congo see Virunga, Parc National des
Alberta prov. Canada 167 H4
Albert Falls Nature Reserve S. Africa 133 O6
Albertinia S. Africa 132 F11
Albertirsa Hungary 49 Q8
Albert Kanaal canal Belgium 51 L2
Albert Lea U.S.A. 174 A3
Albert Nile r. Sudan/Uganda 126 G4
Alberton Canada 169 H4
Alberto Oviedo Mota Mex. 183 I9
Albertshoek S. Africa 133 J4
Albert Town Bahamas 187 E2
Albertville Dem. Rep. Congo see Kalémié
Albertville France 51 M7
Albertville U.S.A. 174 C4
Albeşti Romania 58 I2
Albi France 51 I9
Albia U.S.A. 174 A3
Al Bi'ār Saudi Arabia 104 B3
Al Biḍah Saudi Arabia 105 E2
Albignasego Italy 56 D3
Albina Suriname 199 H3
Albino Italy 56 B3
Albion CA U.S.A. 182 A3
Albion IN U.S.A. 174 C3
Albion MI U.S.A. 173 I8
Albion NY U.S.A. 176 G2
Albion PA U.S.A. 176 E4
Al Bi'r Saudi Arabia 104 B1
also known as Bi'r Ibn Hirmās
Al Birk Saudi Arabia 104 C4
Al Birkah Saudi Arabia 104 C3
Al Biyāḍ reg. Saudi Arabia 105 D3
Alborán, Isla de i. Spain 55 H9
Ålborg Denmark 45 J4
also spelt Aalborg
Ålborg Bugt b. Denmark 45 J4
Alborz, Reshteh-ye mts Iran see Elburz Mountains
Albota Romania 58 F4
Albox Spain 55 I7
Albro Australia 149 E4
Albstadt Germany 48 G7
Albufeira Port. 54 C7
Al Bū Ghars, Sabkhat salt l. Iraq 109 M3
Al Bukayrīyah Saudi Arabia 104 C2
Albula Alpen mts Switz. 51 P6
Albuñol Spain 55 H8
Albuquerque U.S.A. 181 F6
Albuquerque, Cayos de is Caribbean Sea 186 C4
Al Buraymī Oman 105 F2
Alburg U.S.A. 177 L1
Alburno, Monte mt. Italy 57 H8
Alburquerque Spain 54 E5
Albury Australia 147 E4
Albury N.Z. 153 E12
Al Buşayrah Syria 109 L2
also spelt Buseire
Al Buşayţā' plain Saudi Arabia 107 D5
Al Buşayyah Iraq 107 F5
Al Bushūk well Saudi Arabia 107 D5
Al Buţayn plain Saudi Arabia 105 D2
Al Buwi well Oman 105 G4
Alca Peru 200 B3
Alcácer do Sal Port. 54 C6
Alcaçovas r. Port. 54 C6
Alcalá de Chivert Spain 55 L4
Alcalá de Guadaira Spain 54 F7
Alcalá de los Gazules Spain 54 F8
Alcalá de Henares Spain 55 H4
Alcalá la Real Spain 54 H7
Alcalde, Punta pt Chile 204 C3
Alcamo Sicilia Italy 57 E11
Alcanadre r. Spain 55 L3
Alcanar Spain 55 L4
Alcañiz Spain 55 K3
Alcántara Brazil 202 C2
Alcántara Spain 54 E5
Alcántara, Embalse de resr Spain 54 E5
Alcántara I, Embalse de resr Spain 54 E5
Alcantara Lake Canada 167 I2
Alcantarilla Spain 55 J7
Alcaraz Spain 55 I6
Alcaraz, Sierra de mts Spain 55 I6
Alcaria Ruiva hill Port. 54 D7
Alcarrache r. Port./Spain 54 D6
Alcaudete Spain 54 G7
Alcázar de San Juan Spain 55 H5
Alcazarquivir Morocco see Ksar el Kebir
Alchevs'k Ukr. 41 F6
formerly known as Kommunarsk or Voroshilovsk
Alcira Arg. 204 D4
Alcira Spain see Alzira
Alcobaça Brazil 203 E6
Alconchel Spain 54 D6
Alcora Spain 55 L4
Alcorneo r. Port./Spain 54 E5
Alcorta Arg. 204 E4
Alcoy Spain 55 K6
Alcubierre, Sierra de mts Spain 55 K3
Alcúdia Spain 55 P5
Aldabra Atoll Seychelles 129 E7
Aldabra Islands Seychelles 129 E7
Aldama Chihuahua Mex. 184 D2
Aldama Tamaulipas Mex. 185 F4
Aldan Rus. Fed. 39 M4
Aldan r. Rus. Fed. 39 M3
Aldeburgh U.K. 47 N11
Aldeia Velha Brazil 202 B4
Aldeia Viçosa Angola 127 B7
Alder Creek U.S.A. 177 J2
Alderney i. Channel Is 50 D3
also known as Auregny
Alder Peak U.S.A. 182 C6
Aldershot U.K. 47 L12
Alderson U.S.A. 176 E8
Al Dhafrah reg. U.A.E. 105 F3
Aldie U.S.A. 177 O2
Aledo U.S.A. 174 B3
Aleg Mauritania 124 B3
Alegre Brazil 203 D7
Alegre r. Brazil 203 A9
Alegros Mountain U.S.A. 181 E6
Alejandro Korn Arg. 204 F4
Alekhovshchina Rus. Fed. 43 O1
Aleksandra, Mys hd Rus. Fed. 82 E1
Aleksandra Bekovicha-Cherkasskogo, Zaliv b. Kazakh. 102 B3
Aleksandrapol' Armenia see Gyumri
Aleksandriya Ukr. see Oleksandriya
Aleksandrov Rus. Fed. 43 U4
Aleksandrovac Srbija Yugo. 58 C5
Aleksandrov Gay Rus. Fed. 41 J5
Aleksandrovka Rus. Fed. 41 J6
Aleksandrovo Bulg. 58 F6
Aleksandrovsk Rus. Fed. 40 K4
also known as Aleksandrovskaya
Aleksandrovsk Ukr. see Zaporizhzhya
Aleksandrovskiy Rus. Fed. see Aleksandrovsk

Aleksandrovskoye Stavropol'skiy Kray Rus. Fed. 41 G7
Aleksandrovskoye Stavropol'skiy Kray Rus. Fed. 41 H7
Aleksandrovskoye Tomskaya Oblast' Rus. Fed. 38 H3
Aleksandrovsk-Sakhalinskiy Rus. Fed. 82 F2
Aleksandrów Kujawski Poland 49 P3
Aleksandrów Łódzki Poland 49 Q4
Aleksandry, Zemlya i. Rus. Fed. 38 C1
English form Alexandra Land
Alekseyevka Kazakh. see Akkol'
Alekseyevka Kazakh. 103 I2
Alekseyevka Kazakh. see Terekty
Alekseyevka Belgorodskaya Oblast' Rus. Fed. 41 F6
Alekseyevka Belgorodskaya Oblast' Rus. Fed. 41 F6
Alekseyevka Bryanskaya Oblast' Rus. Fed. 43 N8
Alekseyevskaya Rus. Fed. 41 G6
Aleksin Rus. Fed. 43 S7
Aleksinac Srbija Yugo. 58 C5
Aleksino-Shatur Rus. Fed. 43 U6
Alemsō Iraq 109 O1
'Alem Ketema Eth. 128 C2
'Alem Maya Eth. 128 D2
Além Paraíba Brazil 203 D7
Ålen Norway 44 J3
Alençon France 50 G4
Alenquer Brazil 199 H5
Alentejo reg. Port. 54 C6
Alenuihaha Channel U.S.A. 181 [inset] Z1
Alep Syria see Aleppo
Alépé Côte d'Ivoire 124 E5
Aleppo Syria 109 I1
also known as Halab or Yamkhad; also spelt Alep; historically known as Beroea
Aler r. India 94 C1
Alert Canada 165 M1
Alerta Peru 200 C2
Alert Bay Canada 166 E5
Alès France 51 K8
Aleşd Romania 58 D1
Aleshki Ukr. see Tsyurupyns'k
Aleshnya Rus. Fed. 43 O8
Aleşkirt Turkey see Eleşkirt
Alessandria Italy 56 A4
Alessio Albania see Lezhë
Ålesund Norway 44 I3
also spelt Aalesund
Aletrium Italy see Alatri
Aletschhorn mt. Switz. 51 N6
Aleutian Islands U.S.A. 220 G2
Aleutian Range mts U.S.A. 164 D4
Alevina, Mys c. Rus. Fed. 39 P4
Aleviṣik Turkey see Samandağı
Alexander, Cape Antarctica 222 T2
Alexander, Mount hill Australia 148 C4
Alexander Archipelago is U.S.A. 164 F4
Alexander Bay S. Africa 130 C6
Alexander City U.S.A. 175 C5
Alexander Island Antarctica 222 T2
Alexandra Australia 147 E4
Alexandra r. Australia 149 C3
Alexandra N.Z. 153 D13
Alexandra, Cape S. Georgia 205 [inset]
Alexandra Channel India 95 G3
Alexandra Falls Canada 167 G2
Alexandra Land i. Rus. Fed. see Aleksandry, Zemlya
Alexandreia Greece 58 D8
Alexandretta Turkey see Iskenderun
Alexandria Afgh. see Ghazni
Alexandria B.C. Canada 166 F4
Alexandria Ont. Canada 169 F4

▶Alexandria Egypt 121 F2
4th most populous city in Africa. Also known as Al Iskandarīyah; also spelt El Iskandarīya.
world [cities] ▶▶24–25

Alexandria Romania 58 G5
Alexandria S. Africa 133 K10
Alexandria Turkm. see Mary
Alexandria U.K. 46 H8
Alexandria KY U.S.A. 176 A7
Alexandria LA U.S.A. 179 D6
Alexandria MN U.S.A. 178 D2
Alexandria SD U.S.A. 178 C3
Alexandria VA U.S.A. 177 H7
Alexandria Arachoton Afgh. see Kandahār
Alexandria Areion Afgh. see Herāt
Alexandria Bay U.S.A. 177 J1
Alexandria Prophthasia Afgh. see Farāh
Alexandrina, Lake Australia 146 C3
Alexandroupoli Greece 58 G8
Alexânia Brazil 206 B3
Alexis r. Canada 169 J2
Aley r. Rus. Fed. 103 J1
Aleyak Iran 100 D2
Aleysk Rus. Fed. 103 J1
Al Fallūjah Iraq 109 O4
Alfambra r. Spain 55 J4
Al Fardah Yemen 105 E5
Alfaro Spain 55 J2
Al Farūq well Saudi Arabia 105 D2
Al Farwānīyah Kuwait 107 F5
Al Fas Morocco see Fès
Alfatar Bulg. 58 I5
Al Fathah Iraq 107 E4
Al Fatk Yemen 105 F4
Al Fāw Iraq 107 G5
Al Fayyūm Egypt see El Faiyûm
Al Fāzīḩ Yemen 104 C5
Alfeios r. Greece 59 C11
also spelt Alfiós
Alfeld (Leine) Germany 48 G4
Alfenas Brazil 203 C7
Alfios r. Greece see Alfeios
Alföld plain Hungary R9
Alford U.K. 46 J6
Alfred U.S.A. 177 O2
Alfred and Marie Range hills Australia 151 D5
Alfred M. Terrazas Mex. 185 F4
Alfredo Chaves Brazil 207 M7
Alfredton N.Z. 152 J8
Alfta Sweden 45 L3
Al Fujayrah U.A.E. see Fujairah
Al Fuqahā' Libya 120 C3
Al Furāt r. Iraq/Syria see Euphrates
Alga Kazakh. 102 C2
also spelt Algha
Algabas Kazakh. 102 C2
Algar Spain 54 F8
Ålgård Norway 45 I4
Al Şayrahmi Iraq 107 G3
Algbag India 94 B2
Algeciras Spain 54 F8
Algemesí Spain 55 K5
Algena Eritrea 121 H5

▶Algeria country Africa 123 E4
2nd largest country in Africa.
africa [countries] ▶▶114–117

Algha Kazakh. see Alga
Al Ghāfāt Oman 105 G3
Al Ghardaqah Egypt see Hurghada
Al Ghārith Saudi Arabia 104 C3
Al Ghāṭ Saudi Arabia 105 D2

Al Ghawr plain Jordan/West Bank 108 G7
also spelt El Ghor
Al Ghaydah Yemen 105 F4
Al Ghayl Saudi Arabia 105 D3
Al Ghubr reg. Oman 105 G4
Al Ghuwayr well Qatar 105 E2
Al Ghwaybīyah Saudi Arabia 105 E2

▶Algiers Alg. 123 F1
Capital of Algeria. Also known as Al Jazā'ir or Argel or El Djezair; also spelt Alger; historically known as Icosium.

Alginet Spain 55 K5
Algodón r. Peru 198 D4
Algodor r. Spain 54 H5
Algoma U.S.A. 172 F6
Algona U.S.A. 178 D3
Algonac U.S.A. 173 K8
Algonquin Park Canada 168 E4
Algonquin Provincial Park Canada 173 O5
Algorta (Guecho) Spain 55 I1
Al 'grūd Egypt 108 D7
Älgsjö Sweden 44 L2
Algueirao-Mem Martins Port. 54 B6
Al Habakah well Saudi Arabia 107 E4
Al Ḩabbānīyah Iraq 107 E4
Al Ḩabbānīyah, Hawr l. Iraq 107 E4
Al Ḩadaqah well Saudi Arabia 104 D1
Al Ḩaḏbah reg. Saudi Arabia 104 C3
Al Ḩadd Bahrain 105 E2
Al Ḩaddār Saudi Arabia 105 D3
Al Ḩadhālīl plat. Saudi Arabia 107 E4
Al Ḩadīthah Iraq 107 E4
Al Ḩadīthah Saudi Arabia 107 D4
Al Ḩadr Iraq see Hatra
Al Ḩafār Saudi Arabia 104 C1
Al Ḩaffah Syria 108 H2
Al Haggounia W. Sahara 122 B4
Al Ḩā'ir Saudi Arabia 105 D3
Al Hajar Oman 105 G3
Al Hajar al Gharbī mts Oman 105 G2
Al Hajar ash Sharqī mts Oman 105 G3
Al Ḩajr Yemen 105 D4
Al Ḩallāniyah i. Oman 105 G4
Alhama r. Spain 55 J3
Al Ḩamād plain Asia 98 B3
Al Ḩamdānīyah al Ḩamrā' plat. Libya 120 A2
Alhama de Granada Spain 54 H7
Alhama de Murcia Spain 55 J7
Al Ḩāmī Yemen 105 E5
Alhambra U.S.A. 182 G7
Alhamilla, Sierra hills Spain 55 I8
Al Ḩammām Iraq 107 G5
Al Ḩammām Syria 109 L2
Al Ḩanākīyah Saudi Arabia 104 C2
Al Ḩanīsh al Kabīr i. Yemen 104 C5
Al Ḩaniyah esc. Iraq 107 E5
Al Ḩaqlānīyah Iraq 109 N3
Al Ḩaqū Saudi Arabia 104 C4
Al Ḩariq Saudi Arabia 105 D3
Al Ḩarrah reg. Saudi Arabia 107 D4
Al Ḩarūj al Aswad hills Libya 120 C3
Al Ḩasā reg. Saudi Arabia 105 D2
Al Ḩasakah Syria 109 L1
Al Ḩasakah governorate Syria 109 L1
Al Ḩasanī i. Saudi Arabia 104 B2
Al Hāshimīyah Iraq 107 F4
Al Ḩasī i. Saudi Arabia 105 D3
Al Ḩāsikīyah i. Oman 105 G4
Al Ḩaswah reg. Iraq 109 P5
Al Ḩatīfah plain Saudi Arabia 105 D2
Al Ḩawāyā des. Saudi Arabia 104 C4
Al Ḩawī salt pan Saudi Arabia 109 J8
Al Ḩawīyah Iraq 109 O2
Al Ḩawīyah Saudi Arabia 104 C3
Al Ḩawrā Yemen 105 D5
Al Ḩawtah reg. Saudi Arabia 104 C4
Al Ḩayy Iraq 107 F4
Al Ḩayyānīyah waterhole Saudi Arabia 109 N9
Al Hazm Saudi Arabia 104 B1
Al Hazm al-Jawf Yemen 104 D4
Alheit S. Africa 132 E6
Al Ḩibāk des. Saudi Arabia 105 F4
Al Ḩillah Iraq see Hillah
Al Ḩillah governorate Iraq 109 O3
Al Ḩilwah Saudi Arabia 105 D3
Al Ḩimārah well Saudi Arabia 105 E2
Al Hindīyah Iraq 107 F4
Al Ḩinnāh Saudi Arabia 105 E2
Al Ḩinw mt. Saudi Arabia 107 D5
Al Ḩirrah well Saudi Arabia 105 E3
Al Ḩishwah hills Yemen 105 D4
Al Ḩismā plain Saudi Arabia 104 A1
Al Ḩişn Jordan 108 G5
also spelt Husn
Al Ḩişn Yemen 105 D5
Al Hoceima Morocco 122 E2
formerly known as Villa Sanjurjo
Alhuampa Arg. 204 E2
Al Ḩudaydah Yemen see Hodeidah
Al Ḩudaydah governorate Yemen 104 C5
Al Ḩudūd ash Shamālīyah prov. Saudi Arabia 104 C1
Al Ḩufayrah well Saudi Arabia 105 D5
Al Ḩufrah Saudi Arabia 104 B1
Al Ḩufūf Saudi Arabia 105 E2
also spelt Hofuf
Al Ḩulayq al Kabir hills Libya 120 B1
Al Ḩumayshah Yemen 105 D5
Al Ḩumrah reg. U.A.E. 105 F3
Al Ḩunayy Saudi Arabia 105 D2
Al Ḩusayfīn Oman 105 F2
Al Ḩuthul hills Saudi Arabia 109 K8
Al Ḩuwaymī Yemen 105 D5
Al Ḩuwayyit Saudi Arabia 104 C2
Al Ḩuwwah Saudi Arabia 105 D3
Ali China 89 B5
also known as Shiquanhe
'Alīābād Afgh. 101 G2
'Alīābād Golestan Iran 100 C2
'Alīābād Hormozgan Iran 100 C4
'Alīābād Khorāsān Iran 100 D3
'Alīābād Khorāsān Iran 101 E3
'Alīābād Kordestān Iran 100 A3
'Alīābād Qom Iran 100 B3
Aliağa Turkey 106 A3
Aliakmonas r. Greece 59 C8
Aliakmonas, Limni l. Greece 59 C8
Aliambata East Timor 75 C5
Aliartos Greece 59 E10
Alibag India 94 B2
Alibey Adası i. Turkey 59 H9
Alibunar Vojvodina, Srbija Yugo. 58 B3
Alicante Spain 55 K6
also spelt Alacant
Alice Australia 149 D2
Alice watercourse Australia 149 D4
Alice U.S.A. 179 C7
Alice, Punta pt Italy 57 J9
Alice Arm Canada 166 D4
Alicedale S. Africa 133 K10
Alice Springs Australia 148 B4
Alice Town Bahamas 186 D1
Aliceville U.S.A. 175 B5
Alichur Tajik. 101 H2
Alichur r. Tajik. 101 H2
Alichuri Janubí, Qatorkühi mts Tajik. 101 H2
also known as Yuzhno-Alichurskiy, Khrebet

Alicia Phil. 74 B5
Alick Creek r. Australia 149 D4
Alicoto Fr. Guiana 199 H4
Alicudi, Isola i. Isole Lipari Italy 57 G10
Al 'Idd U.A.E. 105 F3
Al 'Idwah well Saudi Arabia 104 C2
Aliero Nigeria 125 G3
Alife Italy 56 G7
Aligarh India 96 C3
Aligūdarz Iran 100 B3
Alihe China 85 I1
also known as Oroqen Zizhiqi
Alijiq, Kūh-e mt. Iran 100 B3
'Ali Kheyl Afgh. 101 G3
Al Ikhwan is Yemen 105 F5
English form The Brothers
Alima r. Congo 126 C5
Al Imām Iraq 109 N5
Al Imārāt al 'Arabīyah al Muttaḩidah country Asia see United Arab Emirates
Alimia i. Greece 59 I12
Alindao Cent. Afr. Rep. 126 D3
Alingar r. Afgh. 101 G3
Alingsås Sweden 45 K4
Alintale well Saudi Arabia 104 C2
Aliova r. Turkey 106 B3
Alipur India 94 C1
Alipur Pak. 101 G4
Alipur Duar India 97 F4
Aliquippa U.S.A. 176 E5
Alirajpur India 96 B5
Ali Sabieh Djibouti 128 D2
Al Iskandarīyah Egypt see Alexandria
Al Iskandarīyah Iraq 109 O4
Aliskerovo Rus. Fed. 39 Q3
Al Ismā'īlīyah Egypt see Ismâ'ilîya
Aliste r. Spain 54 F3
Alitāive mt. Sweden 44 L2
Al Ittiḩab Yemen see Madīnat ash Sha'b
Aliveri Greece 59 F10
Aliwal North S. Africa 133 K7
Alix Canada 167 H4
Aliyah r. Ukr. 58 L3
Al Jafr Jordan 108 H7
Al Jaghbūb Libya 120 E2
Al Jahrah Kuwait 107 F5
Al Jamalīyah Qatar 105 E2
Al Jarāwi well Saudi Arabia 109 J7
Al Jarf Saudi Arabia 104 C3
Al Jawārah well Oman 105 G4
Al Jawb reg. Saudi Arabia 105 E3
Al Jawf Libya 120 D3
Al Jawf al Jawf Saudi Arabia 107 D5
Al Jawf prov. Saudi Arabia 104 B1
Al Jawf governorate Yemen 105 D4
Al Jawlān hills Syria see Golan
Al Jawsh Libya 120 A1
Al Jaza'ir Alg. see Algiers
Al Jaza'ir reg. Iraq/Syria 109 K1
Alj Beyk Iran 100 C2
Aljezur Port. 54 C7
Al Jībān reg. Saudi Arabia 105 E2
Al Jid well Iraq 109 K5
Al Jilh esc. Saudi Arabia 104 D2
Al Jisr Iraq 109 J2
Al Jithāmīyah Saudi Arabia 104 C2
Al Jīzah Egypt see Giza
Al Ju'ayfirah Saudi Arabia 105 D2
Al Jubayl Saudi Arabia 105 E2
Al Jubayl hills Saudi Arabia 105 D3
Al Jubaylah Saudi Arabia 105 D2
Aljucén r. Spain 54 E5
Al Jufra Oasis Libya 120 B2
Al Julaydah well Saudi Arabia 105 D1
Al Jumūm Saudi Arabia 104 B3
Al Junaynah Saudi Arabia 104 C2
Al Jurayd i. Saudi Arabia 105 E2
Al Jurayfah Saudi Arabia 105 D2
Al Jurayr well Saudi Arabia 105 E2
Al Jurdhawīyah Saudi Arabia 104 D2
Al Juwayf depr. Syria 109 J4
Al Juwayfah well Saudi Arabia 105 E3
Al Kahfah Saudi Arabia 104 C2
Al Kalbān Oman 105 G3
Alkali Flat salt flat NV U.S.A. 182 G1
Alkali Flat salt flat NV U.S.A. 183 G3
Alkaliya r. Ukr. 58 L3
Alkamari Niger 125 H3
Al Kāmil Oman 105 G3
Al Karābilah Iraq 109 M3
Al Karak Jordan 108 G6
also known as Karak
Al Karāmah Jordan 108 G6
Al Karmah Iraq 109 O4
Al Kāzimīyah Iraq 107 F4
also known as Kādhimain
Al Khābūrah Oman 105 G3
Al Khadrā' well Saudi Arabia 104 C1
Al Khafaq well Saudi Arabia 105 D2
Al Khafqān salt pan Saudi Arabia 104 C3
Al Khalaf Saudi Arabia 104 C2
Al Khalīl West Bank see Hebron
Al Khālīf Saudi Arabia 104 D2
Al Khalūf Iraq 107 F4
Al Khamāsīn Saudi Arabia 104 C3
Al Khārijah Egypt see El Khârga
Al Kharj Saudi Arabia 105 D3
Al Kharkhayr oasis Saudi Arabia 105 E4
Al Kharrārah Qatar 105 E2
Al Khaṣab Oman 105 G2
Al Khasfah well Saudi Arabia 105 D5
Al Khāşirah Saudi Arabia 104 C3
Al-Khatam reg. U.A.E. 105 F3
Al Khaṭīnī vol. Saudi Arabia 109 J4
Al Khawkhah Yemen 104 C5
Al Khawr Qatar 105 E2
Al Khawtamah i. Yemen 104 C5
Al Khiṣah well Saudi Arabia 105 E2
Al Khizāmī well Saudi Arabia 105 D2
Al Khobar Saudi Arabia 105 E2
Al Khubrah Saudi Arabia 104 C3
Al Khuff reg. Saudi Arabia 104 C2
Al Khufrah Saudi Arabia 120 D3
Al Khufrah Oasis Libya 120 D3
Al Khums Libya 120 B1
also spelt Homs
Al Khunfah sand area Saudi Arabia 104 B1
Al Khunn Saudi Arabia 105 E3
Al Khuwayr Qatar 105 E2
Al Kidan well Saudi Arabia 105 E3
Al Kifl Iraq 107 F4
Al Kir'ānah Qatar 105 E2
Al Kūfah Iraq 107 F4
Al Kufla well Saudi Arabia 105 D2
Al Kumayt Iraq 107 G4
Al Kūrā lava field Saudi Arabia 104 C3
Al Kuşūr hills Saudi Arabia 105 D5
Al Kūt Iraq 107 F4
also known as Kut-al-Imara
Al Kuwayt country Asia see Kuwait
Al Kuwayt Kuwait see Kuwait
Al Labbah plain Saudi Arabia 107 E5
Allada Benin 125 F5
Al Lādhiqīyah Syria see Latakia
Al Lādhiqīyah governorate Syria 108 G2
Allagadda India 94 C3
Allahabad India 97 D4
Al Lajā lava field Syria 109 H5
Allakh-Yun' Rus. Fed. 39 N3
Allanmyo Myanmar 78 A4
Allanridge S. Africa 133 K4
Allapalli India 94 D2
'Allāqi, Wādi el watercourse Egypt 121 G4
Allardt U.S.A. 176 A9
Allariz Spain 54 D2
Al Latakīyah well Yemen 105 E4

Alldays S. Africa 131 F4
Allegan U.S.A. 172 H8
Allegany U.S.A. 176 F3
Alleghe Italy 56 E2
Allegheny r. U.S.A. 176 F5
Allegheny Mountains U.S.A. 176 C9
Allegheny Reservoir U.S.A. 176 F4
Allemanskraaldam resr S. Africa 133 L5
Allen Phil. 74 B3
Allen, Lough r. Rep. of Ireland 47 D9
Allen, Mount U.S.A. 166 F4
Allen, Mount N.Z. 153 B15
Allendale U.S.A. 175 D5
Allende Coahuila Mex. 185 E2
Allende Nuevo León Mex. 185 E3
Allendorf (Lumda) Germany 51 O2
Allenford Canada 173 L6
Allenstein Poland see Olsztyn
Allensville OH U.S.A. 176 C6
Allensville PA U.S.A. 176 H5
Allentown U.S.A. 177 J5
Alleppey India see Alappuzha
Aller r. Germany 48 H3
Alliance NE U.S.A. 178 B3
Alliance OH U.S.A. 176 D5
Al Lībīyah country Africa see Libya
Allier r. France 51 J6
Al Lifīyah well Iraq 107 E5
Alligator Point Australia 149 D3
Al Lihābah well Saudi Arabia 105 D2
Allikher India 94 C3
Allinge-Sandvig Denmark 45 K5
Al Liṣāfah well Saudi Arabia 105 D2
Al Lisān pen. Jordan 108 G6
Alliston Canada 173 N6
Al Lith Saudi Arabia 104 C3
Al Liwā' oasis U.A.E. 105 F3
Alloa U.K. 46 I7
Allonnes Pays de la Loire France 50 G5
Allonnes Pays de la Loire France 50 G5
Allora Australia 147 G2
Allouez U.S.A. 172 E4
Allschwil Switz. 51 N5
Allu Indon. 75 A4
Al Luḩayyah Yemen 104 C5
Allumettes, Île aux i. Canada 173 P5
Allur India 94 D3
Alluru Kottapatnam India 94 D3
Al Lussuf well Iraq 107 E5
Alma Canada 169 G4
formerly known as St-Joseph-d'Alma
Alma KS U.S.A. 178 C4
Alma MI U.S.A. 173 I7
Alma NE U.S.A. 178 C3
Al Ma'ānīyah Iraq 107 E5
Alma-Ata Kazakh. see Almaty
Alma-Ata Oblast admin. div. Kazakh. see Almatinskaya Oblast'
Almaceles Spain 55 L3
Al Machmin waterhole Iraq 109 N6
Almada Port. 54 B6
Al Madāfi' plat. Saudi Arabia 104 B1
Al Madā'in Iraq 109 P4
Al Ma'danīyah well Saudi Arabia 104 C1
Al Maḍāyā Saudi Arabia 104 C4
Almaden Australia 149 E3
Almadén Spain 54 G5
Almadina Brazil 207 N1
Al Madīnah Iraq 107 F5
Al Madīnah Saudi Arabia see Medina
Al Madīnah prov. Saudi Arabia 104 B2
Al Mafraq Jordan 108 H5
also spelt Mafraq
Al Maghrib country Africa see Morocco
Almagro r. Phil. 74 C4
Al Maḩākīk reg. Saudi Arabia 105 D3
Al Maḩāwīl Iraq 109 P5
Al Mahbas W. Sahara 122 C4
Al Maḩḏam Saudi Arabia 104 C3
Al Maḩīā depr. Saudi Arabia 104 D1
Al Maḩmūdīyah Iraq 107 F4
Al Mahrah governorate Yemen 105 E4
Al Mahrah reg. Yemen 105 E5
Al Maḩwīt Yemen 104 C5
Al Maḩwīt governorate Yemen 104 C5
Al Majma'ah Saudi Arabia 105 D2
Almalik Uzbek. 103 G4
also spelt Olmaliq
Al Manādir reg. Oman 105 F3
Al Manāmah Bahrain see Manama
Al Manjūr well Saudi Arabia 105 D3
Almanor, Lake U.S.A. 182 C1
Almansa Spain 55 J6
Al Manşūrah Egypt see El Mansûra
Almanzor mt. Spain 54 F4
Almanzora r. Spain 55 J7
Al Ma'qil Iraq 107 F5
Almar r. Spain 54 F4
Al Mariyyah U.A.E. 105 F3
Al Marj Libya 120 D1
Almas r. Romania 58 E1
Almaş, Rio das r. Brazil 206 D1
Al Masana'a Oman 105 G3
Almatinskaya Oblast' admin. div. Kazakh. 103 I3
English form Almaty Oblast; also known as Almaty Oblysy; formerly known as Alma-Ata Oblast
Al Matmarfag W. Sahara 122 B4

▶Almaty Kazakh. 103 I4
Former capital of Kazakhstan. English form Alma-Ata; formerly known as Vernyy.

Almaty Oblast admin. div. Kazakh. see Almatinskaya Oblast'
Almaty Oblysy admin. div. Kazakh. see Almatinskaya Oblast'
Al Mawşil Iraq see Mosul
Al Mayādīn Syria 109 L3
Almazán Spain 55 I3
Almeida Port. 54 E4
Almeirim Brazil 199 H5
Almeirim Port. 54 C5
Almelo Neth. 48 D3
Almenara Brazil 202 D6
Almenara, Sierra de hills Spain 55 J7
Almendra, Embalse de resr Spain 54 E3
Almendralejo Spain 54 E6
Almere Neth. 48 C3
Almería Spain 55 I8
Almería, Golfo de b. Spain 55 I8
Almetievsk Rus. Fed. see Al'met'yevsk
Al'met'yevsk Rus. Fed. 40 J5
Älmhult Sweden 45 K4
Al Midhnab Saudi Arabia 104 D2
Al Mijrād reg. Saudi Arabia 105 D2
Almina, Punta pt Spain 54 F9
Al Mindak Saudi Arabia 104 C3
Al Mintirib Oman 105 G3
Almirantazgo, Seno del sea chan. Chile 205 C9
Almirante Panama 186 C5
Al-Mirfa U.A.E. 105 F2
Almirós Greece see Almyros
Al Mish'āb Saudi Arabia 105 E1
Al Mishrafah Syria 109 H4
Almodôvar Port. 54 C7
Almodovar del Campo Spain 54 G5
Almoloya Mex. 185 F5
Almont U.S.A. 173 J8
Almonte Canada 173 Q5
Almonte Spain 54 E7
Almonte r. Spain 54 E5

Almora India 96 C3
Almoradí Spain 55 K6
Almorox Spain 54 G4
Al Mota well Niger 125 G3
Almoustarat Mali 125 F2
Al Mu'ayzīlah hill Saudi Arabia 109 J8
Al Mubarrez Saudi Arabia 105 E2
Al Muḍairib Oman 105 G3
Al Mudawwarah Jordan 108 H8
Al Muharraq Bahrain 105 E2
Al Muḥtaṭab depr. Saudi Arabia 109 H9
Al Mukallā Yemen see Mukalla
Al Mukhā Yemen see Mocha
Al Mukhaylī Libya 120 D1
Al Munbaṭiḥ des. Saudi Arabia 105 E3
Al Mundafan pass Saudi Arabia 105 D4
Almuñécar Spain 54 H8 historically known as Sexi
Al Muqdādīyah Iraq 107 F4
Al Murayr well Saudi Arabia 109 K7
Al Mūrītānīyah country Africa see Mauritania
Al Murūt well Saudi Arabia 107 D5
Almus Turkey 107 D2 also known as Tozanlı
Al Musannāh ridge Saudi Arabia 105 D1
Al Musayjīd Saudi Arabia 104 B2
Al Musayyib Iraq 109 P5
Al Muthannā governorate Iraq 107 F5
Al Muwayh Saudi Arabia 104 C3
Al Muwayliḥ Saudi Arabia 104 A2
Almyropotamos Greece 59 F10
Almyros Greece 59 D9 also spelt Almirós
Almyrou, Ormos b. Greece 59 F13
Alness U.K. 46 H6
Alnwick U.K. 46 K8

▶Alofi Niue 145 I3
Capital of Niue.
oceania [countries] ▶ 138–139

Alofi, Île i. Wallis and Futuna Is 145 H3
Aloi Uganda 128 B4
Aloja Latvia 42 F4
Alol' Rus. Fed. 43 K5
Alolya r. Rus. Fed. 43 J5
Along India 97 G3
Alonnisos i. Greece 59 E9
Alonso r. Brazil 206 B11
Alor i. Indon. 75 C5
Alor, Kepulauan is Indon. 75 C5
Alor, Selat sea chan. Indon. 75 B5
Álora Spain 54 G8
Alor Setar Malaysia 76 C1 also spelt Alur Setar; formerly spelt Alor Star
Alor Star Malaysia see Alor Setar
Alosno Spain 54 D7
Alost Belgium see Aalst
Alot India 96 B5
Alota Bol. 200 D5
Alotau P.N.G. 149 F1
Aloysius, Mount Australia 151 E5
Alpachiri Arg. 204 E5
Alpagut Turkey 59 J9
Alpaugh U.S.A. 182 E6
Alpena U.S.A. 173 J5
Alpercatas, Serra das hills Brazil 202 C3
Alpha Australia 149 E4
Alpha S. Africa 133 P4
Alpha U.S.A. 172 C9
Alpi Apuane, Parco Naturale delle nature res. Italy 56 C4
Alpine AZ U.S.A. 183 O8
Alpine CA U.S.A. 183 H9
Alpine NY U.S.A. 177 I3
Alpine TX U.S.A. 179 B6
Alpine WY U.S.A. 180 E4
Alpine National Park Australia 147 E4
Alpinópolis Brazil 206 G7
▶Alps mts Europe 51 M7
europe [landscapes] ▶ 30–31
Al Qā' Saudi Arabia 104 C3
Al Qā'āmīyāt reg. Saudi Arabia 105 D4
Al Qaddāḥīyah Libya 120 B2
Al Qādisīyah governorate Iraq 107 F5 formerly known as Ad Dīwānīyah
Al Qadmūs Syria 108 H2
Al Qaffāy i. U.A.E. 105 F2
Al Qafrah Yemen 105 D5
Al Qāhirah Egypt see Cairo
Al Qahmah Saudi Arabia 104 C4
Al Qā'im Iraq 109 L3
Al Qā'iyah Saudi Arabia 104 C2
Al Qā'iyah well Saudi Arabia 105 D2
Al Qal'a Beni Hammad tourist site Alg. 123 G2
Al Qalībah Saudi Arabia 104 B1
Al Qāmishlī Syria 107 E3
Al Qar'ah well Saudi Arabia 105 D2
Al Qar'ah lava field Syria 109 H5
Al Qarn Yemen 105 D5
Al Qaryatayn Syria 109 I3
Al Qaṣīm prov. Saudi Arabia 104 C2
Al Qaṣr Saudi Arabia 104 C2
Al Qaṭīf Saudi Arabia 105 E2
Al Qaṭn Yemen 105 E5
Al Qaṭrānah Jordan 108 H6
Al Qaṭrūn Libya 120 B3
Al Qawnas reg. Saudi Arabia 105 D3
Al Qayṣūmah Saudi Arabia 105 D1
Al Qāyṣūmah well Saudi Arabia 107 E5
Al Qiblīyah i. Oman 105 G4
Al Qulayyibah waterhole Saudi Arabia 109 N9
Al Qumur country Africa see Comoros
Al Qunayṭirah Syria 108 G4
Al Qunayṭirah governorate Syria 108 G4
Al Qunfidhah Saudi Arabia 104 C4
Al Qurayn Saudi Arabia 104 C2
Al Qurayni oasis Saudi Arabia 105 F3
Al Qurayyah Saudi Arabia 104 C2
Al Qurayyah U.A.E. 105 G2
Al Qurayyāt Saudi Arabia 107 D5
Al Qurnah Iraq 107 F5
Al Quwārah Saudi Arabia 104 C2
Al Quwayi' Saudi Arabia 105 D3
Al Quwayīyah Saudi Arabia 105 D2
Al Quwayrah Jordan 108 G8
Al Quzah Yemen 105 E5
Al Rabbād reg. U.A.E. 105 F3
Alrar Est Alg. 123 H3
Alroy Downs Australia 148 C3
Alsace admin. reg. France 51 N4
Alsace, Plaine d' valley France 51 N5
Al Samha U.A.E. 100 C5
Al Samit well Iraq 107 E5
Alsask Canada 167 I5
Alsek r. U.S.A. 164 F4
Alsfeld Germany 48 G5
Al'skiy Khrebet mt. Rus. Fed. 82 E1
Alston U.K. 47 J9
Alstonville Australia 147 G2
Alsuku Nigeria 125 H5
Alsunga Latvia 42 C5
Alsviķi Latvia 42 H4
Alta Norway 44 M1
Alta, Mount N.Z. 153 C12
Altadena U.S.A. 182 F7
Altaelva r. Norway 44 M1
Altafjorden sea chan. Norway 44 M1
Alta Floresta Brazil 201 F2
Alta Gracia Arg. 204 D3
Alta Gracia Nicaragua 186 B5
Altai Mountains Asia 88 D1 also known as Altayskiy Khrebet
Altamaha r. U.S.A. 175 D6
Altamira Amazonas Brazil 199 E4
Altamira Pará Brazil 199 H5
Altamira Chile 204 C2
Altamira Col. 198 C4
Altamira Costa Rica 186 B5
Altamira Mex. 185 F4
Altamira, Cuevas de tourist site Spain 54 G1
Altamira, Sierra de mts Spain 54 F5
Altamonte Springs City U.S.A. 175 D6
Altamura Italy 57 I8
Altan Rus. Fed. 85 F1
Altanbulag Mongolia 85 E2
Altan Emel China 85 H1 also known as Xin Barag Youqi
Altan Ovoo mt. China/Mongolia 84 A2
Altan Shiret China 85 F4 also known as Ejin Horo Qi; also spelt Altan Xiret
Altan Xiret China see Altan Shiret
Alta Paraiso de Goiás Brazil 202 C5
Altapirire Venez. 199 E2
Altar Mex. 184 C2
Altar r. Mex. 181 E7
Altar, Desierto de des. Mex. 184 B1
Altata Mex. 184 D3
Altavista U.S.A. 176 F8
Altay China 84 A2
Altay Mongolia 84 C2
Altay, Respublika aut. rep. Rus. Fed. 84 A1 English form Altay Republic; formerly known as Gorno-Altayskaya Avtonomnaya Oblast' or Gornyy Altay
Altay Kray admin. div. Rus. Fed. see Altayskiy Kray
Altay Republic aut. rep. Rus. Fed. see Altay, Respublika
Altayskiy Khrebet mts Asia see Altai Mountains
Altayskiy Kray admin. div. Rus. Fed. 88 C1 English form Altay Kray
Altayskiy Zapovednik nature res. Rus. Fed. 84 A1
Altdorf Switz. 51 O6
Altea Spain 55 K6
Alteidet Norway 44 M1
Altenburg Germany 49 J5
Altenkirchen (Westerwald) Germany 48 E5
Altenqoke China 84 B4
Alter do Chão Brazil 199 H5
Alter do Chão Port. 54 D5
Altevatnet l. Norway 44 L1
Altin Köprü Iraq 107 F4
Altınoluk Turkey 59 H9
Altinópolis Brazil 206 F8
Altınova Turkey 59 H9
Altınözü Turkey 108 H1
Altıntaş Turkey 106 B3
Altınyaka Turkey 108 B1
Altiplano plain Bol. 200 C4
Altmühltal park Germany 48 I7
Altnaharra U.K. 46 H5
Alto U.S.A. 172 H8
Alto Araguaia Brazil 203 A6
Alto Cedro Cuba 186 E2
Alto Chicapa Angola 127 C7
Alto Cruz mt. Spain 55 I3
Alto Cuchumatanes mts Guat. 185 H6
Alto de Cabezas mt. Spain 55 H2
Alto de Covelo pass Spain 54 D2
Alto del Moncayo mt. Spain 55 J3
Alto de Pencoso hills Arg. 204 D4
Alto do Trevim mt. Port. 54 C4
Alto Garças Brazil 202 A6
Alto Ligonha Moz. 131 H2
Alto Madidi, Parque Nacional nat. park Bol. 200 C3
Alto Molócuè Moz. 131 H2
Alton U.K. 47 L12
Alton IL U.S.A. 174 B4
Alton KY U.S.A. 176 A7
Alton MO U.S.A. 174 B4
Alton NH U.S.A. 177 N2
Altona B.C. Canada 166 F3
Altona Man. Canada 167 L5
Alto Nevado mt. Chile 205 B7
Altoona PA U.S.A. 176 G5
Altoona WI U.S.A. 172 B6
Alto Pacajá r. Brazil 202 B2
Alto Parnaíba Brazil 202 C4
Alto Purús r. Peru 200 C2
Alto Rio Doce Brazil 207 J8
Alto Río Senguerr Arg. 205 C7
Altos Brazil 202 D3
Altos de Chacaya Chile 200 C4
Altos de Chinchilla mts Spain 55 J6
Alto Sucuriú Brazil 206 A6
Altotero mt. Spain 55 H2
Altotonga Mex. 185 F5
Altötting Germany 49 J7
Alto Uruguai Brazil 203 A8
Altukhovo Rus. Fed. 43 P9
Altun Ha tourist site Belize 185 H5
Altun Shan mt. China 84 B4
Altun Shan mts China 84 B4 also known as Astin Tag
Alturas U.S.A. 180 B4
Altus U.S.A. 179 C5
Altynkul' Uzbek. 102 D4 also spelt Oltinkŭl
Altyn-Topkan Tajik. see Oltintopkan
Alu Estonia 42 F2
Alua Moz. 131 H2
Al 'Ubaydī Iraq 109 M3
Al Ubaylah Saudi Arabia 105 E3
Alucra Turkey 107 D2
Al 'Udayliyah Saudi Arabia 105 E2
Al Udayn Yemen 104 C5
Alūksne Latvia 42 I4
Alūksnes l. Latvia 42 I4
Al 'Ulā Saudi Arabia 104 B2
Al 'Ulayb reg. Yemen 105 D5
Alūm Iran 100 B3
Alum Bridge U.S.A. 176 E6
Alum Creek Lake U.S.A. 176 C5
Alunda Sweden 45 L3
Aluniş Romania 58 F2
Alupka Ukr. 106 C1
Al 'Uqaylah Libya 120 C2
Al 'Uqaylah Saudi Arabia see An Nabk
Al 'Uqayr Saudi Arabia 105 E2
Al Uqṣur Egypt see Luxor
Alur India 94 C3
Al Urayq des. Saudi Arabia 107 D5
Al 'Urdun country Asia see Jordan
Alur Setar Malaysia see Alor Setar
Alushta Ukr. 41 E7
Al Uthaylī Saudi Arabia 104 B1
Aluva India see Alwaye
Al 'Uwayjā' well Saudi Arabia 105 D3
Al 'Uwayjā' well Saudi Arabia 105 E3
Al 'Uwaynah well Saudi Arabia 105 E2
Al 'Uwaynāt Libya 120 E4
Al 'Uwaynāt Libya 120 A3
Al 'Uwaynidhiyah i. Saudi Arabia 104 B2
Al 'Uwayqīlah Saudi Arabia 107 E5
Al Uyainah Saudi Arabia 105 D2
Al 'Uyaynah well Saudi Arabia 108 H9
Al 'Uzaym Saudi Arabia 104 C2
Al 'Uzayr Iraq 107 F5
Alva r. Port. 54 C4
Alva U.S.A. 178 C4
Alvand, Kūh-e mt. Iran 100 B3
Alvão, Parque Natural do nature res. Port. 54 D3
Alvarado Mex. 185 G5
Alvarado U.S.A. 179 C5
Alvarães Brazil 199 E5
Álvares Machado Brazil 206 B9
Älvdalen Sweden 45 K3
Alvdalen valley Sweden 45 K3
Alvedro airport Spain 54 C1
Alverca Port. 54 B6
Alvesta Sweden 45 K4
Alvin TX U.S.A. 179 D6
Alvin WI U.S.A. 172 E5
Alvinópolis Brazil 207 J7
Älvkarleby Sweden 45 L3
Älvsbyn Sweden 44 M2
Al Wafrah Kuwait 107 F5 also spelt Wafra
Al Wajh Saudi Arabia 104 B2
Al Wakrah Qatar 105 E2
Al Wannān Saudi Arabia 105 E2
Al Waqbá well Saudi Arabia 105 D1
Alwar India 96 C4
Al Wari'ah Saudi Arabia 105 D2
Al Waṭīyah Libya 120 A1
Alwaye India 94 C4 also known as Aluva
Al Widyān plat. Iraq/Saudi Arabia 107 E4
Al Wigh Libya 120 B3
Al Wigh, Ramlat des. Libya 120 C3
Al Wusayl Qatar 105 E2
Al Wusayṭ well Saudi Arabia 104 D1
Al Wusṭá admin. reg. Oman 105 G3
Alxa Youqi China see Ehen Hudag
Alxa Zuoqi China see Bayan Hot
Al Yamāmah Saudi Arabia 105 D2
Alyangula Australia 148 C2
Al Yāsāt i. U.A.E. 105 E2
Alyawarra Aboriginal Land res. Australia 148 B4
Alytus Lith. 42 F7
Al Yūsufīyah Iraq 109 P4
Alzada U.S.A. 178 A2
Alzey Germany 48 F6
Alzira Spain 55 K5 also spelt Alcira
Amacayacu, Parque Nacional nat. park Col. 198 D5
Åmådalen Sweden 45 K3
Amadeus, Lake salt flat Australia 148 A5
Amadi Sudan 128 A3
Amadjuak Lake Canada 165 L3
Amadora Port. 54 B6
Amadror plain Alg. 123 G4
Amaga Col. 198 C3
Amagi Japan 91 B8
Amahai Indon. 75 D3
Amakusa-Kami-shima i. Japan 91 B8
Amakusa-nada b. Japan 91 A8
Amakusa-Shimo-shima i. Japan 91 B8
Amal Oman 105 F4
Åmål Sweden 45 K4
Amalaoulaou well Mali 125 F3
Amalapuram India 94 D2
Amalat r. Rus. Fed. 81 J2
Amalia S. Africa 133 J4
Amaliada Greece 59 C11
Amalner India 96 B5
Amamapare Indon. 73 I7
Amambaí Brazil 201 G5
Amambaí, Serra de hills Brazil/Para. 201 G5
Amami-Ō-shima i. Japan 81 L7
Amami-shotō is Japan 81 L7
Amamula Dem. Rep. Congo 126 E5
Åmån r. Sweden 45 K3
Amanã, Lago l. Brazil 199 E5
Amanbidji Aboriginal Land res. Australia 148 A3
Amanda U.S.A. 176 C6
Amandola Italy 56 F6
Amangel'dy Aktyubinskaya Oblast' Kazakh. 102 D2 also spelt Amankeldi
Amangel'dy Kustanayskaya Oblast' Kazakh. 103 F2 also spelt Amankeldi
Amankaragay Kazakh. 103 F1 also spelt Amanqaraghay
Amankeldi Kazakh. see Amangel'dy
Amankeldi Kazakh. see Amangel'dy
Amanotkel' Kazakh. 103 E3
Amanqaraghay Kazakh. see Amankaragay
Amantea Italy 57 I9
Amanzimtoti S. Africa 133 O7
Amapá Brazil 200 C2
Amapá state Brazil 199 I4
Amapala Hond. 186 B4
Amapari r. Brazil 199 I4
Amara Abu Sin Sudan 121 G6
Amaradia r. Romania 58 E4
Amaral Ferrador Brazil 203 A9
Amarante Brazil 202 D3
Amarante do Maranhão Brazil 202 C3
Amarapura Myanmar 78 B3
Amaravati r. India 94 C4
Amardalay Mongolia 85 E2
Amargosa Brazil 202 E5
Amargosa watercourse U.S.A. 181 C5
Amargosa Desert U.S.A. 183 H5
Amargosa Range mts U.S.A. 183 H5
Amargosa Valley U.S.A. 183 H5
Amargura Island Tonga see Fonualei
Amarillo U.S.A. 179 B5
Amarkantak India 97 D5
Amaro, Monte mt. Italy 56 G6
Amarpur India 97 F5
Amarwara India 96 C5
Amasa U.S.A. 172 E4
Amasia Turkey see Amasya
Amasine W. Sahara 122 B4
Amasra Turkey 106 C2
Amassine well Mali 125 F2
Amasya Turkey 106 C2 historically known as Amasia
Amata Australia 148 A5
Amataurá Brazil 199 D5
Amatenango Mex. 185 G5
Amatikulu S. Africa 133 P6
Amatique, Bahía de b. Guat. 185 H6
Amatlán de Cañas Mex. 184 D4

▶Amazon r. S. America 202 B1
Longest river in South America and 2nd in the world. Also spelt Amazonas.
southamerica [landscapes] ▶ 190–191
southamerica [contrasts] ▶ 194–195

Amazon, Mouths of the Brazil 202 B1
Amazon, Source of the Peru 200 C3
Amazonas state Brazil 199 E6
Amazonas dept Col. 198 D5
Amazonas dept Peru 198 B6
Amazonas r. S. America see Amazon
Amazonas state Venez. 199 E4
Amazônia, Parque Nacional nat. park Brazil 199 G6
Āmba Ālagē mt. Eth. 128 C1
Ambad India 94 B2
Amba Farit mt. Eth. 128 C2
Ambahikily Madag. 131 [inset] I4
Ambajogai India 94 C2 also spelt Ambejogai
Ambala India 96 C3
Ambalajanakomby Madag. 131 [inset] J3
Ambalakirajy Madag. 131 [inset] K2
Ambalangoda Sri Lanka 94 D5
Ambalatany Madag. 131 [inset] J4
Ambalavao Madag. 131 [inset] J4
Ambalindum Australia 148 B4
Ambam Cameroon 125 H6
Ambanja Madag. 131 [inset] K2
Ambar Iran 100 D4
Ambarchik Rus. Fed. 39 Q3
Ambarès-et-Lagarve France 50 F8
Ambargasta, Salinas de salt pan Arg. 204 D3
Ambarnyy Rus. Fed. 40 E2
Ambasa India 97 F5
Ambasamudram India 94 C4
Ambathala Australia 149 E5
Ambato Ecuador 198 B5
Ambato Boeny Madag. 131 [inset] J3
Ambato Finandrahana Madag. 131 [inset] J4
Ambatolahy Madag. 131 [inset] J4
Ambatolampy Madag. 131 [inset] J3
Ambatomainty Madag. 131 [inset] J3
Ambatondrazaka Madag. 131 [inset] K3
Ambatosia Madag. 131 [inset] K2
Ambazac France 50 H7
Ambejogai India see Ambajogai
Ambelau i. Indon. 75 C3
Ambelón Greece see Ampelonas
Amberg Germany 48 I6
Amberg U.S.A. 172 F5
Ambergris Cay i. Belize 185 I5
Ambergris Cays is Turks and Caicos Is 187 F2
Ambérieu-en-Bugey France 51 L7
Amberley Canada 173 L6
Amberley N.Z. 153 G11
Ambert France 51 J7
Ambgaon India 94 D1
Ambianum France see Amiens
Ambidédi Mali 124 C3
Ambika r. India 94 B1
Ambikapur India 97 D5
Ambilobe Madag. 131 [inset] K2
Ambition, Mount Canada 166 D3
Amble U.K. 46 K8
Ambleside U.K. 47 J9
Amblève r. Belgium 51 L2
Ambo India 97 E5
Ambo Peru 200 A2
Amboasary Madag. 131 [inset] J5
Amboasary Gara Madag. 131 [inset] K3
Amboavory Madag. 131 [inset] K3
Ambodifotatra Madag. 131 [inset] K3
Ambodiharina Madag. 131 [inset] K4
Ambohidratrimo Madag. 131 [inset] J3
Ambohijanahary Madag. 131 [inset] K3
Ambohimahasoa Madag. 131 [inset] J4
Ambohipaky Madag. 131 [inset] J3
Ambohitra mt. Madag. 131 [inset] K2
Ambohitralanana Madag. 131 [inset] K2
Amboina Indon. see Ambon
Amboise France 50 G5
Ambon Indon. 75 D3 formerly known as Amboina
Ambon i. Indon. 75 C3
Amboró, Parque Nacional nat. park Bol. 201 D4
Amboseli National Park Kenya 128 C5
Ambositra Madag. 131 [inset] J4
Ambovombe Madag. 131 [inset] J5
Amboy CA U.S.A. 183 I7
Amboy IL U.S.A. 172 D9
Ambre, Cap d' c. Madag. see Bobaomby, Tanjona
Ambrim i. Vanuatu see Ambrym
Ambriz Angola 127 B6
Ambriz, Coutada do nature res. Angola 127 B6
Ambrizete Angola see N'zeto
Ambrosio Brazil 198 D5
Ambrym i. Vanuatu 145 F3 also spelt Ambrim
Ambunten Indon. 77 F4
Ambur India 94 C3
Åmdals Verk Norway 45 J4
Am-Dam Chad 120 D6
Amded, Oued watercourse Alg. 123 F5
Amderma Rus. Fed. 40 L1
Amdillis well Mali 125 E2
Am Djéména Chad 120 C6
Amdo China 89 E5 also known as Lharigarbo
Amealco Mex. 185 E4
Ameca Mex. 184 D4
Amecameca Mex. 185 F5
Amedamit mt. Eth. 128 C2
Ameghino Arg. 204 E4
Ameland i. Neth. 48 C2
Amelia Italy 56 E6
Amelia Court House U.S.A. 176 H8
Amellu India 96 D4
Amendolara Italy 57 I9
Amenia U.S.A. 177 L4
American, North Fork r. U.S.A. 182 C3
Americana Brazil 206 F9
American Falls U.S.A. 180 D4
American Falls Reservoir U.S.A. 180 D4
American Fork U.S.A. 183 M1

▶American Samoa terr. S. Pacific Ocean 145 I3
United States Unincorporated Territory. Formerly known as Eastern Samoa.
oceania [countries] ▶ 138–139

Americus U.S.A. 175 C5
Ameringkogel mt. Austria 49 L8
Amersfoort Neth. 48 C3
Amersfoort S. Africa 133 N4
Amery Canada 167 M3
Amery Ice Shelf Antarctica 223 E2
Ames U.S.A. 174 A3
Amesbury U.S.A. 177 O3
Amet India 96 B4
Amethi India 97 D4
Amfilochia Greece 59 C10
Amfissa Greece 59 D10
Amga Rus. Fed. 39 N3
Amgalang China 85 H1 also known as Xin Barag Zuoqi
Amgu Rus. Fed. 82 E3
Amguema Rus. Fed. 39 S3
Amguid Alg. 123 G4
Amgun' r. Rus. Fed. 82 E1
Amhara admin. reg. Eth. 128 C2
Amherst Canada 169 H4
Amherst MA U.S.A. 177 M3
Amherst OH U.S.A. 176 C4
Amherst VA U.S.A. 176 F8
Amherst, Mount hill Australia 150 D3
Amherstburg Canada 173 J8
Amherstdale U.S.A. 176 D8
Amherst Island Canada 173 Q6
Amherstview Canada 173 Q6
Amida Turkey see Diyarbakır
Amidon U.S.A. 178 B2
Amiens France 51 I3 historically known as Ambianum or Samarobriva
'Amīj, Wādī watercourse Iraq 107 E4
Amik Ovası marsh Turkey 107 D3
Amilḥayt, Wādī al r. Oman 105 F4
Amilly France 51 I5
'Amīnābād Iran 100 C4
Amindhaion Greece see Amyntaio
Amindivi i. India see Amini
Amindivi Islands India 94 B4
Amini i. India 94 B4 also known as Amindivi
Amino Japan 91 D7
Aminuis Namibia 130 C4
Amioun Lebanon 108 G3
Amipshahr India 96 C3
Amīrābād Eşfahān Iran 100 E3
Amīrābād Īlām Iran 100 A3
Amirabad Iran see Fūlād Maialleh
Amirante Islands Seychelles 218 K6
Amirli Iraq 109 P3
Amisk Lake Canada 167 K4
Amistad, Represa de resr Mex./U.S.A. see Amistad Reservoir
Amistad Reservoir Mex./U.S.A. 185 E2 also known as Amistad, Represa de
Amisus Turkey see Samsun
Amite U.S.A. 175 B6
Amite Creek r. U.S.A. 175 B6
Amla India 96 C5 also known as Sarni
Amlaḥ, Jabal al hill Saudi Arabia 104 C4
Amlash Iran 100 B2
Amlekhganj Nepal 97 E4
Åmli Norway 45 J4
Amlwch U.K. 47 H10
'Amm Adam Sudan 121 H5
Amman Jordan see 'Ammān

▶'Ammān Jordan 108 G6
Capital of Jordan. English form Amman; historically known as Philadelphia or Rabbath Ammon.

Ammanazar Turkm. 102 C5
Ämmänsaari Fin. 44 O2
'Ammār reg. Yemen 105 D5
'Ammār, Tall hill Syria 109 H5
Ammarnäs Sweden 44 L2
Ammaroodinna watercourse Australia 146 B1
Ammassalik Greenland 165 P3 also known as Tasiilaq; also spelt Angmagssalik
Ammer r. Germany 48 I8
Ammerån r. Sweden 44 L3
Ammersee l. Germany 48 I8
Ammochostos Cyprus see Famagusta
Ammochostos Bay Cyprus 108 F2 also known as Famagusta Bay
Am Nābiyah Yemen 104 C5
Amne Machin Range mts China see A'nyêmaqên Shan
Amnok-kang r. China/N. Korea see Yalu Jiang
Amod India 96 B5
Amo Jiang r. China 86 B4
Amol Iran 100 C2
Amolar Brazil 201 F4
Amoliani i. Greece 59 E8
Amontada Brazil 202 E2
Amor mt. Spain 54 G5
Amorebieta Spain 55 I1
Amores r. Arg. 204 F3
Amorgos i. Greece 59 G12
Amorinópolis Brazil 206 B3
Amory U.S.A. 175 B5
Amos Canada 168 E3
Åmot Buskerud Norway 45 J4
Åmot Telemark Norway 45 I4 also known as Ytre Vinje
Amotape, Cerros de mts Peru 198 A6
Åmotfors Sweden 45 K4
Amourj Mauritania 124 D2
Amoy China see Xiamen
Ampah Indon. 77 F3
Ampanefena Madag. 131 [inset] K2
Ampani India 95 D2
Ampanihy Madag. 131 [inset] J5
Ampanotoamaizina Madag. 131 [inset] K3
Amparafaka, Tanjona pt Madag. 131 [inset] J2
Amparafaravola Madag. 131 [inset] K3
Amparai Sri Lanka 94 D5
Amparo Brazil 206 G9
Ampasimanolotra Madag. 131 [inset] K3 formerly known as Vohibinany
Ampelonas Greece 59 D9 also known as Ambelón
Ampenan Indon. 77 G5
Amper r. Germany 48 I7
Amper Nigeria 125 H4
Amphitrite Group is Paracel Is 72 D3
Ampibaku Indon. 75 B3
Ampisikinana Madag. 131 [inset] K2 formerly spelt Ampitsikinana
Ampitsikinana Madag. see Ampisikinana
Ampoa Indon. 75 B3
Amposta Spain 55 L4
Amqui Canada 169 H3
Amrabad India 94 C2
'Amrah, Jabal hill Saudi Arabia 104 C2
'Amrān Yemen 104 C5
Amraoti India see Amravati
Amravati India 94 C1 formerly spelt Amraoti
Amreli India 96 A5
Am Rijā' Yemen 121 J6
Amritsar India 96 B3
Amroha India 96 C3
Amrum i. Germany 48 F1
Åmsele Sweden 44 L2
Amstelveen Neth. 48 B3

▶Amsterdam Neth. 48 B3
Official capital of the Netherlands.
world [countries] ▶ 10–11

Amsterdam S. Africa 133 O3
Amsterdam NY U.S.A. 177 K3
Amsterdam OH U.S.A. 176 E5
Amsterdam, Île i. Indian Ocean 219 M8 English form Amsterdam Island
Amsterdam Island Indian Ocean see Amsterdam, Île
Amstetten Austria 49 L7
Am Timan Chad 126 D2
Amū r. Col. 198 C4
Amu Co l. China 89 E5
'Amūd, Jabal al mt. Saudi Arabia 109 K7
Amudar'ya r. Asia 99 F1 English form Amu Darya; also known as Dar"yoi Amu; also spelt Amudaryo, Amyderya; historically known as Oxus
Amu Darya r. Asia see Amudar'ya
Amudaryo r. Asia see Amudar'ya
Amund Ringnes Island Canada 165 J2
Amundsen, Mount Antarctica 223 G2
Amundsen Bay Antarctica 223 D2
Amundsen Coast Antarctica 223 O1
Amundsen Glacier Antarctica 223 N1
Amundsen Gulf Canada 164 G2
Amundsen-Scott research station Antarctica 223 A1
Amundsen Sea Antarctica 222 Q2
Amuntai Indon. 77 F3
Amur r. Rus. Fed. 82 F1 also known as Heilong Jiang
'Amur, Wadi watercourse Sudan 121 G5
Amurang Indon. 75 C2
Amur Oblast admin. div. Rus. Fed. see Amurskaya Oblast'
Amursk Rus. Fed. 82 E2 formerly known as Padali
Amurskaya Oblast' admin. div. Rus. Fed. 82 C1 English form Amur Oblast
Amurskiy Rus. Fed. 102 D1
Amurskiy Liman strait Rus. Fed. 82 F1
Amurzet Rus. Fed. 82 C3
Amvrakikos Kolpos b. Greece 59 B10
Amyderya r. Asia see Amudar'ya
Amyntaio Greece 58 C8 also known as Amindhaion
Amyot Canada 173 I2
Amzacea Romania 58 J5
Amzérakad well Mali 125 F2
Am-Zoer Chad 120 D6
Ana r. Turkey 58 I7
Anaa atoll Fr. Polynesia 221 I7
Anabanua Indon. 75 B3
Anabar r. Rus. Fed. 39 L2
Ana Branch r. Australia 146 D3
Anabtā West Bank 108 G5
Anacapa Islands U.S.A. 182 E7
Anaco Venez. 199 E2
Anaconda U.S.A. 180 D3
Anacortes U.S.A. 180 B2
Anadarko U.S.A. 179 C5
Anadolu Dağları mts Turkey 107 D2
Anadyr' Rus. Fed. 39 R3
Anadyr' r. Rus. Fed. 39 R3
Anadyr, Gulf of Rus. Fed. see Anadyrskiy Zaliv
Anadyrskiy Zaliv b. Rus. Fed. 39 S3 English form Anadyr, Gulf of
Anafi Greece 59 G12
Anafi i. Greece 59 G12
Anagé Brazil 202 D5
Anagni Italy 56 F7 historically known as Anagnia
Anagnia Italy see Anagni
'Ānah Iraq 107 E4
Anaheim U.S.A. 182 G8
Anahim Lake Canada 166 E4
Anáhuac Nuevo León Mex. 185 E3
Anáhuac Veracruz Mex. 185 F4
Anahuac U.S.A. 179 D6
Anaimalai Hills India 94 C4
Anai Mudi Peak India 94 C4
Anaiteum i. Vanuatu see Anatom
Anajás Brazil 202 B2
Anajás, Ilha i. Brazil 202 B2
Anajatuba Brazil 202 C2
Anakao Madag. 131 [inset] I4
Anakapalle India 95 D2
Anakie Australia 149 E4
Analalava Madag. 131 [inset] J2
Analavelona mts Madag. 131 [inset] I4
Anamã Brazil 199 F5
Ana María, Golfo de b. Cuba 186 D2
Anambas, Kepulauan is Indon. 77 D2
Anambra state Nigeria 125 G5
Anamosa U.S.A. 174 B3
Anamu r. Brazil 199 G4
Anamur Turkey 106 C3
Anan Japan 91 D8
Anand India 96 B5
Anandapur India 97 E5
Anandpur India 96 C3
Anandpur r. India 97 E5
Ananes i. Greece 59 F12
Anan'ev Kyrg. 103 I4 also known as Anan'yevo
Anangu Pitjantjatjara Aboriginal Lands res. Australia 146 A1
Anantapur India 94 C3
Anantnag Jammu and Kashmir 96 B2 also known as Islamabad
Anant Peth India 96 C4
Ananyev Ukr. see Anan'yiv
Anan'yevo Kyrg. see Anan'ev
Anan'yiv Ukr. 41 D7 also spelt Ananyev
Anapa Rus. Fed. 41 F7
Anápolis Brazil 206 E3
Anapú r. Brazil 199 I5
Anār Fin. see Inari
Anār Iran 100 C4
Anārak Iran 100 C3
Anarbar r. Iran 100 B3
Anardara Afgh. 101 E3
Anare Mountains Antarctica 223 L2
Añasco Puerto Rico 187 G3
Ånäset Sweden 44 M2
Anatahan i. N. Mariana Is 73 K3 formerly spelt Anatajan
Anatajan i. N. Mariana Is see Anatahan
Anatolia reg. Turkey 106 B3
Anatoliki Makedonia kai Thraki admin. reg. Greece 58 G7
Anatom i. Vanuatu 145 F4 also known as Anetchom, Île or Aneytioum, Île or Kéamu; also spelt Aneityum or Anaiteum
Añatuya Arg. 204 E3
Anatye Aboriginal Land res. Australia 148 C4
Anauá r. Brazil 199 F4
Anaurilândia Brazil 206 A9
Anavilhanas, Arquipélago das is Brazil 199 F5
Anaypazari Turkey see Gülnar
Anaz mts Saudi Arabia 109 H9
Anbei China 84 C3
Anbyon N. Korea 83 B5
Ancares, Serra dos mts Spain 54 D2
Ancash dept Peru 200 A2
Ancaster Canada 173 N7
Ancasti, Sierra mts Arg. 204 D3
Ancenis France 50 E5
Anchán Arg. 205 D6
Anchang China see Anxian
Anchau Nigeria 125 H4
Anchieta Brazil 207 M7
Anchodaya Bol. 200 C3
Anchorage U.S.A. 164 E3
Anchorage Island atoll Cook Is see Suwarrow
Anchorage Reefs P.N.G. 149 F1
Anchor Bay U.S.A. 173 K8
Anchuthengu India see Anjengo
Anci China see Langfang
Ančia r. Lith. 42 D6
Anclitas, Cayo i. Cuba 186 D2
An Cóbh Rep. of Ireland see Cóbh
Ancón Peru 200 A2
Ancona Italy 56 F5
Ancuabe Moz. 129 C8
Ancud Chile 205 B6
Ancud, Golfo de g. Chile 205 B6
Ancyra Turkey see Ankara
Anda China see Daqing
Anda China 82 B3
Anda i. Indon. 75 C5
Andacollo Chile 204 C3
Andahuaylas Peru 200 B3
Andal India 97 E5 also spelt Ondal
Andalgalá Arg. 204 D2
Åndalsnes Norway 44 I3
Andalucía aut. comm. Spain 54 G7 English form Andalusia
Andalusia S. Africa see Jan Kempdorp
Andalusia aut. comm. Spain see Andalucía
Andalusia AL U.S.A. 175 C6
Andalusia IL U.S.A. 172 C9
Andām, Wādī r. Oman 105 G3
Andaman and Nicobar Islands union terr. Andaman & Nicobar Is India 95 G4
Andaman and Nicobar Islands union terr. India 93 H9
Andaman Islands India 95 G3
Andaman Sea Indian Ocean 79 A6
Andaman Strait India 95 G3 also known as Middle Strait
Andamooka Australia 146 C2
Andapa Madag. 131 [inset] K2
Andarāb Afgh. 101 G3 also known as Banow
Andarob Tajik. 101 G2 also spelt Anderob
Andeba Ye Midir Zerf Chaf pt Eritrea 104 C5
Andeg Rus. Fed. 40 J2
Andegavum France see Angers
Andelle r. France 50 H3
Andenes Norway 44 L1
Andenne Belgium 51 L2
Andéramboukane Mali 125 F3
Ånderdalen Nasjonalpark nat. park Norway 44 L1
Andermatt Switz. 51 O6
Andernos-les-Bains France 50 E8
Anderob Tajik. see Andarob
Anderson r. Canada 164 G3
Anderson AK U.S.A. 164 E3
Anderson CA U.S.A. 182 B1
Anderson IN U.S.A. 174 C3
Anderson MO U.S.A. 178 D4
Anderson SC U.S.A. 174 D5
Anderson Bay Australia 147 E5
Anderson Reservoir U.S.A. 182 C4
Andes Col. 198 C3
▶Andes mts S. America 200 A2
southamerica [contrasts] ▶ 194–195
Andévalo, Sierra de hills Spain 54 D7
Andfjorden sea chan. Norway 44 L1
Andhíparos i. Greece see Antiparos
Andhra Pradesh state India 94 C2
Andía, Sierra de mts Spain 55 J2
Andijon Uzbek. see Andizhan

index A

Andijon Wiloyati admin. div. Uzbek. see **Andizhanskaya Oblast'**
Andikíra Greece see **Antikyra**
Andikithira i. Greece see **Antikythira**
Andilamena Madag. **131** [inset] K3
Andilanatoby Madag. **131** [inset] K3
Andīmeshk Iran **100** B3
Andímilos i. Greece see **Antimilos**
Andípaxoi i. Greece see **Antipaxoi**
Andípsara i. Greece see **Antipsara**
Andirá Brazil **206** C10
Andir He r. China **89** C4
Andırın Turkey **107** D3
Andirlangar China **89** C4
Andiyskoye Koysu r. Rus. Fed. **102** A4
Andiyur India **94** C4
Andizhan Uzbek. **103** H4
also spelt Andijon
Andizhan Oblast admin. div. Uzbek. see **Andizhanskaya Oblast'**
Andizhanskaya Oblast' admin. div. Uzbek. **103** H4
English form Andizhan Oblast; also known as Andijon Wiloyati
Andkhui r. Afgh. **101** F2
Andkhvoy Afgh. **101** F2
Andoany Madag. **131** [inset] K2
formerly known as Hell-Ville
Andoas Peru **198** B5
Andoas Nuevo Ecuador **198** B5
Andoga r. Rus. Fed. **43** S2
Andogskaya Gryada hills Rus. Fed. **43** S2
Andohahela, Réserve d' nature res. Madag. **131** [inset] J5
Andohajango Madag. **131** [inset] K2
Andol India **94** C2
Andola India **94** C2
Andong China see **Dandong**
Andong S. Korea **83** C5
Andongwei Shandong China **85** H5
Andoom Australia **149** D2
▶**Andorra** country Europe **55** M2
europe [countries] ▶ 32–35
Andorra Spain **55** K4

▶**Andorra la Vella** Andorra **55** M2
Capital of Andorra. Also spelt Andorra la Vieja.

Andorra la Vieja Andorra see **Andorra la Vella**
Andover U.K. **47** K12
Andover MA U.S.A. **177** N3
Andover NH U.S.A. **177** N2
Andover NY U.S.A. **176** H3
Andover OH U.S.A. **176** E4
Andøya i. Norway **44** K1
Andozero, Ozero l. Rus. Fed. **43** S2
Andradas Brazil **206** G9
Andrade U.S.A. **183** J9
Andradina Brazil **206** B7
Andramasina Madag. **131** [inset] J3
Andramy Madag. **131** [inset] J3
Andranomavo Madag. **131** [inset] J3
Andranomena Madag. **131** [inset] K3
Andranopasy Madag. **131** [inset] I4
Andranovondronina Madag. **131** [inset] K2
Andranovory Madag. **131** [inset] J4
Andreanof Islands U.S.A. **221** G2
Andreapol' Rus. Fed. **43** N5
André Félix, Parc National de nat. park Cent. Afr. Rep. **126** D2
André Fernandes Brazil **207** L2
Andrelândia Brazil **203** C7
Andrequicé Brazil **207** I5
Andrew Canada **167** H4
Andrew Bay Myanmar **78** A4
Andrews SC U.S.A. **175** E5
Andrews TX U.S.A. **179** B5
Andreyevka Almatinskaya Oblast' Kazakh. **103** J3
Andreyevka Severnyy Kazakhstan Kazakh. **103** F1
Andreyevka Rus. Fed. **102** B1
Andreyevskoye Rus. Fed. see **Dneprovskoye**
Andreykovichi Rus. Fed. **43** O9
Andreykovo Rus. Fed. **43** P6
Andria Italy **56** I7
Andriba Madag. **131** [inset] J3
Andrieskraal S. Africa **133** I10
Andriesvale S. Africa **132** E3
Andringitra mts Madag. **131** [inset] J4
Androka Madag. **131** [inset] J5
Androna reg. Madag. **131** [inset] K2
Androniki Rus. Fed. **43** U4
Andropov Rus. Fed. see **Rybinsk**
Andros i. Bahamas **186** D1
Andros Greece **59** F11
Andros i. Greece **59** F11
Androscoggin r. U.S.A. **177** P2
Androsovka Rus. Fed. **102** B1
Andros Town Bahamas **186** D1
Andrott i. India **94** B4
Andrushevka Ukr. see **Andrushivka**
Andrushivka Ukr. **41** D6
also spelt Andrushevka
Andrychów Poland **49** Q6
Andselv Norway **44** L1
Andsnes Norway **44** M1
Andújar Spain **54** G6
Andulo Angola **127** C7
Anec, Lake salt flat Australia **150** E4
Anecón Grande mt. Arg. **205** C6
Āneen-Kio terr. N. Pacific Ocean see **Wake Atoll**
Anéfis Mali **125** F2
Anéfis well Mali **125** E2
Anegada i. Virgin Is (U.K.) **187** G3
Anegada, Bahía b. Arg. **204** E6
Anegada Passage Virgin Is (U.K.) **187** H3
Anegam U.S.A. **183** L9
Aného Togo **125** F5
Aneityum i. Vanuatu see **Anatom**
'Aneiza, Jabal hill Iraq see **'Unayzah, Jabal**

Anekal India **94** C3
Añelo Arg. **204** C5
Anemourıon tourist site Turkey **108** D1
Anesbaraka well Alg. **123** G6
Anet France **50** H4
Anetchom, Île i. Vanuatu see **Anatom**
Aneto mt. Spain **55** L2
Aney Niger **125** I2
Aneytioum, Île i. Vanuatu see **Anatom**
Anfile Bay Eritrea **121** I6
Anfu China **87** E3
also known as Pingdu
Angadippuram India **94** C4
Angadoka, Lohatanjona hd Madag. **131** [inset] J2
Angahook Lorne State Park nature res. Australia **147** D4
Angalarri r. Australia **148** A2
Angamma, Falaise d' esc. Chad **120** C5
Angamos, Isla i. Chile **205** B8
Angamos, Punta pt Chile **200** C5
Ang'angxi China **85** I2

▶**Angara** r. Rus. Fed. **84** E1
Part of the Yenisey-Angara-Selenga, 3rd longest river in Asia. English form Upper Tunguska; also known as Verkhnyaya Tunguska.
asia [landscapes] ▶ 62–63

Angaradébou Benin **125** F4
Angarapa Aboriginal Land res. Australia **148** B4
Angarsk Rus. Fed. **80** G2
Angas Downs Australia **148** B5
Angas Range hills Australia **150** E4
Angaston Australia **146** C3
Angat Phil. **74** B3
Angatuba Brazil **206** E10
Angaur i. Palau **73** H5
also spelt Ngeaur or Niaur
Ånge Sweden **44** K3
Ángel, Salto del waterfall Venez. see **Angel Falls**
Angel de la Guarda, Isla i. Mex. **184** B2
Angeles Phil. **74** B3

▶**Angel Falls** Venez. **199** F3
Highest waterfall in the world. Also known as Ángel, Salto del.

Ängelholm Sweden **45** K4
Angelina r. U.S.A. **179** D6
Angellala Creek r. Australia **149** E5
Angelo r. Australia **150** B4
Angels Camp U.S.A. **182** D3
Āngereb Eth. **104** B5
Āngereb Wenz r. Eth. **128** C1
Ångermanälven r. Sweden **44** L3
Angermünde Germany **49** L2
Angers France **50** F5
historically known as Andegavum or Juliomagus
Anggana Indon. **77** G3
Angical Brazil **202** C4
Angicos Brazil **202** E3
Angikuni Lake Canada **167** L2
Angiola U.S.A. **182** E6
Angkor tourist site Cambodia **79** C5
Anglem, Mount hill N.Z. **153** B14
also known as Hananui
Anglesey i. U.K. **47** H10
also known as Ynys Môn
Angleton U.S.A. **179** D6
Angliers Canada **173** N3
Anglin r. France **50** G6
Anglo-Egyptian Sudan country Africa see **Sudan**
Angmagssalik Greenland see **Ammassalik**
Ang Mo Kio Sing. **76** [inset]
Ango Dem. Rep. Congo **126** E3
Angoche Moz. **131** H3
formerly known as António Enes
Angohrān Iran **100** D5
Angol Chile **204** B5
▶**Angola** country Africa **127** C7
formerly known as Portuguese West Africa
africa [countries] ▶ 114–117
Angola IN U.S.A. **174** C3
Angola NY U.S.A. **176** F3
Angonia, Planalto de plat. Moz. **131** G2
Angoon U.S.A. **164** F4
Angora Turkey see **Ankara**
Angostura Mex. **184** C3
Angoulême France **50** G7
historically known as Iculisma
Angra dos Reis Brazil **207** I10
Angren Uzbek. **103** G4
Ängsö naturreservat nature res. Sweden **45** L4
Ang Thong Thai. **79** C5
Angu Dem. Rep. Congo **126** E4
Angualasto Arg. **204** C3
Anguang China **85** I2

▶**Anguilla** terr. West Indies **187** H3
United Kingdom Overseas Territory.
oceania [countries] ▶ 138–139

Anguilla Cays is Bahamas **186** D2
Anguille, Cape Canada **169** J4
Anguli Nur l. China **85** G3
Anguo China **85** G4
Angurugu Australia **148** C2
Angus Canada **173** N6
Angustura Brazil **201** E2
Angwin U.S.A. **182** B3
Anhanguera Brazil **206** E5
Anholt i. Denmark **45** J4
Anhua China **87** D2
also known as Dongping
Anhui prov. China **87** F1
English form Anhwei
Anhumas Brazil **202** A6
Anhwei prov. China see **Anhui**
Aniak U.S.A. **164** D3
Aniakchak National Monument and Preserve nat. park U.S.A. **164** D4
Anicuns Brazil **206** D3
Ánidhros i. Greece see **Anydro**
Anié Togo **125** F5
Anie, Pic d' mt. France **50** F10
Aniene r. Italy **56** E7
Anikhovka Rus. Fed. **103** E2
Anikovo Rus. Fed. **40** G4
Animas r. U.S.A. **181** E5
Anina Romania **58** C3
Anishino Rus. Fed. **43** S7
Añisoc Equat. Guinea **125** H6
Anitaguipan Point Phil. **74** C4
Anıtlı Turkey **108** D1
Aniva Rus. Fed. **82** F3
Aniva, Mys c. Rus. Fed. **82** F3
Aniva, Zaliv b. Rus. Fed. **82** F3
Anivorano Madag. **131** [inset] K3
Anivorano Avaratra Madag. **131** [inset] K2
Aniwa U.S.A. **172** D5
Anjad India **96** B5
Anjafy mt. Madag. **131** [inset] J3
Anjalankoski Fin. **45** N3
Anjangaon India **96** C5
Anjar India **96** A5
Anjengo India **94** C4
also known as Anchuthengu
Anji China **87** F2
also known as Dipu
Anji India **94** C1
Anjiang China see **Qianyang**
Anjihai China **88** D2
Anjir Avand Iran **100** C3
Anjō Japan **91** E7
Anjoman Iran **100** D3

Anjou reg. France **50** F5
Anjou, Val d' valley France **50** F5
Anjouan i. Comoros see **Nzwani**
Anjozorobe Madag. **131** [inset] J3
Anjŭ N. Korea **83** B5
Anjuman reg. Afgh. **101** G3
Anka Nigeria **125** G3
Ankaboa, Tanjona pt Madag. **131** [inset] I4
formerly known as St-Vincent, Cap
Ankang China **87** D1

▶**Ankara** Turkey **106** C3
Capital of Turkey. Historically known as Ancyra or Angora.

Ankaratra mts Madag. **131** [inset] J3
Ankarsrum Sweden **45** L4
Ankatafa Madag. **131** [inset] K2
Ankavandra Madag. **131** [inset] J3
Ankazoabo Madag. **131** [inset] J4
Ankazobe Madag. **131** [inset] J3
Ankeny U.S.A. **174** A3
Ankerika Madag. **131** [inset] J2
An Khê Vietnam **79** E5
formerly known as An Tuc
Ankiliabo Madag. **131** [inset] I4
Anklam Germany **49** K2
Ankleshwar India **96** B5
formerly spelt Anklesvar
Anklesvar India see **Ankleshwar**
Ankofa mt. Madag. **131** [inset] K3
Ankogel mt. Austria **49** K8
Ankola India **94** B3
Ankouzhen China **85** E5
An'kovo Rus. Fed. **43** U5
Ankpa Nigeria **125** G5
Anling China see **Yanling**
Anloga Ghana **125** F5
Anlong China **86** C3
Ânlong Vêng Cambodia **79** D5
Anlu China **87** E2
Anmoore U.S.A. **176** E6
An Muileann gCearr Rep. of Ireland see **Mullingar**
Anmyŏn-do i. S. Korea **83** B5
Ann, Cape Antarctica **223** D2
Ann, Cape U.S.A. **177** O3
Anna Rus. Fed. **41** G6
Anna U.S.A. **176** A5
Anna, Lake U.S.A. **176** H7
Annaba Alg. **123** G1
formerly known as Bône; historically known as Bona or Hippo Regius
Annaberg-Buchholtz Germany **49** K5
An Nabk Saudi Arabia **109** I6
also known as Al 'Uqaylah
An Nabk Syria **109** H3
An Nafūd des. Saudi Arabia **104** C1
Annai Guyana **199** G4
An Nā'ikah, Qarārat depr. Libya **120** C3
An Najaf Iraq **107** F5
An Najaf governorate Iraq **107** E5
An Najaf, Baḩr l. Iraq **109** P6
Annalee r. Rep. of Ireland **47** E9
Annam reg. Vietnam **78** D4
Annam Highlands mts Laos/Vietnam **78** D4
Annan U.K. **47** I9
Annan r. U.K. **47** I9
'Annān, Wādī al watercourse Syria **109** J3
Annandale U.S.A. **177** H7
Anna Plains Australia **150** C3

▶**Annapolis** U.S.A. **177** I7
State capital of Maryland. Historically known as Anne Arundel Town or Providence.

Annapolis Royal Canada **169** H4
Annapurna Conservation Area nature res. Nepal **97** E3

▶**Annapurna I** mt. Nepal **97** D3
10th highest mountain in the world and in Asia.
world [physical features] ▶ 8–9

Annapurna II mt. Nepal **97** E3
Ann Arbor U.S.A. **173** J8
Anna Regina Guyana **199** G3
An Nás Rep. of Ireland see **Naas**
An Nashū, Wādī watercourse Libya **120** B3
An Nāşirīyah Iraq **107** F5
Annaspan imp. l. S. Africa **133** J5
An Nawfalīyah Libya **120** C2
Annean, Lake salt flat Australia **151** B5
Anne Arundel Town U.S.A. see **Annapolis**
Annecy France **51** M7
Annecy, Lac d' l. France **51** M7
Annecy-le-Vieux France **51** M7
Anne Marie Lake Canada **169** I2
Annemasse France **51** M6
Annette Island U.S.A. **166** D4
Annie r. Australia **149** D2
Annikvere Estonia **42** H2
An Nimārah Syria **109** I5
An Nimāş Saudi Arabia **104** C4
Anning China **86** B3
formerly known as Lianran
Anning He r. China **86** B3
Annino Rus. Fed. **43** S2
Anniston U.S.A. **175** C5
Annobón i. Equat. Guinea **125** G7
formerly known as Pagalu
Annonay France **51** K7
Annotto Bay Jamaica **186** D3
An Nu'ayrīyah Saudi Arabia **105** E2
An Nukhaylah waterhole Iraq **109** P4
An Nu'mānīyah Iraq **107** F4
An Nuqay'ah Qatar **105** E2
An Nuşayrīyah, Jabal mts Syria **108** H2
Annville U.S.A. **176** B8
Anogeia Greece **59** F13
also spelt Anóyia
Anoka U.S.A. **174** A2
Anori Brazil **199** F5
Anorontany, Tanjona hd Madag. **131** [inset] I2
Anosibe An'Ala Madag. **131** [inset] K3
Anou I-n-Atei well Alg. **123** G5
Ânou Mellene well Mali **125** F2
Anou-n-Bidek well Alg. **123** G6
Ano Viannos Greece **59** G13
Anóyia Greece see **Anogeia**
Anpu China **87** D4
Anpu Gang b. China **87** D4
Anqing China **87** F2
Anqiu China **85** H4
Anren China **87** E3
Ansai China **85** F4
also known as Zhenwudong
Anse-à-Galets Haiti **187** E3
Anse-à-Pitre Haiti **187** F3
Anse-à-Veau Haiti **187** E3
Anseba Shet watercourse Eritrea **104** B4
Anse d'Hainault Haiti **187** E3
Anser Group is Australia **147** E4
Anserma Col. **198** C3
Anshan China **85** I3
Anshun China **86** C3
Anshunchang China **86** B2
Ansina Uruguay **204** G3
An Sirhān, Wādī watercourse Saudi Arabia **107** D5
Ansjö Sweden **44** L3
Anson U.S.A. **179** C5
Anson Bay Australia **148** A2
Ansongo Mali **125** F3
Ansongo-Ménaka, Réserve Partielle de Faune d' nature res. Mali **125** F3
Ansonia U.S.A. **176** A5
Ansonville Canada **173** M2
Ansted U.S.A. **176** D7

Anstruther U.K. **46** J7
Ansu China see **Xushui**
Anta India **96** C4
Anta Peru **200** B3
Antabamba Peru **200** B3
Antakya Turkey **106** D3
also known as Hatay; historically known as Antioch or Antiochia
Antalaha Madag. **131** [inset] K2
Antalya Turkey **106** B3
also spelt Adalia; historically known as Attalea or Attalia
Antalya prov. Turkey **108** B1
Antalya Körfezi g. Turkey **106** B3
Antanambao Manampotsy Madag. **131** [inset] K3
Antanambe Madag. **131** [inset] K3

▶**Antananarivo** Madag. **131** [inset] J3
Capital of Madagascar. Formerly spelt Tananarive; short form Tana.

Antananarivo prov. Madag. **131** [inset] J3
Antanifotsy Madag. **131** [inset] J3
Antanimora Atsimo Madag. **131** [inset] J5
Antantûr, Râs pt Egypt **108** F9
An tAonach Rep. of Ireland see **Nenagh**

▶**Antarctica** **222**
Most southerly and coldest continent, and the continent with the highest average elevation.
world [land cover] ▶ 18–19
antarctica [features] ▶ 212–213

Antarctic Peninsula Antarctica **222** T2
Antaritarika Madag. **131** [inset] J5
Antelope Island U.S.A. **183** L1
Antelope Range mts U.S.A. **183** H2
Antequera Spain **54** G7
Anthony KS U.S.A. **178** C4
Anthony NM U.S.A. **181** F6
Anthony, Lake salt flat Australia **146** B2
Anthony Lagoon Australia **148** B3
Anti Atlas mts Morocco **122** C3
also known as Petit Atlas
Antibes France **51** N9
Anticosti, Île d' i. Canada **169** I3
English form Anticosti Island
Anticosti Island Canada see **Anticosti, Île d'**
Antifer, Cap d' c. France **50** G3
Antigo U.S.A. **172** D5
Antigonish Canada **169** I4
Antigua i. Antigua and Barbuda **187** H3
Antigua Guat. **185** H6
long form Antigua Guatemala
Antigua country West Indies see **Antigua and Barbuda**
▶**Antigua and Barbuda** country West Indies **187** H3
short form Antigua
northamerica [countries] ▶ 158–159
Antigua Guatemala Guat. see **Antigua**
Antiguo-Morelos Mex. **185** F4
Antikyra Greece **59** D10
also spelt Andikíra
Antikythira i. Greece **59** E13
also spelt Andikithira
Antikythiro, Steno sea chan. Greece **59** E13
Anti Lebanon mts Lebanon/Syria see **Sharqī, Jabal ash**
Antilla Arg. **204** D2
Antilla Cuba **186** E2
Antimilos i. Greece **59** F12
also spelt Andímilos
Antimony U.S.A. **183** M3
An tInbhear Mór Rep. of Ireland see **Arklow**
Antioch Turkey see **Antakya**
Antioch CA U.S.A. **182** C3
Antioch IL U.S.A. **172** E8
Antiocheia ad Cragum tourist site Turkey **108** D1
Antiochia Turkey see **Antakya**
Antioquia Col. **198** C3
Antioquia dept Col. **198** C3
Antiparos i. Greece **59** G11
also spelt Andhíparos
Antipaxoi i. Greece **59** B9
also spelt Andípaxoi
Antipino Rus. Fed. **43** O6
Antipodes Islands N.Z. **145** G6
Antipsara i. Greece **59** G10
also spelt Andípsara
Antitilos i. Greece **59** I12
Antium Italy see **Anzio**
Antlers U.S.A. **179** D5
An t-Ob U.K. see **Leverburgh**
Antofagasta Chile **200** C5
Antofagasta admin. reg. Chile **200** C5
Antofagasta de la Sierra Arg. **204** D2
Antonhibe Madag. **131** [inset] J2
Antônio Carlos Brazil **207** J8
Antonio de Biedma Arg. **205** D7
Antônio Dias Brazil **207** K6
António Enes Moz. see **Angoche**
Antônio Lemos Brazil **202** B2
Antón Recio Cuba **186** C2
Antopal' Belarus **42** F9
Antrim U.K. **47** F9
Antrim Hills U.K. **47** F8
Antrim Plateau Australia **150** E3
Antrodoco Italy **56** F6
Antropovo Rus. Fed. **40** G4
Antsahabe Madag. **131** [inset] K2
Antsalova Madag. **131** [inset] J3
Antsambalahy Madag. **131** [inset] K2
Antseranana Madag. see **Antsirañana**
Antsiferovo Rus. Fed. **43** O3
Antsirabe Madag. **131** [inset] J3
Antsirabe Avaratra Madag. **131** [inset] K2
Antsirañana Madag. **131** [inset] K2
formerly known as Diégo Suarez; formerly spelt Antseranana
Antsirañana prov. Madag. **131** [inset] K2
Antsla Estonia **42** H4
Antsohihy Madag. **131** [inset] J2
Antsohimbondrona Madag. **131** [inset] K2
formerly known as Port St-Louis
Antsondrodava Madag. **131** [inset] J3
Anttis Sweden **44** M2
Anttola Fin. **45** N3
Antu China see **Songjiang**
An Tuc Vietnam see **An Khê**
Antuco Chile **204** C5
Antuco, Volcán vol. Chile **204** C5
Antufash, Jazīrat i. Yemen **104** C5
English form Antufush Island
Antufush Island Yemen see **Antufash, Jazīrat**
Antwerp Belgium **51** K1
also known as Anvers; also spelt Antwerpen
Antwerp U.S.A. **177** J1
Antwerpen Belgium see **Antwerp**
An Uaimh Rep. of Ireland see **Navan**
Anuc, Lac l. Canada **169** F1
Anuchino Rus. Fed. **82** D4
Anueque, Sierra mts Arg. **205** C6
Anugul India **95** E1
Anupgarh India **96** B3
Anuradhapura Sri Lanka **94** D4
Anurrete Aboriginal Land res. Australia **148** B4
Anvers Belgium see **Antwerp**
Anvers Island Antarctica **222** T2
Anvil Range mts Canada **166** C2
Anxi Fujian China **87** F3
also known as Fengcheng
Anxi Gansu China **84** B3
also known as Yuanquan
Anxian China **86** C2
also known as Anchang
Anxiang China **87** E2

Anxin China **85** G4
also known as Xin'an
Anxious Bay Australia **146** B3
Anxur Italy see **Terracina**
Anyang China see **Du'an**
Anyang China **85** G4
also known as Zhangde
Anyang S. Korea **83** B5
Anyar Indon. **77** D4
Anydro i. Greece **59** G12
also known as Ánidhros
A'nyêmaqên Shan mts China **86** A1
English form Amne Machin Range
Anyi China **87** E2
also known as Longjin
Anykščiai Lith. **42** G6
Anyuan Jiangxi China **87** E3
also known as Xinshan
Anyuan Jiangxi China **87** E3
Anyue China **86** C2
also known as Yueyang
Anyuy r. Rus. Fed. **82** E2
Anyuysk Rus. Fed. **39** Q3
Anzac Alta Canada **167** I3
Anzac B.C. Canada **166** F4
Anze China **85** G4
Anzhero-Sudzhensk Rus. Fed. **80** D1
Anzi Dem. Rep. Congo **126** D5
Anzio Italy **56** E7
historically known as Antium
Anzoátegui state Venez. **199** E2
Aoba i. Vanuatu **145** F3
also known as Omba; also spelt Oba
Aob Luang National Park Thai. **78** B4
Aoga-shima i. Japan **91** F8
Aohan Qi China see **Xinhui**
Aomen China see **Macau**
Aomori Japan **90** G4
Aomori pref. Japan **90** G4
Aoos r. Greece **59** B8
Ao Phang Nga National Park Thai. **79** B6
Aoraki N.Z. see **Mount Cook**
Aoraki mt. N.Z. see **Cook, Mount**
Aôral, Phnum mt. Cambodia **79** D5
Aorangi mt. N.Z. see **Cook, Mount**
Aorere r. N.Z. **152** G8
Aosta Italy **51** N7
Aotearoa country Oceania see **New Zealand**
Aouderas Niger **125** H2
Aoufist W. Sahara **122** B4
Aouhinet bel Egra well Alg. **122** D4
Aouk, Bahr r. Cent. Afr. Rep./Chad **126** C2
Aoukalé r. Cent. Afr. Rep./Chad **126** D2
Aoukâr reg. Mali/Mauritania **122** D5
Aoukenek well Mali **125** F2
Aoulef Alg. **123** F4
Aoulime, Jbel mt. Morocco **122** C3
Aourou Mali **124** C3
Aoxi China see **Le'an**
Aoya Japan **91** D7
Aoyang China see **Shanggao**
Aozou Chad **120** C4
Apa r. Brazil **201** F5
Apac Uganda **128** B4
Apache U.S.A. **179** C5
Apache, Lake U.S.A. **183** M8
Apache Junction U.S.A. **183** M8
Apagado, Volcán vol. Bol. **200** D5
Apahida Romania **58** E2
Apaiaí r. Brazil **206** E10
Apaiang atoll Kiribati see **Abaiang**
Apalachee Bay U.S.A. **175** C6
Apalachicola U.S.A. **175** C6
Apalachicola r. U.S.A. **175** C6
Apalachicola Bay U.S.A. **175** C6
Apam Ghana **125** E5
Apamama atoll Kiribati see **Abemama**
Apamea Turkey see **Dinar**
Apan Mex. **185** F5
Apaporis r. Col. **198** D5
Apar, Teluk b. Indon. **77** G3
Aparecida do Rio Doce Brazil **206** B5
Aparecida do Tabuado Brazil **206** B7
Aparima N.Z. see **Riverton**
Aparima r. N.Z. **153** C14
Aparri Phil. **74** B2
Aparurén Venez. **199** F3
Apas, Sierra hills Arg. **205** D6
Apaščia r. Lith. **42** F5
Apatin Vojvodina, Srbija Yugo. **56** K3
Apatity Rus. Fed. **44** P2
Apatou Fr. Guiana **199** H3
Apatzingán Mex. **185** E5
Ape Latvia **42** H4
Apediá r. Brazil **201** E2
Apeldoorn Neth. **48** C3
Apennines mts Italy **53** D3
also known as Appennino
Apere r. Bol. **200** D3
Apex Mountain Canada **166** B2
Aphrodite's Birthplace tourist site Cyprus **108** D3
also known as Petra tou Romiou
Api Dem. Rep. Congo **126** E4
Api mt. Nepal **96** D3
Api, Tanjung pt Indon. **75** B3
Apia Col. **198** C3
Apia atoll Kiribati see **Abaiang**

▶**Apia** Samoa **145** H3
Capital of Samoa.
oceania [countries] ▶ 138–139

Apiacas, Serra dos hills Brazil **201** F2
Apiaí Brazil **203** B8
Apiaú, Serra do mts Brazil **199** F4
Apio Solomon Is **145** F2
Apipilulco Mex. **185** F5
Apishapa r. U.S.A. **178** B4
Apiti N.Z. **152** J7
Apizaco Mex. **185** F5
Apizolaya Mex. **179** B7
Aplao Peru **200** B4
Ap Lei Chau i. Hong Kong China see **Aberdeen Island**
Apo, Mount vol. Phil. **74** C5
Apodi Brazil **202** E3
Apodi, Chapada do hills Brazil **202** E3
Apo East Passage Phil. **74** B3
Apoera Suriname **199** G3
Apolda Germany **48** I4
Apollinopolis Magna Egypt see **Idfu**
Apollo Bay Australia **147** D4
Apollonia Bulg. see **Sozopol**
Apollonia Greece **59** F12
Apolo Bol. **200** C3
Apopka U.S.A. **175** D6
Aporé r. Brazil **206** C6
Apostle Islands U.S.A. **172** C4
Apostle Islands National Lakeshore nature res. U.S.A. **172** C3
Apostolens Tommelfinger mt. Greenland **165** O3
Apóstoles Arg. **204** G2
Apostolos Andreas, Cape Cyprus **108** F2
also known as Zafer Burnu
Apoteri Guyana **199** G3
Apo West Passage Phil. **74** B3
Appalachia U.S.A. **176** C9
▶**Appalachian Mountains** U.S.A. **176** B9
northamerica [landscapes] ▶ 156–157
Appalla i. Fiji see **Kabara**
Appennino mts Italy see **Apennines**
Appennino Abruzzese mts Italy **56** F6
Appennino Lucano mts Italy **57** H8
Appennino Napoletano mts Italy **56** H7
Appennino Tosco-Emiliano mts Italy **56** C5
Appiano sulla Strada del Vino Italy **56** D2
Applecross U.K. **46** G6
Appleton MN U.S.A. **178** C2
Appleton WI U.S.A. **172** E6
Apple Valley U.S.A. **183** G7

Appomattox U.S.A. **176** G8
Aprelevka Rus. Fed. **43** S6
Aprilia Italy **56** E7
Apsheronsk Rus. Fed. **41** F7
formerly known as Apsheronskaya
Apsheronskaya Rus. Fed. see **Apsheronsk**
Apsheronskiy Poluostrov pen. Azer. see **Abşeron Yarımadası**
Apsley Canada **173** O6
Apsley Strait Australia **148** A1
Apt France **51** L9
Apucarana Brazil **206** B10
Apucarana, Serra da hills Brazil **206** B10
Apulum Romania see **Alba Iulia**
Apurahuan Phil. **74** A4
Apure r. Venez. **198** E3
Apure state Venez. **198** D3
Apurímac dept Peru **200** B3
Apurimac r. Peru **200** B3
Apurito Venez. **198** D3
Aq"a Georgia see **Sokhumi**
'Aqaba Jordan see **Al 'Aqabah**
Aqaba, Gulf of Asia **104** A1
'Aqaba, Wâdi el watercourse Egypt **108** E7
Aqadyr Kazakh. see **Agadyr'**
Aqal China **88** B3
Aqbalyq Kazakh. see **Akbalyk**
Aqbeyit Kazakh. see **Akbeit**
Āqchah Afgh. **101** F2
Aq Chai r. Iran **107** F3
Áqdā Iran **100** C3
Aqdoghmish r. Iran **100** A2
Aqiq Sudan **121** H5
Aqiq, Khalîg b. Sudan **104** B4
Aqiq, Wādī al watercourse Saudi Arabia **104** C2
Aqitag mt. China **88** E3
Aqköl Kazakh. see **Akkol'**
Aqköl Kazakh. see **Akkol'**
Aqla well Saudi Arabia **104** B2
Aqmola Kazakh. see **Astana**
Aqmola Oblast admin. div. Kazakh. see **Akmolinskaya Oblast'**
Aqmola Oblysy admin. div. Kazakh. see **Akmolinskaya Oblast'**
Āq Qal'eh Iran **100** C2
formerly known as Pahlavī Dezh
Aqqan China **89** D4
formerly known as Atqan
Aqqikkol Hu salt l. China **89** E4
Aqqystaū Kazakh. see **Akkystau**
Aqra', Wādī al watercourse Saudi Arabia **109** L7
'Aqraba West Bank **108** G5
'Aqrah Iraq **107** E3
'Aqran hill Saudi Arabia **109** J6
Aqsay Kazakh. see **Aksay**
Aqsayqin Hit terr. Asia see **Aksai Chin**
Aqshataū Kazakh. see **Akchatau**
Aqshī Kazakh. see **Akshiy**
Aqshuqyr Kazakh. see **Akshukur**
Aqsū Kazakh. see **Aksu**
Aqsū Kazakh. see **Aksu**
Aqsū Kazakh. see **Aksu**
Aqsūat Kazakh. see **Aksuat**
Aqsū-Ayuly Kazakh. see **Aksu-Ayuly**
Aqtaū Kazakh. see **Aktau**
Aqtöbe Kazakh. see **Aktyubinsk**
Aqtöbe Oblysy admin. div. Kazakh. see **Aktyubinskaya Oblast'**
Aqtoghay Kazakh. see **Aktogay**
Aqtoghay Kazakh. see **Aktogay**
Aquae Grani Germany see **Aachen**
Aquae Gratianae France see **Aix-les-Bains**
Aquae Sextiae France see **Aix-en-Provence**
Aquae Statiellae Italy see **Acqui Terme**
Aquarius Mountains U.S.A. **183** K7
Aquarius Plateau U.S.A. **183** M4
Aquaviva delle Fonti Italy **56** I8
Aquidabánmi r. Para. **201** F5
Aquidauana Brazil **201** G5
Aquidauana r. Brazil **201** F4
Aquila Mex. **184** E5
Aquiles Mex. **184** D2
Aquin Haiti **187** E3
Aquincum Hungary see **Budapest**
Aquiry r. Brazil see **Acre**
Aquisgranum Germany see **Aachen**
Aquitaine admin. reg. France **50** F8
Aqzhal Kazakh. see **Akzhal**
Aqzhar Kazakh. see **Akzhar**
Aqzhayqyn Köli salt l. Kazakh. see **Akzhaykyn, Ozero**
Ara India **97** E4
formerly spelt Arrah
Ara r. Spain **55** L2
Āra Ārba Eth. **128** D3
Arab U.S.A. **174** C5
Arab, Bahr el watercourse Sudan **126** F2
'Arab, Khalîg el b. Egypt **121** F2
'Araba, Wâdi watercourse Egypt **108** D8
'Arabābād Iran **100** D3
Ara Bacalle well Eth. **128** D3
'Arabah, Wādī r. Yemen **105** E4
'Arabah, Wādī al watercourse Israel/Jordan **108** G8
also known as Ha 'Arava
Arabelo Venez. **199** E3
Arabian Gulf Asia see **The Gulf**
Arabian Oryx Sanctuary tourist site Saudi Arabia **105** G4
Arabian Sea Indian Ocean **99** H6
Ara Bonel Eth. **128** D3
Arabopó Venez. **199** F3
Araç Turkey **106** C2
Araça r. Brazil **199** F5
Aracaju Brazil **202** E4
Aracanguy, Montes de hills Para. **201** G6
Aracar, Volcán vol. Arg. **200** D6
Aracati Brazil **202** E3
Aracatu Brazil **202** D5
Araçatuba Brazil **206** C8
Aracena Spain **54** E7
Aracena, Isla i. Chile **205** C9
Aracena, Sierra de hills Spain **54** D7
Arachthos r. Greece **59** C9
also spelt Arakhthos
Aračinovo Macedonia **58** C6
Aracoiaba Brazil **202** E3
Aracruz Brazil **203** D6
Araçuaí Brazil **203** D6
Araçuaí r. Brazil **203** D6
'Arad Israel **108** G6
Arad Romania **58** C2
Arada Chad **120** D6
'Arādah U.A.E. **105** F3
Arādān Iran **100** C3
Aradeib, Wadi watercourse Sudan **120** D6
Arafura Sea Australia/Indon. **144** C2
Aragarças Brazil **206** A2
Aragón aut. comm. Spain **55** K3
Aragón r. Spain **55** J2
Aragoncillo mt. Spain **55** I4
Aragua state Venez. **199** E2
Araguacema Brazil **202** B4
Araguaçu Brazil **202** B5
Aragua de Barcelona Venez. **199** E2
Aragua de Maturín Venez. **199** F2
Araguaia r. Brazil **206** A3
Araguaia, Parque Nacional de nat. park Brazil **202** B4
Araguaiana Brazil **206** B2
Araguaína Brazil **202** B3
Araguana Brazil **202** B3
Araguao, Boca r. mouth Venez. **199** F2
Araguapiche, Punta pt Venez. **199** F2
Araguari Brazil **206** E5
Araguari r. Amapá Brazil **199** I4
Araguari r. Minas Gerais Brazil **206** E5
Araguatins Brazil **202** B3
Aragvi r. Georgia **107** F2
'Ārah, Ra's pt Yemen **104** C5

'Ārah, Wādī r. Oman 105 F4
Arai Japan 90 F6
Araif el Naga, Gebel hill Egypt 108 F7
Araiosos Brazil 202 D2
Arak Alg. 123 F4
Arāk Iran 100 B3
formerly known as Sultanabad
Arak Syria 109 J3
Arakai-yama mt. Japan 90 F6
Arakaka Guyana 199 G3
Arakan state Myanmar 78 A3
also known as Rakhaing or Rakhine or
Yagaing
Arakan Yoma mts Myanmar 78 A3
Arakhthos r. Greece see Arachthos
Arakkonam India 94 C3
formerly spelt Arkonam
Aral China 88 C3
Aral Kazakh. see Aral'sk
Aral Tajik. see Vose

► Aral Sea salt l. Kazakh./Uzbek. 102 D3
2nd largest lake in Asia and 6th in the
world. Formerly known as Aral Tengizi or Orol
Dengizi.
asia [landscapes] ▶▶ 62–63

Aral'sk Kazakh. 103 E3
also known as Aral
Aralsor, Ozero l. Kazakh. 102 B2
Aralsor, Ozero salt l. Kazakh. 102 C2
Aralsul'fat Kazakh. 103 E3
Aral Tengizi salt l. Kazakh./Uzbek. see
Aral Sea
Aramac Australia 149 E4
Aramac Creek watercourse Australia 149 E4
Aramah plat. Saudi Arabia 105 D3
A Ramallosa Spain 54 C2
Aramberri Mex. 185 F3
Arame Brazil 202 C3
Aramia r. P.N.G. 73 J8
Aran r. India 94 B8
Arancibia Arg. 204 C3
Aranda de Duero Spain 55 H3
Arandelovac Srbija Yugo. 58 B4
Arandis Namibia 130 B4
Arang India 94 C3
Arani India 94 C3
Aran Island Rep. of Ireland 47 D9
Aran Islands Rep. of Ireland 47 C10
Aranjuez Spain 55 H4
Aranos Namibia 130 C5
Aransas Pass U.S.A. 179 C12
Arantangi India 94 C4
Arantes r. Brazil 206 C6
Aranuka atoll Kiribati 145 G1
formerly known as Henderville
Aranyaprathet Thai. 79 C6
Arao Japan 91 B8
Araouane Mali 124 E2
Arapaho U.S.A. 179 C5
Arapahoe U.S.A. 178 C3
Arapari Brazil 199 H5
Arapawa Island N.Z. 152 I9
Arapicos Ecuador 198 B5
Arapiraca Brazil 202 E4
Arapis, Akra pt Greece 59 F8
Arapkir Turkey 107 D3
Arapongas Brazil 206 B10
Arapoti Brazil 206 D11
Arapsun Turkey see Gülşehir
Arapuá Brazil 206 B7
Arapuni N.Z. 152 J6
'Ar'ar, Wādī watercourse Iraq/Saudi Arabia
107 E5
Arara r. Brazil 200 D2
Araracuara Col. 198 C5
Araracuara, Cerros de hills Col. 198 C5
Araranguá Brazil 203 B9
Araraquara Brazil 206 E8
Araras Amazonas Brazil 200 C2
Araras Pará Brazil 199 H6
Ararás Brazil 200 D2
Araras São Paulo Brazil 206 F9
Araras, Açude resr Brazil 202 E3
Araras, Serra das hills Brazil 203 A6
Araras, Serra das mts Brazil 203 A8
Ararat Australia 147 D4
Ararat, Mount Turkey 107 F3
also known as Ağrı Dağı
Arari Brazil 202 C2
Araria India 97 E4
Araripe Brazil 202 D3
Araripe, Chapada do hills Brazil 202 D3
Araripina Brazil 202 D3
Araruama Brazil 207 H9
Araruama, Lago de lag. Brazil 207 K9
Aras Turkey 107 E3
also known as Velibaba
Aras r. Turkey see Araz
Ar Asgat Mongolia 85 E1
Aratâne well Mauritania 124 C2
Arataú r. Brazil 202 B2
Aratürük China see Yiwu
Arauá r. Brazil 199 F6
Arauá r. Brazil 200 D2
Arauca Col. 198 D3
Arauca r. Venez. 198 D3
Arauco Chile 204 B5
Arauco, Golfo de b. Chile 204 B5
Arauquita Col. 198 D3
Araure Venez. 198 D2
Aravaipa Creek watercourse U.S.A. 183 N9
Aravalli Range mts India 96 B4
Aravete Estonia 42 G2
Araviana r. Spain 55 I3
Aravissos Greece 58 D3
Arawa P.N.G. 145 E2
Arawale National Reserve nature res.
Kenya 128 D5
Arawata r. N.Z. 153 C12
formerly spelt Arawhata
Arawhana mt. N.Z. 152 L4
Arawhata r. N.Z. see Arawata
Araxá Brazil 206 G6
Araxos, Akra pt Greece 59 C10
Araya, Peninsula de pen. Venez. 199 E2
Arayt Dağı mt. Turkey 106 B3
Araz r. Azer. 107 G2
also spelt Aras
Arba r. Spain 55 J3
Arbailu Iraq see Arbil
Árba Minch Eth. 128 C3
Arbela Iraq see Arbil
Arbil governorate Iraq 107 E4
Arbil Iraq 107 E3
also known as Hawlēr; also spelt Irbil;
historically known as Arbailu or Arbela
Arbil governorate Iraq 107 E4
Arboga Sweden 45 K4
Arbois France 51 L5
Arboletes Col. 198 B2
Arbon Switz. 51 P5
Arborfield Canada 167 K4
Arborg Canada 167 L5
Arbrá Sweden 45 L3
Arbroath U.K. 46 J7
Arbuckle U.S.A. 182 B2
Arbu Lut, Dasht-e des. Afgh. 101 E4
Arc r. France 51 M7
Arcachon France 50 E8
Arcachon, Bassin d' inlet France 50 E8
Arcadia FL U.S.A. 175 D7
Arcadia LA U.S.A. 174 D5
Arcadia WI U.S.A. 172 C6
Arcadia WI U.S.A. 172 G6
Arcalod, Pointe d' mt. France 51 M7
Arcanum U.S.A. 176 A6
Arcas, Cayos is Mex. 185 H4

Arcata U.S.A. 180 A4
Arc Dome mt. U.S.A. 183 G3
Arcelia Mex. 185 E5
Archangel Rus. Fed. 40 G2
also known as Arkhangel'sk; historically
known as Novyj Cholmogory or Novyj
Holmogory or Novyy Kholmogory
Archangel Oblast admin. div. Rus. Fed. see
Arkhangel'skaya Oblast'
Archangelos Greece 59 J12
Archar r. Bulg. 58 D5
Archbold U.S.A. 176 A4
Archena Spain 55 J6
Archer r. Australia 149 D2
Archer Bend National Park Australia 149 D2
Archer City U.S.A. 179 C5
Arches National Park U.S.A. 183 O3
Arch Henda mt. Chad 120 D2
Archidona Spain 54 G7
Archman Turkm. 102 D5
Arci, Monte hill Sardegna Italy 57 A9
Arcidano Italy 56 B7
Arcipélago de la Maddalena, Parco
Nazionale dell' nat. park Sardegna Italy
56 B7
Arçivan Azer. 107 G3
Arckaringa watercourse Australia 146 B2
Arco Italy 56 C3
Arco U.S.A. 180 D4
Arconce r. France 51 K6
Arcos Brazil 207 H7
Arcos de Jalón Spain 55 I3
Arcos de la Frontera Spain 54 F8
Arcos de Valdevez Port. 54 C3
Arcoverde Brazil 202 E4
Arctic Bay Canada 165 K2
Arctic Institute Islands Rus. Fed. see
Arkticheskogo Instituta, Ostrova
► Arctic Ocean 224 C1
arctic [features] ▶▶ 214–215
Arctic Red r. Canada 166 C1
Arctic Red River Canada see Tsiigehtchic
Arctowski research station Antarctica
222 U2
long form Henryk Arctowski
Arda r. Bulg. 58 H7
also known as Ardas
Ardabil Iran 100 B2
Ardabil prov. Iran 100 A2
Ardahan Turkey 107 E2
Ardak Iran 101 D3
Ardakān Fārs Iran 100 C4
Ardakān Yazd Iran 100 C3
Ardal Iran 100 B4
Årdal Norway 45 I3
Årdalstangen Norway 45 I3
Ardas r. Greece 58 H7
Arḍ aş Şawwān plain Jordan 109 I7
Ardatov Respublika Mordoviya Rus. Fed.
40 G5
Ardatov Nizhegorodskaya Oblast' Rus. Fed.
40 G5
Ardbeg Canada 173 M5
Ardèche r. France 51 K8
Ardee Rep. of Ireland 47 F10
Arden, Mount hill Australia 146 C3
Ardennes plat. Belgium 51 K3
also known as l'Ardenne, Plateau de
Ardentes France 50 H6
Arden Town U.S.A. 182 C3
Ardeştān Iran 100 C3
Ardglass U.K. 47 G9
Ardila r. Port. 54 D6
Ardino Bulg. 58 G7
Ardkeen N.Z. 152 L6
Ardlethan Australia 147 E3
Ardmore U.S.A. 179 C5
Ardnamurchan, Point of U.K. 46 F7
Ardon Rus. Fed. 107 F2
Ardrossan Australia 146 C3
Ardrossan U.K. 46 H8
Ards Peninsula U.K. 47 G9
Ardvasar U.K. 46 G7
Åre Sweden 44 K3
Areado Brazil 207 G8
Arealí Dem. Rep. Congo 126 F4
Arecibo Puerto Rico 187 G3
Arefino Rus. Fed. 43 U3
Arefu Romania 58 F3
Areguá Rus. Fed. 43 U3
Areia Branca Brazil 202 E3
Arekhawsk Belarus 43 J7
also spelt Orekhovsk; formerly known as
Orekhi-Vydritsa
Arel Belgium see Arlon
Arelas France see Arles
Arelate France see Arles
Arena reef Phil. 74 B4
Arena, Point U.S.A. 182 A3
Arena de la Ventana, Punta pt Mex. 184 C4
Arenal, Campo del plain Arg. 204 D2
Arenal, Puerto del pass Spain 55 I6
Arenal, Volcán vol. Costa Rica 186 B5
Arenápolis Brazil 201 F3
Arenas, Punta de pt Arg. 205 C9
Arenas de San Pedro Spain 54 F4
Arendal Norway 45 J4
Arendsee (Altmark) Germany 48 I3
Arenys de Mar Spain 55 N3
Arenzano Italy 56 A4
Areopoli Greece 59 D12
Areponapuchi Mex. 181 D7
Arequipa Peru 200 C4
Arequipa dept Peru 200 B3
Arere Brazil 199 H5
Ārero Eth. 128 C3
Ares France 50 E7
Arévalo Spain 54 G3
Areza Eritrea 104 B5
Arezzaf well Mali see Aghezzaf
Arezzo Italy 56 D5
historically known as Arretium
'Arfajah well Saudi Arabia 107 E5
Arfara Greece 59 C11
Arga r. Spain 55 J2
Argadargada Australia 148 C4
Argalasti Greece 59 E9
Argalant Mongolia 85 F2
Argan China 88 E3
Arganda Spain 55 H4
Arganil Port. 54 C4
Argao Phil. 74 B4
Argatay Mongolia 85 E2
Argel Alg. see Algiers
Argelès-Gazost France 50 F9
Argelès-sur-Mer France 51 J10
Argens r. France 51 M9
Argenta Italy 56 D4
Argentan France 50 G5
Argentario, Monte hill Italy 56 D6
Argentat France 50 H7
Argentera, Cima dell' mt. Italy 51 N8

► Argentina country S. America 204 C4
2nd largest country in South America and
8th in the world. 3rd most populous country
in South America. Long form Argentine
Republic.
world [countries] ▶▶ 10–11
southamerica [countries] ▶▶ 192–193

Argentina Range mts Antarctica 223 V1
Argentine Republic country S. America see
Argentina
Argentina, Lago l. Arg. 205 B8
Argenton-sur-Creuse France 50 H6
Argentoratum France see Strasbourg
Argentre France 50 F4
Argeş r. Romania 58 H4

Argeşel r. Romania 58 H4
Arghandab r. Afgh. 101 F4
Arghastan r. Afgh. 101 F4
Argonne U.S.A. 172 E5
Argolikos Kolpos b. Greece 59 D11
Argos Greece 59 D11
Argos U.S.A. 172 H9
Argos Orestiko Greece 59 C8
Argostoli Greece 59 B10
Arguedas Spain 55 J2
Argun' r. China/Rus. Fed. 85 H1
also known as Ergun He
Argun r. Georgia/Rus. Fed. 107 F2
Argun Rus. Fed. 107 F2
Argungu Nigeria 125 G3
Argunsky Khrebet mts Rus. Fed. 85 H1
Arguut Mongolia 84 D2
Argyle r. Australia 148 D3
Argyle l. Australia 148 C5
Argyle WI U.S.A. 172 D8
Argyle, Lake Australia 150 E3
Argyrokastron Albania see Gjirokastër
Arhab reg. Yemen 104 D5
Arhangay prov. Mongolia 84 D2
Århus Denmark 45 J4
also spelt Aarhus
Aria N.Z. 152 I6
Ariaga l. Indon. 75 C1
Ariake-kai b. Japan 91 B8
Ariamsvlei Namibia 130 C6
Ariano Irpino Italy 56 H7
Arias Arg. 204 E4
Ari Atoll Maldives 93 D10
Aribi r. Venez. 199 F2
Aribinda Burkina 125 E3
Arica Chile 200 C4
Arica Col. 198 D5
Aricagua Venez. 198 D2
Arid, Cape Australia 151 C7
Arida Japan 91 D7
Aridaia Greece 58 D3
Aridal, Sabkhat salt pan W. Sahara 122 B4
Arid Island N.Z. see Rakitu Island
Ariège r. France 50 H9
Arieş r. Romania 58 E2
Arieşul Mic r. Romania 58 E2
Ariha Syria 109 H2
Arihā West Bank see Jericho
Arikaree r. U.S.A. 178 B4
Arilje Srbija Yugo. 58 B5
Arima Brazil 199 F6
Ariminum Italy see Rimini
Arimu Mine Guyana 199 G3
'Arin, Wādī al watercourse Saudi Arabia
104 C2
Arinagour U.K. 46 F7
Arinos r. Mato Grosso Brazil 201 G3
Arinos Minas Gerais Brazil 202 C5
Arinos r. Brazil 202 C5
Ario de Rosáles Mex. 185 E5
Ariogala Lith. 42 E6
Aripero r. Col. 198 D3
Aripuanã Brazil 201 F2
Aripuanã r. Brazil 199 F6
Ariquemes Brazil 201 F2
Arirانhá r. Brazil 203 A6
Arisaig U.K. 46 G7
Arisaig, Sound of sea chan. U.K. 46 G7
Arisaru Falls Guyana 199 G3
Arismendi Venez. 198 D2
Aristazabal Island Canada 166 D4
Aristizábal, Cabo c. Arg. 205 D7
Aristóbulo del Valle Arg. 201 G5
Aritwala Pak. 101 H4
Arivonimamo Madag. 131 [inset] J3
Arixang China see Wenquan
Ariya waterhole Kenya 128 C4
Ariyalur India 94 C4
Arizaro, Salar de salt flat Arg. 200 D6
Arizgoiti Spain 55 I1
Arizona Arg. 204 D4
Arizona state U.S.A. 183 M7
Arizpe Mex. 184 C2
'Arjah Saudi Arabia 104 D2
Ārjäng Sweden 45 K4
Arjasa Indon. 77 F4
'Arjawi, Wādi al watercourse Iraq 109 O5
Arjeplog Sweden 44 L2
Arjo r. Venez. 199 E3
Arjona Col. 198 C2
Arjona Spain 54 G6
Arjuni India 96 D5
Arkadak Rus. Fed. 41 G6
Arkadelphia U.S.A. 179 D5
Arkagala Rus. Fed. 39 O3
Arkalgud India 94 C3
Arkalochori Greece 59 G13
also spelt Arqalyq
Arkansas r. U.S.A. 179 E5
Arkansas City AR U.S.A. 175 B5
Arkansas City KS U.S.A. 178 C4
Arkata r. Bulg. 58 G6
Arkatag Shan mts China 89 E4
Arkenu, Jabal mt. Libya 120 E4
Arkhangel'sk Rus. Fed. see Archangel
Arkhangel'skaya Oblast' admin. div.
Rus. Fed. 40 G3
English form Archangel Oblast
Arkhangel'skoye Respublika Bashkortostan
Rus. Fed. 40 K5
Arkhangel'skoye Tul'skaya Oblast' Rus. Fed.
43 S8
Arkhara Rus. Fed. 82 C2
Arkhara r. Rus. Fed. 82 C2
Arkhipovka Rus. Fed. 82 C4
Arkhipovka Rus. Fed. 43 M7
Árki i. Greece 59 H11
Arki India see Ara
Arklow Rep. of Ireland 47 F11
also known as An tInbhear Mór
Arkoi i. Greece 59 H11
also spelt Árki
Arkona Canada 173 L7
Arkona, Kap c. Germany 49 K1
Arkonam India see Arakkonam
Arkosund Sweden 45 L4

► Arkticheskiy, Mys is Rus. Fed. 39 J1
Most northerly point of Asia.

Arkticheskogo Instituta, Ostrova is
Rus. Fed. 39 I2
English form Arctic Institute Islands
Arkul' Rus. Fed. 40 I4
Ārla Sweden 45 L4
Arlanc France 51 J7
Arlanza r. Spain 55 G2
Arlanzón r. Spain 54 G2
Arles France 51 K9
historically known as Arelas or Arelate
Arli Burkina 125 F4
Ar-Ra'abadi al Abyad pt Saudi Arabia 104 C2
also known as Mondragón
Arli Burkina 125 F4
Arlington IA U.S.A. 172 B8
Arlington IL U.S.A. 172 D9
Arlington NY U.S.A. 177 L4
Arlington OH U.S.A. 176 B5
Arlington OR U.S.A. 180 B3
Arlington TX U.S.A. 177 M7
Arlington VA U.S.A. 176 H7
Arlington WI U.S.A. 172 D7
Arlington Heights U.S.A. 174 B3
Arlit Niger 125 G2
Arlon Belgium 51 L3
also known as Aarlen; also spelt Aarlen
Arly France 51 M7
Arlyeya Belarus 43 K8

Arm r. Canada 167 J5
Armadale U.K. 47 J6
Armadale r. Afgh. 101 F4
Armadores i. Indon. 75 C1
Armageddon tourist site Israel see
Tel Megiddo
Armagh U.K. 47 F9
Ar Rifā'ī Iraq 107 F4
Ar Rihāb salt flat Iraq 107 F5
Ar Rimāl des. Saudi Arabia 105 F3
Ar Riyad Saudi Arabia see Riyadh
Ar Riyad prov. Saudi Arabia 104 D3
Arroio Grande Brazil 204 G4
Arronches Port. 54 D5
Arros r. France 50 F9
Arroux r. France 51 J6
Arrow r. Canada 172 D7
Arrow, Lough l. Rep. of Ireland 47 D9
Arrow Lake Canada 172 C2
Arrowsmith, Mount N.Z. 153 E11
Arrowtown N.Z. 153 C12
Arroyo de la Luz Spain 54 E5
Arroyo Grande U.S.A. 182 D6
Arroyo Seco Mex. 185 F4
Ar Rubay'iyah Saudi Arabia 105 D3
Ar Rumādīyat Saudi Arabia 107 F5
Ar Rumaythah Iraq 107 F5
Ar Rummānah Iraq 109 M3
Ar Ruq'i well Saudi Arabia 105 D1
Ar Ruşāfah Syria 109 J2
Ar Rustāq Oman 105 G3
Ar Ruţbah Iraq 107 E4
Ar Ruwaybat well Libya 120 A1
Ar Ruwaydah Saudi Arabia 104 D3
Arruwurra Aboriginal Land res. Australia
148 C3
Armu r. Rus. Fed. 82 E3
Armur India 94 C2
Armutçuk Dağı mts Turkey 106 AC
Armutlu Turkey 58 J8
Armutova Turkey see Gömeç
Armyans'k Ukr. 41 E7
Armyanskaya Wzvyshsha hills Belarus 43 K7
Arnå r. Denmark 48 F1
Arna Greece 59 K12
Arnafjall hill Faroe Is 46 E1
Arnage France 51 H4
Arnaia Greece 58 E8
Arnauti, Cape Cyprus see Arnauti, Cape
Arnarfjörður inlet Iceland 44 [inset] A1
Arnaud r. Canada 169 G1
Arnauti, Cape Cyprus 108 D2
also known as Akama, Akra; also spelt
Arnaoutis, Cape
Arnavutköy Turkey 58 J7
Arnay-le-Duc France 51 K5
Arnedo Spain 55 I2
Arneiroz Brazil 202 D3
Arnemark Sweden 44 M2
Ârnes Norway 45 J3
Arnhem Neth. 48 D4
Arnhem, Cape Australia 148 C2
Arnhem Land reg. Australia 148 B2
Arnhem Land Aboriginal Land res.
Australia 148 B2
Arnijoys 1 Lith. 42 D6
Arnisdale U.K. 46 G6
Arnissa Greece 58 C8
Arno r. Italy 56 C5
Arno Bay Australia 146 C3
Arnoia r. Spain 54 C2
Arnold MD U.S.A. 177 I6
Arnold MI U.S.A. 172 F4
Arnold MO U.S.A. 174 B4
Arnold's Cove Canada 169 K4
Arnoldstein Austria 49 K9
Arnon r. France 51 I5
Arnon r. Jordan see Mawjib, Wādī al
Arnoux, Lac l. Canada 173 N2
Arnoya r. Spain see Arnoia
Arnprior Canada 168 E4
Arnsberg Germany 48 F4
Arnstadt Germany 48 H5
Arnstein Canada 173 N3
Arnstorf Germany 49 J7
Arntfield Canada 173 N2
Aro r. Venez. 199 E3
Aroab Namibia 130 D5
Aroania mt. Greece 59 D11
Aroeira Brazil 203 A7
Aroland Canada 168 C3
Arolsen Germany 48 G4
Aroma Sudan 104 B5
Aron r. France 51 J6
Aron India 96 C4
Arona Italy 56 A3
Aroniadika Greece 59 K13
Aroona Australia 146 C3
Aroorae i. Kiribati 145 G2
also known as Arore; formerly known as Hurd
Island
Arore i. Kiribati see Arorae
Aroroy Phil. 74 B3
Aros r. Mex. 184 C2
Arosa, Ría de est. Spain see Arousa, Ría de
Arossi i. Solomon Is see San Cristobal
Arouca Port. 54 C4
Arouelli well Chad 120 C1
Aru, Kepulauan is Indon. 73 H8
Aru Uganda 128 A4
Aruajá Brazil 199 F6
Aruanã Brazil 206 B1

► Aruba terr. West Indies 198 D1
Self-governing Netherlands Territory.
oceania [countries] ▶▶ 138–139

Arudy France 50 F9
Arumã Brazil 199 F6
Arun r. China 85 I2
Arun r. Nepal 97 F4
Arunachal Pradesh state India 97 G4
historically known as North-East Frontier
Agency
Arun Qi China see Naji
Aruppukkottai India 94 C4
Arus, Tanjung pt Indon. 75 B2
Arusha Tanz. 128 C5
Arusha admin. reg. Tanz. 128 C5
Arusha National Park Tanz. 128 C5
Arut r. Indon. 77 E3
Aruti Brazil 199 F5
Aruwimi r. Dem. Rep. Congo 126 E4
Arvada U.S.A. 180 F5
Arvayheer Mongolia 84 D2
Arvi India 94 C1
Arviat Canada 167 M2
formerly known as Eskimo Point
Arvidsjaur Sweden 44 L2
Arvika Sweden 45 K4
Arviksand Norway 44 M1
Arvin U.S.A. 182 F6
Arvonia U.S.A. 176 G8
Arwā' Saudi Arabia 104 D3
Arwād i. Syria 109 H3
Arwala Indon. 75 C4
Arxan China 85 H2
Aryanah Tunisia see L'Ariana
Arykbalyk Kazakh. 103 G1
also spelt Aryqbayq
Aryqbayq Kazakh. see Arykbalyk
Arys' Kazakh. 103 G4
Arys, Ozero salt l. Kazakh. 103 F3
Arykanyng-Aryg Rus. Fed. 80 H1
Arzamas r. Saudi Arabia 104 D2
Arzamaḥ i. U.A.E. 105 F3
Arzew Alg. 123 E1
Arzew, Golfe d' g. Alg. 55 L9
Arzgir Rus. Fed. 41 H7
Arzila Morocco see Asilah
Arzúa Spain 54 C2
Arzubikha Rus. Fed. 43 V1
Aš Czech Rep. 48 I5
Asa waterhole Kenya 128 C4
Asa r. Namibia 128 C5
Asab Namibia 130 C5
Asaba Nigeria 125 G5
Asad, Buḩayrat al resr Syria 109 J1
Asadābād Afgh. 101 G3
Asadābād Hamadān Iran 100 B3

Asadābād Khorāsān Iran 101 D3
Asagny, Parc National d' nat. park
Côte d'Ivoire 124 D5
Asahan r. Indon. 76 B2
Asahi Chiba Japan 91 G7
Asahi Toyama Japan 91 E6
Asahi-dake mt. Japan 90 H3
Asahi-dake vol. Japan 90 F5
Asahi-gawa r. Japan 91 C7
Asaka Japan 91 F6
Asaka Uzbek. 103 H4
also spelt Assake; formerly known as Leninsk
Asālē l. Iran 100 D1
Asālem Iran 100 B2
Asama-yama vol. Japan 91 F6
Asankranguaa Ghana 124 E5
Asan-man b. S. Korea 83 B5
Asansol India 97 E5
Asanwenso Ghana 124 E5
Āsayita Eth. 128 D2
Asbach Germany 48 E6
Asbestos Canada 169 G4
Asbestos Hill Canada see Purtuniq
Asbestos Mountains S. Africa 132 G4
Āsbe Teferi Eth. 128 D2
Asbury Park U.S.A. 177 K5
Ascalon Israel see Ashqelon
Ascea Italy 57 H8
Ascensión Bol. 201 E4
Ascensión Chihuahua Mex. 184 D2
Ascensión Nuevo León Mex. 185 F3
Ascension atoll Micronesia see Pohnpei

► Ascension i. S. Atlantic Ocean 216 N6
Dependency of St Helena.

Aschaffenburg Germany 48 G6
Ascheberg Germany 48 I4
Aschersleben Germany 48 I4
Asciano Italy 56 D5
Ascoli Piceno Italy 56 F6
historically known as Asculum or Asculum
Picenum
Ascoli Satriano Italy 56 H7
historically known as Ausculum or Ausculum
Apulum
Ascotán Chile 200 C5
Ascotán, Salar de salt flat Chile 200 C5
Asculum Italy see Ascoli Piceno
Asculum Picenum Italy see Ascoli Piceno
Ascutney U.S.A. 177 M2
Åse Norway 44 K1
Åsebyn Sweden 45 K4
Asedjrad plat. Alg. 123 F4
Äsela Eth. 128 C3
Åsele Sweden 44 L2
Asendabo Eth. 128 C3
Asenovgrad Bulg. 58 F6
Åseral Norway 45 I4
Aseri Estonia 42 H2
Aşfāk Iran 100 D3
Aşfar, Jabal mt. Jordan 109 H5
Aşfar, Tall al hill Saudi Arabia 109 M7
Aşfar, Tall al hill Syria 109 H4
Asgårðar Iceland 44 [inset] B2
Asha Rus. Fed. 40 K5
Ashanti admin. reg. Ghana 125 E5
Asharat Saudi Arabia 105 D2
Ashbourne U.K. 47 K10
Ashburn U.S.A. 175 D6
Ashburton watercourse Australia 150 A4
Ashburton N.Z. 153 F11
also known as Hakateree
Ashburton Bay Canada 172 G2
Ashburton Range hills Australia 148 B3
Aschchikol', Ozero salt l. Kazakh. 103 F3
Aschchisay Kazakh. see Achisay
Ashcroft Canada 166 F5
Ashdod Israel 108 F6
historically known as Azotus
Ashdown U.S.A. 179 D5
Asheboro U.S.A. 174 E5
Ashern Canada 167 L5
Asheville U.S.A. 174 C4
Ashevo Rus. Fed. 43 K4
Asheweig r. Canada 168 C2
Ashford Australia 147 F2
Ashford U.K. 47 M12
Ash Fork U.S.A. 183 L6

► Ashgabat Turkm. 102 D5
Capital of Turkmenistan. Formerly known
Ashkhabad; historically known as Poltoratsk.

Ashhurst N.Z. 152 J8
Ashibetsu Japan 90 H3
Ashikaga Japan 91 F6
Ashington U.K. 47 K8
Ashiro Japan 90 G4
Ashizuri-misaki pt Japan 91 C8
Ashizuri-Uwakai National Park Japan 83 D6
Ashkazar Iran 100 C4
Ashkelon Israel see Ashqelon
Ashkhabad Turkm. see Ashgabat
Ashkhabadskaya Oblast' admin. div. Turkm.
see Akhal'skaya Oblast'
Ashkīdah Libya 120 B3
Ashkum U.S.A. 172 F10
Ashkun reg. Afgh. 101 G3
Ashland AL U.S.A. 175 C5
Ashland KS U.S.A. 178 C4
Ashland KY U.S.A. 176 C7
Ashland NE U.S.A. 178 C3
Ashland NH U.S.A. 177 N2
Ashland OH U.S.A. 176 C5
Ashland VA U.S.A. 176 H8
Ashland WI U.S.A. 172 C4
Ashland City U.S.A. 174 C4
Ashley r. N.Z. 153 G11
also known as Rakahuri
Ashley IN U.S.A. 173 H9
Ashley IN U.S.A. 173 I7
Ashley ND U.S.A. 178 C2
Ashley OH U.S.A. 176 C5

► Ashmore and Cartier Islands terr.
Australia 144 C3
Australian External Territory.
oceania [countries] ▶▶ 138–139

Ashmore Reef Australia 150 C2
Ashmūn Egypt 108 B7
Ashmyanskaya Wzvyshsha hills Belarus
42 G7
Ashmyany Belarus 42 G7
Ashmyany r. Belarus 42 H7
Ashoknagar India 96 C4
Ashoro Japan 90 H3
Ashqelon Israel 108 F6
also known as Ashkelon; historically known as
Ascalon
Ash Sha'ar Saudi Arabia 104 C4
Ash Shabakah Iraq 107 E5
Ash Shabrūm waterhole Saudi Arabia
109 O7
Ash Shaddādah Syria 109 L1
Ash Shafa Saudi Arabia 104 C3
Ash Shakk Iraq 109 O2
Ash Sham Syria see Damascus
Ash Sha'm U.A.E. 105 G2
Ash Shanāfiyah Iraq 107 F5
also spelt Shināfiyah
Ash Shaqiq Saudi Arabia 107 E5
Ash Shaqqā Saudi Arabia 104 D2
also spelt Sharqāt; historically known as Ashur
Ash Sharawrah Saudi Arabia 105 E4
Ash Shāriqah U.A.E. see Sharjah
Ash Sharqāt Iraq see Ash Sharqiyah
Ash Sharqiyah admin. reg. Oman 105 G3
Ash Sharqiyah reg. Oman 105 G3

Ash Sharqīyah prov. Saudi Arabia **105** E3
Ash Shaṭrah Iraq **107** F5
Ash Shawbak Jordan **108** G7
  also spelt Shaubak
Ash Shawr hill Iraq **109** L4
Ash Shaykh 'Uthman Yemen **104** D5
  English form Sheikh Othman
Ash Shiblīyat hill Saudi Arabia **109** I8
Ash Shiḥr Yemen **105** E5
Ash Shināş Oman **105** G2
Ash Shiṣar well Oman **105** F4
Ash Shu'aybah Saudi Arabia **104** C2
Ash Shu'bah Saudi Arabia **104** D1
Ash Shubaykiyah Saudi Arabia **104** C2
Ash Shumlūl Saudi Arabia **105** D2
Ash Shuqayq Saudi Arabia **104** B3
Ash Shurayf Saudi Arabia see Khaybar
Ash Shuwayḥiṭīyah waterhole Saudi Arabia **109** L7
Ash Shuwayrif Libya **120** B2
Ashta Madhya Pradesh India **96** C5
Ashta Maharashtra India **94** B2
Ashtabula U.S.A. **176** E4
Ashtarak Armenia **107** F2
Ashti Maharashtra India **94** B2
Ashti Maharashtra India **94** C2
Ashti Maharashtra India **94** C1
Ashton S. Africa **133** E10
Ashton ID U.S.A. **180** E3
Ashton IL U.S.A. **172** D9
Ashuanipi r. Canada **169** H2
Ashuanipi Lake Canada **169** H2
Ashuapmushuan r. Canada **174** F1
  formerly known as Chamouchouane
Ashuapmushuan, Réserve Faunique nature res. Canada **169** F1
Ashur Iraq see Ash Sharqāṭ
Ashusuu pass Kyrg. **103** I4
  also known as Chiyrchik, Pereval
Ashville AL U.S.A. **175** C5
Ashville ME U.S.A. **177** Q1
Ashville PA U.S.A. **176** E4
Ashwabay, Mount U.S.A. **172** C4
Ashwaubenon U.S.A. **172** E6
'Āṣī r. Lebanon/Syria see Orontes
'Āṣī, Nahr al r. Asia see Orontes
Asid Gulf Phil. **74** B3
Asientos Mex. **185** E4
Asifabad India **94** C2
Asika India **95** E2
Asikkala Fin. **45** N3
Asilah Morocco **54** E9
  formerly spelt Arzila
Asillo Peru **200** C3
Asimi Greece **59** G14
Asinara, Golfo dell' b. Sardegna Italy **56** A8
Asinara, Isola i. Sardegna Italy **56** A7
Asind India **96** B4
Asino Rus. Fed. **39** I4
Asintort Belarus **43** J7
Asipovichy Belarus **43** J8
  also spelt Osipovichi
'Asir prov. Saudi Arabia **104** C3
Asisium Italy see Assisi
Askainen Fin. **42** L1
Aşkale Turkey **107** E3
Askarovo Rus. Fed. **102** D1
Asker Norway **45** J4
Askersund Sweden **45** K4
Askim Norway **45** J4
Askino Rus. Fed. **40** K4
Askio mt. Greece **59** C8
Askira Nigeria **125** H4
Askival hill U.K. **46** F7
Askiz Rus. Fed. **80** E2
Askola Fin. **45** N3
Askol'd, Ostrov i. Rus. Fed. **90** C3
Askot India **96** D3
Askvoll Norway **45** I3
Aslam, Wādī watercourse Saudi Arabia **104** C3
Aşlānduz Iran **100** A2
Aşlānköy r. Turkey **108** F1
Aslik r. Belarus **43** K8
Aslözközpont Hungary see Mórahalom
Asmar Afgh. **96** A2
Asmar r. Afgh. **101** G3
Aşmariq Saudi Arabia **104** C3

Asmara Eritrea **121** H6
  Capital of Eritrea. Also spelt Āsmera.

Āsmera Eritrea see Asmara
Åsnen l. Sweden **45** K4
As Neves Spain **54** C2
Asoenangka Brazil **199** G5
Aso-Kuju National Park Japan **91** B8
Asola Italy **56** C3
Asopos r. Greece **59** D11
Asopos r. Greece **59** E10
Åsosa Eth. **128** B2
Asoteriba, Jebel mt. Sudan **121** H4
Asotin U.S.A. **180** C3
Aspang-Markt Austria **49** N8
Aspara Armenia **103** H4
Asparukhovo Bulg. **58** I6
Aspås Sweden **45** K3
Aspe Spain **55** K6
Aspen U.S.A. **180** F5
Aspermont U.S.A. **179** B5

Aspiring, Mount N.Z. **153** C12
  also known as Tititea
As Pontes de García Rodríguez Spain **54** D1
  also known as Puentes de García Rodríguez
Aspro, Cape Cyprus **108** D3
Asprokavos, Akra pt Greece **59** B9
Aspromonte, Parco Nazionale dell' nat. park Italy **57** H10
Aspron, Cape Cyprus see Aspro, Cape
Asprovalta Greece **58** E8
Aspur India **96** B5
Asquith Canada **167** J4
Assa Morocco **122** C3
Assab Eritrea **121** I6
  also spelt Āseb
Assaba admin. reg. Mauritania **124** C2
Aş Şabrīn Saudi Arabia **104** C2
As Sabkhah Syria **109** K2
As Sabsab well Saudi Arabia **105** E2
Assabu Japan **90** G4
Aş Şafā lava field Syria **109** H4
Aş Şafāqis Tunisia see Sfax
Aş Şafī Jordan **108** G6
  also spelt Safi
As Safirah Syria **109** I1
Aş Şaḥāf Saudi Arabia **105** E2
Aş Şaḥīf Yemen **104** C5
Aş Şaḥn hills Iraq/Saudi Arabia **109** N7
Assake Uzbek. see Asaka
Assake-Audan, Vpadina depr. Uzbek. **102** D4
'Assal, Lac l. Djibouti see Assal, Lake

Assal, Lake Djibouti **128** D2
  Lowest point in Africa. Also known as 'Assal, Lac.
  africa (landscapes) >> 112-113

As Salamīyah Saudi Arabia **105** D2
Aş Şāliḥīyah Syria **109** L3
  also known as Dura Europos
As Salmān Iraq **107** F5
As Salṭ Jordan **108** G5
  also spelt Salt
Assam state India **97** F4
Assamakka Niger **125** G2
As Samāwah Iraq **107** F5
Aş Şanam reg. Saudi Arabia **105** E3
As Sarir reg. Libya **120** D3
Assateague Island National Seashore nature res. U.S.A. **177** J3
As Sawādah Iraq **107** F5
As Sawdā' i. Oman **105** F4
Aş Şawrah Saudi Arabia **104** B3
As Şaybīyah waterhole Saudi Arabia **109** M9
Assegaaibos S. Africa **133** I10
Assemini Sardegna Italy **57** B9
Assen Neth. **48** D2
Assen Denmark **45** M5
Assens Denmark **45** M5
Assesse Belgium **51** L2
As Sidrah Libya **120** C2
Assigny, Lac l. Canada **169** H2
As Sikak Saudi Arabia **105** E2
Assiniboia Canada **167** J5
Assiniboine r. Canada **167** L5
Assiniboine, Mount Canada **167** H5
Assinica, Lac l. Canada **168** F3
Assis Brazil **206** C9
Assisi Italy **56** E5
  historically known as Asisium
Assomada Cape Verde **124** [inset]
Assouf Mellene watercourse Alg. **123** F4
Aş Şubayḥīyah Kuwait **107** F5
As Subaykhah Saudi Arabia **104** C4
As Sufāl Yemen **105** E5
Aş Şufayrī well Saudi Arabia **105** D1
As Sukhnah Syria **109** J3
As Sulaymānīyah Iraq **107** F4
As Sulaymānīyah governorate Iraq **107** F4
As Sulaymī Saudi Arabia **104** C3
As Sulayyil Saudi Arabia **105** D3
Aş Şulb reg. Saudi Arabia **105** E2
As Sulṭān Libya **120** C2
Aş Şummān plat. Saudi Arabia **105** E3
Aş Şummān plat. Saudi Arabia **105** E3
As Sūq Saudi Arabia **104** C3
As Sūrīyah country Asia see Syria
Aş Şuwar Syria **109** L2
As Suwaydā' Syria **109** H5
As Suwaydā' governorate Syria **109** H5
As Suwayḥ Oman **105** G3
As Suwayq Oman **105** G3
Aş Şuwayrah Iraq **107** F4
As Suways Egypt see Suez
As Suwwādīyah Yemen **105** D5
Asta r. Norway **45** J3
Asta, Cima d' mt. Italy **56** D2
Astacus Turkey see Kocaeli
Astaffort France **50** F4
Astakida i. Greece **59** H13
Astakos Greece **59** C10
Astalu Island Pak. see Astola Island

Astana Kazakh. **103** G2
  Capital of Kazakhstan. Formerly known as Akmola or Aqmola or Akmolinsk or Tselinograd.

Astaneh Iran **100** B2
Astara Azer. **107** G3
Åsteby Sweden **45** K3
Asterabad Iran see Gorgān
Asti Italy **56** A4
Astica Arg. **204** C3
Astillero Peru **200** C3
Astin Tag mts China see Altun Shan
Astipálaia i. Greece see Astypalaia
Astola Island Pak. **101** E5
  also spelt Astalu Island
Aston Bay S. Africa **133** I11
Astor Jammu and Kashmir **96** B2
Astor r. Pak. **101** H3
Astorga Brazil **206** B10
Astorga Spain **54** E2
  historically known as Asturica Augusta
Astoria U.S.A. **180** B3
Astra Arg. **205** D7
Astrabad Iran see Gorgān
Astrakhan' Kazakh. see Astrakhanka
Astrakhan' Rus. Fed. **102** B3
Astrakhan' Bazar Azer. see Cälilabad
Astrakhanka Kazakh. **103** G2
  also known as Astrakhan'
Astrakhan Oblast admin. div. Rus. Fed. see Astrakhanskaya Oblast'
Astrakhanskaya Oblast' admin. div. Rus. Fed. **102** A3
  English form Astrakhan Oblast
Astravyets Belarus **42** H7
Astrida Rwanda see Butare
Astrolabe, Récifs de l' reef New Caledonia **145** F3
Astros Greece **59** D11
Astryna Belarus **42** H8
Astsyer r. Belarus **43** M8
Asturias aut. comm. Spain **54** E1
Asturica Augusta Spain see Astorga
Astypalaia i. Greece **59** H12
  also spelt Astipálaia
Asubulak Kazakh. **88** C1
  also spelt Asubulag
Asubulaq Kazakh. see Asubulak
Asunción Bol. **200** D2
Asunción r. Mex. **181** D7
Asuncion i. N. Mariana Is **73** K3

Asunción Para. **201** F6
  Capital of Paraguay.

Asunción Mita Guat. **185** H6
Asvyeya Belarus **42** J5
Asvyeyskaye, Vozyera l. Belarus **42** J5
Aswa r. Uganda **128** A4
Aswad Oman **105** H4
Aswad, Wādī watercourse Oman **105** F3
Aswān Egypt **121** G3
Aswān governorate Egypt **104** A2
Aswān Dam Egypt **121** G3
Asyūṭ Egypt **121** F3
  historically known as Lycopolis
Asyūṭ governorate Egypt **106** B6
Ata i. Tonga **145** H4
  formerly known as Sola
Atabapo r. Col./Venez. **199** E3
Atabay Kazakh. **103** J2
Atacama admin. reg. Chile **204** C2
Atacama, Desierto de des. Chile see Atacama Desert
Atacama, Salar de salt flat Chile **200** D5

Atacama Desert Chile **204** C3
  Driest place in the world. Also known as Atacama, Desierto de.
  world (climate and weather) >> 16-17
  southamerica (contrasts) >> 194-195

Atacames Ecuador **198** B4
Ataco Col. **198** C4
Atafaitafa, Djebel mt. Alg. **123** G4
Atafu atoll Tokelau **145** H2
  formerly known as Duke of York
Atakent Turkey **108** F1
Atakor mts Alg. **123** G5
Atakpamé Togo **125** F5
Atalaia Brazil **202** F4
Atalaia hill Port. **54** C6
Atalaia do Norte Brazil **198** D6
Atalaya Panama **186** C5
Atalaya Madre de Dios Peru **200** C3
Atalaya Ucayali Peru **200** B2
Ataléia Brazil **207** I6
Atamanovka Rus. Fed. **85** G1
Atami Japan **91** F7
Atamisqui Arg. **204** D3
Atamyrat Turkm. see Kerki
Ataniya Turkey see Adana
Atapupu Indon. **75** C5
'Ataq Yemen **105** D5
'Atāqa, Gebel hill Egypt **108** D8
Ataran r. Myanmar **78** B4
Atascadero U.S.A. **182** D6
Atascosa watercourse U.S.A. **179** C6
Atasu Kazakh. **103** G2
Atatan He r. China **88** B3
Atatürk Milli Parkı nat. park Turkey **59** J12
Atauro i. East Timor **75** C5
  formerly known as Kambing, Pulau
Atáviros mt. Greece see Attavyros
Atayurt Turkey **108** E1
Atbara r. Sudan **121** G5
Atbara Sudan **121** G5
Atbasar Kazakh. **103** G2
At-Bashy Kyrg. **103** I4
Atchafalaya Bay U.S.A. **175** B6
Atchison U.S.A. **178** D4
Atebubu Ghana **125** E5
Ateca Spain **55** J3
Aten Bol. **200** C3
Atengullo r. Mex. **184** D4
Aternersk Kazakh. see Atyrau
Aterno r. Italy **56** F6
Atessa Italy **56** G6
Atfih Egypt **108** C8
Ath Belgium **51** J2
  also spelt Aath
Athabasca r. Canada **167** H4
Athabasca r. Canada **167** I3
Athabasca, Lake Canada **167** I3
Athagarh India **95** E1
Athalia U.S.A. **176** C7
Athapapuskow Lake Canada **167** K4
Athboy Rep. of Ireland **47** F10
Athenae Greece see Athens
Athenry Rep. of Ireland **47** D10
Athens Canada **173** R6

Athens Greece **59** E11
  Capital of Greece. Also known as Athínai; also spelt Athina; historically known as Athenae.

Athens AL U.S.A. **174** C5
Athens GA U.S.A. **175** D5
Athens NY U.S.A. **177** L3
Athens OH U.S.A. **176** C6
Athens TN U.S.A. **174** C5
Athens TX U.S.A. **179** D5
Atherton Australia **149** E3
Athi r. Kenya **128** C5
Athina Greece see Athens
Athínai Greece see Athens
Athi River Kenya **128** C5
Athlone Rep. of Ireland **47** E10
  also known as Báile Átha Luain
Athna', Wādī al watercourse Jordan **109** J5
Athni India **94** B2
Athol N.Z. **153** C13
Athol U.S.A. **177** M3
Athos mt. Greece **59** F8
Ath Tharthār, Wādī r. Iraq **107** E4
Ath Thāyat hills Saudi Arabia **109** K7
Ath Thāyat mt. Saudi Arabia **108** G8
Ath Thumāmī well Saudi Arabia **105** D2
Athy Rep. of Ireland **47** F11
Ati Chad **120** C6
Ati, Jabal mts Libya **120** B4
Atiābād Iran **100** D3
Atiak Uganda **128** B4
Atiamuri N.Z. **152** K6
Ati Ardébé Chad **120** C6
Atibaia Brazil **206** F9
Atico Peru **200** B4
Atico r. Peru **200** B4
Atiedo Sudan **128** B3
Atikameg Canada **167** H4
Atikameg r. Canada **168** D2
Atik Lake Canada **167** M4
Atikokan Canada **168** B3
Atikonak Lake Canada **169** H2
Atimonan Phil. **74** B3
Atina Italy **56** F7
Atirampattinam India **94** C4
Atitlán, Parque Nacional nat. park Guat. **185** H6
'Atîk, Wâdi al watercourse Saudi Arabia **104** C4
Atka Rus. Fed. **39** Q3
Atkarsk Rus. Fed. **41** H6
Atkri Indon. **75** D3
Atlacomulco Mex. **185** F5
Atlanta GA U.S.A. **175** C5
  State capital of Georgia.

Atlanta TX U.S.A. **179** D5
Atlanti Turkey **106** C3
Atlantic IA U.S.A. **178** D3
Atlantic ME U.S.A. **177** Q1
Atlantic City U.S.A. **177** K6
Atlántico dept Col. **198** C2

Atlantic Ocean **216** K3
  2nd largest ocean in the world.
  oceans (features) >> 210-211

Atlantic Peak U.S.A. **180** E4
Atlantis S. Africa **132** C10
Atlas Bogd mt. Mongolia **84** B3
Atlas Méditerranéen mts Alg. see Atlas Tellien
Atlas Mountains Africa **122** C3
  africa (landscapes) >> 112-113
Atlasova, Ostrov i. Rus. Fed. **39** P4
  formerly known as Alaid, Ostrov
Atlas Saharien mts Alg. **123** F2
  English form Saharan Atlas
Atlas Tellien mts Alg. **123** F2
  also known as Atlas Méditerranéen or Tell Atlas
Atlin Canada **166** C3
Atlin Lake Canada **166** C3
Atlin Provincial Park Canada **166** C3
'Atlit Israel **108** F5
Atlixco Mex. **185** F5
Atmakur Andhra Pradesh India **94** C3
Atmakur Andhra Pradesh India **94** C3
Atmore U.S.A. **175** C6
Atnarko Norway **45** J3
Atner India **96** C5
Atnetye Aboriginal Land res. Australia **148** C4
Atō Japan **91** B7
Atocha Bol. **200** D5
Atoka U.S.A. **179** D5
Atome Angola **127** B7
Atonyia W. Sahara **122** C4
Atotonilco el Alto Mex. **185** E4
Atouat mt. Laos **78** D4
Atoyac de Alvarez Mex. **185** E5
Atpadi India **94** B2
Atqan China see Aqqan
Atqasuk U.S.A. **164** D2
Atrai r. India **97** F4
Atrak, Rūd-e r. Iran/Turkm. see Atrek
Ātran r. Sweden **45** K4
Atranh India **96** C4
Atrato r. Col. **198** B2
Atrek r. Iran/Turkm. **100** C2
  also known as Atrak, Rūd-e or Etrek
Atri Italy **56** F6
Atropatene country Asia see Azerbaijan
Atrūsh Iraq **109** Q1
Atsiki Greece **59** G9
Atsion U.S.A. **177** K6
Atsugi Japan **91** F7
Atsumi Aichi Japan **91** E7
Atsumi Yamagata Japan **90** F5
Atsumi-hantō pen. Japan **91** E7
Atsuta Japan **90** G3
Aṭ Ṭaff reg. U.A.E. **105** F4
Aṭ Ṭā'if Saudi Arabia **104** C3
Aṭ Ṭāji Iraq **109** P4
Attalea Turkey see Antalya
Attalia Turkey see Antalya
Aṭ Ṭallāb oasis Libya **120** D3
Aṭ Ṭa'mīm governorate Iraq **107** F4
At Tamīmī Libya **120** D1
Attapeu Laos **79** D5
  also spelt Attopeu
Attar, Oued el watercourse Alg. **123** G2
Aṭ Ṭarfāt waterhole Iraq **109** L4
Aṭ Ṭārmiyah Iraq **109** P4
Attavyros mt. Greece **59** I12
  also spelt Atáviros
Attawapiskat Canada **168** D2
Attawapiskat r. Canada **168** D2
Attawapiskat Lake Canada **168** C2
Aṭ Ṭawīl mts Saudi Arabia **107** D5
Aṭ Ṭaysīyah plat. Saudi Arabia **104** C1
Aṭ Ṭayyibah Jordan **108** G7
Attendorn Germany **48** E4
Atteridgeville S. Africa **133** M2
Attersee l. Austria **49** K8
At Tibni Syria **109** K2
Attica IN U.S.A. **174** C3
Attica NY U.S.A. **176** G3
Attica OH U.S.A. **176** C4
Attiki admin. reg. Greece **59** E11
Attikamagen Lake Canada **169** H2
At Tin, Ra's pt Libya **120** D1
Attingal India **94** C4
Attleboro U.S.A. **177** N4
Attock City Pak. **101** H3
Attopeu Laos see Attapeu
Attu Greenland **165** N3
Aṭ Ṭubayq reg. Saudi Arabia **107** D5

Attu Island U.S.A. **220** F2
  Most westerly point of North America.

Aṭ Ṭulayḥī well Saudi Arabia **104** D2
Attunga Australia **147** F2
Aṭ Tūnisiyah country Africa see Tunisia
Attur Tamil Nadu India **94** C4
Attur Tamil Nadu India **94** C4
Aṭ Turbah Yemen **104** D5
Aṭ Turbah Yemen **104** D5
Aṭ Tuwayyah well Saudi Arabia **104** D4
Atūd Yemen **105** D5
Atuel r. Arg. **204** D5
Åtvidaberg Sweden **45** K4
Atwari Bangl. **97** F4
Atwater U.S.A. **182** D4
Atwood U.S.A. **178** B4
Atyrau Kazakh. **102** C3
  also known as Ateransk or Gur'yev
Atyrau Oblast admin. div. Kazakh. see Atyrauskaya Oblast'
Atyraū Oblysy admin. div. Kazakh. see Atyrauskaya Oblast'
Atyrauskaya Oblast' admin. div. Kazakh. **102** B3
  English form Atyrau Oblast; also known as Atyraū Oblysy; formerly known as Gur'yevskaya Oblast'
Auati-Paraná r. Brazil **199** E5
Aubagne France **51** L5
Aube r. France **51** J4
Aube dept France **51** K4
Aubenas France **51** K8
Aubergenville France **51** I5
Aubigny-sur-Nère France **51** I5
Aubin France **51** I8
Aubinadong r. Canada **168** D4
Auboué France **51** L3
Aubrey Cliffs mts U.S.A. **183** L6
Aubry Lake Canada **164** G3
Auburn r. Australia **149** F5
Auburn AL U.S.A. **175** C5
Auburn CA U.S.A. **182** C3
Auburn IL U.S.A. **174** B4
Auburn IN U.S.A. **174** C3
Auburn ME U.S.A. **177** O1
Auburn NE U.S.A. **178** D3
Auburn NY U.S.A. **177** I3
Auburn WA U.S.A. **180** B3
Auburn Range hills Australia **149** F5
Aubusson France **51** I7
Auca Mahuida, Sierra de mt. Arg. **204** C5
Auce Latvia **42** E5
Auch France **50** G5
  historically known as Augusta Ausciorum or Elimberrum
Auche Myanmar **78** B2
Auchi Nigeria **125** G5

Auckland N.Z. **152** I4
  5th most populous city in Oceania.
  world (cities) >> 24-25

Auckland admin. reg. N.Z. **152** I4
Auckland Islands N.Z. **220** F9
Aude r. France **51** J5
Auden Canada **168** C3
Audenarde Belgium see Oudenaarde
Audierne, Baie d' b. France **50** B5
Audincourt France **51** M5
Audo Range mts Eth. **128** D3
Audru Estonia **42** F3
Audubon U.S.A. **178** D3
Aue Germany **49** J5
Aue r. Germany **48** I3
Auerbach in der Oberpfalz Germany **48** I6
Auersberg mt. Germany **51** S2
Augathella Australia **149** E5
Augrabies S. Africa **132** E5
Augrabies Falls S. Africa **132** E5
Augrabies Falls National Park S. Africa **132** E5
Au Gres U.S.A. **173** J6
Augsburg Germany **48** H7
  historically known as Augusta Vindelicorum
Augsburg-Westliche Wälder park Germany **48** H7
Augšligatne Latvia **42** G4
Augšzemes Augstiene hills Latvia **42** H5
Augusta Australia **151** A7
Augusta Sicilia Italy **57** H11
Augusta AR U.S.A. **174** B5
Augusta GA U.S.A. **175** D5
Augusta KS U.S.A. **178** C4
Augusta KY U.S.A. **176** A7

Augusta ME U.S.A. **177** P1
  State capital of Maine.

Augusta WI U.S.A. **172** B6
Augusta WV U.S.A. **176** G6
Augusta, Golfo di b. Sicilia Italy **57** H11
Augusta Auscorum France see Auch
Augusta Taurinorum Italy see Turin
Augusta Treverorum Germany see Trier
Augusta Victoria Chile **200** C6
Augusta Vindelicorum Germany see Augsburg
Augustin Cadazzi Col. **198** C2
Augustine Island U.S.A. **164** D4
Augustines, Lac des l. Canada **173** R3
Augusto Cardosa Moz. see Metangula
Augusto de Lima Brazil **207** I5
Augustodunum France see Autun
Augusto Severo Brazil **202** F3
Augustów Poland **49** T2
Augustowski, Kanał canal Poland **49** U2
Augustus, Mount Australia **151** B5
Augustus Island Australia **150** D2
Aukan Island Eritrea **104** C5
Aukštaitijos nacionalinis parkas nat. park Lith. **42** H6
Aukštelkai Lith. **42** E5
Aukštelkė Lith. **42** E6
Auktsjaur Sweden **44** L2
Aulavik National Park Canada **165** H2
Auld, Lake salt flat Australia **150** C4
Auliye Ata Kazakh. see Taraz
Aulla Italy **56** B3
Aulneau Peninsula Canada **167** M5
Aulnoye-Aymeries France **51** J2
Aulon Albania see Vlorë
Ault France **50** H2
Aumale France **50** H3
Aumance r. France **51** I6
Auminzatau, Gory hills Uzbek. **103** E4
  also known as Owminzatow Toghi
Auna Nigeria **125** G4
Aungban Myanmar **78** B3
Auning Denmark **45** J4
Auob watercourse Namibia/S. Africa **132** E3
Aur i. Malaysia **78** D2
Aura Fin. **45** M3
Aurad India **94** C2
Auraiya India **96** C4
Aurajoki r. Fin. **42** D1
Aurangabad Bihar India **97** E4
Aurangabad Maharashtra India **94** B2
Auray France **50** D5
Aurdal Norway **44** J3
Aurich Germany **48** E2
Aurilândia Brazil **206** C7
Aurigny i. Channel Is see Alderney
Aurillac France **51** I8
Aurino r. Italy **56** D2
Auron r. France **51** I5
Auronzo di Cadore Italy **56** E2
Aurora Phil. **74** B5
Aurora S. Africa **132** C9
Aurora CO U.S.A. **180** F5
Aurora IL U.S.A. **174** B3
Aurora IN U.S.A. **176** A6
Aurora MN U.S.A. **172** A3
Aurora MO U.S.A. **174** B4
Aurora NE U.S.A. **178** C3
Aurora OH U.S.A. **176** D4
Aurora UT U.S.A. **183** M3
Aurora Island Vanuatu see Maéwo
Aurukun Australia **149** D2
Aurukun Aboriginal Reserve Australia **149** D2
Aus Namibia **130** C5
Aus Namibia see Ausa
Ausa India **94** C2
Au Sable U.S.A. **173** J6
Au Sable r. U.S.A. **173** J6
Ausable r. U.S.A. **177** L1
Ausable Forks U.S.A. **177** L1
Au Sable Point MI U.S.A. **172** G4
Au Sable Point MI U.S.A. **173** J6
Auschwitz Poland see Oświęcim
Ausculum Italy see Ascoli Satriano
Ausculum Apulum Italy see Ascoli Satriano
Austafjord Norway **44** J4
Aust-Agder county Norway **45** J4
Austari-Jökulsá r. Iceland **44** [inset] C2
Austertana Norway **44** O1
Austin MN U.S.A. **174** A3
Austin NV U.S.A. **183** G2

Austin TX U.S.A. **179** C6
  State capital of Texas.

Austin, Lake salt flat Australia **151** B5
Austral Downs Australia **148** C4
Australes, îles is Fr. Polynesia see Tubuai Islands

Australia country Oceania **144** A4
  Largest country in Oceania and 6th in the world. Most populous country in Oceania. Historically known as New Holland.
  world (countries) >> 10-11
  oceania (countries) >> 138-139

Australian-Antarctic Basin sea feature Indian Ocean **219** N9
Australian Antarctic Territory Antarctica **223** J2
Australian Capital Territory admin. div. Australia **147** F3
Austräsund Australia **151** A7
Austria country Europe **49** J8
  known as Österreich in German
  europe (countries) >> 32-35
Austrumkursas Augstiene hills Latvia **42** D5

Austurland constituency Iceland **44** [inset] D2
Austvågøy i. Norway **44** K1
Autazes Brazil **199** G5
Auterive France **50** H5
Authie r. France **50** H2
Authier Canada **173** O2
Autlán Mex. **184** D5
Autti Fin. **44** N2
Autun France **51** K6
  historically known as Augustodunum
Auvergne admin. reg. France **51** J7
Auvergne, Monts d' mts France **51** I7
Auvézère r. France **50** G7
Auxerre France **51** J5
  historically known as Autesiodorum
Auxonne France **51** L5
Auyama tepui plat. Venez. **199** F3
Auyuittuq National Park Reserve Canada **165** M3
Auzoue r. France **50** G4
Auzzov Kazakh. **103** J2
Ava Myanmar **78** A3
Ava MO U.S.A. **174** B4
Ava NY U.S.A. **177** J2
Avaí Brazil **206** D9
Availles-Limouzine France **50** G6
Avallon France **51** J5
Avalon U.S.A. **182** F8
Avalon Peninsula Canada **169** K4
Avalon Wilderness nature res. Canada **169** K4
Avän Iran **100** A2
Avanashi India **94** C4
Avanganna mt. Guyana **199** G3
Avanigadda India **94** D2
Avanos Turkey **106** C3
Avaré Brazil **206** E10
Avaricum France see Bourges
Avarskoye Koysu r. Rus. Fed. **102** A4

Avarua Cook Is **221** H7
  Capital of the Cook Islands, on Rarotonga island.

Avaträsk Sweden **44** L2
Avawate Mountains U.S.A. **183** H6
Ave r. Port. **54** C3
Aveiro Brazil **199** H5
Aveiro Port. **54** C4
Aveiro admin. dist. Port. **54** C4
Aveiro, Ria de est. Port. **54** C4
Åvej Iran **100** B3
Avellaneda Arg. **204** F3
Avellino Italy **56** G8
  historically known as Abellinum
Avenal U.S.A. **182** D5
Avenio France see Avignon
Avereya i. Norway **44** I3
Aversa Italy **56** G8
Aves i. West Indies **187** H4
Aves is West Indies see Las Aves, Islas
Avesnes-sur-Helpe France **51** J2
Avesta Sweden **45** L3
Aveyron r. France **51** H8
Avezzano Italy **56** F6
  europe (environments) >> 36-37
Avgan Geçidi pass Turkey **108** E1
Avgo i. Kythira Greece **59** E12
Avgo i. Greece **59** G13
Aviá Teraí Arg. **204** E2
Aviemore U.K. **46** I6
Aviemore, Lake N.Z. **153** E12
Avigliano Italy **57** H8
Avignon France **51** K9
  historically known as Avenio
Ávila Spain **54** F3
Ávila, Sierra de mts Spain **54** F3
Avilés Spain **54** F1
Aviño Spain **54** C1
Avinurme Estonia **42** H3
Avión mt. Spain **54** C2
Avis Port. **54** D5
Avisio r. Italy **56** D2
Avize France **51** K4
Avlama Dağı mt. Turkey **108** E1
Avlemonas Greece **59** E12
Avlida Greece **59** E10
Avlona Albania see Vlorë
Avlum Denmark **45** J4
Avnyugskiy Rus. Fed. **40** H3
Avoca Australia **147** D3
Avoca r. Australia **147** D3
Avoca S. Africa **133** P2
Avoca IA U.S.A. **178** D3
Avoca NY U.S.A. **176** H3
Avola Sicilia Italy **57** H12
Avon r. Australia **151** B7
Avon r. England U.K. **47** J11
Avon r. England U.K. **47** J12
Avon r. England U.K. **47** K13
Avon IL U.S.A. **172** C10
Avon NY U.S.A. **176** H3
Avondale U.S.A. **183** L8
Avon Downs Australia **149** E4
Avonmore r. Rep. of Ireland **47** F11
Avon Park U.S.A. **175** D7
Avr S. Africa **132** H10
Avoti Latvia **42** F5
Avram Iancu Romania **58** C2
Avranches France **50** E4
Avre r. France **51** I3
Avrig Romania **58** F3
Avrillé France **50** F5
Avsuyu Turkey **109** H1
Avuavu Solomon Is **145** F2
Avveel Fin. see Ivalo
Avvil Fin. see Ivalo
'A'wa j r. Syria **108** G4
Awaji-shima i. Japan **91** D7
Awakeri N.Z. **152** K6
Awakino N.Z. **152** I6
Awālī Bahrain **105** E2
Awang Indon. **77** G5
Awanui N.Z. **152** H3
Awarawar, Tanjung pt Indon. **77** F4
Awarē Eth. **128** E3
'Awārid, Wādī al watercourse Syria **109** K3
Awarua Point N.Z. **153** C12
Awasa Eth. **128** C3
Āwash Eth. **128** D3
Āwash r. Eth. **128** D2
Awa-shima i. Japan **90** F5

Āwash National Park Eth. **128** C3
Āwash West Wildlife Reserve nature res. Eth. **128** C3

Awat vol. Eth. **128** C3
Āwatā Shet' r. Eth. **128** C3
Awatere r. N.Z. **153** I9
Awbārī Libya **120** B3
Awd reg. Yemen **104** D5
'Awdah well Saudi Arabia **105** E3
'Awdah, Hawr al imp. l. Iraq **107** F5
Aw Dheegle Somalia **128** E4
Awdiinle Somalia **128** D4
Awe, Loch l. U.K. **46** G7
Aweil Sudan **126** E2
Awgu Nigeria **125** G5
Awka Nigeria **125** G5
Awlitis watercourse W. Sahara **122** B4
Awry Lake Canada **167** H2
Awserd W. Sahara **122** B4
Axat France **51** I6
Axe r. U.K. **47** I13
Axel Heiberg Glacier Antarctica **223** N1
Axel Heiberg Island Canada **165** J2
Axente Sever Romania **58** F2
Axim Ghana **125** E5
Axinim Brazil **199** G6

Axioma Brazil **199** E6
Axios r. Greece **58** D8
Axmars naturreservat nature res. Sweden **45** L3
Axum Eth. see Äksum
Ay Kazakh. **103** J3
Ayabe Japan **91** D7
Ayachi, Jbel mt. Morocco **122** D2
Ayacucho Peru **200** B3
Ayacucho dept Peru **200** B3
Ayadaw Myanmar **78** A3
Ayagoz Kazakh. **103** J3
also known as Ayakoz; formerly spelt Ayaguz
Ayagoz watercourse Kazakh. **103** J3
Ayakagytma, Vpadina depr. Uzbek. **103** G3
Ayakkuduk Uzbek. **103** F4
also spelt Oyoqquduq
Ayakkum Hu salt l. China **89** E4
Ayakoz Kazakh. see Ayagoz
Ayamé Côte d'Ivoire **124** E5
Ayamonte Spain **54** D7
Ayan Rus. Fed. **39** N4
Ayancık Turkey **106** C2
Ayang N. Korea **83** B5
Ayangba Nigeria **125** G5
Ayanka Rus. Fed. **39** Q3
Ayapel, Serranía de mts Col. **198** C3
Ayas Turkey **106** C3
Ayaviri Peru **200** C3
Ayayei Eth. **128** C1
Aybak Afgh. **101** G1
Aydabul Kazakh. **103** G1
Aydar r. Ukr. **41** F6
Aydarkul', Ozero l. Uzbek. **103** F3
Aydarly Kazakh. **103** F3
'Aydim, Wādī r. Oman **105** F4
Aydın Turkey **106** A3
Aydıncık Turkey **108** E1
also known as Gilindire
Aydın Dağları mts Turkey **106** A3
Aydıngkol Hu marsh China **88** E3
Ayeat, Gora hill Kazakh. **103** G3
Ayedo mt. Spain **55** I2
Ayelu Terara vol. Eth. **128** D2
Ayer U.S.A. **177** N3
Ayers Rock hill Australia see Uluru
Ayeyarwady r. Myanmar see Irrawaddy
Aygyrzhal Kazakh. **103** J2
Ayía Greece see Agia
Ayiásos Greece see Agiasos
Ayila Ri'gyü mts China **89** B5
Áyios Dhimítrios Greece see
  Agios Dimitrios
Áyios Dhimítrios, Ákra pt Greece see
  Agios Dimitrios, Akra
Áyios Evstrátios i. Greece see
  Agios Efstratios
Áyios Nikólaos Greece see Agios Nikolaos
Áyios Yeóryios i. Greece see
  Agios Georgios
Ayke, Ozero l. Kazakh. **103** E2
Aykhal Rus. Fed. **39** L3
Aykino Rus. Fed. **40** J3
Aykol China **88** C3
Aylesbury U.K. **47** L12
Aylett U.S.A. **177** H8
Ayllón, Sierra de mts Spain **55** H3
Aylmer Canada **173** M8
Aylmer Lake Canada **167** I1
Aymagambetov Kazakh. **103** E2
'Ayn, Ra's al watercourse Oman **105** G4
Ayna Peru **200** B3
Aynabulak Kazakh. **103** I3
'Ayn al 'Abd Libya **120** D2
'Ayn al 'Abd well Saudi Arabia **105** E1
'Ayn al Baydā' well Syria **109** I3
'Ayn al Ghazal spring Libya **120** E4
'Ayn Ba Ma'bad Yemen **105** D5
'Ayn Dibis Iraq **109** O2
'Ayn Hindī oasis Oman **105** G4
Ayni Tajik. **101** G2
'Aynīn well Saudi Arabia **105** E4
'Ayn Sifnī Iraq **109** O1
'Ayn Umm al Banāt waterhole Iraq **109** N3
Ayon, Ostrov i. Rus. Fed. **39** Q3
Ayoquezco Mex. **185** F5
Ayora Spain **55** J5
Ayorou Niger **125** F3
Ayos Cameroon **125** I6
'Ayoûn 'Abd el Mâlek well Mauritania
  122 C4
'Ayoûn el 'Atroûs Mauritania **124** C2
Ayr Australia **149** K4
Ayr U.K. **46** H8
Ayr r. U.K. **46** H8
Ayrag Nuur salt l. Mongolia **84** B1
Ayrancı Turkey **106** C3
Ayrancılar Turkey **59** I10
Ayre, Point of Isle of Man **47** H9
Aysarinskoye Kazakh. see Zaozernyy
Aysary Kazakh. see Zaozernyy
Aysha Eth. **128** D2
Ayteke Bi Kazakh. **103** F3
  formerly known as Novokazalinsk or
  Zhangaqazaly
Aytos Bulg. **58** I6
Aytoska Reka r. Bulg. **58** I6
Aytré France **50** E6
Ayun Oman **105** F4
Ayutla Guerrero Mex. **185** F5
Ayutla Jalisco Mex. **184** D4
Ayutthaya Thai. **79** C5
  also known as Krungkao; long form Phra Nakhon Si
  Ayutthaya; long form Phra Nakhon Si Ayutthaya
Ayvacık Turkey **59** J9
Ayvalı Turkey **107** D3
Ayvalık Turkey **106** A3
Aywat al Manāhil, Wādī r. Yemen **105** E4
Aywat aş Şay'ar, Wādī r. Yemen **105** E4
Azacualpa Hond. **186** B4
Azak Rus. Fed. see Azov
Azambuja Port. **54** C5
Azamgarh India **97** D4
Azangaro Peru **200** C3
Azanja Srbija Yugo. **58** B4
Azaouâd reg. Mali **124** D2
Azaouagh, Vallée de watercourse
  Mali/Niger **124** D3
Azapa Chile **200** C4
Azar watercourse Niger **125** G2
Azaran Iran see Hashtrud
Azärbaycan country Asia see Azerbaijan
Äzärbäyjän-e Gharbī prov. Iran **100** A2
Äzärbäyjän-e Sharqī prov. Iran **100** A2
Azare Nigeria **125** H4
Azarychy Belarus **43** K9
Azatskoye, Ozero l. Rus. Fed. **43** Q2
A'zaz Syria **109** I1
Azazga Alg. **55** P8
Azbine reg Niger see L'Aïr, Massif de
Azdavay Turkey **106** C2
Azélik well Niger **125** H2
Azemmour Morocco **122** C2
▶Azerbaijan country Asia **107** F2
  spelt Azärbaycan in Azeri; formerly known as
  Azerbaydzhanskaya S.S.R.; historically
  known as Atropatene
  asia [countries] ▶▶ 64–67
Azerbaydzhanskaya S.S.R. country Asia
  see Azerbaijan
Azergues r. France **51** K7

Äzezo Eth. **128** C1
Azhu-Tayga, Gora mt. Rus. Fed. **88** E1
Azilal Morocco **122** D2
Azilda Canada **173** L4
Azingo Gabon **126** A5
'Azīzābād Iran **100** D4
Azizbekov Armenia see Vayk'
Āžlam, Wādī watercourse Saudi Arabia
  104 A2
Aznakayevo Rus. Fed. **40** J5
Aznalcóllar Spain **54** E7
Azogues Ecuador **198** B5
Azopol'ye Rus. Fed. **40** H2
▶Azores terr. N. Atlantic Ocean **216** M3
  Autonomous Region of Portugal. Long form
  Arquipélago dos Açores.
  europe [countries] ▶▶ 32–35
Azotus Israel see Ashdod
Azov Rus. Fed. **41** F7
  historically known as Azak
Azov, Sea of Rus. Fed./Ukr. **41** F7
  also known as Azovs'ke More or Azovskoye
  More
Azovo-Sivashskiy Zapovidnyk nature res.
  Ukr. **41** E7
Azovs'ke More sea Rus. Fed./Ukr. see
  Azov, Sea of
Azovskoye More sea Rus. Fed./Ukr. see
  Azov, Sea of
Azpeitia Spain **55** I1
Azraq, Bahr el r. Eth./Sudan **104** A5 see
  Blue Nile
Azrou Morocco **122** D2
Azrou, Oued watercourse Alg. **123** O5
Aztec U.S.A. **181** E5
Azua Dom. Rep. **187** F3
Azuaga Spain **54** F6
Azuay prov. Ecuador **198** B5
Azúcar r. Chile **204** C2
Azūchi-Ō-shima i. Japan **91** A8
Azuer r. Spain **55** H5
Azuero, Península de pen. Panama **186** C6
Azufre, Cerro del mt. Chile **204** C2
Azul Arg. **204** E5
Azul r. Mex. **185** H5
  also known as Blue Creek
Azul, Cordillera mts Peru **200** B2
Azul, Serra hills Brazil **201** G3
Azuma, Wadi watercourse Sudan **120** D3
Azuma-san vol. Japan **90** G6
Azurduy Bol. **201** D5
Azyory Belarus **42** F8
Az Zabadānī Syria **108** H4
Az Zabirah well Saudi Arabia **104** C2
Az Zāfirī reg. Iraq **109** K5
Az Zāhirah admin. reg. Oman **105** G3
Az Zallāf, Wādī watercourse Libya **120** B3
Az Zallāq Bahrain **105** E2
Azzano Decimo Italy **56** E3
Az Zaqāzīq Egypt see Zagazig
Az Zarbah Syria **109** H1
Az Zarqā' Jordan **109** H5
  also known as Zarqā'
Az Zāwiyah Libya **120** B1
Az Zaydīyah Yemen **104** C5
Azzeffâl hills Mauritania/W. Sahara **122** B5
Azzel Matti, Sebkha salt pan Alg. **123** F4
Az Zintān Libya **120** B2
Az Zubayr Iraq **107** F5
Az Zuhrah Yemen **104** C5
Az Zuqur i. Yemen **104** C5
  English form Az Zuqur Island
Az Zuqurī oasis Saudi Arabia **105** E4
Az Zuwaytīnah Libya **120** D2

↓ B

Baa Indon. **75** B5
Baaí r. Indon. **77** G2
Ba'albek Lebanon **108** H3
Ba'al Ḥaẕor mt. West Bank **108** G6
Baardheere Somalia **128** D4
  also known as Bardera
Bab India **96** C4
Baba mt. Bulg. **58** D6
Bâbā, Kūh-e mts Afgh. **101** G3
Baba Burnu pt Turkey **106** A3
Babaçulândia Brazil **202** C3
Babadağ mt. Azer. **107** G2
Babadag Romania **58** J4
Babadağ Turkey **59** K12
Baba Dağ mt. Turkey **59** K12
Babadaygului, Podişul plat. Romania **58** J4
Babadaykhan Akhal'skaya Oblast' Turkm.
  102 E5
  formerly known as Kirovsk
Babadaykhan Akhal'skaya Oblast' Turkm.
  102 E5
  formerly known as Kommuna
Babadurmaz Turkm. **102** D5
Babaeski Turkey **106** A2
Babahoyo Ecuador **198** B5
Babai r. Nepal **97** D3
Babai Gaxun China **84** E3
Babak Phil. **74** C5
Bābā Kalān Iran **100** B4
Babakourimigana well Niger **125** H3
Babana Indon. **75** A3
Babanango S. Africa **133** P5
Babanki Cameroon **125** H5
Babanusa Sudan **126** E2
Babao China see Qilian
Babao China **86** C1
Babar i. Indon. **75** D4
Babar, Kepulauan is Indon. **75** D4
Babati Tanz. **129** B6
Babayevo Rus. Fed. **43** Q2
Babayurt Rus. Fed. **102** A4
Babeldaob i. Palau **73** H5
  also spelt Babelthuap
Babelegi S. Africa **133** M2
Babelthuap i. Palau see Babeldaob
Bābeni Romania **58** F4
Baberu India **96** D4
Bab Ezzouar Alg. **55** O8
Bab Kissingen Germany **48** H5
Bad Königsdorff Poland see
  Jastrzębie-Zdrój
Babi, Pulau i. Indon. **76** B2
Babia Góra mt. Poland **49** Q6
Babian Jiang r. China **86** B3
Bābil governorate Iraq **107** F4
Babīl Egypt **108** C7
Babîle Eth. **128** D3
Babimost Poland **49** M3
Babinavichy Belarus **43** L7
Babinda Australia **149** E3
Babine r. Canada **166** E4
Babine Lake Canada **166** E4
Babine Range mts Canada **166** E4
Babing Dem. Rep. Congo **126** C5
Babite ezers l. Latvia **42** E5
Babo Indon. **75** D3
Bābol Iran **100** C2
Bābol Sar Iran **100** C2
Baboná r. Brazil **199** H4
Babongo Cameroon **125** I5
Baboon Point S. Africa **132** C9

Baboua Cent. Afr. Rep. **126** B3
Babruysk Belarus **43** K8
  also known as Bobruysk
Babstovo Rus. Fed. **82** D3
Babtai Lith. **42** E6
Bab Taza Morocco **54** F9
Babu China see Hexian
Babuna Planina mts Macedonia **58** C7
Babusar Pass Pak. **101** H3
Babushkin Rus. Fed. **85** E1
  formerly known as Mysovsk
Babušnica Srbija Yugo. **58** D5
Babuyan Phil. **74** B4
Babuyan i. Phil. **74** B2
Babuyan Channel Phil. **74** B2
Babuyan Islands Phil. **74** B2
Babylon tourist site Iraq **107** F4
Babynino Rus. Fed. **43** R6
Bač Vojvodina, Srbija Yugo. **58** A3
Bacaadweyn Somalia **128** E3
Bacaba r. Brazil **198** D6
Bacabal Maranhão Brazil **202** C3
Bacabal Pará Brazil **199** G5
Bacajá r. Brazil **199** I5
Bacalar Mex. **185** H5
Bacalar Chico, Boca sea chan. Mex. **185** I5
Bacan i. Indon. **75** C3
Bacanora Mex. **184** C2
Bacarra Phil. **74** B2
Bacău Romania **58** H2
Baccarat France **51** M6
Baccaro Point Canada **169** H5
Bacchiglione r. Italy **56** E3
Bắc Giang Vietnam **78** D3
Bachaquero Venez. **198** D2
Bacheykava Belarus **43** K6
Bachi, Selat sea chan. Indon. **75** C3
Bachinva Mex. **181** F7
Bach Long Vĩ, Đạo i. Vietnam **78** D3
Bachu China **88** B3
  formerly known as Maralbashi or Maralwexi
Bachuma Eth. **128** C3
Back r. Australia **149** D3
Back r. Canada **167** M1
Bačka reg. Hungary/Yugo. **58** A2
Bačka Palanka Vojvodina, Srbija Yugo. **58** A3
Bačka Topola Vojvodina, Srbija Yugo. **58** A3
Backbone Mountain U.S.A. **176** F6
Backbone Ranges mts Canada **166** C1
Backe Sweden **44** L3
Bäckefors Sweden **45** K4
Bäckhammar Sweden **45** K4
Bački Petrovac Vojvodina, Srbija Yugo. **58** A3
Backnang Germany **48** G7
Backo Gradište Vojvodina, Srbija Yugo. **58** A3
Backstairs Passage Australia **146** C3
Bac Lac Vietnam **78** C3
Bagan Datoh Malaysia see Bagan Datuk
Bagan Datuk Malaysia **76** C2
  formerly known as Bagan Datoh
Baga Phil. **74** C5
Bagani Namibia **130** D3
Baganian Peninsula Phil. **74** B5
Bagansiapiapi Indon. **76** C2
Bagar watercourse Kazakh. **88** C2
Bağaras Turkey **59** I11
Bagarē well Niger **125** G3
Bagaroua Niger **125** F3
Bagata Dem. Rep. Congo **126** C5
Bagazán Peru **198** C5
Bagbag Sudan **121** F6
Bagdad U.S.A. **183** K7
Bagé Brazil **204** G3
Bagepalli India **94** C3
Bagerhat Bangl. see Baghe-hat
Bages et de Sigean, Étang de lag. France
  51 J9
Bageshwar India **96** C3
Bagevadi India **94** B2
Baggâ Sweden **45** K4
Baggs U.S.A. **180** F4
Bagh India **96** B5
Baghak Pak. **101** E4
Baghbaghū r. Iran **101** E2

Bad Ragaz Switz. **51** P5
Badr City Egypt **108** D7
Badr Ḥunayn Saudi Arabia **104** B3
Bad Reichenhall Germany **49** J8
Badrinath Peaks China **96** C3
  also known as Badarinath or Chaukhamba
Bad River Indian Reservation res. U.S.A.
  172 C4
Bad Säckingen Germany **48** E8
Bad Salzuflen Germany **48** H5
Bad Salzungen Germany **48** H5
Bad Schwartau Germany **48** I2
Bad Segeberg Germany **48** H2
Badu China **87** F3
Badu Island Australia **73** J8
Badulla Sri Lanka **94** D5
Badvel India **94** C3
Bad Waldsee Germany **48** H8
Bad Windsheim Germany **48** H6
Badzhal'skiy Khrebet mts Rus. Fed. **82** D2
Bae Colwyn U.K. see Colwyn Bay
Bær Iceland **44** [inset]
Baena Spain **54** G7
Baeza Ecuador **198** B5
Baeza Spain **55** H6
Bafang Cameroon **125** H5
Bafatá Guinea-Bissau **124** B3
Baffa Pak. **101** H3
Baffin Bay sea Canada/Greenland **165** M2
▶Baffin Island Canada **165** L2
  2nd largest island in North America and 5th in the world.
  northamerica [landscapes] ▶▶ 156–157
Bafia Cameroon **125** H6
Bafilo Togo **125** F4
Bafing r. Guinea/Mali **124** C3
Bafing, Réserve du nature res. Mali **124** C3
Bafing Makana Mali **124** C3
Bafoulabé Mali **124** C3
Bafoussam Cameroon **125** H5
Bāfq Iran **100** C4
Bafra Turkey **106** C2
Bafra Burnu pt Turkey **106** C2
Bāft Iran **100** D4
Bafwasende Dem. Rep. Congo **126** E4
Bāga r. India **94** B2
Bagā Spain **55** M2
Baga Bogd Uul mt. Mongolia **84** D2
Bagac Bay Phil. **74** B3
Bagaha India **97** E4
Bagahak hill Sabah Malaysia **77** G1
Bagalkot India **94** B2
Bagamoyo Tanz. **129** C6
Bagan China **86** A1

Bahr Saudi Arabia **104** C4
Bahraich India **97** D4
▶Bahrain country Asia **105** E2
  spelt Al Baḩrayn in Arabic
  asia [countries] ▶▶ 64–67
Bahrain, Gulf of Asia **105** E2
Bahrāmābād Iran see Rafsanjān
Bahror Iran **96** C4
Bahuaja-Sonene, Parque Nacional
  nat. park Peru **200** C3
Bāhū Kālāt Iran **101** E5
Baia Romania **58** J3
Baia Romania **58** I4
Baia de Aramă Romania **58** D3
Baia de Arieş Romania **58** E2
Baia dos Tigres Angola **127** A9
Baía Farta Angola **127** B8
Baia Mare Romania **53** G2
Baião Brazil **202** B3
Baiazeh Iran **100** C3
Baïbeli well Chad **120** D5
Baïbokoum Chad **126** B3
Baicheng Jilin China **85** I2
Baicheng Xinjiang China **88** C3
Băicoi Romania **58** G3
Baidoa Somalia see Baydhabo
Baidoi Co l. China **89** D5
Baidunzi China **84** B3
Baie-aux-Feuilles Canada see Tasiujaq
Baie-Comeau Canada **169** G3
Baie de Henne Haiti **187** E3
Baie-du-Poste Canada see Mistissini
Baie-Johan-Beetz Canada **169** H3
Baie-St-Paul Canada **169** G4
Baie-Trinite Canada **169** H3
Baie Verte Canada **169** J3
Baigou r. China **85** H4
Baiguan China **87** E2
Baigura mt. France **50** E9
Baihanchang China **86** A3
Baihar India **96** C5
Baihe Jilin China **82** C4
  formerly known as Erdaobaihe
Baihe Shaanxi China **87** D1
Bai He r. China **87** E2
Baijiantan China **88** D2
Baijnath Himachal Pradesh India **96** C3
  also known as Baijnath
Baijnath Uttaranchal India **96** C3
▶Baikal, Lake Rus. Fed. **81** H2
  Deepest lake in the world and in Asia. 3rd largest lake in Asia and 9th in the world.
  Also known as Baykal, Ozero.
  world [physical features] ▶▶ 8–9
Baikunthpur India **97** D4
Baikunthpur India **97** D5
Bailang China **85** I2
Bailanhe Shuiku resr China **87** E2
Baile Átha Cliath Rep. of Ireland see Dublin
Baile Átha Luain Rep. of Ireland see
  Athlone
Băile Govora Romania **58** F3
Băile Herculane Romania **58** D4
Bailén Spain **54** H6
Băile Olănești Romania **58** F3
Băilești Romania **58** E4
Băile Sigean, Campia plain Romania **58** E4
Băile Tuşnad Romania **58** G2
Bailey S. Africa **133** I8
Bailey Ice Stream Antarctica **223** W1
Bailey Range hills Australia **151** C6
Bailieborough Rep. of Ireland see Bailieborough
Baillie r. Canada **167** J1
Bailong Jiang r. China **86** C1
Bailundo Angola **127** B8
  formerly known as Teixeira da Silva
Baima China **86** B1
  also known as Sêraitang
Baima China see Baoxi
Bainang China **89** E6
Bain-de-Bretagne France **50** E5
Bainduru India **94** B3
Bainet Haiti **187** E3
Baingoin China **89** E6
  also known as Porong
Baini China see Yuqing
Baiona Spain **54** C2
  also spelt Bayona
Baïqên China **86** B1
Baiquan China **82** B3
Bā'ir Jordan **109** H7
Bā'ir, Wādī watercourse
  Jordan/Saudi Arabia **109** H7
Bairab Co l. China **89** C5
Bairagnia India **97** E4
Baird U.S.A. **179** C5
Baird, Mount Canada **166** C1
Baird Mountains U.S.A. **164** C3
▶Bairiki Kiribati **145** G1
  Capital of Kiribati, on Tarawa atoll.
Bairin Qiao China **85** H3
  also known as Balingiao
Bairin Youqi China see Daban
Bairin Zuoqi China see Lindong
Bairkum Kazakh. **103** G4
  also spelt Bayyrqum
Bairnsdale Australia **147** E4
Bais Phil. **74** B4
Baïse r. France **50** G8
Baisha Chongqing China **86** C2
Baisha Hainan China **87** D5
  also known as Yacha
Baishan China see Mashan
Baishan Jilin China **87** A3
Baishan Sichuan China **87** D2
  formerly known as Badaojiang or Hunjiang
Baishui China **85** E4
Baishuijiang China **86** B1
Baisogala Lith. **42** E6
Baitadi Nepal **97** D3
Baitang China **86** A1
Baitou Shan mt. China/N. Korea see
  Paektu-san
Bai Thương Vietnam **78** D4
Baitle r. China **86** B2
Baixa da Banheira Port. **54** B6
Baixi China see Yibin
Baixiang China **85** G4
Baixo Guandu Brazil **207** M6
Baixo-Longa Angola **127** C8
Baiyang Dian resr China **85** H4
Baiyashi China see Dong'an
Baiyin China **84** C4
Baiyü China **86** A2
Baiyuda Desert Sudan **121** G5
Baiyu Shan mts China **85** E4
Baja Hungary **49** P9
Baja, Punta pt Mex. **184** B2
Baja California pen. Mex. **184** B2
  English form Lower California
Baja California Norte state Mex. **184** B2
Baja California Sur state Mex. **184** B3
Bajan Mex. **185** E3
Bajanal Nepal **96** D3
Bajau i. Indon. **77** D2
Bajaur reg. Pak. **101** G3
Bajawa Indon. **75** B5
Baj Baj India **97** F5
Bājgīrān Iran **100** D2
Bājil Yemen **104** C5
Bajitpur Bangl. **97** F4
Bajmok Vojvodina, Srbija Yugo. **58** A3
Bajna India **96** C3
Bajo Baudó Col. **198** B3
Bajo Boquete Panama **186** C5
Bajoga Nigeria **125** H4
Bajo Grande Arg. **205** C7
Bajo Hondo Arg. **204** D3
Bajrakot India **97** E5
Bajram Curri Albania **58** B6
Baka, Bukit mt. Indon. **77** F3
Bakaba Chad **126** C3
Bakala Cent. Afr. Rep. **126** C3
Bakaly Rus. Fed. **40** J5
Bakanas Kazakh. **103** I3
Bakar Croatia **56** G3
Bakau Gambia **124** A3
Bakayan, Gunung mt. Indon. **77** G2
Bakel Senegal **124** B3
Baker CA U.S.A. **183** H6
Baker LA U.S.A. **175** B6
Baker MT U.S.A. **180** F3
Baker OR U.S.A. **180** C3
Baker WV U.S.A. **176** G7
Baker, Mount vol. U.S.A. **180** B2
Baker Butte mt. U.S.A. **183** M7
▶Baker Island N. Pacific Ocean **145** H1
  United States Unincorporated Territory.
  oceania [countries] ▶▶ 138–139
Bakung i. Indon. **76** D2
Bakuny Belarus **42** G8
Bakuriani Georgia **107** E2
Bakutis Coast Antarctica **222** P2
Baky Azer. see Baku
Bakwa Turkey **106** C3
Baky Uyandino r. Rus. Fed. **39** O3
Balâ Turkey **106** C3
Bala U.K. **47** I11
  also known as Y Bala
Bala, Cerros de mts Bol. **200** C3
Balabac i. Phil. **74** A5
Balabac Strait Malaysia/Phil. **77** F1
Balabalagan, Kepulauan atolls Indon. **77** G3
Balābād, Gardaneh-ye pass Iran **100** A3
Balabanovo Rus. Fed. **43** R6
Bălăceanu Romania **58** H3
Bălăcita Romania **58** E4
Balad Iraq **107** F4
Bālā Deh Iran **100** B4
Baladeh Māzandarān Iran **100** B2
Baladeh Māzandarān Iran **100** B2
Balaghat India **96** D5
Balaghat Range mts India **94** B2
Balaguer Spain **55** L3
Bālā Howz̧ Iran **100** D3
Balaikarangan Indon. **77** E2
Balaipungut Indon. **76** C2
Balaïtous mt. France **50** F10
Balakhta Rus. Fed. **80** G2
Balaka Malawi **129** B8
Balakän Azer. **107** F2
Balakhna Rus. Fed. **40** G4
Balakirevo Rus. Fed. **43** T5
Balaklava Australia **146** C3
Balaklava Ukr. **41** E7
Balakleya Ukr. see Balakliya
Balakovo Rus. Fed. **102** A1
  also spelt Balaklya
Balakovo Rus. Fed. **41** I6
Balama Moz. **131** H2
Balambangan i. Sabah Malaysia **77** G1
Bālā Morghāb Afgh. **101** E3
Balan India **96** H4
Bălan Romania **58** G2
Balancán Mex. **185** H5
Balanda Rus. Fed. see Kalininsk
Balanga Phil. **74** B3
Balangala Dem. Rep. Congo **126** C4
Balangir India **95** D1
Balangoda Sri Lanka **94** D5
Balarampur India **97** E5
Balashov Rus. Fed. **41** H6
Balashi India **95** C1
Balasinor India **96** B5
Balassagyarmat Hungary **49** Q7
Balaton l. Hungary see Balaton, Lake

Balaton, Lake Hungary **49** O9
  also known as Balaton
Balatonboglár Hungary **49** O9
Balatonfüred Hungary **49** O9
Balatonlelle Hungary **49** O9
Balauring Indon. **75** B5
Balazote Spain **55** I4
Balbieriškis Lith. **42** E7
Balbina Brazil **199** G5
Balbina, Represa de *resr* Brazil **199** G5
Balbriggan Rep. of Ireland **47** F10
Balcad Somalia **128** E4
Balcanoona Australia **146** C2
Balcarce Arg. **204** F5
Balchik Bulg. **58** J5
Balclutha N.Z. **153** C13
Baldim Brazil **207** J6
Bald Knob *AR* U.S.A. **174** B5
Bald Knob *WV* U.S.A. **176** D8
Bald Mountain **183** I4
Baldwin U.S.A. **175** D6
Baldwinsville U.S.A. **177** I2
Baldwinville U.S.A. **177** M3
Baldock Lake Canada **167** L3
Baldy Mount Canada **166** G5
Baldy Mountain *hill* Canada **167** K5
Baldy Peak U.S.A. **183** O8
Bal'dzhikan Rus. Fed. **85** F1
Bale Indon. **71** G2
Bâle Switz. *see* Basel
Baléa Mali **124** C3
Baleares, Islas *is* Spain *see*
  Balearic Islands
Baleares Insulae *is* Spain *see*
  Balearic Islands
Balearic Islands *is* Spain **55** M5
  also known as Baleares, Islas or Baleares;
  historically known as Baleares Insulae
Baleares, Illes *is* Spain *see* Balearic Islands
Baleh *r.* Sarawak Malaysia **77** F2
Baleia, Ponta da *pt* Brazil **203** E6
Baleines, Pointe des *pt* France **50** D3
Bale Mountains National Park Eth. **128** C3
Băleni Romania **58** G4
Baleno Phil. **74** B3
Baler Phil. **74** B3
Baler Bay Phil. **74** B3
Balesa *well* Kenya **128** C4
Baleshwar India **97** E5
Balestrand Norway **45** I3
Baley Rus. Fed. **85** H1
Baléyara Niger **125** F3
Balezino Rus. Fed. **40** J4
Balfate Hond. **186** B4
Balfe's Creek Australia **149** E4
Balfour Canada **167** G5
Balfour N.Z. **153** C13
Balfour *E. Cape* S. Africa **133** K9
Balfour *Mpumalanga* S. Africa **133** M3
Balfour Downs Australia **150** C4
Balgatay Mongolia **84** C2
  formerly known as Shilüüstey
Balgo Australia **150** D4
Balgo Aboriginal Reserve Australia **150** E4
Balguda *well* Kenya **128** C5
Balguntay China **80** G3
Bâlhaf Yemen **105** E5
Balho Djibouti **128** D1
Bali India **96** B4
Bali *i.* Indon. **77** F5
Bali *prov.* Indon. **77** F5
Bali, Saudi Arabia **104** B2
Bali, Selat *sea chan.* Indon. **77** F5
Baliangao Phil. **74** B4
Baliapal India **97** E5
Bali Barat National Park Indon. **77** F5
Balichak India **97** E5
Balige Indon. **76** B2
Baliguda India **95** D1
Balihan China **85** H3
Balikesir Turkey **106** A3
Balıkesir *prov.* Turkey **106** A3
Balık Gölü *l.* Turkey **107** E3
Balikh *r.* Syria/Turkey **109** K2
Balikpapan Indon. **77** G3
Balikpapan, Teluk *b.* Indon. **77** G3
Bălileşti Romania **58** F3
Balimbing Phil. **74** A5
Balimila Reservoir India **94** D2
Balimo P.N.G. **73** J8
Balin China **85** H3
Balingen Germany **48** F7
Balingian *Sarawak* Malaysia **77** F2
Balingian *r.* Sarawak Malaysia **77** F2
Balingiao China *see* Bairin Qiao
Balintang Channel Phil. **74** B2
Bali Sea Indon. **77** F4
Balitondo Cent. Afr. Rep. **126** D3
Baliungan *i.* Phil. **74** B5
Baljurshi Saudi Arabia **104** B3
▶ Balkan Mountains Bulg./Yugo. **58** D5
  also known as Stara Planina
  europe [issues] ⟩⟩ 34–35
Balkan Oblast *admin. div.* Turkm. *see*
  Balkanskaya Oblast'
Balkanskaya Oblast' *admin. div.* Turkm.
  102 A2
  English form Balkan Oblast; formerly known
  as Krasnovodskaya Oblast'
Balkashino Kazakh. **103** G1
Balkh Afgh. **101** F2
  historically known as Bactra or Zariaspa
Balkh *prov.* Afgh. **101** F2
Balkhab *r.* Afgh. **101** H3
Balkhash India **103** H3
  also spelt Balqash
▶ Balkhash, Lake Kazakh. **103** H3
  4th largest lake in Asia. Also known as
  Balkhash, Ozero or Balqash Köli.
  asia [landscapes] ⟩⟩ 62–63

Balkhash, Ozero *l.* Kazakh. *see*
  Balkhash, Lake
Balkonda India **94** C2
Balkuduk Kazakh. **102** A3
Balla Bangl. **97** F4
Balla Balla Zimbabwe *see* Mbalabala
Ballachulish U.K. **46** G7
Ballaghaderreen Rep. of Ireland **47** D10
Ballangen Norway **44** L1
Ballantrae U.K. **47** H8
Ballarat Australia **147** D4
Ballard, Lake *salt flat* Australia **151** C6
Ballarpur India **94** C2
Ballater U.K. **46** I6
Ballé Mali **124** C3
Ballena, Punta *pt* Chile **204** C2
Ballena, Canal *sea chan.* Chile
  205 C9
Balleny Islands Antarctica **223** K2
Ballia India **97** E4
Ballina Australia **147** G2
Ballina Rep. of Ireland **47** C9
  also spelt Béal an Átha
Ballinasloe Rep. of Ireland **47** D10
  also spelt Béal Átha na Sluaighe
Ballineen Rep. of Ireland **47** D12
Ballinger U.S.A. **179** C6
Ballinrobe Rep. of Ireland **47** C10
Ballons des Vosges, Parc Naturel
  Régional du *nature res.* France **51** M5
Ballsh Albania **58** A8
Ballston Spa U.S.A. **177** L2
Bally U.S.A. **177** J5
Ballybunnion Rep. of Ireland **47** C11
Ballycastle Rep. of Ireland **47** C9
Ballycastle U.K. **47** F8
Ballyhaunis Rep. of Ireland **47** D10
Ballymena U.K. **47** F9
Ballymoney U.K. **47** F8
Ballyshannon Rep. of Ireland **47** D9
Balmaceda Aisén Chile **205** C7
Balmaceda Antofagasta Chile **200** C6
Balmaseda Spain **55** I1
  also spelt Valmaseda
Balmazújváros Hungary **49** S8
Balmer India *see* Barmer
Balmerton Canada **167** M5
Balmoral Australia **146** D4
Balmoral N.Z. **153** G10
Balnearia Arg. **204** E3
Baloa Indon. **75** B3
Balochistan *prov.* Pak. **101** F4
Balochistan reg. Pak. **92** B5
  formerly known as Baluchistan
Balod India **94** D1
Baloda India **97** D5
Baloda Bazar India **97** D5
Balok, Teluk *b.* Indon. **77** D3
Balombo Angola **127** B8
  formerly known as Norton de Matos
Balonne *r.* Australia **147** F2
Balotra India **96** B4
Balpahari Reservoir India **97** E5
Balpyk Bi Kazakh. **103** I3
  formerly known as Kirov or Kirovskiy
Balqash Kazakh. *see* Balkhash
Balqash Köli *l.* Kazakh. *see* Balkhash, Lake
Balrampur India **97** D4
Balranald Australia **147** D3
Balş Romania **58** F4
Balsam Creek Canada **173** N4
Balsam Lake *l.* Canada **173** O6
Balsam Lake U.S.A. **172** A5
Balsapuerto Peru **198** B6
Balsas Brazil **202** C3
Balsas Mex. **185** F5
Balsas *r.* Mex. **185** F5
Balsas, Rio das *r.* Brazil **202** C3
Bal'shavik Belarus **43** L9
Bålsta Sweden **45** L4
Balta Ukr. **41** D7
Baltasi Rus. Fed. **40** I4
Baltasound U.K. **46** L1
Baltay Rus. Fed. **102** A1
Bălţi Moldova **41** C7
  formerly spelt Bel'ts or Bel'tsy
Baltic Sea *g.* Europe **45** L5
Baltim Egypt **121** F2
Baltimore Rep. of Ireland **47** C12
Baltimore *MD* U.S.A. **177** I6
Baltimore *OH* U.S.A. **176** C6
Baltinava Latvia **42** I5
Baltinglass Rep. of Ireland **47** F11
Baltistan reg. Jammu and Kashmir **96** C2
Baltiysk Rus. Fed. **42** A7
  historically known as Pillau
Baltoji Vokė Lith. **42** F7
Baltoro Glacier Jammu and Kashmir **96** C2
Baluarte Brazil **202** D4
Baluch Ab *well* Iran **100** D4
Balüchestän va Sïstän *prov.* Iran **101** F4
Balui *r.* Sarawak Malaysia **77** F2
Balumath India **97** E5
Balumundam Indon. **76** B2
Balupe *r.* Latvia **42** H5
Baluran, Gunung *mt.* Indon. **77** F3
Balurghat India **97** F4
Balut *i.* Phil. **74** C5
Balvatnet *l.* Norway **44** K2
Balvi Latvia **42** I4
Balya Turkey **106** A3
Balyaga Rus. Fed. **85** F1
Balykchy Kyrg. **103** I3
  formerly known as Issyk-Kul' or Ysyk-Köl or
  Rybach'ye
Balykshi Kazakh. **102** B3
  also spelt Balyqshy
Balyktyg-Khem *r.* Rus. Fed. **84** C1
Balyqshy Kazakh. *see* Balykshi
Balzar Ecuador **198** B5
Bam Iran **100** D4
Bäm Iran **100** D2
Bama China **87** D3
Bama Nigeria **125** I4
Bamaga Australia **149** D1
Bamaji Lake Canada **168** B3
▶ Bamako Mali **124** D3
  Capital of Mali.
Bamba *r.* Cent. Afr. Rep. **126** C3
Bamba Dem. Rep. Congo **127** C6
Bamba Mali **125** D2
Bambang Phil. **74** B5
Bambangando Angola **127** D9
Bambanan *r.* Phil. **74** B5
Bambari Cent. Afr. Rep. **126** D3
Bamberg Germany **48** H6
Bamberg U.S.A. **175** D5
Bambesi Eth. **128** B2
Bambey Senegal **124** A3
Bambili Dem. Rep. Congo **126** E4
Bambio Cent. Afr. Rep. **126** C4
Bamboesberg *mts* S. Africa **133** K8
Bamboi Ghana **125** E4
Bambou *well* Mali **125** E2
Bambouti Cent. Afr. Rep. **126** F3
Bambui Brazil **203** C7
Bamda China **86** A2
Bămdezh Iran **100** B4
Bamenda Cameroon **125** H5
Bamendjing, Lac de *l.* Cameroon **125** H5
Bamfield Canada **166** E5

Bami Turkm. **102** D5
  also spelt Bamy
Bämiän Afgh. **101** F3
Bämiän *prov.* Afgh. **101** F3
Bamiancheng China **85** J3
Bamiantong China *see* Muling
Bamingui Cent. Afr. Rep. **126** D3
Bamingui *r.* Cent. Afr. Rep. **126** D3
Bamingui-Bangoran *pref.* Cent. Afr. Rep.
  126 D2
Bamingui-Bangoran, Parc National du
  nat. park Cent. Afr. Rep. **126** C3
Bamiyan *r.* Afgh. **101** G3
Bammo *well* Niger **125** H3
Bamoa Mex. **184** C3
Bamor India **96** C4
Bam Posht *reg.* Iran **101** E5
Bam Posht, Küh-e *mts* Iran **101** E5
Bampūr Iran **101** E5
Bampūr *watercourse* Iran **101** D5
Bamy Turkm. *see* Bami
Bamyili Australia **148** B2
  also known as Barunga
Ban Burkina **124** D3
Bana, Wädi *watercourse* Yemen **105** D5
Banaba *i.* Kiribati **145** G2
  also known as Ocean Island; also spelt
  Paanopa
Banabuiu, Açude *resr* Brazil **202** E3
Bañados del Atuel *marsh* Arg. **204** D5
Bañados del Izozog *swamp* Bol. **201** F4
Bañados de Otuquis *marsh* Bol. **201** F4
Banahao, Mount *vol.* Phil. **74** B3
Banalia Dem. Rep. Congo **126** E4
Banamba Mali **124** C3
Banan China **86** C2
  formerly known as Baxian
Banana Australia **149** F5
Bananal, Ilha do *i.* Brazil **202** B4
Bananga India **95** G5
Banankoro Guinea **124** C4
Banapur India **95** E2
Banarlı Turkey **59** I8
Banas *r.* India **96** C4
Banās, Râs *pt* Egypt **121** G4
Banatski Karlovac *Vojvodina, Srbija* Yugo.
  58 C3
Banawaya *i.* Indon. **75** A4
Banaz Turkey **106** C3
Banaz *r.* Turkey **59** K10
Ban Ban Laos **78** C4
Banbar China **89** E6
  also known as Domartang
Banbridge U.K. **47** F9
Ban Bua Yai Thai. **79** C5
Banbury U.K. **47** K11
Banca Romania **58** I2
Bancoran *i.* Phil. **74** A5
Bancroft Canada **168** E4
Bancroft Zambia *see* Chililabombwe
Band Iran **100** B3
Banda Dem. Rep. Congo **126** E3
Banda *Madhya Pradesh* India **96** C4
Banda *Uttar Pradesh* India **96** D4
Banda, Kepulauan *is* Indon. **75** D4
Banda, Kepulauan *is* Indon. **75** D4
  formerly known as Kutaraja
Banda Banda, Mount Australia **147** G2
Bandahara, Gunung *mt.* Indon. **76** B2
Banda-Asahi National Park Japan **90** F6
Bandama *i.* Côte d'Ivoire **124** D5
Bandama Blanc *r.* Côte d'Ivoire **124** D4
Bandän Iran **101** E4
Bandaneira Indon. **75** D4
Bandän Küh *mts* Iran **101** E4
Bandar India *see* Machilipatnam
Bandar Abbas Iran *see* Bandar-e 'Abbäs
Bandaragung Indon. **76** D4
Bandar-e 'Abbäs Iran **100** D5
  English form Bandar Abbas; historically
  known as Gombroon
Bandar-e Anzali Iran **100** B2
  formerly known as Bandar-e Pahlavï
Bandar-e Chärak Iran **100** C5
Bandar-e Deylam Iran **100** B4
Bandar-e Emäm Khomeynï Iran **100** B4
  formerly known as Bandar-e Shähpür
Bandar-e Lengeh Iran **100** C5
Bandar-e Maqäm Iran **100** C5
Bandar-e Ma'shur Iran **100** B4
Bandar-e Moghüyeh Iran **100** C5
Bandar-e Pahlavï Iran *see* Bandar-e Anzali
Bandar-e Rig Iran **100** B4
Bandar-e Shäh Iran *see*
  Bandar-e Torkeman
Bandar-e Shähpür Iran *see*
  Bandar-e Emäm Khomeynï
Bandar-e Torkeman Iran **100** C2
  formerly known as Bandar-e Shäh
Bandar Lampung Indon. **76** D4
  Tanjungkarang-Telukbetung
Bandar Murcaayo Somalia **128** F2
Bandarpunch *mt.* India **96** C3
▶ Bandar Seri Begawan Brunei **77** F1
  Capital of Brunei. Formerly known as
  Brunei.
Bandar Wanaag Somalia **128** E2
Banda Sea Indon. **75** D4
Bandeira Brazil **207** M2
Bandeirante Brazil **202** B5
Bandeirantes Brazil **206** C10
Bandeiras, Pico de *mt.* Brazil **203** D7
Bandera Arg. **204** E3
Bandera Mex. **184** D2
Banderas, Bahía de *b.* Mex. **184** D4
Bandhi Pak. **101** G5
Bandhogarh India **96** D5
Bandi *r.* India **96** B4
Bandia *r.* India **94** D2
Bandiagara Mali **124** E3
Bandiagara, Falaise de *esc.* Mali **124** E3
Band-i-Amir *r.* Afgh. **101** F3
Band-i-Baba *mts* Afgh. **101** E3
Band-i-Husain Nau *mts* Iran **100** D3
Bandikui India **96** C4
Bandini Iran **101** D5
Bandipur Jammu and Kashmir **96** B2
Bandipur Nepal **97** D3
Bandipur National Park India **94** C4
Band-i-Turkestan *mts* Afgh. **101** E3
Bandjarmasin Indon. *see* Banjarmasin
Bandjer pass Yugo. **58** B5
Bandon Rep. of Ireland **47** D12
Bandon *r.* Rep. of Ireland **47** D12
Ban Don Thai. *see* Surat Thani
Bandon U.S.A. **180** A4
Ban Don, Ao b. Thai. **79** B6
Band Qir Iran **100** B4
Bandra India **94** B2
Bandua Moz. **131** G3
Bandula Moz. **131** G3
Bandundu Dem. Rep. Congo **126** C5
  formerly known as Banningville
Bandundu *prov.* Dem. Rep. Congo **126** C6
Bandung Indon. **77** D4
Bandya Australia **151** C6
Băneasa Romania **58** I4
Băneasa Romania **58** H4
Banemo Indon. **75** D2
Banera India **96** B4
Bäneh Iran **100** A3
Ban Lamduan Thai. **79** C6
Banloc Romania **58** C3
Bañeres Spain **55** K6

Banes Cuba **186** E2
Banff Canada **167** H5
Banff U.K. **46** J6
Banff National Park Canada **167** G5
Banfora Burkina **124** D4
Bang Cent. Afr. Rep. **126** B3
Bang Angola **127** B7
Banga Dem. Rep. Congo **127** D6
Banga *r.* Phil. **74** C5
Bangai Point Phil. **74** C5
Bangall Creek *watercourse* Australia **149** D4
Bangalore India **94** C3
Banganapalle India **94** C3
Banganga *r.* India **96** C4
Bangangté Cameroon **125** H5
Bangaon India **97** F5
Bangar Brunei **77** F1
Bangara *r.* Bangl. **97** F5
Bangarapet India **94** C3
Bangassou Cent. Afr. Rep. **126** D3
Banow Egypt *see* Andaräb
Ban Phaeng Thai. **78** C4
Ban Phai Thai. **78** C4
Ban Phon Laos **79** D5
Banphot Phisai Thai. **78** B5
Ban Pong Thai. **79** B5
Banqiao China **86** B3
Bansang Gambia **124** B3
Ban Saraphi Thai. **78** B4
Ban Sawi Thai. **79** B6
Bansi *Rajasthan* India **96** B4
Bansi *Uttar Pradesh* India **97** D4
Bansi *Uttar Pradesh* India **97** D4
Banská Bystrica Slovakia **49** Q7
Banská Štiavnica Slovakia **49** Q7
Bansko Bulg. **58** E7
Bansloi *r.* India **97** E4
Ban Sut Ta Thai. **78** B4
Banswada India **94** C2
Banswara India **96** B5
Banta *i.* Indon. **77** G5
Bantaeng Indon. **75** A4
Bantayan *i.* Phil. **74** B4
Bantè Benin **125** F4
▶ Bangkok Thai. **79** C5
  Capital of Thailand. Also known as Krung
  Thep.
Bangkok, Bight of *b.* Thai. **79** C5
Bangkor China **89** D6
Bangkulu *i.* Indon. **75** B3
Bangla *state* India *see* West Bengal
▶ Bangladesh country Asia **97** F4
  8th most populous country in the world.
  Formerly known as East Bengal or East
  Pakistan.
  world [population] ⟩⟩ 22–23
  asia [countries] ⟩⟩ 64–67
Bangma Shan *mts* China **86** A4
Bang Mun Nak Thai. **78** C4
Bängnäs Sweden **44** K2
Bangolo Côte d'Ivoire **124** D5
Bangong Co *salt l.*
  China/Jammu and Kashmir **89** B5
  also spelt Pangong Tso
Bangor Gwynedd, Wales U.K. **47** H10
Bangor Northern Ireland U.K. **47** G9
Bangor *ME* U.S.A. **177** Q1
Bangor *MI* U.S.A. **172** G8
Bangor *PA* U.S.A. **177** J5
Bangriposi India **97** E5
Bangs, Mount U.S.A. **183** K5
Bangsalsepulun Indon. **77** G3
Bang Saphan Yai Thai. **79** B6
Bangsund Norway **44** J2
Bangu Dem. Rep. Congo **127** D7
Bangued Phil. **74** B2
▶ Bangui Cent. Afr. Rep. **126** C3
  Capital of Central African Republic.
Bangui Phil. **74** B2
Bangula Malawi **129** B9
Bangunpurba Indon. **76** B2
Bangunu Dem. Rep. Congo **126** E4
Bangweulu, Lake Zambia **127** F7
Banhã Egypt *see* Benha
Banhine, Parque Nacional de *nat. park*
  Moz. **131** G4
Ban Houayxay Laos **78** C3
  also spelt Ban Houei Sai
Ban Houei Sai Laos *see* Ban Houayxay
Bani Burkina **125** E3
Bani Cent. Afr. Rep. **126** D2
Bani Dom. Rep. **187** F3
Bani *r.* Mali **124** D3
Bani Phil. **74** A2
Bani, Jbel *ridge* Morocco **122** C3
Bania Cent. Afr. Rep. **126** C3
Bani Atiyah *reg.* Saudi Arabia **106** C3
Bani-Bangou Niger **125** F3
Banifing *r.* Mali **124** D4
Banihal Pass and Tunnel
  Jammu and Kashmir **96** B2
Bani Khatmah *reg.* Saudi Arabia **105** D4
Bani Khurb *hills* Saudi Arabia **104** D4
Banikoara Benin **125** F4
Bani Ma'äriq *des.* Saudi Arabia **105** D4
Bani Mukassir *des.* Saudi Arabia **105** D4
Bani Suwayf Egypt *see* Beni Suef
Banite Bulg. **58** G7
Bani Thawr Saudi Arabia **104** C4
Banitsa Bulg. **58** D6
Bani Tukhman *reg.* Saudi Arabia **105** D4
Bani Walid Libya **120** B2
Bani Wutayfän *well* Saudi Arabia **105** E2
Bäniyäs Syria **109** H3
  historically known as Caesarea Philippi or
  Paneas
Bani Yas *reg.* U.A.E. **105** F3
Banja *Srbija* Yugo. **58** A5
Banja Luka Bos.-Herz. **56** J4
Banjar India **96** C3
Banjarbaru Indon. **77** F3
Banjarmasin Indon. **77** F3
  formerly spelt Bandjarmasin
▶ Banjul Gambia **124** A3
  Capital of The Gambia. Formerly known as
  Bathurst.
Bankä Azer. **100** B2
Banka India **97** E4
Banka Banka Australia **148** B3
Bankapur India **94** B3
Bankass Mali **124** E3
Ban Khai Thai. **79** C5
Ban Khao Yoi Thai. **79** B5
Banki India **95** E1
Bankim Cameroon **125** H5
Banklop S. Africa **133** O3
Banko, Massif de *mt.* Guinea **124** C4
Bankobankoang *i.* Indon. **77** G4
Bankol India **95** E2
Bankon Guinea **124** C4
Bankura India **97** E5
Bankya India **58** E6
Bankya Bulg. **58** D6
Ban Lamduan Thai. **79** C6
Banlan China **87** D3
Banloc Romania **58** C3
Bañeres Spain **55** K6

Ban Mae Mo Thai. **78** B4
Banmauk Myanmar **78** A2
Bann *r.* U.K. **47** F8
Ban Na San Thai. **79** B6
Banner Hill U.S.A. **176** C9
Bannertown Bahamas **186** D1
Banning U.S.A. **183** H8
Banningville Dem. Rep. Congo *see*
  Bandundu
Bannivka Ukr. **41** E6
Bannockburn U.K. **46** I7
Ban Nol Myanmar **78** B4
Bannu Pak. **101** G3
  formerly known as Edwardesabad
Bañolas Spain *see* Banyoles
Baños Ecuador **198** B5
Baños de Puritama Chile **200** C5
Bánovce nad Bebravou Slovakia **49** P7
Banovići Bos.-Herz. **56** K4
Banow Egypt *see* Andaräb
Bao Angola **127** B7
Ban Phaeng Thai. **78** C4
Ban Phai Thai. **78** C4
Ban Phon Laos **79** D5
Banphot Phisai Thai. **78** B5
Ban Pong Thai. **79** B5
Banqiao China **86** B3
Bansang Gambia **124** B3
Ban Saraphi Thai. **78** B4
Ban Sawi Thai. **79** B6
Bãos de Puritama Chile **200** C5
Bãos Ecuador **198** B5
Bãos Spain *see* Baños
Baño de Melgaço Brazil **207** J6
Barão de Cocais Brazil **207** J6
Barão de Grajaú Brazil **202** D3
Barão de Melgaço Brazil **201** F3
Barão de Melgaço Brazil **201** E2
Baraolt Romania **58** G2
Baraqbay Kazakh. *see* Barakpay
Baramanni Guyana **199** G3
Baramati India **94** B2
Barambah *r.* Australia **147** F5
Barameiya Sudan **121** H5
Baramula Jammu and Kashmir **96** B2
Baran' Belarus **43** L7
Baran India **96** C4
Baran *r.* Pak. **101** G5
Bärän, Küh-e *mts* Iran **101** E3
Baranavichy Belarus **42** H8
  also spelt Baranovichi; formerly spelt
  Baranowicze
Barang, Dasht-i *des.* Afgh. **101** E3
Baranikha Rus. Fed. **39** Q3
Baranivka Ukr. **41** C6
Baranoa Col. **187** E5
Baranof Island U.S.A. **164** C4
Baranovichi Belarus *see* Baranavichy
Baranowicze Belarus *see* Baranavichy
Barão de Cocais Brazil **207** J6

Baramanni Guyana **199** G3
Baramati India **94** B2
Barambah *r.* Australia **147** F5
Barameiya Sudan **121** H5
Baramula Jammu and Kashmir **96** B2
Baran' Belarus **43** L7
Baran India **96** C4
Baran *r.* Pak. **101** G5
Bärän, Küh-e *mts* Iran **101** E3
Baranavichy Belarus **42** H8
  also spelt Baranovichi; formerly spelt
  Baranowicze
Barang, Dasht-i *des.* Afgh. **101** E3
Baranikha Rus. Fed. **39** Q3
Baranivka Ukr. **41** C6
Baranoa Col. **187** E5
Baranof Island U.S.A. **164** C4
Baranovichi Belarus *see* Baranavichy
Baranowicze Belarus *see* Baranavichy
Barão de Cocais Brazil **207** J6
Barão de Grajaú Brazil **202** D3
Barão de Melgaço Brazil **201** F3
Barão de Melgaço Brazil **201** E2
Baraolt Romania **58** G2
Baraqbay Kazakh. *see* Barakpay
Baraqueville France **51** I8
Bararati *r.* Brazil **201** F1
Bârat, Chiyä-e *hill* Iraq **109** P1
Barat Daya, Kepulauan *is* Indon. **75** C4
Baratta Australia **146** C3
Barauaná, Serra *mts* Brazil **199** F4
Baraut India **96** C3
Baraya Col. **198** C4
Barbacena *Minas Gerais* Brazil **203** D7
Barbacena *Pará* Brazil **199** H5
Barbados *country* West Indies **187** I4
  northamerica [countries] ⟩⟩ 158–159
Barbar, Gebel *mt.* Egypt **108** E8
Barbara Lake Canada **168** C3
Barbaria, Cap de *c.* Spain **55** M6
Barbaros Turkey **58** I8
Barbastro Spain **55** L2
Barbate de Franco Spain **54** F8
Bârbele Latvia **42** F5
Barber's Bay Canada **173** M2
Barberspan Nature Reserve S. Africa
  133 J3
Barberton S. Africa **133** O2
Barberton U.S.A. **176** D4
Barbezieux-St-Hilaire France **50** F7
Barbigha India **97** E4
Barbil India **97** E5
Barbosa Col. **198** C3
Barbour Bay Canada **167** M2
Barbours U.S.A. **177** I4
Barboza Phil. **74** B4
Barbuda *i.* Antigua and Barbuda **187** H3
Barca Romania **58** E5
Barcaldine Australia **149** E4
Barcău *r.* Romania **58** D2
Barce Libya *see* Al Marj
Barcellona Pozzo di Gotto *Sicilia* Italy
  57 H10
Barcelona Spain **55** N3
  historically known as Barcino
Barcelona Venez. **199** E2
Barcelonnette France **51** M8
Barcelos Brazil **199** F5
Barcin Poland **49** O3
Barcino Spain *see* Barcelona
Barclay de Tolly *atoll* Fr. Polynesia *see*
  Raroia
Barclayville Liberia **124** C5
Barcoo *watercourse* Australia **149** D5
Barcoo Creek *watercourse* Australia *see*
  Cooper Creek
Barcoo National Park Australia *see*
  Welford National Park
Barcs Hungary **56** J3
Barczewo Poland **49** R2
Bärdä Azer. **107** F2
Barda Rus. Fed. **40** J4
Bardaale Somalia **128** E3
Bárðarbunga *mt.* Iceland **44** [inset] C2
Bardas Blancas Arg. **204** C4
Bardaskan Iran **100** D3
Bardawil, Khabrat al *salt pan* Saudi Arabia
  109 J6
Bardawil, Sabkhet el *lag.* Egypt **108** E6
  formerly spelt Bardawil
Barddhaman India **97** E5
Bardejov Slovakia **49** S6
Bardera Somalia *see* Baardheere
Bardsey Island U.K. **47** H11
Bard Shah India **97** E4
Bardsïr Iran **100** D4
Barðsneshorn *pt* Iceland **165** R3
Bardstown U.S.A. **174** C4
Barduli Italy *see* Barletta
Bardwell U.S.A. **174** B5
Baré Eth. **128** D3
Bareilly India **96** C3
Bareli India **96** C4
Barengapara India **97** F4
Barentin France **50** G3
Barenton France **50** F4
Barentsburg Svalbard **38** B2
Barents Island Svalbard *see* Barentsøya
Barentsøya *i.* Svalbard **38** C2
  English form Barents Island
Barents Sea Arctic Ocean **38** E2
Barentu Eritrea **121** H5
Bareo *Sarawak* Malaysia **77** F2
Barfleur, Pointe de *pt* France **50** E3
Barga China **89** C6
Barga Italy **56** C4
Bargaal Somalia **128** F2
Bärgäh Iran **100** D5
Bargara Australia **149** G5
Bargë China **89** C6
Bargi India **96** C5
Bargïri Turkey *see* Muradiye
Bargteheide Germany **48** H2
Barguna Bangl. **97** F5
Bargur India **94** C4
Barh India **97** E4
Barhaj India **97** D4
Barhalganj India **97** D4
Bar Harbor U.S.A. **177** Q1
Barharwa India **97** E4
Barhi India **97** E4
Bari Dem. Rep. Congo **126** C4
Bari India **96** C4
Bari Italy **56** I7
  historically known as Barium
Bari *admin. reg.* Somalia **128** E2
Ba Ria Vietnam **79** D6
Baridi, Ra's *hd* Saudi Arabia **104** B3
Bari Doab *lowland* Pak. **101** H4
Barik Oman **105** F3
Barika Alg. **123** G1
Barikot Afgh. **101** G3
Barikot Nepal **97** D3
Barima *r.* Guyana **199** G2
Barima *r.* Venez. **187** H5
Barinas Venez. **198** D2
Barinas *state* Venez. **198** D2
Baringa Dem. Rep. Congo **126** D4
Baringo, Lake Kenya **128** C4
Baripada India **97** E5
Bariri Brazil **206** E9
Bari Sadri India **96** B4
Barisal Bangl. **97** F5
Barisal *admin. div.* Bangl. **97** F5
Barisan, Pegunungan *mts* Indon. **76** B3
Barito *r.* Indon. **77** F3
Baritu, Parque Nacional *nat. park* Arg.
  201 D5
Barium Italy *see* Bari

Barjaude, Montagne de *mt.* France 51 M9
Barjols France 51 M9
Barjora India 97 E5
Barjūj, Wādī *watercourse* Libya 120 B3
Barka *prov.* Oman 105 G3
Barkam China 84 E5
Barka, Ra's-e *pt* Iran 100 B4
Barkava Latvia 42 H5
Barker, Lake *salt flat* Australia 151 C6
Barkerville Canada 166 F4
Barkéwel el Abiod Mauritania 124 B2
Barkhan India 97 E4
Barkhan *prov.* India 97 E4
Barkl Saraiya India 97 E4
Bark Lake Canada 173 P5
Barkley East S. Africa 133 L7
Barkley, Lake U.S.A. 174 C4
Barkley Sound *inlet* Canada 166 E5
Barkly East S. Africa 133 L7
Barkly Pass S. Africa 133 L8
Barkly Tableland *reg.* Australia 148 B3
Barkly West S. Africa 133 I5
Barkol China 84 B3
Barkol Hu *salt l.* China 84 B3
Barkot India 96 C3
Bârlad Romania 58 I2
formerly spelt Bîrlad
Bârladului, Podișul *plat.* Romania 58 I2
Barlag Gol *watercourse* Mongolia 84 B2
Bar-le-Duc France 51 L4
Barlee, Lake *salt flat* Australia 151 B6
Barlee Range Australia 150 A4
Barlee Range Nature Reserve Australia 150 A4
Barletta Italy 56 I7
historically known as Barduli
Barlinek Poland 49 M3
Barloew Lake Canada 166 B2
Barmedman Australia 147 E3
Barmen-Elberfeld Germany see Wuppertal
Barmer India 96 A4
also spelt Balmer
Barmera Australia 146 D3
Barm Fīrūz, Kūh-e *mt.* Iran 107 G3
Barmouth U.K. 47 H11
also known as Abermaw
Barmstedt Germany 48 G2
Barnagar India 96 B5
Barnala India 96 B3
Barnard, Mount Canada/U.S.A. 166 B3
Barnard Castle U.K. 47 K9
Barnato Australia 147 E2
Barnaul Rus. Fed. 80 C2
Barnegat U.S.A. 177 K6
Barnegat Bay U.S.A. 177 K6
Barne Inlet Antarctica 223 K1
Barnesboro U.S.A. 176 G5
Barnesville GA U.S.A. 175 D5
Barnesville MN U.S.A. 178 C2
Barnet U.K. 47 M11
Barneveld Neth. 48 C3
Barneville-Carteret France 50 F3
Barney Top *mt.* U.S.A. 183 M4
Barnhart U.S.A. 179 B6
Barnjarn Aboriginal Land *res.* Australia 148 B2
Bârnova, Dealul *hill* Romania 58 I1
Barnsdall U.S.A. 178 C4
Barnsley U.K. 47 K10
Barnstable U.S.A. 177 O4
Barnstaple U.K. 47 H12
Barnstaple Bay U.K. see Bideford Bay
Barnwell U.S.A. 175 D5
Baro Nigeria 125 G5
Baroda India see Vadodara
Baroda India 96 C4
Baroda S. Africa 133 J8
Baroe S. Africa 133 I10
Baroghil Pass Afgh. 101 H2
Barong China 86 A2
Baron'ki Belarus 43 N8
Barons Range *hills* Australia 150 D5
Baroua Cent. Afr. Rep. 126 E3
Baro Wenz *r.* Eth. 128 B2
Barowka Belarus 42 I6
Barpeta India 97 F4
Bar Pla Soi Thai. see Chon Buri
Barqa, Gebel *hill* Egypt see Cheops
Barqā al Ashqar *reg.* Yemen 105 D4
Barqā 'Damaj *well* Saudi Arabia 109 H9
Barques, Point Aux U.S.A. 173 K6
Barquisimeto Venez. 198 D2
Barr, Rās el *pt* Egypt 108 C6
Barra Brazil 202 D4
Barra *i.* U.K. 46 E7
also spelt Barraigh
Barraba Australia 147 F2
Barra Bonita Brazil 206 E9
Barracão do Barreto Brazil 201 F2
Barrackville U.S.A. 176 E6
Barracouta, Cape S. Africa 132 F11
Barra da Estiva Brazil 202 D5
Barra de Navidad Mex. 184 D5
Barra de Santos *inlet* Brazil 206 G11
Barra de São Francisco Brazil 207 M5
Barra de São João Brazil 207 L8
Barra do Bugres Brazil 201 F3
Barra do Corda Brazil 202 C3
Barra do Cuieté Brazil 207 L6
Barra do Cuanza Angola 127 B7
Barra do Garças Brazil 206 A2
Barrado Mendes Brazil 202 D5
Barra do Piraí Brazil 207 J9
Barra do São Manuel Brazil 201 F1
Barra do Una Brazil 206 D2
Barra Falsa, Ponta da *pt* Moz. 131 G4
Barraigh *i.* U.K. see Barra
Barra Kruta Hond. 186 C4
Barra Longa Brazil 207 J7
Barra Mansa Brazil 207 I9
Barrāmīya Egypt 121 G3
Barranca Peru 200 A2
Barranca Venez. 198 D2
Barrancabermeja Col. 198 C3
Barrancas *r.* Arg. 204 C5
Barrancas Barinas Venez. 198 D2
Barrancas Monagas Venez. 199 F2
Barranco de Loba Col. 198 C3
Barranco del Cobre, Parque Natural
nature res. Mex. 184 D3
Barrancos Port. 54 D6
Barranqueras Arg. 204 E3
Barranquilla Atlántico Col. 198 C2
Barranquilla Guaviare Col. 198 C4
Barranquita Peru 198 B6
Barras Brazil 202 D3
Barraute Canada 173 M3
Barrax Spain 55 I5
Barre MA U.S.A. 177 M3
Barre VT U.S.A. 177 M1
Barreal Arg. 204 C3
Barre des Écrins *mt.* France 51 M8
Barreiras Brazil 202 C5
Barreirinha Brazil 199 G5
Barreirinhas Brazil 202 D2
Barreiro *r.* Brazil 206 C4
Barreiro do Nascimento Brazil 202 B4
Barreiros Brazil 202 F4
Barren Island India 95 G3
Barren Island Kiribati see Starbuck Island
Barren Islands U.S.A. 164 C4
Barretos Brazil 206 E7
Barrett U.S.A. 183 H9
Barrett, Mount Australia 150 D3
Barrhead Canada 167 H4
Barrhill N.Z. 153 F11
Barri *i.* Saudi Arabia 104 C4
Barrie Canada 168 E4
Barrie Island Canada 173 K5
Barrier, Cape N.Z. 152 J4

Barrière Canada 166 F5
Barrier Range *hills* Australia 146 D2
Barrier Reef Belize 185 I5
Barrington Canada 169 H5
Barrington S. Africa 132 G10
Barrington, Mount Australia 147 F3
Barrington Lake Canada 167 K3
Barrington Tops National Park Australia 147 F3
Barro Alto Brazil 206 E2
Barrocão Brazil 207 J3
Barrolândia Brazil 207 N3
Barron *r.* U.S.A. 172 B5
Barronett U.S.A. 172 B5
Barroso Brazil 207 J8
Barrow Arg. 204 E5
Barrow *r.* Rep. of Ireland 47 F11
Barrow U.S.A. 164 D2
Barrow, Point U.S.A. 164 D2
Barrow Creek Australia 148 B4
Barrow-in-Furness U.K. 47 I9
Barrow Island Australia 150 A4
Barrow Island Nature Reserve Australia 150 A4
Barrow Range *hills* Australia 151 D5
Barr Smith Range *hills* Australia 151 C5
Barry U.K. 47 I12
Barrydale S. Africa 132 E10
Barry Islands Canada 167 J1
Barry Mountains Australia 147 E4
Barrys Bay Canada 168 E4
Barryton U.S.A. 173 H7
Barryville N.Z. 152 J6
Barryville U.S.A. 177 K4
Barsakel'mes, Ostrov *i.* Kazakh. 102 D3
Barsakel'messkiy Zapovednik nature res. Kazakh. 102 E3
Barsalogo Burkina 125 E3
Barsalpur India 96 B3
Barshatas Kazakh. 103 I2
Barshi India see Barsi
Barsi India 94 B2
formerly spelt Barshi
Barstow U.S.A. 183 G7
Barstyčiai Lith. 42 C5
Barsuki Rus. Fed. 43 S7
Barsur India 94 D2
Bar-sur-Aube France 51 K4
Bar-sur-Seine France 51 K4
Bärta Latvia 42 C5
Bärta *r.* Latvia 42 C5
Bartang *r.* Tajik. 101 G2
Barth Germany 49 J1
Bartholomew, Bayou *r.* U.S.A. 175 A5
Bartica Guyana 199 G3
Bartin Turkey 106 C2
Bartle Frere, Mount Australia 149 E3
Bartles U.S.A. 176 C7
Bartles, Mount U.S.A. 183 N2
Bartlesville U.S.A. 178 C4
Bartlett IL U.S.A. 178 C3
Bartlett NH U.S.A. 177 N1
Bartlett Lake Canada 167 G2
Bartlett Reservoir U.S.A. 183 M8
Bartletts N.Z. 152 L6
Barton U.S.A. 177 M1
Bartonville U.S.A. 172 D10
Bartoszyce Poland 49 R1
Bartow U.S.A. 175 D7
Bartura *r.* Lith. 42 C5
Baru, Isla de *i.* Col. 198 C3
Baruipur India 97 F5
Barüm Yemen 105 E5
Barumun *r.* Indon. 76 C2
Barung *i.* Indon. 77 F5
Barunga Australia see Bamyili
Barun-Torey, Ozero *l.* Rus. Fed. 85 G1
Barus Indon. 76 B2
Baruunharaa Mongolia 85 E1
Baruunsuu Mongolia 85 E3
Baruunturuun Mongolia 84 B1
Baruun Urt Mongolia 85 G2
Baruva India 95 E2
Barwah India 96 C5
Barwala Gujarat India 96 A5
Barwala Haryana India 96 B3
Barwani India 96 B5
Barwar India 96 B5
Barwa Sagar India 96 C4
Barwice Poland 49 N2
Barwon *r.* Australia 147 E2
Baryatino Rus. Fed. 43 P7
Barybino Rus. Fed. 43 S6
Barycz *r.* Poland 49 N4
Barysaw Belarus 43 J7
also spelt Borisov
Barysh Rus. Fed. 41 H5
Basaga Turkm. 101 F2
Basail Arg. 204 E2
Basák, Tônlé *r.* Cambodia 79 D6
Basalt *r.* Australia 149 E3
Basalt Island Hong Kong China 87 [inset]
also known as Sha Tong Hau Shan
Basanga Dem. Rep. Congo 126 E6
Basankusu Dem. Rep. Congo 126 C4
Basantpur India 97 E4
Basarabeasca Moldova 58 J2
formerly known as Romanovka; formerly spelt Bessarabka
Basarabi Romania 58 J4
Basargechar Armenia see Vardenis
Basavilbaso Arg. 204 F4
Basco Phil. 74 B1
Bascom Phil. 74 B1
Bascombe Well Conservation Park nature res. Australia 146 B3
Bas-Congo *prov.* Dem. Rep. Congo 127 B6
formerly known as Bas-Zaïre
Bascuñán, Cabo *c.* Chile 204 C3
Bascuñana, Sierra de *mts* Spain 55 I4
Basedow Range *hills* Australia 148 B5
Basel Switz. 51 N5
English form Basle; also spelt Bâle
Basel-Mulhouse airport France 51 N5
Basentello *r.* Italy 56 I8
Basento *r.* Italy 57 I8
Basey Phil. 74 C4
Bashākerd, Kūhhā-ye *mts* Iran 100 D5
Bashan China see Chongren
Bashanta Rus. Fed. see Gorodovikovsk
Bashaw Canada 167 H4
Bashee *r.* S. Africa 133 M8
Bashee Bridge S. Africa 133 M8
Bashgul *r.* Afgh. 101 G3
Bashi China see Liaizxi
Bashi Channel Taiwan 73 F2
Bashimuke Dem. Rep. Congo 126 E6
Ba'shiqah, Jabal *mt.* Iraq 109 O1
Bashkaus *r.* Rus. Fed. 88 D1
Bashkiria *aut. rep.* Rus. Fed. see Bashkortostan, Respublika
Bashkirskaya A.S.S.R. *aut. rep.* Rus. Fed. see Bashkortostan, Respublika
Bashkirskiy Zapovednik nature res. Rus. Fed. 102 D1
Bashkortostan, Respublika *aut. rep.* Rus. Fed. 102 D1
formerly known as Bashkiria or Bashkirskaya A.S.S.R.
Bashmakovo Rus. Fed. 41 G5
Bāsht Iran 100 B4
Bashtanka Ukr. 41 E7
Bāsi India 96 C4
Basia India 97 E5
Basilaki Island P.N.G. 149 F1

Basilan *i.* Phil. 74 B5
Basilan Strait Phil. 74 B5
Basildon U.K. 47 M12
Basile U.S.A. 179 D6
Basile, Pico *mt.* Equat. Guinea 125 H6
Basilicata *admin. reg.* Italy 57 H8
Basin U.S.A. 180 E3
Basingstoke U.K. 47 K12
Basin Lake Canada 167 J4
Bāsīra *r.* Iraq 107 L5
Basirhat India 97 F5
Basīt, Ra's al *pt* Syria 108 G2
Baskakovka Rus. Fed. 43 P7
Başkale Turkey 107 F3
Baskatong, Réservoir Canada 168 E4
Baskerville, Cape Australia 150 C3
Başkomutan Milli Parkı *nat. park* Turkey 106 B3
Baskunchak, Ozero *l.* Rus. Fed. 102 A2
Basle Switz. see Basel
Basmat India 94 C1
Baso *i.* Indon. 76 C3
Basoko Dem. Rep. Congo 126 D4
Basongo Dem. Rep. Congo 126 D6
Basotu Tanz. 128 B5
Basque Country *aut. comm.* Spain see País Vasco
Basra Iraq 107 F5
also spelt Al Başrah
Bassano Canada 167 H5
Bassano del Grappa Italy 56 D3
Bassar Togo 125 F4
Bassas da India *reef* Indian Ocean 131 H4
Bassas de Pedro Padua Bank *sea feature* India 94 B4
also known as Munyal-Par
Bassawa Côte d'Ivoire 124 D4
Bassein Myanmar 78 A4
also known as Pathein; formerly spelt Pathein
Bassein r. Myanmar 78 A4
Basse-Kotto *pref.* Cent. Afr. Rep. 126 D3
Basse-Normandie *admin. reg.* France 50 F3
Basse Santa Su Gambia 124 B3

▶Basse-Terre Guadeloupe 187 H3
Capital of Guadeloupe.

Basse-Terre *i.* Guadeloupe 187 H3

▶Basseterre St Kitts and Nevis 187 H3
Capital of St Kitts and Nevis.

Bassett NE U.S.A. 178 C3
Bassett VA U.S.A. 176 F9
Bassett Peak U.S.A. 183 N9
Bassikounou Mauritania 124 D3
Bassila Benin 125 F4
Basso, Plateau de Chad 120 D5
Bass Strait Australia 147 E4
Basswood Lake Canada 168 A2
Basswood Lake U.S.A. 172 B2
Båstad Sweden 45 K4
Bastak Iran 100 C5
Bastänäbäd Iran 100 A2
Basti India 97 D4
Bastia Corse France 51 P10
Bastia Italy 56 E5
Bastian U.S.A. 176 D8
Bastogne Belgium 51 L4
Bastos Brazil 206 C8
Bastrop LA U.S.A. 175 B5
Bastrop TX U.S.A. 179 C6
Basuträsk Sweden 44 M2
Basu, Tanjung *pt* Indon. 76 C3
Basul *r.* Pak. 101 F5
Basuo China see Dongfang
Basya *r.* Belarus 43 N6
Bas-Zaïre *prov.* Dem. Rep. Congo see Bas-Congo
Bat *mt.* Croatia 56 I5
Bat, Al-Khutm and Al-Ayn *tourist site* Oman 105 G3
Bata Equat. Guinea 125 H6
Bata Peninsula Phil. 74 B3
Batabanó, Golfo de *b.* Cuba 186 C2
Batac Phil. 74 B2
Batagay Rus. Fed. 39 N3
Batagay-Alyta Rus. Fed. 39 N3
Bataguassu Brazil 206 A8
Batak Bulg. 58 F7
Batakan Indon. 77 F4
Batala India 96 B3
Batalha Brazil 202 D3
formerly known as Belo Monte
Batalha Port. 54 C5
Batam *i.* Indon. 76 C3
Batama Dem. Rep. Congo 126 E4
Batamay Rus. Fed. 39 M3
Batamshinskiy Kazakh. 102 D2
also known as Batamshy
Batamshy Kazakh. see Batamshinskiy
Batan *i.* Phil. 74 B1
Batan *i.* Phil. 74 B1
Batang China 86 A2
also known as Xiaqiong
Batang Indon. 77 E4
Batangafo Cent. Afr. Rep. 126 C3
Batang Ali National Park Sarawak Malaysia 77 F2
Batangas Phil. 74 B3
Batanghari *r.* Indon. 76 D3
Batangnegeri Indon. 75 D3
Batangtoru Indon. 76 B2
Batan Islands Phil. 74 B1
Bátaszék Hungary 49 P9
Batatais Brazil 206 F7
Batavia Indon. see Jakarta
Batavia NY U.S.A. 176 G3
Batavia OH U.S.A. 176 A6
Bataysk Rus. Fed. 41 F7
Batbatan *i.* Phil. 74 B4
Batchawana Canada 173 I4
Batchawana *r.* Canada 173 I4
Batchawana Bay Canada 173 I4
Batchawana Mountain *hill* Canada 168 C4
Batchelor Australia 148 A2
Bätdâmbâng Cambodia 79 C5
also spelt Battambang
Bateemuecica, Gunung *mt.* Indon. 76 A1
Bateké, Plateaux Congo 126 B5
Batemans Bay Australia 147 F3
Batěng Norway 44 N1
Batesburg U.S.A. 175 D5
Bates Range *hills* Australia 151 C5
Batesville AR U.S.A. 174 B5
Batesville MS U.S.A. 174 B5
Batetskiy Rus. Fed. 43 L3
Bath N.B. Canada 169 H4
Bath Canada 173 Q6
Bath U.K. 47 J12
Bath ME U.S.A. 177 P2
Bath NY U.S.A. 177 H3
Bath PA U.S.A. 177 J5
Batha *pref.* Chad 120 C6
Batha *watercourse* Chad 120 C6
Bathgate U.K. 46 I8
Bathinda India 96 B3
also spelt Bhatinda
Bathurst Australia 147 F3
Bathurst Canada 169 H4
Bathurst Gambia see Banjul
Bathurst S. Africa 133 K10
Bathurst, Cape Canada 164 F2
Bathurst Bay Australia 149 E2
Bathurst Inlet Canada 167 I1
Bathurst Inlet *inlet* Canada 167 I1
Bathurst Island Australia 148 A1
Bathurst Island Canada 165 I2
Batī Eth. 128 D2
Batia Benin 125 F4
Batié Burkina 124 E4

Batikala, Tanjung *pt* Indon. 75 B3
Batı Menteşe Dağları *mts* Turkey 59 I11
Bâtin, Wādī al *watercourse* Asia 105 D2
Batista, Serra da Brazil 202 D4
Bati Toroslar *mts* Turkey 106 J3
Batken Kyrg. 103 G5
Batken *admin. div.* Kyrg. 103 H5
Batman Turkey 107 E3
Batna Alg. 123 G2
Batna Alg. 123 G2
Batoka Zambia see Bâtdâmbâng
Batn al Tarfā' *depr.* Saudi Arabia 105 E3
Batočina Srbija Yugo. 58 C4
Batok, Bukit Sing. 76 [inset]
Batok, Bukit *hill* Sing. 76 [inset]
Batote Jammu and Kashmir 9€ B2
Batouri Cameroon 125 I5
Batrā' *tourist site* Jordan see Petra
Batra, Jabal *mt.* Saudi Arabia 104 B2
Batrā', Jabal *mt.* Jordan 103 B4
Ba Tri Vietnam 79 D6
Batroûn Lebanon 108 G3
Batsfjord Norway 44 O1
Bat-Sol Rus. Fed. 84 B1
Battambang Cambodia see Bâtdâmbâng
Batti India 96 B3
Batticaloa Sri Lanka 94 D5
Batti Malv *i.* India 95 G4
Battipaglia Italy 57 G8
Battle *r.* Canada 167 I4
Battle Creek *r.* Australia 148 A2
Battle Creek *r.* Canada/U.S.A. 167 I5
Battle Creek U.S.A. 173 H9
Battlefields Zimbabwe 131 F3
Battleford Canada 167 I4
Battle Mountain U.S.A. 183 G1
Battle Mountain *mt.* U.S.A. 183 G1
Battura Glacier Jammu and Kashmir 96 B1
Batu *mt.* Eth. 128 C3
Batu, Bukit *hill* Sarawak Malaysia *r.* 77 E2
Batu, Pulau-pulau *is* Indon. 76 B3
Batu, Tanjung *pt* Indon. 77 G2
Batuata *i.* Indon. 75 B4
Batuayau, Bukit *mt.* Indon. 77 F3
Batu Bora, Bukit *mt.* Sarawak Malaysia 77 F2
Batudaka *i.* Indon. 75 B3
Batu Gajah Malaysia 76 C1
Batuhitam, Tanjung *pt* Indon. 75 B3
Batui Indon. 75 B3
Batulaki Phil. 74 C5
Batulicin Indon. 77 F3
Batulilangmenang, Gunung *mt.* Indon. 77 F3
Batumi Georgia see Bat'umi
Bat'umi Georgia 107 E2
English form Batum
Batumonga Indon. 76 C3
Batu Pahat Malaysia 76 C2
Batu Puteh, Gunung *mt.* Malaysia 76 C1
Baturaden Indon. 77 E4
Baturino Rus. Fed. 43 N6
Baturité Brazil 202 E3
Batys Qazaqstan Oblysy *admin. div.* Kazakh. see Zapadnyy Kazakhstan
Batz, Île de *i.* France 50 B3
Bau *r.* Brazil 201 G1
Bau Sarawak Malaysia 77 E2
Baubau Indon. 75 B4
Bauchi Nigeria 125 H4
Bauchi *state* Nigeria 125 G5
Bauda India 95 E1
Baudette U.S.A. 178 D1
Baudó, Serranía de *mts* Col. 198 B3
Baudouinville Dem. Rep. Congo see Moba
Bauer *well* Eth. 128 D3
Baugé France 50 F5
Bauges *mts* France 51 M7
Baukau East Timor 75 C5
also known as Baucau
Bauld, Cape Canada 169 K3
Baumann Fiord *inlet* Canada 165 K2
Baume-les-Dames France 51 M5
Baunei Sardegna Italy 57 B8
Bauru Brazil 206 D9
Baús Brazil 206 A8
Baushar Oman 105 G3
Bauska Latvia 42 F5
Bautino Kazakh. 102 B3
Bautzen Germany 49 L4
Bauxrzhan Momysh-Uly Kazakh. 103 G4
also known as Burnoye
Bavaria *land* Germany see Bayern
Bavaria *reg.* Germany 48 I7
historically known as Bayern
Bavda India 94 B2
Båven *l.* Sweden 45 L4
Baviaanskloofberge *mts* S. Africa 132 H10
Bavispe Mex. 184 C2
Bavispe *r.* Mex. 184 C2
Bavla India 96 B5
Bavleny Rus. Fed. 43 U5
Bavly Rus. Fed. 40 J5
Baw Myanmar 78 A3
Bawal India 96 C3
Bawal *i.* Indon. 77 E3
Bawan Indon. 77 F3
Bawang, Tanjung *pt* Indon. 77 E3
Bawdwin Myanmar 78 B3
Bawean *i.* Indon. 77 F4
Bawiti Egypt 121 F2
Bawku Ghana 125 E4
Bawlake Myanmar 78 B4
Bawolung China 86 B2
Baxi China 86 B1
Baxian China see Banan
Baxian China see Bazhou
Baxkorgan China 84 C4
Baxley U.S.A. 175 D6
Baxoi China 86 A2
also known as Baima
Bay admin. reg. Somalia 128 D4
Bay, Laguna de *lag.* Phil. 74 B3
Bay, Réserve de nature res. Mali 124 E3
Bay *r.* Côte d'Ivoire 124 D4
Bayad Alg. 52 A13
Bayamo Cuba 186 D2
Bayamón Puerto Rico 187 G3
Bayan China 82 B3
Bayan China see Hualong
Bayan India 96 C4
Bayan Indon. 77 G4
Bayan Arhangay Mongolia 84 D2
Bayan Govi-Altay Mongolia 84 B2
Bayan Hentiy Mongolia 85 F2
Bayan Gol China see Dengkou
Bayangol Mongolia 84 B2
Bayangol Rus. Fed. 84 D1
Bayan Har Shan *mts* China 84 D5
Bayan Har Shankou *pass* China 85 C5
Bayanhongor Mongolia 84 C2
Bayanhongor *prov.* Mongolia 84 C2
Bayan Hot China 85 G2
also known as Alxa Zuoqi
Bayanhushuu Mongolia 84 B2
Bayan-Kol Respublika Tyva Rus. Fed. 84 B1

Bayan-Kol Rus. Fed. 88 G1
Bayan Mod China 84 E3
also known as Xar Bürd
Bayano, Lago *l.* Panama 186 D5
Bayan Obo Kuangqu China 85 F3
Bayan-Ölgiy *prov.* Mongolia 84 A1
Bayan-Ovoo Govi-Altay Mongolia 84 B2
Bayan-Ovoo Hentiy Mongolia 85 F1
Bayan Qagan China 85 G3
also known as Qahar Youyi Houqi
Bayansayr Mongolia 84 C2
Bayan Shan *mt.* China 84 C4
Bayanteeg Mongolia 84 C2
Bayan Tohoi China 85 H1
Bayan Ul Hot China 85 H2
Bayantöhöm Mongolia 85 E2
Bayan Uul *mts* Mongolia 84 A1
Bayard NE U.S.A. 178 B3
Bayard WV U.S.A. 176 F6
Bayasgalant Mongolia 85 G2
Bayat Turkey 106 C3
Bayawan Phil. 74 B4
Bayāz Iran 100 C4
Baybay Phil. 74 C4
Bay Bulls Canada 169 K4
Bayburt Turkey 107 E2
Baychunas Kazakh. 102 C3
also spelt Bayshonas
Bay City MI U.S.A. 173 J7
Bay City TX U.S.A. 179 C6
Baydā, Jabal al *hill* Saudi Arabia 104 B2
Baydaratskaya Guba *b.* Rus. Fed. 40 M1
Baydhabo Somalia 128 D4
formerly known as Baidoa
Baydrag *r.* Mongolia 84 C2
Baydrag Gol *r.* Mongolia 84 C2
Bay du Nord Wilderness nature res. Canada 169 K3
Bayelsa *state* Nigeria 125 G5
Bayeux France 50 F3
Bayevo Rus. Fed. 103 J1
Bayfield Canada 173 L7
Bayhan al Qisab Yemen 105 D5
Bayhan China 89 F6
Bayi China 107 E4
Bayji Iraq 107 E4
also known as Baiji
Baykadam Kazakh. see Saudakent
Baykal, Ozero *l.* Rus. Fed. see Baikal, Lake
Baykal Range *mts* Rus. Fed. see Baykal'skiy Khrebet
Baykal'sk Rus. Fed. 84 D1
Baykal'skiy Khrebet *mts* Rus. Fed. 81 H2
English form Baykal Range
Baykal'skiy Zapovednik nature res. Rus. Fed. 85 E1
Baykan Turkey 107 E3
Bay-Khaak Rus. Fed. 84 B1
Bay-Khozha Kazakh. 103 E3
Baykibashevo Rus. Fed. 40 K5
Baykit Rus. Fed. 39 J3
Baykonur Karagandinskaya Oblast' Kazakh. 103 F3
Baykonur Kyzyl-Ordinskaya Oblast' Kazakh. 103 E3
also spelt Baykonyr or Bayqongyr; formerly known as Leninsk or Toretam or Tyuratam
Baykonur Kazakh. see Baykonur
Bayley Point Aboriginal Reserve Australia 148 C3
Baymak Rus. Fed. 102 D1
Bay Minette U.S.A. 175 C6
Baynünah *reg.* U.A.E. 105 E3
Bay of Islands Maritime and Historic Park nature res. N.Z. 152 I3
Bay of Plenty *admin. reg.* N.Z. 152 K5
Bayombong Phil. 74 B2
Bayona Spain see Baiona
Bayonne France 50 E5
Bayonne U.S.A. 177 K5
Bayo Point Phil. 74 B4
Bayóvar Peru 198 A6
Bay Port U.S.A. 173 J7
Bayqadam Kazakh. see Saudakent
Bayqongyr Kazakh. see Baykonur
Bayramaly Turkm. 103 F5
Bayramiç Turkey 106 A3
Bayreuth Germany 48 I6
Bayrūt Lebanon see Beirut
Bay St Louis U.S.A. 175 B6
Baysh *watercourse* Saudi Arabia 104 C4
Bayshonas Kazakh. see Baychunas
Bay Springs U.S.A. 175 B6
Baysun Uzbek. 103 F5
also spelt Boysun
Baysuntau, Gory *mts* Uzbek. 103 F5
Bayt al Faqīh Yemen 104 C5
Baytik-Shan *mts* China 84 C1
Bayt Laḩm West Bank see Bethlehem
Baytown U.S.A. 179 D6
Bayu Indon. 75 B3
Bayunglincir Indon. 76 C3
Bay View N.Z. 152 K7
Bayy al Kabīr, Wādī *watercourse* Libya 120 B2
Bayyrqum Kazakh. see Bairkum
Bayzhansay Kazakh. 103 G4
also spelt Baydzhansay
Baza Spain 55 I7
Baza, Sierra de *mts* Spain 55 I7
Bazarchulan Kazakh. 102 C2
formerly spelt Bazarshulan
Bazaruto, Ilha do *i.* Moz. 131 G4
Bazas France 50 F8
Bazdar Pak. 101 F5
Bazhong China 86 C2
Bazhou China 84 H4
formerly known as Baxian
Bazin *r.* Canada 169 F4
Baziwehn Liberia 124 C4
Bazmān Iran 101 E5
Bazmān, Kūh-e *mt.* Iran 101 E4
Bcharre Lebanon 108 G3
Be *r.* Vietnam 79 D6
Bé, Nosy *i.* Madag. 131 [inset] K2
Bé, Nosy *i.* Madag. 131 [inset] K2
formerly spelt Nossi-Bé
Beach U.S.A. 178 B2
Beachburg Canada 173 Q5
Beach City U.S.A. 176 D5

Beach Haven U.S.A. 177 K6
Beachport Australia 146 C4
Beachy Head U.K. 47 M13
Beacon Australia 151 B6
Beacon U.S.A. 177 L4
Beacon Bay S. Africa 133 L9
Beaconsfield Australia 147 E5
Beagle, Canal *sea chan.* Arg. 205 C9
Beagle Bank *reef* Australia 150 C3
Beagle Bay Australia 150 C3
Beagle Bay Aboriginal Reserve Australia 150 C3
Beagle Gulf Australia 148 A2
Beagle Island Australia 151 A6
Béal an Átha Rep. of Ireland see Ballina
Béal Átha na Sluaighe Rep. of Ireland see Ballinasloe
Beampingaratra *mts* Madag. 131 [inset] J5
Beandrarezona Madag. 131 [inset] K2
Bear *r.* U.S.A. 180 D4
Bearalváhki Norway see Berlevåg
Bear Creek Canada 166 B1
Bear Creek *r.* U.S.A. 178 B4
Beardmore Glacier Antarctica 223 L1
Beardmore Reservoir Australia 147 F1
Beardstown U.S.A. 174 B3
Bear Island *i.* Arctic Ocean see Bjørnøya
Bear Island Canada 173 M4
Bear Island Canada 168 D2
Bear Island *i.* Rep. of Ireland 47 C12
Bear Lake *r.* Canada 167 L4
Bear Lake Canada 172 G6
Bear Lake U.S.A. 180 E4
Bearma *r.* India 96 C4
Bear Mountain U.S.A. 178 B3
Bearnaraigh *i.* U.K. see Berneray
Bear Paw Mountain U.S.A. 180 E2
Bearpaw Mountains U.S.A. 180 E2
Bear Peninsula Antarctica 222 Q2
Bearskin Lake Canada 168 B2
Beas *r.* India 96 B3
Beasain Spain 55 I1
Beata, Cabo *c.* Dom. Rep. 187 F3
Beata, Isla *i.* Dom. Rep. 187 F3
Beatrice U.S.A. 178 C3
Beatrice Zimbabwe 131 F3
Beatrice, Cape Australia 148 C2
Beatton *r.* Canada 166 F3
Beatty U.S.A. 183 H5
Beattyville Canada 168 E3
Beattyville U.S.A. 176 B8
Beaucaire France 51 K9
Beauchêne, Lac *l.* Canada 173 O4
Beauchene Island Falkland Is 205 F5
Beaudesert Australia 147 G1
Beaufort Sabah Malaysia 77 F1
Beaufort *r.* Australia 151 C6
Beaufort NC U.S.A. 175 E5
Beaufort SC U.S.A. 175 D5
Beaufort Castle *tourist site* Lebanon 108 G4
Beaufort Island Hong Kong China 87 [inset]
also known as Lo Chau
Beaufort Sea Canada/U.S.A. 164 G2
Beaufort West S. Africa 132 G9
Beaugency France 50 H5
Beaulieu-sur-Dordogne France 50 H8
Beauly U.K. 46 H6
Beauly *r.* U.K. 46 H6
Beaumont Belgium 51 K2
Beaumont TX U.S.A. 179 D6
Beaumont CA U.S.A. 183 H8
Beaumont MS U.S.A. 175 B6
Beaumont TX U.S.A. 179 D6
Beaumont-de-Lomagne France 50 G9
Beaumont-le-Roger France 50 G3
Beaune France 51 K5
Beaune-la-Rolande France 51 I4
Beauraing Belgium 51 K2
Beauséjour Canada 167 L5
Beauvais France 51 I3
Beauvoir-sur-Mer France 50 D6
Beaver r. Alta/Sask. Canada 167 J4
Beaver *r.* Ont. Canada 168 C2
Beaver *r.* Y.T. Canada 166 E3
Beaver OK U.S.A. 178 B4
Beaver *r.* UT U.S.A. 183 I3
Beaver *r.* OK U.S.A. 178 B4
Beaver *r.* UT U.S.A. 183 L2
Beaver City U.S.A. 178 C3
Beaver Creek Canada 166 A2
Beaver Creek *r.* MO U.S.A. 178 D4
Beaver Creek *r.* MT U.S.A. 180 F2
Beaver Creek *r.* ND U.S.A. 178 B2
Beaver Creek *r.* NE U.S.A. 178 C3
Beaver Dam KY U.S.A. 174 C4
Beaver Dam WI U.S.A. 172 E7
Beaver Dam Lake U.S.A. 172 E7
Beaver Falls U.S.A. 176 E5
Beaver Glacier Antarctica 223 D2
Beaverhead *r.* U.S.A. 180 D3
Beaverhill Lake Canada 167 H4
Beaver Hill Lake Canada 167 M4
Beaver Island U.S.A. 172 H5
Beaverlodge Canada 166 G4
Beaver Run Reservoir U.S.A. 176 F5
Beaverton MI U.S.A. 173 I7
Beaverton OR U.S.A. 180 B3
Beawar India 96 B4
Beazley Arg. 204 C4
Bebedero, Salina del *salt pan* Arg. 204 D4
Bébédjia Chad 126 C3
Bebedouro Brazil 206 E7
Beberibe Brazil 202 E3
Bebra Germany 48 G5
Beccles U.K. 47 N11
Bečej Vojvodina, Srbija Yugo. 58 B3
Becerra *r.* Mex. 185 F4
Becerrea Spain 54 D2
Becerril hill Spain 54 F7
Becerro, Cayos *is* Hond. 186 C4
Béchar Alg. 123 E3
formerly known as Colomb-Béchar
Becharof Lake U.S.A. 164 C4
Bechevinka Rus. Fed. 43 S2
Bechuanaland country Africa see Botswana
Beçin Turkey 59 I11
Beckemeyer U.S.A. 174 B4
Becker, Mount Antarctica 222 T1
Beckley U.S.A. 176 D8
Becks N.Z. 153 D12
Becky Peak U.S.A. 183 J3
Beclean Romania 58 F1
Bečva *r.* Czech Rep. 49 O6
Beda Häyk' *l.* Eth. 128 C2
Bédarieux France 51 J9
Bedau Alg. see Ras el Ma
Bedel, Pereval *pass* China/Kyrg. see Bedel Pass
Bedel Pass China/Kyrg. 88 B3
also known as Bedel, Pereval
Bedford Canada 169 I4
Bedford S. Africa 133 K9
Bedford U.K. 47 L11
Bedford IA U.S.A. 178 D3
Bedford IN U.S.A. 174 C4
Bedford KY U.S.A. 174 C4
Bedford NY U.S.A. 177 L4
Bedford PA U.S.A. 176 G6
Bedford VA U.S.A. 176 F8
Bedford, Cape Australia 149 E2
Bedford Downs Australia 150 D3
Bedford Heights U.S.A. 176 D4
Bedi India 96 A5
Bedinggong Indon. 77 D3
Bednja *r.* Croatia 56 I1
Bednodem'yanovsk Rus. Fed. 41 G5

Bedok Sing. 76 [inset]
Bedok, Sungai r. Sing. 76 [inset]
Bedok Jetty Sing. 76 [inset]
Bedok Reservoir Sing. 76 [inset]
Bedouaran well Niger 125 I3
Bedourie Australia 148 G4
Bedrock U.S.A. 183 P3
Bedum Neth. 48 D2
Beechal Creek watercourse Australia 147 E1
Beecher U.S.A. 172 F9
Beech Fork Lake U.S.A. 176 C7
Beechy Canada 167 J5
Beekeepers Nature Reserve Australia 151 A6
Beelitz Germany 49 J3
Beenleigh Australia 147 G1
Beer Somalia 128 E2
Beersheba Israel 108 F6
 also spelt Be'er Sheva'
Be'ér Sheva' Israel see Beersheba
Beer Sheva watercourse Israel 108 F6
Beervlei Dam S. Africa 132 H10
Beeskow Germany 49 L3
Beestekraal S. Africa 133 L2
Beetaloo Australia 148 B3
Beethoven Peninsula Antarctica 222 T2
Beeville U.S.A. 179 C6
Befale Dem. Rep. Congo 126 D4
Befandriana Atsimo Madag. 131 [inset] I4
Befandriana Avaratra Madag. 131 [inset] K2
Befori Dem. Rep. Congo 126 D4
Befotaka Madag. 131 [inset] J4
Bega Australia 147 F4
Bega r. Romania 58 C3
Begamganj Bangl. 97 F5
Bégard France 50 C4
Begari r. Pak. 101 G4
Begicheva, Ostrov i. Rus. Fed. see
 Bol'shoy Begichev, Ostrov
Begovat Uzbek. see Bekabad
Begun India 96 B4
Begusarai India 97 E4
Behäbäd Iran 101 D5
Béhague, Pointe pt Fr. Guiana 199 I3
Behbehän Iran 100 B4
Beheira governorate Egypt 108 B7
Behm Canal sea chan. U.S.A. 166 D4
Behrendt Mountains Antarctica 222 T2
Behshahr Iran 100 C2
Behsüd Afgh. 101 F3
Bei'an China 82 B2
Bei'ao China see Dongtou
Beiba China 86 C1
Beibei China 86 C2
Beichuan China 86 B2
 also known as Qushan
Beida Libya see Al Bayḍā'
Beigang Taiwan see Peikang
Beihai China 87 D4
 historically known as Pakhoi
Bei Hulsan Hu salt l. China 84 B4
Bei Jiang r. China 87 E4
▶Beijing China 85 H4
 Capital of China. Formerly known as Peking;
 historically known as Khanbalik.
 world [countries] ⇒ 10–11
 world [cities] ⇒ 24–25
Beijing municipality China 85 H3
Beilen Neth. 48 D3
Beiliu China 87 D4
Béinamar Chad 126 B2
Beining China 85 I3
 also known as Guangning; formerly known
 as Beizhen
Beinn Bhreac hill U.K. 46 G7
Beinn Mhòr hill U.K. 46 E6
Beinn na Faoghlia i. U.K. see Benbecula
Beipiao China 85 I3
Beira prov. Moz. see Sofala
Beira Alta reg. Port. 54 D3
Beira Baixa reg. Port. 54 D5
Beira Litoral reg. Port. 54 D4
Beiru r. China 87 E1
▶Beirut Lebanon 108 G4
 Capital of Lebanon. Also spelt Bayrût or
 Beyrouth; historically known as Berytus.
Beiseker Canada 167 H5
Beishan China 84 C3
Bei Shan mt. China 84 B3
Bei Shan mts China 84 B3
 formerly spelt Pei Shan
Beitbridge Zimbabwe 131 F4
Beit Jälä West Bank 108 G6
Beitun China 88 D2
Beius Romania 58 D2
Beizhen China see Beining
Beja Brazil 202 B2
Beja Port. 54 D6
Béja admin. dist. Port. 54 C7
Béja Tunisia 123 H1
Bejaïa Alg. 123 G1
 formerly known as Bougie; historically
 known as Saldae
Béjar Spain 54 F4
Bejestän Iran 100 D3
Beji r. Pak. 101 G4
Bejucos Mex. 185 E5
Béka Adamaoua Cameroon 125 I5
Béka Est Cameroon 125 I5
Bekabad Uzbek. 92 C2
 also spelt Bekobod; formerly spelt Begovat
Bekapaika Madag. 131 [inset] J3
Bekasi Indon. 77 D4
Bekdash Turkm. 102 C4
Beke Dem. Rep. Congo 127 E7
Békés Hungary 49 S9
Békéscsaba Hungary 49 S9
Beketovskaya Rus. Fed. 43 U1
Bekilli Turkey 59 K10

Bekily Madag. 131 [inset] J5
Bekitro Madag. 131 [inset] J5
Bekkai Japan 90 I3
Beklemishevo Rus. Fed. 85 G1
Bekobod Uzbek. see Bekabad
Bekopaka Madag. 131 [inset] J3
Bekoropaka-Antongo Madag. 131 [inset] I4
Bekovo Rus. Fed. 41 G5
Bekwai Ghana 125 E5
Bekyem Ghana 125 E5
Bela Bihar India 97 E4
Bela Uttar Pradesh India 97 D4
Bela Pak. 101 F5
Belab r. Pak. 101 G4
Bela-Bela S. Africa 133 M1
Bélabo Cameroon 125 I5
Bela Crkva Vojvodina, Srbija Yugo. 58 C4
Belaga Sarawak Malaysia 77 F2
Bel'agash Kazakh. 103 J2
Bel Air U.S.A. 177 I6
Belalcázar Spain 54 F6
Belang Indon. 75 C2
Belangiran Indon. 77 E3
Bela Palanka Srbija Yugo. 58 D5
Bělá pod Bezdězem Czech Rep. 49 L5
Belapur India 94 B2
▶Belarus country Europe 42 H8
 formerly known as Belorussia or
 Belorusskaya S.S.R. or Byelorussia or White
 Russia
 europe [countries] ⇒ 32–35
Belasica mts Bulg./Macedonia 58 D7
 also known as Kerkini Oros; also spelt
 Belasitsa
Belasitsa mts Bulg./Macedonia see Belasica
Belau country N. Pacific Ocean see Palau
Bela Vista Angola 127 B8
Bela Vista Amazonas Brazil 199 E4
Bela Vista Mato Grosso do Sul Brazil 201 F5
Bela Vista Moz. 133 Q3
Bela Vista de Goiás Brazil 206 C3
Belawan Indon. 76 B2
Belaya r. Rus. Fed. 39 R3
Belaya Glina Rus. Fed. 41 G7
Belaya Kalitva Rus. Fed. 41 G6
Belaya Kholunitsa Rus. Fed. 40 I4
Belayan r. Indon. 77 G3
Belayan, Gunung mt. Indon. 77 G3
Belaya Rechka Rus. Fed. 43 U5
Belaya Tserkva Ukr. see Bila Tserkva
Belbédji Niger 125 G3
Belcesti Romania 58 I1
Bełchatów Poland 49 Q4
Belcher U.S.A. 176 C8
Belcher Islands Canada 168 E1
Belchiragh Afgh. 101 F3
Belcourt Canada 173 P2
Beldanga India 97 F5
Belden U.S.A. 182 C1
Belding U.S.A. 173 H7
Beleapani reef India see Cherbaniani Reef
Belebey Rus. Fed. 40 J5
Beled Hungary 49 O8
Beledweyne Somalia 128 E3
Belek Turkm. 102 C5
Béléko Mali 124 D3
Bélèl Cameroon 125 I5
Bélèl Nigeria 125 I4
Belém Brazil 202 B2
Belén Arg. 204 C2
Belén Para. 201 F5
Belen Antalya Turkey 108 D1
Belen Hatay Turkey 106 D3
Belen U.S.A. 181 F6
Belén, Cuchilla de hills Uruguay 204 F3
Belene Bulg. 58 G5
Bélep, Îles is New Caledonia 145 F3
Belesar, Embalse de resr Spain 54 D2
Belev Rus. Fed. 43 R8
Belevi Turkey 59 I10
Belfast N.Z. 153 G11
Belfast S. Africa 133 O2
▶Belfast U.K. 47 G9
 Capital of Northern Ireland.
Belfast U.K. 47 P1
Belford U.K. 46 K8
Belfort France 51 M5
Belgaum India 94 B3
Belgian Congo country Africa see
 Congo, Democratic Republic of
Belgicafjella mts Antarctica see
 Belgica Mountains
Belgica Mountains Antarctica 223 C2
 also known as Belgicafjella
België country Europe see Belgium
Belgique country Europe see Belgium
▶Belgium country Europe 51 K2
 known as België in Dutch (Flemish) or
 Belgique in French; historically known as
 Spanish Netherlands
 europe [countries] ⇒ 32–35
Belgorod Rus. Fed. 41 F6
Belgorod-Dnestrovskyy Ukr. see
 Bilhorod-Dnistrovs'kyy
Belgorod Oblast admin. div. Rus. Fed. see
 Belgorodskaya Oblast'
Belgorodskaya Oblast' admin. div.
 Rus. Fed. 41 F6
 English form Belgorod Oblast
Belgrade ME U.S.A. 177 P1
Belgrade MT U.S.A. 180 E3
▶Belgrade Srbija Yugo. 58 B4
 Capital of Yugoslavia. Also spelt Beograd;
 historically known as Singidunum.
Belgrano II research station Antarctica
 222 V1
 long form General Belgrano II
Belhirane Alg. 123 G3
Béli Guinea-Bissau 124 B4
Beli Nigeria 125 H5
Belice r. Sicilia Italy 57 E11
Beli Drim r. Yugo. 58 B5
Beli Lom r. Bulg. 58 H5
Beli Manastir Croatia 56 K3
Belin-Béliet France 50 F8
Belington U.S.A. 176 F6
Belingwe Zimbabwe see Mberengwa
Belinskiy Rus. Fed. 41 G5
Belinţ Romania 58 C3
Belinyu Indon. 77 D3
Beli Timok r. Yugo. 58 D5
Belitsa Bulg. 58 E7
Belitung i. Indon. 77 E3
 also spelt Billiton
Belize Angola 126 B6
▶Belize Belize 185 H5
 Former capital of Belize.
▶Belize country Central America 185 H5
 formerly known as British Honduras
 northamerica [countries] ⇒ 158–159
Bélizon Fr. Guiana 199 H3
Beljak Austria see Villach
Beljanica mt. Yugo. 58 C4
Belkina, Mys pt Rus. Fed. 90 E2
Bel'kovskiy, Ostrov i. Rus. Fed. 39 N2
Bell r. Australia 147 F3
Bell r. Canada 168 E3
Bell S. Africa 133 L6
Bell, Point Australia 146 B3
Bella Bella Canada 166 D4
Bellac France 50 H6
Bella Coola Canada 166 E4

Bella Coola r. Canada 166 E4
Bellagio Italy 56 B3
Bellaire MI U.S.A. 173 H6
Bellano Italy 56 E4
Bellaria Italy 56 E4
Bellary India 94 C3
Bellata Australia 147 F2
Bella Unión Uruguay 204 F3
Bella Vista Corrientes Arg. 204 F3
Bella Vista Santa Cruz Arg. 205 C8
Bella Vista Bol. 201 E3
Bella Vista Para. 201 F5
Bellavista Peru 198 C5
Bella Vista U.S.A. 182 B1
Bella Vista, Salar de salt flat Chile 200 C5
Bell Block N.Z. 152 I7
Bell Cay reef Australia 149 G4
Belle U.S.A. 176 D7
Belle-Anse Haiti 187 E3
 formerly known as Saltrou
Belledonne mts France 51 L7
Bellefontaine U.S.A. 176 B5
Belle Fourche U.S.A. 178 B2
Belle Fourche r. U.S.A. 178 B2
Bellegarde-sur-Valserine France 51 L6
Belle Glade U.S.A. 175 D7
Belle-Île i. France 50 C5
Belle Isle i. Canada 169 K3
Belle Isle, Strait of Canada 169 J3
Bellemont U.S.A. 183 M6
Belleoram Canada 169 J4
Belleterre Canada 168 E4
Belleville Canada 168 E4
Belleville France 51 K6
Belleville IL U.S.A. 174 B4
Belleville KS U.S.A. 178 C4
Belleville NJ U.S.A. 177 K5
Bellevue IA U.S.A. 174 B3
Bellevue ID U.S.A. 180 D4
Bellevue OH U.S.A. 176 C4
Bellevue WA U.S.A. 180 B3
Bellin Canada see Kangirsuk
Bellingen Australia 147 G2
Bellingham U.K. 47 J8
Bellingham U.S.A. 180 B2
Bellingshausen research station Antarctica
 222 U1
Bellingshausen Sea Antarctica 222 S2
Bellinzona Switz. 51 P6
Bell Island Canada 169 K3
Bello Col. 198 C3
Bellows Falls U.S.A. 177 M2
Bellpat Pak. 101 G4
Belluno Italy 56 E2
Belluru India 94 C3
Bell Ville Arg. 204 E4
Bellville S. Africa 132 C10
Bellville OH U.S.A. 176 C5
Bellville TX U.S.A. 179 C6
Bellwood U.S.A. 176 G5
Belly r. Canada 167 H5
Bélmez Spain 54 F6
Belmont Australia 147 F3
Belmont S. Africa 133 I6
Belmont NH U.S.A. 177 N2
Belmont NY U.S.A. 176 G3
Belmonte Brazil 202 E5
Belmonte Port. 54 D4
Belmont-sur-Rance France 51 I9
▶Belmopan Belize 185 H5
 Capital of Belize.
Belmore Creek r. Australia 149 D3
Belmullet Rep. of Ireland 47 C9
Belo Madag. 131 [inset] J4
Beloe More Rus. Fed. see Beloye More
Beloe More sea Rus. Fed. see White Sea
Beloevo Rus. Fed. see Beloyevo
Belogorsk Rus. Fed. 82 C2
 formerly known as Kuybyshevka-Vostochnaya
Belogorsk Ukr. see Bilohirs'k
Belogor'ye Kazakh. 103 I2
Belogradchik Bulg. 58 D5
Beloha Madag. 131 [inset] J5
Belo Horizonte Amazonas Brazil 199 E5
Belo Horizonte Minas Gerais Brazil 203 D6
Beloit KS U.S.A. 178 C4
Beloit WI U.S.A. 172 D8
Belo Jardim Brazil 202 E4
Belo Monte Brazil 199 I5
Belomorsk Rus. Fed. 40 E2
Belonia India 97 F5
Beloomut Rus. Fed. 43 U7
Belo Oriente Brazil 207 K6
Belozërsk Belarus see Byelaazyorsk
Belozerskiy Rus. Fed. 43 T6
Belopa Indon. 75 B3
Belorado Spain 55 H2
Belorechensk Rus. Fed. 41 F7
Belorechenskaya Rus. Fed. see Belorechensk
Belören Adıyaman Turkey 107 D3
Belören Konya Turkey 106 C3
 also known as Sarıoğlan
Beloretsk Rus. Fed. 38 F4
Belorussia country Europe see Belarus
Belorusskaya S.S.R. country Europe see
 Belarus
Beloslav Bulg. 58 I5
Belostok Poland see Białystok
Belot, Lac l. Canada 166 E1
Belotintsi Bulg. 58 D5
Belo Tsiribihina Madag. 131 [inset] J4
Belousova Kazakh. 88 C1
Belousovo Rus. Fed. 43 R6
Belo Vale Brazil 207 I7
Belovo Bulg. 58 F6
Belovo Rus. Fed. 80 D2
Beloyarovo Rus. Fed. 82 C2
Beloye, Ozero l. Rus. Fed. 43 S1
Beloye More Rus. Fed. 44 J2
 also spelt Beloe More
Beloye More sea Rus. Fed. see White Sea
Beloyevo Rus. Fed. 40 J4
 also spelt Beloevo
Belozërka Rus. Fed. 102 C1
Belozërsk Rus. Fed. 43 S1
Belpre U.S.A. 176 D6
Beltana Australia 146 C2
Belted Range mts U.S.A. 183 H4
Belterra Brazil 199 H5
Beltes Gol r. Mongolia 84 C1
Belton MO U.S.A. 178 D4
Belton TX U.S.A. 179 C6
Belturbet Rep. of Ireland 47 E9
Belukha, Gora mt. Kazakh./Rus. Fed. 88 D1
Belur India 94 B3
Belush'ya Guba Rus. Fed. 40 J1
Belush'ye Rus. Fed. 40 H2
Beluzhiy Nos, Mys c. Rus. Fed. 40 M1
Belvès France 50 H8
Belvidere IL U.S.A. 174 B3
Belvidere NJ U.S.A. 177 J5
Belyando r. Australia 149 E4
Belyando Crossing Australia 149 E4
Belyayevka Ukr. see Bilyayivka
Belyayevka Ukr. 43 M6
Belye Vody Kazakh. 103 G3
Belyuen Australia 148 A2
Belyy Rus. Fed. 43 N6
Belyy, Ostrov i. Rus. Fed. 38 G2
Belyye Berega Rus. Fed. 43 P8
Belyy Gorodok Rus. Fed. 43 S5
Belyy Yar Rus. Fed. 39 I4
Belzig Germany 49 J3

Belzoni U.S.A. 175 D5
Belżyce Poland 49 T4
Bemaraha, Plateau du Madag. 131 [inset] J3
Bembe Angola 127 B6
Bembérèkè Benin 125 F4
Bembibre Spain 54 E2
Bemidji U.S.A. 178 D2
Béna Burkina 124 D3
Bena Dibele Dem. Rep. Congo 126 D6
Benagin Indon. 77 F3
Ben Alder mt. U.K. 46 H7
Benalla Australia 147 E4
Benalmádena Spain 54 G8
Ben 'Amira well Mauritania 122 B5
Benares India see Varanasi
Ben Arous Tunisia 123 H1
Bénat, Cap c. France 51 M9
Benavente Spain 54 F2
Benavides Bol. 200 D3
Benbecula i. U.K. 46 E7
 also known as Beinn na Faoghlia
Ben Boyd National Park Australia 147 F4
Benbury hill Rep. of Ireland 47 C10
Bencha China 87 G1
Bencheng China see Luannan
Bencubbin Australia 151 B6
Bend U.S.A. 180 B3
Bendearg mt. S. Africa 133 L8
Bendela Dem. Rep. Congo 126 C5
Bender Moldova see Tighina
Bender-Bayla Somalia 128 F2
Benderville U.S.A. 172 F6
Bendery Moldova see Tighina
Bendigo Australia 147 D4
Bendoc Australia 147 F4
Bêne Latvia 42 E5
Bene Moz. 131 G2
Benedict, Mount hill Canada 169 J2
Beneditinos Brazil 202 D3
Benedito Leite Brazil 202 C3
Bénéna Mali 124 D3
Benenitra Madag. 131 [inset] J4
Benešov Czech Rep. 49 L6
Benevento Italy 56 G7
 historically known as Beneventum
Beneventum Italy see Benevento
Benezette U.S.A. 176 G4
Benfeld France 51 N4
Beng r. China 85 H7
Beng, Nam r. Laos 78 C4
Benga Malawi 129 B8
Bengal, Bay of sea Indian Ocean 95 F2
Bengamisa Dem. Rep. Congo 126 E4
Bengbis Cameroon 125 I6
Bengbu China 87 F1
Bengkala Indon. 76 C3
Bengkalis Indon. 76 C2
Bengkayang Indon. 77 E2
Bengkulu Indon. 76 C3
Bengkulu prov. Indon. 76 C3
Bengo prov. Angola 127 B7
Bengtsfors Sweden 45 K4
Benguela Angola 127 B8
Benguela prov. Angola 127 B8
Ben Guerdane Tunisia 123 H2
Benguerir Morocco 122 D2
Benguérua, Ilha i. Moz. 131 G4
Benha Egypt 121 F2
 also spelt Banhā
Ben Hiant hill U.K. 46 F7
Ben Hope hill U.K. 46 H5
Beni Dem. Rep. Congo 126 F4
Beni Nepal 97 D3
Beni-Abbès Alg. 123 E3
Benicarló Spain 55 L4
Benicasim Spain 55 L4
Benicia U.S.A. 182 B3
Benidorm Spain 55 K6
Beni Dourso well Niger 125 I1
Benifaió Spain 55 K5
Benifayo Spain see Benifaió
Beni Guil reg. Morocco 123 E2
Beni Hadifa Morocco 54 G9
Beni Mazar Egypt 106 B5
Beni Mellal Morocco 122 D2
▶Benin country Africa 125 F4
 formerly known as Dahomey
 africa [countries] ⇒ 114–117
Benin r. Nigeria 125 G5
Benin, Bight of g. Africa 125 F5
Benin City Nigeria 125 G5
Beni-Ounif Alg. 123 E3
Beni-Saf Alg. 123 E2
Benishangul admin. reg. Eth. 128 B2
Benisheikh Nigeria 125 I4
Benissa Spain 55 L6
Beni Suef Egypt 121 F2
 also spelt Banī Suwayf
Beni Suef governorate Egypt 108 A9
Benithora r. India 94 C2
Benito r. Equat. Guinea see Mbini
Benito, Islas is Mex. 184 B2
Benito Juárez Arg. 204 F5
Benito Juárez Mex. 185 H5
Benito Soliven Phil. 74 B2
Benjamin U.S.A. 179 C5
Benjamin Constant Brazil 198 D5
Benjamin, Isla i. Chile 205 B7
Benjamin Hill Mex. 184 C2
Benjina Indon. 73 H8
Benkei-misaki pt Japan 90 G3
Benkelman U.S.A. 178 B3
Benken Switz. 51 P5
Benkovac Croatia 56 H4
Benkovski Bulg. 58 I5
Ben Lawers mt. U.K. 46 H7
Ben Lomond mt. Australia 147 F2
Ben Lomond hill U.K. 46 H7
Ben Lomond mt. U.K. 46 H7
Ben Lomond National Park Australia
 147 F5
Ben Macdhui mt. Lesotho 133 L7
Ben Macdui mt. U.K. 46 I6
Benmara Australia 148 C3
Ben More mt. N.Z. 153 F11
Ben More hill U.K. 46 H7
Ben More mt. U.K. 46 H7
Ben More Assynt hill U.K. 46 H5
Bennett Canada 166 C3
Bennett IA U.S.A. 174 B3
Bennett WI U.S.A. 172 B4
Bennett, Lake salt flat Australia 148 A4
Bennetta, Ostrov i. Rus. Fed. 39 O2
 English form Bennett Island
Bennett Island Rus. Fed. see
 Bennetta, Ostrov
Bennett Lake Canada 166 C3
Bennettsville U.S.A. 175 E5
Ben Nevis mt. U.K. 46 G7
Benneydale N.Z. 152 J6
Bennington NH U.S.A. 177 N2
Bennington VT U.S.A. 177 L3
Benoni S. Africa 133 M3
Bénoué r. Cameroon 125 H5
Bénoy Chad 126 C2

Ben Rinnes hill U.K. 46 I6
Bensheim Germany 48 F6
Ben Slimane Morocco 122 D2
 formerly known as Boulhaut
Benson AZ U.S.A. 181 E7
Benson MN U.S.A. 178 D2
Bensonville Liberia 124 C5
Bens Run U.S.A. 176 D6
Bent Iran 101 D5
Benta Seberang Malaysia 76 C1
Benteng Indon. 75 B4
Bentiaba Angola 127 B8
 formerly known as São Nicolau
Bentinck Island Australia 148 C3
Bentinck Island Myanmar 79 B6
Bentiu Sudan 126 F3
Bentley Canada 167 H4
Bentleyville U.S.A. 176 E6
Bento Gomes r. Brazil 201 F4
Benton AR U.S.A. 179 D5
Benton CA U.S.A. 182 F4
Benton IL U.S.A. 174 B4
Benton KY U.S.A. 174 B4
Benton LA U.S.A. 179 D5
Benton MO U.S.A. 174 C4
Benton TN U.S.A. 174 C5
Bentong Malaysia see Bentung
Benton Harbor U.S.A. 172 G8
Bentonville U.S.A. 179 D4
Bên Tre Vietnam 79 D6
 formerly known as Truc Giang
Bentsy Rus. Fed. 43 M5
Bentuang Karimun National Park Indon.
 77 F2
Bentung Malaysia 76 C2
 formerly spelt Bentong
Benua Indon. 75 B4
Benua i. Indon. 75 D5
Benuamartinus Indon. 77 F2
Benue r. Nigeria 125 G5
Benue state Nigeria 125 H5
Benum, Gunung mt. Malaysia 76 C2
Benwa Zambia 127 E7
Benwee Head Rep. of Ireland 47 C9
Benwood U.S.A. 176 E5
Ben Wyvis mt. U.K. 46 H6
Benxi China 82 A4
Ben Zireg Alg. 123 E3
Beograd Srbija Yugo. see Belgrade
Beohari India 97 D4
Béoumi Côte d'Ivoire 124 D5
Bepagut, Gunung mt. Indon. 76 C4
Bepian Jiang r. China 86 C3
Beppu Japan 91 B8
Beppu-wan b. Japan 91 B8
Bequia i. St Vincent 187 H4
Bequimão Brazil 202 C2
Bera Bangl. 97 F4
Berach r. India 96 B4
Beramanja Madag. 131 [inset] K2
Berane Crna Gora Yugo. 58 A3
 formerly known as Ivangrad
Bérard, Lac l. Canada 169 G1
Berasia India 96 C5
Berastagi Indon. 76 B2
Berat Albania 58 A8
Beratus, Gunung mt. Indon. 77 G3
Berau r. Indon. 77 G2
Berau, Teluk b. Indon. 73 H7
 also spelt Berovina
Berbak National Park Indon. 76 C3
Berber Sudan 121 G5
Berbera Somalia 128 E2
Berbérati Cent. Afr. Rep. 126 B3
Berbice r. Guyana 199 G3
Bercel Hungary 49 Q8
Berceto Italy 56 B4
Berchi-Guélé well Chad 120 C5
Berchogur Kazakh. 102 D2
 also spelt Birshoghyr
Berchtesgaden, Nationalpark nat. park
 Germany 49 J8
Berck France 50 H2
Berd Armenia 107 F2
Berdichev Ukr. see Berdychiv
Berdigestyakh Rus. Fed. 39 M3
Berdsk Rus. Fed. 80 C2
Berdyans'k Ukr. 41 F7
 formerly known as Osipenko
Berdychiv Ukr. 41 D6
 also spelt Berdichev
Béré Chad 126 C2
Berea KY U.S.A. 176 A8
Berea OH U.S.A. 176 D4
Berebere Indon. 75 D2
Bereg Rus. Fed. 43 S1
Beregdaróc Hungary 49 T7
Beregovo Ukr. see Berehove
Berehove Ukr. 41 B6
 also spelt Beregovo
Bereketa Madag. 131 [inset] J4
Berekum Ghana 124 E5
Berel' Kazakh. 88 D1
Beremend Hungary 56 K3
Berendeyevo Rus. Fed. 43 U5
Berenguela Bol. 200 C4
Berenice Libya see Benghazi
Berenice Egypt 121 G4
Berens r. Canada 167 L4
Berens Island Canada 167 L4
Berens River Canada 167 L4
Berenty Madag. 131 [inset] J5
Beresford Canada 169 H4
Beresford U.S.A. 178 C3
Beresti Romania 58 I2
Berettyó r. Hungary 49 T8
Berettyóújfalu Hungary 49 S8
Berevo Madag. 131 [inset] J3
Berevo-Ranobe Madag. 131 [inset] J3
Bereza Belarus see Byaroza
Berezayka Rus. Fed. 43 P5
Bereznik Rus. Fed. 40 H3
Berezino Belarus see Byerazino
Berezino Belarus see Byerazino
Berezivka Ukr. 41 D7
 also spelt Berezovka
Berezna Ukr. 41 E6
Berezne Ukr. 41 C6
Bereznik Rus. Fed. 40 H3
Berezniki Rus. Fed. 40 K4
Berezov Rus. Fed. see Berezovo
Berezovaya r. Rus. Fed. 40 K3
Berezovka Amurskaya Oblast' Rus. Fed.
 82 C2
Berezovka Orenburgskaya Oblast' Rus. Fed.
 102 D1
Berezovka Permskaya Oblast' Rus. Fed.
 40 K4
Berezovo Rus. Fed. 38 G3
Berezovyy Rus. Fed. 82 D2
Berezyne Ukr. 58 K2
Berga Spain 55 M2
Bergama Turkey 106 A3
Bergamo Italy 56 B3
 historically known as Bergomum
Bergara Spain 55 I2
Bergby Sweden 45 L3
Bergen Mecklenburg-Vorpommern Germany
 49 K1
Bergen Niedersachsen Germany 48 I3
Bergen Norway 45 I3
Bergen S. Africa 133 Q4
Bergen U.S.A. 176 H2
Bergen op Zoom Neth. 48 B4

Bergerac France 50 G8
Bergerson, Mount Antarctica 223 B2
Berghan Point N.Z. 152 H2
Bergheim (Erft) Germany 48 D5
Bergisch Gladbach Germany 48 E5
Bergland Namibia 130 C4
Bergnäs Sweden 44 L2
Bergnäsviken Sweden 44 L2
Bergomum Italy see Bergamo
Bergsjö Sweden 45 L3
Bergstraße-Odenwald park Germany 48 G6
Bergsviken Sweden 44 M2
Bergues France 51 I2
Berguile S. Africa 133 N5
Berh Mongolia 85 I2
Berhala, Selat sea chan. Indon. 76 C3
Berhampur India see Baharampur
Berheci r. Romania 58 I2
Berikat, Tanjung pt Indon. 77 D3
Berilo Brazil 207 K3
Beringa, Ostrov i. Rus. Fed. 220 D3
Beringarra Australia 151 B5
Beringen Belgium 51 L1
Beringin Indon. 76 C3
Bering Land Bridge National Preserve
 nature res. U.S.A. 164 C3
Beringovskiy Rus. Fed. 39 R3
 formerly known as Ugolnyy
Bering Sea N. Pacific Ocean 39 R4
Bering Strait Rus. Fed./U.S.A. 164 C3
Beris, Ra's pt Iran 101 E5
Berislav Ukr. see Beryslav
Berja Spain 55 I8
Berkåk Norway 44 J3
Berkane Morocco 123 E2
Berkel r. Neth. 48 D3
Berkeley r. Australia 150 D2
Berkeley U.S.A. 182 B4
Berkeley Springs U.S.A. 176 G6
Berkner Island Antarctica 222 U1
Berkovitsa Bulg. 58 E5
Berkshire Hills U.S.A. 177 L3
Berland r. Canada 166 G4
Berlevåg Norway 44 O1
 also known as Bearalváhki
▶Berlin Germany 49 K3
 Capital of Germany.
 europe [countries] ⇒ 32–33
Berlin MD U.S.A. 177 J7
Berlin NH U.S.A. 177 N1
Berlin NJ U.S.A. 177 K6
Berlin OH U.S.A. 176 D5
Berlin PA U.S.A. 176 G6
Berlin WI U.S.A. 172 E7
Berlin, Mount Antarctica 222 O1
Berlins N.Z. 153 F9
Berlişte Romania 58 C4
Bermagui Australia 147 F4
Berm Turkm. 102 D5
Bermeja, Punta pt Arg. 204 E6
Bermejillo Mex. 184 E3
Bermejo r. Arg. 204 D2
Bermejo r. Bol./Arg. 201 F6
Bermejo Bol. 201 D5
Bermeo Spain 55 I1
▶Bermuda terr. N. Atlantic Ocean 216 J3
 United Kingdom Overseas Territory.
 oceania [countries] ⇒ 138–139
▶Bern Switz. 51 N6
 Capital of Switzerland. Also spelt Berne.
Bernalda Italy 57 I8
Bernalillo U.S.A. 181 F6
Bernardino de Campos Brazil 206 D10
Bernard Lake Canada 173 N5
Bernardo O'Higgins, Parque Nacional
 nat. park Chile 205 B8
Bernau Germany 49 K3
Bernau am Chiemsee Germany 49 J8
Bernay France 50 G3
Bernburg (Saale) Germany 48 I4
Berndorf Austria 49 N8
Berne Switz. see Bern
Berne U.S.A. 176 A5
Berner Alpen mts Switz. 51 N6
 English form Bernese Alps
Berneray i. Western Isles, Scotland U.K.
 46 E7
 also known as Bhearnaraigh, Eilean
Berneray i. Western Isles, Scotland U.K.
 46 E7
 also known as Bearnaraigh
Bernese Alps mts Switz. see Berner Alpen
Bernesga r. Spain 54 F2
Bernier Bay Canada 165 K2
Bernier Island Australia 151 A5
Bernina Pass Switz. 51 Q6
Bernina, Piz mt. Switz. 51 Q6
Berninches mt. Spain 55 I4
Bernkastel-Kues Germany 48 E6
Bernstadt U.S.A. 176 A8
Beroea Greece see Veroia
Beroea Syria see Aleppo
Berovina Madag. 131 [inset] J4
Beroun r. Czech Rep. 49 L6
Berounka r. Czech Rep. 49 L6
Berovina Madag. see Beravina
Berovo Macedonia 58 E7
Berre, Étang de l. France 51 L9
Berrechid Morocco 122 D2
Berri Australia 146 D3
Berriane Alg. 123 F2
Berridale Australia 147 F4
Berrigan Australia 147 E3
Berrouaghia Alg. 123 F1
Berry reg. France 51 I6
Berry Creek r. Canada 167 I5
Berryessa, Lake U.S.A. 182 B3
Berry Head hd U.K. 47 I13
Berry Islands Bahamas 186 D1
Berryville AR U.S.A. 179 D4
Berryville VA U.S.A. 176 H6
Berseba Namibia 132 B3
Bersenbrück Germany 48 E3
Bersuat Rus. Fed. 103 E1
Berté, Lac l. Canada 169 G3
Bertinho Brazil 202 B2
Bertolínia Brazil 202 D3
Bertópolis Brazil 207 M4
Bertoua Cameroon 125 I5
Bertraghboy Bay Rep. of Ireland 47 C10
Beru atoll Kiribati 145 G2
Beruri Brazil 199 F5
Beruwala Sri Lanka 94 C5
Berveni Romania 49 T7
Berwick-upon-Tweed U.K. 46 J8
Beryslav Ukr. 41 E7
Berytus Lebanon see Beirut
Berzasca Romania 58 C4
Berzaune Latvia 42 H5
Bērzpils Latvia 42 I5
Bès r. France 51 J8
Besah Indon. 77 G2
Besalampy Madag. 131 [inset] J3
Besalú Spain 55 N2
Besançon France 51 M5
 historically known as Vesontio
Besar r. Indon. 75 B5
Besar, Gunung mt. Indon. 77 F3
Besar, Gunung mt. Malaysia 76 C1
Besbay Kazakh. 102 C3
Besbre r. France 51 J6
Besed' r. Rus. Fed. 43 M9
Beshariq Uzbek. see Besharyk
Besharyk Uzbek. 103 G4
 also spelt Beshariq; formerly known as Kirovo

Beshir Turkm. 103 F5
Beshkent Uzbek. 103 F5
Beshneh Iran 100 C4
Besh-Ter, Gora mt. Kyrg./Uzbek. 103 G4
also known as Besh-Ter Toosu or Beshtor Toghi
Besh-Ter Toosu mt. Kyrg./Uzbek. see Besh-Ter, Gora
Beshtor Toghi mt. Kyrg./Uzbek. see Besh-Ter, Gora
Besikama Indon. 75 C5
Beşiri Turkey 107 E3
Besitang Indon. 76 B1
Beskid Niski hills Poland 49 S6
Beskid Sądecki mts Poland 49 R6
Beskra Alg. see Biskra
Beslan Rus. Fed. 41 H8
Beslet mt. Bulg. 58 E7
Besna Kobila mt. Yugo. 58 D6
Besnard Lake Canada 167 J4
Besni Turkey 107 D3
Besor watercourse Israel 108 F6
Beşparmak Dağları mts Cyprus see Pentadaktylos Range
Béssao Chad 126 B3
Bessarabka Moldova see Basarabeasca
Bessaye, Gora mt. Kazakh. 103 G4
Bessemer AL U.S.A. 175 C5
Bessemer MI U.S.A. 172 C4
Besshoky, Gora hill Kazakh. 102 C3
Bessines-sur-Gartempe France 50 H6
Bessonovka Rus. Fed. 41 H5
Bessou, Mont de hill France 51 I7
Bestamak Aktyubinskaya Oblast' Kazakh. 102 C2
Bestamak Vostochnyy Kazakhstan Kazakh. 103 I2
Bestobe Kazakh. 103 H1
Beswick Australia 148 B2
Beswick Aboriginal Land res. Australia 148 B2
Betafo Madag. 131 [inset] J3
Betanzos Bol. 200 D4
Betanzos Spain 54 C1
Bétaré Oya Cameroon 125 I5
Bete Grise U.S.A. 172 F3
Bete Hor Eth. 128 C2
Bétérou Benin 125 F4
Betet i. Indon. 76 D3
Beth, Oued r. Morocco 122 D2
Bethal S. Africa 133 N3
Bethanie Namibia 130 C5
Bethany MO U.S.A. 178 D3
Bethany OK U.S.A. 179 C5
Bethari Nepal 97 D4
Bethel AK U.S.A. 164 C3
Bethel ME U.S.A. 177 O1
Bethel OH U.S.A. 176 A7
Bethesda MD U.S.A. 177 H6
Bethesda OH U.S.A. 176 D5
Bethesdaweg S. Africa 133 I8
Bethlehem S. Africa 133 M5
Bethlehem U.S.A. 177 J5
Bethlehem West Bank 108 G6
also spelt Bayt Lahm or Bet Lehem
Bethlesdorp S. Africa 133 J10
Bethulie S. Africa 133 J7
Béthune France 51 I2
Betijoque Venez. 198 D2
Betim Brazil 207 I6
Betioky Madag. 131 [inset] J4
Betiri, Gunung mt. Indon. 77 F5
Bet Lehem West Bank see Bethlehem
Betlitsa Rus. Fed. 43 O7
Betma India 96 B5
Betong Thai. 79 C7
Betoota Australia 149 D5
Bétou Congo 126 C4
Betpak-Dala plain Kazakh. 103 G3
Betrandraka Madag. 131 [inset] J3
Betroka Madag. 131 [inset] J4
Bet She'an Israel 108 G5
Betsiamites Canada 169 G3
Betsiamites r. Canada 169 G3
Betsiboka r. Madag. 131 [inset] J2
Betsie, Point U.S.A. 172 G6
Betsy Bay Bahamas 187 E2
Betsy Lake U.S.A. 173 H4
Bettendorf U.S.A. 172 C9
Betul India 96 C5
Betwa r. India 96 C4
Betws-y-coed U.K. 47 I10
Betygala Lith. 42 E6
Béu Angola 127 B6
Beulah U.S.A. 178 B2
Beurfou well Chad 120 B6
Beuthen Poland see Bytom
Beuvron r. France 50 H5
Beverley U.K. 47 L10
Beverly MA U.S.A. 177 O3
Beverly OH U.S.A. 176 D6
Beverly Hills U.S.A. 182 F7
Beverungen Germany 48 G4
Beverwijk Neth. 48 B3
Bex Switz. 51 N6
Bextograk China 88 D4
Beyağaç Turkey 59 J11
Beyazköy Turkey 58 I7
Beyce Turkey see Orhaneli
Beydağ Turkey 59 J10
Bey Dağları mts Turkey 106 B3
Beykonak Turkey 108 B1
Beykoz Turkey 106 B2
Beyla Guinea 124 C4
Beylagan Azer. see Beyläqan
Beyläqan Azer. 107 F3
also spelt Beylagan; formerly known as Zhdanovsk
Beylul Eritrea 121 I6
Beyneu Kazakh. 102 C3
Beyoneisu Retugan i. Japan 91 F9
Beypazarı Turkey 106 B2
Beypınarı Turkey 107 D3
Beypore India 94 B4
Beyra Somalia 128 E3
Beyram Iran 100 C5
Beyrouth Lebanon see Beirut
Beyşehir Turkey 106 B3
Beyşehir Gölü l. Turkey 106 B3
Beytüşşebap Turkey 107 E3
also known as Elki
Bezameh Iran 100 D3
Bezbozhnik Rus. Fed. 40 I4
Bezdan Vojvodina, Srbija Yugo. 56 K3
Bezenjān Iran 100 D4
Bezhanitskaya Vozvyshennost' hills Rus. Fed. 43 K5
Bezhanitsy Rus. Fed. 43 K5
Bezhanovo Bulg. 58 F5
Bezhetsk Rus. Fed. 43 R4
Bezhetskiy Verkh reg. Rus. Fed. 43 R4
Béziers France 51 J9
Bezmein Turkm. see Byuzmeyin
Bezwada India see Vijayawada
Bhabhar India 96 A4
Bhabra India 96 B5
Bhabua India 97 D4
Bhachau India 96 A5
Bhadar r. India 96 A5
Bhadarwah Jammu and Kashmir 96 B2
Bhadaur India 101 H4
Bhadgaon Nepal see Bhaktapur
Bhadohi India 97 D4
Bhadra India 96 B3
Bhadrachalam India 94 D2
Bhadrachalam Road Station India see Kottagudem
Bhadrakh India 97 E5
Bhadra Reservoir India 94 B3
Bhadravati India 94 B3
Bhag Pak. 101 F4
Bhagalpur India 97 E4
Bhagirathi r. India 97 F5
Bhainsa India 94 C2
Bhainsdehi India 96 C5
Bhairab Bazar Bangl. 97 F4
Bhairawa Nepal 97 D4
also known as Siddharthanagar; also spelt Bhairahawa
Bhairahawa Nepal see Bhairawa
Bhairi Hol mt. Pak. 101 F5
Bhakkar Pak. 101 G4
Bhaktapur Nepal 97 E4
also known as Bhadgaon
Bhalki India 94 C2
Bhalwal Pak. 101 H3
Bhamgarh India 96 C5
Bhamo Myanmar 78 B2
Bhandara India 96 C5
Bhander India 96 C4
Bhanjanagar India 95 E2
Bhanpura India 96 B4
Bhanrer Range hills India 96 C5
Bharat country Asia see India
Bharatpur India 96 C4
Bharatpur Nepal 97 E4
Bhareli r. India 97 G4
Bhari r. Pak. 101 E5
Bharthana India 96 C4
Bharuch India 96 B5
formerly known as Broach; historically known as Barygaza or Bhrigukaccha
Bhatapara India 97 D5
Bhatghar Lake India 94 B2
Bhatiapara Ghat Bangl. 97 F5
Bhatinda India see Bathinda
Bhatkal India 94 B3
Bhatnair India see Hanumangarh
Bhatpara India 97 F5
Bhaun Gharibwal Pak. 101 H3
Bhavani India 94 C4
Bhavani r. India 94 C4
Bhavani Sagar l. India 94 C4
Bhavnagar India 96 B5
Bhawana Pak. 101 H4
Bhawanipatna India 95 D2
Bhearnaraigh, Eilean i. U.K. see Berneray
Bheemavaram India see Bhimavaram
Bhekuzulu S. Africa 133 O4
Bhera Pak. 101 H3
Bheri r. Nepal 97 D3
Bhilai India 96 D5
Bhildi India 96 B4
Bhilwara India 96 B4
Bhima r. India 94 C2
Bhimavaram India 94 D2
formerly spelt Bheemavaram
Bhimbar Pak. 101 H3
Bhimnagar India 97 E4
Bhimphedi Nepal 97 E4
Bhind India 96 C4
Bhindar India 96 B4
Bhinga India 97 D4
Bhingar India 94 B2
Bhinmal India 96 B4
Bhiwandi India 94 B2
Bhiwani India 96 C3
Bhogat India 96 A5
Bhojpur Nepal 97 E4
Bhokardan India 94 B1
Bhola Bangl. 97 F5
Bhongaon India 96 C4
Bhongir India 94 C2
Bhongweni S. Africa 133 N7
Bhopal India 96 C5
Bhopalpatnam India 94 D2
Bhor India 94 B2
Bhrigukaccha India see Bharuch
Bhuban India 95 E1
Bhubaneshwar India 95 E1
formerly spelt Bhubaneswar
Bhubaneswar India see Bhubaneshwar
Bhuban Hills India 97 G4
Bhuj India 96 A5
Bhumiphol Dam Thai. 78 B4
Bhunya Swaziland 133 P3
Bhurgaon Bhutan 97 F4
Bhusawal India 96 B5
►Bhutan country Asia 97 F4
known as Druk-Yul in Dzongkha
asia [countries] ▶ 64–67
Bhuttewala India 96 A4
Bhuvanagiri India 94 C4
Biá r. Brazil 199 E5
Bia, Monts mts Dem. Rep. Congo 127 E7
Bia, Phou mt. Laos 78 C4
Biābān mts Iran 100 D5
Biafra, Bight of g. Africa see Benin, Bight of
Biak Irian Jaya Indon. 73 I7
Biak Sulawesi Tengah Indon. 75 B3
Biak i. Indon. 73 I7
Biała r. Poland 49 R5
Biała Piska Poland 49 T2
Biała Podlaska Poland 49 U3
Białobrzegi Poland 49 R4
Białogard Poland 49 M2
Białowieski Park Narodowy nat. park Poland 42 E9
Biały Bór Poland 49 N2
Białystok Poland 49 U2
formerly spelt Belostok
Biancavilla Sicilia Italy 57 G11
Bianco Italy 57 I10
Bianco, Monte mt. France/Italy see Blanc, Mont
Bianga Cent. Afr. Rep. 126 D3
Biankouma Côte d'Ivoire 124 D5
Bianouan Côte d'Ivoire 124 E5
Bianzhuang China see Cangshan
Biaora India 96 C5
Bi'ār Ghabāghib well Syria 109 K2
Bīārjmand Iran 100 C2
Biaro i. Indon. 75 C2
Biarritz France 50 E9
Bi'ār Tabrāk well Saudi Arabia 105 D2
Biasca Switz. 51 O6
Biba Egypt 121 F2
Bibai Japan 90 G3
Bibala Angola 127 B8
formerly known as Vila Arriaga
Bibas Gabon 126 A4
Bibbenluke Australia 147 F4
Bibbiena Italy 56 D5
Biberach an der Riß Germany 48 G7
Bibiani Ghana 124 E5
Bibirevo Rus. Fed. 43 N5
Bibiyana r. Bangl. 97 F4
Biblos Lebanon see Jbail
Bicas Brazil 207 J8
Bicaz Romania 58 H2
Bicheng China see Bishan
Bicheno Australia 147 F5
Bichevaya Rus. Fed. 82 D3
Bichi Nigeria 125 H3
Bichi r. Rus. Fed. 82 E1
Bicholim India 94 B3
Bichraltar Nepal 97 E4
Bichura Rus. Fed. 85 E1
Bichvint'a Georgia 107 E2
also known as Pitsunda
Bickerton Island Australia 148 C2
Bicuari, Parque Nacional do nat. park Angola 127 B8
Bid India 94 B2
also spelt Bir
Bida Nigeria 125 G4
Bidache France 50 E9
Bidadari, Tanjong pt Sabah Malaysia 77 G1
Bidar India 94 C2
Bidasar India 96 B4
Bidbid Oman 105 G3
Biddeford U.S.A. 177 O2
Bideford U.K. 47 H12
Bideford Bay U.K. 47 H12
also known as Barnstaple Bay
Bidente r. Italy 56 E4
Bidjovagge Norway 44 M1
Bidkhan, Kūh-e mt. Iran 100 D4
Bidokht Iran 100 D3
Bidon 5 tourist site Alg. 123 F5
Bidzhan Rus. Fed. 82 C3
Bidzhar r. Rus. Fed. 82 D3
Bié Angola see Kuito
Bié prov. Angola 127 C8
Biebrza r. Poland 49 T2
Biebrzański Park Narodowy nat. park Poland 49 T2
Biedenkopf Germany 48 F5
Biel Switz. 51 N5
also known as Bienne
Bielawa Poland 49 N5
Bielefeld Germany 48 F3
Bielitz Poland see Bielsko-Biała
Biella Italy 56 A3
Bielsko-Biała Poland 49 Q6
historically known as Bielitz
Bielsk Podlaski Poland 49 U3
Bielstein hill Germany 51 P1
Bienenbüttel Germany 48 H2
Biên Hoa Vietnam 79 D6
Bienne r. France 51 L6
Bienne Switz. see Biel
Bienvenida hill Spain 54 E6
Bienvenue Fr. Guiana 199 H4
Bienville, Lac l. Canada 169 F2
Bierbank Australia 149 E5
Bierutów Poland 49 O4
Biesiesvlei S. Africa 133 J3
Biesrespoort S. Africa 132 H8
Bieszczady mts Poland 49 T6
Bieszczadzki Park Narodowy nat. park Poland 49 T6
Bièvre Belgium 51 L3
Biferno r. Italy 56 H7
Bifoun Gabon 126 A5
Bifröst Iceland 44 [inset] B2
Bifuka Japan 90 H2
Big r. U.S.A. 182 A2
Biga Turkey 106 A2
Biga r. Turkey 59 I8
Bigadiç Turkey 106 B3
Biganos France 50 F8
Biga Yarımadası pen. Turkey 59 H9
Big Baldy Mountain U.S.A. 180 E3
Big Bay U.S.A. 172 F4
Big Bay de Noc U.S.A. 172 F5
Big Bear Lake U.S.A. 183 H7
Big Belt Mountains U.S.A. 180 E3
Big Bend Swaziland 133 P3
Big Bend National Park U.S.A. 179 B6
Big Black r. U.S.A. 175 B5
Big Blue r. U.S.A. 178 C4
Big Canyon watercourse U.S.A. 179 B6
Big Cypress National Preserve nature res. U.S.A. 175 D7
Big Desert Wilderness Park nature res. Australia 146 D3
Big Eau Pleine Reservoir U.S.A. 172 D6
Biger Nuur salt l. Mongolia 84 C2
Big Fork r. U.S.A. 174 A1
Biggar Canada 167 J4
Biggar U.K. 46 I8
Biggar, Lac l. Canada 168 F3
Biggarsberg S. Africa 133 N5
Bigge Island Australia 150 D2
Biggenden Australia 149 G5
Bigger, Mount Canada 166 B3
Biggleswade U.K. 47 L11
Biggs U.S.A. 182 C2
Big Hole r. U.S.A. 180 D3
Bighorn r. U.S.A. 180 F3
Bighorn Mountains U.S.A. 180 F3
Bigil'dino Rus. Fed. 43 U8
Big Island i. Nunavut Canada 165 L3
Big Island i. N.W.T. Canada 167 G2
Big Island U.S.A. 176 F8
Big Kalzas Lake Canada 166 C2
Big Lake U.S.A. 179 B6
Big Lake l. U.S.A. 174 H2
Big Muddy Creek r. U.S.A. 180 F2
Bignona Senegal 124 A3
Bigobo Dem. Rep. Congo 127 E6
Big Otter r. U.S.A. 176 F8
Big Pine U.S.A. 182 F4
Big Pine Peak U.S.A. 182 E7
Big Rapids U.S.A. 172 H7
Big Rib r. U.S.A. 172 D6
Big River Canada 167 J4
Big Sable Point U.S.A. 172 G6
Big Salmon Canada 166 C2
Big Salmon r. Canada 166 C2
Big Sand Lake Canada 167 L3
Big Sandy r. U.S.A. 180 E4
Big Sandy watercourse U.S.A. 183 K7
Big Sandy Creek r. U.S.A. 178 B4
Big Sandy Lake Canada 167 J4
Big Sioux r. U.S.A. 178 C3
Big Smokey Valley U.S.A. 183 G3
Big South Cape Island N.Z. 153 B15
Big South Fork National River and Recreation Area park U.S.A. 176 A9
Big Spring U.S.A. 179 B5
Big Stone Canada 167 I5
Big Sur U.S.A. 182 C5
Big Thicket National Preserve nature res. U.S.A. 179 D6
Big Timber U.S.A. 180 E3
Big Trout Lake Canada 168 B2
Big Trout Lake l. Canada 168 B2
Big Valley Canada 167 H4
Big Water U.S.A. 183 M4
Bigwin Canada 173 N5
Bihać Bos.-Herz. 56 H4
Bihar state India 97 E4
Bihariganj India 97 E4
Bihar Sharif India 97 E4
Bihor, Vârful mt. Romania 58 D2
Bihoro Japan 90 I3
Bihpuriagaon India 97 G4
Bijagós, Arquipélago dos is Guinea-Bissau 124 A4
Bijainagar India 96 B4
Bijaipur India 96 C4
Bijapur India 94 B2
Bījār Iran 100 A3
Bijarpur India 94 D2
Bijawar India 96 C4
Bijbehara Jammu and Kashmir 96 B2
Bijeljina Bos.-Herz. 56 L4
Bijelolasica mt. Croatia 56 H3
Bijelo Polje Crna Gora Yugo. 58 A5
Bijie China 86 C3
Bijni India 97 F4
Bijnor India 96 C3
Bijolia India 96 B4
Bijrān well Saudi Arabia 105 E2
Bijrān, Khashm hill Saudi Arabia 105 E2
Bikampur India 96 B4
Bikaner India 96 B3
Bikbauli Kazakh. 103 E3
Bikfaiya Lebanon 108 G4
Bikin Rus. Fed. 82 D3
Bikin r. Rus. Fed. 82 D3
Bikini atoll Marshall Is 220 F5
Bikita Zimbabwe 131 F4
Bikori Sudan 128 B2
Bikoro Dem. Rep. Congo 126 C5
Bikou China 86 C1
Bikramganj India 97 E4
Bilaa Point Phil. 74 C4
Bilād Banī Bū 'Alī Oman 105 G3
Bilād Banī Bū Ḩasan Oman 105 G3
Bilād Ghāmid reg. Saudi Arabia 104 C3
Bilād Zahrān reg. Saudi Arabia 104 C3
Bilanga Burkina 125 E3
Bilangbilangan i. Indon. 77 G2
Bilara India 96 B4
Bilari India 96 C3
Bilaspur Chhattisgarh India 97 D5
Bilaspur Himachal Pradesh India 96 C3
Biläsuvar Azer. 107 G3
formerly known as Pushkino
Bilatan i. Phil. 74 B5
Bila Tserkva Ukr. 41 D6
also spelt Belaya Tserkva
Bilauktaung Range mts Myanmar/Thai. 79 B5
Bilbao Spain 55 I1
also spelt Bilbo
Bilbeis Egypt 121 F2
Bilbo Spain see Bilbao
Bilbor Romania 58 G1
Bildudalur Iceland 44 [inset] B2
Bileća Bos.-Herz. 56 K6
Bilecik Turkey 106 B2
Biled Romania 58 B3
Bilesha Plain Kenya 128 D4
Biłgoraj Poland 49 T5
Bilharamulo Tanz. 128 A5
Bilhaur India 96 D4
Bilhorod-Dnistrovs'kyy Ukr. 41 D7
also spelt Belgorod-Dnestrovskiy; formerly known as Akkerman; historically known as Cetatea Albă or Tyras
Bili Chad 126 C2
Bili r. Dem. Rep. Congo 126 D3
Bilibino Rus. Fed. 39 Q3
Bilibiza Moz. 129 D8
Bīlikōl l. Kazakh. see Biylikol', Ozero
Bilin Myanmar 78 B4
Biliran i. Phil. 74 C4
Bilisht Albania 58 B8
Bilis Qooqaani Somalia 128 D5
Biliu r. China 85 I4
Bill U.S.A. 180 F4
Billabalong Australia 151 A5
Billabong Creek r. Australia see Moulamein Creek
Billdal Sweden 45 J4
Billère France 50 F9
Billiat Conservation Park nature res. Australia 146 D3
Billiluna Australia 150 D3
Billiluna Aboriginal Reserve Australia 150 D3
Billings U.S.A. 180 E3
Billiton i. Indon. see Belitung
Bill of Portland hd U.K. 47 J13
also known as Portland Bill
Billund airport Denmark 45 J5
Bill Williams r. U.S.A. 183 J7
Bill Williams Mountain U.S.A. 183 L6
Bilma Niger 125 I2
Bīlo Eth. 128 C2
Biloela Australia 149 F5
Bilohirs'k Ukr. 41 E7
also spelt Belogorsk; formerly known as Karasubazar
Bilohir"ya Ukr. 41 C6
Biloku Guyana 199 G4
Biloli India 94 C2
Biloluts'k Ukr. 41 F6
Bilovods'k Ukr. 41 F6
Biloxi U.S.A. 175 B6
Bilpa Morea Claypan salt flat Australia 148 C5
Bilqâs Qism Auwal Egypt 108 C6
Bilshausen Germany 48 H4
Bilsi India 96 C3
Biltine Chad 120 D6
Biltine pref. Chad 120 D6
Bilugyun Island Myanmar 78 B4
Bilungala Indon. 75 B2
Bilwascarma Nicaragua 186 C4
Bilyayivka Ukr. 41 D7
also spelt Belyayevka
Bima r. Dem. Rep. Congo 126 E4
Bima Indon. 77 G5
Bima, Teluk b. Indon. 77 G5
Bimbe Angola 127 B7
Bimbila Ghana 125 F4
Bimini Islands Bahamas 186 D1
Bimlipatam India 95 D2
Bina-Etawa India 96 C4
Binaija, Gunung mt. Indon. 75 D3
Binalbagan Phil. 74 B4
Bīnālūd, Kūh-e mts Iran 100 D2
Binatang Sarawak Malaysia 77 E2
Binboğa Daği mt. Turkey 107 D3
Bincheng China 85 H4
formerly known as Binxian
Binchuan China 86 B3
also known as Niujing
Binder Chad 126 B2
Bindki India 96 D4
Bindu Dem. Rep. Congo 127 C6
Bindura Zimbabwe 131 F3
Binefar Spain 55 L3
Binga Zimbabwe 131 E3
Binga, Monte mt. Moz. 131 G3
Bingara Australia 147 F2
Bingaram i. India 94 B4
Bing Bong Australia 148 C2
Bingcaowan China 84 D4
Bingen am Rhein Germany 48 E6
Bingham U.S.A. 174 G2
Binghamton U.S.A. 177 J3
Bin Ghanīmah, Jabal hills Libya 120 B3
Bin Ghashīr Libya 120 B2
Bingmei China see Congjiang
Bingöl Turkey 107 E3
also known as Çapakçur
Bingol Dağı mt. Turkey 107 E3
Bingxi China see Yushan
Bingzhongluo China 86 A2
Binh Son Vietnam 79 E5
Binicuil Phil. 74 B4
Bini Erda well Chad 120 C4
Binika India 97 D5
Binjai Indon. 76 B2
Bin Jawwād Libya 120 C2
Binna, Raas pt Somalia 128 F2
Binnaway Australia 147 F2
Binongko i. Indon. 75 C4
Binpur India 97 E5
Bintan i. Indon. 76 D2
Bintang, Bukit mts Malaysia 76 C1
Bintuan Phil. 74 B3
Bintuhan Indon. 76 C4
Bintulu Sarawak Malaysia 77 F2
Binubusan Phil. 74 B3
Binxian Heilong. China 82 B3
Binxian Shaanxi China 87 D1
also known as Binzhou
Binxian China see Bincheng
Binyang China 87 D4
also known as Binzhou
Bin-Yauri Nigeria 125 G4
Binzhou China see Binyang
Binzhou China see Binxian
Binzhou China 85 H4
Biobío admin. reg. Chile 204 B5
Biobío r. Chile 204 B5
Bioco i. Equat. Guinea 125 H6
also spelt Bioko; formerly known as Fernando Póo or Macías Nguema
Biograd na Moru Croatia 56 H5
Biogradska Gora nat. park Yugo. 58 A6
Bioko i. Equat. Guinea see Bioco
Biokovo park Croatia 56 J5
Biquinhas Brazil 207 H5
Bir India see Bid
Bir, Ras pt Djibouti 128 D2
Bira Rus. Fed. 82 D2
Bira r. Rus. Fed. 82 D2
Bi'r Abā al 'Ajjāj well Saudi Arabia 104 B2
Bîr Abraq well Egypt 121 G4
Bîr Abu Darag well Egypt 108 D8
Bir Abu Garad well Sudan 121 F5
Bîr Abu Hashim well Egypt 121 G4
Bîr Abu Husein well Egypt 121 F4
Bi'r Abū Jady oasis Syria 109 J1
Bîr Abu Minqâr well Egypt 121 E3
Bi'r ad Damar well Libya 120 A3
Bi'r adh Dhakar well Libya 120 D3
Bir Aïdiat well Mauritania 122 C4
Birāk Libya 120 B3
Birakan Rus. Fed. 82 C2
Bi'r al Amīr well Saudi Arabia 104 B2
Bi'r al Aṭbaq well Saudi Arabia 104 B2
Bi'r al 'Awādī well Saudi Arabia 104 B3
Bi'r al Fātiyah well Libya 120 B2
Bi'r al Ghanam Libya 120 B1
Bi'r al Ḩalbā well Syria 109 J3
Bi'r al Ḩisw well Saudi Arabia 104 C2
Bi'r al Ikhwān well Libya 120 D3
Bi'r al Jadīd well Libya 120 B3
Bi'r al Jāhilīyah well Saudi Arabia 104 C3
Bi'r al Marba'ah well Syria 109 K3
Bi'r al Mashī well Saudi Arabia 104 B2
Bi'r al Mastūtah well Libya 120 B3
Bi'r al Mulūsi Iraq 107 E4
Bi'r al Mulūṣī waterhole Iraq 109 L4
Bi'r al Munbaṭiḩ well Syria 109 J3
Bi'r al Mushayqiq well Libya 120 A2
Bi'r al Muwaylih well Libya 120 C2
Bi'r al Qurr well Saudi Arabia 104 B2
Bir 'Amrâne well Mauritania 122 C5
Birandozero Rus. Fed. 40 F3
Bi'r an Nakhīlī waterhole Iraq 109 N3
Bir Anzarane W. Sahara 122 B5
Birao Cent. Afr. Rep. 126 D2
Bir Aouine well Tunisia 123 H2
Bi'r ar 'Alaqah well Libya 120 B2
Bi'r 'Arja well Saudi Arabia 104 C2
Bi'r as Sakhā well Saudi Arabia 104 C3
Biratar Bulak spring China 88 E3
Biratnagar Nepal 97 E4
also known as Morang
Biratori Japan 90 H3
Bi'r at Tarfāwī well Libya 120 E2
Bi'r at Tayyārīyah well Syria 109 K3
Bi'r at Tuwaylah waterhole Iraq 109 L4
Bi'r 'Azīz well Saudi Arabia 105 E3
Bi'raz Zurq well Saudi Arabia 104 C4
Bi'r Başīrī well Syria 109 I3
Bi'r Baydā well Saudi Arabia 104 B2
Bir Bayly well Egypt 120 E2
Bîr Beida well Egypt 108 F7
Bir Bel Guerdâne well Mauritania 122 C4
Bir Ben Takoul well Alg. 123 E4
Bir Bidi well Sudan 121 E5
Bi'r Bū Athlah well Libya 120 D3
Bi'r Budayy well Saudi Arabia 104 B2
Bîr Buerât well Egypt 108 D8
Bi'r Bū Rāḩah well Libya 120 A3
Bi'r Buraym well Saudi Arabia 104 C3
Birch r. Canada 167 H3
Bir Chali well Mali 122 D5
Birch Hills Canada 167 J4
Birchip Australia 147 D3
Birch Lake N.W.T. Canada 167 G2
Birch Lake Sask. Canada 167 I4
Birch Lake U.S.A. 172 B3
Birch Mountains Canada 167 H3
Birch River Canada 167 K4
Birch River U.S.A. 176 E7
Birch Run U.S.A. 173 J7
Birchwood U.S.A. 172 B5
Bircot Eth. 128 D3
Bir Di Sudan 126 F3
Bîr Dibis well Egypt 121 F4
Bîr Dignâsh well Egypt 120 E2
Bird Island N. Mariana Is see Farallon de Medinilla
Bir Dolmane well Alg. 123 H3
Birdsboro U.S.A. 177 J5
Birdseye U.S.A. 183 M2
Birdsville Australia 148 C5
Birdum r. Australia 148 B2
Birecik Turkey 107 D3
Bir ed Deheb well Alg. 123 E4
Bîr el 'Adeid well Egypt 108 F9
Bîr el 'Agramîya well Egypt 108 C8
Bîr el Duweidar well Egypt 108 D7
Bir el Fakama well Sudan 104 A4
Bir el Ghoralia well Tunisia 123 H2
Bir El Hadjaj well Alg. 123 E4
Bîr el Haimur well Egypt 121 G4
Bîr el Istabl well Egypt 121 E2
Bîr el Khamsa well Egypt 121 E2
Bîr el Malha well Egypt 108 E8
Bîr el Nuss well Egypt 121 E3
Bîr el-Obeiyid well Egypt 121 E3
Bîr el Qatrâni well Egypt 121 E2
Bîr el Râbia well Egypt 106 A5
Birendranagar Nepal see Surkhet
Bir en Natrûn well Sudan 121 E5
Bir en Nugeim well Sudan 121 G5
Bir es Smeha well Alg. 123 G2
Bireun Indon. 76 B1
Bi'r Fāḑil well Saudi Arabia 105 E3
Bi'r Fajr well Saudi Arabia 104 B1
Bir Fanoidig well Sudan 104 A4
Bi'r Fardān well Saudi Arabia 105 E3
Bîr Fuâd well Egypt 121 E2
Bir Furawiya well Sudan 120 D6
Bir Gandouz W. Sahara 122 A5
Bi'r Ghawdah well Saudi Arabia 104 D3
Bîr Gifgâfa well Egypt 108 E7
Bîr Gindali well Egypt 108 C8
Bi'r Hādī oasis Saudi Arabia 105 E4
Bi'r Hajal well Syria 109 K3
Birhan mt. Eth. 128 C2
Bi'r Haraqī well Saudi Arabia 104 C3
Bîr Hasana well Egypt 108 E7
Bir Hatab well Sudan 121 G4
Bi'r Haymir well Saudi Arabia 104 B2
Bi'r Hilū well Saudi Arabia 104 B2
Bir Hismet 'Umar well Sudan 121 G4
Bi'r Hudūf well Saudi Arabia 104 C3
Bi'r Humaymah well Syria 109 K3
Bir Huwait well Sudan 121 G4
Bi'r Ḩuwaymidah well Saudi Arabia 104 C2
Bi'r Ibn Ghunayn well Saudi Arabia 104 B2
Bi'r Ibn Hirmās Saudi Arabia see Al Bi'r
Bi'r Ibn Sarrār well Saudi Arabia 104 C4
Bi'r Īdīmah well Saudi Arabia 104 D4
Birigüi Brazil 206 C8
Birin, Col de pass Alg. 55 N9
Birini Cent. Afr. Rep. 126 D3
Bīrjand Iran 101 D3
Bi'r Jaydah well Saudi Arabia 104 B2
Bi'r Jifah well Yemen 105 D5
Bi'r Jubnī well Libya 120 E2
Bi'r Jugjug well Saudi Arabia 104 C3
Birkat Abū Salīm waterhole Saudi Arabia 104 C2
Birkat al 'Aşāfīr waterhole Saudi Arabia 109 O8
Birkat al Ḩamrā well Saudi Arabia 104 C1
Birkat al Haytam waterhole Saudi Arabia 109 O8
Birkat ash Shīḩīyāt waterhole Saudi Arabia 109 O8
Birkat aẓ Ẓafīrī waterhole Saudi Arabia 109 O8
Birkat Zubālah waterhole Saudi Arabia 107 E5
Birkeland Norway 45 J4
Birkenhead U.K. 47 I10
Birket Qârûn l. Egypt 121 F2
Bi'r Khamrān waterhole Iraq 109 O3
Bi'r Khurbah well Saudi Arabia 104 C3
Bi'r Khuwārah well Saudi Arabia 104 C3
Bir Kiau well Sudan 121 G4
Birkim Iraq 107 E3
Birkirkara Malta 57 G13
Birksgate Range hills Australia 146 A1
Bir Labasoi well Sudan 121 G4
Bîrlad Romania see Bârlad
Bîr Lahfân well Egypt 108 E6
Bir Lahmar W. Sahara 122 C4
Birlik Kazakh. 103 H3
formerly spelt Brlik
Birlik Kazakh. see Brlik
Bir Likeit el Fauqani well Sudan 104 A3
Bir Liseila well Sudan 121 G4
Bîr Majal well Egypt 121 G4
Birmal reg. Afgh. 101 G3
Bi'r Malīyah well Saudi Arabia 104 C3
Birmingham U.K. 47 K11
Birmingham U.S.A. 175 C5
Bîr Misâha well Egypt 121 E4
Birmitrapur India 97 E5
Bîr Mogreïn Mauritania 122 C4
formerly known as Fort Trinquet
Bi'r Muḩaymid al Wazwaz well Syria 109 J3
Bi'r Mujayfil well Saudi Arabia 108 G8
Bîr Murra well Egypt 121 G4
Bi'r Muwayliḩ well Syria 109 K3
Bi'r Nabt well Saudi Arabia 104 B2
Bîr Nagib well Egypt 121 G4
Bîr Nâḩid oasis Egypt 121 F2
Bi'r Najib well Syria 109 K3
Bi'r Nasīf Saudi Arabia 104 B2
Bir Nawari well Sudan 121 G4
Birni Benin 125 F4
Birnie i. Kiribati 145 H2
Birnin-Gaouré Niger 125 F3
Birnin-Gwari Nigeria 125 G4
Birnin-Kebbi Nigeria 125 G3
Birnin Konni Niger 125 G3
Birnin Kudu Nigeria 125 H4
Birniwa Nigeria 125 H3
Bir Nukheila well Sudan 121 E5
Birobidzhan Rus. Fed. 82 D2
Birofel'd Rus. Fed. 82 D2
Bir Ounâne well Mali 122 E5
Birpur India 97 E4
Bîr Qasîr el Sirr well Egypt 106 A5
Bîr Quleib well Egypt 121 G3
Birr Rep. of Ireland 47 E10
Birrie r. Australia 147 E2
Birrindudu Australia 148 A3
Birrîyet el Aşeifar Egypt 108 B6
Bîr Rôd Sâlim well Egypt 108 E7
Bir Roumi well Alg. 123 G2
Bi'r Sābil Iraq 107 E4
Bîr Sahara well Egypt 121 F4
Bir Salala well Sudan 121 G4
Birsay U.K. 46 I4
Bîr Shalatein Egypt 121 G4
Bi'r Shamandūr well Syria 109 K1
Birshoghyr Kazakh. see Berchogur
Bi'r Simād waterhole Iraq 109 O3
Birsk Rus. Fed. 40 J5
Bir Sohanit well Sudan 104 A3
Birštonas Lith. 42 F7
Bîr Tâba Egypt 108 F8
Bir Ţalḩah well Saudi Arabia 105 D3
Bir Tanguer well Alg. 123 H3
Bi'r Tānjidar well Libya 120 D2
Bîr Tarfâwi well Egypt 121 F4
Bi'r Ţarūfāwī waterhole Iraq 109 O4
Bîr Thâl well Egypt 108 E8
Birthday Mountain hill Australia 149 D2
Birtle Canada 167 K5
Biru China 89 F6
also known as Biruxiong
Bîr Udeib well Egypt 108 D8
Biruintsa Moldova see Ştefan Vodă
Bir Umm el Gharāniq Libya 120 C2
Bîr Umm Fawâkhir well Egypt 104 A2
Bi'r Umm Missā well Saudi Arabia 104 B2
Bîr Ungât well Egypt 121 G4
Biruni Uzbek. see Beruni
Birur India 94 B3
Bi'r Usaylīlah well Saudi Arabia 105 D3
Biruxiong China see Biru
Bir Wario well Sudan 121 G5
Bi'r Wedeb well Libya 120 B3
Bi'r Wurshah well Saudi Arabia 104 C3
Biryakovo Rus. Fed. 43 V2
Biržai Lith. 42 F5
Bir Zar well Tunisia 123 H3
Bisa i. Indon. 75 C3
Bisalpur India 96 C3
Bisau India 96 B3
Bisbee U.S.A. 181 E7
Biscarrosse France 50 E8
Biscarrosse et de Parentis, Étang de l. France 50 E8
Biscay, Bay of sea France/Spain 50 A7
Biscayne Bay U.S.A. 175 D7
Biscayne National Park U.S.A. 175 D7
Bischofshofen Austria 49 K8
Bischofswerda Germany 49 L4
Biscoe Islands Antarctica 222 T2
Biscotasing Canada 168 D4
Bisert' r. Rus. Fed. 40 K4
Biserti Bulg. 58 H5
Biševo i. Croatia 56 I6
Bisezhai China 86 B4
Bisha Eritrea 121 H6
Bīshah reg. Saudi Arabia 104 C4
Bīshah, Wādī watercourse Saudi Arabia 104 D3
Bishan China 86 C2
also known as Bicheng
Bishbek Kyrg. see Bishkek

►Bishkek Kyrg. 103 H4
Capital of Kyrgyzstan. Also spelt Bishbek or Pishpek; formerly known as Frunze.

Bishnupur India 97 E5
Bisho S. Africa 133 L9
Bishop U.S.A. 182 F4
Bishop Auckland U.K. 47 K9
Bishop Lake Canada 167 G1
Bishop's Stortford U.K. 47 M12
Bishopville U.S.A. 175 D5
Bishrī, Jabal hills Syria 109 K2
Bishti i Pallës pt Albania 58 A7
Bishui China 82 A1
Bishui China see Biyang
Bisi S. Africa 133 N7
Bisinaca Col. 198 D3
Biskra Alg. 123 G2
also spelt Beskra
Biskupiec Poland 49 R2
Bislig Phil. 74 C4
Bislig Bay Phil. 74 C4

►Bismarck U.S.A. 178 B2
State capital of North Dakota.

Bismarck Archipelago is P.N.G. 73 K7
Bismarck Sea P.N.G. 73 K7
Bismil Turkey 107 E3
Bismo Norway 45 J3
Bison U.S.A. 178 B2
Bīsotūn Iran 100 A3
Bispgården Sweden 44 L3
Bissa, Djebel mt. Alg. 55 M8
Bissamcuttak India 95 D2

►Bissau Guinea-Bissau 124 B4
Capital of Guinea-Bissau.

Bissaula Nigeria 125 H5
Bissett Canada 167 M5
Bissikrima Guinea 124 C4
Bissorã Guinea-Bissau 124 B3
Bistcho Lake Canada 166 G3
Bistra mt. Macedonia 58 B7
Bistra mt. Yugo. 58 B6
Bistret Romania 58 E5
Bistreţ, Lacul l. Romania 58 E5

index B

Bistrița Romania 58 F1
Bistrița r. Romania 58 F1
Bistrița r. Romania 58 H2
Bistrița Bârgăului Romania 58 F1
Bistriței, Munții mts Romania 58 G1
Bistrița r. Bulg. 58 E7
Biswan India 96 D4
Bisztynek Poland 49 R1
Bitam Gabon 126 A4
Bitata Eth. 128 C3
Bitburg Germany 48 D6
Bitche France 51 N3
Bitik Kazakh. 102 B2
Bitkine Chad 126 C2
Bitlis Turkey 107 E3
Bitola Macedonia 58 C7
also known as Manastir or Monastir;
formerly spelt Bitolj
Bitolj Macedonia see Bitola
Bitonto Italy 56 H7
Bitrān, Jabal hill Saudi Arabia 105 D3
Bitra Par reef India 94 B4
Bitter Creek r. UT U.S.A. 183 O2
Bitter Creek r. WY U.S.A. 180 E4
Bitterfontein S. Africa 132 C8
Bitterroot r. U.S.A. 180 D3
Bitterwater U.S.A. 182 D5
Bittou Burkina 125 E4
Bituca Brazil 202 A4
Bitung Indon. 75 C2
Bityi S. Africa 133 M8
Bityug r. Rus. Fed. 41 F6
Biula Angola 127 D7
Bivane r. S. Africa 133 P4
Biwabik U.S.A. 172 A3
Biwa-ko l. Japan 91 D7
Bixad Romania 58 E2
Biyala Egypt 108 C6
Biyang China see Yixian
Biyang China 87 E1
also known as Bishui
Biye K'obē Eth. 128 D2
Biylikol, Ozero l. Kazakh. 103 G4
also known as Biylikol
Biyo Ado well Eth. 128 E3
Biysk Rus. Fed. 80 D2
Bizana S. Africa 133 N7
Bizen Japan 91 D7
Bizerta Tunisia see Bizerte
Bizerte Tunisia 123 H1
English form Bizerta; also known as Banzart;
historically known as Hippo Zarytus
Bizhanābād Iran 100 D5

► Bjargtangar hd Iceland 44 [inset] A2
Most westerly point of Europe.

Bjarkøy Norway 44 L1
Bjästa Sweden 44 L3
Bjelasica mts Yugo. 58 A6
Bjelašnica mts Bos.-Herz. 56 K5
Bjelovar Croatia 56 I3
Bjerkvik Norway 44 L1
Bjerringbro Denmark 45 J4
Bjøllånes Norway 44 J3
Bjoneroa Norway 45 J4
Björbo Sweden 45 K3
Bjorkelangen Norway 45 J4
Björkfjället mts Sweden 44 L2
Björkliden Sweden 45 L1
Björklinge Sweden 45 L3
Björksele Sweden 44 L2
Bjorli Norway 44 J3
Björna Sweden 44 L3
Bjernafjorden b. Norway 45 I3
Björneborg Fin. see Pori
Bjørnevatn Norway 44 O1
Bjørnfjell Norway 44 L1

► Bjørnøya i. Arctic Ocean 38 B2
Part of Norway. English form Bear Island.

Bjørnstad Norway 44 O1
Bjurholm Sweden 44 L3
Bjuröklubb pt Sweden 44 M2
Bjursås Sweden 45 K3
Bla Mali 124 D3
Blace Kosovo, Srbija Yugo. 58 B6
Blachownia Poland 49 P5
Black r. Man. Canada 167 L5
Black r. Ont. Canada 168 D2
Black r. Ont. Canada 172 G2
Black r. AR U.S.A. 174 B5
Black r. AZ U.S.A. 183 N8
Black r. MI U.S.A. 173 K9
Black r. SC U.S.A. 175 E5
Black r. WI U.S.A. 172 B6
Blackall Australia 149 E5
Black Bay Ont. Canada 168 B3
Black Bay Sask. Canada 167 I3
Blackbear r. Canada 168 D4
Blackbull Australia 149 D3
Blackburn U.K. 47 J10
Black Butte mt. U.S.A. 182 B2
Black Canyon gorge U.S.A. 183 J6
Black Canyon of the Gunnison National Park U.S.A. 181 F5
Black Coast Antarctica 222 T2
Black Creek r. U.S.A. 172 E6
Black Creek watercourse U.S.A. 183 O6
Black Dome mt. Canada 166 E4
Blackdown Tableland National Park Australia 149 F4
Blackfeet Indian Reservation res. U.S.A. 180 D2
Blackfoot U.S.A. 180 D4
Black Foot r. U.S.A. 180 D3
Blackfoot Reservoir U.S.A. 180 D4
Black Forest mts Germany 48 F8
also known as Schwarzwald
Black Hill Range hills Australia 148 B5

Black Hills SD U.S.A. 180 F3
Black Island Canada 167 L5
Black Lake Canada 167 J3
Black Lake r. Canada 167 J3
Black Lake l. U.S.A. 173 I5
Black Mesa U.S.A. 183 O8
Black Mesa ridge U.S.A. 183 G6
Black Mountain hill U.K. 47 I12
Black Mountain CA U.S.A. 182 G6
Black Mountain KY U.S.A. 176 C9
Black Mountains hills U.K. 47 I12
Black Mountains U.S.A. 183 J6
Black Nossob watercourse Namibia 130 C4
also known as Swart Nossob
Black Pagoda India see Konarka
Black Point Hong Kong China 87 [inset]
also known as Lan Kok Tsui
Blackpool U.K. 47 I10
Black Range State Park nature res. Australia 147 I5
Black River Jamaica 186 D3
Black River r. U.S.A. 177 J1
Black River r. Vietnam 78 D3
also known as Đa, Sông
Black River Falls U.S.A. 172 C6
Black Rock hill Jordan see 'Unāb, Jabal al
Black Rock Desert U.S.A. 182 E1
Blacksburg U.S.A. 176 E8
Black Sea Asia/Europe 41 F8
also known as Chernoye More or Kara Deniz
Backs Port U.S.A. 180 E4
Blackshear U.S.A. 175 D6
Blacksod Bay Rep. of Ireland 47 B9
Black Springs U.S.A. 182 E2
Blackstone r. N.W.T. Canada 166 F2
Blackstone r. Y.T. Canada 166 B1
Blackstone U.S.A. 176 H8
Black Sturgeon r. Canada 172 E2
Black Sugarloaf mt. Australia 147 F2
Black Tickle Canada 169 K2
Black Umfolozi r. S. Africa 133 P5
Black Volta r. Africa 124 E4
also known as Mouhoun; also known as Volta Noire
Blackwater Australia 149 F4
Blackwater watercourse Australia 149 E5
Blackwater r. Canada 166 E2
Blackwater r. Rep. of Ireland 47 E11
Blackwater r. U.S.A. 177 I9
Blackwater watercourse U.S.A. 179 B5
Blackwater Lake Canada 166 F2
Blackwood National Park Australia 149 E4
Bladensburg National Park Australia 149 D4
Blåfjellshatten mt. Norway 44 K2
Blagodarnyy Rus. Fed. 41 G7
Blagodatnoye Kazakh. 103 H2
Blagoevgrad Bulg. 58 E6
formerly known as Gorna Dzhumaya
Blagoveshchenka Rus. Fed. 103 I1
Blagoveshchensk Rus. Fed. 82 D2
Blagoveshchensk Rus. Fed. 40 K5
Blagoveshchenskoye Kazakh. 103 H4
Blaikiston, Mount Canada 167 H5
Blain France 50 E5
Blain U.S.A. 176 H5
Blaine NE U.S.A. 178 C3
Blaine WI U.S.A. 172 A2
Blair NE U.S.A. 178 C3
Blair WI U.S.A. 172 B6
Blair Athol Australia 149 E4
Blair Atholl U.K. 46 I7
Blairbeth S. Africa 133 K2
Blairgowrie U.K. 46 I7
Blairs U.S.A. 176 F9
Blairsden U.S.A. 182 D2
Blairsville U.S.A. 174 D5
Blaj Romania 58 E2
Blak Rus. Fed. 103 E2
Blakang Mati, Pulau i. Sing. see Sentosa
Blakely U.S.A. 175 C6
Blake Point U.S.A. 172 E2
Blakeslee U.S.A. 177 J4
Blama Sierra Leone 124 C5
Blambangan, Semenanjung pen. Indon. 77 F5

Blambangan Nature Reserve Indon. 77 F5

► Blanc, Mont mt. France/Italy 51 M7
5th highest mountain in Europe. Also known as Bianco, Monte.
europe [landscapes] ▶ 30–31

Blanca, Bahía b. Arg. 204 E5
Blanca, Cordillera mts Peru 200 A2
Blanca, Sierra mt. U.S.A. 181 F6
Blanca Peak U.S.A. 181 F5
Blanche, Lake salt flat S.A. Australia 146 C2
Blanche, Lake salt flat W.A. Australia 150 C4
Blanchester U.S.A. 176 B6
Blanchetown Australia 146 C3
Blanco r. Arg. 204 C3
Blanco r. Bol. 201 D3
Blanco r. Peru 198 C6
Blanco S. Africa 132 G10
Blanco r. Spain 54 F7
Blanco, Cabo c. Costa Rica 186 B5
Blanco, Cape U.S.A. 180 A4
Blanc-Sablon Canada 169 J3
Bland r. Australia 147 E3
also known as Yeo Yeo
Bland U.S.A. 176 D8
Blanda r. Iceland 44 [inset] B2
Blandford Forum U.K. 47 J13
Blanding U.S.A. 183 O4
Blanes Spain 55 N3
Blaney Park U.S.A. 172 H4
Blangah, Telok b. Sing. 76 [inset]
Blangkejeren Indon. 76 B2
Blangpidie Indon. 76 B2
Blangy-sur-Bresle France 50 H3
Blānice r. Czech Rep. 49 L6
Blankenheim Germany 48 D5
Blanquefort France 50 F8
Blanquilla, Isla i. Venez. 199 F2
Blansko Czech Rep. 49 N6
Blantyre Malawi 129 B8
Blarney Rep. of Ireland 47 D12
Blåsjø l. Norway 45 I4
Blåskavlen mt. Norway 45 I3
Blåstöten mt. Sweden 44 K3
Blaszki Poland 49 P4
Blåtnå Czech Rep. 49 K6
Blåtinksele Sweden 44 L2
Blau Indon. 75 B2
Blaubeuren Germany 48 G7
Blåvands Huk pt Denmark 45 I5
Blavet r. France 50 C5
Blåviksjön Sweden 40 A2
Blaydon U.K. 47 K9
Blaye France 50 F7
Blayeul Sommet mt. France 51 M8
Blayney Australia 147 F3
Blaze, Point Australia 148 A2
Błażowa Poland 49 T6
Blega Indon. 77 F4
Bleik Norway 44 K1
Bleichtalsperre resr Germany 51 R2
Blekinge county Sweden 45 K4
Blenheim Canada 168 D5
Blenheim N.Z. 152 H9
Blenheim Palace tourist site U.K. 47 K12
Bléré France 50 G5
Blesmanspos S. Africa 132 I4
Bletoppen mt. Norway 45 J4
Bleu, Lac l. Canada 173 O4
Bleus, Monts mts Dem. Rep. Congo 126 F4
Blida Alg. 123 I1
also spelt El Boulaïda
Bligh Sound inlet N.Z. 153 B12
Bligh Water r. Fiji 145 G3
Blind River Canada 168 D4

Blinkwater S. Africa 133 K9
Blinman Australia 146 C2
Bliss U.S.A. 180 D4
Blissfield MI U.S.A. 173 J9
Blissfield OH U.S.A. 176 D5
Blitar Indon. 77 F5
Block Lake Canada 173 Q6
Block Island U.S.A. 177 N4
Block Island i. U.S.A. 177 N4
Block Island Sound sea chan. U.S.A. 177 N4
Bloedrivier S. Africa 133 O4
Bloemfontein S. Africa 133 K4
Bloemhof S. Africa 133 J4
Bloemhof Dam S. Africa 133 J4
Bloemhof Dam Nature Reserve S. Africa 133 J4
Blois France 50 H5
Blomberg se Vloer salt pan S. Africa 132 E7
Blöndulón l. Iceland 44 [inset] C2
Blönduós Iceland 44 [inset] B2
Blongas Indon. 77 E4
Bloods Range mts Australia 148 A5
Bloodsworth Island U.S.A. 177 I7
Bloodvein r. Canada 167 L5
Bloody Foreland pt Rep. of Ireland 47 D8
Bloomer U.S.A. 172 B5
Bloomfield Canada 173 P7
Bloomfield IA U.S.A. 174 A3
Bloomfield IN U.S.A. 174 C4
Bloomfield MO U.S.A. 174 B4
Bloomfield NM U.S.A. 181 F5
Blooming Prairie U.S.A. 174 A3
Bloomington IL U.S.A. 174 B3
Bloomington IN U.S.A. 174 C4
Bloomington MN U.S.A. 174 A2
Bloomsburg U.S.A. 177 I4
Bloomsbury Australia 149 F4
Blora Indon. 77 E4
Blossburg U.S.A. 177 H4
Blosseville Kyst coastal area Greenland 165 Q3
Blossom, Mys pt Rus. Fed. 39 R2
Blouberg Nature Reserve S. Africa 131 F4
Blountstown U.S.A. 175 C6
Blowing Rock U.S.A. 176 D9
Bludenz Austria 48 G8
Blue r. Canada 166 D3
Blue r. U.S.A. 179 D5
Blue watercourse U.S.A. 183 O8
Blue Bell Knoll mt. U.S.A. 183 M3
Blueberry r. Canada 166 F3
Blue Cliff S. Africa 133 J10
Blue Creek r. Mex. see Azul
Blue Diamond U.S.A. 183 I5
Blue Earth U.S.A. 178 D3
Blue Earth r. U.S.A. 178 D2
Bluefield U.S.A. 176 E8
Bluefields Nicaragua 186 C4
Bluegums S. Africa 133 I7
Blue Hill U.S.A. 177 Q1
Blue Hills Turks and Caicos Is 187 E2
Blue Knob hill U.S.A. 176 G5
Blue Lagoon National Park Zambia 127 E8
Blue Mountain hill Canada 169 J3
Blue Mountain India 97 G5
Blue Mountain Pass Lesotho 133 L6
Blue Mountains Australia 147 F3
Blue Mountains N.Z. 153 D14
Blue Mountains U.S.A. 180 C3
Blue Mountains National Park Australia 147 F3
Blue Mud Bay Australia 148 C2
Blue Nile r. Eth./Sudan 104 A5
also known as Ābay Wenz (Ethiopia), Azraq, Bahr el (Sudan)
Blue Nile state Sudan 128 A2
Bluenose Lake Canada 164 H3
Blue Rapids U.S.A. 178 C4
Blue Ridge GA U.S.A. 174 C5
Blue Ridge VA U.S.A. 176 F8
Blue Ridge mts U.S.A. 176 E9
Blue River Canada 166 G4
Blue Stack Mountains hills Rep. of Ireland 47 D9
Bluestone Lake U.S.A. 176 E8
Bluff Australia 149 F4
Bluff City U.S.A. 176 D9
Bluffdale U.S.A. 183 M1
Bluff Face Range hills Australia 150 D3
Bluff Harbour N.Z. 153 C14
Bluff Island Hong Kong China 87 [inset]
also known as Sha Tong Hau Shan
Bluff Knoll mt. Australia 151 B7
Bluffton IN U.S.A. 174 C3
Bluffton OH U.S.A. 176 B5
Blumberg Germany 48 F8
Blumenau Brazil 203 B8
Blustry Mountain Canada 166 F5
Blyde River Nature Reserve S. Africa 133 O1
Blyth r. Australia 148 B2
Blyth Canada 173 L7
Blythdale Beach S. Africa 133 P6
Blythe U.S.A. 183 J8
Blytheville U.S.A. 174 B5
Blyth Range hills Australia 151 E5
Bo Norway 45 J4
Bo Sierra Leone 124 C5
Boac Phil. 74 B3
Boaco Nicaragua 186 B4
Boa Esperança Minas Gerais Brazil 203 C7
Boa Esperança Roraima Brazil 199 F4
Boa Esperança, Açude resr Brazil 202 D3
Boa Esperança do Sul Brazil 206 E8
Boa Hora Brazil 202 D5
Bo'ai Henan China 85 G5
also known as Qinghua
Bo'ai Yunnan China 86 C4
Boal Spain 54 E1
Boali Cent. Afr. Rep. 126 C3
Boalsburg U.S.A. 176 H5
Boane Moz. 133 Q3
Boano i. Indon. 75 C3
Boano, Selat sea chan. Indon. 75 C3
Boa Nova Brazil 202 D5
Boardman U.S.A. 176 E4
Boatlaname Botswana 131 E4
Boatman Australia 147 F1
Boa Viagem Brazil 202 E3
Boa Vista Amazonas Brazil 198 C6
Boa Vista Amazonas Brazil 198 D4
Boa Vista Pará Brazil 199 H5
Boa Vista Roraima Brazil 199 F3
Boa Vista i. Cape Verde 124 [inset]
Boabadah Australia 147 E3
Bobai China 87 D4
Bobaomby, Tanjona c. Madag. 131 [inset] K1
formerly known as Ambre, Cap d'
Bobbili India 95 D2
Bobbio Italy 56 B4
Bobcaygeon Canada 173 O6
Bobia mt. Spain 54 E1
Bobigny France 51 I4
Bobo-Dioulasso Burkina 124 D4
Bobolice Poland 49 N2
Bobon Phil. 74 C4
Boborás Spain 54 C2
Bobotov Kuk mt. Yugo. see Durmitor
Bobotob, Gora mt. Uzbek. 103 G4
Bobr Belarus 43 K7
Bobr r. Belarus 43 J7
Bóbr r. Poland 49 M3
Bobrik r. Belarus see Novomoskovsk
Bobrinets Ukr. see Bobrynets'
Bobrov Rus. Fed. 41 G6
Bobrovitsa Ukr. see Bobrovytsya

Bobrovytsya Ukr. 41 D6
also spelt Bobrovitsa
Bobruysk Belarus see Babruysk
Bobruysk r. Belarus 42 H9
Bobrynets' Ukr. 41 E6
also spelt Bobrinets
Bobso China 86 B1
Bobuk Sudan 128 B2
Bobures Venez. 198 D2
Boby mt. Madag. 131 [inset] J4
Boca Chica Key i. U.S.A. 175 D7
Boca de la Travesía Arg. 204 D6
Boca del Pao Venez. 199 E2
Boca del Río Mex. 185 F5
Boca de Macareo Venez. 199 F2
Boca de Uracoa Venez. 199 F2
Boca do Acre Brazil 200 D2
Boca do Capanã Brazil 199 F6
Boca do Curuquetê Brazil 200 D2
Boca do Jari Brazil 199 I5
Boca do Moaco Brazil 200 C1
Boca Grande r. mouth Trin. and Tob./Venez. 187 H5
Bocaina de Minas Brazil 207 I9
Bocaiúva Brazil 203 D6
Bocaiúva do Sul Brazil 203 B8
Boca Mavaca Venez. 199 E4
Bocanda Côte d'Ivoire 124 D5
Bocaranga Cent. Afr. Rep. 126 B3
Boca Raton U.S.A. 175 D7
Bocas del Toro Panama 186 C5
Bochinche Venez. 199 F3
Bochnia Poland 49 R6
Bocholt Germany 48 D4
Bochum Germany 48 E4
Bochum S. Africa 131 F4
Bockenem Germany 48 H3
Boccio Brazil 127 B8
formerly known as Sousa Lara
Bocșa Romania 58 C3
Boda Cent. Afr. Rep. 126 C3
Böda Sweden 45 L4
Bodalla Australia 147 F4
Bodallin Australia 151 B6
Bodaybo Rus. Fed. 39 L4
Bodden Town Cayman Is 186 C3
Bode r. Germany 48 I4
Bodega Head U.S.A. 182 A3
Bodélé reg. Chad 120 C5
Boden Sweden 44 M2
Bodensee l. Germany/Switz. see Constance, Lake
Bode-Sadu Nigeria 125 G4
Bodeşti Romania 58 H1
Bodfish U.S.A. 182 F6
Bodh Gaya India 97 E4
Bodhan India 94 C2
Bodinayakkanur India 94 C4
Bodión r. Spain 54 E6
Bodmin U.K. 47 H13
Bodø Norway 44 K2
Bodoco Brazil 202 E3
Bodonchiyn Gol watercourse Mongolia 84 A2
Bodoquena Mato Grosso do Sul Brazil 201 F4
Bodoquena, Serra da hills Brazil 201 F5
Bodoukpa Cent. Afr. Rep. 126 C3
Bodrog r. Hungary 49 S7
Bodrum Turkey 106 A3
historically known as Halicarnassus
Bodsjö Sweden 44 K3
Bodva r. Hungary 49 R7
Bodva r. Slovakia 49 R7
Boechout Belgium 51 K1
Boedo r. Spain 54 G2
Boende Dem. Rep. Congo 126 D5
Bo Epinang Indon. 75 B4
Boerne U.S.A. 179 C6
Boesmans r. S. Africa 133 K10
Boesmans hoekpas pass S. Africa 133 K3
Boeuf r. U.S.A. 175 B6
Bofete Brazil 206 E10
Boffa Guinea 124 B4
Boftsay Norway 44 V1
Bogale Myanmar 78 A4
Bogale r. Myanmar 78 A4
Bogalusa U.S.A. 175 B6
Bogan r. Australia 147 E2
Bogandé Burkina 125 E3
Bogan Gate Australia 147 E3
Bogangolo Cent. Afr. Rep. 126 C3
Bogantungan Australia 149 E4
Bogatić Srbija Yugo. 58 A4
Bogazliyan Turkey 106 C3
Bogbonga Dem. Rep. Congo 126 C4
Bogda Feng mt. China 88 E3
Bogdan mt. Bulg. 58 F6
Bogdana Romania 58 G5
Bogdanci Macedonia 58 D7
Bogda Shan mts China 88 E3
Bogembayskiy Kazakh. 103 H1
Bogen Norway 44 L1
Boggeragh Mountains hills Rep. of Ireland 47 C11
Boggola hill Australia 150 B4
Boghar Alg. 55 N9
Boghari Alg. see Ksar el Boukhari
Bogia P.N.G. 73 J7
Bogie r. Australia 149 E4
Bogny-sur-Meuse France 51 K3
Bogo Phil. 74 C4
Bogodukhov Ukr. see Bohodukhiv
Bogodukhovka Kazakh. 103 G1
Bogol Manya Eth. 128 D3
Bogolyubovo Smolenskaya Oblast' Rus. Fed. 43 N6
Bogolyubovo Vladimirskaya Oblast' Rus. Fed. 43 V5
Bogong, Mount Australia 147 E4
Bogopol' Rus. Fed. 90 D2
Bogor Indon. 77 D4
Bogoroditsk Rus. Fed. 43 T8
Bogorodskoye Rus. Fed. 43 Q8
Bogorodskoye Rus. Fed. 82 F1
Bogorodskoye Rus. Fed. 40 I4
Bogoslof Island U.S.A. 164 C4

► Bogotá Col. 198 C3
Capital of Colombia and 5th most populous city in South America. Long form Santa Fé de Bogotá.
world [cities] ▶ 24–25

Bogotol Rus. Fed. 80 D1
Bogovarovo Rus. Fed. 40 H4
Bogoyavlenskoye Rus. Fed. see Pervomayskiy
Bogra Bangl. 97 F4
Boguchany Rus. Fed. 39 J4
Boguchar Rus. Fed. 41 G6
Bogué Mauritania 124 B2
Boh r. Indon. 77 F2
Bo Hai g. China 85 H4
English form Chihli, Gulf of; formerly spelt Po Hai
Bohai Haixia sea chan. China 85 I4
formerly known as Laotieshan Shuidao
Bohain-en-Vermandois France 51 J3
Bohai Wan b. China 85 H4
Bohemia reg. Czech Rep. 49 L5
also known as Böhmen
Bohemia Downs Australia 150 D3
Bohemia Downs Aboriginal Reserve Australia 150 D3
Bohemian Forest mts Germany see Böhmer Wald

Bohicon Benin 125 F5
Bohinjskaya, Vozyera l. Belarus 42 H6
Bohlokong S. Africa 133 M5
Böhmen reg. Czech Rep. see Bohemia
Böhmer Wald mts Germany 49 J6
English form Bohemian Forest
Bohodukhiv Ukr. 41 E6
also spelt Bogodukhov
Bohol i. Phil. 74 C4
Bohol Sea Phil. 74 C4
Bohol Strait Phil. 74 B4
Bohu China 88 D3
also known as Bagrax
Boi, Ponta do pt Brazil 207 H10
Boiaçu Brazil 199 F5
Boichoko S. Africa 132 H5
Boigu Island Australia 73 J8
Boikhutso S. Africa 133 K3
Boila Moz. 131 H3
Boileau, Cape Australia 150 C3
Boinu r. Myanmar 78 A3
Boipeba, Ilha i. Brazil 202 E5
Boiro Spain 54 C2
Bois r. Brazil 206 C5
Bois, Lac des l. Canada 166 E1
Bois Blanc Island U.S.A. 173 I5
Bois de Sioux r. U.S.A. 178 C2

► Boise U.S.A. 180 D4
State capital of Idaho.

Boise r. U.S.A. 180 C4
Boise City U.S.A. 178 B4
Boissevain Canada 167 K5
Boite r. Italy 56 E2
Boitumelong S. Africa 133 J4
Boituva Brazil 206 F10
Bojador, Cape W. Sahara see Boujdour
Bojana r. Albania/Yugo. see Bunë
Bojeador, Cape Phil. 74 B2
Bojnik Srbija Yugo. 58 C5
Bojnūrd Iran 100 D2
Bojonegoro Indon. 77 E4
Bojuru Brazil 204 H3
Bokada Dem. Rep. Congo 126 C3
Bokadaban Feng mt. China 89 E4
Bokajan India 97 G4
Bokanda Congo 126 B5
Bokaro India 97 E5
Bokat Indon. 75 B2
Bokatola Dem. Rep. Congo 126 C5
Boké Guinea 124 B4
Bokfontein S. Africa 133 D9
Bokhara r. Australia 147 E2
Bokhara r. Uzbek. see Bukhoro
Boknafjorden sea chan. Norway 45 I4
Boko Congo 126 B6
Boko Dem. Rep. Congo 127 C6
Bokode Dem. Rep. Congo 126 D4
Bokolo Gabon 126 A5
Bokombayevskoye Kyrg. see Bökönbaev
Bökönbaev Kyrg. 103 I4
also known as Bokombayevskoye or Bokonbayevo
Bokonbayevo Kyrg. see Bökönbaev
Bokong Lesotho 133 M6
Bokoro Chad 120 C6
Bokoro Dem. Rep. Congo 126 C3
Bokote Dem. Rep. Congo 126 D5
Bokovskaya Rus. Fed. 41 G6
Bokpyin Myanmar 79 B6
Boksburg S. Africa 133 M3
Boksitogorsk Rus. Fed. 43 O2
Bokspits S. Africa 132 E3
Boktor Rus. Fed. 82 E2
Bokungu Dem. Rep. Congo 126 D5
Bokurdak Turkm. see Bakhardok
Bokwankusu Dem. Rep. Congo 126 D5
Bol Chad 126 B2
Bola, Bahr watercourse Chad 126 C2
Bolaang Indon. 75 B2
Bolaiti Dem. Rep. Congo 126 E5
Bolama Guinea-Bissau 124 B4
Bolan r. Pak. 101 F4
Bolanda, Jebel mt. Sudan 126 E3
Bolaños de Calatrava Spain 54 H6
Bolan Pass Pak. 101 F4
Bolbec France 50 G3
Boldaji Iran 100 B4
Boldu Romania 58 I3
Boldumsaz Turkm. 102 D4
formerly known as Kalinin
Bole China 88 C2
also known as Bortala
Bole Ghana 124 E4
Boleko Dem. Rep. Congo 126 C5
Bolesławiec Poland 49 M4
Bolgar Rus. Fed. 40 I5
also known as Kuybyshev; also spelt Bulgar
Bolgatanga Ghana 125 E4
Bolgatovo Rus. Fed. 43 J5
Bolgrad Ukr. see Bolhrad
Bolhrad Ukr. 41 D7
also spelt Bolgrad
Boli China 82 C3
Boli Sudan 126 E3
Bolia Dem. Rep. Congo 126 C5
Boliden Sweden 44 M2
Bolinao Phil. 74 A2
Bolintin-Vale Romania 58 G4
Bolívar Antioquia Col. 198 B3
Bolívar Cauca Col. 198 B4
Bolívar dept Col. 198 C2
Bolívar Peru 200 A1
Bolívar MO U.S.A. 178 D4
Bolívar NY U.S.A. 176 G3
Bolívar TN U.S.A. 174 B5
Bolívar state Venez. 199 F3
Bolivia Cuba 175 E4

► Bolivia country S. America 200 D4
5th largest country in South America.
world [land shapes] ▶ 12–13
southamerica [countries] ▶ 192–193
southamerica [impacts] ▶ 196–197

Boljevac Srbija Yugo. 58 C5
Bolkhov Rus. Fed. 43 R8
Bolków Poland 49 N5
Bollène France 51 K8
Bollnäs Sweden 45 L3
Bollon Australia 147 E2
Bollstabruk Sweden 44 L3
Bolmen l. Sweden 45 K4
Bolnisi Georgia 107 F2
Bolobo Dem. Rep. Congo 126 C5
Bolod Islands Phil. 74 B5
Bologna Italy 56 D4
historically known as Bononia or Felsina
Bologoye Rus. Fed. 43 M5
Bolognesi Ucayali Peru 200 B2
Bolokanang S. Africa 133 J6
Bolokhovo Rus. Fed. 43 S7
Bolomba Dem. Rep. Congo 126 C4
Bolombo r. Dem. Rep. Congo 126 D4
Bolon' Rus. Fed. see Achan
Bolonchén de Rejón Mex. 185 H4
Bolondo Dem. Rep. Congo 126 B4
Bolondo Equat. Guinea 125 H6
Bolong Phil. 74 B5
Bolongongo Angola 127 C7
Bolotana Sardegna Italy 57 A8
Bolotnoye Rus. Fed. 80 C1
Bolotovo Rus. Fed. 43 R3
Bolovens, Phoupning plat. Laos 79 D5
Bolozo Dem. Rep. Congo 126 B4
Bolpur India 97 E5

Bolsa, Cerro mt. Arg. 204 C3
Bolsena, Lago di l. Italy 56 D6
Bol'shakovo Rus. Fed. 42 C7
Bol'shaya Rus. Fed. 43 U1
Bol'shaya Bereyka Rus. Fed. 43 T9
Bol'shaya Chernigovka Rus. Fed. 102 B1
Bol'shaya Churakovka Kazakh. 103 F1
Bol'shaya Glushitsa Rus. Fed. 102 B1
Bol'shaya Imandra, Ozero l. Rus. Fed. 40 E2
Bol'shaya Kokshaga r. Rus. Fed. 40 H4
Bol'shaya Kosha Rus. Fed. 43 O5
Bol'shaya Rogovaya r. Rus. Fed. 40 L2
Bol'shaya Synya r. Rus. Fed. 40 L2
Bol'shaya Tsarevshchina Rus. Fed. see Volzhskiy
Bol'shaya Usa Rus. Fed. 40 J4
Bol'shaya Vishera Rus. Fed. 43 N3
Bol'shaya Vladimirovka Rus. Fed. 103 I2
also known as Ülken Vladīmīrovka
Bol'shenarymskoye Kazakh. 88 D1
Bol'she-Ploskoye Rus. Fed. 43 Q4
Bol'sheretsk Rus. Fed. 39 P4
Bol'shevik, Ostrov i. Rus. Fed. 39 K2
Bol'shezemel'skaya Tundra lowland Rus. Fed. 40 J2
Bol'shiye Barsuki, Peski des. Kazakh. 102 D3
Bol'shiye Chirki Rus. Fed. 40 H3
Bol'shiye Kozly Rus. Fed. 40 F2
Bol'shiye Medvedki Rus. Fed. 43 S8
Bol'shiye Peshnyye, Ostrova i. Kazakh. 102 B3
formerly known as Peshnyye, Ostrova
Bol'shoy Aksu Kazakh. 103 I4
Bol'shoy Aksuat, Ozero salt l. Kazakh. 103 F2
also known as Aksuat, Ozero
Bol'shoy Anyuy r. Rus. Fed. 39 P3
Bol'shoy Anyuy r. Rus. Fed. 39 Q3
Bol'shoy Begichev, Ostrov i. Rus. Fed. 39 L2
Bol'shoy Berezovyy, Ostrov i. Rus. Fed. 43 J1
Bol'shoy Bukon' Kazakh. 88 C1
Bol'shoye Alekseyevskoye Rus. Fed. 43 T6
Bol'shoye Beresnevo Rus. Fed. 43 N6
Bol'shoye Korovino Rus. Fed. 43 V6
Bol'shoye Mikhaylovskoye Rus. Fed. 43 T5
Bol'shoye Murashkino Rus. Fed. 40 H5
Bol'shoye Ozerko Rus. Fed. 44 P1
Bol'shoye Polpino Rus. Fed. 43 P8
Bol'shoye Popovo Rus. Fed. 43 U9
Bol'shoye Topol'noye, Ozero salt l. Rus. Fed. 103 I1
Bol'shoye Zaborov'ye Rus. Fed. 43 O3
Bol'shoye Zhokovo Rus. Fed. 43 T7
Bol'shoy Ik r. Rus. Fed. 102 C2
Bol'shoy Irgiz r. Rus. Fed. 102 A2
Bol'shoy Kamen' Rus. Fed. 82 D4
Bol'shoy Kavkaz mts Asia/Europe see Caucasus
Bol'shoy Kokovichi Rus. Fed. 43 O1
Bol'shoy Lyakhovskiy, Ostrov i. Rus. Fed. 39 O2
Bol'shoy Porog Rus. Fed. 39 J3
Bol'shoy Shantar, Ostrov i. Rus. Fed. 82 E1
Bol'shoy Tokmak Kyrg. see Tokmak
Bol'shoy Tokmak Ukr. see Tokmak
Bol'shoy Tuder' r. Rus. Fed. 43 M4
Bol'shoy Uzen' r. Kazakh./Rus. Fed. 102 B2
also known as Ülkenözen
Bol'shoy Yug r. Rus. Fed. 43 T2
Bol'shoy Zelenchuk r. Rus. Fed. 107 E1
Bolsward Neth. 48 C2
Bolton Canada 173 N7
Bolton U.K. 47 J10
Boltutino Rus. Fed. 43 N7
Bolu Turkey 106 B2
Bolungarvik Iceland 44 [inset] B2
Boluntay China 84 B4
Boluo China 87 E4
also known as Luoyang
Bolus Head Rep. of Ireland 47 B12
Bolva r. Rus. Fed. 43 P8
Bolvadin Turkey 106 B3
Bolvanskiy Nos, Mys c. Rus. Fed. 40 K1
Bolyarovo Bulg. 58 H6
Bolzano Italy 56 D2
also known as Bozen
Boma Dem. Rep. Congo 127 B6
Bomaderry Australia 147 F3
Bomai China 86 A2
formerly known as Bowo
Bombala Australia 147 F4
Bombarral Port. 54 B5
Bombay India see Mumbai
Bombay N.Z. 152 I5
Bombay Beach U.S.A. 183 I8
Bomberai, Semenanjung pen. Indon. 73 H7
English form Bomberai Peninsula
Bomberai, Semenanjung
Bomberai Peninsula Indon. see Bomberai, Semenanjung
Bombo r. Dem. Rep. Congo 126 B5
Bombo Uganda 128 B4
Bom Comércio Brazil 200 D2
Bom Despacho Brazil 207 H6
Bomdila India 97 G4
Bomi China 80 D4
also known as Bowo or Zhamo
Bomili Dem. Rep. Congo 126 E4
Bom Jardim Brazil 202 D2
Bom Jardim de Minas Brazil 207 I8
Bom Jardim de Goiás Brazil 206 A3
Bom Jesus Piauí Brazil 202 C4
Bom Jesus Rio Grande do Sul Brazil 203 B9
Bom Jesus da Gurgueia, Serra do hills Brazil 202 D4
Bom Jesus da Lapa Brazil 202 D5
Bom Jesus de Goiás Brazil 206 D5
Bom Jesus do Itabapoana Brazil 203 D7
Bømlo i. Norway 45 I4
Bomokandi r. Dem. Rep. Congo 126 E4
Bompas France 51 I10
Bom Retiro Brazil 203 B8
Bom Sucesso Minas Gerais Brazil 207 I8
Bom Sucesso Paraná Brazil 206 B10
Bon, Cap c. Tunisia 123 H1
Bona Alg. see Annaba
Bona, Mount U.S.A. 166 A2
Bonâb Iran 100 A2
Bonaire i. Neth. Antilles 187 F4
Bonandolok Indon. 76 B2
Bonanza Nicaragua 186 B4
Bonaparte r. Canada 166 F5
Bonaparte Archipelago is Australia 150 D2
Bonaparte Lake Canada 166 F5
Bonarbridge U.K. 46 H7
Bonasse Trin. and Tob. 187 H5
Bonavista Canada 169 K3
Bonavista Bay Canada 169 K3
Bon Bon Australia 146 B2
Bondeno Italy 56 D4
Bondo Orientale Dem. Rep. Congo 126 D5
Bondoc Peninsula Phil. 74 B3
Bondokodi Indon. 75 A5
Bondoukou Côte d'Ivoire 124 E4
Bondowoso Indon. 77 F4
Bonduel U.S.A. 172 E6
Bondyuzhskiy Rus. Fed. see Mendeleyevsk
Bône Alg. see Annaba
Bone Indon. 75 B4
Bone, Teluk b. Indon. 75 B4
Bonekraat S. Africa 132 E6
Bone Lake U.S.A. 172 A5
Bonelipu Indon. 75 B3
Bonerate i. Indon. 75 B4
Bonerate, Kepulauan is Indon. 75 B4

▶**Bonete, Cerro** *mt.* Arg. **204** C2
3rd highest mountain in South America.

Bonfim Brazil **207** I7
Bonfim *r.* Brazil **206** A4
Bonfinópolis de Minas Brazil **202** C6
Bonga Eth. **128** C3
Bongabong Phil. **74** B3
Bongaigaon India **97** F4
Bongandanga Dem. Rep. Congo **126** D4
Bongani S. Africa **132** H6
Bongao Phil. **74** A5
Bongba China **89** C5
Bong Co *l.* China **89** E6
Bongka *r.* Indon. **75** B3
Bongo *i.* Phil. **74** C5
Bongo, Massif des *mts* Cent. Afr. Rep. **126** D2
Bongo, Serra do *mts* Angola **127** B7
Bongolava *mts* Madag. **131** [inset] J3
Bongor Chad **126** B2
Bongouanou Côte d'Ivoire **124** D5
Bông Son Vietnam **79** E5
Bonham U.S.A. **179** C5
Bönhamn Sweden **44** L3
Boni Mali **125** E3
Bonifacio *Corse* France **52** D3
Bonifacio, Bocche di *strait* France/Italy *see* Bonifacio, Strait of
Bonifacio, Bouches de *strait* France/Italy *see* Bonifacio, Strait of
Bonifacio, Strait of France/Italy **56** A7
also known as Bonifacio, Bocche di *or* Bonifacio, Bouches de
Boni National Reserve *nature res.* Kenya **128** D5

▶**Bonin Islands** N. Pacific Ocean **220** D4
Part of Japan. Also known as Ogasawara-shotō.

Bonita Springs U.S.A. **175** D7
Bonito *Mato Grosso do Sul* Brazil **201** F5
Bonito *Minas Gerais* Brazil **207** I2
Bonito *r.* Brazil **206** B3
Bonito *r.* Brazil **206** G2

▶**Bonn** Germany **48** E5
Former capital of Germany. Historically known as Bonna.

Bonna Germany *see* **Bonn**
Bonnat France **51** H6
Bonners Ferry U.S.A. **180** C2
Bonnet, Lac du *resr* Canada **167** M5
Bonnet Plume *r.* Canada **166** C1
Bonneval France **50** H4
Bonneville France **51** M6
Bonney, Lake Australia **146** D4
Bonnie Rock Australia **151** B6
Bonny Glen Aboriginal Holding *res.* Australia **149** E3
Bonny Ridge S. Africa **133** N7
Bonnyville Canada **167** I4
Bono *Sardegna* Italy **57** B8
Bōno-misaki *pt* Japan **91** B9
Bonom Mhai *mt.* Vietnam **79** D6
Bononia Italy *see* **Bologna**
Bonorva *Sardegna* Italy **57** A8
Bonoua Côte d'Ivoire **124** E5
Bonpland, Mount N.Z. **153** C12
Bonsall U.S.A. **183** G8
Bonshaw Australia **147** F2
Bontberg *mt.* S. Africa **132** F9
Bonteberg *mts* S. Africa **132** D10
Bontebok National Park S. Africa **132** E11
Bonthe Sierra Leone **124** B5
Bontoc Phil. **74** B2
Bontomatane Indon. **75** B4
Bontosunggu Indon. **75** A4
Bontrand S. Africa **133** N7
Bontrug S. Africa **133** J10
Bonvouloir Islands P.N.G. **149** F1
Bonyhád Hungary **49** P9
Boo Sweden **45** L4
Boo, Kepulauan *is* Indon. **75** D3
Boodie Boodie Range *hills* Australia **151** C5
Bookabie Australia **146** B2
Book Cliffs *ridge* U.S.A. **183** O2
Booker U.S.A. **178** B4
Boola Guinea **124** C4
Booleroo Centre Australia **146** C3
Booligal Australia **147** E3
Boologooro Australia **151** A5
Boomi Australia **147** F2
Boon U.S.A. **172** H6
Boonah Australia **147** G1
Boone *IA* U.S.A. **174** A3
Boone *NC* U.S.A. **176** D9
Boone Lake U.S.A. **176** C9
Boones Mill U.S.A. **176** F8
Booneville *AR* U.S.A. **179** D5
Booneville *KY* U.S.A. **176** B8
Booneville *MS* U.S.A. **174** B5
Boons S. Africa **133** L2
Boonsboro U.S.A. **176** H6
Böön Tsagaan Nuur *salt l.* Mongolia **84** C2
Boonville *CA* U.S.A. **182** A3
Boonville *IN* U.S.A. **174** C4
Boonville *MO* U.S.A. **178** D4
Boopi *r.* Bol. **200** D3
Boorabin National Park Australia **151** C6
Boorama Somalia **128** D2
Booroorban Australia **147** E3
Boorowa Australia **147** F3
Boosaaso Somalia **128** F2
Boothbay Harbor U.S.A. **177** P2
Boothby, Cape Antarctica **223** D2
Boothia, Gulf of Canada **165** K3
Boothia Peninsula Canada **165** J2
Booué Gabon **126** A5
Bopolu Liberia **124** C5
Boppard Germany **48** E5
Boqê China **89** E6
Boqueirão Brazil **204** G3
Boqueirão, Serra do *hills* Brazil **202** C5
Bor Rus. Fed. **40** H4
Bor Sudan **128** A3
Bor Turkey **106** C3
Bor *Srbija* Yugo. **58** D4
Boragi *waterhole* Kenya **128** C5
Borah Peak U.S.A. **180** D3
Borakalalo Nature Reserve S. Africa **133** L2
Boran Kazakh. *see* **Buran**
Boraraigh *i.* U.K. *see* **Boreray**
Borås Sweden **45** K4
Borasambar India **97** D1
Borāzjān Iran **100** B4
Borba Brazil **199** G6
Borba Port. **54** D6
Borbollón, Embalse del *resr* Spain **54** E4
Borbon Phil. **74** C4
Borborema Brazil **206** D8
Borborema, Planalto da *plat.* Brazil **202** E3
Borca Romania **58** G1
Borcea, Bratul *watercourse* Romania **58** I4
Borchalo Georgia *see* **Marneuli**
Borchgrevink Coast Antarctica **223** K2
Borçka Turkey **107** E2
also known as Yeniyol
Borda, Cape Australia **150** C3
Borda da Mata Brazil **207** G9
Bor Dağı *mt.* Turkey **59** K11
Bordeaux France **50** F8
historically known as Burdigala
Bordehi India **96** C5
Bordein Sudan **121** G6
Borden Canada **169** I4
Borden Island Canada **165** H2
Borden Peninsula Canada **165** K2
Bordentown U.S.A. **177** K5
Border Ranges National Park Australia **147** G2
Bordertown Australia **146** D4
Borðeyri Iceland **44** [inset] B2
Bordj Bou Arréridj Alg. **123** G1
Bordj Bounaama Alg. **55** M9
Bordj Flye Ste-Marie Alg. **123** E4
Bordj Messaouda Alg. **123** H3
Bordj Mokhtar Alg. **123** F5
Bordj Omar Driss Alg. *see* Bordj Omer Driss
Bordj Omer Driss Alg. **123** G3
formerly known as Fort Flatters *or* Zaouet el Kahla; *formerly spelt* Bordj Omar Driss
Bordj Zemoura Alg. **55** P8
Borðoy *i.* Faroe Is **46** F1
Bordu Kyrg. **103** H4
also known as Bordunskiy
Bordunskiy Kyrg. *see* **Bordu**
Bordușani Romania **58** I4
Boré Mali **124** E3
Boreas Nunatak Antarctica **223** X2
Borel *r.* Canada **169** G1
Borensberg Sweden **45** K4
Boreray *i.* U.K. **46** D6
also spelt Boraraigh
Borgå Fin. *see* **Porvoo**
Borgafjäll Sweden **44** K2
Borgarfjörður Iceland **44** [inset] D2
Borgarnes Iceland **44** [inset] B2
Børgefjell Nasjonalpark *nat. park* Norway **44** K2
Borger U.S.A. **179** B5
Borgholm Sweden **45** L4
Borgo *Corse* France **51** P10
Borgo a Mozzano Italy **56** C5
Borgomanero Italy **56** A3
Borgo San Dalmazzo Italy **51** N8
Borgo San Lorenzo Italy **56** D5
Borgosesia Italy **56** A3
Borgo Val di Taro Italy **56** B4
Borgo Valsugana Italy **56** D2
Borgsjåbrotet *mt.* Norway **45** J3
Bori India **94** C1
Bori *r.* India **96** B5
Börili Kazakh. *see* **Burli**
Borilovo Rus. Fed. **43** Q8
Borino Bulg. **58** F7
Borinskoye Rus. Fed. **43** U9
Borisoglebsk Rus. Fed. **41** G6
Borisoglebskiy Rus. Fed. **43** U4
Borisov Belarus *see* **Barysaw**
Borisovka Rus. Fed. **41** F6
Borisovo-Sudskoye Rus. Fed. **43** R2
Borispol' Ukr. *see* **Boryspil'**
Bo River Post Sudan **126** E3
Boriziny Madag. **131** [inset] J2
Borja *mts* Bos.-Herz. **56** J4
Borja Peru **198** B6
Borjas Blancas Spain *see* Les Borges Blanques
Borj Bourguiba Tunisia **123** H2
Borjomis Nakrdzali *nature res.* Georgia **107** E2
Borkavichy Belarus **43** J6
Borken Germany **48** D4
Borkenes Norway **44** L1
Borki Rus. Fed. **43** T9
Borkou-Ennedi-Tibesti *pref.* Chad **120** C5
Borkovskaya Rus. Fed. **40** I2
Borkum Germany **48** D2
Borkum *i.* Germany **48** D2
Borlänge Sweden **45** K3
Borlaug Norway **45** I3
Borlu Turkey **106** B3
Borna Germany **49** J4
Born-Berge *hill* Germany **48** H4
Borne Alg. **123** G4

▶**Borneo** *i.* Asia **77** F2
Largest island in Asia and 3rd in the world.
asia [landscapes] ⟶ 62–63

Bornes *mts* France **51** M7
Bornholm *i.* Denmark **45** K5
Bornholmsgattet *strait* Denmark/Sweden **45** K5
Borno *state* Nigeria **125** I4
Bornova Turkey **106** A3
Borobudur *tourist site* Indon. **77** E4
Borodino *Krasnoyarskiy Kray* Rus. Fed. **39** I3
Borodino *Moskovskaya Oblast'* Rus. Fed. **43** Q6
Borodino Ukr. **58** K2
Borodinskoye Rus. Fed. **43** K1
Borodyanka Ukr. **41** D6
Borogontsy Rus. Fed. **39** N3
Borohoro Shan *mts* China **88** C2
Borok Rus. Fed. **43** T3
Boroko Indon. **75** B2
Borok-Sulezhskiy Rus. Fed. **43** R4
Boromo Burkina **124** E4
Boron Mali **124** D3
Boron U.S.A. **182** G7
Borongan Phil. **74** C4
Bororen Australia **149** F5
Borovan Bulg. **58** E5
Borovenka Rus. Fed. **43** O3
Borovichi Rus. Fed. **43** O3
Borovo Selo Croatia **56** K3
Borovoy *Kirovskaya Oblast'* Rus. Fed. **40** I4
Borovoy *Respublika Kareliya* Rus. Fed. **40** E2
Borovoy *Respublika Komi* Rus. Fed. **40** J3
Borovoye Kazakh. **103** G1
Borovsk Rus. Fed. **43** R6
Borovskoy Kazakh. **103** F1
Borrachudo *r.* Brazil **207** H5
Borrazópolis Brazil **206** B10
Borrego Springs U.S.A. **183** H8
Borroloola Australia **148** C3
Børsa Norway **44** J3
Borșa Romania **58** F1
Borșa Romania **53** G2
Borsad India **96** B5
Borsec Romania **58** G2
Borselv Norway **44** N1
Borshchiv Ukr. **41** C6
Borshchovochnyy Khrebet *mts* Rus. Fed. **85** F1
Borsippa *tourist site* Iraq **107** F4
Borskoye Rus. Fed. **102** B1
Börßum Germany **48** H3
Bortala China *see* **Bole**
Bortala He *r.* China **88** C2
Bort-les-Orgues France **51** I7
Bor-Üdzüür Mongolia **84** B2
Borūjen Iran **100** B4
Borūjerd Iran **100** B3
Bor Ul Shan *mts* China **84** C3
Borun Iran **100** D3
Borushtitsa Bulg. **58** G6
Boryspil' Ukr. **41** D6
also spelt Borispol'
Borzna Ukr. **41** E6
Börzsönyi *park* Hungary **49** P8
Borzya Rus. Fed. **85** H1
Borzya *r.* Rus. Fed. **85** G1
Bosa *Sardegna* Italy **57** A8
Bosaga Kazakh. **103** H3
also spelt Bosagha; *formerly known as* Bosaginskiy
Bosagha Kazakh. *see* **Bosaga**
Bosaginskiy Kazakh. *see* **Bosaga**
Bosanska Dubica Bos.-Herz. **56** I3
also known as Kozarska Dubica
Bosanska Gradiška Bos.-Herz. **56** J3
also known as Gradiška
Bosanska Kostajnica Bos.-Herz. **56** I3
also known as Srpska Kostajnica
Bosanska Krupa Bos.-Herz. **56** I4
also known as Krupa *or* Krupa na Uni
Bosanski Brod Bos.-Herz. **56** K3
also known as Srpski Brod
Bosanski Novi Bos.-Herz. **56** I3
also known as Novi Grad
Bosanski Petrovac Bos.-Herz. **56** I4
also known as Petrovac
Bosanski Šamac Bos.-Herz. **56** K3
also known as Šamac
Bosberg *mt.* S. Africa **133** K5
Bosbokrand S. Africa **133** P1
Boscawen U.S.A. **177** N2
Boscawen Island Tonga *see* **Niuatoputopu**
Bosch Arg. **204** F5
Boscobel U.S.A. **172** C7
Bosduifiaagte *salt pan* S. Africa **132** E6
Bose China **86** C4
Bosencheve, Parque Nacional *nat. park* Mex. **185** E5
Boshchakul' Kazakh. *see* **Bozshakol'**
Boshnyakovo Rus. Fed. **82** F2
Boshoek S. Africa **133** L2
Boshof S. Africa **133** J5
Boshruyeh Iran **100** D3
Bosilegrad *Srbija* Yugo. **58** D6
formerly spelt Bosiljgrad
Bosiljgrad *Srbija* Yugo. *see* **Bosilegrad**
Boskol' Kazakh. **103** E1
also spelt Bozköl; *formerly spelt* Buskul'
Boskovice Czech Rep. **49** N6
Boslanti Suriname **199** H3
Bosna *r.* Bos.-Herz. **56** K3
Bosna *hills* Bulg. **58** I6
Bosna i Hercegovina *country* Europe *see* Bosnia-Herzegovina
Bosna Saray Bos.-Herz. *see* **Sarajevo**
▶**Bosnia-Herzegovina** *country* Europe **56** J4
known as Bosna i Hercegovina *in* Bosnian
europe [countries] ⟶ 32–35
Boso Dem. Rep. Congo **126** D4
Bosobogolo Pan *salt pan* Botswana **132** G2
Bosobolo Dem. Rep. Congo **126** C3
Bōsō-hantō *pen.* Japan **91** G7
Bososama Dem. Rep. Congo **126** D3
Bospoort S. Africa **133** K3
▶**Bosporus** *strait* Turkey **106** B2
also known as İstanbul Boğazı
europe [countries] ⟶ 32–33
Bosque Spain **54** C1
Bossaga Turkm. *see* **Basaga**
Bossangoa Cent. Afr. Rep. **126** C3
Bossembélé Cent. Afr. Rep. **126** C3
Bossemptélé Cent. Afr. Rep. *see* **Bossentélé**
Bossentélé Cent. Afr. Rep. **126** C3
formerly spelt Bossemptélé
Bossiekom S. Africa **132** E6
Bossier City U.S.A. **179** D5
Bossiesvlei Namibia **130** C5
Bossuit S. Africa **133** L2
Bossut, Cape Australia **150** C3
Bostan China **89** D4
Bostān Iran **100** A4
Bosten Hu *l.* China **88** D3
also known as Bagrax Hu
Boston U.K. **47** L11

▶**Boston** U.S.A. **177** N3
State capital of Massachusetts.

Boston Creek Canada **173** N2
Boston Mountains U.S.A. **179** D5
Bosut *r.* Croatia **56** L3
Boswell *IN* U.S.A. **172** F10
Boswell *PA* U.S.A. **176** F5
Botad India **96** A5
Botata Liberia **124** C5
Boteå Sweden **44** L3
Boteler Point S. Africa **133** Q3
Boteni Romania **58** G3
Boteti *r.* Botswana **131** E4
Botev *mt.* Bulg. **58** F6
Botevgrad Bulg. **58** E6
Bothaville S. Africa **133** K4
Bothell U.S.A. **180** B3
Bothnia, Gulf of Fin./Sweden **44** L3
Bothwell Australia **147** E5
Bothwell Canada **173** L8
Boticas Port. **54** D3
Botin *mt.* Bos.-Herz. **56** K5
Botkins U.S.A. **176** A5
Botlikh Rus. Fed. **102** A4
Botna *r.* Moldova **58** K2
Botoșani Romania **53** H2
Botou China **85** H4
Bô Trach Vietnam **78** D4
Botro Côte d'Ivoire **124** D5
Botshabelo S. Africa **133** K6
Botsmark Sweden **44** M2
▶**Botswana** *country* Africa **130** D4
formerly known as Bechuanaland
world [population] ⟶ 22–23
africa [countries] ⟶ 114–117
Bottenviken *g.* Fin./Sweden **44** M2
Bottineau U.S.A. **178** B1
Bottle Creek Turks and Caicos Is **187** E2
Bottom Neth. Antilles **187** H3
Bottrop Germany **48** D4
Botucatu Brazil **206** E9
Botumirim Brazil **207** J3
Bouaflé Côte d'Ivoire **124** D5
Bou Ahmed Morocco **54** G9
Bouaké Côte d'Ivoire **124** D5
Boualem Alg. **123** F2
Bouandougou Côte d'Ivoire **124** D4
formerly spelt Buandougou
Bouanga Congo **126** C5
Bouar Cent. Afr. Rep. **126** B3
Bou Arada Tunisia **57** B12
Bouârfa Morocco **123** E2
Bou Aroua Alg. **123** G2
Bouba Ndjida, Parc National de *nat. park* Cameroon **125** I4
Boubin *mt.* Czech Rep. **49** K6
Boû Bleï'îne *well* Mauritania **124** C2
Boubout *well* Alg. **122** D4
Bouca Cent. Afr. Rep. **126** C3
Boucau France **50** E9
Boucaut Bay Australia **148** B2
Bouchette Canada **173** R4
Bouctouche Canada **169** H4
Boudinar Morocco **54** H9
Boû Djébéha *well* Mali **124** E2
Boudoua Cent. Afr. Rep. **126** C3
Boudry Switz. **51** M6
Bouenza *admin. reg.* Congo **126** B6
Bouenza *r.* Congo **126** B6
Boufore Cent. Afr. Rep. **126** C3
Bougainville, Cape Australia **150** D2
Bougainville Island P.N.G. **145** E2
Bougaroûn, Cap *c.* Alg. **123** G1
Boughessa Mali **125** F2
formerly spelt Bouressa
Bougie Alg. *see* **Bejaïa**
Bougoumen Chad **126** B2
Bougouni Mali **124** D4
Bougtob Alg. **123** F2
Boû Guendoûz *well* Mali **124** D2
Bouguirat Alg. **55** L9
Bougzoul Alg. **55** N9
Bouillon Belgium **51** L3
Bouira Alg. **123** F1
Bou Izakarn Morocco **122** C3
Boujdour W. Sahara **122** B4
Bou Kahil, Djebel *mts* Alg. **123** F2
Boukoumbé Benin **125** F4
Boukta Chad **126** C2
Boulder Australia **151** C6
Boulder *CO* U.S.A. **180** F4
Boulder *MT* U.S.A. **180** D3
Boulder *UT* U.S.A. **183** M4
Boulder Canyon *gorge* U.S.A. **183** J5
Boulder City U.S.A. **183** J6
Bou Legmaden, Oued *watercourse* Alg./Morocco **122** C3
Boulemane Morocco **122** D2
Boulemane Morocco **122** D2
Boulevard U.S.A. **183** H9
Boulhaut Morocco *see* **Ben Slimane**
Boulia Australia **148** C4
Boulogne France *see* **Boulogne-sur-Mer**
Boulogne *r.* France **50** E5
Boulogne-Billancourt France **51** I4
Boulogne-sur-Mer France **50** H2
historically known as Gesoriacum; *short form* Boulogne
Bouloù *r.* Cent. Afr. Rep. **126** E3
Boulouba Cent. Afr. Rep. **126** D3
Boulsupari New Caledonia **145** F4
Boulsa Burkina **125** E3
Boultoum Niger **125** H3
Boumango Gabon **126** B5
Boumba *r.* Cameroon **125** I6
Boumbé I *r.* Cent. Afr. Rep **126** B3
Boumerdes Alg. **123** F1
Bouna Côte d'Ivoire **124** E4
Bou Naceur, Jbel *mt.* Morocco **122** E2
Boû Nâga Mauritania **124** B2
Boundary U.S.A. **166** A1
Boundary Peak U.S.A. **182** F4
Boundiali Côte d'Ivoire **124** D4
Boung *r.* Vietnam **79** E4
Boungou *r.* Cent. Afr. Rep. **126** D3
Bountiful U.S.A. **183** M1
Bounty Islands N.Z. **145** G6
Bourail New Caledonia **145** F4
Bourbince *r.* France **51** K6
Bourbon *terr.* Indian Ocean *see* **Réunion**
Bourbon-Lancy France **51** J6
Bourbonne-les-Bains France **51** L5
Bourbriac France **50** C4
Bourem Mali **125** E2
Bouressa Mali *see* **Boughessa**
Bourg France **50** F7
Bourganeuf France **50** H7
Bourg-en-Bresse France **51** L6
Bourges France **51** I5
historically known as Avaricum
Bourgmont Canada **173** P2
Bourgneuf, Baie de *b.* France **50** D5
Bourgogne *admin. reg.* France **51** K5
Bourgoin-Jallieu France **51** L7
Bourg-St-Andéol France **51** K8
Bourg-St-Maurice France **51** M7
Bourke Australia **147** E2
Bourkes Canada **173** M2
Bournemouth U.K. **47** K13
Bouroum-Bouroum Burkina **124** E4
Bourtoutou Chad **126** D2
Bourzanga Burkina **125** E3
Bou Saâda Alg. **123** G2
Bou Salem Tunisia **57** A12
Bouse U.S.A. **183** J8
Bouse Wash *watercourse* U.S.A. **183** J7
Boussé Burkina **125** E3
Bousso Chad **126** C2
Boû Tezâya *well* Mauritania **124** C2
Boutilimit Mauritania **124** B2
Boutougou Fara Senegal **124** B3
Bouvet Island *terr.* S. Atlantic Ocean *see* **Bouvetøya**

▶**Bouvetøya** *terr.* S. Atlantic Ocean **217** O9
Dependency of Norway. English form Bouvet Island.

Boven Kapuas Mountains Indon./Malaysia *see* **Kapuas Hulu, Pegunungan**
Bow *r.* Australia **150** E3
Bow *r. Alta* Canada **167** I5
Bowa China *see* **Muli**
Bowbells U.S.A. **178** B1
Bowden U.S.A. **176** F7
Bowditch *atoll* Tokelau *see* **Fakaofo**
Bowen Arg. **204** D4
Bowen Australia **149** F4
Bowen *r.* Australia **149** E4
Bowen, Mount Australia **147** F4
Bowen Downs Australia **149** E4
Bowen Strait Australia **148** B1
Bowers Mountains Antarctica **223** K2
Bowie *AZ* U.S.A. **183** O9
Bowie *TX* U.S.A. **179** C5
Bow Island Canada **167** I5
Bowkan Iran **100** A2
Bowling Green *KY* U.S.A. **174** C4
Bowling Green *MO* U.S.A. **174** B4
Bowling Green *OH* U.S.A. **176** B4
Bowling Green *VA* U.S.A. **177** H7
Bowling Green Bay Australia **149** E3
Bowling Green Bay National Park Australia **149** E3
Bowman U.S.A. **178** B2
Bowman, Mount Canada **166** F5
Bowman Coast Antarctica **222** T2
Bowman Island Antarctica **223** G2
Bowman Peninsula Antarctica **222** T2
Bowmanville Canada **173** O7
Bown Somalia **128** D2
Bowo China *see* **Bomai**
Bowo China *see* **Bomi**
Bow River Aboriginal Reserve Australia **150** D3
Bowron *r.* Canada **166** F4
Bowron Lake Provincial Park Canada **166** F4
Bowser Lake Canada **166** D3
Boxberg Germany **48** G6
Box Elder U.S.A. **178** B2
Box Elder *r.* U.S.A. **178** B2
Boxholm Sweden **45** K4
Boxing China **85** H4
Boxtel Neth. **48** C4
Boyabat Turkey **106** C2
Boyaca *dept* Col. **198** C3
Boyadzhik Bulg. **58** H6
Boyalıca Turkey **58** K8
Boyalık Turkey *see* **Çiçekdağı**
Boyana *tourist site* Bulg. **58** E6
Boyang China **87** F2
formerly known as Poyang
Boyanovichi Rus. Fed. **43** P8
Boyanovo Bulg. **58** H6
Boyd *r.* Australia **147** G2
Boyd Lagoon *salt flat* Australia **151** D5
Boyd Lake Canada **167** K2
Boydton U.S.A. **176** G9
Boyer *r.* U.S.A. **178** D3
Boyera Dem. Rep. Congo **126** C5
Boyertown U.S.A. **177** J5
Boykins U.S.A. **177** H9
Boyle Canada **167** H4
Boyle Rep. of Ireland **47** D10
Boyne *r. Qld* Australia **149** F4
Boyne *r. Qld* Australia **149** F5
Boyne *r.* Rep. of Ireland **47** F10
Boyne City U.S.A. **173** H5
Boyni Qara Afgh. **101** F2
Boyo Cent. Afr. Rep. **126** D3
Boyoma, Chutes *waterfall* Dem. Rep. Congo *see* **Boyoma Falls**
Boyoma Falls Dem. Rep. Congo **126** E4
also known as Boyoma, Chutes; *formerly known as* Stanley, Chutes
Boysun Uzbek. *see* **Baysun**
Boyuibe Bol. **201** E5
Böyük Hinaldağ *mt.* Azer. **100** A1
Boyup Brook Australia **151** B7
Bozashy Tübegi *pen.* Kazakh. *see* Buzachi, Poluostrov
Bozburun Turkey **106** B3

▶**Bozcaada** *i.* Turkey **106** A3
Most westerly point of Asia. Also known as Tenedos.

Bozdağ *mt.* Turkey **59** H10
Bozdağ *mt.* Turkey **109** H1
Boz Dağları *mts* Turkey **106** A3
Bozdoğan Turkey **106** B3
Bozeman U.S.A. **180** E3
Bozen Italy *see* **Bolzano**
Bozhou China **87** E1
Bozkır Turkey **106** C3
also known as Silistat
Bozköl Kazakh. *see* **Boskol'**
Bozkurt Turkey **59** K11
Bozoum Cent. Afr. Rep. **126** C3
Bozouls France **51** I8
Bozova Turkey **107** D3
also known as Hüvek
Bozovici Romania **58** D4
Bozqūsh, Kūh-e *mts* Iran **100** A2
Bozshakol' Kazakh. **103** H2
formerly spelt Boshchakul'
Boztumsyk Kazakh. **103** F2
Bozüyük Turkey **106** B3
Bozyazı Turkey **108** D1
Bra Italy **51** N8
Brabant Island Antarctica **222** T2
Brač *i.* Croatia **56** I5
Bracara Port. *see* **Braga**
Bracciano Italy **56** E6
Bracciano, Lago di *l.* Italy **56** E6
Bracebridge Canada **168** E4
Brachet, Lac au *l.* Canada **169** G3
Bräcke Sweden **44** K3
Brackettville U.S.A. **179** B6
Bracki Kanal *sea chan.* Croatia **56** I5
Bracknell U.K. **47** L12
Braço Norte *r.* Brazil **201** G2
Brad Romania **58** D2
Bradano *r.* Italy **57** I8
Bradenton U.S.A. **175** D7
Bradford Canada **173** N6
Bradford U.K. **47** K10
Bradford *PA* U.S.A. **176** G4
Bradford *VT* U.S.A. **177** M2
Bradley U.S.A. **172** F9
Bradner U.S.A. **176** B4
Bradshaw U.S.A. **176** D8
Brady U.S.A. **179** C6
Brady Creek *r.* U.S.A. **179** C6
Brady Glacier U.S.A. **166** B3
Braemar U.K. **46** I6
Braga Port. **54** C3
historically known as Bracara
Braga *admin. dist.* Port. **54** C3
Bragado Arg. **204** E4
Bragança Brazil **202** C2
Bragança Port. **54** E3
Bragança *admin. dist.* Port. **54** E3
Bragança Paulista Brazil **206** G9
Brahin Belarus **41** D6
Brahmakund India **97** H4
Brahmanbaria Bangl. **97** F5
Brahmani *r.* India **95** E1
Brahmapur India **95** E2
Brahmaputra *r.* China/India **89** D6
also known as Dihang (India) *or* Yarlung Zangbo (China)
Braidwood Australia **147** F3
Braidwood U.S.A. **172** E9
Brăila Romania **58** I3
Brăilei, Insula Mare a *i.* Romania **58** I4
Braine France **51** J3
Brainerd U.S.A. **178** D2
Braintree U.K. **47** M12
Braithwaite Point Australia **148** B1
Braives Belgium **51** L2
Brak *r.* S. Africa **132** E10
Brak *watercourse* S. Africa **132** C5
Brake (Unterweser) Germany **48** F2
Brâkna *admin. reg.* Mauritania **124** B2
Brakpoort S. Africa **132** H8
Brakspruit S. Africa **133** K3
Brakwater Namibia **130** C4
Bralorne Canada **166** F5
Bramhapuri India **94** C1
Bramming Denmark **45** J5
Brampton Canada **168** E5
Brampton U.K. **47** J9
Bramsche Germany **48** F3
Bramsöfjärden *l.* Sweden **45** L3
Brancaleone Italy **57** I11
Branch Canada **169** K4
Branco *r. Mato Grosso* Brazil **201** E2
Branco *r. Roraima* Brazil **199** F5
Branco *i.* Cape Verde **124** [inset]
Brandberg *mt.* Namibia **130** B4
Brändbo Sweden **45** L3
Brandbu Norway **45** J3
Brande Denmark **45** J5
Brandenburg Germany **49** J3
Brandenburg *land* Germany **49** K3
Brandenburg U.S.A. **174** C4
Brandenburger Wald- und Seengebiet *park* Germany **49** J3
Brandfort S. Africa **133** K5
Brandkop S. Africa **132** D8
Brändö Fin. **45** M3
Brandon Canada **167** L5
Brandon *MS* U.S.A. **175** B5
Brandon *SD* U.S.A. **178** C3
Brandon *VT* U.S.A. **177** L2
Brandon Head Rep. of Ireland **47** B11
Brandon Mountain *hill* Rep. of Ireland **47** B11
Brandonville U.S.A. **176** F6
Brandvlei S. Africa **132** E8
Brandvlei Dam *resr* S. Africa **132** D10
Brandvoll Norway **44** L1
Brani, Pulau *i.* Sing. **76** [inset]
Braniewo Poland **49** Q1
Brännberg Sweden **44** M2
Brannenburg Germany **48** J8
Bransfield Strait Antarctica **222** T2
Brańsk Poland **49** T3
Brantas *r.* Indon. **77** F4
Brantford Canada **168** D5
Brantôme France **50** G7
Brantwood U.S.A. **172** C5
Brás Brazil **199** G5
Brasalje *Kosovo, Srbija* Yugo. **58** C6
Bras d'Or Lake Canada **169** I4
Brasil Brazil **198** D6
Brasil *country* S. America *see* **Brazil**
Brasil, Planalto do *plat.* Brazil **203** D6
Brasilândia *Mato Grosso do Sul* Brazil **206** A8
Brasilândia *Minas Gerais* Brazil **206** E2
Brasilândia *Minas Gerais* Brazil **207** G4
Brasileia Brazil **200** C2

▶**Brasília** Brazil **206** F2
Capital of Brazil.
southamerica [countries] ⟶ 192–193

Brasília de Minas Brazil **202** C6
Brasília Legal Brazil **199** H5
Brasla *r.* Latvia **42** F4
Braslav Belarus *see* **Braslaw**
Braslaw Belarus **42** I6
also spelt Braslav
Brașov Romania **58** G3
formerly known as Orașul Stalin; *historically known as* Kronstadt
Brasovo Rus. Fed. **43** P9
Brassey, Banjaran *mts Sabah* Malaysia **77** G1
Brassey, Mount Australia **148** B4
Brassey Range *hills* Australia **151** C5
Bratan *mt.* Bulg. **58** G6
Bratca Romania **58** D2

▶**Bratislava** Slovakia **49** O7
Capital of Slovakia. Also known as Pozsony; formerly known as Pressburg.

Bratsk Rus. Fed. **80** G1
Bratskoye Vodokhranilishche *resr* Rus. Fed. **80** G1
Brattleboro U.S.A. **177** M3
Brattmon Sweden **45** K3
Brattvåg Norway **44** I3
Bratunac Bos.-Herz. **56** L4
Braulio Carrillo, Parque Nacional *nat. park* Costa Rica **186** C5
Braúnas Brazil **207** K6
Braunau am Inn Austria **49** K7
Braunsbedra Germany **48** I4
Braunschweig Germany **48** H3
historically known as Brunswick
Brava *i.* Cape Verde **124** [inset]
Brave U.S.A. **176** E6
Bråviken *inlet* Sweden **45** L4
Bravo, Cerro *mt.* Bol. **201** D4
Bravo del Norte, Río *r.* Mex./U.S.A. **185** F3
also known as Rio Grande
Brawley U.S.A. **183** I9
Bray Rep. of Ireland **47** F10
also spelt Bré
Bray S. Africa **132** H2
Braye *r.* France **50** G5
Bray Island Canada **165** L3
Bray-sur-Seine France **51** J4
Brazeau *r.* Canada **167** H4
Brazeau, Mount Canada **167** G4

▶**Brazil** *country* S. America **202** B4
Largest country in South America and 5th in the world. Most populous country in South America and 5th in the world. Spelt Brasil in Portuguese.
world [countries] ⟶ 10–11
world [population] ⟶ 22–23
southamerica [countries] ⟶ 192–193

Brazil U.S.A. **174** C4
Brazos *r.* U.S.A. **179** D6

▶**Brazzaville** Congo **126** B6
Capital of Congo.

Brčko Bos.-Herz. **56** K4
Brda *r.* Poland **49** P2
Brdy *hills* Czech Rep. **49** K6
Bré Rep. of Ireland *see* **Bray**
Breakfast Vlei S. Africa **133** K10
Breaksea Sound *inlet* N.Z. **153** A13
Breaksea Spit Australia **149** G5
Bream Bay N.Z. **152** I3
Bream Head N.Z. **152** I3
Bream Tail *c.* N.Z. **152** I4
Breas Chile **204** C2
Breaza Romania **58** G3
Brebes Indon. **77** E4
Brechin U.K. **46** J7
Brecht Belgium **51** K1
Breckenridge *CO* U.S.A. **180** F5
Breckenridge *MN* U.S.A. **178** C2
Breckenridge *TX* U.S.A. **179** C5
Brecknock, Peninsula *pen.* Chile **205** B9
Břeclav Czech Rep. **49** N7
Brecon U.K. **47** I12
also known as Aberhonddu
Brecon Beacons *reg.* U.K. **47** I12
Brecon Beacons National Park U.K. **47** I12
Breda Neth. **48** B4
Bredasdorp S. Africa **132** E11
Bredbo Australia **147** F3
Bredviken Sweden **44** K2
Bredy Rus. Fed. **103** E1
Breede *r.* S. Africa **132** E11
Bregalnica *r.* Macedonia **58** C7
Bregenz Austria **48** G8
Bregovo Bulg. **58** D4
Bréhal France **50** E4
Breiðafjörður *b.* Iceland **44** [inset] A2
Breiðdalsvík Iceland **44** [inset] D2
Breil-sur-Roya France **51** N9
Breipaal S. Africa **133** K7
Breisach am Rhein Germany **48** E7
Breivikbotn Norway **44** M1
Breivikeidet Norway **44** L1
Brejinho de Nazaré Brazil **202** B4
Brejo Brazil **202** D2
Brejo *r.* Brazil **202** D4
Brejo da Porta Brazil **202** C4
Brekstad Norway **44** J3
Bremen Germany **48** F2
Bremen *GA* U.S.A. **175** C5
Bremen *OH* U.S.A. **176** C6
Bremer Bay Australia **151** B7
Bremerhaven Germany **48** F2
Bremer Range *hills* Australia **151** C7
Bremersdorp Swaziland *see* **Manzini**
Bremerton U.S.A. **180** B3
Bremervörde Germany **48** G2
Breń *r.* Poland **49** S5
Brenham U.S.A. **179** C6
Brenna Norway **44** K2
Brennero Italy **56** D2
Brennero, Passo di *pass* Austria/Italy *see* Brenner Pass
Brennerpaß *pass* Austria/Italy *see* Brenner Pass
Brenner Pass *pass* Austria/Italy **48** I9
also known as Brennero, Passo di *or* Brennerpaß
Breno Italy **56** C3
Brenta *r.* Italy **56** E3
Brenta, Gruppo di *mts* Italy **56** C2
Brentwood U.K. **47** M12
Brenzone Italy **56** C3
Brescia Italy **56** C3
historically known as Brixia
Breslau Poland *see* **Wrocław**
Bresle *r.* France **50** H2
Brésolles, Lac *l.* Canada **169** G2
Bressanone Italy **56** D2
Bressay *i.* U.K. **46** K3
Bressuire France **50** F6
Brest Belarus **42** E9
formerly known as Brest-Litovsk *or* Brześć nad Bugiem
Brest France **50** B4
Brest-Litovsk Belarus *see* **Brest**
Brest Oblast *admin. div.* Belarus *see* Brestskaya Voblasts'
Brestovac *Srbija* Yugo. **58** C5
Brestskaya Oblast' *admin. div.* Belarus *see* Brestskaya Voblasts'
Brestskaya Voblasts' *admin. div.* Belarus **42** G9
English form Brest Oblast; *also known as* Brestskaya Oblast'
Bretagne *admin. reg.* France **50** D4
English form Brittany
Bretagne *reg.* France *see* **Brittany**
Bretana Peru **198** C6
Brețcu Romania **58** H2
Breteuil *Haute-Normandie* France **50** G4
Breteuil *Picardie* France **51** I3
Brétigny-sur-Orge France **51** I4
Breton Canada **167** H4
Breton Sound *b.* U.S.A. **175** B6
Bretten Germany **48** F6
Breu *r.* Brazil/Peru **200** B2
Breueh, Pulau *i.* Indon. **76** A1
Brevard U.S.A. **174** D5
Breves Brazil **202** B2
Brewarrina Australia **147** E2
Brewer U.S.A. **177** Q1
Brewerville Liberia **124** C5
Brewster *NE* U.S.A. **178** C3
Brewster *OH* U.S.A. **176** D5
Brewster *WA* U.S.A. **180** C2
Brewster, Kap *c.* Greenland *see* Kangikajik
Brewster, Lake *imp. l.* Australia **147** E3

index

B
C

Brewton U.S.A. **175** C6
Breyten S. Africa **133** N3
Breytovo Rus. Fed. **43** S3
Brezhnev Rus. Fed. see Naberezhnyye Chelny
Brežice Slovenia **56** H3
Breznik Bulg. **58** D6
Breznita-Motru Romania **58** E4
Breznitsa Bulg. **58** E7
Brezno Slovakia **49** Q7
Brezovo Bulg. **58** G6
Brezovo Polje hill Croatia **56** J3
Bria Cent. Afr. Rep. **126** D3
Briakan Rus. Fed. **82** D1
Briançon France **51** I5
Brian Head mt. U.S.A. **183** L4
Briare France **51** I5
Bribie Island Australia **149** G5
Briceni Moldova **41** C6
  formerly spelt Brichany
Brichany Moldova see Briceni
Bricquebec France **50** E3
Bridgehampton U.S.A. **177** M5
Bridgeman U.S.A. **172** H8
Bridgend U.K. **47** I12
  also known as Pen-y-Bont ar Ogwr
Bridgeport AL U.S.A. **174** C5
Bridgeport CA U.S.A. **182** E3
Bridgeport CT U.S.A. **177** L4
Bridgeport MI U.S.A. **173** J7
Bridgeport NE U.S.A. **178** B3
Bridgeport TX U.S.A. **179** C5
Bridger Peak U.S.A. **180** F4
Bridgeton U.S.A. **177** J6
Bridgetown Australia **151** B7
▶**Bridgetown** Barbados **187** I4
  Capital of Barbados.
Bridgetown Canada **169** H4
Bridgeville U.S.A. **177** J7
Bridgewater Australia **147** E5
Bridgewater Canada **169** H4
Bridgewater MA U.S.A. **177** O4
Bridgewater NJ U.S.A. **177** J3
Bridgewater VA U.S.A. **176** G7
Bridgton U.S.A. **177** O1
Bridgwater U.K. **47** I12
Bridgwater Bay U.K. **47** H12
Bridlington U.K. **47** L9
Bridport Australia **147** E5
Bridport U.K. **47** J13
Brie France **51** I4
Briec France **50** C4
Brie-Comte-Robert France **51** I4
Brieg Poland see Brzeg
Brienne-le-Château France **51** K4
Brienzer See l. Switz. **51** N6
Briery Knob mt. U.S.A. **176** E7
Brig Switz. **51** N6
Briggsville U.S.A. **172** D7
Brigham City U.S.A. **180** D4
Brighton Canada **173** P6
Brighton N.Z. **153** E13
Brighton U.K. **47** L13
Brighton CO U.S.A. **180** F5
Brighton IA U.S.A. **172** B9
Brighton MI U.S.A. **173** J8
Brighton NY U.S.A. **176** H2
Brighton WI U.S.A. **176** C7
Brighton Downs Australia **149** D4
Brignoles France **51** M9
Brihuega Spain **55** I4
Brikama Gambia **124** A3
Brillion U.S.A. **172** E6
Brilon Germany **48** F4
Brimley U.S.A. **173** I4
Brimnes Iceland **44** [inset] D2
Brimson U.S.A. **172** B3
Brindisi Italy **57** J8
  historically known as Brundisium
Brinje Croatia **56** H3
Brinkley U.S.A. **174** B5
Brinkworth Australia **146** C3
Brion, Île i. Canada **169** I4
Brionne France **50** G3
Brioude France **51** J7
Brisay Canada **169** G2
▶**Brisbane** Australia **147** G1
  State capital of Queensland and 3rd most populous city in Oceania.
  world [cities] ▶ 24–25
Brisighella Italy **56** D4
Bristol U.K. **47** J12
Bristol CT U.S.A. **177** M4
Bristol FL U.S.A. **175** C6
Bristol NH U.S.A. **177** N2
Bristol RI U.S.A. **177** N4
Bristol TN U.S.A. **176** D9
Bristol VT U.S.A. **177** L1
Bristol Bay U.S.A. **164** C4
Bristol Channel est. U.K. **47** H12
Bristol Lake U.S.A. **183** I7
Bristol Mountains U.S.A. **183** I7
Britânia Brazil **206** B2
Britannia Island New Caledonia see Maré
British Antarctic Territory Antarctica **222** S2
British Columbia prov. Canada **166** F5
British Empire Range mts Canada **165** K1

British Guiana country S. America see Guyana
British Honduras country Central America see Belize
▶**British Indian Ocean Territory** terr. Indian Ocean **218** L6
  United Kingdom Overseas Territory.
  asia [countries] ▶ 64–67
British Solomon Islands country S. Pacific Ocean see Solomon Islands
Brito Godins Angola see Kiwaba N'zogi
Brits S. Africa **133** L2
Britstown S. Africa **132** H7
Brittany admin. reg. France see Bretagne
Brittany reg. France **50** C4
  also known as Bretagne
Britton U.S.A. **178** C2
Brive-la-Gaillarde France **50** H7
Briviesca Spain **55** H2
Brixham U.K. **47** I13
Brixia Italy see Brescia
Brlik Kazakh. see Birlik
Brlik Kazakh. **103** H4
  also spelt Birlik
Brno Czech Rep. **49** N6
  formerly spelt Brünn
Broach India see Bharuch
Broad r. U.S.A. **174** D5
Broadalbin U.S.A. **177** L2
Broad Arrow Australia **151** C6
Broadback r. Canada **168** E3
Broad Bay U.K. **44** F5
  also known as Tuath, Loch a'
Broadford U.K. **46** G6
Broad Law hill U.K. **46** I8
Broadmere Australia **148** B3
Broad Sound sea chan. Australia **149** F4
Broad Sound Channel Australia **149** F4
Broadsound Range hills Australia **149** F4
Broadus U.S.A. **180** F3
Broadview Canada **167** K5
Broadwater U.S.A. **178** B3
Broadway U.S.A. **176** G7
Broadwood N.Z. **152** H3
Broby Sweden **45** K4
Broceni Latvia **42** D5
Brochet Canada **167** K3
Brocken mt. Germany **48** H4
Brockman, Mount Australia **150** B4
Brockport NY U.S.A. **176** H2
Brockport PA U.S.A. **176** G4
Brockton U.S.A. **177** N3
Brockville Canada **168** F4
Brockway U.S.A. **176** G4
Brod Macedonia **58** B8
Broderick Falls Kenya see Webuye
Brodeur Peninsula Canada **165** K2
Brodhead r. Canada **167** L5
Brodhead WI U.S.A. **176** A8
Brodheadsville U.S.A. **177** J5
Brodick U.K. **46** G8
Brodnax U.S.A. **176** G9
Brodnica Poland **49** Q2
Brody Ukr. **41** C6
Broedersput S. Africa **133** J3
Brok r. Poland **49** S3
Broke Inlet Australia **151** B7
Broken Arrow U.S.A. **179** D4
Broken Bay Australia **147** F3
Broken Bow NE U.S.A. **178** C3
Broken Bow OK U.S.A. **179** D5
Broken Bow Reservoir U.S.A. **179** D5
Brokenburg U.S.A. **176** H7
Brokenhead r. Canada **167** L5
Broken Hill Australia **146** D3
Broken Hill Zambia see Kabwe
Brokopondo Suriname **199** H3
Brokopondo Stuwmeer resr Suriname see Professor van Blommestein Meer
Bromberg Poland see Bydgoszcz
Bromnes Norway **44** L1
Bromo Tengger Semeru National Park Indon. **77** F4
Bromsgrove U.K. **47** J11
Brønderslev Denmark **45** J4
Brong-Ahafo admin. reg. Ghana **125** E5
Bronkhorstspruit S. Africa **133** M2
Bronnitsy Rus. Fed. **43** T6
Brønnøysund Norway **44** K2
Bronson FL U.S.A. **175** D6
Bronson MI U.S.A. **173** H9
Bronte Sicilia Italy **57** G11
Brooke U.S.A. **176** H7
Brookfield MO U.S.A. **178** D4
Brookfield WI U.S.A. **172** E7
Brookhaven U.S.A. **175** B6
Brookings OR U.S.A. **180** A4
Brookings SD U.S.A. **178** C2
Brookline U.S.A. **177** N3
Brooklyn U.S.A. **173** I8
Brooklyn Park U.S.A. **174** A2
Brookneal U.S.A. **176** G8
Brooks Canada **167** I5
Brooks ME U.S.A. **177** P1
Brooks WV U.S.A. **176** C8
Brooks, Cape Antarctica **222** T2
Brooks Brook Canada **166** C2
Brooks Range mts U.S.A. **164** E3
Brookston U.S.A. **172** G10
Brooksville FL U.S.A. **175** D6
Brooksville KY U.S.A. **176** A7
Brookton Australia **151** B7
Brookville IN U.S.A. **176** A6
Broom, Loch inlet U.K. **46** G6
Broome Australia **150** C3
Broomehill Australia **151** B7
Broons France **50** D4
Brora U.K. **46** I5
Brora r. U.K. **46** I5
Brøstadbotn Norway **44** L1
Broşteni Romania **58** G1
Brosville U.S.A. **176** F9
Brotas Brazil **206** D9
Brotas de Macaúbas Brazil **202** D5
Brothers U.S.A. **180** B4
Brou France **50** H4
Broughton Island Canada see Qikiqtarjuaq
Broulkou well Chad **120** C5
Brovary Ukr. **41** D6
Brown, Lake salt flat Australia **151** B6
Brown, Mount hill Australia **146** C3
Brown, Point Australia **146** B3
Brown City U.S.A. **173** K7
Brown Creek r. Australia **149** D3
Brown Deer U.S.A. **172** F7
Browne Range hills Australia **151** D5
Brownfield U.S.A. **179** B5
Brown Mountain U.S.A. **183** G6
Brown's Town Jamaica **186** D3
Brownstown U.S.A. **174** C4
Brownsville PA U.S.A. **176** F6
Brownsville TN U.S.A. **174** B5
Brownsville TX U.S.A. **179** C7
Brownsweg Suriname **199** H3
Brownwood U.S.A. **179** C6
Browse Island Australia **150** C2
Brozas Spain **54** E5
Brozha Belarus **43** K9
Bruay-la-Bussière France **51** I2
Bruce MS U.S.A. **175** B5
Bruce WI U.S.A. **172** B5
Bruce, Mount Australia **150** B4
Bruce Peninsula Canada **173** L6
Bruce Peninsula National Park Canada **173** L5
Bruce Rock Australia **151** B6
Bruchsal Germany **48** F6
Bruck an der Leitha Austria **49** N7

Bruck an der Mur Austria **49** M8
Bruges Belgium see Brugge
Brugge Belgium **51** J1
  also spelt Bruges
Bruhagen Norway **44** I3
Bruin KY U.S.A. **176** B7
Bruin PA U.S.A. **176** F4
Bruin Point mt. U.S.A. **183** N2
Brûk, Wādī el watercourse Egypt **108** E7
Brûk Namibia **130** C5
Brukkaros, Mount Namibia **132** B2
Brûlé Canada **166** G4
Brule U.S.A. **172** B4
Brûlé, Lac l. Canada **169** I2
  also known as Burnt Lake
Brumadinho Brazil **207** I7
Brumado Brazil **202** D5
Brumath France **51** N4
Brumer Islands P.N.G. **149** F1
Brumunddal Norway **45** J3
Brú Na Bóinne tourist site Rep. of Ireland **47** F10
Brundisium Italy see Brindisi
Bruneau r. U.S.A. **180** D4
Bruneau, West Fork r. U.S.A. **180** D4
▶**Brunei** country Asia **77** F1
  asia [countries] ▶ 64–67
Brunei Brunei see Bandar Seri Begawan
Brunei Bay Malaysia **77** F1
Brunette Downs Australia **148** B3
Brunette Island Canada **169** K4
Brunflo Sweden **44** K3
Brunico Sardegna Italy **56** D2
Brünn Czech Rep. see Brno
Brunna Sweden **45** L4
Brunner, Lake N.Z. **153** F10
Bruno U.S.A. **172** A4
Brunsbüttel Germany **48** G2
Brunswick Germany see Braunschweig
Brunswick GA U.S.A. **175** D6
Brunswick MD U.S.A. **176** H6
Brunswick ME U.S.A. **177** P2
Brunswick MO U.S.A. **178** D4
Brunswick OH U.S.A. **176** D4
Brunswick, Península de pen. Chile **205** C9
Brunswick Bay Australia **150** D2
Brunswick Head Australia **147** G2
Brunswick Junction Australia **151** A7
Brunswick Lake Canada **168** D3
Bruntál Czech Rep. **49** O6
Brunt Ice Shelf Antarctica **222** W2
Bruny Island Australia **147** E5
Brus Srbija Yugo. **58** C5
Brusa Turkey see Bursa
Brusartsi Bulg. **58** D5
Brush U.S.A. **178** B3
Brushton U.S.A. **177** K1
Brusovo Rus. Fed. **43** Q4
Brusque Brazil **203** B8
Brussel Belgium see Brussels
▶**Brussels** Belgium **51** K2
  Capital of Belgium. Also spelt Brussel or Bruxelles.
  europe [issues] ▶ 34–35
Brusturi-Drăgănești Romania **58** H1
Brusy Poland **49** O2
Bruthen Australia **147** E4
Bruxelles Belgium see Brussels
Bruyères France **51** M4
Bruzual Venez. **198** D2
Bryan OH U.S.A. **176** A4
Bryan TX U.S.A. **179** C6
Bryan, Mount hill Australia **146** C3
Bryan Coast Antarctica **222** S2
Bryansk Rus. Fed. **43** N8
Bryanskaya Oblast' admin. div. Rus. Fed. **43** O8
  English form Bryansk Oblast
Bryansk Oblast admin. div. Rus. Fed. see Bryanskaya Oblast'
Bryanskoye Rus. Fed. **102** A3
Bryant AR U.S.A. **179** D5
Bryant WI U.S.A. **172** D5
Bryant Creek r. U.S.A. **178** D4
Bryant Pond U.S.A. **177** O1
Bryce Canyon National Park U.S.A. **183** L4
Bryce Mountains U.S.A. **183** O8
Bryher i. U.K. **47** N5
Bryne Norway **45** I4
Bryson, Lac l. Canada **173** P4
Bryukhovetskaya Rus. Fed. **41** F7
Brzava r. Yugo. **58** B3
Brzeg Poland **49** O5
  historically known as Brieg
Brzeg Dolny Poland **49** N4
Brześć nad Bugiem Belarus see Brest
Brzozów Poland **49** T6
Bû well Yemen **105** D4
Bua Angola **127** B6
Bua Sweden **45** K4
Bu'aale Somalia **128** D4
Buad i. Phil. **74** C4
Buala Solomon Is **145** E2
Buandougou Côte d'Ivoire see Bouandougou
Buang i. Indon. **76** C2
Buatan Indon. **76** C2
Bū Athlah well Libya **120** C2
Bu'ayj well Saudi Arabia **105** E2
Bu'ayrāt al Ḥasūn Libya **120** B2
Bubanza Burundi **126** F5
Bubi r. Zimbabwe **131** F4
Būbīyān Island Kuwait **107** G5
Bubuan i. Phil. **74** B5
Buca Turkey **59** I10
Bucak Turkey **59** I11
Bucaramanga Col. **198** C3
Bucas Grande i. Phil. **74** C4
Buccaneer Archipelago is Australia **150** C3
Bucegi, Munţii mts Romania **58** G3
Buchan Australia **147** E4
Buchanan Liberia **124** C5
Buchanan MI U.S.A. **172** G9
Buchanan VA U.S.A. **176** F8
Buchanan, Lake salt flat Australia **149** E4
Buchanan, Lake U.S.A. **179** C6
Buchan Gulf Canada **165** L2
Buchans Canada **169** J3

Buckley U.S.A. **172** E10
Buckley Bay Antarctica **223** J2
Buckskin Mountains U.S.A. **183** K7
Bucks Mountain U.S.A. **182** C2
Bucksport U.S.A. **177** Q1
Bučovice Czech Rep. **49** O6
Bucureşti Romania see Bucharest
Bucyrus U.S.A. **176** C5
Bud Norway **44** I3
Buda Rus. Fed. **43** P8
Buda-Kashalyova Belarus **43** L9
Budai park Hungary **49** P8
Budalin Myanmar **78** A3
▶**Budapest** Hungary **49** Q8
  Capital of Hungary. Historically known as Aquincum.
Budaun India **96** C3
Budayyi'ah well Saudi Arabia **104** C3
Bud Bud Somalia **128** E3
Buddi Eth. **128** D3
Buddusò Sardegna Italy **57** B8
Bude U.K. **47** H13
Budennovsk Rus. Fed. **41** H7
Buderim Australia **149** G5
Budeşti Romania **58** H4
Budhiya, Gebel hills Egypt **108** E8
Budogoshch' Rus. Fed. **43** N2
Budoni Sardegna Italy **57** B8
Budszentmihály Hungary see Tiszavasvári
Budü', Sabkhat al salt pan Saudi Arabia **105** E3
Budureasa Romania **58** D2
Budva Crna Gora Yugo. **56** K6
Budweis Czech Rep. see České Budějovice
Budzilava Belarus **43** K6
Buea Cameroon **125** H5
Buech r. France **51** L8
Buellton U.S.A. **182** D7
Buena Esperanza Arg. **204** D4
Buenaventura Col. **198** B4
Buenaventura Mex. **184** D2
Buena Vista Bol. **201** E4
Buenavista Mex. **185** E5
Buena Vista i. N. Mariana Is see Tinian
Buenavista Phil. **74** B3
Buena Vista CO U.S.A. **180** F5
Buena Vista GA U.S.A. **175** C5
Buena Vista VA U.S.A. **176** F8
Buena Vista, Bahía de b. Cuba **186** D2
Buendia, Embalse de resr Spain **55** I4
Buenga r. Angola **127** B6
Buengas Angola **127** B6
  formerly known as Nova Esperança
Buenópolis Brazil **203** C6
▶**Buenos Aires** Arg. **204** F4
  Capital of Argentina. 2nd most populous city in South America and 10th in the world.
  world [cities] ▶ 24–25
Buenos Aires prov. Arg. **204** E5
Buenos Aires Brazil **200** D2
Buenos Aires Amazonas Col. **198** C5
Buenos Aires Guaviare Col. **198** C4
Buenos Aires Costa Rica **186** C4
Buenos Aires, Lago l. Arg./Chile **205** B7
Buenos Aires National Wildlife Refuge nature res. U.S.A. **181** E7
Buen Pasto Arg. **205** C7
Buen Tiempo, Cabo c. Arg. **205** C8
Buerarema Brazil **202** E5
Buesaco Col. **198** B4
Bueu Spain **54** C2
Buey, Cabeza del mt. Spain **55** H6
Búfalo Mex. **184** D3
Buffalo r. Canada **167** H2
Buffalo MO U.S.A. **178** D4
Buffalo NY U.S.A. **176** D6
Buffalo OK U.S.A. **178** C4
Buffalo SD U.S.A. **178** B2
Buffalo TX U.S.A. **179** C6
Buffalo WY U.S.A. **180** F3
Buffalo r. AR U.S.A. **179** D4
Buffalo r. TN U.S.A. **174** C5
Buffalo r. WI U.S.A. **172** B6
Buffalo Head Hills Canada **167** G3
Buffalo Head Prairie Canada **167** G3
Buffalo Hump mt. U.S.A. **180** D3
Buffalo Lake Alta Canada **167** H4
Buffalo Lake N.W.T. Canada **167** H2
Buffalo Narrows Canada **167** I4
Buffalo Range Zimbabwe **131** F4
Buffalo Valley U.S.A. **183** G1
Buffels r. Kwazulu-Natal S. Africa **133** O5
Buffels r. W. Cape S. Africa **132** E10
Buffels watercourse S. Africa **132** B6
Buffels Drift S. Africa **131** E4
Buford U.S.A. **175** C5
Buftea Romania **58** G4
Bug r. Poland **49** U4
Buga Col. **198** B4
Buga Mongolia **84** B2
Bugala Island Uganda **128** B5
Bugana Nigeria **125** H4
Bugant Mongolia **85** E1
Bugarach, Pic de mt. France **51** I10
Bugaz Ukr. see Zatoka
Bugdayli Turkm. **102** C5
Bugeat France **51** H7
Bugel, Tanjung pt Indon. **77** E4
Bugojno Bos.-Herz. **56** J4
Bugrino Rus. Fed. **40** I1
Bugsuk i. Phil. **74** A4
Bugt China **85** I1
Bugu'ma Rus. Fed. **40** J5
Bugun' Kazakh. **103** F5
Bügür China see Luntai
Buguruslan Rus. Fed. **41** J5
Būhābād Iran **100** C4
Buharkent Turkey **59** J11
Buhera Zimbabwe **131** F3
Buh He r. China **84** C4
Buhi Phil. **74** B3
Buhl ID U.S.A. **180** D4
Buhl MN U.S.A. **172** A3
Buhoci Romania **58** H2
Buhuşi Romania **58** H2
Buia Italy **56** F2
Buick U.S.A. **178** D4
Builth Wells U.K. **47** I11
Buin P.N.G. **145** E2
Bui National Park Ghana **124** E4
Buinsk Rus. Fed. **40** I5
Bu'in Zahrā Iran **100** B3
Buir Nur l. Mongolia **85** H2
Buitepos Namibia **130** C4
Bũyũdžiai Lith. **42** G7
Bujalance Spain **55** H7
Bujanovac Srbija Yugo. **58** C6
Bujaru Romania **58** H5
▶**Bujumbura** Burundi **126** F5
  Capital of Burundi. Formerly known as Usumbura.
Buk Poland **49** N3

Bukachacha Rus. Fed. **81** J2
Buka Island P.N.G. **145** E2
Bukama Dem. Rep. Congo **127** E7
Bukan' Rus. Fed. **43** P8
Būkand Iran **100** C4
Bukanskoye Rus. Fed. **103** J1
Bukantau, Gory hills Uzbek. **103** E4
Bukavu Dem. Rep. Congo **126** F5
  formerly known as Costermansville
Bukedi Dem. Rep. Congo **127** C6
Bukene Tanz. **129** B6
Bukeya Dem. Rep. Congo **127** E7
Bukhara Uzbek. **103** F5
  also spelt Bukhoro
Bukhara Oblast admin. div. Uzbek. see Bukharskaya Oblast'
Bukharskaya Oblast' admin. div. Uzbek. **103** E4
  English form Bukhara Oblast; also known as Bukhoro Wiloyati
Bukhava Belarus **43** K9
Bukhoro Uzbek. see Bukhara
Bukhoro Wiloyati admin. div. Uzbek. see Bukharskaya Oblast'
Bukide i. Indon. **75** C2
Bukima Tanz. **128** B5
Bukit Baka Bukit Raya National Park Indon. **77** F3
Bukit Timah Sing. **76** [inset]
Bukit Timah hill Sing. **76** [inset]
Bukittinggi Indon. **76** C3
  also known as Fort de Kock
Bükk hills Hungary **49** R7
Bukkapatnam India **94** C3
Bükki nat. park Hungary **49** R7
Bükkszérc Hungary **49** R8
Bukoba Tanz. **128** A5
Bukonys Lith. **42** F6
Bukowa r. Poland **49** T5
Bukowo, Jezioro lag. Poland **49** N1
Bükreş Romania see Bucharest
Buku, Tanjung pt Indon. **76** D3
Bula Guinea-Bissau **124** B3
Bula Indon. **73** H7
Bülach Switz. **51** O5
Bulag Mongolia **85** F1
Bulagtay Mongolia **85** E1
Bulahdelal Australia **147** G3
Bulalacao i. Phil. **74** B4
Bulan Phil. **74** B3
Bulan i. Phil. **74** B3
Bulancak Turkey **107** D2
Bulandshahr India **96** C3
Bulanık Turkey **107** E3
Bulanovo Rus. Fed. **102** C1
Bulava Rus. Fed. **82** F2
Bulawa, Gunung mt. Indon. **75** B2
Bulawayo Zimbabwe **131** F4
Bulbula waterhole Kenya **128** C5
Buldan Turkey **106** B3
Buldana India **96** C5
Buldibuyo Peru **200** A2
Buleda reg. Pak. **101** E5
Bulembu Swaziland **133** P2
  formerly known as Havelock
Bulgan Bulgan Mongolia **84** B2
Bulgan Hovd Mongolia **84** A2
  formerly known as Darvi
Bulgan Hövsgöl Mongolia **84** D1
Bulgan Ömnögovi Mongolia **84** D2
Bulgan Övörhangay Mongolia **84** D1
Bulgan prov. Mongolia **84** D1
Bulgan r. Mongolia **84** A2
Bulgar Rus. Fed. see Bolgar
Bülgarevo Bulg. **58** I5
▶**Bulgaria** country Europe **58** F6
  spelt Bŭlgariya in Bulgarian
  europe [countries] ▶ 32–35
Bŭlgariya country Europe see Bulgaria
Bulghah Saudi Arabia **104** C2
Buli Indon. **75** D2
Buli, Teluk b. Indon. **75** D2
Buliluyan, Cape Phil. **74** A4
Bulkley Ranges mts Canada **166** D4
Bullaque r. Spain **54** G6
Bullas Spain **55** J6
Bullaxaar Somalia **128** E2
Bulle Switz. **51** N6
Bullea, Lake salt flat Australia **146** C2
Bullen r. Canada **167** K1
Buller r. N.Z. **153** F9
Bulleringa National Park Australia **149** D3
Bullfinch Australia **151** B6
Bullhead City U.S.A. **183** J6
Bullion Mountains U.S.A. **183** H7
Bullmark Sweden **44** M2
Bullo r. Australia **148** A2
Bulloo watercourse Australia **147** D2
Bulloo Downs Australia **147** D2
Bulloo Lake salt flat Australia **147** D2
Bulls N.Z. **152** J8
Bull Shoals Lake U.S.A. **179** D4
Büllsport Namibia **130** C4
Bully Choop Mountain U.S.A. **182** B1
Bulman Australia **148** B2
Bulman Gorge Australia **148** B2
Bulmer Lake Canada **166** F2
Buloh, Pulau i. Sing. **76** [inset]
Buloke, Lake dry lake Australia **147** D4
Bulolo P.N.G. **73** K8
Bulqizë Albania **58** B7
Bultfontein S. Africa **133** K5
Bulu, Gunung mt. Indon. **77** G2
Buluan Phil. **74** C5
Bulukumba Indon. **75** B4
Bulun Rus. Fed. **39** M2
Bulungu Kasai Occidental Dem. Rep. Congo **126** C6
Bulungu Kasai Occidental Dem. Rep. Congo **127** C6
Bulunqur Uzbek. **103** F5
  formerly known as Krasnogvardeysk
Bulusan Phil. **74** C3
Bulwer S. Africa **133** N5
Bulwark Canada **167** H4
Bumba Bandundu Dem. Rep. Congo **127** C6
Bumba Équateur Dem. Rep. Congo **126** D4
Bumbah, Khalīj b. Libya **120** D1
Bumbat Mongolia **84** B2
Bumbeşti-Jiu Romania **58** E3
Bumbuna Sierra Leone **124** C4
Bumhkang Myanmar **78** B2
Bumpha Bum mt. Myanmar **78** B2
Buna Dem. Rep. Congo **126** C5
Buna Kenya **128** C4
Bunazi Tanz. **128** A5
Bunbury Australia **151** A7
Bunclody Rep. of Ireland **47** F11
  formerly known as Newtownbarry
Buncrana Rep. of Ireland **47** E8
Bunda Tanz. **128** B5
Bundaberg Australia **149** G5
Bundaleer Australia **147** E2
Bundey watercourse Australia **148** B3
Bundi India **96** B4
Bundibugyo Uganda **128** A4
Bundjalung National Park Australia **147** G2
Bundoran Rep. of Ireland **47** D9
Bundu India **97** E5
Bunduqiya Sudan **126** F3
Bunë r. Albania/Yugo. **58** A7
Buner r. Nigeria **125** H3
Bunga r. Nigeria **125** H3
Bungalaut, Selat sea chan. Indon. **76** B3

Bung Boraphet l. Thai. **79** C5
Bungendore Australia **147** F3
Bunger Hills Antarctica **223** G2
Bungi Indon. **75** B4
Bungil Creek r. Australia **149** F5
Bungle Bungle National Park Australia see Purnululu National Park
Bungo Angola **127** B6
Bungoma Kenya **128** B4
Bungo-suidō sea chan. Japan **91** C8
Bungo-takada Japan **91** B8
Bunguran, Pulau is Indon. see Natuna, Kepulauan
Bunguran, Pulau i. Indon. see Natuna Besar
Bunia Dem. Rep. Congo **126** F4
Buningonia well Australia **151** C6
Bunji Jammu and Kashmir **96** B2
Bunker Group atolls Australia **149** G4
Bunkie U.S.A. **179** D6
Bunkris Sweden **45** K3
Bunnell U.S.A. **175** D6
Bunnythorpe N.Z. **152** J8
Buñol Spain **55** K5
Bünsom China **89** C6
Bunsuru watercourse Nigeria **125** G3
Buntok Indon. **77** F3
Buntokecil Indon. **77** F3
Bununu Nigeria **125** G3
Bunya Mountains National Park Australia **149** F5
Bünyan Turkey **106** C3
Bünyu i. Indon. **77** G2
Bunza Nigeria **125** G3
Buoač Bos.-Herz. **56** J4
Buoddobohki Fin. see Patoniva
Buôn Mê Thuột Vietnam **79** E5
Buorkhaya, Guba b. Rus. Fed. **39** N2
Bup r. China **89** D6
Buqayq Saudi Arabia see Abqaiq
Buqbuq Egypt **120** D1
Buqtyrma Bögeni resr Kazakh. see Bukhtarminskoye Vodokhranilishche
Bura Kenya **128** C5
Buraan Somalia **128** F2
Burakin Australia **151** B6
Buram Sudan **126** E2
Buran Kazakh. **88** D1
  also spelt Boran
Buran Darat reef Sing. **76** [inset]
Buranhaém r. Brazil **207** N3
Burannoye Rus. Fed. **102** C2
Burano r. Italy **56** E5
Burao Somalia **128** E2
Burauen Phil. **74** C4
Buraydah Saudi Arabia **104** C2
Burayevo Rus. Fed. **40** J5
Burbach Germany **48** F5
Burbank U.S.A. **182** F7
Burchell Lake Canada **172** C2
Burcher Australia **147** E3
Burdalyk Turkm. **103** F5
Burdekin r. Australia **149** E3
Burdekin Falls Australia **149** E4
Burdigala France see Bordeaux
Burdur Turkey **106** B3
Burdur Gölü l. Turkey **106** B3
Burdwan India see Barddhaman
Burê Eth. **128** C2
Bure r. U.K. **47** N11
Bureå Sweden **44** M2
Bureinskiy Khrebet mts Rus. Fed. **82** D2
  English form Bureya Range
Bureiqa well Sudan **121** F5
Bürenhayrhan Mongolia **84** A2
  formerly known as Bulgan
Bürentsogt Mongolia **85** F2
Bureya r. Rus. Fed. **82** C2
Bureya-Pristan' Rus. Fed. see Novobureyskiy
Bureya Range mts Rus. Fed. see Bureinskiy Khrebet
Bureinski Zapovednik nature res. Rus. Fed. **82** D2
Burgaltay Mongolia **84** E1
Burgas Bulg. **58** I6
Burgaw U.S.A. **174** E5
Burg bei Magdeburg Germany **48** I3
Burgdorf Niedersachsen Germany **48** H3
Burgdorf Niedersachsen Germany **48** H3
Burgdorf Switz. **51** N5
Burg el 'Arab Egypt **108** A7
Burgeo Canada **169** J4
Burgersdorp S. Africa **133** K7
Burgersfort S. Africa **133** N1
Burgerville S. Africa **133** I7
Burges, Mount hill Australia **151** C6
Burgess U.S.A. **177** I8
Burget Tuyur waterhole Sudan **121** E4
Burghausen Germany **49** J7
Burghūth, Sabkhat al salt l. Syria **109** M3
Burgin U.S.A. **176** A8
Burglengenfeld Germany **48** J6
Burg Migheizil Egypt **108** D9
Burgos Mex. **185** F3
Burgos Spain **55** H2
Burgsvik Sweden **45** L4
Burhabalanga r. India **97** E5
Burhan Budai Shan mts China **84** B5
Burhaniye Turkey **106** A3
Burhanpur India **96** C5
Burhar-Dhanpuri India **97** D5
Burhave (Butjadingen) Germany **48** F2
Burhi Gandak r. India **97** E4
Buri Brazil **206** E10
Burias i. Phil. **74** B3
Buriat-Mongol Republic aut. rep. Rus. Fed. see Buryatiya, Respublika
Buribay Rus. Fed. **102** D2
Burica, Punta pt Costa Rica **186** C4
Burin Canada **169** K4
Burin Peninsula Canada **169** K4
Buriram Thai. **79** C5
Buritama Brazil **206** D8
Buriti Brazil **202** D2
Buriti r. Brazil **201** F3
Buriti Alegre Brazil **206** D5
Buriti Bravo Brazil **202** D4
Buritirama Brazil **202** D4
Buritis Brazil **206** F2
Buritizeiro Brazil **207** I4
Burjassot Spain **55** K5
Burkan-Suu r. Kyrg. **103** I4
  also known as Buurakan
Burkburnett U.S.A. **179** C5
Burke watercourse Australia **149** C4
Burke U.S.A. **178** C3
Burke Channel Canada **166** E4
Burke Island Antarctica **222** Q2
Burke Pass N.Z. **153** E12
Burkesville U.S.A. **174** C4
Burketown Australia **148** C3
Burkeville U.S.A. **176** G8
Burkhala Rus. Fed. **39** O3
▶**Burkina** country Africa **125** E3
  also spelt Burkina Faso; formerly known as Upper Volta or Haute-Volta; long form Burkina Faso
  africa [countries] ▶ 114–117
Burkina Faso country Africa see Burkina
Burk's Falls Canada **168** E4
Burla Rus. Fed. **103** I1
Burley U.S.A. **180** D4
Burli Kazakh. **102** C2
  also spelt Börili
Burlin Kazakh. **102** C2
Burlington Canada **168** E5
Burlington CO U.S.A. **178** B4
Burlington IA U.S.A. **174** B3
Burlington KS U.S.A. **178** D4
Burlington NC U.S.A. **176** F9
Burlington VT U.S.A. **177** L1

Burlington *WA* U.S.A. **180** B2
Burlington *WI* U.S.A. **172** E8
Burly Rus. Fed. **40** K5
Burma *country* Asia *see* Myanmar
Burmakino Rus. Fed. **43** V4
Burnaby Canada **166** F5
Burnet U.S.A. **179** C6
Burnett *r.* Australia **149** G5
Burney U.S.A. **182** C1
Burney, Monte *vol.* Chile **205** B9
Burnham U.S.A. **177** P1
Burnie Australia **147** E5
Burning Springs U.S.A. **176** B8
Burnley U.K. **47** J10
Burnoye Kazakh. *see*
  Bauyrzhan Momysh-Uly
Burns U.S.A. **180** C4
Burnside *r.* Canada **167** I1
Burnside U.S.A. **176** A9
Burnside, Lake *salt flat* Australia **151** C5
Burns Junction U.S.A. **180** C4
Burns Lake Canada **166** E4
Burnsville U.S.A. **176** E7
Burnt *r.* U.S.A. **180** C3
Burnt Lake Canada *see* Brûlé, Lac
Burntwood *r.* Canada **167** L4
Burntwood Lake Canada **167** K4
Burog Co *l.* China **89** D5
Buron *r.* Canada **169** G1
Burovoy Uzbek. **103** E4
Burqin China **88** D2
Burqin *r.* China **88** D2
Burqu' Jordan **109** J5
Burra Australia **146** C3
Burra *i.* U.K. **46** K3
Burrel Albania **58** B7
Burrel *i.* **182** E5
Burren *hills* Rep. of Ireland **47** C10
Burrendong Reservoir Australia **147** F3
Burren Junction Australia **147** F2
Burriana Spain **55** K5
Burrinjuck Reservoir Australia **147** F3
Burro, Serranías del *mts* Mex. **185** E2
Burr Oak U.S.A. **172** B7
Burr Oak Reservoir U.S.A. **176** C6
Burrow Creek *watercourse* Australia **183** K7
Burrow Head U.K. **47** H9
Burruyacú Arg. **204** D2
Bursa Turkey **106** B2
  historically known as Brusa *or* Prusa
Bursa *prov.* Turkey **59** J8
Bûr Safâga Egypt **121** G3
Bûr Sa'îd Egypt *see* Port Said
Bûr Sa'îd *governorate* Egypt **108** D6
Bursinskoye Vodokhranilishche *resr*
  Rus. Fed. **82** G2
Bûr Sûdân Sudan *see* Port Sudan
Bur Lake U.S.A. **173** I5
Burton U.K. **173** J8
Burton, Lac *l.* Canada **168** E2
Burton upon Trent U.K. **47** K11
Burträsk Sweden **44** M2
Burtundy Australia **147** D3
Burt Well Australia **148** B4
Buru *i.* Indon. **75** C3
Burubaytal Kazakh. **88** A2
  also known as Bürylbaytal
Burullus, Bahra el *lag.* Egypt *see*
  Burullus, Lake
Burullus, Lake *lag.* Egypt **108** B5
  also known as Burullus, Bahra el
Burultokay China *see* Fuhai
Burûn, Râs *pt* Egypt **108** E6
▶Burundi *country* Africa **126** F5
  formerly known as Urundi
  africa [countries] ➡ 114–117
Burunniy Rus. Fed. *see* Tsagan Aman
Bururi Burundi **126** F5
Burwash Landing Canada **166** B2
Burwell U.S.A. **178** C3
Burwick U.K. **46** J5
Buryatia, *aut. rep.* Rus. Fed. *see*
  Buryatiya, Respublika
Buryatiya, Respublika *aut. rep.* Rus. Fed.
  84 D1
  English form Buryatia; *formerly known as*
  Buriat-Mongol Republic *or* Buryatskaya
  Mongolskaya A.S.S.R.
Buryatskaya Mongolskaya A.S.S.R.
  aut. rep. Rus. Fed. *see*
  Buryatiya, Respublika
Bürylbaytal Kazakh. *see* Burubaytal
Buryn' Ukr. **41** E6
Burynshyk Kazakh. **102** B3
Bury St Edmunds U.K. **47** M11
Burzil Pass Jammu and Kashmir **96** B2
Busalla Italy **56** A4
Busan S. Korea *see* Pusan
Bûs'ân Yemen **104** C5
Busan Bay Phil. **74** B3
Busanga Dem. Rep. Congo **126** D5
Busca Italy **56** A4
Buseire Syria *see* Al Buşayrah
Büsheir Iran **100** B4
  formerly spelt Bushire
Büshehr *prov.* Iran **100** B4
Bushenyi Uganda **128** A5
Bushire Iran *see* Büshehr
Bushkill U.S.A. **177** J4
Bushnell *FL* U.S.A. **175** D6
Bushnell *IL* U.S.A. **172** C9
Bushuika Rus. Fed. **43** V2
Busia Kenya **128** B4
Busing, Pulau *i.* Sing. **76** [inset]
Businga Dem. Rep. Congo **126** D4
Busira *r.* Dem. Rep. Congo **126** C5
Buskerud *county* Norway **45** J3
Busko-Zdrój Poland **49** R5
Buskul' Kazakh. *see* Boskol'
Busobuso Indon. **75** D2
Busselton Australia **151** A7
Bussol', Proliv *strait* Rus. Fed. **81** Q3
Bustamante, Mex. **185** E3
Buşteni Romania **58** H3
Bustillos, Lago *l.* Mex. **184** D2
Busto Arsizio Italy **56** A3
Busuanga Phil. **74** A3
Busuanga *i.* Phil. **74** A3
Busu-Djanoa Dem. Rep. Congo **126** D4
Büsum Germany **48** F1
Busu Modanda Dem. Rep. Congo **126** C4
Buta Dem. Rep. Congo **126** E4
Butajīra Eth. **128** C3
Butang Group *is* Thai. **79** B7
Buta Ranquil Arg. **204** C5
Butare Rwanda **126** F5
  formerly known as Astrida
Butaritari *atoll* Kiribati **220** F6
  also known as Makin
Butauanan *pt* Phil. **74** B3
Bute *i.* U.K. **46** G8
Butedale Canada **166** D4
Bute Inlet Canada **166** F5
Butembo Dem. Rep. Congo **126** F4
Butha Buthe Lesotho **133** M5
Butha Qi China *see* Zalantun
Buthidaung Myanmar **78** A3
Butiá Brazil **203** B9
Butiaba Uganda **128** A4
Butler *AL* U.S.A. **175** B5
Butler *GA* U.S.A. **175** D5
Butler *IN* U.S.A. **176** A4
Butler *KY* U.S.A. **176** A7
Butler *MO* U.S.A. **178** D4
Butler *PA* U.S.A. **176** F4
Buton *i.* Indon. **75** B4
Buton, Selat *sea chan.* Indon. **75** B4
Butrimonys Lith. **42** G7
Butrint, Liqeni i *l.* Albania **59** B9

Buttahatchee *r.* U.S.A. **175** B5
Butte *MT* U.S.A. **180** D3
Butte *NE* U.S.A. **178** C3
Butternut U.S.A. **172** C4
Butterworth Malaysia **76** C1
Butterworth S. Africa **133** M9
Buttes, Sierra *mt.* U.S.A. **182** C2
Butt of Lewis *hd* U.K. **46** F5
  also known as Robhanais, Rubha
Button Bay Canada **167** M3
Button Islands Canada **165** M3
Buttonwillow U.S.A. **182** E6
Butuan Phil. **74** C4
Butuan Bay Phil. **74** C4
Butuo China **86** B3
  also known as Temuli
Buturlinovka Rus. Fed. **41** G6
Butwal Nepal **97** D4
Butzbach Germany **48** F5
Bützow Germany **49** J2
Buubaarde Somalia **128** E4
Buulobarde Somalia **128** E4
Buurakan *r.* Kyrg. *see* Burkan-Suu
Buur Gaabo Somalia **128** D5
Buurhabaka Somalia **128** E4
Buvåg Norway **44** K1
Buvuma Island Uganda **128** B4
Buwārah, Jabal *mt.* Saudi Arabia **108** F9
Buwāţah Saudi Arabia **104** B2
Buxar India **97** E4
Buxtehude Germany **48** G2
Buxton U.K. **47** K10
Buy Rus. Fed. **40** J4
Buy *r.* Rus. Fed. **40** J4
Buyant Bayanhongor Mongolia **84** C2
Buyant Bayan-Ölgiy Mongolia **84** A1
Buyant Hentiy Mongolia **85** F2
Buyant Gol *r.* Mongolia **84** A1
Buyant Gol *r.* Mongolia **84** C1
Buyant-Ovoo Mongolia **85** E2
Buyant-Uhaa Mongolia **85** F2
Buyck U.S.A. **172** A2
Buynaksk Rus. Fed. **102** A4
Buyo Côte d'Ivoire **124** D5
Buyo, Lac de *l.* Côte d'Ivoire **124** D5
Buyuan *Jiang r.* China **86** B4
Büyükada *i.* Turkey **58** I5
Büyük Egri Dağ *mt.* Turkey **108** E1
Büyükkarıştıran Turkey **58** I7
Büyükkonak Turkey **59** K11
Büyükmenderes *r.* Turkey **106** A3
Büyükorhan Turkey **59** J9
Büyükşahinbey Turkey **109** I1
Buyun Shan *mt.* China **85** I3
Buzachi, Poluostrov *pen.* Kazakh. **102** B3
  also known as Bozashy Tübegi
Buzançais France **50** H6
Buzău Romania **58** H3
Buzău *r.* Romania **58** H3
Buzaymah *oasis* Libya **120** D3
Buzha *r.* Rus. Fed. **43** V6
Bûzi Moz. **131** G3
Búzi *r.* Moz. **131** G3
Buziaş Romania **58** C3
Búzios, Cabo dos *c.* Brazil **207** L9
Búzios, Ilha dos *i.* Brazil **207** H10
Büzmeyin Turkm. *see* Byuzmeyin
Buzuluk Rus. Fed. **102** C1
Buzuluk *r.* Rus. Fed. **41** G6
Buzzards Bay U.S.A. **177** O4
Bwagaoia P.N.G. **149** G1
Byadgi India **94** B3
Byahoml' Belarus **42** J7
Byakar Bhutan *see* Jakar
Byala Bulg. **58** G5
Byala Bulg. **58** I6
Byala Slatina Bulg. **58** E5
Byalynichy Belarus **43** K8
Byam Martin Island Canada **165** I2
Byarezina *r.* Belarus **42** J8
Byarezina *r.* Belarus **43** L9
Byaroza Belarus **42** F9
  also spelt Bereza
Byarozawka Belarus **42** G8
  also spelt Berezovka
Byblos *tourist site* Lebanon **108** G3
Bychawa Poland **49** T4
Byczyna Poland **49** P4
Bydgoszcz Poland **49** P2
  historically known as Bromberg
Byelaazyorsk Belarus **42** G9
  also spelt Beloozersk
Byelavyezhskaya Pushcha *park* Belarus
  42 E9
Byelitsk Belarus **43** L7
Byel'ki Belarus **42** I6
Byelorussia *country* Europe *see* Belarus
Byerastavitsa Belarus *see* Pahranichny
Byerazino Belarus **43** J7
Byerazino Belarus **43** J7
  also spelt Berezino
Byeranyaki Belarus **42** I9
Byers U.S.A. **180** F5
Byershty Belarus **42** F8
Byeshankovichy Belarus **43** K6
Byesville U.S.A. **176** D6
Byesyedz' *r.* Belarus **43** M9
Byfield Australia **149** F4
Byfield National Park Australia **149** F4
Bygdeå Sweden **44** M2
Byglandsfjord Norway **45** I4
Bykhaw Belarus **43** L8
  also spelt Bykhov
Bykhov Belarus *see* Bykhaw
Bykle Norway **45** I4
Bykovo Rus. Fed. **41** H6
Bykovskiy Rus. Fed. **39** M2
Bylas U.S.A. **183** N8
Bylot Island Canada **165** L2
Byng Inlet Canada **173** M5
Bynoe *r.* Australia **149** D3
Bynoe Harbour Australia **150** E2
Byramgore Reef India **94** A4
  also known as Chereapani
Byrd Glacier Antarctica **223** K1
Byrka Rus. Fed. **85** H1
Byrkjelo Norway **45** I3
Byrock Australia **147** E2
Byron *IL* U.S.A. **172** D8
Byron *ME* U.S.A. **177** O1
Byron Bay Australia **147** G2
Byron Island Kiribati *see* Nikunau
Byrranga, Gory *mts* Rus. Fed. **39** J2
Byrrne Ukr. **43** O9
Byske Sweden **44** M2
Byskeälven *r.* Sweden **44** M2
Byssa *r.* Rus. Fed. **82** C1
Bystrá *mt.* Slovakia **49** R6
Bystretsovo Rus. Fed. **43** J4
Bystrinskiy Golets, Gora *mt.* Rus. Fed.
  85 F1
Bystrovka Kyrg. *see* Kemin
Bystryy Tanyp *r.* Rus. Fed. **40** J5
Bystrzyca *r.* Poland **49** N4
Bystrzyca *r.* Poland **49** T4
Bytantay *r.* Rus. Fed. **39** N3
Bytča Slovakia **49** P6
Bytom Poland **49** P5
  historically known as Beuthen
Bytosh' Rus. Fed. **43** P8
Bytów Poland **49** O1
Byumba Rwanda **126** F5
Byurgyutli Turkm. **102** C5
Byuzmeyin Turkm. **102** D5
  also spelt Büzmeyin; *formerly spelt* Bezmein

Byxelkrok Sweden **45** L4
Byzantium Turkey *see* İstanbul
Bzura *r.* Poland **49** R3

⬇ C

Ca, Sông *r.* Vietnam **78** D4
Caacupé Para. **201** F6
Caaguazú Para. **201** F6
Caaguazú, Cordillera de *hills* Para. **201** G6
Caála Angola **127** B8
  formerly known as Robert Williams
Caapiranga Brazil **199** F5
Caapucú Para. **201** F6
Caarapó Brazil **203** A7
Caatinga Brazil **207** H4
Caazapá Para. **201** F6
Cabaçal *r.* Brazil **201** F3
Cabaiguán Cuba **186** D2
Caballas Peru **200** B3
Caballo *mt.* Spain **55** H7
Caballococha Peru **198** D5
Cabana *r.* Brazil **199** F5
Cabana Ayacucho Peru **200** B3
Cabanaconde Peru **200** C3
Cabañaquinta Spain **54** F1
Cabanatuan Phil. **74** B3
Cabanès *hill* France **50** H9
Cabano Canada **169** G4
Čabar Croatia **56** G3
Cabdul Qaadir Somalia **128** E2
Cabeceiras Brazil **206** G2
Cabeço Rainha *mt.* Port. **54** D5
Cabedelo Brazil **202** F3
Cabella Ligure Italy **56** B4
Cabeza del Buey Spain **54** F6
Cabeza de Vaca, Punta *pt* Chile **204** C2
Cabeza Prieta National Wildlife Refuge
  nature res. U.S.A. **183** K9
Cabezas Bol. **201** E4
Cabimas Venez. **198** D2
Cabinda Angola **127** B6
Cabinda *prov.* Angola **127** B6
Cabinet Inlet Antarctica **222** T2
Cabinet Mountains U.S.A. **180** D2
Cabingan *i.* Phil. **74** B5
Cabistra Turkey *see* Ereğli
Cable U.S.A. **172** B4
Cabo Brazil **202** F4
Cabo Blanco Arg. **205** D7
Cabo Delgado *prov.* Moz. **131** H2
Cabo Frio Brazil **207** J3
Cabo Frio, Ilha do *i.* Brazil **207** L10
Cabonga, Réservoir Canada **168** E4
Cabool U.S.A. **178** D4
Caboolture Australia **147** G1
Cabo Orange, Parque Nacional de
  nat. park Brazil **199** I4
Cabo Pantoja Peru **198** C5
Cabora Bassa, Lake *resr* Moz. *see*
  Cahora Bassa, Lago de
Cabo Raso Arg. **205** D7
Caborca Mex. **184** B2
Cabot Head Canada **173** L5
Cabot Strait Canada **169** I4
Cabo Verde *country* N. Atlantic Ocean *see*
  Cape Verde
Cabo Verde, Ilhas do *is* N. Atlantic Ocean
  124 [inset]
Cabo Yubi Morocco *see* Tarfaya
Cabra *i.* Phil. **74** B3
Cabra Spain **54** G7
Cabra *r.* Spain **54** G7
Cabral, Serra do *mts* Brazil **203** C6
Cabras *Sardegna* Italy **57** A9
Cabrayıl Azer. **107** F3
Cabred Arg. **204** F3
Cabreira *mt.* Port. **54** C6
Cabrera *i.* Spain **55** N5
Cabrera Dom. Rep. **187** F3
Cabrera *r.* Spain **54** F3
Cabri Canada **167** I5
Cabriel *r.* Spain **55** J5
Cabrobó Brazil **202** E4
Cabruta Venez. **199** E3
Cabugao Phil. **74** B2
Čabulja *mt.* Bos.-Herz. **56** J5
Cabullona Mex. **184** C2
Caçador Brazil **203** B8
Cacagoin China *see* Qagca
Cacahuatepec Mex. **185** F5
Cacao Fr. Guiana **199** H3
Caçapava Brazil **207** H10
Caçapava do Sul Brazil **203** A9
Cacapon *r.* U.S.A. **176** G6
Cácares Col. **198** C3
Caccia, Capo *c. Sardegna* Italy **57** A8
Cacém Port. **54** B6
Cáceres Brazil **201** F3
Cáceres Spain **54** E5
Cachal Bol. **200** D3
Cache U.S.A. **179** B4
Cacheau *r.* Guinea-Bissau **124** A3
Cache Creek Canada **166** F5
Cache Creek *r.* U.S.A. **182** C3
Cache la Poudre *r.* U.S.A. **180** F4
Cacheu Guinea-Bissau **124** A3
Cachi Arg. **204** D2
Cachi, Nevados de *mts* Arg. **200** D6
Cachimbo Brazil **202** A4
Cachimbo, Serra do *hills* Brazil **202** A4
Cachimo Angola **127** D7
Cachina *r.* Chile **204** C2
Cáchira Col. **198** D3
Cachoeira *Bahia* Brazil **202** E5
Cachoeira *Mato Grosso do Sul* Brazil **206** B6
Cachoeira Alta Brazil **206** C3
Cachoeira de Goiás Brazil **206** C3
Cachoeira do Arari Brazil **202** B2
Cachoeira dos Índios Brazil **202** E3
Cachoeiras de Macacu Brazil **207** K9
Cachoeiro de Itapemirim Brazil **203** D7
Cachos, Punta de *pt* Chile **204** C2
Cachuela Esperanza Bol. **200** D2
Cacine Guinea-Bissau **124** B4
Cacolo Angola **127** C7
Caconda Angola **127** B8
Cacongo Angola **127** B6
  formerly known as Guilherme Capelo *or*
  Landana
Cacu Brazil **206** C3
Cacucú Angola **127** B7
Cacula Angola **127** B8
Caculama Angola **127** C7
Caculé Brazil **202** D5
Cacuso Angola **127** B7
Cadca Slovakia **49** P6
Caddabarrawiracanna, Lake *salt flat*
  Australia **146** B2
Cadig Mountains Phil. **74** B3
Cadillac *Que.* Canada **173** N2
Cadillac *Sask.* Canada **167** J5
Cadillac U.S.A. **172** H6
Cadillal, Embalse el *resr* Arg. **204** D2

Cadiz Phil. **74** B4
Cádiz Spain **54** E8
  historically known as Gades
Cadiz *CA* U.S.A. **183** I7
Cadiz *KY* U.S.A. **174** C4
Cadiz *OH* U.S.A. **176** E5
Cádiz, Bahía de *b.* Spain **54** E8
Cadiz Lake U.S.A. **183** I7
Cadomin Canada **167** G4
Cadotte *r.* Canada **167** G3
Caen France **51** G3
Caerdydd U.K. *see* Cardiff
Caere Italy *see* Cerveteri
Caerfyrddin U.K. *see* Carmarthen
Caergybi U.K. *see* Holyhead
Caernarfon U.K. **47** H10
  formerly known as Caernarvon; *historically
  known as* Segontia *or* Segontium
Caernarfon Bay U.K. **47** H10
Caernarfon Castle *tourist site* U.K.
  47 H10
Caernarvon U.K. *see* Caernarfon
Caesaraugusta Spain *see* Zaragoza
Caesarea Alg. *see* Cherchell
Caesarea *tourist site* Israel **108** F5
Caesarea Cappadociae Turkey *see*
  Kayseri
Caesarea Philippi Syria *see* Bāniyās
Caesarodunum France *see* Tours
Caesaromagus U.K. *see* Chelmsford
Caeté Brazil **207** J6
Caeté *r.* Brazil **199** F5
Caetité Brazil **202** D5
Cafayate Arg. **204** D2
Cafelândia Brazil **206** D8
Caffa Ukr. *see* Feodosiya
Cafuini *r.* Brazil **199** G4
Cagayan *r.* Phil. **74** B4
Cagayan *i.* Phil. **74** A4
Cagayan de Oro Phil. **74** C4
Cagayan Islands Phil. **74** B4
Cagli Italy **56** E5
Cagliari *Sardegna* Italy **57** B9
  historically known as Carales *or* Caralis
Cagliari, Golfo di *b. Sardegna* Italy **57** B9
Cagnano Varano Italy **56** H7
Cagnes-sur-Mer France **51** N9
Caguán *r.* Col. **198** C4
Caguas Puerto Rico **187** G3
Cahaba *r.* U.S.A. **175** C5
Cahama Angola **127** B9
Cahersiveen Rep. of Ireland **47** C12
Cahir Rep. of Ireland **47** E11
Cahirciveen Rep. of Ireland *see*
  Cahersiveen
Cahora Bassa, Lago de *resr* Moz. **131** F2
Cahore Point Rep. of Ireland **47** F11
Cahors France **50** H8
Cahuapanas Peru **198** B6
Cahul Moldova **58** J3
  formerly spelt Kagul *or* Kakhul
Caia Moz. **131** G3
  formerly known as Vila Fontes
Caia, Barragem do *resr* Port. **54** C5
Caiabis, Serra dos *hills* Brazil **201** F3
Caianda Angola **127** D7
Caiapó *r.* Brazil **206** C2
Caiapó, Serra do *mts* Brazil **205** A4
Caiaza Brazil **206** B3
Caiapônia Brazil **206** B3
Caibarién Cuba **186** D2
Cai Bau, Đao *i.* Vietnam **78** D3
Cai Be Vietnam **79** D6
Caicara Venez. **199** E3
Caicó Brazil **202** E3
Caicos Islands Turks and Caicos Is **187** F2
Caicos Passage
  Bahamas/Turks and Caicos Is **187** E2
Caidian China **87** E2
  formerly known as Hanyang
Caidu China *see* Shangcai
Caiguna Australia **151** D7
Caihua China **87** E2
Caiine China **87** E2
Caiinyigoin China **86** B1
Caipe Arg. **200** C6
Caird Coast Antarctica **222** W1
Cairngorm Mountains U.K. **46** I6
Cairns Australia **149** E3
Cairnsmore of Carsphairn *hill* U.K. **47** H8
▶Cairo Egypt **121** F2
  Capital of Egypt and 2nd most populous
  city in Africa. Also known as El Qâhira *or*
  Al Qâhirah *or* Le Caire.
  world [cities] ➡ 24–25
  africa [locations] ➡ 118–119
Cairo *GA* U.S.A. **175** C6
Cairo *IL* U.S.A. **174** B4
Cairo, Monte *mt.* Italy **56** F7
Cairo Montenotte Italy **56** A4
Caiscleann an Bharraigh Rep. of Ireland *see*
  Castlebar
Caistor U.K. **47** L10
Caitou Angola **127** B8
Caiundo Angola **127** C8
Caiwarro Australia **147** E2
Caixi China **87** F3
Caiza Bol. **200** D5
Caiza Hu *l.* China **87** F2
Cajabamba Peru **200** A1
Cajamarca Peru **200** A1
Cajamarca *dept* Peru **198** B6
Cajapió Brazil **202** C2
Cajarc France **50** H8
Cajari Brazil **202** C2
Cajàzeiras Brazil **202** E3
Čajetina *Srbija* Yugo. **58** A5
Cajidiocan Phil. **74** B3
Čajniče Bos.-Herz. **56** L5
Čakajna Brazil **206** B3
Čakajna *r.* Romania **58** G4
Čakovec Croatia **56** I2
Çal Turkey **106** B3
Cala S. Africa **133** L8
Cala *r.* Spain **54** E7
Calabar Nigeria **125** H5
Calabogie Canada **173** Q5
Calabozo Venez. **199** E2
Calabria *admin. reg.* Italy **57** I10
Calabria, Parco Nazionale della *nat. park*
  Italy **57** I10
Calaburra, Punta de *pt* Spain **54** G8
Calacoto Bol. **200** C4
Calaf Spain **55** M3
Calafat Romania **58** D5
Calafate Arg. **205** B8
Cala Figuera, Cap de *c.* Spain **55** N5

Calagnaan *i.* Phil. **74** B4
Caltagirone *Sicilia* Italy **57** G11
Calagua Mex. **184** C3
Caltanissetta *Sicilia* Italy **57** G11
Calagua Islands Phil. **74** B3
Calthodzär Turkey **108** E1
Calagurris Spain *see* Calahorra
Calucinga Angola **127** C7
Calahorra Spain **55** J2
Caluire-et-Cuire France **51** K7
  historically known as Calagurris
Calulo Angola **127** B7
Calai Angola **127** C9
Calumet U.S.A. **172** E3
Calais France **51** H2
Calunda Angola **127** D8
Calais U.S.A. **174** H2
Calungua Angola **127** C8
Calais Lake U.S.A. **183** I7
Calusia *i.* Phil. **74** B4
Calalasteo, Sierra de *mts* Arg. **204** D2
Caluula Somalia **128** F2
Calama Chile **200** C5
Caluula, Raas *pt* Somalia **128** F2
Calama *r.* Brazil **199** G5
Calvert *r.* Australia **148** C3
Calamar Col. **198** C4
Calvert Hills Australia **148** C3
Calamar Mex. **181** D7
Calvert Island Canada **166** D5
Calamian Group *is* Phil. **74** A4
Calvert Range *hills* Australia **150** C4
Calamocha Spain **55** J4
Calvi *Corse* France **51** O10
Calañas Spain **54** D7
Calvià Spain **55** N5
Calanda Spain **55** K4
Calvinia S. Africa **132** D8
Calandagan *i.* Phil. **74** B4
Calvitero *mt.* Spain **54** F4
Calang Indon. **76** A1
Calzada de Calatrava Spain **54** H6
Calanque France **51** O10
Cam *r.* U.K. **47** M11
Calanscio Sand Sea *des.* Libya **120** D2
Camabatela Angola **127** B7
Calapan Phil. **74** B3
Camaçari Brazil **207** N2
Calapas *pass* S. Africa **133** L8
Camacho Reservoir U.S.A. **182** D3
Calar Alta *mt.* Spain **55** I7
Camachigama, *r.* Canada **168** E4
Călăraşi Moldova **58** J1
Camachigama, Lac *l.* Canada **173** Q3
  formerly spelt Kalarash
Camacho Mex. **185** E3
Călăraşi Romania **58** I4
Camaçuio Angola **127** B8
Cala Santa Galdana Spain **55** O5
Camacupa Angola **127** C8
Calatafimi *Sicilia* Italy **57** E11
  formerly known as General Machado
Calatayud Spain **55** J3
Camaguán Venez. **199** E3
Calau Germany **49** K4
Camagüey Cuba **186** D2
Calaunag Italy **56** F5
Camagüey, Archipiélago de *is* Cuba
Calavà, Capo *c. Sicilia* Italy **57** G10
  186 D2
Calavite Passage Phil. **74** B3
Camah, Gunung *mt.* Malaysia **76** C1
Calayan *i.* Phil. **74** A3
Camaiú *r.* Brazil **199** G5
Calbayog Phil. **74** C3
Camamu Brazil **202** E5
Calbiga Phil. **74** C4
Camana Peru **200** B3
Calca Peru **200** C3
Camaná *r.* Peru **200** B3
Calcanhar, Ponta do *pt* Brazil **202** F3
Camanongue Angola **127** D7
Calcasieu *r.* U.S.A. **179** D6
  formerly known as Vila Bugaço; *formerly
Calceta Ecuador **198** A5
  spelt* Kamenongue
Calchaqui Arg. **204** E2
Camapuã Brazil **203** A6
Calchaquí Arg. **204** D2
Camaquã Brazil **203** B9
Calcutta India *see* Kolkata
Camaquã *r.* Brazil **203** A9
Căldăraru Romania **58** F4
Camăr Romania **58** C1
Caldas Col. **198** C3
Camará Brazil **199** F5
Caldas da Rainha Port. **54** B5
Camarão Brazil **198** D4
Caldas de Mombuy Spain *see*
Camararé *r.* Brazil **201** F2
  Caldes de Montbui
Camargo Bol. **200** D5
Caldas Novas Brazil **206** E3
Camargo Mex. **185** F3
Calden *r.* Canada **167** G1
Camargo, Parque Natural *nature res.* Mex.
Calderas Mex. **185** H5
  185 F3
Caldera Chile **204** C2
Camargue, Parc Naturel Régional de
Calder *r.* Canada **167** G1
  nat. res. France **51** K9
Caldervale Australia **149** E5
Camarillo U.S.A. **182** E7
Caldes de Montbui Spain **55** N3
Camariñas Spain **54** B1
  also known as Caldes de Mombuy
Camarón, Cabo *c.* Hond. **186** B6
Çaldıran Turkey **107** F3
Camarones Arg. **205** D7
Caldwell *ID* U.S.A. **180** C4
Camarones, Bahía *b.* Arg. **205** D7
Caldwell *KS* U.S.A. **178** C4
Camas U.S.A. **180** B3
Caldwell *OH* U.S.A. **176** D6
Camas *r.* U.S.A. **180** D4
Caldwell *TX* U.S.A. **179** C6
Camas Creek *r.* U.S.A. **180** D4
Caledon *r.* Lesotho/S. Africa **133** K7
Ca Mau Vietnam **79** D6
Caledon S. Africa **132** D11
  formerly known as Quan Long
Caledon Bay Australia **148** C2
Camaxilo Angola **127** C7
Caledonia N.S. Canada **169** H4
Cambalá Brazil **201** F4
Caledonia *Ont.* Canada **173** N7
Camará Brazil **206** D1
Caledonia *admin. div.* U.K. *see* Scotland
Cambay India *see* Khambhat
Caledonia U.S.A. **172** H8
Cambay, Gulf of India *see*
Caledonia *MN* U.S.A. **174** A3
  Khambhat, Gulf of
Caledonia *NY* U.S.A. **176** H3
Cambé Brazil **206** C10
Caledon Nature Reserve S. Africa **133** K6
▶Cambodia *country* Asia **79** C5
Calella Spain **55** N3
  formerly known as Kampuchea *or* Khmer
Calen Australia **149** F4
  Republic
Calera *r.* Spain **54** E7
  asia [countries] ➡ 64–67
Calera France **51** O10
Camborne U.K. **47** G13
Calera y Chozas Spain **54** G5
Cambrai Australia **146** C3
Caleta del Cobre Chile **200** C5
Cambrai France **51** J2
Caleta Josefina Chile **205** C9
Cambre Spain **54** C1
Caleta Lobos Chile **200** C5
Cambria U.S.A. **182** C6
Caleta Pabellón de Pica Chile **200** C5
Cambria *admin. div.* U.K. *see* Wales
Caleufú Arg. **204** D5
Cambrian Canada **168** D5
Calexico U.S.A. **183** I9
Cambrian Mountains *hills* U.K. **47** I11
Calf of Man *i.* Isle of Man **47** F9
Cambridge N.Z. **152** J5
Calgary Canada **167** H5
Cambridge U.K. **47** M11
Calhan U.S.A. **180** F5
Cambridge *IL* U.S.A. **174** B3
Calheta Canada **174** U.5
Cambridge *MD* U.S.A. **177** N3
Cali Col. **198** D4
Cambridge *MA* U.S.A. **177** N3
Cali Turkey **59** J9
Cambridge *MN* U.S.A. **174** A2
Calica U.S.A. **183** J4
Cambridge *NY* U.S.A. **177** L2
Calicut India **94** B3
Cambridge *OH* U.S.A. **176** D5
  also known as Kozhikode
Cambridge *VT* U.S.A. **177** M1
Caliente U.S.A. **183** J4
Cambridge *WI* U.S.A. **172** D7
▶California *state* U.S.A. **182** D4
Cambridge Bay Canada **165** I3
  world [earthquakes] ➡ 14–15
Cambridge Gulf Australia **150** D2
  northamerica [environments] ➡ 162–163
Cambridge Springs U.S.A. **176** E4
California, Golfo de *g.* Mex. *see*
Cambrils Spain **55** M3
  California, Gulf of
Cambul Brazil **209** G9
California, Gulf of Mex. **184** B2
Cambulo Angola **127** D7
  also known as California, Golfo de;
Cambundi-Catembo Angola **127** C7
  historically known as Cortes, Sea of
  formerly known as Nova Gaia
California Aqueduct U.S.A. **182** D5
Cambuquira Brazil **207** H8
California Aqueduct *canal* U.S.A. **182** C4
Cambutal, Cerro *mt.* Panama **186** C6
Călilabad Azer. **107** F3
Cam Co *l.* China **89** C5
  also spelt Dzhalalabad; *formerly known as*
Camden Australia **147** F3
  Astrakhan' Bazar
Camden *AL* U.S.A. **175** C5
Calilegua Arg. **201** D5
Camden *AR* U.S.A. **179** D5
Čalimanești Romania **58** F4
Camden *ME* U.S.A. **177** P1
Căliman, Munţii *mts* Romania **58** F1
Camden *NC* U.S.A. **176** I9
Calingasta Arg. **204** C3
Camden *NY* U.S.A. **177** J2
Calistoga U.S.A. **182** B3
Camden *OH* U.S.A. **176** A6
Calitri Italy **56** H8
Camden *SC* U.S.A. **174** D5
Calitzdorp S. Africa **132** F10
Camden *TN* U.S.A. **174** B4
Çalkara Turkey **108** E1
Camden Bay U.S.A. **164** E2
Calkini Mex. **185** H4
Camden Sound *sea chan.* Australia **150** D2
Callabonna, Lake *salt flat* Australia **146** D2
Camdenton U.S.A. **178** D4
Callabonna Creek *watercourse* Australia
Cameia Angola **127** D7
  146 D2
Cameia, Parque Nacional da *nat. park*
Callac France **50** C4
  Angola **127** D7
Callaghan, Mount U.S.A. **183** H2
  also known as Kameia, Parque Nacional de
Callan Rep. of Ireland **47** E11
Camëll Turkey **59** J10
Callander Canada **168** E4
Cameron *AZ* U.S.A. **183** M6
Callander U.K. **46** H7
Cameron *LA* U.S.A. **179** D6
Callands U.S.A. **176** E9
Cameron *MO* U.S.A. **178** D4
Callang Phil. **74** B2
Cameron *TX* U.S.A. **179** C6
Callao Peru **200** A3
Cameron *WI* U.S.A. **172** B5
Callao *r.* Peru **200** A3
▶Cameroon *country* Africa **125** H5
Callaqui U.S.A. **183** J3
  spelt Cameroun *in French*
Callawa Aboriginal Reserve Australia **150** C4
  africa [countries] ➡ 114–117
Calles Mex. **185** F4
Cameroun *country* Africa *see* Cameroon
Callicoon U.S.A. **177** J4
Cameroun, Mont *vol.* Cameroon **125** H5
Callide Australia **149** F5
Cametá Amazonas Brazil **199** E6
Calling Lake Canada **167** H4
Cametá Pará Brazil **202** C2
Calling Lake *l.* Canada **167** H4
Camfield *r.* Australia **148** A3
Calliope Australia **149** G5
Camiguin *i.* Phil. **74** B2
Callipolis Turkey *see* Gallipoli
Camiguin *i.* Phil. **74** C4
Callosa d'En Sarrià Spain **55** K6
Camilla U.S.A. **175** C6
Callosa de Segura Spain **55** K6
Camiling Phil. **74** B3
Callum Canada **173** M3
Camilla Chile **205** C7
Callyharra Springs Australia **151** B5
Camiranga Brazil **202** C2
Calmar Canada **167** H4
Camiri Bol. **201** E5
Calmar U.S.A. **174** A3
Camisea Peru **200** B2
Čalmâţui *r.* Romania **58** H4
Camisea *r.* Peru **200** B2
Çalıştea *r.* Romania **58** G4
Camissombo Angola **127** D7
Calnali Mex. **185** F4
  formerly known as Veríssimo Sarmento
Calomotul Mex. **185** H4
Calotmul Mex. **185** H4
Caloundra Australia **149** G5
Calovo Slovakia *see* Veľký Meder
Calpe Spain **55** L6
Calpoy's Bay Canada **173** M5
Calpulálpan Mex. **185** F5
Calstock Canada **168** C3

241 ⬅

index

C

Cammarata, Monte mt. Sicilia Italy **57** F11
Cammin Poland see **Kamień Pomorski**
Camocim Brazil **202** D2
Camooweal Australia **148** C3
Camooweal Caves National Park Australia **148** C4
Camopi Brazil **199** H4
Camorta i. India **95** G4
Camotes Sea g. Phil. **74** C4
Campagna Italy **57** H8
Campamento Hond. **186** B4
Campana, Isla i. Chile **205** B8
Campanário Mato Grosso do Sul Brazil **201** G5
Campanário Minas Gerais Brazil **203** D6
Campanella, Punta pt Italy **56** G7
Campania admin. reg. Italy **56** G7
Campania Island Canada **166** F4
Campanquiz, Cerro hills Peru **198** B6
Campaspe r. Australia **149** E4
Campbell S. Africa **132** G6
Campbell U.S.A. **176** C4
Campbell, Cape N.Z. **153** I9
Campbellford Canada **168** E4
Campbell Hill hill U.S.A. **176** B5
Campbell Island N.Z. **79** B6
Campbell Island N.Z. **220** F9
  also known as Motu Ihupuku
Campbell Lake Canada **167** J2
Campbell Range hills Australia **150** D2
Campbell River Canada **166** E5
Campbellsport U.S.A. **172** E7
Campbellstown S. Africa **176** A6
Campbellsville U.S.A. **174** C4
Campbellton Canada **169** H4
Campbelltown Australia **147** F3
Campbell Town Australia **147** F5
Campbeltown U.K. **46** G8
Camp Creek U.S.A. **176** D4
Campeche Mex. **185** H5
Campeche state Mex. **185** H5
Campeche, Bahía de g. Mex. **185** G5
Campechuela Cuba **186** D3
Câmpeni Romania **58** E2
  formerly spelt Cîmpeni
Camperdown Australia **147** D4
Camperdown S. Africa **133** O6
Campestre Brazil **207** G8
Campia Brazil **172** G5
Câmpia Turzii Romania **58** E2
  formerly spelt Cîmpia Turzii
Campiglia Marittima Italy **56** C5
Campillos Spain **54** G7
Campina Brazil **201** H1
Câmpina Romania **58** G3
  formerly spelt Cîmpina
Campinaçu Brazil **202** B5
Campina Grande Brazil **202** F3
Campinas Brazil **206** F9
Campina Verde Brazil **206** D6
Camplong Indon. **75** B5
Campo Cameroon **125** H6
Campo r. Cameroon see **Ntem**
Campo, Réserve de nature res. Cameroon **125** H6
Campoalegre Col. **198** C4
Campo Alegre de Lourdes Brazil **202** D4
Campobasso Italy **56** G7
Campobello di Licata Sicilia Italy **57** F11
Campobello di Mazara Sicilia Italy **57** E11
Campo Belo Brazil **203** C7
Campo de Criptana Spain **55** H5
Campo de Diauarum Brazil **202** A4
Campodólcino Italy **56** B2
Campo Erê Brazil **203** A8
Campo Esperanza Para. **201** F5
Campo Florido Brazil **206** E6
Campo Formoso Brazil **202** D4
Campo Gallo Arg. **204** E2
Campo Grande Amazonas Brazil **201** F2
Campo Grande Mato Grosso do Sul Brazil **203** A7
Campolândia Brazil **206** B3
Campo Largo Brazil **203** B8
Campo Maior Brazil **202** D3
Campo Maior Port. **54** D5
Campomarino Italy **56** H7
Campo Mourão Brazil **206** A11
Campos Brazil **203** D7
Campos Altos Brazil **203** C6
Campos Belos Brazil **202** C4
Campos del Puerto Spain **55** O5
Campos do Jordão Brazil **207** H9
Campo Serio Peru **198** C5
Campos Gerais Brazil **207** H8
Campos Novos Brazil **206** D9
Campos Sales Brazil **202** D3
Campo Tencia mt. Switz. **51** O6
Campo Troco Col. **199** D3
Camprodon Spain **55** N2
Campton U.S.A. **176** B8
Câmpulung Romania **58** G3
  formerly spelt Cîmpulung
Câmpulung Moldovenesc Romania **41** C7
  formerly spelt Cîmpulung Moldovenesc
Campuya Peru **198** C5
Campuya r. Peru **198** C5
Camp Verde U.S.A. **183** M7
Camrose Canada **167** H4
Camsell Lake Canada **167** I2
Camsell Range mts Canada **166** F2
Camulodunum U.K. see **Colchester**
Çamurluk Turkey **109** I1
Can Turkey **106** A2
Canaan U.S.A. **177** L3
Canaan r. Canada **169** H4
Canaan Trin. and Tob. **187** H5
Canaan Peak U.S.A. **183** M4
Canabrava Brazil **207** H4
Cana Brava r. Brazil **202** A3
Cana Brava, Serra da hills Brazil **207** N3
Canabungan i. Phil. **74** A4
Canacona India **94** B3

▶**Canada** country N. America **164** G3
  Largest country in North America and 2nd in the world. 3rd most populous country in North America.
  world (countries) ➤ 10–11
  world (changes) ➤ 20–21
  northamerica (countries) ➤ 158–159
Cañada Honda Arg. **204** C3
Canadian U.S.A. **179** B5
Canadian r. U.S.A. **179** D5
Cañadón de las Vacas Arg. **205** C8
Cañadon Grande, Sierra mts Arg. **205** C7
Canaima, Parque Nacional nat. park Venez. **199** F3
Canajoharie U.S.A. **177** K3
Çanakkale Turkey **106** A2
  formerly known as Chanak
Çanakkale prov. Turkey **59** H8
Çanakkale Boğazı strait Turkey see **Dardanelles**
Canal Flats Canada **167** H5
Canals Spain **55** K6
Canal Winchester U.S.A. **176** C6
Canamari Brazil **200** C2
Canandaigua U.S.A. **177** H3
Canandaigua Lake U.S.A. **177** H3
Cananea Mex. **184** C2
Cananéia Brazil **203** C8
Canapiare, Cerro hill Col. **198** D4
Canápolis Brazil **206** D5
Cañar Ecuador **198** B5
Cañar prov. Ecuador **198** B5
Canarana Brazil **202** A5
Canarias, Islas is N. Atlantic Ocean **122** A3
  also known as Canary Islands
Canarias, Islas terr. N. Atlantic Ocean see **Canary Islands**
Canary Islands is N. Atlantic Ocean see **Canarias, Islas**
▶**Canary Islands** terr. N. Atlantic Ocean **122** A3
  Autonomous Community of Spain. Also known as Canarias, Islas.
  africa (countries) ➤ 114–117
Canasayab Mex. **185** H5
Canaseraga U.S.A. **176** H3
Canastota U.S.A. **177** J2
Canastra, Serra da mts Brazil **206** G6
Canatlán Mex. **184** D3
Canavieiras Brazil **203** E6
Canaveral, Cape U.S.A. **175** D6
  formerly known as Kennedy, Cape
Canaveral National Seashore nature res. U.S.A. **175** D6
Canavieiras Brazil **202** E5
Cañazas Panama **186** C5
Canbelego Australia **147** E2
▶**Canberra** Australia **147** F3
  Capital of Australia.
Canby CA U.S.A. **180** B4
Canby MN U.S.A. **178** C2
Cancale France **50** E4
Canchas Chile **204** C2
Canchyuaya, Cerros de hills Peru **198** C6
Cancún Mex. **185** I4
Çandar Turkey see **Kastamonu**
Candarave Peru **200** C4
Çandarlı Turkey **106** A3
Candás Spain **54** F1
Candé France **50** E5
Candeias Brazil **203** C7
Candeias r. Brazil **201** E2
Candela r. Mex. **179** B7
Candelaria Arg. **204** D2
Candelaria Mex. **185** H5
Candelaria Venez. **199** E3
Candelaro r. Italy **56** H7
Candeleda Spain **54** F4
Candelo Australia **147** F4
Candia Greece see **Iraklion**
Cândido Mendes Brazil **202** C2
Cândido Sales Brazil **207** L2
Çandır Turkey **106** C2
Candle Lake Canada **167** J4
Candle Lake l. Canada **167** J4
Cando U.S.A. **178** C1
Candon Phil. **74** B2
Candover S. Africa **133** P4
Cândrelu, Vârful mt. Romania **58** E3
Cane r. Australia **150** A4
Canea Greece see **Chania**
Canela Baja Chile **204** C3
Canelli Italy **56** A4
Canelones Uruguay **204** F4
Canelos Ecuador **198** B5
Cañete Chile **204** B5
Cañete Spain **55** J4
Caney r. U.S.A. **178** D4
Cangallo Peru **200** B3
Cangalha Brazil **206** G3
Cangamba Angola **127** C7
  formerly known as Vila de Aljustrel
Canganvela Brazil **202** F3
Canguçu Brazil **204** G3
Canguçu, Serra da hills Brazil **204** G3
Cangzhou China **85** H4
Caniapiscau Canada **169** G2
Caniapiscau r. Canada **169** G1
Caniapiscau, Lac l. Canada **169** G2
Canicado Moz. see **Guija**
Canicatti Sicilia Italy **57** E11
Canicattini Bagni Sicilia Italy **57** H11
Canigao Channel Phil. **74** C4
Canigou, Pic de mt. France **51** I10
Caniles Spain **55** I7
Canim Lake Canada **166** F5
Canindé Ceará Brazil **202** E3
Canindé Pará Brazil **202** D3
Canindé r. Brazil **202** D3
Canino Italy **56** D6
Canisteo U.S.A. **176** H3
Canisteo r. U.S.A. **176** H3
Canisteo Peninsula Antarctica **222** R2
Canister Falls Guyana **199** G3
Cañitas de Felipe Pescador Mex. **185** E4
Çankırı Turkey **106** C2
  historically known as Gangra
Cankuzo Burundi **126** F5
Canlaon Phil. **74** B4
Canna i. U.K. **46** F6
Cannanore India **94** B4
  also known as Kannur
Cannanore Islands India **94** B4
Cannes France **51** N9
Cannich U.K. **46** H6
Canning Hill hill Australia **151** B6
Cannobio Italy **56** A2
Cannonball r. U.S.A. **178** B2
Cannon Beach U.S.A. **180** B3
Cannon Rocks S. Africa **133** K10
Cannonsburg U.S.A. **176** C7
Cann River Australia **147** F4
Canoa Ecuador **198** A5
Canoas Brazil **203** B9

Caño Colorado Col. **198** D4
Caño Colorado Venez. **187** H5
Canoeiros Brazil **203** C6
Canoe Lake Canada **167** I4
Canoe Lake l. Canada **167** I4
Canoinhas Brazil **203** B8
Canon City U.S.A. **180** F5
Cañón del Río Blanco, Parque Nacional nat. park Mex. **185** F5
Cañón del Sumidero, Parque Nacional nat. park Mex. **185** G5
Cañon Largo watercourse U.S.A. **181** F5
Canoochia r. U.S.A. **175** D6
Canoona Australia **149** F4
Canora Canada **167** K5
Caño Riecito Venez. **199** D2
Canosa di Puglia Italy **56** I7
  historically known as Canusium
Canouan i. St Vincent **187** H4
Canowindra Australia **147** F3
Canso Canada **169** I4
Canso, Cape Canada **169** I4
Canso, Strait of Canada **169** I4
Canta Peru **200** A2
Cantabria aut. comm. Spain **54** G1
Cantabrian Mountains Spain see **Cantábrica, Cordillera**
Cantabrian Sea Spain see **Cantábrico, Mar**
Cantábrica, Cordillera mts Spain **54** E1
  English form Cantabrian Mountains
Cantábrico, Mar sea Spain **54** E1
  English form Cantabrian Sea
Cantagalo Brazil **199** G6
Cantalejo Spain **54** H3
Cantanhede Port. **54** C4
Canteras hill Spain **55** J3
Canterbury admin. reg. N.Z. **153** G11
▶**Canterbury** U.K. **47** N12
  historically known as Cantuaria or Durovernum
Canterbury Bight b. N.Z. **153** F12
Canterbury Plains N.Z. **153** F11
Cần Thơ Vietnam **79** D6
Cantil U.S.A. **182** G5
Cantilan Phil. **74** C4
Cantillana Spain **54** F7
Canto do Buriti Brazil **202** D4
Canton China see **Guangzhou**
Canton GA U.S.A. **175** C5
Canton IL U.S.A. **174** B3
Canton MO U.S.A. **174** B3
Canton MS U.S.A. **175** B5
Canton NY U.S.A. **177** J1
Canton OH U.S.A. **176** D5
Canton PA U.S.A. **177** I4
Canton SD U.S.A. **178** C3
Canton TX U.S.A. **179** D5
Canton WI U.S.A. **172** B5
Canton Island Kiribati see **Kanton**
Cantu r. Brazil **201** G6
Cantù Italy **56** B3
Cantu, Serra do hills Brazil **203** B8
Cantuaria U.K. see **Canterbury**
Canudos Brazil **202** E4
Cañuelas Arg. **204** F4
Canumã Amazonas Brazil **199** F6
Canumã Amazonas Brazil **199** G6
Canunda National Park Australia **146** D4
Canusium Italy see **Canosa di Puglia**
Canutama Brazil **199** E6
Canvastown N.Z. **152** H9
Canwood Canada **167** J4
Cany-Barville France **50** G3
Cànyoles r. Spain **55** K5
Canyon Canada **166** B2
Canyon U.S.A. **179** B5
Canyon City U.S.A. **180** C3
Canyon Creek r. U.S.A. **182** C2
Canyondam U.S.A. **182** C1
Canyon de Chelly National Monument nat. park U.S.A. **183** O5
Canyon Ferry Lake U.S.A. **180** E3
Canyon Lake U.S.A. **183** M8
Canyonlands National Park U.S.A. **183** O3
Canyon Ranges mts Canada **166** E2
Canyonville U.S.A. **180** B4
Canzar Angola **127** D6
Cao r. China **83** D4
Cao Bằng Vietnam **78** D3
Caocheng China see **Caoxian**
Caohe China see **Qichun**
Caohu China **88** D3
Caojiahe China see **Qichun**
Caojian China **86** A3
Caombo Angola **127** C7
Cao Nguyên Đắc Lắc plat. Vietnam **79** E5
Caorle Italy **56** E3
Caoxian China **87** E1
  also known as Caocheng
Caozhou China see **Heze**
Cap i. Phil. **74** B3
Capac U.S.A. **173** K7
Capaccio Italy **57** H8
Capaci Sicilia Italy **57** F10
Cap-à-Foux c. Haiti **187** I5
Capaia Angola **127** D7
Capakçur Turkey see **Bingöl**
Capalulu, Selat sea chan. Indon. **75** C3
Capana Brazil **198** D5
Capanaparo r. Venez. **199** E3
Capanema Brazil **202** C2
Capanne, Monte mt. Italy **56** C6
Capão Bonito Brazil **206** E11
Caparaó, Serra do mts Brazil **207** L7
Capas Phil. **74** B3
Căpăţânii, Munţii mts Romania **58** F3
Capatárida Venez. **198** D2
Cap-aux-Meules Canada **169** I4
Capbreton France **50** E9
Cap-Chat Canada **169** H3
Cap-de-la-Madeleine Canada **169** F4
Capdenac-Gare France **51** I8
Capdepera Spain **55** O5
Cape r. Australia **149** E4
Cape Arid National Park Australia **151** C7
Cape Bald Canada see **Cap-Pelé**
Cape Barren Island Australia **147** F5
Cape Borda Australia **146** C3
Cape Bougainville Aboriginal Reserve Australia **150** C2
Cape Breton Highlands National Park Canada **169** I4
Cape Breton Island Canada **169** I4
  historically known as Royale, Île
Cape Charles Canada **169** K2
Cape Charles U.S.A. **177** I8
Cape Coast Ghana **125** E5
  also known as Cape Coast Castle
Cape Coast Castle Ghana see **Cape Coast**
Cape Cod Bay U.S.A. **177** O4
Cape Cod National Seashore nature res. U.S.A. **174** I3
Cape Coral U.S.A. **175** D7
Cape Crawford Australia **148** B3
Cape Croker Canada **173** L6
Cape Dorset Canada **165** L3
Cape Elizabeth U.S.A. **177** O2
Cape Fear r. U.S.A. **174** E5
Cape George Canada **169** I4
Cape Girardeau U.S.A. **174** B4
Cape Juby Morocco see **Tarfaya**
Cape Krusenstern National Monument nat. park U.S.A. **164** C3
Capel Australia **151** A7
Cape Le Grand National Park Australia **151** C7
Capelinha Brazil **203** D6
Capella Australia **149** E4

Capelle aan de IJssel Neth. **48** B4
Capelongo Angola **127** B8
  formerly known as Folgares
Capelongo Angola see **Kuvango**
Cape May U.S.A. **177** K6
Cape May Court House U.S.A. **177** K6
Cape May Point U.S.A. **177** K7
Cape Melville National Park Australia **149** E2
Capenda-Camulemba Angola **127** C7
Cape of Good Hope Nature Reserve S. Africa **132** C11
Cape Palmerston National Park Australia **149** F4
Cape Range hills Australia **150** A4
Cape Range National Park Australia **150** A4
Cape Romain National Wildlife Refuge nature res. U.S.A. **175** C5
Cape Sable Island Canada **169** H5
Cape St George Canada **169** J3
Capesterre Guadeloupe **187** H3
▶**Cape Town** S. Africa **132** C10
  Legislative capital of South Africa. Also known as Kaapstad.
  world (countries) ➤ 10–11
  africa (locations) ➤ 118–119
Cape Tribulation National Park Australia **149** E2
Cape Upstart National Park Australia **149** E3
▶**Cape Verde** country N. Atlantic Ocean **124** [inset]
  also known as Cabo Verde
  africa (countries) ➤ 114–117
Cape Vincent U.S.A. **177** I1
Cape Wolfe Canada **169** H4
Cape York Peninsula Australia **149** D2
Cap-Haïtien Haiti **187** E3
Capibara Venez. **199** E4
Capim Brazil **202** C2
Capim r. Brazil **202** B2
Capinópolis Brazil **206** D5
Capinota Bol. **200** D4
Capitán Arturo Prat research station Antarctica **222** U2
Capitão Enéas Brazil **207** J3
Capitari Brazil **199** F6
▶**Capitol Hill** N. Mariana Is. **73** K3
  Capital of the Northern Mariana Islands, on Saipan.
Capitol Reef National Park U.S.A. **183** M3
Capivara, Represa resr Brazil **206** B9
Capivari r. Bahia Brazil **202** E5
Capivari r. São Paulo Brazil **206** F9
Capixaba Brazil **202** D4
Čapljina Bos.-Herz. **56** J5
Capnoyan i. Phil. **74** B4
Capoche r. Moz./Zambia **131** G2
Capo d'Orlando Sicilia Italy **57** G10
Capoeira Brazil **199** G6
Capoeiras, Cachoeira das waterfall Brazil **199** G6
Capoterra Sardegna Italy **57** A9
Cap-Pelé Canada **169** I4
  formerly known as Cape Bald
Capraia, Isola di i. Italy **56** B5
Caprara, Isola i. Sardegna Italy **56** B7
Capri Italy **57** G8
Capri, Isola di i. Italy **57** G8
Capricorn, Cape Australia **149** F4
Capricorn Channel Australia **149** F4
Capricorn Group atolls Australia **149** G4
Caprivi admin. reg. Namibia **130** D3
Caprivi Strip reg. Namibia **130** D2
Caprivi Game Park nature res. Namibia **130** D2
Capsa Tunisia see **Gafsa**
Captain Cook U.S.A. **181** [inset] Z2
Captieux France **50** F7
Capuava Brazil **206** F11
Capuna Angola **127** C8
Capunda Cavilongo Angola **127** B8
  formerly known as Olivença-a-Nova
Caqueta dept Col. **198** C4
Caquetá r. Col. **198** D5
Cáqueza Col. **198** C3
Carabao i. Phil. **74** B3
Carabaya, Cordillera de mts Peru **200** C3
Carabinani r. Brazil **199** F5
Carabobo state Venez. **199** E2
Caracal Romania **58** F4
Caracarai Brazil **199** F4
▶**Caracas** Venez. **199** E2
  Capital of Venezuela.
Caracol Mato Grosso do Sul Brazil **201** F5
Caracol Piauí Brazil **202** D4
Caracol Rondônia Brazil **201** D2
Caracoli Col. **187** K7
Caraga Phil. **74** C5
Caragabal Australia **147** E3
Caraguatatuba Brazil **207** H10
Carahue Chile **204** B5
Caraí Brazil **207** L4
Caraiva Brazil **207** N4
Carajari Brazil **199** H6
Carajás Brazil **199** I6
Carajás, Serra dos hills Brazil **199** I6
Carales Sardegna Italy see **Cagliari**
Caralis Sardegna Italy see **Cagliari**
Caramoan Peninsula Phil. **74** B3
Caramulo mt. Port. **54** C4
Caranavi Bol. **200** D3
Carandaí Brazil **203** D7
Carandaytí Bol. **201** E5
Carandazal Brazil **201** F4
Carangola Brazil **203** D7
Caransebeş Romania **58** D3
Carapajó Brazil **202** B2
Cara-Paraná r. Col. **198** C5
Carapeguá Para. **201** F6
Carapelle r. Italy **56** H7
Caráquez Ecuador **198** A5
Carare r. Col. **198** D5 ?
Caraşova Romania **58** C3
Carat, Tanjung pt Indon. **76** D3
Caratasca Hond. **186** C4
Caratasca, Laguna lag. Hond. **186** C4
Caratinga Brazil **203** D6
Caraúna mt. Brazil see **Grande, Serra**
Caraúbas Brazil **202** E3
Caravaca de la Cruz Spain **55** J6
Caravelas Brazil **203** E6
Caraveli Peru **200** B3
Carballino Spain **54** C2
Carballo Spain **54** C1
Carbó Mex. **184** C2
Carbon, Cap c. Alg. **55** K9
Carbonara, Capo c. Sardegna Italy **57** B9
Carbondale CO U.S.A. **180** F5
Carbondale IL U.S.A. **174** B4
Carbondale PA U.S.A. **177** J4
Carbonear Canada **169** K4
Carboneras Spain **55** J8
Carbonero El Mayor Spain **54** G3
Carbonia Sardegna Italy **57** A9
Carbonita Brazil **207** H9
Carcaixent Spain **55** K5
Carcajou Canada **166** G3
Carcajou r. Canada **166** D1
Carcaliu Romania **58** J3

Carcar Phil. **74** B4
Carcassonne France **51** I9
Carcastillo Spain **55** J2
Çardak Turkey **59** I11
Cardamomes, Chaîne des mts Cambodia see **Cardamom Range**
Cardamom Mountains Cambodia see **Cardamom Range**
Cardamom Range mts Cambodia **79** C5
  also known as Cardamom Chain or Cardamomes, Chaîne des or Cardamom Mountains or Banthat or Krâvanh, Chuŏr Phnum
Cardamon Hills India **94** C4
Cardel Mex. **185** F5
Cárdenas Cuba **186** C2
Cárdenas San Luis Potosí Mex. **185** F4
Cárdenas Tabasco Mex. **185** G5
Cardeña Spain **54** G6
Cardiel, Lago l. Arg. **205** C8
▶**Cardiff** U.K. **47** I12
  Capital of Wales. Also spelt Caerdydd.
Cardigan U.K. **47** H11
  also known as Aberteifi
Cardigan Bay U.K. **47** H11
Cardinal Canada **177** J1
Cardinal Lake Canada **167** G3
Cardington U.S.A. **176** C5
Cardón, Cerro hill Mex. **184** B3
Cardona Spain **55** M3
Cardona Uruguay **204** F4
Cardoner r. Spain **55** M3
Cardoso Brazil **206** D7
Cardoso, Ilha do i. Brazil **203** C8
Cardston Canada **167** H5
Cardwell Australia **149** E3
Careaçu Brazil **207** H9
Careen Lake Canada **167** I3
Carega, Cima mt. Italy **56** D3
Carei Romania **49** T8
Careiro Brazil **199** F5
Careiro do Castanho Brazil **199** F5
Carén Chile **204** C3
Carentan France **50** E3
Carey U.S.A. **176** B5
Carey, Lake salt flat Australia **151** C6
Carey Downs Australia **151** A5
Carey Lake Canada **167** K2
Cargados Carajos Islands Mauritius **218** L7
Carhaix-Plouguer France **50** B4
Carhuamayo Peru **200** A2
Carhué Arg. **204** E5
Cariacica Brazil **203** D7
Cariaco Venez. **187** H5
Cariamanga Ecuador **198** B5
Cariango Angola **127** B7
Cariati Italy **57** I9
Caribbean Sea N. Atlantic Ocean **171** J8
Cariboo Mountains Canada **166** F4
Caribou r. Man. Canada **167** M3
Caribou r. N.W.T. Canada **166** F2
Caribou U.S.A. **174** G2
Caribou Island Canada **172** H3
Caribou Islands Canada **167** H2
Caribou Mountains Canada **167** H3
Carichic Mex. **184** D3
Carigara Phil. **74** C4
Carigara Bay Phil. **74** C4
Carignan France **51** L3
Carinda Australia **147** E2
Cariñena Spain **55** J3
Carinhanha Brazil **202** D5
Carinhanha r. Brazil **202** D5
Caripande Angola **127** D8
Caripe Venez. **199** F2
Caripito Venez. **199** F2
Cariris Novos, Serra dos hills Brazil **202** D3
Caris r. Venez. **199** F2
Caritianas Brazil **201** E1
Carlabhagh U.K. see **Carloway**
Carleton U.S.A. **173** J8
Carleton, Mount hill Canada **169** H4
Carleton Place Canada **168** E4
Carletonville S. Africa **133** L3
Carlin U.S.A. **183** H1
Carlindie Aboriginal Reserve Australia **150** B4
Carlinville U.S.A. **174** B4
Carlisle U.K. **47** J9
Carlisle KY U.S.A. **176** A7
Carlisle NY U.S.A. **177** K3
Carlisle PA U.S.A. **177** H5
Carlisle Bridge S. Africa **133** K10
Carlisle Lakes salt flat Australia **151** D6
Carlit, Pic mt. France **50** H10
Carloforte Sardegna Italy **57** A9
Carlópolis Brazil **206** D10
Carlos Casares Arg. **204** E4
Carlos Chagas Brazil **203** D6
Carlos Tejedor Arg. **204** E4
Carlow Rep. of Ireland **47** F11
  also spelt Ceatharlach
Carloway U.K. **46** F5
  also spelt Carlabhagh
Carlsbad Czech Rep. see **Karlovy Vary**
Carlsbad CA U.S.A. **183** G8
Carlsbad NM U.S.A. **181** F6
Carlsbad TX U.S.A. **179** B6
Carlsbad Caverns National Park U.S.A. **181** F6
Carlson Inlet Antarctica **222** S1
Carlton U.S.A. **174** A2
Carlton Hills S. Africa **133** I8
Carlyle Canada **167** K5
Carlyle U.S.A. **174** B4
Carlyle Lake U.S.A. **174** B4
Carmacks Canada **166** B2
Carmagnola Italy **51** N8
Carman Canada **167** L5
Carmana Iran see **Kermān**
Carmarthen U.K. **47** I12
  also known as Caerfyrddin
Carmarthen Bay U.K. **47** I12
Carmaux France **51** I8
Carmel IN U.S.A. **174** C4
Carmel NY U.S.A. **177** L4
Carmel, Mount hill Israel **108** G5
  also known as Har Karmel
Carmel-by-the-Sea U.S.A. **182** C5
Carmel Head U.K. **47** H10
Carmelita Guat. **185** H5
Carmelo Uruguay **204** E4
Carmel Valley U.S.A. **182** C5
Carmen Col. **198** C2
Carmen r. Mex. **184** D2
Carmen Phil. **74** C4
Carmen, Isla i. Mex. **184** C3
Carmen, Isla del i. Mex. **185** H5
Carmen Alto Chile **200** C5
Carmen de Areco Arg. **204** E4
Carmen de Patagones Arg. **204** E6
Carmi U.S.A. **174** B4
Carmichael U.S.A. **182** C3
Carmila Australia **149** F4
Carmo Brazil **207** I8
Carmo da Cachoeira Brazil **207** H8
Carmo de Minas Brazil **207** H9
Carmo do Paranaíba Brazil **207** G7
Carmody, Lake salt flat Australia **151** B6
Carmona Angola see **Uíge**
Carmona Costa Rica **186** B5

Carmona Spain **54** F7
Carmópolis de Minas Brazil **207** I7
Carnamah Australia **151** A6
Carnarvon Australia **151** A5
Carnarvon S. Africa **132** G7
Carnarvonleegte salt pan S. Africa **132** F7
Carnarvon National Park Australia **149** E5
Carnarvon Range hills Australia **151** C5
Carnarvon Range hills Australia **149** F5
Carnegie Australia **151** C5
Carnegie, Lake salt flat Australia **151** C5
Carn Eighe mt. U.K. **46** G6
Carnero, Bahía del b. Chile **204** B5
Carnes Australia **146** B2
Carnesville U.S.A. **174** D5
Carney U.S.A. **172** F5
Carney Island Antarctica **222** P2
Car Nicobar i. India **95** G4
Carnikava Latvia **42** F4
Carnot Cent. Afr. Rep. **126** B3
Carnot Bay Australia **150** C3
Carnoustie U.K. **46** J7
Carnsore Point Rep. of Ireland **47** F11
Caroço, i. Brazil **199** F4
Caroebe r. Brazil **199** F4
Caroch mt. Spain see **El Caroche**
Carola Cay reef Australia **149** G3
Carol City U.S.A. **175** D7
Carolina Brazil **202** C3
Carolina S. Africa **133** O3
Carolina Beach U.S.A. **175** E5
Caroline Canada **167** H4
Caroline Island Kiribati **221** H6
  also known as Millenium Island
Caroline Islands N. Pacific Ocean **73** J5
Caroline Peak N.Z. **153** B13
Carondelet Ecuador **198** B4
Caroní r. Venez. **199** F2
Carora Venez. **198** D2
C. A. Rosetti Romania **58** K3
Carpathian Mountains Europe **49** Q6
  also known as Carpații or Karpaty
Carpați mts Europe see **Carpathian Mountains**
Carpații Meridionali mts Romania see **Transylvanian Alps**
Carpentaria, Gulf of Australia **148** C2
Carpentaria Downs Australia **149** E3
Carpentras France **51** L8
Carpi Italy **56** C4
Carpina Brazil **202** F3
Cârpiniş Romania **58** B3
Carpinteria U.S.A. **182** E7
Carp Lake Provincial Park Canada **166** F4
Carquefou France **50** E5
Carquesa hill Spain **54** E5
Carrabelle U.S.A. **175** C6
Carraig na Siuire Rep. of Ireland see **Carrick-on-Suir**
Carraipía Col. **198** C2
Carrantuohill mt. Rep. of Ireland **47** C12
Carrara Italy **56** C4
Carrasco, Parque Nacional nat. park Bol. **200** D4
Carrazeda de Ansiães Port. **54** D3
Carr Boyd Range hills Australia **150** E3
Carrbridge U.K. **46** I6
Carregal do Sal Port. **54** C4
Carrhae Turkey see **Harran**
Carriacou i. Grenada **187** H4
Carrickmacross Rep. of Ireland **47** F10
Carrick-on-Shannon Rep. of Ireland **47** D10
Carrick-on-Suir Rep. of Ireland **47** E11
  also known as Carraig na Siuire
Carrieton Australia **146** C3
Carrington U.S.A. **178** C2
Carrión r. Spain **54** G2
Carrión de los Condes Spain **54** G2
Carrizal Col. **198** C2
Carrizal Bajo Chile **204** C3
Carrizo r. U.S.A. **183** N7
Carrizo Creek r. U.S.A. **179** B4
Carrizo Creek watercourse AZ U.S.A. **183** N8
Carrizo Creek watercourse CA U.S.A. **183** I8
Carrizos Mex. **185** F3
Carrizo Springs U.S.A. **179** C6
Carrizo Wash watercourse U.S.A. **183** O7
Carrizozo U.S.A. **181** F6
Carroll U.S.A. **178** D3
Carrollton AL U.S.A. **175** B5
Carrollton GA U.S.A. **175** C5
Carrollton IL U.S.A. **174** B4
Carrollton KY U.S.A. **174** C4
Carrollton MO U.S.A. **178** D4
Carrollton MS U.S.A. **175** B5
Carrollton OH U.S.A. **176** D5
Carron r. Australia **149** D3
Carron r. U.K. **46** H6
Carrot r. Canada **167** K4
Carrot River Canada **167** K4
Carrsville U.S.A. **177** I9
Carruthersville U.S.A. **174** B4
Carry Falls Reservoir U.S.A. **177** K1
Carşamba Turkey **107** D2
Carson r. Australia **150** D2
Carson r. U.S.A. **178** D2
Carson City MI U.S.A. **173** I7
▶**Carson City** NV U.S.A. **182** E2
  State capital of Nevada.
Carson Escarpment Australia **150** D2
Carson Lake U.S.A. **182** F2
Carson River Aboriginal Reserve Australia **150** D2
Carson Sink l. U.S.A. **182** F2
Carsonville U.S.A. **173** K7
Carstensz-top mt. Indon. see **Jaya, Puncak**
Carswell Lake Canada **167** I3
Cartagena Chile **204** C4
Cartagena Col. **198** C2
Cartagena Spain **55** K7
  historically known as Carthago Nova
Cartago Col. **198** C3
Cartago Costa Rica **186** C5
Cártama Spain **54** G8
Cartaya Spain **54** D7
Cartaya, Cap c. France **51** M9
Carter, Mount hill Australia **149** D2
Carteret Group is P.N.G. see **Kilinailau Islands**
Carteret Island Solomon Is. see **Malaita**
Carters Range hills Australia **149** D4
Carterton N.Z. **152** I9
Carthage tourist site Tunisia **123** H1
  historically known as Carthago
Carthage IL U.S.A. **174** B3
Carthage MO U.S.A. **178** D4
Carthage NC U.S.A. **174** E5
Carthage NY U.S.A. **177** J2
Carthage TN U.S.A. **174** C4
Carthage TX U.S.A. **179** D5
Carthago tourist site Tunisia see **Carthage**
Carthago Nova Spain see **Cartagena**
Cartier Canada **173** L4
Cartier Island Australia **150** C2
Cartwright Man. Canada **167** L5
Cartwright Nfld. Canada **169** J2
Caruachi Venez. **199** F2
Carucambaba Brazil **202** D4
Cărunta, Vârful mt. Romania **58** H2
Carúpano Venez. **199** F2
Carutapera Brazil **202** C2
Carvalho Brazil **199** I5
Carver U.S.A. **176** B8
Carvin France **51** I2
Carvoeiro Brazil **199** F5
Carvoeiro, Cabo c. Port. **54** B5

Carwell Australia 149 E5
Cary U.S.A. 174 E5
Caryapundy Swamp Australia 147 D2
Caryville *TN* U.S.A. 176 A9
Caryville *WI* U.S.A. 172 B6
Casabindo, Cerro de *mt.* Arg. 200 D5
Casablanca Chile 204 C4

▶**Casablanca** Morocco 122 D2
5th most populous city in Africa. Also known as Dar el Beida.
world [cities] ➡ 24–25

Casa Branca Brazil 206 F8
Casa de Janos Mex. 184 C2
Casa de Piedra, Embalse *resr* Arg. 204 D5
Casa Grande U.S.A. 183 M9
Casale Monferrato Italy 56 A3
Casalins Arg. 204 F5
Casalmaggiore Italy 56 C4
Casalpusterlengo Italy 56 B3
Casalvasco Brazil 201 E3
Casamance *r.* Senegal 124 A3
Casanare *dept* Col. 198 D3
Casanare *r.* Col. 198 D3
Casares Nicaragua 186 B5
Casas Grandes Mex. 184 D2
Casas Grandes *r.* Mex. 184 D2
Casas-Ibáñez Spain 55 J5
Casbas Arg. 204 E5
Casca Brazil 203 A9
Cascada de Bassaseachic, Parque Nacional *nat. park* Mex. 184 C2
Cascade Australia 151 C7
Cascade *r.* N.Z. 153 C12
Cascade *IA* U.S.A. 174 B3
Cascade *ID* U.S.A. 180 C3
Cascade Point N.Z. 153 C12
Cascade Range *mts* Canada/U.S.A. 164 G5
Cascade Reservoir U.S.A. 180 C3
Cascais Port. 54 B6
Cascal, Paso del *pass* Nicaragua 186 B5
Cascapédia *r.* Canada 169 H3
Cascavel *Ceará* Brazil 202 E3
Cascavel *Paraná* Brazil 203 A8
Căscioarele Romania 58 H4
Casco U.S.A. 172 F6
Casco Bay U.S.A. 177 P2
Caserta Italy 56 G7
Caseville U.S.A. 173 J7
Casey *research station* Antarctica 223 H2
Casey Bay Antarctica 223 D2
Caseyr, Raas *c.* Somalia 128 F2
English form Guardafui, Cape
Cashel Rep. of Ireland 47 E11
Cashmere Australia 147 F1
Cashton U.S.A. 172 C7
Casigua *Falcón* Venez. 198 D2
Casigua *Zulia* Venez. 198 C2
Casiguran Phil. 74 B2
Casiguran Sound *sea chan.* Phil. 74 B2
Casilda Arg. 204 E4
Casimcea Romania 58 J4
Casimcea *r.* Romania 58 J4
Casimiro de Abreu Brazil 207 K9
Casino Australia 147 G2
Casinos Spain 55 K5
Casita Mex. 181 E7
Čáslav Czech Rep. 49 M6
Casma Peru 200 A2
Casnewydd U.K. *see* **Newport**
Casnovia U.S.A. 172 H7
Casogoran Bay Phil. 74 C4
Casoli Italy 56 G6
Caspe Spain 55 K3
Casper U.S.A. 180 F4
Caspian U.S.A. 172 E4
Caspian Lowland Kazakh./Rus. Fed. 102 A3
also known as Kaspīy Mangy Oypaty *or* Prikaspiyskaya Nizmennost'

▶**Caspian Sea** Asia/Europe 102 B4
Largest lake in the world and in Asia/Europe. Lowest point in Europe. Also known as Kaspiyskoye More.
world [physical features] ➡ 8–9

largest lakes

	lake	area sq km	area sq miles	location	page#
1 ▶	Caspian Sea	371 000	*143 243*	Asia/Europe	➡ 102 B4
2 ▶	Lake Superior	82 100	*31 698*	North America	➡ 172 F3
3 ▶	Lake Victoria	68 800	*26 563*	Africa	➡ 128 B5
4 ▶	Lake Huron	59 600	*23 011*	North America	➡ 173 J5
5 ▶	Lake Michigan	57 800	*22 316*	North America	➡ 172 F7
6 ▶	Aral Sea	33 640	*12 988*	Asia	➡ 102 D3
7 ▶	Lake Tanganyika	32 900	*12 702*	Africa	➡ 127 F6
8 ▶	Great Bear Lake	31 328	*12 095*	North America	➡ 166 F1
9 ▶	Lake Baikal	30 500	*11 776*	Asia	➡ 81 H2
10 ▶	Lake Nyasa	30 044	*11 600*	Africa	➡ 129 B7

Cass *r.* U.S.A. 173 J7
Cassacatiza Moz. 131 G2
Cassadaga U.S.A. 176 F3
Cassai Angola 127 D7
Cassamba Angola 127 D8
Cassano allo Ionio Italy 57 I9
Cassara Brazil 201 E3
Cass City U.S.A. 173 J7
Casselman Canada 168 F4
Casselton U.S.A. 178 C2
Cássia Brazil 206 G7
Cassiar Mountains Canada 166 D3
Cassilândia Brazil 206 B6
Cassilis Australia 147 F3
Cassinga Angola 127 C8
also spelt Kassinga
Cassino Brazil 204 G4
Cassino Italy 56 F7
Cassis France 51 L9
Cassley *r.* U.K. 46 H6
Cassongue Angola 127 B7
Cassopolis U.S.A. 172 G9
Cassville *MO* U.S.A. 178 D4
Cassville *WI* U.S.A. 172 C8
Castalla Spain 55 K6
Castanhal *Amazonas* Brazil 199 F6
Castanhal *Pará* Brazil 202 C2
Castanheira de Pêra Port. 54 C4
Castanheiro Brazil 199 E5
Castanho Brazil 201 E1
Castaño Nuevo Arg. 204 C3
Castaños Mex. 185 E3
Castejón, Montes de *mts* Spain 55 J3
Castèl di Sangro Italy 56 G7
Castelfiorentino Italy 56 C5
Castelfranco Emilia Italy 56 D4
Castelfranco Veneto Italy 56 D3
Casteljaloux France 50 G8
Castellammare, Golfo di *b. Sicilia* Italy 57 E10
Castellammare di Stabia Italy 57 G8
Castellane France 51 M9
Castellaneta Italy 57 I8
Castellanos *mt.* Spain 55 I6
Castellar de la Frontera Spain 54 F8
Castelldefels Spain 55 M3
Castell de Ferro Spain 55 H8
Castelli *Buenos Aires* Arg. 204 F5
Castelli *Chaco* Arg. 204 E2
Castell-nedd U.K. *see* **Neath**
Castell Newydd Emlyn U.K. *see* **Newcastle Emlyn**
Castello de Ampurias Spain *see* **Castelló d'Empúries**
Castelló de la Plana Spain 55 K5
also spelt Castellón de la Plana
Castelló d'Empúries Spain 55 O2
also spelt Castello de Ampurias
Castellón de la Plana Spain *see* **Castelló de la Plana**
Castelnaudary France 51 H9
Castelnau-de-Médoc France 50 F7
Castelnovo ne'Monti Italy 56 C4
Castelo Brazil 207 L7
Castelo Branco Port. 54 D5
Castelo Branco *admin. dist.* Port. 54 D4
Castelo de Vide Port. 54 D5
Castelo do Piaui Brazil 202 D3
Castèl San Pietro Terme Italy 56 D4
Castelsardo *Sardegna* Italy 56 A8
Castelsarrasin France 50 H8
Casteltermini *Sicilia* Italy 57 F11
Castelvetrano *Sicilia* Italy 57 E11
Castèl Volturno Italy 56 F7
Casterton Australia 146 D4
Castets France 50 E9
Castiglione dei Pepoli Italy 56 D4
Castiglione del Lago Italy 56 E5
Castiglione della Pescaia Italy 56 C6
Castiglione della Stiviere Italy 56 C3
Castiglion Fiorentino Italy 56 D5
Castile U.S.A. 176 G3
Castilho Brazil 206 B7
Castilla Chile 204 C2
Castilla Peru 198 A6
Castilla - La Mancha *aut. comm.* Spain 55 H5
Castilla y León *aut. comm.* Spain 55 G3
Castillejo Venez. 199 F3
Castilletes Col. 198 D2
Castillo, Canal del *sea chan.* Chile 205 B8
Castillo, Pampa del *hills* Arg. 205 C7
Castillos Uruguay 204 G4
Castillos, Lago de *l.* Uruguay 204 G4
Castlebar Rep. of Ireland 47 C10
also known as Caisleán an Bharraigh
Castleblayney Rep. of Ireland 47 F9
Castle Dale U.S.A. 183 M2
Castle Danger U.S.A. 172 B3
Castle Dome Mountains U.S.A. 183 J8
Castle Douglas U.K. 47 I9
Castlegar Canada 166 G5
Castle Island Bahamas 187 E2
Castleisland Rep. of Ireland 47 C11
Castlemaine Australia 147 E4
Castle Mountain Canada 166 H5
formerly known as Eisenhower, Mount
Castle Mountain U.S.A. 182 D6
Castle Peak *hill Hong Kong* China 87 [inset]
also known as Tsing Shan
Castle Peak Bay *Hong Kong* China 87 [inset]
also known as Tsing Shan Wan
Castlepoint N.Z. 152 K8
Castlepollard Rep. of Ireland 47 E10
Castlerea Rep. of Ireland 47 D10
Castlereagh *r.* Australia 147 E2
Castle Rock *CO* U.S.A. 180 F5
Castle Rock *WA* U.S.A. 180 B3
Castle Rock Lake U.S.A. 172 C7
Castor Canada 167 I4
Castor, Rivière du *r.* Canada 168 E2
Castor Creek *r.* U.S.A. 179 D6
Castra Regina Germany *see* **Regensburg**
Castres France 51 I9
Castricum Neth. 48 B3

▶**Castries** St Lucia 187 H4
Capital of St Lucia.

Castro Brazil 203 B8
Castro Chile 205 B6
Castro Alves Brazil 202 E5
Castrocaro Terme Italy 56 D4
Castro del Río Spain 54 G7
Castro de Rei Spain 54 D1
Castro Marim Port. 54 D7
Castro-Urdiales Spain 55 H1
Castro Verde Port. 54 C7
Castrovillari Italy 57 I9
Castroville U.S.A. 182 C5
Castrovirreyna Peru 200 B3
Castuera Spain 54 F6
Cast Uul *mt.* Mongolia 84 A1
Caswell Sound *inlet* N.Z. 153 B12
Çat Turkey 107 E3
Catabola Angola 127 C8
formerly known as Nova Sintra
Catacamas Hond. 186 B4
Catacaos Peru 198 A6
Catacocha Ecuador 198 B6
Cataguases Brazil 207 K8
Catahoula Lake U.S.A. 179 D6
Cataiñgan Phil. 74 B3
Çatak Turkey 107 E3
Catalão Brazil 206 F5
Çatalca Turkey 58 J7
Çatalca Yarımadası *pen.* Turkey 58 J7
Catalina U.S.A. 183 N9
Catalonia *aut. comm.* Spain *see* **Cataluña**
Cataluña *aut. comm.* Spain 55 M3
English form Catalonia; *also spelt* Catalunya
Catalunya *aut. comm.* Spain *see* **Cataluña**
Çatalzeytin Turkey 106 C2
Catamarca Arg. 204 D3
Catamarca *prov.* Arg. 204 D2
Catambia Moz. *see* **Catandica**
Catana *Sicilia* Italy *see* **Catania**
Catanauan Phil. 74 B3
Catandica Moz. 131 G3
formerly known as Catambia *or* Vila Gouveia
Catanduanes *i.* Phil. 74 C3
Catanduva Brazil 206 D8
Catanduvas Brazil 203 A8
Catania *Sicilia* Italy 57 H11
historically known as Catana
Catania, Golfo di *g. Sicilia* Italy 57 H11
Catán Lil Arg. 204 C5
Catanzaro Italy 57 I10
Cataqueamã Brazil 201 E2
Cataract U.S.A. 172 C6
Cataract Creek *watercourse* U.S.A. 183 L5
Catarina Brazil 202 E3
Catarina U.S.A. 179 C6
Catarino Rodriguez Mex. 185 E3
Catarman Phil. 74 C3
Catarroja Spain 55 K5
Catastrophe, Cape Australia 146 B3
Catata Nova Angola 127 B8
Catatumbo Bari *nat. park* Col. 198 C2
Catavi Bol. 200 D4
Catawba U.S.A. 172 C5
Catawba *r.* U.S.A. 174 D5
Catawissa U.S.A. 177 I5
Cat Ba, Đao *i.* Vietnam 78 D3
Catbalogan Phil. 74 C4
Cateel Phil. 74 C5
Cateel Bay Phil. 74 C5
Catemaco Mex. 185 G5
Catembe Moz. 133 Q3
Catengue Angola 127 B8
Catete Angola 127 B7
Catete *r.* Brazil 199 H6
Cathcart S. Africa 133 L9
Cathedral City U.S.A. 183 H8
Cathedral Peak Lesotho 133 N5
Cathedral Provincial Park Canada 166 F5
Catherine, Mount U.S.A. 183 L3
Catheys Valley U.S.A. 182 D4
Cathlamet U.S.A. 180 B3
Catió Guinea-Bissau 124 B4
Catisimiña Venez. 199 F3
Cat Island Bahamas 187 E1
Catlins Forest Park *nature res.* N.Z. 153 D14
Catoche, Cabo *c.* Mex. 185 I4
Catolé do Rocha Brazil 202 E3
Catolé Grande *r.* Brazil 207 M2
Catolo Angola 127 C7
Catorce Mex. 185 E4
Catota Angola 127 C8
Catoute *mt.* Spain 54 E2
Catria, Monte *mt.* Italy 56 E5
Catriló Arg. 204 E5
Catrimani Brazil 199 F4
Catrimani *r.* Brazil 199 F4
Catskill U.S.A. 177 L3
Catskill Mountains U.S.A. 177 K3
Cattenom France 51 M3
Cattle Creek N.Z. 153 E12
Cattolica Italy 56 E5
Catúa Arg. 200 D5
Catuane Moz. 131 G5
Catur Moz. 129 B8
Cauaxi *r.* Brazil 202 B2
Cauayan Phil. 74 B4
Caubvick, Mount Canada 169 I1
Cauca *dept* Col. 198 B4
Cauca *r.* Col. 198 C2
Caucaia Brazil 202 E2
Caucasia Col. 198 C3
▶**Caucasus** *mts* Asia/Europe 107 E2
also known as Bol'shoy Kavkaz
europe [countries] ➡ 32–33
Caucete Arg. 204 C3
Cauchari, Salar de *salt flat* Arg. 200 D5
Cauchon Lake Canada 167 L4
Caucomgomoc Lake U.S.A. 174 G2
Caudete Spain 55 K6
Caudry France 51 J2
Cauit Point Phil. 74 C4
Caulnes France 50 D4
Caulonia Italy 57 I10
Caunao *r.* Cuba 186 D2
Caungula Angola 127 C7
Cauno Angola 127 C9
Cauquenes Chile 204 B4
Caura *r.* Venez. 199 E3
Caurés *r.* Brazil 199 F5
Causapscal Canada 169 H3
Căușeni Moldova 58 K2
formerly spelt Kaushany
Căușeni *prov.* Moldova 53 H2
Caussade France 50 H8
Cautário *r.* Brazil 201 D3
Caution, Cape Canada 166 E5
Cauto *r.* Cuba 186 D2
Cava de' Tirreni Italy 57 G8
Cávado *r.* Port. 54 C3
Cavaglià Italy 56 A3
Cavaillon France 51 L9
Cavalcante *Goiás* Brazil 202 C5
Cavalcante *Rondônia* Brazil 201 E2
Cavalier U.S.A. 178 C1
Cavalleria, Cap de *c.* Spain 55 P4
Cavalli Islands N.Z. 152 H2
Cavally *r.* Côte d'Ivoire 124 D5
Cavan Rep. of Ireland 47 E10
Çavdarhisar Turkey 59 K9
Çavdır Turkey 106 B3
Cave N.Z. 153 E12
Cave City *AR* U.S.A. 174 B4
Cave City *KY* U.S.A. 174 C4
Cave Creek U.S.A. 183 M8
Caveira Brazil 207 J3
Cavenagh Range *hills* Australia 151 E5
Cavera, Serra do *hills* Brazil 203 A9
Cavernoso, Serra do *mts* Brazil 203 A8
Cave Run Lake U.S.A. 176 B7
Caviana, Ilha *i.* Brazil 202 B1
Cavili *reef* Phil. 74 B4
Cavite Phil. 74 B3
Cavo, Monte *hill* Italy 56 E7
Cavone *r.* Italy 57 I8
Cavongo Angola 127 C8
Çavuşçu Turkey 106 B3
Çavuşköy Turkey 108 B1
Cawndilla Lake *imp. l.* Australia 147 D3
Cawnpore India *see* **Kanpur**
Cawood U.S.A. 176 B9
Caxambu Brazil 207 I8
Caxias *Amazonas* Brazil 198 D6
Caxias *Maranhão* Brazil 202 D3
Caxias do Sul Brazil 203 B9
Caxito Angola 127 B7
Caxiuana, Baía de *l.* Brazil 199 I5
Çay Turkey 106 B3
Cayambe-Coca, Parque Nacional *nat. park* Ecuador 198 B5
Çaybaşı Turkey *see* **Çayeli**
Cayce U.S.A. 175 D5
Çaycuma Turkey 106 C2
Çayeli Turkey 107 E2
also known as Çaybaşı

▶**Cayenne** Fr. Guiana 199 H3
Capital of French Guiana.

Cayey Puerto Rico 187 G3
Çaygören Barajı *resr* Turkey 59 J9
Çayhan Turkey 106 C3
Çayhisar Turkey 59 J12
Çayırhan Turkey 106 B2
Caylus France 50 H8
Cayman Brac *i.* Cayman Is 186 D3

▶**Cayman Islands** *terr.* West Indies 186 C3
United Kingdom Overseas Territory.
oceania [countries] ➡ 138–139

Cay Sal *i.* Bahamas 186 C2
Cay Santa Domingo *i.* Bahamas 186 E2
Cayucos U.S.A. 182 D6
Cayuga Canada 173 N8
Cayuga Heights U.S.A. 177 I3
Cayuga Lake U.S.A. 177 I3
Cazage Angola 127 D7
also spelt Cazaje
Cazaje Angola *see* **Cazage**
Cazalla de la Sierra Spain 54 F7
Căzănești Romania 58 I4
Caza Pava Arg. 204 F3
Cazaux et de Sanguinet, Étang de *l.* France 50 E8
Cazê China 89 D6
Cazenovia U.S.A. 177 J3
Cazères France 50 H9
Cažma Croatia 56 I3
Cazombo Angola 127 D7
Cazorla Spain 55 I7
Cazula Moz. 131 G2
Cea *r.* Spain 54 F2
Ceadâr-Lunga Moldova *see* **Ciadîr-Lunga**
Ceanannus Mór Rep. of Ireland *see* **Kells**
Ceará Brazil *see* **Fortaleza**
Ceará *state* Brazil 202 E3
Ceatalchioi Romania 58 J3
Ceatharlach Rep. of Ireland *see* **Carlow**
Ceballos Mex. 184 D3
Cebireis Dağı *mt.* Turkey 108 D1
Cebollar Arg. 204 D3
Ceboruco, Volcán *vol.* Mex. 184 D4
Cebreros Spain 54 G4
Cebu Phil. 74 B4
Cebu *i.* Phil. 74 B4
Ceccano Italy 56 F7
Cecil U.S.A. 172 E6
Cecil Plains Australia 147 F1
Cecil Rhodes, Mount *hill* Australia 151 C5
Cecilton U.S.A. 177 J6
Cecina Italy 56 C5
Cecina *r.* Italy 56 C5
Ceclavín Spain 54 E5
Cedar *r. MI* U.S.A. 173 I7
Cedar *r. ND* U.S.A. 178 B2
Cedar *r. NE* U.S.A. 178 C3
Cedarberg *mts* S. Africa 132 C9
Cedar Bluff U.S.A. 176 D8
Cedar City U.S.A. 183 K4
Cedar Creek Reservoir U.S.A. 179 C5
Cedaredge U.S.A. 180 F5
Cedar Falls U.S.A. 174 A3
Cedar Grove *CA* U.S.A. 182 F5
Cedar Grove *IN* U.S.A. 176 A6
Cedar Grove *WI* U.S.A. 172 F7
Cedar Grove *WV* U.S.A. 176 D7
Cedar Island U.S.A. 177 J8
Cedar Lake *Man.* Canada 167 K4
Cedar Lake *Ont.* Canada 173 O4
Cedar Point U.S.A. 176 B4
Cedar Rapids U.S.A. 174 B3
Cedar Ridge U.S.A. 183 M5
Cedar River U.S.A. 172 F5
Cedar Run U.S.A. 177 K6
Cedar Springs Canada 173 K8
Cedar Springs U.S.A. 172 H7
Cedarville S. Africa 133 N7
Cedarville *IL* U.S.A. 172 D8
Cedarville *MI* U.S.A. 173 I5
Cedarville *OH* U.S.A. 176 B6
Cedegolo Italy 56 C2
Cedeira Spain 54 C1
Cedeño Hond. 186 B4
Cedral *Quintana Roo* Mex. 185 I4
Cedral *San Luis Potosí* Mex. 185 E4
Cedro Brazil 202 E3
Cedros Hond. 186 B4
Cedros Mex. 185 E3
Cedros, Cerro *mt.* Mex. 181 D7
Cedros, Isla *i.* Mex. 184 B2
Ceduna Australia 146 B3
Cée Spain 54 B2
Ceelayo Somalia 128 F2
Ceelbuur Somalia 128 E3
Ceel Dhaab Somalia 128 E2
Ceeldheere Somalia 128 E4
Ceel Gaal *Bari* Somalia 128 F2
Ceel Gaal *Woqooyi Galbeed* Somalia 128 D2
Ceel Huur Somalia 128 F3
Ceel Walaaq *well* Somalia 128 D4
Ceerigaabo Somalia 128 E2
Cefalù *Sicilia* Italy 57 G10
historically known as Cephaloedium
Cega *r.* Spain 54 G3
Cegléd Hungary 49 Q8
Čegrane Macedonia 58 B7
Ceheng China 86 C3
also known as Zhelou
Cehu Silvaniei Romania 58 E1
Ceira *r.* Port. 54 C4
Çekerek Turkey 106 C2
also known as Hacıköy
Celah, Gunung *mt.* Malaysia 76 C1
Celano Italy 56 F6
Celaque, Parque Nacional *nat. park* Hond. 186 A4
Celaya Mex. 185 E4
Celbridge Rep. of Ireland 47 F10
Célé *r.* France 50 H8

▶**Celebes** *i.* Indon. 75 B3
4th largest island in Asia. Also known as Sulawesi.
asia [landscapes] ➡ 62–63

Celebes Sea Indon./Phil. 75 B2
Celendín Peru 198 B6
Celina *OH* U.S.A. 176 A5
Celina *TN* U.S.A. 174 C4
Celje Slovenia 56 H2
Cella Spain 55 J4
Celldömölk Hungary 49 O8
Celle Germany 48 H3
Celles-sur-Belle France 50 F6
Cellina *r.* Italy 56 E2
Celone *r.* Italy 56 H7
Celovec Austria *see* **Klagenfurt**
Celtic Sea Rep. of Ireland/U.K. 47 F13
Cemaru, Gunung *mt.* Indon. 77 F2
Cemilbey Turkey 106 C2
Çemişgezek Turkey 107 D3
Čempi, Teluk *b.* Indon. 77 G5
Cenad Romania 58 B2
Cenajo, Embalse del *resr* Spain 55 J6
Cencenighe Agordino Italy 56 D2
Cenderawasih, Teluk *b.* Indon. 73 I7
also known as Irian, Teluk
Cenei Romania 58 B3
Cenis, Col du Mont *pass* France 51 M7
Ceno *r.* Italy 56 C4
Cenon France 50 F8
Čenta *Vojvodina, Srbija* Yugo. 58 B3
Centane S. Africa *see* **Kentani**
Centenário do Sul Brazil 206 B9
Centenary Zimbabwe 131 F3
Centennial Wash *watercourse* U.S.A. 183 L8
Center *ND* U.S.A. 178 B2
Center *NE* U.S.A. 178 C3
Center *TX* U.S.A. 179 D6
Centerburg U.S.A. 176 C5
Center City U.S.A. 178 D2
Centereach U.S.A. 177 L5
Center Hill Lake *resr* U.S.A. 174 C5
Center Point U.S.A. 175 C5
Centerville *AL* U.S.A. 175 C5
Centerville *IA* U.S.A. 174 A3
Centerville *MO* U.S.A. 174 B4
Centerville *NC* U.S.A. 176 G9
Centerville *OH* U.S.A. 176 C7
Centerville *PA* U.S.A. 176 F4
Centerville *TN* U.S.A. 174 C5
Centerville *TX* U.S.A. 179 D6
Centerville *WV* U.S.A. 176 E6
Cento Italy 56 D4
Centrafricaine, République *country* Africa *see* **Central African Republic**
Central *admin. dist.* Botswana 131 E4
Central Brazil 202 D4
Central Chile 200 C5
Central *admin. reg.* Ghana 125 E5
Central *prov.* Kenya 128 C5
Central *admin. reg.* Malawi 129 B8
Central U.S.A. 181 E6
Central *prov.* Zambia 127 F8
Central, Cordillera *mts* Bol. 200 D4
Central, Cordillera *mts* Col. 198 E4
Central, Cordillera *mts* Dom. Rep. 187 F3
Central, Cordillera *mts* Panama 186 C5
Central, Cordillera *mts* Peru 200 A2
Central, Cordillera *mts* Phil. 74 B2
Central African Empire *country* Africa *see* **Central African Republic**
▶**Central African Republic** *country* Africa 126 C3
known as Centrafricaine, République in French; *formerly known as* Central African Empire *or* Ubangi-Shari
africa [countries] ➡ 114–117
Central Australia Aboriginal Reserve Australia 150 E4
Central Brahui Range *mts* Pak. 101 F4
Central Butte Canada 167 J5
Central City *IA* U.S.A. 174 B3
Central City *NE* U.S.A. 178 C3
Central City *PA* U.S.A. 176 G5
Central de Minas Brazil 207 L5
Central Desert Aboriginal Land *res.* Australia 148 A4
Central Falls U.S.A. 177 N4
Centralia *IL* U.S.A. 174 B4
Centralia *WA* U.S.A. 180 B3
Central Islip U.S.A. 177 L5
Central Kalahari Game Reserve *nature res.* Botswana 131 D4
Central Makran Range *mts* Pak. 101 F5
Central Mount Wedge Australia 148 A4
Central'noolesnoy Zapovednik *nature res.* Rus. Fed. 43 N5
Central Plateau Conservation Area *nature res.* Australia 147 E5
Central Provinces *state* India *see* **Madhya Pradesh**
Central Range *mts* Lesotho 133 M6
Central Range *mts* P.N.G. 73 J7
Central Russian Upland *hills* Rus. Fed. 43 R7
also known as Sredne-Russkaya Vozvyshennost'
Central Siberian Plateau Rus. Fed. 39 L3
also known as Siberia *or* Sredne-Sibirskoye Ploskogor'ye
Central Square U.S.A. 177 I2
Central Valley U.S.A. 182 B1
Centre *prov.* Cameroon 125 H5
Centre *admin. reg.* France 50 H5
Centre U.S.A. 175 C5
Centreville *MD* U.S.A. 177 I6
Centreville *VA* U.S.A. 176 H7
Centurion S. Africa 133 M2
formerly known as Verwoerdburg
Cenxi China 87 D4
Ceos *i.* Greece *see* **Kea**
Céou *r.* France 50 H8
Cephaloedium *Sicilia* Italy *see* **Cefalù**
Cephalonia *i.* Greece 59 B10
also known as Kefallinía; *also spelt* Kefallonia
Čepin Croatia 56 K3
Čepkelių *nature res.* Lith. 42 F8
Ceprano Italy 56 F7
Cepu Indon. 77 E4
Cer *hills* Yugo. 58 A4
Ceram *i.* Indon. *see* **Seram**
Ceram Sea Indon. *see* **Seram Sea**
Cerbat Mountains U.S.A. 183 J6
Cerbol *r.* Spain *see* **Servol**
Cercal *hill* Port. 54 C7
Čerchov *mt.* Czech Rep. 49 J6
Cère *r.* France 51 H8
Cerea Italy 56 D3
Cereal Canada 167 I5
Cereales Arg. 204 E5
Ceres Arg. 204 E3
Ceres Brazil 206 D2
Ceres S. Africa 132 D10
Ceres U.S.A. 182 D4
Céret France 51 I10
Cereté Col. 198 C2
Cerf, Lac du *l.* Canada 173 R4
Cerignola Italy 56 H7
Cerigo *i.* Greece *see* **Kythira**
Çerikli Turkey 106 C3
Cêringgolêb China *see* **Dongco**
Çerkeş Turkey 106 C2
Çerkezköy Turkey 58 J7
Cerknica Slovenia 56 G3
Cermei Romania 58 C2
Çermik Turkey 107 D3
Cerna Romania 58 J3
Cerna *r.* Romania 58 D3
Cerna *r.* Romania 58 D4
Cerna *r.* Romania 58 F4
Cernat Romania 58 H3
Cernăuți Ukr. *see* **Chernivtsi**
Cernavodă Romania 58 J4
Cernay France 51 N5
Cerqueira César Brazil 206 D10
Cerralvo Mex. 185 F3
Cerralvo, Isla *i.* Mex. 184 C3
Cërrik Albania 58 A7
Cerrillos Arg. 200 D6
Cerritos Mex. 185 E4
Cerro Azul Brazil 203 B8
Cerro Azul Mex. 185 F4
Cerro de Pasco Peru 200 A2
Cerro Hoya, Parque Nacional *nat. park* Panama 186 C6
Cerro Manantiales Chile 205 C9
Cerrón *mt.* Spain 55 H8
Cerrón, Cerro *mt.* Venez. 198 D2
Cerro Negro Chile 200 C5
Cerros Colorados, Embalse *resr* Arg. 204 C5
Cerros de Amotape, Parque Nacional *nat. park* Peru 198 A5
Certaldo Italy 56 D5
Certeju de Sus Romania 58 D3
Cervantes Australia 151 A6
Cervantes, Cerro *mt.* Arg. 205 B8
Cervaro *r.* Italy 56 H7
Cervati, Monte *mt.* Italy 57 H8
Cervenia Romania 58 G5
Cervera Spain 55 M3
Cervera de Pisuerga Spain 54 G2
Cerveteri Italy 56 E7
historically known as Caere
Cervia Italy 56 E4
Cervialto, Monte *mt.* Italy 57 H8
Cervignano del Friuli Italy 56 F3
Cervina, Punta *mt.* Italy 56 D2
Cervione *Corse* France 51 P10
Cervo Spain 54 D1
César *dept* Col. 198 C2
César *r.* Col. 198 C2
Cesarò *Sicilia* Italy 57 G11
Cesena Italy 56 E4
Cesenatico Italy 56 E4
Cēsis Latvia 42 G4
historically known as Wenden
Česká Lípa Czech Rep. 49 L5
Česká Republika *country* Europe *see* **Czech Republic**
České Budějovice Czech Rep. 49 L7
formerly known as Budweis
České Středohoří *hills* Czech Rep. 49 K5
Českomoravská Vysočina *hills* Czech Rep. 49 L6
Český Krumlov Czech Rep. 49 L7
Český Les *mts* Czech Rep./Germany 49 J6
Český Těšín Czech Rep. 49 P6
Česma *r.* Croatia 56 I3
Çeşme Turkey 106 A3
Cessnock Australia 147 F3
Cesson-Sévigné France 50 E4
Cestas France 50 F8
Cestos *r.* Liberia 124 C5
Cesuras Spain 54 C1
Cesvaine Latvia 42 H5
Cêtar China 84 D4
formerly known as Qaidar
Cetate Romania 58 E4
Cetatea Albă Ukr. *see* **Bilhorod-Dnistrovs'kyy**
Cetina *r.* Croatia 56 I5
Cetinje *Crna Gora* Yugo. 56 K6
Cetraro Italy 57 H9

▶**Ceuta** N. Africa 54 F9
Spanish Territory.
africa [countries] ➡ 114–117

Ceva-i-Ra *reef* Fiji 145 G4
also spelt Theva-i-Ra
Cévennes *mts* France 51 J9
Cévennes, Parc National des *nat. park* France 51 J8
Čevetjävri Fin. *see* **Sevettijärvi**
Cevizli Turkey 109 I1
Cevizlik Turkey *see* **Maçka**
Ceyhan Turkey 106 C3
Ceyhan *r.* Turkey 107 C3
Ceyhan Boğazı *r. mouth* Turkey 108 G1
Ceylanpınar Turkey 107 E3
also known as Resülayn
Ceylon *country* Asia *see* **Sri Lanka**
Cèze *r.* France 51 K8
Chaacha Turkm. 102 E5
also spelt Chäche
Chābahār Iran 101 E5
Chablais *mts* France 51 M6
Chablé Mex. 185 H5
Chablis France 51 J5
Chabre *ridge* France 51 L8
Chabrol *i.* New Caledonia *see* **Lifou**
Chabyêr Caka *salt l.* China 89 D6
Chaca Chile 200 C4
Chacabuco Arg. 204 E4
Chacarilla Bol. 200 C4
Chachahuén, Sierra *mt.* Arg. 204 C5
Chachapoyas Peru 198 B6
Chachaura-Binaganj India 96 C4
Chäche Turkm. *see* **Chaacha**
Chachersk Belarus 43 L9
Chachevichy Belarus 43 K8
Chachoengsao Thai. 79 C5
Chaco *prov.* Arg. 204 E2
formerly known as Presidente Juan Perón
Chaco Boreal *reg.* Para. 201 F5
Chaco Culture National Historical Park *nat. park* U.S.A. 181 F5
Chacon, Cape U.S.A. 166 C4
Chacorão, Cachoeira da *waterfall* Brazil 199 G6
Chacra de Piros Peru 200 B2

▶**Chad** *country* Africa 120 C6
5th largest country in Africa. Also spelt Tchad or Tshad.
africa [countries] ➡ 114–117

▶**Chad, Lake** Africa 120 B6
4th largest lake in Africa.
africa [landscapes] ➡ 112–113

Chadaasan Mongolia 84 D2
Chadan Rus. Fed. 84 A1
Chadileo *r.* Arg. 204 D5
Chadron U.S.A. 178 B3
Chadyr-Lunga Moldova *see* **Ciadîr-Lunga**
Chae Hom Thai. 78 B4
Chaek Kyrg. 103 H4
also spelt Chayek
Chaeryŏng N. Korea 83 B5
Chae Son National Park Thai. 78 B4
Chaffee U.S.A. 174 B4
Chaffers, Isla *i.* Chile 205 B7
Chaffey U.S.A. 172 A4
Chafurray Col. 198 C4
Chagai Pak. 101 F4
Chagai Hills Afgh./Pak. 101 E4
Chagalamarri India 94 C3
Chagan *Kzyl-Ordinskaya Oblast'* Kazakh. 103 F3
Chagan *Vostochnyy Kazakhstan* Kazakh. 103 I2
also spelt Shaghan
Chaganuzun Rus. Fed. 84 A1
Chagdo Kangri *reg.* China 89 D5
Chaghā Khūr *mt.* Iran 100 B4
Chaghcharān Afgh. 101 F3
Chaglinka *r.* Kazakh. 103 G1
Chagny France 51 K6
Chagoda Rus. Fed. 43 Q2
Chagoda *r.* Rus. Fed. 43 Q2
Chagodoshcha *r.* Rus. Fed. 43 R3
Chagos Archipelago *is* Indian Ocean 218 L6
Chagoyan Rus. Fed. 82 C1
Chagra *r.* Rus. Fed. 102 B1
Chagrayskoye Plato *plat.* Kazakh. *see* **Shagyray, Plato**
Chagres, Parque Nacional *nat. park* Panama 186 D5
Chaguanas Trin. and Tob. 187 H5
Chaguaramas Venez. 199 E2
Chagyl Turkm. 102 C4
Chagyllyshor, Vpadina *depr.* Turkm. 102 C4
Chaha *r.* Ukr. 58 K3
Chahah Burjal Afgh. 101 E4
Chāh Ākhvor Iran 101 D3
Chaharbagh Afgh. 101 G3
Chahār Maḩāll vā Bakhtīārī *prov.* Iran 100 B3
Chah Baba *well* Iran 100 C3
Chāh Bahār, Khalīj-e *b.* Iran 101 E5
Chahbounia Alg. 55 N9
Chāh-e'Asalū *well* Iran 100 C4
Chāh-e Bābā *well* Iran 100 D3
Chāh-e Gonbad *well* Iran 100 C3
Chāh-e Kavīr *well* Iran 100 D3
Chāh-e Khorāsān *well* Iran 100 C3
Chāh-e Malek *well* Iran 100 C3
Chāh-e Malek Mīrzā *well* Iran 100 C4
Chāh-e Mirzā *well* Iran 100 C3
Chāh-e Mūjān *well* Iran 100 C3
Chāh-e Nūklok Iran 100 C3
Chāh-e Nūklok *well* Iran 100 C3
Chāh-e Pansu *well* Iran 100 C3
Chāh-e Qeyşar *well* Iran 100 C4
Chāh-e Qobād *well* Iran 100 C3
Chāh-e Raḩmān *well* Iran 101 D4
Chāh-e Shūr *well* Iran 100 C3
Chāh-e Ţāqestān *well* Iran 100 C4
Chāh-e Tūnī *well* Iran 100 D3
Chāh Haji Abdulla *well* Iran 100 C3
Chāh Ḩaqq Iran 100 C4
Chah-i-Ab Afgh. 101 G2
Chāh Pās *well* Iran 100 C3
Chāh Ru'ī *well* Iran 101 D4
Chah Sandan Pak. 101 E4
Chahuites Mex. 185 G5
Chai *r.* China 82 A4
Chaibasa India 97 E5
Chaigneau, Lac *l.* Canada 169 H2
Chaigoubu China *see* **Huai'an**
Chaillu, Massif du *mts* Gabon 126 A5
Chainat Thai. 79 C5
Chainjoin Co *l.* China 89 D5
Chai Si *r.* Thai. 79 C5
Chaitén Chile 205 B6
Chai Wan *Hong Kong* China 87 [inset]
Chaiwopu China 88 D3
Chaiya Thai. 79 B6
Chaiyaphum Thai. 79 C5
Chajarí Arg. 204 F3
Chakai India 97 E4
Chakar *r.* Pak. 101 G4
Chakari Zimbabwe 131 F3
Chake Chake Tanz. 129 C6
Chakhānsūr Afgh. 101 E4
Chakia India 97 D4
Chak Jhumra Pak. 101 H4
Chakonipau, Lake Canada 169 G1
Chakradharpur India 97 E5
Chakulia India 97 E5
Chakwal Pak. 101 H3
Chala Peru 200 B3
Chala Tanz. 129 A6
Chalais France 50 G7
Chalap Dalan *mts* Afgh. 101 F3
Chalatenango El Salvador 185 H6
Chaláua Moz. 131 H3
Chalaxung China 86 A1
Chalbi Desert Kenya 128 C4
Chalcedon Turkey *see* **Kadıköy**
Chalengkou China 84 B4
Chaleur Bay *inlet* Canada 169 H3
also known as Chaleurs, Baie de

index C

Chaleurs, Baie de inlet Canada see Chaleur Bay
Chalia r. Arg. 205 C8
Chalib Abū Munţār watercourse Iraq 109 L5
Chaling China 87 E3
Chalinze Tanz. 129 C6
Chalisgaon India 94 B1
Chalisseri India 94 C4
Chalkar, Ozero salt l. Kazakh. see Shalkar, Ozero
Chalki Greece 59 I12
Chalki i. Greece 59 I12
also spelt Khálki
Chalkudysu India 103 I4
Chalky Inlet N.Z. 153 A14
Challakere India 94 C3
Challans France 50 E6
Challapata Bol. 200 D4

▶Challenger Deep sea feature
N. Pacific Ocean 220 D5
Deepest point in the world (Mariana Trench).
oceans [features] ➠➠ 210–211

Challis U.S.A. 180 D3
Chalmette U.S.A. 175 B6
Chal'mny-Varre Rus. Fed. 40 F2
Chalons-en-Champagne France 51 K4
formerly known as Châlons-sur-Marne
Châlons-sur-Marne France see Châlons-en-Champagne
Chalon-sur-Saône France 51 K6
Chalt Jammu and Kashmir 96 B1
Chalumna S. Africa 133 L10
Chālus France 50 G7
Chālūs Iran 100 B2
Cham Germany 49 J6
Chama U.S.A. 181 F5
Chama r. U.S.A. 181 F5
Chamamba Tanz. 129 B6
Chaman Pak. 101 F4
Chaman Bid Iran 100 D2
Chamao, Khao mt. Thai. 79 C5
Chamba India 96 C2
Chamba r. Tanz. 129 C6
Chambal r. India 96 C4
Chambas Cuba 186 D2
Chambeaux, Lac l. Canada 169 G2
Chamberlain r. Australia 150 D3
Chamberlain Canada 167 J5
Chamberlain U.S.A. 178 C3
Chamberlain Lake U.S.A. 174 G2
Chambers U.S.A. 183 O6
Chambers Bay Australia 148 A3
Chambersburg U.S.A. 176 H6
Chambers Island U.S.A. 172 F5
Chambéry France 51 L7
Chambeshi Zambia 127 F7
Chambeshi r. Zambia 127 F8
Chambi, Jebel mt. Tunisia 123 H2
Chambira r. Peru 198 C6
Chambord Canada 169 F3
Chambri Lake P.N.G. 73 J7
Chamdo China see Qamdo
Chame Panama 186 D5
Chamela Mex. 184 D5
Chamical Arg. 204 D3
Chamili i. Greece 59 H13
Cham'o Häyk' l. Eth. 128 C3
Chamoli India see Gopeshwar
Chamonix-Mont-Blanc France 51 M7
Chamouchouane r. Canada see Ashuapmushuan
Chamouse, Montagne de mt. France 51 L8
Champa India 97 D5
Champagne Castle mt. S. Africa 133 N6
Champagne-Ardenne admin. reg. France 51 K4
Champagny Islands Australia 150 D2
Champagnole France 51 L6
Champaign U.S.A. 174 B3
Champaqui, Cerro mt. Arg. 204 D3
Champasak Laos 79 D5
Champdôré, Lac l. Canada 169 H2
Champhai India 97 G5
Champion Canada 167 H5
Champion U.S.A. 172 F4
Champlain NY U.S.A. 177 L1
Champlain VA U.S.A. 177 I7
Champlain, Lake Canada/U.S.A. 174 F2
Champlain Canal U.S.A. 177 L2
Champlitte France 51 L5
Champneuf Canada 173 P2
Champotón Mex. 185 H5
Champrajnagar India see Chamrajnagar
Cham Siyāh Iran 100 B4
Chamusca Port. 54 C5
Chamzinka Rus. Fed. 41 H5
Chan, Ko i. Thai. 79 B6
Chana Thai. 79 C7
Chanak Turkey see Çanakkale
Chanal Mex. 185 G5
Chañar Arg. 204 C4
Chañar Chile see Chañaral
Chañaral Chile 204 C3
Chañaral, Isla i. Chile 204 C3
Chañarán Iran 101 D2
Chañaro, Cerro mt. Venez. 199 F3
Chança r. Port./Spain see Chanza
Chancay Peru 200 A3
Chanco Chile 204 B4
Chancos Peru 200 A2
Chanda India see Chandrapur
Chandalar r. U.S.A. 164 E3
Chandama Tanz. 129 C6
Chandausi India 96 C3
Chandbali India 97 E5
Chandeleur Islands U.S.A. 175 B6

Chanderi India 96 C4
Chandia India 96 D5
Chandigarh India 96 C3
Chandil India 97 E5
Chandler Canada 169 H3
Chandler AZ U.S.A. 183 M8
Chandler OK U.S.A. 179 C5
Chandless r. Brazil 200 C2
Chandmany Mongolia 84 B1
Chandos Lake Canada 173 P6
Chandpur Bangl. 97 F5
Chandpur India 96 C3
Chandragiri India 94 C3
Chandrapur India 94 C2
formerly known as Chanda
Chandvad India 94 B1
Chandyr r. Turkm. 102 C5
also spelt Chendir
Chang, Ko i. Thai. 79 C5
Changalane Moz. 133 Q3
Chang'an China see Rong'an
Chang'an China 87 D1
also known as Weiqu
Chang-an S. Korea 91 A7
Changane r. Moz. 131 G5
Changara Moz. 131 G3
Changbai China 82 B4
Changbai Shan mts China/N. Korea 82 B4
also known as Ch'ang-pai Shan
Changchow China see Zhangzhou
Changchow China see Changzhou
Changchun China 82 B4
historically known as Hsinking
Changdao China 85 I4
also known as Nanchangshan; formerly known as Sihou
Changde China 87 D2
formerly spelt Changsha
Changfeng China 87 F1
also known as Shuihu
Changge China 87 E1
Changgi-ap pt S. Korea 83 C5
Changgo China 89 D6
Changhai China 85 I4
also known as Sikuaishi
Chang Hu l. China 87 E2
Changhua Taiwan 87 G3
also spelt Zhanghua
Changhua Jiang r. China 87 D5
also known as Shiliu
Changhŭng S. Korea 83 B6
Changi Sing. 76 [inset]
Changjiang China 87 D5
also known as Shilu
Chang Jiang r. China see Yangtze
Changjiang Kou r. mouth China see Yangtze, Mouth of the
Changjin N. Korea 83 B4
Changjin-gang r. N. Korea 83 B4
Changkiang China see Zhanjiang
Changle China 87 F3
Changleng China see Xinjian
Changli China 85 H4
Changling China 85 J2
Changliushui China 84 B3
Changning Jammu and Kashmir 96 C2
Changning Hunan China 87 E3
Changning China see Xunwu
Changning Sichuan China 86 C2
Changnyon N. Korea 83 B5
Ch'ang-pai Shan mts China/N. Korea see Changbai Shan
Changping China 85 H4
Changpu China see Suining
Changsan-got pt N. Korea 83 B5
Changsha China 87 E3
Changshan China 87 F2
Changshou China 86 C2
Changshoujie China 87 E2
Changshu China 87 G2
Changsŏng S. Korea 83 B6
Changtai China 87 F3
also known as Wu'an
Changteh China see Changde
Changting Fujian China 87 F3
also known as Tingzhou
Changtu China 82 B4
Changuinola Panama 186 C5
Ch'angwŏn S. Korea 83 C6
Changwu China 85 E5
also known as Zhaoren
Changxing China 87 F2
also known as Zhicheng
Changyang China 87 D2
also known as Longzhouping
Changyi China 85 H4
Changyŏn N. Korea 83 B5
Changyuan China see Rongchang
Changyuan China 85 H5
Changzhi Shanxi China 85 G4
Changzhi Shanxi China 85 G4
also known as Handian
Changzhou China 87 F2
also known as Wujin; formerly spelt Changchow
Chanf Iran see Chang
Chani, Nevado de mt. Arg. 200 D6
Chania Greece 59 F13
also spelt Khaniá; historically known as Canea or Cydonia
Chanion, Kolpos b. Greece 59 E13
Chankou China 84 E5
Channagiri India 94 B3
Channapatna India 94 C3
Channel Islands English Chan. 50 D3
also known as Normandes, Îles
Channel Islands U.S.A. 182 E8
Channel Islands National Park U.S.A. 182 E7
Channel-Port-aux-Basques Canada 169 J4
Channel Rock i. Bahamas 186 D2
Channel Tunnel France/U.K. 50 H1
Channing U.S.A. 172 E4
Chantada Spain 54 D2
Chantal'skiy mt. Rus. Fed. 39 R3
Chanthaburi Thai. 79 C5
Chantilly France 51 I3
Chantonnay France 50 E6
Chanumla India 95 D4
Chanute U.S.A. 178 D4
Chany, Ozero salt l. Rus. Fed. 80 B2
Chanza r. Port./Spain 54 D7
also known as Chança
Chao Peru 200 A2
Chaobai Xinhe r. China 85 H4
Chaohu China 87 F2
Chao Hu l. China 87 F2
Chao Phraya r. Thai. 79 C5
Chaor China 85 I1
Chaor r. China 85 I1
Chaouèn Morocco 122 D2
Chaoyang Guangdong China 87 F4
Chaoyang China see Jiayin
Chaoyang Liaoning China 85 I3
Chaozhong China 85 I1
Chaozhou China 87 F4
Chapada Diamantina, Parque Nacional da nat. park Brazil 202 D5
Chapada dos Guimarães Brazil 201 G3
Chapada dos Veadeiros, Parque Nacional da nat. park Brazil 202 C5
Chapadão do Céu Brazil 206 A5
Chapadão do Sul Brazil 206 A5
Chapadinha Brazil 202 D2
Chapais Canada 169 F3
Chapak Guzar Afgh. 101 F2

Chapala Mex. 185 E4
Chapala, Laguna de l. Mex. 185 E4
Chapare r. Bol. 200 D3
Cháparra Peru 200 B3
Chaparral Col. 198 C4
Chapayevo Kazakh. 102 B2
Chapayevsk Rus. Fed. 102 B1
Chapayevskoye Kazakh. 103 H1
Chapecó Brazil 203 A8
Chapecó r. Brazil 203 A8
Chapel Hill U.S.A. 174 E5
Chapicuy Uruguay 204 F3
Chapimarca Peru 200 B3
Chapleau Canada 168 D4
Chapleau Crown Game Reserve nature res. Canada 168 D3
Chaplin Cameroon 167 J5
Chaplin Rus. Fed. 39 S3
Chaplin Lake dry lake Canada 167 J5
also spelt Chendir
Chaplino Rus. Fed. 39 S3
Chaplygin Rus. Fed. 41 F5
Chapman, Mount Canada 166 G5
Chapmanville PA U.S.A. 176 F4
Chapmanville WV U.S.A. 176 C8
Chappell U.S.A. 178 B3
Chappell Islands Australia 147 E5
Chapra India see Chhapra
Chapri Pass Afgh. 101 F3
Charadai Arg. 204 F2
Charagua Bol. 201 E4
Charana Bol. 200 D4
Charapita Col. 198 C5
Charata Arg. 204 E2
Charbonnel, Pointe de mt. France 51 N7
Charcas Mex. 185 E4
Charcot Island Antarctica 222 S2
Chard Canada 167 I4
Chard U.K. 47 J12
Chardara Kazakh. see Shardara
Chardarinskoye Vodokhranilishche resr Kazakh./Uzbek. 103 G4
also known as Shardara Bögeni
Chardon U.S.A. 176 D4
Chardzhev Turkm. 103 E5
also known as Turkmenabat; also spelt Chärjew; formerly spelt Chardzhou
Chardzhou Turkm. see Chardzhev
Chardzhouskaya Oblast' admin. div. Turkm. see Lebapskaya Oblast'
Char Chu r. Xizang China 89 F6
Charente r. France 50 E7
Charg Iran 100 C4
Chari r. Cameroon/Chad 125 I3
also spelt Shari
Chari-Baguirmi pref. Chad 126 C2
Chārīkār Afgh. 101 G3
Charikov U.S.A. 176 A6
Chariton U.S.A. 174 A3
Chariton r. U.S.A. 174 A4
Chärjew Turkm. see Chardzhev
Charkayuvom Rus. Fed. 40 J2
Charkhari India 96 C4
Charkhi Dadri India 96 C3
Charkhlik China see Ruoqiang
Charleroi Belgium 51 K2
Charles, Cape U.S.A. 177 J8
Charlesbourg Canada 169 G4
Charles City IA U.S.A. 174 A3
Charles City VA U.S.A. 177 H8
Charles de Gaulle airport France 51 I3
Charles Lake Canada 167 J3
Charles M. Russell National Wildlife Refuge nature res. U.S.A. 180 F3
Charles Point Australia 148 A2
Charleston N.Z. 153 F9
Charleston IL U.S.A. 174 B4
Charleston MO U.S.A. 174 B4
Charleston MS U.S.A. 174 B5
Charleston SC U.S.A. 175 E5

▶Charleston WV U.S.A. 176 D7
State capital of West Virginia.

Charleston Peak U.S.A. 183 I5
Charlestown St Kitts and Nevis 187 H3
Charlestown NH U.S.A. 177 M2
Charlestown RI U.S.A. 177 N4
Charles Town U.S.A. 176 H6
Charleville Australia 149 E5
Charleville Rep. of Ireland see Rathluirc
Charleville-Mézières France 51 K3
Charlevoix U.S.A. 172 H5
Charlie Lake Canada 166 F3
Charlotte MI U.S.A. 173 I8
Charlotte NC U.S.A. 174 D5

▶Charlotte Amalie Virgin Is (U.S.A.) 187 G3
Capital of the U.S. Virgin Islands.

Charlotte Bank sea feature S. China Sea 77 D1
Charlotte Court House U.S.A. 176 G8
Charlotte Harbor b. U.S.A. 175 D7
Charlotte Lake Canada 166 E4
Charlottenberg Sweden 45 K4
Charlottesville U.S.A. 176 F7

▶Charlottetown Canada 169 I4
Provincial capital of Prince Edward Island.

Charlotteville Trin. and Tob. 187 H5
Charlton Australia 147 D4
Charlton Island Canada 168 E2
Charmes France 51 M4
Charmitsa r. Belarus 43 T7
Charnley r. Australia 150 D3
Charomkhava Belarus 42 I6
Charomskoye Rus. Fed. 43 T2
Charozero Rus. Fed. 43 T1
Charron Lake Canada 167 M4
Charsadda Pak. 101 G3
Charshanga Turkm. 103 F5
Charsk Kazakh. see Shar
Charters U.S.A. 176 B7
Charters Towers Australia 149 E4
Chartres France 50 H4
Charvakskoye Vodokhranilishche resr Kazakh./Uzbek. 103 G4
Charyn Kazakh. 103 I4
also spelt Sharyn
Charyn r. Kazakh. 103 I4
Charysh r. Rus. Fed. 103 J1
Charyshskoye Rus. Fed. 88 C1
Chas India 97 E5
Chās mt. Port. 54 C4
Chascomús Arg. 204 F4
Chascos Canada 166 G5
Chase U.S.A. 172 H7
Chase City U.S.A. 176 G9
Chashkent Turkm. 103 F5
Chashmeh-ye Ab-e Garm spring Iran 100 D3
Chashmeh-ye Garm Ab spring Iran 100 D3
Chashmeh-ye Magu well Iran 100 D3
Chashmeh-ye Safid spring Iran 100 B3
Chashmeh-ye Shotoran well Iran 100 C3
Chashniki Belarus 43 K7
Chasŏng N. Korea 82 B4
Chashiri reg. Greece 59 C9
Chaska U.S.A. 178 D2
Chaslands Mistake c. N.Z. 153 D14
Chasovenkaya Rus. Fed. 43 O1
Chasovenkaya Rus. Fed. 43 T2
Chassezac r. France 51 J8
Chassiron, Pointe de pt France 50 E6
Chastab, Küh-e mts Iran 100 D3
Chastyye Rus. Fed. 40 J4
Chasuta Peru 198 B6
Chāt Iran 100 D2
Château-Arnoux France 51 L8

Châteaubriant France 50 E5
Château-Chinon France 51 J5
Château-du-Loir France 50 G5
Chateaugay U.S.A. 177 K1
Châteaugiron France 50 E4
Chateauguay r. Canada 169 G1
Château-Gontier France 50 F5
Chateauguay, Lac l. Canada 169 G1
Châteaulin France 50 B3
Châteauneuf-en-Thymerais France 50 H4
Châteauneuf-sur-Loire France 51 I5
Chateau Pond l. Canada 169 J2
Châteauponsac France 50 H6
Châteaurenard France 51 K9
Château-Renault France 50 G5
Châteauroux France 51 H6
Château-Salins France 51 M4
Châte_u-Thierry France 51 J3
Châtelaillon-Plage France 50 E6
Châtelet Belgium 51 K2
Châtellerault France 50 G6
Châtenois France 51 L4
Chatfield U.S.A. 178 B3
Chatham N.B. Canada 169 H4
Chatham Ont. Canada 168 D5
Chatham U.K. 47 M12
Chatham MA U.S.A. 177 P4
Chatham MI U.S.A. 172 G4
Chatham NY U.S.A. 177 L3
Chatham VA U.S.A. 176 F9
Chatham, Isla i. Chile 205 B8
Chatham Island Samoa see Savai'i
Chatham Island S. Pacific Ocean 145 H6
also known as Rekohua
Chatham Islands S. Pacific Ocean 145 H6
Chatham Sound sea chan. Canada 166 D4
Chatham Strait U.S.A. 166 C3
Châtillon-sur-Indre France 50 H6
Châtillon-sur-Loire France 51 I5
Châtillon-sur-Seine France 51 K5
Chatkal mts Kyrg. 103 G4
Chatom U.S.A. 175 B6
Chatra India 97 E4
Chatra Nepal 97 E4
Chatsu India 96 B4
Chatsworth Australia 149 D4
Chatsworth Canada 173 M6
Chatsworth GA U.S.A. 174 C5
Chatsworth IL U.S.A. 172 E10
Chatsworth NJ U.S.A. 177 K6
Chatsworth Zimbabwe 131 F3
Chattagam Bangl. see Chittagong
Chattahoochee U.S.A. 175 C6
Chattahoochee r. U.S.A. 179 F6
Chattanooga U.S.A. 174 C5
Chatto Creek N.Z. 153 D13
Chatturat Thai. 79 C5
Chatyr-Kёl', Ozero l. Kyrg. see Chatyr-Köl
Chatyr-Köl l. Kyrg. 88 B3
also known as Chatyrkёl', Ozero
Chatyr-Tash Kyrg. 103 I4
Châu Độc Vietnam 79 D6
formerly known as Chau Phu
Chauffailles France 51 K6
Chauk Myanmar 78 A3
Chauka r. India 96 D4
Chaukhamba mts India see Badrinath Peaks
Chau Kung To i. Hong Kong China see Sunshine Island
Chaumont France 51 L4
Chauncey U.S.A. 176 C6
Chaungwabyin Myanmar 79 B5
Chaunskaya Guba b. Rus. Fed. 39 Q3
Chauny France 51 J3
Chau Phu Vietnam see Châu Độc
Chaural India 96 C5
Chausey, Îles is France 50 E4
Chausy Belarus see Chavusy
Chautauqua, Lake U.S.A. 176 F3
Chauvay Kyrg. 103 H4
Chauvigny France 50 G6
Chauvin Canada 167 I4
Chaval Brazil 202 D2
Chavan'ga r. Rus. Fed. 40 F2
Chavār Iran 100 A3
Chaves Brazil 202 B2
Chaves Port. 54 D3
Chaves Valdivia Peru 198 B6
Chavigny, Lac l. Canada 169 F1
Chaviva Col. 198 D3
Chavusy Belarus 43 L8
also spelt Chausy
Chawal r. Pak. 101 G4
Chay, r. Vietnam 78 D3
Chayan Kazakh. see Shayan
Chayanta r. Bol. 200 D4
Chayatyn, Khrebet ridge Rus. Fed. 82 E1
Chayek Kyrg. see Chaek
Chayevo Rus. Fed. 43 S3
Chaykovskiy Rus. Fed. 40 J4
Chazhegovo Rus. Fed. 40 J3
Chazón Arg. 204 E4
Chazy U.S.A. 177 L1
Cheat r. U.S.A. 176 F6
Cheb Czech Rep. 49 J5
Chebanse U.S.A. 172 F9
Chebbi salt l. Alg. 123 F4
Cheboksary Rus. Fed. 40 H4
Cheboygan U.S.A. 173 I5
Chebsara Rus. Fed. 43 T2
Chechen', Ostrov i. Rus. Fed. 102 A4
Chechenskaya Respublika aut. rep. Rus. Fed. 41 H8
short form Chechnya; English form Chechenia or Chechnia; also known as Ichkeria
Cheche Pass Lesotho 133 M6
Chechnia, aut. rep. Rus. Fed. see Chechenskaya Respublika
Chechnya aut. rep. Rus. Fed. see Chechenskaya Respublika
Chech'ŏn S. Korea 83 C5
Chęciny Poland 49 R5
Checotah U.S.A. 179 D5
Cheder Rus. Fed. 84 B1
Cheduba Island Myanmar 78 A4
also known as Man-aung Kyun
Cheduba Strait Myanmar 78 A4
Chée r. France 51 K4
Cheepash r. Canada 168 D3
Cheepie Australia 149 E5
Cheetham, Cape Antarctica 223 K2
Chef-Boutonne France 50 F6
Cheffadène well Niger 125 I2
Chegga Mauritania 122 D4
Cheggué watercourse Mauritania 124 C2
Cheguti Zimbabwe 131 F3
Chehalis U.S.A. 180 B3
Chehalis r. U.S.A. 180 B3
Chehardeh Iran 100 D3
Chehariz tourist site Iraq 107 F4
Chehel Chashmeh, Küh-e hill Iran 100 A3
Chehel Dokhtarān, Küh-e mt. Iran 101 E4
Chehell'āyeh Iran 100 C4
Cheikria well Alg. 122 D4
Cheil Nerei-Beuşniţa nat. park Romania 58 C3

Cheiron, Cime du mt. France 51 M9
Cheju S. Korea 83 B6
Cheju-do i. S. Korea 83 B6
English form Quelpart Island
Cheju-haehyŏp sea chan. S. Korea 83 B6
Chekalin Rus. Fed. 43 R7
Chek Chau i. Hong Kong China see Port Island
Chek Chue Hong Kong China see Stanley
Chekhov Rus. Fed. 43 S6
formerly known as Lopasnya
Chekhov Rus. Fed. 82 F3
Chekiang prov. China see Zhejiang
Chek Jawa, Tanjong pt Sing. 76 [inset]
Chek Lap Kok i. Hong Kong China 87 [inset]
Chek Mun Hoi Hap sea chan. Hong Kong China see Tolo Channel
Chekshino Rus. Fed. 43 V2
Chela, Serra da mts Angola 127 B9
Chelan U.S.A. 180 B3
Chelan, Lake U.S.A. 180 B2
Cheleken Turkm. 102 C5
Chelforó Arg. 204 D5
Chélif, Oued r. Alg. 55 L8
Cheline Moz. 131 G4
Chelkar Kazakh. 102 D3
also spelt Shalqar
Chellal Alg. 55 P9
Chelm Poland 53 G1
historically known as Kholm
Chelmer r. U.K. 47 M12
Chelmno Poland 49 P2
Chelmsford U.K. 47 M10
historically known as Caesaromagus
Chelmsford U.S.A. 177 N3
Chelmsford Dam S. Africa 133 N4
Chelmsford Public Resort Nature Reserve S. Africa 133 N4
Chelmża Poland 49 P2
Chelsea U.S.A. 173 I8
Cheltenham N.Z. 152 J8
Cheltenham U.K. 47 J12
Chelva Spain 55 K5
Chelyabinskaya Oblast' admin. div. Rus. Fed. 103 I1
English form Chelyabinsk Oblast
Chelyabinsk Oblast admin. div. Rus. Fed. see Chelyabinskaya Oblast'
Chelyan U.S.A. 176 D7
Chelyuskin Rus. Fed. 39 K2
Chelyuskin, Mys c. Rus. Fed. 39 K2
Chemaia Morocco 122 C2
Chembe Zambia 127 F7
Chemcham, Sebkhet salt flat Mauritania 122 B5
Chem Co l. China 89 B5
Chemillé France 50 F5
Chemmis Egypt see Akhmim
Chemnitz Germany 49 J5
formerly known as Karl-Marx-Stadt
Chemulpo S. Korea see Inch'ŏn
Chemult U.S.A. 180 B4
Chemung r. U.S.A. 177 I4
Chenab r. India/Pak. 96 A3
Chenachane Alg. 122 D4
Chenachane, Oued watercourse Alg. 122 D4
Chenango r. U.S.A. 177 J3
Chenango Bridge U.S.A. 177 J3
Ch'ench'a Eth. 128 C3
Chendir r. Turkm. see Chandyr
Cheney U.S.A. 180 C3
Cheney Reservoir U.S.A. 178 C4
Chengalpattu India 94 D3
also known as Chingleput
Chengam India 94 C3
Cheng'an China 85 G4
Chengbihe Shuiku resr China 86 C3
Chengbu China 87 D3
also known as Rulin
Chengcheng China 85 F5
Chengchow China see Zhengzhou
Chengde China 85 H3
Chengdu China 86 C2
formerly spelt Chengtu
Chengel'dy Kazakh. see Shengel'dy
Chenggong China 86 B3
also known as Longcheng
Chenghai China 87 F4
Cheng Hai l. China 86 B3
Chengjiang China see Taihe
Chengjiang China 86 B3
Chengkou China 87 D2
also known as Gecheng
Chengmai China 87 D5
also known as Jinjiang
Chengqiao China see Chongming
Chengshou China see Yingshan
Chengtu China see Chengdu
Chengwu China 87 E1
Chengxian China 86 C1
Chengxiang China see Wuxi
Chengxiang China see Quannan
Chengxiang China see Tianquan
Chengxiang China see Mianning
Chengyang China see Juxian
Chengzhong China see Ningming
Chenhu Shan i. China 85 H5
Chennai India 94 D3
formerly known as Madras
Chenoa U.S.A. 172 E10
Chenstokhov Poland see Częstochowa
Chenting, Tanjong pt Sing. 76 [inset]
Chenxi China 87 D3
also known as Chenyang
Chenyang China see Wannian
Chenzhou China 87 E3
Cheom Ksan Cambodia see Chôâm Khsant
Chepelare Bulg. 58 F7
Chepén Peru 200 A1
Chepes Arg. 204 D3
Chepo Panama 186 D5
Chepstow U.K. 47 J12
Cheptsa r. Rus. Fed. 40 I4
Chequamegon Bay U.S.A. 172 C4
Cher r. France 51 G5
Chera state India see Kerala
Cherán Mex. 185 E5
Cherangany Hills Kenya 128 B4
Cheraw U.S.A. 174 E5
Cherbaniani Reef India 94 A3
Cherbourg France 50 F2
historically known as Caesaris
Cherchen China see Qiemo
Cherdakly Rus. Fed. 40 K3
Cherdyn' Rus. Fed. 40 K3
Chère r. France 50 E5
Chereapani reef India see Byramgore Reef
Cherekha r. Rus. Fed. 43 J4
Cheremisinovo Rus. Fed. 41 F6
Cheremkhovo Rus. Fed. 80 E2
Cheremshany Rus. Fed. 82 D4
formerly known as Sinancha
Cheremukhovka Rus. Fed. 40 I4
Cherepanovo Rus. Fed. 80 C2
Cherepovets Rus. Fed. 43 S3
Cherevkovo Rus. Fed. 40 H3
Chergui, Chott ech imp. l. Alg. 123 E2
Chéria Alg. 123 G2
Cherial India see Cheriyal
Cheriton U.S.A. 177 J8
Cheriyam i. India 94 B4
Cherkasy Ukr. 41 E6
also known as Cherkassy

Cherkasy Ukr. see Cherkassy
Cherkessk Rus. Fed. 41 G7
Cherkutino Rus. Fed. 43 U5
Cherla India 94 D2
Chermenze Angola 127 D8
Chermoz Rus. Fed. 40 K4
Chern' Rus. Fed. 43 R8
Chern' r. Rus. Fed. 43 R8
Chernak Kazakh. 103 G4
also spelt Shornaq
Chernava Lipetskaya Oblast' Rus. Fed. 43 T9
Chernava Ryazanskaya Oblast' Rus. Fed. 43 U8
Chernaya Rus. Fed. 40 K1
Chernaya Rus. Fed. 40 K1
Chernaya r. Rus. Fed. 42 I3
Chernaya Kholunitsa Rus. Fed. 40 I4
Chernevo Pskovskaya Oblast' Rus. Fed. 43 J3
Chernevo Moskovskaya Oblast' Rus. Fed. 43 T7
Chernigov Ukr. see Chernihiv
Chernigovka Rus. Fed. 82 D3
Chernihiv Ukr. 41 D6
also known as Chernigov
Cherni Lom r. Bulg. 58 G5
Cherninivka Ukr. 41 F7
Cherni Vrŭkh mt. Bulg. 58 E6
Chernivtsi Ukr. 41 C6
also known as Czernowitz; also spelt Chernovtsy; historically known as Cernăuţi
Chernobyl' Ukr. see Chornobyl'
Chernogorsk Rus. Fed. 80 E2
Chernoostrovskoye Rus. Fed. 39 I3
Chernorechenskiy Rus. Fed. 40 J3
Chernoretskoye Kazakh. 103 I1
Chernushevo Rus. Fed. 43 N1
Chernovskoye Rus. Fed. 40 H4
Chernovtsy Ukr. see Chernivtsi
Chernoye More sea Asia/Europe see Black Sea
Chernukha Rus. Fed. 40 K4
Chernyakhiv Ukr. 41 D6
Chernyakhovsk Rus. Fed. 42 C7
historically known as Insterburg
Chernyanka Rus. Fed. 41 F6
Chernyayeve Rus. Fed. 82 B1
Chernysheva, Zaliv b. Kazakh. 102 D3
Chernyshevsk Rus. Fed. 81 J2
Chernyshevskiy Rus. Fed. 39 L3
Chernyshkovskiy Rus. Fed. 41 G6
Chernyy, Mys c. Rus. Fed. 40 J1
Chernyye Zemli reg. Rus. Fed. 41 H7
Chernyy Irtysh r. China/Kazakh. see Ertix He
Chernyy Otrog Rus. Fed. 102 C2
Chernyy Porog Rus. Fed. 40 E3
Chernyy Rynok Rus. Fed. see Kochubey
Chernyy Yar Rus. Fed. 102 A2
Cherokee IA U.S.A. 178 D3
Cherokee OK U.S.A. 178 C4
Cherokee Lake U.S.A. 176 B9
Cherokees, Lake o' the U.S.A. 178 D4
Cherokee Sound Bahamas 186 D1
Cherpessa Rus. Fed. 43 L5

▶Cherrapunji India 97 F4
Highest recorded annual rainfall in the world.
world [climate and weather] ➠➠ 16–17

Cherry Creek r. U.S.A. 178 B2
Cherry Creek Mountains U.S.A. 183 J1
Cherryfield U.S.A. 177 R1
Cherry Hill U.S.A. 177 J6
Cherry Island Solomon Is 145 F3
Cherry Lake U.S.A. 182 E3
Cherry Valley Canada 173 P7
Cherskaya Rus. Fed. 43 J4
Cherskiy Rus. Fed. 39 Q3
formerly known as Nizhniye Kresty
Cherskiy Range mts Rus. Fed. see Cherskogo, Khrebet
Cherskogo, Khrebet mts Rus. Fed. 85 F1
English form Cherskiy Range
Cherskogo, Khrebet mts Rus. Fed. 39 O3
Chersonisos Methano pen. Greece 59 E11
Cherthala India see Shertally
Chertkov Ukr. see Chortkiv
Chertkovo Rus. Fed. 41 G6
Chertolino Rus. Fed. 43 O5
Chertsey N.Z. 153 F11
Cherusti Rus. Fed. 43 V6
Cherven Bryag Bulg. 58 F5
Chervonoarmeyskoye Ukr. see Vil'nyans'k
Chervonoarmiys'k Ukr. see Krasnoarmiys'k
Chervonograd Ukr. see Chervonohrad
Chervonohrad Ukr. 41 C6
also spelt Chervonograd; formerly known as Chervonograd or Krystynopol'
Chervonoozavods'ke Ukr. 41 E6
Chervonoznam"yanka Ukr. 58 L1
Chervyen' Belarus 43 J8
Cherykaw Belarus 43 M8
Chesaning U.S.A. 173 I7
Chesapeake U.S.A. 177 I9
Chesapeake Bay U.S.A. 177 I7
Chesapeake Beach U.S.A. 177 I7
Cheshire U.S.A. 177 L3
Cheshme Vtoroy Turkm. 102 E5
Cheshskaya Guba b. Rus. Fed. 40 H2
Chesht-e Sharif Afgh. 101 E3
Chesma Rus. Fed. 103 I1
Chesnokovka Rus. Fed. see Novoaltaysk
Chester Canada 169 H4
Chester U.K. 47 J10
historically known as Deva
Chester CA U.S.A. 182 C1
Chester IL U.S.A. 174 B4
Chester MT U.S.A. 180 E2
Chester NJ U.S.A. 177 K5
Chester OH U.S.A. 176 D7
Chester PA U.S.A. 177 J6
Chester SC U.S.A. 174 D5
Chester VA U.S.A. 176 H8
Chester r. U.S.A. 177 I7
Chesterfield U.K. 47 K10
Chesterfield MO U.S.A. 174 B4
Chesterfield SC U.S.A. 174 D5
Chesterfield VA U.S.A. 176 H8
Chesterfield, Îles is New Caledonia 145 E3
Chesterfield Inlet Canada 167 N2
also known as Igluligaarjuk
Chesterfield Inlet inlet Canada 167 N2
Chestertown U.S.A. 177 I6
Chesterville U.S.A. 176 F5
Chesuncook Lake U.S.A. 174 G2
Chetek U.S.A. 172 B5
Chéticamp Canada 169 I4
Chetlat i. India 94 B4
Chetopa U.S.A. 178 D4
Chetumal Mex. 185 H5
Chetwode Islands N.Z. 152 I8
Chetwynd Canada 166 F4
Cheviot N.Z. 153 H10
Cheviot U.S.A. 176 A6
Cheviot Hills U.K. 47 J8
Cheviot Range hills Australia 149 D5
Chevreulx r. Canada 169 F2
Che'w Bahir salt l. Eth. 128 C3
Che'w Bahir Wildlife Reserve nature res. Eth. 128 C3
Chewelah U.S.A. 180 C2
Cheyenne OK U.S.A. 179 C5

▶Cheyenne WY U.S.A. 180 F4
State capital of Wyoming.

Cheyenne r. U.S.A. 178 B2

Cheyenne River Indian Reservation res.
U.S.A. 178 B2
Cheyenne Wells U.S.A. 178 B4
Cheyne Bay Australia 151 B6
Cheyur India 94 D3
Chezacut Canada 166 E4
Chhabra India 96 C4
Chhaapar India 96 B4
Chhapra India 97 E4
formerly spelt Chapra
Chhata India 96 C4
Chhatak Bangl. 97 F4
Chhatarpur Jharkhand India 97 E4
Chhatarpur Madhya Pradesh India 96 C4
Chhatrapur India 95 E2
Chhattisgarh state India 97 D5
Chhay Arêng, Stœng r. Cambodia 79 C6
Chhindwara India 96 C4
Chhlong, Prêk r. Cambodia 79 D5
Chhota Chhindwara India 96 C5
Chhota Udepur India 96 B5
Chhuk Cambodia see Phumĭ Chhuk
Chhukha Bhutan 97 F4
Chiai Taiwan 87 F4
also spelt Jiayi
Ch'iak-san National Park S. Korea 83 B5
Chiang Dao Thai. 78 B4
Chiange Angola 127 B8
formerly known as Vila de Almoster
Chiang Kham Thai. 78 C4
Chiang Khan Thai. 78 C4
Chiang Mai Thai. 78 B4
also spelt Chiengmai
Chiang Rai Thai. 78 B4
Chiani r. Italy 56 E5
Chiapa Mex. 185 G5
Chiapas state Mex. 185 G5
Chiat'ura Georgia 107 E2
Chiautla Mex. 185 F5
Chiavari Italy 56 B4
Chiavenna Italy 56 B2
Chiba Japan 91 G7
Chiba pref. Japan 90 G7
Chibemba Angola 127 B8
Chibi China 87 E2
Chibia Angola 127 B8
formerly known as João de Almeida
Chibit Rus. Fed. 88 D1
Chibizovka Rus. Fed. see Zherdevka
Chiboma Moz. 131 G4
Chibougamau Canada 169 F3
Chibougamau, Lac l. Canada 169 F3
Chibu-Sangaku National Park Japan 91 E6
English form Japan Alps National Park
Chibuto Moz. 131 G5
Chibuzhang Hu l. China 89 E5
Chibwe Zambia 127 F8
Chicacole India see Srikakulam
▶ Chicago U.S.A. 174 C3
4th most populous city in North America.
world [cities] ▶▶ 24–25

Chicago Heights U.S.A. 172 F9
Chicala Angola 127 C7
Chicamba Moz. 131 G3
Chicapa r. Angola 127 D6
Chic-Chocs, Monts mts Canada 169 H3
Chic-Chocs, Réserve Faunique des
nature res. Canada 169 H3
Chicha well Chad 120 C5
Chichagof Island U.S.A. 164 F4
Chichak r. Pak. 101 F5
Chichaoua Morocco 122 C3
Chicheng China see Pengxi
Chichén Itzá tourist site Mex. 185 H4
Chichester U.K. 47 L13
Chichester Range mts Australia 150 B4
Chichgarh India 94 D1
Chichijima-rettō is Japan 73 H7
Chichirivichie Venez. 199 D2
Chicholi India 96 C5
Chickahominy r. U.S.A. 177 I8
Chickasawhay r. U.S.A. 175 B6
Chickasha U.S.A. 179 C5
Chiclana de la Frontera Spain 54 E8
Chiclayo Peru 198 B6
Chico r. Chubut Arg. 205 C6
Chico r. Chubut Arg. 205 D7
Chico r. Santa Cruz Arg. 205 C8
Chico U.S.A. 182 C2
Chicoa Moz. 131 G2
Chicobea r. Fiji see Cikobia
Chicobi, Lac l. Canada 173 O2
Chicomba Angola 127 B8
Chicomo Moz. 131 G4
Chicomucelo Mex. 185 G6
Chiconono Moz. 129 B8
Chicopee U.S.A. 177 M3
Chico Sapocoy, Mount Phil. 74 B2
Chicoutimi Canada 169 G3
Chicualacuala Moz. 131 F4
formerly known as Malvérnia
Chicuma Angola 127 B8
Chidambaram India 94 C4
Chido S. Korea 83 B6
Chiede Angola 127 C9
Chiefland U.S.A. 175 D6
Chiemsee l. Germany 49 J8
Chiengi Zambia 127 F7
Chiengmai Thai. see Chiang Mai
Chienti r. Italy 56 F5
Chieo Lan Reservoir Thai. 79 B6
Chieri Italy 51 N7
Chiers r. France 51 L3
Chiese r. Italy 56 C3
Chieti Italy 56 G6
historically known as Teate
Chifeng China 85 H3
also known as Ulanhad
Chifre, Serra do mts Brazil 203 D6
Chifunda Moz. 131 G2
formerly known as Tembué
Chiganak Kazakh. 103 H3
also spelt Shyganaq
Chiginagak, Mount vol. U.S.A. 164 C4
Chignecto Bay Canada 169 H4
Chignecto Game Sanctuary nature res.
Canada 169 H4
Chignik U.S.A. 164 D4
Chigorodó Col. 198 B3
Chigu China 89 E6
Chigu Co l. China 89 E6
Chihli, Gulf of China see Bo Hai
Chihuahua Mex. 184 D2
Chihuahua state Mex. 184 D2
Chiili Kazakh. 103 F3
also spelt Shieli
Chijinpu China 84 B4
Chikalda India 96 C5
Chikan China 87 D4
Chikaskia r. U.S.A. 178 C4
Chik Ballapur India 94 C3
Chikhli India 94 C1
Chikmagalur India 94 B3
Chikodi India 94 B2
Chikodi Road India 94 B2
Chikoy r. Rus. Fed. 85 E1

Chikoy r. Rus. Fed. 85 E1
Chikugo Japan 91 B8
Chikuma-gawa r. Japan 90 F6
Chikushino Japan 91 A8
Chikwa Zambia 129 B7
Chikwawa Malawi 129 B9
Chikyū-misaki pt Japan 90 G3
Chila Angola 127 B8
Chilanko r. Canada 166 E4
Chilanko Forks Canada 166 E4
Chilapa Mex. 185 F5
Chilas Jammu and Kashmir 96 B2
Chilaw Sri Lanka 94 C5
Chilca Peru 200 A3
Chilcaya Chile 200 C4
Chilcotin r. Canada 166 F5
Chilcott Island Australia 149 F3
Childers Australia 149 G5
Childress U.S.A. 179 B5
▶ Chile country S. America 205 B7
southamerica [countries] ▶▶ 192–193
Chile Chico Chile 205 C7
Chilecito Arg. 204 C3
Chilengue, Serra de mts Angola 127 B8
Chilete Peru 200 A1
Chilhowie U.S.A. 176 D9
Chilia-Nouă Ukr. see Kiliya
Chilia Veche Romania 58 K3
Chilik Kazakh. 103 I4
also spelt Shelek
Chilik r. Kazakh. 103 I4
Chilika Lake India 95 I2
Chililabombwe Zambia 127 E8
formerly known as Bancroft
Chiliomodi Greece 59 D11
also known as Khiliomódhion
Chilko r. Canada 166 F4
Chilko Lake Canada 166 E5
Chilkoot Trail National Historic Site
U.S.A. 164 F4
Chillagoe Australia 149 E3
Chillán Chile 204 B5
Chillar Arg. 204 F5
Chillicothe IL U.S.A. 172 D10
Chillicothe MO U.S.A. 178 D4
Chillicothe OH U.S.A. 176 C6
Chilliculco Peru 200 C4
Chillinji Jammu and Kashmir 96 B1
Chilliwack Canada 166 F5
Chil'mamedkum, Peski des. Turkm. 102 C4
Chilmari Bangl. 97 F4
Chiloé, Isla de i. Chile 205 B6
long form Chiloé, Isla Grande de
Chiloé, Isla Grande de i. Chile see
Chiloé, Isla de
Chilombo Angola 127 D8
Chilonga Zambia 127 F8
Chiloquin U.S.A. 180 B4
Chilpancingo Mex. 185 F5
Chiltern Australia 147 E4
Chiltern Hills U.K. 47 L12
Chilton U.S.A. 172 E6
Chiluage Angola 127 D7
Chilubi Zambia 127 F8
Chilumba Malawi 129 B7
Chilung Taiwan 87 G3
English form Keelung; also spelt Jilong
Chilung Pass Jammu and Kashmir 96 C2
Chilwa, Lake Malawi 129 B9
Chimala Tanz. 129 B7
Chimaltenango Guat. 185 H6
Chimán Panama 186 D5
Chimanimani Zimbabwe 131 G3
formerly known as Mandidzuzure or
Melsetter
Chi Ma Wan Hong Kong China 87 [inset]
Chimba Zambia 127 F7
Chimbas Arg. 204 C3
Chimbay Uzbek. 102 D4
also spelt Chimboy
Chimborazo mt. Ecuador 198 B5
Chimborazo prov. Ecuador 198 B5
Chimbote Peru 200 A2
Chimboy Uzbek. see Chimbay
Chimian Pak. 101 H4
Chimichaguá Col. 187 E5
Chimion Uzbek. 103 G4
Chimishliya Moldova see Cimişlia
Chimkent Kazakh. see Shymkent
Chimkentskaya Oblast' admin. div. Kazakh.
see Yuzhnyy Kazakhstan
Chimoio Moz. 131 G3
formerly known as Vila Pery
Chimorra hill Spain 54 G6
Chimpay Arg. 204 D5
Chimtargha, Qullai mt. Tajik. 101 G2
also known as Chimtorga, Gora
Chimtorga, Gora mt. Tajik. see
Chimtargha, Qullai
Chin state Myanmar 78 A3
▶ China country Asia 80 D5
Most populous country in the world and in
Asia. 2nd largest country in Asia and 4th
largest in the world. Known in Chinese as
Zhongguo; long form Zhongguo Renmin
Gongheguo or Chung-hua Jen-min Kung-
ho-kuo.
world [countries] ▶▶ 10–11
world [population] ▶▶ 22–23
asia [countries] ▶▶ 64–67

	country	population	location	page#
1 ▶	China	1 260 137 000	Asia	▶▶ 80 D5
2 ▶	India	1 008 937 000	Asia	▶▶ 96
3 ▶	USA	283 230 000	North America	▶▶ 170 E3
4 ▶	Indonesia	212 092 000	Asia	▶▶ 72 D8
5 ▶	Brazil	170 406 000	South America	▶▶ 202 B4
6 ▶	Russian Federation	145 491 000	Asia/Europe	▶▶ 38 F3
7 ▶	Pakistan	141 256 000	Asia	▶▶ 101 F4
8 ▶	Bangladesh	137 439 000	Asia	▶▶ 97 F4
9 ▶	Japan	127 096 000	Asia	▶▶ 90 E5
10 ▶	Nigeria	113 862 000	Africa	▶▶ 125 G4

largest populations

China Mex. 185 F3
China, Republic of country Asia see Taiwan
China Bakir r. Myanmar see To
Chinacates Mex. 184 D3
China Lake U.S.A. 177 P1
Chinandega Nicaragua 186 B4
China Point U.S.A. 182 F9
Chinati Peak U.S.A. 181 F7
Chinaz Uzbek. 103 G4
also spelt Chinoz
Chincha Alta Peru 200 A3
Chinchaga r. Canada 166 F3
Chinchal, Nahr r. Iraq 109 J3
Chinchilla Australia 149 F5
Chincholi India 94 C2
Chinchorro, Banco sea feature Mex. 185 I5
Chincolco Chile 204 C4
Chincoteague U.S.A. 177 J8
Chincoteague Bay U.S.A. 177 J8
Chinde Moz. 131 H3
Chin-do i. S. Korea 83 B6
Chindu China 86 A1
Chindwin r. Myanmar 78 A3
Chineni Jammu and Kashmir 96 B2
Chinese Turkestan aut. reg. China see
Xinjiang Uygur Zizhiqu
Chingaza, Parque Nacional nat. park Col.
198 C3
Chinghai prov. China see Qinghai

Chinghwa N. Korea 83 B5
Chingirlau Kazakh. 102 C2
also spelt Shynggyrlaū
Chingleput India see Chengalpattu
Chingola Zambia 127 E8
Chinguar Angola 127 C8
Chinguetti Mauritania 122 B5
Chinguil Chad 120 C6
Chinhae S. Korea 83 C6
Chinhanda Moz. 131 G2
Chinhoyi Zimbabwe 131 F3
formerly spelt Sinoia
Chini India see Kalpa
Chiniâk Bol. 200 C4
Chining China see Jining
Chiniot Pak. 101 H4
Chinipas Mex. 184 C2
Chinit, Stœng r. Cambodia 79 D5
Chinju S. Korea 83 C6
Chinko r. Cent. Afr. Rep. 126 D3
Chinle U.S.A. 183 O5
Chinle Valley U.S.A. 183 L7
Chinle Wash watercourse U.S.A. 183 O5
Chinmen Taiwan 87 F3
also spelt Jinmen or Kinmen
Chinmen Tao i. Taiwan 87 F3
English form Quemoy
Chinna Ganjam India 94 D3
Chinnamanur India 94 C4
Chinnampo N. Korea see Namp'o
Chinna Salem India 94 C4
Chinnur India 94 C2
Chino Japan 91 F7
Chino U.S.A. 183 L6
Chino Creek watercourse U.S.A. 183 L7
Chinocup, Lake salt flat Australia 151 B7
Chinocup Nature Reserve Australia
151 B7
Chinon France 50 G5
Chinook U.S.A. 180 E2
Chino Valley U.S.A. 183 L7
Chinoz Uzbek. see Chinaz
Chinsali Zambia 127 F7
Chintalnar India 94 D2
Chintamani India 94 C3
Chinteni Romania 58 E2
Chiñú Col. 198 C2
Chinyama Litapi Zambia 127 D8
Chin'yavoryk Rus. Fed. 40 J3
Chioco Moz. 131 G3
Chioggia Italy 56 E3
Chiona Tanz. 129 B6
Chios Greece 59 H10
Chios i. Greece 59 G10
also spelt Khíos
Chios Strait Greece 59 H10
English form Khíos Strait
Chipanga Moz. 131 G2
Chipata Zambia 129 B8
Chipchihua, Sierra de mts Arg. 205 C6
Chipili Zambia 127 F7
Chipindo Angola 127 B8
Chipinga Zimbabwe see Chipinge
Chipinge Zimbabwe 131 G4
formerly spelt Chipinga
Chipiona Spain 54 E8
Chipley U.S.A. 175 C6
Chiplun India 94 B2
Chipman Canada 169 H4
Chipoia Angola 127 C8
Chipperone, Monte mt. Moz. 131 G2
Chippewa r. MN U.S.A. 178 D2
Chippewa r. WI U.S.A. 172 B6
Chippewa, Lake U.S.A. 172 B5
Chippewa Falls U.S.A. 172 B6
Chipping Norton U.K. 47 K12
Chiprovtsi Bulg. 58 D5
Chipundu Zambia 127 F8
Chipurupalle Andhra Pradesh India 95 D2
Chipurupalle Andhra Pradesh India 95 D2
Chiquian Peru 200 A2
Chiquibul, Parque Nacional nat. park
Belize 185 H5
Chiquilá Mex. 185 I4
Chiquimula Guat. 185 H6
Chiquinquira U.S.A. 198 C3
Chiquintirca Peru 200 B3
Chiquita, Mar l. Arg. 204 E4
Chiquitos, Llanos de plain Bol. 201 E4
Chiquitos Jesuit Missions tourist site
Brazil 201 E4
Chir r. Rus. Fed. 41 G6
Chirada India 94 D3
Chiradzulu Malawi 129 B8
Chirala India 94 D3
Chiramba Moz. 131 G3
Chirambirá, Punta pt Col. 198 B3
Chiras Afgh. 101 F3
Chirawa India 89 A6
Chirchik Uzbek. 103 G4
Chirchik r. Uzbek. 103 G4
Chiredzi Zimbabwe 131 F4
Chire Wildlife Reserve nature res. Eth.
128 C1
Chirfa Niger 125 I1
Chirgua r. Venez. 199 E2

Chisholm MN U.S.A. 178 D2
Chishtian Mandi Pak. 101 H4
Chishui China 86 C2
Chishui He r. China 86 C2
Chisimaio Somalia see Kismaayo
▶ Chişinău Moldova 58 J1
Capital of Moldova. Formerly spelt Kishinev.

Chişineu-Criş Romania 58 C2
Chisone r. Italy 51 N8
Chistopol' Rus. Fed. 40 I5
Chistopol'ye Kazakh. 103 F1
Chistyakovskoye Kazakh. 103 G1
Chita Bol. 200 C3
Chita Col. 198 C3
Chita r. Rus. Fed. 85 G1
Chita Tanz. 129 B7
Chitado Angola 127 B9
Chitaldrug India see Chitradurga
Chitalwana India 96 B4
Chita Oblast admin. div. Rus. Fec. see
Chitinskaya Oblast'
Chitato Angola 127 D6
Chitek Lake Canada 167 I4
Chitek Lake l. Canada 167 L4
Chitembo Angola 127 C8
Chitina U.S.A. 164 E3
Chitipa Malawi 129 A7
Chitobe Moz. 131 G4
formerly known as Machaze
Chitokoloki Zambia 127 D8
Chitongo Zambia 127 F8
Chitor India see Chittaurgarh
Chitose Japan 90 H3
Chitradurga India 94 C3
formerly known as Chitaldrug
Chitrakut India 96 D4
Chitral Pak. 101 G3
Chitral r. Pak. 101 G3
Chitravati r. India 94 C3
Chitré Panama 186 C6
Chitrod India 96 A5
Chittagong Bangl. 97 F5
also spelt Chattagam
Chittagong admin. div. Bangl. 97 F5
Chittaranjan India 97 E5
formerly known as Mihidjan
Chittaurgarh India 96 B4
formerly known as Chitor; formerly spelt
Chittorgarh
Chittoor India 94 C3
Chittur India 94 C4
Chitungulu Zambia 129 B8
Chitungwiza Zimbabwe 131 F3
Chiu Lung Hong Kong China see Kowloon
Chiume Angola 127 D8
Chiûre Novo Moz. 131 H2
Chiusa Sclafani Sicilia Italy 57 F11
Chiuta Moz. 131 G2
Chiva Spain 55 K5
Chivasso Italy 56 A3
Chivato, Punta pt Mex. 184 C3
Chivay Peru 200 C3
Chive Bol. 200 C3
Chivela Mex. 185 G5
Chivhu Zimbabwe 131 F3
formerly known as Enkeldoorn
Chivilcoy Arg. 204 E4
Chiyirchik, Pereval pass Kyrg. see Ashusuu
Chizarira Hills Zimbabwe 131 E3
Chizarira National Park Zimbabwe 131 E3
Chizha Vtoraya Kazakh. 102 C2
Chizu Japan 91 D7
Chkalov Rus. Fed. see Orenburg
Chkalovo Kazakh. 103 G1
Chkalovsk Rus. Fed. 40 G4
Chkalovskaya Oblast' admin. div. Rus. Fed.
see Orenburgskaya Oblast'
Chkalovsk Rus. Fed. 44 G4
Chkalovskoye Rus. Fed. 82 D3
Chlef Alg. see Ech Chélif
Chloride U.S.A. 183 I6
Chlumec nad Cidlinou Czech Rep. 49 M6
Chlya, Ozero l. Rus. Fed. 82 F1
Chmielnik Poland 49 R5
Choa Chu Kang Sing. 76 [inset]
Choa Chu Kang hill Sing. 76 [inset]
Chôâm Khsant Cambodia 79 D5
formerly known as Cheom Ksan
Choapa r. Chile 204 C3
Chobe admin. dist. Botswana 131 E3
Chobe National Park Botswana 131 E3
Choch'iwŏn S. Korea 83 B5
Chociańów Poland 49 M4
Choco col. U.S.A. 198 B3
Chocolate Mountains U.S.A. 183 I8
Chocontá Col. 198 C3
Choctawhatchee r. U.S.A. 175 C6
Chodavaram India 94 D2
Chodecz Poland 49 Q3
Chodel r. Poland 49 S4
Chodo i. N. Korea 83 B5
Chodov Czech Rep. 49 K5
Chodoralyg Rus. Fed. 84 C1
Chodzież Poland 49 N3
Choele Choel Arg. 204 D5
Chofombo Moz. 131 F2
Choghâdak Iran 100 B4
Chogo Lungma Glacier
Jammu and Kashmir 96 B2
Chograyskoye Vodokhranilishche resr
Rus. Fed. 41 H7
Choiceland Canada 167 J4
Choique Arg. 204 D5
Choiseul i. Solomon Is 145 E2
also known as Chrysochou, Kolpos; also
spelt Khrysokhou Bay
Choiseul Sound sea chan. Falkland Is
205 F8
Choix Mex. 184 C3
Chojna Poland 49 L3
Chojnice Poland 49 O2
Chojnów Poland 49 M4
Chōkai-san vol. Japan 90 G5
Chok'ē Mountains Eth. 128 C1
also spelt Shokpar or Shoqpar
Chokpar Kazakh. 103 H4
also spelt Shokpar or Shoqpar
Chokue Moz. see Chókwé
Chokurdakh Rus. Fed. 39 O2
Chókwé Moz. 131 G5
formerly known as Vila de Trego Morais;
formerly spelt Chokwe
Cho La pass China 86 A2
Cholame U.S.A. 182 D6
Cholame Creek r. U.S.A. 182 D6
Chola Shan mts China 86 A1
Cholet France 50 F5
Choloma Hond. 186 B4
Cholpon-Ata Kyrg. 103 I4
Choluteca Hond. 186 B4
Choma Zambia 127 E9
Chomo China see Yadong
Chomo Ganggar mt. China 89 E6
Chomo Lhari mt. Bhutan 97 F4
Chomun India 96 B4
Chomutov Czech Rep. 49 K5
Chona r. Rus. Fed. 39 K3
Chŏnan S. Korea 83 B5
also spelt Chŏnju
Chone Ecuador 198 A5
Chong'an China see Wuyishan
Ch'ŏngch'ŏn-gang r. N. Korea 83 B5
Ch'ongdo S. Korea 83 C6
Chonggye China see Qonggyai
Chongji N. Korea 82 C4
Chongjin N. Korea 82 C4
Ch'ŏngjin N. Korea 82 C4
Ch'ŏngju S. Korea 83 B5
Chongkü China 86 A2
Chongli China 85 G3
also known as Xiwanzi
Chonglong China see Zizhong
Chongming municipality China 87 G2
Chongming Dao i. China 87 G2
Chongoroi Angola 127 B8
Ch'ŏngp'yŏng N. Korea 83 B5
Chongqing China 86 C2
formerly known as Chungking
Chongqing municipality China 87 C2
Chongqing China see Chongzhou
Chongren China 87 F3
Chongup S. Korea 83 B6
Chongwe Zambia 127 F8
Chongyang China 87 E2
Chongyang Xi r. China 87 F3
Chongyi China 87 E3
also known as Hengshui
Chongzuo China 87 C4
also known as Taiping
Chŏnju S. Korea 83 B5
Chonogol Mongolia 85 G2
Chontalpa Mex. 185 G5
Chom Thanh Vietnam 79 D6
Cho Oyu mt. China/Nepal 97 E3
6th highest mountain in the world and in
Asia.
world [physical features] ▶▶ 8–9

Chop Ukr. 49 T7
Chopan India 97 D4
Chopda India 96 B5
Cho Phuoc Hai Vietnam 79 D6
Chopim r. Brazil 203 A8
Chopimzinho Brazil 203 A8
Choptank r. U.S.A. 177 I7
Choquecamata Bol. 200 D4
Chor Pak. 101 G5
Chora Greece 59 C11
also known as Khóra
Chorley U.K. 47 J10
Chornobyl' Ukr. see Chernobyl'
Chornomors'ke Ukr. 41 E7
Chornomors'kyy Zapovidnyk nature res.
Ukr. 41 D7
Choroszcz Poland 49 T2
Chorrochó Brazil 202 E4
Chortkiv Ukr. 41 C6
also spelt Chertkov
Chorwad India 94 A1
Ch'ŏrwŏn S. Korea 83 B5
Chorzele Poland 49 R2
Ch'osan N. Korea 83 B4
Chŏsen-kaikyō sea chan. Japan/S. Korea
see Nishi-suidō
Chōshi Japan 91 G7
Choshuenco, Volcán vol. Chile 204 B5
Chosica Peru 200 A3
Chos Malal Arg. 204 C5
Chosmes Arg. 204 C3
Choszczno Poland 49 M2
Chota Peru 198 B6
Chota Nagpur reg. India 97 D5
Choteau U.S.A. 180 D3
Chotila India 96 A5
Choûm Mauritania 122 B5
Chowan r. U.S.A. 177 I9
Chowchilla U.S.A. 182 D4
Chowgham India 94 B4
Chowilla Regional Reserve nature res.
Australia 146 C3
Chown, Mount Canada 166 G4
Choya Arg. 204 D3
Choybalsan Mongolia 85 G2
Choyr Mongolia 85 F2
Chozi Zambia 129 B7
Chreïrik well Mauritania 122 B5
Chřiby hills Czech Rep. 49 O6
Chrisman U.S.A. 174 C4
Chrissiesmeer S. Africa 133 O3
Christchurch N.Z. 153 G11
Christiana S. Africa 133 J4
Christiana Norway see Oslo
Christian Island Canada 173 M6
Christianshåb Greenland see Qasigiannguit
Christian Sound sea chan. U.S.A. 166 C4
Christiansted Virgin Is (U.S.A.) 187 G3
Christie r. U.S.A. 172 C4
Christie Bay Canada 167 I3
Christina r. Canada 167 I3
Christina S. Africa 133 J4
Christmas Creek Australia 150 D3
Christmas Creek r. Australia 150 D3
▶ Christmas Island terr. Indian Ocean 218 O6
Australian External Territory.
asia [countries] ▶▶ 64–67

Christopher, Lake salt flat Australia 151 D5
Christos Greece 59 H11
also spelt Hristós
Chrudim Czech Rep. 49 M6
Chrysi i. Greece 59 G14
Chrysochou Bay Cyprus 108 D2
also known as Chrysochou, Kolpos; also
spelt Khrysokhou Bay
Chrysochou, Kolpos b. Cyprus see
Chrysochou Bay
Chrysoupoli Greece 58 F8
also known as Khrisoúpolis
Chu Kazakh. see Shu
Chu r. Kazakh. 103 F3
Chuadanga Bangl. 97 F5
Chuali, Lago l. Moz. 133 Q1
Chuanbu China see Jinxi
Chuansha China 87 G2
Chubalung China 86 A2
Chubarovka Ukr. see Polohy
Chubartau Kazakh. see Barshatas
Chubbuck U.S.A. 180 D4
Chubut prov. Arg. 205 C6
Chubut r. Arg. 205 C6
Chuchkovo Rus. Fed. 41 G5
Chucul Arg. 204 D4
Chucunaque r. Panama 186 D5
Chudniv Ukr. 41 D6
Chudovo Rus. Fed. 43 M2
Chudskoye, Ozero l. Estonia/Rus. Fed. see
Peipus, Lake
Chudz'yavr, Ozero l. Rus. Fed. 44 P1
Chugach Mountains U.S.A. 164 E3
Chūgoku-sanchi mts Japan 91 C7
Chugqênsumdo China see Jigzhi
Chuguchak China see Tacheng
Chuguyev Ukr. see Chuhuyiv
Chuguyevka Rus. Fed. 82 D3
Chuhai China see Zhuhai
Chuhuyiv Ukr. 41 F6
also known as Chuguyev
Chu-Iliyskiye Gory mts Kazakh. 103 H4
also spelt Shu-Ile
Chukai Malaysia see Cukai
Chukchagirskoye, Ozero l. Rus. Fed. 82 E1

Chukchi Peninsula Rus. Fed. see
Chukotskiy Poluostrov
Chukchi Sea Rus. Fed./U.S.A. 164 B3
Chukhloma Rus. Fed. 40 G4
Chukotskiy, Mys c. Rus. Fed. 39 S3
Chukotskiy Poluostrov pen. Rus. Fed. 39 S3
English form Chukchi Peninsula
Chulakkurgan Kazakh. see Shollakorgan
Chulaktau Kazakh. see Karatau
Chulasa Rus. Fed. 40 H2
Chula Vista U.S.A. 183 G9
Chulkovo Rus. Fed. 43 R9
Chulucanas Peru 198 A6
Chulung Pass 96 C2
Chulym Rus. Fed. 80 C1
Chulyshman r. Rus. Fed. 88 D2
Chulyshmanskoye Ploskogor'ye plat.
Rus. Fed. 84 A1
Chum Rus. Fed. 40 L2
Chuma Bol. 200 C3
Chumba Eth. 128 C3
Chumbicha Arg. 204 D3
Chumda China 86 A1
Chumerna mt. Bulg. 58 G6
Chumikan Rus. Fed. 82 D1
Chum Phae Thai. 78 C4
Chumphon Thai. 79 B5
Chum Saeng Thai. 78 C5
Chumphon Thai. 78 B5
Chuna r. Rus. Fed. 39 J4
Chuña Huasi Arg. 204 D3
Chun'an China see Pailing
Chuna-Tundra plain Rus. Fed. 44 P2
Ch'unch'ŏn S. Korea 83 B5
Chundzha Kazakh. 103 I4
also spelt Shonzha
Chunga Zambia 127 E8
Chung-hua Jen-min Kung-ho-kuo country
Asia see China
Chung-hua Min-kuo country Asia see
Taiwan
Ch'ungju S. Korea 83 B5
Chungking China see Chongqing
Ch'ungmu S. Korea see T'ongyŏng
Chungsan N. Korea 83 B5
also known as Taiwan Shan
Chunhua China 86 D1
Chunxi China see Gaochun
Chunya r. Rus. Fed. 39 J3
Chunya Tanz. 129 B7
Chu Oblast admin. div. Kyrg. see Chüy
Chuôr Phnum Dângrêk mts
Cambodia/Thai. 79 D5
Chuosijia China see Guanyinqiao
Chupa Rus. Fed. 44 P2
Chuprovo Rus. Fed. 40 J3
Chuquibamba Peru 200 C4
Chuquicamata Chile 200 C5
Chuquisaca dept Bol. 201 D5
Chuqung China see Chindu
Chur Switz. 51 R4
also spelt Coire; historically known as Curia
Churachandpur India 97 G4
Chūrān Iran 100 C4
Churapcha Rus. Fed. 39 N3
Churayevo Rus. Fed. 40 K3
Church Hill MD U.S.A. 177 J6
Church Hill TN U.S.A. 176 C8
Churchill Canada 167 M3
Churchill r. Man. Canada 167 M3
Churchill r. Nfld. Canada 169 I2
formerly known as Hamilton
Churchill, Cape Canada 167 M3
Churchill Falls Canada 169 I2
Churchill Lake Canada 167 I4
Churchill Mountains Antarctica 223 K1
Churchill Peak Canada 166 E3
Churchill Sound sea chan. Canada 168 E1
Churchville U.S.A. 176 F7
Churen-Tag, Gora mt. Rus. Fed. 84 A1
Churia Ghati Hills Nepal 97 E4
Churilovo Rus. Fed. 43 L6
Churin Peru 200 A2
Churov Rus. Fed. 40 H4
Churovichi Rus. Fed. 43 N9
Churu India 96 B3
Churubay Nura Kazakh. see Abay
Churuguara Venez. 198 D2
Chürür Japan 90 H3
Churumuco Mex. 185 E5
Chushul Jammu and Kashmir 96 C2
Chuska Mountains U.S.A. 183 O5
Chusovaya r. Rus. Fed. 40 K4
Chusovoy Rus. Fed. 40 K4
Chust Ukr. see Khust
Chust Uzbek. 103 G4
Chute-Rouge Canada 173 N3
Chutung Taiwan 87 G3
Chuuk is Micronesia 220 E5
Chuvashia aut. rep. Rus. Fed. see
Chuvashskaya Respublika
Chuvashskaya A.S.S.R. aut. rep. Rus. Fed.
see Chuvashskaya Respublika
Chuvashskaya Respublika aut. rep.
Rus. Fed. 40 H5
English form Chuvashia; formerly known as
Chuvashskaya A.S.S.R.
Chuwang-san National Park S. Korea 83 C5
Chüy admin. div. Kyrg. 103 H4
English form Chu Oblast; also known as
Chuyskaya Oblast'
Chuy Uruguay 204 G4
Chư Yang Sin mt. Vietnam 79 E6
Chuyskaya Oblast' admin. div. Kyrg. see Chüy
Chuzhou China 87 F1
Chyganak Kazakh. 103 G3
Chyhyrynskaye Vodaskhovishcha resr
Belarus 43 K8
Chymyshliya Moldova see Cimişlia
Chyrvonaya Slabada Belarus 43 J9
Chyrvonaye, Vozyera l. Belarus 42 J9
Chyulu Range mts Kenya 128 C5
Ciacova Romania 58 C3
Ciadâr-Lunga Moldova see Ciadir-Lunga
Ciadir-Lunga Moldova 58 J2
also known as Ceadâr-Lunga or Ciadâr-
Lunga or Chadyr-Lunga
Ciamis Indon. 77 E4
Ciampino airport Italy 56 E7
Cianjur Indon. 77 D4
Cianorte Brazil 206 A10
Cibadak Indon. 77 D4
Cibatu Indon. 77 D4
Cibecue U.S.A. 183 N7
Cibinong Indon. 77 D4
Cibitoke Burundi 126 F5
Cibolo Creek r. U.S.A. 179 C6
Ci Buni r. Indon. 77 D4
Cibuta Mex. 184 C2
Cibuta, Sierra mt. Mex. 184 C2
Čićarija mts Croatia 56 F3
Çiçekdaği Turkey 106 C3
also known as Boyalık
Çiçekli Turkey 106 C3
Çiçekli Turkey 109 J1
Cicero U.S.A. 172 F9
Cicero Dantas Brazil 202 E4
Ćićevac Srbija Yugo. 58 C4
Cidacos r. Spain 55 J2
Cide Turkey 106 C2
Cidlina r. Czech Rep. 49 M5
Ciechanów Poland 49 R3
Ciechanowiec Poland 49 T3
Ciechocinek Poland 49 P3
Ciego de Ávila Cuba 186 D2
Ciénaga Col. 198 C2

Ciénagas del Catatumbo nat. park Venez. 198 D2
Cienfuegos Cuba 186 C2
Cies, Illas i. Spain 54 C2
Cieszanów Poland 49 U5
Cieszyn Poland 49 P6
Cieza Spain 55 J6
Çiflikköy Turkey 109 I1
Çiftlik Turkey 58 J7
Çiftlikköy Turkey 58 J7
Cifuentes Spain 55 I4
Cigeulis Indon. 77 D4
Cigüela r. Spain 55 H5
also known as Inevi
Cihangazi Turkey 59 K9
Cihuatlán Mex. 184 D5
Cijara, Embalse de resr Spain 54 G5
Cikai China see Gongshan
Çikes, Maja e mt. Albania 59 A8
Cikobia i. Fiji 145 H3
also spelt Thikombia; formerly spelt Chicobea or Ticumbia or Tikumbia
Čikola r. Croatia 56 I5
Cilacap Indon. 77 E4
Cilangkahan Indon. 77 D4
Çıldır Turkey 107 E2
also known as Zurzuna
Çıldır Gölü l. Turkey 107 E2
Çıldıroba Indon. 77 E4
Çiledug Indon. 77 E4
Cilento e del Vallo di Diano, Parco Nazionale del nat. park Italy 57 H8
Cili China 87 D2
Cilician Gates pass Turkey see Gülek Boğazı
Cilieni Romania 58 F5
Cill Airne Rep. of Ireland see Killarney
Cill Chainnigh Rep. of Ireland see Kilkenny
Cill Mhantáin Rep. of Ireland see Wicklow
Cilo Dağı mt. Turkey 107 F3
Çiloy Adası i. Azer. 107 I2
Cima U.S.A. 183 I6
Cimahi Indon. 77 D4
Cimarron KS U.S.A. 178 B4
Cimarron NM U.S.A. 181 F5
Cimarron r. U.S.A. 179 C4
Cimarron Creek r. U.S.A. 181 F5
Cimino, Monte mt. Italy 56 E6
Cimişlia Moldova 58 J2
formerly spelt Chimishliya or Chymyshliya
Cimone, Monte mt. Italy 56 C4
Cimpeni Romania see Câmpeni
Cimpia Turzii Romania see Câmpia Turzii
Cimpina Romania see Câmpina
Cimpulung Romania see Câmpulung
Cimpulung Moldovenesc Romania see Câmpulung Moldovenesc
Cina, Tanjung i. Indon. 76 D4
Çınar Turkey 107 E3
also known as Hanakpınar
Çınarcık Turkey 58 K8
Cinaruco r. Venez. 199 E3
Cinaruco-Capanaparo, Parque Nacional nat. park Venez. 199 E3
Cinca r. Spain 55 L3
Cincar mt. Bos.-Herz. 56 J5
Cincinnati U.S.A. 176 A6
Cincinnatus U.S.A. 177 J3
Cinco-Balas, Cayos is Cuba 186 D2
Cinco de Outubro Angola see Xá-Muteba
Cincu Romania 58 F2
Çine Turkey 106 B3
Çine r. Turkey 59 I11
Cinfães Port. 54 C3
Cingoli Italy 56 F5
Cinque Island India 95 G4
Cintalapa Mex. 185 G5
Cinto, Monte mt. France 51 O10
Cintruénigo Spain 55 J2
Cinzas r. Brazil 206 C9
Ciolpani Romania 58 H4
Čiovo i. Croatia 56 I5
Cipatuja Indon. 77 D4
Ciping China see Jinggangshan
Cipó Brazil 207 K6
Cipó r. Brazil 206 E2
Cipolletti Arg. 204 D5
Cipotânea Brazil 207 J2
Circeo, Monte hill Italy 56 F7
Circeo, Parco Nazionale del nat. park Italy 56 E7
Circle AK U.S.A. 164 E3
Circle MT U.S.A. 180 F3
Circleville OH U.S.A. 176 C6
Circleville UT U.S.A. 183 L3
Cirebon Indon. 77 D4
formerly spelt Tjirebon
Cirencester U.K. 47 K12
historically known as Corinium
Cirene Italy see Cyrene
Cirié Italy 51 N7
Ciriš l. Latvia 42 H5
Cirò Marina Italy 57 J9
Ciron r. France 50 F8
Cirque Mountain Canada 169 I1
Cirta Alg. see Constantine
Cisco U.S.A. 183 O3
Cisnădie Romania 58 F3
Cisterna di Latina Italy 56 E7
Cisterna Spain 54 F2
Citadelle Laferrière tourist site Haiti 187 E3
Citlaltépetl vol. Mex. see Orizaba, Pico de
Citluk Bos.-Herz. 56 J5
Citronelle U.S.A. 175 C6
Citrus Heights U.S.A. 182 C3
Citrusdal S. Africa 132 D9
Cittadella Italy 56 D3
Città di Castello Italy 56 E5
Cittanova Italy 57 I10
Ciucaş, Vârful mt. Romania 58 G3
Ciucea Romania 58 D2
Ciudad Acuña Mex. 185 E2

Ciudad Altamirano Mex. 185 E5
Ciudad Bolívar Venez. 199 F2
Ciudad Camargo Mex. 184 D3
Ciudad Constitución Mex. 184 C3
also known as Villa Constitución
Ciudad Cuauhtémoc Mex. 185 H6
Ciudad del Carmen Mex. 185 H5
Ciudad del Este Para. 201 G6
formerly known as Puerto Presidente Stroessner
Ciudad Delicias Mex. 184 D2
Ciudad del Maíz Mex. 185 F4
Ciudad de Valles Mex. 185 F4
Ciudad Guayana Venez. 199 F2
Ciudad Guzmán Mex. 184 E5
Ciudad Hidalgo Mex. 185 E5
Ciudad Ixtepec Mex. 185 G5
Ciudad Juárez Mex. 184 D2
Ciudad Lerdo Mex. 184 D3
Ciudad Madero Mex. 185 F4
Ciudad Mante Mex. 185 F4
Ciudad Mendoza Mex. 185 F5
Ciudad Mier Mex. 185 F3
Ciudad Obregón Mex. 184 C3
Ciudad Piar Venez. 199 F3
Ciudad Real Spain 54 H6
Ciudad Río Bravo Mex. 185 F3
Ciudad Rodrigo Spain 54 E4
Ciudad Trujillo Dom. Rep. see Santo Domingo
Ciudad Victoria Mex. 185 F4
Ciudanovița Romania 58 C3
Ciumani Romania 58 G2
Ciutadella de Menorca Spain 55 O4
Civa Burnu pt Turkey 107 D2
Civetta, Monte mt. Italy 56 E2
Cividale del Friuli Italy 56 F2
Civita Castellana Italy 56 E6
historically known as Falerii
Civitanova Marche Italy 56 F5
Civitavecchia Italy 56 D6
Civitella Roveto Italy 56 F7
Civray France 50 G6
Çivril Turkey 106 B3
Cixi China 87 G2
also known as Hushan
Cixian China 85 G4
also known as Cizhou
Ciyao China 85 H5
Cizhou China see Cixian
Cizre Turkey 107 F3
Clackamas U.S.A. 180 B3
Clacton-on-Sea U.K. 47 N12
Clain r. France 50 G6
Claire, Lake Canada 167 H3
Clair Engle Lake resr U.S.A. 180 B4
Clairmont Canada 166 G4
Clairton r. France 50 G6
Clam Lake U.S.A. 172 C4
Clan Alpine Mountains U.S.A. 182 G2
Clanton U.S.A. 175 C5
Clanville S. Africa 133 L8
Clanwilliam S. Africa 132 C9
Clanwilliam Dam S. Africa 132 C9
Clara r. Australia 149 D3
Clara S.A. Australia 146 C3
Clare r. Rep. of Ireland 47 C10
Clare U.S.A. 173 I7
Claremont Australia 147 G2
Claremont U.S.A. 177 M2
Claremont Isles Australia 149 D2
Claremore U.S.A. 179 D4
Claremorris Rep. of Ireland 47 D10
Clarence r. Australia 147 G2
Clarence r. N.Z. 153 H10
Clarence U.S.A. 172 B9
Clarence, Isla i. Chile 205 C9
Clarence Island Antarctica 222 U2
Clarence Strait Australia 148 A1
Clarence Strait U.S.A. 166 C3
Clarence Town Bahamas 187 E2
Clarendon N.Z. 153 E14
Clarendon AR U.S.A. 174 B5
Clarendon PA U.S.A. 176 F4
Clarendon TX U.S.A. 179 B5
Clarinda U.S.A. 178 D3
Clarington U.S.A. 176 E6
Clarion IA U.S.A. 174 A3
Clarion PA U.S.A. 176 F4
Clarion r. U.S.A. 176 F4
Clarión, Isla i. Mex. 184 B5
Claris N.Z. 152 J4
Clark U.S.A. 178 C2
Clark, Mount Canada 166 F1
Clarkdale U.S.A. 183 L7
Clarke r. Australia 149 E3
Clarkebury S. Africa 133 M8
Clarke Range mts Australia 149 E3
Clarkes Creek r. Australia 149 E4
Clarke's Head Canada 169 K3
Clark Fork r. ID U.S.A. 180 C2
Clark Fork r. MT U.S.A. 180 C3
Clark Hill Reservoir U.S.A. 175 D5
Clark Mountain U.S.A. 183 I6
Clark Mountains Antarctica 222 N1
Clark Point Canada 168 D4
Clarksburg U.S.A. 176 E6
Clarksdale U.S.A. 174 B5
Clark's Fork Yellowstone r. U.S.A. 180 E3
Clarks Junction N.Z. 153 E13
Clarkson S. Africa 133 I11
Clarkston U.S.A. 180 C3
Clarksville AR U.S.A. 179 D5
Clarksville TN U.S.A. 174 C4
Clarksville TX U.S.A. 179 D5
Claro r. Goiás Brazil 206 C6
Claro r. Mato Grosso Brazil 206 B2
Clatskanie U.S.A. 180 B3
Claude U.S.A. 179 B5
Cláudio Brazil 203 C7
Claveria Phil. 74 B2
Clavering Ø i. Greenland 165 Q2
Claxton U.S.A. 175 D5
Clay U.S.A. 176 D7
Clayburg U.S.A. 177 L1
Clay Center KS U.S.A. 178 C4
Clay Center NE U.S.A. 178 C3
Clay City U.S.A. 176 B8
Clayhole Wash watercourse U.S.A. 183 K4
Claypool U.S.A. 183 N8
Claypool U.S.A. 183 N7
Clay Springs U.S.A. 183 N7
Clayton DE U.S.A. 177 J6
Clayton GA U.S.A. 175 D5
Clayton NM U.S.A. 178 B4
Clayton NY U.S.A. 177 I3
Claytor Lake U.S.A. 176 E8
Clearco U.S.A. 176 E7
Clear Creek Canada 173 M8
Clear Creek U.S.A. 183 N6
Clear Creek r. AZ U.S.A. 183 N7
Clearfield PA U.S.A. 176 G4
Clearfield UT U.S.A. 180 D4
Clear Fork Brazos r. U.S.A. 179 C5
Clear Hills Canada 166 G3
Clear Island Rep. of Ireland 47 C12
Clear Lake I. Canada 167 K4
Clear Lake IA U.S.A. 174 A3
Clear Lake SD U.S.A. 178 C2
Clear Lake WI U.S.A. 172 A5
Clear Lake l. CA U.S.A. 182 B2
Clear Lake l. UT U.S.A. 183 L2
Clearlake Oaks U.S.A. 182 B2
Clear Lake Reservoir U.S.A. 180 B4

Clearmont U.S.A. 180 F3
Clear Spring U.S.A. 176 H6
Clearwater Canada 166 G5
Clearwater r. Alta Canada 167 H4
Clearwater r. Alta/Sask. Canada 167 I3
Clearwater r. ID U.S.A. 180 C3
Clearwater r. MN U.S.A. 178 D2
Clear Water Bay Hong Kong China 87 [inset]
also known as Tsing Shui Wan
Clearwater Lake l. Canada 167 K4
Clearwater Lake U.S.A. 172 G5
Clearwater Lake Provincial Park Canada 167 K4
Clearwater Mountains U.S.A. 180 D3
Clearwater River Provincial Park Canada 167 I3
Cleburne U.S.A. 179 C5
Cle Elum U.S.A. 180 B3
Cléguérec France 50 C4
Clemency Lux. 51 M5
Clementina Brazil 206 C8
Clemmons U.S.A. 176 E9
Clemson U.S.A. 174 D5
Clendenin U.S.A. 176 D7
Clendening Lake l. U.S.A. 176 D5
Cleopatra Needle mt. Phil. 74 A4
Clères France 50 H3
Clerf Lux. see Clervaux
Clericy Canada 173 O2
Clerke Reef Australia 150 B3
Clermont Australia 149 E4
Clermont France 51 I3
Clermont U.S.A. 175 D6
Clermont-en-Argonne France 51 L3
Clermont-Ferrand France 51 J7
Clermont-l'Hérault France 51 J9
Clervaux Lux. 51 M2
also known as Clerf
Cles Italy 56 D2
Cleve Australia 146 C3
Cleveland r. Canada 167 O1
Cleveland GA U.S.A. 174 D5
Cleveland MS U.S.A. 175 B5
Cleveland OH U.S.A. 176 D4
Cleveland TN U.S.A. 174 C5
Cleveland TX U.S.A. 179 D6
Cleveland UT U.S.A. 183 N2
Cleveland VA U.S.A. 176 C9
Cleveland WI U.S.A. 172 F7
Cleveland, Cape Australia 149 E3
Cleveland, Mount U.S.A. 180 D2
Cleveland Bay Australia 149 E3
Cleveland Hills U.K. 47 K9
Cleverlândia do Norte Brazil 199 I4
Cleveland Peninsula U.S.A. 166 C3
Cleves Germany see Kleve
Clew Bay Rep. of Ireland 47 C10
Clewiston U.S.A. 175 D7
Clifden Rep. of Ireland 47 B10
Cliffdale r. Australia 148 C3
Clifford S. Africa 133 L8
Clifftop U.S.A. 176 E7
Clifton Australia 147 F1
Clifton AZ U.S.A. 183 O8
Clifton IL U.S.A. 172 F10
Clifton Beach Australia 149 E3
Clifton Forge U.S.A. 176 F8
Clifton Hills Australia 146 C1
Clifton Park U.S.A. 177 L3
Climax Canada 167 I5
Climax U.S.A. 172 H8
Clinch r. U.S.A. 176 B9
Clinchco U.S.A. 176 C9
Clinch Mountain mts U.S.A. 176 C9
Clinchport U.S.A. 176 C9
Cline River Canada 167 G4
Clinton Canada 168 D5
Clinton N.Z. 153 D14
Clinton AR U.S.A. 179 D5
Clinton IA U.S.A. 172 B9
Clinton KY U.S.A. 174 B4
Clinton LA U.S.A. 175 B6
Clinton ME U.S.A. 177 P1
Clinton MI U.S.A. 173 J8
Clinton MO U.S.A. 178 D4
Clinton MS U.S.A. 175 B5
Clinton NC U.S.A. 174 E5
Clinton OK U.S.A. 179 C5
Clinton TN U.S.A. 176 A9
Clinton-Colden Lake l. Canada 167 J1
Clinton Creek Canada 166 A1
Clintonville U.S.A. 172 E6
Clintonville WV U.S.A. 176 E8
Clintwood U.S.A. 176 C8
Clio U.S.A. 173 J7
▶ Clipperton, Île terr. N. Pacific Ocean 221 K5
French Overseas Territory. Most easterly point of Oceania. English form Clipperton Island.
oceania [countries] ▶▶ 138–139
Clipperton Island terr. N. Pacific Ocean see Clipperton, Île
Clishham hill U.K. 46 F6
Clisson France 50 E5
Clitheroe U.K. 47 J10
Clive N.Z. 152 K7
Clive Lake Canada 167 G2
Cliza Bol. 200 D4
Cloates, Point Australia 150 A4
Cloclan S. Africa 133 L5
Clonagh Australia 149 D4
Cloncurry Australia 149 D4
Cloncurry r. Australia 149 D3
Clones Rep. of Ireland 47 E9
Clonmel Rep. of Ireland 47 E11
also known as Cluain Meala
Cloppenburg Germany 48 F3
Cloquet U.S.A. 174 A2
Cloquet r. U.S.A. 174 A2
Clorinda Arg. 204 F2
Cloud Bay Canada 172 D2
Cloud Peak WY U.S.A. 180 F3
Cloudy Bay N.Z. 152 I9
Clova Canada 168 E3
Clover U.S.A. 183 L1
Cloverdale S. Africa 132 A3
Clovis CA U.S.A. 182 E4
Clovis NM U.S.A. 179 B5
Cloyes-sur-le-Loir France 50 H5
Cloyne Canada 173 N6
Cluain Meala Rep. of Ireland see Clonmel
Cluanie, Loch l. U.K. 46 G6
Cluff Lake Mine Canada 167 I3
Cluj-Napoca Romania 58 E2
also known as Kolozsvár
Cluny Australia 148 C5
Cluny France 51 K6
Cluses France 51 M6
Cluster Springs U.S.A. 176 G9
Clutha r. N.Z. 153 D14
Clut Lake Canada 167 G1
Clutterbuck Hills hill Australia 151 D5
Clwydian Range hills U.K. 47 I10
Clyde Canada 167 H4
Clyde r. U.K. 46 H8
Clyde NY U.S.A. 177 I2
Clyde OH U.S.A. 176 C5
Clyde, Firth of est. U.K. 46 H8
Clydebank U.K. 46 H8
Clyde River Canada 165 M2
Clydevale N.Z. 153 D14
Clyman U.S.A. 172 E7
Clymer U.S.A. 176 F3
Cnossus tourist site Greece see Knossos

Côa r. Port. 54 D3
Coachelia Canal U.S.A. 183 I9
Coachella U.S.A. 183 H8
Coahuayutla de Guerrero Mex. 185 E5
Coahuila state Mex. 185 E3
Coal r. Canada 166 E3
Coal City U.S.A. 172 E9
Coaldale Canada 167 H5
Coalgate U.S.A. 179 C5
Coal Grove U.S.A. 176 C7
Coal Harbour Canada 166 E5
Coalinga U.S.A. 182 D5
Coalport U.S.A. 176 G5
Coal River Canada 166 E3
Coal Valley U.S.A. 183 I4
Coalville Australia 147 E3
Coamo Puerto Rico 187 G3
Coaraci Brazil 207 N1
Coari Brazil 199 F5
Coari r. Brazil 199 F6
Coari, Lago l. Brazil 199 F6
Coast prov. Kenya 128 D5
Coast admin. reg. Tanz. see Pwani
Coastal Plain U.S.A. 175 A6
Coast Mountains Canada 166 E4
Coast Range hills Australia 149 F5
Coast Ranges mts U.S.A. 182 A1
Coatepec Mex. 185 F5
Coatepeque Guat. 185 H6
Coatesville U.S.A. 177 J6
Coaticook Canada 169 G4
Coats Island Canada 165 K3
Coats Land reg. Antarctica 222 V1
Coatzacoalcos Mex. 185 G5
formerly known as Puerto México
Coatzintla Mex. 185 F4
Cobadin Romania 58 J4
Coban Guat. 185 H6
Cobán Guat. 185 H6
Cobar Australia 147 E3
Cobargo Australia 147 F4
Cobb, Lake salt flat Australia 150 D3
Cobden Canada 173 O5
Cóbh Rep. of Ireland 47 D12
also known as An Cóbh; formerly known as Queenstown
Cobija Bol. 200 C2
Cobija Chile 200 C5
Coblenz Germany see Koblenz
Cobleskill U.S.A. 177 K3
Cobos Mex. 185 F4
Cobourg Canada 168 E5
Cobourg Peninsula Australia 148 B1
Cobquecura Chile 204 B5
Cobra Australia 150 B5
Cobram Australia 147 E3
Cobres Arg. 200 D3
Côbue Moz. 129 B8
Coburg Germany 48 H5
Coburg Island Canada 165 L2
Coca r. Australia 149 E2
Cocachacra Peru 200 C4
Cocal Brazil 202 D2
Cocalinho Brazil 202 B5
Cocanada India see Kakinada
Cocapata Bol. 200 D4
Cocentaina Spain 55 K6
Cochabamba Bol. 200 D4
Cochabamba dept Bol. 200 D4
Cochamó Chile 205 B6
Coche, Isla i. Venez. 199 F2
Cochem Germany 48 E5
Co Chiên, Sông r. mouth Vietnam 79 D6
Cochin India 94 C4
also known as Kochi
Cochin reg. Vietnam 79 D6
Cochinos, Bahía de b. Cuba see Pigs, Bay of
Cochise U.S.A. 183 O9
Cochise Head mt. U.S.A. 183 O9
Cochran U.S.A. 175 D5
Cochrane Alta Canada 167 H5
Cochrane Ont. Canada 168 D3
Cochrane r. Canada 167 K3
Cochrane Chile 205 B7
Cochrane, Lago l. Arg./Chile 205 B7
Cockaleechie Australia 146 C3
Cockburn Australia 146 D3
Cockburn Harbour Turks and Caicos Is 187 F2
Cockburn Island Canada 168 D4
Cockburn Town Bahamas 187 E1
Cockburn Town Turks and Caicos Is see Grand Turk
Cockermouth U.K. 47 I8
Cocklebiddy Australia 151 D7
Cocks comb mt. S. Africa 133 I10
Coclé del Norte Panama 186 C5
Coco r. Brazil 202 B4
Coco r. Hond./Nicaragua 186 C4
also known as Segovia
Coco, Cayo i. Cuba 186 D2
Coco, Isla de i. N. Pacific Ocean 221 M5
Cocobeach Gabon 126 A4
Coco Channel India 95 G3
Coconino Plateau U.S.A. 183 K6
Cocoparra National Park Australia 147 E3
Cocorná Col. 198 C3
▶ Cocos Brazil 202 B5
▶ Cocos Islands terr. Indian Ocean 218 N6
Australian External Territory. Also known as Keeling Islands.
asia [countries] ▶▶ 64–67

Cocula Mex. 184 E4
Cod, Cape U.S.A. 177 O4
Codăeşti Romania 58 I2
Codajás Brazil 199 F5
Codera, Cabo c. Venez. 199 E2
Coderre Canada 167 J5
Codigoro Italy 56 E4
Cod Island Canada 169 I1
Codlea Romania 58 G3
Codó Brazil 202 D3
Codogno Italy 56 B3
Codrington Antigua and Barbuda 187 H3
Codrington, Mount Antarctica 223 E2
Codroipo Italy 56 E3
Codru Moldova 58 J2
Coen Australia 149 D2
Coen r. Australia 149 D2
Coenwijk S. Africa 133 I9
Coesfeld Germany 48 E3
Coetzeesberg mts S. Africa 133 I9
Coetzersdam S. Africa 133 I3
Coeur d'Alene U.S.A. 180 C3
Coeur d'Alene r. U.S.A. 180 C3
Coeur d'Alene Indian Reservation res. U.S.A. 180 C3
Coffee Bay S. Africa 133 N8
Coffee Creek Canada 166 B2
Coffeyville U.S.A. 178 D4
Coffin Bay Australia 146 B3
Coffin Bay b. Australia 146 B3
Coffin Bay National Park Australia 146 B3
Coffs Harbour Australia 147 G2
Cofimvaba S. Africa 133 M8
formerly known as St Mark's
Cofre de Perote, Parque Nacional nat. park Mex. 185 F5

Cogălniceanu airport Romania see Kogălniceanu
Cogealac Romania 58 J4
Coggon U.S.A. 172 B8
Coghinas r. Sardegna Italy 57 A8
Coghlan S. Africa 133 N8
Coghlan, Mount hill Australia 150 D3
Cognac France 50 F7
Cogo Equat. Guinea 125 H6
Cogolin France 51 M9
Cogollos Spain 54 F1
Cohocton U.S.A. 177 I3
Cohoes U.S.A. 177 L3
Cohuna Australia 147 E3
Coiba, Isla i. Panama 186 C6
Coihaique Chile 205 B7
Coihueco Chile 204 B5
Coimbatore India 94 C4
Coimbra Port. 54 C4
Coimbra admin. dist. Port. 54 C4
Coin Spain 54 G8
Coipasa, Salar de salt flat Bol. 200 C4
Cojata Peru 200 C3
Cojedes state Venez. 198 D2
Cojojoro Venez. 187 F5
Cojudo Blanco, Cerro mt. Arg. 205 C7
Colac Australia 147 D4
Colac N.Z. 153 B14
Colair Lake India see Kolleru Lake
Çolaklı Turkey 108 C1
Çolares Brazil 202 B2
Colatina Brazil 203 D6
Colbinabbin Australia 147 E3
Colborne Canada 173 P7
Colby KS U.S.A. 178 B4
Colby WI U.S.A. 172 C6
Colca r. Peru 200 C3
Colceag Romania 58 H4
Colchester S. Africa 133 J10
Colchester U.K. 47 M12
historically known as Camulodunum
Colchester U.S.A. 177 M4
Cold Bay U.S.A. 164 C4
also known as Fort Randall
Cold Lake Canada 167 I4
Cold Lake l. Canada 167 I4
Coldspring U.S.A. 179 D6
Cold Springs U.S.A. 182 G2
Coldstream Canada 166 G5
Coldstream U.K. 46 J8
Coldwater Canada 173 N6
Coldwater KS U.S.A. 178 B4
Coldwater MI U.S.A. 173 I9
Coldwater r. U.S.A. 179 B4
Coldwell Canada 172 G2
Colebrook U.S.A. 177 N1
Coleford U.K. 47 J12
Coleman r. Australia 149 D2
Coleman MI U.S.A. 173 I7
Coleman TX U.S.A. 179 C6
Coleman WI U.S.A. 172 E5
Çölemerik Turkey see Hakkâri
Colenso S. Africa 133 N5
Colentina r. Romania 58 G4
Coleraine Australia 146 D4
Coleraine U.K. 47 F8
Coleroon r. India 94 C4
Coles, Punta de pt Peru 200 C4
Colesberg S. Africa 133 J7
Coleville U.S.A. 182 E3
Coleville CA U.S.A. 182 D2
Colfax CA U.S.A. 182 C2
Colfax LA U.S.A. 179 D6
Colfax WA U.S.A. 180 C3
Colfax WI U.S.A. 172 B6
Colhué Huapi, Lago l. Arg. 205 C7
Colibaşi Romania 58 F4
Colico Italy 56 B2
Coligny S. Africa 133 L3
Colima Mex. 184 E5
Colima state Mex. 184 E5
Colima, Nevado de vol. Mex. 184 E4
Colina Brazil 206 E7
Colinas Brazil 202 C3
Coliseu r. Brazil 202 A5
Coll i. U.K. 46 F7
Collado Bajo mt. Spain 55 J4
Collado Villalba Spain 54 H4
Collahuasi Chile 200 C5
Collalto mt. Austria/Italy 48 J9
also known as Hochgall
Collarenebri Australia 147 F2
Collecchio Italy 56 C4
Colle di Val d'Elsa Italy 56 D5
Colleen Bawn Zimbabwe 131 F4
College U.S.A. 164 E3
College Corner U.S.A. 176 A6
College Hill U.S.A. 176 B6
College Park U.S.A. 175 C5
College Station U.S.A. 179 C6
Colleria Australia 147 E2
Collesalvetti Italy 56 C5
Collie Australia 151 B7
Collier Bay Australia 150 D3
Collier Range hills Australia 151 B5
Collier Range National Park Australia 151 B5
Collierville U.S.A. 174 B5
Collingwood Canada 168 D4
Collingwood N.Z. 152 G8
Collins r. U.S.A. 172 C6
Collins Glacier Antarctica 223 E2
Collins Lake U.S.A. 182 C2
Collinson Peninsula Canada 165 I2
Collinsville U.S.A. 149 E4
Collinsville OK U.S.A. 179 D4
Collinsville VA U.S.A. 176 F9
Collipulli Chile 204 B5
Collmberg hill Germany 49 K4
Colloney Rep. of Ireland 47 D9
Colmar France 51 N4
Colmena Arg. 204 E3
Colmenar de Oreja Spain 55 H4
Colmenar Viejo Spain 54 H4
Colne U.K. 47 J10
Colo r. Australia 147 F3
Cologne Germany 48 D5
also known as Köln; historically known as Colonia Agrippina
Coloma MI U.S.A. 172 G8
Coloma WI U.S.A. 172 D6
Colomb-Béchar Alg. see Béchar
Colômbia Brazil 206 D7
Colombia Col. 198 C4
Colombia Mex. 185 F3
▶ Colombia country S. America 198 C4
2nd most populous and 4th largest country in South America.
southamerica [countries] ▶▶ 192–193

▶ Colombo Sri Lanka 94 C5
Former capital of Sri Lanka.

Colombourg Canada 173 N2
Colomiers France 50 H9
Colón Buenos Aires Arg. 204 E4
Colón Entre Ríos Arg. 204 F4
Colón Cuba 186 C2
Colon U.S.A. 173 H9
Colón Panama 186 D5
Colona Australia 146 A3
Colonelganj India 97 D4
Colonel Hill Bahamas 187 F2
Colonet, Cabo c. Mex. 184 A2

Colonia Arg. 204 E2
Colônia r. Brazil 207 N1
Colonia Micronesia 73 I5
Colonia Agrippina Germany see Cologne
Colonia del Sacramento Uruguay 204 F4
Colonia Dora Arg. 204 E3
Colonia Emilio Mitre Arg. 204 D5
Colonia Julia Fenestris Italy see Fano
Colonia Las Heras Arg. 205 C7
Colonial Heights U.S.A. 176 H8
Colonia Suiza Uruguay 204 F4
Colonna, Capo c. Italy 57 J9
Colonsay i. U.K. 46 F7
Colorado r. La Rioja Arg. 204 D3
Colorado r. San Juan Arg. 204 C3
Colorado r. Arg. 204 E5
Colorado r. Mex./U.S.A. 184 B2
Colorado r. U.S.A. 179 C6
Colorado state U.S.A. 180 F5
Colorado City AZ U.S.A. 183 K5
Colorado City TX U.S.A. 179 B5
Colorado Desert U.S.A. 183 H8
Colorado National Monument nat. park U.S.A. 183 P2
Colorado Plateau U.S.A. 183 O4
Colorado River Aqueduct canal U.S.A. 183 J7
Colorado River Indian Reservation res. U.S.A. 183 J8
Colorados, Cerro mt. Arg. 204 C2
Colorado Springs U.S.A. 180 F5
Colorno Italy 56 C4
Colossae Turkey see Honaz
Colotlán Mex. 185 E4
Colquechaca Bol. 200 D4
Colquiri Bol. 200 D4
Colquitt U.S.A. 175 C6
Colson U.S.A. 176 C8
Colstrip U.S.A. 180 F3
Colton CA U.S.A. 183 G7
Colton NY U.S.A. 177 K1
Colton UT U.S.A. 183 M2
Columbia KY U.S.A. 174 C4
Columbia LA U.S.A. 179 D5
Columbia MD U.S.A. 177 I6
Columbia MO U.S.A. 178 D4
Columbia MS U.S.A. 175 B6
Columbia NC U.S.A. 174 E5
Columbia PA U.S.A. 177 I5
▶ Columbia SC U.S.A. 175 D5
State capital of South Carolina.
Columbia TN U.S.A. 174 C5
Columbia r. U.S.A. 180 B3
Columbia, Cape Canada 165 L1
Columbia, Mount Canada 167 G4
Columbia, Sierra mts Mex. 184 C3
Columbia City U.S.A. 174 C5
Columbia Falls ME U.S.A. 177 R1
Columbia Falls MT U.S.A. 180 D2
Columbia Mountains Canada 166 F4
Columbia Plateau U.S.A. 180 C3
Columbine, Cape S. Africa 132 B9
Columbretes, Islas is Spain 55 L5
Columbus GA U.S.A. 175 C5
Columbus IN U.S.A. 174 C4
Columbus KS U.S.A. 178 D4
Columbus MS U.S.A. 175 B5
Columbus MT U.S.A. 180 E3
Columbus NC U.S.A. 174 D5
Columbus NE U.S.A. 178 C3
▶ Columbus OH U.S.A. 176 B6
State capital of Ohio.
Columbus PA U.S.A. 176 F4
Columbus TX U.S.A. 179 C6
Columbus WI U.S.A. 172 D7
Columbus Grove U.S.A. 176 A5
Columbus Junction U.S.A. 172 B9
Columbus Salt Marsh U.S.A. 182 F3
Coluna Brazil 207 K5
Colunga Spain 54 F1
Cousa U.S.A. 182 B2
Colville N.Z. 152 J4
Colville r. U.S.A. 164 D2
Colville, Cape N.Z. 152 J4
Colville Channel N.Z. 152 J4
Colville Indian Reservation res. U.S.A. 180 C2
Colville Lake Canada 166 E1
Colwyn Bay U.K. 47 I10
also known as Bae Colwyn
Comacchio Italy 56 E4
Comacchio, Valli di lag. Italy 56 E4
Comai China see Damxoi
Comalcalco Mex. 185 G5
Comallo Arg. 204 C6
Comana Romania 58 H4
Comanche U.S.A. 179 C6
Comandante Ferraz research station Antarctica 222 U2
Comandante Fontana Arg. 204 F2
Comănești Romania 58 H2
Comarnic Romania 58 G3
Comayagua Hond. 186 B4
Combahee r. U.S.A. 175 D5
Combarbalá Chile 204 C3
Comber U.K. 47 G9
Combermere Canada 173 P5
Combermere Bay Myanmar 78 A4
Comboi i. Indon. 76 C2
Combourg France 50 E4
Comcomércio Brazil 206 D6
Comercinho Brazil 207 L3
Comet Australia 149 F4
Comet r. Australia 149 F4
Comfort TX U.S.A. 179 C6
Comfort WV U.S.A. 176 D7
Comilla Bangl. 97 F5
Comino i. Malta see Kemmuna
Comino, Capo c. Sardegna Italy 57 B8
Comiso Sicilia Italy 57 G12
Comitán de Domínguez Mex. 185 G5
Commanda Canada 173 N5
Commentry France 51 I6
Commissioner's Salt Pan S. Africa 132 D7
Committee Bay Canada 165 K3
Commodale S. Africa 133 C5
Commonwealth Bay Antarctica 223 J2
Commonwealth Territory admin. div.
Australia see Jervis Bay Territory
Como Italy 56 B3
Como, Lago di l. Italy see Como, Lake
Como, Lake Italy 56 B3
also known as Como, Lago di
Como Chamling l. China 89 E6
Comodoro Rivadavia Arg. 205 D7
Comoé r. Côte d'Ivoire see Komoé
Comonfort Mex. 185 E4
Comores country Africa see Comoros
Comorin, Cape India 94 C4
also known as Kanniya Kumari
▶ Comoros country Africa 129 D7
known as Al Qumur in Arabic; also spelt Comores in French
africa [countries] ▶▶ 114–117
Comox Canada 166 E5
Compiègne France 51 I3
Compostela Mex. 184 D4
Compostela Phil. 74 C5
Compridia, Ilha i. Brazil 203 C8
Compton CA U.S.A. 182 F8
Compton IL U.S.A. 172 D9

Comrat Moldova 58 J2
formerly spelt Komrat
Con, Sông r. Vietnam 78 D4
Cona China 89 E7
also spelt Tsona

▶ Conakry Guinea 124 B4
Capital of Guinea.

Conambo Ecuador 198 B5
Conambo r. Ecuador 198 B5
Cona Niyeo Arg. 205 D6
Conay Chile 204 C3
Concarneau France 50 C5
also spelt Konk-Kerne
Conceição Amazonas Brazil 199 F5
Conceição Mato Grosso Brazil 201 F1
Conceição Paraíba Brazil 202 E3
Conceição Rondônia Brazil 201 E2
Conceição Roraima Brazil 199 F4
Conceição r. Brazil 207 I5
Conceição da Barra Brazil 203 E6
Conceição das Alagoas Brazil 206 E6
Conceição do Araguaia Brazil 202 B4
Conceição do Coité Brazil 202 E4
Conceição do Mato Dentro Brazil 203 D6
Conceição do Maú Brazil 199 G4
Concepción Corrientes Arg. 204 F3
Concepción Tucumán Arg. 204 D2
Concepción Beni Bol. 201 E3
Concepción Santa Cruz Bol. 201 E4
Concepción Chile 204 B5
Concepción r. Mex. 184 B2
Concepción Mex. 185 E3
Concepción Panama 186 C5
Concepción Para. 201 F5
Concepción, Canal sea chan. Chile 205 B8
Concepción, Punta pt Mex. 184 C3
Concepción del Uruguay Arg. 204 F4
Conception, Point U.S.A. 182 B7
Conception Bay Namibia 130 B4
Concesio Italy 56 C3
Concession Zimbabwe 131 F3
Concha Mex. 184 D4
Conchas Brazil 206 E9
Conchas Lake U.S.A. 181 F6
Conches-en-Ouche France 50 G4
Concho Mex. 184 D3
Concho U.S.A. 183 O7
Concho r. U.S.A. 179 C6
Conchos r. Chihuahua Mex. 184 D2
Conchos r. Nuevo León/Tamaulipas Mex. 185 F3
Concord CA U.S.A. 182 B4
Concord NC U.S.A. 173 I8
Concord NC U.S.A. 174 D5

▶ Concord NH U.S.A. 177 N2
State capital of New Hampshire.

Concord PA U.S.A. 176 H5
Concord VA U.S.A. 176 G8
Concord VT U.S.A. 177 N1
Concordia Arg. 204 F3
Concórdia Amazonas Brazil 199 E6
Concórdia Santa Catarina Brazil 203 A8
Concordia Antioquia Col. 198 C4
Concordia Meta Col. 198 C4
Concordia Peru 198 C6
Concórdia S. Africa 132 B6
Concordia U.S.A. 178 C4
Concord Peak Afgh. 101 H2
Con Cuông Vietnam 78 D4
Conda Angola 127 B7
Condamine Australia 149 F5
Condamine r. Australia 147 F1
Conde Brazil 202 E4
Condega Nicaragua 186 B4
Condeixa Brazil 202 D2
Condé-sur-Noireau France 50 F4
Condeúba Brazil 202 D5
Condobolin Australia 147 E3
Condoe Moz. 131 G3
Condom France 50 G9
Condon U.S.A. 180 B3
Condor, Cordillera del mts Ecuador/Peru 198 B6
Conecuh r. U.S.A. 175 C6
Conejos Mex. 184 D3
Conejos U.S.A. 181 F5
Conejos r. U.S.A. 181 F5
Conemaugh r. U.S.A. 176 F5
Conero, Monte hill Italy 56 F6
Conesus Lake U.S.A. 176 H3
Conesville IA U.S.A. 172 B9
Conesville OH U.S.A. 176 D5
Coney Island Sing. see Serangoon, Pulau
Coney Island U.S.A. 177 L5
Conflict Group is P.N.G. 149 F1
Confluence U.S.A. 176 F6
Confoederatio Helvetica country Europe see Switzerland
Confolens France 50 G6
Confusion Range mts U.S.A. 183 K3
Confuso r. Para. 201 F6
Congdü China see Nyalam
Conghua China 87 E4
Congjiang China 87 D3
also known as Bingmei
Congleton U.K. 47 J10

▶ Congo country Africa 126 B5
formerly known as Congo (Brazzaville) or French Congo or Middle Congo or Moyen Congo; long form Congo, Republic of
africa [countries] ▶▶▶ 114–117

▶ Congo r. Congo/Dem. Rep. Congo 127 B6
2nd longest river in Africa and 8th in the world. Formerly known as Zaïre.
africa [landscapes] ▶▶▶ 112–113

Congo (Brazzaville) country Africa see Congo
Congo (Kinshasa) country Africa see Congo, Democratic Republic of

▶ Congo, Democratic Republic of country Africa 126 D5
3rd largest and 4th most populous country in Africa. Formerly known as Zaire or Belgian Congo or Congo (Kinshasa) or Congo Free State.
africa [countries] ▶▶▶ 114–117

Congo, Republic of country Africa see Congo
Congo Basin Dem. Rep. Congo 126 D5
Congo Free State country Africa see Congo, Democratic Republic of
Congonhas Brazil 207 J7
Congonhinhas Brazil 206 C10
Congress U.S.A. 183 L7
Conguillo, Parque Nacional nat. park Chile 204 C5
Conhuas Mex. 185 H5
Cónico, Cerro mt. Arg. 205 C6
Conil de la Frontera Spain 54 E8
Coniston Canada 173 M4
Coniston U.K. 47 I9
Conjuboy Australia 149 E3
Conkal Mex. 185 H4
Conklin Canada 167 I4
Conlara r. Arg. 204 D4
Conn r. Canada 168 E2
Conn, Lough l. Rep. of Ireland 47 C9
Connacht reg. Rep. of Ireland see Connaught

Connaught Canada 173 M2
Connaught reg. Rep. of Ireland 47 C10
also spelt Connacht
Conneaut U.S.A. 176 E4
Conneaut Lake U.S.A. 176 F4
Conneautville U.S.A. 176 E4
Connecticut r. U.S.A. 177 M4

▶ Connecticut state U.S.A. 177 M4
Connell U.S.A. 46 G7
Connells Lagoon Conservation Reserve nature res. Australia 148 C3
Connemara reg. Rep. of Ireland 47 C10
Connemara Australia 149 D5
Connemara National Park Rep. of Ireland 47 C10,C10
Conner, Mount hill Australia 148 A5
Connersville U.S.A. 174 C4
Connolly, Mount Canada 166 C2
Connors Range hills Australia 149 F4
Cononaco Ecuador 198 C5
Cononaco r. Ecuador 198 C5
Conover U.S.A. 172 D4
Conquista Bol. 200 D2
Conquista Brazil 206 F6
Conrad U.S.A. 180 E2
ConrADO r. Australia 149 D6
Conroe U.S.A. 179 D6
Conroe, Lake U.S.A. 179 D6
Consecon Canada 168 E4
Consejo Belize 186 A3
Conselheiro Lafaiete Brazil 203 D7
Conselheiro Pena Brazil 203 D6
Conselice Italy 56 D4
Consett U.K. 47 K9
Consolación del Sur Cuba 186 C2
Côn Son i. Vietnam 79 D6
Consort Canada 167 I4
Constance Germany see Konstanz
Constance, Lake Germany/Switz. 51 P5
also known as Bodensee
Constância dos Baetas Brazil 199 F6
Constanța Romania 58 J4
also spelt Küstence; historically known as Tomi or Tomis
Constantia tourist site Cyprus see Salamis
Constantia Germany see Konstanz
Constantine Alg. 123 G1
also known as Qacentina; historically known as Cirta
Constantine, Cape Canada 164 D4
Constitución de 1857, Parque Nacional nat. park Mex. 184 B1
Consuelo Australia 149 F5
Consuelo Brazil 201 E3
Consul Canada 167 I5
Consul r. Canada 167 K1
Contagem Brazil 207 I6
Contamana Peru 200 B1
Contarina Italy 56 D4
Contas r. Brazil 202 E5
Conthey Switz. 51 N6
Contoocook r. U.S.A. 177 N2
Contoy, Isla i. Mex. 186 B2
Contratación Col. 198 C3
Contreras, Embalse de resr Spain 55 J5
Contreras, Isla i. Chile 205 B8
Contres France 50 H5
Contria Brazil 207 I5
Contwoyto Lake Canada 167 I1
Convención Col. 198 C2
Convent U.S.A. 175 D6
Convoy U.S.A. 176 A5
Conway S. Australia 133 J8
Conway AR U.S.A. 179 D5
Conway KY U.S.A. 176 A8
Conway NC U.S.A. 177 H9
Conway NH U.S.A. 177 N2
Conway SC U.S.A. 175 E5
Conway, Cape Australia 149 F4
Conway, Lake salt flat Australia 146 B2
Conway National Park Australia 149 F4
Conway Springs U.S.A. 178 C4
Coober Pedy Australia 146 B2
Cooch Behar India see Koch Bihar
Coogoon r. Australia 147 F1
Cook Australia 146 A2
Cook r. U.S.A. 172 A3
Cook, Bahía de b. Chile 205 C9
Cook, Cape Canada 166 E5
▶ Cook, Mount Canada/U.S.A. 166 B2
oceania [landscapes] ▶▶▶ 136–137

▶ Cook, Mount N.Z. 153 I11
Highest mountain in New Zealand. Also known as Aoraki or Aorangi.

Cook Atoll Kiribati see Tarawa
Cookes Peak U.S.A. 181 F6
Cookeville U.S.A. 174 C4
Cookhouse S. Africa 133 J9
Cook Ice Shelf Antarctica 223 K2
Cook Inlet sea chan. U.S.A. 164 D3

▶ Cook Islands S. Pacific Ocean 221 H7
Self-governing New Zealand Territory.
oceania [countries] ▶▶▶ 138–139

Cooksburg U.S.A. 177 K3
Cooks Passage Australia 149 E2
Cookstown U.K. 47 F9
Cook Strait N.Z. 152 H8
Cooktown Australia 149 E2
Coolabah Australia 147 E2
Coolah Australia 147 F2
Coolamon Australia 147 E3
Coolgardie Australia 151 C6
Coolibah Australia 148 A3
Coolimba Australia 151 A6
Cooloola National Park Australia 149 G5
Coolum Beach Australia 149 G5
Cooma Australia 147 F4
Coombabarabran Australia 147 F2
Coonalpyn Australia 146 C3
Coonamble Australia 147 F2
Coonana Aboriginal Reserve Australia 151 C6
Coondambo Australia 146 B2
Coondapoor India see Kundapura
Coongan r. Australia 150 B4
Coongan Aboriginal Reserve Australia 150 B4
Coongoola Australia 147 E1
Coon Rapids U.S.A. 174 A2
Cooper r. Australia 148 B2
Cooper U.S.A. 179 D5
Cooper Creek watercourse Australia 146 C2
also known as Barcoo Creek
Cooperdale U.S.A. 176 D5
Coopernook Australia 147 G2
Coopersburg U.S.A. 177 J5
Coopers Mills U.S.A. 177 P1
Cooperstown ND U.S.A. 178 C2
Cooperstown NY U.S.A. 177 K3
Coopracambra National Park Australia 147 F4
Coorabie Australia 146 A2
Coor-de-Wandy hill Australia 151 B5
Coorong National Park Australia 146 C4
Coorow Australia 151 A6
Cooroy Australia 149 G5
Coosa r. U.S.A. 175 C5
Coosada Australia 149 D3
Coosawhatchie r. U.S.A. 149 E4
Coos Bay U.S.A. 180 A4
Coos Bay b. U.S.A. 180 A4
Cootamundra Australia 147 F3
Cooum r. India 94 C3
Copahue, Volcán vol. Chile 204 C5
Copainalá Mex. 185 G5

Copala Mex. 185 F5
Copal Urcu Peru 198 C5
Copán tourist site Hond. 186 A4
Cope, Cabo c. Spain 55 J7
Copemish U.S.A. 172 H6

▶ Copenhagen Denmark 45 K5
Capital of Denmark. Also known as København.

Copere Bol. 201 E4
Copetonas Arg. 204 E5
Copeton Reservoir Australia 147 F2
Cô Pi, Phou mt. Laos/Vietnam 78 D4
Copiapó Chile 204 C2
Copiapó, Volcán vol. Chile 204 C2
Copley Australia 146 C2
Coporaque Peru 200 C3
Coppano Italy 56 D4
Coppename r. Suriname 199 G3
Copparo Italy 56 D4
Copperbelt prov. Zambia 127 E8
formerly known as Western Province
Copperfield r. Australia 149 D3
Copper Harbor U.S.A. 172 F3
Coppermine r. Canada see Kugluktuk
Coppermine r. Canada 167 I1
Coppermine Point Canada 168 C4
Copperton S. Africa 132 F6
Copperton S.A. 183 L1
Copp Lake Canada 167 H2
Copşa Mică Romania 58 F2
Coqên China 89 D6
Coquilhatville Dem. Rep. Congo see Mbandaka
Coquille i. Micronesia see Pikelot
Coquille r. U.S.A. 180 A4
Coquimbo Chile 204 C3
Coquimbo admin. reg. Chile 204 C3
Coquitlam Canada 166 F5
Corabia Romania 58 F5
Coração de Jesus Brazil 202 C6
Coracora Peru 200 C3
Coracesium Turkey see Alanya
Coral Bay Australia 150 A4
Coral Harbour Canada 165 K3

▶ Coral Sea S. Pacific Ocean 145 E3

▶ Coral Sea Islands Territory terr. Australia 145 E3
Australian External Territory.
oceania [countries] ▶▶▶ 138–139

Coralville U.S.A. 172 B9
Corangamite, Lake Australia 147 C4
Coranzuli Arg. 200 D5
Coraopolis U.S.A. 176 E5
Corato Italy 56 I7
Corbett National Park India 96 C3
Corbie France 51 J3
Corbin U.S.A. 176 A9
Corbones r. Spain 54 F7
Corbu Romania 58 J4
Corby U.K. 47 L11
Corcaigh Rep. of Ireland see Cork
Córcoles r. Spain 55 H5
Corcoran U.S.A. 182 E5
Corcovado Brazil 202 C5
Corcovado, Golfo de sea chan. Chile 205 B6
Corcovado, Parque Nacional nat. park Costa Rica 186 C5
Corcyra i. Greece see Corfu
Cordeiro Brazil 207 K9
Cordele U.S.A. 175 D6
Cordelia U.S.A. 182 B3
Cordell U.S.A. 179 C5
Cordillera de los Picachos, Parque Nacional nat. park Col. 198 C4
Cordilleras Range mts Phil. 74 B2
Cordillo Downs Australia 146 C5
Cordisburgo Brazil 207 I6
Córdoba Córdoba Arg. 204 D3
Córdoba Río Negro Arg. 204 C6
Córdoba prov. Arg. 204 E4
Córdoba dept Col. 198 C2
Córdoba Durango Mex. 185 E3
Córdoba Veracruz Mex. 185 F5
Córdoba Spain 54 G7
historically known as Cordova or Corduba or Karmona
Córdoba, Sierras de mts Arg. 204 D3
Cordova Peru 200 B3
Cordova Spain see Córdoba
Cordova AK U.S.A. 164 E3
Cordova IL U.S.A. 172 C9
Cordova Bay U.S.A. 166 C4
Corduba Spain see Córdoba
Coreaú Brazil 202 D2
Corella r. Australia 149 D3
Corella Lake salt flat Australia 148 B3
Corfield Australia 149 D4

▶ Corfu i. Greece 59 A9
also known as Kerkyra; also spelt Kérkira; historically known as Corcyra

Corguinho Brazil 201 F3
Coria Spain 54 E5
Coria del Río Spain 54 E7
Coribe Brazil 202 C5
Coricudgy mt. Australia 147 F3
Corigliano, Golfo di b. Italy 57 I9
Corigliano Calabro Italy 57 I9
Coringa Islands Australia 149 F3
Corinium U.K. see Cirencester
Corinth Canada 167 J5
Corinth Greece 59 D11
also known as Korinthos; historically known as Corinthus
Corinth MS U.S.A. 174 B5
Corinth NY U.S.A. 177 L2
Corinth, Gulf of sea chan. Greece 59 D10
also known as Korinthiakos Kolpos
Corinthus Greece see Corinth
Corinto Brazil 203 C6
Corinto Nicaragua 186 B4
Corixa Grande r. Bol./Brazil 201 F4
Corixinha r. Brazil 201 F4
Cork Rep. of Ireland 47 D12
also spelt Corcaigh
Corlay France 50 C4
Corleone Sicilia Italy 57 F11
Çorlu Turkey 106 A2
Çorlu r. Turkey 58 I7
Cormàcchia, Monte mt. Italy 56 H7
Cormeilles France 50 G3
Cormorant Canada 167 K4
Cormorant Lake Canada 167 K4
Cormorant Provincial Forest nature res. Canada 167 K4
Corn r. Australia 148 B2
Cornacchia, Monte mt. Italy 56 H7
Cornelia S. Africa 133 M4
Cornelio Procópio Brazil 206 C10
Corneliskondre Suriname 199 G3
Cornell U.S.A. 172 C5
Cornell U.S.A. 179 G5
Cornellà de Llobregat Spain 55 N3
Corner Brook Canada 169 J3
Corneto Italy see Tarquinia
Cornetto mt. Italy 56 B2
Cornélio Procópio Brazil 206 C10
Cornia r. Italy 56 C6
Corning AR U.S.A. 174 B4
Corning CA U.S.A. 182 B2
Corning IA U.S.A. 178 D3
Corning NY U.S.A. 177 H3
Corning OH U.S.A. 176 C6
Corno, Monte mt. Italy 56 F6
Cornouaille reg. France 50 B4
Cornucopia U.S.A. 172 B3
Cornwall Ont. Canada 169 F4

Cornwall P.E.I. Canada 169 I4
Cornwall U.K. 47 I15
Cornwallis Island Canada 165 J2
Corny Point Australia 146 C3
Coro Venez. 198 D1
Coroaci Brazil 203 D6
Coroatá Brazil 202 D6
Corocoro Bol. 200 D4
Corocoro, Isla i. Venez. 199 F2
Coroglen N.Z. 152 J4
Coroico Bol. 200 D4
Corolla U.S.A. 177 J9
Coromandel Brazil 206 F5
Coromandel N.Z. 152 J4
Coromandel Coast India 94 D4
Coromandel Forest Park nature res. N.Z. 152 J5
Coromandel Peninsula N.Z. 152 J4
Coromandel Range hills N.Z. 152 J4
Coron Phil. 74 B3
Corona CA U.S.A. 182 G8
Corona NM U.S.A. 181 F6
Coronado U.S.A. 183 L1
Coronado, Bahía de b. Costa Rica 186 C5
Coronation Canada 167 I4
Coronation Gulf Canada 165 H3
Coronation Island Australia 150 D2
Coronation Island S. Atlantic Ocean 222 U2
Coronation Islands Australia 150 D2
Coronda Arg. 204 E3
Coronel Brandsen Arg. 204 F4
Coronel Dorrego Arg. 204 E5
Coronel Fabriciano Brazil 203 D6
Coronel Francisco Sosa Arg. 204 D6
Coronel Moldes Arg. 204 D4
Coronel Murta Brazil 207 K3
Coronel Oviedo Para. 201 F6
Coronel Portillo Peru 198 C5
Coronel Pringles Arg. 204 E5
Coronel Sapucaia Brazil 201 G5
Coronel Suárez Arg. 204 E5
Coronel Vidal Arg. 204 F5
Corovodë Albania 58 B8
Corowa Australia 147 E3
Corozal Belize 185 H5
Corozal Venez. 187 H7
Corozo Pando Venez. 199 E2
Corpen Aike Arg. 205 C8
Corpus Christi U.S.A. 179 C7
Corpus Christi, Lake U.S.A. 179 C6
Corque Bol. 200 D4
Corral Chile 204 B5
Corral de Almaguer Spain 55 H5
Corral de Cantos mt. Spain 54 G5
Corralillo Cuba 186 C2
Corralitos U.S.A. 182 C5
Corrandibby Range hills Australia 151 A5
Corrane Moz. 131 H2
Córrego do Ouro Brazil 206 C3
Córrego Novo Brazil 207 C3
Corrente Brazil 202 C4
Corrente r. Bahia Brazil 202 D5
Corrente r. Minas Gerais Brazil 206 A6
Corrente Grande r. Brazil 207 K6
Correntes Brazil 203 A6
Correntes r. Brazil 201 G4
Correntina Brazil 202 C5
Correntina r. Brazil see Éguas
Corrèze France 50 H7
Corrèze r. France 51 H7
Corrib, Lough l. Rep. of Ireland 47 C10
Corrientes Arg. 204 F3
Corrientes prov. Arg. 204 F3
Corrientes r. Arg. 204 F3
Corrientes r. Peru 198 C5
Corrientes, Cabo c. Arg. 204 F5
Corrientes, Cabo c. Col. 198 B3
Corrientes, Cabo c. Cuba 186 B2
Corrientes, Cabo c. Mex. 184 C4
Corrigan U.S.A. 179 D6
Corrigin Australia 151 B7
Corriverton Guyana 199 G3
Corrubedo, Cabo c. Spain 54 B2
Corry U.S.A. 176 F4
Corryong Australia 147 E4
Corsaglia r. Italy 51 N9
Corse admin. reg. France 56 B6
Corse i. France see Corsica
Corse, Cap c. Corse France 51 P3
Corsica i. France 51 O10
also known as Corse
europe [environments] ▶▶▶ 36–37
Corsicana U.S.A. 179 C5
Corsico, Baie de b. Gabon 126 A4
Cort Adelaer, Kap c. Greenland see Kangeq
Corte Corse France 51 P10
Cortegana Spain 54 E7
Cortes Spain 55 J3
Cortes, Sea of g. Mex. see California, Gulf of
Cortes de la Frontera, Reserva Nacional de nature res. Spain 54 E8
Cortez U.S.A. 181 I5
Cortez Mountains U.S.A. 183 H1
Cortina d'Ampezzo Italy 56 E2
Cortland NY U.S.A. 177 I3
Cortland OH U.S.A. 176 E4
Cortona Italy 56 D6
Çoruh Turkey see Artvin
Çoruh r. Turkey 107 E2
Çorum Turkey 106 C2
Corumbá Brazil 201 F4
Corumbá r. Brazil 206 E5
Corumbá de Goiás Brazil 206 D3
Corumbaíba Brazil 206 B10
Corumbataí r. Brazil 206 E5
Corumbaú, Ponta pt Brazil 207 N3
Corunna r. Canada 173 J3
Corunna Spain 54 B2
Corunna Spain see A Coruña
Corunna U.S.A. 173 I8
Coruripe Brazil 202 E4
Corvallis U.S.A. 180 B3
Corven U.K. 47 I11
Coruche Port. 54 C6
Cos i. Greece see Kos
Cosalá Mex. 184 D3
Cosamaloapan Mex. 185 G5
Coscaya Chile 200 C4
Cosentia Italy see Cosenza
Cosenza Italy 57 I9
historically known as Cosentia
Coşereni Romania 58 H3
Coshocton U.S.A. 176 D5
Cosmédica Atoll Seychelles 129 E7
Cosmo Newberry Aboriginal Reserve Australia 151 C6
Cosmópolis Brazil 206 F9
Cosne-Cours-sur-Loire France 51 I5
Cosquín Arg. 204 D3
Cossato Italy 56 A3
Cossé-le-Vivien France 50 F5
Costa Bol. 202 D3
Costa Blanca coastal area Spain 55 K6
Costa Brava coastal area Spain 55 O3
Costache Negri Romania 58 I3
Costa de la Luz coastal area Spain 54 D7
Costa, Alpi mts France/Italy see Cottian Alps
Costa del Azahar coastal area Spain 55 K5
Costa del Sol coastal area Spain 54 G8
Costa Dorada coastal area Spain 55 N3
Costa Marques Brazil 201 D5
Costa Rica Brazil 203 A6

Costa Rica country Central America 186 B5
northamerica [countries] ▶▶▶ 158–159
Costa Rica Mex. 184 D3
Costa Verde coastal area Spain 54 E1
Costermansville Dem. Rep. Congo see Bukavu
Costeşti Brazil 206 D6
Costeşti Romania 58 G4
Costigan Lake Canada 167 J3
Costilla U.S.A. 181 F5
Cotabambas Peru 200 B3
Cotabato Phil. 74 C5
Cotacachi, Cerro vol. Ecuador 198 B4
Cotacajes r. Bol. 200 D4
Cotagaita Bol. 200 D4
Cotahuasi Peru 200 C3
Cotaxé r. Brazil 203 D6
Cote, Mount U.S.A. 166 D3
Cote des Prairies slope U.S.A. 178 C3
Coteau des Prairies slope U.S.A. 178 B1
Coteau du Missouri slope ND U.S.A. 178 B1
Coteau du Missouri slope SD U.S.A. 178 B2
Coteaux Haiti 187 E3
Côte d'Azur coastal area France 51 N9

Côte d'Ivoire country Africa 124 C4
formerly known as Ivory Coast
africa [countries] ▶▶▶ 114–117

Côte Française de Somalis country Africa see Djibouti
Cotegipe Brazil 202 C5
Côtes de Meuse ridge France 51 K3
Cotiella mt. Spain 55 L2
Cotigao r. Brazil 200 D2
Cotiaeum Turkey see Kütahya
Cotiella mt. Spain 55 L2
Cotingo r. Brazil 199 F4
Cotmeana r. Romania 58 G4
Cotonou Benin 125 F5
Cotopaxi prov. Ecuador 198 B5
Cotovisc Moldova see Hîncești
Cotswold Hills U.K. 47 J12
Cottage Grove U.S.A. 180 B4
Cottbus Germany 49 L4
Cottenham U.K. 47 L11
Cottian Alps mts France/Italy 51 M8
Cottica Suriname 199 H3
Cottiennes, Alpes mts France/Italy see Cottian Alps
Cotton U.S.A. 172 A3
Cottonbush Creek watercourse Australia 148 C4
Cottonwood AZ U.S.A. 183 L7
Cottonwood CA U.S.A. 182 B1
Cottonwood r. KS U.S.A. 178 C4
Cottonwood r. MN U.S.A. 178 D2
Cottonwood Creek watercourse U.S.A. 181 G7
Cottonwood Falls U.S.A. 178 C4
Cottonwood Wash watercourse U.S.A. 183 N7
Cotui Dom. Rep. 187 F3
Cotulla U.S.A. 179 C6
Couchman Range hills Australia 150 D2
Coudersport U.S.A. 176 G4
Coudres, Île aux i. Canada 169 G4
Couëron France 50 E4
Couesnon r. France 50 E4
Couhé France 51 I10
Coulee Dam U.S.A. 180 C2
Coulman Island Antarctica 223 L2
Coulogne France 51 H7
Coulonge r. Canada 168 E4
Coulommiers France 51 J4
Coulonge r. Canada 168 E4
Coulterville U.S.A. 182 D4
Council U.S.A. 180 C3
Council Bluffs U.S.A. 178 D3
Council Grove U.S.A. 178 C4
Councillor Island Australia 147 E4
Coupeville U.S.A. 180 B2
Courageous Lake Canada 167 I1
Courantyne r. Guyana 199 G3
Courland Lagoon b. Lith./Rus. Fed. 42 C6
also known as Kurshskiy Zaliv or Kurskiy Zaliv or Kuršiu marios
Cournon-d'Auvergne France 51 J7
Coursan France 51 J9
Courtenay Canada 166 E5
Courthézon France 51 K8
Courtland U.S.A. 177 H9
Courtrai Belgium see Kortrijk
Coushatta U.S.A. 179 D5
Coutances France 50 E3
Coutinho Moz. see Ulongue
Couto de Magalhães de Minas Brazil 207 J5
Coutras France 50 F7
Coutts Canada 167 I5
Couvin Belgium 51 K2
Couzeix France 50 H7
Coval$eda Spain 55 I3
Covasna Romania 58 H3
Cove Fort U.S.A. 183 L3
Cove Island Canada 173 L5
Covelo U.S.A. 182 A2
Cove Mountains hills U.S.A. 176 G6
Covendo Bol. 200 D3
Coventry U.K. 47 K11
Covesville U.S.A. 176 G8
Covilhã Port. 54 D4
Covington GA U.S.A. 175 D5
Covington IN U.S.A. 174 C3
Covington KY U.S.A. 176 A6
Covington OH U.S.A. 176 A5
Covington TN U.S.A. 174 B5
Covington VA U.S.A. 176 E8
Cow r. Canada 173 J3
Cowal, Lake dry lake Australia 147 E3
Cowan, Lake salt flat Australia 151 C6
Cowcowing Lakes salt flat Australia 151 B6
Cowdenbeath U.K. 46 I7
Cowell Australia 146 C3
Cowen U.S.A. 176 E7
Cowes Australia 147 E4
Cowley Australia 149 E5
Cowlitz r. U.S.A. 180 B3
Cowpasture r. U.S.A. 176 F8
Cowra Australia 147 F3
Cox r. Australia 148 B2
Coxá r. Brazil 207 J4
Coxen Hole Hond. see Roatán
Coxilha de Santana hills Brazil/Uruguay 204 G3
Coxilha Grande hills Brazil 203 A9
Coxim Brazil 201 G3
Coxim r. Brazil 203 A6
Coxoacatlán Mex. 185 F4
Cox's Bazar Bangl. 97 F5
Coyah Guinea 124 B4
Coy Aike Arg. 205 C8
Coyame Mex. 181 F7
Coyanosa Creek watercourse U.S.A. 179 B6
Coyote r. Mex. 181 D7
Coyote, Punta pt Mex. 184 C3
Coyote Lake U.S.A. 183 H6
Coyote Peak hill U.S.A. 182 F5
Coyotitán Mex. 184 D4
Coyuca de Benítez Mex. 185 E5
Coyuca de Catalán Mex. 185 E5
Cozad U.S.A. 178 C3
Cozia, Vârful mt. Romania 58 F3
Cozie, Alpi mts France/Italy see Cottian Alps
Cozumel Mex. 185 I4
Cozumel, Isla de i. Mex. 185 I4
Cozzo del Pellegrino mt. Italy 57 I9
Crab Island Australia 149 D1
Crab Orchard U.S.A. 176 A8

Cracovia Poland see Kraków
Cracow Poland see Kraków
Cracow Australia 149 F5
Cradle Mountain Lake St Clair National Park Australia 147 E5
Cradock S. Africa 133 J9
Craftbole S. Africa 132 I3
Craig U.S.A. 166 C4
Craig CO U.S.A. 180 F4
Craigavon U.K. 47 F9
Craigieburn Australia 147 E4
Craigieburn N.Z. 153 F11
Craigieburn Forest Park nature res. N.Z. 153 F11
Craignure U.K. 46 G7
Craigsville VA U.S.A. 176 F7
Craigsville WV U.S.A. 176 E7
Crail U.K. 46 J7
Crailsheim Germany 48 H6
Craiova Romania 58 E4
Cramlington U.K. 47 K8
Cramond S. Africa 132 F4
Cranberry Junction Canada 166 D4
Cranberry Lake U.S.A. 177 K1
Cranberry Portage Canada 167 K4
Cranbourne Australia 147 E4
Cranbrook Canada 167 H5
Cranbrook Australia 151 C6
Crane OR U.S.A. 180 C4
Crane TX U.S.A. 179 B6
Crane Lake l. Canada 167 I5
Crane Lake U.S.A. 172 A2
Cranston KY U.S.A. 176 B7
Cranston RI U.S.A. 177 N4
Cranz Rus. Fed. see Zelenogradsk
Craolândia Brazil 202 C3
Craon France 50 F5
Crary Ice Rise Antarctica 223 M1
Crary Mountains Antarctica 222 P1
Crasna Romania 58 D1
Crasna r. Romania 58 C1
Crater Lake National Park U.S.A. 180 B4
Crater Peak U.S.A. 182 C1
Craters of the Moon National Monument nat. park U.S.A. 180 D4
Crateús Brazil 202 D3
Crato Brazil 202 E3
Crato Port. 54 D5
Cravari r. Brazil 201 F3
Cravinhos Brazil 206 F8
Cravo Norte Col. 198 D3
Crawford U.S.A. 178 B3
Crawford Point Phil. 74 A4
Crawford Range hills Australia 148 B4
Crawfordsville U.S.A. 174 C3
Crawfordville U.S.A. 175 C6
Crawley U.K. 47 L12
Crazy Mountains U.S.A. 180 E3
Crean Lake Canada 167 J4
Crécy-en-Ponthieu France 51 H2
Crediton U.K. 47 I13
Cree r. Canada 167 J3
Creede U.S.A. 181 F5
Creedmoor U.S.A. 176 G9
Creel Mex. 184 D3
Cree Lake Canada 167 J3
Creighton Canada 167 K4
Creighton S. Africa 133 N7
Creil France 51 I3
Crema Italy 56 B3
Cremona Canada 167 H5
Cremona Italy 56 C3
Crepori r. Brazil 199 G6
Crépy-en-Valois France 51 I3
Cres Croatia 56 G4
Cres i. Croatia 56 G4
Crescent City U.S.A. 180 A4
Crescent Head Australia te 72 C3
Crescent Head Australia 147 G2
Crescent Junction U.S.A. 183 O3
Crescent Lake National Wildlife Refuge nature res. U.S.A. 178 B3
Crescent Peak U.S.A. 183 I6
Crescent Valley U.S.A. 183 H1
Cresco U.S.A. 174 A3
Crespo Arg. 204 E4
Cresswell watercourse Australia 148 A3
Cresswell Downs Australia 148 B3
Crest France 51 L8
Crest Hill hill Hong Kong China 87 [inset]
also known as Tai Shek Mo
Crestline U.S.A. 176 C5
Creston Canada 167 G5
Creston IA U.S.A. 178 D3
Creston WY U.S.A. 180 F4
Crestview U.S.A. 175 C6
Creta i. Greece see Crete
Crêt de la Neige mt. France 51 L6
Crete i. Greece see Kriti; historically known as Creta
Crete U.S.A. 178 C3
Crêt Monniot mt. France 51 M5
Creus, Cap de c. Spain 55 O2
Creuse r. France 51 I5
Crevacore Italy 56 D3
Crevasse Valley Glacier Antarctica 222 O1
Crevillente Spain 55 K6
Crewe U.K. 47 J10
Crewe U.S.A. 176 G8
Crianlarich U.K. 46 H7
Criccieth U.K. 47 H11
Criciúma Brazil 203 B8
Cricova Moldova 58 J2
Cricovu Sărat r. Romania 58 H4
Cridersville U.S.A. 176 A5
Crieff U.K. 46 I7
Criffell hill U.K. 47 I9
Crikvenica Croatia 56 G3
Crillon, Mount U.S.A. 166 B3
Crimea pen. Ukr. 41 E7
also known as Kryms'kyy Pivostriv; short form Krym'
Crimmitschau Germany 49 J5
Cripple Creek U.S.A. 180 F5
Crişan Romania 58 K3
Crisfield U.S.A. 177 J8
Cristais, Serra dos mts Brazil 206 F4
Cristal, Monts de mts Equat. Guinea/Gabon 126 H5
Cristalândia Brazil 202 B4
Cristalina Brazil 206 D3
Cristalina r. Brazil 201 G2
Cristalino r. Brazil see Mariembero
Cristianópolis Brazil 206 D3
Cristino Brazil 207 I7
Cristino Castro Brazil 202 C4
Cristuru Secuiesc Romania 58 F5
Criterion, Mt. Peru 200 B3
Crişul Alb r. Romania 58 C2
Crişul Negru r. Romania 58 C2
Crişul Repede r. Romania 58 C1
Crişurilor, Câmpia plain Romania 58 C2
Criuleni Moldova 58 K1
formerly spelt Kriulyany
Crivitz Germany 48 I2
Crixás Brazil 206 C2
Crixás Açu r. Brazil 202 B2
Crixás Mirim r. Brazil 202 B3
Crna r. Macedonia 58 C7
Crna Gora aut. rep. Yugo. 58 A6
English form Montenegro
Crna Glava mt. Yugo. 58 A4
Crna Gora mts Macedonia/Yugo. 58 C6
Crni Drim r. Macedonia 58 B7
Crni Timok r. Srbija Yugo. 58 D5
Crna Trava Srbija Yugo. 58 D6
Crni vrh mt. Slovenia 56 F2
Crnomelj Slovenia 56 H3

Crnook mt. Yugo. 58 D6
Croajingolong National Park Australia 147 F4
▶Croatia country Europe 56 H3
  known as Hrvatska in Croatian
  europe [countries] 32–35
Crocco, Monte mt. Italy 57 I10
Crocker, Banjaran mts Malaysia 77 F1
Crocker Range National Park Sabah Malaysia 77 G1
Crockett U.S.A. 179 D6
Croghan U.S.A. 177 J2
Croisette, Cap c. France 51 L9
Croisic, Pointe de pt France 50 D5
Croisilles France 51 I2
Croker, Cape Australia 148 B1
Croker, Cape Canada 173 M6
Croker Island Australia 148 B1
Cromarty U.K. 46 H6
Cromer U.K. 47 N11
Cromwell N.Z. 153 C13
Cromwell U.S.A. 172 A4
Cronadun N.Z. 153 F10
Crooked r. U.S.A. 180 B3
Crooked Creek U.S.A. 166 A1
Crooked Harbour b. Hong Kong China 87 [inset]
  also known as Kat O Hoi
Crooked Island Bahamas 187 E2
Crooked Island Hong Kong China 87 [inset]
  also known as Kat O Chau
Crooked Island Passage Bahamas 187 E2
Crooked Lake Canada/U.S.A. 172 D2
Crooked River Canada 167 K4
Crookston U.S.A. 178 C2
Crooksville U.S.A. 176 C6
Crookwell Australia 147 F3
Crosbie r. Australia 151 B5
Crosby U.K. 47 I10
Crosby MN U.S.A. 174 A2
Crosby ND U.S.A. 178 B1
Crosbyton U.S.A. 179 B5
Cross r. Nigeria 125 H5
Cross Bay Canada 167 M2
Cross City U.S.A. 175 D6
Crosse, Île-à-la- Canada 167 J4
Crossett U.S.A. 175 A5
Cross Fell hill U.K. 47 J9
Crossfield Canada 167 H5
Cross Lake Canada 167 L4
Cross Lake l. Canada 167 L4
Cross Lake l. U.S.A. 173 Q7
Crossman Peak U.S.A. 183 J7
Cross River state Nigeria 125 H5
Cross Sound sea chan. U.S.A. 166 B3
Croswell U.S.A. 173 K7
Crotch Lake Canada 173 Q6
Croton Italy see Crotone
Crotone Italy 57 I9
  historically known as Croton
Crow r. Canada 166 E3
Crow Agency U.S.A. 180 F3
Crowal watercourse Australia 147 E2
Crow Creek r. U.S.A. 180 F4
Crow Creek Indian Reservation res. U.S.A. 178 C2
Crowdy Bay National Park Australia 147 G2
Crowell U.S.A. 179 C5
Crow Indian Reservation res. U.S.A. 180 F3
Crowl watercourse Australia 147 E3
Crowley U.S.A. 179 D6
Crowley, Lake U.S.A. 182 F4
Crown Point IN U.S.A. 181 E6
Crownpoint U.S.A. 181 G7
Crown Point NY U.S.A. 177 L2
Crown Prince Olav Coast Antarctica 223 C2
Crown Princess Martha Coast Antarctica 223 W1
Crows Nest Australia 147 G1
Crowsnest Pass Canada 167 H5
Crowsnest Pass pass Canada 167 H5
Crow Wing r. U.S.A. 178 D2
Croydon Australia 149 D3
Crozet U.K. 70 Ngu...
Crozet, Îles is Indian Ocean 219 K9
  English form Crozet Islands
Crozet Islands Indian Ocean see Crozet, Îles
Crozier Channel Canada 165 G2
Crozon France 50 B4
Crucea Romania 58 G1
Crucero Peru 200 C3
Cruces Cuba 186 C2
Cruces, Punta c. Col. 198 B3
Cruillas Mex. 185 F3
Crum U.S.A. 176 C8
Cruz r. Spain 55 I5
Cruz Venez. 199 E2
Cruz Alta Brazil 203 A9
Cruz, Cabo c. Cuba 186 D3
Cruz del Eje Arg. 204 D4
Cruzeiro Brazil 203 D7
Cruzeiro do Sul Brazil 200 B1
Cruzen Island Antarctica 222 Q2
Cruz Grande Mex. 185 F5
Crvenka Vojvodina, Srbija Yugo. 58 A3
Cry Lake Canada 166 E3
Crysdale, Mount Canada 166 F4
Crystal U.S.A. 183 P5
Crystal Brook Australia 146 C3
Crystal City Canada 167 L5

Crystal City MO U.S.A. 174 B4
Crystal City TX U.S.A. 179 C6
Crystal Falls U.S.A. 172 E4
Crystal Lake U.S.A. 172 E8
Crystal River U.S.A. 175 D6
Crystal Springs U.S.A. 175 B6
Csabrendek Hungary 49 O8
Csanádpalota Hungary 49 R9
Csépa Hungary 49 R8
Cserhát hills Hungary 49 Q7
Csesznek Tomaj Hungary 49 O9
Csongrád Hungary 49 R9
Csorna Hungary 49 N8
Csorvás Hungary 49 R9
Csóványos hill Hungary 49 P8
Csurgó Hungary 49 O9
Ctesiphon tourist site Iraq 107 F4
  also known as Tayspun
Cua r. Spain 54 E2
Cu'a Dinh An r. mouth Vietnam 79 D6
Cuadrada, Sierra hills Arg. 205 C7
Cuale Angola 127 B8
Cualedro Spain 54 D3
Cuamato Angola 127 B9
Cuamba Moz. 131 H2
  formerly known as Nova Freixa
Cuando r. Angola/Zambia 127 D9
Cuando Cubango prov. Angola 127 C8
Cuangar Angola 127 C9
Cuango Cuando Cubango Angola 127 C8
Cuango Lunda Norte Angola 127 C7
Cuango Uíge Angola 127 C6
Cuango r. Angola 127 C6
  also spelt Kwango
Cuanza r. Angola 127 B7
  also spelt Kwanza
Cuanza Norte prov. Angola 127 B7
Cuanza Sul prov. Angola 127 B7
Cuareim r. Uruguay 204 F3
Cuaró r. Uruguay 204 F3
Cuarto r. Arg. 204 E4
Cuatir r. Angola 127 C9
Cuatro Ciénegas Mex. 185 E3
Cuatro Ojos Bol. 201 E4
Cuauhtémoc Mex. 184 D2
Cuautla Mex. 185 F5
Cuba Port. 54 D6
Cuba NY U.S.A. 176 G3
Cuba OH U.S.A. 176 B6
▶Cuba country West Indies 186 C2
  5th largest island and 5th most populous country in North America.
  northamerica [landscapes] 156–157
  northamerica [landscapes] 158–159
Cubagua, Isla i. Venez. 199 E2
Cubal Angola 127 B8
Cubal r. Angola 127 B7
Cubango r. Angola/Namibia 127 D9
Cubara Col. 198 C2
Cubatão Brazil 206 G10
Cub Hills Canada 167 J4
Cubillas r. Spain 55 H7
Çubuk Turkey 106 C2
Cucao Chile 205 B6
Cuchi Angola 127 C8
Cuchilla Grande hills Uruguay 204 F4
Cuchilla Grande Inferior hills Uruguay 204 F4
Cuchillo-Có Arg. 204 D5
Cucu, Vârful mt. Romania 58 G2
Cucuí Brazil 199 E4
Cucumbi Angola 127 C7
Cucurrupí Col. 198 D3
Cúcuta Col. 198 D3
Cucutas hill Spain 55 K3
Cudalbi Romania 58 I3
Cuddalore India 94 C4
Cuddapah India 94 C3
Cuddapan, Lake salt flat Australia 149 D5
Cuddeback Lake U.S.A. 182 G6
Cudi watercourse Turkey 109 K1
Cudi Dağı hill Turkey 109 J1
Cudillero Spain 54 E1
Cue Australia 151 B5
Cue r. Angola 127 D8
Cuebe r. Angola 127 C8
Cuéllar Spain 54 G3
Cuemba Angola 127 C8
Cuenca Ecuador 198 B5
Cuenca Phil. 74 B3
Cuenca Spain 55 I4
Cuenca, Serranía de mts Spain 55 I4
Cuencamé Mex. 184 E3
Cuernavaca Mex. 185 F5
Cuero U.S.A. 179 C6
Cuers France 51 M9
Cuervos Mex. 183 J9
Cueto Cuba 186 E2
Cuevo Bol. 201 E5
Cugir Romania 58 E3
Cugir r. Romania 58 E3
Cuglieri Sardegna Italy 57 A8
Cugo r. Angola 127 C6
Cugnaux France 50 H9
Cuiabá Brazil 201 F4
Cuiabá r. Brazil 201 F4
Cuiaés r. Brazil 202 A3
Cuicatlan Mex. 185 F5
Cuihua China see Daguan
Cuijiang China see Ninghua
Cuilapa Guat. 185 H6
Cuilcagh hill Rep. of Ireland/U.K. 47 E9
Cuillin Hills U.K. 46 F6
Cuillin Sound sea chan. U.K. 46 F6
Cuilo Angola 127 C7
Cuilo-Futa Angola 127 B6
Cuíma Angola 127 B8
Cuiseaux France 51 L6
Cuité r. Brazil 207 L6
Cuito r. Angola 127 C9
Cuito Cuanavale Angola 127 C8
Cuitzeo, Laguna de l. Mex. 185 C5
Cuiuni r. Brazil 199 F5
Cujangan i. Phil. 74 B5
Cujmir Romania 58 D4
Cukai Malaysia 76 C1
  also spelt Chukai
Çuke Albania 59 B9
Çukurca Turkey 107 E3
  also known as Çal
Çukurova plat. Turkey 108 G1
Çula r. Moldova 58 J1
  formerly spelt Kula
Culai Shan mt. China 85 H4
Cu Lao Cham i. Vietnam 78 E5
Cu Lao Re i. Vietnam 78 E5
Cu Lao Thu i. Vietnam 79 E6
Culasi Phil. 74 B4
Culbertson U.S.A. 180 F2
Culcairn Australia 147 E3
Culebras Peru 200 A1
Culfa Azer. 107 F3
  also spelt Dzhul'fa
Culiacan Mex. 184 D3
Culion Phil. 74 A4
Culion i. Phil. 74 A4
Cúllar-Baza Spain 55 I7
Cullen U.S.A. 179 D5
Cullen Point Australia 149 D1
Cullera Spain 55 K5
Cullinan S. Africa 133 N4
Cullman U.S.A. 174 C5
Cul Mor hill U.K. 46 G5
Culpeper U.S.A. 176 H7
Culuene r. Brazil 202 A2
Culverden N.Z. 153 G10
Culvert Point Australia 151 D7
Cumã, Baía de inlet Brazil 202 C2

Cumaná Venez. 199 E2
Cumbal, Nevado de vol. Col. 198 B4
Cumberland KY U.S.A. 176 C9
Cumberland MD U.S.A. 176 G6
Cumberland OH U.S.A. 176 D6
Cumberland WI U.S.A. 172 A5
Cumberland r. U.S.A. 176 B9
Cumberland Bay S. Georgia 205 [inset]
  also spelt Kikládhes or Kyklades
Cumberland House Canada 167 K4
Cumberland Islands Australia 149 F4
Cumberland Mountain mts U.S.A. 176 B9
Cumberland Peninsula Canada 165 M3
Cumberland Plateau U.S.A. 174 C5
Cumberland Point U.S.A. 172 D3
Cumberland Sound sea chan. Canada 165 M3
Cumbernauld U.K. 46 I8
Cumbre Alta mt. Spain 54 G5
Cumbre Negro mt. Arg. 205 C7
Cumbres de Majalca, Parque Nacional nat. park Mex. 184 D2
Cumbum India 94 C3
Cuminá Brazil 199 G5
Cuminapanema r. Brazil 199 H5
Cummins Australia 146 B3
Cummins Range hills Australia 150 D3
Cumnock U.K. 46 H8
Cumpas Mex. 184 C2
Çumra Turkey 106 C3
Çumuruxatiba Brazil 207 N4
Çumani Brazil 199 I4
Cuñaré Col. 198 C4
Cundeelee Aboriginal Reserve Australia 151 C6
Cunderdin Australia 151 B6
Cundinamarca dept Col. 198 C3
Cunene prov. Angola 127 B9
Cunene r. Angola 127 A9
  also spelt Kunene
Cuneo Italy 51 N7
Cung Son Vietnam 79 E5
Çüngüş Turkey 107 D3
Cunha Brazil 207 I10
Cunhinga Angola 127 C8
  formerly known as Vouga
Cunnamulla Australia 147 E2
Cunshamayo Peru 200 B1
Cununa mt. Romania 58 C4
Ćuokkaraš'ša mt. Norway 44 N1
Cuorgné Italy 51 N7
Cupar U.K. 46 I7
Cupari r. Brazil 199 H5
Cupica Col. 198 B3
Cupra Marittima Italy 56 F5
Cúprija Srbija Yugo. 58 B5
Cupula, Pico mt. Mex. 184 C3
Curaça Brazil 199 F6
Curaçá Brazil 202 E4
Curaçá r. Brazil 198 D6
Curaçao i. Neth. Antilles 187 F4
Curacó r. Arg. 204 D5
Curaculo r. Angola 127 B8
Curahuara de Carangas Bol. 200 C4
Curanilahue Chile 204 B5
Curanja r. Peru 200 C2
Curaray r. Ecuador 198 C5
Curatabaca Venez. 199 F3
Curaya r. Arg. 204 C4
Curdlawidny Lagoon salt flat Australia 146 C2
Curé r. Col. 198 D5
Cure r. France 51 J5
Curiapo Venez. 199 F2
Curicó Chile 204 C4
Curitiari, Serra hill Brazil 199 E5
Curieuntari r. Brazil 199 E5
Curimata Brazil 202 C4
Curiplaya Col. 198 C4
Curitiba Brazil 203 B8
Curitibanos Brazil 203 B8
Curiúva Brazil 206 C10
Curnamona Australia 146 C2
Curoca r. Angola 127 A8
Curral de Dentro Brazil 207 L2
Curralinho Brazil 202 B2
Curral Velho Cape Verde 124 [inset]
Currawilla Australia 149 D5
Currawinya National Park Australia 147 E2
Current Bahamas 186 D1
Current r. U.S.A. 174 B4
Currie Australia 147 D4
Currie U.S.A. 183 J1
Currituck U.S.A. 177 I9
Currituck Sound inlet U.S.A. 177 J9
Curtea de Argeş Romania 58 F3
Curtici Romania 58 C2
Curtis Channel Australia 149 G5
Curtis Group is Australia 147 E4
Curtis Island Australia 149 F4
Curtis Island N.Z. 145 H5
Curuá Brazil 199 H5
Curuá r. Brazil 199 H6
Curuaés r. Brazil 202 A3
Curuai Brazil 199 H5
Curuapanema r. Brazil 199 H5
Curuá Una r. Brazil 199 H6
Curuçá Brazil 202 C2
Curumu Brazil 199 J5
Curupira Brazil 199 F5
Curupira, Serra mts Brazil/Venez. 199 E4
Cururú Bol. 201 E3
Cururu r. Brazil 201 F1
Cururupu Brazil 202 C2
Curutú, Cerro mt. Venez. 199 F3
Curuzú Cuatiá Arg. 204 F3
Curvelo Brazil 203 C6
Curwood, Mount hill U.S.A. 172 E4
Cusco Peru 200 C3
Cushendun U.K. 47 F8
Cushing U.S.A. 179 C4
Cusseta U.S.A. 175 C5
Custer MT U.S.A. 180 F3
Custer SD U.S.A. 178 B3
Cut Bank U.S.A. 180 D2
Cut Bank Creek r. U.S.A. 180 D2
Cuthbert U.S.A. 175 C6
Cuthbertson Falls Australia 148 B2
Cutler U.S.A. 182 E5
Cutler Ridge U.S.A. 175 D7
Cut Off U.S.A. 175 B6
Cutral-Co Arg. 204 C5
Cutro Italy 57 I9
Cuttaburra Creek r. Australia 147 E2
Cuttack India 95 E5
Cuvelai Angola 127 B8
Cuvette admin. reg. Congo 126 B5
Cuvette Ouest admin. reg. Congo 126 B4
Cuvier, Cape Australia 151 A5
Cuvier Island N.Z. 152 I4
Cuvillier, Lac l. Canada 173 Q2
Cuxhaven Germany 48 F2
Cuya Chile 200 C5
Cuyahoga Valley National Recreation Area park U.S.A. 176 D4
Cuyama U.S.A. 182 E7
Cuyama r. U.S.A. 182 D7
Cuyapo Phil. 74 B3
Cuyo Phil. 74 B4
Cuyo East Passage Phil. 74 B4
Cuyo Islands Phil. 74 B4
Cuyo West Passage Phil. 74 B4
Cuyuni r. Guyana 199 G3

Cumaná Venez. 199 E2
Cuzco Peru see Cusco
Cuzco Peru 200 A1
Cuzna r. Spain 54 G6
Cwmbran U.K. 47 I12
Cyangugu Rwanda 126 F5
Cybinka Poland 49 L3
Cyclades is Greece 59 F11
  also spelt Kikládhes or Kyklades
Cydonia Greece see Chania
Cygnet U.K. 178 B4
Cymru admin. div. U.K. see Wales
Cynthiana U.S.A. 176 A7
Cypress Hills Canada 167 I5
Cypress Hills Provincial Park Canada 167 I5
▶Cyprus country Asia 108 D3
  spelt Kypros in Greek or Kibris in Turkish; historically known as Alashiya
  asia [countries] 64–67
Cyrenaica reg. Libya 120 D1
Cyrene tourist site Libya 120 D1
  also spelt Cirene
Cythera i. Greece see Kythira
Czaplinek Poland 49 N2
Czar Canada 167 I4
Czarna r. Poland 49 Q6
Czarna r. Poland 49 S5
Czarna Białostocka Poland 49 U2
Czarna Nida r. Poland 49 R5
Czarna Struga r. Poland 49 O3
Czarne Poland 49 N2
Czarnków Poland 49 N3

▶Czechoslovakia
  Divided in 1993 into the Czech Republic and Slovakia.
Czechowice-Dziedzice Poland 49 Q6
▶Czech Republic country Europe 49 K6
  also known as Česká Republika
  europe [countries] 32–35
Czempiń Poland 49 N3
Czermejewo Poland 49 O3
Czernowitz Ukr. see Chernivtsi
Czersk Poland 49 O2
Czerwieńsk Poland 49 M3
Częstochowa Poland 49 Q5
  formerly known as Chenstokhov
Człopa Poland 49 N2
Człuchów Poland 49 O2

▼ D

Ða, Sông r. Vietnam see Black River
Da'an China 85 J2
  formerly known as Dalai
Daanbantayan Phil. 74 B4
Ðabãb, Jabal ad mt. Jordan 108 G6
Dabaga Tanz. 129 B7
Dabajuro Venez. 198 D2
Dabakala Côte d'Ivoire 124 D4
Daban China 85 H3
  also known as Bairin Youqi
Daban Shan mts China 84 D4
Dabao China 86 B2
Dabas Hungary 49 Q8
Daba Shan mts China 87 D1
Dabat Eth. 104 B5
Dabba China see Daocheng
Dabeiba Col. 198 B3
Dabein Myanmar 78 B4
Dabhoi India 96 B5
Dabhol India 94 B2
Ðab'i, Wãdi ad watercourse Jordan 109 H6
Ðąbie, Jezioro l. Poland 49 L2
Dabie Shan mts China 87 E2
Dąbki Poland 49 N1
Dabl, Wãdi watercourse Saudi Arabia 109 H8
Daboh India 96 C4
Dabola Guinea 124 C4
Dabou Côte d'Ivoire 124 D5
Daboya Ghana 125 E4
Dabqig China 85 F4
Dabra India 96 C4
Dabrasławka Belarus 42 H9
Dąbrowa Białostocka Poland 49 U2
Dąbrowa Górnicza Poland 49 Q5
  formerly known as Dombrowa; historically known as Dombrau
Dąbrowa Tarnowska Poland 49 R5
Dabsan Hu salt l. China 84 B4
Dabu China 87 F3
  also known as Huliao
Dăbuleni Romania 58 F5
Dacca Bangl. see Dhaka
Dachau Germany 48 I7
Dachengfeng mt. China 84 D4
Dachengzi China 85 H4
  also known as Harqin Zuoqi Mongolzu Zizhixian
Dachepalle India 94 C2
Dacre Canada 173 Q5
Dadaj, Jezioro l. Poland 49 R2
Dadanawa Guyana 199 G4
Dadatoto Djibouti 128 D1
Dade City U.S.A. 175 D6
Dadeville U.S.A. 175 C5
Dadhar Pak. 101 F4
Ðadkãn Iran 101 E5
Dadong China see Donggang
Dadou r. France 51 H9
Dadra India see Achalpur
Dadra and Nagar Haveli union terr. India 94 B1
Dadu Pak. 101 F5
Dadu He r. China 86 B2
Ða Dung r. Vietnam 79 D6
Daedalus Reef Saudi Arabia 104 B2
Daet Phil. 74 B3
Dafang China 86 C3
Dafdaf, Jabal mt. Saudi Arabia 108 G9
Dafeng China 87 G1
  formerly known as Dazhongji
Dafir U.A.E. 105 F3
Dafla Hills India 97 G4
Dafni Greece 59 F8
Dafnoudi, Akra pt Greece 59 B10
Dafoe r. Canada 167 M4
Dafra Chad 126 C2
Dafter U.S.A. 173 I4
Dag India 96 B5
Daga Medo Eth. 128 D3
Dagana Senegal 124 A2
Daga Post Sudan 128 B2
Dagash Sudan 121 G5
Dagcanglhamo China 86 B1
  also known as Langmusi
Dagda Latvia 42 I5
Dage China see Fengning
Dagezhen China see Fengning
Daghestan aut. rep. Rus. Fed. see Dagestan, Respublika
Daghmar Oman 105 G3
Dağlıq Qarabağ aut. reg. Azer. 107 F3
  English form Nagorno-Karabakh; also known as Nagornyy Karabakh or Artsakh
Daglung China 89 E6
Dagmersellen Switz. 51 N5

Dagö i. Estonia see Hiiumaa
Dagon Myanmar see Rangoon
Dagon mt. N.Z. 153 C12
Dagrag Zangbo r. China 89 D6
Dagu China 85 H4
Dagu r. China 85 I4
Daguan China 86 B3
  also known as Cuihua
Dagupan Phil. 74 B3
Daguragu Aboriginal Land res. Australia 148 A3
Dagwin Myanmar 78 B4
Dagxoi China see Yidun
Dagxoi China see Sowa
Dagzê China 89 E6
  also known as Dêqên
Dagzê Co salt l. China 89 D6
Dagzhuka China 89 E6
Dahab Egypt 121 G2
Dahab, Marsa b. Egypt 108 F9
Dahabān Saudi Arabia 104 B3
Dahadinni r. Canada 166 E2
Dahalach, Isole is Eritrea see Dahlak Archipelago
Dahana des. Saudi Arabia see Ad Dahnā'
Dahanu India 94 B2
Dahe China see Ziyuan
Dahei Shan mt. China 84 B3
Dahei Shan mts China 82 B4
Daheng China 87 F3
Daheyan China see Turpan Zhan
Dahezhen China 82 D3
Dahin, Ḥarrāt ad lava field Saudi Arabia 104 C4
Da Hinggan Ling mts China 85 H3
  English form Greater Khingan Mountains
Dahivadi India 94 B2
Dahlak Archipelago is Eritrea 121 I6
  formerly known as Dahalach, Isole
Dahlak Marine National Park Eritrea 121 I5
Dahl al Furayy well Saudi Arabia 105 D2
Dahlem Germany 48 D5
Dahlia Zimbabwe 131 E3
Dahl Iftākh well Saudi Arabia 105 D2
Dahlonega U.S.A. 174 D5
Dahme Germany 49 K4
Dahod India 96 B5
  also spelt Dohad
Dahomey country Africa see Benin
Dahongliutan Aksai Chin 89 C3
Dahra Senegal see Dara
Dahshūr Egypt 108 C7
Dahūk Iraq 107 E3
Dahūk governorate Iraq 107 E3
Ðahyah, Wãdi r. Yemen 105 E4
Dai i. Indon. 75 D4
Daicheng China 85 H4
  also known as Pingshu
Daido r. N. Korea see Taedong-gang
Dai Hai l. China 85 G3
Daik Indon. 76 D3
Daikanvik Sweden 44 L2
Daik-u Myanmar 78 B4
Dailekh Nepal 97 D3
Dailey U.S.A. 176 F7
Daim Iran 91 C6
Daimanji-san hill Japan 83 D5
Daimiel Spain 55 H5
Daingerfield U.S.A. 179 D5
Dainichiga-take vol. Japan 91 E6
Dainkog China 86 A1
Daintree Australia 149 E3
Daintree National Park Australia 149 E3
Daiō-zaki pt Japan 91 E7
Daiquiri Cuba 186 E3
Daireaux Arg. 204 E5
Dairen China see Dalian
Dairût Egypt 121 F3
Dairyland U.S.A. 172 A4
Dai-sen vol. Japan 91 C6
Daisen-Oki National Park Japan 91 C7
Daisetsu-zan National Park Japan 90 H3
Daishan China 87 G2
  also known as Gaotingzhen
Daiyue China see Shanyin
Daiyun Shan mts China 87 F3
Dajarra Australia 148 C4
Dajie China see Jiangchuan
Dajin Chuan r. China 86 B2
Dajing China 86 B2
Da Juh China 84 B4
Dakahlia prov. Egypt 108 B4
Dakar Senegal 124 A3
  Capital of Senegal.
Dakar el Arak well Sudan 121 F5
Dakhal, Wãdi r. watercourse Egypt 108 D9
Dakhin Shahbazpur Island Bangl. 97 F5
Dakhla W. Sahara see Ad Dakhla
Dakhla Oasis Egypt 121 F3
Dakhlet Nouâdhibou admin. reg. Mauritania 122 A5
Dakingari Nigeria 125 G4
Dak Kon Vietnam 79 D5
Dak Nghe r. Vietnam 79 D5
Dakoank India 95 G5
Dakol'ka r. Belarus 43 J9
Dakor India 96 B5
Dakoro Niger 125 G3
Dakota City IA U.S.A. 178 D3
Dakota City NE U.S.A. 178 D3
Ðakovica Kosovo, Srbija Yugo. 58 A3
  also spelt Djakovica
Ðakovo Croatia 56 K3
Dala Angola 127 D8
Dalaba Guinea 124 B4
Dalai China see Da'an
Dala-Jokna watercourse Eth. 128 D3
Dalai Lake l. China see Shulinzhao
Dalai China see Da'an
Dalain Hob China 84 D3
  also known as Ejin Qi
Dalai Nur l. China 85 H3
Dàlà Khãnī, Kūh-e mt. Iran 100 A3
Ðãlaki Iran 100 B4
Dalalven r. Sweden 45 L3
Dalaman Turkey 106 B3
Dalaman r. Turkey 106 B3
Dalandzadgad Mongolia 84 D3
Dalaoba China 85 G3
Dalap-Uliga-Darrit Marshall Is see Delap-Uliga-Djarrit
Dalarna county Sweden 45 K3
  formerly known as Kopparberg
Dalarna reg. Sweden 45 K3
Dalat Sarawak Malaysia 77 E2
Ða Lat Vietnam 79 E6
Dalatando Angola see N'dalatando
Dalay Mongolia 84 D3
Dalbandin Pak. 101 F4
Dalbeg Australia 149 E4
Dalbosjön l. Sweden 45 K4
Dalby Australia 147 F1
Dalby Sweden 45 K5
Dalcahue Chile 205 B6
Dale Hordaland Norway 45 I3
Dale Sogn og Fjordane Norway 45 I3
Dale City U.S.A. 177 H7
Dale Hollow Lake U.S.A. 174 C4
Daletme Myanmar 78 A3
Dalfors Sweden 45 K3
Dalgan Australia 148 B3
Dalgaranger, Mount hill Australia 151 B5
Dalgety r. Australia 151 A5
Dalhart U.S.A. 179 B4
Dalhousie Canada 169 H3

Dalhousie, Cape Canada 164 G2
Dali Shaanxi China 87 D1
Dali Yunnan China 86 B3
  also known as Xiaguan
Dali r. China 85 F4
Dalian China 85 I4
  formerly known as Dairen or Dalny or Lüda
Daliang China see Shunde
Daliang China 86 B3
Daliang Shan mts China 86 B2
Dalian Wan b. China 85 I4
Dalin China 85 I3
Daling r. China 85 I3
Dalinghe China see Linhai
Dalizi China 82 B4
Dalj Croatia 56 K3
Dalkola India 97 E4
Dallas OR U.S.A. 180 B3
Dallas TX U.S.A. 179 C5
Dallas City U.S.A. 172 B10
Dalles City U.S.A. see The Dalles
Dall Island U.S.A. 164 F4
Dallol Bosso watercourse Mali/Niger 125 F3
Dalmā i. U.A.E. 105 F2
Dalmacija reg. Croatia see Dalmatia
Dalmally U.K. 46 H7
Dalman India 96 D4
Dalmas, Lac l. Canada 169 G2
▶Dalmatia reg. Croatia 56 H4
  also spelt Dalmacija
  europe [landscapes] 30–31
Dalmellington U.K. 46 H8
Dalmeny Canada 167 J4
Dal'negorsk Rus. Fed. 82 D3
  formerly known as Tetyukhe
Dal'nerechensk Rus. Fed. 82 D3
  formerly known as Iman
Dal'niye Zelentsy Rus. Fed. 40 F1
Dalny China see Dalian
Daloa Côte d'Ivoire 124 D5
▶Daloi Eth. 128 D1
  Highest recorded annual mean temperature in the world.
  world [climate and weather] 16–17
Dalou Shan mts China 86 C3
Dalqān well Saudi Arabia 105 D2
Dalrymple, Lake Australia 149 E4
Dalrymple, Mount Australia 149 E4
Dalsbruk Fin. 42 D1
Daltenganj India 97 E4
  formerly spelt Daltonganj
Dalton Canada 168 C3
Dalton S. Africa 133 O6
Dalton GA U.S.A. 174 C5
Dalton MA U.S.A. 177 L3
Dalton OH U.S.A. 176 D5
Dalton PA U.S.A. 177 J4
Dalton Iceberg Tongue Antarctica 223 H2
Dalton Mills Canada 173 I2
Daludalu Indon. 76 C2
Daluo China see Daxin
Dalupiri i. Phil. 74 B2
Dalvík Iceland 44 [inset] C2
Dalwallinu Australia 151 B6
Dalwhinnie U.K. 46 H7
Daly r. Australia 148 A2
Daly City U.S.A. 182 B4
Daly River/Port Keats Aboriginal Land res. Australia 148 A2
Daly Waters Australia 148 B3
Damagaram Takaya Niger 125 H3
Damalisques de Leshwe nature res. Dem. Rep. Congo 127 E8
Daman India 94 B1
  formerly spelt Damão
Daman and Diu union terr. India 94 A1
Damanava Belarus 42 G9
Damāne well Mauritania 124 B2
Dāmaneh Iran 100 B3
Damanhūr Egypt 121 F2
Damão India see Daman
Damaqun Shan mts China 85 G3
Damar Indon. 75 C2
Damar i. Moluccas Indon. 75 D3
Damar i. Moluccas Indon. 75 D3
Damara Cent. Afr. Rep. 126 C3
Damaraland reg. Namibia 130 C4
Damariscotta Lake U.S.A. 174 G2
Damar Laut, Pulau i. Sing. 76 [inset]
Damas Syria see Damascus
Damasak Nigeria 125 I3
Damascus Syria 109 H4
  Capital of Syria. Also known as Ash Sham or Damas; also spelt Dimashq.
Damascus MD U.S.A. 177 H6
Damascus VA U.S.A. 176 D9
Damaturu Nigeria 125 H4
Damāvand Iran 100 C3
Damāvand, Mount Iran 100 C3
  English form Demavend
Damba Angola 127 B6
Dambai Ghana 125 F4
Dambatta Nigeria 125 H3
Dambo Nigeria 125 I4
Dâmbovița r. Romania 58 G4
Damchara India 97 G4
Damdy Kazakh. 103 F2
  formerly known as Zhalanash
Dame Marie Haiti 187 E3
Damghan Iran 100 C2
Damietta Egypt see Dumyât
Daming China 85 G4
Daming Shan mt. China 87 C3
Damjong China 87 G2
Damlasu Turkey 109 K1
Dammai i. Phil. 74 B5
Dammam Saudi Arabia 105 E2
  also spelt Ad Dammām
Dammastock mt. Switz. 51 O6
Damme Germany 48 F3
Damoh India 96 C5
Damongo Ghana 125 E4
Damour Lebanon 108 G4
Dampelas, Tanjung pt Indon. 75 A2
Dampier Australia 150 B5
Dampier Archipelago is Australia 150 B4
Dampier Island P.N.G. see Karkar Island
Dampier Land reg. Australia 150 C3
Dampierre-sur-Salon France 51 L5
Dampier Strait P.N.G. see D25
Dampir, Selat sea chan. Indon. 73 H7
Dampit Indon. 77 F5
Damqoq Zangbo r. China see Maquan He
Dam Qu r. China 92 C2
Dâmrei, Chuôr Phnum mts Cambodia 79 D6
Damroh India 97 G3
Damxoi China see Comai
Damxung China 89 E6
  also known as Gongtang
Dan r. U.S.A. 176 F9
Dana i. Indon. 75 B5
Dana Nepal 97 E3
Danakil Eritrea/Eth. see Denakil
Danané Côte d'Ivoire 124 C5
Ða Nāng Vietnam 78 E4
  formerly known as Tourane
Ða Nang, Vinh b. Vietnam 78 E4
Danao Phil. 74 B4
Danao China 86 B2
  also known as Rongzhag or Zhangu
Danata Turkm. 102 C5
Danba China 86 B2
Dandeli India 94 B3

Danbury CT U.S.A. 177 L4
Danbury NC U.S.A. 176 E9
Danbury NH U.S.A. 177 N2
Danbury WI U.S.A. 172 A4
Danby U.S.A. 177 M2
Danby Lake U.S.A. 183 I7
Dancheng China 87 E1
Dancheng China see Xiangshan
Dande r. Angola 127 B7
Dande Eth. 128 C3
Dandel'dhura Nepal 96 D3
Dandeli India 94 B3
Dando Angola 127 C7
Dandong China 83 B4
formerly known as Andong
Dandridge U.S.A. 174 D4
Danė r. Lith. 42 C6
Daneborg Greenland 165 Q2
Daneți Romania 58 F5
Dānew Turkm. see Dyanev
Danfeng China 87 D1
also known as Longjuzhai
Danfeng China see Shizong
Dangan Liedao i. China 87 E4
Dangara Tajik. see Danghara
Dangbizhen Rus. Fed. 82 C3
Dangchang China 86 C1
Dangchengwan China see Subei
Dange Angola 127 B6
formerly known as Quitexe
Danger Islands atoll Cook Is see Pukapuka
Danger Point S. Africa 132 D11
Dangé-St-Romain France 50 G6
Danggali Conservation Park nature res. Australia 146 D3
Danghara Tajik. 101 G2
also spelt Dangara
Danghe Nanshan mts China 84 B4
Dangila Eth. 128 C2
Dangjin Shankou pass China 84 B4
Dangla Shan mts China see Tanggula Shan
Dan Gorayo Somalia 128 F2
Dangori India 97 G4
Dangqên China 89 E6
Dangriga Belize 185 H5
formerly known as Stann Creek
Dangshan China 87 F1
Dangtu China 87 F2
Dan-Gulbi Nigeria 125 G4
Dangur Eth. 128 B2
Dangur Mountains Eth. 128 B2
Dangyang China 87 D2
Daniel's Harbour Canada 169 J3
Danielskuil S. Africa 132 H5
Danielson U.S.A. 177 N4
Danielsrus S. Africa 133 M4
Danielsville U.S.A. 175 D5
Danilkovo Rus. Fed. 43 S2
Danilov Rus. Fed. 43 V3
Danilovgrad Crna Gora Yugo. 58 A6
Danilovka Kazakh. 103 G1
Danilovka Rus. Fed. 41 H6
Danilovskaya Vozvyshennost' hills Rus. Fed. 40 F4
Daning China 85 F4
Dānizkānarı Azer. 107 G2
Danjiang China see Leishan
Danjiangkou China 87 D1
formerly known as Junxian
Danjiangkou Shuiku resr China 87 D1
Danjo-guntō is Japan 91 A8
Dank Oman 105 G3
Dankalia prov. Eritrea 104 C5
Dankov Rus. Fed. 43 U8
Dankova, Pik mt. Kyrg. 103 I4
Danleng China 86 B2
Danlí Hond. 186 B4
Danmark Fjord inlet Greenland 165 Q1
English form Denmark Fjord
Dannebrog Ø i. Greenland see Qillak
Dannemora U.S.A. 177 L1
Dannenberg (Elbe) Germany 48 I2
Dannet well Niger 125 G2
Dannevirke N.Z. 152 K8
Dannhauser S. Africa 133 O5
Dan Sai Thai. 78 C4
Danshui Taiwan see Tanshui
Dansville U.S.A. 176 H3
Danta Gujarat India 96 B4
Danta Rajasthan India 89 A7
Dantewara India 94 D2
Dantu China 87 F1
also known as Zhenjiang

▶Danube r. Europe 58 J3
2nd longest river in Europe. Also spelt Donau (Austria/Germany) or Duna (Hungary) or Dunaj (Slovakia) or Dunărea (Romania) or Dunav (Bulgaria/Croatia/Yugoslavia) or Dunay (Ukraine).
europe [landscapes] ➡ 30–31

Danube Delta Romania 58 K3
also known as Dunării, Delta
Danubyu Myanmar 78 A4
Danumparai Indon. 77 F2
Danum Valley Conservation Area nature res. Sabah Malaysia 77 G1
Danville AR U.S.A. 179 D5
Danville IL U.S.A. 174 C3
Danville IN U.S.A. 174 C4
Danville KY U.S.A. 176 A8
Danville OH U.S.A. 176 C5
Danville PA U.S.A. 177 I5
Danville VA U.S.A. 176 F9
Danville VT U.S.A. 177 M1
Danxian China see Danzhou
Danyang China 87 F2
Danzhai China 87 C3
also known as Longquan
Danzhou Guangxi China 87 D3
Danzhou Hainan China 87 D5
also known as Nada; formerly known as Danxian
Danzhou China see Yichuan
Danzig Poland see Gdańsk
Danzig, Gulf of Poland/Rus. Fed. see Gdańsk, Gulf of
Dao Phil. 74 B4
Dão r. Port. 54 C4
Daocheng China 86 B2
also known as Dabba or Jinzhu
Daojiang China see Daoxian
Daokou China see Huaxian
Daoshiping China 87 D2
Daotanghe China 84 D4
Dao Tay Sa is S. China Sea see Paracel Islands
Dao Timmi Niger 125 I1
Daoud Alg. see Aïn Beïda
Daoudi well Mauritania 124 D3
Daoukro Côte d'Ivoire 124 E5
Daoxian China 87 D3
also known as Daojiang
Daozhen China 87 C2
also known as Yuxi
Dapa Phil. 74 C4
Dapaong Togo 125 F4
Dapchi Nigeria 125 H3
Daphabum mt. India 97 H4
Daphnae tourist site Egypt 108 D7
also known as Kawm Dafanah
Daphne U.S.A. 175 C6
Dapiak, Mount Phil. 74 B4
Dapingdi China see Yanbian
Dapitan Phil. 74 B4
Daqahlīya governorate Egypt 108 C6
Da Qaidam Zhen China 84 B4
Daqiao China 86 B3
Daqing China 82 B3
also known as Anda; formerly known as Sartu
Daqing Shan mts China 85 F3
Daqin Tal China 85 I3
also known as Naiman Qi
Daqiu China 87 F3
Daqq-e Patargān salt flat Iran 101 E3
Daqq-e-Tundi, Dasht-e imp. l. Afgh. 101 E3
Daquan China 84 B3
Daquanwan China 84 B3
Dāqūq Iraq 107 F4
Daqu Shan i. China 87 G2
Dara Senegal 124 B3
formerly spelt Dahra
Dar'ā Syria 108 H5
Dar'ā governorate Syria 108 H5
Dâra, Gebel mt. Egypt 106 C6
Daraá r. Brazil 199 E5
Dārāb Iran 100 C4
Daraga Phil. 74 B3
Darahanava Belarus 43 J8
Daraim Afgh. 96 A1
Daraina Madag. 131 [inset] K2
Daraj Libya 120 A2
Daram i. Phil. 74 C4
Dārān Iran 100 B3
Đa Răng, Sông r. Vietnam 79 E5
Darasun Rus. Fed. 85 G1
Daraut-Kurgan Kyrg. see Daroot-Korgan
Đaravica mt. Yugo. 58 B6
Darazo Nigeria 125 H4
Darb Saudi Arabia 104 C4
Darband Iran 100 D4
Darband Uzbek. see Derbent
Darband, Kūh-e mt. Iran 100 D4
Darb-e Behesht Iran 100 D4
Darbėnai Lith. 42 C5
Dar Ben Karricha el Behri Morocco 54 F9
Darbhanga India 97 E4
Darcang China 86 A1
Dar Chabanne Tunisia 57 C12
Dar Chaoui Morocco 54 F9
D'Arcy Canada 166 F5
Darda Croatia 56 K3
Dardanelle AR U.S.A. 179 D5
Dardanelle CA U.S.A. 182 E3
Dardanelle, Lake U.S.A. 179 D5
Dardanelles strait Turkey 106 A2
also known as Çanakkale Boğazı; historically known as Hellespont
Dardo China see Kangding
Dar el Beida Morocco see Casablanca
Darende Turkey 107 D3

▶Dar es Salaam Tanz. 129 C6
Former capital of Tanzania.

Dārestān Iran 100 C4
Darfield N.Z. 153 G11
Darfo Boario Terme Italy 56 C3
Dargai Pak. 101 G3
Darganata Turkm. 103 E4
Dargaville N.Z. 152 H3
Dargin, Jezioro l. Poland 49 S1
Dargo Australia 147 E4
Darhan Mongolia 85 E1
Darhan Muminggan Lianheqi China see Bailingmiao
Darıca Turkey 58 K8
Darıcı Turkey 59 J9
Darien CT U.S.A. 177 L4
Darien GA U.S.A. 175 D6
Darién, Golfo del g. Col. 198 B2
Darién, Parque Nacional de nat. park Panama 186 D6
Darién, Serranía del mts Panama 186 D5
Dar'inskiy Kazakh. 103 H2
also known as Dariya
Dar'inskoye Kazakh. 102 B2
Dario Nicaragua 186 B4
Dariya Kazakh. see Dar'inskiy
Dariz Oman 105 G3
Darjeeling India 97 F4
also spelt Darjiling
Darjiling India see Darjeeling
Dārkhovin Iran 100 B4
Darlag China 86 A1
also known as Gyümai

▶Darling r. Australia 147 D3
2nd longest river in Oceania. Part of the longest (Murray-Darling).
oceania [landscapes] ➡ 136–137

Darling S. Africa 132 C10
Darling Downs hills Australia 147 F1
Darling Range hills Australia 151 A7
Darlington U.K. 47 K9
Darlington SC U.S.A. 175 E5
Darlington WI U.S.A. 172 C8
Darlington Dam resr S. Africa 133 J10
Darlington Point Australia 147 E3
Darlot, Lake salt flat Australia 151 C5
Darłowo Poland 49 N1
Dărmănești Romania 58 H2
Darma Pass China/India 89 C6
Darmaraopet India 94 C2
Darmstadt Germany 48 F6
Darna r. India 94 B1
Darnah Libya 120 D1
also spelt Derna
Darnall S. Africa 133 P6
Darnick Australia 147 D3
Darnley, Cape Antarctica 223 E2
Darnley Bay Canada 164 G3
Daroca Spain 55 J3
Daroot-Korgan Kyrg. 103 H5
also spelt Daraut-Kurgan
Darovskoy Rus. Fed. 40 H4
Dar Pahn Iran 100 D5
Darr watercourse Australia 149 D4
Darregueira Arg. 204 E5
Darreh Bīd Iran 100 D3
Darreh Gaz Iran 101 D2
also known as Moḩammadābād
Darreh Gozaru r. Iran see Gīzeh Rūd
Darreh-ye Bāhābād Iran 100 C4
Darreh-ye Shahr Iran 100 A3
Darreh-ye Shekārī r. Afgh. 101 G3
Darreh-ye Shekārī r. Afgh. 101 G3
Darro watercourse Eth. 128 D3
Darsa i. Yemen 105 F5
Darsi India 94 C3
Darß pen. Germany 49 J1
Darßer Ort c. Germany 49 J1
Darta Turkm. 102 C4
formerly known as Kianly; formerly spelt Tarta
Dār Ta'izzah Syria 109 H1
Dartang China see Baqên
Dartford U.K. 47 M12
Dartmoor Australia 146 D4
Dartmoor hills U.K. 47 H13
Dartmoor National Park U.K. 47 I13
Dartmouth Canada 169 I4
Dartmouth U.K. 47 I13
Dartmouth, Lake salt flat Australia 149 E5
Dartmouth Reservoir Australia 147 E4
Daru P.N.G. 73 J8
Daru waterhole Sudan 121 G5
Daruba Indon. 75 D2
Daruvar Croatia 56 J3
Darvaza Turkm. 102 D4
also spelt Derweze
Darvi Mongolia 84 B2
Darvi Mongolia see Bulgan
Darvinskiy Gosudarstvennyy Zapovednik nature res. Rus. Fed. 43 S3
Darvoz, Qatorkŭhi mts Tajik. 101 G2
Darwendale Zimbabwe 131 F3
Darwha India 94 C1

▶Darwin Australia 148 A2
Capital of Northern Territory. Historically known as Palmerston.

Darwin Falkland Is 205 F8
Darwin, Canal sea chan. Chile 205 B7
Darwin, Monte mt. Chile 205 C9
Darya Khan Pak. 101 G4
Dar'yalyktakyr, Ravnina plain Kazakh. 103 F3
Daryānah Libya 120 D1
Dar"yoi Amu r. Asia see Amudar'ya
Dar"yoi Sir r. Asia see Syrdar'ya
Dārzīn Iran 100 D4
Dās i. U.A.E. 105 F2
Dasada India 96 A5
Dasha r. China 85 G4
Dashbalbar Mongolia 85 G1
Dashhowuz Turkm. see Dashkhovuz
Dashiqiao China 85 I3
formerly known as Yingkou
Dashitou China 88 E3
Dashizhai China 85 I2
Dashkawka Belarus 43 L8
Dashkesan Azer. see Daşkäsän
Dashkhovuz Turkm. 102 D4
also known as Dashoguz; also spelt Dashhowuz; formerly known as Tashauz
Dashkhovuz Oblast admin. div. Turkm. see Dashkhovuzskaya Oblast'
Dashkhovuzskaya Oblast' admin. div. Turkm. 102 D4
English form Dashkhovuz Oblast; formerly known as Tashauzskaya Oblast'
Dashköpri Turkm. see Tashkepri
Dashoguz Turkm. see Dashkhovuz
Dasht Iran 100 D2
Dasht r. Pak. 101 E5
Dashtak Qal'ehsi Iran 100 D2
formerly spelt Dashtak Qal'ehsi
Dashtak Qal'ehsi Iran see Dashtak Qaléhsi
Dasht-e Bar Iran 100 D4
Dasht-e Palang r. Iran 100 C4
Dashtiari Iran 101 E5
Dashuikeng China 85 E4
Dashuiqiao China 84 C4
Dashuitou China 84 E4
Daska Pak. 101 H3
Daşkäsän Azer. 107 F2
also spelt Dashkesan
Daskop S. Africa 132 G10
Dasongshu China 86 C3
Daspar mt. Pak. 101 H2
Dassa Benin 125 F5
Dassalan i. Phil. 74 B5
Dassen Island S. Africa 132 C10
Dastakān, Ra's-e pt Iran 100 C5
Da Suifen He r. China 82 C4
Dasuya India 96 B3
Dasville S. Africa 133 M3
Datadian Indon. 77 F2
Datça Turkey 106 A3
Date Japan 90 G3
Date Creek watercourse U.S.A. 183 K7
Dateland U.S.A. 183 K9
Datha India 96 B5
Datia India 96 C4
Datian China 87 F3
also known as Junxi
Datian Ding mt. China 87 D4
Datong China see Tong'an
Datong Heilong. China 82 B3
Datong Qinghai China 84 D4
also known as Qiaotou
Datong Shanxi China 85 G3
Datong He r. China 84 D4
Datong Shan mts China 84 C4
Datta Rus. Fed. 82 F2
Datu i. Indon. 77 E2
Datu, Tanjung c. Indon./Malaysia 77 E2
Datuk, Tanjung pt Indon. 76 C3
Datu Piang Phil. 74 C5
also known as Dulawan
Daudkandi Bangl. 97 F5
Daud Khel Pak. 101 G3
Daudnagar India 97 E4
Daudzeva Latvia 42 G5
Daugai Lith. 42 F7
Daugailiai Lith. 42 G6
Daugava r. Latvia 42 F4
Daugavpils Latvia 42 H6
also known as Dvinsk; formerly known as Dünaburg
Daugyvenė r. Lith. 42 E5
Daulatabad Afgh. 101 F2
Daulatabad Iran see Malāyer
Daulatpur Bangl. 97 F5
Daule Ecuador 198 B5
Daun Germany 48 D5
Daund India 94 B2
Daung Kyun i. Myanmar 79 B5
also known as Ross Island
Daungyu r. Myanmar 78 A3
Dauphin Canada 167 K5
Dauphiné reg. France 51 L7
Dauphiné, Alpes du mts France 51 L8
Dauphin Island U.S.A. 175 B6
Dauphin Lake Canada 167 L5
Daura Nigeria 125 H3
Daurie Creek r. Australia 151 A5
Dauriya Rus. Fed. 85 H1
Daurskiy Khrebet mts Rus. Fed. 85 F1
Dausa India 96 C4
Dầu Tiêng, Hồ resr Vietnam 79 D6
Däväçi Azer. 107 G2
also spelt Divichi
Davangere India 94 B3
Davao Phil. 74 C5
Davao Gulf Phil. 74 C5
Dāvarān Iran 100 D4
Dāvar Panāh Iran 101 E5
also known as Dizak
Davel S. Africa 133 N3
Davenport IA U.S.A. 174 B3
Davenport NY U.S.A. 177 K3
Davenport WA U.S.A. 180 C3
Davenport Downs Australia 149 D5
Davenport Range hills Australia 148 B4
Daveyton S. Africa 133 M3
David Panama 186 C5
David City U.S.A. 178 C3
Davidson Canada 167 J5
Davidson, Mount hill Australia 148 A4
Davidson Lake Canada 167 L4
Davies, Mount Australia 146 A1
Davinópolis Brazil 206 F5
Davis research station Antarctica 223 F2
Davis r. Australia 150 C4
Davis i. Myanmar see Than Kyun
Davis CA U.S.A. 182 C3
Davis WV U.S.A. 176 F6
Davis, Mount hill U.S.A. 176 F6
Davis Bay Antarctica 223 I2
Davis Dam U.S.A. 183 J6
Davis Dam dam U.S.A. 183 J6
Davis Inlet Canada 169 I2
Davison U.S.A. 173 J7
Davis Sea Antarctica 223 G2
Davis Strait Canada/Greenland 165 N3
Davlekanovo Rus. Fed. 40 J5
Davlia Greece 59 D10
also spelt Dhavlia
Davos Switz. 51 P6
Davutlar Turkey 59 I11
Davy U.S.A. 176 D8
Davyd-Haradok Belarus 42 I9
Davydkovo Rus. Fed. see Tolbukhino
Davydovo Rus. Fed. 43 T4
Davy Lake Canada 167 I3
Dawa China 85 I3
Dawa Co l. China 89 D6
Dawāsir reg. Saudi Arabia 104 D3
Dawāsir, Wādī ad watercourse Saudi Arabia 104 D3
Dawa Wenz r. Eth. 128 D3
Dawaxung China 89 D6
Dawê China 86 B2
Dawei Myanmar see Tavoy
Dawei b. Myanmar see Tavoy
Dawen r. China 85 H5
Dawera i. Indon. 75 D4
Dawhat Bilbul b. Saudi Arabia 105 E2
Dawhinava Belarus 42 I7
Dawna Range mts Myanmar/Tha. 78 B4
Dawqah Oman 105 F4
Dawqah Saudi Arabia 104 C4
Dawrān Yemen 104 D5
Dawson r. Australia 149 F4
Dawson Canada 166 B1
Dawson GA U.S.A. 175 C6
Dawson ND U.S.A. 180 H3
Dawson, Isla i. Chile 205 C9
Dawson, Mount Canada 167 G5
Dawson Bay Canada 167 K4
Dawson Creek Canada 166 F4
Dawson Inlet Canada 167 M2
Dawson Range mts Canada 166 A2
Dawsons Landing Canada 166 E5
Dawu Hubei China 87 E2
Dawu China see Maqên
Dawu Sichuan China 86 B2
also known as Xianshui
Dawu Taiwan see Tawu
Dawukou China see Shizuishan
Dawu Shan hill China 87 E2
Dawwah Oman 105 G3
Dax France 50 E9
Daxian China see Dazhou
Daxiang Ling mts China 86 B2
Daxihaizi Shuiku l. China 88 D3
Daxin China 87 C4
also known as Taocheng
Daxing China see Ninglang
Daxing China see Lüchun
Daxue China see Wencheng
Daxue Shan mts China 86 B2
Dayan China see Lijiang
Dayang r. China 85 I4
Dayangshu China 85 J1
Dayan Nuur l. Mongolia 84 A1
Dayao China 86 B3
also known as Jinbi
Dayao Shan mts China 87 D4
Dāyat en Nahārāt well Mali 124 E2
Daye China 87 E2
Dayi China 86 B2
also known as Jinyuan
Daying Jiang r. China 86 A3
Dayishan China see Guanyun
Dayl Oman 105 G2
Daylesford Australia 147 E4
Dayong China 87 D2
formerly known as Zhangjiajie
Dayr Abū Sa'īd Jordan 108 G5
Dayr az Zawr Syria 109 L2
also spelt Deir-ez-Zor
Dayr az Zawr governorate Syria 109 L2
Dayr Ḥāfir Syria 109 I1
Daysland Canada 167 H4
Dayton OH U.S.A. 176 A6
Dayton TN U.S.A. 174 C5
Dayton TX U.S.A. 179 D6
Dayton VA U.S.A. 176 G7
Dayton WA U.S.A. 180 C3
Daytona Beach U.S.A. 175 D6
Dayu China 87 E3
also known as Nan'ao
Dayu Indon. 77 F3
Dayu Ling mts China 87 E3
Da Yunhe canal China 87 F1
English form Grand Canal
Dayyina i. U.A.E. 105 F2
Dazaifu Japan 91 B8
Dazhe China see Pingyuan
Dazhongji China see Dafeng
Dazhou China 87 C2
formerly known as Daxian
Dazhou Dao i. China 87 D5
Dazhu China 87 C2
also known as Zhuyang
Dazu China 86 C2
also known as Longgang
De Aar S. Africa 132 I7
Dead r. U.S.A. 172 F4
Deadman's Cay Bahamas 187 E2
Dead Mountains U.S.A. 183 J7

▶Dead Sea salt l. Asia 98 B3
Lowest point in the world and in Asia. Also known as Bahrat Lut or HaMelah, Yam.

Deadwood U.S.A. 178 B2
Deakin Australia 151 E6
Deal U.K. 47 N12
Dealesville S. Africa 133 J5
Dean r. Canada 166 E4
De'an China 87 E2
also known as Puting
Dean Channel Canada 166 E4
Deán Funes Arg. 204 D3
Deanuvuotna inlet Norway see Tanafjorden
Dearborn U.S.A. 173 J8
Dease r. B.C. Canada 166 D3
Dease r. N.W.T. Canada 167 G1
Dease Arm b. Canada 166 F1
Dease Lake Canada 166 D3
Dease Lake l. Canada 166 D3
Dease Strait Canada 165 I3
Death Valley U.S.A. 183 H5

▶Death Valley depr. U.S.A. 183 G5
Lowest point in the Americas.
northamerica [landscapes] ➡ 156–157

Death Valley Junction U.S.A. 183 H5
Death Valley National Park U.S.A. 183 G5
Deaver U.S.A. 180 E3
Debagram India 97 F5
Debak Sarawak Malaysia 77 E2
Debao China 86 C4
Debar Macedonia 58 B7
Debark Eth. 128 C1
Debay well Yemen 105 E4
Debden Canada 167 J4
De Beers Pass S. Africa 133 N5
Debert Canada 169 I4
Debesy Rus. Fed. 40 J4
Dębica Poland 49 S5
De Biesbosch, Nationaal Park nat. park Neth. 48 B4
Debila Alg. 123 G2
Debin Rus. Fed. 39 P3
Dęblin Poland 49 S4
Dębno Poland 49 L3
Débo, Lac l. Mali 124 D3
Deborah East, Lake salt flat Australia 151 B6
Deborah West, Lake salt flat Australia 151 B6
Deboyne Islands P.N.G. 149 G1
Debre Birhan Eth. 128 C2
Debrecen Hungary 49 S8
Debre Markos Eth. 128 C2
Debre Sīna Eth. 128 C2
Debre Tabor Eth. 128 C2
Debre Werk' Eth. 128 C2
Debre Zeyit Eth. 128 C2
Debrzno Poland 49 O2
Deçan Kosovo, Srbija Yugo. see Dečani
Dečani Kosovo, Srbija Yugo. 58 B6
also spelt Deçan
Decatur AL U.S.A. 174 C5
Decatur GA U.S.A. 175 C5
Decatur IL U.S.A. 174 B4
Decatur IN U.S.A. 176 A5
Decatur MI U.S.A. 172 H8
Decatur MS U.S.A. 175 B5
Decatur TN U.S.A. 174 C5
Decatur TX U.S.A. 179 C5
Decazeville France 51 I8

▶Deccan plat. India 94 C2
Plateau making up most of southern and central India.

Deception watercourse Botswana 130 E4
Deception Bay Australia 147 G1
Dechang China 86 B3
also known as Dezhou
Decheng China see Deqing
Děčín Czech Rep. 49 L5
Decize France 51 J6
Decorah U.S.A. 174 B3
Dedap i. Indon. see Penasi, Pulau
Dedaye Myanmar 78 A4
Dedebağı Turkey 59 K11
Dedegöl Dağları mts Turkey 106 B3
Deder Eth. 128 D2
Dedinovo Rus. Fed. 43 U6
Dedo de Deus mt. Brazil 206 F11
Dedop'listsqaro Georgia 107 F2
formerly known as Tsiteli Tskaro
Dédougou Burkina 124 E3
Dedovichi Rus. Fed. 43 K4
Dedu China 82 B2
also known as Qingshan
Dedurovka Rus. Fed. 102 C2
Dedza Malawi 129 B8
Dedza Mountain Malawi 131 G2
Dee r. England/Wales U.K. 47 I10
Dee r. Scotland U.K. 46 J6
Deeg India 96 C4
Deelfontein S. Africa 132 H7
Deep Bay Hong Kong China 87 [inset]
also known as Shenzhen Wan
Deep Bight inlet Australia 150 D2
Deep Creek Lake U.S.A. 176 F6
Deep Creek Range mts U.S.A. 183 K2
Deep Gap U.S.A. 176 D9
Deep River Canada 168 E4
Deep River U.S.A. 177 M4
Deer Creek r. U.S.A. 182 B2
Deer Creek Reservoir U.S.A. 183 M1
Deeri Somalia 128 E3
Deering, Mount Australia 151 E5
Deer Island Canada 169 H4
Deer Island AK U.S.A. 164 C4
Deer Island ME U.S.A. 177 Q1
Deer Isle U.S.A. 177 Q1
Deer Lake Nfld. Canada 169 J3
Deer Lake Ont. Canada 167 M4
Deer Lake l. Canada 167 M4
Deer Lodge U.S.A. 180 D3
Deer Park U.S.A. 180 C3
Deerpass Bay Canada 166 F1
Deesa India see Disa
Defeng China see Liping
Defensores del Chaco, Parque Nacional nat. park Para. 201 E5
Defiance U.S.A. 176 A4
Defiance Plateau U.S.A. 183 O6
Défirou well Niger 125 I1
De Funiak Springs U.S.A. 175 C6
Degana India 96 B4
Degano r. Italy 56 E2
Dêgê China 86 A2
also known as Gengqing
Degebe r. Port. 54 D6
Degeberga Sweden 45 K5
Degeh Bur Eth. 128 D2
Dégelis Canada 169 G4
formerly known as Ste-Rose-du-Dégelé
Degema Nigeria 125 G5
Degerfors Sweden 45 K4
Deggendorf Germany 49 J7
Degh r. Pak. 101 H4
Değirmencik r. Turkey 59 J9
Değirmenlik Cyprus see Kythrea
Degodia reg. Eth. 128 D3
De Grey Australia 150 B4
De Grey r. Australia 150 B4
Degtevo Rus. Fed. 41 G6
Degtyarevka Rus. Fed. 43 N8
Dehaj Iran 100 C4
Dehak Iran 101 E5
Dehalak Deset i. Eritrea 121 I6
Deh Bakrī Iran 100 D4
Deh Barez Iran see Fāryāb
Deh Bīd Iran 100 C4
Deh-Dasht Iran 100 B4
Dehdez Iran 100 B4
Dehej India 96 B5
Deh-e Khalīfeh Iran 100 B4
Deh-e Kohneh Iran 100 B4
Dehel Island Eritrea 104 B5
Dehgāh Iran 100 B2
Deh Golān Iran 100 A3
Dehi Afgh. 101 F3
Deh Khvājeh Iran 100 C4
Dehkūyeh Iran 100 C5
Dehlorān Iran 100 A3
Deh Mollā Iran 100 B4
De Hoge Veluwe, Nationaal Park nat. park Neth. 48 C3
De Hoop Nature Reserve S. Africa 132 E11
De Hoop Vlei l. S. Africa 132 E11
Dehqonobod Uzbek. see Dekhkanabad
Dehra Dun India 96 C3
Dehri India 97 E4
Deh Shū Afgh. 101 E4
Dehua China 87 F3
also known as Longxun
Dehui China 82 B3
Deim Zubeir Sudan 126 E3
Deinze Belgium 51 J2
Deir el Qamar Lebanon 108 G4
Deir-ez-Zor Syria see Dayr az Zawr
Dej Romania 58 E1
Dejë, Mal mt. Albania 58 B7
Dejen Eth. 128 C2
Deji China see Rinbung
Dejiang China 87 D2
also known as Jiangsi
Deka Drum Zimbabwe 131 E3
De Kalb IL U.S.A. 174 B3
De Kalb MS U.S.A. 175 B5
De Kalb TX U.S.A. 179 D5
De Kalb Junction U.S.A. 177 J1
De-Kastri Rus. Fed. 81 O2
Dekemhare Eritrea 121 H6
Dekese Dem. Rep. Congo 126 D5
Dekhkanabad Uzbek. 103 F5
also spelt Dehqonobod
Dékoa Cent. Afr. Rep. 126 C3
Delaki Indon. 75 C5
Delamar Lake U.S.A. 183 J4
Delami Sudan 128 A2
De Land U.S.A. 175 D6
Delano U.S.A. 182 E6
Delano Peak U.S.A. 183 L3

▶Delap-Uliga-Djarrit Marshall Is 220 F5
Capital of the Marshall Islands, on Majuro atoll. Also spelt Dalap-Uliga-Darrit or Djarrit-Uliga-Dalap.

Delārām Afgh. 101 E3
Delareyville S. Africa 133 J3
Delaronde Lake Canada 167 J4
Delavan U.S.A. 172 E8
Delaware U.S.A. 176 B5
Delaware r. KS U.S.A. 178 D4
Delaware r. NJ/PA U.S.A. 177 J6
Delaware state U.S.A. 177 J7
Delaware, East Branch r. U.S.A. 177 J4
Delaware, West Branch r. U.S.A. 177 J4
Delaware Bay U.S.A. 177 J6
Delaware City U.S.A. 177 J6
Delaware Water Gap National Recreational Area park U.S.A. 177 K4
Delay r. Canada 169 G1
Delbarton U.S.A. 176 C8
Delbeng Sudan 126 F3
Del Bonita Canada 167 H5
Delburne Canada 167 H4
Delčevo Macedonia 58 D7
Delegate Australia 147 F4
Delémont Switz. 51 N5
Delevan CA U.S.A. 182 B2
Delevan NY U.S.A. 176 G3
Delfinópolis Brazil 206 G7
Delft Neth. 48 B3
Delft Island Sri Lanka 94 C4
Delfzijl Neth. 48 D2
Delgado, Cabo c. Moz. 129 D7
Delgermörön Mongolia 84 C2
Delger Mörön r. Mongolia 84 D1
Delgo Sudan 121 F4
Delhi Canada 173 M8
Delhi China 84 C4
formerly known as Delingha
▶Delhi India 96 C3
world [cities] ➡ 24–25
Delhi admin. div. India 89 B6
Delhi CA U.S.A. 182 D4
Delhi LA U.S.A. 175 B5
Delhi NY U.S.A. 177 K3
Deli i. Indon. 77 D4
Deli r. Turkey 107 E3
Delice Turkey 106 C3
Delice r. Turkey 106 C2
Délices Fr. Guiana 199 H3
Delījān Iran 100 B3
Deliktaş Turkey 59 H10
Déline Canada 166 F1
formerly known as Fort Franklin
Delingha China see Delhi
Delisle Canada 167 J5
Delitua Indon. 76 B2
Delitzsch Germany 49 J4
Dell Rapids U.S.A. 178 C3
Dellys Alg. 123 F1
Del Mar U.S.A. 183 G9
Delmar DE U.S.A. 177 J7
Delmar IA U.S.A. 172 C8
Delmas S. Africa 133 M3
Delmenhorst Germany 48 F2
Delmont U.S.A. 176 F5
Delmore Downs Australia 148 B4
Delnice Croatia 56 G3
Del Norte U.S.A. 181 F5
Delong China 86 C4
De-Longa, Ostrova is Rus. Fed. 39 P2
English form De Long Islands
De Long Islands Rus. Fed. see De-Longa, Ostrova
De Long Mountains U.S.A. 164 C3
De Long Strait Rus. Fed. see Longa, Proliv
Deloraine Australia 147 E5
Deloraine Canada 167 K5
Delphi tourist site Greece 59 D10
Delphi U.S.A. 174 C3
Delphos U.S.A. 176 A5
Delportshoop S. Africa 133 I5
Delray Beach U.S.A. 175 D7
Del Río Mex. 184 C2
Del Rio U.S.A. 179 B6
Delsbo Sweden 45 L3
Delta state Nigeria 125 G5
Delta CO U.S.A. 181 E5
Delta OH U.S.A. 176 A4
Delta UT U.S.A. 183 L2
Delta Amacuro state Venez. 199 F2
Delta du Saloum, Parc National du nat. park Senegal 124 A3
Delta Junction U.S.A. 164 E3
Delta National Wildlife Refuge nature res. U.S.A. 175 B6
Delta Reservoir U.S.A. 177 J2
Deltona U.S.A. 175 D6
Delungra Australia 147 F2
Delvada India 94 A1
Delvinë Albania 59 B9
Dema r. Rus. Fed. 102 C1
Demak Indon. 77 E4
Demavend mt. Iran see Damāvand, Qolleh-ye
Demba Dem. Rep. Congo 127 D6
Dembava Lith. 42 F6
Dembia Cent. Afr. Rep. 126 E3
Dembī Dolo Eth. 128 B2
Demerara Guyana see Georgetown
Demidov Rus. Fed. 43 M6
Deming U.S.A. 181 F6
Demini r. Brazil 199 F5
Demini, Serras do mts Brazil 199 F4
Demirci Turkey 106 B3
Demir Hisar Macedonia 58 C7
Demirköprü Barajı resr Turkey 106 B3
Demirköy Turkey 58 I7
Demirler r. Turkey 59 K10
Demistkraal S. Africa 133 I10
Demmin Germany 49 K2
Democracia Brazil 199 F6
Demopolis U.S.A. 175 C5
Dempo, Gunung vol. Indon. 76 C4
Dempster Highway Canada 166 B1
Dêmqog Jammu and Kashmir 96 C2
Demyakhi Rus. Fed. 43 N6
Dem'yanovo Rus. Fed. 40 H3
Demyansk Rus. Fed. 43 N4
De Naawte S. Africa 132 F7
Denair U.S.A. 182 D4
Denakil reg. Eritrea/Eth. 121 I6
also spelt Danakil
Denali National Park and Preserve U.S.A. 164 D3
formerly known as Mount McKinley National Park
Denan Eth. 128 D3
Denare Beach Canada 167 K4
Denau Uzbek. 103 F5
also spelt Denow
Denbigh Canada 168 E4
Denbigh U.K. 47 I10
also spelt Dinbych
Den Bosch Neth. see 's-Hertogenbosch
Den Burg Neth. 48 B2
Den Chai Thai. 78 C4
Dendang Indon. 77 D3
Dendâra Mauritania 124 D2
Dendermonde Belgium 51 K1
also known as Termonde
Đeneral Janković Kosovo, Srbija Yugo. 58 C6
also spelt Djeneral Janković
Denezhkin Kamen', Gora mt. Rus. Fed. 40 K3
Dengas Niger 125 H3
Denge Nigeria 125 G3
Dengfeng China 87 E1
Dênggar China 89 D6
Dengjiabu China see Yujiang
Dêngka China see Têwo
Dêngkagoin China see Têwo
Dengkou China 85 E3
also known as Bayan Gol
Dêngqên China 97 G3
also known as Gyamotang
Dengta China 87 E4
Dengtu Cent. Afr. Rep. 126 D3
Dengxian China see Dengzhou
Dengzhou China 87 E1
formerly known as Dengxian
Dengzhou China see Penglai
Den Haag Neth. see The Hague
Denham Australia 151 A5
Denham r. Australia 150 E2
Denham Range mts Australia 149 F4
Denham Sound sea chan. Australia 151 A5
Den Helder Neth. 48 B3
Denholm Canada 167 I4
Denia Spain 55 L6

index D

Denial Bay Australia 146 B3
Deniliquin Australia 147 E3
Deniskovichi Rus. Fed. 43 M9
Denison IA U.S.A. 178 D3
Denison TX U.S.A. 179 C5
Denison, Cape Antarctica 223 J2
Denison Plains Australia 150 E3
Denisovka Kazakh. see Ordzhonikidze
Denizli Turkey 106 B3 historically known as Laodicea or Laodicea ad Lycum
Denizli prov. Turkey 59 K11
Denman Australia 147 F3
Denman Glacier Antarctica 223 G2
Denmark Australia 151 B7
▶Denmark country Europe 45 J5 europe [countries] ➡ 32–35
Denmark U.S.A. 172 F6
Denmark Fjord inlet Greenland see Danmark Fjord
Denmark Strait Greenland/Iceland 165 Q3
Dennilton S. Africa 133 N2
Dennis, Lake salt flat Australia 150 E4
Dennison U.S.A. 176 D5
Dennisville U.S.A. 177 K6
Denow Uzbek. see Denau
Denpasar Indon. 77 F5
Densongi Indon. 75 B3
Denton MD U.S.A. 177 J7
Denton TX U.S.A. 179 C5
D'Entrecasteaux, Point Australia 151 A7
D'Entrecasteaux, Récifs reef New Caledonia 145 F3
D'Entrecasteaux Islands P.N.G. 145 E2
D'Entrecasteaux National Park Australia 151 A7
Dents du Midi mt. Switz. 51 M6
▶Denver U.S.A. 180 F5 State capital of Colorado.
Denys r. Canada 168 E2
Deo India 97 E4
Deoband India 96 C3
Deobhog India 95 D2
Deogarh Orissa India 97 E5
Deogarh Rajasthan India 96 B4
Deogarh mt. India 97 D5
Deoghar India 97 E4 also spelt Devghar
Deoli India 94 C1
Déols France 50 H6
Deori India 96 C5
Deoria India 97 D4
Deosai, Plains of Jammu and Kashmir 96 B2
Dep r. Rus. Fed. 82 B1
Depalpur India 96 B5
De Pas, Rivière r. Canada 169 H2
De Pere U.S.A. 172 E6
Depew U.S.A. 176 G3
Deposit U.S.A. 177 J3
Depot-Forbes Canada 173 Q3
Depot-Rowanton Canada 173 P4
Depsang Point hill Aksai Chin 89 B5
Depue U.S.A. 172 D9
Deputatskiy Rus. Fed. 39 N3
Dêqên Xizang China 89 E6
Dêqên Xizang China 89 E6
Dêqên China see Dagzê
Dêqên Yunnan China 86 A2 also known as Kaiping
Deqing Guangdong China 87 D4 also known as Decheng
Deqing Zhejiang China 87 G2
De Queen U.S.A. 179 D5
De Quincy U.S.A. 179 D6
Der, Lac du l. France 51 K4
Dera Eth. 128 C2
Dera Bugti Pak. 101 G4
Dera Ghazi Khan Pak. 101 G4
Deraheib reg. Sudan 121 G4
Dera Ismail Khan Pak. 101 G4
Derajat reg. Pak. 101 G4
Deram, Mount Antarctica 223 C2
Derbent Rus. Fed. 102 B4
Derbent Turkey 59 J10
Derbent Uzbek. 103 F5 formerly spelt Darband
Derbesiye Turkey see Şenyurt
Derby Australia 150 C3
Derby S. Africa 133 L2
Derby U.K. 47 K11
Derby CT U.S.A. 177 L4
Derby KS U.S.A. 178 C4 formerly known as El Paso
Derby Line U.S.A. 177 M1
Derecske Hungary 49 S8
Dereköy Turkey 108 D1
Dereköy Turkey 59 K11
Dereva Rus. Fed. 43 N2
Derg, Lough l. Rep. of Ireland 47 D11
Dergachi Rus. Fed. 102 B2
Dergachi Ukr. see Derhachi
Dergholm State Park nature res. Australia 146 D4
Derhachi Ukr. 41 F6 also spelt Dergachi
De Ridder U.S.A. 179 D6
Derik Turkey 107 E3
Derinkuyu Turkey 106 C3
Derkali well Kenya 128 D4
Derna Libya see Darnah
Dêrong China 86 A2 also known as Songmai
Derow Iran 102 B5
Derre Moz. 131 H3
Derry U.K. see Londonderry
Derry U.S.A. 177 N3
Derryveagh Mountains hills Rep. of Ireland 47 D9
Derstei China 84 D3
Dêrub China see Rutog
Derudeb Sudan 121 H5
De Rust S. Africa 132 G10
Deruta Italy 56 E6
Derventa Bos.-Herz. 56 J4
Derwent r. Australia 147 E5
Derwent r. Derbyshire, England U.K. 47 K11
Derwent r. England U.K. 47 L10
Derweze Turkm. see Darvaza
Deryugino Rus. Fed. 43 Q9
Derza r. Rus. Fed. 43 P5
Derzhavino Rus. Fed. 102 C1
Derzhavinsk Kazakh. 103 F2 formerly known as Derzhavinskiy
Derzhavinskiy Kazakh. see Derzhavinsk
Desa Romania 58 E5
Desaguadero r. Arg. 204 D4
Desaguadero r. Bol. 200 C4
Désappointement, Îles du is Fr. Polynesia 221 I6 English form Disappointment Islands
Des Arc U.S.A. 174 B5
Desatoya Mountains U.S.A. 182 G2
Desbarats Canada 173 J4
Descalvado Mato Grosso Brazil 201 F4
Descalvado São Paulo Brazil 206 F8
Descartes France 50 G6
Deschambault Lake Canada 167 K4
Deschambault Lake l. Canada 167 K4
Deschutes r. U.S.A. 170 B2
Desē Eth. 128 C2 formerly spelt Dessye
Deseada Chile 200 C5
Deseado Arg. 205 D7
Deseado r. Arg. 205 D7
Desembarco Del Granma National Park tourist site Cuba 186 D3
Desemboque Mex. 184 B2
Desengaño, Punta pt Arg. 205 D8
Deseret U.S.A. 183 L2
Deseret Peak U.S.A. 183 L1
Deseronto Canada 173 P6
Désert, Lac l. Canada 173 Q4
Desertas, Ilhas is Madeira 122 A2
Desert Canal Pak. 101 G4
Desert Center U.S.A. 183 I8
Desert Hot Springs U.S.A. 183 H8
Désertines France 51 I6
Desert Lake U.S.A. 183 I5
Desert National Wildlife Refuge nature res. U.S.A. 183 I5
Desert View U.S.A. 183 M5
Deshler U.S.A. 176 B4
Deshnok India 96 B4
Desiderio Tello Arg. 204 D3
Desierto Central de Baja California, Parque Natural del nature res. Mex. 184 B2
Desierto de Sechura des. Peru 198 A6
Deskati Greece 59 C9 also spelt Dheskáti
De Smet U.S.A. 178 C2
▶Des Moines IA U.S.A. 174 A3 State capital of Iowa.
Des Moines NM U.S.A. 178 B4
Des Moines r. U.S.A. 174 A3
Desna r. Rus. Fed./Ukr. 41 D6
Desnăţui r. Romania 58 E5
Desnogorsk Rus. Fed. 43 O7
Desnogorskoye Vodokhranilishche resr Rus. Fed. 43 O7
Desnudo, Cerro mt. Arg. 205 C7
Desolación, Isla i. Chile 205 B9
Desolation Point Phil. 74 C4
DeSoto U.S.A. 172 B7
Despatch S. Africa 133 J10
Despen Rus. Fed. 84 B1
Des Plaines U.S.A. 172 F8
Despotovac Srbija Yugo. 58 C4
Dessau Germany 49 J4
Dessye Eth. see Desē
Destor Canada 173 O2
D'Estrees Bay Australia 146 C3
Destruction Bay Canada 166 B2
Desvres France 51 H2
Deta Romania 58 C3
Detah Canada 167 H2
Detchino Rus. Fed. 43 R7
Dete Zimbabwe 131 E3 formerly spelt Dett
De Teut Natuurreservaat nature res. Belgium 51 L2
Deti Jon b. Albania/Greece 59 A8
Đetinja r. Yugo. 58 B5
Detmold Germany 48 F4
Detour, Point U.S.A. 172 G5
De Tour Village U.S.A. 173 J5
Detrital Wash watercourse U.S.A. 183 J5
Detroit U.S.A. 173 J8
Detroit Lakes U.S.A. 178 D2
Dett Zimbabwe see Dete
Det Udom Thai. 79 D5
Detva Slovakia 49 Q7
Deua National Park Australia 147 F3
Deurne Neth. 48 C4
Deutschland country Europe see Germany
Deutschlandsberg Austria 49 M9
Deutsch-Luxemburgischer Naturpark nature res. Germany 48 D6
Deux-Rivières Canada 173 O4
Deva Romania 58 D3
Deva U.K. see Chester
Devadurga India 94 C2
Devakottai India 94 C4
Devana U.K. see Aberdeen
Devanhalli India 94 C3
Devarkonda India 94 C2
Deve Bair pass Macedonia see Velbuzhdki Prokhod
Devecser Hungary 49 O8
Develi Turkey 106 C3 also known as Everek
Deveron r. U.K. 46 J6
Devesel Romania 58 D4
Devét Skal hill Czech Rep. 49 N6
Devgadh Bariya India 96 B5
Devghar India see Deoghar
Devikot India 96 A4
Devil River Peak N.Z. 152 G8
Devils r. U.S.A. 179 B6
Devil's Gate pass U.S.A. 182 E3
Devil's Island U.S.A. 172 C3
Devils Lake U.S.A. 178 C1
Devil's Lake l. U.S.A. 179 B6
Devil's Paw mt. U.S.A. 164 F4
Devil's Peak U.S.A. 182 E4
Devil's Point Bahamas 187 E1
Devil's Thumb mt. Canada/U.S.A. 166 C3
Devin Bulg. 58 F7
Devine U.S.A. 179 C6
Devizes U.K. 47 K12
Devli India 96 B4
Devnya Bulg. 58 I5
Devoll r. Albania 58 A8
Dévoluy mts France 51 L8
Devon Alta Canada 180 D1
Devon Ont. Canada 173 J3
Devon S. Africa 133 M3
Devon Island Canada 165 J2
Devonport Australia 147 E5
Devrek Turkey 106 B2
Devrez r. Turkey 106 C2
Devrukh India 94 B2
Dewa, Tanjung pt Indon. 76 A2
Dewakang Besar i. Indon. 77 G4
Dewanganj Bangl. 97 F4
Dewangiri Bhutan 97 F4
Dewas India 96 C5
De Weerribben, Nationaal Park nat. park Neth. 48 D3
Dewelē Eth. 128 D2
Dewetsdorp S. Africa 133 K6
De Witt AR U.S.A. 174 B5
De Witt IA U.S.A. 174 B3
Dexing China 87 F2 formerly known as Yincheng
Dexter MI U.S.A. 173 J8
Dexter MO U.S.A. 174 B4
Dexter NM U.S.A. 181 F6
Dexter NY U.S.A. 177 I1
Deyang China 86 C2
Dey-Dey Lake salt flat Australia 146 A2
Deyhuk Iran 100 D3
Deynau Turkm. see Dyanev
Deyong, Tanjung pt Indon. 73 I8
Dêyü Co l. China 89 D5
Deyyer Iran 100 B5
Dez r. Iran 100 B3
Dez, Sadd-e resr Iran 107 G4 formerly known as Mohammad Reza Shah Pahlavi Dam
Dezadeash Canada 166 B2
Dezadeash Lake Canada 166 B2
Dezfūl Iran 100 B3
▶Dezhneva, Mys c. Rus. Fed. 39 T3 Most easterly point of Asia. English form East Cape.
Dezhou China 85 H4
Dezhou China see Dechang
Dezh Shāhpūr Iran see Marīvān
Dhading Nepal 97 E4
Dhahab, Wādī adh r. Syria 108 G5
Dhāhiriya West Bank 108 F6
Dhahlān, Jabal hill Saudi Arabia 104 D2
Dhahran Saudi Arabia 105 E2 also spelt Az Zahrān
▶Dhaka Bangl. 97 F5 Capital of Bangladesh and 5th most populous city in Asia. Formerly spelt Dacca. world [cities] ➡ 24–25
Dhaka admin. div. Bangl. 97 F5
Dhalbhum reg. India 97 E5
Dhaleswari r. Bangl. 97 F5
Dhaleswari r. India 97 G4
Dhalgaon India 94 B2
Dhamār Yemen 104 D5
Dhamār governorate Yemen 104 D5
Dhamnod India 96 B5
Dhampur India 96 C3
Dhamtari India 94 D1
Dhanbad India 97 E5
Dhandhuka India 96 B5
Dhanera India 96 B4
Dhangarhi Nepal 96 D3
Dhang Range mts Nepal 97 D3
Dhankuta Nepal 97 E4
Dhar India 96 B5
Dhar Adrar hills Mauritania 124 B2
Dharampur India 94 B1
Dharan Bazar Nepal 97 E4
Dharapuram India 94 C4
Dhari India 96 A5
Dharmanagar India 97 G4
Dharmapuri India 94 C3
Dharmavaram India 94 C3
Dharmjaygarh India 97 D5 also known as Rabkob
Dharmkot India 96 B3
Dharoor watercourse Somalia 128 F2
Dhar Oualâta hills Mauritania 124 D2
Dhar Tîchît hills Mauritania 124 C2
Dharug National Park Australia 147 F3
Dharur India 94 C2
Dharwad India 94 B3 formerly known as Dharwar
Dharwar India see Dharwad
Dhasa India 96 A5
Dhasan r. India 96 C4
▶Dhaulagiri mt. Nepal 97 D3 7th highest mountain in the world and in Asia. Also spelt Dhawlagiri. world [physical features] ➡ 8–9
Dhaulpur India 96 C4
Dhaurahra India 96 D4
Dhávlia Greece see Davlia
Dhawlagiri mt. Nepal see Dhaulagiri
Dhebar Lake India 96 B4
Dhekelia Sovereign Base Area military base Cyprus 108 E2
Dhekiajuli India 97 G4
Dhenkanal India 95 E1
Dheskáti Greece see Deskati
Dhiafánion Greece see Diafani
Dhībān Jordan 108 G6
Dhidhimótikhon Greece see Didymoteicho
Dhing India 97 G4
Dhī Qār governorate Iraq 107 F5
Dhirwāh, Wādī adh watercourse Jordan 109 H6
Dhodhekánisos is Greece see Dodecanese
Dhofar admin. reg. Oman see Ẓufār
Dhokós i. Greece see Dokos
Dhola India 96 A5
Dholka India 96 B5
Dhomokós Greece see Domokos
Dhone India 94 C3
Dhoomadheere Somalia 128 D4
Dhoraji India 96 A5
Dhori India 96 A5
Dhragonádha i. Greece see Dragonada
Dhragónisos i. Greece see Dragonisi
Dhrangadhra India 96 A5
Dhrol India 96 A5
Dhrosiá Greece see Drosia
Dhubāb Yemen 104 C5
Dhubri India see Dhuburi
Dhuburi India 97 F4 also spelt Dhubri
Dhule India 94 B1 formerly known as Dhulia
Dhulia India see Dhule
Dhulian India 97 E4
Dhuma India 96 C5
Dhunche Nepal 97 E4
Dhuudo Somalia 128 F2
Dhuusa Marreeb Somalia 128 E3
Dhuwaybān basin Saudi Arabia 104 B2
Dhytikí Ellás admin. reg. Greece see Dytiki Ellas
Dhytikí Makedhonía admin. reg. Greece see Dytiki Makedonia
Dia i. Greece 59 G13
Diablo, Mount U.S.A. 182 C4
Diablo Range mts U.S.A. 182 C4
Diaca Moz. 129 C7
Diafani Greece 59 I13 also known as Dhiafánion
Diafarabé Mali 124 D3
Diaka r. Mali 124 D3
Dialakoto Senegal 124 B3
Diallassagou Mali 124 E3
Diamante Arg. 204 E4
Diamante r. Arg. 204 D4
Diamante Italy 57 H9
Diamantina watercourse Australia 149 C5
Diamantina Amazonas Brazil 199 F6
Diamantina Minas Gerais Brazil 203 D6
Diamantina, Chapada plat. Brazil 202 D5
Diamantina Gates National Park Australia 149 D4
Diamantina Lakes Australia 149 D4
Diamantino Mato Grosso Brazil 201 F3
Diamantino Mato Grosso Brazil 202 A6
Diamantino r. Brazil 206 A3
Diamond Harbour India 97 F5
Diamond Islets Australia 149 F3
Diamond Peak U.S.A. 183 I2
Diamond Springs U.S.A. 182 D3
Diamondville U.S.A. 180 E4
Diamou Mali 124 C3
Diamounguél Senegal 124 B3
Dianbai China 87 D4 also known as Shuidong
Dianbu China see Feidong
Diancang Shan mt. China 86 B3
Dian Chi l. China 86 B3
Diandioumé Mali 124 C3
Diane Bank sea feature Australia 149 F2
Diangounté Kamara Mali 124 C3
Diani r. Guinea 124 C5
Dianjiang China 87 C2 also known as Guixi
Diano Marina Italy 56 A5
Dianópolis Brazil 202 C4
Dianra Côte d'Ivoire 124 D4
Diaobingshan China see Tiefa
Diaokou China 85 H4
Diaoling China 82 C3
Diapaga Burkina 125 F3
Diaporioi i. Greece 59 E11
Diarizos r. Cyprus 108 D3
Diatifèrè Guinea 124 C4
Diavolo, Mount hill India 95 G3
Diaz Point Namibia 130 B5
Dib, Râs pt Egypt 108 E9
Dibā al Ḥiṣn U.A.E. 105 G2
Ḍibab Oman 105 G3
Dibang r. India see Dingba Qu
Dibaya Dem. Rep. Congo 127 D6
Dibbis Sudan 120 E6
Dibek Dağı mt. Turkey 59 J10
Dibella well Niger 125 I2
Dibeng S. Africa 132 G4
Dībilē Eth. 128 D2
Dibis Iraq 109 P2
Ḍibīy, Jabal hills Saudi Arabia 104 C2
Dibrugarh India 97 G4
Dibulla Col. 198 C2
Dickens U.S.A. 179 B5
Dickeyville U.S.A. 172 C8
Dickinson U.S.A. 178 B2
Dickson U.S.A. 174 C4
Dicle r. Turkey 107 E3 see Tigris
Dida Galgalu reg. Kenya 128 C4
Dīdah well Saudi Arabia 104 D2
Dīdī, Jabal ad hill Syria 109 K2
Didicas i. Phil. 74 B2
Didiéni Mali 124 C3
Didinga Hills Sudan 128 B3
Dido waterhole Kenya 128 D5
Didsbury Canada 167 H5
Didwana India 96 B4
Didymoteicho Greece 58 H7 also known as Dhidhimótikhon
Didžiasalis Lith. 42 I6
Didžiulis l. Lith. 42 F7
Die France 51 L8
Die Berg mt. S. Africa 133 O2
Diébougou Burkina 124 E4
Dieburg Germany 48 F6
Diedenhofen France see Thionville
Diefenbaker, Lake Canada 167 I5
Diège r. France 51 I7
Diego de Almagro, Isla i. Chile 205 B8
Diego Garcia i. British Indian Ocean Terr. 218 L6
Diego Martin Trin. and Tob. 187 H5
Diégo Suarez Madag. see Antsirañana
Diégrâga well Mauritania 124 C3
Diéké Guinea 124 C5
Diekirch Lux. 51 M3
Diéma Mali 124 C3
Diemelsee park Germany 48 F4
Điên Châu Vietnam 78 D4
Dienvidsusēja r. Latvia 42 F5
Diepholz Germany 48 F3
Dieppe France 50 H3
Dierks U.S.A. 179 D5
Di'er Nonchang Qu r. China 85 E4
Di'er Songhua Jiang r. China 82 B3
Diest Belgium 51 L2
Dietikon Switz. 51 O5
Dieveniškės Lith. 42 G7
Diffa Niger 125 I3
Diffa dept Niger 125 I2
Difnein Island Eritrea 104 B4
Dig well Eth. 128 E3
Diga Diga well Niger 125 F3
Digapahandi India 95 E2
Digba Dem. Rep. Congo 126 E3
Digboi India 97 G4
Digby Canada 169 H4
Digerbergen hill Sweden 45 K3
Digerberget hill Sweden 45 K3
Diggi India 96 B4
Dighton U.S.A. 178 B4
Diglur India 94 C2
Digne-les-Bains France 51 M8
Digoin France 51 J6
Digos Phil. 74 C5
Digras India 94 C1
Digri Pak. 101 G5
Digul r. Indon. 73 I8
Digya National Park Ghana 125 E5
Dihang r. India 97 G3 see Brahmaputra
Diib, Wadi watercourse Sudan 104 B3
Diinsoor Somalia 128 D4
Dijlah, Nahr r. Iraq/Syria 107 F4 see Tigris
Dijlah - Ath Tharthār, Qanāt canal Iraq 109 O4 English form Tharthār Canal
Dijon France 51 L5
Dik Chad 126 C2
Dikanäs Sweden 44 L2
Diken India 96 B4
Dikhil Djibouti 128 D2
Dikho r. India 97 G4
Dikili Turkey 106 A3
Diksal India 94 B2
Diksmuide Belgium 51 I1
Dikson Rus. Fed. 39 I2
Dikwa Nigeria 125 I3
Dīla Eth. 128 C3
Dilaram Iran 100 D4
Dilek Yarımadası Milli Parkı nat. park Turkey 59 I11
Dili Dem. Rep. Congo 126 E4
▶Dili East Timor 75 C5 Capital of East Timor.
Dilia watercourse Niger 125 I3
Dilijan Armenia 107 F2 also spelt Dilizhan
Dilijan Argelanots' nature res. Armenia 107 F2
Di Linh Vietnam 79 E6
Dilion Cone mt. N.Z. 153 H10
Dilizhan Armenia see Dilijan
Dillenburg Germany 48 F5
Dilley U.S.A. 179 C6
Dilli Mali 124 D3
Dilling Sudan 121 F6
Dillingen an der Donau Germany 48 H7
Dillingham U.S.A. 164 D4
Dillinya Aboriginal Land res. Australia 148 B2
Dillon Canada 167 I4
Dillon r. Canada 167 I4
Dillon MT U.S.A. 180 D3
Dillon SC U.S.A. 174 E5
Dillsburg U.S.A. 177 H5
Dillwyn U.S.A. 176 G8
Dilolo Dem. Rep. Congo 127 D7
Dilos i. Greece 59 G11
Diltāwa Iraq 107 F4
Dimako Cameroon 125 I5
Dimapur India 97 G4
Dimas Mex. 184 D4
Dimashq Syria see Damascus
Dimashq governorate Syria 109 I4
Dimbelenge Dem. Rep. Congo 127 D6
Dimbokro Côte d'Ivoire 124 D5
Dimboola Australia 147 D4
Dimbulah Australia 149 E3
Dimitrovgrad Bulg. 58 G6
Dimitrovgrad Rus. Fed. 41 I5 formerly known as Melekess
Dimitrovgrad Srbija Yugo. 58 D5 formerly known as Tsaribrod
Dimitrovo Bulg. see Pernik
Dimmitt U.S.A. 179 B5
Dīmona Israel 108 G6
Dinagat i. Phil. 74 C4
Dinagat Sound sea chan. Phil. 74 C4
Dinajpur Bangl. 97 F4
Dinan France 50 D4
Dinanagar India 96 B2
Dinangourou Mali 125 E3
Dinant Belgium 51 K2
Dinapur India 97 E4
Dinar Turkey 106 B3 historically known as Apamea
Dīnār, Kūh-e mt. Iran 100 B4
Dinara mt. Bos.-Herz. 56 I4
Dinara Planina mts Bos.-Herz./Croatia see Dinaric Alps
Dinard France 50 D4
Dinaric Alps mts Bos.-Herz./Croatia 56 I4 also known as Dinara Planina
Dinas well Kenya 128 C4
Dinbych U.K. see Denbigh
Dinbych-y-Pysgod U.K. see Tenby
Dinder r. Sudan 121 G6
Dinder el Agaliyin r. Sudan 104 A5
Dinder National Park Sudan 121 G6
Dindi r. India 94 C2
Dindigul India 94 C4
Dindima Nigeria 125 H4
Dindiza Moz. 131 G4
Dindori Madhya Pradesh India 96 D5
Dindori Maharashtra India 94 B1
Dinek Turkey 106 C3
Dinga Dem. Rep. Congo 127 C6
Dinga Pak. 101 H3
Dingalan Bay Phil. 74 B3
Dingba Qu r. India 97 G4 also known as Dibang
Dingbian China 85 E4
Dingbujie China 87 E2
Dingelstädt Germany 48 H4
Dingin, Bukit mt. Indon. 76 C3
Dingla Nepal 97 E4
Dingle Rep. of Ireland 47 B11
Dingle Bay Rep. of Ireland 47 B11
Dingnan China 87 E3 also known as Lishi
Dingo Australia 149 F4
Dingolfing Germany 49 J7
Dingping China see Linshui
Dingras Phil. 74 B2
Dingtao China 85 G5
Dinguiraye Guinea 124 C4
Dingwall Canada 169 I4
Dingwall U.K. 46 H6
Dingxi China 84 E5
Dingxian China see Dingzhou
Dingxiang China 85 G4
Dingxin China 84 C3
Dingxing China 85 G4
Dingyuan China 87 F1
Dingzhou China 85 G4 formerly known as Dingxian
Dingzi Gang b. China 85 I4
Dingzikou China 84 B4
Dinhata India 97 F4
Dinh Lâp Vietnam 78 D3
Dinkel r. Neth. 48 D3
Dinkelsbühl Germany 48 H6
Dinnebito Wash watercourse U.S.A. 183 M6
Dinngyê China 89 D6 also known as Gyangkar
Dinokwe Botswana 131 E4
Dinosaur U.S.A. 183 O1
Dinosaur National Monument nat. park U.S.A. 183 O1
Dintiteladas Indon. 77 D4
Dinuba U.S.A. 182 E5
Dinwiddie U.S.A. 176 H8
Dioïla Mali 124 D3
Diois, Massif du mts France 51 L8
Dion r. Guinea 124 C4
Dionisio Brazil 207 K6
Dionísio Cerqueira Brazil 203 A8
Diorama Brazil 206 B3
Dioscurias Georgia see Sokhumi
Diosig Romania 58 D1
Diospolis Magna tourist site Egypt see Thebes
Diouloulou Senegal 124 A3
Dioumara Mali 124 C3
Dioundiou Niger 125 F3
Dioura Mali 124 D3
Diourbel Senegal 124 A3
Dipalpur Pak. 101 H4
Dipayal Nepal 96 D3
Diphu India 97 G4
Dipkarpaz Cyprus see Rizokarpason
Diplo Pak. 101 G5
Dipolog Phil. 74 B4
Dipperu National Park Australia 149 F4
Dipton N.Z. 153 C13
Dipu China see Anji
Dir Pak. 101 G3
Dir reg. Pak. 101 H3
Dīrah U.A.E. 105 F2
Dirang India 97 G4
Diré Mali 124 E2
Direction, Cape Australia 149 D2
Dirē Dawa Eth. 128 D2
Dirfys mts Greece 59 E10
Dirhami Estonia 42 E2
Diriamba Nicaragua 186 B5
Dirico Angola 127 D9
Dirillo r. Sicilia Italy 57 G11
Dirimli Geçidi pass Turkey 108 A1
Dirk Hartog Island Australia 151 A5
Dirkou Niger 125 I2
Dirranbandi Australia 147 F2
Dirs Saudi Arabia 104 C4
Dirschau Poland see Tczew
Dirty Devil r. U.S.A. 183 N4
Disa India 96 B4 formerly spelt Deesa
Disang r. India 97 G4
Disappointment, Cape Antarctica 222 T2
Disappointment, Cape S. Georgia 205 [inset]
Disappointment, Cape U.S.A. 180 A3
Disappointment, Lake salt flat Australia 150 C4
Disappointment Islands Fr. Polynesia see Désappointement, Îles du
Disappointment Lake Canada 169 I2
Discovery Bay Australia 146 D4
Discovery Bay Hong Kong China 87 [inset] also known as Tai Pak Wan
Discovery Bay Coastal Park nature res. Australia 146 D4
Disentis Muster Switz. 51 O6
Disgrazia, Monte mt. Italy 56 B2
Dishna Egypt 121 G3
Disko i. Greenland see Qeqertarsuaq
Disko Bugt b. Greenland see Qeqertarsuup Tunua
Dismal Lakes Canada 167 G1
Dismal Mountains Antarctica 223 D2
Dismal Swamp U.S.A. 177 I9
Disneyland Paris tourist site France 51 I4
Dispur India 97 F4
Disputanta U.S.A. 177 H8
Disraëli Canada 169 G4
Diss U.K. 47 N11
Dissān Island Saudi Arabia 104 C4
Distrito Federal admin. dist. Brazil 206 F2 English form Federal District
Distrito Federal admin. dist. Mex. 185 F5
Distrito Federal admin. dist. Venez. 199 E2 English form Federal District
Disūq Egypt 108 B6
Ditloung S. Africa 132 G5
Dittaino r. Sicilia Italy 57 H11
Diu India 94 A1
Diuata Mountains Phil. 74 C4
Diuata Point Phil. 74 C4
Dīvān Darreh Iran 100 A3
Divehi country Indian Ocean see Maldives
Divénié Congo 126 B5
Dives r. France 50 F3
Divichi Azer. see Däväçi
Divide Mountain U.S.A. 166 A2
Divilacan Bay Phil. 74 B2
Divinésia Brazil 207 J7
Divinópolis Brazil 203 C7
Divisões, Serra das mts Brazil 206 B4 also known as Santa Marta, Serra de
Divisor, Sierra de mts Peru see Ultraoriental, Cordillera
Divjaka nat. park Albania 58 A8
Divnoye Rus. Fed. 41 G7
Divo Côte d'Ivoire 124 D5
Divo Rus. Fed. 43 M6
Divor r. Port. 54 C6
Divounia i. Greece 59 H13
Divriği Turkey 107 D3
Divuma Dem. Rep. Congo 127 D7
Div'ya Rus. Fed. 40 K4
Diwaniyah Iraq see Ad Dīwānīyah
Dixcove Ghana 125 E5
Dixfield U.S.A. 177 O1
Dix Milles, Lac des l. Canada 173 S3
Dixmont U.S.A. 177 P1
Dixon CA U.S.A. 182 C3
Dixon IL U.S.A. 174 B3
Dixon Entrance sea chan. Canada/U.S.A. 164 F4
Dixon's Bahamas 175 F7
Dixonville Canada 167 G3
Diyadin Turkey 107 E3
Diyālá governorate Iraq 107 F4
Diyarbakır Turkey 107 E3 historically known as Amida
Diyodar India 96 A4
Diz Pak. 101 E5
Dizak Iran see Dāvar Panāh
Dizangué Cameroon 125 H6
Diz Chah Iran 100 C3
Dize Turkey see Yüksekova
Dizney U.S.A. 176 B9
Dja r. Cameroon 125 I6
Dja, Réserve du nature res. Cameroon 125 I6
Djado Niger 125 I1
Djado, Plateau du Niger 125 I1
Djakarta Indon. see Jakarta
Djakovica Kosovo, Srbija Yugo. see Đakovica
Djamâa Alg. 123 G2
Djamba Dem. Rep. Congo 127 D7
Djambala Congo 126 B5
Djampie Dem. Rep. Congo 126 C5
Djampiel Cameroon 125 I5
Djanet Alg. 123 H4 formerly known as Fort Charlet
Djarrit-Uliga-Dalap Marshall Is see Delap-Uliga-Djarrit
Djebr mt. Alg. 123 F4
Djébrène Chad 126 C2
Djédaa Chad 120 C6
Djedid well Alg. 123 F4
Djelfa Alg. 123 F2
Djéma Cent. Afr. Rep. 126 E3
Djèmber Chad 126 C2
Djeneral Janković Kosovo, Srbija Yugo. see Đeneral Janković
Djenné Mali 124 D3 also spelt Jenne
Djerdap nat. park Yugo. 58 D4
Djermaya Chad 120 B6
Djia Dem. Rep. Congo 126 D5
Djibo Burkina 125 E3
Djiboroso Côte d'Ivoire 124 D4
▶Djibouti country Africa 128 D3 spelt Jībūtī in Arabic; formerly known as Côte Française de Somalis in French or French Somaliland or French Territory of the Afars and Issas africa [countries] ➡ 114–117
▶Djibouti Djibouti 128 D2 Capital of Djibouti. Also spelt Jibuti.
Djidjelli Alg. see Jijel
Djiguéni Mauritania 124 C3
Djinet, Cap c. Alg. 55 O8
Djoli-Kera, Forêt classée de nature res. Chad 126 C2
Djolu Dem. Rep. Congo 126 D4
Djombo Kibbit Chad 120 C6
Djoua r. Congo/Gabon 126 B4
Djoubissi Cent. Afr. Rep. 126 D3
Djougou Benin 125 F4
Djoum Cameroon 125 I6
Djugu Dem. Rep. Congo 126 F4
Djuma Dem. Rep. Congo 126 C6
Djúpivogur Iceland 44 [inset] D2
Djurås Sweden 45 K3
Djurdjura National Park Alg. 55 P8
Djurö nationalpark nat. park Sweden 45 K4
Dlairi India 96 B3
Dmitriya Lapteva, Proliv sea chan. Rus. Fed. 39 O2
Dmitriyevka Primorskiy Kray Rus. Fed. 90 C2
Dmitriyevka Samarskaya Oblast' Rus. Fed. 102 B1
Dmitriyev-L'govskiy Rus. Fed. 43 Q9
Dmitriyevsk Ukr. see Makiyivka
Dmitriyevskoye Rus. Fed. 43 S7
Dmitrov Rus. Fed. 43 S5
Dmitrovo Rus. Fed. 43 O8
Dmitrovskiy Pogost Rus. Fed. 43 U6
Dmitrovsk-Orlovskiy Rus. Fed. 43 Q9
Dmytriyevs'k Ukr. see Makiyivka
Dnepr r. Rus. Fed. see Dnieper
Dneprodzerzhinsk Ukr. see Dniprodzerzhyns'k
Dnepropetrovsk Ukr. see Dnipropetrovs'k
Dneprorudnoye Ukr. see Dniprorudne
Dneprovskoye Rus. Fed. 43 O6 formerly known as Andreyevskoye
Dnestrovsc Moldova 58 K2
▶Dnieper r. Europe 41 D6 3rd longest river in Europe. Also spelt Dnepr (Rus. Fed.) or Dnipro (Ukraine) or Dnyapro (Belarus). europe [landscapes] ➡ 30–31
Dniester r. Moldova 58 L2 also spelt Nistru
Dniester r. Ukr. 41 D6 also spelt Dnister (Ukraine) or Nistru (Moldova)
Dnipro r. Ukr. 41 D6 see Dnieper
Dniprodzerzhyns'k Ukr. 41 E6 also spelt Dneprodzerzhinsk; formerly known as Kamenskoye
Dnipropetrovs'k Ukr. 41 E6 also spelt Dnepropetrovsk; formerly known as Yekaterinoslav
Dniprorudne Ukr. 41 E7 also spelt Dneprorudnoye
Dnister r. Ukr. 41 C6 see Dniester
Dnistrov'ky Lyman l. Ukr. 58 L2
Dno Rus. Fed. 43 K4

Dnyapro *r.* Belarus **41** D5 *see* **Dnieper**
Dnyaprowska-Buhskì, Kanal *canal* Belarus **42** F9
Doa Moz. **131** G3
Doabi Mekh-i-Zarin Afgh. **101** F3
Doaktown Canada **169** H4
Doangdoangan Besar *i.* Indon. **77** G4
Doangdoangan Kecil *i.* Indon. **77** G4
Doany Madag. **131** [inset] K2
Doba Chad **126** C2
Doba China *see* **Toiba**
Dobasna *r.* Belarus **43** L9
Dobbertiner Seenlandschaft *park* Germany **49** J2
Dobbs, Cape Canada **167** O1
Dobczyce Poland **49** R6
Dobele Latvia **42** E5
Döbeln Germany **49** K4
Doberai, Jazirah *pen.* Indon. **73** H7
English form Doberai Peninsula; *formerly known as* Vogelkop Peninsula
Doberai Peninsula Indon. *see* **Doberai, Jazirah**
Döbern Germany **49** L4
Dobiegniew Poland **49** M3
Doblas Arg. **204** D5
Dobo Indon. **73** H8
Doboj Bos.-Herz. **56** K4
Do Borjī Iran **100** C4
Dobra Poland **49** P4
Dobre Miasto Poland **49** R2
Dobreşti Romania **58** D2
Dobrich Bulg. **58** I5
formerly known as Tolbukhin
Dobrinka Rus. Fed. **41** G5
Dobříš Czech Rep. **49** L6
Dobromyl' Ukr. **49** T6
Dobroteşti Romania **58** F4
Dobrovăţ Romania **58** I2
Dobrovol'sk Rus. Fed. **42** D7
Dobroye Rus. Fed. **43** U9
Dobruchi Rus. Fed. **42** I3
Dobrudzhansko Plato *plat.* Bulg. **58** I5
Dobrun Romania **58** F4
Dobrush Belarus **43** M9
Dobryanka Rus. Fed. **40** K4
Dobryanka Ukr. **43** M9
Dobrynikha Rus. Fed. **43** S6
Dobskie, Jezioro *l.* Poland **49** S1
Dobson N.Z. **153** F10
Dobson *r.* N.Z. **153** D12
Dobzha China **89** E6
Doc Can *reef* Phil. **74** A5
Doce *r. Espírito Santo* Brazil **203** E6
Doce *r. Goiás* Brazil **206** B5
Do China Qala Afgh. **101** G4
Doctor Arroyo Mex. **185** E4
Doctor Belisario Domínguez Mex. **184** D2
Doctor Hicks Range *hills* Australia **151** D6
Doctor Petru Groza Romania *see* **Ştei**
Doda Tanz. **129** C6
Dod Ballapur India **94** C3
Dodecanese *is* Greece **59** I13
also spelt Dodekanisos *or* Dhodhekánisos
Dodekanisos *is* Greece *see* **Dodecanese**
Dodge Center U.S.A. **174** A2
Dodge City U.S.A. **178** B4
Dodgeville U.S.A. **172** C8
Dodman Point U.K. **47** H13
Dodola Eth. **128** C3

▶**Dodoma** Tanz. **129** B6
Capital of Tanzania.

Dodoma *admin. reg.* Tanz. **129** B6
Dodori National Reserve *nature res.* Kenya **128** D5
Dodsonville U.S.A. **176** B6
Doetinchem Neth. **48** D4
Dofa Indon. **75** C3
Doftana *r.* Romania **58** G3
Dog *r.* Canada **168** B3
Dogai Coring *salt l.* China **89** E5
Dogaicoring Qangco *salt l.* China **89** E5
Doğanbey *Aydın* Turkey **59** I11
Doğanbey *İzmir* Turkey **59** H10
Doğanşehir Turkey **107** D3
Dog Creek Canada **166** F5
Doghārūn Iran **101** E3
Dog Island Canada **169** I1
Dog Lake *Man.* Canada **167** L5
Dog Lake *Ont.* Canada **168** B3
Dog Lake *Ont.* Canada **168** C3
Dognecea Romania **58** C3
Dōgo *i.* Japan **91** C6
Dogoble *well* Somalia **128** E2
Dogondoutchi Niger **125** G3
Dogoumbo Chad **126** C2
Dōgo-yama *mt.* Japan **91** C7
Dog Rocks *is* Bahamas **186** D1
Doğubeyazıt Turkey **107** F3
Doğu Menteşe Dağları *mts* Turkey **106** B3
Dogxung Zangbo *r.* China **89** D6
also known as Raka Zangbo

▶**Doha** Qatar **105** E2
Capital of Qatar. Also spelt Ad Dawḩah

Dohad India *see* **Dahod**
Dohazari Bangl. **78** A3
Dohrighat India **89** C7
Doi *i.* Fiji **145** H4
also spelt Ndoi
Doi Inthanon National Park Thai. **78** B4
Doi Luang National Park Thai. **78** B4
Doilungdêqên China **89** E6
also known as Namka
Doïranis, Limni *l.* Greece/Macedonia *see* **Dojran, Lake**
Doire U.K. *see* **Londonderry**
Doi Saket Thai. **78** B4
Doisanagar India **97** E5
Dois Córregos Brazil **206** E9
Dois Irmãos, Serra dos *hills* Brazil **202** D4
Dojran, Lake Greece/Macedonia **58** D7
also known as Doïranis, Limni *or* Dojransko, Ezero
Dojransko Ezero *l.* Greece/Macedonia *see* **Dojran, Lake**
Doka Sudan **121** G6
Dokali Iran **100** C3
Dokhara, Dunes de *des.* Alg. **123** G2
Dokkum Neth. **48** C2
Dokos *i.* Greece **59** E11
also spelt Dhokós
Dokri Pak. **101** G5
Dokshukino Rus. Fed. *see* **Nartkala**
Dokshytsy Belarus **42** I7
Doksy Czech Rep. **49** L5
Dokuchayeva, Mys *c.* Rus. Fed. **90** J2
Dokuchayevka Kazakh. **103** F2
Dokuchayevs'k Ukr. **41** F7
formerly known as Olenivs'ki Kar"yery *or* Yelenovskiye Kar"yery
Dolak, Pulau *i.* Indon. **73** I8
also known as Yos Sudarso
Dolan Springs U.S.A. **183** J6
Dolavón Arg. **205** D6
Dolbeau Canada **169** F3
Dol-de-Bretagne France **50** E4
Dole France **51** L5
Dolgellau U.K. **47** I11
Dolgeville U.S.A. **177** K2
Dolgiy, Ostrov *i.* Rus. Fed. **40** K1
Dolgorukovo Rus. Fed. **43** T9
Dolgoye *Lipetskaya Oblast'* Rus. Fed. **43** U8
Dolgoye *Orlovskaya Oblast'* Rus. Fed. **43** S9
Dolgusha Rus. Fed. **43** T9
Dolhasca Romania **58** H1
Dolianova *Sardegna* Italy **57** B9
Dolinsk Rus. Fed. **82** F3
Dolisie Congo *see* **Loubomo**
Dolit Indon. **75** C3
Doljevac *Srbija* Yugo. **58** C5
Dolleman Island Antarctica **222** T2
Dolna Lipnitska Bulg. **58** G5
Dolni Chiflik Bulg. **58** I6
formerly known as Georgi Traykov
Dolni Dŭbnik Bulg. **58** F5
Dolno Kamartsi Bulg. **58** E6
Dolno Levski Bulg. **58** F6
Dolný Kubín Slovakia **49** Q6
Dolo Indon. **75** A3
Dolomites *mts* Italy **56** D3
also known as Dolomiti *or* Dolomitiche, Alpi
Dolomiti *mts* Italy *see* **Dolomites**
Dolomiti Bellunesi, Parco Nazionale delle *nat. park* Italy **56** D2
Dolomitiche, Alpi *mts* Italy *see* **Dolomites**
Dolon, Pereval *pass* Kyrg. *see* **Dolon Ashuusu**
Dolon Ashuusu *pass* Kyrg. **103** H4
also known as Dolon, Pereval
Dolonnur China *see* **Duolun**
Dolo Odo Eth. **128** D3
Doloon Mongolia **85** E2
Dolores Arg. **204** F5
Dolores Guat. **185** H5
Dolores Mex. **184** C3
Dolores Uruguay **204** F4
Dolores *r.* U.S.A. **183** O3
Dolores Hidalgo Mex. **185** E4
Dolovo *Vojvodina, Srbija* Yugo. **58** B4
Dolphin, Cape Falkland Is **205** F8
Dolphin and Union Strait Canada **164** H3
Dolphin Head Namibia **130** B5
Dolphin Island Nature Reserve Australia **150** B4
Đô Lương Vietnam **78** D4
Dolzhitsy Rus. Fed. **43** K3
Dom, Gunung *mt.* Indon. **73** I7
Domaniç Turkey **106** B3
also known as Hisarköy
Domar Bangl. **97** F4
Domartang China *see* **Banbar**
Domažlice Czech Rep. **49** J6
Domba China **97** G2
Dombarovskiy Rus. Fed. **102** D2
Dombås Norway **45** J3
Dombe Moz. **131** G3
Dombe Grande Angola **127** B8
Dombegyház Hungary **49** S9
Dombóvár Hungary **49** P9
Dombra Angola **127** C8
Dombrau Poland *see* **Dąbrowa Górnicza**
Dombrovitsa Ukr. *see* **Dubrovytsya**
Dombrowa Poland *see* **Dąbrowa Górnicza**
Dom Cavati Brazil **207** K6
Domda China *see* **Qingshuihe**
Dome Argus *ice feature* Antarctica **223** F1
Dome Charlie *ice feature* Antarctica **223** H2
also known as Dome Circe
Dome Circe *ice feature* Antarctica *see* **Dome Charlie**
Dome Fuji *research station* Antarctica **223** C1
Domeikava Lith. **42** E7
Domel Island Myanmar *see* **Letsok-aw Kyun**
Dome Rock Mountains U.S.A. **183** J8
Domett, Cape Australia **150** E2
Domett, Mount N.Z. **152** G9
Domeyko Chile **204** C3
Dom Feliciano Brazil **203** A9
Domfront France **50** F4
Domingos Martins Brazil **207** M7
▶**Dominica** *country* West Indies **187** H4
northamerica [countries] ⟶ 158–159
Dominical Costa Rica **186** C5
Dominicana, República *country* West Indies *see* **Dominican Republic**
▶**Dominican Republic** *country* West Indies **187** F3
also known as Dominicana, República; *historically known as* Santo Domingo
northamerica [countries] ⟶ 158–159
Dominica Passage Dominica/Guadeloupe **187** H4
Dominion, Cape Canada **165** L3
Dominique *i.* Fr. Polynesia *see* **Hiva Oa**
Domiongo Dem. Rep. Congo **126** D6
Dom Joaquim Brazil **207** J5
Domka Bhutan **97** F4
Domneşti Romania **58** F3
Domneşti Romania **58** G4
Domo Eth. **128** E3
Domodedovo Rus. Fed. **43** S6
Domodossola Italy **56** A2
Domokos Greece **59** D9
also spelt Dhomokós
Domoni Comoros **129** E8
Domozhirovo Rus. Fed. **43** O1
Dom Pedrito Brazil **203** A9
Dom Pedro Brazil **202** C3
Dompu Indon. **77** G5
Domula China **89** C5
Domusnovas *Sardegna* Italy **57** A9
Domuyo, Volcán *vol.* Arg. **204** C5
Domville, Mount *hill* Australia **147** F2
Domžale Slovenia **56** G2
Don *r.* Australia **149** F3
Don *r.* India **94** C2
Don Mex. **184** C3

▶**Don** *r.* Rus. Fed. **43** U9
5th longest river in Europe.
europe [landscapes] ⟶ 30–31

Don *r.* U.K. **46** J6
Don, Xé *r.* Laos **79** D5
Donadeu Arg. **204** E2
Donald Australia **147** D4
Donaldsonville U.S.A. **175** B6
Donalnes, Cerro *mt.* Chile **204** C2
Donalsonville U.S.A. **175** C6
Doñana, Parque Nacional de *nat. park* Spain **54** E8
Donau *r.* Austria/Germany **49** L7 *see* **Danube**
Donaueschingen Germany **48** F8
Donauwörth Germany **48** H7
Don Benito Spain **54** F6
Doncaster U.K. **47** K10
Dondo Angola **127** B7
Dondo Moz. **131** G3
Dondo, Tanjung *pt* Indon. **75** B2
Dondo, Teluk *b.* Indon. **75** B2
Dondonay *i.* Phil. **74** B4
Dondra Head Sri Lanka **94** D5
Donegal Rep. of Ireland **47** D9
Donegal Bay Rep. of Ireland **47** D9
Dönenbay Kazakh. *see* **Dunenbay**
Donets'k Ukr. **41** F7
formerly known as Stalino *or* Yuzovka
Donets'kyy Kryazh *hills* Rus. Fed./Ukr. **41** F6
Dønfoss Norway **45** J3
Donga *r.* Cameroon/Nigeria **125** H4
Donga Nigeria **125** H5
Dong'an China **87** D3
also known as Baiyashi
Dongara Australia **151** A6
Dongargaon India **94** D1
Dongargarh India **96** D5
Dongbatu China **84** B3
Dongbo China *see* **Mêdog**
Dongchuan China **86** B3
formerly known as Xincun
Dongchuan China *see* **Yao'an**
Dongco China **89** D5
also known as Cêringgolêb
Dong Co *l.* China **89** D5
Dongcun China *see* **Haiyang**
Dongcun China *see* **Lanxian**
Dong'e China **85** H4
also known as Tongcheng
Dongfang China **87** D5
also known as Basuo
Dongfanghong China **82** D3
Dongfeng China **82** B4
Donggala Indon. **75** A3
Donggang China **83** B5
formerly known as Dadong *or* Donggou
Donggi Cona *l.* China **84** C5
Donggou China *see* **Donggang**
Donggu China **87** E3
Dongguan China **87** E4
Đông Hà Vietnam **78** D4
Donghai China **87** F1
also known as Niushan
Dong Hai *sea* N. Pacific Ocean *see* **East China Sea**
Donghai Dao *i.* China **87** D4
Dong He *r.* China **86** C2
Dong He *watercourse* China **84** D3
Đông Hới Vietnam **78** D4
Dong Jiang *r.* China **87** E4
Dongjingcheng China **82** C3
Dongkait, Tanjung *pt* Indon. **75** A3
Dongkou China **87** D3
Donglan China **87** C3
Dongle China **84** D4
Dongliao *r.* China **85** I3
Donglük China **88** E4
Dongmen China *see* **Luocheng**
Dongming China **85** G5
Dongning China **82** C3
Dongo Angola **127** B8
Dongo Italy **56** B2
Dongobesh Tanz. **129** B6
Dongola Sudan **121** F5
Dongotona Mountains Sudan **128** B3
Dongou Congo **126** C4
Dong Phraya Fai *mts* Thai. **78** C4
Dong Phraya Yen *esc.* Thai. **79** C5
Dongping *Guangdong* China **87** E4
Dongping China *see* **Anhua**
Dongping *Shandong* China **85** H5
Dongping Hu *l.* China **85** H4
Dongpo China *see* **Meishan**
Dongqiao China **89** E6
Dongshan *Fujian* China **87** F4
also known as Xibu
Dongshan China *see* **Jiangning**
Dongshan *Jiangsu* China **87** G2
Dongshan China *see* **Shangyou**
Dongshao China **87** E3
Dongsha Qundao *is* China **81** J8
English form Pratas Islands
Dongsheng China **85** F4
Dongshuan China *see* **Tangdan**
Dongtai China **87** G1
Dongtai *r.* China **87** G1
Dong Taijnar Hu *l.* China **84** B4
Dongting Hu *l.* China **87** E2
Dongtou China **87** G3
also known as Bei'ao
Donguena Angola **127** B9
Donguila Gabon **126** A4
Dong Ujimqin Qi China *see* **Uliastai**
Dongxiang China *see* **Xuanhan**
Dongxiangzu China *see* **Xiaonan**
Dongxing China **82** B3
Dongyang China **87** G2
Dongying China **85** H4
Dongzhen China **84** D4
Dongzhi China **87** F2
also known as Yaodu
Doniphan U.S.A. **174** B4
Donja Dubnica *Kosovo, Srbija* Yugo. **58** C6
Donjek *r.* Canada **166** A2
Donji Miholjac Croatia **56** K3
Donji Milanovac *Srbija* Yugo. **58** D4
Donji Vakuf Bos.-Herz. **56** J4
also known as Srbobran
Donji Zemunik Croatia **56** H4
Donkerpoort S. Africa **133** J8
Donmanick Islands Bangl. **97** F5
Dønna *i.* Norway **44** K2
Donnacona Canada **169** G4
Donnelly Canada **167** G4
Donnellys Crossing N.Z. **152** H3
Donner Pass U.S.A. **182** D2
Donnersberg *hill* Germany **48** E6
Donnybrook Australia **151** A7
Donostia - San Sebastián Spain **55** J1
Donoussa Greece **59** G11
Donoussa *i.* Greece **59** G11
Donovan U.S.A. **172** F10
Donskoy Rus. Fed. **43** T8
Donskoye *Lipetskaya Oblast'* Rus. Fed. **43** T9
formerly known as Vodopyanovo
Donskoye *Stavropol'skiy Kray* Rus. Fed. **41** G7
Donsol Phil. **74** B3
Donthami *r.* Myanmar **78** B4
Donzenac France **50** H7
Doomadgee Australia **148** C3
Doomadgee Aboriginal Reserve Australia **148** C3
Doon Doon Aboriginal Reserve Australia **150** E3
Door Peninsula U.S.A. **172** F6
Dooxo Nugaaleed *valley* Somalia **128** F2
Do Qu *r.* China **86** B2
Dor *watercourse* Afgh. **101** E4
also known as Pudai
Dor Rus. Fed. **43** Q6
Dora, Lake *salt flat* Australia **150** C4
Dorado Mex. **184** D3
Do Rāhak Iran **100** B5
Dorah Pass Pak. **101** G2
Doramarkog China **86** A1
Doran Lake Canada **167** I2
Dora Riparia *r.* Italy **51** N7
D'Orbigny Bol. **201** E5
Dorbiljin China *see* **Emin**
Dorbod China *see* **Taikang**
Dorbod Qi China *see* **Ulan Hua**
Đorče Petrov Macedonia **58** C6
Dorchester U.K. **47** J13
Dordabis Namibia **130** C4
Dordogne *r.* France **51** F7
Dordrecht Neth. **48** B4
Dordrecht S. Africa **133** L8
Doré Lake Canada **167** J4
Doré Lake *l.* Canada **167** J4
Dores de Guanhães Brazil **207** K6
Dores do Indaiá Brazil **203** C6
Dorey Mali **125** E3
Dorfen Germany **48** J7
Dorfmark Germany **48** G3
Dorgali *Sardegna* Italy **57** B8
Dörgön Mongolia **84** B1
Dori *r.* Afgh. **101** F4
Dori Burkina **125** E3
Doring *r.* S. Africa **132** C8
Doring *r.* S. Africa **132** D9
Doringbaai S. Africa **132** C8
Doringbos S. Africa **132** D8
Dorisvale Australia **148** A2
Dormaa-Ahenkro Ghana **124** E5
Dormans France **51** J3
Dormidontovka Rus. Fed. **82** D3
Dornakal India **94** D2
Dornbirn Austria **48** G8
Dornoch U.K. **46** H6
Dornoch Firth *est.* U.K. **46** H6
Dornod *prov.* Mongolia **85** G1
Dornogovĭ *prov.* Mongolia **85** F2
Doro Mali **125** E2
Dorobanţu Romania **58** H4
Dorobino Rus. Fed. **43** S8
Dorog Hungary **49** P8
Dorogobuzh Rus. Fed. **43** O7
Dorohoi Romania **53** H2
Dorokhovo Rus. Fed. **43** R6
Dorokhsh Iran **101** D3
Döröö Nuur *salt l.* Mongolia **84** B2
Dorostol Bulg. *see* **Silistra**
Dorotea Sweden **44** L2
Dorowa Zimbabwe **131** F3
Dorpat Estonia *see* **Tartu**
Dorre Island Australia **151** A5
Dorrigo Australia **147** G2
Dorris U.S.A. **180** B4
Dorsale Camerounaise *slope* Cameroon/Nigeria **125** H5
Dorset Canada **173** O5
Dorsoidong Co *l.* China **89** E5
Dortmund Germany **48** E4
Dorton U.S.A. **176** C8
Dörtyol Turkey **106** D3
Doruma Dem. Rep. Congo **126** E3
Dorūneh Iran **100** D3
Dorylaeum Turkey *see* **Eskişehir**
Do Sārī Iran **100** D4
Dos Bahías, Cabo *c.* Arg. **205** D7
Dos Cabezas Mountains U.S.A. **183** O9
Dos de Mayo Peru **198** C6
Doshakh, Koh-i- *mt.* Afgh. **101** E3
Dos Hermanas Spain **54** F7
Dos Lagunos Guat. **185** H5
Đo Son Vietnam **78** D3
Dos Palos U.S.A. **182** D5
Dospat Bulg. **58** F7
Dospat *r.* Bulg. **58** F7
Dos Pozos Arg. **205** D6
Dosse *r.* Germany **49** J3
Dosso Niger **125** F3
Dosso *dept* Niger **125** F3
Dosso, Réserve Partielle de *nature res.* Niger **125** F3
Dossor Kazakh. **102** C3
Dostyk Kazakh. **88** C2
also spelt Dostyq; *formerly known as* Druzhba
Dostyq Kazakh. *see* **Dostyk**
Dothan U.S.A. **175** C6
Dötlingen Germany **48** F3
Douai France **51** J2
Douako Guinea **124** C4
Douala Cameroon **125** H5
Douala-Edéa, Réserve *nature res.* Cameroon **125** H6
Douarnenez France **50** B4
Douarnenez, Baie de *b.* France **50** B4
Double Headed Shot Cays *is* Bahamas **186** C2
Double Island *Hong Kong* China **87** [inset]
also known as Wong Wan Chau
Double Island Point Australia **149** G5
Double Mountain Fork *r.* U.S.A. **179** B5
Double Peak U.S.A. **182** F6
Double Point Australia **149** E3
Double Springs U.S.A. **174** C5
Doubs *r.* France/Switz. **51** L6
Doubtful Bay Australia **150** D2
Doubtful Island Bay Australia **151** B7
Doubtful Sound N.Z. **153** B13
Doué-la Fontaine France **50** F5
Douentza Mali **124** E3
Dougga *tourist site* Tunisia **123** H1
Doughboy Bay N.Z. **153** B15

▶**Douglas** Isle of Man **47** H9
Capital of the Isle of Man.

Douglas N.Z. **152** I7
Douglas S. Africa **132** H6
Douglas *AZ* U.S.A. **181** E7
Douglas *GA* U.S.A. **175** D6
Douglas *WY* U.S.A. **180** F4
Douglas Apsley National Park Australia **147** F5
Douglas Channel Canada **166** D4
Douglas City U.S.A. **182** B1
Douglas Creek *watercourse* Australia **146** C2
Douglas Creek *r.* U.S.A. **183** P1
Douglas Range *mts* Antarctica **222** T2
Douglas Reef *i.* Japan *see* **Okino-Tori-shima**
Douglasville U.S.A. **175** C5
Dougoulé *well* Niger **125** H3
Douhi Chad **120** C5
Douhudi China *see* **Gong'an**
Doukato, Akra *pt* Greece **59** B10
Doulaincourt-Saucourt France **51** L4
Douliu Taiwan *see* **Touliu**
Doullens France **51** I2
Doumè Benin **125** F4
Doumé Cameroon **125** I5
Doumé *r.* Cameroon **125** I5
Doumen China **87** E4
also known as Jing'an
Douna Mali **125** E3
Dounkassa Benin **125** F4
Doupovské Hory *mts* Czech Rep. **49** K5
Dourada, Cachoeira *waterfall* Brazil **206** D5
Dourada, Serra *hills* Brazil **206** C3
Dourada, Serra *mts* Brazil **202** B5
Dourados Brazil **203** A7
Dourados *r.* Brazil **203** A7
Dourados, Serra dos *hills* Brazil **203** A7
Dourbali Chad **126** B2
Dourdou *r.* France **51** I8
Dourdoura Chad **126** D2
Douro *r.* Port. **54** C3
also spelt Duero (Spain)
Doushi China *see* **Gong'an**
Doushui Shuiku *resr* China **87** E3
Doutor Camargo Brazil **206** A10
Douve *r.* France **50** E3
Douz Tunisia **123** H2
Douze *r.* France **50** F9
Douziat Chad **120** C6
Dove *r.* U.K. **47** K11
Dove Brook Canada **169** J2
Dove Bugt *b.* Greenland **165** Q2
Dove Creek U.S.A. **183** P4
Dover U.K. **47** N12
historically known as Dubris

▶**Dover** *DE* U.S.A. **177** J6
State capital of Delaware.

Dover *NH* U.S.A. **177** O2
Dover *NJ* U.S.A. **177** K5
Dover *OH* U.S.A. **176** D5
Dover *TN* U.S.A. **174** C4
Dover, Point Australia **151** D7
Dover, Strait of France/U.K. **50** H2
also known as Pas de Calais
Dover-Foxcroft U.S.A. **174** G2
Dover Plains U.S.A. **177** L4
Dovey *r.* U.K. *see* **Dyfi**
Doveyrīch, Rūd-e *r.* Iran/Iraq **107** G5
Dovnsklint *cliff* Denmark **48** I1
Dovrefjell *mts* Norway **44** J3
Dovrefjell Nasjonalpark *nat. park* Norway **44** J3
Dow, Lake Botswana *see* **Xau, Lake**
Dowa Malawi **129** B8
Dowagiac U.S.A. **172** G9
Dowgha'ī Iran **100** D2
Dowi, Tanjung *pt* Indon. **76** E2
Dowlatābād Afgh. **101** F2
Dowlatābād *Fārs* Iran **100** B4
Dowlatābād *Fārs* Iran **100** C4
Dowlatābād *Khorāsan* Iran **100** D2
Dowlatābād *Khorāsan* Iran **101** D3
Dowlatābād *Khorāsan* Iran **101** E2
Dowl at Yār Afgh. **101** F3
Downey *CA* U.S.A. **182** F8
Downey *IA* U.S.A. **172** B9
Downham Market U.K. **47** M11
Downieville U.S.A. **182** D2
Downpatrick U.K. **47** G9
Downs U.S.A. **178** C4
Downsville *NY* U.S.A. **177** K3
Downsville *WI* U.S.A. **172** B6
Downton, Mount Canada **166** E4
Dow Rūd Iran **100** B3
Dow Sar Iran **100** A3
Dowshī Afgh. **101** G3
Dowsk Belarus **43** L8
Dowzha Belarus **43** L6
Doyle U.S.A. **182** D1
Doyles Canada **169** J4
Doyrentsi Bulg. **58** F5
Dozdān *r.* Iran **100** D5
Dōzen *is* Japan **91** C6
Dozois, Réservoir Canada **168** E4
Dozulé France **50** F3
Drâa, Oued *watercourse* Morocco **122** C3
Dracena Brazil **206** B8
Drachkava Belarus **42** J8
Drachten Neth. **48** D2
Dragalina Romania **58** I4
Dragan *l.* Sweden **44** K2
Drăgăneşti-Olt Romania **58** F4
Drăgăneşti-Vlaşca Romania **58** G4
Drăgăşani Romania **58** F4
Draghoender S. Africa **132** G6
Dragoman Bulg. **58** D6
Dragonada *i.* Greece **59** H13
also spelt Dhragonádha
Dragonera, Isla *i.* Spain *see* **Sa Dragonera**
Dragones Arg. **201** E5
Dragonisi *i.* Greece **59** G11
also known as Dhragónisos
Dragon Rocks Nature Reserve Australia **151** B7
Dragon's Mouths *strait* Trin. and Tob./Venez. **187** H5
Dragoon U.S.A. **183** N9
Dragør Denmark **45** K5
Dragoş Vodă Romania **58** I4
Dragsfjärd Fin. **45** M3
Draguignan France **51** M9
Drăguşeni Romania **58** I3
Drahichyn Belarus **42** G9
also spelt Drogichin
Drakensberg *mts* Lesotho/S. Africa **133** M6
Drakensberg *mts* S. Africa **131** F5
Drakensberg Garden S. Africa **133** N6
Draken's Rock *mt.* S. Africa **133** M7
Drakes Bay U.S.A. **182** A4
Drakulya *r.* Ukr. **58** K3
Drama Greece **58** F7
Drammen Norway **45** J4
Drang, Prêk *r.* Cambodia **79** D5
Drangajökull *ice cap* Iceland **44** [inset] B2
Drangedal Norway **45** J4
Drangme Chhu *r.* Bhutan **97** F4
Dranov, Lacul *l.* Romania **58** K4
Dranske Germany **49** K1
Draper U.S.A. **183** M1
Draper, Mount U.S.A. **166** B3
Drapsaca Afgh. *see* **Kondūz**
Dras Jammu and Kashmir **96** B2
Drau *r.* Austria **49** L9
also spelt Drava *or* Dráva
Drava *r.* Croatia/Slovenia **49** N9
also spelt Drau *or* Dráva
Dráva *r.* Hungary **56** K3
also spelt Drau *or* Drava
Dravinja *r.* Slovenia **56** H2
Dravograd Slovenia **56** H2
Drawa *r.* Poland **49** M3
Drawieński Park Narodowy *nat. park* Poland **49** M2
Drawno Poland **49** M2
Drawsko, Jezioro *l.* Poland **49** N2
Drawsko Pomorskie Poland **49** M2
Drayton Valley Canada **167** H4
Drebber Germany **48** F3
Dreieich Germany **48** F5
Dreistelzberge *hill* Germany **48** G5
Drenovci Croatia **56** K4
Drenovets Bulg. **58** D5
Drepano, Akra *pt* Greece **59** E9
Dresden Canada **173** K8
Dresden Germany **49** K4
Dresden U.S.A. **174** B4
Dretun' Belarus **43** K6
Dreux France **50** H4
Drevsjø Norway **45** K3
Drewryville U.S.A. **177** H9
Drezdenko Poland **49** M3
Dricēni Latvia **42** I5
Dridža *l.* Latvia **42** I6
Driftwood U.S.A. **176** G4
Driggs U.S.A. **180** E4
Drillham Australia **149** F5
Drin *r.* Albania **58** A6
Drina *r.* Bos.-Herz./Yugo. **56** L4
Drincea *r.* Romania **58** D4
Drini i Zi *r.* Albania **58** B6
Drinit, Gjiri i *b.* Albania **58** A7
Drino *r.* Albania **59** B8
Driscoll Island Antarctica **222** O1
Drissa Belarus *see* **Vyerkhnyadzvinsk**
Drniš Croatia **56** I5
Drobeta - Turnu Severin Romania **58** D4
also known as Turnu Severin
Drochtersen Germany **48** G2
Drogheda Rep. of Ireland **47** F10
also spelt Droichead Átha
Drogichin Belarus *see* **Drahichyn**
Drogobych Ukr. *see* **Drohobych**
Drohiczyn Poland **49** T3
Drohobych Ukr. **53** G2
also spelt Drogobych
Droichead Átha Rep. of Ireland *see* **Drogheda**
Droitwich U.K. **47** J11
Dronne *r.* France **50** F7
Dronning Ingrid Land *reg.* Greenland **165** O3
Dronning Louise Land *reg.* Greenland **165** Q2
Dronning Maud Land *reg.* Antarctica *see* **Queen Maud Land**
Droogmakerij de Beemster *tourist site* Neth. **48** B3
Dropt *r.* France **50** F8
Drosh Pak. **101** G3
Drosia Greece **59** E10
also spelt Dhrosiá
Droskovo Rus. Fed. **43** S9
Drovyanaya Rus. Fed. **85** G1
Drowning *r.* Canada **168** C3
Drūkšių ežeras *l.* Belarus/Lith. **42** H6
also known as Drysvyaty Vozyera
Druk-Yul *country* Asia *see* **Bhutan**
Drumheller Canada **167** H5
Drummond *atoll* Kiribati *see* **Tabiteuea**
Drummond, Lake U.S.A. **177** I9
Drummond Island Kiribati *see* **McKean**
Drummond Island U.S.A. **173** J5
Drummond Range *hills* Australia **149** E5
Drummondville Canada **169** F4
Drummore U.K. **47** H9
Drumnadrochit U.K. **46** H6
Drury Lake Canada **166** C2
Druskieniki Lith. *see* **Druskininkai**
Druskininkai Lith. **42** F8
formerly known as Druskieniki
Drusti Latvia **42** G4
Druts' *r.* Belarus **43** L8
Druya Belarus **42** I6
Druzhba Kazakh. *see* **Dostyk**
Druzhba Ukr. **43** O9
Druzhina Rus. Fed. **39** O3
Druzhinnoye, Ozero *l.* Rus. Fed. **43** S1
Druzhnaya Gorka Rus. Fed. **43** L2
Druzhylavichy Belarus **42** G9
Drwęca *r.* Poland **49** P2
Dry *r.* Australia **148** B2
Dryanovo Bulg. **58** G6
Dryazhno Rus. Fed. **43** J3
Dry Bay U.S.A. **166** B3
Dryberry Lake Canada **168** A3
Drybin Belarus **43** M7
Dry Cimarron *r.* U.S.A. **178** B4
Dryden Canada **168** A3
Dryden *NY* U.S.A. **177** I3
Dryden *VA* U.S.A. **176** C9
Dry Fork *r.* U.S.A. **180** F4
Drygalski Fjord *inlet* S. Georgia **205** [inset]
Drygalski Ice Tongue Antarctica **223** L1
Drygalski Island Antarctica **223** G2
Drygarn Fawr *hill* U.K. **47** I11
Dry Harts *r.* S. Africa **133** I4
Dry Lake U.S.A. **183** J5
Dry Lake *l.* U.S.A. **182** G2
Dry Ridge U.S.A. **176** A7
Drysa *r.* Belarus **43** I6
Drysdale *r.* Australia **150** D2
Drysdale Island Australia **148** B1
Drysdale River National Park Australia **150** D2
Drysvyaty Vozyera *l.* Belarus/Lith. *see* **Drūkšių ežeras**
Dry Tortugas *is* U.S.A. **175** D7
Drzewica Poland **49** R4
Dschang Cameroon **125** H5
Dua *r.* Dem. Rep. Congo **126** D4
Dūāb *r.* Iran **100** B3
Du'an China **87** D4
also known as Anyang
Duancun China *see* **Wuxiang**
Duaringa Australia **149** F4
Duars *reg.* India **97** F4
Duarte, Pico *mt.* Dom. Rep. **187** F3
formerly known as Trujillo, Monte
Ḍubā Saudi Arabia **104** A2
Dubai U.A.E. **105** F2
also spelt Dubayy
Dubakella Mountain U.S.A. **182** A1
Dubăsari Moldova **58** K1
formerly spelt Dubesar' *or* Dubossary
Dubăsari *prov.* Moldova **53** H2
Dubawnt *r.* Canada **167** L2
Dubawnt Lake Canada **167** K2
Dubayy U.A.E. *see* **Dubai**
Dubbagh, Jabal ad *mt.* Saudi Arabia **104** A2
Dubbo Australia **147** F3
Dube *r.* Liberia **124** D5
Dübendorf Switz. **51** O5
Dübener Heide *park* Germany **49** J4
Dubesar' Moldova *see* **Dubăsari**
Dubets Rus. Fed. **43** T3
Dubičiai Lith. **42** F7
Dubinës, Maja e *mt.* Albania **58** A6
Dubingiai Lith. **42** G6
Dublán Mex. **184** D2
Dublin Canada **172** F2

▶**Dublin** Rep. of Ireland **47** F10
Capital of the Republic of Ireland. Also known as Baile Átha Cliath.

Dublin *GA* U.S.A. **175** D5
Dublin *VA* U.S.A. **176** E8
Dubna *r.* Latvia **42** H5
Dubna *Moskovskaya Oblast'* Rus. Fed. **43** S5
Dubna *Tul'skaya Oblast'* Rus. Fed. **43** R7
Dubnica nad Váhom Slovakia **49** P7
Dubno Ukr. **41** C6
Dubois U.S.A. **180** D3
Du Bois U.S.A. **176** G4
Dubossary Moldova *see* **Dubăsari**
Dubovaya Roshcha Rus. Fed. **43** R8
Dubovka *Tul'skaya Oblast'* Rus. Fed. **43** T8
Dubovka *Volgogradskaya Oblast'* Rus. Fed. **41** H6
Dubovoye, Ozero *l.* Rus. Fed. **43** V6
Dubovskoye Rus. Fed. **41** G7
Dübrar Pass Azer. **107** G2
Dubréka Guinea **124** B4
Dubris U.K. *see* **Dover**
Dubrovichi Rus. Fed. **43** U7
Dubrovka *Bryanskaya Oblast'* Rus. Fed. **43** O8
Dubrovka *Pskovskaya Oblast'* Rus. Fed. **43** J5
Dubrovka *Pskovskaya Oblast'* Rus. Fed. **43** K4
Dubrovnik Croatia **56** K6
historically known as Ragusa
Dubrovytsya Ukr. **41** C6
formerly known as Dombrovitsa
Dubrowna Belarus **43** L7
Dubun Kazakh. **103** J4
Dubuque U.S.A. **174** B3
Dubysa *r.* Lith. **42** E6
Duc de Gloucester, Îles du *is* Fr. Polynesia **221** I7
English form Duke of Gloucester Islands
Ducey France **50** E4
Duchang China **87** F2
Duchateau Entrance *sea chan.* P.N.G. **149** G1
Ducherow Germany **49** K2
Duchesne U.S.A. **183** N1
Duchesne *r.* U.S.A. **183** O1
Duchess Australia **148** C4
Duchess Canada **167** I5
Ducie Island Pitcairn Is **221** J7
Duck *r.* U.S.A. **174** C4
Duck Bay Canada **167** K4
Duck Creek *r.* Australia **150** B4
Duck Lake Canada **167** J4
Duck Valley Indian Reservation *res.* U.S.A. **180** C4
Duckwater U.S.A. **183** I3
Duckwater Peak U.S.A. **183** I3
Đuc Trong Vietnam **79** E6
Duda *r.* Col. **198** C4
Duderstadt Germany **48** H4
Dudeştii Vechi Romania **58** B2
Dudhi India **97** D4
Dudinka Rus. Fed. **39** I3
Dudley U.K. **47** J11
Dudleyville U.S.A. **183** N9
Dudna *r.* India **94** C2
Dudorovskiy Rus. Fed. **43** Q8
Duduza S. Africa **133** M3
Duékoué Côte d'Ivoire **124** D5
Duen, Bukit *vol.* Indon. **76** C3
Dueré Brazil **202** B4
Duerna *r.* Spain **54** F2
Duero *r.* Spain **55** E3
also spelt Douro (Portugal)
Dufault, Lac *l.* Canada **173** O2
Dufferin, Cape Canada **168** E1
Duffer Peak U.S.A. **180** C4
Duffield U.S.A. **176** C9
Duff Islands Solomon Is **145** F2
Duffreboy, Lac *l.* Canada **169** G1
Dufftown U.K. **46** I6
Dufourspitze *mt.* Italy/Switz. **56** A3
Dufrost Canada **167** L5
Dugab Uzbek. **103** F5
also spelt Dughoba
Dugald *r.* Australia **149** D3
Duga Resa Croatia **56** H3
Duga-Zapadnaya, Mys *c.* Rus. Fed. **39** O4
Dughdash *mts* Saudi Arabia **109** H8
Dughoba Uzbek. *see* **Dugab**
Dugi Otok *i.* Croatia **56** H4
Dugi Rat Croatia **56** I5
Dugna Rus. Fed. **43** R7
Dugopolje Croatia **56** I5
Dugo Selo Croatia **56** I3
Dugui Qarag China **85** F4
Düğüncübaşı Turkey **58** I7
Dugway U.S.A. **183** L1
Du He *r.* China **87** D1

index

D E

Duhūn Tārsū *mts* Chad/Libya **120** C4
Duida-Marahuaca, Parque Nacional *nat. park* Venez. **199** E4
Duifken Point Australia **149** D2
Duisburg Germany **48** D4
Duitama Col. **198** C3
Dujiangyan China **86** B2
formerly known as Guanxian
Dukan Dam Iraq **107** F3
Dukat Rus. Fed. **39** P3
Dukat *mt.* Yugo. **58** D6
Dukathole S. Africa **133** K7
Duke Island U.S.A. **166** I5
Duke of Clarence *atoll* Tokelau *see* Nukunonu
Duke of Gloucester Islands Fr. Polynesia *see* Duc de Gloucester, Îles du
Duke of York *atoll* Tokelau *see* Atafu
Duk Fadiat Sudan **128** A3
Duk Faiwil Sudan **128** A3
Dukhān Qatar **105** E2
Dukhnah Saudi Arabia **104** C2
Dukhovnitskoye Rus. Fed. **102** B1
Dukhovshchina Rus. Fed. **43** N6
Dukhovshehinskaya Vozvyshennost' *hills* Rus. Fed. **43** M6
Duki Rus. Fed. **82** D2
Duki *r.* Rus. Fed. **82** D2
Dukku Nigeria **125** H4
Dukla Poland **49** S6
Dukou China *see* Panzhihua
Dūkštas Lith. **42** H4
Dukwe Botswana **131** E4
Dulaanhaan Mongolia **85** E1
Dulac U.S.A. **175** D6
Dulan China **84** C4
also known as Qagan Us
Dulawan Phil. *see* Datu Piang
Dulce *r.* Arg. **204** E3
Dulce *r.* Spain **55** I4
Dulce U.S.A. **181** F5
Dulce, Golfo *b.* Costa Rica **186** C5
Dulce Nombre de Culmí Hond. **186** B4
Dulcinea Chile **204** C2
Dul'durga Rus. Fed. **85** G1
Dulgalakh *r.* Rus. Fed. **39** N3
Dûlgopol Bulg. **58** I5
Dulhunty *r.* Australia **149** D1
Dulishi Hu *salt l.* China **89** C5
Dulit, Pegunungan *mts* Sarawak Malaysia **77** F2
Duliu Jiang *r.* China **87** D3
Duljugan Point Phil. **74** C4
Dullabchara India **97** G4
Dullstroom S. Africa **133** O2
Dülmen Germany **48** E4
Dulovka Rus. Fed. **43** J4
Dulovo Bulg. **58** I5
Duluth U.S.A. **174** A2
Dulyapino Rus. Fed. **43** V4
Dūmā Syria **109** H4
Dumago Bone National Park Indon. **75** B2
Dumaguete Phil. **74** B4
Dumai Indon. **76** C2
Dumanquilas Bay Phil. **74** B5
Dumaran *i.* Phil. **74** B4
Dumarchen *i.* Indon. **75** C1
Dumaresq *r.* Australia **147** F2
Dumas *AR* U.S.A. **174** B5
Dumas *TX* U.S.A. **179** B5
Dumayr Syria **107** H3
Dumayr, Jabal *mts* Syria **109** H4
Dumbarton U.K. **46** H8
Dumbe S. Africa **133** O4
Dumbéa New Caledonia **145** F4
Dumbier *mt.* Slovakia **49** Q7
Dumbleyung Australia **151** B7
Dumbleyung, Lake *salt flat* Australia **151** B7
Dumbo Cameroon **125** H5
Dumbrăveni Romania **58** F2
Dumbrăveni Romania **58** I3
Dumbrăvita Romania **58** G3
Dumdum *i.* Indon. **75** C1
Dum Duma India **97** G4
Dumeşti Romania **58** I2
Dumfries U.K. **47** I8
Duminichi *Kaluzhskaya Oblast'* Rus. Fed. **43** Q8
Duminichi *Kaluzhskaya Oblast'* Rus. Fed. **43** Q8
Dumitra Romania **58** F1
Dumka India **97** E4
Dummagudem India **94** C2
Dümmer, Naturpark *nature res.* Germany **48** F3
Dummerstorf Germany **49** J2
Dumoga Indon. **75** C2
Dumoine, r. Canada **168** E4
Dumoine, Lac *l.* Canada **173** Q4
Dumont d'Urville *research station* Antarctica **223** J2
Dumraon India **97** E4
Dumsuk *i.* Saudi Arabia **104** C4
Dumyāt Egypt **121** F2
English form Damietta
Dumyāt *governorate* Egypt **108** C6
Dumyāt, Masabb *est.* Egypt **108** C6
Duna *r.* Hungary **49** P9 *see* Danube
Dünaburg Latvia *see* Daugavpils
Dunaföldvár Hungary **49** P9

Dunaj *r.* Slovakia **49** O8 *see* Danube
Dunajec *r.* Poland **49** R5
Dunajská Streda Slovakia **49** O8
Dunajs'ki Plavni *nature res.* Ukr. **58** K3
Dunakeszi Hungary **49** Q8
Dunanbay Kazakh. *see* Dunenbay
Dunany Point Rep. of Ireland **47** F10
Dunapataj Hungary **49** Q9
Dunărea *r.* Romania **58** J3 *see* Danube
Dunării, Delta Romania *see* Danube Delta
Dunaszekcső Hungary **49** P9
Dunaújváros Hungary **49** P9
formerly known as Sztálinváros
Dunav *r.* Bulg./Croatia/Yugo. **58** H5 *see* Danube
Dunavtsi Bulg. **58** D5
Dunay Rus. Fed. **90** C3
Dunay *r.* Ukr. **58** J3 *see* Danube
Dunay, Ostrova *is* Rus. Fed. **39** M2
Dunayivtsi Ukr. **41** C6
Dunback N.Z. **153** E13
Dunbar Australia **149** D3
Dunbar *PA* U.S.A. **176** F6
Dunbar *WI* U.S.A. **172** E5
Dunbar *WV* U.S.A. **176** D7
Dunbeath U.K. **46** I5
Dunblane Canada **166** F5
Duncan *AZ* U.S.A. **181** E6
Duncan *OK* U.S.A. **179** C5
Duncan, Lake Canada **168** D2
Duncan Lake *l. N.W.T.* Canada **167** G5
Duncannon U.S.A. **177** H5
Duncan Passage India **95** G4
Duncansby Head U.K. **46** I5
Duncan Town Bahamas **186** E2
Dundaga Latvia **42** D4
Dundalk Rep. of Ireland **47** F9
also called Dún Dealgan
Dundalk U.S.A. **177** I6
Dundalk Bay Rep. of Ireland **47** F10
Dundas Canada **173** N7
Dundas Greenland **165** M2
also known as Uummannaq
Dundas, Lake *salt flat* Australia **151** C7
Dundas Island Canada **166** D4
Dundas Nature Reserve Australia **151** C7
Dundas Peninsula Canada **165** H2
Dundas Strait Australia **148** A1
Dundbürd Mongolia **85** F2
Dún Dealgan Rep. of Ireland *see* Dundalk
Dundee S. Africa **133** O5
Dundee U.K. **46** J7
Dundee U.S.A. **177** I3
Dundgovĭ *prov.* Mongolia **85** E2
Dund Hot China **85** H3
also known as Xulun Hoh Qi or Zhenglan Qi
Dundoo Australia **149** E5
Dundrum Bay U.K. **47** G9
Dundwa Range *mts* India/Nepal **97** D4
Dune, Lac *l.* Canada **169** F1
Dunedin N.Z. **153** E13
Dunedin U.S.A. **175** D6
Dunenbay Kazakh. **103** J2
also spelt Dönenbay; formerly spelt Dunanbay
Dunfermline U.K. **46** I7
Dungannon U.K. **47** F9
Dún Garbhán Rep. of Ireland *see* Dungarvan
Dungargarh India **96** B3
Dungarpur India **96** B5
Dungarvan Rep. of Ireland **47** E11
also spelt Dún Garbhán
Dungeness *hd* U.K. **47** M13
Dungeness, Punta *pt* Arg. **205** C9
Dungu Dem. Rep. Congo **126** F4
Dungun Malaysia **76** C1
formerly known as Kuala Dungun
Dungunab Sudan **104** B3
Dunhou China *see* Ji'an
Dunhua China **82** C4
Dunhuang China **84** B3
Dunkeld Australia **149** F5
Dunkeld U.K. **46** I7
Dunkerque France *see* Dunkirk
Dunkirk France **51** I1
Dunkirk U.S.A. **176** F3
Dunkwa Ghana **125** E5
Dún Laoghaire Rep. of Ireland **47** F10
Dunlap *IA* U.S.A. **178** D3
Dunlap *IN* U.S.A. **172** H9
Dunlap *TN* U.S.A. **174** C5
Dunluce *tourist site* U.K. **47** F8
Dunmanway Rep. of Ireland **47** C12
Dunmarra Australia **148** B3
Dunmore *PA* U.S.A. **177** J4
Dunmore *WV* U.S.A. **176** F7
Dunmore Town Bahamas **186** D1
Dunn U.S.A. **174** E5
Dunnet Head U.K. **46** I5
Dunnigan U.S.A. **182** C3
Dunning U.S.A. **178** B3
Dunn Rock Nature Reserve Australia **151** B7
Dunnville Canada **173** N8
Dunolly Australia **147** D4
Dunphy U.S.A. **183** H1
Dunragit U.K. see Dunkerque
Dunsandel N.Z. **153** G11
Dunsborough Australia **151** A7
Dunsmuir U.S.A. **180** B4
Dunstan Mountains N.Z. **153** D13
Duntroon N.Z. **153** E12
Dunvegan U.K. **46** F6
Dunvegan Lake Canada **167** J2
Dunyapur Pak. **101** G4
Duobukur *r.* China **85** J1
Duolun China **85** H3
also known as Dolonnur
Dupado India **94** C3
Dupang Ling *mts* China **87** D3
Duparquet Canada **173** N2
Duparquet, Lac *l.* Canada **173** N2
Duperré Alg. *see* Aïn Defla
Dupnitsa Bulg. **58** E6
formerly known as Stanke Dimitrov
Dupree U.S.A. **178** B2
Dupuy, Cape Australia **150** A4
Duque de Bragança Angola *see* Calandula
Duque de Caxias Brazil **207** J9
Duque de York, Isla *i.* Chile **205** B8
Duquette U.S.A. **172** A4
Dura *r.* Eth. **128** C2
Dura West Bank **108** G6
Durack *r.* Australia **150** D3
Durack Range *hills* Australia **150** D3
Durağan Turkey **106** C2
Durance *r.* France **51** K9
Durand *MI* U.S.A. **173** J8
Durand *WI* U.S.A. **172** B6
Duranes *r.* Indon. **75** B3
Durango *Baja California Norte* Mex. **183** O9
Durango *Durango* Mex. **184** D3
Durango *state* Mex. **184** D3
Durango Spain **55** I1
Durango U.S.A. **181** F5
Durani *reg.* Afgh. **101** F4
Dúrankulak Bulg. **58** J5
Duranno, Monte *mt.* Italy **56** E2
Durant *IA* U.S.A. **172** B9
Durant *MS* U.S.A. **175** B5
Durant *OK* U.S.A. **179** C5
Duratón *r.* Spain **54** G3
Durazno Arg. **204** C3
Durazno Uruguay **204** F4
Durazzo Albania *see* Durrës
Durban S. Africa **133** P6

Durban-Corbières France **51** I10
Durbanville S. Africa **132** C10
Durbin U.S.A. **176** F7
Durbuy Belgium **51** L2
Đurđevac Croatia **56** J2
Durdura, Raas *pt* Somalia **128** F2
Düre China **84** A2
Düren Germany **48** D5
Düren Iran **100** D3
Duren, Kūh-e *mt.* Iran **100** D3
Durg India **97** D5
Durgapur Bangl. **97** F4
Durgapur India **97** E5
Durham Canada **173** M6
Durham U.K. **47** K9
Durham *CA* U.S.A. **182** C2
Durham *NC* U.S.A. **174** E5
Durham *NH* U.S.A. **177** O2
Durham Downs Australia **146** D1
Durhi *well* Eth. **128** D3
Duri Indon. **76** C2
Durlas Rep. of Ireland *see* Thurles
Durleşti Moldova **58** J1
Durmitor *mt.* Yugo. **58** A5
also known as Bobotov Kuk
Durmitor *nat. park* Yugo. **58** A5
Durness U.K. **46** H4
Durocortorum France *see* Reims
Durostorum Bulg. *see* Silistra
Durovernum U.K. *see* Canterbury
Durrës Albania **58** A7
formerly spelt Durazzo; historically known as Dyrrhachium or Epidamnus
Dursey Island Rep. of Ireland **47** B12
Dursunbey Turkey **106** B3
Durtal France **50** F5
Duru China *see* Wuchuan
Duru *r.* Dem. Rep. Congo **126** F4
Duru *reg.* Oman **105** G3
Dürüb Iran **101** E3
Durukhsi Somalia **128** E2
Durusu Gölü *l.* Turkey **58** J7
Durūz, Jabal ad *mt.* Syria **109** H5
D'Urville, Tanjung *pt* Indon. **73** I7
D'Urville Island N.Z. **152** H8
Durzab Afgh. **101** F3
Dusetos Lith. **42** G6
Dushan China **87** D3

▶**Dushanbe** Tajik. **101** G2
Capital of Tajikistan. Formerly known as Stalinabad.

Dushanzi China **88** D2
also known as Maytag
Dushore U.S.A. **177** I4
Dusia *l.* Lith. **42** E7
Dusky Sound *inlet* N.Z. **153** A13
Dussejour, Cape Australia **150** E2
Düsseldorf Germany **48** D4
Dusti Tajik. **101** G2
formerly known as Pyandzh
Dustlik Uzbek. **103** G4
Dusty U.S.A. **180** C3
Duszniki-Zdrój Poland **49** N5
Dutch East Indies *country* Asia *see* Indonesia
Dutch Guiana *country* S. America *see* Suriname
Dutch Mountain U.S.A. **183** K1
Dutch New Guinea *prov.* Indon. *see* Irian Jaya
Dutch West Indies *terr.* West Indies *see* Netherlands Antilles
Dutsan-Wai Nigeria **125** H4
Dutse Nigeria **125** H4
Dutsin-Ma Nigeria **125** G3
Dutton *r.* Australia **149** D4
Dutton Canada **173** L8
Dutton, Lake *salt flat* Australia **146** C2
Dutton, Mount U.S.A. **183** L3
Duval Canada **167** J5
Duved Sweden **44** K3
Duvergé Dom. Rep. **187** F3
Duvert, Lac *l.* Canada **169** G1
Duvno Bos.-Herz. *see* Tomislavgrad
Duweihin *well* Saudi Arabia **100** D5
Duweihin, Khor *b.* Saudi Arabia/U.A.E. **105** E2
Duwin Iraq **107** F3
Duyinzeik Myanmar **78** B4
Duyun China **87** C3
Duzab Pak. **101** E5
Düzce Turkey **106** B2
Duzdab Iran *see* Zāhedān
Dvaretsa Belarus **42** H9
Dve Mogili Bulg. **58** G5
Dviete Latvia **42** H5
Dvinitsa *r.* Rus. Fed. **43** V2
Dvinsk Latvia *see* Daugavpils
Dvinskaya Guba *g.* Rus. Fed. **40** F2
Dvin'ye, Ozero *l.* Rus. Fed. **43** M5
Dvor Croatia **56** I3
Dvoriki Rus. Fed. **43** T5
Dvoryanka Rus. Fed. **90** B2
Dvoyni *r.* Rus. Fed. **43** U6
Dwangwa Malawi **129** B8
Dwarka India **96** A5
Dwarsberg S. Africa **133** K1
Dwellingup Australia **151** B7
Dwesa Nature Reserve S. Africa **133** M9
Dweshula S. Africa **133** O7
Dwight U.S.A. **172** E9
Dwingelderveld, Nationaal Park *nat. park* Neth. **48** D3
Dwyka S. Africa **132** H9
Dwyka *r.* S. Africa **132** F10
D'yakonovo Rus. Fed. **43** V3
Dyanev Turkm. **103** E5
also spelt Danew; formerly spelt Deynau
Dyankovo Bulg. **58** H5
Dyat'kovo Rus. Fed. **43** P8
Dyce U.K. **46** J6
Dyer, Cape Canada **165** M3
Dyer Bay Canada **173** L5
Dyer Plateau Antarctica **222** T2
Dyersburg U.S.A. **174** B4
Dyersville U.S.A. **172** B8
Dyfi *r.* U.K. **47** I11
also spelt Dovey
Dyje *r.* Austria/Czech Rep. **49** N7

▶**Dzaoudzi** Mayotte **129** E8
Capital of Mayotte.

Dzaudzhikau Rus. Fed. *see* Vladikavkaz
Dzavhan *prov.* Mongolia **84** B1
Dzavhan Gol *r.* Mongolia **84** B1
Džbán *mts* Czech Rep. **49** K5
Dzegstey Mongolia **84** D2
Dzeni Latvia **42** H4
Dzerzhinsk Belarus *see* Dzyarzhynsk
Dzerzhinsk Rus. Fed. **40** G4
Dzerzhinskoye Kazakh. *see* Kabanbay
Dzhagdy, Khrebet *mts* Rus. Fed. **82** C1
Dzhaki-Unakhta Yakbyyana, Khrebet *mts* Rus. Fed. **82** D2
Dzhaksy Kazakh. *see* Zhaksy
Dzhakul', Gora *mt.* Rus. Fed. **84** B1
Dzhalagash Kazakh. **103** F3
also spelt Zhalaghash
Dzhalal-Abad Kyrg. *see* Jalal-Abad
Dzhalal-Abadskaya Oblast' *admin. div.* Kyrg. *see* Jalal-Abad
Dzhalil' Rus. Fed. **40** J5
Dzhalinda Rus. Fed. **82** A1
Dzhaltyr Kazakh. *see* Zhaltyr
Dzhambeyty Kazakh. *see* Zhympity
Dzhambul Kazakh. *see* Taraz
Dzhambulskaya Oblast' *admin. div.* Kazakh. *see* Zhambylskaya Oblast'
Dzhanga Turkm. **102** C4
Dzhangala Kazakh. **102** B2
formerly known as Kisykkamys
Dzhangel'dy Uzbek. **103** E4
formerly known as Jangeldi; formerly spelt Dzhankel'dy or Dzhingil'dy
Dzhankoy Ukr. **41** E7
Dzhansugurov Kazakh. **103** I3
also spelt Zhansügirov
Dzhanybek Kazakh. **102** A2
also known as Zhänibek
Dzharkent Kazakh. *see* Zharkent
Dzharkurgan Uzbek. **103** F5
Dzhebariki-Khaya Rus. Fed. **39** N3
Dzhebel Bulg. **58** G7
Dzhebel Turkm. **102** C5
Dzheksona, Ostrov *i.* Rus. Fed. **38** F1
English form Jackson Island
Dzhelondi Tajik. *see* Dzhilandy
Dzheltulak Rus. Fed. **82** B1
Dzhergalan Kyrg. *see* Jyrgalang
Dzhetygara Kazakh. *see* Zhitikara
Dzhetysay Kazakh. *see* Zhetysay
Dzheykhun Turkm. **103** E5
also spelt Jeyhun; formerly known as Farab-Pristan'
Dzhezdy Kazakh. *see* Zhezdy
Dzhezkazgan Kazakh. *see* Zhezkazgan
Dzhida Rus. Fed. **85** F1
Dzhida *r.* Rus. Fed. **84** E1
Dzhidinskiy, Khrebet *mts* Mongolia/Rus. Fed. **84** D1
Dzhigirbent Turkm. **103** E4
Dzhilandy Tajik. **101** H2
also spelt Dzhelondi or Jelondi
Dzhingil'dy Uzbek. *see* Dzhangel'dy
Dzhirgatal' Tajik. *see* Jirgatal
Dzhizak Uzbek. *see* Jizzakh
also spelt Jizzakh
Dzhizak Oblast *admin. div.* Uzbek. *see* Dzhizakskaya Oblast'
Dzhizakskaya Oblast' *admin. div.* Uzbek. **103** F5
English form Dzhizak Oblast; also known as Jizzakh Wiloyati
Dzhokhar Ghala Rus. Fed. *see* Groznyy
Dzhubga Rus. Fed. **41** F7
Dzhugdzhur, Khrebet *mts* Rus. Fed. **39** N4
Dzhul'fa Azer. *see* Culfa
Dzhuma Uzbek. **103** F5
also spelt Juma
Dzhungarskiy Alatau, Khrebet *mts* China/Kazakh. **88** D2
Dzhurun Kazakh. *see* Zhuryn
Dzhusaly Kazakh. **103** F3
also spelt Zhosaly
Działdowo Poland **49** R2
Dzibalchén Mex. **185** H5
Dzierzoniów Poland **49** N5
Dzilam de Bravo Mex. **185** H4
Dzioua Alg. **123** G2
Dzisna Belarus **43** J6
Dzitás Mex. **185** F5
Dzitva *r.* Belarus **42** G8
Dzodze Ghana **125** F5
Dzogsool Mongolia **85** E2
Dzöölön Mongolia **84** C1
Dzūkija *nat. park* Lith. **42** F7
Dzungaria *reg.* China *see* Junggar Pendi
Dzungarian Gate *pass* China/Kazakh. **88** C2
also known as Alataw Shankou
Dzur Mongolia **84** B1
Dzüünbayan Mongolia **85** F2
Dzüünharaa Mongolia **85** F1
Dzuunmod Mongolia **85** E1
Dzüyl Mongolia **84** B2
formerly known as Tonhil
Dzyaniskavichy Belarus **42** H9
Dzyarzhnya *r.* Belarus **43** M8
Dzyarechyn Belarus **42** F9
Dzyarzhynsk Belarus **42** I9
also spelt Dzerzhinsk; formerly known as Kaydanovo
Dzyatlava Belarus **42** G9
Dzyatlavichy Belarus **42** H9
Dzyerkawshchyna Belarus **42** I6

↓ E

Eabamet Lake Canada **168** C3
Eads U.S.A. **178** B4
Eagar U.S.A. **183** O7
Eagle *r.* Canada **169** J3
Eagle *AK* U.S.A. **166** A1
Eagle *CO* U.S.A. **180** F5
Eagle Cap *mt.* U.S.A. **180** C3
Eagle Crags *mt.* U.S.A. **183** G6
Eagle Creek *r.* Canada **167** J4
Eagle Lake *CA* U.S.A. **182** C1
Eagle Lake *ME* U.S.A. **174** G2
Eagle Mountain U.S.A. **183** I8
Eagle Mountain *hill* U.S.A. **174** B2
Eagle Pass U.S.A. **179** B6
Eagle Passage Falkland Is **205** F9
Eagle Peak U.S.A. **181** F7
Eagle Plain Canada **164** F3
Eaglesham Canada **167** G4
Eagle Tail Mountains U.S.A. **183** K8
Eagle Village U.S.A. **166** A1
Eap *i.* Micronesia *see* Yap
Earaheedy Australia **151** C5
Earl Falls Canal Pak. **101** H4
Earlimart U.S.A. **182** E6
Earl Mountains N.Z. **153** B13
Earlton Canada **173** N3
Earn *r.* U.K. **46** I7
Earn, Loch *l.* U.K. **46** H7
Earnscleugh N.Z. **153** D13
Earnslaw, Mount N.Z. **153** C12
also known as Pikirakatahi
Earp U.S.A. **183** J7
Earth U.S.A. **179** B5
Easley U.S.A. **174** D5
East, Mount *hill* Australia **151** C6
East Alligator *r.* Australia **148** A1
East Antarctica *reg.* Antarctica **223** H1
East Ararat U.S.A. **177** J4
East Aurora U.S.A. **176** G3
East Baines *r.* Australia **148** A2
East Bay U.S.A. **175** B6
East Bay *inlet* U.S.A. **175** I6
East Bengal *country* Asia *see* Bangladesh
East Berlin U.S.A. **177** I6
Eastbourne N.Z. **152** I9
Eastbourne U.K. **47** M13
East Brady U.S.A. **176** F5
East Branch Clarion River Reservoir U.S.A. **176** G4
East Branch U.S.A. **177** J4
East Caicos *i.* Turks and Caicos Is **187** F2
East Cape N.Z. **152** M5
East Cape Rus. Fed. *see* Dezhneva, Mys
East Carbon City U.S.A. **183** N2
East Chicago U.S.A. **172** G9
East China Sea N. Pacific Ocean **81** L6
also known as Dong Hai
East Coast Bays N.Z. **152** I4
East Dereham U.K. **47** M11
East Dubuque U.S.A. **172** C8
Eastend Canada **167** I5
Easter Group *is* Australia **151** A6

▶**Easter Island** S. Pacific Ocean **221** K7
Part of Chile. Also known as Pascua, Isla de.

Eastern *admin. reg.* Ghana **125** E5
Eastern *prov.* Kenya **128** C5
Eastern *prov.* Sierra Leone **124** C4
Eastern *prov.* Zambia **127** F8
Eastern Cape *prov.* S. Africa **133** K8
Eastern Desert Egypt **121** G3
also known as Sahara el Sharqīya
Eastern Equatoria *state* Sudan **128** B3
Eastern Ghats *mts* India **94** C4

▶**Eastern Island** *HI* U.S.A. **220** G4
Most northerly point of Oceania.

Eastern Lesser Sunda Islands *prov.* Indon. *see* Nusa Tenggara Timur
Eastern Nara *canal* Pak. **101** G5
Eastern Samoa *terr.* S. Pacific Ocean *see* American Samoa
Eastern Sayan *mts* Rus. Fed. *see* Vostochnyy Sayan
Eastern Taurus *plat.* Turkey *see* Güneydoğu Toroslar
Eastern Transvaal *prov.* S. Africa *see* Mpumalanga
Easterville Canada **167** L4
East Falkland *i.* Falkland Is **205** F9
East Frisian Islands Germany **48** E3
also known as Ostfriesische Inseln
East Grand Forks U.S.A. **178** D2
East Grand Rapids U.S.A. **172** H8
Easthampton U.S.A. **177** M3
East Hampton U.S.A. **177** M4
East Hartford U.S.A. **177** M4
East Haydon Australia **149** D3
East Holden U.S.A. **177** Q1
East Island P.N.G. **149** G1
East Jamaica U.S.A. **177** M2
East Jordan U.S.A. **173** H5
East Kazakhstan Oblast *admin. div.* Kazakh. *see* Vostochnyy Kazakhstan
East Kilbride U.K. **46** H8
East Lamma Channel Hong Kong China **87** [inset]
also known as Tung Pok Liu Hoi Hap
Eastland U.S.A. **179** C5
East Lansing U.S.A. **173** I8
Eastleigh U.K. **47** K13
East Linton U.K. **46** J8
East Liverpool U.S.A. **176** E5
East London S. Africa **133** L10
also known as Oos-Londen
East Longmeadow U.S.A. **177** M3
Eastmain Canada **168** E2
Eastmain *r.* Canada **168** E2
Eastman U.S.A. **175** D5
East Middlebury U.S.A. **177** L2
East Millinocket U.S.A. **174** G2
East Naples U.S.A. **175** D7
Easton *CA* U.S.A. **182** E5
Easton *PA* U.S.A. **177** J5
Easton *MD* U.S.A. **177** I7
East Pakistan *country* Asia *see* Bangladesh
East Park Reservoir U.S.A. **182** B2
East Peoria U.S.A. **172** D10
East Point Canada **169** I4
Eastport *ME* U.S.A. **174** I2
Eastport *MI* U.S.A. **172** H5
East Range *mts* U.S.A. **183** H1
East Retford U.K. *see* Retford
East Ridge U.S.A. **174** C5
East St Louis U.S.A. **174** B4
East Sea N. Pacific Ocean *see* Japan, Sea of
East Shoal Lake Canada **167** L5
East Siberian Sea Rus. Fed. **39** Q2
also known as Vostochno-Sibirskoye More
East Side Canal *r.* U.S.A. **182** E6
East Tavaputs Plateau U.S.A. **183** O2
East Tawas U.S.A. **173** J6

▶**East Timor** *terr.* Asia **75** C5
Former Portuguese territory. Part of Indonesia 1976–1999, awaiting independence. Formerly known as Portuguese Timor or Timor Timur.
asia [countries] ➡➡ 64–67

East Tons *r.* India **97** E4
East Troy U.S.A. **172** E8
East Verde *r.* U.S.A. **183** M7
Eastville Canada *see* Vanier
East Walker *r.* U.S.A. **182** E3
East York Canada **173** N7
Eateringinna Creek *watercourse* Australia **148** B5
Eaton *CO* U.S.A. **180** F4
Eaton *OH* U.S.A. **176** A6
Eatonia Canada **167** I5
Eaton Rapids U.S.A. **173** I8
Eatonton U.S.A. **175** D5
Eatonville U.S.A. **180** B3
Eau Claire U.S.A. **172** B6
Eau Claire *r.* U.S.A. **172** B6
Eauripik *atoll* Micronesia **73** J5
also spelt Eaurypyg
Eaurypyg *atoll* Micronesia *see* Eauripik
Eauze France **50** G8
Ebagoola Australia **149** D2
Eban Nigeria **125** G4
Ebano Mex. **185** F4
Ebbw Vale U.K. **47** I12
Ebebiyin Equat. Guinea **125** I6
Ebeltoft Denmark **45** J4
Ebenerde Namibia **130** C5
Ebensburg U.S.A. **176** G5
Ebensee Austria **49** L9
Eberswalde-Finow Germany **49** K3
Ebetsu Japan **90** G3
Ebian China **86** B2
also known as Shaping
Ebino Japan **91** B8
Ebi Nor *salt l.* China *see* Ebinur Hu

Ebinur Hu *salt l.* China **88** C2
Ebla *tourist site* Syria **109** H2
Ebnat-Kappel Switz. **51** P5
Ebo Angola **127** B7
Ebola *r.* Dem. Rep. Congo **126** D4
Ebolowa Cameroon **125** H6
Ebony Namibia **130** B4
Ebonyi *state* Nigeria **125** H5
Ebre *r.* Spain *see* Ebro
Ebro *r.* Spain **55** L4
also spelt Ebre
Ebro, Embalse del *resr* Spain **54** H1
Eburacum U.K. *see* York
Ebusus *i.* Spain *see* Ibiza
Ecbatana Iran *see* Hamadān
Eccles U.S.A. **176** D8
Eceabat Turkey **59** H8
also known as Maydos
Echague Phil. **74** B2
Echarri-Aranaz Spain **55** I2
also known as Etxarri-Arantza
Ech Chélif Alg. **123** F1
also spelt Chlef; formerly known as El Asnam or Orléansville
Ech Cherita, Sebkhet *salt pan* Tunisia **57** C13
Echeng China *see* Ezhou
Echinades *i.* Greece **59** B10
Echinos Greece **58** F7
also spelt Ekhínos
Echizen-misaki *pt* Japan **91** D7
Echmiadzin Armenia *see* Ejmiatsin
Echo Bay *N.W.T.* Canada **167** G1
also known as Port Radium
Echo Bay *Ont.* Canada **168** C4
Echo Cliffs *esc.* U.S.A. **183** M5
Echoing *r.* Canada **167** M4
Échouani, Lac *l.* Canada **173** R3
Echternach Lux. **51** M3
Echuca Australia **147** E4
Écija Spain **54** F7
Ečka *Vojvodina, Srbija* Yugo. **58** B3
Eckernförde Germany **48** H1
Eckerman U.S.A. **173** H4
Eckerö Fin. **45** L3
Eckerö *i.* Fin. **42** L1
Eckman U.S.A. **176** D8
Eclipse Sound *sea chan.* Canada **165** K2
Ecoporanga Brazil **207** M5
Écrins, Parc National des *nat. park* France **51** M8

▶**Ecuador** *country* S. America **198** B5
southamerica [countries] ➡➡ 192–193
southamerica [contrasts] ➡➡ 194–195

Écueillé France **50** H5
Ed Eritrea **121** I6
Ed Sweden **45** J4
Eday *i.* U.K. **46** J4
Ed Da'ein Sudan **126** E2
Ed Dair, Jebel *mt.* Sudan **121** F6
Ed Damazin Sudan **128** B2
Ed Damer Sudan **121** G5
also spelt Ad Damir
Ed Debba Sudan **121** F5
Eddeki *well* Chad **120** C4
Eddies Cove Canada **169** J3
Ed Dueim Sudan **121** G6
also spelt Ad Duwaym
Eddystone Point Australia **147** F5
Eddyville U.S.A. **174** B4
Ede Neth. **48** C3
Ede Cameroon **125** H6
Edehon Lake Canada **167** L2
Edéia Brazil **206** D4
Eden Australia **147** F4
Eden *r.* U.K. **47** I9
Eden *NC* U.S.A. **176** F9
formerly known as Leaksville
Eden *TX* U.S.A. **179** C6
Edenburg S. Africa **133** J6
Edendale N.Z. **153** C14
Edendale S. Africa **133** O6
Edenderry Rep. of Ireland **47** E10
Edenhope Australia **146** D4
Edenton U.S.A. **177** I9
Edenvale S. Africa **133** M3
Edenville S. Africa **133** L4
Eder *r.* Germany **48** G4
Eder-Stausee *resr* Germany **51** O1
Edessa Greece **58** D8
also spelt Edhessa
Edessa Turkey *see* Şanlıurfa
Edevik Sweden **44** K3
Edfu Egypt *see* Idfu
Edgar Ranges *hills* Australia **150** C3
Edgartown U.S.A. **177** O4
Edgcumbe N.Z. **152** K5
Edgecumbe Island Solomon Is *see* Utupua
Edgefield U.S.A. **175** D5
Edge Island Svalbard *see* Edgeøya
Edgeøya *i.* Svalbard **38** C2
English form Edge Island
Edgerton Canada **167** I4
Edgerton *OH* U.S.A. **176** A4
Edgerton *WI* U.S.A. **176** H9
Edgewood U.S.A. **177** I6
Édhessa Greece *see* Edessa
Edievale N.Z. **153** D13
Edigan Rus. Fed. **88** F2
Édikel *well* Niger **125** H2
Edina U.S.A. **174** A3
Edinboro U.S.A. **176** E4
Edinburg *TX* U.S.A. **179** C7
Edinburg *VA* U.S.A. **176** G7

▶**Edinburgh** U.K. **46** I8
Capital of Scotland.

Edincik Turkey **59** I8
Edinet *Edinet* Moldova **41** D7
Edinet *prov.* Moldova **53** H2
Edingeni Malawi **129** B8
Edirne Turkey **106** A2
historically known as Adrianople or Adrianopolis
Edirne *prov.* Turkey **58** H8
Edisto *r.* U.S.A. **175** D5
Edith, Mount U.S.A. **180** E3
Edithburgh Australia **146** C3
Edith Cavell, Mount Canada **166** G4
Edith Ronne Land *ice feature* Antarctica *see* Ronne Ice Shelf
Edith Withnell, Lake *salt flat* Australia **151** C5
Edjeleh Libya **120** B4
Edjudina Australia **151** C6
Édjérir *watercourse* Mali **125** F2
Edmond U.S.A. **179** C5
Edmonds U.S.A. **180** B3
Edmonton Australia **149** E3

▶**Edmonton** Canada **167** H4
Provincial capital of Alberta.

Edmonton U.S.A. **174** C4
Edmundston Canada **169** G4
Edna U.S.A. **179** C6
Edo Japan *see* Tōkyō
Edo *state* Nigeria **125** G5
Edolo Italy **56** C2
Edom *reg.* Israel/Jordan **108** G7
Edremit Turkey **106** H3
historically known as Adramyttium
Edremit Körfezi *b.* Turkey **106** A3
historically known as Adramyttium, Gulf of
Edrengiyn Nuruu *mts* Mongolia **84** C2
Edsbro Sweden **45** L4

Edsbyn Sweden **45** K3
Edsele Sweden **44** L3
Edson Canada **167** G4
Eduardo Castex Arg. **204** D4
Eduni, Mount Canada **166** D1
Edward r. N.S.W. Australia **147** E3
Edward r. Qld Australia **149** D2
Edward, Lake Dem. Rep. Congo/Uganda **126** F5
  also known as Rutanzige, Lake; formerly known as Idi Amin Dada, Lake
Edward, Mount Antarctica **222** T1
Edwardesabad Pak. see Bannu
Edward Island Australia **148** B2
Edward Island Canada **172** E2
Edward River Aboriginal Reserve Australia **149** D2
Edwards U.S.A. **177** J1
Edwards Plateau U.S.A. **179** B6
Edwardsville U.S.A. **174** B4
Edward VIII Bay Antarctica **223** D2
Edward VII Peninsula Antarctica **223** N1
Edwin B. Forsythe National Wildlife Refuge nature res. U.S.A. **177** K6
Edzell Canada see Rae-Edzo
Eel r. U.S.A. **182** A1
Eel, South Fork r. U.S.A. **182** A1
Eendekuil S. Africa **132** C9
Eenzaamheid Pan salt pan S. Africa **132** E4
Eesti country Europe see Estonia
Efaté i. Vanuatu **145** F3
  also known as Vaté; formerly known as Sandwich Island
Efes tourist site Turkey see Ephesus
Effingham U.S.A. **174** B4
Eflâni Turkey **106** C2
Efsus Turkey see Afşin
Eftimie Murgu Romania **58** D4
Eg Mongolia **85** F1
Ega r. Spain **55** J2
Egadi, Isole is Sicilia Italy **57** D10
  English form Egadi Islands
Egadi Islands is Sicilia Italy see Egadi, Isole
Egan Range mts U.S.A. **183** J3
Eganville Canada **173** P5
Egbe Nigeria **125** G5
Egedesminde Greenland see Aasiaat
Egentliga Finland reg. Fin. see Varsinais-Suomi
Eger r. Germany **49** J5
Eger Hungary **49** R8
Egersund Norway **45** I4
Egerton, Mount hill Australia **151** B5
Eggenfelden Germany **49** J7
Egg Harbor U.S.A. **172** F5
Egg Harbor City U.S.A. **177** K6
Egg Lake Canada **167** J4
Eggum Norway **44** K1
Egilsstaðir Iceland **44** [inset] D2
Eğin Turkey see Kemaliye
Eginbula Australia **150** B4
Egindibulaq Kazakh. see Yegindybulak
Egindy Kazakh. **103** H2
Eğirdir Turkey **106** B3
Eğirdir Gölü l. Turkey **106** B3
Egiyn Gol r. Mongolia **84** D1
Egletons France **51** I7
Eglinton Island Canada **165** H2
Eglisau Switz. **51** O5
Egmont, Cape N.Z. **152** H7
Egmont, Mount vol. N.Z. see Taranaki, Mount
Egmont National Park N.Z. **152** I7
Egmont Village N.Z. **152** I7
Egua Col. **199** D3
Éguas r. Brazil **202** C5
Egvekinot Rus. Fed. **39** S3

▶Egypt country Africa **121** F3
  2nd most populous country in Africa.
  Known as Misr or Mudraya in Arabic; formerly known as United Arab Republic; historically known as Aegyptus.
  africa [countries] ▶▶ 114–117

Ehcel well Mali see Agous-n-Ehsel
Ehen Hudag China **84** D4
Ehime pref. Japan **91** C8
Ehingen (Donau) Germany **48** G7
Ehrenberg U.S.A. **183** J8
Ehrenberg Range hills Australia **148** A4
Eibar Spain **55** I1
Eibergen Neth. **48** D3
Eichstätt Germany **48** I7
Eide Norway **44** I1
Eidfjord Norway **45** I3
Eidsvåg Norway **44** J3
Eidsvold Australia **149** F5
Eidsvoll Norway **45** J3
Eifel hills Germany **48** D5
Eigg i. U.K. **46** F7
Eight Degree Channel India/Maldives **94** B5
Eighty Mile Beach Australia **150** C3
Eilat Israel **108** F8
  also spelt Elat
Eildon, Lake Australia **147** E4
Eildon State Park nature res. Australia **147** E4
Eileen Lake Canada **167** J2
Eilenburg Germany **49** J4
Eilerts de Haan, Natuurreservaat nature res. Suriname **199** G4
Eilerts de Haan Gebergte mts Suriname **199** G4
Eil Malk i. Palau **73** H5
  also known as Mecherchar
Einasleigh Australia **149** E3
Einasleigh r. Australia **149** D3
Einbeck Germany **48** G4
Eindhoven Neth. **48** C4
Eindpaal Namibia **132** D2
Einme Myanmar **78** A4
Einsiedeln Switz. **51** O5
Éire country Europe see Ireland, Republic of
Eiriosgaigh i. U.K. see Eriskay
Eiru r. Brazil **198** D6
Eirunepé Brazil **198** D6
Eisberg hill Germany **48** G4
Eiseb watercourse Namibia **130** D3
Eisenach Germany **48** H5
Eisenerz Austria **49** L8
Eisenerzer Alpen mts Austria **49** L8
Eisenhower, Mount Canada see Castle Mountain
Eisenhüttenstadt Germany **49** L3
Eisenstadt Austria **49** N8
Eišiškes Lith. **42** I7
Eistow N.Z. **152** J5
Eitape P.N.G. see Aitape
Eivinvik Norway **45** I3
Eivissa Spain see Ibiza
Eivissa i. Spain see Ibiza
Ejea de los Caballeros Spain **55** J2
Ejeda Madag. **131** [inset] J5
Ejin Horo Qi China see Altan Shiret
Ejin Qi China see Dalain Hob
Ej Jill, Sebkhet salt flat Mauritania **122** C3
Ejmiadzin Armenia see Ejmiatsin
Ejmiatsin Armenia **107** F2
  formerly spelt Echmiadzin or Ejmiadzin
Ejura Ghana **125** H5
Ekalaka U.S.A. **180** F3
Ekang Nigeria **125** H6
Ekangala S. Africa **133** M2
Ekata Gabon **126** B4

Ekawasaki Japan **91** C8
Ekenäs Fin. **45** M4
  also known as Tammisaari
Ekenäs Sweden **45** K4
Ekenäs skärgårds Nationalpark nat. park Fin. **45** M4
  also known as Tammisaaren Saariston Kansallispuisto
Ekerem Turkm. see Okarem
Eket Nigeria **125** G5
Eketahuna N.Z. **152** J8
Ekhinos Greece see Echinos
Ekhmîm Egypt see Akhmim
Ekibastuz Kazakh. **103** H2
Ekimchan Rus. Fed. **82** D1
Ekinyazi Turkey **109** K1
Ekiti state Nigeria **125** G5
Ekka Island Canada **166** F1
Ekoli Dem. Rep. Congo **126** D5
Ekonda Rus. Fed. **39** K3
Ekondo Titi Cameroon **125** H5
Ekostrovskaya Imandra, Ozero l. Rus. Fed. **44** P2
Ekouamou Congo **126** B4
Ekpoma Nigeria **125** G5
Eksere Turkey see Gündoğmuş
Ekshärad Sweden **45** K3
Eksjö Sweden **45** K4
Ekskavatornyy Rus. Fed. **82** A1
Eksteenfontein S. Africa **132** B5
Ektrask Sweden **44** L2
Ekwan r. Canada **168** D2
Ekwan Point Canada **168** D2
Ela Myanmar **78** B4
El Aaiún W. Sahara see Laâyoune
El 'Abbasiya Sudan **121** F6
Elafonisos i. Greece **59** D12
Elafonisou, Steno sea chan. Greece **59** D12
El 'Agrûd well Egypt **108** F7
Elaia, Cape Cyprus see Elaia, Cape
  also known as Zeytin Burnu; also spelt Elea, Cape
El Ejido Spain **55** H5
El 'Alamein Egypt **121** F2
El 'Alamein Egypt **121** F2
  also spelt Al 'Alamayn
El Alamo Mex. **184** A2
El Alia Alg. **123** G2
El Alia Tunisia **57** B11
El Alto Peru **198** A6
El 'Amiriya Egypt **108** B8
El 'Arish Egypt **121** G2
Elasa i. Greece **59** H13
El Ashmheein Egypt **121** F3
  historically known as Hermopolis Magna
El Asnam Alg. see Ech Chélif
Elassona Greece **59** D9
El Astillero Spain **54** H1
Elat Israel see Eilat
El 'Atf reg. W. Sahara **122** B5
Elati mt. Greece **59** B10
Elato atoll Micronesia **73** K5
Elazığ Turkey **107** D3
Elba U.S.A. **175** C6
Elba, Isola d' i. Italy **56** C6
  historically known as Ilva
El Bahr El Ahmar governorate Egypt **108** C9
El'ban Rus. Fed. **82** E2
El Banco Col. **198** C2
El Bânoûn well Mauritania **124** C2
El Barco de Ávila Spain **54** F4
El Barco de Valdeorras Spain see O Barco
El Barreal salt l. Mex. **184** D2
El Barun Sudan **128** B2
Elbasan Albania **58** B7
Elbaşı Turkey **106** C3
El Bauga Sudan **121** G5
El Baúl Venez. **199** D2
El Bayadh Alg. **123** F2
  formerly known as Géryville
Elbe r. Germany **48** G2
  also known as Labe (Czech Republic)
'Elb el Faʿl plat. Mauritania **124** C2
El Beqaʿa valley Lebanon **109** H3
El Berié well Mauritania **124** C2
Elberta U.S.A. **183** M2
Elberton U.S.A. **175** D5
El Beru Hagia Somalia **128** D4
Elbeuf France **50** H3
Elbeyli Turkey **109** I1
El Beyyed well Mauritania **122** C5
El Beyyed well Mauritania **122** D5
El Billete, Cerro mt. Mex. **185** E5
Elbing Poland see Elbląg
Elbistan Turkey **107** D3
Elbląg Poland **49** Q1
  historically known as Elbing
Elbląski, Kanal canal Poland **49** Q1
El Bluff Nicaragua **186** C4
El Bolsón Arg. **205** C6
El Bordj Alg. **55** L9
El Borma Tunisia **123** H3
El Boulaïda Alg. see Blida
Elbow Canada **167** J5
Elbow Lake U.S.A. **178** C2
El Bozal Mex. **185** E4

▶Elbrus mt. Rus. Fed. **41** G8
  Highest mountain in Europe.
  europe [landscapes] ▶▶ 30–31

El Buheyrat state Sudan **126** F3
El Buitre mt. Spain **55** J6
El Burg Egypt **108** C5
El Burgo de Osma Spain **55** H3
El Burumbul Egypt **108** D8
El Cain Arg. **205** C6
El Cajon U.S.A. **183** H9
El Callao Venez. **199** F3
El Campo U.S.A. **179** C6
El Canton Venez. **198** D2
El Capulin r. Mex. **179** D7
El Carmelo Venez. **198** D2
El Carmen Arg. **200** D6
El Carmen Beni Bol. **201** E3
El Carmen Santa Cruz Bol. **201** F4
El Carmen Ecuador **198** B5
El Carmen Venez. **199** E4
El Caroche mt. Spain **55** K5
  also spelt Caroch
El Casco Mex. **184** D3
El Cebu, Cerro mt. Mex. **185** G6
El Centro U.S.A. **183** I9
El Cerro Bol. **201** F4
El Chaparro Venez. **199** E2
Elche Spain **55** K6
  historically known as Ilici
El Chichónal vol. Mex. **185** G5
El Chilicote Mex. **184** D2
Elcho U.S.A. **172** D5
Elcho Island Australia **148** B1
El Coca Ecuador see Puerto Francisco de Orellana
El Cocuy, Parque Nacional nat. park Col. **198** C3

El Collado hill Spain **54** G6
El Contador, Puerto de pass Spain **55** I7
El Cotorro Cuba **186** D2
El Cuy Arg. **204** C5
El Cuyo Mex. **185** I4
Elda Spain **55** K6
El Dabʿa Egypt **53** H5
El Daheir Egypt **108** B7
Eldama Ravine Kenya **128** B4
Elde r. Germany **49** I2
El Debb well Egypt **108** C7
El Deir Egypt **108** C7
Eldena U.S.A. **172** D9
Elderon U.S.A. **172** D6
El Desemboque Mex. **181** D7
El Diamante Mex. **184** D2
El Dificil Col. **198** C2
El'dikan Rus. Fed. **39** N3
El Diviso Col. **198** B4
El Djezair Alg. see Algiers
El Doctor Mex. **184** B2
Eldon U.S.A. **178** D4
Eldorado Arg. **204** G3
Eldorado Brazil **203** B8
El Dorado Col. **198** D4
El Dorado Mex. **184** D3
El Dorado AR U.S.A. **179** D5
El Dorado KS U.S.A. **178** C4
Eldorado U.S.A. **179** F3
Eldorado Mountains U.S.A. **183** J6
Eldoret Kenya **128** B4
Eldridge U.S.A. **172** C9
Eldridge, Mount U.S.A. **166** A1
Elea, Cape Cyprus see Elaia, Cape
Eleanor U.S.A. **176** D7
Electric Peak U.S.A. **180** E3
El Eglab plat. Alg. **122** D4
El 'Ein well Sudan **121** F5
Eleja Latvia **42** E5
El Ejido Spain **55** H5
Elek r. Rus. Fed. see Ilek
Elektrėnai Lith. **42** F7
Elektrogorsk Rus. Fed. **43** T6
Elektrostal' Rus. Fed. **43** T6
Elektrougli Rus. Fed. **43** T6
Elele Nigeria **125** G5

▶Elemi Triangle terr. Africa **128** B3
  Disputed territory (Ethiopia/Kenya/Sudan) administered by Kenya.

Elena Bulg. **58** G6
El Encanto Col. **198** C5
El Encinal Mex. **183** I9
Elephanta Caves tourist site India **94** B2
Elephant Butte Reservoir U.S.A. **181** F6
Elephant Island Antarctica **222** U2
Éléphants de Kaniama, Réserve des nature res. Dem. Rep. Congo **127** E6
Éléphants de Sakania, Réserve Partielle aux nature res. Dem. Rep. Congo **127** F7
Eleshnitsa Bulg. **58** E7
Eleşkirt Turkey **107** F3
El Espinar Spain **54** G4
El Estor Guat. **185** H6
Eleuthera i. Bahamas **186** D1
Eleva U.S.A. **172** B6
Eleven Point r. U.S.A. **178** E4
El Fahs Tunisia **57** B12
El Faiyûm Egypt **121** F2
  also spelt Al Fayyûm
El Faiyûm governorate Egypt **108** B8
El Faouar Tunisia **123** H2
El Fasher Sudan **121** E6
El Fashn Egypt **106** B5
El Fendek Morocco **54** E9
El Ferrol Spain see Ferrol
El Ferrol del Caudillo Spain see Ferrol
El Fud Eth. **128** D3
El Fuerte Mex. **184** C3
El Fula Sudan **121** E6
Elgå Norway **45** J3
Elgal waterhole Kenya **128** C4
El Gamaliya Egypt **108** C6
El Gçaib well Mali **122** C5
  formerly known as El Ksaib Ounane
El Geili Sudan **121** G6
El Geneina Sudan **120** D6
El Geteina Sudan **121** G6
El Gezira state Sudan **121** G6
El Ghaba Sudan **121** F5
El Ghalla, Wadi watercourse Sudan **126** E1
El Ghallâouîya well Mauritania **122** C5
El Gheddiya Mauritania **124** C2
El Ghor plain Jordan/West Bank see Al Ghawr
Elgin U.K. **46** I6
Elgin IL U.S.A. **172** E8
Elgin NV U.S.A. **183** J4
Elgin OR U.S.A. **180** C3
Elgin TX U.S.A. **179** C6
Elgin Down Australia **149** E4
El'ginskiy Rus. Fed. **39** O3
El Gir well Sudan **121** F5
El Gîza Egypt see Giza
El Gîza governorate Egypt **108** A9
El Gogorrón, Parque Nacional nat. park Mex. **185** E4
El Goléa Alg. **123** F3
El Guante Mex. **184** D2
El Guetar Tunisia **123** H2
El Guettâra well Mali **123** E5
El'gyay Rus. Fed. **39** L3
El Haddâgi Egypt **108** B6
El Hamma Tunisia **123** H2
El Hammam Egypt **121** F2
El Hammâmi reg. Mauritania **122** C5
El Hamûl Egypt **108** C6
El Hank r. Mali **123** E4
El Hank esc. Mali/Mauritania **122** C5
El Haouaria Tunisia **57** D11
El Harra Egypt **121** F2
El Hasira Sudan **104** A5
El Hato del Volcán Panama **186** C5
El Hawata Sudan **121** G6
El Heiz Egypt **106** B5
El Hierro i. Canary Is **122** A4
El Higo Mex. **185** F4
El Hilla Sudan **121** E6
El Homr Alg. **123** F3
El Homra Sudan **121** F6
El Houeïrat well Mauritania **124** C2
El Huecu Arg. **204** C5
El Huseiniya Egypt **108** C6
Eli well Niger **125** H3
Elias Garcia Angola **127** B7
Elías Piña Dom. Rep. **187** F3
Elichpur India see Achalpur
El'ichun India **78** A2
Elila r. Dem. Rep. Congo **126** E5
Elila r. Dem. Rep. Congo **126** E5
El 'Ilw el Ahmar el Qibli hill Egypt **108** B9
Elim S. Africa **132** D11
Elim U.S.A. **164** C3
Elimäki Fin. **42** I1
Elimberrum France see Auch
Elin Pelin Bulg. **58** E6
Eliot, Mount Canada **169** I1
Eliozondo Spain **55** J1
Elipa Dem. Rep. Congo **126** E5
Elisabetha Dem. Rep. Congo **126** D4
  also known as Lokutu

Élisabethville Dem. Rep. Congo see Lubumbashi
Eliseu Martins Brazil **202** D4
El Iskandariya Egypt see Alexandria
El Iskandariya governorate Egypt **108** A6
Elista Rus. Fed. **41** H7
  formerly known as Stepnoy
Elizabeth U.S.A. **177** K5
Elizabeth, Mount Australia **150** D3
Elizabeth City U.S.A. **177** I9
Elizabeth Creek r. Australia **148** C3
Elizabeth Island Pitcairn Is see Henderson Island
Elizabeth Islands U.S.A. **177** O4
Elizabeth Point Namibia **130** B5
Elizabeth Reef Australia **145** E4
Elizabethton U.S.A. **176** C9
Elizabethtown KY U.S.A. **174** C4
Elizabethtown NC U.S.A. **174** C3
Elizabethtown NY U.S.A. **177** L1
Elizavety, Mys c. Rus. Fed. **39** O4
El Jadida Morocco **122** C2
  formerly known as Mazagan
El Jaralito Mex. **184** D3
El Jebelein Sudan **121** G6
El Jem Tunisia **123** H2
El Julie Mex. **185** G5
Elk r. Canada **167** H5
Elk r. MD U.S.A. **177** J6
Elk r. TN U.S.A. **174** C5
El Kaa Lebanon see Qaa
El Kab Sudan **121** G5
Elkader U.S.A. **174** B3
El Kala Alg. **123** H1
  formerly spelt La Calle
El Kamlin Sudan **121** G6
El Karabi Sudan **121** G5
Elkas salt l. Latvia **42** G4
Elk City U.S.A. **179** C5
Elk Creek U.S.A. **182** B2
Elkedra Australia **148** B4
Elkedra watercourse Australia **148** C4
Elkford Canada **167** H5
Elk Grove U.S.A. **182** C3
El Khalil West Bank see Hebron
El Khandaq Sudan **121** F5
El Khârga Egypt **121** F3
  also spelt Al Khârijah
Elkhart IN U.S.A. **172** H9
Elkhart KS U.S.A. **178** B4
El Khartûm Sudan see Khartoum
El Khatatba Egypt **108** B7
El Khenachich esc. Mali see El Khnâchîch
El Khnâchîch esc. Mali **122** D5
  also known as El Khenachich
El Khili Turkey see Beytüşşebap
Elkhorn U.S.A. **178** C3
Elkhorn r. U.S.A. **178** C3
Elkhorn City U.S.A. **176** C8
Elkhovo Bulg. **58** H6
Elki Turkey see Beytüşşebap
El Kkala U.S.A. **176** E9
Elkin U.S.A. **176** D9
Elkins U.S.A. **176** F7
Elk Island National Park Canada **167** H4
Elk Lake Canada **168** D4
Elk Lake l. U.S.A. **172** H5
Elkland U.S.A. **177** H4
Elk Mountain U.S.A. **180** F4
Elko Canada **167** H5
Elko U.S.A. **183** I1
El K'oran Eth. **128** E3
Elk Park U.S.A. **176** D9
Elk Point Canada **167** I4
Elk Point U.S.A. **178** C3
El Koran Eth. see El K'oran
El Ksaib Ounane well Mali see El Gçaib
El Ksour Tunisia **57** A13
Elk Springs U.S.A. **183** P1
Elkton KY U.S.A. **174** C4
Elkton MD U.S.A. **177** J6
Elkton VA U.S.A. **176** F7
Elkview U.S.A. **176** D7
El Lagowa Sudan **126** F2
Ellaló Australia **151** B7
Ellaville U.S.A. **175** C5
Ell Bay Canada **167** O1
Ellef Ringnes Island Canada **165** I2
El Lêh Eth. **128** C4
Ellen well Kenya **128** D5
Elleker Australia **151** B7
Ellen, Mount U.S.A. **183** N3
Ellenabad India **96** B3
Ellenboro U.S.A. **176** D6
Ellenburg Depot U.S.A. **177** L1
Ellendale DE U.S.A. **177** J7
Ellendale ND U.S.A. **178** C2
Ellensburg U.S.A. **180** B3
Ellenville U.S.A. **177** K4
Ellery, Mount Australia **149** E4
Ellesmere N.Z. **153** G11

▶Ellesmere Island Canada **165** K2
  4th largest island in North America and 10th in the world.
  northamerica [landscapes] ▶▶ 156–157

Ellesmere Island National Park Reserve Canada **165** L1
Ellesmere Port U.K. **47** J10
Ellice r. Canada **167** K1
Ellice Island atoll Tuvalu see Funafuti
Ellice Islands country S. Pacific Ocean see Tuvalu
Ellicott City U.S.A. **177** I6
Ellicottville U.S.A. **176** G3
Ellijay U.S.A. **174** C5
El Limón Mex. **185** F4
Elliot Australia **148** B3
Elliot S. Africa **133** L8
Elliot, Mount Australia **149** E3
Elliotdale S. Africa **133** M8
  also known as Xhora
Elliot Knob mt. U.S.A. **176** F7
Elliot Lake Canada **168** D4
Elliot Price Conservation Park nature res. Australia **146** C2
Ellis U.S.A. **178** C4
Ellisras S. Africa **131** E4
Elliston Australia **146** B3
Elliston U.S.A. **176** E8
Ellon U.K. **46** J6
Ellore India see Eluru
Ellsworth KS U.S.A. **178** C4
Ellsworth ME U.S.A. **177** Q1
Ellsworth WI U.S.A. **174** A2
Ellsworth Land Antarctica **222** R1
Ellsworth Mountains Antarctica **222** S1
Ellwangen (Jagst) Germany **48** H7
El Macao Dom. Rep. **187** F3
El Mahala el Kubra Egypt **108** C7
El Mahâriq Egypt **121** F3
El Maharraqa Egypt **108** C7
El Mahia reg. Mali **123** E4
El Maitén Arg. **205** B6
El Makhari hill Egypt **121** F3
El Makzun Dağı mt. Turkey **108** I1
Elmalı Turkey **106** B3
El Mallâha marsh Egypt **108** E9
El Malpais National Monument nat. park U.S.A. **181** F6
El Ma'mûra Egypt **108** B6
El Manaqil Sudan **121** G6

El Mango Venez. **199** E4
El Mansûra Egypt **121** F2
  also known as Al Manşûrah
El Mansûriya Egypt **108** C7
El Manteco Venez. **199** F3
El Manzla Morocco **54** F9
El Marsa Tunisia **57** C12
El Matariya Egypt **108** D6
El Medo Eth. **128** D3
El Meghaier Alg. **123** H2
El Melemm Sudan **121** F6
El Melhes well Mauritania **124** D3
El Meselhemiya Sudan **121** G6
El Messir well Chad **121** I5
El Mex Egypt **108** A6
El Miamo Venez. **199** F3
El Mina Lebanon **108** G3
El Minya Egypt **108** C8
El Minya Egypt **108** C8
El Minya governorate Egypt **108** B9
Elmira Germany **48** G2
Elmira Ont. Canada **173** M7
Elmira P.E.I. Canada **169** I4
Elmira MI U.S.A. **173** I5
Elmira NY U.S.A. **177** I3
El Mirage U.S.A. **183** L8
El Moînane well Mauritania **124** C2
Elmore Australia **147** E4
El Morro mt. Arg. **204** D4
El Mraîfig well Mauritania **124** C3
El Mraîti well Mali **122** E5
El Mreyyé reg. Mauritania **124** D2
Elmshorn Germany **48** G2
El Muglad Sudan **126** E2
El Mugrón mt. Spain **55** J6
Elmwood U.S.A. **172** D10
El Mzereb well Mali **122** D4
Elne France **51** I10
Elnesvågen Norway **44** I3
El Nido Phil. **74** A4
El Oasis Mex. **183** I9
El Obeid Sudan **121** F6
El Ocote, Parque Natural nature res. Mex. **185** G5
El Odaiya Sudan **121** F6
El Oro prov. Ecuador **198** B5
El Oro Mex. **184** E3
Elos Greece **59** E13
El Oued Alg. **123** G2
Eloy U.S.A. **183** M9
El Palmar Venez. **199** F3
El Palmito Mex. **184** D3
El Pao Bolívar Venez. **199** F2
El Pao Cojedes Venez. **199** D2
Elpaputih, Teluk b. Indon. **75** C3
El Paraíso Hond. **186** B4
El Paso r. U.S.A. **172** D9
El Paso U.S.A. see Derby
El Peñón Arg. **204** D3
El Perelló Spain **55** L4
Elphinstone i. Myanmar see Thayawthadangyi Kyun
El Pilar Venez. **199** F2
El Pino, Sierra mts Mex. **185** E2
El Pintado Arg. **201** D6
El Pluma Arg. **205** C7
El Pocito Bol. **201** E3
El Portele Bol. **198** C1
El Porvenir Col. **198** D3
El Porvenir Mex. **183** H9
El Porvenir Mex. **184** D3
El Porvenir Panama **186** D5
El Prat de Llobregat Spain **55** N3
  also known as Prat de Llobregat
El Progreso Guat. **185** H6
El Progreso Mex. see Guastatoya
El Puente Bol. **200** D5
El Puente Nicaragua **186** B4
El Puerto de Santa María Spain **54** E8
El Qâ' valley Egypt **108** D9
El Qâhira Egypt see Cairo
El Qâhira governorate Egypt **108** C8
El Qanâtir el Qahîriya Egypt **108** C7
El Qantara Egypt **106** C5
El Qantara el Sharqîya Egypt **108** D7
El Qasimîye r. Lebanon **108** G3
El Qasr Egypt **121** E3
El Quds Israel/West Bank see Jerusalem
El Quebrachal Arg. **204** D2
El Quss Abû Saîd plat. Egypt **121** E3
El Real Panama **186** D5
El Regocijo Mex. **184** D4
El Reno U.S.A. **179** C5
El Retorno Mex. **185** E4
El Rey, Parque Nacional nat. park Arg. **201** D5
El Ridisîya Bahari Egypt **121** G3
El Río U.S.A. **182** E7
El Rôda Egypt **108** B9
El Rosario watercourse Mex. **181** D7
Elrose Canada **167** I5
Elroy U.S.A. **172** C7
El Rucio Mex. **185** E4
Elsa Canada **173** K2
El Saff Egypt **121** F2
El Sahuaro Mex. **184** B2
El Salado Arg. **205** C8
El Salado Mex. **185** E3
El Sâlhiya Egypt **108** D7
El Salto Mex. **184** D4

▶El Salvador country Central America **185** H6
  also known as Salvador
  northamerica [countries] ▶▶ 158–159

El Salvador Chile **204** C2
El Salvador Mex. **185** E3
El Salvador Phil. **74** C4
El Samán de Apure Venez. **198** D3
Elsas Canada **173** K2
El Sauz Mex. **184** D2
El Seibo Dom. Rep. **187** F3
Elsen Nur l. China **84** B5
El Serrat Andorra **55** M2
El Shab well Egypt **121** E4
El Shâyib hill Egypt **108** B8
El Shuhada Egypt **108** C7
Elsie U.S.A. **173** I7
Elsinore Denmark see Helsingør
Elsinore CA U.S.A. **183** G8
Elsinore UT U.S.A. **183** M3
Elsnes Norway **44** M1
El Sosneado Arg. **204** C4
Elsterniederung und Westliche Oberlausitzer Heide park Germany **49** K4
Elsterwerda Germany **49** K4
El Sueco Mex. **184** D2
El Suweis Egypt see Suez
El Suweis governorate Egypt **108** C8
El Tajin tourist site Mex. **185** F4
El Tama, Parque Nacional nat. park Venez. **198** C3
El Tarabil hill Egypt **108** D8
El Tarf Alg. **123** H1
El Teleno mt. Spain **54** E2
El Temascal Mex. **185** F5
Eltham N.Z. **152** I7
El Thamad Egypt **121** G2
El Tigre Venez. **199** E2
El Tigre, Parque Nacional nat. park Guat. **185** H5
El Tocuyo Venez. **198** D2
El'ton Rus. Fed. **102** A2
El'ton, Ozero l. Rus. Fed. **102** A2
El Toro Spain **55** K4
El Toro Chile **204** C3
Eltopia U.S.A. **180** C3
El Trébol Arg. **204** E4
El Tren Arg. **204** D5
El Tunal Arg. **204** D2

El Tuparro, Parque Nacional nat. park Col. **198** D3
El Tûr Egypt **121** G2
El Turbio Chile **205** B8
El Turbón mt. Spain **55** L2
El Uqsur Egypt see Luxor
Eluru India **94** D2
El 'Uteishan well Sudan **121** G5
Elva Estonia **42** H3
El Vallecillo Mex. **184** C2
Elvanli Turkey see Tömük
Elvas Port. **54** D6
Elvebakken Norway **44** M1
Elven France **50** D5
El Vendrell Spain **55** M3
  also spelt Vendrell
Elvenes Norway **44** O1
Elverum Norway **45** J3
El Viejo mt. Col. **198** C3
El Viejo Nicaragua **186** B4
El Viejo, Cerro mt. Mex. **184** D4
Elvira Brazil **198** D5
Elvira r. Australia **150** C3
Elvire Aboriginal Reserve Australia **150** D3
Elvo r. Italy **56** A3
El Wâdi El Jadid governorate Egypt **106** A6
El Wak Kenya **128** D4
El Wasta Egypt **108** C8
El Watya well Egypt **121** F6
Elwood Australia **147** E4
Elwood NE U.S.A. **178** C3
Elwood NJ U.S.A. **177** K6
El Wuz Sudan **121** F6
Ely U.K. **47** M11
Ely MN U.S.A. **174** B2
Ely NV U.S.A. **183** J2
El Yagual Venez. **198** D3
El Yibo well Kenya **128** C3
Elyria U.S.A. **176** C4
Elysburg U.S.A. **177** I5
El Zacatón, Cerro mt. Mex. **185** F5
El Zape Mex. **184** D3
El Zawâmil Egypt **108** C7
Emajõgi r. Estonia **42** I3
Emâm Qoli Iran **100** D2
Emâmrûd Iran **100** C3
Emām-e Shahr Iran see Shahrud
Emām Şaheb Afgh. **101** G2
Emām Taqi Iran **100** D2
  formerly known as Shāh Taqi
Emangusi S. Africa **133** Q4
E. Martínez Mex. see Emiliano Martínez
Emas, Parque Nacional das nat. park Brazil **206** A5
Emazar Kazakh. **88** C2
Emba Kazakh. **102** D2
Emba r. Kazakh. **102** D3
Embalenhle S. Africa **133** N3
Embarcación Arg. **201** D5
Embarras Portage Canada **167** I3
Embarrass r. U.S.A. **172** A3
Embetsu Japan see Enbetsu
Embi Kazakh. see Emba
Embiah, Mount hill Sing. **76** [inset]
Embira r. Brazil see Envira
Émbonas Greece see Emp. Emponas
Emborcação, Represa de resr Brazil **206** F5
Emborion Greece see Emporeio
Embu Brazil **206** G10
Embu Kenya **128** C5
Emdundo Angola **127** C9
Emden Germany **48** E2
Emecik Turkey **59** I12
Emei China see Emeishan
Emeishan China **86** B2
  formerly known as Emei
Emei Shan mt. China **86** B2
Emel' r. Kazakh. **88** C2
Emerald Australia **149** F4
Emeril Canada **169** I2
Emerita Augusta Spain see Mérida
Emerson Canada **167** L5
Emery U.S.A. **183** M3
Emesa Syria see Homs
Emet Turkey **106** B3
Emigrant Gap U.S.A. **182** D2
Emigrant Pass U.S.A. **183** H1
Emigrant Valley U.S.A. **183** I4
Emijindini S. Africa **133** P2
Emi Koussi mt. Chad **120** C5
Emile r. Canada **167** G2
Emiliano Martínez Mex. **184** D3
  short for E. Martínez
Emiliano Zapata Mex. **185** H5
Emilia-Romagna admin. reg. Italy **56** D4
Emin China **88** C2
  also known as Dorbiljin
Emine, Nos pt Bulg. **58** I6
Eminence U.S.A. **174** C4
Emin He r. China **88** C2
Eminska Planina hills Bulg. **58** I6
Emirdağ Turkey **106** B3
Emir Dağı mt. Turkey **106** B3
Emlenton U.S.A. **176** F4
Emmabodna Sweden **45** K4
Emmahaven Indon. see Telukbayur
Emmaste Estonia **42** D3
Emmaus Rus. Fed. **43** R5
Emmaus U.S.A. **177** J5
Emmeloord Neth. **48** C3
Emmelshausen Germany **48** E5
Emmen Neth. **48** D3
Emmen Switz. **51** O5
Emmendingen Germany **48** E7
Emmerich Germany **48** D4
Emmet Australia **149** E5
Emmetsburg U.S.A. **178** D3
Emmett U.S.A. **180** D4
Emmiganuru India **94** C3
  formerly spelt Yemmiganur
Emmitsburg U.S.A. **177** H6
Emo Canada **168** A3
Emőd Hungary **49** R8
Emona Slovenia see Ljubljana
Emory U.S.A. **179** D5
Emory Peak U.S.A. **179** B6
Empada Guinea-Bissau **124** B3
Empalme Mex. **184** C3
Empanadas mt. Spain **55** I7
Empangeni S. Africa **133** P5
Empedrado Arg. **204** F3
Empexa, Salar de salt flat Bol. **200** C5
Empingham U.S.A. **172** G6
Emponas Greece **59** I12
Emporeio Greece **59** G12
  also known as Emborion
Emporia KS U.S.A. **178** C4
Emporia VA U.S.A. **176** H9
Emporium U.S.A. **176** G4
Empress Canada **167** I5
Empress Mine Zimbabwe **131** F3
Empty Quarter des. Saudi Arabia see Rub' al Khālī
'Emrâni Iran Iran **100** D2
Ems r. Germany **48** E2
Emsdetten Germany **173** N5
Ems-Jade-Kanal canal Germany **48** E2
Emsworth U.K. **47** L12
Emu China **82** B3
Emu Creek r. Australia **149** E4
Emumägi hill Estonia **42** H3
Emu Park Australia **149** F4
Emur r. China **82** B1
Emur Shan mts China **82** A1
Emzinoni S. Africa **133** N3
Ena Japan **91** E7
Enafors Sweden **44** K3
Enambú Col. **198** D4

Enamuna Brazil 199 F3
Enarotali Indon. 73 I7
Ena-san *mt.* Japan 91 E7
Enbetsu Japan 90 G2
  also spelt Embetsu
Encanadé *mt.* Spain 55 L4
Encantadas, Serra das *hills* Brazil 203 A9
Encanto, Cape Phil. 74 B3
Encarnación Mex. 185 E4
Encarnación Para. 201 G6
Enchi Ghana 124 C5
Encinas *mt.* Spain 54 H6
Encinitas U.S.A. 183 G8
Encino U.S.A. 181 F6
Encón Arg. 204 D4
Encontrados Venez. 198 C2
Encounter Bay Australia 146 C3
Encruzilhada Brazil 202 D5
Encruzilhada do Sul Brazil 203 A9
Encs Hungary 49 S7
Endako Canada 166 E4
Endau Malaysia 76 C2
Endau *r.* Malaysia 76 C2
Endeavour Strait Australia 149 D1
Endeh Indon. 75 B5
Enderbury *i.* Kiribati 145 H2
Enderby Canada 166 G5
Enderby Land *reg.* Antarctica 223 D2
Endicott Mountains U.S.A. 164 D3
Endimari *r.* Brazil 200 D2
Endla riiklik looduskaitseala *nature res.*
  Estonia 42 H3
Endom Cameroon 125 I6
Endwell U.S.A. 177 I3
Endzele Latvia 42 G4
Ene *r.* Peru 200 B2
Eneabba Australia 151 A6
Enebakk Norway 45 J4
Enemutu Brazil 199 G3
EnenKio *terr.* N. Pacific Ocean *see* Wake Atoll
Energeticheskiy Kazakh. 103 I4
Energetik Rus. Fed. 102 D2
Energía Arg. 204 F5
Enewetak *atoll* Marshall Is 220 E5
Enez Turkey 106 A2
  historically known as Aenus
Enfiǎo, Ponta do *pt* Angola 127 A8
Enfidaville Tunisia 57 C12
Enfield Canada 169 I4
Enfield U.S.A. 174 E4
Engan Norway 44 J3
Engaño, Cabo *c.* Dom. Rep. 187 F3
Engaños, Río de los *r.* Col. *see* Yarí
Engaru Japan 90 H2
Engcobo S. Africa 133 L8
Engelhard U.S.A. 174 F5
Engel's Rus. Fed. 102 A2
  also known as Pokrovsk
Engelschmangat *sea chan.* Neth. 48 B2
Engenheiro Beltrão Brazil 206 A10
Engenheiro Navarro Brazil 207 J4
Engenina *watercourse* Australia 146 B2
Engerdal Norway 45 J3
Enghershatu *mt.* Eritrea 121 H5
Engineer Canada 166 C3
Engkilili Sarawak Malaysia 77 F2
England *admin. div.* U.K. 47 K11
Englee Canada 169 K3
Englehart Canada 168 E4
Englewood FL U.S.A. 175 D7
Englewood OH U.S.A. 176 A6
English *r.* Canada 167 M5
English Bazar India *see* Ingraj Bazar
English Channel France/U.K. 47 K14
  also known as la Manche
English Coast Antarctica 222 S2
Engozero Rus. Fed. 40 E2
Engstingen Germany 48 G7
Engure Latvia 42 E4
Engures ezers *l.* Latvia 42 E4
Enguri *r.* Georgia 107 E2
Enhlalakahle S. Africa 133 O6
Enid U.S.A. 179 C4
Enipefs *r.* Greece 59 D9
Eniwa Japan 90 G3
eNjesuthi *mt.* S. Africa 133 N6
Enkan, Mys *pt* Rus. Fed. 39 O4
Enkeldoorn Zimbabwe *see* Chivhu
Enkhuizen Neth. 48 D3
Enköping Sweden 45 L4
Enle China *see* Zhenyuan
Enna Sicilia Italy 57 G11
Ennadai Canada 167 K2
Ennadai Lake Canada 167 K2
En Nahud Sudan 121 F6
En Namous, Oued *watercourse* Alg. 123 E3
E-n-Nassamé *well* Niger 125 H3
Ennedi, Massif *mts* Chad 120 C5
Ennedi Acheloma *watercourse* Chad 120 C5
Enneri Maro *watercourse* Chad 120 C5
Enneri Yebigué *watercourse* Chad 120 C5
Ennery Haiti 187 F3
Engongia Australia 147 E2
Ennis Rep. of Ireland 47 D11
  also spelt Inis
Ennis MT U.S.A. 180 E3
Ennis TX U.S.A. 179 C5
Enniscorthy Rep. of Ireland 47 F11
  also spelt Inis Córthaidh
Enniskerry Rep. of Ireland 47 F10
Enniskillen U.K. 47 E9

Ennistymon Rep. of Ireland 47 C11
Enn Nâqoûra Lebanon 108 G4
Enns Austria 49 L7
Enns *r.* Austria 49 L7
Eno Fin. 44 O3
Enoch U.S.A. 183 K4
Enonkoski Fin. 44 O3
Enontekiö Fin. 44 M1
Enoree *r.* U.S.A. 174 D5
Enosburg Falls U.S.A. 177 M1
Enping China 87 E4
Enrekang Indon. 75 A3
Enrile Phil. 74 B2
Enriquillo Dom. Rep. 187 F3
Enriquillo, Lago de *l.* Dom. Rep. 187 F3
Enschede Neth. 48 D3
Ensenada *Baja California Norte* Mex. 184 C3
Ensenada *Baja California Sur* Mex. 184 C4
Ensenada de Utria *nat. park* Col. 198 B3
Enshi China 87 D2
Ensley U.S.A. 175 C6
Entebbe Uganda 128 B4
Enterprise U.S.A. 167 G2
Enterprise AL U.S.A. 175 C6
Enterprise OR U.S.A. 180 C3
Enterprise UT U.S.A. 183 K4
Enterprise Point Phil. 74 A4
Entrance Canada 167 G4
Entrepeñas, Embalse de *resr* Spain 55 I4
Entre Rios Arg. 204 F4
Entre Rios Bol. 201 D5
Entre Rios *Bahia* Brazil 202 E4
Entre Rios *Pará* Brazil 199 H6
Entre Rios de Minas Brazil 203 C7
Entre Rios Moz. *see* Malema
Entroncamento Port. 54 C5
Entuba Zimbabwe 131 E3
Entumeni S. Africa 133 P5
Enugu Nigeria 125 G5
Enugu *state* Nigeria 125 G5
Enurmino Rus. Fed. 39 S3
Envigado Col. 198 C3
Envira Brazil 200 C1
Envira *r.* Brazil 200 C1
  also known as Embira
Enying Hungary 49 P9
Enys, Mount N.Z. 153 F11
Enzan Japan 91 F7
Eo *r.* Spain 54 D1
Eochaill Rep. of Ireland *see* Youghal
Eokuk Lake Canada 167 H1
Eooa *i.* Tonga *see* Eua
Epe Nigeria 125 F5
Épernay France 51 J3
Epena Congo 126 C4
Épernay France 51 J3
Ephesus *tourist site* Turkey 59 I11
  also known as Efes
Ephraim U.S.A. 183 M2
Ephrata PA U.S.A. 177 I5
Ephrata WA U.S.A. 180 C3
Epidamnus Albania *see* Durrës
Epidavros *tourist site* Greece 59 E11
Epidavrou Limiras, Kolpos *b.* Greece 59 E12
Épila Spain 55 J3
Épinac France 51 K6
Épinal France 51 M4
Epirus *admin. reg.* Greece *see* Ipeiros
Episkopi Cyprus 108 D3
Episkopi Bay Cyprus 108 D3
  also known as Episkopis, Kolpos
Episkopis, Kolpos *b.* Cyprus *see*
  Episkopi Bay
Epping U.K. 47 M12
Epping U.S.A. 177 N2
Epping Forest National Park Australia
  149 F4
Eppynt, Mynydd *hills* U.K. 47 I11
Epsom U.K. 47 L12
Epte *r.* France 50 H3
Epu-pel Arg. 204 D5
Epuyén Arg. 205 C6
Eqlid Iran 100 C4
Équateur *prov.* Dem. Rep. Congo 126 D4
▶**Equatorial Guinea** *country* Africa 125 H6
  known as Guinea Ecuatorial in Spanish;
  formerly known as Spanish Guinea
Equeipa Venez. 199 F3
Equerdreville-Hainneville France 50 D4
Era *r.* Italy 56 C5
Erac Creek *watercourse* Australia 149 E5
Eraclea Italy 56 E3
Erakurri *mt.* Spain 55 J1
Eran Bay Phil. 74 A4
Erandol India 94 B1
Erawadi *r.* Myanmar *see* Irrawaddy
Erawan National Park Thai. 79 B5
Erba, Jebel *mt.* Sudan 121 H4
Erbaa Turkey 107 D2
Erbendorf Germany 48 J6
Erbeskopf *hill* Germany 48 E6
Ercan *airport* Cyprus 108 E2
Erçek Turkey 107 F3
Erciş Turkey 107 F3
Erciyes Dağı *mt.* Turkey 106 C3
Ercsi Hungary 49 P8
Érd Hungary 49 P8
Erdalsfjellet *hill* Norway 44 N1
Erdaobaihe China *see* Baihe
Erdaogou China 84 B5
Erdao Jiang *r.* China 82 B4
Erdek Turkey 106 A2
Erdemli Turkey 106 C3
  also known as Yağda
Erdenet *Hövsgöl* Mongolia 84 C1
Erdenet *Orhon* Mongolia 84 E1
Erdenetsogt *Bayanhongor* Mongolia 84 D2
Erdenetsogt *Ömnögovi* Mongolia 85 E3
Erding Germany 48 I7
Erdniyevskiy Rus. Fed. 102 A3
Erdre *r.* France 50 E5
Eré Peru 198 D5
Eré, Campos *hills* Brazil 206 A11
Erebato *r.* Venez. 199 E3
Erebus, Mount *vol.* Antarctica 223 L1
Erech *tourist site* Iraq 107 F5
  also spelt Uruk
Erechim Brazil 203 A8
Ereentsav Mongolia 85 G1
Ereğli *Konya* Turkey 106 C3
  historically known as Cabistra or Heraclea
Ereğli *Zonguldak* Turkey 106 B2
  historically known as Heraclea Pontica
Erego Moz. *see* Errego
Erei, Monti *mts* Sicilia Italy 57 G11
  also spelt Ereikoussa
Ereikoussa *i.* Greece 59 A9
Erementaú Kazakh. *see* Yereymentau
Eréndira Mex. 185 E5
Erenhaberga Shan *mts* China 88 D3
Erenhot China 85 G3
Erenik *r.* Yugo. 58 B6
Erenköy Cyprus *see* Kokkina
Eresk Iran 100 D3
Eresma *r.* Spain 54 G3
Eressos Greece 59 G10
Eretria Greece 59 E10
Erevan Armenia *see* Yerevan
Erfenis Dam *r.* S. Africa 133 K5
Erfenis Dam Nature Reserve S. Africa 133 K5
Erfoud Morocco 122 D2
Erfurt Germany 48 I5
Ergani Turkey 107 D3
Erganu China 85 F3
Ergel Mongolia 85 F3
Érgeme Latvia 42 G4

Ergene *r.* Turkey 106 A2
Erg Iabès *des.* Alg. 123 E4
Erg Iguidi *des.* Alg./Mauritania 122 D4
'Erg I-n-Sâkâne *des.* Mali 123 E5
Erg Issaouane *des.* Alg. 123 G3
Erg Kilian *des.* Alg. 123 H5
Ergli Latvia 42 G5
Erg Mehedjibat *des.* Alg. 123 G4
Erg Tassedjefit *des.* Alg. 123 F4
Erguig *r.* Chad 126 B2
Ergun China 85 I1
  formerly known as Ergun Youqi or Labudalin
Ergun He *r.* China/Rus. Fed. *see* Argun'
Er Hai *l.* China 86 B3
Erheib Sudan 104 B4
Eria *r.* Spain 54 F2
Eric Sicilia Italy 57 E10
Ericht, Loch *l.* U.K. 46 H7
Erickson Man. Canada 167 L5
Erie KS U.S.A. 178 D4
Erie PA U.S.A. 176 E4
Erie, Lake Canada/U.S.A. 173 M8
'Erigāt *des.* Mali 122 D4
Erik Eriksenstretet *sea chan.* Svalbard 38 C2
Erikoússa *i.* Greece *see* Ereikoussa
Eriksdale Canada 167 L5
Erikslund Sweden 45 L4
Erimo Japan 90 H3
Erimo-misaki *c.* Japan 90 H4
Erin Canada 173 M7
Erin U.S.A. 174 C4
Eriskay *i.* U.K. 46 E6
  also spelt Eiriosgaigh
Erithraí Greece *see* Erythres
Erithrópotamos *r.* Greece *see* Erydropotamos
▶**Eritrea** *country* Africa 121 H6
  africa [countries] ▶▶ 114–117
Erkech-Tam Kyrg. 103 H5
  formerly known as Irkeshtam
Erkner Germany 49 K3
Erkowit Sudan 104 B4
Erlangen Germany 48 I6
Erlangping China 87 D1
Erldunda Australia 148 B5
Erlong Shan *mt.* China 82 C4
Ermak Kazakh. *see* Aksu
Ermana, Khrebet *mts* Rus. Fed. 85 G1
Ermelo S. Africa 133 N3
Ermenek Turkey 106 C3
Ermenek *r.* Turkey 108 E1
Ermil Sudan 121 F6
Ermioni Greece 59 E11
Ermoupoli Greece 59 F11
Ernakulam India 94 C4
Erne *r.* Rep. of Ireland/U.K. 47 D9
Ernée France 50 F4
Ernest Giles Range *hills* Australia 151 C5
Ernest Sound *sea chan.* U.S.A. 166 C4
Erode India 94 C4
Eromanga Australia 149 D5
Erongo *admin. reg.* Namibia 130 B4
Erongo China 84 B3
Erqu China *see* Zhouzhi
Errabiddy Hills Australia 151 A5
Er Rachidia Morocco 122 D3
  formerly known as Ksar-es-Souk
Er Rahad Sudan 121 F6
Erramala Hills India 94 C3
Er Raoui *des.* Alg. 123 E3
Errego Moz. 131 H2
  formerly spelt Erego
Er Renk Sudan 128 B2
Errigal *hill* Rep. of Ireland 47 D8
Erris Head *hd* Rep. of Ireland 47 B9
Er *r.* Spain 55 I2
Er Rogel Sudan 121 G5
Erromango *i.* Vanuatu 145 F3
Erronan *i.* Vanuatu *see* Futuna
Er Roseires Sudan 128 B2
Er Rua'at Sudan 121 G6
Ersekë Albania 59 B8
Erskine U.S.A. 178 D2
Ertai China 84 A2
Ertil' Rus. Fed. 41 G6
Ertis *r.* Kazakh./Rus. Fed. *see* Irtysh
Ertis He *r.* China/Kazakh. 88 D1
  also known as Chernyy Irtysh or Qara Ertis
Erufu Nigeria 125 G4
Eruh Turkey 107 F3
Eruwa Nigeria 125 F5
Erval Brazil 204 G4
Ervália Brazil 207 K7
Erve *r.* France 50 F5
Erwin U.S.A. 178 D4
Erwitte Germany 48 F4
Erydropotamos *r.* Greece 58 H7
  also spelt Erythropotamos
Erythres Greece 59 E10
  also known as Erithraí
Eryuan China 86 A3
  also known as Yuhu
Erzen *r.* Albania 58 A7
Erzgebirge *mts* Czech Rep./Germany 49 K5
  historically known as Ore Mountains
Erzhan China 82 B2
Erzin Rus. Fed. 84 B1
Erzin Turkey 106 C3
Erzincan Turkey 107 D3
Erzurum Turkey 107 E3
  also spelt Erzerum
Erzvilkas Lith. 42 D6
Esa-ala P.N.G. 145 E2
Esan-misaki *pt* Japan 90 H2
Esashi *Hokkaido* Japan 90 H2
Esashi *Iwate* Japan 90 G5
Esbjerg Denmark 45 J5
Esbo Fin. *see* Espoo
Escada Brazil 202 F4
Escalante Phil. 74 B4
Escalante *r.* U.S.A. 183 N4
Escalante Desert U.S.A. 183 K4
Escalón Mex. 184 D3
Escambia *r.* U.S.A. 175 C6
Escandón, Puerto de *pass* Spain 55 K4
Escárcega Mex. 185 H5
Escarpada Point Phil. 74 B2
Escaut *r.* Belgium 51 J2
Eschede Germany 48 H3
Esch-sur-Alzette Lux. 51 L5
Eschwege Germany 48 H4
Eschweiler Germany 48 D4
Escocesa, Bahía *b.* Dom. Rep. 187 F3
Escoma Bol. 200 C3
Escondido Mex. 179 B6
Escondido *r.* Nicaragua 186 C4
Escondido U.S.A. 183 G8
Escudilla *mt.* U.S.A. 183 O7
Escuinapa Mex. 184 D4
Escuintla Guat. 185 H6
Escuintla Mex. 185 G6
Escuque Venez. 198 D2
Escurso *r.* Brazil 206 G4
Escusa *mt.* Spain 54 D4
Ese-Khayya Rus. Fed. 39 N3
Eşen Turkey 106 B3
Eşen *r.* Turkey 59 K12
Esence Dağı *mt.* Turkey 107 D3
Esenguly Turkm. 102 C5
  also spelt Esenkuli
Esenkuli Turkm. *see* Esenguly
Esenköy Turkey 58 I7
Esenyurt Turkey 58 J7
Eşfahân Iran 100 B3

Eşfahân *prov.* Iran 100 C3
Esfandak Iran 101 E5
Esfarayen, Reshteh-ye Iran 100 D2
Esfideh Iran 101 D3
Esgueva *r.* Spain 54 G3
Eshan China 86 B3
  also known as Shuangjiang
Eshanguzar Kyrg. 103 I4
Eshimba Dem. Rep. Congo 127 E6
Eshkamesh Afgh. 101 G2
Eshowe S. Africa 133 P5
Esigodini Zimbabwe 131 F4
  formerly known as Essexvale
Esikhawini S. Africa 133 Q5
Esil Kazakh. *see* Yesil'
Esil *r.* Kazakh./Rus. Fed. *see* Ishim
Esino *r.* Italy 56 F5
eSizameleni S. Africa 133 O4
Esk Australia 147 G1
Esk *r.* Australia 147 E5
Esk *r.* U.K. 47 I9
Eskdale U.K. 47 I9
Esker Canada 169 H2
Eski Gediz Turkey 106 B3
Eskilstuna Sweden 45 L4
Eskimo Lakes Canada 164 F3
Eskimo Point Canada *see* Arviat
Eski-Nookat Kyrg. 103 H4
  formerly spelt Iski-Naukat
Eskipazar Turkey 106 C2
Eskişehir Turkey 106 B3
  historically known as Dorylaeum
Esla *r.* Spain 54 F2
Esla, Embalse de *resr* Spain *see*
  Ricobayo, Embalse de
Eslâmâbâd-e Gharb Iran 100 A3
  formerly known as Shâhâbâd
Esler Dağı *mt.* Turkey 59 K11
Eslöv Sweden 45 K5
Esmâ'ili-ye Soflá Iran 100 D4
Eşme Turkey 106 B3
Esmeralda Cuba 186 D2
Esmeralda, Isla *i.* Chile 205 B8
Esmeraldas Brazil 207 I6
Esmeraldas Ecuador 198 B4
Esmeraldas *prov.* Ecuador 198 B4
Esmeraldo *r.* Bol. 200 D3
Esmont U.S.A. 176 G8
Esnagi Lake Canada 173 I2
Espakeh Iran 101 E5
Espalha *r.* Brazil *see* São Francisco
Espalmador, Isla *i.* Spain *see* S'Espalmador
España *country* Europe *see* Spain
Espanola Canada 168 D4
Espanola U.S.A. 181 F5
Esparreguera Spain 55 M3
Esparta Hond. 186 B4
Espe Kazakh. 103 H4
Espelette France 50 E9
Esperance Australia 151 C7
Esperance Bay Australia 151 C7
Esperantinópolis Brazil 202 C3
Esperanza *research station* Antarctica 222 U2
Esperanza *Santa Cruz* Arg. 205 C8
Esperanza *Santa Fé* Arg. 204 E4
Esperanza Mex. 184 C3
Esperanza Peru 200 C2
Esperanza Phil. 74 C4
Espichel, Cabo *c.* Port. 54 B6
Espiel Spain 54 G6
Espigão, Serra de *mts* Brazil 203 D6
Espinazo Mex. 185 E3
Espinhaço, Serra do *mts* Brazil 203 D6
Espinheira Angola 127 B9
Espinho Port. 54 C4
Espinilho, Serra do *hills* Brazil 203 A9
Espino Venez. 199 E2
Espinosa Brazil 202 D5
Espinosa de los Monteros Spain 55 H1
Espírito Santo Brazil *see* Vila Velha
Espírito Santo *state* Brazil 203 D6
Espíritu Phil. 74 B3
Espíritu Santo Bol. 200 D4
Espíritu Santo *i.* Vanuatu 145 F3
Espíritu Santo, Bahía del *b.* Mex. 185 I5
Espíritu Santo, Isla *i.* Mex. 184 C4
Espita Mex. 185 H4
Esplanada Brazil 202 E4
Espoo Fin. 45 N3
  also spelt Esbo
Espungabera Moz. 131 G4
Esquel Arg. 205 C6
Esquina Arg. 204 F3
Esquipulas Guat. 185 H6
Esquiú Arg. 204 D3
Essaouira Morocco 122 C2
  formerly known as Mogador
Essé Cameroon 125 H5
Es Semara W. Sahara 122 C4
▶**Essen** Germany 48 E4
  4th most populous city in Europe.
  world [cities] ▶▶ 24–25
Essendon, Mount *hill* Australia 151 C5
Essex Canada 173 K8
Essex CA U.S.A. 183 J7
Essex MA U.S.A. 177 O3
Essex MD U.S.A. 177 I6
Essex NY U.S.A. 177 L1
Essex Junction U.S.A. 177 L1
Essexvale Zimbabwe *see* Esigodini
Essexville U.S.A. 173 J7
Esslingen am Neckar Germany 48 G7
Esso Rus. Fed. 39 P4
Essonne *r.* France 51 I4
Est *prov.* Cameroon 125 I5
Est Estonia 42 I4
Es Suki Sudan 128 B2
Es Suwais Egypt *see* Suez
Esta *prov.* Cameroon 125 I5
Estaca de Bares, Punta da *pt* Spain 54 D1
Estagno Point Phil. 74 B2
Eşţahbân Iran 100 C4
Estância *Goiás* Brazil 206 B4
Estância *Sergipe* Brazil 202 E4
Estância U.S.A. 181 F6
Estância Camerón Chile 205 C9
Estância Carmen Arg. 205 C9
Estarreja Port. 54 C4
Estats, Pic d' *mt.* France/Spain 55 M2
Estcourt S. Africa 133 N6
Este Italy 56 D3
Este, Parque Nacional del *nat. park*
  Dom. Rep. 187 F3
Esteban Iraq 107 F5
Esteban de Urizar Arg. 201 D5
Esteli Nicaragua 186 B4
Estella Spain 55 I2
  also known as Lizarra
Estena *r.* Spain 54 G5
Estepa Spain 54 G7
Estepona Spain 54 F8
Esteras *r.* Spain 54 H5
Esterel *reg.* France 51 M9
Estero Bay U.S.A. 182 C5
Esteros Para. 201 E5
Estes Park U.S.A. 180 F4

Este Sudeste, Cayos del *is* Col. 198 A1
Estevan Canada 167 K5
Esteven Group *i.* Canada 166 D4
Estherville U.S.A. 178 D3
Estill U.S.A. 175 D5
Estiva Brazil 207 G9
Estiva *r.* Brazil 202 C3
Eston Canada 167 I5
▶**Estonia** *country* Europe 42 F3
  known as Eesti in Estonian; formerly known
  as Estonskaya S.S.R.
  europe [countries] ▶▶ 32–35
Estonskaya S.S.R. *country* Europe *see*
  Estonia
Estreito Brazil 204 H3
Estrela, Serra da *mts* Port. 54 D4
Estrela do Indaiá Brazil 207 H6
Estrela do Sul Brazil 206 H5
Estrella *mt.* Spain 55 H6
Estrella, Punta *pt* Mex. 184 B2
Estrella, Sierra *mts* U.S.A. 183 L8
Estrema Brazil 200 D3
Estremadura *reg.* Port. 54 B5
Estremoz Port. 54 D6
Estrondo, Serra *hills* Brazil 202 B3
Estuaire *prov.* Gabon 126 A4
Estuario do Sado, Reserva Natural do
  nature res. Port. 54 C6
Estuario do Tejo, Reserva Natural
  nature res. Port. 54 C6
Estūh Iran 100 B3
Esztergom Hungary 49 P8
  also known as Gran
Étables-sur-Mer France 50 D4
Etadunna Australia 146 C2
Etah India 96 C4
Étain France 51 L3
Etamamiou Canada 169 J3
Étampes France 51 I4
Etamunbanie, Lake *salt flat* Australia 148 C5
Étaples France 50 H2

	mountain	height	location	page#
1 ▶	Mount Everest	8 848m / 29 028ft	China/Nepal Asia ▶▶	97 E4
2 ▶	K2	8 611m / 28 251ft	China/Jammu and Kashmir Asia ▶▶	96 C4
3 ▶	Kangchenjunga	8 586m / 28 169ft	India/Nepal Asia ▶▶	97 F4
4 ▶	Lhotse	8 516m / 27 939ft	China/Nepal Asia ▶▶	97 E3
5 ▶	Makalu	8 463m / 27 765ft	China/Nepal Asia ▶▶	97 F4
6 ▶	Cho Oyu	8 201m / 26 906ft	China/Nepal Asia ▶▶	97 E3
7 ▶	Dhaulagiri	8 167m / 26 794ft	Nepal Asia ▶▶	97 D3
8 ▶	Manaslu	8 163m / 26 781ft	Nepal Asia ▶▶	97 E3
9 ▶	Nanga Parbat	8 126m / 26 660ft	Jammu and Kashmir Asia ▶▶	96 B2
10 ▶	Annapurna I	8 091m / 25 545ft	Nepal Asia ▶▶	97 D3

highest mountains

Etawah *Rajasthan* India 96 C4
Etawah *Uttar Pradesh* India 96 C4
Etchojoa Mex. 184 C3
Etelä-Suomi *prov.* Fin. 45 N3
eThandukukhanya S. Africa 133 O3
Ethelbert Canada 167 K5
Ethel Creek Australia 150 C4
E'Thembini S. Africa 132 G4
Etheridge *r.* Australia 149 D3
▶**Ethiopia** *country* Africa 128 C2
  3rd most populous country in Africa. Spelt
  Ityopia in Amharic; historically known as
  Abyssinia.
  africa [countries] ▶▶ 114–117
Ethiopian Highlands *mts* Eth. 128 C2
Etili Turkey 59 H9
  also known as Gölçük
Etimeşğut Turkey 106 C3
Etna *r.* Norway 45 J3
Etna, Monte *vol.* Sicilia Italy *see* Etna, Mount
Etna, Mount *vol.* Sicilia Italy 57 H11
  also known as Etna, Monte
Etna, Parco dell' *park* Sicilia Italy 57 G11
Etne Norway 45 I4
Etobicoke Canada 173 N7
Etolin Island U.S.A. 164 F3
Eton Australia 149 F4
Etorofu-tō *i.* Rus. Fed. *see* Iturup, Ostrov
Etosha National Park Namibia 130 B3
Etosha Pan *salt pan* Namibia 130 C3
Etoumbi Congo 126 B4
Etrek *r.* Iran/Turkm. *see* Atrek
Étrépagny France 50 H3
Etropole Bulg. 58 F6
Etsha Botswana 130 D3
Ettelbruck Lux. 51 L4
Etten-Leur Neth. 48 B4
Ettlingen Germany 48 F7
Ettumanur India 94 C4
Etxarri-Aranatz Spain *see* Echarri-Aranaz
Etzatlán Mex. 184 D4
Etzicom Coulee *r.* Canada 167 I5
Eua *i.* Tonga 145 H4
  formerly spelt Eooa
Euabalong Australia 147 E3
Eubank U.S.A. 176 A8
Euboea *i.* Greece *see* Evvoia
Eucla U.S.A. 176 E6
Euclid U.S.A. 176 D4
Euclides da Cunha Brazil 202 E4
Eucumbene, Lake Australia 147 E3
Eudora U.S.A. 175 B5
Eudunda Australia 146 C3
Eufaula AL U.S.A. 175 C6
Eufaula OK U.S.A. 179 D5
Eufaula Lake *resr* U.S.A. 179 D5
Eugene U.S.A. 180 B3
Eugenia, Punta *pt* Mex. 184 B3
Eulo Australia 147 E2
Eungella Australia 149 F4
Eungella National Park Australia 149 F4
Eunice LA U.S.A. 179 D6
Eunice NM U.S.A. 179 B5
▶**Euphrates** *r.* Asia 107 F5
  Longest river in western Asia. Also known
  as Al Furāt (Iraq/Syria) or Firat (Turkey).
Eupora U.S.A. 175 B5
Eura Fin. 45 M3
Eure *r.* France 50 H3
Eureka N.W.T. Canada 172 D10
Eureka CA U.S.A. 180 A4
Eureka IL U.S.A. 168 B5
Eureka KS U.S.A. 178 C4
Eureka MT U.S.A. 180 D2
Eureka NV U.S.A. 182 G2
Eureka OH U.S.A. 176 C2
Eureka SD U.S.A. 178 B2
Eureka UT U.S.A. 183 L2
Eureka Sound *sea chan.* Canada 165 K2
Eureka Springs U.S.A. 179 D4
Eureka Valley U.S.A. 182 G4
Eurinilla *watercourse* Australia 146 D2
Euriowie Australia 147 D2
Euroa Australia 147 E4
Eurombah Australia 149 F5
Eurombah Creek *r.* Australia 149 F5
Europa, Île *i.* Indian Ocean *see* Europa, Île
  English form Europa Island
Europa, Picos de *mts* Spain 54 F1
Europa, Punta de *pt* Gibraltar *see*
  Europa Point
Europa Island Indian Ocean *see* Europa, Île

Europa Point Gibraltar 54 F8
  also known as Europa, Punta de
Eustis U.S.A. 175 D6
Euston Australia 147 D3
Eutaw U.S.A. 175 C5
Eutin Germany 48 H1
Eutsuk Lake Canada 166 E4
Evale Angola 127 B9
Evans, Lac *l.* Canada 168 E3
Evansburg Canada 167 H4
Evans City U.S.A. 176 E5
Evans Ice Stream Antarctica 222 S1
Evans Strait Canada 165 K3
Evanston IL U.S.A. 174 C3
Evanston WY U.S.A. 180 E4
Evansville Canada 168 D4
Evansville IN U.S.A. 174 C4
Evansville WI U.S.A. 172 D8
Evansville WY U.S.A. 180 F4
Eva Perón Arg. *see* La Plata
Eva Perón *prov.* Arg. *see* La Pampa
Evart U.S.A. 173 H7
Evaton S. Africa 133 L3
Evaz Iran 100 C5
Evcili Turkey 108 F1
Eveleth U.S.A. 174 A2
Evening Shade U.S.A. 174 B4
Evensk Rus. Fed. 39 P3
Evenskjær Norway 44 L1
Everard, Cape Australia 147 F4
Everard, Lake *salt flat* Australia 146 B2
Everard, Mount N.T. Australia 148 B4
Everard, Mount S.A. Australia 148 B5
Everard Range *hills* Australia 146 B1
Everek Turkey *see* Develi
▶**Everest, Mount** China/Nepal 97 E4
  Highest mountain in the world and in Asia.
  Also known as Qomolangma Feng or
  Sagarmatha.
  world [physical features] ▶▶ 8–9
Everett PA U.S.A. 176 G5
Everett WA U.S.A. 180 B2
Evergem Belgium 51 J1
▶**Everglades** *swamp* U.S.A. 175 D7
  world [land cover] ▶▶ 18–19
Everglades National Park U.S.A. 175 D7
Evergreen U.S.A. 175 C6
Everman, Volcán *vol.* Mex. 184 C6
Everson U.S.A. 180 B2
Evertsberg Sweden 45 K3
Evesham Australia 149 D4
Evesham U.K. 47 K11
Évian-les-Bains France 51 M6
Evijärvi Fin. 44 M3
Evinayong Equat. Guinea 125 H6
Evington U.S.A. 176 F8
Evinos *r.* Greece 59 C10
Evje Norway 45 I4
Evolène Switz. 51 N6
Évora Port. 54 D6
Evoron, Ozero *l.* Rus. Fed. 82 E2
Evosmo Greece 58 D8
Evowghlí Iran 100 A2
Évreux France 50 H3
Évron France 50 F5
Evros *r.* Greece/Turkey 58 H8
  also known as Meriç; also spelt Hebros
Evrotas *r.* Greece 59 D12
Évry France 51 I4
Evrychou Cyprus 108 D2
  also spelt Evrykhou
Evrykhou Cyprus *see* Evrychou
Evvoia *i.* Greece 59 F10
  English form Euboea; also known as
  Negroponte
Ewa Beach U.S.A. 181 [inset] Z1
Ewan Australia 149 E3
Ewaso Ngiro *r.* Kenya 128 D4
Ewbank S. Africa 132 H4
Ewe, Loch *b.* U.K. 46 G6
Ewen U.S.A. 172 C4
Ewenkizu Zizhiqi China *see* Bayan Tohoi
Ewing Island Antarctica 222 T2
Ewirgol China 88 D3
Ewo Congo 126 B5
Exaltación Bol. 200 D3
Excelsior S. Africa 133 L5
Excelsior Mountain U.S.A. 182 F3
Excelsior Mountains U.S.A. 182 F3
Excelsior Springs U.S.A. 178 D4
Exe *r.* U.K. 47 I13
Executive Committee Range *mts*
  Antarctica 222 P1
Exeland U.S.A. 172 B5
Exeter Canada 173 L7
Exeter U.K. 47 I13
Exeter CA U.S.A. 182 E5
Exeter NH U.S.A. 177 O3
Exmoor *hills* U.K. 47 I12
Exmoor National Park U.K. 47 I12
Exmore U.S.A. 177 J8
Exmouth Australia 150 A4
Exmouth U.K. 47 I13
Exmouth, Mount Australia 147 F2
Exmouth Gulf Australia 150 A4
Exmouth Lake Canada 167 H1
Expedition National Park Australia 149 F5
Expedition Range *mts* Australia 149 F5
Exploits *r.* Canada 169 K3
Exton U.S.A. 177 J5
Extremadura *aut. comm.* Spain 54 H5
Extrême-Nord *prov.* Cameroon 125 I4
Exuma Cays *is* Bahamas 186 D1
Exuma Sound *sea chan.* Bahamas 186 E1
Eya *r.* Rus. Fed. 41 F7
Eyangu Dem. Rep. Congo 126 D5
Eyasi, Lake *salt l.* Tanz. 129 B5
Eyawadi *r.* Myanmar *see* Irrawaddy
Eydehavn Norway 45 J4
Eyeberry Lake Canada 167 K2
Eyelemebbresk Rus. Fed. 40 L2
Eyemouth U.K. 46 J8
Eyjafjallajökull *ice cap* Iceland 44 [inset] C3
Eyl Somalia 128 F3
Eylau Rus. Fed. *see* Bagrationovsk
Eymet France 50 G8
Eymir Turkey 59 J11
Eymoutiers France 50 H7
Eyre *r.* France 50 E8
Eyre (South), Lake *salt flat* Australia 146 C2
▶**Eyre, Lake** *salt flat* Australia 146 C2
  Largest lake in Oceania and lowest point.
  oceania [landscapes] ▶▶ 136–137
  oceania [features] ▶▶ 142–143
Eyre Creek *watercourse* Australia 148 C5

Eyre Mountains N.Z. 153 C13
Eyre Peak N.Z. 153 C13
Eyre Peninsula Australia 146 B3
Eyrieux r. France 51 K8
Eysturoy i. Faroe Is 46 F1
Eyuku waterhole Kenya 128 C5
Eyumojok Cameroon 125 H5
Eyvānaki Iran 100 C3
Ezakheni S. Africa 133 O5
eZamokuhle S. Africa 133 N3
'Ezbet el Burg Egypt 108 C6
Ezbet el Gezîra Egypt 108 C6
Ezbet Gamasa el Gharbîya Egypt 108 C6
Ezel U.S.A. 176 B8
Ezenzeleni S. Africa 133 M4
Ezequiel Ramos Mexía, Embalse resr Arg. 204 C5
Ezernieki Latvia 42 I5
Ezhou China 87 E2
formerly known as Echeng
Ezhva Rus. Fed. 40 I3
formerly known as Sloboda
Ezine Turkey 106 A3
Ezinepazar Turkey 106 D2
Ezo i. Japan see Hokkaidō
Ezousa r. Cyprus 108 D3
Ezra's Tomb tourist site Iraq 107 F5

↓ F

Faadhippolhu Atoll Maldives 94 B5
Fabens U.S.A. 181 F7
Faber, Mount hill Sing. 76 [inset]
Faber Lake Canada 167 G2
Fabero Spain 54 E2
Fåborg Denmark 45 J5
Fabriano Italy 56 E5
Facatativá Col. 198 C3
Fachi Niger 125 H2
Factoryville U.S.A. 177 J4
Facundo Arg. 205 C7
Fada Chad 120 D5
Fada-Ngourma Burkina 125 F3
Faḍīlah well Saudi Arabia 105 E3
Faḍli reg. Yemen 105 D5
Fadnoun, Plateau du Alg. 123 H4
Faenza Italy 56 D4
Færingehavn Greenland see Kangerluarsoruseq
Færoerne terr. N. Atlantic Ocean see Faroe Islands
Faeroes terr. N. Atlantic Ocean see Faroe Islands
Fafa r. Cent. Afr. Rep. 126 C3
Fafanlap Indon. 73 H7
Fafe Port. 54 C3
Fafen Shet' watercourse Eth. 128 E3
Fafi waterhole Kenya 128 D5
Faga watercourse Burkina 125 F3
Făgăraş Romania 58 F3

▶Fagatogo American Samoa 145 H3
Capital of American Samoa.

Fagersta Sweden 45 K4
Făget Romania 58 D3
Fagnano, Lago l. Arg./Chile 205 C9
Fagne reg. Belgium 51 K2
Fagochia well Niger 125 G2
Faguibine, Lac l. Mali 124 D2
Fagurhólsmýri Iceland 44 [inset] C3
Fagwir Sudan 128 A2
Fahlīān, Rūdkhāneh-ye watercourse Iran 100 B4
Fahraj Iran 100 C4
Fahūd, Jabal hill Oman 105 G3
Faillon, Lac l. Canada 173 Q2
Fairbanks U.S.A. 164 E3
Fairborn U.S.A. 176 A6
Fairbury U.S.A. 178 C3
Fairchild U.S.A. 172 C6
Fairfax N.Z. 153 C14
Fairfax IA U.S.A. 172 B9
Fairfax VA U.S.A. 177 H7
Fairfax VT U.S.A. 177 L1
Fairfield CA U.S.A. 182 B3
Fairfield IA U.S.A. 174 B3
Fairfield ID U.S.A. 180 D4
Fairfield IL U.S.A. 174 B4
Fairfield OH U.S.A. 176 A6
Fairfield TX U.S.A. 179 C6
Fairfield UT U.S.A. 183 L1
Fairfield VA U.S.A. 176 F8
Fairgrove U.S.A. 173 J7
Fairhaven U.S.A. 177 O4
Fair Haven U.S.A. 177 L2
Fair Head U.K. 47 F8
Fair Hill U.S.A. 177 J6
Fair Isle i. U.K. 46 K4
Fairlee U.S.A. 177 M2
Fairlie N.Z. 153 E12
Fairmont MN U.S.A. 178 D3
Fairmont WV U.S.A. 176 E6
Fairmont Hot Springs Canada 167 H5
Fairplay U.S.A. 180 F5
Fairview Australia 149 E2
Fairview Canada 166 G3
Fairview IL U.S.A. 172 C10
Fairview KY U.S.A. 176 B7
Fairview MI U.S.A. 173 I6
Fairview OK U.S.A. 179 C4
Fairview PA U.S.A. 176 E3
Fairview UT U.S.A. 183 M2
Fairview WI U.S.A. 172 C7
Fairview Park Hong Kong China 87 [inset]
Fairweather, Cape U.S.A. 166 B3
Fairweather, Mount Canada/U.S.A. 164 F4
Fais i. Micronesia 73 J5
formerly known as Tromelin Island
Faisalabad Pak. 101 H4
formerly known as Lyallpur
Faizabad Afgh. see Feyzābād
Faizabad Afgh. 101 F2
Faizabad India 97 D4
Fāj aş Şulubī watercourse Saudi Arabia 109 M7
Fajj, Wādī al watercourse Iraq 109 O5
Fajr, Wādī watercourse Saudi Arabia 107 D5
Fakaofo atoll Tokelau 145 H2
also spelt Fakaofu; formerly known as Bowditch
Fakaofu atoll Tokelau see Fakaofo
Fakel Rus. Fed. 40 J4
formerly known as Sergiyevskiy
Fakenham U.K. 47 M11
Fåker Sweden 44 K3
Fakfak Indon. 73 H7
Fakhrabad Iran 100 C4
Fakiragram India 97 F4
Fakiyska Reka r. Bulg. 58 I6
Fakse Denmark 45 K5
Fakse Bugt b. Denmark 45 K5
Faku China 85 I3
Falaba Sierra Leone 124 C4
Falagountou Burkina 125 F3
Falaise France 50 F4
Falaise Lake Canada 167 G2
Falakata India 97 F4
Falam Myanmar 78 A3
Falavarjan Iran 100 B3
Falcarragh Rep. of Ireland 47 D8
Falces Spain 55 J2
Fălciu Romania 58 J2
Falcón state Venez. 198 D2
Falcon, Cap c. Alg. 55 K9
Falconara Marittima Italy 56 F5
Falcone, Capo del c. Sardegna Italy 56 A8
Falcon Island Tonga see Fonuafo'ou
Falcon Lake Canada 167 M5
Falcon Lake l. Mex./U.S.A. 185 F3
Falelima Samoa 145 H3
Falémé r. Mali/Senegal 124 B3
Falerii Italy see Civita Castellana
Falfurrias U.S.A. 179 C7
Falher Canada 167 G4
Falkat watercourse Eritrea 104 B4
Falkenberg Germany 49 K4
Falkenberg Sweden 45 K4
Falkensee Germany 49 K3
Falkirk U.K. 46 I8

▶Falkland Islands terr. S. Atlantic Ocean 205 F8
United Kingdom Overseas Territory. Also known as Malvinas, Islas.
southamerica [countries] ▶ 192–193

Falkland Sound sea chan. Falkland Is 205 E9
Falkner Arg. 204 D6
Falkonera i. Greece 59 E12
Falköping Sweden 45 K4
Fall r. U.S.A. 178 D4
Fall Branch U.S.A. 176 C9
Fallbrook U.S.A. 183 G8
Fall Creek U.S.A. 172 B6
Fallieres Coast Antarctica 222 T2
Fallon U.S.A. 182 F2
Fall River U.S.A. 177 N4
Fall River Pass U.S.A. 180 F4
Falls City U.S.A. 178 D3
Falls Creek U.S.A. 176 G4
Falmouth Antigua and Barbuda 187 H3
Falmouth Jamaica 186 D3
Falmouth U.K. 47 G13
Falmouth KY U.S.A. 176 A7
Falmouth MA U.S.A. 177 O4
Falmouth ME U.S.A. 177 O2
Falmouth VA U.S.A. 176 H7
Falou Mali 124 D3
False r. Canada 169 G1
False Bay S. Africa 132 C11
False Bay Park S. Africa 133 Q4
False Point India 95 E1
Falso, Cabo c. Dom. Rep. 187 F3
Falso, Cabo c. Hond. 186 C4
Falso Cabo de Hornos c. Chile 205 C9
Falster i. Denmark 45 J5
Fălticeni Romania 58 H1
Falun Sweden 45 K3
Falzarego, Passo di pass Italy 56 E2
Famagusta Cyprus 108 E2
also known as Ammochostos or Gazimağusa or Magosa
Famagusta Bay Cyprus see Ammochostos Bay
Famatina Arg. 204 D3
Famatina, Sierra de mts Arg. 204 C3
Famenin Iran 100 B3
Fame Range hills Australia 151 C5
Family Lake Canada 167 M5
Family Well Australia 150 D4
Fana Mali 124 D3
Fanad Head Rep. of Ireland 47 E8
Fanambana Madag. 131 [inset] K2
Fanandrana Madag. 131 [inset] K3
Fanari, Akra pt Greece 59 H11
Fanchang China 87 F2
Fandriana Madag. 131 [inset] J4
Fang Thai. 78 B4
Fangak Sudan 128 A2
Fangcheng China see Fangchenggang
Fangcheng China 87 E1
Fangchenggang China 87 D4
formerly known as Fangcheng
Fangdou Shan mts China 87 D2
Fangliao Taiwan 87 G4
Fangshan Taiwan 87 G4
Fangxian China 87 D1
Fangzheng China 82 C3
Fani i Vogël r. Albania 58 A7
Fanipal' Belarus 42 I8
Fankuai China 87 D2
formerly known as Fankuaidian
Fankuaidian China see Fankuai
Fanling Hong Kong China 87 [inset]
Fannrem Norway 44 J3
Fannūj Iran 101 D5
Fanø i. Denmark 45 J5
Fano Italy 56 F5
historically known as Colonia Julia Fenestris or Fanum Fortunae
Fanoualie i. Tonga see Fonualei
Fanshan Anhui China 87 F2
Fanshan Zhejiang China 87 G3
Fanshi China 85 G4
Fan Si Pan mt. Vietnam 78 C3
Fanum Fortunae Italy see Fano
Fanxian China 85 G5
also known as Yingtaoyuan
Farab Turkm. see Farap
Faraba Mali 124 C3
Farab-Pristan' Turkm. see Dzheykhun
Faradje Dem. Rep. Congo 126 F4
Faradofay Madag. see Tôlañaro
Farafangana Madag. 131 [inset] J4
Farafenni Gambia 124 B3
Farafra Oasis Egypt 121 F3
Farāgheh Iran 100 C4
Farāh Afgh. 101 E3
historically known as Alexandria Prophthasia
Farāh prov. Afgh. 101 E3
Faraḩābād Iran see Khezerābād
Farah Rūd watercourse Afgh. 101 E4
Farakhulm Afgh. 101 G3
Farallon de Medinilla i. N. Mariana Is 73 K3
also known as Bird Island
Farallon de Pajaros vol. N. Mariana Is 73 J2
Farallones de Cali, Parque Nacional nat. park Col. 198 B4
Farallon National Wildlife Refuge nature res. U.S.A. 182 A4
Faramuti I. Sudan 126 E2
Faranah Guinea 124 C4
Faraoani Romania 58 H2
Far'aoun well Mauritania 124 B2
Farap Turkm. 103 E5
formerly spelt Farab
Fararah Oman 105 F4
Farasān Saudi Arabia 104 C4
Farasān, Jazā'ir is Saudi Arabia 104 C4
Faratsiho Madag. 131 [inset] J3
Faraulep atoll Micronesia 73 J5
also known as Fattoilep; also spelt Foraulep; formerly known as Gardner
Fardes r. Spain 55 I7
Farewell, Cape Greenland 165 O3
also known as Farvel, Kap or Nunap Isua or Uummannarsuaq
Farewell, Cape N.Z. 152 G8
Farewell Spit N.Z. 152 G8
Färgelanda Sweden 45 K4
Farghona Uzbek. see Fergana
Farghona Wiloyati admin. div. Uzbek. see Ferganskaya Oblast'
Fargo U.S.A. 178 C2
Faribault U.S.A. 174 A2
Faribault, Lac l. Canada 169 G1
Faridabad India 96 C3
Faridkot India 96 B3
Faridpur Bangl. 97 F5
Faridpur India 96 C3
Fārīġ Iran 100 D2
Fārigh, Wādī al watercourse Libya 120 C2
Färila Sweden 45 K3
Farim Guinea-Bissau 124 B3
Farīmān Iran 101 D3
Farinha r. Brazil 202 C3
Farish Uzbek. 103 F4
also spelt Forish
Fâriskûr Egypt 108 C6
Färjestaden Sweden 45 L4
Farkadhon Greece 59 D9
Farkhar Afgh. see Farkhato
Farkhato Afgh. 101 G2
also known as Farkhar
Farkhor Tajik. 101 G2
also spelt Parkhar
Farley U.S.A. 172 B8
Farmahin Iran 100 B3
Farmakonisi i. Greece 59 I11
Farmer City U.S.A. 174 B3
Farmer Island Canada 168 D1
Farmerville U.S.A. 179 D5
Farmington Canada 166 F4
Farmington IA U.S.A. 172 B10
Farmington IL U.S.A. 172 C10
Farmington ME U.S.A. 177 O1
Farmington MO U.S.A. 174 B4
Farmington NH U.S.A. 177 N2
Farmington NM U.S.A. 181 E5
Farmington UT U.S.A. 180 E4
Farmington Hills U.S.A. 173 J8
Far Mountain Canada 166 E4
Farmville U.S.A. 176 G8
Farne Islands U.K. 46 K8
Farnham U.S.A. 177 I8
Farnham, Lake salt flat Australia 151 D5
Farnham, Mount Canada 167 G5
Faro Brazil 199 G5
Faro r. Cameroon 125 I4
Faro Canada 166 C2
Faro Port. 54 D7
Faro admin. dist. Port. 54 C7
Fårö i. Sweden 45 L4
Faro, Réserve du nature res. Cameroon 125 I4
Faro, Serra do mts Spain 54 D2

▶Faroe Islands terr. N. Atlantic Ocean 46 E2
Self-governing Danish Territory. Also spelt Faeroes; also known as Færoerne or Føroyar.
europe [countries] ▶ 32–35

Fårösund Sweden 45 L4
Farquhar Atoll Seychelles 129 F7
Farquhar Islands Seychelles 129 F7
Farquharson Tableland hills Australia 151 C5
Farrandsville U.S.A. 176 H4
Farrars Creek watercourse Australia 149 D5
Farrāsh, Jabal al hill Saudi Arabia 104 C4
Farrāshband Iran 100 C4
Farr Bay Antarctica 223 G2
Farrellton Canada 173 R5
Farrokhī Iran 101 D3
Farrukhabad India see Fatehgarh
Fārs prov. Iran 100 C4
historically known as Pars or Parsa or Persis
Farsakh Iran 100 C3
Farsala Greece 59 D9
Farsaliotis r. Greece 59 D9
Fārsī, Jazīreh-ye i. Iran 107 G6
Farson U.S.A. 180 E4
Farsund Norway 45 I4
Fartak, Jabal mts Yemen 105 E5
Fartak, Ra's c. Yemen 105 F5
Fărţăneşti Romania 58 I3
Fartura r. Brazil 206 C3
Fartura, Serra da mts Brazil 203 A8
Farvel, Kap c. Greenland see Farewell, Cape
Farwell MI U.S.A. 173 I7
Farwell TX U.S.A. 179 B5
Fāryāb prov. Afgh. 101 F2
Fāryāb Hormozgan Iran 100 D5
also known as Deh Barez
Fāryāb Kerman Iran 100 D4
Farynava Belarus 43 J6
Fasā Iran 100 C4
Fasano Italy 56 J8
Fåset Norway 45 J3
Faşikan Geçidi pass Turkey 108 D1
Fasil Ghebbi and Gonder Monuments tourist site Eth. 128 C1
Fāsteh, Ra's-e pt Iran 101 E5
Fastiv Ukr. 41 D6
also spelt Fastov
Fastov Ukr. see Fastiv
Fatehabad India 96 B3
Fatehgarh Madhya Pradesh India 96 C4
Fatehgarh Uttar Pradesh India 96 C4
formerly known as Farrukhabad
Fatehnagar India 96 B4
Fatehpur Rajasthan India 96 B4
Fatehpur Uttar Pradesh India 96 D4
Fatehpur Sikri India 96 C4
Fateyevka Rus. Fed. 43 P9
Fatezh Rus. Fed. 43 Q9
Fatḩābād Iran 100 C4
Fathai Sudan 128 A2
Fati, Lac l. Mali 124 E2
Fatick Senegal 124 A3
Fattoilep atoll Micronesia see Faraulep
Fatuma Dem. Rep. Congo 127 F6
Faulkton U.S.A. 178 C2
Faulquemont France 51 M3
Fauquier Canada 166 G5
Fauresmith S. Africa 133 J6
Fauske Norway 44 K2
Faust Canada 167 H4
Favalto, Monte mt. Italy 56 E5
Favignana Sicilia Italy 57 E11
Favignana, Isola i. Sicilia Italy 57 E11
Fawcett Canada 167 H4
Fawn r. Canada 168 B2
Fawnleas S. Africa 133 O6
Fawwārah Saudi Arabia 104 C2
Faxaflói b. Iceland 44 [inset] B2
Faxälven r. Sweden 44 L3
Faxian Hu l. China 86 B3
Faya Chad 120 C5
also known as Largeau
Fayaoué New Caledonia 145 F4
Fayḍat al Adyān waterhole Iraq 109 M6
Fayḍat al Habbārīyah waterhole Iraq 109 N5
Fayette AL U.S.A. 175 C5
Fayette IA U.S.A. 172 B8
Fayette MI U.S.A. 172 G5
Fayette MO U.S.A. 178 D4
Fayette MS U.S.A. 175 B6
Fayette OH U.S.A. 176 A4
Fayetteville AR U.S.A. 179 D4
Fayetteville GA U.S.A. 175 C5
Fayetteville NC U.S.A. 174 E5
Fayetteville NY U.S.A. 177 I2
Fayetteville PA U.S.A. 176 H6
Fayetteville TN U.S.A. 174 C5
Fayetteville WV U.S.A. 176 D7
Fayfā Saudi Arabia 104 C4
Fayḩālah, Wādī watercourse Saudi Arabia 109 O8
Fâyid Egypt 108 D7
Faylakah i. Kuwait 107 G5
Fayl-la-Forêt France 51 L5
Fazair al Ghrazi watercourse Saudi Arabia 109 H8
Fazao Malfakassa, Parc National de nat. park Togo 125 F4
Fazeï well Niger 125 H2
Fazilka India 96 B3
Fazrān, Jabal hill Saudi Arabia 105 E2
Fdérik Mauritania 122 B5
formerly known as Fort Gouraud
Fead Group is P.N.G. see Nuguria Islands
Feale r. Rep. of Ireland 47 C11
Fear, Cape U.S.A. 175 E5
Feather r. U.S.A. 182 C3
Feather, North Fork r. U.S.A. 182 C2
Featherston N.Z. 152 J9
Fécamp France 50 G3
Federacija Bosna i Hercegovina aut. div. Bos.-Herz. 56 K4
English form Federation of Bosnia and Herzegovina; also known as Muslim-Croat Federation
Federal Arg. 204 F3
Federal Capital Territory admin. div. Nigeria 125 G4
Federal District admin. dist. Brazil see Distrito Federal
Federal District admin. dist. Venez. see Distrito Federal
Federalsburg U.S.A. 177 J7
Federated Malay States country Asia see Malaysia
Federation of Bosnia and Herzegovina aut. div. Bos.-Herz. see Federacija Bosna i Hercegovina
Fedorov Kazakh. see Fedorovka
Fedorovka Kustanayskaya Oblast' Kazakh. 103 E1
Fedorovka Pavlodarskaya Oblast' Kazakh. 103 I1
Fedorovka Zapadnyy Kazakhstan Kazakh. 102 B2
also known as Fedorov
Fedorovka Rus. Fed. 102 C1
Fedorovskoye Rus. Fed. 43 U5
Fehérgyarmat Hungary 49 T8
Fehet Lake Canada 167 M1
Fehmarn i. Germany 48 I1
Fehmarn Belt strait Denmark/Germany 45 J5
also known as Femer Bælt
Fehrbellin Germany 49 J3
Feia, Lagoa lag. Brazil 203 D7
Feicheng China see Feixian
Feidong China 87 F2
also known as Dianbu
Feijó Brazil 200 C2
Feilding N.Z. 152 J8
Fei Ngo Shan hill Hong Kong China see Kowloon Peak
Feio r. Brazil see Aguapeí
Feira Zambia see Luangwa
Feira de Santana Brazil 202 E5
Feira do Monte Spain 54 D1
Feirân well Egypt 108 E9
Feirân, Wâdi watercourse Egypt 108 E9
Feirâni, Gebel mt. Egypt 108 F9
Feixi China 87 F2
also known as Shangpai; formerly known as Shangpaihe
Feixian China 85 H5
also known as Feicheng
Feixiang China 85 G4
Fejaj, Chott el salt l. Tunisia 123 H2
Fejø i. Denmark 48 I1
Feke Turkey 106 C3
Felanitx Spain 55 O5
Felaou well Alg. 125 G2
Feldberg mt. Ger. 51 N5
Feldkirch Austria 48 G8
Feldkirchen in Kärnten Austria 49 L9
Feldru Romania 58 F1
Feliciano r. Arg. 204 F3
Felicity U.S.A. 176 A7
Felidhu Atoll Maldives 93 D10
Felipe C. Puerto Mex. 185 H5
Felixlândia Brazil 203 C6
Felixstowe U.K. 47 N12
Felletin France 51 I7
Fellowsville U.S.A. 176 F6
Felsberg Germany 48 G4
Felsina Italy see Bologna
Feltre Italy 56 D2
Femeas r. Brazil 202 C5
Femer Bælt strait Denmark/Germany see Fehmarn Belt
Femminamorta, Monte mt. Italy 57 I9
Femø i. Denmark 48 I1
Femundsmarka Nasjonalpark nat. park Norway 44 K3
Fen r. China 85 F5
Fenambosy, Lohatanjona pt Madag. 131 [inset] J5
Fenelon Falls Canada 173 O6
Fener Burnu hd Turkey 108 G1
also known as Karataş Burnu
Fénérive Madag. see Fenoarivo Atsinanana
Fengari mt. Greece 59 G8
Fengcheng China see Lianjiang
Fengcheng China see Yongding
Fengcheng China see Anxi
Fengcheng China see Xinfeng
Fengcheng China see Fengshan
Fengcheng Jiangxi China 87 E2
Fengcheng Liaoning China 83 B4
Fengchuan China see Fengxin
Fengdu China 87 C2
also known as Xiucaiwan; formerly known as Mingshan
Fenggang China see Shaxian
Fenggang China 87 C3
also known as Longquan
Fenggang China see Yihuang
Fenggeling China 86 C1
Fenghua China 87 G2
Fenghuang China 87 D3
also known as Tuojiang
Fengjiaba China see Wangcang
Fengjie China 87 D2
also known as Yong'an
Fengkai China 87 D4
also known as Jiangkou
Fenglin Taiwan 87 G4
Fengming China see Qishan
Fengnan China 85 H4
Fengning China 85 H3
also known as Dage or Dagezhen
Fengqi China see Luochuan
Fengqing China 86 A3
also known as Fengshan
Fengqiu China 87 E1
Fengrun China 85 H4
Fengshan China see Luoyuan
Fengshan China 86 C3
also known as Fengcheng
Fengshan China see Luotian
Fengshan China see Fengqing
Fengshuba Shuiku resr China 87 E3
Fengshui Shan mt. China 82 A1
Fengtai China 87 F1
Fengtongzai Giant Panda Reserve nature res. China 86 B2
Fengxian Jiangsu China 87 F1
Fengxian Shaanxi China 86 C1
also known as Shuangshipu
Fengxian Shanghai China 87 G2
also known as Nanqiao
Fengxiang China see Luobei
Fengxiang China see Lincang
Fengxin China 87 E2
also known as Fengchuan
Fengyang China 87 F1
also known as Fucheng
Fengyi China see Zheng'an
Fengyi China see Maoxian
Fengyüan Taiwan 87 G3
Fengzhen China 85 G3
Fenhe Shuiku resr China 85 F4
Feni Bangl. 97 F5
Feni Islands P.N.G. 145 E2
Fenny r. Bangl./India 97 F5
Feno, Capo di c. Corse France 56 A7
Fenoarivo Atsinanana Madag. 131 [inset] K3
formerly known as Fénérive
Fenoarivo Be Madag. 131 [inset] J3
Fenton U.S.A. 173 J8
Fenua Ura atoll Fr. Polynesia see Manuae
Fenwick U.S.A. 176 E7
Fenyang China 85 F4
Fenyi China 87 E3
Feodosiya Ukr. 41 E7
also known as Caffa or Kafa or Kefe; historically known as Theodosia
Fer, Cap de c. Alg. 123 G1
Férai Greece see Feres
Ferapontovo Rus. Fed. 43 T2
Ferdinandshof Germany 49 K2
Ferdows Iran 100 D3
Fère-Champenoise France 51 J4
Feres Greece 58 H8
also known as Férai
Fërfër Somalia 128 E3
Fergana Uzbek. 103 G4
also spelt Farghona; formerly known as Novyy Margelan or Skobelev
Fergana Oblast admin. div. Uzbek. see Ferganskaya Oblast'
Fergana Range mts Kyrg. see Fergana Too Tizmegi
Fergana Too Tizmegi mts Kyrg. 103 H4
English form Fergana Range; also known as Ferganskiy Khrebet
Ferganskaya Oblast' admin. div. Uzbek. 103 G4
English form Fergana Oblast; also known as Farghona Wiloyati
Ferganskiy Khrebet mts Kyrg. see Fergana Too Tizmegi
Fergus Canada 173 M7
Fergus Falls U.S.A. 178 C2
Ferguson Lake Canada 167 L2
Fergusson r. Australia 148 A2
Fergusson Island P.N.G. 145 E2
Fériana Tunisia 123 H2
Ferjukot Iceland 44 [inset] B2
Ferkessédougou Côte d'Ivoire 124 D4
Ferlach Austria 49 L9
Ferlo, Vallée du watercourse Senegal 124 B3
Ferlo-Nord, Réserve de Faune du nature res. Senegal 124 B3
Ferlo-Sud, Réserve de Faune du nature res. Senegal 124 B3
Fermo Italy 56 F5
historically known as Firmum or Firmum Picenum
Fermont Canada 169 H2
Fermoselle Spain 54 E3
Fermoy Rep. of Ireland 47 D11
Fernandina Beach U.S.A. 175 D6
Fernando de Magallanes, Parque Nacional nat. park Chile 205 B9
Fernando de Noronha i. Brazil 216 L6
Fernandópolis Brazil 206 C7
Fernando Poó i. Equat. Guinea see Bioco
Fernán Núñez Spain 54 G7
Fernão Dias Brazil 207 I3
Fernão Veloso Moz. 131 I2
Ferndale U.S.A. 180 B2
Ferndown U.K. 47 K13
Fernhill N.Z. 152 K7
Fernie Canada 167 H5
Fernley U.S.A. 182 E2
Ferns Rep. of Ireland 47 F11
Ferozepore India see Firozpur
Ferrara Italy 56 D4
Ferrato, Capo c. Sardegna Italy 57 B9
Ferreira Spain 54 D1
Ferreira do Alentejo Port. 54 C6
Ferrellsburg U.S.A. 176 C7
Ferreñafe Peru 198 B6
Ferriday U.S.A. 175 B6
Ferro, Capo c. Sardegna Italy 56 B7
Ferrol Spain 54 C1
also known as El Ferrol; long form El Ferrol del Caudillo
Ferron U.S.A. 183 M2
Ferros Brazil 203 D6
Ferrum U.S.A. 176 E9
Ferryland Canada 169 K4
Ferryville Tunisia see Menzel Bourguiba
Fertő-tavi nat. park Hungary 49 N8
Ferzikovo Rus. Fed. 43 R7
Fès Morocco 122 D2
also spelt Al Fas or Fez
Feshi Dem. Rep. Congo 127 C6
Fessenden U.S.A. 178 C2
Fet Dom, Tanjung pt Indon. 75 D3
Fété Bowé Senegal 124 B3
Feteşti Romania 58 I4
Feteşti-Gară Romania 58 I4
Fethard Rep. of Ireland 47 E11
Fethiye Turkey see Yazıhan
Fethiye Turkey 106 B3
Fetisovo Kazakh. 102 C4
Fetlar i. U.K. 46 L3
Feuilles, Rivière aux r. Canada 169 G1
Feurs France 51 K7
Fevral'sk Rus. Fed. 82 C1
Fevzipaşa Turkey 107 D3
Feyzābād Afgh. 101 G2
also spelt Faizabad
Feyẕābād Iran 100 C4
Fez Morocco see Fès
Fiambalá Arg. 204 D2
Fiambala r. Arg. 204 D2
Fian Ghana 124 E4
Fianarantsoa Madag. 131 [inset] J4
Fianarantsoa prov. Madag. 131 [inset] J4
Fianga Chad 126 B2
Fiano Romano Italy 56 E6
Ficalho hill Port. 54 D7
Fichē Eth. 128 C2
Fichtelgebirge hills Germany 51 S2
Fichtelgebirge park Germany 48 J5
Ficksburg S. Africa 133 L5
Fidā oasis Saudi Arabia 105 F4
Fidenza Italy 56 C4
Fidîmîn Egypt 108 B8
Fidjeland Norway 45 I4
Fidlův Kopec hill Czech Rep. 49 O6
Field B.C. Canada 167 G5
Field Ont. Canada 173 M4
Field U.S.A. 176 B9
Field Island Australia 148 B2
Fiemanka r. Latvia 42 H5
Fieni Romania 58 G3
Fier Albania 58 A8
Fiery Creek r. Australia 148 C3
Fierzes, Liqeni i resr Albania 58 B6
Fife Lake U.S.A. 172 H6
Fife Ness pt U.K. 46 J7
Fifield U.S.A. 172 C5
Fifteenth of May City Egypt see Medinet 15 Mayo
Fifth Cataract rapids Sudan see 5th Cataract
Fifth Meridian Canada 167 H3
Figalo, Cap c. Alg. 55 J9
Figari, Capo c. Sardegna Italy 56 B8
Figeac France 51 I8
Figueira r. Port. 54 C6
Figueira da Foz Port. 54 C4
Figueiró dos Vinhos Port. 54 C5
Figueras Spain see Figueres
Figueres Spain 55 N2
also spelt Figueras
Figuig Morocco 123 E2
Figuil Cameroon 125 I4

▶Fiji country S. Pacific Ocean 145 G3
4th most populous and 5th largest country in Oceania.
oceania [countries] ▶ 138–139

Fik' Eth. 128 D2
Filabusi Zimbabwe 131 F4
Filadelfia Costa Rica 186 B5
Filadelfia Italy 57 I10
Filadelfia Para. 201 E5
Fiľakovo Slovakia 49 Q7
Filamana Mali 124 D4
Filchner Ice Shelf Antarctica 222 V1
Filey U.K. 47 L9
Filiaşi Romania 58 E4
Filiates Greece 59 B9
Filiatra Greece 59 C11
Filibe Bulg. see Plovdiv
Filicudi, Isola i. Isole Lipari Italy 57 G10
Filingué Niger 125 F3
Filiouri r. Greece 58 G8
Filipinas country Asia see Philippines
Filippa, Mys hd Rus. Fed. 82 E1
Filippiada Greece 59 B9
Filippoi tourist site Greece 58 F7
Filipstad Sweden 45 K4
Fillan Norway 44 J3
Fillíra Greece see Fillyra
Fillmore CA U.S.A. 182 F7
Fillmore UT U.S.A. 183 L3
Fillyra Greece 58 G7
also spelt Fillíra
Filtu Eth. 128 D3
Fimbull Ice Shelf Antarctica 223 A2
Fina, Réserve de nature res. Mali 124 C3
Finale Ligure Italy 56 A4
Fincastle U.S.A. 176 F8
Finch'a'ā Hāyk' l. Eth. 128 C2
Findhorn r. U.K. 46 I6
Fındık Turkey 107 E3
also known as Parona
Findlay U.S.A. 176 B4
Fine U.S.A. 177 J1
Finger Lake Canada 167 M4
Finger Lakes U.S.A. 177 I3
Fingeshwar India 94 D1
Fingoè Moz. 131 F2
Finiels, Sommet de mt. France 51 J8
Finike Turkey 106 B3
Finike Körfezi b. Turkey 106 B3
Finisterre Spain see Fisterra
Finisterre, Cabo c. Spain see Finisterre, Cape
Finisterre, Cape Spain 54 B2
also known as Finisterre, Cabo or Fisterra, Cabo
Finke Australia 148 B5
Finke watercourse Australia 148 B5
Finke, Mount hill Australia 146 B2
Finke Aboriginal Land res. Australia 148 C5
Finke Bay Australia 148 A2
Finke Flood Flats lowland Australia 148 B5
Finke Gorge National Park Australia 148 B5
▶Finland country Europe 44 M3
known as Suomi in Finnish
europe [countries] ▶ 32–35
europe [environments] ▶ 36–37
Finland U.S.A. 172 B3
Finland, Gulf of Europe 42 D2
Finlay r. Canada 166 E3
Finlay, Mount Canada 166 E3
Finlay Forks Canada 166 F4
Finlayson U.S.A. 172 A4
Finley Australia 147 E3
Finley U.S.A. 178 C2
Finmark Canada 172 D2
Finn r. Rep. of Ireland 47 E9
Finne ridge Germany 48 I4
Finnigan, Mount Australia 149 E2
Finniss r. Australia 148 A2
Finniss, Cape Australia 146 B3
Finnis Springs Aboriginal Land res. Australia 146 C2
Finnmark county Norway 44 N1
Finnmarksvidda reg. Norway 44 M1
Finnskog Norway 45 K3
Finnsnes Norway 44 L1
Finschhafen P.N.G. 73 K8
Finspång Sweden 45 K4
Finsteraarhorn mt. Switz. 51 O6
Finsterwalde Germany 49 K4
Finström Fin. 42 A1
Fintona U.K. 47 E9
Finucane Range hills Australia 149 D4
Fiora r. Italy 56 D6
Fiordland National Park N.Z. 153 B13
Fiorenzuola d'Arda Italy 56 B4
Fir reg. Saudi Arabia 105 D1
Fırat r. Turkey 107 D3 see Euphrates
Firavahana Madag. 131 [inset] J3
Firebaugh U.S.A. 182 D5
Firedrake Lake Canada 167 J2
Firenze Italy see Florence
Fire River Canada 173 J2
Fireside Canada 166 E3
Firesteel Creek r. U.S.A. 178 C3
Firiña Venez. 199 E3
Firk, Sha'īb watercourse Iraq 107 F5
Firkachi well Niger 125 I3
Firmat Arg. 204 E4
Firmino Alves Brazil 207 N1
Firminópolis Brazil 206 C3
Firminy France 51 K7
Firmum Italy see Fermo
Firmum Picenum Italy see Fermo
Firovo Rus. Fed. 43 O4
Firozabad India 96 C4
Firozkoh reg. Afgh. 101 F3
Firozpur Haryana India 96 C4
Firozpur Punjab India 96 B3
formerly spelt Ferozepore
First Cataract rapids Egypt see 1st Cataract
First Three Mile Opening sea chan. Australia 149 E2
Firuzabad Iran see Rāsk
Firūzābād Iran 100 C4
Firūzeh Iran 100 D2
Fīrūzkūh Iran 100 C3
Fischersbrunn Namibia 130 B5
Fish watercourse Namibia 130 C6
Fish r. S. Africa 132 E7
Fisher Australia 146 A2
Fisher Bay Antarctica 223 J2
Fisher Glacier Antarctica 223 E2
Fisher River Canada 167 L5
Fisher Strait Canada 165 K3
Fishersville U.S.A. 176 G7
Fishguard U.K. 47 H12
also known as Abergwaun
Fishing Creek U.S.A. 177 I7
Fishing Lake Canada 167 M4
Fish Lake Canada 166 F2
Fish Lake MN U.S.A. 172 A4
Fish Lake UT U.S.A. 183 M3
Fish Point U.S.A. 173 J7
Fiskå Norway 44 I3
Fiske, Cape Antarctica 222 T2
Fiskebøl Norway 44 K1
Fiskenæsset Greenland see Qeqertarsuatsiaat
Fismes France 51 J3
Fisterra Spain 54 B2
also spelt Finisterre
Fisterra, Cabo c. Spain see Finisterre, Cape
Fitampito Madag. 131 [inset] J4
Fitchburg MA U.S.A. 177 N3
Fitchburg WI U.S.A. 172 D8
Fitchville U.S.A. 176 C4
Fitíai Greece see Fyteies
Fitjar Norway 45 I4
Fitri, Lac l. Chad 120 C6
Fitzcarrald Peru 200 B2
Fitzgerald U.S.A. 175 D6
Fitzgerald River National Park Australia 151 B7
Fitz Hugh Sound sea chan. Canada 166 D5
Fitzmaurice r. Australia 148 A2
Fitz Roy Arg. 205 D7
Fitzroy r. Qld Australia 149 F4
Fitzroy r. W.A. Australia 150 C3
Fitz Roy, Cerro mt. Arg. 205 B8
Fitzroy Aboriginal Land res. Australia 148 A2
Fitzroy Crossing Australia 150 D3
Fitzwilliam Island Canada 168 D4
Fiume Croatia see Rijeka
Fiumefreddo di Sicilia Sicilia Italy 57 H11
Five Fingers Peninsula N.Z. 153 A13
Five Forks N.Z. 153 E13
Five Points U.S.A. 182 D5
Fivizzano Italy 56 C4
Fizi Dem. Rep. Congo 126 F6
Fizuli Azer. see Füzuli
Fjällsjönäs Sweden 44 L2
Fjellbu Norway 44 L1
Fjerritslev Denmark 45 J4
Fkih Ben Salah Morocco 122 D2
Flå Norway 45 J3
Flaga Iceland 44 [inset] C3

Flagstaff S. Africa 133 N8
also known as Siphaqeni
Flagstaff U.S.A. 183 M6
Flagstaff Lake U.S.A. 174 G2
Flaherty Island Canada 168 E1
Flakaberg Sweden 44 M2
Flåm Norway 45 I3
Flambeau r. U.S.A. 172 B5
Flamborough Head U.K. 47 L9
Flamenco, Isla i. Arg. 204 E6
Fläming hills Germany 49 J3
Flaming Gorge Reservoir U.S.A. 180 E4
Flaminksvlei salt pan S. Africa 132 F7
Flanagan U.S.A. 167 M4
Flandreau U.S.A. 178 C2
Flannagan Lake U.S.A. 176 C8
Flannan Isles U.K. 46 E5
Flåsjön i. Sweden 44 K2
Flat r. Canada 166 E2
Flat r. U.S.A. 172 I4
Flateyjardalsheiði reg. Iceland 44 [inset] C2
Flathead r. U.S.A. 180 D2
Flathead, Middle Fork r. U.S.A. 167 H5
Flathead Indian Reservation res. U.S.A. 180 D3
Flathead Lake U.S.A. 180 D3
Flatiron mt. Antarctica 222 P1
Flat Island Mauritius 72 E4
Flat Lick U.S.A. 176 B9
Flat Point N.Z. 152 J9
Flattery, Cape Australia 149 E2
Flattery, Cape U.S.A. 180 A2
Flat Top mt. Canada 166 E4
Flatwillow Creek r. U.S.A. 180 F3
Flatwoods KY U.S.A. 176 C7
Flatwoods WV U.S.A. 176 E7
Flechtinger Höhenzug park Germany 48 I3
Fleetwood U.K. 47 I10
Fleetwood U.S.A. 177 J5
Flekkefjord Norway 45 I4
Flemingsburg U.S.A. 176 B7
Flemington U.S.A. 177 K5
Flen Sweden 45 L4
Flensborg Fjord inlet Denmark/Germany 45 J7
also known as Flensburger Förde
Flensburg Germany 48 G1
Flensburger Förde inlet Denmark/Germany see Flensborg Fjord
Flers France 50 F4
Flesherton Canada 173 N6
Flesko, Tanjung pt Indon. 75 C2
Fletcher Lake Canada 167 I2
Fletcher Peninsula Antarctica 222 S2
Fletcher Pond i. U.S.A. 173 I6
Fleurance France 50 G9
Fleur de Lys Canada 169 J3
Fleur-de-May, Lac i. Canada 169 H3
Fleury-les-Aubrais France 51 H5
Flinders r. Australia 149 D3
Flinders Bay Australia 151 A7
Flinders Chase National Park Australia 146 C3
Flinders Group is Australia 149 E2
Flinders Group National Park Australia 149 E2
Flinders Island S.A. Australia 146 C3
Flinders Island Tas. Australia 147 E4
Flinders Passage Australia 149 E3
Flinders Ranges mts Australia 146 C3
Flinders Ranges National Park Australia 146 C2
Flinders Reefs Australia 149 F3
Flin Flon Canada 167 K4
Flint U.K. 47 I10
also known as Y Fflint
Flint r. U.S.A. 173 J7
Flint r. GA U.S.A. 175 C6
Flint r. MI U.S.A. 173 J7
Flint Island Kiribati 221 H6
Flintstone U.S.A. 176 G6
Flisa Norway 45 K3
Flisa r. Norway 45 K3
▶ Flissingskiy, Mys c. Rus. Fed. 38 G2
Most easterly point of Europe.
Flix Spain 55 L3
Flöha Germany 49 K5
Flood Range mts Antarctica 222 P1
Flora r. Australia 148 A2
Flora U.S.A. 172 G10
Florala U.S.A. 175 C6
Florac France 51 J8
Flora Reef Australia 149 E3
Floraville Australia 148 C3
Florence Italy 56 D5
also known as Firenze; historically known as Florentia
Florence AL U.S.A. 174 C4
Florence AZ U.S.A. 183 M8
Florence CO U.S.A. 181 F5
Florence KY U.S.A. 176 A7
Florence OR U.S.A. 180 A4
Florence SC U.S.A. 175 E5
Florence Junction U.S.A. 183 M8
Florencia Arg. 204 F3
Florencia Col. 198 C4
Florentia Italy see Florence
Florentino Ameghino Arg. 205 D6
Florentino Ameghino, Embalse resr Arg. 205 D6
Flores Brazil 202 D3

Flores Guat. 185 H5
Flores i. Indon. 75 B5
Florescência Brazil 200 C2
Flores de Goiás Brazil 202 C5
Flores Island Canada 166 E5
Flores Sea Indon. 75 A4
Floresta Brazil 202 E4
Floresville U.S.A. 179 C6
Floriano Brazil 202 D3
Floriano Peixoto Brazil 200 D2
Florianópolis Brazil 203 B8
Florida Bol. 201 E4
Florida Chile 204 B5
Florida Cuba 186 D2
Florida Uruguay 204 F4
Florida state U.S.A. 175 D6
Florida, Straits of Bahamas/U.S.A. 186 D2
Florida Bay U.S.A. 175 D7
Florida Keys is U.S.A. 175 D7
Florida Negra Arg. 205 D8
Flórida Paulista Brazil 206 B8
Floridia Sicilia Italy 57 H11
Florii, Vârful hill Romania 58 E1
Florin U.S.A. 182 C3
Florina Greece 58 C8
Florínia Brazil 206 C6
Floriskraaldam i. S. Africa 132 F10
Florissant U.S.A. 174 B4
Florø Norway 45 I3
Flour Lake Canada 169 H2
Floyd U.S.A. 176 E9
Floyd, Mount U.S.A. 183 L6
Floydada U.S.A. 179 B5
Fluchthorn mt. Austria/Switz. 51 Q6
Fluk Indon. 75 C3
Flums Switz. 51 P5
Flushing Neth. see Vlissingen
Flushing OH U.S.A. 176 D5
Fluvià r. Spain 55 O2
Fly r. P.N.G. 73 J8
Flying Fish, Cape Antarctica 222 R2
Flying Fox Creek r. Australia 148 B2
Foam Lake Canada 167 K4
Foča Bos.-Herz. 56 K5
also known as Srbinje
Foça Turkey 106 A3
Focșani Romania 58 I3
Focuri Romania 58 I1
Fodé Cent. Afr. Rep. 126 D3
Foelsche r. Australia 148 C2
Fogang China 87 E4
Fog Bay Australia 148 A2
Fogelsville U.S.A. 177 J5
Foggâret el Arab Alg. 123 F4
Foggia Italy 56 H7
Foglia r. Italy 56 E5
Föglö Fin. 45 M3
Fogo i. Cape Verde 124 [inset]
Fogo Island Canada 169 K3
Fogoleva Kazakh. 103 G4
Föhr i. Germany 48 F1
Foix France 50 H10
Fokino Rus. Fed. 43 P8
formerly known as Tsementnyy
Fokku Nigeria 125 G4
Folarskarnuten mt. Norway 45 I3
Folda i. Nord. Norway 44 K2
Folda i. N.-Trøndel. Norway 44 J2
Foldereid Norway 44 K2
Foldfjorden sea chan. Norway 44 J2
Folegandros Greece 59 F12
Folegandros i. Greece 59 F12
Foley U.S.A. 175 C6
Foley AL U.S.A. 175 C6
Foley MN U.S.A. 174 A2
Foleyet Canada 168 D3
Foley Island Canada 165 L3
Folgares Angola see Capelongo
Folger, Cape Antarctica 223 H2
Foligno Italy 56 E6
Folkestone U.K. 47 N12
Folkston U.S.A. 175 D6
Folldal Norway 45 J3
Follett U.S.A. 179 C9
Follonica Italy 56 C6
Folsom U.S.A. 176 E6
Folsom Lake U.S.A. 182 C3
Fomboni Comoros 129 D8
Fómento Cuba 186 D2
Fomin Rus. Fed. 41 Q7
Fominskoye Rus. Fed. 40 G4
Fonda U.S.A. 177 K3
Fond-du-Lac Canada 167 J3
Fond du Lac r. Canada 167 J3
Fond du Lac U.S.A. 172 E7
Fond du Lac Indian Reservation res. U.S.A. 174 A2
Fonde U.S.A. 176 B9
Fondevila Spain 54 C3
Fondi Italy 56 F7
historically known as Fundi
Fon Going ridge Guinea 124 C4
Fonni Sardegna Italy 57 B8
Fonsagrada Spain see A Fonsagrada
Fonseca Col. 198 C2
Fontainebleau France 51 I4
Fontanges Canada 169 G2
Fontas r. Canada 166 F3
Fontas r. Canada 166 F3
Fonte Boa Brazil 199 E5
Fonte do Pau-d'Água Brazil 201 F3
Fontenay-le-Comte France 50 F6
Fonteneau, Lac i. Canada 169 I3
Fontur pt Iceland 44 [inset] D2
Fonuafo'ou i. Tonga 145 H4
also known as Falcon Island; also spelt Fonuafu'u
Fonuafu'u i. Tonga see Fonuafo'ou
Fonualei i. Tonga 145 H3
also spelt Fanoualie; formerly known as Amargura Island
Fonyód Hungary 49 O9
Foochow China see Fuzhou
Fool Creek Reservoir U.S.A. 183 L2
Foot's Bay Canada 173 N5
Foping China 87 D1
also known as Yuanjiazhuang
Foraker, Mount U.S.A. 164 D3
Forat Iran 100 C3
Forauleg atoll Micronesia see Faraulep
Forbes Australia 147 F3
Forbes Reef Swaziland 133 P3
Forchheim Germany 48 I5
Ford r. Canada 169 H1
Ford r. U.S.A. 172 F5
Ford City CA U.S.A. 182 E6
Ford City PA U.S.A. 176 F5
Førde Hordaland Norway 45 I4
Førde Sogn og Fjordane Norway 45 I3
Fordell U.S.A. 182 B2
Fordingbridge U.K. 50 E2
Ford Range mts Antarctica 222 O1
Fords Bridge Australia 147 E2
Fordyce U.S.A. 179 D5
Forécariah Guinea 124 B4
Forel, Mont mt. Greenland 165 P3
Foreman U.S.A. 179 D5
Foremost Canada 167 I5
Foresight Mountain Canada 166 E4
Forest Canada 168 D5
Forest MS U.S.A. 175 B5
Forest OH U.S.A. 176 B5
Forest VA U.S.A. 176 F8
Forestburg Canada 167 H4
Forest City U.S.A. 174 E3
Forest Creek r. Australia 149 D3
Foresthill U.S.A. 182 D3

Forest Junction U.S.A. 172 E6
Forest Lake U.S.A. 172 A5
Forest Lakes U.S.A. 183 N7
Forest Park U.S.A. 175 C5
Forest Ranch U.S.A. 182 C2
Forestville Canada 169 G3
Forestville CA U.S.A. 182 A3
Forestville MI U.S.A. 173 K7
Forestville NY U.S.A. 176 F3
Forêt des Deux Balé nat. park Burkina 124 E4
Forêt de Togodo nature res. Togo 125 F5
Forfar U.K. 46 J7
Forges-les-Eaux France 50 H3
Forillon, Parc National de nat. park Canada 169 H3
Forish Uzbek. see Farish
Forked River U.S.A. 177 K6
Forks U.S.A. 180 A3
Fork Union U.S.A. 176 G8
Forlì Italy 56 E4
Forman U.S.A. 178 C2
Formby U.K. 47 I10
Formentera i. Spain 55 M6
Formentor, Cap de c. Spain 55 O5
Formerie France 50 H3
Former Yugoslav Republic of Macedonia country Europe see Macedonia
Formia Italy 56 F7
Formiga Brazil 203 C7
Formigine Italy 56 C4
Formosa Arg. 204 F2
Formosa r. Arg. 204 F2
Formosa country Asia see Taiwan
Formosa prov. Arg. 204 F2
Formosa, Serra hills Brazil 201 G3
Formoso Brazil 202 B4
Formoso r. Bahia Brazil 202 C5
Formoso r. Goiás Brazil 206 A5
Formoso r. Tocantins Brazil 202 B4
also known as Javaés
Fornos Moz. 131 G4
Forolshogna mt. Norway 44 J3
Føroyar terr. N. Atlantic Ocean see Faroe Islands
Forres U.K. 46 I5
Forrest Australia 151 E6
Forrest r. Australia 150 E2
Forrest U.S.A. 174 B3
Forrestal Range mts Antarctica 222 U1
Forrest City U.S.A. 174 B5
Forrest Lakes salt flat Australia 151 E4
Forreston U.S.A. 172 D8
Forsand Norway 45 I4
Forsayth Australia 149 D3
Forsbakken Norway 44 L1
Forshaga Sweden 45 K4
Forssa Fin. 45 M3
Forst Germany 49 L4
Forster Australia 147 G3
Forsyth GA U.S.A. 175 D5
Forsyth MO U.S.A. 178 D4
Forsyth MT U.S.A. 180 F3
Forsythe Canada 173 Q2
Forsyth Islands Australia 148 C3
Forsyth Range hills Australia 149 D4
Fort Abbas Pak. 101 H4
Fort Albany Canada 168 D2
Fortaleza Pando Bol. 200 C2
Fortaleza Pando Bol. 200 D3
Fortaleza Brazil 202 E2
formerly known as Ceará
Fortaleza de Santa Teresa Uruguay 204 G4
Fort Apache Indian Reservation res. U.S.A. 183 N8
Fort Archambault Chad see Sarh
Fort Ashby U.S.A. 176 G6
Fort Assiniboine Canada 167 H4
Fort Atkinson U.S.A. 172 E8
Fort Augustus U.K. 46 H6
Fort Beaufort S. Africa 133 K9
Fort Belknap Indian Reservation res. U.S.A. 180 E2
Fort Benton U.S.A. 180 E3
Fort Berthold Indian Reservation res. U.S.A. 178 B2
Fort Black Canada 167 J4
Fort Brabant Canada see Tuktoyaktuk
Fort Bragg U.S.A. 182 A2
Fort Carillon U.S.A. see Ticonderoga
Fort Carnot Madag. see Ikongo
Fort Charlet Alg. see Djanet
Fort Chimo Canada see Kuujjuaq
Fort Chipewyan Canada 167 I3
Fort Collins U.S.A. 180 F4
Fort Constantine Australia 149 D4
Fort-Coulonge Canada 168 E4
Fort Covington U.S.A. 177 K1
Fort Crampel Cent. Afr. Rep. see Kaga Bandoro
Fort-Dauphin Madag. see Tôlañaro
Fort Davis U.S.A. 179 B6

▶ Fort-de-France Martinique 187 H4
Capital of Martinique.

Fort de Kock Indon. see Bukittinggi
Fort de Polignac Alg. see Illizi
Fort Deposit U.S.A. 175 C5
Fort Dodge U.S.A. 178 D3
Fort Donald S. Africa 133 O1
Fort Duchesne U.S.A. 183 O1
Forte, Monte hill Sardegna Italy 57 A8
Forte Edward U.S.A. 177 L2
Forte Nordeste Angola 127 D6
Forte Veneza Brazil 199 H6
Fortezza, Monte della hill Italy 56 C6
Fort Flatters Alg. see Bordj Omer Driss
Fort Foureau Cameroon see Kousséri
Fort Franklin Canada see Déline
Fort Gaines U.S.A. 175 C6
Fort Gardel Alg. see Zaouatallaz
Fort Garland U.S.A. 181 F5
Fort Gay U.S.A. 176 C7
Fort Gibson Lake U.S.A. 179 D5
Fort Good Hope Canada 166 D1
Fort Gouraud Mauritania see Fdérik
Forth r. U.K. 46 I7
Forth, Firth of est. U.K. 46 I7
Fort Hall Kenya see Muranga
Fort Hall Indian Reservation res. U.S.A. 180 D4
Fort Hertz Myanmar see Putao
Fortification Range mts U.S.A. 183 J3
Fortín Aroma Para. 201 F5
Fortín Ávalos Sánchez Para. 201 E5
Fortín Boquerón Para. 201 F5
Fortín Capitán Demattei Para. 201 E5
Fortín Carlos Antonio López Para. 201 F5
Fortín Coronel Bogado Para. 201 F5
Fortín Coronel Eugenio Garay Para. 201 E4
Fortín Galpón Para. 201 F4
Fortín General Caballero Para. 201 F6
Fortín General Díaz Para. 201 E5
Fortín General Mendoza Para. 201 E5
Fortín Hernandarias Para. 201 F5
Fortín Infante Rivarola Para. 201 E5
Fortín Juan de Zalazar Para. 201 F5
Fortín Lagerenza Para. 201 E4
Fortín Lavalle Arg. 204 E2
Fortín Leonardo Britos Para. 201 F5
Fortín Leonida Escobar Para. 201 E4
Fortín Linares Para. 201 E5
Fortín Madrejón Para. 201 F4
Fortín May Alberto Gardel Para. 201 E4
Fortín Nueva Asunción Para. 201 E5
Fortín Pilcomayo Para. 201 E5
Fortín Presidente Ayala Para. 201 F5

Fortín Ravelo Bol. 201 E4
Fortín Suárez Arana Bol. 201 E4
Fortín Teniente Juan Echauri López Para. 201 E5
Fortín Teniente Montania Para. 201 E5
Fortín Teniente Primero hill Mendoza Para. 201 F4
Fortín Teniente Rojas Silva Para. 201 E6
Fort Jameson Zambia see Chipata
Fort Johnston Malawi see Mangochi
Fort Kent U.S.A. 174 H1
Fort Laperrine Alg. see Tamanrasset
Fort Lauderdale U.S.A. 175 D7
also known as Port Everglades
Fort Liard Canada 166 F2
Fort Liberté Haiti 187 F3
Fort Loudon U.S.A. 176 H6
Fort Mackay Canada 167 I3
Fort Macleod Canada 167 H5
formerly known as MacLeod
Fort Madison U.S.A. 174 B3
Fort Manning Malawi see Mchinji
Fort McCoy U.S.A. 172 C6
Fort McMurray Canada 167 I3
Fort McPherson Canada 164 C3
Fort Myers U.S.A. 175 D7
Fort Nelson Canada 166 F3
Fort Nelson r. Canada 166 F3
Fort Norman Canada see Tulít'a
Fort Orange U.S.A. see Albany
Fort Payne U.S.A. 174 C5
Fort Peck Reservoir U.S.A. 180 F3
Fort Pierce U.S.A. 175 D7
Fort Pierre U.S.A. 178 B2
Fort Portal Uganda 128 A4
Fort Providence Canada 167 G2
Fort Qu'Appelle Canada 167 K5
Fort Randall U.S.A. see Cold Bay
Fort Recovery U.S.A. 176 A5
Fortress N.Z. 153 C14
Fortrose N.Z. 153 C14
Fortrose U.K. 46 H6
Fort Rosebery Zambia see Mansa
Fort Rousset Congo see Owando
Fort Rupert Canada see Waskaganish
Fort St James Canada 166 E4
Fort St John Canada 166 F3
Fort Sandeman Pak. see Zhob
Fort Saskatchewan Canada 167 H4
Fort Scott U.S.A. 178 D4
Fort Severn Canada 168 C1
Fort-Shevchenko Kazakh. 102 B3
Fort Simpson Canada 166 F2
Fort Smith Canada 167 H2
Fort Smith U.S.A. 179 D5
Fort Stockton U.S.A. 179 B6
Fort Sumner U.S.A. 181 F6
Fort Totten (Devils Lake Sioux) Indian Reservation res. U.S.A. 178 C2
Fort Trinquet Mauritania see Bîr Mogreïn
Fortuna U.S.A. 180 A4
Fortune Bay Canada 169 K4
Fort Valley U.S.A. 175 D5
Fort Vermilion Canada 167 G3
Fort Victoria Zimbabwe see Masvingo
Fort Walton U.S.A. see Fort Walton Beach
Fort Walton Beach U.S.A. 175 C6
formerly known as Fort Walton
Fort Ware Canada see Ware
Fort Wayne U.S.A. 174 C3
Fort Wellington Guyana 199 G3
Fort White Myanmar 78 A3
Fort William U.K. 46 G7
Fort Worth U.S.A. 179 C5
Fort Yates U.S.A. 178 B2
Fortymile r. Canada/U.S.A. 166 A1
Forty Mile Scrub National Park Australia 149 E3
Forty-Second Hill S. Africa see 42nd Hill
Fort Yukon U.S.A. 164 E3
Forum Iulii France see Fréjus
Forûr, Jazîreh-ye i. Iran 100 C5
Forvik Norway 44 K3
Fos, Golfe de b. France 51 K9
Foshan China 87 E4
Fo Shek Chau i. Hong Kong China see Basalt Island
Foskvallen Sweden 45 K3
Fosna pen. Norway 44 J3
Foso Ghana 125 E5
Foss Iceland 44 [inset] C3
Fossano Italy 51 N3
Fosshóll Iceland 44 [inset] C2
Fossil U.S.A. 180 B3
Fossil Downs Australia 150 D3
Fossombrone Italy 56 E5
Fos-sur-Mer France 51 K9
Foster Australia 147 E4
Foster r. Canada 167 J3
Foster U.S.A. 176 A7
Foster, Mount Canada/U.S.A. 166 C3
Foster Bugt b. Greenland 165 Q2
Foster Lakes Canada 167 J3
Fostoria U.S.A. 176 B4
Fotadrevo Madag. 131 [inset] J5
Fotuna i. Vanuatu see Futuna
Fouesnant France 50 B5
Fougamou Gabon 126 A5
Fougères France 50 E4
Foula i. U.K. 46 J3
Foulata U.S.A. 174 [inset]
Foul Bay Egypt 121 G4
Foulenzem Gabon 126 A5
Foulpointe Madag. see Mahavelona
Foulwind, Cape N.Z. 153 F9
Foumban Cameroon 125 H5
Foumbot Cameroon 125 H5
Foum Zguid Morocco 122 D3
Foundation Ice Stream glacier Antarctica 222 T1
Founougo Benin 125 F4
Fount U.S.A. 176 B9
Fountain Green U.S.A. 183 M2
Fountains Abbey tourist site U.K. 47 K9
Four, Pointe de pt Alg. 55 N8
Fourchambault France 51 I5
Fourches, Mont des hill France 51 L4
Four Corners U.S.A. 183 O3
Fourdou Madag. see Tôlañaro
Fourier, Lac i. Canada 169 H3
Fournoi Greece 59 H11
Fournoi i. Greece 59 H11
Fourteen Mile Point U.S.A. 172 D4
Fourth Cataract rapids Sudan see 4th Cataract
Fouta Djallon reg. Guinea 124 B4
Foveaux Strait N.Z. 153 B14
Fowl Cay i. Bahamas 175 E7
Fowler CA U.S.A. 182 D5
Fowler CO U.S.A. 181 F5
Fowler MI U.S.A. 173 I7
Fowler Ice Rise Antarctica 222 S1
Fowlers Bay Australia 146 B2
Fowlers Bay b. Australia 146 B3
Fowlerville U.S.A. 173 I8
Fox r. Man. Canada 167 M3
Fox r. IL U.S.A. 174 B3
Fox r. WI U.S.A. 172 D7
Foxas Spain 54 C1
Fox Creek Canada 167 H4
Foxe Basin g. Canada 165 L3
Foxe Channel Canada 165 K3
Foxen i. Sweden 45 J4
Foxe Peninsula Canada 165 L3

Fox Glacier N.Z. 153 E11
Fox Islands U.S.A. 164 C4
Fox Lake Canada 167 H3
Fox Mountain Canada 166 C2
Foxton N.Z. 152 J8
Foxton Beach N.Z. 152 J8
Fox Valley Canada 167 I5
Foyle, Lough est. Rep. of Ireland/U.K. 47 E9
Foyle, Lough b. Rep. of Ireland/U.K. 47 E8
Foz Spain 54 D1
Foz de Areia, Represa de resr Brazil 203 B8
Foz de Gregório Brazil 198 D6
Foz do Copeá Brazil 199 F5
Foz do Cunene Angola 127 A9
Foz do Iguaçu Brazil 203 A8
Foz do Jamari Brazil 201 E2
Foz do Jutaí Brazil 199 E5
Foz do Mamoriá Brazil 199 E5
Foz do Riosinho Brazil 200 C1
Frackville U.S.A. 177 I5
Fraga Arg. 204 D4
Fraga Spain 55 L3
Fraile Muerto Uruguay 204 G4
Frakes, Mount Antarctica 222 Q1
Framingham U.S.A. 177 N3
Framnes Mountains Antarctica 223 E2
Fram Peak Antarctica 223 D2
Franca Brazil 206 F7
Francavilla al Mare Italy 56 G6
Francavilla Fontana Italy 57 J8
▶ France country Europe 50 F5
3rd largest and 4th most populous country in Europe. Historically known as Gallia or Gaul.
europe [countries] ▶▶▶ 32–35
France, Île de i. Greenland 165 R2
Frances Australia 146 D4
Frances r. Canada 166 D2
Francés, Punta pt Cuba 186 C2
Frances Lake Canada 166 D2
Frances Lake i. Canada 166 D2
Francesville U.S.A. 172 G10
Franceville Gabon 126 B5
also known as Masuku
Franche-Comté admin. reg. France 51 M5
Francis Canada 167 K5
Francis atoll Kiribati see Beru
Francisco de Orellana Ecuador see Puerto Francisco de Orellana
Francisco de Orellana Peru 198 C5
Francisco I. Madero Coahuila Mex. 185 E3
Francisco I. Madero Durango Mex. 184 D3
Francisco Meeks Arg. 204 E5
Francisco Sá Brazil 202 D6
Francisco Zarco Mex. 184 A1
Francistown Botswana 131 E4
Franco da Rocha Brazil 206 G10
Francofonte Sicilia Italy 57 G11
François Lake Canada 166 E4
Francois Peron National Park Australia 151 A5
Francs Peak U.S.A. 180 E4
Frankenberg (Eder) Germany 48 F4
Frankenhöhe park Germany 48 H6
Frankenmuth U.S.A. 173 J7
Frankenthal (Pfalz) Germany 48 F6
Frankenwald mts Germany 48 I5
Frankenwald park Germany 48 I5
Frankford Canada 173 P6
Frankfort S. Africa 133 M4
Frankfort S. Africa 133 N7
▶ Frankfort KY U.S.A. 176 A7
State capital of Kentucky.
Frankfort MI U.S.A. 172 G6
Frankfort OH U.S.A. 176 B6
Frankfurt am Main Germany 48 F5
Frankfurt an der Oder Germany 49 L3
Frank Hann National Park Australia 151 C7
Frank Hutte Lake U.S.A. 183 I1
Fränkische Alb hills Germany 48 H7
Fränkische Schweiz reg. Germany 48 I5
Fränkische Schweiz Veldensteiner Forst park Germany 48 I5
Frankland r. Australia 151 B7
Frankland, Cape Australia 147 E4
Franklin S. Africa 133 N7
Franklin AZ U.S.A. 183 O9
Franklin IN U.S.A. 174 C4
Franklin KY U.S.A. 174 C4
Franklin LA U.S.A. 175 B6
Franklin MA U.S.A. 177 N3
Franklin ME U.S.A. 177 Q1
Franklin NC U.S.A. 174 D5
Franklin NE U.S.A. 178 C3
Franklin NH U.S.A. 177 N2
Franklin NJ U.S.A. 177 J4
Franklin OH U.S.A. 176 A6
Franklin PA U.S.A. 176 F4
Franklin TN U.S.A. 174 C5
Franklin TX U.S.A. 179 C6
Franklin VA U.S.A. 177 I9
Franklin WI U.S.A. 172 F8
Franklin WV U.S.A. 176 F7
Franklin Bay Canada 164 G3
Franklin D. Roosevelt Lake U.S.A. 180 C2
Franklin Furnace U.S.A. 176 C7
Franklin-Gordon National Park Australia 147 E5
Franklin Grove U.S.A. 172 D9
Franklin Island Antarctica 223 L1
Franklin Lake Canada 167 M1
Franklin Mountains Canada 166 F2
Franklin Mountains N.Z. 153 B12
Franklin Sound sea chan. Australia 147 E4
Franklin Strait Canada 165 I2
Franklinton LA U.S.A. 175 B6
Franklinton NC U.S.A. 176 G9
Frankston Australia 147 E4
Fransenhof S. Africa 132 G6
Fransfontein Namibia 130 B4
Franske Øer is Greenland 165 R2
Frantsa-Iosifa, Zemlya is Rus. Fed. 38 F2
English form Franz Josef Land
Franz Canada 168 C3
Franz Josef Glacier N.Z. 153 E11
Franz Josef Land is Rus. Fed. see Frantsa-Iosifa, Zemlya
Frasca, Capo della c. Sardegna Italy 57 A9
Frascati Italy 56 E7
Fraser r. Australia 150 C3
Fraser r. B.C. Canada 166 F5
Fraser r. Nfld. Canada 169 I1
Fraser, Mount Australia 151 B5
Fraserburg S. Africa 132 F8
Fraserburgh U.K. 46 J5
Fraserdale Canada 168 D3
Fraser Island Australia 151 A5
also known as Great Sandy Island
Fraser Island National Park Australia 149 G5
Fraser Lake Canada 166 E4
Fraser National Park Australia 147 E4
Fraser Plateau Canada 166 E4
Fraser Range hills Australia 151 C7
Frasertown N.Z. 152 K8
Frauenfeld Switz. 51 O3
Frätești Romania 58 G5
Frauenfeld Switz. 51 O3
Fray Bentos Uruguay 204 F4
Fray Marcos Uruguay 204 F4
Frazeysburg U.S.A. 176 C5
Frazier Downs Aboriginal Reserve Australia 150 C3
Frazier Park U.S.A. 182 F7

Frecăței Romania 58 J4
Frederic MI U.S.A. 173 I6
Frederic WI U.S.A. 172 A5
Frederica U.S.A. 177 J6
Fredericia Denmark 45 J5
Frederick MD U.S.A. 176 H6
Frederick OK U.S.A. 179 C5
Frederick E. Hyde Fjord inlet Greenland 165 P1
Frederick Hills Australia 148 B2
Frederick Reef Australia 149 G4
Fredericksburg TX U.S.A. 179 C6
Fredericksburg VA U.S.A. 176 H7
Frederick Sound sea chan. U.S.A. 166 C3
Fredericktown MO U.S.A. 174 B4
Fredericktown OH U.S.A. 176 C5
▶ Fredericton Canada 169 H4
Provincial capital of New Brunswick.
Fredericton airport Canada 174 H2
Frederikshåb Greenland see Paamiut
Frederikshavn Denmark 45 J4
Frederikssund Denmark 45 K5
Frederiksted Virgin Is (U.S.A.) 187 G3
Frederiksværk Denmark 45 K5
Fredonia AZ U.S.A. 183 L5
Fredonia KS U.S.A. 178 D4
Fredonia NY U.S.A. 176 F3
Fredonia PA U.S.A. 176 E4
Fredonia WI U.S.A. 172 F7
Fredrika Sweden 44 L2
Fredriksberg Sweden 45 K3
Fredrikshamn Fin. see Hamina
Fredrikstad Norway 45 J4
Freedonyer Peak U.S.A. 182 D1
Freehold U.S.A. 177 K5
Freeland U.S.A. 177 J4
Freeling Heights hill Australia 146 C2
Freel Peak U.S.A. 182 E3
Freels, Cape Canada 169 K3
Freeman U.S.A. 178 C3
Freeman, Lake U.S.A. 172 G10
Freeport IL U.S.A. 174 B3
Freeport ME U.S.A. 177 O2
Freeport PA U.S.A. 176 F5
Freeport TX U.S.A. 179 D6
Freeport City Bahamas 186 D1
Freer U.S.A. 179 C7
Freesoil U.S.A. 172 G6
Free State prov. S. Africa 133 K5
formerly known as Orange Free State
▶ Freetown Sierra Leone 124 B4
Capital of Sierra Leone.
Freewood Acres U.S.A. 177 K5
Fregenal de la Sierra Spain 54 E6
Fregon Australia 146 B1
Fréhel, Cap c. France 50 D4
Freiberg Germany 49 K5
Freiburg im Breisgau Germany 48 E7
Freiburg Switz. see Fribourg
Frei Gonzaga Brazil 207 L4
Frei Inocêncio Brazil 207 L5
Freising Germany 48 I7
Freistadt Austria 49 L7
Freital Germany 49 K5
Freixo de Espada à Cinta Port. 54 E3
Fréjus France 51 M9
also known as Forum Iulii
Frekhaug Norway 45 I3
Fremantle Australia 151 A7
Fremont CA U.S.A. 182 C4
Fremont IN U.S.A. 176 A4
Fremont MI U.S.A. 172 H7
Fremont NE U.S.A. 178 C3
Fremont OH U.S.A. 176 B4
Fremont WI U.S.A. 172 E6
Fremont r. U.S.A. 183 M3
Fremont Junction U.S.A. 183 M3
Frenchburg U.S.A. 176 B8
French Congo country Africa see Congo
French Creek r. U.S.A. 176 E4
▶ French Guiana terr. S. America 199 H4
French Overseas Department. Known as Guyane Française in French.
southamerica [countries] ▶▶▶ 192–193
French Guinea country Africa see Guinea
French Island Australia 147 E4
Frenchman r. U.S.A. 180 F2
Frenchman Bay U.S.A. 177 Q1
Frenchman Creek r. U.S.A. 178 B3
Frenchman Lake CA U.S.A. 182 D2
Frenchman Lake NV U.S.A. 183 I5
French Pass N.Z. 152 H8
▶ French Polynesia terr. S. Pacific Ocean 221 I7
French Overseas Territory. Known as Polynésie Française in French.
world [large] ▶▶▶ 12–13
oceania [countries] ▶▶▶ 138–139
oceania [issues] ▶▶▶ 140–141
French Somaliland country Africa see Djibouti
▶ French Southern and Antarctic Lands terr. Indian Ocean 218 L8
French Overseas Territory. Known as Terres Australes et Antarctiques Françaises in French.
asia [countries] ▶▶▶ 64–67
French Sudan country Africa see Mali
French Territory of the Afars and Issas country Africa see Djibouti
Frenchtown U.S.A. 177 J5
Frenda Alg. 123 F2
Frenštát pod Radhoštěm Czech Rep. 49 P6
Frere S. Africa 133 N5
Fresco r. Brazil 199 I6
Fresco Côte d'Ivoire 124 D5
Freshfield, Cape Antarctica 223 K2
Fresnillo Mex. 185 E4
Fresno U.S.A. 182 E5
Fresno r. U.S.A. 182 D5
Fressel, Lac i. Canada 169 G2
Fresvikbreen glacier Norway 45 I3
Freu, Cap des c. Spain 55 O5
Freudenstadt Germany 48 F7
Frew watercourse Australia 148 B4
Frewsburg U.S.A. 176 F3
Freycinet Estuary inlet Australia 151 A5
Freycinet Peninsula Australia 147 F5
Freyming-Merlebach France 51 M3
Freyre Arg. 204 E3
Freyung Germany 49 K7
Fria Guinea 124 B4
Fria, Cape Namibia 130 B3
Friant U.S.A. 182 E5
Friant-Kern Canal U.S.A. 182 E5
Frias Arg. 204 D3
Fribourg Switz. 51 N6
also known as Freiburg
Frick Switz. 51 O3
Friday Harbor U.S.A. 180 B2
Fridtjof Nansen, Mount Antarctica 223 M1
Friedberg Germany 48 H7
Friedens U.S.A. 176 G5
Friedland Germany 49 K2
Friedland Rus. Fed. see Pravdinsk
Friedrichshafen Germany 48 G8
Friend U.S.A. 178 C3
Friendly Islands country S. Pacific Ocean see Tonga
Friendship U.S.A. 176 G3
Friesach Austria 49 L9

Friesack Germany 49 J3
Friesoythe Germany 48 E2
Friggesund Sweden 45 L3
Frio r. TX U.S.A. 179 C6
Frio watercourse U.S.A. 179 B5
Friol Spain 54 D1
Frisco U.S.A. 180 F5
Frisco Mountain U.S.A. 183 K3
Frissell, Mount hill U.S.A. 177 L3
Friuli - Venezia Giulia admin. reg. Italy 56 F2
Friza, Proliv strait Rus. Fed. 81 P3
Froan nature res. Norway 44 J2
Frobisher Bay Canada see Iqaluit
Frobisher Bay b. Canada 165 M3
Frobisher Lake Canada 167 I3
Frohavet b. Norway 44 J3
Frohburg Germany 49 J4
Frohnleiten Austria 49 M8
Frolovo Rus. Fed. 41 G6
Frombork Poland 49 Q1
Frome watercourse Australia 146 C2
Frome U.K. 47 J12
Frome, Lake salt flat Australia 146 C2
Fromveur, Passage du strait France 50 A4
Fronteira Port. 54 D5
Fronteiras Brazil 202 D3
Frontera Coahuila Mex. 185 E3
Frontera Tabasco Mex. 185 G5
Frontera, Punta pt Mex. 185 G5
Fronteras Mex. 184 C2
Frontignan France 51 J9
Front Royal U.S.A. 176 G7
Frosinone Italy 56 F7
historically known as Frusino
Frosta Norway 44 J3
Frostburg U.S.A. 176 G6
Frost Glacier Antarctica 223 I2
Frøya i. Norway 44 J3
Fruges France 51 I2
Fruita U.S.A. 183 P2
Fruitland IA U.S.A. 172 B9
Fruitland MD U.S.A. 177 J7
Fruitland UT U.S.A. 183 N1
Fruitport U.S.A. 172 G7
Fruitvale U.S.A. 183 P2
Fruktovaya Rus. Fed. 43 U7
Frunze Kyrg. 103 G4
also known as Frunzenskoye
Frunze Kyrg. see Bishkek
Frunzenskoye Kyrg. see Frunze
Frunzivka Ukr. 58 K1
Frusino Italy see Frosinone
Fruska Gora nat. park Yugo. 58 A3
Frutigen Switz. 51 N6
Frutillar Chile 205 B6
Frutuoso Brazil 201 E3
Fryanovo Rus. Fed. 43 T5
Fryazino Rus. Fed. 43 T6
Frýdek-Místek Czech Rep. 49 P6
Fryeburg U.S.A. 177 O1
Fu'an China 87 F3
Fucheng China see Fengyang
Fucheng China see Fuxian
Fuchū Japan 91 C7
Fuchuan China 87 D3
also known as Fuyang
Fuchun Jiang r. China 87 G2
Fudai Japan 90 G4
Fude China 87 F3
Fuding China 87 G3
Fudua waterhole Kenya 128 C5
Fudul reg. Saudi Arabia 105 D3
Fuengirola Spain 54 G8
Fuenlabrada Spain 54 H4
Fuente-Álamo Spain 55 J6
Fuente Álamo Spain 55 J7
Fuente Albilla, Cerro de mt. Spain 55 J6
Fuente de Cantos Spain 54 E6
Fuente Obejuna Spain 54 F6
Fuentesaúco Spain 54 F3
Fuentes de Ebro Spain 55 K3
Fuerte Olimpo Para. 201 F5
Fuerteventura i. Canary Is 122 B3
Fuga i. Phil. 74 B2
Fugloy i. Faroe Is 46 F1
Fuglstad Norway 44 K2
Fugou China 87 E1
Fugu China 85 F4
Fuguo China see Zhanhua
Fuhai China 88 D2
also known as Burultokay
Fuhaymī Iraq 109 N3
Fujairah U.A.E. 105 G2
also spelt Al Fujayrah or Fujeira
Fujeira U.A.E. see Fujairah
Fuji China see Luxian
Fuji Japan 91 F7
Fujian prov. China 87 F3
English form Fukien
Fu Jiang r. China 86 C2
Fujieda Japan 91 F7
Fuji-Hakone-Izu National Park Japan 91 F7
Fujiidera Japan 91 D7
Fujin China 82 C3
Fujinomiya Japan 91 F7
Fujioka Japan 91 F6
Fuji-san vol. Japan 91 F7
Fujiyoshida Japan 91 F7
Fūka Egypt 106 A5
Fukagawa Japan 90 H3
Fukang China 88 D2
Fukaura Japan 90 F4
Fukaya Japan 91 F6
Fukien prov. China see Fujian
Fukuchiyama Japan 91 D7
Fukue Japan 91 A8
Fukue-jima i. Japan 91 A8
Fukui Japan 91 E6
Fukui pref. Japan 91 E7
Fukuno Japan 91 E6
Fukuoka Japan 91 B8
Fukuoka pref. Japan 91 B8
Fukushima Fukushima Japan 90 G6
Fukushima Hokkaidō Japan 90 G4
Fukushima pref. Japan 90 G6
Fukuyama Japan 91 C7
Fūl, Gebel hill Egypt 108 D8
Fulacunda Guinea-Bissau 124 B4
Fūlād Maïalleh Iran 100 C2
also known as Amirabad
Fulayj Oman 105 G3
Fulchhari Bangl. 97 F4
Fulda Germany 48 G5
Fulda r. Germany 48 G4
Fule China 86 C3
Fuli China see Jixian
Fuliji China 87 F1
Fulin China see Hanyuan
Fuling China 87 C2
Fulitun China see Jixian
Fullerton CA U.S.A. 182 G8
Fullerton NE U.S.A. 178 C3
Fullerton, Cape Canada 167 N2
Fulnek Czech Rep. 49 O6
Fulton KY U.S.A. 174 B4
Fulton MO U.S.A. 174 B4
Fulton MS U.S.A. 174 B5
Fulton NY U.S.A. 177 I2
Fulufjället naturreservat nature res. Sweden 45 K3
Fulunäs Sweden 45 K3
Fumay France 51 K3
Fumel France 50 G8
Fumin China 86 B3
also known as Yongding
Funabashi Japan 91 F7
Funafuti atoll Tuvalu 145 G2
formerly known as Ellice Island
Funan China 87 E1
Funan China see Fusui
Funäsdalen Sweden 44 K3

▶Funchal Madeira 122 A2
Capital of Madeira.

Fundación Col. 198 C2
Fundão Brazil 203 D6
Fundão Port. 54 D4
Fundi Italy see Fondi
Fundición Mex. 184 C3
Fundo das Figuerias Cape Verde 124 [inset]
Fundulea Romania 58 H4
Fundy, Bay of g. Canada 169 H4
Fünen i. Denmark see Fyn
Funeral Peak U.S.A. 183 H5
Fünfkirchen Hungary see Pécs
Fung Wong Shan hill Hong Kong China see Lantau Peak
Funhalouro Moz. 131 G4
Funing Jiangsu China 87 F1
Funing Yunnan China 86 C4
also known as Xinhua
Funiu Shan mts China 87 D1
Funnel Creek r. Australia 149 F4
Funsi Ghana 125 E4
Funtua Nigeria 125 G4
Funzie U.K. 46 L3
Fuping China 85 G4
Fuqing China 87 F3
Fuquan China 87 C3
also known as Chengxian
Furancungo Moz. 131 G2
Furano Japan 90 H3
Fürgun, Kūh-e mt. Iran 100 D5
Furmanov Rus. Fed. 40 G4
Furmanovka Kazakh. see Moyynkum
Furmanovo Kazakh. see Zhalpaktal
Furmanovo Rus. Fed. 90 D3
Furnas, Represa resr Brazil 207 G8
Furneaux Group is Australia 147 F5
Furnes Belgium see Veurne
Furong China see Wan'an
Fürstenau Germany 48 E3
Fürstenberg Germany 49 K2
Fürstenfeld Austria 49 N8
Fürstenfeldbruck Germany 48 I7
Fürstenwalde Germany 49 L3
Fürth Germany 48 H6
Furth im Wald Germany 49 J6
Furubira Japan 90 G3
Furudal Sweden 45 K3
Furukawa Japan 90 G5
Fury and Hecla Strait Canada 165 K3
Fusagasugá Col. 198 C3
Fusan S. Korea see Pusan
Fushan Shandong China 85 I4
Fushan Shanxi China 85 F5
Fushë-Krujë Albania 58 A7
Fushun Liaoning China 82 A4
Fushun Sichuan China 86 C2
Fusong China 82 B4
Fusui China 87 C4
also known as Xinning; formerly known as Funan
Futago-san vol. Japan 91 B8
Futaleufú Chile 205 C6
Fu Tau Pun Chau i. Hong Kong China 87 [inset]
Futog Vojvodina, Srbija Yugo. 58 A3
Futtsu Japan 91 F7
Futuna i. Vanuatu 145 G3
also spelt Fotuna; formerly known as Erronan
Futuna, Île i. Wallis and Futuna Is 145 H3
Futuna Islands Wallis and Futuna Is 145 H3
English form Hoorn Islands; also known as Hoorn, Îles de or Horne, Îles de.
Futun Xi r. China 87 F3
Fuwa Egypt 108 B6
Fuwayrit Qatar 105 E2
Fuxian China see Wafangdian
Fuxian China 85 F5
also known as Fucheng
Fuxin Liaoning China 85 I3
also known as Fuxinzhen
Fuxin Liaoning China 85 I3
Fuxing China see Wangmo
Fuxinzhen China see Fuxin
Fuya Japan 90 F5
Fuyang Anhui China 87 E1
Fuyang China see Fuchuan
Fuyang Zhejiang China 87 F2
Fuyang r. China 85 H4
Fuying Dao i. China 87 G3
Fuyu Heilong. China 85 J2
Fuyu China see Songyuan
Fuyu Jilin China 82 B3
formerly known as Sanchahe
Fuyuan Heilong. China 82 D2
Fuyuan Yunnan China 86 C3
also known as Zhong'an
Fuyun China 84 A2
also known as Koktokay
Füzesabony Hungary 49 R8
Füzesgyarmat Hungary 49 S8
Fuzhou China 87 F3
formerly spelt Foochow
Fuzhou China see Linchuan
Füzuli Azer. 107 F3
also spelt Fizuli; formerly known as Karyagino
Fwamba Dem. Rep. Congo 127 D6
Fyn county Denmark 45 J5
Fyn i. Denmark 38 B4
also known as Fünen
Fyne, Loch inlet U.K. 46 G8
Fyresvatn l. Norway 45 J4
F.Y.R.O.M. country Europe see Macedonia
Fyteies Greece 59 C10
also known as Fitiái

↓ G

Gaâfour Tunisia 57 B12
Gaalkacyo Somalia 128 E3
Ga'ara, Birket el salt l. Egypt 108 B7
Gaat r. Sarawak Malaysia 77 F2
Gab watercourse Namibia 132 B4
Gabakly Turkm. see Kabakly
Gabangab well Eth. 128 E3
Gabas r. France 50 F9
Gabasumdo China see Tongde
Gabbac, Raas pt Somalia 128 F2
Gabbs Valley Range mts U.S.A. 182 F3
Gabd Pak. 101 E5
Gabela Angola 127 B7
Gaberones Botswana see Gaborone
Gabès Tunisia 123 H2
Gabès, Golfe de g. Tunisia 123 H2
English form Gabès, Gulf of
Gabès, Gulf of Tunisia see Gabès, Golfe de
Gabgaba, Wadi watercourse Sudan 121 G4
Gable End Foreland hd N.Z. 152 M6
▶Gabon country Africa 126 A5
africa [countries] ➡ 114–117
Gabon, Estuaire du est. Gabon 126 A4

▶Gaborone Botswana 131 E5
Capital of Botswana. Formerly spelt Gaberones.

Gabou Senegal 124 B3
Gabriel Vera Bol. 200 D4
Gabriel y Galán, Embalse de resr Spain 54 E4
Gābrik Iran 100 D5
Gābrik watercourse Iran 100 D5
Gabrovnitsa Bulg. 58 E5
Gabrovo Bulg. 58 G6
Gabú Guinea-Bissau 124 B3
Gabuli vol. Eth. 128 D1
Gacé France 50 G4
Gacko Bos.-Herz. 56 K5
Gädäbäy Azer. 107 F2
Gadabedji, Réserve Totale de Faune de nature res. Niger 125 G3
Gadag India 94 B3
Gadaisu P.N.G. 149 F1
Gäddede Sweden 44 K2
Gadê China 86 A1
also known as Pagqên
Gadebusch Germany 48 I2
Gades Spain see Cádiz
Gadhada India 96 A5
Gadhra India 94 A1
Gadsden U.S.A. 175 C5
Gadwal India 94 C2
Gadyach Ukr. see Hadyach
Gadyn Turkm. 103 E5
Gadzi Cent. Afr. Rep. 126 C3
Gadžin Han Srbija Yugo. 58 D5
Gæi'dnuvuop'pi Norway 44 M1
Gael Hamke Bugt b. Greenland 165 Q2
Găeşti Romania 58 G4
Gaeta Italy 56 F7
Gaeta, Golfo di g. Italy 56 F7
Gafanha da Nazaré Port. 54 C4
Gaferut i. Micronesia 73 K5
Gaffney U.S.A. 174 D5
Gafra, Wâdi el watercourse Egypt 108 C7
Gafsa Tunisia 123 H2
historically known as Capsa
Gag i. Indon. 75 D3
Gagal Chad 126 B2
Gagaon India 96 B5
Gagarin Rus. Fed. 43 Q6
formerly known as Gzhatsk
Gagarin Uzbek. 103 G4
formerly known as Yerzhar
Gagere watercourse Nigeria 125 G3
Gagliano del Capo Italy 57 K9
Gagnoa Côte d'Ivoire 124 D5
Gagnon Canada 169 G3
Gago Coutinho Angola see Lumbala N'guimbo
Gagra Georgia 107 E2
Gaià r. Spain 55 M3
also spelt Gayá
Gaiab watercourse Namibia 130 C6
Gaibandha Bangl. 97 F4
Găiceana Romania 58 I2
Gaifi, Wâdi el watercourse Egypt 108 F7
Gail r. Austria 49 K9
Gail U.S.A. 179 B5
Gaillac France 50 H9
Gaillimh Rep. of Ireland see Galway
Gaillon France 50 H3
Gaindaingoinkor China see Lhünzhub
Gainesboro U.S.A. 178 F4
Gainesville FL U.S.A. 175 D6
Gainesville GA U.S.A. 174 D5
Gainesville MO U.S.A. 178 D4
Gainesville TX U.S.A. 179 C5
Gainsborough U.K. 47 L10
Gairdner r. Australia 151 B7
Gairdner, Lake salt flat Australia 146 B2
Gairloch U.K. 46 G6
Gairo Tanz. 129 C6
Gaixian China see Gaizhou
Gaizhou China 85 I3
formerly known as Gaixian
Gaizinkalns hill Latvia 42 G5
Gaja r. Hungary 49 P8
Gajah Hutan, Bukit hill Malaysia 76 C1
Gajapatinagaram India 95 D2
Gaji r. Nigeria 125 H4
Gajiram Nigeria 125 I3
Gajol India 97 F4
Gajos well Kenya 128 C4
Gakarosa mt. S. Africa 132 H4
Gakem Nigeria 125 H5
Gakuch Jammu and Kashmir 96 B1
Gala China 89 E6
Galaasiya Uzbek. 103 F5
also spelt Galaosiyo
Galâla el Baḥarîya, Gebel el plat. Egypt 108 C8
Galán, Cerro mt. Arg. 204 D2
Galana r. Kenya 128 D5
Galand Iran 100 C2
Galang Besar i. Indon. 76 D2
Galangue Angola 127 C8
Galanta Slovakia 49 O7
Galaosiyo Uzbek. see Galaasiya
Galápagos, Islas is Pacific Ocean see Galapagos Islands

▶Galapagos Islands is Pacific Ocean 221 M6
Part of Ecuador. Most westerly point of South America. Also known as Galápagos, Islas or Colón, Archipiélago de.
southamerica [contrasts] ➡ 194–195

Galashiels U.K. 46 J8
Galata Bulg. 58 I5
Galatea N.Z. 152 K6
Galați Romania 58 J3
Galatina Italy 57 K8
Galatini Greece 59 C8
Galatista Greece 59 E8
Galatone Italy 57 K8
Galax U.S.A. 176 E9
Galaymor Turkm. see Kala-I-Mor
Galdhøpiggen mt. Norway 45 J3
Galeana Chihuahua Mex. 184 D2
Galeana Nuevo León Mex. 185 E3
Galegu Sudan 121 G6
Galela Indon. 75 C2
Galena AK U.S.A. 164 D3
Galena IL U.S.A. 174 B3
Galena KS U.S.A. 178 D4
Galena MD U.S.A. 177 J6
Galena MO U.S.A. 178 D4
Galena Bay Canada 166 G5
Galera, Punta pt Chile 204 B6
Galera, Punta pt Ecuador 198 A4
Galera, Punta pt Mex. 185 F6
Galera Point Trin. and Tob. 187 H5
Galeras vol. Col. 198 B4
Galesburg IL U.S.A. 174 B3
Galesburg MI U.S.A. 172 H8
Galeshewe S. Africa 133 I5
Galesville U.S.A. 172 B6
Galeton U.S.A. 176 H4
Galga r. Hungary 49 Q8
Galguduud admin. reg. Somalia 128 E3
Gal Hareeri Somalia 128 E3
Gália Brazil 206 D9
Galicea Mare Romania 58 E4
Galich Rus. Fed. 40 G4
Galichskaya Vozvyshennost' hills Rus. Fed. 40 G4
Galicia aut. comm. Spain 54 D2
Galičica nat. park Macedonia 58 B7
Galilee, Sea of l. Israel 108 G5
also known as Tiberias, Lake or Kinneret, Yam
Galiléia Brazil 207 L6
Galissas Greece 59 F11
Galitsa Rus. Fed. 43 S8
Galiuro Mountains U.S.A. 183 N9
Galiwinku Australia 148 B2
Gallabat Sudan 121 H6
Gallarate Italy 56 A3
Gallatin MO U.S.A. 178 D4
Gallatin TN U.S.A. 174 C4
Gallatin r. U.S.A. 180 E3
Galle Sri Lanka 94 D5
Gállego r. Spain 55 K3
Gallegos r. Arg. 205 C8
Gallegos, Cabo c. Chile 205 B7
Gallia country Europe see France

▶Gallinas, Punta pt Col. 198 D1
Most northerly point of South America.

Gallipoli Italy 57 K8
Gallipoli Turkey 106 A2
also spelt Gelibolu; historically known as Callipolis
Gallipolis U.S.A. 176 C7
Gällivare Sweden 44 M2
Gallneukirchen Austria 49 L7
Gallo r. Spain 55 I4
Gällö Sweden 44 K3
Gallo, Capo c. Sicilia Italy 57 F10
Gallup KY U.S.A. 176 C7
Gallup NM U.S.A. 181 E6
Gallur Spain 55 J3
Gallura reg. Sardegna Italy 56 A8
Gallyaaral Uzbek. 103 F4
also spelt Ghallaorol
Galma watercourse Nigeria 125 G4
Galoya Sri Lanka 94 D4
Gal Oya National Park Sri Lanka 94 D5
Gal Shiikh Somalia 128 E2
Galt U.S.A. 182 C3
Gal Tardo Somalia 128 E4
Galtat Zemmour W. Sahara 122 C4
Galtee Mountains hills Rep. of Ireland 47 D11
Galtymore hill Rep. of Ireland 47 D11
Galūgāh, Kūh-e mts Iran 100 C4
Galūgāh-e Āsīyeh Iran 101 D3
Galunggung, Gunung vol. Indon. 77 E4
Galva U.S.A. 172 C9
Galveias Port. 54 D5
Galveston IN U.S.A. 172 G10
Galveston TX U.S.A. 179 D6
Galveston Bay U.S.A. 179 D6
Gálvez Arg. 204 E4
Galwa Nepal 97 D3
Galway Rep. of Ireland 47 C10
also spelt Gaillimh
Galway Bay Rep. of Ireland 47 C10
Gâm r. Vietnam 78 D3
Gamá Brazil 206 E3
Gama, Isla i. Arg. 204 E6
Gamaches France 50 H3
Gamagōri Japan 91 E7
Gamalakhe S. Africa 133 O7
Gamalama vol. Indon. 75 C2
Gamarra Col. 198 C2
Gámas Fin. see Kaamanen
Gamawa Nigeria 125 H3
Gamay Bay Phil. 74 C3
Gamba China 89 E6
also known as Gongbalou
Gamba Gabon 126 A5
Gambēla Eth. 128 B2
Gambēla admin. reg. Eth. 128 B3
Gambēla National Park Eth. 128 B3
Gambell U.S.A. 164 B3
▶Gambia country Africa 124 A3
africa [countries] ➡ 114–117
Gambia r. Gambia 124 A3
Gambie r. Senegal 124 B3
Gambier, Îles is Fr. Polynesia 221 J7
English form Gambier Islands; also known as Mangareva Islands
Gambier Islands Australia 146 C3
Gambier Islands Fr. Polynesia see Gambier, Îles
Gambo Canada 169 K3
Gamboma Congo 126 B5
Gamboola Australia 149 D3
Gamboula Cent. Afr. Rep. 126 B3
Gamda China see Zamtang
Gamka r. S. Africa 132 F10
Gamkunoro, Gunung vol. Indon. 75 C2
Gamlakarleby Fin. see Kokkola
Gamleby Sweden 45 L4
Gammams well Sudan 121 G5
Gammelstaden Sweden 44 M2
Gammon Ranges National Park Australia 146 C2
Gamoep S. Africa 132 C6
Gamova, Mys pt Rus. Fed. 82 C4
Gampaha Sri Lanka 94 C5
Gampola Sri Lanka 94 D5
Gams Switz. 51 P5
Gamshadzai Kūh mts Iran 101 E4
Gamtog China 86 A2
Gamtoos r. S. Africa 133 J10
Gamud mt. Eth. 128 C3
Gamvik Norway 44 O1
Gan r. China 85 J1
Gana China see Gengda
Ganado U.S.A. 183 O6
Ganāg Egypt 108 B7
Gananoque Canada 168 E4
Ganāveh Iran 100 B4
Gäncä Azer. 107 F2
also spelt Gandzha; formerly known as Kirovabad; formerly spelt Gyandzha
Gand Belgium see Ghent
Ganda Angola 127 B8
formerly known as Mariano Machado
Gandadiwata, Bukit mt. Indon. 75 A3
Gandai India 96 D5
Gandajika Dem. Rep. Congo 127 D6
Gándara Spain 54 C1
Gandarbal Jammu and Kashmir 96 B2
Gandari Mountain Pak. 101 G4
Gandava Pak. 101 F4
Gander Canada 169 K3
Gander r. Nfld. Canada 169 K3
Ganderkesee Germany 48 F2
Gander Lake Canada 169 K3
Gandesa Spain 55 L3
Gandevi India 94 B1
Gandhidham India 96 A5
Gandhinagar India 96 B5
Gandhi Sagar resr India 96 B4
Gandi, Wadi watercourse Sudan 126 E2
Gandía Spain 55 K6
Gand-i-Zureh plain Afgh. 101 E4
Gandomān Iran 100 B4
Gandu Brazil 202 E5
Gandvik Norway 44 O1
Gandzha Azer. see Gäncä
Ganëb well Mauritania 124 C2
Ganga r. Bangl./India see Ganges
Ganga Nigeria 125 G4
Ganga r. Sri Lanka 94 D5
Gangakher India 94 C2
Gangán Arg. 205 C6
Gangán, Pampa de plain Arg. 205 C6
Ganganagar India 96 B3
Gangapur Maharashtra India 94 B2
Gangapur Rajasthan India 96 B4
Gangapur Rajasthan India 96 C4
Gangara Niger 125 H3
Gangavali r. India 94 B3
Gangaw Myanmar 78 A3
Gangawati India 94 C3
Gangaw Range mts Myanmar 78 B3
Gangca China 84 D4
also known as Shaliuhe
Gangdhar India 96 B5
Gangdisê Shan mts China 89 C6
English form Kailas Range
Ganges r. Bangl./India 96 F5
also known as Ganga or Padma (Bangl.)
Ganges France 51 J9
▶Ganges, Mouths of the Bangl./India 97 F5
asia [landscapes] ➡ 62–63
Gangi Sicilia Italy 57 G11
Ganglota Liberia 124 C5
Gangouyi China 84 E5
Gangra Turkey see Çankırı
Gangrar India 96 B4
Gangtok India 97 F4
Gangu China 86 C1
Gangziyao China 85 G4
Ganhezi China 88 E2
Gani Indon. 75 D3
Ganiakali Guinea 124 C4
Ganjam India 95 E2
Gan Jiang r. China 87 F2
Ganjig China 85 I3
also known as Horqin Zuoyi Houqi
Gankovo Rus. Fed. 43 O2
Ganluo China 86 B2
also known as Xinshiba
Gannan China 85 I2
Gannat France 51 J6
Gannett Peak U.S.A. 180 E4
Ganq China 84 B4
Ganquan China 85 F4
Gansbaai S. Africa 132 D11
Gänserndorf Austria 49 N7
Ganshui China 86 C2
Ganskuil S. Africa 133 K1
Gansu prov. China 84 C3
English form Kansu
Gantamaa Somalia 128 D4
Gantapara India 95 D1
Gantheaume Point Australia 150 C3
Gant'iadi Georgia 107 E2
formerly known as Pilenkovo
Ganting China see Huxian
Gantsevichi Belarus see Hantsavichy
Ganxian China 87 E3
also known as Meilin
Ganyal r. India 94 C1
Ganye Nigeria 125 I4
Ganyesa S. Africa 132 I3
Ganyu China 87 F1
also known as Qingkou
Ganyushkino Kazakh. 102 B3
Ganzhe China see Minhou
Ganzhou China 87 E3
Ganzi Sudan 128 A3
Ganzurino Rus. Fed. 85 E1
Gao Mali 125 E2
Gao admin. reg. Mali 125 F2
Gao'an China 87 E2
Gaocheng China 85 G4
Gaocheng China see Litang
Gaochun China 87 F2
also known as Chunxi
Gaocun China see Mayang
Gaohebu China 87 F2
Gaojian China 87 G2
Gaolan China 84 D4
formerly known as Shidongsi
Gaoleshan China see Xianfeng
Gaoliangjian China see Hongze
Gaoligong Shan mts China 86 A3
Gaoling China 87 D1
also known as Luyuan
Gaomi China 85 H4
Gaomutang China 87 D3
Gaoping China 85 G5
Gaoqing China 85 H4
also known as Tianzhen
Gaotai China 84 C4
Gaotang China 85 H4
Gaotangling China see Wangcheng
Gaotingzhen China see Daishan
Gaotouyao China 85 F4
Gaoua Burkina 124 E4
Gaoual Guinea 124 B4
Gaoxian China 86 C2
also known as Wenjiang
Gaoxiong Taiwan see Kaohsiung
Gaoyang China 85 G4
Gaoyi China 85 G4
Gaoyou China 87 F1
Gaoyou Hu l. China 87 F1
Gaozhou China 87 D4
Gap France 51 M8
Gapan Phil. 74 B3
Gapuwiyak Australia 148 B2
Gaqoi China 89 C6
Gar China 99 K3
also known as Gargunsa or Shiquanhe
Gar Pak. 101 E5
Gar' r. Rus. Fed. 82 C1
Garaa Tebourt well Tunisia 123 H3
Garabekevyul Turkm. 103 F5
formerly spelt Karabekaul
Garabil Belentligi hills Turkm. see Karabil', Vozvyshennost'
Garabinzam Congo 126 B4
Garabogazköl Aylagy b. Turkm. see Kara-Bogaz-Gol, Zaliv
Garabogazköl Bogazy sea chan. Turkm. see Kara-Bogaz-Gol, Proliv
Garacad Somalia 128 F3
Garachiné Panama 186 D5
Garachiné, Punta pt Panama 186 D5
Garadag Somalia 128 E2
Gara Ekar hill Alg. 123 G6
Garagoa Col. 198 C3
Garagum des. Kazakh. see Karakum Desert
Garagum des. Turkm. see Karakum Desert
Garah Australia 147 F2
Garalo Mali 124 D4
Garamätnyyaz Turkm. see Karamet-Niyaz
Garamba r. Dem. Rep. Congo 126 F4
Garanhuns Brazil 202 E4
Ga-Rankuwa S. Africa 133 L2
Garapu Brazil 202 A5
Garapuava Brazil 206 G3
Garar, Plaine de plain Chad 126 D2
Garawa Aboriginal Land res. Australia 148 C3
Garba Cent. Afr. Rep. 126 D2
Garbahaarey Somalia 128 D4
Garba Tula Kenya 128 C4
Garberville U.S.A. 182 A1
Garbo China see Lhozhag
Garbosh, Kūh-e mt. Iran 100 B3
Gârbova, Vârful hill Romania 58 H3
Garbsen Germany 48 G3
Garça Brazil 206 D9
Garças, Rio das r. Brazil 206 A2
Gârceni Romania 58 I2
Garcias Brazil 206 A7
Garcia Sola, Embalse de resr Spain 54 F5
Gârcina Romania 58 H2
Gard r. France 51 K9
Garda Italy 56 C3
Garda, Lago di l. Italy see Garda, Lake
Garda, Lake Italy 56 C3
also known as Garda, Lago di
Gardabani Georgia 107 F2
Gârda de Sus Romania 58 D2
Garde Lake Canada 167 J2
Gardelegen Germany 48 I3
Garden City U.S.A. 178 B4
Garden Corners U.S.A. 172 G5
Garden Grove U.S.A. 182 G8
Garden Hill Canada 167 M4
Garden Island U.S.A. 172 H5
Garden Mountain U.S.A. 176 D8
Gardermoen airport Norway 45 J3
also known as Oslo
Gardez Afgh. 101 G3
Gardinas Belarus see Hrodna
Gardiner U.S.A. 177 P1
Gardiner, Mount Australia 148 B4
Gardiner Range hills Australia 148 A3
Gardiners Island U.S.A. 177 M4
Gardiner's Range mts Australia 148 B4
Gardner atoll Micronesia see Faraulep
Gardner IL U.S.A. 172 E9
Gardner MA U.S.A. 177 N3
Gardner Inlet Antarctica 222 T1
Gardner Island Kiribati see Nikumaroro
Gardner Pinnacles is U.S.A. 221 G4
formerly known as Man-of-War Rocks or Pollard Islands
Gardnerville U.S.A. 182 E3
Gardno, Jezioro lag. Poland 49 O1
Gárdony Hungary 49 P8
Gardsjönäs Sweden 44 L2
Gärdslösa Sweden 45 L4
Gåregasnjárga Fin. see Karigasniemi
Gares Spain see Puente la Reina
Garešnica Croatia 56 I3
Garet El Djenoun mt. Alg. 123 G4
Gare Tigre Fr. Guiana 199 H3
Garfield U.S.A. 181 F5
Garforth U.K. 47 K10
Gargalianoi Greece 59 C11
Gargáligas r. Spain 54 F5
Gargano, Parco Nazionale del nat. park Italy 56 H7
Gargantua, Cape Canada 168 C4
Gargunsa China see Gar
Gargždai Lith. 42 C6
Garhakota India 96 C5
Garhbeta India 97 E5
Garhchiroli India 94 D1
Garhi India 96 B5
Garhi Khairo Pak. 101 F4
Garhi Malehra India 96 C4
Garhmuktesar India 96 C3
Garhshankar India 96 C3
Garibaldi Brazil 203 B9
Garibaldi Canada 166 F5
Garibaldi, Mount Canada 166 F5
Garibaldi Provincial Park Canada 166 F5
Gariep Dam resr S. Africa 133 J7
Gariep Dam Nature Reserve S. Africa 133 J7
Garies S. Africa 132 B7
Garissa Kenya 128 C5
Garkalne Latvia 42 F4
Garkung Caka l. China 89 D5
Garland U.S.A. 179 C5
Garliava Lith. 42 E7
Gârliciu Romania 58 J4
Garlin France 50 F9
Garm Tajik. see Gharm
Garmab Afgh. 101 F3
Garmdasht Iran 100 B4
Garmeh Iran 100 D2
Garmī Iran 100 B2
Garmisch-Partenkirchen Germany 48 I8
Garmo, Qullai mt. Tajik. 101 G2
also known as Kommunizma, Pik or Kommunizm, Qullai
Garmsar Iran 100 C3
Garmsel reg. Afgh. 101 E4
Garner IA U.S.A. 174 A3
Garner KY U.S.A. 176 C8
Garnett U.S.A. 178 D4
Garnpung Lake imp. l. Australia 147 D3
Garo Hills India 97 F4
Garonne r. France 50 F8
Garoowe Somalia 128 F2
Garoth India 96 B4
Garou, Lac l. Mali 124 E2
Garoua Cameroon 125 I4
Garoua Boulai Cameroon 125 I5
Garqêntang China see Sog
Garrett U.S.A. 173 H9
Garrison KY U.S.A. 176 B7
Garrison ND U.S.A. 178 B2
Garrucha Spain 55 J7
Garrygala Turkm. 102 D5
formerly spelt Kara-Kala
Garry Lake Canada 167 K1
Garryowen S. Africa 133 L8
Garsen Kenya 128 D5
Garshy Turkm. see Karshi
Garsila Sudan 120 D6
Gartar China see Qianning
Gartempe r. France 50 G6
Gartog China see Markam
Gartok China see Garyarsa
Garut Indon. 77 D4
Garvie Mountains N.Z. 153 C13
Garwa India 97 D4
Garwolin Poland 49 S4
Gar Xincun China 89 C5
Gary IN U.S.A. 174 C3
Gary WV U.S.A. 176 D8
Garyarsa China 89 C6
also known as Gartok
Garyi China 86 A2
Garyū-zan mt. Japan 91 C7
Garza Arg. 204 E3
Gar Zangbo r. China 89 B5
Garzê China 86 A2
Garzón Col. 198 C4
Gasan-Kuli Turkm. see Esenguly
Gasan-Kuliyskiy Zapovednik nature res. Turkm. 102 C5
Gascogne reg. France see Gascony
Gascogne, Golfe de g. France/Spain see Gascony, Gulf of
Gasconade r. U.S.A. 174 B4
Gascony reg. France 50 F9
also spelt Gascogne
Gascony, Gulf of France/Spain 50 D9
also known as Gascogne, Golfe de or Gascuña, Golfo de
Gascoyne r. Australia 151 A5
Gascoyne, Mount hill Australia 151 B5
Gascoyne Junction Australia 151 A5
Gascuña, Golfo de g. France/Spain see Gascony, Gulf of
Gash and Setit prov. Eritrea 104 B5
Gasherbrum mt. Jammu and Kashmir 96 C2
Gash Setit Wildlife Reserve nature res. Eritrea 121 H6
Gasht Iran 101 E5
Gas Hu salt l. China 88 E4
Gashua Nigeria 125 H3
Gaspar Cuba 186 D2
Gaspar, Selat sea chan. Indon. 77 D3
Gaspé Canada 169 H3
Gaspé, Baie de b. Canada 169 H3
Gaspé, Cap c. Canada 169 H3
Gaspé, Péninsule de pen. Canada 169 H3
Gassan Burkina 124 E3
Gassan vol. Japan 90 G5
Gassane Senegal 124 B3
Gassaway U.S.A. 176 E7
Gassol Nigeria 125 H4
Gass Peak U.S.A. 183 I5
Gasteiz Spain see Vitoria-Gasteiz
Gastello Rus. Fed. 82 F2
Gaston U.S.A. 176 H9
Gaston, Lake U.S.A. 176 H9
Gastonia U.S.A. 174 D5
Gastouni Greece 59 C11
Gastre Arg. 205 C6
Gata, Cabo de c. Spain 55 I8
Gata, Cape Cyprus 108 E3
also known as Gatas, Akra
Gata, Sierra de mts Spain 54 E4
Gataga r. Canada 166 E3
Gătaia Romania 58 C3
Gatas, Akra c. Cyprus see Gata, Cape
Gatchina Rus. Fed. 43 L2
Gateshead U.K. 47 K9
Gates of the Arctic National Park and Preserve U.S.A. 164 D3
Gatesville U.S.A. 179 C6
Gateway U.S.A. 183 P3
Gatico Chile 200 C5
Gatineau Canada 168 F4
Gatineau r. Canada 168 F4
Gatlinburg U.S.A. 179 G5
Gatong China see Jomda
Gatooma Zimbabwe see Kadoma
Gatton Australia 147 G1
Gatún Panama 186 D5
Gatún, Lago l. Panama 186 C5
Gatvand Iran 100 B3
Gatwick airport U.K. 47 L12
Gaúcha do Norte Brazil 202 A5
Gaud-i-Zirreh depr. Afgh. 101 E4
Gauer Lake Canada 167 L3
Gauhati India see Guwahati
Gauja r. Latvia 42 F4
Gaujas nacionālais parks nat. park Latvia 42 G4
Gaul country Europe see France
Gaula r. Norway 44 J3
Gauley Bridge U.S.A. 176 D7
Gaupne Norway 45 I3
Gaurdak Turkm. see Govurdak

Gaurella India 97 D5
Gauribidanur India 94 C3
Gaurnadi Bangl. 97 F5
Gauteng prov. S. Africa 133 M3
also known as Pretoria-Witwatersrand-
Vereeniging
Gavà Spain 55 N3
Gavarr Armenia see Kamo
Gavâter Iran 101 E5
Gâvbandi Iran 100 C4
Gâvbûs, Kûh-e mts Iran 100 C5
Gavdopoula i. Greece 59 F14

▶Gavdos i. Greece 59 F14
Most southerly point of Europe.

Gave r. France 50 E9
Gâveh Rûd r. Iran 100 A3
Gavião r. Brazil 202 D5
Gavião Port. 54 D5
Gävle Sweden 45 L3
Gävleborg county Sweden 45 K3
Gävlebukten b. Sweden 45 L3
Gavrilovka Vtoraya Rus. Fed. 41 G5
Gavrilov-Yam Rus. Fed. 43 U4
Gavrio Greece 59 F11
Gawachab Namibia 130 C5
Gawai Myanmar 78 B2
Gawan India 97 E4
Gawat well Libya 120 B3
Gawilgarh Hills India 96 C5
Gawler Australia 146 C3
Gawler Ranges hills Australia 146 B3
Gâwûr watercourse Turkm. see Gyaur
Gaxun Nur salt l. China 84 C3
Gay Rus. Fed. 102 D2
Gay U.S.A. 172 E1
Gaya r. China 82 C4
Gaya India 97 E4
Gaya i. Sabah Malaysia 77 G1
Gaya Niger 125 F3
Gayà r. Spain see Gaià
Gaya, Pulau i. Sabah Malaysia 77 G1
Gayam Indon. 77 F4
G'Aydat al Jhoucha ridge W. Sahara 122 C4
Gayéri Burkina 125 F3
Gaylord MI U.S.A. 173 I5
Gaylord MN U.S.A. 178 D2
Gayndah Australia 149 F5
Gaynovo Rus. Fed. 43 R4
Gayny Rus. Fed. 40 J3
Gaysin Ukr. see Haysyn
Gayutino Rus. Fed. 43 T3
Gaz Iran 100 D3

▶Gaza terr. Asia 108 F6
Semi-autonomous region.
asia [countries] ▶▶ 64–67

▶Gaza Gaza 108 F6
Capital of Gaza. Also spelt 'Azza.

Gaza prov. Moz. 131 G4
Gaz-Achak Turkm. 103 F4
also spelt Gazojak
Gazalkent Uzbek. 103 G4
also spelt Ghazalkent
Gazandzhyk Turkm. 102 C5
formerly spelt Kazandzhik
Gazawa Cameroon 125 I4
Gaziantep Turkey 107 D3
also known as Aintab
Gazibenli Turkey see Yahyalı
Gazik Iran 101 E3
Gazimağusa Cyprus see Famagusta
Gazimuro-Ononskiy Khrebet mts Rus. Fed.
85 F1
Gazimurskiy Zavod Rus. Fed. 85 H1
Gazipaşa Turkey 106 C3
Gazivode Jezero l. Yugo. 58 B6
Gazojak Turkm. see Gaz-Achak
Gbaaka Liberia 124 C5
Gbangbatok Sierra Leone 124 B5
Gbarnga Liberia 124 C5
Gbatala Liberia 124 C5
Gbéroubouè Benin 125 F4
Gboko Nigeria 125 H5
Gbwado Dem. Rep. Congo 126 D4
Gdańsk Poland 49 P1
historically known as Danzig
Gdańsk, Gulf of Poland/Rus. Fed. 49 Q3
also known as Gdańska, Zatoka; formerly
known as Danzig, Gulf of
Gdańska, Zatoka g. Poland/Rus. Fed. see
Gdańsk, Gulf of
Gdingen Poland see Gdynia
Gdov Rus. Fed. 42 I3
Gdyel Alg. 55 K9
Gdynia Poland 49 P1
historically known as Gdingen or
Gotenhafen
Gearhart Mountain U.S.A. 180 B4
Gebe i. Indon. 75 D2
Gebeit Sudan 121 H5
Gebeit Mine Sudan 121 H4
Gebel Iweibid Egypt 108 D7
Gebre Guracha Eth. 128 C2
Gebze Turkey 58 K8
Gech'a Eth. 128 B3
Gecheng China see Chengkou
Gedang, Gunung mt. Indon. 76 C3
Gedaref Sudan 121 G6
Gedaref state Sudan 121 G6
Gedern Germany 48 G5
Gediz Turkey 59 L9
Gediz r. Turkey 106 A3
Gedlegubē Eth. 128 D3
Gêdo Eth. 128 C2
Gedo admin. reg. Somalia 128 D4
Gedong, Tanjong pt Sing. 76 [inset]
Gedser Denmark 45 J5

Gedungpakuan Indon. 76 D4
Geel Belgium 51 L1
Geelong Australia 147 E4
Geelvink Channel Australia 151 A6
Geel Vloer salt pan S. Africa 132 E6
Geesthacht Germany 48 H2
Gefersa Eth. 128 C2
Gêgê r. Lith. 42 C6
Gegužinė Lith. 42 F7
Ge Hu l. China 87 F2
Geidam Nigeria 125 H3
Geiersberg hill Germany 48 G6
Geikie r. Canada 167 K3
Geikie Island Canada 168 B3
Geikie Range hills Australia 149 D2
Geilo Norway 45 J3
Geiselhöring Germany 49 J7
Geislingen an der Steige Germany 48 G7
Geisûm, Gezâ'ir is Egypt see
Qeisûm, Gezâ'ir
Geita Tanz. 128 B5
Gejiu China 86 B4
Gekdepe Turkm. 102 D5
also spelt Gökdepe; formerly spelt Geok-Tepe
Gel r. Sudan 128 A3
Gel watercourse Sudan 126 F2
Gela Sicilia Italy 57 G11
Gela r. Sicilia Italy 57 G11
Gela, Golfo di g. Sicilia Italy 57 G11
Geladaindong mt. China 89 E5
Geladī Eth. 128 E3
Gelai vol. Tanz. 128 C5
Gelam i. Indon. 77 E3
Geldern Germany 48 D4
Gelembe Turkey 59 I9
Gelemso Eth. 128 D3
Gelendzhik Rus. Fed. 41 F7
Gelephu Bhutan 97 F4
also known as Hatisar
Gelibolu Turkey see Gallipoli
Gelibolu Yarımadası pen. Turkey 59 H8
Gelibolu Yarımadası Tarihi Milli Parkı
nat. park Turkey 59 H8
Gelidonya Burnu pt Turkey see
Yardımcı Burnu
Gelincik Dağı mt. Turkey 106 B3
Gelinsoor Somalia 128 E3
Gelmord Iran 100 D3
Gelnica Slovakia 49 R7
Gelsenkirchen Germany 48 E4
Gemas Malaysia 76 C2
Gembu Nigeria 125 H5
Gemena Dem. Rep. Congo 126 C4
Gemenci park Hungary 49 P9
Gemerek Turkey 106 D3
Gemlik Turkey 106 D2
Gemlik Körfezi b. Turkey 58 J8
Gemlufall Iceland 44 [inset] B2
Gemona del Friuli Italy 56 F7
Gémozac France 50 F7
Gemsa Egypt 121 G3
Gemsbok National Park Botswana 130 D5
Gemsbokfein well S. Africa 132 E3
Gemsbokvlakte S. Africa 133 I3
Gen r. China 85 H1
Genal r. Spain 54 F8
Genalē Wenz r. Eth. 128 D3
Gençay France 50 G6
Gendoa r. Eth. 104 B5
General Acha Arg. 204 D6
General Alvear Buenos Aires Arg. 204 E5
General Alvear Mendoza Arg. 204 D4
General Artigas Para. 201 F6
General Belgrano Arg. 204 F4
General Belgrano II research station
Antarctica see Belgrano II
General Cabrera Arg. 204 D4
General Carneiro Brazil 206 A2

▶General Carrera, Lago l. Arg./Chile 205 B7
Deepest lake in South America.

General Conesa Arg. 204 D6
General Escobedo Mex. 185 E3
General Freire Angola see Muxaluando
Generalísimo, Embalse del resr Spain
55 J5
General José de San Martín Arg. 204 F2
General Juan Madariaga Arg. 204 F5
General Lagos Chile 200 C4
General La Madrid Arg. 204 E5
General Luna Phil. 74 C4
General MacArthur Phil. 74 C4
General Machado Angola see Camacupa
General Martín Miguel de Güemes Arg.
200 D6
General Paz Arg. 204 F2
General Pico Arg. 204 E5
General Pinto Arg. 204 E4
General Roca Arg. 204 D5
General Saavedra Bol. 201 E4
General Salgado Brazil 206 C7
General San Martín research station
Antarctica see San Martín
General Santos Phil. 74 C5
General Simón Bolívar Mex. 185 E3
General Terán Mex. 185 F3
General Toshevo Bulg. 58 J5
General Trias Mex. 184 D2
General Villegas Arg. 204 E4
Genesee U.S.A. 176 H4
Genesee r. U.S.A. 176 H2
Geneseo IL U.S.A. 172 C9
Geneseo NY U.S.A. 176 H3
Genet Eth. 128 C2
Geneva Switz. 51 M6
also known as Genève or Genf
Geneva IL U.S.A. 175 C6
Geneva NE U.S.A. 178 C3
Geneva NY U.S.A. 177 H3
Geneva OH U.S.A. 176 E4 [inset]
Geneva, Lake France/Switz. 51 M6
also known as Léman, Lac
Genève Switz. see Geneva
Genf Switz. see Geneva
Gengda China 86 B1
formerly known as Gana
Gengenbach Germany 48 F7
Gengpaga India 94 B3
Gengqing China 86 A1
also known as Dêgê
Genil r. Sudan 128 B3
Genil r. Spain 54 F7
Genisea Greece 58 F7
also spelt Yenísea
Genk Belgium 51 L1
Genkai-nada b. Japan 91 B8
Gennargentu, Monti del mts Sardegna Italy
57 B9
Gennes France 50 F5
Genoa Australia 147 F4
Genoa Italy 56 A4
also spelt Genova; historically known as Genua
Genoa U.S.A. 172 E8
Genoa, Gulf of Italy 56 A4 [inset]
also known as Genova, Gulf of
Genova Italy see Genoa
Genova, Gulf of Italy see Genoa, Gulf of
Gênt Belgium see Ghent
Genteng Indon. 77 E3
Genteng i. Indon. 77 F4
Genthin Germany 49 J3
Gentio do Ouro Brazil 202 D4
Genua Italy see Genoa
Genzano di Roma Italy 56 E7

Geographical Society Ø i. Greenland
165 Q2
Geok-Tepe Turkm. see Gekdepe
Georga, Zemlya i. Rus. Fed. 38 E1
English form George Land
George r. Canada 169 H1
George S. Africa 132 G10
George, Lake N.S.W. Australia 147 F3
George, Lake S.A. Australia 146 C4
George, Lake salt flat Australia 150 A4
George, Lake Uganda 128 A4
George, Lake FL U.S.A. 175 D6
George, Lake NY U.S.A. 177 L2
George Gills Range mts Australia 148 A4
George Land i. Rus. Fed. see
Georga, Zemlya
Georges Mills U.S.A. 177 M2
George Sound inlet N.Z. 153 B12
George Town Australia 149 D3
George Town Bahamas 186 D2
Georgetown Canada 173 N7

▶George Town Cayman Is 186 C3
Capital of the Cayman Islands.

Georgetown Gambia 124 B3

▶Georgetown Guyana 199 G3
Capital of Guyana. Formerly known as
Demerara; historically known as Stabroek.

George Town Malaysia 76 C1
also known as Pinang
Georgetown DE U.S.A. 177 J7
Georgetown GA U.S.A. 175 C6
Georgetown KY U.S.A. 176 A7
Georgetown OH U.S.A. 176 B7
Georgetown SC U.S.A. 175 E5
Georgetown TX U.S.A. 179 C6
George VI Sound sea chan. Antarctica
222 T2
George V Land reg. Antarctica 223 K2
George West U.S.A. 179 C6

▶Georgia country Asia 107 E2
known as Sakartvelo in Georgian; formerly
known as Gruzinskaya S.S.R.
asia [countries] ▶▶ 64–67

Georgia, Strait of Canada 166 E5
Georgian Bay Canada 168 D4
Georgian Bay Islands National Park
Canada 173 N6
Georgi Dimitrov, Yazovir resr Bulg. see
Koprinka, Yazovir
Georgina watercourse Australia 148 C5
Georgi Traykov Bulg. see Dolni Chiflik
Georgiu-Dezh Rus. Fed. see Liski
Georgiyevka Aktyubinskaya Oblast' Kazakh.
102 D2
Georgiyevka Vostochnyy Kazakhstan Kazakh.
103 D2
Georgiyevka Kazakh. see Korday
Georgiyevskoye Kostromskaya Oblast'
Rus. Fed. 40 H4
Georgiyevskoye Vologod. Obl. Rus. Fed.
43 R7
Georg von Neumayer research station
Antarctica see Neumayer
Gera Germany 48 J5
Gerakarou Greece 58 E8
also known as Yerakaroú
Geraki Greece 59 D12
also known as Yeràkion
Geraki, Akra pt Greece 59 B11
also spelt Yeràki
Geral de Goiás, Serra hills Brazil 202 C4
Geraldine U.S.A. 180 E3
Geral do Paraná, Serra hills Brazil 206 C4
Geraldton Australia 151 A6
Gerama i. Indon. 75 C3
Geraneia mts Greece 59 E11
Gerar watercourse Israel 108 F6
Gérardmer France 51 N4
Gerash Iran 100 C5
Gerber U.S.A. 182 B1
Gerçüş Turkey 107 E3
Gerdau S. Africa 133 K3
Gerdauen Rus. Fed. see Zheleznodorozhnyy
Gerdine, Mount U.S.A. 164 D3
Gerede Turkey 106 C2
Gerede r. Turkey 106 C2
Gereshk Afgh. 101 F4
Geretsried Germany 48 I8
Gergovie tourist site France 51 J7
Gerik Malaysia 76 C1
formerly spelt Grik
Gerimenj Iran 100 D3
Gering U.S.A. 178 B3
Gerlach U.S.A. 182 E1
Gerlachovský štít mt. Slovakia 49 R6
Gerlospaß pass Austria 48 J8
Germaine, Lac l. Canada 169 H2
Germania country Europe see Germany
Germania Land reg. Greenland 165 P2
Germanicea Turkey see Kahramanmaraş
Germansen Landing Canada 166 E4
German South-West Africa country Africa
see Namibia
Germantown MD U.S.A. 177 H6
Germantown TN U.S.A. 174 B5
Germantown WI U.S.A. 172 E7

▶Germany country Europe 48 F5
2nd most populous country in Europe.
Known as Deutschland in German;
historically known as Germania.
europe [countries] ▶▶ 32–35

Germencik Turkey 59 I11
Germersheim Germany 48 F6
Germiston S. Africa 133 M3
Gernika-Lumo Spain 55 I1
also known as Guernica
Gerolstein Germany 48 D5
Gerolzhofen Germany 48 H5
Gerona Spain see Girona
Gerrit Denys is P.N.G. see Lihir Group
Gers r. France 50 G5
Gersfeld (Rhön) Germany 48 G5
Gersoppa India 94 B3
Géryville Alg. see El Bayadh
Gêrzê China 89 D5
also known as Luring
Gerze Turkey 106 C2
Geschriebenstein hill Austria 49 N8
Gesoriacum France see Boulogne-sur-Mer
Gessler Arg. 204 E3
Geta Fin. 45 L3
Getafe Spain 55 H4
Getchen, Küh-e hills Iran 100 C3
Gete r. Belgium 51 L1
Getic, Podişul plat. Romania 58 E4
Getlina Brazil 206 D8
Getúlio Vargas Brazil 203 A8
Getúlio Vargas Brazil 206 D8
Getu He r. China 86 C3
Getz Ice Shelf Antarctica 222 P2
Geumapang r. Indon. 76 B2
Geureudong, Gunung vol. Indon. 76 B1
Geva r. Vietnam 78 D4
Gevaş Turkey 107 E3
also known as Vastan
Gevgelija Macedonia 58 D7
Gevrai India 94 B2
Gevrey-Chambertin France 51 K5
Gewanê Wildlife Reserve nature res. Eth.
128 D2

Gex France 51 M6
Gexianzhuang China see Qinghe
Gey Iran see Nikshahr
Geydik Dağları mts Turkey 108 D1
Geyikli Turkey 59 H9
Geylang Sing. 76 [inset]
Geylang r. Sing. 76 [inset]
Geyserville U.S.A. 182 B3
Gezarina Brazil 206 B5
Ghaap Plateau S. Africa 132 H4
Ghabeish Sudan 126 E2
Ghadaf, Wādī al watercourse Iraq 107 E4
Ghadaf, Wādī al watercourse Jordan
109 H6
Ghadamés Libya see Ghadāmis
Ghadāmis Libya 120 A2
also known as Ghudamis; formerly spelt
Ghadamés
Ghaddūwah Libya 120 B3
Ghadīr al Khayl waterhole Iraq 109 N6
Ghadir al Mulūsī well Iraq 109 K4
Ghaem Shahr Iran 100 C2
Ghaggar, Dry Bed of watercourse Pak. 101 H4
Ghaghara r. India 97 E4
Ghaghra India 97 E5
formerly spelt Gogra
Ghāidah watercourse Iraq 109 M5
Ghalkarteniz, Solonchak salt marsh
Kazakh. 103 E3
Ghallaorol Uzbek. see Gallyaaral

▶Ghana country Africa 125 E4
formerly known as Gold Coast
africa [countries] ▶▶ 114–117

Ghanādah, Rās al i. U.A.E. 105 F2
Ghānah well Oman 105 G4
Ghanim well Saudi Arabia 105 F4
Ghanliala India 96 B4
Ghantwar India 94 A1
Ghanwā Saudi Arabia 105 E2
Ghanzi Botswana 130 D4
Ghanzi admin. dist. Botswana 130 D4
Ghap'an Armenia see Kapan
Gharāmil, Jabal al hill Saudi Arabia 104 C3
Gharandal Jordan 108 G7
Gharandal, Wādī watercourse Egypt 108 D8
Gharbarāt Tāris hill Syria 109 M2
Gharbīya governorate Egypt 108 C7
Ghardaïa Alg. 123 F2
Ghardimaou Tunisia 57 A12
Ghar el Melh Tunisia 57 C11
Gharghoda India 97 D5
Ghārib, Gebel hill Egypt 121 G2
Ghârib, Râs pt Egypt 108 D7
Gharm Tajik. 101 H2
also spelt Garm
Gharo Pak. 101 F5
Gharyān Libya 120 B1
Gharz, Wādī al watercourse Syria 109 I5
Ghāt Libya 120 A3
Ghatampur India 96 D4
Ghatgan India 97 E5
Ghatol India 96 B5
Ghatsila India 97 E5
Ghauspur Pak. 101 G4
Ghawdex i. Malta see Gozo
Ghawr, Wādī al watercourse Syria 109 L3
Ghaymān Yemen 104 D5
Ghazal, Bahr al watercourse Chad 120 C5
Ghazal, Bahr el r. Sudan 128 A3
Ghazalkent Uzbek. see Gazalkent
Ghaziabad India 96 C3
Ghazilah, Wādī al watercourse Iraq 109 O3
Ghazipur India 97 D4
Ghazira, Ghubbat al inlet Oman 105 G2
English form Malcolm Inlet
Ghazna Afgh. see Ghazni
Ghazni Afgh. 101 G3
also spelt Ghazna; historically known as
Alexandria
Ghazni r. Afgh. 101 F3
Ghazni r. Afgh. 101 F3
Ghazzālah Saudi Arabia 104 C3
Ghelari Romania 58 D3
Ghelinţa Romania 58 H3
Ghemeis, Ras ar U.A.E. 105 F2
Ghent Belgium 51 J1
also spelt Gent or Gand
Ghent U.S.A. 176 B8
Gheorghe Gheorghiu-Dej Romania see
Oneşti
Gheorghe Lazār Romania 58 I4
Gheorgheni Romania 58 G2
Gherdi India 94 B2
Gherla Romania 58 E1
formerly known as Armenopolis
Ghijduwan Uzbek. see Gizhduvan
Ghilzai reg. Afgh. 101 F4
Ghīnah, Wādī al watercourse Saudi Arabia
107 D5
Ghioroiu Romania 58 E4
Ghisonaccia Corse France 52 D3
Ghizao Afgh. 101 F3
Ghizar Jammu and Kashmir 96 B1
Ghizri Creek inlet Pak. 101 F5
Ghod India 94 B2
Ghod r. India 94 B2
Gholvad India 94 B2
Ghoraghat Bangl. 97 F4
Ghorak Afgh. 101 F3
Ghorband r. Afgh. 101 G3
Ghost Lake Canada 167 H2
Ghotaru India 96 A4
Ghotki Pak. 101 G5
Ghowr prov. Afgh. 101 F3
Ghuari r. India 97 E4
Ghubbah Yemen 105 F5
Ghudamis Libya see Ghadāmis
Ghugus India 94 C2
Ghulam Mohammed Barrage Pak. 101 G5
Ghurayfah hill Saudi Arabia 109 I6
Ghurian Afgh. 101 E3
Ghurrab, Jabal hill Saudi Arabia 104 D2
Ghūrūb, Jabal hill Saudi Arabia 104 C3
Ghuzayn Oman 105 F4
Ghuzayyil, Sabkhat salt marsh Libya 120 C2
Ghuzor Uzbek. see Guzar
Gia Dinh Vietnam 79 D6
Giaginskaya Rus. Fed. 41 G7
Gia Nghia Vietnam 79 D5
Giannitsa Greece 58 D8
also known as Yenije-i-Vardar; also spelt
Yiannitsá
Giannutri, Isola di i. Italy 56 D6
Giant's Causeway lava field U.K. 47 F3
Gianyar Indon. 77 F5
Gianysada i. Greece 59 H13
Giarabub Libya see Al Jaghbûb
Giardini-Naxos Sicilia Italy 57 H11
Giarmata Romania 58 C3
Giarre Sicilia Italy 57 H11
Giaveno Italy 51 N7
Gibara Cuba 186 D2
Gibarrayo hill Spain 54 F7
Gibb r. Australia 150 D3
Gibbon U.S.A. 178 C3
Gibb River Aboriginal Reserve Australia
150 D3
Gibeon Namibia 130 C5
Gibraleón Spain 54 E7

▶Gibraltar Europe 54 F8
United Kingdom Overseas Territory.
europe [countries] ▶▶ 32–35

▶Gibraltar, Strait of Morocco/Spain 54 E9
europe [countries] ▶▶ 32–33

Gibraltar Range National Park Australia
147 G2
Gibson Australia 151 C7
Gibson City U.S.A. 174 B3
▶Gibson Desert Australia 150 C5
oceania [landscapes] ▶▶ 136–137
Gibson Desert Nature Reserve Australia
151 C5
Gibsons Canada 166 F5
Gichgeniyn Nuruu mts Mongolia 84 B2
Gidami Eth. 128 B2
Gidda Eth. 128 B2
Giddalur India 94 C3
Giddi, Gebel el hill Egypt 121 G2
English form Giddi Pass
Giddings U.S.A. 179 C6
Giddi Pass hill Egypt see Giddi, Gebel el
Gideāhwn r. Sweden 44 L3
Gīdolē Eth. 128 C3
Gien France 51 I5
Giesecke Isfjord inlet Greenland see
Kangerlussuaq
Gießen Germany 48 F5
Gifan Iran 100 D2
Gifatin, Geziret i. Egypt 104 A2
English form Gifatin Island
Giffou r. France 51 I8
Gifhorn Germany 48 H3
Gift Lake Canada 167 H4
Gifu Japan 91 E7
Gifu pref. Japan 91 E7
Gigant Rus. Fed. 41 G7
Giganta, Cerro mt. Mex. 184 C3
Gigante Col. 198 C4
Gigante i. U.K. 46 G8
Gighera Romania 58 E5
Giglio, Isola dei i. Italy 56 C6
also spelt Xixón
Gijón Spain 54 F1
Gikongoro Rwanda 126 F5
Gila r. U.S.A. 183 I9
Gila Bend U.S.A. 183 L9
Gila Bend Mountains U.S.A. 183 K8
Gila Mountains U.S.A. 183 J9
Gilān prov. Iran 100 B2
Gīlān-e Gharb Iran 100 A3
Gilardaïa Alg. 123 F2
Ghardimaou Tunisia 57 A12
Gila River Indian Reservation res. U.S.A.
183 M8
Gilău Romania 58 E2
Gīlāzī Azer. 107 G2
also spelt Kilyazi
Gilbert r. Australia 149 D3
Gilbert AZ U.S.A. 183 M8
Gilbert MN U.S.A. 172 A3
Gilbert WV U.S.A. 176 D8
Gilbert Islands country Pacific Ocean see
Kiribati
Gilbert Range mts Australia 149 D3
Gilbert River Australia 149 D3
Gilbués Brazil 202 C4
Gilé Moz. 131 H3
Gilead reg. Jordan see Jil'ād
Giles Creek r. Australia 148 A3
Giles Meteorological Station Australia
151 E5
Gilf Kebir Plateau Egypt 121 E4
also known as Jilf al Kabīr, Haḍabat al
Gilgandra Australia 147 F2
Gil Gil Creek r. Australia 147 F2
Gilgit Jammu and Kashmir 96 B2
Gilgit r. Jammu and Kashmir 96 B2
Gilgunnia Australia 147 E3
Gili Iyang i. Indon. 77 F4
Gilimanuk Indon. 77 F5
Gillam Canada 167 M3
Gillen watercourse Australia 148 B4
Gillen, Lake salt flat Australia 151 D5
Gilles, Lake salt flat Australia 146 C3
Gillespies Point N.Z. 153 D11
also known as Kōhaihai
Gillett PA U.S.A. 177 I4
Gillett WI U.S.A. 172 E6
Gillette U.S.A. 180 F3
Gillhov Sweden 44 K3
Gilliat Australia 149 D4
Gilliat r. Australia 149 D4
Gillingham U.K. 47 M12
Gilman IL U.S.A. 174 C3
Gilman WI U.S.A. 172 C5
Gilmer U.S.A. 179 D5
Gilort r. Romania 58 E4
Gilroy U.S.A. 182 C4
Giluwe, Mount P.N.G. 73 J8
Gimbī Eth. 128 B2
Gimli Canada 167 L5
Gimo Sweden 45 L3
Gimont France 50 G9
Gin Gin Australia 149 F5
Gingin Australia 151 A6
Gingindlovu S. Africa 133 P6
Gingoog Phil. 74 C4
Ginir Eth. 128 D3
Ginkūnai Lith. 42 E5
Ginzo de Limia Spain see Xinzo de Limia
Gioia, Golfo di b. Italy 57 H10
Gioia del Colle Italy 57 I8
Gioia Tauro Italy 57 H10
Gioura i. Greece 59 F9
also spelt Yioúra
Giouloux r. Canada 169 F2
Gippsland reg. Australia 147 E4
Girâ, Wādī watercourse Egypt 108 E8
Girab India 96 A4
Girân Rīg mt. Iran 101 D4
Girar India 94 C1
Girard KS U.S.A. 178 D4
Girard OH U.S.A. 176 E4
Girard PA U.S.A. 176 E3
Girardin, Lac l. Canada 169 H1
Girdar Dhor r. Pak. 101 F5
Girga Egypt 121 G3
Girga Egypt 121 F3
Girgenti Sicilia Italy see Agrigento
Giri r. Dem. Rep. Congo 126 C4
Giridih India 97 E4
Girilambone Australia 147 E2
Girna r. India 96 B5
Gir National Park India 96 A5
Girne Cyprus see Kyrenia
Giromagny France 51 M5
Giron Ecuador 198 B5
Giron Sweden see Kiruna
Girona Spain 55 N3
also spelt Gerona
Gironde est. France 50 F7
Girou r. France 50 H9
Girua r. Brazil 203 A9
Girvan U.K. 47 H8
Girvas Rus. Fed. 40 E3
Gisborne N.Z. 152 M6
Gisborne admin. reg. N.Z. 152 M6
Giscome Canada 166 F4
Gisenyi Rwanda 126 F5
Gislaved Sweden 45 K4
Gisors France 50 H3
Gissar Tajik. see Hisor
Gissar Range mts Tajik./Uzbek.
101 F2
also known as Gissarskiy Khrebet or Hisor
Tizmasi
Gissarskiy Khrebet mts Tajik./Uzbek. see
Gissar Range

Gissarskiy Zapovednik nature res. Uzbek.
103 F5
Gitarama Rwanda 126 F5
Gitega Burundi 126 F5
Giuba r. Somalia see Jubba
Giubega Romania 58 E4
Giubiasco Switz. 51 P6
Giugliano in Campania Italy 56 G8
Giulianova Italy 56 F6
Giurgeului, Munţii mts Romania 58 G2
Giurgiu Romania 58 G5
Giurgiu r. Romania 58 G5
Givar Iran 100 D2
Give Denmark 45 J5
Givors France 51 K7
Giyani S. Africa 131 F4
Giyon Eth. 128 C2
Giza Egypt 121 F2
also spelt El Gîza or Al Jîzah
▶Giza Pyramids tourist site Egypt 121 F2
also known as Ahrâmât el Jîzah
africa [locations] ▶▶ 118–119
Gizeh Egypt 121 F2
also known as Darreh Gozaru
Gizhduvan Uzbek. 103 F4
also spelt Ghijduwan
Gizhiga Rus. Fed. 39 Q3
Gizo Solomon Is 145 E2
Giżycko Poland 49 S1
Gjalicë e Lumës, Mal mt. Albania 58 B6
Gjerde Norway 45 J3
Gjerstad Norway 45 J4
Gjirokastër Albania 59 B8
formerly known as Argyrokastron
Gjoa Haven Canada 165 J3
Gjøgur Iceland 44 [inset] B2
Gjøra Norway 44 J3
Gjøvik Norway 45 J3
Gjuhëzës, Kepi i pt Albania 58 A8
Glace Bay Canada 169 J4
Glacier Bay U.S.A. 166 C3
Glacier Bay National Park and Preserve
U.S.A. 164 E4
Glacier National Park Canada 167 G5
Glacier National Park U.S.A. 180 D2
Glacier Peak vol. U.S.A. 180 B2
Glade Spring U.S.A. 176 D9
Gladstone Qld Australia 149 F4
Gladstone S.A. Australia 146 C3
Gladstone Canada 167 L5
Gladstone MI U.S.A. 172 J9
Gladstone VA U.S.A. 176 G8
Gladwin U.S.A. 173 I7
Gladys U.S.A. 176 F8
Gladys Lake Canada 166 C3
Glamis U.K. 46 I7
Glamoč Bos.-Herz. 56 I4
Glan r. Austria 49 L9
Glan r. Germany 48 E6
Glan Phil. 74 C5
Glan l. Sweden 45 K4
Glarner Alpen mts Switz. 51 O6
Glarus Switz. 51 P5
Glasfjorden l. Sweden 45 K4
Glasford U.S.A. 172 D10
Glasgow U.K. 46 H8
Glasgow KY U.S.A. 174 C4
Glasgow MT U.S.A. 180 F2
Glasgow VA U.S.A. 176 F8
Glaskogens naturreservat nature res.
Norway 45 K4
Glaslyn Canada 167 I4
Glassboro U.S.A. 177 J6
Glass Mountain U.S.A. 182 F4
Glass Peninsula U.S.A. 166 C3
Glauchau Germany 49 J5
Glavacioc r. Romania 58 F4
Glavan Bulg. 58 H6
Glavinitsa Bulg. 58 H5
Glåvångsi Romania 58 I2
Glavnik Kosovo, Srbija Yugo. 58 C6
Glazoué Benin 125 F5
Glazov Rus. Fed. 40 J4
Glazunovka Rus. Fed. 43 R9
Glazunovo Rus. Fed. 43 T6
Gleason U.S.A. 172 D5
Gleichen Canada 167 H5
Gleisdorf Austria 49 M8
Glen Sweden 44 K3
Glen U.S.A. 177 N1
Glen Afton Canada 173 M4
Glen Afton N.Z. 152 J5
Glen Allen U.S.A. 176 H8
Glénan, Îles de is France 50 C5
Glen Arbor U.S.A. 172 H6
Glenavy N.Z. 153 F12
Glenboro Canada 167 L5
Glen Burnie U.S.A. 177 I6
Glen Canyon gorge U.S.A. 183 M4
Glen Canyon Dam U.S.A. 183 M5
Glencoe S. Africa 133 O5
Glencoe KY U.S.A. 176 A7
Glencoe MN U.S.A. 178 D2
Glenconnor S. Africa 133 J10
Glen Cove U.S.A. 177 L5
Glendale Canada 173 L4
Glendale AZ U.S.A. 183 L8
Glendale CA U.S.A. 182 F7
Glendale UT U.S.A. 183 L4
Glendale Lake U.S.A. 176 G5
Glendale Springs U.S.A. 176 D9
Glendambo Australia 146 B2
Glendive U.S.A. 180 F3
Glendon Canada 167 I4
Glendo Reservoir U.S.A. 180 F4
Glenelg r. Australia 146 D4
Glenfield U.S.A. 177 J2
Glenfinnan U.K. 46 G7
Glengarry Range hills Australia 151 B5
Glengyle Australia 148 C5
Glen Hill Aboriginal Reserve Australia
150 D3
Glen Innes Australia 147 F2
Glenlyon Peak Canada 166 C2
Glen Massey N.Z. 152 I5
Glen More valley U.K. 46 H6
Glenmorgan Australia 147 F1
Glen Murray N.Z. 152 I5
Glenn U.S.A. 182 B2
Glennallen U.S.A. 164 E3
Glennie U.S.A. 173 J6
Glenns U.S.A. 177 I8
Glenns Ferry U.S.A. 180 D4
Glenora Canada 166 D3
Glenore Australia 149 D3
Glenormiston Australia 148 C4
Glenorn Aboriginal Reserve Australia
151 C6
Glen Rock U.S.A. 177 I6
Glen Rogers U.S.A. 176 D8
Glen Rose U.S.A. 179 C5
Glenrothes U.K. 46 I7
Glens Falls U.S.A. 177 L2
Glen Shee valley U.K. 46 I7
Glenties Rep. of Ireland 47 D3
Glentunnel N.Z. 153 F11
Glenveagh National Park Rep. of Ireland
47 E2
Glenville U.S.A. 176 E7
Glenwater Canada 172 D2
Glen Wilton U.S.A. 176 F8
Glenwood AR U.S.A. 179 D5
Glenwood IA U.S.A. 178 D3
Glenwood MN U.S.A. 178 D2
Glenwood NM U.S.A. 183 I8
Glenwood UT U.S.A. 183 M3
Glenwood WV U.S.A. 176 C7
Glenwood City U.S.A. 172 A5
Glenwood Springs U.S.A. 180 F5

Glevum U.K. see Gloucester
Glina r. Bos.-Herz./Croatia 56 I3
Glina Croatia 56 I3
Glinka Rus. Fed. 43 N7
Glittertinden mt. Norway 45 J3
Gliwice Poland 49 P5
historically known as Gleiwitz
Globe U.S.A. 183 N8
Glodeanu-Sărat Romania 58 H4
Glodeni Romania 58 F2
Glogau Poland see Głogów
Gloggnitz Austria 49 M8
Glogovac Kosovo, Srbija Yugo. 58 B6
Głogów Poland 49 N4
historically known as Glogau
Głogówek Poland 49 O5
Głogów Małopolski Poland 49 S5
Glomfjord Norway 44 K2
Glomma r. Norway 45 J4
Glommersträsk Sweden 44 L2
Glória Brazil 202 E4
Glorieuses, Îles is Indian Ocean 129 E7
English form Glorioso Islands
Glorioso Islands Indian Ocean see Glorieuses, Îles
Gloucester Australia 147 F2
Gloucester P.N.G. 145 D2
Gloucester U.K. 47 J12
historically known as Glevum
Gloucester MA U.S.A. 177 O3
Gloucester VA U.S.A. 177 I8
Gloucester Island Australia 149 F4
Gloucester Point U.S.A. 177 I8
Glover Reef Belize 185 I5
Gloversville U.S.A. 177 K2
Glovertown Canada 169 K3
Glöwen Germany 48 J3
Głowno Poland 49 Q4
Glubczyce Poland 49 O5
Glubinnoye Rus. Fed. 82 D3
Glubokiy Rus. Fed. 41 G6
Glubokoye Belarus see Hlybokaye
Glubokoye Kazakh. 88 C1
Glubokoye, Ozero l. Rus. Fed. 43 K1
Glücksburg (Ostsee) Germany 48 G1
Glückstadt Germany 48 G2
Gluggarnir hill Faroe Is 46 F2
Glukhov Ukr. see Hlukhiv
Gmelinka Rus. Fed. 102 A2
Gmünd Austria 49 L7
Gmunden Austria 49 K8
Gnadenhutten U.S.A. 176 D5
Gnarp Sweden 45 L3
Gnarrenburg Germany 48 G2
Gnesen Poland see Gniezno
Gniew Poland 49 P2
Gniewkowo Poland 49 P3
Gniezno Poland 49 O3
historically known as Gnesen
Gnisvärd Sweden 45 L4
Gnjilane Kosovo, Srbija Yugo. 58 C6
Gnoien Germany 49 J2
Gnowangerup Australia 151 B7
Gnows Nest Range hills Australia 151 B6
Goa state India 94 B3
Goageb Namibia 130 C5
Goalpara India 97 F4
Goang Indon. 75 A5
Goaso Ghana 124 E5
Goat Fell hill U.K. 46 G8
Goba Eth. 128 D3
Gobabis Namibia 130 C4
Gobannium U.K. see Abergavenny
Gobas Namibia 130 C5
Gobernador Crespo Arg. 204 E3
Gobernador Duval Arg. 204 D5
Gobernador Gregores Arg. 205 C8
Gobernador Mayer Arg. 205 C8
Gobernador Virasoro Arg. 204 F3
Gobi des. China/Mongolia 85 E2
English form Gobi Desert
Gobi Desert China/Mongolia see Gobi
Gobiki Rus. Fed. 43 O8
Göblberg hill Austria 49 K7
Gobō Japan 91 D8
Goch Germany 48 D4
Gochas Namibia 130 C5
Go Công Vietnam 79 D6
Godagari Bangl. 97 F4
Godavari r. India 94 D2
Godbout Canada 169 H3
Godbout r. Canada 169 H3
Godda India 97 E4
Goddard, Mount U.S.A. 182 F4
Godē Eth. 128 D3
Godech Bulg. 58 E5
Goderich Canada 168 D5
Goderville France 50 G3
Godhavn Greenland see Qeqertarsuaq
Godhra India 96 B5
Godinlabe Somalia 128 E3
Godo, Gunung mt. Indon. 75 C3
Gödöllő Hungary 49 Q8
Gods r. Canada 167 M3
Gods Lake Canada 167 M4
God's Mercy, Bay of Canada 167 O2
Godthåb Greenland see Nuuk
Godučohkka mt. Sweden 44 L1
also spelt Kåtotjåkka
Godwin-Austen, Mount China/Jammu and Kashmir see K2
Goedemoed S. Africa 133 K7
Goedgegun Swaziland see Nhlangano
Goéland, Lac au l. Canada 168 E3
Goélands, Lac aux l. Canada 169 I2
Goes Neth. 48 A4
Goetzville U.S.A. 173 I4
Goffstown U.S.A. 177 N2
Gogama Canada 168 D4
Gogebic, Lake U.S.A. 172 D4
Gogebic Range hills U.S.A. 172 D4
Göğeç Turkey 109 K1
Gogland, Ostrov i. Rus. Fed. 42 H1
Gogoi Moz. 131 G4
Gogolevka Rus. Fed. 43 M7
Gogoşu Romania 58 D4
Gogounou Benin 125 F4
Gogra India see Ghaghra
Gogra r. India see Ghaghara
Gogrial Sudan 126 F2
Gogunda India 96 B4
Gohad India 96 C4
Gohana India 96 C3
Goharganj India 96 C5
Goiana Brazil 202 F3
Goianésia Brazil 206 D2
Goiânia Brazil 206 D3
Goianinha Brazil 202 F3
Goianira Brazil 206 D3
Goiás Brazil 206 C2
Goiás state Brazil 206 C3
Goiatuba Brazil 206 D5
Goincang China 86 B1
Goio-Erê Brazil 203 A8
Goi-Pula Dem. Rep. Congo 127 E6
Goito Italy 56 C3
Gojeb Wenz r. Eth. 128 C3
Gojra Pak. 101 H4
Gokak India 94 B2
Gokarn India 94 B3
Gök Çay r. Turkey 108 D1
Gökçeada i. Turkey 106 A2
also known as Imroz
Gökçedağ Turkey 106 B3
Gökçen Turkey 59 I10
Gökçeören Turkey 59 J10
Gökdepe Turkm. see Gekdepe
Gökdere r. Turkey 108 D1
Gökirmak r. Turkey 106 C2
Goklenkuy, Solonchak salt l. Turkm. 102 D4
Gökova Turkey see Ula
Gökova Körfezi b. Turkey 106 A3
Gokprosh Hills Pak. 101 E5
Göksun Turkey 107 D3
Göksu Nehri r. Turkey 106 C3
Goksu Parkı Turkey 108 E1
Gokteik Myanmar 78 B3
Göktepe Turkey 108 D1
Gokwe Zimbabwe 131 F3
Gol Norway 45 J3
Gola India 96 D3
Golaghat India 97 G4
Golakganj India 97 F4
Golan hills Syria 108 G4
also spelt Al Jawlān or HaGolan
Golāncz Poland 49 O3
Golbāf Iran 100 D4
Golbahār Afgh. 101 G3
Gölbaşı Turkey 107 D3
Golconda India 94 C2
Golconda IL U.S.A. 174 B4
Golconda NV U.S.A. 183 G1
Gölcük Turkey 59 I9
Gölcük Turkey 106 B2
Gölçük Turkey see Etili
Gölcük r. Turkey 59 J9
Golczewo Poland 49 L2
Gold U.S.A. 176 H4
Gołdap Poland 49 T1
Gołdapa r. Poland 49 S1
Gold Beach U.S.A. 180 A4
Goldberg Germany 49 J2
Gold Coast country Africa see Ghana
Gold Coast Australia 147 G2
formerly known as South Coast Town
Gold Coast coastal area Ghana 125 E5
Golden Canada 167 G5
Golden Bay N.Z. 152 G8
Goldendale U.S.A. 180 B3
Golden Downs N.Z. 153 G9
Golden Ears Provincial Park Canada 166 F5
Golden Gate Highlands National Park S. Africa 133 M5
Golden Hinde mt. Canada 166 E5
Golden Lake Canada 168 E4
Golden Meadow U.S.A. 175 B6
Golden Valley S. Africa 133 J9
Golden Valley Zimbabwe 131 F3
Goldfield U.S.A. 183 G4
Gold River Canada 166 E5
Goldsand Lake Canada 167 K3
Goldsboro U.S.A. 174 E5
Goldstone Lake U.S.A. 183 H6
Goldsworthy Australia 150 B4
Goldthwaite U.S.A. 179 C6
Goldvein U.S.A. 176 H7
Göle Turkey 107 E2
also known as Merdenik
Goleniów Poland 49 L2
Golestān Afgh. 101 E3
Golestān prov. Iran 100 C2
Goleta U.S.A. 182 E7
Golfito Costa Rica 186 C5
Golfo de Tehuantepec g. Mex. see Tehuantepec, Gulf of
Golfo di Orosei Gennargentu e Asinara, Parco Nazionale del nat. park Sardegna Italy 57 B8
Gölgeli Dağları mts Turkey 106 B3
Gölhisar Turkey 59 K11
Goliad U.S.A. 179 C6
Golija nat. park Yugo. 58 B5
Golija Planina mts Yugo. 58 B5
Golingka China see Gongbo'gyamda
Golitsyno Rus. Fed. 43 S6
Gölköy Turkey 107 D2
also known as Kuşluyan
Gollel Swaziland see Lavumisa
Gölmarmara Turkey 59 I10
Golmberg hill Germany 49 K3
Golmud China 84 B4
Golmud He r. China 84 B4
Golo i. Phil. 74 B3
Golobino Rus. Fed. 43 V6
Golodnaya Step' plain Uzbek. 103 F4
Golondrina Arg. 204 E3
Gölova Turkey 108 A1
Gölovası Turkey 108 G1
Golovnino Rus. Fed. 90 I3
Golpāyegān Iran 100 B3
Gölpazarı Turkey 106 B2
Golspie U.K. 46 I6
Golub-Dobrzyń Poland 49 Q2
Golubovka Kazakh. 103 H1
Golungo Alto Angola 127 B7
Goluzino Rus. Fed. 43 V2
Gol Vardeh Iran 101 E3
Golweyn Somalia 128 E4
Golyama Syutkya mt. Bulg. 58 F7
Golyama Zhelyazna Bulg. 58 F6
Golyam Perelik mt. Bulg. 58 F7
Golyam Persenk mt. Bulg. 58 F7
Golyashi Belarus see Sasnovy Bor
Gölyazı Turkey 59 J8
Golyshi Rus. Fed. 43 M7
Golyshi Rus. Fed. see Vetluzhskiy
Goma Dem. Rep. Congo 126 F5
Goma Uganda 128 A5
Gomang Co salt l. China 89 E6
Gomati r. India 96 D4
Gombak, Bukit hill Sing. 76 [inset]
Gombari Dem. Rep. Congo 126 F4
Gombe Nigeria 125 H4
Gombe state Nigeria 125 H4
Gombe r. Tanz. 129 A6
Gombi Nigeria 125 I4
Gombroon Iran see Bandar-e 'Abbās
Gömeç Turkey 59 H9
also known as Armutova
Gomel' Belarus see Homyel'
Gomel Oblast admin. div. Belarus see Homyel'skaya Voblasts'
Gomel'skaya Oblast' admin. div. Belarus see Homyel'skaya Voblasts'
Gómez Palacio Mex. 184 E3
Gómez Rendón Ecuador 198 A5
Gömil, Rūbār-e r. Iraq 109 O1
Gomīshān Iran 100 C2
Gomo China 89 D5
Gomo Co salt l. China 89 D5
Gomorovichi Rus. Fed. 43 P1
Gomumu i. Indon. 75 C3
Gonabad Iran see Jüymand
Gonaïves Haiti 187 E3
Gonarezhou National Park Zimbabwe 131 F4
Gonbad-e Kavus Iran 100 C2
Gonda India 97 D4
Gondal India 96 A5
Gonda Libah well Eth. 128 E2
Gondar Col. 198 C5
Gondar Eth. see Gonder
Gonder Eth. 128 C1
formerly spelt Gondar
Gondey Chad 126 C2
Gondia India 96 D5
Gondomar Spain 54 C2
Gönen Turkey 106 A2
Gönen r. Turkey 59 I8
Gonfreville-l'Orcher France 50 G3
Gong'an China 87 E2
also known as Douhudi; formerly known as Doushi
Gongbalou China see Gamba
Gongbo'gyamda China 89 F6
also known as Golingka
Gongcheng China 87 D3
Gonggar China 89 E6
also known as Gyixong
Gongga Shan mt. China 86 B2
also known as Minya Konka
Gonghe China 84 D4
also known as Qabqa
Gonghe China see Mouding
Gonghui China 85 G3
Gongjiang China see Yudu
Gongliu China 88 C3
also known as Tokkuztara
Gongola r. Nigeria 125 I4
Gongolgon Australia 147 E2
Gongoué Gabon 126 A5
Gongpoquan China 84 C3
Gongqen China see Gongxian
Gongshan China 86 A3
also known as Cikai
Gongtang China see Damxung
Gongwang Shan mts China 86 B3
Gongxian China see Gongyi
Gongxian China 86 C2
also known as Gongquan
Gongyi China 87 E1
formerly known as Gongxian or Xiaoyi
Gongzhuling China 82 B4
formerly known as Huaide
Goniądz Poland 49 T2
Goniri Nigeria 125 I4
Gonjo China 86 A2
also known as Kasha
Gonjog China 89 D6
Gonnesa Sardegna Italy 57 A9
Gonnoi Greece 59 D9
Gonnosfanadiga Sardegna Italy 57 A9
Gōnoura Japan 91 A8
Gonubie S. Africa 133 M9
Gonzáles Mex. 185 F4
Gonzales CA U.S.A. 182 C5
Gonzales TX U.S.A. 179 C6
González Moreno Arg. 204 E4
Gonzalo Vásquez Panama 186 D5
Goochland U.S.A. 176 H8
Goode U.S.A. 176 F8
Goodenough, Cape Antarctica 223 I2
Goodenough Island P.N.G. 145 E2
Gooderham Canada 173 O6
Good Harbor Bay U.S.A. 172 H5
Good Hart U.S.A. 173 H5
Good Hope Botswana 133 J2
Good Hope U.S.A. 172 C10
Good Hope, Cape of S. Africa 132 C11
Good Hope Mountain Canada 166 E5
Goodland U.S.A. 178 B4
Goodman U.S.A. 172 E5
Goodooga Australia 147 E2
Goodparla Australia 148 B2
Goodrich U.S.A. 172 C5
Goodspeed Nunataks Antarctica 223 E2
Goodwood r. Canada 169 G2
Goole U.K. 47 L10
Goolgowi Australia 147 E3
Goolwa Australia 146 C3
Goomadeer r. Australia 148 B1
Goomalling Australia 151 B6
Goombalie Australia 147 E2
Goomeri Australia 149 G5
Goonda Moz. 131 G3
Goondiwindi Australia 147 F2
Goongarrie, Lake salt flat Australia 151 C6
Goongarrie National Park Australia 151 C6
Goonyella Australia 149 E4
Goorly, Lake salt flat Australia 151 B6
Goose r. Canada 169 I2
Goose r. U.S.A. 178 C2
Goose Bay Canada see Happy Valley - Goose Bay
Goose Creek U.S.A. 175 D5
Goose Creek r. U.S.A. 180 D4
Goose Green Falkland Is 205 F8
Goose Lake U.S.A. 180 B4
Goose Lake Canal r. U.S.A. 182 E6
Gooty India 94 C3
Gop India 95 E2
Gopalganj Bangl. 97 F5
Gopalganj India 97 E4
Gopeshwar India 96 C3
formerly known as Chamoli
Gopichettipalayam India 94 C4
Gopiganj India 97 D4
Göppingen Germany 48 G7
Góra Poland 49 N4
Goradiz Azer. see Horadiz
Goragorskiy Rus. Fed. 41 H8
Góra Kalwaria Poland 49 S4
Gorakhpur India 97 D4
Goražde Bos.-Herz. 56 K5
Gorbachevo Rus. Fed. 43 S8
Gorchukha Rus. Fed. 40 G4
Gorczański Park Narodowy nat. park Poland 49 R6
Gorda, Banco sea feature Hond. 186 C4
Gorda, Punta pt Nicaragua 186 C4
Gorda, Punta pt U.S.A. 180 A4
Gorda, Sierra mts Spain 54 G7
Gördalen Sweden 45 K3
Gördes Turkey 106 B3
Gordeyevka Rus. Fed. 43 M9
Gordon r. Canada 167 O1
Gordon NE U.S.A. 178 B3
Gordon WI U.S.A. 172 B4
Gordon, Isla i. Chile 205 C9
Gordon, Lake Australia 147 E5
Gordon Bay Australia 148 A1
Gordon Downs Australia 150 E3
Gordon Lake Canada 167 H2
Gordonsville U.S.A. 176 G7
Gordonvale Australia 149 E3
Goré Chad 126 C3
Gorē Eth. 128 B2
Gore N.Z. 153 C14
Gore U.S.A. 176 G6
Gore Bay Canada 173 K5
Gorelki Rus. Fed. 43 S7
Goreloye Rus. Fed. 41 G5
Gore Point U.S.A. 164 D4
Goretovo Rus. Fed. 43 Q6
Gorey Rep. of Ireland 47 F11
Gorg Iran 101 D4
Gorgān Iran 100 C2
also spelt Gurgan; formerly known as Asterabad or Astrabad; historically known as Hyrcania or Varkana
Gorgan Bay Iran 100 C2
Gorge Range hills Australia 150 B4
Gorge Range mts Australia 149 E3
Gorge Road N.Z. 153 C14
Gorges Namibia 132 B4
Gorgol admin. reg. Mauritania 124 B2
Gorgona, Isola di i. Italy 56 B5
Gorgora Eth. 128 C1
Gorgoram Nigeria 125 H3
Gorgova, Lacul l. Romania 58 K3
Gorham U.S.A. 177 N1
Gori Georgia 107 F2
Gorinchem Neth. 48 B4
Goris Armenia 107 F3
Goritsa Bulg. 58 I6
Goritsy Rus. Fed. 43 R4
Gorizia Italy 56 F3
Gorka Rus. Fed. 43 T5
Gorkhā Nepal 97 E4
Gorki Belarus see Horki
Gor'kiy Rus. Fed. see Nizhniy Novgorod
Gor'kovskaya Oblast' admin. div. Rus. Fed. see Nizhegorodskaya Oblast'
Gor'kovskoye Vodokhranilishche resr Rus. Fed. 43 V4
Gor'koye, Ozero salt l. Rus. Fed. 103 J1
Gor'koye, Ozero salt l. Rus. Fed. 103 J1
Gorlice Poland 49 S6
Görlitz Germany 49 L4
Gorlovka Ukr. see Horlivka
Gorlovo Rus. Fed. 43 U8
Gormi India 96 C4
Gorna Dzhumaya Bulg. see Blagoevgrad
Gorna Oryakhovitsa Bulg. 58 G5
Gorni Dŭbnik Bulg. 58 F5
Gornja Radgona Slovenia 56 H2
Gornja Toponica Srbija Yugo. 58 C5
Gornji Matejevac Srbija Yugo. 58 C5
Gornji Milanovac Srbija Yugo. 58 B4
Gornji Vakuf Bos.-Herz. 56 J5
also known as Uskoplje
Gorno Ablanovo Bulg. 58 G5
Gorno-Altaysk Rus. Fed. 80 D2
Gorno-Altayskaya Avtonomnaya Oblast' aut. rep. Rus. Fed. see Altay, Respublika
Gorno-Badakhshan aut. rep. Tajik. see Kŭhistoni Badakhshon
Gornopravdinsk Rus. Fed. 38 G3
Gornotrakiyska Nizina lowland Bulg. 58 G6
Gornozavodsk Rus. Fed. 40 K4
formerly known as Novopashiyskiy
Gornozavodsk Rus. Fed. 82 F3
Gornyak Rus. Fed. 88 C1
Gornyak Rus. Fed. 43 U8
Gornye Klyuchi Rus. Fed. 82 D3
Gornyy Khabarovskiy Kray Rus. Fed. 82 E2
formerly known as Solnechnyy
Gornyy Primorskiy Kray Rus. Fed. 90 C2
Gornyy Saratovskaya Oblast' Rus. Fed. 102 B2
Gornyy Altay aut. rep. Rus. Fed. see Altay, Respublika
Gornyy Badakhshan aut. rep. Tajik. see Kŭhistoni Badakhshon
Gornyy Balykley Rus. Fed. 41 H6
Goro Eth. 128 D3
Goro i. Fiji see Koro
Goroch'an mt. Eth. 128 C2
Gorodenka Ukr. see Horodenka
Gorodets Rus. Fed. 40 G4
Gorodishche Penzenskaya Oblast' Rus. Fed. 41 H5
Gorodishche Volgogradskaya Oblast' Rus. Fed. 41 H6
Gorodok Belarus see Haradok
Gorodok Belarus see Haradok
Gorodok Rus. Fed. see Zakamensk
Gorodok Ukr. see Horodok
Gorodovikovsk Rus. Fed. 41 G7
formerly known as Bashanta
Goroka P.N.G. 73 K8
Goroke Australia 146 D4
Gorokhovets Rus. Fed. 40 G4
Gorom Gorom Burkina 125 E3
Gorong, Kepulauan is Indon. 73 H7
Gorongosa Moz. 131 G3
formerly known as Vila Paiva de Andrada
Gorongosa mt. Moz. 131 G3
Gorongosa, Parque Nacional de nat. park Moz. 131 G3
Gorontalo Indon. 75 B2
Goronyo Nigeria 125 G3
Goroubi watercourse Niger 125 F3
Gorouol r. Burkina/Niger 125 F3
Górowo Iławeckie Poland 49 R1
Gorshechnoye Rus. Fed. 41 F6
Gór Stołowych, Park Narodowy nat. park Poland 49 N5
Goru, Vârful mt. Romania 58 H3
Görükle Turkey 59 J8
Gorumna Island Rep. of Ireland 47 C10
Gorutuba r. Brazil 207 J2
Goryachiy Klyuch Rus. Fed. 41 F7
Górzno Poland 49 Q2
Gorzów Wielkopolski Poland 49 M3
historically known as Landsberg
Gosainthan mt. China see Xixabangma Feng
Goschen Strait P.N.G. 149 F1
Gosford Australia 147 F3
Goshen CA U.S.A. 182 E5
Goshen IN U.S.A. 174 C3
Goshen NH U.S.A. 177 M2
Goshen VA U.S.A. 176 F8
Goshoba Turkm. see Koshoba
Goshogawara Japan 90 G4
Goslar Germany 48 H4
Gospić Croatia 56 H4
Gossas Senegal 124 A3
Gosse watercourse Australia 148 B3
Gossi Mali 125 E3
Gossinga Sudan 126 E2
Gostivar Macedonia 58 B7
Gostyń Poland 49 O4
Gostynin Poland 49 Q3
Gosu China 86 A1
Gota Eth. 128 D2
Götaälven r. Sweden 45 J4
Göteborg Sweden see Gothenburg
Gotel Mountains Cameroon/Nigeria 125 H5
Gotemba Japan see Gotenba
Gotenba Japan 91 F7
also spelt Gotemba
Götene Sweden 45 K4
Gotenhafen Poland see Gdynia
Gotha Germany 48 H5
Gothem Sweden 45 L4
Gothenburg Sweden 45 J4
also spelt Göteborg
Gothenburg U.S.A. 178 B3
Gothèye Niger 125 F3
Gotland i. Sweden 45 L4
Gotō-rettō is Japan 91 A8
Gotse Delchev Bulg. 58 E7
Gotska Sandön Sweden 45 L4
Gotska Sandön i. Sweden 45 L4
Gōtsu Japan 91 C7
Gottero, Monte mt. Italy 56 B4
Göttingen Germany 48 G4
Gottne Sweden 44 L3
Gott Peak Canada 166 F5
Gottwaldov Czech Rep. see Zlín
Gotval'd Ukr. see Zmiyiv
Gouako Cent. Afr. Rep. 126 D3
Gouda Neth. 48 B3
Gouda S. Africa 132 D10
Goudiri Senegal 124 B3
Goudoumaria Niger 125 H3
Goudreau Canada 173 I2
Gouéké Guinea 124 C4
Goûgaram Niger 125 G2

Gough Island S. Atlantic Ocean 217 N8
Dependency of St Helena.

Gouin, Réservoir Canada 169 F3
Goukamma Nature Reserve S. Africa 132 G11
Goulais River Canada 173 I4
Goulburn Australia 147 F3
Goulburn r. Australia 147 E4
Goulburn Islands Australia 148 B1
Goulburn River National Park Australia 147 F3
Gould, Mount hill Australia 151 B5
Gould City U.S.A. 172 H4
Gould Coast Antarctica 223 O1
Goulféy Cameroon 125 I3
Goulia Côte d'Ivoire 124 D4
Goulou atoll Micronesia see Ngulu
Goumbou Mali 124 D3
Goumenissa Greece 58 D8
Gouna Cameroon 125 I4
Goundam Mali 124 E2
Goundi Chad 126 C2
Gounou-Gaya Chad 126 B2
Gouraya Alg. 55 M8
Gouraye Mauritania 124 B3
Gourcy Burkina 124 E3
Gourdon France 50 H8
Gouré Niger 125 H3
Gourin France 50 C4
Gouripur Bangl. 97 F4
Gourits r. S. Africa 132 F11
Gourlay Lake Canada 173 I2
Gourma-Rharous Mali 125 E2
Goûrmél well Mauritania 124 C2
Gourmeur well Chad 120 D5
Gournay-en-Bray France 50 H3
Gouro Chad 120 C5
Goûr Oulad Ahmed reg. Mali 122 D5
Goussainville France 51 I3
Gouvêa Brazil 207 J5
Gouveia Port. 54 D4
Gouverneur U.S.A. 177 J1
Gove U.S.A. 178 B4
Gove, Barragem do resr Angola 127 B8
Govedartsi Bulg. 58 E6
Govena, Mys hd Rus. Fed. 39 Q4
Gove Peninsula Australia 148 C2
Governador Valadares Brazil 203 D6
Governor Generoso Phil. 74 C5
Governor's Harbour Bahamas 186 D1
Govĭ-Altay prov. Mongolia 84 B2
Govĭ Altayn Nuruu mts Mongolia 84 C2
Govind Ballash Pant Sagar resr India 97 D4
Govindgarh India 97 D4
Govind Sagar resr India 96 C3
Govurdak Turkm. 103 F5
also spelt Gowurdak; formerly spelt Gaurdak
Gowanbridge N.Z. 153 G9
Gowanda U.S.A. 176 G3
Gowan Range hills Australia 149 E5
Gowd-e Ahmar Iran 100 C4
Gowd-e Rūd-e watercourse Iran 100 C5
Gowd-e Hasht Tekkeh waterhole Iran 100 D3
Gowganda Canada 173 M3
Gowganda Lake Canada 173 M3
Gowmal Kalay Afgh. 101 G3
Gowurdak Turkm. see Govurdak
Goya Arg. 204 F3
Göyçay Azer. 107 F2
Goyder r. Australia 148 B2
Goyder watercourse Australia 148 B5
Goyder Lagoon salt flat Australia 146 C1
Goymatdag hills Turkm. see Koymatdag, Gory
Göynük Antalya Turkey 108 B1
Göynük Bingöl Turkey 107 E3
also known as Oğnut
Göynük Bolu Turkey 106 B2
Göynükbelen Turkey 59 K9
Goyō-zan mt. Japan 90 G5
Göytäpä Azer. 107 G3
Gözareh Afgh. 101 E3
Goz-Beïda Chad 120 D6
Gözcüler Turkey 108 F1
Gözene Turkey 107 D3
Gözne Turkey 108 F1
Gozo i. Malta 57 G12
also known as Ghawdex
Goz Regeb Sudan 121 G5
Graaf-Reinet S. Africa 133 I9
Graafwater S. Africa 132 C9
Grabia r. Poland 49 P4
Grabo Côte d'Ivoire 124 D5
Grabouw S. Africa 132 D11
Grabovica Srbija Yugo. 58 D4
Grabovo Kazakh. 103 H1
Grabow Germany 48 I2
Grabów r. Poland 49 N1
Grabów nad Prosną Poland 49 P4
Gračac Croatia 56 H4
Gračanica Bos.-Herz. 56 K4
Gračanica Jezero l. Yugo. 58 A6
Graçay France 50 H5
Grace, Lake salt flat Australia 151 B7
Gracefield Canada 168 E4
Gracemere Australia 149 F4
Grachevka Rus. Fed. 102 C1
Grachi Kazakh. 103 I2
Gracias Hond. 186 A4
Gradačac Bos.-Herz. 56 K4
Gradaús Brazil 202 B3
Gradaús, Serra dos hills Brazil 202 B4
Gradets Bulg. 58 H6
Gradignan France 50 F8
Gradishte hill Bulg. 58 H6
Gradiška Bos.-Herz. see Bosanska Gradiška
Gradište Croatia 56 K3
Grădiștea Romania 58 H4
Grado Italy 56 F3
Grado Spain 54 E1
Grady U.S.A. 179 B5
Gräfenhainichen Germany 49 J4
Gräftåvallen Sweden 44 K3
Grafton Australia 147 G2
Grafton ND U.S.A. 178 C1
Grafton WI U.S.A. 172 F7
Grafton WV U.S.A. 176 E6
Grafton, Cape Australia 149 E3
Grafton, Mount U.S.A. 183 J3
Grafton Passage Australia 149 E3
Graham NC U.S.A. 176 F9
Graham TX U.S.A. 179 C5
Graham, Mount U.S.A. 183 O9
Graham Bell Island Rus. Fed. see Greem-Bell, Ostrov
Graham Island B.C. Canada 166 C4
Graham Island Nunavut Canada 165 J2
Graham Lake U.S.A. 177 Q1
Graham Land reg. Antarctica 222 T2
Graham Moore, Cape Canada 165 L2
Grahamstown S. Africa 133 K10
Graiguenamanagh Rep. of Ireland 47 F11
Grajagan Indon. 77 F5
Grajaú Brazil 202 C3
Grajaú r. Brazil 202 C2
Grajewo Poland 49 T2
Gram Denmark 45 J5
Gramada mt. Yugo. 58 D6
Gramat France 50 H8
Gramatikovo Bulg. 58 I6
Grammichele Sicilia Italy 57 G11
Grámmos mt. Greece 59 B8
Gramoz, Mal mt. Albania/Greece 59 B8
Grampian U.S.A. 176 G5
Grampian Mountains U.K. 46 H7
Grampians, The mts Australia 147 D4
Grampians National Park Australia 147 D4
Gramsh Albania 58 B8
Gran Hungary see Esztergom
Granaatboskolk S. Africa 132 D7
Granada Col. 198 C4
Granada Nicaragua 186 B5
Granada Spain 55 H7
Granado hill Spain 54 D7
Granado U.S.A. 178 B4
Gran Altiplanicie Central plain Arg. 205 C8
Granard Rep. of Ireland 47 E10
Gran Baja San Julián valley Arg. 205 C8
Gran Bajo depr. Arg. 205 D7
Gran Bajo Salitroso salt flat Arg. 204 D5
Granbury U.S.A. 179 C5
Granby Canada 169 F4
Granby U.S.A. 180 F4
Gran Canaria i. Canary Is 122 B4
English form Grand Canary
Gran Chaco reg. Arg./Para. 201 E6
Grand r. MO U.S.A. 174 C3
Grand r. SD U.S.A. 178 B2
Grand, North Fork r. U.S.A. 178 B2
Grand, South Fork r. U.S.A. 178 B2
Grand Atlas mts Morocco see Haut Atlas
Grand Bahama i. Bahamas 186 D1
Grand Bank Canada 169 K4
Grand-Bassam Côte d'Ivoire 124 E5
Grand Bay Canada 169 H4
Grand Bay U.S.A. 175 B6
Grand Bend Canada 173 L7
Grand Bérard mt. France 51 M8
Grand Bourg Guadeloupe 187 H4
Grand Caicos i. Turks and Caicos Is 187 F2
Grand Canal China see Da Yunhe
Grand Canal Rep. of Ireland 47 E10
Grand Canary i. Canary Is see Gran Canaria
Grand Canyon U.S.A. 183 L5
Grand Canyon gorge U.S.A. 183 L5
world [land images] 12–13
northamerica [landscapes] 156–157
Grand Canyon National Park U.S.A. 183 L5
Grand Cayman i. Cayman Is 186 C3
Grand Centre Canada 167 I4
Grand Combin mt. Switz. 51 N7
Grand Detour U.S.A. 172 D9
Grande r. Arg. 204 C5
Grande r. Santa Cruz Bol. 201 E4
Grande r. Santa Cruz Bol. 201 E4
also known as Guapay
Grande r. Bahia Brazil 202 D4
Grande r. São Paulo Brazil 206 C7
Grande r. Peru 200 B3
Grande, Bahía b. Arg. 205 C8
Grande, Cayo i. Cuba 186 D2
Grande, Cerro mt. Mex. 185 F5
Grande, Ciénaga lag. Col. 198 C2
Grande, Ilha i. Brazil 203 C7
Grande, Serra hills Brazil 201 E2
Grande, Serra mt. Brazil 199 F4
also known as Carauná
Grande Cache Canada 166 G4
Grande Comore i. Comoros see Njazidja
Grande de Manacapuru, Lago l. Brazil 199 F5
Grande-Entree Canada 169 I4
Grande Leyre r. France 50 F8
Grande Prairie Canada 166 G4
Grand Erg de Bilma des. Niger 125 I2
Grand Erg Occidental des. Alg. 123 E3
English form Great Western Erg
Grand Erg Oriental des. Alg. 123 G3
English form Great Eastern Erg
Grande-Rivière Canada 169 H3
Grande Ronde r. U.S.A. 180 C3
Grandes, Salinas salt marsh Arg. 200 D5
Grandes, Salinas salt marsh Arg. 204 D3
Gran Desierto del Pinacate, Parque Natural del nature res. Mex. 184 B2
Grande-Terre i. Guadeloupe 187 H3
Grande Terre i. Mayotte 129 E8
Grande Tête de l'Obiou mt. France 51 L8
Grande-Vallée Canada 169 H3
Grand Falls N.B. Canada 169 H4
Grand Falls Nfld. Canada 169 K3
Grandfather Mountain U.S.A. 176 D9
Grand Forks Canada 166 G5
Grand Forks U.S.A. 178 C2
Grand-Fougeray France 50 E5
Grand Gorge U.S.A. 177 K3
Grand Gosier Haiti 187 E3
Grand Harbour Canada 169 H4
Grand Haven U.S.A. 172 G7
Grandin, Lac l. Canada 167 G1
Grand Island U.S.A. 178 C3
Grand Island i. U.S.A. 172 G4
Grand Isle U.S.A. 175 B6
Grand Junction CO U.S.A. 183 P2
Grand Junction MI U.S.A. 172 G8
Grand-Lahou Côte d'Ivoire 124 D5
Grand Lake N.B. Canada 169 H4
Grand Lake Nfld. Canada 169 I2
Grand Lake Nfld. Canada 169 J3
Grand Lake LA U.S.A. 179 D6
Grand Lake LA U.S.A. 179 E6
Grand Lake MI U.S.A. 173 J5
Grand Lake St Marys U.S.A. 176 A5
Grand Ledge U.S.A. 173 I8
Grand Manan Island Canada 169 H4
Grand Marais MI U.S.A. 172 H4
Grand Marais MN U.S.A. 174 B2
Grand Marsh U.S.A. 172 D7
Grand-Mère Canada 169 F4
Grândola Port. 54 C6
Grândola, Serra de mts Port. 54 C6
Grand Pacific Glacier Canada 166 B3
Grand Passage New Caledonia 145 F3
Grand Rapids Canada 167 L4
Grand Rapids MI U.S.A. 172 H8
Grand Rapids MN U.S.A. 174 A2
Grand Récif de Cook reef New Caledonia 145 F3
Grand Récif du Sud reef New Caledonia 145 F4
Grand St Bernard, Col du pass Italy/Switz. see Great St Bernard Pass
Grand Santi Fr. Guiana 199 H3
Grand Teton mt. U.S.A. 180 E4
Grand Teton National Park U.S.A. 180 E4
Grand Traverse Bay U.S.A. 172 H6

Grand Turk Turks and Caicos Is 187 F2
Capital of the Turks and Caicos Islands. Also known as Cockburn Town.

Grand Turk i. Turks and Caicos Is 187 F2
Grand Valley Swaziland 133 P3
Grand View U.S.A. 172 B4
Grandville U.S.A. 172 H8
Grandvilliers France 51 H3
Grand Wash watercourse U.S.A. 183 J5
Grand Wash Cliffs mts U.S.A. 183 J6
Grañén Spain 55 K3
Graneros Chile 204 C4
Granger U.S.A. 180 E4
Grängesberg Sweden 45 K3
Grangeville U.S.A. 180 C3
Granhult Sweden 44 M2
Granisle Canada 166 E4
Granite U.S.A. 180 C3
Granite City U.S.A. 174 B4
Granite Falls U.S.A. 178 D2
Granite Mountain U.S.A. 182 G1
Granite Mountains CA U.S.A. 183 I7
Granite Mountains CA U.S.A. 183 I8
Granite Peak MT U.S.A. 180 E3
Granite Peak UT U.S.A. 183 K1
Granite Range mts U.S.A. 182 E1
Granitogorsk Kazakh. 103 H4
Granitola, Capo c. Sicilia Italy 57 E11
Granity N.Z. 153 F9
Granja Brazil 202 D2
Gran Laguna Salada l. Arg. 205 D7
Gran Morelos Mex. 181 F7
Granollers Spain 55 N3
Gran Pajonal plain Peru 200 B2
Gran Paradiso mt. Italy 51 N7
Gran Paradiso, Parco Nazionale del nat. park Italy 51 N7
Gran Pilastro mt. Austria/Italy 48 I9
also known as Hochfeiler
Gran San Bernardo, Colle del pass Italy/Switz. see Great St Bernard Pass
Gran Sasso d'Italia mts Italy 56 F6
Gran Sasso e Monti della Laga, Parco Nazionale del nat. park Italy 56 F6
Gransee Germany 49 K2
Grant U.S.A. 178 B3
Grant, Mount NV U.S.A. 182 F3
Grant, Mount NV U.S.A. 182 G2
Grant City U.S.A. 178 D3
Grantham U.K. 47 L11
Grant Island Antarctica 222 P2
Grant Lake Canada 167 G1
Granton U.S.A. 172 C6
Grantown-on-Spey U.K. 46 I6
Grant Park U.S.A. 172 F9
Grant Range mts U.S.A. 183 I3
Grants U.S.A. 181 F6
Grantsburg U.S.A. 172 A5
Grants Pass U.S.A. 180 B4
Grantsville U.S.A. 183 L1
Granville Canada 166 B2
Granville France 50 E4
Granville AZ U.S.A. 183 O8
Granville IL U.S.A. 172 D9
Granville NY U.S.A. 177 L2
Granville OH U.S.A. 176 C5
Granville Lake Canada 167 K3

Great Falls U.S.A. **180** E3
Great Fish r. S. Africa **133** L10
Greatford N.Z. **152** J8
Great Gandak r. India **97** E4
Great Ganges atoll Cook Is see Manihiki
Great Guana Cay i. Bahamas **186** D1
Great Harbour Cay i. Bahamas **186** D1
Great Inagua i. Bahamas **187** E2
Great Karoo plat. S. Africa **132** H9
also known as Karroo
Great Kei r. S. Africa **133** M9
Great Lake Australia **147** E5

▶Great Lakes Canada/U.S.A. **172**
Consist of Lakes Erie, Huron, Michigan,
Ontario and Superior.

Great Mercury Island N.Z. **152** J4
Great Miami r. U.S.A. **176** A6
Great Namaqualand reg. Namibia **130** C5
Great Nicobar i. India **95** G6
Great North East Channel Australia/P.N.G. **144** D2
Great Ouse r. U.K. **47** M11
Great Oyster Bay Australia **147** F5
Great Palm Island Australia **149** E3
Great Peconic Bay U.S.A. **177** M5
Great Plain of the Koukdjuak Canada **165** L1
Great Plains U.S.A. **178** B3
Great Point U.S.A. **177** O4
Great Rift Valley Africa **128** C5
Great Ruaha r. Tanz. **129** C6
Great Sacandaga Lake U.S.A. **177** K2
Great St Bernard Pass Italy/Switz. **51** N7
also known as Grand St Bernard, Col du or
Gran San Bernardo, Colle del
Great Salt Lake U.S.A. **183** L1
Great Salt Lake Desert U.S.A. **183** K1
Great Sand Hills Canada **167** I5
Great Sand Sea des. Egypt/Libya **120** E2
Great Sandy Desert Australia **150** C4
Great Sandy Island Australia see Fraser Island
Great Sandy Island Nature Reserve Australia **150** A4
Great Sea Reef Fiji **145** G3

▶Great Slave Lake Canada **167** H2
Deepest and 5th largest lake in North America.
northamerica [landscapes] ▶ 156-157

Great Smoky Mountains U.S.A. **174** C5
Great Smoky Mountains National Park U.S.A. **174** D5
Great Snow Mountain Canada **166** E3
South South Bay U.S.A. **177** L3
Great Usutu r. Africa see Usutu
Great Victoria Desert Australia **151** E6
Great Victoria Desert Conservation Park nature res. Australia **146** A2
Great Victoria Desert Nature Reserve Australia **151** F6
Great Wall research station Antarctica **222** U2
also known as Chang Cheng
▶Great Wall tourist site China **85** H3
asia [countries] ▶ 64-65
Great Western Erg des. Alg. see Grand Erg Occidental
Great West Torres Islands Myanmar **79** B6
Great Winterhoek mt. S. Africa **132** D10
Great Yarmouth U.K. **47** N11
short form Yarmouth
Great Zab r. Iraq see Zāb al Kabīr, Nahr az
Great Zimbabwe National Monument tourist site Zimbabwe **131** F4
short form Zimbabwe
Grebbestad Sweden **45** J4
Grebenkovskiy Ukr. see Hrebinka
Grebnevo Rus. Fed. **43** U7
Grebyonka Ukr. see Hrebinka
Greci, Vârful hill Romania **58** J3
Greco, Cape Cyprus see Greko, Cape
Greco, Monte mt. Italy **56** F7
Gredos, Sierra de mts Spain **54** F4
▶Greece country Europe **59** C10
known as Ellas in Greek; historically known as Hellas
europe [countries] ▶ 32-35
Greece U.S.A. **176** H2
Greeley U.S.A. **180** F4
Greely Center U.S.A. **178** C3
Greely Fiord inlet Canada **165** K1
Greem-Bell, Ostrov i. Rus. Fed. **39** G1
English form Graham Bell Island
Green r. Canada **171** M2
Green r. KY U.S.A. **174** C4
Green r. ND U.S.A. **178** B2
Green r. WY U.S.A. **183** O3
Green Bay U.S.A. **172** E6
Green Bay b. U.S.A. **172** F5
Greenbrier r. U.S.A. **176** E8
Greenbushes Australia **151** B7
Greencastle Rep. of Ireland **47** I4
Greencastle U.K. **47** J4
Greencastle IN U.S.A. **174** C4
Greencastle PA U.S.A. **176** H6
Green Cove Springs U.S.A. **175** D6
Greendale IN U.S.A. **176** A6
Greendale KY U.S.A. **176** A7
Greene ME U.S.A. **177** O1
Greene NY U.S.A. **177** J3
Greeneville U.S.A. **176** C9
Greenfield CA U.S.A. **182** C5
Greenfield IA U.S.A. **178** D3
Greenfield IN U.S.A. **174** C4
Greenfield MA U.S.A. **177** M3
Greenfield MO U.S.A. **178** D4
Greenfield OH U.S.A. **176** B6
Greenfield WI U.S.A. **172** E6
Green Head Australia **151** A6
Greenhill Island Australia **148** B1
Greenhills U.S.A. **153** C14
Greening Canada **173** S2
Green Island i. Taiwan see Lü Tao
Green Island U.S.A. **172** C8
Green Island Bay Phil. **74** A4
Green Islands P.N.G. **145** E2
Green Lake i. Canada **166** F5
Green Lake U.S.A. **172** F4

▶Greenland terr. N. America **165** O2
Self-governing Danish Territory. Largest island in the world and 3rd largest political entity in North America.
Known as Grønland in Danish or Kalaallit Nunaat in Greenlandic.
world [physical features] ▶ 8-9
world [land images] ▶ 12-13
oceania [countries] ▶ 138-139
northamerica [environments] ▶ 162-163

Greenland U.S.A. **172** D4
Greenly Island Australia **146** B3
Green Mountains U.S.A. **177** M1
Greenock U.K. **46** H8
Greenough Australia **151** A6
Greenough r. Australia **151** A6
Greenport U.S.A. **177** M4
Green River WY U.S.A. **180** E4
Greensboro GA U.S.A. **175** D5
Greensboro MD U.S.A. **177** J7
Greensboro NC U.S.A. **176** F9
Greensburg IN U.S.A. **174** C4
Greensburg KS U.S.A. **178** C4
Greensburg KY U.S.A. **174** C4
Greensburg LA U.S.A. **175** B6
Greensburg PA U.S.A. **176** F5
Greens Peak U.S.A. **183** O7
Green Swamp U.S.A. **175** E5
Greenup IL U.S.A. **174** B4
Greenup KY U.S.A. **176** C7
Greenvale Australia **149** E3
Green Valley U.S.A. **181** E7
Greenville Canada **166** C4
Greenville Liberia **124** C5
Greenville AL U.S.A. **175** C6
Greenville CA U.S.A. **182** D1
Greenville IL U.S.A. **174** B4
Greenville KY U.S.A. **174** C4
Greenville ME U.S.A. **177** M2
Greenville MI U.S.A. **172** I7
Greenville MO U.S.A. **174** B4
Greenville MS U.S.A. **175** B5
Greenville NC U.S.A. **174** E5
Greenville NH U.S.A. **177** N3
Greenville OH U.S.A. **176** A5
Greenville PA U.S.A. **176** E4
Greenville SC U.S.A. **174** D5
Greenville TX U.S.A. **179** C5
Greenwater Lake Canada **172** C2
Greenwater Provincial Park Canada **167** K4
Greenwich atoll Micronesia see Kapingamarangi
Greenwich CT U.S.A. **177** L4
Greenwich NY U.S.A. **177** M2
Greenwich OH U.S.A. **176** C4
Greenwood AR U.S.A. **175** C4
Greenwood IN U.S.A. **174** C4
Greenwood MS U.S.A. **175** B5
Greenwood SC U.S.A. **175** D5
Greenwood WI U.S.A. **172** C6
Greer U.S.A. **174** D5
Greers Ferry Lake U.S.A. **179** D5
Gregório r. Brazil **198** D6
Gregory r. Australia **148** C3
Gregory AR U.S.A. **175** B4
Gregory SD U.S.A. **178** C3
Gregory, Lake salt flat S.A. Australia **146** C2
Gregory, Lake salt flat W.A. Australia **150** D4
Gregory, Lake salt flat W.A. Australia **151** B5
Gregory Downs Australia **148** C3
Gregory National Park Australia **148** A3
Gregory Range hills Qld Australia **149** D3
Gregory Range hills W.A. Australia **150** C4
Greifswald Germany **49** K1
Greifswalder Bodden b. Germany **49** K1
Greifswalder Oie i. Germany **49** K1
Greiz Germany **49** J5
Greko, Cape Cyprus **108** F3
also spelt Greco, Cape
Gremikha Rus. Fed. **40** F1
Gremyachev Rus. Fed. **43** T7
Gremyachinsk Rus. Fed. **40** M4
Gremyachinsk Rus. Fed. **81** H2
Grenå Denmark **45** J4
Grenada U.S.A. **175** B5
▶Grenada country West Indies **187** H4
northamerica [countries] ▶ 158-159
Grenade France **50** H9
Grenade-sur-l'Adour France **50** E9
Grenchen Switz. **51** N5
Grenen spit Denmark **45** J4
English form The Skaw
Grenfell Australia **147** F3
Grenfell Canada **167** K5
Grense-Jakobselv Norway **44** O1
Grenville Grenada **187** H4
Grenville, Cape Australia **149** F1
Grenville Island Fiji see Rotuma
Gresham U.S.A. **180** B3
Gresik Indon. **77** F4
Gressåmoen Nasjonalpark nat. park Norway **44** J2
Gretna LA U.S.A. **175** B6
Gretna VA U.S.A. **176** F9
Grevelingen sea chan. Neth. **48** A4
Greven Germany **48** E3
Grevena Greece **59** C8
Grevenbroich Germany **48** D4
Grevenmacher Lux. **51** M3
Grevesmühlen Germany **48** I2
Grey r. N.Z. **153** F10
also known as Māwheranui
Grey, Cape Australia **148** C2
Greybull U.S.A. **180** E3
Greybull r. U.S.A. **180** E3
Grey Hunter Peak Canada **166** C2
Greylock, Mount U.S.A. **177** L3
Greymouth N.Z. **153** F10
Grey Range hills Australia **147** D2
Grey's Plains Australia **151** A5
Greystone Zimbabwe **131** F4
Greystones Rep. of Ireland **47** F10
Grez-Doiceau Belgium **51** K2
Gria, Akra pt Greece **59** F11
Gribanovskiy Rus. Fed. **41** G6
Gribingui r. Cent. Afr. Rep. **126** C2
Gribingui-Bamingui, Réserve de Faune du nature res. Cent. Afr. Rep. **126** C2
Gridley CA U.S.A. **182** C2
Gridley IL U.S.A. **172** E10
Griekwastad S. Africa **132** H5
Griesbach Germany **49** K5
Griffin U.S.A. **175** C5
Griffith Australia **147** E3
Griffith Canada **173** P5
Griffiths Point Canada **165** G2
Griffithsville U.S.A. **176** D7
Grigan i. N. Mariana Is see Agrihan
Grigiškes Lith. **42** G7
Grignols France **50** F8
Grigoriopol Moldova **58** K1
Grik Malaysia see Gerik
Grim, Cape Australia **147** D5
Grimari Cent. Afr. Rep. **126** D3
Grimma Germany **49** J4

Greenland U.S.A. **172** D4

Grimmen Germany **49** K1
Grimsby Canada **173** N7
Grimsby U.K. **47** L10
Grímsey i. Iceland **44** [inset] C2
Grimshaw Canada **167** G3
Grímsstaðir Iceland **44** [inset] C2
Grimstad Norway **45** J4
Grindaheim Norway **45** J3
Grindavík Iceland **44** [inset] B3
Grindsted Denmark **45** J5
Grindu Romania **58** H4
Grindu Romania **58** J3
Grindul Chituc spit Romania **58** J4
Grindușu, Vârful mt. Romania **58** H2
Grinevo Rus. Fed. **43** O9
Grinnell U.S.A. **174** A3
Grinnell Peninsula Canada **165** J2
Grintieș Romania **58** H1
Grintovec mt. Slovenia **56** G2
Griquae East reg. S. Africa **133** N7
Griqualand East reg. S. Africa **133** N7
Griqualand West reg. S. Africa **132** H5
Griquatown S. Africa **132** H5
Grise Fiord Canada **165** K2
Grishino Ukr. see Krasnoarmiys'k
Grisík Indon. **76** C3
Gris Nez, Cap c. France **50** H2
Grisolles France **50** H8
Grisslehamn Sweden **45** L3
Gritley U.K. **46** J5
Grizim well Alg. **123** G4
Grizzly Bear Mountain hill Canada **166** F1
Grmeč mts Bos.-Herz. **56** I4
Groais Island Canada **169** K3
Grobbendonk Belgium **51** K1
Grobiņa Latvia **42** C5
Groblersdal S. Africa **133** N2
Groblershoop S. Africa **132** G5
Gröbming Austria **49** K8
Grocka Srbija Yugo. **58** B4
Grodekovo Rus. Fed. **82** C3
Grodkow Poland **49** O5
Grodno Belarus see Hrodna
Grodno Oblast admin. div. Belarus see Hrodzyenskaya Voblasts'
Grodzisk Mazowiecki Poland **49** R3
Grodzisk Wielkopolski Poland **49** N3
Groen watercourse N. Cape S. Africa **132** H7
Groen watercourse W. Cape/W. Cape S. Africa **132** B7
Groesbeck U.S.A. **179** C6
Gröf Iceland **44** [inset] B2
Grogarville Australia **149** C3
Groix, Île de i. France **50** C5
Grójec Poland **49** R4
Grömitz Germany **48** H1
Gronau (Westfalen) Germany **48** E3
Grong Norway **44** J2
Groningen Neth. **48** D2
Groningen Suriname **199** H3
Grønland terr. N. America see Greenland
Grønnedal Greenland see Kangilinnguit
Groom Lake U.S.A. **183** I4
Groot r. S. Africa **132** I10
Groot r. W. Cape S. Africa **132** C8
Groot r. W. Cape S. Africa **132** C9
Groot-Aar Pan salt pan S. Africa **132** F4
Groot Berg r. S. Africa **132** C9
Groot Brak r. S. Africa **133** J8
Groot Brakrivier S. Africa **132** G10
Groote Eylandt i. Australia **148** C2
Groote Eylandt Aboriginal Land res. Australia **148** C2
Grootfontein Namibia **130** C3
Groot-Grannapan salt pan S. Africa **133** J3
Groot Karas Berg plat. Namibia **130** C5
Grootmis S. Africa **132** B6
Grootpan S. Africa **133** K2
Grootrivierhoogte mts S. Africa **132** H10
Groot Swartberge mts S. Africa **132** F10
Grootvlaograspan salt pan Namibia **132** C3
Grootvloer salt pan S. Africa **132** E6
Groot Winterberg mt. S. Africa **133** K9
Groot-Winterhoekberge mts S. Africa **133** I10
Gropeni Romania **58** I3
Grosa, Isla i. Spain **55** K7
Gros Islet St Lucia **187** H4
Grosne r. France **51** K6
Gross Barmen Namibia **130** C4
Grossenhain Germany **49** K4
Großenkneten Germany **48** F2
Großenlüder Germany **48** G5
Großer Arber mt. Germany **49** K6
Großer Beerberg hill Germany **48** H5
Grösser Bösenstein mt. Austria **49** K8
Grosser Priel mt. Austria **49** L8
Großer Rachel mt. Germany **49** K6
Grosser Speikkofel mt. Austria **49** K9
Grosser Speikkogel mt. Austria **49** L9
Grosseto Italy **56** D6
Groß-Gerau Germany **48** F6
Großglockner mt. Austria **49** J8
Groß-Hesepe Germany **48** E3
Großräschen Germany **49** K4
Groß Schönebeck Germany **49** K3
Gross Ums Namibia **130** C4
Großvenediger mt. Austria **49** J8
Grosuplje Slovenia **56** H3
Grosvenor Mountains Antarctica **223** L1
Gros Ventre Range mts U.S.A. **180** E4
Groswater Bay Canada **169** J2
Groton CT U.S.A. **177** M4
Groton NY U.S.A. **177** I3
Groton SD U.S.A. **178** C2
Grottoes U.S.A. **176** G7
Grouard Lake Canada **167** G1
Grouard Mission Canada **167** G4
Grouin, Pointe du pt France **50** E4
Groumania Côte d'Ivoire **124** E5
Groundhog r. Canada **168** D3
Grove U.S.A. **178** D4
Grove City OH U.S.A. **176** B6
Grove City PA U.S.A. **176** E4
Grove Hill U.S.A. **175** C6
Grövelsjön Sweden **45** K3
Grove Mountains Antarctica **223** F2
Grover Beach U.S.A. **182** D6
Groveton NH U.S.A. **177** N1
Groveton TX U.S.A. **179** D6
Grovfjord Norway **44** L1
Growler Mountains U.S.A. **183** K9
Grozd'ovo Bulg. **58** I3
Groznyy Rus. Fed. **41** H8
also known as Dzhokhar Ghala
Grubišno Polje Croatia **56** J3
Grudovo Bulg. see Sredets
Grudziądz Poland **49** P2
historically known as Graudenz
Grumăzeşti Romania **58** H1
Grums Sweden **45** K4
Grünau Namibia **130** C5
Grünau-Grünheider Wald und Seengebiet park Germany **49** K3
Grünberg Germany **48** F5
Grünberg Poland see Zielona Góra
Grundagssätern Sweden **45** K3
Grundarfjörður Iceland **44** [inset] A2
Grundforsen Sweden **45** K3
Grundlsee nature res. Austria **49** K8
Grundsuna Sweden **44** L3
Grune r. Brazil **207** L6
Grünidora Mex. **185** E3
Gruver U.S.A. **179** B4
Gruzdžiai Lith. **42** E5

Gruzinskaya S.S.R. country Asia see Georgia
Gryazi Rus. Fed. **41** F5
Gryaznoye Rus. Fed. **43** U7
Gryazovets Rus. Fed. **43** V3
Grybów Poland **49** R6
Gryfice Poland **49** M2
Gryfino Poland **49** L2
Gryfów Śląski Poland **49** M4
Grytlefjord Norway **44** L1
Grytviken S. Georgia **205** [inset]
Gua India **97** E5
Guà r. Italy **56** D3
Guabito Panama **186** C5
Guacanayabo, Golfo de b. Cuba **186** D2
Guacara Venez. **187** G5
Guacharía r. Col. **198** D3
Guaçu Brazil **203** A7
Guaçuí Brazil **207** L7
Guadaíra r. Spain **54** E6
Guadajoz r. Spain **54** F6
Guadalajara Mex. **185** E4
Guadalajara Spain **55** H4
Guadalaviar r. Spain **55** J4
Guadalcacín, Embalse de resr Spain **54** F8
Guadalcanal i. Solomon Is **145** F2
Guadalcanal Spain **54** F6
Guadalén r. Spain **55** H6
Guadales Arg. **204** D4
Guadalhorce r. Spain **55** H7
Guadalhorce, Embalse de resr Spain **54** G8
Guadalimar r. Spain **55** H7
Guadalmez r. Spain **54** F6
Guadalope r. Spain **55** K3
Guadalquivir r. Spain **54** E8
Guadalupe Brazil **202** D3
Guadalupe Nuevo León Mex. **185** E3
Guadalupe Zacatecas Mex. **185** E4
Guadalupe i. Mex. **170** C6
Guadalupe Peru **200** A1
Guadalupe Spain **54** F5
Guadalupe AZ U.S.A. **183** M8
Guadalupe CA U.S.A. **182** D6
Guadalupe r. TX U.S.A. **179** C6
Guadalupe, Sierra de mts Spain **54** F5
Guadalupe Aguilera Mex. **184** D3
Guadalupe Mountains National Park U.S.A. **181** F7
Guadalupe Victoria Baja California Norte Mex. **183** I9
Guadalupe Victoria Durango Mex. **184** D3
Guadarrama r. Spain **54** G5
Guadarrama r. Spain **54** G5
Guadarrama, Puerto de pass Spain **54** G4
Guadarrama, Sierra de mts Spain **54** G4
Guadazaón r. Spain **55** J5

▶Guadeloupe terr. West Indies **187** H3
French Overseas Department.
oceania [countries] ▶ 138-139

Guadeloupe Passage Caribbean Sea **187** H3
Guadiamar r. Spain **54** D7
Guadiana r. Port./Spain **54** D7
Guadiana, Bahía de b. Cuba **186** B2
Guadiana Menor r. Spain **55** H7
Guadiaro r. Spain **54** F8
Guadiato r. Spain **54** F7
Guadiela r. Spain **54** I4
Guadiervas r. Spain **54** F4
Guadix Spain **55** H7
Guafo, Isla i. Chile **205** B6
Guagua Phil. **74** C3
Guaíba Brazil **203** A9
Guaira Brazil **206** A9
Guairaçá Brazil **206** B8
Guaitecas, Islas is Chile **205** B6
Guajará Açu Brazil **202** B2
Guajará Mirim Brazil **200** D2
Guajaratuba Brazil **199** F6
Guajarraá Brazil **200** D1
Guaje, Laguna de l. Mex. **185** E2
Guaje, Llano de plain Mex. **185** E3
Guajira dept Col. **198** C2
Gualaceo Ecuador **198** B5
Gualala U.S.A. **182** A3
Gualán Guat. **185** H6
Gualaquiza Ecuador **198** B5
Gualdo Tadino Italy **56** E5
Gualeguay Arg. **204** F4
Gualeguay r. Arg. **204** F4
Gualeguaychu Arg. **204** F4
Gualicho, Salina salt flat Arg. **204** D6
Gualjaina Arg. **205** C6
Guallatiri vol. Chile **200** C4

▶Guam terr. N. Pacific Ocean **73** J4
United States Unincorporated Territory.
oceania [countries] ▶ 138-139

Guamblin, Isla i. Chile **205** B7
Guamini Arg. **204** E5
Guamo Cuba **186** D2
Guampí, Sierra de mts Venez. **199** E3
Guamúchil Mex. **184** D3
Gu'an China **85** H4
Guan r. China **87** D1
Guanabacoa Cuba **186** C2
Guanabara Brazil **200** C2
Guanabara, Baía de b. Brazil **207** J9
Guanacaste, Parque Nacional nat. park Costa Rica **186** B5
Guanacevi Mex. **184** D3
Guanahacabibes, Península de pen. Cuba **186** B2
Guanaja Hond. **186** B3
Guanajay Cuba **186** C2
Guanajuato Mex. **185** E4
Guanajuato state Mex. **185** E4
Guanambi Brazil **202** D5
Guanare Venez. **198** D2
Guanare Viejo r. Venez. **198** D2
Guanarito Venez. **198** D2
Guanay Bol. **200** D3
Guandacol Arg. **204** C3
Guandi China **87** D1
Guandu r. Brazil **207** L6
Guandu China **87** F1
Guane Cuba **186** B2
Guan'an China **86** B2
Guangchang China **87** F3
Guangde China **87** F2
also known as Taoshan
Guangdong prov. China **87** E4
English form Kwangtung
Guangfeng China **87** F2
also known as Yongfeng
Guanghai China **87** E4
Guanghan China **86** B2
Guanghua China see Laohekou
Guangji China **85** G4
Guangming China see Xide
Guangming Ding mt. China **87** F2

Guangnan China **86** C3
also known as Liancheng
Guangning China **87** E4
also known as Nanjie
Guangning China see Beining
Guangrao China **85** H4
Guangshan China **87** E2
Guangshui China **87** E2
Guangxi aut. reg. China see Guangxi Zhuangzu Zizhiqu
▶Guangxi Zhuangzu Zizhiqu aut. reg. China **87** D4
short form Guangxi; English form Kwangsi or Kwangsi Chuang Autonomous Region
Guangyuan China **86** C1
Guangze China **87** F3
also known as Hangchuan
Guangzhou China **87** E4
English form Canton; formerly spelt Kwangchow
Guanhães Brazil **203** D6
Guanhães r. Brazil **207** K6
Guanhe Kou r. mouth China **87** F1
Guánica Puerto Rico **187** G3
Guanipa r. Venez. **199** F3
Guanling China **86** C3
also known as Guansuo
Guanpo China **87** D1
Guansuo China see Guanling
Guanta Venez. **199** F2
Guantánamo Cuba **187** E2
Guantao China **85** G4
Guanxian China see Dujiangyan
Guanyang China **87** D3
Guanyinqiao China **86** B2
formerly known as Chuosijia
Guanyun China **87** F1
also known as Yishan; formerly known as Dayishan
Guapay r. Bol. see Grande
Guapé Brazil **203** C7
Guapi Col. **198** B4
Guapiara Brazil **206** E11
Guápiles Costa Rica **186** C5
Guaporé r. Bol./Brazil **200** D2
Guaporé Brazil **203** B9
Guaporé state Brazil see Rondônia
Guaqui Bol. **200** C4
Guará r. Brazil **206** F7
Guará r. Brazil **202** C5
Guara, Sierra de mts Spain **55** K2
Guarabira Brazil **202** F3
Guaranda Ecuador **198** B5
Guarani Brazil **207** K8
Guaranta Brazil **206** D8
Guarapari Brazil **203** D7
Guarapuava Brazil **203** B8
Guararapes Brazil **206** C8
Guaratinga Brazil **202** E6
Guaratinguetá Brazil **207** H9
Guaratuba Brazil **203** B8
Guarayos Bol. **200** C3
Guarda admin. dist. Port. **54** D3
Guarda Port. **54** D3
Guardafui, Cape Somalia see Caseyr, Raas
Guardal r. Spain **55** I7
Guardamar del Segura Spain **55** K6
Guardatinajas Venez. **199** E2
Guardia Escolta Arg. **204** E3
Guardiagrele Italy **56** F6
Guardianes de la Patria Mex. **183** I9
Guardo Spain **54** G2
Guardunha, Serra de mts Port. **54** D3
Guareña Spain **54** E6
Guariba r. Brazil **201** E1
Guárico state Venez. **199** E2
Guarico, Punta c pt Cuba **187** E2
Guarrojo r. Col. **198** D3
Guarujá Brazil **207** G10
Guarulhos Brazil **206** C10
Guasare r. Venez. **187** F5
Guasave Mex. **184** C3
Guasdualito Venez. **198** D3
Guasipati Venez. **199** F3
Guastatoya Guat. see El Progreso
Guasuba r. India **97** F5

▶Guatemala country Central America **185** H6
4th most populous country in North America.

Guatemala Guat. see Guatemala City

▶Guatemala City Guat. **185** H6
Capital of Guatemala. Also known as Guatemala.
northamerica [countries] ▶ 158-159

Guatimozin Arg. **204** E4
Guatrache Arg. **204** E5
Guatrochi Arg. **206** D3
Guaviare dept Col. **198** D4
Guaviare r. Col. **198** D3
Guaxupé Brazil **206** G8
Guayabal Col. **198** B3
Guayabal Cuba **186** D2
Guayaguas, Sierra da mts Arg. **204** C4
Guayama Puerto Rico **187** G3
Guayapo, Serranía mts Venez. **199** E3
Guayaquil Ecuador **198** B5
Guayaquil, Golfo de g. Ecuador **198** A5
Guayaramerin Bol. **200** D2
Guayas prov. Ecuador **198** A5
Guayatayoc, Lago de imp. l. Arg. **200** D5
Guaymas Mex. **184** C3
Guayquiraró r. Arg. **204** F3
Guazacapán Guat. **185** H6
Guba Dem. Rep. Congo **127** F8
Guba Eth. **128** C2
Gubadag Turkm. **102** D4
formerly known as Tel'man
Guba Dolgaya Rus. Fed. **40** K1
Gubakha Rus. Fed. **40** K4
Gübâl, Geziret i. Egypt **104** A2
English form Gûbâl Island
Gûbâl Island Egypt see Gûbâl, Geziret
Guban plain Somalia **128** D2
Gubat Phil. **74** C3
Gubbi India **94** C3
Gubbio Italy **56** E5
historically known as Iguvium
Gubdor Rus. Fed. **40** K3
Gubed Binna b. Somalia **128** F2
Guben Germany **49** L4
formerly known as Wilhelm-Pieck-Stadt
Gübene Bulg. **58** G6
Gubin Poland **49** L4
Gubio Nigeria **125** I3
Gubino Rus. Fed. **43** Q6
Gubkin Rus. Fed. **41** F6
Gucheng Hebei China **85** G4
also known as Zhengkou; formerly known as Zhengjiang
Gucheng Hubei China **87** D1
Gudalur India **94** C4
Gudar, Sierra de mts Spain **55** K4
Gudari India **95** D2
Gudaut'a Georgia **107** E2
Gudbrandsdalen valley Norway **45** J3
Guddu Barrage Pak. **101** G4
Gudermes Rus. Fed. **102** A3
Gudi India **94** C3
Gudivada India **94** D2
Gudiyattam India **94** C3
Gudong China **82** C4
Gudri r. Pak. **101** F5
Güdül Turkey **106** C2
Gudur Andhra Pradesh India **94** C3
Gudur Andhra Pradesh India **94** C3
Gudvangen Norway **45** I3
Gudzhal r. Rus. Fed. **82** D2

Granvin Norway **45** I3
Grão Mogol Brazil **202** D6
Grapevine Mountains U.S.A. **183** G5
Gras, Lac de l. Canada **167** I1
Graskop S. Africa **133** O1
Gräsö i. Sweden **45** L3
Grasplatz Namibia **130** B5
Grasse r. Canada **167** L3
Grasse France **51** M9
Grassflat U.S.A. **176** G4
Grass Lake U.S.A. **173** I8
Grasslands National Park Canada **167** J5
Grass Patch Australia **151** C7
Grassridgedam I. S. Africa **133** J8
Grass River Provincial Park Canada **167** K4
Grassy Australia **147** E5
Grassy Creek r. Bahamas **186** D2
Grästorp Sweden **45** K4
Gratiot U.S.A. **172** C8
Gratkorn Austria **49** M8
Graulhet France **51** H9
Graus Spain **55** L2
Gravata Brazil **202** F4
Gravatai Brazil **203** B9
Gravdal Norway **44** K1
Grave, Pointe de pt France **50** E7
Gravelbourg Canada **167** J5
Gravenhurst Canada **168** E4
Grave Peak U.S.A. **180** D3
Gräveri Latvia **42** I5
Gravesend Australia **147** F2
Gravette U.S.A. **179** D4
Gravina in Puglia Italy **57** I8
Gravina Island U.S.A. **166** D4
Gravois, Pointe-à- pt Haiti **187** E3
Grawn U.S.A. **172** H6
Gray France **51** L5
Gray GA U.S.A. **175** D5
Gray KY U.S.A. **176** A9
Gray ME U.S.A. **177** O2
Gray TN U.S.A. **176** C9
Grayback Mountain U.S.A. **180** B4
Gray Lake i. Canada **167** I2
Grayling r. Canada **166** E3
Grayling U.S.A. **173** I6
Grays Harbor inlet U.S.A. **180** A3
Grays Lake U.S.A. **180** E4
Grayville U.S.A. **174** C4
Graz Austria **49** M8
Grdelica Srbija Yugo. **58** D6
Greasy Lake Canada **166** F2
Great Abaco i. Bahamas **186** D1
Great Australian Bight g. Australia **146** A4
Great Bahama Bank sea feature Bahamas **186** D1
Great Barrier Island N.Z. **152** J4

▶Great Barrier Reef Australia **149** E1
oceania [landscapes] ▶ 136-137
oceania [landscapes] ▶ 142-143

Great Barrier Reef Marine Park (Cairns Section) Australia **149** E2
Great Barrier Reef Marine Park (Capricorn Section) Australia **149** F4
Great Barrier Reef Marine Park (Central Section) Australia **149** E3
Great Barrier Reef Marine Park (Far North Section) Australia **149** E2
Great Barrington U.S.A. **177** L3
Great Basalt Wall National Park Australia **149** E3
Great Basin U.S.A. **183** H2
Great Basin National Park U.S.A. **183** J3
Great Bear r. Canada **166** E1

▶Great Bear Lake Canada **166** F1
4th largest lake in North America and 8th in the world.
northamerica [landscapes] ▶ 156-157

Great Belt sea chan. Denmark **45** J5
also known as Store Bælt
Great Bend KS U.S.A. **178** C4
Great Bend PA U.S.A. **177** J4
Great Bitter Lake Egypt **121** G2
known as Murrat el Kubra, Buheirat
Great Blasket Island Rep. of Ireland **47** B11

▶Great Britain i. U.K. **47** J9
Largest island in Europe and 8th in the world.
europe [landscapes] ▶ 30-31

Great Coco Island Cocos Is **79** A5
Great Dismal Swamp National Wildlife Refuge nature res. U.S.A. **177** I9
Great Dividing Range mts Australia **145** D5
Great Driffield U.K. **47** L9
Great Duck Island Canada **173** K5
Great Eastern Erg des. Alg. see Grand Erg Oriental
Great Egg Harbor Inlet U.S.A. **177** K6
Greater Accra admin. reg. Ghana **125** F5
Greater Antilles is Caribbean Sea **174** J7
Greater Khingan Mountains China see Da Hinggan Ling
Greater Tunb i. The Gulf **105** F3
also known as Tonb-e Bozorg, Jazīreh-ye or Tunb al Kubrā
Great Exhibition Bay N.Z. **152** H2
Great Exuma i. Bahamas **186** E2

	island	area sq km	area sq miles	location	page#
1 ▶	Greenland	2 175 600	840 004	North America	▶ 165 O2
2 ▶	New Guinea	808 510	312 167	Oceania	▶ 73 J8
3 ▶	Borneo	745 561	287 863	Asia	▶ 77 F2
4 ▶	Madagascar	587 040	226 657	Africa	▶ 131 J4
5 ▶	Baffin Island	507 451	195 927	North America	▶ 165 L2
6 ▶	Sumatra	473 606	182 860	Asia	▶ 76 B2
7 ▶	Honshū	227 414	87 805	Asia	▶ 91 F6
8 ▶	Great Britain	218 476	84 354	Europe	▶ 47 J9
9 ▶	Victoria Island	217 291	83 897	North America	▶ 165 H2
10 ▶	Ellesmere Island	196 236	75 767	North America	▶ 165 K2

largest islands

Gudžiūnai Lith. 42 E6
Guè, Rivière du r. Canada 169 G1
Guebwiller France 51 N5
Guéckédou Guinea 124 C4
Guéguen, Lac l. Canada 173 P2
Guelb er Rîchât hill Mauritania 122 C5
Guélengdeng Chad 126 B2
Guelma Alg. 123 G1
Guelmine Morocco 122 C3
Guelph Canada 168 D5
Guémez Mex. 185 F4
Guendour well Mauritania 122 C6
Guené Benin 125 F4
Guènt Paté Senegal 124 B3
Guer France 50 D5
Guéra pref. Chad 126 C2
Guéra, Massif du mts Chad 126 C2
Guérande France 50 D5
Guerara Alg. 123 G3
Guérard, Lac l. Canada 169 H1
Guercif Morocco 123 E2
Guéré watercourse Chad 120 C5
Guerende Libya 120 B1
Guéret France 51 H6
Guerneville U.S.A. 182 B3
Guernica Spain see Gernika-Lumo

▶Guernsey terr. Channel Is 50 D3
United Kingdom Crown Dependency.
europe [countries] ▶ 32–35

Guernsey U.S.A. 180 F4
Guérou Mauritania 124 C2
Guerrero Coahuila Mex. 179 B6
Guerrero Tamaulipas Mex. 185 F3
Guerrero state Mex. 185 E5
Guerrero Negro Mex. 184 B3
Guers, Lac l. Canada 169 H1
Guerzim Alg. 123 E3
Gueţăţira well Mali 122 D4
Gueugnon France 51 K6
Guéyo Côte d'Ivoire 124 C5
Gufeng China see Pingnan
Gufu China see Xingshan
Gugë mt. Eth. 128 C3
Gügerd, Küh-e mts Iran 100 C3
Guglieri Arg. 204 E3
Guguan i. N. Mariana Is 73 K3
Guidari Chad 126 C2
Guide China 84 D5
also known as Heyin
Guidel France 50 C5
Guider Cameroon 125 I4
Guidford U.S.A. 174 C2
Guidimaka admin. reg. Mauritania 124 B3
Guiding China 87 D3
Guidong China 87 E3
Guidonia-Montecelio Italy 56 E7
Guier, Lac de l. Senegal 124 B2
Guietsou Gabon 126 A5
Guigang China 87 D4
Guiglo Côte d'Ivoire 124 D5
Güigüe Venez. 187 F3
Guija Moz. 131 G5
formerly known as Caniçado or Vila Alferes
Chamusca
Gui Jiang r. China 87 D4
Guiji Shan mts China 87 G2
Guijuelo Spain 54 F4
Guildford U.K. 47 L12
Guildford U.S.A. 174 G2
Guilherand France 51 K8
Guilherme Capelo Angola see Cacongo
Guilin China 87 D3
Guillaume-Delisle, Lac l. Canada 168 E1
Guillestre France 51 M8
Guimarães Brazil 202 C2
Guimarães Port. 54 C3
Guimaras i. Phil. 74 B4
Guimaras Strait Phil. 74 B4
Guimeng Ding mt. China 85 H5
Guinagourou Benin 125 F4
Guinan China 84 D5
also known as Mangra
Guindulman Phil. 74 C4
▶Guinea country Africa 124 B4
also spelt Guinea-Conakry; spelt Guinée
in French; formerly known as French Guinea
africa [countries] ▶ 114–117
Guinea, Gulf of Africa 125 G6
▶Guinea-Bissau country Africa 124 B3
also spelt Guiné-Bissau; formerly known as
Portuguese Guinea
africa [countries] ▶ 114–117
Guinea-Conakry country Africa see Guinea
Guinea Ecuatorial country Africa see
Equatorial Guinea
Guiné-Bissau country Africa see
Guinea-Bissau
Guinée country Africa see Guinea
Guinée-Forestière admin. reg. Guinea
124 C4
Guinée-Maritime admin. reg. Guinea
124 B4
Güines Cuba 186 C2
Guines France 51 H2
Guingamp France 50 C4
Guiones, Punta pt Costa Rica 186 B4
Guipavas France 50 B4
Guiping China 87 D4
Güira de Melena Cuba 186 C2
Guiratinga Brazil 206 A2
Güiria Venez. 199 F2
Guisanbourg Fr. Guiana 199 I3
Guisborough U.K. 47 K9
Guise France 51 J3
Guishan China see Xinping
Guissefa well Mali 125 F3
Guitiriz Spain 54 D1
Guitri Côte d'Ivoire 124 D5
Guiuan Phil. 74 C4
Guivi hill Fin. 44 N1
Guixi China see Dianjiang
Guixian China see Guiping
Guiyang Guizhou China 86 C3
formerly known as Kweiyang
Guiyang Hunan China 87 E3
Guizhou prov. China 87 D3
English form Kweichow
Guizi China 87 D4
Gujan-Mestras France 50 E8
Gujar Khan Pak. 101 H3
Gujarat state India 96 B5
formerly spelt Gujerat
Gujba Nigeria 125 H4
Gujerat state India see Gujarat
Gujranwala Pak. 101 H3
Gujrat Pak. 101 H3
Gukou China 87 F3
Gukovo Rus. Fed. 41 F6
Gulabgarh Jammu and Kashmir 96 C2
Gulabie China 84 D4
Gülan Islands Egypt see Qul'ān, Gezā'ir
Gülbahçe Turkey 59 H10

Gulbarga India 94 C2
Gul Basin dock Sing. 76 [inset]
Gulbene Latvia 42 H4
Gul'cha Kyrg. see Gülchö
Gülchö Kyrg. 103 H4
also spelt Gul'cha
Gülek Turkey 106 C3
also known as Çamalan
Gülek Boğazı pass Turkey 106 C3
English form Cilician Gates
Gulf, The Asia 105 E4
also known as Persian Gulf or Arabian Gulf
Gulfport U.S.A. 175 B6
Gulf Shores U.S.A. 175 C6
Gulgong Australia 147 F3
Gulian China 82 A1
Gulin China 86 C3
Gulistan Pak. 101 F4
Gulistan Uzbek. 103 G4
also known as Guliston; formerly known as
Mirzachul
Guliston Uzbek. see Gulistan
Guliya Shan mt. China 85 I1
Gulja China see Yining
Gul Kach Pak. 101 G4
Gul'kevichi Rus. Fed. 41 G7
Gull r. Canada 169 G1
Gullbrå Norway 45 I3
Gullkrona fjärd b. Fin. 45 M4
Gull Lake Canada 167 I5
Gullrock Lake Canada 167 M5
Gullspång Sweden 45 K4
Gullträsk Sweden 44 M2
Güllübahçe Turkey 59 I11
Güllük Turkey 59 I11
Güllük Körfezi b. Turkey 106 A3
Gülmar Turkey 106 C3
also known as Anayazari
Gülpınar Turkey 59 H10
Gulrip'shi Georgia 107 E2
Gülşehir Turkey 106 C3
also known as Arapsun
Gul'shad Kazakh. 103 H3
Gulu China see Xincai
Gulu Uganda 128 B4
Gülübovo Bulg. 58 G6
Gulumba Gana Nigeria 125 I4
Gulwe Tanz. 129 C6
Gulyantsi Bulg. 58 F5
Gulyayevskiye Koshki, Ostrova is
Rus. Fed. 40 J1
Guma China see Pishan
Gumal r. Pak. 101 G4
Gumare Botswana 130 D3
Gumbiri mt. Sudan 128 A3
Gumdag Turkm. 102 C5
formerly known as Kushka
Gumel Nigeria 125 G3
Gümeldi China see Varto
Gumla India 97 E5
Gumma pref. Japan see Gunma
Gummersbach Germany 48 E4
Gumpang r. Indon. 76 B1
Gumsi Nigeria 125 H4
Gümüşhane Turkey 107 D2
Gümüşsuyu Turkey 59 I10
Gümüşyaka Turkey 58 J7
Guna India 96 C4
Gunan China see Qijiang
Guna Terara mt. Eth. 128 C2
Gunci r. Tajik. 101 G2
also spelt Gunt
Gundagai Australia 147 F3
Gunderi India 94 C2
Gundji Dem. Rep. Congo 126 D4
Gundlakamma r. India 94 D3
Gundlupet India 94 C4
Gündoğmuş Turkey 106 C3
Güneşli Turkey 59 J9
Güney Denizli Turkey 59 K10
Güney Kütahya Turkey 59 J9
Güneyoğlu Toroslar plat. Turkey 107 E3
English form Eastern Taurus
Güneyyurt Turkey 108 D1
Gunglilap Myanmar 78 E2
Gungu Dem. Rep. Congo 127 C6
Gungue Angola 127 B8
Gunib Rus. Fed. 102 A4
Gunisao r. Canada 167 L4
Gunja Croatia 56 K4
Günlüce Turkey 59 K9
Gunma pref. Japan 91 F6
also spelt Gumma
Gunna, Gebel mts Egypt 108 F9
Gunnarn Sweden 44 L2
Gunnbjørn Fjeld nunatak Greenland 165 Q3
Gunnedah Australia 147 F2
Gunnison CO U.S.A. 181 F5
Gunnison UT U.S.A. 183 M2
Gunnison r. U.S.A. 183 P2
Gunn Point Australia 148 A2
Gunong Ayer Sarawak Malaysia see
Gunung Ayer
Gunpowder Creek r. Australia 148 C3
Guns Hungary see Kőszeg
Gun Sangari India 94 C2
Gunt r. Tajik. see Gunci
Guntakal India 94 C3
Guntersville U.S.A. 174 C5
Guntur India 94 D2
Gununa Australia 148 C3
Gunungapi i. Indon. 75 C4
Gunung Ayer Sarawak Malaysia 77 E2
formerly spelt Gunong Ayer
Gunung Gading National Park Sarawak
Malaysia 77 E2
Gunung Leuser National Park Indon. 76 B2
Gunung Mulu National Park Sarawak
Malaysia 77 F1
Gunung Niyut Reserve nature res. Indon.
77 E2
Gunung Palung National Park Indon. 77 E3
Gunung Rinjani National Park Indon.
77 G5
Gunungsitoli Indon. 76 B2
Gunungsugih Indon. 76 D4
Gunungtua Indon. 76 B2
Gunupur India 95 D2
Günyüzü Turkey 106 B3
also known as Kozağaç
Gunza Angola see Porto Amboim
Günzburg Germany 48 H7
Gunzenhausen Germany 48 H6
Guochengyi China 84 C4
Guo He r. China 87 F1
Guoluezhen China see Lingbao
Guozhen China see Baoji
Gupis Jammu and Kashmir 96 B2
Gura Caliței Romania 58 H3
Gurais Jammu and Kashmir 96 B2
Gura Portiței sea chan. Romania 58 J4
Gurara r. Nigeria 125 G4
Gura Şuţii Romania 58 G4
Gura Teghii Romania 58 H3
Gurba r. Dem. Rep. Congo 126 E4
Gurban Obo China 85 F3
Gurbantünggüt Shamo des. China 88 D2
Gurdaspur India 96 B3
Gurdim Iran see Sepahani
Gürdür India 94 C2
Güre Turkey 59 H9
Güre Turkey 106 B3
Gürgan Azer. 100 B1
Gurgan Iran see Gorgān
Gurgei, Jebel mt. Sudan 120 E6
Gurghiu r. Romania 58 F2

Gurghiului, Munţii mts Romania 58 F2
Gurgueia r. Brazil 202 D3
Gurha India 96 A4
Guri, Embalse de resr Venez. 199 F3
Gurig National Park Australia 148 B1
Gurinhatã Brazil 206 C2
Gurjaani Georgia 107 F2
Gurk r. Austria 49 K9
Gurktaler Alpen mts Austria 49 K9
Gurlan Uzbek. see Gurlen
Gurlen Uzbek. 102 E4
also spelt Gurlan
Gurmatkal India 94 C2
Gurnee U.S.A. 172 F8
Guro Moz. 131 G3
Gürpınar Turkey 107 E3
also known as Kasrik
Gurramkonda India 94 C3
Gurué Moz. 131 H2
formerly known as Vila de Junqueiro
Gürün Turkey 107 D3
Gurupá Brazil 199 I5
Gurupá, Ilha Grande de i. Brazil 199 I5
Gurupi r. Brazil 202 C2
Gurupi, Cabo c. Brazil 202 C2
Gurupi, Serra do hills Brazil 202 B3
Guru Sikhar mt. India 96 B4
Guruve Zimbabwe 131 F3
also spelt Guruwe; formerly known as
Chipuriro or Sipolilo
Guruwe Zimbabwe see Guruve
Guruzala India 97 G5
Gurvan Sayan Uul mts Mongolia 84 C3
Gur'yev Kazakh. see Atyrau
Gur'yevskaya Oblast' admin. div. Kazakh.
see Atyrauskaya Oblast'
Gusau Nigeria 125 G3
Gusev Rus. Fed. 42 D7
historically known as Gumbinnen
Gushgy Turkm. 101 E2
formerly spelt Kushka
Gushi r. Turkm. 101 E2
Gushiegu Ghana 125 E4
Gusinoozersk Rus. Fed. 85 E1
formerly known as Shakhty
Gusinoye, Ozero l. Rus. Fed. 85 E1
Guskara India 97 E5
Gus'-Khrustal'nyy Rus. Fed. 40 G5
Guspini Sardegna Italy 57 A9
Güssing Austria 49 N8
Gustav Holm, Kap c. Greenland see
Tasiilap Karra
Gustavia West Indies 187 H3
Gustavo Sotelo Mex. 184 B2
Gustine U.S.A. 182 D4
Güstrow Germany 49 J2
Gütersloh Germany 48 F4
Guthrie AZ U.S.A. 183 O9
Guthrie KY U.S.A. 174 C5
Guthrie OK U.S.A. 179 C5
Guthrie TX U.S.A. 179 B5
Guthrie Center U.S.A. 178 D3
Gutian Fujian China 87 F3
Gutian Fujian China 87 F3
Gutian Shuiku resr China 87 F3
also known as Xincheng
Gutian Shuiku resr China 87 F3
Gutiérrez Bol. 201 E4
Gutting China see Yutai
Guttenberg U.S.A. 174 B3
Gutu Zimbabwe 131 F3
Guwahati India 97 F4
also spelt Gauhati
Guwēr Iraq 107 L4
Guwlumayak Turkm. see Kuuli-Mayak
Guxian China 87 E2
▶Guyana country S. America 199 G3
formerly known as British Guiana
southamerica [countries] ▶ 192–193
Guyane Française terr. S. America see
French Guiana
Guyang China see Guzhang
Guyang China 85 F3
Guyenne reg. France 50 F8
Guy Fawkes River National Park Australia
147 G2
Guyi China see Sanjiang
Guymon U.S.A. 178 B4
Guyong China see Jiangle
Guyot Glacier Canada/U.S.A. 166 A2
Guyra Australia 147 F2
Guysborough Canada 169 I4
Guyu Zimbabwe 131 F4
Guyuan Hebei China 85 G3
also known as Pingcingbu
Guyuan Ningxia China 85 G3
Guzar Uzbek. 103 F5
also spelt Ghuzor
Güzelbağ Turkey 108 C1
Güzelhisar Baraji resr Turkey 59 I10
Güzeloluk Turkey 108 F1
Güzelyurt Cyprus see Morfou
Guzhang China 87 D2
also known as Guyang
Guzhen China 87 F1
Guzhou China see Rongjiang
Guzmán Mex. 184 D2
Guzmán, Lago de l. Mex. 184 D2
Gvardeysk Rus. Fed. 42 C7
historically known as Tapiau
Gvasyugi Rus. Fed. 82 E3
Gwa Myanmar 78 A4
Gwada Nigeria 125 G4
Gwadabawa Nigeria 125 G3
Gwadar Pak. 101 E5
formerly spelt Gwadur
Gwadar West Bay b. Pak. 101 E5
Gwador Pak. see Gwadar
Gwaii Haanas National Park Reserve
Canada 166 D4
Gwalior India 96 C4
Gwanda Zimbabwe 131 F4
Gwarzo Nigeria 125 G3
Gwatar Bay Pak. 101 E5
Gwayi Zimbabwe 131 E3
Gwayi r. Zimbabwe 131 E3
Gwda r. Poland 49 N2
Gweebarra Bay Rep. of Ireland 47 D3
Gweedore Rep. of Ireland 47 D8
Gwelo Zimbabwe see Gweru
Gweru Zimbabwe 131 F3
formerly known as Gwelo
Gweta Botswana 131 E4
Gwinn U.S.A. 172 F4
Gwoza Nigeria 125 I4
Gwydir r. Australia 147 F2
Gyablung China 89 F6
Gyaca China 89 F6
also known as Ngarrab
Gyagartang China 86 B1
Gya'gya China see Saga
Gyaijêpozhanggê China see Zhidoi
Gyai Qu r. China 89 E6
Gyaisi China see Jiulong
Gyali i. Greece 59 I12
also spelt Yiali
Gyamotang China see Dêngqên
Gyamug China 89 C5
Gyandzha Azer. see Gäncä
Gyangkar China see Dinngyê
Gyangnyi Caka salt l. China 89 D5
Gyangrang China 89 D6
Gyangtse China see Gyangzê

Gyangzê China 89 E6
also spelt Gyangtse
Gyaring China 89 E6
Gyaring Co l. China 89 E6
Gyaring Hu l. China 86 A1
Gyaros i. Greece 59 F11
Gyaros i. Greece 59 F11
Gyaur watercourse Turkm. 102 C5
Gyaurs Turkm. see Sakhra
Gyda Rus. Fed. see Gydan
▶Gdan, Khrebet mts Rus. Fed. see
Kolymskiy, Khrebet
Gydan Peninsula Rus. Fed. 39 H2
Gydopas pass S. Africa 132 D10
Gyêgu China see Yushu
Gyêmdong China 89 F6
also known as Zhongba
Gyêsar Co l. China 89 D5
Gyêwa China 89 D6
also known as Zabqung
Gyigang China 89 F6
Gyimda China 89 F6
Gyirong Xizang China 89 D6
Gyirong Xizang China 89 D6
also known as Zonggga
Gyitang China 86 A2
Gyixong China see Gonggar
Gyiza China 97 G2
Gyldenløve Fjord inlet Greenland see
Umiiviip Kangertiva
Gyljen Sweden 44 M2
Gympie Australia 149 G5
Gyobingauk Myanmar 78 A4
Gyomaendröd Hungary 49 R9
Gyöngyös Hungary 49 Q8
Györ Hungary 49 O8
historically known as Raab
Györszentmárton Hungary see
Pannonhalma
Gypsum Point Canada 167 H2
Gypsumville Canada 167 L5
Gytheio Greece 59 D12
Gyula Hungary 49 S9
Gyulafehérvár Romania see Alba Iu ia
Gyümai China see Darlag
Gyumri Armenia 107 E2
also known as Kumayri; formerly known as
Aleksandropol or Leninakan
Gyurgen Bair hill Turkey 58 H7
Gyzylarbat Turkm. 102 D5
formerly spelt Kizyl-Arbat
Gyzyletrek Turkm. 102 C5
Gyzylsuw Turkm. see Kizyl-Su
Gzhat' r. Rus. Fed. 43 P6
Gzhatsk Rus. Fed. see Gagarin

🔽 H

Ha Bhutan 97 F4
Haabneeme Estonia 42 F2
Häädemeeste Estonia 42 F3
Haag Austria 49 L7
Haanhöhiy Uul mts Mongolia 84 B1
Haanja Estonia 42 I4
Ha'ano i. Tonga 145 H3
Ha'apai Group is Tonga 145 H3
also spelt Habai Group
Haapajärvi Fin. 40 C3
Haapavesi Fin. 44 N2
Ha 'Arava watercourse Israel/Jordan see
'Arabah, Wādī al
Haarlem Neth. 48 B3
Haarlem S. Africa 132 H10
Haarstrang ridge Germany 48 E4
Haast N.Z. 153 D11
Haast r. N.Z. 153 D11
Haasts Bluff Aboriginal Land res. Australia
148 A4
Haaway Somalia 128 D4
Hab r. Pak. 101 F5
Habahe China 88 D1
also known as Kaba
Habai Group is Tonga see Ha'apai Group
Habana Cuba see Havana
Habarön well Saudi Arabia 105 E3
Habarut Oman 105 F4
Habaswein Kenya 128 C4
Habawnah, Wādī watercourse Saudi Arabia
104 D4
Habay Canada 166 G3
Habay-la-Neuve Belgium 51 L5
Habbān Yemen 105 E5
Ḩabbānīyah, Hawr al l. Iraq 107 E4
Ḩabbānīyah, Hawr al l. Iraq 107 E4
Habay Canada 166 G3
Habeit China 82 B3
Hailong China see Meihekou
Hailin China 82 B3
Hailun China 82 B3
Hailuoto i. Fin. 44 N2
Haimen China 87 G2
Hainan i. China 87 D5
Hainan prov. China 87 D5
Hainan Strait China see Qiongzhou Haixia
Hainaut reg. France 51 J2
Hainburg an der Donau Austria 49 N7
Haindi Liberia 124 C5
Haines U.S.A. 166 C3
Haines City U.S.A. 175 D6
Haines Junction Canada 166 B2
Haines Road Canada/U.S.A. 166 B2
Hainich ridge Germany 48 H4
Hainleite ridge Germany 48 H4
Haiphong Vietnam 109 H1
English form Haiphong
Haiqing China 82 D3
Hainan Namag China 84 D3
Haitan Dao i. China 87 F3
formerly known as Pingtan Dao
▶Haiti country West Indies 187 E3
historically known as St-Domingue
northamerica [countries] ▶ 158–159
Haiwee Reservoir U.S.A. 182 G5
Haiya Sudan 121 H5
Haiyan Qinghai China 84 D4
also known as Sanjiaocheng
Haiyan Zhejiang China 87 G2
also known as Wuyuan
Haiyang China 85 I4
also known as Dongcun
Haiyou China see Sanmen
Haiyuan China 85 E4
Haizhou Wan b. China 87 F1
Hajar, Jibāl mts Saudi Arabia 104 C4
Hajdú, Oued el well Mali 124 E2
Hajdúböszörmény Hungary 49 S8
Hajdúhadház Hungary 49 S8
Hajdúnánás Hungary 49 S8
Hajdúszoboszló Hungary 49 S8
Hajeb El Ayoun Tunisia 57 B13
Hajhir mt. Yemen 105 F5
Hajipur India 97 E4
Hajir reg. Saudi Arabia 105 E3
Hajjah Yemen 104 C5
Hajī Ali Qoli, Kavīr-e salt l. Iran 100 C3
Hājī, Jibāl mts Saudi Arabia 104 C4
Hajiki-zaki pt Japan 90 F5
Hajipur India 97 E4
Hajir reg. Saudi Arabia 105 E3
Ḩajjah governorate Yemen 104 C5
Hajjah Yemen 104 C5
Ḩajjiabad Fars Iran 100 C4
Ḩājjīābād Hormozgan Iran 100 C4
Hajnówka Poland 49 U3
Hajo India 97 F4
Hakari Turkey see Hakkâri
Hakas Japan 91 A8
Hakase-yama mt. Japan 91 F6
Hakataramea N.Z. 153 E12
Hakatere N.Z. see Ashburton
Hakatere r. N.Z. see Ashburton
Hakelhuincul, Altiplanicie de plat. Arg.
204 C6
Hakha Myanmar see Haka
Hakippa, Har hill Israel 108 G7
Hakkâri Turkey 107 F3
also known as Çölemerik
Hakkas Sweden 44 M2
Hakken-zan mt. Japan 91 D7
Hakkōda-san mt. Japan 90 G4
Hako-dake mt. Japan 90 H2
Hakodate Japan 90 G4
Hakodate-wan b. Japan 90 G4
Hakos Mountains Namibia 130 C4
Hakseen Pan salt pan S. Africa 132 E3
Hakui Japan 91 E6
Haku-san vol. Japan 91 E6
Haku-san National Park Japan 91 E6
Hal Belgium see Halle
Hala Pak. 101 G5
Hala r. China 84 C4
Halab governorate Syria 109 I1
Halab Syria see Aleppo
Halab l. China 82 B3
Halaban Saudi Arabia 104 D3
Halabja Iraq 107 F4
Halach Turkm. see Khalach
Halachó Mex. 185 H4
Halahai China 82 B3
Halaib Sudan 121 H4

▶Halaib Triangle terr. Egypt/Sudan 121 G4
Disputed territory (Egypt/Sudan)
administered by Sudan.

Halāl, Gebel hill Egypt 108 E7
Ḩalānīyāt, Juzur al is Oman 105 G4
English form Kuria Muria Islands
Ḩalānīyāt, Khalīj al b. Oman 105 F4
English form Kuria Muria Bay
Ḩālat 'Ammār Saudi Arabia 106 D5
Hălăuceşti Romania 58 H1
Halawa U.S.A. 181 [inset] Z1
Halba', Wādī al watercourse Saudi Arabia
109 M8
Halban Mongolia 84 C2
Halberstadt Germany 48 I4
Halcon, Mount Phil. 74 B3
Halcyon Drift S. Africa 133 M7
Haldane r. Canada 166 F1
Halden Norway 45 J4
Haldensleben Germany 48 I3
Haldi r. India 97 F5
Haldia India 97 F5
Haldibari India 97 F4
Haldwani India 96 C3
Hale watercourse Australia 148 B5
Hale China 85 F3
Hale r. China 173 J6
Hale, Mount hill Australia 151 B5
Haleakala National Park U.S.A.
181 [inset] Z1
Hāleh Iran 100 C5
Haleiwa U.S.A. 181 [inset] Y1
Halénia well Chad 120 C5
Haleparki Deresi r. Syria/Turkey
Quwayq, Nahr
Half Assini Ghana 124 D5
Halfeti Turkey 107 D3
Halfmoon Bay N.Z. 153 B14
Half Moon Bay U.S.A. 182 B4
Half Moon Bay salt flat Australia 146 B2
Halfway r. Canada 166 F3
Halfway U.S.A. 176 H6
Halfweg S. Africa 132 E7
Halghol Mongolia 85 H2
Haliburton Canada 173 O5
Haliburton Highlands hills Canada 168 E4
Halicarnassus Turkey see Bodrum
Halichy Rus. Fed. 43 N8

▶Halifax Canada 169 I4
Provincial capital of Nova Scotia.

Halifax U.K. 47 K10
Halifax NC U.S.A. 176 H9
Halifax VA U.S.A. 176 G9
Halifax, Mount Australia 149 E3
Halifax Bay Australia 149 E3
Halikko Fin. 42 E1
Halīl r. Iran 100 D4
Halilulik Indon. 75 C5
Halīmah mt. Lebanon/Syria 109 H3
Halimun National Park Indon. 77 D4
Halinor Lake salt flat Australia 146 C4
Haliut China see Urad Zhongqi
Ḩaliya well Yemen 105 E4
Haliyal India 94 B3
Hall atoll Kiribati see Maiana
Hall U.S.A. 176 A8
Hälla Sweden 44 L3
Halland county Sweden 45 K4
Halla-san mt. S. Korea 83 B6
Halla-san National Park S. Korea 83 B6
Hall Beach Canada 165 K3
Halle Belgium 51 K2
also spelt Hal
Halleck U.S.A. 180 E4
Hällefors Sweden 45 K4
Hälleforsnäs Sweden 45 L4
Hallein Austria 49 K8
Hallencourt France 51 H3
Hallett, Cape Antarctica 223 L2
Hallettsville U.S.A. 179 C6
Hälleviksstrand Sweden 45 J4
Halley research station Antarctica 222 W1
Hallgreen, Mount Antarctica 223 X2
Halliday Lake Canada 167 I2
Halligen is Germany 48 F1
Hallingdal valley Norway 45 J3
Hallingdalselva r. Norway 45 J3
Hall in Tirol Austria 48 I8
Hall Islands Micronesia 220 E5
Halliste r. Estonia 42 G3
Hällnäs Sweden 44 L2
Hallock U.S.A. 178 C1
Hall Peninsula Canada 165 M3
Hallsberg Sweden 45 K4
Halls Creek Australia 150 D3
Halls Lake Canada 173 O5
Hallstavik Sweden 45 L3
Hällvik Sweden 44 L2
Hallviken Sweden 44 K2
Hallyŏ Haesang National Park S. Korea
83 C6
Halmahera i. Indon. 75 D2
Halmahera i. Indon. see Jailolo Gilolo
Halmahera Sea Indon. 75 D3
Halmstad Sweden 45 K4
Halol India 96 B5
Halozer reg. Slovenia 56 H2
Hals Denmark 45 J4
Hal Saflieni Hypogeum tourist site Malta
57 G13
Hälsingborg Sweden see Helsingborg
Halsua Fin. 44 N3
Haltern Germany 48 E4
Haltwhistle U.K. 47 J9
Halūl i. Qatar 105 F2
Halvad India 96 A5
Halvmåneoya i. Svalbard 38 G2
Halwan Iran see Sarah-e
Halwan bin' S. Africa 109 K9
Ham France 51 J3
Ham watercourse Namibia 132 D5

index

H

Ham, Oued el r. Alg. **55** O9
Hamab Namibia **132** D5
Hamada Japan **91** C7
Hamada ed Douakel plat. Mali **122** D5
Hamada El Haricha des. Mali **122** D5
Hamadan Iran **100** B3
  also known as Itagmatana; historically
  known as Ecbatana
Hamadat Murzuq plat. Libya **120** B3
Hamada Tounassine des. Alg. **122** D3
Hamaguir Alg. **123** E3
Hamah Syria **109** H2
Hamah governorate Syria **109** I2
Hamakita Japan **91** E7
Hamamasu Japan **90** G3
Hamamatsu Japan **91** E7
Hamapega hill Spain **54** F6
Hamar Norway **45** J3
Hamar Nafur i. Oman **105** G4
Hamaroy i. Norway **44** K1
Hamasaka Japan **91** D7
Hamasien prov. Eritrea **104** B5
Hamata, Gebel mt. Egypt **121** G3
Hambantota Sri Lanka **94** D5
Hambidge Conservation Park nature res.
  Australia **146** B3
Hambleton U.S.A. **176** F6
Hamburg Germany **48** G2
Hamburg S. Africa **133** L10
Hamburg AR U.S.A. **175** B5
Hamburg IA U.S.A. **178** D3
Hamburg NY U.S.A. **177** K4
Hamburg PA U.S.A. **177** J5
Hamburgisches Wattenmeer,
  Nationalpark nat. park Germany **48** F2
Hamd, Wadi al watercourse Saudi Arabia
  104 B2
Hamdah Saudi Arabia **104** C4
Hamdallay Niger **125** F3
Hamdanah Saudi Arabia **104** C4
Hamden U.S.A. **177** M4
Hamdibey Turkey **59** I9
Hamdili Turkey **108** G1
Hameenkangas moorland Fin. **45** M3
Hameenkoski Fin. **42** E1
  formerly known as Koski
Hameenkyro Fin. **45** M3
  also known as Tavastehus
Hameenlinna Fin. **45** N3
  also known as Tavastehus
HaMelah, Yam salt l. Asia see Dead Sea
Hamelin Germany **48** H3
Hamelin Pool b. Australia **151** A5
Hameln Germany **48** G3
Hamerov Hadad Eth. **128** D3
Hamersley Australia **150** B4
Hamersley Lakes salt flat Australia **151** B6
Hamersley Range mts Australia **150** B4
Hamgyong-sanmaek mts N. Korea **82** C4
Hamhung N. Korea **83** B5
Hami China **84** B3
  also known as Kumul
Hamid Iran **100** B4
Hamid Sudan **121** F4
Hamidiye Turkey **58** H7
Hamilton Australia **149** D4
Hamilton S.A. Australia **148** B5
Hamilton Vic. Australia **147** D4
Hamilton watercourse Qld Australia **149** C4
Hamilton watercourse S.A. Australia **146** B1
▶Hamilton Bermuda **171** N5
  Capital of Bermuda.
Hamilton Canada **168** E5
Hamilton r. Canada see Churchill
Hamilton N.Z. **152** J5
Hamilton U.K. **46** H1
Hamilton AL U.S.A. **174** C5
Hamilton MT U.S.A. **180** D3
Hamilton NY U.S.A. **177** J3
Hamilton OH U.S.A. **176** A6
Hamilton TX U.S.A. **179** C6
Hamilton, Mount CA U.S.A. **182** C4
Hamilton, Mount NV U.S.A. **183** I2
Hamilton Burn N.Z. **153** C13
Hamilton City U.S.A. **182** B2
Hamilton Downs Australia **148** B4
Hamilton Inlet U.S.A. **177** K2
Hamilton Sound sea chan. Canada **169** K3
Hamim, Wadi al watercourse Libya **120** D2
Hamina Fin. **45** N3
  also known as Fredrikshamn
Hamir, Wadi al watercourse Saudi Arabia
  107 E5
Hamirpur Himachal Pradesh India **96** C3
Hamirpur Uttar Pradesh India **96** D4
Hamitabat Turkey see Isparta
Hamlet U.S.A. **174** E5
Hamley Bridge Australia **146** C3
Hamlin PA U.S.A. **177** J4
Hamlin TX U.S.A. **179** B5
Hamlin U.S.A. **176** C3
Ham Luong, Song r. mouth Vietnam **79** D6
Hamm Germany **48** E4
Hammada du Draa plat. Alg. **122** C3
Hammadat Tingharat des. Libya **120** A2
Hammam Boughrara Alg. **55** L9
Hammamet, Golfe de g. Tunisia **57** C12
Hammamet Tunisia **57** C12
Hammam al 'Alil Iraq **107** E3
Hammam-Lif Tunisia **57** C12
Hammar, Hawr al imp. l. Iraq **107** F5
Hammarland Fin. **42** A1
Hammarsdale S. Africa **133** O6
Hammarstrand Sweden **44** L3
Hammelburg Germany **48** G5
Hammerdal Sweden **44** L3
Hammerfest Norway **44** M1
Hammond IN U.S.A. **174** C4

Hammond LA U.S.A. **175** B6
Hammond Bay U.S.A. **173** I5
Hammondsport U.S.A. **177** H3
Hammonton U.S.A. **177** K6
Hambukt Norway **44** N1
Ham Ninh Vietnam **79** D6
Hamorton U.S.A. **177** J6
Hampden N.Z. **153** E13
Hampden Highlands U.S.A. **177** Q1
Hampden Sydney U.S.A. **176** G8
Hampi India **94** C3
  also known as Vijayanagar
Hampjakk Sweden **44** M2
Hampstead U.K. **47** L12
Hampton Canada **169** H4
Hampton AR U.S.A. **177** D5
Hampton IA U.S.A. **174** A3
Hampton NH U.S.A. **177** O3
Hampton SC U.S.A. **175** D5
Hampton TN U.S.A. **176** C8
Hampton VA U.S.A. **177** I8
Hampton Bays U.S.A. **177** M5
Hampton Tableland reg. Australia **151** D7
Hamra, Wadi al watercourse Syria/Turkey see
  Himar, Wadi al
Hamrat esh Sheikh Sudan **121** E6
Hamrin, Jabal hills Iraq **107** F4
Hams Fork r. U.S.A. **180** E4
Ham Tan Vietnam **79** D6
Hamta Pass India **96** C3
Hamun-e-Chah Gheybi salt pan Iran
  101 E4
Hamun-e Jaz Murian salt marsh Iran
  100 D5
Hamun Helmand salt l. Afgh./Iran **101** E4
Hamun-i-Lora dry lake Pak. **101** F4
Hamun-i-Mashkel salt flat Pak. **101** E4
Hamun Pu marsh Afgh. **101** E4
Hamur Turkey **107** E3
Hamwic U.K. see Southampton
Hamza Uzbek. see Khamza
Hana U.S.A. **181** [inset] Z1
Hana r. Czech Rep. **49** N7
▶Hanabana r. Cuba **186** D2
Hanahai watercourse Botswana/Namibia
  130 D4
Hanakpinar Turkey see Cinar
Hanalc Saudi Arabia **104** B3
Hanamaki Japan **90** G5
Hanamanioa, Cape U.S.A. **181** [inset] Z1
Hanam Plateau Namibia **132** B2
Hanang mt. Tanz. **129** B6
Hananui hill N.Z. see Anglem, Mount
Hanapepe U.S.A. **181** [inset] Y1
Hanau Germany **48** F5
Hancheng China **85** F5
Hanchuan China **87** E2
Hancock MD U.S.A. **176** G6
Hancock MI U.S.A. **172** E4
Hancock NY U.S.A. **177** J4
Handa Japan **91** E7
Handan China **85** G4
Handeni Tanz. **129** C6
Handian China see Changzhi
Handlova Slovakia **49** P7
HaNegev des. Israel see Negev
Haneqarot watercourse Israel **108** G7
Hanerau-Hademarschen Germany **48** G1
Hanfeng China see Kaixian
Hanford U.S.A. **182** E5
Hangal India **94** B3
Hangan Myanmar **79** B5
Han-gang r. S. Korea **83** B5
Hangay Nuruu mts Mongolia **84** C1
Hangchow China see Hangzhou
Hangchuan China see Guangze
Hanggin Houqi China see Xamba
Hanggin Qi China see Xin
Hango Fin. see Hanko
Hango östra fjärd i. Fin. **42** E2
Hango västra fjärd i. Fin. **42** D2
Hangu Pak. **101** G3
Hangya China **84** C4
Hangzhou China **87** G2
  formerly spelt Hangchow
Hangzhou Wan b. China **87** G2
Hani Turkey **107** E3
Hanidh Saudi Arabia **105** E2
Hanife r. Turkey **59** J8
Hanish Kabir i. Yemen **104** C5
Hanjiang China **87** F3
  also known as Yangzhou
Han Jiang r. China **87** F4
Hanjiaoshui China **85** E4
Hankasalmi Fin. **44** N3
Hankey S. Africa **133** I10
Hanko Fin. **45** M4
  also spelt Hango
Hanksville U.S.A. **183** N3
Hanle Jammu and Kashmir **96** C2
Hanley Canada **167** J5
Hanmer Forest Park nature res. N.Z.
  153 G10
Hanmer Springs N.Z. **153** G10
Hann r. Qld Australia **149** E2
Hann r. W.A. Australia **150** D2
Hanna Canada **167** I5
Hannagan Meadow U.S.A. **183** O8
Hannah Bay Canada **168** D3
Hannibal MO U.S.A. **174** B4
Hannibal NY U.S.A. **177** I2
Hannibal OH U.S.A. **176** E6
Hannik well Sudan **120** E5
Hannover Germany **48** G3
  English form Hanover
Hannoversch Münden Germany **48** G4
Hann Range mts Australia **148** B4
Hanöbukten b. Sweden **45** K5
▶Ha Noi Vietnam **78** D3
  Capital of Vietnam. English form Hanoi.
Hanoi Vietnam see Ha Noi
Hanover Canada **168** D4
Hanover Germany see Hannover
Hanover S. Africa **133** I8
Hanover NH U.S.A. **177** M2
Hanover OH U.S.A. **176** C5
Hanover PA U.S.A. **177** H5
Hanover VA U.S.A. **176** H8
Hanover, Isla i. Chile **205** B8
Hanover Road S. Africa **133** I7
Hansen Mountains Antarctica **223** N4
Hanshou China **87** E2
Han Shui r. China **87** E2
Hansi India **96** C3
Hansnes Norway **44** L1
Hanson watercourse Australia **148** A3
Hanson, Lake salt flat Australia **146** C2
Hanstholm Denmark **45** J4
Han Sum China **85** I3
Hantengri Feng mt. Kazakh./Kyrg. see
  Khan-Tengri, Pik
Hantsavichy Belarus **42** H9
  also spelt Gantsevichi
Hanumana India **97** D4
Hanumangarh India **96** B3
  also known as Bhatnair
Hanun well Oman **105** F4
Hanuy Gol r. Mongolia **84** D1
Hanyin China **87** D1
Hanyuan China **86** B2
  also known as Fulin
Hanzhong China **86** C1

Hao atoll Fr. Polynesia **221** I7
Haomen China see Menyuan
Haora India **97** F5
  formerly spelt Howrah
Haoud el Hamra Alg. **123** G2
Haouza W. Sahara **122** C4
Haparanda Sweden **44** N2
Haparanda skärgård nationalpark
  nat. park Sweden **44** N2
Hapch'on S. Korea **91** A7
Hapoli India **97** G4
Happy Jack U.S.A. **183** M7
Happy Valley - Goose Bay Canada **169** I2
  also known as Goose Bay
Hapsu N. Korea **83** C4
Hapur India **96** C3
Haql Saudi Arabia **106** C5
Haqshah well Saudi Arabia **105** E3
Hara Alol mt. Djibouti **128** D2
Harad well Saudi Arabia **105** E2
Harad Yemen **104** C4
Harad, Jabal al mt. Jordan **108** G8
Haradah Saudi Arabia **105** D3
Haradh Saudi Arabia **105** E2
Haradok Belarus **42** H7
  also spelt Gorodok
Haradok Belarus **43** K6
  also spelt Gorodok
Haradskaye Wzvyshsha hills Belarus
  43 K6
Harads Sweden **44** M2
Haradzishcha Belarus **42** H8
Haradzishcha Belarus **43** K8
Haradzyeya Belarus **42** H8
Haraiya India **96** C5
Haraja Saudi Arabia **104** C4
Haramachi Japan **90** G6
Haramukh mt. Jammu and Kashmir **96** B2
Haran Turkey see Harran
Harany Belarus **43** L6
Harappa Road Pak. **101** H4
▶Harare Zimbabwe **131** F3
  Capital of Zimbabwe. Formerly known as
  Salisbury.
Ha Rasebi S. Africa **133** J6
Harasis, Jiddat al des. Oman **105** F4
  also known as a-Jiddet
Harat Iran **100** C4
Harat Island Eritrea **121** H5
Haraym well Saudi Arabia **105** F4
Har-Ayrag Mongolia **85** F2
Haraz-Djombo Chad **120** C6
Haraze-Mangueigne Chad **126** D2
Harbacheva Belarus **43** J7
Harbel Liberia **124** C5
Harbin China **82** B3
Harbke-Allertal park Germany **48** I3
Harboi Hills Pak. **101** F4
Harbor Beach U.S.A. **173** K7
Harbor Springs U.S.A. **173** I5
Harbour Breton Canada **169** K4
Harbutt Range hills Australia **150** C4
Harcuvar Mountains U.S.A. **183** K8
Harda Khas India **96** C5
Hardangerfjorden sea chan. Norway **45** I4
Hardangervidda Nasjonalpark nat. park
  Norway **45** I3
Hardap reg. Namibia **130** C5
Hardap Dam Namibia **130** C5
Hardbakke Norway **45** I3
Harden, Bukit mt. Indon. **77** F1
Hardenberg Neth. **48** D3
Harderwijk Neth. **48** C3
Hardeveld mts S. Africa **132** C8
Hardey r. Australia **150** B4
Hardin IL U.S.A. **174** B4
Hardin MT U.S.A. **180** F3
Harding r. Australia **150** B4
Harding S. Africa **133** N7
Harding Range hills W.A. Australia **150** D3
Harding Range hills W.A. Australia **151** B5
Hardoi India **96** D4
Hardwar India see Haridwar
Hardwick GA U.S.A. **175** D5
Hardwick VT U.S.A. **177** M1
Hardwicke Bay Australia **146** C3
Hardy U.S.A. **174** B4
Hardy, Mount N.Z. see Rangipoua
Hardy, Peninsula pen. Chile **205** C9
Hare Bay Canada **169** K3
Hareid Norway **44** I3
Hareidin, Wadi watercourse Egypt **108** E7
Hare Indian r. Canada **166** D1
Haren (Ems) Germany **48** E3
Hareøen i. Greenland see Qeqertarsuatsiaq
Härer Eth. **128** D2
Härer Wildlife Sanctuary nature res. Eth.
  128 D2
Harf el Mreffi mt. Lebanon **108** G4
Hargant China **85** H1
Hargeisa Somalia see Hargeysa
Hargele Eth. **128** D3
Hargeysa Somalia **128** D3
  also spelt Hargeisa
Harghita, Muntii mts Romania **58** G2
Harghita-Mădăraş, Vârful mt. Romania
  58 G2
Hargigo Eritrea **104** B5
Harhal Dağları mts Turkey **107** E3
Harhatan China **85** E4
Harhorin Mongolia **84** D2
Har Hu l. China **84** C4
Harib Yemen **105** D5
Haribomo, Lac l. Mali **124** E2
Haridwar India **96** C3
  formerly spelt Hardwar
Harif, Har mt. Israel **108** F7
  also known as Kharuf, Ra's
Harihar India **94** B3
Harihari N.Z. **153** E11
Hariharpur India **94** B3
Harij India **96** A5
Hari kurk sea chan. Estonia **42** D2
Härim Syria **109** H1
Harima-nada b. Japan **91** D7
Haringhat r. Bangl. **97** F5
Haringvliet est. Neth. **48** B4
Haripad India **94** C4
Haripur Pak. **101** H3
Hari, Wadi al r. Syria **108** H5
Hari Rud r. Afgh./Iran **101** E3
Harj reg. Saudi Arabia **105** E3
Harjavalta Fin. **45** M3
Härjedalen reg. Sweden **45** K3
Harjufjärden b. Sweden **44** M2
Härkan r. Sweden **44** K3
Har Karmel hill Israel see Carmel, Mount
Harlan U.S.A. **176** B9
Harlan County Lake U.S.A. **178** C3
Hârlău Romania **58** H1
  also spelt Hîrlău
Harlem U.S.A. **180** F2
Harlingen Neth. **48** C2
Harlingen U.S.A. **179** C7
Harlow U.K. **47** M12
Harlowton U.S.A. **180** E3
Harman U.S.A. **176** F7
Harmancik Turkey **106** B3
Harmil i. Eritrea **121** I5
Harmony U.S.A. **177** O2
Harnai Pak. **101** F4
Harney Basin U.S.A. **180** C4
Harney Lake U.S.A. **180** C4
Härnösand Sweden **44** L3
Har Nur China **85** I2
Har Nuur l. Mongolia **84** B1

Har Nuur l. Mongolia **84** C1
Haro Spain **55** I2
Harochychy Belarus **43** K9
Harold U.S.A. **176** C8
Haroldswick U.K. **46** L3
Harpanahalli India **94** B3
Harper Liberia **124** D5
Harper r. U.S.A. **178** C4
Harper, Mount Canada **166** B1
Harper Creek r. Canada **167** H3
Harper Lake U.S.A. **183** H7
Harpers Ferry U.S.A. **176** H6
Harqin Qi China see Jinshan
Harqin Zuoqi Mongolzu Zizhixian China
  see Dachengzi
Harquahala Mountains U.S.A. **183** K8
Harrai India **96** C5
Harran Turkey **109** K1
  also spelt Haran; historically known as
  Carrhae
Harras of Dhamar vol. Yemen **104** D5
Harrat Kishb lava field Saudi Arabia **104** C3
Harricanaw r. Canada **168** E3
Harriman U.S.A. **177** K4
Harriman Reservoir U.S.A. **177** M3
Harrington Australia **147** G3
Harrington DE U.S.A. **177** J7
Harrington ME U.S.A. **177** R1
Harris reg. U.K. **46** F6
Harris, Lake salt flat Australia **146** B2
Harris, Mount Australia **148** A5
Harris, Sound of sea chan. U.K. **46** E6
Harrisburg AR U.S.A. **174** B5
Harrisburg IL U.S.A. **174** B4
Harrisburg NE U.S.A. **178** B3
▶Harrisburg PA U.S.A. **177** I5
  State capital of Pennsylvania.
Harrismith S. Africa **133** N5
Harris Mountains N.Z. **153** C12
Harrison AR U.S.A. **179** D4
Harrison NE U.S.A. **178** B3
Harrison, Cape Canada **169** J2
Harrison Bay U.S.A. **164** D2
Harrisonburg VA U.S.A. **176** G7
Harrison Lake Canada **166** F5
Harrisonville U.S.A. **178** D4
Harrisville NY U.S.A. **177** J1
Harrodsburg U.S.A. **176** A8
Harrodsville N.Z. see Otorohanga
Harrogate U.K. **47** K10
Harrowsmith Canada **173** Q6
Harry S. Truman Reservoir U.S.A. **178** D4
Harsa Sweden **45** K3
Har Sai Shan mt. China **84** C5
Hârsova Romania **58** I4
  formerly spelt Hîrşova
Harstad Norway **44** L1
Harsud India **96** C5
Harsvik Norway **44** J2
Hart r. Canada **166** B1
Hart U.S.A. **172** G7
Hart, Lake salt flat Australia **146** C2
Hart, Mount hill Australia **150** D3
Hartao China **85** I3
Hartbees r. S. Africa **132** E5
Hartbeesfontein S. Africa **133** L3
Hartbeespoort S. Africa **133** L2
Hartberg Austria **49** M8
Harteigan mt. Norway **45** I3
Hartford Liberia **124** C5
▶Hartford CT U.S.A. **177** M4
  State capital of Connecticut.
Hartford KY U.S.A. **174** C4
Hartford MI U.S.A. **172** G8
Hartford SD U.S.A. **178** C3
Hartford WI U.S.A. **172** E7
Hartford City U.S.A. **174** C3
Hârtibaciu r. Romania **58** F3
Hartington U.S.A. **178** C3
Hartland Canada **169** H4
Hartland U.S.A. **177** O1
Hartland Point U.K. **47** H12
Hartlepool U.K. **47** K9
Hartley r. Australia **151** G6
Hartley Zimbabwe see Chegutu
Hartley Bay Canada **166** D4
Hart Mountain National Wildlife Refuge
  nature res. U.S.A. **180** C4
Hartola Fin. **45** N3
Harts r. S. Africa **133** I5
Hartselle U.S.A. **174** C5
Hartsfield hills Germany **48** H7
Hartshorne U.S.A. **179** D5
Harts Range Australia **148** B4
Hartsville SC U.S.A. **174** D5
Hartsville TN U.S.A. **174** C4
Hartswater S. Africa **133** I4
Hartville MO U.S.A. **178** D4
Hartville OH U.S.A. **176** D5
Hartwell U.S.A. **175** D5
Hartwell Reservoir U.S.A. **174** D5
Haruku i. Indon. **75** D3
Harur India **94** C4
Har Us Nuur l. Mongolia **84** B1
Har Us Nuur l. Mongolia **84** B1
Harut watercourse Afgh. **101** E4
Harut Yemen **105** E5
Haruuhin Gol r. Mongolia **84** E1
Harūz-e Bālā Iran **100** D3
Harvard U.S.A. **172** E8
Harvard, Mount U.S.A. **180** F5
Harvey Canada **169** H4
Harvey MI U.S.A. **172** F4
Harvey ND U.S.A. **178** B2
Harvey Mountain U.S.A. **182** C1
Harwich U.K. **47** N12
Harwich Port U.S.A. **177** O4
Haryana state India **96** C3
Harz hills Germany **48** H4
Har Zin Israel **108** G7
Hasah, Wadi al watercourse Jordan
  108 G7
Hasalbag China **88** B3
Hasan, Wadi watercourse Egypt **108** E7
Hasana India **96** C3
Hasan Dağı mts Turkey **106** C3
Hasankeyf Turkey **107** E3
Hasan Langi Iran **100** D5
Hasan Sālārān Iran **100** A2
Hasanur India **94** C4
Hasbaiya Lebanon **108** G4
Hasbani r. Lebanon **106** C4
Hasbek Turkey **106** C3
Hasdo r. India **94** B2
Hase r. Germany **48** E3
Haselünne Germany **48** E3
HaSharon plain Israel see Sharon, Plain of
Hashimoto Japan **91** D7
Hashish, Ghubbat b. Oman **105** G4
Hashtgerd Iran **100** B3

Hashtpar Iran **100** B2
  formerly known as Tālesh
Hashtrud Iran **100** A2
  formerly known as Azaran or Sar Eskandar
Hasic B.-Herz. see Srnice
Hasik Oman **105** F5
Hasilpur Pak. **101** H4
Hasle Denmark **45** M5
Haslemere U.K. **47** L12
Haslev Denmark **45** J5
Hâşmaşul Mare mt. Romania **58** G2
Hasparren France **50** E9
Hassan India **94** B3
Hassankadam well Libya **120** A3
Hass, Jabal al hills Syria **109** I1
Hassa Turkey **109** H1
Hassassampa watercourse U.S.A. **183** L8
Haßberge park Germany **49** M6
Hasselt Belgium **51** L2
Hassi Aridal well W. Sahara **122** B4
Hassi Bahbah Alg. **55** O9
Hassi Bedjedjene well Alg. **123** H4
Hassi Bel Guebbour Alg. **123** G4
Hassi Bou Bernous well Alg. **123** E4
Hassi Bourahla well Alg. **123** F4
Hassi Chebbaba well Alg. **123** F3
Hassi Dalaa Alg. **123** F3
Hassi el Ahmar well Alg. **123** F3
Hassi el Krenig well Alg. **123** F4
Hassi Fahl well Alg. **123** F3
Hassi Habadra well Alg. **123** G4
Hassi Ifertas well Libya **120** A2
Hassi I-n-Akeouet well Alg. **123** H4
Hassi I-n-Belrem well Alg. **123** G4
Hassi Inifel Alg. **123** F3
Hassi Khanem well Alg. **123** G4
Hassi Mdakene well Alg. **123** G3
Hassi Messaoud Alg. **123** G3
Hassi Mseguem well Alg. **123** F4
Hassi Nebka well Alg. **123** F3
Hassi Ntsel well Alg. **123** G4
Hassi Sebbakh well Alg. **123** G3
Hassi Tabelbalet well Alg. **123** H4
Hassi Tiguentourine well Alg. **123** F4
Hassi Ti-n Fouchaye well Alg. **123** H3
Hässleholm Sweden **45** K4
Hastière-Lavaux Belgium **51** K2
Hastings Australia **147** E4
Hastings Canada **173** P6
Hastings N.Z. **152** K7
Hastings U.K. **47** M13
Hastings MI U.S.A. **172** H8
Hastings MN U.S.A. **174** A2
Hastings NE U.S.A. **178** C3
Hastings Island P.N.G. **149** F1
Hasvik Norway **44** M1
Haswayl Yemen **105** F5
Hasy Haghe well Libya **120** A3
Hat India **97** D4
Hatanbuulag Mongolia **84** D2
Hatay Turkey see Antakya
Hatay prov. Turkey **108** H1
Hatch U.S.A. **183** L4
Hatches Creek Australia **148** B4
Hatchie r. U.S.A. **174** B5
Hat Creek U.S.A. **182** C1
Hateg Romania **58** D3
Hatepe N.Z. **152** K6
Hatfield Australia **147** D3
Hatgal Mongolia **84** D1
Hat Head National Park Australia **147** G2
Hathras India **96** C4
Hatia Bangl. **97** F5
Hatia Nepal **97** E4
Hātibah, Ra's pt Saudi Arabia **104** B3
Ha Tiên Vietnam **79** D6
Ha Tinh Vietnam **78** D4
Hatisar Bhutan see Gelephu
Hato Corozal Col. **198** D3
Hato la Vergareña Venez. **199** F3
Hato Mayor Dom. Rep. **187** F3
Hat Piplia India **96** C4
Hatta Madhya Pradesh India **96** C4
Hatta Madhya Pradesh India **96** D5
Hattah Australia **147** D3
Hatteras, Cape U.S.A. **174** F5
Hattfjelldal Norway **44** K2
Hatti r. India **95** D2
Hattiesburg U.S.A. **175** B6
Hattingen Germany **48** E4
Hatton, Gunung hill Sabah Malaysia **77** G1
Hattras Passage Myanmar **79** B5
Hattula Fin. **45** N3
Hatvan Hungary **49** Q8
Hat Yai Thai. **79** C7
Haud reg. Eth. **128** E2
HaugNorway **45** I4
Haugesund Norway **45** I4
Hâu Giang, Sông r. Vietnam **79** D6
Hauho Fin. **45** N3
Hauhungaroa Range mts N.Z. **152** J6
Haukeligrend Norway **45** I4
Haukipudas Fin. **44** N2
Haukivesi l. Fin. **44** O3
Haukivuori Fin. **45** N3
Haultain r. Canada **167** J3
Haungpa Myanmar **78** B2
Haupttrus S. Africa **133** K3
Hauraki Gulf N.Z. **152** J4
Hauraki Gulf Maritime Park nature res.
  N.Z. **152** I4
Hauroko, Lake N.Z. **153** B14
Hausach Germany **48** F7
Hausjärvi Fin. **42** F1
Haut, Isle au U.S.A. **177** Q1
Hautajärvi Fin. **44** O2
Haut Atlas mts Morocco **122** C3
  English form High Atlas; also known as
  Grand Atlas
Haut-Congo prov. Dem. Rep. Congo see
  Orientale
Hautefort France **50** H7
Haute-Guinée admin. reg. Guinea **124** C4
Haute-Kotto pref. Cent. Afr. Rep. **126** D3
Haute-Normandie admin. reg. France **50** H3
Hauterive Canada **169** G3
Hauteurs de la Gâtine reg. France **50** F6
Haute-Volta country Africa see Burkina
Haut Jura, Parc Naturel Régional du
  nature res. France **51** L6
Haut-Languedoc, Parc Naturel Régional
  nature res. France **51** I8
Haut-Mbomou pref. Cent. Afr. Rep. **126** E3
Haut-Ogooué prov. Gabon **126** B5
Hauts Plateaux Alg. **123** E2
Haut-Zaïre prov. Dem. Rep. Congo see
  Orientale
Hauvo Fin. see Nagu
Hauwai N.Z. **153** I9
Hauzenberg Germany **49** K7
▶Havana Cuba **186** C2
  Capital of Cuba. Also spelt Habana or La
  Habana.
Havana U.S.A. **174** B3
Havant U.K. **47** L13
Havasu, Lake U.S.A. **183** J7
Havel r. Germany **48** J3
Havelberg Germany **49** J3
Havelock Canada **173** P6
Havelock N.Z. **152** H9
Havelock Swaziland see Bulembu
Havelock U.S.A. **174** E5
Havelock Falls Australia **148** B2
Havelock Island India **95** G4
Havelock North N.Z. **152** K7
Haven U.S.A. **178** C4
Haverdal Sweden **45** K4
Haverfordwest U.K. **47** H12
  also known as Hwlffordd
Haverhill U.K. **47** M11
Haverhill U.S.A. **177** N3
Haveri India **94** B3
Haverstraw U.S.A. **177** L4
Havličkuv Brod Czech Rep. **49** M6
Havøysund Norway **44** N1
Havran Turkey **59** I9
Havran r. Turkey **59** H9
Havre U.S.A. **180** E2
Havre Aubert Canada **169** I4
Havre Aubert, Île de i. Canada **169** I4
Havre de Grace U.S.A. **177** I6
Havre Rock i. N.Z. **145** I5
Havre-St-Pierre Canada **169** I3
Havsa Turkey **58** H7
Havutlu Turkey **108** G1
Havza Turkey **106** C2
Hawaii i. U.S.A. **181** [inset] Z1
▶Hawaii state U.S.A. **181** [inset] Z1
  northamerica [environments] ▶▶ 162–163
Hawaii Volcanoes National Park U.S.A.
  181 [inset] Z2
Hawalli Kuwait **107** G5
Hawar i. The Gulf see Huwar
Hawashiya, Wadi watercourse Egypt **108** D9
Hawea, Lake N.Z. **153** D12
Hawea Flat N.Z. **153** D12
Hawera N.Z. **152** I7
Hawes U.K. **47** J9
Hawesville U.S.A. **174** C4
Hawick U.K. **46** I4
Hawke Bay N.Z. **152** L7
Hawke Island Canada **169** K2
Hawker Australia **146** C2
Hawkers Gate Australia **146** D2
Hawkes Bay Canada **169** J3
Hawke's Bay admin. reg. N.Z. **152** K7
Hawkins Peak U.S.A. **183** K4
Hawk Junction Canada **173** J2
Haw Knob mt. U.S.A. **174** C5
Hawkesbill Cay i. Bahamas **175** E7
Hawksnest Point Bahamas **186** E1
Hawkswood N.Z. **153** H10
Hawler U.K. see Arbil
Hawley U.S.A. **177** J4
Hawng Luk Myanmar **78** B3
Hawra' Yemen **105** E5
Haw River U.S.A. **176** F9
Hawşal hills Saudi Arabia **108** G9
Hawshah, Jibal al mts Saudi Arabia
  104 D3
Hawthorne U.S.A. **182** F3
Hawya r. Belarus **42** G8
Hawzên Eth. **104** B5
Hay Australia **147** E3
Hay watercourse Australia **148** B4
Hay r. Canada **167** H2
Hay r. U.S.A. **172** B6
Haya China **84** D3
Haya Indon. **75** D3
Hayachine-san mt. Japan **90** G5
Hayakita Japan **90** G3
Hayang S. Korea **91** A7
Haydan, Wadi al r. Jordan **108** G7
  also known as Heidan
Haydarabad Iran **100** A2
Haydaroba Turkey **59** I9
Hayden CO U.S.A. **180** F4
Hayden ID U.S.A. **180** C3
Hayes r. Man. Canada **167** M3
Hayes r. Nunavut Canada **165** J3
Hayes Center U.S.A. **178** B3
Hayes Creek Australia **148** A2
Hayes Halvø pen. Greenland **165** M2
Hayesville U.S.A. **174** C5
Hayf Yemen **105** F5
Hayfield Reservoir U.S.A. **183** I8
Hayfork U.S.A. **182** A1
Haykel Oman **105** G2
Hayl, Wādī watercourse Syria **109** I4
Hayl, Wādī al watercourse Oman **109** K3
Haylaastay Mongolia **85** G2
Hayma' Oman **105** G4
Haymana Turkey **106** C3
Haymarket U.S.A. **176** H7
Hayna r. Belarus **42** J7
Haynesville U.S.A. **179** D5
Haysville U.S.A. **175** C5
Hayotboshi Toghi mt. Uzbek. see
  Khayatbashi, Gora
Hayrabolu Turkey **106** A2
Hay River Canada **167** H2
Hay River Reserve Canada **167** H2
Hays U.S.A. **178** C4
Hays Yemen **104** C5
Hayshah, Sabkhat al salt pan Libya **120** C2
Haysi U.S.A. **176** C8
Hays Mountains Antarctica **223** N1
Haysville U.S.A. **178** C4
Haysyn Ukr. **41** D6
  also spelt Gaysin
Hayti U.S.A. **174** B4
Hayward CA U.S.A. **182** B4
Hayward WI U.S.A. **172** B4
Haywards Heath U.K. **47** L13
Hayy well Oman **105** G3
Hazarajat reg. Afgh. **101** F3
Hazar Masjed, Küh-e mts Iran **101** D2
Hazárán, Küh-e mt. Iran **100** D4
Hazaribagh Range mts India **97** D5
Hazár Masjed, Küh-e mts Iran **101** D2
Hazebrouck France **51** I2
Hazel Green U.S.A. **172** C8
Hazelhurst U.S.A. **172** D5
Hazelton Canada **166** E4
Hazen, Lake Canada **165** L1
Hazen Strait Canada **165** H2
Hazhdanahr reg. Afgh. **101** F2
Hazlehurst GA U.S.A. **175** D6
Hazlehurst MS U.S.A. **175** B6
Hazleton U.S.A. **177** J5
Hazlett, Lake salt flat Australia **150** E4
Hazorasp Uzbek. see Khazarasp
Hazrat Sultan Afgh. **101** F3
Hazro r. Turkey **107** E3
Hazro Turkey **107** E3
H. Bouchard Arg. **204** E4
Headingly Australia **148** C4
Head of Bight b. Australia **146** A2
Healdsburg U.S.A. **182** B3
Healdton U.S.A. **179** C5
Healesville Australia **147** E4
Healing Springs U.S.A. **176** F8
▶Heard and McDonald Islands terr.
  Indian Ocean **219** L9
  Australian External Territory.
  asia [countries] ▶▶ 64–67
Heard Island Indian Ocean **219** L9
Hearne U.S.A. **179** C6
Hearne Lake Canada **167** H2
Hearst Canada **168** D3

Hearst Island Antarctica 222 T2
Heart r. U.S.A. 178 B2
Heath r. Bol./Peru 200 C3
Heathcote Australia 147 E4
Heathfield U.K. 47 M13
Heathrow airport U.K. 47 L12
Heathsville U.S.A. 177 I8
Heavener U.S.A. 179 D5
Hebbronville U.S.A. 179 C7
Hebei prov. China 85 G4
English form Hopei
Hebel Australia 147 E2
Heber AZ U.S.A. 183 N7
Heber CA U.S.A. 183 I9
Heber City U.S.A. 183 M1
Heber Springs U.S.A. 179 D5
Hebgen Lake U.S.A. 180 E3
Hebi China 85 G5
Hebian China 85 G4
Hebron Canada 169 I1
Hebron IN U.S.A. 172 F9
Hebron MD U.S.A. 177 J7
Hebron NE U.S.A. 178 C3
Hebron West Bank 108 G6
also known as Al Khalil or El Khalil; also spelt Hevron
Hebron Fiord inlet Canada 169 I1
Hebros r. Greece/Turkey see Evros
Heby Sweden 45 L4
Hecate Strait Canada 166 D4
Hecelchakán Mex. 185 H4
Hecheng China see Zixi
Hecheng China see Qingtian
Hechi China 87 D3
also known as Jinchengjiang
Hechingen Germany 48 F7
Hechuan China 86 C2
Hechuan China see Yongxing
Hecla Island Canada 167 L5
Hector U.S.A. 178 D2
Hector Mountain mts N.Z. 153 C13
Hedberg Sweden 44 L2
Hede China see Sheyang
Hédé France 50 E4
Hede Sweden 44 K3
Hedemora Sweden 45 K3
Hedenäset Sweden 44 M2
Hede Shuiku resr China 87 D4
Hedesunda Sweden 45 L3
He Devil Mountain U.S.A. 180 C3
Hedgehope N.Z. 153 C14
Hedmark county Norway 45 J3
Heerenveen Neth. 48 C3
Heerhugowaard Neth. 48 B3
Heerlen Neth. 48 C5
Ḥefa Israel see Haifa
Ḥefa, Mifraz b. Israel see Haifa, Bay of
Hefei China 87 F2
Hefeng China 87 D2
also known as Rongmei
Heflin U.S.A. 175 C5
Hegang China 82 C3
Heggadadevankote India 94 C3
Heggenes Norway 45 J3
Hegura-jima i. Japan 90 E6
Heguri-jima i. Japan 91 C8
Heho Myanmar 78 B3
Heiban Sudan 128 A2
Heidan r. Jordan see Haydān, Wādī al
Heide Germany 48 G1
Heidelberg Germany 48 F6
Heidelberg Gauteng S. Africa 133 M3
Heidelberg W. Cape S. Africa 132 E11
Heidenheim an der Brenz Germany 48 H7
Heihe China 82 B2
formerly known as Aihui
Heilbron S. Africa 133 L4
Heilbronn Germany 48 G6
Heiligenbeil Rus. Fed. see Mamonovo
Heiligenhafen Germany 48 H1
Hei Ling Chau i. Hong Kong China 87 [inset]
Heilongjiang prov. China 85 I2
English form Heilungkiang
Heilong Jiang r. China 82 D2
also known as Amur
Heilungkiang prov. China see Heilongjiang
Heimaey i. Iceland 44 [inset] B3
Heinävesi Fin. 44 O3
Heinola Fin. 45 N3
Heinrichswalde Rus. Fed. see Slavsk
Heinz Bay Myanmar 79 B5
Heinze Islands Myanmar 79 B5
Heishan China 85 I3
Heishantou China 85 H1
Heishi Beihu l. China 89 C5
Heishui China 86 B1
also known as Luhua
Heisker Islands U.K. see Monach Islands
Heitān, Gebel hill Egypt 108 E7
Heituo Shan mt. China 85 G4
Hejaz reg. Saudi Arabia see Hijaz
Hejian China 85 H4
Hejiang China 86 C2
He Jiang r. China 87 D4
Hejin China 85 F5
Hejing China 88 D3
Heka China 84 C5
Hekimhan Turkey 107 D3
Hekla vol. Iceland 44 [inset] C3
Hekou Gansu China 84 D4
Hekou Hubei China 87 E2
Hekou China see Yanshan
Hekou China see Yajiang
Hekou Yunnan China 86 B4
Hekpoort S. Africa 133 L2
Hel Poland 49 P1
Helagsfjället mt. Sweden 44 K3
Helan Shan mts China 85 E4
Helegiu Romania 58 H2
Helem India 97 G4
Helen i. Palau 73 H6
Helen, Mount U.S.A. 183 H4
Helena AR U.S.A. 174 B5

▶Helena MT U.S.A. 180 D3
State capital of Montana.

Helena OH U.S.A. 176 B4
Helen Reef Palau 73 H6
Helensburgh U.K. 46 H7
Helensville N.Z. 152 I4
Helenwood U.S.A. 176 A9
Helgoland i. Germany 48 E1
English form Heligoland
Helgoländer Bucht b. Germany 48 F1
English form Heligoland Bight
Helgum Sweden 44 L3
Heligoland i. Germany see Helgoland
Heligoland Bight b. Germany see Helgoländer Bucht
Helixi China see Ningguo
Hella Iceland 44 [inset] B3
Hellas country Europe see Greece
Helleh r. Iran 100 B4
Hellertown U.S.A. 177 J5
Hellespont strait Turkey see Dardanelles
Hellevoetsluis Neth. 48 B4
Hellhole Gorge National Park Australia 149 E5
Helligskogen Norway 44 M1
Hellín Spain 55 J6
Hells Canyon gorge U.S.A. 180 C3
Hell-Ville Madag. see Andoany
Helm U.S.A. 182 D5
Helmand prov. Afgh. 101 E4
Helmand r. Afgh. 101 E4
Helmantica Spain see Salamanca
Helmbrechts Germany 48 I5
Helme r. Germany 48 I4
Helmeringhausen Namibia 130 C5
Helmond Neth. 48 C4
Helmsdale U.K. 46 I5
Helmsdale r. U.K. 46 I5
Helmsley U.K. 47 K9
Helmsley Aboriginal Holding res. Australia 149 D2
Helmstedt Germany 48 I3
Helodrano Antongila b. Madag. 131 [inset] K2
Helong China 82 C4
Helper U.S.A. 183 N2
Helpmekaar S. Africa 133 O5
Helsingborg Sweden 45 K4
formerly spelt Hälsingborg
Helsingfors Fin. see Helsinki
Helsingør Denmark 45 K4
historically known as Elsinore

▶Helsinki Fin. 45 N3
Capital of Finland. Also known as Helsingfors.

Helston U.K. 47 G13
Heltermaa Estonia 42 E3
Helvacı Turkey 59 I10
Helvécia Brazil 203 E6
Helvetic Republic country Europe see Switzerland
Helvetinjärven kansallispuisto nat. park Fin. 45 M3
Helwân Egypt 121 F2
also spelt Ḩulwān
Hemel Hempstead U.K. 47 L12
Hemet U.S.A. 183 H8
Hemlo Canada 172 H2
Hemlock Lake U.S.A. 176 H3
Hemmoor Germany 48 G2
Hemnesberget Norway 44 K2
Hemphill U.S.A. 179 D6
Hempstead U.S.A. 179 C6
Hemse Sweden 45 L4
Hemsedal Norway 45 J3
Hemsedal valley Norway 45 J3
Henan China 86 B1
also known as Yêgainnyin
Henan prov. China 87 E1
English form Honan
Hen and Chickens Islands N.Z. 152 I3
Henares r. Spain 55 H4
Henashi-zaki pt Japan 90 F4
Henbury Australia 148 B5
Hendawashi Tanz. 129 B5
Henderson KY U.S.A. 174 C4
Henderson LA U.S.A. 179 E6
Henderson NC U.S.A. 176 G9
Henderson NV U.S.A. 183 J5
Henderson NY U.S.A. 177 I2
Henderson TN U.S.A. 174 B5
Henderson TX U.S.A. 179 D5
Henderson Island Antarctica 223 G2
Henderson Island Pitcairn Is 221 J7
historically known as Elizabeth Island
Hendersonville NC U.S.A. 174 D5
Hendersonville TN U.S.A. 174 C4
Henderville atoll Kiribati see Aranuka
Hendījān Iran 100 B4
Hendorābī i. Iran 100 C5
Hendriksdal S. Africa 133 O2
Hendrina S. Africa 133 N3
Hengām, Jazīreh-ye i. Iran 100 C5
Hengch'un Taiwan 87 G4
Hengdong China 87 E3
Hengduan Shan mts China 86 A2
Hengelo Neth. 48 D3
Hengnan China see Hengyang
Hengshan Heilong. China 82 C3
Hengshan Hunan China 87 E3
Hengshan Shaanxi China 85 F4
Heng Shan mt. China 87 E3
Heng Shan mts China 85 G4
Hengshui China 85 G4
Hengshui China see Chongyi
Hengxian China 87 D4
also known as Hengzhou
Hengyang Hunan China 87 E3
also known as Hengnan
Hengyang Hunan China 87 E3
also known as Xidu
Hengzhou China see Hengxian
Henlopen, Cape U.S.A. 177 J7
Hennebont France 50 C5
Hennef (Sieg) Germany 48 E5
Hennenman S. Africa 133 L4
Hennessey U.S.A. 179 C4
Hennigsdorf Berlin Germany 49 K3
Henniker U.S.A. 177 N2
Henrichemont France 51 I5
Henrietta U.S.A. 179 C5
Henrietta Maria, Cape Canada 168 D2
Henrique de Carvalho Angola see Saurimo
Henry r. Australia 150 A4
Henry U.S.A. 172 D9
Henry, Cape U.S.A. 177 I9
Henryetta U.S.A. 179 D5
Henry Ice Rise Antarctica 222 T1
Henryk Arctowski research station Antarctica see Arctowski
Henry Kater, Cape Canada 165 M3
Henry Mountains U.S.A. 183 N3
Henrys Fork r. U.S.A. 180 E4
Hensall Canada 173 L7
Henshaw, Lake U.S.A. 183 H8
Henstedt-Ulzburg Germany 48 G2
Hentiesbaai Namibia 130 B4
Hentiy prov. Mongolia 85 F2
Henzada Myanmar 78 A4
also spelt Hinthada
Heping China see Huishui
Heping China see Yanhe
Hepo China see Jiexi
Heppner U.S.A. 180 C3
Hepu China 87 D4
also known as Lianzhou
Heqiaoyi China 84 D4
Heqing Guangdong China 87 E4
Heqing Yunnan China 86 B3
also known as Yunhe
Hequ China 85 F4
Heraclea Turkey see Ereğli
Heraclea Pontica Turkey see Ereğli
Heraklion Greece see Iraklion
Herald Cays atolls Australia 149 F3
Herāt Afgh. 101 E3
historically known as Alexandria Areion
Herāt prov. Afgh. 101 E3
Hérault r. France 51 J9
Herbagat Sudan 104 B4
Herbert r. Australia 149 E3
Herbert watercourse Australia 148 C3
Herbert Canada 167 J5
Herbert N.Z. 153 E13
Herbert Downs Australia 148 C4
Herberton Australia 149 E3
Herbert River Falls National Park Australia 149 E3
Herbertsdale S. Africa 132 F11
Herbertville N.Z. 152 K8
Herbert Wash salt flat Australia 151 D5
Herbignac France 50 D5
Herbstein Germany 48 G5
Herceg-Novi Crna Gora Yugo. 56 K6
Herculândia Brazil 206 C8
Hercules Dome ice feature Antarctica 223 Q1
Heredia Costa Rica 186 B5
Hereford U.K. 47 J11
Hereford U.S.A. 179 B5
Herekino N.Z. 152 H3
Heretaniwha Point N.Z. 153 D11
Héricourt France 51 M5
Herington U.S.A. 178 C4
Heriot N.Z. 153 D13
Herisau Switz. 51 P5
Heritage Range mts Antarctica 222 S1
Herkimer U.S.A. 177 K2
Herlen Mongolia 85 F2
Herlen Gol r. China/Mongolia see Kerulen
Herlen He r. China/Mongolia see Kerulen
Herlong U.S.A. 182 D1
Hermagor Austria 49 K9
Herma Ness hd U.K. 46 L3
Hermann U.S.A. 174 B4
Hermannsburg Australia 148 B4
Hermanus S. Africa 132 D11
Hermel Lebanon 109 H3
Hermes, Cape S. Africa 133 N8
Hermidale Australia 147 E2
Hermitage MO U.S.A. 178 D4
Hermitage PA U.S.A. 176 E4
Hermitage Bay Canada 169 J4
Hermite, Islas is Chile 205 D9
Hermit Islands P.N.G. 73 K7
Hermon, Mount Lebanon/Syria 108 G4
also known as Sheikh, Jebel esh
Hermonthis Egypt see Armant
Hermopolis Magna Egypt see El Ashmûnein
Hermosa, Valle valley Arg. 205 C7
Hermosillo Mex. 184 C2
Hernád r. Hungary 49 R8
also spelt Hornád (Slovakia)
Hernandarias Para. 201 G6
Hernando U.S.A. 174 B5
Hernani Spain 55 J1
Herndon CA U.S.A. 182 E5
Herndon WV U.S.A. 176 D8
Herne Germany 48 E4
Herning Denmark 45 J4
Heroica Nogales Mex. see Nogales
Heron Bay Canada 172 G2
Herong China 87 E2
Hérouville-St-Clair France 50 F3
Herowābād Iran see Khalkhāl
Herradura Mex. 185 E4
Herrenberg Germany 48 F7
Herrera Arg. 204 E3
Herrera del Duque Spain 54 F5
Herrero, Punta pt Mex. 185 I5
Herrieden Germany 48 H6
Herrin U.S.A. 174 B4
Herrljunga Sweden 45 K4
Hervik Sweden 45 L4
Hers r. France 50 H9
Herschel S. Africa 133 L7
Herschel Island Canada 164 F3
Hershey U.S.A. 177 I5
Hertel U.S.A. 172 A5
Hertford U.K. 47 L12
Hertford U.S.A. 177 I9
Hertzogville S. Africa 133 J5
Hervey Bay Australia 149 G5
Hervey Islands Cook Is 221 H7
Herzberg Germany 49 K4
Herzliyya Israel 108 F5
Herzogenaurach Germany 48 H6
Herzogenburg Austria 49 M7
Heşār Iran 100 B4
Heşār Iran 100 B3
Hesdin France 51 I2
Heshan China 87 D4
Heshengqiao China 87 E2
Heshui China 85 F5
also known as Xihuachi
Heshun China 85 G4
Hesperia CA U.S.A. 183 G7
Hesperia MI U.S.A. 172 G7
Hesquiat Canada 166 E5
Hess r. Canada 166 C2
Hesse land Germany see Hessen
Hessel U.S.A. 173 I4
Hesselberg hill Germany 48 H6
Hessen land Germany 48 G5
English form Hesse
Hessischer Spessart, Naturpark nature res. Germany 48 G5
Hessisch Lichtenau Germany 48 G4
Hess Mountains Canada 166 C2
Hester Malan Nature Reserve S. Africa 132 C6
Hestvika Norway 44 J3
Het r. Laos 78 D3
Hetch Hetchy Aqueduct canal U.S.A. 182 B4
Hettinger U.S.A. 178 B2
Hettstedt Germany 48 I4
Heung Kong Tsai Hong Kong China see Aberdeen
Heuningneskloof S. Africa 133 I6
Heuningspruit S. Africa 133 L4
Heuningvlei salt pan S. Africa 132 H3
Heuvelton U.S.A. 177 J1
Heves Hungary 49 R8
Hevron West Bank see Hebron
Hewlett U.S.A. 176 H8
Hexenkopf mt. Austria 48 H8
Hexham U.K. 47 J9
Hexian China 87 F2
Hexigten Qi China see Jingpeng
Hexipu China 84 D4
Hexrivierberg mts S. Africa 132 D10
Heyang China see Nanhe
Heyang China 85 F5
Heydebreck Poland see Kędzierzyn-Koźle
Heydon S. Africa 133 I8
Heygali well Eth. 128 E3
Heyin China see Guide
Heyshope Dam S. Africa 133 O3
Heyuan China 87 E4
Heywood Australia 146 D4
Heze China 85 G5
also known as Caozhou
Hezhang China 86 C3
Hezheng China 84 D5
Hezhou China 87 D3
also known as Babu
Hezuozhen China 84 D5
Hhohho reg. Swaziland 133 P3
Hialeah U.S.A. 175 D7
Hiawassee U.S.A. 174 D5
Hiawatha U.S.A. 178 D4
Hibata reg. Saudi Arabia 104 C4
Hibbing U.S.A. 174 A2
Hibberdene S. Africa 133 O7
Hibbs, Point Australia 147 E5
Hibernia Reef Australia 150 C2
Hibiki-nada b. Japan 91 B7
Hichān Iran 101 E5
Hickman U.S.A. 174 B4
Hickory U.S.A. 174 D5
Hicks Bay N.Z. 152 M5
Hicks Cays is Belize 185 H5
Hicksville NY U.S.A. 177 L5
Hicksville OH U.S.A. 176 A4
Hico U.S.A. 179 C5
Hidaka Japan 90 H3
Hidaka-sanmyaku mts Japan 90 H3
Hidalgo Coahuila Mex. 185 F3
Hidalgo Tamaulipas Mex. 185 F3
Hidalgo state Mex. 185 F4
Hidalgo del Parral Mex. 184 D3
Hidalgo Yalalag Mex. 185 F5
Hidasnémeti Hungary 49 S7
Hiddensee i. Germany 49 K1
Hidişelu de Sus Romania 58 D2
Hidrolândia Brazil 206 D3
Hierosolyma Israel/West Bank see Jerusalem
Hietaniemi Fin. 44 O2
Higashi-Hiroshima Japan 91 C7
Higashi-matsuyama Japan 91 F6
Higashine Japan 90 G5
Higashi-ōsaka Japan 91 D7
Higashi-suidō sea chan. Japan 91 A8
Higgins Bay U.S.A. 177 K2
Higgins Lake U.S.A. 173 I6
Higg's Hope S. Africa 132 H6
High Atlas mts Morocco see Haut Atlas
High Desert U.S.A. 180 B4
High Falls Reservoir U.S.A. 172 E5
Highflats S. Africa 133 O7
High Island i. Hong Kong China 87 [inset]
also known as Leung Shuen Wan Chau
High Island U.S.A. 179 D6
High Island i. U.S.A. 172 H5
High Island Reservoir Hong Kong China 87 [inset]
Highland CA U.S.A. 183 G7
Highland MN U.S.A. 172 B3
Highland NY U.S.A. 177 L4
Highland WI U.S.A. 172 C7
Highland Beach U.S.A. 177 I7
Highland Peak CA U.S.A. 182 E3
Highland Peak NV U.S.A. 183 J4
Highlands U.S.A. 177 L5
Highland Springs U.S.A. 177 H8
High Level Canada 167 G3
High Level Canal India 95 E1
Highline Canal U.S.A. 183 I9
Highmore U.S.A. 178 C2
High Point U.S.A. 174 E5
High Point hill U.S.A. 177 K4
High Prairie Canada 167 G4
High River Canada 167 H5
High Rock Bahamas 186 D1
Highrock Lake Canada 167 K4
High Rocky Point Australia 147 E5
High Springs U.S.A. 175 D6
High Tatras mts Poland/Slovakia see Tatra Mountains
Hightstown U.S.A. 177 K5
High Wycombe U.K. 47 L12
Higlale well Eth. 128 E3
Higuera de Abuya Mex. 184 D3
Higuera de Zaragoza Mex. 184 C3
Higüey Dom. Rep. 187 F3
Hihifo Tonga 145 H3
Hihnavaara Fin. 44 O2
Hiidenportin kansallispuisto nat. park Fin. 44 O3
Hiidenvesi l. Fin. 42 F1
Hiiraan Somalia 128 E3
Hiiraan admin. reg. Somalia 128 E3
Hiiumaa i. Estonia 42 D3
also known as Dagö; historically known as Oesel or Ösel
Hijānah, Buḩayrat al imp. l. Syria 109 H4
Hijānah, Wādī watercourse Syria 109 K3
Hijau, Gunung mt. Indon. 76 C3
Hijaz reg. Saudi Arabia 104 B2
English form Hejaz
Hiji Japan 91 B8
Hijo Phil. 74 C5
Hikari Japan 91 B8
Hiketa Japan 91 D7
Hikone Japan 91 E7
Hikurangi mt. N.Z. 152 M5
Hila Indon. 75 C4
Hilahila Indon. 75 B4
Hilarios Chile 200 C5
Hilary Coast Antarctica 223 K1
Hildale U.S.A. 183 K4
Hildburghausen Germany 48 H5
Hilders Germany 48 H5
Hildesheim Germany 48 G3
Ḩilf, Ra's c. Oman 105 G3
Hili Bangl. 97 F4
Hillah Iraq 107 F4
also spelt Al Ḩillah
Hillandale S. Africa 132 E10
Hillard U.S.A. 176 B5
Hill City U.S.A. 178 C4
Hill Creek r. U.S.A. 183 O2
Hillerød Denmark 45 K5
Hillersden N.Z. 153 H9
Hillerse Germany 48 H3
Hillerstorp Sweden 45 K4
Hillesheim Germany 48 D5
Hillgrove Australia 149 E3
Hill Island Lake Canada 167 I2
Hillman U.S.A. 173 J5
Hillman, Lake salt flat Australia 151 B6
Hillsboro IL U.S.A. 174 B4
Hillsboro MO U.S.A. 174 B4
Hillsboro ND U.S.A. 178 C2
Hillsboro NH U.S.A. 177 N2
Hillsboro OH U.S.A. 176 B6
Hillsboro OR U.S.A. 180 B3
Hillsboro TX U.S.A. 179 C5
Hillsboro WI U.S.A. 172 C7
Hillsboro Canal U.S.A. 175 D7
Hillsborough Grenada 187 H4
Hillsborough U.S.A. 176 F9
Hillsborough, Cape Australia 149 F4
Hillsdale MI U.S.A. 173 I9
Hillsdale NY U.S.A. 177 L3
Hillsgrove U.S.A. 177 I4
Hillside Australia 150 B4
Hillsport Canada 168 C3
Hillston Australia 147 E3
Hillsville U.S.A. 176 E9
Hillswick U.K. 46 K3
Hilo U.S.A. 181 [inset] Z2
Hilton Australia 148 C4
Hilton U.S.A. 176 H2
Hilton Beach Canada 173 J4
Hilton Head Island U.S.A. 175 D5
Hilvan Turkey 107 D3
also known as Karacurun
Hilversum Neth. 48 C3
Ḩimā well Saudi Arabia 104 D4
Himachal Pradesh state India 96 C3
Ḩimā Ḑarīyah, Jabal mt. Saudi Arabia 104 C2
▶Himalaya mts Asia 97 C2
world [physical features] ⟶ 8–9
asia [landscapes] ⟶ 62–63
Himalchuli mt. Nepal 97 E3
Himanka Fin. 44 M2
Ḩimār, Wādī al watercourse Syria/Turkey 109 K1
also known as Hamra, Vâdii
Himarë Albania 59 A8
Ḩimār Umm Khunşur hill Saudi Arabia 109 M7
Himatangi Beach N.Z. 152 J8
Himatnagar India 96 B5
Himbirti Eritrea 104 B5
Himeji Japan 91 D7
Himekami-dake mt. Japan 90 G5
Himeville S. Africa 133 N6
Hime-zaki pt Japan 90 F5
Himi Japan 91 E6
Himora Eth. 128 C1
Ḩimş Syria see Homs
Ḩimş governorate Syria 109 J2
Ḩimş, Baḩrat resr Syria see Qaţţīnah, Buḩayrat
Hinako i. Indon. 76 B2
Hinakura N.Z. 152 J9
Hinatuan Phil. 74 C4
Hinatuan Passage Phil. 74 C4
Hînceşti Moldova 58 J2
formerly known as Cotovsc or Kotovsk; formerly spelt Hânceşti or Khynchest' or Khynchesty
Hinche Haiti 187 E3
Hinchinbrook Island Australia 149 E3
Hinckley U.K. 47 K11
Hinckley IL U.S.A. 172 E9
Hinckley ME U.S.A. 177 P1
Hinckley MN U.S.A. 174 A2
Hinckley UT U.S.A. 183 L2
Hinckley Reservoir U.S.A. 177 J2
Hind, Wādī al watercourse Saudi Arabia 108 G8
Hinda Congo 126 B6
Hindan r. India 89 B6
Hindaun India 96 C4
Hindelang Germany 48 H8
Hindenburg Poland see Zabrze
Hindman U.S.A. 176 C8
Hindmarsh, Lake dry lake Australia 146 D4
Hindola India 95 E1
Hindoli India 96 B4
Hindoria India 96 C5
Hindri r. India 94 C3
Hinds N.Z. 153 F12
Hindu Kush mts Afgh./Pak. 101 F3
Hindupur India 94 C3
Hines Creek Canada 166 G3
Hinesville U.S.A. 175 D6
Hinganghat India 94 C1
Hingol r. Pak. 101 F5
Hingol r. Pak. see Girdar Dhor
Hınıs Turkey 107 E3
Hinks Conservation Park nature res. Australia 146 C3
Hinnøya i. Norway 44 K1
Hino Japan 91 C7
Hinobaan Phil. 74 B4
Hinojedo mt. Spain 55 I3
Hinojosa del Duque Spain 54 F6
Hino-misaki pt Japan 91 C7
Hinsdale U.S.A. 177 M3
Hinterzarten Germany 48 F8
Hinthada Myanmar see Henzada
Hinton KY U.S.A. 176 A7
Hinton OK U.S.A. 179 C5
Hinton WV U.S.A. 176 E8
Hinuera N.Z. 152 J5
Hiort i. U.K. see Hirta
Hipólito Mex. 185 E3
Hipponium Italy see Vibo Valentia
Hippopotames, Réserve de nature res. Dem. Rep. Congo 126 F6
Hippopotames, Réserve de Faune des nature res. Dem. Rep. Congo 126 E5
Hippopotames de Sakania, Réserve de nature res. Dem. Rep. Congo 127 F8
Hippo Regius Alg. see Annaba
Hippo Zarytus Tunisia see Bizerte
Hirabit Dağ mt. Turkey 107 F3
Hirado Japan 91 A8
Hirado-shima i. Japan 91 A8
Hirafok Alg. 123 G5
Hirakud Reservoir India 97 D5
Hiraman watercourse Kenya 128 C5
Hirata Japan 91 C7
Hiré-Watta Côte d'Ivoire 124 D5
Hiriyur India 94 C3
Hîrlău Romania see Hârlău
Hiroo Japan 90 H3
Hirosaki Japan 90 G4
Hirose Japan 91 C7
Hiroshima Japan 91 C7
Hiroshima airport Japan 91 C7
Hiroshima pref. Japan 91 C7
Hirota-wan b. Japan 90 G5
Hirschaid Germany 48 I6
Hirschberg Germany 48 I5
Hirschberg Poland see Jelenia Góra
Hirson France 51 K3
Hîrşova Romania see Hârşova
Hirta i. U.K. 46 D6
also known as Hiort
Hirtshals Denmark 45 J4
Hisai Japan 91 E7
Hisaka-jima i. Japan 91 A8
Hisar India 96 B3
also spelt Hissar
Hisar, Koh-i- mts Afgh. 101 F3
Hisarcık Turkey 59 K9
Hisarköy Turkey see Domaniç
Hisarönü Turkey 106 C2
Hisarönü Körfezi b. Turkey 59 I12
Ḩisb, Sha'īb watercourse Iraq 107 F5
Ḩişn al Fuḑūl Yemen 105 E4
Hisor Tajik. 101 G2
also known as Gissar
Hisor Tizmasi mts Tajik./Uzbek. see Gissar Range
Hispalis Spain see Seville
Hispania country Europe see Spain

▶Hispaniola i. Caribbean Sea 171 L7
Consists of the Dominican Republic and Haiti.

Hispur Glacier Jammu and Kashmir 96 B1
Hissar India see Hisar
Hisua India 97 E4
Hīt Iraq 107 E4
Hita Japan 91 B8
Hitachi Japan 91 G6
Hitachinaka Japan 91 G6
Hitachi-ōta Japan 91 G6
Hitoyoshi Japan 91 B8
Hitra i. Norway 44 J3
Hiuchi-nada b. Japan 91 C7
Hiva Oa i. Fr. Polynesia 221 I6
formerly known as Dominique
Hiwasa Japan 91 D8
Hixon Canada 166 F4
Hixson Cay reef Australia 149 G4
Hixton U.S.A. 172 B6
Hiyon watercourse Israel 108 G7
Hizan Turkey 107 E3
also known as Karasu
Hjallerup Denmark 45 J4
Hjälmaren l. Sweden 45 K4
Hjelle Norway 45 I3
Hjellestad Norway 46 R3
Hjelmeland Norway 45 I4
Hjerkinn Norway 44 J3
Hjo Sweden 45 K4
Hjørring Denmark 45 J4
Hjuvik Sweden 45 J4
Hka, Nam r. Myanmar 78 B3
Hkakabo Razi mt. Myanmar 78 B1
Hkok r. Myanmar 78 B3
Hkring Bum mt. Myanmar 78 B2
Hlabisa S. Africa 133 P5
Hlaing r. Myanmar 78 B4
Hlako Kangri mt. China see Lhagoi Kangri
Hlane Game Sanctuary nature res. Swaziland 133 P3
Hlatikulu Swaziland 133 P3
Hlazove Ukr. 43 O9
Hlegu Myanmar 78 B4
Hlinsko Czech Rep. 49 M6
Hlohlowane S. Africa 133 L5
Hlohovec Slovakia 49 O7
Hlotse Lesotho 133 M5
Hlučín Czech Rep. 49 P6
Hluhluwe S. Africa 133 Q5
Hluhluwe Game Reserve nature res. S. Africa 133 Q5
Hlukhiv Ukr. 41 E6
also spelt Glukhov
Hlung-Tan Myanmar 78 B3
Hlusha Belarus 43 J8
Hlusk Belarus 43 J9
Hlybokaye Belarus 42 I6
also spelt Glubokoye
Hnilec r. Slovakia 49 R7
Hnúšťa Slovakia 49 Q7
Ho Ghana 125 F5
Hoa Binh Vietnam 78 D3
Hoachanas Namibia 130 C4
Hoang Liên Son mts Vietnam 78 C3
Hoang Sa is S. China Sea see Paracel Islands
Hoanib watercourse Namibia 130 B3
Hoarusib watercourse Namibia 130 B3

▶Hobart Australia 147 E5
State capital of Tasmania.

Hobart U.S.A. 179 C5
Hobbs U.S.A. 179 B5
Hobbs Coast Antarctica 222 P1
Hobe Sound U.S.A. 175 D7
Hobhouse S. Africa 133 L6
Hobo Col. 198 C4
Hoboksar China 88 D2
Hobor China 85 G3
also known as Qahar Youyi Zhongqi
Hobot Xar Qi China see Xin Bulag
Hobro Denmark 45 J4
Hoburg Sweden 45 L4
Hoburgen pt Sweden 45 L4
Hobyo Somalia 128 F3
formerly spelt Obbia
Hochfeiler mt. Austria/Italy see Gran Pilastro
Hochfeld Namibia 130 C4
Hochgall mt. Austria/Italy see Collalto
Hochgolling mt. Austria 49 K8
Hochharz nat. park Germany 48 H4
Hô Chi Minh Vietnam see Ho Chi Minh City
Ho Chi Minh City Vietnam 79 D6
also known as Hô Chi Minh; formerly known as Saigon
Hochobir mt. Austria 49 L9
Hochschwab mt. Austria 49 M8
Hochtaunus nature res. Germany 48 F5
Hochtor mt. Austria 49 L8
Hōd reg. Mauritania 124 C2
Hodal India 96 C4
Hodda mt. Somalia 128 F2
Hodeidah Yemen 104 C5
also spelt Al Ḩudaydah
Hodein, Wâdi watercourse Egypt 121 G4
Hodgesville U.S.A. 176 E6
Hodgson Downs Australia 148 B2
Hodgson Downs Aboriginal Land res. Australia 148 B2
Hodh Ech Chargui admin. reg. Mauritania 124 D2
Hodh El Gharbi admin. reg. Mauritania 124 C2
Hódmezővásárhely Hungary 49 R9
Hodmo watercourse Somalia 128 E2
Hodna, Chott el salt l. Alg. 123 G2
Hodonín Czech Rep. 49 O7
Hodoşa Romania 58 F2
Hödrögö Mongolia 84 C1
Hodsons Peak Lesotho 133 N6
Hoek van Holland Neth. see Hook of Holland
Hoeryŏng N. Korea 82 C4
Hoeyang N. Korea 83 B5
Hof Germany 48 I5
Hoffman Mountain U.S.A. 177 L2
Hoffman's Cay i. Bahamas 186 D1
Hofmeyr S. Africa 133 J8
Höfn Iceland 44 [inset] D2
Hofors Sweden 45 L3
Hofsjökull ice cap Iceland 44 [inset] C2
Hofsós Iceland 44 [inset] C2
Hōfu Japan 91 B7
Hofūf Saudi Arabia see Al Hufūf
Höganäs Sweden 45 K4
Hogan Group is Australia 147 E4
Hogansburg U.S.A. 177 K1
Hoganthulla Creek r. Australia 149 E5
Hogg, Mount Canada 166 C2
▶Hoggar plat. Alg. 123 G5
also spelt Ahaggar
world [land cover] ⟶ 18–19
Hog Island U.S.A. 177 J8
Högsby Sweden 45 L4
Høgste Breakulen mt. Norway 45 I3
Hogsty Reef Bahamas 187 E2
Högyész Hungary 49 P9
Hoh r. U.S.A. 180 A3
Hohenems Austria 48 G8
Hohenloher Ebene plain Germany 48 G6
Hohe Nock mt. Austria 49 L8
Hohensalza Poland see Inowrocław
Hohenwald U.S.A. 174 C5
Hohenwartetalsperre resr Germany 51 R2
Hoher Dachstein mt. Austria 49 K8
Hoh Ereg China see Wuchuan
Hoher Göll mt. Austria/Germany 49 K8
Hohe Rhön mts Germany 48 G5
Hohe Tauern mts Austria 49 J8
Hohe Tauern, Nationalpark nat. park Austria 49 J8
Hohe Venn moorland Belgium 51 M2
Hohhot China 85 F3
also spelt Huhhot; formerly spelt Huhehot
Hohoe Ghana 125 F5
Ho Hok Shan Hong Kong China 87 [inset]
Hōhoku Japan 91 B7
Hoh Xil Hu salt l. China 89 E5
Hoh Xil Shan mts China 80 D5
Hôi An Vietnam 78 E5
Hoima Uganda 128 A4
Hoisdorf Germany 48 H2
Hoisington U.S.A. 178 C4
Hoit Taria China 84 C4
Hôi Xuân Vietnam 78 D3
Hojagala Turkm. see Khodzha-Kala
Hojai India 97 G4
Hojambaz Turkm. see Khodzhambaz
Hōjo Japan 91 C8
Hökensås hills Sweden 45 K4
Hokio Beach N.Z. 152 J8
Hokitika N.Z. 153 E10
Hokkaidō i. Japan 81 O4
historically known as Ezo or Yezo
Hokkaidō pref. Japan 90 H3
Hokksund Norway 45 J4
Hokmābād Iran 100 D2
Hokonui N.Z. 153 C14
Hokonui Hills N.Z. 153 C13
Hokota Japan 91 G6
Hoktemberyan Armenia 107 F2
formerly spelt Oktemberyan
Hol Buskerud Norway 45 J3
Hol Nordland Norway 44 L1
Hola Kenya 128 C5
Holalkere India 94 C3
Holanda Bol. 200 D3
Holbæk Denmark 45 J5
Holberg Canada 166 D5
Holbrook Australia 147 E3
Holbrook U.S.A. 183 N7
Holcombe U.S.A. 172 B5
Holcombe Flowage resr U.S.A. 172 B5
Holden Canada 167 H4
Holden U.S.A. 183 L2
Holdenville U.S.A. 179 C5
Holdich Arg. 205 C7
Holdrege U.S.A. 178 C3
Hole Narsipur India 94 C3
Holgat watercourse S. Africa 132 A5
Holgate U.S.A. 176 A4
Holguín Cuba 186 D2
Holíč Slovakia 49 O7
Höljes Sweden 45 K3
Hollabrunn Austria 49 N7
Holland country Europe see Netherlands
Holland MI U.S.A. 172 G8
Holland NY U.S.A. 176 G3
Hollandale U.S.A. 175 B5
Hollandia Indon. see Jayapura
Hollands Diep est. Neth. 48 B4
Hollick-Kenyon Peninsula Antarctica 222 T2
Hollick-Kenyon Plateau Antarctica 222 Q1
Hollis U.S.A. 179 C5
Hollister U.S.A. 182 C5
Hollóháza Hungary 49 S7
Hollola Fin. 45 N3
Hollum Neth. 48 C2
Holly U.S.A. 173 J8
Holly Springs U.S.A. 174 B5

Hollywood U.S.A. 175 D7
Holm Norway 44 K2
Holman Canada 165 H2
  also known as Uluqsaqtuuq
Holmes Reef Australia 149 E3
Holmdene S. Africa 133 N3
Holmestrand Norway 45 J4
Holmgard Rus. Fed. see Velikiy Novgorod
Holm Ø i. Greenland see Kiatassuaq
Holmöarna naturreservat nature res. Sweden 44 M3
Holmön i. Sweden 44 M3
Holmsund Sweden 44 M3
Holmudden pt Sweden 45 L4
Holod r. Romania 58 D2
Holon Israel 108 F5
  also spelt Kholon
Holoog Namibia 130 C5
Holothuria Banks reef Australia 150 D2
Holroyd r. Australia 150 D2
Holroyd Bluff hills Australia 151 C5
Holspruit r. S. Africa 133 M4
Holstebro Denmark 45 J4
Holsted Denmark 45 J5
Holstein U.S.A. 178 B9
Holston r. U.S.A. 176 D9
Holston Lake U.S.A. 176 D9
Holt U.S.A. 173 I8
Holton KS U.S.A. 178 D4
Holton MI U.S.A. 172 G7
Holtville U.S.A. 183 I9
Holtwood U.S.A. 177 I6
Holy Cross, Mount of the U.S.A. 180 F4
Holyhead U.K. 47 H10
  also known as Caergybi
Holy Island England U.K. 46 K8
  also known as Lindisfarne
Holy Island Wales U.K. 47 H10
Holyoke CO U.S.A. 178 B3
Holyoke MA U.S.A. 177 M3
Holy See Europe see Vatican City
Holzkirchen Germany 48 I8
Holzminden Germany 48 H4
Hom watercourse Namibia 132 C5
Homa Bay Kenya 128 B5
Homalin Myanmar 78 A2
Homathko r. Canada 166 E5
Homāyūnshahr Iran see Khomeynīshahr
Homberg (Efze) Germany 48 H4
Hombetsu Japan see Honbetsu
Hombori Mali 125 E3
Hombre Muerto, Salar del salt flat Arg. 204 D2
Homburg Germany 48 E6
Home Bay Canada 165 M3
Home Hill Australia 149 E3
Home Point U.S.A. 152 I3
Homer AK U.S.A. 164 D4
Homer GA U.S.A. 174 D5
Homer LA U.S.A. 179 D5
Homer MI U.S.A. 173 I8
Homer City U.S.A. 176 F5
Homerville U.S.A. 175 D6
Homestead Australia 149 E4
Homestead U.S.A. 175 D7
Homewood N.Z. 152 J9
Homewood U.S.A. 175 D7
Hommelvik Norway 44 J3
Homnabad India 94 C2
Homoca Romania 58 I2
Homoine Moz. 131 G4
Homoodji well Niger 125 I2
Homs Libya see Al Khums
Homs Syria 109 H3
  also known as Hims; historically known as Emesa
Homyel' Belarus 43 M9
  also spelt Gomel
Homyel' Oblast admin. div. Belarus see Homyel'skaya Voblasts'
Homyel'skaya Voblasts' admin. div. Belarus 43 K9
  English form Homyel Oblast or Gomel Oblast; also known as Gomel'skaya Oblast'
Honaker U.S.A. 176 D8
Honan prov. China see Henan
Honavar India 94 B3
Honaz Turkey 59 K11
  historically known as Colossae
Hon Bai Canh i. Vietnam 79 D6
Honbetsu Japan 90 H3
  also spelt Hombetsu
Hon Chông Vietnam 79 D6
Hon Chuối r. Vietnam 79 D6
Honda Col. 198 C3
Honda India 97 E5
Honda, Bahía b. Col. 198 C1
Honda Bay Phil. 74 A4
Hondapa India 95 E1
Hondeblaf r. S. Africa 133 I7
Hondeklipbaai S. Africa 132 B7
Hondo Japan 91 B8
Hondo NM U.S.A. 181 F6
Hondo TX U.S.A. 179 C6
Hondo r. U.S.A. 181 F6
Honduras country Central America 186 B4
  northamerica [countries] ▶▶ 158–159
Honduras, Gulf of Belize/Hond. 186 B3
Honefoss Norway 45 J3
Honesdale U.S.A. 177 J4
Honey Brook U.S.A. 177 J5

Honey Lake U.S.A. 182 D1
Honfleur France 50 G3
Hông, Sông r. Vietnam see Red River
Hong'an China 87 E2
Hongch'ŏn S. Korea 83 B5
Hongde China 85 E4
Hông Gai Vietnam 78 D3
Honggouzi China 88 E4
Honggu China 84 D4
  formerly known as Yaojie
Honghai Wan b. China 87 E4
Honghe China 86 B4
  also known as Yisa
Hong He r. China 87 E1
Honghu China 87 E2
  formerly known as Xindi
Hong Hu l. China 87 E2
Hongjialou China see Licheng
Hongjiang China 87 D3
Hongjiang China see Wangcang
Hong Kong Hong Kong China 87 [inset]
  also known as Hsiang Kang or Xianggang
  world [cities] ▶▶ 24–25
Hong Kong special admin. reg. China 87 [inset]
  long form Xianggang Tebie Xingzhengqu
Hong Kong Harbour sea chan. Hong Kong China 87 [inset]
  also known as Victoria Harbour
Hong Kong Island Hong Kong China 87 [inset]
  also known as Hsiang Chang
Hongliu r. China 85 F4
Hongliu Daquan well China 84 C3
Hongliuwan China see Aksay
Hongliuyuan Gansu China 84 B3
Hongliuyuan Gansu China 84 D4
Hông Ngư Vietnam 79 D6
Hongor Mongolia 85 G2
Hongqiao China see Qidong
Hongqizhen China see Tongshi
Hongshan China 86 B3
  formerly known as Mabating
Hongshui He r. China 87 D4
Hongtong China 85 F4
Hongū Japan 91 D8
Honguedo, Détroit d' sea chan. Canada 169 I3
Hongwansi China see Sunan
Hongwŏn N. Korea 83 B4
Hongyuan China 86 B1
  also known as Qiongxi
Honze China 87 F1
  also known as Gaoliangjian
Hongze Hu l. China 87 F1

Honiara Solomon Is 145 E2
  Capital of the Solomon Islands.

Honiton U.K. 47 I13
Honjō Japan 90 G5
Honkajoki Fin. 45 M3
Hon Khoai i. Vietnam 79 D6
Hon Mê i. Vietnam 79 D6
Hon Minh Hoa i. Vietnam 79 D6
Honnali India 94 B3
Honningsvåg Norway 44 N1
Honokaa U.S.A. 181 [inset] Z1

Honolulu U.S.A. 181 [inset] Z1
  State capital of Hawaii.

Honor U.S.A. 172 G6
Hon Rai r. Vietnam 79 D6

Honshū i. Japan 91 F6
  3rd largest island in Asia and 7th in the world.
  asia [landscapes] ▶▶ 62–63

Honwad India 94 B2
Hood r. Canada 167 I1
Hood, Mount vol. U.S.A. 180 B3
Hood Point Australia 151 B7
Hood River U.S.A. 180 B3
Hoogeveen Neth. 48 D3
Hoogezand-Sappemeer Neth. 48 D2
Hooghly r. mouth India see Hugli
Hooker U.S.A. 178 B4
Hooker Creek Aboriginal Land res. Australia 148 A3
Hook Head Rep. of Ireland 47 F11
Hook of Holland Neth. 48 B4
  also known as Hoek van Holland
Hook Reef Australia 149 F3
Hoonah U.S.A. 164 F4
Hoopa Valley Indian Reservation res. U.S.A. 180 B4
Hooper Bay U.S.A. 164 C3
Hooper Island U.S.A. 177 I7
Hoopstad S. Africa 133 J4
Hoorn Neth. 48 C3
Hoorn, Îles de is Wallis and Futuna Is see Futuna Islands
Hoorn Islands Wallis and Futuna Is see Futuna Islands
Hoosick U.S.A. 177 L3
Hoover Dam U.S.A. 183 J5
Hoover Memorial Reservoir U.S.A. 176 C5
Höövör Mongolia 84 D2
Hóp lag. Iceland 44 [inset] B2
Hopa Turkey 107 E2
Hope Canada 166 F5
Hope r. N.Z. 152 H9
Hope U.S.A. 179 D5
Hope, Lake salt flat S.A. Australia 146 C2
Hope, Lake salt flat W.A. Australia 151 C7
Hope, Point U.S.A. 164 C2
Hopedale Canada 169 I2
Hopefield S. Africa 132 C10
Hopelchén Mex. 185 H5
Hope Mountains Canada 169 I2
Hopen i. Svalbard 38 C2
Hopes Advance, Baie b. Canada 169 G1
Hopes Advance, Cap c. Canada 169 G1
Hopes Advance Bay Canada see Aupaluk
Hopetoun Vic. Australia 147 D3
Hopetoun W.A. Australia 151 C7
Hopetown S. Africa 132 I6
Hope Vale Aboriginal Reserve Australia 149 E2
Hope Valley U.S.A. 177 N4
Hopewell U.S.A. 177 H8
Hopewell Islands Canada 168 E1
Hopi Indian Reservation res. U.S.A. 183 N6
Hopin Myanmar 78 B2
Hopkins r. Australia 147 D4
Hopkins, Lake salt flat Australia 150 E5
Hopkinsville U.S.A. 174 C4
Hopland U.S.A. 182 A3
Hopong Myanmar 78 B3
Hopseidet Norway 44 N1
Hopquiam U.S.A. 180 B3
Hor Qinghai China 84 D5
Hor Xizang China 89 C6
  also spelt Huoer
Horadiz Azer. 107 F3
  also spelt Goradiz
Horasan Turkey 107 F2
Horažďovice Czech Rep. 49 K6
Horb am Neckar Germany 48 F7
Hörby Sweden 45 K5
Horcajo de Santiago Spain 55 I5
Horcasitas Mex. 184 C2
Horcón Chile see Horcones
Horcones r. Arg. 204 D2
Horda Norway 45 I4
Horezu Romania 58 E3
Horgo Mongolia 84 C1

Horgoš Vojvodina, Srbija Yugo. 58 A2
Hörh Uul mts Mongolia 85 E3
Horia Romania 58 J3
Horicon U.S.A. 172 E7
Horinger China 85 F3
Horiult Mongolia 84 D2

Horizon Deep sea feature
  S. Pacific Ocean 220 G7
  2nd deepest point in the world (Tonga Trench).

Horki Belarus 43 L7
  also known as Gorki
Horlick Mountains Antarctica 223 Q1
Horlivka Ukr. 41 F6
  also spelt Gorlovka
Hormak Iran 101 E4
Hormoz i. Iran 100 D5
Hormoz, Küh-e mt. Iran 100 C5
Hormozgan prov. Iran 100 D5
Hormūd-e Bāgh Iran 100 D5
Hormūd-e Mīr Khūnd Iran 100 C5
Hormuz, Strait of Iran/Oman 105 G2
Horn Austria 49 M7
Horn r. Canada 167 G2
Horn c. Iceland 44 [inset] B2
  also known as Nord Kap
Horn, Cape Chile 205 D9
  Most southerly point of South America. Also known as Hornos, Cabo de.

Hornád r. Slovakia 49 R7
  also spelt Hernád (Hungary)
Hornavan l. Sweden 44 L2
Hornbrook U.S.A. 180 B4
Horndal Sweden 45 L3
Horne, Îles de is Wallis and Futuna Is see Futuna Islands
Hörnefors Sweden 44 L3
Hornell U.S.A. 176 H3
Hornepayne Canada 168 C3
Hornindal Norway 45 I3
Hornkranz Namibia 130 C4
Horn Island U.S.A. 175 B6
Horn Mountains Canada 166 F2
Hornos, Cabo de c. Chile see Horn, Cape
Hornos, Parque Nacional de nat. park Chile 205 D9
Hornoy-le-Bourg France 51 H3
Horn Peak Canada 166 D2
Hornsby Australia 147 F3
Hornsea U.K. 46 L10
Hornslandet pen. Sweden 45 L3
Hornslet Denmark 45 J4
Hornstrandir reg. Iceland 44 [inset] B2
Horodenka Ukr. 41 C6
  also spelt Gorodenka
Horodnya Ukr. 41 D6
Horodok Ukr. 41 C6
  also spelt Gorodok
Horokanai Japan 90 H2
Horo Shan mts China 88 C3
Horoshiri-dake mt. Japan 90 H3
Horqin Shadi reg. China 85 I3
Horqin Youyi Qianqi China see Ulanhot
Horqin Zuoyi Houqi China see Ganjig
Horqin Zuoyi Zhongqi China see Baokang
Horqueta Para. 201 F5
Horru China 89 E6
Horse Creek r. U.S.A. 180 F4
Horsefly Canada 166 F4
Horseheads U.S.A. 177 I3
Horse Lake U.S.A. 182 D1
Horsens Denmark 45 J4
Horseshoe Bend Australia 148 B5
Horseshoe Reservoir U.S.A. 183 M7
Horsham Australia 147 F3
Horsham U.K. 47 L12
Horten Norway 45 J4
Hortobágyi nat. park Hungary 49 S8
Horton r. Canada 164 G3
Horwood Lake Canada 168 D3
Ho Sai Hu l. China 84 B5
Hosa'ina Eth. 128 C3
Hosdurga India 94 C3
Hose, Pegunungan mts Sarawak Malaysia 77 F2
Hosenofu well Libya 120 D4
Hoseynābād Iran 100 A3
Hoseynīyeh Iran 100 B4
Hoshab Pak. 101 E5
Hoshangabad India 96 C5
Hoshiarpur India 96 B3
Hoshō'isa Egypt 108 B7
Höshööt Arhangay Mongolia 84 D1
Höshööt Bayan-Ölgiy Mongolia 84 A1
Hoskins P.N.G. 145 E2
Hoşköy Turkey 58 I8
Hospet India 94 C3
Hossévé Vokre mt. Cameroon 125 I4
Hosszúpályi Hungary 49 S8
Hoste, Isla i. Chile 205 C9
Hosur India 94 C3
Hotan China 89 C4
  formerly spelt Khotan
Hotan r. China 88 C3
Hotazel S. Africa 132 G4
Hot Creek r. U.S.A. 183 H3
Hot Creek Range mts U.S.A. 183 I3
Hotham r. Australia 151 B7
Hotham, Cape Australia 148 A2
Hoting Sweden 44 L2
Hot Springs AR U.S.A. 179 D5
Hot Springs SD U.S.A. 178 B3
  Truth or Consequences
Hot Sulphur Springs U.S.A. 180 F4
Hottah Lake Canada 167 G1
Hottentots-Holland Nature Reserve S. Africa 132 C11
Hottentots Point Namibia 130 B5
Houaïlu New Caledonia 145 F4
Houdan France 50 H4
Houffalize Belgium 51 L2
Hougang Sing. 76 [inset]
Houghton MI U.S.A. 172 E3
Houghton NY U.S.A. 176 H3
Houghton Lake U.S.A. 173 I6
Houghton Lake l. U.S.A. 173 I6
Houghton le Spring U.K. 47 K9
Houie Moc, Phou mt. Laos 78 C3
Houlton U.S.A. 174 H2
Houma China 85 F5
Houma U.S.A. 179 D6
Houmen China 87 [inset]
Houmt Souk Tunisia 123 H2
Houndé Burkina 124 E4
Hourtin et Carcans, Étang d' l. France 50 E7
Housatonic U.S.A. 177 L3
Housatonic r. U.S.A. 177 L4
House Range mts U.S.A. 183 K2
Housesteads tourist site U.K. 47 J8
  historically known as Vercovicium
Houston Canada 166 E4
Houston MN U.S.A. 172 B7
Houston MO U.S.A. 178 E4
Houston MS U.S.A. 175 B5
Houston TX U.S.A. 179 D6
Hout Bay S. Africa 132 C11
Houtkraal S. Africa 132 G6
Houtman Abrolhos is Australia 151 A6
Houtskär Fin. 42 C1
Houwater S. Africa 132 H7
Houxia China 88 D3
Houzhai China see Nan'ao
Hov Denmark 45 J5
Hov Norway 45 J3

Hova Sweden 45 K4
Hovd Hovd Mongolia 84 A2
  also known as Jargalant
Hovd Övörhangay Mongolia 84 D2
Hovd prov. Mongolia 84 B2
Hovden park Norway 45 I4
Hovden Norway 45 I4
Hoveyzeh Iran 107 G5
Hovland U.S.A. 172 D3
Hövsgöl Mongolia 85 F3
Hövsgöl prov. Mongolia 84 D1
Hövsgöl Nuur l. Mongolia 84 D1
Hövüün Mongolia 84 D3
Howa, Ouadi watercourse Chad/Sudan 120 D5
Howakil Bay Eritrea 104 C5
Howakil Island Eritrea 104 C5
Howar, Wadi watercourse Sudan 120 E5
Howard Australia 149 G5
Howard KS U.S.A. 178 C4
Howard SD U.S.A. 178 C3
Howard WI U.S.A. 172 E6
Howard City U.S.A. 172 H7
Howard Island Australia 148 B2
Howard Springs Australia 148 A2
Howden U.K. 47 L10
Howe, Cape Australia 147 F4
Howe, Mount Antarctica 223 O1
Howell U.S.A. 173 J8
Howes U.S.A. 180 G3
Howick S. Africa 133 O6
Howitt, Lake salt flat Australia 146 C1
Howland U.S.A. 174 G2

Howland Island N. Pacific Ocean 145 H1
  United States Unincorporated Territory.
  oceania [countries] ▶▶ 138–139

Howlong Australia 147 E3
Howrah India see Haora
Howz well Iran 100 D3
Howz-e Panj Iran 100 D4
Howz-e Panj waterhole Iran 100 C3
Howz-i-Khan well Iran 100 D3
Howz i-Mian i-Tak Iran 100 C3
Hoxie U.S.A. 178 B4
Höxter Germany 48 H4
Hoxtolgay China 88 D2
Hoxud China 88 D3
Hoy i. U.K. 46 I5
Hoyang Norway 45 I3
Hoyerswerda Germany 49 L4
Høylandet Norway 44 K2
Hoyle Canada 173 L2
Höytiäinen l. Fin. 44 O3
Hoyt Peak U.S.A. 183 M1
Hozha Belarus 42 F8
Hpa-an Myanmar see Pa-an
Hradec Králové Czech Rep. 49 M5
Hradiště hill Czech Rep. 49 K5
Hradzyanka Belarus 43 J8
Hrasnica Bos.-Herz. 56 K5
Hraun Iceland 44 [inset] D2
Hraun slope Iceland 44 [inset] D2
Hrawzhyshki Belarus 42 G7
Hrazdan Armenia 107 F2
  also spelt Razdan; formerly known as Akhta
Hrazený hill Czech Rep. 49 L5
Hrebinka Ukr. 41 E6
  also spelt Grebyonka; formerly known as Grebenkovskiy
Hrem"yach Ukr. 43 O9
Hristós Greece see Christos
Hrodna Belarus 42 E8
  also known as Gardinas; also spelt Grodno
Hrodna Oblast admin. div. Belarus see Hrodzyenskaya Voblasts'
Hrodzyenskaya Voblasts' admin. div. Belarus 42 G8
  English form Hrodna Oblast or Grodno Oblast; also known as Grodnenskaya Oblast'
Hron r. Slovakia 49 P8
Hrvatska country Europe see Croatia
Hrvatska Kostajnica Croatia 56 I3
Hsenwi Myanmar 78 B3
Hsiang i. Hong Kong China see Hong Kong Island
Hsiang Kang Hong Kong China see Hong Kong
Hsi-hseng Myanmar 78 B3
Hsin, Nam r. Myanmar 78 B3
Hsin-chia-p'o country Asia see Singapore
Hsin-chia-p'o Sing. see Singapore
Hsinchu Taiwan 87 G3
  also spelt Xinzhu
Hsinking China see Changchun
Hsinying China 87 G4
  also spelt Xinying
Hsi-sha Ch'un-tao is S. China Sea see Paracel Islands
Hsiyüp'ing Yü i. Taiwan 87 F4
Hsüeh Shan mt. Taiwan 87 G3
Hua'an China 87 F3
Huab watercourse Namibia 130 B4
Huacaibamba Peru 200 A2
Huacaraje Bol. 201 E3
Huacaya Bol. 201 E5
Huacheng China 87 E3
Huachi Bol. 201 E3
Huachi China 85 E4
  also known as Rouyuan; formerly known as Rouyuanchengzi
Huachinera Mex. 184 C2
Huachou China 87 E4
Huacho Peru 200 A3
Huachón Peru 200 B3
Huachuan China 82 C3
  also known as Yuelai
Huacrachuco Peru 200 A2
Huacullani Peru 200 C4
Huade China 85 G3
Huadian China 82 B4
Huadu China 87 E4
  formerly known as Huaxian or Xinhua
Huafeng China see Hua'an
Huahine i. Fr. Polynesia 221 I7
Hua Hin Thai. 79 B5
Hua'an Hebei China 85 G3
Huai'an Jiangsu China 87 F1
Huaibei China 87 E1
Huaibin China 87 E1
  formerly known as Wulongji
Huaicheng China see Huaiji
Huaide China see Gongzhuling
Huaidian China see Shenqiu
Huai Nam Dang National Park Thai. 78 B4
Huai He r. China 87 E1
Huaihua China 87 D3
  also known as Yushuwan
Huaiji China 87 E4
  also known as Huaicheng
Huai-kha-khaeng Wildlife Reserve nature res. Thai. 79 B5
Huailai China 85 G3
Huai Luang r. Thai. 78 C4
Huainan China 87 F1
Huaining China 87 F2
Huairen China 85 G4
Huairou China 85 H3
Huai Sanri r. Thai. 79 D5
Huaiyang China 87 E1
  also known as Wangying
Huaiyin China 87 F1
  formerly known as Qingjiang
Huaiyuan Anhui China 87 F1

Huaiyuan Guangxi China 87 D3
Huajialing China 84 E5
Huajuápan de León Mex. 185 F5
Huaki Indon. 75 C4
Hualahuises Mex. 185 F3
Hualapai Indian Reservation res. U.S.A. 183 K6
Hualapai Peak U.S.A. 183 K6
Hualfín Arg. 204 D2
Hualien Taiwan 87 G3
Hualla Peru 200 B3
Huallaga r. Peru 198 C6
Hualong China 84 D4
  also known as Bayan
Huamachuco Peru 200 A1
Huamani Peru 200 B3
Huambo Angola 127 B8
  formerly known as Nova Lisboa
Huambo prov. Angola 127 B8
Huams watercourse Namibia 132 B3
Huanan China 82 C3
Huancabamba Peru 198 B6
Huancache, Sierra mts Arg. 205 C6
Huancapi Peru 200 B3
Huancavelica Peru 200 B3
Huancavelica dept Peru 200 B3
Huancayo Peru 200 B3
Huancheng China see Huanxian
Huangbei China 87 E3
Huangcaoba China see Xingyi
Huangchuan China 87 E2
Huanggang China 87 E2
  also known as Huangzhou
Huang He r. China see Yellow River
Huanghe Kou r. mouth China 85 H4
Huanghua China 85 H4
Huangjiajian China 87 G1
Huangling China 85 F5
  also known as Qiaoshan
Huangliu China 87 D5
Huanglong China 85 F5
Huanglongsi China see Kaifeng
Huangmao Jian mt. China 87 F3
Huangmei China 87 E2
Huangnihe China 82 B4
Huangpi China 87 E2
Huangping China 87 C3
  also known as Xinzhou
Huangqi China 87 F3
Huangshan China 87 F2
  also known as Tunxi
Huang Shan mts China 87 F2
Huangshengguan China 86 B1
Huangshi China 87 E2
Huang Shui r. China 84 D4
Huangtu Gaoyuan plat. China 85 F4
Huangxian China 85 I4
Huangyan China 87 G2
Huangyangzhen China 84 D4
Huangyuan China 84 D4
Huangzhong China see Lushar
Huangzhou China see Huanggang
Huaning China 86 B3
Huanjiang China 87 D3
  also known as Si'en
Huan Jiang r. China 85 E4
Huanren China 82 B4
Huanshan China see Yuhuan
Huanta Peru 200 B3
Huantai China 85 H4
  also known as Suozhen
Huánuco Peru 200 A2
Huánuco dept Peru 200 A2
Huanuhuanu Peru 200 B3
Huanuni Bol. 200 D3
Huanxian China 85 E4
  also known as Huancheng
Huaping China 86 B3
  also known as Zhongxin
Huap'ing Yü i. Taiwan 87 G3
Huar Bol. 200 D3
Huaral Peru 200 A2
Huaráz Peru 200 A2
Huari Peru 200 A2
Huariaca Peru 200 A2
Huarmey Peru 200 A3
Huarochiri Peru 200 A3
Huaron Peru 200 A2
Huarong China 87 E2
Huasaga r. Peru 198 C5
Huascarán, Parque Nacional nat. park Peru 200 A2
Huasco Chile 204 C3
Hua Shan mt. China 87 D1
Huashaoying China 85 G3
Huashixia China 85 A5
  also known as Zogainrawar
Huashugou China see Jingtieshan
Huatabampo Mex. 184 C3
Huatusco Mex. 185 F5
Huauchinango Mex. 185 F4
Huauru, Islas de is Peru 200 A2
Huautla Mex. 185 F5
Huaxian China see Huadu
Huaxian Henan China 85 G5
  also known as Daokou
Huaxian Shaanxi China 87 D1
Huayacocotla Mex. 185 F4
Huayang China see Jixi
Huayin China 87 D1
Huayllay Peru 200 A2
Huayuan China 87 D2
Huazangsi China see Tianzhu
Huazhaizi China 84 D4
Huazhou China 87 E4
Hubbard, Mount Canada/U.S.A. 166 B3
Hubbard, Pointe pt Canada 169 H1
Hubbard Lake U.S.A. 173 J6
Hubbart Point Canada 167 M3
Hubei prov. China 87 E2
  English form Hupeh
Hubli India 94 B3
Hucal Arg. 204 D5
Huch'ang N. Korea 82 B4
Hückelhoven Germany 48 D4
Hudag Humar mts Saudi Arabia 104 B2
Huddersfield U.K. 47 K10
Hudiksvall Sweden 45 L3
Hudson MA U.S.A. 177 N3
Hudson MI U.S.A. 173 I9
Hudson NH U.S.A. 177 N3
Hudson NY U.S.A. 177 L3
Hudson r. U.S.A. 177 L3
Hudson, Baie d' sea Canada see Hudson Bay
Hudson, Cerro mt. Chile 205 B7
Hudson, Détroit d' strait Canada see Hudson Strait
Hudson Bay Canada 167 K4
Hudson Bay sea Canada 165 K4
  also known as Hudson, Baie d'
Hudson Falls U.S.A. 177 L2
Hudson Island Tuvalu see Nanumanga
Hudson Land reg. Greenland 165 Q2
Hudson's Hope Canada 166 F3
Hudson Strait Canada 165 L3
  also known as Hudson, Détroit d'
Huê Vietnam 78 D4
Huebra r. Spain 54 E4
Huechucuicui, Punta pt Chile 205 B6
Huedin Romania 58 E2
Huehuetán Mex. 185 G6
Huehuetenango Guat. 185 H6
Huehueto, Cerro mt. Mex. 184 D3
Huejuquilla Mex. 184 E4
Huejutla Mex. 185 F4
Huelgoat France 50 C4

Huelma Spain 55 H7
Huelva Spain 54 E7
Huelva r. Spain 55 K3
Huentelauquén Chile 204 C4
Huépac Mex. 184 C2
Huércal-Overa Spain 55 J7
Huerfano r. U.S.A. 181 F5
Huerva r. Spain 55 K2
Huesca Spain 55 K2
Huéscar Spain 55 I7
Huétamo Mex. 185 E5
Huete Spain 55 I4
Hueytown U.S.A. 175 C5
Huftarøy i. Norway 46 R3
Hugeilig r. Sudan 126 E2
Hugh watercourse Australia 148 B5
Hughenden Australia 149 E4
Hughes Australia 146 A4
Hughes r. Canada 167 K3
Hughes Bay Antarctica 222 T2
Hughesville MD U.S.A. 177 I4
Hughesville PA U.S.A. 177 I4
Hughson U.S.A. 182 D4
Hugli r. mouth India 97 E5
  also spelt Hooghly
Hugli-Chunchura India 97 F5
Hugo CO U.S.A. 178 B4
Hugo OK U.S.A. 179 D5
Hugoton U.S.A. 178 B4
Huhehot China see Hohhot
Huhhot China see Hohhot
Huhudi S. Africa 133 I3
Hui Fin. 44 O3
Hui'an China 87 F3
  also known as Luocheng
Hui'anpu China 85 E4
Huiarau Range mts N.Z. 152 K6
Huib-Hoch Plateau Namibia 130 C5
Huichang China 87 E3
Huichapán Mex. 185 F4
Huicheng China see Shexian
Huicheng China see Huilai
Huich'ŏn N. Korea 83 B4
Huidong Guangdong China 87 E4
  also known as Pingshan
Huidong Sichuan China 86 B3
Huifa r. China 82 B4
Huíla Angola 127 B8
Huíla prov. Angola 127 B8
Huila dept Col. 198 C4
Huila, Nevado de vol. Col. 198 C4
Huilai China 87 F4
  also known as Huicheng
Huili China 86 B3
Huilong China see Qidong
Huimanguillo Mex. 185 G5
Huimin China 85 H4
Huinahuaca Arg. 200 D5
Huiñaimarca, Lago de l. Bol./Peru 200 C4
Huinan China see Nanhui
Huinan China see Chaoyang
Huinca Renancó Arg. 204 D4
Huining China 84 E5
  also known as Huishi
Huishi China see Huining
Huishui China 86 C3
  also known as Heping
Huisne r. France 50 F5
Huiten Nur l. China 89 E5
Huitong China 87 D3
  also known as Lincheng
Huittinen Fin. 45 M3
Huixian Gansu China 86 C1
Huixian Henan China 85 G5
Huixtla Mex. 185 G6
Huiyang China see Huizhou
Huize China 86 B3
  also known as Zhongping
Huizhou China 87 E4
  also known as Huiyang
Hujir Arhangay Mongolia 84 D1
Hujirt Övörhangay Mongolia 84 D2
Hujirt Töv Mongolia 84 E2
Hukanui N.Z. 152 I7
Hukawng Valley Myanmar 78 B2
Hukou China 87 F2
Hukuntsi Botswana 130 D4
Hulan r. China 82 B3
Hulan Ergi China 85 I2
Hulayfah Saudi Arabia 104 C3
Hulayhilah well Syria 109 J3
Hulbert U.S.A. 173 I4
Hulbert Lake U.S.A. 173 I4
Hulen U.S.A. 176 B9
Huliao China see Dabu
Hulin China 82 D3
Hull Canada 168 F4
Hull U.K. see Kingston upon Hull
Hull U.S.A. 177 O3
Hull Island Kiribati see Orona
Hulo Estonia 42 E3
Hultsfred Sweden 45 K4
Hulu r. China 85 E4
Huludao China 85 I3
Hulun China see Hailar
Hulun Nur l. China 85 H1
Hulwān Egypt see Helwân
Hulyaypole Ukr. 41 F7
Huma China 82 B2
Huma r. China 82 B2
Humacao Puerto Rico 187 G3
Humaitá Bol. 200 D3
Humaitá Brazil 201 E1
Humaitá Para. 201 F6
Humansdorp S. Africa 133 I11
Humay Peru 200 B3
Humaym well U.A.E. 105 F3
Humayyan, Jabal hill Saudi Arabia 104 D2
Humbe Angola 127 B9
Humber, Serra do mts Angola 127 B8
Humber, Mouth of the U.K. 47 M10
Humberside airport U.K. 47 L10
Humberstone Chile 200 C5
Humberto de Campos Brazil 202 D2
Humboldt Canada 167 J4
Humboldt AZ U.S.A. 183 L7
Humboldt NE U.S.A. 178 D3
Humboldt TN U.S.A. 174 B5
Humboldt r. U.S.A. 182 F1
Humboldt, Mont mt. New Caledonia 145 F4
Humboldt Bay U.S.A. 180 A4
Humboldt Gletscher glacier Greenland see Sermersuaq
Humboldt Lake U.S.A. 182 F1
Humboldt Mountain mt. N.Z. 153 C12
Humboldt Range mts U.S.A. 182 F1
Humbolt Salt Marsh U.S.A. 182 G1
Hume r. Canada 166 D1
Humeburn Australia 147 E1
Humeda plain Arg. 204 D5
Humenné Slovakia 49 S7
Hume Reservoir Australia 147 F3
Humícha r. Bos.-Herz. 56 I5
Humina, Gora hill Croatia 56 I3
Humos, Cabo c. Chile 204 B4
Humpata Angola 127 B8
Humphrey Island atoll Cook Is see Manihiki
Humphreys, Mount U.S.A. 182 E4
Humphreys Peak U.S.A. 183 M6
Humpolec Czech Rep. 49 M6
Humppila Fin. 45 M3
Humpty Doo Australia 148 A2

Hun r. China 85 I3
Hūn Libya 120 B2
Húnaflói b. Iceland 44 [inset] B2
Hunan prov. China 87 D3
Hunchun China 82 C4
Hunchun r. China 82 C4
Hundorp Norway 45 J3
Hundred U.S.A. 176 E6
Hunedoara Romania 58 D3
Hünfeld Germany 48 G5
▶Hungary country Europe 49 P8
known as Magyar Köztársaság in Hungarian
europe [countries] → 32–35
Hungerford Australia 147 E2
Hungerford U.K. 47 K12
Hung Fa Leng hill Hong Kong China see Robin's Nest
Hüngiy Gol r. Mongolia 84 B1
Hŭngnam N. Korea 83 B5
Hungry Horse Reservoir U.S.A. 180 D2
Hung Shui Kiu Hong Kong China 87 [inset]
Hungund India 94 C2
Hunissout Pan salt pan S. Africa 132 D7
Hunjiang China see Baishan
Hun Jiang r. China 82 B4
Hunnebostrand Sweden 45 J4
Huns Mountains Namibia 132 B4
Hunstanton U.K. 47 M11
Hunsur India 94 C3
Hunta Canada 173 L1
Hunte r. Germany 48 F2
Hunter r. Australia 147 F3
Hunter N.Z. 153 F12
Hunter r. N.Z. 153 D12
Hunterganj India 97 E4
Hunter Island Australia 147 E5
Hunter Island Canada 166 D5
Hunter Island S. Pacific Ocean 145 G4
Hunter Islands Australia 147 E5
Hunter Mountains N.Z. 153 B13
Hunter's Bay Myanmar 78 A4
Huntingdon U.K. 47 L11
Huntingdon PA U.S.A. 176 H5
Huntingdon TN U.S.A. 174 B4
Huntington IN U.S.A. 174 C3
Huntington UT U.S.A. 183 N2
Huntington WV U.S.A. 176 C7
Huntington Beach U.S.A. 182 F8
Huntington Creek r. U.S.A. 183 I1
Huntly N.Z. 152 J5
Huntly U.K. 46 J6
Hunt Mountain U.S.A. 180 F3
Hunt Peninsula Australia 146 C2
Huntsville Canada 168 E4
Huntsville AL U.S.A. 174 C5
Huntsville AR U.S.A. 179 D4
Huntsville MO U.S.A. 178 D4
Huntsville TX U.S.A. 179 D6
Hunucmá Mex. 185 H4
Hunyani r. Moz./Zimbabwe see Manyame
Hunyuan China 85 G4
Hunza Jammu and Kashmir 96 B1
Hunza reg. Jammu and Kashmir 96 B1
Hunza r. Pak. 101 H3
Hunze r. Neth. 48 D2
Huocheng China 88 C2
also known as Shuiding
Huoer China see Hor
Huojia China 85 G5
Huolin r. China 85 J2
Huolongmen China 82 B2
Huolu China see Luquan
Hương Thuy Vietnam 78 D4
Huon Peninsula P.N.G. 73 K8
Huonville Australia 147 E5
Huoqiu China 87 F1
Huoshan China 87 F2
Huo Shan mt. China 87 F2
Huoshao Tao i. Taiwan see Lü Tao
Huotsaus waterhole Namibia 130 B4
Huoxian China see Huozhou
Huozhou China 85 F4
formerly known as Huoxian
Hupeh prov. China see Hubei
Hupnik r. Turkey 109 H1
Ḥūr Iran 100 D4
Hurault, Lac l. Canada 169 G2
Huraymilā Saudi Arabia 105 D2
Huraysān reg. Saudi Arabia 105 D3
Hurbanovo Slovakia 49 P8
Hurd, Cape Canada 168 D4
Hurd Island Kiribati see Arorae
Hurdiyo Somalia 128 F2
Hure China 85 I3
also known as Hure Qi
Hüremt Mongolia 84 D1
Hürent Mongolia 84 D2
Hure Qi China see Hure
Hurghada Egypt 121 G3
also known as Al Ghardaqah
Huri mt. Kenya 128 C4
Huriel France 51 I6
Hurkett Canada 172 E2
Hurley U.S.A. 177 K4
Hurlock U.S.A. 177 J7
Huron CA U.S.A. 182 D5
Huron SD U.S.A. 178 C2

▶Huron, Lake Canada/U.S.A. 173 J5
2nd largest lake in North America and 4th in the world.
northamerica [landscapes] → 156–157

Huron Bay U.S.A. 172 E4
Huron Beach U.S.A. 173 I5
Huronian Canada 172 C2
Huron Mountains hills U.S.A. 172 F4
Hurricane U.S.A. 183 K4
Hurricane Flats sea feature Bahamas 175 E8
Hurtado Chile 204 C3
Hurung, Gunung mt. Indon. 77 F2
Hurunui r. N.Z. 153 H10
Hurup Denmark 45 J4
Husain Nika Pak. 101 G4
Húsavík Norðurland eystra Iceland 44 [inset] C2
Húsavík Vestfirðir Iceland 44 [inset] B2
Husayn reg. Yemen 105 D4
Huseyinabat Turkey see Alaca
Huseyinli Turkey see Kızılırmak
Hushan China see Wuyi
Hushan China see Cixi
Husheib Sudan 121 G6
Huşi Romania 58 J2
Huskvarna Sweden 45 K4
Husn Jordan see Al Ḥiṣn
Ḥuṣn Āl 'Abr Yemen 105 D4
Husnes Norway 45 I4
Husøy i. Norway 46 Q2
Hussainabad India 97 E4
Hustopeče Czech Rep. 49 N7
Husum Germany 48 G1
Husum Sweden 44 L3
Husvik S. Georgia 205 [inset]
Hutag Mongolia 84 D1
Hūtak Iran 100 D4
Hutanopan Indon. 76 B2
Hutaym, Ḥarrat lava field Saudi Arabia 104 C2
Hutchinson S. Africa 132 H8
Hutchinson KS U.S.A. 178 C4
Hutchinson MN U.S.A. 178 D2
Hutch Mountain U.S.A. 183 M7
Ḥūth Yemen 104 C4
Hutou China 82 D3
Huttah Kulkyne National Park Australia 147 D3
Hutton, Mount hill Australia 149 F5
Hutton Range hills Australia 151 C5
Hutubi China 88 D2
Hutubi He r. China 88 D2
Hutuo r. China 85 H4
Hutup watercourse Namibia 132 B2
Huu Đô Vietnam 78 D3
Huvadhu Atoll Maldives 93 D10
Hūvār Iran 101 E5
Hüvek Turkey see Bozova
Hūvīān, Kūh-e mts Iran 101 D5
Huwār i. The Gulf 105 E2
also spelt Hawar
Ḥuwaymī, Sha'īb al watercourse Iraq 109 P7
Huwaytat reg. Saudi Arabia 107 D5
Huxi China 87 E3
Huxian China 87 D1
also known as Ganting
Huxley, Mount hill Australia 150 D3
Huxley, Mount N.Z. 153 D12
Huy Belgium 51 L2
Hūzgān Iran 100 B4
Huzhen China 87 G2
Huzhou China 87 G2
formerly known as Wuxing
Huzhu China 84 D4
also known as Weiyuan
Huzurnagar India 94 C2
Hvalnes Iceland 44 [inset] D2
Hvammsfjörður inlet Iceland 44 [inset] B2
Hvannadalshnúkur vol. Iceland 44 [inset] C2
Hvar Croatia 56 I5
Hvar i. Croatia 56 I5
Hvardiys'ke Ukr. 41 E7
Hvarski Kanal sea chan. Croatia 56 I5
Hveragerði Iceland 44 [inset] B2
Hvide Sande Denmark 45 J4
Hvíta r. Iceland 44 [inset] B3
Hvítárvatn l. Iceland 44 [inset] C2
Hwadae N. Korea 83 C4
Hwange Zimbabwe 131 E3
formerly spelt Wankie
Hwange National Park Zimbabwe 131 E3
Hwang Ho r. China see Yellow River
Hwangju N. Korea 83 B5
Hwayang S. Korea 91 A7
Hwedza Zimbabwe 131 F3
Hwlffordd U.K. see Haverfordwest
Hyannis MA U.S.A. 177 O4
Hyannis NE U.S.A. 178 B3
Hyargas Nuur salt l. Mongolia 84 B1
Hyco Lake U.S.A. 176 F9
Hyde N.Z. 153 E13
Hyden Australia 151 B7
Hyden U.S.A. 176 B8
Hyderabad India 94 C2
Hyderabad Pak. 101 G5
Hydra i. Greece see Ydra
Hyères France 51 M9
Hyères, Îles d' is France 51 M10
Hyermanavichy Belarus 42 I6
Hyesan N. Korea 82 C4
Hyland r. Canada 166 D3
Hyland, Mount Australia 147 G2
Hyland Bay Australia 148 A2
Hyland Post Canada 166 D3
Hyllekrog i. Denmark 48 I1
Hyllestad Norway 45 I3
Hyltebruk Sweden 45 K4
Hyndman U.S.A. 176 G6
Hyndman Peak U.S.A. 180 D4
Hyōgo pref. Japan 91 D7
Hyōno-sen mt. Japan 91 D7
Hyrcania Iran see Gorgān
Hyrra Banda Cent. Afr. Rep. see Ira Banda
Hyrynsalmi Fin. 44 O2
Hysham U.S.A. 180 F3
Hythe Canada 166 G4
Hyūga Japan 91 B8
Hyvinkää Fin. 45 N3

↓ I

Ia A Dun r. Vietnam 79 E5
Iacanga Brazil 206 D8
Iaciara Brazil 202 C5
Iaco r. Brazil 200 C2
Iacobeni Romania 58 F2
Iacobeni Romania 58 G1
Iacri Brazil 206 C8
Iaçu Brazil 202 D5
Iadera Croatia see Zadar
Iaeger U.S.A. 176 D8
Iakora Madag. 131 [inset] J4
Ialomița r. Romania 58 I4
Ialomiței, Balta marsh Romania 58 I4
Ialoveni Moldova 58 J2
formerly known as Kutuzov; formerly spelt Yaloven'
Ialpug r. Moldova 58 J2
formerly spelt Yalpukh
Ianca Romania 58 I3
Ian Calder Lake Canada 167 L1
Iancu Jianu Romania 58 F4
Iapu Brazil 207 K6
Iara r. Romania 58 E2
Iarauarune, Serra mts Brazil 199 F4
Iargara Moldova 58 J2
formerly spelt Yargara
Iași Romania 58 I1
also known as Jassy; also spelt Yaş
Iasmos Greece 58 G7
Iba Phil. 74 A3
Ibadan Nigeria 125 F5
Ibagué Col. 198 C3
Ibaiti Brazil 206 C10
Ibanda Uganda 128 A5
Ibănești Romania 58 F2
Ibañeta, Puerto de pass Spain 55 J1
Ibanga Kasai Occidental Dem. Rep. Congo 127 D6
Ibanga Sud-Kivu Dem. Rep. Congo 126 E5
Ibapah U.S.A. 183 K1
Ibar r. Yugo. 58 B5
Ibara Japan 91 C7
Ibaraki pref. Japan 91 G6
Ibarra Ecuador 198 B4
Ibarreta Arg. 204 F2
Ibaté Brazil 206 F8
Ibb Yemen 104 D5
Ibb governorate Yemen 104 D5
Ibba watercourse Sudan 126 F3
Ibbenbüren Germany 48 E3
Ibdeqqene watercourse Mali 125 F2
Iberá, Esteros del marsh Arg. 204 F3
Iberá, Lago l. Arg. 204 F3
Iberia Loreto Peru 198 C6
Iberia Madre de Dios Peru 200 C2

▶Iberian Peninsula Europe 54
Consists of Portugal, Spain and Gibraltar.

Ibertioga Brazil 207 J8
Iberville, Lac d' l. Canada 169 F2
also known as Upper Seal Lake
Ibestad Norway 44 L1
Ibeto Nigeria 125 G4
Ibi Indon. 76 B1
Ibi Nigeria 125 H4
Ibi Spain 55 K6
Ibiá Brazil 206 G6
Ibiapaba, Serra da hills Brazil 202 D2
Ibias r. Spain 54 E1
Ibicaraí Brazil 202 E5
Ibicuí Bahia Brazil 207 N1
Ibicuí Rio Grande do Sul Brazil 204 F3
Ibicuí r. Brazil 203 A9
Ibigawa Japan 91 E7
Ibimirim Brazil 202 E4
Ibina r. Dem. Rep. Congo 126 F4
Ibiporã Brazil 206 B10
Ibirá Brazil 206 D8
Ibiraçu Brazil 207 M6
Ibiranhém Brazil 207 M4
Ibitiara Brazil 202 D5
Ibitinga Brazil 206 E8
Ibiúna Brazil 206 F10
Ibiza Spain 55 M6
also spelt Eivissa
Ibiza i. Spain 55 M5
also spelt Eivissa; formerly spelt Iviza; historically known as Ebusus
Iblei, Monti mts Sicilia Italy 57 G11
İblis Burnu pt Turkey 59 J12
Ibn Buşayyiş well Saudi Arabia 105 D2
Ibn Ḥādī Saudi Arabia 104 C4
Ibotirama Brazil 202 D5
Iboundji, Mont hill Gabon 126 A5
Ibrā' Oman 105 G3
Ibra, Wadi watercourse Sudan 126 E2
Ibrāt, Wādī watercourse Iraq 109 N2
Ibresi Rus. Fed. 40 H5
Ibrī Oman 105 G3
Ibu Indon. 75 C2
Ibuhos i. Phil. 74 B1
Ibusuki Japan 91 B9
Içá r. Brazil 198 E5
Ica Peru 200 B3
Ica dept Peru 200 B3
Icabarú Venez. 199 F3
Icaiché Mex. 185 H5
Içana Brazil 199 E4
Içana r. Brazil 198 E4
Icaraí Brazil 202 E2
Icaria i. Greece see Ikaria
Icatu Brazil 202 C2
Iceberg Canyon gorge U.S.A. 183 J5
İçel Turkey 106 C3
also known as Mersin
İçel prov. Turkey 108 E1

▶Iceland country Europe 44 [inset] B2
2nd largest island in Europe. Known as Ísland in Icelandic.
europe [landscapes] → 30–31
europe [countries] → 32–35
europe [environments] → 36–37

Icem Brazil 206 D7
Ichak India 97 E4
Ichalkaranji India 94 B2
Ichchapuram India 95 E2
Ichihara Japan 91 G7
Ichilo r. Bol. 201 D4
Ichinoseki Japan 90 G5
Ichinskiy, Vulkan vol. Rus. Fed. 39 P4
Ichkeria aut. rep. Rus. Fed. see Chechenskaya Respublika
Ichkeul National Park Tunisia 57 B11
Ichnya Ukr. 41 E6
Ich'ŏn N. Korea 83 B5
Ich'ŏn S. Korea 83 B5
Ichuña Peru 200 C4
İçikler Turkey 59 J10
İçmeler Turkey 59 J12
Icó Brazil 202 E3
Iconha Brazil 207 M7
Iconium Turkey see Konya
Icosium Alg. see Algiers
Iculisma France see Angoulême
Icy Bay U.S.A. 166 A3
Icy Strait U.S.A. 166 C3
Ida, Mount N.Z. 153 E12
Idabdaba well Niger 125 H2
Idabel U.S.A. 179 D5
Idaga Hamus Eth. 104 B5
Ida Grove U.S.A. 178 D3
Idah Nigeria 125 G5
Idaho state U.S.A. 180 D3
Idaho City U.S.A. 180 D4
Idaho Falls U.S.A. 180 D4
Idalia National Park Australia 149 E5
Idanha-a-Nova Port. 54 D5
Idar India 96 B5
Idar-Oberstein Germany 48 E6
Ida Valley N.Z. 153 D13
Iday well Niger 125 H3
Iddan Somalia 128 F3
Idd el Asoda well Sudan 121 F6
Idd el Chanam Sudan 126 E2
Idd esh Shurak well Sudan 121 F5
Idefjorden inlet Norway/Sweden 45 J4
Ider Mongolia 84 C1
Ideriyn Gol r. Mongolia 84 D1
Idfina Egypt 108 B6
Idfu Egypt 121 G3
also spelt Edfu; historically known as Apollinopolis Magna
Idhān Awbārī des. Libya 120 A3
Idhān Murzūq des. Libya 120 B3
Idhra i. Greece see Ydra
Idhras, Kólpos sea chan. Greece see Ydras, Kolpos
Idi Amin Dada, Lake Dem. Rep. Congo/Uganda see Edward, Lake
Idice r. Italy 56 D4
Idiofa Dem. Rep. Congo 126 C6
Idku Egypt 121 F2
Idlib Syria 109 H2
Idlib governorate Syria 109 H2
Idra i. Greece see Ydra
Idracowra Australia 148 B5
Idre Sweden 45 K3
Idrija Slovenia 56 G2
Idrijca r. Slovenia 56 F2
Idritsa Rus. Fed. 43 J5
Idstein Germany 48 F5
Idugala Tanz. 129 B6
Idukki India 94 C4
Idutywa S. Africa 133 M9
Idyllwild U.S.A. 183 H8
Idzhevan Armenia see Ijevan
Iecava Latvia 42 F5
Iecava r. Latvia 42 E5
Iepê Brazil 206 B9
Ieper Belgium 51 I2
also spelt Ypres
Ier r. Romania 49 T8
Ierapetra Greece 59 G13
Ierissou, Kolpos b. Greece 59 E8
Ifakara Tanz. 129 C7
'Ifāl, Wādī watercourse Saudi Arabia 104 A1
also known as Afal
Ifalik atoll Micronesia 73 J5
also spelt Ifaluk; formerly known as Wilson
Ifaluk atoll Micronesia see Ifalik
Ifanadiana Madag. 131 [inset] J4
Ifanirea Madag. 131 [inset] J4
Ife Nigeria 125 G5
Ifenat Chad 120 C6
Iferouâne Niger 125 H2
Ifetesene mt. Alg. 123 G4
Iffley Australia 149 D3
Ifjord Norway 44 N1
Ifôghas, Adrar des hills Mali 125 F2
also known as Iforas, Adrar des; short form Adrar
Ifon Nigeria 125 G5
Iforas, Adrar des hills Mali see Ifôghas, Adrar des
Ifould Lake salt flat Australia 146 B2
Ifrane Morocco 122 D2
Ifumo Dem. Rep. Congo 126 D5
Ifunda Tanz. 129 B7
Igan Sarawak Malaysia 72 D6
Igan r. Sarawak Malaysia 77 E2
Iganga Uganda 128 B4
Igarapava Brazil 206 F7
Igarapé Açu Brazil 202 C2
Igarapé Grande Brazil 202 C3
Igarapé Miri Brazil 202 B2
Igaratá Brazil 207 G10
Igarité Brazil 202 D4
Igarka Rus. Fed. 39 I3
Igatpuri India 94 B2
Igbeti Nigeria 125 G4
Igboho Nigeria 125 F4
Iğdır Turkey 107 F3
Iggesund Sweden 45 L3
Ighiu Romania 58 E2
Iglesia Arg. 204 C3
Iglesias Sardegna Italy 57 A9
Igli Alg. 123 E3
Iglino Rus. Fed. 40 K5
Igloolik Canada 165 K3
Igluligaarjuk Canada see Chesterfield Inlet
'Igma, Gebel el plat. Egypt 108 E8
Ignace Canada 168 B3
Ignacio Zaragosa Mex. 184 D2
Ignacio Zaragoza Mex. 185 F4
Ignalina Lith. 42 H6
İğneada Turkey 106 A2
İğneada Burnu pt Turkey 106 B2
Igoma Tanz. 129 B6
Igombe r. Tanz. 129 A6
Igorevskaya Rus. Fed. 43 O6
Igoumenitsa Greece 59 B9
Igra Rus. Fed. 40 J4
Igrim Rus. Fed. 38 G3
Iguaçu r. Brazil 203 A8
Iguaçu, Parque Nacional do nat. park Brazil 203 A8
Iguaçu, Saltos do waterfall Arg./Brazil see Iguaçu Falls
Iguaçu Falls Arg./Brazil 204 G2
also known as Iguazú, Cataratas do or Iguaçu, Saltos do
Iguaí Brazil 202 D5
Iguaje, Mesa de hills Col. 198 C4
Iguala Mex. 185 F5
Igualada Spain 55 M3
Iguape Brazil 203 C8
Iguaraçu Brazil 206 B10
Iguarapé Brazil 207 I7
Iguatemi Brazil 203 A7
Iguatemi r. Brazil 203 A7
Iguatu Brazil 202 E3
Iguazú, Cataratas do waterfall Arg./Brazil see Iguaçu Falls
Iguazú, Parque Nacional del nat. park Arg. 204 G2
Iguéla Gabon 126 A5
Igueña Spain 54 E2
Iguetti, Sebkhet salt flat Mauritania 122 C4
Igunga Tanz. 129 B6
Iguobazuwa Nigeria 125 G5
Igusule Tanz. 129 B5
Iguvium Italy see Gubbio
Iharaña Madag. 131 [inset] K2
formerly known as Vohémar or Vohimarina
Ihavandhippolhu Atoll Maldives 94 B5
Ihbulag Mongolia 85 E3
Ihhayrhan Mongolia 85 E2
Ihiala Nigeria 125 G5
Ihirène, Oued watercourse Alg. 123 G5
Ihosy Madag. 131 [inset] J4
Ihsuuj Mongolia 85 E1
Ih Tal China 85 I3
Iida Japan 91 E7
Iide-san mt. Japan 90 F6
Iijoki r. Fin. 44 N2
Iisalmi Fin. 44 N3
Iitti Fin. 42 H1
Iiyama Japan 91 F6
Iizuka Japan 91 B8
Ijâfene des. Mauritania 122 C5
Ijara Kenya 128 D5
Ijebu-Ode Nigeria 125 F5
Ijevan Armenia 107 F2
also spelt Idzhevan
IJmuiden Neth. 48 B3
Ijnâouene well Mauritania 124 B2
Ijoubbâne des. Mali 122 D5
IJssel r. Neth. 48 C3
IJsselmeer l. Neth. 48 C3
formerly known as Zuider Zee
Ijuí Brazil 203 A9
Ijuí r. Brazil 203 A8
Ijzer r. Belgium 51 I2
also known as Yser (France)
Ikaahuk Canada see Sachs Harbour
Ikaalinen Fin. 45 M3
Ikageleng S. Africa 133 K2
Ikageng S. Africa 133 L3
Ikahavo hill Madag. 131 [inset] J3
Ikalamavony Madag. 131 [inset] J4
Ikamatua N.Z. 153 F10
Ikang Nigeria 125 H5
Ikare Nigeria 125 G5
Ikaria i. Greece 59 H11
English form Icaria
Ikast Denmark 45 J4
Ikawai N.Z. 153 E12
Ikawhenua Range mts N.Z. 152 K6
Ikeda Hokkaidō Japan 90 H3
Ikeda Tokushima Japan 91 C7
Ikeja Nigeria 125 F5
Ikela Dem. Rep. Congo 126 D5
Ikelemba r. Dem. Rep. Congo 126 C4
Ikelenge Zambia 127 E7
Ikengo Dem. Rep. Congo 126 C5
Ikéngue Gabon 126 A5
Ikere Nigeria 125 G5
also spelt Ikerre
Ikerre Nigeria see Ikere
Ikhtiman Bulg. 58 E6
Ikhutseng S. Africa 133 I5
Iki i. Japan 91 A8
Iki-Burul Rus. Fed. 41 H7
Ikimba, Lake Tanz. 128 A5
Ikire Nigeria 125 G5
Iki-suidō sea chan. Japan 91 A8
Ikla Estonia 42 F4
Ikom Nigeria 125 H5
Ikona r. Tanz. 128 B5
Ikongo Madag. 131 [inset] J4
formerly known as Fort Carnot
Ikopa r. Madag. 131 [inset] J3
Ikorodu Nigeria 125 F5
Ikosi Dem. Rep. Congo 126 E5
Ikot Ekpene Nigeria 125 G5
Ikouhaouene, Adrar mt. Alg. 123 H4
Iksan S. Korea 83 B6
formerly known as Iri
Ikungu Tanz. 129 B6
Ila Nigeria 125 G4
Ilaferh, Oued watercourse Alg. 123 F5
Ilagala Tanz. 129 A6
Ilagan Phil. 74 B2
Ilaisamis Kenya 128 C4
Ilaiyankudi India 94 C4
Ilaka Atsinanana Madag. 131 [inset] K3
Īlām Iran 100 A3
Īlām prov. Iran 100 A3
Ilam Nepal 97 E4
Ilan Taiwan 87 G3
also spelt Yilan
Ilanz Switz. 51 P6
Ilaro Nigeria 125 F5
Ilave Peru 200 C4
Iława Poland 49 Q2
Ilazārān, Kūh-e mt. Iran 100 D4
Il Bogd Uul mts Mongolia 84 C2
Ile r. China/Kazakh. 88 B3
Île-à-la-Crosse, Lac l. Canada 167 J4
Ilebo Dem. Rep. Congo 126 D6
formerly known as Port Francqui
Île-de-France admin. reg. France 51 I4
Ileje Tanz. 129 B7
Ilek Kazakh. 102 C2
Ilek r. Rus. Fed. 102 C2
also spelt Elek
Ilen r. Rep. of Ireland 47 C12
Ileret Kenya 128 C3
Ilesa Nigeria 125 G5
also spelt Ilesha
Ilesha Nigeria see Ilesa
Ilet' r. Rus. Fed. 40 I5
Ileza Rus. Fed. 40 G3
Ilford Canada 167 M3
Ilfracombe Australia 149 E4
Ilfracombe U.K. 47 H12
Ilgaz Turkey 106 C2
Ilgaz Dağları mts Turkey 106 C2
Ilgın Turkey 106 B3
Ilhabela Brazil 203 C7
Ilha Grande Brazil 199 E5
Ilha Grande, Baía da b. Brazil 207 I10
Ilha Grande, Represa resr Brazil 203 A7
Ilha Solteira, Represa resr Brazil 206 B7
Ílhavo Port. 54 C4
Ilhéus Brazil 202 E5
Ili Kazakh. see Kapchagay
Ilia Romania 58 D3
Iliamna Lake U.S.A. 164 D4
İliç Turkey 107 D3
Il'ich Kazakh. 103 G4
Il'ichevsk Azer. see Şärur
Ilici Spain see Elche
Ilig, Raas pt Somalia 128 F3
Iligan Phil. 74 C4
Iligan Bay Phil. 74 C4
Iligan Point Phil. 74 B2
Ilijaš Bos.-Herz. 56 K5
Ilimananngip Nunaa i. Greenland 165 Q2
also known as Milne Land
Ilimpeya r. Rus. Fed. 39 K3
Il'inka Kazakh. 102 D2
Il'inka Kaluzhskaya Oblast' Rus. Fed. 43 R7
Il'inka Respublika Altay Rus. Fed. 88 D1
Il'inka Respublika Buryatiya Rus. Fed. 85 E1
Il'inka Respublika Tyva Rus. Fed. 84 B1
Il'ino Rus. Fed. 43 M6
Il'inskiy Permskaya Oblast' Rus. Fed. 40 J4
Il'inskiy Respublika Kareliya Rus. Fed. 43 N1
Il'inskiy Sakhalin Rus. Fed. 82 F3
Il'insko-Podomskoye Rus. Fed. 40 H3
Il'inskoye Orlovskaya Oblast' Rus. Fed. 43 Q8
Il'inskoye Tverskaya Oblast' Rus. Fed. 43 S5
Il'inskoye Yaroslavskaya Oblast' Rus. Fed. 43 T4
Il'inskoye-Khovanskoye Rus. Fed. 43 U5
Ilin Strait Phil. 74 B3
Iliomar East Timor 75 C5
Ilion U.S.A. 177 J2
Ilirska Bistrica Slovenia 56 G3
Ilium tourist site Turkey see Troy
Iliya r. Belarus 42 I7
Iliysk Kazakh. see Kapchagay
Ilk Hungary 49 T7
Il'ka Rus. Fed. 85 F1
Ilkal India 94 C3
Ill r. France 51 N4
Illana Bay Phil. 74 B5
Illapel Chile 204 C3
Illapel r. Chile 204 C3
Illbillee, Mount hill Australia 146 B1
Ille r. France 50 E4
Illela Nigeria 125 G3
Iller r. Germany 48 G7
Illertissen Germany 48 H7
Illescas Spain 54 H4
Illescas Uruguay 204 G4
Illimani, Nevado de mt. Bol. 200 D4
Illinois r. U.S.A. 174 B4
Illinois state U.S.A. 174 B4
Illinois and Mississippi Canal U.S.A. 172 D9
Illizi Alg. 123 H4
formerly known as Fort de Polignac
Illogwa watercourse Australia 148 B5
Illueca Spain 55 J3
Ilm r. Germany 48 I4
Ilma, Lake salt flat Australia 151 D6
'Ilmān, Jabal al hill Saudi Arabia 104 D4
Il'men', Ozero l. Rus. Fed. 43 M3
Ilmenau Germany 48 H5
Ilmtal park Germany 48 I5
Ilo Peru 200 C4
Ilobu Nigeria 125 G5
Iloc i. Phil. 74 A4
Iloilo Phil. 74 B4
Iloilo Strait Phil. 74 B4
Ilomantsi Fin. 44 O3
Ilongero Tanz. 129 B6
Ilorin Nigeria 125 G4
Ilova r. Croatia 56 I3
Ilovatka Rus. Fed. 41 H6
Ilovik i. Croatia 56 G4
Ilovlya Rus. Fed. 41 G6
Ilovlya r. Rus. Fed. 41 G6
Iłowa Poland 49 M4
Il-Ponta ta' Benghajsa pt Malta see Benghisa Point
Il'pyrskiy Rus. Fed. 39 Q3
formerly known as Il'pyrskoye
Il'pyrskoye Rus. Fed. see Il'pyrskiy
Ilūkste Latvia 42 H6
Ilulissat Greenland 165 N3
also known as Jakobshavn
Ilunde Tanz. 129 B6
Ilungu Tanz. 129 B6
Ilva i. Italy see Elba, Isola d'
Il'ya Belarus 42 I7
Il'yaly Turkm. see Yylanly
Ilych r. Rus. Fed. 40 K3
Iłża r. Poland 49 S4
Imabari Japan 91 C7
Imabetsu Japan 90 G4
Imabū r. Brazil 199 G5
Imagane Japan 90 G3
Imaichi Japan 91 F6
Imala Moz. 131 H2
Imām al Ḥamzah Iraq 107 F5
Imam-baba Turkm. 103 E5
Imamoğlu Turkey 106 C3
Iman Rus. Fed. see Dal'nerechensk
Iman r. Rus. Fed. 82 D3
Imantau, Ozero l. Kazakh. 103 G1
Imari Japan 91 A8
Imasgo Burkina 125 E3
also spelt Imassogo
Imassogo Burkina see Imasgo
Imata Peru 200 C3
Imataca, Serranía de mts Venez. 199 F3
Imatra Fin. 45 O3
Imavere Estonia 42 G3
Imazu Japan 91 E7
Imbabura prov. Ecuador 198 B4
Imbaimadai Guyana 199 F3
Imbituba Brazil 203 B9
imeni 26 Bakinskikh Komissarov Azer. see 26 Bakı Komissarı
imeni 26 Bakinskikh Komissarov Turkm. 102 C5
imeni Babushkina Rus. Fed. 40 G4
imeni C. A. Niyazova Turkm. 103 E5
formerly known as imeni Chapayevka
imeni Chapayevka Turkm. see imeni C. A. Niyazova
imeni Gastello Rus. Fed. 39 O3
imeni Kalinina l. Tajik. 101 H2
imeni Karbabayeva Turkm. 102 E5
formerly known as Karrychirla
imeni Khamzy Khakikmzade Uzbek. see Khamza
imeni Kirova Kazakh. see Kopbirlik
imeni Kuybysheva Turkm. 103 E5
also known as Kuybyshev Adyndaky
imeni Petra Stuchki Latvia see Aizkraukle
imeni Poliny Osipenko Rus. Fed. 82 E1
imeni Voroshilova Kyrg. see Eshanguzar
imeni Zhelyabova Rus. Fed. 43 R3
Imeni, Serra mts Brazil 199 E4
Imese Dem. Rep. Congo 126 C4
Īmī Eth. 128 D3
Imishli Azer. see İmişli
İmişli Azer. 107 G3
also spelt Imishli
Imit Jammu and Kashmir 96 B1
Imja-do i. S. Korea 83 B6
Imjin-gang r. N. Korea/S. Korea 83 B5
Imlay U.S.A. 182 F1
Imlay City U.S.A. 173 J7
Imlili W. Sahara 122 B5
Immokalee U.S.A. 175 D7
Imo state Nigeria 125 G5
Imola Italy 56 D4
Imotski Croatia 56 J5
Imperatriz Brazil 202 C3
Imperia Italy 56 A5
Imperial Peru 200 A3
Imperial CA U.S.A. 183 I9
Imperial NE U.S.A. 178 B3
Imperial Beach U.S.A. 183 G9
Imperial Dam U.S.A. 183 J9
Imperial Valley plain U.S.A. 183 I9
Imperieuse Reef Australia 150 B3
Impfondo Congo 126 C4
Imphal India 97 G4
formerly known as Manipur
İmralı Adası i. Turkey 58 J8
Imrān Yemen 104 D5
İmroz Turkey 106 A2
İmroz i. Turkey see Gökçeada
Imrun Turkey see Pütürge
Imsil S. Korea 83 B6
Imst Austria 48 H8
Imtān Syria 109 H5
Imuris Mex. 184 C2
Imuruan Bay Phil. 74 A4
Imzouren Morocco 54 H9
In r. Rus. Fed. 82 D2
Ina Japan 91 E7
Ina r. Poland 49 L2
I-n-Abangharit well Niger 125 G2
Inabu Japan 91 E7
In Afaleleh well Alg. 123 H5
Inagauan Phil. 74 A4
Inago Moz. 131 H2
Inahuaya Peru 200 B1
Inajá Brazil 202 E4
Inaja, Serra do hills Brazil 201 H2
I-n-Akhmed well Mali 125 E2
I-n-Alchi well Mali 125 E2
I-n-Aleï well Mali 124 E2
Inamba-jima i. Japan see Inanba-jima
Inambari Peru 200 C3
Inambari r. Peru 200 C3
I-n-Ameddé well Mali 124 D2
In Aménas Alg. 123 H3
In Amguel Alg. 123 G5
Inanba-jima i. Japan 91 F8
also spelt Inamba-jima
Inanda S. Africa 133 O6
Inangahua Junction N.Z. 153 F9
Inanwatan Indon. 73 H7
Iñapari Peru 200 C2
Inari Fin. 44 N1
also known as Aanaar or Anár
Inarigda Rus. Fed. 39 K3
Inarijärvi l. Fin. 44 N1
Inarijoki r. Fin./Norway 44 N1
I-n-Arouinat well Niger 125 G2
I-n-Atankarer well Mali 125 F2
Inauini r. Brazil 200 D2
Inawashiro-ko l. Japan 90 G6
I-n-Azaoua well Alg. 123 G4
In-Azaoua well Alg. 123 G5
I-n-Azaoua watercourse Niger 125 G1
In Azar well Libya 120 A2
In Azâwah well Libya 120 A3
I-n-Azerraf well Mali 125 F2
In Belbel Alg. 123 F4
Inca Spain 55 N5
Inca de Oro Chile 204 C2
İnce Burnu pt Turkey 58 I8
İnce Burun pt Turkey 106 C2
İnceler Turkey 59 K11
Inchbonnie N.Z. 153 F10
Incheh Iran 100 D2
Inch'inī Terara mt. Eth. 128 C3
Inchiri admin. reg. Mauritania 122 B5
Inch'ŏn S. Korea 83 B5
also known as Jinsen; formerly known as Chemulpo
Inchope Moz. 131 G3
I-n-Choumaguene well Mali 125 F2
Incirli Turkey see Karasu
İncirlik Turkey 108 G1
Incomati r. Moz. 131 G5
Incudine, Monte mt. France 56 B7
Inčukalns Latvia 42 F4
Indaiá r. Brazil 207 H5
Indaiá Grande r. Brazil 206 A6
Indaiatuba Brazil 206 F10
Indalsälven r. Sweden 44 L3
Indalstø Norway 45 I3
Indargarh Madhya Pradesh India 96 C4
Indargarh Rajasthan India 96 C4
Inda Silasē Eth. 128 C1
Indawgyi, Lake Myanmar 78 B2
Indé Mex. 184 D3
I-n-Délimane well Mali 125 F3
Independence CA U.S.A. 182 F5
Independence IA U.S.A. 174 B3
Independence KS U.S.A. 178 D4
Independence KY U.S.A. 176 A7
Independence MO U.S.A. 178 D4
Independence VA U.S.A. 176 D9
Independence WI U.S.A. 172 B6
Independence Fjord inlet Greenland 165 Q1
Independence Mountains U.S.A. 180 C4
Independencia Bol. 200 D4
Independența Romania 58 I4
Independența Romania 58 J5
Independența Romania 58 I3
Inder China 85 I2
also known as Jalaid
Inder, Ozero salt l. Kazakh. 102 B2
Inderborskiy Kazakh. 102 B2
Indi India 94 C2

▶India country Asia 93 E6
2nd most populous country in the world and in Asia. 3rd largest country in Asia and 7th in the world. Known as Bharat in Hindi.
world [countries] → 10–11
world [population] → 22–23
asia [landscapes] → 62–63
asia [countries] → 64–67

Indian r. U.S.A. 172 G4
Indiana U.S.A. 176 F5
Indiana state U.S.A. 174 C3

▶Indianapolis U.S.A. 174 C4
State capital of Indiana.

Indian Cabins Canada 167 G3
Indian Desert India/Pak. see Thar Desert
Indian Fields U.S.A. 176 B8
Indian Harbour Canada 169 J2
Indian Head Canada 167 K5
Indian Lake U.S.A. 177 K2
Indian Lake l. MI U.S.A. 172 G5
Indian Lake l. NY U.S.A. 177 K2
Indian Lake l. OH U.S.A. 176 B5
Indian Lake l. PA U.S.A. 176 G5

▶Indian Ocean 218 M7
3rd largest ocean in the world.
oceans [features] → 210–211

Indianola IA U.S.A. 174 A3
Indianola MS U.S.A. 175 B5
Indian Peak U.S.A. 183 K3
Indian Springs U.S.A. 183 I5

index

J

Indian Wells U.S.A. 183 N6
Indiara Brazil 206 C4
Indiaroba Brazil 202 E4
Indibir Eth. 128 C2
Indiga Rus. Fed. 40 I2
Indigirka r. Rus. Fed. 39 O2
Indigskaya Guba b. Rus. Fed. 40 I2
Inđija Vojvodina, Srbija Yugo. 58 B3
Indin Myanmar 78 A3
Indin Lake Canada 167 H1
Indio r. Nicaragua 186 C5
Indio U.S.A. 183 H8
Indispensable Reefs Solomon Is 145 F3
Indo-China reg. Asia 72 C3
Indomanka r. Rus. Fed. 43 S1

▶Indonesia country Asia 72 D8
4th most populous country in the world and Asia. 5th largest country in Asia. Formerly known as Dutch East Indies.
world [population] ▶ 22–23
asia [countries] ▶ 64–67

Indore India 96 B5
Indragiri r. Indon. 76 C3
Indramayu Indon. 77 E4
Indramayu, Tanjung pt Indon. 77 E4
Indrapura, Gunung vol. Indon. see Kerinci, Gunung
Indrapura, Tanjung pt Indon. 76 C3
Indravati r. India 95 D2
Indre r. France 51 G5
Indulkana Australia 146 B1
Indur India see Nizamabad
Indura Belarus 42 E8
Indurti India 94 C2
Indus r. China/Pakistan 89 C5
also known as Shiquan He
Indus, Mouths of the Pak. 101 F5
Indwe S. Africa 133 L8
Indwe r. S. Africa 133 L9
Indzhe Voyvoda Bulg. 58 I6
In Ebeggi well Alg. 123 G5
İnebolu Turkey 106 C2
I-n-Échaï well Mali 123 E5
İnegöl Turkey 106 B2
In Ekker Alg. 123 G4
Inerie vol. Indon. 75 B5
Ineu Romania 58 C2
Inevi Turkey see Cihanbeyli
Inez U.S.A. 176 C8
In Ezzane well Alg. 123 H5
Infanta, Cape S. Africa 132 E11
Infantas Col. 187 E6
Infantes Spain see Villanueva de los Infantes
Infernao, Cachoeira waterfall Brazil 201 E2
Infielés, Punta pt Chile 204 C2
Infiernillo, Presa resr Mex. 185 E5
Infiesto Spain 54 F1
Ing, Mae Nam r. Thai. 78 C3
Inga Dem. Rep. Congo 127 B6
Ingå Fin. 45 N3
Ingabu Myanmar 78 A4
Ingal Niger 125 G2
Ingallanna watercourse Australia 148 B4
Ingalls, Mount U.S.A. 182 D2
Inganda Dem. Rep. Congo 126 D5
Ingelstad Sweden 45 K4
Ingende Dem. Rep. Congo 126 C5
Ingeniero Guillermo Nueva Juárez Arg. 201 E5
Ingeniero Jacobacci Arg. 204 C6
Ingenika r. Canada 166 E3
Ingenio r. Peru 200 B3
Ingersoll Canada 173 M7
Ingessana Hills Sudan 128 B2
Ingettolgoy Mongolia 84 D1
Ingezi Zimbabwe see Ngezi
Ingham Australia 149 E3
Ingichka Uzbek. 103 F5
formerly known as Rudnik Ingichka
Inglefield Land reg. Greenland 165 L2
Inglewood Qld Australia 147 F2
Inglewood Vic. Australia 147 D4
Inglewood N.Z. 152 I7
Inglewood U.S.A. 182 F8
Ingoda r. Rus. Fed. 85 G1
Ingoka Pum mt. Myanmar 78 B2
Ingolf Fjord inlet Greenland 165 R1
Ingolstadt Germany 48 I7
Ingomar Australia 146 B2
Ingonish Canada 169 I4
Ingraj Bazar India 97 F4
formerly known as English Bazar
Ingram VA U.S.A. 176 F9
Ingram WI U.S.A. 172 C5
Ingray Lake Canada 167 G1
Ingrid Christensen Coast Antarctica 223 F2
I-n-Guezzam Alg. 123 G6
I-n-Guita well Mali 125 F3
Ingulets Ukr. see Inhulets'
Ingulsvatn Norway 44 K2
Ingushetia aut. rep. Rus. Fed. see Ingushetiya, Respublika
Ingushetiya, Respublika aut. rep. Rus. Fed. 41 H8
English form Ingushetia or Ingush Republic
Ingush Republic aut. rep. Rus. Fed. see Ingushetiya, Respublika
Ingwavuma S. Africa 133 Q4
Ingwavuma r. Swaziland see Ngwavuma
Ingwe Zambia 127 E8
Inhaca Moz. 133 Q2
Inhaca, Península pen. Moz. 131 G5
Inhafenga Moz. 131 G4
Inhambane Moz. 131 G4
Inhambane prov. Moz. 131 G4
Inhambupe Brazil 202 E4
Inhamitanga Moz. 131 G3
Inhapim Brazil 203 D6
Inharrime Moz. 131 G5
Inhassoro Moz. 131 G4
Inhaúmas Brazil 202 C5
I-n-Hihaou, Adrar hills Alg. 123 F5
Inhobim Brazil 207 M2
Inhulets' Ukr. 41 E7
also spelt Ingulets
Inhumas Brazil 206 D3
Inielika vol. Indon. 75 B5
Iniesta Spain 55 J5
Inimutaba Brazil 207 I5
Iniö Fin. 42 C1
Inírida r. Col. 198 E4
Inis Rep. of Ireland see Ennis
Inis Córthaidh Rep. of Ireland see Enniscorthy
Inishark i. Rep. of Ireland 47 B10
Inishbofin i. Rep. of Ireland 47 B10
Inishmore i. Rep. of Ireland 47 C10
Inishmurray i. Rep. of Ireland 47 D9
Inishowen pen. Rep. of Ireland 47 E8
Inishowen Head Rep. of Ireland 47 F8
Inishtrahull i. Rep. of Ireland 46 E8
Inishturk i. Rep. of Ireland 47 B10
Injgan Sum China 85 H2
Injibara Eth. 128 C2
Injune Australia 149 F5
Inkardar'ya Kazakh. 103 F3
I-n-Kerchef well Mali 124 D2
Inkerman Australia 149 D3
Inklin Canada 166 C3
Inklin r. Canada 166 C3
Inkylap Turkm. 103 E5
Inland Kaikoura Range mts N.Z. 153 H10
Inland Sea Japan see Seto-naikai
Inlet U.S.A. 177 K2
I-n-Milach well Mali 125 E2
Inn r. Europe 48 H9
Innaanganeq c. Greenland 165 M2
also known as York, Kap
Innai Japan 91 B8
Innamincka Australia 146 D1
Innamincka Regional Reserve nature res. Australia 146 D1
Inndyr Norway 44 K2
Inner Mongolia aut. reg. China see Nei Mongol Zizhiqu
Inner Sound sea chan. U.K. 46 G6
Innes National Park Australia 146 C3
Innisfail Australia 149 E3
Innisfail Canada 167 H4
Innokent'yevka Rus. Fed. 82 C2
Innoshima Japan 91 C7
Innsbruck Austria 48 I8
Innuksuak r. Canada 168 E1
Inny r. Rep. of Ireland 47 E10
Ino Japan 91 C8
Inobonto Indon. 75 C2
Inocência Brazil 206 B6
Inongo Dem. Rep. Congo 126 C5
Inoni Congo 126 B5
Inonias Peru 198 C5
İnönü Turkey 106 B3
Inosu Col. 198 D1
Inoucdjouac Canada see Inukjuak
Inovec mt. Slovakia 49 P7
Inowrocław Poland 49 P3
historically known as Hohensalza
Inquisivi Bol. 200 D4
In Salah Alg. 123 F4
also spelt Ain Salah

▶Inscription, Cape Australia 151 A5
Most westerly point of Oceania.

Insein Myanmar 78 B4
Insel Usedom park Germany 49 L2
Ińsko Poland 49 M2
In Sokki, Oued watercourse Alg. 123 F3
Insterburg Rus. Fed. see Chernyakhovsk
Instruch r. Rus. Fed. 42 C7
Însurăţei Romania 58 I4
Insuza r. Zimbabwe 131 E3
Inta Rus. Fed. 40 L2
I-n-Tadéra well Niger 125 H1
I-n-Tadrof well Niger 125 H2
In Takoufi, Oued watercourse Alg. 123 G4
I-n-Tassit well Mali 125 F2
I-n-Tebezas Mali 125 F2
I-n-Téguift well Mali 125 F2
I-n-Telli well Mali 125 F2
I-n-Témegui well Mali 125 F2
İntepe Turkey 59 H8
Interamna Italy see Teramo
Interlaken Switz. 51 N6
International Falls U.S.A. 174 A1
Interview Island India 95 G3
Intich'o Eth. 104 B5
Întorsura Buzăului Romania 58 H3
I-n-Touft well Mali 125 F2
Intracoastal Waterway canal U.S.A. 179 D6
Intutu Peru 198 C5
Inubō-zaki pt Japan 91 G7
Inukai Japan 91 B8
Inukjuak Canada 168 E1
formerly known as Port Harrison; formerly spelt Inoucdjouac
Inútil, Bahía b. Chile 205 C9
Inuvik Canada 164 F3
Inuya r. Peru 200 B2
In'va r. Rus. Fed. 40 K4
Inveraray U.K. 46 G7
Inverbervie U.K. 46 J7
Invercargill N.Z. 153 C14
Inverell Australia 147 F2
Inverleigh Australia 149 D3
Inverness Canada 169 I4
Inverness U.K. 46 H6
Inverness CA U.S.A. 182 B3
Inverness FL U.S.A. 175 D6
Inverurie U.K. 46 J6
Inverway Australia 148 A3
Investigator Channel Myanmar 79 B5
Investigator Group is Australia 146 B3
Investigator Strait Australia 146 C3
Inwood U.S.A. 176 G6
Inxu r. S. Africa 133 M8
Inya Rus. Fed. 88 D1
Inyanga Zimbabwe see Nyanga
Inyanga Mountains Zimbabwe 131 G3
Inyanga National Park Zimbabwe see Nyanga National Park
Inyangani mt. Zimbabwe 131 G3
Inyati Zimbabwe see Nyathi
Inyazura Zimbabwe see Nyazura
Inyokern U.S.A. 182 G6
Inyo Mountains U.S.A. 182 F4
Inyonga Tanz. 129 B6
Inza Rus. Fed. 41 H5
Inzer r. Rus. Fed. 40 K5
Inzhavino Rus. Fed. 41 G5
Ioannina Greece 59 B9
also spelt Yannina
Ioanninon, Limni l. Greece 59 B9
Iôf di Montasio mt. Italy 56 F2
Iō-jima i. Kazan-rettō Japan 73 J2
also known as Iō-tō; also spelt Iwo Jima
Iō-jima i. Japan 91 B9
also spelt Iō-shima
Iokanga r. Rus. Fed. 40 F2
Iola KS U.S.A. 178 D4
Iola WI U.S.A. 172 D6
Iolgo, Khrebet mts Rus. Fed. 88 D1
Iolotan' Turkm. see Yeloten
Iona Angola 127 B9
Iona Canada 169 I4
Iona i. U.K. 46 F7
Iona, Parque Nacional do nat. park Angola 127 B9
Iona Abbey tourist site U.K. 46 F7
Ione U.S.A. 182 G3
Ioneşti Romania 58 F4
Ionia U.S.A. 173 H8
Ionian Islands admin. reg. Greece see Ionioi Nisoi
Ionian Islands reg. Greece 59 A9
also known as Ionioi Nisoi
Ionian Sea Greece/Italy 59 A11
Ionioi Nisoi admin. reg. Greece 59 A10
English form Ionian Islands
Ionioi Nisoi reg. Greece see Ionian Islands
Iony, Ostrov i. Rus. Fed. 39 O4
Iordan Uzbek. 101 G1
also spelt Yordon; formerly spelt Yardan
Iori r. Georgia 107 F2
Ios Greece 59 G12
Ios i. Greece 59 G12
Iō-shima i. Japan see Iō-jima
Iō-tō i. Japan see Iō-jima
Iouîk Mauritania 124 A2
Iowa r. U.S.A. 174 B3
Iowa state U.S.A. 174 A3
Iowa City U.S.A. 174 B3
Iowa Falls U.S.A. 174 A3
Ipameri Brazil 206 E4
Ipanema Brazil 203 D6
Ipanema r. Brazil 202 E4
Iparía Peru 200 B2
Ipatinga Brazil 203 D6
Ipatovo Rus. Fed. 41 G7
Ipauçu Brazil 206 D10
Ipeiros admin. reg. Greece 59 B9
English form Epirus; also spelt Ípiros
Ipeľ r. Slovakia 49 P8
Ipelegeng S. Africa 133 J4
Ipiaçu Brazil 206 D5
Ipiales Col. 198 B4
Ipiaú Brazil 202 E5
Ipirá Brazil 202 E5
Ipiranga Amazonas Brazil 198 D5
Ipiranga Amazonas Brazil 199 F6
Ípiros admin. reg. Greece see Ipeiros
Ipixuna Brazil 200 B1
Ipixuna r. Amazonas Brazil 199 F6
Ipixuna r. Amazonas Brazil 200 B1
Ipoh Malaysia 76 C1
Ipoly r. Hungary/Slovakia 49 P8
Ipopeng S. Africa 133 J6
Iporá Brazil 206 B3
Ippy Cent. Afr. Rep. 126 D3
İpsala Turkey 58 H8
Ipswich Australia 147 G1
Ipswich U.K. 47 N11
Ipswich U.S.A. 178 C2
Ipu Brazil 202 D3
Ipuã Brazil 206 E7
Ipueiras Brazil 202 D3
Ipuh Indon. 76 C3
Ipupiara Brazil 202 D4
Iput' r. Rus. Fed. 43 M9

▶Iqaluit Canada 165 M3
Territorial capital of Nunavut. Formerly known as Frobisher Bay.

Iqe He r. China 84 B4
Iquê r. Brazil 201 F3
also known as Languiaru
Iquique Chile 200 C5
Iquiri r. Brazil see Ituxi
Iquitos Peru 198 C5
Ira Banda Cent. Afr. Rep. 126 D3
formerly spelt Hyrra Banda
Iracoubo Fr. Guiana 199 H3
Īrafshān reg. Iran 101 E5
Irai Brazil 203 A8
Irai Island P.N.G. 149 F1
Irakleia Greece 58 E7
Irakleia i. Greece 59 G12
also spelt Iráklia
Irakleio Greece see Iraklion
Irakleiou, Kolpos b. Greece 59 G13
Iráklia i. Greece see Irakleia
Iraklion Greece 59 G13
also spelt Heraklion or Irakleio; historically known as Candia
Irala Para. 201 G6
Iramaia Brazil 202 D5
▶Iran country Asia 100 C4
formerly known as Persia
asia [countries] ▶ 64–67
Iran, Pegunungan mts Indon. 77 F2
Īrānshāh Iran 100 A2
Īrānshahr Iran 101 E5
Irapuato Mex. 185 E4
▶Iraq country Asia 107 E4
asia [countries] ▶ 64–67
Irarrarene reg. Alg. 123 G4
Irasville U.S.A. 177 M1
Iratapuru r. Brazil 199 H5
Irati Brazil 203 B8
Irati r. Spain 55 J2
Irayel' Rus. Fed. 40 J2
Irazu, Volcán vol. Costa Rica 186 C5
Irbe r. Latvia 42 D4
Irbes šaurums sea chan. Estonia/Latvia see Irbe Strait
Irbe Strait Estonia/Latvia 42 D4
also known as Irbe väin or Irbes šaurums or Kura kurk or Sõrve väin
Irbe väin sea chan. Estonia/Latvia see Irbe Strait
Irbid Jordan 108 G5
Irbil Iraq see Arbīl
Irbit Rus. Fed. 38 G4
Irebu Dem. Rep. Congo 126 C5
Irecê Brazil 202 D4
Iregua r. Spain 55 I2

▶Ireland i. International Feature 47 C11
4th largest island in Europe.
europe [landscapes] ▶ 30–31

▶Ireland, Republic of country Europe 47 D10
known as Éire in Irish; formerly known as Irish Free State
europe [countries] ▶ 32–35
Iren' r. Rus. Fed. 40 K4
Irene Arg. 204 E5
Irene, Mount N.Z. 153 B13
Ireng r. Guyana/Venez. 199 G4
Iretama Brazil 206 A11
Irgiz Kazakh. 103 E2
also spelt Yrghyz
Irgiz r. Kazakh. 102 E2
Irharrhar, Oued watercourse Alg. 123 G3
Irharrhar, Oued watercourse Alg. 123 G5
Irherm Morocco 122 C3
Irhil M'Goun mt. Morocco 122 D3
Irhzer Ediessane watercourse Alg. 120 A3
Iri S. Korea see Iksan
Irian, Teluk b. Indon. see Cenderawasih, Teluk
Irian Barat prov. Indon. see Irian Jaya
Irian Jaya prov. Indon. 75 D3
also known as West Papua; formerly known as Dutch New Guinea or Irian Barat or West Irian
Irian Jaya reg. Indon. 73 I7
Iriba Chad 120 D6
Iricoumé, Serra hills Brazil 199 G4
Īrī Dāgh mt. Iran 100 A2
Iriga Phil. 74 B3
Iriklinskiy Rus. Fed. 102 D2
Iriklinskoye Vodokhranilische resr Rus. Fed. 102 D2
Iringa Tanz. 129 B6
Iringa admin. reg. Tanz. 129 B7
Iriri r. Brazil 199 H5
Iriri Novo r. Brazil 202 A4
Irish Free State country Europe see Ireland, Republic of
Irish Sea Rep. of Ireland/U.K. 47 G10
Irituia Brazil 202 C2
'Irj well Saudi Arabia 105 E2
Irkeshtam Kyrg. see Erkech-Tam
Irkut r. Rus. Fed. 84 D1
Irkutsk Rus. Fed. 80 G2
Irkutskaya Oblast' admin. div. Rus. Fed. 84 D1
English form Irkutsk Oblast
Irkutsk Oblast admin. div. Rus. Fed. see Irkutskaya Oblast'
Irma U.S.A. 172 D5
Irmak Turkey 106 C3
Irminio r. Sicilia Italy 57 G12
Irmo U.S.A. 175 D5
Irnijärvi l. Fin. 44 O2
Iro, Lac l. Chad 126 C2
Iroise, Mer d' g. France 50 B4
Iron Baron Australia 146 C3
Iron Bridge Canada 173 J4
Irondequoit U.S.A. 176 H2
Iron Junction U.S.A. 172 A3
Iron Knob Australia 146 C3
Iron Mountain U.S.A. 172 E5
Iron Mountain mt. U.S.A. 183 K4
Iron Range National Park Australia 149 D2
Iron River MI U.S.A. 172 E4
Iron River WI U.S.A. 172 B4
Ironton MO U.S.A. 174 B4
Ironton OH U.S.A. 176 C7
Ironwood U.S.A. 172 C4
Iroquois Canada 177 J1
Iroquois r. U.S.A. 172 F9
Iroquois Falls Canada 168 D3
Irosin Phil. 74 C3
Irō-zaki pt Japan 91 F7
Irpen' Ukr. see Irpin'
Irpin' Ukr. 41 D6
also spelt Irpen'
Īrqah Yemen 105 D5
'Irq al Ḩarūrī des. Saudi Arabia 105 D2
Irq al Maẓhūr des. Saudi Arabia 104 C2
'Irq Banbān des. Saudi Arabia 105 D2
'Irq Jahām des. Saudi Arabia 105 D2
'Irq Subay des. Saudi Arabia 104 C3
Irramarne Aboriginal Land res. Australia 148 C4
Irrawaddy admin. div. Myanmar 78 A4
Irrawaddy r. Myanmar 78 A5
also spelt Ayeyarwady or Erawadi or Eyawadi
Irrawaddy, Mouths of the Myanmar 79 A5
Irsarybaba, Gory hills Turkm. 102 C4
also known as Ärsarybaba Erezi
Irshad Pass Afgh./Pak. 101 H2

▶Irtysh r. Kazakh./Rus. Fed. 38 G3
5th longest river in Asia and 10th in the world. Part of the 2nd longest river in Asia (Ob'-Irtysh). Also spelt Ertis.
asia [landscapes] ▶ 62–63

Irtyshsk Kazakh. 103 H1
also known as Ertis; formerly known as Irtyshskoye
Irtyshskoye Kazakh. see Irtyshsk
Iruma Japan 91 F7
Irumu Dem. Rep. Congo 126 F4
Irún Spain 55 J1
Iruña Spain see Pamplona
Irupana Bol. 200 D4
Irvine U.K. 46 H8
Irvine CA U.S.A. 182 G8
Irvine KY U.S.A. 176 B8
Irvine Glacier Antarctica 222 T2
Irving U.S.A. 179 C5
Irwin r. Australia 151 A6
Irwinton U.S.A. 175 D5
Isa Nigeria 125 G3
'Īsá, Ra's pt Yemen 104 C5
Isaac r. Australia 149 F4
Isaac Lake Canada 166 F4
Isabela Negros Phil. 74 B4
Isabela Phil. 74 B5
Isabela, Cabo c. Dom. Rep. 187 F3
Isabelia, Cordillera mts Nicaragua 186 B4
Isabella U.S.A. 172 B3
Isabella Indian Reservation res. U.S.A. 173 I7
Isabella Lake U.S.A. 182 F6
Isabelle, Point U.S.A. 172 F3
İsabey Turkey 59 K11
Isaccea Romania 58 J3
Isachenko, Ostrov i. Rus. Fed. 39 I2
Isachsen, Cape Canada 165 I2
Ísafjarðardjúp est. Iceland 44 [inset] B2
Ísafjörður Iceland 44 [inset] B2
Isagarh India 96 C4
Isahaya Japan 91 B8
Isai Kalat Pak. 101 F5
Isà Khel Pak. 101 G3
Isakogorka Rus. Fed. 40 G2
Isakovo Rus. Fed. 43 P6
Işalniţa Romania 58 E4
Isana r. Col. 198 D4
Isanga Dem. Rep. Congo 126 D5
Isangano National Park Zambia 127 F7
Isaouane-n-Tifernine des. Alg. 123 G4
Isar r. Germany 48 J7
Isbister U.K. 46 K3
Íscar Spain 54 G3
Iscayachi Bol. 200 D5
Ischia Italy 57 F8
Ischia, Isola d' i. Italy 57 F8
Isdell r. Australia 150 D3
Ise Japan 91 E7
formerly known as Ujiyamada
Isefjord b. Denmark 45 J5
Iseke Tanz. 129 B6
Isel r. Austria 49 J9
Isengi Dem. Rep. Congo 126 E4
Iseo, Lago d' l. Italy 56 C3
Isère r. France 51 K8
Isère, Pointe pt Fr. Guiana 199 H3
Iserlohn Germany 48 E4
Isernhagen Germany 48 G3
Isernia Italy 56 G7
historically known as Aesernia
Ise-shima National Park Japan 91 E7
Ise-wan b. Japan 91 E7
Iseyin Nigeria 125 F5
Isfahan Iran see Eşfahān
Isfana Kyrg. 103 G5
Isfandaqeh Iran see Sangū'īyeh
Isfara Tajik. 101 G1
Isherim, Gora mt. Rus. Fed. 40 K3
Isherton Guyana 199 G4
Isheyevka Rus. Fed. 41 I5
Ishikari Japan 90 G3
Ishikari-gawa r. Japan 90 G3
Ishikari-wan b. Japan 90 G3
Ishikawa pref. Japan 91 E6
Ishim r. Kazakh./Rus. Fed. 103 F1
also known as Esil
Ishim Rus. Fed. 38 G4
Ishimbay Rus. Fed. 102 D1
Ishinomaki Japan 90 G5
Ishioka Japan 91 G6
Ishizuchi-san mt. Japan 91 C8
Ishkaft, Jabal hill Iraq 109 N1
Ishkoshim Tajik. 101 G2
Ishkuman Jammu and Kashmir 96 B1
Ishnya Rus. Fed. 43 U4
Ishpeming U.S.A. 172 F4
Ishtikhon Uzbek. see Ishtykhan
Ishtragh Afgh. 101 G2
Ishtykhan Uzbek. 103 F5
also spelt Ishtikhon
Ishurdi Bangl. 97 F4
Isiboro r. Bol. 200 D3
Isiboro Sécure, Parque Nacional nat. park Bol. 200 D4
Isigny-sur-Mer France 50 E3
Işıklı Turkey 106 B3
Isil'kul' Rus. Fed. 38 H4
Isimbira Tanz. 129 B6
Isinliví Ecuador 198 B5
Isiolo Kenya 128 C4
Isipingo S. Africa 133 O6
Isiro Dem. Rep. Congo 126 E4
formerly known as Paulis
Isisford Australia 149 E5
Iskabad Canal Afgh. 101 F2
Iskateley Rus. Fed. 40 J2
İskele Cyprus see Trikomon
İskenderun Turkey 106 D3
historically known as Alexandretta
İskenderun Körfezi b. Turkey 106 C3
İskilip Turkey 106 C2
Iski-Naukat Kyrg. see Eski-Nookat
Iskine Kazakh. 102 C3
Iskitim Rus. Fed. 80 C2
Iskra Rus. Fed. 43 U7
Iskŭr r. Bulg. 58 F5
Iskŭr, Yazovir resr Bulg. 58 E6
Iskushuban Somalia 128 F2
Iskut r. Canada 166 D3
Isla r. U.K. 46 I7
Isla, Wâdi watercourse Egypt 108 E9
Isla Cristina Spain 54 D7
Isla de Salamanca, Parque Nacional nat. park Col. 198 C2
Isla Gorge National Park Australia 149 F5
İslahiye Turkey 107 D3
Islamabad Jammu and Kashmir see Anantnag

▶Islamabad Pak. 101 H3
Capital of Pakistan.

Isla Magdalena, Parque Nacional nat. park Chile 205 B7
Islamkot Pak. 101 G5
Islamorada U.S.A. 175 D7
Islampur India 97 E4
Island r. Canada 166 F2
Ísland country Europe see Iceland
Island Bay Phil. 74 A4
Island Lagoon salt flat Australia 146 C2
Island Lake Canada 167 M4
Island Lake l. Canada 167 M4
Island Lake l. U.S.A. 172 A3
Island Magee pen. U.K. 47 G9
Island Pond U.S.A. 177 N1
Islands, Bay of N.Z. 152 I3
Islas Baleares aut. comm. Spain 55 N5
Islas de Bahá, Parque Nacional nat. park Hond. 186 B3
Islay i. U.K. 46 F8
Islaz Romania 58 F5
Isle r. France 50 F8

▶Isle of Man i. Irish Sea 47 H9
United Kingdom Crown Dependency.
europe [countries] ▶ 32–35

Isle of Wight U.S.A. 177 I9
Isle Royale National Park U.S.A. 172 E3
Isluga, Parque Nacional nat. park Chile 200 C4
Ismail Ukr. see Izmayil
Ismâ'ilîya Egypt 121 G2
also spelt Al Ismā'īlīyah
Ismâ'ilîya governorate Egypt 108 D7
Ismâ'ilîya, Tir'at el canal Egypt 108 D7
Ismailly Azer. see İsmayıllı
İsmayıllı Azer. 107 G2
also spelt Ismailly
Isna Egypt 121 G3
Isoanala Madag. 131 [inset] J4
Isojoki Fin. 45 M3
Isoka Zambia 129 B7
Isokylä Fin. 44 N2
Isokyrö Fin. 44 M3
Isola del Liri Italy 56 F7
Isola di Capo Rizzuto Italy 57 J10
Isonzo r. Italy 56 F3
also known as Soča
Isopa Tanz. 129 A7
Isorana Madag. 131 [inset] J4
Iso-Syöte hill Fin. 44 N2
Ispahan Iran see Eşfahān
Isparta Turkey 106 B3
also known as Hamitabat
Isperikh Bulg. 58 H5
Ispica Sicilia Italy 57 G12
İspir Turkey 107 E2
Ispisar Tajik. see Khŭjand
▶Israel country Asia 108 F5
spelt Yizra'el in Hebrew or Isra'īl in Arabic
asia [countries] ▶ 64–67
Israelândia Brazil 206 C3
Israelite Bay Australia 151 C7
Isra'īl country Asia see Israel
Issa Croatia see Vis
Issa r. Rus. Fed. 43 J5
Issano Guyana 199 G3
Issia Côte d'Ivoire 124 D5
Issimu Indon. 75 B2
Issin tourist site Iraq 107 F5
Issoire France 51 J7
Issoudun France 51 H6
Issuna Tanz. 129 B6
Is-sur-Tille France 51 L5
Issyk-Kul' Kyrg. see Balykchy
Issyk-Kul', Ozero salt l. Kyrg. see Ysyk-Köl
Issyk-Kul Oblast admin. div. Kyrg. see Ysyk-Köl
Issyk-Kul'skaya Oblast' admin. div. Kyrg. see Ysyk-Köl
Ista r. Rus. Fed. 43 R8
Iştabl 'Antar Saudi Arabia 104 B2
Iştablāt tourist site Iraq 107 E4
İstanbul Turkey 106 B2
historically known as Byzantium or Constantinople
İstanbul prov. Turkey 58 J7
İstanbul Boğazı sea chan. Turkey see Bosporus
İstanbul Boğazı strait Turkey see Bosporus
Isten dombja hill Hungary 49 N9
Īstgāh-e Eznā Iran 100 B3
Isthilart Arg. 204 F3
Istiaia Greece 59 E10
Istik r. Tajik. 101 H2
Istmina Col. 198 B3
Istok Kosovo, Srbija Yugo. 58 B6
Istokpoga, Lake U.S.A. 175 D7
Istra pen. Croatia see Istria
Istra Rus. Fed. 43 R6
Istres France 51 K9
Istria pen. Croatia 56 F3
also spelt Istra
Istria Romania 58 J4
Istriţa, Dealul hill Romania 58 H3
Ist'ya r. Rus. Fed. 43 V7
Isuela r. Spain 55 J3
Iswaripur Bangl. 97 F5
Iswepe S. Africa 133 O3
Isyangulovo Rus. Fed. 102 D1
Isyk Kazakh. 103 I4
Itabaianinha Brazil 202 E4
Itabapoana Brazil 207 M8
Itabapoana r. Brazil 207 M8
Itaberá Brazil 206 D10
Itaberaba Brazil 202 D5
Itaberaí Brazil 206 D3
Itabira Brazil 203 D6
Itabirito Brazil 203 D7
Itaboca Brazil 199 F6
Itaboraí Brazil 207 K9
Itabuna Brazil 202 E5
Itacaiuna r. Brazil 202 B3
Itacajá Brazil 202 C4
Itacambira Brazil 207 J4
Itacarambi Brazil 202 C5
Itacaré Brazil 202 E5
Itacayunas, Serra hills Brazil 201 H1
Itacoatiara Brazil 199 G5
Itacuaí r. Brazil 198 D6
Itaetê Brazil 202 D5
Itagmatana Iran see Hamadān
Itagmirim Brazil 207 N3
Itaguaçu Brazil 203 D6
Itaguaí Brazil 207 J9
Itaguajé Brazil 206 B9
Itaguara Brazil 207 I7
Itahuania Peru 200 C3
Itaí Brazil 206 D10
Itaim r. Brazil 202 D3
Itaiópolis Brazil 203 B8
Itaipu, Represa de resr Brazil 203 A8
Itäisen Suomenlahden kansallispuisto nat. park Fin. 45 N3
Itaituba Brazil 199 G6
Itajá Brazil 206 B6
Itajaí Brazil 203 B8
Itajobi Brazil 206 D8
Itajubá Brazil 203 C7
Itaju de Colônia Brazil 207 N2
Itajuipe Brazil 202 E5
Itaki India 97 E5
Itala Nature Reserve S. Africa 133 P4
Italia country Europe see Italy

▶Italy country Europe 56 C4
5th most populous country in Europe. Known as Italia in Italian.
europe [countries] ▶ 32–35

Itamaracá, Ilha de i. Brazil 202 F3
Itamaraju Brazil 203 E6
Itamarandiba Brazil 203 D6
Itamataré Brazil 202 C2
Itambacuri Brazil 207 L5
Itambacuri r. Brazil 207 L5
Itambé Brazil 202 D5
Itambé, Pico de mt. Brazil 203 D6
Itami airport Japan 91 D7
Itamirim Brazil 207 K1
Itampolo Madag. 131 [inset] I5
Itanagar India 97 G4
Itanguari r. Brazil 207 H1
Itanhaém Brazil 206 G11
Itanhauã r. Brazil 199 F6
Itanhém Brazil 203 D6
Itanhém r. Brazil 203 E6
Itanhomi Brazil 207 L6
Itany r. Fr. Guiana/Suriname 199 H4
Itaobím Brazil 202 D6
Itaocara Brazil 207 K8
Itapaci Brazil 206 D1
Itapajipe Brazil 206 D6
Itaparaná r. Brazil 199 F6
Itaparica, Represa de resr Brazil 202 E4
Itapé Brazil 207 N1
Itapebi Brazil 202 E5
Itapebí Uruguay 204 F3
Itapecerica Brazil 207 H7
Itapemirim Brazil 203 D7
Itaperuna Brazil 203 D7
Itapetinga Brazil 202 D5
Itapetininga Brazil 206 E10
Itapeva Brazil 206 E10
Itapeva, Lago l. Brazil 203 B9
Itapi r. Brazil 199 G5
Itapicuru Brazil 202 D4
Itapicuru r. Brazil 202 C2
Itapicuru r. Brazil 202 E4
Itapicuru, Serra de hills Brazil 202 C3
Itapicuru Mirim Brazil 202 C2
Itapicuru Mirim r. Brazil 202 E4
Itapinima Brazil 199 F6
Itapipoca Brazil 202 E2
Itapira Brazil 206 G9
Itapiranga Brazil 199 G5
Itapirapuã Brazil 206 C2
Itapiúna Brazil 202 E3
Itápolis Brazil 206 E8
Itaporanga Paraíba Brazil 202 E3
Itaporanga São Paulo Brazil 206 D10
Itapuã Brazil 203 B9
Itapuranga Brazil 206 D2
Itaquaquecetuba Brazil 207 G10
Itaqui Brazil 204 F3
Itarana Brazil 207 M6
Itarantim Brazil 207 M2
Itararé Brazil 206 D11
Itararé r. Brazil 206 D10
Itarsi India 96 C5
Itarumã Brazil 206 B5
Itä-Suomi prov. Fin. 44 O3
Itatiba Brazil 206 G10
Itatinga Brazil 206 E10
Itatuba Brazil 199 F6
Itatupã Brazil 199 I5
Itauçu Brazil 206 D3
Itaueira r. Brazil 202 D3
Itaúna Amazonas Brazil 199 E5
Itaúna Minas Gerais Brazil 203 C7
Itaúnas r. Brazil 207 N5
Itbayat i. Phil. 74 B1
Itchen Lake Canada 167 H1
Ite Peru 200 C4
Itea Greece 59 D10
Itebero Dem. Rep. Congo 126 F5
Itemger, Ozero l. Kazakh. 103 G1
Itende Tanz. 129 B6
Itezhi-Tezhi Dam Zambia 127 E8
Ithaca Greece see Ithaki
Ithaca i. Greece see Ithaki
Ithaca MI U.S.A. 173 I7
Ithaca NY U.S.A. 177 I3
Ithaki Greece 59 B10
English form Ithaca; also known as Vathi
Ithaki i. Greece 59 B10
English form Ithaca
Ithakis, Steno sea chan. Greece 59 B10
Ith Hils ridge Germany 48 G3
Ithil, Wādī al watercourse Saudi Arabia 109 H9
Itigi Tanz. 129 B6
Itihusa-yama mt. Japan 91 B8
Itilleq Greenland 165 N3
Itimbiri r. Dem. Rep. Congo 126 D4
Itinga Brazil 202 D6
Itiquira Brazil 203 A6
Itiquira r. Brazil 201 F4
Itirapina Brazil 206 F9
Itirapuã Brazil 206 F7
Itiúba Brazil 202 E4
Itiúba, Serra de hills Brazil 202 E4
Itiyura r. Arg. 201 E5
Itkhari India 97 E4
Itmurinkol', Ozero l. Kazakh. 102 C2
Itō Japan 91 F7
Itoculo Moz. 131 I2
Itoigawa Japan 90 E6
Itoko Dem. Rep. Congo 126 D5
Iton r. France 50 H3
Itongafeno mt. Madag. 131 [inset] J4
Itororó Brazil 207 M2
Itsuki Japan 91 B8
Itsukushima Shrine tourist site Japan 91 C7
Ittiri Sardegna Italy 57 A8
Ittoqqortoormiit Greenland 165 Q2
also known as Scoresbysund

Itu Brazil **206** F10
Itu Nigeria **125** G5
Itu Abu Island S. China Sea **72** D4
Ituaçu Brazil **202** D5
Ituberá Brazil **202** E5
Ituí r. Brazil **198** D6
Ituiutaba Brazil **206** D5
Itula Dem. Rep. Congo **126** E5
Itumba Tanz. **129** B7
Itumbiara Brazil **206** D5
Itumbiara, Barragem resr Brazil **206** D5
Itungi Port Malawi **129** B7
Ituni Guyana **199** G3
Ituporanga Brazil **206** B11
Iturbe Para. **201** F6
Iturbide Campeche Mex. **185** H5
Iturbide Nuevo León Mex. **185** F3
Ituri r. Dem. Rep. Congo **126** E4
Iturup, Ostrov i. Rus. Fed. **82** G3
also known as Etorofu-tō
Itutinga Brazil **207** F8
Ituverava Brazil **206** F7
Ituxi r. Brazil **200** D1
also known as Iquiri
Ituzaingó Arg. **204** F2
Ityopia country Africa see Ethiopia
Itzehoe Germany **48** G2
Iuaretê Brazil **39** S3
Iuka U.S.A. **174** B5
Iul'tin Rus. Fed. **39** S3
Iuluti Moz. **131** D5
Iúna Brazil **207** L7
Ivaí r. Brazil **198** A10
Ivaí r. Brazil **206** A10
Ivaiporã Brazil **206** B11
Ivalo Fin. **44** N1
also known as Avveel or Avvil
Ivalojoki r. Fin. **44** N1
also spelt Avveel
Ivanava Belarus **42** G9
also spelt Ivanovo
Ivanec Croatia **56** I2
Ivangorod Rus. Fed. **43** J2
Ivangrad Crna Gora Yugo. see Berane
Ivanhoe N.S.W. Australia **147** E3
Ivanhoe W.A. Australia **150** E2
Ivanhoe r. Canada **168** D1
Ivanhoe CA U.S.A. **182** D4
Ivanhoe MN U.S.A. **178** C2
Ivanhoe VA U.S.A. **176** E8
Ivanhoe Lake N.W.T. Canada **167** J2
Ivanhoe Lake Ont. Canada **173** N2
Ivanić-Grad Croatia **56** I3
Ivanishchi Rus. Fed. **43** V6
Ivanivka Ukr. **58** L2
Ivanjica Croatia **56** K3
Ivankiv Ukr. **41** D6
Ivankovo Croatia **56** K3
Ivan'kovo Rus. Fed. **43** S7
Ivan'kovskiy Rus. Fed. **43** V5
Ivan'kovskoye Vodokhranilishche resr Rus. Fed. **43** R5
Ivankovtsy Rus. Fed. **82** D2
Ivano-Frankivs'k Ukr. **41** C6
also spelt Ivano-Frankovsk; formerly known as Stanislav
Ivano-Frankovsk Ukr. see Ivano-Frankivs'k
Ivanovka Kazakh. see Kokzhayyk
Ivanovka Amurskaya Oblast' Rus. Fed. **82** B2
Ivanovka Orenburgskaya Oblast' Rus. Fed. **102** C1
Ivanovo tourist site Bulg. **58** G5
Ivanovo Ivanova
Ivanovo Ivanovskaya Oblast' Rus. Fed. **40** G4
Ivanovo Pskovskaya Oblast' Rus. Fed. **43** L5
Ivanovo Tverskaya Oblast' Rus. Fed. **43** S3
Ivanovo Oblast admin. div. Rus. Fed. see Ivanovskaya Oblast'
Ivanovskaya Oblast' admin. div. Rus. Fed. **43** U4
English form Ivanovo Oblast
Ivanovskiy Khrebet mts Kazakh. **88** C1
Ivanovskoye Orlovskaya Oblast' Rus. Fed. **43** R8
Ivanovskoye Yaroslavskaya Oblast' Rus. Fed. **43** U5
Ivanpah Lake U.S.A. **183** I6
Ivanšćica mts Croatia **56** H2
Ivanski Bulg. **58** I5
Ivanteyevka Rus. Fed. **102** B1
Ivantsevichi Belarus see Ivatsevichy
Ivato Madag. **131** [inset] J4
Ivatsevichy Belarus **42** G9
also spelt Ivantsevichi
Ivaylovgrad Bulg. **58** H7
Ivaylovgrad, Yazovir resr Bulg. **58** G7
Ivdel' Rus. Fed. **38** G3
Iveşti Romania **58** I3
Iveşti Romania **58** I2
Ivi, Cap c. Alg. **55** L8
Ivindo r. Gabon **126** B4
Ivinheima Brazil **203** A7
Ivittuut Greenland **165** O3
Iviza i. Spain see Ibiza
Ivohibe Madag. **131** [inset] J4
Ivolândia Brazil **206** C4
Ivolginsk Rus. Fed. **85** E1
Ivón Bol. **200** D2
Ivor U.S.A. **177** I9
Ivory Coast country Africa see Côte d'Ivoire
Ivösjön l. Sweden **45** K4
Ivot Rus. Fed. **43** P9
Ivrea Italy **51** N7
Ivrindi Turkey **59** I9
Ivris Ugheltekhili pass Georgia **107** F2
Ivujivik Canada see Ivujivik
Ivujivik Canada **165** L3
formerly spelt Ivugivik
Ivuna Tanz. **129** B7
Ivvavik National Park Canada **164** F3
Ivyanyets Belarus **42** H9
Ivydale U.S.A. **176** D7
Iwaizumi Japan **90** G5
Iwaki Japan **90** G6
Iwakuni Japan **91** C7
Iwamizawa Japan **90** G3
Iwan r. Indon. **77** F2
Iwanai Japan **90** G3
Iwanda Tanz. **129** B7
Iwanuma Japan **90** G5
Iwata Japan **91** E7
Iwate Japan **90** G5
Iwate pref. Japan **90** G5
Iwate-san vol. Japan **90** G5
Iwo Nigeria **125** F5
Iwo Jima i. Japan see Iō-jima
Iwupataka Aboriginal Land res. Australia **148** B4
Iwye Belarus **42** G8
Ixcamilpa Mex. **185** F5
Ixiamas Bol. **200** C3
Ixmiquilpán Mex. **185** F4
Ixopo S. Africa **133** O7
Ixtacomitán Mex. **185** G5
Ixtlán Nayarit Mex. **184** D4
Ixtlán Oaxaca Mex. **185** F5
Iya r. Indon. **75** B5
Iya r. Rus. Fed. **80** G1
Iyayi Tanz. **129** A7
Iyirmi Alti Baki Komissari Azer. see 26 Baki Komissari
Iyo Japan **91** C8
Iyomishima Japan **91** C8
Iyo-nada b. Japan **91** C8
Izabal, Lago de l. Guat. **185** H6
Izamal Mex. **185** H4
Izapa tourist site Mex. **185** G6
Izari-dake mt. Japan **90** G4
Izazi Tanz. **129** B6

Izbăşeşti hill Romania **58** F3
Izberbash Rus. Fed. **102** A4
Izdeshkovo Rus. Fed. **43** O6
Iżeh Iran **100** B4
Izgagane well Niger **125** H2
Izgrev hill Bulg. see Sosnogorsk
Izhevsk Rus. Fed. **40** J4
formerly known as Ustinov
Izhma Rus. Fed. **40** J2
Izhma r. Rus. Fed. **40** J2
Izki Oman **105** G3
Izmail Ukr. see Izmayil
Izmalkovo Rus. Fed. **43** S9
Izmayil Ukr. **41** D7
also spelt Izmail; formerly spelt Ismail
Izmeny, Proliv sea chan. Japan/Rus. Fed. see Notsuke-suidō
İzmir Turkey **106** A3
historically known as Smyrna
İzmir prov. Turkey **106** A3
İzmir Körfezi g. Turkey **106** A3
İzmit Turkey see Kocaeli
İzmit Körfezi b. Turkey **106** B2
Izmorene Morocco **54** H9
Iznajar, Embalse de resr Spain **54** G7
Iznalloz Spain **55** H7
İznik Turkey **58** K9
historically known as Nicaea
İznik Gölü l. Turkey **106** B2
Iznoski Rus. Fed. **43** Q7
Izobil'noye Rus. Fed. see Izobil'nyy
Izobil'nyy Rus. Fed. **41** G7
formerly known as Izobil'noye
Izola Slovenia **56** F3
Izoplit Rus. Fed. **43** R5
Izozog Bajo Bol. **201** E4
Izra' Syria **108** H5
Iztochni Rodopi mts Bulg. **58** G7
Izúcar de Matamoros Mex. **185** F5
Izuhara Japan **91** A7
Izumi Japan **91** B8
Izumisano Japan **91** D7
Izumo Japan **91** C7

Izu-Ogasawara Trench sea feature N. Pacific Ocean **220** D3
5th deepest trench in the world.

Izu-shotō is Japan **91** F7
Izu-tobu vol. Japan **91** F7
Izvestiy Tsentral'nogo Ispolnitel'nogo Komiteta, Ostrova Rus. Fed. **39** I2
Izvestkovyy Rus. Fed. **82** C2
Izvoarele Romania **58** G5
Izvoarele Romania **58** G6
Izvoarele Romania **58** H3
Izvoru Romania **58** F4
Izyaslav Ukr. **41** C6
Iz"yayu Rus. Fed. **40** K2
Izyndy Kazakh. **102** D3
Izyum Ukr. **41** F6

↓ J

Jaama Estonia **42** I2
Ja'ar Yemen **105** E5
Jaba watercourse Iran **100** D3
Jabal as Sirāj Afgh. **101** G3
Jabal Dab Saudi Arabia **105** E3
Jabalón r. Spain **54** G6
Jabalpur India **96** C5
Jabbārah Fara Islands Saudi Arabia **104** C4
Jabbūl, Sabkhat al salt flat Syria **109** I2
Jabiluka Aboriginal Land res. Australia **148** B2
Jabir reg. Oman **105** G3
Jabiru Australia **148** B2
Jablah Syria **108** G2
Jablanica Bos.-Herz. **56** J5
Jablanica r. Yugo. **58** C5
Jablonec nad Nisou Czech Rep. **49** M5
Jabłonowo Pomorskie Poland **49** Q2
Jablunkov Czech Rep. **49** P6
Jaboatical Brazil **206** E8
Jaboticatubas Brazil **207** J6
Jabuka i. Croatia **56** H5
Jabuka Vojvodina, Srbija Yugo. **58** B4
Jabung, Tanjung pt Indon. **76** D3
Jaburu Brazil **199** E6
Jabuti Brazil **199** G6
Jaca Spain **55** K2
Jacala Mex. **185** F4
Jacaraci Brazil **207** K1
Jacaré Mato Grosso Brazil **202** A5
Jacaré Rondônia Brazil **201** D2
Jacaré r. Brazil **199** F6
Jacaré r. Brazil **202** D4
Jacareacanga Brazil **199** G6
Jacareí Brazil **207** G10
Jacaretinga Brazil **201** D2
Jacarèzinho Brazil **206** D10
Jáchal r. Arg. **204** D3
Jaciara Brazil **202** B3
Jacinto Brazil **202** D6
Jaciparaná Brazil **201** D2
Jaciparaná r. Brazil **201** D2
Jack r. Australia **149** E2
Jackfish Canada **172** G2
Jackfish Lake Canada **167** I4
Jack Lee, Lake resr U.S.A. **179** D5
Jacksboro TN U.S.A. **176** A9
Jacksboro TX U.S.A. **179** C5
Jackson Australia **149** F5
Jackson AL U.S.A. **175** C6
Jackson CA U.S.A. **182** D3
Jackson GA U.S.A. **175** D5
Jackson KY U.S.A. **176** B8
Jackson MI U.S.A. **173** I8
Jackson MN U.S.A. **178** D3
Jackson MO U.S.A. **174** B4

Jackson MS U.S.A. **175** B5
State capital of Mississippi.

Jackson NC U.S.A. **176** H9
Jackson OH U.S.A. **176** C6
Jackson TN U.S.A. **174** B5
Jackson WI U.S.A. **172** E7
Jackson WY U.S.A. **180** E4
Jackson, Cape N.Z. **152** I8
Jackson, Mount Antarctica **222** T2
Jackson Bay N.Z. **153** C11
also known as Okahu
Jackson Head N.Z. **153** C11
Jackson Island Rus. Fed. see Dzheksona, Ostrov
Jacksonburg U.S.A. **180** E4
Jacksonport U.S.A. **172** F6
Jacksons N.Z. **153** F10
Jacksonville AL U.S.A. **175** C5
Jacksonville AR U.S.A. **179** D5
Jacksonville FL U.S.A. **175** D6
Jacksonville IL U.S.A. **174** B4
Jacksonville NC U.S.A. **174** E5
Jacksonville OH U.S.A. **176** C6
Jacksonville TX U.S.A. **179** D6
Jacksonville Beach U.S.A. **175** D6
Jack Wade U.S.A. **166** A1
Jacmel Haiti **187** F3
Jaco i. East Timor see Jako
Jacobabad Pak. **101** G4
Jacobina Brazil **202** D4
Jacob Lake U.S.A. **183** L5

Jacquesdal S. Africa **133** I6
Jacques-Cartier, Détroit de sea chan. Canada **169** H3
also known as Jacques Cartier Passage
Jacques Cartier, Mont mt. Canada **169** H3
Jacques Cartier Passage Canada see Jacques-Cartier, Détroit de
Jacquet River Canada **169** H4
Jacuba r. Brazil **206** A5
Jacuí r. Brazil **203** B9
Jacuípe r. Brazil **202** E4
Jacunda Brazil **202** B2
Jacundá r. Brazil **202** B2
Jacupemba Brazil **207** M6
Jacupiranga Brazil **203** C8
Jacura Venez. **198** D2
Jadar r. Bos.-Herz. **56** L4
Jadar r. Yugo. **58** A4
Jadcherla India **94** C2
Jaddangi India **95** D2
Jaddi, Ras pt Pak. **101** E5
Jadebusen b. Germany **48** F2
Jadhdhanah Saudi Arabia **104** C4
Jadib Yemen **105** F4
Jadotville Dem. Rep. Congo see Likasi
Jadova r. Croatia **56** H4
Jaén Peru **198** B5
Jaén Phil. **74** B3
Jaén Spain **54** H7
Ja'farābād Ardabil Iran **100** B2
Ja'farābād Khorāsan Iran **100** D2
Jaffa Israel see Tel Aviv-Yafo
Jaffa, Cape Australia **146** C4
Jaffna Sri Lanka **94** C4
Jaffrey U.S.A. **177** M3
Jafr, Qa' al imp. l. Jordan **109** H7
Jagadhri India **96** C3
Jägala r. Estonia **42** G2
Jagalur India **94** C3
Jagdalak Afgh. **101** G3
Jagdalpur India **94** D2
Jagdaqi China **85** J1
Jagdishpur India **97** E4
Jagersfontein S. Africa **133** J6
Jaggang China **89** B5
Jaggayyapeta India **94** D2
Jaghin Iran **100** D5
Jaghjaghah, Nahr r. Syria/Turkey **109** M1
Jagin watercourse Iran **100** D5
Jagkolk Vloer salt pan S. Africa **132** E6
Jagodina Srbija Yugo. **58** C5
formerly known as Svetozarevo
Jagok Tso salt l. China see Urru Co
Jagsamka China see Luding
Jagst r. Germany **48** G6
Jagtial India **94** C2
Jaguapitã Brazil **206** B10
Jaguarão r. Brazil/Uruguay **204** G4
also known as Yaguarón
Jaguarão Uruguay **204** G4
Jaguarari Brazil **202** D3
Jaguaretama Brazil **202** E3
Jaguari Brazil **203** A9
Jaguaribe Brazil **202** E3
Jaguaribe r. Brazil **202** E3
Jaguaruana Brazil **202** E3
Jagüe Arg. **204** C3
Jagüey Grande Cuba **186** C2
Jahanabad India **97** E4
formerly spelt Jehanabad
Jahān Dāgh mt. Iran **100** B2
Jahleel, Point Australia **148** A1
Jahmah well Iraq **107** F5
Jahrom Iran **100** C4
Jāhyad Iran **100** D5
Jaicós Brazil **202** D3
Jaigarh India **94** B2
Jailolo Indon. **75** C2
Jailolo, Selat sea chan. Indon. **75** D3
Jailolo Gilolo i. Indon. see Halmahera
Jaíña Chile **200** C4
Jainca China **84** D5
Jaintiapur Bangl. **97** G4
Jaipur India **96** B4
Jaipurhat Bangl. **97** F4
Jais India **97** D4
Jaisalmer India **96** A4
Jaisinghnagar India **97** D5
Jaitaran India **96** B4
Jaitgarh hill India **94** C1
Jaipur India **96** C4
Jajarkot Nepal **97** D3
Jajce Bos.-Herz. **56** J4
Jajnagar state India see Orissa
Jakar Bhutan **97** F4
also known as Byakar

Jakarta Indon. **77** D4
Capital of Indonesia. Formerly spelt Djakarta; historically known as Batavia or Sunda Kalapa.
world [cities] ➤ 24–25

Jakhan India **101** G6
Jakharrah Libya **120** C2
Jakin mt. Afgh. **101** F4
Jakkalsberg Namibia **130** C3
Jakkalsberg hills Namibia **132** A5
Jakki Kowr Iran **101** E5
Jäkkvik Sweden **44** L2
Jakliat India **96** B3
Jako i. East Timor **75** C5
also known as Jaco
Jakobshavn Greenland see Ilulissat
Jakobstad Fin. **44** M3
also known as Pietarsaari
Jakupica mts Macedonia **58** C7
Jal U.S.A. **179** B5
Jalaid China see Inder
Jalājil Saudi Arabia **105** D2
Jalālābād Afgh. **101** G3
Jalalabad Punjab India **96** B3
Jalalabad Uttar Pradesh India **96** C3
Jalalabad Uttar Pradesh India **96** C4
also spelt Dzhalal-Abad
Jalal-Abad Kyrg. **103** H4
English form Dzhalal-Abad; also known as Dzhalal-Abadskaya Oblast'
Jalal-Abad admin. div. Kyrg. **103** H4
English form Dzhalal-Abad; also known as Dzhalal-Abadskaya Oblast'
Jalal-Abad Oblast admin. div. Kyrg. see Jalal-Abad
Jalalpur Gujarat India **94** B1
Jalalpur Uttar Pradesh India **97** D4
formerly spelt Jullundur
Jalalpur Pirwala Pak. **101** G4
Jalan Kayu Sing. **76** [inset]
Jalapa Guat. **185** H6
Jalapa Mex. see Xalapa
Jalapa Nicaragua **186** B4
Jalapa Enríquez Mex. **185** F5
also known as Xalapa
Jalapur Pak. **101** H4
Jalasjärvi Fin. **44** M3
Jalaun India **96** C4
Jalawlā' Iraq **107** F4
Jalboi r. Australia **148** B3
Jaldak Afgh. **101** F4
Jaldhaka r. Bangl. **97** F4
Jaldrug India **94** C2

Jales Brazil **206** C7
Jalesar India **96** C4
Jaleshwar Nepal see Jaleswar
Jaleswar Nepal **97** F4
also spelt Jaleshwar
Jalgaon India **96** B5
Jalībah Iraq **107** G5
Jalingo Nigeria **125** H5
Jalísco state Mex. **184** D5
Jallābī Iran **100** D5
Jalna India **94** B2
Jalón r. Spain **55** J3
Jalor India **96** A4
Jalostotitlán Mex. **185** E4
Jalpa Mex. **185** E4
Jalpaiguri India **97** F4
Jalpan Mex. **185** F4
Jalrez Afgh. **101** G3
Jālū Libya **120** D2
Jālū Oasis Libya **120** D2
Jālūlā' Iraq see Jalawlā'
Jam r. Iran **101** E3
Jām reg. Iran **101** E3
Jamaica Cuba **187** E3

Jamaica country West Indies **186** D3
northamerica [countries] ➤ 158–159

Jamaica Channel Haiti/Jamaica **187** E3
Jamāja Estonia **42** D3
Jamalpur Bangl. **97** F4
Jamalpur India **97** F4
Jamanxim r. Brazil **199** G6
Jamari Brazil **201** D2
Jamba Angola **127** C8
Jambi Indon. **76** D3
also known as Telanaipura
Jambi prov. Indon. **76** D3
Jāmbīn Australia **149** F5
Jambo India **96** B4
Jambō India **96** B4
Jamboaye r. Indon. **76** B1
Jambongan i. Sabah Malaysia **77** G1
Jambuair, Tanjung pt Indon. **76** B1
Jambūr Iraq **109** P2
Jambusar India **96** A5
Jamekunte India **94** C2
James r. Canada **167** I1
James r. MO U.S.A. **178** D4
James r. ND/SD U.S.A. **178** C3
James r. VA U.S.A. **177** I8
James, Isla i. Chile **205** B7
James Bay Canada **168** D2
James Cistern Bahamas **186** D1
Jameson Land reg. Greenland **165** Q2
Jameson Range mts Australia **151** D5
James Peak N.Z. **153** C13
James Ross Island Antarctica **222** U2
James Ross Strait Canada **165** J3
Jamestown Australia **146** C3
Jamestown Canada see Wawa

Jamestown St Helena **216** N7
Capital of St Helena and Dependencies.

Jamestown CA U.S.A. **182** D4
Jamestown KY U.S.A. **176** A9
Jamestown ND U.S.A. **178** C2
Jamestown NY U.S.A. **176** F3
Jamestown RI U.S.A. **177** M4
Jamestown TN U.S.A. **176** A9
Jāmījārvi Fin. **45** M3
Jamiltepec Mex. **185** F5
Jamkhandi India **94** B2
Jamkhed India **94** B2
Jammalamadugu India **94** C3
Jammerbugten b. Denmark **45** J4

Jammu Jammu and Kashmir **96** B2

Jammu and Kashmir terr. Asia **96** C2
Disputed territory (India/Pakistan). Short form Kashmir.
asia [countries] ➤ 64–67

Jamnagar India **96** A5
formerly known as Navanagar
Jamner India **94** B1
Jamni r. India **96** C4
Jamno, Jezioro lag. Poland **49** N1
Jampang Kulon Indon. **77** D4
Jampur Pak. **101** G4
Jāmsā Fin. **45** N3
Jämsänkoski Fin. **45** N3
Jamshedpur India **97** E5
Jamtara India **97** E5
Jamtari Nigeria **125** H5
Jämtland county Sweden **44** K3
Jamui India **97** E4
Jamuna r. Bangl. **97** F4
Jamuna r. India **97** E4
Janá i. Saudi Arabia **105** E2
Janāb, Wādī al watercourse Jordan **109** H6
Janakpur Nepal **97** D3
Janakpur Nepal **97** E4
Janaúba Brazil **207** J2
Jāndaq Iran **100** C3
Jandaia Brazil **206** C4
Jandaia do Sul Brazil **206** B10
Jandiala India **96** B3
Jandiatuba r. Brazil **198** D5
Jandongi Dem. Rep. Congo **126** D4
Jandowae Australia **149** F5
Jándula r. Spain **54** H6
Jandullīa r. Spain **55** H7
Janeiro r. Brazil **202** C5
Janesville CA U.S.A. **182** D1
Janesville WI U.S.A. **172** D8
Jang, Tanjung pt Indon. **76** D3
Jangal Iran **101** D3
Jangamo Moz. **131** G5
Jangaon India **94** C2
Jangeru Indon. **77** G3
Jangi Afgh. see Dzhangel'dy
Jangipur India **97** F4
Jangngai Ri mts China **89** D5
Jāni Beyglū Iran **100** A2
Janikowo Poland **49** P3
Janiópolis Brazil **206** A11
Janja Bos.-Herz. **56** L4
Janjevo Kosovo, Srbija Yugo. **58** C6
Jan Kempdorp S. Africa **133** I4
formerly known as Andalusia
Jankov Crna Gora Yugo. **58** B5

Jan Mayen i. Arctic Ocean **224** X2
Part of Norway.

Jāņmuiža Latvia **42** G4
Jannatābād Iran **100** D3
Jañona mt. Spain **54** E4
Janos Mex. **184** C2
Jánoshalma Hungary **49** Q8
Jánossomorja Hungary **49** O8
Janów Lubelski Poland **49** T5
Jansenville S. Africa **133** I8
Jans Bay Canada **167** I4
Jānua Coeli Brazil **202** B2
Jānubia Brazil **202** C5
Jānūb Sīnā' governorate Egypt **108** E8
English form South Sinai; also known as Sinai al Janūbīya

Janwada India **94** C2
Janzar mt. Pak. **101** E5
Janzé France **50** E5
Jaora India **96** B5

Japan country Asia **90** E5
9th most populous country in the world. Known as Nihon or Nippon in Japanese.
world [population] ➤ 22–23
asia [countries] ➤ 64–67

Japan, Sea of N. Pacific Ocean **83** D5
also known as East Sea or Nippon Hai
Japan Alps National Park Japan see Chūbu-Sangaku National Park
Japón Hond. **186** B4
Japurá r. Brazil **198** E4
Japvo Mount India **97** G4
Jaqué Panama **187** F3
Jarabacoa Dom. Rep. **187** F3
Jarābulus Syria **109** M1
Jarad Saudi Arabia **104** C4
Jaraguá Brazil **206** D3
Jaraguá do Sul Brazil **203** B8
Jaraguari Brazil **203** A7
Jaraiz de la Vera Spain **54** F4
Jarama r. Spain **55** H4
Jarash Jordan **108** G5
Jaraucu r. Brazil **199** H5
Järbo Sweden **45** L3
Jarboesville U.S.A. see Lexington Park
Jar-bulak Kazakh. see Kabanbay
Jardim Brazil **206** G3
Jardim Mato Grosso do Sul Brazil **201** D1
Jardín r. Spain **55** I6
Jardine River National Park Australia **149** D1
Jardinópolis Brazil **206** F8
Jargalant Arhangay Mongolia **84** D2
Jargalant Bayanhongor Mongolia **84** C2
Jargalant Bayan-Ölgiy Mongolia **84** A2
Jargalant Dornod Mongolia **85** G2
Jargalant Govĭ-Altay Mongolia **84** B2
Jargalant Töv Mongolia **85** E1
Jargalant Hayrhan mt. Mongolia **84** B2
Jargalthaa Mongolia **85** F2
Jari r. Brazil **199** I5
Jarmen Germany **49** K2
Järna Dalarna Sweden **45** K3
Järna Stockholm Sweden **45** L4
Jarnac France **50** F7
Jarocin Poland **49** O4
Jaroměř Czech Rep. **49** M5
Jarosław Poland **49** T5
Järpen Sweden **44** J3
Jarqūrghon Uzbek. see Dzharkurgan
Jarrāh, Wādī watercourse Syria **109** M1
Jarrahi watercourse Iran **100** B4
Jarratt U.S.A. **176** H9
Jarrettsville U.S.A. **177** I6
Jartai China **85** E4
Jartai Yanchi salt l. China **84** E4
Jaru Brazil **201** E2
Jārūb Yemen **105** F4
Jarud China see Lubei
Jarut mt. Iran **100** D3
Järvakandi Estonia **42** F3
Järvenpää Fin. **45** N3

Jarvis Island terr. N. Pacific Ocean **221** H6
United States Unincorporated Territory.
oceania [countries] ➤ 138–139

Järvsand Sweden **44** K2
Järvsö Sweden **45** L3
Jarwa India **97** D4
Jasdan India **96** A5
Jashpurnagar India **97** E5
Jasień Poland **49** M4
Jasiołka r. Poland **49** S6
Jāsk Iran **100** D5
Jāsk-e Kohneh Iran **100** D5
Jasliq Uzbek. see Zhaslyk
Jasło Poland **49** S6
Jason Islands Falkland Is **205** E8
Jason Peninsula Antarctica **222** T2
Jasper Canada **166** G4
Jasper AL U.S.A. **175** C5
Jasper AR U.S.A. **179** D4
Jasper FL U.S.A. **175** D6
Jasper GA U.S.A. **174** C5
Jasper IN U.S.A. **174** C4
Jasper NY U.S.A. **176** H3
Jasper OH U.S.A. **176** B7
Jasper TN U.S.A. **174** C5
Jasper TX U.S.A. **179** D6
Jasper National Park Canada **167** G4
Jaşşān Iraq **107** F4
Jassy Romania see Iaşi
Jastarnia Poland **49** P1
Jastrebarsko Croatia **56** H3
Jastrowie Poland **49** N2
Jastrzębie-Zdrój Poland **49** P6
historically known as Bad Königsdorff
Jászapáti Hungary **49** R8
Jászárokszállás Hungary **49** Q8
Jászberény Hungary **49** Q8
Jatai Brazil **206** C3
Jatapu r. Brazil **199** G5
Jati Pak. **101** G5
Jatibarang Indon. **77** D4
Jatibonico Cuba **186** D2
Játiva Spain see Xátiva
Jatiwangi Indon. **77** D4
Jatobá Brazil **202** D3
Jatoí Pak. **101** G4
Jättendal Sweden **45** L3
Jatuarana Brazil **201** E1
Jaú Brazil **206** D9
Jaú r. Brazil **199** F5
Jaú, Parque Nacional do nat. park Brazil **199** F5
Jauaperi r. Brazil **199** F5
Jauari Brazil **199** E6
Jaua Sarisariñama, Parque Nacional nat. park Venez. **199** E3
Jaúco Cuba **187** E2
Jauja Peru **200** B2
Jaumave Mex. **185** F4
Jauna r. Brazil **199** F6
Jaunanna Latvia **42** I4
Jaunay-Clan France **50** G6
Jaunjelgava Latvia **42** G5
Jaunkalsnava Latvia **42** H5
Jaunlutrini Latvia **42** D5
Jaunmärupe Latvia **42** G4
Jaunpiebalga Latvia **42** H4
Jaunpils Latvia **42** E5
Jaunpur India **97** D4
Jaupaci Brazil **206** C3
Jauru Brazil **201** D4
Jauru r. Brazil **201** E4
Jauru r. Brazil **201** F4

Janwada India **94** C2

Java i. Indon. **77** E4
5th largest island in Asia. Also spelt Jawa.
asia [landscapes] ➤ 62–63

Javaés r. Brazil see Formoso
Javaés, Serra dos hills Brazil **202** B4
Javalambre mt. Spain **55** K4
Javalambre, Sierra de mts Spain **55** J3
Javand Afgh. **101** F3
Javari r. Brazil **198** D6
Javarthushuu Mongolia **85** G1

Java Trench sea feature Indian Ocean **218** N6
Deepest point in the Indian Ocean.
oceans [features] ➤ 210–211

Jávea Spain **55** L6
Javier, Isla i. Chile **205** B7
Javor mt. Yugo. **58** B5
Javořice hill Czech Rep. **49** M6
Javorie mt. Slovakia **49** Q7
Javornik mt. Slovenia **56** H2
Javorníky mts Slovakia **49** P6
Jawa i. Indon. see Java
Jawad India **96** B4
Jawai r. India **96** A4
Jawala Mukhi India **96** C3
Jawar India **96** C5
Jawhar Somalia **128** E4
Jawhar India **94** B2
Jawor Poland **49** N4
Jaworzno Poland **49** Q5
Jawoyn Aboriginal Land res. Australia **148** B2
Jay U.S.A. **179** D4

Jaya, Puncak mt. Indon. **73** I7
Highest mountain in Oceania. Formerly known as Carstensz-top or Puntjak Sukarno.
oceania [landscapes] ➤ 136–137

Jayanca Peru **198** B6
Jayanti India **97** F4
Jayapura Indon. **73** J7
formerly known as Hollandia or Sukarnapura
Jayb, Wādī al watercourse Israel/Jordan **108** G6
Jaynagar Bihar India **97** F4
Jaynagar W. Bengal India **97** F5
Jaypur India **95** D2
Jayrūd Syria **109** H4
Jayton U.S.A. **179** B5
Jazirat al Hamrā U.A.E. **105** F2
Jarmen Germany **49** K2
Jbail Lebanon **108** G3
historically known as Biblos
J. C. Murphey Lake U.S.A. **172** F9
Jdaïdé Syria **109** H4
Jeanerette U.S.A. **175** B6
Jean Marie River Canada **166** F2
Jebāl Bārez, Kūh-e mts Iran **100** D4
Jebba Nigeria **125** F4
Jebel Libya **120** C2
Jebel Turkm. see Dzhebel
Jebel, Bahr el r. Sudan/Uganda see White Nile
Jebel Ali U.A.E. see Mina Jebel Ali
Jeberos Peru **198** B6
Jebha Morocco **54** G9
Jebus Indon. **77** D3
Jedburgh U.K. **46** J8
Jeddah Saudi Arabia **104** B3
also spelt Jiddah
Jeddore Lake Canada **169** K3
Jędrzejów Poland **49** R5
Jedwabne Poland **49** T2
Jeetze r. Germany **48** I2
Jefferson IA U.S.A. **178** D3
Jefferson NC U.S.A. **176** D9
Jefferson OH U.S.A. **176** E4
Jefferson TX U.S.A. **179** D5
Jefferson WI U.S.A. **172** E7
Jefferson r. U.S.A. **180** E3
Jefferson, Mount U.S.A. **180** B3
Jefferson, Mount vol. U.S.A. **180** B3

Jefferson City MO U.S.A. **178** D4
State capital of Missouri.

Jefferson City TN U.S.A. **176** B8
Jeffersonton U.S.A. **176** H7
Jeffersonville IN U.S.A. **174** C4
Jeffersonville OH U.S.A. **176** B6
Jeffersonville KY U.S.A. **176** B8
Jeffrey U.S.A. **176** D8
Jeffrey's Bay S. Africa **133** I11
Jega Nigeria **125** F4
Jehanabad India see Jahanabad
Jekabpils Latvia **42** G5
Jelbart Ice Shelf Antarctica **223** X2
Jelcz-Laskowice Poland **49** O4
Jeldėsa Eth. **128** D2
Jelenia Góra Poland **49** M5
historically known as Hirschberg
Jelep La pass China/India **89** E7
Jelgava Latvia **42** E5
Jellico U.S.A. **176** A9
Jelloway U.S.A. **176** C5
Jellicoe Canada **168** C3
Jelondi Tajik. see Dzhilandy
Jelow Gir Iran **100** A3
Jemaja i. Indon. **77** D2
Jember Indon. **77** F5
Jemez Pueblo U.S.A. **181** F5
Jeminay China **88** D2
also known to Topterek
Jemma Bauchi Nigeria **125** H4
Jemma Kaduna Nigeria **125** H4
Jemmel Tunisia **57** C12
Jemnice Czech Rep. **49** M6
Jempang, Danau l. Indon. **77** G3
Jena Germany **48** I5
Jena U.S.A. **179** D6
Jenda Malawi **129** B8
Jendouba Tunisia **123** H1
Jengish Chokusu mt. China/Kyrg. see Pobeda Peak
Jenin West Bank **108** G5
Jenipapo Brazil **199** G5
Jenkinjones U.S.A. **176** D8
Jenkins U.S.A. **176** C8
Jenkintown U.S.A. **177** J5
Jenne Mali see Djenné
Jenner Canada **167** I5
Jennersdorf Austria **49** N9
Jennings U.S.A. **179** D6
Jennings r. Canada **166** C3
Jenpeg Canada **167** L4
Jepara Indon. **77** E4
Jeparit Australia **147** C4
Jeppo Fin. **44** M3
Jequié Brazil **202** D5
Jequitaí Brazil **207** I4
Jequitaí r. Brazil **207** I4
Jequitinhonha Brazil **202** D6
Jequitinhonha r. Brazil **207** O2
Jerba, Île de i. Tunisia **123** H2
Jerbar Sudan **128** A3
Jereh Iran **107** G5
Jérémie Haiti **187** E3
Jeremoabo Brazil **202** E4
Jerer Shet' watercourse Eth. **128** D3
Jeremoabo Brazil **202** E4
Jerez Mex. **185** E4
Jerez, Rus. Fed. **80** G1
Jerez de la Frontera Spain **54** E8
Jerez de los Caballeros Spain **54** E6
Jerfojaur Sweden **44** L2
Jergul Norway **44** N1
Jericho Australia **149** E4
Jericho West Bank **108** G6
also known as Arīḥā; also spelt Yeriho; historically known as Tell es-Sultan

index

J K

Jerid, Chott el *salt l.* Tunisia **123** H2
Jerijih, Tanjong *pt* Sarawak Malaysia **77** E2
Jerilderie Australia **147** E3
Jermyn U.S.A. **177** J4
Jerome *AZ* U.S.A. **183** L7
Jerome *ID* U.S.A. **180** D4
Jerramungup Australia **151** B7
▶ Jersey *terr.* Channel Is **50** D3
  United Kingdom Crown Dependency.
  europe [countries] ➡ 32–35
Jersey City U.S.A. **177** K5
Jerseyville U.S.A. **174** B4
Jerte *r.* Spain **54** E5
Jerumenha Brazil **202** D3
▶ Jerusalem Israel/West Bank **108** G6
  Capital of Israel. Also known as El Quds;
  also spelt Yerushalayim; historically known
  as Aelia Capitolina or Hierosolyma.
  asia [issues] ➡ 66–67
Jerusalem N.Z. **152** J7
Jervis Bay Australia **147** F3
Jervis Bay Territory *admin. div.* Australia
  147 F3
  also known as Commonwealth Territory
Jervois Range *hills* Australia **148** B4
Jesenice Slovenia **56** G2
Jeseník Czech Rep. **49** O5
Jesi Italy **56** F5
Jesmond Canada **166** F5
Jesolo Italy **56** E3
Jesselton *Sabah* Malaysia *see*
  Kota Kinabalu
Jessen Germany **49** J4
Jessheim Norway **45** J3
Jessore Bangl. **97** F5
Jesu Maria Island P.N.G. *see*
  Rambutyo Island
Jesup U.S.A. **175** D6
Jesús Carranza Mex. **185** G5
Jesús María Arg. **204** D3
Jesús Maria, Barra *spit* Mex. **185** F3
Jetalsar India **96** A5
Jethro *tourist site* Saudi Arabia **104** A1
  also known as Maghā'ir Shu'ayb
Jetmore U.S.A. **178** C4
Jevnaker Norway **45** J3
Jewett City U.S.A. **177** N4
Jewish Autonomous Oblast *admin. div.*
  Rus. Fed. *see*
  Yevreyskaya Avtonomnaya Oblast'
Jeyhun Turkm. *see* Dzheykhun
Jeziorak, Jezioro *l.* Poland **49** Q2
Jeziorany Poland **49** R2
Jeziorka *r.* Poland **49** S3
Jeziorsko, Jezioro *l.* Poland **49** P4
Jezzine Lebanon **108** G4
Jhabua India **96** B5
Jha Jha India **97** F4
Jhajjar India **96** C3
Jhajju India **96** B4
Jhal Pak. **101** F4
Jhalakati Bangl. **97** F5
Jhalawar India **97** E5
Jhalida India **97** E5
Jhalrapatan India **96** C4
Jhang Pak. **101** H4
Jhanjharpur India **97** E4
Jhansi India **96** C4
Jhanzi *r.* India **97** G4
Jhapa Nepal **97** F4
Jharia India **97** E5
Jharkhand *state* India **97** E5
Jharsuguda India **97** E5
Jhatpat Pak. **101** G4
Jhawani Nepal **97** E4
Jhelum Pak. **101** H3
Jhelum *r.* India/Pak. **96** B3
Jhenaidaha Bangl. *see* Jhenida
Jhenida Bangl. **97** F5
  also known as Jhenaidaha
Jhinjhuvada India **96** A5
Jhinkpani India **97** E5
Jhudo Pak. **101** G5
Jhumritilaiya India **97** E4
Jhunjhunun India **96** B3
Jhusi India **97** D4
Jiachuan China **86** C3
  formerly known as Jiachuanzhen
Jiachuanzhen China *see* Jiachuan
Jiading China **87** G2
Jiahe China **87** E3
Jiajiang China **86** B2
Jialing Jiang *r.* China **86** C2
Jialu China **87** E1
Jialu *r.* China **87** E1
Jiamusi China **82** C3
Ji'an *Jiangxi* China **87** E3
  also known as Dunhou
Ji'an *Jiangxi* China **87** E3
Ji'an China **83** D4
Jianchang China *see* Nancheng
Jianchang China **85** H3
Jianchuan China **86** A3
Jiandaoyu China *see* Zigui
Jiande China **87** F2
Jiang'an China **86** C2

Jiangbei China *see* Yubei
Jiangcheng China **86** B4
  also known as Menglie
Jiangchuan China **86** B3
  also known as Dajie
Jiangcun China **87** D3
Jiangdu China **87** F1
  formerly known as Xiannümiao
Jiange China **86** C2
  also known as Pu'an
Jiangjiehe China **87** E3
Jiangjin China **86** C2
Jiangjunmiao China **88** E2
Jiangjunmu China **85** G4
Jiangjuntai China **84** B4
Jiangkou China *see* Fengkai
Jiangkou *Guizhou* China **87** D3
  also known as Shuangjiang
Jiangkou *Shaanxi* China **86** C1
Jiangkou China *see* Pingchang
Jiangle China **87** F3
  also known as Guyong
Jiangling China *see* Jingzhou
Jiangluozhen China **86** C1
Jiangmen China **87** E4
Jiangna China *see* Yanshan
Jiangning China **87** F2
  also known as Dongshan
Jiangshan China **87** F2
Jiangsi China *see* Dejiang
Jiangsu *prov.* China **87** F1
  English form Kiangsu
Jiangtaibu China **85** E5
Jiangxi *prov.* China **87** E3
  English form Kiangsi
Jiangxia China *see* Wuchang
Jiangxian China **85** F5
Jiangxigou China **84** D4
Jiangyan China **87** G1
  formerly known as Taixian
Jiangyin China **87** G2
Jiangyong China **87** D3
  also known as Xiaopu
Jiangyou China **86** C2
  formerly known as Zhongba
Jiangyu China **85** H4
Jiangzhesongrong China **89** D6
Jianhu China **87** F1
Jian Jiang *r.* China **87** D4
Jianjun China *see* Yongshou
Jianli China **87** E2
  also known as Rongcheng
Jianning China **87** F3
Jian'ou China **87** F3
Jianping *Liaoning* China **85** H3
  also known as Yebaishou
Jianping *Liaoning* China **85** H3
Jianshe China **86** A1
Jianshe China *see* Baiyü
Jianshi China **87** D2
  also known as Yezhou
Jianshui China **86** B3
  also known as Lin'an
Jianxing China **86** C2
Jianyang *Fujian* China **87** F3
Jianyang *Sichuan* China **86** C2
Jiaochang China **86** B1
Jiaochangba China *see* Jiaochang
Jiaocheng China *see* Jiaoling
Jiaocheng China **85** G4
Jiaohe *Hebei* China **85** H4
Jiaojiang China *see* Taizhou
Jiaokou China **85** F4
Jiaokou China *see* Yiliang
Jiaolai *r.* China **85** H4
Jiaolai *r.* China **85** I3
Jiaoling China **87** F3
  also known as Jiaocheng
Jiaonan China **85** H5
  formerly known as Wanggezhuang
Jiaowei China **87** F3
Jiaozhou China **85** I4
Jiaozhou Wan *b.* China **85** I4
Jiaozuo China **85** G5
Jiapigou China **82** B4
Jiasa China **86** B3
Jiashan China *see* Mingguang
Jiashi China **88** B4
  also known as Payzawat
Jia Tsuo La *pass* China **89** D6
Jiaxian *Henan* China **87** E1
Jiaxian *Shaanxi* China **85** F4
  also known as Jialu
Jiaxiang China **85** H5
Jiaxing China **87** G2
Jiayi Taiwan *see* Chiai
Jiayin China **82** C2
  also known as Chaoyang
Jiayu China **87** E2
Jiayuguan China **84** C4
  also known as Yuyue
Jiazi China **87** F4
Jibou Romania **58** F1
Jibsh, Ra's *c.* Oman **105** G3
Jibuti country Africa *see* Djibouti
Jibuti Djibouti *see* Djibouti
Jicarilla Apache Indian Reservation *res.*
  U.S.A. **181** F5
Jičín Czech Rep. **49** M5
Jiddah Saudi Arabia *see* Jeddah
Jidong China **82** C3
Jiehkkevárri *mt.* Norway **44** L1
Jiehu China *see* Yinan
Jieshi China **87** E4
Jieshou China **87** E1
Jieshi Wan *b.* China **87** E4
Jiesjavrre *l.* Norway **44** N1
Jiexi China **87** E4
Jiexiu China **85** F4
Jieyang China **87** F4
Jieznas Lith. **42** F7
Jigalong Aboriginal Reserve Australia
  150 C4
Jigawa *state* Nigeria **125** H3
Jigerbent Turkm. *see* Dzhigirbent
Jiggalong Australia **150** C4
Jiggs U.S.A. **183** I1
Jiguaní Cuba **186** D2
Jigzhi China **86** B1
Jihar, Wadi al *watercourse* Syria **109** I3
Jihlava Czech Rep. **49** M6
Jihlava *r.* Czech Rep. **49** N7
Jijel Alg. **123** G1
  formerly spelt Djidjelli
Jijia *r.* Romania **58** J2
Jijiga Eth. **128** D2
Jijona Spain **55** K6
Jiju China **86** B2
Jil'ad *reg.* Jordan **108** G5
  English form Gilead
Jilan ash Shuwayhitiyah *esc.* Saudi Arabia
  109 K7
Jilava Romania **58** H4
Jilbadji Nature Reserve Australia **151** B6
Jilf al Kabir, Hadabat al *plat.* Egypt *see*
  Gilf Kebir Plateau
Jilga *r.* Afgh. **101** G3
Jilh al 'Ishar *plain* Saudi Arabia **105** D3
Jilib Somalia **128** D4
Jili Hu *l.* China **88** D2
Jilin China **82** B4
Jilin *prov.* China **85** J3
  English form Kirin
Jiling China **84** D4
Jilin Hada Ling *mts* China **82** B4
Jiloca *r.* Spain **55** J3
Ji-Paraná Brazil **201** E2
Ji-Paraná *r.* Brazil **201** E2
Jiparaná Ecuador **198** A5
Jiquilisco El Salvador **186** B4
Jiquipilas Mex. **185** F5
Jiquiritaia Brazil **207** N4

Jilong Taiwan *see* Chilung
Jima Eth. **128** C3
Jima Ali *well* Eth. **128** E3
Jimani Haiti **187** F3
Jimbo Tanz. **129** C6
Jimbolia Romania **58** B3
Jimda China *see* Zindo
Jimena de la Frontera Spain **54** F8
Jiménez *Chihuahua* Mex. **184** D3
Jiménez *Coahuila* Mex. **185** E2
Jiménez *Tamaulipas* Mex. **185** F3
Jimeta Nigeria **125** I4
Jimi *r.* P.N.G. **73** J7
Jim Jim Creek *r.* Australia **148** B2
Jimo China **85** I4
Jimsar China **88** E3
Jina Romania **58** E3
Jinan China **85** H4
  formerly spelt Tsinan
Jin'an China *see* Songpan
Jinbi China *see* Dayao
Jinchang China **84** D4
  formerly known as Jinchuan
Jincheng China **85** G5
Jincheng China *see* Leibo
Jincheng China *see* Yilong
Jincheng China *see* Wuding
Jinchengjiang China *see* Hechi
Jinchuan China *see* Jinchang
Jinchuan China *see* Xingan
Jinchuan China **85** J4
  also known as Quqên
Jind India **96** C3
Jindrichuv Hradec Czech Rep. **49** M6
Jin'e China *see* Longchang
Jinfosi China **84** C4
Jing China *see* Jinghe
Jing *r.* China **87** D1
Jing'an China *see* Doumen
Jingbian China **85** F4
  also known as Zhangjiapan
Jingchuan China **85** E5
Jingde China **87** F2
Jingdezhen China **87** F2
Jingdong China **86** B3
  also known as Jinping
Jinggangshan China **87** E3
  formerly known as Ciping
Jinggang Shan *hill* China **87** E3
Jinggongqiao China **87** F2
Jinggu China **86** B4
  also known as Weiyuan
Jinghai China **85** H4
Jinghe China **88** C2
  also known as Jing
Jinghong China **86** B4
  formerly known as Yunjinghong
Jingjiang China **87** G1
Jingle China **85** G4
Jingmen China **87** E2
Jingning China **85** E5
Jingpeng China **85** H3
  also known as Hexigten Qi
Jingpo Hu *resr* China **82** C4
Jingshan China **87** E2
  also known as Xinshi
Jingtai China **84** D4
  also known as Yitiaoshan
Jingtieshan China **84** C4
  formerly known as Huashugou
Jingxi China **86** C4
  also known as Xinjing
Jingxian China **87** F2
Jingxian China *see* Jingzhou
Jingxin China **82** C4
  also known as Yongshan
Jingyan China **86** C2
Jingyang China *see* Yancheng
Jingyang China *see* Jingde
Jingyu China **82** B4
Jingyuan China **85** E4
Jingzhou *Hubei* China **87** E2
  formerly known as Jiangling
Jingzhou *Hubei* China **87** E2
  also known as Shashi
Jingzhou *Hunan* China **87** D3
  also known as Quyang; formerly known as
  Jingxian
Jinhe China *see* Jinping
Jinhua China *see* Jianchuan
Jinhua China **87** F2
Jining *Nei Mongol* China **85** G3
  also spelt Tsining
Jining *Shandong* China **85** H5
  formerly known as Chining
Jinja Uganda **128** B4
Jinjiang *Fujian* China **87** F3
Jinjiang China *see* Chengmai
Jinjiang *Yunnan* China **86** B3
Jin Jiang *r.* China **87** D3
Jin Jiang *r.* China **87** E2
Jinka Eth. **128** C3
Jinkouhe China **86** B2
Jinmen Taiwan *see* Chinmen
Jinmu Jiao *pt* China **87** D5
Jinning China **86** B3
Jinotega Nicaragua **186** B4
Jinotepe Nicaragua **186** B5
Jinping *Guizhou* China **87** D3
  also known as Sanjiang
Jinping China *see* Jinghe
Jinping *Yunnan* China **86** B4
  also known as Jinhe
Jinping China *see* Qiubei
Jinping Shan *mts* China **86** B3
Jinsen S. Korea *see* Inch'ŏn
Jinsha China **87** D3
Jinsha Jiang *r.* China **78** D3
  also known as Yangtze
Jinshan *Nei Mongol* China **85** H3
  also known as Harqin Qi
Jinshan *Shanghai* China **87** G2
  also known as Zhujing
Jinshan China *see* Lufeng
Jinshi China **87** D2
Jinshi China *see* Xinning
Jinta China **84** C4
Jintan China **87** F2
Jintang China **86** C2
  also known as Zhaozhen
Jintotolo Channel Phil. **74** B4
Jintur India **94** C2
Jinxi China **87** F3
  also known as Xiugu
Jinxi China *see* Lianshan
Jin Xi *r.* China **87** F3
Jinxian China **87** F2
  also known as Minhe
Jinxian China *see* Linhai
Jinxiang *Shandong* China **85** H5
Jinxiang *Zhejiang* China **87** G3
Jinxiu China **87** D3
Jinyang China *see* Dayi
Jinyun China **87** G2
  also known as Wuyun
Jinzhai China **87** E2
  also known as Meishan
Jinzhong China **85** G4
Jinzhou *Liaoning* China **85** I3
Jinzhou *Liaoning* China **85** I4
Jinzhou Wan *b.* China **85** I4
Jinzhu China *see* Daocheng

Jírau Brazil **200** D2
Jirgatol Tajik. **101** G2
  also known as Gatong
Jiri *r.* India **97** G4
Jirin Gol China **85** H2
Jirkov Czech Rep. **49** K5
Jiroft Iran **100** D4
  also known as Sabzvārān
Jirriban Somalia **128** E3
Jirwān Saudi Arabia **105** E3
Jirzah Egypt **108** C8
Jishan China **85** F5
Jishi China *see* Xunhua
Jishou China **87** D2
Jishui China *see* Yongfeng
Jisr ash Shughūr Syria **108** H2
Jitian China *see* Lianshan
Jitra Malaysia **76** C1
Jiu *r.* Romania **58** E5
Jiudengkou China **85** E4
Jiuding Shan *mt.* China **86** B2
Jiugong Shan *mt.* China **87** E2
Jiujiang *Jiangxi* China **87** E2
  also known as Shahejie; formerly known as
  Shahezhen
Jiujiang *Jiangxi* China **87** E2
Jiuling Shan *mts* China **87** E2
Jiulong *Hong Kong* China *see* Kowloon
Jiulong China **86** B2
Jiulong China *see* Yuechi
Jiuquan China **84** C4
  formerly known as Suzhou
Jiutai China **85** J3
Jiuxian China **85** F4
Jiuxu China **87** D3
Jiuzhen China **87** F3
Jiwani Pak. **101** E5
Jiwen China **85** I1
Jixi *Anhui* China **87** F2
  also known as Huayang
Jixi *Heilong.* China **82** C3
Jixian China *see* Jizhou
Jixian *Heilong.* China **82** C3
  also known as Fuli; formerly known as Fulitun
Jixian *Shanxi* China **85** F5
Jiyuan China **85** G5
Jiz, Wādī al *r.* Yemen **105** F4
Jīzān Saudi Arabia **104** C4
Jīzān *prov.* Saudi Arabia **104** C4
Jizera *r.* Czech Rep. **49** L5
Jizerské Hory *mts* Czech Rep. **49** M5
Jizhou China **85** G5
  formerly known as Jixian
Jizl *watercourse* Saudi Arabia **104** B2
Jizō-zaki *pt* Japan **91** C7
Jizzakh Uzbek. *see* Dzhizak
Jizzakh Wiloyati *admin. div.* Uzbek. *see*
  Dzhizakskaya Oblast'
Joaçaba Brazil **203** B8
Joachimsthal Germany **49** K3
Joaíma Brazil **202** D6
Joal-Fadiout Senegal **124** A3
Joana Peres Brazil **202** B2
João Belo Moz. *see* Xai-Xai
João de Almeida Angola *see* Chibia
João Monlevade Brazil **207** J6
João Pessoa Brazil **202** F3
João Pinheiro Brazil **203** C6
Joaquim Felício Brazil **207** I5
Joaquín V. González Arg. **204** D2
Jobabo Cuba **186** D2
Jobat India **96** B5
Job Peak U.S.A. **182** F2
Jockfall Sweden **44** M2
Jocoli Arg. **204** C4
Joda India **97** E5
Jodhpur India **96** A4
Jodiya India **96** A5
Joe Batt's Arm Canada **169** K3
Joensuu Fin. **44** O3
Joesjö Sweden **44** K2
Jœtsu Japan **90** F6
Jofane Moz. **131** F4
Joffre, Mount Canada **167** H5
Jogbani India **97** E4
Jogbura Nepal **96** D3
Jõgeva Estonia **42** H3
Jogighopa India **97** F4
Jogindarnagar India **96** C3
Jogjakarta Indon. *see* Yogyakarta
Jõgua Estonia **42** I2
Johannesburg S. Africa **133** L3
Johan Peninsula Canada **165** L2
Jõhen Japan **91** C8
Johilla *r.* India **96** D5
John Day U.S.A. **180** C3
John Day *r.* U.S.A. **180** C3
John Day, Middle Fork *r.* U.S.A. **180** C3
John Day, North Fork *r.* U.S.A. **180** C3
John d'Or Prairie Canada **167** H3
John F. Kennedy *airport* U.S.A. **177** L5
John hill Kerr Reservoir U.S.A. **176** G9
John Jay, Mount Canada/U.S.A. **166** C3
Johnny Hoe *r.* Canada **166** F1
John o'Groats U.K. **46** I5
Johnson U.S.A. **177** M1
Johnson City *NY* U.S.A. **177** J3
Johnson City *TN* U.S.A. **176** C9
Johnson City *TX* U.S.A. **179** C6
Johnsondale U.S.A. **182** F6
Johnsonville U.S.A. **175** D5
Johnston, Lake *salt flat* Australia **151** C7
Johnston and Sand Islands *atoll*
  N. Pacific Ocean *see* Johnston Atoll
▶ Johnston Atoll N. Pacific Ocean **220** G4
  United States Unincorporated Territory. Also
  known as Johnston and Sand Islands.
  oceania [countries] ➡ 138–139
Johnstone Lake Canada *see*
  Old Wives Lake
Johnstone Strait Canada **166** E5
Johnstone Range *hills* Australia **151** B6
Johnstown *NY* U.S.A. **177** K2
Johnstown *OH* U.S.A. **176** C5
Johnstown *PA* U.S.A. **176** G5
Johor *state* Malaysia **76** C2
Johor, Selat *strait* Malaysia/Sing. **76** [inset]
Johor, Sungai Malaysia **76** C2
Johor Bahru Malaysia **76** C2
Jõhvi Estonia **42** I2
Joigny France **51** J5
Joinville Brazil **203** B8
Joinville Island Antarctica **222** U2
Jõjutla Mex. **185** F5
Jokela Fin. **45** N3
Jokkmokk Sweden **44** M2
Jøkelbugten *b.* Greenland **165** Q2
Jokioinen Fin. **45** M3
Jokiperä Fin. **44** M3
Jökulbunga *hill* Iceland **44** [inset] B2
Jökulfirðir *inlet* Iceland **44** [inset] B2
Jökulsá á Dál *r.* Iceland **44** [inset] D2
Jökulsá á Fjöllum *r.* Iceland **44** [inset] C2
Jolarpettai India **94** C3
Jolfa Iran **107** G4
Joliet U.S.A. **174** B4
Joliette Canada **169** F4
Jolly Lake Canada **167** H1
Jolo Phil. **74** B5
Jolo *i.* Phil. **74** B5
Jomala Fin. **45** K3
Jomalig *i.* Phil. **74** B3
Jomard Entrance *sea chan.* P.N.G. **149** F1

Jombang Indon. **77** F4
Jomda China **86** A2
  also known as Gatong
Jømna Norway **45** J3
Jomsom Nepal **97** D3
Jonāh Iran **100** C5
Jonancy U.S.A. **176** C8
Jonathán Point Belize **185** H5
Jonava Lith. **42** F6
Jonê China **86** B1
  also known as Liulin
Jonesboro *AR* U.S.A. **174** B5
Jonesboro *IL* U.S.A. **174** B4
Jonesboro *LA* U.S.A. **179** D5
Jonesboro *TN* U.S.A. **176** C9
Jones Mills U.S.A. **176** F5
Jones Mountains Antarctica **222** R2
Jones Sound *sea chan.* Canada **165** K2
Jonestown *KY* U.S.A. **176** A8
Jonestown *PA* U.S.A. **177** I5
Jonesville *NC* U.S.A. **176** E9
Jonesville *VA* U.S.A. **176** B9
Jonglei Sudan **128** B3
Jonglei *state* Sudan **128** B3
Jonglei Canal Sudan **128** A3
Joniškėlis Lith. **42** E5
Joniškis Lith. **42** E5
Jönköping Sweden **45** K4
Jönköping *county* Sweden **45** K4
Jonquière Canada **169** G3
Jonuta Mex. **185** G5
Jonzac France **50** E4
Joplin U.S.A. **178** D4
Joppa Israel *see* Tel Aviv-Yafo
Jora India **96** C4
▶ Jordan *country* Asia **108** G7
  known as Al 'Urdun in Arabic
  asia [countries] ➡ 64–67
Jordan *r.* Asia **108** G6
Jordan *MT* U.S.A. **180** F3
Jordan *NY* U.S.A. **177** I2
Jordan *r.* OR U.S.A. **180** C4
Jordan *r.* UT U.S.A. **183** L1
Jordânia Brazil **207** M2
Jordet Norway **45** K3
Jorge Montt, Isla *i.* Chile **205** B8
Jorhat India **97** G4
Jorm Afgh. **101** G2
Jormvattnet Sweden **44** K2
Jörn Sweden **44** M2
Joroinen Fin. **44** N3
Jørpeland Norway **45** I4
Jos Nigeria **125** H4
Jose Abad Santos Phil. **74** C5
José Bonifácio *Rondônia* Brazil **201** E3
José Bonifácio *São Paulo* Brazil **206** D8
José Cardel Mex. **185** F5
José de Freitas Brazil **202** D3
José de San Martin Arg. **205** C7
José Enrique Rodó Uruguay **204** F4
Joselândia Brazil **201** F4
José Pañganiban Phil. **74** B3
José Pedro Varela Uruguay **204** G4
Joseph, Lac *l.* Canada **169** H3
Joseph Bonaparte Gulf Australia **150** D2
Joseph City U.S.A. **183** N7
Joshimath India **96** C3
Jōshin-etsu-kōgen National Park Japan
  91 F6
Joshipur India **97** E5
Joshua Tree U.S.A. **183** H7
Joshua Tree National Park U.S.A. **183** I8
Jos Plateau Nigeria **125** H4
Josselin France **50** C5
Jossund Norway **44** J2
Jostedalsbreen *glacier* Norway **45** I3
Jostedalsbreen Nasjonalpark *nat. park*
  Norway **45** I3
Josvainiai Lith. **42** E6
Jotunheimen *mts* Norway **45** J3
Jotunheimen Nasjonalpark *nat. park*
  Norway **45** J3
Joubertina S. Africa **132** H10
Jouberton S. Africa **133** K3
Joué-lès-Tours France **50** G5
Joukokylä Fin. **44** N2
Jourdanton U.S.A. **179** C6
Joussard Canada **167** H4
Joutsa Fin. **45** N3
Joutseno Fin. **45** O3
Joutsijärvi Fin. **44** N2
Joux, Lac de *l.* Switz. **51** M6
Jovellanos Cuba **186** C2
Jowai India **97** G4
Jowzjān *prov.* Afgh. **101** F2
Joy, Mount Canada **166** C2
Joya de Cerén *tourist site* El Salvador
  185 H6
Jozini S. Africa **133** Q4
Jrayfiya *well* W. Sahara **122** B4
Jreïda Mauritania **124** A2
Juan Aldama Mex. **185** E3
Juancheng China **85** G5
Juan de Fuca Strait Canada/U.S.A. **164** G5
Juan de Garay Arg. **204** E4
Juan de Nova *i.* Indian Ocean **129** D9
Juan E. Barra Arg. **204** E5
Juan Escutia Mex. **184** D4
Juan Fernández, Archipiélago *is*
  S. Pacific Ocean *see*
  Juan Fernández Islands
Juan Fernández Islands S. Pacific Ocean
  221 M8
  also known as Juan Fernández, Archipiélago
Juangriego Venez. **199** F2
Juan Jorge Arg. **204** F3
Juankoski Fin. **44** O3
Juan Mata Ortíz Mex. **184** C2
Juanshui China *see* Tongcheng
Juan Stuven, Isla *i.* Chile **205** B7
Juara Brazil **201** F3
Juárez Mex. **185** F3
Juárez, Sierra *de mts* Mex. **184** A1
Juatinga, Ponta da *pt* Brazil **207** I10
Juazeiro Brazil **202** D4
Juazeiro do Norte Brazil **202** E3
Juazohn Liberia **124** C5
Juba *r.* Somalia *see* Jubba
Juba Sudan **128** B3
Juban Yemen **104** D5
Jubany *research station* Antarctica **222** U2
  long form Teniente Jubany
Jubba *r.* Somalia **128** D5
  also spelt Juba; formerly spelt Giuba
Jubbada Dhexe *admin. reg.* Somalia **128** D4
Jubbada Hoose *admin. reg.* Somalia **128** D4
Jubbah Saudi Arabia **104** C1
Jubbulpore India *see* Jabalpur
Jubilee Lake *salt flat* Australia **151** D6
Jubing Nepal **97** E4
Juby, Cap *c.* Morocco **122** B4
Júcar *r.* Spain **55** K5
Juçara Brazil **206** C2
Júcaro Cuba **186** D2
Juchatengo Mex. **185** F5
Juchitán Mex. **184** D4
Juchitlán Mex. **184** D4
Jucurucu Brazil **203** E6
Jucuruçu *r.* Brazil **207** N4
Judaberg Norway **45** I4
Judaidah *watchole* Iraq **109** M5
Judaydah Syria **109** J2
Judayyidat 'Ar'ar *well* Iraq **107** C4
Judenburg Austria **49** L8
Judian China **86** A3
Judith *r.* U.S.A. **180** E3

Judith Gap U.S.A. **180** E3
Juegang China *see* Rudong
Juego de Bolos *mt.* Spain **55** H6
Juelsminde Denmark **45** J5
Juerana Brazil **207** N4
Jufari *r.* Brazil **199** F5
Jugon-les-Lacs France **50** D4
Jugoslavija country Europe *see* Yugoslavia
Juh China **85** G3
Juhaynah *reg.* Saudi Arabia **104** B2
Juigalpa Nicaragua **186** B4
Juillac France **50** H7
Juillet, Lac *l.* Canada **169** I2
Juína Brazil **201** F2
Juina *r.* Brazil **201** F3
Juína Brazil **201** F3
Juist *i.* Germany **48** E2
Juiz de Fora Brazil **203** D7
Jujuhan *r.* Indon. **76** C3
Jujuy *prov.* Arg. **200** D5
Jukkasjärvi Sweden **44** M2
  also known as Čohkkiras
Julaca Bol. **200** D5
Julesburg U.S.A. **178** B3
Juli Peru **200** C4
Julia Brazil **199** F5
Juliaca Peru **200** C3
Julia Creek Australia **149** D4
Julian U.S.A. **183** H8
Julian, Lac *l.* Canada **168** E2
Julian Alps *mts* Slovenia *see* Julijske Alpe
Julianatop *mt.* Indon. *see* Mandala, Puncak
Juliana Top *mt.* Suriname **199** G4
Julianehåb Greenland *see* Qaqortoq
Julijske Alpe *mts* Slovenia **56** F3
  English form Julian Alps
Julimes Mex. **184** D2
Juliomagus France *see* Angers
Júlio Mesquita Brazil **206** D9
Julius, Lake Australia **149** C4
Jullundur India *see* Jalandhar
Juma *r.* Brazil **199** E6
Juma *r.* China **85** H4
Juma Uzbek. *see* Dzhuma
Jumaggoin China **86** A1
Jumba Somalia **128** D5
Jumilla Spain **55** J6
Jumla Nepal **97** D3
Jumna *r.* India *see* Yamuna
Jump *r.* U.S.A. **172** B5
Jumprava Latvia **42** F5
Junagadh India **96** A5
Junagarh India **94** D2
Junan China **85** H5
  also known as Shizilu
Jun Bulen China **85** H2
Junction *TX* U.S.A. **179** C6
Junction *UT* U.S.A. **183** L3
Junction Bay Australia **148** B1
Junction City *KS* U.S.A. **178** C4
Junction City *KY* U.S.A. **176** A8
Junction City *OR* U.S.A. **180** B3
Jundah Australia **149** D5
Jundiaí Brazil **206** G10
▶ Juneau U.S.A. **164** F3
  State capital of Alaska.
Juneau Icefield Canada **166** C3
Junee Australia **147** F3
Jūn el Khudr *b.* Lebanon **108** G4
Jungar Qi China *see* Shagedu
Jungfrau *mt.* Switz. **51** O6
Junggar Pendi *basin* China **88** D2
  English form Dzungarian Basin
Jungshahi Pak. **101** F5
Junguls Sudan **128** B2
Juniata *r.* U.S.A. **177** H5
Junik *Kosovo, Srbija* Yugo. **58** B6
Junín Arg. **204** E4
Junín Peru **200** A2
Junín *r.* Peru **200** B2
Junior U.S.A. **176** F7
Juniper Mountains U.S.A. **183** K6
Junípero Serro Peak U.S.A. **182** C5
Junkerdalen Balvatnet *nature res.* Norway
  44 K2
Junlian China **86** B2
Junnar India **94** B2
Junosuando Sweden **44** M2
Junsele Sweden **44** L3
Junshan Hu *l.* China **87** F2
Juntura U.S.A. **180** C4
Juntusranta Fin. **44** O2
Junxi China *see* Datian
Junxian China *see* Danjiangkou
Ju'nyung China **86** A1
  formerly known as Ju'nyunggoin
Ju'nyunggoin China *see* Ju'nyung
Juodkrantė Lith. **42** C6
Juodšiliai Lith. **42** G7
Juodupė Lith. **42** G5
Juoksengi Sweden **44** M2
Juosta *r.* Lith. **42** F6
Juostinikai Lith. **42** G6
Juozapinės kalnas *hill* Lith. **42** G7
Jupägi Iran **100** D4
Juparanã, Lagoa *l.* Brazil **207** M6
Jupiá, Represa *resr* Brazil **206** B8
Jupiter U.S.A. **175** D7
Juquiá Brazil **206** F11
Juquiá *r.* Brazil **206** F11
Juquitiba Brazil **206** F10
Jur *r.* Sudan **126** E3
Jura *mts* France/Switz. **51** L7
Jūra *r.* Lith. **42** D6
Jura *i.* U.K. **46** G7
Jura, Sound of *sea chan.* U.K. **46** G8
Juradó Col. **198** B3
Juramento Brazil **207** J3
Juranda Brazil **206** A11
Juré Estonia **42** F2
Juremal Brazil **202** D4
Jurf ad Darāwīsh Jordan **108** G7
Jurgurra *r.* Australia **150** C3
Jurh China **85** I2
Jürhen Ul Shan *mts* China **97** G3
Jūrī Estonia **42** F2
Jurien Australia **151** A6
Jurien Bay Australia **151** A6
Jurilovca Romania **58** J4
Juriti Velho Brazil **199** G5
Jūrmala Latvia **42** E5
Jurmu Fin. **44** N2
Jurong China **87** F2
Jurong, Selat *strait* Sing. **76** [inset]
Jurong Island *reg.* Sing. **76** [inset]
Juruá Brazil **198** D5
Juruá *r.* Brazil **198** E5
Juruena Brazil **201** F1
Juruena *r.* Brazil **201** F3
Jurumirim, Represa de *resr* Brazil **206** E10
Juruparí *r.* Brazil **199** E4
Juruti Brazil **199** G5
Juruti Velho Brazil **199** G5
Justice U.S.A. **176** D8
Justo Daract Arg. **204** D4
Jutaí Brazil **198** D5
Jutaí *r.* Brazil **198** E5
Jüterbog Germany **49** K4
Juti Brazil **203** A7
Jutiapa Guat. **185** H6
Jutiapa Hond. **186** B4

Juticalpa Hond. 186 B4
Jutis Sweden 44 L2
Jutland pen. Denmark 45 J4
also spelt Jylland
Juuka Fin. 44 O3
Juupajoki Fin. 45 N3
Juurikorpi Fin. 42 H1
Juva Fin. 45 N3
Juwain Afgh. 101 E4
Juwana Indon. 77 E4
Juxian China 85 H5
also known as Chengyang
Juye China 85 H5
Jūymand Iran 100 D3
also known as Gonabad
Jūyom Iran 100 C4
Južnoukrajinsk Ukr. see Yuzhnoukrayinsk
Jwaneng Botswana 131 E5
Jylland pen. Denmark see Jutland
Jyrgalang Kyrg. 103 I4
also spelt Dzhergalan
Jyväskylä Fin. 44 N3

↓ K

▶K2 mt. China/Jammu and Kashmir 96 C2
2nd highest mountain in the world and in
Asia. English form Godwin-Austen, Mount;
also known as Qogir Feng.
world [physical features] ➤➤ 8–9

Ka r. Nigeria 125 G4
Kaabong Uganda 128 B4
Kaa-Iya, Parque Nacional nat. park Bol.
201 E4
Kaakhka Turkm. see Kaka
Kaalpan salt pan S. Africa 132 I4
Kaalrug S. Africa 133 P2
Kaamanen Fin. 44 N1
also known as Gámas
Kaambooni Kenya 128 D5
Kääpa Estonia 42 I4
Kaapamuiden S. Africa 133 P2
Kaapstad S. Africa see Cape Town
Kaarina Fin. 45 M3
Kaarta r. Mali 124 C3
Kaavi Fin. 44 O3
Kaba China see Habahe
Kaba r. China/Kazakh. 88 D2
Kabakly Turkm. 103 E5
also spelt Gabakly
Kabala Sierra Leone 124 C4
Kabale Uganda 128 A5
Kabalega Falls National Park Uganda see
Murchison Falls National Park
Kabalo Dem. Rep. Congo 126 E6
Kabambare Dem. Rep. Congo 126 E6
Kabambay Kazakh. 88 C2
Kabanga Dem. Rep. Congo 127 C6
Kabangu Dem. Rep. Congo 127 D7
Kabanjahe Indon. 76 B2
Kabansk Rus. Fed. 85 E1
Kabara r. Fiji 145 H3
also spelt Kambara; formerly known as
Appalla
Kabardino-Balkarskaya A.S.S.R. aut. rep.
Rus. Fed. see
Kabardino-Balkarskaya Respublika
Kabardino-Balkarskaya Respublika
aut. rep. Rus. Fed. 41 G8
formerly known as Kabardino-Balkarskaya
A.S.S.R.
Kabardino-Balkarskiy Zapovednik
nature res. Rus. Fed. 41 G8
Kabare Dem. Rep. Congo 126 F5
Kabarega National Park Uganda see
Murchison Falls National Park
Kabasalan Phil. 74 B5
Kabaung r. Myanmar 78 B4
Kabaw Valley Myanmar 78 A3
Kabba Nigeria 125 G5
Kabbani r. India 94 C3
Kåbdalis Sweden 44 M2
Kabd aş Şārim reg. Syria 109 K3
Kabd Warqah reg. Syria 109 K3
Kabélawa Niger 125 I3
Kabenung Lake Canada 173 I2
Kaberneeme Estonia 42 G2
Kabertene Alg. 123 F3
Kab-hegy hill Hungary 49 O8
Kabinakagami r. Canada 168 C3
Kabinakagami Lake Canada 168 C3
Kabinda Dem. Rep. Congo 127 D6
Kabir r. Syria 108 G2
Kabīrkūh mts Iran 100 A3
Kabirwala Pak. 101 G4
Kabli Estonia 42 F3
Kabneshwar India 96 C5
Kabo Cent. Afr. Rep. 126 C3
Kabompo Zambia 127 D8
Kabompo r. Zambia 127 C8
Kabondo-Dianda Dem. Rep. Congo 127 E7
Kabongo Dem. Rep. Congo 127 E6
Kabosa Island Myanmar 79 B5
Kabou Cent. Afr. Rep. 126 D3
Kabou Togo 125 F4
Kabozha Rus. Fed. 43 R3
Kabrousse Senegal 124 A3
Kabshah, Jabal hills Saudi Arabia 104 C2
Kabūdeh Iran 101 E3
Kabūd Gonbad Iran 101 D2
also known as Kalāt
Kabul r. Afgh. 101 H3
Kabugao Phil. 74 B2

▶Kābul Afgh. 101 G3
Capital of Afghanistan. Historically known
as Ortospana.

Kābul prov. Afgh. 101 G3
Kabul r. Afgh. 101 H3
Kabunda Dem. Rep. Congo 127 F8
Kabunduk Indon. 75 A5
Kaburuang r. Indon. 75 C2
Kabushiya Sudan 121 G5
Kabūtar Khān Iran 100 C4
Kabwe Zambia 127 F8
formerly known as Broken Hill
Kabyrga r. Kazakh. 103 E2
also spelt Qabyrgha
Kačanik Kosovo, Srbija Yugo. 58 C4
Kacepi Indon. 75 D3
Kacha Kuh mts Iran/Pak. 101 E4
Kachalinskaya Rus. Fed. 41 H6
Kachchh, Gulf of India 96 A5
formerly known as Kutch, Gulf of
Kachchh, Rann of marsh India 96 A4
also spelt Kutch, Rann of
Kachh Pak. 101 F5
Kachhola India 96 B4
Kachhwa India 97 D4
Kachia Nigeria 125 G4
Kachin state Myanmar 78 B2
Kachiry Kazakh. 103 I1
Kachisi Eth. 128 C2
Kacholola Zambia 127 F8
Kachug Rus. Fed. 85 E1
Kachung Uganda 128 B4
Kaçkar Dağı mt. Turkey 107 E2
Kaczawa r. Poland 49 N4
Kada Japan 91 D7
Kadaingti Myanmar 78 B4

Kadaiyanallur India 94 C4
Kadam mt. Uganda 128 B4
Kadana Chad 120 D6
Kadanai r. Afgh./Pak. 101 F4
Kadan Kyun i. Myanmar 79 B5
also known as King Island
Kadapongan i. Indon. 77 F4
Kadaura India 96 D4
Kadavu i. Fiji 145 G3
also known as Kantavu
Kadavu Passage Fiji 145 G3
also known as Kedairu Passage; also spelt
Kandavu Passage
Kadaya Rus. Fed. 85 H1
Kaddam r. India 94 C2
Kade Ghana 125 E5
Kadéï r. Cent. Afr. Rep. 125 J6
Kadgo, Lake salt flat Australia 151 D5
Kādhimain Iraq see Al Kāzimīyah
Kadi India 96 B5
Kadiana Mali 124 D4
Kadiapattanam India 94 C4
Kadijica mt. Bulg. see Kadiytsa
Kadiköy Turkey 58 H8
Kadiköy Turkey 58 H8
historically known as Chalcedon
Kadina Australia 146 C3
Kading r. Laos 78 C4
Kadınhanı Turkey 106 C3
Kadiolo Mali 124 D4
Kadiri India 94 C3
Kadiri Turkey 106 D3
Kadiyevka Ukr. see Stakhanov
Kadiytsa mt. Bulg. 58 D7
also known as Kadijica
Kadmat i. India 94 B4
Kadnikov Rus. Fed. 43 V2
Kado Nigeria 125 G4
Kadok Malaysia 76 C1
Kadoka U.S.A. 178 B3
Kadoma Zimbabwe 131 F3
formerly spelt Gatooma
Kadonkani Myanmar 78 A5
Kadrina Estonia 42 H2
Kadugli Sudan 126 E2
Kaduna Nigeria 125 G4
Kaduna r. Nigeria 125 G4
Kaduna state Nigeria 125 G4
Kadur India 94 C3
Kaduy Rus. Fed. 43 S2
Kadyy Rus. Fed. 43 V4
Kadzherom Rus. Fed. 40 J2
Kadzhi-Say Kyrg. see Kajy-Say
Kaechon N. Korea 83 B5
Kaédi Mauritania 124 B3
Kaegudeck Lake Canada 169 K3
Kaélé Cameroon 125 I4
Kaena Point U.S.A. 181 [inset] Y1
Kaeng Krachan National Park Thai. 79 B5
Kaeo N.Z. 152 H3
Kaesŏng N. Korea 83 B5
Kafa Ukr. see Feodosiya
Kafakumba Dem. Rep. Congo 127 D7
Kafan Armenia see Kapan
Kafanchan Nigeria 125 H4
Kafferrivier S. Africa 133 K6
Kaffin-Hausa Nigeria 125 H3
Kaffir r. S. Africa 133 J6
Kafia Kingi Sudan 126 D2
Kafiau i. Indon. 75 D3
Kafireas, Akra pt Greece 59 F10
Kafireos, Steno sea chan. Greece 59 F11
Kafiristan reg. Pak. 101 G3
Kafirnigan r. Tajik. see Kofarnihon
Kåfjordbotn Norway 44 M1
Kafolo Côte d'Ivoire 124 E4
Kafr el Battikh Egypt 108 C6
Kafr el Dauwâr Egypt 108 B6
Kafr el Garâyda Egypt 108 C6
Kafr el Sheikh Egypt 121 F2
Kafr el Sheikh governorate Egypt 108 B6
Kafr el Zaiyât Egypt 108 B6
Kafret Rihama Egypt 121 E2
Kafr Silīm Egypt 108 B6
Kafu r. Uganda 128 B4
Kafue Zambia 127 F8
Kafue r. Zambia 127 F8
Kafue Flats marsh Zambia 127 E8
Kafue National Park Zambia 127 E8
Kaga Japan 91 E6
Kaga Bandoro Cent. Afr. Rep. 126 C3
formerly known as Fort Crampel
Kagan Uzbek. 103 F5
also spelt Kagon
Kaganovich Rus. Fed. see Tovarkovskiy
Kaganovichabad Tajik. see Kolkhozobod
Kaganovichi Pervyye Ukr. see Polis'ke
Kagarlyk Ukr. see Kaharlyk
Kagawa pref. Japan 91 D7
Kagawong Canada 173 K5
Kåge Sweden 44 M2
Kagera admin. reg. Tanz. 128 C5
Kagera, Parc National de la nat. park
Rwanda see Akagera National Park
Kagera r. S. Africa 133 L4
Kağızman Turkey 107 E2
Kagmar Sudan 121 F6
Kagologolo Indon. 76 B3
Kagoshima Japan 91 B9
Kagoshima airport Japan 91 B9
Kagoshima pref. Japan 91 B9
Kagoshima-wan b. Japan 91 B9
Kāhak Iran 100 B3
Kahalaiya, Gebel hill Egypt 108 D8
Kahama Tanz. 129 B5
Kaharlyk Ukr. 41 D6
also spelt Kagarlyk
Kahatola i. Indon. 75 C2
Kahawero waterhole Namibia 130 B4
Kahayan r. Indon. 77 F3
Kahemba Dem. Rep. Congo 127 C6
Kaherekoau Mountains N.Z. 153 B13
Kahla Germany 48 I5
Kahntah Canada 166 F3
Kahnu Iran see Kahnūj
Kahnūj Iran 100 D5
also known as Kahnu
Kahoe N.Z. 152 H3
Kahoka U.S.A. 174 B3
Kahoolawe i. U.S.A. 181 [inset] Z1
also spelt Kahulaui; formerly known as
Tahaurawe
Kahperusvaarat mts Fin. 38 C3
Kahramanmaraş Turkey 107 D3
also known as Maraş; historically known
as Germanicia
Kahror Pak. 101 G4
Kahta Turkey 107 D3
Kahuku Japan 90 G6
Kakus r. Sarawak Malaysia 77 F2
Kahuku U.S.A. 181 [inset] Y1
Kahului U.S.A. 181 [inset] Z1
also known as Kaholawe
Kahūrak Iran 101 D4
Kahurangi National Park N.Z. 152 G9
formerly known as North West Nelson
Forest Park
Kahuta Pak. 101 H3
Kahuzi-Biega, Parc National du nat. park
Dem. Rep. Congo 126 F5
Kai, Kepulauan is Indon. 73 H8
Kaiama Nigeria 125 F4

Kaiapit P.N.G. 73 K8
Kaiapoi N.Z. 153 G11
Kaibab U.S.A. 183 L5
Kaibamardang China 84 C4
Kaibara India 91 A5
Kai Besar i. Indon. 73 H8
Kaibito Plateau U.S.A. 183 M5
Kaidu He r. China 88 D3
Kaieteur Falls Guyana 199 G3
Kaifeng Henan China 87 E1
also known as Huanglongsi
Kaifeng Henan China 87 E1
also known as Kaifeng
Kaihu r. N.Z. 152 H3
Kaihua China see Wenshan
Kaihua China 87 C2
Kaijiang China 87 C2
also known as Xinning
Kai Kecil i. Indon. 73 H8
Kai Keung Leng Hong Kong China
87 [inset]
Kaikohe N.Z. 152 H3
Kaikoura N.Z. 153 H10
Kaikoura Peninsula N.Z. 153 H10
Kailahun Sierra Leone 124 C4
Kailas mt. China see Kangrinboqê Feng
Kailas Range mts China see Gangdisê Shan
Kaili China 85 I3
Kailong China see Hanyuan
Kailu China 85 J3
Kailua U.S.A. 181 [inset] Z1
Kailua Kona U.S.A. 181 [inset] Z2
Kailua r. Indon. 75 A3
Kaimai-Mamaku Forest Park nature res.
N.Z. 152 J5
Kaimana Indon. 73 H7
Kaimanawa Forest Park nature res. N.Z.
152 K6
Kaimanawa Mountains N.Z. 152 J7
Kaimar China 84 C4
Kaimganj India 96 C4
Kaimon-dake hill Japan 91 B9
Kaimur Range hills India 97 D4
Käina Estonia 42 D3
Kainan Tokushima Japan 91 D8
Kainan Wakayama Japan 91 D7
Kainda Kyrg. see Kayyngdy
Kaindy Kyrg. see Kayyngdy
Kaingaroa Forest N.Z. 152 K6
Kaingiwa Nigeria 125 G4
Kainji Lake National Park Nigeria 125 G4
Kainji Reservoir Nigeria 125 G4
Kaintaragarh India 95 E1
Kaipara Harbour N.Z. 152 H3
Kaiparowits Plateau U.S.A. 183 M4
Kaiping China 87 E4
Kaiping China see Dêqên
Kaipokok Bay Canada 169 J2
Kaira India see Kheda
Kairakau Beach N.Z. 152 K7
Kairana India 96 C3
Kairatu Indon. 75 D3
Kairouan Tunisia 123 H2
Kaiserslautern Germany 48 E6
Kaiser Wilhelm II Land reg. Antarctica
223 F2
Kaishantun China 82 C4
Kaišiadorys Lith. 42 F7
Kait, Tanjung pt Indon. 77 D3
Kaitaia N.Z. 152 H3
Kaitangata N.Z. 153 D14
Kaitawa N.Z. 152 L6
Kaitha India 96 C5
Kaithal India 96 C3
Kaitong China see Tongyu
Kaitum Sweden 44 M2
Kaitumälven r. Sweden 44 M2
Kaiwatu Indon. 75 C5
Kaiwi Channel U.S.A. 181 [inset] Z1
also known as Hanfeng
Kaixian China 87 D2
Kaiyang Liaoning China 85 J3
Kaiyuan Yunnan China 86 B3
Kaijaani Fin. 44 N2
Kajabbi Australia 149 D4
Kajaki Afgh. 101 F3
Kajang Malaysia 76 C2
Kajdar Iran 101 E5
Kajiado Kenya 128 C5
Kajo Kaji Sudan 128 A4
Kaju Iran 100 A2
Kajuligah Nature Reserve Australia 147 E3
Kajy-Say Kyrg. 103 I4
also known as Kadzhi-Say
Kak, Ozero salt l. Kazakh. 103 F1
also known as Qay Köli
Kaka Sudan 128 A2
Kaka Turkm. 102 D5
formerly spelt Kaakhka
Kakaban i. Indon. 77 G2
Kakabeka Falls Canada 168 B3
Kakabia i. Indon. 75 B4
Kakadu Aboriginal Land res. Australia
148 A2
Kakadu National Park Australia 148 A2
Kakagi Lake Canada 168 A3
Kakal r. Phil. 74 C5
Kakamas S. Africa 132 E5
Kakamega Kenya 128 B4
Kakamigahara Japan 91 E7
Kakana Indon. 95 H6
Kakanj Bos.-Herz. 56 K4
Kakanui Mountains N.Z. 153 E13
Kakarahil well Niger 125 H3
Kakaramea r. N.Z. 152 I7
Kakaramea vol. N.Z. 152 J6
Kakata Liberia 124 C5
Kakatahi N.Z. 152 J7
Kake Japan 91 C7
Kakel-Dawa well Eth. 128 D3
Kakenge Dem. Rep. Congo 126 D6
Kakesio Tanz. 128 B5
Kakhi Azer. see Qax
Kakhovka Ukr. 41 E7
Kakhovs'ke Vodoskhovyshche resr Ukr.
41 E7
Kakhul Moldova see Cahul
Kāki Iran 100 B4
Kakinada India 95 D2
also known as Cocanada
Kakinjēs, Maja e mt. Albania 58 A6
Kakisa r. Canada 167 G2
Kakisa Lake Canada 167 G2
Kakkalpur India 94 B3
Kakkaik r. India 94 B4
Kaklik Turkey 106 B3
Kaklimo Indon. 77 F4
Kakogawa Japan 91 D7
Kakonko Tanz. 128 B5
Kakpin Côte d'Ivoire 124 E4
Kakrala India 96 C4
Kakrima r. Guinea 124 B4
Kakshaal-Too mts China/Kyrg. see
Kokshaal-Tau
Kakuda Japan 90 G6
Kakuma Kenya 128 B4
Kakus r. Sarawak Malaysia 77 F2
Kakwa r. Canada 166 G4
Kala Tanz. 129 A7
Kalaä Kebira Tunisia 123 H2
Kalaallit Nunaat terr. N. America see
Greenland
Kalabagh Pak. 101 G3
Kalabahi Indon. 75 C5
Kalabakan Sabah Malaysia 77 G1
Kalabáka Greece see Kalampaka
Kalabaydh Togdheer Somalia 128 E2
Kalabaydh Woqooyi Galbeed Somalia 128 D2

Kalabo Zambia 127 D8
Kalach Rus. Fed. 41 G6
Kalacha Dida Kenya 128 C4
Kaladan r. India/Myanmar 95 G1
Kaladar Canada 168 E4
Kaladgi India 94 B2
Kaladaena r. Indon. 75 B3
Kalagwe Myanmar 78 B3
Kalahandi India 95 B2
▶Kalahari Desert Africa 130 D4
world [population] ➤➤ 22–23
Kalahari Gemsbok National Park S. Africa
132 E2
Kalaikhum Tajik. see Qal'aikhum
Kalai-Khumb Tajik. see Qal'aikhum
Kala-I-Mor Turkm. 101 E3
also spelt Galaymor
Kalaiya Nepal 97 E4
Kalajoki Fin. 44 M2
Kalajoki r. Fin. 44 M2
Kalak Norway 44 N1
Kalakoch hill Bulg. 58 H5
Kalalé Benin 125 F4
Kalalok Indon. 75 C1
Kalalusu i. Indon. 75 C1
Kalam India 94 C1
Kalam Pak. 101 H3
Kalāmai Greece see Kalamata
Kalamaria Greece 58 D8
Kalamata Greece 59 D11
Kalamazoo U.S.A. 172 H8
Kalamazoo r. U.S.A. 172 G8
Kalambau i. Indon. 77 F4
Kalamnuri India 94 C2
Kalamos i. Greece 59 B10
Kalamos, Akra pt Greece 59 G12
Kalampaka Greece 59 C9
also spelt Kalabáka
Kalana Estonia 42 D3
Kalana Mali 124 D4
Kalanaur Haryana India 89 B3
Kalanaur Punjab India 96 B3
Kalanchak Ukr. 41 E7
Kalandula Angola see Calandula
Kalangala Tanz. 129 B6
Kalanguru Rus. Fed. 85 H1
Kalannie Australia 151 B6
Kalanwali India 96 B3
Kalao i. Indon. 75 B4
Kalaoa U.S.A. 181 [inset] Z2
Kalaong Phil. 74 C5
Kalaotoa i. Indon. 75 B4
Kala Oya r. Sri Lanka 94 C4
Kalapana U.S.A. 181 [inset] Z2
Kalar r. watercourse Iran 101 E5
Kalār Iraq 107 F4
Kalarash Moldova see Călărași
Kalashnikovo Rus. Fed. 43 Q5
Kalasin Thai. 78 C4
Kalāt Iran 101 D3
Kalāt Iran see Kabūd Gonbad
Kalat Balochistan Pak. 101 F4
Kalat, Küh-e mt. Iran 100 D3
Kalaus r. Rus. Fed. 41 H7
Kalavad India 96 A5
Kalavryta Greece 59 D10
Kalaw Myanmar 78 B3
Kalbā U.A.E. 105 G2
Kälbäcär Azer. 107 F2
Kalbar Indon. see Kalimantan Barat
Kalbarri Australia 151 A5
Kalbarri National Park Australia 151 A5
Kalbinskiy Khrebet mts Kazakh. 88 C1
Kalbu Iran see Qalbi Zhotasy
Kaldırım Turkey 108 G1
Kaldygayty r. Kazakh. 102 C2
Kale r. India 94 B2
Kalecik Turkey 106 C2
Kaledupa i. Indon. 75 B4
Kalefeld Germany 48 H4
Kalega r. Indon. 77 G4
Kalegauk Island Myanmar 79 B5
Kaleidnung inlet Myanmar 78 A4
Kalémié Dem. Rep. Congo 127 F6
formerly known as Albertville
Kalemyo Myanmar 78 A3
Kalenoye Kazakh. 102 C2
Kalesija Bos.-Herz. 56 K4
Kalevala Rus. Fed. 44 O2
formerly known as Ukhta
Kalewa Myanmar 78 A3
Kaleybar Iran 100 A2
Kalga Rus. Fed. 85 H1
Kalgan r. Australia 151 B7
Kalgan China see Zhangjiakou
Kalghatgi India 94 B3
Kalgoorlie Australia 151 C6
Kalguéri Niger 125 H3
Kali Croatia 56 H4
Kali r. India/Nepal 96 D3
Kaliakra, Nos pt Bulg. 58 J5
Kalianda Indon. 77 D4
Kalibo Phil. 74 B4
Kaliet Indon. 76 B3
Kali Gandaki r. Nepal 97 E4
Kaligiri India 94 C3
Kalij Indon. 75 A3
Kalima Dem. Rep. Congo 126 E5
Kalimantan reg. Indon. 77 F2
Kalimantan Barat prov. Indon. 77 E2
Kalimantan Selatan prov. Indon. 77 F3
Kalimantan Tengah prov. Indon. 77 F3
Kalimantan Timur prov. Indon. 77 F2
Kalimedence park Hungary 49 O9
Kálimnos i. Greece see Kalymnos
Kalimpang India 97 F4
Kalinadi r. India 94 B3
Kali Nadi r. India 96 D3
Kalingapatnam India 95 E2
Kalinin Rus. Fed. see Tver'
Kalinin Turkm. see Boldumsaz
Kalininabad Tajik. see Kalininobod
Kaliningrad Rus. Fed. 42 B7
historically known as Königsberg
Kaliningrad Oblast admin. div. Rus. Fed.
see Kaliningradskaya Oblast'
Kaliningradskaya Oblast' admin. div.
Rus. Fed. 42 C7
English form Kaliningrad Oblast
Kaliningradskiy Zaliv b. Rus. Fed. 42 A7
Kalinino Armenia see Tashir
Kalinino Kostromskaya Oblast' Rus. Fed.
40 I4
Kalinino Omskaya Oblast' Rus. Fed. 103 H1
Kalinino Permskaya Oblast' Rus. Fed. 40 K4
Kalininobod Tajik. 101 G2
also known as Kalininabad
Kalininsk Rus. Fed. 41 H6
formerly known as Balanda
Kalininskaya Rus. Fed. 41 F7
also known as Popovicheskaya
Kalininskaya Oblast' admin. div.
Rus. Fed. see Tverskaya Oblast'
Kalinjara India 96 B5
Kalinkavichy Belarus 43 K9
also spelt Kalinkovichi
Kalinkovichi Belarus see Kalinkavichy
Kalinovka Kazakh. 102 C2
Kalinovik Bos.-Herz. 56 J4
Kaliningbalik Turkey 106 A3
Kalis Somalia 128 E2
Kalisat Indon. 77 F5
Kalisch Poland see Kalisz
Kalispell U.S.A. 180 D2
Kalisz Poland 49 P4
historically known as Kalisch
Kalisz Pomorski Poland 49 M2
Kalitva r. Rus. Fed. 41 G6

Kaliua Tanz. 129 A6
Kalix Sweden 44 M2
Kalixälven r. Sweden 44 M2
Kalka India 96 C3
Kalkan Turkey 106 B3
Kalkaringi Australia 148 A3
Kalkaska U.S.A. 173 H6
Kalkfeld Namibia 130 C4
Kalkfonteindam dam S. Africa 133 J6
Kalkfontein Dam Nature Reserve S. Africa
133 J6
Kalkwerf S. Africa 132 F5
Kallakurichi India see Kallakkurichi
Kallakoopah Creek watercourse Australia
146 C2
Kallang Sing. 76 [inset]
Kallang r. Sing. 76 [inset]
Kallaste Estonia 42 I3
Kallavesi l. Fin. 44 N3
Källberget Sweden 44 L4
Kalldorf Germany 48 G3
Kållfjärden b. Sweden 44 M2
Kallfoni Greece 59 I11
Kallonis, Kolpos b. Greece 59 H9
Kalloni Greece 59 G11
Kallur India see Kallür
Kallur India 94 C3
Kalmakkyrgan watercourse Kazakh. 103 F3
Kalmar Sweden 45 L4
Kalmar county Sweden 45 L4
Kalmarsund sea chan. Sweden 45 L4
Kalmthoutse Heide Natuurreservaat
nature res. Belgium 51 K1
Kalmücke India 96 C5
Kalmükh Qaleh Iran 101 D2
Kalmunai Sri Lanka 94 D5
Kalmykia - Khalm'g-Tangch, Republika
aut. rep. Rus. Fed. see
Kalmykiya - Khalm'g-Tangch, Respublika
Kalmykiya - Khalm'g-Tangch, Respublika
aut. rep. Rus. Fed. 41 H7
English form Kalmykia; formerly known as
Kalmytskaya Avtonomnaya Oblast'
Kalmykovo Kazakh. see Taypak
Kalmytskaya Avtonomnaya Oblast'
aut. rep. Rus. Fed. see
Kalmykiya - Khalm'g-Tangch, Respublika
Kalnai India 97 D5
Kalnciems Latvia 42 E5
Kalni r. Bangl. 97 F4
Kalnik mts Croatia 56 I2
Kalo Chório Greece 59 G13
Kalocsa Hungary 49 P9
Kalodnaye Belarus 41 H6
Kaloko Dem. Rep. Congo 127 E6
Kalol Gujarat India 96 B5
Kalol Gujarat India 96 B5
Kaloma i. Indon. 75 C4
Kaloma Tanz. 129 A6
Kalomo Zambia 127 E8
Kalone Peak Canada 166 E4
Kalopanagiotis Cyprus 108 D8
Kalozhnoye, Ozero l. Rus. Fed. 44 O2
Kalpa India 96 C3
Kalpakkam India see Chini
Kalpeni i. India 94 B4
Kalpetta India 94 C4
Kalpi India 96 C4
Kalpin China 88 D3
Kalqudug Uzbek. see Kulkuduk
Kāl-Shūr, Rūd-e r. Iran 100 D3
Kaltanėnai Lith. 42 G6
Kaltenkirchen Germany 48 G2
Kaltukatjara Australia 148 A5
Kaltungo Nigeria 125 H4
Kalu India 96 B3
Kalu r. Indon. 75 A3
Kaluderica Srbija Yugo. 58 B4
Kaluga Rus. Fed. 43 R7
Kaluga Oblast admin. div. Rus. Fed. see
Kaluzhskaya Oblast'
Kalukalukuang i. Indon. 77 G4
Kaluku Indon. 75 A3
Kalulushi Zambia 127 F8
Kalumburu Australia 150 D2
Kalumburu Aboriginal Reserve Australia
150 D2
Kalundborg Denmark 45 J5
Kalupis Falls Sabah Malaysia 77 G1
Kalur Kot Pak. 101 G3
Kalush Ukr. 41 C6
Kalutara Sri Lanka 94 C5
Kaluzhskaya Oblast' admin. div. Rus. Fed.
43 R7
English form Kaluga Oblast
Kalvan India 94 B1
Kalvarija Lith. 42 E7
Kalveliai Lith. 42 G7
Kälviä Fin. 40 D3
Kalvitsa Fin. 45 N3
Kalvola Fin. 45 N3
Kalwakurti India 94 C2
Kalyan India 94 B2
Kalyandurg India 94 C3
Kalyani India 94 C2
Kalyansingapuram India 95 D2
Kalyazin Rus. Fed. 43 S4
Kalymnos Greece 59 H12
Kalymnos i. Greece 59 H11
also spelt Kálimnos
Kalyshki Belarus 43 L5
Kama Dem. Rep. Congo 126 E5
▶Kama r. Rus. Fed. 40 J4
4th longest river in Europe.
europe [landscapes] ➤➤ 30–31
Kamaishi Japan 90 G5
Kamakura Japan 91 F7
Kamakusa Guyana 199 G3
Kamakwie Sierra Leone 124 B4
Kamal Chad 120 C2
Kamalapuram India 94 C3
Kamalia Pak. 101 H4
Kamamaung Myanmar 78 B3
Kaman Turkey 106 C3
Kamananassie r. S. Africa 132 G10
Kamanassieberg mts S. Africa 132 G10
Kamaniskeg Lake Canada 173 P5
Kamanjab Namibia 130 B3
Kamaran Yemen 104 C5
Kamarān i. Yemen 104 C5
English form Kamaran Island
Kamarang Guyana 199 F3
Kamaran Island Yemen see Kamarān
Kamard reg. Afgh. 101 F3
Kamareddi India see Kamareddy
Kamareddy India 94 C2
Kamares Dytiki Ellas Greece 59 C10
Kamares Sifnos Greece 59 F12
Kamaria Falls Guyana 199 G3
Kamarlu Armenia see Artashat
Kamas U.S.A. 183 M1
Kamashi Uzbek. 103 F5
also spelt Qamashi
Kamativi Zimbabwe 131 E3
Kamba Nigeria 125 F4
Kamba Cent. Afr. Rep. 126 C3
Kambalda Australia 151 C6
Kambam India 94 C4
Kambara i. Fiji see Kabara
Kambara Rus. Fed. 40 J4
Kambarka Rus. Fed. 40 J4
Kambayan Phil. 74 B4
Kambia Sierra Leone 124 B4
Kambing, Pulau i. East Timor see Atauro
Kambo-san mt. N. Korea see Kwanmo-bong
Kamburovo Bulg. 58 H5
Kambut Libya 120 E2
Kamchatka r. Rus. Fed. 39 Q4
Kamchatka, Poluostrov pen. Rus. Fed. see
Kamchatka Peninsula
▶Kamchatka Peninsula Rus. Fed. 39 P4
also known as Kamchatka, Poluostrov
asia [threats] ➤➤ 70–71
Kamchatskiy Proliv strait Rus. Fed. 39 Q4
Kamchatskiy Zaliv b. Rus. Fed. 39 Q4
Kamchiya r. Bulg. 58 I5
Kamchiya Planina hills Bulg. 58 I6
Kamdesh Afgh. 101 H3
Kamel r. Rus. Fed. 102 B1
Kamen' Bulg. 58 H5
Kamen Dem. Rep. Congo 127 E6
Kamen', Gory mts Rus. Fed. 39 J3
Kamende Dem. Rep. Congo 127 E6
Kamenets-Podol'skiy Ukr. see
Kam"yanets'-Podil's'kyy
Kamenitsa r. Bulg. 58 F5
Kamenjak, Rt pt Croatia 56 F4
Kamenka Kazakh. 102 B2
Kamenka Arkhangel'skaya Oblast' Rus. Fed.
40 H2
Kamenka Kaluzhskaya Oblast' Rus. Fed.
43 Q7
Kamenka Leningradskaya Oblast' Rus. Fed.
43 K1
Kamenka Lipetskaya Oblast' Rus. Fed. 43 T9
Kamenka Penzenskaya Oblast' Rus. Fed.
41 H5
Kamenka Primorskiy Kray Rus. Fed. 82 E3
Kamenka Smolenskaya Oblast' Rus. Fed.
43 N6
Kamenka-Bugskaya Ukr. see
Kam"yanka-Buz'ka
Kamenka-Strumilovskaya Ukr. see
Kam"yanka-Buz'ka
Kamenki Rus. Fed. 43 S5
Kamenniki Rus. Fed. 43 T3
Kamennogorsk Rus. Fed. 43 K1
Kamennomostskiy Rus. Fed. 41 G8
Kamennoye, Ozero l. Rus. Fed. 44 O2
Kameno Bulg. 58 I5
Kamenongue Angola see Camanongue
Kamen'-Rybolov Rus. Fed. 82 D3
Kamenskiy Rus. Fed. 41 H6
Kamenskoye Koryakskiy Avtonomnyy Okrug
Rus. Fed. 39 Q3
Kamenskoye Lipetskaya Oblast' Rus. Fed.
43 T9
Kamenskoye Ukr. see Dniprodzerzhyns'k
Kamensk-Shakhtinskiy Rus. Fed. 41 G6
Kamensk-Ural'skiy Rus. Fed. 38 G4
Kamenz Germany 49 L4
Kameoka Japan 91 D7
Kamet mt. China 89 B6
Kameyama Japan 91 E7
Kamëz Albania 58 A7
Kamiah U.S.A. 180 C3
Kamienna r. Poland 49 S4
Kamienna Gora Poland 49 N5
Kamień Pomorski Poland 49 L2
historically known as Cammin
Kamiesberg S. Africa 132 C7
Kamiesberg mts S. Africa 132 C7
Kamieskroon S. Africa 132 C7
Kamifurano Japan 90 H3
Kamikawa Japan 90 H3
Kamiiti Nigeria 149 D3
Kamina Dem. Rep. Congo 127 E7
Kaminak Lake Canada 167 M2
Kaminokuni Japan 90 G4
Kaminoyama Japan 90 G5
Kaminške in Savinjske Alpe mts Slovenia
56 I2
Kaminuriak Lake Canada see
Qamanirjuaq Lake
Kamioka Japan 91 E6
Kamiros Greece 59 I12
Kamishihoro Japan 90 H3
Kamitsushima Japan 91 A7
Kamituga Dem. Rep. Congo 126 F5
Kamkaly Kazakh. 103 G3
Kamla r. India 97 E4
Kamla r. India 97 E4
Kamloops Canada 166 F5
Kamloops Lake Canada 166 F5
Kammuri-yama mt. Japan see
Kanmuri-yama
Kamo Armenia 107 F2
Kamo N.Z. 152 I3
▶Kampala Uganda 128 B4
Capital of Uganda.
Kampanos, Akra pt Greece 59 F10
Kampar r. Indon. 76 C2
Kampar Malaysia 76 C1
Kamparkalns hill Latvia 42 D4
Kamparkiri r. Indon. 76 C2
Kampen Neth. 48 D3
Kampene Dem. Rep. Congo 126 E5
Kamphaeng Phet Thai. 78 B4
Kampi Katoto Tanz. 129 B6
Kampinoski Park Narodowy nat. park
Poland 49 R3
Kampli India 94 C3
Kampo N. Korea 91 A7
Kampolombo, Lake Zambia 127 F7
Kâmpóng Cham Cambodia 79 D5
also spelt Kompong Cham
Kâmpóng Chhnang Cambodia 79 D5
also spelt Kompong Chhnang
Kâmpóng Khleang Cambodia 79 D5
also spelt Kompong Kleang
Kâmpóng Saôm Cambodia see
Sihanoukville
Kâmpóng Spoe Cambodia 79 D6
also spelt Kompong Speu
Kâmpóng Thum Cambodia 79 D6
also spelt Kompong Thom
Kâmpôt Cambodia 79 D6
Kampuchea country Asia see Cambodia
Kamrau, Teluk b. Indon. 73 H7
Kamromskoye, Ozero l. Rus. Fed. 43 V1
Kamsack Canada 167 K5
Kamsar Latvia 42 E4
Kamskoye Vodokhranilishche resr
Rus. Fed. 40 K4
Kamsuuma Somalia 128 D4
Kamtha India 96 D5
Kamui-dake mt. Japan 90 H3
Kamui-misaki c. Japan 90 G3
Kamuli Uganda 128 B4
Kamuna Dem. Rep. Congo 127 E6
Kam"yanets'-Podil's'kyy Ukr. 41 C6
Kam"yanka-Buz'ka Ukr. 41 C6
formerly known as Kamenka-Bugskaya;
formerly known as Kamenka-Strumilovskaya
Kam"yanets-Podil's'kyy Ukr. see
Kamenets-Podol'skiy
Kam"yanka-Buz'ka Ukr. see
Kamenka-Bugskaya
Kamyanyets Belarus 42 E9
Kamyārān Iran 100 A3
Kamyen' Belarus 43 J6
Kamyshin Rus. Fed. 41 H6

index

K

Kamyshla Rus. Fed. 41 J5
Kamyshlybash Kazakh. 103 E3 also spelt Qamystybas; formerly spelt Kamyslybas
Kamysh-Samarskiye Ozera l. Kazakh. 102 B2
Kamysknoye Kazakh. 103 E2
Kamyslybas Kazakh. see **Kamyshlybash**
Kamyslybas, Ozero l. Kazakh. 103 E3
Kamyzyak Rus. Fed. 102 B3
Kamzar Oman 105 G2
Kan r. Rus. Fed. 80 F2
Kan Sudan 128 A2
Kana r. Zimbabwe 131 E3
Kana, Bukit mt. Sarawak Malaysia 77 F2
Kanaaupscow r. Canada 169 E2
Kanab U.S.A. 183 L4
Kanab Creek r. U.S.A. 183 L5
Kanagawa pref. Japan 90 F7
Kanagi Japan 90 G4
Kanaima Falls Guyana 199 F3
Kanairiktok r. Canada 169 J2
Kanakapura India 94 C3
Kanala Greece 59 F11
Kanallaki Greece 59 B9
Kanan Sweden 44 K2
Kanana S. Africa 133 K3
Kananga Dem. Rep. Congo 127 D6 formerly known as Luluabourg
Kanangra-Boyd National Park Australia 147 F3
Kanarak India see **Konarka**
Kanarraville U.S.A. 183 K4
Kanas watercourse Namibia 132 B4
Kanash Rus. Fed. 40 H5
Kanas Köl l. China 88 D1
Kanawha r. U.S.A. 176 C7
Kanazawa Japan 91 E6
Kanbalu Myanmar 78 A3
Kanchanaburi Thai. 79 B5
Kanchanjanga mt. India/Nepal see Kangchenjunga
Kanchipuram India 94 C3
Kańczuga Poland 49 T6
Kand mt. Pak. 101 F4
Kandahār Afgh. 101 F4 also spelt Qandahar; historically known as Alexandria Arachoton
Kandahār prov. Afgh. 101 F4
Kandahar India 94 C2
Kandalaksha Rus. Fed. 44 P2
Kandalakshskiy Zaliv g. Rus. Fed. 40 E2
Kandalakshskiy Zapovednik nature res. Rus. Fed. 44 P2
Kandang Indon. 76 B2
Kandangan Indon. 77 F3
Kandava Latvia 42 D4
Kandavu Passage Fiji see **Kadavu Passage**
Kandé Togo 125 F4
Kandhkot Pak. 101 G4
Kandi Benin 125 F4
Kandi, Tanjung pt Indon. 75 B2
Kandiaro Pak. 101 G5
Kandila Dytiki Ellas Greece 59 B10
Kandila Peloponnisos Greece 59 D11
Kandil Bouzou well Niger 125 H3
Kandıra Turkey 106 B2
Kandja Cent. Afr. Rep. 126 D3
Kandla India 96 A5
Kandos Australia 147 F3
Kandra India 95 E1
Kandreho Madag. 131 [inset] J3
Kandri India 97 D5
Kandrian P.N.G. 145 D2
Kandukur India 94 C3
Kandy Sri Lanka 94 D5
Kandyagash Kazakh. 102 D2 also spelt Qandyaghash; formerly known as Oktyabr' or Oktyabr'sk
Kane U.S.A. 176 G4
Kane Basin b. Greenland see **Kane Bassin**
Kane Bassin b. Greenland 165 M2 English form Kane Basin
Kaneh watercourse Iran 100 C5
Kanem pref. Chad 120 B6
Kaneohe U.S.A. 181 [inset] Z1
Kanevskaya Rus. Fed. 41 F7
Kaneyama Japan 90 G5
Kang Botswana 130 D4
Kanga r. Bangl. 97 F5
Kangaamiut Greenland 165 N3
Kangaarsussuaq c. Greenland 165 L2 also known as Parry, Kap
Kangaatsiaq Greenland 165 N3
Kangaba Mali 124 C4
Kangal Turkey 107 D3
Kangalassy Rus. Fed. 39 M3
Kangān Būshehr Iran 100 C5
Kangān Hormozgan Iran 100 D5
Kangan Aboriginal Reserve Australia 150 B4
Kangandala, Parque Nacional de nat. park Angola see Cangandala, Parque Nacional de
Kangar Malaysia 76 C1
Kangaré Mali 124 C4
Kangaroo Island Australia 146 C3
Kangaroo Point Australia 148 C3
Kangaruma Guyana 199 G3
Kangasala Fin. 45 N3
Kangaslampi Fin. 44 O3
Kangasniemi Fin. 45 N3
Kangāvar Iran 100 A3
Kangayam India 94 C4
Kangbao China 85 G3

▶**Kangchenjunga** mt. India/Nepal 97 F4
3rd highest mountain in the world and in Asia. Also spelt Kanchanjanga.
world [physical features] ➡ 8–9

Kangding China 86 B2 also known as Dardo or Lucheng
Kangean, Kepulauan is Indon. 77 F4
Kangen r. Sudan 128 B3
Kangeq c. Greenland 165 O3 also known as Cort Adelaer, Kap
Kangerluarsoruseq Greenland 165 N3 also known as Færingehavn
Kangerlussuaq Greenland 165 N3 also known as Søndre Strømfjord
Kangerlussuaq inlet Greenland 165 N2 also known as Giesecke Isfjord
Kangerlussuaq inlet Greenland 165 N3 also known as Søndre Strømfjord
Kangerlussuaq inlet Greenland 165 P3
Kangerlussuatsiaq inlet Greenland 165 O3 also known as Lindenow Fjord
Kangersuatsiaq Greenland 165 N2 also known as Prøven
Kangertittivaq sea chan. Greenland 165 Q2 also known as Scoresby Sund
Kangertittivatsiaq inlet Greenland 165 P3
Kangetet Kenya 128 C4
Kanggye N. Korea 83 B4
Kangikajik c. Greenland 165 Q2 also known as Brewster, Kap
Kangilinnguit Greenland 165 O3 also known as Grønnedal
Kangiqsualujjuaq Canada 169 H1 formerly known as Port-Nouveau-Québec
Kangiqsujuaq Canada 165 L3 formerly known as Maricourt or Wakeham
Kangirsuk Canada 165 L3 formerly known as Bellin or Payne
Kang Krung National Park Thai. 79 B6
Kangle China 84 D5
Kangle China see **Wanzai**
Kanglong China 86 A1
Kangmar China 89 E6
Kangnŭng S. Korea 83 C5
Kango Gabon 126 A4
Kangping China 85 I3
Kangra India 96 C2
Kangri Karpo Pass China/India 86 A2
Kangrinboqê Feng mt. China 89 C6 also known as Kailas
Kangsangdobdê China see **Xainza**
Kang Tipayan Dakula i. Phil. 74 B5
Kangto mt. China/India 89 F7
Kangtog China 89 D5
Kangxian China 86 C1 also known as Zuitai; formerly known as Zuitaizi
Kangxiwar China 89 B4
Kangyidaung Myanmar 78 A4
Kanhan r. India 96 C5
Kanhar r. India 97 D4
Kanhargaon India 94 C2
Kani Côte d'Ivoire 124 D4
Kani Myanmar 78 A3
Kaniama Dem. Rep. Congo 127 E6
Kanibadam Tajik. 101 G1 also spelt Konibodom
Kanibongan Sabah Malaysia 77 G1
Kaniere N.Z. 153 F10
Kanifing Gambia 124 A3
Kanigiri India 94 C3
Kanimekh Uzbek. 103 F4 also spelt Konimekh
Kanin, Poluostrov pen. Rus. Fed. 40 H2
Kanin Nos Rus. Fed. 40 G1
Kanin Nos, Mys c. Rus. Fed. 40 G1
Kaninskiy Bereg coastal area Rus. Fed. 40 G2
Kanita Japan 90 G4
Kaniva Australia 146 D4
Kanjiroba mt. Nepal 97 D3
Kanjiža Vojvodina, Srbija Yugo. 58 B2 also known as Magyarkanizsa
Kankaanpää Fin. 45 M3
Kankakee U.S.A. 174 C3
Kankakee r. U.S.A. 174 B3
Kankan Guinea 124 C4
Kankan, Réserve Naturelle de nature res. Guinea 124 C4
Kanker India 94 D1
Kankesanturai Sri Lanka 94 D4
Kankiya Nigeria 125 G3
Kankossa Mauritania 124 C3
Kanmaw Kyun i. Myanmar 79 B6 also known as Kisseraing Island
Kanmuri-yama mt. Japan 91 C7 also spelt Kammuri-yama
Kannad India 94 B1
Kannapolis U.S.A. 174 D5
Kannauj India 96 C4 also known as Kanyakubja
Kanniyakumari India 94 C4
Kanniya Kumari c. India see **Comorin, Cape**
Kannod India 96 C5
Kannonkoski Fin. 44 N3
Kannur India see **Cannanore**
Kannus Fin. 44 M3
Kannuskoski Fin. 42 I1
Kano Nigeria 125 H3
Kano r. Nigeria 125 H4
Kano state Nigeria 125 H4
Kanona Zambia 127 F8
Kanonerka Kazakh. 103 I2
Kan-onji Japan 91 C7
Kanonpunt pt S. Africa 132 F11
Kanor India 96 B4
Kanosh U.S.A. 183 L3
Kanovlei Namibia 130 C3
Kanowit Sarawak Malaysia 77 F2
Kanoya Japan 91 B9
Kanpur India 96 D4 formerly spelt Cawnpore
Kanpur Pak. 101 G4
Kanrach reg. Pak. 101 F5
Kansai airport Japan 91 D7
Kansanshi Zambia 127 E8
Kansas r. U.S.A. 178 D4
Kansas state U.S.A. 178 C4
Kansas City KS U.S.A. 178 D4
Kansas City MO U.S.A. 178 D4
Kansenia Dem. Rep. Congo 127 E7
Kansk Rus. Fed. 80 F1
Kansu China 88 A4
Kansu prov. China see **Gansu**
Kanta mt. Eth. 128 B3
Kantala Fin. 44 N3
Kantang Thai. 79 B7
Kantara hill Cyprus 108 E2
Kantaralak Thai. 79 D5
Kantavu i. Fiji see **Kadavu**
Kantchari Burkina 125 F3
Kantemirovka Rus. Fed. 41 F6
Kanth India 96 C3
Kanti India 97 E4
Kantilo India 95 E1
Kantishna r. U.S.A. 164 D3
Kanton i. Kiribati 145 H2 also known as Abariringa; formerly spelt Canton Island
Kan-Too, Pik mt. Kazakh./Kyrg. see **Khan-Tengri, Pik**
Kanto-sanchi mts Japan 91 F7
Kantserava Belarus 45 O5
Kanttaji Aboriginal Land res. Australia 148 B3
Kanturk Rep. of Ireland 47 D11
Kanturrpa Aboriginal Land res. Australia 148 B3
Kanuku Mountains Guyana 199 G4
Kanuma Japan 91 F6
Kanur India 94 C3 also known as Vajrakarur
Kanus Namibia 132 C4
Kanuwe r. P.N.G. 73 J8
Kanyakubja India see **Kannauj**
KaNyamazane S. Africa 133 P2
Kanye Botswana 131 E5
Kanyemba Zimbabwe 131 F2
Kanyutino Rus. Fed. 43 O6
Kao Indon. 75 C2
Kao Niger 125 G3
Kao i. Tonga 145 H3
Kao, Teluk b. Indon. 75 C2
Kaohsiung Taiwan 87 G4 also spelt Gaoxiong
Kaôh Tang i. Cambodia 79 C6
Kaokoveld plat. Namibia 130 B3
Kaolack Senegal 124 A3
Kaoma Zambia 127 E8
Kaouadja Cent. Afr. Rep. 126 D3
Kapaa U.S.A. 181 [inset] Y1
Kapaau U.S.A. 181 [inset] Z1
Kapal Kazakh. 103 I3 also spelt Qapal
Kapalabuaya Indon. 75 C3
Kapa Moračka mt. Yugo. 58 A6
Kapan Armenia 107 F3 formerly spelt Ghap'an or Kafan
Kapanga Dem. Rep. Congo 127 D7
Kapareli Greece 59 E10
Kapatkyevichy Belarus 43 J9
Kapatu Zambia 127 F7
Kapchagay Kazakh. 103 I4 also spelt Qapshagay; formerly known as Ili or Iliysk
Kapchagayskoye Vodokhranilishche resr Kazakh. 103 I4 also known as Qapshagay Bögeni
Kapchorwa Uganda 128 B4
Kapčiamiestis Lith. 42 E8
Kap Dan Greenland see **Kulusuk**
Kapellen Belgium 51 K1
Kapello, Akra pt Greece 59 E12
Kapellskär Sweden 45 L4 also spelt Kapelskär
Kapelskär Sweden see **Kapellskär**
Kapfenberg Austria 49 M8
Kapıdağı Yarımadası pen. Turkey 58 I8
Kapili r. India 97 F4
Kapingamarangi atoll Micronesia 145 E1 formerly known as Greenwich
Kapıorman Dağları mts Turkey 106 B2
Kapiri Mposhi Zambia 127 F8
Kāpīsā prov. Afgh. 101 G3
Kapisillit Greenland 165 N3
Kapiskau r. Canada 168 D2
Kapiskong Lake Canada 173 L3
Kapit Sarawak Malaysia 77 F2
Kapiti Island N.Z. 152 I8
Kapiting Brazil 199 H4
Kapka well Chad 120 D5
Kapka, Massif du mts Chad 120 D6
Kaplamada, Gunung mt. Indon. 75 C3
Kaplankyr, Chink hills Turkm./Uzbek. 102 C4
Kaplankyrskiy Gosudarstvennyy Zapovednik nature res. Turkm. 102 D4
Kaplice Czech Rep. 49 L7
Kapoe Thai. 79 B6
Kapoeta Sudan 128 B3
Kapondai, Tanjung pt Indon. 75 B5
Kaponga N.Z. 152 I7
Kapos r. Romania 49 P9
Kaposvár Hungary 49 O9
Kappar Pak. 101 E5
Kappeln Germany 48 G1
Kapran India 96 C4
Kapsabet Kenya 128 B4
Kap Salt Swamp Pak. 101 E5
Kapsan N. Korea 83 C4
Kapsha r. Rus. Fed. 43 O2
Kapsukas Lith. see **Marijampolė**
Kaptai Bangl. 97 G5
Kaptsegaytuy Rus. Fed. 85 H1
Kaptsevichy Belarus 43 J9
Kapuas r. Indon. 77 E3
Kapuas r. Indon. 77 F3
Kapuas Hulu, Pegunungan mts Indon./Malaysia 77 F2 also known as Boven Kapuas Mountains
Kapunda Australia 146 C3
Kapuriya India 96 B4
Kapurthala India 96 B3
Kapuskasing Canada 168 D3
Kapuskasing r. Canada 168 D3
Kapustin Yar Rus. Fed. 41 H6
Kaputa Zambia 127 F7
Kaputar mt. Australia 147 F2
Kaputir Kenya 128 B4
Kapuvár Hungary 49 O8
Kapydzhik, Gora mt. Armenia/Azer. see **Qazangödağ**
Kapyl' Belarus 42 I8 also spelt Kopyl'
Kap'yŏng S. Korea 83 B5
Kapyrevshchina Rus. Fed. 43 N6
Ka Qu r. China 89 F6
Kaqung China 88 B4
Kara India 97 D4
Kara r. Rus. Fed. 40 M1
Kara Togo 125 F4
Kara r. Turkey 107 E3
Kara Ada i. Turkey 59 H10
Karaali Turkey 106 C3
Kara Art Pass China 88 A4
Karaaul Kazakh. see **Karaul**
Kara-Balta Kyrg. 103 H4
Karabanovo Rus. Fed. 43 T5
Karabas Kazakh. 103 H2 also spelt Qarabas
Karabekaul Turkm. see **Garabekevyul**
Karabiga Turkey 106 A2
Karabil', Vozvyshennost' hills Turkm. 103 E5 also known as Garabil Belentligi
Kara-Bogaz-Gol Turkm. see **Karabogazkel'**
Kara-Bogaz-Gol, Proliv sea chan. Turkm. 102 C4 also known as Garabogazköl Bogazy
▶**Kara-Bogaz-Gol, Zaliv** b. Turkm. 102 C4 also known as Garabogazköl Aylagy
asia [changes] ➡ 68–69
Karabogazkel' Turkm. 102 C4 formerly spelt Kara-Bogaz-Gol
Karabük Turkey 106 C2
Karabulak Almatinskaya Oblast' Kazakh. 103 I3 also spelt Qarabulaq
Karabulak Vostochnyy Kazakhstan Kazakh. 88 D2
Karabulakskaya Kazakh. 103 H2
Karabura China see **Yumin**
Karaburun Turkey 106 A3
Karabutak Kazakh. 102 E2 also spelt Qarabutaq
Karacabey Turkey 106 B2
Karacadağ mts Turkey 106 C3
Karacakılavuz Turkey 58 I7
Karacaköy Turkey 106 B2
Karacalı Dağ mt. Turkey 107 D3
Karaçal Tepe mt. Turkey 108 D1
Karacasu Turkey 59 J11
Karaca Yarımadası pen. Turkey 108 B1
Karachay-Cherkess Republic aut. rep. Rus. Fed. see Karachayevo-Cherkesskaya Respublika
Karachayevo-Cherkesskaya A.S.S.R. aut. rep. Rus. Fed. see Karachayevo-Cherkesskaya Respublika
Karachayevo-Cherkesskaya Respublika aut. rep. Rus. Fed. 41 G8 English form Karachay-Cherkess Republic; formerly known as Karachayevo-Cherkesskaya A.S.S.R.
Karachayevsk Rus. Fed. 41 G8 formerly known as Klukhori
Karachev Rus. Fed. 43 P8
▶**Karachi** Pak. 101 F5
world [cities] ➡ 24–25
Karaçoban Turkey 107 E3 also known as Karaköprü
Karaçulha Turkey 59 K12
Karacurun Turkey see **Hilvan**
Karad India 94 B2
Kara Dağ hill Turkey 59 H8
Kara Dağ hill Turkey 109 J1
Kara Dağ mt. Turkey 106 C3
Kara-Darya r. Kyrg. 103 H4 also spelt Qoradaryo
Kara-Dar'ya Uzbek. see **Payshanba**
Kara Deniz sea Asia/Europe see **Black Sea**
Karaga Ghana 125 E4
Karaganda Kazakh. 103 H2 also spelt Qaraghandy
Karaganda Oblast admin. div. Kazakh. see Karagandinskaya Oblast'
Karagandinskaya Oblast' admin. div. Kazakh. 103 H2 English form Karaganda Oblast; also known as Qaraghandy Oblysy
Karagash Kazakh. 103 I3
Karagay Rus. Fed. 40 J4
Karagayly Kazakh. 103 H2 also spelt Qaraghayly
Karagez Turkm. 102 C5
Karaginskiy, Ostrov i. Rus. Fed. 39 Q4
Karagiye, Vpadina depr. Kazakh. 102 B4
Karaguzhikha Kazakh. 88 C1 also known as Qaraqozha
Karagwe Tanz. 128 A5
Karahalil Turkey 58 I7
Karahallı Turkey 59 K10
Karahasanlı Turkey 106 C3
Karahisar Turkey 59 J11
Karaidel' Rus. Fed. 40 K5
Karaikal India 94 C4
Karaikkudi India 94 C4
Kara Irtysh r. Kazakh. 88 D2
Karaisalı Turkey 106 C3
Karaj Iran 100 B3
Karak Jordan see **Al Karak**
Kara-Kala Turkm. see **Garrygala**
Karakalli Turkey see **Özalp**
Karakalpakistan, Respublika aut. rep. Uzbek. 102 D4 also known as Karakalpakskaya Respublika or Karakalpakstan or Qaraqalpaqstan Respublikasy or Qoraqalpoghiston Respublikasi
Karakalpakiya Uzbek. 102 D3 also known as Qoraqalpoghiston
Karakalpakskaya Respublika aut. rep. Uzbek. see **Karakalpakistan, Respublika**
Karakalpakstan aut. rep. Uzbek. see **Karakalpakistan, Respublika**
Kara Kara State Park nature res. Australia 147 D4
Karakatinskaya, Vpadina depr. Uzbek. 103 F4
Karakax China see **Moyu**
Karakax He r. China 89 C4
Karakax Shan mts China 89 C5
Karakeçi Turkey 107 D3 also known as Mizar
Karakeçili Turkey 106 C3
Karakelong i. Indon. 75 C1
Kara-Khol' Rus. Fed. 88 E1
Karaki China 89 C4
Karakitang i. Indon. 75 C2
Karaklis Armenia see **Vanadzor**
Karakoçan Turkey 107 E3 also known as Tepeköy
Karakoin salt l. Kazakh. see **Karakoyyn, Ozero**
Karakol' Kazakh. 102 C2 also spelt Qaraköl
Kara-Köl Kyrg. 103 H4 also spelt Kara Kul'
Karakol Ysyk-Köl Kyrg. 103 I4 also known as Karakolka
Karakol Ysyk-Köl Kyrg. 103 I4 formerly known as Przheval'sk
Karakolka Kyrg. see **Karakol**
Karaköprü Turkey see **Karaçoban**
Karakoram mts Asia 99 J2
Karakoram Pass China/Jammu and Kashmir 89 B5
Kara K'orē Eth. 128 C2
Karakoro r. Mali/Mauritania 124 B3
Karaköse Turkey see **Ağrı**
Karakoyyn, Ozero salt l. Kazakh. 103 G3 also known as Karakoin or Qaraqoyyn Köli
Karaksar Rus. Fed. 85 G1
Karakubbud Ukr. see **Komsomol's'ke**
Kara Kul' Kyrg. see **Kara-Köl**
Karakul' Bukharskaya Oblast' Uzbek. 103 E5
Karakul' Bukharskaya Oblast' Uzbek. 103 E5
Karakul', Ozero l. Tajik. see **Qarokŭl**
Kara-Kul'dzha Kyrg. see **Kara-Kulja**
Karakulino Rus. Fed. 40 J4
Kara-Kulja Kyrg. 103 H4 also spelt Kara-Kul'dzha
Karakum Kazakh. 103 I3
Karakum Desert Kazakh. 102 C3 also known as Garagum or Peski Karakum or Qaraqum
Karakum Desert Turkm. 102 E5 also known as Garagum or Peski Karakumy or Qaraqum
Karakumskiy Kanal canal Turkm. 103 E5
Karakurt Turkey 107 E2
Karakurt Turkey 59 I9
Karala Estonia 42 C3
Karalı Turkey 108 H1
Karalundi Australia 151 B5
Karama r. Indon. 75 A3
Karaman Turkey 106 C3 historically known as Laranda
Karaman prov. Turkey 108 D1
Karamanbeyli Geçidi pass Turkey 108 B1
Karamanlı Turkey 106 B3
Karamay China 88 D2
Karambar Pass Afgh./Pak. 101 H2
Karamea N.Z. 152 G9
Karamea r. N.Z. 152 G9
Karamea Bight b. N.Z. 152 F9
Karamet-Niyaz Turkm. 103 F5 also spelt Garamätnyyaz
Karamian i. Indon. 77 F4
Karamiran China 89 D4
Karamiran He r. China 89 D4
Karamiran Shankou pass China 89 D4
Karamken Rus. Fed. 39 P3
Karamürsel Turkey 58 K8
Karamyshevo Rus. Fed. 43 J4
Karan r. Afgh. 101 G2
Karan state Myanmar see **Kayin**
Karān i. Saudi Arabia 105 E2
Karang Senegal 124 A3
Karang, Tanjung pt Indon. 75 A3
Karangagung Indon. 76 D3
Karangan Indon. 76 D4
Karangarua N.Z. 153 D11
Karangasem Indon. 77 F5
Karangetang vol. Indon. 75 C2
Karangoua r. Congo 126 B4
Karanja India 94 C1
Karanja r. India 94 C2
Karanjia India 97 E5
Karanpura India 96 B3
Karaoba Kazakh. 103 I1
Karaova Turkey 59 I11
Karaoy Almatinskaya Oblast' Kazakh. 103 H3
Karaoy Almatinskaya Oblast' Kazakh. 103 H3 also spelt Qaraoy
Karapelit Bulg. 58 I5
Karapınar Turkey 106 C3 also known as Sultanıye
Karapürçek Turkey 59 J9
Karaqi China 88 B3
Karas admin. reg. Namibia 130 C5
Karas mts Namibia 132 B4
Karaşar Turkey 106 B2
Karasay China 89 C4
Kara-Say Kyrg. 103 I4
Karasburg Namibia 130 C6
Kara Sea Rus. Fed. 39 H2 also known as Karskoye More
Karash Rus. Fed. 43 U5
Karashoky Kazakh. 103 H2
Karašica r. Croatia 56 K3
Karasica r. Hungary/Romania 56 K3
Kárášjohka Norway 44 N1 also spelt Karasjok
Kárášjohka r. Norway 44 N1 also spelt Karasjokka
Karasjok Norway see **Kárášjohka**
Karasjokka r. Norway see **Kárášjohka**
Karasor, Ozero salt l. Karagandinskaya Oblast' Kazakh. 103 H2
Karasor, Ozero salt l. Pavlodarskaya Oblast' Kazakh. 103 H2
Kara Strait Rus. Fed. see **Karskiye Vorota, Proliv**
Karasu Karagandinskaya Oblast' Kazakh. 103 H3
Karasu Kustanayskaya Oblast' Kazakh. 103 E2
Karasu Kustanayskaya Oblast' Kazakh. 103 F1 also spelt Qarasū
Karasu r. Kazakh. 103 H1
Karasu r. Syria/Turkey 109 H1 also known as Qara Şū Chāy
Karasu Turkey see **Hizan**
Karasu Turkey 106 B2 also known as Incirli
Karasu r. Turkey 107 E3
Karasubazar Ukr. see **Bilohirs'k**
Kara-Sug Rus. Fed. 84 B1
Karasuk Rus. Fed. 80 B2
Karasulak r. Ukr. 58 J3
Kara-Suu Kyrg. 103 H4
Karāt Iran 101 E3
Karatan Kazakh. 88 D2
Karataş Turkey 106 C3
Karataş Burnu hd Turkey see **Fener Burnu**
Karatau Kazakh. 103 G4 also spelt Qarataū; formerly known as Chulaktau
Karatau, Khrebet mts Kazakh. 103 F3 also known as Qarataū Zhotasy
Karatayka Rus. Fed. 40 L1
Karathuri Myanmar 79 B6
Karativu i. Sri Lanka 94 C4
Karatj l. Sweden 44 L2
Karatobe Kazakh. 102 C2 also spelt Qaratöbe
Karatobe, Mys pt Kazakh. 102 D3
Karatogay Kazakh. 102 D2 also spelt Qaratoghay
Karatol r. Kazakh. 103 I3
Karatomarskoye Vodokhranilishche resr Kazakh. 103 E1 also known as Qaratomar Bögeni
Karaton Kazakh. 102 C3 also spelt Qaraton
Karatsu Japan 91 A8
Karatünggü China 84 A2
Karatup, Poluostrov pen. Kazakh. 102 D3
Kara-Turgey r. Kazakh. 103 F2
Karaul Kazakh. 103 I2 also spelt Qaraūyl; formerly known as Abay; formerly spelt Karaaul
Karaulbazar Uzbek. 103 F5 also spelt Qorowulbozor
Karauli India 96 C4
Karaulkel'dy Kazakh. see **Bayganin**
Karaurgan Turkey 107 E2
Karauzyak Uzbek. 102 D4 also spelt Qara Özek or Qoraŭzak
Karavan Kyrg. see **Kerben**
Karavas Greece 59 D12
Karavastasë, Gjiri i b. Albania 58 A8
Karavastasë, Laguna e lag. Albania 58 A8
Karavatsichy Belarus 43 L9
Karavayevo Rus. Fed. 43 V4
Karavi i. Greece 59 E12
Karavonisia i. Greece 59 H13
Karawa Dem. Rep. Congo 126 D4
Karawang Indon. 77 D4
Karaxahar r. China see **Kaidu He**
Karayılan Turkey 108 H1
Karayulgan China 88 C3
Karazhal Kazakh. 103 G2 also spelt Qarazhal
Karazhar Uzbek. 102 D4
Karazhingil Kazakh. 103 H3
Karbalā' Iraq 107 F4 also spelt Kerbela
Karbalā' governorate Iraq 107 E4
Karbushevka Kazakh. 103 H2
Karcag Hungary 49 R8
Kardam Bulg. 58 J5
Kardamaina Greece 59 I12 also spelt Kardhaámaina
Kardeljevo Croatia see **Ploče**
Kardhaámaina Greece see **Kardamaina**
Kardhítsa Greece see **Karditsa**
Kardis Sweden 44 M2
Karditsa Greece 59 C9 also spelt Kardhítsa
Kärdla Estonia 42 D3
Kardymovo Rus. Fed. 43 N7
Karee S. Africa 133 K5
Kareeberge mts S. Africa 132 F7
Kareebospoort pass S. Africa 132 G7
Kareedouw S. Africa 133 I10
Kareha, Jebel mt. Morocco 54 F9
Kareima Sudan 121 F5
Karelaksha Rus. Fed. 44 P2
Kareli India 96 C5
Karelia aut. rep. Rus. Fed. see **Kareliya, Respublika**
Karelichy Belarus 42 H8
Kareliya, Respublika aut. rep. Rus. Fed. 44 P3 English form Karelia; formerly known as Karel'skaya A.S.S.R.
Karel'skaya A.S.S.R. aut. rep. Rus. Fed. see **Kareliya, Respublika**
Karel'skiy Bereg coastal area Rus. Fed. 40 E2
Karema Dodoma Tanz. 129 B6
Karema Rukwa Tanz. 129 A6
Karen state Myanmar see **Kayin**
Karenga r. Rus. Fed. 81 J2
Karera India 96 C4
Karesuando Sweden 44 M1
Kārevāndar Iran 101 E5
Kargala Rus. Fed. 102 C2
Kargalinskaya Rus. Fed. 102 A4 also known as Kargalinski
Kargalinski Rus. Fed. see **Kargalinskaya**
Kargalinskoye Kazakh. 102 D2 formerly known as Zhilyanka
Kargapazarı Dağları mts Turkey 107 E3
Karghalik China see **Yecheng**
Kargı Turkey 106 C2
Kargil Jammu and Kashmir 96 C2
Kargilik China see **Yecheng**
Kargıpınarı Turkey 108 F1
Kargopol' Rus. Fed. 40 F3
Kargowa Poland 49 M3
Kargūshkī Iran 100 D5
Karhal India 96 C4
Kari Nigeria 125 H4
Karīān Iran 100 D5
Kariba Zimbabwe 131 F3
Kariba, Lake resr Zambia/Zimbabwe 127 E9
Kariba Dam Zambia/Zimbabwe 127 F9
Kariba-yama vol. Japan 90 F3
Karibib Namibia 130 B4
Kariega r. S. Africa 132 H10
Karīf Salāsil well Yemen 105 E4
Karigasniemi Fin. 44 N1 also known as Gáregasnjárga
Karijini National Park Australia 150 B4
Karikari, Cape N.Z. 152 H2
Karīmābād Iran 100 C3
Karimata i. Indon. 77 E3
Karimata, Pulau-pulau is Indon. 77 E3
Karimata, Selat strait Indon. 77 E3
Karimganj India 97 G4
Karim Khanch Iran 100 B3
Karimnagar India 94 C2
Karimun Besar i. Indon. 76 C2
Karimunjawa i. Indon. 77 E4
Karimunjawa, Pulau-pulau is Indon. 77 E4
Karin Somalia 128 E2
Karinainen Fin. 45 M3
Käringsjön Sweden 44 K3
Karino S. Africa 133 P2
Karioi hill N.Z. 152 I5
Karis Fin. 45 M3 also known as Karjaa
Karisimbi, Mont vol. Rwanda 126 F5
Káristos Greece see **Karystos**
Karit Iran 100 D3
Karitsa Greece 59 D8
Kariya Japan 91 E7
Kariyangwe Zimbabwe 131 E3
Karjaa Fin. see **Karis**
Karjalohja Fin. 42 E1
Karjan India 96 B5
Karjat India 94 B2
Karkai r. India 97 E5
Karkal India 94 B3
Karkamb India 94 B2
Karkams S. Africa 132 B7
Karkaralinsk Kazakh. 103 H2 also known as Qarqaraly
Karkaralong, Kepulauan is Indon. 75 C1
Karkar Island P.N.G. 73 K7 also known as Dampier Island
Karkas, Kūh-e mts Iran 100 B3
Karkh Pak. 101 F5
Karkheh, Rūdkhāneh-ye r. Iran 100 A4
Karkinits'ka Zatoka g. Ukr. 41 E7
Karkkila Fin. 45 N3
Kärkölä Fin. 45 N3
Karkonoski Park Narodowy nat. park Czech Rep./Poland see **Krkonošský narodní park**
Karksi-Nuia Estonia 42 G3
Karkūmā, Ra's hd Saudi Arabia 104 B2
Karlantijpa North Aboriginal Land res. Australia 148 B3
Karlantijpa South Aboriginal Land res. Australia 148 B4
Karlik Shan mt. China 84 B3
Karlino Poland 49 M1
Karlıova Turkey 107 E3
Karlivka Ukr. 41 E6 also spelt Karlovka
Karl Marks, Qullai mt. Tajik. 101 H2
Karl-Marx-Stadt Germany see **Chemnitz**
Karlovac Croatia 56 H3
Karlovka Ukr. see **Karlivka**
Karlovo Bulg. 58 F6 formerly known as Levskigrad
Karlovy Vary Czech Rep. 49 J5 historically known as Carlsbad
Karlsberg Sweden 45 K3
Karlsborg Sweden 45 K4
Karlsburg Romania see **Alba Iulia**
Karlshamn Sweden 45 K4
Karlskoga Sweden 45 K4
Karlskrona Sweden 45 K4
Karlsruhe Germany 48 F6
Karlstad Sweden 45 K4
Karlstadt Germany 48 G6
Karlyuk Turkm. 103 F5
Karma Belarus 43 L8
Karma Niger 125 F3
Karma, Ouadi watercourse Chad 120 C6
Karmala India 94 B2
Karmanovka Kazakh. 102 B2
Karmanovo Rus. Fed. 43 P6
Karmas Sweden 44 L2
Karmona Spain see **Córdoba**
Karnabchul', Step' plain Uzbek. 103 F5
Karnafuli Reservoir Bangl. 97 G5
Karnal India 96 C3
Karnali r. Nepal 97 D3
Karnaprayag India 96 C3
Karnataka state India 94 B3 formerly known as Mysore
Karnes City U.S.A. 179 C6
Karnobat Bulg. 58 H6 formerly known as Polyanovgrad
Karodi Pak. 101 F5
Karoi Zimbabwe 131 F3
Karokpi Myanmar 78 B5
Karo La pass China 89 E6
Karong India 97 G4
Karonga Malawi 129 B7
Karonie Australia 151 C6
Karoo National Park S. Africa 132 G9
Karoonda Australia 146 C3
Karor Pak. 101 G4
Karora Eritrea 121 H5
Káros i. Greece see **Keros**
Karossa Indon. 75 A3
Karossa, Tanjung pt Indon. 77 G5
Karotis Greece 58 H7
Karouassa well Mali 125 E2
Karpasia pen. Cyprus 108 F2 also known as Karpas Peninsula; also spelt Kırpaşa
Karpas Peninsula Cyprus see **Karpasia**
Karpathos Greece 59 I13
Karpathos i. Greece 59 I13 formerly known as Scarpanto
Karpathou, Steno sea chan. Greece 59 I12
Karpaty mts Europe see **Carpathian Mountains**
Karpenisi Greece 59 C10
Karpilovka Belarus see **Aktsyabrski**
Karpinsk Rus. Fed. 38 G4
Karpogory Rus. Fed. 40 H2
Karpovychi Ukr. 43 N9
Karpuz r. Turkey 108 C1
Karpuzlu Aydın Turkey 59 I11
Karpuzlu Edirne Turkey 58 H8
Karratha Australia 150 B4
Karrats Fjord inlet Greenland see **Nuugaatsiaap Imaa**
Karrī Iran 100 B4
Karringmelkspruit S. Africa 133 L7
Karroo plat. S. Africa see **Great Karoo**
Karroun Hill Nature Reserve Australia 151 B6
Karrukh Afgh. 101 E3
Karrychirla Turkm. see **imeni Kerbabayeva**
Kars Turkey 107 E2
Karsakpay Kazakh. 103 F3 also spelt Qarsaqbay
Kärsämäki Fin. 44 N3
Kārsava Latvia 42 I5
Karshi Turkm. 102 C4 also spelt Garshy
Karshi Uzbek. 103 F5 also spelt Qarshi; historically known as Nautaca
Karshinskaya Step' plain Uzbek. 103 F5 also known as Qarshi Chŭli
Karşıyaka Balıkesir Turkey 58 J8
Karşıyaka İzmir Turkey 59 I10
Karsiyang India 97 F4
Karskiye Vorota, Proliv strait Rus. Fed. 40 K1 English form Kara Strait
Karskoye More sea Rus. Fed. see **Kara Sea**
Karstädt Germany 48 I2
Karsu Turkey 109 H1
Karsun Rus. Fed. 41 H5
Kartal Turkey 106 B2
Kartala vol. Comoros 129 D7
Kartaly Rus. Fed. 103 E1

Kartarpur India 96 B3
Kartena Lith. 42 C6
Karthaus U.S.A. 176 G4
Kartsino, Akra pt Greece 59 F10
Karttula Fin. 44 N3
Kartuni Guyana 199 G3
Karubwe Zambia 127 F8
Karumai Japan 90 G4
Karumba Australia 149 D3
Karun, Kūh-e hill Iran 100 B4
Kārūn, Rūd-e r. Iran 100 B4
Karunagapalli India 94 C4
Karungi Sweden 44 M2
Karungu Kenya 128 B5
Karuni Indon. 75 A5
Karup Denmark 45 J4
Karuzi Burundi 126 F5
Karvetnagar India 94 C3
Karvia Fin. 45 M3
Karviná Czech Rep. 49 P6
Karwar India 94 B3
Karwendelgebirge nature res. Austria 48 I8
Karwi India 96 D4
Karya Greece 59 B10
Karyagino Azer. see Füzuli
Karyes Greece 59 E11
Karymskoye Rus. Fed. 85 G1
Karynzharyk, Peski des. Kazakh. 102 C4
Karystos Greece 59 F10
Kaş Turkey 106 B3
Kasa India 94 B2
Kasaba Turkey see Turgutlu
Kasaba Lodge Zambia 127 F7
Kasabonika Canada 168 C3
Kasai r. Dem. Rep. Congo 127 C5
Kasai Japan 91 D7
Kasai, Plateau du Dem. Rep. Congo 127 D6
Kasai Occidental prov. Dem. Rep. Congo 126 F1
Kasai Oriental prov. Dem. Rep. Congo 126 F1
Kasaji Dem. Rep. Congo 127 D7
Kasama Japan 91 G6
Kasama Zambia 127 F7
Kasan Uzbek. 103 F5
also spelt Koson
Kasane Botswana 131 E3
Kasanga Tanz. 129 A7
Kasangulu Dem. Rep. Congo 126 B4
Kasanka National Park Zambia 127 F8
Kasansay Uzbek. 103 G4
also spelt Kosonsoy
Kasar, Ras pt Sudan 121 H5
Kasaragod India 94 B3
Kasari r. Estonia 42 F3
Kasatkino Rus. Fed. 82 C2
Kasba Lake Canada 167 K2
Kasba Tadla Morocco 122 D2
Kasbi Uzbek. 103 F5
Kaseda Japan 91 B9
Kasempa Zambia 127 E8
Kasenga Katanga Dem. Rep. Congo 127 D7
Kasenga Katanga Dem. Rep. Congo 126 F4
Kasenye Dem. Rep. Congo 126 F4
Kasese Dem. Rep. Congo 126 F5
Kasese Uganda 128 A4
Kasevo Rus. Fed. see Neftekamsk
Kasganj India 96 C3
Kasha China see Gonjo
Kasha waterhole Namibia 128 D5
Kashabowie Canada 168 B3
Kāshān Iran 100 B3
Kashary Rus. Fed. 41 G6
Kashechewan Canada 168 D2
Kashgar China see Kashi
Kashi China 88 B4
formerly known as Kashgar or Kaxgar
Kashihara Japan 91 D7
Kashima Japan 91 B8
Kashima-nada b. Japan 91 G6
Kashin Rus. Fed. 43 S4
Kashinka r. Rus. Fed. 43 S4
Kashiobwe Dem. Rep. Congo 127 F7
Kashipur India 96 C3
Kashira Rus. Fed. 43 T7
Kashirka r. Rus. Fed. 43 T7
Kashiwazaki Japan 90 F6
Kashkadar'inskaya Oblast' admin. div. Uzbek. 103 F5
English form Kashkadarya Oblast; also known as Qashqadaryo Wiloyati
Kashkadar'ya r. Uzbek. 103 F5
also known as Qashqadaryo
Kashkadarya Oblast admin. div. Uzbek. see Kashkadar'inskaya Oblast'
Kashkanteniz Kazakh. 103 H3
also spelt Kashken-Teniz or Qashqantengiz
Kashken-Teniz Kazakh. see Kashkanteniz
Kashkurino Rus. Fed. 43 M6
Kashmar Iran 100 D3
Kashmir terr. Asia see Jammu and Kashmir
Kashmir, Vale of valley India 96 B2
Kashmor Pak. 101 G4
Kashmund reg. Afgh. 101 G3
Kashyukulu Dem. Rep. Congo 127 E6
Kasi India 97 E4
Kasia India 97 E4
Kasilovo Rus. Fed. 43 O8
Kasimov Rus. Fed. 40 G5
Kasingi Dem. Rep. Congo 126 F4
Kasinga i. Indon. 75 C3
Kaskaskia r. U.S.A. 174 B4
Kaskattama r. Canada 167 N3
Kaskelen Kazakh. 103 I4
also spelt Qaskelen
Kaskinen Fin. 44 M3
Kas Klong i. Cambodia see Kŏng, Kaôh
Kaskö Fin. see Kaskinen
Kaslo Canada 167 G5
Kasmere Lake Canada 167 K3
Kasnya r. Rus. Fed. 43 P6
Kasomeno Dem. Rep. Congo 127 E6
Kasongan Indon. 77 F3
Kasongo Dem. Rep. Congo 126 E6
Kasongo-Lunda Dem. Rep. Congo 127 C6
Kasonguele Dem. Rep. Congo 127 C6
Kasos i. Greece 59 H13
Kasou, Steno sea chan. Greece 59 I13
Kaspi Georgia 107 F2
Kaspiy Mangy Oypaty lowland Kazakh./Rus. Fed. see Caspian Lowland
Kaspiysk Rus. Fed. 102 A4
Kaspiyskiy Rus. Fed. see Lagan'
Kaspiyskoye More sea Asia/Europe see Caspian Sea
Kasplya Rus. Fed. 43 M7
Kasplya r. Rus. Fed. 43 L6
Kasrawad India 96 B5
Kasrik Turkey see Gürpınar
Kassa Slovakia see Košice
Kassaare laht b. Estonia 42 D3
Kassala Sudan 121 H6
Kassala state Sudan 121 G6
Kassandra pen. Greece 59 E8
Kassandras, Akra pt Greece 59 E9
Kassandras, Kolpos b. Greece 59 E9
Kassandreia Greece 59 E8
Kassel Germany 48 G4
Kasserine Tunisia 123 H2
Kassouloua well Niger 125 H3
Kastamonu Turkey 106 C2
also known as Çandar

Kastelli Kriti Greece 59 E13
also known as Kastéllion
Kastelli Kriti Greece 59 G13
also known as Kastéllion
Kastéllion Greece see Kastelli
Kastellorizon i. Greece see Megisti
Kastellou, Akra pt Greece 59 J13
Kastoria Greece 58 C8
Kastorias, Limni l. Greece 58 C8
Kastornoye Rus. Fed. 41 F6
Kastos i. Greece 59 B10
Kastre Estonia 42 I3
Kastrova Belarus 43 L4
Kastsyukovichy Belarus 43 N8
also spelt Kostyukovichi
Kastsyukowka Belarus 43 L9
also spelt Kostyukovka
Kasugai Japan 91 E7
Kasuku Dem. Rep. Congo 126 E5
Kasulu Tanz. 129 A6
Kasumiga-ura l. Japan 91 G6
Kasumkent Rus. Fed. 107 G2
Kasungu Malawi 129 B8
Kasungu National Park Malawi 129 B8
Kasur Pak. 101 H4
Kataba Zambia 127 E9
Katagum Nigeria 125 H3
Katahdin, Mount U.S.A. 174 G2
Kataklik Jammu and Kashmir 96 C2
Katako-Kombe Dem. Rep. Congo 126 E5
Katakolo, Akra pt Greece 59 C11
Katakwi Uganda 128 B4
Katanda Dem. Rep. Congo 126 E6
Katangi India 94 D3
Katanga prov. Dem. Rep. Congo 127 D6
formerly known as Shaba
Katangi Madhya Pradesh India 96 C5
Katangi Madhya Pradesh India 96 C5
Katangli Rus. Fed. 82 F2
Katanning Australia 151 B7
Kata Pusht Iran 100 B4
Katashin Rus. Fed. 43 N9
Katastari Greece 59 B11
Katavi National Park Tanz. 129 A6
Katawaz Afgh. 101 G3
Katawaz reg. Afgh. 101 F3
Katchall i. India 95 G5
Katchamba Togo 125 F4
Katerini Greece 58 D7
Katesh Tanz. 129 B6
Kate's Needle mt. Canada/U.S.A. 164 F4
Katete Zambia 129 B8
Katghora India 97 D5
Katha Myanmar 78 B3
Katherîna, Gebel mt. Egypt 121 G2
Katherine Australia 148 B2
Katherine r. Australia 148 A2
Katherine Gorge National Park Australia see Nitmiluk National Park
Kathi India 96 B5
Kathiawar pen. India 96 A5
Kathib, Ra's al pt Yemen 104 C5
Kathib el Henu hill Egypt 108 D7
Kathib el Makhâzin des. Egypt 108 A7
Kathleen Falls Australia 148 A2
Kathlehong S. Africa 133 M3
Kathmandu Nepal 97 E4
Capital of Nepal. English form Katmandu.
Kathu S. Africa 132 H4
Kathua Jammu and Kashmir 96 B2
Kathua watercourse Kenya 128 C5
Kati Mali 124 C3
Katibas r. Sarawak Malaysia 77 F2
Kati-ér r. Hungary 49 S8
Katihar India 97 E4
Katikati N.Z. 152 I5
Kati-Kati S. Africa 133 L9
Katima Mulilo Namibia 131 E3
Katimik Lake Canada 167 L4
Katiola Côte d'Ivoire 124 D4
Kā Tiritiri o te Moana mts N.Z. see Southern Alps
Katiti Aboriginal Land res. Australia 148 A5
Katkop Hills S. Africa 132 E7
Katlabukh, Ozero l. Ukr. 58 J3
Katma China 88 D4
Katmai National Park and Preserve U.S.A. 164 D4
Katmandu Nepal see Kathmandu
Kato Achaïa Greece 59 C10
Kat O Chau i. Hong Kong China see Crooked Island
Katochi Greece 59 C10
Kato Figaleia Greece 59 C11
Kat O Hoi b. Hong Kong China see Crooked Harbour
Katol India 96 C5
Katombe Dem. Rep. Congo 127 D6
Katompi Dem. Rep. Congo 127 E6
Katondwe Zambia 127 F8
Kato Nevrokopi Greece 58 E7
Katong Sing. 76 [inset]
Katonga r. Uganda 128 A4
Katon-Karagay Kazakh. 88 D1
also spelt Katonqaraghay
Katonqaraghay Kazakh. see Katon-Karagay
Katoomba Australia 147 F3
Katoposa, Gunung mt. Indon. 75 B3
Katosan India 96 B5
Kato Tithorea Greece 59 D10
Kátotjåkka mt. Sweden see Godučohkka
Katowice Poland 49 Q5
formerly known as Stalinogród; historically known as Kattowitz
Katoya India 97 F5
formerly spelt Katwa
Katpur India 96 B5
Katrineholm Sweden 45 L4
Katse Dam Lesotho 133 M6
Katsepy Madag. 131 [inset] J2
Katsikas Greece 58 B9
Katsina Nigeria 125 G3
Katsina state Nigeria 125 G3
Katsina-Ala r. Nigeria 125 H5
Katsumoto Japan 91 A8
Katsuura Japan 91 G7
Katsuyama Japan 91 E6
Kattakurgan Uzbek. 103 F5
also spelt Kattaqürghon
Kattamudda Well Australia 150 D4
Kattaqürghon Uzbek. see Kattakurgan
Kattasang Hills Afgh. 101 F3
Kattavia Greece 59 I13
Kattegat strait Denmark/Sweden 45 J4
Kattisavan Sweden 44 L2
Kattowitz Poland see Katowice
Kattuputtur India 94 C4
Katumbi Malawi 129 B7
Katun' r. Rus. Fed. 88 D1
Katunino Rus. Fed. 40 H4
Katunskiy Khrebet mts Rus. Fed. 88 D1
Katwa India see Katoya
Katwijk aan Zee Neth. 48 B3
Katyk Ukr. see Shakhtars'k
Katyn' Rus. Fed. 43 M7
Katy Wrocławskie Poland 49 N4
Kauai i. U.S.A. 181 [inset] Y1
Kauai Channel U.S.A. 181 [inset] Y1
Kaudom Game Park nature res. Namibia 130 D3
Kaufbeuren Germany 48 H8
Kaufman U.S.A. 179 D5
Kauhajoki Fin. 44 M3
Kauhanevan-Pohjankankaan kansal-lispuisto nat. park Fin. 45 M3
Kauhava Fin. 44 M3

Kaukauna U.S.A. 172 E6
Kaukkwè Hills Myanmar 78 B2
Kaukonen Fin. 44 N2
Kauksi Estonia 42 I2
Kaulinranta Fin. 44 M2
Kaumajet Mountains Canada 169 I1
Kaunakakai U.S.A. 181 [inset] Z1
Kaunas Lith. 42 E7
formerly known as Kovno
Kaunata Latvia 42 I5
Kaundy, Vpadina depr. Kazakh. 102 C4
Kaupiri N.Z. 153 F10
Kauno marios i. Lith. 42 F7
Kaura-Namoda Nigeria 125 G3
Kau Sai Chau i. Hong Kong China 87 [inset]
Kaushany Moldova see Căuşeni
Kaustinen Fin. 44 M3
Kautokeino Norway 44 M1
Kau-ye Kyun i. Myanmar 79 B6
Kavacha r. Rus. Fed. 39 Q3
Kavadarci Macedonia 58 D7
Kavajë Albania 58 A7
Kavak Turkey 58 H8
Kavak Turkey 106 C2
Kavak Dağı hill Turkey 59 H9
Kavaklıdere Manisa Turkey 59 J10
Kavaklıdere Muğla Turkey 59 J11
Kavala Greece 58 F8
Kavalas, Kolpos b. Greece 58 F8
Kavalerovo Rus. Fed. 82 D3
Kavali India 94 D3
Kavalpatnam India 94 C4
Kavaratti India 94 B4
Kavaratti i. India 94 B4
Kavār Iran 100 C4
Kavarna Bulg. 58 J5
Kavarskas Lith. 42 F6
Kavendou, Mont mt. Guinea 124 B4
Kaveri r. India 94 C3
Kaveripatnam India 94 C3
Kavi India 96 B5
Kavieng P.N.G. 145 E2
Kavir Iran 100 B3
Kavir, Dasht-e des. Iran 100 C3
Kavir-e Abarkuh des. Iran 100 C3
Kavir-i-Namak salt flat Iran 100 D3
Kavir Küshk well Iran 100 D3
Kavirondo Gulf Kenya see Winam Gulf
Kavkazskiy Zapovednik nature res. Rus. Fed. 41 G8
Kaw Fr. Guiana 199 H3
Kawabe Japan 90 G5
Kawachi-nagano Japan 91 D7
Kawagama Lake Canada 168 E4
Kawagoe Japan 91 F7
Kawaguchi Japan 91 F7
Kawahara Japan 91 D7
Kawaihae U.S.A. 181 [inset] Z1
Kawaihoa Point U.S.A. 181 [inset] Y1
Kawakawa N.Z. 152 I3
Kawamata Japan 90 G5
Kawambwa Zambia 127 F7
Kawaminami Japan 91 B8
Kawana Japan 91 F7
Kawangkoan Indon. 75 C2
Kawanishi Japan 90 G5
Kawardha India 96 D5
Kawartha Lakes Canada 168 E4
Kawasa Dem. Rep. Congo 127 F7
Kawasaki Japan 91 F7
Kawashiri-misaki pt Japan 91 B7
Kawato Indon. 75 B3
Kawaura Japan 91 B8
Kawawachikamach Canada 169 H2
Kawei i. Indon. 75 D2
Kaweah, Lake U.S.A. 182 F5
Kaweka Forest Park nature res. N.Z. 152 K7
Kaweka Range mts N.Z. 152 K7
Kawerau N.Z. 152 I6
Kawhia N.Z. 152 I6
Kawich Peak U.S.A. 183 H4
Kawich Range mts U.S.A. 183 H4
Kawinaw Lake Canada 167 L4
Kawio i. Indon. 75 C1
Kawkabān Yemen 104 C5
Kawkareik Myanmar 78 B4
Kaw Lake U.S.A. 178 C4
Kawlin Myanmar 78 A3
Kawludo Myanmar 78 B4
Kawmapyin Myanmar 79 B5
Kawm Umbū Egypt 121 G3
Kawng-hmu Myanmar 78 B3
Kawthaung Myanmar 79 B6
Kawthoolei state Myanmar see Kayin
Kawthule state Myanmar see Kayin
Kaxgar China see Kashi
Kaxgar He r. China 88 B3
Kax He r. China 89 C4
Kaya Burkina 125 E3
Kaya S. Korea 91 F7
Kayacı Dağı hill Turkey 59 H9
Kayadibi Turkey 107 D3
Kayah state Myanmar 78 B4
Kayambi Zambia 129 F1
Kayan r. Indon. 77 F2
Kayan Myanmar 78 B4
Kayanaza Burundi 126 F5
Kayangel atoll Palau 73 H5
Kayankulam India 94 C4
Kayar India 94 C2
Kayasa Indon. 75 C2
Kaya-san National Park S. Korea 91 A7
Kaybagar, Ozero l. Kazakh. see Koybagar, Ozero
Kaydanovo Belarus see Dzyarzhynsk
Kayenta U.S.A. 183 N5
Kayes Mali 124 C3
Kayes admin. reg. Mali 124 C3
Kaygy Kazakh. 103 F2
also known as Qayghy; formerly known as Kaygy
Kayin state Myanmar 78 B4
formerly spelt Kayah; historically known as Karen or Kawthoolei or Kawthule
Kaymanachikha Kazakh. 103 H1
Kaymaz Turkey 106 B3
Kaynar Kazakh. 103 I2
Kaynar Turkey 107 D3
Kaynarca Turkey 58 I7
Kayoa i. Indon. 75 C2
Kayrakkum Tajik. see Qayroqqum
Kayrakkumskoye Vodokhranilishche resr Tajik. see Qayroqqum Vodokhranilishche
Kayrakty Kazakh. 103 H2
also spelt Qayraqty
Kayseri Turkey 106 C3
historically known as Caesarea Cappadociae or Mazaca
Kaysersberg France 51 N4
Kayuadi i. Indon. 75 B4
Kayuagung Indon. 76 D3
Kayyerkan Rus. Fed. 39 I3
Kayyngdy Kyrg. 103 H4
formerly spelt Kaindo or Kaindy; formerly known as Molotovsk
Kazachka Rus. Fed. 41 H6
Kazach'ye Rus. Fed. 39 N2
Kazakdar'ya Uzbek. 102 C4
also spelt Qozoqdaryo

Kazakhskaya S.S.R. country Asia see Kazakhstan
Kazakhskiy Melkosopochnik plain Kazakh. 103 G2
Kazakhskiy Zaliv b. Kazakh. 102 C4
also known as Qazaq Shyghanaghy
▶Kazakhstan country Asia 102 C2
4th largest country in Asia and 7th in the world. Also spelt Kazakstan or Qazaqstan in Kazakh; formerly known as Kazakhskaya S.S.R.
world [countries] ➤➤ 10–11
asia [countries] ➤➤ 64–67
Kazakhstan Kazakh. see Aksay
Kazaki Rus. Fed. 43 T9
Kazakstan country Asia see Kazakhstan
Kazalinsk Kazakh. 103 E3
also known as Qazaly
Kazan r. Canada 167 M2
Kazan' Rus. Fed. 40 I5
Kazanchunkur Kazakh. 103 I3
Kazancı Turkey 106 C3
Kazandzhik Turkm. see Gazandzhyk
Kazanje, Mal mt. Albania 59 39
Kazanka r. Rus. Fed. 40 I5
Kazanketken Uzbek. 102 D4
also spelt Qozonketkan
Kazanlı Turkey 108 F1
Kazanlŭk Bulg. 58 G6
Kazanovo Rus. Fed. 85 G1
Kazan-rettō is N. Pacific Ocean see Volcano Islands
Kazatin Ukr. see Kozyatyn
Kazatskiy Kazakh. 102 D2
Kaza Wenz r. Eth. 128 C1
▶Kazbek mt. Georgia/Rus. Fed. 107 F2
4th highest mountain in Europe. Also known as Mqinvartsveri.
europe [landscapes] ➤➤ 30–31
Kāzerūn Iran 100 B4
Kazgorodok Kazakh. 103 G1
Kazhim Rus. Fed. 40 I3
Kazhmak r. Pak. 101 E5
Kazikbeli Geçidi pass Turkey 59 K11
Kazi Magomed Azer. see Qazimämmäd
Kazimierza Wielka Poland 49 R5
Kazimierz Dolne Poland 49 S4
Kazincbarcika Hungary 49 F7
Kazinka Lipetskaya Oblast' Rus. Fed. 43 U9
formerly known as Novaya D
Kazinka Ryazanskaya Oblast' Rus. Fed. 43 U7
Kaziranga National Park India 97 G4
Kazlowshchyna Belarus 42 38
Kazlowshchyna Belarus 42 J6
Kazlu Rŭda Lith. 42 E7
Kazo Japan 91 F6
Katalovka Kazakh. 102 B2
Kazuma Pan National Park Zimbabwe 131 E3
Kazumba Dem. Rep. Congo 127 D6
Kazungula Zambia 127 D6
Kazuno Japan 90 G4
Kazy Turkm. 102 D5
Kazyany Belarus 43 K6
Kazygurt Kazakh. 103 G4
Kazym r. Rus. Fed. 38 G3
Kazymskiy Mys Rus. Fed. 38 G3
Kçirë Albania 58 A6
Kea i. Greece 59 F11
English form Ceos
Keaau U.S.A. 181 [inset] Z2
Keahole Point U.S.A. 181 [inset] Z2
Kealakekua Bay U.S.A. 181 [inset] Z2
Kealia U.S.A. 181 [inset] Y1
Keams Canyon U.S.A. 183 N6
Kéamu i. Vanuatu see Anatom
Kearney U.S.A. 178 C3
Kearneysville U.S.A. 176 H6
Kearny U.S.A. 183 N8
Keas, Steno sea chan. Greece 59 F11
Keate's Drift S. Africa 133 O5
Keban Turkey 107 D3
Keban Baraji resr Turkey 107 D3
Kebatu i. Indon. 77 E3
Kebbi state Nigeria 125 F3
Kébémèr Senegal 124 A3
Kébi r. Cameroon 125 I4
Kébi Côte d'Ivoire 124 D4
Kebili Tunisia 123 H2
Kebir, Nahr al r. Lebanon/Syria 108 G3
Kebkabiya Sudan 120 E6
Kebnekaise mt. Sweden 44 L2
K'ebrī Dehar Eth. 128 D3
Kebumen Indon. 77 E4
Kecel Hungary 49 Q9
Kechika r. Canada 166 E2
Kecskemét Hungary 49 Q9
Kedah state Malaysia 76 C1
Kedainiai Lith. 42 E6
Kedarnath India see Kadavu Passage
Kédédéssé Chad 126 C2
Kedgwick Canada 169 H4
Kediri Indon. 77 F4
Kedong China 82 B3
Kedougou Senegal 124 B3
Kedva r. Rus. Fed. 40 J2
Kędzierzyn-Koźle Poland 49 P5
historically known as Heydebreck
Keele r. Canada 166 E2
Keele Peak Canada 166 D2
Keeley Lake Canada 167 I4
Keeling Islands terr. Indian Ocean see Cocos Islands
Keelung Taiwan see Chilung
Keenapusan i. Phil. 74 A5
Keene Canada 168 E4
Keene NH U.S.A. 177 M3
Keene OH U.S.A. 176 D5
Keep r. Australia 148 A2
Keepit, Lake resr Australia 147 F2
Keep River National Park Australia 148 A2
Keeroongooloo Australia 147 C5
Keer-weer, Cape Australia 149 D2
Keetmanshoop Namibia 130 C5
Keewatin Canada 167 M5
Keewatin U.S.A. 174 A2
Kefallinia i. Greece see Cephalonia
Kefallonia i. Greece see Cephalonia
Kefalos Greece 59 H12
Kefalos, Akra pt Greece 59 F11
Kefamenanu Indon. 75 C5
Kefe Ukr. see Feodosiya
Keflavik Iceland 44 [inset] B2
Kegalla Sri Lanka 94 D5
Kegayli Uzbek. see Kegeyli
Kegen Kazakh. 103 I4
Kegeyli Uzbek. 102 D4
also spelt Kegayli
Kegul'ta Rus. Fed. 41 H7
Keg River Canada 169 H1
Kegul'ta Rus. Fed. 41 H7
Kegums Latvia 42 F5
Kehl Germany 48 E7
Kehra Estonia 42 G2
Kehtna Estonia 42 F3
Kei r. S. Africa 133 M9
Keighley U.K. 47 K10
Keihoku Japan 91 D6
Keila Estonia 42 F2
Keila r. Estonia 42 F2
Keilak Sudan 128 E2
Keili Sudan 128 B2
Kei Ling Ha Hoi b. Hong Kong China see Three Fathoms Cove
Keimoes S. Africa 132 E5
Kei Mouth S. Africa 133 M9
Kei Road S. Africa 133 L9
Keiskama r. S. Africa 133 L9
Keiskammahoek S. Africa 133 L10
Keïta Niger 125 G3
Keïta, Bahr r. Chad 126 C2
Keitele Fin. 44 N3
Keitele l. Fin. 44 N3
Keith Australia 146 D4
Keith, Cape Australia 148 A1
Keith U.K. 46 J6
Keith Arm b. Canada 166 F1
Keithley Creek Canada 166 F4
Keith Australia 148 A1
Kejimkujik National Park Canada 169 H4
Kekaha U.S.A. 181 [inset] Y1
Kék-Art Kyrg. see Alaykuu
Kekava Latvia 42 F5
Kekes mt. Hungary 49 R8
Kekova Adasi i. Turkey 108 A1
Kekra Rus. Fed. 39 O4
Kekri India 96 B4
Kék-Tash Kyrg. see Kök-Tash
K'elafo Eth. 128 D3
Kelai atoll Maldives 94 B5
Kelan r. Indon. 75 C3
Kelang Malaysia 76 C2
formerly known as Kelang
Kelang r. Malaysia 76 C1
Kelantan r. Malaysia 76 C1
Kelantan state Malaysia 76 C1
Kelârdasht Iran 100 B2
Kelawar r. Iran 100 A2
Kelbia, Sebkhet salt pan Tunisia 57 C13
Kelberg Germany 48 D5
Kelbia r. U.S.A. 174 G2
Kelekçi Turkey 59 K11
Keles Uzbek. 103 G4
Keles Turkey 59 K9
Kelheim Germany 48 I7
Kelibia Tunisia 123 I1
Kelif Turkm. 103 F5
Kelifskiy Uzboy marsh Turkm. 103 E5
Kelkit Turkey 107 D2
Kelkit r. Turkey 107 D2
Kellé Congo 126 B5
Kellerberrin Australia 151 B6
Kellett, Cape Canada 164 G2
Kelleys Island U.S.A. 176 C4
Kelliher Canada 167 K5
Kellogg U.S.A. 180 D3
Kelloselkä Fin. 44 O2
Kells Rep. of Ireland 47 F10
also known as Ceanannus Mór
Kelly Lake Canada 166 F1
Kelly Range hills Australia 151 C5
Kelmė Lith. 42 D6
Kelo Chad 126 C2
Kelowna Canada 166 G5
Kelp Head Canada 166 E5
Kelsey Canada 167 L4
Kelseyville U.S.A. 182 B3
Kelso N.Z. 153 D13
Kelso U.K. 46 J8
Kelso CA U.S.A. 183 I6
Kelso WA U.S.A. 180 B3
Keltan S. Africa 133 M9
Kelti, Jebel mt. Morocco 54 F7
Keluang Malaysia 76 C2
formerly spelt Kluang
Kelujärvi Fin. 44 N2
Kelvington Canada 167 K4
Kelvin Island Canada 168 C3
Kelwara India 96 B4
Kem' Rus. Fed. 40 D2
Kem' r. Rus. Fed. 40 D2
Kema r. Rus. Fed. 43 S1
Ke Macina Mali see Massina
Kemah Turkey 107 D3
Kemaliye Turkey 107 D3
Kemalpaşa Turkey 59 I10
Kemano Canada 166 E4
Kembé Cent. Afr. Rep. 126 D3
Kembolcha Eth. 128 D2
Kemen Indon. 77 E4
Kemer Antalya Turkey 106 B3
Kemer Muğla Turkey 106 B3
Kemer Baraji resr Turkey 106 B3
Kemerovo Rus. Fed. 80 D1
Kemerovskaya Oblast' admin. div. Rus. Fed. 80 D2
English form Kemerovo Oblast
Kemerovskaya Oblast' admin. div. Rus. Fed. 80 D2
Kemi Fin. 44 N2
Kemihaara r. Fin. 44 O2
Kemijärvi Fin. 44 N2
Kemijärvi l. Fin. 44 N2
Kemijoki r. Fin. 44 N2
Kemin Kyrg. 103 H4
formerly known as Bystrovka
Keminmaa Fin. 44 N2
Kemiö Fin. see Kimito
Kemir Turkm. 102 D5
formerly spelt Keymir
Kemlya Rus. Fed. 40 H5
Kemmerer U.S.A. 180 E4
Kemmuna i. Malta 57 G12
also known as Comino
Kemp, Lake U.S.A. 179 C5
Kempele Fin. 44 N2
Kempen reg. Belgium 51 K1
Kempisch Kanaal canal Belgium 51 L1
Kempsey Australia 147 G2
Kempt, Lac l. Canada 173 N5
Kempten (Allgäu) Germany 48 H8
Kempton Australia 147 E5
Kempton Park S. Africa 133 M3
Kemptville Canada 173 R5
Kemujan i. Indon. 77 E4
Ken r. India 96 D4
Kenabeek Canada 173 N3
Kenai U.S.A. 164 D3
Kenai Fjords National Park U.S.A. 164 D4
Kenai Mountains U.S.A. 164 D4
Kenamu r. Canada 169 J2
Kenamuke Swamp Sudan 128 B3
Kenansville U.S.A. 174 E6
Kenawang, Bukit mt. Sarawak Malaysia 77 F2
Kenâyis, Râs el pt Egypt 121 E2

Kendall, Cape Canada 167 O2
Kendall, Mount N.Z. 152 G9
Kendallville U.S.A. 172 H9
Kendari Indon. 75 B3
Kendawangan Indon. 77 E3
Kendégué Chad 126 C2
Kendraparha India 95 E1
Kendrew S. Africa 133 I9
Kendrick Peak U.S.A. 183 M6
Kendua Bangl. 97 F4
Kendujhargarh India 97 E5
Kendyktas mts Kazakh. 103 H4
Kendyrli-Kayasanskoye, Plato plat. Kazakh. 102 C4
Kenedy U.S.A. 179 C6
Keneka r. S. Africa 133 N7
Kenema Sierra Leone 124 C4
Kenepai, Gunung mt. Indon. 77 E2
Keneurgench Turkm. 102 D4
also known as Köneürgench; formerly spelt Kunya-Urgench
Kenge Dem. Rep. Congo 126 C5
Kengere Dem. Rep. Congo 127 E7
Keng Hkam Myanmar 78 B3
Kengis Sweden 44 M2
Keng Lap Myanmar 78 C3
Keng Lon Myanmar 78 B3
Keng-Peli Uzbek. 102 D4
Keng Tawng Myanmar 78 B3
Kengtung Myanmar 78 B3
Kenhardt S. Africa 132 F6
Kéniéba Mali 124 C3
Kéniéboulé, Réserve de nature res. Mali 124 C3
Kénitra Morocco 122 D2
formerly known as Port-Lyautrey
Kenli China 85 H4
Kenmare Rep. of Ireland 47 C12
Kenmare U.S.A. 178 B1
Kenmare River inlet Rep. of Ireland 47 B12
Kenmaur Zimbabwe 131 F3
Kenmore U.S.A. 176 G3
Kenn Germany 48 D5
Kennebec U.S.A. 178 C3
Kennebec r. U.S.A. 174 G2
Kennebunk U.S.A. 177 O2
Kennebunkport U.S.A. 177 O2
Kennedy Australia 149 E3
Kennedy r. Australia 149 E2
Kennedy, Cape U.S.A. see Canaveral, Cape
Kennedy Range hills Australia 151 A5
Kennedy Range National Park Australia 151 A5
Kennedy's Vale S. Africa 133 O1
Kennedy Town Hong Kong China 87 [inset]
Kennedyville U.S.A. 177 J6
Kennet r. U.K. 47 L12
Kenneth Range hills Australia 150 B4
Kennett U.S.A. 174 B4
Kennewick U.S.A. 180 C3
Kenogami r. Canada 168 C3
Kenogami Lake Canada 173 M2
Kenogamissi Lake Canada 173 L2
Keno Hill Canada 166 C2
Kenora Canada 167 M5
Kenosha U.S.A. 172 F8
Kenova U.S.A. 176 C7
Kenozero, Ozero l. Rus. Fed. 40 F3
Kensington Canada 169 I4
Kent OH U.S.A. 176 D4
Kent TX U.S.A. 181 F7
Kent VA U.S.A. 176 D8
Kent WA U.S.A. 180 B3
Kentani S. Africa 133 M9
also spelt Centane
Kentau Kazakh. 103 G4
Kent Group is Australia 147 E4
Kentland U.S.A. 174 C3
Kenton MI U.S.A. 172 E4
Kenton OH U.S.A. 176 B5
Kenton-on-Sea S. Africa 133 K10
Kent Peninsula Canada 165 I3
Kentriki Makedonia admin. reg. Greece 58 E8
also spelt Kendhriki Makedonia
Kentucky r. U.S.A. 176 B8
Kentucky state U.S.A. 176 A8
Kentucky Lake U.S.A. 174 B4
Kentwood U.S.A. 175 B6
Kentwood MI U.S.A. 172 H8
▶Kenya country Africa 128 C4
africa [countries] ➤➤ 114–117
▶Kenya, Mount Kenya 128 C5
2nd highest mountain in Africa. Also known as Kirinyaga.
africa [landscapes] ➤➤ 112–113
Kenyir, Tasik resr Malaysia 76 C1
Kenzingen Germany 48 E7
Keokuk U.S.A. 174 B3
Keonjhar National Park India 96 C5
Keosauqua U.S.A. 174 B3
Keowee, Lake resr U.S.A. 174 D5
Kepa Rus. Fed. 44 P2
Kepahiang Indon. 76 C3
Kepina r. Rus. Fed. 40 G2
Kepler Mountains N.Z. 153 B13
Kepno Poland 49 O4
Keppel Bay Australia 149 F4
Keppel Harbour sea chan. Sing. 76 [inset]
Keppel Island Tonga see Tafahi
Kepsut Turkey 106 B3
Kerala state India 94 B4
historically known as Chera
Kerang Australia 147 D3
Kerava Fin. 45 N3
Kerba Alg. 55 M8
Kerbau, Tanjung pt Indon. 76 C3
Kerbela Iraq see Karbalā'
Kerben Kyrg. 103 G4
also spelt Karavan
Kerbi r. Rus. Fed. 82 E1
Kerch Ukr. 41 F7
historically known as Panticapaeum
Kerchem'ya Rus. Fed. 40 J3
Kerchevskiy Rus. Fed. 40 K4
Kere Eth. 128 C3
Kerema P.N.G. 73 K8
Keremeos Canada 166 G5
Kerempe Burun pt Turkey 106 C2
Keren Eritrea 121 H6
Kerend-e Gharb Iran 100 A3
Kerepehi N.Z. 152 I5
Kerest' r. Rus. Fed. 43 M3
Keret' Rus. Fed. 44 P2
Keret', Ozero l. Rus. Fed. 44 P2
Kerewan Gambia 124 A3
Kerey watercourse Kazakh. 103 G2
Kerey, Ozero l. Kazakh. 103 G2
formerly spelt Kirey, Ozero
Kerguelen, Îles is Indian Ocean 219 L9
English form Kerguelen Islands
Kerguelen Islands Indian Ocean see Kerguelen, Îles
Kericho Kenya 128 C5
Kerihun mt. Indon. 77 F2
Kerikeri N.Z. 152 H3
Kerimäki Fin. 45 O3
Kerinci, Danau l. Indon. 76 C3

Kerinci, Gunung *vol.* Indon. 76 C3
formerly known as Gunung Indrapura or Kerintji
Kerintji *vol.* Indon. *see* Kerinci, Gunung
Kerio *watercourse* Kenya 128 C2
Keriya China *see* Yutian
Keriya He *watercourse* China 88 C4
Keriya Shankou *pass* China 89 C5
Kerka *r.* Romania 49 N9
Kerkebet Eritrea 104 B4
Kerki Turkm. 103 F5
Kerkichi Turkm. 103 F5
Kerkini Oros *mts* Bulg./Macedonia *see* Belasica
Kerkinitis, Limni *l.* Greece 58 E7
Kérkira *i.* Greece *see* Corfu
Kerkouane *tourist site* Tunisia 123 H1
Kerkyra *i.* Greece *see* Corfu
Kerma Sudan 121 F5
Kermadec Islands S. Pacific Ocean 145 H5
▶**Kermadec Trench** *sea feature* S. Pacific Ocean 220 G8
4th deepest trench in the world.
Kermān Iran 100 D4
also spelt Kirman; historically known as Carmana
Kermān *prov.* Iran 100 D4
Kerman U.S.A. 182 D5
Kermān Desert Iran 101 D4
Kermānshāh Iran 100 A3
formerly known as Bākhtarān or Qahremānshahr
Kermānshāh *prov.* Iran 100 A3
formerly known as Bākhtarān or Qahremānshahr
Kermānshāhān *prov.* Iran *see* Kermānshāh
Kermine Uzbek. *see* Navoi
Kermit U.S.A. 179 B6
Kern *r.* U.S.A. 182 E6
Kern, South Fork *r.* U.S.A. 182 F6
Kernersville U.S.A. 176 E9
Kernertut, Cap *c.* Canada 169 H1
Kernot Range *hills* Australia 148 B5
Kernville U.S.A. 182 F6
Keros *i.* Greece 59 G12
Kerpen Germany 48 D5
Kerr, Cape Antarctica 223 K1
Kerrobert Canada 167 I5
Kerrville U.S.A. 179 C6
Kerry Head Rep. of Ireland 47 C11
Kersa Dek Eth. 128 C3
Kershaw U.S.A. 180 D4
Kert, Oued *r.* Morocco 55 H9
Kerteminde Denmark 45 J5
Kertosono Indon. 77 F4
Kerulen *r.* China/Mongolia 85 H1
also known as Herlen Gol or Herlen He
Kerumutan Reserve *nature res.* Indon. 76 C3
Kerur India 94 B2
Kerva Rus. Fed. 43 U6
Keryneia Cyprus *see* Kyrenia
Kerzaz Alg. 123 E3
Kerzhenets *r.* Rus. Fed. 40 H4
Kesagami *r.* Canada 168 E3
Kesagami Lake Canada 168 D3
Kesälahti Fin. 44 O3
Keşan Turkey 106 A2
Keşap Turkey 107 D2
Kesarevo Bulg. 58 G5
Kesariya India 97 E4
Kesennuma Japan 90 G5
Keshan China 82 B2
Keshem Afgh. 101 G2
Keshod India 96 A5
Keshorai Patan India 96 C4
Keskin Turkey 106 C3
Keskozero Rus. Fed. 40 E3
Kes'ma Rus. Fed. 43 S3
Kesova Gora Rus. Fed. 43 S4
Kesra Tunisia 57 B13
Kestel Turkey *see* Gürsu
Kestel Turkey 59 K8
Kestell S. Africa 133 M5
Kesten'ga Rus. Fed. 44 O2
Kestilä Fin. 44 N2
Keswick U.K. 47 I9
Keswick U.S.A. 182 B1
Keszthely Hungary 49 O9
Ket' *r.* Rus. Fed. 39 I4
Keta Ghana 125 F5
Ketahun Indon. 76 C3
Ketam, Pulau *i.* Sing. 76 [inset]
Ketapang *Jawa Timur* Indon. 77 F4
Ketapang *Kalimantan Barat* Indon. 77 E3
Ketchikan U.S.A. 166 D4
Ketchum U.S.A. 180 D4
Kete Krachi Ghana 125 E5
Ketmen', Khrebet *mts* China/Kazakh. 88 C3
Kétou Benin 125 F5
Ketoy, Ostrov *i.* Rus. Fed. 81 Q3
Kętrzyn Poland 49 S1
Kette Cameroon 125 I5
Kettering U.K. 47 L11
Kettering U.S.A. 176 A6
formerly known as Van Buren
Kettle *r.* Canada 166 G5
Kettle *r.* U.S.A. 174 A2
Kettle Creek *r.* U.S.A. 176 H4
Kettle Falls U.S.A. 180 C2
Kettleman City U.S.A. 182 E5
Kettle River *r.* U.S.A. 172 A4
Kettle River Range *mts* U.S.A. 180 C2
Ketungau *r.* Indon. 77 E2
Keuka U.S.A. 177 H3
Keuka Lake U.S.A. 177 H3

Keumgang, Mount N. Korea *see* Kumgang-san
Keumgang, Mount N. Korea *see* Kumgang-san
Keur Massène Mauritania 124 A2
Keurusselkä *l.* Fin. 45 N3
Keuruu Fin. 44 N3
Kevelaer Germany 48 D4
Kevo luonnonpuisto *nature res.* Fin. 44 N1
Kew Turks and Caicos Is 187 E2
Kewanee U.S.A. 174 B3
Kewaskum U.S.A. 172 E7
Kewaunee U.S.A. 172 F6
Keweenaw Bay U.S.A. 172 E4
Keweenaw Bay *b.* U.S.A. 172 E4
Keweenaw Peninsula U.S.A. 172 E3
Keweenaw Point U.S.A. 172 F3
Keyala Sudan 128 B3
Keya Paha *r.* U.S.A. 178 C3
Keyi China 88 I1
Keyihe China 85 I1
Key Largo U.S.A. 175 D7
Key Largo National Marine Sanctuary *nature res.* U.S.A. 175 D7
Keyling Inlet Australia 148 A2
Keymir Turkm. *see* Kemir
Keyser U.S.A. 176 G6
Keysers Ridge U.S.A. 176 F6
Keystone Lake *OK* U.S.A. 179 C4
Keystone Lake *PA* U.S.A. 176 F5
Keysville U.S.A. 176 G8
Keytesville U.S.A. 178 D4
Keytü Iran 100 D3
Keyvy, Vozvyshennost' *hills* Rus. Fed. 40 F2
Key West *FL* U.S.A. 175 D7
Key West *IA* U.S.A. 174 A3
Kez Rus. Fed. 40 J4
Kezar Falls U.S.A. 177 O2
Kezi Zimbabwe 131 F4
Kežmarok Slovakia 49 R6
Kgakala S. Africa 133 K4
Kgalagadi *admin. dist.* Botswana 130 D5
Kgatleng *admin. dist.* Botswana 131 E5
Kgotsong S. Africa 133 K4
Khabari al Hajm *salt pan* Saudi Arabia 109 K6
Khabari al Khubub *salt pan* Iraq 109 K4
Khabarikha Rus. Fed. 40 J2
Khabarovo Rus. Fed. 40 L1
Khabarovsk Rus. Fed. 82 D3
Khabarovskiy Kray *admin. div.* Rus. Fed. 82 D2
English form Khabarovsk Kray
Khabarovskiy Kray *admin. div.* Rus. Fed. *see* Khabarovskiy Kray
Khabb, Wādī *watercourse* Yemen 104 D4
Khabis Iran *see* Shahdād
Khabody Pass Afgh. 101 E3
Khabra al'Arn *salt pan* Saudi Arabia 104 C3
Khabrah Şāfiyah *hill* Saudi Arabia 109 K6
Khābūr, Nahr al *r.* Syria 109 L1
Khachmas Azer. *see* Xaçmaz
Khachrod India 96 B5
Khadar, Jabal *mt.* Oman 105 G3
Khaḍārah Saudi Arabia 104 C4
Khadari *watercourse* Sudan 126 E2
Khadun *r.* Belarus 43 M8
Khadyzhensk Rus. Fed. 41 F7
Khadzhidimovo Bulg. 58 E7
Khadzhybey's'kyy Lyman *l.* Ukr. 58 L2
Khafi, Sha'ib al *watercourse* Iraq 109 N6
Khafs Banbān *well* Saudi Arabia 105 D2
Khaga India 97 E4
Khagaria India 97 E4
Khagaul India 97 E4
Khagrachari Bangl. 97 F5
also known as Khagrachhari
Khagrachhari Bangl. *see* Khagrachari
Khairagarh *Chhattisgarh* India 96 C1
Khairagarh *Uttar Pradesh* India 89 B7
Khaïrpur Pak. 101 F4
Khairpur Pak. 101 G5
Khairwara India 96 B5
Khāiz, Kūh-e *mt.* Iran 100 B4
Khaja du Koh *hill* Afgh. 103 E5
Khakasiya, Respublika *aut. rep.* Rus. Fed. 80 E2
English form Khakassia; formerly known as Khakasskaya A.S.S.R.
Khakassia *aut. rep.* Rus. Fed. *see* Khakasiya, Respublika
Khakasskaya A.S.S.R. *aut. rep.* Rus. Fed. *see* Khakasiya, Respublika
Khalach Turkm. 103 F5
also spelt Halach
Khalajestan *reg.* Iran 100 B3
Khalamyer"ye Belarus 43 K6
Khalatse Jammu and Kashmir 96 C2
Khalidabad Iran 100 C3
Khalilabad India 97 D4
Khalilabad Iran 100 D3
Khalilovo Rus. Fed. 102 C2
Khalkabad Turkm. 103 E4
Khalkabad Uzbek. 102 D4
also spelt Kalkqobod
Khalkhāl Iran 100 B2
formerly known as Herowābād
Khálki *i.* Greece *see* Chalki
Khalkís Greece *see* Chalkida
Khallikot India 95 E2
Khal'mer-Yu Rus. Fed. 40 M2
Khalopyenichy Belarus 43 J7
Khaloboot Uzbek. *see* Khalkabad
Khalte Nepal 97 E4
Khalturin Rus. Fed. *see* Orlov
Khamar-Daban, Khrebet *mts* Rus. Fed. 84 D1
Khamaria India 96 C5
Khambhaliya India 96 A5
Khambhat India 96 B5
formerly known as Cambay
Khambhat, Gulf of India 94 A2
also known as Cambay, Gulf of
Khamgaon India 94 C1
Khamīr Iran 100 C5
Khamir Yemen 104 C4
Khami Ruins National Monument *tourist site* Zimbabwe 131 F4
Khamis Mushayt Saudi Arabia 104 C4
Khamma *well* Saudi Arabia 105 D2
Khammam India 94 D2
Khampa Rus. Fed. 39 M3
Khampat Myanmar 78 A2
Khamra Rus. Fed. 39 L3
Khamra *r.* Iran 100 B3
Khamza Uzbek. 103 G4
also spelt Hamza; formerly known as imeni Khamzy Khakimzade
Khan Afgh. 101 G3
Khan, Nam *r.* Laos 78 C4
Khānābād Afgh. 101 G2
Khanabad Uzbek. 103 H4
also spelt Khonobod; formerly known as Sovetabad
Khān al Baghdādī Iraq 107 F4
Khān al Ḩammād Iraq 107 F4
Khān al Maḩāwil Iraq 107 F4
Khanapur *Karnataka* India 94 B3
Khanapur *Maharashtra* India 94 B2
Khānaqāh Iran 100 A3
Khān ar Raḩbah Iraq 107 F5
also spelt Khan Ruhābah
Khanasur Pass Iran/Turkey 107 F3

Khanbalik China *see* Beijing
Khānch Iran 100 A2
Khandagayty Rus. Fed. 84 B1
Khandala India 94 B2
Khandud Afgh. 101 H2
Khandwa India 96 C1
Khandyga Rus. Fed. 39 N3
Khaneh Khowreh Iran 100 C4
Khanewal Pak. 101 G4
Khangarh Pak. 101 G4
Khanh Duong Vietnam 79 E5
Khan Hung Vietnam *see* Soc Trăng
Khani Rus. Fed. 39 M4
Khaniá Greece *see* Chania
Khaniadhana India 96 C4
Khanino Rus. Fed. 43 R7
Khānī Yek Iran 100 C4
Khanka Uzbek. 102 E4
also spelt Khonqa; formerly spelt Khanki
Khanka, Lake China/Rus. Fed. 82 D3
also known as Ozero Khanka or Xingkai Hu
Khanka, Ozero *l.* China/Rus. Fed. 39 J3
see Khanka, Lake
Khankendi Azer. *see* Xankändi
Khanki Uzbek. *see* Khanka
Khanna India 96 C3
Khanna, Qā' *salt pan* Jordan 109 H5
Khannfoussa *hill* Alg. 123 G4
Khanovey Rus. Fed. 40 L2
Khanpur Pak. 101 G4
Khān Ruḩābah Iraq *see* Khān ar Raḩbah
Khān Shaykhūn Syria 109 H2
Khansiir, Raas *pt* Somalia 128 E2
Khantau Kazakh. 103 H3
Khantayskoye, Ozero *l.* Rus. Fed. 39 J3
Khantayskoye Vodokhranilishche *resr* Rus. Fed. 39 I3
Khanty-Mansiysk Rus. Fed. 38 G3
Khanty-Mansiyskiy Avtonomnyy Okrug *admin. div.* Rus. Fed. 40 L3
English form Khanty-Mansy Autonomous Okrug
Khanty-Mansy Autonomous Okrug *admin. div.* Rus. Fed. *see* Khanty-Mansiyskiy Avtonomnyy Okrug
Khān Yūnis Gaza 108 F6
Khao-ang-runai Wildlife Reserve *nature res.* Thai. 79 C5
Khao Banthat Wildlife Reserve *nature res.* Thai. 79 B7
Khao Chum Thong Thai. 79 B6
Khaoen Si Nakarin National Park Thai. 79 B5
Khao Laem National Park Thai. 79 B5
Khao Laem Reservoir Thai. 79 B5
Khao Luang National Park Thai. 79 B5
Khao Pu-Khao Ya National Park Thai. 79 B7
Khao-soi-dao Wildlife Reserve *nature res.* Thai. 79 C5
Khao Sok National Park Thai. 79 B6
Khao Yai National Park Thai. 79 C5
Khapa India 96 C1
Khapcheranga Rus. Fed. 85 G1
Khaptad National Park Nepal 96 D3
Kharabali Rus. Fed. 102 A3
Kharaghoda India 96 A5
Kharagpur *Bihar* India 97 E4
Kharagpur *W. Bengal* India 97 E5
Kharakī Iran 100 C3
Kharampur Rus. Fed. 38 H3
Kharan Pak. 101 F4
Kharari India *see* Abu Road
Khardi India 94 B2
Khardung La *pass* Jammu and Kashmir 96 C2
also known as Laowohi
Kharfiyah Iraq 107 F5
Kharga *r.* Rus. Fed. 82 D1
Kharga Oasis Egypt 121 F3
also known as The Great Oasis
Khargapur India 96 C4
Khargon India 96 B5
Kharī *r.* India 96 B4
Khariar India 97 D5
Kharian Pak. 101 H3
Kharim, Gebel *hill* Egypt 108 E7
Kharkhara *r.* India 96 D5
Kharkhauda India 96 C3
Kharkiv Ukr. 41 F6
formerly known as Khar'kov
Khar'kov Ukr. *see* Kharkiv
Khār Kūh *mt.* Iran 100 C3
Kharu Rus. Fed. 40 D3
Kharmah, Ghubbat *b.* Yemen 105 F5
Kharmanli Bulg. 58 G7
Kharora India 97 D5
Kharoti *reg.* Afgh. 101 G3
Kharovsk Rus. Fed. 43 V2
Kharovskaya Gryada *hills* Rus. Fed. 43 V2
Kharsawan India 97 E5
Kharsia India 97 D5

▶**Khartoum** Sudan 121 G6
Capital of Sudan. Also spelt El Khartûm.
Khartoum *state* Sudan 121 G6
Khartoum North Sudan 121 G6
Kharuf, Ra's *mt.* Israel *see* Harif, Har
Kharwar *reg.* Afgh. 101 G3
Khasab, Khor *b.* Oman 105 F2
Khasardag, Gora *mt.* Turkm. 102 D5
Khash Afgh. 101 E4
Khāsh Iran 101 E4
also known as Vāsht
Khash Desert Afgh. 101 E4
Khashgort Rus. Fed. 38 G3
Khashm el Girba Sudan 121 G6
Khashm el Girba Dam Sudan 121 G6
Khash Rūd *r.* Afgh. 101 E4
Khashuri Georgia 107 E2
Khasi Hills India 97 F4
Khaskovo Bulg. 58 G7
Khasm al Mu'aydil *hill* Saudi Arabia 105 E2
Khatam, Jabal al *hill* Saudi Arabia 104 B2
Khatanga Rus. Fed. 39 K2
Khatanga *r.* Rus. Fed. 39 K2
Khatanga, Gulf of Rus. Fed. *see* Khatangskiy Zaliv
Khatangskiy Zaliv *b.* Rus. Fed. 39 K2
English form Khatanga, Gulf of
Khategaon India 96 C5
Khatinza Pass Pak. 101 G2
Khatlon *admin. div.* Tajik. 101 G2
English form Khatlon Oblast
Khatlon Oblast *admin. div.* Tajik. *see* Khatlon
Khatmat al Malāha Oman 105 G2
Khatmia Pass Egypt 108 D7
Khātūnābād Iran 100 C4
Khatyrka Rus. Fed. 39 R3
Khavast Uzbek. 103 G4
formerly known as Khowos; formerly known as Ursat'yevskaya
Khavda India 96 A5
Khawak Pass Afgh. 101 G3
Khawlaf, Ra's *pt* Yemen 105 F5
Khawr Shiban *well* Saudi Arabia 105 F4
Khawsh Saudi Arabia 104 C2
Khayamnami S. Africa 133 J8
Khayatbashi, Gora *mt.* Uzbek. 103 F4
also known as Hayotboshi Toghi
Khaybar Saudi Arabia 104 B2
also known as Ash Shurayf
Khaydarken Kyrg. 103 G5
Khayelitsha S. Africa 132 C11
Khaypudyrskaya Guba *b.* Rus. Fed. 40 K1

Khayrān, Ra's al *pt* Oman 105 G3
Khazarasp Uzbek. 103 E4
also spelt Hazorasp
Khē Bo Vietnam 78 D4
Khed *Maharashtra* India 94 B2
Khed *Maharashtra* India 94 B2
Kheda India 96 B5
formerly known as Kaira
Khedbrahma India 96 B4
Khedrī Iran 100 D3
Khefa Israel *see* Haifa
Khehuene, Ponta *pt* Moz. 131 G4
Khelari India 97 E5
Khelyulya Rus. Fed. 44 O3
Khemchik *r.* Rus. Fed. 88 F1
Khemis Beni Arous Morocco 54 F9
Khemis Miliana Alg. 123 H1
formerly known as Affreville
Khemisset Morocco 122 D2
Khenchela Alg. 123 G2
Khenifra Morocco 122 D2
Khenjan Afgh. 101 G3
Kheralu India 96 B4
Kherämeh Iran 100 C4
Kherli India 96 C4
Kherreh Iran 100 C5
Kherson Ukr. 41 E7
Khe Sanh Vietnam 78 D4
Kheta Rus. Fed. 39 K2
Khetolambina Rus. Fed. 44 P2
Kheyrābād Iran 100 C4
Khezerābād Iran 100 C2
formerly known as Farahābād
Khiaw, Khao *mt.* Thai. 79 C5
Khibiny *mts* Rus. Fed. 44 P2
Khiḑā, Jabal *hill* Saudi Arabia 104 D3
Khilchipur India 96 C4
Khiliomódhion Greece *see* Chiliomodi
Khilok *r.* Rus. Fed. 85 F1
Khilok *r.* Rus. Fed. 85 E1
Khimki Rus. Fed. 43 S6
Khingansk Rus. Fed. 82 C2
Khinganskiy Zapovednik *nature res.* Rus. Fed. 82 C2
Khios *i.* Greece *see* Chios
Khios Strait Greece *see* Chios Strait
Khirbat Isrīyah Syria 109 I2
Khirkiya India 96 C5
Khirr, Wādī al *watercourse* Iraq 109 L4
Khisarya Bulg. 58 F6
Khislavichi Rus. Fed. 43 N7
Khitai Pass Aksai Chin 89 B5
Khiva Uzbek. 102 D4
also spelt Khiwa
Khiwa Uzbek. *see* Khiva
Khīyāv Iran 100 A2
Khiytola Rus. Fed. 45 O3
Khlepen' Rus. Fed. 43 P6
Khlevnoye Rus. Fed. 43 U9
Khlong, Mae *r.* Thai. 79 C5
Khlong-saeng Wildlife Reserve *nature res.* Thai. 79 B6
Khlong Wang Chao National Park Thai. 78 B4
Khlung Thai. 79 C5
Khmelezero Rus. Fed. 43 P1
Khmelinets Rus. Fed. 43 T9
Khmelita Rus. Fed. 43 O6
Khmel'nik Ukr. *see* Khmil'nyk
Khmel'nitskiy Ukr. *see* Khmel'nyts'kyy
Khmel'nyts'kyy Ukr. 41 C6
also spelt Khmel'nitskiy; formerly known as Proskurov
Khmer Republic *country* Asia *see* Cambodia
Khmes, Jebel *mt.* Morocco 54 F9
Khmil'nyk Ukr. 41 C6
also spelt Khmel'nik
Khobda Kazakh. 102 C2
formerly known as Novoalekseyevka
Khodā Āfarīd *spring* Iran 100 D3
Khodasy Belarus 43 M8
Khodzha Davlet Uzbek. 103 E5
Khodzha-Kala Turkm. 102 D5
also spelt Hojagala
Khodzhambaz Turkm. 103 F5
also spelt Hojambaz
Khodzhaolen Turkm. 102 D5
Khodzhapir'yakh, Gora *mt.* Uzbek. 92 C3
Khodzhavend Azer. *see* Xocavänd
Khodzhent Tajik. *see* Khŭjand
Khodzheyli Uzbek. *see* Khŭjayli
Khodzhyder *r.* Ukr. 58 K3
Khogali Uzbek. 103 F5
Khojand Tajik. *see* Khŭjand
Khokhlovo Rus. Fed. 43 S2
Khokhol'skiy Rus. Fed. 41 F6
Kholapur India 94 C1
Kholbon Rus. Fed. 85 H1
Kholm Afgh. 101 F2
Kholm *Novgorodskaya Oblast'* Rus. Fed. 43 N4
also known as Chelm
Kholm *Smolenskaya Oblast'* Rus. Fed. 43 M6
Kholmogory Rus. Fed. 40 H3
Kholmsk Rus. Fed. 82 F2
Kholm-Zhirkovskiy Rus. Fed. 43 O6
Kholon Israel *see* Holon
Kholova *r.* Rus. Fed. 43 N3
Kholzun, Khrebet *mts* Kazakh./Rus. Fed. 88 D1
Khoman Iran 100 B2
Khomas *admin. reg.* Namibia 130 C4
Khomas Highland *hills* Namibia 130 B4
Khomeyn Iran 100 B3
Khomeynishahr Iran 100 B3
formerly known as Homāyūnshahr
Khomutovo Rus. Fed. 43 S9
Khong, Mae Nam *r.* Myanmar *see* Salween
Khonj Iran 100 C5
Khon Kaen Thai. 78 C4
Khonobod Uzbek. *see* Khanabad
Khonqa Uzbek. *see* Khanka
Khonsa India 97 G4
Khonuu Rus. Fed. 39 O3
Khoper *r.* Rus. Fed. 41 G6
Khor Rus. Fed. 82 D3
Khor *r.* Rus. Fed. 82 D3
Khóra Greece *see* Chora
Khorāsan *prov.* Iran *see* Khorāsān
Khorat Plateau Thai. 78 C4
Khorazm Wiloyati *admin. div.* Uzbek. *see* Khorezm Oblast'
Khordha India 95 E1
Khoreyver Rus. Fed. 40 K2
Khorezm Oblast' *admin. div.* Uzbek. *see* Khorezmskaya Oblast'
Khorezmskaya Oblast' *admin. div.* Uzbek. 102 E4
English form Khorezm Oblast; also known as Khorazm Wiloyati
Khorinsk Rus. Fed. 81 H2
Khorixas Namibia 130 B4
formerly known as Welwitschia
Khor-Pkhur, Kuh-e *mt.* Iran 100 B4
Khorog Tajik. *see* Khorugh
Khorol Rus. Fed. 82 D3
Khorol Ukr. 41 E6
Khorramābād Iran 100 B3
Khorram Darreh Iran 100 B3
Khorramshahr Iran 100 B3
formerly known as Khūninshahr or Muhammarah

Khorugh Tajik. 101 G2
also spelt Khorog
Khosedayu *r.* Rus. Fed. 40 K2
Khosf Iran 100 D3
Khosheutovo Rus. Fed. 102 A3
Khosravī Iran 100 B4
Khosrovi Argelanots' *nature res.* Armenia 107 F2
Khosta Rus. Fed. 41 F8
Khosūyeh Iran 100 C4
Khotang Nepal 97 E4
Khotetovo Rus. Fed. 43 R9
khot'kovo Rus. Fed. 43 T5
Khotsimsk Belarus 43 O8
Khotynets Rus. Fed. 43 Q8
Khouribga Morocco 122 D2
Khovaling Tajik. 101 G2
Khowai India 97 F5
Khowos Uzbek. *see* Khavast
Khowrjan Iran 100 C4
Khowrnag, Kūh-e *mt.* Iran 100 C3
Khowst Afgh. 101 G3
Khowst *reg.* Afgh./Pak. 101 G3
Khozap'ini, Tba *l.* Georgia 107 F2
Khozor Anghar Djibouti 104 C4
Khram, Ko *i.* Thai. 79 C5
Khri *r.* India 97 F4
Khrisoúpolis Greece *see* Chrysoupoli
Khristoforovo Rus. Fed. 40 H3
Khroma *r.* Rus. Fed. 39 O2
Khromtau Kazakh. 102 C2
Khru *r.* India 97 G4
Khrushchev Ukr. *see* Svitlovods'k
Khrushchovo Rus. Fed. 43 V7
Khrustalnyy Rus. Fed. 82 D3
Khrysokhou Bay Cyprus *see* Chrysochou Bay
Khubbāz, Wādī *watercourse* Iraq 109 N4
Khubelu *r.* Lesotho 133 M6
Khudan *r.* Rus. Fed. 85 F1
Khudat Azer. *see* Xudat
Khude Hills Pak. 101 F4
Khudian Pak. 101 H4
Khudrah, Wādī *r.* Yemen 105 E4
Khudzhand Tajik. *see* Khŭjand
Khufaysah, Khashm al *hill* Saudi Arabia 105 D3
Khuff Saudi Arabia 104 C2
Khugiana Afgh. *see* Pirzada
Khŭh lale, Ra's *pt* Iran 101 E5
Khuis Botswana 132 F3
Khŭjand Tajik. 101 G1
also spelt Khodzhent or Khojand or Khudzhand; formerly known as Ispisar or Leninabad or Leninobod
Khŭjand *admin. div.* Tajik. *see* Leninobod
Khŭjayli Uzbek. *see* Khodzheyli
Khu Khan Thai. 79 D5
Khulays Saudi Arabia 104 B3
Khuldabad India 94 B2
also known as Rauza
Khulga *r.* Rus. Fed. 40 L2
Khulkhuta Rus. Fed. 102 A3
Khulm *r.* Afgh. 101 F2
Khulna Bangl. 97 F5
Khulna *admin. div.* Bangl. 97 F5
Khuma S. Africa 133 K3
Khunayzir, Jabal al *mts* Syria 109 I3
Khŭnd, Koh-i- *mt.* Afgh. 101 G3
Khurd, Koh-i- *mt.* Afgh. 101 F3
Khuneiqa *watercourse* Sudan 121 F6
Khŭnik Bālā Iran 101 D3
Khŭninshahr Iran *see* Khorramshahr
Khunjerab Pass China/Jammu and Kashmir 89 A4
Khunsar Iran 100 B3
Khunti India 97 E5
Khŭr Iran 100 D3
Khurai India 96 C4
Khūran *sea chan.* Iran 100 C5
Khurays Saudi Arabia 105 E2
Khureit Sudan 121 F6
Khuria Tank *resr* India *see* Maniari Tank
Khurja India 96 C3
Khurmalik Afgh. 101 E3
Khurmuli Rus. Fed. 82 E2
Khurr, Wādī al *watercourse* Saudi Arabia 107 F5
Khurvatan Uzbek. 103 F5
Khushab Pak. 101 H3
Khushshah, Wādī al *watercourse* Jordan/Saudi Arabia 109 H8
Khust Ukr. 53 G2
also spelt Chust
Khutar Belarus 43 J8
Khutgaon India 94 D1
Khutse Game Reserve *nature res.* Botswana 131 E4
Khutsong S. Africa 133 L3
Khutu *r.* Tanz. 82 E2
Khuwei Sudan 121 F6
Khuzdar Pak. 101 F4
Khūzestān *prov.* Iran 100 B4
Khvājeh Iran 100 A2
Khvalynsk Rus. Fed. 102 B1
Khvashchevka Rus. Fed. 43 Q6
Khvastovichi Rus. Fed. 43 Q8
Khvor Iran 100 C3
Khvord Nārvan Iran 100 D3
Khvormūj Iran 100 B4
Khvorostyanka Rus. Fed. 102 B1
Khvosh Maqām Iran 100 A2
Khvoshna Belarus 43 L6
Khvoy Iran 100 A2
Khvoynaya Rus. Fed. 43 P3
Khvoynyy Rus. Fed. 82 B1
Khwae Noi *r.* Thai. 79 B5
Khwahan Afgh. 101 G2
Khwaja Amran *mt.* Pak. 101 F4
Khwaja-i-Ghar Afgh. 101 G2
Khwaja Muhammad Range *mts* Afgh. 101 G2
Khyber Pass Afgh./Pak. 101 G3
Khynchest' Moldova *see* Hînceşti
Khynchesty Moldova *see* Hînceşti
Kia'i Iran 100 D5
Kiama Australia 147 F3
Kiamba Phil. 74 C5
Kiambi Dem. Rep. Congo 127 F6
Kiamichi *r.* U.S.A. 179 D5
Kiamika, Lac *l.* Canada 173 P5
Kiangsi *prov.* China *see* Jiangxi
Kiangsu *prov.* China *see* Jiangsu
Kiang West National Park Gambia 124 A3
Kianly Turkm. *see* Darta
Kiantajärvi *l.* Fin. 44 O2
Kiaseh Iran 100 C2
Kiatassuaq *i.* Greenland 165 N2
also known as Holm Ø
Kiato Greece 59 D10
Kibaha Tanz. 129 C6
Kibala Angola 127 B6
Kibale National Park Uganda 128 A4
Kibali *r.* Dem. Rep. Congo 126 F4
Kibangou Congo 126 B6
Kibara, Monts *mts* Dem. Rep. Congo 127 E7
Kibawe Phil. 74 C5
Kibaya Tanz. 129 C6
Kiberashi Tanz. 129 C6
Kiberege Tanz. 129 C6
Kiboga Uganda 128 A4
Kibombo Dem. Rep. Congo 126 E5
Kibondo Tanz. 128 A5

Kibray Uzbek. 103 G4
also spelt Qibray
Kibre Mengist Eth. 128 C3
Kibris *country* Asia *see* Cyprus
Kibrīt, Jabal al *hill* Saudi Arabia 108 F9
Kibungo Rwanda 126 F5
Kibuye Rwanda 126 F5
Kibwesa Tanz. 129 A6
Kičevo Macedonia 58 B7
Kichi-Kichi *well* Chad 120 C5
Kichmengskiy Gorodok Rus. Fed. 40 H4
Kichwamba Uganda 128 A5
Kicking Horse Pass Canada 167 G5
Kid, Wādī *watercourse* Egypt 108 F9
Kidal Mali 125 F2
Kidal *admin. reg.* Mali 125 F2
Kidatu Tanz. 129 C6
Kidderminster U.K. 47 J11
Kidepo Valley National Park Uganda 128 B4
Kidete Tanz. 129 C6
Kidira Senegal 124 B3
Kidmang Jammu and Kashmir 96 C2
Kidnappers, Cape N.Z. 152 L7
Kiel Germany 48 H1
Kiel U.S.A. 172 E7
Kiel Canal Germany 48 G1
also known as Nord-Ostsee-Kanal
Kielce Poland 49 R5
Kielder Water *r.* U.K. 47 J8
Kieler Bucht *b.* Germany 48 H1
Kieler Förde *g.* Germany 48 H1
Kiembara Burkina 124 E3
Kienge Dem. Rep. Congo 127 E7
Kietrz Poland 49 P5
Kiev Kazakh. *see* Kiyevka
Kiev Ukr. 41 D6
Capital of Ukraine. Also spelt Kiyev or Kyiv or Kyyev or Kyyiv; historically known as Könugard or Sambat.
Kiffa Mauritania 124 C2
Kifisia Greece 59 E10
Kifisos *r.* Greece 59 D10
Kifrī Iraq 107 F4
Kifwanzondo Dem. Rep. Congo 127 C6
Kigali Rwanda 126 F5
Capital of Rwanda.
Kiǧi Turkey 107 E3
Kiglapait Mountains Canada 169 I1
Kiglikavik Lake Canada 167 H1
Kignan Mali 124 D4
Kigoma Tanz. 129 A6
Kigoma *admin. reg.* Tanz. 129 A6
Kigwe Tanz. 129 B6
Kihambatang Indon. 77 F3
Kihei U.S.A. 181 [inset] Z1
Kihikihi N.Z. 152 J6
Kihlanki Fin. 44 M2
Kihniö Fin. 45 M3
Kihnu *i.* Estonia 42 E3
Kiik Kazakh. 103 H3
Kiikala Fin. 42 E1
Kiiminki Fin. 44 N2
Kii-nagashima Japan 91 E7
Kii-sanchi *mts* Japan 91 D8
Kii-suidō *sea chan.* Japan 91 D8
Kijungu *well* Tanz. 129 C6
Kikerino Rus. Fed. 43 K2
Kikládhes *is* Greece *see* Cyclades
Kiknur Rus. Fed. 40 H4
Kikonai Japan 90 G4
Kikondja Dem. Rep. Congo 127 E7
Kikongo Dem. Rep. Congo 126 C6
Kikori P.N.G. 73 J8
Kikori *r.* P.N.G. 73 J8
Kikuchi Japan 91 B8
Kikwit Dem. Rep. Congo 126 C6
Kil Sweden 45 K4
Kilafors Sweden 45 L3
Kilakkarai India 94 C4
Kilan Iran 100 C3
Kilauea U.S.A. 181 [inset] Y1
Kilauea Crater U.S.A. 181 [inset] Z2
world [volcanoes] ▶▶ 14–15
Kilbogham Norway 44 K2
Kilbotn Norway 44 L1
Kilchu N. Korea 83 C4
Kilcock Rep. of Ireland 47 F10
Kilcoy Australia 149 G5
Kildare Rep. of Ireland 47 F10
Kil'dinstroy Rus. Fed. 44 P1
Kildonan Zimbabwe 131 F3
Kilekale Lake Canada 166 F1
Kilemary Rus. Fed. 40 H4
Kilembe Dem. Rep. Congo 127 C6
Kilgore U.S.A. 179 D5
Kilgour *r.* Australia 148 B3
Kilia Ukr. *see* Kiliya
Kiliba Dem. Rep. Congo 126 F5
Kilibo Benin 125 F4
Kilifi Kenya 128 C5
Kilik Pass China 89 A4
Kilimanjaro *admin. reg.* Tanz. 129 C5
▶**Kilimanjaro** *vol.* Tanz. 128 C5
Highest mountain in Africa.
africa [landscapes] ▶▶ 112–113
Kilimanjaro National Park Tanz. 128 C5
Kilimatinde Tanz. 129 B6
Kilinailau Islands P.N.G. 145 E2
formerly known as Carteret Group or Nine Islands
Kilindoni Tanz. 129 C6
Kilingi-Nõmme Estonia 42 F3
Kılıs Turkey 107 D3
Kılıs *prov.* Turkey 109 I1
Kiliya Ukr. 58 K3
also known as Chilia-Nouă; also spelt Kilia
Kilkee Rep. of Ireland 47 C11
Kilkenny Rep. of Ireland 47 E11
also spelt Cill Chainnigh
Kilkis Greece 58 D7
Killala Rep. of Ireland 47 C9
Killala Bay Rep. of Ireland 47 C9
Killala Lake Canada 172 E2
Killaloe Rep. of Ireland 47 D11
Killaloe Station Canada 173 P5
Killam Canada 167 I4
Killarney Australia 147 G2
Killarney Canada 168 D4
Killarney Rep. of Ireland 47 C11
also spelt Cill Airne
Killarney National Park Rep. of Ireland 47 C12
Killarney Provincial Park Canada 173 L4
Killary Harbour *b.* Rep. of Ireland 47 C10
Killeen U.S.A. 179 C6
Killin U.K. 46 H7
Killinek Island Canada *see* Killiniq Island
Killini *mt.* Greece *see* Kyllini
Killiniq Canada 165 M3
Killiniq Island Canada 165 M3
also spelt Killinek Island
Killorglin Rep. of Ireland 47 C11
Killybegs Rep. of Ireland 47 D9
Kilmarnock U.K. 46 H8
Kilmez' Rus. Fed. 40 I4
Kilmez' *r.* Rus. Fed. 40 I4
Kilmore Australia 147 E4
Kilosa Tanz. 129 C6
Kilpisjärvi Fin. 44 M1
Kilpua Fin. 44 N2

Kilrush Rep. of Ireland 47 C11
Kilttan i. India 94 B4
Kilwa Dem. Rep. Congo 127 F7
Kilwa Masoko Tanz. 129 C7
Kilyazi Azer. see Giläzi
Kim Chad 126 B2
Kimambi Tanz. 129 C7
Kimanis, Teluk b. Sabah Malaysia 77 F1
Kimasozero Rus. Fed. 44 O2
Kimasozero, Ozero l. Rus. Fed. 44 O2
Kimba Australia 146 C3
Kimba Congo 126 B5
Kimball NE U.S.A. 178 B3
Kimbe P.N.G. 145 E2
Kimberley Canada 167 H5
Kimberley S. Africa 133 I5
Kimberley Downs Australia 150 D3
Kimberley Plateau Australia 150 D3
Kimberley Range hills Australia 151 B5
Kimbirila-Sud Côte d'Ivoire 124 D4 formerly known as Kinbirila
Kimch'aek N. Korea 83 C4 also known as Sŏngjin
Kimch'ŏn S. Korea 83 C5
Kimhae S. Korea 83 C6
Kimi Greece see Kymi
Kimito Fin. 45 M3 also known as Kemiö
Kimje S. Korea 83 B6
Kimmirut Canada 165 M3 formerly known as Lake Harbour
Kimobetsu Japan 90 G3
Kimolos i. Greece 59 F12
Kimolou-Sifnou, Steno sea chan. Greece 59 F12
Kimongo Congo 126 B6
Kimovaara Rus. Fed. 44 O3
Kimovsk Rus. Fed. 43 T8 formerly known as Mikhaylovka
Kimpanga Dem. Rep. Congo 127 E6
Kimpangu Dem. Rep. Congo 127 B6
Kimparana Mali 124 D3
Kimper U.S.A. 176 C8
Kimpese Dem. Rep. Congo 127 B6
Kimpoko Dem. Rep. Congo 126 B6
Kimpoku-san mt. Japan see Kinpoku-san
Kimry Rus. Fed. 43 S5
Kimsquit Canada 166 E4
Kimvula Dem. Rep. Congo 127 B6
Kinabalu, Gunung mt. Sabah Malaysia 77 G1
Kinabalu National Park Sabah Malaysia 77 G1
Kinabatangan r. Sabah Malaysia 77 G1
Kınalıada i. Turkey 58 K8
Kinango Kenya 129 C6
Kinaros i. Greece 59 H12
Kinaskan Lake Canada 166 D3
Kinbasket Lake Canada 166 G4 also known as McNaughton Lake
Kinbirila Côte d'Ivoire see Kimbirila-Sud
Kinbrace U.K. 46 I5
Kincaid Canada 167 J5
Kincardine Canada 168 D4
Kinchang Myanmar 78 B2
Kinchega National Park Australia 147 D3
Kincolith Canada 166 D4
Kinda Dem. Rep. Congo 127 E7
Kindamba Congo 126 B5
Kindat Myanmar 78 A3
Kinde U.S.A. 173 K7
Kindembe Dem. Rep. Congo 127 C6
Kinder U.S.A. 179 D6
Kindersley Canada 167 I5
Kindia Guinea 124 B4
Kindongo-Mbe Dem. Rep. Congo 126 C5
Kindu Dem. Rep. Congo 126 E5
Kinel' Rus. Fed. 41 I5
Kinel'-Cherkasy Rus. Fed. 41 I5
Kineshma Rus. Fed. 40 G4
King r. N.T. Australia 148 B2
King r. W.A. Australia 150 E2
King U.S.A. 176 E9
King, Canal sea chan. Chile 205 B7
King, Lake salt flat Australia 151 C5
King and QueenCourthouse U.S.A. 177 I8
Kingaroy Australia 149 F5
King City U.S.A. 182 C5
Kingcome r. Canada 166 E5
King Creek watercourse Australia 148 C5
King Edward r. Australia 150 D2
Kingfisher U.S.A. 179 C5
King George Bay Falkland Is 205 E8
King George Island Antarctica 222 U2
King George Islands Canada 168 E1
King George Islands Fr. Polynesia see Roi Georges, Îles du
King George Sound b. Australia 151 B7
King George VI Falls Guyana 199 F3
Kingimbi Dem. Rep. Congo 126 B6
Kingisepp Rus. Fed. 43 J2
King Island Australia 147 D4
King Island Canada 166 E4
King Island Myanmar see Kadan Kyun
Kingissepa Estonia see Kuressaare
King Kirkland Canada 173 N2
Kinglake National Park Australia 147 E4
King Leopold and Queen Astrid Coast Antarctica 223 F2
King Leopold Range National Park Australia 150 D3
King Leopold Ranges hills Australia 150 D3
Kingman AZ U.S.A. 183 J6
Kingman KS U.S.A. 178 C4

▶Kingman Reef N. Pacific Ocean 221 H5
United States Unincorporated Territory.
oceania [countries] ▶ 138–139

King Mountain Canada 166 D3
King Mountain hill U.S.A. 179 B6
Kingombe Mbali Dem. Rep. Congo 126 E5
Kingondji Dem. Rep. Congo 127 C6
Kingoonya Australia 146 B2
King Peak Antarctica 223 S1
King Peninsula Antarctica 222 R2
Kingri Pak. 101 G4
Kings r. CA U.S.A. 182 D5
Kings r. NV U.S.A. 180 C4
Kingsburg U.S.A. 182 E5
Kings Canyon Australia 148 A5
Kings Canyon National Park U.S.A. 182 F5
Kingscote Australia 146 C3
Kingscourt Rep. of Ireland 47 F10
Kingseat N.Z. 152 I5
King Sejong research station Antarctica 222 U2
Kingsford U.S.A. 172 E5
Kingsland GA U.S.A. 175 D6
Kingsland IN U.S.A. 173 H10
Kingsley S. Africa 133 O4
Kingsley U.S.A. 172 H6
King's Lynn U.K. 47 M11 short form Lynn
Kingsmill Group is Kiribati 145 G2
King Sound b. Australia 150 C3
Kings Peak U.S.A. 183 N1
Kingsport U.S.A. 176 C9
Kingston Australia 147 E5
Kingston Canada 168 E4

▶Kingston Jamaica 186 D3
Capital of Jamaica.

▶Kingston Norfolk I. 220 F7
Capital of Norfolk Island.

Kingston N.Z. 153 C13
Kingston MA U.S.A. 177 O4
Kingston MO U.S.A. 178 D4
Kingston NY U.S.A. 177 K4
Kingston OH U.S.A. 176 C6
Kingston PA U.S.A. 177 J4
Kingston TN U.S.A. 174 C5
Kingston Peak U.S.A. 183 I6
Kingston South East Australia 146 C4
Kingston upon Hull U.K. 47 L10 short form Hull

▶Kingstown St Vincent 187 H4
Capital of St Vincent.

Kingstree U.S.A. 175 E5
Kingsville U.S.A. 179 C7
Kingswood U.K. 47 J12
Kington U.K. 47 I11
Kingungi Dem. Rep. Congo 127 C6
Kingurutik r. Canada 169 I1
Kingussie U.K. 46 H6
King William Island Canada 165 J3
King William's Town S. Africa 133 L9
Kingwood TX U.S.A. 179 D6
Kingwood WV U.S.A. 176 F6
Kiniama Dem. Rep. Congo 127 F7
Kınık Antalya Turkey 59 K12
Kınık İzmir Turkey 59 I9
Kinkala Congo 126 B6
Kinka-san i. Japan 90 G5
Kinleith N.Z. 152 J6
Kinloch N.Z. 153 C12
Kinlochleven U.K. 46 H7
Kinmen Taiwan see Chinmen
Kinmount Canada 173 O6
Kinna Sweden 45 K4
Kinnarasani r. India 94 D2
Kinnarodden pt Norway 44 N1
Kinnegad Rep. of Ireland 47 E10
Kinneret, Yam l. Israel see Galilee, Sea of
Kinniyai Sri Lanka 94 D4
Kinnula Fin. 44 N3
Kinoje r. Canada 168 D2
Kino-kawa r. Japan 91 D7
Kinomoto Japan 91 E7
Kinoosao Canada 167 K3
Kinpoku-san mt. Japan 90 F5 also spelt Kimpoku-san
Kinross S. Africa 133 N3
Kinsale Rep. of Ireland 47 D12
Kinsale U.S.A. 177 I7
Kinsarvik Norway 45 I3
Kinsele Dem. Rep. Congo 126 C6

▶Kinshasa Dem. Rep. Congo 126 B6
Capital of the Democratic Republic of Congo and 3rd most populous city in Africa. Formerly known as Léopoldville.
world [cities] ▶ 24–25

Kinshasa municipality Dem. Rep. Congo 126 C6
Kinsley U.S.A. 178 C4
Kinston U.S.A. 174 E5
Kintai Lith. 42 C6
Kintampo Ghana 125 E4
Kintata Dem. Rep. Congo 127 B6
Kintinian Guinea 124 C4
Kintom Indon. 75 B3
Kintop Indon. 77 F3
Kintore Australia 148 A4
Kintore, Mount Australia 146 A1
Kintyre pen. U.K. 46 G8
Kinu Myanmar 78 A3
Kinushseo r. Canada 168 D2
Kinuso Canada 167 H4
Kinwat India 94 C2
Kinyangiri Tanz. 129 B6
Kinyeti mt. Sudan 128 B4
Kinzhaly Kazakh. 102 D2
Kiomboi Tanz. 129 B6
Kiosk Canada 173 O4
Kiowa CO U.S.A. 180 F5
Kiowa KS U.S.A. 178 C4
Kipahigan Lake Canada 167 K4
Kipahulu U.S.A. 181 [inset] Z1
Kiparissia Greece see Kyparissia
Kipawa, Lac l. Canada 168 E4
Kipchak Pass China 88 B3
Kipelovo Rus. Fed. 43 U2
Kipen' Rus. Fed. 43 K2
Kipengere Range mts Tanz. 129 B7
Kipili Tanz. 129 A6
Kipini Kenya 128 D5
Kipling Canada 167 K5 formerly known as Kipling Station
Kipling Station Canada see Kipling
Kiptopeke U.S.A. 177 J8
Kipungo Angola see Quipungo
Kipushi Dem. Rep. Congo 127 E7
Kipushia Dem. Rep. Congo 127 F8
Kirakat India 97 D4
Kirakira Solomon Is 145 F3
Kiran Dağları hills Turkey 59 H10
Kirandul India 94 D2
Kirané Mali 124 C3
Kirawsk Belarus 43 K8
Kiraz Turkey 59 J10
Kirbla Estonia 42 E3
Kirbyville U.S.A. 179 D6
Kirchdorf an der Krems Austria 49 L8
Kirdimi Chad 120 C5
Kirenga r. Rus. Fed. 81 H1
Kirensk Rus. Fed. 81 H1
Kirey watercourse Kazakh. see Kerey
Kirey, Ozero salt l. Kazakh. see Kerey, Ozero
Kireyevsk Rus. Fed. 43 S8
Kirghizia country Asia see Kyrgyzstan
Kirghiz Range mts Asia 88 A3 also known as Kirgizskiy Khrebet
Kirgiziya Kazakh. 103 I2
Kirgiz-Miyaki Rus. Fed. 102 C1
Kirgizskaya S.S.R. country Asia see Kyrgyzstan
Kirgizskiy Khrebet mts Asia see Kirghiz Range
Kirgizstan country Asia see Kyrgyzstan
Kiri Dem. Rep. Congo 126 C5
Kiria Greece see Kyria
Kiriákion Greece see Kyriaki
▶Kiribati country Pacific Ocean 145 G2 formerly known as Gilbert Islands
oceania [countries] ▶ 138–139
Kiridh Somalia 128 E2
Kırıkhan Turkey 106 D3
Kırıkkale Turkey 106 C3
Kirikkuduk China 84 A2
Kirikopuni N.Z. 152 I3
Kirillov Rus. Fed. 43 T2
Kirillovo Rus. Fed. 82 F3
Kirillovskoye Rus. Fed. 43 K1
Kirin China see Jilin
Kirin prov. China see Jilin
Kirinyaga mt. Kenya see Kenya, Mount
Kirishi Rus. Fed. 43 N2
Kirishima-Yaku National Park Japan 91 B9
Kirishima-yama vol. Japan 91 B9
Kiritimati i. Kiribati 221 H5
Kiriwina Islands P.N.G. see Trobriand Islands
Kırkağaç Turkey 59 I9
Kirk Bulāg Dāgh mt. Iran 100 A2
Kirkby U.K. 47 J10
Kirkby Stephen U.K. 47 J9
Kirkcaldy U.K. 46 I7
Kirkcudbright U.K. 47 H9
Kirkenær Norway 45 K3
Kirkenes Norway 44 O1
Kirkfield Canada 173 O6
Kirkkonummi Fin. 45 N3
Kirkland AZ U.S.A. 183 L7
Kirkland IL U.S.A. 172 E8
Kirkland Lake Canada 168 D3
Kırklareli Turkey 106 A2
Kırklareli prov. Turkey 59 I7
Kırklareli Barajı resr Turkey 58 I7
Kirkliston Range mts N.Z. 153 E12
Kirkonmaanselkä b. Fin. 42 I1
Kirkovo Bulg. 58 G7
Kirkpatrick, Mount Antarctica 223 L1
Kirksville U.S.A. 174 A3
Kirkuk Iraq see Kirkūk
Kirkūk Iraq 107 F4 English form Kirkuk
Kirkwall U.K. 46 J5
Kirkwood S. Africa 133 J10
Kirkwood U.S.A. 172 C10
Kirman Iran see Kermān
Kırmır r. Turkey 106 B2
Kirobasi Turkey see Mağara
Kirov Kazakh. see Balpyk Bi
Kirov Kyrg. see Kyzyl-Adyr
Kirov Kaluzhskaya Oblast' Rus. Fed. 43 P7
Kirov Kirovskaya Oblast' Rus. Fed. 40 I4 also known as Vyatka
Kirova, Zaliv b. Azer. see Qızılağac Körfäzi
Kirovabad Azer. see Gäncä
Kirovabad Tajik. see Panj
Kirovakan Armenia see Vanadzor
Kirovo Kazakh. 102 C2
Kirovo Ukr. see Kirovohrad
Kirovo Uzbek. see Besharyk
Kirov Oblast admin. div. Rus. Fed. see Kirovskaya Oblast'
Kirovo-Chepetsk Rus. Fed. 40 I4 formerly spelt Kirovo-Chepetskiy
Kirovo-Chepetskiy Rus. Fed. see Kirovo-Chepetsk
Kirovograd Ukr. see Kirovohrad
Kirovohrad Ukr. 41 E6 also spelt Kirovograd; formerly known as Kirovo or Yelizavetgrad or Zinovyevsk
Kirovsk Leningradskaya Oblast' Rus. Fed. 43 L2 formerly known as Nevdubstroy
Kirovsk Murmanskaya Oblast' Rus. Fed. 44 P2
Kirovsk Turkm. see Babadaykhan
Kirovskaya Oblast' admin. div. Rus. Fed. 40 I4 English form Kirov Oblast
Kirovskiy Kazakh. see Balpyk Bi
Kirovskiy Rus. Fed. 82 D3
Kirovskoye Kyrg. see Kyzyl-Adyr
Kirpaşa pen. Cyprus see Karpasia
Kirpili Turkm. 102 D5
Kirriemuir U.K. 46 I7
Kirs Rus. Fed. 40 J4
Kirsanov Rus. Fed. 41 G5
Kirsanovo Kazakh. 102 C2
Kırşehir Turkey 106 C3
Kirtachi Niger 125 F3
Kirthar National Park Pak. 101 F5
Kirthar Range mts Pak. 101 F5
Kiruna Sweden 44 M2 also spelt Giron
Kirundo Burundi 126 F5
Kirundu Dem. Rep. Congo 126 E5
Kirwan Escarpment Antarctica 223 X2
Kirya Rus. Fed. 40 H5
Kiryū Japan 91 F6
Kirzhach Rus. Fed. 43 T5
Kisa Sweden 45 K4
Kisakata Japan 90 F5
Kisaki Tanz. 129 C6
Kisama, Parque Nacional de nat. park Angola see Quiçama, Parque Nacional do
Kisangani Dem. Rep. Congo 126 E4 formerly known as Stanleyville
Kisar i. Indon. 75 C5
Kisaran Indon. 76 B2
Kisarawe Tanz. 129 C6
Kisarazu Japan 91 F7
Kis-Balaton park Hungary 49 O9
Kisbér Hungary 49 P8
Kiselevsk Rus. Fed. 80 D2
Kiseljak Bos.-Herz. 56 K5
Kisel'nya Rus. Fed. 43 N1
Kisel'ovka Rus. Fed. 82 E2
Kishanganj India 97 E4
Kishangarh Rajasthan India 96 A4
Kishangarh Rajasthan India 96 B4
Kishen Ganga r. India/Pak. 96 B2
Kishi-Karoy, Ozero salt l. Kazakh. 103 G1
Kishika-zaki pt Japan 91 B9
Kishinev Moldova see Chişinău
Kishiözen r. Kazakh./Rus. Fed. see Malyy Uzen'
Kishiwada Japan 91 D7
Kishkenekol' Kazakh. 103 H1 formerly known as Kzyltu or Qyzyltū
Kishorganj Bangl. 97 F4
Kishtwar Jammu and Kashmir 96 B2
Kisi Nigeria 125 F4
Kisi Tanz. 129 A6
Kisigo r. Tanz. 129 B6
Kisii Kenya 128 B5
Kisiju Tanz. 129 C6
Kiskittogisu Lake Canada 167 L4
Kiskitto Lake Canada 167 L4
Kisko Fin. 45 M3
Kiskőrös Hungary 49 Q9
Kiskunfélegyháza Hungary 49 Q9
Kiskunhalas Hungary 49 Q9
Kiskunlacháza Hungary 49 Q8
Kiskunmajsa Hungary 49 Q9
Kiskunsági nat. park Hungary 49 Q8
Kislovodsk Rus. Fed. 41 G8
Kismaayo Somalia 128 D5 formerly spelt Chisimaio or Kismayu
Kismayu Somalia see Kismaayo
Kisofukushima Japan 91 E7
Kisoro Uganda 128 A5
Kiso-sanmyaku mts Japan 91 E7
Kispiox Canada 166 E4
Kispiox r. Canada 166 E4
Kissamou, Kolpos b. Greece 59 E13
Kisseraing Island Myanmar see Kanmaw Kyun
Kissidougou Guinea 124 C4
Kissimmee U.S.A. 175 D6
Kissimmee r. U.S.A. 175 D7
Kissimmee, Lake U.S.A. 175 D7
Kississing Lake Canada 167 K4
Kissu, Jebel mt. Sudan 120 E4
Kistanje Croatia 56 H5
Kistelek Hungary 49 Q9
Kistna r. India see Krishna
Kistrand Norway 44 N1
Kisújszállás Hungary 49 R8
Kisumu Kenya 128 B5
Kisvárda Hungary 49 T7
Kisykkamys Kazakh. see Dzhangala
Kit r. Sudan 128 A3
Kita Mali 124 C3
Kitab Uzbek. 103 F5 also spelt Kitob
Kita-Daitō-jima i. Japan 81 M7
Kitagawa Japan 91 B8
Kitahiyama Japan 90 F3
Kitaibaraki Japan 90 G6
Kita-Iō-jima vol. Japan 73 J1
Kitakami Japan 90 G5
Kitakami-gawa r. Japan 90 G5
Kitakata Japan 90 F6
Kita-Kyūshū Japan 91 B8
Kitale Kenya 128 B4
Kitami Japan 90 H3
Kitami-sanchi mts Japan 90 H2
Kitanda Dem. Rep. Congo 127 E6
Kitaura Japan 91 B8
Kitchener Canada 168 D5
Kitchigama r. Canada 168 E3
Kiteba Dem. Rep. Congo 127 E6
Kitee Fin. 44 O3
Kitendwe Dem. Rep. Congo 127 F6
Kitgum Uganda 128 B4
Kithira i. Greece see Kythira
Kithnos i. Greece see Kythnos
Kithnou, Stenón sea chan. Greece see Kythnou, Steno
Kiti, Cape Cyprus see Kition, Cape
Kitimat Canada 166 D4
Kitinen r. Fin. 44 N2
Kition, Cape Cyprus 108 E3 also known as Kiti, Cape or Kitiou, Akra
Kitiou, Akra c. Cyprus see Kition, Cape
Kitkatla Canada 166 D4
Kitob Uzbek. see Kitab
Kitriani i. Greece 59 F12
Kitsa Rus. Fed. 44 P1
Kitsault Canada 166 D4
Kitscoty Canada 167 I4
Kitsuki Japan 91 B8
Kittanning U.S.A. 176 F5
Kittatinny Mountains hills U.S.A. 177 K5
Kittilä Fin. 44 N2
Kittur India 94 B3
Kitty Hawk U.S.A. 177 J9
Kitui Kenya 128 C5
Kitumbeine vol. Tanz. 128 C5
Kitumbini Tanz. 129 C7
Kitunda Tanz. 129 B6
Kitwanga Canada 166 D4
Kitwe Zambia 127 F8
Kitzbühel Austria 49 J8
Kitzbüheler Alpen mts Austria 49 J8
Kitzingen Germany 48 H6
Kiu Kenya 128 C5
Kiu Lom Dam Thai. 78 B4
Kiunga P.N.G. 73 J8
Kiunga Marine National Reserve nature res. Kenya 128 D5
Kiuruvesi Fin. 44 N3
Kivalo ridge Fin. 44 N2
Kiverichi Rus. Fed. 43 R4
Kivijärvi Fin. 44 N3
Kivijärvi l. Fin. 42 I1
Kivijärvi l. Fin. 44 N3
Kivilompolo Norway 44 M1
Kiviõli Estonia 42 H2
Kivivaara Fin. 44 O3
Kivi-Vigala Estonia 42 F3
Kivu, Lake Dem. Rep. Congo/Rwanda 126 F5
Kiwaba N'zogi Angola 127 C7 formerly known as Brito Godins
Kiwai Island P.N.G. 73 J8
Kiwawa Tanz. 129 C7
Kiwirrkurra Aboriginal Reserve Australia 150 D4
Kiyakty, Ozero salt l. Kazakh. 103 G2
Kiyāt Saudi Arabia 104 C4
Kiyev Ukr. see Kiev
Kiyevka Kazakh. 103 G2 also known as Kiev
Kiyevka Rus. Fed. 90 C3
Kiyevskiy Rus. Fed. 43 R6
Kiyevskoye Vodokhranilishche resr Ukr. see Kyyivs'ke Vodoskhovyshche
Kıyıköy Turkey 58 J7 also known as Midye
Kiyma Kazakh. 103 F2 also spelt Qima
Kizel Rus. Fed. 40 K4
Kizema Rus. Fed. 40 H3
Kizhi, Ostrov i. Rus. Fed. 40 E3
Kizhinga Rus. Fed. 85 F1
Kiziba-Baluba, Réserve de nature res. Dem. Rep. Congo 127 E7
Kizigo Game Reserve nature res. Tanz. 129 B6
Kizil China 88 C3
Kızılcadağ Turkey 106 B3
Kızılca Dağ mt. Turkey 106 B3
Kızılcahamam Turkey 106 C2 also known as Yabanabat
Kızıldağ mt. Turkey 108 E1
Kızıldağ mt. Turkey 108 G1
Kızıl Dağı mt. Turkey 107 D3
Kızılırmak Turkey 106 C2 also known as Huseyınli
Kızılırmak r. Turkey 107 C2
Kızılören Turkey 106 C3
Kizil'skoye Rus. Fed. 102 D1
Kızıltepe Turkey 107 E3 also known as Koçhisar
Kizil"yurt Rus. Fed. 102 A4
Kızkalesi Turkey 108 F1
Kizlyar Rus. Fed. 102 A4
Kizlyarskiy Zaliv b. Rus. Fed. 102 A3
Kizner Rus. Fed. 40 I4
Kizreka Rus. Fed. 44 O2
Kizyl-Arbat Turkm. see Gyzylarbat
Kizyl-Atrek Turkm. see Gyzyletrek
Kizylayak Turkm. 103 F5
Kizyl Jilga Aksai Chin 89 B5
Kizyl-Su Turkm. 102 C5 also known as Gyzylsuw
Kjøllefjord Norway 44 N1
Kjøpsvik Norway 44 L1
Klaarstroom S. Africa 132 G10
Kladanj Bos.-Herz. 56 K4
Kladno Czech Rep. 49 L5
Kladovo Srbija Yugo. 58 D4
Klagan Sabah Malaysia 77 G1
Klagenfurt Austria 49 L9 also known as Celovec
Klagetoh U.S.A. 183 O6
Klaipėda Lith. 42 C6 historically known as Memel
Klaksvig Faroe Is see Klaksvík
Klaksvík Faroe Is 46 F1 also spelt Klaksvig
Klamath r. U.S.A. 180 A4
Klamath Falls U.S.A. 180 B4
Klamath Mountains U.S.A. 180 B4
Klampo Indon. 77 G2
Klang Malaysia see Kelang
Klappan r. Canada 166 D3
Klášterec nad Ohří Czech Rep. 49 K5
Klaten Indon. 77 E4
Klatovy Czech Rep. 49 K6
Klawer S. Africa 132 C8
Klawock U.S.A. 164 F4
Klazienaveen Neth. 48 D3
Kłecko Poland 49 O3
Kleczew Poland 49 P3
Kleides Islands Cyprus 108 F2 also known as Zafer Adaları; also spelt Klidhes Islands
Kleinbegin S. Africa 132 F5
Klein Doring r. S. Africa 132 D8
Kleinegga mt. Norway 44 J3
Klein Karas Namibia 132 C4
Kleinmachnow Germany 49 K3
Kleinmond S. Africa 132 D11
Klein Roggeveldberge mts S. Africa 132 E10
Kleinsee S. Africa 132 B6
Kleinseenplatte Neustrelitz park Germany 49 J2
Klein Swartberg mt. S. Africa 132 F10
Klein-Vet r. S. Africa 133 K5
Kleitoria Greece 59 D11 also spelt Klitória
Klekovača mt. Bos.-Herz. 56 I4
Klemtu Canada 166 D4
Kleppesto Norway 45 I3
Klerksdorp S. Africa 133 K3
Klerkskraal S. Africa 133 L3
Kleszczele Poland 49 U3
Kletnya Rus. Fed. 43 O8
Kletsk Belarus see Klyetsk
Kletskaya Rus. Fed. 41 G6 formerly known as Kletskiy
Kletskiy Rus. Fed. see Kletskaya
Kleve Germany 48 D4 historically known as Cleves
Klichaw Belarus 43 K8
Klichka Rus. Fed. 85 H1
Klidhes Islands Cyprus see Kleides Islands
Klienpoort S. Africa 133 I10
Klimatino Rus. Fed. 43 S4
Klimavichy Belarus 43 M8 also spelt Klimovichi
Klimawka Belarus 43 M9
Kliment Bulg. 58 I5
Klimovichi Belarus see Klimavichy
Klimovo Rus. Fed. 43 N9
Klimovsk Rus. Fed. 43 S6
Klimov Zavod Rus. Fed. 43 P7
Klimpfjäll Sweden 44 K2
Klin Rus. Fed. 43 R5
Klina Kosovo, Srbija Yugo. 58 B6
Klinaklini r. Canada 166 E5
Kling Phil. 74 C5
Klingkang, Banjaran mts Indon./Malaysia 77 E2
Klinsko-Dmitrovskaya Gryada ridge Rus. Fed. 43 R5
Klintehamn Sweden 45 L4
Klintsovka Rus. Fed. 102 B2
Klintsy Rus. Fed. 43 N9
Klip r. S. Africa 133 N4
Klipdale S. Africa 132 D11
Klipfontein S. Africa 133 J10
Klippan Sweden 45 K4
Klipplaat S. Africa 133 I10
Kliprand S. Africa 132 C7
Klipskool S. Africa 133 O2
Klipvoor Dam S. Africa 133 L2
Klis Croatia 56 I5
Klishino Moskovskaya Oblast' Rus. Fed. 43 T7
Klishino Novgorodskaya Oblast' Rus. Fed. 43 O2
Klitmøller Denmark 45 J4
Klitória Greece see Kleitoria
Ključ Bos.-Herz. 56 I4
Kłobuck Poland 49 P5
Kłodawa Poland 49 P3
Kłodzko Poland 49 N5
Klondike r. Canada 166 B1
Klondike Goldrush National Historical Park nat. park U.S.A. 166 C3
Klooga Estonia 42 F2
Klosterneuburg Austria 49 N7
Klosters Switz. 51 P6
Klötze (Altmark) Germany 48 I3
Kluane r. Canada 166 B2
Kluane Game Sanctuary nature res. Canada 166 A2
Kluane Lake Canada 166 B2
Kluane National Park Canada 166 B2
Kluang Malaysia see Keluang
Kluang, Tanjung pt Indon. 77 E3
Kluczbork Poland 49 P5
Klukhori Rus. Fed. see Karachayevsk
Klumpang, Teluk b. Indon. 77 G3
Klungkung Indon. 77 F5
Klupro Pak. 101 G5
Klyastsitsy Belarus 43 J6
Klyava r. Belarus 43 J8
Klyavlino Rus. Fed. 40 J5
Klyaz'ma r. Rus. Fed. 43 U5
Klyetsk Belarus 42 H8 also spelt Kletsk
▶Klyuchevskaya, Sopka vol. Rus. Fed. 39 Q4
asia [threats] ▶ 70–71
Klyuchi Rus. Fed. 103 I1
Klyuchi Rus. Fed. 39 Q4
Knapdaar S. Africa 133 K7
Knapp Mound hill U.S.A. 172 C6
Knaresborough U.K. 47 K9
Knee Lake Man. Canada 167 M4
Knee Lake Sask. Canada 167 J4
Knesebeck Germany 48 H3
Knetzgau Germany 48 H6
Kneževi Vinogradi Croatia 56 K3
Knezha Bulg. 58 F5
Knić Srbija Yugo. 58 B5
Knife r. U.S.A. 178 B2
Knife River U.S.A. 172 B4
Knight Inlet Canada 166 E5
Knighton U.K. 47 I11
Knights Landing U.S.A. 182 C3
Knin Croatia 56 I4
Knittelfeld Austria 49 L8
Knivsta Sweden 45 L4
Knizhovnik Bulg. 58 G7
Knjaževac Srbija Yugo. 58 D5
Knob Lake Canada see Schefferville
Knob Peak hill Australia 150 E2
Knockaboy hill Rep. of Ireland 47 C12
Knock Hill hill U.K. 46 J6
Knockmealdown Mountains hills Rep. of Ireland 47 D11
Knokke-Heist Belgium 51 J1
Knosos tourist site Greece see Knossos
Knossos tourist site Greece 59 G13 also spelt Knosos or Knossós; historically known as Cnossus
Knossós tourist site Greece see Knossos
Knowles, Cape Antarctica 222 T2
Knox IN U.S.A. 172 G9
Knox PA U.S.A. 176 F4
Knox, Cape Canada 166 C4
Knox Atoll Kiribati see Tarawa
Knox Coast Antarctica 223 G2
Knoxville GA U.S.A. 175 D5
Knoxville IA U.S.A. 174 A3
Knoxville IL U.S.A. 172 C10
Knoxville TN U.S.A. 174 D5
Knud Rasmussen Land reg. Greenland 165 M2
Knyahinin Belarus 42 I7
Knyazevo Rus. Fed. 43 J5
Knyazhikha Rus. Fed. 43 R4
Knyazhitsy Rus. Fed. 43 J3
Knyazhytsy Belarus 43 L7
Knysna S. Africa 132 H11
Knyszyn Poland 49 T2
Ko, Gora mt. Rus. Fed. 82 E3
Koani Tanz. 129 C6
Koartac Canada see Quaqtaq
Koa Valley watercourse S. Africa 132 D6
Koba Indon. 77 D3
Kobayashi Japan 91 B9
Kobbfoss Norway 44 O1
Kobe Indon. 75 C2
▶Kōbe Japan 91 D7
world [earthquakes] ▶ 14–15
København Denmark see Copenhagen
Kobenni Mauritania 124 C3
Kobi Indon. 75 D3
Koblenz Germany 48 E5 formerly spelt Coblenz
K'obo Eth. 128 C1
Koboldo Rus. Fed. 82 D1
Kobozha r. Rus. Fed. 43 R3
Kobrin Belarus see Kobryn
Kobroör i. Indon. 73 H8
Kobryn Belarus 42 F9 also spelt Kobrin
Kobuk Valley National Park U.S.A. 164 D3
K'obulet'i Georgia 107 E2
Kobyay Rus. Fed. 39 M3
Kocaafşar r. Turkey 59 J8
Koca Dağ mt. Turkey 59 K10
Kocaeli Turkey 106 B2 also known as İzmit; historically known as Astacus or Nicomedia
Kocaeli prov. Turkey 58 K8
Kocaeli Yarımadası pen. Turkey 58 K7
Kočani Macedonia 58 D7
Koçarlı Turkey 59 I11
Kocasu r. Turkey 106 B2
Kocatepe Turkey 109 I1
Koceljevo Srbija Yugo. 58 A4
Kočevje Slovenia 56 G3
Koch'ang S. Korea 83 B6
Koch Bihar India 97 F4 formerly spelt Cooch Behar
Kocher r. Germany 48 G6
Kocherinovo Bulg. 58 E6
Kochevo Rus. Fed. 40 J4
Kochi India see Cochin
Kōchi Japan 91 C8
Kōchi pref. Japan 91 C8
Koçhisar Turkey see Kızıltepe
Kochkor Kyrg. 103 H4 also known as Kochkorka
Kochkorka Kyrg. see Kochkor
Kochkurovo Rus. Fed. 41 H5
Kochubey Rus. Fed. 102 A3 formerly known as Chernyy Rynok
Kochylas hill Greece 59 F10
Kock Poland 49 T4
Kocs Hungary 49 P8
Kod India 94 B3
Kodaikanal India 94 C4
Kodala India 95 E2
Kodari Nepal 97 E4
Kodarma India 97 E4
Kodavere Estonia 42 I3
Kodiak U.S.A. 164 D4
Kodiak Island U.S.A. 164 D4
Kodinar India 94 A1
Kodino Rus. Fed. 40 F3
Kodiyakkarai India 94 C4
Kodok Sudan 128 B2
Kodomari Japan 90 G4
Kodori r. Georgia 107 E2
Kodumuru India 94 C3
Kodyma Ukr. 41 D6
Kodzhaele mt. Bulg./Greece 58 G7
Koedoesberg mts S. Africa 132 E9
Koedoeskop S. Africa 133 L1
Koegrabie S. Africa 132 F6
Koekenaap S. Africa 132 C8
Koës Namibia 130 C5
Kofa Mountains U.S.A. 183 K8
Kofa National Wildlife Refuge nature res. U.S.A. 183 J8
Kofarnihon Tajik. 101 G2 also spelt Kafirnigan; formerly known as Ordzhonikidzeabad or Orjonikidzeobod
Kofarnihon r. Tajik. 101 G2
Kofçaz Turkey 58 I7
Koffiefontein S. Africa 133 J6
Kofinas, Oros mt. Greece 59 G14
Köflach Austria 49 M8
Koforidua Ghana 125 E5
Kōfu Tottori Japan 91 C7
Kōfu Yamanashi Japan 91 F7
Kogălniceanu airport Romania 58 J4 also known as Cogălniceanu or Constanța
Kogaluc r. Canada 168 E1
Kogaluc, Baie de b. Canada 168 E1
Kogaluk r. Canada 169 I1
Kögart Kyrg. see Alaykuu
Køge Denmark 45 K5
Kogel' r. Rus. Fed. 40 K3
Kogi state Nigeria 125 G4
Kogon Uzbek. see Kagan
Kogoni Mali 124 D3
Kōhaihai pt N.Z. see Gillespies Point
Kohat Pak. 101 G3
Kohila Estonia 42 F2
Kohima India 97 G4
Kohistan reg. Pak. 101 H3
Kohkīlūyeh va Būyer Ahmadī prov. Iran 100 B4
Kohler Range mts Antarctica 222 Q2
Kohls Ranch U.S.A. 183 M7
Kohlu Pak. 101 G4
Kohouro well Chad 120 D5
Kohrener Land park Germany 49 J4
Kohsan Afgh. 101 E3
Kohtla-Järve Estonia 42 I2
Kohyl'nyk r. Ukr. 58 K3
Koide Japan 90 F6
Koidern Canada 166 A2
Koidern Mountain Canada 166 A2
Koidu Sierra Leone see Sefadu
Koigi Estonia 42 G3
Koihoa India 95 G4
Koiingnaas S. Africa 132 B7
Koilkonda India 94 C2
Koilkuntla India 94 C3
Koin r. Rus. Fed. 40 I3
Koi Sanjaq Iraq 107 F4
Koitere l. Fin. 44 O3
Koivu Fin. 44 N2
Kŏje-do i. S. Korea 83 C6
Ko-jima i. Japan 90 F4
Ko-jima i. Japan 91 F8
Kojonup Australia 151 B7
Kok r. Thai. 78 C3
Kokalaat Kazakh. 103 F2
Kokand Uzbek. 103 G4 also spelt Qŭqon
Kokankishlak Uzbek. see Pakhtaabad
Kökar Fin. 45 M4
Kökar i. Fin. 42 B2
Kök-Art Kyrg. see Alaykuu
Kokatahi N.Z. 153 F10
Kök-Aygyr Kyrg. 103 H4 also spelt Kökaygyr
Kokcha r. Afgh. 101 G2
Kokchetav Kazakh. see Kokshetau
Kokemäki Fin. 45 M3
Kokerboom Namibia 130 C6
Kokhanava Belarus 43 K7
Koki Senegal 124 B3
Kök-Janggak Kyrg. 103 H4 also spelt Kok-Yangak
Kokkina Cyprus 108 D2 also known as Erenköy
Kokkola Fin. 44 M3 also known as Gamlakarleby
Kok Kuduk well China 88 D2
Koknese Latvia 42 G5
Koko Nigeria 125 G4
Kokofata Mali 124 C3
Kokolo-Pozo Côte d'Ivoire 124 D5
Kokomo U.S.A. 174 C3
Kokong Botswana 130 D5
Kokonoe Japan 91 B8
Kokora Estonia 42 I3
Kokorevka Rus. Fed. 43 P9
Kokorevo Rus. Fed. 43 K4
Kokoro Benin 125 F4
Kokoshkino Rus. Fed. 43 S6
Kokosi S. Africa 133 L3
Kokou mt. Guinea 124 B4
Kokpekti Kazakh. 88 C1
Koksan N. Korea 83 B5
Koksaray Kazakh. 103 G4
Kokshaal-Tau mts China/Kyrg. 88 B3 also known as Kakshaal-Too
Kokshetau Kazakh. 103 G1 formerly spelt Kokchetav
Koksoak r. Canada 169 G1
Kokstad S. Africa 133 N7
Koksu Almatinskaya Oblast' Kazakh. 103 I3
Koksu Yuzhnyy Kazakhstan Kazakh. 103 G4
Koktal Kazakh. 103 I3
Kök-Tash Kyrg. 103 H4 also spelt Kěk-Tash
Kokterek Kazakh. 103 I3
Koktokay China 84 A2
Koktuma Kazakh. 88 C2
Koku, Tanjung pt Indon. 75 B4
Kokubu Japan 91 B9
Kok-Yangak Kyrg. see Kök-Janggak
Kokyar China 88 B4

Kolymskiy, Khrebet mts Rus. Fed. **39** Q3
English form Kolyma Range; also known as Gydan, Khrebet
Kolymskoye Vodokhranilische resr Rus. Fed. **39** O3
Kolyshley Rus. Fed. **41** H5
Kolyuchinskaya Guba b. Rus. Fed. **39** S3
Kolyvan' Rus. Fed. **88** C1
Kom mt. Bulg. **58** E7
Kom China **88** D1
Komadugu-gana watercourse Nigeria **125** I3
Komaga-take mt. Japan **90** F6
Komaga-take vol. Japan **90** G4
Komaggas S. Africa **132** B6
Komaggas Mountains S. Africa **132** B6
Komagvær Norway **44** O1
Komaki Japan **91** E7
Komandnaya, Gora mt. Rus. Fed. **82** E2
Komandorskiye Ostrova is Rus. Fed. **39** Q4
Komárno Slovakia **49** P8
Komarichi Rus. Fed. **43** P9
Komarno Ukr. see Komarno
Komary Rus. Fed. **43** O6
Komati r. Swaziland **133** P2
Komatipoort S. Africa **133** P2
Komatsu Japan **91** E6
Komatsushima Japan **91** D7
Komba Dem. Rep. Congo **126** D4
Komba i. Indon. **75** B4
Kombakomba Indon. **75** B3
Kombat Namibia **130** D3
Kombe Dem. Rep. Congo **126** E6
Kombe Tanz. **129** A6
Kombissiri Burkina **125** E3
Komering r. Indon. **75** B4
Komga S. Africa **133** L9
Kôm Hamâda Egypt **108** B7
Komi, Respublika aut. rep. Rus. Fed. **40** I3
English form Komi Republic; formerly known as Komi A.S.S.R.
Komi A.S.S.R. aut. rep. Rus. Fed. see Komi, Respublika
Kominato Japan **90** G4
Komintern Ukr. see Marhanets'
Kominternivs'ke Ukr. **41** D7
Komi-Permyak Autonomous Okrug admin. div. Rus. Fed. see Komi-Permyatskiy Avtonomnyy Okrug
Komi-Permyatskiy Avtonomnyy Okrug admin. div. Rus. Fed. **40** J3
English form Komi-Permyak Autonomous Okrug
Komi Republic aut. rep. Rus. Fed. see Komi, Respublika
Komiža Croatia **56** I5
Komkans S. Africa **132** C8
Komló Hungary **49** P9
Kommandokraal S. Africa **132** G10
Kommetjie S. Africa **132** C11
Kommissiepoort S. Africa **133** L6
Kommuna Turkm. see Babadaykhan
Kommunar Kostromskaya Oblast' Rus. Fed. **40** G4
Kommunar Leningradskaya Oblast' Rus. Fed. **43** L2
Kommunarsk Ukr. see Alchevs'k
Kommunizm, Qullai mt. Tajik. see Garmo, Qullai
Kommunizma, Pik mt. Tajik. see Garmo, Qullai
Komodo i. Indon. **75** A5
Komodo National Park Indon. **75** A5
Komodou Guinea **124** C4
Komoé r. Côte d'Ivoire **124** E5
also spelt Comoé
Kôm Ombo Egypt **121** G3
Komono Congo **126** B5
Komoran i. Indon. **73** I8
Komoro Japan **91** F7
Komotini Greece **58** G7
Kompong Cham Cambodia see Kâmpóng Cham
Kompong Chhnang Cambodia see Kâmpóng Chhnang
Kompong Kleang Cambodia see Kâmpóng Khleăng
Kompong Som Cambodia see Sihanoukville
Kompong Som Bay Cambodia see Sihanoukville, Chhâk
Kompong Speu Cambodia see Kâmpóng Spœ
Kompong Thom Cambodia see Kâmpóng Thum
Komrat Moldova see Comrat
Komsberg mt. S. Africa **132** F9
Komsberg mts S. Africa **132** E9
Komsomol Kazakh. see Komsomol'skiy
Komsomol Kazakh. see Komsomolets
Komsomol Turkm. see Komsomol'sk
Komsomolets Kazakh. **103** D1
also known as Komsomol
Komsomolets, Ostrov i. Rus. Fed. **39** J1
Komsomolets, Zaliv b. Kazakh. **102** C3
Komsomol'sk Ivanovskaya Oblast' Rus. Fed. **43** V3
Komsomol'sk Kaliningradskaya Oblast' Rus. Fed. **42** B7
Komsomol'sk Turkm. **103** E5
also known as Komsomol
Komsomol's'ke Ukr. **41** F7
formerly known as Karakubbud
Komsomol'skiy Kazakh. **102** C3
Komsomol'skiy Chukotskiy Avtonomnyy Okrug Rus. Fed. **39** R3
Komsomol'skiy Rus. Fed. see Yugorsk
Komsomol'skiy Respublika Kalmykiya - Khalm'g-Tangch Rus. Fed. **41** H7
formerly known as Krasnyy Kamyshanik
Komsomol'skiy Respublika Mordoviya Rus. Fed. **41** H5
formerly known as Zavodskoy
Komsomol'sk-na-Amure Rus. Fed. **82** E2
Komsomol'skoye Kazakh. **103** E2
Komuniga Bulg. **58** G7
Kömürlü Turkey **107** E2
Kon India **97** D4
Konacık Turkey **108** G1
Konada India **95** D2
Konaklı Turkey **108** C1
Konakovo Rus. Fed. **43** R5
Konar prov. Afgh. **101** D3
Konarak India **95** E2
Konarka India see Konarka
Konarka India **95** E2
also known as Black Pagoda; formerly known as Kanarak or Konarak
Konch India **96** C4
Konchanskoye-Suvorovskoye Rus. Fed. **43** P3
Konchezero Rus. Fed. **40** E3
Konchytsy Belarus **42** G9
Konda Rus. Fed. **44** P2
Kondagaon India **94** D2
Kondapalle India **94** D2
Kondaparinga Aboriginal Holding res. Australia **149** E3
Kondavid India **94** D2
Kondiaronk, Lac l. Canada **173** Q4
Kondinin Australia **151** B7
Kondinskoye Rus. Fed. see Oktyabr'skoye
Kondinskoye Rus. Fed. **38** G3
formerly known as Nakhrachi
Kondoa Tanz. **129** B5
Kondol' Rus. Fed. **41** H5
Kondopoga Rus. Fed. **40** E3
Kondoros Hungary **49** R9
Kondrat'yevo Rus. Fed. **43** J1

Kondrovo Rus. Fed. **43** Q7
Kondūz Afgh. **101** G2
also spelt Kunduz; historically known as Drapsaca
Kondūz prov. Afgh. **101** G2
Konečka Planina mts Macedonia **58** D7
Konetsbor Rus. Fed. **40** K2
Köneürgench Turkm. see Keneurgench
Konevits, Ostrov i. Rus. Fed. **43** L1
Kong Cameroon **125** I5
Kong Côte d'Ivoire **124** D4
Kŏng, Kaôh i. Cambodia **79** C6
formerly known as Kas Klong
Kŏng, Tônlé r. Cambodia **79** D5
Kong, Xé r. Laos **79** D5
Kongassambougou, Réserve de nature res. Mali **124** C3
Kong Christian IX Land reg. Greenland **165** P3
Kong Christian X Land reg. Greenland **165** Q2
Kongelab atoll Marshall Is see Rongelap
Kong Frederik IX Land reg. Greenland **165** N3
Kong Frederik VIII Land reg. Greenland **165** Q2
Kong Frederik VI Kyst coastal area Greenland **165** O3
Kong Karls Land is Svalbard **38** C2
Kong Kat hill Indon. **77** G2
Kongkemul mt. Indon. **77** G2
Kongola Namibia **130** D3
Kong Oscars Fjord inlet Greenland **165** Q2
Kongolo Dem. Rep. Congo **127** E6
Kongoussi Burkina **125** E3
Kongsberg Norway **45** J4
Kongsfjord Norway **44** O1
Kongsøya i. Svalbard **38** C2
Kongsvinger Norway **45** K3
Kongur Shan mt. China **88** A4
also known as Kungur
Kong Wilhelm Land reg. Greenland **165** Q2
Konibodom Tajik. see Kanibadam
Koniecpol Poland **49** Q5
Königsberg Rus. Fed. see Kaliningrad
Königsbrunn Germany **48** H7
Königswartha Germany **49** L4
Königswinter Germany **48** E5
Königs Wusterhausen Germany **49** K3
Konimekh Uzbek. see Kanimekh
Konin Poland **49** P3
Konin r. Rus. Fed. **82** E2
Koniningen, Qullai mt. Tajik. see Garmo, Qullai
Kōnis mt. Japan **91** F6
Konitsa Greece **59** B8
Köniz Switz. **51** N6
Konj mt. Bos.-Herz. **56** I5
Konjic Bos.-Herz. **56** K4
Konjuh mts Bos.-Herz. **56** K4
Könkämäeno r. Fin./Sweden **44** M1
Konkiepe watercourse Namibia **130** C6
Kon'-Kolodez' Rus. Fed. **43** U9
Konkwesso Nigeria **125** G4
Konna Mali **124** E3
Konnarock U.S.A. **176** D9
Konnevesi Fin. **44** N3
Konongo Ghana **125** E5
Konoplyane Ukr. **58** L1
Konosha Rus. Fed. **40** G3
Kōnosu Japan **91** F6
Konotop Ukr. **41** E6
Kon Plong Vietnam **79** E5
Konqi He r. China **88** E3
Konskie Poland **49** R4
Konso Eth. **128** C3
Konstantinograd Ukr. see Krasnohrad
Konstantinovka Rus. Fed. **82** B2
Konstantinovka Ukr. see Kostyantynivka
Konstantinovsk Rus. Fed. **43** T5
Konstantinovskiy Rus. Fed. **43** U4
Konstanz Germany **48** G8
English form Constance; historically known as Constantia
Kontagora Nigeria **125** G4
Kontcha Cameroon **125** I5
Kontiolahti Fin. **44** O3
Kontiomäki Fin. **44** O2
Kontos, Akra pt Greece **59** F12
Konttila Fin. **44** N2
Kon Tum Vietnam **79** D5
Kontum, Plateau du Vietnam **79** E5
Kõnugard Ukr. see Kiev
Konushin, Mys pt Rus. Fed. **40** G2
Konya Turkey **106** C3
historically known as Iconium
Konyrat Kazakh. **103** H3
also spelt Qongyrat; formerly known as Kounradskiy
Konyrolen Kazakh. **103** I3
also spelt Qongyröleng
Konystanu Kazakh. **102** C2
also spelt Qonystanū
Konz Germany **48** D6
Konzhakovskiy Kamen', Gora mt. Rus. Fed. **40** K4

Koocanusa, Lake resr Canada/U.S.A. **167** H5
Kookynie Australia **151** C6
Kooline Australia **150** B4
Koolivoo, Lake salt flat Australia **148** C5
Koolkootinnie, Lake salt flat Australia **146** C2
Koolyanobbing Australia **151** B6
Koonga Estonia **42** F3
Koongie Park Aboriginal Reserve Australia **150** D3
Koonibba Australia **146** B2
Koopan-Suid S. Africa **132** E4
Koorawatha Australia **147** F3
Koorda Australia **151** B6
Koordarrie Australia **150** A4
Koorküla Estonia **42** G4
Koosa Estonia **42** I3
Koosharem U.S.A. **183** M3
Kooskia U.S.A. **180** C3
Kootenay r. Canada **167** G5
Kootenay Bay Canada **167** G5
Kootenay Lake Canada **167** G5
Kootenay National Park Canada **167** G5
Kootingal Australia **147** F2
Kootjieskolk S. Africa **132** E8
Kopa Kazakh. **103** H4
Kopa Zambia **127** F7
Kopanovka Rus. Fed. **41** I6
Kopaonik mts Yugo. **58** B5
Kopaonik nat. park Yugo. **58** B5
Kopargaon India **94** B2
Köpasker Iceland **44** [inset] D1
Kopbirlik Kazakh. **103** I3
formerly known as imeni Kirova
Koper Slovenia **56** F3
Kopet Dag mts Iran/Turkm. **100** D2
also known as Kopet-Dag, Khrebet; also spelt Koppeh Dāgh
Kopet-Dag, Khrebet mts Iran/Turkm. see Kopet Dag
Köping Sweden **45** L4
Koplik Albania **58** A6
Köpmanholmen Sweden **44** L3
Koporikha Rus. Fed. **43** P6
Koppa India **94** B3
Koppal India **94** C3
Koppang Norway **45** J3
Kopparberg county Sweden see Dalarna
Kopparberg Sweden **45** K4
Koppeh Dāgh mts Iran/Turkm. see Kopet Dag
Koppi r. Rus. Fed. **82** F2
Koppies S. Africa **133** L4
Koppies Dam Nature Reserve S. Africa **133** L4

Koppieskraal Pan salt pan S. Africa **132** E3
Koprinka, Yazovir resr Bulg. **58** G6
formerly known as Georgi Dimitrov, Yazovir
Koprivnica Croatia **56** I2
Köprü r. Turkey **106** B3
Köprübaşı Turkey **59** J10
Köprülü Turkey **106** C3
Köprülü Kanyon Milli Parkı nat. park Turkey **106** B3
Kopshorn mt. S. Africa **133** L8
Koptsi Belarus **43** L6
Kopu r. Estonia **42** G3
Kōpu N.Z. **152** J5
Kopyl' Belarus see Kapyl'
Kora India **96** D4
Korab mts Albania/Macedonia **58** B7
Korablino Rus. Fed. **43** V8
Koraf well Eth. **128** D3
K'orahē Eth. **128** E3
Koramlik China **89** D4
Korana r. Bos.-Herz./Croatia **56** H3
Korangal India **94** C2
Koraput India **95** D2
Korat Thai. see Nakhon Ratchasima
Koratla India **94** C2
Korba India **97** D5
Korba Tunisia **57** C12
Korbach Germany **48** F4
Korbenichi Rus. Fed. **43** P1
Korbous Tunisia **57** C12
Korbu, Gunung mt. Malaysia **76** C1
Korçë Albania **58** B8
formerly known as Koritsa
Korchino Rus. Fed. **103** J1
Korčula Croatia **56** J6
Korčula i. Croatia **56** I6
Korčulanski Kanal sea chan. Croatia **56** I5
Korday Kazakh. **103** H4
formerly known as Georgiyevka
Kordestān prov. Iran **100** A3
Kord Kūy Iran **100** C2
Kordon Rus. Fed. **40** K4
Korea, North country Asia **83** B4
asia [countries] ➤ 64–67
Korea, South country Asia **83** B5
asia [countries] ➤ 64–67
Korea Bay g. China/N. Korea **83** B5
Korea Strait Japan/S. Korea **83** C6
also known as Tsushima-kaikyō
Koregaon India **94** B2
Korem Eth. **128** C1
Korenovsk Rus. Fed. **41** F7
formerly known as Korenovskaya
Korenovskaya Rus. Fed. see Korenovsk
Korets' Ukr. **41** C6
Korf Rus. Fed. **39** Q3
Körfez Turkey **106** B2
also known as Yarımca
Korff Ice Rise Antarctica **222** T1
Korfovskiy Rus. Fed. **82** D2
Korgas China **88** C2
Korgen Norway **44** K2
Korhogo Côte d'Ivoire **124** D4
Koriabo Guyana **199** G3
Koribundu Sierra Leone **124** C5
Kori Creek inlet India **96** A5
Koringberg S. Africa **132** C10
Koringplaas S. Africa **132** E9
Koriniti N.Z. **152** J7
Korinos Greece **59** D8
Korinthiakos Kolpos sea chan. Greece see Corinth, Gulf of
Korinthos Greece see Corinth
Korissia Greece **59** F11
Koritsa Albania see Korçë
Kōriyama Japan **90** G6
Korkana Fin. **44** O2
Korkī Iran **100** D2
Korkino Rus. Fed. **38** G4
Korkodon r. Rus. Fed. **39** P3
Korkuteli Turkey **106** C3
Körkvere Estonia **42** E3
Korla China **88** D3
Kormakitis, Cape Cyprus **108** D2
Korman mt. Rus. Fed. **58** A5
Körmend Hungary **49** N8
Körmör Iraq **107** L8
Kornat i. Croatia **56** H5
Kornat nat. park Croatia **56** H5
Korneyevka Karagandinskaya Oblast' Kazakh. **103** H2
Korneyevka Severnyy Kazakhstan Kazakh. **103** G1
Korneyevka Rus. Fed. **102** B2
Kornsjø Norway **45** J4
Koro Côte d'Ivoire **124** D3
Koro r. Indon. **75** B3
also spelt Goro
Koro Mali **124** E3
Korobets Rus. Fed. **43** O7
Koroc r. Canada **169** H1
Köroğlu Dağları mts Turkey **106** C2
Köroğlu Tepesi mt. Turkey **106** C2
Korogo well Eth. **128** C2
Korogwe Tanz. **129** C6
Korom, Bahr watercourse Chad **126** C2
Koroni Greece **59** C11
Koronowo Poland **49** O2
Koropi Greece **59** E11

Kos i. Greece **59** I12
English form Cos
Kosa Rus. Fed. **40** J4
Kosa r. Rus. Fed. **40** J3
Kosagal Kazakh. **103** E2
Kosaka Japan **90** G4
Kosan N. Korea **83** B5
formerly known as Sin'gosan
Kosava Belarus **42** G9
Kosaya Gora Rus. Fed. **43** S7
Koschagyl Kazakh. **102** C3
also known as Qosshaghyl
Kościan Poland **49** N3
Kościerzyna Poland **49** O1
Kosciusko U.S.A. **175** B5
Kosciusko, Mount Australia see Kosciuszko, Mount
Kosciusko Island U.S.A. **166** C3
Kosciuszko, Mount Australia **147** F4
formerly spelt Kosciusko, Mount
Kosciuszko National Park Australia **147** F4
Kose Estonia **42** G2
Kösecobanlı Turkey **108** E1
Köse Dağı mt. Turkey **107** D2
Kösedere Turkey **59** H9
Kosgi India **94** C2
Kosha Sudan **121** F4
Kosh-Agach Rus. Fed. **84** A1
Koshankol' Kazakh. **102** B2
Koshbulakskoye Vodokhranilische resr Turkm. **103** E4
Kosh-Döbö Kyrg. **103** H4
Koshikijima-rettō is Japan **91** A9
Koshiki-kaikyō sea chan. Japan **91** A9
Koshimizu Japan **90** I3
Koshk Afgh. **101** E3
Koshkak Iran **101** E3
Koshkarkol', Ozero l. Kazakh. **88** C2
Koshk-e Kohneh Afgh. **101** E3
Koshki Rus. Fed. **41** I5
Koshkonong, Lake U.S.A. **172** E8
Koshkupyr Uzbek. **102** D4
also spelt Qūshkŭpir
Koshoba Turkm. **102** C4
Koshrabad Uzbek. **103** G4
also spelt Qūshrabot
Koshoku Japan **91** F6
Koshoku Japan **91** F6
Koshtēbē Kyrg. see Kosh-Döbö
Kosi India **96** C3
Kosi r. India **96** D3
Kosi Bay S. Africa **133** Q3
Kosi Bay Nature Reserve S. Africa **133** Q3
Košice Slovakia **49** S7
also known as Kassa
Kosigi India **94** C3
Kosi Reservoir Nepal **97** E4
Kos-Istek Kazakh. **102** D2
Kosjerić Srbija Yugo. **58** A5
Kōşk Turkey **59** J11
Koski Fin. see Hämeenkoski
Koski Fin. **45** M3
Koskol' Kazakh. **103** F2
Kos'kovo Rus. Fed. **43** O1
Koskuduk Kazakh. **103** I3
Koskullskulle Sweden **44** M2
Koslan Rus. Fed. **40** I3
Köslin Poland see Koszalin
Kosma r. Rus. Fed. **40** I2
Kosmynino Rus. Fed. **43** V4
Kosnica r. Croatia **56** I3
Koson Uzbek. see Kasan
Kosŏng N. Korea **82** C4
Kosŏng N. Korea **83** C5
Kosŏng S. Korea **91** A7
Kosonsoy Uzbek. see Kasansay
Kosorzha Rus. Fed. **43** R9
Kosova prov. Yugo. see Kosovo
Kosovo prov. Yugo. **58** B6
also known as Amselfeld; also spelt Kosovë; long form Kosovo-Metohija
europe [issues] ➤ 34–35
Kosovo-Metohija prov. Yugo. see Kosovo
Kosovo Polje Kosovo, Srbija Yugo. **58** C6
Kosovo Polje Kosovo, Srbija Yugo. **58** C6
Kosovska Kamenica Kosovo, Srbija Yugo. **58** C6
Kosovska Mitrovica Kosovo, Srbija Yugo. **58** B6
formerly known as Titova Mitrovica; short form Mitrovica
Kosrae atoll Micronesia **220** E5
also known as Ualan; formerly spelt Kusaie
Kossa well Mauritania **124** D3
Kossatori well Niger **125** I3
Kösseine hill Germany **48** I5
Kossol Reef Palau **73** H5
Kossou, Lac de l. Côte d'Ivoire **124** D5
Kosta-Khetagurovo Rus. Fed. see Nazran'
Kostanay Kazakh. **103** E1
also spelt Qostanay; formerly spelt Kustanay
Kostenets Bulg. **58** E6
Koster S. Africa **133** K2
Kosterevo Rus. Fed. **43** U6
Kosti Sudan **128** B1
Kostinbrod Bulg. **58** E6
Kostino Rus. Fed. **43** V4
Kostobobriv Ukr. **43** N9
Kostolac Srbija Yugo. **58** C3
Kostomuksha Rus. Fed. **44** O2
Kostomukshskiy Zapovednik nature res. Rus. Fed. **44** O2
Kostopil' Ukr. **41** C6
also spelt Kostopol'
Kostopol' Ukr. see Kostopil'
Kostroma r. Rus. Fed. **43** V3
Kostroma Rus. Fed. **43** V4
Kostroma Oblast admin. div. Rus. Fed. see Kostromskaya Oblast'
Kostromskaya Oblast' admin. div. Rus. Fed. **40** G4
English form Kostroma Oblast
Kostrzyn Poland **49** L3
Kostrzyn r. Poland **49** T3
Kostyantynivka Ukr. **41** F6
Kostyukovichi Belarus see Kastsyukovichy
Kostyzhitsy Rus. Fed. **43** K4
Kosubosu Nigeria **125** F4
Kos'yu Rus. Fed. **40** K2
Kos'yu r. Rus. Fed. **40** K2
Koszalin Poland **49** N1
historically known as Köslin
Kőszeg Hungary **49** N8
also known as Güns
Kota Andhra Pradesh India **94** D3
Kota Chhattisgarh India **97** D5
Kota Rajasthan India **96** C4
Kotaagung Indon. **76** D4
Kota Baharu Malaysia see Kota Bharu
Kotabaru Kalimantan Barat Indon. **77** G3
Kotabaru Kalimantan Selatan Indon. **77** G3
Kotabaru Sumatra Indon. **76** B2
Kota Belud Sabah Malaysia **77** G1
Kota Bharu Malaysia **76** C1
also spelt Kota Baharu
Kotabumi Indon. **76** D4
Kot Addu Pak. **101** G4
Kota Kinabalu Sabah Malaysia **77** G1
formerly known as Jesselton
Kotala Fin. **44** O2
Kotamobagu Indon. **75** C2
Kotaneli Gora mt. Kazakh. **103** I3
Kotapinang Indon. **76** C2
Kotar India **96** D4
Kotari r. India **96** B4
Kota Samarahan Sarawak Malaysia **77** F2
also known as Muara Tuang
Kota Tinggi Malaysia **76** C2

Kotawaringin Indon. **77** E3
Kotchandpur Bangl. **97** F5
Kotcho r. Canada **166** F3
Kotcho Lake Canada **166** F3
Kot Diji Pak. **101** G5
Kotdwara India **96** C3
Koteasro Afgh. **101** E4
Kotel Bulg. **58** H6
Kotel'nich Rus. Fed. **40** I4
Kotel'nikovo Rus. Fed. **41** G7
Kotel'nyy, Ostrov i. Rus. Fed. **39** N2
Kotemaori N.Z. **152** L7
Kotgar India **95** D2
Kotgarh India **96** C3
Kothagudem India see Kottagudem
Köthen (Anhalt) Germany **48** I4
Kothi India **96** D4
Kotiari Naoude Senegal **124** B3
Kotido Uganda **128** B4
Kotka Fin. **45** N3
Kot Kapura India **96** B3
Kotkino Rus. Fed. **40** I2
Kotlas Rus. Fed. **40** H3
Kotli Pak. **101** H3
Kotlik U.S.A. **164** C3
Kotlina Sandomierska basin Poland **49** S5
Kotlovan Rus. Fed. **43** P3
Kötlutangi pt Iceland **44** [inset] C3
Kotly Rus. Fed. **42** I1
Koton-Karifi Nigeria **125** G4
Kotooka Japan **90** G4
Kotorkoshi Nigeria **125** G3
Kotorosl' r. Rus. Fed. **43** U4
Kotorsko Bos.-Herz. **56** K4
Kotor Varoš Bos.-Herz. **56** J4
Kotouba Côte d'Ivoire **124** E4
Kotovo Rus. Fed. **41** H6
Kotovsk Moldova see Hînceşti
Kotovsk Rus. Fed. **41** H5
Kotovs'k Ukr. **41** D7
Kot Putli India **96** C4
Kotra r. Belarus **42** F8
Kotri r. India **94** D2
Kotri Pak. **101** G5
Kotronas Greece **59** D12
Kotsk Kazakh. **102** D2
Kot Sarae Pak. **101** F6
Kottagudem India **94** D2
also known as Bhadrachalam Road Station; short Kothagudem
Kottayam Kerala India **94** C4
Kottayam Pondicherry India **94** B4
Kotte Sri Lanka see Sri Jayewardenepura Kotte
Kotto r. Cent. Afr. Rep. **126** D3
Kotturu India **94** C3
Kotuy r. Rus. Fed. **39** K2
Kotwar Peak India **97** D5
Kotzebue U.S.A. **164** C3
Kotzebue Sound sea chan. U.S.A. **164** C3
Kotzehoop S. Africa **132** B5
Kotzesrus S. Africa **132** B7
Kouango Cent. Afr. Rep. **126** D3
Kouba Olanga Chad **120** C6
Koubia Guinea **124** C3
Kouchibouguac National Park Canada **169** H4
Koudougou Burkina **124** E3
Kouebokkeveld mts S. Africa **132** D9
Kouéré Burkina **124** E4
Koueveldberge mts S. Africa **132** H9
Koufalia Greece **58** D8
Koufonisi i. Kriti Greece **59** H14
Koufonisi i. Greece **59** G12
Koufos Greece **59** E9
Kouga r. S. Africa **133** I10
Kougaberge mts S. Africa **132** H10
Koui Cent. Afr. Rep. **126** B3
Kouilou admin. reg. Congo **126** A6
Kouilou r. Cent. Afr. Rep. **126** C3
Koukourou r. Cent. Afr. Rep. **126** C3
Koukourou-Bamingui, Réserve de Faune du nature res. Cent. Afr. Rep. **126** C3
Koulamoutou Gabon **126** B5
Koulbo Chad **120** D6
Koulikoro Mali **124** D3
Koulikoro admin. reg. Mali **124** D3
Kouloudia Chad **120** B6
Koum Cameroon **125** I4
Kouma r. Cent. Afr. Rep. **126** C3
Koumac New Caledonia **145** F4
Koumala Australia **149** F4
Koumameyong Gabon **126** A4
Koumbala Cent. Afr. Rep. **126** D2
Koumbia Burkina **124** D3
Koumbia Guinea **124** B3
Koumogo Chad **126** C3
Koumra Chad **126** C3
Koundâra Guinea **124** B3
Koundian Mali **124** C3
Koundougou Burkina **124** D4
Koundoual Senegal **124** B3
Kounoupoi i. Greece **59** H12
Kounradskiy Kazakh. see Konyrat
Kounsitél Guinea **124** B3
Kountchi well Niger **125** H3
Kountze U.S.A. **179** D6
Koup S. Africa **132** F10
Koupéla Burkina **125** E3
Kouridinga well Niger **125** I2
Kournas Greece **59** F13
Kourou Fr. Guiana **199** H3
Kourou r. Greece **58** G7
Koûroudjél Mauritania **124** C2
Kouroussa Guinea **124** C4
Koussanar Senegal **124** B3
Koussané Mali **124** C3
Kousséri Cameroon **125** I3
formerly known as Fort Foureau
Koussountou Togo **125** F4
Koutiala Mali **124** D3
Kouto Côte d'Ivoire **124** D4
Kouvola Fin. **45** N3
Kouyou r. Congo **126** C5
Kovačica Vojvodina, Srbija Yugo. **58** B3
Kovarzino Rus. Fed. **43** T1
Kovda Rus. Fed. **44** P2
Kovdor Rus. Fed. **44** P2
Kovdozero, Ozero l. Rus. Fed. **44** P2
Kovel' Ukr. **41** C6
Kovernino Rus. Fed. **40** G4
Kovilj Vojvodina, Srbija Yugo. **58** B3
Kovilpatti India **94** C4
Kovin Vojvodina, Srbija Yugo. **58** B3
Kovno Lith. see Kaunas
Kovriga, Gora hill Rus. Fed. **40** I2
Kovrov Rus. Fed. **40** G4
Kovylkino Rus. Fed. **41** G5
Kovzha canal Rus. Fed. **43** S1
Kovzhskoye, Ozero l. Rus. Fed. **43** S1
Kowanyama Australia **149** D2
Kowanyama Aboriginal Reserve Australia **149** D2
Kowares waterhole Namibia **130** B3
Kowary Poland **49** M5
Kowhia Belarus **43** K8
Kowhitirangi N.Z. **153** F10
Kowli Kosh, Gardaneh-ye pass Iran **100** C3
Kowloon Hong Kong China **87** [inset]
also known as Chiu Lung or Jiulong
Kowloon Peak hill Hong Kong China **87** [inset]
also known as Fei Ngo Shan
Kowloon Peninsula Hong Kong China **87** [inset]

Kowr-e-Koja *watercourse* Iran **101** E5
Kox Kuduk *well* China **84** B3
Kōya Japan **91** D7
Kōyama-misaki *pt* Japan **91** B7
Koybagar, Ozero *l.* Kazakh. **103** F1
formerly known as Kaybagar, Ozero
Köyceğiz Turkey **106** B3
Köyceğiz Gölü *l.* Turkey **59** J12
Koygorodok Rus. Fed. **40** I3
Koymatdag, Gory *hills* Turkm. **102** C4
also known as Goymatdag
Koynare Bulg. **58** F5
Koyna Reservoir India **94** B2
Koyp, Gora *mt.* Rus. Fed. **40** K3
Koyukuk *r.* U.S.A. **164** D3
Koyulhisar Turkey **107** D2
Koza Rus. Fed. **43** U3
Kozağacı Turkey *see* **Günyüzü**
Kō-zaki *pt* Japan **91** A7
Kozan Turkey **106** C3
also known as Sis
Kozani Greece **59** C8
Kozar, Ras *pt* Eritrea **104** C5
Kozara *mts* Bos.-Herz. **56** I3
Kozara *nat. park* Bos.-Herz. **56** J3
Kozarska Dubica Bos.-Herz. *see* **Bosanska Dubica**
Kozel'sk Rus. Fed. **43** Q7
Kozen *well* Chad **120** C4
Kozhabakhy Kazakh. **103** E3
Kozhakol', Ozero *l.* Kazakh. **103** G2
also known as Qozhaköl
Kozhevnikovo Rus. Fed. **39** L2
Kozhikode India *see* **Calicut**
Kozhim-Iz, Gora *mt.* Rus. Fed. **40** K3
Kozhva Rus. Fed. **40** K2
Kozhva *r.* Rus. Fed. **40** K2
Kozhym *r.* Rus. Fed. **40** K2
Kozienice Poland **49** S4
Kozlikha Rus. Fed. **43** V1
Kozloduy Bulg. **58** E5
Kozlovka *Chuvashskaya Respublika* Rus. Fed. **40** I5
Kozlovka *Voronezhskaya Oblast'* Rus. Fed. **41** G6
Kozlovo Rus. Fed. **43** R5
Kozlu Turkey **106** B2
Kozluk Bos.-Herz. **56** L4
Koźmin Poland **49** O4
Koz'modem'yansk Rus. Fed. **40** H4
Kozmoldak Kazakh. **103** G4
Koznitsa *mt.* Bulg. **58** E6
Kożuchów Poland **49** M4
Kožuf *mts* Greece/Macedonia **58** D7
Kōzu-shima *i.* Japan **91** F7
Kozyatyn Ukr. **41** D6
also spelt Kazatin
Kozyörük Turkey **58** H7
Kpalimé Togo **125** F5
Kpandae Ghana **125** E4
Kpandu Ghana **125** F5
Kpungan Pass India/Myanmar **97** H4
Kra, Isthmus of Thai. **79** B6
Kraai *r.* S. Africa **133** K7
Kraankuil S. Africa **132** I6
Krabi Estonia **42** H4
Krabi Thai. **79** B6
Kra Buri Thai. **79** B6
Krâchéh Cambodia **79** D5
also spelt Kratie
Kräckelbäcken Sweden **45** K3
Kraftino, Ozero *l.* Rus. Fed. **43** P4
Kragan Indon. **77** E4
Kragerø Norway **45** J4
Kragujevac *Srbija* Yugo. **58** B4
Krajenka Poland **49** O2
Krakatau *i.* Indon. **77** D4
Krakatau Volcano National Park Indon. **76** D4
Krakau Poland *see* **Kraków**
Kråklivollen Norway **44** J3
Kraków Poland **49** Q5
historically known as Cracovia *or* Cracow *or* Krakau
Krakow U.S.A. **172** E6
Kralendijk Neth. Antilles **187** F4
Kraljeviča Croatia **56** G3
Kraljevo *Srbija* Yugo. **58** B5
formerly known as Rankovićevo
Kráľova hoľa *mt.* Slovakia **49** R7
Kráľovský Chlmec Slovakia **49** S7
Kralupy nad Vltavou Czech Rep. **49** L5
Kramators'k Ukr. **41** F6
Kramfors Sweden **44** L3
Krammer *est.* Neth. **48** B4
Kranidi Greece **59** E11
Kranj Slovenia **56** G2
Kranji Reservoir Sing. **76** [inset]
Kransfontein S. Africa **133** M5
Kranskop S. Africa **133** O5
Kranskop *mt.* S. Africa **133** N4
Krapanj Croatia **56** H5
Krapina Croatia **56** H2
Krapinske Toplice Croatia **56** H2
Krapivna *Kaluzhskaya Oblast'* Rus. Fed. **43** Q8
Krapivna *Smolenskaya Oblast'* Rus. Fed. **43** O7
Krapkowice Poland **49** O5
Krasavino Rus. Fed. **40** H3
Krasilov Ukr. *see* **Krasyliv**
Krasino Rus. Fed. **40** J1
Kraskino Rus. Fed. **82** C4
Krāslava Latvia **42** I6
Kraslice Czech Rep. **49** J5
Krasnapollye Belarus **43** M8
Krasnasyel'ski Belarus **42** F8
Krasnaya Gora Rus. Fed. **43** M8
Krasnaya Gorbatka Rus. Fed. **40** G5
Krasnaya Polyana Kazakh. **103** H2
Krasnaya Polyana Rus. Fed. **41** G8
Krasnaya Slabada Belarus **42** I9
Krasnaya Zarya Rus. Fed. **43** S9
Kraśnik Poland **49** T5
Krasnoarmeysk Kazakh. *see* **Tayynsha**
Krasnoarmeysk *Moskovskaya Oblast'* Rus. Fed. **43** T5
Krasnoarmeysk *Saratovskaya Oblast'* Rus. Fed. **41** H6
Krasnoarmeysk Ukr. *see* **Krasnoarmiys'k**
Krasnoarmeyskaya Rus. Fed. *see* **Poltavskaya**
Krasnoarmeyskiy *Chukotskiy Avtonomnyy Okrug* Rus. Fed. **39** R3
Krasnoarmeyskiy *Rostovskaya Oblast'* Rus. Fed. **41** G7
formerly known as Kuberle
Krasnoarmiys'k Ukr. **41** F6
also spelt Krasnoarmeysk; *formerly known as* Chervonoarmiys'k *or* Grishino *or* Postysheve
Krasnobarskiy Rus. Fed. **43** Q2
Krasnoborsk Rus. Fed. **40** H3
Krasnodar Rus. Fed. **41** F7
formerly known as Yekaterinodar
Krasnodar Kray *admin. div.* Rus. Fed. *see* **Krasnodarskiy Kray**
Krasnodarskiy Kray *admin. div.* Rus. Fed. **41** F7
English form Krasnodar Kray
Krasnodon Ukr. **41** F6
Krasnofarfornyy Rus. Fed. **43** M2
Krasnogorka Kazakh. *see* **Ul'ken Sulutar**
Krasnogorodskoye Rus. Fed. **43** J5
Krasnogorsk Rus. Fed. **43** S6
Krasnogorsk Rus. Fed. **82** F2
Krasnogorskoye Rus. Fed. **40** J4
Krasnograd Ukr. *see* **Krasnohrad**
Krasnogvardeysk Uzbek. *see* **Bulungur**
Krasnogvardeyskiy Rus. Fed. **43** V5
Krasnogvardeyskoye Rus. Fed. **41** G7
formerly known as Yevdokimovskoye
Krasnohrad Ukr. **41** E6
also spelt Krasnograd; *formerly known as* Konstantinograd
Krasnohvardiys'ke Ukr. **41** E7
Krasnokamensk Rus. Fed. **85** H1
Krasnokamsk Rus. Fed. **40** J4
Krasnokholm Rus. Fed. **102** C2
Krasnokutsk Kazakh. *see* **Aktogay**
Krasnokutskoye Kazakh. *see* **Aktogay**
Krasnolesnyy Rus. Fed. **41** F6
Krasnoles'ye Rus. Fed. **42** D7
Krasnomayskiy Rus. Fed. **43** P4
Krasnoostrovskiy Rus. Fed. **43** J1
Krasnoperekops'k Ukr. **41** E7
Krasnopol'ye Rus. Fed. **82** F2
Krasnorechenskiy Rus. Fed. **82** D3
Krasnosel'kup Rus. Fed. **39** I3
Krasnosel'skoye Rus. Fed. **43** K1
Krasnoslobodsk Rus. Fed. **41** G5
Krasnotur'insk Rus. Fed. **38** G4
Krasnoufimsk Rus. Fed. **40** K4
Krasnousol'skiy Rus. Fed. **40** K5
Krasnovishersk Rus. Fed. **40** K3
Krasnovodsk Turkm. *see* **Turkmenbashi**
Krasnovodskaya Oblast' *admin. div.* Turkm. *see* **Balkanskaya Oblast'**
Krasnovodskiy Gosudarstvenny Zapovednik *nature res.* Turkm. **102** C5
Krasnovodskiy Zaliv *b.* Turkm. **102** C5
Krasnovodskoye Plato *plat.* Turkm. **102** C4
Krasnoyar Kazakh. **102** C2
Krasnoyarovo Rus. Fed. **82** C2
Krasnoyarsk Rus. Fed. **80** E1
Krasnoyarskiy Rus. Fed. **102** D2
Krasnoyarskiy Kray *admin. div.* Rus. Fed. **80** E1
English form Krasnoyarsk Kray
Krasnoyarsk Kray *admin. div.* Rus. Fed. *see* **Krasnoyarskiy Kray**
Krasnoye *Belgorodskaya Oblast'* Rus. Fed. **41** F6
Krasnoye *Bryanskaya Oblast'* Rus. Fed. **43** O8
Krasnoye *Lipetskaya Oblast'* Rus. Fed. **43** T9
Krasnoye *Pskovskaya Oblast'* Rus. Fed. **43** K5
Krasnoye Rus. Fed. *see* **Ulan Erge**
Krasnoye *Smolenskaya Oblast'* Rus. Fed. **43** M7
Krasnoye, Ozero *l.* Rus. Fed. **39** R3
Krasnoye Plamya Rus. Fed. **43** T5
Krasnoye Znamya Rus. Fed. **43** Q4
Krasnozatonskiy Rus. Fed. **40** I3
Krasnozavodsk Rus. Fed. **43** T5
Krasnoznamensk Rus. Fed. **42** D7
Krasnoznamenskiy Kazakh. *see* **Krasnoznamenskoye**
Krasnoznamenskoye Kazakh. **103** G2
formerly known as Krasnoznamenskiy
Krasnystaw Poland **49** U5
Krasnyy Rus. Fed. **43** M7
Krasnyy Chikoy Rus. Fed. **85** F1
Krasnyye Baki Rus. Fed. **40** H4
Krasnyye Barrikady Rus. Fed. **102** A3
Krasnyye Tkachi Rus. Fed. **43** U4
Krasnyy Kamyshanik Rus. Fed. *see* **Komsomol'skiy**
Krasnyy Kholm Rus. Fed. **43** S3
Krasnyy Kut Rus. Fed. **102** A2
Krasnyy Luch Rus. Fed. **43** L4
Krasnyy Luch Ukr. **41** F6
Krasnyy Lyman Ukr. **41** F6
Krasnyy Oktyabr' Rus. Fed. **43** T5
Krasnyy Profintern Rus. Fed. **43** V4
Krasnyy Rog *Bryanskaya Oblast'* Rus. Fed. **43** O8
Krasnyy Rog *Bryanskaya Oblast'* Rus. Fed. **43** O9
Krasnyy Tekstil'shchik Rus. Fed. **41** H6
Krasnyy Yar Kazakh. **103** G1
Krasnyy Yar Rus. Fed. **102** B3
Krasyliv Ukr. **41** C6
also spelt Krasilov
Kratie Cambodia *see* **Krâchéh**
Kratovo Macedonia **58** D6
Krauja Latvia **42** H6
Kraul Mountains Antarctica **223** X2
Kraulshavn Greenland *see* **Nuussuaq**
Krâvanh, Chuŏr Phnum *mts* Cambodia *see* **Cardamom Range**
Kraynovka Rus. Fed. **102** A4
Krechevitsy Rus. Fed. **43** M3
Krefeld Germany **48** D4
Krekenava Lith. **42** F6
Kremaston, Techniti Limni *resr* Greece **59** C10
Kremen *mt.* Croatia **56** H4
Kremenchug Ukr. *see* **Kremenchuk**
Kremenchuk Ukr. **41** E6
also spelt Kremenchug
Kremenchuts'ka Vodoskhovyshche *resr* Ukr. **41** E6
Kremenki Rus. Fed. **43** S7
Kremenskoye Rus. Fed. **43** Q6
Kremges Ukr. *see* **Svitlovods'k**
Kreml' Rus. Fed. *see* **Solovetskiy**
Kremmidi, Akra *pt* Greece **59** E12
Kremmling U.S.A. **180** F4
Krems an der Donau Austria **49** M7
Kremsmünster Austria **49** L7
Krenitzin Islands U.S.A. **164** C4
Krepoljin *Srbija* Yugo. **58** C4
Kresna Bulg. **58** E7
Kresta, Zaliv *g.* Rus. Fed. **39** S3
Krestena Greece **59** C11
Krest-Khal'dzhayy Rus. Fed. **39** N3
Krestovka Rus. Fed. **40** J2
Kresttsy Rus. Fed. **43** N3
Kresty *Moskovskaya Oblast'* Rus. Fed. **43** S6
Kresty *Pskovskaya Oblast'* Rus. Fed. **43** M6
Kresty *Tul'skaya Oblast'* Rus. Fed. **43** T8
Krestyakh Rus. Fed. **39** L3
Kretinga Lith. **42** C6
Kreuth Germany **48** I8
Kreuzau Germany **48** D5
Kreuzeck Gruppe *mts* Austria **49** K9
Kreuzlingen Switz. **51** P5
Kreuztal Germany **48** E5
Kreva Belarus **42** H7
Kribi Cameroon **125** H6
Krichev Belarus *see* **Krychaw**
Krichim Bulg. **58** F6
Krieglach Austria **49** M8
Kriel S. Africa **133** N3
Krievukalns *hill* Latvia **42** C5
Krieza Greece **59** F10
Krikellos Greece **59** C10
Krikelos, Akra *pt* Greece **59** H12
Krikovo Moldova *see* **Cricova**
Kril'on, Mys *c.* Rus. Fed. **82** F3
Krios, Akra *pt* Greece **59** E13
Krishna *r.* India **94** D2
formerly known as Kistna
Krishnagiri India **94** C3
Krishnai *r.* India **97** F4
Krishnanagar India **97** F5
Krishnaraja Sagara *l.* India **94** C3
Krishnarajpet India **94** C3
Kristdala Sweden **45** L4
Kristiania Norway *see* **Oslo**
Kristiansand Norway **45** I4
Kristianstad Sweden **45** K4
Kristiansund Norway **44** I3
Kristiinankaupunki Fin. *see* **Kristinestad**
Kristinehamn Sweden **45** K4
Kristinestad Fin. **45** M3
also known as Kristiinankaupunki
Kristinopol' Ukr. *see* **Chervonohrad**
Kriti *admin. reg.* Greece **59** F14
Kriti *i.* Greece *see* **Crete**
Kriūkai Lith. **42** E6
Kriulyany Moldova *see* **Criuleni**
Kriusha Rus. Fed. **43** U7
Krivača *mt.* Yugo. **58** B5
Krivaja *r.* Bos.-Herz. **56** K4
Krivandino Rus. Fed. **43** U6
Kriva Palanka Macedonia **58** D6
Kriva Reka *r.* Macedonia **58** C6
Křivoklátská Vrchovina *hills* Czech Rep. **49** K6
Krivoles Rus. Fed. **43** N8
Krivoy Porog Rus. Fed. **40** E2
Krivoy Rog Ukr. *see* **Kryvyy Rih**
Križevci Croatia **56** I2
Krk *mt.* Bos.-Herz. **56** L4
Krk Croatia **56** G3
Krk *i.* Croatia **56** G3
Krka *r.* Croatia **56** H5
Krka *r.* Slovenia **56** H3
Krkonošský narodní park *nat. park* Czech Rep./Poland **49** M5
also known as Karkonoski Park Narodowy
Krnjača *Srbija* Yugo. **58** B4
Krnov Czech Rep. **49** O5
Krobia Poland **49** N4
Krohnwodoke Liberia **124** D5
Kroknes Norway **44** O1
Krokom Sweden **44** K3
Króksfjarðarnes Iceland **44** [inset] B2
Krokstadøra Norway **44** J3
Krolevets' Ukr. **41** E6
Kroma *r.* Rus. Fed. **43** Q9
Kromdraai S. Africa **133** N2
Kromy Rus. Fed. **43** Q9
Kronach Germany **48** I5
Kronfjell *hill* Norway **45** J4
Krŏng Kaôh Kŏng Cambodia **79** C6
Kronli India **97** G3
Kronoberg *county* Sweden **45** K4
Kronoby Fin. **44** M3
Kronotskiy Poluostrov *pen.* Rus. Fed. **39** Q4
Kronotskiy Zaliv *b.* Rus. Fed. **39** Q4
Kronotskoye Ozero *l.* Rus. Fed. **39** Q4
Kronprins Christian Land *reg.* Greenland **165** Q1
Kronprins Frederik Bjerge *nunataks* Greenland **165** P3
Kronshagen Germany **48** H1
Kronshtadt Rus. Fed. **43** K2
English form Kronstadt
Kronstadt Romania *see* **Braşov**
Kronstadt Rus. Fed. *see* **Kronshtadt**
Kroonstad S. Africa **133** L4
Kropotkin Rus. Fed. **41** G7
Kropp Germany **48** G1
Krosno Poland **49** S6
Krosno Odrzańskie Poland **49** M3
Krossen Norway **45** J4
Krotoszyn Poland **49** O4
Krotz Springs U.S.A. **175** B6
Krousonas Greece **59** F13
Kroya Indon. **77** E4
Krško Slovenia **56** H3
Krstača *mt.* Yugo. **58** B6
Krugerdrifdam *resr* S. Africa **133** K5
Kruger National Park S. Africa **133** P2
Krugersdorp S. Africa **133** L3
Krugerspos S. Africa **133** O1
Kruglyakov Rus. Fed. *see* **Oktyabr'skiy**
Kruhlaye Belarus **43** K7
Krui Indon. **76** C4
Kruidfontein S. Africa **132** F9
Kruisfontein S. Africa **133** I11
Krujë Albania **58** A7
Krumë Albania **58** B6
Krumovgrad Bulg. **58** G7
Krungkao Thai. *see* **Ayutthaya**
Krung Thep Thai. *see* **Bangkok**
Kruoja *r.* Lith. **42** E5
Krupa Bos.-Herz. *see* **Bosanska Krupa**
Krupa na Uni Bos.-Herz. *see* **Bosanska Krupa**
Krupanj *Srbija* Yugo. **58** A4
Krupina Slovakia **49** Q7
Krupki Belarus **43** K7
Kruševac *Srbija* Yugo. **58** C5
Kruševo Macedonia **58** C7
Krušné Hory *mts* Czech Rep. **49** J5
Krustkalnu rezervāts *nature res.* Latvia **42** H5
Kruszwica Poland **49** P3
Krutoye *Orlovskaya Oblast'* Rus. Fed. **43** S9
Krutoye *Smolenskaya Oblast'* Rus. Fed. **43** M6
Kruzof Island U.S.A. **166** C3
Krybinka *r.* Belarus **43** K6
Krychaw Belarus **43** M8
also spelt Krichev
Kryezi Albania **58** B6
Krym' *pen.* Ukr. *see* **Crimea**
Krymsk Rus. Fed. **41** F7
formerly known as Krymskaya
Krymskaya Rus. Fed. *see* **Krymsk**
Kryms'kyy Pivostriv *pen.* Ukr. *see* **Crimea**
Kryms'kyy Zapovidnyk *nature res.* Ukr. **106** C1
Krynica Poland **49** R6
Krynica Morska Poland **49** Q1
Krynki Belarus **43** L6
Krystynopol Ukr. *see* **Chervonohrad**
Krytiko Pelagos *sea* Greece **59** G12
Kryvichy Belarus **42** I7
Kryvyy Rih Ukr. **41** E7
also spelt Krivoy Rog
Krzepice Poland **49** P5
Krzna *r.* Poland **49** U3
Krzna Południowa *r.* Poland **49** T4
Krzyż Wielkopolski Poland **49** N3
Ksabi Alg. **123** E3
Ksar Chellala Alg. **55** N9
formerly known as Reïbell
Ksar el Boukhari Alg. **123** F2
formerly known as Boghari
Ksar el Hirane Alg. **123** F2
Ksar el Kebir Morocco **122** D2
formerly spelt Alcazarquivir
Ksar-es-Souk Morocco *see* **Er Rachidia**
Ksenofontova Rus. Fed. **40** J3
Kshen' *r.* Rus. Fed. **43** S9
Kskyrbulak Yuzhnyy, Gora *hill* Turkm. **102** C4
Ksour, Monts des *mts* Alg. **120** A1
Ksour, Monts des *mts* Tunisia **123** H2
Ksour Essaf Tunisia **123** H2
Kstovo Rus. Fed. **40** H4
Ktsyn' Rus. Fed. **43** Q8
Kū', Jabal al *hill* Saudi Arabia **105** D2
Ku, Wadi el *watercourse* Sudan **121** E6
Kuaidamao China *see* **Tonghua**
Kuala Belait Brunei **77** F1
Kuala Dungun Malaysia *see* **Dungun**
Kualajelai Indon. **77** E3
Kuala Kangsar Malaysia **76** C1
Kualakapuas Indon. **77** F3
Kuala Kerai Malaysia **76** C1
Kuala Kinabatangan *r. mouth Sabah* Malaysia **77** G1
Kualakuayan Indon. **77** F3
Kuala Kubu Baharu Malaysia **76** C2
Kualakurun Indon. **77** F3
Kuala Lipis Malaysia **76** C1

▶**Kuala Lumpur** Malaysia **76** C2
Capital of Malaysia.

Kualapembuang Indon. **77** F3
Kuala Penyu *Sabah* Malaysia **77** F1
Kuala Pilah Malaysia **76** C2
Kualapuu U.S.A. **181** [inset] Z1
Kualasampit Indon. **77** F3
Kualasimpang Indon. **76** B1
Kuala Terengganu Malaysia **76** C1
Kualatungal Indon. **76** C3
Kuamut *Sabah* Malaysia **77** G1
Kuamut *r. Sabah* Malaysia **77** G1
Kuancheng China **85** H3
Kuandian China **83** B4
Kuangyuan China *see* **Yiliang**
Kuanshan Taiwan **87** G4
Kuantan Malaysia **76** C2
Kuaotuou N.Z. **152** J4
Kuba Azer. *see* **Quba**
Kuban' *r.* Rus. Fed. **41** F7
Kubār *Dayr az Zawr* Syria **109** K2
Kubārah Oman **105** G3
Kūbassaare poolsaar *pen.* Estonia **42** E3
Kubaysah Iraq **107** E4
Kubbum Sudan **126** D2
Kubena *r.* Rus. Fed. **43** U2
Kubenskoye Rus. Fed. **43** U2
Kubenskoye, Ozero *l.* Rus. Fed. **43** U2
Kuberle Rus. Fed. *see* **Krasnoarmeyskiy**
Kubinka Rus. Fed. **43** R6
Kubitzer Bodden *b.* Germany **49** K1
Kubnya *r.* Rus. Fed. **40** I5
Kubokawa Japan **91** C8
Kubor, Mount P.N.G. **73** J8
Kubrat Bulg. **58** H5
Kubrinsk Rus. Fed. **43** T5
Kubumesaäi Indon. **77** F2
Kučevo *Srbija* Yugo. **58** C4
Kuchaman India **96** B4
Kuchema Rus. Fed. **40** G2
Kuchera India **96** B4
Kuching *Sarawak* Malaysia **77** E2
also spelt Kucing
Kuchinotsu Japan **91** B8
Kuchukskoye, Ozero *salt l.* Rus. Fed. **103** I1
Kuchurhan *r.* Ukr. **58** K2
Kucing *Sarawak* Malaysia *see* **Kuching**
Kuçovë Albania **58** A8
formerly known as Qyteti Stalin
Küçükköy Turkey **59** H9
Küçükmenderes *r.* Turkey **59** H8
Küçükmenderes *r.* Turkey **59** [illegible]
Kuda India **96** A5
Kudachi India **94** B2
Kudal India **94** B3
Kudamatsu Japan **91** B8
Kudap Indon. **76** C2
Kudara-Somon Rus. Fed. **85** E1
Kudev *r.* Rus. Fed. **42** J4
Kudever' Rus. Fed. **43** K5
Kudirkos Naumiestis Lith. **42** D7
Kudligi India **94** C3
Kudremukh *mt.* India **94** B3
Kudrinskaya Rus. Fed. **43** Q7
Kudu Nigeria **125** G4
Kudus Indon. **77** E4
Kudymkar Rus. Fed. **40** J4
Kueishan Tao *i.* Taiwan **87** G3
Kufstein Austria **48** J8
Kugaly Kazakh. **103** I3
also spelt Qoghaly
Kugesi Rus. Fed. **40** H4
Kugka Lhai China **89** E6
Kugluktuk Canada **165** H3
formerly known as Coppermine
Kugmallit Bay Canada **164** F3
Kūh, Ra's-al- *pt* Iran **100** D5
Kūhak Iran **101** E5
Kūhbonān Iran **100** D4
Kūhdasht Iran **100** A3
Kūhestak Iran **100** D5
Kūhīn Iran **100** B2
Kūhīrī Iran **101** E5
Kŭhistoni Badakhshon *aut. rep.* Tajik. **101** H2
also known as Gorno-Badakhshan *or* Gornyy Badakhshan; *formerly known as* Badakhshoni Kŭhí; *short form* Badakhshan
Kühlung *park* Germany **48** I1
Kuhmo Fin. **44** O2
Kuhmoinen Fin. **45** N3
Kūhpāyeh Iran **100** C3
Kūhpāyeh *mt.* Iran **100** D4
Kūhrān, Kūh-e *mt.* Iran **100** D5
Kūhrang *r.* Iran **100** B4
Kui Buri Thai. **79** B5
Kuimetsa Estonia **42** G2
Kuis Namibia **130** C5
Kuiseb *watercourse* Namibia **130** B4
Kuitan China **87** E4
Kuitin China *see* **Kuytun**
Kuito Angola **127** C8
formerly known as Bié
Kuiu Island U.S.A. **166** C3
Kuivaniemi Fin. **44** N2
Kuivastu Estonia **42** E3
Kuja *r.* Latvia **42** H5
Kujang India **95** E1
Kujang N. Korea **83** B5
Kuji Japan **90** G4
Kuji-wan *b.* Japan **90** G4
Kujū-san *vol.* Japan **91** B8
Kukālār, Kūh-e *hill* Iran **100** B4
Kukan Rus. Fed. **82** D2
Kukatush Canada **173** K2
Kukawa Nigeria **125** I3
Kukerin Australia **151** B7
Kukës Albania **58** B6
Kuki Japan **91** F6
Kukkola Fin. **44** N2
Kukmor Rus. Fed. **40** I4
Kukoboy Rus. Fed. **43** U3
Kukruse Estonia **42** I2
Kukshi India **96** B5
Kukunuru India **94** D2
Kukup Malaysia **76** C2
Kukurtli Turkm. **102** D5
formerly known as Sernyy Zavod
Kukusan, Gunung *hill* Indon. **77** F3
Kukushtan Rus. Fed. **40** K4
Kūl *r.* Iran **100** C5
Kula Bulg. **58** D5
Kula *r.* Moldova *see* **Cula**
Kula Nigeria **125** G5
Kula Turkey **106** B3
Kula *Vojvodina, Srbija* Yugo. **58** A3
Kula *mt.* Yugo. **58** A6
Kulabu, Gunung *mt.* Indon. **76** B2
Kulachi Pak. **101** G4
Kulagi Rus. Fed. **43** N9
Kulagino Kazakh. **102** B2
Kula Kangri *mt.* Bhutan **97** F3
Kulal, Mount Kenya **128** C4
Kulaly, Ostrov *i.* Kazakh. **102** E3
also known as Qulaly Araly
Kulandy Kazakh. **102** D3
also spelt Qulandy
Kulaneh *reg.* Pak. **101** E5
Kulanotpes *watercourse* Kazakh. **103** G2
also spelt Qulanötpes
Kulao *r.* Pak. **101** F4
Kular Rus. Fed. **39** N2
Kulassein *i.* Phil. **74** B5
Kulat, Gunung *mt.* Indon. **77** G2
Kulautuva Lith. **42** E7
Kulawi Indon. **75** A3
Kulb Sudan **121** F4
Kuldīga Latvia **42** C5
Kuldja China *see* **Yining**
Kul'dur Rus. Fed. **82** C2
Kul'dzhuktau, Gory *hills* Uzbek. **103** E4
also known as Quljuqtow Toghi
Kule Botswana **130** D4
Kulebaki Rus. Fed. **40** G5
Kuleshi Rus. Fed. **43** S9
Kûlet el Qrein *hill* Egypt **108** C3
Kulgera Australia **148** B5
Kulgunino Rus. Fed. **102** D1
Kuliai Lith. **42** C6
Kuligi Rus. Fed. **40** J4
Kulikovo *Arkhangel'skaya Oblast'* Rus. Fed. **40** H3
Kulikovo *Lipetskaya Oblast'* Rus. Fed. **43** U9
Kulim Malaysia **76** C1
Kulittalai India **94** C4
Kulkuduk Uzbek. **103** E4
also spelt Kalquduq
Kulkyne *watercourse* Australia **147** E2
Kullamaa Estonia **42** F3
Kullu India **96** C3
Kulmbach Germany **48** I5
Kŭlob Tajik. **101** G2
also spelt Kulyab
Kulotino Rus. Fed. **43** O3
Kuloy Rus. Fed. **40** G3
Kuloy *r.* Rus. Fed. **40** G2
Kulp Turkey **107** E3
also known as Pasur
Kul'sary Kazakh. **102** C3
also spelt Qulsary
Kulshabi Sudan **126** F2
Kultuk Rus. Fed. **84** D1
Kulu Turkey **106** C3
Kulübe Tepe *mt.* Turkey **106** B3
Kulunda Rus. Fed. **103** I1
Kulunda *r.* Rus. Fed. **103** I1
Kulundinskaya Step' *plain* Kazakh./Rus. Fed. **103** H1
Kulundinskoye, Ozero *salt l.* Rus. Fed. **103** I1
Kulusuk Greenland **165** P3
also known as Kap Dan
Kūlvand Iran **100** C4
Kulwin Australia **147** D3
Kulyab Tajik. *see* **Kŭlob**
Kuma *r.* Rus. Fed. **44** O2
Kuma *r.* Rus. Fed. **102** A3
Kumagaya Japan **91** F6
Kumai, Teluk *b.* Indon. **77** E3
Kumaishi Japan **90** F3
Kumak *r.* Rus. Fed. **102** D2
Kumaka Guyana **199** G4
Kumalar Dağı *mts* Turkey **106** B3
Kumamoto Japan **91** B8
Kumamoto *pref.* Japan **91** B8
Kumano Japan **91** E8
Kumanovo Macedonia **58** C6
Kumara N.Z. **153** F10
Kumara Junction N.Z. **153** F10
Kumarkhali Bangl. **97** F5
Kumasi Ghana **125** E5
Ku-Mayima S. Africa **133** M8
Kumayri Armenia *see* **Gyumri**
Kumba Cameroon **125** H5
Kumbağ Turkey **58** I8
Kumbakonam India **94** C4
Kümbet Turkey **106** B3
Kumbharli Ghat *mt.* India **94** B2
Kumbher Nepal **97** D3
Kumbla India **94** B3
Kumbo Cameroon **125** H5
Kumbri Latvia **42** D5
Kumchuru Botswana **130** D4
Kum-Dag Turkm. *see* **Gumdag**
Kumdah Saudi Arabia **105** D3
Kumel *well* Iran **100** C3
Kumertau Rus. Fed. **102** C1
Kŭm-gang *r.* S. Korea **83** B6
Kumgang-san *mt.* N. Korea **83** C5
English form Keumgang, Mount; *formerly known as* Keumsang, Mount
Kumguri India **97** F4
Kumharsain India **89** B6
Kumher India **96** C4
Kŭmho-gang *r.* S. Korea **83** C6
Kumi S. Korea **83** C5
Kumi Uganda **128** B4
Kumkale Turkey **59** H9
Kum Kuduk *well* China **88** E3
Kumla Sweden **45** K4
Kumlinge Fin. **45** M3
Kumlu Turkey **109** H1
Kumluca Turkey **108** B1
Kummerower See *l.* Germany **49** J2
Kumo Nigeria **125** H4
Kŭmŏ-do *i.* S. Korea **83** B6
Kumola *watercourse* Kazakh. **103** F3
also spelt Qumola
Kumon Range *mts* Myanmar **78** B2
Kumphawapi Thai. **78** C4
Kumputunturi *hill* Fin. **44** N2
Kumta India **94** B3
Kumu Dem. Rep. Congo **126** E4
Kumukahi, Cape U.S.A. **181** [inset] Z2
Kumul China *see* **Hami**
Kumund India **95** D1
Kümüx China **88** E3
Kumylzhenskaya Rus. Fed. *see* **Kumylzhenskiy**
Kumylzhenskiy Rus. Fed. **41** G6
formerly known as Kumylzhenskaya
Kumyshtag, Pik *mt.* Kyrg. *see* **Kyumyush-Tak, Pik**
Kun *r.* Myanmar **78** B4
Kunar *r.* Afgh. **101** G3
Kunashir, Ostrov *i.* Rus. Fed. **82** G3
Kunashirskiy Proliv *sea chan.* Japan/Rus. Fed. *see* **Nemuro-kaikyō**
Kunchaung Myanmar **78** B3
Kunda Dem. Rep. Congo **126** E5
Kunda Estonia **42** H2
Kunda *r.* Estonia **42** H2
Kunda India **97** D4
Kunda-dia-Baze Angola **127** C7
Kunda laht *b.* Estonia **42** H2
Kundapura India **94** B3
formerly spelt Coondapoor
Kundar *r.* Afgh./Pak. **101** G3
Kundat *Sabah* Malaysia **77** G1
Kundelungu, Parc National de *nat. park* Dem. Rep. Congo **127** E7
Kundelungu Ouest, Parc National de *nat. park* Dem. Rep. Congo **127** E7
Kundgol India **94** B3
Kundian Pak. **101** G3
Kundur *i.* Indon. **76** C2
Kunduz Afgh. *see* **Kondūz**
Kunene *admin. reg.* Namibia **130** B3
Kunene *r.* Namibia **127** A9
also spelt Cunene
Künes China *see* **Xinyuan**
Künes Chang China **88** C3
Künes He *r.* China **88** C3
Künes Linchang China **88** D3
Kungälv Sweden **45** J4
Kungei Alatau *mts* Kazakh./Kyrg. **103** I4
also spelt Küngöy Ala-Too
Kunggar China *see* **Maizhokunggar**
Kunghit Island Canada **166** D4
Küngöy Ala-Too *mts* Kazakh./Kyrg. *see* **Kungei Alatau**
Kungrad Uzbek. **102** D4
also spelt Qongrat *or* Qŭnghirot; *formerly known as* Zheleznodorozhnyy
Kungradkol' Uzbek. **102** E4
Kungsbacka Sweden **45** K4
Kungshamn Sweden **45** J4
Kungsör Sweden **45** L4
Kungu Dem. Rep. Congo **126** C4
Kungur *mt.* China *see* **Kongur Shan**
Kungur Rus. Fed. **40** K4
Kungyangon Myanmar **78** A4
Kunhegyes Hungary **49** R8
Kuni *r.* India **94** C2
Kunié *i.* New Caledonia *see* **Pins, Île des**
Kunigai India **94** C3
Kunimi-dake *mt.* Japan **91** B8
Kuningaküla Estonia **42** I2
Kuningan Indon. **77** E4
Kunisaki Japan **91** B8
Kunjabar India **95** E1
Kunlavav India **96** A5
Kunlong Myanmar **78** B3
Kunlui *r.* India/Nepal **97** F4
Kunlun Shan *mts* China **84** B5
Kunlun Shankou *pass* China **84** B5
Kunmadaras Hungary **49** R8
Kunming China **86** B3
Kunmunya Aboriginal Reserve Australia **150** D2
Kuno *r.* India **96** C4
Kunoy *i.* Faroe Is **46** F1
Kunsan S. Korea **83** B6
Kunshan China **87** G2
Kunszentmárton Hungary **49** R9
Kunszentmiklós Hungary **49** Q8
Kuntshankoie Dem. Rep. Congo **126** D5
Kununurra Australia **150** E2
Kunwak *r.* Canada **167** L2
Kunwari *r.* India **96** C4
Kun'ya Rus. Fed. **43** L5
Kun'ya *r.* Rus. Fed. **43** M4
Kunyang China *see* **Yexian**
Kunyang China *see* **Jinning**
Kunyang China *see* **Pingyang**
Kunya-Urgench Turkm. *see* **Keneurgench**
Kunyu Shan *mts* China **85** I4
Künzelsau Germany **48** G6
Kuocang Shan *mts* China **87** G2
Kuolayarvi Rus. Fed. **44** O2
Kuopio Fin. **44** N3
Kuosku Fin. **44** O2
Kupa *r.* Croatia/Slovenia **56** I3
Kupang Indon. **75** B5
Kupang, Teluk *b.* Indon. **75** B5
Kupanskoye Rus. Fed. **43** T5
Kupari India **97** E5
Kupiškis Lith. **42** F6
Kuprava Latvia **42** I4
Kupreanof Island U.S.A. **164** F4
Kupreanof Point U.S.A. **164** D4
Kupuy Rus. Fed. **43** L5
Kupwara Jammu and Kashmir **96** B2
Kup"yans'k Ukr. **41** F6
Kuqa China **88** C3
Kür *r.* Azer. **107** G3
Kür *r.* Georgia **107** F2
Kur *r.* Rus. Fed. **82** D2
Kura *r.* Azer./Georgia **107** F2
Kura *r.* Rus. Fed. **41** G8
Kurabuka *r.* Australia **150** B5
Kuragaty Kazakh. **103** H4
also spelt Qoraghaty
Kuragwi Nigeria **125** H4
Kurakh Rus. Fed. **102** A4
Kura kurk *sea chan.* Estonia/Latvia *see* **Irbe Strait**
Kuramā, Ḩarrat *lava field* Saudi Arabia **104** C2
Kurashasayskiy Kazakh. **102** D2
Kurashiki Japan **91** C7
Kurasia India **97** D5
Kura Soak *well* Australia **150** D3
Kurayn *i.* Saudi Arabia **105** E2
Kurayoshi Japan **91** C7
Kurayskiy Khrebet *mts* Rus. Fed. **84** A1
Kurba Rus. Fed. **43** U4
Kurban Dağı *mt.* Turkey **58** K8
Kurbin *r.* China **82** C2
Kurca *r.* Romania **58** B2
Kurchatov Rus. Fed. **41** E6
Kurchum Kazakh. **88** C1
also spelt Kürshim; *formerly known as* Kurmashkino
Kurchum *r.* Kazakh. **88** C1
Kürdämir Azer. **107** G2
also spelt Kyurdamir
Kurday Kazakh. **103** H4
also spelt Qorday
Kür Dili *pt* Azer. **107** G3
Kurduvadi India **94** B2
Kŭrdzhali Bulg. **58** G7
Kure Japan **91** C7
Küre Turkey **106** C2
Kure Atoll U.S.A. **220** G4
also known as Ocean Island
Kuressaare Estonia **42** D3
formerly known as Kingisseppa
Kureya *r.* Rus. Fed. **43** K3
Kureyskoye Vodokhranilische *resr* Rus. Fed. **39** I3
Kurgal'dzhino Kazakh. *see* **Kurgal'dzhinskiy**
Kurgal'dzhinskiy Kazakh. **103** G2
also known as Qorghalzhyn; *formerly known as* Kurgal'dzhino
Kurgan Rus. Fed. **38** G4
Kurganinsk Rus. Fed. **41** G7
formerly known as Kurgannaya
Kurgannaya Rus. Fed. *see* **Kurganinsk**
Kurgantyube Tajik. *see* **Qŭrghonteppa**
Kuri India **96** A4
Kuria *is* Kiribati **145** G1
Kuria Muria Bay Oman *see* **Ḩalāniyāt, Khalīj al**
Kuria Muria Islands Oman *see* **Ḩalāniyāt, Juzur al**
Kuridala Australia **149** D4
Kurigram Bangl. **97** F4
Kurikka Fin. **44** M3
Kurikoma-yama *vol.* Japan **90** G5
Kurile, Mal *mt.* Albania **58** A6
Kuril Islands Rus. Fed. **82** G3
also known as Kuril'skiye Ostrova *or* Chishima-retto
Kurilovka Rus. Fed. **102** B2
Kuril'sk Rus. Fed. **81** P3
Kuril'skiye Ostrova *is* Rus. Fed. *see* **Kuril Islands**
Kuriyama Japan **90** G3
Kurkino Rus. Fed. **43** T8
Kurkurabazhi, Gora *mt.* Rus. Fed. **84** A1
Kurlkuta Aboriginal Reserve Australia **150** D4
Kurlovskiy Rus. Fed. **40** G5
Kurmanayevka Rus. Fed. **102** B1
Kurmashkino Kazakh. *see* **Kurchum**
Kurmene Latvia **42** F5
Kurmuk Sudan **128** B2
Kurnool India **94** C3
Kurobe Japan **91** E6
Kuroishi Japan **90** G4
Kuroiso Japan **90** G6
Kuromatsunai Japan **90** G3
Kuror, Jebel *mt.* Sudan **121** F4
Kuro-shima *i.* Japan **91** A9
Kurovskiy Rus. Fed. **82** B1
Kurovskoy Rus. Fed. **43** R7
Kurovskoye Rus. Fed. **43** T6
Kurow N.Z. **153** E12
Kurram *r.* Afgh./Pak. **101** G3
Kurri Kurri Australia **147** F3
Kuršėnai Lith. **42** D5
Kursh, Jabal *hill* Saudi Arabia **104** C3
Kürshim Kazakh. *see* **Kurchum**
Kurshskiy Zaliv *b.* Lith./Rus. Fed. *see* **Courland Lagoon**
Kurshynavichy Belarus **42** H9
Kursīši Latvia **42** D5
Kuršių marios *b.* Lith./Rus. Fed. *see* **Courland Lagoon**
Kuršių neringos nacionalinis parkas *nat. park* Lith. **42** B6
Kursk Rus. Fed. **41** F6
Kurskaya Rus. Fed. **41** H7
Kurskaya Oblast' *admin. div.* Rus. Fed. **41** F6
English form Kursk Oblast
Kurskiy Zaliv *b.* Lith./Rus. Fed. *see* **Courland Lagoon**
Kursk Oblast *admin. div.* Rus. Fed. *see* **Kurskaya Oblast'**
Kuršumlija *Srbija* Yugo. **58** C5
Kurşunlu Turkey **106** C2
Kurtalan Turkey **107** E3
also known as Misraç
Kürti *r.* Kazakh. *see* **Kurtty**
Kurtoğlu Burnu *pt* Turkey **106** B3

index

K

L

Kurtpınar Turkey **108** G1
Kurttepe Turkey **108** G1
Kurtty r. Kazakh. **103** I3
also spelt Kürti or Kurty
Kurty r. Greece see Kourou
Kuru Fin. **45** M3
Kurú r. Greece see Kourou
Kuru India **97** E5
Kuru watercourse Sudan **126** E2
Kurucaspie Turkey **106** C2
Kurud India **94** D1
Kurukshetra India **96** C3
Kuruman S. Africa **132** H4
Kuruman watercourse S. Africa **132** E3
Kuruman Hills S. Africa **132** H4
Kurume Japan **91** B8
Kurun r. Sudan **128** B2
Kurun watercourse Australia **148** B4
Kurundvad India **94** B2
Kurunegala Sri Lanka **94** D5
Kurunzulay Rus. Fed. **85** H1
Kurupam India **95** D2
Kurupukari Guyana **199** G3
Kurush, Jebel hills Sudan **121** F4
Kur'ya Rus. Fed. **43** J2
Kur'ya Rus. Fed. **40** K3
Kuryk Kazakh. **102** E4
formerly known as Yeraliyev
Kuryongp'o S. Korea **91** A7
Kuşadası Turkey **106** A3
Kuşadası Körfezi b. Turkey **106** A3
Kusaie atoll Micronesia see Kosrae
Kusary Azer. see Qusar
Kusawa Lake Canada **166** B2
Kuşcenneti Milli Parkı nat. park Turkey **59** I8
Kuse Japan **91** C7
Kuş Gölü l. Turkey **106** A2
formerly known as Manyas Gölü
Kushalgarh India **96** B5
Kushalino Rus. Fed. **43** R4
Kusheriki Nigeria **125** G4
Kushida-gawa r. Japan **91** E7
Kushikino Japan **91** B9
Kushima Japan **91** B9
Kushimoto Japan **91** D8
Kushiro Japan **90** I3
Kushiro-Shitsugen National Park Japan **90** I3
Kushka Turkm. see Gushgy
Kushmurun Kazakh. **103** F1
also spelt Qusmuryn
Kushmurun, Ozero l. Kazakh. **103** F1
also known as Qusmuryn Köli
Kushnarenkovo Rus. Fed. **40** J4
Kushtagi India **94** C3
Kushtia Bangl. **97** F5
also spelt Kustia
Kushtih Iran **101** D4
Kushtozero, Ozero l. Rus. Fed. **43** R1
Kushui r. China **88** E4
Kushum r. Kazakh. **102** B2
Kuskan Turkey **108** E1
Kuskokwim r. U.S.A. **164** C3
Kuskokwim Bay U.S.A. **164** C4
Kuskokwim Mountains U.S.A. **164** D3
Kuskovo Rus. Fed. **43** Q6
Kuşluyan Turkey see Gölköy
Kusöng N. Korea **83** B5
Kussharo-ko l. Japan **90** I3
Kustanay Kazakh. see Kostanay
Kustanay Oblast admin. div. Kazakh. see Kustanayskaya Oblast'
Kustanayskaya Oblast' admin. div. Kazakh. **103** E1
English form Kustanay Oblast; also known as Qostanay Oblysy
Kustavi Fin. **45** M3
Küstence Romania see Constanţa
Kustia Bangl. see Kushtia
Kusu Indon. **75** C2
Kut, Ko i. Thai. **79** C6
Kutacane Indon. **76** B2
Kütahya Turkey **106** B3
historically known as Cotiaeum
Kütahya prov. Turkey **59** K9
Kutai National Park Indon. **77** G2
K'ut'aisi Georgia **107** E2
Kut-al-Imara Iraq see Al Kūt
Kutan Rus. Fed. **102** A3
Kutaraja Indon. see Banda Aceh
Kutarere N.Z. **152** L6
Kutayfat Turayf vol. Saudi Arabia **109** J6
Kutch, Gulf of India see Kachchh, Gulf of
Kutch, Rann of marsh India see Kachchh, Rann of
Kutchan Japan **90** G3
Kūt-e Gapu tourist site Iran **100** B3
Kutina Croatia **56** J3
Kutjevo Croatia **56** J3
Kutkai Myanmar **78** B3
Kutloanong S. Africa **133** K4
Kutná Hora Czech Rep. **49** M6
Kutno Poland **49** Q3
Kuttainen Sweden **44** M1
Kutu Dem. Rep. Congo **126** C5
Kutubdia Island Bangl. **97** F5

Kutum Sudan **120** E6
Kutuzov Moldova see Ialoveni
Kutztown U.S.A. **177** J5
Kuujjua r. Canada **165** H2
Kuujjuaq Canada **169** G1
formerly known as Fort Chimo
Kuujjuarapik Canada **168** E2
also known as Poste-de-la-Baleine
Kuuli-Mayak Turkm. **102** C4
also spelt Guwlumaýak
Kuusajoki Fin. **44** N2
Kuusalu Estonia **42** G2
Kuusamo Fin. **44** O2
Kuusankoski Fin. **45** N3
Kuusjoki Fin. **42** E1
Kutse mägi hill Estonia **42** H3
Kuvandyk Rus. Fed. **102** D2
Kuvango Angola **127** C8
formerly known as Artur de Paiva or Capelongo or Vila da Ponte
Kuvshinovo Rus. Fed. **43** P4
▶**Kuwait** country Asia **107** F5
spelt Al Kuwayt in Arabic
world [changes] ▶ 20–21
asia [countries] ▶ 64–67

▶**Kuwait** Kuwait **107** F5
Capital of Kuwait. Also spelt Al Kuwayt.

Kuwait Jun b. Kuwait **107** F5
Kuwajleen atoll Marshall Is see Kwajalein
Kuwana Japan **91** E7
Küybyshev Kazakh. see Kuybyshevskiy
Kuybyshev Rus. Fed. **80** B1
Kuybyshev Rus. Fed. see Bolgar
Kuybyshev Rus. Fed. see Samara
Kuybysheve Ukr. **41** F7
Kuybyshevka-Vostochnaya Rus. Fed. see Belogorsk
Kuybyshevo Kazakh. see Zhyngyldy
Kuybyshevskaya Oblast' admin. div. Rus. Fed. see Samarskaya Oblast'
Kuybyshevskiy Kazakh. **103** F1
also known as Küybyshev; formerly known as Trudovoy
Kuybyshevskoye Vodokhranilishche resr Rus. Fed. **40** I5
Kuybyshew Adyndaky Turkm. see imeni Kuybysheva
Kuye r. China **85** F4
Kuyeda Rus. Fed. **40** J4
Kuygan Kazakh. **103** H3
also spelt Quyghan
Küysu China **84** B3
Kuytun China **88** D2
Kuytun He r. China **88** C2
Kuyucak Turkey **59** J11
Kuyukkol', Ozero salt l. Kazakh. **103** F2
Kuyus Rus. Fed. **88** D1
Kuyu Tingni Nicaragua **186** C4
also known as Cuyuntingni
Kuyuwini r. Guyana **199** G4
Kuyvozi Rus. Fed. **43** L1
Kuzino Rus. Fed. **43** T2
Kuz'minichi Rus. Fed. **43** O7
Kuz'minskoe Rus. Fed. **43** O5
Kuz'molovskiy Rus. Fed. **43** L1
Kuznechnoye Rus. Fed. **43** L1
Kuznetsk Rus. Fed. **41** H5
Kuznetsovo Rus. Fed. **90** F1
Kuznetsovs'k Ukr. **41** L4
Kuzomen' Rus. Fed. **40** F2
Kuzovatovo Rus. Fed. **41** H5
Kuzovka Rus. Fed. **43** T8
Kuzumaki Japan **90** F5
Kvaenangen sea chan. Norway **44** M1
Kvalaya i. Norway **44** L1
Kvaleya i. Norway **44** M1
Kvalsund Norway **44** M1
Kvareli Georgia see Qvareli
Kvarkeno Rus. Fed. **102** D1
Kvarnberg Sweden **45** K3
Kvarner g. Croatia **56** G4
Kvarnerić sea chan. Croatia **56** G4
Kvedarna Lith. **42** C6
Kvernen Norway **44** J3
Kvichak Bay U.S.A. **164** D4
Kvikkjokk Sweden **44** L2
Kvisseleby Sweden **45** L3
Kvitanosi Norway **45** I3
Kvitegga mt. Norway **44** I3
Kvitoya ice feature Svalbard **38** C1
Kvitsøy Norway **45** I4
Kwa r. Dem. Rep. Congo **126** C5
Kwabhaca S. Africa see Mount Frere
KwaChibukhulu S. Africa **133** O3
Kwadacha Wilderness Provincial Park Canada **166** E3
KwaDela S. Africa **133** N3
Kwadelen atoll Marshall Is see Kwajalein
Kwaga Tanz. **129** A6
KwaGuga S. Africa **133** N2
Kwajalein atoll Marshall Is **220** F5
also known as Kwajalein or Kwadelen
Kwakoegron Suriname **199** G3
Kwakwani Guyana **199** G3
Kwakwatse S. Africa **133** L4
Kwale Kenya **129** C6
Kwale Nigeria **125** G5
Kwa-Mashu S. Africa **133** O6
Kwa-Mbonambi S. Africa **133** Q5
KwaMhlanga S. Africa **133** N3
Kwamouth Dem. Rep. Congo **126** C5
Kwandang Indon. **75** B2
Kwangchow China see Guangzhou
Kwangju S. Korea **83** B6
Kwango r. Dem. Rep. Congo **126** C5
also spelt Cuango
Kwangsi aut. reg. China see Guangxi
Kwangsi Chuang Autonomous Region aut. reg. China see Guangxi Zhuangzu Zizhiqu
Kwangtung prov. China see Guangdong
Kwangwazi Tanz. **129** C6
Kwania, Lake Uganda **128** A4
Kwanmo-bong mt. N. Korea **82** C4
also known as Kambo-san
Kwanobuhle S. Africa **133** J10
KwaNojoli S. Africa **133** J9
Kwanonqubela S. Africa **133** K10
Kwanonzame S. Africa **133** J10
Kwanza r. Angola see Cuanza
Kwa-Pita S. Africa **133** J9
Kware state Nigeria see Kebbi
KwaThandeka S. Africa **133** O3
Kwatinidubu S. Africa **133** J10
Kwawr Umm Wu'al depr. Saudi Arabia
Kwazamokuhle S. Africa **133** N3
Kwazamukuso S. Africa **133** I9
Kwazamuxolo S. Africa **133** I8
KwaZanele S. Africa **133** N3
Kwazulu-Natal prov. S. Africa **133** O5
formerly known as Natal
Kweichow prov. China see Guizhou
Kweiyang China see Guiyang
Kwekwe Zimbabwe **131** F3
formerly spelt Que Que
Kwena Dam S. Africa **133** N2
Kweneng admin. dist. Botswana **131** E4
Kwenge r. Dem. Rep. Congo **126** C5
Kwetabohigan r. Canada **168** D3
Kwezi-Naledi S. Africa **133** L7
Kwiambana Nigeria **125** G4

Kwidzyn Poland **49** P2
historically known as Marienwerder
Kwiha Eth. **104** B5
Kwikila P.N.G. **73** K8
Kwilu r. Angola/Dem. Rep. Congo **127** C5
Kwisa r. Poland **49** M4
Kwitaro r. Guyana **199** G4
Kwo Chau Kwan To is Hong Kong China see Ninepin Group
Kwoka mt. Indon. **73** H7
Kwoungo, Mont mt. Cent. Afr. Rep. **126** E3
Kwun Tong Hong Kong China **87** [inset]
Kyabé Chad **126** C2
Kyabra Australia **149** D5
Kyabra watercourse Australia **149** D5
Kyabram Australia **147** E4
Kyadet Myanmar **78** A3
Kyaiklat Myanmar **78** A4
Kyaikto Myanmar **78** B4
Kya-in Seikkyi Myanmar **78** B4
Kyakhta Rus. Fed. **85** F1
Kyalite Australia **147** D3
Kyancutta Australia **146** B3
Kyangin Irrawaddy Myanmar **78** A4
Kyangin Mandalay Myanmar **78** B4
Kyaukhnyat Myanmar **78** B4
Kyaukkyi Myanmar **78** B4
Kyaukme Myanmar **78** B3
Kyaukmyaung Myanmar **78** A3
Kyaukpadaung Myanmar **78** A4
Kyaukpyu Myanmar **78** A4
Kyaukse Myanmar **78** B3
Kyauktan Myanmar **78** B4
Kyauktaw Myanmar **78** A3
Kyaunggon Myanmar **78** A4
Kybartai Lith. **42** D6
Kybeyan Range mts Australia **147** F4
Ky Cung, Sông r. Vietnam **78** D3
Kyeburn N.Z. **153** E13
Kyeintali Myanmar **78** A4
Kyela Tanz. **129** B7
Kyelang India **96** C2
Kyenjojo Uganda **128** A4
Kyeraa Ghana **125** E4
Kyeyibelen, Gora hill Kazakh. **103** H3
Kyidaunggan Myanmar **78** B4
Kyikug China **84** D4
Kyinderi Ghana **125** E4
Kyiv Ukr. see Kiev
Kyjov Czech Rep. **49** O6
Kyklades is Greece see Cyclades
Kyle Canada **167** I5
Kyle of Lochalsh U.K. **46** G6
Kyll r. Germany **48** D6
Kyllíni mt. Greece **59** D11
also spelt Killíni
Kyllínis, Akra pt Greece **59** C11
Kymi Greece **59** F10
also spelt Kími
Kymijoki r. Fin. **42** H1
Kymis, Akra pt Greece **59** F10
Kynna r. Norway **45** K3
Kynuna Australia **149** D4
Kyoga, Lake Uganda **128** B4
Kyōga-misaki pt Japan **91** D7
Kyogle Australia **147** G2
Kyom watercourse Sudan **126** F2
Kyondo Myanmar **78** B4
Kyŏngju-man b. S. Korea **83** B5
Kyŏngju S. Korea **83** C6
Kyongju National Park S. Korea **83** C6
Kyonpyaw Myanmar **78** A4
Kyōto Japan **91** D7
Kyōto pref. Japan **91** D7
Kyōwa Japan **90** G5
Kyparissia Greece **59** C11
Kyparissiakos Kolpos b. Greece **59** C11
Kypros country Asia see Cyprus
Kypshak, Ozero salt l. Kazakh. **103** G2
also known as Qypshaq Köli
Kyra Rus. Fed. **85** G1
Kyra Panagia i. Greece **59** F9
Kyren Rus. Fed. **84** D1
Kyrenia Cyprus **108** E2
also known as Girne; also spelt Keryneia
Kyrenia Mountains Cyprus see Pentadaktylos Range
▶**Kyrgyzstan** country Asia **103** H4
also spelt Kirgizstan; formerly known as Kirghizia or Kirgizskaya S.S.R.
asia [countries] ▶ 64–67
Kyrhyzh-Kytay r. Ukr. **58** K3
Kyria Greece **58** F7
also spelt Kíria
Kyriaki Greece **59** D10
Kyritz Germany **49** J3
Kyritz-Ruppiner Heide park Germany **49** J2
Kyrnychky Ukr. **58** K3
Kyrta Rus. Fed. **40** K3
Kysucké Nové Mesto Slovakia **49** P6
Kytay, Ozero l. Ukr. **58** K3
Kythira Greece **59** D12
Kythira i. Greece **59** D12
English form Cerigo; also spelt Kíthira; historically known as Cythera
Kythnos i. Greece **59** F11
also spelt Kíthnos
Kythnou, Steno sea chan. Greece **59** F11
also spelt Kíthnou; Stenón
Kytlrea Cyprus **108** E2
also known as Değirmenlik
Kyumyush-Tak, Pik mt. Kyrg. **103** I4
also spelt Kumyshtag, Pik
Kyunglung China **89** C6
Kyungyaung Myanmar **79** B5
Kyunhla Myanmar **78** A3
Kyuquot Canada **166** E5
Kyurdamir Azer. see Kürdämir
Kyushe Kazakh. **102** D3
Kyūshū i. Japan **91** B8
Kyūshū-sanchi mts Japan **91** B8
Kyustendil Bulg. **58** D6
Kywebwe Myanmar **78** B4
Kywong Australia **147** E3
Kyyiv Ukr. see Kiev
Kyyivs'ke Vodoskhovyshche resr Ukr. **41** D6
also known as Kiyevskoye Vodokhranilishche
Kyyjärvi Fin. **44** N3
Kyyvesi l. Fin. **45** N3
Kyzan Kazakh. **102** C3
also spelt Qyzan
Kyzketken Uzbek. **102** D4
also spelt Qizqetkan
Kyzyl Rus. Fed. **80** G1
Kyzyl-Adyr Kyrg. **103** G4
also known as Kirov or Kirovskoye
Kyzylagash Kazakh. **103** I3
Kyzyl-Art, Pereval pass Kyrg./Tajik. see Kyzylart Pass
Kyzylart Pass Kyrg./Tajik. **101** H2
also known as Kyzyl-Art, Pereval or Qizil-Art, Aghbai
Kyzyl-Burun Azer. see Siyäzän
Kyzylkesek Kazakh. **88** D2
also spelt Qyzylkesek; formerly known as Kyzylkesken
Kyzylkesken Kazakh. see Kyzylkesek
Kyzyl-Khem r. Rus. Fed. **84** C1
Kyzyl-Kiya Kyrg. see Kyzyl-Kyya
Kyzylkoga Kazakh. **102** C2
Kyzyl'kol', Ozero l. Kazakh. **103** E2
also known as Qyzylkol
Kyzylkol Kazakh. **103** E2
Kyzylkum, Peski des. Kazakh./Uzbek. see Kyzylkum Desert

Kyzylkum Desert Kazakh./Uzbek. **103** F4
historically known as Kyzylkum, Peski
Kyzyl-Kyya Kyrg. **103** H4
also spelt Kyzyl-Kiya
Kyzyl-Mazhalyk Rus. Fed. **84** A1
Kyzylorda Kazakh. **103** F3
also spelt Kyzl-Orda or Qyzylorda; formerly known as Ak-Mechet
Kyzyl-Orda Oblast admin. div. Kazakh. see Kyzyl-Ordinskaya Oblast'
Kyzylrabot Tajik. see Qizilrabot
Kyzylsay Kazakh. **102** C4
formerly known as Ozen or Uzen'
Kyzyl-Suu r. Kyrg. **103** I4
formerly known as Pokrovka
Kyzyl-Suu r. Kyrg. **103** I4
also spelt Qyzylsu
Kyzyltam Kazakh. **103** G2
also spelt Qyzyltam; formerly spelt Kyzl-Dzhar
Kyzyl-Dzhar Kazakh. see Kyzylzhar
Kyzyl-Orda Kazakh. see Kyzylorda
Kyzyl-Ordinskaya Oblast' admin. div. Kazakh. **103** F3
English form Kyzyl-Orda Oblast; also known as Qyzylorda Oblysy
Kzyl-Ordinskoye Vodokhranilishche resr Kazakh. **103** F3
Kzyltu Kazakh. see Kishkenekol'

↓ **L**

Laage Germany **49** J2
Laagri Estonia **42** F2
La Almunia de Doña Godina Spain **55** J3
La Amistad, Parque Internacional nat. park Costa Rica/Panama **186** C5
La Angostura, Presa de resr Mex. **185** G6
Lääniste Estonia **42** I3
Laanle well Somalia **128** E2
La Antigua, Salina salt pan Arg. **204** D3
La Araucania admin. reg. Chile **204** B5
La Ardilla, Cerro mt. Mex. **185** E4
Laas Aano Somalia **128** F3
Laascaanood Somalia **128** E3
formerly known as Las Anod
La Ascensión, Bahía de b. Mex. **185** I5
Laas Dawaco Somalia **128** F3
Laasgoray Somalia **128** F2
La Asunción Venez. **199** F2
Laau Point U.S.A. **181** [inset] Z1

▶**Laâyoune** W. Sahara **122** B4
Capital of Western Sahara. Formerly spelt El Aaiún.

Lab r. Yugo. **58** C6
Laba r. Rus. Fed. **41** G7
La Babia Mex. **185** E2
La Bahía, Islas de is Hond. **186** B3
English form Bay Islands
La Baie Canada **169** G3
formerly known as Port-Alfred
Labala Indon. **75** B5
La Baleine, Grande Rivière de r. Canada **168** E2
La Baleine, Petite Rivière de r. Canada **168** E2
La Baleine, Rivière à r. Canada **169** H1
also known as Whale
La Banda Arg. **204** D2
La Bañeza Spain **54** E3
Labang Sarawak Malaysia **77** F2
Labanoras Lith. **42** G6
Labao China see Liujiang
La Barthe-de-Neste France **50** G9
Labasa Fiji **145** G3
La Baule-Escoublac France **50** D5
Labaz, Ozero l. Rus. Fed. **39** J2
Labazhskoye Rus. Fed. **40** J2
Labe r. Czech Rep. **49** L5
English form Elbe (Germany)
Labé Guinea **124** B4
Labelle Canada **169** F4
La Belle U.S.A. **175** D7
Labengke i. Indon. **75** B3
La Bénoué, Parc National de nat. park Cameroon **125** I4
Laberge, Lake Canada **166** C2
La Bernarde, Sommet de mt. France **51** M9
Labi Brunei **77** F2
La Biche r. Canada **166** F3
La Biche, Lac l. Canada **167** H4
Labin Croatia **56** G3
Labinsk Rus. Fed. **41** G7
Labis Malaysia **76** C2
La Bisbal d'Empordà Spain **55** O3
La Biznaga Mex. **184** D4
Labo Phil. **74** B3
La Bobia, Sierra de mts Spain **54** E1
Labobo i. Indon. **75** B3
La Bodera mt. Spain **55** I3
La Bomu, Réserve de Faune de nature res. Dem. Rep. Congo **126** E3
La Boquilla Mex. **184** D3
Labora Namibia **132** C1
Laboubouere France **50** F8
Labouchere, Mount hill Australia **151** B5
La Boucle du Baoulé, Parc National de nat. park Mali **124** C3
Laboué Lebanon **109** H3
Labouheyre France **50** F8
Laboulaye Arg. **204** E4
Labrador reg. Canada **169** I2
Labrador City Canada **169** H2
Labrador Sea Canada/Greenland **165** N3
Labrang China see Xiahe
Lábrea Brazil **200** D1
La Brea Peru **198** A6
La Brède France **50** F8
La Brenne, Parc Naturel Régional de nature res. France **50** H6
Labruguière France **51** I9
Labuan Malaysia **77** F1
formerly known as Victoria
Labuan i. Malaysia **77** F1
Labuanbajo Indon. **75** B5
Labudalin China see Ergun
La Bufa, Cerro mt. Mex. **185** E5
Labuhan Indon. **77** D4
Labuhanbajo Indon. **75** A5
Labuhanbilik Indon. **76** B2
Labuhanmeringgai Indon. **77** D4
Labuhanruku Indon. **76** B2
Labuk r. Sabah Malaysia **77** G1
Labuk, Telukan b. Sabah Malaysia **77** G1
Labuna Indon. **75** D4
Labutta Myanmar **78** A4
Labyrinth, Lake salt flat Australia **146** A2
Labytnangi Rus. Fed. **38** G3
Lac Albania **58** A7
Lac pref. Chad **120** B6
La Cabrera, Sierra de mts Spain **54** E2
La Cadena Mex. **184** D3
La Calderina mt. Spain **54** H5
La Calera Chile **204** C4
La Calle Alg. see El Kala
La Campana Spain **54** F7
Lacanau, Étang de l. France **50** E8
Lacandón, Parque Nacional nat. park Guat. **185** H5
Lacantún r. Mex. **185** H5
La Capelle France **51** J3
Laçara Vojvodina, Srbija Yugo. **58** A3
La Carlota Arg. **204** E4
La Carlota Phil. **74** B4
La Carlota Spain **54** G7
Laferté Canada **173** O2

La Carolina Spain **55** H6
Laccadive, Minicoy and Amindivi Islands union terr. India see Lakshadweep
Laccadive Islands India **94** B4
also known as Lakshadweep
Lac du Bonnet Canada **167** L5
Lac du Flambeau U.S.A. **172** C4
Lacedaemon Greece see Sparti
La Ceiba Hond. **186** B4
Lacepede Bay Australia **146** C4
Lacepede Islands Australia **150** C3
Lacha, Ozero l. Rus. Fed. **40** E4
La Charité-sur-Loire France **51** J6
La Chartre-sur-le-Loir France **50** G5
La Chartreuse, Massif de mts France **51** L7
La Châtaigneraie France **50** F6
La Châtre France **51** H6
La Chaux-de-Fonds Switz. **51** M5
Lachine U.S.A. **173** J5
▶**Lachlan** r. Australia **147** D3
5th longest river in Oceania.
oceania [landscapes] ▶ 136–137
La Chorrera Col. **198** C5
La Chorrera Panama **186** D5
Lachung India **97** F4
Lachute Canada **169** F4
Lāçi Latvia **42** H6
Laçin Azer. **107** F3
La Ciotat France **51** L9
La Ciudad Mex. **184** D4
Lackawanna U.S.A. **176** G3
Lac La Biche Canada **167** I4
Lac la Martre Canada see Wha Ti
Lac La Ronge Provincial Park Canada **167** J4
Lac-Mégantic Canada **169** G4
La Cocha Arg. **204** D2
La Cogulla mt. Spain **55** L3
La Colorada Sonora Mex. **184** C2
La Colorada Zacatecas Mex. **185** E4
Lacombe Canada **167** H4
La Comoé, Parc National de nat. park Côte d'Ivoire **124** E4
La Concordia Mex. **185** G5
La Corey Canada **167** I4
La Corne Canada **173** F2
La Corse, Parc Naturel Régional de nature res. Corse France **56** A6
La Coruña Spain see A Coruña
La Coubre, Pointe de pt France **50** E7
La Crescent U.S.A. **172** B4
La Crete Canada **167** G3
La Croix, Lac l. Canada/U.S.A. **172** B2
La Crosse KS U.S.A. **178** C4
La Crosse VA U.S.A. **176** G9
La Crosse WI U.S.A. **172** B7
La Cruz Arg. **204** F3
La Cruz Col. **198** B4
La Cruz Costa Rica **186** B5
La Cruz Chihuahua Mex. **184** D3
La Cruz Sinaloa Mex. **184** D4
La Cruz Tamaulipas Mex. **185** F3
La Cruz Nicaragua **186** B4
La Cruz Uruguay **204** F4
La Cruz, Cerro mt. Mex. **185** I5
La Cuenca Alta del Manzanares, Parque Regional de park Spain **54** H4
La Culebra, Sierra de mts Spain **54** E3
La Curva Mex. **181** F7
La Cygne U.S.A. **178** D4
Ladainha Brazil **207** L4
Ladak reg. Jammu and Kashmir **96** C2
English form Little Tibet
Ladakh Range mts India **96** C2
Ladang i. Thai. **79** B7
Ladd U.S.A. **172** D9
Lądek-Zdrój Poland **49** N5
La Demajagua Cuba **186** D2
also known as Santa Bárbara
La Demanda, Sierra de mts Spain **55** H3
La Déroute, Passage de strait Channel Is/France **50** D3
La Désirade i. Guadeloupe **187** H3
Ladik Turkey **106** C2
Ladismith S. Africa **132** F10
Ladispoli Italy **56** E6
Lādīz Iran **101** E4
Ladnun India **96** B4
▶**Ladoga, Lake** Rus. Fed. **43** M1
2nd largest lake in Europe. Also known as Ladozhskoye Ozero.
europe [landscapes] ▶ 30–31
La Dôle mt. Switz. **51** M6
Ladon r. Greece **59** C11
Ladong China **87** D3
Ladozhskoye Ozero l. Rus. Fed. see Ladoga, Lake
Ladra r. Spain **54** D1
Ladrillero, Canal sea chan. Chile **205** A8
also known as Ladrones, Canal
Ladrones terr. N. Pacific Ocean see Northern Mariana Islands
Ladrones, Islas is Panama **186** C6
Ladu mt. Indon. **75** A3
Ladue r. Canada/U.S.A. **166** A2
Ladushkin Rus. Fed. **42** B7
historically known as Ludwigsort
Ladva Rus. Fed. **40** E3
Ladva-Vetka Rus. Fed. **40** E3
Ladwa India **96** C3
Lady Ann Strait Canada **165** K2
Lady Barron Australia **147** F5
Ladybrand S. Africa **133** L6
Lady Evelyn Lake Canada **173** M3
Lady Frere S. Africa **133** L7
Lady Grey S. Africa **133** L7
Lady Newnes Bay Antarctica **223** L4
Ladysmith Canada **166** F5
Ladysmith S. Africa **133** N5
Ladysmith U.S.A. **172** B5
Ladyzhenka Kazakh. **103** G2
Ladzhanurges Georgia see Lajanurpekhi
Lae P.N.G. **73** K8
Lae i. Thai. **78** C4
Laem Ngop Thai. **79** C6
La Encrucijada Venez. **187** G5
La Escala Spain see L'Escala
La Esmeralda Arg. **204** E2
La Esmeralda Bol. **201** E5
La Esmeralda Venez. **199** E4
Læsø i. Denmark **45** J4
La Esperanza Arg. **204** D5
La Esperanza Santa Cruz Bol. **201** E3
La Esperanza Hond. **186** B4
La Estrella Bol. **201** E4
Laeva Estonia **42** H3
Lævvajåkka Norway **44** N1
La Falda Arg. **204** D3
La Farge U.S.A. **172** C7
La Fargeville U.S.A. **177** J1
Lafayette CO U.S.A. **180** F5
Lafayette GA U.S.A. **175** C5
Lafayette IN U.S.A. **174** C3
Lafayette LA U.S.A. **179** D6
Lafayette OH U.S.A. **176** B5
Lafayette TN U.S.A. **174** C4
Laferté Canada **173** O2

Laferte r. Canada **167** G2
La Ferté-Bernard France **50** G4
La Ferté-Gaucher France **51** J4
La Ferté-Macé France **50** F4
La Ferté-St-Aubin France **51** H5
La Ferté-sous-Jouarre France **51** J4
Lafia Nigeria **125** H5
Lafiagi Nigeria **125** G4
Laflamme r. Canada **173** P1
La Flèche France **50** F5
Lafleche Canada **167** J5
La Follette U.S.A. **176** B8
La Fontaine U.S.A. **172** H10
Lafnitz r. Austria **49** N9
Laforce Canada **173** O3
Laforest Canada **173** L3
La Forest, Lac l. Canada **169** G2
La Forêt-d'Orient, Parc Naturel Régional de nature res. France **51** K4
Laforge Canada **169** F2
Laforge r. Canada **169** F2
Lafourche, Bayou r. U.S.A. **175** B6
La Française France **50** H8
La Frégate, Lac l. Canada **169** F2
Läft Iran **100** C5
▶**La Galite** i. Tunisia **123** H1
Most northerly point of Africa.

La Galite, Canal de sea chan. Tunisia **123** H1
La Gallareta Arg. **204** E3
Lagamar Brazil **206** G5
Lagan' Rus. Fed. **102** A3
formerly known as Kaspiyskiy
Lagan r. Sweden **45** K4
Lagana, Kolpos b. Greece **59** B11
Lagané well Niger **125** I3
La Garamba, Parc National de nat. park Dem. Rep. Congo **126** F3
Lagarto Brazil **202** E4
Lagarto, Serra do hills Brazil **206** A10
Lagbar Senegal **124** B3
Lagdo, Lac de l. Cameroon **125** I4
Lågen r. Norway **45** J3
Lågen r. Norway **45** J4
Lagh Bogal watercourse Kenya/Somalia **128** D4
Lagh Bor watercourse Kenya/Somalia **128** D4
Lagh Kutulo watercourse Kenya/Somalia **128** D4
Laghmän prov. Afgh. **101** G3
Laghouat Alg. **123** F2
La Gineta Spain **55** J5
Lagkadas Greece **58** E8
also spelt Langadhás
Lagkor Co salt l. China **89** D5
La Gloria Col. **198** C2
La Gloria Mex. **185** F3
Lago prov. Moz. see Niassa
Lagoa da Prata Brazil **207** H7
Lagoa Dourada Brazil **207** I7
Lagoa Formosa Brazil **206** G5
Lagoa Santa Brazil **207** I6
Lagoa Vermelha Brazil **203** B9
Lago Belgrano Arg. **205** C7
Lago Cardiel Arg. **205** C8
Lago da Pedra Brazil **202** C3
Lagodekhi Georgia **107** F2
Lagolândia Brazil **206** D3
La Gomera i. Canary Is **122** A3
La Gomera Guat. **185** H6
La Gonâve, Île de i. Haiti **187** E3
Lagong i. Indon. **77** E2
Lagoon Creek r. Australia **148** C3
Lago Posadas Arg. **205** C7
▶**Lagos** Nigeria **125** F5
Former capital of Nigeria. Most populous city in Africa and 6th in the world.
world [cities] ▶ 24–25

Lagos state Nigeria **125** F5
Lagos Port. **54** C7
Lagosa Tanz. **129** A6
Lagos de Moreno Mex. **185** E4
Lago Verde Brazil **202** C2
Lagran Spain **55** I2
La Grande r. Canada **168** E2
La Grande U.S.A. **180** C3
La Grande 2, Réservoir Canada **168** E2
La Grande 3, Réservoir Canada **169** F2
La Grande 4, Réservoir Que. Canada **169** F2
La Grande Casse, Pointe de mt. France **51** M7
La Grande-Combe France **51** K8
La Grange Australia **150** C4
La Grange CA U.S.A. **182** D4
La Grange GA U.S.A. **175** C5
La Grange KY U.S.A. **174** C4
La Grange TX U.S.A. **179** C6
Lagrange Bay Australia **150** C3
La Gran Sabana plat. Venez. **199** F3
La Grita Venez. **198** D2
La Guadeloupe Canada **169** G4
La Guaira Chile **204** C2
La Guardia Spain see A Guardia
Laguna Brazil **203** B9
Laguna U.S.A. **181** F6
Laguna, Ilha da i. Brazil **202** B2
Laguna Beach U.S.A. **182** G8
Laguna Dam U.S.A. **183** J9
Laguna de Laja, Parque Nacional nat. park Chile **204** C5
Laguna de Perlas Nicaragua **186** C4
Laguna de Temascal, Parque Natural nature res. Mex. **185** F5
Laguna Grande Arg. **205** C8
Laguna Lachua, Parque Nacional nat. park Guat. **185** H6
Laguna Mountains U.S.A. **183** H9
Lagunas Chile **200** C5
Lagunas Peru **198** B5
Laguna San Rafael, Parque Nacional nat. park Chile **205** B7
Lagunas de Catemaco, Parque Natural nature res. Mex. **185** G5
Lagunas de Chacahua, Parque Nacional nat. park Mex. **185** F6
Lagunas de Montebello, Parque Nacional nat. park Mex. **185** H5
Laguna Yema Arg. **201** E6
Lagunillas Bol. **201** E4
Lagunillas Venez. **198** D2
Laha China **85** J1
La Habana Cuba see Havana
La Habra U.S.A. **182** G8
Lahad Datu Malaysia **77** G1
Lahad Datu, Telukan b. Sabah Malaysia **77** G1
La Hague, Cap de c. France **50** E3
Lahar India **96** C4
La Harpe U.S.A. **172** C10
Laharpur India **96** D4
Lahat Indon. **76** C3
Lahemaa rahvuspark nat. park Estonia **42** G2
Lahepera laht b. Estonia **42** H2
La Hève, Cap de c. France **50** G3
Lahewa Indon. **76** B2
Lahij Yemen **104** D5
Lahij governorate Yemen **104** D5
Lahishyn Belarus **42** G10
Lahn r. Germany **48** F5
Lahnstein Germany **48** E5
Laholm Sweden **45** K4

Laholmsbukten b. Sweden **45** K4
Lahontan Reservoir U.S.A. **182** E2
Lahore Pak. **101** H4
La Horqueta Venez. **199** F3
La Hotte, Massif de mts Haiti **187** E3
Lahr (Schwarzwald) Germany **48** E7
Lahri Pak. **101** G4
Lahti Fin. **45** N3
La Huerta Mex. **184** D5
L'Ahzar, Vallée de watercourse Niger **125** F3
Laï Chad **126** C2
Lai'an China **87** F1
also known as Xin'an
Laibach Slovenia see **Ljubljana**
Laibin China **87** D4
Laie U.S.A. **181** [inset] Z1
also known as Xiangfeng
Laifeng China **87** D3
Laihia Fin. **44** M2
Lai-hka Myanmar **78** B3
Lai-Hsak Myanmar **78** B3
Laingsburg S. Africa **132** E10
Laingsburg U.S.A. **173** I8
Lainioälven r. Sweden **44** M2
Lainsitz r. Austria **49** M7
Lair U.S.A. **176** A7
L'Aïr, Massif de mts Niger **125** H2
also known as Azbine
L'Aïr et du Ténéré, Réserve Naturelle Nationale de nature res. Niger **125** H2
Lairg U.K. **46** H5
Lais Indon. **76** C3
La Isabela Cuba **186** C2
Laisälven r. Sweden **44** L2
Laishevo Rus. Fed. **40** I5
La Isla Col. **198** B3
Laitila Fin. **45** M3
Laivera well Tanz. **129** C6
Laives Italy **56** D2
Laiwu China **85** H4
Laiwui Indon. **75** C3
Laixi China **85** I4
formerly known as Shuiji
Laiyang China **85** I4
Laiyuan China **85** G4
Laizhou China **85** H4
formerly known as Yexian
Laizhou Wan b. China **85** H4
La Jagua Col. **198** C2
Lajamanu Australia **148** A3
Lajanurpekhi Georgia **107** E2
also known as Ladzhanurges
Lajeado Brazil **203** A9
Lajedo Brazil **202** E4
Laje dos Santos i. Brazil **207** G11
Lajes Brazil **203** B8
Lajinha Brazil **207** L7
Lajkovac Srbija Yugo. **58** B4
La Jolla U.S.A. **182** F7
Lajosmizse Hungary **49** Q8
La Joya Mex. **184** B3
La Joya Peru **200** C4
La Joya de los Sachas Ecuador **198** B5
Lajta r. Austria/Hungary **49** O8
La Junta Bol. **201** E3
La Junta Mex. **184** D2
La Junta U.S.A. **178** B4
La Juventud, Isla de i. Cuba **186** C2
formerly known as Pines, Isle of or Pinos, Isla de
Lakadiya India **96** A5
L'Akagera, Parc National de nat. park Rwanda see **Akagera National Park**
Lakathah Saudi Arabia **104** C4
Lakatrâsk Sweden **44** M2
Lake KY U.S.A. **176** B8
Lake WY U.S.A. **180** E3
Lake Alice N.Z. **152** J8
Lake Andes U.S.A. **178** C3
Lake Arthur U.S.A. **179** D6
Lake Butler U.S.A. **175** D6
Lake Cargelligo Australia **147** E3
Lake Charles U.S.A. **179** D6
Lake City AR U.S.A. **174** B5
Lake City CO U.S.A. **181** F5
Lake City FL U.S.A. **175** D6
Lake City IA U.S.A. **178** D3
Lake City MN U.S.A. **168** A4
Lake City SC U.S.A. **175** E5
Lake City TN U.S.A. **176** A9
Lake Clark National Park and Preserve U.S.A. **164** D3
Lake Clear U.S.A. **177** K1
Lake Coleridge N.Z. **153** F11
Lake Cowichan Canada **166** E5
Lake District National Park U.K. **47** I9
Lake Eyre National Park Australia **146** C2
Lakefield Australia **149** E2
Lakefield Canada **168** E4
Lakefield National Park Australia **149** E2
Lake Fork r. U.S.A. **183** O1
Lake Frome Regional Reserve nature res. Australia **146** C2
Lake Gairdner National Park Australia **146** B2
Lake Geneva U.S.A. **172** E8
Lake Gilles Conservation Park nature res. Australia **146** C2
Lake Grace Australia **151** B7
Lake Gregory Aboriginal Reserve Australia **150** D4
Lake Harbour Canada see **Kimmirut**
Lake Havasu City U.S.A. **183** J7
Lake Hurst U.S.A. **177** K5
Lake Isabella U.S.A. **182** F6
Lake Jackson U.S.A. **179** D6
Lake King Australia **151** B7
Lake King Nature Reserve Australia **151** B7
Lakeland Australia **149** E2
Lakeland FL U.S.A. **175** D6
Lakeland GA U.S.A. **175** D6
Lake Linden U.S.A. **172** E3
Lake Louise Canada **167** G5
Lake Mackay Aboriginal Land res. Australia **148** A4
Lake Magenta Nature Reserve Australia **151** B7
Lake Manyara National Park Tanz. **128** B5
Lake Mburo National Park Uganda **128** A5
Lake Mills U.S.A. **174** A3
Lake Nash Australia **148** C4
Lake Paringa N.Z. **153** D11
Lake Placid U.S.A. **177** L1
Lakeport CA U.S.A. **182** B4
Lakeport MI U.S.A. **173** K7
Lake Pukaki N.Z. **153** E12
Lakeview OH U.S.A. **176** B5
Lakeview OR U.S.A. **180** B4
Lake Village U.S.A. **175** B5
Lakeville U.S.A. **174** A2
Lake Wales U.S.A. **175** D7
Lakewood CO U.S.A. **180** F5
Lakewood OH U.S.A. **176** D4
Lakewood WI U.S.A. **172** E5
Lakhdaria Alg. **55** O8
Lakhdenpokh'ya Rus. Fed. **45** O3
Lakheri India **96** C4
Lakhimpur India **96** D4
Lakhipur India **97** G4
Lakhisarai India see **Luckeesarai**
Lakhish r. Israel **108** F6
Lakhnadon India **96** C5
Lakhpat India **96** A5
Lakhtar India **96** A5
Lakhva r. Belarus **43** L8
Lakin U.S.A. **178** B4
Lakinsk Rus. Fed. **43** U5
formerly known as Lakinskiy
Lakinskiy Rus. Fed. see **Lakinsk**
Lakitusaki r. Canada **168** D2
Lakki Pak. **101** G3
Lakkoma Greece **59** G8
Lakonikos Kolpos b. Greece **59** D12
Lakor i. Indon. **75** C5
Laksefjorden sea chan. Norway **44** N1
Lakselv Norway **44** N1
Laksfors Norway **44** K2
Lakshadweep is India see **Laccadive Islands**
Lakshadweep union terr. India **94** B4
formerly known as Laccadive, Minicoy and Amindivi Islands
Laksham Bangl. **97** F5
Lakshettipet India **94** C2
Lakshmeshwar India **94** B3
Lakshmikantapur India **97** F5
Lakshmipur India **97** F5
Laktyshy Vodaskhovishcha resr Belarus **42** H9
Lala Phil. **74** C5
Lalago Tanz. **128** B5
La Laguna Arg. **204** E4
La Laguna, Picacho de mt. Mex. **184** C4
La Laguna Ojo de Liebre, Parque Natural de nature res. Mex. **184** B3
Lala Musa Pak. **101** H3
Lalapanzi Zimbabwe **131** F3
Lalapaşa Turkey **58** H7
Lalara Gabon **126** A4
Lalaua Moz. **131** H2
L'Albufera l. Spain **55** K5
La Libertad Ecuador **198** A5
La Libertad El Salvador **185** H6
La Libertad Guat. **185** H5
La Libertad Nicaragua **186** B4
La Libertad dept Peru **200** A2
La Ligua Chile **204** C3
Laliki Indon. **75** B3
Lalimboee Indon. **75** B3
Lalin China **82** B3
Lalín r. China **82** B3
Lalín Spain **54** C2
Lalinde France **50** G4
La Línea de la Concepción Spain **54** F8
Lalitpur India **96** C4
Lalitpur Nepal see **Patan**
Lal-Lo Phil. **74** B2
Lalmanirhat Bangl. **97** F4
Lalmikor Uzbek. see **Lyal'mikar**
La Loche Canada **167** I3
La Loche, Lac l. Canada **167** I3
La Loire et de l'Allier, Plaines de plain France **51** J6
La Loma Bol. **201** D5
La Loma Negra, Planicie de plain Arg. **204** D5
La Loupe France **50** H4
La Louvière Belgium **51** K2
Lalpur India **96** A5
Lal'sk Rus. Fed. **40** H3
Lalsot India **96** C4
La Lufira, Lac de retenue de resr Dem. Rep. Congo **127** E7
Laluni r. Indon. **75** C3
Lalung La pass China **89** D6
Lama Bazar India **97** G5
La Macarena, Parque Nacional nat. park Col. **198** C4
La Maddalena Sardegna Italy **56** B7
La Madeleine, Îles de is Canada **169** I4
Lamag Sabah Malaysia **77** G1
La Maiko, Parc National de nat. park Dem. Rep. Congo **126** D5
Lamaing Myanmar **79** B5
La Malbaie Canada **169** G4
La Malinche, Parque Nacional nat. park Mex. **185** F5
La Mancha Mex. **185** F5
La Mancha strait France/U.K. see **English Channel**
La Manga del Mar Menor Spain **55** K7
La Manika, Plateau de Dem. Rep. Congo **127** E7
Landes de Gascogne, Parc Naturel Régional des nature res. France **50** F8
Landes de Lanvaux reg. France **50** D5
Landes du Mené reg. France **50** D4
Landfall Island India **95** G3
Landi, Gunung mt. Indon. **76** C3
Landis Canada **167** I4
Landivisiau France **50** B4
Landless Corner Zambia **127** F8
Land O' Lakes U.S.A. **172** C4
Landón Sweden **44** K3
Landor Australia **151** B5
Landquart Switz. **51** P5
Landrienne Canada **173** P2
La Mauricie, Parc National de nat. park Canada **169** F4
La Matanzilla, Pampa de plain Arg. **204** C5
La Maya Cuba **186** D2
Lamballe France **50** D4
Lambaréné Gabon **126** A5
Lambayeque Peru **198** B6
Lambayeque dept Peru **198** B6
Lambay Island Rep. of Ireland **47** G10
Lambeng Indon. **77** F3
Lambert atoll Marshall Is see **Ailinglapalap**
Lambert, Cape Australia **150** B4
► Lambert Glacier Antarctica **223** E2
Largest of glaciers in the world.
Lambert's Bay S. Africa **132** C9
Lamberville U.S.A. **177** K5
Lambeth Canada **173** L8
Lambi India **96** B3
Lambina Australia **146** B1
Lambro r. Italy **56** B3
Lam Chi r. Thai. **78** D5
Lam Chi r. Thai. **79** C5
La Media Luna, Arrecife de reef Hond. **186** C4
La Medjerda, Monts de mts Alg. **57** A12
Lamego Port. **54** D3
La Mejorada Peru **200** B3
Lamen Vanuatu **145** F3
Lamèque, Île l. Canada **169** H4
Lameroo Australia **146** D3
La Mesa U.S.A. **183** G9
Lamesa U.S.A. **179** B5
L'Ametlla de Mar Spain **55** L4
Lamezia Italy **57** I10
Lamhar Touil, Sabkhet imp. l. W. Sahara **122** A5
Lamia Greece **59** D10
Lamigan Point Phil. **74** C5
Lamington National Park Australia **147** G2
Lamir Iran **100** B2
La Mirada U.S.A. **182** F8
formerly known as Mirada Hills
La Misa Mex. **184** C2
La Misión Mex. **183** H9
Lamitan Phil. **74** B5
Lamma Island Hong Kong China **87** [inset]
also known as Pok Liu Chau
Lammerkop S. Africa **133** N2
Lammerlaw Range mts N.Z. **153** D13
Lammermuir Hills U.K. **46** J8
Lammhult Sweden **45** K4
Lammi Fin. **45** N3
Lammijärv lake channel Estonia/Rus. Fed. **42** I3
La Moille U.S.A. **172** D9
Lamoille r. U.S.A. **177** L1
La Mojonera Spain **55** I8
Lamon Bay Phil. **74** B3
Lamone r. Italy **56** E4
Lamongan Indon. **77** F4
Lamoni U.S.A. **174** A3
Lamont U.S.A. **182** F6
La Montagne d'Ambre, Parc National de nat. park Madag. **131** [inset] K2
La Montagne de Reims, Parc Naturel Régional de nature res. France **51** J3
La Morita Mex. **184** D2
La Morita Coahuila Mex. **179** B6
La Motte France **51** M6
La Motte Canada **173** O2
Lamotek atoll Micronesia **73** L5
Lamotte-Beuvron France **51** I5
La Motte-Servolex France **51** L7
La Mougalaba, Réserve de nature res. Gabon **126** A5
La Moure U.S.A. **178** C2
Lampa Peru **200** C3
Lampang Thai. **78** B4
Lam Pao Reservoir Thai. **78** C4
Lampasas U.S.A. **179** C6
Lampasas r. U.S.A. **179** C6
Lampazos Mex. **185** E3
Lampedusa, Isola di i. Sicilia Italy **57** E13
Lampeland Norway **45** J4
Lampeter U.K. **47** H11
Lamphun Thai. **78** B4
Lam Plai Mat r. Thai. **79** C5
Lampozhnya Rus. Fed. **40** H2
Lampsacus Turkey see **Lâpseki**
Lampung prov. Indon. **76** C4
Lampung, Teluk b. Indon. **76** D4
Lamu Kenya **128** D5
Lamu Myanmar **78** A4
Lana Australia **149** D4
Lana r. Albania **58** A8
Lanai i. U.S.A. **181** [inset] Z1
also known as Ranai
Lanai City U.S.A. **181** [inset] Z1
Lanak La pass China **89** C5
Lanao, Lake Phil. **74** C5
Lanark Canada **173** Q5
Lanark U.K. **46** I8
Lanark U.S.A. **172** D8
Lanas Sabah Malaysia **77** G1
Lanbi Kyun i. Myanmar **79** B6
Lanboyan Point Phil. **74** B4
Lancang China **86** A4
also known as Menglang
Lancang Jiang r. China see **Mekong**
Lancaster U.K. **47** J9
Lancaster CA U.S.A. **182** F7
Lancaster KY U.S.A. **176** A8
Lancaster MO U.S.A. **174** A4
Lancaster NH U.S.A. **177** N1
Lancaster OH U.S.A. **176** C6
Lancaster PA U.S.A. **177** I5
Lancaster SC U.S.A. **174** D5
Lancaster VA U.S.A. **177** I8
Lancaster WI U.S.A. **172** C8
Lancaster Sound strait Canada **165** J2
Lancelin Australia **151** A6
L'Anse U.S.A. **172** E3
L'Anse-St-Jean Canada **169** G4
Lansford U.S.A. **177** J5
Lansing r. Canada **166** C2
Lansing IA U.S.A. **172** B7
► Lansing MI U.S.A. **173** I8
State capital of Michigan.
Länsi-Suomi prov. Fin. **44** M3
Lansjärv Sweden **44** M2
Lanta, Ko i. Thai. **79** B6
Lantau Island Hong Kong China **87** [inset]
also known as Tai Yue Shan
Lantau Peak hill Hong Kong China **87** [inset]
also known as Fung Wong Shan
Lanterne r. France **51** M5
Lantian China **87** D1
also known as Languan
Lanusei Sardegna Italy **57** B9
Lanuza Phil. **74** C4
Lanuza Bay Phil. **74** C4
Lanxi Heilong. China **82** B3
Lanxi Zhejiang China **87** F2
Lanxi China **85** I4
also known as Dongcun
Lanya Sudan **128** A3
Lanyi r. China **85** F4
Lan Yü i. Taiwan **87** G4
Lanzarote i. Canary Is **122** B3
Lanzhou China **84** D4
also spelt Lanchow
Lanzijing China **85** I2
Lanzo Torinese Italy **51** N7
Lao r. Italy **57** H9
Lao, Mae r. Thai. **78** B4
Laoag Phil. **74** B2
Laoang Phil. **74** C3
Laobie Shan mts China **86** A4
Laocheng China see **Yumen**
Lao Cai Vietnam **78** D3
Laodicea Syria see **Latakia**
Laodicea Turkey see **Denizli**
Laodicea ad Lycum Turkey see **Denizli**
Laodicea ad Mare Syria see **Latakia**
Laofengkou China **88** C2
Laoha He r. China **85** I3
Laoheishan China **82** C4
Laohekou China **87** D1
formerly known as Guanghua
Laojunmiao China see **Yumen**
Lao Ling mts China **82** B4
Laolong China see **Longchuan**
Laon France **51** J3
Laona U.S.A. **172** E5
La Oroya Peru **200** B2
Laos country Asia **78** C4
Laoshan China **85** I4
also known as Licun
Laotieshan Shuidao sea chan. China see **Bohai Haixia**
Laotougou China **82** C4
Laoximiao China **84** D3
Laoye Ling mts China **82** C4
Lapa Brazil **203** B8
Lapac i. Phil. **74** B5
Lapai Nigeria **125** G4
Lapalisse France **51** J6
La Palma i. Canary Is **122** A3
La Palma Panama **186** D5
La Palma U.S.A. **183** M9
La Palma del Condado Spain **54** E7
La Paloma Uruguay **204** G4
La Pampa prov. Arg. **204** D5
formerly known as Eva Perón
La Panza Range mts U.S.A. **182** D6
La Paragua Venez. **199** F3
La Paramera, Puerto de pass Spain **54** F4
La Paramera, Sierra de mts Spain **54** F4
Laparan i. Phil. **74** B5
La Parata, Pointe de pt Corse France **56** A7
La Paya, Parque Nacional nat. park Col. **198** C4
La Paz Entre Ríos Arg. **204** F3
La Paz Mendoza Arg. **204** D4
► La Paz Bol. **200** C4
Official capital of Bolivia.
world [countries] ▶▶▶ 10–11
southamerica [contrasts] ▶▶▶ 194–195
La Paz dept Bol. **200** C3
La Paz Hond. **186** B4
La Paz Mex. **184** C3
La Paz Nicaragua **186** B4
Lapaz U.S.A. **172** G9
La Paz, Bahía b. Mex. **184** C3
La Pedrera Col. **198** D5
Lapeer U.S.A. **173** J7
La Pelada Arg. **204** E3
La Peña Panama **186** C5
La Pendjari, Parc National de nat. park Benin **125** F4
La Perla Mex. **184** D2
La Pérouse Strait Japan/Rus. Fed. **90** G2
also known as Sõya-kaikyõ
La Pesca Mex. **185** F4
La Piedad Mex. **185** E4
La Pila, Sierra de mts Spain **55** J6
La Pine U.S.A. **180** B4
Lapinig Phil. **74** C4
Lapinlahti Fin. **44** N3
La Pintada Panama **186** C5
Laplace U.S.A. **175** B6
Lap Lae Thai. **78** C4
La Plaine Dominica **187** H4
La Plata Arg. **204** F4
formerly known as Eva Perón
La Plata MD U.S.A. **177** I7
La Plata MO U.S.A. **174** B4
La Plata, Río de sea chan. Arg./Uruguay **204** F4
La Plonge, Lac l. Canada **167** J4
Lapmezciems Latvia **42** E4
La Pobla de Segur Spain **55** L2
La Pola de Gordón Spain **54** F2
La Poma Arg. **200** D6
Lapominka Rus. Fed. **40** G2
La Porte U.S.A. **174** C4
Laporte U.S.A. **177** I4
Laposo, Bukit mt. Indon. **75** A4
La Potherie, Lac l. Canada **169** F1
Lapovo Srbija Yugo. **58** C4
La Poyata Col. **198** C3
Lappajärvi Fin. **44** M3
Lappajärvi l. Fin. **44** M3
Lappi Fin. **45** M3
Lappi reg. Fin. **44** L2
Lappohja Fin. **42** E1
Lappträsk Sweden **44** M2
Laprida Arg. **204** E5
La Pryor U.S.A. **179** C6
Lâpseki Turkey **106** A2
historically known as Lampsacus
Laptev Sea Rus. Fed. **39** M2
also known as Laptevykh, More
Laptevykh, More sea Rus. Fed. see **Laptev Sea**
Lapua Fin. **44** M3
Lapuanjoki r. Fin. **44** M3
La Puebla Spain see **Sa Pobla**
La Puebla del Río Spain **54** E7
La Puebla de Montalbán Spain **54** G5
La Puerta Catamarca Arg. **204** D3
La Puerta Córdoba Arg. **204** D3
La Puerta Venez. **198** D2
Lapu-Lapu Phil. **74** B4
La Punilla, Cordillera de mts Chile **204** C3
Lapurdum France see **Bayonne**
La Push U.S.A. **180** A3
La Quiaca Arg. **200** D6
La Quinta U.S.A. **183** H8
Lâr Iran **100** C5
Lara Australia **147** E4
Lara state Venez. **198** D2
Laracha Spain **54** C1
Larache Morocco **122** C1
formerly spelt El Araïche; historically known as Lixus
Laragne-Montéglin France **51** L8
Lārak i. Iran **100** D5
Laramie U.S.A. **180** F4
Laramie r. U.S.A. **180** F4
Laramie Mountains U.S.A. **180** F4
Laranda Turkey see **Karaman**
Laranjal Brazil **199** G6
Laranjal Paulista Brazil **206** F10
Laranjeiras Brazil **202** E5
Laranjeiras do Sul Brazil **203** A8
Laranjinha r. Brazil **206** D9
Larantuka Indon. **75** B5
Larat i. Indon. **73** H8
Larat Indon. **73** I8
Larba Alg. **55** O8
L'Arbresle France **51** K7
Lårbro Sweden **45** L4
L'Archipélago de Mingan, Réserve du Parc National de nat. park Canada **169** I3
Larder r. Plateau de Belgium see **Ardennes**
Larder Lake Canada **173** N2
Larder Lake l. Canada **173** N2
Laredo Spain **55** H1
Laredo U.S.A. **179** C7
La Reforma Sonora Mex. **181** F7
La Reforma Veracruz Mex. **185** F4
La Reina Adelaida, Archipiélago de is Chile **205** B9
English form Queen Adelaide Islands
La Reine Canada **173** N2
La Réole France **50** F8
Largeau Chad see **Faya**
L'Argentière-la-Bessée France **51** M8
Largo U.S.A. **175** D7
Largo, Cayo i. Cuba **186** C2
Largs U.K. **46** H8
Lārī Iran **100** A2
Laoximiao China **84** D3
Laoye Ling mts China **82** C4
Laowohi pass Jammu and Kashmir see **Khardung La**
Laoximiao China **84** D3
Laoye Ling strait China **82** C4
Lapa Brazil **203** B8
Lapac i. Phil. **74** B5
Lapachito Arg. **204** F2
La Rinconada Spain **54** F7
Larino Italy **56** G7
La Rioja Arg. **204** D3
La Rioja prov. Arg. **204** D3
La Rioja aut. comm. Spain **55** I2
Larionovo Rus. Fed. **43** L1
Larisa Greece **59** D9
also known as Yenişehir; also spelt Larissa
Larissa Greece see **Larisa**
Laristan reg. Iran **100** D5
Larkana Pak. **101** G5
Lark Harbour Canada **169** J3
Lar Koh mt. Afgh. **101** E3
Lark Passage Australia **149** E2
L'Arli, Parc National de nat. park Burkina **125** F4
L'Arli, Réserve Partielle de nature res. Burkina **125** F4
Larnaca Cyprus **108** E3
also spelt Larnaka
Larnaka Cyprus see **Larnaca**
Larne U.K. **47** G9
Larned U.S.A. **178** C4
Laro Cameroon **125** I4
La Robe Noire, Lac de l. Canada **169** I3
La Robla Spain **54** F2
La Roche-en-Ardenne Belgium **51** L2
La Rochelle France **50** E6
La Roche-sur-Yon France **50** E6
La Roda Spain **55** I5
La Romana Dom. Rep. **187** F3
La Ronge Canada **167** J4
La Ronge, Lac l. Canada **167** J4
La Rosa Mex. **185** E3
La Rosa de Castilla Mex. **183** H9
La Rosita Mex. **185** E2
Larouco, Serra do mts Spain **54** D3
Larrey Point Australia **150** B4
Larrimah Australia **148** B2
Larrimah Aboriginal Land res. Australia **148** B2
Lars Christensen Coast Antarctica **223** E2
► Larsen Ice Shelf Antarctica **222** T2
antarctica [features] ▶▶▶ 212–213
Larsnes Norway **44** I3
La Rubia Arg. **204** E3
Larvik Norway **45** J4
Lar'yak Rus. Fed. **39** I3
Larzac, Causse du plat. France **51** J8
La Sabana Arg. **204** F2
La Sabana Col. **198** D3
Las Adjuntas, Presa de resr Mex. **185** F4
La Sal U.S.A. **183** O3
La Sal, Cerros de mts Peru **200** B2
La Sal Junction U.S.A. **183** O3
La Salle Canada **169** J3
La Salle U.S.A. **174** C3
La Salonga Nord, Parc National de nat. park Dem. Rep. Congo **126** D5
La Salonga Sud, Parc National de nat. park Dem. Rep. Congo **126** D5
Las Animas U.S.A. **178** B4
Las Animas, Punta pt Mex. **184** B2
Las Anod Somalia see **Laascaanood**
La Sarre Canada **168** E3
La Sauvette hill France **51** M9
Las Aves, Islas is West Indies **187** G5
short form Aves
Las Avispas Mex. **184** C2
La Savonnière, Lac l. Canada **169** F2
Las Bonitas Venez. **199** E3
Las Breñas Arg. **204** E2
Las Chapas Arg. **205** D6
La Scie Canada **169** J3
Las Conchas Bol. **182** D7
Las Cruces Mex. **184** C2
Las Cruces CA U.S.A. **182** D7
Las Cruces NM U.S.A. **181** F6
La Selle mt. Haiti **187** E3
La Serena Chile **204** C3
Las Serena, Embalse de resr Spain **54** F6
Las Esperanzas Mex. **185** E3
Las Estancias, Sierra de mts Spain **55** I7
Las Flores Buenos Aires Arg. **204** F5
Las Flores Salta Arg. **200** D6
Lashburn Canada **167** I4
Las Heras Arg. **204** D4
Las Hermosas, Parque Nacional nat. park Col. **198** C3
Las Herreras Mex. **184** D3
Las Martinetas Arg. **205** D7
Lashio Myanmar **78** B3
Lashkar Gāh Afgh. **101** F4
Las Horquetas Arg. **205** C8
La Sila reg. Italy **57** I9
Łasin Poland **49** Q2
Las Juntas Chile **204** C2
Las Lajas Arg. **204** C5
Las Lajitas Venez. **199** E3
Las Lavaderos Mex. **185** F4
Las Lomas Peru **198** A4
Las Lomitas Arg. **201** E5
Las Marismas marsh Spain **54** E7
Las Martinetas Arg. **205** D7
Las Médulas tourist site Spain **54** E2
Las Mercedes Venez. **199** E2
Las Mesteñas Mex. **184** D2
Las Minas Venez. **199** E2
Las Minas, Sierra de mts Guat. **185** H6
Las Mulatas is Panama see **San Blas, Archipiélago de**
Las Nieves Mex. **184** D3
Las Nopaleras, Cerro mt. Mex. **185** E3
La Solana Spain **55** H6
Lasolo, r. Indon. **75** B3
Las Orquideas, Parque Nacional nat. park Col. **198** B3
La Souterraine France **50** H6
Las Ovejas Arg. **204** C5
Las Palmas watercourse Mex. **183** G9
Las Palmas Panama **186** C5
► Las Palmas de Gran Canaria Canary Is **122** A3
Joint capital of the Canary Islands.
Las Perlas, Archipiélago de is Panama **186** D5
Las Petas Bol. **201** F4
La Spezia Italy **56** B4
Las Piedras Uruguay **204** F4
Las Piedras, Río de r. Peru **200** C3
Las Pipinas Arg. **204** F4
Las Planchas Hond. **186** B4
Las Plumas Arg. **205** D6
Laspur Pak. **101** H3
Las Rosas Arg. **204** E3
Las Rozas de Madrid Spain **54** H4
Las Salinas, Pampa de salt pan Arg. **204** D3
Lassance Brazil **207** I4
Lassay-les-Châteaux France **50** F4
Lassen Peak vol. U.S.A. **182** C1
Lassen Volcanic National Park U.S.A. **182** C1
Las Tablas Panama **186** C6
Las Tablas de Daimiel, Parque Nacional nat. park Chile **205** C9
Last Chance U.S.A. **178** B4
Las Termas Arg. **204** D2
Last Mountain Lake Canada **167** J5
Las Torres de Cotillas Spain **55** J6
Las Tórtolas, Cerro mt. Chile **204** C3

index

L

Lastoursville Gabon 126 B5
Lastovo i. Croatia 56 I6
Lastovski Kanal sea chan. Croatia 56 I6
Las Tres Vírgenes, Volcán vol. Mex. 184 B3
Las Trincheras Venez. 199 E3
Las Tunas Cuba 186 D2
Lasva Estonia 42 G5
Las Varas Col. 199 D3
Las Varas Chihuahua Mex. 184 D2
Las Varas Nayarit Mex. 184 D4
Las Varas Venez. 198 D3
Las Varillas Arg. 204 E3
Las Vegas NM U.S.A. 181 F6
Las Vegas NV U.S.A. 183 I5
Las Villuercas mt. Spain 54 E5
Las Yaras Peru 200 C4
Lata Solomon Is 145 F3
Latacunga Ecuador 198 B5
La Tagua Col. 186 C5
Latakia Syria 108 G2
  also known as Lattaquié; also spelt
  Al Lādhiqīyah; historically known as
  Laodicea or Laodicea ad Mare
Latalata i. Indon. 75 C3
Latchford Canada 173 N3
Latehar India 97 E5
La Teignouse, Passage de strait France 50 C5
Latemar mt. Italy 56 D2
La Teste France 50 E8
La Tetilla, Cerro mt. Mex. 184 D4
Latgales Augstiene reg. Latvia 42 I5
Latham Australia 151 B6
Lathi India 96 A5
Lathrop U.S.A. 182 C4
Lātīdān Iran 100 C5
Latimojong Mountains Reserve nature res. Indon. 75 B3
Latina Italy 56 I6
Latisana Italy 56 F3
La Toma Arg. 204 D4
La Tortue, Île de i. Haiti 187 E2
La Tortuga, Isla i. Venez. 199 E2
Latoritsya r. Ukr. 49 T7
Latouche Treville, Cape Australia 150 C3
Latouma well Niger 123 I3
La Tour-du-Pin France 51 L7
La Tranquera, Embalse de resr Spain 55 J3
La Tremblade France 50 E7
La Trinidad Nicaragua 186 B4
La Trinidad Phil. 74 B2
La Trinitaria Mex. 185 G5
La Trinité France 51 N9
Latrobe Australia 147 E5
Latrobe U.S.A. 176 F5
Latronico Italy 57 I8
La Troya r. Arg. 204 D3
La Truite, Lac à l. Canada 173 O3
Latskoye Rus. Fed. 43 T3
Lattaquié Syria see Latakia
Latte Island Tonga see Late Island
Lattes France 51 J9
Latulipe Canada 173 N3
La Tuque Canada 169 F4
Latur India 94 C2
Latvia country Europe 42 E5
  spelt Latvija in Latvian; also known as
  Latviyskaya S.S.R.
  europe [countries] 32–35
Latvija country Europe see Latvia
Latviyskaya S.S.R. country Europe see Latvia
Lau Nigeria 125 H4
Lau r. Sudan 128 A3
Laua r. India 97 E5
Lauban waterhole Namibia 130 D3
Lauca, Parque Nacional nat. park Chile 200 C4
Lauenburg (Elbe) Germany 48 H2
Lauf an der Pegnitz Germany 48 I6
Laufen Germany 49 J8
Laufen Switz. 51 N5
Laugarbakki Iceland 44 [inset] B2
Lauge Koch Kyst reg. Greenland 165 M2
Laughland Lake Canada 167 M1
Laughlin, Mount Australia 148 B4
Laughlin Peak U.S.A. 181 F5
Lauhanvuoren kansallispuisto nat. park Fin. 45 M3
Lauka Estonia 42 D3
Laukaa Fin. 44 N3
Laukuva Lith. 42 D6
Laun Thai. 79 B6
Launay Canada 173 O2
Launceston Australia 147 E5
Launceston U.K. 47 H13
Launglon Myanmar 79 B5
Launglon Bok Islands Myanmar 79 B5
La Unidad Mex. 185 G6
La Unión Bol. 201 E3
La Unión Chile 204 B6
La Unión Col. 198 C4
La Unión El Salvador 185 I6
La Unión Hond. 186 B4
La Unión Mex. 185 E5
La Unión Huánuco Peru 200 A2
La Unión Piura Peru 198 A6
Laur Phil. 74 B3
Laura Australia 149 E2
La Urbana Venez. 199 E3
Laurel DE U.S.A. 177 J7
Laurel MS U.S.A. 175 B6
Laurel MT U.S.A. 180 E3
Laureldale U.S.A. 177 J5
Laureles Para. 201 F4
Laurel Hill U.S.A. 176 F6
Laurencekirk U.K. 46 J7
Laurens IA U.S.A. 178 C3
Laurens SC U.S.A. 174 D5

Laurentides, Réserve Faunique des nature res. Canada 169 G4
Lauri India 96 D4
Lauria Italy 57 H8
Laurie Island S. Atlantic Ocean 222 V2
Laurinburg U.S.A. 174 E5
Lauriston N.Z. 153 F11
Laurium U.S.A. 172 E3
Lauru i. Solomon Is see Choiseul
Lausanne Switz. 51 M6
Lausitzer Grenzwall park Germany 49 L6
Laut i. Indon. 77 E1
Laut i. Indon. 77 E3
Laut i. Indon. 77 E3
Laut, Selat sea chan. Indon. 77 F3
Lauta Germany 49 L4
Lautaro Chile 204 B5
Lautaro, Cerro vol. Chile 205 B8
Lautem East Timor 75 C5
Lauterbrunnen Switz. 51 N6
Lauterbach (Hessen) Germany 48 G5
Lauvuskylä Fin. 44 P3
Lauwersmeer l. Neth. 48 D2
Lava r. Rus. Fed. 49 S1
Lava Beds National Monument nat. park U.S.A. 180 B4
Lavaca r. U.S.A 179 C6
Laval Canada 169 F4
Laval France 50 F4
Lavalette U.S.A. 176 C7
Lāvān i. Iran 100 C5
La Vanoise, Massif de mts France 51 M7
La Vanoise, Parc National de nat. park France 51 M7
Lavant r. Austria/Slovenia 49 L9
Lavapié, Punta pt Chile 204 B5
Lāvar Iran 100 C4
Lavara Greece 58 H7
Lavaray Madag. 131 [inset] J4
Lavardac France 50 G8
Lävar Meydān salt marsh Iran 100 C4
La Vassako-Bolo, Réserve National Intégral de nature res. Cent. Afr. Rep. 126 C2
Lavaur France 50 H9
Laveaga Peak U.S.A. 182 C5
La Vega Dom. Rep. 187 F3
La Vela Venez. 187 F5
La Vela, Cabo de c. Col. 198 C1
Lavello Italy 56 H7
La Venada r. Mex. 179 B6
Laveno Italy 56 A3
La Venta Hond. 186 B4
La Ventana, Sierra de mts Arg. 204 E5
Laventie France 51 N7
La Venturosa Col. 198 D3
La Vérendrye, Réserve Faunique de nature res. Canada 168 E4
Laverne U.S.A. 178 C4
Laverton Australia 151 C6
Lavia Fin. 45 M3
La Vibora Mex. 185 E3
La Victoria Venez. 187 G5
Lavieille, Lake Canada 173 O5
Lavigne Canada 173 M4
La Viña Arg. 204 D2
La Viña Peru 198 B6
Lavina U.S.A. 180 E3
La Virgen, Sierra de mts Spain 55 J3
Lavit France 50 G8
La Vôge reg. France 51 M8
Lavongai i. P.N.G. see New Hanover
Lavoriškes Lith. 42 G7
La Voulte-sur-Rhône France 51 K8
Lavras Brazil 203 C7
Lavrov Orlovskaya Oblast' Rus. Fed. 43 R9
Lavrovo Vologod. Obl. Rus. Fed. 43 S2
Lavumisa Swaziland 133 P4
  formerly known as Gollel
Lavushi-Manda National Park Zambia 127 F8
Lawa r. Liberia 124 C5
Lawa Myanmar 78 B2
Lawagamau r. Canada 168 E3
Lawan India 97 D5
Lawang i. Indon. 77 G5
Lawashi r. Canada 168 D2
Lawdar Yemen 105 D5
Law Dome ice feature Antarctica 223 H2
Lawele Indon. 75 B4
Lawik Reef P.N.G. 149 G1
Lawit, Gunung mt. Indon./Malaysia 77 F2
Lawit, Gunung mt. Malaysia 76 C1
Lawksawk Myanmar 78 B3
Lawn Hill Australia 148 C3
Lawn Hill Creek r. Australia 148 C3
Lawn Hill National Park Australia 148 C3
Lawqah Saudi Arabia 107 E5
Lawra waterhole Saudi Arabia 121 I2
Lawra Ghana 124 E4
Lawrence N.Z. 153 D13
Lawrence KS U.S.A. 178 D4
Lawrence MA U.S.A. 177 N3
Lawrenceburg KY U.S.A. 176 A7
Lawrenceburg TN U.S.A. 174 C5
Lawrenceville IL U.S.A. 174 C4
Lawrenceville NJ U.S.A. 177 K5
Lawrenceville PA U.S.A. 177 H4
Lawrenceville VA U.S.A. 176 H9
Lawrence Wells, Mount hill Australia 151 C5
Lawton U.S.A. 179 C5
Lawu, Gunung vol. Indon. 77 E4
Lawz, Jabal al mt. Saudi Arabia 104 A1
Laxá Sweden 45 K4
Laxey U.K. 47 J10
Lax Kw'alaams Canada 166 D4
  formerly known as Port Simpson
Laya r. France 50 E6
Laya r. Rus. Fed. 40 K2
Layar, Tanjung pt Indon. 77 G4
La Yarada Peru 200 C4
La Yata-Ngaya, Réserve de Faune de nature res. Cent. Afr. Rep. 126 D2
Laydennyy, Mys c. Rus. Fed. 40 H1
Layeni Indon. 75 D4
Laylá Saudi Arabia 105 D3
Layla salt pan Saudi Arabia 109 J6
Laylān Iraq 100 A3
Layon r. France 50 F5
L'Ayrolle, Étang de lag. France 51 J9
Laysan Island U.S.A. 221 G4
Laytonville U.S.A. 182 A1
La Zacatosa, Picacho mt. Mex. 184 C4
Lazarev Rus. Fed. 82 F1
  formerly known as Mys Lazareva
Lazarevac Srbija Yugo. 58 B4
Lazarevo Rus. Fed. 43 S4
Lazarevskoye Rus. Fed. 107 D2
Lázaro, Sierra de San mts Mex. 184 C4
Lázaro Cárdenas Baja California Norte Mex. 184 B2
Lázaro Cárdenas Baja California Norte Mex. 184 B2
Lázaro Cárdenas Michoacán Mex. 185 E5
Lazcano Uruguay 204 G4
Lazdijai Lith. 42 E7
Lazinki Rus. Fed. 43 P7
Lazio admin. reg. Italy 56 E6
Lazise Italy 56 C3
Lazo r. Arg. 204 F4
Lazo Rus. Fed. 82 D4
Lazo Rus. Fed. 39 N3
La Zorra watercourse Mex. 179 B6

Leach Island Canada 173 I3
Leader Canada 167 I5
Leadville U.S.A. 180 F5
Leaf r. U.S.A. 175 B6
Leaf Bay Canada see Tasiujaq
Leaf Rapids Canada 167 K3
Leahy, Mount hill Australia 150 D3
Leakesville U.S.A. 175 B6
Leakey U.S.A. 179 C6
Leal, Mount hill Australia 150 B4
Leales Arg. 204 D2
Leamington Canada 168 D5
Leamington Spa, Royal U.K. 47 K11
Le'an China 87 E3
  also known as Aoxi
Leandra S. Africa 133 M3
Leandro N. Alem Arg. 204 G2
Leanja Madag. 131 [inset] J2
Leasburg U.S.A. 176 F9
L'Eau Claire, Lac à l. Canada 169 F1
Leava Wallis and Futuna Is see Sigave
Leavenworth KS U.S.A. 178 D4
Leavenworth WA U.S.A. 180 B3
Leavitt Peak U.S.A. 182 E3
Łeba Poland 49 O1
Lebach Germany 48 D6
Lebak Phil. 74 C5
Lebaleng S. Africa 133 J4
Lebamba Gabon 126 A5
Lebane Srbija Yugo. 58 C6
Lebanon country Asia 108 G3
  spelt Lubnān in Arabic or Liban in French
  asia [countries] 64–67
Lebanon IN U.S.A. 174 C4
Lebanon MO U.S.A. 178 D4
Lebanon NH U.S.A. 177 M2
Lebanon NJ U.S.A. 177 K5
Lebanon OR U.S.A. 180 B3
Lebanon PA U.S.A. 177 I5
Lebanon TN U.S.A. 174 C4
Lebanon VA U.S.A. 176 C9
Lebap Turkm. 103 E4
Lebap Oblast admin. div. Turkm. see Lebapskaya Oblast'
Lebapskaya Oblast' admin. div. Turkm. 103 E5
  English form Lebap Oblast; formerly known as Chardzhouskaya Oblast'
Lebda tourist site Libya see Leptis Magna
Lebec U.S.A. 182 F7
Lebedin Ukr. see Lebedyn
Lebedyan' Rus. Fed. 43 U8
Lebedyn Ukr. 41 E6
  also spelt Lebedin
Lebel-sur-Quévillon Canada 168 E3
Lebioli ali well Eth. 128 E3
Le Blanc France 50 H6
Lebo Dem. Rep. Congo 126 D3
Lebomboberg hills Moz. see Lebombomtsberg
Lebombomtsberg hills Moz. 133 Q3
  also known as Lebomboberg
Lebonang S. Africa 133 M3
Lebork Poland 49 O1
Le Bourg-d'Oisans France 51 M7
Lebowakgomo S. Africa 131 F5
Lebrija Spain 54 E8
Łebsko, Jezioro lag. Poland 49 O1
Lebu Chile 204 B5
Le Bugue France 50 G8
Lebyazh'ye Kazakh. see Akku
Lebyazh'ye Kirovskaya Oblast' Rus. Fed. 40 I4
Lebyazh'ye Leningradskaya Oblast' Rus. Fed. 43 K2
Le Caire Egypt see Cairo
Lecce Italy 57 K8
Lecco Italy 56 B3
Lech r. Austria/Germany 48 H8
Lechaina Greece 59 C11
  also spelt Lekhainá
Lechang China 87 E3
Le Chasseron mt. Switz. 51 M6
Le Château-d'Oléron France 50 E7
Lechința Romania 58 F1
Lechtaler Alpen mts Austria 48 H8
Leck Germany 48 F1
Lecompte U.S.A. 179 D6
L'Écorce, Lac de l. Canada 173 Q3
Le Coteau France 51 K6
Le Creusot France 51 K6
Lectoure France 50 G8
Lecumberri Spain 55 J1
Łęczyca Poland 49 Q3
Ledang, Gunung mt. Malaysia 76 C2
Ledava r. Slovenia 56 I2
Ledbury U.K. 47 J11
Ledeč nad Sázavou Czech Rep. 49 M6
Ledengskoye Rus. Fed. 40 H4
Ledesma Spain 54 F3
Lediba Dem. Rep. Congo 126 C5
Ledmozero Rus. Fed. 44 P3
Ledong Hainan China 87 D5
  also known as Baoyou
Le Dorat France 50 H6
Ledu China 84 D4
  also known as Nianbai
Le Duffre mt. France 51 L8
Ledyanaya, Gora mt. Rus. Fed. 39 R3
Lee r. Rep. of Ireland 47 D12
Leechburg U.S.A. 176 F5
Leech Lake U.S.A. 178 D2
Leech Lake Indian Reservation res. U.S.A. 174 A2
Leeds U.K. 47 K10
Leenane Rep. of Ireland 47 C10
Leeper U.S.A. 176 F4
Leer (Ostfriesland) Germany 48 E2
Leesburg FL U.S.A. 175 D6
Leesburg GA U.S.A. 175 C6
Leesburg KY U.S.A. 176 A7
Leesburg OH U.S.A. 176 B6
Leesburg VA U.S.A. 176 H6
Lee Steere Range hills Australia 151 C5
Leeston N.Z. 153 G11
Leesville U.S.A. 179 D6
Leesville Lake U.S.A. 176 F8
Leeton Australia 147 E3
Leeudoringstad S. Africa 133 K4
Leeu-Gamka S. Africa 132 G8
Leeukop mt. S. Africa 133 J5
Leeuw r. S. Africa 133 L1
Leeuwarden Neth. 48 C2
Leeuwin, Cape Australia 151 A7
Lee Vining U.S.A. 182 E4
Leeward Islands Caribbean Sea 187 G3
Leewin-Naturaliste National Park Australia 151 A7
Le Faouët France 50 C4
Lefedha r. Bulg. 58 G5
Lefka Cyprus 108 D2
  also spelt Lefke
Lefkada Greece 59 B10
Lefkada i. Greece 59 B10
  also known as Lefkás; formerly known as
  Leukas; historically known as Leucas
Lefkás Greece see Lefkada
Lefke Cyprus see Lefka
Lefkimmi Greece 59 B9
  also spelt Levkími
Lefkosia Cyprus see Nicosia
Lefkoşa Cyprus see Nicosia

Lefroy, Lake salt flat Australia 151 C6
Leg r. Poland 49 S5
Legarde r. Canada 168 C3
Legaspi Phil. 74 B3
Legé France 50 E6
Leghorn Italy see Livorno
Legionowo Poland 49 R3
Legnago Italy 56 D3
Legnica Poland 49 N4
  historically known as Liegnitz
Legnone, Monte mt. Italy 56 B2
Le Grand U.S.A. 182 D4
Le Grand, Cape Australia 151 C7
Le Grand Coyer mt. France 51 M8
Le Grau-du-Roi France 51 K9
Leguena Chile 200 C5
Legune Australia 148 A2
Legwe r. Dem. Rep. Congo 126 E4
Leh Jammu and Kashmir 96 C2
Le Havre France 50 G3
Lehi U.S.A. 183 M1
Lehighton U.S.A. 177 J5
Lehliu-Gară Romania 58 H4
Lehlohonolo S. Africa 133 M7
Lehrte Germany 48 G3
Lehtimäki Fin. 44 N3
Leiah Pak. 101 G4
Leibnitz Austria 49 M9
Leibo China 86 B2
Leicester U.K. 47 K11
  historically known as Ratae
Leichhardt r. Australia 148 C3
Leichhardt Falls Australia 148 C3
Leichhardt Range mts Australia 149 E4
Leiden Neth. 48 B3
  historically known as Leyden
Leie r. Belgium 51 J1
Leie Estonia 42 H3
Leigh watercourse Australia 146 C2
Leigh Creek Australia 146 C2
Leighlinbridge Rep. of Ireland 47 F11
Leikanger Norway 45 I3
Leiktho Myanmar 78 B4
Leine r. Germany 48 G3
Leinefelde Germany 48 H4
Leinster Australia 151 C6
Leinster reg. Rep. of Ireland 47 F10
Leinster, Mount hill Rep. of Ireland 47 F11
Leipalingis Lith. 42 E7
Leipojärvi Sweden 44 M2
Leipsic U.S.A. 176 B4
Leipsoi i. Greece 59 H11
  also spelt Lipsoi
Leipzig Germany 49 K4
Leipzig-Halle airport Germany 49 J4
Leira Møre og Romsdal Norway 44 I3
Leira Oppland Norway 45 J3
Leiria Port. 54 C5
Leirbotn Norway 44 N1
Leirvik Sogn og Fjordane Norway 45 I3
Leishan China 87 D3
  also known as Danjiang
Lei Shui r. China 87 E3
Leisi Estonia 42 D3
Leisler, Mount hill Australia 148 A4
Leister Hills Australia 146 A2
Leitchfield U.S.A. 174 C5
Leithfield N.Z. 153 G11
Leivonmäki Fin. 45 N3
Leiyang China 87 E3
Leizhou China 87 D4
  formerly known as Haikang
Leizhou Bandao pen. China 87 D4
  English form Luichow Peninsula
Leizhou Wan b. China 87 D4
Lek r. Neth. 48 B4
Leka i. Norway 44 J2
Lékana Congo 126 B5
Le Kef Tunisia 123 H1
  historically known as Sicca Veneria
Lékéti r. Congo 126 B5
Lekhaina Greece see Lechaina
Lekhcheb Mauritania 124 C2
Lekkersing S. Africa 132 B6
Lekoes Norway 44 K1
Lékoni Gabon 126 B5
Lékoumou admin. reg. Dem. Rep. Congo 126 B5
Leksand Sweden 45 K3
Leksozero, Ozero l. Rus. Fed. 44 O3
Lek'suiri Georgia see Lentekhi
Leksura Georgia see Lentekhi
Leksvik Norway 44 J3
Lelai, Tanjung pt Indon. 75 D2
Le Lamentin Martinique 187 H4
Leland IL U.S.A. 172 E9
Leland MS U.S.A. 175 B5
Lélâng l. Sweden 45 K4
Le Lavandou France 51 M9
Leleque Arg. 205 C6
Leli China see Tianlin
Lelija mt. Bos.-Herz. 56 K5
Le Locle Switz. 51 M5
Lelogama Indon. 75 B5
Lélouma Guinea 124 B4
Le Lude France 50 G5
Lelydorp Suriname 199 H3
Lelystad Neth. 48 C3
Le Maire, Estrecho de sea chan. Arg. 205 D9
Léman, Lac l. France/Switz. see Geneva, Lake
Le Mans France 50 G4
Le Mars U.S.A. 178 C3
LeMay Range mts Antarctica 222 T2
Lembeh i. Indon. 75 C2
Lemberg mt. Germany 48 F7
Lemberg Ukr. see L'viv
Lembu Indon. 77 G1
Lembu, Gunung mt. Indon. 76 B1
Lembubut Indon. 77 G1
Lemdiyya Alg. see Médéa
Leme Brazil 203 B7
Le Merlu Rocher mt. France 51 L8
Lemeshivka Ukr. 43 M9
Lemesos Cyprus see Limassol
Lemförde Germany 48 F3
Lemhi r. U.S.A. 180 D3
Lemhi Range mts U.S.A. 180 D3
Lemieux Islands Canada 165 M3
Lemmenjoen kansallispuisto nat. park Fin. 44 N1
Lemmer Neth. 48 C3
Lemmon U.S.A. 178 B2
Lemmon, Mount U.S.A. 183 N9
Lemnos i. Greece see Limnos
Le Môle St Nicolas Haiti 187 E3
Le Mont-Dore New Caledonia 145 G4
Le Mont-St-Michel tourist site France 50 E4
  also known as Mont St Michel
Lemoore U.S.A. 182 E5
Lempäälä Fin. 45 M3
Lemro r. Myanmar 78 A3
Lemukutan i. Indon. 77 E2
Le Murge hills Italy 56 I7
Lemva r. Rus. Fed. 40 L2
Lemvig Denmark 45 J4
Lemyethna Myanmar 78 A4
Lem'yu r. Rus. Fed. 40 K3
Lena Norway 45 J3

Lena r. Rus. Fed. 80 H1
Lena IL U.S.A. 172 D8
Lena, Mount U.S.A. 183 O1
Lénakel Vanuatu 145 F3
Lēnas Latvia 42 C5
Lencloître France 50 G6
Lençóis Maranhenses, Parque Nacional dos nat. park Brazil 202 D2
Lençóis Paulista Brazil 206 E9
Lenda r. Dem. Rep. Congo 126 F4
Lendeh Iran 100 B4
Lendery Rus. Fed. 44 O3
Lendinara Italy 56 D3
Le Neubourg France 50 G3
Lengbrüt Iran 101 D3
Lenger Kazakh. 103 G4
Lengerich Germany 48 E3
Lenggries Germany 48 I8
Lenghuzhen China 84 D4
Lenglong Ling mts China 84 D4
Lengoué r. Congo 126 B4
Lengshuijiang China 87 E3
Lengshuitan China 87 D3
Lengulu Dem. Rep. Congo 126 E4
Lenhovda Sweden 45 K4
Lenin Kazakh. see Kazygurt
Lenin Tajik. 101 G2
Lenin, Qullai mt. Kyrg./Tajik. see Lenin Peak
Lenina, Kanal canal Rus. Fed. 41 H8
Lenina, Pik mt. Kyrg./Tajik. see Lenin Peak
Leninabad Tajik. see Khŭjand
Leninabad Uzbek. 102 D4
Leninakan Armenia see Gyumri
Lenin Atyndagy Choku mt. Kyrg./Tajik. see Lenin Peak
Lenine Ukr. 41 E7
  also spelt Lenino; formerly known as Sem Kolodezy
Leningori Georgia see Akhalgori
Leningrad Rus. Fed. see St Petersburg
Leningrad Tajik. 101 G2
  also known as Leningradskiy or Mŭ'minobod; formerly known as Muminabad
Leningrad Oblast admin. div. Rus. Fed. see Leningradskaya Oblast'
Leningradskaya Oblast' admin. div. Rus. Fed. 43 N2
  English form Leningrad Oblast
Leningradskiy Rus. Fed. see Leningrad
Lenino Ukr. see Lenine
Leninobod admin. div. Tajik. see Khŭjand
  English form Leninabad Oblast; also known as Muminobod
Leninobod Uzbek. see Leninabad
Leninogor Kazakh. see Leninogorsk
Leninogorsk Kazakh. 88 C1
  also known as Leninogor or Ridder
Leninogorsk Rus. Fed. 40 J5
  formerly known as Novaya Pismyanka
Lenin Peak Kyrg./Tajik. 101 G2
  also known as Lenina, Pik or Lenin, Qullai or Lenin Atyndagy Choku
Leninpol' Kyrg. 103
Leninsk Kazakh. see Baykonur
Leninsk Rus. Fed. 41 H6
Leninsk Turkm. see Akdepe
Leninsk Uzbek. see Asaka
Leninskiy Kazakh. 102 D2
Leninskiy Rus. Fed. 43 U7
Leninsk-Kuznetskiy Rus. Fed. 80 D2
Leninskoye Kazakh. see Kazygurt
Leninskoye Kazakh. 102 D2
Leninskoye Rus. Fed. 82 D3
Leninskoye Rus. Fed. 40 J4
Lenkoran' Azer. see Länkäran
Lennard r. Australia 150 D3
Lenne r. Germany 51 N1
Lennox, Isla i. Chile 205 D9
Lennox-King Glacier Antarctica 223 L1
Lenoir U.S.A. 174 D5
Lenoir City U.S.A. 174 C5
Lenore U.S.A. 176 C8
Lenore Lake Canada 167 J4
Lenox U.S.A. 177 L3
Lens France 52 C1
Lensk Rus. Fed. 39 L3
  formerly known as Mukhtuya
Lentekhi Georgia 107 E2
  formerly known as Lek'suiri or Leksura
Lenti Hungary 49 N9
Lentini Sicilia Italy 57 H11
Lentua l. Fin. 44 O2
Lentvaravas Lith. see Lentvaris
Lentvaris Lith. 42 G7
  also spelt Lentvaravas
Lent'yevo Rus. Fed. 43 R3
Lenya Myanmar 79 B6
Léo Burkina 124 E4
Leoben Austria 49 M8
Leodhais, Eilean i. U.K. see Lewis, Isle of
Léogâne Haiti 187 E3
Leok Indon. 75 B2
Leola U.S.A. 178 C2
Leominster U.K. 47 J11
Leominster U.S.A. 177 N3
León Mex. 185 E4
León Nicaragua 186 B4
León Spain 54 F2
León U.S.A. 178 D3
León, Montes de mts Spain 54 E2
Leonard U.S.A. 179 C5
Leonardo da Vinci airport Italy 56 E6
Leonardtown U.S.A. 177 I7
Leonardville Namibia 130 C4
Leona Vicario Mex. 185 I4
Leonforte Sicilia Italy 57 G11
Leongatha Australia 147 E4
Leonidi Greece 59 D11
Leonidovo Rus. Fed. 82 F2
Leonora Australia 151 C6
Léopold l. Australia 150 D3
Léopold II, Lac l. Dem. Rep. Congo see Mai-Ndombe, Lac
Leopoldina Brazil 203 D7
Leopoldo de Bulhões Brazil 206 E3
Léopoldville Dem. Rep. Congo see Kinshasa
Leoti U.S.A. 178 B4
Leova Moldova 58 J2
  also spelt Leovo
Leoville Canada 167 J4
Leovo Moldova see Leova
Lepar i. Indon. 77 D3
Le Péage-de-Roussillon France 51 K7
Lepel' Belarus see Lyepyel'
Lepenou Greece 59 C10
Lephalale S. Africa 131 E4
Lephepe Botswana 131 E4
Lephoi S. Africa 133 J6
Leping China 87 F3
Le Poiré-sur-Vie France 50 E6
Le Pontet France 51 K8
Lepontine, Alpi mts Italy/Switz. 56 A2
Lepsa Kazakh. see Lepsy
Leposavić Kosovo, Srbija Yugo. 58 B5

Leppävirta Fin. 44 N3
Lepreau, Point Canada 169 H4
Lepsa Kazakh. see Lepsy
Lepsa r. Kazakh. see Lepsy
Lepsi Kazakh. see Lepsinsk
Lepsinsk Kazakh. 103 J3
  also known as Lepsi
Lepsy Kazakh. 103 I3
  also known as Lepsa
Lepsy r. Kazakh. 103 I3
  formerly known as Lepsa
Leptis Magna tourist site Libya 120 B1
Leptokarya Greece 59 D8
Le-Puy-en-Velay France 51 J7
Leqceïba Mauritania 124 B2
Léraba r. Burkina/Côte d'Ivoire 124 D4
Lerala Botswana 131 E4
Leratswana S. Africa 133 L5
Lercara Friddi Sicilia Italy 57 F11
Léré Chad 126 B2
Léré Mali 124 D3
Lere Nigeria 125 H4
Lereh, Tanjung pt Indon. 77 G3
Le Relecq-Kerhuon France 50 B4
Lérida Col. 198 D5
Lérida Spain see Lleida
Lerik Azer. 107 G3
Lerma Mex. 185 H5
Lerma Spain 54 H2
Lermontov Rus. Fed. 107 E1
  formerly known as Lermontovskiy
Lermontovka Rus. Fed. 82 D3
Lermontovskiy Rus. Fed. see Lermontov
Lermo, Monte mt. Sardegna Italy 57 B8
Le Robert Martinique 187 H4
Leros i. Greece 59 H11
Le Roy U.S.A. 176 H3
Lerum Sweden 45 K4
Lerwick U.K. 46 K3
Ler Zerai well Sudan 126 E2
Les Agudes mt. Spain 55 N3
Les Borges Blanques Spain 55 L3
  also known as Borjas Blancas
Lesbos i. Greece 59 G9
  also known as Mytilene; also spelt Lesvos
L'Escala Spain 55 O2
  also known as La Escala
Les Cayes Haiti 187 E3
Le Sentier Switz. 51 M6
Les Escaldes Andorra 55 M2
Les Escoumins Canada 169 G3
La Seu d'Urgell Spain 55 M2
  also spelt Seo de Urgell
Leshan China 86 B2
Les Herbiers France 50 E6
Leshou China see Xianxian
Leshukonskoye Rus. Fed. 40 H2
Lésina, Lago di lag. Italy 56 H7
Leśna Poland 49 M4
Lesjöfors Sweden 45 K4
Leskhimstroy Ukr. see Syeverodonets'k
Lesko Poland 49 T6
Leskovac Srbija Yugo. 58 C6
Leskovik Albania 59 B8
Leskov Island Antarctica 223 F2
Leslie U.S.A. 173 I8
Les Méchins Canada 169 H3
Les Mées France 51 L8
Les Minquiers is Channel Is 50 D4
Lesneven France 50 B4
Lesnoy Kirovskaya Oblast' Rus. Fed. 40 J4
Lesnoy Rus. Fed. see Umba
Lesnoy Smolenskaya Oblast' Rus. Fed. 43 M6
Lesnoy, Ostrov i. Rus. Fed. 43 J1
Lesnoye Rus. Fed. 43 R3
Lesnyye Polyany Rus. Fed. 40 J4
Lesogorsk Rus. Fed. 82 F2
Lesogorskiy Rus. Fed. 43 J1
Lesopil'noye Rus. Fed. 82 D3
Lesosibirsk Rus. Fed. 39 J4
Lesotho country Africa 133 L6
  formerly known as Basutoland
  africa [countries] 114–117
Lesotho Highlands Water Scheme Lesotho 133 M6
Lesozavodsk Rus. Fed. 82 D3
Lesozavodskiy Rus. Fed. 44 P2
Lesparre-Médoc France 50 F7
Les Pieux France 50 E3
L'Espérance Rock i. N.Z. 145 H5
Les Ponts-de-Cé France 50 F5
L'Espina mt. Spain 55 L4
Les Sables-d'Olonne France 50 E6
Lesse r. Belgium 51 K2
Les Sept-Îles is France 50 C4
Lesser Antilles is Caribbean Sea 187 G4
Lesser Caucasus mts Asia 41 G2
  also known as Malyy Kavkaz
Lesser Himalaya mts India/Nepal 96 C3
Lesser Khingan Mountains China see Xiao Hinggan Ling
Lesser Slave Lake Canada 167 H4
Lesser Slave Lake Provincial Park Canada 167 H4
Lesser Tunb i. The Gulf see Tunb
  also known as Tonb-e Kūchek, Jazīreh-ye or Ţunb aş Şughrá
Lessingskop mt. S. Africa 133 K6
L'Est, Île de i. Canada 169 I4
L'Est, Pointe de pt Canada 169 I3
Lester U.S.A. 176 D8
Lestijärvi Fin. 44 N3
Lestijoki r. Fin. 44 M3
Les Triagoz is France 50 C4
Les Trois Rivières Cent. Afr. Rep. 126 D3
Lesung, Bukit mt. Indon. 77 F2
Les Vans France 51 K8
Lesvos i. Greece see Lesbos
Leszno Poland 49 N4
  historically known as Lissa
Le Teil France 51 K8
Le Télégraphe hill France 51 K5
Letenye Hungary 49 N9
Leteri India 96 C4
Lethabile S. Africa 133 L2
Letha Range mts Myanmar 78 A3
Lethbridge Alta Canada 167 H5
Lethbridge Nfld. Canada 169 K3
Lethem Guyana 199 G4
Le Thillot France 51 M5
Leti i. Indon. 75 D5
Leti, Kepulauan is Indon. 75 C5
Leticia Col. 198 D5
Leting China 85 H4
Letjiesbos S. Africa 132 G9
Letlhakane Botswana 131 E4
Letlhakeng Botswana 131 E4
Letnerechenskiy Rus. Fed. 40 F2
Letniy Navolok Rus. Fed. 40 G2
Le Touquet-Paris-Plage France 50 H2
Letpadan Myanmar 78 A4
Le Tréport France 50 H2
Letsok-aw Kyun i. Myanmar 79 B6
  also known as Domel Island
Letsopa S. Africa 133 J3
Lette Island Tonga see Late Island
Letterkenny Rep. of Ireland 47 E9
Letung Indon. 77 D2
Letwurung Indon. 75 D5
Lëtzebuerg country Europe see Luxembourg
Leu Romania 58 F4
Léua Angola 127 D7
Leucas Greece see Lefkada
Leucate, Étang de l. France 51 J10
  also known as Salses, Étang de

Leukas Greece see **Lefkada**
Leung Shuen Wan Chau i. Hong Kong China see **High Island**
Leunovo Rus. Fed. 40 G2
Leupp U.S.A. 183 N6
Leura Australia 149 F4
Leuser, Gunung mt. Indon. 76 B2
Leutkirch im Allgäu Germany 48 H8
Leuven Belgium 51 K2
also spelt Louvain
Levadeia Greece 59 D10
Levan Albania 58 A8
Levanger Norway 44 J3
Levante, Riviera di coastal area Italy 56 A4
Levanto Italy 56 B4
Levanzo, Isola di i. Sicilia Italy 57 E10
Levashi Rus. Fed. 102 A4
Levelland U.S.A. 179 B5
Levels N.Z. 153 F12
Leven U.K. 46 J7
Levens France 51 N9
Lévêque, Cape Australia 150 C3
Leverburgh U.K. 46 E6
also known as An t-Ob
Levering U.S.A. 173 I5
Leverkusen Germany 48 D4
Leverville Dem. Rep. Congo see **Lusanga**
Lévézou mts France 51 I8
Levice Slovakia 49 P7
Levidi Greece 59 D11
Levin N.Z. 152 J8
Lévis Canada 169 G4
Levitha i. Greece 59 H12
Levittown U.S.A. 177 K5
Levka Bulg. 58 H7
Levkás i. Greece see **Lefkada**
Levkímmi Greece see **Lefkimmi**
Levoča Slovakia 49 R6
Levočské vrchy mts Slovakia 49 R6
Levroux France 50 H6
Levski Bulg. 58 G5
Levskigrad Bulg. see **Karlovo**
Lev Tolstoy Rus. Fed. 43 U8
Levuka Fiji 145 G3
Lėvuo r. Lith. 42 F5
Lewa Indon. 75 A5
Lewe Myanmar 78 B4
Lewer watercourse Namibia 132 B2
Lewerberg mt. S. Africa 132 B6
Lewes U.K. 47 M13
Lewes U.S.A. 177 J7
Lewin Brzeski Poland 49 O5
Lewis U.S.A. 183 P4
Lewis r. U.S.A. 180 B3
Lewis, Isle of i. U.K. 46 F5
also known as Leodhais, Eilean
Lewis, Lake salt flat Australia 148 B4
Lewisburg OH U.S.A. 176 A6
Lewisburg PA U.S.A. 177 I5
Lewisburg TN U.S.A. 174 C5
Lewisburg WV U.S.A. 176 E8
Lewis Cass, Mount Canada/U.S.A. 166 D3
Lewis Hills hill Canada 169 J3
Lewis Inlet India 95 G3
Lewis Pass N.Z. 153 G10
Lewis Pass National Reserve nature res. N.Z. 153 G10
Lewisporte Canada 169 K3
Lewis Range hills Australia 150 E4
Lewis Range mts U.S.A. 180 D2
Lewis Smith, Lake U.S.A. 175 C5
Lewiston CA U.S.A. 182 B1
Lewiston ID U.S.A. 180 C3
Lewiston ME U.S.A. 177 O1
Lewiston MN U.S.A. 172 B7
Lewistown IL U.S.A. 174 B3
Lewistown MT U.S.A. 180 E3
Lewistown PA U.S.A. 176 H5
Lewisville U.S.A. 179 D5
Lewisville, Lake U.S.A. 179 C5
Lewitz park Germany 48 I2
Lewotobi, Gunung vol. Indon. 75 B5
Lexington GA U.S.A. 175 D5
Lexington IL U.S.A. 172 E10
Lexington KY U.S.A. 176 A7
Lexington MI U.S.A. 173 K7
Lexington MO U.S.A. 178 D4
Lexington MS U.S.A. 175 B5
Lexington NC U.S.A. 174 D5
Lexington NE U.S.A. 178 C3
Lexington OH U.S.A. 176 C5
Lexington SC U.S.A. 175 D5
Lexington TN U.S.A. 174 B5
Lexington VA U.S.A. 176 F8
Lexington Park U.S.A. 177 I7
formerly known as Jarboesville
Leyden Neth. see **Leiden**
Leye China 86 C3
also known as Tongle
Leyla Dāgh mt. Iran 100 A2
Leyte i. Phil. 74 C4
Leyte Gulf Phil. 74 C4
Leżajsk Poland 49 T5
Lèze r. France 50 H9
Lezha Rus. Fed. 43 V3
Lezha r. Rus. Fed. 43 V2
Lezhë Albania 58 A7
formerly known as Alessio
Lezhi China 86 C2
also known as Tianchi
Lézignan-Corbières France 51 I9
Lezuza Spain 55 I6
L'gov Rus. Fed. 41 E6
Lhagoi Kangri mt. China 89 D6
also known as Hlako Kangri
Lhari China 89 F6
also known as Sirdingka
Lharidon Bight b. Australia 151 A5
Lharigarbo China see **Amdo**
Lhasa China 89 E6
Lhasa He r. China 89 E6
Lhasoi China 89 F6
Lhatog China 86 A2
Lhazê Xizang China 89 D6
also known as Quxar
Lhazê Xizang China 97 G3
L'Herbaudière, Pointe de pt France 50 D5
Lhokseumawe Indon. 76 B1
Lhoksukon Indon. 76 B1
Lhorong China 97 G3
also known as Zito

▶**Lhotse** mt. China/Nepal 97 E3
4th highest mountain in the world and in Asia.
world [physical features] ➤ 8–9

Lhozhag China 89 E6
also known as Garbo
Lhuentse Bhutan 97 F4
Lhünzê China 89 F6
also known as Xingba
Lhünzhub China 89 E6
also known as Gaindaingoinkor
Liancheng China 87 F3
also known as Lianfeng
Liancheng China see **Qinglong**
Liancheng China see **Guangnan**
Liancourt Rocks i. N. Pacific Ocean 91 B6
also known as Take-shima or Tokdo or Tok-tō or Tokto-ri
Lianfeng China see **Liancheng**
Liang Indon. 75 B3
Lianga Phil. 74 C4
Lianga Bay Phil. 74 C4
Liangaz Hu l. China 87 E2
Liangcheng China 85 G3
Liangdang China 86 C1
Liangfeng China 87 D3
Lianghe China 86 A3
also known as Zhedao
Lianghekou Gansu China 86 C1
Lianghekou Sichuan China 86 B2
Liangjiayoufang China see **Youyu**
Liangping China 87 C2
also known as Liangshan
Liangpran, Bukit mt. Indon. 77 F2
Liangshan China see **Liangping**
Liang Shan mt. Myanmar 78 B2
Liangshi China see **Shaodong**
Liang Timur, Gunung mt. Malaysia 76 C2
Liangwang Shan mts China 86 B3
Liangzhen China 85 F4
Liangzhou China see **Wuwei**
Lianhe China see **Qianjiang**
Lianhua China 87 E3
also known as Qinting
Lianhua Shan mts China 87 E4
Lianjiang Fujian China 87 F3
also known as Fengcheng
Lianjiang Guangdong China 87 D4
Lianjiang China see **Xingguo**
Lianjiangkou China 87 E3
Lian Jianng r. China 78 D2
Liannan China 87 E3
also known as Sanjiang
Lianping China 87 E3
also known as Yuanshan
Lianran China see **Anning**
Lianshan Guangdong China 87 E3
also known as Jitian
Lianshan Liaoning China 85 I3
formerly known as Jinxi
Liant, Cape pt Thai. see **Samae San, Laem**
Liantang China see **Nanchang**
Liantuo China 87 D2
Lianxian China see **Lianzhou**
Lianyin China 82 A1
Lianyuan China 87 D3
formerly known as Lantian
Lianyungang China 87 F1
Lianzhou China 87 E3
formerly known as Lianxian
Lianzhou China see **Hepu**
Lianzhushan China 82 C3
Liao r. China 85 I3
Liaocheng China 85 G4
Liaodong Bandao pen. China 85 I3
Liaodong Wan b. China 85 I3
Liaodun China 84 B3
Liaodunzhan China 84 B3
Liaoning prov. China 85 I3
Liaoyang China 85 I3
Liaoyuan China 82 B4
Liaozhong China 85 I3
Liapades Greece 59 A9
Liaqatabad Pak. 101 G3
Liard r. Canada 166 F2
Liard Highway Canada 166 F2
Liard Plateau Canada 166 E2
Liard River Canada 166 E3
Liari Pak. 101 F5
Liat i. Indon. 77 D3
Liathach mt. U.K. 46 G6
Liban country Asia see **Lebanon**
Liban, Jebel mts Lebanon 108 H3
Libano Col. 198 C3
Libau Latvia see **Liepāja**
Libby U.S.A. 180 D2
Libenge Dem. Rep. Congo 126 C4
Liberal U.S.A. 178 B4
Liberdade Brazil 207 I9
Liberdade r. Amazonas Brazil 200 C1
Liberdade r. Mato Grosso Brazil 202 A4
Liberec Czech Rep. 49 M5
▶**Liberia** country Africa 124 C5
africa [countries] ➤ 114–117
Liberia Costa Rica 186 B5
Libertad Venez. 198 D2
Libertador General San Martin Arg. 201 D5
Liberty AK U.S.A. 166 A1
Liberty IN U.S.A. 176 A6
Liberty KY U.S.A. 176 A8
Liberty ME U.S.A. 177 P1
Liberty MO U.S.A. 178 D4
Liberty NY U.S.A. 177 K4
Liberty TX U.S.A. 179 D6
Libertyville U.S.A. 172 F8
Libmanan Phil. 74 B3
Libni, Gebel hill Egypt 108 E7
Libo China 87 C3
also known as Yuping
Libobo, Tanjung pt Indon. 75 D3
Libode S. Africa 133 N8
Libohovë Albania 59 B8
Liboi Kenya 128 D4
Libong, Ko i. Thai. 79 B7
Libourne France 50 F8
Libral Well Australia 150 D4
Librazhd Albania 58 B7
Libre, Sierra mts Mex. 184 C2

▶**Libreville** Gabon 126 A4
Capital of Gabon.

Libuganon r. Phil. 74 C5

▶**Libya** country Africa 120 B3
4th largest country in Africa. Spelt Al Lībīyah in Arabic.
africa [countries] ➤ 114–117

Libyan Desert Egypt/Libya 120 E3
Libyan Plateau Egypt 121 E2
Licantén Chile 204 B4
Licata Sicilia Italy 57 F11
Lice Turkey 107 E3
Lichas pen. Greece 59 D10
also spelt Likhás
Licheng China see **Xianyou**
Licheng China see **Lipu**
Licheng Shandong China 85 H4
also known as Hongjialou
Licheng Shanxi China 85 G4
Lichfield N.Z. 152 J6
Lichfield U.K. 47 K11
Lichinga Moz. 129 B8
formerly known as Vila Cabral
Lichte Germany 48 I5
Lichtenburg S. Africa 133 K3
Lichtenfels Germany 48 I5
Lichuan Hubei China 87 D2
Lichuan Jiangxi China 87 F3
also known as Rifeng
Licínio de Almeida Brazil 207 K1
Liciro Moz. 131 H3
Licking r. U.S.A. 176 A6
Lički Osik Croatia 56 H4
Licun China see **Laoshan**
Lid' r. Rus. Fed. 43 Q2
Lida Belarus 42 G8
Lidjombo Cent. Afr. Rep. 126 C4
Lidköping Sweden 45 K4
Lidsjöberg Sweden 44 K2
Lidumnieki Latvia 42 I5
Lidzbark Poland 49 Q2
Lidzbark Warmiński Poland 49 R1
Liebenbergs Vlei r. S. Africa 133 M4
Liebenwalde Germany 49 K3
Liebig, Mount Australia 148 A4
Liebling Romania 58 C3
▶**Liechtenstein** country Europe 51 P5
europe [countries] ➤ 32–35
Liège Belgium 51 L2
also known as Luik
Liegnitz Poland see **Legnica**
Lieksa Fin. 44 O3
Lielais Ludzas l. Latvia 42 I5
Lielupe r. Latvia 42 F4
Lielvārde Latvia 42 F5
Lien Sweden 44 L3
Lienz Austria 49 J9
Liepāja Latvia 42 C5
also spelt Liepaya; formerly spelt Libau
Liepaya Latvia see **Liepāja**
Liepna Latvia 42 I4
Liesjärven kansallispuisto nat. park Fin. 42 E1
Liestal Switz. 51 N5
Lieto Fin. 42 D1
Liétor Spain 55 J6
Lietuva country Europe see **Lithuania**
Liévin France 51 I2
Lièvre r. Canada 168 F4
Liezen Austria 49 L8
Lifamatola i. Indon. 75 C3
Lifanga Dem. Rep. Congo 126 D4
Liffey r. Rep. of Ireland 47 F10
Lifford Rep. of Ireland 47 E9
Liffré France 50 E4
Lifi Mahuida mt. Arg. 205 C6
Lifou i. New Caledonia 145 F4
also spelt Lifu; formerly known as Chabrol
Lifu i. New Caledonia see **Lifou**
Lifudzin Rus. Fed. see **Rudnyy**
Ligao Phil. 74 B3
Līgatne Latvia 42 G4
Lighthouse Reef Belize 185 I5
Lightning Ridge Australia 147 E2
Ligny-en-Barrois France 51 L4
Ligonha r. Moz. 131 H3
Ligonier IN U.S.A. 172 H9
Ligonier PA U.S.A. 176 F5
Ligoúrion Greece see **Lygourio**
Ligui Mex. 184 C3
Ligure, Mar sea France/Italy see **Ligurian Sea**
Liguria admin. reg. Italy 56 A4
Ligurian Sea France/Italy 51 O9
also known as Ligure, Mar or Ligurienne, Mer
Ligurienne, Mer sea France/Italy see **Ligurian Sea**
Ligurta U.S.A. 183 J9
Lihir Group is P.N.G. 145 E2
formerly known as Gerrit Denys
Lihou Reef and Cays Australia 149 F3
Lihue U.S.A. 181 [inset] Y1
Lihula Estonia 42 E3
Liivi laht b. Estonia/Latvia see **Riga, Gulf of**
Lijiang China 86 B3
also known as Dayan
Lijiang China see **Yuanjiang**
Lijiazhai China 87 E2
Lik, Nam r. Laos 78 C4
Lika reg. Croatia 56 H4
Likak Iran 100 B4
Likala Dem. Rep. Congo 126 C4
Likasi Dem. Rep. Congo 127 E7
formerly known as Jadotville
Likati Dem. Rep. Congo 126 D4
Likati r. Dem. Rep. Congo 126 E4
Likely Canada 166 F4
Likhachevo Ukr. see **Pervomays'kyy**
Likhachyovo Ukr. see **Pervomays'kyy**
Likhás pen. Greece see **Lichas**
Likhoslavl' Rus. Fed. 43 Q4
Likimi Dem. Rep. Congo 126 D4
Likino-Dulevo Rus. Fed. 43 T6
Likisia East Timor 75 C5
also spelt Liquiçá or Liquissa
Likma India 94 D1
Likolia Dem. Rep. Congo 126 D5
Likouala admin. reg. Congo 126 C4
Likouala r. Congo 126 C5
Likouala aux Herbes r. Congo 126 C5
Liku Indon. 77 E2
Liku Sarawak Malaysia 77 F1
Likupang Indon. 75 C2
L'Île d'Anticosti, Réserve Faunique de nature res. Canada 169 I3
L'Île-Rousse Corse France 51 O10
Lilienfeld Austria 49 M7
Lilienthal Germany 48 F2
Liling China 87 E3
Liljendal Fin. 42 H1
Lilla Pak. 101 H3
Lilla Edet Sweden 45 K4
Lilla Luleälven r. Sweden 44 M2
Lillblaiken hill Sweden 44 L2
Lille Belgium 51 K1
Lille France 51 J2
Lille Bælt sea chan. Denmark see **Little Belt**
Lillebonne France 50 G3
Lillehammer Norway 45 J3
Lillesand Norway 45 J4
Lillestrøm Norway 45 J4
Lilley U.S.A. 172 H7
Lillian, Point hill Australia 151 D5
Lillie Glacier Antarctica 223 L2
Lillington U.S.A. 174 E5
Lillooet Canada 166 F5
Lillooet r. Canada 166 F5
Lillooet Range mts Canada 166 F5
Lilo r. Dem. Rep. Congo 126 E5
Lilong India 97 G4

▶**Lilongwe** Malawi 129 B8
Capital of Malawi.

Lilo Viejo Arg. 204 E2
Liloy Phil. 74 B4
Lily U.S.A. 172 E5
Lim r. Yugo. 58 A5

▶**Lima** Peru 200 A3
Capital of Peru and 4th most populous city in South America.
world [cities] ➤ 24–25

Lima dept Peru 200 A2
Lima MT U.S.A. 180 D3
Lima NY U.S.A. 176 H3
Lima OH U.S.A. 176 A5
Limaão Brazil 199 F4
Lima Duarte Brazil 207 J8
Līmah Oman 105 G2
Lima Islands China see **Wanshan Qundao**
Liman Rus. Fed. 102 A3
Limanowa Poland 49 R6
Limar Indon. 75 C4
Limarí r. Chile 204 C3
Limas Indon. 76 D2
Limassol Cyprus 108 E3
also known as Lemesos
Limavady U.K. 47 F8
Limay r. Arg. 204 D5
Limay Mahuida Arg. 204 D5
Limbach-Oberfrohna Germany 49 J5
Limbang r. Sarawak Malaysia 77 F1
Limbani Peru 200 C3
Limbaži Latvia 42 F4
Limbdi India 96 A5
Limbe Cameroon 125 H5
formerly known as Victoria
Limboto Indon. 75 B2
Limboto, Danau l. Indon. 75 B2
Limbuè Moz. 131 H3
Limbungan Indon. 77 F3
Limbunya Australia 148 A3
Limburg an der Lahn Germany 48 F5
Lim Chu Kang Sing. 76 [inset]
Lim Chu Kang hill Sing. 76 [inset]
Lime Acres S. Africa 132 H5
Limehills N.Z. 153 C14
Limeira Brazil 206 F9
Limenaria Greece 58 F8
Limerick Rep. of Ireland 47 D11
also spelt Luimneach
Limestone U.S.A. 176 C9
Limestone Point Canada 167 L4
Limfjorden sea chan. Denmark 45 J4
Limia r. Spain 54 C3
Limin Chersonisou Greece 59 G13
Limingen Norway 44 K2
Limingen l. Norway 44 K2
Liminka Fin. 44 N2
Limmen Bight b. Australia 148 C2
Limmen Bight River r. Australia 148 B2
Limni Greece 59 E10
Limnos i. Greece 59 G9
also spelt Lemnos
Limoeiro Brazil 202 F3
Limoges France 50 H7
Limón Costa Rica 186 C5
Limón Hond. 186 B4
Limon U.S.A. 178 B4
Limonum France see **Poitiers**
Limoquije Bol. 200 D3
Limousin admin. reg. France 50 H7
Limousin, Plateaux du France 50 H7
Limoux France 51 I9
Limpopo r. S. Africa/Zimbabwe 131 G5
Limu China 87 D3
Limulunga Zambia 127 D8
Linaälven r. Sweden 44 M2
Līnah Saudi Arabia 104 C1
Linakeng Lesotho 133 M6
Linakhamari Rus. Fed. 44 O1
Lin'an China see **Jianshui**
Lin'an China 87 F2
Linao Bay Phil. 74 C5
Linapacan i. Phil. 74 A4
Linapacan Strait Phil. 74 A4
Linares Chile 204 C4
Linares Mex. 185 F3
Linares Spain 55 H6
Linas, Monte mt. Sardegna Italy 57 A9
Linau Balui plat. Sarawak Malaysia 77 F2
Lincang China 86 B4
also known as Fengxiang
Lincheng China see **Lingao**
Lincheng China see **Huitong**
Linchuan China 87 F3
formerly known as Fuzhou
Linck Nunataks Antarctica 222 R1
Lincoln Arg. 204 E4
Lincoln U.K. 47 L10
historically known as Lindum
Lincoln CA U.S.A. 182 C3
Lincoln IL U.S.A. 174 B3
Lincoln KS U.S.A. 178 C4
Lincoln ME U.S.A. 174 G2
Lincoln MI U.S.A. 173 J6

▶**Lincoln** NE U.S.A. 178 C3
State capital of Nebraska.

Lincoln City U.S.A. 180 A3
Lincoln Island Paracel Is 72 D3
Lincoln National Park Australia 146 B3
Lincoln Sea Canada/Greenland 165 O1
Lincolnshire Wolds hills U.K. 47 L10
Linda, Serra hills Brazil 202 D5
Lindas Norway 46 R3
Lindau (Bodensee) Germany 48 G8
Lindeman Group is Australia 149 F4
Linden Canada 167 H5
Linden Guyana 199 G3
formerly known as Mackenzie
Linden AL U.S.A. 175 C5
Linden CA U.S.A. 182 C3
Linden NJ U.S.A. 177 K5
Linden TN U.S.A. 174 C5
Linden TX U.S.A. 179 D5
Lindenow Fjord inlet Greenland see **Kangerlussuatsiaq**
Lindesberg Sweden 45 K4
Líndhos Greece see **Lindos**
Lindi r. Dem. Rep. Congo 126 E4
Lindi Tanz. 129 C7
Lindi admin. reg. Tanz. 129 C7
Lindian China 85 J2
Lindisfarne i. U.K. see **Holy Island**
Lindley S. Africa 133 L4
Lindóia Brazil 206 G9
Lindome Sweden 45 K4
Lindong China 85 H3
also known as Bairin Zuoqi
Lindos Greece 59 J12
also spelt Líndhos
Lindos, Akra pt Greece 59 J12
Lindsay Canada 168 E4
Lindsay CA U.S.A. 182 E5
Lindsborg U.S.A. 178 C4
Lindsdal Sweden 45 L4
Lindside U.S.A. 176 E8
Lindum U.K. see **Lincoln**
Line Islands S. Pacific Ocean 221 H5
Linets Rus. Fed. 43 Q9
Linfen China 85 F4
Lingamparti India 94 D2
Linganamakki Reservoir India 94 B3
Lingao China 87 D5
also known as Lincheng
Lingayen Phil. 74 B2
Lingayen Gulf Phil. 74 B2
Lingbao China 87 D1
formerly known as Guoluezhen
Lingbi China 87 F1
Lingcheng China see **Lingshan**
Lingcheng China see **Lingshui**
Lingcheng China see **Lingxian**
Lingchuan Guangxi China 87 D3
Lingchuan Shanxi China 85 G5
Lingelethu S. Africa 133 K9
Lingelihle S. Africa 133 J9
Lingen (Ems) Germany 48 E3
Lingga i. Indon. 76 D3
Lingga, Kepulauan is Indon. 76 D3
Linggo Co l. China 89 E5
Lingig Phil. 74 C5
Lingle U.S.A. 180 F4
Lingomo Dem. Rep. Congo 126 D4
Lingqiu China 85 G4
Lingshan China 87 D4
also known as Lingcheng
Lingshan Wan b. China 85 I5
Lingshi Bhutan see **Lingzhi**
Lingshi China 85 F4
Lingshui China 87 D5
also known as Lingcheng
Lingsugur India 94 C2
Lingtai China 85 E5
also known as Zhongtai
Linguère Senegal 124 B3
Lingui China 87 D3
Lingxi China see **Yongshun**
Lingxian China see **Yanling**
Lingxian China 85 H4
also known as Lingcheng
Lingxiang China 87 E2
Lingyuan China 85 H3
Lingyun China 86 C3
also known as Sicheng
Lingzhi Bhutan 97 F4
also spelt Lingshi
Lingzi Thang Plains l. Aksai Chin 89 B5
Linhai Liaoning China 85 I3
also known as Dalinghe; formerly known as Jinxian
Linhai Zhejiang China 87 G2
Linhares Brazil 203 D6
Linh Cam Vietnam 78 D4
Linhe China 85 E3
Linhpa Myanmar 78 A2
Linidis Valley N.Z. 153 D12
Linjiang China see **Shanghang**
Linjiang China 82 B4
Linköping Sweden 45 K4
Linkou China 82 C3
Linksness U.K. 46 I5
Linkuva Lith. 42 E5
Linli China 87 D2
Linlű Shan mt. China 85 G4
Linmingguan China see **Yongnian**
Linn U.S.A. 174 B4
Linn, Mount U.S.A. 182 B1
Linnansaaren kansallispuisto nat. park Fin. 44 O3
Linnhe, Loch inlet U.K. 46 G7
Linosa, Isola di i. Sicilia Italy 57 E13
Linova Belarus 42 F9
Linqing China 85 G4
Linru China see **Ruzhou**
Lins Brazil 206 D8
Linsan Guinea 124 B4
Linshui China 86 C2
also known as Dingping
Linta r. Madag. 131 [inset] J5
Lintah, Selat sea chan. Indon. 75 A5
Lintan China 86 B1
Lintao China 84 D5
also known as Taoyang
Linth r. Switz. 51 P5
Linthal Switz. 51 P6
Linton U.S.A. 178 B2
Lintong China 87 D1
also known as Lishan
Linville U.S.A. 176 D9
Linxi China 85 H3
Linxia China 84 D5
Linxian China see **Linzhou**
Linxian China 85 F4
Linxiang China 87 E2
Linyanti r. Botswana/Namibia 131 E3
Linyanti Swamp Namibia 130 D3
Linyi Shandong China 85 H4
Linyi Shandong China 85 H5
Linyi Shanxi China 85 F5
Linying China 87 E1
Linz Austria 49 L7
Linze China 84 D4
formerly known as Shahepu or Shahezhen
Linzhou China 85 G4
formerly known as Linxian
Lioma Moz. 131 H2
Lion, Golfe du g. France 51 J10
English form Lions, Gulf of
Lions, Gulf of France see **Lion, Golfe du**
Lions Den Zimbabwe 131 F3
Lion's Head Canada 173 L6
Lioua Chad 120 B6
Liouesso Congo 126 B4
Lipa Phil. 74 B3
Lipari Isole Lipari Italy 57 G10
Lipari, Isola i. Isole Lipari Italy 57 G10
Lipari, Isole is Italy 57 G10
Lipatkain Indon. 76 C2
Lipawki Belarus 42 I6
Liperi Fin. 44 O3
Lipetsk Rus. Fed. 43 U9
Lipetskaya Oblast' admin. div. Rus. Fed. 43 T9
English form Lipetsk Oblast
Lipetsk Oblast admin. div. Rus. Fed. see **Lipetskaya Oblast'**
Lipez, Cordillera de mts Bol. 200 D5
Lipiany Poland 49 L2
Lipin Bor Rus. Fed. 43 S1
Liping China 87 D3
also known as Defeng
Lipitsy Rus. Fed. 43 S8
Lipki Rus. Fed. 43 S8
Lipljan Kosovo, Srbija Yugo. 58 C6
Lipnaya Gorka Rus. Fed. 43 O2
Lipník nad Bečvou Czech Rep. 49 O6
Lipno Poland 49 Q3
Lipno, Vodní nádrž resr Czech Rep. 49 L7
Lipova Romania 58 C2
Lipovtsy Rus. Fed. 90 B2
Lipovu Romania 58 E4
Lippe r. Germany 48 D4
Lippstadt Germany 48 F4
Lipscomb U.S.A. 179 B4
Lipsk Poland 49 U2
Lipsko Poland 49 S4
Lipsoí i. Greece see **Leipsoi**
Lipti Lekh pass Nepal 96 D3
Liptovská Mara, Vodná nádrž resr Slovakia 49 Q6
Liptovský Hrádok Slovakia 49 Q6
Liptovský Mikuláš Slovakia 49 Q6
Liptrap, Cape Australia 147 E4
Liptsy Rus. Fed. 43 P6
Lipu China 87 D3
also known as Licheng
Lipusz Poland 49 O1
Liquiçá East Timor see **Likisia**
Liquissa East Timor see **Likisia**
Lira Uganda 128 B4
Liran i. Indon. 75 C4
Liranga Congo 126 C5
Liri r. Italy 56 F7
Liri, Jebel el mt. Sudan 128 A2
Lirung Indon. 75 C2
Lis Albania 58 B7
Lisa Romania 58 F3
Lisakovsk Kazakh. 103 E1
Lisala Dem. Rep. Congo 126 D4
L'Isalo, Massif de mts Madag. 131 [inset] J4
L'Isalo, Parc National de nat. park Madag. 131 [inset] J4
Lisboa Port. see **Lisbon**
Lisboa admin. dist. Port. 54 B5

▶**Lisbon** Port. 54 B6
Capital of Portugal. Also spelt Lisboa; historically known as Olisipo.

Lisbon IL U.S.A. 172 E9
Lisbon ME U.S.A. 177 O1
Lisbon ND U.S.A. 178 C2
Lisbon NH U.S.A. 177 N1
Lisbon OH U.S.A. 176 E5
Lisbon Falls U.S.A. 177 O2
Lisburn U.K. 47 F9
Liscannor Bay Rep. of Ireland 47 C11
Liscomb Game Sanctuary nature res. Canada 169 I4
Lisdoonvarna Rep. of Ireland 47 C10
Lisec mt. Macedonia 58 D7
L'Iseran, Col de pass France 51 N7
Lishan China see **Lintong**
Lishan Taiwan 87 G3
Lishe Jiang r. China 86 B3
Lishi China see **Dingnan**
Lishi China 85 F4
Līshtar-e Bālā Iran 100 B4
Lishu China 82 B4
Lishui Jiangsu China 87 F2
Lishui Zhejiang China 87 F2
Li Shui r. China 87 D2
Lisichansk Ukr. see **Lysychans'k**
Lisieux France 50 G3
Lisiy Nos Rus. Fed. 43 L1
Liskeard U.K. 47 H13
Liski Rus. Fed. 41 F6
formerly known as Georgiu-Dezh
L'Isle-en-Dodon France 50 G9
L'Isle-Jourdain France 50 H9
L'Isle-sur-la-Sorgue France 51 L9
L'Isle-sur-le-Doubs France 51 M5
Lismore Australia 147 G2
Lismore N.Z. 153 F11
Lismore Rep. of Ireland 47 E11
Lisne Ukr. 58 K2
Liss mt. Saudi Arabia 109 J6
Lissa Croatia see **Vis**
Lissa Poland see **Leszno**
Lisseri, Oued watercourse Tunisia 123 H2
Listafjorden b. Norway 45 I4
Lister, Mount Antarctica 223 K1
Listore watercourse Australia 148 C5
Listowel Canada 168 D5
Listowel Rep. of Ireland 47 C11
Listowel Downs Australia 149 E5
Listvyaga, Khrebet mts Kazakh./Rus. Fed. 88 D1
Listvyanka Rus. Fed. 84 E1
Liswarta r. Poland 49 P4
Lit Sweden 44 K3
Litang Guangxi China 87 D4
Litang Sichuan China 86 B2
also known as Gaocheng
Litang Qu r. China 86 B2
Litani r. Fr. Guiana/Suriname 199 H4
Lītāni r. Lebanon 108 G4
Litchfield CA U.S.A. 182 D1
Litchfield IL U.S.A. 174 B4
Litchfield MI U.S.A. 173 I8
Litchfield MN U.S.A. 178 D2
Litembe Tanz. 129 D7
Litene Latvia 42 I4
Līth, Wādī al watercourse Saudi Arabia 104 C3
Lithgow Australia 147 F3
Lithino, Akra pt Greece 59 F14
▶**Lithuania** country Europe 42 E6
known as Lietuva in Lithuanian; formerly known as Litovskaya S.S.R.
europe [countries] ➤ 32–35
Litija Slovenia 56 G2
Lititz U.S.A. 177 I5
Litke, Mys c. Rus. Fed. 39 S2
Litochoro Greece 59 D8
Litoměřice Czech Rep. 49 L5
Litomyšl Czech Rep. 49 N6
Litovel Czech Rep. 49 O6
Litovko Rus. Fed. 82 D2
Litovskaya S.S.R. country Europe see **Lithuania**
Little r. LA U.S.A. 179 D6
Little r. OK U.S.A. 179 D5
Little r. TX U.S.A. 179 C6
Little Abaco i. Bahamas 186 D1
Little Abitibi r. Canada 168 D3
Little Abitibi Lake Canada 168 D3
Little Aden Yemen see **'Adan as Sughra**
Little Andaman i. India 95 G4
Little Bahama Bank sea feature Bahamas 186 D1
Little Barrier i. N.Z. 152 J4
Little Bay de Noc U.S.A. 172 F5
Little Belt sea chan. Denmark 45 J5
also known as Lille Bælt
Little Belt Mountains U.S.A. 180 E3
Little Bighorn r. U.S.A. 180 F3
Little Bitter Lake Egypt 108 D7
also known as Murrat el Sughra, Buheirat
Little Blue r. U.S.A. 178 C4
Little Bow r. Canada 167 H5
Little Buffalo r. Canada 167 H2
Little Cayman i. Cayman Is 186 C3
Little Churchill r. Canada 167 M3
Little Coco Island Cocos Is 79 A5
Little Colorado r. U.S.A. 183 M5
Little Creek Peak U.S.A. 183 L4
Little Current Canada 168 D4
Little Current r. Canada 168 C3
Little Desert National Park Australia 146 D4
Little Egg Harbor inlet U.S.A. 177 K6
Little Exuma i. Bahamas 186 E2
Little Falls MN U.S.A. 178 D2
Little Falls NY U.S.A. 177 K2
Littlefield AZ U.S.A. 183 K5
Littlefield TX U.S.A. 179 B5
Little Fish r. S. Africa 133 K10
Little Fork r. U.S.A. 174 A1
Little Fort Canada 166 F5
Little Grand Rapids Canada 167 M4
Little Grass Valley Reservoir U.S.A. 182 C2
Little Inagua Island Bahamas 187 E2
Little Kanawha r. U.S.A. 176 D6
Little Karas Berg plat. Namibia 132 C4
Little Karoo plat. S. Africa 132 E10
Little Lake U.S.A. 182 G6
Little Mecatina r. Canada 169 I3
also known as Petit Mécatina
Little Mecatina Island Canada see **Petit Mécatina, Île du**
Little Miami r. U.S.A. 176 A6
Little Minch sea chan. U.K. 46 E6
Little Missouri r. U.S.A. 178 B2
Little Muskingum r. U.S.A. 176 D6
Little Nicobar i. India 95 G5
Little Olifants r. S. Africa 133 N2
Little Pamir mts Afgh. 101 H2
Little Pic r. Canada 172 G2
Little Powder r. U.S.A. 180 F3
Little Rann marsh India 96 A5
Little Red r. U.S.A. 179 E5
Little Red River Canada 167 H3
Little River N.Z. 153 G11
Little River U.S.A. 175 E5

▶**Little Rock** U.S.A. 179 D5
State capital of Arkansas.

Littlerock U.S.A. 182 G7
Little Sable Point U.S.A. 172 G7
Little Sachigo Lake Canada 168 A2
Little Salmon Lake Canada 166 C2
Little Salt Lake U.S.A. 183 L4
Little Sandy Desert Australia 150 B4
Little San Salvador i. Bahamas 186 E1
Little Sioux r. U.S.A. 178 C3
Little Smoky Canada 167 G4
Little Smoky r. Canada 167 G4
Little Snake r. U.S.A. 180 E4
Littlestown U.S.A. 177 H6
Little Tibet reg. Jammu and Kashmir see **Ladakh**
Littleton NC U.S.A. 176 H9
Littleton NH U.S.A. 177 N1
Littleton WV U.S.A. 176 E6
Little Traverse Bay U.S.A. 173 H5
Little Tupper Lake U.S.A. 177 K1
Little Turtle Lake Canada 172 A2
Little Valley U.S.A. 176 G3
Little Wabash r. U.S.A. 174 B4
Little Wanganui N.Z. 152 G9
Little White r. U.S.A. 178 B3
Little Wichita r. U.S.A. 179 C5
Little Wind r. U.S.A. 180 E4
Little Wood r. U.S.A. 180 D4
Little Zab r. Iraq see **Zāb aş Şaghīr, Nahr az**
Littoral prov. Cameroon 125 H5
Litunde Moz. 129 B8
Lituya Bay U.S.A. 166 B3
Litvínov Czech Rep. 49 K5
Liu r. China 85 H3
Liu r. China 85 I3
Liu Estonia 42 F3
Liuba China 86 C1
Liuchiu Yü i. Taiwan 87 G4
Liuchong He r. China 86 C3
Liuchow China see **Liuzhou**
Liugong Dao i. China 85 I4
Liugu r. China 85 I3
Liuhe China 82 B4
Liuheng Dao i. China 87 G2
Liujiachang China 87 D2
Liujiang China 87 D3
also known as Labao
Liujiaxia China see **Yongjing**
Liujiaxia Shuiku resr China 84 D5
Liulin China see **Jonê**
Liulin China 85 F4
Liupai China see **Tian'e**
Liupan Shan mts China 85 E5
Liupanshui China see **Lupanshui**
Liupo Moz. 131 H2
Liure Hond. 186 B4
Liushuquan China 84 B3
Liuwa Plain Zambia 127 D8
Liuwa Plain National Park Zambia 127 D8
Liuyang China 87 E2
Liuyang He r. China 87 E2
Liuzhangzhen China see **Yuanqu**

index

L

Liuzhou China 87 D3
formerly known as Liuchow
Livada, Akra pt Greece 59 G11
Livadi i. Greece 59 H12
Livadiya Rus. Fed. 82 D4
Līvāni Latvia 42 H5
Livanjsko Polje plain Bos.-Herz. 56 I4
Livarot France 50 G3
Līvbērze Latvia 42 E5
Live Oak CA U.S.A. 182 C2
Live Oak FL U.S.A. 175 D6
Liveringa Australia 150 D3
Livermore U.S.A. 182 C4
Livermore, Mount U.S.A. 181 F7
Liverpool Australia 147 F3
Liverpool Canada 169 H4
Liverpool U.K. 47 J10
Liverpool U.S.A. 177 I3
Liverpool Bay Canada 164 F3
Liverpool Plains Australia 147 F2
Liverpool Range mts Australia 147 F2
Livingston U.K. 46 I8
Livingston AL U.S.A. 175 B5
Livingston CA U.S.A. 182 D4
Livingston KY U.S.A. 176 A8
Livingston LA U.S.A. 175 B6
Livingston MT U.S.A. 180 E3
Livingston NJ U.S.A. 177 K5
Livingston TX U.S.A. 179 D6
Livingston WI U.S.A. 172 C8
Livingston, Lake U.S.A. 179 D6
Livingstone Zambia 127 E9
also known as Maramba
Livingstonia Malawi 129 B7
Livingston Island Antarctica 222 T2
Livingston Manor U.S.A. 177 K4
Livingston Mountains N.Z. 153 C12
Livno Bos.-Herz. 56 I5
Livny Rus. Fed. 43 S9
Livo r. Fin. 44 O2
Livonia MI U.S.A. 173 J8
Livonia NY U.S.A. 176 H3
Livorno Italy 56 C5
historically known as Leghorn
Livradois, Monts du France 51 J7
Livradois Forez, Parc Naturel Régional du nature res. France 51 J7
Livramento do Brumado Brazil 202 D5
Livron-sur-Drôme France 51 K8
Liwā Oman 105 F3
Liwā', Wādī al watercourse Syria 109 H5
Liwale Tanz. 129 C7
Liwiec r. Poland 49 S3
Liwonde Malawi 129 B8
Liwonde National Park Malawi 129 B8
Liwu China i. see Lixian
Lixian Gansu China 86 C1
Lixian Hebei China 85 G4
also known as Liwu
Lixian Hunan China 87 D2
Lixian Sichuan China 86 B2
also known as Zagunao
Lixin China 87 E1
Lixouri Greece 59 B10
Lixus Morocco see Larache
Liyang China 87 F2
Liyuan China see Sangzhi
Liz r. Port. 54 C5
Lizarda Brazil 202 C4
Lizard Island Australia 149 E2
Lizard Point U.K. 47 G14
Lizarra Spain see Estella
Lizemores U.S.A. 176 D7
Liziping China 86 B2
Lizonne r. France 50 G7
Ljig Srbija Yugo. 58 B4
Ljubija Bos.-Herz. 56 I4

▶ Ljubljana Slovenia 56 G2
Capital of Slovenia. Historically known as Emona or Laibach.

Ljubuški Bos.-Herz. 56 J5
Ljugarn Sweden 45 L4
Ljunga r. Sweden 44 L3
Ljungan r. Sweden 44 L3
Ljungby Sweden 45 K4
Ljungskile Sweden 45 K4
Ljusdal Sweden 45 L3
Ljusnan r. Sweden 45 L3
Ljusne Sweden 45 L3
Ljutomer Slovenia 56 I2
Llagostera Spain 55 N3
Llaima, Volcán vol. Chile 204 C5
Llanbedr U.K. see Lampeter
Llançà Spain 55 O2
also spelt Llansá
Llancanelo, Salina salt flat Arg. 204 C4
Llandeilo U.K. 47 I12
Llandovery U.K. 47 I12
also known as Llanymddyfri
Llandrindod Wells U.K. 47 I11
Llandudno U.K. 47 I10
Llanelli U.K. 47 H12
Llanes Spain 54 G1
Llangollen U.K. 47 I11
Llangurig U.K. 47 I11
Llano Mex. 184 C2
Llano U.S.A. 179 C6
Llano r. U.S.A. 179 C6
Llano Estacado plain U.S.A. 179 B5
Llanos plain Col./Venez. 198 D3

Llanquihue, Lago l. Chile 205 B6
Llansá Spain see Llançà
Llanymddyfri U.K. see Llandovery
Llata Peru 200 A2
Lleida Spain 55 L3
also spelt Lérida
Llerena Spain 54 E6
Lliria Spain 55 M3
Llobregat r. Spain 55 M3
Llodio Spain 55 I1
Lloret de Mar Spain 55 N3
Llorgara nat. park Albania 59 A8
Lloyd Bay Australia 149 D2
Lloyd George, Mount Canada 166 E3
Lloyd Lake Canada 167 I3
Lloydminster Canada 167 I4
Lluchmayor Spain see Llucmajor
Llucmajor Spain 55 N5
also spelt Lluchmayor
Llullaillaco, Volcán v. Chile 200 C6
Loa r. Chile 200 C5
Loa U.S.A. 183 M3
Loagan Bunut National Park Sarawak Malaysia 77 F2
Loakulu Indon. 77 G3
Loanda Brazil 203 A7
Loano Italy 56 A4
Loay Phil. 74 C4
Lob' r. Rus. Fed. 43 Q5
Loban' r. Rus. Fed. 40 I4
Lobanovo Rus. Fed. 43 T8
Lobata Indon. 75 B3
Lobatse Botswana 131 E5
Löbau Germany 49 L4
Lobaye pref. Cent. Afr. Rep. 126 C3
Lobaye r. Cent. Afr. Rep. 126 C4
Löbenberg hill Germany 49 J4
Loberia Arg. 204 F5
Łobez Poland 49 M2
Lobito Angola 127 B8
Lobitos Peru 198 A6
Lobnya Rus. Fed. 43 S5
Loboko Dem. Rep. Congo 126 C5
Lobón Spain 54 E6
Lobos Arg. 204 F4
Lobos, Cabo c. Mex. 184 B2
Lobos, Isla de i. Mex. 185 F4
Lobos de Afuera, Islas is Peru 198 A6
Lobos de Tierra, Isla i. Peru 198 A6
Loburg Germany 48 J3
Łobżenica Poland 49 O2
Locarno Switz. 51 O6
Lochaline U.K. 46 G7
Lochalsh Canada 173 I2
Lo Chau i. Hong Kong China see Beaufort Island
Loch Baghasdail U.K. see Lochboisdale
Lochboisdale U.K. 46 E6
also spelt Loch Baghasdail
Lochern National Park Australia 149 D3
Loches France 50 G5
Loch Garman Rep. of Ireland see Wexford
Lochgilphead U.K. 46 G7
Lochiel S. Africa 133 O3
Lochinver U.K. 46 G5
Lochmaddy U.K. 46 E6
also known as Loch nam Madadh
Loch nam Madadh U.K. see Lochmaddy
Lochnagar mt. U.K. 46 I7
Łochów Poland 49 S3
Lochranza U.K. 46 G8
Lochsa r. U.S.A. 180 D3
Lochy, Loch l. U.K. 46 H7
Lock Australia 146 B3
Lockbourne U.S.A. 176 C6
Lockeford U.S.A. 182 C3
Lockerbie U.K. 47 I8
Lockhart Australia 147 E3
Lockhart U.S.A. 179 C6
Lockhart River Australia 149 D2
Lockhart River Aboriginal Reserve Australia 149 D2
Lock Haven U.S.A. 176 H4
Löcknitz r. Germany 48 L2
Lockport U.S.A. 176 G2
Locminé France 50 D5
Loc Ninh Vietnam 79 D6
Locorotondo Italy 57 J8
Locri Italy 57 I11
Locumba r. Peru 200 C4
Lod Israel 108 F6
also known as Lydda
Loddon r. Australia 147 D3
Lode Latvia 42 G4
Lodève France 51 J9
Lodeynoye Pole Rus. Fed. 43 O1
Lodge, Mount Canada/U.S.A. 166 B3
Lodge Creek r. Canada/U.S.A. 167 I5
Lodhikheda India 96 C5
Lodhran Pak. 101 G4
Lodi Italy 56 B3
Lodi CA U.S.A. 182 C3
Lodi OH U.S.A. 176 C5
Lodi WI U.S.A. 172 D7
Loding Norway 44 K2
Lodingen Norway 44 K1
Lodja Dem. Rep. Congo 126 D5
Lodomeria Rus. Fed. see Vladimir
Lodosa Spain 55 I2
Łodrani India 96 A5
Lodwar Kenya 128 B4
Lodz Poland see Łódź
Łódź Poland 49 Q4
English form Lodz
Loei Thai. 78 C4
Loeriefontein S. Africa 132 D7
Lofoten is Norway 44 K1
Lofsdalen Sweden 45 K3
Lofter S. Africa 133 J7
Lofty Range hills Australia 150 B5
Log Rus. Fed. 41 G6
Loga Niger 125 F3
Logageng S. Africa 133 I2
Logan IA U.S.A. 178 C3
Logan NM U.S.A. 181 G6
Logan OH U.S.A. 176 C6
Logan UT U.S.A. 180 E4
Logan WV U.S.A. 176 D8

▶ Logan, Mount Canada 166 A2
2nd highest mountain in North America.
northamerica [landscapes] >>> 156-157

Logan, Mount U.S.A. 180 C3
Logan Creek r. Australia 149 E4
Logan Creek r. U.S.A. 178 C3
Logandale U.S.A. 183 J5
Logan Lake Canada 166 F5
Logan Mountains Canada 166 D2
Logansport IN U.S.A. 172 G9
Logansport LA U.S.A. 179 D6
Logatec Slovenia 56 G3
Lögdeälven r. Sweden 44 L3
Loge r. Angola 127 B6
Logan'an China 87 E4
Logone r. Africa 126 B1
Logone Birni Cameroon 125 I4
Logone Occidental pref. Chad 126 B2
Logone Oriental pref. Chad 126 C2
Logrești Romania 58 E4
Logroño Spain 55 I2
Løgstør Denmark 45 J4
Logtak Lake India 97 G4
Logudoro reg. Sardegna Italy 57 A8
Lohardaga India 97 E5
Loharu India 96 B3
Lohatlha S. Africa 132 H5

Lohawat India 96 B4
Lohi r. China/India see Zayü Qu
Lohilahti Fin. 45 O3
Lohiniva Fin. 44 N2
Lohja Fin. 45 N3
Lohjanjärvi l. Fin. 42 E1
Löhne (Oldenburg) Germany 48 F3
Lohne (Oldenburg) Germany 48 F3
Lohtaja Fin. 44 M2
Lohusuu Estonia 42 I3
Loi, Nam r. Myanmar 78 C3
Loikaw Myanmar 78 B4
Loi Lan mt. Myanmar/Thai. 78 B4
Loimaa Fin. 45 M3
Loimaan kunta Fin. 42 D1
Loipyet Hills Myanmar 78 B2
Loir r. France 50 F5
Loir, Les Vaux du valley France 50 G5
Loire r. France 51 D5
Loisach r. Germany 48 I8
Loi Sang mt. Myanmar 78 B3
Loi Song mt. Myanmar 78 B3
Loita Plains Kenya 128 B5
Loja Ecuador 198 B6
Loja prov. Ecuador 198 B6
Loja Spain 54 G7
Lokan r. Sabah Malaysia 77 G1
Lokandu Dem. Rep. Congo 126 E5
Lokan tekojärvi l. Fin. 44 N2
Lokchim r. Rus. Fed. 40 I3
Lokeren Belgium 51 K1
Lokichar Kenya 128 B4
Lokichokio Kenya 128 B3
Lokilalaki, Gunung mt. Indon. 75 B3
Lokka Fin. 44 N2
Løkken Denmark 45 J4
Løkken Norway 44 J3
Loknya Rus. Fed. 43 L5
Lokofe Dem. Rep. Congo 126 D5
Lokoja Nigeria 125 G5
Lokolama Dem. Rep. Congo 126 C5
Lokolo r. Dem. Rep. Congo 126 C5
Lokomo Cameroon 125 I6
Lokoro r. Dem. Rep. Congo 126 C5
Lokosafa Cent. Afr. Rep. 126 C3
Lokossa Benin 125 F5
Lokot' Rus. Fed. 43 P9
Loksa Estonia 42 G2
Løksebotn Norway 44 L1
Loks Land i. Canada 165 M3
Lokutu Dem. Rep. Congo see Elisabetha
Lol r. Sudan 126 F2
Lol watercourse Sudan 126 F2
Lola Angola 127 B8
Lola Guinea 124 C5
Lola, Mount U.S.A. 182 D2
Lolland i. Denmark 45 J5
Lolle watercourse Sudan 128 A2
Lollondo Tanz. 128 B5
Lolo Dem. Rep. Congo 126 D4
Lolo U.S.A. 180 D3
Loloda Indon. 75 C2
Loloda Utara, Kepulauan is Indon. 75 C2
Lolodorf Cameroon 125 H6
Lolo Pass U.S.A. 180 D3
Lolowau Indon. 76 B2
Lolwane S. Africa 132 H3
Lom Bulg. 58 E5
Lom r. Bulg. 58 E5
Lom Norway 45 J3
Lom Rus. Fed. 43 U4
Loma U.S.A. 180 E3
Loma Alta Bol. 200 D4
Lomako r. Dem. Rep. Congo 126 D4
Lomaloma Fiji 145 H3
Lomami r. Dem. Rep. Congo 126 E4
Loma Mountains Sierra Leone 124 C4
Lomar Pass Afgh. 101 F3
Lomas Peru 200 B3
Lomas Coloradas hills Arg. 205 D6
Lomas de Zamora Arg. 204 F4
Lomati r. S. Africa see Mlumati
Lombarda, Serra hills Brazil 199 H4
Lombardia admin. reg. Italy 56 B3
Lombardy admin. reg. Italy see Lombardia
Lomblen i. Indon. 75 B5
Lombok Indon. 77 G5
Lombok i. Indon. 77 G5
Lombok, Selat sea chan. Indon. 77 F5

▶ Lomé Togo 125 F5
Capital of Togo.

Lomela r. Dem. Rep. Congo 126 D5
Lomié Cameroon 125 I6
Lomira U.S.A. 172 E7
Lommel Belgium 51 L1
Lomond Canada 167 H5
Lomond, Loch l. U.K. 46 H7
Lomonosov Rus. Fed. 43 K2
Lomont hills France 51 M5
Lomovoye Rus. Fed. 40 G2
Lomphat Cambodia see Lumphăt
Lompobattang, Gunung mt. Indon. 75 A4
Lompoc U.S.A. 182 D7
Lom Sak Thai. 78 C4
Lomsjö Sweden 44 L2
Łomża Poland 49 S2
Lonar India 94 C2
Lonavale India 94 B2
Loncopue Arg. 204 C5
Londa Bangl. 97 F5
Londa India 94 B3
Londinium U.K. see London
Londoko Rus. Fed. 82 D2
London Canada 168 D5

▶ London U.K. 47 L12
Capital of the United Kingdom and of England. 3rd most populous city in Europe. Historically known as Londinium.
world [cities] >>> 24-25
europe [environments] >>> 36-37

London KY U.S.A. 176 A8
London OH U.S.A. 176 B6
London City airport U.K. 47 M12
Londonderry U.K. 47 I9
also known as Derry or Doire
Londonderry U.S.A. 177 N2
Londonderry, Cape Australia 150 D2
Londres Arg. 204 D2
Londrina Brazil 206 B10
Lone Mountain U.S.A. 176 A9
Lone Pine U.S.A. 182 F5
Long Thai. 78 B4
Longa Angola 127 C8
Longa r. Bengo/Cuanza Sul Angola 127 B7
Longa r. Cuando Cubango Angola 127 C9
Longa, Proliv sea chan. Rus. Fed. 39 R2
English form De Long Strait
Longagung Indon. 77 F2
Long Akah Sarawak Malaysia 77 F2
Long'an China 87 D4
Long'an China see Pingwu
Longarone Italy 56 E2
Longavi, Nevado de mt. Chile 204 C4
Long Bay U.S.A. 175 E5
Long Beach N.Z. 153 F12
Long Beach CA U.S.A. 182 F8
Long Beach WA U.S.A. 180 A3
Longbia Indon. 77 G2
Longboh Indon. 77 F2
Long Branch U.S.A. 177 L5
Longburn N.Z. 152 J8

Long Cay i. Bahamas 187 E2
Longchang China see Xiaoxian
also known as Jin'e
Longcheng China see Longmen
Longcheng China see Pengze
Longcheng China see Chenggong
Longchuan China 87 E3
also known as Laolong
Longchuan China see Nanhua
Longde China 85 F4
Longfellow, Mount N.Z. 153 G10
Longford Rep. of Ireland 47 E10
Longgang China see Dazu
Longgang China 87 E4
Longgi r. Indon. 77 G2
Long Harbour Hong Kong China 87 [inset]
also known as Tai Tan Hoi Hap
Longhope U.K. 46 I5
Longhua China 85 H3
Longhui China 87 D3
also known as Taohong; formerly known as Taohuaping
Longhurst, Mount Antarctica 223 K1
Longibau Indon. 77 G2
Longido Tanz. 128 C5
Longikis Indon. 77 G3
Longing, Cape Antarctica 222 U2
Longiram Indon. 77 F3
Long Island Bahamas 187 E2
Long Island N.S. Canada 169 H4
Long Island Nunavut Canada 168 E2
Long Island P.N.G. 73 K8
Long Island U.S.A. 177 M5
Long Island Sound sea chan. U.S.A. 177 L4
Longjiang China 85 I2
Long Jiang r. China 87 D3
Longjin China see Qingliu
Longjin China see Anyi
Longjuzhai China see Danfeng
Longkou China 85 I4
Longkou Wan b. China 85 I4
Longlac Canada 168 C3
Long Lake l. U.S.A. 177 K2
Long Lake l. MI U.S.A. 172 H6
Long Lake l. MI U.S.A. 173 J5
Long Lake l. NY U.S.A. 177 K1
Longli China 86 C3
also known as Longshan
Longlin China 86 C3
also known as Xinzhou
Longmeadow U.S.A. 177 M3
Longmen China 87 E4
also known as Longcheng
Longmen Shan mts China 86 C1
Longming China 86 C4
Longmont U.S.A. 180 F4
Longnan China 87 E3
Longnawan Indon. 77 F2
Longobucco Italy 57 I9
Longonjo Angola 127 B8
Longotoma Chile 204 C4
Longpahangai Indon. 77 F2
Long Phu Vietnam 79 D6
Longping China see Luodian
Longqing China see Danzhai
Longquan China see Fenggang
Longquan China 87 F2
Longquan Xi r. China 87 G2
Long Range Mountains Nfld. Canada 169 J3
Longreach Australia 149 E4
Long Reef Australia 150 E2
Long Reef P.N.G. 149 F1
Longriba China 86 B1
Long Ridge U.S.A. 176 A7
Longshan China see Longli
Longshan China 87 D2
Longsheng China 87 D3
Longshou Shan mts China 84 D4
Longs Peak U.S.A. 180 F4
Long Teru Sarawak Malaysia 77 F2
Longtian China 87 D2
Longtom Lake Canada 167 G1
Long Tompas pass S. Africa 133 C2
Longtown U.K. 47 J8
Longué-Jumelles France 50 F5
Longue-Pointe Canada 169 H3
Longueuil Canada 169 F4
Longuyon France 51 L3
Longvale U.S.A. 182 A2
Long Valley U.S.A. 183 M7
Longview TX U.S.A. 179 D5
Longview WA U.S.A. 180 B3
Longwangmiao China 90 C2
Longwei Co l. China 89 E5
Longxi China 84 E5
Long Xian r. China 87 F3
Longxian China see Dehua
Long Xuyen Vietnam 79 D6
Longyan China 87 F3
Longyao China 85 G4

Longzhen China 82 B2
Longzhou China 86 C4
Longzhouping China see Changyang
Lonigo Italy 56 D3
Lonja r. Croatia 56 I3
Lonjsko Polje plain Croatia 56 I3
Lonkimtsy Madag. 131 [inset] K4
Lonoke U.S.A. 174 B5
Lönsboda Sweden 45 K4
Lønsdalen valley Norway 44 K2
Lons-le-Saunier France 51 L6
Lontar i. Indon. 75 D4
Lonton Myanmar 78 B2
Lontra Brazil 199 I6
Lontra r. Mato Grosso do Sul Brazil 203 A7
Lontra r. Tocantins Brazil 202 B3
Looc Phil. 74 B3
Looc Phil. 74 B3
Looking Glass r. U.S.A. 173 I8
Lookout, Cape Canada 168 D2
Lookout, Cape U.S.A. 174 E5
Lookout, Point U.S.A. 173 J6
Lookout Mountain U.S.A. 182 F5
Lookout Point W.A. Australia 151 B7
Loolmalasin vol. crater Tanz. 128 B5
Looma Australia 150 B3
Loon Canada 168 B3
Loon r. Canada 167 H3
Loongana Australia 151 D6
Loon Lake Canada 167 I4
Loop Head Rep. of Ireland 47 C11
Lootsberg Pass S. Africa 133 I8
Lop China 89 C4
Lopandino Rus. Fed. 43 P9
Lopary Madag. 131 [inset] J4
Lopasnya r. Rus. Fed. 43 S7
Lopatina, Gora mt. Rus. Fed. 82 F2
Lopatino Rus. Fed. 41 I5

Lopatinskiy Rus. Fed. 43 T6
Lopatka, Cape Rus. Fed. see Lopatka, Mys
Lopatka, Mys c. Kamchatskaya Oblast' Rus. Fed. 39 P4
Lopatka, Mys c. Respublika Sakha (Yakutiya) Rus. Fed. 39 P2
English form Lopatka, Cape
Lopatovo Rus. Fed. 43 J4
Lopazna Rus. Fed. 43 N8
Lop Buri Thai. 79 C5
Lopburi r. Indon. 73 I8
Lopé-Okanda, Réserve de nature res. Gabon 126 A5
Lopez Phil. 74 B3
Lopez, Cap c. Gabon 126 A5
Lopnur China see Yuli
Lop Nur salt l. China 88 E3
Lop r. Dem. Rep. Congo 126 C4
Lopphavet b. Norway 44 M1
Loppi Fin. 45 N3
Lora r. Afgh. 101 F4
Lora watercourse Australia 146 B2
Lora Norway 45 J3
Lora del Rio Spain 54 F7
Lorain U.S.A. 176 C4
Loralai Pak. 101 G4
Loralai r. Pak. 101 G4
Lorca Spain 55 J7
Lord Howe Atoll Solomon Is see Ontong Java Atoll
Lord Howe Island Australia 145 E5
Lord Loughborough Island Myanmar 79 B6
Lordsburg U.S.A. 181 E6
Lore Lindu National Park Indon. 75 B3
Lorena Brazil 203 C7
Lorengau P.N.G. 73 K7
Lorentz r. Indon. 73 I8
Lorentz National Park Indon. 73 I7
Lorenzo del Real Mex. 185 F4
Lorenzo Geyres Uruguay 204 F4
Lorestan prov. Iran 100 B3
Loreto Brazil 202 C3
Loreto Italy 56 F5
Loreto Mex. 184 C3
Loreto Para. 201 F5
Loreto dept Peru 198 C5
Loreto Phil. 74 C5
Loretta U.S.A. 172 C5
Lorian Swamp Kenya 128 C4
Lorica Col. 198 B2
Lorient France 50 C5
Lorillard r. Canada 167 N1
Lormi r. India 97 D5
Lorne, Firth of est. U.K. 46 G7
Lorne Qld Australia 149 E5
Lorne Vic. Australia 147 D4
Loro r. China 89 F6
Loropéni Burkina 124 E4
Lörrach Germany 48 E8
Lorrain r. Australia 151 C7
Lorraine Australia 148 C3
Lorraine admin. reg. France 51 M4
Lorraine, Parc Naturel Régional de park France 51 L4
Lort r. Australia 151 C7
Lorut i. Indon. 75 C5
Los, Îles de is Guinea 124 B4
Losai National Reserve nature res. Kenya 128 C4
Losal India 96 B4
Los Alamitos, Sierra de mt. Mex. 185 E4
Los Alamos CA U.S.A. 182 D7
Los Alamos NM U.S.A. 181 F5
Los Alerces, Parque Nacional nat. park Arg. 205 C6
Los Amores Arg. 204 F3
Los Andes Chile 204 C4

▶ Los Angeles U.S.A. 182 F7
3rd most populous city in North America and 7th in the world.
world [cities] >>> 24-25
northamerica [threats] >>> 160-161

Los Angeles Aqueduct canal U.S.A. 182 F6
Los Antiguos Arg. 205 C7
Los Arabos Cuba 186 C2
Los Argallanes, Sierra de hills Spain 54 F6
Los Banos U.S.A. 182 D4
Los Barreros mt. Spain 55 I6
Los Barrios Spain 54 F8
Los Blancos Arg. 201 E5
Los Caballos Mesteños, Llano de plain Mex. 184 D2
Los Canarreos, Archipiélago de is Cuba 186 C2
Los Chiles Costa Rica 186 B5
Los Chonos, Archipiélago de is Chile 205 B7
Los Choros, Islas de los Arg. 204 C3
Los Cisnes, Lagunas de lakes Arg. 204 E4
Los Corales del Rosario, Parque Nacional nat. park Col. 198 C2
Los Coronados, Golfo de b. Chile 205 B6
Los Coronados, Islas is Mex. 183 G9
Los Corrales de Buelna Spain 54 G1
Los Cusis Beni Bol. 200 D3
Los Cusis Beni Bol. 201 D3
Los Difuntos, Lago de l. Uruguay see Negra, Lago
Los Desventurados, Islas de is S. Pacific Ocean 221 M7
Los Estados, Isla de i. Arg. 205 D9
historically known as Staten Island
Losevo Rus. Fed. 41 G6
Los Gatos U.S.A. 182 C4
Los Glaciares, Parque Nacional nat. park Arg. 205 B8
Los Haitises nat. park Dom. Rep. 187 F3
Los Hoyos Mex. 184 C2
Los Huemules, Parque Nacional nat. park Chile 205 B7
Los Huicholes, Sierra de mts Mex. 184 D4
Los Idolos Mex. 185 G5
Lošinj i. Croatia 56 G4
Los Jardines de la Reina, Archipiélago de is Cuba 186 D2
Los Juries Arg. 204 E3
Loskop S. Africa 133 N5
Loskop Dam Nature Reserve S. Africa 133 N2
Los Lagos Chile 204 B5
Los Lagos admin. reg. Chile 204 B6
Loslau Poland see Wodzisław Śląski
Los Leones Mex. 184 D2
Los Lunas U.S.A. 181 F6
Los Mármoles, Parque Nacional nat. park Mex. 185 F4
Los Menucos Arg. 205 C6
Los Mexicanos, Lago de l. Mex. 184 D2
Los'mino Rus. Fed. 43 P6
Los Mochis Mex. 184 C3
Los Molinos U.S.A. 182 B1
Los Mosquitos, Golfo de b. Panama 186 C5
Los Navalmorales Spain 54 G5
Los Nevados, Parque Nacional nat. park Col. 198 C3
Los Nodales, Bahía de b. Arg. 205 D8
Los Organos, Sierra de hills Cuba 175 C8
Los Palacios Cuba 186 C2
Los Palacios y Villafranca Spain 54 F7
Lospatos East Timor 75 C5
Los Pedroches plain Spain 54 F6
Los Picos de Europa, Parque Nacional de nat. park Spain 54 G1
Los Reyes Mex. 185 E5
Los Riachos, Islas de is Arg. 204 E6
Los Rios prov. Ecuador 198 B5

Los Roques, Islas is Venez. 199 E2
Los Sauces Chile 204 B5
Lossiemouth U.K. 46 I6
Los Taques Venez. 198 D2
Lost Creek U.S.A. 176 B8
Los Telares Arg. 204 E3
Los Teques Venez. 199 E2
Los Testigos is Venez. 199 F2
Lost Hills U.S.A. 182 E6
Lost Trail Pass U.S.A. 180 D3
Losvida, Vozyera l. Belarus 43 L6
Los Vientos Chile 200 C6
Los Vilos Chile 204 B4
Lot r. France 51 G8
Lota Chile 204 B5
Lotagipi Swamp Kenya 128 B3
Lote Norway 45 J3
Loten Norway 45 J3
Lotfābād Turkm. 102 D5
Loth U.K. 46 J4
Lothagum Hills Sudan 128 B3
Lothair S. Africa 133 O3
L'Oti, Réserve de Faune de nature res. Togo 125 F4
Lotikipi Plain Kenya 128 B3
Loto Dem. Rep. Congo 126 D5
Lotoi r. Dem. Rep. Congo 126 C5
Lotoshino Rus. Fed. 43 Q5
Lot's Wife i. Japan see Sōfu-gan
Lotta r. Fin./Rus. Fed. 44 O1
also spelt Lutto
Louang Namtha Laos 78 C3
also spelt Luang Nam Tha
Louangphrabang Laos 78 C4
also spelt Luang Prabang
Louang Phrabang Range mts Laos/Thai. 78 C4
Loubomo Congo 126 B6
also known as Dolisie
Loučná hill Czech Rep. 49 K5
Loudéac France 50 D4
Loudi China 87 D3
Loudima Congo 126 B6
Loudon U.S.A. 174 C5
Loudonville U.S.A. 176 C5
Loudun France 50 G5
Louésse r. Congo 126 B6
L'Ouest, Pointe de pt Canada 169 H3
Louga Senegal 124 A3
Lougborough U.K. 47 K11
Loughborough Island Canada 165 I2
Loughrea Rep. of Ireland 47 D10
Louhans France 51 L6
Louisa KY U.S.A. 176 C7
Louisa VA U.S.A. 176 H7
Louisa Downs Aboriginal Reserve Australia 150 D3
Louisbourg Canada 169 J4
formerly spelt Louisburg
Louisburg U.S.A. 176 G9
Louisburg Canada see Louisbourg
Louise Falls Canada 167 G2
Louis-Gentil Morocco see Youssoufia
Louisiade Archipelago is P.N.G. 149 G3
Louisiana U.S.A. 174 B4
Louisiana state U.S.A. 175 B6
Louis Trichardt S. Africa 131 F3
Louisvale S. Africa 132 F5
Louisville GA U.S.A. 175 D5
Louisville IL U.S.A. 174 B4
Louisville KY U.S.A. 174 C4
Louisville MS U.S.A. 175 B5
Louisville OH U.S.A. 176 D5
Louis-XIV, Pointe pt Canada 168 E2
Loukhi Rus. Fed. 44 P2
Loukoléla Congo 126 C5
Loukouo Congo 126 B6
Loulé Port. 54 C7
Loulouni Mali 124 D4
Louny Czech Rep. 49 K5
Loup r. U.S.A. 178 C3
Loup City U.S.A. 178 C3
Loups-Marins, Lacs des lakes Canada 169 F1
Lourdes Canada 169 J3
Lourdes France 50 F9
Lourenço Brazil 199 I4
Lourenço Marques Moz. see Maputo
Lourinhã Port. 54 B5
Lousã Port. 54 C4
Louterwater S. Africa 132 H10
Louth Australia 147 E2
Louth U.K. 47 L10
Loutra Greece 59 F11
Loutra Aidipsou Greece 59 E10
Loutraki Greece 59 D11
Louvain Belgium see Leuven
Louviers France 50 H3
Louwsburg S. Africa 133 P3
Lövånger Sweden 44 M2
Lövberga Sweden 44 K3
Lovat' r. Rus. Fed. 43 M3
Lovćen mts Yugo. 56 K6
Lovech Bulg. 58 F5
Loveland U.S.A. 180 F4
Lovell WY U.S.A. 180 F4
Lovell ME U.S.A. 177 O1
Lovelock U.S.A. 182 F1
Lovenia, Mount U.S.A. 183 N1
Lovere Italy 56 C3
Lovers' Leap mt. U.S.A. 176 E9
Loves Park U.S.A. 172 E8
Loviisa Fin. 45 N3
Lovington U.S.A. 181 G6
Lovosice Czech Rep. 49 K5
Lovozero Rus. Fed. 40 E1
Lovran Croatia 56 G3
Lovrin Romania 58 C3
Lovua Angola 127 D6
Lövvik Sweden 45 L6
Lovtsy Rus. Fed. 43 U6
Lôvua Angola 127 D6
Lôvua Angola 127 D7
Low Canada 173 R5
Lowa Dem. Rep. Congo 126 E5
Lowa r. Dem. Rep. Congo 126 E5
Lowani Pass Pak. 101 G3
Lowarai Pass Pak. 101 G3
Lowell IN U.S.A. 172 F9
Lowell MA U.S.A. 177 N3
Lowell MI U.S.A. 172 H8
Lowell OH U.S.A. 176 C6
Lowell VT U.S.A. 177 M1
Lowelli Sudan 128 B3
Löwen watercourse Namibia 132 B4
Lower Arrow Lake Canada 166 G5
Lower Brule Indian Reservation res. U.S.A. 178 C2
Lower California pen. Mex. see Baja California
Lower Garry Lake Canada 167 L1
Lower Glenelg National Park Australia 146 D4
Lower Granite Gorge U.S.A. 183 K6
Lower Hutt N.Z. 152 I9
Lower Klamath National Wildlife Refuge nature res. U.S.A. 180 B4
Lower Laberge Canada 166 C2
Lower Lake U.S.A. 182 B3
Lower Loteni S. Africa 133 N6
Lower Lough Erne l. U.K. 47 E9
Lower Peirce Reservoir Sing. 76 [inset]
Lower Pitsong S. Africa 133 M7
Lower Red Lake U.S.A. 178 D2
Lower Sabie S. Africa 133 P2
Lower Saxony land Germany see Niedersachsen
Lower Tunguska r. Rus. Fed. see Nizhnyaya Tunguska
Lower Zambezi National Park Zambia 127 F8

Lowestoft U.K. 47 N11
Lowgar prov. Afgh. 101 G3
Łowicz Poland 49 Q3
Low Island Kiribati see Starbuck Island
Lowmoor U.S.A. 176 F8
Lowsville U.S.A. 176 E6
Lowville U.S.A. 177 J2
Loxton Australia 146 D3
Loxton S. Africa 132 G8
Loyalsock Creek r. U.S.A. 177 I4
Loyalton U.S.A. 182 D2
Loyalty Islands New Caledonia see Loyauté, Îles
Loyang China see Luoyang
Loyauté, Îles is New Caledonia 145 F4
English form Loyalty Islands
Loyd U.S.A. 172 C7
Loyengo Swaziland 133 P3
Loyev Belarus see Loyew
Loyew Belarus 41 D6
also spelt Loyev
Loyno Rus. Fed. 40 J4
Loyola, Punta pt Arg. 205 C8
Løypskardtinden mt. Norway 44 K2
Lozère, Mont mt. France 51 J8
Loznica Srbija Yugo. 58 A4
Loznitsa Bulg. 58 H5
Lozova Ukr. 41 F6
also spelt Lozovaya
Lozovaya Kazakh. see Lozovoye
Lozovaya Ukr. see Lozova
Lozovik Srbija Yugo. 58 C4
Lozovoye Kazakh. 103 I1
formerly known as Lozovaya
Loz'va r. Rus. Fed. 40 L3
Ltyentye Apurte Aboriginal Land res. Australia 148 B5
also known as Santa Teresa Aboriginal Land
Lu r. China 85 F4
Luabo Moz. 131 H3
Luacano Angola 127 D7
Luachimo r. Angola/Dem. Rep. Congo 127 D6
Lua Dekere r. Dem. Rep. Congo 126 C4
Luakila Dem. Rep. Congo 126 E6
Luala r. Moz. 131 H3
Luambe National Park Zambia 129 B8
Luampa r. Zambia 127 E8
Lu'an China 87 F2
Luanchun China 87 D1
Luanco Spain 54 F1

▶Luanda Angola 127 B7
Capital of Angola.

Luanda prov. Angola 127 B7
Luando Angola 127 C7
Luando r. Angola 127 C7
Luando, Reserva Natural Integral do nature res. Angola 127 C7
Luang, Khao mt. Thai. 79 B6
Luanginga r. Zambia 127 D8
Luang Nam Tha Laos see Louang Namtha
Luang Prabang Laos see Louangphrabang
Luanguinga r. Angola 127 D8
Luangwa Zambia 127 F8
formerly known as Feira
Luangwa r. Zambia 127 F8
Luanhaizi China 84 B5
Luan He r. China 85 H4
Luannan China 85 H4
also known as Bencheng
Lua Nova Brazil 199 G6
Luanping China 85 H3
Luanshya Zambia 127 F8
Luanxian China 85 H4
also known as Luanzhou
Luanza Dem. Rep. Congo 127 F7
Luanzhou China see Luanxian
Luao Angola see Luau
Luapula prov. Zambia 127 F7
Luar, Danau l. Indon. 77 F2
Luarca Spain 54 E1
Luashi Dem. Rep. Congo 127 D7
Luatamba Angola 127 D8
Luau Angola 127 D7
formerly known as Teixeira de Sousa or Vila Teixeira de Sousa; formerly spelt Luao
Luba Equat. Guinea 125 H6
formerly known as San Carlos
Lubaczów Poland 49 U5
Lubalo Angola 127 C7
Lubań Poland 49 M4
Lubāna Latvia 42 H5
Lubānas ezers l. Latvia 42 H5
Lubang Phil. 74 B3
Lubang i. Phil. 74 B3
Lubang Islands Phil. 74 A3
Lubango Angola 127 B8
formerly known as Sá da Bandeira
Lubao Dem. Rep. Congo 127 E6
Lubartów Poland 49 T4
Lubawa Poland 49 Q2
Lübbecke Germany 48 F3
Lübben Germany 49 K4
Lübbenau Germany 49 K4
Lubbeskolk salt pan S. Africa 132 D6
Lubbock U.S.A. 179 B5
Lübeck Germany 48 H2
Lubeck U.S.A. 176 D6
Lübecker Bucht b. Germany 48 H1
Lubefu Dem. Rep. Congo 126 E6
Lubei China 85 I2
also known as Jarud
Lubelska, Wyżyna hills Poland 49 T4
Lüben Poland see Lubin
Lubenka Kazakh. 102 C2
Lubero Dem. Rep. Congo 126 F5
Lubéron, Montagne du ridge France 51 L9
Lubéron, Parc Naturel Régional du nature res. France 51 L9
Lubersac France 50 H7
Lubie, Jezioro l. Poland 49 M2
Lubienka r. Poland 49 P3
Lubień Kujawski Poland 49 Q3
Lubin Poland 49 N4
historically known as Lüben
Lubisi Dam resr S. Africa 133 L8
Lublin Poland 49 T4
Lubliniec Poland 49 P5
Lubnān country Asia see Lebanon
Lubny Ukr. 41 E6
Lubok Antu Sarawak Malaysia 77 E2
Luboń Poland 49 N3
Lubosalma Rus. Fed. 44 O3
Lubraniec Poland 49 P3
Lubrín Spain 55 I7
Lübtheen Germany 48 I2
Lubuagan Phil. 74 B2
Lubudi Dem. Rep. Congo 127 E7
Lubudi r. Dem. Rep. Congo 127 E7
Lubuklinggau Indon. 76 C3
Lubukpakam Indon. 76 B2
Lubuksikaping Indon. 76 C2
Lubumbashi Dem. Rep. Congo 127 E7
formerly known as Élisabethville
Lubunda Dem. Rep. Congo 127 E6
Lubungu Zambia 127 E8
Lubuta Zambia 127 D9
Lubutu Dem. Rep. Congo 126 E5
Lubutu r. Dem. Rep. Congo 126 E5
Lubwe Zambia 127 F7
Lubyanki Rus. Fed. 43 Q9
Lucala Angola 127 B7
Lucan Canada 173 L7
Lucanas Peru 200 B3
Lučani Srbija Yugo. 58 B5
Lucania, Mount Canada 166 A2
Lücaoshan China 84 B4
Lucapa Angola 127 D7
formerly known as Lukapa
Lucas Brazil 201 G3
Lucasville U.S.A. 176 C7
Lucca Italy 56 C5
Lucé France 50 H4
Lucea Jamaica 186 D3
Luce Bay U.K. 47 H9
Lucedale U.S.A. 175 B6
Lucélia Brazil 206 B8
Lucena Phil. 74 B3
Lucena Spain 54 G7
Lučenec Slovakia 49 Q7
Lucera Italy 56 H7
Lucerna Peru 200 C3
Lucerne Switz. 51 O5
also spelt Luzern
Lucerne U.S.A. 182 B2
Lucerne Valley U.S.A. 183 H7
Lucero Mex. 184 D2
Lucha r. Rus. Fed. 82 C1
Luchay Belarus 42 I6
Luchegorsk Rus. Fed. 82 D3
Lucheng China see Luchuan
Lucheng China 85 G4
Lucheng China see Kangding
Lucheringo r. Moz. 129 C7
Luchki Rus. Fed. 43 U5
Luchosa r. Belarus 43 L7
Lüchow Germany 48 I3
Luchuan China 87 D4
also known as Lucheng
Lüchun China 86 B4
also known as Daxing
Lucinda Australia 149 E3
Lucipara, Kepulauan is Indon. 75 C4
Lucira Angola 127 B8
Luciu Romania 58 I4
Luck Ukr. see Luts'k
Luck U.S.A. 172 A5
Luckau Germany 49 K4
Luckeesarai India 97 E4
also spelt Lakhisarai
Luckenwalde Germany 49 K3
Luckhoff S. Africa 133 I6
Lucknow Canada 173 L7
Lucknow India 96 D4
Luçon France 50 E6
Lücongpo China 87 D2
Lucunga Angola 127 B6
Lucusse Angola 127 D8
Lucy Creek Australia 148 C4
Lüda China see Dalian
Luda Kamchiya r. Bulg. 58 I5
Ludbreg Croatia 56 I2
Lüdenscheid Germany 48 E4
Lüderitz Namibia 130 B5
Ludewa Tanz. 129 B7
Ludhiana India 96 B3
Ludian China 86 B3
also known as Wenping
Luding China 86 B2
also known as Jagsamka or Luqiao
Ludington U.S.A. 172 G7
Ludlow U.K. 47 J11
Ludlow CA U.S.A. 183 H7
Ludlow VT U.S.A. 177 M2
Ludogorie reg. Bulg. 58 H5
Ludogorsko Plato plat. Bulg. 58 H5
Ludoni Rus. Fed. 43 K3
Ludowici U.S.A. 175 D6
Luduș Romania 58 F2
Ludvika Sweden 45 K3
Ludwigsburg Germany 48 G7
Ludwigsfelde Germany 49 K3
Ludwigshafen am Rhein Germany 48 F6
Ludwigslust Germany 48 I2
Ludwigsort Rus. Fed. see Ladushkin
Ludza Latvia 42 I5
Luebo Dem. Rep. Congo 127 D6
Lueki Dem. Rep. Congo 126 E5
Lueki r. Dem. Rep. Congo 126 E5
Luembe Zambia 127 F8
Luena Angola 127 C7
formerly known as Luso
Luena Dem. Rep. Congo 127 E7
Luena Zambia 127 F7
Luena r. Zambia 127 D8
Luena Flats plain Zambia 127 D8
Luengé, Coutada Pública do nature res. Angola 127 D9
Luengue r. Angola 127 D9
Luenha r. Moz./Zimbabwe 131 G3
Luepa Venez. 199 F3
Lüeyang China 86 C1
Lufeng Guangdong China 87 E4
Lufeng China see Xupu
Lufeng Yunnan China 86 B3
also known as Jinshan
Lufira r. Dem. Rep. Congo 127 E7
Lufkin U.S.A. 179 D6
Lufu China see Lunan
Lug r. Yugo. 58 C4
Luga Rus. Fed. 43 K3
Luga r. Rus. Fed. 43 J2
Lugano Switz. 51 O6
Lugansk Ukr. see Luhans'k
Luganville Vanuatu 145 F3
Lugdunum France see Lyon
Lugela Moz. 131 H3
Lugela r. Moz. 131 H3
Lugenda r. Moz. 131 H1
Lugg r. U.K. 47 J11
Luggate N.Z. 153 D12
Luggudontsen mt. China 89 E6
Lughaye Somalia 128 D2
Lugo Italy 56 D4
Lugo Spain 54 D1
Lugoj Romania 58 C3
Lugovaya Rus. Fed. 43 S5
Lugovaya Proleyka Rus. Fed. see Primorsk
Lugovoy Kazakh. 103 H4
Lugovoye Kazakh. 103 H4
Lugus i. Phil. 74 B5
Luhanka Fin. 45 N3
Luhans'k Ukr. 41 F6
also spelt Lugansk; formerly known as Voroshilovgrad
Luhawskiya Belarus 43 L6
Luhe China 87 F1
Luḩfī, Wādī watercourse Jordan 109 H5
Luhin Sum China 85 H2
Luhit r. China/India see Zayü Qu
Luhit r. India 97 G3
Luhombero Tanz. 129 C7
Luhua China see Heishui
Luhuo China 86 B2
also known as Xindu or Zhaggo
Luhyny Ukr. 41 D6
Lui r. Angola 127 C7
Luia Angola 127 D7
Luia r. Angola 127 D6
Luia r. Moz. 131 G3
Luiana Angola 127 D9
Luiana r. Angola 127 D9
Luiana, Coutada Pública do nature res. Angola 127 D9
Luica Romania 58 H4
Luichow Peninsula China see Leizhou Bandao
Luik Belgium see Liège
Luilaka r. Dem. Rep. Congo 126 D5
Luimneach Rep. of Ireland see Limerick
Luing i. U.K. 46 G7
Luino Italy 56 A3
Luio r. Angola 127 D8
Luiro r. Fin. 44 N2
Luís Correia Brazil 202 D2
Luís Echeverría Álvarez Mex. 183 H9
Luís Gomes Brazil 202 E3
Luishia Dem. Rep. Congo 127 E7
Luís L. León, Presa resr Mex. 184 D2
Luís Moya Durango Mex. 184 E3
Luís Moya Zacatecas Mex. 185 E4
Luitpold Coast Antarctica 222 V1
Luiza Dem. Rep. Congo 127 D6
Luizi Dem. Rep. Congo 127 E6
Luján Arg. 204 F4
Luján de Cuyo Arg. 204 C4
Lujiang China 87 F2
Lukackek Rus. Fed. 82 D1
Lukala Dem. Rep. Congo 127 B6
Lukanga Dem. Rep. Congo 126 C6
Lukanga Swamps Zambia 127 E8
Lukapa Angola see Lucapa
Lukavac Bos.-Herz. 56 K4
Luke, Mount hill Australia 151 B5
Lukenga, Lac l. Dem. Rep. Congo 127 E7
Lukenie r. Dem. Rep. Congo 126 C5
Lukh r. Rus. Fed. 40 G4
Lukhovitsy Rus. Fed. 43 U7
Lŭki Bulg. 58 F7
Lukinskaya Rus. Fed. 43 P1
Luk Keng Hong Kong China 87 [inset]
Lukolela Équateur Dem. Rep. Congo 126 C5
Lukolela Kasai Oriental Dem. Rep. Congo 127 E6
Lukomskaye, Vozyera l. Belarus 43 K7
Lukou China see Zhuzhou
Lukovac r. Bos.-Herz. 56 L4
Lukovë Albania 59 A9
Lukovit Bulg. 58 F5
Lukovnikovo Rus. Fed. 43 P5
Łuków Poland 49 T4
Lukoyanov Rus. Fed. 40 H5
Luksagu Indon. 75 B3
Lukšiai Lith. 42 E7
Lukuga r. Dem. Rep. Congo 127 E6
Lukula Dem. Rep. Congo 127 B6
Lukuledi Tanz. 129 C7
Lukulu Zambia 127 D8
Lukumburu Tanz. 129 B7
Lukuni Dem. Rep. Congo 127 C6
Lukusashi r. Zambia 127 F8
Lukusuzi National Park Zambia 129 B8
Lula r. Dem. Rep. Congo 126 D5
Luleå Sweden 44 M2
Luleälven r. Sweden 44 M2
Lüleburgaz Turkey 106 A2
Lules Arg. 204 D2
Luliang China 86 B3
also known as Zhongshu
Lüliang Shan mts China 85 F4
Lulimba Dem. Rep. Congo 126 F6
Luling U.S.A. 179 C6
Lulong China 85 H4
Lulonga Dem. Rep. Congo 126 C4
Lulonga r. Dem. Rep. Congo 126 C4
Lulu r. Dem. Rep. Congo 126 D4
Luluabourg Dem. Rep. Congo see Kananga
Lülung China 89 D6
Lulworth, Mount hill Australia 151 B5
Lumachomo China 89 D6
Lumai Angola 127 D8
Lumajang Indon. 77 F5
Lumajangdong Co salt l. China 89 C5
Lūmanda Estonia 42 D3
Lūmār Iran 107 F4
Lumbala Angola see Lumbala N'guimbo
Lumbala Angola see Lumbala Kaquengue
Lumbala Kaquengue Angola 127 D8
formerly known as Lumbala
Lumbala N'guimbo Angola 127 D8
formerly known as Gago Coutinho or Lumbala
Lumber r. U.S.A. 174 E5
Lumberton U.S.A. 174 E5
Lumbis Indon. 77 G1
Lumbrales Spain 54 E4
Lumding India 97 G4
Lumecha Tanz. 129 B7
Lumezzane Italy 56 C3
Lumi P.N.G. 73 J7
Lumijoki Fin. 44 N2
Lumina Romania 58 J4
Luminárias Brazil 207 I8
Lum-nan-pai Wildlife Reserve nature res. Thai. 78 B4
Lumparland Fin. 45 M3
Lumphăt Cambodia 79 D5
also spelt Lomphat
Lumpkin U.S.A. 175 C5
Lumsden Canada 167 J5
Lumsden N.Z. 153 C13
Lumut, Gunung mt. Indon. 77 F3
Lumut, Tanjung pt Indon. 77 D3
Lumwana Zambia 127 E7
Lün Mongolia 85 E2
Luna Phil. 74 B2
Luna hill Spain 54 F8
Luna r. Spain 54 F2
Lunan China 86 B3
also known as Lufu
Lunan Lake Canada 167 M1
Lunan Shan mts China 86 B3
Luna Pier U.S.A. 173 J9
Lunavada India 96 B5
Lunayyir, Ḩarrat lava field Saudi Arabia 104 B2
Lunca Romania 58 F5
Lunca Bradului Romania 58 G2
Lunca Ilvei Romania 58 F1
Luncavăț r. Romania 58 F4
Lund Sweden 45 K5
Lund NV U.S.A. 183 I3
Lund UT U.S.A. 183 K3
Lunda Norte prov. Angola 127 C7
Lundar Canada 167 L5
Lunda Sul prov. Angola 127 D7
Lundazi Zambia 129 B8
Lundbreck Canada 167 H5
Lundi r. Zimbabwe see Runde
Lunds U.S.A. 172 E6
Lundu Tanz. 129 B7
Lundy Island U.K. 47 H12
Lune r. U.K. 47 J9
Lüneburg Germany 48 H2
Lüneburger Heide reg. Germany 48 H2
Lüneburger Heide, Naturpark nature res. Germany 48 H2
Lunel France 51 K9
Lünen Germany 48 E4
Lunenburg U.S.A. 176 G9
Lunestedt Germany 48 F2
Lunéville France 51 M4
Lunga Moz. 131 I2
Lunga r. Zambia 127 E8
Lunggar China 89 C6
Lunggar Shan mts China 89 C6
Lung Kwu Chau i. Hong Kong China 87 [inset]
Lunglei India see Lunglei
Lunglei India 97 G5
formerly spelt Lungleh
Lungmari mt. China 89 D6
Lungmu Co salt l. China 89 C5
Lungnaquilla Mountain hill Rep. of Ireland 47 F11
Lungro Italy 57 I9
Lungué-Bungo r. Angola 127 D8
Lungwebungu r. Zambia 127 D8
Lunh Nepal 97 D3
Luni r. India 96 A4
Luni r. Pak. 101 G4
Luninets Belarus see Luninyets
Luning U.S.A. 182 F3
Luninyets Belarus 42 H9
also spelt Luninets
L'Union France 50 H9
Lunkaransar India 96 B3
Lunkha India 96 B3
Lunkho mt. Afgh./Pak. 101 H2
Lunkkaus Fin. 44 N2
Lunna Belarus 42 F8
Lunna Island P.N.G. 149 F1
Lunsar Sierra Leone 124 B4
Lunsemfwa r. Zambia 127 F8
Lunsklip S. Africa 131 F5
Luntai China 88 D3
also known as Bügür
Lunxhërisë, Mali i ridge Albania 59 B8
Lunyuk Indon. 77 G5
Lunzua Zambia 127 F7
Luo r. Henan China 87 E1
Luo r. Shaanxi China 87 D1
Luobei China 82 C3
also known as Fengxiang
Luobuzhuang China 88 E4
Luocheng China see Hui'an
Luocheng Gansu China 84 C4
Luocheng Guangxi China 87 D3
also known as Dongmen
Luochuan China 85 F5
also known as Fengqi
Luodian China 86 C3
also known as Longping
Luoding China 87 D4
Luodonselkä sea chan. Fin. 44 N2
Luodou Sha i. China 87 D4
Luohe China 87 E1
Luoma Hu l. China 87 F1
Luonan China 87 D1
Luoning China 87 D1
Luonnonsuojelualue nature res. Fin. 44 M3
Luonteri l. Fin. 45 N3
Luoping China 86 C3
also known as Luoxiong
Luopioinen Fin. 45 N3
Luoshan China 87 E1
Luotian China 87 E2
also known as Fengshan
Luovtejohk Norway 44 O1
Luoxiao Shan mts China 87 E3
Luoxiong China see Luoping
Luoyang China see Boluo
Luoyang China 87 E1
formerly known as Loyang
Luoyang China see Taishun
Luoyuan China 87 F3
also known as Fengshan
Luozi Dem. Rep. Congo 126 B6
Luozigou China 82 C4
Lupa Market Tanz. 129 B7
Lupane Zimbabwe 131 E3
Lupanshui China 86 C3
also known as Shuicheng or Xiaoyingpan or Zhongshan; formerly spelt Liupanshui
Lupar r. Sarawak Malaysia 77 E2
Łupawa r. Poland 49 O1
L'Upemba, Parc National de nat. park Dem. Rep. Congo 127 E7
Lupeni Romania 58 G2
Lupeni Romania 58 E3
Luperón Dom. Rep. 187 F3
Lupilichi Moz. 129 B7
formerly known as Olivença
Lupire Angola 127 C8
Lupiro Tanz. 129 C7
Lupon Phil. 74 C5
Luppa Germany 49 J4
Lupton U.S.A. 183 O6
Lup'ya r. Rus. Fed. 40 J3
Luqiao China see Luding
Luqu China 86 B1
also known as Ma'ngê
Lu Qu r. China see Tao He
Luquan Hebei China 85 G4
formerly known as Huolu
Luquan Yunnan China 86 B3
also known as Pingshan
Luquembo Angola 127 C7
Lūrā Shīrīn Iran 107 F3
Luray U.S.A. 176 G7
Lure France 51 M5
Lure, Sommet de mt. France 51 L8
Lureco r. Moz. 129 C8
Luremo Angola 127 C7
Lurgan U.K. 47 F9
Lūrg-e Shotorān salt pan Iran 101 D3
Luribay Bol. 200 D4
Lurín Peru 200 A3
Luring China see Gêrzê
Lúrio Moz. 131 I2
Lurio r. Moz. 131 I2
Lusaheia park Norway 45 I4
Lusahunga Tanz. 128 A5
Lusaka Dem. Rep. Congo 127 F6

▶Lusaka Zambia 127 F8
Capital of Zambia.

Lusaka prov. Zambia 127 F8
Lusambo Dem. Rep. Congo 126 D6
Lusancay Islands and Reefs P.N.G. 145 E2
Lusanga Dem. Rep. Congo 126 C6
formerly known as Leverville
Lusangi Dem. Rep. Congo 126 E6
Luseland Canada 167 I4
Lusenga Plain National Park Zambia 127 F7
Lusewa Tanz. 129 C7
Lush, Mount hill Australia 150 D3
Lushan China 86 B2
also known as Luyang
Lushar China see Huangzhong
Lushi China 87 D1
Lushnjë Albania 58 A8
Lushoto Tanz. 129 C6
Lüshun China 85 I4
formerly known as Port Arthur or Ryojun
Lüsi China 87 G1
Lusi r. Indon. 77 E4
Lusignan France 50 G6
Lusikisiki S. Africa 133 N8
Lusiwasi Zambia 127 F8
Lusk U.S.A. 180 F4
Luso Angola see Luena
Lussac-les-Châteaux France 50 G6
Lussusso Angola 127 B7
Lusushwana r. Swaziland 133 P3
Lusutufu r. Africa see Usutu
Lut, Bahrat salt l. Asia see Dead Sea
Lut, Dasht-e des. Iran 100 D4
Lü Tao i. Taiwan 87 G4
English form Green Island; also known as Huoshao Tao
Lutécia Brazil 206 C9
Luterskie, Jezioro l. Poland 49 R2
Lutetia France see Paris
Lüt-e Zangī Aḩmad des. Iran 100 D4
Luther Lake Canada 173 M7
Luthersburg U.S.A. 176 G4
Lutherstadt Wittenberg Germany 49 J4
also known as Wittenberg
Lutiba Dem. Rep. Congo 126 F5
Lütjenburg Germany 48 H1
Luton U.K. 47 L12
Lutong Sarawak Malaysia 77 F1
Lutope r. Zimbabwe 131 F3
Łutselk'e Canada 167 I2
formerly known as Snowdrift
Lutshi Dem. Rep. Congo 126 E5
Luts'k Ukr. 41 C6
formerly spelt Luck
Luttig S. Africa 132 G9
Lutto r. Fin./Rus. Fed. see Lotta
Lutuai Angola 127 D8
Lutynia r. Poland 49 O3
Lutz U.S.A. 175 D6
Lützow-Holm Bay Antarctica 223 C2
Lutzputs S. Africa 132 E5
Lutzville S. Africa 132 C8
Luumäki Fin. 45 N3
Luuq Somalia 128 D4
Luve Swaziland 133 P3
Luverne AL U.S.A. 175 C6
Luverne MN U.S.A. 178 C3
Luvia Fin. 45 M3
Luvo Angola 127 B6
Luvozero Rus. Fed. 44 O2
Luvua r. Dem. Rep. Congo 127 E6
Luvuei Angola 127 D8
Luvuvhu r. S. Africa 131 F4
Luwegu r. Tanz. 129 C7
Luwero Uganda 128 B4
Luwingu Zambia 127 F7
Luwo i. Indon. 75 D2
Luwuk Indon. 75 B3
▶Luxembourg country Europe 51 L3
Letzebuergish form Lëtzebuerg; also spelt Luxemburg
europe [countries] 32–35

▶Luxembourg Lux. 51 M3
Capital of Luxembourg.

Luxemburg country Europe see Luxembourg
Luxemburg IA U.S.A. 172 B8
Luxemburg WI U.S.A. 172 F6
Luxeuil-les-Bains France 51 M5
Luxi Hunan China 87 D2
also known as Wuxi
Luxi Yunnan China 86 A3
also known as Mangshi
Luxi Yunnan China 86 B3
also known as Zhongshu
Luxian China 86 C2
also known as Fuji
Luxolweni S. Africa 133 J8
Luxor Egypt 121 G3
also spelt El Uqşur or Al Uqşur
Luyang China see Lushan
Luya Shan mts China 85 F4
Luy de France r. France 50 F9
Luyi China 87 E1
Luyuan China see Gaoling
Luz Brazil 207 H6
Luza Rus. Fed. 40 H3
Luza r. Rus. Fed. 40 H3
Luza r. Rus. Fed. 40 I3
Luzech France 50 H8
Luzern Switz. see Lucerne
Luzha r. Rus. Fed. 43 R7
Luzhai China 87 D3
Luzhi China 86 C3
also known as Xiayingpan
Luzhou China 86 C2
Luziânia Brazil 206 F3
Lužické Hory mts Czech Rep. 49 L5
Luzilândia Brazil 202 D2
Lūžņas Latvia 42 C4
Lužnice r. Czech Rep. 49 L6
Luzon i. Phil. 74 B3
Luzon Strait Phil. 74 B1
Luzy France 51 J6
Luzzi Italy 57 I9
L'viv Ukr. 41 C6
English form Lvov; also spelt L'vov; formerly spelt Lwów; historically known as Lemberg
L'vov Ukr. see L'viv
Lvov Ukr. see L'viv
L'vovskiy Rus. Fed. 43 S6
Lwów Ukr. see L'viv
Lwówek Poland 49 N3
Lyady Belarus 43 M7
Lyady Rus. Fed. 43 J3
Lyakhavichy Belarus 42 H8
also spelt Lyakhovichi
Lyakhovichi Belarus see Lyakhavichy
Lyakhovskiye Ostrova is Rus. Fed. 39 O2
Lyallpur Pak. see Faisalabad
Lyal'mikar Uzbek. 103 F5
also spelt Lalmikor
Lyamtsa Rus. Fed. 40 F2
Lyangar Uzbek. see Langar
Lyangar Uzbek. 103 F4
also spelt Langar
Lyapin r. Rus. Fed. 40 L3
Lyaskelya Rus. Fed. 44 O3
Lyaskovets Bulg. 58 G5
Lyasnaya Belarus 42 G9
Lyasnaya r. Belarus 42 E9
Lybster U.K. 46 I5
Lychkovo Rus. Fed. 43 N4
Lyck Poland see Ełk
Lycksele Sweden 44 L2
Lycopolis Egypt see Asyūt
Lydda Israel see Lod
Lyddan Island Antarctica 222 W2
Lydenburg S. Africa 133 O2
Lydia reg. Turkey 59 I10
Lydynia r. Poland 49 R3
Lyebyada r. Belarus 42 G8
Lyel'chytsy Belarus 41 D6
Lyell, Mount U.S.A. 182 E4
Lyell Island Canada 166 D4
Lyell Range mts N.Z. 153 G9
Lyenina Belarus 43 M9
Lyepyel' Belarus 43 K7
also spelt Lepel'
Lygourio Greece 59 E11
also known as Ligoúrion
Lygumai Lith. 42 E5
Lykens U.S.A. 177 I5
Lykoshino Rus. Fed. 43 O3
Lykso S. Africa 132 I4
Lyman Ukr. 58 K3
Lyman U.S.A. 180 E4
Lyman's'ke Ukr. 58 K2
Lyme Bay U.K. 47 J13
Lymington U.K. 47 K13
Łyna r. Poland 49 S1
Lynch U.S.A. 176 C9
Lynchburg TN U.S.A. 174 C5
Lynchburg VA U.S.A. 176 F8
Lynches r. U.S.A. 175 E5
Lynch Station U.S.A. 176 F8
Lynchville U.S.A. 177 O1
Lynd r. Australia 149 D3
Lyndhurst Qld Australia 149 E3
Lyndhurst S.A. Australia 146 C2
Lyndon Australia 150 A4
Lyndon r. Australia 150 A4
Lyndon U.S.A. 178 D4
Lyndonville NY U.S.A. 176 G2
Lyndonville VT U.S.A. 177 M1
Lyngdal Norway 45 I4
Lyngen sea chan. Norway 44 M1
Lyngseidet Norway 44 M1
Lynher Reef Australia 150 C2
Lynn U.K. see King's Lynn
Lynn IN U.S.A. 176 A5
Lynn MA U.S.A. 177 O3
Lynn Canal sea chan. U.S.A. 166 C3
Lynndyl U.S.A. 183 L2
Lynn Haven U.S.A. 175 C6
Lynn Lake Canada 167 K3
Lynton U.K. 47 I12
Lyntupy Belarus 42 H6
Lynx Lake Canada 167 J2
Lynxville U.S.A. 172 B7
Lyon France 51 K7
English form Lyons; historically known as Lugdunum
Lyon Mountain U.S.A. 177 L1
Lyonnais, Monts du hills France 51 K7
Lyons Australia 146 B2
Lyons r. Australia 151 A5
Lyons France see Lyon
Lyons GA U.S.A. 175 D5
Lyons KS U.S.A. 178 C4
Lyons NY U.S.A. 177 I2
Lyons Falls U.S.A. 177 J2
Lyozna Belarus 43 L6
Lyra Reef P.N.G. 145 E2
Lysá Hora mt. Czech Rep. 49 P6
Lysekil Sweden 45 J4
Lyshchichi Rus. Fed. 43 N9
Łysica hill Poland 49 R5
Lyskovo Rus. Fed. 40 H4
Lys'va Rus. Fed. 40 K4
Lysychans'k Ukr. 41 F6
also spelt Lisichansk
Lysyye Gory Rus. Fed. 41 H6
Lytham St Anne's U.K. 47 I10
Lytkarino Rus. Fed. 43 S6
Lyttelton N.Z. 153 G11
Lytton Canada 166 F5
Lyuban' Belarus 42 J9
Lyuban' Rus. Fed. 43 M2
Lyubanskaye Vodaskhovishcha resr Belarus 42 J9
Lyubavichi Rus. Fed. 43 L7
Lyubazh Rus. Fed. 43 Q9
Lyubcha Belarus 42 H8
Lyubertsy Rus. Fed. 43 S6
Lyubeshiv Ukr. 41 C6
Lyubim Rus. Fed. 43 V3
Lyubimets Bulg. 58 H7
Lyubimovka Rus. Fed. 43 T8
Lyubishchytsy Belarus 42 G9
Lyubitovo Rus. Fed. 43 P3
Lyubokhna Rus. Fed. 43 P8
Lyubomirovo Rus. Fed. 43 T2
Lyubotin Ukr. see Lyubotyn
Lyubotyn Ukr. 53 J2
also spelt Lyubotin
Lyubyacha Belarus 42 I8
Lyubytino Rus. Fed. 43 O3
Lyudinovo Rus. Fed. 43 P8
Lyugovichi Rus. Fed. 43 O1
Lyulyakovo Bulg. 58 I6
Lyunda r. Rus. Fed. 40 H4
Lyusina Belarus 42 H9
Lyzha r. Rus. Fed. 40 K2
Lža r. Latvia 42 J4
Lzha r. Rus. Fed. 43 J4

↓ M

Ma r. Myanmar 78 B3
Ma, Nam r. Laos 78 C3
Ma, Sông r. Vietnam 78 D4
Maalhosmadulu Atoll Maldives 94 B5
Maamakundhoo i. Maldives see Makunudhoo
Maamba Zambia 127 E9
Ma'an Cameroon 125 H6
Ma'an Jordan 108 G7
Maaninka Fin. 44 N3
Maaninkavaara Fin. 44 O2
Maanselkä Fin. 44 O3
Ma'anshan China 87 F2
Maanyt Bulgan Mongolia 84 D1
Maanyt Töv Mongolia 85 E2
Maardu Estonia 42 G2
Maarianhamina Fin. see Mariehamn
Ma'arrat an Nu'mān Syria 109 H2
Maartenshoop S. Africa 133 O1
Maas r. Neth. 48 B4
also spelt Meuse (Belgium/France)
Maaseik Belgium 51 L1
Maasin Phil. 74 C4
Maas-Schwalm-Nette nat. park Germany/Neth. 48 D4
Maastricht Neth. 48 C5
Maatsuyker Group is Australia 147 E5
Maba China 87 F1
Maba Indon. 75 D2
Maba, Ouadi watercourse Chad 120 D6
Mabalacat Phil. 74 B3
Mabalane Moz. 131 G4
Mabana Dem. Rep. Congo 126 F4
Mabanda Gabon 126 A5
Ma'bar Yemen 104 D5
Mabaruma Guyana 199 G2
Mabating China see Hongshan
Mabein Myanmar 78 B3
Mabel Creek Australia 146 B2
Mabel Downs Australia 150 D3
Mabella Canada 168 B3
Maberly Canada 173 Q6
Mabian China 86 B2
also known as Minjian
Mablethorpe U.K. 47 M10
Mably France 51 K6
Mabopane S. Africa 133 M2
Mabote Moz. 131 G4
Mabou Canada 169 I4
Mabrak, Jabal mt. Jordan 108 G7
Mabrouk well Mali 125 E2
Mabrous well Niger 125 I1
Mabuasehube Game Reserve nature res. Botswana 130 D5
Mabudis i. Phil. 74 B1
Mabula S. Africa 133 L1
Ma'būs Yūsuf oasis Libya 120 D3
Mabutsane Botswana 130 D5
Macá, Monte mt. Chile 205 B7
Macachín Arg. 204 E5
Macadam Plains Australia 151 B5
Macadam Range hills Australia 148 A2
Macaé Brazil 203 D7
Macael Spain 55 I7
Macaíba Brazil 202 F3
Macajalar Bay Phil. 74 C4
Macajuba Brazil 202 D5
Macaloge Moz. 129 B8
formerly known as Miranda or Vila Miranda
MacAlpine Lake Canada 167 K1
Macamic Canada 168 E3
Macan, Kepulauan atolls Indon. see Taka'Bonerate, Kepulauan
Macandze Moz. 131 G4
Macaneta, Ponta de pt Moz. 133 Q2
Macao China see Macau
Macapá Amapá Brazil 199 I4
Macapá Amazonas Brazil 200 D2
Macará Ecuador 198 B6
Macaracas Panama 186 C6
Macarani Brazil 202 D5
Macarena, Cordillera mts Col. 198 C4
Macareo, Caño r. Venez. 199 F2
Macas Ecuador 198 B5
Macassar Indon. see Ujung Pandang
Macassar Strait Indon. see Makassar Strait
Macau Brazil 202 E3
Macau China 87 E4
also known as Aomen; also spelt Macao
Macaúba Brazil 202 B4
Macaúbas Brazil 202 D5
Macauley Island N.Z. 145 H5
Macayari Col. 198 C4
Macbride Head Falkland Is 205 F8
Maccaretane Moz. 131 G5
Macclenny U.S.A. 175 D6
Macclesfield U.K. 47 J10
Macclesfield Bank sea feature S. China Sea 72 D3
also known as Zhongsha Qundao
Macdiarmid Canada 168 B3
Macdonald, Lake salt flat Australia 150 E4
MacDonnell Creek watercourse Australia 146 C2
Macdonnell Ranges mts Australia 148 A4
MacDowell Lake Canada 167 M4
Macedo de Cavaleiros Port. 54 E3
Macedon country Europe see Macedonia
▶Macedonia country Europe 58 C7
spelt Makedonija in Macedonian; historically known as Macedon; long form Former Yugoslav Republic of Macedonia; short form F.Y.R.O.M.
europe [countries] 32–35
Maceió Brazil 202 F4
Maceio, Ponta da pt Brazil 202 E3
Macenta Guinea 124 C4
Macerata Italy 56 F5
Macfarlane, Lake salt flat Australia 146 C3

index

M

Macgillycuddy's Reeks mts Rep. of Ireland 47 C12
Mach Pak. 101 F4
Macha Rus. Fed. 39 L3
Machacalis Brazil 207 M4
Machacamarca Bol. 200 D4
Machachi Ecuador 198 B5
Machadinho r. Brazil 201 F3
Machado Brazil 207 H8
Machadodorp S. Africa 133 O2
Machai Zambia 127 E8
Machaila Moz. 131 G4
Machakos Kenya 128 C5
Machala Ecuador 198 B5
Machali China see Madoi
Machanga Moz. 131 G4
Machareti Bol. 201 E5
Machar Marshes Sudan 128 A2
Machatuine Moz. 133 Q2
Machaze Moz. see Chitobe
Machecoul France 50 E6
Macheng China 87 E2
Macherla India 94 C2
Machesney Park U.S.A. 172 D8
Machhiwara India 96 C3
formerly spelt Machiwara
Machhlishahr India 97 D4
Machias ME U.S.A. 174 H2
Machias NY U.S.A. 176 A3
Machico Madeira 122 B2
Machilipatnam India 94 D2
also known as Masulipatam; formerly known as Bandar
Machina Malawi 129 B8
Machiques Venez. 198 C2
Machiwara India see Machhiwara
Mach Kowr Iran 101 E5
Macho, Arroyo del watercourse U.S.A. 181 F6
Machupicchu tourist site Peru 200 B3
Machupo r. Bol. 201 D3
Machynlleth U.K. 47 I11
Macia Moz. 131 G5
Macias Nguema i. Equat. Guinea see Bioco
Măcin Romania 58 J3
Macintyre r. Australia 147 F2
Macintyre Brook r. Australia 147 F2
Macizo de Tocate mts Peru 200 B3
Maçka Turkey 107 D2
also known as Cevizlik
MacKay r. Australia 149 F4
MacKay r. Canada 167 I3
Mackay, Lake salt flat Australia 150 E4
MacKay Lake Canada 167 I2
Mackay Mountains Antarctica 222 O1
Mackenzie r. Australia 149 F4
Mackenzie B.C. Canada 166 F4
Mackenzie Ont. Canada 172 E2
▶**Mackenzie** r. Canada 166 E2
northamerica [landscapes] ▶ 156–157
Mackenzie Guyana see Linden
Mackenzie atoll Micronesia see Ulithi
Mackenzie Bay Antarctica 223 E2
Mackenzie Bay Canada 164 F3
Mackenzie Bison Sanctuary nature res. Canada 167 G2
Mackenzie Highway Canada 167 G2
Mackenzie King Island Canada 165 H2
Mackenzie Mountains Canada 166 C1
▶**Mackenzie-Peace-Finlay** r. Canada 166
2nd longest river in North America.
northamerica [landscapes] ▶ 156–157
Mackillop, Lake salt flat Australia see Yamma Yamma, Lake
Mackinac, Straits of lake channel U.S.A. 173 H5
Mackinac Island U.S.A. 173 I5
Mackinaw r. U.S.A. 174 B3
Macklin Canada 167 I4
Macksville Australia 147 G2
Mackunda Creek watercourse Australia 149 D4
Maclean Australia 147 G2
Macleantown S. Africa 133 L9
Maclear S. Africa 133 M8
Macleay r. Australia 147 G2
MacLeod Canada see Fort Macleod
MacLeod, Lake imp. l. Australia 150 A4
Macmillan r. Canada 166 C2
Macmillan Pass Canada 166 D2
Macobere Moz. 131 G4
Macocola Angola 127 C6
Macomb U.S.A. 174 B3
Macomer Sardegna Italy 57 A8
Mâcon France 51 K6
Macon GA U.S.A. 175 D5
Macon MO U.S.A. 178 D4
Macon MS U.S.A. 175 B5
Macon OH U.S.A. 176 B7
Macon, Bayou r. U.S.A. 175 B6
Macondo Angola 127 D8
Macossa Moz. 131 G3
Macotera Spain 54 F4
Macoun Lake Canada 167 K3
Macovane Moz. 131 G4
Macpherson Robertson Land reg. Antarctica see Mac. Robertson Land
Macquarie r. N.S.W. Australia 147 E2
Macquarie r. Tas. Australia 147 E5
Macquarie Harbour Australia 147 E5
▶**Macquarie Island** S. Pacific Ocean 220 E9
Part of Australia. Most southerly point of Oceania.
Macquarie Marshes Australia 147 E2
Macquarie Marshes Nature Reserve Australia 147 E2
Macquarie Mountain Australia 147 F3
Macraes Flat N.Z. 153 E13

MacRitchie Reservoir Sing. 76 [inset]
Mac. Robertson Land reg. Antarctica 223 E2
long form Macpherson Robertson Land
Macroom Rep. of Ireland 47 D12
Mactún Mex. 185 H5
Macú Brazil 198 D1
Macuira, Parque Nacional nat. park Col. 198 D1
Macuje Col. 198 C4
Macukull Albania 58 B7
Macumba Australia 146 B1
Macumba watercourse Australia 146 C1
Macururé Brazil 202 E4
Macusani Peru 200 C3
Macuspana Mex. 185 G5
Macuzari, Presa resr Mex. 184 C3
Macuze Moz. 131 H3
Mādabā Jordan 108 G6
Madadeni S. Africa 133 O4
▶**Madagascar** country Africa 131 [inset] J4
Largest island in Africa and 4th in the world.
africa [landscapes] ▶ 112–113
africa [countries] ▶ 114–117
Madagli Nigeria 125 I4
Madā'in Şāliḥ Saudi Arabia 104 B2
Madalena Brazil 202 E3
Madama Niger 123 I5
Madan Bulg. 58 F7
Madana Chad 126 C2
Madana well Chad 120 C5
Madanapalle India 94 C3
Madang P.N.G. 73 K8
Madaora India 96 C4
Madaoua Niger 125 G3
Mādāraş Romania 68 C2
Madaripur Bangl. 97 F5
Madarounfa Niger 125 G3
Madau Turkm. 102 C5
also spelt Madaw; formerly known as Suidzhikurmsy
Madaw Turkm. see Madau
Madawaska Canada 167 K4
Madawaska r. Canada 168 E4
Madaya Myanmar 78 B3
Maddalena, Isola i. Sardegna Italy 56 B7
Maddaloni Italy 56 G7
Madded India 94 D2
Maddur India 94 C3
Madeir Sudan 126 F3
▶**Madeira** r. Brazil 199 G5
4th longest river in South America.
southamerica [landscapes] ▶ 190–191
▶**Madeira** terr. N. Atlantic Ocean 122 A2
Autonomous Region of Portugal. Long form Madeira, Arquipélago da.
africa [countries] ▶ 114–117
Madeira, Arquipélago da terr. N. Atlantic Ocean see Madeira
Madeirinha r. Brazil 201 F2
Madeley U.K. 47 J11
Madeline Island U.S.A. 172 C4
Madel Ouèï Chad 126 C2
Maden Turkey 107 D3
Madenïyet Kazakh. 103 I3
Madera Mex. 184 C2
Madera U.S.A. 182 D5
Madgaon India 94 B3
formerly known as Margao
Madgoul Djibouti 128 D1
Madhapur India 96 A5
Madhepura India 97 E4
Madhogani India 89 C7
Madhubani India 97 E4
Madhugiri India 94 C3
Madhya Pradesh state India 96 C5
formerly known as Central Provinces
Madi, Dataran Tinggi plat. Indon. 77 F2
Madibogo S. Africa 133 J3
Madikeri India 94 B3
Madill U.S.A. 179 C5
Madimba Angola 127 B6
Madimba Dem. Rep. Congo 126 B6
Madinani Côte d'Ivoire 124 D4
Madīnat al 'Abīd Yemen 104 C5
Madīnat ash Sha'b Yemen 104 D5
formerly known as Al Ittihad
Madīnat ath Thawrah Syria 109 J2
also known as Ṭabaqah
Madingo-Kayes Congo 126 A6
Madingou Congo 126 B6
Madingrin Cameroon 125 I4
Madinī r. Bol. 200 D3
Madirovalo Madag. 131 [inset] J3
Madison AL U.S.A. 174 C5
Madison FL U.S.A. 175 D6
Madison GA U.S.A. 175 D5
Madison IN U.S.A. 174 C4
Madison ME U.S.A. 177 P1
Madison MN U.S.A. 178 C2
Madison NC U.S.A. 176 F9
Madison NE U.S.A. 178 C3
Madison OH U.S.A. 176 D4
Madison SD U.S.A. 178 C3
Madison VA U.S.A. 176 G7
▶**Madison** WI U.S.A. 172 D7
State capital of Wisconsin.
Madison WV U.S.A. 176 D7
Madison r. U.S.A. 180 E3
Madison Heights U.S.A. 176 F8
Madisonville KY U.S.A. 174 C4
Madisonville TN U.S.A. 174 C4
Madisonville TX U.S.A. 179 D6
Madīta Indon. 75 B5
Madiun Indon. 77 E4
Madjingo Gabon 126 B4
Madley, Mount hill Australia 150 C5
Madliena Latvia 42 G5
Mado Dem. Rep. Congo 126 F4
Madoc Canada 168 E4
Mado Gashi Kenya 128 C4
Madoi China 86 A1
also known as Machali
Madona Latvia 42 H5
Madongo Pan salt pan Botswana 130 D4
Madonie mts Sicilia Italy 57 F11
Madra Dağı mts Turkey 106 A3
Madrakah Saudi Arabia 104 B3
Madrakah, Ra's c. Oman 105 G4
Madras India see Chennai
Madras state India see Tamil Nadu
Madras U.S.A. 180 B3
Madre, Laguna lag. Mex. 185 F3
Madre, Laguna lag. U.S.A. 179 C7
Madre, Sierra mts Mex. 185 G5
also known as Madre de Chiapas, Sierra or Soconusco, Sierra de
Madre, Sierra mt. Phil. 74 B2
Madre de Chiapas, Sierra mts Mex. see Madre, Sierra
Madre de Dios dept Peru 200 C2
Madre de Dios, Isla i. Chile 205 B8
Madre del Sur, Sierra mts Mex. 185 E5
Madre Occidental, Sierra mts Mex. 184 C2
Madre Oriental, Sierra mts Mex. 185 E3
Madrès, Pic de mt. France 51 I10
Madrid Phil. 74 B4
▶**Madrid** Spain 54 H4
Capital of Spain.
Madrid aut. comm. Spain 54 H4
Madridejos Phil. 74 B4
Madridejos Spain 55 H5

Madrona, Sierra mts Spain 54 G6
Madruga Cuba 186 C2
Madrūsah Libya 120 B3
Maduda Dem. Rep. Congo 126 B6
Madugula India 95 D2
Madura Australia 151 D6
Madura i. Indon. 77 F4
Madura, Selat sea chan. Indon. 77 F4
Madurai India 94 C4
Madurantakam India 94 C3
Madvār, Kūh-e mt. Iran 100 C4
Madwas India 97 D4
Madyan Saudi Arabia see Al Bad'
Madzhalis Rus. Fed. 102 A4
Madzharovo Bulg. 58 G7
Madziwadzido Zimbabwe 131 F3
Madziwa Mine Zimbabwe 131 F3
Maebashi Japan 91 F6
Mae Hong Son Thai. 78 B4
Maelang Indon. 75 B2
Maella Spain 55 L3
Mae Ping National Park Thai. 78 B4
Mae Ramat Thai. 78 B4
Mae Rim Thai. 78 B4
Mae Sariang Thai. 78 B4
Maeser U.S.A. 183 O1
Maes Howe tourist site U.K. 46 I8
Mae Sot Thai. 78 B4
Maestra, Sierra mts Cuba 186 D3
Mae Suai Thai. 78 B4
Mae Tuen Wildlife Reserve nature res. Thai. 78 B4
Maevatanana Madag. 131 [inset] J3
Maéwo i. Vanuatu 145 F3
also spelt Maiwo; formerly known as Aurora Island
Mae Wong National Park Thai. 78 B5
Mae Yom National Park Thai. 78 C4
Mafa Indon. 75 C2
Mafeking Canada 167 K4
Mafeking S. Africa see Mafikeng
Mafeteng Lesotho 133 L6
Mafia Channel Tanz. 129 C7
Mafia Island Tanz. 129 C6
Mafikeng S. Africa 133 J2
formerly spelt Mafeking
Mafinga Tanz. 129 B7
Mafra Brazil 201 H6
Mafra Jordan see Al Mafraq
Mafungabusi Plateau Zimbabwe 131 F3
Magabeni S. Africa 133 O7
Magacela hill Spain 54 F6
Magadan Rus. Fed. 39 P4
Magadi Kenya 128 C5
Magallanes Chile see Punta Arenas
Magallanes, Estrecho de sea chan. Chile see Magellan, Strait of
Magallanes y Antártica Chilena admin. reg. Chile 205 C8
Magangue Col. 198 C2
Maganik mt. Yugo. 56 J6
Maġara Turkey 106 C3
also known as Kırobası
Maġarali Turkey 109 J1
Magaramkent Rus. Fed. 102 B4
Magaria Niger 125 H3
Magas Iran see Zāboli
Magas Rus. Fed. 107 G2
Magat r. Phil. 74 B2
Magazine Mountain hill U.S.A. 179 D5
Magbakele Dem. Rep. Congo 126 D4
Magburaka Sierra Leone 124 C4
Magdagachi Rus. Fed. 82 B1
Magdalena Bol. 201 D3
Magdalena dept Col. 198 C2
Magdalena r. Col. 198 C2
Magdalena Mex. 184 C2
Magdalena r. Mex. 184 C2
Magdalena, Bahía b. Col. 198 B3
Magdalena, Bahía b. Mex. 184 C3
Magdalena, Isla i. Chile 205 B7
Magdalena, Isla i. Mex. 184 B3
Magdalena, Gunung mt. Sabah Malaysia 77 G1
Magdeburg Germany 48 I3
Magdelaine Cays atoll Australia 149 F3
Magee U.S.A. 175 B5
Magelang Indon. 77 E4
Magellan, Strait of Chile 205 C9
also known as Magallanes, Estrecho de
Magenta Italy 56 A3
Magenta, Lake salt flat Australia 151 B7
Magereya i. Norway 44 N1
Mage-shima i. Japan 91 B9
Maggia r. Switz. 51 O6
Maggiorasca, Monte mt. Italy 56 B4
Maggiore, Lago l. Italy see Maggiore, Lake
Maggiore, Lake Italy 56 A3
also known as Maggiore, Lago
Maggiore, Monte hill Sardegna Italy 57 B8
Maghāgha Egypt 121 F2
Maghā'ir Shu'ayb tourist site Saudi Arabia see Jethro
Maghama Mauritania 124 B3
Maghāra, Gebel hill Egypt 108 E7
Maghera U.K. 47 F9
Maghnia Alg. 123 E2
Maghor Afgh. 101 E3
Mágina, Sierra mts Spain 55 H7
Magingo Tanz. 129 B7
Magione Italy 56 E5
Magitang China see Jainca
Maglaj Bos.-Herz. 56 K4
Maglavit Romania 58 E4
Maglie Italy 57 J8
Magma U.S.A. 183 M8
Magna Grande hill Italy 57 E12
Magnet Bay Antarctica 223 D2
Magnetic Island Australia 149 E3
Magnetic Passage Australia 149 E3
Magnitnyy Rus. Fed. 102 D1
Magnolia AR U.S.A. 179 D5
Magnolia MS U.S.A. 175 B6
Magnor Norway 45 K4
Magny-en-Vexin France 50 H3
Mago Rus. Fed. 82 F1
Mágocs-er r. Hungary 49 R9
Mago Moz. 131 F2
Magog Canada 169 F4
Magoïe Tanz. 129 C6
Mago National Park Eth. 128 C3
Magosa Cyprus see Famagusta
Magoye Zambia 127 E8
Magozal Mex. 185 F4
Magpie Canada 169 H3
Magpie r. Ont. Canada 168 C4
Magpie, Lac l. Que. Canada 169 H3
Magpie r. Que. Canada 169 H3
Magpie-Ouest r. Canada 169 H3
Magrath Canada 167 H5
Magre r. Spain 55 K5
Maguarinho, Cabo c. Brazil 202 C2
Magude Moz. 131 G4
Magudu S. Africa 133 P4
Magué Moz. 131 G2
Maguse Lake Canada 167 M2
Magwa S. Africa 133 N5
Magway Myanmar see Magwe

Magway admin. div. Myanmar see Magwe
Magwe Myanmar 78 A3
also spelt Magway
Magwe admin. div. Myanmar 78 A3
also spelt Magway
Magwegqana watercourse Botswana 130 D3
Magyarkanizsa Vojvodina, Srbija Yugo. see Kanjiža
Magyar Köztársaság country Europe see Hungary
Magyichaung Myanmar 78 A3
Mahābād Iran 100 A2
also known as Sāūjbolāgh
Mahabaleshwar India 94 B2
Mahabe Madag. 131 [inset] J3
Mahabharat Range mts Nepal 97 E4
Mahabo Toliara Madag. 131 [inset] J4
Mahabo Toliara Madag. 131 [inset] J4
Mahaboboka Madag. 131 [inset] J4
formerly known as Maneva
Mahad India 94 B2
Mahaddayweyne Somalia 128 E4
Mahadeo Hills India 96 C5
Mahadeopur India 94 C2
Mahaffey U.S.A. 176 G5
Mahagi Dem. Rep. Congo 126 F4
Mahagi Port Dem. Rep. Congo 126 F4
Mahaicony Guyana 199 G3
Mahajan India 96 B3
Mahajanga Madag. 131 [inset] J2
formerly spelt Majunga
Mahajanga prov. Madag. 131 [inset] J2
Mahakam r. Indon. 77 G3
Mahalapye Botswana 131 E4
Mahale Mountain National Park Tanz. 129 A6
also known as Makari Mountain National Park
Mahalevona Madag. 131 [inset] J3
Mahallāt Iran 100 B3
Maham India 96 C3
Mahān Iran 100 D4
Mahanadi r. India 95 E1
Mahanoro Madag. 131 [inset] K3
also spelt Mahdia
Maharajganj Bihar India 97 E4
Maharajganj Uttar Pradesh India 97 D4
Maharajpur India 96 C4
Maharashtra state India 94 B2
Mahārlū, Daryācheh-ye salt l. Iran 100 C4
Maha Sarakham Thai. 78 C4
Mahasham, Wādī el watercourse Egypt 108 F7
Mahatalaky Madag. 131 [inset] J5
Maḥaṭṭat Dab'ah Jordan 108 H6
Mahavavy r. Madag. 131 [inset] J3
Mahavelona Madag. 131 [inset] K3
formerly known as Foulpointe
Mahaweli r. Sri Lanka 94 D4
Mahazoma Madag. 131 [inset] J3
Mahbubabad India 94 D2
Mahbubnagar India 94 C2
Mahd adh Dhahab Saudi Arabia 104 C3
Mahdah Oman 105 F2
Mahdia Guyana 199 G3
Mahdia Tunisia 123 H2
also spelt Mehdia
Mahe China 84 E5
Mahe India 94 B4
Mahé i. Seychelles 218 K6
Mahendragarh India 96 C3
Mahendragiri mt. India 95 E2
Mahenge Tanz. 129 C7
Maheno N.Z. 153 E13
Mahesana India 96 B5
formerly spelt Mahsana
Maheshwar India 96 B4
Mahesh India 96 C3
Mahi r. China 85 H4
Mahi r. India 96 B4
Māhī watercourse Iran 101 D4
Mahia Peninsula N.Z. 152 L7
Mahilyow Belarus 43 L8
also spelt Mogilev
Mahilyow Oblast admin. div. Belarus see Mahilyowskaya Voblasts'
Mahilyowskaya Voblasts' admin. div. Belarus 43 L8
English form Mahilyow Oblast or Mogilev Oblast; also known as Mogilevskaya Oblast'
Mahim India 94 B2
Mahina Mali 124 C3
Mahkene mt. Sweden 44 K2
Mahlabatini S. Africa 133 O5
Mahlaing Myanmar 78 A3
Mahlangasi S. Africa 133 P3
Mahlatswetsa S. Africa 133 L5
Mahmudabad India 96 D4
Mahmudabad Iran 100 C2
Mahmudia Romania 58 K3
Mahmudiye Turkey 59 H9
Mahmutlar Turkey 108 D1
Mahmutşevketpaşa Turkey 58 K7
Mahnomen U.S.A. 178 C2
Mahoba India 96 C4
Mahoenui N.Z. 152 I6
Maholi India 96 C3
Mahón Spain 55 P5
Mahone Bay Canada 169 H4
Mahongo Game Park nature res. Namibia 130 D3
Mahony Lake Canada 166 E1
Mahou Mali 124 D3
Mahrāt, Jabal mt. Yemen 105 E4
Mahrāt, Wādī r. Yemen 105 E4
Mahrauni India 96 C4
Mähren reg. Czech Rep. see Moravia
Mahrès Tunisia 123 H2
Māhrūd Iran 101 E3
Mahsana India see Mahesana
Mahuangou China 84 B4
Mahur Assam India 97 G4
Mahur Maharashtra India 94 C2
Mahuta Tanz. 129 C7
Mahuva India 96 A5
Mahwa India 96 C4
Mahya Daği mt. Turkey 58 I7
Mahyār Iran 100 B3
Mai i. Indon. 75 C4
Maia Port. 54 C3
Maia American Samoa 145 I3
Maiaia Moz. see Nacala
Maiana atoll Kiribati 145 G1
also known as Hall
Maibang India 97 G4
Maicao Col. 198 C2
Maicasagi r. Canada 168 E3
Maicasagi, Lac l. Canada 168 E3
Maîche France 51 M5
Maici r. Brazil 199 F5
Maicuru r. Brazil 199 H5
Maidens U.K. 46 H8
Maidi Indon. 75 C2
Maidstone Canada 167 I4
Maidstone U.K. 47 M12
Maiduguri Nigeria 125 I3
Maïeru Romania 58 F1
Maigh Nuad Rep. of Ireland see Maynooth
Mai Gudo mt. Eth. 128 C3
Maihar India 96 D4
Maihihi N.Z. 152 J6
Maïji China see Maijishan
Maiji Shan mt. China 86 C1
Maikala Range hills India 96 D5

Maiko r. Dem. Rep. Congo 126 E4
Mailan Hill mt. India 97 D5
Mailani India 96 D3
Mailao Chad 126 B2
Mailsi Pak. 101 H4
Ma'in tourist site Yemen 104 C5
Main Brook Canada 169 K3
Maindargi India 94 C2
Mai-Ndombe, Lac l. Dem. Rep. Congo 126 C5
formerly known as Léopold II, Lac
Maine state U.S.A. 177 O1
Maine, Gulf of U.S.A. 177 P2
Mainé Hanari, Cerro hill Col. 198 C5
Maïné-Soroa Niger 125 I3
Maingkwan Myanmar 78 B2
Maingy Island Myanmar 79 B5
Mainit Phil. 74 C4
Mainit, Lake Phil. 74 C4
Mainkung China 86 A2
Mainland i. Orkney, Scotland U.K. 46 I4
Mainland i. Shetland, Scotland U.K. 46 K3
Mainling China 89 F6
also known as Tungdor
Mainoru Australia 148 B2
Mainoru r. Australia 148 B2
Mainpat reg. India 97 D5
Mainpuri India 96 C4
Main Range National Park Australia 147 G2
Maintenon France 50 H4
Maintirano Madag. 131 [inset] J3
Mainua Fin. 44 N2
Mainz Germany 48 F5
historically known as Mogontiacum
Maio i. Cape Verde 124 [inset]
Maipó, Volcán vol. Chile 204 C4
Maipú Buenos Aires Arg. 204 F5
Maipú Mendoza Arg. 204 C4
Maipures Col. 199 D3
Maipuri Landing Guyana 199 G3
Maiquetía Venez. 199 E2
Maiquinique Brazil 207 M2
Maiqu Zangbo r. China 89 D6
Mairabari India 97 F4
Mairaga Brazil 202 D4
Mairiporã Brazil 206 G10
Mairipotaba Brazil 206 D4
Maisí Cuba 187 E2
Maišiagala Lith. 42 G7
Maiskhal Island Bangl. 97 F5
Maisons-Laffitte France 51 I4
Maitencillo Chile 204 C3
Maitengwe Botswana 131 E4
Maithon India 97 E5
Maitland N.S.W. Australia 147 F3
Maitland S.A. Australia 146 C3
Maitland r. Australia 150 B4
Maitland, Banjaran mts Sabah Malaysia 77 G1
Maitland salt flat Australia 151 C5
Maitri research station Antarctica 223 C2
Maiwo i. Vanuatu see Maéwo
Maiwok r. Australia 148 B1
Maiz, Islas del i. Nicaragua 186 C4
also known as Corn Islands
Maizhokunggar China 89 E6
also known as Kunggar or Medu Kongkar
Maïzuru Japan 91 D7
Maja Jezercë mt. Albania 58 A6
Majalgaon India 94 C2
Majari r. Brazil 199 F4
Majdahah Yemen 105 E5
Majdanpek Srbija Yugo. 58 C4
Majé Brazil 207 J9
Majene Indon. 75 A3
Majevica mts Bos.-Herz. 56 K4
Majhgawan India 96 D4
Majholi India 96 C5
Maji Eth. 128 C3
Majia r. China 85 H4
Majiang Guangxi China 87 D3
Majiang Guizhou China 87 C3
also known as Xingshan
Majōl country N. Pacific Ocean see Marshall Islands
Major, Puig mt. Spain 55 N5
also spelt Mayor, Puig
Majorca i. Spain see Mallorca
Mājro atoll Marshall Is see Majuro
Majuli Island India 97 G4
Majunga Madag. see Mahajanga
Majurá Brazil 200 D1
Majuro atoll Marshall Is 220 F5
also known as Mājro; formerly spelt Meduro
Majwemasweu S. Africa 133 K5
Maka Senegal 124 B3
Makabana Congo 126 B5
Makahuena Point U.S.A. 181 [inset] Y1
Makak Cameroon 125 H6
Makale Indon. 75 A3
Makalehi i. Indon. 75 C2
▶**Makalu** mt. China/Nepal 89 E4
5th highest mountain in the world and in Asia.
world [physical features] ▶ 8–9
Makalu Barun National Park Nepal 97 E4
Makamba Burundi 126 F5
Makanchi Kazakh. 88 C2
also spelt Maqanshy
Makanjila Malawi 129 B7
Makanza Dem. Rep. Congo 126 C4
Makanza Tanz. 129 C6
also spelt Mankanza; formerly known as Nouvelle Anvers
Makaraingo Madag. 131 [inset] J3
Makarewa N.Z. 153 C14
Makari Cameroon 125 I3
Makari Mountain National Park Tanz. see Mahale Mountain National Park
Makarov Rus. Fed. 82 F3
Makarska Croatia 56 I5
Makar'ye Rus. Fed. 40 I4
Makassar Indon. see Ujung Pandang
Makassar Strait Indon. 75 A3
also spelt Macassar Strait
Makat Kazakh. 102 C3
also spelt Maqat
Makatini Flats lowland S. Africa 133 Q4
Makaw Myanmar 78 B2
Makay, Massif du mts Madag. 131 [inset] J4
Makedonija country Europe see Macedonia
Makeleketla S. Africa 133 K5
Makeni Sierra Leone 124 B4
Makete Tanz. 129 B7
Makeyevka Ukr. see Makiyivka
Makgadikgadi salt pan Botswana 131 E4
Makgadikgadi Pans National Park Botswana 131 E4
Makhachkala Rus. Fed. 102 A4
Makhaleng r. Lesotho 133 L7
Makhambet Kazakh. 102 B3
formerly known as Yamankhalinka
Makhmūr, Jabal al hill Saudi Arabia 104 C2
Makharadze Georgia see Ozurget'i
Makheka mt. Lesotho 133 N6
Makhfar al Ḥammām Syria 109 J2
Makhmal Turkm. 102 E5
Makhmūr Iraq 107 E4
Makhtal India 94 C2
Makhyah, Wādī r. Yemen 105 E4
Makian vol. Indon. 75 C2
Makikihi N.Z. 153 F12
Makin atoll Kiribati see Butaritari
Makindu Kenya 128 C5
Makinsk Kazakh. 103 G1

Makira i. Solomon Is see San Cristobal
Makiyivka Ukr. 41 F6
also spelt Makeyevka; formerly known as Dmitriyevsk or Dmytriyevs'k
Makkah Saudi Arabia see Mecca
Makkah prov. Saudi Arabia 104 C3
Makkaurhalvøya Naturreservat nature res. Norway 44 O1
Makkovik Canada 169 J2
Makkovik, Cape Canada 169 J2
Maklaki Rus. Fed. 43 P7
Makljen pass Bos.-Herz. 56 J5
Makó Hungary 53 G2
Makoa, Serra hills Brazil 199 G4
Makokou Gabon 126 B4
Makokskraal S. Africa 133 K3
Makonde Plateau Tanz. 129 C7
Makongolosi Tanz. 129 B7
Makopong Botswana 130 D5
Makoro Dem. Rep. Congo 126 F4
Makotipoko Congo 126 B5
Makoua Congo 126 B5
Makovnik mt. Croatia 56 H3
Maków Mazowiecki Poland 49 S3
Makra i. Greece 59 G12
Makrakomi Greece 59 D10
Makran r. Iran/Pak. 101 E5
Makrana India 96 B4
Makran Coast Range mts Pak. see Talar-i-Band
Makronisi i. Greece 59 F11
Makronisi i. Greece 59 H11
Maksatikha Rus. Fed. 43 Q4
Maksi India 96 C5
Maksimovka Rus. Fed. 82 E3
Makstag Iran 101 E4
Maksudangarh India 96 C5
Makthar Tunisia 57 B13
Mākū Iran 100 A2
Makum India 97 G4
Makumbako Tanz. 129 B7
Makumbi Dem. Rep. Congo 127 D6
Makundu i. Maldives see Makunudhoo
Makunduchi Tanz. 129 C6
Makung Taiwan 87 F4
Makunguwiro Tanz. 129 C7
Makunudhoo i. Maldives 94 B5
also known as Maamakundhoo; also spelt Makundu
Makurazaki Japan 91 B9
Makurdi Nigeria 125 H5
Makuri N.Z. 152 J8
Makuungo Somalia 128 D4
Makuyuni Tanz. 128 C5
Makwassie S. Africa 133 J4
Mal India 97 F4
Mala Peru 200 A3
Mala Rep. of Ireland see Mallow
Mala i. Solomon Is see Malaita
Malå Sweden 44 L2
Mala, Punta pt Panama 186 C6
Mala Aboriginal Land res. Australia 148 A4
Mal'ab, Ra's pt Egypt 108 D3
Malabang Phil. 74 C4
Malabar Coast India 94 B3
▶**Malabo** Equat. Guinea 125 H6
Capital of Equatorial Guinea. Formerly known as Santa Isabel.
Malabuñgan Phil. 74 A4
Malaca Spain see Málaga
Malacacheta Brazil 207 K4
Malacca Malaysia see Melaka
Malacca state Malaysia see Melaka
Malacca, Strait of Indon./Malaysia 76 B1
Malacky Slovakia 49 O7
Malad r. U.S.A. 180 D4
Malad City U.S.A. 180 D4
Maladzyechna Belarus 42 H7
also spelt Molodechno
Malá Fatra nat. park Slovakia 49 Q6
Málaga Spain 54 G8
also spelt Malaca
Malaga NJ U.S.A. 177 J6
Malaga NM U.S.A. 181 F6
Malaga OH U.S.A. 176 D6
Malagarasi r. Burundi/Tanz. 129 A6
Malagarasi Tanz. 129 A6
Malagón Spain 54 H5
Malagon r. Spain 54 D7
Malahar Indon. 75 B3
Mala Ina r. Poland 49 M2
Malaita i. Solomon Is 145 F2
also known as Mala; historically known as Carteret Island
Malaja i. Indon. 77 G5
Malakal Sudan 128 A2
Malakanagiri India 94 C3
Mala Kapela mts Croatia 56 H3
Malakheti Nepal 96 D3
Malak Malak Aboriginal Land res. Australia 148 A2
Malakula i. Vanuatu 145 F3
Malakwal Pak. 101 H3
Malali Guyana 199 G3
Malamala Indon. 75 B3
Malamaui i. Phil. 74 B5
Malampaya Sound sea chan. Phil. 74 A4
Malan, Ras c. Pak. 101 F5
Malang Indon. 77 F4
Malanga Moz. 129 C8
Malangali Tanz. 129 B7
Malangana Nepal see Malangwa
Malange Angola see Malanje
Malangseidet Norway 44 L1
Malangwa Nepal 97 E4
Malanipa i. Phil. 74 B5
Malanje Angola 127 C7
formerly spelt Malange
Malanje prov. Angola 127 C7
Malanut Bay Phil. 74 A4
Malanville Benin 125 F4
Malanzán Arg. 204 D3
Malanzán, Sierra de mts Arg. 204 D3
Malappuram India 94 C4
Mälaren l. Sweden 45 L4
Malargüe Arg. 204 C4
Malaripo Brazil 199 H4
Malartic Canada 168 E3
Malartic, Lac l. Canada 173 O2
Malasoro, Teluk b. Indon. 75 A4
Malaspina Arg. 205 D7
Malaspina Glacier U.S.A. 166 A3
Malaspina Strait Canada 166 F5
Malatayur, Tanjung pt Indon. 77 F3
Malatya Turkey 107 D3
historically known as Melitene or Milid
Malaut India 96 B3
Malavalli India 94 C3
Malavate Fr. Guiana 199 H4
Malawali i. Sabah Malaysia 77 G1
▶**Malawi** country Africa 129 B7
formerly known as Nyasaland
africa [countries] ▶ 114–117
Malawi, Lake Africa see Nyasa, Lake
Malawi National Park Zambia see Nyika National Park
Malawiya Sudan 121 H6
Malax Fin. 44 M3
Malaya pen. Malaysia see Peninsular Malaysia
Malaya Byeraztavitsa Belarus 42 E8
Malaya Pera Rus. Fed. 40 J2
Malaya Vishera Rus. Fed. 43 N3
Malaybalay Phil. 74 C4
Malāyer Iran 100 B3
also known as Daulatabad
Malay Reef Australia 149 F3

Malay Sary Kazakh. 103 I3
▶**Malaysia** *country* Asia 76 C1
formerly known as Federated Malay States
asia [countries] ▶ 64–67
Malaysia, Semenanjung *pen.* Malaysia *see* **Peninsular Malaysia**
Malazgirt Turkey 107 E3
Malbaie *r.* Canada 169 G4
Malbaza Niger 125 G3
Malbon Australia 149 D4
Malbork Poland 49 Q1
historically known as Marienburg
Malbrán Arg. 204 E3
Malchin Germany 49 J2
Malcolm Australia 151 C6
Malcolm, Point Australia 151 C7
Malcolm Inlet Oman *see* **Ghazira, Ghubbat al**
Maldegem Belgium 51 J1
Malden U.S.A. 174 B4
Malden Island Kiribati 221 H6
▶**Maldives** *country* Indian Ocean 93 D10
also known as Divehi
asia [countries] ▶ 64–67
Maldon U.K. 47 M12
Maldonado Uruguay 204 G4
Maldonado, Punta *pt* Mex. 185 F5

▶**Male** Maldives 93 D10
Capital of the Maldives.
world [countries] ▶ 10–11

Male Myanmar 78 B3
Maléa Guinea 124 C4
Maleas, Akra *pt Lesbos* Greece 59 H9
Maleas, Akra *pt* Greece 59 E12
Male Atoll Maldives 93 D10
Malebogo S. Africa 133 J5
Malegaon *Maharashtra* India 94 B1
Malegaon *Maharashtra* India 94 C2
Malei Moz. 131 H3
Malé Karpaty *hills* Slovakia 49 O7
Malek Sīāh, Kūh-e *mt.* Afgh. 101 E4
Malela *Maniema* Dem. Rep. Congo 126 E5
Malela *Maniema* Dem. Rep. Congo 126 E6
Malélé Congo 126 B6
Malele Dem. Rep. Congo 127 B6
Malema Moz. 131 H2
formerly known as Entre Rios
Malendo *watercourse* Nigeria 125 G4
Malente Germany 48 H1
Maleoskop S. Africa 133 N2
Målerås Sweden 45 K4
Maler Kotla India 96 B3
Maleševske Planine *mts* Bulg./Macedonia 58 D7
Malesherbes France 51 I4
Malesina Greece 59 E10
Mālestān Afgh. 101 F3
Malestroit France 50 D5
Maleta Rus. Fed. 85 F1
Malevka Rus. Fed. 43 T8
Malgas S. Africa 132 E11
Malgobek Rus. Fed. 41 H8
Malgomaj *l.* Sweden 44 L2
Malha Sudan 121 E6
Malhada Brazil 202 D5
Malham Saudi Arabia 105 D2
Malhargarh India 96 B4
Malheur *r.* U.S.A. 180 C3
Malheur Lake U.S.A. 180 C4
Malheur National Wildlife Refuge *nature res.* U.S.A. 180 C4
▶**Mali** *country* Africa 124 E2
formerly known as French Sudan
africa [countries] ▶ 114–117
Mali Dem. Rep. Congo 126 E5
Mali Guinea 124 B3
Malia Greece 59 G13
also spelt Mallia
Malian *r.* China 85 E5
Maliana East Timor 75 C5
Malianjing *Gansu* China 84 B3
Malianjing *Gansu* China 84 D4
Malibamatso *r.* Lesotho 133 M6
Malibu U.S.A. 182 F7
Maligay Bay Phil. 74 B5
Malihabad India 89 C7
Mali Hka *r.* Myanmar 78 B2
Malikdin Afgh. 101 G3
Malik Naro *mt.* Pak. 101 E4
Maliku Indon. 75 B3
Mali Kyun *i.* Myanmar 79 B5
also known as Tavoy Island
Malili Indon. 75 B3
Mali Lošinj Croatia 56 G4
Malimba, Monts *mts* Dem. Rep. Congo 127 F6
Malin Rep. of Ireland 47 E8
Malin Ukr. *see* **Malyn**
Malindi Kenya 128 D5
Malines Belgium *see* **Mechelen**
Malinga Gabon 126 B5
Malin Head Rep. of Ireland 46 E8
Mălini Romania 58 H1
Malino Indon. 75 A4
Malino Rus. Fed. 43 T6
Malino, Gunung *mt.* Indon. 75 B2
Malinovka *r.* Rus. Fed. 82 D3
Malinovoye Ozero Rus. Fed. 103 I2
formerly known as Mikhaylovskiy
Malinyi Tanz. 129 C7
Malipo China 86 C4
Maliq Albania 58 B8
Mali Raginac *mt.* Croatia 56 H4
Malit, Qafa e *pass* Albania 58 B6
Malita Phil. 74 C5
Malitbog Phil. 74 C4
Maliwun Myanmar 79 B6
Maliya India 96 A5
Malka *r.* Rus. Fed. 41 H8
Malka Mary Kenya 128 D3
Malkapur *Maharashtra* India 94 B2
Malkapur *Maharashtra* India 94 C1
Malkara Turkey 106 A2
Mal'kavichy Belarus 42 H9
Malkhanskiy Khrebet *mts* Rus. Fed. 85 F1
Malko Tŭrnovo Bulg. 58 I7
Mallacoota Australia 147 F4
Mallacoota Inlet *b.* Australia 147 F4
Mallaig U.K. 46 G7
Mallanga *well* Chad 120 D5
Mallani *reg.* India 96 A4
Mallawi Egypt 121 F3
Mallee Cliffs National Park Australia 147 D3
Mållejus *hill* Norway 44 M1
Mallery Lake Canada 167 L1
Mallét Brazil 203 B8
Mallia Greece *see* **Malia**
Mallorca *i.* Spain *see* **Majorca**
Mallow Rep. of Ireland 47 D11
also spelt Mala
Mallowa Well Australia 150 D4
Malm Norway 44 J2
Malmberget Sweden 44 M2
Malmédy Belgium 51 M2
Malmesbury S. Africa 132 C10
Malmesbury U.K. 47 J12
Malmköping Sweden 45 L4
Malmö Sweden 45 K5
Malmö-Sturup *airport* Sweden 45 K5
Malmslätt Sweden 45 K4
Malmyzh Rus. Fed. 40 I4
Malo *i.* Indon. 75 C1
Maloarkhangel'sk Rus. Fed. 43 R9
Maloca *Amazonas* Brazil 199 F5
Maloca *Pará* Brazil 199 H4
Maloca Salamaim Brazil 201 E3
Malo Crniće *Srbija* Yugo. 58 C4
Malolos Phil. 74 B3
Malolotja Nature Reserve Swaziland 133 P3
Maloma Swaziland 133 P4
Malombe, Lake Malawi 129 B8
Malone U.S.A. 177 K1
Malong China 86 B3
also known as Tongquan
Malonga Dem. Rep. Congo 127 D7
Małopolska, Wyżyna *hills* Poland 49 R5
Maloshuyka Rus. Fed. 40 F3
Malovan *pass* Bos.-Herz. 56 J5
Malovăț Romania 58 D4
Malowera Moz. 131 F2
formerly spelt Maluera
Måløy Norway 44 I3
Maloyaroslavets Rus. Fed. 43 R6
Maloye Borisovo Rus. Fed. 43 R2
Malozemel'skaya Tundra *lowland* Rus. Fed. 40 I2
Malpelo, Isla de *i.* N. Pacific Ocean 198 A4
Malpica Spain 54 C1
Mālpils Latvia 42 F4
Malprabha *r.* India 94 C2
Malpura India 96 B4
Malše *r.* Czech Rep. 49 L7
Malsiras India 94 B2
▶**Malta** *country* Europe 57 G13
europe [countries] ▶ 32–35
Malta Latvia 42 I5
Malta *r.* Latvia 42 I5
Malta *i.* Malta 57 G13
Malta U.S.A. 180 F2
Maltahöhe Namibia 130 C5
Maltam Cameroon 125 I3
Maltion luonnonpuisto *nature res.* Fin. 44 O2
Malton U.K. 47 L9
Maluera Moz. *see* **Malowera**
Malukken *is* Indon. *see* **Moluccas**
Maluku *is* Indon. *see* **Moluccas**
Maluku *prov.* Indon. 75 D3
Ma'lūlā, Jabal *mts* Syria 109 H4
Malului, Vârful *hill* Romania 58 D2
Malumfashi Nigeria 125 G4
Malundano Zambia 127 E9
Malung Sweden 45 K3
Maluti Mountains Lesotho 133 M6
Malu'u Solomon Is 145 F2
Malvan India 94 B2
Malvasia Greece *see* **Monemvasia**
Malvern *AR* U.S.A. 179 D5
Malvern *OH* U.S.A. 176 D5
Malvérnia Moz. *see* **Chicualacuala**
Malvinas, Islas *terr.* S. Atlantic Ocean *see* **Falkland Islands**
Malwa *reg.* India 96 C5
Malwal Sudan 128 A2
Malxe *r.* Germany 49 L4
Malý Dunaj *r.* Slovakia 49 P8
Malykay Rus. Fed. 39 L3
Malyn Ukr. 41 D6
also spelt Malin
Malyy, Ostrov *i.* Rus. Fed. 43 J1
Malyy Anyuy *r.* Rus. Fed. 39 Q3
Malyye Soli Rus. Fed. 43 V4
Malyy Irgiz *r.* Rus. Fed. 41 I5
Malyy Kavkaz *mts* Asia *see* **Lesser Caucasus**
Malyy Kunaley Rus. Fed. 85 E1
Malyy Lyakhovskiy, Ostrov *i.* Rus. Fed. 39 O2
Malyy Taymyr, Ostrov *i.* Rus. Fed. 39 K2
Malyy Uzen' *r.* Kazakh./Rus. Fed. 102 B2
also known as Kishiözen
Malyy Yenisey *r.* Rus. Fed. 84 B1
Malyy Zelenchuk *r.* Rus. Fed. 107 E1
Mama *r.* Rus. Fed. 39 O3
Mamadysh Rus. Fed. 40 I5
Mamafubedu S. Africa 133 M4
Mamahabane S. Africa 133 L5
Mamaranui N.Z. 152 H3
Mamasa Indon. 75 A3
Mambahenauhan *i.* Phil. 74 A5
Mambai Brazil 202 C5
Mambajao Phil. 74 C4
Mambal Cameroon 125 I5
Mambali Tanz. 129 B6
Mambasa Dem. Rep. Congo 126 F4
Mambéré *r.* Cent. Afr. Rep. 126 C4
Mambéré-Kadéï *pref.* Cent. Afr. Rep. 126 B3
Mambi Indon. 75 A3
Mambili *r.* Congo 126 C4
Mambolo Sierra Leone 124 B4
Mamborê Brazil 206 A11
Mambrui Kenya 128 D5
Mamburao Phil. 74 B3
Mamelodi S. Africa 133 M2
Mamers France 50 G4
Mamfé Cameroon 125 H5
Mamiá Brazil 199 F6
Mamili National Park Namibia 130 D3
Mamiña Chile 200 C5
Mamison Pass Georgia/Rus. Fed. 107 E2
Mammoth U.S.A. 183 N9
Mammoth Cave National Park U.S.A. 174 C4
Mammoth Lakes U.S.A. 182 F4
Mammoth Reservoir U.S.A. 182 E4
Mamonas Brazil 207 K2
Mamonovo *Kaliningradskaya Oblast'* Rus. Fed. 42 A7
historically known as Heiligenbeil
Mamonovo *Ryazanskaya Oblast'* Rus. Fed. 43 U8
Mamontovo Rus. Fed. 103 J1
Mamoré *r.* Bol./Brazil 200 D2
Mamori Brazil 199 E5
Mamori, Lago *l.* Brazil 199 F5
Mamoriá Brazil 200 D1
Mamou Guinea 124 B4
Mamoudzou Mayotte 129 E8
also spelt Mamoutsou *or* Mamutzu
Mamoutsou Mayotte *see* **Mamoudzou**
Mampikony Madag. 131 [inset] J3
Mampong Ghana 125 E5
Mamre S. Africa 132 C10
Mamry, Jezioro *l.* Poland 49 S1
Mamuju Indon. 75 A3
Ma'mūl Oman 105 F4
Mamuno Botswana 130 D4
Mamuras Albania 58 A7
Mamurogawa Japan 90 G5
Mamutzu Mayotte *see* **Mamoudzou**
Man Côte d'Ivoire 124 D5
Man *r.* India 94 B2
Man U.S.A. 176 D8

▶**Man, Isle of** *i.* Irish Sea 47 H9
United Kingdom Crown Dependency.
europe [countries] ▶ 32–35

Mana Fr. Guiana 199 H3
Mana U.S.A. 181 [inset] Y1
Mana Bárbara Venez. 198 C2
Manabí *prov.* Ecuador 198 B5
Manacacias *r.* Col. 198 C3
Manacapuru Brazil 199 F5
Manacor Spain 55 O5
Manado Indon. 75 C2

▶**Managua** Nicaragua 186 B4
Capital of Nicaragua.

Managua, Lago de *l.* Nicaragua 186 B4
Manah Oman 105 G3
Manaia N.Z. 152 I7
Manakara Madag. 131 [inset] J4
Manakau *mt.* N.Z. 153 H10
Manākhah Yemen 104 C5
Manali India 96 C2

▶**Manama** Bahrain 105 E2
Capital of Bahrain. Also spelt Al Manāmah.
world [countries] ▶ 10–11

Manamadurai India 94 C4
Manambaho *r.* Madag. 131 [inset] J3
Manambondro Madag. 131 [inset] J4
Manamelkudi India 94 C4
Manam Island P.N.G. 73 K7
also known as Vulcan Island
Manamo, Caño *r.* Venez. 199 F2
Manamoc *i.* Phil. 74 B4
Mananantañana *r.* Madag. 131 [inset] J4
Mananara *r.* Madag. 131 [inset] J4
Mananara, Parc National de *nat. park* Madag. 131 [inset] K3
Mananara Avaratra Madag. 131 [inset] K3
Manangoora Australia 148 C3
Mananjary Madag. 131 [inset] K4
Manankoliva Madag. 131 [inset] J5
Manankoro Mali 124 D4
Manantali, Lac de *l.* Mali 124 C3
Manantavadi India 94 C4
Manantenina Madag. 131 [inset] J5
Mana Pass China/India 89 B6
Mana Pools National Park Zimbabwe 131 F3
Manapouri N.Z. 153 B13

▶**Manapouri, Lake** N.Z. 153 B13
Deepest lake in Oceania.

Manapparai India 94 C4
Manarantsandry Madag. 131 [inset] J3
Manas China 88 D2
Manas *r.* India 97 F4
Manas, Gora *mt.* Uzbek. 103 G4
Manasa India 96 B4
Manas He *r.* China 88 D2
Manas Hu *l.* China 88 D2
Manāṣīr *reg.* U.A.E. 105 F3

▶**Manaslu** *mt.* Nepal 97 E3
8th highest mountain in the world and in Asia.
world [physical features] ▶ 8–9

Manasquan U.S.A. 177 K5
Manassas U.S.A. 176 H7
Manastir Macedonia *see* **Bitola**
Manas Wildlife Sanctuary *nature res.* Bhutan 97 F4
Manatang Indon. 75 C5
Manatuto East Timor 75 C5
Man-aung Kyun *i.* Myanmar *see* **Cheduba Island**
Manaus Brazil 199 F5
Manavgat Turkey 106 B3
Manavgat *r.* Turkey 108 C1
Manawa U.S.A. 172 E6
Manawar India 96 B5
Manawaru N.Z. 152 J5
Manawashei Sudan 120 E6
Manawatu *r.* N.Z. 152 J8
Manawatu-Wanganui *admin. reg.* N.Z. 152 J7
Manay Phil. 74 C5
Manayenki Rus. Fed. 43 R8
Manbazar India 97 E5
Manbij Syria 109 I1
Mancelona U.S.A. 173 H6
Manchar India 94 B2
Manchester U.K. 47 J10
Manchester *CT* U.S.A. 177 M4
Manchester *IA* U.S.A. 174 B3
Manchester *KY* U.S.A. 176 B8
Manchester *MD* U.S.A. 177 I6
Manchester *MI* U.S.A. 173 I8
Manchester *NH* U.S.A. 177 N3
Manchester *OH* U.S.A. 176 B7
Manchester *TN* U.S.A. 174 C5
Manchhar Lake Pak. 101 F5
Manciano Italy 56 D6
Mancılık Turkey 107 D3
Mancınık Dağı *mts* Turkey 59 I9
Mancos *r.* U.S.A. 183 P5
Mand Pak. 101 E5
Mand, Rūd-e *r.* Iran 100 B4
also known as Qara Āghach
Manda Bangl. 97 F4
Manda Malawi 129 B7
Manda Tanz. 129 B6
Manda, Jebel *mt.* Sudan 126 E2
Manda, Parc National de *nat. park* Chad 126 C2
Mandabe Madag. 131 [inset] J4
Mandaguaçu Brazil 206 A10
Mandaguari Brazil 206 B10
Mandai Sing. 76 [inset]
Mandal Afgh. 101 E3
Mandal *Gujarat* India 96 A5
Mandal *Rajasthan* India 96 B4
Mandal *Bulgan* Mongolia 84 D1
Mandal *Töv* Mongolia 85 E1
Mandal Norway 45 I4

▶**Mandala, Puncak** *mt.* Indon. 73 J7
3rd highest mountain in Oceania. Formerly known as Julianatop.
oceania [landscapes] ▶ 136–137

Mandalay Myanmar 78 B3
also spelt Mandale
Mandalay *admin. div.* Myanmar 78 A3
also spelt Mandale
Mandale Myanmar *see* **Mandalay**
Mandale *admin. div.* Myanmar *see* **Mandalay**
Mandalgarh India 96 B4
Mandalgovĭ Mongolia 85 E2
Mandalī Iraq 107 F4
Mandalt China 85 G3
also known as Sonid Zuoqi
Mandan U.S.A. 178 B2
Mandaon Phil. 74 B3
Mandapam India 94 C4
Mandar, Teluk *b.* Indon. 75 A3
Mandas *Sardegna* Italy 57 B9
Mandav Hills India 96 A5
Mandé, Mont de *hill* France 51 K6
Mandelieu-la-Napoule France 51 M9
Mandello del Lario Italy 56 B3
Mandera Kenya 128 D4
Manderfield U.S.A. 183 L3
Mandeville Jamaica 186 D3
Mandeville N.Z. 153 C13
Mandha India 96 A4
Mandheera Somalia 128 E2
Mandhoúdhion Greece *see* **Mantoudi**
Mandi India 96 C3
Mandiakui Mali 124 D3
Mandiana Guinea 124 C4
Mandi Burewala Pak. 101 H4
Mandidzuzure Zimbabwe *see* **Chimanimani**
Mandié Moz. 131 G3
Mandimba Moz. 131 G2
Manding, Monts *mts* Mali 124 C3
Mandioli *i.* Indon. 75 C3
Mandji Gabon 126 A5
Mandla India 96 D5
Mandor India 96 B4
Mandorah Australia 148 A2
Mandoro Dem. Rep. Congo 126 F3
Mandoro Madag. 131 [inset] J3
Mandor Reserve *nature res.* Indon. 77 E2
Mandouri Togo 125 F4
Mandra Greece 59 E10
Mandraki Greece 59 I12
Mandrare *r.* Madag. 131 [inset] J5
Mandrenska *r.* Bulg. *see* **Sredetska Reka**
Mandritsara Madag. 131 [inset] K2
Mandsaur India 96 B4
Mandul *i.* Indon. 77 G2
Mandurah Australia 151 A7
Manduria Italy 57 J8
Mandvi *Gujarat* India 96 A5
Mandvi *Gujarat* India 96 B5
Mandya India 94 C3
Manekwara India 96 A5
Manendragarh India 97 D5
Maner India 97 E4
Maner *r.* India 94 C2
Manerbio Italy 56 C3
Maneromango Tanz. 129 C6
Manesht Kūh *mt.* Iran 100 A3
Mănești Romania 58 G4
Maneva Madag. *see* **Mahaboboka**
Manevychi Ukr. 41 C6
Manfalût Egypt 121 F3
Manfredonia Italy 56 H7
Manfredonia, Golfo di *g.* Italy 56 I7
Manga Brazil 202 D5
Manga Burkina 125 E4
Mangabeiras, Serra das *hills* Brazil 202 C4
Manga Grande Angola 127 B6
Mangai Dem. Rep. Congo 126 C5
Mangai, Réserve de Faune des Hippopotames de *nature res.* Dem. Rep. Congo 126 C5
Mangaia *i.* Cook Is 221 H7
also spelt Mangea
Mangakino N.Z. 152 J6
Mangalagiri India 94 D2
Mangaldai India 97 G4
Mangalia Romania 58 J5
Mangalmé Chad 120 C6
Mangalore India 94 B3
Mangalvedha India 94 B2
Mangamaunu N.Z. 153 H10
Mangamuka N.Z. 152 H3
Mangania Dem. Rep. Congo 126 D4
Manganui *r.* N.Z. 152 H3
Mangaon India 94 B2
Mangapet India 94 D2
Mangarakau N.Z. 152 G8
Mangaratiba Brazil 207 I9
Mangareva Islands Fr. Polynesia *see* **Gambier, Îles**
Mangatainoka N.Z. 152 J8
Mangatawhiri N.Z. 152 J5
Mangaung S. Africa 133 K6
Mangawan India 97 D4
Mangaweka N.Z. 152 J7
Mangawhai N.Z. 152 I4
Mangde Chhu *r.* Bhutan *see* **Trongsa Chhu**
Ma'ngê China *see* **Luqu**
Mangea *i.* Cook Is *see* **Mangaia**
Mangembe Dem. Rep. Congo 126 E6
Manger Norway 45 I3
Manggar Indon. 77 E3
Mangghyshlaq Kazakh. *see* **Mangistau**
Mangghystaū Kazakh. *see* **Mangistau**
Mangghystaū Oblysy *admin. div.* Kazakh. *see* **Mangistauskaya Oblast'**
Mangghyt Uzbek. *see* **Mangit**
Manghit Uzbek. *see* **Mangit**
Mangistau Kazakh. 102 B4
also spelt Mangghystaū; *formerly known as* Mangghyshlaq *or* Mangyshlak
Mangistau, Gory *hills* Kazakh. 102 B3
Mangistauskaya Oblast' *admin. div.* Kazakh. 102 C4
also known as Mangghystaū Oblysy; *formerly known as* Mangyshlak Oblast *or* Mangyshlakskaya Oblast'
Mangit Uzbek. 102 E4
also spelt Mangghyt *or* Manghit
Mangkalihat, Tanjung *pt* Indon. 77 G2
Mangkutup *r.* Indon. 77 F3
Manglares, Punta *pt* Col. 198 B4
Mangnai China 88 E4
Mangnai Zhen China 88 E4
Mangoaka Madag. 131 [inset] K2
Mangochi Malawi 129 B8
formerly known as Fort Johnston
Mangodara Burkina 124 D4
Mangoky *r. Toliara* Madag. 131 [inset] I4
Mangoky *r. Toliara* Madag. 131 [inset] J4
Mangole *i.* Indon. 75 C3
Mangole, Selat *sea chan.* Indon. 75 C3
Mangoli India 94 B2
Mangombe Dem. Rep. Congo 126 E5
Mangonui N.Z. 152 H3
Mangoro *r.* Madag. 131 [inset] K3
Mangqystaū Shyghanaghy *b.* Kazakh. *see* **Mangyshlakskiy Zaliv**
Mangra China *see* **Guinan**
Mangral India 96 A5
Mangrol India 96 C4
Mangrul India 94 C1
Mangshi China *see* **Luxi**
Mangualde Port. 54 D4
Manguari Brazil 198 D5
Manguchar Pak. 101 F4
Mangueira, Lago *l.* Brazil 204 G4
Mangueirinha Brazil 203 A8
Manguéni, Plateau du Niger 123 H5
Mangui China 82 A2
Manguinha, Pontal do *pt* Brazil 202 E4
Mangula Zimbabwe *see* **Mhangura**
Mangum U.S.A. 179 C5
Mangunça, Ilha *i.* Brazil 202 C2
Mangut Rus. Fed. 85 G1
Mangyshlak Kazakh. *see* **Mangistau**
Mangyshlak, Poluostrov *pen.* Kazakh. 102 B3
also known as Tüpqaraghan Tübegi
Mangyshlak Oblast *admin. div.* Kazakh. *see* **Mangistauskaya Oblast'**
Mangyshlakskaya Oblast' *admin. div.* Kazakh. *see* **Mangistauskaya Oblast'**
Mangyshlakskiy Zaliv *b.* Kazakh. 102 B3
also known as Mangqystaū Shyghanaghy
Manhan Mongolia *see* **Tögrög**
Manhan Mongolia 84 C1
Manhattan U.S.A. 178 C4
Manhattan Beach U.S.A. 182 F8
Manhica Moz. 133 Q2
Manhoca Moz. 133 Q3
Manhuaçu Brazil 203 D7
Manhuaçu *r.* Brazil 207 L6
Manhumirim Brazil 207 L7
Mani Chad 120 B6
Mani *well* Chad 120 C5
Mani China 89 D5
Mani Col. 198 C3
Mani Nigeria 125 G3
Mānī', Wādī al *watercourse* Iraq 109 M3
Mania *r.* Madag. 131 [inset] J3
Maniago Italy 56 E2
Maniakoi Greece 58 C8
Maniari Tank *resr* India 97 D5
also known as Khuria Tank
Manica Moz. 131 G3
Manica *prov.* Moz. 131 G3
Manicaland *prov.* Zimbabwe 131 G3
Manicoré Brazil 199 F6
Manicoré *r.* Brazil 199 F6
Manicouagan Canada 169 G3
Manicouagan *r.* Canada 169 G3
Manicouagan, Réservoir Canada 169 G3
Manic Trois, Réservoir Canada 169 G3
Maniema *prov.* Dem. Rep. Congo 126 E5
Manīfah Saudi Arabia 105 E2
Maniganggo China 86 A2
Manigotagan Canada 167 L5
Manihari India 97 E4
Manihiki *atoll* Cook Is 221 H6
formerly known as Great Ganges *or* Humphrey Island
Maniitsoq Greenland 165 N3
also known as Sukkertoppen
Maniji *r.* Pak. 101 F5
Manikchhari Bangl. 97 G5
Manikganj Bangl. 97 F5
Manikgarh India *see* **Rajura**
Manikpur India 96 D4

▶**Manila** Phil. 74 B3
Capital of the Philippines.
world [cities] ▶ 24–25

Manila U.S.A. 180 E4
Manila Bay Phil. 74 B3
Manilaid *i.* Estonia 42 F3
Manilla Australia 147 F2
Manily Rus. Fed. 39 Q3
Manimbaya, Tanjung *pt* Indon. 75 A3
Maningrida Australia 148 B2
Maninjau, Danau *l.* Indon. 76 C3
Manipa *i.* Indon. 75 C3
Manipa, Selat *sea chan.* Indon. 75 C3
Manipur India *see* **Imphal**
Manipur *state* India 97 G4
Manipur *r.* India/Myanmar 97 G5
Manisa Turkey 106 A3
Manisa *prov.* Turkey 59 J10
Manises Spain 55 K5
Manissauá Missu *r.* Brazil 202 A4
Manistee U.S.A. 172 G6
Manistee *r.* U.S.A. 172 G6
Manistique U.S.A. 172 G5
Manistique Lake U.S.A. 172 H4
Manitoba *prov.* Canada 167 L4
Manitoba, Lake Canada 167 L5
Manito Lake Canada 167 I4
Manitou Canada 167 L5
Manitou *r.* Canada 169 H3
Manitou, Lake Canada 168 D4
Manitou Beach U.S.A. 176 H2
Manitou Falls Canada 168 A3
Manitou Island U.S.A. 172 F3
Manitou Islands U.S.A. 172 G5
Manitoulin Island Canada 168 D4
Manitouwadge Canada 168 C3
Manitowaning Canada 173 L5
Manitowik Lake Canada 173 I2
Manitowish Waters U.S.A. 172 D4
Manitowoc U.S.A. 172 F6
Maniwaki Canada 168 F4
Manizales Col. 198 C3
Manja Madag. 131 [inset] J4
Manjacaze Moz. 131 G5
Manjak Madag. 131 [inset] J3
Manjam Umm Qurayyât *waterhole* Egypt 104 A3
Manjarabad India 94 B3
Manjeri India 94 C4
Manjhand Pak. 101 G5
Man Jiang *r.* China 82 B4
Manjil Iran 100 B2
Manjimup Australia 151 B7
Manjo Cameroon 125 H5
Manjra *r.* India 94 C2
Man Kabat Myanmar 78 B2
Mankachar India 97 F4
Mankanza Dem. Rep. Congo *see* **Makanza**
Mankato *KS* U.S.A. 178 C4
Mankato *MN* U.S.A. 178 D2
Mankono Côte d'Ivoire 124 D4
Mankota Canada 167 J5
Manlleu Spain 55 N3
Manly U.S.A. 174 A3
Manmad India 94 B1
Mann *r.* Australia 148 B2
Mann, Mount Australia 148 A5
Manna Indon. 76 C4
Mannahill Australia 146 C3
Mannar Sri Lanka 94 C4
Mannar, Gulf of India/Sri Lanka 94 C4
Mannargudi India 94 C4
Manneru *r.* India 94 D3
Mannheim Germany 48 F6
Mannicolo Islands Solomon Is *see* **Vanikoro Islands**
Männikuste Estonia 42 F3
Manning Canada 167 G3
Manning *ND* U.S.A. 178 B2
Manning *SC* U.S.A. 175 D5
Manning Provincial Park Canada 166 F5
Mannington U.S.A. 176 E6
Männlifluh *mt.* Switz. 51 N6
Mann Ranges *mts* Australia 148 A5
Mannsville U.S.A. 177 I2
Mannu *r. Sardegna* Italy 57 A8
Mannu *r. Sardegna* Italy 57 A9
Mannu *r. Sardegna* Italy 57 B9
Mannu, Capo *c. Sardegna* Italy 57 A8
Mannville Canada 167 I4
Mano *r.* Liberia/Sierra Leone 124 C5
Manoa Bol. 200 D2
Man-of-War Rocks *is* U.S.A. *see* **Gardner Pinnacles**
Manoharpur India 89 B7
Manohar Thana India 96 C4
Manokotak U.S.A. 164 D4
Manokwari Indon. 73 H7
Manombo Atsimo Madag. 131 [inset] I4
Manompana Madag. 131 [inset] K3
Manono Dem. Rep. Congo 127 E6
Manora Head Pak. 101 F5
Mano River Liberia 124 C5
Manosque France 51 L9
Manouane, Lac *l.* Canada 169 G3
Mano-wan *b.* Japan 90 F6
Man Pan Myanmar 78 B3
Manp'o N. Korea 83 B4
Manpur India 96 B5
Manra *i.* Kiribati 145 H2
formerly known as Sydney Island
Manresa Spain 55 M3
Mansa *Gujarat* India 96 B5
Mansa *Punjab* India 96 B3
Mansa Zambia 127 F7
formerly known as Fort Rosebery
Mansabá Guinea-Bissau 124 B3
Mansa Konko Gambia 124 B3
Man Sam Myanmar 78 B3
Mansehra Pak. 101 H3
Mansel Island Canada 165 L3
Mansel'kya *ridge* Fin./Rus. Fed. 44 O2
Mansfield Australia 147 E4
Mansfield U.K. 47 K10
Mansfield *AR* U.S.A. 179 D5
Mansfield *LA* U.S.A. 179 D5
Mansfield *MA* U.S.A. 177 N3
Mansfield *OH* U.S.A. 176 C5
Mansfield *PA* U.S.A. 177 H4
Mansfield, Mount U.S.A. 177 M1
Man Si Myanmar 78 B2
Mansi Myanmar 78 A2
Mansidão Brazil 202 D4
Manso *r.* Brazil *see* **Mortes, Rio das**
Manso-Nkwanta Ghana 125 E5
Mansuela Indon. 75 D3
Mansurlu Turkey 106 C3
also known as Tapan
Manta Ecuador 198 A5
long form San Pablo de Manta
Mantalingajan, Mount Phil. 74 A4
Mantantale Dem. Rep. Congo 126 D5
Mantaro *r.* Peru 200 B3
Manteca U.S.A. 182 C4
Mantecal Venez. 198 D3
Mantehage *i.* Indon. 75 C2
Manteigas Port. 54 D4
Mantena Brazil 203 D6
Manteno U.S.A. 172 F9
Manteo U.S.A. 174 F5
Mantes-la-Jolie France 50 H4
Manthani India 94 C2
Manti U.S.A. 183 M2
Mantiqueira, Serra da *mts* Brazil 203 C7
Manto Hond. 186 B4
Manton U.S.A. 172 H6
Mantorville U.S.A. 168 A4
Mantos Blancos Chile 200 C5
Mantoudi Greece 59 E10
also known as Mandhoúdhion
Mantova Italy *see* **Mantua**
Mäntsälä Fin. 45 N3
Mänttä Fin. 45 N3
Mantua Cuba 186 B2
Mantua Italy 56 C3
also spelt Mantova
Mantua U.S.A. 176 D4
Mantuan Downs Australia 149 E5
Manturovo Rus. Fed. 40 H4
Mäntyharju Fin. 45 N3
Mäntyjärvi Fin. 44 N2
Manu *r.* Bol. *see* **Mapiri**
Manú *r.* Peru 200 C3
Manu, Parque Nacional *nat. park* Peru 200 B3
Manuae *atoll* Fr. Polynesia 221 H7
also known as Fenua Ura; *formerly known as* Scilly, Île
Manua Islands American Samoa 145 I3
Manubi S. Africa 133 M9
Manuel Alves *r.* Brazil 202 B4
Manuel J. Cobo Arg. 204 F4
Manuel Rodriguez, Isla *i.* Chile 205 B9
Manuel Urbano Brazil 200 C2
Manuel Vitorino Brazil 202 D5
Manuelzinho Brazil 202 A3
Manui *i.* Indon. 75 B3
Manūjān Iran 100 D5
Manukan Phil. 74 B4
Manukau N.Z. 152 I4
Manukau Harbour N.Z. 152 I5
Manuk Manka *i.* Phil. 74 A5
Manunda *watercourse* Australia 146 C3
Manupari *r.* Bol. 200 D2
Manurimi *r.* Bol. 200 D2
Manuripi *r.* Bol. 200 D2
Manusela National Park Indon. 75 D3
Manus Island P.N.G. 73 K7
Manutuke N.Z. 152 L6
Manvi India 94 C3
Manwat India 94 C2
Many U.S.A. 179 D6
Manyallaluk Aboriginal reserve *res.* Australia 148 B2
Manyame *r.* Moz./Zimbabwe 131 F2
formerly known as Hunyani
Manyara, Lake *salt l.* Tanz. 129 B5
Manyas Turkey 59 I8
Manyas Gölü *l.* Turkey *see* **Kuş Gölü**
Manyatseng S. Africa 133 L6
Manyberries Canada 167 I5
Manych-Gudilo, Ozero *l.* Rus. Fed. 41 G7
Many Farms U.S.A. 183 O5
Manyinga Zambia 127 E8
Many Island Lake Canada 167 I5
Manyoni Tanz. 129 B6
Many Peaks, Mount *hill* Australia 151 B7
Manzala, Bahra el *lag.* Egypt *see* **Manzala, Lake**
Manzala, Lake *lag.* Egypt 108 D6
also known as Manzala, Bahra el
Manzanal, Puerto del *pass* Spain 54 E2
Manzanares Spain 55 H5
Manzaneda, Cabeza de *mt.* Spain 54 D2
Manzanillo Cuba 186 D2
Manzanillo Mex. 184 D5
Manzanillo, Punta *pt* Panama 186 D5
Manzanza Dem. Rep. Congo 126 F6
Manzariyeh Iran 100 B3
Manzengele Dem. Rep. Congo 127 C6
Manzhouli China 85 H1
Manzini Swaziland 133 P3
formerly known as Bremersdorp
Manzini *admin. dist.* Swaziland 133 P3
Manzovka Rus. Fed. *see* **Sibirtsevo**
Mao Chad 120 B6
Mao Dom. Rep. 187 F3
formerly known as Valverde
Maó Spain *see* **Mahón**
Mao, Nam *r.* Myanmar *see* **Shweli**
Maoba *Guizhou* China 86 C3
Maoba *Hubei* China 87 D2
Maocifan China 87 E2
Mao'ergai China 86 B1
Maoke, Pegunungan *mts* Indon. 73 I7
Maokeng S. Africa 133 L4
Maokui Shan *mt.* China 83 A4
Maomao Shan *mt.* China 84 D4
Maoming China 87 D4
Ma On Shan *hill Hong Kong* China 87 [inset]
Maopi Cape Taiwan *see* **Maopi T'ou**
Maopi T'ou *c.* Taiwan 87 G4
English form Maopi Cape
Maopora *i.* Indon. 75 C4
Maotou Shan *mt.* China 86 B3
Maowen China *see* **Maoxian**
Maoxian China 86 B2
also known as Fengyi; *formerly known as* Maowen
Mapai Moz. 131 F4
Mapam Yumco *l.* China 89 C6
Mapane Indon. 75 B3
Mapanza Zambia 127 E9
Mapastepec Mex. 185 G6
Maphodi S. Africa 133 J7
Mapi *r.* Indon. 73 I8
Mapiche, Serranía *mts* Venez. 199 E3
Mapimí Mex. 184 E3
Mapimí, Bolsón de *des.* Mex. 184 D3
Mapin *i.* Phil. 74 A5
Mapinhane Moz. 131 G4
Mapire Venez. 199 E3
Mapireme Brazil 199 H4
Mapiri Bol. 200 C3
Mapiri *r.* Bol. 200 D2
also known as Manu
Mapirpán Col. 198 C4
Mapiu N.Z. 152 J6
Maple *r. IA* U.S.A. 178 D3
Maple *r. MI* U.S.A. 173 I8
Maple *r. ND* U.S.A. 178 C2
Maple *r. ND* U.S.A. 178 C2
Maple Creek Canada 167 I5
Maple Peak U.S.A. 183 O8
Mapleton *IA* U.S.A. 178 D3
Mapleton *UT* U.S.A. 183 M1
Maplewood U.S.A. 172 F6
Mapoon Australia 149 D1
Mapoon Aboriginal Reserve Australia 149 D2
Mapor *i.* Indon. 76 D2
Mapoteng Lesotho 133 L6
Maprik P.N.G. 73 J7
Mapuca India 94 B3
Mapuera *r.* Brazil 199 G5
Mapulanguene Moz. 131 G5
Mapunda Dem. Rep. Congo 127 E7

▶**Maputo** Moz. 131 G5
Capital of Mozambique. Formerly known as Lourenço Marques.

Maputo *prov.* Moz. 131 G5
Maputo *r.* Moz./S. Africa 133 Q3
Maputo, Baía de *b.* Moz. 133 Q3
Maputo Elephant Reserve *nature res.* Moz. 133 Q3
Maputsoe Lesotho 133 L5
Maqanshy Kazakh. *see* **Makanchi**
Maqar an Na'am *well* Iraq 107 E5
Maqat Kazakh. *see* **Makat**
Maqên China 86 B1
also known as Dawu
Maqên Gangri *mt.* China 86 A1
Maqla, Jabal al *mt.* Saudi Arabia 108 G9

Maqnā Saudi Arabia **108** F9
Maqrat Yemen **105** E5
Maqteïr reg. Mauritania **122** C5
Maqu China **86** B1
also known as Nyinma
Ma Qu r. China see Yellow River
Maquan He r. China **89** D6
also known as Damqog Zangbo
Maqueda Channel Phil. **74** B3
Maquela do Zombo Angola **127** B6
Maquinchao Arg. **204** C6
Maquoketa r. U.S.A. **174** B4
Maquoketa U.S.A. **174** B4
Maquon U.S.A. **172** C10
Mar r. Pak. **101** F5
Mar, Serra do mts Rio de Janeiro/São Paulo
Brazil **203** C7
Mar, Serra do mts Rio Grande do Sul/Santa
Catarina Brazil **203** B8
Mar, Serra do mts Brazil **207** J9
Mara r. Canada **167** I1
Mara Guyana **199** G4
Mara India **97** D5
Mara admin. reg. Tanz. **128** D5
Maraã Brazil **199** E5
Maraba Brazil **202** B3
Marabahan Indon. **77** F3
Marabatua r. Indon. **77** F3
Marabitanas Brazil **199** E4
Maracá r. Brazil **199** I5
Maracá, Ilha i. Brazil **199** F4
Maracaí Brazil **206** C9
Maracaibo Venez. **198** D2
Maracaibo, Lago de l. Venez. see
Maracaibo, Lake
Maracaibo, Lake l. Venez. **198** D2
also known as Maracaibo, Lago de
Maracaju Brazil **201** G5
Maracaju, Serra de hills Brazil **201** G5
Maracanã Brazil **202** C2
Maracanaquará, Planalto plat. Brazil
199 H5
Maracanda Uzbek. see Samarkand
Maracás Brazil **202** D5
Maracás, Chapada de hills Brazil **202** D5
Maracay Venez. **199** E2
Marachkova Belarus **43** J6
Marādah Libya **120** E2
Maradi Niger **125** G3
Maradi dept Niger **125** G3
Marāgheh Iran **100** A3
Maragogi Brazil **202** F4
Maragondon Phil. **74** B3
Marah Saudi Arabia **105** D2
Marahuaca, Cerro mt. Venez. **199** E4
Marais des Cygnes r. U.S.A. **178** D4
Marais du Cotentin et du Bessin, Parc
Naturel Régional du nature res. France
50 E3
Marais Poitevin, Val de Sèvre et Vendée,
Parc Naturel Régional nature res. France
50 F6
Marajó, Baía de est. Brazil **202** B2
Marajó, Ilha de i. Brazil **202** B2
Marakei atoll Kiribati **145** G1
also spelt Maraki; formerly known as
Matthew
Maraki atoll Kiribati see Marakei
Marakkanam India **94** C3
Maralal Kenya **128** C4
Maralbashi China see Bachu
Maraldy Kazakh. **103** I1
Maraldy, Ozero salt l. Kazakh. **103** I1
Maralinga Australia **146** E4
Maralinga-Tjarutja Aboriginal Lands res.
Australia **146** E4
Maralwexi China see Bachu
Maramasike i. Solomon Is **145** F2
Marambio research station Antarctica **222** U2
long form Vicecomodoro Marambio
Marampit i. Indon. **75** C1
Maran mt. Pak. **101** F4
Marana U.S.A. **183** M9
Marand Iran **100** A2
Marandellas Zimbabwe see Marondera
Marang Myanmar **79** B6
Maranguape Brazil **202** E2
Maranhão r. Brazil **206** E1
Maranhão state Brazil **202** C4
Maranoa r. Australia **147** F1
Marañón r. Peru **198** C4
Marans France **50** F6
Marão Moz. **131** G5
formerly known as Mauê-ele
Marão mt. Port. **54** D3
Maraoué r. Côte d'Ivoire **124** D5
Marapanim Brazil **202** C2
Marape Brazil **201** F4
Marapi, Gunung vol. Indon. **76** C3
Marari Brazil **199** E6
Mararoa r. N.Z. **153** B13
Mara Rosa Brazil **202** B5
Maraş Cyprus see Varosia
Maraş Turkey see Kahramanmaraş
Marasende i. Indon. **77** G4
Mărăşeşti Romania **58** I3
Marateca r. Port. **54** C6
Maratea Italy **57** H9
Mărăşeşti Romania **58** I4
Mărăşu Romania **58** I3
Marathia, Akra pt Greece **59** B11
Marathokampos Greece **59** H11
Marathon Canada **168** C3
Marathón Greece see Marathonas
Marathon FL U.S.A. **175** D8
Marathon TX U.S.A. **179** B6
Marathon WI U.S.A. **172** D6
Marathonas Greece **59** E10
also known as Marathon
Maratua i. Indon. **77** G2
Marauá Brazil **199** E5
Marauiá r. Brazil **199** E5
Maravatío Mex. **185** E5
Maravillas Creek watercourse U.S.A.
179 B6

Marāwah Libya **120** D1
Marawi Phil. **74** C4
Marayes Arg. **204** D3
Maray Lake Pak. **101** G4
Mar'ayt Yemen **105** E4
Marbella Spain **54** G8
Marble Bar Australia **150** B4
Marble Canyon U.S.A. **183** M5
Marble Canyon gorge U.S.A. **183** M5
Marble Hall S. Africa **133** N1
Marble Hill U.S.A. **174** B4
Marble Island Canada **167** N2
Marbul Pass Jammu and Kashmir **96** B2
Marburg S. Africa **133** O7
Marburg Slovenia see Maribor
Marburg an der Lahn Germany **48** F5
Marca Peru **200** A2
Marca, Ponta do pt Angola **127** A9
Marçal r. Hungary **49** O8
Marcali Hungary **49** O9
Marcapata Peru **200** C3
Marcelino Brazil **199** E5
Marcellus MI U.S.A. **172** H8
Marcellus NY U.S.A. **177** I3
March r. Austria/Slovakia see Morava
March U.K. **47** M11
Marchant Hill hill Australia **146** C3
Marche reg. France **50** H6
Marche admin. reg. Italy **56** E5
Marche-en-Famenne Belgium **51** L2
Marchena Spain **54** F7
Mar Chiquita, Lag. l. Arg. **204** E3
Marchtrenk Austria **49** L7
Mărciena Latvia **42** H5
Marcona Peru **200** B3
Marcos Juárez Arg. **204** E4
Marcoule France **51** L8
Marcus Island N. Pacific Ocean see
Minami-Tori-shima
Marcy, Mount U.S.A. **177** L1
Mardan Pak. **101** H3
Mar de Ajó Arg. **204** F5
Mar del Plata Arg. **204** F5
Mardiān Afgh. **101** F2
Mardin Turkey **107** E3
Mardzad Mongolia **84** D2
Maré i. New Caledonia **145** F4
formerly known as Britannia Island
Mare de Déu del Toro hill Spain **55** P5
Maree, Loch l. U.K. **46** G6
Mare di Gioiosa Ionica Italy **57** I10
Mar'ina Gorka Belarus see Mar'ina Horka
Mar''ina Horka Belarus **42** J8
also spelt Mar'ina Gorka
Marinduque i. Phil. **74** B3
Marine City U.S.A. **173** K8
Marinella, Golfo di b. Sardegna Italy **56** B7
Mariner Glacier Antarctica **223** L2
Marinette U.S.A. **172** F5
Maringá Brazil **206** B10
Maringa r. Dem. Rep. Congo **126** C4
Maringue Moz. **131** G3
Marinha Grande Port. **54** C5
Marinjab Iran **100** B3
Mar'insko Rus. Fed. **43** J3
Marion AL U.S.A. **175** C5
Marion AR U.S.A. **174** B5
Marion IA U.S.A. **172** B8
Marion IL U.S.A. **174** B4
Marion IN U.S.A. **174** C3
Marion KS U.S.A. **178** C4
Marion KY U.S.A. **174** B4
Marion NC U.S.A. **174** D5
Marion OH U.S.A. **176** B5
Marion SC U.S.A. **175** E5
Marion VA U.S.A. **176** D9
Marion WI U.S.A. **172** E6
Marion, Lake U.S.A. **175** D5
Marion Bay Australia **146** C3
Marion Lake U.S.A. **178** C4
Marion Reef Australia **149** G3
Mariou, Adrar mt. Alg. **123** H5
Maripa r. Venez. **199** E3
Maripasoula Fr. Guiana **199** H4
Maripipi i. Phil. **74** C4
Mariposa r. U.S.A. **182** E4
Mariposa U.S.A. **182** D4
Mariquita Col. **198** C3
Marir, Gezīret i. Egypt **104** A3
English form Mirear Island
Marisa Indon. **75** B2
Mariscal Estigarribia Para. **201** E5
Mărişel Romania **58** H1
Mărişelu Romania **58** F1
Marite S. Africa **133** P1
Maritime Alps mts France/Italy **51** M8
also known as Maritimes, Alpes or
Marittime, Alpi
Maritimes, Alpes mts France/Italy see
Maritime Alps
Maritsa Bulg. see Simeonovgrad
Maritsa r. Bulg. **58** H7
also spelt Marica
Marittime, Alpi mts France/Italy see
Maritime Alps
Mari-Turek Rus. Fed. **40** I4
Mariupol' Ukr. **41** F7
formerly known as Zhdanov
Mariusa r. Venez. **199** F2
Mariusa, Isla i. Venez. **199** F2
Marīvān Iran **107** F4
formerly known as Dezh Shāhpūr
Mariy, Respublika aut. rep. Rus. Fed.
40 I4
English form Mari El; formerly known as
Mariyskaya A.S.S.R. or Mary A.S.S.R.
Mariyskaya A.S.S.R. aut. rep. Rus. Fed. see
Mariy, Respublika
Mārjamaa Estonia **42** F3
Marjan Afgh. see Wazi Khwa
Marjayoûn Lebanon **108** G4
Markā i. Saudi Arabia **104** C4
Marka Somalia **128** E4
formerly spelt Merca
Markakol', Ozero l. Kazakh. see Markakol
Markala Mali **124** D3
Markam China **86** A2
also known as Gartog
Markapur India **94** C3
Markaryd Sweden **45** K4
Markawene well Eth. **128** E3
Markaz, Ra's pt Oman **105** G4
Markazi prov. Iran **100** B3
Markdale Canada **173** M6
Marken S. Africa **131** F3
Markermeer l. Neth. **48** C3
Market Harborough U.K. **47** L11
Market Rasen U.K. **47** L10
Market Weighton U.K. **47** L10
Markha r. Rus. Fed. **39** L3
Markham Canada **168** F5
Markham, Mount Antarctica **223** K1
Markit China **88** B3
Markitta Sweden **44** M2
Markleeville U.S.A. **182** E3
Marklohe Germany **48** G3
Markounda Cent. Afr. Rep. **126** C2
Markovo Chukotskiy Avtonomnyy Okrug
Rus. Fed. **39** R3
Markovo Ivanovskaya Oblast' Rus. Fed.
43 V4
Markoye Burkina **125** F3
Marks Rus. Fed. **102** A2
Marks U.S.A. **174** B5
Marksville U.S.A. **175** A6
Marktheidenfeld Germany **48** G6
Marktoberdorf Germany **48** H8

Maribo Denmark **48** I1
Maribor Slovenia **56** H2
historically known as Marburg
Maricá Brazil **207** K9
Marica r. Bulg. see Maritsa
Marico r. S. Africa **133** K1
Marico Bosveld Nature Reserve S. Africa
133 K2
Maricopa AZ U.S.A. **183** L8
Maricopa CA U.S.A. **182** E6
Maricopa Mountains U.S.A. **183** L8
Maricourt Canada see Kangiqsujuaq
Maridi watercourse Sudan **126** F3
Maridi Sudan **126** F3
Marié r. Brazil **199** E5
Marie Byrd Land reg. Antarctica **222** P1
Marie-Galante i. Guadeloupe **187** H4
Mariehamn Fin. **45** L3
also spelt Maarianhamina
Mari El aut. rep. Rus. Fed. see
Mariy El, Respublika
Mariembero r. Brazil **202** B5
also known as Cristalino
Marienbad Poland see Malbork
Marienburg Poland see Malbork
Mariental Namibia **130** C4
Marienville U.S.A. **176** F4
Marienwerder Poland see Kwidzyn
Mariestad Sweden **45** K4
Mariet r. Canada **168** E1
Marietta GA U.S.A. **175** C5
Marietta OH U.S.A. **176** D6
Marietta OK U.S.A. **179** C5
Mariga r. Nigeria **125** G4
Marigliano Italy **56** G8
Marignane France **51** L9
Marigot Dominica **187** H4
Marigot West Indies **187** H3
Marili, Mys pt Rus. Fed. **82** F1
Mariinsk Rus. Fed. **80** D1
Mariinskoye Rus. Fed. **103** E1
Marijampolė Lith. **42** D7
formerly known as Kapsukas
Marikostinovo Bulg. **58** D7
Marília Brazil **206** D9
Marillana Australia **150** B4
Marimba Angola **127** C7
Marín Spain **54** C2
Marina U.S.A. **182** C4
Marine City U.S.A. **173** K8
Marinela, Golfo di b. Sardegna Italy **56** B7
Mariner Glacier Antarctica **223** L2
Marinette U.S.A. **172** F5
Maringá Brazil **206** B10
Maringa r. Dem. Rep. Congo **126** C4
Maringue Moz. **131** G3
Marinha Grande Port. **54** C5
Marinjab Iran **100** B3
Mar'insko Rus. Fed. **43** J3
Marion AL U.S.A. **175** C5
Marion AR U.S.A. **174** B5
Marion IA U.S.A. **172** B8
Marion IL U.S.A. **174** B4
Marion IN U.S.A. **174** C3
Marion KS U.S.A. **178** C4
Marion KY U.S.A. **174** B4
Marion NC U.S.A. **174** D5
Marion OH U.S.A. **176** B5
Marion SC U.S.A. **175** E5
Marion VA U.S.A. **176** D9
Marion WI U.S.A. **172** E6
Marion, Lake U.S.A. **175** D5
Marion Bay Australia **146** C3
Marion Lake U.S.A. **178** C4
Marion Reef Australia **149** G3
Mariou, Adrar mt. Alg. **123** H5
Maripa r. Venez. **199** E3
Maripasoula Fr. Guiana **199** H4
Maripipi i. Phil. **74** C4
Mariposa r. U.S.A. **182** E4
Mariposa U.S.A. **182** D4
Mariquita Col. **198** C3
Marir, Gezīret i. Egypt **104** A3
English form Mirear Island
Marisa Indon. **75** B2
Mariscal Estigarribia Para. **201** E5
Mărişel Romania **58** H1
Mărişelu Romania **58** F1
Marite S. Africa **133** P1
Maritime Alps mts France/Italy **51** M8
also known as Maritimes, Alpes or
Marittime, Alpi
Maritimes, Alpes mts France/Italy see
Maritime Alps
Maritsa Bulg. see Simeonovgrad
Maritsa r. Bulg. **58** H7
also spelt Marica
Marittime, Alpi mts France/Italy see
Maritime Alps
Mari-Turek Rus. Fed. **40** I4
Mariupol' Ukr. **41** F7
formerly known as Zhdanov
Mariusa r. Venez. **199** F2
Mariusa, Isla i. Venez. **199** F2
Marīvān Iran **107** F4
formerly known as Dezh Shāhpūr
Mariy, Respublika aut. rep. Rus. Fed.
40 I4
English form Mari El; formerly known as
Mariyskaya A.S.S.R. or Mary A.S.S.R.
Mariyskaya A.S.S.R. aut. rep. Rus. Fed. see
Mariy, Respublika
Mārjamaa Estonia **42** F3
Marjan Afgh. see Wazi Khwa
Marjayoûn Lebanon **108** G4
Markā i. Saudi Arabia **104** C4
Marka Somalia **128** E4
formerly spelt Merca
Markakol', Ozero l. Kazakh. **88** D1
also spelt Markakol'
Markala Mali **124** D3
Markam China **86** A2
also known as Gartog
Markapur India **94** C3
Markaryd Sweden **45** K4
Markawene well Eth. **128** E3
Markaz, Ra's pt Oman **105** G4
Markazi prov. Iran **100** B3
Markdale Canada **173** M6
Marken S. Africa **131** F3
Markermeer l. Neth. **48** C3
Market Harborough U.K. **47** L11
Market Rasen U.K. **47** L10
Market Weighton U.K. **47** L10
Markha r. Rus. Fed. **39** L3
Markham Canada **168** F5
Markham, Mount Antarctica **223** K1
Markit China **88** B3
Markitta Sweden **44** M2
Markleeville U.S.A. **182** E3
Marklohe Germany **48** G3
Markounda Cent. Afr. Rep. **126** C2
Markovo Chukotskiy Avtonomnyy Okrug
Rus. Fed. **39** R3
Markovo Ivanovskaya Oblast' Rus. Fed.
43 V4
Markoye Burkina **125** F3
Marks Rus. Fed. **102** A2
Marks U.S.A. **174** B5
Marksville U.S.A. **175** A6
Marktheidenfeld Germany **48** G6
Marktoberdorf Germany **48** H8

Marktotis Canada **166** E5
Marktredwitz Germany **48** J5
Marl Germany **48** E4
Marla Australia **146** B1
Marlboro U.S.A. **177** L4
Marlborough Australia **149** F4
Marlborough admin. reg. N.Z. **153** H9
Marlborough MA U.S.A. **177** N3
Marlborough NH U.S.A. **177** M3
Marle France **51** J3
Marlin U.S.A. **179** C6
Marlinton U.S.A. **176** E7
Marlo Australia **147** F4
Marloth Nature Reserve S. Africa **132** E11
Marlton U.S.A. **177** K6
Marmagao India **94** B3
formerly spelt Mormugao
Marmande France **50** G4
Marmara Turkey **58** I8
Marmara, Sea of g. Turkey **106** B2
also known as Marmara Denizi
Marmara Adası i. Turkey **58** I8
Marmara Denizi g. Turkey see
Marmara, Sea of
Marmaraereğlisi Turkey **59** J8
Marmara Gölü l. Turkey **59** J10
Marmarica reg. Libya **120** E2
Marmaris Turkey **106** C3
Marmaro Greece **59** H10
Marmelos r. Brazil **201** E1
Marmet U.S.A. **176** D7
Marmion, Lake salt l. Australia **151** C6
Marmion Lake Canada **168** B3
Marmolada mt. Italy **56** D2
Marmolejo Spain **54** G6
Marne r. France **51** I4
Marne Germany **48** G2
Marne, Source de la tourist site France
48 C8
Marne-la-Vallée France **51** I4
Marneuli Georgia **107** F2
formerly known as Borchalo or Sarvani
Maro Chad **126** C2
Maroambihy Madag. **131** [inset] K3
Maroantsetra Madag. **131** [inset] K3
Maroba r. Brazil **207** N4
Marofandilia Madag. **131** [inset] J4
Marokopa N.Z. **152** I6
Marol Jammu and Kashmir **96** C2
Marolambo Madag. **131** [inset] K4
Maroldsweisach Germany **48** H5
Marolles-les-Braults France **50** G4
Maromokotro mt. Madag. **131** [inset] K2
formerly spelt Marandellas
Marondera Zimbabwe **131** [inset] F3
Maroni r. Fr. Guiana **199** H3
Maronne r. France **51** H7
Maroochydore Australia **149** G5
Maroonah Australia **150** A4
Maroon Peak U.S.A. **180** F5
Maros Indon. **75** A4
Maros r. Romania **58** D2
Maroseranana Madag. **131** [inset] K3
Maros-Körös Köze plain Hungary **49** R9
Maroslele Hungary **49** R9
Marosvásárhely Romania see Târgu Mureş
Marotandrano Madag. **131** [inset] K3
Marotolana Madag. **131** [inset] K2
Maroua Cameroon **125** I4
Marovato Antsirañana Madag. **131** [inset] K2
Marovato Toliara Madag. **131** [inset] J5
Marovoay Mahajanga Madag. **131** [inset] K3
Marovoay Atsimo Madag. **131** [inset] K3
Marowali Indon. **75** B3
Marowijne r. Suriname **199** H3
Marqaba al Khubbāz hill Iran **109** N4
Marqādah Syria **109** L2
Marqakōl l. Kazakh. see Markakol', Ozero
Mar Qu r. China **86** B1
Marquard S. Africa **133** L5
Marquesas Islands Fr. Polynesia **221** I6
also known as Marquises, Îles
Marquesas Keys is U.S.A. **175** D7
Marquês de Valença Brazil **207** J9
Marquette U.S.A. **172** F4
Marquise France **51** H2
Marquises, Îles is Fr. Polynesia see
Marquesas Islands
Marra r. Australia **147** E2
Marra, Jebel mt. Sudan **120** E6
Marra, Wādī watercourse Egypt **108** F9
Marra Aboriginal Land res. Australia
148 B2
Marracuene Moz. **133** Q2
formerly known as Vila Luísa
Marradi Italy **56** D4
Marrah i. Saudi Arabia **104** C4
Marrakech Morocco **122** D3
English form Marrakesh
Marrakesh Morocco see Marrakech
Marra Plateau Sudan **120** E6
Marrawah Australia **147** D5
Marree Australia **146** C2
Marresale Rus. Fed. **40** M1
Marromeu Moz. **131** G3
Marromeu, Reserva de nature res. Moz.
131 G3
Marrupa Moz. **129** C8
Marryat Australia **148** B5
Mars r. France **51** I7
Mars U.S.A. **176** F5
Marsá Alam Egypt **121** G3
Marsa al Burayqah Libya **120** C2
Marsabit Kenya **128** C4
Marsabit National Reserve nature res.
Kenya **128** C4
Marsa Darur Sudan **121** H5
Marsa Delwein Sudan **121** H4
Marsala Sicilia Italy **57** E11
Marsa Mar'ob Sudan **104** C4
Marsa Matrûh Egypt **121** E2
historically known as Paraetonium
Marsa Oseif Sudan **104** B3
Marsa Shin'ab Sudan **104** C4
Marsa Tundaba Egypt **104** A2
Marsberg Germany **48** F4
Marsciano Italy **56** E6
Marsden Australia **147** E3
Marsden Canada **167** I4
Marseille France **51** L9
English form Marseilles; historically known
as Massilia
Marseilles France see Marseille
Marshall r. Australia **148** B4
Marshall watercourse Australia **148** C4
Marshall AR U.S.A. **179** D5
Marshall IL U.S.A. **174** C4
Marshall MI U.S.A. **173** I8
Marshall MN U.S.A. **178** D2
Marshall MO U.S.A. **178** D4
Marshall TX U.S.A. **179** D5
Marshall VA U.S.A. **176** H7
Marshall Islands country
N. Pacific Ocean **220** G5
also known as Majôl
oceania [countries] ▶▶ 138–139
Marshalltown U.S.A. **174** A3
Marshfield WI U.S.A. **172** C6
Marsh Harbour Bahamas **186** D1
Mars Hill U.S.A. **174** H2
Marsh Island U.S.A. **175** B6

Marsh Lake Canada **166** C2
Marsh Lake l. Canada **166** C2
Marsh Peak U.S.A. **183** O1
Marshūn Iran **100** B2
Marsyangdi r. Nepal **97** E4
Marta Italy **56** D6
Marta r. Italy **56** D6
Martaban Myanmar **78** B4
also known as Môktama
Martaban, Gulf of Myanmar **78** B4
Martapura Kalimantan Indon. **77** F3
Martapura Sumatra Indon. **76** D4
Martel France **51** H8
Marten River Canada **168** E4
Marte R. Gómez, Presa resr Mex. **185** F3
English form Meshed
Martés mt. Spain **55** K5
Martés, Serra mts Spain **55** J5
Martha's Vineyard i. U.S.A. **177** O4
Martí Cuba **186** D2
Martigny Switz. **51** N6
Martim Vaz, Ilhas is S. Atlantic Ocean see
Martin Vas, Ilhas
Martin r. Canada **166** F2
Martin Slovakia **49** P6
Martin r. Spain **55** K3
Martin U.S.A. **178** B3
Martin, Lake U.S.A. **175** C5
Martina Franca Italy **57** J8
Martinborough N.Z. **152** J9
Martinet Spain **55** M2
Martínez Mex. **185** F4
Martínez CA U.S.A. **182** B3
Martínez GA U.S.A. **175** D5
Martínez Lake U.S.A. **183** J9
Martinho Campos Brazil **203** C6

▶ Martinique terr. West Indies **187** H4
French Overseas Department.
oceania [countries] ▶▶ 138–139

Martinique Passage Dominica/Martinique
187 H4
Martino Greece **59** E10
Martinópolis Brazil **206** B9
Martin Peninsula Antarctica **222** Q2
Martins Bay N.Z. **153** B11
Martinsburg OH U.S.A. **176** C5
Martinsburg PA U.S.A. **176** G5
Martinsburg WV U.S.A. **176** H6
Martinsville IN U.S.A. **174** C4
Martinsville VA U.S.A. **176** F9

▶ Martin Vas, Ilhas is S. Atlantic Ocean
217 M7
Most easterly point of South America.
English form Martin Vaz Islands; also spelt
Martim Vaz, Ilhas

Martin Vaz Islands S. Atlantic Ocean see
Martin Vas, Ilhas
Martók Kazakh. see Martuk
Marton N.Z. **152** J8
Martorell Spain **55** M3
Martos Spain **54** H7
Martuk Kazakh. **102** D2
also spelt Martók
Martuni Armenia **107** F2
Maru Nigeria **125** G3
Maruchak Afgh. **101** E3
Marudi Sarawak Malaysia **77** F1
Marudu, Teluk b. Sabah Malaysia **77** G1
Marugame Japan **91** C7
Maruia r. N.Z. **153** G9
Maruim Brazil **202** F4
Marukhis Ugheltekhili pass
Georgia/Rus. Fed. **107** E2
Marum, Mount vol. Vanuatu **145** F3
Mārūn r. Iran **100** B4
Marunga Angola **127** D9
Marusthali reg. India **96** A4
Maruwa Aboriginal Reserve Australia
150 D4
Maruwa Hills Sudan **128** B3
Marvast Iran **100** C4
Marv Dasht Iran **100** C4
Marvejols France **51** J8
Marvine, Mount U.S.A. **183** M3
Marwar Junction India **96** B4
Marwayne Canada **167** I4
Mary r. N.T. Australia **148** A2
Mary r. Qld Australia **149** G5
Mary r. W.A. Australia **150** D3
Mary Turkm. **103** E5
historically known as Alexandria or Merv
Mary A.S.S.R. aut. rep. Rus. Fed. see
Mariy El, Respublika
Mary's Harbour Canada **169** K2
Marystown Canada **169** K4
Marysvale U.S.A. **183** L3
Marysville CA U.S.A. **182** C2
Marysville KS U.S.A. **178** C4
Marysville MI U.S.A. **173** K8
Marysville OH U.S.A. **176** B5
Marysville WA U.S.A. **180** B2
Maryvale r. N.T. Australia **148** B5
Maryvale Qld Australia **149** E3
Maryville MO U.S.A. **178** D3
Maryville TN U.S.A. **174** D5
Maryyskaya Oblast' admin. div. Turkm.
see Mary Oblast
Mary Oblast admin. div. Turkm. see
Maryyskaya Oblast'
Marzagão Brazil **203** B6
Marzo, Cabo c. Col. **198** B3
Masachapa Nicaragua **186** B5
Masada tourist site Israel **108** G6
also known as Metsada or Mezada
Masaff, Wādī watercourse Syria/Turkey
109 L1
Masagüon Tanz. **129** C7
Masāhūn, Kūh-e mt. Iran **100** C4
Masai Mara National Reserve nature res.
Kenya **128** B5
Masai Steppe plain Tanz. **129** C6
Masaka Uganda **128** A5
Masakhane S. Africa **133** K8
Masalanyane Pan salt pan Botswana
130 D7
Masalembu Besar i. Indon. **77** F4
Masalembu Kecil i. Indon. **77** F4
Masallı Azer. **107** G3
Masamba Indon. **75** B3
Masan S. Korea **83** C6
Masan r. Indon. **75** B3
Masanasa Spain **55** K5
Masasi Tanz. **129** C7
Masavi Bol. **201** E4
Masaya Nicaragua **186** B5
Masaya, Volcán vol. Nicaragua **186** B5
Masbate Phil. **74** B3
Masbate i. Phil. **74** B3
Mascara Alg. **123** F2
also spelt Mouaskar
Mascot U.S.A. **176** B9
Mascote Brazil **207** N2
Mascouche Canada **169** F4
Mascoutah U.S.A. **174** B4
Masela Indon. **75** D5
Masela i. Indon. **75** D5

Masères, Lac l. Canada **173** Q2

▶ Maseru Lesotho **133** L6
Capital of Lesotho.

Masfjorden Norway **45** I3
Mashaba Zimbabwe see Mashava
Mashābih i. Saudi Arabia **104** B2
Mashai Lesotho **133** M6
Mashala Dem. Rep. Congo **126** D6
Mashan China **87** D4
also known as Baishan
Mashava Zimbabwe **131** F4
formerly spelt Mashaba
Masherbrum mt. Jammu and Kashmir **96** C2
Masheve Ukr. **43** N9
Mashhad Iran **101** D2
English form Meshed
Mashi r. India **96** B4
Mashike Japan **90** F3
Mashket r. Pak. **101** E5
Mashki Chah Pak. **101** E5
Māshkīd r. Iran **101** E5
Mashonaland Central prov. Zimbabwe
131 F3
Mashonaland East prov. Zimbabwe **131** F3
Mashonaland West prov. Zimbabwe **131** F3
Mashtagi Azer. see Maştağa
Masiáca Mex. **184** C3
Masi-Manimba Dem. Rep. Congo **126** C5
Masindi Uganda **128** A4
Masinloc Phil. **74** A3
Masinyusane S. Africa **132** H8
Masira, Gulf of Oman see Maşīrah, Khalīj
Masira Channel Oman see Maşīrah, Tur'at
Maşīrah, Jazīrat i. Oman **105** G3
English form Masira Island
Maşīrah, Khalīj b. Oman **105** G4
English form Masira, Gulf of
Maşīrah, Tur'at sea chan. Oman **105** G3
English form Masira Channel
Masira Island Oman see Maşīrah, Jazīrat
Masis Armenia **107** F2
Masisea Peru **200** B2
Masjaing S. Africa **133** L8
Masjed Soleymān Iran **100** B4
Mask, Lough l. Rep. of Ireland **47** C10
Maskanah Syria **109** L1
Maskūtān Iran **101** D5
Maslti Pak. **101** F4
Masna'ah Yemen **105** E5
Masoala, Tanjona c. Madag. **131** [inset] K2
Masoala, Parc National nat. park Madag.
131 [inset] K2
Masohi Indon. **75** D3
Mason KY U.S.A. **176** A7
Mason MI U.S.A. **173** I8
Mason OH U.S.A. **176** A6
Mason TX U.S.A. **179** C6
Mason WV U.S.A. **176** D6
Mason, Lake salt flat Australia **151** B5
Mason City N.Z. **153** B14
Mason City U.S.A. **174** A3
Masoni i. Indon. **75** C3
Masontown PA U.S.A. **176** F6
Masontown WV U.S.A. **176** F6
Masqat Oman see Muscat
Masqat governorate Oman **105** G3
Masqaţ Oman see Muscat
Massa Italy **56** C4
Massachusetts state U.S.A. **177** M3
Massachusetts Bay U.S.A. **177** O3
Massadona U.S.A. **183** P1
Massafra Italy **57** J8
Massaguet Chad **120** B6
Massakory Chad **120** B6
Massa Marittima Italy **56** C5
Massambará Brazil **204** G3
Massana Gabon **126** A5
Massangena Moz. **131** G4
Massango Angola **127** C7
Massaroca Brazil **202** D4
Massarosa Italy **56** C5
Massau Guyá **127** C7
Massawa Eritrea **121** H5
also known as Mits'iwa
Massawa Channel Eritrea **121** H5
Massena U.S.A. **177** K1
Massenya Chad **126** C2
Masset Canada **166** C4
Masset Inlet Canada **166** C4
Masseube France **50** G9
Massey Canada **168** D4
Massiac France **51** J7
Massieville U.S.A. **176** C6
Massigued Mali **124** D2
Massilia France see Marseille
Massina Mali **124** D3
Massinga Moz. **131** G4
Massingir Moz. **131** G4
Massintonto r. Moz./S. Africa **133** Q2
Masson Canada **173** R5
Masson Island Antarctica **223** G2
Maştağa Azer. **107** H2
also spelt Mashtagi
Mastchoh Tajik. **101** G2
also known as Matcha
Masterton N.Z. **152** J8
Masticho, Akra pt Greece **59** H10
Mastic Point Bahamas **186** D1
Mastigouche, Réserve Faunique de
nature res. Canada **169** F4
Mastrevik Norway **46** J3
Mastuj Pak. **101** H2
Mastung Pak. **101** F4
Mastūrah Saudi Arabia **104** B3
Masty Belarus **42** F8
also spelt Mosty
Masuda Japan **91** B7
Masuika Dem. Rep. Congo **127** D6
Masuku Gabon see Franceville
Masuleh Iran **100** B2
Masulipatam India see Machilipatnam
Masuna i. American Samoa see Tutuila
Masurai, Bukit mt. Indon. **76** C3
Masvingo Zimbabwe **131** F4
formerly known as Fort Victoria or Nyande
Masvingo prov. Zimbabwe **131** F4
Maswe Tanz. **128** B5
Maswe Game Reserve nature res. Tanz.
128 B5
Maşyāf Syria **109** H2
Mat r. Albania **58** A7
Mata r. N.Z. **152** M5
Mata Amarilla Arg. **205** C8
Mataba Zambia **127** C8
Mataba Zambia **127** C8
Matabaan Somalia **128** E3
Matabeleland North prov. Zimbabwe **131** E3
Matabeleland South prov. Zimbabwe
131 F4
Matabhanga India **97** F4
Matachewan Canada **168** D4
Matachic Mex. **184** D2
Matad Mongolia **85** I2
Matadi Dem. Rep. Congo **127** B6
Matador U.S.A. **179** B5
Matagalpa Nicaragua **186** B4
Matagami Canada **168** E3
Matagorda, Lac l. Canada **168** E3
Matagorda U.S.A. **179** C6
Mata Grande Brazil **202** E4

Mataigou China see Taole
Matak i. Indon. 77 D2
Matak Kazakh. 103 H2
Matakana Island N.Z. 152 K5
Matakaoa Point N.Z. 152 M5
Matakitaki N.Z. 153 G9
Matala Angola 127 B8
Matale Sri Lanka 94 D5
Mataleng S. Africa 133 I5
Maṭālī', Jabal hill Saudi Arabia 104 C2
Matam Senegal 124 B3
Matamata N.Z. 152 J5
Mata-Mata S. Africa 132 E2
Matamau N.Z. 152 K8
Matamey Niger 125 H3
Matamoras U.S.A. 177 K4
Matamoros Campeche Mex. 185 H5
Matamoros Coahuila Mex. 185 E3
Matamoros Tamaulipas Mex. 185 F3
Ma'ta Moûlana well Mauritania 124 B2
Matana, Danau l. Indon. 75 B3
Matanal Point Phil. 74 B5
Ma'ṭan as Sārah well Libya 120 D4
Ma'ṭan Bishrah well Libya 120 D4
Matandu r. Tanz. 129 C7
Matane Canada 169 H3
Matane, Réserve Faunique de nature res. Canada 169 H3
Mata Negra Venez. 199 F2
Matanga Madag. 131 [inset] J4
Matangi N.Z. 152 J5
Matanzas Cuba 186 C2
Matão Brazil 206 E8
Matão, Serra do hills Brazil 202 B4
Matapalo, Cabo c. Costa Rica 186 C5
Matapan, Cape pt Greece see Tainaro, Akra
Mata Panew r. Poland 49 P5
Matapédia, Lac l. Canada 169 H3
Mataporquera Spain 54 G2
Maṭār well Saudi Arabia 105 D2
Matará Arg. 204 E3
Matara Sri Lanka 94 D5
also known as Matturai
Mataragka Greece 59 C10
also spelt Mataránga
Mataram Indon. 77 G5
Mataránga Greece see Mataragka
Mataranka Australia 148 B2
Matarinao Bay Phil. 74 C4
Matarka Morocco 123 E2
Matarma, Râs pt Egypt 108 D8
Mataró Spain 55 N3
Mataroa N.Z. 152 J7
Matarombea r. Indon. 75 B3
Matarraña r. Spain 55 L3
Mataruška Banja Srbija Yugo. 58 B5
Matasiri i. Indon. 77 F4
Matassi well Sudan 121 F5
Matassi Tanz. 129 C6
Matatiele S. Africa 133 M7
Matatila Dam India 96 C4
Matau N.Z. 152 I7
Mataura N.Z. 153 C14
Mataura r. N.Z. 153 C14

▶Matā'utu Wallis and Futuna Is 145 H3
Capital of Wallis and Futuna.

Matawai N.Z. 152 L6
Matawaia N.Z. 152 H3
Matawin r. Canada 169 F4
Matay Kazakh. 103 I3
Maṭbakh, Ra's al pt Qatar 105 E2
Matcha Tajik. see Mastchoh
Matchi-Manitou, Lac l. Canada 173 P2
Mategua Bol. 201 E3
Matehuala Mex. 185 E4
Matei Romania 58 F2
Mateke Hills Zimbabwe 131 F4
Matelica Italy 56 F5
Matelot Trin. and Tob. 187 H5
Matemanga Tanz. 129 C7
Matende Angola 127 C9
Matera Italy 57 I8
Matese, Monti del mts Italy 56 G7
Mátészalka Hungary 49 T8
Matetsi Zimbabwe 131 E3
Mateur Tunisia 57 B11
Mateus Leme Brazil 207 I6
Matewan U.S.A. 176 C8
Matha France 50 F7
Matheson Canada 168 D3
Mathews U.S.A. 177 I8
Mathias U.S.A. 176 G7
Mathis U.S.A. 179 C6
Mathraki i. Greece 59 A9
Mathura India 96 C4
Mati Phil. 74 C5
Matiacoali Burkina 125 F3
Matianxu China 87 E3
Matiari Pak. 101 G5
Matias Barbosa Brazil 207 J8
Matias Cardoso Brazil 202 D5
Matías Romero Mex. 185 G5
Matibane Moz. 131 I2
Matimekosh Canada 169 H2
Matina Costa Rica 186 C5
Matinicus Island U.S.A. 177 Q2
Matizi China 86 B1
Matjiesfontein S. Africa 132 E10
Matla r. India 97 F5
Matli Pak. 101 G5
Matlock U.K. 47 K10
Matlwangtlwang S. Africa 133 L4
Matna Sudan 104 A5
Mato r. Venez. 199 E3
Mato, Cerro mt. Venez. 199 E3
Matoaka U.S.A. 176 D8
Matobo Hills Zimbabwe 131 F4
also spelt Matopo Hills
Matobo National Park Zimbabwe 131 F4
formerly known as Rhodes Matopos National Park
Matogrossense, Pantanal marsh Brazil 201 G4
Mato Grosso Brazil 201 F3
▶Mato Grosso state Brazil 206 A2
southamerica [contrasts] 194–195
Mato Grosso, Planalto do plat. Brazil 202 A5
Mato Grosso do Sul state Brazil 206 A6
Matola Moz. 131 G5
Matondo Moz. 131 G3
Matope Malawi 129 B8
Matopo Hills Zimbabwe see Matobo Hills
Matos r. Bol. 200 D3
Matosinhos Port. 54 C3
Matou China see Pingguo
Mato Verde Brazil 207 K2
Matozinhos Brazil 207 I6
Mátra mts Hungary 49 Q8
Maṭraḥ Oman 105 G3
Matrai park Hungary 49 R8
Matrei in Osttirol Austria 49 J9
Matroosberg S. Africa 132 D10
Matroosberg mt. S. Africa 132 D10
Matrooster S. Africa 133 K2
Maṭrūḥ governorate Egypt 108 A8
Matsalu riiklik looduskaitseala nature res. Estonia 42 E3
Matsap S. Africa 132 G5
Matsesta Rus. Fed. 107 D2
Matsitama Botswana 131 E4
Matsudo Japan 91 F7
Matsue Japan 91 C7
Matsumae Japan 90 G4
Matsumoto Japan 91 E6
Matsusaka Japan 91 E7
Matsu Tao i. Taiwan 87 G3
Matsuura Japan 91 A8
Matsuyama Japan 91 C8
Matsuzaki Japan 91 F7
Mattagami r. Canada 168 D3
Mattamuskeet, Lake U.S.A. 174 E5
Mattawa Canada 168 E4
Matterhorn mt. Italy/Switz. 51 N7
Matterhorn mt. U.S.A. 180 D4
Mattersburg Austria 49 N8
Matthew atoll Kiribati see Marakei
Matthews U.S.A. 174 D5
Matthews Peak Kenya 128 C4
Matthews Ridge Guyana 199 F3
Matthew Town Bahamas 187 E2
Maṭṭī, Sabkhat salt pan Saudi Arabia 105 F3
Mattituck U.S.A. 177 M5
Mattmar Sweden 44 K3
Mattō Japan 91 E6
Mattoon U.S.A. 174 B4
Måttsund Sweden 44 M2
Matturai Sri Lanka see Matara
Matu Sarawak Malaysia 77 E2
Matua, Ostrov i. Rus. Fed. 81 Q3
Matucana Peru 200 A2
Matugama Sri Lanka 94 D5
Matuku i. Fiji 145 G3
Matumbo Angola 127 C8
Matun Afgh. see Khowst
Maturín Venez. 199 F2
Maturuca Brazil 199 F3
Matusadona National Park Zimbabwe 131 F3
Matutuang i. Indon. 75 C1
Matveyev, Ostrov i. Rus. Fed. 40 K1
Matveyevka Rus. Fed. 102 C1
Matwabeng S. Africa 133 L5
Matxitxako, Cabo c. Spain 55 I1
Maty Island P.N.G. see Wuvulu Island
Matyrskiy Rus. Fed. 43 U9
Mau Madhya Pradesh India 96 C4
Mau Uttar Pradesh India 97 D4
Mau Uttar Pradesh India 97 D4
Mau Aimma India 97 D4
Maubermé, Pic de mt. France/Spain 55 L2
Maubeuge France 51 J2
Maubin Myanmar 78 A4
Ma-ubin Myanmar 78 B2
Maubourguet France 50 G9
Mauchsberg S. Africa 133 O2
Maudaha India 96 D4
Maude Australia 147 E3
Mau-é-ele Moz. see Marão
Maués Brazil 199 G5
Maués r. Brazil 199 G5
Mauganj India 97 D4
Maug Islands N. Mariana Is 73 K2
Mauguio France 51 K9
Maui i. U.S.A. 181 [inset] Z1
Maukkadaw Myanmar 78 A3
Maule admin. reg. Chile 204 B4
Maule r. Chile 204 B4
Mauléon France 50 F6
Mauléon-Licharre France 50 F9
Maullín Chile 205 B6
Maulvi Bazar Bangl. 97 F4
also spelt Moulavibazar
Maumaupaki hill N.Z. 152 J5
Maumee U.S.A. 176 B4
Maumee r. U.S.A. 176 B4
Maumee Bay U.S.A. 176 B4
Maumere Indon. 75 B5
Maun Botswana 130 D3
Mauna Kea vol. U.S.A. 181 [inset] Z2
Mauna Loa vol. U.S.A. 181 [inset] Z2
Maun Game Sanctuary nature res. Botswana 130 D3
Maungataniwha mt. N.Z. 152 K6
Maungatapere N.Z. 152 I3
Maungaturoto N.Z. 152 I4
Maungdaw Myanmar 78 A3
Maungmagan Islands Myanmar 79 B5
Maungmagon Myanmar 79 B5
Maupin U.S.A. 180 B3
Mau Rampur India 96 C4
Maurawan India 96 D4
Maurepas, Lake U.S.A. 175 B6
Maures, Massif des hills France 51 M9
Mauri r. Bol. 200 C4
Mauriac France 51 I7
Maurice country Indian Ocean see Mauritius
Maurice, Lake salt flat Australia 146 A2
▶Mauritania country Africa 122 B6
spelt Al Mūrītānīyah in Arabic or Mauritanie in French
world [countries] 10–11
africa [countries] 114–117
Mauritanie country Africa see Mauritania
▶Mauritius country Indian Ocean 218 K7
also known as Maurice
africa [countries] 114–117
Mauro, Monte mt. Italy 56 G7
Mauron France 50 D4
Mauros mt. Spain 54 D3
Maurs France 51 I8
Mauston U.S.A. 172 C7
Mauvezin France 50 G9
Mauzé-sur-le-Mignon France 50 F6
Mava Dem. Rep. Congo 126 E4
Mavaca r. Venez. 199 E4
Mavago Moz. 129 C8
Mavasjaure l. Sweden 44 L2
Mavengue Angola 127 C9
Mavinga Angola 127 D8
Mavisdale U.S.A. 176 C8
Mavita Moz. 131 G3
Mavra i. Greece 59 H12
Mavrothalassa Greece 58 E8
Mavrovo nat. park Macedonia 58 B7
Mavume Moz. 131 G4
Mavuya S. Africa 133 L8
Mawa, Bukit mt. Indon. 77 F2
Ma Wan i. Hong Kong China 87 [inset]
Māwān, Khashm hill Saudi Arabia 105 D3
Mawana India 96 C3
Mawanga Dem. Rep. Congo 127 C6
Mawasangka Indon. 75 B4
Mawdaung Pass Myanmar/Thai. 79 B6
Mawei China 87 F3
Mawhai Point N.Z. 152 M6
Mawheraiti N.Z. 153 F10
Māwheranui r. N.Z. see Grey
Māwiyah Yemen 104 D5
Mawjib, Wādī al r. Jordan 108 G6
also known as Arnon
Mawkhi Myanmar 78 B4
Mawkmai Myanmar 78 B3
Mawlaik Myanmar 78 A3
also known as Upper Chindwin
Mawlamyaing Myanmar see Moulmein
Mawlamyine Myanmar see Moulmein
Mawphlang India 97 F4
Mawqaq Saudi Arabia 104 C2
Mawshij Yemen 104 C5
Mawson research station Antarctica 223 E2
Mawson Coast Antarctica 223 E2
Mawson Escarpment Antarctica 223 E2
Mawson Peninsula Antarctica 223 K2
Maw Taung mt. Myanmar 79 B6
Mawza Yemen 104 C5
Maxaanss Somalia 128 E3
Maxán Arg. 204 D3
Maxcanú Mex. 185 H4
Maxhamish Lake Canada 166 F3
Maxia, Punta mt. Sardegna Italy 57 A9
Măxineni Romania 58 I3
Maxixe Moz. 131 G4
Maxmo Fin. 44 M3
Maxwell N.Z. 152 I7
Maxwelton Australia 149 D4
Maya Chad 126 C3
Maya i. Indon. 77 E3
Maya r. Rus. Fed. 39 N3
Mayaguana i. Bahamas 187 E2
Mayaguana Passage Bahamas 187 E2
Mayagüez Puerto Rico 187 G3
Mayahi Niger 125 G3
Mayak Rus. Fed. 102 C2
Mayakovskogo mt. Tajik. 101 G2
also known as Mayakovskogo, Pik
Mayakovskogo, Pik mt. Tajik. see Mayakovskogo
Mayakum Kazakh. 103 G4
also spelt Mayaqum
Mayala Dem. Rep. Congo 127 C6
Mayama Congo 126 B5
Mayamba Dem. Rep. Congo 126 C6
Mayamey Iran 100 C2
Maya Mountains Belize/Guat. 185 H5
Mayan China see Mayanhe
Mayang China 87 D3
also known as Gaocun
Mayanhe China 86 C1
formerly known as Mayan
Mayaqum Kazakh. see Mayakum
Mayarí Cuba 186 E2
Maya-san mt. Japan 90 F5
Maybeury U.S.A. 176 D8
Maybole U.K. 46 H8
Maych'ew Eth. 128 C1
Maydā Shahr Afgh. 101 G3
Maydh Somalia 128 E2
Maydos Turkey see Eceabat
Mayen Germany 48 E5
Mayenne France 50 F4
Mayenne r. France 50 F5
Mayer U.S.A. 183 L7
Mayêr Kangri mt. China 89 D5
Mayersville U.S.A. 175 B5
Mayerthorpe Canada 167 H4
Mayet France 50 G5
Mayfa'ah Yemen 105 D5
Mayfield N.Z. 153 F11
Mayfield KY U.S.A. 174 B4
Mayfield UT U.S.A. 183 M2
Mayhan Mongolia 84 D2
Mayi r. China 82 C3
Maykain Kazakh. 103 H2
also spelt Mayqayyng
Maykamys Kazakh. 103 I3
Maykhura Tajik. 101 G2
Maykop Rus. Fed. 41 G7
Mayluu-Suu Kyrg. 103 H4
formerly known as Mayly-Say
Mayly-Say Kyrg. see Mayluu-Suu
Maymak Kazakh. 103 G4
Maymyo Myanmar 78 B3
Mayna Rus. Fed. 80 E2
Mayna Rus. Fed. 41 H5
Maynardville U.S.A. 174 D4
Mayne watercourse Australia 149 D4
Mayni India 94 B2
Maynooth Canada 173 P5
Mayo Canada 166 C2
formerly known as Mayo Landing
Mayo r. Mex. 181 E8
Mayo r. Peru 198 B6
Mayo U.S.A. 175 D6
Mayo Alim Cameroon 125 I4
Mayo-Belwa Nigeria 125 I4
Mayo Darlé Cameroon 125 H5
Mayo-Kébbi pref. Chad 126 B2
Mayoko Congo 126 B5
Mayo Lake Canada 166 C2
Mayo Landing Canada see Mayo
Mayo Lara Cent. Afr. Rep. 126 B3
Mayon vol. Phil. 74 B3
Mayor, Puig mt. Spain see Major, Puig
Mayor Buratovich Arg. 204 E5
Mayor Island N.Z. 152 K5
Mayor Pablo Lagerenza Para. 201 E4

▶Mayotte terr. Africa 129 E8
French Territorial Collectivity.
africa [countries] 114–117

May Pen Jamaica 186 D3
Mayqayyng Kazakh. see Maykain
Mayraira Point Phil. 74 B2
Maysah, Tall al mt. Jordan 108 G6
Maysān governorate Iraq 107 F5
Mayskiy Amurskaya Oblast' Rus. Fed. 82 C1
Mayskiy Kabardino-Balkarskaya Respublika Rus. Fed. 41 H8
Mayskiy Permskaya Oblast' Rus. Fed. 40 J4
Mayskiy, Khrebet mt. Rus. Fed. 82 D1
Mayskoye Kazakh. 103 I2
Mays Landing U.S.A. 177 K6
Mayson Lake Canada 167 J3
Maysville KY U.S.A. 176 B7
Maysville MO U.S.A. 178 D4
Maytag China see Dushanzi
Mayu i. Indon. 75 C2
Mayu r. Myanmar 78 A3
Mayumba Gabon 126 A5
Mayum La pass China 89 C6
Mayuram India 94 C4
Mayville MI U.S.A. 173 J7
Mayville ND U.S.A. 178 C2
Maywood U.S.A. 178 B3
Mayya Rus. Fed. 39 N3
Maza Arg. 204 E5
Maza Rus. Fed. 43 R2
Mazabuka Zambia 127 E8
Mazaca Turkey see Kayseri
Mazagan Morocco see El Jadida
Mazagão Brazil 199 I5
Ma'zah, Jabal hill Syria 109 L2
Mazaka Jugla r. Latvia 42 F5
Mazamet France 51 I9
Mazán Peru 198 C5
Māzandarān prov. Iran 100 B2
Mazao Dem. Rep. Congo 127 D7
Mazapil Mex. 185 E3
Mazar China 89 B4
Mazar, Koh-i- mt. Afgh. 101 F3
Mazāra Oman 105 G3
Mazara, Val di valley Sicilia Italy 57 E11
Mazara del Vallo Sicilia Italy 57 E11
Mazār-e Sharīf Afgh. 101 F2
Mazarrón Spain 55 J7
Mazartag mt. China 88 B4
Mazaruni r. Guyana 199 G3
Mazatán Mex. 184 C2
Mazatenango Guat. 185 H6
Mazatlán Mex. 184 D4
Mazatzal Peak U.S.A. 183 M7
Mazāvī watercourse Iran 100 D5
Mazeepa Bay S. Africa 133 M9
Mažeikiai Lith. 42 D5
Mazelet well Niger 125 H2
Mazı Turkey 59 I11
Mazie U.S.A. 176 C7
Mazirbe Latvia 42 D4
Mazocahui Mex. 184 C2
Mazocruz Peru 200 C4
Mazomanie U.S.A. 172 D7
Mazomeno Dem. Rep. Congo 126 E6
Mazomora Tanz. 129 C6
Mazong Shan mt. China 84 C3
Mazong Shan mts China 84 B3
Mazowe r. Zimbabwe 131 G3
Mazrub well Sudan 121 F6
Mazsalaca Latvia 42 G4
Māzū Iran 100 B3
Mazunga Zimbabwe 131 F4
Mazurskie, Pojezierze reg. Poland 49 R2
Mazyr Belarus 43 K9
also spelt Mozyr'
Mazzouna Tunisia 123 H2
Mba Cameroon 125 H5

▶Mbabane Swaziland 133 P3
Capital of Swaziland.

Mbacké Senegal 124 B3
Mbaéré r. Cent. Afr. Rep. 126 C4
Mbagne Mauritania 124 B2
Mbahiakro Côte d'Ivoire 124 D5
Mbaïki Cent. Afr. Rep. 126 C4
Mbakaou Cameroon 125 I5
Mbakaou, Lac de l. Cameroon 125 I5
Mbala Zambia 127 F7
formerly known as Abercorn
Mbalabala Zimbabwe 131 F4
formerly spelt Balla Balla
Mbalam Cameroon 125 I6
Mbale Uganda 128 B4
Mbalmayo Cameroon 125 H6
Mbam r. Cameroon 125 H5
Mbamba Bay Tanz. 129 B7
Mbandaka Dem. Rep. Congo 126 C5
formerly known as Coquilhatville
Mbandjok Cameroon 125 H5
Mbang Cameroon 125 I6
Mbanga Cameroon 125 H5
M'banza Congo Angola 127 B6
formerly known as São Salvador or São Salvador do Congo
Mbanza-Ngungu Dem. Rep. Congo 127 B6
formerly known as Songololo or Thysville
Mbar Senegal 124 B3
Mbarangandu Tanz. 129 C7
Mbarara Uganda 128 A5
Mbari r. Cent. Afr. Rep. 126 D3
Mbarika Mountains Tanz. 129 C7
Mbaswana S. Africa 133 Q4
Mbata Cent. Afr. Rep. 126 C4
Mbati Zambia 127 F7
Mbé Cameroon 125 I5
Mbé Congo 126 B5
Mbemba Moz. 129 B8
Mbembesi Zimbabwe 131 F3
Mbemkuru r. Tanz. 129 C7
Mbéni Comoros 129 D7
Mbénqué Côte d'Ivoire 124 D4
Mberengwa Zimbabwe 131 F4
formerly known as Belingwe
Mbereshi Zambia 127 F7
Mbeya Tanz. 129 B7
Mbeya admin. reg. Tanz. 129 B7
Mbi r. Cameroon 125 I5
Mbi r. Cent. Afr. Rep. 126 C3
Mbigou Gabon 126 A5
Mbinda Congo 126 B5
Mbinga Tanz. 129 B7
Mbini Equat. Guinea 125 H6
Mbini r. Equat. Guinea 125 H6
formerly known as Benito
Mbizi Zimbabwe 131 F4
Mbizi Mountains Tanz. 129 A7
Mbo Cent. Afr. Rep. 126 C2
Mboki Cent. Afr. Rep. 126 E3
Mbomo Congo 126 B4
Mbomou pref. Cent. Afr. Rep. 126 D3
Mbomou r. Cent. Afr. Rep./Dem. Rep. Congo 126 D3
Mbon Congo 126 B5
Mbouda Cameroon 125 H5
Mbour Senegal 124 A3
Mbout Mauritania 124 B2
Mbowela Zambia 127 E8
Mbozi Tanz. 129 B7
Mbrès Cent. Afr. Rep. 126 C3
Mbrostar Albania 58 A8
Mbuji-Mayi Dem. Rep. Congo 127 D6
Mbulu Tanz. 129 B5
Mbuluzi r. Swaziland 133 Q3
Mburucuyá Arg. 204 F3
Mbutini Hills Swaziland 133 P3
Mbuyuni Tanz. 129 C6
Mbwewe Tanz. 129 C6
McAdam Canada 169 H4
McAdoo U.S.A. 177 J5
McAlester U.S.A. 179 D5
McAllen U.S.A. 179 C7
McAllister U.S.A. 172 F5
McArthur r. Australia 148 C2
McArthur U.S.A. 176 C6
McArthur Mills Canada 173 P5
McArthur Wildlife Sanctuary nature res. Canada 166 C2
McBain U.S.A. 173 H6
McBride Canada 166 F4
McCall U.S.A. 180 C3
McCamey U.S.A. 179 B6
McCammon U.S.A. 180 D4
McCaslin Mountain hill U.S.A. 172 E5
McCauley Island Canada 166 D4
McClintock, Mount Antarctica 223 K1
McClintock Channel Canada 165 I2
McClintock Range hills Australia 150 D3
McClure, Lake U.S.A. 182 D4
McClure Strait Canada 165 H2
McClusky U.S.A. 178 B2
McComb MS U.S.A. 175 B6
McComb OH U.S.A. 176 B4
McConaughy, Lake U.S.A. 178 B3
McConnellsburg U.S.A. 176 H6
McConnelsville U.S.A. 176 D6
McCook U.S.A. 178 B3
McCormick U.S.A. 175 D5
McCoy U.S.A. 176 E8
McCrea r. Canada 167 H2
McCreary Canada 167 L5
McCullough Range mts U.S.A. 183 I6
McCullum, Mount Canada 166 B1
McCutchenville U.S.A. 176 B5
McDame Canada 166 D3
McDonald Islands Indian Ocean 219 L9
McDonald Peak U.S.A. 180 D3
McDouall Range hills Australia 148 B3
McDowell Peak U.S.A. 183 M8
McFarland CA U.S.A. 182 E6
McFarland WI U.S.A. 172 D7
McFarlane r. Canada 167 J3
McFarlane, Mount N.Z. 153 D11
McGill U.S.A. 183 J2
McGivney Canada 169 H4
McGrath AK U.S.A. 164 D3
McGrath MN U.S.A. 174 A2
McGregor r. Canada 166 F4
McGregor, Lake Canada 167 H5
McGregor Bay Canada 173 L4
McGregor Range hills Australia 147 D1
McGuire, Mount U.S.A. 180 D3
Mcherrah reg. Alg. 122 D4
Mchinga Tanz. 129 C7
Mchinji Malawi 129 B8
formerly known as Fort Manning
McIlwraith Range hills Australia 149 D2
McInnes Lake Canada 167 M4
McIntosh U.S.A. 178 B2
McKay Range hills Australia 150 C4
McKean i. Kiribati 145 H2
formerly known as Drummond Island
McKee U.S.A. 176 A8
McKeesport U.S.A. 176 F5
McKees Rocks U.S.A. 176 E5
McKenney U.S.A. 176 H9
McKenzie U.S.A. 174 B4
McKenzie r. U.S.A. 180 B3
McKinlay Australia 149 D4
McKinlay r. Australia 149 D4

▶McKinley, Mount U.S.A. 164 D3
Highest mountain in North America.
northamerica [landscapes] 156–157

McKinney U.S.A. 179 C5
McKittrick U.S.A. 182 E6
McLeansboro U.S.A. 174 B4
McLennan Canada 167 G4
McLeod r. Canada 167 H4
McLeod Bay Canada 167 I2
McLeod Lake Canada 166 F4
McLeods Island Myanmar 79 B6
McMinns Creek watercourse Australia 148 B5
McMinnville OR U.S.A. 180 B3
McMinnville TN U.S.A. 174 C5
McMurdo research station Antarctica 223 L1
McMurdo Sound b. Antarctica 223 L1
McNary U.S.A. 183 O7
McNaughton U.S.A. 172 D5
McNaughton Lake Canada see Kinbasket Lake
McPhadyen r. Canada 169 H2
McPherson U.S.A. 178 C4
McPherson Range mts Australia 147 G2
McQuesten r. Canada 166 B2
McRae U.S.A. 175 D5
McTavish Arm b. Canada 167 G1
McVeytown U.S.A. 176 H5
McVicar Arm b. Canada 166 F1
McWhorter U.S.A. 176 E6
Mda r. Rus. Fed. 43 N3
Mdantsane S. Africa 133 L9
M'Daourouch Alg. 123 G1
Mdiq Morocco 54 F9
formerly known as Rincon
Mead, Lake resr U.S.A. 183 J5
Meade U.S.A. 178 B4
Meade r. U.S.A. 164 D2
Meadow Australia 151 A5
Meadow U.S.A. 183 L3
Meadowbank r. Canada 167 L1
Meadow Bridge U.S.A. 176 E8
Meadow Lake Canada 167 I4
Meadow Lake Provincial Park Canada 167 I4
Meadow Valley Wash r. U.S.A. 183 J5
Meadowview U.S.A. 176 D9
Meadville MS U.S.A. 175 B6
Meadville PA U.S.A. 176 E4
Meaford Canada 173 M6
Meaken-dake vol. Japan 90 I3
Mealhada Port. 54 C4
Mealy Mountains Canada 169 J2
Meandarra Australia 147 F1
Meander River Canada 167 G3
Meares i. Indon. 75 C1
Mearim r. Brazil 202 C2
Meaux France 51 I4
Mebridege r. Angola 127 B6
Mebtoun, Oued El watercourse Alg. 55 K9
Mebu India 97 G3
Mebulu, Tanjung pt Indon. 77 F5
Mecanhelas Moz. 131 G2
Mecca Saudi Arabia 104 B3
also spelt Makkah
Mecca U.S.A. 181 C6
Mechanic Falls U.S.A. 177 O1
Mechanicsburg OH U.S.A. 176 B5
Mechanicsburg VA U.S.A. 176 E8
Mechanicsville U.S.A. 176 H8
Mechanicville U.S.A. 177 L3
Mechelen Belgium 51 K1
also known as Malines
Mecherchar i. Palau see Eil Malk
Mecheria Alg. 123 E2
Mechernich Germany 48 D5
Mechimeré Chad 120 B6
Mechka r. Bulg. 58 G6
Mecidiye Edirne Turkey 58 H8
Mecidiye Manisa Turkey 59 I10
Mecitözü Turkey 106 C2
Meckenheim Germany 48 E5
Mecklenburger Bucht b. Germany 48 I1
Mecklenburg-Vorpommern land Germany 49 J2
English form Mecklenburg - West Pomerania
Mecklenburg - West Pomerania land Germany see Mecklenburg-Vorpommern
Meconta Moz. 131 H2
Mecubúri Moz. 131 H2
Mecubúri r. Moz. 131 I2
Mecufi Moz. 131 I2
Mecula Moz. 129 C8
Meda r. Australia 150 C3
Meda Port. 54 D4
Meda mt. Spain 54 D2
Medak India 94 C2
Medan Indon. 76 B2
Medang i. Indon. 77 G5
Médanos Buenos Aires Arg. 204 E5
Médanos Entre Ríos Arg. 204 F4
Médanosa, Punta pt Arg. 205 D8
Médanos de Coro, Parque Nacional nat. park Venez. 198 D2
Medaryville U.S.A. 172 G9
Medchal India 94 C2
Médéa Alg. 123 F1
also known as Lemdiyya
Medeiros Neto Brazil 207 M4
Medellín Col. 198 C3
Medenine Tunisia 123 H2
Meder Eritrea 104 C5
Mederdra Mauritania 124 B2
Medford NY U.S.A. 177 M5
Medford OK U.S.A. 178 C4
Medford OR U.S.A. 180 B4
Medford WI U.S.A. 172 C5
Medgidia Romania 58 J4
Mediadilet well Mali 125 E2
Media Luna Arg. 204 D4
Mediapolis U.S.A. 172 B9
Mediaș Romania 58 F2
Medicine Bow r. U.S.A. 180 F4
Medicine Bow Mountains U.S.A. 180 F4
Medicine Bow Peak U.S.A. 180 F4
Medicine Hat Canada 167 I5
Medicine Lake U.S.A. 180 F2
Medicine Lodge U.S.A. 178 C4
Medina Brazil 202 D6
Medina Col. 198 C3
Medina Saudi Arabia 104 B2
also spelt Al Madīnah
Medina NY U.S.A. 176 G2
Medina OH U.S.A. 176 D4
Medina r. U.S.A. 179 C6
Medinaceli Spain 55 I3
Medina del Campo Spain 54 G3
Medina de Pomar Spain 55 H2
Medina de Rioseco Spain 54 F3
Medina Gounas Senegal 124 B3
Medina-Sidonia Spain 54 F8
Medinet 15 Mayo Egypt 108 C8
English form 15th of May City
Medinet el Amal Egypt 108 C8
Medînet el Obour Egypt 108 C7
Medinet el Sadat Egypt 108 B7
Medinipur India 97 E5
formerly spelt Midnapore
Mediolanum Italy see Milan
Mediterranean Sea 53 C4
Medje Dem. Rep. Congo 126 E4
Medjedel Alg. 55 O9
Mednogorsk Rus. Fed. 102 D2
Mednoye Rus. Fed. 43 Q5
Mednyy, Ostrov i. Rus. Fed. 220 F2
Médoc reg. France 50 E7
Mêdog China 97 G3
also known as Dongbo
Medora U.S.A. 178 B2
Médouneu Gabon 126 A4
Medstead Canada 167 I4
Medu Kongkar China see Maizhokunggar
Meduro atoll Marshall Is see Majuro
Medveđa Srbija Yugo. 58 C6
Medvedevo Rus. Fed. 40 H4
Medveditsa r. Rus. Fed. 41 G6
Medvednica mts Croatia 56 H3
Medvedok Rus. Fed. 40 I4
Medvėgalio kalnis hill Lith. 42 D6
Medvezh'i, Ostrova is Rus. Fed. 39 Q2
Medvezh'yegorsk Rus. Fed. 40 E3
Medyn' Rus. Fed. 43 Q7
Medzilaborce Slovakia 49 S6
Meeberrie Australia 151 A5
Meekatharra Australia 151 B5
Meeker CO U.S.A. 180 F4
Meeker OH U.S.A. 176 C5
Meeks Bay U.S.A. 182 D2
Meeladeen Somalia 128 F2
Meelberg mt. S. Africa 132 I9
Meelpaeg Reservoir Canada 169 J3
Meerane Germany 49 J5
Meerapalu Estonia 42 I3
Meerut India 96 C3
Mefta Sidi Boubekeur Alg. 55 K9
Mēga Eth. 128 C3
Mega i. Indon. 76 C3
Mega Escarpment Eth./Kenya 128 C3
Megali Panagia Greece 59 E8
Megalo Eth. 128 D3
Megalo Chorio Greece 59 I12
Megalopoli Greece 59 D11
Megalos Anthropofas i. Greece 59 H11
Meganisi i. Greece 59 B10
Mégantic, Lac l. Canada 169 G4
Megara Greece 59 E10
Megezez mt. Eth. 128 C2

▶Meghalaya state India 97 F4
Highest mean annual rainfall in the world.
world [climate and weather] 16–17

Meghasani mt. India 97 E5
Meghna r. Bangl. 97 F5
Meghri Armenia 107 F3
also spelt Megri
Megion Rus. Fed. 38 H3
Mégiscane, Lac l. Canada 173 R2
Megisti i. Greece 59 K12
formerly known as Kastellorizon
Megletsy Rus. Fed. 43 P3
Meglino, Ozero l. Rus. Fed. 43 Q3
Megra r. Rus. Fed. 43 Q1
Megrega Rus. Fed. 43 O1
Megri Armenia see Meghri
Megrozero Rus. Fed. 43 O1
Mehadica Romania 58 D3
Mehamn Norway 44 N1
Mehar Pak. 101 F5
Meharry, Mount Australia 150 B4
Mehdia Tunisia see Mahdia
Mehedeby Sweden 45 L3
Mehekar India 94 C1
Meherpur Bangl. 97 F5
Meherrin U.S.A. 176 G8
Meherrin r. U.S.A. 176 I9
Mehidpur India 96 B5
Mehlville U.S.A. 174 B4
Mehmadabad India 96 B5
Mehndawal India 97 D4
Mehrābān Iran 100 A2
Mehrān Iran 100 A3
Mehrān watercourse Iran 100 C5
Mehrān Iraq 107 F4
Mehtar Lām Afgh. 101 G3
Mehun-sur-Yèvre France 51 I5
Meia Ponte r. Brazil 206 D5
Meicheng China see Qianshan
Meicheng China see Minqing
Meichengzhen China 87 D2
Meidougou Cameroon 125 I5
Meiganga Cameroon 125 I5
Meighen Island Canada 165 J2
Meigu China 86 B2
also known as Bapu
Meihekou China 82 B4
formerly known as Hailong
Meijiang China see Ningdu
Mei Jiang r. China 87 E3
Meikeng China 87 E3
Meikle r. Canada 166 G3
Meiktila Myanmar 78 A3
Meilen Switz. 51 O5
Meilin China see Ganxian
Meilleur r. Canada 166 E2
Meilü China see Wuchuan
Meiningen Germany 48 H5
Meira Spain 54 D1
Meiringen Switz. 51 O6
Meiringspoort pass S. Africa 132 G10
Meishan China see Jinzhai
Meishan China 86 B2
also known as Dongpo
Meißen Germany 49 K4
Meißner-Kaufunger Wald, Naturpark nature res. Germany 48 G4
Meister r. Canada 166 D2
Meitan China 87 C3
also known as Yiquan
Meitingen Germany 48 H7
Meixi China 82 C3
Meixian China see Meizhou
Meixian China 87 C1
Meixing China see Xiaojin
Meizhou China 87 F3
formerly known as Meixian
Mej r. India 96 C4
Méjan, Sommet de mt. France 51 K8
Mejaouda well Mauritania 122 D5
Mejez el Bab Tunisia 57 B12
Mejicana mt. Arg. 204 D3
Mejillones Chile 200 C5
Mejillones del Sur, Bahía de b. Chile 200 C5
Mekadio well Sudan 121 G5
Mékambo Gabon 126 B4
Mek'elē Eth. 128 C1
Mekhbaza Rus. Fed. 43 O1
Mékhé Senegal 124 A3
Mekhtar Pak. 101 G4
Mekkaw Nigeria 125 F5
Meknès Morocco 122 D2
Mekong r. Asia 78 D4
also known as Lancang Jiang (China) or Mènam Khong (Laos/Thailand)
Mekong, Mouths of the Vietnam 79 D6
Méla, Mont hill Cent. Afr. Rep. 126 D2
Melaka Malaysia 76 C2
formerly spelt Malacca
Melaka state Malaysia 76 C2
formerly spelt Malacca
Melalo, Tanjung pt Indon. 77 D3
Melanesia is Oceania 220 E6
Melar Iceland 44 [inset] B2
Melawi r. Indon. 77 E2

▶Melbourne Australia 147 E4
State capital of Victoria. 2nd most populous city in Oceania.
world [cities] 24–25

Melbourne AR U.S.A. 174 B4
Melbourne FL U.S.A. 175 D6
Melbu Norway 44 K1
Melchor, Isla i. Chile 205 B7
Melchor de Mencos Guat. 185 H5
Melchor Ocampo Mex. 185 E3
Meldal Norway 44 J3
Meldola Italy 56 E4
Meldorf Germany 48 G1
Meldrum U.S.A. 176 B9
Meldrum Bay Canada 168 D4
Mele, Capo c. Italy 56 A5
Melech r. Rus. Fed. 43 R4
Melekess Rus. Fed. see Dimitrovgrad
Melenci Vojvodina, Srbija Yugo. 58 B3
Melendiz Dağı mt. Turkey 106 C3
Melenki Rus. Fed. 40 G5
Melet Turkey see Mesudiye
Meleuz Rus. Fed. 102 C1
Mélèzes, Rivière aux r. Canada 169 G1
Melfa U.S.A. 177 J8
Mélfi Chad 126 C2
Melfi Italy 56 H8
Melfort Canada 167 J4
Melgaço Brazil 202 B2
Melgar de Fernamental Spain 54 G2

Melhus Norway **44** J3
Meliadine Lake Canada **167** M2
Melimoyu, Monte *mt.* Chile **205** B7
Melina, Mount N.Z. **153** D12
Melintang, Danau *l.* Indon. **77** G3
Melipilla Chile **204** C4
Melita Canada **167** K5
Melitene Turkey *see* Malatya
Melito di Porto Salvo Italy **57** H11
Melitopol' Ukr. **41** E7
Melk Austria **49** M7
Melka Guba Eth. **128** C3
Melkosele Fin. **44** N2
Mellansel Sweden **44** L3
Mellansjö Sweden **45** K3
Mellanström Sweden **44** L2
Melle Germany **48** F3
Mellègue, Barrage *dam* Tunisia **57** A12
Mellerud Sweden **45** K4
Mellid Spain *see* Melide
Mellit Sudan **121** E6
Mellizo Sur, Cerro *mt.* Chile **205** B8
Mellor Glacier Antarctica **223** E2
Mellrichstadt Germany **48** H5
Mellum *i.* Germany **48** F3
Melmele *watercourse* Chad **120** C6
Melmoth S. Africa **133** K5
Melnik Bulg. Fed. **82** D3
Mel'nichoye Rus. Fed. **82** D3
Mělník Czech Rep. **49** L5
Mel'nikovo Rus. Fed. **43** K1
Melo Arg. **204** E4
Melo Uruguay **204** G4
Meloding S. Africa **133** K5
Melolo Indon. **75** B5
Melovoye Ukr. *see* Milove
Melozitna *r.* U.S.A. **164** D3
Melrose Australia **151** C5
Melrose U.K. **46** J8
Melrose U.S.A. **179** C6
Melsetter Zimbabwe *see* Chimanimani
Melsungen Germany **48** H3
Melta, Mount *Sabah* Malaysia *see* Meliau, Gunung
Meltaus Fin. **44** N2
Melton Australia **147** E4
Melton Mowbray U.K. **47** L11
Meluan *Sarawak* Malaysia **77** E2
Melun France **51** I4
Melur India **94** C4
Melut Sudan **128** B2
Melville Canada **167** K5
Melville, Cape Australia **149** E2
Melville, Lake Canada **169** J2
Melville, Cape Phil. **74** A5
Melville Bay Australia **148** C1
Melville Bugt *b.* Greenland *see* Qimusseriarsuaq
Melville Island Australia **148** A1
Melville Island Canada **165** H2
Melville Peninsula Canada **165** K3
Melvin, Lough *l.* Rep. of Ireland/U.K. **47** D9
Mélykút Hungary **49** Q9
Memaliaj Albania **59** H4
Mêmar Co *salt l.* China **89** C5
Memba Moz. **131** I2
Memba, Baía de *b.* Moz. **131** I2
Memberamo *r.* Indon. **73** I7
Memel Lith. *see* Klaipėda
Memel S. Africa **133** N4
Mêmele *r.* Latvia **42** F5
Memiakalnis *hill* Lith. **42** H6
Memmingen Germany **48** H8
Mempakul *Sabah* Malaysia **77** F1
Memphis *tourist site* Egypt **121** F2
Memphis *MI* U.S.A. **173** K8
Memphis *MO* U.S.A. **174** A4
Memphis *TN* U.S.A. **179** J9
Memphis *TX* U.S.A. **179** B5
Memuro-dake *mt.* Japan **90** H3
Mena Eth. **128** C3
Mena Indon. **75** C5
Mena Ukr. **41** E6
Mena U.S.A. **179** D5
Menabe *mts* Madag. **131** [inset] J4
Mênaka Mali **125** F3
Mênam Khong *r.* Asia **78** D4 *see* Mekong
Menanga Indon. **75** C3
Menarandra *r.* Madag. **131** [inset] J5
Menard U.S.A. **179** C6
Menasha U.S.A. **172** E6
Mencal *mt.* Spain **55** H7
Mencué *arg.* Arg. **204** C6
Mendanau *i.* Indon. **77** D3
Mendarda India **96** A5
Mendarik *i.* Indon. **77** D2
Mendawai Indon. **77** F3
Mendawai *r.* Indon. **77** E3
Mende France **51** J8
Mendebo Mountains Eth. **128** C3
Mendefera Eritrea **121** H6
also known as Adi Ugri
Mendeleyevsk Rus. Fed. **40** J5
formerly known as Bondyuzhskiy
Menden (Sauerland) Germany **48** E4
Mendenhall U.S.A. **175** D6
Mendenhall, Cape U.S.A. **164** C4
Mendenhall Glacier U.S.A. **166** C3
Menderes Turkey **59** I10
Méndez Mex. **185** F3
Méndez-Nuñez Phil. **74** B3

Mendi P.N.G. **73** J8
Mendip Hills U.K. **47** J12
Mendocino U.S.A. **182** A2
Mendocino, Cape U.S.A. **180** A4
Mendocino, Lake U.S.A. **182** A2
Mendota *CA* U.S.A. **182** D5
Mendota *IL* U.S.A. **174** B3
Mendota, Lake U.S.A. **172** D7
Mendoza Arg. **204** C4
Mendoza *prov.* Arg. **204** C4
Mendoza Bol. **200** D4
Mene de Mauroa Venez. **198** D2
Menemen Turkey **59** I10
Menez Bré *hill* France **50** C4
Menfi *Sicilia* Italy **57** E11
Menga, Puerto de *pass* Spain **54** F4
Mengalum *i.* Malaysia **77** F1
Mengban China **86** B4
Mengcheng China **87** F1
Mengen Turkey **106** C2
Menggala Indon. **76** D4
Menghai China **86** A4
also known as Xiangshan
Mengibar Spain **54** H6
Mengkiang *r.* Indon. **77** E2
Mengkoka, Gunung *mt.* Indon. **75** B3
Menglang China *see* Lancang
Menglie China *see* Jiangcheng
Mengmeng China *see* Shuangjiang
Mengong Cameroon **125** H6
Mengshan China **87** D3
Mengxian China *see* Mengzhou
Mengyang China *see* Mingshan
Mengyin China **85** H5
Mengzhou China **87** E1
formerly known as Mengxian
Mengzi China **86** B4
also known as Wenlan
Menihek Canada **169** H2
Menindee Australia **147** D3
Menindee Aboriginal Reserve Australia **147** D3
Menindee Lake Australia **147** D3
Meningie Australia **146** C3
Menkere Rus. Fed. **39** M3
Menna *r.* Eth. **104** B5
Mennecy France **51** I4
Mennonite Colony *res.* Para. **201** F5
Menominee *r.* U.S.A. **172** F5
Menominee U.S.A. **172** E5
Menomonee Falls U.S.A. **172** E7
Menomonie U.S.A. **172** E6
Menongue Angola **127** C8
formerly known as Serpa Pinto
Menor, Mar *lag.* Spain **55** K7
Menorca *i.* Spain *see* Minorca
Mensalong Indon. **77** G2
Men'shikova, Mys *c.* Rus. Fed. **40** K1
Mentakab Malaysia *see* Mentekab
Mentarang *r.* Indon. **77** G2
Mentawai, Kepulauan *is* Indon. **76** B3
Mentawai, Selat *sea chan.* Indon. **76** C3
Mentaya *r.* Indon. **77** F3
Mentekab Malaysia **76** C2
formerly spelt Mentakab
Mentiras *hill* Port. **54** D6
Mentiras *mt.* Spain **55** I6
Mentok Indon. **76** D3
Menton France **51** N9
Mentone U.S.A. **179** B6
Mentor U.S.A. **176** C4
Mentuba *r.* Indon. **77** F3
Menufia *governorate* Egypt *see* Minūfiya
Menukung Indon. **77** F3
Menumu Indon. **75** B2
Menyapa, Gunung *mt.* Indon. **77** G2
Menyuan China **84** D4
also known as Haomen
Menza *r.* Rus. Fed. **85** F1
Menzel Bourguiba Tunisia **123** H1
formerly known as Ferryville
Menzelet Baraji *resr* Turkey **107** D3
Menzelinsk Rus. Fed. **40** J4
Menzel Temime Tunisia **57** D12
Menzies Australia **151** C6
Menzies, Mount Antarctica **223** E2
Meobbaai *b.* Namibia **130** B5
Meoqui Mex. **184** D2
Mepala Angola **127** B6
Meponda Moz. **131** G1
Meppel Neth. **48** D3
Meppen Germany **48** E2
Meqheleng S. Africa **133** L5
Mequéns *r.* Brazil **201** E3
Mequinenza, Embalse de *resr* Spain **55** L3
Mequon U.S.A. **172** F7
Mer France **50** H5
Merah Indon. **77** G3
Merak Indon. **77** D4
Meräker Norway **44** J3
Meramangye, Lake *salt flat* Australia **146** B2
Meramec *r.* U.S.A. **178** E4
Merano Italy **56** D2
Merapi, Gunung *vol.* Java Indon. **77** E4
Merapi, Gunung *vol.* Java Indon. **77** F5
Merari, Serra *mt.* Brazil **199** F3
Meratswe *r.* Botswana **131** E4
Meratus, Pegunungan *mts* Indon. **77** F3
Merauke Indon. **73** J8
Merawwah *i.* U.A.E. **105** F2
Merbau Indon. **76** C2
Merbein Australia **147** D3
Merca Somalia *see* Marka
Mercadal Spain **55** P5
Mercantour, Parc National du *nat. park* France **51** M8
Merced *r.* U.S.A. **182** D4
Merced *r.* U.S.A. **182** D4
Mercedario, Cerro *mt.* Arg. **204** C4
Mercedes *Corrientes* Arg. **204** F3
Mercedes *San Luis* Arg. **204** D4
Mercedes Uruguay **204** F4
Mercedes *Acre* Brazil **200** C2
Mercedes *Minas Gerais* Brazil **203** D7
Mercês *Acre* Brazil **200** C2
Mercier Bol. **202** C5
Mercury *r.* N.Z. **152** J7
Mercury Bay N.Z. **152** J4
Merden Turkey *see* Göle
Merdja Zerga, Réserve de *nature res.* Morocco **122** D2
Meredith U.S.A. **177** N2
Meredith, Cape Falkland Is **205** E9
Meredith, Lake U.S.A. **179** B5
Meredoua Alg. **123** F4
Mereeg Somalia **128** E4
Merefa Ukr. **41** F6
Meremä Estonia **42** I4
Meremere N.Z. **152** J7
Merenkurkku *strait* Fin./Sweden **44** M3
Merepah Aboriginal Holding *res.* Australia **149** D2
Merezha Rus. Fed. **43** R2
Merga Oasis Sudan **121** E5
Mergenevo Kazakh. **102** B2
Mergui Myanmar **79** B5
also known as Myeik
Mergui Archipelago *is* Myanmar **79** B6
Merhei, Lacul *l.* Romania **58** K3
Meribah Australia **146** D3
Meriç *r.* Greece/Turkey *see* Evros
Meriç *r.* Greece/Turkey **58** H8
Meriç Turkey **58** H7
Merichas Greece **59** F11

Mérida Mex. **185** H4
Mérida Spain **54** E6
historically known as Emerita Augusta
Mérida Venez. **198** D2
Mérida *state* Venez. **198** D2
Mérida, Cordillera de *mts* Venez. **198** D3
Meriden U.S.A. **177** M4
Meridian *MS* U.S.A. **175** B5
Meridian *TX* U.S.A. **179** C6
Mérignac France **50** F8
Merijärvi Fin. **44** N2
Merikarvia Fin. **45** M3
Merimbula Australia **147** F4
Merin, Laguna *l.* Brazil/Uruguay *see* Mirim, Lagoa
Merinda Australia **149** F4
Meringur Australia **146** D3
Merir *i.* Palau **73** H6
historically known as Warren Hastings Island
Merirumã Brazil **199** H4
Merivale *r.* Australia **149** E5
Merke Kazakh. **103** H4
Merkel U.S.A. **179** B5
Merkinė Lith. **42** F7
Merlimau, Pulau *reg.* Sing. **76** [inset]
Mermaid Reef Australia **150** B3
Merolia Australia **151** C6
Meron, Har *mt.* Israel **108** G5
Merošina *Srbija* Yugo. **58** C5
Merowe Sudan **121** F5
Merredin Australia **151** B6
Merrick *hill* U.K. **47** H8
Merrickville Canada **173** R6
Merrill *MI* U.S.A. **173** I7
Merrill *WI* U.S.A. **172** D5
Merrill, Mount Canada **166** E2
Merrillan U.S.A. **172** C6
Merrillville U.S.A. **172** F9
Merriman S. Africa **132** H8
Merriman *r.* Australia **148** D3
Merritt Canada **166** F5
Merritt Island U.S.A. **175** D6
Merrygoen Australia **147** F2
Mersa Fatma Eritrea **121** I6
Mersa Gulbub Eritrea **121** H5
Mersa Teklay Eritrea **121** H5
Mersch Lux. **51** M3
Merse *r.* Italy **56** D5
Merseburg (Saale) Germany **48** I4
Mersey *r.* U.K. **47** J10
Mersin Turkey *see* İçel
Mersing Malaysia **76** C2
Mersing, Bukit *mt.* *Sarawak* Malaysia **77** F2
Mersin Galgalo Eth. **128** E3
Mërsrags Latvia **42** E4
Mërsrags *pt* Latvia **42** E4
Merta India **96** B4
Merta Road India **96** B4
Merthyr Tydfil U.K. **47** I12
Merti Kenya **128** C4
Merti Plateau Kenya **128** C4
Mértola Port. **54** D7
Mertoutek Alg. **123** G4
Mertz Glacier Antarctica **223** J2
Mertz Glacier Tongue Antarctica **223** J2
Mertzon U.S.A. **179** B6
Méru France **51** I3
Meru Kenya **128** C4

▶ Meru *vol.* Tanz. **128** C5
4th highest mountain in Africa.
africa [landscapes] ▶▶▶ 112–113

Meru Betiri National Park Indon. **77** F5
Merui Pak. **101** E4
Meru National Park Kenya **128** C4
Merv Turkm. *see* Mary
Merweville S. Africa **132** F9
Merzifon Turkey **106** C2
Merzig Germany **48** D6
Merz Peninsula Antarctica **222** T2
Mesa S. Africa **133** K3
Mesa U.S.A. **183** M8
Mesabi Range *hills* U.S.A. **174** A2
Mesa Bolivar Venez. **198** D3
Mesagne Italy **57** J8
Mesara, Ormos *b.* Greece **59** F13
Mesa Verde National Park U.S.A. **181** E5
Mescalero Apache Indian Reservation *res.* U.S.A. **181** F6
Meschede Germany **48** F4
Meselefors Sweden **44** L2
Mesfinto Eth. **128** C1
Meshchersk Rus. Fed. **43** Q7
Meshchovsk Rus. Fed. **43** Q7
Meshed Iran *see* Mashhad
Meshekli Uzbek. **103** F4
Meshkän Iran **100** D2
Meshoppen U.S.A. **177** J4
Mesimeri Greece **59** E8
Meslay-du-Maine France **50** F5
Mesola Italy **56** E4
Mesolongi Greece **59** C10
English form Missolonghi; *also known as* Mesolóngion
Mesolóngion Greece *see* Mesolongi
Mesquita Brazil **203** D6
Mesquite U.S.A. **179** C5
Mesquite Lake U.S.A. **183** N6
Messaad Alg. **123** G2
Messak Mellet *hills* Libya **120** A3
Messalo *r.* Moz. **129** D7
Messana *Sicilia* Italy *see* Messina
Messaoud, Oued *watercourse* Alg. **123** E4
Messier, Canal *sea chan.* Chile **205** B8
Messina *Sicilia* Italy **57** H10
historically known as Messana *or* Zancle
Messina S. Africa **133** P4
Messina, Strait of Italy **57** H10
also known as Stretta di Messina
Messines Canada **173** Q5
Messini Greece **59** D11
Messiniakos Kolpos *b.* Greece **59** D12
Meßkirch Germany **48** G8
Messlingen Sweden **44** K3
Mesta *r.* Greece *see* Nestos
Mestghanem Alg. *see* Mostaganem
Meston, Akra *pt* Greece **59** G10
Mesudiye Turkey **107** D2
Mesuji *r.* Indon. **77** D4
Meta *dept* Col. **198** C4
Meta *r.* Col./Venez. **198** E3
Métabetchouan Canada **169** G3
Metagama Canada **173** L3
Metairie U.S.A. **175** B6
Metaliferi, Munţii *mts* Romania **58** C2
Metallifere, Colline *mts* Italy **56** C5
Metallostroy Rus. Fed. **43** N4
Metamora U.S.A. **172** D10
Metan Arg. **204** C2
Metanara Eth. **128** C2
Metangula Moz. **129** B8
formerly known as Augusto Cardosa
Metapan El Salvador **185** H6
Meteghan Canada **169** H4
Metelys *l.* Lith. **42** F7
Metema Eth. **128** C1
Meteor Creek *r.* Australia **149** F5
Meteora *tourist site* Greece **59** C9
Methoni Greece **59** C12
Methuen, Mount U.S.A. **164** E3
Methven N.Z. **153** F11
Metiononga Lake Canada **168** B3
Metković Croatia **56** J5
Metlakatla U.S.A. **166** D4

Metlaoui Tunisia **123** H2
Metlika Slovenia **56** H3
Metoro Moz. **131** H2
Metro Indon. **76** D4
Metropolis U.S.A. **174** B5
Metsada *tourist site* Israel *see* Masada
Metsäkylä Fin. **44** O2
Metsovo Greece **59** C9
Metter U.S.A. **175** D5
Mettler U.S.A. **182** F6
Mettuppalaiyam India **94** C4
Mettur India **94** C4
Metu Eth. **128** B2
Metz France **51** M4
Metzingen Germany **48** G7
Meu *r.* France **50** E4
Meulaboh Indon. **76** B1
Meung-sur-Loire France **50** H5
Meurthe *r.* France **51** M4
Meuse *r.* Belgium/France **51** L1
also known as Maas (Netherlands)
Mêwa China **86** B1
Mexcala Mex. **185** F5
Mexia U.S.A. **179** C6
Mexiana, Ilha *i.* Brazil **202** B1
Mexicali Mex. **184** B1
Mexican Hat U.S.A. **183** O4
Mexican Water U.S.A. **183** O5

▶ Mexico *country* Central America **184** D4
2nd most populous and 4th largest country in North America.
northamerica [countries] ▶▶▶ 158–159

México Mex. *see* Mexico City
México *state* Mex. **185** F5
Mexico *ME* U.S.A. **177** O1
Mexico *MO* U.S.A. **174** B4
Mexico *NY* U.S.A. **177** I2
Mexico, Gulf of Mex./U.S.A. **171** G7

Mexico City Mex. **185** F5
Capital of Mexico. Most populous city in North America and 2nd in the world. Also known as México.
world [cities] ▶▶▶ 24–25

Meybod Iran **100** C3
Meydanī, Ra's-e *pt* Iran **100** D5
Meyenburg Germany **49** J2
Meyersdale U.S.A. **176** F6
Meyerton S. Africa **133** M3
Meylan France **51** L7
Meymac France **51** I7
Meymaneh Afgh. **101** F3
Meymeh Iran **100** B3
Meynypil'gyno Rus. Fed. **39** R3
Meyo Centre Cameroon **125** H6
Meyssac France **50** H7
Meza *r.* Rus. Fed. **43** V3
Mezcala *r.* Mex. **185** G5
Mezcalapa *r.* Mex. **185** G5
Mezdra Bulg. **58** E5
Mèze France **51** J9
Mezen' Rus. Fed. **40** H2
Mezen' *r.* Rus. Fed. **40** H2
Mézenc, Mont *mt.* France **51** K8
Mezenskaya Guba *b.* Rus. Fed. **40** G2
Mezha *r.* Rus. Fed. **43** M6
Mezhdurechensk Rus. Fed. **80** D2
Mezhdurechenskiy Rus. Fed. **38** G4
Mezhdurechye Rus. Fed. *see* Shali
Mezhdusharskiy, Ostrov *i.* Rus. Fed. **40** J1
Mezhgorye Ukr. *see* Mizhhir"ya
Mezin France **50** F8
Mézin France **50** G8
Mezinovskiy Rus. Fed. **43** V6
Mezitli Turkey **108** F1
Mezőberény Hungary **49** S9
Mezőcsát Hungary **49** S8
Mezőhegyes Hungary **49** R9
Mezőkovácsháza Hungary **49** R9
Mezőkövesd Hungary **49** S8
Mezőtúr Hungary **49** R9
Mezquital Mex. **184** D4
Mezquital *r.* Mex. **184** D4
Mezquitic Mex. **184** D4
Mežvidi Latvia **42** I5
Mezzolombardo Italy **56** D2
Mfouati Congo **126** B6
Mfuwe Zambia **127** F8
Mgachi Rus. Fed. **82** F2
Mgbidi Nigeria **125** G5
Mglin Rus. Fed. **43** N8
Mgwali *r.* S. Africa **133** M8
Mhail, Rubh' a' *pt* U.K. **46** F8
Mhangura Zimbabwe **131** F3
formerly spelt Mangula
Mhasvad India **94** B2
Mhlambanyatsi Swaziland **133** P3
Mhlume Swaziland **133** P3
Mhluzi S. Africa **133** N3
Mhow India **96** B5
Mi *r.* China **87** E2
Mi *r.* Myanmar **78** A3
Miahuatlán Mex. **185** F5
Miajadas Spain **54** F5
Miaméré Cent. Afr. Rep. **126** C2
Miami *AZ* U.S.A. **183** N8
Miami *FL* U.S.A. **175** D7
Miami *OK* U.S.A. **179** D4
Miami *TX* U.S.A. **179** B5
Miami Beach U.S.A. **175** D7
Miamisburg U.S.A. **176** A6
Miamitown U.S.A. **176** A6
Miānāb Iran **100** C4
Mianaz Pak. **101** E5
Mianchaowan China **84** C5
Mianchi China **87** D1
Miändasht Iran **100** D2
Miandowāb Iran **100** A2
Miandrivazo Madag. **131** [inset] J3
Miangas *i.* Phil. **74** C5
Miani Hor *b.* Pak. **101** F5
Mianmian Shan *mts* China **86** B3
Mianning China **86** B2
Mianwali Pak. **101** G3
Mianxian China **86** C1
Mianyang China *see* Xiantao
Mianyang China **86** C2
Mianzhu China **86** C2
Miaodao Qundao *is* China **85** I4
Miao'ergou China **88** D2
also known as Utu
Miaogao China *see* Suichang
Miaoli Taiwan **87** G3
Miarinarivo *Antananarivo* Madag. **131** [inset] J3
Miarinarivo *Toamasina* Madag. **131** [inset] J3
Miass Rus. Fed. **38** G4
Miastko Poland **49** N1
Mica, Cerro de *mt.* Chile **200** C5
Mica Creek Canada **166** G4
Mica Mountain U.S.A. **183** N9
Micaune Moz. **131** H3
Micang Shan *mts* China **86** C1
Michalovce Slovakia **49** S7
Michel Canada **167** I4
Michelson, Mount U.S.A. **164** E3
Micheng China *see* Midu
Miches Dom. Rep. **187** F3
Michigamme Lake U.S.A. **172** E4
Michigamme Reservoir U.S.A. **172** E4
Michigan *state* U.S.A. **173** E4

▶ Michigan, Lake U.S.A. **172** F7
3rd largest lake in North America and 5th in the world.
northamerica [landscapes] ▶▶▶ 156–157

Michigan City U.S.A. **174** C3
Michipicoten Bay Canada **168** C4
Michipicoten Island Canada **168** C4
Michipicoten River Canada **168** C4
Michoacán *state* Mex. **185** E5
Michurin Bulg. *see* Tsarevo
Michurinsk Rus. Fed. **41** G5
Micos Mex. **185** F4
Micoud St Lucia **187** H4
Micronesia *is* Pacific Ocean **220** D5

▶ Micronesia, Federated States of *country* N. Pacific Ocean **220** D5
oceania [countries] ▶▶▶ 138–139

Midai *i.* Indon. **77** D2
Midal *well* Niger **125** G2
Midale Canada **167** K5
Middelberg Pass S. Africa **132** D9
Middelburg Neth. **48** A4
Middelburg *E. Cape* S. Africa **133** J8
Middelburg *Mpumalanga* S. Africa **133** N2
Middelfart Denmark **45** J5
Middelharnis Neth. **48** B4
Middelpos S. Africa **132** E8
Middelwit S. Africa **133** L1
Middle Alkali Lake U.S.A. **180** B4
Middle Andaman *i.* India **95** H3
Middle Atlas *mts* Morocco *see* Moyen Atlas
Middle Bay Canada **169** J3
Middleboro U.S.A. **177** O4
Middlebury *VA* U.S.A. **176** F7
Middleburg S. Africa **133** J9
Middleburgh U.S.A. **177** K3
Middlebury *IN* U.S.A. **172** H9
Middlebury *VT* U.S.A. **177** L1
Middle Concho *r.* U.S.A. **179** B6
Middle Congo *country* Africa *see* Congo
Middle Creek *r.* U.S.A. **149** C3
Middle Island U.S.A. **177** M5
Middle Loup *r.* U.S.A. **178** C3
Middlemount Australia **149** F4
Middleport U.S.A. **176** C6
Middle Raccoon *r.* U.S.A. **178** D3
Middle Ridge Wildlife Reserve *nature res.* Canada **169** K3
Middle River U.S.A. **177** I6
Middlesboro U.S.A. **176** B9
Middlesbrough U.K. **47** K9
Middlesex U.S.A. **177** H3
Middle Strait India *see* Andaman Strait
Middleton Australia **149** D4
Middleton Canada **169** H4
Middleton S. Africa **133** J9
Middleton U.S.A. **172** D7
Middletown *CA* U.S.A. **182** B3
Middletown *CT* U.S.A. **177** M4
Middletown *DE* U.S.A. **177** J6
Middletown *MD* U.S.A. **176** H6
Middletown *NY* U.S.A. **177** K4
Middletown *OH* U.S.A. **176** A6
Middletown *PA* U.S.A. **177** I5
Middletown *VA* U.S.A. **176** G6
Middleville *MI* U.S.A. **172** H8
Middleville *NY* U.S.A. **177** L6
Midelt Morocco **122** D2
Midhisho *well* Somalia **128** E2
Midhurst U.K. **47** L13
Midi *r.* Yemen **104** C4
Midi, Canal du France **50** I9
Midi de Bigorre, Pic du *mt.* France **50** G10
Midi-Pyrénées *admin. reg.* France **50** I8
Midland Canada **168** E4
Midland *CA* U.S.A. **183** J8
Midland *MI* U.S.A. **173** I7
Midland *TX* U.S.A. **179** B5
Midland Junction Australia **151** A6
Midlands *prov.* Zimbabwe **131** F3
Midleton Rep. of Ireland **47** D12
Midlothian *TX* U.S.A. **179** C5
Midlothian *VA* U.S.A. **176** H8
Midmar Nature Reserve S. Africa **133** O6
Midmay Canada **173** L6
Midnapore India *see* Medinipur
Midongy Atsimo Madag. **131** [inset] J4
Midou *r.* France **50** F9
Midouze *r.* France **50** F9
Midsayap Phil. **74** C5
Midu China **86** B3
also known as Micheng
Midvale U.S.A. **183** M1
Midway Oman *see* Thamarīt
Midway *KY* U.S.A. **176** A7
Midway *UT* U.S.A. **183** M1

▶ Midway Islands N. Pacific Ocean **220** G4
United States Unincorporated Territory.
oceania [countries] ▶▶▶ 138–139

Midway Well Australia **150** C4
Midwest U.S.A. **180** F4
Midwest City U.S.A. **179** C5
Midyan *reg.* Saudi Arabia **104** A2
Midyat Turkey **107** E3
Midye Turkey *see* Kıyıköy
Midzhur *mt.* Bulg./Yugo. **58** D5
Mie *pref.* Japan **91** E7
Miechów Poland **49** R5
Miedwie, Jezioro *l.* Poland **49** L2
Międzychód Poland **49** N4
Międzylesie Poland **49** N5
Międzyrzec Podlaski Poland **49** T4
Międzyrzecz Poland **49** M3
Międzyzdroje Poland **49** L2
Miehikkälä Fin. **42** I1
Miekojärvi *l.* Fin. **44** N2
Mielec Poland **49** S5
Mień *r.* Poland **49** P3
Mienga Angola **127** C9
Miengwe Zambia **127** F8
Mienhua Yü *i.* Taiwan **87** G3
Mieraslompolo Fin. **44** N1
also known as Mierašluoppal
Mierašluoppal Fin. *see* Mieraslompolo
Miercurea-Ciuc Romania **58** G2
Mieron Norway **44** M1
Mieres del Camín Spain *see* Mieres
Mieres del Camino Spain *see* Mieres
Mieres Spain **54** G1
long form Mieres del Camín *or* Mieres del Camino
Mieron Spain **54** G1
Mierojohka *r.* Norway **44** M1
Mieron Spain **54** G1
Mierzeja Helska *pen.* Poland **49** P1
Mierzeja Wiślana *spit* Poland **49** Q1
Miesbach Germany **48** I8
Mi'èso Eth. **128** D2
Mieste Germany **48** I3
Mietoinen Fin. **45** N3
Mifah Saudi Arabia **104** C4
Mifflin U.S.A. **176** C5
Mifflinburg U.S.A. **177** H5
Mifflintown U.S.A. **177** H5
Migang Shan *mt.* China **85** E5
Migdol S. Africa **133** K3
Migennes France **51** J5
Mignone *r.* Italy **56** D6
Miguel Alemán, Presa *resr* Mex. **185** F5
Miguel Alves Brazil **202** D2
Miguel Auza Mex. **184** E3
Miguel Calmon Brazil **202** D4
Miguel de la Borda Panama **186** C5
Miguel Hidalgo, Presa *resr* Mex. **184** C3
Migushino Rus. Fed. **43** K6
Migyaunye Myanmar **78** A4
Mihail Kogălniceanu Romania **58** J4
Mihăilești Romania **58** G4
Mihalıççık Turkey **106** B3

Mihara Japan **91** C7
Mihara-yama *vol.* Japan **91** F7
Mihdjam India **97** E5
Mihijam India **97** E5
Mijares *r.* Spain **55** K4
Mijas *mt.* Spain **54** G8
Mikasa Japan **90** G3
Mikashevichy Belarus **42** I9
Mikawa-wan *b.* Japan **91** E7
Mikhali Rus. Fed. **43** U6
Mikhalishki Belarus **42** H7
Mikhanivichy Belarus **42** I9
Mikha Tskhakaia Georgia *see* Senaki
Mikhaylov Rus. Fed. **43** U7
Mikhaylovgrad Bulg. *see* Montana
Mikhaylovka Kazakh. *see* Sarykemer
Mikhaylovka *Amurskaya Oblast'* Rus. Fed. **82** C2
Mikhaylovka *Kurskaya Oblast'* Rus. Fed. **85** H1
Mikhaylovka *Volgogradskaya Oblast'* Rus. Fed. **43** Q9
Mikhaylovka *Primorskiy Kray* Rus. Fed. **82** D4
Mikhaylovka Rus. Fed. *see* Kimovsk
Mikhaylovka *Volgogradskaya Oblast'* Rus. Fed. **41** I6
Mikhaylovo Bulg. **58** E5
Mikhaylovskiy Rus. Fed. **103** I2
Mikhaylovskiy Rus. Fed. *see* Malinovoye Ozero
Mikhaylovskoye Rus. Fed. *see* Shpakovskoye
Mikhaylovskoye Rus. Fed. *see* Shpakovskoye
Mikhaylovskoye Rus. Fed. **43** V2
Mikhaylovskoye Island Antarctica **223** F2
Mikhnevo Rus. Fed. **43** S6
Miki Japan **91** D7
Mikines *tourist site* Greece *see* Mycenae
Mikir Hills India **97** G4
Mikkeli Fin. **45** N3
Mikkelin mlk Fin. **45** N3
Mikkwa *r.* Canada **167** H3
Mikonos *i.* Greece *see* Mykonos
Mikoyan Armenia *see* Yeghegnadzor
Mikropoli Greece **58** E7
Mikulkin, Mys *c.* Rus. Fed. **40** H2
Mikulov Czech Rep. **49** N7
Mikumi Tanz. **129** C6
Mikumi National Park Tanz. **129** C6
Mikun' Rus. Fed. **40** I3
Mikuni Japan **91** E6
Mikuni-sanmyaku *mts* Japan **91** F6
Mikura-jima *i.* Japan **91** F8
Mila Alg. **123** G1
Miladhunmadulu Atoll Maldives **94** B5
Milagres Brazil **202** D3
Milagro Arg. **204** D3
Milagro Ecuador **198** B5
Milan Italy **56** B3
also known as Milano; *historically known as* Mediolanum
Milan *TN* U.S.A. **173** J8
Milan *MO* U.S.A. **174** A3
Milan *OH* U.S.A. **176** C4
Milando Angola **127** C7
Milando, Reserva Especial do *nature res.* Angola **127** C7
Milang Australia **146** C3
Milange Moz. **131** G3
Milano Italy *see* Milan
Milano (Malpensa) *airport* Italy **51** O7
Milas Turkey **106** A3
historically known as Mylasa
Milavidy Belarus **42** G9
Milazzo, Capo di *c.* *Sicilia* Italy **57** H10
Milazzo *Sicilia* Italy **57** H10
historically known as Mylae
Milbank U.S.A. **178** C2
Milbridge U.S.A. **177** R1
Mildura Australia **147** D3
Mile China **86** B3
also known as Miyang
Mile Eth. **128** D2
Miles Australia **149** F5
Milesburg U.S.A. **176** H5
Miles City U.S.A. **180** F3
Milë Serdo Reserve *nature res.* Eth. **128** D2
Miletin *r.* Romania **58** I1
Mileura Australia **151** B5
Milevsko Czech Rep. **49** L6
Mileyevo Rus. Fed. **43** Q8
Milford *CT* U.S.A. **177** L4
Milford *DE* U.S.A. **177** J7
Milford *IL* U.S.A. **172** F10
Milford *NE* U.S.A. **178** C3
Milford *NH* U.S.A. **177** N3
Milford *PA* U.S.A. **177** K4
Milford *UT* U.S.A. **183** K3
Milford *VA* U.S.A. **176** H7
Milford Haven U.K. **47** G12
also known as Aberdaugleddau
Milford Lake U.S.A. **178** C4
Milford Sound N.Z. **153** B12
Milford Sound *inlet* N.Z. **153** B12
also known as Piopiotahi
Milgarra Australia **149** D3
Milgun Australia **151** B5
Milh, Bahr al *l.* Iraq *see* Razāzah, Buhayrat ar
Milh, Wādī al *watercourse* Iraq **109** P5
Milhat Ashqar *salt l.* Iraq **109** N3
Milia Alg. **55** N8
Milicz Poland **49** O4
Milili Turkey *see* Malatya
Milikapiti Australia **148** A1
Miling Australia **151** B6
Milingimbi Australia **148** B2
Milip Vanuatu **145** F3
Milk *r.* U.S.A. **180** D2
Milk, Wadi el *watercourse* Sudan **121** F5
Mil'kovo Rus. Fed. **39** P4
Milk River Canada **167** H5
Millaa Millaa Australia **149** E3
Millárs *r.* Spain **55** K4
Millau France **51** J8
Millboro U.S.A. **176** F8
Millbrook Canada **173** O6
Millbrook U.S.A. **177** L4
Mill City U.S.A. **180** B3
Mill Creek *r.* U.S.A. **182** B1
Milledgeville *GA* U.S.A. **175** D5
Milledgeville *IL* U.S.A. **179** O9
Mille Lacs *lakes* U.S.A. **174** A2
Mille Lacs, Lac des *l.* Canada **168** B3
Milledgeville U.S.A. **175** D5
Millennium Island Kiribati *see* Caroline Island
Miller S. Africa **132** H10
Miller U.S.A. **178** C2
Miller Dam Flowage *resr* U.S.A. **172** C5
Miller Lake Canada **173** L5
Millerovo Rus. Fed. **41** G6
Millersburg *MI* U.S.A. **173** I5
Millersburg *OH* U.S.A. **176** D5
Millers Creek Australia **146** C2
Millers Falls U.S.A. **177** M3
Millers Flat N.Z. **153** D13
Millerton U.S.A. **177** L4
Millerton Lake U.S.A. **182** E4
Milleur Point U.K. **47** G8
Mill Glacier Antarctica **223** L1
Mill Hall U.S.A. **176** H4
Millicent Australia **146** D4

Millijiddie Aboriginal Reserve Australia 150 D3
Millington *MI* U.S.A. **173** J7
Millington *TN* U.S.A. **174** B5
Mill Inlet Antarctica **222** T2
Millinocket U.S.A. **174** G2
Milliri, Cerro *mt.* Bol. **200** D5
Mill Island Antarctica **223** G2
Mill Island Canada **165** L1
Millmerran Australia **147** F1
Milom U.K. **47** I9
Millsboro U.S.A. **177** J7
Mills Creek *watercourse* Australia **149** D3
Mills Lake Canada **167** G2
Millston U.S.A. **172** C6
Millstone U.S.A. **173** J7
Millstream Australia **150** B4
Millstream-Chichester National Park Australia **150** B4
Milltown U.S.A. **172** A5
Millungera Australia **149** D3
Millvale S. Africa **133** K2
Millville *CA* U.S.A. **182** B1
Millville U.S.A. **177** J6
Millwood Lake U.S.A. **179** D5
Milly-la-Forêt France **51** I4
Milly Milly Australia **151** B5
Milne Bay P.N.G. **149** F1
Milne Land *i.* Greenland *see*
  Ilimananngip Nunaa
Milo *r.* Guinea **124** C4
Milo U.S.A. **174** G2
Milogradovo Rus. Fed. **82** D4
Milolii U.S.A. **181** [inset] J4
Milos *i.* Greece **59** D11
Miloslavskoye Rus. Fed. **43** U8
Miloslaw Poland **49** O3
Miloud *well* Alg. **122** D4
Milove Ukr. **41** G6
  also spelt Melovoye
Milparinka Australia **146** D2
Milpitas U.S.A. **182** C4
Milroy U.S.A. **176** H5
Milton Canada **173** N7
Milton N.Z. **153** D14
Milton *DE* U.S.A. **177** J7
Milton *FL* U.S.A. **175** C6
Milton *VT* U.S.A. **177** L1
Milton *WV* U.S.A. **176** C7
Milton-Freewater U.S.A. **180** C3
Milton Keynes U.K. **47** L11
Miluo China **87** E2
Milverton Canada **173** M7
Milwaukee U.S.A. **172** F7

▶ Milwaukee Deep *sea feature*
  Caribbean Sea **216** J4
  Deepest point in the Atlantic Ocean
  (Puerto Rico Trench).
  oceans [features] ➤ 210–211

Mily Kazakh. **103** E2
Milybulabk Kazakh. **103** H2
  formerly spelt Myylybulak
Milyushino Rus. Fed. **43** T3
Milyutinskaya Rus. Fed. **41** H7
Mimbelly Congo **126** C4
Mimbres *watercourse* U.S.A. **181** F6
Mimili Australia **146** B1
Mimisal India **94** C4
Mimizan France **50** E8
Mimizan Czech Rep. **49** L5
Mimongo Gabon **126** B5
Mimosa Rocks National Park Australia **147** F4
Mimoso Brazil **206** E2
Mimoso do Sul Brazil **207** L8
Mina Mex. **185** E3
Mina U.S.A. **182** F3
Mina, Oued *watercourse* Alg. **55** L9
Mināb Iran **100** E5
Mināb *r.* Iran **100** E5
Mina Japan **91** E6
Mina Clavero Arg. **204** D3
Minaçu Brazil **202** B5
Minago *r.* Canada **167** L4
Minahasa, Semenanjung *pen.* Indon. **75** B2
  English form Minahasa Peninsula
Minahassa Peninsula Indon. *see*
  Minahasa, Semenanjung
Mina Jebel Ali U.A.E. **105** F2
  short form Jebel Ali
Minaker Canada *see* Prophet River
Minaki Canada **167** M5
Minamata Japan **91** B8
Minamata Australia **148** B2
Minami Alps National Park Japan **91** F7
Minami-Daitō-jima *i.* Japan **81** M7
Minami-Iō-jima *vol.* Japan **73** J2
  also known as Longshan
Min'an China *see* Longshan
Minaret Peaks N.Z. **153** D12
Minas Cuba **186** D2
Minas Indon. **76** C2
Minas Uruguay **204** G4
Minā' Sa'ūd Kuwait **107** G5
Minas Basin *b.* Canada **169** H4
Minas Channel Canada **169** H4
Minas de Matahambre Cuba **186** C2
Minas Gerais *state* Brazil **207** K4
Minas Novas Brazil **207** K4
Minatitlán Mex. **185** G5
Minbu Myanmar **78** A3
Minbya Myanmar **78** A3
Minchinabad Pak. **101** H4
Minchinmávida *vol.* Chile **205** B6
Mincio *r.* Italy **56** C3
Mincivan Azer. **107** F3
  also spelt Mindzhivan
Mindanao *i.* Phil. **74** C5
Mindanao *r.* Phil. **74** C5
Mindat Sakan Myanmar **78** A3
Mindelheim Germany **48** H7
Mindelo Cape Verde **124** [inset]
Minden Germany **48** F3
Minden *LA* U.S.A. **179** D5
Minden *NE* U.S.A. **178** C4
Minden *NV* U.S.A. **182** E3
Minden City U.S.A. **173** K7
Mindoro Australia **150** A4
Mindon Myanmar **78** A4
Mindona Lake *imp. l.* Australia **147** D3
Mindoro *i.* Phil. **74** B3
Mindoro Strait Phil. **74** A3
Mindouli Congo **126** B6
Mindszent Hungary **49** R9
Minduri Brazil **207** I8
Mindzhivan Azer. *see* Mincivan
Mine Japan **91** B7
Mine Centre Canada **172** A4
Minehead U.K. **47** I12
Mineiga, Gebel *mts* Egypt/Sudan **104** A3
Mineola U.S.A. **179** D5
Mineral U.S.A. **176** H7
Mineral'nyye Vody Rus. Fed. **41** G7
Mineral Point U.S.A. **172** C8
Mineral Wells U.S.A. **179** C5
Mineralwells U.S.A. **176** D6
Minersville U.S.A. **183** L3
Minerva Reefs Fiji **145** H4
Minfeng China **89** C4
  also known as Niya
Minga Dem. Rep. Congo **127** E7
Mingäçevir Azer. **107** F2
  also spelt Mingechaur
Mingäçevir Su Anbarı *resr* Azer. **107** F2
  also known as Mingechaurskoye
  Vodokhranilishche
Mingala Cent. Afr. Rep. **126** D3

Mingan Canada **169** H3
Mingan, Îles de *is* Canada **169** I3
Mingbulak Uzbek. **103** G4
Mingela Australia **149** E3
Mingenew Australia **151** A6
Mingera Creek *watercourse* Australia **148** C4
Mingfeng China *see* Yuan'an
Minggang China **87** E1
Mingguang China **87** F1
  formerly known as Jiashan
Mingin Myanmar **78** A3
Mingin Range *mts* Myanmar **78** A3
  also spelt Min-Kush
Minglanilla Spain **55** I4
Mingo Junction U.S.A. **176** E5
Mingoyo Tanz. **129** C7
Mingshan China *see* Fengdu
Mingshan China **86** B2
Mingshui *Gansu* China **84** D3
Mingshui *Heilong.* China **82** B3
Mingteke China **89** A4
Minguez, Puerto *de pass* Spain **55** J4
Mingulay *i.* U.K. **46** E7
  also known as Miughalaigh
Mingxi China **87** F3
  also known as Xuefeng
Mingzhou China *see* Weixian
Mingzhou China *see* Suide
Minhe China *see* Jinxian
Minhla *Magwe* Myanmar **78** A4
Minhla *Pegu* Myanmar **78** A4
Minho *reg.* Port. **54** C3
Minho *r.* Port. **54** C3
  also known as Ganzhe
Minhou China **87** F3
Minḩ Vale Australia **149** G6
Minicoy *i.* India **94** B4
Minigwal, Lake *salt flat* Australia **151** C6
Minija *r.* Lith. **42** C6
Minilya Australia **150** A4
Minilya *r.* Australia **150** A4
Minімiñe China **200** C4
Minian Côte d'Ivoire **124** D4
Minipi Lake Canada **169** I2
Ministra, Sierra *mts* Spain **55** I3
Minitonas Canada **167** K4
Minitskaya Rus. Fed. **43** P1
Minjian China *see* Mabian
Min Jiang *r. Sichuan* China **86** C2
Min Jiang *r.* China **87** F3
Minjilang Australia **148** B1
Minkamen Japan **91** E7
Minlaton Australia **146** C3
Minle China **84** D4
Minna Nigeria **125** G4
Minna Bluff *pt* Antarctica **223** L1
Minne Sweden **45** K3
Minneapolis *KS* U.S.A. **178** C4
Minneapolis *MN* U.S.A. **174** A2
Minnedosa Canada **167** L5
Minnehaha Springs U.S.A. **176** F7
Minnesota *state* U.S.A. **174** A2
Minnesota *r.* U.S.A. **178** D2
Minnesota City U.S.A. **172** B6
Minnewaukan U.S.A. **178** C1
Minnie Creek Australia **150** A4
Minnipa Australia **146** B3
Minnitaki Lake Canada **168** B3
Miño *r.* Port./Spain **54** C3
Minokamo Japan **91** E7
Minonk U.S.A. **172** D10
Minorca *i.* Spain **55** P4
  also spelt Menorca
Minot U.S.A. **178** B1
Minqār, Ghadīr *imp. l.* Syria **109** I5
Minqār Khurayyit *hill* Egypt **108** B7
Minqin China **84** D4
Minqing China **87** F3
  also known as Meicheng
Minquan China **87** E1
Min Shan *mts* China **86** B1
Minsin Myanmar **78** A2

▶ Minsk Belarus **42** I8
  Capital of Belarus.

Minskaya Oblast' *admin. div.* Belarus *see*
  Minskaya Voblasts'
Minskaya Voblasts' *admin. div.* Belarus **42** I8
  English form Minsk Oblast; also known as
  Minskaya Oblast'
Mińsk Mazowiecki Poland **49** S3
Minsk Oblast *admin. div.* Belarus *see*
  Minskaya Voblasts'
Minster U.S.A. **176** A5
Mintaka Pass China/Jammu and Kashmir **89** A4
Mintang China **86** B1
Mintlaw U.K. **46** K6
Minto *N.B.* Canada **169** H4
Minto *Y.T.* Canada **166** B2
Minto, Lac *l.* Canada **169** F1
Minto, Mount Antarctica **223** L2
Minto Inlet Canada **165** H2
Mintom Cameroon **125** I6
Minton Canada **167** J5
Minturn U.S.A. **180** F5
Minturnae Italy *see* Minturno
Minturno Italy **56** F7
  historically known as Minturnae
Minudasht Iran **100** D2
Minūf Egypt **108** B7
  also spelt Menûfîya
Minūfîya *governorate* Egypt **108** B7
  also spelt Menûfîya
Minusinsk Rus. Fed. **80** E2
Minutang India **86** A2
Minvoul Gabon **126** B4
Minxian China **86** B2
Minya Konka *mt.* China *see* Gongga Shan
Minyar Rus. Fed. **40** K5
Minywa Myanmar **78** A3
Minzong India **91** H4
Mio *well* Niger **125** H2
Mio U.S.A. **173** I6
Mionica *Srbija* Yugo. **58** B4
Mipia, Lake *salt flat* Australia **148** C5
Miquan China **88** D3
Miquelon Canada **168** E3
Miquelon *i.* St Pierre and Miquelon **169** J4
Mir Belarus **42** H8
Mi'r, Wādī *watercourse* Egypt **108** D9
Mira *r.* Col. **198** B4
Mira Port. **54** C4
Mira, Sierra de *mts* Spain **55** J5
Mirabela Brazil **202** C6
Miracema Brazil **207** K8
Miracema do Norte Brazil *see*
  Miracema do Tocantins
Miracema do Tocantins Brazil **202** B4
  formerly known as Miracema do Norte
Mirada Hills U.S.A. *see* La Mirada
Mirador Brazil **206** A10
Mirador, Parque Nacional de *nat. park*
  Brazil **202**
Mirador-Dos Lagunos-Río Azul, Parque
  Nacional *nat. park* Guat. **185** H5
Miradouro Brazil **207** K7
Miraflores *Boyaca* Col. **198** C3
Miraflores *Guaviare* Col. **198** C4
Mirah, Wādī al *watercourse*
  Iraq/Saudi Arabia **107** E4
Mirai Brazil **207** K8
Miraj India **94** B2
Miralta Brazil **207** J3

Mingan Canada **169** H3

Miramar Arg. **204** F5
Miramar, Canal *sea chan.* Chile **205** B8
Miramas France **51** L9
Miramichi Bay Canada **169** H4
Miram Shah Pak. **101** G3
Miraña Col. **198** D5
Miranda Brazil **201** F5
Miranda *r.* Brazil **201** F4
Miranda Moz. *see* Macaloge
Miranda *state* Venez. **199** E2
Miranda, Lake *salt flat* Australia **151** C5
Miranda de Ebro Spain **55** I2
Miranda do Douro Port. **54** E3
Mirande France **50** G9
Mirandela Port. **54** E3
Mirandola Italy **56** C3
Mirante, Serra do *hills* Brazil **206** C9
Mirante do Paranapanema Brazil **206** B9
Mirapinima Brazil **199** F5
Miras Albania **59** B8
Mirassol Brazil **206** D7
Mir Bacheh Kowt Afgh. **101** G3
Mir-Bashir Azer. *see* Tärtär
Mirbāţ Oman **105** F4
Mirbāţ, Ra's *c.* Oman **105** F4
Mirear Island Egypt *see* Marīr, Geziret
Mirebalais Haiti **187** E3
Mirebeau France **50** G6
Mirecourt France **51** M4
Miréméné Chad **120** B6
Mirepoix France **50** H9
Mirganj India **97** E4
Miri *mt.* Pak. **101** F4
Miria Niger **125** H3
Miri Hills India **97** G4
Miri *Sarawak* Malaysia **77** F1
Miriam Vale Australia **149** G5
Mirim, Lagoa *l.* Brazil/Uruguay **204** G4
  also known as Merín, Laguna
Mirim, Lagoa do *l.* Brazil **203** B9
Mirimire Venez. **198** D2
Mirina Greece *see* Myrina
Mirjan India **94** B3
Mīrjāveh Iran **101** E4
Mirkovo Bulg. **58** F6
Mirna *r.* Croatia **56** F3
Mirny *research station* Antarctica **223** G2
Mirnyy *Arkhangel'skaya Oblast'* Rus. Fed.
  40 G3
Mirnyy *Bryanskaya Oblast'* Rus. Fed. **43** M9
Mirnyy *Respublika Sakha (Yakutiya)* Rus. Fed.
  39 L3
Miroč *hills* Yugo. **58** D4
Miromiro *mt.* N.Z. **153** G10
Mirond Lake Canada **167** K4
Mironovka *r.* Rus. Fed. **43** O7
Mirosławiec Poland **49** N2
Mirow Germany **49** J2
Mirpur Pak. **101** H3
Mirpur Batoro Pak. **101** G5
Mirpur Khas Pak. **101** G5
Mirpur Sakro Pak. **101** F5
Mirsale Somalia **128** E3
Mirsali China **88** B3
Mirs Bay *Hong Kong* China **87** [inset]
  also known as Tai Pang Wan
Mirtoan Sea Greece *see* Mirtoö Pelagos
Mirtoö Pelagos *sea* Greece **59** E12
  English form Mirtoan Sea
Miruro Moz. **129** A4
Miryalaguda India *see* Mirialguda
Miryang S. Korea **83** C6
Mirzachirla Turkm. *see* Murzechirla
Mirzachul Uzbek. *see* Gulistan
Mirzapur India **97** D4
Misaki Japan **91** C8
Misakubo Japan **91** E7
Misantla Mex. **185** F5
Misau Nigeria **125** H4
Misawa Japan **90** G4
Miscou Island Canada **169** H4
Misehkow *r.* Canada **168** B3
Misery, Mount St Kitts and Nevis **187** H3
Misgar Jammu and Kashmir **96** B1
Mish, Kūh-e *hill* Iran **100** D3
Mīsh Yazīd Egypt **108** C7
Misha India **95** G5
Mishaf, Rujm al *hill* Iraq **109** O6
Mishamattawa *r.* Canada **168** C2
Mishāsh al Ashāwī *well* Saudi Arabia **105** E2
Mishāsh aẕ Ẕuayyini *well* Saudi Arabia **105** E2
Mishawaka U.S.A. **172** G9
Misheronsky Rus. Fed. **43** U6
Mishibishu Lake Canada **172** F2
Mishima Japan **91** F7
Mi-shima *i.* Japan **91** B7
Mishlah, Khashm *hill* Saudi Arabia **105** D3
Mishmi Hills India **97** G3
Misilmeri *Sicilia* Italy **57** F10
Misima Island P.N.G. **149** G1
Misiones *prov.* Arg. **204** G2
Misis Dağ *hills* Turkey **108** G1
Miskah Saudi Arabia **104** D2
Miskitos, Cayos *is* Nicaragua **186** C4
Miskitos, Costa de *coastal area* Nicaragua
  see Mosquitos, Costa de
Miskolc Hungary **49** R7
Mislinja *r.* Slovenia **56** H2
Mismā, Jibāl al *mts* Saudi Arabia **104** C2
Mismā, Tall al *hill* Jordan **109** I5
Mīsōsī *r.* Rus. Fed. *see* Panlian
Misquah Hills U.S.A. **174** B2
Misr *country* Africa *see* Egypt
Misraq-Gojam Eth. **128** C2
Misr country Africa *see* Egypt
Misrāẕ Libya **120** B1
  also spelt Misurata
Misrīkh India **96** D4
Missanabie Canada **173** I2
Missinaibi *r.* Canada **168** D3
Missinaibi Lake Canada **168** D3
Missinipe Canada **167** J4
Mission *r.* Canada **168** D2
Mission *SD* U.S.A. **178** B3
Mission *TX* U.S.A. **179** C7
Mission Beach Australia **149** E3
Mission Viejo U.S.A. **182** G8
Missisa *r.* Canada **168** C2
Missisa Lake Canada **168** C2
Missisicabi *r.* Canada **168** E3
Mississagi *r.* Canada **168** D4
Mississauga Canada **168** E5

▶ Mississippi *r.* Canada **173** Q5
  world [changes] ➤ 20–21

▶ Mississippi *r.* U.S.A. **179** E6
  4th longest river in North America. Part of
  the longest (Mississippi-Missouri).
  northamerica [landscapes] ➤ 156–157

Mississippi *state* U.S.A. **175** B5
Mississippi Delta U.S.A. **175** B6
Mississippi Lake Canada **173** Q5

▶ Mississippi-Missouri *r.* U.S.A. **179** E6
  Longest river in North America and in the
  world.
  northamerica [landscapes] ➤ 156–157

Mississippi Sound *sea chan.* U.S.A. **175** B6
Missolonghi Greece *see* Mesolongi
Missoula U.S.A. **180** D3
Missour Morocco **122** E2

▶ Missouri *r.* U.S.A. **178** E4
  3rd longest river in North America. Part of
  the longest (Mississippi-Missouri)
  northamerica [landscapes] ➤ 156–157

Missouri *state* U.S.A. **174** A4
Missouri Valley U.S.A. **178** D3
Mistake Creek *r.* Australia **149** E4
Mistanipisipou *r.* Canada **169** I3
Mistassibi *r.* Canada **169** F3
Mistassini *r.* Canada **169** F3
Mistassini Canada **169** F3
  also known as Lomati
Mistassini, Lac *l.* Canada **169** F3
Mistastin Lake Canada **169** I2
Mistelbach Austria **49** N7
Mistissini Canada **169** F3
  formerly known as Baie-du-Poste
Misterbianco *Sicilia* Italy **57** H11
Mistissini Canada **169** F3
Mistras *tourist site* Greece **59** D11
Misty Fiords National Monument
  Wilderness *nat. park* U.S.A. **164** F4
Misuratah Libya *see* Mişrātah
Misvær Norway **44** K2
Mita, Punta de *pt* Mex. **184** D4
Mitaraca *hill* Suriname **199** H4
Mitatib Sudan **121** H6
Mitchell *r. N.S.W.* Australia **147** G2
Mitchell *r. Qld* Australia **149** D2
Mitchell *r. Vic.* Australia **147** E4
Mitchell Australia **149** E5
Mitchell *OR* U.S.A. **180** B3
Mitchell *SD* U.S.A. **178** C3
Mitchell, Lake Australia **149** E3
Mitchell, Lake U.S.A. **172** H6
Mitchell, Mount U.S.A. **174** D5
Mitchell and Alice Rivers National Park
  Australia **149** D2
Mitchell Island Cook Is *see* Nassau
Mitchell Island Tuvalu *see* Nukulaelae
Mitchell Point Australia **148** A1
Mitchell Range *hills* Australia **148** B2
Mitchelstown Rep. of Ireland **47** D11
Mitchinamécus, Lake Canada **173** R3
Mit Fāris Egypt **108** C5
Mit Ghamr Egypt **108** C7
Mithi Pak. **101** G5
Mithimna Greece *see* Mythimna
Mithrani Can *canal* Pak. **101** G5
Mithymna Greece **59** H9
  also spelt Mithimna
Mitilg, Gebel *hill* Egypt **104** A2
Mitilini Greece *see* Mytilini
Mitishkino Rus. Fed. **43** O7
Mitkof Island U.S.A. **166** C3
Mito Japan **91** G6
Mitomoni Tanz. **129** B7
Mitre *mt.* N.Z. **153** J8
Mitre, Península *pen.* Arg. **205** D9
Mitre Island Solomon Is **145** G3
Mitrofanovka Rus. Fed. **41** F6
Mitrovica *Kosovo, Srbija* Yugo. **58** B5
  formerly known as Kosovska Mitrovica
Mitsamiouli Comoros **129** D7
Mitsikeli *mt.* Greece **59** B9
Mits'iwa Eritrea *see* Massawa
Mitsuke Japan **90** F6
Mittagong Australia **147** F3
Mittelebe *park* Germany **49** I4
Mittenwald Germany **48** I8
Mittersill Austria **49** J8
Mitterteich Germany **49** J6
Mittet Norway **44** I3
Mittimatalik Canada *see* Pond Inlet
Mittleres Saaletal *park* Germany **49** I5
Mitú Col. **198** D4
Mituas Col. **198** D4
Mitumba, Chaîne des *mts*
  Dem. Rep. Congo **127** E6
Mitumba, Monts *mts* Dem. Rep. Congo
  126 F5
Mitwaba Dem. Rep. Congo **127** E7
Mitzic Gabon **126** A4

Mlaula *r.* Swaziland **133** Q3
Mlava *r.* Yugo. **58** C4
Mława Poland **49** R2
Mlawula Nature Reserve Swaziland **133** Q3
Mlilwane Nature Reserve Swaziland **133** P3
Mljet *i.* Croatia **56** J6
Mljet *nat. park* Croatia **56** J6
Mljetski Kanal *sea chan.* Croatia **56** J6
Mlowoka Tanz. **129** C7
Mlumati *r.* S. Africa **133** P2
Mlungisi S. Africa **133** K8
Mmabatho S. Africa **133** K2
Mmadinare Botswana **131** E4
Mmashoro Botswana **131** E4
Mmathethe Botswana **131** E5
Mnjoli Dam Swaziland **133** P3
Mnogovershinnyy Rus. Fed. **82** E1
Mo Norway **45** I3
Moa *r.* Brazil **200** D5
Moa Cuba **187** E3
Moa *i.* Indon. **75** D5
Moab *reg.* Jordan **108** G6
Moab U.S.A. **183** O3
Moabi Gabon **126** A5
Moaco *r.* Brazil **200** D5
Moa Island Australia **73** J9
Moala *i.* Fiji **145** H4
Moana N.Z. **153** F10
Moanda Gabon **126** B5
Moate Rep. of Ireland **47** E10
Moatize Moz. **131** G3
Moba Dem. Rep. Congo **127** F6
  formerly known as Baudouinville
Mobaye Cent. Afr. Rep. **126** D3
Mobayembongo Dem. Rep. Congo *see*
  Mobayi-Mbongo
Mobayi-Mbongo Dem. Rep. Congo **126** D3
  also spelt Mobayembongo; *formerly known
  as* Banzyville
Mobeka Dem. Rep. Congo **126** C4
Moberly U.S.A. **178** D4
Moberly Lake Canada **166** F4
Mobert Canada **172** F2
Mobile *AL* U.S.A. **175** B6
Mobile *AZ* U.S.A. **183** L8
Mobile Bay U.S.A. **175** B6
Mobile Point U.S.A. **175** C6
Moble *watercourse* Australia **147** E1
Mobo Phil. **74** B3
Mobridge U.S.A. **178** B2
Mobutu, Lake Dem. Rep. Congo/Uganda
  see Albert, Lake
Mobutu Sese Seko, Lake
  Dem. Rep. Congo/Uganda *see* Albert, Lake
Moca Gepidi *plain* Turkey **108** E1
Mocajuba Brazil **202** B2
Mocambicano, Planalto *plat.* Moz. **131** G4
Moçambique *country* Africa *see*
  Mozambique
Moçambique Moz. **131** I2
Mocambo, Porto *b.* Moz. **131** J2
Moçâmedes Angola *see* Namibe
Moccasin U.S.A. **182** D4
Moccasin Gap U.S.A. **176** C9
Mocha, Isla *i.* Chile **204** B5
Mocha Yemen **104** C5
  also spelt al Mukhā
Mochirma, Parque Nacional *nat. park*
  Venez. **199** F2
Mochudi Botswana **131** E5
Mochily Rus. Fed. **43** T7
Mochowo Poland **49** Q2
Möckeln *l.* Sweden **45** K4
Möckern-Magdeburger Forst *park*
  Germany **49** I3
Mocksville U.S.A. **174** D5
Mocó *r.* Brazil **199** G5
Mocoa Col. **198** B4
Mococa Brazil **206** G8
Mocorito Mex. **184** D3
Moctezuma Chihuahua Mex. **184** D2
Moctezuma San Luis Potosí Mex. **185** E4
Moctezuma Sonora Mex. **184** C2
Moctezuma *r.* Mex. **181** E7
Mocuba Moz. **131** H3
Mocun China **87** E4
Modane France **51** M7
Modasa India **96** B5
Modder *r.* S. Africa **133** I6
Modena Italy **56** C3
  historically known as Mutina
Modena U.S.A. **183** K4
Modesto U.S.A. **182** C4
Modica *Sicilia* Italy **57** G12
Mödling Austria **49** N7
Modot Mongolia **85** F2
Modrīča Bos.-Herz. **56** K4
Modung Italy **56** I7
Moe Australia **147** E4
Moebase Moz. **131** H3
Moel Sych *hill* U.K. **47** J11
Moelv Norway **45** J3
Moen Norway **44** L1
Moengo Suriname **199** H3
Moenkopi U.S.A. **183** M5
Moenkopi Wash *r.* U.S.A. **183** M6
Moerewa N.Z. **152** I3
Moero, Lake Dem. Rep. Congo/Zambia *see*
  Mweru, Lake
Moers Germany **48** D4
Moeswal S. Africa **132** G4
Moffat U.K. **46** I8

▶ Mogadishu Somalia **128** E4
  Capital of Somalia. Also spelt Muqdisho.

Mogador Morocco *see* Essaouira
Mogadouro Port. **54** E3
Mogadouro, Serra de *mts* Port. **54** E3
Mogalo Dem. Rep. Congo **126** C4
Mogalturru India **94** D2
Mogami-gawa *r.* Japan **90** F5
Mogandjo Dem. Rep. Congo **126** D4
Moganyaka S. Africa **133** N1
Mogareb *watercourse* Eritrea **104** B3
Mogaung Myanmar **78** B2
Mogdy Rus. Fed. **82** D1
Moggar Alg. **123** G2

▶ Mogadishu Somalia **128** E4

Mogollon Plateau U.S.A. **183** M7
Mogontiacum Germany *see* Mainz
Mogor Eth. **128** D3
Mogoro *r. Sardegna* Italy **57** A9
Mogoşeşti Romania **58** H2
Mogroum Chad **126** B2
Moguer Spain **54** E7
Mogui China **83** B3
Mogwase S. Africa **133** L2
Mogzon Rus. Fed. **85** G1
Mohács Hungary **49** P9
Mohaka *r.* N.Z. **152** K7
Mohala India **94** D1
Mohale's Hoek Lesotho **133** L7
Mohall U.S.A. **178** B1
Mohammad Iran **100** D3
Mohammadābād Iran *see* Darreh Gaz
Mohammadia Alg. **123** F2
  formerly known as Perrégaux
Mohammad Reza Shah Pahlavi Dam *resr*
  Iran *see* Dez, Sadd-e
Mohan *r.* India/Nepal **96** D3
Mohana India **95** D2
Mohanganj Bangl. **97** F4
Mohave, Lake U.S.A. **183** J6
Mohave Mountains U.S.A. **183** J7
Mohawk U.S.A. **172** E3
Mohawk *r.* U.S.A. **177** L3
Mohe China **82** A1
  also known as Xilinji
Mohed Sweden **45** K3
Moheda Sweden **45** K4
Mohéli *i.* Comoros *see* Mwali
Mohembo Botswana **130** D3
Mohenjo Daro *tourist site* Pak. **101** G5
Möhkö Fin. **44** O3
Möhne *r.* Germany **48** E4
Mohnyin Myanmar **78** B2
Moho Peru **200** C3
Mohol India **94** B2
Mohon Peak U.S.A. **183** K7
Mohoro Tanz. **129** C7
Mohyliv Podil's'kyy Ukr. **41** C6
  also spelt Mogilev Podol'skiy
Moi *Rogaland* Norway **45** I4
Moi *Vest-Agder* Norway **45** I4
Moijabana Botswana **131** E5
Moinda China **89** E6
  also known as Zara
Moine Moz. **133** P1
Moineşti Romania **58** H2
Moinkum *des.* Kazakh. *see*
  Moyynkum, Peski
Mointy Kazakh. *see* Moyynty
Moírai Greece *see* Moires
Moi i Rana Norway **44** K2
Moirang India **97** G4
Moires Greece **59** F13
  also known as Moírai
Moisaküla Estonia **42** G3
Moisie Canada **169** I3
Moisie *r.* Canada **169** I3
Moissac France **50** H8
Moïssala Chad **126** C2
Moitaco Venez. **199** F2
Mojácar Spain **55** J7
Mojados Spain **54** G3
Mojave U.S.A. **182** F6
Mojave *r.* U.S.A. **183** G7
Mojave Desert U.S.A. **183** G6
Mojiang China **86** B3
  also known as Jiulian
Moji das Cruzes Brazil **207** G10
Moji-Guaçu *r.* Brazil **206** E7
Mojikō Japan **91** B8
Mojkovac Crna Gora Yugo. **58** A6
Mojo Bol. **200** D5
Mojo Eth. **128** C3
Mojokerto Indon. **77** F4
Mojones, Cerro *mt.* Arg. **204** D2
Mojos, Llanos de *plain* Bol. **200** D3
Moju Brazil **202** B2
Mōka Japan **91** G6
Mokai N.Z. **152** J6
Mokama India **97** E4
Mokambo Dem. Rep. Congo **127** F6
Mokaria Dem. Rep. Congo **126** D4
Mokau N.Z. **152** I6
Mokeo Congo **126** B4
Mokelumne *r.* U.S.A. **182** C3
Mokelumne Aqueduct *canal* U.S.A. **182** C3
Mokhoabong Pass Lesotho **133** M6
Mokhotlong Lesotho **133** N6
Mokhovoye Rus. Fed. **43** P9
Mokhsogollokh Rus. Fed. **39** M3
Mokimbo Dem. Rep. Congo **127** F6
Moknine Tunisia **57** D13
Mokohinau Islands N.Z. **152** I3
Mokokchung India **97** G4
Mokolo Cameroon **125** I4
Mokolo *r.* S. Africa **131** E4
Mokoreta N.Z. **153** C14
Mokotua N.Z. **153** C14
Mokp'o S. Korea **83** B6
Mokra Gora *mts* Yugo. **58** B5
Mokrin *Vojvodina, Srbija* Yugo. **58** B3
Mokrous Rus. Fed. **41** H6
Moksha *r.* Rus. Fed. **40** G5
Mokshan Rus. Fed. **41** H5
Möktama Myanmar *see* Martaban
Mokundurra India *see* Mukandwara
Mokwa Nigeria **125** G4
Mokwalo S. Africa **133** J3
Mola di Bari Italy **56** J7
Molaly Kazakh. *see* Mulaly
Molango Mex. **185** F4
Molaoi Greece **59** D12
Molat *i.* Croatia **56** G4
Moldavia *country* Europe *see* Moldova
Moldavskaya S.S.R. *country* Europe *see*
  Moldova
Molde Norway **44** I3
Moldefjorden *inlet* Norway **44** I3
Moldjord Norway **44** K2

▶ Moldova *country* Europe **41** C6
  formerly known as Moldavia or
  Moldavskaya S.S.R.
  europe [countries] ➤ 32–35

Moldova *r.* Romania **58** H2
Moldova Nouă Romania **58** C4
Moldoveanu, Vârful *mt.* Romania **58** F3
Moldovei Centrale, Podişul *plat.* Moldova
  58 I1
Moldovei de Sud, Cîmpia *plain* Moldova
  58 I1
Molega Lake Canada **169** H4
Molegbe Dem. Rep. Congo **126** C4
Molen *r.* S. Africa **133** M4
Mole National Park Ghana **125** E4
Molepolole Botswana **131** E5
Molétai Lith. **42** G6
Molfetta Italy **56** I7
Molières France **50** H8
Molina Arg. **204** C4
Molina de Aragón Spain **55** J3
Molina de Segura Spain **55** J6
Moline U.S.A. **174** B3
Molinella Italy **56** D3
Molinos Arg. **204** D2
Molins de Rei Spain **55** N3

Molot *i.* Croatia **56** G4
Mira Port. **54** C4
Moliro Dem. Rep. Congo **127** F7

Molise *admin. reg.* Italy **56** G7
Molkom Sweden **45** K4
Molledo Spain **54** G1
Mol Len *mt.* India **97** G4
Mollendo Peru **200** C4
Mollerin, Lake *salt flat* Australia **151** B6
Mollerussa Spain **55** L3
Mölln Germany **48** H2
Mölnlycke Sweden **45** K4
Molochnoye Rus. Fed. **43** U2
Molodechno Belarus *see* Maladzyechna
Molodezhnaya *research station* Antarctica **223** D2
Molod'kovo Rus. Fed. **43** N8
Molodoy Tud Rus. Fed. **43** O5
Mologa *r.* Rus. Fed. **43** S3
Molokai *i.* U.S.A. **181** [inset] Z1
Molokovo Rus. Fed. **43** Q6
Moloma *r.* Rus. Fed. **40** I4
Molong China *see* Zhaosu
Molopo *watercourse* Botswana/S. Africa **132** C5
Moloporivier Botswana **133** I2
Molos Greece **59** D10
Molotov Rus. Fed. *see* Perm'
Molotovsk Kyrg. *see* Kayyngdy
Molotovsk Rus. Fed. *see* Severodvinsk
Molotovsk Rus. Fed. *see* Nolinsk
Molotovskaya Oblast' *admin. div.* Rus. Fed. *see* Permskaya Oblast'
Moloundou Cameroon **125** I6
Molsheim France **51** N4
Molson Lake Canada **167** L4
Molteno S. Africa **133** M6
Moltenopass *pass* S. Africa **132** G9
Molu *i.* Indon. **73** H8
Moluccas *is* Indon. **75** C3
also known as Malukken *or* Maluku; *historically known as* Spice Islands
Molucca Sea Indon. **75** C3
Moluengo *mt.* Spain **55** J5
Molumbo Moz. **131** H2
Molvotitsy Rus. Fed. **43** N4
Molwe Dem. Rep. Congo **127** E7
Moma Moz. **131** H1
Momba Australia **147** D2
Mombaça Brazil **202** E4
Mombasa Kenya **129** D5
Mombenzélé Dem. Rep. Congo **126** C4
Mombetsu Japan *see* Monbetsu
Mombetsu Japan *see* Monbetsu
Momboyo *r.* Dem. Rep. Congo **126** C5
Mombuca, Serra da *hills* Brazil **206** A5
Momchilgrad Bulg. **58** G7
Momeik Myanmar *see* Möng Mir
Momence U.S.A. **172** F9
Momi, Ra's *pt* Yemen **105** F5
Momotombo, Volcán *vol.* Nicaragua **186** B4
Mompog Passage Phil. **74** B3
Mompono Dem. Rep. Congo **126** D4
Mompós Col. **198** C2
Momskiy Khrebet *mts* Rus. Fed. **39** O3
Møn *i.* Denmark **45** K5
Mon India **97** G4
Mon *state* Myanmar **78** B4
Mona U.S.A. **183** M2
Mona, Isla *i.* Puerto Rico **187** G3
Monaca U.S.A. **176** E5
Monach Islands U.K. **46** E6
also known as Heiskeir Islands
▶Monaco *country* Europe **51** N9
historically known as Portus Herculis Monoeci
europe [countries] ▶ ▶ 32–35
Monadhliath Mountains U.K. **46** H6
Monagas *state* Venez. **199** F2
Monaghan Rep. of Ireland **47** F9
also known as Muineachán
Monahans U.S.A. **179** B6
Mona Passage Dom. Rep./Puerto Rico **187** F3
Monapo Moz. **131** I2
Mona Quimbundo Angola **127** C7
Monar, Loch *l.* U.K. **46** G6
Monarch Mountain Canada **166** E5
Monarch Pass U.S.A. **181** F5
Monashee Mountains Canada **166** G5
Monastero del Suso *tourist site* Spain **55** I2
Monastir Macedonia *see* Bitola
Monastir Tunisia **123** H2
Monastyryshche Ukr. *see* Monastyryshche
Monastyrshchina Rus. Fed. **43** M7
Monastyryshche Ukr. **41** D6
also spelt Monastyrishche
Monavale N.Z. **153** E12
Monbetsu *Hokkaidō* Japan **90** H2
also spelt Mombetsu
Monbetsu *Hokkaidō* Japan **90** H3
also spelt Mombetsu
Monbré Cameroon **125** I4
Moncalieri Italy **51** N7
Moncalvo *mt.* Italy **51** N7
Monchegorsk Rus. Fed. **44** P2
Mönchengladbach Germany **48** D4
formerly spelt München-Gladbach
Monchique Port. **54** C7
Monchique, Serra de *mts* Port. **54** C7
Moncks Corner U.S.A. **175** D5
Monclova Mex. **185** E3
Moncton Canada **169** I4
Mondai Brazil **203** A8
Mondego *r.* Port. **54** C4
Mondego, Cabo *c.* Port. **54** C4
Mondimbi Dem. Rep. Congo **126** D4
Mondim de Basto Port. **54** D3
Mondlo S. Africa **133** O4

Mondo Chad **120** B6
Mondolfo Italy **56** F5
Mondoñedo Spain **54** D1
Mondovi Italy **51** N8
Mondovi U.S.A. **172** B6
Mondragón Spain *see* Arrasate
Mondragone Italy **56** F7
Mondsee *l.* Austria **49** K8
Mondúver *hill* Spain **55** K5
Monee U.S.A. **172** F9
Monemvasia Greece **59** E12
also known as Malvasia
Moneron, Ostrov *i.* Rus. Fed. **82** F3
Monessen U.S.A. **176** F5
Monesterio Spain **54** E6
Monet Canada **173** F2
Moneta U.S.A. **176** F8
Monéteau France **51** J5
Monfalcone Italy **56** F3
Monflanquin France **50** G4
Monfort Col. **198** D4
Monforte Port. **54** D6
Monforte Spain **54** D2
Monfurado *hill* Port. **54** C6
Monga *Katanga* Dem. Rep. Congo **127** E5
Monga *Orientale* Dem. Rep. Congo **126** D3
Mongaguá Brazil **206** G11
Mongala *r.* Dem. Rep. Congo **126** C4
Mongar Bhutan **97** F4
Mông Cai Vietnam **78** D3
Mongemputu Dem. Rep. Congo **126** D5
Mongers Lake *salt flat* Australia **151** B6
Mong Hang Myanmar **78** B3
Monghidoro Italy **56** D4
▶Mongolia *country* Asia **84** C2
known as Mongol Uls *in Mongolian; formerly known as* Outer Mongolia
asia [countries] ▶ ▶ 64–67
Mong Hpayak Myanmar **78** B3
Mong Hsat Myanmar **78** B3
Monghyr India *see* Munger
Mong Kung Myanmar **78** B3
Mong Kyawt Myanmar **78** B4
Mong La Myanmar **78** C3
Mong Lin Myanmar **78** C3
Mong Loi Myanmar **78** C3
Mong Long Myanmar **78** B3
Möng Mir Myanmar **78** B3
also known as Momeik
Mong Nai Myanmar **78** B3
Mong Nawng Myanmar **78** B3
Mongo Chad **120** C6
Mongolküre China *see* Zhaosu
Mongomo Equat. Guinea **125** H6
Mongonu Nigeria **125** I3
Mongora Pak. **101** H3
Mongoumba Cent. Afr. Rep. **126** C4
Mong Pan Myanmar **78** C3
Mong Pat Myanmar **78** B3
Mong Ping Myanmar **78** B3
Mongu Zambia **127** D8
Mongua Angola **127** B9
Mong Un Myanmar **78** C3
Mong Yai Myanmar **78** B3
Mong Yang Myanmar **78** B3
Mong Yawng Myanmar **78** C3
Mong Yu Myanmar **78** B3
Monhbulag Mongolia **84** C2
Mönh Hayrhan Uul *mt.* Mongolia **84** A2
Monhegan Island U.S.A. **177** P2
Moniquirá Col. **198** C3
Monistrol-sur-Loire France **51** K7
Monitor Mountain U.S.A. **183** H3
Monitor Range *mts* U.S.A. **183** H3
Moñitos Col. **198** B2
Monjolos Brazil **207** I5
Monkey Bay Malawi **129** B8
Monkey Mia Australia **151** A5
Mońki Poland **49** T2
Monkira Australia **149** D5
Monkoto Dem. Rep. Congo **126** D5
Monkton Canada **173** L7
Monmouth U.K. **47** J12
also known as Trefynwy
Monmouth *CA* U.S.A. **182** C4
Monmouth *IL* U.S.A. **174** B3
Monmouth Mountain Canada **166** F5
Monnett U.S.A. **176** B5
Mono *r.* Togo **125** F5
Mono, Punta del *pt* Nicaragua **186** C5
Monolithos Greece **59** I12
Monon U.S.A. **172** G10
Monona U.S.A. **172** B7
Monongahela *r.* U.S.A. **176** F5
Monor Hungary **49** Q8
Monorgahela *r.* U.S.A. **176** F5
Monou Chad **120** D5
Monóvar Spain **55** K6
Monowai, Lake N.Z. **153** B13
Monreal del Campo Spain **55** J4
Monreale Sicilia Italy **57** F10
Monroe *GA* U.S.A. **175** D5
Monroe *IA* U.S.A. **174** A3
Monroe *LA* U.S.A. **179** D5
Monroe *MI* U.S.A. **173** J9
Monroe *NC* U.S.A. **174** D5
Monroe *NY* U.S.A. **177** K4
Monroe *UT* U.S.A. **183** L3
Monroe *VA* U.S.A. **176** F8
Monroe *WA* U.S.A. **180** B3
Monroe *WI* U.S.A. **172** D8
Monroe Center U.S.A. **172** D6
Monroe City U.S.A. **174** B4
Monroe Lake U.S.A. **174** C4
Monroeton U.S.A. **177** I4
Monroeville *AL* U.S.A. **175** C6
Monroeville *IN* U.S.A. **176** A5
Monroeville *OH* U.S.A. **176** C4
▶Monrovia Liberia **124** C5
Capital of Liberia.
Mons Belgium **51** J2
Monsaràs, Ponta de *pt* Brazil **207** N6
Monselice Italy **56** D3
Mons Klint *cliff* Denmark **45** J1
Mönsterås Sweden **45** L4
Montabaur Germany **48** E5
Montague Canada **169** I4
Montague U.S.A. **179** C5
Montague Island U.S.A. **164** E3
Montague Range *hills* Australia **151** B5
Montague Sound *b.* Australia **150** D3
Montaigu France **50** E6
Montaigu-de-Quercy France **50** H8
Montaiguët *r.* Indon. **77** F3
Montalto *mt.* Italy **57** H10
Montalto di Castro Italy **56** D6
Montalto Uffugo Italy **57** I9
Montalvo Ecuador **198** B5
Montana Bulg. **58** E5
Montana *state* U.S.A. **180** E3
northamerica [environments] ▶ ▶ 162–163
Montaña de Comayagua, Parque Nacional *nat. park* Hond. **186** B4
Montaña de Cusuco, Parque Nacional *nat. park* Hond. **186** A4
Montaña de Yoro *nat. park* Hond. **186** B4
Montánchez *hill* Spain **54** E5
Montánchez, Sierra de *mts* Spain **54** E5
Montanha Brazil **207** N5
Montargis France **51** I5
Montauban France **50** H8
Montauk U.S.A. **177** N4
Montauk Point U.S.A. **177** N4

Mont-aux-Sources *mt.* Lesotho **133** M5
Montbard France **51** K5
Montbéliard France **51** M5
▶Mont Blanc *mt.* France/Italy **51** M7
5th highest mountain in Europe.
europe [landscapes] ▶ ▶ 30–31
Montblanc Spain **55** M3
also spelt Montblanch
Montblanch Spain *see* Montblanc
Montbrison France **51** K7
Montcalm U.S.A. **176** D8
Montceau-les-Mines France **51** K6
Montchanin France **51** K6
Montcuq France **50** H8
Mont-de-Marsan France **50** F9
Montdidier France **51** I3
Monte, Lago del *l.* Arg. **204** E5
Monte Alban *tourist site* Mex. **185** F5
Monte Alegre *r.* Brazil **206** C4
Monte Alegre Brazil **199** H5
Monte Alegre de Goiás Brazil **202** C5
Montealegre del Castillo Spain **55** J6
Monte Alegre de Minas Brazil **206** E5
Monte Aprazível Brazil **206** D7
Monte Azul Brazil **207** I2
Monte Azul Paulista Brazil **206** E7
Montebello Canada **169** F4
Montebello Islands Australia **150** A4
Montebelluna Italy **56** E3
Monte Buey Arg. **204** E4
Monte-Carlo Monaco **51** N9
English form Monte Carlo
Monte Carlo Monaco *see* Monte-Carlo
Monte Carmelo Brazil **206** E5
Monte Caseros Arg. **204** F3
Montecatini Terme Italy **56** C5
Montecchio Maggiore Italy **56** D3
Montech France **50** H9
Monte Christo S. Africa **131** E4
Montecito U.S.A. **182** E7
Monte Cotugna, Lago di *l.* Italy **57** I8
Monte Cristi Dom. Rep. **187** F3
Monte Cristi *nat. park* Dom. Rep. **187** F3
Monte Cristo Bol. **201** E3
Montecristo, Isola di *i.* Italy **56** C6
Monte da Rocha, Barragem do *resr* Port. **54** C7
Monte Dinero Arg. **205** C9
Monte Dourado Brazil **199** H5
Monte Escobedo Mex. **184** D4
Monte Falterona, Campigna e delle Foreste Casentinesi, Parco Nazionale del *nat. park* Italy **56** D5
Montefiascone Italy **56** E6
Montegiorgio Italy **56** F5
Montego Bay Jamaica **186** D3
Monte Hermoso Arg. **204** E5
Montehermoso Spain **54** E4
Monteiro Brazil **202** E3
Montejinnie Australia **148** A3
Montejunto, Serra de *hill* Port. **54** B6
Monte León Arg. **205** C8
Monte Libano Col. **198** C2
Montélimar France **51** K8
historically known as Acunum Acusio
Monte Lindo *r.* Para. **201** F5
Montellano Spain **54** F7
Montello Bol. **201** E4
Montemayor, Meseta de *plat.* Arg. **205** D7
Montemorelos Mex. **185** F3
Montemor-o-Novo Port. **54** C6
Montendre France **50** F7
Montenegro *aut. rep.* Yugo. *see* Crna Gora
Montenegro Brazil **203** B9
Monte Patria Chile **204** C3
Montepuez Moz. **129** D8
Montepuez *r.* Moz. **129** D8
Monte Quemado Arg. **204** E2
Montereau-faut-Yonne France **51** I4
Monterey Mex. *see* Monterrey
Monterey *CA* U.S.A. **182** C5
Monterey *KY* U.S.A. **176** B7
Monterey *VA* U.S.A. **176** F7
Monterey Bay U.S.A. **182** B5
Monterey Bay National Marine Sanctuary *nature res.* U.S.A. **182** B5
Montería Col. **198** C2
Monteriggioni Italy **56** D5
Montero Bol. **201** E4
Monteros Arg. **204** D2
Monterotondo Italy **56** E6
Monterrey *Baja California Norte* Mex. **183** I9
Monterrey *Nuevo León* Mex. **185** E3
also spelt Monterey
Montes Altos Brazil **202** C3
Montesano U.S.A. **180** B3
Montesano sulla Marcellana Italy **57** H8
Monte Sant'Angelo Italy **56** H7
Monte Santo Brazil **202** E4
Monte Santo de Minas Brazil **206** G6
Monte Santu, Capo di *c.* Sardegna Italy **57** B8
Montes Claros Brazil **202** D6
Montesilvano Italy **56** G6
Montesquieu-Volvestre France **50** H9
▶Montevideo Uruguay **204** F4
Capital of Uruguay.
Montevideo U.S.A. **178** D2
Monte Vista U.S.A. **181** F5
Montezinho, Parque Natural de *nature res.* Port. **54** D3
Montezuma U.S.A. **174** A3
Montezuma Creek U.S.A. **183** O4
Montezuma Creek *r.* U.S.A. **183** O4
Montezuma Peak U.S.A. **183** G4
Montfort-le-Gesnois France **50** G4
Montfragüe, Parque Natural de *nature res.* Spain **54** F5
▶Montgomery AL U.S.A. **175** C5
State capital of Alabama.
Montgomery U.K. **47** I11
also known as Trefaldwyn
Montgomery *PA* U.S.A. **177** I4
Montgomery *WV* U.S.A. **176** D7
Montgomery City U.S.A. **174** B4
Montgomery Islands Australia **150** C3
Monthey Switz. **51** M6
Monti *Sardegna* Italy **57** B8
Monticello *AR* U.S.A. **175** B5
Monticello *FL* U.S.A. **175** D6
Monticello *GA* U.S.A. **175** D5
Monticello *IA* U.S.A. **172** B8
Monticello *IL* U.S.A. **174** B3
Monticello *IN* U.S.A. **174** C3
Monticello *KY* U.S.A. **176** A8
Monticello *MS* U.S.A. **175** B6
Monticello *NY* U.S.A. **177** K4
Monticello *UT* U.S.A. **183** O4
Monticello *WI* U.S.A. **172** D8
Montichiari Italy **56** C3
Montiel, Cuchilla de *hills* Arg. **204** F3
Montier-en-Der France **51** K4
Montignac France **50** G3
Montigny, Lac de *l.* Canada **173** P2
Montijo Port. **54** C6
Montijo Spain **54** E6
Montilla Spain **54** G7
Monti Sibillini, Parco Nazionale dei *nat. park* Italy **56** F6
Montivilliers France **50** G3
Mont-Joli Canada **169** H3
Mont-Laurier Canada **168** F3
Mont Louis Canada **169** H3
Montluçon France **51** I6

Montmagny Canada **169** G4
Montmélian France **51** M7
Montmirail France **51** J4
Montmoreau-St-Cybard France **50** G7
Montmorillon France **50** G6
Monto Australia **149** F5
Montoire-sur-le-Loir France **50** G5
Montoro Spain **54** G6
Montour Falls U.S.A. **177** I3
Montoursville U.S.A. **177** I4
Mont Peko, Parc National du *nat. park* Côte d'Ivoire **124** D3
Montpelier *ID* U.S.A. **180** E4
Montpelier *IN* U.S.A. **172** H10
Montpelier *OH* U.S.A. **176** A4
▶Montpelier *VT* U.S.A. **177** M1
State capital of Vermont.
Montpellier France **51** J9
Montpezat-de-Quercy France **50** H8
Montpon-Ménestérol France **50** G7
Montréal Canada **169** F4
English form Montreal; *historically known as* Ville-Marie
Montreal *r.* Ont. Canada **168** C4
Montreal *r.* Ont. Canada **168** E3
Montreal Island Canada **173** I3
Montreal Lake *l.* Canada **167** J4
Montreal Lake Canada **167** J4
Montréal-Mirabel *airport* Canada **169** F4
Montreal River Canada **168** C4
Montreuil France **50** H2
Montreux Switz. **51** M6
Montrose *well* S. Africa **132** E3
Montrose U.K. **46** J7
Montrose *CO* U.S.A. **181** F5
Montrose *MI* U.S.A. **173** J7
Montrose *PA* U.S.A. **177** J4
Montrose *WV* U.S.A. **176** F6
Monts France **50** G5
Mont-St-Aignan France **50** H3
Mont-St-Michel, Baie du *b.* France **50** E4
Montsalvy France **51** I8
Montsant, Parc Natural del *nat. park* Côte d'Ivoire **124** D3
Montseny, Parque Natural del *nature res.* Spain **55** N3
▶Montserrat *terr.* West Indies **187** H3
United Kingdom Overseas Territory.
oceania [countries] ▶ ▶ 138–139
Mont St Michel *tourist site* France *see* Le Mont-St-Michel
Montuosa, Isla *i.* Panama **186** C6
Montvale U.S.A. **176** F8
Montviel, Lac *l.* Canada **169** G2
Monument Draw *watercourse* U.S.A. **179** B5
Monument Valley *reg.* U.S.A. **183** N5
Monveda Dem. Rep. Congo **126** D4
Monyakeng S. Africa **133** K4
Monywa Myanmar **78** A3
Monza Italy **56** B3
Monza *r.* Rus. Fed. **43** V3
Monze Zambia **127** E8
Monze, Cape *pt* Pak. *see* Muari, Ras
Monzhukly Turkm. **102** C5
Monzón Peru **200** A2
Monzón Spain **55** L3
Mooi *r.* Kwazulu-Natal S. Africa **133** O5
Mooi *r.* North West S. Africa **133** K3
Mooifontein Namibia **132** A3
Mooirivier S. Africa **133** O6
Mookane Botswana **131** F4
Moolawatana Australia **146** C2
Moomba Australia **147** C2
Moomin Creek *r.* Australia **147** F2
Moonbi Range *mts* Australia **147** F2
Moonda Lake *salt flat* Australia **149** D5
Moonie Australia **147** F1
Moonie *r.* Australia **147** F2
Moonta Australia **146** C3
Moora Australia **151** B6
Mooraberree Australia **149** D5
Moorcroft U.S.A. **180** F3
Moordenaarsnek *pass* S. Africa **133** M7
Moordorf (Südbrookmerland) Germany **48** E2
Moore *r.* Australia **151** A6
Moore U.S.A. **180** E3
Moore, Lake *salt flat* Australia **151** B6
Moore Embayment *b.* Antarctica **223** K1
Moorefield U.S.A. **176** G6
Moore Haven U.S.A. **175** D7
Moore Reef Australia **149** E3
Moore River National Park Australia **151** A6
Moorfoot Hills U.K. **46** I8
Moorhead U.S.A. **178** D2
Moornanyah Lake *imp. l.* Australia **147** D3
Mooroopna Australia **147** E4
Moorpark U.S.A. **182** F7
Moorreesburg S. Africa **132** C10
Moorrinya National Park Australia **149** E4
Moosburg an der Isar Germany **48** I7
Moose *r.* Canada **168** D3
Moose Factory Canada **168** D3
Moosehead Lake U.S.A. **174** G2
Moose Jaw Canada **167** J5
Moose Jaw *r.* Canada **167** J5
Moose Lake U.S.A. **178** E2
Moose Mountain Creek *r.* Canada **167** K5
Moose River Canada **168** D3
Moosilauke, Mount U.S.A. **177** N1
Moosomin Canada **167** K5
Moosonee Canada **168** D3
Mootwingee National Park Australia **147** D2
Mopane S. Africa **131** F3
Mopeia Moz. **131** G3
Mopipi Botswana **131** E4
Mopti Mali **124** D3
Mopti *admin. reg.* Mali **124** D3
Moquata Sudan **104** A5
Moquegua Peru **200** C4
Moquegua *dept* Peru **200** C4
Mor Hungary **49** P8
Mora Cameroon **125** I4
Mora Port. **54** C6
Mora Sweden **45** K3
Mora *MN* U.S.A. **174** A2
Mora *NM* U.S.A. **181** F6
Mora *r.* U.S.A. **181** F6
Mora, Cerro *mt.* Arg./Chile **204** C4
Morača *r.* Yugo. **58** A4
Morach *r.* Belarus **42** J9
Moradabad India **96** C3
Morada Nova *Amazonas* Brazil **200** G1
Morada Nova *Ceará* Brazil **202** E3
Morada Nova de Minas Brazil **207** H5
Morafenobe Madag. **131** [inset] J3
Morag Poland **49** Q2
Mórahalom Hungary **49** Q9
formerly known as Alsóközpont
Moraine Lake Canada **173** I1
Moraleda, Canal *sea chan.* Chile **205** B7
Moralejo Spain **54** E4
Morales Guat. **185** H6
Moram India **94** C2
Moramanga Madag. **131** [inset] K3
Moran *MI* U.S.A. **173** I5
Moran *WY* U.S.A. **180** E4
Moranbah Australia **149** F4
Morang Nepal *see* Biratnagar
Morangas Brazil **206** A6
Moranhat India **97** G4

Morant Cays *is* Jamaica **186** E3
Morant Point Jamaica **186** D3
Morappur India **94** C3
Morar, Loch *l.* U.K. **46** G7
Moratalla Spain **55** J6
Moratuwa Sri Lanka **94** C5
Morava *r.* Czech Rep. *see* Moravia
Morava *r.* Europe **49** N7
also known as March
Moravatou Madag. **131** [inset] K2
Moravia *reg.* Czech Rep. **49** O6
also known as Morava; *formerly known as* Mähren
Moravia U.S.A. **177** I3
Moravian Falls U.S.A. **176** D9
Moravica *r.* Yugo. **58** B5
Moravica *r.* Czech Rep. **49** O6
Moravské Třebová Czech Rep. **49** N6
Moravské Budějovice Czech Rep. **49** M6
Moravskoslezské Beskydy *mts* Czech Rep. **49** P6
Morawa Australia **151** A6
Morawhanna Guyana **199** G2
Moray Firth *b.* U.K. **46** H6
Moray Range *hills* Australia **148** A2
Morbach Germany **48** E6
Morbegno Italy **56** B2
Morbi India **96** A5
formerly spelt Morvi
Morcenx France **50** F8
Morcillo Mex. **184** D3
Mordaga China **85** I1
Mor Dağı *mt.* Turkey **107** F3
Mordelles France **50** E4
Morden Canada **167** L5
Mordovia *aut. rep.* Rus. Fed. *see* Mordoviya, Respublika
Mordoviya, Respublika *aut. rep.* Rus. Fed. **41** H5
English form Mordovia *or* Mordvinia; *formerly known as* Mordovskaya A.S.S.R.
Mordovo Rus. Fed. **41** G5
Mordovskaya A.S.S.R. *aut. rep.* Rus. Fed. *see* Mordoviya, Respublika
Mordves Rus. Fed. **43** T7
Mordvinia *aut. rep.* Rus. Fed. *see* Mordoviya, Respublika
Mordy Poland **49** T3
Moreau *r.* U.S.A. **178** B2
Moreau, South Fork *r.* U.S.A. **178** B2
Morecambe U.K. **47** I9
Morecambe Bay U.K. **47** I9
Moree Australia **147** F2
Morehead P.N.G. **73** J8
Morehead U.S.A. **176** B7
Morehead City U.S.A. **174** E5
Moreira Brazil **199** F5
Morel-Iz, Gora *hill* Rus. Fed. **40** L1
Morel *r.* India **96** C4
Moreland U.S.A. **176** A8
Morelia Col. **198** C4
Morelia Mex. **185** E5
Morella Australia **149** E4
Morella Spain **55** K4
Morelos *state* Mex. **185** F5
Morena India **96** C4
Morena, Sierra *mts* Spain **54** E7
formerly known as Mariánica, Cordillera
Morenci U.S.A. **183** O8
Moreni Romania **58** G4
Moreno Mex. **184** C2
Moreno Valley U.S.A. **183** G8
Morerú *r.* Brazil **201** F2
Mores *Sardegna* Italy **57** A8
Moresby, Mount Canada **166** D4
Moresby Island Canada **166** C4
Moreton Bay Australia **147** G2
Moreton Island Australia **147** G1
Moreuil France **51** I3
Moreyu *r.* Rus. Fed. **40** K1
Morez France **51** M6
Morfou Cyprus **108** D2
also known as Güzelyurt; *also spelt* Morphou
Morfou Bay Cyprus **108** D2
Morgam-Viibus *hill* Fin. **44** N1
Morgan Australia **146** C3
Morgan U.S.A. **176** A7
Morgan, Mount U.S.A. **182** F4
Morgan City U.S.A. **175** B6
Morgan Hill U.S.A. **182** C4
Morgans Corner U.S.A. **177** I9
Morganton U.S.A. **174** D5
Morgantown *KY* U.S.A. **174** C4
Morgantown *WV* U.S.A. **176** F6
Morgenzon S. Africa **133** N3
Morges Switz. **51** M6
Morgex Italy **51** N7
Morhar *r.* India **97** E4
Mori China **88** E3
Mori *r.* Japan **90** G3
Moriah, Mount U.S.A. **183** J2
Moriarty U.S.A. **181** F6
Moriarty's Range *hills* Australia **147** E3
Moribaya Guinea **124** C4
Morice Lake Canada **166** E4
Moricetown Canada **166** E4
Morichal Col. **198** D4
Morija Lesotho **133** L6
Morik Nigeria **125** H3
Morkiny Gory Rus. Fed. **43** R4
Morlaix France **50** C4
Morley Canada **167** H5
Mormal' Belarus **43** K9
Mormant France **51** I4
Mormon Lake U.S.A. **183** M7
Mormugao India *see* Marmagao
Morney *watercourse* Australia **149** D5
Mornington, Isla *i.* Chile **205** B8
Mornington Island Australia **148** C3
Moro Pak. **101** F5
Moro *r.* U.S.A. **181** F6
Moro P.N.G. **73** K8
▶Morocco *country* Africa **122** C3
africa [countries] ▶ ▶ 114–117
Morocco U.S.A. **172** F10
Moro Creek *r.* U.S.A. **179** D5
Morogoro Tanz. **129** C6
Morogoro *admin. reg.* Tanz. **129** C7
Moro Gulf Phil. **74** B5
Morojaneng S. Africa **133** K6
Morokweng S. Africa **132** H3
Moroleón Mex. **185** E4
Morombe Madag. **131** [inset] I4
Moromoro Bol. **201** D4
Moron Arg. **204** E6
Morón Cuba **186** D2
Mörön Mongolia **84** D1
Morona Ecuador **198** B5
Morona *r.* Peru **198** B5
Morona-Santiago *prov.* Ecuador **198** B5

Morondava Madag. **131** [inset] I4
Morón de la Frontera Spain **54** F7
Morondo Côte d'Ivoire **124** D4
Morongo Valley U.S.A. **183** H7
▶Moroni Comoros **129** D7
Capital of the Comoros.
Moroni U.S.A. **183** M2
Moron Us He *r.* China **84** B5
Moros *r.* Spain **54** G3
Morotai *i.* Indon. **75** D2
Morotai, Selat *sea chan.* Indon. **75** C2
Moroto Uganda **128** B4
Moroto, Mount Uganda **128** B4
Morotsuka Japan **91** B8
Morowali N.Z. **153** B13
Morowali Reserve *nature res.* Indon. **75** B3
Morozova Rus. Fed. **43** L2
Morozovo Rus. Fed. **43** V5
Morozovsk Rus. Fed. **41** G6
Morpara Brazil **202** D5
Morpeth Canada **173** L8
Morpeth U.K. **47** K8
Morphou Cyprus *see* Morfou
Morretes Brazil **203** B8
Morrill U.S.A. **178** B3
Morrilton U.S.A. **179** D5
Morrin Canada **167** H5
Morrinhos Brazil **206** D4
Morrinsville N.Z. **152** J5
Morris Canada **167** L5
Morris *IL* U.S.A. **172** E9
Morris *MN* U.S.A. **178** D2
Morris *PA* U.S.A. **177** I4
Morrisburg Canada **177** J1
▶Morris Jesup, Kap *c.* Greenland **165** P1
Most northerly point of North America.
Morrison U.S.A. **174** B3
Morrisons N.Z. **153** E13
Morristown *AZ* U.S.A. **183** L8
Morristown *NJ* U.S.A. **177** K5
Morristown *NY* U.S.A. **177** J1
Morristown *TN* U.S.A. **176** B9
Morrisville *NC* U.S.A. **177** I3
Morrisville *PA* U.S.A. **177** J5
Morrisville *VT* U.S.A. **177** M1
Morr Morr Aboriginal Holding *res.* Australia **149** E3
Morro Brazil **207** I3
Morro, Punta *pt* Chile **204** C2
Morro Agudo Brazil **206** E6
Morro Bay U.S.A. **182** D6
Morro d'Anta Brazil **203** E6
Morro de Papanoa *hd* Mex. **185** E5
Morro de Petatlán *hd* Mex. **185** E5
Morro do Chapéu Brazil **202** D5
Morro do Coco Brazil **207** L8
Morro do Sinai *hills* Brazil **201** G2
Morros Brazil **202** C2
Morrosquillo, Golfo de *b.* Col. **198** C2
Morrumbala Moz. **131** G3
Morrumbene Moz. **131** G4
Mors *reg.* Denmark **45** J4
Morse Canada **167** J5
Morse U.S.A. **172** C4
Morse, Cape Antarctica **223** I2
Morshi India **96** C5
Morsott Alg. **57** A13
Mersvikbotn Norway **44** K2
Mort *watercourse* Australia **149** D4
Mortagne-au-Perche France **50** G4
Mortagne-sur-Sèvre France **50** F5
Mortain France **50** E4
Mortara Italy **56** B3
Morteau France **51** M5
Morteros Arg. **204** E3
Mortes, Rio das *r.* Minas Gerais Brazil **207** I8
Mortes, Rio das *r.* Tocantins Brazil **202** B4
also known as Manso
Mortimer's Bahamas **187** E2
Mortlach Canada **167** J5
Mortlake Australia **147** D4
Mortlock Islands Micronesia **220** E5
also known as Nomoi Islands
Mortlock Islands P.N.G. *see* Tauu Islands
Morton *IL* U.S.A. **174** B3
Morton *TX* U.S.A. **179** B5
Morton *WA* U.S.A. **180** B3
Morton National Park Australia **147** F3
Mortugaba Brazil **207** K1
Morundah Australia **147** E3
Moruroa *atoll* Fr. Polynesia *see* Mururoa
Moruya Australia **147** F3
Morvan, Parc Naturel Régional du *nature res.* France **51** K5
Morven Australia **149** E5
Morven N.Z. **153** F12
Morven *hill* U.K. **46** I5
Morvi India *see* Morbi
Morwell Australia **147** E4
Mor'ye Rus. Fed. **43** M1
Morzhovets, Ostrov *i.* Rus. Fed. **40** G2
Mosal'sk Rus. Fed. **43** P7
Mosbach Germany **48** F6
Mosby U.S.A. **180** F3
Moscarter, Punta des *pt* Spain **55** M5
▶Moscow Rus. Fed. **43** S6
Capital of the Russian Federation and 2nd most populous city in Europe. Also known as Moskva.
world [cities] ▶ ▶ 24–25
Moscow *IA* U.S.A. **172** B9
Moscow *ID* U.S.A. **180** C3
Moscow *PA* U.S.A. **177** J4
Moscow Oblast *admin. div.* Rus. Fed. *see* Moskovskaya Oblast'
Moscow University Ice Shelf Antarctica **223** I2
Mosel *r.* Germany **48** E5
Moselebe *watercourse* Botswana **130** D5
Moseley U.S.A. **176** H8
Moselle *r.* France **51** M3
Moses, Mount U.S.A. **183** G1
Moses Lake U.S.A. **180** C3
Mosgiel N.Z. **153** E13
Moshannon U.S.A. **176** G4
Moshaweng *watercourse* S. Africa **132** G3
Moshchnyy, Ostrov *i.* Rus. Fed. **42** I2
Moshenskoye Rus. Fed. **43** P3
Moshi Tanz. **129** C6
Moshi *r.* Nigeria **125** G4
Mosina Poland **49** N3
Mosinee U.S.A. **172** D6
Mosi-oa-Tunya National Park Zimbabwe *see* Victoria Falls National Park
Mosita S. Africa **133** I3
Mosjøen Norway **44** J4
Moskal'vo Rus. Fed. **82** F1
Moskenesøya *i.* Norway **44** K2
Moskenstraumen *sea chan.* Norway **44** K2
Moskkugáisi *mt.* Norway **44** L2
Moskosel Sweden **44** L3
Moskovskaya Oblast' *admin. div.* Rus. Fed. **43** T6
English form Moscow Oblast
Moskovskiy Uzbek. *see* Shakhrikhan
Moskva *r.* Rus. Fed. **43** T6
Moskva Tajik. **101** G2
Moskvy, Kanal imeni *canal* Rus. Fed. **43** S5
Moșna Romania **58** I2
Mosonmagyaróvár Hungary **49** O8

Mosopo Botswana 133 J1
Mosor mts Croatia 56 I5
Mosquera Col. 198 B4
Mosquero U.S.A. 181 F6
Mosquitia reg. Hond. 186 C4
Mosquito Creek Lake U.S.A. 176 E4
Mosquito Lake Canada 167 K2
Mosquitos, Costa de coastal area Nicaragua 186 C4
also spelt Miskitos, Costa de
Moss Norway 45 J4
Mossaka Congo 126 C5
Mossâmedes Angola see Namibe
Mossâmedes Brazil 206 C3
Mossburn N.Z. 153 C13
Mosselbaai S. Africa see Mossel Bay
Mossel Bay S. Africa 132 G11
also spelt Mosselbaai
Mossel Bay b. S. Africa 132 G11
Mossendjo Congo 126 B5
Mossgiel Australia 147 E3
Mossman Australia 149 E3
Mossoró Brazil 202 E3
Moss Vale Australia 147 F3
Mossy r. Canada 167 K4
Most Bulg. 58 G7
Most Czech Rep. 49 K5
Mostaganem Alg. 123 F2
also spelt Mestghanem
Mostar Bos.-Herz. 56 J5
Mostardas Brazil 204 H3
Moşteni Romania 58 G4
Mostiştea r. Romania 58 H4
Móstoles Spain 54 H4
Mostoos Hills Canada 167 I4
Mostovskoy Rus. Fed. 41 G7
Mosty Belarus see Masty
Mosul Iraq 107 E3
also spelt Al Mawşil
Møsvatn Austfjell park Norway 45 J4
Møsvatnet l. Norway 45 J4
Mosvik Norway 44 J3
Mot'a Eth. 128 C2
Motaba r. Congo 126 C4
Mota del Cuervo Spain 55 I5
Motagua r. Guat. 185 H6
Motal' Belarus 42 G9
Motala Sweden 45 K4
Mota Lava i. Vanuatu 145 F3
also known as Saddle Island or Valua
Motaze Moz. 131 G5
Moţca Romania 58 H1
Motenge-Boma Dem. Rep. Congo 126 C4
Moteng Pass Lesotho 133 M5
Moth India 96 C4
Motherwell U.K. 46 I8
Mothibistat S. Africa 132 H4
Mothonaio, Akra pt Greece 59 E12
Motihari India 97 E4
Motilla hill Spain 54 F6
Motilla del Palancar Spain 55 J5
Motiti Island N.Z. 152 K5
Motlan Ling hill China 83 A4
Motloutse r. Botswana 131 F4
Motokwe Botswana 130 D5
Motovskiy Zaliv sea chan. Rus. Fed. 44 P1
Motoyoshi Japan 90 G5
Motozintla Mex. 185 G6
Motril Spain 55 H8
Motru Romania 58 D4
Motru r. Romania 58 E4
Motshikiri S. Africa 133 L2
Mott U.S.A. 178 B2
Motueka N.Z. 152 H9
Motuhora Island N.Z. 152 K5
also known as Whale Island; formerly known as Moutohora Island
Motu Ihupuku i. N.Z. see Campbell Island
Motukarara N.Z. 153 G11
Motul Mex. 185 H4
Motupipi N.Z. 152 G8
Mouali Gbangba Congo 126 C4
Mouan, Nam r. Laos 78 D4
Mouaskar Alg. see Mascara
Moubray Bay Antarctica 223 L2
Mouchalagane r. Canada 169 G3
Mouchet, Mont mt. France 51 J8
Mouchoir Bank sea feature Turks and Caicos Is 187 F2
Mouchoir Passage Turks and Caicos Is 187 F2
Mouding China 86 B3
also known as Gonghe
Moudjéria Mauritania 124 B2
Moudon Switz. 51 M6
Moudros Greece 59 G9
Mougri well Mauritania 124 B2
Mouhijärvi Fin. 45 M3
Mouhoun r. Africa 124 E4 see Black Volta
Mouila Gabon 126 A5
Moul well Niger 125 I3
Moulamein Australia 147 E3
Moulamein Creek r. Australia 147 D3
also known as Billabong Creek
Moulavibazar Bangl. see Maulvi Bazar
Moule Guadeloupe 187 H3
Moulèngui Binza Gabon 126 A5
Moulentâr well Mali 124 D2
Moulhoulé Djibouti 128 D1
Moulins France 51 J6
Moulins-Engilbert France 51 J6
Moulle de Jaut, Pic du mt. France 50 F9
Moulmein Myanmar 78 B4
also known as Mawlamyaing or Mawlamyine
Moulmeingyun Myanmar 78 A4
Moulouya, Oued r. Morocco 122 E2
Moultrie U.S.A. 174 C5
Moulton, Mount Antarctica 222 P1
Moultonborough U.S.A. 177 N2
Moultrie U.S.A. 175 D6
Moultrie, Lake U.S.A. 175 E5
Mounana Gabon 126 B5
Mound City KS U.S.A. 178 D4
Mound City MO U.S.A. 178 D3
Mound City SD U.S.A. 178 B2
Moundou Chad 126 C2
Moundsville U.S.A. 176 E6
Mounta, Akra pt Greece 59 B10
Mount Abu India 96 B4
Mountainair U.S.A. 181 F6
Mountain Brook U.S.A. 175 C5
Mountain City U.S.A. 176 D9
Mountain Grove U.S.A. 178 D4
Mountain Home AR U.S.A. 179 D4
Mountain Home ID U.S.A. 180 D4
Mountain Home UT U.S.A. 183 N1
Mountain Iron U.S.A. 172 A3
Mountain Lake Park U.S.A. 176 F6
Mountain Pass U.S.A. 183 I6
Mountain View AR U.S.A. 179 D5
Mountain View CA U.S.A. 182 B4
Mountain View HI U.S.A. 181 [inset] Z2
Mountain Village U.S.A. 164 C3
Mountain Zebra National Park S. Africa 133 J9
Mount Airy MD U.S.A. 177 H6
Mount Airy NC U.S.A. 176 E9
Mount Anderson Aboriginal Reserve Australia 150 C3
Mount Arapiles-Tooan State Park nature res. Australia 146 D4
Mount Aspiring National Park N.Z. 153 C12
Mount Assiniboine Provincial Park Canada 167 H5
Mount Augustus Australia 150 B5
Mount Ayliff S. Africa 133 N7
Mount Ayr U.S.A. 178 D3
Mount Baldy U.S.A. 182 G7
Mount Barker S.A. Australia 146 C3
Mount Barker W.A. Australia 151 B7
Mount Barnett Australia 150 D3
Mount Barnett Aboriginal Reserve Australia 150 D3
Mount Beauty Australia 147 E4
Mount Bellew Rep. of Ireland 47 D10
Mount Bruce N.Z. 152 J8
Mount Brydges Canada 173 L8
Mount Buffalo National Park Australia 147 E4
Mount Carmel IL U.S.A. 174 C4
Mount Carmel TN U.S.A. 176 C9
Mount Carmel Junction U.S.A. 183 L4
Mount Carroll U.S.A. 174 B3
Mount Clere Australia 151 B5
Mount Cook N.Z. 153 E11
also known as Aoraki
Mount Cook National Park N.Z. 153 E11
Mount Coolon Australia 149 E4
Mount Currie Nature Reserve S. Africa 133 N7
Mount Darwin Zimbabwe 131 F3
Mount Denison Australia 148 B4
Mount Desert Island U.S.A. 177 Q1
Mount Eba Australia 146 B2
Mount Eccles National Park Australia 146 D4
Mount Edziza Provincial Park Canada 166 D3
Mount Etna U.S.A. 172 H10
Mount Field National Park Australia 147 E5
Mount Fletcher S. Africa 133 M7
Mount Forest Canada 168 D5
Mount Frankland National Park Australia 151 B7
Mount Frere S. Africa 133 M7
also known as Kwabhaca
Mount Gambier Australia 146 D4
Mount Garnet Australia 149 E3
Mount Hagen P.N.G. 73 J8
Mount Holly U.S.A. 177 K6
Mount Holly Springs U.S.A. 177 H5
Mount Hope N.S.W. Australia 147 E3
Mount Hope S.A. Australia 146 B3
Mount Hope U.S.A. 176 D8
Mount Horeb U.S.A. 172 D7
Mount House Australia 150 D3
Mount Howitt Australia 149 D5
Mount Hutt N.Z. 153 F11
Mount Ida U.S.A. 179 D5
Mount Isa Australia 148 C4
Mount Jackson U.S.A. 176 G7
Mount James Aboriginal Reserve Australia 151 B5
Mount Jewett U.S.A. 176 G4
Mount Kaputar National Park Australia 147 F2
Mount Keith Australia 151 C5
Mount Kenya National Park Kenya 128 C5
Mount Lebanon U.S.A. 176 E5
Mount Lofty Range mts Australia 146 C3
Mount MacDonald Canada 173 M3
Mount Magnet Australia 151 B6
Mount Manara Australia 147 D3
Mount Manning Nature Reserve Australia 151 B6
Mount Maunganui N.Z. 152 K5
Mount McKinley National Park U.S.A. see Denali National Park and Preserve
Mount Meadows Reservoir U.S.A. 182 D1
Mount Molloy Australia 149 E3
Mount Moorosi Lesotho 133 L7
Mount Morgan Australia 149 F4
Mount Morris IL U.S.A. 172 D8
Mount Morris MI U.S.A. 173 J7
Mount Morris NY U.S.A. 176 H3
Mount Nebo U.S.A. 176 E7
Mount Olivet U.S.A. 176 A7
Mount Orab U.S.A. 176 B6
Mount Pearl Canada 169 K4
Mount Perry Australia 149 F5
Mount Pierre Aboriginal Reserve Australia 150 D3
Mount Pleasant Canada 169 H4
Mount Pleasant IA U.S.A. 174 B3
Mount Pleasant MI U.S.A. 173 I7
Mount Pleasant PA U.S.A. 176 F5
Mount Pleasant SC U.S.A. 175 E5
Mount Pleasant TX U.S.A. 179 D5
Mount Pleasant UT U.S.A. 183 M2
Mount Rainier National Park U.S.A. 180 B3
Mount Remarkable National Park Australia 146 C3
Mount Revelstoke National Park Canada 166 G5
Mount Richmond Forest Park nature res. N.Z. 152 H9
Mount Robson Provincial Park Canada 166 G4
Mount Rogers National Recreation Area park U.S.A. 176 D9
Mount Rupert S. Africa 133 I5
Mount St Helens National Volcanic Monument nat. park U.S.A. 180 B3
Mount Sanford Australia 148 A3
Mount's Bay U.K. 47 G13
Mount Shasta U.S.A. 180 B4
Mount Somers N.Z. 153 F11
Mount Sterling IL U.S.A. 174 B4
Mount Sterling KY U.S.A. 176 B7
Mount Sterling OH U.S.A. 176 B6
Mount Stewart S. Africa 133 I10
Mount Storm U.S.A. 176 F6
Mount Surprise Australia 149 E3
Mount Upton U.S.A. 177 J3
Mount Vernon Australia 150 B5
Mount Vernon GA U.S.A. 175 D5
Mount Vernon IA U.S.A. 172 B9
Mount Vernon IL U.S.A. 174 B4
Mount Vernon IN U.S.A. 174 C4
Mount Vernon KY U.S.A. 176 A8
Mount Vernon MO U.S.A. 178 D4
Mount Vernon OH U.S.A. 176 C5
Mount Vernon TX U.S.A. 179 D5
Mount Vernon WA U.S.A. 180 B2
Mount Wedge Australia 148 B4
Mount Welcome Aboriginal Reserve Australia 150 B4
Mount William National Park Australia 147 F5
Mount Willoughby Australia 146 B1
Moura Australia 149 F5
Moura Brazil 199 F5
Moura r. Brazil 200 B1
Moura Port. 54 D6
Mourão Port. 54 D6
Mourdiah Mali 124 D3
Mourdi, Dépression du depr. Chad 120 D5
Mourenx France 50 F9
Mourne Mountains hills U.K. 47 F9
Mourre de Chanier mt. France 51 M9
Mourtzeflos, Akra pt Greece 59 G9
Mousa i. U.K. 46 K3
Mouscron Belgium 51 J2
Mousgougou Chad 126 C2
Mousie U.S.A. 176 C8
Moussafoyo Chad 126 C2
Moussoro Chad 120 C6
Moutamba Congo 126 B5
Mouth of Wilson U.S.A. 176 D9
Moutiers France 51 M7
Moutohora Island N.Z. see Motuhora Island
Moutong Indon. 75 B2
Moutourwa Cameroon 125 I4
Mouydir, Monts du plat. Alg. 123 F4
Mouyondzi Congo 126 B5
Mouzaki Greece 59 C9
Mouzarak Chad 120 B6
Mouzon France 51 L3
Movas Mex. 184 C2
Movila Miresii Romania 58 I3
Movileni Romania 58 F4
Mowanjum Aboriginal Reserve Australia 150 C3
Mowbullan, Mount Australia 149 F5
Mowchadz' Belarus 42 G8
Moxahala U.S.A. 176 C6
Moxey Town Bahamas 186 D1
Moxico prov. Angola 127 C8
Moy r. Rep. of Ireland 47 C9
Moyahua Mex. 185 E4
Moyale Eth. 128 C4
Moyamba Sierra Leone 124 B4
Moyen Atlas mts Morocco 122 D2
English form Middle Atlas
Moyen-Chari pref. Chad 126 C2
Moyen Congo country Africa see Congo
Moyeni Lesotho 133 L7
also known as Quthing
Moyenne-Guinée admin. reg. Guinea 124 B4
Moyen-Ogooué prov. Gabon 126 A5
Moynalyk Rus. Fed. 88 F1
Moynaq Uzbek. see Muynak
Moyo i. Indon. 77 G5
Moyo Uganda 128 A4
Moyobamba Peru 198 B6
Moyowosi r. Tanz. 129 A6
Moysalen mt. Norway 44 K1
Moyto Chad 120 C6
Moyu China 89 B4
formerly known as Karakax
Moyum waterhole Kenya 128 C4
Moyynkum Kazakh. 103 H3
formerly known as Furmanovka
Moyynkum, Peski des. Kazakh. 103 F3
also known as Moinkum
Moyynty Kazakh. 103 H3
formerly spelt Mointy
▶Mozambique country Africa 131 G4
spelt Moçambique in Portuguese; historically known as Portuguese East Africa
africa [countries] 114–117
Mozambique Channel Africa 131 I4
Mozarlândia Brazil 206 C1
Mozdok Rus. Fed. 41 H8
Mozdūrān Iran 101 E2
Mozelle U.S.A. 176 B8
Mozhaysk Rus. Fed. 43 R6
Mozhga Rus. Fed. 40 J4
Mozhong China 86 A1
Mozo Myanmar 78 A3
Mozyr' Belarus see Mazyr
Mpal Senegal 124 A3
formerly spelt Pal
Mpanda Tanz. 129 A6
Mpandamatenga Botswana 131 E3
Mpande Zambia 127 F7
Mpé Congo 126 B5
Mpemvana S. Africa 133 O4
Mpessoba Mali 124 D3
Mpigi Uganda 128 B4
Mpika Zambia 127 F7
Mpoko r. Cent. Afr. Rep. 126 C3
Mpolweni S. Africa 133 O6
Mpongwe Zambia 127 F8
Mporokoso Zambia 127 F7
Mposa S. Africa 133 Q5
Mpouya Congo 126 C5
Mpui Tanz. 129 A7
Mpulungu Zambia 127 F7
Mpumalanga S. Africa 133 O6
Mpumalanga prov. S. Africa 133 N3
formerly known as Eastern Transvaal
Mpwapwa Tanz. 129 C6
Mqanduli S. Africa 133 M8
Mqinvartsveri mt. Georgia/Rus. Fed. see Kazbek
Mrągowo Poland 49 S2
Mrewa Zimbabwe see Murehwa
Mrežnica r. Croatia 56 H3
Mrkonjić-Grad Bos.-Herz. 56 J4
Mrocza Poland 49 O2
Mroga r. Poland 49 Q4
M'Saken Tunisia 57 C13
Msambweni Kenya 129 C6
Msata Tanz. 129 C6
Mshinskaya Rus. Fed. 43 K2
M'Sila Alg. 123 G2
Msta Rus. Fed. 43 P4
Msta r. Rus. Fed. 43 M3
Mstinskiy Most Rus. Fed. 43 N3
Mstislavl' Belarus see Mstsislaw
Mstsislaw Belarus 43 M7
also spelt Mstislavl'
Msunduze r. S. Africa 133 Q4
Mszana Dolna Poland 49 R6
Mtama Tanz. 129 C7
Mt'at'ushet'is Nakrdzali nature res. Georgia 107 F2
Mtelo Kenya 128 B4
Mtera Reservoir Tanz. 129 B6
Mtoko Zimbabwe see Mutoko
Mtonjaneni S. Africa 133 P5
Mtorashanga Zimbabwe see Mutorashanga
Mtsensk Rus. Fed. 43 R8
Mts'khet'a Georgia 107 F2
Mtukula Tanz. 129 C6
Mtunzini S. Africa 133 P5
Mtwara Tanz. 129 D7
Mtwara admin. reg. Tanz. 129 C7
Mu r. Myanmar 78 A3
Mu hill Port. 54 C7
Mu'āb, Jibāl reg. Jordan see Moab
Muaguide Moz. 129 C8
Mualama Moz. 131 H3
Muana Brazil 202 B2
Muanda Dem. Rep. Congo 127 B6
Muang Khammouan Laos 78 D4
Muang Không Laos 79 D5
Muang Khôngxédôn Laos 79 D5
Muang Luang r. Thai. 79 B6
Muang Pakbeng Laos 78 C4
Muang Pakxan Laos 78 C4
Muang Phin Laos 78 D4
Muang Phôn-Hông Laos 78 C4
Muang Sam Sip Thai. 79 D5
Muang Sing Laos 78 C3
Muang Thai country Asia see Thailand
Muang Vangviang Laos 78 C4
Muang Xaignabouri Laos 78 C4
also known as Sayabouri
Muanza Moz. 131 G3
Muar Malaysia 76 C2
Muar r. Malaysia 76 C2
Muara Brunei 77 F1
Muaraancalong Indon. 77 G2
Muarabeliti Indon. 76 C3
Muarabungo Indon. 76 C3
Muaradua Indon. 76 D4
Muaraenim Indon. 76 C3
Muarainu Indon. 77 F3
Muarakaman Indon. 77 G3
Muaralesan Indon. 77 G2
Muararupit Indon. 76 C3
Muarasoma Indon. 76 B2
Muaras Reef Indon. 75 A2
Muaratebo Indon. 76 C3
Muaratembesi Indon. 76 C3
Muarateweh Indon. 77 F3
Muara Tuang Sarawak Malaysia see Kota Samarahan
Muarawahau Indon. 77 G2
Muarwari, Ras pt Pak. 101 F5
also known as Monze, Cape
Mu'aylā, Wādī al watercourse Iraq 109 M5
Muazzam India 96 B3
Mubārak, Jabal mt. Jordan/Saudi Arabia 108 G8
Mubarakpur India 97 D4
Mubarek Uzbek. 103 F5
also spelt Muborak
Mubarraz well Saudi Arabia 107 E5
Mubende Uganda 128 A4
Mubi Nigeria 125 I4
Muborak Uzbek. see Mubarek
Mubur i. Indon. 77 D2
Mucabа Angola 127 B6
Mucajá Brazil 199 G5
Mucajaí r. Brazil 199 F4
Mucajaí, Serra do mts Brazil 199 F4
Mucalic r. Canada 169 H1
Mučanj mt. Yugo. 58 B5
Mucheng China see Wuzhi
Muchinga Escarpment Zambia 127 F8
Muchiri Bol. 201 E4
Muchuan China 86 B2
also known as Muxi
Muck i. U.K. 46 F7
Muckadilla Australia 149 F5
Muckaty Aboriginal Land res. Australia 148 B3
Muco r. Col. 198 D3
Mucojo Moz. 129 D8
Muconda Angola 127 D7
formerly known as Nova Chaves
Mucope Angola 127 B9
Mucubela Moz. 131 H3
Mucucuaú r. Brazil 199 F5
Mucuim r. Brazil 199 E6
Mucumbura Moz. 131 F3
Mucundi Angola 127 C9
Mucunha Angola 127 C8
Mucupia Moz. 131 H3
Mucur Turkey 106 C3
Mucura Brazil 199 F5
Mucuri Brazil 203 E6
Mucuri r. Brazil 207 N5
Mucurici Brazil 207 M5
Mucuripe Brazil 198 D5
Mucuripe, Ponta de pt Brazil 202 E2
Mucusso, Coutada Pública do nature res. Angola 127 D9
Mucussueje Angola 127 D7
Muda r. Malaysia 76 C1
Mudabidri India 94 B3
Mudanjiang China 82 C3
Mudan Jiang r. China 82 C3
Mudan Ling mts China 82 B4
Mudanya Turkey 106 B2
Mudayrah Kuwait 107 F5
Mudaysisāt, Jabal al hill Jordan 108 H6
Muddebihal India 94 C2
Muddus nationalpark nat. park Sweden 44 L2
Muddy r. U.S.A. 183 J5
Muddy Boggy Creek r. U.S.A. 179 D5
Muddy Creek r. U.S.A. 183 N3
Muddy Gap Pass U.S.A. 180 F
Muddy Peak U.S.A. 183 J5
Mūd-e-Dahanāb Iran 101 D3
Muden S. Africa 133 O5
Mudgal India 94 C3
Mudgee Australia 147 F3
Mudhol India 94 B2
Mudigere India 94 B3
Mudjatik r. Canada 167 J3
Mudkhed India 94 C2
Mudki India 96 B3
Mud Lake U.S.A. 183 G4
Mudon Myanmar 78 B4
Mudraya country Africa see Egypt
Mudug admin. reg. Somalia 128 E3
Mudukani Tanz. 129 B5
Mudumu National Park Namibia 130 D3
Mudurnu Turkey 106 B2
Mud'yuga Rus. Fed. 40 F3
Muecate Moz. 131 H2
Mueda Moz. 129 C7
Muela de Arés mt. Spain 55 K4
Mueller Range hills Australia 150 D3
Muende Moz. 131 G2
formerly known as Vila Caldas Xavier
Muerto, Mar lag. Mex. 185 G5
Muertos Cays is Bahamas 186 C1
Muftah well Sudan 121 G4
Muftyuga Rus. Fed. 40 H2
Mufulira Zambia 127 F8
Mufumbwe Zambia 127 E8
Mufu Shan mts China 87 E2
Muğan Düzü lowland Azer. 107 G3
Muge r. Port. 54 C5
Mugeba Moz. 131 H3
Mughalbhin Pak. see Jati
Mughal Sarai India 97 D4
Mūghār Iran 100 C3
Mughayrā' Saudi Arabia 107 D5
Mughayrā' well Saudi Arabia 105 D2
Mughshin Oman 105 F4
Mughsu r. Tajik. 101 G2
also spelt Muksu
Mugia Spain see Muxia
Mugila, Monts mts Dem. Rep. Congo 127 F6
Muğla Turkey 106 B3
Muğla prov. Turkey 59 J11
Mugodzharskaya Kazakh. 102 D2
Mugodzhary, Gory mts Kazakh. 102 D3
Mug Qu r. China 80 E6
Muguia Moz. 129 C8
Mugu Karnali r. Nepal 97 E3
Mugur-Aksy Rus. Fed. 84 A1
Muguxung China 89 F5
Muḩ, Sabkhat imp. l. Syria 109 J3
Muhagiriya Sudan 126 E2
Muhala China see Yutian
Muhala Dem. Rep. Congo 127 F6
Muhammad, Râs pt Egypt 121 G3
Muhammadabad India 97 D4
Muhammad Qol Sudan 121 H4
Muhammarah Iran see Khorramshahr
Muhayriqah Saudi Arabia 105 D3
Muhaysh, Wādī al watercourse Jordan 108 H8
Muhaywīr tourist site Iraq 109 M4
Muheza Tanz. 129 C6
Mühlacker Germany 48 F7
Mühlberg Germany 49 K
Mühldorf am Inn Germany 49 J7
Mühlhausen (Thüringen) Germany 48 H4
Mühlig-Hofmann Mountains Antarctica 223 A2
Muhos Fin. 44 N2
Muhradah Syria 109 H2
Muhu i. Estonia 42 E3
Muhukuru Tanz. 129 B7
Muhula Moz. 131 H2
Muhulu Dem. Rep. Congo 126 E5
Mui Eth. 128 B3
Mui Bai Bung c. Vietnam see Mui Ca Mau
Mui Ca Mau c. Vietnam 79 D6
also known as Mui Bai Bung
Mui Dinh hd Vietnam 79 E5
Mui Độc pt Vietnam 78 D4
Muidumbe Moz. 129 C7
Mui Ké pt Vietnam 79 E5
Muiliyk i. Indon. 75 D3
Muineachán Rep. of Ireland see Monaghan
Muine Bheag Rep. of Ireland 47 F11
Muir U.S.A. 173 I8
Muir Glacier Canada/U.S.A. 166 B3
Muirkirk U.K. 46 H8
Mui Ron hd Vietnam 78 D4
Muisne Ecuador 198 B4
Muite Moz. 131 H2
Mujeres, Isla i. Mex. 185 I4
Muji China 88 B4
Mujong r. Sarawak Malaysia 77 F2
Muju S. Korea 83 B5
Mujui Joboti Brazil 199 H5
Mukačevo Ukr. see Mukacheve
Mukacheve Ukr. 49 T7
also spelt Mukachevo or Mukačevo; historically known as Munkács
Mukachevo Ukr. see Mukacheve
Mukah Sarawak Malaysia 77 F2
Mukah r. Sarawak Malaysia 77 F2
Mukalla Yemen 105 E5
also spelt Al Mukallā
Mukandgarh India 96 B4
Mukandwara India 96 C4
also spelt Mokundurra
Mukanga Dem. Rep. Congo 127 D6
Mukawa Japan 90 G3
Mu-kawa r. Japan 90 G3
Mukawwar, Gezirat i. Sudan 121 H4
Mukdahan Thai. 78 D4
Mukden China see Shenyang
Mukerian India 96 B3
Muketei r. Canada 168 C2
Mukhen Rus. Fed. 82 E2
Mukhino Rus. Fed. 82 B1
Mukhorshibir' Rus. Fed. 85 F1
Mukhtuya Rus. Fed. see Lensk
Mukinbudin Australia 151 B6
Mu Ko Chang National Park Thai. 79 C6
Mukomuko Indon. 76 C3
Mukono Uganda 128 B4
Mukoshi Zambia 127 F7
Mukry Turkm. 103 F5
Muksu r. Tajik. see Mughsu
Muktinath Nepal 97 D3
Muktsar India 96 B3
Mukuku Zambia 127 F8
Mukumbura Zimbabwe 131 F3
formerly spelt Mkumvura
Mukunsa Zambia 127 F7
Mukur Atyrauskaya Oblast' Kazakh. 102 C3
also spelt Muqyr
Mukur Vostochnyy Kazakhstan Kazakh. 103 J2
Mukutawa r. Canada 167 L4
Mukwonago U.S.A. 172 E8
Mul India 94 C1
Mula r. India 94 B2
Mula r. Pak. 101 F4
Mula Spain 55 J6
Mulakatholhu Maldives 93 D10
formerly known as Mulaku
Mulaku atoll Maldives see Mulakatholhu
Mulaly Kazakh. 103 I3
also spelt Molaly
Mulan China 82 C3
Mulanay Phil. 74 B3
Mulanje Malawi 129 B9
Mulapula, Lake salt flat Australia 146 C2
Mula-tupo Panama 186 D5
Mulayh salt pan Saudi Arabia 109 J8
Mulayjah Saudi Arabia 105 E2
Mulbagal India 94 C3
Mulbekh Jammu and Kashmir 96 C2
Mulberry AR U.S.A. 179 D5
Mulberry NC U.S.A. 176 D9
Mulchatna r. U.S.A. 164 D3
Mulchén Chile 204 B5
Mulde r. Germany 49 J4
Muleba Tanz. 128 A5
Mule Creek U.S.A. 180 F4
Mulegé Mex. 184 B3
Mulekatembo Zambia 129 B7
Mules i. Indon. 75 B5
Muleshoe U.S.A. 179 B5
Mulevala Moz. 131 H3
Mulga Park Australia 148 A5
Mulgathing Australia 146 B2
Mulhacén mt. Spain 55 H7
Mülhausen France see Mulhouse
Mülheim an der Ruhr Germany 48 D4
Mulhouse France 51 N5
also known as Mülhausen
Muli China 86 B3
also known as Qiaowa; formerly known as Bowa
Muli Rus. Fed. see Vysokogorniy
Mulilansolo Zambia 129 B7
Muling Heilong. China 82 C3
formerly known as Bamiantong
Muling Heilong. China 82 C3
Muling r. China 82 D3
Mull i. U.K. 46 G7
Mulla Ali Iran 100 B2
Mullaaxe Beyle Somalia 128 E2
Mullaittivu Sri Lanka 94 D4
Muller watercourse Australia 148 B4
Muller, Pegunungan mts Indon. 77 F2
Mullett Lake U.S.A. 173 I5
Mullewa Australia 151 A6
Müllheim Germany 48 E8
Mullica r. U.S.A. 177 K6
Mullingan watercourse Australia 148 C5
Mullingar Rep. of Ireland 47 E10
also known as An Muileann gCearr
Mullins U.S.A. 175 E5
Mull of Galloway c. U.K. 47 H9
Mull of Kintyre hd U.K. 47 G8
Mull of Oa hd U.K. 46 F8
Müllrose Germany 49 L3
Mullsjö Sweden 45 K4
Mullutu laht l. Estonia 42 D3
Mulobezi Zambia 127 E9
Mulondo Angola 127 B8
Mulonga Plain Zambia 127 D9
Mulongo Dem. Rep. Congo 127 E6
Mulsanne France 50 G5
Mulshi Lake India 94 B2
Multai India 96 C5
Multān Iran 101 E5
Multan Pak. 101 G4
Multia Fin. 44 N3
Mulu, Gunung mt. Sarawak Malaysia 77 F1
Mulug India 94 C2
Mulumbe, Monts mts Dem. Rep. Congo 127 E7
Mulurulu Lake Australia 147 D3
Mulūşī, Wādī al watercourse Iraq 109 K4
Muma Dem. Rep. Congo 126 D4
Mūmān Iran 101 E5
▶Mumbai India 94 B2
2nd most populous city in Asia and 3rd in the world. Formerly known as Bombay.
world [cities] 24–25
Mumbeji Zambia 127 D8
Mumbondo Angola 127 B7
Mumbwa Zambia 127 E8
Mumbwi Tanz. 129 C6
Mume Dem. Rep. Congo 127 E7
Muminabad Tajik. see Leningrad
Mu'minobod Tajik. see Leningrad
Mumoma Dem. Rep. Congo 127 D6
Mumra Rus. Fed. 102 A3
Mun, Mae Nam r. Thai. 79 D5
Muna i. Indon. 75 B4
Muna Mex. 185 H4
Muna r. Rus. Fed. 39 M3
Munabao Pak. 101 G5
Munaðarnes Iceland 44 [inset] B2
Munagala India 94 C2
Munakata Japan 91 B8
Munayly Kazakh. 102 C3
Munayshy Kazakh. 102 C4
Münchberg Germany 48 I5
München Germany see Munich
München-Gladbach Germany see Mönchengladbach
Munchique, Parque Nacional nat. park Col. 198 B4
Muncho Lake Canada 166 E3
Muncho Lake Provincial Park Canada 166 E3
Munch'ŏn N. Korea 83 B5
Muncie U.S.A. 174 C3
Muncoonie West, Lake salt flat Australia 148 C5
Muncy U.S.A. 177 I4
Munda Solomon Is 145 E2
Mundel Lake Sri Lanka 94 C5
Mundemba Cameroon 125 H5
Mundiwindi Australia 150 C4
Mundjura Creek r. Australia 149 D3
Mundo r. Spain 55 J6
Mundo Novo Brazil 202 D4
Mundra India 96 A5
Mundrabilla Australia 151 D6
Munds Park U.S.A. 183 M7
Mundubbera Australia 149 F5
Mundwa India 96 B4
Muneru r. India 94 D2
Munfordville U.S.A. 174 C4
Mungallala Australia 149 E5
Mungallala Creek r. Australia 147 E2
Mungana Australia 149 E3
Mungaoli India 96 C4
Mungári Moz. 131 G3
Mungaroona Range Nature Reserve Australia 150 B4
Mungbere Dem. Rep. Congo 126 F4
Mungeli India 97 D5
Munger India 97 E4
formerly spelt Monghyr
Munger U.S.A. 173 J7
Mungeranie Australia 146 C2
Mu Nggava i. Solomon Is see Rennell
Munggaresak, Tanjung pt Indon. 77 E2
Mungili Aboriginal Reserve Australia 151 D5
Mungindi Australia 147 F2
Mungkarta Aboriginal Land res. Australia 148 B4
Mungla Bangl. 97 F5
Mungo Angola 127 C7
Mungo, Lake Australia 147 D3
Mungo National Park Australia 147 D3
Mungwi Zambia 127 F7
Mun'gyŏng S. Korea 83 B5
Munhango Angola 127 C8
Munhino Angola 127 B8
Munich Germany 48 I7
also known as München
Munising U.S.A. 172 G4
Muniz Freire Brazil 207 L7
Munkács Ukr. see Mukacheve
Munkedal Sweden 45 J4
Munkflohögen Sweden 44 K3
Munku-Sardyk, Gora mt. Mongolia/Rus. Fed. 84 D1
Munro, Mount Australia 147 F5
Munse Indon. 75 B4
Munshiganj Bangl. 97 F5
Münsingen Switz. 51 N6
Münster Niedersachsen Germany 48 H3
Münster Nordrhein-Westfalen Germany 48 E4
Munster reg. Rep. of Ireland 47 D11
Münsterland reg. Germany 48 E4
Münster-Osnabrück airport Germany 48 E3
Muntadgin Australia 151 B6
Munte Indon. 75 A2
Muntele Mare, Vârful mt. Romania 58 E2
Munteni Romania 58 I3
Mununga Zambia 127 F7
Munyal-Par sea feature India see Bassas de Pedro Padua Bank
Munyati r. Zimbabwe 131 F3
Munyu S. Africa 133 M8
Munzur Vadisi Milli Parkı nat. park Turkey 107 D3
Muodoslompolo Sweden 44 M2
Muojärvi l. Fin. 44 O2
Muonio Fin. 44 M2
Muonioälven r. Fin./Sweden 44 M2
also known as Muonionjoki
Muonionjoki r. Fin./Sweden see Muonioälven
Mupa Angola 127 B9
Mupa, Parque Nacional da nat. park Angola 127 B8
Mupfure r. Zimbabwe 131 F3
formerly known as Umfuli
Muping China 85 I4
Muqaddam watercourse Sudan 121 F5
Muqaybirah Yemen 105 D5
Muqaynimah well Saudi Arabia 105 E3
Muqdisho Somalia see Mogadishu
Muqnīyāt Oman 105 G3
Muqshin, Wādī r. Oman 105 F4
Muquem Brazil 202 B5
Muqui Brazil 203 D7
Muqyr Kazakh. see Mukur
Mur r. Austria 49 N9
also spelt Mura
Mura r. Croatia/Slovenia 49 N9
also spelt Mur
Muradiye Turkey 59 I10
Muradiye Turkey 107 E3
also known as Bargiri
Murai, Tanjong pt Sing. 76 [inset]
Murai Reservoir Sing. 76 [inset]
Murakami Japan 90 F5
Murallón, Cerro mt. Chile 205 B8
Muramvya Burundi 126 F5
Muráň r. Slovakia 49 R7
Muranga Kenya 128 C5
formerly known as Fort Hall
Muras Spain 54 D1
Murashi Rus. Fed. 40 I4
Murat France 51 I7
Murat r. Turkey 107 D3
Muratlı Turkey 106 A2
Murayama Japan 90 G5
Murayr, Jabal hill Saudi Arabia 104 C2
Muraysah, Ra's al pt Libya 120 E2
Murça Port. 54 D3
Murcheh Khvort Iran 100 B3
Murchison Australia 147 E4
Murchison watercourse Australia 151 A5
Murchison N.Z. 153 G9
Murchison, Mount Antarctica 223 L2
Murchison, Mount hill Australia 151 B5
Murchison Falls Uganda 128 A4
Murchison Falls National Park Uganda 128 A4
also known as Kabalega Falls National Park or Kabarega National Park
Murchison Island Canada 168 B3
Murchison Mountains N.Z. 153 B13
Murchison Range hills Australia 148 B4
Murcia Spain 55 J7
Murcia aut. comm. Spain 55 J7
Murcielagos Bay Phil. 74 B4
Mûr-de-Bretagne France 50 D4
Murdo U.S.A. 178 B3
Murdochville Canada 169 H3
Mürefte Turkey 106 A2
Muregi Nigeria 125 G4
Murehwa Zimbabwe 131 F3
formerly spelt Mrewa or Murewa
Mureş r. Romania 58 B2
Muret France 50 H9
Murewa Zimbabwe see Murehwa
Murfjället mt. Norway 44 K2
Murfreesboro AR U.S.A. 179 D5
Murfreesboro NC U.S.A. 177 H9
Murfreesboro TN U.S.A. 174 C5
Murgab Tajik. see Murghob
Murgab r. Tajik. 101 H2
Murgab Turkm. see Murgap
Murgab r. Turkm. see Murgap
Murgap Turkm. 103 E5
also spelt Murgab
Murgap r. Turkm. 103 E5
formerly spelt Murgab
Murgeni Romania 58 J2
Murge Tarantine hills Italy 57 J8
Murghab r. Afgh. 101 E3
Murghab reg. Afgh. 101 E3
Murgha Kibzai Pak. 101 G4

Murghob Tajik. 101 H2
also spelt Murgab
Murgh Pass Afgh. 101 G3
Murgon Australia 149 F5
Murgoo Australia 151 B4
Muri Qinghai China 84 C4
Muri Qinghai China 84 D4
Muri Iran 97 E5
Muria, Gunung mt. Indon. 77 E4
Muriaé Brazil 203 D7
Muriege Angola 127 E7
Murii-dake mt. Japan 90 H3
Murillo Canada 172 G2
Müritz l. Germany 49 J2
Müritz, Nationalpark nat. park Germany
49 K2
Muriwai N.Z. 152 L6
Murjek Sweden 44 M2
Murkong Selek India 97 G4
Murmansk Rus. Fed. 44 P1
Murmanskaya Oblast' admin. div. Rus. Fed.
44 P1
English form Murmansk Oblast
Murmanskiy Bereg coastal area Rus. Fed.
40 E1
Murmansk Oblast admin. div. Rus. Fed. see
Murmanskaya Oblast'
Murmashi Rus. Fed. 44 P1
Murmino Rus. Fed. 43 V7
Muro, Capo di c. Corse France 56 A7
Muro Lucano Italy 57 H8
Murom Rus. Fed. 40 G5
Murongo Tanz. 128 A5
Muros Spain 54 B2
Muros e Noia, Ría de est. Spain 54 B2
Muroto Japan 91 D8
Muroto-zaki pt Japan 91 D8
Murowana-Goślina Poland 49 O3
Murphy ID U.S.A. 180 C4
Murphy NC U.S.A. 174 D5
Murphys U.S.A. 182 D3
Murrah reg. Saudi Arabia 105 E3
Murra Murra Australia 147 F2
Murranji Aboriginal Land res. Australia
148 B3
Murrat el Kubra, Buheirat l. Egypt see
Great Bitter Lake
Murrat el Sughra, Buheirat l. Egypt see
Little Bitter Lake
▶Murray r. S.A. Australia 147 C3
3rd longest river in Oceania. Part of the
longest (Murray-Darling).
oceania (landscapes) ▶▶ 136–137
Murray r. W.A. Australia 151 A7
Murray r. Canada 166 F3
Murray KY U.S.A. 174 B4
Murray UT U.S.A. 183 M1
Murray, Lake P.N.G. 73 J8
Murray, Lake U.S.A. 175 D5
Murray, Mount Canada 166 D2
Murray Bridge Australia 146 C4
Murray City U.S.A. 176 C6
▶Murray-Darling r. Australia 144 D5
Longest river in Oceania.
oceania (landscapes) ▶▶ 136–137
Murray Downs Australia 148 B4
Murray Harbour Canada 169 I4
Murray Range Australia 151 E5
Murraysburg S. Africa 132 H8
Murray Sunset National Park Australia
146 D3
Murrayville Australia 146 D3
Murree Pak. 101 H3
Murrieta U.S.A. 183 G8
Murroa Moz. 131 H3
▶Murrumbidgee r. Australia 147 D3
4th longest river in Oceania.
oceania (landscapes) ▶▶ 136–137
Murrupula Moz. 131 H2
Murrurundi Australia 147 F2
Murshidabad India 97 F4
Murska Sobota Slovenia 56 I2
Murtajapur India 94 C1
Murten Switz. 51 N6
Murter Croatia 56 H5
Murter i. Croatia 56 H5
Murtoa Australia 147 D4
Murtovaara Fin. 44 O2
Muru r. Brazil 200 C2
Murua i. P.N.G. see Woodlark Island
Murud India 94 B2
Murud, Gunung mt. Indon. 77 F2
Murui r. Indon. 77 F3
Murung r. Indon. 77 F3
Muruntau Uzbek. 103 F4
Murupara N.Z. 152 K6
Mururoa atoll Fr. Polynesia 221 I7
also spelt Moruroa; historically known as
Osnaburg
Muruti, Ilha i. Brazil 199 I4
Murviedro Spain see Sagunto
Murwāni, Wādī watercourse Saudi Arabia
104 B3

Murwara India 96 D5
Murwillumbah Australia 147 G2
Murygino Kirovskaya Oblast' Rus. Fed. 40 I4
Murygino Smolenskaya Oblast' Rus. Fed.
43 N7
Mürz r. Austria 49 M8
Murzechirla Turkm. 102 E5
formerly spelt Mirzachirla
Murzūq Libya 120 B3
Muş Turkey 107 E3
Musa Dem. Rep. Congo 126 C4
Mūsa r. Latvia/Lith. 42 F5
Mūsa r. Latvia/Lith. 42 F5
Mūsa, Gebel mt. Egypt see Sinai, Mount
Mūsá, Khowr-e b. Iran 100 B4
Musa Ali Terara vol. Africa 128 D1
Musabani India 97 E5
Musabeyli Turkey 109 H1
Muşabih Saudi Arabia 104 C4
Musa Khel Bazar Pak. 101 G4
Musala mt. Bulg. 58 E6
Musala i. Indon. 76 B2
Musali Turkey 108 F1
Musan N. Korea 82 C4
Musandam admin. reg. Oman 105 G2
Musandam Peninsula Oman/U.A.E. 105 G2
Musa Qala, Rūd-i r. Afgh. 101 F3
Musay'īd Qatar see Umm Sa'id
Musaymir Yemen 104 D3
Musbat well Sudan 120 E6

▶Muscat Oman 105 G3
Capital of Oman. Also spelt Masqaţ.

Muscat reg. Oman 105 G2
also spelt Masqaţ
Muscat and Oman country Asia see Oman
Muscatine U.S.A. 174 B3
Muscoda U.S.A. 172 C7
Muscongus Bay U.S.A. 177 P2
Musé r. Lith. 42 F7
Musgrave Australia 149 D2
Musgrave, Mount U.S.A. 153 E11
Musgrave Harbour Canada 169 K3
Musgrave Ranges mts Australia 148 A5
Mūshakī Afgh. 101 F3
Mushandike Sanctuary nature res.
Zimbabwe 127 F10
Mushāsh al Kabid well Jordan 109 H8
Mushash Dabl well Saudi Arabia 109 H9
Mushash Mudayyan well Saudi Arabia
109 J9
Mushayniqah well Yemen 105 D4
Mushayyish, Wādī al watercourse Jordan
108 H7
Mushenge Dem. Rep. Congo 126 D6
Mushie Dem. Rep. Congo 126 C5
Mushin Nigeria 125 F5
Musi r. India 94 C2
Musi r. Indon. 76 C3
Música mt. Macedonia 58 C7
Myadzyel Belarus 42 H7
Myadzyel, Vozyera l. Belarus 42 H7
Myaing Myanmar 78 A3
Myajlar India 96 A4
Myakishevo Rus. Fed. 43 J5
Myakit Rus. Fed. 39 P3
Myaksa Rus. Fed. 43 T3
Myall Lakes National Park Australia 147 G3
Myamoura-dake mt. Japan 91 B9
Myanaung Myanmar 78 A4
▶Myanmar country Asia 78 A3
also known as Burma
asia [countries] ▶▶ 64–67
Myaretskiya Belarus 42 I6
Myatlevo Rus. Fed. 43 Q7
Myaundzha Rus. Fed. 39 O3
Myaungmya Myanmar 78 A4
Myawadi Thai. 78 B4
Mycenae tourist site Greece 59 D11
also known as Mikines or Mykines
Myeik Myanmar see Mergui
Myerkulavichy Belarus 43 L9
Myers U.S.A. 176 B7
Myingyan Myanmar 78 A3
Myinmoletkat mt. Myanmar 79 B5
Myinmu Myanmar 78 A3
Myitkyina Myanmar 78 A1
Myitson Myanmar 78 B3
Myitta Myanmar 79 B5
Myittha Myanmar 78 B3
Myittha r. Myanmar 95 G1
Myjava Slovakia 49 O7
Mykines i. Faroe Is 46 E1
Mykines tourist site Greece see Mycenae
Myklebostad Norway 44 K2
Mykolayiv Ukr. 41 E7
formerly spelt Nikolayev
Mykolayivka Chernihivs'ka Oblast' Ukr. 43 M9
Mykolayivka Odes'ka Oblast' Ukr. 58 L2
Mykolayivka-Novorosiys'ka Ukr. 58 K2
Mykonos Greece 59 G11
Mykonos i. Greece 59 G11
also spelt Mikonos
Myla Rus. Fed. 40 I3
Myla r. Rus. Fed. 40 I2
Mylae Sicilia Italy see Milazzo
Mylasa Turkey see Milas
Myllykoski Fin. 42 H1
Mymensingh Bangl. see Mymensingh
Mymensingh Bangl. 97 F4
also spelt Mymensing; formerly known as
Nasirabad
Mynäjoki r. Fin. 42 C1
Mynämäki Fin. 45 M3
also spelt Myngaral
Mynfontein S. Africa 132 H7
Myngaral Kazakh. see Mynaral
Myohaung Myanmar 78 A3
Myŏnggan N. Korea 82 C4
Myory Belarus 42 I6
Myôzin-sho i. Japan 91 G9
Myrdalsjökull ice cap Iceland 44 [inset] C3
Myrdalssandur sand area Iceland
44 [inset] C3
Myre Norway 44 K1
Myrheden Sweden 44 M2
Myrhorod Ukr. 41 E6
also spelt Mirgorod
Myrina Greece 59 G9
also spelt Mírina
Myrlandshaugen Norway 44 L1
Myrnam Canada 167 I4
Myrnopillya Ukr. 58 K2
Myronivka Ukr. 41 D6
also spelt Mironovka
Myrskylä Fin. 45 N3
Myrtle Beach U.S.A. 175 E5
Myrtle Creek U.S.A. 180 B4
Myrtleford Australia 147 E4
Myrtle Point U.S.A. 180 A4
Myrzakent Kazakh. 103 G4
formerly spelt Slavyanka
Mysen Norway 45 J4
Myshanka r. Belarus 42 G9
Myshkin Rus. Fed. 43 T4
formerly known as Myshkino
Myshkino Rus. Fed. see Myshkin
Mys Lazareva Rus. Fed. see Lazarev
Myślenice Poland 49 R6
Myślibórz Poland 49 L3
My Son tourist site Vietnam 78 E5
Mysore India 94 C3
Mysore state India see Karnataka
Mysovsk Rus. Fed. see Babushkin
Mys Shmidta Rus. Fed. 39 S3
Myszków Poland 49 Q5
Myszyniec Poland 49 S2
Myt Rus. Fed. 40 G4
My Tho Vietnam 79 D6
Mytilene i. Greece see Lesbos

Myuombe Zambia 129 B7
Myuka Cameroon 125 H5
Muyumba Dem. Rep. Congo 127 E6
Muyunkum, Peski des. Kazakh. 103 G3
Muyunkym Kazakh. 103 H4
Muyuping China 87 D2
Muzaffarabad Pak. 101 H3
Muzaffargarh Pak. 101 G4
Muzaffarnagar India 96 C3
Muzaffarpur India 97 E4
Muzamane Moz. 131 G4
Muzambinho Brazil 206 G8
Muzat He r. China 88 C3
Muze Moz. 131 F2
Muzillac France 50 D5
Mūzīn Iran 101 E5
Muzon, Cape U.S.A. 166 C4
Múzquiz Mex. 185 E3
Muztag mt. Xinjiang China 89 C5
Muztag mt. Xinjiang China 89 D4
Muztagata mt. China 88 A4
Muztor Kyrg. see Toktogul
Mvadi Gabon 126 B4
Mvangan Cameroon 125 H6
Mvolo Sudan 126 F3
Mvomero Tanz. 129 C6
Mvoung r. Gabon 126 B4
Mvouti Congo 126 B6
Mvuma Zimbabwe 131 F3
formerly known as Umvuma
Mwali i. Comoros 129 D8
also spelt Mohéli
Mwanisenga Tanz. 129 B6
Mwanza Malawi 129 B8
Mwanza Tanz. 128 B5
Mwanza admin. reg. Tanz. 128 B5
Mweho Dem. Rep. Congo 126 E6
Mweka Dem. Rep. Congo 126 D6
Mwenda Zambia 127 F7
Mwene-Biji Dem. Rep. Congo 126 D6
Mwene-Ditu Dem. Rep. Congo 127 D6
Mwenezi Zimbabwe 131 F4
Mwenezi r. Zimbabwe 131 F4
formerly known as Nuanetsi
Mwenga Dem. Rep. Congo 126 F5
Mwereni Kenya 129 C6
Mweru, Lake Dem. Rep. Congo/Zambia
127 F7
formerly known as Moero, Lake
Mweru Plateau Tanz. 129 C7
Mweru Wantipa, Lake Zambia 127 F7
Mweru Wantipa National Park Zambia
127 F7
Mwewa Zambia 129 A7
Mwimba Dem. Rep. Congo 127 D7
Mwingi Kenya 128 C5
Mwinilunga Zambia 127 E7
Mya, Oued watercourse Alg. 123 G3
Myaing Myanmar 78 A3

Na, Nam r. China/Vietnam 86 B4
Naab r. Germany 48 J6
Naalehu U.S.A. 181 [inset] Z2
Naam Sudan 126 F2
Naama Alg. 123 E2
Naantali Fin. 45 M3
also known as Nådendal
Naas Rep. of Ireland 47 F10
also spelt An Nás
Näätämö Fin. 44 O1
Naba Japan 81 L7
Nababeep S. Africa 132 B4
Nabadwip India see Navadwip
Nabão r. Port. 54 C5
Nabarangapur India 95 D2
Nabas Phil. 74 B4
Nabatiyet et Tahta Lebanon 108 G4
Nabberu, Lake salt flat Australia 151 C5
Nabéré, Réserve Partielle de nature res.
Burkina 124 E4
Naberera Tanz. 129 C6
Naberezhnyye Chelny Rus. Fed. 40 J5
formerly known as Brezhnev
Nabha India 96 C3
Nabibleng r. Brazil 201 F5
Nabinagar India 97 E4
Nabire Indon. 73 I7
Nabi Younés, Ras en pt Lebanon 108 G4
Nāblus West Bank 108 G5
English form Nablus; also known as
Shekhem; also spelt Nābulus
Nablus West Bank see Nāblus
Nabolo Ghana 125 E4
Naboomspruit S. Africa 131 F5
Nabra r. India 96 C2
Nabule Myanmar 79 B5
Nābulus West Bank see Nāblus
Nacajuca Mex. 185 G5
Nacala Moz. 131 I2
formerly known as Maiaia
Nacaome Hond. 186 B4
Nacaroa Moz. 131 H2
Nacebe Bol. 200 D2
Nacha Belarus 42 F7
Nacha r. Belarus 43 J7
Nachalovo Rus. Fed. 102 B3
Nachingwea Tanz. 129 C7
Náchod Czech Rep. 49 N5
Nachuge India 95 G4
Nacimiento Chile 204 B5
Nacimiento Reservoir U.S.A. 182 D5
Nacogdoches U.S.A. 179 D6
Nacozari de García Mex. 184 C2
Nada China see Danzhou
Nadaleen r. Canada 166 C2
Nādendal Fin. see Naantali
Nadezhdinka Kazakh. 103 E1
formerly known as Nadezhdinskiy
Nadezhdinskiy Kazakh. see Nadezhdinka
Nadi Fiji 145 G3
Nadiad India 96 B5
Nădlac Romania 58 B2
Nador Morocco 123 E2
Nadporozh'ye Rus. Fed. 43 P1
Nādūshan Iran 100 C3
Nadvirna Ukr. 41 C6
also spelt Nadvornaya
Nadvornaya Ukr. see Nadvirna
Nadym Rus. Fed. 38 H3
Naenwa India 96 B4
Næstved Denmark 45 J5
Naf r. Bangl./Myanmar 97 G5
Nafas, Rās el r. en pt Egypt 108 F8
Nafha, Har hill Israel 108 F7
Nafpaktos Greece 59 C10
also spelt Návpaktos
Nafplio Greece 59 D11
also known as Návplion
Naft r. Iraq see Āb Naft
Naftalan Azer. 107 F2
Naft-e Safid Iran 100 B4
Naft-e Shāh Iran see Naft Shahr
Naft Shahr Iran 107 F3
formerly known as Naft-e Shāh
Nafūd ad Dahl des. Saudi Arabia 105 D3
Nafūd al Ghuwayṭah des. Saudi Arabia
109 J8
Nafūd al Jur'ā des. Saudi Arabia 105 D3
Nafūd al 'Urayq des. Saudi Arabia 104 C2
Nafūd as Sirr des. Saudi Arabia 104 C3
Nafūd as Surrah des. Saudi Arabia 104 C3
Nafūd Qunayfidhah des. Saudi Arabia
105 D2
Nafūsah, Jabal hills Libya 120 A2
Nafy Saudi Arabia 104 C2
Nag, Co l. China 89 D5
Naga Phil. 74 B3
Naga r. Canada 168 D2
Nagagami Lake Canada 168 C3
Nagahama Ehime Japan 91 C8
Nagahama Shiga Japan 91 E7
Naga Hills India 97 G4
Naga Hills state India see Nagaland
Nagai Japan see Nai
Nagaland state India 97 G4
formerly known as Naga Hills
Nagambie Australia 147 E4
Nagano Japan 91 F6
Nagano pref. Japan 91 E6
Nagaoka Japan 90 F6
Nagaon India 97 G4
also known as Nowgong
Nagappattinam India see Nagappattinam
Nagappattinam India 94 C4
formerly spelt Negapatam
Nagar r. Bangl./India 97 F4
Nagar Himachal Pradesh India 96 C3
Nagar Karnataka India 94 B3
Nagar Rajasthan India 96 B4
Nagarjuna Sagar Reservoir India 94 C2
Nagarote Nicaragua 186 B4
Nagar Parkar Pak. 96 A4
Nagasaki Japan 91 A8
Nagasaki pref. Japan 91 A8
Naga-shima i. Japan 91 B8
Naga-shima i. Japan 91 C8
Nagato Japan 91 B7
Nagaur India 96 B4
Nagavali r. India 95 D2
Nagda India 96 B4
Nagercoil India 94 C4
Nagha Kalat Pak. 101 F5

Myombe Zambia 129 B7
Mzamomhle S. Africa 133 K8
Mze r. Czech Rep. 49 J6
Mziha Tanz. 129 C6
Mzimba Malawi 129 B7
Mzimvubu r. S. Africa 133 N6
Mzingwani r. Zimbabwe 131 F4
also spelt Umzingwani
Mzuzu Malawi 129 B7

↓ N

Nagina India 96 C3
Nagineh Iran 100 D3
Nagma Nepal 97 D3
Nagod India 96 D4
Nagold Germany 48 F7
Nagong Chu r. China see Parlung Zangbo
Nagornyy Rus. Fed. 81 K1
Nagorno-Karabakh aut. reg. Azer. see
Dağlıq Qarabağ
Nagornyy Rus. Fed. 43 T5
Nag'oye Japan 91 E7
Nagpur India 96 C5
Nagqu China 89 F6
Nag Qu r. China 89 F6
Nagu Fin. 45 M3
also known as Hauvo
Nagua Dom. Rep. 187 F3
Nagurskoye Rus. Fed. 38 E1
Nagyatád Hungary 49 O9
Zrenjanin
Nagyecsed Hungary 49 T8
Nagyenyed Romania see Aiud
Nagyhalász Hungary 49 S7
Nagykanizsa Hungary 49 N9
Nagykáta Hungary 49 Q8
Nagykörös Hungary 49 Q8
Nagykunság reg. Hungary 49 R9
Nagyvárad Romania see Oradea
Naha Estonia 42 I3
Naha Japan 81 L7
Nahan India 96 C3
Nahang r. Iran/Pak. 101 E5
Nahanni Butte Canada 166 F2
also known as Tthenaagoo
Nahanni National Park Canada 166 E2
Nahanni Range mts Canada 166 E2
Nahari Japan 91 D8
Nahariyya Israel 108 G3
Nahāvand Iran 100 B3
N'Ahnet, Adrar mts Alg. 123 F5
Nahr, Jabal salt flat Saudi Arabia 104 B2
Nahr Ouassel, Oued watercourse Alg. 55 N9
Nahr 'Umr Iraq 100 A4
Nahuel Huapi Arg. 204 C6
Nahuel Huapi, Parque Nacional nat. park
Arg. 204 C6
Nahuel Mapá Arg. 204 D4
Nahuel Niyeu Arg. 204 D6
Nahunta U.S.A. 175 D6
Naic Phil. 74 B3
Naica Mex. 184 D3
Naidor well Tanz. 129 C6
Naikliu Indon. 75 B5
Naik Murad Bangl. 97 F4
Nailung China 89 F6
Na'ima Sudan 121 G6
Naiman Qi China see Daqin Tal
Naimin Bulak well China 84 C4
Nain Canada 169 I1
Nā'īn Iran 100 C3
Naina India 96 D4
Nainpur India 96 D5
Naiopué Moz. 131 H3
Nairn U.K. 46 I6
Nairn Centre Canada 173 L4
▶Nairobi Kenya 128 C5
Capital of Kenya.
Naissaar i. Estonia 42 F2
Naissus Srbija Yugo. see Niš
Naivasha Kenya 128 C5
Naizishan China 82 B4
Najafābād Iran 100 B3
Najasa r. Cuba 186 D2
Najd reg. Saudi Arabia 104 C2
English form Nejd
Nájera Spain 55 I2
Najerilla r. Spain 55 I2
Naji China 85 I1
also known as Arun Qi; formerly known as
Najitun
Najibabad India 96 C3
Najin China 82 D4
Najitun China see Naji
Najmah Saudi Arabia 105 E2
Najrān Saudi Arabia 104 D4
Najrān prov. Saudi Arabia 105 D4
Najrān, Wādī watercourse Saudi Arabia
104 D4
Nakadōri-shima i. Japan 91 A8
Naka-gawa r. Japan 91 G6
Nakalele Point U.S.A. 181 [inset] Z1
Nakama Japan 91 B7
Nakamba watercourse Burkina/Ghana
125 E3 see White Volta
Nakamura Japan 91 C8
Nakanbe watercourse Burkina/Ghana
125 E3 see White Volta
Nakanno Rus. Fed. 39 K3
Nakano Japan 91 F6
Nakanojō Japan 91 F6
Nakano-shima i. Japan 83 C7
Nakapanya Tanz. 129 C7
Nakasatsunai Japan 90 H3
Nakashibetsu Japan 90 I3
Nakasongola Uganda 128 B4
Nakatonbetsu-chō hill Japan 90 H2
Nakatsu Japan 91 B7
Nakatsugawa Japan 91 E7
Nakfa Eritrea 121 H5
Nakfa Wildlife Reserve nature res. Eritrea
121 H5
Nakhichevan' Azer. see Naxçivan
Nakhl Egypt 121 F3
Nakhl-e Taqī Iran 100 C5
Nakhodka Rus. Fed. 82 D4
Nakhola India 97 F4
Nakhon Nayok Thai. 79 C5
Nakhon Pathom Thai. 79 C5
Nakhon Phanom Thai. 78 D4
Nakhon Ratchasima Thai. 79 C5
also known as Korat
Nakhon Sawan Thai. 79 C5
also known as Paknampho
Nakhon Si Thammarat Thai. 79 B6
Nakhrachi Rus. Fed. see Kondinskoye
Nakhtarana India 96 A5
Nakina r. Canada 166 C3
Nakło nad Notecią Poland 49 O2
Naknek U.S.A. 164 C4
Nakodar India 96 B3
Nakonde Zambia 129 B7
Nakop Namibia 132 D6
Nakskov Denmark 45 J5
Näkten l. Sweden 44 K3
Naktong-gang r. S. Korea 83 C6
Nakuru Kenya 128 C5
Nakusp Canada 166 G5
Na-lang Myanmar 78 B3
Nalayh Mongolia 85 F2
Nalázi Moz. 131 G5
Nalbari India 97 F4
Nal'chik Rus. Fed. 41 G8
Naldurg India 94 C2
Nalerigu Ghana 125 E4
Nalgonda India 94 C2
Nalhati India 97 E4
Nalitabari Bangl. 97 F4
Nalkhera India 96 C4
Nallamala Hills India 94 C3
Nallıhan Turkey 106 C2
Nalolo Zambia 127 D8

Nalón r. Spain 50 A9
Nālūt Libya 120 A2
Namaa, Tanjung pt Indon. 75 D3
Namaacha Moz. 131 G5
Namacala Moz. 131 I3
Namacunde Angola 127 B9
Namacurra Moz. 131 H3
Namadgi National Park Australia 147 F3
Namahadi S. Africa 133 M4
Namak, Daryācheh-ye salt flat Iran 100 B3
Namak-e Miqhān, Kavir-e salt flat Iran
100 B3
Namaki watercourse Iran 100 C4
Namakkal India 94 C4
Namakzar-e Shadad salt flat Iran 100 D4
Namanga Kenya 128 C5
Namangan Uzbek. 103 G4
Namangan Oblast admin. div. Uzbek. see
Namanganskaya Oblast'
Namanganskaya Oblast' admin. div. Uzbek.
103 G4
English form Namangan Oblast; also known
as Namangan Wiloyati
Namangan Wiloyati admin. div. Uzbek. see
Namanganskaya Oblast'
Namanyere Tanz. 129 A6
Namapa Moz. 131 I2
Namaponda Moz. 131 H2
Namaqualand reg. S. Africa 132 A6
Namarrói Moz. 131 H2
Namasale Uganda 128 B4
Namatanai P.N.G. 145 E2
Namba Angola 127 B7
Nambol India 97 G4
Nambour Australia 149 G5
Nambucca Heads Australia 147 G2
Nambung National Park Australia 151 A6
Năm Căn Vietnam 79 D6
Namcha Barwa mt. China see
Namjagbarwa Feng
Namche Bazar Nepal 97 E4
Namch'ŏn N. Korea 83 B5
Namco China 89 E6
Nam Co salt l. China 89 E6
Namdalen valley Norway 44 K2
Namdaleseid Norway 44 J2
Nam Đinh Vietnam 78 D3
Namekagon r. U.S.A. 172 B5
Namen Belgium see Namur
Námestovo Slovakia 49 Q6
Nametil Moz. 131 H2
Namew Lake Canada 167 K4
Nam-gang r. N. Korea 83 B5
Namhkam Myanmar 78 B3
Namhsan Myanmar 78 B3
Namialo Moz. 131 H2
▶Namib Desert Namibia 130 B5
world [land images] ▶▶ 12–13
Namibe Angola 127 B8
formerly known as Moçâmedes or
Mossâmedes
Namibe prov. Angola 127 B7
Namibe, Reserva de nature res. Angola
127 B7
▶Namibia country Africa 130 B4
formerly known as South-West Africa;
historically known as German South-West
Africa
africa [countries] ▶▶ 114–117
Namib-Naukluft Game Park nature res.
Namibia 130 B5
Namichiga Tanz. 129 C7
Namicunde Moz. 131 H2
Namidobe Moz. 131 H3
Namie Japan 90 G5
Namies S. Africa 132 D6
Namin Iran 100 B2
Namina Moz. 131 H2
Namitete Malawi 129 B8
Namjagbarwa Feng mt. China 80 E7
also known as Namcha Barwa
Namji S. Korea 91 A7
Namka China see Doilungdêqên
Namlan r. Myanmar 78 B3
Namlang r. Myanmar 78 B3
Namlea Indon. 75 C3
Namling China 89 E6
also known as Nanmulingzue
Nam Nao National Park Thai. 78 C4
Nam Ngum Reservoir Laos 78 C4
Namoi r. Australia 147 F2
Namoluk Canada 167 G3
Nampa mt. Nepal 96 D3
Nampa U.S.A. 180 C4
Nampala Mali 124 D3
Namp'o N. Korea 83 B5
formerly known as Chinnamp'o
Nampuecha Moz. 131 I2
Nampula Moz. 131 H2
Nampula prov. Moz. 131 H2
Nam Pung Reservoir Thai. 78 C4
Namrole Indon. 75 C3
Namrup India 97 G4
Namsai Myanmar 78 B3
Namsang Myanmar 78 B3
Nam She Tsim hill Hong Kong China see
Sharp Peak
Namsos Norway 44 J2
Namsskogan Norway 44 K2
Namtari Nigeria 125 I4
Namtok Myanmar 78 B4
Nam Tok Thai. 79 B5
Namtok Chattakan National Park Thai.
78 C4
Namtok Mae Surin National Park Thai.
78 B4
Namton Myanmar 78 B3
Namtsy Rus. Fed. 39 M3
Namu Canada 166 E5
Namuli, Monte mt. Moz. 131 H2
Namuno Moz. 131 H2
Namur Belgium 51 K2
also known as Namen
Namutoni Namibia 130 C3
Namwala Zambia 127 E8
Namwera Malawi 129 B8
Namwŏn S. Korea 83 B6
Namya Ra Myanmar 78 B2
Namyit Island S. China Sea 72 D4
Nan, Mae Nam r. Thai. 78 C5
Nana r. Cent. Afr. Rep. 126 C3
Nana Bakassa Cent. Afr. Rep. 126 C3
Nana Barya r. Cent. Afr. Rep./Chad 126 C3
Nana-Mambéré pref. Cent. Afr. Rep. 126 C3
Nan'an China 87 F3
Nanango Australia 149 G5
Nanānib Plateau Namibia 130 C3
Nan'ao China 87 F4
also known as Houzhai
Nanao Japan 91 E6
Nanatsu-shima i. Japan 90 E6
Nanay r. Peru 198 C5
Nanbai China see Zunyi
Nanbaxian China 84 B4
Nanbin China see Shizhu
Nanbu China 86 C2
also known as Nanlong
Nancha China 82 C3
also known as Liantang
Nanchang Jiangxi China 87 E3
also known as Xiangtang
Nanchang Jiangxi China 87 E3
Nanchangshan China see Changdao
Nancheng China 87 F3
Nanchong China 86 C2
Nanchuan China 86 C2

Ñancorainza Bol. 201 E5
Nancowry i. India 95 G5
Nancut Canada 166 E4
Nancy France 51 M4
Nancy U.S.A. 176 A8
Nanda Devi mt. India 96 D3
Nanda Kot mt. India 96 D3
Nandan China 87 C3
Nanded India 94 C2
formerly known as Nander
Nander India see Nanded
Nandewar Range mts Australia 147 F2
Nandgaon India 94 B1
Nandi Zimbabwe 131 F4
Nandigama India 94 D2
Nandikotkur India 94 C3
Nanding He r. China 86 A4
Nandod India 96 B5
Nandu Jiang r. China 87 D4
Nandura India 94 C1
Nandurbar India 96 B5
Nandyal India 94 C3
Năneşti Romania 58 I3
Nanfeng Guangdong China 87 D4
Nanfeng Jiangxi China 87 F3
also known as Qincheng
Nang China 89 F6
Nangade Moz. 129 C7
Nanga Eboko Cameroon 125 I5
Nangah Dedai Indon. 77 E3
Nangahembaloh Indon. 77 F2
Nangahkemangai Indon. 77 F3
Nangahmau Indon. 77 E3
Nangahpinoh Indon. 77 E3
Nangahsuruk Indon. 77 F2
Nangahtempuai Indon. 77 F2
Nangalala Australia 148 B2
Nanganga Tanz. 129 C7
Nangang Shan mts China 82 C4

▶Nanga Parbat mt. Jammu and Kashmir 96 B2
9th highest mountain in the world and in Asia.
world [physical features] ▶ 8–9

Nangarhār prov. Afgh. 101 G3
Nangatayap Indon. 77 E3
Nangbéto, Retenue de resr Togo 125 F5
Nangin Myanmar 79 B6
Nangis France 51 J4
Nangnim N. Korea 83 B4
Nangnim-sanmaek mts N. Korea 83 B4
Nangō Japan 90 F6
Nangong China 85 G4
Nangqên China 86 A1
also known as Xangda
Nangulangwa Tanz. 129 C7
Nanguneri India 94 C4
Nanhe China 85 G4
also known as Heyang
Nanhu China 84 B4
Nanhua Gansu China 84 C4
Nanhua Yunnan China 86 B3
also known as Longchuan
Nanhui China 87 G2
also known as Huinan
Nani Afgh. 101 G3
Nanisivik Canada 165 K2
Nanjangud India 94 C3
Nanjian China 86 B3
Nanjiang China 86 C1
Nanjie China see Guangning
Nanjing Fujian China 87 F3
also known as Shancheng
Nanjing Jiangsu China 87 F1
formerly spelt Nanking
Nanji Shan i. China 87 G3
Nanka Jiang r. China 86 A4
Nankang China 87 E3
formerly known as Rongjiang
Nankang China see Xingzi
Nanking China see Nanjing
Nankoku Japan 91 C8
Nankova Angola 127 C9
Nanlan He r. China 86 A4
Nanle China 85 G4
Nanling China 87 F2
Nan Ling mts China 87 D3
Nanliu Jiang r. China 87 D4
Nanlong China see Nanbu
Nanma China see Yiyuan
Nanmulingzue China see Namling
Nannine Australia 151 B5
Nanning China 87 D4
Nannup Australia 151 A7
Na Noi Thai. 78 C4
Nanortalik Greenland 165 O3
Nanouki atoll Kiribati see Nonouti
Nanouti atoll Kiribati see Nonouti
Nanpan Jiang r. China 86 C3
Nanpara India 97 D4
Nanpi China 85 H4
Nanpiao China 85 I3
Nanping Fujian China 87 F3
Nanping Sichuan China 86 C1
also known as Yongle
Nanpu China see Pucheng
Nanpu Xi r. China 87 F3
Nanqiao China see Fengxian
Nanri Dao i. China 87 F3
Nansa r. Spain 54 G1
Nansebo Eth. 128 C3
Nansei-shotō is Japan see Ryukyu Islands
Nansenga Zambia 127 E8
Nansen Land reg. Greenland 165 O1
Nansen Sound sea chan. Canada 165 J1
Nanshan Island S. China Sea 72 E4
Nanshankou China 84 B3
Nansha Qundao is S. China Sea see Spratly Islands
Nansio Tanz. 128 B5
Nantawarrina Aboriginal Land res. Australia 146 C2
Nantes France 50 E5
Nantes à Brest, Canal de France 50 D5
Nanthi Kadal lag. Sri Lanka 94 D4
Nantiat France 50 H6
Nanticoke Canada 168 D5
Nanticoke MD U.S.A. 177 J7
Nanticoke PA U.S.A. 177 I4
Nanticoke r. U.S.A. 177 J7
Nanton Canada 167 H5
Nantong Jiangsu China 87 G1
Nantong Jiangsu China 87 G1
Nantou China 87 [inset]
Nant'ou Taiwan 87 G4
Nantucket U.S.A. 177 O4
Nantucket Island U.S.A. 177 P4
Nantucket Sound g. U.S.A. 177 O4
Nantulo Moz. 129 C8
Nanty Glo U.S.A. 176 G5
Nanumaga i. Tuvalu see Nanumanga
Nanumanga i. Tuvalu 145 G2
also spelt Nanumaga; formerly known as Hudson Island
Nanumea i. Tuvalu 145 G2
Nanuque Brazil 203 D6
Nanusa, Kepulauan is Indon. 75 C1
Nanutarra Roadhouse Australia 150 A4
Nanxi China 86 C2
Nanxian China 87 E2
also known as Nanzhou
Nanxiong China 87 E3
formerly known as Xiongzhou
Nanyandang Shan mt. China 87 G3
Nanyang China 87 E1
Nanyō Japan 90 G5
Nanyuki Kenya 128 C5
Nanzamu China 82 B4
Nanzhang China 87 D2
Nanzhao China see Zhao'an
Nanzhao China 87 E1
Nanzheng China 86 C1
also known as Zhoujiaping
Nanzhou China see Nanxian
Naogaon Bangl. 97 F4
Naokot Pak. 101 G5
Naoli r. China 82 D3
Naomid, Dasht-e des. Afgh./Iran 101 E3
Naousa Greece 58 D8
Napa U.S.A. 182 B3
Napak mt. Uganda 128 B4
Napaktulik Lake Canada 167 H1
also known as Takijuq Lake
Napanee Canada 168 E4
Napasar India 96 B4
Napasoq Greenland 165 N3
Naperville U.S.A. 174 B3
Napier N.Z. 152 K7
Napier S. Africa 132 D11
Napier Broome Bay Australia 150 D2
Napier Mountains Antarctica 223 D2
Napier Peninsula Australia 148 B2
Napier Range hills Australia 150 D3
Naples Italy 57 G8
also known as Napoli; historically known as Neapolis
Naples FL U.S.A. 175 D7
Naples ME U.S.A. 177 O2
Naples NY U.S.A. 177 H3
Naples UT U.S.A. 183 O1
Napo China 86 C4
Napo prov. Ecuador 198 B5
Napo r. Ecuador 198 C5
Napoleon ND U.S.A. 178 C2
Napoleon OH U.S.A. 176 A4
Napoleonville U.S.A. 175 B6
Napoli Italy see Naples
Napoli, Golfo di b. Italy 57 G8
Naposta Arg. 204 E5
Nappanee U.S.A. 172 H9
Napperby Australia 148 B4
Naqadeh Iran 100 A2
Naqb Malha mt. Egypt 108 D8
Naqūb Yemen 105 D5
Nara Japan 91 D7
Nara pref. Japan 90 D7
Nara Mali 124 D3
Nara r. Rus. Fed. 43 S7
Narach Belarus 42 H7
Narach r. Belarus 42 H7
Narach, Vozyera l. Belarus 42 H7
Naracoorte Australia 146 D4
Naradhan Australia 147 E3
Narail Bangl. 97 F5
Naraina India 96 B4
Naranbulag Dornod Mongolia 85 G1
Naranbulag Uvs Mongolia 84 B1
Narang Afgh. 101 G3
Naranjal Ecuador 198 B5
Naranjal Peru 198 C6
Naranjos Mex. 185 F4
Naran Sebstein Bulag spring China 84 C3
Narao Japan 91 A8
Naraq Iran 100 B3
Narasannapeta India 95 E2
Narasapatnam, Point India 94 D2
Narasapur India 94 D2
Narasaraopet India 94 D2
Narasinghapur India 95 E1
Narasun Rus. Fed. 85 G1
Narat China 88 D3
Narathiwat Thai. 79 C7
Narat Shan mts China 88 C3
Nara Visa U.S.A. 179 B5
Narayanganj Bangl. 97 F5
Narayanganj India 96 D5
Narayangaon India 94 B2
Narayanpet India 94 C2
Naray Kelay Afgh. 101 G3
Narbada r. India see Narmada
Narbo France see Narbonne
Narbonne France 51 J9
historically known as Narbo
Narbuvoll Norway 44 J3
Narcea r. Spain 54 E1
Narcondam Island India 95 G3
Nardin Iran 100 C2
Nardò Italy 57 K8
Nare Arg. 204 E3
Narechi r. Pak. 101 G4
Naregal India 94 B3
Narembeen Australia 151 B7
Nares Strait Canada/Greenland 165 L2
Naretha Australia 151 D6
Narew r. Poland 49 R3
Narewka r. Poland 42 E9
Nari r. Pak. 101 F4
Naria Bangl. 97 F5
Narib Namibia 130 C5
Narie, Jezioro l. Poland 49 R2
Nariep S. Africa 132 B7
Narimanov Rus. Fed. 102 A3
formerly known as Nizhnevolzhsk
Narimskiy Khrebet mts Kazakh. 88 D1
Narin Afgh. 101 G2
Narin reg. Afgh. 101 G2
Narin China 85 F4
Narince Turkey 107 D3
Narin Gol watercourse China 84 B4
Nariño dept Col. 198 B4
Narita Japan 91 G7
Nariu-misaki pt Japan 91 D7
Nariwa Japan 91 C7
Narizon, Punta pt Mex. 184 C3
Narkaus Fin. 44 N2
Narken Sweden 44 M2
Narmada r. India 96 B5
also known as Narbada
Narnaul India 96 C3
Narni Italy 56 E6
historically known as Narnia
Narnia Italy see Narni
Narodnaya, Gora mt. Rus. Fed. 40 L2
Naro-Fominsk Rus. Fed. 43 R6
Narok Kenya 128 B5
Narooma Australia 147 F4
Narowlya Belarus 41 D6
Närpes Fin. 44 M3
Narrabri Australia 147 F2
Narragansett Bay U.S.A. 177 N4
Narran r. Australia 147 E2
Narrandera Australia 147 E3
Narran Lake Australia 147 E2
Narrogin Australia 151 B7
Narromine Australia 147 F3
Narrow Hills Provincial Park Canada 167 J4
Narrows U.S.A. 176 E8
Narrowsburg U.S.A. 177 J4
Narsalik Greenland 165 O3
Narsapur India 94 C2
Narsaq Greenland 165 O3
Narsarsuaq Greenland 165 O3
Narsimhapur India 96 C5
Narsingdi Bangl. 97 F5
Narsinghgarh India 96 C5
Narsipatnam India 95 D2
Nart China 85 G3
Nart Mongolia 85 E1
Nartë Albania 58 A8
Nartkala Rus. Fed. 107 E2
formerly known as Dokshukino
Naruko Japan 90 G5
Naruto Japan 91 D7
Narva Estonia 43 J2
Narva r. Estonia/Rus. Fed. 42 J2
Narva Bay Estonia/Rus. Fed. 42 I2
also known as Narva laht or Narvskiy Zaliv
Narvacan Phil. 74 B2
Narva-Jõesuu Estonia 43 J2
Narva laht b. Estonia/Rus. Fed. see Narva Bay
Narva Reservoir Estonia/Rus. Fed. see Narvskoye Vodokhranilishche
Narva veehoidla resr Estonia/Rus. Fed. see Narvskoye Vodokhranilishche
Narvik Norway 44 L1
Narvskiy Zaliv b. Estonia/Rus. Fed. see Narva Bay
Narvskoye Vodokhranilishche resr Estonia/Rus. Fed. 43 J2
English form Narva Reservoir; also known as Narva veehoidla
Narwana India 96 C3
Narwar India 96 C4
Narwinbi Aboriginal Land res. Australia 148 C3
Nar'yan-Mar Rus. Fed. 40 J2
Naryn Kyrg. 103 H4
Naryn admin. div. Kyrg. 103 H4
English form Naryn Oblast; also known as Narynskaya Oblast'; formerly known as Tien Shan Oblast or Tyanshanskaya Oblast'
Naryn r. Kyrg./Uzbek. 103 H4
Naryn Rus. Fed. 84 B1
Narynkol Kazakh. 88 C3
also spelt Narynqol
Naryn Oblast admin. div. Kyrg. see Naryn
Narynqol Kazakh. see Narynkol
Narynskaya Oblast' admin. div. Kyrg. see Naryn
Naryshkino Rus. Fed. 43 Q9
Năsăud Romania 58 F1
Näsby Sweden 45 L4
Naseby N.Z. 153 E13
Nashik India 94 B1
also spelt Nasik
Nashua U.S.A. 177 N3
Nashville AR U.S.A. 179 D5
Nashville GA U.S.A. 175 D6
Nashville IL U.S.A. 174 B4
Nashville NC U.S.A. 174 E5
Nashville OH U.S.A. 176 C5

▶Nashville TN U.S.A. 174 C4
State capital of Tennessee.

Našice Croatia 56 K3
Nasielsk Poland 49 R3
Näsijärvi l. Fin. 45 M3
Nasik India see Nashik
Nasir Sudan 128 B2
Nasirabad Bangl. see Mymensingh
Nasirabad India 96 B4
Nasirabad Pak. 101 G4
Naskaupi r. Canada 169 I2
Nasmganj India 97 E4
Nasondoye Dem. Rep. Congo 127 E7
Nasonville U.S.A. 172 C6
Nasosnyy Azer. see Hacı Zeynalabdin
Nasr Egypt 108 B7
Naṣrābād Eṣfahān Iran 100 B3
Naṣrābād Khorāsan Iran 101 D3
Naṣrānī, Jabal an mts Syria 109 I4
Nasratabad Iran see Zābol
Naṣrīan-e-Pā'īn Iran 100 A3
Nass r. Canada 166 D4
Nassarawa Nigeria 125 G4
Nassarawa state Nigeria 125 H4
Nassau r. Australia 149 D2

▶Nassau Bahamas 186 D1
Capital of The Bahamas.

Nassau i. Cook Is 221 G6
formerly known as Mitchell Island
Nassau U.S.A. 177 L3
Nassau, Naturpark nature res. Germany 48 E5
Nassawadox U.S.A. 177 J8
Nasser, Lake resr Egypt 121 G4
Nassian Côte d'Ivoire 124 E4
Nässjö Sweden 45 K4
Nassuttooq inlet Greenland 165 N3
also known as Nordre Strømfjord
Nastapoca r. Canada 169 E1
Nastapoka Islands Canada 168 E1
Nastola Fin. 42 G1
Nasu-dake vol. Japan 90 F6
Nasugbu Phil. 74 B3
Nasva Rus. Fed. 43 L5
Nasva r. Rus. Fed. 43 L5
Nata Botswana 131 E4
Nata watercourse Botswana/Zimbabwe 131 E4
Natabu Indon. 75 C3
Natal Amazonas Brazil 201 E1
Natal Rio Grande do Norte Brazil 202 F3
Natal Indon. 76 B2
Natal prov. S. Africa see Kwazulu-Natal
Natal Drakensberg National Park S. Africa 133 N6
Natanz Iran 100 B3
Natashquan Canada 169 I3
Natashquan r. Canada 169 I3
Natchez U.S.A. 175 B6
Natchitoches U.S.A. 179 D6
Nathalia Australia 147 E4
Nathana India 96 B3
Nathdwara India 96 B4
Nati, Punta pt Spain 55 O4
Natiaboani Burkina 125 F4
National City U.S.A. 183 G9
National Park N.Z. 152 J7
National West Coast Tourist Recreation Area park Namibia 130 B4
Natitingou Benin 125 F4
Natividad, Isla i. Mex. 184 B3
Natividade Rio de Janeiro Brazil 207 L8
Natividade Tocantins Brazil 202 C4
Natla r. Canada 166 D2
Natmauk Myanmar 78 A3
Natogyi Myanmar 78 A3
Nator Bangl. 97 F4
Nátora Mex. 181 E7
Natori Japan 90 G5
Natron, Lake salt l. Tanz. 128 C5
Nattai National Park Australia 147 F3
Nattalin Myanmar 78 A4
Nattam India 94 C4
Nattaung mt. Myanmar 78 B4
Nattavaara Sweden 44 M2
Natū Iran 101 E3
Natuna, Kepulauan is Indon. 77 D1
also known as Bunguran, Kepulauan
Natuna Besar i. Indon. 77 E1
also known as Bunguran, Pulau
Natural Bridge U.S.A. 176 F8
Natural Bridges National Monument nat. park U.S.A. 183 N4
Naturaliste, Cape Australia 151 A7
Naturaliste Channel Australia 151 A5
Nature's Valley S. Africa 132 H10
Nau Tajik. see Nov
Naubinway U.S.A. 172 H4
Naucelle France 51 I8
Nauchas Namibia 130 C4
Nau Co l. China 89 C5
Naudesberg Pass S. Africa 133 I9
Nauen Germany 49 J3
Naugatuck U.S.A. 177 L4
Nau Hissar Pak. 101 F4
Naujan Phil. 74 B3
Naujoji Akmenė Lith. 42 D5
Naukh India 96 B4
Naulila Angola 127 B9
Naumburg (Saale) Germany 48 I4
Naungpale Myanmar 78 B4
Na'ūr Jordan 106 C5
Naurskaya Rus. Fed. 107 F2
Nauru i. Nauru 145 F2
▶Nauru country S. Pacific Ocean 145 F2
oceania [countries] ▶ 138–139
Naushahro Firoz Pak. 101 G5
Naushara Pak. 101 G5
Naushki Rus. Fed. 85 E1
Naustdal Norway 45 I3
Nauta Peru 198 C6
Nautaca Uzbek. see Karshi
Naute Dam Namibia 132 B3
Nautla Mex. 185 F4
Nautonwa India 97 D4
Nautsi Rus. Fed. 44 O1
Nauvoo U.S.A. 172 B10
Nava r. Dem. Rep. Congo 126 E4
Navabad Tajik. see Novobod
Navacerrada, Puerto de pass Spain 54 H4
Navachica mt. Spain 54 H8
Navadrutsk Belarus 42 I6
Navadwip India 97 F5
formerly spelt Nabadwip
Navahermosa Spain 54 G5
Navahrudak Belarus 42 G8
also spelt Novogrudok
Navahrudskaye Wzvyshsha hills Belarus 42 G8
Navajo r. U.S.A. 181 F5
Navajo Indian Reservation res. U.S.A. 183 O6
Navajo Lake U.S.A. 181 F5
Navajo Mountain U.S.A. 183 N4
Naval Phil. 74 C4
Navalmoral de la Mata Spain 54 F5
Navalvillar de Pela Spain 54 F5
Navan Rep. of Ireland 47 F10
also known as An Uaimh
Navangar India see Jamnagar
Navapolatsk Belarus 43 J6
also spelt Novopolotsk
Navarin, Mys c. Rus. Fed. 39 R3
Navarino, Isla i. Chile 205 D9
Navarra aut. comm. Spain 55 J2
English form Navarre
Navarre aut. comm. Spain see Navarra
Navarrenx France 50 F9
Navarro Peru 198 C6
Navarro r. U.S.A. 182 A2
Navashino Rus. Fed. 40 G5
Navasota U.S.A. 179 C6
Navasota r. U.S.A. 179 C6

▶Navassa Island terr. West Indies 187 E3
United States Unincorporated Territory.
oceania [countries] ▶ 138–139

Navasyolki Belarus 43 J9
Navayel'nya Belarus 42 G8
Naver r. U.K. 46 H5
Navesnoye Rus. Fed. 43 S9
Navesti r. Estonia 42 F3
Navia Spain 54 E1
Navia r. Spain 54 E1
Navidad Chile 204 C4
Navidad r. U.S.A. 179 C6
Naviraí Brazil 203 A7
Navlakhi India 96 A5
Navlya Rus. Fed. 43 P9
Navlya r. Rus. Fed. 43 P9
Năvodari Romania 58 J4
Navoi Uzbek. 103 F4
also spelt Nawoiy; formerly known as Kermine
Navoiyskaya Oblast' admin. div. Uzbek. 103 E4
English form Navoy Oblast; also known as Nawoiy Wiloyati
Navojoa Mex. 184 C3
Navolato Mex. 184 D3
Navoy Oblast admin. div. Uzbek. see Navoiyskaya Oblast'
Návpaktos Greece see Nafpaktos
Návplion Greece see Nafplio
Nävragöl Sweden 45 K4
Navrongo Ghana 125 E4
Navşar Turkey see Şemdinli
Navsari India 94 B1
Navua Fiji 145 G3
Nawa India 96 B4
Nawá Syria 108 H5
Nawabganj Bangl. 97 F4
Nawabganj India 97 D4
Nawabshah Pak. 101 G5
Nawada India 97 E4
Nāwah Afgh. 101 F3
Nawakot Nepal 97 E4
Nawalgarh India 96 B4
Nawar, Dasht-i- imp. l. Afgh. 101 F3
Nawashahr India 89 B6
Nawāṣīf, Ḥarrāt lava field Saudi Arabia 104 C3
Nawnghkio Myanmar 78 B3
Nawngleng Myanmar 78 B3
Nawoiy Uzbek. see Navoi
Nawoiy Wiloyati admin. div. Uzbek. see Navoiyskaya Oblast'
Naws, Ra's c. Oman 105 F4
Naxçıvan Azer. 107 F3
also spelt Nakhichevan'
Naxi China 86 C2
Naxos Greece 59 G11
Naxos i. Greece 59 G11
Naya Col. 198 B4
Nayagarh India 95 E1
Nayak Afgh. 101 F3
Nayarit state Mex. 184 D4
Nāy Band, Kūh-e mt. Iran 100 D3
Nayfah oasis Saudi Arabia 105 E4
Nayong China 86 C3
also known as Yongxi
Nayoro Japan 90 H2
Nayt Yemen 105 F5
Nayuchi Malawi 129 B8
Nayudupeta India 94 C3
Nayyāl, Wādī watercourse Saudi Arabia 104 B1
Nazare Brazil 199 E4
Nazaré Brazil 199 H6
Nazareno Mex. 184 E3
Nazareth India 94 C4
Nazareth Israel 108 G5
Nazareth U.S.A. 177 J5
Nazário Brazil 206 D3
Nazas Mex. 184 D3
Nazas r. Mex. 184 D3
Nazca Peru 200 B3
Nāzīk Iran 100 A2
Nazilli Turkey 106 B3
Nazımiye Turkey 107 D3
Nazinon r. Burkina/Ghana 125 E4 see Red Volta
Nazira India 97 G4
Nazir Hat Bangl. 97 F5
Naziya Rus. Fed. 43 M2
Nazko Canada 166 F4
Nazko r. Canada 166 F4
Nazran' Rus. Fed. 41 H8
formerly known as Kosta-Khetagurovo
Nazrēt Eth. 128 C2
Nazwá Oman 105 G3
also spelt Nizwá
Nazyvayevsk Rus. Fed. 38 H4
formerly known as Novonazyvayevka
Nbâk Mauritania 124 B2
Ncanaha S. Africa 133 J10
Nchelenge Zambia 127 F7
Ncheu Malawi see Ntcheu
Ncora S. Africa 133 L8
Ncue Equat. Guinea 125 H6
Ndala Tanz. 129 B6
N'dalatando Angola 127 B7
formerly known as Salazar or Vila Salazar; formerly spelt Dalatando
Ndali Benin 125 F4
Ndanda Cent. Afr. Rep. 126 D3
Ndao i. Indon. 75 B5
Ndareda Tanz. 129 B6
Ndélé Cent. Afr. Rep. 126 D2
Ndélélé Cameroon 125 I5
Ndendé Gabon 126 A5
Ndende i. Solomon Is see Ndeni
Ndeni i. Solomon Is 145 F3
also spelt Ndende or Nitendi
Ndiael, Réserve de Faune du nature res. Senegal 124 A2
Ndikiniméki Cameroon 125 H5
Ndim Cent. Afr. Rep. 126 B3
N'Djamena Chad see Ndjamena

▶Ndjamena Chad 120 B6
Capital of Chad. Also spelt N'Djamena; formerly known as Fort Lamy.

Ndji r. Cent. Afr. Rep. 126 D3
Ndjim r. Cameroon 125 H5
Ndjolé Gabon 126 A5
Ndjouani i. Comoros see Nzwani
Ndjounou Gabon 126 B5
Ndofane Senegal 124 B3
Ndogo, Lagune lag. Gabon 126 A5
Ndoi i. Fiji see Doi
Ndok Cameroon 125 I5
Ndola Zambia 127 F8
Ndoto mt. Kenya 128 C4
Ndougou Gabon 126 A5
Nduke i. Solomon Is see Kolombangara
Ndumbwe Tanz. 129 C7
Ndumu S. Africa 133 Q3
Ndumu Game Reserve nature res. Moz. 133 Q3
Nduye Dem. Rep. Congo 126 F4
Ndwedwe S. Africa 133 O6
Nea Anchialos Greece 59 D9
Nea Apollonia Greece 58 E8
Nea Artaki Greece 59 E10
Neabul Creek r. Australia 147 E1
Neagh, Lough l. U.K. 47 F9
Neah Bay U.S.A. 180 A2
Neajlov r. Romania 58 G4
Nea Karvali Greece 58 F8
Neale, Lake salt flat Australia 148 A5
Neale Junction Nature Reserve Australia 151 D6
Neales watercourse Australia 146 C2
Nea Liosia Greece 59 E10
Nea Makri Greece 59 E10
Nea Moudania Greece 59 E8
Neamț r. Romania 58 H1
Nea Peramos Greece 58 F8
Neapoli Kriti Greece 59 G13
Neapoli Peloponnisos Greece 59 E12
Neapolis Italy see Naples
Nea Roda Greece 59 E8
Nea Santa Greece 58 D8
Neath U.K. 47 I12
also known as Castell-nedd
Nea Zichni Greece 58 E7
Nebbi Uganda 128 A4
Nebbou Burkina 125 E4
Nebesnaya, Gora mt. Rus. Fed. 88 C3
Nebine Creek r. Australia 147 E2
Nebitdag Turkm. 102 C5
Nebo Australia 149 F4
Nebo, Mount U.S.A. 183 M2
Nebolchi Rus. Fed. 43 O2
Nebraska state U.S.A. 178 B3
Nebraska City U.S.A. 178 D3
Nebrodi, Monti mts Sicilia Italy 57 G11
Nebyloye Rus. Fed. 43 U5
Necedah U.S.A. 172 C6
Necedah National Wildlife Refuge nature res. U.S.A. 172 C6
Neches r. U.S.A. 179 D6
Nechí r. Col. 198 C2
Nechisar National Park Eth. 128 C3
Neckarsulm Germany 48 G6
Neckartal-Odenwald, Naturpark nature res. Germany 48 G6
Necker Island U.S.A. 221 H4
Necochea Arg. 204 F5
Necoclí Col. 198 B2
Nedelino Bulg. 58 G7
Nedelišće Croatia 56 I2
Nedel'noye Rus. Fed. 43 R7
Nederland country Europe see Netherlands
Nederlandse Antillen terr. West Indies see Netherlands Antilles
Neder Rijn r. Neth. 48 C4
Nedlouc, Lac l. Canada 169 F1
also known as Nedluk Lake
Nedluk Lake Canada see Nedlouc, Lac
Nédong China 89 E6
Nedre Soppero Sweden 44 M1
Nédroma Alg. 55 J9
Nedstrand Norway 45 I4
Needham U.S.A. 177 N3
Needles U.S.A. 183 J7
Neemuch India 96 B4
Neemuch India see Nimach
Neenah U.S.A. 172 E6
Neepawa Canada 167 L5
Neergaard Lake Canada 165 K2
Nefta Tunisia 123 G2
Neftçala Azer. 107 G3
also spelt Neftechala
Neftechala Azer. see 26 Bakı Komissarı
Neftechala Azer. see Neftçala
Neftegorsk Sakhalin Rus. Fed. 82 F1
formerly known as Vostok
Neftegorsk Samarskaya Oblast' Rus. Fed. 102 B1
Neftekamsk Rus. Fed. 40 J4
formerly known as Kasevo
Neftekumsk Rus. Fed. 41 H7
Nefteyugansk Rus. Fed. 38 H3
formerly known as Ust'-Balyk
Neftezavodsk Turkm. see Seydi
Nefza Tunisia 57 B11
Negada Weyn well Eth. 128 E3
Negage Angola 127 B6
Négala Mali 124 C3
Negār Iran 100 D4
Negara Bali Indon. 77 F5
Negara Kalimantan Selatan Indon. 77 F3
Negara r. Indon. 77 F3
Negaunee U.S.A. 172 F4
Negēlē Oromīa Eth. 128 C3
Negēlē Oromīa Eth. 128 C3
Negeri Sembilan state Malaysia 76 C2
formerly spelt Negri Sembilan
Negev des. Israel 108 G7
also spelt HaNegev
Negomane Moz. 129 C7
Negombo Sri Lanka 94 C5
Negotin Srbija Yugo. 58 D4
Negotino Macedonia 58 D7
Negra, Cordillera mts Peru 200 A2
Negra, Lago l. Uruguay 204 G4
also known as Los Difuntos, Lago de
Negra, Punta pt Peru 198 A6
Negra, Serra mts Brazil 203 D6
Negra, Serranía de mts Bol. 201 E3
Negrais, Cape Myanmar 78 A5
Negratín, Embalse de resr Spain 55 I7
Negreira Spain 54 C2
Negreiros Chile 200 C4
Nègrepelisse France 50 H8
Negrești Romania 58 I2
Negri r. Australia 148 A3
Negri Romania 58 H2
Négrine Alg. 123 G2
Negri Sembilan state Malaysia see Negeri Sembilan
Negritos Peru 198 A6
Negro r. Arg. 204 E6
Negro r. Brazil 201 F4
Negro r. Para. 201 F6
Negro r. S. America 199 G5
Negro r. Uruguay 204 G4
Negro, Cabo c. Morocco 54 F9
Negroponte i. Greece see Evvoia
Negros i. Phil. 74 B4
Negru Vodă Romania 58 J5
Nehalem r. U.S.A. 180 B3
Nehavand Iran 100 B3
Nehbandān Iran 101 E4
Nehe China 85 J1
Nehoiu Romania 58 H3
Nehone Angola 127 C9
Neiafu Tonga 145 H3
Neiba Dom. Rep. 187 F3
Neijiang China 86 C2
Neilersdrif S. Africa 132 E5
Neill Island India 95 G4
Neillsville U.S.A. 172 C6
Nei Mongol Zizhiqu aut. reg. China 85 D3
English form Inner Mongolia
Neiqiu China 85 G4
Neiße r. Germany/Poland 49 L3
also known as Nysa Łużycka
Neiva Col. 198 C4
Neixiang China 87 D1
Nejanilini Lake Canada 167 L3
Nejapa Mex. 185 G5
Nejd reg. Saudi Arabia see Najd
Neka Iran 100 C2
Neka r. Iran 100 C2
Nek'emtē Eth. 128 C2
Nekhayevskaya Rus. Fed. 41 G6
formerly known as Nekhayevskiy
Nekhayevskiy Rus. Fed. see Nekhayevskaya
Neklyudovo Rus. Fed. 43 V6
Nekrasovskiy Rus. Fed. 43 S5
Nekrasovskoye Rus. Fed. 43 V4
Nekse Denmark 45 K5
Nela r. Spain 54 H2
Nelamangala India 94 C3
Nelas Port. 54 D4
Nelazskoye Rus. Fed. 43 S2
Nelia Australia 149 D4
Nelidovo Rus. Fed. 43 N5
Neligh U.S.A. 178 C3
Nel'kan Khabarovskiy Kray Rus. Fed. 39 N4
Nel'kan Respublika Sakha (Yakutiya) Rus. Fed. 39 O3
Nellie Lake Canada 173 M2
Nellim Fin. 44 O1
also spelt Njellim
Nellore India 94 C3
Nelluz watercourse Turkey 109 K1
Nelshoogte pass S. Africa 133 O2
Nelson Arg. 204 E3
Nelson Canada 166 G5
Nelson r. Canada 167 M3
Nelson N.Z. 152 H9
Nelson admin. reg. N.Z. 152 H9
Nelson AZ U.S.A. 183 K6
Nelson NE U.S.A. 178 C3
Nelson NV U.S.A. 183 J6
Nelson, Cape Australia 146 D4
Nelson, Estrecho strait Chile 205 B8
Nelson Bay Australia 147 G3
Nelson Creek N.Z. 153 F10
Nelson Forks Canada 166 F3
Nelson House Canada 167 L4
Nelson Lakes National Park N.Z. 153 G10
Nelspoort S. Africa 132 H9
Nelspruit S. Africa 133 O2
Nem r. Rus. Fed. 40 J3
Néma Mauritania 124 D2
Nema Rus. Fed. 40 I4
Nemadji r. U.S.A. 172 A4
Neman r. Belarus/Lith. see Nyoman
Neman Rus. Fed. 42 D6
Neman r. Rus. Fed. 42 D6
Ne'matābād Iran 100 D4
Nemausus France see Nîmes
Nembe Nigeria 125 G5
Nemda r. Rus. Fed. 40 G4
Nemea Greece 59 D11
Nemed Rus. Fed. 40 J3
Nemegos Canada 173 J3
Nemegosenda Lake Canada 173 J2
Nemenčinė Lith. 42 G7
Nemetocenna France see Arras
Nemetskiy, Mys c. Rus. Fed. 44 O1
Nemirov Ukr. see Nemyriv
Némiscau r. Canada 168 E3
Nemor r. China 85 J1
Nemours Alg. see Ghazaouet
Nemours France 51 I4
Nemrut Dağı mt. Turkey 107 E3
Nemta r. Rus. Fed. 42 C6
Nemunas r. Lith. 42 C6
Nemunėlio Radviliškis Lith. 42 F5
Nemunėlis r. Lith. 42 G5
Nemuro Japan 90 I3
Nemuro-hantō pen. Japan 90 I3
Nemuro-kaikyō sea chan. Japan/Rus. Fed. 90 I3
also known as Kunashirskiy Proliv
Nemuro-wan b. Japan 90 I3
Nemyriv Ukr. 41 D6
also spelt Nemirov
Nenagh Rep. of Ireland 47 D11
also known as An tAonach
Nenana U.S.A. 164 E3
Nenashevo Rus. Fed. 43 S7
Nene r. U.K. 47 M11
Nenets Autonomous Okrug admin. div. Rus. Fed. see Nenetskiy Avtonomnyy Okrug
Nenetskiy Avtonomnyy Okrug admin. div. Rus. Fed. 40 J2
English form Nenets Autonomous Okrug
Nenjiang China 85 J1
Nen Jiang r. China 85 J2
also known as Nonni
Neo Japan 91 E7
Neochori Greece 59 C9
also known as Neokhórion
Neo Karlovasi Greece 59 H11
also known as Néon Karlovásion
Neokhórion Greece see Neochori
Neola U.S.A. 183 N1
Neo Monastiri Greece 59 D9
Néon Karlovásion Greece see Neo Karlovasi
Neopit U.S.A. 172 E6
Neosho U.S.A. 178 D4
Neosho r. U.S.A. 178 D4
Neos Marmaras Greece 59 E8
▶Nepal country Asia 97 D3
asia [countries] ▶ 64–67
Nepalganj Nepal 97 D3
Nepanagar India 96 C5
Nepean Canada 168 F4
Nephi U.S.A. 183 M2
Nephin hill Rep. of Ireland 47 C9
Nephin Beg Range hills Rep. of Ireland 47 C9
Nepisiguit r. Canada 169 H4
Nepryadva r. Rus. Fed. 43 T8
Neptune U.S.A. 177 K5
Ner r. Poland 49 P3
Nera r. Italy 56 E6
Nérac France 50 G8
Neral India 94 B2
Nerang Australia 147 G1
Nera Tso l. Xizang China 89 F6
Neravai Lith. 42 F7
Nerchinsk Rus. Fed. 85 H1
Nerchinskiy Zavod Rus. Fed. 85 H1
Nereju Romania 58 H3
Nerekhta Rus. Fed. 43 V4
Nereta Latvia 42 G5
Neretva r. Bos.-Herz./Croatia 56 J5
Neretvanski Kanal sea chan. Croatia 56 J5
Neri India 94 C1
Nêri Pünco l. China 89 E6
Neriquinha Angola 127 D8
Neris r. Lith. 42 E7

Nerka, Lake U.S.A. 164 D4
Nerl' r. Ivanovskaya Oblast' Rus. Fed. 43 V5
Nerl' Tverskaya Oblast' Rus. Fed. 43 T4
Nerl' r. Rus. Fed. 43 S4
Nero, Ozero l. Rus. Fed. 43 U4
Nerópolis Brazil 206 D3
Neroyka, Gora mt. Rus. Fed. 40 K2
Ner Pinglai India 96 C5
Neruch' r. Rus. Fed. 43 R9
Nerussa r. Rus. Fed. 43 O9
Neryungri Rus. Fed. 39 M4
Nes Norway 45 J3
Nes' Rus. Fed. 40 H2
Nes' r. Rus. Fed. 40 H2
Nes' Iran 100 B2
Nesbyen Norway 45 J3
Nesebūr Bulg. 58 I6
Neskaupstaður Iceland 44 [inset] D2
Nesna Norway 44 K4
Nesque r. France 51 K8
Nesri India 94 B2
Ness, Loch l. U.K. 46 H6
Ness City U.S.A. 178 C4
Nesse r. Germany 48 H5
Nesselrode, Mount Canada/U.S.A. 166 C3
Nesselwang Germany 48 H8
Neste r. France 50 G9
Nesterov Rus. Fed. 42 D7
Nesterovo Rus. Fed. 43 O7
Nestery Rus. Fed. 43 O7
Nestore r. Italy 56 E6
Nestor Falls Canada 168 A3
Nestoria U.S.A. 172 E4
Nestos r. Greece 58 F8
also known as Mesta
Nesvizh Belarus see Nyasvizh
Netanya Israel 108 F5
Netarhat India 97 E5
Netcong U.S.A. 177 K5
▶Netherlands country Europe 48 J3
also known as Holland; known as Nederland in Dutch
europe [countries] ▶▶▶ 32–35
▶Netherlands Antilles terr. West Indies 187 F4
Self-governing Netherlands Territory. Also known as Nederlandse Antillen; formerly known as Dutch West Indies.
oceania [countries] ▶▶▶ 138–139
Neto r. Italy 57 J9
Netrakona Bangl. 97 F4
Netrang India 96 B5
Nettilling Lake Canada 165 L3
Nettuno Italy 56 E7
Neubari r. Sudan 128 B3
Neubrandenburg Germany 49 K2
Neubukow Germany 48 I1
Neuburg an der Donau Germany 48 I7
Neuchâtel Switz. 51 M6
Neuchâtel, Lac de l. Switz. 51 M6
Neuenhagen Berlin Germany 49 K3
Neuenkirchen Germany 48 I4
Neuenkirchen-Seelscheid Germany 48 E5
Neufchâteau Belgium 51 L5
Neufchâteau France 51 L4
Neufchâtel-en-Bray France 50 H3
Neuhausen Rus. Fed. see Gur'yevsk
Neuillé-Pont-Pierre France 50 G5
Neukuhren Rus. Fed. see Pionerskiy
Neumarkt in der Oberpfalz Germany 48 I6
Neumayer research station Antarctica 223 X2
long form Georg von Neumayer
Neumünster Germany 48 G1
Neun, Nam r. Laos 78 D4
Neunkirchen Austria 49 N8
Neunkirchen Germany 48 E6
Neuquén Arg. 204 C5
Neuquén prov. Arg. 204 C5
Neuquén r. Arg. 204 D5
Neuruppin Germany 49 J3
Neu Sandez Poland see Nowy Sącz
Neuse r. U.S.A. 174 E5
Neusiedl am See Austria 49 N8
Neusiedler See l. Austria/Hungary 49 N8
Neusiedler See Seewinkel, Nationalpark nat. park Austria 49 N8
Neuss Germany 48 D4
Neustadt (Wied) Germany 48 E5
Neustadt an der Rübenberge Germany 48 G3
Neustadt an der Aisch Germany 48 H6
Neustadt an der Hardt Germany see Neustadt an der Weinstraße
Neustadt an der Weinstraße Germany 48 F6
formerly known as Neustadt an der Hardt
Neustadt in Holstein Germany 48 H1
Neustadt in Sachsen Germany 49 L4
Neustift im Stubaital Austria 56 D1
Neustrelitz Germany 49 K2
Neuves-Maisons France 51 M4
Neuville-aux-Bois France 51 I4
Neuville-lès-Dieppe France 50 H3
Neuwerk i. Germany 48 F1
Neuwied Germany 48 E5
Nevada IA U.S.A. 174 A3
Nevada MO U.S.A. 178 D4
Nevada state U.S.A. 183 G2
Nevada, Sierra mts. Arg. 204 C2
Nevada, Sierra mts Spain 205 H7
Nevada, Sierra nature res. Spain 55 H7
Nevada, Sierra mts U.S.A. 182 C1
Nevada City U.S.A. 182 C2
Nevado, Cerro mt. Arg. 204 C4
Nevado de Colima, Parque Nacional nat. park Mex. 184 E5
Nevado de Toluca, Parque Nacional nat. park Mex. 185 F5
Nevasa India 94 B2
Nevdol'sk Rus. Fed. 43 P9
Nevdubstroy Rus. Fed. see Kirovsk
Neve, Serra da mts Angola 127 B8
Nevel' Rus. Fed. 43 K5

Nevel', Ozero l. Rus. Fed. 43 K6
Nevel'sk Rus. Fed. 82 F3
Neverkino Rus. Fed. 41 H5
Neveronys Lith. 42 F7
Nevers France 51 J5
Nevertire Australia 147 E2
Neves Brazil 207 J9
Nevėžis r. Lith. 42 E6
Nevinnomyssk Rus. Fed. 41 G7
Nevis i. St Kitts and Nevis 187 H3
Nevşehir Turkey 106 C3
Nevskoye Rus. Fed. 43 K5
New r. CA U.S.A. 183 I8
New r. WV U.S.A. 176 D8
New Aiyansh Canada 166 D4
Newala Tanz. 129 C7
New Albany IN U.S.A. 174 C4
New Albany MS U.S.A. 174 B5
Newald U.S.A. 172 E5
New Amsterdam Guyana 199 G3
New Angledool Australia 147 E2
Newark CA U.S.A. 182 B4
Newark DE U.S.A. 177 J6
Newark NJ U.S.A. 177 K5
Newark NY U.S.A. 177 I2
Newark OH U.S.A. 176 C5
Newark airport U.S.A. 177 K5
Newark Lake U.S.A. 183 I2
Newark-on-Trent U.K. 47 L10
Newark Valley U.S.A. 177 I3
New Augusta U.S.A. 175 B6
Newaygo U.S.A. 172 H7
New Bedford U.S.A. 177 O4
Newberg U.S.A. 180 B3
New Berlin U.S.A. 177 J3
New Bern U.S.A. 174 E5
Newberry MI U.S.A. 172 H4
Newberry SC U.S.A. 175 D5
Newberry National Volcanic Monument nat. park U.S.A. 180 B4
Newberry Springs U.S.A. 183 H7
New Bethlehem U.S.A. 176 F4
New Bight Bahamas 187 E1
New Bloomfield U.S.A. 177 H5
Newboro Canada 168 E4
New Boston IL U.S.A. 172 C9
New Boston OH U.S.A. 176 C7
New Boston TX U.S.A. 179 D5
New Braunfels U.S.A. 179 C6
New Brighton U.K. 47 I10
New Brighton U.S.A. 176 E5
New Britain i. P.N.G. 145 D2
New Britain U.S.A. 177 M4
New Brunswick prov. Canada 169 H4
New Brunswick U.S.A. 177 K5
New Buffalo U.S.A. 172 G9
Newburg U.S.A. 176 H5
Newburgh Canada 173 Q6
Newburgh U.K. 46 J6
Newburgh U.S.A. 177 K4
Newbury U.K. 47 K12
Newburyport U.S.A. 177 O3
▶New Caledonia i. S. Pacific Ocean see Nouvelle-Calédonie
▶New Caledonia terr. S. Pacific Ocean 145 F4
French Overseas Territory. Also known as Nouvelle Calédonie.
oceania [countries] ▶▶▶ 138–139
oceania [features] ▶▶▶ 142–143
New Carlisle Canada 169 H3
Newcastle Australia 147 F3
Newcastle N.B. Canada 169 H4
Newcastle Ont. Canada 168 E5
Newcastle S. Africa 133 N4
Newcastle U.K. 47 G9
Newcastle CA U.S.A. 182 C3
New Castle DE U.S.A. 177 J6
New Castle IN U.S.A. 174 C4
New Castle KY U.S.A. 174 C4
Newcastle ME U.S.A. 177 P1
New Castle PA U.S.A. 176 E4
New Castle UT U.S.A. 183 K4
Newcastle VA U.S.A. 176 E8
Newcastle WY U.S.A. 180 F4
Newcastle Creek r. Australia 148 B3
Newcastle Emlyn U.K. 47 H11
also known as Castell Newydd Emlyn
Newcastle Range hills Australia 149 D3
Newcastle-under-Lyme U.K. 47 J10
Newcastle upon Tyne U.K. 47 K9
New Church U.S.A. 177 J8
Newchwang China see Yingkou
New City U.S.A. 177 L4
Newcomerstown U.S.A. 176 D5
New Concord U.S.A. 176 D6
Newdegate Australia 151 B7
▶New Delhi India 96 C3
Capital of India.
New Don Pedro Reservoir U.S.A. 182 D4
Newell, Lake salt flat Australia 151 D5
Newell, Lake Canada 167 I5
New England Range mts Australia 147 F2
Newenham, Cape U.S.A. 164 C4
New Era U.S.A. 172 G7
New Falls U.S.A. 176 G3
Newfound Lake U.S.A. 177 N2
Newfoundland i. Canada 169 J3
historically known as Vinland
Newfoundland prov. Canada 169 H3
Newfoundland U.S.A. 177 J4
Newfoundland Evaporation Basin salt l. U.S.A. 183 K1
New Freedom U.S.A. 177 I6
New Galloway U.K. 47 H8
New Georgia i. Solomon Is 145 E2
New Georgia Islands Solomon Is. 145 E2
New Georgia Sound sea chan. Solomon Is. 145 E2
also known as The Slot
New Glarus U.S.A. 172 D8
New Glasgow Canada 169 I4
Newgrange Tomb tourist site Rep. of Ireland 47 F10
▶New Guinea i. Indon./P.N.G. 73 J8
Largest island in Oceania and 2nd in the world.
oceania [landscapes] ▶▶▶ 136–137
New Halfa Sudan 121 G6
Newhall U.S.A. 182 F7
New Hampshire state U.S.A. 177 N1
New Hanover i. P.N.G. 145 E2
New Hanover S. Africa 133 O6
New Hartford U.S.A. 177 J2
New Haven CT U.S.A. 177 M4
New Haven IN U.S.A. 173 H9
New Haven MI U.S.A. 173 K8
New Haven WV U.S.A. 176 C6
New Hazelton Canada 166 E4
New Hebrides country S. Pacific Ocean see Vanuatu
New Hogan Reservoir U.S.A. 182 D3
New Holland country Oceania see Australia
New Holland U.S.A. 177 I5
New Iberia U.S.A. 175 B6
Newington S. Africa 133 P1
New Ireland i. P.N.G. 145 E2
New Jersey state U.S.A. 177 K6
New Kandla India 96 A5
New Kensington U.S.A. 176 F5
New Kent U.S.A. 177 H8
Newkirk U.S.A. 178 C4
New Lanark tourist site U.K. 46 I8
Newland Range hills Australia 151 C6
New Lexington U.S.A. 176 C6
New Lisbon U.S.A. 172 C7
New Liskeard Canada 168 E4

New London CT U.S.A. 177 M4
New London IA U.S.A. 172 B10
New London OH U.S.A. 176 C4
New London WI U.S.A. 172 E6
New Madrid U.S.A. 174 B4
Newman Australia 150 B4
Newman U.S.A. 182 C4
Newman Island Antarctica 222 O1
Newmarket Canada 168 E4
Newmarket Rep. of Ireland 47 C11
Newmarket U.K. 47 M11
Newmarket U.S.A. 177 O2
New Market TN U.S.A. 174 B9
New Market VA U.S.A. 176 G7
Newmarket-on-Fergus Rep. of Ireland 47 D11
New Martinsville U.S.A. 176 E6
New Meadows U.S.A. 180 C3
New Mexico state U.S.A. 181 F6
New Miami U.S.A. 176 A6
New Milford CT U.S.A. 177 L4
New Milford PA U.S.A. 177 J4
Newnan U.S.A. 175 C5
New Norcia Australia 151 B6
New Norfolk Australia 147 E5
New Orleans U.S.A. 175 B6
New Oxford U.S.A. 177 H6
New Paltz U.S.A. 177 K4
New Paris IN U.S.A. 172 H9
New Paris OH U.S.A. 176 A6
New Philadelphia U.S.A. 176 D5
New Plymouth N.Z. 152 I7
Newport Isle of Wight, England U.K. 47 K13
Newport Newport, Wales U.K. 47 I12
also known as Casnewydd
Newport DE U.S.A. 177 J6
Newport IN U.S.A. 174 C4
Newport ME U.S.A. 177 P1
Newport NH U.S.A. 177 M2
Newport NJ U.S.A. 177 J6
Newport OR U.S.A. 180 A3
Newport PA U.S.A. 177 H5
Newport RI U.S.A. 177 N4
Newport TN U.S.A. 174 D5
Newport VT U.S.A. 177 M1
Newport Beach U.S.A. 182 G8
Newport News U.S.A. 177 I8
New Port Richey U.S.A. 175 D6
New Providence i. Bahamas 186 D1
Newquay U.K. 47 G13
New Richmond Canada 169 H3
New Richmond U.S.A. 172 A5
New River U.S.A. 183 L8
New Roads U.S.A. 175 B6
New Rockford U.S.A. 178 C2
New Ross Canada 169 H4
New Ross Rep. of Ireland 47 F11
Newry Australia 148 A3
Newry U.K. 47 F9
Newry U.S.A. 172 C7
New Sharon U.S.A. 174 A3
New Siberia Islands Rus. Fed. 39 O2
also known as Novosibirskiye Ostrova
New Smyrna Beach U.S.A. 175 D6
New South Wales state Australia 147 E3
New Stanton U.S.A. 176 F5
New Tazewell U.S.A. 176 B9
Newton GA U.S.A. 175 C6
Newton IA U.S.A. 174 A3
Newton IL U.S.A. 174 B4
Newton KS U.S.A. 178 C4
Newton MA U.S.A. 177 N3
Newton MS U.S.A. 175 B5
Newton NJ U.S.A. 177 K4
Newton TX U.S.A. 179 D6
Newton Abbot U.K. 47 I13
Newton Falls U.S.A. 176 E4
Newton Stewart U.K. 47 H9
Newtontoppen mt. Svalbard 38 B2
Newtown U.K. 47 I11
also known as Y Drenewydd
New Town U.S.A. 178 B1
Newtown U.S.A. 177 K5
Newtownabbey U.K. 47 G9
Newtownards U.K. 47 G9
Newtownbarry Rep. of Ireland see Bunclody
Newtownbutler U.K. 47 E9
Newtown St Boswells U.K. 46 J8
Newtownstewart U.K. 47 E9
New Ulm U.S.A. 178 D2
New Vienna U.S.A. 176 B6
Newville U.S.A. 176 H5
New Vineyard U.S.A. 177 O1
New Woodstock U.S.A. 177 J3
▶New York U.S.A. 177 L5
2nd most populous city in North America and 5th in the world.
world [land cover] ▶▶▶ 18–19
world [cities] ▶▶▶ 24–25
New York state U.S.A. 177 J2
New York Mountains U.S.A. 183 I6
▶New Zealand country Oceania 152 E7
3rd largest and 3rd most populous country in Oceania. Known as Aotearoa in Maori.
oceania [countries] ▶▶▶ 138–139
Neya Rus. Fed. 40 G4
Neya r. Rus. Fed. 40 G4
Ney Bid Iran 100 D3
Neyestānak Iran 100 C3
Neyriz Iran 100 C4
Neyshābūr Iran 100 D2
also spelt Nīshāpūr; historically known as Abarshahr
Neyyattinkara India 94 C4
Nezahualcóyotl, Presa resr Mex. 185 G5
Nezhin Ukr. see Nizhyn
Nezperce U.S.A. 180 C3
Nez Perce Indian Reservation res. U.S.A. 180 D3
Ngabang Indon. 77 E2
Ngabé Congo 126 C6
Nga Chong, Khao mt. Myanmar/Thai. 79 B5
Ngagala watercourse Nigeria 125 I3
Ngagahtawng Myanmar 78 B2
Ngagli Rus. Fed. 82 B1
Ngaiotonga N.Z. 152 I3
Ngajira Tanz. 129 B6
Ngala Nigeria 125 I3
Ngalipaëng Indon. 75 C2
Ngalu Indon. 75 B5
Ngam Chad 126 C2
Ngama Chad 126 C2
Ngamaseri watercourse Botswana 130 D3
Ngamatapouri N.Z. 152 I7
Ngambé Cameroon 125 I6
Ngamda China 86 A2
Ngamiland admin. dist. Botswana 130 D3
Ngamring China 89 D6
Ngangala Sudan 128 A3
Ngangla Ringco salt l. China 89 C6
Nganglong Kangri mt. China 89 C5
Nganglong Kangri mts China 89 C5
N'gangula Angola 127 B7
Ngangzê Co salt l. China 89 D6
Ngangzê Shan mts China 89 D6
Ngan Hei Shui Tong resr Hong Kong China see Shing Mun Reservoir
Nganjuk Indon. 77 E4
Ngan Sau, Sông r. Vietnam 86 C5
Ngao Thai. 78 B4
Ngaoundéré Cameroon 125 I5
Ngapuke N.Z. 152 I6
Ngara Malawi 129 B7
Ngara Tanz. 128 A5

Ngarkat Conservation Park nature res. Australia 146 D3
Ngarrab China see Gyaca
Ngaruawahia N.Z. 152 J5
Ngaruroro r. N.Z. 152 K7
Ngatea N.Z. 152 L6
Ngathainggyaung Myanmar 78 A3
Ngawa China see Aba
Ngawan Chaung r. Myanmar 79 B5
Ngawi Indon. 77 E4
Ngayok Bay Myanmar 78 A4
Ngcheangel atoll Palau see Kayangel
Ngeaur i. Palau see Angaur
Ngegera Tanz. 129 A6
Ngeruangel i. Palau 73 H5
Ngezi Zimbabwe 131 F4
formerly spelt Ingezi
Nggelelevu i. Fiji see Qelelevu
Nghabe r. Botswana 130 D4
Ngiap r. Laos 78 C4
Ngilmina Indon. 75 C5
Ngimbang Indon. 77 F4
Ngiva Angola see Ondjiva
Ngo Congo 126 B5
Ngoc Linh mt. Vietnam 79 D5
Ngofakiaha Indon. 75 C2
Ngoïla Cameroon 125 I6
Ngoin, Co salt l. China 89 E6
Ngoko r. Cameroon/Congo 125 I6
Ngola Shankou pass China 84 C5
Ngol Bembo Angola 125 I6
Ngoma Zambia 127 E7
Ngoma Bridge Botswana 131 E3
Ngoma Tsé-Tsé Congo 126 B6
Ngomba Tanz. 129 B7
Ngome S. Africa 133 P4
Ngom Qu r. China 80 F6
Ngong Cameroon 125 I4
Ngongola Angola 127 C8
Ngongotaha N.Z. 152 K6
Ngong Shuen Chau pen. Hong Kong China see Stonecutters' Island
Ngoqumaima China 89 D5
Ngoring China 86 A1
Ngoring Hu l. China 86 A1
▶Ngorongoro Conservation Area nature res. Tanz. 128 B5
world [land cover] ▶▶▶ 18–19
Ngorongoro Crater Tanz. 128 B5
Ngoumou Cameroon 125 H6
Ngounié r. Gabon 126 A5
Ngouoni Gabon 126 A5
Ngoura Chad 120 C6
Ngouri Chad 120 B6
Ngourti Niger 125 I3
Ngoutchey well Chad 120 C5
Ngozi Burundi 126 F5
Ngozi S. Africa 133 N8
Ngqeleni S. Africa 133 N7
Nguigmi Niger 125 I3
Nguini well Niger 125 H3
Nguiu Australia 148 A1
Ngukurr Australia 148 B2
Ngulu atoll Micronesia 73 I5
also spelt Goulou
Ngum, Nam r. Laos 78 C4
Ngundu Zimbabwe 131 F4
Ngunguru Bay N.Z. 152 I3
Ngunju, Tanjung pt Indon. 75 B5
Nguna Angola see Sumbe
Ngunza-Kabolu Angola see Sumbe
Nguru Nigeria 125 H3
Nguru Mountains Tanz. 129 C6
Nguyên Binh Vietnam 78 C3
Ngwaketse admin. dist. Botswana 131 E5
Ngwako Pan salt pan Botswana 130 D4
Ngwane country Africa see Swaziland
Ngwathe S. Africa 133 L4
Ngwavuma r. Swaziland 133 Q3
also spelt Ingwavuma
Ngwelezana S. Africa 133 P5
Ngwempisi r. S. Africa 133 P3
Ngwezi r. Zambia 127 E9
Nhamatanda Moz. 131 G3
Nhamundá Brazil 199 G5
Nhamundá r. Brazil 199 G5
Nhandeara Brazil 206 C7
N'harea Angola 127 C7
Nha Trang Vietnam 79 E5
Nhecolândia Brazil 201 F4
Nhill Australia 146 D4
Nhlangano Swaziland 133 P4
also known as Goedgegun
Nhlazatshe S. Africa 133 P5
Nhoma Namibia 130 D3
Nho Quan Vietnam 78 D3
Nhulunbuy Australia 148 C2
Niabembe Dem. Rep. Congo 126 E5
Niablé Ghana 124 E5
Niacam Canada 167 J4
Niafounké Mali 124 E3
Niagara U.S.A. 172 F5
Niagara Falls Canada 168 E5
Niagara Falls waterfall Canada/U.S.A. 176 G2
Niagara Falls U.S.A. 176 F2
Niagara-on-the-Lake Canada 173 N7
Niagassola Guinea 124 C3
Niagouelé, Mont du hill Guinea 124 C4
Niagzu Aksai Chin 89 B5
Niah Sarawak Malaysia 77 F2
Niak Nepal 97 E3
Niakaramandougou Côte d'Ivoire 124 D4
Niamina Mali 124 D3
Nianbai China see Ledu
Niandan r. Guinea 124 C4
Niandankoro Guinea 124 C4
Niangandu Tanz. 129 C6
Niangara Dem. Rep. Congo 126 E4
Niangay, Lac l. Mali 124 E3
Niangoloko Burkina 124 D4
Niangua r. U.S.A. 174 A4
Niangxi China see Xinshao
Nia-Nia Dem. Rep. Congo 126 E4
Nianzishan China 85 I2
Niari admin. reg. Congo 126 B5
Nias i. Indon. 76 B2
Niassa prov. Moz. 131 H2
formerly known as Lago
Niassa, Lago l. Africa see Nyasa, Lake
Niassa, Reserva do nature res. Moz. 129 C8
Niauri i. Palau see Angaur
Nibil Well Australia 150 C4
Nica Latvia 42 C5
Nicaea Turkey see Iznik
▶Nicaragua country Central America 186 B4
5th largest country in North America.
northamerica [countries] ▶▶▶ 158–159
Nicaragua, Lago de l. Nicaragua see Nicaragua, Lake
Nicaragua, Lake Nicaragua 186 B5
also known as Nicaragua, Lago de
Nicaro Cuba 187 E2
Nicastro Italy 57 I10
Nice France 51 N9
also known as Nizza
Nice U.S.A. 182 B2
Nicephorium Syria see Ar Raqqah
Niceville U.S.A. 175 C6
Nichicun, Lac l. Canada 169 G2
Nichihara Japan 91 B7

Nichinan Japan 91 B9
Nichlaul India 97 D4
Nicholas Channel Bahamas/Cuba 186 C2
Nicholasville U.S.A. 176 A8
Nicholl's Town Bahamas 186 D1
Nichols IA U.S.A. 172 B9
Nichols NY U.S.A. 177 I3
Nicholson Australia 150 E3
Nicholson r. Australia 148 C3
Nicholson Canada 173 J3
Nicholson Lake Canada 167 K2
Nicholson Range hills Australia 151 B5
Nichollville U.S.A. 177 K1
Nickol Bay Australia 150 B4
Nicobar Islands India 95 G4
Nicolae Bălcescu Romania 58 J4
Nicolás Bravo Mex. 185 H5
Nicolaus U.S.A. 182 C3
Nicomedia Turkey see Kocaeli
Nico Pérez Uruguay 204 G4
Nicopolis Bulg. see Nikopol
▶Nicosia Cyprus 108 E2
Capital of Cyprus. Also known as Lefkosia or Lefkoşa.
Nicosia Sicilia Italy 57 G11
Nicotera Italy 57 H10
Nicoya Costa Rica 186 B5
Nicoya, Golfo de b. Costa Rica 186 B5
Nicoya, Península de pen. Costa Rica 186 B5
Nicuadala Moz. 131 H3
Niculiţel Romania 58 J3
Nida Lith. 42 C6
Nida r. Poland 49 R5
Nidadavole India 94 D2
Nidagunda India 94 C2
Nidym Rus. Fed. 39 J3
Nidze mt. Greece/Macedonia 58 C4
Nidzica Poland 49 R2
Nidzkie, Jezioro l. Poland 49 S2
Niebüll Germany 48 F1
Nied r. France 51 M3
Niederaula Germany 48 G5
Niederer Fläming park Germany 49 J3
Niedere Tauern mts Austria 49 K8
Niederlausitz reg. Germany 49 K4
Niedersachsen land Germany 48 F3
English form Lower Saxony
Niedersächsisches Wattenmeer, Nationalpark nat. park Germany 48 D2
Niefang Equat. Guinea 125 H6
Niekerkshoop S. Africa 132 G5
Niellé Côte d'Ivoire 124 D4
Niem Cent. Afr. Rep. 126 B3
Niemba Dem. Rep. Congo 127 F6
Niemegk Germany 49 J3
Niemisel Sweden 44 M2
Niéna Mali 124 D3
Nienburg (Weser) Germany 48 G3
Niéri Ko watercourse Senegal 124 B3
Niers r. Germany 48 C4
Niesky Germany 49 L4
Nietverdiend S. Africa 133 K2
Nieu Amsterdam Suriname 199 H3
Nieuw Nickerie Suriname 199 G3
Nieuwoudtville S. Africa 132 D8
Nieuwpoort Belgium 51 I1
Nieves Spain see As Neves
Niğde Turkey 106 C3
Nigel S. Africa 133 M3
▶Niger country Africa 125 G2
africa [countries] ▶▶▶ 114–117
▶Niger r. Africa 124 G5
3rd longest river in Africa.
africa [landscapes] ▶▶▶ 112–113
Niger state Nigeria 125 G4
Niger, Mouths of the Nigeria 125 G5
Niger, Source of the tourist site Guinea 124 C4
▶Nigeria country Africa 125 G4
Most populous country in Africa and 10th in the world.
world [population] ▶▶▶ 22–23
africa [countries] ▶▶▶ 114–117
Nighasan India 96 D3
Nightcaps N.Z. 153 C13
Nighthawk Lake Canada 168 D3
Nigrande Latvia 42 D5
Nigrita Greece 58 E8
Nihing Pak. 101 F4
Nihommatsu Japan see Nihonmatsu
Nihon country Asia see Japan
Nihonmatsu Japan 90 G6
also spelt Nihommatsu
Niigata Japan 90 F6
Niigata pref. Japan 90 F6
Niigata-yake-yama vol. Japan 91 F5
Niihama Japan 91 C7
Niihau i. U.S.A. 181 [inset] Y1
Nii-jima i. Japan 91 F7
Niikappu Japan 90 H3
Niimi Japan 91 C7
Niitsu Japan 90 F6
Nijar Spain 55 I7
Nijerāne well Mauritania 124 C2
Nijil, Wādī watercourse Jordan 108 G7
Nijmegen Neth. 48 D4
formerly known as Nimwegen
Nijverdal Neth. 48 D3
Nikaia Greece 59 D9
Nikel' Rus. Fed. 44 O1
Nikel'tau Kazakh. 102 D2
Nikiniki Indon. 75 C5
Nikininka Kazakh. 88 C1
Nikkaluokta Sweden 44 L2
Nikki Benin 125 F4
Nikkō Japan 91 F6
Nikkō National Park Japan 90 F6
Nikolaevo Bulg. 58 H6
Nikolayev Ukr. see Mykolayiv
Nikolayevka Chelyabinskaya Oblast' Rus. Fed. 103 I1
Nikolayevka Khabarovskiy Kray Rus. Fed. 82 D2
Nikolayevka Ul'yanovskaya Oblast' Rus. Fed. 41 H5
Nikolayevsk Rus. Fed. 41 H6
Nikolayevsk-na-Amure Rus. Fed. 82 F1
Nikolayevskiy Rus. Fed. see Nikolayevsk
Nikol'sk Penzenskaya Oblast' Rus. Fed. 41 H5
formerly known as Nikol'skaya Pestravka

Nikol'sk Vologod. Obl. Rus. Fed. 40 H4
Nikol'skaya Pestravka Rus. Fed. see Nikol'sk
Nikol'skiy Kazakh. see Satpayev
Nikol'skiy Rus. Fed. 43 P1
Nikol'skiy Torzhok Rus. Fed. 43 T2
Nikol'skoye Kamchatskaya Oblast' Rus. Fed. 39 Q4
Nikol'skoye Lipetskaya Oblast' Rus. Fed. 43 U9
Nikol'skoye Orenburgskaya Oblast' Rus. Fed. 102 C1
Nikol'skoye Vologod. Obl. Rus. Fed. 43 S2
Nikol'skoye Rus. Fed. see Sheksna
Nikopol Bulg. 58 H5
historically known as Nicopolis
Nikopol' Ukr. 41 E7
Nik Pey Iran 100 B2
Niksar Turkey 107 D2
Nikshahr Iran 101 E5
also known as Gey
Nikšić Crna Gora Yugo. 56 K6
Nikumaroro i. Kiribati 145 H2
formerly known as Gardner Island
Nīl, Bahr el r. Africa see Nile
Nila vol. Indon. 75 D4
Nilagiri India 97 E5
Nilakka l. Fin. 44 N3
Nilakkottai India 94 C4
Nilambur India 94 C3
Niland U.S.A. 183 I8
Nilandhoo Atoll Maldives 93 D10
Nilanga India 94 C2
Nilaveli Sri Lanka 94 D4
▶Nile r. Africa 121 F2
Longest river in the world and in Africa. Also known as Nīl, Bahr el.
world [physical features] ▶▶▶ 8–9
africa [issues] ▶▶▶ 116–117
Nile state Sudan 121 G5
▶Nile Delta Egypt 108 C6
world [physical features] ▶▶▶ 8–9
africa [issues] ▶▶▶ 116–117
Niles MI U.S.A. 172 G9
Niles OH U.S.A. 176 E4
Nileswaram India 94 B3
Nilgiri Hills India 94 C4
Nili r. Eth. 104 B5
Nilka China 88 C3
Nilópolis Brazil 207 J9
Nil Pass Afgh. 101 F3
Nilphamari Bangl. 97 F4
Nilsiä Fin. 44 N3
Nimach India 96 B4
formerly spelt Neemuch
Nimaj India 96 B4
Niman r. Rus. Fed. 82 D2
Nimba, Monts mts Africa see Nimba Mountains
Nimbahera India 96 B4
also spelt Nimbhera
Nimbal India 94 B2
Nimba Mountains Africa 124 C5
also known as Nimba, Monts
Nimberra Well Australia 150 C4
Nimbhera India see Nimbahera
Nimelen r. Rus. Fed. 82 E1
Nîmes France 51 K9
historically known as Nemausus
Nimka Thana India 96 B4
Nimmitabel Australia 147 F4
Nimos i. Greece 59 I12
Nimpkish r. Canada 166 E5
Nimrod Glacier Antarctica 223 K1
Nimrūz prov. Afgh. 101 E4
Nimu Jammu and Kashmir 96 C2
Nimule Sudan 128 B4
Nimwegen Neth. see Nijmegen
Nina Estonia 42 I3
Ninawá governorate Iraq 107 E4
Ninawá tourist site Iraq see Nineveh
Ninda Angola 127 D8
Nindai Tanz. 129 C7
Nindigully Australia 147 F2
Nine Degree Channel India 94 B4
Nine Islands P.N.G. see Kilinailau Islands
Nine Mile Lake salt flat Australia 147 D2
Ninemile Peak U.S.A. 183 H2
Ninepin Group is Hong Kong China 87 [inset]
also known as Kwo Chau Kwan To
Ninety Mile Beach Australia 147 E4
Ninety Mile Beach N.Z. 152 G3
Nineveh tourist site Iraq 107 E3
also spelt Ninawá
Ninfas, Punta pt Arg. 205 D6
Ningaloo Marine Park nature res. Australia 150 A4
Ning'an China 82 C3
Ningbo China 87 G2
also known as Yinxian
Ningcheng China 85 H3
also known as Tianyi
Ningde China 87 F3
Ningdu China 87 E3
also known as Meijiang
Ning'er China see Pu'er
Ningguo China 87 F2
also known as Helixi
Ninghai China 87 G2
Ninghe China 85 H4
also known as Lutai
Ninghsia Hui Autonomous Region aut. reg. China see Ningxia Huizu Zizhiqu
Ninghua China 87 E3
also known as Cuijiang
Ningi Nigeria 125 H4
Ningjiang China see Songyuan
Ningjing Shan mts China 86 A2
Ninglang China 86 B3
also known as Daxing
Ningling China 87 E1
Ningming China 86 C4
also known as Chengzhong
Ningnan China 86 B3
Ningqiang China 86 C1
Ningshan China 87 D1
Ningwu China 85 G4
Ningxia aut. reg. China see Ningxia Huizu Zizhiqu
▶Ningxia Huizu Zizhiqu aut. reg. China 85 H4
short form Ningxia; English form Ningsia or Ninghsia Hui Autonomous Region

longest rivers	river	length	location	page#
1 ▶	Nile	6 695km / 4 160miles	Africa	121 F2
2 ▶	Amazon	6 516km / 4 049miles	South America	202 B1
3 ▶	Yangtze	6 380km / 3 964miles	Asia	87 G2
4 ▶	Mississippi-Missouri	5 969km / 3 709miles	North America	179 E6
5 ▶	Ob'-Irtysh	5 568km / 3 459miles	Asia	38 G3
6 ▶	Yenisey-Angara-Selenga	5 550km / 3 445miles	Asia	39 I2
7 ▶	Yellow	5 464km / 3 395miles	Asia	85 H4
8 ▶	Congo	4 667km / 2 900miles	Africa	127 B6
9 ▶	Rio de la Plata-Paraná	4 500km / 2 796miles	South America	204 F4
10 ▶	Irtysh	4 440km / 2 759miles	Asia	38 G3

Ningxian China 85 E5
also known as Xinning
Ningxiang China 87 E2
Ningyang China 85 H5
Ningyuan China 87 D3
Ningzhou China *see* Huaning
Ninh Binh Vietnam 78 D4
Ninh Hoa Vietnam 79 E5
Ninigo Group *is* P.N.G. 73 J7
Ninnis Glacier Antarctica 223 J2
Ninnis Glacier Tongue Antarctica 223 K2
Ninohe Japan 90 G4
Ninualac, Canal *sea chan.* Chile 205 B7
Nioaque Brazil 201 E5
Niobrara *r.* U.S.A. 178 C3
Nioghalvfjerdsfjorden *inlet* Greenland 165 R2
Nioki Dem. Rep. Congo 126 C5
Niokolo Koba, Parc National du *nat. park* Senegal 124 B3
Niono Mali 124 C3
Nioro Mali 124 C3
Niort France 50 F6
Nioût *well* Mauritania 124 D3
Nipa P.N.G. 73 J8
Nipani India 94 B2
Nipanipa, Tanjung *pt* Indon. 75 B3
Niphad India 94 B1
Nipigon Canada 168 B3
Nipigon, Lake Canada 168 B3
Nipigon Bay Canada 172 F2
Nipiodi Moz. 131 H3
Nipishish Lake Canada 169 I2
Nipissing Canada 173 N4
Nipissing, Lake Canada 168 E4
Nipomo U.S.A. 182 C6
Nippon *country* Asia *see* Japan
Nippon Hai *see* N. Pacific Ocean *see* Japan, Sea of
Nippur *tourist site* Iraq 107 F4
Niquelândia Brazil 202 B5
Niquero Cuba 186 D3
Nir *Ardabil* Iran 100 A2
Nir *Yazd* Iran 100 C3
Nir, Jabal an *hills* Saudi Arabia 104 C2
Nira *r.* India 94 B2
Nirasaki Japan 91 F7
Nirji China 85 J1
also known as Morin Dawa
Nirmal India 94 C2
Nirmali India 97 E4
Nirmal Range *hills* India 94 C2
Nirzas *r.* Latvia 42 I5
Niš Srbija Yugo. 58 C6
historically known as Naissus
Nisa Port. 54 D5
Nişāb Yemen 105 D5
Nisah, Wādī *watercourse* Saudi Arabia 105 D2
Nišava *r.* Yugo. 58 C5
Niscemi *Sicilia* Italy 57 G11
Niseko Japan 90 G3
Nīshābūr Iran *see* Neyshābūr
Nischa *r.* Belarus 43 J6
Nishibetsu-gawa *r.* Japan 90 I3
Nishikawa Japan 90 G5
Nishinomiya Japan 91 D7
Nishino-omote Japan 91 B9
Nishino-shima *i.* Japan 91 B9
Nishino-shima *vol.* Japan 81 O7
Nishi-Sonogi-hantō *pen.* Japan 91 A8
Nishi-suidō *sea chan.* Japan/S. Korea 91 A7
also known as Chōsen-kaikyō
Nishiwaki Japan 91 D7
Nísia Floresta Brazil 202 F4
Nisibis Turkey *see* Nusaybin
Nisi-mera Japan 91 B8
Nísiros *i.* Greece *see* Nisyros
Niskankselkä *l.* Fin. 44 N2
Niskayuna U.S.A. 177 L3
Niskibi *r.* Canada 168 B1
Nisko Poland 49 T5
Nisling *r.* Canada 166 B2
Nispoeni Moldova 58 J1
Nissan *r.* Sweden 45 K4
Nisser *l.* Norway 45 J4
Nissum Bredning *b.* Denmark 45 J4
Nistru *r.* Moldova *see* Dniester
Nistrului Inferior, Cîmpia *lowland* Moldova 58 K1
Nisutlin *r.* Canada 166 C2
Nisyros *i.* Greece 59 I12
also spelt Nísiros
Nita Japan 91 C7
Nitchequon Canada 169 G2
Nitendi *i.* Solomon Is. *see* Ndeni
Niterói Brazil 203 D7
Nith *r.* U.K. 47 I8
Niti Pass China 96 C3
Nitmiluk National Park Australia 148 B2
formerly known as Katherine Gorge National Park
Nitra Slovakia 49 P7
Nitra *r.* Slovakia 49 P8
Nitro U.S.A. 176 D7
Nittedal Norway 45 J3
Niuafo'ou *i.* Tonga 145 H3
also spelt Niuafu
Niuafu *i.* Tonga *see* Niuafo'ou
Niuatoputapu *i.* Tonga 145 I3
formerly known as Boscawen Island

► Niue *terr.* S. Pacific Ocean 145 I3
Self-governing New Zealand Overseas Territory.
oceania [countries] ➤ 138–139

Niujing China *see* Binchuan
Niulakita *i.* Tuvalu 145 G3
formerly spelt Nurakita
Niulan Jiang *r.* China 86 B3
Niur, Pulau *i.* Indon. 76 C3
Niushan China *see* Donghai
Niutao *i.* Tuvalu 145 G2
Niutoushan China 87 F2
Niuzhuang China 85 I3
Nivala Fin. 44 N3
Nivastroy Rus. Fed. 44 P2
Nive *watercourse* Australia 149 E5
Nive *r.* France 50 E9
Nive Downs Australia 149 E5
Nivelles Belgium 51 K2
Nivnoye Rus. Fed. 43 N8
Nivskiy Rus. Fed. 44 P2
Niwai India 96 B4
Niwari India 96 C4
Nixia China *see* Sêrxu
Nixon U.S.A. 182 C5
Niya China *see* Minfeng
Niya He *r.* China 89 C4
Niyut, Gunung *mt.* Indon. 77 E2
Niz Rus. Fed. 43 O2
Nizamabad India 94 C2
also known as Indur
Nizampatnam India 94 D3
Nizam Sagar *l.* India 94 C2
Nizh Aydere Turkm. 102 D5
Nizhegorodskaya Oblast' *admin. div.* Rus. Fed. 40 H4
English form Nizhniy Novgorod Oblast;
formerly known as Gor'kovskaya Oblast'
Nizhneangarsk Rus. Fed. 81 H1
Nizhnedevitsk Rus. Fed. 41 F6
Nizhnekamsk Rus. Fed. 40 I5
Nizhnekamskoye Vodokhranilishche *resr* Rus. Fed. 40 J5
Nizhne-Svirskiy Zapovednik *nature res.*

Nizhneudinsk Rus. Fed. 80 F2
Nizhnevartovsk Rus. Fed. 38 H3
Nizhnevolzhsk Rus. Fed. *see* Narimanov
Nizhneye Kuyto, Ozero *l.* Rus. Fed. 44 O2
Nizhniy Irginsk Rus. Fed. 40 K4
Nizhniy Chir Rus. Fed. 41 G6
Nizhniy Kresty Rus. Fed. *see* Cherskiy
Nizhniye Ustriki Poland *see* Ustrzyki Dolne
Nizhniy Lomov Rus. Fed. 41 G5
Nizhniy Novgorod Rus. Fed. 40 G4
formerly known as Gor'kiy
Nizhniy Novgorod Oblast' *admin. div.* Rus. Fed. *see* Nizhegorodskaya Oblast'
Nizhniy Odes Rus. Fed. 40 J3
Nizhniy Pyandzh Tajik. *see* Panji Poyon
Nizhniy Tagil Rus. Fed. 38 F4
Nizhniy Yenangsk Rus. Fed. 40 H4
Nizhnyaya Mola Rus. Fed. 40 H2
Nizhnyaya Omra Rus. Fed. 40 J3
Nizhnyaya Pesha Rus. Fed. 40 H2
Nizhnyaya Pirenga, Ozero *l.* Rus. Fed. 44 P2
Nizhnyaya Poyma Rus. Fed. 80 F1
Nizhnyaya Suyetka Rus. Fed. 103 I1
Nizhnyaya Tunguska *r.* Rus. Fed. 39 I3
English form Lower Tunguska
Nizhnyaya Tura Rus. Fed. 38 F4
Nizhnyaya Zolotitsa Rus. Fed. 40 G2
Nizhyn Ukr. 41 D6

Nizina Mazowiecka *reg.* Poland 49 R3
Nizip Turkey 107 D3
Nizkabor"ye Belarus 43 L6
Nízke Beskydy *hills* Slovakia 49 S6
Nízke Tatry *mts* Slovakia 49 Q7
Nízke Tatry *nat. park* Slovakia 49 Q7
Nizmennyy, Mys *pt* Rus. Fed. 90 D3
Nizwá Oman *see* Nazwá
Nizza France *see* Nice
Nizza Monferrato Italy 56 A4
Njavve Sweden 44 L2
Njazidja *i.* Comoros 129 D7
also known as Grande Comore
Njegoš *mts* Yugo. 56 K6
Njellim Fin. *see* Nellim
Njinjo Tanz. 129 C7
Njombe Tanz. 129 B7
Njombe *r.* Tanz. 129 B6
Njutånger Sweden 45 L3
Nkai Zimbabwe *see* Nkayi
Nkambe Cameroon 125 H5
Nkandla S. Africa 133 P5
Nkasi Tanz. 129 A6
Nkawkaw Ghana 125 H5
Nkayi Zimbabwe 131 F3
formerly known as Nkai
Nkhaïlé *well* Mauritania 124 D2
Nkhata Bay Malawi 129 B7
Nkhotakota Malawi 129 B8
Nkhotakota Game Reserve *nature res.* Malawi 129 B8
Nkomfap Nigeria 125 H5
Nkomi, Lagune *lag.* Gabon 126 A5
Nkondwe Tanz. 129 A6
Nkongsamba Cameroon 125 H5
Nkoranza Ghana 125 H5
Nkoteng Cameroon 125 I5
Nkululeko S. Africa 133 L7
Nkundi Tanz. 129 A6
Nkungwi Tanz. 129 A6
Nkurenkuru Namibia 130 C3
Nkwalini S. Africa 133 P5
Nkwanta Ghana 125 F4
Nkwenkwezi S. Africa 133 K10
Nmai Hka *r.* Myanmar 78 B2
Noa China *r.* India 97 H4
Noakhali Bangl. 97 F5
Noamundi India 97 E5
Noatak *r.* U.S.A. 164 C3
Noatak National Preserve *nature res.* U.S.A. 164 C3
Nobeoka Japan 91 B8
Nobleford Canada 167 H5
Nobleville U.S.A. 174 C3
Nobokwe S. Africa 133 L8
Noboribetsu Japan 90 G3
Nobres Brazil 201 F4
Noccundra Australia 147 D1
Noce *r.* Italy 56 D2
Nocera Terinese Italy 57 I9
Nochistlán Mex. 185 F4
Nochixtlán Mex. 185 F5
Noci Italy 57 J8
Nockatunga Australia 147 D1
Nocona U.S.A. 179 C5
Noda Japan 91 F7
Nodaway *r.* U.S.A. 178 D4
Nodeland Norway 45 I4
Noel Kempff Mercado, Parque Nacional *nat. park* Bol. 201 E3
Noelville Canada 173 M4
Noenieput S. Africa 132 E4
Nogales Mex. 184 C2
also known as Heroica Nogales
Nogales U.S.A. 181 E7
Nogat *r.* Poland 49 Q1
Nōgata Japan 91 B8
Nogayty Kazakh. 102 C2
Nogent-le-Rotrou France 50 G4
Nogent-sur-Oise France 51 I4
Nogent-sur-Seine France 51 J4
Noginsk *Evenkiyskiy Avtonomnyy Okrug* Rus. Fed. 39 J3
Noginsk *Moskovskaya Oblast'* Rus. Fed. 43 T6
Nogliki Rus. Fed. 82 F2
Nogo *r.* Australia 149 F5
Nogoa *r.* Australia 149 F4
Nogohaku-san *mt.* Japan 91 E7
Nogoyá Arg. 204 F4
Nohar India 96 B3
Noheji Japan 90 G4
Nohfelden Germany 48 E6
Nohili Point U.S.A. 181 [inset] Y1
Nohur Turkm. *see* Nokhur
Noia Spain 54 C2
also spelt Noya
Noidore *r.* Brazil 206 A1
Noire *r.* Canada 173 Q5
Noire, Montagne *mts* France 51 I9
Noire, Pointe *pt* Morocco 55 H9
Noires, Montagnes *hills* France 50 C4
Noirmoutier, Île de *i.* France 50 D6
Noirmoutier-en-l'Île France 50 D5
Nojima-zaki *c.* Japan 91 F7
Nokesville U.S.A. 176 H7
Nokha India 96 B4
Nokhowch, Kūh-e *mt.* Iran 101 E5
Nokhur Turkm. 102 D5
also spelt Nohur
Nokia Fin. 45 M3
Nökis Uzbek. *see* Nukus
Nok Kundi Pak. 101 E4
Nokomis Canada 167 J5
Nokomis Lake Canada 167 K3
Nokou Chad 120 B6
Nokrek Peak India 97 F4
Nola Cent. Afr. Rep. 126 C4
Nolichucky *r.* U.S.A. 176 B9
Nolinsk Rus. Fed. 40 I4
formerly known as Molotovsk
Noll S. Africa 132 G10
Nólsoy *i.* Faroe Is. 46 F1
Noma-misaki *pt* Japan 91 B9
Nomgon Mongolia 85 F3
Nomhon China 84 C4
Nomoi Islands Micronesia *see* Mortlock Islands
Nomonde S. Africa 133 K8
Nomo-zaki *pt* Japan 91 A8

Nomto Rus. Fed. 84 E1
Nomuka Tonga 145 H4
Nomuka Rus. Fed. 40 G4
Nomwache Lake Canada 167 I2
Nong'an China 82 B3
Nong Hong Thai. 79 C5
Nonghui China *see* Guang'an
Nong Khai Thai. 78 D4
Nongoma S. Africa 133 P4
Nongstoin India 97 F4
Nonni *r.* China *see* Nen Jiang
Nonoai Brazil 203 A8
Nonoava Mex. 184 D3
Nonouti *atoll* Kiribati 145 G2
also spelt Nanouki *or* Nanouti; *formerly known as* Sydenham
Nonsan S. Korea 83 B5
Nonthaburi Thai. 79 C5
Nonzwakazi S. Africa 132 I7
Nóo Estonia 42 I3
Nookawarra Australia 151 B5
Nooldanye U.S.A. 182 I5
Noonamah Australia 148 A2
Noondie, Lake *salt flat* Australia 151 B6
Noonkanbah Australia 150 D3
Noonkanbah Aboriginal Reserve Australia 150 D3
Noonthorangee Range *hills* Australia 147 D2
Noorama Creek *watercourse* Australia 147 E1
Noordbeveland *i.* Neth. 48 A4
Noorderhaaks *i.* Neth. 48 B3
Noordkaap S. Africa 133 P2
Noordkuil S. Africa 132 C9
Noordoewer Namibia 132 B6
Noordoost Polder Neth. 48 C3
Noordpunt *pt* Neth. Antilles 187 F4
Noormarkku Fin. 45 M3
Noorvik U.S.A. 164 C3
Nootka Island Canada 166 E5
Nóqui Angola 127 B6
Nora *r.* Rus. Fed. 82 C2
Norak Tajik. 101 G2
also spel: Nurek
Norala Phil. 74 C5
Noranda Canada 168 E3
Nor-Bayazet Armenia *see* Kamo
Norberg Sweden 45 K3
Nord Cameroon 125 I4
Nord Greenland *see* Station Nord
Nord, Canal du France 48 A5
Nordaustlandet *i.* Svalbard 38 C2
Nordborg Denmark 45 J5
Nordbotn Norway 44 M1
Nordegg Canada 167 G4
Norden Germany 48 E2
Nordenshel'da, Arkhipelag *is* Rus. Fed. 39 J2
English form Nordenskjold Archipelago
Nordenskiold *r.* Canada 166 B2
Nordenskjold Archipelago *is* Rus. Fed. *see* Nordenshel'da, Arkhipelag
Norder Hever *sea chan.* Germany 48 F1
Norderney Germany 48 E2
Norderney *i.* Germany 48 E2
Norderstedt Germany 48 H2
Nordfjord Norway 44 O1
Nordfjord *inlet* Norway 45 I3
Nordfjordeid Norway 45 I3
Nordfold Norway 44 M2
Nordfriesische Inseln *is* Germany *see* North Frisian Islands
Nordhausen Germany 48 I4
Nordholz Germany 48 F2
Nordhorn Germany 48 E3
Nordhuglo Norway 45 I3
Nordinghå naturreservat *nature res.* Sweden 44 L3
Nord Kap *c.* Iceland *see* Horn
Nordkapp *c.* Norway *see* North Cape
Nord-Kivu *prov.* Dem. Rep. Congo 126 F5
Nordkynhalvøya *i.* Norway 44 N1
Nordland *county* Norway 44 K2
Nordli Norway 44 K2
Nördliches Harzvorland *park* Germany 48 H4
Nördlingen Germany 48 H7
Nordmaling Sweden 44 L3
Nordmannvik Norway 44 M1
Nord- og Østgrønland, Nationalparken i *nat. park* Greenland 165 P2
Nordstrundingen *c.* Greenland *see* Northeast Foreland
Nord-Ostsee-Kanal *canal* Germany *see* Kiel Canal
Nord *prov.* Cameroon 125 H5
Nord - Pas-de-Calais *admin. reg.* France 51 I2
Nord-Pas-de-Calais, Parc Naturel Régional de *nature res.* France 51 J2
Nordre Strømfjord *inlet* Greenland *see* Nassuttooq
Nordrhein-Westfalen *land* Germany 48 E4
English form North Rhine - Westphalia
Nordstrand *i.* Germany 48 F1
Nord-Trøndelag *county* Norway 44 K2
Nord-Trøndelag *state* Norway *see* Nord-Trøndelag
Nørdurland vestra *constituency* Iceland 44 [inset] B2
Nørðurland vestra *constituency* Iceland 44 [inset] B2
Nordvik Rus. Fed. 39 L2
Nordvika Norway 44 J1
Nore *r.* Rep. of Ireland 47 F11
Nore, Pic de *mt.* France 51 I9
Noreg *country* Europe *see* Norway
Noreikiškės Lith. 42 E7
Norema *r.* Australia 149 F4
Norfolk *i.* Australia 145 F4
Norfolk *NE* U.S.A. 178 C3
Norfolk *NY* U.S.A. 177 K1
Norfolk *VA* U.S.A. 177 I8

► Norfolk Island *terr.* S. Pacific Ocean 145 F4
Australian External Territory.
oceania [countries] ➤ 138–139

Norfork Lake U.S.A. 179 D4
Norge *country* Europe *see* Norway
Norheimsund Norway 45 I3
Noria Chile 200 C5
Norikura-dake *vol.* Japan 91 E6
Noril'sk Rus. Fed. 39 I3
Norkyung China *see* Banang
Norland Canada 173 O6
Norlina U.S.A. 176 G9
Normal U.S.A. 174 B3
Norman *r.* Australia 149 D3
Norman U.S.A. 179 C5
Norman, Lake *resr* U.S.A. 174 D5
Normanby *r.* Australia 149 E2
Normanby N.Z. 152 I7
Normanby Island P.N.G. 145 E2
Normanby Range *hills* Australia 149 F4
Normandes, Îles *is* English Chan. *see* Channel Islands
Normandia Brazil 199 G4
Normandie *reg.* France *see* Normandy
Normandie, Collines de *hills* France 50 E4
Normandie-Maine, Parc Naturel Régional *nature res.* France 50 F4
Normandien S. Africa 133 N4
Normandy *reg.* France 50 F4
also spelt Normandie
Normanton Australia 149 D3
Norman Wells Canada 166 E1
Normétal Canada 173 N2
Nornachus Mex. 184 F5
Norquay Canada 167 K5
Norquinco Arg. 205 C6
Norra Kvarken *strait* Fin./Sweden 44 M3

Norrbotten *county* Sweden 44 L2
Norre Nebel Denmark 45 J5
Norrent-Fontes France 51 I2
Nörrfjärden Sweden 44 M2
Norrhult-Klavreström Sweden 45 K4
Norris U.S.A. 176 K9
Norris Lake U.S.A. 176 B8
Norristown U.S.A. 177 J5
Norrköping Sweden 45 L4
Norrsundet Sweden 45 L3
Nörrtälje Sweden 45 L4
Norseman Australia 151 C7
Norsewood N.Z. 152 K8
Norsk Rus. Fed. 82 C1
Norske Øer *is* Greenland 165 R2
Norsjø *l.* Norway 45 J4
Norsjö Sweden 44 L2
Norte, Punta *pt* Buenos Aires Arg. 204 F5
Norte, Punta *pt* Arg. 205 C8
Norte, Serra *hills* Brazil 201 F5
Norte de Santander *dept* Col. 198 C2
Nortelândia Brazil 201 F3
North, Cape Canada 169 I4
North Adams U.S.A. 177 L3
Northallerton U.K. 47 K9
Northam Australia 151 A6
Northam S. Africa 133 L1
Northampton Australia 151 A6
Northampton U.K. 47 L11
Northampton *MA* U.S.A. 177 M3
Northampton *PA* U.S.A. 177 J5
Northampton Downs Australia 149 E5
North Andaman *i.* India 95 G3
North Anna *r.* U.S.A. 176 H7
North Anson U.S.A. 177 O1
North Arm *b.* Canada 167 H2
North Balabac Strait Phil. 74 A4
North Baltimore U.S.A. 176 B4
North Battleford Canada 167 I4
North Bay Canada 168 E4
North Bend *OR* U.S.A. 180 A4
North Bend *PA* U.S.A. 176 H4
North Bennington U.S.A. 177 L3
North Berwick U.K. 46 J7
North Berwick U.S.A. 177 O2
North Borneo *state* Malaysia *see* Sabah
North Bosque *r.* U.S.A. 179 C6
North Branch *r.* U.S.A. 173 J7
North Branch *MN* U.S.A. 172 A5
North Caicos *i.* Turks and Caicos Is 187 F2
North Canadian *r.* U.S.A. 179 D5
North Cape Canada 169 H4
North Cape Norway 44 N1
also known as Nordkapp
North Cape S. Georgia 205 [inset]
North Cape N.Z. 152 H2
North Caribou Lake Canada 168 B2
North Carolina *state* U.S.A. 176 F9
North Cascades National Park U.S.A. 180 B2
North Central Aboriginal Reserve Australia 150 D4
North Channel *lake channel* Canada 168 D4
North Channel *str.* Northern Ireland/Scotland U.K. 47 G8
North Charleston U.S.A. 175 E5
North Cheyenne Indian Reservation *res.* U.S.A. 180 F3
Northcliffe Australia 151 B7
Northcliffe Glacier Antarctica 223 G2
North Collins U.S.A. 176 G3
North Concho *r.* U.S.A. 179 B6
North Conway U.S.A. 177 N1
North Cowichan Canada 166 F5
North Creek U.S.A. 177 L2
North Dakota *state* U.S.A. 178 B2
North Downs *hills* U.K. 47 L12
North East *admin. dist.* Botswana 131 E4
North East *MD* U.S.A. 177 J6
North East *PA* U.S.A. 176 F4
North East Cay *reef* Australia 149 G4
North-Eastern *prov.* Kenya 128 D5

► Northeast Foreland *c.* Greenland 165 R1
Most easterly point of North America. Also known as Nordostrundingen.

North-East Frontier Agency *state* India *see* Arunachal Pradesh
Northeast Point Bahamas 175 F8
Northeast Providence Channel Bahamas 186 D1
North Edwards U.S.A. 182 G6
Northeim Germany 48 G4
North End Point Bahamas 175 F7
Northern *admin. reg.* Ghana 125 E4
Northern *prov.* Malawi 129 B7
Northern *prov.* S. Africa 133 N1
formerly known as Northern Transvaal
Northern *prov.* Sierra Leone 124 C4
Northern *state* Sudan 121 F4
Northern *prov.* Zambia 127 F7
Northern Aegean *admin. reg.* Greece *see* Voreio Aigaio
Northern Areas *admin. div.* Pak. 101 H2
Northern Bahr el Ghazal *state* Sudan 126 E2
Northern Cape *prov.* S. Africa 132 D6
Northern Darfur *state* Sudan 121 E6
Northern Donets *r.* Rus. Fed./Ukr. *see* Severskiy Donets
Northern Dvina *r.* Rus. Fed. *see* Severnaya Dvina
Northern Indian Lake Canada 167 L3
Northern Ireland *prov.* U.K. 47 F9
Northern Kordofan *state* Sudan 121 F6
Northern Lau Group *is* Fiji 145 H3
Northern Light Lake Canada 168 B3

► Northern Mariana Islands *terr.* N. Pacific Ocean 73 J3
United States Commonwealth. Historically known as Ladrones.
oceania [countries] ➤ 138–139

Northern Rhodesia *country* Africa *see* Zambia
Northern Sporades *is* Greece *see* Voreioi Sporades
Northern Territory *admin. div.* Australia 148 B3
Northern Transvaal *prov.* S. Africa *see* Northern
North Fabius *r.* U.S.A. 174 B4
Northfield *MN* U.S.A. 174 A2
Northfield *VT* U.S.A. 177 M1
North Foreland *c.* U.K. 47 N12
North Fork U.S.A. 182 E4
North Fork Pass Canada 166 C2
North Fox Island U.S.A. 172 H5
North French *r.* Canada 168 D3
North Frisian Islands Germany 48 F1
also known as Nordfriesische Inseln
North Geomagnetic Pole Arctic Ocean 224 T1
North Haven U.S.A. 177 M4
North Head *r.* U.S.A. 152 I4
North Henik Lake Canada 167 L1
North Hero U.S.A. 177 L1
North Highlands U.S.A. 182 C3
North Horr Kenya 128 C4
North Hudson U.S.A. 177 L2
North Island India 94 B4

► North Island N.Z. 152 H6
3rd largest island in Oceania.
oceania [landscapes] ➤ 136–137

North Island Phil. 74 B1
English form Southern Aegean; *also spelt* Nótion Aiyaíon
Nótion Aiyaíon *admin. reg.* Greece *see* Notio Aigaio
Notios Evvoïkos Kolpos *sea chan.* Greece 59 E10
Notio Steno Kerkyras *sea chan.* Greece 59 B9
Noto *Sicilia* Italy 57 H12
Noto Japan 90 E6
Noto, Golfo di g. *Sicilia* Italy 57 H12
Notodden Norway 45 J4
Noto-hantō *pen.* Japan 90 E6
Notre Dame, Monts *mts* Canada 169 G4
Notre Dame Bay Canada 169 K3
Notre-Dame-de-Koartac Canada *see* Quaqtaq
Notre-Dame-de-la-Salette Canada 173 R4
Notre-Dame-du-Laus Canada 173 R4
Notre-Dame-du-Nord Canada 173 N3
Notsé Togo 125 F5
Notsu Japan 91 B8
Notsuke-saki *pt* Japan 90 I3
Notsuke-suidō *sea chan.* Japan/Rus. Fed. 90 I3
also known as Izmeny, Proliv
Nottawasaga Bay Canada 173 M6
Nottaway *r.* Canada 168 E3
Nottingham U.K. 47 K11
Nottingham Island Canada 165 L3
Nottingham Road S. Africa 133 O6
Nottoway U.S.A. 176 G8
Nottoway *r.* U.S.A. 176 I9

► Nouâdhibou Mauritania 122 A5
formerly known as Port Étienne
Nouâdhibou, Râs *c.* Mauritania 122 A5

► Nouakchott Mauritania 124 B2
Capital of Mauritania.

Noual *well* Mauritania 124 D2
Nouâmghâr Mauritania 124 A2
Nouei Vietnam 79 D5

► Nouméa New Caledonia 145 G4
Capital of New Caledonia.

Noun *r.* Cameroon 125 H5
Nouna Burkina 124 D3
Noupoort S. Africa 133 I8
Nousu Fin. 44 O2
Nouveau-Comptoir Canada *see* Wemindji
Nouvelle Anvers Dem. Rep. Congo *see* Makanza
Nouvelle Calédonie *i.* S. Pacific Ocean 145 F4
also known as New Caledonia
Nouvelle Calédonie *terr.* S. Pacific Ocean *see* New Caledonia
Nouvelles Hébrides *country* S. Pacific Ocean *see* Vanuatu
Nov Tajik. 101 G2
also spelt Nau
Nôva Estonia 42 E2
Nova Almeida Brazil 207 M7
Nova América Brazil 206 D2
Nova Aurora Brazil 206 B5
Nova Era Brazil 207 K6
Nova Friburgo Brazil 203 D7
Nova Gaia Angola *see* Cambundi-Catembo
Nova Goa India *see* Panaji
Nova Gorica Slovenia 56 F3
Nova Gradiška Croatia 56 J3
Nova Granada Brazil 206 D7
Nova Iguaçu Brazil 203 D7
Nova Kakhovka Ukr. 41 E7
also spelt Novaya Kakhovka
Nova Lima Brazil 203 D6
Nova Lisboa Angola *see* Huambo
Nova Londrina Brazil 206 A9
Novalukoml' Belarus 43 K7
also spelt Novolukoml'
Nova Mambone Moz. 131 G4
Nova Nabúri Moz. 131 H3
Nova Odesa Ukr. 41 D7
also spelt Novaya Odessa
Nová Paka Czech Rep. 49 M5
Nova Paraiso Brazil 199 F4
Nova Pazova Vojvodina, Srbija Yugo. 58 B4
Nova Pilão Arcado Brazil 202 D4
Nova Ponte Brazil 206 F6
Nova Ponte, Represa *resr* Minas Gerais Brazil 206 F6
Nova Ponte, Represa *resr* Brazil 203 C6
Novara Italy 56 A3
Nova Remanso Brazil 202 D4
Nova Resende Brazil 206 G9
Nova Russas Brazil 202 D3
Nova Scotia *prov.* Canada 169 H5
historically known as Acadia
Nova Sento Sé Brazil 202 D4
Nova Serrana Brazil 207 I6
Nova Sintra Angola *see* Catabola
Nova Soure Brazil 202 E4
Novate Mezzola Italy 56 B2
Novato U.S.A. 182 B3
Nova Topola Bos.-Herz. 56 J3
Novator Rus. Fed. 40 I3
Nova Vanduzi Moz. 131 G3
Nova Venécia Brazil 207 L4
Nova Viçosa Brazil 207 N4
Nova Vida *r.* Amazonas Brazil 199 E5
Nova Vida *r.* Rondônia Brazil 201 F2
Nova Xavantino Brazil 206 A2
Novaya Kakhovka Ukr. *see* Nova Kakhovka
Novaya Kazanka Kazakh. 102 B2
also known as Zhanga Qazan
Novaya Ladoga Rus. Fed. 43 N1
Novaya Odessa Ukr. *see* Nova Odesa
Novaya Pismyanka Rus. Fed. *see* Leninogorsk
Novaya Sibir', Ostrov *i.* Rus. Fed. 39 O2

► Novaya Zemlya *is* Rus. Fed. 40 J1
3rd largest island in Europe.
europe [landscapes] ➤ 30–31
arctic [features] ➤ 214–215

Novaya Zhizn' Rus. Fed. *see* Kazinka
Nova Zagora Bulg. 58 H6
Novelda Spain 55 K6
Novellara Italy 56 C3
Nové Město nad Metují Czech Rep. 49 N5
Nové Mlýny, Vodní nádrž *resr* Czech Rep. 49 N7
Nové Zámky Slovakia 49 P8
Novgorod Rus. Fed. *see* Velikiy Novgorod
Novgorodka Rus. Fed. 43 J4
Novgorod Oblast' *admin. div.* Rus. Fed. *see* Novgorodskaya Oblast'
Novgorod-Severskiy Ukr. *see* Novhorod-Sivers'kyy
Novgorodskaya Oblast' *admin. div.* Rus. Fed. 43 N2
English form Novgorod Oblast
Novhorod-Sivers'kyy Ukr. 41 E6
Novhorod-Volynskiy Ukr. *see* Novohrad-Volyns'kyy
Novgradets Bulg. *see* Suvorovo

Novhorod-Sivers'kyy Ukr. 41 E6
also spelt Novgorod-Severskiy
Novi U.S.A. 173 J8
Novi Bečej Vojvodina, Srbija Yugo. 58 B3
Novi Grad Bos.-Herz. see Bosanski Novi
Novi Iskür Bulg. 58 E6
Novikovo Rus. Fed. 82 F3
Novi Kozarci Vojvodina, Srbija Yugo. 58 B3
Novi Kritsim Bulg. see Stamboliyski
Novi Ligure Italy 56 A4
Novillero Mex. 184 D4
Novi Marof Croatia 56 I2
Novi Pazar Bulg. 58 I5
Novi Pazar Srbija Yugo. 58 B5
Novi Sad Vojvodina, Srbija Yugo. 58 A3
also known as Újvidék
Novi Travnik Bos.-Herz. 56 J4
formerly known as Pucarevo
Novi Vinodolski Croatia 56 G3
Novlenskoye Rus. Fed. 43 U4
Novoaleksandropov Rus. Fed. 82 F3
Novoaleksandrovsk Rus. Fed. 41 G7
Novoaleksandrovskiy Rus. Fed. 43 P7
Novoalekseyevka Kazakh. see Khobda
Novoaltaysk Rus. Fed. 80 C2
formerly known as Chesnokovka
Novoanninskiy Rus. Fed. 41 H6
Novo Aripuanã Brazil 199 F6
Novoazov's'k Ukr. 41 F7
Novo Beograd Srbija Yugo. 58 B4
Novobod Tajik. 101 G2
also spelt Navabad
Novobod Tajik. 101 G2
also spelt Navabad; formerly known as
Shul'mak; formerly spelt Novabad
Novobogatinskoye Kazakh. see
Novobogatinskoye
Novobogatinskoye Kazakh. 102 B3
also known as Novobogatinsk
Novobureyskiy Rus. Fed. 82 C2
formerly known as Bureya-Pristan'
Novocheboksarsk Rus. Fed. 40 H4
Novocherkassk Rus. Fed. 41 G7
Novo Cruzeiro Brazil 203 D6
Novodolinka Kazakh. 103 H2
Novodugino Rus. Fed. 43 P6
Novodvinsk Rus. Fed. 40 G2
formerly known as Pervomayskiy
Novogeorgiyevka Rus. Fed. 82 B2
Novogezdilovo Rus. Fed. 43 Q9
Novogrudok Belarus see Navahrudak
Novogurovskiy Rus. Fed. 43 S7
Novo Hamburgo Brazil 203 B9
Novo Horizonte Brazil 206 D8
Novohrad-Volyns'kyy Ukr. 41 D6
also spelt Novograd-Volynskiy
Novoigorshok Rus. Fed. 85 F1
Novokazalinsk Kazakh. see Ayteke Bi
Novokhopersk Rus. Fed. 41 G6
Novokhovansk Rus. Fed. 43 K6
Novokiyevskiy Uval Rus. Fed. 82 C2
Novokizhinginsk Rus. Fed. 85 F1
Novokubansk Rus. Fed. 41 H7
formerly known as Novokubanskiy
Novokubanskiy Rus. Fed. see Novokubansk
Novokuybyshevsk Rus. Fed. 102 B1
Novokuznetsk Rus. Fed. 80 D2
formerly known as Stalinsk
Novolazarevskaya research station
Antarctica 223 A2
Novolukoml' Belarus see Novalukoml'
Novol'vovsk Rus. Fed. 43 T8
Novo Marapi Brazil 199 G5
Novomarkovka Rus. Fed. 103 H2
Novo Mesto Slovenia 56 H3
Novomichurinsk Rus. Fed. 43 U7
Novomikhaylovskiy Rus. Fed. 41 F7
Novo Miloševo Vojvodina, Srbija Yugo.
58 B3
Novomirgorod Ukr. see Novomyrhorod
Novomoskovs'k Ukr. 41 E6
Novomoskovsk Rus. Fed. 43 T7
Novomyrhorod Ukr. 41 D6
also spelt Novomirgorod
Novonazyvayevka Rus. Fed. see
Nazyvayevsk
Novonikolayevka Kazakh. 103 G4
Novonikolayevsk Rus. Fed. see Novosibirsk
Novonikolayevskiy Rus. Fed. 41 G6
Nóvooleksiyivka Ukr. 41 E7
Novo Olinda do Norte Brazil 199 G5
Novo Oriente Brazil 202 D3
Novoorsk Rus. Fed. 102 D2
Novo Parnarama Brazil 202 D3
Novopashiyskiy Rus. Fed. see
Gornozavodsk
Novopavlovsk Rus. Fed. 85 G2
Novopokrovka Kustanayskaya Oblast'
Kazakh. 103 F3
Novopokrovka Severnyy Kazakhstan Kazakh.
103 F1
Novopokrovka Vostochnyy Kazakhstan
Kazakh. 103 J2
Novopokrovskaya Rus. Fed. 41 G7
Novopolotsk Belarus see Navapolatsk
Novopskov Ukr. 41 F6
Novo Redondo Angola see Sumbe
Novorepnoye Rus. Fed. 102 B2
Novorossiysk Rus. Fed. 41 F7

Novorossiyskiy Kazakh. see
Novorossiyskoye
Novorossiyskoye Kazakh. 102 D2
formerly known as Novorossiyskiy
Novoryabnaya Rus. Fed. 39 K2
Novorzhev Rus. Fed. 43 K4
Novoselki Moskovskaya Oblast' Rus. Fed.
43 T7
Novoselki Tverskaya Oblast' Rus. Fed. 43 M6
Novoselovo Rus. Fed. 43 U5
Novoselskoye Rus. Fed. see
Achkhoy-Martan
Novosel'ye Rus. Fed. 43 J3
Novosergiyevka Rus. Fed. 102 C1
Novoshakhtinsk Rus. Fed. 41 F7
Novoshakhtinskiy Rus. Fed. 82 D3
Novosheshminsk Rus. Fed. 40 I5
Novosibirsk Rus. Fed. 80 C1
formerly known as Novonikolayevsk
Novosibirskaya Oblast' admin. div.
Rus. Fed. 80 C1
English form Novosibirsk Oblast
Novosibirskiye Ostrova is Rus. Fed. see
New Siberia Islands
Novosibirsk Oblast admin. div. Rus. Fed.
see Novosibirskaya Oblast'
Novosil' Rus. Fed. 43 S9
Novosokol'niki Rus. Fed. 43 L5
Novospasskoye Rus. Fed. 41 H6
Novotroitsk Rus. Fed. 102 D2
Novotroitskoye Kazakh. see Tole Bi
Novotroitskoye Rus. Fed. 43 O8
Novotroyits'ke Ukr. 41 E7
Novoukrainka Ukr. see Novoukrayinka
Novoukrayinka Ukr. 41 D6
also spelt Novoukrainka
Novoural'sk Rus. Fed. 102 D2
Novouzensk Rus. Fed. 102 B2
Novovasylivka Ukr. 43 O9
Novovolyns'k Ukr. 41 C6
Novovoronezh Rus. Fed. 41 F6
formerly known as Novovoronezhskiy
Novovoronezhskiy Rus. Fed. see
Novovoronezh
Novo-Voskresenovka Rus. Fed. 82 B1
Novovoznesenovka Kyrg. 103 I4
Novoyamskoye Rus. Fed. 43 P9
Novoye Leushino Rus. Fed. 43 V5
Novozavidovskiy Rus. Fed. 43 R5
Novozhilovskaya Rus. Fed. 40 I2
Novozybkov Rus. Fed. 43 M9
Novska Croatia 56 I3
Novy Boletsk Belarus 43 L8
Nový Bor Czech Rep. 49 L5
Novy Bykhaw Belarus 43 L8
Nový Dvor Belarus 42 F9
Nový Jičín Czech Rep. 49 O6
Novyya Kruki Belarus 42 I6
Novyya Zhuravichy Belarus 43 L8
Novyy Bor Rus. Fed. 40 J2
Novyye Burasy Rus. Fed. 102 A1
Novyye Ivatynki Rus. Fed. 43 V6
Novyye Petushki Rus. Fed. see Petushki
Novyy Izborsk Rus. Fed. 42 I4
Novyy Nekouz Rus. Fed. 43 T4
Novyy Oskol Rus. Fed. 41 F6
Novyy Port Rus. Fed. 38 H3
Novyy Ropsk Rus. Fed. 43 N9
Novyy Sinets Rus. Fed. 43 R8
Novyy Urengoy Rus. Fed. 38 H3
Novyy Urgal Rus. Fed. 82 D2
formerly known as Raz"yezd 3km
Novyy Uzen' Kazakh. see Zhanaozen
Novyy Zay Rus. Fed. 40 J5
Now Iran 100 C2
Nowa Deba Poland 49 S5
Nowa Ruda Poland 49 N5
Nowa Sarzyna Poland 49 T5
Nowa Sól Poland 49 M4
Nowata U.S.A. 178 D4
Nowdi Iran 100 B2
Nowe Poland 49 P2
Nowe Miasteczko Poland 49 M4
Nowe Miasto Lubawskie Poland 49 Q3
Nowe Miasto nad Pilicą Poland 49 R4
Nowe Skalmierzyce Poland 49 O4
Nowgong India see Nagaon
Nowgong India 96 C4
Now Kharegan Iran 100 C2
Noweye Lake Canada 167 K2
Nowgard Poland 49 M2
Nowogród Poland 49 S2
Nowogród Bobrzański Poland 49 M4
Nowood r. U.S.A. 180 F3
Noworadomsk Poland see Radomsko
Nowra Australia 147 F3
Nowshahr Iran 100 B2
Now Shahr Iran 100 B2
Nowshera Pak. 101 H3
Nowsüd Iran 100 A3
Nowy Dwór Gdański Poland 49 Q1
Nowy Dwór Mazowiecki Poland 49 R3
Nowy Sącz Poland 49 R6
historically known as Neu Sandez
Nowy Staw Poland 49 Q1
Nowy Targ Poland 49 R6
Nowy Tomyśl Poland 49 N3
Noxen U.S.A. 177 I4
Noxubee National Wildlife Refuge
nature res. U.S.A. 175 B5
Noy, Xé r. Laos 78 D4
Noy, Xé r. Laos 78 D4
Noya Spain see Noia
Noyabr'sk Rus. Fed. 38 H3
Noyant France 50 G5
Noyes Island U.S.A. 166 C4
Noyil r. India 94 C4
Noyon France 51 I3
Nozay France 50 E5
Nozizwe S. Africa 133 J7
Npitamaiong mt. Kenya 128 B4
Nqabeni S. Africa 133 O7
Nqamakwe S. Africa 133 L9
Nqutu S. Africa 133 O5
Nsalamu Zambia 127 F8
Nsambi Dem. Rep. Congo 126 C5
Nsanje Malawi 129 B9
formerly known as Port Herald
Nsawam Ghana 125 E5
Nseluka Zambia 127 F7
Nsoc Equat. Guinea 125 H6
Nsoko Swaziland 133 P4
Nsombo Zambia 127 F7
Nsukka Nigeria 125 G5
Nsumbu National Park Zambia see
Sumbu National Park
Ntalfa well Mauritania 122 B5
Ntambu Zambia 127 E8
Ntandembele Dem. Rep. Congo 126 C5
Ntcheu Malawi 129 B8
formerly spelt Ncheu
Ntchisi Malawi 129 B8
Ntem r. Cameroon 125 H6
formerly known as Campo
Ntha S. Africa 133 M5
Ntiona Chad 120 B6
Ntomba, Lac l. Dem. Rep. Congo 126 C4
Ntoroko Uganda 128 A4
Ntoum Gabon 126 A4
Ntui Cameroon 125 H5
Ntungamo Uganda 128 A5
Ntwetwe Pan salt pan Botswana 131 E4
Ntywenka S. Africa 133 M8
Nuakata Island P.N.G. 149 F1
Nuanetsi r. Zimbabwe see Mwenezi

Nuangan Indon. 75 C2
Nu'aym reg. Oman 105 F3
Nuba, Lake resr Sudan 121 F4
Nuba Mountains Sudan 128 A2
Nubian Desert Sudan 121 G4
Nucet Romania 58 D2
Nudol' Rus. Fed. 43 R5
Nueces r. U.S.A. 179 C6
Nueltin Lake Canada 167 L2
Nueva, Isla i. Chile 205 D9
Nueva Alejandría Peru 198 C6
Nueva Arcadia Hond. 186 A4
Nueva Ciudad Guerrero Mex. 179 C7
Nueva Esparta state Venez. 199 E2
Nueva Florida Venez. 198 D2
Nueva Germania Para. 201 F5
Nueva Gerona Cuba 186 C2
Nueva Harberton Arg. 205 D9
Nueva Lubecka Arg. 205 C7
Nueva Loja Ecuador 198 B4
Nueva Palmira Uruguay 204 F4
Nueva Rosita Mex. 185 E3
Nueva San Salvador El Salvador 185 H6
Nueva Villa de Padilla Mex. 185 F3
Nueve de Julio Arg. see 9 de Julio
Nuevitas Cuba 186 D2
Nuevo, Cayo i. Mex. 185 H4
Nuevo, Golfo g. Arg. 205 D6
Nuevo Casas Grandes Mex. 184 C2
Nuevo Ideal Mex. 184 D3
Nuevo Laredo Mex. 185 F3
Nuevo León Mex. 183 I9
Nuevo León state Mex. 185 F3
Nuevo Mamo Venez. 187 H5
Nufayyid Sabhah des. Saudi Arabia
104 D3
Nuga Mongolia 84 B1
Nugaal admin. reg. Somalia 128 F2
Nugaal watercourse Somalia 128 F3
Nuga Nuga, Lake Australia 149 F5
Nugget Point N.Z. 153 D14
Nugr' r. Rus. Fed. 43 R8
Nugrus, Gebel mt. Egypt 121 G3
Nugu r. India 94 C3
Nguru Islands P.N.G. 145 E2
formerly known as Red Group
Nuh, Ras pt Pak. 101 E5
Nuhaka N.Z. 152 L7
Nui i. Tuvalu 145 G2
Nui Con Voi r. Vietnam see Red River
Nuijamaa Fin. 43 J1
Nui Ti On mt. Vietnam 79 D5
Nuits-St-Georges France 51 K5
Nu Jiang r. China 86 A3 see Salween
Nukey Bluff hill Australia 146 B3
Nukha Azer. see Şäki

Nuku'alofa Tonga 145 H4
Capital of Tonga.
world [countries] ➤ 10–11

Nukufetau i. Tuvalu 145 G2
Nukulaelae i. Tuvalu 145 G2
also spelt Nukulailai; formerly known as
Mitchell Island
Nukulailai i. Tuvalu see Nukulaelae
Nukumanu Islands P.N.G. 145 E2
Nukunau i. Kiribati see Nikunau
Nukunonu atoll Tokelau see Nukunonu
Nukunonu atoll Tokelau 145 H2
also spelt Nukonono; formerly known as
Duke of Clarence
Nukus Uzbek. 102 D4
also known as Nökis
Nulato U.S.A. 164 D3
Nules Spain 55 K5
Nullagine Australia 150 C4
Nullagine r. Australia 150 C4
Nullarbor Australia 146 A2
Nullarbor National Park Australia 146 A2
Nullarbor Plain Australia 146 A2
Nullarbor Regional Reserve park Australia
146 A2
Nuluarniavik, Lac l. Canada 168 E1
Nulu'erhu Shan mts China 85 H3
Num i. Indon. 73 I7
Num Nepal 97 E4
Numalla, Lake salt flat Australia 147 E2
Numan Nigeria 125 I4
Nu'mān i. Saudi Arabia 104 A2
Numata Gunma Japan 91 F6
Numata Hokkaidō Japan 90 G3
Numazu Japan 91 F7
Numbi Gate S. Africa 133 P2
Numbulwar Australia 148 B2
Numfoor i. Indon. 73 H7
Numin r. China 82 B3
Numkaub Namibia 130 C3
Nummi Fin. 45 M3
Numurkah Australia 147 E4
Nunaksaluk Island Canada 169 I2
Nunakuluut i. Greenland 165 O3
also known as Nunarsuit
Nunap Isua c. Greenland see
Farewell, Cape
Nunarsuit i. Greenland see Nunakuluut
Nunavik reg. Canada 169 E1
Nunavut admin. div. Canada 167 L2
Nuneaton U.K. 47 K11
Nungatta National Park Australia 147 F4
Nungesser Lake Canada 167 M5
Nungnain Sum China 85 H2
Nungo Moz. 131 H2
Nunivak Island U.S.A. 164 C4
Nunkapasi India 95 I1
Nunkun mt. Jammu and Kashmir 96 C3
Nunligran Rus. Fed. 39 S3
Nuñoa Peru 200 C3
Nuñomoral Spain 54 E4
Nunukan i. Indon. 77 G2
Nuojiang China see Tongjiang
Nuomin r. China 85 J1
Nuoro Sardegna Italy 57 B8
Nupani i. Solomon Is 145 F3
Nuqayy, Jabal mts Libya 120 C4
Nuqrah Saudi Arabia 104 C3
Nuqui Col. 198 B3
Nur r. Iran 100 C2
Nura r. Kazakh. 103 G2
Nūrābād Iran 100 B4
Nurakita i. Tuvalu see Niulakita
Nurata Uzbek. 103 F4
also spelt Nurota
Nurdağ mts Turkey 107 C3
Nure r. Italy 56 B3
Nurek Tajik. see Norak
Nuremberg Germany 48 I6
also known as Nürnberg
Nūr Gal Afgh. 101 G3
Nuri Mex. 184 C2
Nuri Sudan 121 G5
Nuri, Teluk b. Indon. 77 E3
Nuristan reg. Afgh. 101 G3
Nurla Jammu and Kashmir 96 C2
Nurmes Fin. 44 O3
Nurmijärvi Fin. 45 N3
Nurmo Fin. 44 M3
Nürnberg Germany see Nuremberg
Nurota Uzbek. see Nurata
Nurpur Pak. 101 G4
Nurrai Lakes salt flat Australia 146 A2
Nurri, Mount hill Australia 147 E2
Nursfjellet mt. Norway 44 K2
Nurste Estonia 42 D3
Nürtingen Germany 48 G7
Nurzec r. Poland 49 T3

Nusa Tenggara Barat prov. Indon. 77 G5
English form Western Lesser Sunda Islands
Nusa Tenggara Timur prov. Indon. 75 B5
English form Eastern Lesser Sunda Islands
Nusaybin Turkey 107 E3
historically known as Nisibis
Nusela, Kepulauan is Indon. 75 D3
Nu Shan mts China 86 A3
Nushki Pak. 101 F4
Nutak Canada 169 I1
Nutarawit Lake Canada 167 L2
Nutrioso U.S.A. 183 O8
Nutwood Downs Australia 148 B2
Nuugaatsiaap Imaa inlet Greenland 165 N2
also known as Karrats Fjord
Nuugaatsiaq Greenland 165 N2

Nuuk Greenland 165 N3
Capital of Greenland. Also known as
Godthåb.
world [countries] ➤ 10–11

Nuuksion kansallispuisto nat. park Fin.
42 F1
Nuupas Fin. 44 N2
Nuussuaq Greenland 165 N2
also known as Kraulshavn
Nuussuaq pen. Greenland 165 N2
Nuwakot Nepal 97 D3
Nuweiba el Muzeina Egypt 121 G2
Nuwekloof pass S. Africa 132 H10
Nuwerus S. Africa 132 C8
Nuweveldberge mts S. Africa 132 F9
Nuyts, Point Australia 146 B5
Nuyts Archipelago is Australia 146 B3
Nuyts Archipelago Conservation Park
nature res. Australia 146 B3
Nuytsland Nature Reserve Australia
151 D7
Nuzvid India 94 D2
Nxai Pan National Park Botswana 131 E3
Nxaunxau Botswana 130 D3
Nyaän, Bukit hill Indon. 77 F2
Nyabessan Cameroon 125 H6
Nyabing Australia 151 B7
Nyack U.S.A. 177 L4
Nyagan' Rus. Fed. 38 H3
formerly known as Nyakh
Nyaguguka China see Yajiang
Nyagrong China see Xinlong
Nyahua Tanz. 129 B6
formerly known as Thompson's Falls
Nyainqêntanglha Feng mt. China 89 E6
Nyainqêntanglha Shan mts China 89 E6
English form Nyenchen Tanglha Range
Nyainrong China 89 E5
Nyakahura Kagera Tanz. 128 A5
Nyakahura Kagera Tanz. 128 A5
Nyakaliro Tanz. 128 B5
Nyakallong S. Africa 133 K4
Nyakanazi Tanz. 128 A5
Nyäker Sweden 44 L3
Nyakh Rus. Fed. see Nyagan'
Nyakhachava Belarus 42 G9
Nyakrom Ghana 125 E5
Nyala Sudan 120 E6
Nyalam China 89 D6
also known as Congdü
Nyamandhlovu Zimbabwe 131 F3
Nyamapanda Zimbabwe 131 G3
Nyambiti Tanz. 128 B5
Nyamlell Sudan 126 E2
Nyamtumbo Tanz. 129 C7
Nyande Dem. Rep. Congo see Masvingo
Nyandoma Rus. Fed. 40 G3
Nyandomskiy Vozvyshennost' hills
Rus. Fed. 40 F3
Nyanga Congo 126 B5
Nyanga Gabon 126 A5
Nyanga prov. Gabon 126 A5
Nyanga Zimbabwe 131 G3
formerly spelt Inyanga
Nyanga National Park Zimbabwe 131 G3
formerly known as Rhodes Inyanga National
Park; formerly spelt Inyanga National Park
Nyang Qu r. China 89 E6
Nyang Qu r. China 89 D6
Nyankpala Ghana 125 E4
Nyanza prov. Kenya 128 B5
Nyapa, Gunung mt. Indon. 77 G2
Nyapongeth Sudan 128 B3
Nyar r. India 96 C3
Nyarling r. Canada 167 H2

Nyasa, Lake Africa 129 B7
3rd largest lake in Africa and 10th in the
world. Also known as Malawi, Lake or
Niassa, Lago.
africa [landscapes] ➤ 112–113

Nyasaland country Africa see Malawi
Nyashabozh Rus. Fed. 40 J2
Nyasvizh Belarus 42 H8
also spelt Nesvizh
Nyathi Zimbabwe 131 F3
formerly known as Inyati
Nyaunglebin Myanmar 78 B4
Nyaungu Myanmar 78 A3
Nyays r. Rus. Fed. 40 L3
Nyazura Zimbabwe 131 G3
formerly spelt Inyazura
Nyborg Denmark 45 J5
Nyborg Norway 44 O1
Nyborg Sweden 44 M2
Nybro Sweden 45 K4
Nyeboe Land reg. Greenland 165 N1
Nyeharelaye Belarus 42 I8
Nyêmo China 89 E6
also known as Tarrong
Nyenchen Tangla Range mts China see
Nyainqêntanglha Shan
Nyeri Kenya 128 C5
Nyeshcharda, Vozyera l. Belarus 43 K6
Nyhammar Sweden 45 K3
Nyi, Co l. China 89 D5
Nyika Zambia 127 E8
also known as Malawi National Park
Nyima China 89 D5
Nyimba Zambia 127 F8
Nyingchi China 89 F6
also known as Pula
Nyinma China see Maqu
Nyirbátor Hungary 49 T8
Nyírbéltek Hungary 49 T8
Nyíregyháza Hungary 49 S8
Nyiru, Mount Kenya 128 C4
Nykarleby Fin. 44 M3
also known as Uusikaarlepyy
Nykøbing Denmark 45 J5
Nykøbing Mors Denmark 45 J4
Nykøbing Sjælland Denmark 45 J5
Nyköping Sweden 45 L4
Nylstroom S. Africa 133 M1
Nylsvley nature res. S. Africa 133 M1
Nymagee Australia 147 E3
Nymboida National Park Australia 147 G2
Nymburk Czech Rep. 49 M5
Nynäshamn Sweden 45 L4
Nyngan Australia 147 E2
Nyogzê China 89 C6
Nyoman r. Belarus/Lith. 42 E8
also spelt Neman
Nyomanskaya Nizina lowland Belarus
42 G8
Nyon Switz. 51 M6

Nyong r. Cameroon 125 H6
Nyons France 51 L8
Nyřany Czech Rep. 49 K6
Nyrob Rus. Fed. 40 K3
Nyrud Norway 44 O1
Nysa Poland 49 O5
Nysa Kłodzka r. Poland 49 O5
Nysa Łużycka r. Germany/Poland see Neiße
Nysäter Sweden 45 K3
Nysätern Sweden 44 K3
Nysh Rus. Fed. 82 F2
Nyssa U.S.A. 180 C4
Nystad Fin. see Uusikaupunki
Nyūdō-zaki pt Japan 90 F5
Nyuk, Ozero l. Rus. Fed. 44 O2
Nyuksenitsa Rus. Fed. 40 H3
Nyunzu Dem. Rep. Congo 127 F6
Nyurba Rus. Fed. 39 L3
Nyuvchim Rus. Fed. 40 I3
Nyuya Rus. Fed. 39 L3
Nyuya r. Rus. Fed. 39 L3
Nyyskiy Zaliv lag. Rus. Fed. 82 F1
Nyzh'ohirs'kyy Ukr. 41 E7
Nzambi Congo 126 A5
Nzara Sudan 126 F3
Nzébéla Guinea 124 C4
Nzega Tanz. 129 B6
Nzérékoré Guinea 124 C5
N'zeto Angola 127 B6
formerly known as Ambrizete
Nzi r. Côte d'Ivoire 124 D5
Nzilo, Lac l. Dem. Rep. Congo 127 E7
Nzingu Dem. Rep. Congo 126 E5
Nzo r. Côte d'Ivoire 124 C5
N'Zo, Réserve de Faune du nature res.
Côte d'Ivoire 124 D5
Nzobe Dem. Rep. Congo 127 B6
Nzoia r. Kenya 128 B4
Nzoro r. Dem. Rep. Congo 126 F4
Nzwani i. Comoros 129 E8
also known as Anjouan; also spelt Ndjouani

↓ O

Oahe, Lake U.S.A. 178 B2
Oahu i. U.S.A. 181 [inset] Y1
northamerica [environments] ➤ 162–163
Oaitupu i. Tuvalu see Vaitupu
Oakbank Australia 146 D3
Oak Bluffs U.S.A. 177 N4
Oak City U.S.A. 183 L2
Oak Creek U.S.A. 172 F8
Oakdale CA U.S.A. 182 D4
Oakdale LA U.S.A. 179 D6
Oakes U.S.A. 178 C2
Oakey Australia 147 F1
Oakfield U.S.A. 176 G2
Oak Grove LA U.S.A. 175 B5
Oak Grove MI U.S.A. 173 I6
Oakham U.K. 47 L11
Oak Harbor OH U.S.A. 176 B4
Oak Harbor WA U.S.A. 180 B2
Oak Hill OH U.S.A. 176 C7
Oak Hill WV U.S.A. 176 D8
Oakhurst U.S.A. 182 E4
Oak Island U.S.A. 182 E4
Oak Knolls U.S.A. 182 D7
Oak Lake Canada 167 K5
Oakland CA U.S.A. 182 B4
Oakland MD U.S.A. 176 F7
Oakland ME U.S.A. 177 P1
Oakland NE U.S.A. 178 C3
Oakland airport U.S.A. 182 B4
Oakland City U.S.A. 174 C4
Oaklands Australia 147 E3
Oak Lawn U.S.A. 174 C3
Oakley KS U.S.A. 178 B4
Oakley MI U.S.A. 173 I7
Oakover r. Australia 150 C4
Oak Park U.S.A. 172 F9
Oakridge U.S.A. 180 B4
Oak Ridge U.S.A. 176 A9
Oakura N.Z. 152 H7
Oak View U.S.A. 182 E7
Oakville Canada 168 E5
Oamaru N.Z. 153 E13
Oaonui N.Z. 152 H7
Oaro N.Z. 153 H10
Oasis U.S.A. 182 G4
Oates Coast reg. Antarctica see Oates Land
Oates Land reg. Antarctica 223 K2
also known as Oates Coast
Oatlands Australia 147 E5
Oatlands S. Africa 133 I9
Oaxaca Mex. 185 F5
Oaxaca state Mex. 185 F5
Ob' r. Rus. Fed. 38 G3
Ob, Gulf of sea chan. Rus. Fed. see
Obskaya Guba
Oba Canada 168 D3
Oba i. Vanuatu see Aoba
Obaghan r. Kazakh. see Ubagan
Obaluat' Belarus 43 K6
Obal' canal Belarus 43 K6
Obala Cameroon 125 H5
Oba Lake Canada 173 G4
Obama Japan 91 D7
Oban Nigeria 125 H5
Oban U.K. 46 G7
Obanazawa Japan 90 G5
Obanbori Qayroqqum resr Tajik. 101 G3
also known as Kayrakkumskoye
Vodokhranilishche
Oban Hills mt. Nigeria 125 H5
O Barco Spain see El Barco de Valdeorras
Obbia Somalia see Hobyo
Obbola Sweden 44 M3
Obdorsk Rus. Fed. see Salekhard
Obed Canada 167 G4
Obeliai Lith. 42 G6
Obelisk mt. N.Z. 153 D13
Oberá Arg. 204 G2
Oberau Germany 48 I8
Obere Donau park Germany 48 F7
Obere Saale park Germany 48 I5
Oberes Westerzgebirge park Germany
49 L4
Oberlin KS U.S.A. 178 B4
Oberlin OH U.S.A. 176 C4
Obernai France 51 N4
Oberndorf am Neckar Germany 48 F7
Oberon Australia 147 F3
Oberpfälzer Wald mts Germany 48 J6
Oberpullendorf Austria 49 N8
Oberstdorf Germany 48 H8
Oberviechtach Germany 49 J6
Oberwart Austria 49 N8
Obi i. Indon. 75 C3
Obi, Kepulauan is Indon. 75 C3
Obi, Selat sea chan. Indon. 75 C3
Óbidos Brazil 199 H5
Obigarm Tajik. 101 G2
Obihiro Japan 90 H3
Obilatu i. Indon. 75 C3
Obilić Kosovo, Srbija Yugo. 58 C6
Obil'noye Rus. Fed. 41 H7
Obion r. U.S.A. 174 B4
Obira Japan 90 G2

Ob'-Irtysh r. Asia 38 G3
2nd longest river in Asia and 5th in the world.
asia [landscapes] ➤ 62–63

Obispos Venez. 198 D3
Obluch'ye Rus. Fed. 82 C2

Obninsk Rus. Fed. 43 R6
Obnora r. Rus. Fed. 43 V3
Obo Cent. Afr. Rep. 126 E3
Obo China 84 D4
Obogorap S. Africa 132 E4
Obock Djibouti 128 D2
Obokote Dem. Rep. Congo 126 E5
Obolo Nigeria 125 G5
Obong, Gunung mt. Sarawak Malaysia 77 E2
Oborniki Poland 49 N3
Obouya Congo 126 B5
Oboyan' Rus. Fed. 41 F6
Obozerskiy Rus. Fed. 40 G3
Obra India 97 D4
Obra r. Poland 49 M3
Obrage Arg. 204 F3
Obregón, Presa resr Mex. 184 C3
Obrenovac Srbija Yugo. 58 B4
O'Brien U.S.A. 180 B4
Obrochishte Bulg. 58 J5
Obruk Turkey 106 C3
Obrzycko Poland 49 N3
Observatory Hilet Canada 166 C4
Obsha r. Rus. Fed. 43 N6
Obshchiy Syrt hills Rus. Fed. 102 B2
Obskaya Guba sea chan. Rus. Fed. 38 H3
English form Ob, Gulf of
Obuasi Ghana 125 E5
Obubra Nigeria 125 H5
Obudovac Bos.-Herz. 56 K4
Obudu Nigeria 125 H5
Obukhovo Rus. Fed. 40 I3
Ob"yachevo Rus. Fed. 40 I3
Ocala U.S.A. 175 D6
Ocampo Mex. 185 E3
Ocaña Col. 198 C2
Ocaña Peru 200 B3
Ocaña Spain 55 H5
Occidental, Cordillera mts Chile 200 C4
Occidental, Cordillera mts Col. 198 B4
Occidental, Cordillera mts Peru 200 C4
Oceana U.S.A. 176 D8
Ocean Cape U.S.A. 166 B3
Ocean City MD U.S.A. 177 J7
Ocean City NJ U.S.A. 177 K6
Ocean Falls Canada 166 E4
Ocean Island Kiribati see Banaba
Ocean Island atoll U.S.A. see Kure Atoll
Oceano U.S.A. 182 D6
Oceans Cay i. Bahamas 186 D1
Oceanside U.S.A. 183 G8
Ocean Springs U.S.A. 175 B6
Ochakiv Ukr. 41 D7
Och'amch'ire Georgia 107 E2
Ocher Rus. Fed. 40 J4
Ochi mt. Greece 59 F10
also known as Ókhi Óros
Ochiishi-misaki pt Japan 90 I3
Ochil Hills U.K. 46 I7
Ochkyne Ukr. 43 O9
Ochlockonee r. U.S.A. 175 C6
Ochrida, Lake Albania/Macedonia see
Ohrid, Lake
Ochsenfurt Germany 48 H6
Ochthonia Greece 59 F10
also spelt Okhthonia
Ochthonia, Akra cr Greece 59 F10
Ocilla U.S.A. 175 D6
Ockelbo Sweden 45 L3
Ocland Romania 58 G2
Ocmulgee r. U.S.A. 175 D6
Ocna Mureş Romania 58 E2
Ocna Sibiului Romania 58 F2
Ocolaşul Mare, Vârful mt. Romania 58 G2
Ocoña Peru 200 C3
O'Connell Creek r. Australia 149 D4
Oconomowoc U.S.A. 172 E7
Oconto U.S.A. 172 F6
Oconto Falls U.S.A. 172 E6
O Corgo Spain 54 D2
Ocoruro Peru 200 C3
Ocos Guat. 185 G6
Ocosingo Mex. 185 G5
Ocotal Nicaragua 186 B4
Ocotlán Mex. 185 F5
Ocozocoautla Mex. 185 G5
October Revolution Island Rus. Fed. see
Oktyabr'skoy Revolyutsii, Ostrov
Ocurri Bol. 200 D4
Ocussi East Timor see Pantemakassar
Ocussi enclave East Timor 75 C5
Oda Ghana 125 E5
Oda Japan 91 C7
Oda, Jebel mt. Sudan 121 H4
Ódáðahraun lava field Iceland 44 [inset] C2
Ödaejin N. Korea 82 C4
Odae-san National Park S. Korea 83 C5
Ódaigahara-zan mt. Japan 91 D7
Odanah U.S.A. 172 C4
Ödate Japan 90 G4
Odawara Japan 91 F7
Odda Norway 45 I3
Odder Denmark 45 J5
Odei r. Canada 167 L3
Odell U.S.A. 172 E9
Odem U.S.A. 179 C7
Odemira Port. 54 C7
Ödemiş Turkey 106 A3
Ödenburg Hungary see Sopron
Odendaalsrus S. Africa 133 K4
Odensbacken Sweden 45 K4
Odense Denmark 45 J5
Oder r. Germany 48 I4
also spelt Odra (Poland)
Oderbucht b. Germany 49 L1
Oderhaff b. Germany 49 L1
also known as Stettiner Haff
Oderzo Italy 56 E3
Odesa Ukr. 41 D7
also spelt Odessa
Ódeshog Sweden 45 K4
Odes'ka Oblast' admin. div. Ukr. 58 K1
English form Odessa Oblast; also spelt
Odes'ka Oblast'
Odessa Ukr. see Odesa
Odessa U.S.A. 179 B6
Odessa Oblast admin. div. Ukr. see
Odes'ka Oblast'
Odesskaya Oblast' admin. div. Ukr. see
Odes'ka Oblast'
Odessus Bulg. see Varna
Odi watercourse Sudan 121 H5
Odiel r. Spain 54 E7
Odienné Côte d'Ivoire 124 D4
Odintsovo Rus. Fed. 43 S6
Odobeşti Romania 58 I3
Odobeştii, Măgura mt Romania 58 H3
Odolanów Poland 49 O4
Odom Inlet Antarctica 222 T1
Odorheiu Secuiesc Romania 58 G2
Odoyev Rus. Fed. 43 R8
Odra r. Poland 49 P6
Odra r. Spain 54 G2
Odžaci Vojvodina, Srbija Yugo. 58 A3
Odzala, Parc National d' nat. park Congo
126 B4
Odzi Zimbabwe 131 G3
Odzi r. Zimbabwe 131 G3
Oea Libya see Tripoli
Oedong S. Korea 91 A7
Oeiras Brazil 202 D3
Oelde Germany 48 F4
Oelrichs U.S.A. 178 B3
Oelsnitz Germany 49 J5
Oenpelli Australia 148 B2

Oesel i. Estonia see Hiiumaa
Oeufs, Lac des l. Canada 169 F2
Oeversee Germany 48 G1
Of Turkey 107 E2
O'Fallon r. U.S.A. 180 F3
Ofanto r. Italy 57 I7
Offa Nigeria 125 G4
Offenbach am Main Germany 48 F5
Offenburg Germany 48 E7
Offerdal Sweden 44 K3
Ofidoussa i. Greece 59 H12
Ofotfjorden sea chan. Norway 44 L1
Oga Japan 90 G5
Ogachi Japan 90 G5
Ogaden reg. Eth. 128 E3
Oga-hantō pen. Japan 90 F5
Ōgaki Japan 91 E7
Ogallala U.S.A. 178 B3
Ogan r. Indon. 76 C3
Ogasawara-shotō is N. Pacific Ocean see
  Bonin Islands
Ogawa Japan 90 G6
Ogascanane, Lac l. Canada 173 O3
Ogbomosho Nigeria see Ogbomoso
Ogbomoso Nigeria 125 G4
  also spelt Ogbomosho
Ogden IA U.S.A. 178 D3
Ogden UT U.S.A. 180 E4
Ogdensburg U.S.A. 177 J1
Ogeechee r. U.S.A. 175 D6
Ogema U.S.A. 172 C5
Ogi Japan 90 F6
Ogidaki Canada 168 C4
Ogilvie r. Canada 164 F3
Ogilvie Mountains Canada 166 A1
'Oglât el Khnâchich well Mali 122 C1
Oglat Sbot well Alg. 122 C4
Oglio r. Italy 56 C3
Ogmore Australia 149 F4
Ognon r. France 51 L5
Oğnut Turkey see Göynük
Ogoamas, Gunung mt. Indon. 75 B3
Ogoja Nigeria 125 H5
Ogoki r. Canada 168 C3
Ogoki Lake Canada 168 C3
Ogooué r. Gabon 126 A5
Ogooué-Ivindo prov. Gabon 126 B5
Ogooué-Lolo prov. Gabon 126 B5
Ogooué-Maritime prov. Gabon 126 A5
Ogoron Rus. Fed. 82 C1
Ogosta r. Bulg. 58 E5
Ogou r. Togo 125 F5
O'Grady, Lake salt flat Australia 151 B6
Ograżden mts Bulg./Macedonia see
  Ograzhden
Ograżden mts Bulg./Macedonia 58 D7
  also spelt Ograzhden
Ogre Latvia 42 F5
Ogre r. Latvia 42 F5
Ogudnevo Rus. Fed. 43 T5
Ogulin Croatia 56 H3
Ogun state Nigeria 125 F5
Ogurchinskiy, Ostrov i. Turkm. 102 C2
  also known as Ogurjaly Adasy or
  Turkmen Adasy
Ogurjaly Adasy i. Turkm. see
  Ogurchinskiy, Ostrov
Oğuz Azer. 107 F2
  formerly known as Vartashen
Ohafia Nigeria 125 G5
Ohai N.Z. 153 B13
Ohakune N.Z. 152 J7
Ohanet Alg. 123 H3
Ohangwena admin. reg. Namibia 130 C3
Ōhara Japan 91 G7
O'Hare airport U.S.A. 172 F9
Ōhata Japan 90 G4
Ohau N.Z. 152 J8
Ohau, Lake N.Z. 153 D12
Ohcejohka Fin. see Utsjoki
O'Higgins Chile 200 C5
O'Higgins, admin. reg. Chile 204 C4
O'Higgins, Lago l. Chile 205 B8
Ohio r. U.S.A. 172 D9
Ohio r. U.S.A. 178 E4
Ohio state U.S.A. 176 C5
Ohio Range mts Antarctica 223 Q1
Öhm r. Germany 48 G5
Ohře r. Germany 42 I3
'Ohonua Tonga 145 H4
Ohope N.Z. 152 L5
Ohrdruf Germany 48 I5
Ohře r. Germany 48 I3
Ohrid Macedonia 58 B7
Ohrid, Lake Albania/Macedonia 58 B7
  also known as Ochrida, Lake or Ohridsko
  Ezero or Ohrit, Liqeni i
Ohridsko Ezero l. Albania/Macedonia see
  Ohrid, Lake
Ohrigstad S. Africa 133 O1
Ohrigstad Dam Nature Reserve S. Africa
  133 O1
Öhringen Germany 48 G6
Ohrit, Liqeni i l. Albania/Macedonia see
  Ohrid, Lake
Ohura N.Z. 152 I6
Oiapoque Brazil 199 I4
Oiapoque r. Brazil/Fr. Guiana 199 I3
Oiba Col. 198 C3
Oich r. U.K. 46 H6
Oik Kazakh. see Uyuk
Oil City U.S.A. 176 F4
Oildale U.S.A. 182 E6
Oi Qu r. China 86 A2
Oirase-gawa r. Japan 90 G4
Oise r. France 51 I4
Oiseaux du Djoudj, Parc National des
  nat. park Senegal 124 A2
Ōita Japan 91 B8
Oiti mt. Greece 59 D10
Oiti nat. park Greece 59 D10
Oituz r. Romania 58 H2
Oiuru well Libya 120 C4
Oiwake Japan 90 G4
Ojai U.S.A. 182 F5
Ojailén r. Spain 54 H6
Ojalava i. Samoa see Upolu
Ojamaa r. Estonia 42 I2
Ojcowski Park Narodowy nat. park Poland
  49 Q5
Öje Sweden 45 K3
Ojika-jima i. Japan 91 A8
Ojinaga Mex. 184 D2
Ojitlán Mex. 185 F5
Ojiya Japan 90 F6
Ojobo Nigeria 125 G5
Ojo de Laguna Mex. 184 D2
Ojo de Liebre, Lago b. Mex. 184 B3
Ojos del Salado, Nevado mt. Arg./Chile
  204 C2
  2nd highest mountain in South America.
  south america [landscapes] 190–191
Ojuelos de Jalisco Mex. 185 E4
Ojung Sweden 45 K3
Oka Nigeria 125 G5
Oka r. Rus. Fed. 43 R9
Okahandja Namibia 130 C4
Okahu b. N.Z. see Jackson Bay
Okahukura N.Z. 152 H6
Okains Bay N.Z. 153 H11
Okains Bay b. N.Z. 153 H11
Okaka Nigeria 125 F4

Okakarara Namibia 130 C4
Okak Islands Canada 169 I1
Okanagan Falls Canada 166 G5
Okanagan Lake Canada 166 G5
Okanagan U.S.A. 180 C2
Okanogan r. U.S.A. 180 C2
Okanogan Range mts U.S.A. 180 B2
Okaputa Namibia 130 C4
Okara Pak. 101 H4
Okarem Turkm. 100 C2
  also spelt Ekerem
Okarito Lagoon N.Z. 153 E11
Okaukuejo Namibia 130 B3
Okavango r. Botswana/Namibia 130 D3
  world [land cover] 18–19
  africa [issues] 116–117
Okavango admin. reg. Namibia 130 C3
Okavango Delta swamp Botswana 130 D3
  Largest oasis in the world.
Ōkawa Japan 91 B8
Okaya Japan 91 F6
Okayama Japan 91 C7
Okayama pref. Japan 91 C7
Okazaki Japan 91 E7
Okeechobee U.S.A. 175 D7
Okeechobee, Lake U.S.A. 175 D7
Okehampton U.K. 47 H13
Okemah U.S.A. 179 C5
Okene Nigeria 125 G5
Oker r. Germany 48 H3
Oketo Japan 90 H3
Okha India 96 A5
Okha Rus. Fed. 82 F1
Okhadunga Nepal see Okhaldhunga
Okhaldhunga Nepal 97 E4
  also spelt Okhadunga
Okhansk Rus. Fed. 40 J4
Ókhi Óros mt. Greece see Ochi
Okhotino Rus. Fed. 43 T4
Okhotka r. Rus. Fed. 39 O4
Okhotsk Rus. Fed. 39 O4
Okhotsk, Sea of Japan/Rus. Fed. 90 I2
Okhotskoye More sea Japan/Rus. Fed. see
  Okhotsk, Sea of
Okhthonía Greece see Ochthonia
Okhtyrka Ukr. 41 E6
  also spelt Akhtyrka
Okhvat Rus. Fed. 43 N5
Okiep S. Africa 132 B5
Okinawa i. Japan 81 L7
Okinawa-guntō is Japan see
  Okinawa-shotō
Okinawa-shotō is Japan 81 L7
  also known as Okinawa-guntō
Okino-Daitō-jima i. Japan 81 M8
Okino-shima i. Japan 91 B7
Okino-shima i. Japan 91 C6
Okino-Tori-shima i. Japan 81 N8
  also known as Parece Vela; formerly known
  as Douglas Reef
Oki-shotō is Japan 91 C6
Okitipupa Nigeria 125 G5
Okkan Myanmar 78 A4
Oklahoma state U.S.A. 179 C5
Oklahoma City U.S.A. 179 C5
  State capital of Oklahoma.
Oklawaha r. U.S.A. 175 D6
Okmulgee U.S.A. 179 C5
Oko, Wadi watercourse Sudan 121 H4
Okola Cameroon 125 H5
Okolona MS U.S.A. 174 B5
Okolona OH U.S.A. 176 A4
Okondja Gabon 126 B5
Okonek Poland 49 N2
Okotoks Canada 167 H5
Okotusu well Namibia 130 A3
Okovskiy Les for. Rus. Fed. 43 N7
Okoyo Congo 126 B5
Okpety, Gora mt. Kazakh. 88 C2
Oksbøl Denmark 45 J5
Øksfjord Norway 44 M1
Oksovskiy Rus. Fed. 40 F3
Øksskolten mt. Norway 44 K2
Oksu r. Tajik. 101 H2
Oktemberyan Armenia see Hoktemberyan
Oktumkum, Peski des. Turkm. 102 C2
Oktwin Myanmar 78 B4
Oktyabr' Kazakh. see Kandyagash
Oktyabr' Rus. Fed. 43 S4
Oktyabr' Kazakh. see Kandyagash
Oktyabr' Rus. Fed. 41 I5
Oktyabr'skiy Belarus see Aktsyabrski
Oktyabr'skiy Belarus see Aktsyabrski
Oktyabr'skiy Kazakh. 103 E1
Oktyabr'skiy Amurskaya Oblast' Rus. Fed.
  82 C1
Oktyabr'skiy Arkhangel'skaya Oblast'
  Rus. Fed. 40 G3
Oktyabr'skiy Ivanovskaya Oblast' Rus. Fed.
  43 V4
Oktyabr'skiy Kaluzhskaya Oblast' Rus. Fed.
  43 R7
Oktyabr'skiy Kamchatskaya Oblast'
  Rus. Fed. 39 P4
Oktyabr'skiy Murmanskaya Oblast' Rus. Fed.
  44 P2
Oktyabr'skiy Respublika Bashkortostan
  Rus. Fed. 40 J5
Oktyabr'skiy Ryazanskaya Oblast' Rus. Fed.
  43 T7
Oktyabr'skiy Sverdlovskaya Oblast' Rus. Fed.
  40 K4
Oktyabr'skiy Volgogradskaya Oblast'
  Rus. Fed. 41 G7
  formerly known as Kruglyakov
Oktyabr'skoye Kazakh. 103 F1
Oktyabr'skoye Rus. Fed. 38 G3
  formerly known as Kondinskoye
Oktyabr'skoye Rus. Fed. 102 C1
Oktyabr'skoy Revolyutsii, Ostrov i.
  Rus. Fed. 39 J2
  English form October Revolution Island
Oktyb'sk Turkm. 102 C2
Okučani Croatia 56 J3
Ōkuchi Japan 91 B8
Okulovka Rus. Fed. 43 N4
Okuru N.Z. 153 C11
Okushiri-kaikyō sea chan. Japan 90 F3
Okushiri-tō i. Japan 90 E3
Okutango-hantō pen. Japan 91 D7
Okwa watercourse Botswana 130 E4
Ola Rus. Fed. 39 P4
Ola U.S.A. 179 D5
Olafsfjörður Iceland 44 [inset] B2
Ólafsvík Iceland 44 [inset] B2
Olan, Pic d' mt. France 51 M8
Olancha U.S.A. 182 F5
Olanchito Hond. 186 B4
Öland i. Sweden 45 L5
Olanga Rus. Fed. 44 O2
Olary Australia 146 D3
Olary watercourse Australia 146 C3
Olathe U.S.A. 178 D4
Olavakod India 94 C4
Olavarría Arg. 204 E5
Oława Poland 49 N5
Olbernhau Germany 49 K5
Olbia Sardegna Italy 56 B8

Olbia, Golfo di b. Sardegna Italy 56 B8
Ol'chan Rus. Fed. 39 O3
Olcott U.S.A. 176 G2
Old Bahama Channel Bahamas/Cuba
  186 D2
Old Bastar India 94 D2
Old Cherrabun Australia 150 D3
Old Cork Australia 149 D4
Old Crow Canada 164 F3
Oldeide Norway 45 I3
Oldenburg Germany 48 F2
Oldenburg in Holstein Germany 48 H1
Oldenzaal Neth. 48 D2
Olderdalen Norway 44 M1
Oldfield r. Australia 151 C7
Old Forge U.S.A. 177 K2
Old Gidgee Australia 151 B5
Oldham U.K. 47 J10
Old Head of Kinsale Rep. of Ireland
  47 D12
Oldmeldrum U.K. 46 J6
Old Mkushi Zambia 127 F8
Old Morley S. Africa 133 N8
Old Orchard Beach U.S.A. 177 O2
Old Perlican Canada 169 K4
Old River U.S.A. 182 E6
Olds Canada 167 H5
Old Saybrook U.S.A. 177 M4
Old Speck Mountain U.S.A. 177 O1
Old Station U.S.A. 182 C1
Oldtown U.S.A. 176 G7
Old Town U.S.A. 174 G2
Olduvai Gorge tourist site Tanz. 128 B5
Old Washington U.S.A. 176 D5
Old Wives Lake Canada 167 J5
Olean U.S.A. 176 G3
Ölekert r. Kazakh. 103 H1
Olecko Poland 49 T1
Oleggio Italy 56 B3
Olekma r. Rus. Fed. 39 M3
Olekminsk Rus. Fed. 39 M3
Oleksandriya Ukr. 41 E6
  also spelt Aleksandriya
Ölen Norway 45 I4
Olenegorsk Rus. Fed. 44 P1
  formerly known as Olenya
Olenek r. Rus. Fed. 39 L2
Olenek Bay Rus. Fed. see Olenekskiy Zaliv
Olenekskiy Zaliv b. Rus. Fed. 39 M2
  English form Olenek Bay
Oleniy, Ostrov i. Rus. Fed. 39 H2
Olenino Rus. Fed. 43 O5
Olenitsa Rus. Fed. 40 E2
Olenivs'ki Kar"yery Ukr. see
  Dokuchayevs'k
Olenti r. Kazakh. 102 C2
Olenti r. Kazakh. see Ölengi
Oleńti r. Kazakh. 103 H1
Olentuy Rus. Fed. 85 G2
Olenya Rus. Fed. see Olenegorsk
Oléron, Île d' i. France 50 E7
Oleśnica Poland 49 O4
Olesno Poland 49 P5
Olet Tongo mt. Indon. 77 G5
Olevs'k Ukr. 41 C6
Ol'ga Rus. Fed. 82 D4
Olga, r. Canada 168 F3
Olga, Mount Australia 148 A5
Ólgiy Mongolia 84 A1
Olhão Port. 54 D7
Olhava Fin. 44 N2
Olhos d'Agua Brazil 207 J4
Olia Chain mts Australia 148 A5
Oliana Spain 55 M2
Oliena Sardegna Italy 57 B8
Olib i. Croatia 56 G4
Olifants watercourse Namibia 130 C5
Olifants r. S. Africa 132 C8
Olifants r. W. Cape S. Africa 132 F10
Olifants r. W. Cape S. Africa 132 B5
Olifants r. S. Africa 131 F4
Olifantshoek S. Africa 132 G4
Olifantsrivierberge mts S. Africa 132 C9
Olimarao atoll Micronesia 73 K5
Olimbos hill Greece see Olympus, Mount
Olimbos mt. Greece see Olympus, Mount
Olimpia Brazil 206 E7
Olimpos Beydağları Milli Parkı nat. park
  Turkey 106 B3
Olinalá Mex. 185 F5
Olinda Entrance sea chan. Australia 149 E1
Olinga Moz. 131 H3
Olio Australia 149 D4
Oliosi Brazil 207 I3
Olite Spain 55 J2
Oliva Arg. 204 E4
Oliva Spain 55 K6
Oliva Hill Spain 55 J6
Oliva, Cordillera de mts Arg./Chile 204 C3
Oliva de la Frontera Spain 54 E6
Olivares, Cerro de mt. Arg./Chile 204 C3
Olive Hill U.S.A. 176 B7
Olivehurst U.S.A. 182 C2
Oliveira Brazil 203 D7
Oliveira de Douro Port. 54 C3
Oliveira dos Brejinhos Brazil 202 D5
Olivença Moz. see Lupilichi
Olivença-a-Nova Angola see
  Capunda Cavilongo
Oliver Canada 166 G5
Oliver Lake Canada 167 K3
Olivet France 51 H5
Olivet U.S.A. 178 D2
Olivia U.S.A. 178 D2
Oljoro Wells Tanz. 129 C6
Ol'keyek r. Kazakh. see Ul'kayak
Ol'khovatka Rus. Fed. 41 F6
Ol'khovets Rus. Fed. 43 U6
Olkusz Poland 49 Q5
Ollachea Peru 200 C3
Ollagüe Chile 200 C5
Ollioules France 51 L9
Ollita, Cordillera de mts Arg./Chile 204 C3
Ollitas mt. Arg. 204 C3
Öllölä Fin. 44 O3
Ollon Congo 126 D5
Olmaliq Uzbek. see Almalyk
Olmedo Spain 54 G3
Olmeto Corse France 56 A7
Olmos Peru 198 B6
Olmütz Czech Rep. see Olomouc
Olney IL U.S.A. 174 B4
Olney MD U.S.A. 177 H6
Olney TX U.S.A. 179 C5
Olochi Rus. Fed. 85 H1
Olofström Sweden 45 K4
Ol'oinka Kazakh. 103 I1
Olomane r. Canada 169 J3
Olomouc Czech Rep. 49 O6
  also known as Olmütz
Olonets Rus. Fed. 40 E3
Olonetskaya Vozvyshennost' hills
  Rus. Fed. 40 D3
Olongapo Phil. 74 B3
Olongliko Indon. 77 B3
Olonne-sur-Mer France 50 E6
Oloron-Ste-Marie France 50 F9
Olosenga i. American Samoa see
  Swains Island
Olot Spain 55 N2

Olot Uzbek. see Alat
Olovo Bos.-Herz. 56 K4
Olovyannaya Rus. Fed. 85 G1
Oloy, Qatorkŭhi mts Asia see Alai Range
Olpad Rus. Fed. 96 B5
Olpe Germany 48 E4
Ol'sa r. Belarus 43 M7
Olše r. Czech Rep. 49 P6
Ol'sha Rus. Fed. 43 M7
Olsztyn Poland 49 R2
  historically known as Allenstein
Olsztynek Poland 49 R2
Olt r. Romania 58 F5
Olta Arg. 204 D3
Olte, Sierra de mts Arg. 205 C6
Olten Switz. 51 N5
Oltenița Romania 58 H4
Oltet r. Romania 58 F4
Oltina Romania 58 I4
Oltinkŭl Uzbek. see Altynkul'
Oltintopkan Tajik. 101 G1
Oltu Turkey 107 E2
Oluan Cape Taiwan see Oluan Pi
Oluan Pi c. Taiwan 87 G4
  English form Oluan Cape
Olutanga i. Phil. 74 B5
Olvega Spain 55 J3
Olvera Spain 54 F8
Ol'viopol' Ukr. see Pervomays'k
Olym r. Rus. Fed. 43 T9
Olymbos hill Cyprus see Olympos
Olympia tourist site Greece 59 C11
Olympia U.S.A. 180 B3
  State capital of Washington.
Olympic National Park U.S.A. 180 B3
Olympos hill Cyprus 108 A3
  also spelt Olimbos or Olymbos
Olympos mt. Greece see Olympus, Mount
Olympos nat. park Greece 59 D8
Olympus, Mount Greece see Olympus, Mount
Olympus, Mount U.S.A. 180 B3
Olyutorskiy, Mys c. Rus. Fed. 39 R4
Olyutorskiy Zaliv b. Rus. Fed. 39 R4
Olzheras Rus. Fed. see Mezhdurechensk
Oma China 89 C3
Oma Japan 90 G4
Oma r. Rus. Fed. 40 H2
Omachi Japan 91 E6
Omae-zaki pt Japan 91 F7
Ōmagari Japan 90 G5
Omagh U.K. 47 E9
Omaguas Peru 198 C6
Omaha U.S.A. 178 D3
Omaha Indian Reservation res. U.S.A.
  178 C3
Omaheke admin. reg. Namibia 130 C4
Omakere N.Z. 152 L8
Omal'skiy Khrebet mts Rus. Fed. 82 E1
Omalur India 94 C4
Oman country Asia 105 F4
  spelt 'Umān in Arabic; formerly known as
  Muscat and Oman
  asia [countries] 64–67
Oman, Gulf of Asia 105 F4
Omangambo Namibia 130 B4
Omarama N.Z. 153 D12
Omaruru Namibia 130 B4
Omaruru r. Namibia 130 B4
Omas Peru 200 A3
Omatako watercourse Namibia 130 D3
Omate Peru 200 C4
Omatjette Namibia 130 B4
Omawewozo Botswana 132 G2
Omba i. Vanuatu see Aoba
Ombai, Selat sea chan. Indon. 75 C5
Ombalantu Namibia see Uutapi
Ombella-Mpoko pref. Cent. Afr. Rep. 126 C3
Ombika watercourse Namibia 130 B3
Ombouè Gabon 126 A5
Ombu China 89 D3
Omdraaisvlei S. Africa 132 H7
Omdurman Sudan 121 G6
Ōme Japan 91 F7
Omedu Estonia 42 I3
Omegna Italy 56 A3
Omeo Australia 147 E4
Ömerler Turkey 59 K9
Ometepe, Isla de i. Nicaragua 186 B5
Ometepec Mex. 185 F5
Omgoy Wildlife Reserve nature res. Thai.
  78 B4
Om Hajēr Eritrea 121 H6
Omidiyeh Iran 100 B4
Ōmihachiman Japan 91 E7
Omihi N.Z. 153 G11
Omineca Mountains Canada 166 E3
Omiš Croatia 56 I5
Omitara Namibia 130 C4
Ōmiya Japan 91 F7
Ommaney, Cape U.S.A. 166 C4
Ommen Neth. 48 D3
Ömnögovi prov. Mongolia 84 D3
Omodeo, Lago l. Sardegna Italy 57 B8
Omoku Nigeria 125 G5
Omolon Rus. Fed. 39 Q3
Omolon r. Rus. Fed. 39 Q3
Omo National Park Eth. 128 B3
Omono-gawa r. Japan 90 G5
Omro U.S.A. 172 E6
Omsk Rus. Fed. 80 A1
Omskaya Oblast' admin. div. Rus. Fed. 80 A1
  English form Omsk Oblast
Omsk Oblast admin. div. Rus. Fed. see
  Omskaya Oblast'
Omsukchan Rus. Fed. 39 P3
Ōmū Japan 90 H2
Omu, Vârful mt. Romania 58 G3
Omu-Aran Nigeria 125 G4
Omulew r. Poland 49 S3
Ōmura Japan 91 A8
Omura-wan b. Japan 91 A8
Omurtag Bulg. 58 H5
Omusati admin. reg. Namibia 130 B3
Omutninsk Rus. Fed. 40 J4
Onalaska U.S.A. 172 B7
Onaman Lake Canada 168 C3
Onancock U.S.A. 177 J8
Onang Indon. 75 A3
Onangué, Lac l. Gabon 126 A5
Onarga U.S.A. 172 E10
Onavas Mex. 184 C2
Onawa U.S.A. 178 C3
Onbingwin Myanmar 79 B5
Oncativo Arg. 204 E3
Öncocua Angola 130 A2
Öncül Turkey 109 K1
Onda Spain 55 K5
Ondangwa Namibia 130 B3
Ondarroa Spain 55 I1
Ondava r. Slovakia 49 S7
Ondjiva Angola 127 B9
Ondo Nigeria 125 G5
Ondo state Nigeria 125 G5
Öndörhaan Mongolia 85 F2
Öndörhushuu Mongolia 85 F2
Ondor Mod China 85 G3
Ondor Sum China 85 G3

One and a Half Degree Channel Maldives
  93 D10
One and a Half Mile Opening sea chan.
  Australia 149 E2
Onega Rus. Fed. 40 F3
Onega r. Rus. Fed. 40 F3
Onega, Lake Rus. Fed. 43 Q1
  3rd largest lake in Europe. Also known as
  Onezhskoye Ozero.
  europe [landscapes] 30–31
Onega Bay g. Rus. Fed. see
  Onezhskaya Guba
One Hundred and Fifty Mile House
  Canada see 150 Mile House
One Hundred Mile House Canada see
  100 Mile House
Oneida IL U.S.A. 172 C9
Oneida NY U.S.A. 177 J2
Oneida TN U.S.A. 176 A9
Oneida Lake U.S.A. 177 J2
O'Neill U.S.A. 178 C3
Onekaka N.Z. 152 G8
Onekama U.S.A. 172 G6
Onekotan, Ostrov i. Rus. Fed. 39 P5
Oneonta AL U.S.A. 175 C5
Oneonta NY U.S.A. 177 J3
Oneroa N.Z. 152 I4
Oneşti Romania 58 H2
  formerly known as Gheorghiu-Dej
Onet-le-Château France 51 I8
Onezhskaya Guba g. Rus. Fed. 40 F2
Onezhskiy Kanal canal Rus. Fed. 43 Q3
Onezhskoye Ozero l. Rus. Fed. see
  Onega, Lake
Onga r. India 95 D1
Onga Gabon 126 B5
Ongandjera N.Z. 152 K7
Ongeri Dem. Rep. Congo 126 F6
Ông Đốc, Sông r. Vietnam 79 D6
Ongerup S. Africa 132 C8
Ongi Dundgovĭ Mongolia 84 D2
Ongi Övörhangay Mongolia 84 D2
Ongjin N. Korea 83 B5
Ongniud Qi China see Wudan
Ongole India 94 D3
Ongon Mongolia 84 D2
Ongtüstik Qazaqstan Oblysy admin. div.
  Kazakh. see Yuzhnyy Kazakhstan
Onguday Rus. Fed. 88 D1
Oni Georgia 107 E2
Onida U.S.A. 178 B2
Onilahy r. Madag. 131 [inset] I4
Onistagane, Lac l. Canada 169 G3
Onitsha Nigeria 125 G5
Onjati Mountain Namibia 130 C4
Onjiva Angola see Ondjiva
Onkamo Fin. 44 O3
Onkivesi l. Fin. 44 N3
Onmakere N.Z. see Omakere
Onna Japan 81 L7
Onnes Rus. Fed. 39 N3
Ōno Fukui Japan 91 E7
Ōno Hokkaidō Japan 90 G4
Onoda Japan 91 B8
Onomichi Japan 91 C7
Onon Mongolia 85 F1
Onon Gol r. Mongolia 85 G1
Onon, Gora mt. Rus. Fed. 82 B2
Onotoa atoll Kiribati 145 G2
  also spelt Onatu
Ons, Illa de i. Spain 54 C2
Onsan S. Korea 91 A7
Onseepkans S. Africa 132 D5
Onslow Australia 150 A4
Onslow Bay U.S.A. 174 E5
Onsŏng N. Korea 82 C4
Ontake-san vol. Japan 83 F6
Ontario prov. Canada 167 N5
Ontario CA U.S.A. 182 G7
Ontario OR U.S.A. 180 C3
Ontario WI U.S.A. 172 C7
Ontario, Lake Canada/U.S.A. 173 P7
Onteniente Spain see Ontinyent
Ontinyent Spain 55 K6
  also spelt Onteniente
Ontojärvi l. Fin. 44 O2
Ontong Java Atoll Solomon Is 145 E2
  formerly known as Lord Howe Atoll
Ontur Spain 55 J6
Onud i. Kiribati see Onotoa
Onverwacht Suriname 199 H3
Onyx U.S.A. 182 F6
Oodnadatta Australia 146 B1
Oodweyne Somalia 128 E2
Ooldea Australia 146 A2
Ooldea Range hills Australia 146 A2
Oologah Lake resr U.S.A. 178 D4
Oombulg Aboriginal Reserve Australia
  150 D2
Ooratippra r. Australia 148 C4
Oorindi Australia 149 D4
Oos-Londen S. Africa see East London
Oostanaula r. U.S.A. 174 C5
Oostende Belgium see Ostend
Oosterhout Neth. 48 B4
Oosterschelde est. Neth. 48 A4
Oostvleteren Belgium 51 I2
Ootacamund India see Udagamandalam
Ootsa Lake Canada 166 E4
Ootsa Lake l. Canada 166 E4
Opala Dem. Rep. Congo 126 E5
Oparau N.Z. 152 I5
Opari r. N.Z. 152 J8
Opari Sudan 128 B4
Oparino Rus. Fed. 40 I4
Oparo i. Fr. Polynesia see Rapa
Opasatika r. Canada 168 D3
Opasatika Lake Canada 168 D3
Opasquia Canada 167 M4
Opasquia Provincial Park Canada 167 M4
Opataca, Lac l. Canada 169 G3
Opatija Croatia 56 G3
Opatów Poland 49 R5
Opava Czech Rep. 49 O6
Opava r. Czech Rep. 49 O6
Opelika U.S.A. 175 C5
Opelousas U.S.A. 179 D6
Opeongo Lake Canada 168 E4
Opheim U.S.A. 180 F2
Ophir N.Z. 153 D13
Ophir, Gunung vol. Indon. 76 C2
Opihikao U.S.A. 181 [inset] Z2
Opinaca r. Canada 168 E2
Opinaca, Réservoir resr Canada 168 E2
Opinnagau r. Canada 168 D2
Opis tourist site Iraq 107 F4
Opiscotéo, Lac l. Canada 169 H2
Opobo Nigeria 125 G5
Opochka Rus. Fed. 43 J5
Opoco Bol. 200 D5
Opocopa Mun. Ecuador 198 B5
Opoczno Poland 49 R4
Opole Poland 49 O5
  historically known as Oppeln
Opole Lubelskie Poland 49 S4
Opononi N.Z. 152 H3
O포чинай Kazakh. 102 C2
Oporto Port. 54 C3
Öөндörшхушуу see
Opotiki N.Z. 152 L6
Opovo Vojvodina, Srbija Yugo. 58 B3
Opp U.S.A. 175 C6
Oppdal Norway 44 J3

Oppedal Norway 45 I3
Oppeln Poland see Opole
Oppido Lucano Italy 57 H8
Oppland county Norway 45 J3
Opportunity U.S.A. 180 C3
Oprişor Romania 58 E4
Optaşi-Măgura Romania 58 F4
Opua N.Z. 152 I3
Opunake N.Z. 152 G7
Opuwo Namibia 130 B3
Opytnoye Rus. Fed. 102 B3
Oqqal"a Uzbek. see Akkala
Oqtosh Uzbek. see Aktash
Oquawka U.S.A. 174 B3
Or r. Rus. Fed. 102 D2
Øra Norway 44 M1
Oracle U.S.A. 183 N9
Oradea Romania 58 D2
  also known as Nagyvárad
Orahovac Kosovo, Srbija Yugo. 58 B6
Orahovica Croatia 56 J3
Orai India 96 C4
Oraibi U.S.A. 183 N6
Oraibi Wash watercourse U.S.A. 183 N6
Orain r. France 51 L6
Oral Kazakh. see Ural'sk
Orajärvi Fin. 44 N2
Oral Kazakh. see Ural'sk
Oran Alg. 123 E2
  also spelt Ouahran or Wahran
Orán Arg. 201 D5
Oran, Sebkha d' salt pan Alg. 55 K9
Orange France 51 K8
Orange r. Namibia/S. Africa 132 A5
Orange r. Namibia/S. Africa 132 A5
  also spelt Oranje
Orange CA U.S.A. 182 G8
Orange TX U.S.A. 179 D6
Orange VA U.S.A. 176 G7
Orange, Cabo c. Brazil 199 I3
Orangeburg U.S.A. 175 D5
Orange Cay i. Bahamas 186 D1
Orange City U.S.A. 178 C3
Orange Cove U.S.A. 182 E5
Orange Free State prov. S. Africa see
  Free State
Orange Park U.S.A. 175 D6
Orangerie Bay P.N.G. 149 F1
Orangevale U.S.A. 182 C3
Orangeville Canada 168 D5
Orangeville U.S.A. 183 M2
Orange Walk Belize 185 H5
Orani Sardegna Italy 57 B8
Orani Phil. 74 B3
Oranienburg Germany 49 K3
Oranje r. Namibia/S. Africa see Orange
Oranje Gebergte hills Suriname 199 H4
Oranjemund Namibia 130 C6
Oranjerivier S. Africa 132 H5
Oranjestad Aruba 187 E4
  Capital of Aruba.
Oranjestad Neth. Antilles 187 H3
Oranjeville S. Africa 133 M3
Orantjugurr, Lake salt flat Australia 150 E4
Oranzherei Rus. Fed. 102 A3
Orapa Botswana 131 E4
Oras Phil. 74 C3
Orašac Bos.-Herz. 56 I4
Orăştie Romania 58 E3
Orašje Bos.-Herz. 56 K3
Oraș Stalin Romania see Braşov
Orava r. Slovakia 49 Q6
Orava, Vodná nádrž resr Slovakia 49 Q6
Oravais Fin. 44 M3
Oravița Romania 58 C4
Oravská Magura mts Slovakia 49 Q6
Orawia N.Z. 153 B14
Orba Co l. China 89 C5
Orbassano Italy 51 N7
Orbeasca Romania 58 G4
Orbec France 50 G3
Orbetello Italy 56 D6
Orbieu r. France 51 I9
Orbost Australia 147 F4
Örbyhus Sweden 45 L3
Orbost Australia 147 F4
Orcadas research station S. Atlantic Ocean
  222 V2
Orcera Spain 55 I6
Orchard Mesa U.S.A. 183 P2
Orchha India 96 C4
Orchila, Isla i. Venez. 199 E2
Orchomenos Greece 59 D10
Orchy r. U.K. 46 G7
Orco r. Italy 56 D3
Orco r. Italy 51 N7
Ord r. Australia 150 E3
Ord, Mount hill Australia 150 D3
Ord Mountain U.S.A. 183 H7
Ord River Dam Australia 150 E3
Ord River Nature Reserve Australia
  150 E2
Ordu Turkey see Yayladağı
Ordu Turkey 107 D2
Ordubad Azer. 107 F3
Ordway U.S.A. 178 B4
Ordzhonikidze Kazakh. 103 E1
  formerly known as Denisovka
Ordzhonikidze Rus. Fed. see Vladikavkaz
Ordzhonikidze Ukr. 41 E7
Ordzhonikidzeabad Tajik. see Kofarnihon
Ordzhonikidzevskaya Rus. Fed. see
  Sleptsovskaya
Ore Nigeria 125 G5
Öreälven r. Sweden 44 L3
Öreälven r. Sweden 45 K3
Örebro Sweden 45 K4
Örebro county Sweden 45 K4
Oredezh r. Rus. Fed. 43 L3
Oregon IL U.S.A. 174 B3
Oregon OH U.S.A. 176 B4
Oregon WI U.S.A. 172 D8
Oregon state U.S.A. 180 B4
Oregon City U.S.A. 180 B3
Orekhi-Vydritsa Belarus see Arekhawsk
Orekhov Ukr. see Orikhiv
Orekhovno Rus. Fed. 43 L4
Orekhovo Belarus see Arekhawsk
Orekhovo-Zuyevo Rus. Fed. 43 T6
Orel Permskaya Oblast' Rus. Fed. 40 K4
Orel Rus. Fed. 82 D1
Orel Oryol'skaya Oblast' Rus. Fed. see Oryol
Orel, Gora mt. Rus. Fed. 82 E1
Orel', Ozero l. Rus. Fed. 82 E1
Orelek mt. Bulg. 58 E7
Orellana Peru see Ucayali
Orellana prov. Ecuador 198 C5
Orellana Peru 198 B6
Orellana, Embalse de resr Spain 54 F5
Orel Oblast admin. div. Rus. Fed. see
  Orlovskaya Oblast'
Orem U.S.A. 183 M1
Ore Mountains Czech Rep./Germany see
  Erzgebirge
Ören Turkey 59 K12
Ören Turkey 106 A3
Orenburg Rus. Fed. 102 C2
  formerly known as Chkalov

Orenburg Oblast *admin. div.* Rus. Fed. *see*
Orenburgskaya Oblast'
Orenburgskaya Oblast' *admin. div.*
Rus. Fed. **102** B2
English form Orenburg Oblast; formerly known as Chkalovskaya Oblast'
Orense Arg. **204** F5
Orense Spain *see* Ourense
Oreón, Dhíavlos *sea chan.* Greece *see* Oreon, Diavlos
Oreon, Diavlos *sea chan.* Greece **59** D10
also spelt Oreón, Dhíavlos
Oreor Palau *see* Koror
Orepuki N.Z. **153** B14
Oresh Bulg. **58** G5
Öreskilsälven *r.* Sweden **45** J4
Orestiada Greece **58** H7
also known as Orestiás
Orestiás Greece *see* Orestiada
Öresund *strait* Denmark/Sweden **45** K5
Oretana, Cordillera *mts* Spain *see* Toledo, Montes de
Oreti *r.* N.Z. **153** C14
Orewa N.Z. **152** I4
Orfane *well* Niger **125** G2
Orfanou, Kolpos *b.* Greece **58** E8
Orford Bay Australia **149** D1
Orford Ness *hd* U.K. **47** N11
Organabo Fr. Guiana **199** H3
Organ Pipe Cactus National Monument *nat. park* U.S.A. **183** N9
Orgeyev Moldova *see* Orhei
Orgil Mongolia **84** C1
Orgiva Spain **55** H8
Orgon Tal China **85** J3
Orgtrud Rus. Fed. **43** V5
Orgün Afgh. **101** G3
Orhaneli Turkey **106** B3
also known as Beyce
Orhangazi Turkey **58** K8
Orhei Moldova **58** J1
formerly spelt Orgeyev or Orkhey
Orhei *prov.* Moldova **58** H2
Orhontuul Mongolia **84** E1
Orhy, Pic d' *mt.* France/Spain **55** J2
Oria Spain **55** I7
Orichi Rus. Fed. **40** J4
Oriental, Cordillera *mts* Bol. **200** D4
Oriental, Cordillera *mts* Col. **198** C2
Oriental, Cordillera *mts* Peru **200** C3
Orientale *prov.* Dem. Rep. Congo **126** C4
formerly known as Haut-Congo or Haut-Zaïre
Oriente Brazil **201** D2
Orient Island U.S.A. **177** M4
Orihuela Spain **55** K6
Orikhiv Ukr. **41** E7
also spelt Orekhov
Orikum Albania **59** A8
Orillia Canada **168** E4
Orimattila Fin. **45** N3
Orin U.S.A. **180** F4
▶**Orinoco** *r.* Col./Venez. **199** F2
world (land images) ➡ 12–13
Orinoco Delta Venez. **199** F2
Orion U.S.A. **172** C9
Oripää Fin. **45** M3
Oriskany U.S.A. **177** J2
Orissa *state* India **95** E1
formerly known as Jajnagar
Orissaare Estonia **42** E3
Oristano *Sardegna* Italy **57** A9
Oristano, Golfo di *b. Sardegna* Italy **57** A9
Orivesi Fin. **45** N3
Orivesi *l.* Fin. **44** O3
Oriximiná Brazil **199** H5
▶**Orizaba** Mex. **185** F5
Orizaba, Pico de *vol.* Mex. **185** F5
3rd highest mountain in North America. Also known as Citlaltépetl.
northamerica (landscapes) ➡ 156–157
Orizona Brazil **206** D6
Orjonikidzeobod Tajik. *see* Kofarnihon
Örkelljunga Sweden **45** K4
Orkhey Moldova *see* Orhei
Orkhomenós Greece *see* Orchomenos
Orkney S. Africa **133** K3
Orkney *is* U.K. **46** I4
Orla *r.* Poland **49** O5
Orla Poland **49** O2
Orland U.S.A. **182** B2
Orlândia Brazil **206** F7
Orlando U.S.A. **175** D6
Orleaes Brazil **203** B9
Orléans France **51** H5
Orleans *MA* U.S.A. **177** P4
Orleans *VT* U.S.A. **177** M1
Orléans, Île d' *i.* Canada **169** G4
Orléansville Alg. *see* Ech Chélif
Orlické Hory *mts* Czech Rep. **49** N5
Orlik Rus. Fed. **80** F2
Orlik, Vodní nádrž *resr* Czech Rep. **49** L6
Orljava *r.* Croatia **56** I3
Orlov Rus. Fed. **40** I4
formerly known as Khalturin
Orlov Gay Rus. Fed. **102** C3
Orlovo Rus. Fed. **43** R9
Orlovskaya Oblast' *admin. div.* Rus. Fed. **43** R8
English form Orel Oblast
Orlovskiy Rus. Fed. **41** G7

Orly *airport* France **51** I4
Ormankans *hill* Latvia **42** G5
Ormara Pak. **101** F5
Ormara, Ras *hd* Pak. **101** F5
Ormília Greece *see* Ormylia
Ormoc Phil. **74** C4
Ormond N.Z. **152** L6
Ormond Beach U.S.A. **175** D6
Ormskirk U.K. **47** J10
Ormylia Greece **59** E8
also spelt Ormilia
Ornans France **51** M5
Orne *r.* France **50** F3
Orne *r.* France **50** G4
Ørnes Norway **44** K2
Orneta Poland **49** R1
Örnö *i.* Sweden **45** L4
Örnsköldsvik Sweden **44** L3
Örö *i.* Fin. **42** D2
Oro N. Korea **83** B4
Oro, Lac *l.* Mali **124** E2
Orobayaya Bol. **201** E3
Orobie, Alpi *mts* Italy **56** B2
Orocó Brazil **202** E4
Orocué Col. **198** D3
Orodara Burkina **124** D4
Orofino U.S.A. **180** C3
Orog Nuur *salt l.* Mongolia **84** D2
Oro Grande U.S.A. **183** G7
Orol Dengizi *salt l.* Kazakh./Uzbek. *see* Aral Sea
Oromia *admin. reg.* Eth. **128** C2
Oromocto Canada **169** H4
Oromocto Lake Canada **169** H4
Oron Israel **108** F7
Oron Nigeria **125** H5
Orona *i.* Kiribati **145** H2
formerly known as Hull Island
Orono U.S.A. **174** G7
Oronoque Guyana **199** G4
Oronoque *r.* Guyana **199** G4
Orontes *r.* Lebanon/Syria **109** H3
also known as ʿĀṣī or ʿĀṣī, Nahr al
Orope Venez. **198** D2
Oropesa, Cabo de *c.* Spain **55** L4
Oroqen Zizhiqi China *see* Alihe
Oroquieta Phil. **74** B4
Ororbia Spain **55** J2
Orós Brazil **202** E3
Orós, Açude *resr* Brazil **202** E3
Orosei *Sardegna* Italy **57** B8
Orosei, Golfo di *b. Sardegna* Italy **57** B8
Orosháza Hungary **49** R9
Oroszlány Hungary **49** P8
Orotukan Rus. Fed. **39** P3
Oro Valley U.S.A. **183** N9
Oroville *CA* U.S.A. **182** C2
Oroville *WA* U.S.A. **180** C2
Oroville, Lake *resr* U.S.A. **182** C2
Orqohan China **85** I1
Orrefors Sweden **45** K4
Orri, Monte *hill Sardegna* Italy **57** A9
Orkjelen *hill* Norway **45** J3
Orroroo Australia **146** C3
Orsa Sweden **45** K3
Örsági Tájvédelmi Körzet *nature res.* Hungary **49** N9
Orsha Belarus **43** L7
Orsha Rus. Fed. **43** R5
Orshanka Rus. Fed. **40** H4
Orsjön *l.* Sweden **45** L3
Orsk Rus. Fed. **102** D2
Ørsta Norway **44** I3
Örsundsbro Sweden **45** L4
Ortaca Turkey **59** J12
Orta Nova Italy **56** H7
Orta Toroslar *plat.* Turkey **108** E1
Orte Italy **56** E6
Ortegal, Cabo *c.* Spain **54** D1
Orteguaza *r.* Col. **198** C4
Orthez France **50** F5
Ortholmen Sweden **45** K3
Ortigueira Brazil **206** C11
Ortigueira Spain **54** D1
Ortişoara Romania **58** C2
Ortíz Mex. **184** C2
Ortiz Venez. **199** E2
Ortles *mt.* Italy **56** C2
Ortona Italy **56** G6
Ortonville U.S.A. **173** J8
Ortonville *MN* U.S.A. **178** C2
Ortospana Afgh. *see* Kābul
Örträsk Sweden **44** L2
Örtülü Turkey *see* Şenkaya
Oru Estonia **42** I2
Orulgan, Khrebet *mts* Rus. Fed. **39** M3
Orumbo Namibia **130** C4
Orumbo Boka *hill* Côte d'Ivoire **124** D5
Orūmīyeh Iran *see* Urmia
Orūmīyeh, Daryācheh-ye *salt l.* Iran *see* Urmia, Lake
Oruro Bol. **200** D4
Oruro *dept* Bol. **200** D4
Orūzgān *prov.* Afgh. **101** F3
Orvault France **50** E4
Orvieto Italy **56** E6
historically known as Urbs Vetus or Velsuna or Volsinii
Orville Coast Antarctica **222** T1
Orwell *OH* U.S.A. **176** E4
Orwell *VT* U.S.A. **177** L2
Orxon Gol *r.* China **85** H1
Oryahovo Bulg. **58** E5
Oryol Rus. Fed. *see* Orel
Orzinuovi Italy **56** B3
Orzyc *r.* Poland **49** S3
Orzysz Poland **49** S2
Orzyce, Jezioro *l.* Poland **49** T2
Os Norway **44** J3
Osa *r.* Latvia **42** H5
Osa *r.* Poland **49** Q4
Osa Rus. Fed. **40** J4
Osa, Península de *pen.* Costa Rica **186** C5
Osage *IA* U.S.A. **174** A3
Osage *WV* U.S.A. **176** E6
Osage *r.* U.S.A. **178** D4
Osage City U.S.A. **178** D4
▶**Ōsaka** Japan **91** D7
world (cities) ➡ 24–25
Ōsaka *pref.* Japan **90** D7
Osakarovka Kazakh. **103** H2
Ōsaka-wan *b.* Japan **91** D7
Osasco Brazil **206** G10
Osawatomie U.S.A. **178** D4
Osborn S. Africa **133** P5
Osborne U.S.A. **178** C4
Oscar Fr. Guiana **199** H4
Oscar Range *hills* Australia **150** D3
Osceola *AR* U.S.A. **174** B5
Osceola *IA* U.S.A. **174** A3
Osceola *MO* U.S.A. **178** D4
Osceola *WI* U.S.A. **172** A5
Oschersleben (Bode) Germany **48** I3
Oschiri *Sardegna* Italy **57** B8
Oscoda U.S.A. **173** J6
Osečina *Srbija* Yugo. **58** A4
O Seixo Spain **54** C3
Ösel *i.* Estonia *see* Hiiumaa
Osensjøen *l.* Norway **45** J3
Osetr *r.* Rus. Fed. **43** T6
Ōse-zaki *pt* Japan **91** A8
Osgode Canada **168** F4
O'Sullivan, Lac *l.* Canada **173** Q4
Osh Kyrg. **103** H4
Osh *admin. div.* Kyrg. **103** H4
English form Osh Oblast; also known as Oshskaya Oblast'
Oshakati Namibia **130** B3
Oshamambe Japan *see* Oshamanbe
Oshamanbe Japan **90** G3
also spelt Oshamambe

Oshana *admin. reg.* Namibia **130** B3
Oshika Japan **90** G5
Oshika-hantō *pen.* Japan **90** G5
Oshikango Namibia **130** B3
Oshikoto *admin. reg.* Namibia **130** C3
Oshikuku Namibia **130** B3
Ō-shima *i.* Japan **90** F4
Ō-shima *i.* Japan **91** D8
Ō-shima *i.* Japan **91** F7
Oshima-hantō *pen.* Japan **90** F3
Oshin *r.* Nigeria **125** G4
Oshivelo Namibia **130** C3
Oshkosh *NE* U.S.A. **178** B3
Oshkosh *WI* U.S.A. **172** E6
Oshmyany Belarus *see* Ashmyany
Oshnovīyeh Iran **100** A3
Osh Oblast *admin. div.* Kyrg. *see* Osh
Oshogbo Nigeria **125** F4
also spelt Osogbo
Oshper Rus. Fed. **40** L2
Oshskaya Oblast' *admin. div.* Kyrg. *see* Osh
Oshtorān Kūh *mt.* Iran **100** B3
Oshun *state* Nigeria *see* Osun
Oshwe Dem. Rep. Congo **126** C5
Osijek Croatia **56** K3
Osikovitsa Bulg. **58** F6
Osilinka *r. B.C.* Canada **166** E3
Osimo Italy **56** F5
Osipaonica *Srbija* Yugo. **58** C4
Osipenko Ukr. *see* Berdyans'k
Osipovichi Belarus *see* Asipovichy
Osire Namibia **130** C4
Osiyan India **96** B4
Osizweni S. Africa **133** O4
Osječenica *mts* Bos.-Herz. **56** I4
Oskaloosa *IA* U.S.A. **174** A3
Oskaloosa *KS* U.S.A. **178** D4
Oskarshamn Sweden **45** K4
Oskarström Sweden **45** K4
Oskélanéo Canada **173** P2
Öskemen Kazakh. *see* Ust'-Kamenogorsk
Oskil *r.* Ukr. *see* Oskol
Oskol *r.* Rus. Fed. **41** F6
also known as Oskil
Oskuya *r.* Rus. Fed. **43** M2
Oslava *r.* Czech Rep. **49** N6
Oslawa *r.* Poland **49** T6
▶**Oslo** Norway **45** J4
Capital of Norway. Historically known as Christiania or Kristiania.
Oslo *airport* Norway *see* Gardermoen
Oslob Phil. **74** C4
Oslofjorden *sea chan.* Norway **45** J4
Osmanabad India **94** C2
Osmancık Turkey **106** C2
Osmaneli Turkey **106** B2
Osmaniye Turkey **106** C3
Osmannagar India **94** C2
also known as Sultanabad
Os'mino Rus. Fed. **43** K2
Ōsmo Sweden **45** L4
Osmussaar *i.* Estonia **42** E2
Osnabrück Germany **48** F3
Osnaburg *atoll* Fr. Polynesia *see* Mururoa
Osno Lubuskie Poland **49** L3
Oso *r.* Dem. Rep. Congo **126** E5
Osogbo Nigeria *see* Oshogbo
Osogovske Planine *mts* Bulg./Macedonia **58** D6
Osor *hill* Croatia **56** G4
Osório Brazil **203** B9
Osorno Chile **204** B6
Osorno Spain **54** G2
Osoyoos Canada **166** G5
Oseyri *Hordaland* Norway **46** P3
Osprey Reef Australia **149** E2
Oss Neth. **48** C4
Ossa *hill* Port. **54** D6
Ossa, Mount Australia **147** E5
Osse *r.* Nigeria **125** G5
Osseo U.S.A. **172** B6
Ossi *Sardegna* Italy **57** A8
Ossineke U.S.A. **173** J6
Ossining U.S.A. **177** L4
Ossipee Lake U.S.A. **177** N2
Ossora Rus. Fed. **39** Q4
Ossu East Timor **75** C5
Ostashevo Rus. Fed. **43** Q6
Ostashkov Rus. Fed. **43** O4
Oste *r.* Germany **48** G2
Osten Germany **48** G2
Ostend Belgium **51** I1
also spelt Oostende or Ostende
Ostende Belgium *see* Ostend
Oster Rus. Fed. **43** N7
Oster *r.* Rus. Fed. **43** N8
Oster Ukr. **41** D6
Osterburg (Altmark) Germany **48** I3
Österbybruk Sweden **45** L3
Österbymo Sweden **45** K4
Österdalälven *l.* Sweden **45** K3
Österfärnebo Sweden **45** L3
Osterholz-Scharmbeck Germany **48** F2
Ostermundigen Switz. **51** N6
Osterode am Harz Germany **48** H4
Östersund Sweden **44** K3
Östervåla Sweden **45** L3
Osterzgebirge *park* Germany **49** K5
Ostfold *county* Norway **45** J4
Ostfriesische Inseln *is* Germany *see* East Frisian Islands
Ostfriesland *reg.* Germany **48** E2
Östhammar Sweden **45** L3
Östra Kvarken *strait* Fin./Sweden **44** M3
Ostrava Czech Rep. **49** P6
Ostróda Poland **49** Q2
Ostrogozhsk Rus. Fed. **41** F6
Ostro Koplje *mt.* Yugo. **58** D6
Ostrołęka Poland **49** S2
Ostrov Czech Rep. **49** J5
Ostrov Romania **58** J4
Ostrov Romania **58** J4
Ostrov Rus. Fed. **43** J4
Ostrovets Poland *see* Ostrowiec Świętokrzyski
Ostrovskoye Rus. Fed. **40** H4
formerly known as Semyonovskoye
Ostrów Poland *see* Ostrów Wielkopolski
Ostrowiec Poland *see* Ostrowiec Świętokrzyski
Ostrowiec Świętokrzyski Poland **49** S5
formerly known as Ostrowiec; short form Ostrowiec
Ostrów Lubelski Poland **49** T4
Ostrów Mazowiecka Poland **49** S3
Ostrowo Poland *see* Ostrów Wielkopolski
Ostrów Wielkopolski Poland **49** O4
formerly known as Ostrowo; short form Ostrow
Ostrzeszów Poland **49** O4
Ostuni Italy **57** J8
Osuga *r.* Rus. Fed. **43** P4
Osuga *r.* Rus. Fed. **43** P5
Osun *state* Nigeria **125** G5
also spelt Oshun
Osuna Spain **54** F7

Osvaldo Cruz Brazil **206** C8
Oswego *IL* U.S.A. **172** E9
Oswego *KS* U.S.A. **178** D4
Oswego *NY* U.S.A. **177** I2
Oswego *r.* U.S.A. **177** I2
Oswestry U.K. **47** I11
Oświęcim Poland **49** Q5
historically known as Auschwitz
Osyno Rus. Fed. **43** J5
Ōta Japan **91** F6
Otago *admin. reg.* N.Z. **153** D13
Otago Peninsula N.Z. **153** E13**
Otahiti *i.* Fr. Polynesia *see* Tahiti
Otairi N.Z. **152** J7
Otama N.Z. **153** C13
Otamauri N.Z. **152** K7
Otar Kazakh. **103** H4
Otaru Japan **90** G3
Otatara N.Z. **153** C14
Otava *r.* Czech Rep. **49** L6
Otava Fin. **45** N3
Otavalo Ecuador **198** B4
Otavi Namibia **130** C3
Otawara Japan **90** G6
Otchinjau Angola **127** B9
Otdia *atoll* Marshall Is *see* Wotje
Otekaieke N.Z. **153** C13
Otelnuc, Lac *l.* Canada **169** G1
Oţelu Roşu Romania **58** D3
Otematata N.Z. **153** C12
Otepää Estonia **42** I3
Otepää kõrgustik *hills* Estonia **42** H3
Oteren Norway **44** L1
Oteros *r.* Mex. **181** E8
Otgon Tenger Uul *mt.* Mongol a **84** C2
Othe, Forêt d' *for.* France **51** J4
Othello U.S.A. **180** C3
Othonoi *i.* Greece **59** A9
Oti *r.* Ghana/Togo **125** F4
Oti Sudan **121** F7
Otimati S. Africa **133** P6
Otinapa Mex. **184** D3
Otira N.Z. **153** F10
Otisco Lake U.S.A. **177** I3
Otish, Monts *hills* Canada **169** G3
Otjikondo Namibia **130** B3
Otjinene Namibia **130** C4
Otjitambi Namibia **130** B3
Otjiwarongo Namibia **130** C4
Otjovasandu *waterhole* Namibia **130** B3
Otjozondjupa *admin. reg.* Nam ibia **130** C4
Otobe Japan **90** G4
Otobe-dake *mt.* Japan **90** G4
Otočac Croatia **56** H4
Otofuke Japan **90** H3
Otog Qi China *see* Ulan
Otoineppu Japan **90** H2
Otok China **84** B4
Otoka Bos.-Herz. **56** I4
Otoko N.Z. **152** L6
Otonga N.Z. **152** J6
Otoro, Jebel *mt.* Sudan **121** F7
Otorohanga N.Z. **152** J6
Otoskwin *r.* Canada **168** B3
Ōtoyo Japan **91** C8
Otpan, Gora *hill* Kazakh. **102** E3
Otpor Rus. Fed. *see* Zabaykal'sk
Otradinskiy Rus. Fed. **43** R8
Otradnoye Rus. Fed. **43** L2
also known as Otradnyy
Otradnoye, Ozero *l.* Rus. Fed. **43** L1
Otradnyy Rus. Fed. **41** I5
formerly known as Otradnoye
Otranto Italy **57** K8
Otranto, Strait of Albania/Italy **56** K7
Otrogovo Rus. Fed. *see* Stepnoye
Otrokovice Czech Rep. **49** O6
Otrozhnyy Rus. Fed. **39** T3
Ötscher-Tormäuer *nature res.* Austria **49** M8
Otsego U.S.A. **172** H8
Otsego Lake U.S.A. **177** K3
Ōtsu Japan **91** D7
Otta N.Z. **152** J3
▶**Ottawa** Canada **168** F4
Capital of Canada.
Ottawa *r.* Canada **168** F4
also known as Outaouais, Rivière des
Ottawa *IL* U.S.A. **174** B3
Ottawa *KS* U.S.A. **178** D4
Ottawa *OH* U.S.A. **176** A4
Ottawa Islands Canada **168** D1
Otter *r.* U.K. **47** I13
Otterburn U.K. **47** J8
Otter Creek U.S.A. **172** C8
Otterstad Sweden **45** K4
Ottignies Belgium **51** K2
Ottosdal S. Africa **133** J3
Ottoshoop S. Africa **133** J2
Ottumwa U.S.A. **174** A3
Otukpa Nigeria **125** G5
Otukpo Nigeria **125** H5
Otuyo Bol. **200** D4
Otway U.S.A. **176** B7
Otway, Bahía *b.* Chile **205** B9
Otway, Cape Australia **147** D5
Otway, Seno *b.* Chile **205** C9
Otway National Park Australia **147** D4
Otway Range *mts* Australia **147** D4
Otwock Poland **49** S3
Ötztaler Alpen *mts* Austria **48** H3
Ou *r.* Laos **78** C3
Ou, Nam *r.* Laos **78** C3
Ouacha Chad **120** C6
Ouachita *r.* U.S.A. **179** E6
Ouachita, Lake U.S.A. **179** D5
Ouachita Mountains U.S.A. **179** D5
Ouadâne Mauritania **122** C5
Ouadda Cent. Afr. Rep. **126** D2
Ouaddaï *pref.* Chad **120** D5
Ouadjinkarem *well* Niger **125** G1
Ouâd Nâga Mauritania **124** B2
Ouadou *watercourse* Mauritania **124** C3
Ouagadougou Burkina **125** E3
Capital of Burkina.
Ouahigouya Burkina **124** E3
Ouahran Alg. *see* Oran
Ouaka *pref.* Cent. Afr. Rep. **126** D3
Ouaka *r.* Cent. Afr. Rep. **126** D3
Oualâta Mauritania **124** D2
Oualé *r.* Burkina **124** E4
Oualia Mali **124** C3
Ouallam Niger **125** F3
Ouallene Alg. **123** F4
Ouanary Fr. Guiana **199** I3
Ouanda *well* Chad **120** C5
Ouanda-Djallé Cent. Afr. Rep. **126** D2
Ouandago Cent. Afr. Rep. **126** C2
Ouandja *Haute-Kotto* Cent. Afr. Rep. **126** D2
Ouandja *Vakaga* Cent. Afr. Rep. **126** D2
Ouando Cent. Afr. Rep. **126** D3
Ouango Cent. Afr. Rep. **126** D3
Ouangolodougou Côte d'Ivoire **124** D4
formerly known as Wangolodougou
Ouani Kalaoua *well* Niger **125** G3
Ouanne *r.* France **51** I5
Ouaqui Fr. Guiana **199** H4
Ouara *r.* Cent. Afr. Rep. **126** E3
Ouarâne *reg.* Mauritania **122** C5
Ouargaye Burkina **125** F4
Ouargla Alg. **123** G2
Ouarissibtil *well* Mali **125** F2
Ouaritoufoulout *well* Mali **125** F2
Ouarkziz, Jbel *ridge* Alg./Morocco **122** C2

Ouarsenis, Massif de l' Alg. **55** M9
Ouarzazate Morocco **122** D3
Ouatagouna Mali **125** F3
Oubangui *r.* Cent. Afr. Rep./Dem. Rep. Congo *see* Ubangi
Oubergpas *pass* S. Africa **133** I9
Oudenaarde Belgium **51** J2
also spelt Audenarde
Oudon *r.* France **50** F5
Oudtshoorn S. Africa **132** G10
Oued Laou Morocco **54** H9
Oued Rhiou Alg. **55** L9
Oued Tlélat Alg. **55** K9
Oued Zem Morocco **122** D2
Ouéléssébougou Mali **124** D4
Ouémé *r.* Benin **125** F5
Ouessa Burkina **124** E4
Ouessant, Île d' *i.* France **50** A4
historically known as Ushant
Ouésso Congo **126** C4
Ouest *prov.* Cameroon **125** H5
Ouezzane Morocco **122** D2
Oughterard Rep. of Ireland **47** C10
Ougnat, Jbel Morocco **122** D3
Ouham *pref.* Cent. Afr. Rep. **126** C2
Ouham *r.* Cent. Afr. Rep./Chad **126** C2
Ouham Pendé *pref.* Cent. Afr. Rep. **126** C3
Ouidah Benin **125** F5
historically known as Whydah
Ouinardene Mali **125** F2
Ouirigo Mex. **184** C3
Ouistreham France **50** F3
Oujâf *well* Mauritania **124** D2
Oujda Morocco **123** E2
Oujeft Mauritania **124** B2
Oulad Teïma Morocco **122** C3
Oulainen Fin. **44** N2
Oulangan kansallispuisto *nat. park* Fin. **44** O2
Ould Yenjé Mauritania **124** C3
Ouled Djellal Alg. **123** G2
Ouled Farès Alg. **55** M8
Ouled Naïl, Monts des *mts* Alg. **123** F2
Ouled Saïd *well* Alg. **123** F3
Ouli Cameroon **125** I5
Oullins France **51** K7
Oulu Fin. **44** N2
also known as Uleåborg
Oulu *prov.* Fin. **44** N2
Oulujärvi *l.* Fin. **44** N2
Oulujoki *r.* Fin. **44** N2
Oulunsalo Fin. **44** N2
Oulx Italy **51** M7
Oum-Chalouba Chad **120** D6
Oumé Côte d'Ivoire **124** D5
Oum-Hadjer Chad **120** C6
Oum el A'sel *well* Mali **122** D5
Oumm ed Droûs Guebli, Sebkhet *salt flat* Mauritania **122** C5
Oumm ed Droûs Telli, Sebkha *salt flat* Mauritania **122** C5
Oumm el A'sel *well* Mali **122** D5
Ounara Morocco **122** C3
Ounasjoki *r.* Fin. **44** N2
Oungre Canada **167** K5
Ounianga Kébir Chad **120** D5
Ounianga Sérir Chad **120** D5
Ounissoul *well* Niger **125** I2
Oupeye Belgium **51** L2
Our *r.* Lux. **51** M3
Ouray U.S.A. **181** F5
Ourcq *r.* France **51** J3
Ouré Kaba Guinea **124** C4
Ourém Brazil **202** C2
Ourense Spain **54** D2
also spelt Orense
Ouricuri Brazil **202** E4
Ourinhos Brazil **206** D9
Ourini Chad **120** D5
Ourique Port. **54** C7
Ouro Branco Brazil **207** J7
Ouro Fino Brazil **206** F9
Ouro Preto Brazil **203** D7
Ourthe *r.* Belgium **51** L2
Ouse *r.* U.K. **47** L10
Oust *r.* France **50** D5
Outamba Kilimi National Park Sierra Leone **124** B4
Outaouais, Rivière des *r.* Canada *see* Ottawa
Outardes *r.* Canada **169** G3
Outardes Quatre, Réservoir Canada **169** G3
Outat Oulad el Haj Morocco **122** E2
Outeniekwaberge *mts* S. Africa **132** G10
Outer Hebrides *is* U.K. **46** F6
Outer Island U.S.A. **172** C3
Outer Mongolia *country* Asia *see* Mongolia
Outer Santa Barbara Channel U.S.A. **182** F8
Outjo Namibia **130** C4
Outlook Canada **167** J5
Outokumpu Fin. **40** D3
Outoul Alg. **123** G5
Outram N.Z. **153** D13
Out Skerries *is* U.K. **46** L3
Ouvéa *i.* New Caledonia **145** F4
also spelt Uéa or Uvéa
Ouyanghai Skuiku *resr* China **87** D3
Ouyen Australia **147** D3
Ova *r.* Turkey **59** I11
Ovacık Turkey **107** D3
Ovada Italy **56** A4
Ovayemiri Turkey **59** I11
Ovalle Chile **204** C3
Ovamboland *reg.* Namibia **130** B3
Ovan Gabon **126** B4
Ovar Port. **54** C4
Ovejas Col. **187** E5
Oveng Cameroon **125** I6
Ovens *r.* Australia **147** E4
Øvergard Norway **44** L1
Overhalla Norway **44** J2
Överkalix Sweden **44** M2
Overlander Roadhouse Australia **151** A5
Overland Park U.S.A. **178** D4
Övermark Fin. **44** M3
Overo, Volcán *vol.* Arg. **204** C4
Overton *NV* U.S.A. **183** J5
Overton *TX* U.S.A. **179** D6
Övertorneå Sweden **44** M2
Överum Sweden **45** K4
Ovid *MI* U.S.A. **173** I7
Ovid *NY* U.S.A. **177** I3
Ovidiopol' Ukr. **58** J1
Ovidiu Romania **58** J4
Oviedo Spain **54** F1
Ovinishchenskaya Vozvyshennost' *hills* Rus. Fed. **43** R3
Oviŝtrags *hd* Latvia **42** D5
Oviston Nature Reserve S. Africa **133** J7
Övögdiy Mongolia **84** C1
Ovoot Mongolia **85** G2
Övörhangay *prov.* Mongolia **84** D2
Ovruch Ukr. **41** D6
Övt Mongolia **84** D2
Owahanga N.Z. **152** K8
Owaka N.Z. **153** D14

Owakonze Canada **172** C2
Owando Congo **126** B5
formerly known as Fort Rousset
Owasco Lake U.S.A. **177** I3
Owase Japan **91** E7
Owasso U.S.A. **179** D4
Owatonna U.S.A. **174** A2
Owbeh Afgh. **101** E3
Oweh U.S.A. **177** I3
Owen, Mount N.Z. **152** H9
Owendale S. Africa **132** H5
Owen Falls Dam Uganda **128** B4
Owen Island Myanmar **79** B6
Owen River N.Z. **152** H9
Owens *r.* U.S.A. **182** G5
Owensboro U.S.A. **174** C4
Owens Lake U.S.A. **182** G5
Owen Sound Canada **168** D4
Owen Sound *inlet* Canada **173** M6
Owen Stanley Range *mts* P.N.G. **145** D2
Owensville U.S.A. **174** C4
Owenton U.S.A. **176** A6
Owerri Nigeria **125** G5
Owhango N.Z. **152** J7
Owikeno Lake Canada **166** E5
Owings U.S.A. **177** I7
Owingsville U.S.A. **176** B7
Owl *r.* Canada **167** M3
Owl Creek *r.* U.S.A. **180** E4
Owminzatow Toghi *hills* Uzbek. *see* Auminzatau, Gory
Owo Nigeria **125** G5
Owosso U.S.A. **173** I8
Owyhee U.S.A. **180** C4
Owyhee *r.* U.S.A. **180** C4
Owyhee Mountains U.S.A. **180** C4
Owyhee North Fork *r.* U.S.A. **180** C4
Owyhee South Fork *r.* U.S.A. **180** C4
Oxapampa Peru **200** B2
Öxarfjörður *b.* Iceland **44** [inset] C2
Oxbow Canada **167** K5
Ox Creek *r.* U.S.A. **178** B1
Oxelösund Sweden **45** L4
Oxford N.Z. **153** G11
Oxford U.K. **47** K12
Oxford *IA* U.S.A. **172** B9
Oxford *MA* U.S.A. **177** N3
Oxford *ME* U.S.A. **177** O1
Oxford *MI* U.S.A. **173** J8
Oxford *MS* U.S.A. **174** B5
Oxford *NC* U.S.A. **176** G9
Oxford *NY* U.S.A. **177** J3
Oxford *OH* U.S.A. **176** A6
Oxford *PA* U.S.A. **177** J6
Oxford *WI* U.S.A. **172** D7
Oxford House Canada **167** M4
Oxford Junction U.S.A. **172** C9
Oxford Lake Canada **167** M4
Oxkutzcab Mex. **185** H4
Oxley Australia **147** E3
Oxleys Peak Australia **147** L3
Oxley Wild Rivers National Park Australia **147** L2
Ox Mountains *hills* Rep. of Ireland *see* Slieve Gamph
Oxnard U.S.A. **182** E7
Oxtongue Lake Canada **173** O5
Oxus *r.* Asia *see* Amudar'ya
Oxylithos Greece **59** F10
Oya *r.* Sarawak Malaysia **77** E2
Øya Norway **44** K2
Oyabe Japan **91** E6
Oyama Japan **91** F6
Ō-yama *mt.* Japan **91** F7
Ō-yama *vol.* Japan **83** E6
Oyapock *r.* Brazil/Fr. Guiana **199** I3
Oyapock, Baie d' *b.* Fr. Guiana **199** I3
Oyem Gabon **126** A4
Oyen Canada **167** I5
Øyeren *r.* Norway **45** J4
Oygon Mongolia **84** C1
Oykel *r.* U.K. **46** H6
Oymapınar Turkey **108** C1
Oymyakon Rus. Fed. **39** O3
Oyo Congo **126** B5
Oyo Nigeria **125** F4
Oyo *state* Nigeria **125** F4
Oyón Peru **200** A2
Oyonnax France **51** L6
Oyoqquduq Uzbek. *see* Ayakkuduk
Oyster Bay S. Africa **133** I11
Oytal Kazakh. **103** H4
Oytograk China **89** C4
Oyukludağı *mt.* Turkey **108** C1
Oyyl Kazakh. *see* Uil
Oyyq Kazakh. *see* Uyuk
Özalp Turkey **107** F3
formerly known as Karakalli
Ozamiz Phil. **74** B4
Ozark *AL* U.S.A. **175** C6
Ozark *AR* U.S.A. **179** D5
Ozark *MO* U.S.A. **178** D4
Ozark Plateau U.S.A. **178** D4
Ozarks, Lake of the U.S.A. **178** D4
Ożarów Poland **49** S5
Ożbaşı Turkey **59** I11
Ozbekiston *country* Asia *see* Uzbekistan
Ózd Hungary **49** P7
Özdere Turkey **59** I11
Ozen Kazakh. *see* Kyzylsay
Özerdere Rus. Fed. **43** P3
Ozerne Ukr. **58** J3
Ozerninskoye Vodokhranilishche *resr* Rus. Fed. **43** R6
Ozernovskiy Rus. Fed. **39** O4
Ozernoye Kazakh. **103** I1
formerly known as Ozernyy
Ozernoye Rus. Fed. **102** B2
Ozernyy Kazakh. *see* Shashubay
Ozernyy Kazakh. *see* Ozernoye
Ozernyy *Ivanovskaya Oblast'* Rus. Fed. **43** V4
Ozernyy *Orenburgskaya Oblast'* Rus. Fed. **103** D2
Ozernyy *Smolenskaya Oblast'* Rus. Fed. **43** N6
Ozerpakh Rus. Fed. **82** F1
Ozersk Rus. Fed. **42** D7
Ozerskiy Rus. Fed. **82** F3
Ozery Rus. Fed. **43** T7
Ozeryane Rus. Fed. **82** C5
Özgön Kyrg. **103** H4
also spelt Uzgen
Ozherel'ye Rus. Fed. **43** T7
Ozhogina *r.* Rus. Fed. **39** P3
Ozieri *Sardegna* Italy **57** B8
Ozimek Poland **49** P5
Ozinki Rus. Fed. **102** B2
Ozolnieki Latvia **42** G5
Ozona U.S.A. **179** B6
Ozorków Poland **49** Q4
Ōzu *Ehime* Japan **91** C8
Ōzu *Kumamoto* Japan **91** B8
Ozuki Japan **91** B7
Ozuluama Mex. **185** F4
Ozurget'i Georgia **107** E2
formerly known as Makharadze

Pã Burkina **124** E4
Paakkola Fin. **44** N2
Paamiut Greenland **165** O3
also known as Frederikshåb
Pa-an Myanmar **78** B4
also spelt Hpa-an
Paanopa *i.* Kiribati *see* Banaba

P

Paarl S. Africa 132 C10
Paasvere Estonia 42 H2
Paatsjoki r. Europe see Patsoyoki
Paauilo U.S.A. 181 [inset] Z1
Pabaigh i. U.K. see Pabbay
P'abal-li N. Korea 83 C4
Pabbay i. Western Isles, Scotland U.K. 46 E6
Pabbay i. Western Isles, Scotland U.K. 46 E7
also spelt Pabaigh
Pabianice Poland 49 Q4
historically known as Pabianitz
Pabna Bangl. 97 F4
Pabradė Lith. 42 G7
Pab Range mts Pak. 101 F5
Pacaás, Serra dos hills Brazil 201 D2
Pacaás Novos, Parque Nacional nat. park Brazil 201 E2
Pacaembu Brazil 206 B8
Pacahuaras r. Bol. 200 D2
Pacajus Brazil 202 E3
Pacaraima, Serra mts S. America see Pakaraima Mountains
Pacaraima Mountains S. America see Pakaraima Mountains
Pacarán Peru 200 B3
Pacasmayo Peru 200 A1
Pacatuba Brazil 202 E3
Pacaya r. Peru 198 C6
Pacaya, Volcán de vol. Guat. 185 H6
Pacaya Samiria, Reserva Nacional nature res. Peru 198 C6
Paceco Sicilia Italy 57 E11
Pacheco Chihuahua Mex. 184 C2
Pacheco Zacatecas Mex. 185 E3
Pachia i. Greece 59 G12
also spelt Pakhiá
Pachía Peru 200 C4
Pachino Sicilia Italy 57 H12
Pachitea r. Peru 200 B2
Pachiza Peru 200 A1
Pachmarhi India 96 C5
Pachor India 96 C5
Pachora India 94 B1
Pachpadra India 96 B4
Pachuca Mex. 185 F4
Pacifica U.S.A. 182 B4
Pacific Grove U.S.A. 182 C5
Pacific Ocean 220
Largest ocean in the world.
oceans [features] ➤ 210–211

oceans
	ocean	area sq km	area sq miles	greatest depth	page#
1 ▶	Pacific	166 241 000	64 186 000	10 920m / 35 826ft	➤ 220–221
2 ▶	Atlantic	86 557 000	33 420 000	8 605m / 28 231ft	➤ 216–217
3 ▶	Indian	73 427 000	28 350 000	7 125m / 23 376ft	➤ 218–219
4 ▶	Arctic	9 485 000	3 662 000	5 450m / 17 880ft	➤ 224

Pacific Rim National Park Canada 166 E5
Pacijan i. Phil. 74 C4
Pacinan, Tanjung pt Indon. 77 F4
Pačir Vojvodina, Srbija Yugo. 58 A3
Pacitan Indon. 77 F4
Packsattel pass Austria 49 L9
Pacov Czech Rep. 49 M6
Pacoval Brazil 199 H5
Pacuí r. Brazil 207 I3
Paczków Poland 49 O5
Padada Phil. 74 C5
Padali Rus. Fed. see Amursk
Padamarang i. Indon. 75 B4
Padampur India 96 D3
Padang Kalimantan Barat Indon. 77 E3
Padang i. Indon. 76 C2
Padangpanjang Indon. 76 C3
Padangsidimpuan Indon. 76 B2
Padangtikar Indon. 77 E3
Padangtikar i. Indon. 77 E3
Padany Rus. Fed. 40 E3
Padarosk Belarus 42 F7
Padasjoki Fin. 45 N3
Padatha, Kūh-e mt. Iran 100 B3
Padauiri r. Brazil 199 E5
Padaung Myanmar 78 A4
Padcaya Bol. 201 D5
Paddington Australia 147 E3
Paden City U.S.A. 176 E6
Paderborn Germany 48 F4
Padeşu, Vârful mt. Romania 58 D3
Padilla Bol. 201 D4
Padina Romania 58 I4
Padina Vojvodina, Srbija Yugo. 58 B3
Padinska Skela Srbija Yugo. 58 B4
Padjelanta nationalpark nat. park Sweden 44 L2
Padluzhha Belarus 43 M8
Padma r. Bangl. see Ganges
Padmanabhapuram India 94 C4
Padmapur India 96 D5
Padra India 96 B5
Padrão, Ponta pt Angola 127 B6
Padrauna India 97 E4
Padre Bernardo Brazil 206 E2
Padre Caro hill Spain 54 E7
Padre Island U.S.A. 179 C7
Padre Island National Seashore nature res. U.S.A. 179 C7
Padre Paraíso Brazil 207 L4
Padrón Spain 54 C2
Padsvillye Belarus 42 I6
Padua India 95 D2
Padua Italy 56 D3
also spelt Padova; historically known as Patavium
Paducah KY U.S.A. 174 B4
Paducah TX U.S.A. 179 B5
Padul Spain 55 H7
Padum Jammu and Kashmir 96 C2
Pădurea Craiului, mts Romania 58 D2
Paekakariki N.Z. 152 I8
Paekdu-san mt. China/N. Korea 82 C4
Paengnyŏng-do i. S. Korea 83 B5
Paeroa N.Z. 153 D13
Paeroa i. N.Z. 152 I5
Paestum tourist site Italy 57 G8
historically known as Poseidonia
Paete Phil. 74 B3
Pafos Cyprus see Paphos
Pafúri Moz. 131 F3
Pag Croatia 56 H4
Pag i. Croatia 56 G4
Paga r. Rus. Fed. 40 L2
Paga Conta Brazil 199 H6
Pagadenburu Indon. 77 D4
Pagadian Phil. 74 B5
Pagai Selatan i. Indon. 76 C3
Pagai Utara i. Indon. 76 C3
Pagan i. N. Mariana Is 73 K3
also spelt Pagon
Pagaralam Indon. 76 C4
Pagasitikos Kolpos b. Greece 59 D9
Pagatan Kalimantan Selatan Indon. 77 F3
Pagatan Kalimantan Tengah Indon. 77 F3
Page U.S.A. 183 M5
Pagėgiai Lith. 42 C6
Pagerdewa Indon. 76 D3

Paget, Mount S. Georgia 205 [inset]
Paget Cay reef Australia 149 G3
Paghman mt. Afgh. 101 G3
Pagiriai Lith. 42 F6
Pagiriai Lith. 42 G7
Pagon i. N. Mariana Is see Pagan
Pagosa Springs U.S.A. 181 F5
Pagouda Togo 125 F4
Pagri China 89 E7
Pagwachuan r. Canada 168 C3
Pagwi P.N.G. 73 J7
Pahala U.S.A. 181 [inset] Z2
Pahang r. Malaysia 76 C2
Pahang state Malaysia 76 C2
Paharpur tourist site Bangl. 97 F4
Paharpur Pak. 101 G3
Pahauman Indon. 77 E2
Pahia Point N.Z. 153 B14
Pahiatua N.Z. 152 J8
Pahlavi Dezh Iran see Āq Qal'eh
Pahlgam Jammu and Kashmir 96 C2
Pahokee U.S.A. 175 D7
Pahost Vodaskhovishcha resr Belarus 42 H9
Pahra Kariz Afgh. 101 E3
Pahranagat Range mts U.S.A. 183 I4
Pahranichny Belarus 42 E8
formerly known as Byerastavitsa
Pahrump U.S.A. 183 I5
Pahuj r. India 96 C4
Pahute Mesa plat. U.S.A. 183 H4
Paiaguás Brazil 201 F4
Paicines U.S.A. 182 C5
Paide Estonia 42 G3
Paignton U.K. 47 I13
Paihia N.Z. 152 I3
Paiján Peru 200 A1
Päijänne r. Fin. 45 N3
Paikü Co l. China 89 D6
Paila r. Bol. 201 D4
Pailing China see Chun'an
Paillaco Chile 204 B6
Paimio Fin. 45 M3
Paimpol France 50 C4
Painan Indon. 76 C3
Painavu India 94 C4
Paine Chile 204 C4
Paine, Cerro mt. Chile 205 B8
Paineiras Brazil 207 H5
Painesdale U.S.A. 172 C3
Painesville U.S.A. 176 D4
Pains Brazil 207 H7
Painted Desert U.S.A. 183 M5
Painted Rock Dam U.S.A. 183 K8
Paint Hills Canada see Wemindji
Paint Lake Canada 167 L4
Paint Lake Provincial Recreation Park Canada 167 L4
Paint Lick U.S.A. 176 A8
Paint Rock U.S.A. 179 C6
Paintsville U.S.A. 176 C8
Paipa Col. 198 C3
Pairi r. India 94 D1
Paisley Canada 173 L6
Paisley U.K. 46 H11
País Vasco aut. comm. Spain 55 I1
English form Basque Country
Paita Peru 198 A6
Paitan, Teluk b. Sabah Malaysia 77 G1
Paithan India 94 B2
Paitou China 87 G2
Paiva r. Port. 54 C3
Paiva Couceiro Angola see Quipungo
Paixban Mex. 185 H5
Paizhou China 87 E2
Pajala Sweden 44 M2
Pajan Ecuador 198 A5
Pajarito Col. 198 C3
Pájaros, Islotes Chile 204 C3
Pajęczno Poland 49 P4
Pakala India 94 C3
Pakapë Lith. 42 E6
Pakaraima Mountains S. America 199 F4
English form Pacaraima Mountains; also known as Pacaraimã, Serra de or Paracaima, Sierra
Pakashkan Lake Canada 168 B3
Pakaur India 97 F4
Pakawau N.Z. 152 G8
Pakch'ŏn N. Korea 83 B5
Pakesley Canada 168 D4
Pakhachi Rus. Fed. 39 Q3
Pakhar' Kazakh. 102 D2
Pakhia i. Greece see Pachia
Pakhoi China see Beihai
Pakhomovo Rus. Fed. 43 S7
Pakhtaabad Uzbek. 103 H4
formerly known as Kokankishlak
Pakistan country Asia 101 F4
5th most populous country in Asia and 7th in the world.
world [population] ➤ 22–23
asia [countries] ➤ 64–67
Pak Ka Shan hill Hong Kong China see Parker, Mount
Pakkat Indon. 76 B2
Paklenica nat. park Croatia 56 H4
Paknampho Thai. see Nakhon Sawan
Pakokku Myanmar 78 A3
Pakoktaii N.Z. 152 I5
Pakowki Lake imp. l. Canada 167 I5
Pakpattan Pak. 101 H4
Pak Phanang Thai. 79 C6
Pak Phayun Thai. 79 C7
Pakra r. Croatia 56 I3
Pakrac Croatia 56 I3
Pakruojis Lith. 42 E6
Paks Hungary 49 P9
Pakse Laos see Pakxé
Paktīkā prov. Afgh. 101 G3
Paktīā prov. Afgh. 101 G3
Paku r. Sarawak Malaysia 77 F2
Pakue Indon. 75 B3
Pakwash Lake Canada 167 M5
Pakxé Laos 79 D5
also spelt Pakse
Pal Senegal see Mpal
Pala Chad 126 B2
Pala Myanmar 79 B5
Palabuhanratu Indon. 77 D4
Palabuhanratu, Teluk b. Indon. 77 D4
Palacios Bol. 200 D3
Palaestinia area see Palestine
Palafrugell Spain 55 O3
Palagiano Italy 57 J8
Palagruža i. Croatia 56 I6
Palaia Fokaia Greece 59 E11
Palaikastro Greece 59 H13
also known as Palaiókastron
Palaiochora Greece 59 E13
Palaiókastron Greece see Palaikastro
Palairos Greece 59 B10

Palaiseau France 51 I4
Palakkat India see Palghat
Palamakoloi Botswana 130 D4
Palamas Greece 59 D9
Palamós Spain 55 O3
Palam Pur India 96 C2
Palana India 96 B4
Palana Rus. Fed. 39 P4
Palanan Phil. 74 B2
Palanan Point Phil. 74 B2
Palandur India 96 C1
Palanga Lith. 42 C6
Palani India 94 C4
Palanpur India 96 B4
Palapag Phil. 74 C3
Palapye Botswana 131 E4
Palar r. India 94 C3
Palasa Indon. 75 B2
Palasbari India 97 F4
Palas de Rei Spain 54 D2
Palata r. Belarus 43 J6
Palata Rus. Fed. 43 J1
Palatka U.S.A. 175 D6
Palau Sardegna Italy 56 C7
Palau country N. Pacific Ocean 73 H5
also spelt Belau
asia [countries] ➤ 64–67
Palaui i. Phil. 74 B1
Palauig Phil. 74 A3
Palau Islands Palau 73 H5
Palauk Myanmar 79 B5
Palaw Myanmar 79 B5
Palawan i. Phil. 74 A4
historically known as Paragua
Palawan Passage strait Phil. 74 A3
Palayan N.Z. 74 B3
Palayankottai India 94 C4
Palazzo, Punta pt Corse France 51 O10
Palazzolo Acreide Sicilia Italy 57 H11
Paldiski Estonia 42 F2
Pale Bos.-Herz. 56 K5
Paleleh Indon. 75 B2
Palembang Indon. 76 C3
Palena r. Aisén Chile 205 B6
Palena Los Lagos Chile 205 C6
Palencia Spain 54 G2
Palenque Mex. 185 G5
Palermo Arg. 201 D6
Palermo Sicilia Italy 57 F10
historically known as Panormus
Palermo Punta Raisi airport Sicilia Italy 57 F10
Palestine reg. Asia 108 G5
historically known as Palaestinia
Palestine U.S.A. 179 D6
Paletwa Myanmar 78 A3
Palghar India 94 B2
Palghat India 94 C4
also spelt Palakkat
Palgrave, Mount hill Australia 150 A4
Pali Madhya Pradesh India 96 D5
Pali Maharashtra India 94 B2
Pali Rajasthan India 96 B4
Palik Belarus 43 J7
Palikir Micronesia 220 E5
Capital of Micronesia.
Palimbang Phil. 74 C5
Palinuro, Capo c. Italy 57 H8
Paliouri Greece 59 E9
Paliouri, Akra pt Greece 59 E9
Palisade U.S.A. 180 E5
Palitana India 96 A5
Palja hill Sweden 44 L2
Paljakka hill Fin. 44 O2
Pālkāne Fin. 45 N3
Palk Bay Sri Lanka 94 C4
Palkino Rus. Fed. 42 J4
Palkohda India 95 D2
Palkonda Range mts India 94 C3
Palkot India 97 E5
Palk Strait India/Sri Lanka 94 C4
Palladam India 94 C4
Pallapalla mt. Peru 200 C3
Pallas ja Ounastunturin kansallispuisto nat. park Fin. 44 M1
Pallasovka Rus. Fed. 41 H6
Pallavaram India 94 D3
Palleru r. India 94 C2
Pallinup r. Australia 151 B7
Pallisa Uganda 128 B4
Palliser, Îles is Fr. Polynesia 221 I7
Palliser Bay N.Z. 152 J9
Pallu India 96 B3
Palma r. Brazil 202 C5
Palma Moz. 129 D7
Palma del Río Spain 54 F7
Palma de Mallorca Spain 55 N5
Palma di Montechiaro Sicilia Italy 57 F11
Palmaner India 94 C3
Palmanova Italy 56 F3
Palmares Acre Brazil 200 D3
Palmares Pernambuco Brazil 202 F4
Palmares do Sul Brazil 203 B9
Palmarito Venez. 198 D3
Palmarola, Isola i. Italy 56 F8
Palmarolle Canada 173 N2
Palmas Paraná Brazil 203 B8
Palmas Tocantins Brazil 202 B4
Palmas, Cape Liberia 124 D5
Palmas, Golfo di b. Sardegna Italy 57 A10
Palma Soriano Cuba 186 E2
Palm Bay U.S.A. 175 D7
Palmdale U.S.A. 182 F7
Palmeira Brazil 203 B8
Palmeira das Missões Brazil 203 A8
Palmeira dos Índios Brazil 202 E4
Palmeirais Brazil 202 C3
Palmeiras r. Brazil 202 C5
Palmeiras de Goiás Brazil 206 D3
Palmeirinhas, Ponta das pt Angola 127 B7
Palmer research station Antarctica 222 T2
Palmer r. Australia 149 D3
Palmer watercourse Australia 148 B5
Palmer U.S.A. 164 E3
Palmer Land reg. Antarctica 222 T2
Palmerston Australia see Darwin
Palmerston Australia 148 A2
Palmerston, Cape Australia 149 F4
Palmerston atoll Cook Is 221 H7
also known as Avarau
Palmerston North N.Z. 152 J8
Palmerton U.S.A. 177 J5
Palmerville Australia 149 E2
Palmetto U.S.A. 175 D7
Palmi Italy 57 H10
Palmillas Mex. 185 F4
Palmira Cuba 186 C2
Palmital Brazil 206 C9
Palmnicken Rus. Fed. see Yantarnyy
Palm Springs U.S.A. 183 H8
Palm Tree Creek r. Australia 149 F5
Palm Valley Australia 148 B5
oceania [landscapes] ➤ 142–143
Palmyra Syria see Tadmur
Palmyra NY U.S.A. 177 H2
Palmyra PA U.S.A. 177 I5
Palmyra VA U.S.A. 176 G8

Palmyra Atoll N. Pacific Ocean 221 H5
United States Unincorporated Territory.
oceania [countries] ➤ 138–139
Palmyras Point India 95 E1
Palni Hills India 94 C4
Palo Phil. 74 C4
Palo Alto U.S.A. 182 B4
Palo Blanco Arg. 204 D2
Palo Chino watercourse Mex. 181 D7
Palo de las Letras Col. 198 B3
Palo de vol. watercourse U.S.A. 179 B5
Paloh Sarawak Malaysia 77 E2
Paloich Sudan 128 B2
Palojoensuu Fin. 44 M1
Palomaa Fin. 44 N1
Palomani mt. Peru 200 C3
Palomares Mex. 185 G5
Palomar Mountain U.S.A. 183 H8
Palomera, Sierra mts Spain 55 J4
Palomitas Arg. 200 D6
Paloncha India 94 D2
Palo Pinto U.S.A. 179 C5
Palopo Indon. 75 B3
Palos, Cabo de c. Spain 55 K7
Palo Santo Arg. 204 F2
Palouse r. U.S.A. 180 C3
Palo Verde U.S.A. 183 J8
Palo Verde, Parque Nacional nat. park Costa Rica 186 B5
Palovesi l. Fin. 45 M3
Palpa Ica Peru 200 B3
Palpa Lima Peru 200 A2
Palpetu, Tanjung pt Indon. 75 C3
Palsana India 96 B5
Paltamo Fin. 44 N2
Paltaselkä l. Fin. 44 N2
Pal'tsevo Rus. Fed. 43 J1
Pal'tso Rus. Fed. 43 P8
Pal'vart Turkm. 103 F5
Palwal India 96 C3
Palwancha India see Paloncha
Pal'yanovo Rus. Fed. 38 H3
Palyatskishki Belarus 42 G7
Palyavaam r. Rus. Fed. 39 S3
Palyeskaya Nizina marsh Belarus/ Ukr. see Pripet Marshes
Palyessye Belarus 43 K9
Palyessye Belarus 43 M8
Pama Austria 49 O7
Pama Burkina 125 F4
Pama r. Cent. Afr. Rep. 126 C3
Pama, Réserve Partielle de nature res. Burkina 125 F4
Pamamaroo Lake Australia 147 C3
Pamana i. Indon. 75 B5
Most southerly point of Asia.
Pamar Col. 198 D5
Pamban Channel India 94 C4
Pambarra Moz. 131 G4
Pambula Australia 147 F4
Pamekasan Indon. 77 F4
Pameungpeuk Indon. 77 D4
Pamidi India 94 C3
Pamiers France 50 H9
Pamir r. Afgh./Tajik. 101 H2
Pamir mts Asia 99 I2
Pamlico r. U.S.A. 174 E5
Pamlico Sound sea chan. U.S.A. 174 E5
Pampa U.S.A. 179 B5
Pampa Chica Arg. 205 C7
Pampachiri Peru 200 C3
Pampa de Infierno Arg. 204 E2
Pampa Grande Bol. 201 D4
Pampanua Indon. 75 B4
Pampas reg. Arg. 204 E5
southamerica [landscapes] ➤ 190–191
Pampas Peru 200 B3
Pampas r. Peru 200 B3
Pampierstad S. Africa 133 I4
Pamplona Spain see Pamplona
Pamplona Col. 198 C3
Pamplona Phil. 74 B3
Pamplona Spain 55 J2
also known as Iruña; historically known as Pampeluna
Pamukan, Teluk b. Indon. 77 G3
Pamukçu Turkey 59 I9
Pamukkale Turkey 59 K11
Pamukova Turkey 106 B2
Pamunkey r. U.S.A. 177 I8
Pamzal Jammu and Kashmir 96 C2
Pana Gabon 126 B5
Pana r. Rus. Fed. 44 N1
Panabá Mex. 185 H4
Panabo Phil. 74 C5
Panabutan Bay Phil. 74 B5
Panaca U.S.A. 183 J4
Panache, Lake Canada 168 D4
Panaci Romania 58 G1
Panaeati P.N.G. 149 G1
Panagar India 96 C5
Panagia i. Greece 58 F8
also spelt Panayia
Panagiri India 94 C3
Panagtaran Point Phil. 74 A4
Panagyurishte Bulg. 58 F6
Panaitan i. Indon. 76 D4
Panaji India 94 B3
formerly known as Panjim; historically known as Nova Goa
Panama country Central America 186 D5
central america [countries] ➤ 158–159
Panama Panama see Panamá
Panamá Panama 186 D5
Panamá, Bahía de b. Panama 186 D5
Panamá, Golfo de g. Panama see Panama, Gulf of
Panama, Gulf of Panama 186 D6
also known as Panamá, Golfo de
Panama Canal Panama 186 D5
Panama City Panama 186 DE
Capital of Panama. Also known as Panamá.
Panama City U.S.A. 175 C6
Panamint Range mts U.S.A. 183 G5
Panamint Valley U.S.A. 183 G5
Panao Peru 200 A2
Panaon i. Phil. 74 C4
Panapompom Island P.N.G. 149 G1
Panar r. India 97 F4
Panarea, Isola i. Isole Lipari Italy 57 H10
Panarik Indon. 77 D2
Panaro r. Italy 56 C3
Panarukan Indon. 77 F4
Panatinane Island P.N.G. 149 G1
Panay i. Phil. 74 B4
Panay Gulf Phil. 74 B4
Panayia i. Greece see Panagia
Panbult S. Africa 133 O3
Pancake Range mts U.S.A. 183 I3
Pancas Brazil 207 M6
Pančevo Vojvodina, Srbija Yugo. 58 B4
also spelt Pancsova

Panchagarh Bangl. 97 F4
Panch'iao Taiwan 87 G3
Pancingapan, Bukit mt. Indon. 77 F2
Panciu Romania 58 I3
Pâncota Romania 58 C2
formerly spelt Pincota
Pancsova Vojvodina, Srbija Yugo. see Pančevo
Panda Moz. 131 G5
Pandan Panay Phil. 74 B4
Pandan Phil. 74 C3
Pandan Bay Phil. 74 B4
Pandan Reservoir Sing. 76 [inset]
Pandaria India 97 D5
Pandavapura India 94 C3
Pan de Azúcar Chile 204 D2
Pan de Azúcar, Parque Nacional nat. park Chile 204 C2
Pandeglang Indon. 77 D4
Pandeiros r. Brazil 207 I2
Pandélys Lith. 42 G5
Pandhana India 96 C5
Pandharpur India 94 B2
Pandhurna India 96 C5
Pando dept Bol. 200 C2
Pando Uruguay 204 G4
Pandokrátor hill Greece see Pantokratoras
Pandora Entrance sea chan. Australia 149 E1
Pandrup Denmark 45 J4
Panduranga India 94 C4
Panduranga Tamil Nadu India 94 C4
Pandwaha India 95 D3
Paparoa r. Brazil 207 I2
Pandharkawada India see Pandharkaoda
Paneas Syria see Bāniyās
Panelas Brazil 201 E2
Panevėžys Lith. 42 F6
Panfilov Kazakh. see Zharkent
Pang r. China 82 B1
Pang, Nam r. Myanmar 78 B3
Panga Dem. Rep. Congo 126 E4
Panga Estonia 42 D3
Pangai Tonga 145 H3
Pangal Andhra Pradesh India 94 C2
Pangandaran Indon. 77 E4
Pangani Tanz. 129 C6
also known as Ruvu
Pangani r. Tanz. 129 C6
Panganiban Phil. 74 C3
Pangar Djerem, Réserve du nature res. Cameroon 125 I5
Pangean Indon. 75 A3
Panghsang Myanmar 78 B3
Pangi Dem. Rep. Congo 126 E5
Pangi Range mts Pak. 101 H3
Pangjiabu China 85 G3
Pangkah, Tanjung pt Indon. 77 F4
Pangkalanbuun Indon. 77 E3
Pangkalanlunang Indon. 76 B2
Pangkalansusu Indon. 76 B1
Pangkal Kalong Malaysia 76 C1
Pangkalpinang Indon. 77 D3
Pangkalsiang, Tanjung pt Indon. 75 B3
Panglang Myanmar 78 B2
Panglao i. Phil. 74 B4
Pangman Canada 167 J5
Pango Aluquém Angola 127 B7
Pangody Rus. Fed. 38 H3
Pangonda Cent. Afr. Rep. 126 D3
Pangrango vol. Indon. 77 D4
Pang Sida National Park Thai. 79 C5
Pang Sua, Sungai r. Sing. 76 [inset]
Pangtara Myanmar 78 B3
Panguipulli Chile 204 B5
Panguru N.Z. 152 H3
Pangururan Indon. 76 B2
Panhandle U.S.A. 179 B5
Pania-Mwanga Dem. Rep. Congo 127 F6
Pani Mines India 96 B5
Panino Tverskaya Oblast' Rus. Fed. 43 P5
Panino Voronezhskaya Oblast' Rus. Fed. 41 G6
Panipat India 96 C3
Panitan Phil. 74 B4
Panizowye Belarus 43 L7
Panj r. Afgh./Tajik. 101 G2
Panj Tajik. 101 G2
Panjab Afgh. 101 F3
Panjakent Tajik. 101 F2
also spelt Pendzhikent
Panjang i. Indon. 77 E2
Panjang i. Indon. 77 E3
Panjang, Bukit Sing. 76 [inset]
Panjang, Selat sea chan. Indon. 76 C2
Panjgur Pak. 101 F5
Panjim India see Panaji
Panji China 85 I3
also known as Banshe
Panji Poyon Tajik. 101 G2
Panjkora r. Pak. 101 G3
Panjnad r. Pak. 101 H4
Pankakoski Fin. 44 O3
Pankova Rus. Fed. 43 J9
Panlian China see Miyi
Pan Ling mts China 82 C4
Panlong China see Queshan
Panna India 96 D4
Pannawonica Australia 150 A4
Pannonhalma Hungary 49 O8
formerly known as Győrszentmárton
Pano Aqil Pak. 101 G5
Panopah Indon. 77 E3
Panorama Brazil 206 C8
Panormus Sicilia Italy see Palermo
Panruti India 94 C4
Panshan China see Panjin
Panshi China 82 B4
Panshui China see Pu'an
Pantaicermin, Gunung mt. Indon. 76 C3
Pantanal marsh S. America 201 F4
Largest area of wetlands in the world.
Pantanal de São Lourenço marsh Brazil 201 F4
Pantanal do Taquari marsh Brazil 201 F4
Pantanal Matogrossense, Parque Nacional do nat. park Brazil 201 F4
Pantar i. Indon. 75 B5
Pantelleria Sicilia Italy see Pantelleria
Pantelleria, Isola di i. Sicilia Italy 57 E12
Pantemakassar East Timor 75 C5
formerly known as Ocussi
Pantha Myanmar 78 A3
Panticapaeum Ukr. see Kerch
Pantijan Aboriginal Reserve Australia 150 D3
Pantokratoras hill Greece 59 A9
also known as Pandokrátor
Pantoowarinna, Lake salt flat Australia 146 C1
Pantukan Phil. 74 C5
Panu Dem. Rep. Congo 126 C5
Pánuco Mex. 185 F4
Pánuco r. Mex. 185 F4

Panvel India 94 B2
Panwari India 96 C4
Panxian China 86 B3
Panyu China 87 E4
also known as Shiqiao
Panzhihua China 86 B3
Panzos Guat. 185 H6
Pao r. Venez. 199 E2
Pão de Açúcar Brazil 202 E4
Paola Italy 57 I9
Paola U.S.A. 178 D4
Paoli U.S.A. 174 C4
Paoni Indon. 75 D3
Paonia U.S.A. 180 F5
Paoua Cent. Afr. Rep. 126 C3
Paôy Pêt Cambodia 79 C5
Pap Uzbek. 103 G4
also spelt Pop
Pápa Hungary 49 O8
Papa, Monte del mt. Italy 57 H8
Papa Guat. 185 H6
Papadianika Greece 59 D12
Papagaio r. Brazil see Sauêruiná
Papagaios Minas Gerais Brazil 207 I6
Papagaios Rôndonia Brazil 201 G2
Papagni r. India 94 C3
Papakura N.Z. 152 I5
Papallacta Ecuador 198 B5
Papamoa Beach N.Z. 152 K6
Papanasam Tamil Nadu India 94 C4
Papanasam Tamil Nadu India 94 C4
Papantla Mex. 185 F4
Paparhahandi India 95 D2
Paparoa N.Z. 152 I4
Paparoa National Park N.Z. 153 F10
Paparoa Range mts N.Z. 153 F10
Papas, Akra pt Greece 59 G11
Papa Stour i. U.K. 46 K9
Pápateszér Hungary 49 O8
Papatoetoe N.Z. 152 I4
Papatowai N.Z. 153 D14
Papa Westray i. U.K. 46 J4
also known as Papay
Papay i. U.K. see Papa Westray
Papeete Fr. Polynesia 221 I7
Capital of French Polynesia.
Papenburg Germany 48 E2
Papendorp S. Africa 132 C8
Paphos Cyprus 108 D3
also spelt Pafos; historically known as Paphus
Paphus Cyprus see Paphos
Papigochic r. Mex. 184 C2
Papikio mt. Bulg./Greece 58 F7
Papilė Lith. 42 D5
Papillion U.S.A. 178 C3
Papineau-Labelle, Réserve Faunique de nature res. Canada 168 F4
Papoose Lake U.S.A. 183 I4
Paposo Chile 204 C2
Papua, Gulf of P.N.G. 73 J8
Papua New Guinea country Oceania 144 D2
2nd largest and 2nd most populous country in Oceania.
oceania [countries] ➤ 138–139
Papun Myanmar 78 B4
Papunya Australia 148 A4
Pará r. Brazil 203 C6
Pará state Brazil 199 I5
Para i. Indon. 75 C2
Para r. Rus. Fed. 41 G5
Pará, Rio do r. Brazil 202 B2
Paraburdoo Australia 150 B4
Paracaima, Sierra mts S. America see Pakaraima Mountains
Paracale Phil. 74 C3
Paracambi Brazil 207 J9
Paracas Peru 200 A3
Paracas, Península pen. Peru 200 A3
Paracatu Brazil 206 G4
Paracatu r. Minas Gerais Brazil 206 H3
Paracel Islands S. China Sea 72 D3
also known as Dao Tây Sa or Hoang Sa or Hsi-sha Ch'un-tao or Quan Dao Hoang Sa or Xisha Qundao
Parachilna Australia 146 C2
Parachinar Pak. 101 G3
Paráčin Srbija Yugo. 58 C5
Parada, Punta pt Peru 200 B3
Pará de Minas Brazil 207 I6
Paradis Canada 168 E3
Paradise r. Canada 169 J2
Paradise Guyana 199 G3
Paradise CA U.S.A. 182 C2
Paradise NV U.S.A. 173 H4
Paradise NV U.S.A. 183 I5
Paradise Gardens Canada 167 H2
Paradise Hill Canada 167 I4
Paradise Peak U.S.A. 182 G3
Paradise River Canada 169 J2
Paradise Valley U.S.A. 183 M8
Paradwip India 95 E1
Paraetonium Egypt see Marsa Matrûh
Paragominas Brazil 202 C2
Paragua r. Bol. 201 E3
Paragua r. Phil. see Palawan
Paragua r. Venez. 199 F3
Paraguaçu r. Brazil 207 H8
Paraguaçu Paulista Brazil 206 C9
Paraguaná, Península de pen. Venez. 198 D2
Paraguari Para. 201 F6
Paraguay r. Arg./Para. 201 F6
Paraguay country S. America 201 F5
southamerica [countries] ➤ 192–193
Paraíba r. Brazil 202 F3
Paraíba state Brazil 202 F3
Paraíba do Sul Brazil 207 J9
Paraíba do Sul r. Brazil 207 K9
Paraibuna Brazil 207 H10
Parainen Fin. see Pargas
Paraíso Brazil 206 A6
Paraíso Mex. 185 G5
Paraíso do Norte Brazil 202 B4
Paraisópolis Brazil 207 H9
Parakka Sweden 44 M2
Parakou Benin 125 F4
Parakylia Australia 146 C2
Paralakhemundi India 95 D2
formerly spelt Parlakimedi
Paralia Greece 59 D10
Paramagudi India see Paramakkudi
Paramakkudi India 94 C4
formerly spelt Paramagudi
Paramaribo Suriname 199 H3
Capital of Suriname.
Paramillo, Col. 198 C3
Paramillo, Parque Nacional nat. park Col. 198 B3
Paramirim Brazil 202 D5
Paramirim r. Brazil 202 D5
Páramo hill Spain 54 C2
Páramo de Masa, Puerto del pass Spain 54 H2
Paramonga Peru 200 A2
Paramushir, Ostrov i. Rus. Fed. 39 P4
Paramythia Greece 59 B9
Paran watercourse Israel 108 G7
Paraná Arg. 204 E4
Paraná r. Brazil 202 B5
Paraná state Brazil 206 B11

index

P

Paraná r. S. America 206 B7
Part of the Río de la Plata - Paraná, 2nd longest river in South America.
southamerica [landscapes] ➤ 190–191

Paranaguá Brazil 203 B8
Paranaiba Brazil 206 B6
Paranaíba r. Brazil 206 B7
Paraná Ibicuy r. Arg. 204 F4
Paranaiguara Brazil 206 C5
Paranaíta r. Brazil 201 F2
Paranapanema r. Brazil 206 B9
Paranapiacaba, Serra mts Brazil 203 B8
Paranapura Peru 198 B6
Paranari Brazil 199 G5
Parandak Iran 100 B3
Parang i. Indon. 77 E4
Parang Phil. 74 B5
Parangi Aru r. Sri Lanka 94 D4
Parangipettai India 94 C4
historically known as Porto Novo
Parang Pass India 96 C2
Pârângul Mare, Vârful mt. Romania 58 E3
Parantij India 96 B5
Paraopeba Brazil 203 C6
Paraopeba r. Brazil 203 C6
Parapanda mt. Spain 54 H7
Parapara Indon. 75 C2
Pârãpãra Iraq 107 F4
Paraparaumu N.Z. 152 I8
Parapuã Brazil 206 C8
Paraque, Cerro mt. Venez. 199 E3
Paras Mex. 185 E3
Paraspori, Akra pt Greece 59 I13
Parati Brazil 203 C7
Paratinga Brazil 202 D5
Paratoo Australia 146 C3
Parãú, Küh-e mt. Iraq 107 F4
Parauapebas r. Brazil 202 B3
Parauaquara, Serra hill Brazil 199 H5
Parauari r. Brazil 199 G5
Paraúna Brazil 206 C5
Paray-le-Monial France 51 K6
Parbati r. India 96 C4
Parbatipur Bangl. 97 F4
Parbhani India 94 C2
Parchim Germany 48 I2
Parchment U.S.A. 172 H8
Parczew Poland 49 T4
Pardee Reservoir U.S.A. 182 D3
Pardeeville U.S.A. 172 D7
Pardina Romania 58 J3
Pardo r. Arg. 204 F5
Pardo r. Bahia Brazil 207 O2
Pardo r. Mato Grosso do Sul Brazil 206 A8
Pardo r. Minas Gerais Brazil 207 I2
Pardo r. São Paulo Brazil 206 E7
Pardoo Australia 150 B4
Pardubice Czech Rep. 49 M5
Pare r. Brazil 199 G5
Parece Vela i. Japan see Okino-Tori-shima
Parechcha Belarus 42 G7
Pare Chu r. China 89 B5
Parecis Brazil 201 F3
Parecis r. Brazil 201 F3
Paredes de Nava Spain 54 G2
Paredón Mex. 185 F5
Paremata N.Z. 152 I9
Parenda India 94 B2
Parent Canada 169 F4
Parentis-en-Born France 50 E8
Pareora N.Z. 153 E12
Parepare Indon. 75 A4
Parfino Rus. Fed. 43 M4
Parga Greece 59 B9
also known as Parainen
Parghelia Italy 57 H10
Pargi India 94 C2
Pargolovo Rus. Fed. 43 L1
Paria Bol. 200 D4
Paria r. U.S.A. 183 M5
Paria, Gulf of Trin. and Tob./Venez. 187 H5
Paria, Península de pen. Venez. 199 F3
Pariaman Indon. 76 B3
Paria Plateau U.S.A. 183 L5
Paricatuba Brazil 199 F6
Parida, Isla i. Panama 186 C5
Parigi Indon. 75 B3
Parikkala Fin. 45 O3
Parikud Islands India 95 E2
Parima r. Brazil 199 F4
Parima, Serra mts Brazil 199 E4
Parima-Tapirapecó, Parque Nacional
nat. park Venez. 199 E4
Parinari Peru 198 C6
Pariñas, Punta c. Peru 198 A6
Parintins Brazil 199 G5
Paris Canada 173 M7

Paris France 51 I4
Capital of France and most populous city in Europe. Historically known as Lutetia.
world [cities] ➤ 24–25

Paris U.S.A. 180 G4
Paris IL U.S.A. 174 C4
Paris KY U.S.A. 176 A7
Paris ME U.S.A. 177 O1
Paris MO U.S.A. 178 D4
Paris TN U.S.A. 174 A7
Paris TX U.S.A. 179 D5
Paris U.S.A. 177 I2
Parisienne, Île i. Canada 173 I4
Pãriz Iran 100 D4
Park Iran 101 E5
Park r. U.S.A. 178 C1
Parka Dem. Rep. Congo 126 E3
Parkajoki Sweden 44 M2
Parkal India 94 C2

Park City U.S.A. 183 M1
Parke Lake Canada 169 J2
Parkent Uzbek. 103 G4
Parker U.S.A. 183 J7
Parker, Mount hill Hong Kong China 87 [inset]
also known as Pak Ka Shan
Parker Dam U.S.A. 183 J7
Parker Lake Canada 167 M2
Parker Range hills Australia 151 B7
Parkersburg U.S.A. 176 D6
Parkers Lake U.S.A. 176 A9
Parkes Australia 147 F3
Park Falls U.S.A. 172 C5
Park Forest U.S.A. 172 F9
Parkhar Tajik. see Farkhor
Parkhill Canada 173 L7
Parkinson Canada 173 J4
Parkman U.S.A. 176 D4
Park Rapids U.S.A. 178 D2
Parksley U.S.A. 177 J8
Parkston U.S.A. 178 C3
Parksville Canada 166 E5
Parkutta Jammu and Kashmir 96 C2
Parla Spain 54 H4
Parlakimedi India see Paralakhemundi
Parla Kimedi India 95 E2
Parli Vaijnath India 94 B2
Parma Italy 56 C4
Parma r. Italy 56 C4
Parma Rus. Fed. 40 K2
Parma ID U.S.A. 180 C4
Parma MI U.S.A. 173 I8
Parma OH U.S.A. 176 D4
Parmana Venez. 199 E3
Parmaguá Brazil 202 C4
Parnaíba Brazil 202 D2
Parnaíba r. Brazil 202 A4
Parnaíba r. Brazil 202 D2
Parnaibinha r. Brazil 202 C4
Parnarama Brazil 202 D3
Parnassos mt. Greece 59 D10
Parnassos nat. park Greece 59 D10
Parnassus N.Z. 153 H10
Parndana Australia 146 C3
Parner India 94 B2
Parnitha nat. park Greece 59 E10
Parnon mts Greece 59 D11
Pärnu Estonia 42 F3
formerly known as Pernov
Pärnu r. Estonia 42 F3
Pärnu-Jaaguri Estonia 42 F3
Pärnu laht b. Estonia 42 F3
Paro Bhutan 97 F4
Paroa N.Z. 153 F10
Parona Turkey see Fındık
Paroo watercourse Australia 147 D2
Paroo Channel watercourse Australia 147 D2
Paropamisus mts Afgh. 101 E3
also known as Safīd Kūh
Paroreang, Bukit mt. Indon. 75 A3
Paros Greece 59 G11
Paros i. Greece 59 G11
Parow S. Africa 132 C10
Parowan U.S.A. 183 L4
Parral Chile 204 C5
Parral r. Mex. 181 F7
Parramatta Australia 147 F3
Parramore Island U.S.A. 177 J8
Parras Mex. 185 E3
Parrett r. U.K. 47 J12
Parris Island U.S.A. 175 D5
Parrsboro Canada 169 H4
Parry, Kap c. Greenland see Kangaarsussuaq
Parry Bay Canada 165 K3
Parry Channel Canada 165 H2
Parry Islands Canada 165 H2
Parry Lagoons Nature Reserve Australia 150 E2
Parry Range hills Australia 150 A4
Parry Sound Canada 168 D4
Parsnip Peak U.S.A. 183 J3
Parsons KS U.S.A. 178 D4
Parsons WV U.S.A. 176 F6
Parsons Range hills Australia 148 B2
Partabgarh India 94 B2
Partabpur Chhattisgarh India 94 D2
Partabpur Chhattisgarh India 97 D5
Partakko Fin. 44 N1
Partanna Sicilia Italy 57 E11
Pârte mt. Sweden 44 L2
Partenstein Germany 48 I5
Parthenay France 50 F6
Partida, Isla i. Mex. 184 C3
Partinico Sicilia Italy 57 F10
Partizansk Rus. Fed. 82 D4
formerly known as Suchan
Partizánske Slovakia 49 P7
Partridge r. Canada 168 D3
Paru r. Brazil 199 H5
Parú, Serranía mts Venez. 199 E3
Paru de Oeste r. Brazil 199 G4
Parur India 94 C4
Parvãn prov. Afgh. 101 G3
Parvãreh Iran 100 D3
Parvatipuram India 95 D2
Parvatsar India 96 A4
Paryang China 89 C6
Parychy Belarus 43 K9
Parygino Kazakh. 88 D1
Parys S. Africa 133 L3
Pas r. Spain 54 H1
Pasa Daği mt. Turkey 106 C3
Pasadena CA U.S.A. 182 F7
Pasadena TX U.S.A. 179 D6
Pasado, Cabo c. Ecuador 198 A5
Pasaje Ecuador 198 B5
Pa Sak, Mae Nam r. Thai. 79 C5
Paşalimanı Adası i. Turkey 58 I8
Pasan India 97 D5
Pasarwajo Indon. 75 B4
Pasawng Myanmar 78 B4
Pascagoula r. Canada 168 F3
Pascagoula U.S.A. 175 B6
Pascagoula r. U.S.A. 175 B6
Pascalis Canada 173 P2
Paşcani Romania 58 H1
Pasco dept Peru 200 B3
Pasco U.S.A. 180 C3
Pascoag U.S.A. 177 N4
Pascoal, Monte hill Brazil 203 E6
Pascoe r. Australia 149 D2
Pascua, Isla de i. S. Pacific Ocean see Easter Island
Pascual Phil. 74 B3
Pas de Calais strait France/U.K. see Dover, Strait of
Pasewalk Germany 49 L2
Pasfield Lake Canada 167 J3
Pasha Rus. Fed. 43 O1
Pasha r. Rus. Fed. 43 N1
Pashkovo Rus. Fed. 82 C3
Pashozero Rus. Fed. 43 O1
Pashtun Zarghun Afgh. 101 E3
Pãsíg Phil. 74 B3
Pasi Ga Myanmar 78 B2
Pasighat India 97 G3
Pasinler Turkey 107 E3
Pasir Gudang Malaysia 76 [inset]
Pasirian Indon. 77 F5
Pasir Laba, Tanjong pt Sing. 76 [inset]
Pasir Mas Malaysia 76 C1
Pasirpangarayan Indon. 76 C2
Pasir Panjang Sing. 76 [inset]

Pasir Panjang hill Sing. 76 [inset]
Pasir Putih Malaysia 76 C1
Paskevicha, Zaliv l. Kazakh. see Shevchenko, Zaliv
Paskúh Iran 101 E5
Pasłęk Poland 49 Q1
Pasłęka r. Poland 49 Q1
Pasley, Cape Australia 151 C7
Pas!kaya Turkey 108 H1
Pašman i. Croatia 56 H5
Pasni Pak. 101 E5
Paso de Caballo Venez. 199 E2
Paso de Indios Arg. 205 C6
Paso del Limay Arg. 204 C6
Paso de los Libres Arg. 204 F3
Paso de los Toros Uruguay 204 F4
Paso del Sapo Arg. 205 C6
Paso de Patria Para. 201 F6
Paso de San Antonio Mex. 179 B6
Paso Real Hond. 186 B4
Paso Rio Mayo Arg. 205 C7
Paso Robles U.S.A. 182 D6
Pasquia Hills Canada 167 K4
Pasrur Pak. 101 H3
Passage Island U.S.A. 172 E2
Passagem Franca Brazil 202 D3
Passaic U.S.A. 177 K5
Passa Quatro Brazil 207 I9
Passa Tempo Brazil 207 I7
Passau Germany 49 K7
Passi Phil. 74 B4
Passo Fundo Brazil 203 A9
Passo Real, Barragem resr Brazil 203 A9
Passos Brazil 206 G7
Passu Jammu and Kashmir 96 B1
Pastavy Belarus 42 H6
also spelt Postavy
Pastaza prov. Ecuador 198 B5
Pastaza r. Peru 198 B6
Pasteur Arg. 204 E4
Pasto Col. 198 B4
Pasto Grande Brazil 201 E1
Pastora Peak U.S.A. 183 O5
Pastos Bons Brazil 202 D3
Pasu Jammu and Kashmir 96 B1
Pasuquin Phil. 74 B2
Pasur Turkey see Kulp
Pasuruan Indon. 77 F4
Pasvalys Lith. 42 F5
Pasvikelva r. Europe see Patsoyoki
Pásztó Hungary 49 Q8
Pata Bol. 200 C3
Pata i. Phil. 74 B5
Pata r. Senegal 124 B3
Patagonia reg. Arg. 205 C8
southamerica [contrasts] ➤ 194–195

Pataliputra India see Patna
Patan India see Somnath
Patan Gujarat India 96 B5
Patan Madhya Pradesh India 96 C5
Patan Maharashtra India 94 B2
Patan Nepal 97 E4
also known as Lalitpur
Patancheru India 94 C2
Patandar, Koh-i- mt. Pak. 101 F5
Patani Indon. 75 D2
Patani Nigeria 125 G5
Patan Saongi India 96 C5
Pataudi India 96 C3
Patay Arg. 204 E2
Patchewollock Australia 147 D3
Patch Grove U.S.A. 172 C8
Patchogue U.S.A. 177 L5
Patea N.Z. 152 I7
Patea r. N.Z. 152 I7
Pate Island Kenya 128 D5
Patensie S. Africa 133 I10
Paternion Austria 49 K9
Paternò Sicilia Italy 57 G11
Paterson r. Australia 147 E2
Paterson S. Africa 133 J10
Paterson U.S.A. 177 K5
Paterson Inlet N.Z. 153 B14
also known as Whaka a Te Wera
Paterson Range hills Australia 150 C4
Pathalgaon India 97 D5
Pathanamthitta India 94 C4
Pathankot India 96 B2
Patharia India 96 C5
Pathein Myanmar see Bassein
Pathfinder Reservoir U.S.A. 180 F4
Pathiu Thai. 79 B6
Pathri India 94 C2
Pathum Thani Thai. 79 C5
Pati India 96 B5
Pati Indon. 77 E4
Patía r. Col. 198 B4
Patiala India 96 C3
Patinti, Selat sea chan. Indon. 75 C3
Patitiri Greece 59 E9
Pativilca r. Peru 200 A2
Pätkai Bum mts India/Myanmar 78 A2
Patkaklik China 89 D4
Patnagar Turkey 59 K12
Patmos i. Greece 59 H11
Patna India 97 E4
historically known as Pataliputra
Patnagarh India 95 D1
Patnanongan i. Phil. 74 B3
Patnos Turkey 107 F3
Pato, Cerro mt. Chile 205 B7
Pato Branco Brazil 203 A8
Patoda India 94 B2
Patoka r. U.S.A. 174 C4
Patomskoye Nagor'ye mts Rus. Fed. 39 L4
Patoniva Fin. 44 N1
also known as Buoddobohki
Patos Albania 58 A8
Patos Brazil 202 E3
Patos, Lagoa dos l. Brazil 203 B9
Patos, Rio dos r. Brazil 206 E1
Patos de Minas Brazil 206 G5
Patquía Arg. 204 D3
Patra Greece see Patras
Patrae Greece see Patras
Pátrai Greece see Patras
Patraïkos Kolpos b. Greece 59 C10
Patras Greece 59 C10
also known as Patra or Pátrai; historically known as Patrae
Patrasaer India 97 E5
Patratu India 97 E5
Patreksfjörður Iceland 44 [inset] B2
Patri India 96 B5
Patricio Lynch, Isla i. Chile 205 B8
Patrick Creek watercourse Australia 149 C4
Patrick Springs U.S.A. 176 E8
Patrimônio Brazil 206 F6
Patrocínio Brazil 206 F5
Patsoyoki r. Europe 44 O1
also known as Pasvikelva; also spelt Paatsjoki
Pattadakal tourist site India 94 B3
Pattanapuram India 94 C4
Pattani Thai. 79 C7
Pattani r. Thai. 79 C7
Pattaya Thai. 79 C5
Patten U.S.A. 174 G2
Patterson CA U.S.A. 182 C4
Patterson LA U.S.A. 175 B6
Patterson r. U.S.A. 176 C6
Patterson, Mount Canada 166 C1
Patterson, Point U.S.A. 172 H5
Patterson Mountain U.S.A. 182 E5
Patti India 97 E4
Patti Indon. 75 C5
Patti Sicilia Italy 57 G10
Pattikonda India 94 C3
Pattukkottai India 94 C4

Pattullo, Mount Canada 166 D3
Patu Brazil 202 E3
Patuakhali Bangl. 97 F5
Patuanak Canada 167 J4
Patuca, Parque Nacional nat. park Hond. 186 B4
Patuca, Punta pt Hond. 186 B4
Patur India 94 C1
Patutu mt. N.Z. 152 J7
Patuxent r. U.S.A. 177 I7
Patuxent Range mts Antarctica 223 S1
Patvinsuon kansallispuisto nat. park Fin. 44 O3
Pátzcuaro Mex. 185 E5
Pau France 50 F9
Pau-Brasil Brazil 207 N2
Paucartambo Peru 200 B2
Paucartambo r. Peru see Yavero
Paud'Arco Brazil 202 B3
Pau d'Arco r. Brazil 201 H1
Pauhunri mt. China/India 89 E7
Pauillac France 50 F7
Pauini Brazil 200 D1
Pauini r. Brazil 199 F5
Pauini r. Brazil 200 D1
Pauk Myanmar 78 A3
Paukkaung Myanmar 78 A4
Paulatuk Canada 164 G3
Paulden U.S.A. 183 L7
Paulding Bay Antarctica 223 I2
Paulicéia Brazil 206 B8
Paulis Dem. Rep. Congo see Isiro
Pauliş Romania 58 C2
Pauljig r. U.S.A. 181 [inset] Z1
Paulista Brazil 202 F3
Paulistana Brazil 202 D4
Paulo Afonso Brazil 202 E4
Paulo de Faria Brazil 206 D7
Paulpietersburg S. Africa 133 O4
Pauls Valley U.S.A. 179 C5
Paumotu is Fr. Polynesia see Tuamotu Islands
Păuneşti Romania 58 H2
Paung Myanmar 78 B4
Paungbyin Myanmar 78 A2
Paungde Myanmar 78 A4
Pauni India 94 C1
Pauni India 96 C1
Pausa Peru 200 B3
Pauto r. Col. 198 D3
Pauträsk Sweden 44 L2
Pauwela U.S.A. 181 [inset] Z1
Pavagada India 94 C3
Pavão Brazil 203 D6
Pavarandocito Col. 198 B3
Păveh Iran 100 A3
Pavelets Rus. Fed. 43 U8
Pavia Italy 56 B3
historically known as Ticinum
Pavilion U.S.A. 176 G3
Pāvilosta Latvia 42 C5
Pavino Rus. Fed. 40 H4
Pavištytčio kalnas hill Lith. 42 D7
Pavlikeni Bulg. 58 G5
Pavlinovo Rus. Fed. 43 O7
Pavlivka Ukr. 58 J1
Pavlodar Kazakh. 103 I1
Pavlodar Oblast admin. div. Kazakh. see Pavlodarskaya Oblys'
Pavlodar Oblysy admin. div. Kazakh. see Pavlodarskaya Oblast'
Pavlodarskaya Oblast' admin. div. Kazakh. 103 I1
English form Pavlodar Oblast; also known as Pavlodar Oblysy
Pavlof Volcano U.S.A. 164 C4
Pavlograd Ukr. see Pavlohrad
Pavlohrad Ukr. 41 E6
also spelt Pavlograd
Pavlovka Akmolinskaya Oblast' Kazakh. 103 H2
Pavlovka Kustanayskaya Oblast' Kazakh. 103 I2
Pavlovka Respublika Bashkortostan Rus. Fed. 40 K5
Pavlovka Ul'yanovskaya Oblast' Rus. Fed. 41 H5
Pavlovsk Leningradskaya Oblast' Rus. Fed. 43 L2
Pavlovsk Voronezhskaya Oblast' Rus. Fed. 41 G6
Pavlovskaya Rus. Fed. 41 F7
Pavlovskiy Kazakh. 103 I1
Pavlovskiy Posad Rus. Fed. 43 T6
Pavlovskoye Rus. Fed. 43 V5
Pavlovskoye Vodokhranilishche resr Rus. Fed. 40 K5
Pavullo nel Frignano Italy 56 C4
Pavy Rus. Fed. 43 K3
Pawai India 96 C5
Pawan r. Indon. 77 E3
Pawarenga N.Z. 152 H3
Pawayan India 96 D3
Pawhuska U.S.A. 178 D4
Pawling U.S.A. 177 L4
Pawn r. Myanmar 78 B4
Pawnee r. U.S.A. 178 C4
Pawnee r. U.S.A. 178 C4
Pawnee City U.S.A. 178 C3
Paw Paw WV U.S.A. 176 G6
Pawu Aboriginal Land res. Australia 148 B4
Paxaro mt. Spain 54 C2
Paximada i. Greece 59 H13
Paximada i. Greece 59 H13
Paxoi i. Greece 59 B9
Paxson U.S.A. 164 E3
Paxton U.S.A. 174 B3
Payahe Indon. 75 D2
Payakumbuh Indon. 76 C3
Paya Lebar Sing. 76 [inset]
Payette U.S.A. 180 C3
Payette r. U.S.A. 180 C3
Pay-Khoy, Khrebet hills Rus. Fed. 40 L1
Payne Canada see Kangirsuk
Payne r. Canada see Arnaud
Payne, Lac l. Canada 168 F1
Payne's Creek U.S.A. 182 C1
Payne's Find Australia 151 B6
Paynesville Australia 147 E4
Paynesville U.S.A. 178 D2
Paysandú Uruguay 204 F4
Pays de la Loire admin. reg. France 50 E5
Pays de Léon reg. France 50 B4
Payshanba Uzbek. 103 F4
formerly known as Kara-Dar'ya
Payson U.S.A. 183 M7
Payún, Cerro vol. Arg. 204 C5
Payyer, Gora mt. Rus. Fed. 40 M2
Payzawat China see Jiashi
Paz, Rio de r. Brazil 202 B4
Pazar Turkey 107 E2
Pazarcık Turkey 107 D3
Pazardzhik Bulg. 58 F6
Pazarköy Turkey 59 I9
Pazarlar Turkey 59 K10
Paz de Ariporo Col. 198 D3
Paz de Río Col. 198 D3
Pazin Croatia 56 F3
Pazña Bol. 200 D4
Pchelva r. Rus. Fed. 43 M2
Pčinja r. Macedonia 58 C7
Pe Myanmar 79 B5
Peabiru Brazil 206 A10
Peabody KS U.S.A. 178 C4
Peabody MA U.S.A. 177 O3
Peace r. Canada 167 I3
Peace r. U.S.A. 175 D7

Peace Point Canada 167 H3
Peace River Canada 167 G3
Peach Creek U.S.A. 176 D8
Peachland Canada 166 G5
Peach Springs U.S.A. 183 K6
Peacock Hills Canada 167 I1
Peaima Falls Guyana 199 F3
Pea Island National Wildlife Refuge nature res. U.S.A. 174 F5
Peak Charles hill Australia 151 C7
Peak Charles National Park Australia 151 C7
Peak District National Park U.K. 47 K10
Peaked Mountain hill U.S.A. 174 H2
Peake watercourse Australia 146 C2
Peak Hill N.S.W. Australia 147 F3
Peak Hill W.A. Australia 151 B5
Peak Mountain hill U.S.A. 174 F3
Peak Range hills Australia 149 F4
Peaks Mill U.S.A. 176 A7
Peale, Mount U.S.A. 183 O3
Pearblossom U.S.A. 182 A1
Pearce Point Australia 148 A2
Pearisburg U.S.A. 176 E8
Pearl Canada 172 E2
Pearl r. U.S.A. 175 B6
Pearsall U.S.A. 179 C6
Pearson U.S.A. 175 D6
Pearson Islands Australia 146 B3
Pearston S. Africa 133 J9
Peary Channel Canada 165 J2
Pease r. U.S.A. 179 C5
Peawah r. Australia 150 B4
Peawanuck Canada 168 C2
Pebane Moz. 131 H3
Pebas Peru 198 D5
Pebengko Indon. 75 B3
Pebble Island Falkland Is 205 F8
Pebworth U.S.A. 181 [inset] Z1
Peć Kosovo, Srbija Yugo. 58 B6
also known as Peje
Pecan Bayou r. U.S.A. 179 C6
Pecatonica U.S.A. 172 D8
Péccel Hungary 49 Q8
Pecha r. Rus. Fed. 44 O1
Pechenga Rus. Fed. 44 O1
formerly known as Petsamo
Pechenga r. Rus. Fed. 44 O1
Pechenitsy Rus. Fed. 43 P1
Pecherniki Rus. Fed. 43 U7
Pechersk Rus. Fed. 43 N7
Pechora Rus. Fed. 40 K2
Pechora r. Rus. Fed. 40 J1
Pechora Sea Rus. Fed. see Pechorskoye More
Pechoro-Ilyskiy Zapovednik nature res. Rus. Fed. 40 K3
Pechorskaya Guba b. Rus. Fed. 40 J1
Pechorskoye More sea Rus. Fed. 40 J1
English form Pechora Sea
Pechory Rus. Fed. 42 I4
Pecica Romania 58 C2
Pecineaga Romania 58 J5
Peck U.S.A. 173 K7
Pecora, Capo c. Sardegna Italy 57 A9
Pecos U.S.A. 179 B6
Pecos r. U.S.A. 179 B6
Pécs Hungary 49 P9
formerly known as Fünfkirchen
Pécsvárad Hungary 49 P9
Pedasi Panama 186 C6
Peddapuram r. India 94 C2
Pedder, Lake Australia 147 E5
Peddie S. Africa 133 L10
Pededze Latvia 42 I4
Pededze r. Latvia 42 H5
Pedernales Haiti 187 F3
Pedernales Mex. 181 F7
Pedernales r. U.S.A. 179 C6
Pedernales Venez. 199 F3
Pedernales, Salar de salt flat Chile 204 C2
Pedernales r. U.S.A. 179 C6
Pederneiras Brazil 206 D9
Pedersöre Fin. 44 M3
Pediva Angola 127 B9
Pedra Azul Brazil 207 L6
Pedra Badejo Cape Verde 124 [inset]
Pedrada mt. Port. 54 C3
Pedrafita do Cebreiro Spain 54 D2
Pedra Lume Cape Verde 124 [inset]
Pedra Preta, Serra da mts Brazil 202 C3
Pedras r. Brazil 204 D3
Pedras de Maria da Cruz Brazil 207 I2
Pedras Negras Brazil 201 E3
Pedregal Panama 186 C5
Pedregal Venez. 198 D2
Pedregulho Brazil 206 F7
Pedreiras Maranhão Brazil 202 C3
Pedreiras São Paulo Brazil 206 G9
Pedriceña Mex. 177 E3
Pedro, Point Sri Lanka 94 D4
Pedro Afonso Brazil 202 B3
Pedro Avelino Brazil 202 E3
Pedro Bank sea feature Jamaica 186 D3
Pedro Barros Brazil 206 H10
Pedro Betancourt Cuba 175 D8
Pedro Cays is Jamaica 186 D3
Pedro Chico Col. 198 D4
Pedro Gomes Brazil 203 A6
Pedro Gómez mt. Spain 54 F5
Pedro II Brazil 202 D3
Pedro II, Ilha reg. Brazil/Venez. 199 E4
Pedro Juan Caballero Para. 201 F5
Pedro Leopoldo Brazil 203 C6
Pedroll Brazil 202 C3
Pedro Luro Arg. 204 E5
Pedro Muñoz Spain 55 I5
Pedro Osório Brazil 204 G3
Pedroso Port. 54 C3
Pedro Toledo Brazil 206 F11
Peebinga Australia 146 D3
Peebles U.K. 46 I8
Peebles U.S.A. 176 B7
Peedamulla Aboriginal Reserve Australia 150 A4
Peekskill U.S.A. 177 L4
Peel r. Australia 147 F2
Peel r. Canada 166 C1
Peel Isle of Man 47 H9
Peene r. Germany 49 K2
Peera Peera Poolanna Lake salt flat Australia 148 C3
Peerless Lake Canada 167 H3
Peerless Lake l. Canada 167 H3
Peery Lake salt flat Australia 147 D2
Pegasus Bay N.Z. 153 G11
Pegnitz Germany 48 I6
Pego Spain 55 K6
Pegu Myanmar 78 B4
also known as Bago
Pegu admin. div. Myanmar 78 A4
Pegu Yoma mts Myanmar 78 A4
also spelt Beigong
Pegunungan Range mts Sarawak Malaysia see Tama Abu, Banjaran
Peña Mira mt. Spain 54 E3
Peña Nevada, Cerro mt. Mex. 185 F4
Penang state Malaysia see Pinang
Penaranda de Bracamonte Spain 54 F4
Pen Argyl U.S.A. 177 J5
Penarie Australia 147 D3
Peñarroya mt. Spain 55 K4
Peñarroya-Pueblonuevo Spain 54 F6
Peñas, Cabo de c. Spain 54 F1
Penas, Golfo de g. Chile 205 B7
Peñas Blancas Nicaragua 186 B5

Pei Shan mts China see Bei Shan
Peitz Germany 49 L4
Peixe Brazil 202 B5
Peixe r. Goiás Brazil 206 C1
Peixe r. Goiás Brazil 206 E3
Peixe r. São Paulo Brazil 206 B8
Peixe, Rio do r. Brazil 206 A3
Peixes r. Brazil 207 J3
Peixes, Rio dos r. Brazil 201 B1
Peixian China see Pizhou
Peixian China 87 F1
Peixoto, Represa resr Brazil 206 G7
Peixoto de Azevedo Brazil 202 A4
Peixoto de Azevedo r. Brazil 201 G3
Pejantan i. Indon. 77 D2
Peje Kosovo, Srbija Yugo. see Peć
Pek r. Yugo. 58 C4
Pekabata Indon. 75 A3
Pekalongan Indon. 77 E4
Pekan Malaysia 76 C2
Pekanbaru Indon. 76 C2
also spelt Pakanbaru
Pékans, Rivière aux r. Canada 169 H2
Peki Ghana 125 F5
Pekin U.S.A. 174 B3
Peking China see Beijing
Peklino Rus. Fed. 43 O8
Pelabuhan Kelang Malaysia 76 C2
formerly known as Port Klang or Port Swettenham
Pelabuhan Sandakan inlet Sabah Malaysia 77 G1
Pelada, Pampa hills Arg. 205 C7
Pelado mt. Spain 55 J5
Pelagie, Isole is Sicilia Italy 57 E13
Pelagonija plain Macedonia 58 C7
Pelagonija, Diavlos sea chan. Greece 59 F9
Pelaihari Indon. 77 F3
Pelalawan Indon. 76 C2
Pelapis i. Indon. 77 E3
Pelasgia Greece 59 D10
also known as Pelasyía
Pelasgía Greece see Pelasgia
Pelat, Mont mt. France 51 M8
Pelatsoeu mt. Lesotho 133 M5
Pelawanbesar Indon. 77 G2
Pełczyce Poland 49 M2
Peleaga, Vârful mt. Romania 58 D3
Pelechuco Bol. 200 C3
Peleči Latvia 42 H5
Pelée, Montagne vol. Martinique 187 H4
Pelee Island Canada 168 D5
Pelee Point Canada 168 D5
Peleliu i. Palau 73 H5
also spelt Beliliou
Peleng i. Indon. 75 B3
Peleng, Selat sea chan. Indon. 75 B3
Peleng, Teluk b. Indon. 75 B3
Peles Rus. Fed. 40 I3
Pelhřimov Czech Rep. 49 M6
Pelican Creek r. Australia 149 D3
Pelican Lake l. Canada 167 K4
Pelican Lake U.S.A. 172 D5
Pelican Lake l. U.S.A. 178 D1
Pelican Narrows Canada 167 K4
Pelican Point Canada 168 C3
Pelister mt. Macedonia 58 C8
Pelister nat. park Macedonia 58 C8
Pelješac pen. Croatia 56 J6
Pelkosenniemi Fin. 44 N2
Pella S. Africa 132 C5
Pellat Lake Canada 167 I1
Pellegrue France 50 G8
Pelleluhu Islands P.N.G. 73 J7
Pello Fin. 44 M2
Pellworm i. Germany 48 F1
Pelly r. Canada 166 B2
Pelly Bay Canada 165 K3
Pelly Crossing Canada 166 B2
Pelly Lake Canada 167 K1
Pelly Mountains Canada 166 C2
Pelokang is Indon. 77 G4
Peloponnese admin. reg. Greece see Peloponnisos
Peloponnese reg. Greece 59 C11
also known as Peloponnisos; historically known as Peloponnesus
Peloponnese reg. Greece see Peloponnisos
Peloponnisos admin. reg. Greece see Peloponnese
Peloponnisos reg. Greece 59 C11
English form Peloponnese; historically known as Peloponnesus
Peloponnisos reg. Greece see Peloponnese
Peloritani, Monti mts Sicilia Italy 57 G11
Pelotas Brazil 204 G3
Pelotas, Rio das r. Brazil 203 B8
Pelovo Bulg. 58 F5
Pelplin Poland 49 P2
Pelsart Group is Australia 151 A6
Peltovuoma Fin. 44 N1
Pelusium tourist site Egypt 108 D6
Pelusium, Bay of Egypt see Tina, Khalig el
Pelvoux, Massif du mts France 51 M8
Pemache r. Canada 173 J3
Pemadumcook Lake U.S.A. 174 G2
Pemalang Indon. 77 E4
Pemangkat Indon. 77 E2
Pemarung, Pulau i. Indon. 77 G3
Pematangsiantar Indon. 76 B2
Pemba Moz. 131 I2
formerly known as Porto Amélia
Pemba Zambia 127 E9
Pemba, Baia de b. Moz. 129 D8
Pemba Channel Tanz. 129 C6
Pemba Island Tanz. 129 C6
Pemba North admin. reg. Tanz. 129 C6
Pemba South admin. reg. Tanz. 129 C6
Pemberton Australia 151 A7
Pemberton Canada 166 F5
Pemberton U.S.A. 177 K6
Pembina r. Canada 167 H4
Pembina r. U.S.A. 178 C1
Pembroke Canada 168 E4
Pembroke U.K. 47 H12
also known as Penfro
Pembroke U.S.A. 175 D5
Pembroke, Cape Falkland Is 205 F8
Pembroke, Mount N.Z. 153 B12
Pembroke Pines U.S.A. 175 D7
Pembrokeshire Coast National Park U.K. 47 G12
Pembuanghulu Indon. 77 F3
Pemuco Chile 204 B5
Pen India 94 B2
Pen r. Myanmar 78 A3
Pena Barrosa Bol. 200 D5
Peña Cabollera mt. Spain 55 H3
Peña de Francia mt. Spain 54 E4
Peña de Izaga mt. Spain 55 J2
Peña de Oroel mt. Spain 55 K2
Peñafiel Spain 54 H3
Peñaflor Spain 54 F7
Peñagolosa mt. Spain 55 K4
Peñalara mt. Spain 54 H4
Peñalba de Santiago tourist site Spain 54 E2
Peñalsordo Spain 54 F6
Penamacor Port. 54 D4
Penambo Range mts Sarawak Malaysia see Tama Abu, Banjaran

Penasi, Pulau i. Indon. 76 A1
also known as Dedap
Peña Ubiña mt. Spain 54 F1
Peña Utrera hill Spain 54 E6
Pench r. India 96 C5
Pencheng China see Ruichang
Pench National Park India 96 C5
Penck, Cape Antarctica 223 F2
Pendé r. Cent. Afr. Rep. 126 C3
Pendembu Sierra Leone 124 B4
Pender U.S.A. 178 C3
Pender Bay Australia 150 C3
Pender Bay Aboriginal Reserve Australia 150 C3
Pendik Turkey 58 K8
Pendleton U.S.A. 180 C3
Pendleton Bay Canada 166 E4
Pendopo Indon. 76 C3
Pend Oreille r. U.S.A. 180 C2
Pend Oreille Lake U.S.A. 180 C2
Pendra India 97 D5
Penduv India 94 B2
Pendzhikent Tajik. see Panjakent
Penebangan i. Indon. 77 E3
Peneda Gerês, Parque Nacional da nat. park Port. 54 C3
Pene-Mende Dem. Rep. Congo 126 F6
Pénessoulou Benin 125 F4
Penetanguishene Canada 173 N6
Penfield U.S.A. 176 G4
Penfro U.K. see Pembroke
Peng'an China 86 C2
also known as Zhoukou
Penganga r. India 94 C2
Peng Chau i. Hong Kong China 87 [inset]
P'engchia Yü i. Taiwan 87 G3
Penge Dem. Rep. Congo 127 E6
P'enghu Ch'üntao is Taiwan 87 F4
English form Pescadores; also known as P'enghu Liehtao
P'enghu Liehtao is Taiwan see P'enghu Ch'üntao
P'enghu Tao i. Taiwan 87 F4
Pengiki i. Indon. 77 E2
Peng Kang hill Sing. 76 [inset]
Penglai China 85 I4
formerly known as Dengzhou
Pengshan China 86 B2
Pengshui China 87 D2
also known as Hanjia
Peng Siang, Sungai r. Sing. 76 [inset]
Pengwa Myanmar 78 A3
Pengxi China 86 C2
also known as Chicheng
Pengxian China see Pengzhou
Pengze China 87 F2
also known as Longcheng
Pengzhou China 86 B2
formerly known as Pengxian
Penhalonga Zimbabwe 131 G3
Penhoek Pass S. Africa 133 K8
Penhook U.S.A. 176 F9
Peniche Port. 54 B5
Penicuik U.K. 46 I8
Penida i. Indon. 77 F5
Peninga Rus. Fed. 40 E3
Peninsular Malaysia Malaysia 76 C2
also known as Malaya or Semenanjung Malaysia; formerly known as West Malaysia
Penitente, Serra do hills Brazil 202 C4
Pênjwîn Iraq 107 F4
Penmarch France 50 B5
Penmarch, Pointe de pt France 50 B5
Penn U.S.A. see Penn Hills
Penna, Punta della pt Italy 56 G6
Penne Italy 56 F6
Pennell Coast Antarctica 223 L2
Penner r. India 94 D3
Penneshaw Australia 146 C3
Penn Hills U.S.A. 176 F5
formerly known as Penn
Pennine, Alpi mts Italy/Switz. 51 N7
English form Pennine Alps
Pennine Alps mts Italy/Switz. see Pennine, Alpi
Pennines hills U.K. 47 J9
Pennington S. Africa 133 O7
Pennington Gap U.S.A. 176 B9
Pennsboro U.S.A. 176 E6
Penns Grove U.S.A. 177 J6
Pennsville U.S.A. 177 J6
Pennsylvania state U.S.A. 176 G4
Penny Icecap Canada 165 M3
Penny Point Antarctica 223 K1
Peno Rus. Fed. 43 N5
Penobscot r. U.S.A. 177 Q1
Penobscot Bay U.S.A. 177 Q1
Penola Australia 146 D4
Peñón Blanco Mex. 184 D3
Penong Australia 146 B2
Penonomé Panama 186 C5
Penrhyn atoll Cook Is 221 H6
also known as Tongareva
Penrith Australia 147 F3
Penrith U.K. 47 J9
Pensacola U.S.A. 175 C6
Pensacola Bay i. U.S.A. 175 C6
Pensacola Mountains Antarctica 223 T1
Pensamiento Bol. 201 E3
Pensaukee U.S.A. 172 F6
Pentadaktylos Range mts Cyprus 108 E2
also known as Kyrenia Mountains or Beşparmak Dağları
Pentakota India 95 D2
Pentecost Island Vanuatu 145 F3
also known as Pentecôte, Île; formerly known as Whitsun Island
Pentecôte r. Canada 169 H3
Pentecôte, Île i. Vanuatu see Pentecost Island
Penteleu, Vârful mt. Romania 58 H3
Penticton Canada 166 G5
Pentire Point U.K. 47 G13
Pentland Australia 149 E4
Pentland Firth sea chan. U.K. 46 I5
Pentland Hills U.K. 46 I8
Pentwater U.S.A. 172 G7
Penukonda India 94 C3
Penunjok, Tanjong pt Malaysia 76 C1
Penwegon Myanmar 78 B4
Pen-y-Bont ar Ogwr U.K. see Bridgend
Penygadair hill U.K. 47 I11
Penylan Lake Canada 167 J2
Penyu, Kepulauan is Indon. 75 C4
Penza Rus. Fed. 41 H5
Penzance U.K. 47 G13
Penza Oblast admin. div. Rus. Fed. see Penzenskaya Oblast'
Penzenskaya Oblast' admin. div. Rus. Fed. 41 H5
English form Penza Oblast
Penzhinskaya Guba b. Rus. Fed. 39 Q3
Peoples Creek r. U.S.A. 180 E2
Peoria AZ U.S.A. 183 L8
Peoria IL U.S.A. 174 B3
Peoria Heights U.S.A. 172 D10
Pepeekeo U.S.A. 181 [inset] Z2
Pepel Sierra Leone 124 B4
Peper Sudan 128 B3
Pepworth S. Africa 133 N5
Pëqin Albania 58 A7
Pequi Brazil 207 I6
Pequop Mountains U.S.A. 183 J1
Pera Head Australia 149 D2
Peraitepuy Venez. 199 F3
Perak i. Malaysia 76 B1
Perak r. Malaysia 76 C1
Perak state Malaysia 76 C1
Perama Greece 59 F13
Perambalur India 94 C4
Perämeren kansallispuisto nat. park Fin. 44 N2
Perä-Posio Fin. 44 N2
Percé Canada 169 H3
Perche, Collines du hills France 50 G4
Percival Lakes salt flat Australia 150 D4
Percy France 50 E4
Percy U.S.A. 177 N1
Percy Isles Australia 149 F4
Percy Reach l. Canada 173 P6
Perdekop S. Africa 133 N4
Perdepoort pass S. Africa 132 H10
Perdida r. Brazil 202 C4
Perdido r. Brazil 201 F5
Perdido, Monte mt. Spain 55 L2
Perdiguère, Pic mt. France/Spain 55 L2
Perdika Greece 59 B9
Perdizes Brazil 206 F6
Perdões Brazil 207 H8
Perdu, Lac l. Canada 169 G3
Perechyn Ukr. 49 T7
Peregrebnoye Rus. Fed. 38 G3
Pereira Col. 198 C3
Pereira Barreto Brazil 206 B7
Pereira de Eça Angola see Ondjiva
Pereiro Brazil 202 E3
Perekhoda r. Rus. Fed. 43 M3
Perelyub Rus. Fed. 102 B2
Pere Marquette r. U.S.A. 172 G7
Peremetnoye Kazakh. 102 B2
Peremul Par reef India 94 B4
Peremyshl' Rus. Fed. 43 R7
Peremyshlyany Ukr. 41 C6
Perené r. Peru 200 B2
Perenjori Australia 151 B6
Pereshnoye, Ozero l. Rus. Fed. 43 T1
Pereslavl'-Zalesskiy Rus. Fed. 43 T5
Pereslavskiy Natsional'nyy Park nat. park Rus. Fed. 43 T5
Peretu Romania 58 G4
Perevolotskiy Rus. Fed. 102 C2
Pereyaslavka Rus. Fed. 82 D3
Pereyaslav-Khmel'nitskiy Ukr. see Pereyaslav-Khmel'nyts'kyy
Pereyaslav-Khmel'nyts'kyy Ukr. 41 D6
also spelt Pereyaslav-Khmel'nitskiy
Pérez Chile 204 C2
Perg Austria 49 L7
Pergamino Arg. 204 E4
Perge tourist site Turkey 108 B1
Pergine Valsugana Italy 56 D2
Pergola Italy 56 E5
Perhentian Besar i. Malaysia 76 C1
Perho Fin. 44 N3
Periam Romania 58 B2
Péribonca r. Canada 169 F3
Perico Arg. 200 D6
Pericos Mex. 184 D3
Peridot U.S.A. 183 N8
Perieni Romania 58 I2
Périers France 50 E3
Perigoso, Canal sea chan. Brazil 202 B2
Périgueux France 50 G7
Perijá, Parque Nacional nat. park Venez. 198 C2
Perija, Sierra de mts Venez. 198 C2
Perim Island Yemen see Barīm
Peringat Malaysia 76 C1
Periprava Romania 58 K3
Perişoru Romania 58 I4
Peristera i. Greece 59 E9
Peristerio Greece 59 E10
Periteasca-Gura Portiței nature res. Romania 58 K4
Perito Moreno Arg. 205 C7
Perito Moreno, Parque Nacional nat. park Arg. 205 B7
Perivar r. India 94 C4
Perlas, Laguna de lag. Nicaragua 186 C4
Perlas, Punta de pt Nicaragua 186 C4
Perleberg Germany 48 I2
Perlis state Malaysia 76 C1
Perm' Rus. Fed. 40 K4
formerly known as Molotov
Permas Rus. Fed. 40 H4
Përmet Albania 59 B8
Perm Oblast admin. div. Rus. Fed. see Permskaya Oblast'
Permskaya Oblast' admin. div. Rus. Fed. 40 K4
English form Perm Oblast; formerly known as Molotovskaya Oblast'
Permuda i. Croatia 56 G4
Pernå Fin. 42 H1
Pernambuco Brazil see Recife
Pernambuco state Brazil 202 E4
Pernatty Lagoon salt flat Australia 146 C2
Pernem India 94 B3
Pernik Bulg. 58 E6
formerly known as Dimitrovo
Perniö Fin. 45 M3
Pernov Estonia see Pärnu
Perolândia Brazil 206 A4
Peron, Cape Australia 151 A5
Peron Islands Australia 148 A2
Péronnas France 51 L6
Péronne France 51 I3
Peron Peninsula Australia 151 A5
Perote Mex. 185 F5
Perpignan France 51 I10
Perrégaux Alg. see Mohammadia
Perris U.S.A. 183 G8
Perros-Guirec France 50 C4
Perry Canada 173 I3
Perry r. Canada 167 K1
Perry FL U.S.A. 175 D6
Perry GA U.S.A. 175 D5
Perry IA U.S.A. 178 D3
Perry MI U.S.A. 173 I8
Perry OK U.S.A. 179 C4
Perry Hall U.S.A. 177 I6
Perrymennyy, Cape Antarctica 223 G2
Perrysburg U.S.A. 176 B4
Perryton U.S.A. 179 B4
Perryville AR U.S.A. 179 D5
Perryville KY U.S.A. 176 A8
Persepolis tourist site Iran 100 C4
Persia country Asia see Iran
Persian Gulf Asia see The Gulf
Persis prov. Iran see Fārs
Pertek Turkey 107 D3
Perth Tas. Australia 147 E5
▶Perth W.A. Australia 151 A6
State capital of Western Australia. 4th most populous city in Oceania.
world [cities] → 24–25
Perth Canada 168 E4
Perth U.K. 46 I7
Perth-Andover Canada 169 H4
Pertominsk Rus. Fed. 40 F2
Pertteli Fin. 42 E1
Pertuis France 51 L9
Pertuis Breton sea chan. France 50 E6
Pertuis d'Antioche sea chan. France 50 E6
Pertunmaa Fin. 45 N3
Pertusato, Capo c. Corse France 56 B7
Perú Bol. 200 D3
Peru atoll Kiribati see Beru
▶Peru country S. America 200 B2
3rd largest and 4th most populous country in South America.
southamerica [countries] → 192–193
Peru IL U.S.A. 172 D9
Peru IN U.S.A. 174 C3
Peru NY U.S.A. 177 L1
Peručko Jezero l. Croatia 56 I5
Perugia Italy 56 E5
historically known as Perusia
Perugorria Arg. 204 F3
Peruhumpenai Mountains Reserve nature res. Indon. 75 B3
Peruíbe Brazil 206 G11
Peruru India 94 C3
Perushtitsa Bulg. 58 F6
Perusia Italy see Perugia
Péruwelz Belgium 51 J2
Pervoavgustovskiy Rus. Fed. 43 Q9
Pervomaisc Moldova 58 K2
Pervomay Kyrg. 103 H4
also known as Pervomayskoye; formerly known as Pervomayskiy
Pervomaysk Rus. Fed. 40 G5
formerly known as Tashino
Pervomays'k Ukr. 41 D6
formerly known as Ol'viopol'
Pervomayskiy Kazakh. 103 J2
Pervomayskiy Kyrg. see Pervomay
Pervomayskiy Rus. Fed. see Novodvinsk
Pervomayskiy Chitinskaya Oblast' Rus. Fed. 85 G1
Pervomayskiy Orenburgskaya Oblast' Rus. Fed. 102 C2
Pervomayskiy Smolenskaya Oblast' Rus. Fed. 43 N7
Pervomayskiy Tambovskaya Oblast' Rus. Fed. 41 G5
formerly known as Bogoyavlenskoye
Pervomayskiy Tul'skaya Oblast' Rus. Fed. 43 S7
Pervomayskoye Kyrg. see Pervomay
Pervomayskoye Rus. Fed. 82 B1
Pervomayskoye Rus. Fed. 43 K1
Pervomays'kyy Ukr. 41 F6
formerly known as Likhachevo or Likhachyovo
Pervorechenskiy Rus. Fed. 39 Q3
Per'yevo Rus. Fed. 43 U2
Pes' Rus. Fed. 43 P3
Pes' r. Rus. Fed. 43 Q2
Pesa r. Italy 56 D5
Pesaguan r. Indon. 77 E3
Pesaro Italy 56 E5
historically known as Pisaurum
Pescadero U.S.A. 182 B4
Pescadores is Taiwan see P'enghu Ch'üntao
Pescadores, Punta pt Peru 200 B4
Pescara Italy 56 G6
Pescara r. Italy 56 G6
Peschanokopskoye Rus. Fed. 41 G7
Peschanoye Rus. Fed. see Yashkul'
Peschanyy, Mys pt Kazakh. 102 B4
Peschici Italy 56 I7
Pescia Italy 56 C5
Pesebre, Punta pt Canary Is 122 B3
Pesha r. Rus. Fed. 40 H2
Peshanjan Afgh. 101 E3
Peshawar Pak. 101 G3
Peshkopi Albania 58 B7
Peshnyye, Ostrova is Kazakh. see Bol'shiye Peshnyye, Ostrova
Peshtera Bulg. 58 F6
Peshtigo U.S.A. 172 F5
Peshtigo r. U.S.A. 172 F6
Peski Kazakh. 103 F1
Peski Moskovskaya Oblast' Rus. Fed. 43 T6
Peski Voronezhskaya Oblast' Rus. Fed. 41 G6
Peski Turkm. 103 E5
Peski Karakum des. Kazakh. see Karakum Desert
Peski Karakumy des. Turkm. see Karakum Desert
Peskovka Rus. Fed. 40 J4
Pesnica Slovenia 56 H2
Pesochnoye Rus. Fed. 43 U3
Pesochnya Rus. Fed. 43 O8
Peso da Régua Port. 54 D3
Pespire Hond. 186 B4
Pesqueira Brazil 202 E4
Pesqueira Mex. 184 C2
Pessac France 50 F8
Pessinki naturreservat nature res. Sweden 40 B2
Pestovo Rus. Fed. 43 Q3
Pestravka Rus. Fed. 102 B1
Pestyaki Rus. Fed. 40 G4
Petah Tiqwa Israel 108 F5
Petaihari Martapura Reserve nature res. Indon. 77 F3
Petäjävesi Fin. 44 N3
Petalidi Greece 59 C12
Petalioi i. Greece 59 F10
Petaluma U.S.A. 182 B3
Pétange Lux. 51 L3
Petangis Indon. 77 F3
Petare Venez. 199 E2
Petas Greece 59 C9
Petatlán Mex. 185 E5
Petauke Zambia 127 F8
Petawaga, Lac l. Canada 173 R4
Petawawa Canada 173 P5
Petén Itzá, Lago l. Guat. 185 H5
Petenwell Lake U.S.A. 172 D6
Peterbell Canada 168 D3
Peterborough S.A. Australia 146 C3
Peterborough Vic. Australia 147 D4
Peterborough Canada 168 E4
Peterborough U.K. 47 L11
Peterborough U.S.A. 177 N3
Peterhead U.K. 46 K6
Peter I Island Antarctica 222 R2
also known as Peter I Øy
Peter I Øy i. Antarctica see Peter I Island
Peter Lougheed Provincial Park Canada 167 H5
Petermann Aboriginal Land res. Australia 148 A5
Petermann Bjerg nunatak Greenland 165 Q2
Petermann Ranges mts Australia 148 A5
Peter Pond Lake Canada 167 I4
Petersburg S. Africa 133 I9
Petersburg AK U.S.A. 164 F4
Petersburg IL U.S.A. 174 B4
Petersburg IN U.S.A. 174 C4
Petersburg NY U.S.A. 177 L3
Petersburg OH U.S.A. 176 E5
Petersburg VA U.S.A. 176 H8
Petersburg WV U.S.A. 176 F7
Petershagen Germany 48 F3
Peters Mine Guyana 199 G3
Peterstown U.S.A. 176 E8
Petersville U.S.A. 164 D3
Peter the Great Bay Rus. Fed. see Petra Velikogo, Zaliv
Pétervárad Vojvodina, Srbija Yugo. see Petrovaradin
Peterwardein Vojvodina, Srbija Yugo. see Petrovaradin
Peth India 94 B2
Petilia Policastro Italy 57 I9
Petit Atlas mts Morocco see Anti Atlas
Petitcodiac Canada 169 H4
Petite Creuse r. France 51 H6
Petite-Goâve Haiti 187 E3
Petitjean Morocco see Sidi Kacem
Petit Lac Manicouagan l. Canada 169 H2
Petit-Loango, Réserve de nature res. Gabon 126 A5
Petit Maine r. France 50 E5
Petit Mécatina r. Canada see Little Mecatina
Petit Mécatina r. Canada 169 J3
Petit Mécatina, Île du i. Canada 169 J3
also known as Little Mecatina Island
Petit Morin r. France 51 J4
Petitot r. Canada 166 F2
Petit St-Bernard, Col du pass France 51 M7
Petkino Rus. Fed. 43 U7
Petkula Fin. 44 N2
Petlad India 96 B5
Petlawad India 96 B5
Peto Mex. 185 H4
Petoskey U.S.A. 173 I5
Petra tourist site Jordan 108 G7
also spelt Batrā'
Petras, Mount Antarctica 222 P1
Petra tou Romiou tourist site Cyprus see Aphrodite's Birthplace
Petra Velikogo, Zaliv b. Rus. Fed. 82 C4
English form Peter the Great Bay
Petre, Point Canada 173 P7
Petrich Bulg. 58 E7
Petrified Forest National Park U.S.A. 183 O6
Petrijevci Croatia 56 K3
Petrikau Poland see Piotrków Trybunalski
Petrikov Belarus see Pyetrykaw
Petrila Romania 58 E3
Petrinja Croatia 56 I3
Petro, Cerro de mt. Chile 204 C3
Petroaleksandrovsk Uzbek. see Turtkul'
Petrodvorets Rus. Fed. 43 K2
Petrograd Rus. Fed. see St Petersburg
Petrokov Poland see Piotrków Trybunalski
Petrokrepost' Rus. Fed. see Shlissel'burg
Petrokrepost', Bukhta b. Rus. Fed. 43 M1
Petrolândia Brazil 202 E4
Petrolia Canada 173 K8
Petrolina Amazonas Brazil 199 E5
Petrolina Pernambuco Brazil 202 D4
Petrolina de Goiás Brazil 206 D3
Petron, Limni l. Greece 58 C8
Petropavl Kazakh. see Petropavlovsk
Petropavlovka Kazakh. 103 J3
Petropavlovka Rus. Fed. 85 E1
Petropavlovka Rus. Fed. 41 G6
Petropavlovsk Kazakh. 38 G4
also known as Petropavl
Petropavlovsk Rus. Fed. see Petropavlovsk-Kamchatskiy
Petropavlovsk-Kamchatskiy Rus. Fed. 39 P4
historically known as Petropavlovsk
Petrópolis Brazil 207 J9
Petroşani Romania 58 E3
Petrovac Bos.-Herz. see Bosanski Petrovac
Petrovac Srbija Yugo. 58 C4
Petrovaradin Vojvodina, Srbija Yugo. 58 A3
also known as Pétervárad; historically known as Peterwardein
Petrovichi Rus. Fed. 43 N8
Petrovsk Rus. Fed. 41 H5
Petrovsk Rus. Fed. 43 V5
Petrovskoye Moskovskaya Oblast' Rus. Fed. 43 R5
Petrovskoye Rus. Fed. see Svetlograd
Petrovskoye Yaroslavskaya Oblast' Rus. Fed. 43 U4
Petrovsk-Zabaykal'skiy Rus. Fed. 85 F1
Petrov Val Rus. Fed. 41 H6
Petrozavodsk Rus. Fed. 40 E3
Petru Rareş Romania 58 F1
Petrusburg S. Africa 133 J6
Petrus Steyn S. Africa 133 M4
Petrusville S. Africa 133 I7
Petsamo Rus. Fed. see Pechenga
Petsana S. Africa 133 M4
Pettau Slovenia see Ptuj
Petukhovo Rus. Fed. 38 G4
Petushki Rus. Fed. 43 U6
formerly known as Novyye Petushki
Peuetsagu, Gunung vol. Indon. 76 B1
Peurasuvanto Fin. 44 N2
Pevek Rus. Fed. 39 R3
Pêxung China 89 F5
Peza r. Rus. Fed. 40 H2
Pézenas France 51 J9
Pezinok Slovakia 49 O7
Pfaffenhofen an der Ilm Germany 48 I7
Pfälzer Wald hills Germany 48 E6
Pfälzer Wald park Germany 48 E6
Pfarrkirchen Germany 49 J7
Pforzheim Germany 48 F7
Pfullendorf Germany 48 G8
Pfungstadt Germany 48 F6
Phagwara India 96 B3
Phahameng S. Africa 133 K5
Phalaborwa S. Africa 131 F4
Phalia Pak. 101 H3
Phalodi India 96 B4
Phalsbourg France 51 N4
Phalsund India 96 A4
Phaltan India 94 B2
Phalut Peak India/Nepal 97 F4
Phangan, Ko i. Thai. 79 C6
Phangnga Thai. 79 B6
Phan Rang Vietnam 79 E6
Phan Ri Vietnam 79 E6
Phan Thiêt Vietnam 79 E6
Phan Thiêt, Vinh b. Vietnam 79 E6
Phaphund India 96 C4
Phaplu Nepal 97 E4
Phat Diêm Vietnam 78 D3
Phatthalung Thai. 79 C7
Phayao Thai. 78 B4
Phek India 97 G4
Phelp r. Australia 148 B2
Phelps NY U.S.A. 177 H3
Phelps WI U.S.A. 172 D4
Phen Thai. 78 C4
Phenix U.S.A. 176 G8
Phenix City U.S.A. 175 C5
Phephane watercourse S. Africa 132 G2
Phet Buri Thai. 79 B5
Phetchabun Thai. 78 C4
Phichit Thai. 78 C4
Philadelphia Jordan see 'Ammān
Philadelphia S. Africa 132 C10
Philadelphia Turkey see Alaşehir
Philadelphia MS U.S.A. 175 B5
Philadelphia NY U.S.A. 177 J1
Philadelphia PA U.S.A. 177 J6
Philae tourist site Egypt 121 G4
Philip U.S.A. 178 B2
Philip Atoll Micronesia see Sorol
Philippeville Alg. see Skikda
Philippeville Belgium 51 K2
Philippi U.S.A. 176 E6
Philippi, Lake salt flat Australia 148 C5
▶Philippines country Asia 74 A3
spelt Filipinas or Pilipinas in Filipino
asia [countries] → 64–67
Philippine Sea N. Pacific Ocean 74 B2
▶Philippine Trench sea feature N. Pacific Ocean 220 C5
3rd deepest trench in the world.
Philippolis S. Africa 133 J7
Philippolis Road S. Africa 133 J7
Philippopolis Bulg. see Plovdiv
Philipsburg Neth. Antilles 187 H3
Philipsburg U.S.A. 180 D3
Philip Smith Mountains U.S.A. 164 E3
Philipstown S. Africa 133 I7
Phillip Island Australia 147 E4
Phillips r. Australia 151 C7
Phillips ME U.S.A. 177 O1
Phillips WI U.S.A. 172 C5
Phillips Arm Canada 166 E5
Phillipsburg KS U.S.A. 178 C4
Phillipsburg NJ U.S.A. 177 J5
Phillips Inlet Canada 165 K1
Phillips Range hills Australia 150 D3
Phillipston U.S.A. 176 F5
Philmont U.S.A. 177 L3
Philomelium Turkey see Akşehir
Philpott Reservoir U.S.A. 176 E9
Phimun Mangsahan Thai. 79 D5
Phiritona S. Africa 133 L4
Phitsanulok Thai. 78 C4
Phlox U.S.A. 172 D5
▶Phnom Penh Cambodia 79 D6
Capital of Cambodia. Also spelt Phnum Pénh.
Phnum Pénh Cambodia see Phnom Penh
Pho, Laem pt Thai. 79 C7
Phoenicia U.S.A. 177 K3
▶Phoenix AZ U.S.A. 183 L8
State capital of Arizona.
Phoenix NY U.S.A. 177 I2
Phoenix Island Kiribati see Rawaki
Phoenix Islands Kiribati 145 H2
Phoenixville U.S.A. 177 J5
Phokwane S. Africa 133 N1
Phola S. Africa 133 N3
Phomolong S. Africa 133 L4
Phon Thai. 78 C5
Phong Nha Vietnam 78 D4
Phôngsali Laos 78 C3
also spelt Phong Saly
Phong Saly Laos see Phôngsali
Phong Thô Vietnam 78 C3
Phosphate Hill Australia 149 D4
Phrae Thai. 78 C4
Phra Nakhon Si Ayutthaya Thai. see Ayutthaya
Phrao Thai. 78 B4
Phra Saeng Thai. 79 B6
Phra Thong, Ko i. Thai. 79 B6
Phuchong-Nayoi National Park Thai. 79 D5
Phu Cuong Vietnam see Thu Dâu Môt
Phuduhudu Botswana 131 E4
Phuentsholing Bhutan 97 F4
also spelt Phuntsholing
Phuket Thai. 79 B7
Phuket, Ko i. Thai. 79 B7
Phu-khieo Wildlife Reserve nature res. Thai. 78 C4
Phulabani India 95 E1
Phulpur India 97 D4
Phu Luang Wildlife Reserve nat. park Thai. 78 C4
Phu Ly Vietnam 78 D3
Phumĭ Chhuk Cambodia 79 D6
also known as Chhuk
Phumĭ Kâmpóng Trâlach Cambodia 79 D5
Phumĭ Mlu Prey Cambodia 79 D5
Phumĭ Prâmaôy Cambodia 79 C5
Phumĭ Sâmraông Cambodia 79 C5
also known as Samrong
Phuntsholing Bhutan see Phuentsholing
Phu Phac Mo mt. Vietnam 78 C3
Phu Phan National Park Thai. 78 C4
Phu Quôc, Đao i. Vietnam 79 C6
formerly known as Quan Phu Quoc
Phuthaditjhaba S. Africa 133 M5
Phu Tho Vietnam 78 D3
Phu Vinh Vietnam see Tra Vinh
Pia Aboriginal Reserve Australia 151 B5
Piabung, Gunung mt. Indon. 77 F2
Piaca Brazil 202 C3
Piacatu Brazil 206 C8
Piacenza Italy 56 B3
historically known as Placentia
Piacouadie, Lac l. Canada 169 G3
Piadena Italy 56 C3
Piagochioui r. Canada 168 E2
Pian r. Australia 147 F2
Piana di Catania plain Sicilia Italy 57 G11
Piangil Australia 147 D3
Pianguan China 85 F4
Pianoro Italy 56 D4
Pianosa, Isola i. Italy 56 C6
Piaseczno Poland 49 S3
Piaski Poland 49 T4
Piassabussu Brazil 202 E4
Piatã Brazil 202 D5
Piatra Romania 58 G5
Piatra Neamţ Romania 58 H2
Piatra Olt Romania 58 F4
Piatra Şoimului Romania 58 H2
Piauí r. Brazil 202 D3
Piauí state Brazil 202 D3
Piauí, Serra de hills Brazil 202 D4
Piave r. Italy 56 E3
Piazza Armerina Sicilia Italy 57 G11
Piazzi, Cima de' mt. Italy 56 C2
Piazzi, Isla i. Chile 205 B8
Pibor r. Sudan 128 B2
Pibor Post Sudan 128 B3
Pic r. Canada 168 C3
Pica Chile 200 C5
Picacho U.S.A. 183 M9
Picachos, Cerro dos mt. Mex. 184 B2
Picardie admin. reg. France 51 I3
Picardie reg. France see Picardy
Picardy reg. France 50 H3
also spelt Picardie
Picassent Spain 55 K5
Picayune U.S.A. 175 B6
Pichácho Mex. 184 D2
Pichanal Arg. 201 D5
Pichilemu Chile 204 B4
Pichilingue Mex. 184 C3
Pichi Mahuida Arg. 204 D5
Pichincha prov. Ecuador 198 B5
Pichor India 96 C4
Pichucalco Mex. 185 G5
Pic Island Canada 172 G2
Pickens U.S.A. 176 E7
Pickerel Lake Canada 172 B2
Pickering Canada 173 N7
Pickering U.K. 47 L9
Pickford U.S.A. 173 I4
Pickle Lake Canada 168 B3
Pico Bonito, Parque Nacional nat. park Hond. 186 B4
Pico da Neblina, Parque Nacional do nat. park Brazil 199 E4
Pico de Orizaba, Parque Nacional nat. park Mex. 185 F5
Pico de Tancítaro, Parque Nacional nat. park Mex. 185 E5
Picos Brazil 202 D3
Picos, Punta dos pt Spain 54 C3
Picota Peru 198 B6
Pico Truncado Arg. 205 D7
Pic River Canada 172 G2
Picton Australia 147 F3
Picton Canada 168 E5
Picton N.Z. 152 I9
Picton, Mount Australia 147 E5
Pictou Canada 169 I4
Picture Butte Canada 167 H5
Pictured Rocks National Lakeshore nature res. U.S.A. 172 G4
Picuí Brazil 202 E3
Picún Leufú Arg. 204 C5
Pidarak Pak. 101 E5
Pidurutalagala mt. Sri Lanka 94 D5
Piedade Brazil 206 F10
Pie de Palo, Sierra mts Arg. 204 C3
Piedimonte Matese Italy 56 G7
Piedmont admin. reg. Italy see Piemonte
Piedmont MO U.S.A. 174 B4
Piedmont OH U.S.A. 176 D5
Piedmont Lake U.S.A. 176 D5
Piedra r. Spain 55 J3
Piedrabuena Spain 54 G5
Piedra de Aguila Arg. 204 C6
Piedrafita Spain see Pedrafita do Cebreiro
Piedrahita Spain 54 F4
Piedralaves Spain 54 G4
Piedras, Punta pt Arg. 204 F4
Piedras Blancas Spain 54 F1
Piedras Blancas Point U.S.A. 182 C6
Piedras Negras Guat. 185 H5
Piedras Negras Coahuila Mex. 185 E2
Piedras Negras Veracruz Mex. 185 F5
Pie Island Canada 172 D2
Pieksämäki Fin. 44 N3
Pielavesi Fin. 44 N3
Pielavesi l. Fin. 44 N3
Pielinen l. Fin. 44 O3
Pieljekaise nationalpark nat. park Sweden 44 L2
Piemonte admin. reg. Italy 56 A4
English form Piedmont
Pienaarsrivier S. Africa 133 M2
Pieniężno Poland 49 R1
Pieniński Park Narodowy nat. park Poland 49 R6
Pieninský nat. park Slovakia 49 R6
Pieńsk Poland 49 M4
Pierce U.S.A. 178 C3
Pierce Lake Canada 167 M4
Pierceland Canada 167 I4
Pierceton U.S.A. 172 H9
Pieria mts Greece 59 D8
▶Pierre U.S.A. 178 B2
State capital of South Dakota.
Pierre, Bayou r. U.S.A. 175 B6
Pierre Bayou r. U.S.A. 179 D6
Pierrelatte France 51 K8
Pieskehaure l. Sweden 44 L2
Piešťany Slovakia 49 O7
Pietermaritzburg S. Africa 133 O6
Pietersaari Fin. see Jakobstad
Pietersburg S. Africa 131 F4
also known as Polokwane
Piet Plessis S. Africa 133 I3
Pietraperzia Sicilia Italy 57 G11
Pietrasanta Italy 56 C5
Pietra Spada, Passo di pass Italy 57 I10
Piet Retief S. Africa 133 O4
Pietrosu, Vârful mt. Romania 58 G1
Pieve di Cadore Italy 56 E2
Pievepelago Italy 56 C4
Pigeon r. Canada/U.S.A. 174 B1
Pigeon Bay Canada 173 K9
Pigeon Lake Canada 167 H4
Pigeon River U.S.A. 172 D2
Pigg r. U.S.A. 176 F8
Piggott U.S.A. 174 B4
Pigg's Peak Swaziland 133 P2
Pigon, Limni l. Greece 59 C9
Pigs, Bay of b. Cuba 186 C2
also known as Cochinos, Bahía de
Pigüé Arg. 204 E5
Piguicas mt. Mex. 185 F4
Piha N.Z. 152 I4
Pihama N.Z. 152 H7
Pihani India 96 D4
Pi He r. China 87 F1
Pihkva järv l. Estonia/Rus. Fed. see Pskov, Lake
Pihlajavesi l. Fin. 45 O3
Pihlava Fin. 45 M3
Pihtipudas Fin. 44 N3
Piikkiö Fin. 42 D1
Piippola Fin. 44 N2
Piirissaar i. Estonia 42 I3
Piirsalu Estonia 42 F2
Piispajärvi Fin. 44 O2
Piji China see Puge
Pijijiapan Mex. 185 G6
Pikalevo Rus. Fed. 43 P2
Pike NY U.S.A. 176 G3
Pike WV U.S.A. 176 D6
Pikelot i. Micronesia 73 K5
formerly known as Coquille
Pikes Peak U.S.A. 180 F5
Piketberg S. Africa 132 C9
Piketon U.S.A. 176 B6
Pikeville KY U.S.A. 176 C8
Pikeville TN U.S.A. 174 C5
Pikihatiti b. N.Z. see Port Pegasus
Pikirakatahi mt. N.Z. see Earnslaw, Mount
Pikou China 85 I4
Pikounda Congo 126 C4
Pila Arg. 204 F5
Piła Poland 49 N2
historically known as Schneidemühl
Pila mt. Spain 55 J6
Pilagá r. Arg. 204 F2
Pilanesberg National Park S. Africa 133 L2
Pilani India 96 B3
Pilar Buenos Aires Arg. 204 F4
Pilar Córdoba Arg. 204 E3
Pilar Para. 201 F6
Pilar Phil. 74 C4
Pilar, Cabo c. Chile 205 B9
Pilar do Sul Brazil 206 F10
Pilas i. Phil. 74 B5
Pilas Spain 54 E7
Pilas Channel Phil. 74 B5
Pilat, Mont mt. France 51 K7
Pilat, Parc Naturel Régional du nature res. France 51 K7
Pilaya r. Bol. 201 D5
Pilcaniyeu Arg. 204 C6
Pilcomayo r. Bol./Para. 201 F6
Pilenkovo Georgia see Gant'iadi
Piler India 94 C3
Pili Greece see Pyli
Pili Phil. 74 B3
Pili, Cerro mt. Chile 200 D5
also known as Acamarachi
Piliakalnis hill Lith. 42 G6
Pilibangan India 96 B3
Pilibhit India 96 C3
Pilica r. Poland 49 S4
Piliga Nature Reserve Australia 147 F2
Pilipinas country Asia see Philippines
Pilisi park Hungary 49 P8
Pillau Rus. Fed. see Baltiysk
Pillcopata Peru 200 C3
Pilliga Australia 147 F2
Pillo, Isla del i. Arg. 204 E4
Pillsbury, Lake U.S.A. 182 B2
Pil'na Rus. Fed. 40 H5
Pil'nya, Ozero l. Rus. Fed. 40 K1
Pilões, Serra dos mts Brazil 206 F4
Pilón Cuba 186 D3
Pilón r. Mex. 179 C7
Pilos Greece see Pylos
Pilot Mountain hill U.S.A. 176 E9
Pilot Peak U.S.A. 182 G3
Pilot Point U.S.A. 164 D4
Pilot Rock U.S.A. 180 C3
Pilot Station U.S.A. 164 C3
Pilsen Czech Rep. see Plzeň
Pilsen U.S.A. 172 F6
Piltene Latvia 42 C4
Pilu, Nam r. Myanmar 78 B4
Pilvė r. Lith. 42 E7
Pilviškiai Lith. 42 E7
Pima U.S.A. 183 O9
Pimenta Bueno Brazil 201 E2
Pimpalner India 94 B1
Pimpri India 94 B1
Pimu Dem. Rep. Congo 126 D4
Pin r. Myanmar 78 A3
Pina r. Belarus 42 H9
Pinahat India 96 C4
Pinaleno Mountains U.S.A. 183 N9
Pinamalayan Phil. 74 B3
Pinamar Arg. 204 F5
Pinang Malaysia see George Town
Pinang i. Malaysia 76 C1
Pinang state Malaysia 76 C1
also known as Pulau Pinang; formerly spelt Penang
Pinar mt. Spain 54 F8
Pinar, Puerto del pass Spain 55 I6
Pınarbaşı Turkey 107 D3
also known as Aziziye
Pinar del Río Cuba 186 C2
Pinarhisar Turkey 106 A2

Piñas Ecuador 198 B5
Pinatubo, Mt *vol* Phil. 73 F3
Pincher Creek Canada 167 H5
Pinckneyville U.S.A. 174 F4
Pinconning U.S.A. 172 J7
Pincota Romania *see* Pâncota
Pińczów Poland 49 R5
Pindaíba Brazil 206 A1
Pindamonhangaba Brazil 207 H9
Pindar Australia 151 A6
Pindar *r.* India 96 C3
Pindaré *r.* Brazil 202 C2
Pind Dadan Khay Pak. 101 I3
Pindhos Óros *mts* Greece *see* Pindus Mountains
Pindi Batiau Pak. 101 H4
Pindi Gheb Pak. 101 H3
Pindobal Brazil 202 B2
Pindos *mts* Greece *see* Pindus Mountains
Pindus Mountains Greece 59 B9
also known as Pindhos Óros;
also spelt Pindos
Pindwara India 96 B4
Pine *watercourse* Australia 146 D3
Pine *r.* MI U.S.A. 172 H6
Pine *r.* MI U.S.A. 173 I7
Pine *r.* WI U.S.A. 172 C7
Pine *r.* WI U.S.A. 172 E5
Pine, Cape Canada 169 K4
Pine Bluff U.S.A. 174 A5
Pine Bluffs U.S.A. 180 F4
Pine City U.S.A. 178 D2
Pine Creek Australia 148 A2
Pine Creek *r.* U.S.A. 176 H4
Pine Creek *watercourse* U.S.A. 183 H1
Pinecrest U.S.A. 182 D3
Pinedale U.S.A. 180 E4
Pine Dock Canada 167 L5
Pine Falls Canada 167 L5
Pinega Rus. Fed. 40 G2
Pinega *r.* Rus. Fed. 40 G2
Pinegrove Australia 151 A5
Pine Grove CA U.S.A. 176 A7
Pine Grove PA U.S.A. 177 I5
Pine Grove WV U.S.A. 176 E6
Pine Hills U.S.A. 182 G7
Pine Hills FL U.S.A. 175 D6
Pinehouse Lake Canada 167 J4
Pinehouse Lake *l.* Canada 167 J4
Pineimuta *r.* Canada 168 B2
Pineios *r.* Greece 59 D9
also spelt Piniós
Pineiou, Techniti Limni *resr* Greece 59 C11
Pine Island Bay Antarctica 222 R2
Pine Island Glacier Antarctica 222 R1
Pine Islands FL U.S.A. 175 D7
Pine Islands FL U.S.A. 175 D7
Pine Knot U.S.A. 176 A9
Piñellas Park U.S.A. 175 D7
Pine Mountain U.S.A. 182 C6
Pine Peak U.S.A. 183 K7
Pine Point Canada 167 H2
Pine Point *pt* Canada 167 H2
Pineridge U.S.A. 182 E4
Pine Ridge U.S.A. 178 B3
Pine Ridge Indian Reservation *res.* U.S.A. 178 B3
Pinerolo Italy 51 N8
Pines, Isle of *i.* Cuba *see* La Juventud, Isla de
Pines, Isle of *i.* New Caledonia *see* Pins, Île des
Pines, Lake o' the U.S.A. 179 D5
Pineto Italy 56 G6
Pinetop U.S.A. 183 O7
Pinetown S. Africa 133 O6
Pinetown U.S.A. 177 I3
Pineville KY U.S.A. 176 B9
Pineville LA U.S.A. 179 D8
Pineville MO U.S.A. 176 D8
Ping, Mae Nam *r.* Thai. 78 C5
Pingal Jammu and Kashmir 96 B1
Ping'an China 84 D4
formerly known as Ping'anyi
Ping'anyi China *see* Ping'an
Pingba China 86 C3
Pingbian China 86 B4
also known as Yupin
Pingchang China 86 C2
also known as Jiangkou
Ping Dao *i.* China 85 H5
Pingding China 85 G4
Pingdingbu China *see* Guyuan
Pingdingshan China 87 D1
Pingdong Taiwan *see* P'ingtung
Pingdu China 85 H4
Pinggu China 85 H3
Pingguo China 87 E4
Pinghai China 87 E4
Pinghe China 87 F3
Pinghu China 87 G2
Pingjiang China 87 E2
Pingle China 87 D3
Pingli China 87 C1
Pingliang China 85 E5
Pinglu China 87 D1
formerly known as Shengrenjian
Pingluo China 85 E4
Pingma China *see* Tiandong
Pingnan Fujian China 87 F3
also known as Gufeng
Pingnan Guangxi China 87 D4
Pingquan China 85 H3
Pingshan China *see* Huidong
Pingshan Hebei China 85 G4
Pingshan Sichuan China 86 C2
Pingtan China *see* Luquan
Pingshi China *see* Daicheng
Pingshu China *see* Daicheng
Pingtan China 87 F3

Pingtan Dao *i.* China *see* Haitan Dao
P'ingtung Taiwan 87 G4
also spelt Pingdong
Pingwu China 86 C1
also known as Long'an
Pingxi China *see* Yuping
Pingxiang China *see* Tongwei
Pingxiang Guangxi China 86 C4
Pingxiang Jiangxi China 87 E3
Pingyang Heilong. China 85 J1
Pingyang Zhejiang China 87 G3
also known as Kunyang
Pingyao China 85 G4
Pingyi China 85 H5
Pingyin China 85 H4
Pingyu China 87 E1
also known as Guhuai
Pingyuan Guangdong China 87 E3
also known as Dazhe
Pingyuan Shandong China 85 H4
Pingzhai China 85 D3
Pinhal Brazil 206 G9
Pinhal Novo Port. 54 C6
Pinheiro Brazil 202 C2
Pinheiro Machado Brazil 204 G3
Pinheiros Brazil 207 M5
Pinhel Port. 54 E4
Pinhuã *r.* Brazil 199 E6
Pini *i.* Indon. 76 B3
Pinilla *r.* Spain 55 I6
Piniós *r.* Greece *see* Pineios
Pinjarra Australia 151 A7
Pinjin Aboriginal Reserve Australia 151 C6
Pinkafeld Austria 49 N8
Pinkawilinie Conservation Park *nature res.* Australia 146 C3
Pinkerton Range *hills* Australia 148 A2
Pink Mountain Canada 166 F3
Pinlaung Myanmar 78 B3
Pinlebu Myanmar 78 A2
Pinnacle U.S.A. 176 F5
Pinnacle *hill* U.S.A. 176 G6
Pinnacles National Monument *nat. park* U.S.A. 182 C5
Pinnaroo Australia 146 D3
Pinneberg Germany 48 G2
Pinnes, Akra *pt* Greece 59 F8
Pinofranqueado Spain 54 E4
Pinoh *r.* Indon. 77 E3
Pinos, Isla *i.* Cuba *see* La Juventud, Isla de
Pinos, Mount U.S.A. 182 E7
Pinoso Spain 55 J6
Pinoso *mt.* Spain 55 J6
Pinos-Puente Spain 54 H7
Pinotepa Nacional Mex. 185 F5
Pinrang Indon. 75 A3
Pins, Île des *i.* New Caledonia 145 F4
English form Pines, Isle of;
also known as Kunié
Pins, Pointe aux *pt* Canada 173 L8
Pinsk Belarus 42 H9
Pinta, Sierra *mt* U.S.A. 183 K9
Pintados Chile 200 C5
Pintasan Sabah Malaysia 77 G1
Pinto Spain 55 H4
Pintura U.S.A. 183 K4
Pinzolo Italy 56 D2
Pioche U.S.A. 183 J4
Pio IX Brazil 202 D3
Piombino Italy 56 C6
Pioneer OH U.S.A. 176 A4
Pioneer TN U.S.A. 176 A9
Pioneer Mountains U.S.A. 180 D3
Pioner, Ostrov *i.* Rus. Fed. 39 J2
Pionerskiy Kaliningradskaya Oblast' Rus. Fed. 42 B7
historically known as Neukuhren
Pionerskiy Khanty-Mansiyskiy Avtonomnyy Okrug Rus. Fed. 38 H3
Pionki Poland 49 S4
Piopio N.Z. 152 J6
Piopiotahi *inlet* N.Z. *see* Milford Sound
Piorini *r.* Brazil 199 F5
Piorini, Lago *l.* Brazil 199 F5
Piotrków Trybunalski Poland 49 Q4
formerly known as Petrokov; *historically known as* Petrikau
Piove di Sacco Italy 56 E3
Pip Iran 101 E5
Pipa Dingzi *mt.* China 82 C4
Pipanaco, Salar de *salt flat* Arg. 204 D3
Pipar India 96 B4
Pipar Road India 96 B4
Piperi *i.* Greece 59 F9
Piper Peak U.S.A. 182 G4
Pipestone Canada 167 K5
Pipestone *r.* Canada 168 B2
Pipestone U.S.A. 178 C3
Pipiriki N.Z. 152 J7
Pipli India 96 B3
Pipmuacan, Réservoir Canada 169 G3
Pippingarra Aboriginal Reserve Australia 150 B4
Pipriac France 50 E5
Piqan China *see* Shanshan
Piqanlik China 88 C3
Piqua U.S.A. 176 A5
Piqueras, Puerto de *pass* Spain 55 I2
Piquet Carneiro Brazil 202 E3
Piquete Brazil 207 H9
Piquiri *r.* Mato Grosso do Sul Brazil 201 G4
Piquiri *r.* Paraná Brazil 203 A8
Piracaia Brazil 207 H9
Piracanjuba Brazil 206 D5
Piracanjuba *r.* Brazil 206 D5
Piracicaba Brazil 206 E9
Piracicaba *r.* Minas Gerais Brazil 203 D6
Piracicaba *r.* São Paulo Brazil 206 E9
Piraçununga Brazil 206 F8
Piracuruca Brazil 202 D2
Piraeus Greece 59 E11
also spelt Peiraias *or* Piraiévs
Piraí do Sul Brazil 203 B8
Piraiévs Greece *see* Piraeus
Piraju Brazil 206 D10
Pirajuba Brazil 206 D8
Pirajuí Brazil 206 D8
Pirallahı Adası Azer. 107 G2
Pirané Arg. 204 F2
Piranga Brazil 207 J7
Piranga *r.* Brazil 207 I7
Piranhas Alagoas Brazil 202 E4
Piranhas Amazonas Brazil 199 F6
Piranhas Goiás Brazil 206 C5
Piranhas *r.* Goiás Brazil 206 C5
Piranhas *r.* Rio Grande do Norte Brazil 202 E3
Pirapemas Brazil 202 C2
Pirapetinga Amazonas Brazil 201 E1
Pirapetinga Minas Gerais Brazil 207 K8
Pirapó *r.* Brazil 206 A9
Pirapora Brazil 203 C6
Pirapozinho Brazil 206 B9
Piraputangas Brazil 201 F4
Pirara Guyana 199 G4
Pirarajá Uruguay 204 G4
Pirari Nepal 97 E4
Piratini Brazil 204 G3
Piratininga Brazil 206 D9
Piratininga *r.* Brazil 199 F5
Pirawa India 96 C4
Pirchevan Azer. *see* Zängilan
Pire Mahuida, Sierra *mts* Arg. 205 C6
Pirenópolis Brazil 206 E3
Pires do Rio Brazil 206 D4
Pirganj Bangl. 97 F4
Pirgos Greece *see* Pyrgos
Pirgovo Bulg. 58 G5
Piriaka N.Z. 152 J6

Piriápolis Uruguay 204 G4
Pirin *mts* Bulg. 58 E7
Pirin *nat. park* Bulg. 58 E7
Pirineos *mts* Europe *see* Pyrenees
Piripá Brazil 207 L1
Piripiri Brazil 202 D2
Pirita *r.* Estonia 42 F2
Piritu Falcón Venez. 198 D2
Piritu Portuguesa Venez. 198 D2
Pirmasens Germany 48 E6
Pirmed India 94 C4
Pirna Germany 49 K5
Pirojpur Bangl. 97 F5
Pirón *r.* Spain 54 G3
Pirongia N.Z. 152 J5
Pirongia *vol.* N.Z. 152 J5
Pirongia Forest Park *nature res.* N.Z. 152 J5
Piros, Ozero *l.* Rus. Fed. 43 O3
Pirot Srbija Yugo. 58 E6
Pirpainti India 97 E4
Pir Panjal Pass Jammu and Kashmir 96 B2
Pir Panjal Range *mts* India/Pak. 96 B2
Pirrasisit Dağ *mt.* Turkey 107 E3
Pirsaat Azer. 100 B2
Pirsaatçay *r.* Azer. 107 G2
Piru Indon. 75 D3
Piru, Teluk *b.* Indon. 75 D3
Pir'yakh, Gora *mt.* Tajik. 101 G2
also known as Piryakh, Kŭhi
Piryakh, Kŭhi *mt.* Tajik. *see* Pir'yakh, Gora
Piryatin Ukr. *see* Pyryatyn
Piryetós Greece *see* Pyrgetos
Piryion Greece *see* Pyrgi
Pirzada Afgh. 101 F4
also known as Khugiana
Pisa Italy 56 C5
historically known as Pisae
Pisa *r.* Poland 49 S2
Pisac Peru 200 C3
Pisae Italy *see* Pisa
Pisagua Chile 200 C4
Pisang *i.* Indon. 75 D3
Pisa Range *mts* N.Z. 153 D12
Pisau, Tanjong *pt* Malaysia 77 G1
Pisaurum Italy *see* Pesaro
Pisba, Parque Nacional *nat. park* Col. 198 C3
Pisco Peru 200 A3
Pisco *r.* Peru 200 A3
Piseco Lake U.S.A. 177 K2
Pisek Czech Rep. 49 L6
Pisha China *see* Ningnan
Pishan China 88 C4
also known as Guma
Pishin Iran 101 E5
Pishin Pak. 101 F4
Pishin Lora *r.* Pak. 101 F4
Pishpek Kyrg. *see* Bishkek
Pising Indon. 75 B4
Pisinimo U.S.A. 183 L9
Piskent Uzbek. *see* Pskent
Pismo Beach U.S.A. 182 D6
Piso Firme Bol. 201 E3
Pisogne Italy 56 C3
Pissa *r.* Rus. Fed. 42 C7

▶ Pissis, Cerro *mt.* Arg. 204 C2
4th highest mountain in South America.
southamerica [landscapes] ▶▶▶ 190–191

Pista *r.* Rus. Fed. 44 O2
Pisté Mex. 185 H4
Pisticci Italy 57 I8
Pistoia Italy 56 C5
historically known as Pistoriae
Pistoriae Italy *see* Pistoia
Pistsovo Rus. Fed. 43 V4
Pisuerga *r.* Spain 54 G3
Pisz Poland 49 S2
Pit *r.* U.S.A. 180 B4
Pita Guinea 124 B4
Pitaga Canada 169 H2
Pital Mex. 185 H5
Pitalito Col. 198 B4
Pitanga Brazil 203 A8
Pitangueiras Brazil 206 E8
Pitangui Brazil 203 C6
Pitarpunga Lake *imp. l.* Australia 147 D3

▶ Pitcairn Islands *terr.* S. Pacific Ocean 221 J7
United Kingdom Overseas Territory.
oceania [countries] ▶▶▶ 138–139

Piteå Sweden 44 M2
Piteälven *r.* Sweden 44 M2
Pitelino Rus. Fed. 41 G5
Piterka Rus. Fed. 102 A2
Pitești Romania 58 F4
Pithiviers France 51 I5
Pithoragarh India 96 D3
Pitiquito Mex. 184 B2
Pitkul' Rus. Fed. 44 P2
Pitkyaranta Rus. Fed. 40 D3
Pitlochry U.K. 46 I7
Pitoa Cameroon 125 I4
Pitomača Croatia 56 J3
Pitong China *see* Pixian
Pitrufquén Chile 204 B5
Pitsane Siding Botswana 133 J2
Pitseng Lesotho 133 M6
Pitsunda Georgia *see* Bichvint'a
Pitti *i.* India 94 B4
Pitt Island Canada 166 D4
Pitt Island S. Pacific Ocean 145 H6
also known as Rangiauria
Pitt Islands Solomon Is. *see* Vanikoro Islands
Pittsboro U.S.A. 174 E5
Pittsburg CA U.S.A. 182 C3
Pittsburg KS U.S.A. 178 D4
Pittsburg TX U.S.A. 179 D5
Pittsburgh U.S.A. 176 F5
Pittsfield IL U.S.A. 174 B4
Pittsfield MA U.S.A. 177 L3
Pittsfield ME U.S.A. 177 P1
Pittsfield NH U.S.A. 177 N2
Pittsfield VT U.S.A. 177 M2
Pittsville U.S.A. 172 C6
Pittsworth Australia 147 F1
Pituri Creek *watercourse* Australia 148 C4
Pitz Lake Canada 167 L2
Piui Brazil 202 B4
Pium Brazil 202 B4
Piumhi Brazil 207 H7
Piura Peru 198 A6
Piura *r.* Peru 198 A6
Piusa *r.* Estonia 42 I4
Piute Peak U.S.A. 182 F6
Piute Mountains U.S.A. 183 I7
Piuthan Nepal 97 D3
Pivabiska *r.* Canada 168 D3
Pivijay Col. 198 C2
Pivka Slovenia 56 H3
Piwniczna Poland 49 R6
Pixaria *mt.* Greece *see* Pyxaria
Pixian China 86 B2
also known as Pitong
Pixley U.S.A. 182 E6
Pixoyal Mex. 185 H5
Pizacoma Peru 200 C4
Pizhanka Rus. Fed. 40 I4
Pizhi Nigeria 125 G4
Pizhma Rus. Fed. 40 H4
Pizhma *r.* Rus. Fed. 40 J4
Pizhou China 87 F1
formerly known as Peixian *or* Yunhe
Piz Kesch *mt.* Switz. 51 P6
Pizol *mt.* Switz. 51 P6
Piz Pisoc *mt.* Switz. 51 Q6

Piz Platta *mt.* Switz. 51 P6
Pizzo Italy 57 I10
Pizzo Carbonara *mt.* Sicilia Italy 57 G11
Pizzuto, Monte *mt.* Italy 56 E6
Placentia Canada 169 K4
Placentia Italy *see* Piacenza
Placentia Bay Canada 169 K4
Placer Masbate Phil. 74 B4
Placer Mindanao Phil. 74 C4
Placerville CA U.S.A. 182 D3
Placerville CO U.S.A. 181 E5
Placetas Cuba 186 D2
Plácido de Castro Brazil 200 D2
Plain Dealing U.S.A. 179 D5
Plainfield IN U.S.A. 174 C4
Plainfield NJ U.S.A. 177 K5
Plainfield VT U.S.A. 177 M1
Plainfield WI U.S.A. 172 D6
Plains U.S.A. 179 B5
Plainview NE U.S.A. 178 C3
Plainview NY U.S.A. 177 L5
Plainview TX U.S.A. 179 B5
Plainville U.S.A. 178 C4
Plainwell U.S.A. 172 H8
Plaisance France 50 G9
Plaisance Haiti 187 E3
Plaistow U.S.A. 177 N3
Plaju Indon. 76 D3
Plaka, Akra *pt* Greece 59 H13
Plakoti, Cape Cyprus 108 F2
Plampang Indon. 77 G5
Plana Cays *is* Bahamas 187 E2
Planada U.S.A. 182 D4
Planaltina Brazil 200 D2
Planalto Brazil 207 M1
Plancoët France 50 D4
Plandište Vojvodina, Srbija Yugo. 58 C3
Plane *r.* Germany 49 J3
Plankinton U.S.A. 178 C3
Plano IL U.S.A. 172 E9
Plano TX U.S.A. 179 D5
Plant City U.S.A. 175 D7
Planura Brazil 206 E7
Plaquemine U.S.A. 175 B6
Plasencia Spain 54 E4
Plaški Croatia 56 H3
Plaster City U.S.A. 183 I9
Plaster Rock Canada 169 H4
Plaston S. Africa 133 P2
Plastun Rus. Fed. 82 E3
Platamon, Rt *pt* Yugo. 56 K6
Platamonas Greece 59 D9
Platanal Peru 200 C4
Platani *r.* Sicilia Italy 57 F11
Platanistos Greece 59 F10
Platanos Greece 59 C13
Platbakkies S. Africa 132 C7
Platberg *mt.* S. Africa 133 N5

Plateau *state* Nigeria 125 G4
Plateaux *admin. reg.* Congo 126 B5
Plateliai Lith. 42 C5
Plateros Mex. 185 E4
Plathuis S. Africa 132 E10
Platičevo Vojvodina, Srbija Yugo. 58 A4
Platina U.S.A. 182 B1
Platinum U.S.A. 164 C4
Plato Col. 198 C2
Plato de Sopa Chile 204 C2
Platrand S. Africa 133 N4
Platte *r.* MO U.S.A. 178 D3
Platte *r.* NE U.S.A. 178 D3
Platte City U.S.A. 178 D3
Plattenberg *hill* Austria 49 L7
Platteville CO U.S.A. 180 F4
Platteville WI U.S.A. 172 C8
Plattling Germany 49 J7
Plattsburgh U.S.A. 177 L1
Plattsmouth U.S.A. 178 D3
Platy Greece 58 D8
Plau Germany 49 J2
Plauen Germany 49 I5
Plauer See *l.* Germany 49 J2
Plav Crna Gora Yugo. 58 A6
Plava *r.* Rus. Fed. 43 S8
Plavinas Latvia 42 G5
Plavna *r.* Croatia 56 G4
Plavsk Rus. Fed. 43 S8
Playa de Castilla *coastal area* Spain 54 E7
Playa del Carmen Mex. 185 I4
Playas Ecuador 198 A5
Plây Cu Vietnam 79 E5
Playgreen Lake Canada 167 L4
Playón Mex. 184 D4
Playones de Santa Ana *l.* Col. 198 C3
Plaza del Judío *mt.* Spain 54 G6
Plaza Huincul Arg. 204 C5
Pleasant, Lake U.S.A. 183 L8
Pleasant Bay U.S.A. 177 J7
Pleasant Grove U.S.A. 183 M1
Pleasanton CA U.S.A. 182 C4
Pleasanton TX U.S.A. 179 C6
Pleasant Point N.Z. 153 F12
Pleasantville U.S.A. 177 K6
Pleaux France 51 I7
Plechý *mt.* Czech Rep. 49 K7
Plei Doch Vietnam 79 D5
Pleiße *r.* Germany 51 S1
Plenty *watercourse* Australia 148 C5
Plenty, Bay of *g.* N.Z. 152 K5
Plentywood U.S.A. 180 F2
Plesetsk Rus. Fed. 40 G3
Pleshanovo Rus. Fed. 102 C1
Pleshchentsy Belarus *see* Plyeshchanitsy
Pleshcheyevo, Ozero *l.* Rus. Fed. 43 T5
Pleso Rus. Fed. 43 Q2
Pleszew Poland 49 O4
Pleternica Croatia 56 J3
Pletipi, Lac *l.* Canada 169 G3
Plettenberg Germany 48 E4
Plettenberg Bay S. Africa 132 H11
Pleven Bulg. 58 F5
formerly known as Plevna
Plevlja Crna Gora Yugo. *see* Pljevlja
Plevna Bulg. *see* Pleven
Pleyben France 50 C4
Plieran *r.* Sarawak Malaysia 77 F2
Plinkšių ežeras *l.* Lith. 42 D5
Pliska Bulg. 58 H5
Plješevica *mts* Croatia 56 H4
Pljevlja Crna Gora Yugo. 58 A5
Ploaghe Sardegna Italy 57 A8
Ploče Croatia 56 J5
formerly known as Kardeljevo
Płock Poland 49 Q3
formerly spelt Plozk; *historically known as* Schröttersburg
Plöckenpass *pass* Austria/Italy 49 J9
Plocno *mt.* Bos.-Herz. 56 J5
Plodovoye Rus. Fed. 43 L1
Ploemeur France 50 C5
Ploeşti Romania *see* Ploiești
Plœuc-sur-Lié France 50 D4
Ploiești Romania 58 H4
formerly spelt Ploesti
Plomari Greece 59 H10
Plomb du Cantal *mt.* France 51 I7
Plombières-les-Bains France 51 M5
Plön Germany 48 H1
Płońsk Poland 49 R3
Plopiş Romania 58 D1
Ploskoš' Rus. Fed. 43 M6
Ploskoye Rus. Fed. *see* Stanovoye
Ploskoye Rus. Fed. 43 V3
Plotnitsa Belarus 42 H9
Płoty Poland 49 M2

Ploudalmézeau France 50 B4
Ploufragan France 50 D4
Plouguerneau France 50 B4
Plouha France 50 D4
Plouzané France 50 B4
Plouzévédé France 50 B4
Plovdiv Bulg. 58 F6
also known as Filibe; *historically known as* Philippopolis
Plover U.S.A. 172 D6
Plover *r.* U.S.A. 172 D6
Plover Cove Reservoir Hong Kong China 87 [inset]
Plozk Poland *see* Płock
Pluckemin U.S.A. 177 K5
Plum U.S.A. 176 F5
Plum Coulee Canada 167 L5
Plummer U.S.A. 180 C3
Plumridge Lakes *salt flat* Australia 151 D6
Plumridge Lakes Nature Reserve Australia 151 D6
Plumtree Zimbabwe 131 E4
Plungė Lith. 42 C6
Plutarco Elías Calles, Presa *resr* Mex. 181 E7
Plutarco Elis Calles, Presa *resr* Mex. 184 C2
Pluto, Lac *l.* Canada 169 G2
Plužine Crna Gora Yugo. 56 K5
Plyeshchanitsy Belarus 42 I7
also spelt Pleshchentsy
Ply Huey Wati, Khao *mt.* Myanmar/Thai. 78 B4

▶ Plymouth Montserrat 187 H3
Capital of Montserrat, largely abandoned in 1997 owing to volcanic activity.

Plymouth Trin. and Tob. 187 H5
Plymouth U.K. 47 H13
Plymouth CA U.S.A. 182 D3
Plymouth IN U.S.A. 172 G9
Plymouth NC U.S.A. 174 E5
Plymouth NH U.S.A. 177 N2
Plymouth WI U.S.A. 172 F7
Plymouth Bay U.S.A. 177 J3
Plynlimon *hill* U.K. 47 I11
Plyusa Rus. Fed. 43 K3
Plyussa *r.* Rus. Fed. 43 J2
Plzeň Czech Rep. 49 K6
historically known as Pilsen
Pmere Nyente Aboriginal Land *res.* Australia 148 B5
Pniewy Poland 49 N3
Pô *r.* Italy 56 E3
Pô Burkina 125 E4
Pô, Parc National de *nat. park* Burkina 125 E4
Po, Tanjong *pt* Sarawak Malaysia 77 E2
Poás, Volcán *vol.* Costa Rica 186 B5
Poat *i.* Indon. 75 B3
Pobeda, Gora *mt.* Rus. Fed. 39 O3
also known as Jengish Chokusu *or* Tomur Feng; *formerly known as* Pobedy, Pik *or* Shengli Feng
Pobedinskiy Rus. Fed. *see* Zarechnyy
Pobedy, Pik *mt.* China/Kyrg. *see* Pobeda Peak
Pobiedziska Poland 49 O3
Pobla de Segur Spain 55 L2
Poblado Poland 49 M2
Poção Brazil 202 E4
Poções Brazil 202 D5
Poço Fundo Brazil 207 H8
Pocomoke City U.S.A. 177 J7
Pocomoke Sound *b.* U.S.A. 177 J8
Pocona Bol. 200 D4
Poconé Brazil 201 F4
Pocono Mountains *hills* U.S.A. 177 J4
Pocono Summit U.S.A. 177 J4
Poco Ranakah *vol.* Indon. 75 B5
Poços de Caldas Brazil 206 F8
Pocrane Brazil 207 L6
Poddębice Poland 49 P4
Poddor'ye Rus. Fed. 43 M4
Podensac France 51 I4
Podgorac Srbija Yugo. 58 C5
Podgorenskiy Rus. Fed. 41 F6
Podgorica Crna Gora Yugo. 58 A6
formerly known as Titograd
Podgorie Albania 58 B8
Podgornoye Rus. Fed. 39 I4
Podile Rus. Fed. 43 P9
Podişul Transilvaniei *plat.* Romania *see* Transylvanian Basin
Podkamennaya Tunguska Rus. Fed. 39 J3
Podkamennaya Tunguska *r.* Rus. Fed. 39 J3
Podkhozheye Rus. Fed. 43 T7
Podlesnoye Rus. Fed. 102 A2
Podocarpus, Parque Nacional *nat. park* Ecuador 198 B5
Podoleni Romania 58 I2
Podol'sk Rus. Fed. 43 S6
Podor Senegal 124 B2
Podosinki Rus. Fed. 43 M6
Podozerskiy Rus. Fed. 43 V4
Podporozh'ye Rus. Fed. 43 P1
Podu Turcului Rus. Fed. 43 V3
Podujevo Kosovo, Srbija Yugo. 58 C5
Poduyuga Rus. Fed. 40 G3
Podyut'ye Rus. Fed. 43 P9
Poel *i.* Germany 48 I1
Poeppel Corner *salt flat* Australia 148 C5
Poetovio Slovenia *see* Ptuj
Pofadder S. Africa 132 C6
Pogamasing Canada 173 L4
Pogar Rus. Fed. 43 O9
Poggibonsi Italy 56 D5
Poggio Ballone *hill* Italy 56 C6
Poggio di Montieri *mt.* Italy 56 D5
Poggio Rusco Italy 56 D3
Pogled *mt.* Yugo. 58 B6
Pogoreloye-Gorodishche Rus. Fed. 43 P5
Pogradec Albania 58 B8
Pogrebishche Ukr. *see* Pohrebyshche
Po Hai *g.* China *see* Bo Hai
Pohang S. Korea 83 C5
Pohja Fin. 45 M3
Pohnpei *atoll* Micronesia 220 E5
formerly spelt Ponape; *historically known as* Ascension
Pohrebyshche Ukr. 41 D6
also spelt Pogrebishche
Pohri India 96 C4
Poiana Mare Romania 58 E6
Poiana Ruscă, Munţii *mts* Romania 58 D3
Poiana Stampei Romania 58 G1
Poienești Romania 58 I2
Poienţia, Vârful *mt.* Romania 58 G1
Poindimié New Caledonia 145 F4
Poinsett, Cape Antarctica 223 H2
Point au Fer Island U.S.A. 175 B6
Point-Comfort Canada 173 R4
Pointe à la Hache U.S.A. 175 B6
Pointe-à-Pitre Guadeloupe 187 H3
Pointe au Baril Station Canada 173 M5

Pointe Aux Pins U.S.A. 173 I5
Pointe-Noire Congo 126 A6
Pointe Noire Guadeloupe 187 H3
Point Hope U.S.A. 164 C3
Point Kenny Australia 146 B3
Point Lake Canada 167 H1
Point Nepean National Park Australia 147 E4
Point of Rocks MD U.S.A. 176 H6
Point of Rocks WY U.S.A. 180 E4
Point Pelee National Park Canada 173 K9
Point Pleasant U.S.A. 177 K5
Point Reyes National Seashore *nature res.* U.S.A. 182 B3
Point Salvation Aboriginal Reserve Australia 151 C6
Point Samson Australia 144 A4
Poisevo Rus. Fed. 40 J5
Poisson Blanc, Lac du *l.* Canada 173 R5
Poissonnier Point Australia 150 B3
Poitiers France 50 G6
historically known as Limonum
Poitou, Plaines et Seuil du *plain* France 50 G6
Poitou-Charentes *admin. reg.* France 50 F6
Poix-de-Picardie France 51 H3
Pojo Bol. 200 D4
Pojuca Brazil 202 E5
Pokaran India 96 A4
Pokataroo Australia 147 F2
Pokat's' *r.* Belarus 43 L9
Pokcha Rus. Fed. 40 K3
Pokeno N.Z. 152 J5
Pokhara Nepal 97 D3
Pokhvistnevo Rus. Fed. 41 J5
Pokigron Surinam 199 H3
Pokka Fin. 44 N1
Pok Liu Chau *i.* Hong Kong China *see* Lamma Island
Poko Dem. Rep. Congo 126 E4
Pokrov Smolenskaya Oblast' Rus. Fed. 43 Q6
Pokrov Vladimirskaya Oblast' Rus. Fed. 43 U6
Pokrovka Kazakh. 103 G2
Pokrovka Kyrg. 103 G4
Pokrovka Kyrg. *see* Kyzyl-Suu
Pokrovka Moskovskaya Oblast' Rus. Fed. 43 S6
Pokrovka Orenburgskaya Oblast' Rus. Fed. 102 C2
Pokrovka Primorskiy Kray Rus. Fed. 82 C4
Pokrovka Primorskiy Kray Rus. Fed. 90 C2
Pokrovka Rus. Fed. *see* Priamurskiy
Pokrovsk Rus. Fed. 39 M3
Pokrovsk Rus. Fed. *see* Engel's
Pokrovskoye Lipetskaya Oblast' Rus. Fed. 43 T9
Pokrovskoye Orlovskaya Oblast' Rus. Fed. 43 S9
Pokrovskoye Rostovskaya Oblast' Rus. Fed. 41 F7
Pokrovsk-Ural'skiy Rus. Fed. 40 K3
Pokshen'ga *r.* Rus. Fed. 40 H3
Pol' *r.* Rus. Fed. 43 V6
Pola Croatia *see* Pula
Pola Phil. 74 B3
Pola Rus. Fed. 43 M4
Polacca U.S.A. 183 N6
Polacca Wash *watercourse* U.S.A. 183 N6
Pola de Allande Spain 54 E1
Pola de Laviana Spain 54 F1
Pola de Lena Spain 54 F1
Pola de Siero Spain 54 F1
Pola de Somiedo Spain 54 E1
Polān Iran 101 E5
Polán Spain 54 G5
Poľana *mt.* Slovakia 49 Q7
▶ Poland *country* Europe 49
known as Polska *in Polish*
europe [countries] ▶▶▶ 32–35
Połaniec Poland 49 S5
Polanów Poland 49 N1
Polar Bear Provincial Park Canada 168 D2
Polar Plateau Antarctica 223 V1
Polar Times Glacier Antarctica 223 I4
Polatlı Turkey 106 C3
Polatsk Belarus 43 J6
also spelt Polotsk
Polatskaya Nizina *lowland* Belarus 42 J6
Polavaram India 94 D2
Polazna Rus. Fed. 40 K4
Poleirkeln Sweden 44 N2
Połczyn Zdrój Poland 49 N2
Poldarsa Rus. Fed. 40 H3
Pol-e Fāsā Iran 100 C4
Pole-Khatum Iran 101 E2
Pol-e Khomri Afgh. 101 G3
Pol-e Safid Iran 100 C2
Polessk Rus. Fed. 42 C7
Poles'ye *marsh* Belarus/Ukr. *see* Pripet Marshes
Polewali Indon. 75 A3
Poli Cameroon 125 I4
Poli Cyprus *see* Polis
Poliaigos *i.* Greece *see* Polyaigos
Polican Albania 58 B8
Policastro, Golfo di *b.* Italy 57 H9
Police Poland 49 L2
Polichnitos Greece 59 H9
also spelt Polikhnitos
Policoro Italy 57 I8
Polidhrosos Greece *see* Polydroso
Polignano a Mare Italy 56 J8
Poligny France 51 L6
Polikastron Greece *see* Polykastro
Polikhnitos Greece *see* Polichnitos
Polikrayshte Bulg. 58 G5
Polillo *i.* Phil. 74 B3
Polillo Islands Phil. 74 J
Polillo Strait Phil. 74 B3
Polis Cyprus 108 D2
also known as Poli
Polis'ke Ukr. 41 D6
formerly known as Kaganovichi Pervyye
Polis'kyy Zapovidnyk *nature res.* Ukr. 41 D6
Polist' *r.* Rus. Fed. 43 M3
Polistena Italy 57 I10
Polisto, Ozero *l.* Rus. Fed. 43 L4
Polítovo Rus. Fed. 40 I2
Poliyiros Greece *see* Polygyros
Polk U.S.A. 176 F4
Polkorona Latvia 42 H5
Polkowice Poland 49 N4
Polla Italy 57 H8
Pollachi India 94 C4
Pollard Islands U.S.A. *see* Gardner Pinnacles
Pöllauer Tal *nature res.* Austria 49 M8
Pollença Spain 55 O5
also spelt Pollensa
Pollensa Spain *see* Pollença
Pollino, Monte *mt.* Italy 57 I9
Pollino, Parco Nazionale del *nat. park* Italy 57 I9
Polloc Harbour *b.* Phil. 74 B5
Pollock Pines U.S.A. 182 D3
Pollock Reef Australia 151 C7
Pollok N.Z. 152 I5
Polmak Norway 44 N1
Polnovat Rus. Fed. 38 G3
Polo Fin. 44 O2
Polo U.S.A. 172 D9
Polog Ukr. *see* Polohy
Polohy Ukr. 41 F7
also spelt Pology; *formerly known as* Chubarovka
Polokwane S. Africa *see* Pietersburg
Polomet' *r.* Rus. Fed. 43 N4
Polomoloc Phil. 74 C5
Polonnaruwa Sri Lanka 94 D5
Polonne Ukr. 41 C6
also spelt Polonnoye

Polonnoye Ukr. see Polonne
Polotnyanyy Zavod Rus. Fed. 43 Q7
Polotsk Belarus see Polatsk
Polovinka Rus. Fed. see Ugleural'skiy
Polovragi Romania 58 E3
Pöls r. Austria 49 L8
Polska country Europe see Poland
Polski Trŭmbesh Bulg. 58 G5
Polson U.S.A. 180 D3
Polta r. Rus. Fed. 40 G2
Poltár Slovakia 49 Q7
Poltava Ukr. 41 E6
Poltavka Rus. Fed. 82 C3
Poltavskaya Rus. Fed. 41 F7
formerly known as Krasnoarmeyskaya
Poltoratsk Turkm. see Ashgabat
Põltsamaa Estonia 42 G3
Põltsamaa r. Estonia 42 H3
Polur India 94 C3
Põlva Estonia 42 I3
Polvadera U.S.A. 181 F6
Polvijärvi Fin. 44 O3
Polya r. Rus. Fed. 43 U6
Polyaigos i. Greece 59 F12
also spelt Políaigos
Polyanovgrad Bulg. see Karnobat
Polyany Rus. Fed. 43 K1
Polyarnoye Rus. Fed. see Russkoye Ust'ye
Polyarnyy Chukotskiy Avtonomnyy Okrug Rus. Fed. 39 R3
Polyarnyy Murmanskaya Oblast' Rus. Fed. 44 P1
Polyarnyye Zori Rus. Fed. 44 P2
Polyarnyy Krug Rus. Fed. 44 P2
Polyarnyy Ural mts Rus. Fed. 40 L2
Polydroso Greece 59 D10
also known as Polídhrosos
Polygyros Greece 59 E8
also spelt Políyiros
Polyiagou-Folegandrou, Steno sea chan. Greece 59 F12
Polykastro Greece 58 D8
also known as Políkastron
Polynesia is Oceania 220 G5
Polynésie Française terr. S. Pacific Ocean see French Polynesia
Pomabamba Peru 200 A2
Pomahaka r. N.Z. 153 D14
Pomarance Italy 56 C5
Pomarkku Fin. 45 M3
Pomba r. Brazil 203 D7
Pombal Pará Brazil 199 H5
Pombal Paraíba Brazil 202 E3
Pombal Port. 54 C5
Pombas r. Brazil 199 F6
Pombas Cape Verde 124 [inset]
Pombo r. Brazil 206 A7
Pomene Moz. 131 G4
Pomeroy S. Africa 133 O5
Pomeroy OH U.S.A. 176 C6
Pomeroy WA U.S.A. 180 C3
Pomezia Italy 56 E7
Pomfret S. Africa 132 H2
Pomio P.N.G. 145 E2
Pomokaira reg. Fin. 44 N2
Pomona Namibia 130 B5
Pomona U.S.A. 182 G7
Pomorie Bulg. 58 I6
Pomorska, Zatoka b. Poland 49 L1
Pomorskie, Pojezierze reg. Poland 49 O2
Pomorskiy Bereg coastal area Rus. Fed. 40 E2
Pomorskiy Proliv sea chan. Rus. Fed. 40 I1
Pomos Point Cyprus 108 D2
also known as Pomou, Akra
Pomo Tso l. China see Puma Yumco
Pomou, Akra pt Cyprus see Pomos Point
Pompei Italy 57 G8
historically known as Pompeii
Pompéia Brazil 206 C9
Pompeii Italy see Pompei
Pompéu Brazil 203 C6
Pompton Lakes U.S.A. 177 K4
Ponape atoll Micronesia see Pohnpei
Ponask Lake Canada 167 M4
Ponazyrevo Rus. Fed. 40 H4
Ponca U.S.A. 178 C3
Ponca City U.S.A. 178 C4
Ponce Puerto Rico 187 G3
Ponce de Leon Bay U.S.A. 175 D7
Poncha Springs U.S.A. 181 F5
Ponda India 94 B3
Pondicherry India 94 C4
also spelt Pondichéry or Puducheheri
Pondicherry union terr. India 95 C4
Pondichéry India see Pondicherry
Pond Inlet Canada 165 L2
also known as Mittimatalik; formerly known as Ponds Bay
Pondoland reg. S. Africa 133 N8
Ponds, Island of Canada 169 K2
Ponds Bay Canada see Pond Inlet
Poneloya Nicaragua 186 B4
Ponente, Riviera di coastal area Italy 56 A5
Ponferrada Spain 54 E2
Pongakawa N.Z. 152 K5
Pongara, Pointe pt Gabon 126 A4
Pongaroa N.Z. 152 K8
Pongo watercourse Sudan 126 E3
Pongo de Manseriche gorge Peru 198 B6
Pongola S. Africa 133 P4
Pongola r. S. Africa 133 Q3
Pongolapoort Dam l. S. Africa 133 P4
Pongolapoort Public Resort Nature Reserve S. Africa 133 P4
Poniatowa Poland 49 T4
Poniki, Gunung mt. Indon. 75 B2
Ponindilisa, Tanjung pt Indon. 75 B3
Ponizov'ye Rus. Fed. 43 M6
Ponnagyun Myanmar 78 A3
Ponnaivar r. India 94 C4
Ponnampet India 94 B3
Ponnani India 94 B4
Ponnani r. India 94 B4
Ponneri India 94 D3
Ponnyadaung Range mts Myanmar 78 A3
Ponoka Canada 167 H4
Ponomarevka Rus. Fed. 102 C1
Ponorogo Indon. 77 E4
Ponoy r. Rus. Fed. 40 G2
Pons r. Canada 169 G1
Pons France 50 F7
Pons Spain see Ponts
Ponsacco Italy 56 C5
Ponsul r. Port. 54 D5
Pontacq France 50 F9

▶Ponta Delgada Azores 216 M3
Capital of the Azores.

Ponta de Pedras Brazil 202 B2
Ponta dos Índios Brazil 199 I3
Ponta do Sol Cape Verde 124 [inset]
Ponta Grossa Brazil 203 B8
Pontal do Ipiranga Brazil 207 N6
Pontalina Brazil 206 D4
Pont-à-Mousson France 51 M4
Pontant Arg. 204 E5
Pontão Brazil 202 B3
Ponta Porã Brazil 201 G5
Pontarlier France 51 M6
Pontassieve Italy 56 D5
Pont-Audemer France 50 G3
Pont-Aven France 50 C5
Pontax r. Canada 168 E3
Pontchartrain, Lake U.S.A. 175 B6
Pontchâteau France 50 D5
Pont-d'Ain France 51 L6
Pont-de-Roide France 51 M5
Pont de Suert Spain 55 L2
Ponte Alta do Norte Brazil 202 C4
Ponteareas Spain 54 C2
also spelt Puenteareas
Pontebba Italy 56 F2
Ponte Branca Brazil 206 A3
Ponte-Ceso Spain 54 C1
Pontecorvo Italy 56 F7
Ponte de Pedra Brazil 201 F3
Pontedera Italy 56 C5
Ponte de Sor Port. 54 C5
Ponte do Rio Verde Brazil 203 A6
Ponte Firme Brazil 206 G5
Ponteix Canada 167 J5
Ponteland U.K. 47 K8
Ponte Nova Brazil 203 D7
Pontes-e-Lacerda Brazil 201 F3
Pontevedra Spain 54 C2
Pontevedra, Ría de est. Spain 54 C2
Ponthierville Dem. Rep. Congo see Ubundu
Pontiac IL U.S.A. 174 B3
Pontiac MI U.S.A. 173 J8
Pontiae is Italy see Ponziane, Isole
Pontianak Indon. 77 E3
Pontine Islands is Italy see Ponziane, Isole
Pontivy France 50 D4
Pont-l'Abbé France 50 B5
Pontoetoe Suriname 199 H4
Pontoise France 51 I3
Ponton watercourse Australia 151 C6
Ponton Canada 167 L4
Pontotoc U.S.A. 174 B5
Pontremoli Italy 56 B4
Ponts Spain 55 M3
also spelt Pons
Pont-St-Esprit France 51 K8
Pont-sur-Yonne France 51 J4
Pontypool Canada 173 O6
Pontypool U.K. 47 I12
Pontypridd U.K. 47 I12
Ponui Island N.Z. 152 J4
Ponyatovka Rus. Fed. 43 N8
Ponyri Rus. Fed. 43 R9
Ponza Italy 57 E8
Ponza, Isola di i. Italy 56 E8
Ponziane, Isole is Italy 56 E8
English form Pontine Islands; historically known as Pontiae
Poochera Australia 146 B3
Pool admin. reg. Congo 126 B5
Poole U.K. 47 K13
Poolowanna Lake salt flat Australia 148 C5
Poona India see Pune
Pooncarie Australia 147 D3
Poopelloe Lake Australia 147 E2
Poopó Bol. 200 D4
Poopó, Lago de l. Bol. 200 D4
Poor Knights Islands N.Z. 152 I3
Pop Uzbek. see Pap
Popa Mountain Myanmar 78 A3
Popayán Col. 198 B4
Pope Latvia 42 C4
Popes Creek U.S.A. 177 I7
Popigay r. Rus. Fed. 39 K2
Popilta Lake imp. l. Australia 146 D3
Popio Lake Australia 146 D3
Poplar r. Man. Canada 167 L4
Poplar r. N.W.T. Canada 166 G2
Poplar U.S.A. 172 B4
Poplar r. U.S.A. 180 F2
Poplar, West Fork r. U.S.A. 180 F2
Poplar Bluff U.S.A. 174 B4
Poplar Camp U.S.A. 176 E9
Poplar Plains U.S.A. 176 B7
Poplarville U.S.A. 175 B6
Poplevinskiy Rus. Fed. 43 U8

▶Popocatépetl, Volcán vol. Mex. 185 F5
5th highest mountain in North America.
northamerica [landscapes] ▶▶ 156–157
northamerica [threats] ▶▶ 160–161

Popoh Indon. 77 E5
Popokabaka Dem. Rep. Congo 127 C6
Popoli Italy 56 F6
Popondetta P.N.G. 145 D2
Popovača Croatia 56 I3
Popovichskaya Rus. Fed. see Kalininskaya
Popovka Vologod. Obl. Rus. Fed. 43 S2
Popovka Vologod. Obl. Rus. Fed. 43 U1
Popovo Bulg. 58 H5
Popovo Polje plain Bos.-Herz. 56 J6
Popovska Reka r. Bulg. 58 H6
Poppberg hill Germany 48 I6
Poppenberg hill Germany 48 H4
Poprad r. Poland 49 R6
Poprad Slovakia 49 R6
Poquis, Nevado de mt. Chile 200 D5
Poquoson U.S.A. 177 I8
Por r. Poland 49 U5
Porali r. Pak. 101 F5
Porangahau N.Z. 152 K8
Porangatu Brazil 202 B5
Porazava Belarus 42 F9
Porbandar India 96 A5
Porcher Island Canada 166 D4
Porciúncula Brazil 207 K7
Porco Bol. 200 D4
Porcsalma Hungary 49 T8
Porcuna Spain 54 G7
Porcupine r. Canada/U.S.A. 164 E3
Porcupine, Cape Canada 169 J2
Porcupine Creek r. U.S.A. 180 F2
Porcupine Gorge National Park Australia 149 E4
Porcupine Hills Canada 167 K4
Porcupine Mountains U.S.A. 172 D4
Porcupine Plain Canada 167 K4
Porcupine Provincial Forest nature res. Canada 167 K4
Pordenone Italy 56 E3
Pordim Bulg. 58 F5
Pore Col. 198 D3
Poreč Croatia 56 F3
Porecatu Brazil 206 B9
Porech'ye Moskovskaya Oblast' Rus. Fed. 43 Q6
Porech'ye Pskovskaya Oblast' Rus. Fed. 43 L5
Porech'ye Tverskaya Oblast' Rus. Fed. 43 R3
Porech'ye-Rybnoye Rus. Fed. 43 U4
Poretskoye Rus. Fed. 40 H5
Porga Benin 125 F4
Pori Fin. 45 M3
also known as Björneborg
Porirua N.Z. 152 I9
Porjus Sweden 44 L2
Porkhov Rus. Fed. 43 K4
Porkkalafjärden b. Fin. 42 F2
Porlamar Venez. 199 F2
Porma r. Spain 54 F2
Pormpuraaw Australia 149 D2
Pornainen Fin. 45 N3
Pornic France 50 D5
Poro i. Phil. 74 C4
Poro, Monte hill Italy 57 H10
Poronaysk Rus. Fed. 82 F2
Porong China see Baingoin
Pŏrŏng, Stœ̆ng r. Cambodia 79 D5
Poros Greece 59 E11
Poros i. Greece 59 E11
Porosozero Rus. Fed. 40 E3
Porpoise Bay Antarctica 223 G2
Porquerolles, Île de i. France 51 M10
Porquis Junction Canada 173 M2
Porrentruy Switz. 51 N5
Porriño Spain 54 C2
Porsangen sea chan. Norway 44 N1
Porsangerhalvøya pen. Norway 44 N1
Porsgrunn Norway 45 J4
Porsuk r. Turkey 106 B3
Portadown U.K. 47 F9
Portaferry U.K. 47 G9
Portage IN U.S.A. 172 F9
Portage MI U.S.A. 172 H8
Portage PA U.S.A. 176 G5
Portage WI U.S.A. 172 D7
Portage Lakes U.S.A. 176 D5
Portage la Prairie Canada 167 L5
Portal U.S.A. 178 B1
Port Alberni Canada 166 E5
Port Albert Australia 147 E4
Portalegre Port. 54 D5
Portalegre admin. dist. Port. 54 D5
Portales U.S.A. 179 B5
Port-Alfred Canada see La Baie
Port Alfred S. Africa 133 K10
Port Alice Canada 166 E5
Port Allegany U.S.A. 176 G4
Port Allen U.S.A. 175 B6
Port Alma Australia 149 F4
Port Angeles U.S.A. 180 B2
Port Antonio Jamaica 186 D3
Port-à-Piment Haiti 187 E3
Portarlington Rep. of Ireland 47 E10
Port Arthur Australia 147 E5
Port Arthur China see Lüshun
Port Arthur U.S.A. 179 D6
Port Askaig U.K. 46 F8
Port Augusta Australia 146 C3
Port-au-Port Bay Canada 169 J3

▶Port-au-Prince Haiti 187 E3
Capital of Haiti.

Port aux Choix Canada 169 J3
Port Beaufort S. Africa 132 E11
Port Blair India 95 G4
Port Bolster Canada 173 N6
Portbou Spain 55 O2
Port Bradshaw b. Australia 148 C2
Port Broughton Australia 146 C3
Port Burwell Canada 173 M8
Port Campbell Australia 147 D4
Port Campbell National Park Australia 147 D4
Port Canning India 97 F5
Port Carling Canada 173 N5
Port-Cartier Canada 169 H3
formerly known as Shelter Bay
Port Chalmers N.Z. 153 E13
Port Charles N.Z. 152 J4
Port Charlotte U.S.A. 175 D7
Port Clements Canada 166 C4
Port Clinton OH U.S.A. 176 C4
Port Clyde U.S.A. 177 P2
Port Colborne Canada 168 E5
Port Credit Canada 173 N7
Port Darwin b. Australia 148 A2
Port Davey b. Australia 147 E5
Port-de-Paix Haiti 187 E3
Port de Pollença Spain 55 O5
also spelt Puerto de Pollensa
Port Dickson Malaysia 76 C2
Port Douglas Australia 149 E3
Port Dover Canada 173 M8
Port Easington inlet Australia 148 A1
Porte des Morts lake channel U.S.A. 172 G5
Port Edward Canada 166 D4
Port Edward S. Africa 133 O8
Port Edwards U.S.A. 172 D6
Porteira Brazil 199 G5
Porteirinha Brazil 202 D5
Portel Brazil 202 B2
Portel Port. 54 D6
Portelândia Brazil 206 A4
Port Elgin N.B. Canada 169 H4
Port Elgin Ont. Canada 168 D4
Port Elizabeth S. Africa 133 J10
Port Ellen U.K. 46 F8
Port Erin Isle of Man 47 H9
Porter Lake N.W.T. Canada 167 J2
Porter Lake Sask. Canada 167 J3
Porter Landing Canada 166 D3
Porterville S. Africa 132 C10
Porterville U.S.A. 182 E5
Portes-lès-Valence France 51 K8
Port Étienne Mauritania see Nouâdhibou
Port Everglades U.S.A. see Fort Lauderdale
Port Fairy Australia 147 D4
Port Fitzroy N.Z. 152 J4
Port Francqui Dem. Rep. Congo see Ilebo
Port-Gentil Gabon 126 A5
Port Gibson U.S.A. 175 B6
Port Grosvenor S. Africa 133 N8
Port Harcourt Nigeria 125 G5
Port Hardy Canada 166 E5
Port Harrison Canada see Inukjuak
Port Hawkesbury Canada 169 I4
Porthcawl U.K. 47 I12
Port Hedland Australia 150 B4
Port Henry U.S.A. 177 L1
Port Herald Malawi see Nsanje
Porthmos Zakynthou sea chan. Greece 59 B11
Port Hope Canada 173 O7
Port Hope U.S.A. 173 K7
Port Hope Simpson Canada 169 K2
Port Hueneme U.S.A. 182 E7
Port Huron U.S.A. 173 K8
Port-Iliç Azer. 107 G3
Portillo Cuba 186 D3
Portimão Port. 54 C7
Port Island Hong Kong China 87 [inset]
also known as Chek Chau
Port Jackson Australia see Sydney
Port Jackson inlet Australia 147 F3
Port Jefferson U.S.A. 177 L5
Port Kaituma Guyana 199 G3
Port Keats Australia see Wadeye
Port Kent U.S.A. 177 L1
Port Klang Malaysia see Pelabuhan Kelang
Port Láirge Rep. of Ireland see Waterford
Portland Australia 146 D4
Portland IN U.S.A. 176 A5
Portland ME U.S.A. 177 O2
Portland MI U.S.A. 173 I8
Portland OR U.S.A. 180 B3
Portland, Isle of pen. U.K. 47 J13
Portland Bay Australia 146 D4
Portland Bill hd U.K. see Bill of Portland
Portland Canal inlet Canada 166 D4
Portland Creek Pond l. Canada 169 J3
Portland Inlet Canada 166 D4
Portland Point Jamaica 186 D3
Portland Roads Australia 149 D2
Portlaoise Rep. of Ireland 47 E10
Port Lavaca U.S.A. 179 C6
Port Lincoln Australia 146 B3
Port Loko Sierra Leone 124 B4
Port Louis Guadeloupe 187 H3

▶Port Louis Mauritius 219 K7
Capital of Mauritius.

Port-Lyautrey Morocco see Kénitra
Port MacDonnell Australia 146 D4
Port Macquarie Australia 147 G2
Port Manvers inlet Canada 169 I1
Port McArthur b. Australia 148 C2
Port McNeill Canada 166 E5
Port-Menier Canada 169 H3
Port Moller b. U.S.A. 164 C4
Port Morant Jamaica 186 D3

▶Port Moresby P.N.G. 73 K8
Capital of Papua New Guinea.

Port Musgrave b. Australia 149 D1
Portnacroish U.K. 46 G7
Portnahaven U.K. 46 F8
Port Neches U.S.A. 179 D6
Port Neill Australia 146 C3
Port Nelson Bahamas 187 E2
Portneuf r. Canada 169 G3
Portneuf, Réserve Faunique de nature res. Canada 169 F4
Port Nis U.K. 46 F5
Port Nolloth S. Africa 132 A6
Port Norris U.S.A. 177 J6
Port-Nouveau-Québec Canada see Kangiqsualujjuaq
Porto Brazil 202 D2
Porto Port. see Oporto
Porto admin. dist. Port. 54 C3
Porto, Golfe de b. Corse France 51 O10
Porto Acre Brazil 200 D2
Porto Alegre Amazonas Brazil 200 C2
Porto Alegre Mato Grosso do Sul Brazil 203 A7
Porto Alegre Pará Brazil 199 H6
Porto Alegre Rio Grande do Sul Brazil 203 B9
Porto Alencastro Brazil 206 C6
Porto Alexandre Angola see Tombua
Porto Amarante Brazil 201 E3
Porto Amboim Angola 127 B7
also known as Gunza
Porto Amélia Moz. see Pemba
Porto Artur Brazil 201 G3
Porto Azzurro Italy 56 C6
Porto Belo Brazil 203 B8
Portobelo Panama 186 D5
Portobelo, Parque Nacional nat. park Panama 186 D5
Porto Camargo Brazil 203 A7
Porto Calvo Brazil 202 F4
Porto da Fôlha Brazil 202 E4
Porto da Lontra Brazil 199 H6
Porto de Meinacos Brazil 202 A5
Porto de Moz Brazil 199 H5
Porto de Santa Cruz Brazil 207 L2
Porto do Barka Brazil 199 H6
Porto do Massacas Brazil 201 E3
Porto dos Gaúchos Óbidos Brazil 201 F2
Porto do Son Spain 54 B2
also spelt Puerto del Son
Porto Empedocle Sicilia Italy 57 F11
Porto Esperança Brazil 201 F4
Porto Esperidião Brazil 201 F3
Porto Estrêla Brazil 201 F3
Porto Feliz Brazil 206 F10
Portoferraio Italy 56 C6
Porto Ferreira Brazil 206 F8
Porto Firme Brazil 207 J7
Porto Franco Brazil 202 C3

▶Port of Spain Trin. and Tob. 187 H5
Capital of Trinidad and Tobago.

Porto Grande Brazil 199 I4
Portogruaro Italy 56 E3
Porto Inglês Cape Verde 124 [inset]
Porto Jofre Brazil 201 F4
Portola U.S.A. 182 D2
Porto Luceno Brazil 203 A8
Portomaggiore Italy 56 D4
Porto Mauá Brazil 203 A8
Porto Murtinho Brazil 201 F5
Porto Nacional Brazil 202 B4

▶Porto-Novo Benin 125 F5
Capital of Benin.

Porto Novo Cape Verde 124 [inset]
Porto Novo India see Parangipettai
Portopalo di Capo Passero Sicilia Italy 57 H12
Porto Primavera, Represa resr Brazil 206 A8
Port Orange U.S.A. 175 D6
Port Orchard U.S.A. 180 B3
Port Orford U.S.A. 180 A4
Porto Rincão Cape Verde 124 [inset]
Porto San Giorgio Italy 56 F5
Porto Santana Brazil 199 I5
Porto Sant'Elpidio Italy 56 F5
Porto Santo, Ilha de i. Madeira 122 A2
Portoscuso Sardegna Italy 57 A9
Porto Seguro Brazil 202 E6
Porto Tolle Italy 56 E4
Porto Torres Sardegna Italy 56 A8
historically known as Turris Libisonis
Porto Triunfo Brazil 201 E3
Porto União Brazil 203 B8
Porto-Vecchio Corse France 52 D3
Porto Velho Brazil 201 E2
Portoviejo Ecuador 198 A5
Porto Wálter Brazil 200 B2
Portpatrick U.K. 47 G9
Port Pegasus b. N.Z. 153 B15
also known as Pikihatiti
Port Perry Canada 173 O6
Port Phillip Bay Australia 147 E4
Port Pirie Australia 146 C3
Portree U.K. 46 F6
Port Renfrew Canada 166 E5
Port Rexton Canada 169 K3
Port Roper b. Australia 148 B2
Port Rowan Canada 173 M8
Port Royal U.S.A. 177 H7
Port Royal Sound inlet U.S.A. 175 D5
Port Said Egypt 121 G2
also known as Bûr Sa'îd
Port St Joe U.S.A. 175 C6
Port St Johns S. Africa 133 N8
Port St-Louis Madag. see Antsohimbondrona
Port-St-Louis-du-Rhône France 51 K9
Port Saint Lucie City U.S.A. 175 D7
Port Salvador Falkland Is 205 F8
Ports de Beseit mts Spain 55 L4
also spelt Puertos de Beceite
Port Severn Canada 173 N6
Port Shelter b. Hong Kong China 87 [inset]
also known as Ngau Mei Hoi
Port Shepstone S. Africa 133 O7
Port Simpson Canada see Lax Kw'alaams
Portsmouth Dominica 187 H4
Portsmouth U.K. 47 K13
Portsmouth NH U.S.A. 177 O2
Portsmouth OH U.S.A. 176 C7
Portsmouth VA U.S.A. 177 I9
Port Stanley Falkland Is see Stanley
Port Stephens Falkland Is 205 E9
Port Sudan Sudan 121 H5
also known as Bûr Sûdân
Port Sulphur U.S.A. 175 B6
Port-sur-Saône France 51 M5
Port Swettenham Malaysia see Pelabuhan Kelang
Port Talbot U.K. 47 I12
Port Tambang b. Phil. 74 B3
Porttipahdan tekojärvi l. Fin. 44 N1
Port Townsend U.S.A. 180 B2
▶Portugal country Europe 54 C7
europe [countries] ▶▶ 32–35
Portugalete Spain 55 H1
Portugália Angola see Chitato
Portuguesa state Venez. 198 D2
Portuguese East Africa country Africa see Mozambique
Portuguese Guinea country Africa see Guinea-Bissau
Portuguese Timor terr. Asia see East Timor
Portuguese West Africa country Africa see Angola
Portumna Rep. of Ireland 47 D10
Portus Herculis Monoeci country Europe see Monaco
Port-Vendres France 51 J10
Port Victoria Australia 146 C3

▶Port Vila Vanuatu 145 F3
Capital of Vanuatu. Also known as Vila.

Portville U.S.A. 176 G3
Port Vladimir Rus. Fed. 44 P1
Port Waikato N.Z. 152 I5
Port Wakefield Australia 146 C3
Port Warrender Australia 150 D2
Port Washington U.S.A. 172 F7
Port Wing U.S.A. 172 B4
Porumamilla India 94 C3
Porus'ya r. Rus. Fed. 43 M4
Porvenir Pando Bol. 200 C2
Porvenir Santa Cruz Bol. 201 E3
Porvenir Chile 205 C9
Porvoo Fin. 45 N3
also known as Borgå
Porvoonjoki r. Fin. 42 G1
Por'ya Guba Rus. Fed. 44 P2
Poryŏng S. Korea 83 B5
formerly known as Taech'ŏn
Porzuna Spain 54 G5
Posada Sardegna Italy 57 B8
Posada r. Sardegna Italy 57 B8
Posada Spain 54 F1
Posadas Arg. 204 G2
Posadas Spain 54 F7
Posadowsky Bay Antarctica 223 G2
Posavina reg. Bos.-Herz./Croatia 56 I3
Poschiavo Switz. 51 Q6
Poseidonia Greece 59 F11
Poseidonia tourist site Italy see Paestum
Posen Poland see Poznań
Posen U.S.A. 173 J5
Poshekhon'ye Rus. Fed. 43 U3
formerly known as Poshekhon'ye-Volodarsk
Poshekhon'ye-Volodarsk Rus. Fed. see Poshekhon'ye
Posht watercourse Iran 100 D4
Posht-e Badam Iran 100 C3
Poshteh-ye Chaqvir hill Iran 100 D4
Posht-e Kūh mts Iran 100 A3
Posht Kūh hill Iran 100 B2
Posio Fin. 44 O2
Poskam China see Zepu
Poso Indon. 75 B3
Poso r. Indon. 75 B3
Poso, Danau l. Indon. 75 B3
Poso, Teluk b. Indon. 75 B3
Posof Turkey 107 E2
Posorja Ecuador 198 A5
Pospelikha Rus. Fed. 103 J1
Posse Brazil 202 C5
Possession Islands Antarctica 223 L2
Pößneck Germany 48 I5
Post U.S.A. 179 B5
Poşta Călnău Romania 58 H3
formerly spelt Poşta Cîlnău
Poşta Cîlnău Romania see Poşta Călnău
Postavy Belarus see Pastavy
Poste-de-la-Baleine Canada see Kuujjuarapik
Postmasburg S. Africa 132 H5
Postojna Slovenia 56 G3
Poston U.S.A. 183 J7
Postville Canada 169 J2
Postville U.S.A. 174 B3
Post Weygand Alg. 123 F4
Postysheve Ukr. see Krasnoarmiys'k
Posušje Bos.-Herz. 56 J5
Pos'yet Rus. Fed. 82 C4
Pota Indon. 75 B5
Potamia Greece 58 F8
Potamos Greece 59 D12
Potanino Rus. Fed. 43 N1
Potchefstroom S. Africa 133 L3
Potcoava Romania 58 F4
Poté Brazil 203 D6
Poteau U.S.A. 179 D5
Potegaon India 94 D2
Potentia Italy see Potenza
Potenza Italy 57 H8
historically known as Potentia
Potenza r. Italy 56 F5
Poteriteri, Lake N.Z. 153 B14
Potfontein S. Africa 132 I7
Potgietersrus S. Africa 131 F5
Poti r. Brazil 202 D3
P'ot'i Georgia 107 E2
Potikal India 94 D2
Potiraguá Brazil 202 E5
Potiskum Nigeria 125 H4
Potnarvin Vanuatu 145 F3
Poto Peru 200 C3
Po Toi i. Hong Kong China 87 [inset]
also spelt Putoi
Potomac r. U.S.A. 177 I7
Potomac, South Branch r. U.S.A. 176 G6
Potomac, South Fork South Branch r. U.S.A. 176 F7
Potomana, Gunung mt. Indon. 75 C5
Potoru Sierra Leone 124 C5
Potosí Bol. 200 D4
Potosí dept Bol. 200 D5
Potosi U.S.A. 174 B4
Potosi Mountain U.S.A. 183 I6
Pototan Phil. 74 B4
Potrerillos Chile 204 C2
Potrero del Llano Mex. 184 D2
Potro r. Peru 198 B6
Potsdam Germany 49 K3
Potsdam U.S.A. 177 K1
Potsdamer Havelseengebiet park Germany 49 J3
Pottangi India 95 D2
Pottendorf Austria 49 N8
Potter U.S.A. 178 B3
Potter Valley U.S.A. 182 A2
Potterville U.S.A. 176 A3
Pottsville U.S.A. 177 I5
Potwar reg. Pak. 101 H3
Pouancé France 50 E5
Pouce Coupe Canada 166 F4
Pouch Cove Canada 169 K4
Poughkeepsie U.S.A. 177 L4
Poultney U.S.A. 177 L2
Pouma Cameroon 125 H6
Pound U.S.A. 176 C8
Poupan S. Africa 132 I7
Pourerere N.Z. 152 K8
Pouso Alegre Brazil 207 H9
Pouso Alegre, Serra mts Brazil 206 D2
Pouso Alto Brazil 206 A3
Poutasi Samoa 145 H3
Poŭthĭsăt Cambodia 79 C5
also spelt Pursat
Pouto N.Z. 152 I4
Pouzauges France 50 F6
Povarovo Rus. Fed. 43 S5
Považská Bystrica Slovakia 49 P6
Poved' r. Rus. Fed. 43 P4
Povenets Rus. Fed. 40 E3
Povlen mt. Yugo. 58 A4
Povoação Brazil 207 N6
Póvoa de Varzim Port. 54 C3
Povorino Rus. Fed. 41 G6
Povorotnyy, Mys hd Rus. Fed. 82 D4
Poway U.S.A. 183 G9
Powder r. MT U.S.A. 180 F3
Powder r. OR U.S.A. 180 C3
Powder, South Fork r. U.S.A. 180 F4
Powder River U.S.A. 180 F4
Powell U.S.A. 180 E3
Powell r. U.S.A. 176 B9
Powell, Lake resr U.S.A. 183 N4
Powell Creek watercourse Australia 149 D5
Powell Mountain U.S.A. 182 F3
Powell River Canada 166 E5
Powellsville U.S.A. 177 I9
Powers U.S.A. 172 F5
Powhatan U.S.A. 176 H8
Powhatan Point U.S.A. 176 E6
Powidzkie, Jezioro l. Poland 49 O3
Powo China 86 A1
Poxoréu Brazil 202 A5
Poyan, Sungai r. Sing. 76 [inset]
Poyang China see Boyang
Poyang Hu l. China 87 F2
Poyan Reservoir Sing. 76 [inset]
Poyarkovo Rus. Fed. 82 C2
Poygan, Lake U.S.A. 172 E6
Poynette U.S.A. 172 D7
Poyo, Cerro mt. Spain 55 I7
Poysdorf Austria 49 N7
Pöytyä Fin. 45 M3
Pozantı Turkey 106 C3
Požarevac Srbija Yugo. 58 C4
Poza Rica Mex. 185 F4
Požega Croatia 56 J3
formerly known as Slavonska Požega
Požega Srbija Yugo. 58 B5
Pozharskoye Rus. Fed. 90 D1
Pozhnya Rus. Fed. 43 M5
Pozhva Rus. Fed. 40 K4
Poznań Poland 49 N3
historically known as Posen
Pozo Alcón Spain 55 I7
Pozo Betbeder Arg. 204 D2
Pozoblanco Spain 54 G6
Pozo Colorado Para. 201 F5
Pozo del Tigre Arg. 201 E6
Pozo Hondo Arg. 204 D2
Pozohondo Spain 55 J6
Pozo Nuevo Mex. 184 C2
Pozos, Punta pt Arg. 205 D7
Pozo San Martin Arg. 204 E2
Pozsony Slovakia see Bratislava
Pozuzo Peru 200 B2
Pozzallo Sicilia Italy 57 G12
Pozzuoli Italy 57 G8
historically known as Puteoli
Pra r. Ghana 125 E5
Prabumulih Indon. 76 D3
Prabuty Poland 49 Q2
Prachatice Czech Rep. 49 L6
Prachi r. India 95 E2
Prachin Buri Thai. 79 C5
Prachuap Khiri Khan Thai. 79 B6
Pradairo mt. Spain 54 D1
Praděd mt. Czech Rep. 49 O5
Pradera Col. 198 B4
Prades France 51 I10
Prado Brazil 203 E6
Pradópolis Brazil 206 E8

▶Prague Czech Rep. 49 L5
Capital of the Czech Republic. Also known as Praha.

Praha Czech Rep. see Prague
Prahova r. Romania 58 H4

▶Praia Cape Verde 124 [inset]
Capital of Cape Verde.

Praia a Mare Italy 57 H9
Praia do Bilene Moz. 131 G5
Praia Grande Brazil 206 G11
Praia Rica Brazil 201 G3
Prainha Amazonas Brazil 201 E1
Prainha Pará Brazil 199 H5
Prairie Australia 149 E4
Prairie r. U.S.A. 174 A2
Prairie City U.S.A. 180 C3
Prairie Dog Town Fork r. U.S.A. 179 B5
Prairie du Chien U.S.A. 172 B7
Prairie River Canada 167 K4
Prakhon Chai Thai. 79 C5
Pram r. Austria 49 K7
Pramanta Greece 59 C9
Pran r. Thai. 79 C5
Pran Buri Thai. 79 B5
Prangli i. Estonia 42 G2
Pranhita r. India 94 C2
Prapat Indon. 76 B2
Prasonisi, Akra pt Greece 59 I13
Praszka Poland 49 P4
Prat i. Chile 205 B8
Prata Brazil 206 E6
Prata r. Goiás Brazil 206 A5
Prata r. Minas Gerais Brazil 206 D5
Prata r. Minas Gerais Brazil 207 G4
Pratapgarh India 96 B4
Pratas Islands China see Dongsha Qundao
Prat de Llobregat Spain see El Prat de Llobregat
Prathes Thai country Asia see Thailand
Pratinha Brazil 206 G6
Prato Italy 56 D5
Pratt U.S.A. 178 C4
Prattville U.S.A. 175 C5
Pravara r. India 94 B2
Pravda Bulg. 58 I5
Pravdinsk Rus. Fed. 42 C7
historically known as Friedland
Pravia Spain 54 E1
Praya Indon. 77 G5
Prazaroki Belarus 45 O5
Preah, Prêk r. Cambodia 79 D5
Preăh Vihear Cambodia 79 D5
Prechistoye Smolenskaya Oblast' Rus. Fed. 43 N6
Prechistoye Yaroslavskaya Oblast' Rus. Fed. 43 V3
Precipice National Park Australia 149 F5
Predazzo Italy 56 D2
Predeal Romania 58 G3
Preeceville Canada 167 K5
Pré-en-Pail France 50 F4
Preetz Germany 48 H1
Pregolya r. Rus. Fed. 42 B7
Preiļi Latvia 42 I5
Preissac, Lac l. Canada 173 O2
Prekornica mts Yugo. 58 A6
Prelate Canada 167 I5
Prémery France 51 J5
Premnitz Germany 49 J3
Prenj mts Bos.-Herz. 56 J5
Prentiss U.S.A. 175 B6
Prenzlau Germany 49 K2
Preobrazheniye Rus. Fed. 82 D4
Preparis Island Cocos Is 79 A5
Preparis North Channel Cocos Is 79 A5
Preparis South Channel Cocos Is 79 A5
Přerov Czech Rep. 49 O6
Presa de la Amistad, Parque Natural nature res. Mex. 185 E2
Presanella, Cima mt. Italy 56 C2
Presa San Antonio Mex. 185 E3
Prescott Canada 168 F4
Prescott AR U.S.A. 179 D5
Prescott AZ U.S.A. 183 L7
Prescott Valley U.S.A. 183 L7
Preservation Inlet N.Z. 153 A14
Preševo Srbija Yugo. 58 C6
Presidencia Roca Arg. 204 F2
Presidencia Roque Sáenz Peña Arg. 204 E2
Presidente Bernardes Brazil 206 B9
Presidente de la Plaza Arg. 204 F2
Presidente Dutra Brazil 202 C3
Presidente Eduardo Frei research station Antarctica 222 U2
Presidente Epitácio Brazil 206 A8
Presidente Hermes Brazil 201 E2
Presidente Jânio Quadros Brazil 207 L1
Presidente Juan Perón prov. Arg. see Chaco
Presidente Juscelino Brazil 207 I5
Presidente Olegário Brazil 206 G5
Presidente Prudente Brazil 206 B9
Presidente Venceslau Brazil 206 B8
Presidio U.S.A. 181 F7
Preslav Bulg. see Veliki Preslav
Prešov Slovakia 49 S7
Prespa, Lake Europe 58 C8
also known as Prespansko Ezero or Prespës, Liqeni i
Prespansko Ezero l. Europe see Prespa, Lake

Prespes nat. park Greece 58 C8
Prespës, Liqeni i. Europe see Prespa, Lake
Presque Isle ME U.S.A. 174 G2
Presque Isle MI U.S.A. 173 J5
Presque Isle WI U.S.A. 172 F4
Presque Isle Point U.S.A. 172 F4
Pressbaum Austria 49 N7
Pressburg Slovakia see Bratislava
Prestea Ghana 125 E5
Presteigne U.K. 47 I11
Přeštice Czech Rep. 49 K6
Preston U.K. 47 J10
Preston GA U.S.A. 175 C5
Preston IA U.S.A. 172 C8
Preston ID U.S.A. 180 E4
Preston MD U.S.A. 177 J7
Preston MN U.S.A. 174 A3
Preston, Cape Australia 150 B4
Prestonsburg U.S.A. 176 C8
Prestwick U.K. 46 H8
Preto r. Amazonas Brazil 199 F5
Preto r. Bahia Brazil 202 D4
Preto r. Goiás Brazil 206 C5
Preto r. Minas Gerais Brazil 206 G3
Preto r. Rondônia Brazil 201 E2
Preto r. São Paulo Brazil 206 D7

▶ Pretoria S. Africa 133 M2
Official capital of South Africa.
world [countries]   ▶ ▶ 10–11

Pretoria-Witwatersrand-Vereeniging prov.
S. Africa see Gauteng
Preussisch-Eylau Rus. Fed. see
Bagrationovsk
Preußisch Stargard Poland see
Starogard Gdański
Preveza Greece 59 B10
Prey Vêng Cambodia 79 D6
Priamurskiy Rus. Fed. 82 D2
formerly known as Pokrovka
Priaral'skiye Karakumy, Peski des.
Kazakh. 103 E3
Priargunsk Rus. Fed. 85 H1
formerly known as Tsurukhaytuy
Pribinić Bos.-Herz. 56 J4
Priboj Srbija Yugo. 58 A5
Příbram Czech Rep. 49 L6
Price r. Australia 148 A2
Price Canada 169 G3
Price NC U.S.A. 176 F9
Price UT U.S.A. 183 N2
Price r. U.S.A. 183 N2
Prichaly Rus. Fed. 42 G6
Prichard AL U.S.A. 175 B6
Prichard WV U.S.A. 176 C7
Priego de Córdoba Spain 54 G7
Priekule Latvia 42 C5
Priekulė Lith. 42 C6
Priekuļi Latvia 42 G4
Prienai Lith. 42 E7
Prienai Lith. 42 G7
Prieska S. Africa 132 G6
Prieskapoort pass S. Africa 132 G6
Priest Lake U.S.A. 180 F2
Prieto hill Spain 55 H6
Prievidza Slovakia 49 P7
Prigor'ye Rus. Fed. 43 O8
Prijedor Bos.-Herz. 56 I4
Prijepolje Srbija Yugo. 58 A5
Prikaspiyskaya Nizmennost' lowland
Kazakh./Rus. Fed. see Caspian Lowland
Prikro Côte d'Ivoire 124 E5
Prilep Macedonia 58 C7
Priluki Rus. Fed. 43 U2
Priluki Ukr. see Pryluky
Primavera Bol. 200 D3
Primavera do Leste Brazil 202 A5
Primeira Cruz Brazil 202 D2
Primero de Enero Cuba 186 D2
Primghar U.S.A. 178 D3
Primorsk Leningradskaya Oblast'
Rus. Fed. 43 J1
Primorsk Volgogradskaya Oblast'
Rus. Fed. 41 H6
formerly known as Lugovaya Proleyka
Primorsk Ukr. see Prymors'k
Primorskiy Rus. Fed. 82 C4
formerly known as Ust'-Mongunay
Primorskiy Khrebet mts Rus. Fed. 85 E1
Primorskiy Kray admin. div. Rus. Fed. 82 D3
Primorsko-Akhtarsk Rus. Fed. 41 F7
Primrose r. Canada 166 B2
Primrose Lake Canada 167 I4
Prince Albert Canada 167 J4
Prince Albert S. Africa 132 G10
Prince Albert Mountains Antarctica
223 K1
Prince Albert National Park Canada
167 J4
Prince Albert Peninsula Canada 165 H2
Prince Albert Road S. Africa 132 F9
Prince Albert Sound sea chan. Canada
165 H2
Prince Alfred, Cape Canada 164 G2
Prince Charles Island Canada 165 L3
Prince Charles Mountains Antarctica
223 E2
Prince Edward Island prov. Canada 169 I4

▶ Prince Edward Islands Indian Ocean
219 J9
Part of South Africa.

Prince Edward Point Canada 173 Q7
Prince Frederick U.S.A. 177 I7
Prince Frederick Harbour Australia 150 D2
Prince George Canada 166 F4
Prince Gustaf Adolf Sea Canada 165 I2
Prince Harald Coast Antarctica 223 C2
also known as Prins Harald Kyst
Prince Karl Foreland i. Svalbard see
Prins Karls Forland
Prince of Wales, Cape U.S.A. 164 C3
Prince of Wales Island Australia 149 D1
Prince of Wales Island Canada 165 J2
Prince of Wales Island U.S.A. 166 C4
Prince of Wales Strait Canada 165 H2
Prince Patrick Island Canada 165 H2
Prince Regent r. Australia 150 D2
Prince Regent Inlet sea chan. Canada
165 J2
Prince Regent Nature Reserve Australia
150 D2
Prince Rupert Canada 166 D4
Princess Anne U.S.A. 177 J7
Princess Astrid Coast Antarctica 223 B2
Princess Charlotte Bay Australia 149 D2
Princess Elizabeth Land reg. Antarctica
223 F2
Princess Mary Lake Canada 167 L1
Princess May Range hills Australia 150 D2
Princess Mountains N.Z. 153 B13
Princess Ragnhild Coast Antarctica 223 B2
Princess Royal Island Canada 166 D4
Princeton Canada 166 F5
Princeton CA U.S.A. 182 B2
Princeton IL U.S.A. 174 B3
Princeton IN U.S.A. 174 C4
Princeton KY U.S.A. 174 C4
Princeton MO U.S.A. 174 A3
Princeton NJ U.S.A. 177 K5
Princeton WV U.S.A. 176 D8
Prince William Sound b. U.S.A. 164 E3
Príncipe i. São Tomé and Príncipe 125 G6
Prineville U.S.A. 180 B3
Prinos Greece 58 F7
Prins Harald Kyst coastal area Antarctica
see Prince Harald Coast
Prins Karls Forland i. Svalbard 38 B2
English form Prince Karl Foreland
Prinzapolca Nicaragua 186 C4
Priolo Gargallo Sicilia Italy 57 H11
Prior, Cabo c. Spain 54 C1
Priozernyy Kazakh. see Tugyl
Priozersk Rus. Fed. 43 L1
also spelt Priozyorsk
Priozyorsk Rus. Fed. see Priozersk
Pripet r. Belarus/Ukr. 41 C5
also spelt Pryp"yat' (Ukraine) or Prypyats'
(Belarus)
Pripet Marshes Belarus/Ukr. 41 C6
also known as Palyeskaya Nizina or Poles'ye
Pripolyarnyy Ural mts Rus. Fed. 40 M2
Priponeşti Romania 58 I2
Prirechnyy Rus. Fed. 44 O1
Prisăcani Romania 58 I1
Priseka hill Croatia 56 I3
Pristan' Przheval'sk Kyrg. see
Przheval'sk Pristany
Priština Kosovo, Srbija Yugo. 58 C6
Prithvipur India 96 C4
Pritzwalk Germany 49 J2
Privas France 51 K8
Privlaka Croatia 56 H4
Privokzal'nyy Rus. Fed. 43 Q6
Privolzhsk Rus. Fed. 40 G4
Privolzhskaya Vozvyshennost' hills
Rus. Fed. 41 H6
English form Volga Upland
Privolzh'ye Rus. Fed. 41 I5
Priyutnoye Rus. Fed. 41 G7
Prizren Kosovo, Srbija Yugo. 58 B6
Prizzi Sicilia Italy 57 F11
Prnjavor Bos.-Herz. 56 J4
Probištip Macedonia 58 D6
Probolinggo Indon. 77 F4
Prochowice Poland 49 N4
Proctor MN U.S.A. 172 A4
Proctor VT U.S.A. 177 L2
Proctorville U.S.A. 176 C7
Proddatur India 94 C3
Prokuplje Srbija Yugo. 58 C5
Proletariy Rus. Fed. 43 L4
Proletarsk Rus. Fed. 41 G7
formerly known as Proletarskaya
Proletarskaya Rus. Fed. see Proletarsk
Prome Myanmar see Pyè
Promissão Brazil 201 E8
Promissão, Represa resr Brazil 206 C8
Promontorio del Gargano plat. Italy 56 H7
Pronino Rus. Fed. 40 G4
Pronsk Rus. Fed. 43 U7
Pronya r. Belarus 43 M8
Prophet r. Canada 166 F3
Prophet River Canada 166 F3
formerly known as Minaker
Prophetstown U.S.A. 172 D9
Propriá Brazil 202 E4
Proserpine Australia 149 F4
Proskhava Belarus 42 I8
Proskurov Ukr. see Khmel'nyts'kyy
Prosna r. Poland 49 O3
Prosotsani Greece 58 E7
Prospect NY U.S.A. 177 J2
Prospect OH U.S.A. 176 B5
Prospect OR U.S.A. 180 B4
Prospect PA U.S.A. 176 E5
Prosperidad Phil. 74 C4
Prosser U.S.A. 180 C3
Prostějov Czech Rep. 49 O6
Proston Australia 149 F5
Proszowice Poland 49 R5
Protem S. Africa 132 E11
Proti i. Greece 59 C11
Protva r. Rus. Fed. 43 S6
Provadiya Bulg. 58 I5
Proven Greenland see Kangersuatsiaq
Provence-Alpes-Côte-d'Azur admin. reg.
France 51 M9
Providence U.S.A. see Annapolis

▶ Providence U.S.A. 177 N4
State capital of Rhode Island.

Providence, Cape N.Z. 153 A14
Providence Atoll Seychelles 129 D7
Providence Bay Canada 173 K5
Providence Ecuador 198 C4
Providence, Isla de i. Caribbean Sea
186 C4
Providência, Serra de hills Brazil 201 F2
Providenciales Island Turks and Caicos Is
187 E2

Providencia Col. 198 C3
Provincia Col. 198 C3
Provins France 51 J4
Provo U.S.A. 183 M1
Provost Canada 167 I4
Prozor Bos.-Herz. 56 J5
Prozorovo Rus. Fed. 43 S3
formerly known as Mikhaykovsky
Prrenjas Albania 58 B7
Pru r. Ghana 125 E4
Prubi r. Rus. Fed. 40 J3
Prudentópolis Brazil 203 B8
Prudhoe Bay U.S.A. 164 E2
Prudhoe Island Australia 149 F4
Prudki Rus. Fed. 43 N7
Prudnik Poland 49 O5
Prudzinki Belarus 43 J6
Prüm Germany 48 D5
Prundeni Romania 58 F4
Prundu Romania 58 H4
Prundu Bârgăului Romania 58 F1
formerly spelt Prundu Birgăului
Prundu Birgăului Romania see
Prundu Bârgăului
Prusa Turkey see Bursa
Prushkov Poland see Pruszków
Pruszcz Gdański Poland 49 P1
Pruszków Poland 49 R3
historically known as Prushkov
Prut r. Europe 58 J3
Pruzhany Belarus 42 F9
Prvić i. Croatia 56 H4
Prydz Bay Antarctica 223 F2
Pryelbrussky Natsional'nyy Park nat. park
Rus. Fed. 41 G8
Pryluky Ukr. 41 E6
also spelt Priluki
Prymors'k Ukr. 41 F7
also spelt Primorsk
Prymors'ke Ukr. see Sartana
Prymors'ke Ukr. 58 K3
Pryor U.S.A. 179 C4
Pryp"yat' r. Ukr. see Pripet
Prypyats' r. Belarus 41 C5 see Pripet
Przasnysz Poland 49 R2
Przedbórz Poland 49 Q4
Przeworsk Poland 49 T5
Przheval'sk Kyrg. see Karakol
Przheval'skoye Rus. Fed. 43 M6
formerly known as Sloboda
Przheval'sk Pristany Kyrg. 103 I4
also known as Pristan' Przheval'sk
Przysucha Poland 49 R4
Psachna Greece 59 E10
Psakhná Greece see Psachna
Psalidis, Akra pt Greece 59 F12
Psara Greece 59 G10
Psara i. Greece 59 F9
Psathoura i. Greece 59 F9
Psebay Rus. Fed. 41 G7
Pserimos i. Greece 59 I12
Pskent Uzbek. 103 G4
Pskov Rus. Fed. 43 J4
Pskov, Lake Estonia/Rus. Fed. 42 I3
also known as Pihkva järv
or Pskovskoye Ozero
Pskova r. Rus. Fed. 43 J4
Pskov Oblast admin. div. Rus. Fed. see
Pskovskaya Oblast'
Pskovskaya Oblast' admin. div.
Rus. Fed. 43 K4
English form Pskov Oblast
Pskovskoye Ozero l. Estonia/Rus. Fed. see
Pskov, Lake
Psunj mts Croatia 56 J3
Ptan' r. Rus. Fed. 43 T8
Ptich' Belarus see Ptsich
Ptolemaïda Greece 58 C8
Ptolemais Israel see 'Akko
Ptsich r. Belarus 42 J9
also spelt Ptich'
Ptsich r. Belarus 42 J9
Ptuj Slovenia 56 H2
also known as Pettau; historically
known as Poetovio
Pu r. China 85 E5
Pu r. Indon. 76 C3
Puaka hill Sing. 76 [inset]
Pu'an China 86 C3
also known as Panshui
Pu'an China see Jiange
Pucacuro Peru 198 C5
Pucacuro r. Peru 198 C5
Pucalá Peru 198 B6
Pucallpa Peru 198 C6
Pucará Bol. 201 E4
Pucara Peru 200 C3
Pucarani Bol. 200 C4
Pucarevo Bos.-Herz. see Novi Travnik
Puca Urco Peru 198 D5
Pucheng Fujian China 87 F3
also known as Nanpu
Pucheng Shaanxi China 87 D1
Puchezh Rus. Fed. 40 G4
Puch'ŏn S. Korea 83 B5
Puchŏ S. Korea 83 B5
Pucioasa Romania 58 G3
Pucka, Zatoka b. Poland 49 P1
Puckford, Mount hill Australia 151 B5
Puçol Spain 55 K5
also spelt Puzol
Pucón Chile 204 C5
Pudai watercourse Afgh. see Dor
Pūdanū Iran 100 C3
Pudasjärvi Fin. 44 N2
Pudimoe S. Africa 133 I4
Puding China 86 C3
Pudozh Rus. Fed. 40 F3
Puebla Baja California Norte Mex. 183 I9
Puebla Puebla Mex. 185 F5
long from Puebla de Zaragoza
Puebla state Mex. 185 F5
Puebla de Don Fadrique Spain 55 I7
Puebla de Obando Spain 54 E5
Puebla de Zaragoza Mex. see Puebla
Pueblo U.S.A. 181 F5
Pueblo Hundido Chile 204 C2
Pueblo Viejo Col. 199 E4
Pueblo Viejo, Laguna de lag. Mex. 185 F4
Pueblo Yaqui Mex. 184 C3
Puech de Rouet hill France 51 I8
Puelches Arg. 204 D5
Puelén Arg. 204 D5
Puenteareas Spain see Ponteareas
Puente de Ixtla Mex. 185 F5
Puente del Inca Arg. 204 C4
Puente la Reina Spain 55 J2
also spelt Gares
Puentes de García Rodríguez Spain see
As Pontes de García Rodríguez
Puente Torres Venez. 198 D2
Pu'er China 86 B4
also known as Ning'er
Puerco watercourse AZ U.S.A. 183 N7
Puerco watercourse NM U.S.A. 181 G5
Puerto Acosta Bol. 200 C3
Puerto Adela Para. 201 F4
Puerto Aisén Chile 205 B7
Puerto Alegre Bol. 201 E3
Puerto Alejandría Bol. 200 D2
Puerto Alfonso Col. 198 D5
Puerto America Peru 198 B6

Providencia Rus. Fed. 39 S3
Providential Channel Australia 149 D2
Provincetown U.S.A. 177 O3

Puerto Ángel Mex. 185 F6
Puerto Antequera Para. 201 F6
Puerto Arista Mex. 185 G6
Puerto Armuelles Panama 186 C5
Puerto Asís Col. 198 B4
Puerto Ayacucho Venez. 199 E3
Puerto Bajo Pisagua Chile 205 B7
Puerto Berrío Col. 198 C3
Puerto Boyaca Col. 198 C3
Puerto Cabello Venez. 199 E2
Puerto Cabezas Nicaragua 186 C4
Puerto Cabo Gracias á Dios Nicaragua
186 D4
Puerto Carreño Col. 199 E3
Puerto Casado Para. 201 F5
Puerto Cavinas Bol. 200 D3
Puerto Cerpera Peru 198 C5
Puerto Ceticayo Peru 200 C2
Puerto Chacabuco Chile 205 B7
Puerto Chicama Peru 200 A1
Puerto Cisnes Chile 205 B7
Puerto Coig Arg. 205 C8
Puerto Córdoba Col. 198 D5
Puerto Cortés Costa Rica 186 C5
Puerto Cortés Hond. 186 B3
Puerto Cortés Mex. 184 C3
Puerto Cuarebo Venez. 198 D2
Puerto Cuemaní Col. 198 C4
Puerto de Cabras Canary Is see
Puerto del Rosario
Puerto de Cayo Ecuador 198 A5
Puerto Definitivo Peru 200 C3
Puerto de Hierro Venez. 187 H5
Puerto de los Ángeles, Parque Natural
nature res. Mex. 184 D4
Puerto del Rosario Canary Is 122 B3
formerly known as Puerto de Cabras
Puerto del Son Spain see Porto do Son
Puerto de Morelos Mex. 185 I4
Puerto de Nutrias Venez. 198 D3
Puerto de Pollensa Spain see
Port de Pollença
Puerto Escondido Mex. 185 F6
Puerto Estrella Col. 198 D1
Puerto Flamenco Chile 204 C2
Puerto Francisco de Orellana
Ecuador 198 B5
also known as El Coca; short form
Francisco de Orellana
Puerto Génova Bol. 200 D3
Puerto Grether Bol. 201 E4
Puerto Guaraní Para. 201 F5
Puerto Harberton Arg. 205 D9
Puerto Heath Bol. 200 C3
Puerto Huitoto Col. 198 C4
Puerto Inca Peru 200 B2
Puerto Ingeniero Ibáñez Chile 205 B7
Puerto Inírida Col. 199 E4
Puerto Irigoyen Arg. 201 E5
Puerto Isabel Bol. 201 F4
Puerto Jesús Costa Rica 186 B5
Puerto Juárez Mex. 185 I4
Puerto La Paz Arg. 201 E5
Puerto Leguizamo Col. 198 C5
Puerto Libertad Mex. 184 B2
Puertollano Spain 54 G6
Puerto Lobos Arg. 205 D6
Puerto López Col. 198 D2
Puerto López Col. 198 C3
Puerto Lumbreras Spain 55 J7
Puerto Madero Mex. 185 G6
Puerto Madryn Arg. 205 D6
Puerto Magdalena Mex. 184 B3
Puerto Maldonado Peru 200 C3
Puerto Mamoré Bol. 200 D4
Puerto Mancha Cuba 186 D2
Puerto Máncora Peru 198 A6
Puerto María Auxiliadora Para. 201 F5
Puerto Marquez Bol. 200 D3
Puerto Melinka Chile 205 B7
Puerto Mercedes Col. 198 C4
Puerto México Mex. see Coatzacoalcos
Puerto Mihanovich Para. 201 F5
Puerto Miranda Venez. 199 E3
Puerto Montt Chile 205 B6
Puerto Morazán Nicaragua 186 B4
Puerto Natáles Chile 205 B8
Puerto Nuevo Col. 198 D3
Puerto Olaya Col. 187 E6
Puerto Ordaz Venez. 199 F2
Puerto Ospina Col. 198 C4
Puerto Padre Cuba 186 D2
Puerto Páez Venez. 199 E3
Puerto Pando Bol. 200 D3
Puerto Pardo Peru 200 B5
Puerto Pariamana Peru 200 C3
Puerto Peñasco Mex. 184 B2
Puerto Pinasco Para. 201 F5
Puerto Pirámides Arg. 205 D6
Puerto Piritu Venez. 199 E2
Puerto Pizarro Col. 198 C5
Puerto Portillo Peru 200 B2
Puerto Prado Peru 200 B2
Puerto Presidente Stroessner Para. see
Ciudad del Este
Puerto Princesa Phil. 74 A4
Puerto Quepos Costa Rica 186 B5
Puerto Quetzal Guat. 185 H6
Puerto Real Spain 54 E8
Puerto Rico Arg. 204 G2
Puerto Rico Bol. 200 D2

▶ Puerto Rico terr. West Indies 187 G3
United States Commonwealth.
oceania [countries] ▶ ▶ 138–139

▶ Puerto Rico Trench sea feature
Caribbean Sea 216 J4
Deepest trench in the Atlantic Ocean.

Puerto Saavedra Chile 204 B5
Puerto Salgar Col. 198 C3
Puerto Sama Cuba see Samá
Puerto San Agustín Peru 198 D5
Puerto San Carlos Chile 205 B7
Puerto Sandino Nicaragua 186 B4
formerly known as Puerto Somoza
Puerto San José Guat. 185 H6
Puerto Santa Cruz Arg. 205 C8
Puerto Sastre Para. 201 F5
Puerto Saucedo Bol. 201 E3
Puerto Serrano Spain 54 F8
Puerto Siles Bol. 200 D3
Puerto Socorro Peru 198 D5
Puerto Somoza Nicaragua see
Puerto Sandino
Puerto Suárez Bol. 201 F4
Puerto Supe Peru 200 A3
Puerto Tahuantisuyo Peru 200 C2
Puerto Tejado Col. 198 B4
Puerto Tunigrama Peru 198 B5
Puerto Vallarta Mex. 184 D4
Puerto Victoria Peru 200 B2
Puerto Villazon Bol. 201 E3
Puerto Visser Arg. 205 D7
Puerto Wilches Col. 198 C3
Puerto Yartou Chile 205 C9
Puesto Arturo Peru 198 C5
Puga Brazil 201 F4
Pugachev Rus. Fed. 102 B1
Pugachevo Rus. Fed. 40 J4
Pugal India 96 B3

Puga Puga, Ilha i. Moz. 131 H2
Puge China 86 B3
also known as Piji
Puger Indon. 77 F5
Pugwash Canada 169 I4
Puha N.Z. 152 L6
Pühäl-e Khamir, Kūh-e mts Iran 100 C5
Puhiwaero c. N.Z. see South West Cape
Puhja Estonia 42 H3
Pui Romania 58 D3
Puieşti Romania 58 I1
Puig de Comanegra mt. Spain 55 N2
Puig des Galatzó mt. Spain 55 N5
Puigmal mt. France/Spain 55 N2
Pui O Wan b. Hong Kong China 87 [inset]
Puiseaux France 51 I4
Puits 29 well Chad 120 C6
Puits 30 well Chad 120 C6
Pujada Bay Phil. 74 C5
Puji China see Wugong
Pujiang China 87 F2
also known as Puyang
Pukaki, Lake N.Z. 153 E12
Puk'an-san National Park S. Korea 83 B5
also known as Danger Islands
Pukapuka atoll Cook Is 221 G6
Pukaskwa r. Canada 172 H2
Pukaskwa National Park Canada 168 C3
Pukatawagan Canada 167 K4
Pukchin N. Korea 83 B4
Pukch'ŏng N. Korea 83 C4
Pukë Albania 58 A6
Pukeamaru N.Z. 152 L5
Pukekohe N.Z. 152 I5
Pukekura N.Z. 152 H2
Pukeokahu N.Z. 152 J7
Pukekau N.Z. 152 I9
Pukerau N.Z. 153 D14
Pukerua Bay N.Z. 152 I9
Puketeraki Range mts N.Z. 153 G11
Puketitiri N.Z. 152 K7
Puketoi Range hills N.Z. 152 K8
Puketutu N.Z. 152 J6
Pukeuri Junction N.Z. 153 F13
Pukhnovo Rus. Fed. 43 M6
Pukkila Fin. 42 G1
Puksoozero Rus. Fed. 40 G3
Puksubaek-san mt. N. Korea 83 B4
Pula China see Nyingchi
Pula Croatia 56 F4
formerly spelt Pola
Pula Sardegna Italy 57 B9
Pulacayo Bol. 200 D5
Pulandian China 85 I4
formerly known as Xinjin
Pulandian Wan b. China 85 I4
Pulangi r. Phil. 74 C5
Pulangpisau Indon. 77 F3
Pular, Cerro mt. Chile 200 C6
Pulasi i. Indon. 75 B4
Pulaski NY U.S.A. 177 I2
Pulaski TN U.S.A. 174 C5
Pulaski VA U.S.A. 176 E8
Pulaski WI U.S.A. 172 E6
Pulau r. Indon. 73 I8
Pulau Pinang state Malaysia see Pinang
Pulawy Poland 49 S4
Pulheim Germany 48 D4
Pulicat India 94 D3
Pulicat Lake inlet India 94 D3
Pulivendla India 94 C3
Pulkau r. Austria 49 N7
Pulkkila Fin. 44 N2
Pullman U.S.A. 180 C3
Pulo Anna i. Palau 73 H6
Pulog, Mount Phil. 74 B2
Pulozero Rus. Fed. 40 E1
Púlpito, Punta pt Mex. 184 C3
Pulsano Italy 57 J8
Pultusk Poland 49 R3
Pulu China 89 C5
Pülümür Turkey 107 D3
Pulutan Indon. 75 C1
Pulyatin Rus. Fed. 90 C3
Puma Tanz. 129 B6
Puma Yumco l. China 89 E6
also spelt Pomo Tso
Pumiao China see Yongning
Pumpkin Creek r. U.S.A. 180 F3
Puná, Isla i. Ecuador 198 A5
Puna de Atacama plat. Arg. 204 D3
Punakaiki N.Z. 153 F10
Punakha Bhutan 97 F4
Punaluu U.S.A. 181 [inset] Z2
Punata Bol. 200 D4
Punch Pak. 101 H3
Punchaw Canada 166 F4
Punda Maria S. Africa 131 F4
Pundri India 96 C3
Pune India 94 B2
formerly spelt Poona
Punganuru India 94 C3
Punggol Sing. 76 [inset]
Punggol, Sungai r. Sing. 76 [inset]
P'ungsan N. Korea 83 C4
Púnguè r. Moz. 131 G3
Punia Dem. Rep. Congo 126 E5
Punitaqui Chile 204 C3
Punjab state India 96 B3
Punjab prov. Pak. 101 G4
Punkaharju Fin. 45 O3
Punmah Glacier China/Jammu and Kashmir
89 B5
Puno Peru 200 C3
Puno dept Peru 200 C3
Punpun r. India 97 E4
Punta, Cerro de mt. Puerto Rico 187 G3
Punta Alta Arg. 204 E5
Punta Arenas Chile 205 C9
formerly known as Magallanes
Punta Balestrieri mt. Sardegna Italy 57 B8
Punta de Bombón Peru 200 C4
Punta de Díaz Chile 204 C2
Punta Delgada Arg. 205 E6
Punta de los Llanos Arg. 204 D3
Punta Gorda Belize 185 H5
Punta Gorda Nicaragua 186 C5
Punta Gorda U.S.A. 175 D7
Punta Negra, Salar salt flat Chile 200 C6
Punta Norte Arg. 205 E6
Punta Prieta Mex. 184 B2
Puntarenas Costa Rica 186 B5
Puntas Negras, Cerro mt. Chile 200 C5
Punta Umbría Spain 54 E7
Puntón de Guara mt. Spain 55 K2
Punxsutawney U.S.A. 176 G5
Puokio Fin. 44 N2
Puolanka Fin. 44 N2
Puquio Peru 200 B3
Puquios Chile 200 C4
Pur r. Rus. Fed. 39 H3
Puracé, Parque Nacional nat. park Col.
198 B4
Puranpur India 96 D3
Purari r. P.N.G. 73 J8
Purbalingga Indon. 77 E4
Purcell U.S.A. 179 C5
Purcell Mountains Canada 167 G5
Purcellville U.S.A. 176 H6
Pureba Conservation Park nature res.
Australia 146 B2
Purekkari neem pt Estonia 42 G2
Purén Chile 204 B5
Pureora Forest Park nature res. N.Z.
152 J6
Purgatoire r. U.S.A. 178 B4
Purgstall an der Erlauf Austria 49 M7

▶ Purus r. Peru 199 F5
3rd longest river in South America.
southamerica [landscapes] ▶ ▶ 190–191

Puruvesi l. Fin. 45 O3
Purvis U.S.A. 175 B6
Pürvomay Bulg. 58 G6
Purwa India 96 D3
Purwakarta Indon. 77 D4
Purwareja Indon. 77 E4
Purwodadi Indon. 77 E4
Purwokerto Indon. 77 E4
Puryŏng N. Korea 82 C4
Pus r. India 94 C2
Puša Latvia 42 I5
Pusa r. Spain 54 G5
Pusad India 94 C2
Pusan S. Korea 83 C6
also spelt Busan or Fusan
Pusan Point Phil. 74 C5
Pusatdamai Indon. 77 E3
Pusatlı Dağı mt. Turkey 108 E1
Pushchino Rus. Fed. 43 S7
Pushemskiy Rus. Fed. 40 H3
Pushkar India 96 B4
Pushkin Rus. Fed. 43 L2
Pushkino Azer. see Bilāsuvar
Pushkino Rus. Fed. 102 A2
Pushkinskaya, Gora mt. Rus. Fed. 82 F3
Pushkinskiye Gory Rus. Fed. 43 J4
Pusht-i Āsmān spring Iran 100 D3
Pusht-i-Rud reg. Afgh. 101 E4
Püspökladány Hungary 49 S8
Püssi Estonia 42 I2
Pusti Lisac mt. Yugo. 56 K6
Pusula Fin. 42 E1
Puszcza Augustowska for. Poland 49 U2
Puszcza Natecka for. Poland 49 M3
Pusztaszeri park Hungary 49 R9
Putahow Lake Canada 167 K3
Putao Myanmar 78 B2
formerly known as Fort Hertz
Putaruru N.Z. 152 J6
Putbus Germany 49 K1
Puteoli Italy see Pozzuoli
Puteran i. Indon. 77 F4
Putere N.Z. 152 L6
Puteyets Rus. Fed. 40 K2
Puthein Myanmar see Bassein
Putian China 87 F3
Putignano Italy 56 J8
Putilovo Rus. Fed. 40 H4
Putimets Rus. Fed. 43 R9
Putina Peru 200 C3
Putivl' Ukr. 41 E6
Puula i. Fin. 45 N3
Puumala Fin. 45 O3
Puuwai U.S.A. 181 [inset] Y1
Puvurnitug Canada 165 L3
Puxian China 85 F4
Puyallup U.S.A. 180 B3
Puyang China see Pujiang
Puy de Dôme mt. France 51 I7
Puy de Montoncel mt. France 51 J7
Puy de Sancy mt. France 51 I7
Puyehue, Parque Nacional nat. park Chile
204 C6
Puyel Arg. 205 C6
Puy Gris mt. France 51 M7
Puylaurens France 51 I9
Puyo Ecuador 198 B5
Puysegur Point N.Z. 153 A14
Puzol Spain see Puçol
Pwani admin. reg. Tanz. 129 C6
Pweto Dem. Rep. Congo 127 F7
Pwllheli U.K. 47 H11
Pyalitsa Rus. Fed. 40 F2
Pyal'ma Rus. Fed. 40 F3
Pyamalaw r. Myanmar 78 A5
Pyandzh r. Afgh./Tajik. 101 G2
also known as Ab-i-Panja; also spelt Panj
Pyandzh Tajik. see Dusti
Pyandzh Tajik. see Panj
Pyaozero, Ozero l. Rus. Fed. 44 O2
Pyaozerskiy Rus. Fed. 44 O2
Pyapon Myanmar 78 A4
Pyasina r. Rus. Fed. 39 I2
Pyasino, Ozero l. Rus. Fed. 39 I3
Pyasinskiy Zaliv b. Rus. Fed. 39 I2
Pyasüchnik r. Bulg. 58 F6
Pyatigorsk Rus. Fed. 41 G8
Pyatikhatki Ukr. see P"yatykhatky
Pyatimar Kazakh. see Pyatimarskoye
Pyatimarskoye Kazakh. 102 B2
formerly known as Pyatimarskoye
P"yatykhat'ye Rus. Fed. 43 R7
P"yatykhatky Ukr. 41 E6
also spelt Pyatikhatki
Pyatovskiy Rus. Fed. 43 R7
Pyawbwe Myanmar 78 B3
Pyazhelka Rus. Fed. 43 Q1
Pyazhozero, Ozero l. Rus. Fed. 43 Q1
Pyè Myanmar 78 A4
also known as Pyin; formerly
known as Prome
Pyeramyshski Belarus 42 G7
Pyeski Belarus 42 F8
Pyes Pa N.Z. 152 K5
Pyetrykaw Belarus 43 J9
also spelt Petrikov
Pygmalion Point India 95 G5

Pyhäjärvi l. Fin. 44 N3
Pyhäjärvi l. Fin. 44 N3
Pyhäjärvi l. Fin. 44 O3
Pyhäjärvi l. Fin. 45 M3
Pyhäjoki Fin. 44 N2
Pyhäjoki r. Fin. 44 N2
Pyhältö Fin. 42 I1
Pyhäntä Fin. 44 N2
Pyhäranta Fin. 45 M3
Pyhäselmi Fin. 44 N3
Pyhäselkä Fin. 44 O3
Pyhäselkä l. Fin. 44 O3
Pyhätunturin kansallispuisto nat. park Fin. 44 N2
Pyhtää Fin. 45 N3
Pyin Myanmar see Pyè
Pyingaing Myanmar 78 A3
Pyinmana Myanmar 78 B4
Pyli Greece 59 I12 also spelt Pili
Pyl'karamo Rus. Fed. 39 I3
Pylos Greece 59 C12 also spelt Pílos
Pymatuning Reservoir U.S.A. 176 E4
Pyŏksŏng N. Korea 83 B5
Pyŏktong N. Korea 83 B4
P'yŏnggang N. Korea 83 B5
P'yŏngsong N. Korea 83 B5
P'yŏngt'aek S. Korea 83 B5

▶P'yŏngyang N. Korea 83 B5
Capital of North Korea.

Pyŏnsan Bando National Park S. Korea 83 B6
Pyramid Lake U.S.A. 182 E1
Pyramid Lake Indian Reservation res. U.S.A. 182 E1
Pyramid Range mts U.S.A. 182 E2
Pyrenees mts Europe 55 N2 also spelt Pyrénées or Pirineos
Pyrénées mts Europe see Pyrenees
Pyrénées Occidentales, Parc National des nat. park France/Spain 55 K2
Pyrgetos Greece 59 D9 also spelt Pirgetós
Pyrgi Greece 59 G10 also known as Piryíon
Pyrgos Greece 59 C11 also spelt Pirgos
Pyrton, Mount hill Australia 150 B4
Pyryatyn Ukr. 41 E6 also spelt Piryatin
Pyrzyce Poland 49 L2
Pyshchug Rus. Fed. 40 H4
Pyshna Belarus 43 J7
Pyszna r. Poland 49 P4
Pytalovo Rus. Fed. 42 I4
Pythonga, Lac l. Canada 173 Q4
Pyu Myanmar 78 B4
Pyxaria mt. Greece 59 E10 also spelt Pixariá

↓ Q

Qā', Wādī al watercourse Saudi Arabia 104 B2
Qaa Lebanon 109 H3 formerly spelt El Kaa
Qaanaaq Greenland see Thule
Qabanbay Kazakh. see Kabanbay
Qabātiya West Bank 108 G5
Qābil Oman 105 F3
Qabka China see Xaitongmoin
Qabnag China 89 F6
Qabqa China see Gonghe
Qabr Bandar tourist site Iraq 107 E5
Qabr Hūd Oman 105 E4
Qabyrgha r. Kazakh. see Kabyrga
Qacentina Alg. see Constantine
Qacha's Nek Lesotho 133 M7
Qadā' Chāy watercourse Iraq 109 P3
Qadamgāh Iran 100 D2
Qādes Afgh. 101 E3
Qadīmah Saudi Arabia 104 B3
Qādir Karam Iraq 107 F4
Qādisīyah, Buḩayrat al resr Iraq 109 N3
Qādisīyah, Sadd dam Iraq 107 E4 English form Qadisiyah Dam
Qadisiyah Dam Iraq see Qādisīyah, Sadd
Qādub Yemen 105 F5
Qa'emabad Iran 101 E4
Qā'emiyeh Iran 100 B4
Qagan China 85 H1
Qagan Ders China 85 E3
Qagan Nur Nei Mongol China 85 F4
Qagan Nur Nei Mongol China 85 G3 also known as Xulun Hobot Qagan Qi or Zhengxiangbai Qi
Qagan Nur Nei Mongol China 85 G3
Qagan Nur Qinghai China 84 C4
Qagan Nur l. China 85 J2
Qagan Nur resr China 85 G3
Qagan Teg China 85 G3
Qagan Tohoi China 84 B5
Qagan Us China see Dulan
Qagan Us He r. China 84 C4
Qagca China 86 A1 formerly known as Cacagoin
Qagchêng China see Xiangcheng
Qahar Youyi Houqi China see Bayan Qagan
Qahar Youyi Qianqi China see Togrog Ul
Qahar Youyi Zhongqi China see Hobor
Qā' Ḩazawzā' depr. Saudi Arabia 107 D5
Qahd, Wādī watercourse Saudi Arabia 104 C2
Qahr, Jibāl al hills Saudi Arabia 104 D4
Qahremānshahr Iran see Kermānshāh
Qaḩṭān reg. Saudi Arabia 104 C3
Qaidam He r. China 84 B4
Qaidam Pendi basin China 84 B4 English form Tsaidam Basin
Qaidar China see Cêtar
Qainaqangma China 89 E5
Qaisar Afgh. 101 F3
Qaisar r. Afgh. 101 F2
Qaisar, Koh-i- mt. Afgh. 101 F3
Qalabotjha S. Africa 133 M4
Qalā Diza Iraq 107 F3
Qala'en Nahl Sudan 121 G6
Qala-i-Fateh Afgh. 101 E4
Qala-i-Kang Afgh. 101 E4
Qal'aikhum Tajik. 101 G2 also spelt Kalaikhum; formerly spelt Kalai-Khumb
Qalamat Abū Shafrah Saudi Arabia 105 F3
Qalamat Al Juḩaysh oasis Saudi Arabia 105 E3
Qalamat ar Rakabah oasis Saudi Arabia 105 F3
Qalamat Fāris oasis Saudi Arabia 105 E4
Qalamat Nadqān well Saudi Arabia 105 E3
Qalamat Shutfah well Saudi Arabia 105 E3
Qalansīyah Yemen 105 F5
Qala Shinia Takht Afgh. 101 F3
Qalāt Afgh. 101 F3
Qal'at al Azlam Saudi Arabia 104 A2
Qal'at al Ḩişn tourist site Syria 109 H3
Qal'at al Marqab tourist site Syria 108 G2
Qal'at al Mu'aẓẓam Saudi Arabia 104 B2
Qal'at Bīshah Saudi Arabia 104 C3
Qal'at Muqaybirah, Jabal mt. Syria 109 J2
Qal'at Şāliḩ Iraq 107 F5
Qala Vali Afgh. 101 E3
Qalbī Zhotasy mts Kazakh. see Kalbinskiy Khrebet
Qal'eh Iran 100 C2
Qal'eh Dāgh mt. Iran 100 A2
Qal'eh Tirpul Afgh. 101 E3
Qal 'eh-ye Bost Afgh. 101 F4
Qal 'eh-ye Now Afgh. 101 E3
Qal'eh-ye Shūrak well Iran 100 D3
Qalhāt Oman 105 G3
Qalīb Bāqūr well Iraq 107 F5
Qalqīlya West Bank 108 F5
Qalqutan Kazakh. see Koluton
Qalti el Adusa well Sudan 121 E5
Qalyūb Egypt 121 F2
Qalyūbīya governorate Egypt 108 C7
Qamalung China 86 A1
Qamanirjuaq Lake Canada 167 M2 also known as Kaminuriak Lake
Qamanittuaq Canada see Baker Lake
Qamar, Ghubbat al b. Yemen 105 F4 English form Qamar Bay
Qamar, Jabal al mts Oman 105 F4
Qamar Bay Yemen see Qamar, Ghubbat al
Qamashi Uzbek. see Kamashi
Qamdo China 86 A2 also spelt Chamdo
Qam Hadīl Saudi Arabia 104 C4
Qamīnis Libya 120 C2
Qamruddin Karez Pak. 101 G4
Qamşar Iran 100 B3
Qamystybas Kazakh. see Kamyshlybash
Qanawt Oman 105 F4
Qandahar Afgh. see Kandahār
Qandala Somalia 128 F2
Qandaranbashi mt. Iran 100 A2
Qandyaghash Kazakh. see Kandyagash
Qangzê China 89 B6
Qanţara, Gebel hill Egypt 108 B7
Qapal Kazakh. see Kapal
Qapan Iran 100 C2
Qapqal China 88 C3
Qapshagay Kazakh. see Kapchagay
Qapshagay Bögeni resr Kazakh. see Kapchagayskoye Vodokhranilishche
Qaq Köli salt l. Kazakh. see Kak, Ozero
Qaqortoq Greenland 165 O3 also known as Julianehåb
Qara Egypt 106 A5
Qarā', Jabal al mts Oman 105 F4
Qara Āghach r. Iran see Mand, Rūd-e
Qara Anjīr Iraq 109 P2
Qaraaoun Lebanon 108 G4
Qarabas Kazakh. see Karabas
Qarabulaq Kazakh. see Karabulak
Qarabutaq Kazakh. see Karabutak
Qaraçala Azer. 100 B2
Qarachōq, Jabal mts Iraq 107 E4
Qara Ertis r. China/Kazakh. see Ertix He
Qaraghandy Kazakh. see Karaganda
Qaraghandy Oblysy admin. div. Kazakh. see Karagandinskaya Oblast'
Qaraghayly Kazakh. see Karagayly
Qārah Saudi Arabia 107 E5
Qārah, Jabal al hill Saudi Arabia 104 D4
Qarah Bāgh Ghaznī Afgh. 101 G3
Qarah Bāgh Kābul Afgh. 101 G3
Qarak China 88 B4
Qaraköl Kazakh. see Karakol'
Qaranqu r. Iran 100 A2
Qaraoy Kazakh. see Karaoy
Qara Özek Uzbek. see Karauzyak
Qaraqalpaqstan Respublikasy aut. rep. Uzbek. see Karakalpakistan, Respublika
Qara Qōsh Iraq 109 O1
Qaraqoyyn Köli salt l. Kazakh. see Karakoyyn, Ozero
Qaraqozha Kazakh. see Karaguzhikha
Qaraqum des. Kazakh. see Karakum Desert
Qaraqum des. Turkm. see Karakum Desert
Qarasū Kazakh. see Karasu
Qara Şū Chāy r. Syria/Turkey see Karasu
Qara Tarai mt. Afgh. 101 F3
Qarataū Kazakh. see Karatau
Qarataū Zhotasy mts Kazakh. see Karatau, Khrebet
Qaratöbe Kazakh. see Karatobe
Qaratoghay Kazakh. see Karatogay
Qaratomar Bögeni resr Kazakh. see Karatomarskoye Vodokhranilishche
Qaraton Kazakh. see Karaton
Qaraūyl Kazakh. see Karaul
Qarazhal Kazakh. see Karazhal
Qardho Somalia 128 F2
Qardud Sudan 126 F2
Qareh Chāy r. Iran 100 B3
Qareh Dāgh mts Iran 100 A2
Qareh Qāch, Kūh-e mts Iran 100 C3
Qareh Sū r. Iran 100 A2
Qāret Gahannam hill Egypt 108 B8
Qarhan China 84 B4
Qarkilik China see Ruoqiang
Qarnayt, Jabal hill Saudi Arabia 104 C3
Qarnein i. U.A.E. 105 F2
Qarn el Kabsh, Gebel mt. Egypt 121 G2
Qarokŭl l. Tajik. 101 H2 also known as Karakul', Ozero
Qarqan China see Qiemo
Qarqan He r. China 88 D4
Qarqaraly Kazakh. see Karkaralinsk
Qarqi Xinjiang China 88 C3
Qarqi Xinjiang China 88 D3
Qārqi Iran 102 C5
Qarqīn Afgh. 101 F2
Qarrit, Qafa e pass Albania 58 B8
Qarsaqbay Kazakh. see Karsakpay
Qarshi Uzbek. see Karshi
Qarshi Chŭli plain Uzbek. see Karshinskaya Step'
Qartaba Lebanon 108 G3
Qārūh, Jazīrat i. Kuwait 107 G5
Qārūn Egypt 108 B8
Qaryat al Ulyā Saudi Arabia 105 D2
Qaşab, Wādī al watercourse Iraq 109 O2
Qasamī Iran 100 D3
Qasa Murg mts Afgh. 101 E3
Qasba India 97 E4
Qaşbah, Ras al pt Saudi Arabia 108 F9
Qāsemābād Khorāsan Iran 100 D3
Qāsemābād Khorāsan Iran 101 D2
Qashqadaryo r. Uzbek. see Kashkadar'ya
Qashqadaryo Wiloyati admin. div. Uzbek. see Kashkadar'inskaya Oblast'
Qash Qai reg. Iran 100 B4
Qashqantengiz Kazakh. see Kashkanteniz
Qasigiannguit Greenland 165 N3 also known as Christianshåb
Qasīm reg. Saudi Arabia 104 C2
Qaskelen Kazakh. see Kaskelen
Qasq China 85 F3 also known as Tumd Zuoqi
Qaşr ad Dayr, Jabal mt. Jordan 108 G7
Qaşr al Azraq Jordan 109 H6
Qaşr al Ḩayr tourist site Syria 109 I3
Qaşr al Khubbāz Iraq 107 E4
Qaşr 'Amij Iraq 109 M4
Qaşr 'Amrah tourist site Jordan 109 H6
Qaşr aş Şabīyah Kuwait 107 G5
Qaşr Burqu' tourist site Jordan 109 I5
Qaşr-e Qand Iran 101 E5
Qaşr-e Shīrīn Iran 107 F4
Qaşr Farafra Egypt 121 E3
Qaşr Ḩimām Saudi Arabia 105 D3
Qaşr Larocu Libya 120 B3
Qaşr Shaqrah tourist site Iraq 107 F5
Qassimiut Greenland 165 O3
Qa'tabah Yemen 104 D5
Qatanā Syria 108 H4
▶Qatar country Asia 105 E2
asia [countries] ▶▶ 64–67
Qatlish Iran 100 D2
Qatrâni, Gebel esc. Egypt 121 F2
Qatrūyeh Iran 100 C4
Qaţţāfī, Wādī al watercourse Jordan 109 I6
Qaţţâra, Râs esc. Egypt 121 E2
Qaţţâra Depression Egypt 121 E2 also known as Qaţţārah, Munkhafaḑ al
Qaţţārah, Munkhafaḑ al depr. Egypt see Qaţţâra Depression
Qaţţīnah, Buḩayrat resr Syria 109 H3 also known as Ḩimş, Baḩrat
Qavāmābād Iran 100 D4
Qax Azer. 107 F2 also spelt Kakhi
Qāyen Iran 100 D3
Qayghy Kazakh. see Kayga
Qaynar Kazakh. see Kaynar
Qayraqty Kazakh. see Kayrakty
Qayroqqum Tajik. 101 G1 formerly spelt Kayrakkum
Qaysīyah, Qa' al imp. l. Jordan 109 H6
Qayyārah Iraq 107 E4
Qazaly Kazakh. see Kazalinsk
Qazangödağ mt. Armenia/Azer. 107 F3 also known as Kapydzhik, Gora
Qazaq Shyghanaghy b. Kazakh. see Kazakhskiy Zaliv
Qazaqstan country Asia see Kazakhstan
Qazax Azer. 107 F2 also spelt Kazakh
Qazi Ahmad Pak. 101 G5
Qazımämmäd Azer. 107 G2 also spelt Kazi Magomed
Qazvīn Iran 100 B2
Qazvin prov. Iran 100 B2
Qazyqurt Kazakh. see Kazygurt
Qedir China 88 D3
Qeh China 84 D3
Qeisûm, Gezâ'ir is Egypt 104 A2 English form Qeisûm Islands; also spelt Qeisūm, Gezā'ir
Qeisûm Islands Egypt see Qeisûm, Gezâ'ir
Qelelevu i. Fiji 145 H3 also spelt Nggelelevu
Qena Egypt 121 G3 also spelt Qinā
Qena governorate Egypt 104 A2
Qena, Wâdi watercourse Egypt 121 G3
Qeqertarsuaq Greenland 165 N3 also known as Godhavn
Qeqertarsuaq i. Greenland 165 N3 also known as Disko
Qeqertarsuatsiaat Greenland 165 N3 also known as Fiskenæsset
Qeqertarsuatsiaq i. Greenland 165 N2 also known as Hareøen
Qeqertarsuup Tunua b. Greenland 165 N3 also known as Disko Bugt
Qeshlāq Iran 100 A3
Qeshm Iran 100 D5
Qeshm i. Iran 100 D5
Qeydār Iran 100 B2
Qeys i. Iran 100 C5
Qezel Owzan, Rūdkhāneh-ye r. Iran 100 B2
Qezi'ot Israel 108 F7
Qi r. China 85 G5
Qian r. China 87 C1
Qian'an Hebei China 85 H4
Qian'an Jilin China 85 J2
Qiancheng China 87 D3
Qiang r. China 87 F1
Qian Gorlos China see Qianguozhen
Qianguozhen China 82 B3 also known as Qian Gorlos
Qianjiang Chongqing China 87 D2 also known as Lianhe
Qianjiang Hubei China 87 E2
Qianjin China 82 D3 formerly known as Weidongmen
Qianning China 86 B2 also known as Gartar
Qianqihao China 85 I2
Qianshan China 87 F2 also known as Meicheng
Qian Shan mts China 85 I3
Qianshanlaoba China 88 D2
Qianwei China 86 B2 also known as Yujin
Qianxi Guizhou China 86 C3
Qianxi Hebei China 85 H3 also known as Xingcheng
Qianxian China 87 D1
Qianyang Hunan China 87 D3 also known as Anjiang
Qianyang Shaanxi China 86 C1
Qianyang Zhejiang China 87 F2
Qianyou China see Zhashui
Qiaocun China 85 G4
Qiaojia China 86 B3
Qiaoshan China see Huangling
Qiaotou China see Datong
Qiaotou China 86 B3
Qiaowa China see Muli
Qiaowan China 84 C3
Qiaozhuang China see Qingchuan
Qibā' Saudi Arabia 104 D2
Qibing S. Africa 133 L6
Qibray Uzbek. see Kibray
Qichun China 87 E2 also known as Caohe; formerly known as Caojiahe
Qidong Hunan China 87 E3 formerly known as Hongqiao
Qidong Jiangsu China 87 G2 also known as Huilongzhen
Qiemo China 88 D4 formerly known as Cherchen or Qarqan
Qihe China 85 H4 also known as Yancheng
Qijiang China 86 C2 also known as Gunan
Qijiaojing China 88 E3
Qikiqtarjuaq Canada 165 M3 formerly known as Broughton Island
Qiktim China 88 E3
Qila Ladgasht Pak. 101 E5
Qilaotu Shan mts China 85 H3
Qila Safed Pak. 101 E4
Qila Saifullah Pak. 101 G4
Qili China see Shitai
Qilian China 84 D4 also known as Babao
Qilian Shan mt. China 84 C4
Qilian Shan mts China 84 C4
Qillak i. Greenland 165 P3 also known as Dannebrog Ø
Qima Kazakh. see Kiyma
Qiman el 'Arûs Egypt 108 C8
Qimantag mts China 89 E4
Qimen China 87 F2 also known as Qishan
Qimusseriarsuaq b. Greenland 165 M2 also known as Melville Bugt
Qin r. China 87 E1
Qinā Egypt see Qena
Qināb, Wādī r. Yemen 105 E4
Qin'an China 86 C1 also known as Xingguo
Qincheng China see Nanfeng
Qing r. China 82 A4
Qing'an China 82 B3
Qingcheng China see Qingyang
Qingchengzi China 83 A4
Qingchuan China 86 C1 also known as Qiaozhuang
Qingdao China 85 I4 formerly spelt Tsingtao
Qinggang China 82 B3
Qinggil China see Qinghe
Qingguandu China 87 D2
Qinghai prov. China 84 C4 English form Tsinghai; formerly known as Chinghai
Qinghai Hu salt l. China 84 D4
Qinghai Nanshan mts China 84 C4
Qinghe Hebei China 85 G4 also known as Gexianzhuang
Qinghe Xinjiang China 84 A2 also known as Qinggil
Qinghua China see Bo'ai
Qingjian China 85 F4 also known as Xiuyan
Qingjiang China see Huaiyin
Qingjiang China see Zhangshu
Qing Jiang r. China 87 D2
Qingkou China see Ganyu
Qingliu China 87 F3 also known as Longjin
Qinglong Guizhou China 86 C3 also known as Liancheng
Qinglong Hebei China 85 H3
Qinglong r. China 85 H4
Qingpu China 87 G2
Qingquan China see Xishui
Qingshan China see Dedu
Qingshizui China 84 D4
Qingshui China see Qingshuipu
Qingshui China 86 C1
Qingshuihe Nei Mongol China 85 F4
Qingshuihe Qinghai China 86 A1 also known as Domda
Qingshuihezi China 88 C2
Qingshuilang Shan mts China 86 A3
Qingshuipu China 84 C4 formerly known as Qingshui
Qingtian China 87 G2
Qingtongxia China 85 E4
Qingxi China 87 D3 also known as Xiaoba
Qingxian China 85 H4
Qingxu China 85 G4 also known as Qingyuan
Qingyang Anhui China 87 F2 also known as Rongcheng
Qingyang Gansu China 85 E4 also known as Qingcheng
Qingyang China see Sihong
Qingyuan China see Weiyuan
Qingyuan Guangdong China 87 E4
Qingyuan China see Yizhou
Qingyuan Liaoning China 82 B4
Qingyuan China see Qingxu
Qingyuan Zhejiang China 87 F3
Qingyun China 85 H4 formerly known as Xiejiaji
Qingzang Gaoyuan plat. China see Tibet, Plateau of
Qingzhen China 86 C3
Qingzhou China see Qingxian
Qingzhou Hubei China 87 D2
Qingzhou Shandong China 85 H4 formerly known as Yidu
Qinhuangdao China 85 H4
Qinjiang China see Shicheng
Qin Ling mts China 87 C1
Qinshui China 85 G5
Qinting China see Lianhua
Qinxian China 85 G4
Qinyang China 85 G5
Qinyuan China 85 G4
Qinzhou China 87 D4
Qinzhou Wan b. China 87 D4
Qionghai China 87 D5
Qiongjiexue China see Qonggyai
Qionglai China 86 B2
Qionglai Shan mts China 86 B2
Qiongshan China 87 D5
Qiongxi China see Hongyuan
Qiongzhou Haixia strait China see Hainan Strait
Qiqihar China 85 I2 formerly spelt Tsitsihar
Qiquanhu China 88 E3
Qīr Iran 100 C4
Qira China 89 C4
Qiraîya, Wâdi watercourse Egypt 108 F7
Qiryat Gat Israel 108 F6
Qiryat Shemona Israel 108 G4
Qishan China see Qimen
Qishan China 87 C1 also known as Fengming
Qishn Yemen 105 E5
Qishon r. Israel 108 G5
Qishrān Island Saudi Arabia 104 C3
Qitab ash Shāmah vol. crater Saudi Arabia 107 D5
Qitai China 88 E3
Qitaihe China 82 C3
Qitbīt, Wādī r. Oman 105 F4
Qiubei China 86 C3 also known as Jinping
Qiujin China 87 E2
Qixia China 85 I4
Qixian Henan China 85 G5 formerly known as Zhaoge
Qixian Henan China 87 E1
Qixian Shanxi China 85 G4
Qixing r. China 82 D3
Qiyang China 87 D3
Qiying China 85 E4
Qizhou Liedao i. China 87 D5
Qızılağac Körfäzi b. Azer. 100 B2 formerly known as Kirova, Zaliv
Qizil-Art, Aghbai pass Kyrg./Tajik. see Kyzylart Pass
Qizilrabot Tajik. 101 H2 also spelt Kyzylrabot
Qizqetkan Uzbek. see Kyzketken
Qoboqobo S. Africa 133 M9
Qoghaly Kazakh. see Kugaly
Qogir Feng mt. China/Jammu and Kashmir see K2
Qog Qi China 85 E3
Qojūr Iran 100 A2
Qolora Mouth S. Africa 133 M9
Qoltag mts China 88 E3
Qom Iran 100 B3
Qom prov. Iran 100 B3
Qomdo China see Qumdo
Qomisheh Iran 100 B3 formerly known as Shahrezā
Qomolangma Feng mt. China/Nepal see Everest, Mount
Qonaqkänd Azer. 107 G2
Qonggyai China 89 E6 also known as Qiongjiexue; also spelt Chonggye
Qongj China 85 F3
Qongkol China 88 D3
Qongrat Uzbek. see Kungrad
Qongyrat Kazakh. see Kounradskiy
Qongyrat Kazakh. see Konyrat
Qongyröleng Kazakh. see Konyrolen
Qonj China 84 C4
Qonystanū Kazakh. see Konystanu
Qooriga Neegro b. Somalia 128 F3
Qoornoq Greenland 165 N3
Qoqek China see Tacheng
Qoqodala S. Africa 133 K8
Qoradaryo r. Kyrg. see Kara-Darya
Qorağhaty Kazakh. see Kuragaty
Qoraqalpoghiston Uzbek. see Karakalpakiya
Qoraqalpoghiston Respublikasi aut. rep. Uzbek. see Karakalpakistan, Respublika
Qoraūzak Uzbek. see Karauzyak
Qorday Kazakh. see Kurday
Qorghalzhyn Kazakh. see Kurgal'dzhinskiy
Qornet es Saouda mt. Lebanon 108 H3
Qorowulbozor Uzbek. see Karaulbazar
Qoroy, Gardaneh-ye pass Iran 100 B2
Qorveh Iran 100 A3
Qosh Tepe Iraq 107 E3
Qosshaghyl Kazakh. see Koschagyl
Qostanay Kazakh. see Kostanay
Qostanay Oblysy admin. div. Kazakh. see Kustanayskaya Oblast'
Qoţbābād Iran 100 D5
Qoţūr Iran 100 A2
Qozhaköl l. Kazakh. see Kozhakol', Ozero
Qozonketkan Uzbek. see Kazanketken
Qozoqdaryo Uzbek. see Kazakhdar'ya
Quabbin Reservoir U.S.A. 177 M3
Quadra Island Canada 166 E5
Quadros, Lago dos l. Brazil 203 B9
Quaggasfontein Poort pass S. Africa 132 E8
Quail Mountains U.S.A. 183 G6
Quairading Australia 151 B7
Quakenbrück Germany 48 E3
Quamby Australia 149 D4
Quanah U.S.A. 179 C5
Quanbao Shan mt. China 87 D1
Quân Đao Cô Tô is Vietnam 78 D3
Quan Dao Hoang Sa is S. China Sea see Paracel Islands
Quân Đao Nam Du i. Vietnam 79 D6
Quan Dao Truong Sa is S. China Sea see Spratly Islands
Quang Ngai Vietnam 79 E5
Quang Tri Vietnam 78 D4
Quang Yen Vietnam 78 D3
Quan He r. China 87 E1
Quanjiang China see Suichuan
Quan Long Vietnam see Ca Mau
Quannan China 87 E3 also known as Chengxiang
Quan Phu Quoc i. Vietnam see Phu Quôc, Đao
Quanshang China 87 F3
Quanwan Hong Kong China see Tsuen Wan
Quanzhou Fujian China 87 F3
Quanzhou Guangxi China 87 D3
Qu'Appelle r. Canada 167 K5
Quaqtaq Canada 165 M3 formerly known as Notre-Dame-de-Koartac; formerly spelt Koartac
Quaraí Brazil 204 F3
Quarry Bay Hong Kong China 87 [inset]
Quarryville U.S.A. 177 I6
Quarteira Port. 54 C7
Quartu Sant'Elena Sardegna Italy 57 B9
Quartzite Mountain U.S.A. 183 H4
Quartzsite U.S.A. 183 J8
Quaryat al Faw tourist site Saudi Arabia 105 D4
Quba Azer. 107 G2 also spelt Kuba
Quchan Iran 100 D2
Qudaysah well Oman 105 G4
Qudeni S. Africa 133 O5
Queanbeyan Australia 147 F3

▶Québec Canada 169 G4
Provincial capital of Québec.

Québec prov. Canada 169 F2
Quebra Anzol r. Brazil 206 F6
Quedas Moz. 131 G3
Quedlinburg Germany 48 I4
Queen Adelaide Islands Chile see La Reina Adelaida, Archipiélago de
Queen Alia airport Jordan 108 G6
Queen Anne U.S.A. 177 J7
Queen Bess, Mount Canada 166 E5
Queen Charlotte Canada 166 C4
Queen Charlotte Bay Falkland Is 205 E8
Queen Charlotte Islands Canada 166 C4
Queen Charlotte Sound sea chan. Canada 166 D5
Queen Charlotte Strait Canada 166 E5
Queen Creek U.S.A. 183 M8
Queen Elizabeth Islands Canada 165 I2
Queen Elizabeth National Park Uganda 128 A5 formerly known as Rwenzori National Park
Queen Elizabeth Range mts Antarctica 223 K1
Queen Fabiola Mountains Antarctica 223 C2
Queen Mary Land reg. Antarctica 223 G2
Queen Maud Bird Sanctuary nature res. Canada 167 K1
Queen Maud Gulf Canada 165 I3
Queen Maud Land reg. Antarctica 223 A2 also known as Dronning Maud Land
Queen Maud Mountains Antarctica 223 O1
Queensburgh S. Africa 133 O6
Queens Channel Australia 148 A2
Queenscliff Australia 147 E4
Queensland state Australia 149 E4
Queenstown Australia 147 E5
Queenstown N.Z. 153 C13
Queenstown Rep. of Ireland see Cóbh
Queenstown S. Africa 133 K8
Queenstown Sing. 76 [inset]
Queenstown U.S.A. 177 I7
Queen Victoria Spring Nature Reserve Australia 151 C6
Quehua Bol. 200 D4
Quehué Arg. 204 D5
Queiba well Chad 120 D5
Queimada Brazil 201 E2
Queimada, Ilha i. Brazil 202 B2 also known as Serraria, Ilha
Queimadas Brazil 202 E4
Queiroz Brazil 206 C8
Quela Angola 127 C7
Quelimane Moz. 131 H3
Quelite Mex. 184 D4
Quellón Chile 205 B6
Quelpart Island S. Korea see Cheju-do
Queluz Brazil 207 I9
Quemada Grande, Ilha i. Brazil 206 G11
Quemado U.S.A. 181 E6
Quembo r. Angola 127 D8
Quemchi Chile 205 B6
Quemoy i. Taiwan see Chinmen Tao
Quemú-Quemú Arg. 204 E5
Quepem India 94 B3
Que Que Zimbabwe see Kwekwe
Quequén Arg. 204 F5
Querência Brazil 202 A5
Querétaro Mex. 185 E4
Querétaro state Mex. 185 F4
Querfurt Germany 48 I4
Querobabi Mex. 184 C2
Querpon Peru 198 B6
Quesada Spain 55 H7
Quesat watercourse W. Sahara 122 C4
Queshan China 87 E1 also known as Panlong
Quesnel Canada 166 F4
Quesnel r. Canada 166 F4
Quesnel Lake Canada 166 F4
Questembert France 50 D5
Quetena de Lipez r. Bol. 200 D5
Quetico Provincial Park Canada 172 B2
Quetta Pak. 101 F4
Queuco Chile 204 C5
Queulat, Parque Nacional nat. park Chile 205 B7
Queupán Arg. 204 D6
Queyras, Parc Naturel Régional du nature res. France 51 M8
Quezaltenango Guat. 185 H6
Quezaltepeque El Salvador 185 H6
Quezon Negros Phil. 74 B4
Quezon Palawan Phil. 74 A4

▶Quezon City Phil. 74 B3
Former capital of the Philippines.

Qufu China 85 H5
Qugayatang China 89 E6
Quibala Angola 127 B7
Quibaxe Angola 127 B7
Quibdó Col. 198 B3
Quiberon France 50 C5
Quiberon, Baie de b. France 50 C5
Quíbor Venez. 198 D2
Quicama, Parque Nacional do nat. park Angola 127 B7 also spelt Kisama, Parque Nacional de
Quiet Lake Canada 166 C2
Quihita Angola 127 B8
Quiindy Para. 201 F6
Quilá Mex. 184 D3
Quilalí Nicaragua 186 B4
Quilán, Cabo c. Chile 205 B6
Quilandi India 94 B4
Quilca Peru 200 B4
Quilenda Angola 127 B7
Quilengues Angola 127 B8
Quillacollo Bol. 200 D4
Quillan France 51 I10
Quill Lakes Canada 167 J5
Quillota Chile 204 C4
Quilmes Arg. 204 F4
Quilon India 94 C4 also known as Kollam
Quilpie Australia 149 E5
Quilpué Chile 204 C4
Quimbele Angola 127 C6
Quimilí Arg. 204 E2
Quimome Bol. 201 E4
Quimper France 50 C5
Quimperlé France 50 C5
Quinault r. U.S.A. 180 A3
Quinault Indian Reservation res. U.S.A. 180 A3
Quince Mil Peru 200 C3
Quincinetto Italy 51 N7
Quincy CA U.S.A. 182 D2
Quincy FL U.S.A. 175 C6
Quincy IL U.S.A. 174 B4
Quincy MI U.S.A. 173 I9
Quincy OH U.S.A. 176 B5
Quindio dept Col. 198 C3
Quines Arg. 204 D4
Quinga Moz. 131 I2
Quinhagak U.S.A. 164 C4
Quinhámel Guinea-Bissau 124 B4
Qui Nhon Vietnam 79 E5
Quinigua, Cerro mts Venez. 199 E3
Quiniluban i. Phil. 74 B4
Quinkan Aboriginal Holding res. Australia 149 E2
Quinn r. U.S.A. 180 C4
Quinn Canyon Range mts U.S.A. 183 I4
Quinnimont U.S.A. 176 D8
Quiñones Bol. 200 D2
Quintana Brazil 206 C9
Quintana de la Serena Spain 54 F6
Quintanar de la Orden Spain 55 H5
Quintanar del Rey Spain 55 J5
Quintana Roo state Mex. 185 H5
Quintin France 50 D4
Quinto r. Arg. 204 D4
Quinto Spain 55 K3
Quinzau Angola 127 B6
Quinze, Lac des l. Canada 173 N3
Quionga Moz. 129 D7
Quiotepec Mex. 185 F5
Quipapá Brazil 202 F4
Quipungo Angola 127 B8 formerly known as Paiva Couceiro; formerly spelt Kipungo
Quiquive r. Bol. 200 D3
Quiriguá tourist site Guat. 185 H6
Quirihue Chile 204 B5
Quirima Angola 127 C7
Quirindi Australia 147 F2
Quirinópolis Brazil 206 C5
Quirke Lake Canada 173 K4
Quiroga Bol. 200 D4
Quiroga Spain 54 D2
Quisiro Venez. 198 D2
Quissac France 51 K9
Quissamã Brazil 207 L9
Quitapa Angola 127 C7
Quita Sueño Bank sea feature Caribbean Sea 186 C4
Quiterajo Moz. 129 D7
Quitéria r. Brazil 206 B7
Quitexe Angola see Dange
Quitilipi Arg. 204 E2
Quitman GA U.S.A. 175 D6
Quitman MS U.S.A. 175 B5

▶Quito Ecuador 198 B5
Capital of Ecuador.

Quitovac Mex. 184 B2
Quitralco, Parque Nacional nat. park Chile 205 B7
Quixadá Brazil 202 E3
Quixeramobim Brazil 202 E3
Qujiang China see Quxian
Qu Jiang r. China 86 C2
Qujing China 86 B3
Quko S. Africa 133 M9
Qulaly Araly i. Kazakh. see Kulaly, Ostrov
Qul'ân, Gezâ'ir i. Egypt 104 A2 English form Gulân Islands
Qulandy Kazakh. see Kulandy
Qulanötpes watercourse Kazakh. see Kulanotpes
Qulbān Layyah well Iraq 107 F5
Quljuqtow Toghi hills Uzbek. see Kul'dzhuktau, Gory
Qulsary Kazakh. see Kul'sary
Qulūsana Egypt 106 B5
Qulzum, Baḩr el b. Egypt see Suez Bay
Qumar He r. China 84 B5
Qumarheyan China 84 B5
Qumarlêb China 84 B5 also known as Yiggêtang
Qumbu S. Africa 133 M8
Qumdo China 97 G3 formerly spelt Qomdo
Qumola watercourse Kazakh. see Kumola
Qumrha S. Africa 133 L9
Qunayy well Saudi Arabia 105 D3
Qunayyin, Sabkhat al salt marsh Libya 120 D2
Qunfudh Yemen 105 E4
Qŭnghirot Uzbek. see Kungrad
Qu'nyido China 86 A2
Quoich r. Canada 167 M1
Quoin Island Australia 148 A2
Quoin Point S. Africa 132 D11
Quong Muztag mt. China 89 C5
Quorn Australia 146 C3
Quoxo r. Botswana 131 E4
Qupên China see Jinchuan
Qŭqon Uzbek. see Kokand
Qurayat Oman 105 G3
Qurayyah tourist site Saudi Arabia 108 H9
Qurayyat al Milḩ l. Jordan 109 I6
Qŭrghontepa Tajik. 101 G2 also spelt Kurgantyube
Qus Egypt 121 G3
Qusar Azer. 107 G2 also spelt Kusary
Quşay'ir Saudi Arabia 105 E5
Quseir Egypt 121 G3
Qushan China see Beichuan
Qūshchī Iran 100 A2
Qūshēh Dāgh mts Iran 100 A2
Qŭshkŭpir Uzbek. see Koshkupyr
Qŭshrabot Uzbek. see Koshrabad
Qusmuryn Kazakh. see Kushmurun
Qusmuryn Köli salt l. Kazakh. see Kushmurun, Ozero
Qusum Xizang China 89 B5
Qusum Xizang China 89 F6 also known as Xiajiang
Quthing Lesotho see Moyeni
Quthing r. Lesotho 133 L7
Quţn, Jabal hill Saudi Arabia 104 C2

index

Q R

Qutü' Island Saudi Arabia 104 C4
Quwayq, Nahr r. Syria/Turkey 109 I2
  also known as Haleparki Deresi
Qü' Wishām reg. Oman 105 F4
Quwu Shan mts China 85 E4
Quxar China see Lhazê
Quxian China 86 C2
  also known as Qujiang
Qüxü China 89 E6
  also known as Xoi
Quyang China see Jingzhou
Quyghan Kazakh. see Kuygan
Quyon Canada 173 Q5
Qüyün Eshek i. Iran 100 A2
Qüz Saudi Arabia 104 C4
Quzhou Hebei China 85 G4
Quzhou Zhejiang China 87 F2
Quzi China 85 E4
Qvareli Georgia 107 F2
  also spelt Kvareli
Qypshaq Köli salt l. Kazakh. see Kypshak, Ozero
Qyteti Stalin Albania see Kuçovë
Qyzan Kazakh. see Kyzan
Qyzylaghash Kazakh. see Kyzylagash
Qyzylkesek Kazakh. see Kyzylkesek
Qyzylköl l. Kazakh. see Kyzylkol', Ozero
Qyzylorda Kazakh. see Kyzylorda
Qyzylorda Oblysy admin. div. Kazakh. see Kyzyl-Ordinskaya Oblast'
Qyzyltaū Kazakh. see Kyzyltau
Qyzyltū Kazakh. see Kishkenekol'
Qyzylzhar Kazakh. see Kyzylzhar

↓ R

Raab r. Austria 49 N9
Raab Hungary see Győr
Raahe Fin. 44 N2
Rääkkylä Fin. 44 O3
Raalte Neth. 48 D3
Ra'an, Khashm ar hill Saudi Arabia 104 C2
Raanujärvi Fin. 44 N2
Raas i. Indon. 77 F4
Raasay i. U.K. 46 F6
Raasiku Estonia 42 G2
Rab i. Croatia 56 G4
Rába r. Hungary 49 O8
Raba Indon. 77 G5
Raba r. Poland 49 R5
Rabaale Somalia 128 F2
Rabak Sudan 121 G6
Rabang China 89 C5
Rabat Gozo Malta see Victoria
Rabat Malta 53 E4
▶ Rabat Morocco 122 D2
  Capital of Morocco.
Rabatakbaytal Tajik. see Akbaytal
Rabāt-e Kamah Iran 100 D3
Rabaul P.N.G. 145 F2
Rabaul P.N.G. 145 E2
Rabbath Ammon Jordan see 'Ammān
Rabbi r. Italy 56 E4
Rabbit r. Canada 166 E3
Rabbitskin r. Canada 166 F2
Rábca r. Hungary 49 O8
Rabezha Rus. Fed. 43 Q4
Rabidine well Niger 125 H3
Rabigh Saudi Arabia 104 B3
Rabinal Guat. 185 H6
Rabka Poland 49 Q6
Rabkob India see Dharmjaygarh
Rabnabad Islands Bangl. 97 F5
Rābnița Moldova see Rîbnița
Râbor Iran 100 D4
Rabotoqbaytal Tajik. see Akbaytal
Rabt Sbayta des. W. Sahara 122 B5
Rabyānah oasis Libya 120 D3
Rača Srbija Yugo. 58 B4
Racalmuto Sicilia Italy 57 F11
Racconigi Italy 51 N8
Raccoon Cay i. Bahamas 186 E2
Raccoon Creek r. U.S.A. 176 C7
Raceland U.S.A. 175 B6
Race Point U.S.A. 177 O3
Rachaïya Lebanon 108 G4
Rachel U.S.A. 183 I4
Rachevo Rus. Fed. 43 S3
Rach Gia Vietnam 79 D6
Rach Gia, Vinh b. Vietnam 79 D6
Raciąż Poland 49 R3
Racibórz Poland 49 P5
  historically known as Ratibor
Racine WI U.S.A. 172 F7
Racine WV U.S.A. 176 D7
Racine Lake Canada 173 J2
Râciu Romania 58 G2
Racoş Romania 58 G2
Racovita Romania 58 G3
Radă' Yemen 104 D5
Radashkovichy Belarus 42 I7
  also spelt Radoshkovichi
Rădăuţi Romania 58 H1
Radbuza r. Czech Rep. 49 K6
Radchenko Rus. Fed. 43 R5
Radcliff U.S.A. 174 C4
Radd, Wādī ar watercourse Syria 109 M1

Radde Rus. Fed. 82 C2
Rade Norway 45 J4
Radebeul Germany 49 K4
Radenthein Austria 49 K9
Radew r. Poland 49 M1
Radford U.S.A. 176 E8
Radford Point Australia 148 A1
Radhanpur India 96 A5
Radishchevo Rus. Fed. 102 A1
Radisson Que. Canada 168 E2
Radisson Sask. Canada 167 J4
Raditsa-Krylovka Rus. Fed. 43 P8
Radium S. Africa 133 M2
Radium Hot Springs Canada 167 G5
Radlinski, Mount Antarctica 222 R1
Radnevo Bulg. 58 G6
Rado de Tumaco inlet Col. 198 B4
Radolfzell am Bodensee Germany 48 F8
Radom Poland 49 S4
Radom Sudan 126 E2
Radomir Bulg. 58 D6
Radomir mt. Bulg./Greece 58 E7
  formerly known as Kalabak
Radomka r. Poland 49 S4
Radom National Park Sudan 126 D2
Radomsko Poland 49 Q4
Radomyshl' Ukr. 41 D6
Radoshkovichi Belarus see Radashkovichy
Radovets Bulg. 58 H7
Radoviš Macedonia 58 D7
Radovitskiy Rus. Fed. 43 U6
  formerly known as Tsentral'nyy
Radovljica Slovenia 56 G2
Radøy i. Norway 46 J4
Radstock, Cape Australia 146 B3
Rădučăneni Romania 58 I2
Radun' Belarus 42 F7
Radunia r. Poland 49 P1
Radviliškis Lith. 42 E6
Radwá, Jabal mt. Saudi Arabia 104 B2
Radymno Poland 49 T6
Radziejów Poland 49 P3
Radzyń Podlaski Poland 49 T4
Rae Bareli India 96 D4
Raecreek r. Canada 166 B1
Rae-Edzo Canada 167 G2
  also known as Edzo
Raeford U.S.A. 174 E5
Rae Lakes Canada 167 G1
Raeside, Lake salt flat Australia 151 C6
Raetihi N.Z. 152 J7
Rāf hill Saudi Arabia 107 D5
Rafaela Arg. 204 E3
Rafah Gaza see Rafiah
Rafaï Cent. Afr. Rep. 126 D3
Raffadali Sicilia Italy 57 F11
Rafhā' Saudi Arabia 107 E5
Rafiah Gaza 108 F6
  also spelt Rafah
Rafina Greece 59 F10
Rafsanjān Iran 100 C4
  also known as Bahāmābād
Raft r. U.S.A. 180 D4
Raga Sudan 126 E2
Ragag Sudan 126 E2
Ragana Latvia 42 F4
Ragang, Mount vol. Phil. 74 C5
Ragay Gulf Phil. 74 B3
Ragged, Mount hill Australia 151 C7
Ragged Island Bahamas 186 D2
Ragged Island U.S.A. 177 Q2
Raghogarh India 96 C4
Raghwah waterhole Saudi Arabia 109 P9
Raghwān, Wādī watercourse Yemen
  104 D5
Raglan N.Z. 152 I5
Rago Nasjonalpark nat. park Norway 44 L2
Ragueneau Canada 169 G3
Ragusa Croatia see Dubrovnik
Ragusa Sicilia Italy 57 G12
Raha Indon. 75 B4
Rahachow Belarus 43 L8
  also spelt Rogachev
Rahad r. Sudan 121 G6
Rahad Canal Sudan 121 G6
Rahad al Berdi Sudan 126 D2
Rahad Wahal well Sudan 120 E6
Rahaeng Thai. see Tak
Raḥaṭ, Ḥarrat lava field Saudi Arabia 104 C3
Rahatgaon India 96 C5
Rahimyar Khan Pak. 101 G4
Rähjerd Iran 100 B3
Rahotu N.Z. 152 H7
Rahouia Alg. 55 M9
Rahumäe Estonia 42 I3
Rahuri India 94 B2
Rahzanak Afgh. 101 E3
Raiatea i. Fr. Polynesia 221 H7
  also known as Uliatea
Raibu i. Indon. see Air
Raichur India 94 C2
Raiganj India 97 F4
Raigarh Chhattisgarh India 97 D5
Raigarh Orissa India 94 D2
Raijua i. Indon. 75 B5
Raikot India 96 B3
Railroad Valley U.S.A. 183 I3
Raimangal r. Bangl. 97 F5
Raimbault, Lac l. Canada 169 G2
Rainbow Lake Canada 166 G3
Raine Entrance sea chan. Australia 149 E1
Raine Island Australia 149 E1
Rainelle U.S.A. 176 E8
Rainī r. Pak. 101 G4
Rainier, Mount vol. U.S.A. 180 B3
Rainy r. U.S.A. 174 A1
Rainy Lake Canada 168 A3
Raipur Bangl. 97 F5
Raipur Chhattisgarh India 97 D5
Raipur Rajasthan India 96 B4
Raipur W. Bengal India 97 E5
Rairangpur India 97 E5
Raisen India 96 C5
Raisinghnagar India 96 B3
Raisio Fin. 45 M3
Raistakka Fin. 44 O2
Raitalai India 96 C5
Raith Canada 172 D2
Rai Valley N.Z. 152 H9
Raivavae i. Fr. Polynesia 221 I7
  also known as Vavitao
Raiwind Pak. 101 H4
Raja, Ujung pt Indon. 76 B2
Rajaampat, Kepulauan is Indon. 75 D3
Rajabasa, Gunung vol. Indon. 77 D4
Raja-Jooseppi Fin. 44 O1
  also known as Räijjosseppi
Rajahmundry India 94 D2
Raja-Jooseppi Fin. see Räijjosseppi
Rajamäki Fin. 42 F1
Rajampet India 94 C3
Rajang r. Sarawak Malaysia 77 F2
Rajanpur Pak. 101 G4
Rajapalaiyam India 94 C4
Rajapur India 94 B2
Rajasthan state India 96 B4
  historically known as Rajputana Agency
Rajasthan Canal India 96 B3
Rajauli India 97 E4
Rajbari Bangl. 97 F5
Rajgarh Madhya Pradesh India 96 C4
Rajgarh Maharashtra India 94 B2
Rajgarh Rajasthan India 96 B3
Rajgarh Rajasthan India 96 C4
Rajgir India 97 E4

Rajgród Poland 49 T2
Räijjosseppi Fin. see Raja-Jooseppi
Rajim India 94 D1
Rajince Srbija Yugo. 58 C6
Rajkot India 96 A5
Rajmahal India 97 E4
Rajmahal Hills India 97 E4
Raj Nandgaon India 96 D5
Rajpipla India 96 B5
Rajpur India 96 B5
Rajpura India 96 B3
Rajputana Agency state India see
  Rajasthan
Rajsamand India 96 B4
Rajshahi Bangl. 97 F4
  also known as Rampur Boalia
Rajshahi admin. div. Bangl. 97 F4
Rajula India 96 A5
Rajur India 96 C5
Rajura India 94 C2
  also known as Manikgarh
Rajura India see Ahmadpur
Raka China 89 D6
Rakahuri r. N.Z. see Ashley
Rakai Uganda 128 A5
Rakaia r. N.Z. 153 G11
Rakan, Ra's pt Qatar 105 E2
Rakaposhi mt. Jammu and Kashmir 96 B1
Raka Zangbo r. China see Dogxung Zangbo
Rakeahua, Mount hill N.Z. 153 B14
Rakhaing state Myanmar see Arakan
Rakhine state Myanmar see Arakan
Rakhiv Ukr. 53 G2
Rakhshan r. Pak. 101 E5
Rakiraki Fiji 145 G3
Rakit i. Indon. 77 F4
Rakitnitsa r. Bulg. 58 G6
Rakitnoye Rus. Fed. 41 E6
Rakitnoye Rus. Fed. 82 D3
Rakitu Island N.Z. 152 J4
  formerly known as Arid Island
Rakiura i. N.Z. see Stewart Island
Rakke Estonia 42 H3
Rakkestad Norway 45 J4
Rakmanovskie Klyuchi Kazakh. 88 D1
Rakni r. Pak. 101 G4
Rakoniewice Poland 49 N3
Rakops Botswana 131 E4
Rakovitsa Bulg. 58 D5
Rakovník Czech Rep. 49 K5
Rakovski Bulg. 58 F6
Rakushechnyy, Mys pt Kazakh. 102 C4
Rakvere Estonia 42 H2
Ralebona Lesotho 133 M7
Raleigh MS U.S.A. 175 B5
▶ Raleigh NC U.S.A. 174 E5
  State capital of North Carolina.
Raleighvallen Voltsberg, Natuurreservaat
  nature res. Suriname 199 G3
Ralla Indon. 75 A4
Ralph U.S.A. 172 F4
Ralston Canada 167 I5
Ralston U.S.A. 177 I4
Ram r. Canada 166 F2
Rama Israel 108 G5
Rama Nicaragua 186 B4
Ramacca Sicilia Italy 57 G11
Ramādī, Saddat ar dam Iraq 109 O4
Ramaditas Chile 200 D3
Ramah Canada 169 I1
Ramales de la Victoria Spain 55 H1
Ramalho, Serra do hills Brazil 202 C5
Ramallah West Bank 108 G6
Ramallo Arg. 204 E4
Ramanagaram India 94 C3
Ramanathapuram India 94 C4
Ramanuj Ganj India 97 D5
Ramas, Cape India 94 B3
Ramasukha Rus. Fed. 43 O9
Ramatlabama watercourse
  Botswana/S. Africa 133 J2
Ramat r. Sudan 121 G6
Ramayampet India 94 C2
Ramberg Norway 44 K1
Rambervillers France 51 M4
Rambouillet France 50 H4
Rambutyo Island P.N.G. 73 K7
  historically known as Jesu Maria Island
Ramdurg India 94 B2
Ramechhap Nepal 97 E4
Rame Head S. Africa 133 N8
Rame Head U.K. 47 H13
Ramenskoye Rus. Fed. 43 T6
Rameshki Rus. Fed. 43 R4
Rameswaram India 94 C4
Ramezān Kalak Iran 101 E5
Ramgarh Bangl. 97 F5
Ramgarh Jharkhand India 97 E5
Ramgarh Rajasthan India 96 A4
Ramgarh Rajasthan India 96 C4
Ramgul reg. Afgh. 101 G3
Rämhormoz Iran 100 B4
Ramingining Australia 148 B2
Ramit Tajik. see Romit
Ramitan Uzbek. see Romiton
Ramla Israel 108 F6
Ramlat al Ghāfah des. Saudi Arabia 105 F3
Ramlat al Wahibah des. Oman 105 G3
Ramlat Amilhayt des. Oman 105 G3
Ramlat as Sab'atayn des. Yemen 105 D5
Ramlat Dahm des. Saudi Arabia/Yemen
  105 D4
Ramlat Rabyānah des. Libya see
  Rebiana Sand Sea
Ramm, Jabal mts Jordan 108 G4
Ramnad India see Ramanathapuram
Ramnagar Madhya Pradesh India 96 D4
Ramnagar Uttaranchal India 96 C3
Ramnagar Jammu and Kashmir 96 B2
Ramni Belarus 43 L6
Râmnicu Sărat r. Romania 58 I3
Râmnicu Sărat Romania 58 I3
  formerly spelt Rimnicu Sărat
Râmnicu Vâlcea Romania 58 F3
  formerly spelt Rimnicu Vîlcea
Ramo Eth. 128 D3
Ramokgwebane Botswana 131 E4
Ramona U.S.A. 183 H8
Ramón Lista Arg. 205 D7
Ramonville-St-Agne France 50 H9
Ramore Canada 173 M2
Ramos r. Nigeria 125 G5
Ramos Arizpe Mex. 185 E3
Ramotswa Botswana 133 K3
Rampart of Genghis Khan tourist site Asia
  85 G1
Ramparts r. Canada 166 D1
Rampur Himachal Pradesh India 89 B6
Rampur Uttar Pradesh India 96 C3
Rampur Uttar Pradesh India 96 C3
Rampura India 96 B4
Rampur Boalia Bangl. see Rajshahi
Rampur Hat India 97 E4
Ramree Myanmar 78 A4
Ramree Island Myanmar 78 A4
Ramsele Sweden 44 L4
Ramsey Canada 168 D3
Ramsey Isle of Man 47 H9
Ramsey Lake Canada 168 D3
Ramsgate S. Africa 133 O7
Ramsgate U.K. 47 N12
Ramshai Hat India 97 F4
Rāmshīr Iran 100 B4
Ramsing mt. India 97 G3

Ramsjö Sweden 45 K3
Ramtek India 96 C5
Ramu Bangl. 97 G5
Ramu r. P.N.G. 73 J7
Ramusio, Lac l. Canada 169 I2
Ramvik Sweden 44 L3
Rana, Cerro hill Col. 199 D4
Rañadoiro, Puerto de pass Spain 54 E2
Rañadoiro, Sierra de mts Spain 54 E1
Ranaghat India 97 F5
Ranai i. U.S.A. see Lanai
Rana Pratap Sagar resr India 96 B4
Ranapur India 96 B5
Rânăsfoss Norway 45 J3
Ranau Sabah Malaysia 77 G1
Ranau, Danau l. Indon. 76 C4
Rancagua Chile 204 C4
Rance r. France 50 D4
Rancharia Brazil 206 C9
Rancheria Canada 166 D2
Rancheria r. Canada 166 D2
Ranchester U.S.A. 180 F3
Ranchi India 97 E5
Rancho Cordova U.S.A. 182 C3
Rancho de Caçados Tapiúnas Brazil
  201 F2
Ranchos de Taos U.S.A. 181 F5
Rancho Veloz Cuba 175 D8
Ranco, Lago l. Chile 204 B6
Randallstown U.S.A. 177 I6
Randan France 51 J6
Randazzo Sicilia Italy 57 G11
Randburg S. Africa 133 L3
Randers Denmark 45 J4
Randfontein S. Africa 133 L3
Randijaure l. Sweden 44 L2
Randolph MA U.S.A. 177 N3
Randolph ME U.S.A. 177 P1
Randolph NY U.S.A. 176 G3
Randolph UT U.S.A. 180 E4
Randolph VT U.S.A. 177 M2
Randow r. Germany 49 L2
Randsburg U.S.A. 182 G6
Randsfjorden l. Norway 45 J3
Randsverk Norway 45 J3
Randvaal S. Africa 133 M3
Rânea Sweden 44 M2
Ranfurly N.Z. 153 E13
Ranga r. India 78 A2
Rangae Thai. 79 C7
Rangamati Bangl. 97 G5
Rangapara North India 97 G4
Rangas, Tanjung pt Indon. 75 A3
Rangasa, Tanjung pt Indon. 75 A3
Rangaunu Bay N.Z. 152 H2
Rangeley Lake U.S.A. 177 O1
Rangely U.S.A. 183 P1
Ranger Lake Canada 168 D3
Ranger Lake l. Canada 173 J4
Rangi India 94 D1
Rangia Patharughat India 97 F4
Rangiauria i. S. Pacific Ocean see
  Pitt Island
Rangiora N.Z. 153 G11
Rangipoua mt. N.Z. 152 L5
  also known as Hardy, Mount
Rangitaiki r. N.Z. 152 K6
Rangitata N.Z. 153 F12
Rangitata r. N.Z. 153 F12
Rangitikei r. N.Z. 152 J8
Rangitoto Islands N.Z. 152 H4
Rangiwaea Junction N.Z. 152 J7
Rangiwahia N.Z. 152 J7
Rangkasbitung Indon. 77 D4
Rangke China see Zamtang
Rangkül Tajik. 101 H2
Rangôn Myanmar see Rangoon
Rangôn admin. div. Myanmar see Yangôn
Rangôn r. Myanmar 78 B4
Rangpur Bangl. 97 F4
Rangsang i. Indon. 76 C2
Rangse Myanmar 78 A3
Rani India 96 B4
Rania India 96 B3
Ranibennur India 94 B3
Raniganj India 97 E5
Ranijula Peak India 97 D5
Ranikhet India 96 C3
Ranipur Pak. 101 G5
Raniwara India 96 A5
Ranken watercourse Australia 148 C4
Rankin U.S.A. 179 B6
Rankin Inlet Canada 167 M2
Rankin Inlet inlet Canada 167 M2
Rankin's Springs Australia 147 E3
Rankovićevo Srbija Yugo. see Kraljevo
Ranna Estonia 42 I3
Rannes Australia 149 F5
Ranneye Rus. Fed. 102 C2
Rannoch, Loch l. U.K. 46 H7
Rannu Estonia 42 H3
Rano Nigeria 125 H4
Ranobe r. Madag. 131 [inset] J3
Ranohira Madag. 131 [inset] J4
Ranomafana Madag. 131 [inset] K3
Ranomatana Madag. 131 [inset] J5
Ranong Thai. 79 B6
Ranongga i. Solomon Is 145 E2
Ranot Thai. 79 C7
Ranotsara Avaratra Madag. 131 [inset] J4
Ranova r. Rus. Fed. 43 V7
Ranpur India 96 A5
Ransiki Indon. 75 D3
Ransom U.S.A. 172 E9
Ranta Fin. 44 N1
Rantabe Madag. 131 [inset] K2
Rantasalmi Fin. 44 O3
Rantau Indon. 77 F3
Rantau i. Indon. 76 C2
Rantaukampar Indon. 76 C2
Rantaupanjang Kalimantan Tengah Indon.
  77 F3
Rantaupanjang Kalimantan Timur Indon.
  77 G2
Rantauprapat Indon. 76 B2
Rantaupulut Indon. 77 F3
Rantemario, Gunung mt. Indon. 75 B3
Rantepao Indon. 75 A3
Rantoul U.S.A. 174 B3
Rantsevo Rus. Fed. 43 P5
Rantsila Fin. 44 N2
Ranua Fin. 44 N2
Ranxë Albania 58 A7
Rānya Iraq 107 F3
Ranyah, Wādī watercourse Saudi Arabia
  104 C3
Rao Go mt. Laos/Vietnam 78 D4
Raohe China 82 D3
Raon-l'Étape France 51 M4
Raoul Island N.Z. 145 H4
Rapa i. Fr. Polynesia 221 I7
  also known as Oparo or Rapa-iti
Rapa-iti i. Fr. Polynesia see Rapa
Rapallo Italy 56 B4
Rapar Gujarat India 96 A5
Rapar Punjab India 96 B3
Rapch watercourse Iran 101 D5
Raper, Cape Canada 165 M3
Rapid r. U.S.A. 172 D3
Rapid Bay Australia 146 C3

Rapid City U.S.A. 178 B2
Rapide-Deux Canada 173 O3
Rapide-Sept Canada 173 O3
Räpina Estonia 42 I3
Rapirrān r. Brazil 200 D2
Rapla Estonia 42 F3
Rappahannock r. U.S.A. 177 I8
Rappang Indon. 75 A3
Rapti r. India 97 D4
Rapulo r. Bol. 200 D3
Rapur Andhra Pradesh India 94 C3
Rapur Gujarat India 96 A5
Rapurapu i. Phil. 74 C3
Raqqa Syria see Ar Raqqah
Raqqah Syria see Ar Raqqah
Raquette r. U.S.A. 177 K1
Raquette Lake U.S.A. 177 K2
Rara National Park Nepal 97 D3
Raroia atoll Fr. Polynesia 221 I7
Rarotonga i. Cook Is 221 H7
  historically known as Barclay de Tolly
Ras India 96 B4
Rasa r. Croatia 56 G3
Rasa i. Phil. 74 A4
Rasa, Punta pt Arg. 204 E6
Ra's ad Daqm Oman 105 G4
Ra's al 'Ayn Syria 109 L1
Ra's al Ḥadd Oman 105 G3
Ras al Khaimah U.A.E. see
  Ra's al Khaymah
Ra's al Khaymah U.A.E. 105 F2
  English form Ras al Khaimah
Ra's al Mish'āb Saudi Arabia 105 E1
Raşan, Jabal hill Saudi Arabia 104 C3
Ra's an Naqb Jordan 108 G7
Ra's ash Shaykh Humayd Saudi Arabia
  104 A1
▶ Ras Dashen mt. Eth. 128 C1
  5th highest mountain in Africa.
  africa [landscapes] ▶▶▶ 112–113
Raseiniai Lith. 42 E6
Ras el Ma Alg. 123 E2
  formerly known as Bedeau
Râs el Mâ Mali 124 D2
Ras Ghārib Egypt 121 G2
Rashaant Bayan-Ölgiy Mongolia 84 A2
Rashaant Dundgovi Mongolia 85 F2
Rashad Sudan 128 A2
Rashid Egypt 121 F2
  historically known as Rosetta
Râshid reg. Saudi Arabia 105 F3
Rashid Qala Afgh. 101 F3
Rashsham Yemen 105 D5
Rasht Iran 100 B2
Rasina r. Yugo. 58 C5
Rasina r. Yugo. 58 C5
Rasjön Sweden 44 K3
Rask Iran 101 E5
  also known as Firuzabad
Raška Srbija Yugo. 58 B5
Raskam mts China 89 A4
Ras Koh mt. Pak. 101 F4
Raskoh mts Pak. 101 F4
Râs Muhammad National Park Egypt
  104 A2
Rasmussen Basin sea feature Canada
  165 J3
Rasna Belarus 43 M7
Rasna Belarus 43 K7
Râşnov Romania 58 H3
  formerly spelt Rîşnov
Raso i. Cape Verde 124 [inset]
Raso da Catarina hills Brazil 202 E4
Rason Lake salt flat Australia 151 D6
Rasony Belarus 43 J6
  also spelt Rossony
Rasova Romania 58 I4
Rasovo Bulg. 58 E5
Rasra India 97 D4
Ra's Săq, Jabal hill Saudi Arabia 104 B2
Ra's Sharwayn c. Yemen 105 E5
Rasshua, Ostrov i. Rus. Fed. 81 Q3
Ra's Şirāb Oman 105 G3
Rass Jebel Tunisia 57 C11
Rasskazovo Rus. Fed. 41 G6
Rast Romania 58 E5
Rasta r. Belarus 43 L8
Ras Tannūrah Saudi Arabia 105 E2
Rastatt Germany 48 F7
Rastede Germany 48 F2
Rastojaure l. Sweden 44 M1
Rastorguyevo Rus. Fed. see Vidnoye
Rata N.Z. 152 J7
Ratae U.K. see Leicester
Ratai, Gunung mt. Indon. 76 D4
Ratanda S. Africa 133 M3
Ratangarh Madhya Pradesh India 96 B4
Ratangarh Rajasthan India 96 B3
Ratanpur Chhattisgarh India 97 D5
Ratanpur Gujarat India 96 B5
Ratansbyn Jämtland Sweden 44 K3
Rat Buri Thai. 79 B5
Ratchaburi Thai. see Rat Buri
Ratcliffe, Mount Canada 166 E4
Ratelfontein S. Africa 132 C8
Rath India 96 C4
Rathbun Lake U.S.A. 174 A3
Rathedaung Myanmar 78 A3
Rathenow Germany 49 J3
Rathenower Wald- und Seengebiet park
  Germany 49 J3
Rathlin Island U.K. 47 F8
Rathluirc Rep. of Ireland 47 D11
  also known as Charleville
Ratibor Poland see Racibórz
Ratisbon Germany see Regensburg
Ratitovec mt. Slovenia 56 G2
Ratiya India 96 B3
Raṭiyah, Wādī watercourse Jordan 108 H8
Rat Lake Canada 167 L3
Ratlam India 96 B5
Ratnagiri India 94 B2
Ratnapura Sri Lanka 94 D5
Ratne Ukr. 41 C6
  also spelt Ratno
Ratno Ukr. see Ratne
Rato Dero Pak. 101 G5
Raton U.S.A. 181 F5
Ratqah, Wādī ar watercourse Iraq 109 L4
Rattray Head U.K. 46 K6
Ratz, Mount Canada 166 C3
Ratzeburg Germany 48 H2
Rau i. Indon. 75 D2
Raub Malaysia 76 C2
Rauch Arg. 204 F5
Rauðamýri Iceland 44 [inset] B2
Raudanjoki r. Fin. 44 N2
Rău de Mori Romania 58 E3
Raudhatain Kuwait 107 F5
Raudna r. Estonia 42 H3
Raudondvaris Lith. 42 E7
Raufarhöfn Iceland 44 [inset] D2
Raukokore N.Z. 152 L5
Raukumara r. N.Z. 152 L6
Raukumara Forest Park nature res. N.Z.
  152 L5
Raukumara Range mts N.Z. 152 L6
Rauland Norway 45 I4
Rauma Fin. 45 L3
Rauna Latvia 42 G4
Raurimu N.Z. 152 J7
Raurkela India 97 E5
Rauschen Rus. Fed. see Svetlogorsk
Rausu Japan 90 I2
Rausu-dake mt. Japan 90 I2
Rautalampi Fin. 44 N3

Rautavaara Fin. 44 O3
Rautjärvi Fin. 45 O3
Rauza Rus. Fed. see Khuldabad
Ravalli U.S.A. 180 D3
Ravänsar Iran 100 A3
Ravanusa Sicilia Italy 57 F11
Rāvar Iran 100 D3
Ravat Kyrg. 101 G2
Ravena U.S.A. 177 L3
Ravenna Italy 56 E4
Ravenna NE U.S.A. 178 C3
Ravenna OH U.S.A. 176 D4
Ravensburg Germany 48 G8
Ravenshoe Australia 149 E3
Ravensthorpe Australia 151 B7
Ravenswood Australia 149 E4
Ravenswood U.S.A. 176 D7
Raver India 96 C5
Ravi r. Pak. 101 G4
Ravna Gora Croatia 56 G3
Ravna Gora hill Croatia 56 J3
Ravnina Turkm. 103 F5
  also spelt Rawnina
Ravshan Uzbek. 102 D4
Rawa Aopa Watumohe National Park
  Indon. 75 B4
Râwah Iraq 107 E4
Rawai well Sudan 104 A4
Rawaki i. Kiribati 145 H2
  formerly known as Phoenix Island
Rawala Kot Pak. 101 H3
Rawalpindi Pak. 101 H3
Rawalpindi Lake Canada 167 H1
Rawāndiz Iraq 107 F3
Rawándiz, Rūbār-i r. Iraq 109 P1
Rawas r. Indon. 76 C3
Rawatsar India 96 B3
Rawdah Yemen 104 D5
Rawdah, Sabkhat ar salt marsh Syria 109 M2
Rawghah watercourse Saudi Arabia 109 I9
Rawhide Lake Canada 173 K4
Rawi i. Thai. 79 B7
Rawicz Poland 49 N4
Rawka r. Poland 49 R4
Rawlinna Australia 151 D6
Rawlins U.S.A. 180 F4
Rawlinson, Mount hill Australia 151 D5
Rawlinson Range hills Australia 151 E5
Rawnina Turkm. see Ravnina
Rawson Arg. 205 D6
Rawu China 86 A2
Raxaul India 97 E4
Ray, Cape Canada 169 J4
Raya, Bukit mt. Kalimantan Indon. 77 F3
Raya, Bukit mt. Kalimantan Indon. 77 F3
Rayachoti India 94 C3
Rayadurg India 94 C3
Rayagarha India 95 D2
Rayak Lebanon 108 H4
Raychikhinsk Rus. Fed. 82 C2
Rayda Rus. Fed. 43 R3
Raydah Yemen 104 D5
Raydär Iraq 109 P2
Räyen Iran 100 D4
Rayes Peak U.S.A. 182 E7
Rayevskiy Rus. Fed. 40 J5
Raymän i. Saudi Arabia 108 G9
Raymond Canada 167 H5
Raymond NH U.S.A. 177 N2
Raymond WA U.S.A. 180 B3
Raymond Terrace Australia 147 F3
Raymondville U.S.A. 179 C7
Raymore Canada 167 J5
Rayna India 97 E5
Rayner Glacier Antarctica 223 D2
Rayón Mex. 185 E3
Rayones Mex. 185 E3
Rayong Thai. 79 C5
Raystown Lake U.S.A. 176 G5
Raysūt Oman 105 F4
Rayth al Khayl watercourse Saudi Arabia
  109 I9
Rayton S. Africa 133 M2
Rayville U.S.A. 175 B5
Raz, Pointe du pt France 50 B4
Razam India 95 D2
Razan Iran 100 B3
Ražanj Srbija Yugo. 58 C5
Razāzah, Buḥayrat ar l. Iraq 107 E4
  formerly known as Milḥ, Baḥr al
Razdan Armenia see Hrazdan
Razdel'naya Ukr. see Rozdil'na
Razdol'noye Rus. Fed. 82 C4
Razdzyalavichy Belarus 42 H9
Razeh Iran 100 B3
Razgrad Bulg. 58 H5
Razhëng Zangbo r. China 89 E6
Razim, Lacul lag. Romania 58 J4
Razlog Bulg. 58 E7
Räznas i. Latvia 42 I5
Raz"yezd 3km Rus. Fed. see Novyy Urgal
R. D. Bailey Lake U.S.A. 176 D8
Ré, Île de i. France 50 D6
Reading U.K. 47 L12
Reading MI U.S.A. 173 H9
Reading OH U.S.A. 176 A6
Reading PA U.S.A. 177 J5
Readsboro U.S.A. 177 M3
Readstown U.S.A. 172 C7
Reagile S. Africa 133 K2
Real r. Brazil 202 E4
Real Spain 54 C1
Reales mt. Spain 54 F8
Realicó Arg. 204 D4
Reálmont France 51 I9
Reăng Kesei Cambodia 79 C5
Reata Mex. 185 E3
Reate Italy see Rieti
Rebaa Alg. 123 H3
Rebbenesøy i. Norway 44 L1
Rebecca, Lake salt flat Australia 151 C6
Rebiana Sand Sea des. Libya 120 D3
  also known as Ramlat Rabyānah
Rebollera mt. Spain 54 G6
Reboly Rus. Fed. 44 O3
Rebrebti Dhubo well Eth. 128 C3
Rebrikha Rus. Fed. 103 J1
Rebun-tō i. Japan 90 G2
Recanati Italy 56 F5
Recaş Romania 58 C3
Recco Italy 56 B4
Rechane Rus. Fed. 43 M5
Recherche, Archipelago of the is Australia
  151 C7
Rechitsa Belarus see Rechytsa
Rechna Doab lowland Pak. 101 H4
Rechytsa Belarus 43 L9
  also spelt Rechitsa
Recife Brazil 202 F4
  formerly known as Pernambuco
Recife, Cape S. Africa 133 J11
Recinto Chile 204 B5
Recklinghausen Germany 48 E4
Recknitz r. Germany 49 J1
Reconquista Arg. 204 E3
Recovery Glacier Antarctica 223 V1
Recreio Mato Grosso Brazil 201 F2
Recreio Minas Gerais Brazil 207 K8
Recreo Arg. 204 D3
Rectorville U.S.A. 176 B7
Recz Poland 49 M2
Red r. Australia 149 D3
Red r. Canada 166 G3
Red r. Canada/U.S.A. 167 L5
Red r. U.S.A. 179 E6
Red, North Fork r. U.S.A. 179 C5
Redang i. Malaysia 76 C1

Red Bank NJ U.S.A. 177 K5
Red Bank TN U.S.A. 174 C5
Red Basin China see Sichuan Pendi
Red Bay Canada 169 J3
Redberry Lake Canada 167 J4
Red Bluff hill Australia 151 B5
Red Bluff U.S.A. 182 B1
Red Bluff Lake U.S.A. 179 B6
Red Butte mt. U.S.A. 183 L6
Redcar U.K. 47 K9
Redcliff Canada 167 I5
Red Cliff U.S.A. 172 C4
Redcliff Zimbabwe 131 F3
Redcliffe, Mount hill Australia 151 C6
Red Cliffs Australia 147 D3
Red Cloud U.S.A. 178 C3
Red Deer Canada 167 H4
Red Deer r. Alta/Sask. Canada 167 I5
Red Deer r. Man./Sask. Canada 167 K4
Red Deer Lake Canada 167 K4
Reddersburg S. Africa 133 K6
Redding U.S.A. 182 B1
Redditch U.K. 47 K11
Red Earth Creek Canada 167 H3
Redelinghuys S. Africa 132 C9
Redenção Pará Brazil 202 B3
Redenção Piauí Brazil 202 C4
Redeyef Tunisia 123 H2
Redfield U.S.A. 178 C2
Red Granite Mountain Canada 166 B2
Redhill Australia 146 C3
Red Hills U.S.A. 178 C4
Red Hook U.S.A. 177 L4
Red Idol Gorge China 89 E6
Red Indian Lake Canada 169 J3
Redkino Rus. Fed. 43 R5
Redknife r. Canada 166 G2
Red Lake Canada 167 M5
Red Lake l. Canada 167 M5
Red Lake U.S.A. 183 L6
Red Lake r. U.S.A. 178 C2
Red Lake Falls U.S.A. 178 C2
Red Lake Indian Reservation res. U.S.A. 178 D1
Red Lakes U.S.A. 178 D1
Redlands U.S.A. 183 G7
Red Lion NJ U.S.A. 177 K6
Red Lion PA U.S.A. 177 I6
Red Lodge U.S.A. 180 E3
Red Mercury Island N.Z. 152 J4
Redmond OR U.S.A. 180 B3
Redmond UT U.S.A. 183 M2
Red Oak U.S.A. 178 D3
Redojari waterhole Kenya 128 C5
Redon France 50 D5
Redonda i. Antigua and Barbuda 187 H3
Redondela Spain 54 C2
Redondo Port. 54 D6
Redondo Beach U.S.A. 182 F8
Red Peak U.S.A. 180 D3
Red River r. Vietnam 78 D3
also known as Hông, Sông or Nui Con Voi
Red Rock Canada 168 B3
Red Rock AZ U.S.A. 183 M9
Red Rock PA U.S.A. 177 I4
Red Rock r. U.S.A. 180 D3
Red Sea Africa/Asia 104 A2
Red Sea state Sudan 121 G5
Redstone Canada 166 F4
Redstone r. N.W.T. Canada 166 E1
Redstone r. Ont. Canada 173 L2
Red Volta r. Burkina/Ghana 125 E4
also known as Nazinon (Burkina)
Redwater r. U.S.A. 180 F2
Redway U.S.A. 182 A1
Red Willow Creek r. U.S.A. 178 B3
Red Wine r. Canada 169 J2
Red Wing U.S.A. 174 A2
Redwood City U.S.A. 182 B4
Redwood Falls U.S.A. 178 D2
Redwood National Park U.S.A. 180 A4
Redwood Valley U.S.A. 182 A2
Ree, Lough l. Rep. of Ireland 47 E10
Reed City U.S.A. 172 H7
Reed Lake Canada 167 K4
Reedley U.S.A. 182 E5
Reedsburg U.S.A. 172 D7
Reedsport U.S.A. 180 A4
Reedsville OH U.S.A. 176 D6
Reedsville PA U.S.A. 176 H5
Reedville U.S.A. 177 I8
Reedy U.S.A. 176 D7
Reedy Creek watercourse Australia 149 E4
Reedy Glacier Antarctica 223 P1
Reefton N.Z. 153 F10
Reese U.S.A. 173 J7
Reese r. U.S.A. 183 H1
Refahiye Turkey 107 D3
Reform U.S.A. 175 B5
Reforma Mex. 185 G5
Refugio U.S.A. 179 C6
Rega r. Poland 49 M1
Regen Germany 49 K7
Regência Brazil 207 N6
Regensburg Germany 48 J6
historically known as Castra Regina or Ratisbon
Regenstauf Germany 51 S3
Regente Feijó Brazil 206 B9
Reggane Alg. 123 F4
Reggio Italy see Reggio di Calabria
Reggio Italy see Reggio nell'Emilia
Reggio di Calabria Italy 57 H10
historically known as Rhegium; short form Reggio
Reggio Emilia Italy see Reggio nell'Emilia
Reggio nell'Emilia Italy 56 C4
also known as Reggio Emilia; historically known as Regium Lepidum; short form Reggio
Reghin Romania 58 F2
Regi Afgh. 101 F3

▶Regina Canada 167 J5
Provincial capital of Saskatchewan.

Régina Fr. Guiana 199 H3
Registan reg. Afgh. 101 F4
Registro Brazil 206 F11
Registro do Araguaia Brazil 206 B2
Regium Lepidum Italy see Reggio nell'Emilia
Regozero Rus. Fed. 44 O2
Rehli India 96 C5
Rehoboth Namibia 130 C4
Rehoboth Bay U.S.A. 177 J7
Rehoboth Beach U.S.A. 177 J7
Rehovot Israel 108 F6
Reibell Alg. see Ksar Chellala
Reichenbach Germany 49 J5
Reichshoffen France 51 N4
Reid Australia 151 E6
Reidsville GA U.S.A. 175 D5
Reidsville NC U.S.A. 176 F9
Reigate U.K. 47 L12
Reiley Peak U.S.A. 183 N9
Reims France 51 K3
English form Rheims; historically known as Durocortorum or Remi
Reinach Switz. 51 N5
Reinbek Germany 48 H2
Reindeer r. Canada 167 K4
Reindeer Island Canada 167 L4
Reindeer Lake Canada 167 K3
Reine Norway 44 K2
Reinersville U.S.A. 176 D6
Reineskarvet mt. Norway 45 J3
Reinga, Cape N.Z. 152 G2
Reinosa Spain 54 G2
Reinsfeld Germany 48 D6
Reiphólsfjöll hill Iceland 44 [inset] B2
Reisa Nasjonalpark nat. park Norway 44 M1
Reisjärvi Fin. 44 N3
Reisterstown U.S.A. 177 I6
Reitz S. Africa 133 M4
Reitzburg S. Africa 133 L4
Reiu r. Estonia 42 F3
Reivilo S. Africa 132 I4
Rejowiec Fabryczny Poland 49 U4
Rekapalle India 94 D2
Rekohua i. S. Pacific Ocean see Chatham Island
Rekovac Srbija Yugo. 58 C5
Rėkyvos ežeras l. Lith. 42 E6
Reliance Canada 167 I2
Relizane Alg. 123 F2
Rellano Mex. 184 D3
Relli India 95 D2
Remada Tunisia 123 H2
Remarkable, Mount hill Australia 146 C3
Rembang Indon. 77 E4
Remedios Cuba 186 D2
Remedios, Punta pt El Salvador 185 H6
Remel el Abiod des. Tunisia 123 H3
Remennikovo Rus. Fed. 43 J5
Remeshk Iran 100 D5
Remeskylä Fin. 44 N3
Remi France see Reims
Remington U.S.A. 176 H7
Rémire Fr. Guiana 199 H3
Remiremont France 51 M4
Remmel Mountain U.S.A. 180 B2
Remo Glacier Jammu and Kashmir 96 C2
Remontnoye Rus. Fed. 41 G7
Rempang i. Indon. 76 D2
Remscheid Germany 48 E4
Remus U.S.A. 173 H7
Rena Norway 45 J3
Rena r. Norway 45 J3
Renabie Canada 173 J2
Renaix Belgium see Ronse
Renapur India 94 C2
Renard Islands P.N.G. 149 G1
Rende China see Xundian
Rende Italy 57 I9
Rend Lake U.S.A. 174 B4
Rendsburg Germany 48 G1
Renedo Spain 54 H1
René-Levasseur, Île i. Canada 169 G3
Renens Switz. 51 M6
Renews Canada 169 K4
Renfrew Canada 168 E4
Rengat Indon. 76 C3
Rengo Chile 204 C4
Ren He r. China 87 D1
Renheji China 87 E2
Renhou China see Tangxian
Renhua China 87 E3
Renhuai China 86 C3
Reni Ukr. 41 D7
Renick U.S.A. 176 E8
Renigunta India 94 C3
Renko Fin. 42 F1
Renland reg. Greenland see Tuttut Nunaat
Renmark Australia 146 D3
Rennell i. Solomon Is 145 F3
also known as Mu Nggava
Rennell, Islas is Chile 205 B8
Rennerod Germany 48 F5
Renner Springs Australia 148 B3
Rennes France 50 E4
Rennes, Bassin de basin France 50 E4
Rennick Glacier Antarctica 223 K2
Rennie Canada 167 M5
Reno r. Italy 56 E4
Reno MN U.S.A. 172 B7
Reno NV U.S.A. 182 E2
Renoster r. S. Africa 133 K3
Renoster watercourse S. Africa 132 E8
Renosterkop S. Africa 132 G9
Renovo U.S.A. 176 H4
Renqiu China 85 H4
Renshou China 86 C2
also known as Wenlin
Rensselaer IN U.S.A. 174 C3
Rensselaer NY U.S.A. 177 L3
Rentjärn Sweden 44 L2
Renton U.S.A. 180 B3
Renukut India 97 D4
Renwick N.Z. 152 H9
Renya r. Rus. Fed. 43 S3
Réo Burkina 124 E3
Reo Indon. 75 B5
Repartimento Brazil 199 G5
Repembe r. Moz. 131 G4
Repetek Turkm. 103 E5
Repetekskiy Zapovednik nature res. Turkm. 103 E5
Repino Rus. Fed. 43 N6
Repokaira reg. Fin. 44 N1
Repolka Rus. Fed. 43 K2
Reporoa N.Z. 152 K6
Reposaari Fin. 45 M3
Republic OH U.S.A. 176 B4
Republic WA U.S.A. 180 C2
Republican r. U.S.A. 178 C4
Republican, South Fork r. U.S.A. 178 B3
Republika Srpska aut. div. Bos.-Herz. 56 J4
Repulse Bay b. Australia 149 F4
Repulse Bay Canada 165 K3
Repvåg Norway 44 N1
Requena Peru 198 C6
Requena Spain 55 J5
Réquista France 51 I8
Reriutaba Brazil 202 D3
Reşadiye Turkey 107 E3
also known as Sorp
Reşadiye Turkey 107 D2
Reşadiye Yarımadası pen. Turkey 59 I12
Resag, Gunung mt. Indon. 76 D4
Resava r. Yugo. 58 C4
Resavica Srbija Yugo. 58 C4
Resen Macedonia 58 C7
Resende Brazil 207 I9
Reserva Brazil 203 B8
Reserve U.S.A. 181 E6
Reshetnikovo Rus. Fed. 43 R5
Reshi China 87 D2
Resia, Passo di pass Austria/Italy 48 H9
Resistencia Arg. 204 F2
Reşiţa Romania 58 C3
Resko Poland 49 M2
Resolute Bay Canada 165 J2
Resolution Island Canada 165 M3
Resolution Island N.Z. 153 A13
Resplendor Brazil 207 L6
Ressa r. Rus. Fed. 43 Q7
Ressango Garcia S. Africa 133 P2
Resseta r. Rus. Fed. 43 Q8
Restefond, Col de pass France 51 M8
Restelica Kosovo, Srbija Yugo. 58 B7
Restinga de Marambaia coastal area Brazil 207 I10
Restinga Seca Brazil 203 A9
Restrepo Col. 198 C3
Resülayn Turkey see Ceylanpınar
Retalhuleu Guat. 185 H6
Retem, Oued er watercourse Alg. 123 G2
Retén Llico Chile 204 B4
Retezat, Parcul Naţional nat. park Romania 58 D3
Retford U.K. 47 L10
also known as East Retford
Rethel France 51 K3
Réthimnon Greece see Rethymno
Rethymno Greece 59 F13
also known as Réthimnon
Retiers France 50 E5
Retortillo tourist site Spain 54 G2
Rettikhovka Rus. Fed. 90 C2
Retuerta mt. Spain 55 J4

▶Réunion terr. Indian Ocean 218 K7
French Overseas Department. Historically known as Bourbon.
africa [countries] ▶▶ 114–117

Reus Spain 55 M3
Reusam, Pulau i. Indon. 76 B2
Reutlingen Germany 48 G7
Reutov Rus. Fed. 43 S6
Reval Estonia see Tallinn
Revda Rus. Fed. 44 P2
Reveille Peak U.S.A. 183 H4
Revel Estonia see Tallinn
Revel France 51 I9
Revelganj India 97 E4
Revelstoke Canada 166 G5
Reventazón Peru 198 A6
Revermont reg. France 51 L7
Reviga Romania 58 I4
Reviga r. Romania 58 I4
Revigny-sur-Ornain France 51 K4
Revillagigedo, Islas is Mex. 184 B5
Revillagigedo Island U.S.A. 164 F4
Revna r. Rus. Fed. 43 P9
Revolyutsii, Pik mt. Tajik. see Revolyutsiya, Qullai
Revolyutsiya, Qullai mt. Tajik. 101 H2
also known as Revolyutsii, Pik
Revsnes Norway 44 L1
Revúca Slovakia 49 R7
Revuè r. Moz. 131 G3
Revyakino Rus. Fed. 43 S7
Rewa India 97 D4
Rewari India 96 C3
Rex, Mount Antarctica 222 S2
Rexburg U.S.A. 180 E4
Rexton Canada 169 H4
Rey, Isla del i. Panama 186 D5
Reyes Bol. 200 C3
Reyes, Point U.S.A. 182 A3
Reyes, Punta pt Col. 198 B4
Reyhanlı Turkey 109 H1
Reykir Iceland 44 [inset] C2
Reykjanes constituency Iceland 44 [inset] B3
Reykjanestá pt Iceland 44 [inset] B3

▶Reykjavík Iceland 44 [inset] B2
Capital of Iceland. English form Reykjavik.

Reykjavik Iceland see Reykjavík
Reynolds Range mts Australia 148 B4
Reynosa Mex. 185 F3
Reyssouze r. France 51 K6
Rezā, Kūh-e hill Iran 100 B3
Rezā'īyeh Iran see Urmia
Rezā'īyeh, Daryācheh-ye salt l. Iran see Urmia, Lake
Rēzekne Latvia 42 I5
Rēzekne r. Latvia 42 I5
Rezinjski vrh mt. Slovenia 56 G3
Rezovska Reka r. Bulg./Turkey 58 J7
Rezvāndeh Iran see Rezvānshahr
Rezvānshahr Iran 100 B2
also known as Rezvāndeh
R. F. Magón Mex. see Ricardo Flores Magón
Rgotina Srbija Yugo. 58 D4
Rharbi, Oued el watercourse Alg. 123 F3
Rhegium Italy see Reggio di Calabria
Rheims France see Reims
Rhein r. Germany 48 D4 see Rhine
Rheine Germany 48 E3
Rheinland-Pfalz land Germany 48 E6
English form Rhineland-Palatinate
Rheinsberg Germany 49 J2
Rhein-Taunus, Naturpark nature res. Germany 48 F5
Rheinwaldhorn mt. Switz. 51 P6
Rhemilès well Alg. 122 D3
Rheris, Oued watercourse Morocco 122 D3
Rhin r. France 51 N4 see Rhine
Rhine r. Europe 48 D4
also spelt Rhein (Germany) or Rhin (France)
Rhinebeck U.S.A. 177 L4
Rhinelander U.S.A. 172 D5
Rhineland-Palatinate land Germany see Rheinland-Pfalz
Rhinluch marsh Germany 49 J3
Rhino Camp Uganda 128 A4
Rhinow Germany 49 J3
Rhir, Cap c. Morocco 122 C3
Rho Italy 56 B3
Rhode Island state U.S.A. 177 N4
Rhodes Greece 59 J12
also spelt Rodos
Rhodes i. Greece 59 J12
also spelt Rodos or Ródhos; formerly known as Rodi; historically known as Rhodus
Rhodesia country Africa see Zimbabwe
Rhodes Inyanga National Park Zimbabwe see Nyanga National Park
Rhodes Matopos National Park Zimbabwe see Matobo National Park
Rhodes Peak U.S.A. 180 D3
Rhodope Mountains mts Bulg. 58 E7
Rhodope Mountains Bulg./Greece 58 E7
also known as Rodopi Planina
Rhodus i. Greece see Rhodes
Rhône r. France/Switz. 51 K9
Rhône-Alpes admin. reg. France 51 L7
Rhube, Oasis of Syria see Ruḥbah
Rhuthun U.K. see Ruthin
Rhyl U.K. 47 I10
Riaba Equat. Guinea 125 H6
Riachão Brazil 202 C3
Riachão das Neves Brazil 202 C4
Riacho de Santana Brazil 202 D5
Riacho dos Machados Brazil 207 J2
Ri'al Fuhah hill Saudi Arabia 108 H9
Rialma Brazil 206 D2
Rialp, Pantà de resr Spain 55 M3
Rialto U.S.A. 183 G7
Riangnom Sudan 126 F2
Riaño, Embalse de resr Spain 54 F2
Rianópolis Brazil 206 D2
Riansáres r. Spain 55 H5
Riasi Jammu and Kashmir 96 B2
Riau prov. Indon. 76 C2
Riau, Kepulauan is Indon. 76 D2
Riaza r. Spain 55 H3
Ribadavia Spain 54 C2
Ribadeo Spain 54 D1
Ribadesella Spain 54 F1
Ribas de Fresser Spain see Ribes de Freser
Ribas do Rio Pardo Brazil 203 A7
Ribat Afgh. 101 G2
Ribat-i-Shur waterhole Iran 100 D3
Ribáuè Moz. 131 H2
Ribble r. U.K. 47 J10
Ribe Denmark 45 J5
Ribeirão Branco Brazil 206 E11
Ribeirão das Neves Brazil 207 I6
Ribeirão do Pinhal Brazil 206 C10
Ribeirão Preto Brazil 206 F8
Ribera Sicilia Italy 57 F11
Ribérac France 50 G7
Riberalta Bol. 200 D2
Ribes de Freser Spain 55 N2
also spelt Ribas de Fresser
Ribnica Slovenia 56 G3
Rîbniţa Moldova 41 D7
formerly spelt Râbniţa or Rybnitsa
Ribnitz-Damgarten Germany 49 J1
Ribnovo Bulg. 58 E7
Rica Aventura Chile 200 C5
Říčany Czech Rep. 49 L6
Ricardo Flores Magón Mex. 184 D2
short form R. F. Magón
Riccione Italy 56 E4
Rice CA U.S.A. 183 J7
Rice VA U.S.A. 176 G8
Rice Lake l. Ont. Canada 168 E4
Rice Lake l. Ont. Canada 173 K3
Rice Lake U.S.A. 172 B5
Riceville U.S.A. 176 C8
Richards Bay S. Africa 133 Q5
Richards Inlet Antarctica 223 L1
Richards Island Canada 164 F3
Richardson r. Canada 167 I3
Richardson Island Canada 167 G1
Richardson Lakes U.S.A. 177 O1
Richardson Mountains Canada 164 F3
Richardson Mountains N.Z. 153 C12
Richard Toll Senegal 124 B2
Richelieu France 50 G5
Richfield U.S.A. 183 L3
Richfield Springs U.S.A. 177 K3
Richford NY U.S.A. 177 I3
Richford VT U.S.A. 177 M1
Richgrove U.S.A. 182 E6
Richibucto Canada 169 H4
Rich Lake Canada 167 I4
Richland U.S.A. 180 C3
Richland Center U.S.A. 172 C7
Richlands U.S.A. 176 D8
Richmond N.S.W. Australia 147 F3
Richmond Qld Australia 149 D4
Richmond Ont. Canada 173 R5
Richmond Que. Canada 169 F4
Richmond N.Z. 152 H9
Richmond KwaZulu-Natal S. Africa 133 O6
Richmond N. Cape S. Africa 132 H8
Richmond U.K. 47 K9
Richmond CA U.S.A. 182 B4
Richmond IL U.S.A. 172 E8
Richmond IN U.S.A. 176 A6
Richmond KY U.S.A. 176 A8
Richmond ME U.S.A. 177 P1
Richmond MI U.S.A. 173 K8
Richmond TX U.S.A. 179 D6

▶Richmond VA U.S.A. 176 H8
State capital of Virginia.

Richmond VT U.S.A. 177 M1
Richmond, Mount N.Z. 152 H9
Richmond Dale U.S.A. 176 C6
Richmond Hill Canada 168 E5
Richmond Hill U.S.A. 175 D6
Richmond Range hills Australia 147 G2
Richmond Range mts N.Z. 152 H9
Richmondville U.S.A. 177 K3
Rich Square U.S.A. 177 H9
Richtersveld National Park S. Africa 132 B5
Richvale U.S.A. 182 C2
Richwood OH U.S.A. 176 B5
Richwood WV U.S.A. 176 E7
Rickleån r. Sweden 44 M2
Ricobayo, Embalse de resr Spain 54 F3
also known as Esla, Embalse de
Ricomagus France see Riom
Riddell Nunataks Antarctica 223 E2
Ridder Kazakh. see Leninogorsk
Riddlesburg U.S.A. 176 G5
Rideau r. Canada 173 R5
Rideau Lakes Canada 168 E4
Ridge r. Canada 168 C3
Ridgecrest U.S.A. 182 G6
Ridgefield U.S.A. 177 L4
Ridgeland MS U.S.A. 175 B5
Ridgeland SC U.S.A. 175 D5
Ridgeland WI U.S.A. 172 B5
Ridgetown Canada 173 L8
Ridgeway U.S.A. 176 F9
Ridgway U.S.A. 176 G4
Riding Mountain National Park Canada 167 K5
Ridley r. Australia 150 B4
Riebeek-Kasteel S. Africa 132 C10
Riebeek-Oos S. Africa 133 K10
Riebeek Wes S. Africa 132 C10
Riecito Venez. 198 D2
Ried im Innkreis Austria 49 K7
Riedlingen Germany 48 G7
Riekertsdam S. Africa 133 K2
Rieppesgai'sa mt. Norway 44 M1
Riesa Germany 49 K4
Riesco, Isla i. Chile 205 B9
Riesi Sicilia Italy 57 G11
Rieste Germany 48 F3
Riet r. S. Africa 133 H6
Riet watercourse S. Africa 132 E8
Rietavas Lith. 42 C6
Rietberg Germany 48 F4
Rietbron S. Africa 132 H9
Rietfontein S. Africa 132 E3
Riethuiskraal S. Africa 132 F11
Rieti Italy 56 E6
historically known as Reate
Rietpoort S. Africa 132 C7
Rietschen Germany 49 L4
Riet se Vloer salt pan S. Africa 132 E7
Rietvlei S. Africa 133 O6
Rieumes France 50 H9
Rifā'ī, Tall mt. Jordan/Syria 109 H5
Rifaina Brazil 206 F7
Rifeng China see Lichuan
Rifle U.S.A. 180 F5
Rift Valley prov. Kenya 128 B4
Rift Valley Lakes National Park Eth. see Abijatta-Shalla National Park

▶Rīga Latvia 42 F5
Capital of Latvia. English form Riga.

Riga Latvia see Rīga
Riga, Gulf of Estonia/Latvia 42 E4
also known as Liivi laht or Rīgas jūras līcis or Riia laht
Rigacikun Nigeria 125 G4
Rigaio Greece 59 D9
Rīgān Iran 100 D4
Rīgas jūras līcis b. Estonia/Latvia see Riga, Gulf of
Rigby U.S.A. 180 E4
Rig-Rig Chad 120 B6
Riguel r. Spain 55 J2
Riia laht b. Estonia/Latvia see Riga, Gulf of
Riihimäki Fin. 45 N3
Riiser-Larsen Ice Shelf Antarctica 223 W2
Riisipere Estonia 42 F2
Riisitunturin kansallispuisto nat. park Fin. 44 O2
Riito Mex. 184 B1
Rijau Nigeria 125 G4
Riječki Zaliv b. Croatia 56 G3
Rijeka Croatia 56 G3
formerly known as Fiume
Rijm al Mudharī hill Iraq 109 K5
Rikā, Wādī ar watercourse Saudi Arabia 104 D3
Rikubetsu Japan 90 H3
Rikuchū-kaigan National Park Japan 90 H5
Rikuzen-takata Japan 90 G5
Rila Bulg. 58 E6
Rila mts Bulg. 58 E6
Rila China 89 D6
Riley U.S.A. 180 C4
Rileyville U.S.A. 176 G7
Rillieux-la-Pape France 51 K7
Rillito U.S.A. 183 M9
Rima watercourse Niger/Nigeria 125 G3
Rimah, Wādī al watercourse Saudi Arabia 104 C2
Rimau, Pulau i. Indon. 76 D3
Rimava r. Slovakia 49 R7
Rimavská Sobota Slovakia 49 R7
Rimbey Canada 167 H4
Rimbo Sweden 45 L4
Rimersburg U.S.A. 176 F4
Rimetea Romania 58 E2
Rimforsa Sweden 45 K4
Rimini Italy 56 E4
historically known as Ariminum
Rîmnicu Sărat Romania see Râmnicu Sărat
Rîmnicu Vîlcea Romania see Râmnicu Vâlcea
Rimouski Canada 169 G3
Rimouski, Réserve Faunique de nature res. Canada 169 G3
Rimutaka Forest Park nature res. N.Z. 152 J9
Rinbung China 89 E6
also known as Deji
Rinca i. Indon. 75 A5
Rincão Brazil 206 E8
Rincon Morocco see Mdiq
Rincón, Cerro del mt. Chile 200 D6
Rinconada Arg. 200 D5
Rincón del Bonete, Lago Artificial de resr Uruguay 204 F4
Rincón de los Sauces Arg. 204 C5
Rincón de Romos Mex. 185 E4
Rind r. India 96 D4
Rinda r. Latvia 42 C4
Rindal Norway 44 J3
Rineia i. Greece 59 G11
also spelt Rinia
Riner U.S.A. 176 E8
Ringarooma Bay Australia 147 E5
Ringas India 96 B4
Ringe Denmark 45 J5
Ringebu Norway 45 J3
Ringgold U.S.A. 174 C5
Ringim Nigeria 125 H3
Ringkøbing Denmark 45 J4
Ringkøbing Fjord lag. Denmark 45 J5
Ringsted Denmark 45 J5
Ringvassøy i. Norway 44 L1
Ringwood U.K. 47 K13
Ringwood U.S.A. 177 K4
Rinia i. Greece see Rineia
Rinópolis Brazil 206 C8
Rinteln Germany 48 G3
Rinya r. Romania 49 O9
Rio IL U.S.A. 172 C9
Rio WI U.S.A. 172 D7
Rio Alegre Brazil 201 F4
Riobamba Ecuador 198 B5
Rio Bananal Brazil 207 M6
Rio Blanco U.S.A. 180 F5
Rio Bonito Brazil 207 K9
Rio Branco Brazil 200 D2
Rio Branco state Brazil see Roraima
Rio Branco, Parque Nacional do nat. park Brazil 199 F4
Rio Bravo, Parque Internacional del nat. park Mex. 185 E2
Rio Brilhante Brazil 203 A7
Rio Bueno Chile 204 B6
Rio Caribe Venez. 199 F2
Rio Casca Brazil 203 D7
Rio Chico Arg. 205 C8
Rio Chico Venez. 199 E2
Rio Claro Rio de Janeiro Brazil 207 I9
Rio Claro São Paulo Brazil 206 F9
Rio Claro Trin. and Tob. 187 H5
Rio Claro Venez. 187 F5
Rio Colorado Arg. 204 D5
Rio Corrientes Ecuador 198 B5
Rio Cuarto Arg. 204 D4
Rio das Almas r. Brazil 201 H3
Rio das Pedras Moz. 131 G4

▶Rio de Janeiro Brazil 203 D7
3rd most populous city in South America. Former capital of Brazil.
world [cities] ▶▶ 24–25

Rio de Janeiro state Brazil 203 D7
Rio de Jesús Panama 186 C6

▶Rio de la Plata - Paraná r. S. America 204 F4
2nd longest river in South America and 9th in the world.
southamerica [landscapes] ▶▶ 190–191

Rio Dell U.S.A. 180 A4
Rio do Sul Brazil 203 B8
Rio Formoso Brazil 202 F4
Rio Frio Costa Rica 186 C5
Rio Gallegos Arg. 205 C8
Rio Grande Arg. 205 D9
Rio Grande Bol. 200 D5
Rio Grande Brazil 204 G4
Rio Grande Mex. 185 E4
Rio Grande r. Mex./U.S.A. 185 F3
also known as Bravo del Norte, Río
Rio Grande, Salar de salt flat Arg. 204 C2
Rio Grande City U.S.A. 179 C7
Rio Grande do Norte state Brazil 202 E3
Rio Grande do Sul state Brazil 203 A9
Riohacha Col. 198 C2
Rio Hato Panama 186 C5
Rio Hondo, Embalse resr Arg. 204 D2
Rioja Peru 198 B6
Rio Lagartos Mex. 185 H4
Rio Largo Brazil 202 F4
Riom France 51 J7
historically known as Ricomagus
Rio Maior Port. 54 C5
Riom-ès-Montagnes France 51 I7
Rio Muerto Arg. 204 E2
Rio Mulatos Bol. 200 D4
Rio Muni reg. Equat. Guinea 125 H6
Rio Negro prov. Arg. 204 D5
Rio Negro Brazil 203 B8
Rio Negro Chile 204 B6
Rionero in Vulture Italy 56 H8
Rioni r. Georgia 107 E2
Rio Novo Brazil 207 J8
Rio Novo do Sul Brazil 207 M7
Rio Pardo de Minas Brazil 202 D5
Rio Plátano, Reserva Biósfero del nature res. Hond. 186 B4
Rio Pomba Brazil 207 J8
Rio Preto Brazil 207 J9
Rio Preto, Serra do hills Brazil 206 G3
Rio Rancho U.S.A. 181 F6
Rios Spain 54 D3
Riosucio Col. 198 B3
Rio Tercero Arg. 204 D4
Rio Tigre Ecuador 198 B5
Rio Tinto Brazil 202 F3
Rio Tuba Phil. 74 A4
Riou, Oued watercourse Alg. 55 L9
Riou Lake Canada 167 J3
Rio Verde Brazil 206 C4
Rio Verde Chile 205 C9
Rioverde Ecuador 198 B4
Rio Verde Quintana Roo Mex. 185 H5
Rio Verde San Luis Potosí Mex. 185 F4
Rio Verde de Mato Grosso Brazil 203 A6
Rio Vermelho Brazil 207 J5
Rio Vista U.S.A. 182 C3
Riozinho Brazil 200 D2
Riozinho r. Amazonas Brazil 199 E5
Riozinho r. Mato Grosso do Sul Brazil 201 F4
Ripanj Srbija Yugo. 58 B4
Ripats Sweden 44 M2
Ripky Ukr. 41 D6
Ripley MS U.S.A. 174 B5
Ripley NY U.S.A. 176 F3
Ripley OH U.S.A. 176 B7
Ripley TN U.S.A. 174 B5
Ripley WV U.S.A. 176 D7
Ripoll Spain 55 N2
Ripon U.K. 47 K9
Ripon CA U.S.A. 182 C4
Ripon WI U.S.A. 172 E7
Riposto Sicilia Italy 57 H11
Risalpur Pak. 101 H3
Risān 'Aneiza hill Egypt 108 E7
Risaralda dept Col. 198 C3
Risasi Dem. Rep. Congo 126 E5
Risbäck Sweden 44 K2
Riscle France 50 F9
Risco Plateado mt. Arg. 204 C4
Risha, Birkat Umm salt l. Egypt 108 B7
Rishā', Wādī ar watercourse Saudi Arabia 104 D2
Rishikesh India 96 C3
Rishiri-Rebun-Sarobetsu National Park Japan 90 G2
Rishiri-tō i. Japan 90 G2
Rishiri-zan vol. Japan 82 F3
Rishon Le Ziyyon Israel 108 F6
Rising Sun IN U.S.A. 176 A7
Rising Sun MD U.S.A. 177 I6
Risle r. France 50 G3
Risnjak nat. park Croatia 56 G3
Rîşnov Romania see Râşnov
Rison U.S.A. 179 D5
Risør Norway 45 J4
Rissa Norway 44 J3
Rissington N.Z. 152 K7
Rissu, Gebel hill Egypt 108 B8
Ristiina Fin. 45 N3
Ristijärvi Fin. 44 O2
Ristikent Rus. Fed. 44 O1
Risum China 89 B5
Ritan r. Indon. 77 F2
Ritausma Latvia 42 F5
Ritchie S. Africa 133 I6
Ritchie's Archipelago is India 95 G3
Ritch Island Canada 167 G1
Ritscher Upland mts Antarctica 223 X2
Ritsem Sweden 44 L2
Ritsis Nakrdzali nature res. Georgia 107 E2
Ritter, Mount U.S.A. 182 E4
Ritupe r. Latvia 42 I5
Ritzville U.S.A. 180 C3
Riu, Mount hill P.N.G. 149 G1
Riva r. Latvia 42 C5
Rivadavia Buenos Aires Arg. 204 E4
Rivadavia Mendoza Arg. 204 C4
Rivadavia Salta Arg. 201 E6
Rivadavia Chile 204 C3
Riva del Garda Italy 56 C3
Riva Palacio Mex. 181 F7
Rivarolo Canavese Italy 51 N7
Rivas Nicaragua 186 B5
Rīvash Iran 100 D3
Rive-de-Gier France 51 K7
Rivera Arg. 204 E5
Rivera Uruguay 204 G3
River Cess Liberia 124 C5
Riverdale U.S.A. 182 E5
Riverhead U.S.A. 177 M5
Riverina Australia 151 C6
Riverina reg. Australia 147 E3
Rivero, Isla i. Chile 205 B7
Rivers state Nigeria 125 G5
Riversdale N.Z. 153 C13
Riversdale S. Africa 132 F11
Riversdale Beach N.Z. 152 K9
Riverside S. Africa 133 N7
Riverside CA U.S.A. 182 G8
Riverside IA U.S.A. 172 B9
Riversleigh Australia 148 C3
Riverton Canada 167 L5
Riverton N.Z. 153 C14
also known as Aparima
Riverton S. Africa 133 I5
Riverton UT U.S.A. 183 M1
Riverton VA U.S.A. 176 G7
Riverton WY U.S.A. 180 E4
Riverview Canada 169 H4
River View S. Africa 133 Q5
Rives France 51 L7
Rivesaltes France 51 I10
Rivesville U.S.A. 176 E6
Rivière-au-Renard Canada 169 H3
Rivière Bleue Canada 169 G4
Rivière-du-Loup Canada 169 G4
Rivière-Pentecote Canada 169 H3
Rivière-Pigou Canada 169 H3
Rivière-Pilote Martinique 187 H4
Riviersonderend S. Africa 132 D11
Riviersonderend Mountains S. Africa 132 D11
Rivne Ukr. 41 C6
also spelt Rovno; formerly spelt Równe
Rivoli Italy 51 N7
Rivulets S. Africa 133 O2
Rivungo Angola 127 D9
Riwaka N.Z. 152 G9
Riwoqê China 86 A2

▶Riyadh Saudi Arabia 105 D2
Capital of Saudi Arabia. Also spelt Ar Riyāḍ.

Riyan Yemen 105 E5
Riyue Shankou pass China 84 D4
Riza well Iran 100 C3
Rizal Phil. 74 B3
Rize Turkey 107 E2
Rizhao Shandong China 85 H5
formerly known as Shijiusuo
Rizhao Shandong China 85 H5
Rizokarpaso Cyprus see Rizokarpason
Rizokarpason Cyprus 108 F2
also known as Dipkarpaz or Rizokarpaso
Rīzū well Iran 100 D3
Rīzū'īyeh Iran 100 D4
Rjukan Norway 45 J4
Rkîz, Lac l. Mauritania 124 B2
Roa Norway 45 J3
Roa Spain 54 H3
Roach Lake U.S.A. 183 I6
Roads U.S.A. 176 C6

▶Road Town Virgin Is (U.K.) 187 G3
Capital of the British Virgin Islands.

Roan Norway 44 J2
Roan Cliffs ridge U.S.A. 183 O2
Roan Fell hill U.K. 47 J8
Roan Mountain U.S.A. 176 C9
Roanne France 51 K6
Roanoke AL U.S.A. 175 C5
Roanoke IL U.S.A. 172 D10
Roanoke VA U.S.A. 176 F8
Roanoke r. U.S.A. 176 I9
Roanoke Rapids U.S.A. 176 H9
Roan Plateau U.S.A. 183 O2
Roaringwater Bay Rep. of Ireland 47 C12
Roatán Hond. 186 B3
also known as Coxen Hole
Robāt r. Afgh. 101 E4
Robāţ Iran 100 D4
Robāţ-e Khān Iran 100 D3
Robāţ-e Shahr-e Bābak Iran 100 C4
Robāţe Tork Iran 100 B3
Robāţ-e Ţoroq Iran 100 C3
Robāţ Karīm Iran 100 B3
Robāţ-Sang Iran 101 D3
Robat Thana Pak. 101 E4
Robb Canada 167 G4
Robben Island S. Africa 132 C10
Robbins U.S.A. 176 A9
Robbins Island Australia 147 E5
Robbinsville U.S.A. 174 D5
Robe r. Australia 150 A4
Robe, Mount hill Australia 146 D2
Robel Germany 49 J2
Robert Glacier Antarctica 223 D2
Robert Lee U.S.A. 179 B6
Roberts U.S.A. 180 D4
Roberts, Mount Australia 147 G2
Robertsburg U.S.A. 176 D7
Roberts Butte mt. Antarctica 223 K2
Roberts Creek Mountain U.S.A. 183 H2
Robertsfors Sweden 44 M2
Robertsganj India 97 D4

Robert S. Kerr Reservoir U.S.A. 179 D5
Robertson r. Australia 149 D3
Robertson S. Africa 132 D10
Robertson Bay Antarctica 223 L2
Robertson Island Antarctica 222 U2
Robertson Point N.Z. 152 I9
Robertson Range hills Australia 150 C4
Robertsport Liberia 124 C5
Robertstown Australia 146 C3
Roberval Canada 169 F3
Robeson Channel Canada/Greenland 165 M1
Robhanais, Rubha hd U.K. see Butt of Lewis
Robin's Nest hill Hong Kong China 87 [inset]
also known as Hung Fa Leng
Robinson r. N.T. Australia 148 C3
Robinson r. W.A. Australia 150 D3
Robinson Canada 166 C2
Robinson IL U.S.A. 174 C9
Robinson KY U.S.A. 176 A7
Robinson Creek r. Australia 149 F5
Robinson Range hills Australia 151 B5
Robinvale Australia 147 D3
Robles La Paz Col. 198 C2
Roblin Canada 167 K5
Robore Bol. 201 F4
Robsart Canada 167 I5
Robson, Mount Canada 166 G4
Robstown U.S.A. 179 C7
Roby U.S.A. 179 B5
Roçadas Angola see Xangongo
Roca Partida, Isla i. Mex. 184 B5
Rocas, Atol das atoll Brazil 202 F2
Rocas Alijos is Mex. 184 B3
Rocca Busambra mt. Sicilia Italy 57 F11
Rocca Imperiale Italy 57 I8
Roccastrada Italy 56 D5
Roc de Montalet mt. France 51 I9
Roc d'Enfer mt. France 51 M6
Rocha Uruguay 204 G4
Rochdale U.K. 47 J10
Rochechouart France 50 G7
Roche de Vic hill France 50 H7
Rochefort Belgium 51 K5
Rochefort France 50 F7
Rochefort, Lac l. Canada 169 F1
Rochegda Rus. Fed. 40 G3
Rochelle U.S.A. 172 D9
Rochester IN U.S.A. 174 C3
Rochester MN U.S.A. 174 A2
Rochester NH U.S.A. 177 O2
Rochester NY U.S.A. 176 H2
Roc'h Trévezel hill France 50 C4
Rocina r. Spain 54 E18
Rock r. Canada 166 E2
Rock r. IA U.S.A. 174 B3
Rock r. IL U.S.A. 174 B3
Rock and Pillar Range mts N.Z. 153 D13
Rock Bay Canada 166 E5
Rock Creek Canada 166 B1
Rock Creek r. U.S.A. 180 F2
Rockdale U.S.A. 179 C6
Rockefeller National Wildlife Refuge nature res. U.S.A. 179 D6
Rockefeller Plateau Antarctica 222 Q1
Rockford AL U.S.A. 175 C5
Rockford IL U.S.A. 172 D8
Rockford NC U.S.A. 176 E9
Rockford OH U.S.A. 176 A5
Rockglen Canada 167 J5
Rock Hall U.S.A. 177 I6
Rockhampton Australia 149 F4
Rockhampton Downs Australia 148 B3
Rock Hill U.S.A. 174 D5
Rockingham Australia 151 A7
Rockingham U.S.A. 174 E5
Rockingham Bay Australia 149 E3
Rockinghorse Lake Canada 167 H1
Rocklake U.S.A. 178 C1
Rockland MA U.S.A. 177 O3
Rockland ME U.S.A. 177 P1
Rocklands Reservoir Australia 147 C4
Rocklea Australia 150 B4
Rocklin U.S.A. 182 C3
Rockmart U.S.A. 175 C5
Rock Point U.S.A. 183 O5
Rockport IN U.S.A. 174 C4
Rockport MA U.S.A. 177 O3
Rockport TX U.S.A. 179 C7
Rockport WV U.S.A. 176 D6
Rock Rapids U.S.A. 178 B3
Rock River U.S.A. 180 F4
Rock Sound Bahamas 186 D1
Rock Springs MT U.S.A. 180 F3
Rocksprings U.S.A. 179 B6
Rock Springs WY U.S.A. 180 E4
Rockstone Guyana 199 G3
Rockton U.S.A. 172 D8
Rockville IN U.S.A. 174 C4
Rockville MD U.S.A. 177 H6
Rockwall U.S.A. 179 C5
Rockwood U.S.A. 173 J8
Rocky Boy's Indian Reservation res. U.S.A. 180 E2
Rockyford Canada 167 H5
Rocky Ford U.S.A. 178 A4
Rocky Fork Lake U.S.A. 176 B6

Rocky Harbour Canada 169 J3
Rocky Hill U.S.A. 176 C7
Rocky Lane Canada 167 G3
Rocky Mount NC U.S.A. 174 E5
Rocky Mount VA U.S.A. 176 F9
Rocky Mountain House Canada 167 H4
Rocky Mountain National Park U.S.A. 180 F4
Rocky Mountains U.S.A. 170 D3
Rocky Mountains Forest Reserve nature res. Canada 167 G4
Rocroi France 51 K3
Rodberg Norway 45 J3
Rødbyhavn Denmark 45 J5
Roddickton Canada 169 K3
Rode S. Africa 133 N7
Rødeby Sweden 45 K4
Rodeo Mex. 184 D3
Roderick r. Australia 151 B5
Rodez France 51 I8
Rodholivos Greece see Rodolivos
Rodhópolis Greece see Rodopoli
Ródhos i. Greece see Rhodes
Rodi i. Greece see Rhodes
Roding Germany 49 J6
Rodino Rus. Fed. 103 J1
Rodna Romania 58 F1
Rodnichek Rus. Fed. see Rodnichok
Rodnichok Rus. Fed. 41 G6
also spelt Rodnichek
Rodnya Belarus 43 M7
Rodnykovka Kazakh. 102 D2
Rodolfo Sanchez Toboada Mex. 184 A2
Rodolivos Greece 58 E8
also spelt Rodholivos
Rodonit, Kepi i pt Albania 58 A7
Rodopi Planina mts Bulg./Greece see Rhodope Mountains
Rodopoli Greece 58 E7
also known as Rodhópolis
Rodopos Greece 59 E13
Rodos Greece see Rhodes
Rodosto Turkey see Tekirdağ
Rodovoye Rus. Fed. 42 I4
Rodøya i. Norway 44 K2
Rodrigues Peru 198 C6
Rodrigues Island Mauritius 218 L7
Redsand Norway 44 O1
Roe r. Australia 150 B4
Roebourne Australia 150 B4
Roebuck Bay Australia 150 C3
Reedtan S. Africa 133 F5
Roe Plains Australia 151 D6
Roermond Neth. 48 C4
Roeselare Belgium 51 J2
also known as Roulers
Roes Welcome Sound sea chan. Canada 167 O2
Rogachev Belarus see Rahachow
Rogachevo Rus. Fed. 43 S5
Rogagua, Laguna l. Bol. 200 D3
Rogaland county Norway 45 I4
Rogaška Slatina Slovenia 49 M9
Rogatica Bos.-Herz. 56 L5
Roger, Lac l. Canada 173 O3
Rogers U.S.A. 179 D4
Rogers, Mount U.S.A. 176 D9
Rogers City U.S.A. 173 J5
Rogers Lake U.S.A. 182 G7
Rogersville U.S.A. 176 B9
Roggan r. Canada 168 E2
Roggan, Lac l. Canada 168 E2
Roggeveld plat. S. Africa 132 E9
Roggeveldberge esc. S. Africa 132 E9
Rogliano Italy 57 I9
Rognan Norway 44 K2
Rognedino Rus. Fed. 43 O8
Rognitz r. Germany 48 H2
Rogoźno Poland 49 O3
Rogue r. U.S.A. 180 A4
Roha India 94 B2
Rohnert Park U.S.A. 182 B3
Rohrbach in Oberösterreich Austria 49 K7
Rohri Pak. 101 G5
Rohtak India 96 C3
Roi Et Thai. 78 C4
Roi Georges, Îles du is Fr. Polynesia 221 I6
English form King George Islands
Roine l. Fin. 45 N3
Roing India 97 G3
Roja Latvia 42 D4
Rojas Arg. 204 E4
Röjdåfors Sweden 45 K3
Rojhan Pak. 101 G4
Rojo, Cabo c. Mex. 185 F4
Rojo, Cabo c. Puerto Rico 187 G3
Rojo Aguado, Laguna l. Bol. 200 D3
Rokan r. Indon. 76 C2
Rokeby Australia 149 D2
Rokeby National Park Australia 149 D2
Rokiškis Lith. 42 G6
Rokkasho Japan 90 G4
Rokkō-zaki pt Japan 90 E6
Rokland Norway 44 K2
Roknäs Sweden 44 M2
Rokycany Czech Rep. 49 K6
Rokytne Ukr. 44 C6
Rola Kangri mt. China 89 E5
Rolândia Brazil 206 B10
Rolas, Ilha das i. São Tomé and Principe 125 G7
Rolim de Moura Brazil 201 E2
Roll U.S.A. 183 K9
Rolla U.S.A. 174 B4
Rolla MO U.S.A. 174 B4
Rolla ND U.S.A. 178 C1
Rollag Norway 45 J3
Rolleston Australia 149 F5
Rolleston N.Z. 153 G11
Rollet Canada 173 N3
Rolleville Bahamas 186 E2
Rolling Fork U.S.A. 175 B5
Rollinsford U.S.A. 177 O2
Rolphton Canada 173 N3
Rolvsøya i. Norway 44 N1
Roma Australia 149 F5
Roma i. Indon. 75 C4
Roma Italy see Rome
Roma Lesotho 133 L6
Roma U.S.A. 179 C7
Romain, Cape U.S.A. 171 K5
Romaine r. Canada 169 I3
Roman Romania 58 H2
Română, Câmpia plain Romania 58 G2
Romanat, Lac l. Canada 169 H1
Români Egypt 108 D7
Romania country Europe 58 E3
also spelt Roumania or Rumania
europe [countries] ▶ 32–35
Roman-Kosh mt. Ukr. 41 E7
Romanche, Cayo i. Cuba 186 D2
Romang, Selat sea chan. Indon. 75 C5
Romanovka Moldova see Basarabeasca
Romanovka Rus. Fed. 41 I2
Romanovka Rus. Fed. 41 G6
Romanovo Rus. Fed. 103 J1
Romanovo Rus. Fed. 42 I4
Romans-sur-Isère France 51 L7
Romanzof, Cape U.S.A. 164 C3
Romão Brazil 199 F5
Rombas France 51 M3
Romblon Phil. 74 B3
Romblon i. Phil. 74 B3
Romblon Passage Phil. 74 B3
Rombo, Ilhéus do is Cape Verde see Secos, Ilhéus

Rome Italy 56 E7
Capital of Italy. Also spelt Roma.
Rome GA U.S.A. 179 F5
Rome ME U.S.A. 177 P1
Rome NY U.S.A. 177 J2
Romeo U.S.A. 173 J8
Romford U.K. 47 M12
Romilly-sur-Seine France 51 J4
Romit Tajik. 101 G2
also spelt Ramit
Romitan Uzbek. 103 F5
formerly spelt Ramitan
Romney U.S.A. 176 F6
Romny Ukr. 41 E6
Rømø i. Denmark 45 J5
Romorantin-Lanthenay France 50 H5
Rompin r. Malaysia 76 C2
Romppala Fin. 44 O3
Romsey U.K. 47 K13
Romu mt. Indon. 77 G5
Romulus U.S.A. 173 J8
Ron India 94 B3
Rona i. U.K. 46 I5
also known as North Rona
Ronas Hill hill U.K. 46 K3
Roncador, Serra do hills Brazil 202 A4
Roncador Cay i. Caribbean Sea 186 C4
Roncador Reef Solomon Is 145 E2
Ronceverte U.S.A. 176 D8
Ronciglione Italy 56 E6
Ronco r. Italy 56 E4
Ronda Spain 54 F8
Ronda, Serranía de mts Spain 54 F8
Ronda, Serranía de nature res. Spain 54 G8
Ronda das Salinas Brazil 201 E3
Rondane Nasjonalpark nat. park Norway 45 J3
Ronde i. Grenada 187 H4
Rondon Brazil 206 A10
Rondón Col. 198 D3
Rondônia state Brazil 201 E2
formerly known as Guaporé
Rondonópolis Brazil 202 A6
Rondout Reservoir U.S.A. 177 K4
Rong'an China 87 D3
also known as Chang'an
Rongbaca China 86 B2
also known as Changyuan
Rongcheng China see Qingyang
Rongcheng China see Rongxian
Rongcheng China see Jianli
Rongcheng China 85 I4
formerly known as Yatou
Rongcheng Wan b. China 85 I4
Rong Chu r. China 89 E6
Rong'e China see Nangqên
Rongjiang China 87 D3
also known as Guzhou
Rongjiang China see Nankang
Rong Jiang r. China 87 D4
Rongjiawan China see Yueyang
Rongklang Range mts Myanmar 78 A3
Rongmei China see Hefeng
Rongshui China 87 D3
Rongwo China see Tongren
Rongxian Guangxi China 87 D4
also known as Rongcheng
Rongxian Sichuan China 86 C2
also known as Xuyang
Rongzhag China see Danba
Rönlap atoll Marshall Is see Rongelap
Renne Denmark 45 K5
Ronneby Sweden 45 K4
Ronne Entrance strait Antarctica 222 S2
Ronne Ice Shelf Antarctica 222 T1
formerly known as Edith Ronne Land
Ronnenberg Germany 48 G3
Ronse Belgium 51 J2
also known as Renaix
Ronuro r. Brazil 202 A5
Roodebank S. Africa 133 N3
Rooiberg mt. Free State S. Africa 133 M5
Rooiberg mt. W. Cape S. Africa 132 F10
Rooikloof pass S. Africa 132 E9
Rooikraal S. Africa 133 N2
Rooke Island P.N.G. see Umboi
Rookh Aboriginal Reserve Australia 150 B4
Roorkee India 96 C3
Roosboom S. Africa 133 N5
Roosendaal Neth. 48 B4
Roosevelt AZ U.S.A. 183 M8
Roosevelt UT U.S.A. 183 O1
Roosevelt, Mount Canada 166 E3
Roosevelt Island Antarctica 223 N1
Roosna-Alliku Estonia 42 G2
Roossenekal S. Africa 133 N2
Root r. Canada 166 F2
Root r. U.S.A. 174 B3
Ropa r. Poland 49 S6
Ropaži Latvia 42 F5
Roper r. Australia 148 B2
Roper Bar Australia 148 B2
Roper Bar Aboriginal Land res. Australia 148 B2
also known as Yutpundji Djindiwinrritj
Roper Creek r. Australia 149 F4
Ropinsalmi Fin. 44 M1
Roquebrune-sur-Argens France 51 M9
Roquefort France 50 F8
Roquetas de Mar Spain 55 I8
Roraima state Brazil 199 F4
formerly known as Rio Branco
Roraima, Mount Guyana 199 F3
Rorey Lake Canada 166 D1
Rori India 96 B3
Roros Norway 44 J3
Rorschach Switz. 51 P5
Rorvik Norway 44 J2
Ros' r. Belarus 42 H9
Ros, Jezioro l. Poland 49 S2
Ros, Punta pt Mex. 184 C3
Rosa, Lake Bahamas 187 E2
Rosa, Punta pt Mex. 184 C3
Rosal de la Frontera Spain 54 D7
Rosales Mex. 184 D2
Rosal U.S.A. 180 C3
Rosamond U.S.A. 182 F7
Rosamond Lake U.S.A. 182 F7
Rosamorada Mex. 184 D4
Rosario Arg. 204 E4
Rosario Jujuy Arg. 200 D5
Rosario Santa Fé Arg. 204 E4
Rosário Brazil 202 C2
Rosario Baja California Norte Mex. 184 A1
Rosario Baja California Norte Mex. 184 B2
Rosario Baja California Sur Mex. 184 C3
Rosario Sinaloa Mex. 184 D4
Rosario Sonora Mex. 184 C2
Rosario Venez. 198 C2
Rosario, Cayo i. Cuba 186 C2
Rosario, Cayo del i. Cuba 186 C2
Rosario, Sierra del hills Cuba 175 D8
Rosario de la Frontera Arg. 204 D2
Rosario de Lerma Arg. 200 D3
Rosário do Sul Brazil 203 A9
Rosário Oeste Brazil 201 F3
Rosarito Baja California Norte Mex. 184 A1
Rosarito Baja California Norte Mex. 184 B2
Rosarito Baja California Sur Mex. 184 C3
Rosarno Italy 57 H10
Rosas Spain see Roses
Rosas, Golfo de b. Spain see Roses, Golfo de
Rosa Zárate Ecuador 198 B4

Roscoff France 50 C4
Roscommon Rep. of Ireland 47 D10
Roscommon U.S.A. 173 I6
Roscrea Rep. of Ireland 47 E11
Rose r. Australia 148 B2
Rose, Mount U.S.A. 182 E2
Roseau Dominica 187 H4
Capital of Dominica.
Roseau r. U.S.A. 178 D1
Roseau U.S.A. 178 C1
Roseberth Australia 148 C5
Rosebery Australia 147 E5
Rose Blanche Canada 169 J4
Rosebud r. Canada 167 H5
Rosebud Creek r. U.S.A. 180 F3
Rosebud Indian Reservation res. U.S.A. 178 B3
Roseburg U.S.A. 180 B4
Rose City U.S.A. 173 I6
Rosedale MS U.S.A. 174 B5
Rosedale TN U.S.A. 176 A9
Rosedene S. Africa 132 G9
Rosehall Guyana 199 G3
Roseires Reservoir Sudan 128 B2
Rosemary Island Australia 150 B4
Rosenberg U.S.A. 179 D6
Rosendal Norway 45 I4
Rosendale U.S.A. 172 E7
Rosengarten Germany 48 G2
Rosenheim Germany 48 J8
Rose Peak U.S.A. 183 O8
Rose Point Canada 166 D4
Roses Spain 55 O2
also spelt Rosas
Roses, Golf de b. Spain 55 O2
also known as Rosas, Golfo de
Roseto degli Abruzzi Italy 56 G6
Rosetown Canada 167 J5
Rosetta Egypt see Rashid
Rosetta Creek r. Australia 149 E4
Rouyn Canada 168 E3
Rouyuan China see Huachi
Rouyuanchengzi China see Huachi
Rovaniemi Fin. 44 N2
Rovato Italy 56 C3
Roven'ki Rus. Fed. 41 F6
Rovereto Italy 56 D3
Roversi Arg. 204 E2
Rovigo Italy 56 D3
Rovinari Romania 58 E4
Rovinj Croatia 56 F3
Rovno Ukr. see Rivne
Rovnoye Rus. Fed. 102 A2
Rovuma r. Moz./Tanz. see Ruvuma
Rowena Australia 147 F2
Rowesville U.S.A. 175 D5
Rowland U.S.A. 176 F6
Rowlesburg U.S.A. 176 F6
Rowley r. Canada 165 K3
Rowley Island Canada 165 L3
Rowley Shoals sea feature Australia 150 B3
Rownaye Belarus 43 K6
Rowra Ukr. see Rivne
Row Polski r. Poland 49 N4
Rowsburg U.S.A. 176 D5
Roxas Luzon Phil. 74 B2
Roxas Mindanao Phil. 74 B4
Roxas Mindoro Phil. 74 B3
Roxas Palawan Phil. 74 A4
Roxas Panay Phil. 74 B4
Roxboro U.S.A. 176 F8
Roxborough Downs Australia 148 C4
Roxburgh Island Cook Is see Rarotonga
Roxby Downs Australia 146 C2
Roxen l. Sweden 45 K4
Roxo r. Port. 54 C7
Roxo, Barragem do resr Port. 54 C7
Royal Canal Rep. of Ireland 47 E10
Royal Center U.S.A. 172 G10
Royal Chitwan National Park Nepal 97 E4
Royale, Île i. Canada see Cape Breton Island
Royale, Isle i. U.S.A. 172 E2
Royal Natal National Park S. Africa 133 M5
Royal Oak U.S.A. 173 J8
Royal Society Range mts Antarctica 223 K1
Royalton U.S.A. 172 E6
Royan France 50 E7
Roye France 51 I3
Roy Hill Australia 150 B4
Royston U.K. 47 L11
Röyttä Fin. 44 N2
Rožaje Crna Gora Yugo. 58 B6
Rožan Poland 49 S3
Rozdil'na Ukr. 41 M2
also known as Razdel'naya
Rozdol'ne Ukr. 41 E7
Rozhdestvenka Kazakh. 103 G2
Rozhdestveno Tverskaya Oblast' Rus. Fed. 43 R5
Rozhdestveno Yaroslavskaya Oblast' Rus. Fed. 43 V3
Rozhdestvenskoye Rus. Fed. 40 H4
Rozhdestvo Rus. Fed. 43 P9
Rozhkovychi Rus. Fed. 43 P9
Rozino Bulg. 58 F6
Rozivka Ukr. 41 F7
Rožňava Slovakia 49 R7
Rozoy-sur-Serre France 51 K3
Roztoczański Park Narodowy nat. park Poland 49 U5
Rozveh Iran 100 B3
Rozzano Italy 56 B3
Rrëshen Albania 58 A7
Rrogozhinë Albania 58 A7
Rtishchevo Rus. Fed. 41 G5
Ruacana Namibia 130 B3
Ruaha National Park Tanz. 129 B6
Ruahine Forest Park nature res. N.Z. 152 K7
Ruahine Range mts N.Z. 152 K8
Ruakaka N.Z. 152 I3
Ruapehu, Mount vol. N.Z. 152 J7
Ruapuke Island N.Z. 153 C14
Ruarwe Malawi 129 B7
Ruatangata N.Z. 152 I3
Ruatapu N.Z. 153 E10
Ruatoria N.Z. 152 M5
Ruba Belarus 43 L5
formerly known as Vyarkhowye
Rub' al Khālī des. Saudi Arabia 105 D4
Largest uninterrupted stretch of sand in the world. English form Empty Quarter.
Rubaydā reg. Saudi Arabia 105 D2
Rubeho Mountains Tanz. 129 C6
Rubelita Brazil 207 K3
Rubeshibe Japan 90 H3
Rubezhnoye Ukr. see Rubizhne
Rubi r. Dem. Rep. Congo 126 E4
Rubiácea Brazil 206 C8
Rubiataba Brazil 206 D2
Rubicon r. U.S.A. 182 C3
Rubim Brazil 207 M3
Rubinéia Brazil 206 C7
Rubio Venez. 198 C3
Rubizhne Ukr. 41 F6
formerly known as Rubezhnoye
Rubondo National Park Tanz. 128 A5
Rubtsovsk Rus. Fed. 103 J1
Rubuga Tanz. 129 B6
Rubū', Jabal ar hill Saudi Arabia 104 C4
Ruby U.S.A. 164 D3
Ruby Dome mt. U.S.A. 183 I1
Ruby Lake U.S.A. 183 I1
Ruby Lake National Wildlife Refuge nature res. U.S.A. 183 I1
Ruby Mountains U.S.A. 183 I1
Rubys Inn U.S.A. 183 L4

Ruby Valley U.S.A. 183 I1
Rucăr Romania 58 G3
Ruchay Belarus 42 I6
Rucheng China see Ruyuan
Rucheng China 87 E3
Ruciane-Nida Poland 49 S2
Ruckersville U.S.A. 176 G7
Rudall watercourse Australia 150 C4
Rudall River National Park Australia 150 C4
Rudarpur India 97 D4
Ruda Śląska Poland 49 P5
Rudauli India 97 D4
Rudbar Afgh. 101 E4
Rudbar Iran 100 B2
Rüdbär Iran 100 D3
Rudina pass Yugo. 58 A5
Rüd-e Kor watercourse Iran 100 C4
Rüdersdorf Berlin Germany 49 K3
Rudhumatal Hiri hill Iraq 109 K4
Rudina pass Yugo. 58 A5
Rudka r. Poland 49 U4
Rudkøbing Denmark 45 J5
Rudna Glava Srbija Yugo. 58 D4
Rudna Poland 49 T5
Rudnaya Pristan' Primorskiy Kray Rus. Fed. 82 D3
formerly known as Tetyukhe-Pristan'
Rudnaya Pristan' Primorskiy Kray Rus. Fed. 82 D4
Rudnichnyy Kazakh. 103 I3
Rudnichnyy Rus. Fed. 40 J4
Rudnik Poland 49 T5
Rudnik Ingichka Uzbek. see Ingichka
Rudnya Smolenskaya Oblast' Rus. Fed. 43 M7
Rudnya Tverskaya Oblast' Rus. Fed. 43 M5
Rudnya Volgogradskaya Oblast' Rus. Fed. 41 H6
Rudnyy Kazakh. 103 E1
Rudnyy Rus. Fed. 82 D3
formerly known as Lifudzin
Rudolf, Lake l. Eth./Kenya see Turkana, Lake
Rudol'fa, Ostrov i. Rus. Fed. 38 F1
Most northerly point of Europe. English form Rudolph Island.
Rudolph Island Rus. Fed. see Rudol'fa, Ostrov
Rudolstadt Germany 48 I5
Rudong China 87 G1
also known as Juegang
Rudozem Bulg. 58 F7
Rüdsar Iran 100 B2
Rudzyensk Belarus 42 I8
Rue France 50 H2
Ruecas r. Spain 54 F5
Ruel Canada 173 L2
Ruen mt. Macedonia see Rujen
Ruenya r. Zimbabwe 131 G3
Rufa'a Sudan 121 G5
Ruffec France 50 G6
Rufiji r. Tanz. 129 C7
Rufino Arg. 204 E4
Rufisque Senegal 124 A3
Rufunsa Zambia 127 E2
Rugāji Latvia 42 I4
Rugao China 87 G1
Rugby U.K. 47 K11
Rugby ND U.S.A. 178 B1
Rugby TN U.S.A. 176 A9
Rügen i. Germany 49 K1
Rügen, Naturpark park Germany 49 K1
Rugged Mountain Canada 166 E5
Rugheiwa well Sudan 121 F5
Rugles France 50 G4
Ruhango Tanz. 129 C7
Ruhayyat al Ḩamr'a' waterhole Saudi Arabia 105 D2
Ruhbah oasis Syria 109 I5
English form Rhube, Oasis of
Ruhengeri Rwanda 126 F5
Ruhla Germany 48 H5
Ruhnu i. Estonia 42 E4
Ruhpolding Germany 49 J8
Ruhr r. Germany 48 D4
Ruhudji r. Tanz. 129 B7
Ruhuna National Park Sri Lanka 94 D5 see Yala National Park
Rui'an China 87 G3
Ruichang China 87 E2
formerly known as Pencheng
Ruidoso U.S.A. 181 F6
Ruiz Mex. 184 D4
Ruiz, Nevado del vol. Col. 198 C3
Ruj mt. Bulg. 58 D6
Rūja r. Latvia 42 G4
Rujaylah, Ḩarrat ar lava field Jordan 109 I5
Rujen mt. Macedonia 58 D6
also spelt Ruen
Rūjiena Latvia 42 G4
Ruki r. Dem. Rep. Congo 126 C4
Rukumkot Nepal 97 D3
Rukwa admin. reg. Tanz. 129 A6
Rukwa Indon. 75 C4
Rukwa, Lake Tanz. 129 B7
Rūl Dadnah U.A.E. 105 G2
Ruleville U.S.A. 175 B5
Rulin China see Chengbu
Rulong China see Xinlong
Rūm Iran 100 B3
Rum i. U.K. 46 F7
Rum r. U.S.A. 174 A2
Rum, Jebel mts Jordan see Ramm, Jabal
Ruma Nigeria 125 G3
Rumādah Yemen 104 C5
Rumāh Saudi Arabia 105 D2
Rumania country Europe see Romania
Rumaylah waterhole Iraq 109 O4
Rumaylah, Wādī watercourse Syria 109 M1
Rumayn r. Saudi Arabia 104 C3
Rumbek Sudan 126 F3
Rumblar r. Spain 54 H6
Rumburk Czech Rep. 49 L5
Rum Cay i. Bahamas 187 E2
Rumford U.S.A. 177 O1
Rumia Poland 49 P1
Rumilly France 51 L7
Rummān, Jabal ar mts Saudi Arabia 104 C2
Rummānah hill Syria 109 J4
Rumoi Japan 90 G3
Runan China 87 E1
also known as Runing
Runanga N.Z. 153 F10
Runaway, Cape N.Z. 152 L5
Runcorn U.K. 47 J10
Runcu Romania 58 E4
Runde r. Zimbabwe 131 G4
Rundu Namibia 130 C3
Rundvik Sweden 44 M3
Rŭng, Kaôh i. Cambodia 79 C6
Rungu Dem. Rep. Congo 126 E4
Rungwa Rukwa Tanz. 129 A6
Rungwa Singida Tanz. 129 B6
Rungwa Game Reserve nature res. Tanz. 129 B6
Runing China see Runan
Runize-Bālā Iran see Rūdbār
Runni i. Sweden 45 K3
Running Springs U.S.A. 183 G7
Running Water watercourse U.S.A. 179 B5
Runton Range hills Australia 150 C4
Ruokolahti Fin. 45 O3
Ruoqiang China 88 D3
formerly known as Charkhlik or Qarkilik

Ruoqiang He r. China 88 E4
Ruo Shui watercourse China 84 D3
Ruotsinpyhtää Fin. 42 H1
Rupa India 97 G4
Rupat i. Indon. 76 C2
Rupea Romania 58 G2
Rupert r. Canada 168 E3
Rupert ID U.S.A. 180 D4
Rupert WV U.S.A. 176 E8
Rupert Bay Canada 168 E3
Rupert Coast Antarctica 222 O1
Rupert Creek r. Australia 149 D4
Rupnagar India 96 B4
Rupshu reg. Jammu and Kashmir 96 C2
Ruqaytah Saudi Arabia 104 C3
Ruqqad, Wādi ar watercourse Israel 108 G5
Rural Hall U.S.A. 176 E9
Rural Retreat U.S.A. 176 D9
Rurrenabaque Bol. 200 D3
Rus Romania 58 E1
Rusaddir N. Africa see Melilla
Rusape Zimbabwe 131 G3
Rusca Montană Romania 58 D3
Ruschuk Bulg. see Ruschuk
Ruse Bulg. 58 G5
  historically known as Ruschuk
Rusera India 97 E4
Ruşeţu Romania 58 I4
Rushan China 85 I4
  formerly known as Xiacun
Rushan Tajik. see Rushon
Rushanskiy Khrebet mts Tajik. see
  Rushon, Qatorkŭhi
Rush Creek r. U.S.A. 178 B4
Rushford U.S.A. 174 B3
Rush Lake U.S.A. 172 E7
Rushon Tajik. 101 G2
  also spelt Rushan
Rushon, Qatorkŭhi mts Tajik. 101 G2
  also known as Rushanskiy Khrebet
Rushui r. China 85 E5
Rushville IL U.S.A. 174 B3
Rushville IN U.S.A. 174 C4
Rushville NE U.S.A. 178 B3
Rushworth Australia 147 E4
Rusk U.S.A. 179 D6
Ruskele Sweden 44 L2
Ruskin U.S.A. 175 D7
Rusné Lith. 42 C6
Rusokastro Bulg. 58 I6
Rușona Latvia 42 H5
Rūsonu ezers l. Latvia 42 H5
Russaró i. Fin. 42 D2
Russas Brazil 202 E3
Russell Man. Canada 167 K5
Russell Ont. Canada 173 R5
Russell N.Z. 152 I3
Russell KS U.S.A. 178 C4
Russell PA U.S.A. 176 F4
Russell Bay Antarctica 222 P2
Russell Island Canada 165 J2
Russell Lake Man. Canada 167 K3
Russell Lake N.W.T. Canada 167 H2
Russellville AL U.S.A. 174 C5
Russellville AR U.S.A. 174 B5
Russellville KY U.S.A. 174 C4
Russellville OH U.S.A. 176 B7
Rüsselsheim Germany 48 F5
Russi Italy 56 E4
Russia country Asia/Europe see
  Russian Federation

▶ Russian Federation country Asia/Europe
38 F3
Largest country in the world, Europe and
Asia. Most populous country in Europe, 3rd
in Asia and 6th in the world. Formerly
known as Russian Soviet Federal Socialist
Republic or Rossiyskaya Sotsialisticheskaya
Federativnaya Sotsialisticheskaya
Respublika; short form Russia.
world [countries]   ▶ 10—11
world [population]   ▶ 22—23
europe [countries]   ▶ 32—35
asia [countries]   ▶ 64—67

		country	area sq km	area sq miles	location	page#
1	▶	Russian Federation	17 075 400	6 592 864	Asia/Europe	38 F3
2	▶	Canada	9 970 610	3 849 674	North America ▶	164 G3
3	▶	USA	9 809 378	3 787 422	North America ▶	170 E3
4	▶	China	9 584 492	3 700 593	Asia	80 D5
5	▶	Brazil	8 547 379	3 300 161	South America ▶	202 B4
6	▶	Australia	7 682 395	2 966 189	Oceania	144 A4
7	▶	India	3 065 027	1 183 414	Asia	93 E6
8	▶	Argentina	2 766 889	1 068 302	South America ▶	204 C4
9	▶	Kazakhstan	2 717 300	1 049 155	Asia	102 C2
10	▶	Sudan	2 505 813	967 500	Africa	121 E5

largest countries

Russian Soviet Federal Socialist Republic
country Asia/Europe see Russian Federation
Russkaya-Polyana Rus. Fed. 103 H1
Russkiy, Ostrov i. Rus. Fed. 90 B3
Russkiy Kameshkir Rus. Fed. 41 H5
Russkiy Zavorot, Poluostrov pen.
  Rus. Fed. 40 J1
Russkoye Rus. Fed. 43 N8
Russkoye Ust'ye Rus. Fed. 39 O2
  formerly known as Polyarnoye
Rust'avi Georgia 107 F2
Rustburg U.S.A. 176 F8
Rust de Winter S. Africa 133 M2
Rust de Winter Nature Reserve S. Africa
  133 M2
Rustenburg S. Africa 133 L2
Rustenburg Nature Reserve S. Africa
  133 L2
Rustfontein Dam l. S. Africa 133 K6
Rustig S. Africa 133 L4
Ruston U.S.A. 179 D5
Rut' r. Rus. Fed. 43 R6
Ruta Indon. 75 C3
Rutana Burundi 126 F5
Rutanzige, Lake Dem. Rep. Congo/Uganda
  see Edward, Lake
Rute Spain 54 G7
Ruteng Indon. 75 B5
Rutenga Zimbabwe 131 F4
Rutherfordton U.S.A. 174 D5
Ruther Glen U.S.A. 176 H8
Ruthin U.K. 47 I10
  also spelt Rhuthun
Rutland U.S.A. 177 M2
Rutland Island India 95 G4
Rutledge U.S.A. 176 B9
Rutledge Lake Canada 167 I2
Rutog Xizang China 89 D6
Rutog Xizang China 89 F6
  also known as Dêrub
Rutter Canada 173 M4
Rutul Rus. Fed. 102 A4
Ruukki Fin. 44 N4
Ruusa Estonia 42 I3
Ruvaslahti Fin. 44 O3
Ruvo di Puglia Italy 56 I7
Ruvozero Rus. Fed. 44 O2

Ruvozero, Ozero l. Rus. Fed. 44 O2
Ruvu Tanz. see Pangani
Ruvuma r. Moz./Tanz. 129 D7
Ruvuma admin. reg. Tanz. 129 C7
Ruwais pt Saudi Arabia 108 F8
Ruweis U.A.E. 105 F2
Ruwenzori mts Dem. Rep. Congo/Uganda
  126 F5
Ruwenzori National Park Uganda see
  Queen Elizabeth National Park
Ruya r. Zimbabwe 131 G3
Ruyigi Burundi 126 F5
Ruyuan China 87 E3
  also known as Rucheng
Ruza Rus. Fed. 43 R6
Ruzayevka Kazakh. 103 F1
Ruzayevka Rus. Fed. 41 H5
Ruzbugino Rus. Fed. 43 V3
Ruzhany Belarus 42 F9
Ruzhou China 87 E1
  formerly known as Linru
Ružomberok Slovakia 49 Q6
Rwanda country Africa 126 F5
  formerly spelt Ruanda
africa [countries]   ▶ 114—117
Ryābād Iran 100 C2
Ryabovo Rus. Fed. 43 J1
Ryal Bush N.Z. 153 C14
Ryall, Mount N.Z. 153 F10
Ryan, Loch b. U.K. 47 G8
Ryazan' Rus. Fed. 43 T6
Ryazan Oblast admin. div. Rus. Fed. see
  Ryazanskaya Oblast'
Ryazanovskiy Rus. Fed. 43 U6
Ryazanskaya Oblast' admin. div. Rus. Fed.
  43 V7
  English form Ryazan Oblast
Ryazantsevo Rus. Fed. 43 U5
Ryazhsk Rus. Fed. 41 G5
Rybache Kazakh. 88 C2
Rybachiy, Poluostrov pen. Rus. Fed. 44 P1
Rybachiy Poselok Uzbek. 102 D3
Rybach'ye Kyrg. see Balykchy
Rybinsk Rus. Fed. 43 T3
  formerly known as Andropov or
  Shcherbakov
Rybinskoye Vodokhranilishche resr
  Rus. Fed. 43 T3
Rybnik Poland 49 P5
Rybnitsa Moldova see Rîbniţa
Rybnoye Rus. Fed. 43 U7
Rybreka Rus. Fed. 40 E3
Rychnov nad Kněžnou Czech Rep. 49 N5
Rycroft Canada 166 G4
Ryd Sweden 45 K4
Rydberg Peninsula Antarctica 222 S2
Ryde U.K. 47 K13
Rye Beach U.S.A. 177 O3
Ryegate U.S.A. 180 E3
Rye Patch Dam U.S.A. 182 F1
Rye Patch Reservoir U.S.A. 182 F1
Ryki Poland 49 S4
Rykovo Ukr. see Yenakiyeve
Ryl'sk Rus. Fed. 41 E6
Rymanów Poland 49 S6
Rýmařov Czech Rep. 49 O6
Rymättylä Fin. 45 M3
Ryn Poland 49 S2
Ryn-Peski des. Kazakh. 102 B3
Ryńskie, Jezioro l. Poland 49 S2
Ryōtsu Japan 90 F5
Rypin Poland 49 Q3
Rysjedal Norway 45 I3
Rytterknægten hill Denmark 45 K5
Ryttylä Fin. 42 H1
Ryukhovo Rus. Fed. 43 N9
Ryukyu Islands Japan 81 K8
  also known as Ryūkyū-rettō or Nansei-shotō;
  historically known as Loochoo Islands
Ryūkyū-rettō is Japan see Ryukyu Islands
Ryzhikovo Rus. Fed. 43 M7
Ryzhkawka Belarus 43 L8
Rzadza r. Poland 49 S3

Rzav r. Bos.-Herz. 56 L5
Rzepin Poland 49 L3
Rzeszów Poland 49 T5
Rzhaksa Rus. Fed. 41 G5
Rzhanitsa Rus. Fed. 43 O8
Rzhavets r. Belarus 43 L9
Rzhev Rus. Fed. 43 P5

↓ S

▶ Sa'ābād Iran 100 C2
Saacow Somalia 128 D4
Sa'ādah al Barṣā' pass Saudi Arabia
  109 H8
Sa'ādatābād Fārs Iran 100 C4
Sa'ādatābād Hormozgan Iran 100 C4
Saaifontein S. Africa 132 F8
Saalach r. Germany 49 K8
Saale park Germany 48 I4
Saale r. Germany 48 I4
Saalfeld Germany 48 I5
Saalfelden am Steinernen Meer Austria
  49 J8
Saanen Switz. 51 N6
Saanich Canada 166 F5
Saar land Germany see Saarland
Saar r. Germany 48 D6
Saarbrücken Germany 48 D6
Saare Estonia 42 H3
Sääre Estonia 42 E3
Saaremaa i. Estonia 42 D3
Saarenkylä Fin. 44 N2
Saar-Hunsrück, Naturpark nature res.
  Germany 48 D6
Saari Fin. 45 O3
Saarijärvi Fin. 44 N3
Saari-Kämä Fin. 44 N2
Saariselkä Fin. 44 N1
  also known as Suoločielgi
Saaristomeren Kansallispuisto nat. park
  Fin. see Skärgårdshavets Nationalpark
Saarland land Germany 48 D6
  English form Saar
Saarlouis Germany 48 D6
Saatlı Azer. 107 G3
  also spelt Saatly
Saatly Azer. see Saatlı
Saatse Estonia 42 I4

Saba i. Neth. Antilles 187 H3
Saba, Wādī watercourse Saudi Arabia
  104 B1
Šabac Srbija Yugo. 58 A4
Sabadell Spain 55 N3
Sabae Japan 91 E7
Sabah state Malaysia 77 G1
  formerly known as North Borneo
Sabak Malaysia 76 C2
Sabaki r. Kenya 128 D5
Sabalan, Kūhhā-ye mts Iran 100 A2
Sabalana i. Indon. 75 A4
Sabalana, Kepulauan is Indon. 75 A4
Sabalgarh India 96 C4
Sabamagrande Hond. 186 B4
Sabana, Archipiélago de is Cuba 186 C2
Sabana de la Mar Dom. Rep. 187 F3
Sabanalarga Col. 198 C2
Sabaneta Dom. Rep. 187 F3
Sabang Sulawesi Selatan Indon. 75 B3
Sabang Sulawesi Tengah Indon. 75 A2
Sabang Indon. 76 A1
Sabano Col. 193 C5
Sabanözü Turkey 106 C2
Šābāoani Romania 58 H1
Sabará Brazil 203 D6
Sabari r. India 94 D2
  also known as Kolab
Sabarmati r. India 96 B5
Sabaru i. Indon. 75 A4
Sabastiya West Bank 108 G5
Sabaudia Italy 56 F7
Sabaya Bol. 200 C4
Sabāyā Island Saudi Arabia 104 C4
Sabelo S. Africa 132 H8
Sabena Desert Kenya 128 C4
Sabetha U.S.A. 178 D4
Sabha Libya 120 B3
Şabḥā' Saudi Arabia 104 C3
Sabhrai India 96 A5
Sabi r. Moz./Zimbabwe see Save
Sabi r. Moz. 131 G5
Sabie r. Moz./S. Africa 133 Q2
Sabie S. Africa 133 Q2
Sabile Latvia 42 D4
Sabina U.S.A. 176 B6
Sabinal Mex. 184 D2
Sabinal, Cayo i. Cuba 186 D2
Sabiñánigo Spain 55 K2
Sabinar, Punta del mt. Spain 55 I8
Sabinas Mex. 185 E3
Sabinas r. Coahuila Mex. 179 B7
Sabinas r. Nuevo León Mex. 179 C7
Sabinas Hidalgo Mex. 185 E3
Sabine r. U.S.A. 179 D6
Sabine Lake U.S.A. 179 D6
Sabine National Wildlife Refuge
  nature res. U.S.A. 179 D6
Sabinópolis Brazil 207 L5
Sabinov Slovakia 49 S6
Sabirabad Azer. 107 G2
Sablayan Phil. 74 B3
Sable, Cape Canada 169 H5
Sable, Cape U.S.A. 175 D7
Sable, Lac du l. Canada 169 H2
Sable, Rivière du r. Canada 168 G2
Sable Island Canada 169 J5
Sables, River aux r. Canada 173 K4
Sablé-sur-Sarthe France 50 F5
Sablon, Pointe du pt France 51 K9
Saboeiro Brazil 202 E3
Sabon Kafi Niger 125 H3
Sabou Burkina 124 E3
Sabourin, Lac l. Canada 173 O3
Sabres France 50 F8
Sabrina Coast Antarctica 223 H2
Sabtang i. Phil. 74 B1
Sabugal Port. 54 D4
Sabula U.S.A. 172 C8
Sabulu Indon. 75 B3
Sabunten i. Indon. 77 F4
Şabyā Saudi Arabia 104 C4
Sabzawar Afgh. see Shīndand
Sabzevār Iran 100 D2
Sabzvārān Iran see Jīroft
Saca, Vârful mt. Romania 58 G2
Sacaba Bol. 200 D4
Sa Cabaneta Spain 55 N5
Sacaca Bol. 200 D4
Sacalinul Mare, Insula i. Romania 58 K4
Sacandaga r. U.S.A. 177 K2
Sacaton U.S.A. 183 N8
Saccarel, Mont mt. France/Italy 51 N8
Sac City U.S.A. 178 D3
Sacco r. Italy 56 F7
Săcel Romania 58 G3
Săcele Romania 58 G3
Săcele Romania 58 J4
Săceni Romania 58 G4
Sachanga Angola 127 C8
Sachigo r. Canada 168 B2
Sachigo Lake Canada 167 M4
Sachin India 96 B5
Sach'on S. Korea 83 C6
  formerly known as Samch'ŏnp'o
Sach'ŏn S. Korea 91 A7
Sach Pass India 96 C2
Sachsen land Germany 49 K4
Sachsen-Anhalt land Germany 48 I3
  English form Saxony-Anhalt
Sachs Harbour Canada 164 G2
Sächsische Schweiz park Germany 49 L5
Saciçuyu r. Syria/Turkey see Säjür, Nahr
Sackpfeife hill Germany 48 F5
Sackville Canada 169 H4
Saco r. U.S.A. 177 O2
Sacol i. Phil. 74 B5
Sacramento Brazil 206 F6

▶ Sacramento U.S.A. 182 C3
State capital of California.

Sacramento r. U.S.A. 182 C3
Sacramento, Pampa del plain Peru 200 A1
Sacramento Mountains U.S.A. 181 F6
Sacramento Valley U.S.A. 182 B3
Sacrifilà r. Spain 55 H8
Sacriç, Cabo c. Spain 55 H8
Săcueni Romania 58 D1
Sacuriuiná r. Brazil 201 T3
Sacxán Mex. 185 H5
Sada S. Africa 133 K9
Sa'dābād Iran 100 B2
Sá da Bandeira Angola see Lubango
Saḍad watercourse Yemen 104 C4
Şa'dah Yemen 104 C4
Sa'dah governorate Yemen 104 C4
Sada-misaki pt Japan 91 C8
Sadang r. Indon. 75 A3
Sadani Tanz. 129 C6
Sadao Thai. 79 C7
Şadārah Yemen 105 E4
Sadaseopet India 94 C2
Saddat al-Hindīyah Iraq 107 F4
Saddleback pass S. Africa 133 P2
Saddleback Mesa mt. U.S.A. 179 B5
Saddle Hill hill Australia 149 E2
Saddle Island Vanuatu see Mota Lava
Saddle Peak India 95 G3
Sa Đéc Vietnam 79 D6
Sadh Oman 105 F4
Sadhaura India 96 C3
Sadiba India 94 B4
Sadi Eth. 128 B2
Sadieville U.S.A. 176 A7
Sadiqabad Pak. 101 G4
Sadiya India 80 F7
Sa'diya r. Iran 100 D3
Sa'diya Saudi Arabia 104 B3
Sa'diyah, Hawr as imp. l. Iraq 107 F4

Sa'diyyat i. U.A.E. 105 F2
Sadjoavato Madag. 131 [inset] K2
Sad-Kharv Iran 100 D2
Sado r. Port. 54 C6
Sadoga-shima i. Japan 90 F6
Sadon Rus. Fed. 41 H8
Sadovoye Rus. Fed. 41 H7
Sa Dragonera i. Spain 55 N5
  also known as Dragonera, Isla
Sadri India 96 B4
Sadujudu India 94 B4
Sādūs Saudi Arabia 105 D2
Sæby Denmark 45 J4
Saegertown U.S.A. 176 E4
Saena Julia Italy see Siena
Safad Israel see Zefat
Safaga, Geziret i. Egypt 104 A2
  English form Safaga Island
Safaga Island Egypt see Safaga, Geziret
Safané Burkina 124 E3
Šafárikovo Slovakia see Tornal'a
Safayal Maqūf well Iraq 107 F5
Safed Khirs mts Afgh. 101 G2
Safed Koh mts Afgh. 101 E3
Safed Koh mts Afgh./Pak. 101 F3
  also known as Paropamisus
Safed Sagak Iran 101 E3
Säffle Sweden 45 K4
Safford U.S.A. 183 N9
Safi Jordan see Aṣ Şāfī
Safi Morocco 122 C2
  also known as Aş Şāfī
Safīd r. Iran 100 B2
Safīdār, Kūh-e mt. Iran 100 C4
Safid Dasht Iran 100 B3
Safīd Kuh mts Afgh. see Paropamisus
Safīd Sagak Iran 101 E3
Safīr Yemen 105 D5
Safiras, Serra das mts Brazil 203 D6
Şafītā Syria 108 H3
Sailyugem Mountains Rus. Fed. 84 A1
Safonovo Arkhangel'skaya Oblast' Rus. Fed.
  40 I2
Safonovo Smolenskaya Oblast' Rus. Fed.
  43 O6
Safotu Samoa 145 H3
Safra' al Asyāh esc. Saudi Arabia 104 C2
Safra' al Sark esc. Saudi Arabia 104 C2
Safranbolu Turkey 106 C2
Safwān Iraq 107 F5
Şağ Romania 58 C3
Saga China 89 D6
  also known as Gya'gya
Saga Japan 91 B8
Saga pref. Japan 91 B8
Saga Kazakh. 103 F2
Sāgae Japan 90 G5
Sagaing Myanmar 78 A3
Sagaing admin. div. Myanmar 78 A3
Sagala Mali see Saghala
Sagamihara Japan 91 F7
Sagami-nada g. Japan 91 F7
Sagami-wan b. Japan 91 F7
Sagamu Nigeria 125 F5
  also spelt Shagamu
Saganash Lake Canada 173 K1
Saganoseki Japan 91 B8
Saganthit Kyun i. Myanmar 79 B5
  also known as Sellore Island
Sagar Karnataka India 94 B3
Sagar Karnataka India 94 B3
Sagar Madhya Pradesh India 96 C5
Sagaredzho Georgia see Sagarejo
Sagarejo Georgia 107 F2
  also spelt Sagaredzho
Sagaria Bangl. 97 F4
Sagar Island India 97 F5
Sagarmatha mt. China/Nepal see
  Everest, Mount
Sagarmatha National Park Nepal 97 E4
Sagastyr Rus. Fed. 39 M2
Sagauli India 97 E4
Sagavanirktok r. U.S.A. 164 E2
Sage U.S.A. 180 E4
Sage Creek r. U.S.A. 180 E3
Saggi, Har mt. Israel 108 F7
Saghand Iran 100 D3
Saghyz Kazakh. see Sagiz
Sagil r. Hong Kong China 87 [inset]
Sagil Mongolia 84 C2
Saginaw MI U.S.A. 173 J7
Saginaw MN U.S.A. 172 A4
Saginaw Bay U.S.A. 173 J7
Sağırlar Turkey 59 J9
Sagiz Atyrauskaya Oblast' Kazakh. 102 C2
Sagiz r. Kazakh. see Sagyz
Sağlamtaş Turkey 58 I8
Saglek Bay Canada 169 I1
Saglouc Canada see Salluit
Sagly Rus. Fed. 88 E1
Sagone, Golfe de b. Corse France 56 A6
Sagra r. Italy 56 I9
Sagra mt. Spain 55 I7
Sagres Port. 54 C7
Sagres, Ponta de pt Port. 54 C8
Sagsay watercourse Mongolia 84 C2
Sagu Myanmar 78 A3
Saguache U.S.A. 181 F5
Saguache r. U.S.A. 181 F5
Sagua de Tánamo Cuba 187 E2
Sagua la Grande Cuba 186 C2
Saguaro National Park U.S.A. 183 N9
Saguenay r. Canada 169 G3
Sagunt Spain see Sagunto
Saguntum Spain see Sagunto
Sagunto Spain 55 K5
  also spelt Sagunt; historically known as
  Murviedro or Saguntum
Sagwara India 96 B5
Sagyndyk, Mys pt Kazakh. 102 B3
Sagyz r. Kazakh. 102 C2
  formerly spelt Saghyz
Sagzī Iran 100 C3

Sahu China see Zadoi
Sahuaripa Mex. 184 C2
Sahuayo Mex. 185 E4
Şāḥūq reg. Saudi Arabia 104 C2
Şāḥūq, Wādī watercourse Saudi Arabia
  104 C2
Sahyadri mts India see Western Ghats
Sahyadriparvat Range hills India 94 B1
  also known as Ajanta Range
Sai r. India 96 D4
Saibai Island Australia 73 J8
Sai Buri Thai. 79 C7
Sai Buri r. Thai. 79 C7
Saïda Alg. 123 F2
Saïda Lebanon see Sidon
Saïda, Monts de mts Alg. 55 L9
Saïdabad Iran see Sīrjān
Sa'id Bin Sahrān Oman 105 G3
Saïdia Morocco 55 I9
Saidpur Bangl. 97 F4
Saidpur India 97 D4
Saidu Pak. 101 H3
Saigō Japan 91 C6
Saigon Vietnam see Ho Chi Minh City
Saiha India 96 B5
Saihan Tal China 85 G3
  also known as Sonid Youqi
Saihan Toroi China 84 D3
Saija Fin. 44 O2
Saijō Japan 91 A8
Saikanosy Masoala pen. Madag.
  131 [inset] K3
Saiki Japan 91 B8
Sai Kung Hong Kong China 87 [inset]
Sailana India 96 B5
Sailyugem Mountains Rus. Fed. 84 A1
Saimaa l. Fin. 45 O3
Saimaankanava r. Fin. 45 O3
Saimbeyli Turkey 106 D3
Sain Alto Mex. 185 E4
Saindak Pak. 101 E4
Sa'īndezh Iran 100 A2
  also known as Sa'in Qal'eh; formerly known
  as Shāhīn Dezh
Sa'in Qal'eh Iran see Sa'īndezh
Saïnsoubou Senegal 124 C3
Saint r. U.S.A. 178 C4
St Abb's Head U.K. 46 J8
St-Affrique France 51 I9
St-Aignan France 50 H5
St Alban's Canada 169 K4
St Albans U.K. 47 L12
  historically known as Verulamium
St Albans VT U.S.A. 177 L1
St Albans WV U.S.A. 176 D7
St Alban's Head U.K. 47 J13
  also known as St Aldhelm's Head
St Albert Canada 167 H4
St Aldhelm's Head U.K. see
  St Alban's Head
St-Amand-les-Eaux France 51 I6
St-Amand-Montrond France 51 I6
St-Ambroise Canada 169 G3
St-Amour France 51 L6
St-André, Cap st Madag. see
  Vilanandro, Tanjona
St-André-de-Cubzac France 50 F8
St Andrews N.Z. 153 G12
St Andrews U.K. 46 J7
St Andrew Sound inlet U.S.A. 175 D6
St Anne U.S.A. 172 F9
St Ann's Bay Jamaica 186 D3
St Anthony Canada 169 K3
Saint Anthony U.S.A. 180 E4
St Arnaud Australia 147 D4
St Arnaud N.Z. 153 H10
St-Arnoult-en-Yvelines France 51 H4
St Asaph Bay Australia 148 A1
St-Astier France 50 G8
St-Aubin-du-Cormier France 50 E4
St Augustin r. Canada 169 J3
St Augustine U.S.A. 175 D6
  historically known as San Agostín
St-Aulaye France 50 G7
St Austell U.K. 47 H13
St-Avé France 50 D5
St Barbe Canada 169 J3
St-Barthélemi Canada 169 F4
St-Barthélemy i. West Indies 187 H3
St-Barthélemy, Pic de mt. France 50 H10
St Bathans N.Z. 153 D12
St Bees Head U.K. 47 I9
St Bernard mt. N.Z. 153 H10
St-Blaise Switz. 51 M5
St-Brice-en-Coglès France 50 E4
St Bride's Bay U.K. 47 G12
St-Brieuc France 50 D4
St-Brieuc, Baie de b. France 50 D4
St-Calais France 50 G5
St Catharines Canada 168 E5
St Catherine's Canada 169 K4
St Catherine's Point U.K. 47 K13
St-Céré France 50 H8
St-Chamond France 51 K7
St Charles Canada 173 M4
St Charles ID U.S.A. 180 E4
St Charles MD U.S.A. 177 I7
St Charles MO U.S.A. 174 B4
Saint Charles MI U.S.A. 173 I7
St-Chély-d'Apcher France 51 J8
St-Christol-lès-Alès France 51 K8
St Christopher i. St Kitts and Nevis see
  St Kitts
St Christopher and Nevis country
  West Indies see St Kitts and Nevis
St-Ciers-sur-Gironde France 50 F7
St Clair r. Canada/U.S.A. 173 J8
St Clair, Lake Canada/U.S.A. 173 J8
St Clairsville U.S.A. 176 E5
St-Claude France 51 L6
Saint Cloud U.S.A. 175 D6
St Cloud U.S.A. 178 D2
St-Coeur-de-Marie Canada 169 G3
St Croix r. Canada/U.S.A. 165 M5
St Croix r. U.S.A. 172 A5
St Croix Falls U.S.A. 172 B5
St Croix Island Virgin Is (U.S.A.) 187 G3
St-Cyr-sur-Loire France 50 G5
St David's U.K. 47 G12
St David's Head U.K. 47 G12
St-Denis France see Sig

▶ St-Denis Réunion 219 K7
Capital of Réunion.

St-Denis-du-Sig Alg. see Sig
St-Dié France 51 M4
St-Dizier France 51 K4
St-Domingue country West Indies see Haiti
Sainte Anne Canada 167 L5
Sainte Anne, Lac l. Alta Canada 167 H4
Sainte Anne, Lac l. Que. Canada 169 H3
Ste-Anne-de-Beaupré Canada 169 G4
Ste-Anne-de-Portneuf Canada 169 H3
Ste-Anne-des-Monts Canada 169 H3
St-Égrève France 51 L7
Ste-Émélie-de-l'Énergie Canada 169 F4
Ste-Foy-La-Grande France 50 G8
Sainte Genevieve U.S.A. 174 B4
St Elias, Cape U.S.A. 164 E4

▶ St Elias, Mount U.S.A. 166 A2
4th highest mountain in North America.
northamerica [landscapes]   ▶ 156—157

St Elias Mountains Canada 166 A2
St-Élie Fr. Guiana 199 H3
St-Éloy-les-Mines France 51 I6
Ste-Marie r. Canada 169 F4
Ste-Marie Martinique 187 H4
Ste-Marie, Cap c. Madag. see
  Vohimena, Tanjona
Ste-Maure-de-Touraine France 50 G5
Ste-Maxime France 51 M9
Ste-Rose Guadeloupe 187 H3
Ste-Rose-du-Dégelis Canada see Dégelis
Sainte Rose du Lac Canada 167 L5
Saintes France 50 F7
Saintes, Îles des is Guadeloupe 187 H4
Sainte Thérèse, Lac l. Canada 166 F1
St-Étienne France 51 K7
St-Étienne-de-Tinée France 51 M8
St-Étienne-du-Rouvray France 50 H3
St Eustatius i. Neth. Antilles 187 H3
St-Fabien Canada 169 H3
St Faith's S. Africa 133 O7
St-Félicien Canada 169 F3
St-Félix-de-Dalquier Canada 173 O2
St-Florentin France 51 J4
St-Florent-sur-Cher France 51 I6
St Floris, Parc National nat. park
  Cent. Afr. Rep. 126 D2
St-Flour France 51 J8
St Francesville U.S.A. 175 B6
St Francis r. Canada/U.S.A. 174 G2
St Francis r. U.S.A. 174 B5
St Francis U.S.A. 178 B4
St Francis, Cape S. Africa 133 I11
St Francis Bay S. Africa 133 J11
St Francis Isles Australia 146 B3
St-François r. Canada 169 F4
St-François, Lac l. Canada 169 G4
St-Gaudens France 50 G9
St-Gély-du-Fesc France 51 J9
St-Geniez-d'Olt France 51 J8
St George Australia 147 F2
St George r. Australia 149 E4
St George AK U.S.A. 164 C4
St George SC U.S.A. 175 D5
St George UT U.S.A. 183 K4
St George, Cape P.N.G. 145 E2
St George, Point U.S.A. 180 A4
St George Head Australia 147 F3
St George Island AK U.S.A. 164 C4
St George Island FL U.S.A. 175 C6
St George Range hills Australia 150 D3
St George's Canada 169 J3
St-Georges Canada 169 G4
St Georges Fr. Guiana 199 I4

▶ St George's Grenada 187 H4
Capital of Grenada.

St George's Bay Nfld. Canada 169 J3
St George's Bay N.S. Canada 169 I4
St George's Cay i. Belize 185 I5
St George's Channel Canada 169 G5
St George's Channel P.N.G. 145 E2
St George's Channel Rep. of Ireland/U.K.
  47 F12
St Germain Canada 172 C5
St-Germain-du-Puy France 51 I5
St-Germain-des-Belles France 50 H7
St-Gildas, Pointe de pt France 50 D5
St-Gildas-des-Bois France 50 D5
St-Gilles France 51 K9
St-Gilles-Croix-de-Vie France 50 E6
St Govan's Head U.K. 47 H12
St Helen U.S.A. 173 I6

▶ St Helena terr. S. Atlantic Ocean 216 N7
United Kingdom Overseas Territory.

St Helena U.S.A. 182 B3
St Helena Bay S. Africa 132 C9
St Helena Bay b. S. Africa 132 C9
St Helena Sound inlet U.S.A. 175 D5
St Helens Australia 147 F5
St Helens U.K. 47 J10
St Helens U.S.A. 180 B3

▶ St Helens, Mount vol. U.S.A. 180 B3
northamerica [threats]   ▶ 160—161

St Helens Point Australia 147 F5
St Helier Channel Is 50 D3
Capital of Jersey.

St-Hilaire-du-Harcouët France 50 E4
St Hilaria India 97 E5
St-Hubert Belgium 51 L2
St-Hyacinthe Canada 169 F4
St Ignace U.S.A. 173 I5
St Ignace Island Canada 168 C3
St Ignatius Guyana 199 G4
St Ives U.K. 47 G13
St Jacques, Cap Vietnam see Vung Tau
St-Jacques-de-Dupuy Canada 168 E3
St-Jacques-de-la-Lande France 50 E4
St-James France 50 E4
St James MI U.S.A. 173 H5
St James MN U.S.A. 178 D3
St James MO U.S.A. 174 B4
St James NY U.S.A. 177 L5
St James, Cape Canada 166 C4
St-Jean r. Que. Canada 169 I3
St-Jean, Lac l. Que. Canada 169 G3
St Jean Fr. Guiana 199 I3
St-Jean-d'Angély France 50 F7
St-Jean-de-la-Ruelle France 50 H5
St-Jean-de-Luz France 50 E9
St-Jean-de-Maurienne France 51 M7
St-Jean-de-Monts France 50 D6
St-Jean-Lac l. Que. Canada 169 F4
St-Jean-de-Port-Joli Canada 169 G4
St-Jean-sur-Richelieu Canada 169 F4
St-Jérôme Canada 169 F4
St Joe r. U.S.A. 180 D3
Saint John Canada 169 H4
St John r. Liberia 124 C5
St John r. U.S.A. 178 C4
St John U.S.A. 174 H2
St John, Cape Canada 169 K3
St John Bay Canada 169 J3
St John Island Virgin Is (U.S.A.) 187 G3

▶ St John's Antigua and Barbuda 187 H3
Capital of Antigua and Barbuda.

▶ St John's Canada 169 K4
Provincial capital of Newfoundland.

St Johns AZ U.S.A. 183 O7
St Johns MI U.S.A. 173 I7
St Johns OH U.S.A. 176 A5
St John's r. U.S.A. 175 D6
St Johnsbury U.S.A. 177 M1
St Johnsville U.S.A. 177 K3
St Joseph LA U.S.A. 175 B6
St Joseph MI U.S.A. 172 G8
St Joseph MO U.S.A. 178 D4
St Joseph, Lake Canada 168 B3
St-Joseph-d'Alma Canada see Alma
St Joseph Island Canada 168 D4
St Joseph Island U.S.A. 179 C7
St Jovité Canada 169 F4
St-Juéry France 51 I9
St-Julien-de-Concelles France 50 E5
St-Julien-en-Genevois France 51 M6
St-Junien France 50 G7
St-Just-en-Chaussée France 51 I3

index

S

St-Just-St-Rambert France **51** K7
St Kilda i. U.K. **46** D6
St Kitts i. St Kitts and Nevis **187** H3
also known as St Christopher
▶St Kitts and Nevis country West Indies
187 H3
also known as St Christopher and Nevis
northamerica [countries] ➤ 158–159
St-Laurent, Golfe du g. Canada see
St Lawrence, Gulf of
St-Laurent-du-Maroni Fr. Guiana **199** H3
St Lawrence Australia **149** F4
St Lawrence Canada **169** K4
St Lawrence inlet Canada **169** G3
St Lawrence, Cape Canada **169** I4
St Lawrence, Gulf of Canada **169** I3
also known as St-Laurent, Golfe du
St Lawrence Island U.S.A. **164** C3
St Lawrence Islands National Park
Canada **173** R6
St Lawrence Seaway sea chan.
Canada/U.S.A. **174** F2
St Lazare Canada **167** K5
St-Léonard N.B. Canada **169** H4
St-Léonard Que. Canada **169** F4
St-Léonard mt. France **51** J7
St-Léonard-de-Noblat France **50** H7
St Lewis Canada **169** K3
St Lewis r. Canada **169** J3
St-Lô France **50** E3
St-Louis France **51** N5
St Louis MI U.S.A. **173** I7
St Louis MO U.S.A. **174** B4
St Louis r. U.S.A. **174** A2
St-Louis du Nord Haiti **187** E3
St-Loup-sur-Semouse France **51** M5
▶St Lucia country West Indies **187** H4
northamerica [countries] ➤ 158–159
St Lucia, Lake S. Africa **133** Q5
St Lucia Channel Martinique/St Lucia
187 H4
St Lucia Estuary S. Africa **133** Q5
St Lucia Game Reserve nature res.
S. Africa **133** Q5
St Lucia Park nature res. S. Africa **133** Q5
St Luke's Island Myanmar see
Zadetkale Kyun
St-Macaire-en-Mauges France **50** F5
St Magnus Bay U.K. **46** K3
St-Maixent-l'École France **50** F6
St-Malo France **50** D4
St-Malo, Golfe de g. France **50** D3
St-Mandrier-sur-Mer France **51** L9
St Marc Haiti **187** E3
St-Marc, Canal de sea chan. Haiti **187** E3
St-Marcellin France **51** L7
St Margaret's Hope U.K. **46** J5
Saint Maries U.S.A. **180** C3
St Marks S. Africa **133** L4
St Mark's S. Africa see Cofimvaba
St Marks National Wildlife Refuge
nature res. U.S.A. **175** C6
▶St Martin i. West Indies **187** H3
Dependency of Guadeloupe (France). The
southern part of the island is the Dutch
territory of Sint Maarten.

St Martin, Lake Canada **167** L5
St-Martin-de-Crau France **51** K9
St-Martin-de-Ré France **50** E6
St-Martin-d'Hères France **51** L7
St Mary r. Canada **167** H5
St Mary, Mount N.Z. **153** D12
St Mary Peak Australia **146** C3
St Marys Australia **147** F5
St Marys Canada **173** L7
St Mary's i. U.K. **47** F14
Saint Marys U.S.A. **178** C4
St Marys OH U.S.A. **173** I6
St Marys PA U.S.A. **176** G3
St Marys WV U.S.A. **176** D6
St Marys r. U.S.A. **176** A5
St Mary's, Cape Canada **169** K4
St Mary's Bay Canada **169** I4
St Marys City U.S.A. **177** I7
St-Mathieu Canada **173** O2
St-Mathieu, Pointe de pt France **50** B4
St Matthew Island U.S.A. **164** B3
St Matthews U.S.A. **175** D5
St Matthew's Island Myanmar see
Zadetkyi Kyun
▶St Matthias Group is P.N.G. **145** D2
St Maurice r. Canada **169** F4
St-Maurice, Réserve Faunique du
nature res. Canada **169** F4
St-Maximin-la-Ste-Baume France **51** L9
St-Médard-en-Jalles France **50** F8
St Michaels U.S.A. **177** I7
St Michael's Bay Canada **169** K3
St-Michel-de-Maurienne France **51** M7
St-Michel-des-Saints Canada **169** F4
St Mihiel France **51** L4
St-Nazaire France **50** D5
St Nicolas Belgium see Sint-Niklaas
St-Nicolas-de-Port France **51** M4
St Niklaus Switz. **51** N6
St-Omer France **51** J2
Saintonge reg. France **50** F7
St-Pacôme Canada **169** G4
St-Palais France **50** E9
St Paris U.S.A. **176** B5
St Pascal Canada **169** G4
St-Patrice, Lac l. Canada **173** P4
St Paul r. Canada **167** I4
St Paul r. Liberia **124** C5
St Paul IA U.S.A. **172** B10
▶St Paul MN U.S.A. **174** A2
State capital of Minnesota.

St Paul NE U.S.A. **178** C3

St Paul VA U.S.A. **176** C9
St Paul, Île i. Indian Ocean **219** M8
English form St Paul Island
St-Paul-de-Fenouillet France **51** I10
St Paul Island Canada **169** I4
St Paul Island Indian Ocean see St Paul, Île
St-Paul-lès-Dax France **51** J9
St Paul Subterranean River National Park
Phil. **74** A4
St Peter U.S.A. **174** A2
St Peter and St Paul Rocks is
N. Atlantic Ocean see São Pedro e São Paulo
▶St Peter Port Channel Is **50** D3
Capital of Guernsey.

St Peter's Canada **169** I4
St Peters Canada **169** I4
▶St Petersburg Rus. Fed. **43** L2
5th most populous city in Europe. Also
known as Sankt-Peterburg; formerly known as
Leningrad; historically known as Petrograd.
world [cities] ➤ 24–25

St Petersburg U.S.A. **175** D7
St Petrus i. Indon. **77** E2
St-Philbert-de-Grand-Lieu France **50** E5
St-Pierre mt. France **51** L9
St Pierre Mauritius **129** F7
▶St-Pierre St Pierre and Miquelon **169** K4
Capital of St Pierre and Miquelon.

St-Pierre, Lac l. Canada **169** F4

▶St Pierre and Miquelon terr. N. America
169 J4
French Territorial Collectivity.
oceania [countries] ➤ 138–139

St-Pierre-des-Corps France **50** G5
St-Pierre-d'Oléron France **50** E7
St-Pierre-le-Moûtier France **51** J6
St-Pol-sur-Ternoise France **51** I2
St-Pons-de-Thomières France **51** I9
St-Pourçain-sur-Sioule France **51** J6
St-Quentin Canada **169** H4
St-Quentin France **51** J3
St-Raphaël France **51** M9
St Regis r. U.S.A. **177** K1
St Regis Falls U.S.A. **177** K1
St-Renan France **50** B4
St-Rigaud, Mont mt. France **51** K6
St-Sauveur-des-Monts Canada **169** F4
St-Savin France **50** F7
St-Savinien France **50** F7
St-Sébastien-sur-Loire France **50** E5
St-Siméon Canada **169** G4
St-Sorlin, Mont de mt. France **51** M6
St Stephen U.S.A. **175** E5
St-Symphorien France **50** F8
St Terese U.S.A. **166** C3
St Theresa Point Canada **167** M4
St Thomas Canada **168** D5
St Thomas i. Virgin Is (U.S.A.) **187** G3
St-Tite-des-Caps Canada **169** G4
St-Tropez France **51** M9
St-Tropez, Cap de c. France **51** M9
St-Valery-en-Caux France **50** G2
St-Valery-sur-Somme France **50** H2
St-Vallier Bourgogne France **51** K6
St-Vallier Rhône-Alpes France **51** K7
St-Vaury France **50** H6
St-Vincent Italy **51** N7
St Vincent i. West Indies **199** F1
St-Vincent, Cap pt Madag. see
Ankaboa, Tanjona
St Vincent, Cape Australia **147** E5
St Vincent, Cape Port. see
São Vicente, Cabo de
St Vincent, Gulf Australia **146** C3
▶St Vincent and the Grenadines i.
West Indies **187** H4
northamerica [countries] ➤ 158–159
St-Vincent-de-Tyrosse France **50** E9
St Vincent Island U.S.A. **175** C6
St Vincent Passage St Lucia/St Vincent
187 H4
St Walburg Canada **167** I4
St-Yrieix-la-Perche France **50** H7
Saipal mt. Nepal **97** D3
Saipan i. N. Mariana Is **73** K3
also known of Seypan
Saison r. France **50** F9
Saitama pref. Japan **90** F7
Saiteli Turkey see Kadınhanı
Saito Japan **91** B8
Saittanulkki hill Fin. **40** O2
Saivomuotka Sweden **44** M1
Sai Yok National Park Thai. **79** B5
Sajama, Nevado mt. Bol. **200** C4
Sajid Saudi Arabia **104** C4
Sâjir Saudi Arabia **104** D2
Sâjir, Ra's c. Oman **105** F4
Sajó r. Hungary **49** R8
Sajóhídvég Hungary **49** R7
Sájur, Nahr r. Syria/Turkey **109** J1
Sajzi Iran **100** C3
Sak watercourse S. Africa **132** E6
Saka Eth. **128** C2
Sakai Japan **91** D7
Sakaide Japan **91** C7
Sakaiminato Japan **91** C7
Sakākah Saudi Arabia **107** E5
also known as Sikaka
Sakakawea, Lake U.S.A. **178** B2
Sakala i. Indon. **77** F4
Sakalile Tanz. **129** A7
Sakami Canada **168** F2
Sakami r. Canada **169** E2
Sakami Lake Canada **168** E2
Sakania Dem. Rep. Congo **127** F8
Sakar mts Bulg. **58** H7
Sakar Turkm. **103** E5
Sakaraha Madag. **131** [inset] J4
Sakar-Chaga Turkm. **103** E5
Sakartvelo country Asia see Georgia
Sakarya Turkey **106** B2
also known as Adapazarı; formerly known as
Adabazar
Sakarya r. Turkey **106** B2
Sakassou Côte d'Ivoire **124** D5
Sakata Japan **90** F5
Sakawa Japan **91** C8
Sakchu N. Korea **83** B4
Saken Seyfullin Kazakh. **103** H2
also known as Zhárvk
Sa Keo r. Thai. **79** C5
Sakété Benin **125** F5
Sakhalin i. Rus. Fed. **82** F2
Sakhalin Oblast admin. div. Rus. Fed. see
Sakhalinskaya Oblast'
Sakhalinskaya Oblast' admin. div.
Rus. Fed. **82** F2
English form Sakhalin Oblast
Sakhalinskiy Zaliv b. Rus. Fed. **82** F1
Sakhnin Israel **108** G5
Sakhnovshchyna Ukr. **41** F6
Sakharovo Rus. Fed. **43** R5
Sakhile S. Africa **133** N3
Sakhra Turkm. **102** D3
formerly known as Gyaurs
Sakht-Sar Iran **100** B2
Şäki Azer. **107** F2
also spelt Sheki; formerly known as Nukha
Saki Nigeria **125** F4
Saki Ukr. see Saky
Šakiai Lith. **42** E7
Sakiet Sidi Youssef Tunisia **57** A12

Sakir mt. Pak. **101** F4
Sakishima-shotō is Japan **81** K8
Sakleshpur India **94** B3
Sakmara Rus. Fed. **102** C2
Sako Nakhon Thai. **78** D4
Sakol India **96** C5
Sakon Nakhon Thai. **78** D4
Sakra, Pulau reg. Sing. **76** [inset]
Sakrand India **101** G5
Sakrivier S. Africa **132** E5
Saksaul'skiy Kazakh. **103** E3
also known as Sekseuil; formerly known
as Saksaul'skoye
Saksaul'skoye Kazakh. see Saksaul'skiy
Sakshaug Norway **44** J3
Sakti India **97** D5
Saku Estonia **42** F2
Saku Japan **91** F6
Sakura Japan **91** G7
Sakura-jima vol. Japan **91** B9
Saky Ukr. **41** E7
also known as Saki
Säkylä Fin. **45** M3
Sal i. Cape Verde **124** [inset]
Sal r. Rus. Fed. **53** K2
Sal, Punta pt Hond. **186** B4
Sala Latvia **42** G4
Sala Latvia **42** F5
Šala Slovakia **49** O7
Sala Sweden **45** L4
Salabangka, Kepulauan is Indon. **75** B3
Salaberry-de-Valleyfield Canada **169** F4
Salaca r. Latvia **42** F4
Salacea Romania **58** D1
Salacgriva Latvia **42** F4
Sala Consilina Italy **57** H8
Salada, Bahía b. Chile **204** C2
Salada, Laguna salt l. Mex. **184** B1
Şalādīh, Wādī watercourse Jordan **108** G8
Saladas Arg. **204** F3
Saladillo r. Córdoba Arg. **204** D3
Saladillo r. Santiago del Estero Arg. **204** F4
Salado r. Buenos Aires Arg. **204** F4
Salado r. Formosa Arg. **204** F2
Salado r. La Rioja Arg. **204** C3
Salado r. Río Negro Arg. **204** D6
Salado r. Santa Fe Arg. **204** E4
Salado r. Arg. **204** D5
Salado r. Cuba **186** D2
Salado r. Mex. **185** F3
Salado r. Spain **54** F8
Salado watercourse U.S.A. **181** D4
Saladou Guinea **124** C4
Salaga Ghana **125** E4
Şalah Saudi Arabia **104** C4
Şalah, Tall hill Jordan **109** J4
Şalāh ad Dīn governorate Iraq **107** E4
Salahuddin Iraq **107** F3
Salajwe Botswana **131** E4
Salakh, Jabal mt. Oman **105** G3
Salal Chad **120** C1
Salālā Sudan **104** H4
Şalālah Oman **105** F4
Salalé well Niger **125** I3
Salamá Guat. **185** H6
Salamá Hond. **186** B4
Salamajärven kansallispuisto nat. park Fin.
44 N3
Salamanca Chile **204** C3
Salamanca Mex. **185** E4
Salamanca Spain **54** F4
historically known as Helmantica or
Salamantica
Salamanca U.S.A. **176** G3
Salamango Moz. **131** G5
Salamantica Spain see Salamanca
Salamat pref. Chad **126** D2
Salamat, Bahr r. Chad **126** C2
Salāmatābād Iran **100** A3
Salamban Indon. **77** F3
Salamina Col. **198** B3
Salamina i. Greece see Salamina
Salamina i. Greece **59** E11
Salamina i. Greece **59** E11
also known as Salamís
Salamis tourist site Cyprus **108** E2
also known as Constantia
Salamís i. Greece see Salamina
Salamīyah Syria **109** I2
Salamonie r. U.S.A. **172** H10
Salamonie Lake U.S.A. **172** H10
Salandi r. India **95** E1
Salantai Lith. **42** C5
Salaqi China **85** F3
also known as Tumd Youqi
Sălard Romania **58** D1
Salar de Pocitos Arg. **200** D6
Salas Spain **54** E1
Salas de los Infantes Spain **55** H2
Salaspils Latvia **42** F5
Salat r. France **50** G9
Sălāuța r. Romania **58** F1
Salavat Rus. Fed. **102** C1
Salaverry Peru **200** A2
Salawati i. Indon. **73** H7
Salawin Wildlife Reserve nature res. Thai.
78 A3
Salaya Phil. **74** C4
Salaya India **96** A5
Salayar i. Indon. **75** B4
Salayar, Selat sea chan. Indon. **75** B4
Sala y Gómez, Isla i. S. Pacific Ocean
221 K7
Salazar Angola see N'dalatando
Salazar Arg. **204** E5
Salbris France **51** I5
Salcantay, Cerro mt. Peru **200** B3
Salcedo Dom. Rep. **187** F3
Sălciile Romania **58** H4
Šalčininkai Lith. **42** G7
Sălcioara Romania **58** H4
Saldae Alg. see Bejaïa
Salda Gölü l. Turkey **59** K11
Saldana Col. **198** C3
Saldaña Spain **54** G2
Saldanha S. Africa **132** B10
Saldanha Bay S. Africa **132** B10
Saldus Latvia **42** C5
Sale Australia **147** E4
Sale Indon. **77** E3
Sale Myanmar **78** A3
Salé Morocco **122** D2
Sale r. Indon. **75** B3
Saleh, Teluk b. Indon. **77** G5
Şālehābād Hamadān Iran **100** B3
Şālehābād Khorāsān Iran **101** C3
Salekhard Rus. Fed. **38** G3
historically known as Obdorsk
Salem India **94** C4
Salem S. Africa **133** K10
Salem AR U.S.A. **174** B4
Salem IL U.S.A. **172** B10
Salem IN U.S.A. **174** C4
Salem MA U.S.A. **177** O3
Salem MO U.S.A. **174** B4
Salem NJ U.S.A. **177** J6
Salem NY U.S.A. **177** L2
▶Salem OR U.S.A. **180** B3
State capital of Oregon.

Salem SD U.S.A. **178** C3
Salem UT U.S.A. **183** M1
Salem VA U.S.A. **176** E8
Salem WV U.S.A. **176** E6
Salem i. U.S.A. **174** C3
Sălen Sweden **45** K3
Salerno Italy **57** G8
Salerno, Golfo di g. Italy **57** G8
Salernum Italy see Salerno
Sales Oliveira Brazil **206** F7

Salesópolis Brazil **207** H10
Salford U.K. **47** J10
Salgada Brazil **207** H5
Salgado Brazil **202** E5
Salgado r. Brazil **202** E4
Salgótarján Hungary **49** Q7
Salgueiro Brazil **202** E4
Sali r. Azer. **107** G2
Sali India **96** C5
Salian Afgh. **101** E4
Salibabu i. Indon. **75** C2
Salida U.S.A. **181** F5
Saliena Latvia **42** H5
Salignac-Eyvignes France **50** H8
Salihli Turkey **106** B3
also spelt Soligorsk
Salihorsk Belarus **42** I9
also known as Sol'gorsk
Saliharskaye Vodaskhovishcha resr
Belarus **42** I9
Salikénié Senegal **124** B3
Salimi Dem. Rep. Congo **127** D7
Salimo Moz. **129** C8
Salina KS U.S.A. **178** C4
Salina UT U.S.A. **183** M3
Salina Cruz Mex. **185** G5
Salinas Brazil **202** D6
Salinas Ecuador **198** A5
Salinas Mex. **185** E4
Salinas U.S.A. **182** C5
Salinas r. U.S.A. **182** C5
Salinas, Cabo de c. Spain see
Ses Salines, Cap de
Salinas, Ponta das pt Angola **127** B8
Salinas, Punta pt Dom. Rep. **187** F3
Salinas de Garci Mendoza Bol. **200** D4
Salinas Peak U.S.A. **181** F6
Saline r. AR U.S.A. **179** D5
Saline r. KS U.S.A. **178** C4
English form Little, Cape
Saline Valley depr. U.S.A. **182** G5
Salineville U.S.A. **176** E5
Salingyi Myanmar **78** A3
Salinópolis Brazil **202** C2
Salinosó Lachay, Punta pt Peru **200** A2
Salisbury U.K. **47** K12
Salisbury MD U.S.A. **177** J7
Salisbury NC U.S.A. **174** D5
Salisbury PA U.S.A. **176** F6
Salisbury Zimbabwe see Harare
Salisbury Island Canada **165** L3
Salisbury Plain U.K. **47** J12
Sălişte Romania **58** E3
Salkhad Syria **109** H5
Salki r. India **95** E1
Salla Fin. **44** P2
Salliqueló Arg. **204** E5
Sallisaw U.S.A. **179** D5
Sallom Sudan **104** B4
Salluit Canada **165** L3
formerly known as Saglouc
Sallyana Nepal **97** D3
Salmā Syria **108** H1
Salmäs Iran **100** A2
Salme Estonia **42** C3
Salmi Rus. Fed. **40** D3
Salmivaara Fin. **44** O2
Salmo r. Canada **167** G5
Salmon r. U.S.A. **180** D3
Salmon, Middle Fork r. U.S.A. **180** D3
Salmon Arm Canada **166** G5
Salmon Falls Creek r. U.S.A. **180** D4
Salmon Reservoir U.S.A. **177** J2
Salmon River Mountains U.S.A. **180** D3
Salmonsdam Nature Reserve S. Africa
132 D11
Salmtal Germany **48** D6
Sal'nyye Tundry, Khrebet mts Rus. Fed.
44 O1
Salo Cent. Afr. Rep. **126** C4
Salo Fin. **45** M3
Salò Italy **56** C3
Saloinen Fin. **44** N2
Salome U.S.A. **183** K8
Salon India **97** D4
Salon-de-Provence France **51** L9
Salonga r. Dem. Rep. Congo **126** D5
Salonica Greece see Thessaloniki
Salonika Greece see Thessaloniki
Salonta Romania **58** C2
Salor r. Spain **54** D5
Salou Spain **55** M3
Salou, Cap de c. Spain **55** M3
Saloum watercourse Senegal **124** A3
Salpausselkä reg. Fin. **45** N3
Salsacate Arg. **204** D3
Salsbruket Norway **44** J2
Salses, Étang de l. France see
Leucate, Étang de
Sal'sk Rus. Fed. **41** G7
Salso r. Sicilia Italy **57** F11
Salso r. Sicilia Italy **57** G11
Salsomaggiore Terme Italy **56** B4
Salt Jordan see As Salt
Salt watercourse S. Africa **132** H10
Salt r. Spain **55** N3
Salt r. AZ U.S.A. **183** L8
Salt r. MO U.S.A. **178** D4
Salt r. WY U.S.A. **180** E4
Salta Arg. **200** D5
Salta prov. Arg. **204** D2
Saltanovka Rus. Fed. **43** P9
Saltash U.K. **47** H13
Salt Creek r. U.S.A. **176** C6
Saltee Islands Rep. of Ireland **47** F11
Saltery Bay Canada **166** E5
Saltfjellet Svartisen Nasjonalpark
nat. park Norway **44** K2
Salt Fork r. U.S.A. **178** C4
Salt Fork Arkansas r. U.S.A. **178** C4
Salt Fork Brazos r. U.S.A. **179** B5
Salt Fork Red r. U.S.A. **179** C5
Saltillo Mex. **185** E3
Salt Lake salt l. India **89** A7
Salt Lake salt l. India **96** [inset] G2
▶Salt Lake City U.S.A. **183** M1
State capital of Utah.

Salt Lick U.S.A. **176** B7
Salt Marsh Lake salt l. U.S.A. **183** K2
Salto Arg. **204** E4
Salto Brazil **206** F10
Salto Uruguay **204** F3
Salto da Divisa Brazil **202** E6
Salto de Agua Mex. **185** G5
Salto del Guairá Para. **201** G6
Salto Grande Brazil **206** D9
Salto Grande, Embalse de resr Uruguay
204 F3
Salton City U.S.A. **183** H8
Salton Sea salt l. U.S.A. **183** I8
Saltpond Ghana **125** E5
Salt River Canada **167** H2
Saltrou Haiti see Belle-Anse
Saltville U.S.A. **176** D8
Saltykovka Rus. Fed. **43** U8
Saluda SC U.S.A. **175** D5
Saluda r. U.S.A. **174** D5
Saluebesar i. Indon. **75** B3
Salue Timpaus, Selat sea chan. Indon.
75 B3
Salūm Egypt **106** A5
Salūm, Gulf of g. Egypt **121** E2
Salumbar India **96** B4
Saluq, Kūh-e mt. Iran **100** D2

Salur India **95** D2
Saluzzo Italy **51** N8
Salvador Brazil **202** E5
formerly known as Bahia
Salvador country Central America see
El Salvador
Salvador, Lake U.S.A. **175** B6
Salvador Mazza Arg. **201** E5
Salvaterra Brazil **202** C2
Salvatierra Mex. **185** E4
Salvatierra Spain see Agurain
Salviac France **50** H8
Salwah Saudi Arabia **105** E2
Salwah, Dawhat b. Qatar/Saudi Arabia
105 E2
Salween r. China/Myanmar **78** B4
also known as Mae Nam Khong or Thanlwin
(Myanmar) or Nu Jiang (China)
Salyan Azer. **107** G3
also spelt Sal'yany
Sal'yany Azer. see Salyan
Sal'yany Azer. see Salyan
Salzach r. Austria/Germany **49** J7
Salzbrunn Namibia **130** C5
Salzburg Austria **49** K8
Salzgitter Germany **48** I3
formerly known as Watenstadt-Salzgitter
Salzkotten Germany **48** F4
Salzwedel Germany **48** I3
Salzwedel-Diesdorf park Germany **48** H3
Sam Gabon **126** A4
Sam India **96** A4
Sam r. Laos/Vietnam **78** D4
Samā Cuba **186** E2
also known as Puerto Sama
Samā r. India **96** C4
Samae San, Laem pt Thai. **79** C5
Samagaltay Rus. Fed. **84** B1
Samāh well Saudi Arabia **105** D1
Samaida Iran see Someydeh
Samaipata Bol. **201** E4
Samak, Tanjung pt Indon. **77** D3
Samakoulou Mali **124** C3
Samal i. Phil. **74** C4
Samalayuca Mex. **184** D2
Samales Group is Phil. **74** B5
Samalkot India **95** D2
Samālūt Egypt **121** F2
Samana India **96** C3
Samaná, Cabo c. Dom. Rep. **187** F3
Samana Cay i. Bahamas **187** F2
Samandağı Turkey **106** C3
also known as Alevişik; historically known as
Seleucia Pieria
Samangan prov. Afgh. **101** F2
Samangan Iran **101** E3
Samani Japan **90** H3
Samar Kazakh. see Samarskoye
Samar i. Phil. **74** C4
Samara r. Canada **169** E2
Samara Rus. Fed. **102** B1
formerly known as Kuybyshev
Samara r. Rus. Fed. **102** B1
Samarahan Sarawak Malaysia see Sri Aman
Samarai P.N.G. **149** F1
Samara Oblast admin. div. Rus. Fed. see
Samarskaya Oblast'
Samarga Rus. Fed. **82** E3
Samaria nat. park Greece **59** E13
Samariapo Venez. **199** E3
Samarinda Indon. **77** G3
Sal'nyye Tundry, Khrebet mts Rus. Fed.
44 O1
Samarkand Uzbek. **103** F5
also spelt Samarqand; historically known as
Maracanda
Samarkand, Pik mt. Tajik. **101** G2
also known as Samarqand, Qullai
Samarkand Oblast admin. div. Uzbek. see
Samarkandskaya Oblast'
Samarkandskaya Oblast' admin. div.
Uzbek. **103** F5
English form Samarkand Oblast; also known
as Samarqand Wiloyati
Samarobriva France see Amiens
Samarqand Uzbek. see Samarkand
Samarqand, Qullai mt. Tajik. see
Samarkand, Pik
Sāmarrā' Iraq **107** E4
Sāmarrā', Saddat dam Iraq **109** M3
Samar Sea g. Phil. **74** C4
Samarskaya Oblast' admin. div. Rus. Fed.
102 B1
English form Samara Oblast; formerly known
as Kuybyshevskaya Oblast'
Samarskoye Kazakh. **88** C1
also known as Samar
Samasata Pak. **101** G4
Samastipur India **97** E4
Samaúma Brazil **199** F6
Şamaxı Azer. **107** G2
also spelt Shemakha
Samba Dem. Rep. Congo **126** E6
Samba r. Indon. **77** E3
Samba Jammu and Kashmir **96** B2
Samba Cajú Angola **127** B7
Sambaliung mts Indon. **77** G2
Sambalpur India **97** D5
Sambar, Tanjung pt Indon. **77** E3
Sambas Indon. **77** D2
Sambat Ukr. see Kiev
Sambava Madag. **131** [inset] K2
Sambhal India **96** C3
Sambhar Lake India **96** B4
Sambir Ukr. **53** I2
Sambit i. Indon. **77** G2
Sambo Angola **127** C8
Sambo Indon. **75** C3
Samboja Indon. **77** G3
Sâmbor Ukr. see Sambir
Sâmbor Dam Cambodia **79** D5
Samborombón, Bahía b. Arg. **204** F4
Samch'ŏk S. Korea **83** C5
Samch'ŏnp'o S. Korea see Sach'on
Sameikkon Myanmar **78** A3
Samer France **51** H2
Samet' Rus. Fed. **43** V4
Samet', Ko i. Thai. **79** C5
Samfya Zambia **127** F7
Samhah i. Yemen **105** F5
Samhān, Jabal mts Oman **105** F4
Sami India **96** A5
Sami Pak. **101** E5
Samirah Saudi Arabia **104** C2
Samiria r. Peru **198** C6
Samirum Iran see Yazd-e Khvāst
Samka Myanmar **78** B3
Sāmkir Azer. **107** F2
also known as Shamkhor
Samnah oasis Saudi Arabia **104** C3
Samnan va Damghan reg. Iran **100** C3
Sam Neua Laos see Xam Hua
Samnū Libya **120** B3
▶Samoa country S. Pacific Ocean **145** H3
formerly known as Western Samoa or
Samoa i Sisifo
oceania [countries] ➤ 138–139
Samoa i Sisifo country S. Pacific Ocean see
Samoa

Samobor Croatia **56** H3
Samoded Rus. Fed. **40** G3
Samokov Bulg. **58** E6
Šamorín Slovakia **49** O7
Samos Greece **59** H11
Samos i. Indon. **76** B2
Samosir i. Greece see Samothraki
Samothrace i. Greece see Samothraki
Samothraki Greece **58** G8
Samothraki i. Greece **59** G8
English form Samothrace
Samovodene Bulg. **58** G6
Samoylovka Rus. Fed. **41** G6
Sampa Côte d'Ivoire **124** D4
Sampacho Arg. **204** D4
Sampaga Indon. **75** A3
Sampang Indon. **77** F4
Sampit Indon. **77** F3
Sampit, Teluk b. Indon. **77** F3
Sampit r. Indon. **77** F3
Sampur Rus. Fed. **41** G5
Sampwe Dem. Rep. Congo **127** E7
Samreboe Ghana **124** E5
Samr el 'Abd, Gebel mt. Egypt **108** D9
Samro, Ozero l. Rus. Fed. **43** J3
Samrong Cambodia see Phumĭ Sâmraông
Samsang China **89** D6
Sam Sao, Phou mts Laos/Vietnam **78** C3
Samsø i. Denmark **45** J5
Samsø Bælt sea chan. Denmark **45** J5
Samson Vietnam **78** D4
Samsun Turkey **107** D2
historically known as Amisus
Samsy Kazakh. **103** I4
Samtens Germany **49** K1
Samthar India **96** C4
Samtredia Georgia **107** E2
Samui, Ko i. Thai. **79** C6
Samulun, Pulau i. Sing. **76** [inset]
Samundri Pak. **101** H4
Samur r. Azer./Rus. Fed. **107** G2
Samutik Turkey see Demirli
Samut Prakan Thai. **79** C5
Samut Sakhon Thai. **79** C5
Samut Songkhram Thai. **79** C5
San Mali **124** D3
San r. Poland **49** S5
San, Phou mt. Laos **78** C4
San, Tônlé r. Cambodia **79** D5
Sana r. Bos.-Herz. **56** I3

▶Şan'ā' Yemen **104** D5
Capital of Yemen.

Şan'ā' governorate Yemen **104** D5
Sanaag admin. reg. Somalia **128** E2
San Adrián, Cabo de c. Spain **54** C1
Sanae research station Antarctica **223** X2
Sanaga r. Cameroon **125** H6
San Agostín U.S.A. see St Augustine
San Agustín Col. **198** B4
San Agustin, Cape Phil. **74** C5
Sanak Island U.S.A. **164** C5
Sanām Saudi Arabia **104** D3
San Ambrosio i. S. Pacific Ocean **200** A6
Sanandaj Iran **100** A3
also known as Sinneh
Sanando Mali **124** D3
San Andreas U.S.A. **182** C3
San Andrés Bol. **201** E3
San Andrés Col. **198** C3
San Andres Phil. **74** C3
San Andrés, Isla de i. Caribbean Sea
186 C4
San Andrés del Rabanedo Spain **54** F2
San Andres Mountains U.S.A. **181** F6
San Andrés Tuxtla Mex. **185** G5
San Angelo U.S.A. **179** B6
Sanankoroba Mali **124** D3
San Antolín de Ibias Spain **54** E1
San Antonio Arg. **204** D3
San Antonio Belize **185** H5
San Antonio Bol. **201** F3
San Antonio Chile **204** C2
San Antonio Hond. **186** B4
San Antonio Peru **198** C5
San Antonio Phil. **74** B3
San Antonio NM U.S.A. **181** F6
San Antonio TX U.S.A. **179** C6
San Antonio r. CA U.S.A. **182** D6
San Antonio r. TX U.S.A. **179** C6
San Antonio Venez. **187** H5
San Antonio, Cabo c. Arg. **204** F5
San Antonio, Cabo c. Cuba **186** B2
San Antonio, Mount U.S.A. **182** G7
San Antonio Abad Spain **55** M6
San Antonio Bay Phil. **74** A4
San Antonio de Caparo Venez. **198** D3
San Antonio del Mar Mex. **184** A2
San Antonio de los Cobres Arg. **200** D5
San Antonio de Palé Equat. Guinea **125** G7
San Antonio de Tamanaco Venez. **199** E2
San Antonio Este Arg. **204** D6
San Antonio Oeste Arg. **204** D6
San Antonio Reservoir U.S.A. **182** D6
San Augustín Arg. **204** D5
San Agustín de Valle Fértil Arg. **204** D3
San Augustine U.S.A. **179** D6
Sanaw Yemen **105** E4
Sanawad India **96** C5
San Bartolo Mex. **185** E4
San Bartolomeo in Galdo Italy **56** H7
San Benedetto del Tronto Italy **56** F6
San Benedicto, Isla i. Mex. **184** C5
San Benito Guat. **185** H5
San Benito U.S.A. **179** C7
San Benito r. U.S.A. **182** C5
San Benito Mountain U.S.A. **182** D5
San Bernardino U.S.A. **183** G7
San Bernardino, Passo di pass Switz.
51 P6
San Bernardino Mountains U.S.A. **183** G7
San Bernardino Strait Phil. **74** C3
San Bernardo Chile **204** C3
San Bernardo Mex. **184** D3
San Blas Arg. **204** D6
San Blas Nayarit Mex. **184** D4
San Blas Sinaloa Mex. **184** C3
San Blas, Archipiélago de is Panama **186** D5
formerly known as Las Mulatas
San Blas, Cape U.S.A. **175** C6
San Blas, Cordillera de mts Panama
186 D5
San Borja Bol. **200** D3
Sanborn U.S.A. **178** C3
Sanbornville U.S.A. **177** N2
San Buenaventura Mex. **185** E3
Sanca Moz. **131** G3
San Candido Italy **56** E2
historically known as Agatunum
San Caprasio hill Spain **55** J3
San Carlos Mendoza Arg. **204** C4
San Carlos Salta Arg. **204** D2
San Carlos Chile **204** C5
San Carlos Equat. Guinea see Luba
San Carlos Coahuila Mex. **185** E2
San Carlos Tamaulipas Mex. **185** F3
San Carlos Nicaragua **186** B5
San Carlos Para. **201** F5
San Carlos r. Para. **201** F5
San Carlos Luzon Phil. **74** B3
San Carlos Negros Phil. **74** B4
San Carlos Uruguay **204** G4
San Carlos U.S.A. **183** N8
San Carlos Amazonas Venez. **199** E4
San Carlos Cojedes Venez. **198** D2
San Carlos de Bariloche Arg. **204** C6
San Carlos de Bolívar Arg. **204** E5

San Carlos de la Rápita Spain see Sant Carles de la Ràpita
San Carlos del Zulia Venez. 198 D2
San Carlos Indian Reservation res. U.S.A. 183 N8
San Carlos Lake U.S.A. 183 N8
San Cataldo Sicilia Italy 57 F11
San Cayetano Arg. 204 F5
San Celoni Spain see Sant Celoni
Sancerre France 51 I5
Sancerrois, Collines du hills France 51 I5
San Cesario di Lecce Italy 57 K8
Sancha Gansu China 86 C1
Sancha Shanxi China 85 F4
Sanchahe China see Fuyu
Sancha He r. China 86 C3
Sanchakou China 88 B4
Sanchi India 96 C5
San Chien Pau mt. Laos 78 C3
Sanchor India 96 A4
Sanchuan r. China 85 F4
Sanchursk Rus. Fed. 40 H4
San Ciro de Acosta Mex. 185 F4
San Clemente Chile 204 C4
San Clemente Spain 55 I5
San Clemente U.S.A. 182 G8
San Clemente del Tuyú Arg. 204 F5
San Clemente Island U.S.A. 182 F9
Sancoins France 51 I6
Sanco Point Phil. 74 C4
San Cristóbal Arg. 204 E3
San Cristóbal Potosí Bol. 200 D5
San Cristóbal Santa Cruz Bol. 201 E3
San Cristóbal Col. 198 C5
San Cristóbal Dom. Rep. 187 F3
San Cristobal i. Solomon Is 145 F3
also known as Arossi, or Makira
San Cristóbal Venez. 198 C3
San Cristóbal, Volcán vol. Nicaragua 186 B4
San Cristóbal de las Casas Mex. 185 G5
San Cristobal Wash watercourse U.S.A. 183 K9
Sancti Spíritus Cuba 186 D2
Sand Norway 45 I4
Sand r. Free State S. Africa 133 K5
Sand r. Northern S. Africa 131 F4
Sanda Japan 91 D7
Sandagou Rus. Fed. 90 D3
Sandai Indon. 77 E3
Sandakan Sabah Malaysia 77 G1
Sandakphu Peak India 97 F4
Sandane Norway 45 I3
Sandanski Bulg. 58 E7
Sandaohezi China see Shawan
Sandaré Mali 124 C3
Sanday i. U.K. 46 J4
Sandberg S. Africa 132 C9
Sandbukt Norway 44 M1
Sand Cay reef India 94 B4
Sande Sogn og Fjordane Norway 45 I3
Sande Vestfold Norway 45 J4
Sandefjord Norway 45 J4
Sandefjord (Torp) airport Norway 45 J4
Sandercock Nunataks Antarctica 223 D2
Sanders U.S.A. 183 O6
Sanderson U.S.A. 179 B6
Sandersville U.S.A. 175 D5
Sandfire Roadhouse Australia 150 C3
Sandfloeggi mt. Norway 45 I4
Sand Hill r. U.S.A. 178 C2
Sand Hills U.S.A. 178 B3
Sandhornøy i. Norway 44 K2
Sandi India 96 D4
Sandia Peru 200 C3
San Diego Mex. 181 E7
San Diego CA U.S.A. 183 G9
San Diego TX U.S.A. 179 C7
San Diego, Cabo c. Arg. 205 D9
San Diego, Sierra mts Mex. 184 C2
San Diego de Cabrutica Venez. 199 E2
Sandıklı Turkey 106 B3
Sandila India 96 D4
Sanding i. Indon. 76 C3
Sand Island U.S.A. 172 C4
Sandivey r. Rus. Fed. 40 K2
Sand Lake U.S.A. 168 C4
Sand Lake l. Canada 167 M5
Sandnes Norway 45 I4
Sandnessjøen Norway 44 K2
Sandø i. Faroe Is see Sandoy
Sandoa Dem. Rep. Congo 127 D7
Sandomierz Poland 49 S5
Sândominic Romania 58 G2
formerly spelt Sîndominic
San Domino, Isole i. Italy 56 H6
Sandoná Col. 198 B4
San Donà di Piave Italy 56 E3
Sandover watercourse Australia 148 C4
Sandovo Rus. Fed. 43 R3
Sandow, Mount Antarctica 223 G2
Sandoway Myanmar 78 A4
also known as Thandwè
Sandoy i. Faroe Is 46 F2
also spelt Sandø
Sandpoint U.S.A. 180 C2
Sandray i. U.K. 46 E7
also spelt Sanndraigh
Sandringham Australia 148 C5
Sand River Reservoir Swaziland 133 P3
Sandsele Sweden 44 L2
Sandspit Canada 166 D4
Sand Springs IA U.S.A. 172 B8
Sand Springs OK U.S.A. 179 C4
Sand Springs Salt Flat U.S.A. 182 F2
Sandspruit r. S. Africa 133 K4
Sandstone Australia 151 B5
Sandstone U.S.A. 174 A2
Sand Tank Mountains U.S.A. 183 L9
Sandton S. Africa 133 M3
Sandu Guizhou China 87 C3
also known as Sanhe
Sandu Hunan China 87 E3
Sandur India 94 C3
Sandusky MI U.S.A. 173 K7
Sandusky OH U.S.A. 176 C4
Sandusky Bay U.S.A. 176 C4
Sandveld mts S. Africa 132 C8
Sandveld Nature Reserve S. Africa 133 J4
Sandverhaar Namibia 132 B3
Sandvika Akershus Norway 45 J4
Sandvika Nord-Trøndelag Norway 44 K3
Sandviken Sweden 45 L3
Sandvlakte S. Africa 133 I10
Sandwich U.S.A. 177 O4
Sandwich Bay Canada 169 J2
Sandwich Island Vanuatu see Éfaté
Sandwip Bangl. 97 F5
Sandwip Channel Bangl. 97 F5
Sandy U.S.A. 183 M1
Sandy r. U.S.A. 177 P1
Sandy Bay Canada 167 K4
Sandy Bight b. Australia 151 C7
Sandy Cape Qld Australia 149 G5
Sandy Cape Tas. Australia 147 E5
Sandy Creek r. Australia 148 C3
Sandy Island Australia 150 C2
Sandykachi Turkm. 103 E5
Sandykly Gumy des. Turkm. see Sundukli, Peski
Sandy Lake Alta Canada 167 H4
Sandy Lake Ont. Canada 167 M4
Sandy Lake l. Canada 167 M4
Sandy Springs U.S.A. 175 C5
Sandyville U.S.A. 176 D7
Sân el Hagar Egypt 108 C7
San Estanislao Para. 201 F6
San Esteban Hond. 186 B4
San Esteban, Isla i. Mex. 184 B2
San Fabián de Alico Chile 204 C5
San Felipe Chile 204 C4
San Felipe Baja California Norte Mex. 184 B2
San Felipe Chihuahua Mex. 184 D3
San Felipe Guanajuato Mex. 185 E4
San Felipe mt. Spain 55 J4
San Felipe Venez. 198 D2
San Felipe, Cayos de is Cuba 186 C2
San Feliú de Guíxols Spain see Sant Feliu de Guíxols
San Félix, Isla i. S. Pacific Ocean 221 M7
San Fernando Arg. 204 F4
San Fernando Chile 204 C4
San Fernando Baja California Norte Mex. 184 B2
San Fernando Tamaulipas Mex. 185 F3
San Fernando Luzon Phil. 74 B2
San Fernando Luzon Phil. 74 B3
San Fernando Spain 54 E8
San Fernando Trin. and Tob. 187 H5
San Fernando U.S.A. 182 F7
San Fernando de Apure Venez. 199 E3
San Fernando de Atabapo Venez. 199 E3
San Filipe Creek watercourse U.S.A. 183 I8
Sånfjället nationalpark nat. park Sweden 45 K3
Sanford r. Australia 151 A5
Sanford FL U.S.A. 175 D6
Sanford ME U.S.A. 177 O2
Sanford MI U.S.A. 173 I7
Sanford NC U.S.A. 174 E5
San Francisco Arg. 204 E3
San Francisco Bol. 200 D3
San Francisco Mex. 184 B2
▶San Francisco U.S.A. 182 B4
world [cities] 24–25
world [communications] 26–27
San Francisco r. U.S.A. 181 E6
San Francisco, Paso de pass Arg. 204 C2
San Francisco, Sierra mts Mex. 184 B3
San Francisco Bay inlet U.S.A. 182 B4
San Francisco del Oro Mex. 184 D3
San Francisco de Macorís Dom. Rep. 187 F3
San Francisco de Paula, Cabo c. Arg. 205 D8
San Francisco Gotera El Salvador 185 H6
San Francisco Javier Spain 55 M6
Sanga Dem. Rep. Congo 127 F6
San Gabriel Ecuador 198 B4
San Gabriel, Punta pt Mex. 184 B2
San Gabriel Mountains U.S.A. 182 F7
Sangachaly Azer. see Sanqaçal
Sangai, Parque Nacional nat. park Ecuador 198 B5
Sangaigerong Indon. 76 D3
Sa'ngain China 86 A2
San Gallan, Isla i. Peru 200 A3
Sangam India 94 C3
Sangameshwar India 94 B2
Sangamner India 94 B2
Sangamon r. U.S.A. 174 B3
Sangān Iran 101 D3
Sangan, Koh-i- mt. Afgh. 101 F3
Sangar r. Pak. 101 G4
Sangar Rus. Fed. 39 M3
Sangaréa Guinea 124 B4
Sangareddi India 94 C2
Sangarédi Guinea 124 B4
Sangaria India 96 B3
Sangasanga Indon. 77 G3
Sanga Sanga i. Phil. 74 A5
Sangasso Mali see Zangasso
Sangaste Estonia 42 H4
San Gavino Monreale Sardegna Italy 57 A9
Sangay, Volcán vol. Ecuador 198 B5
Sang Bast Iran 101 D3
Sangbé Cameroon 125 I5
Sangboy Islands Phil. 74 B5
Sangbur Afgh. 101 E3
Sangeang i. Indon. 77 G5
Sangejing China 85 E3
Sângeorgiu de Pădure Romania 58 F2
formerly spelt Sîngeorgiu de Pădure
Sângeorz-Băi Romania 58 F1
formerly spelt Sîngeorz-Băi
Sangequanzi China 88 E3
Sânger Romania 58 F2
Sanger U.S.A. 182 E5
Sângera Moldova see Sîngera
Sangerfield U.S.A. 177 J3
Sangerhausen Germany 48 I4
San Germán Puerto Rico 187 G3
Sanggan r. China 85 G3
Sanggar, Teluk b. Indon. 77 G5
Sanggarmai China 86 B1
Sanggau Indon. 77 E2
Sanggou Wan b. China 85 I4
Sangha admin. reg. Congo 126 B4
Sangha r. Congo 126 C5
Sangha-Mbaéré pref. Cent. Afr. Rep. 126 C4
Sanghar Pak. 101 G5
San Gil Col. 198 C3
Sangilen, Nagor'ye mts Rus. Fed. 84 B1
San Giovanni in Fiore Italy 57 I9
San Giovanni Rotondo Italy 56 H7
San Giovanni Suegiu Sardegna Italy 57 A9
Sangir India 96 B5
Sangir i. Indon. 75 C2
Sangir, Kepulauan is Indon. 75 C2
Sangiran tourist site Indon. 77 E4
San Giuliano Terme Italy 56 C5
San Giustino Italy 56 E5
Sangiyn Dalay Mongolia 84 E2
Sangiyn Dalay Nuur salt l. Mongolia 84 C1
Sangju S. Korea 83 C5
Sangkapura Indon. 77 F4
Sangkarang, Kepulauan is Indon. 75 A4
Sângke, Stœng r. Cambodia 79 C5
Sangkulirang Indon. 77 G2
Sangkulirang, Teluk b. Indon. 77 G2
Sangla Pak. 101 H4
Sangli India 94 B2
San Glorio, Puerto de pass Spain 54 G1
Sangmélima Cameroon 125 H6
Sango Zimbabwe 131 F4
formerly known as Vila Salazar or Villasalazar
Sangod India 96 C4
Sangole India 94 B2
San Gorgonio Mountain U.S.A. 183 H7
Sangowo Indon. 75 D2
Sangpi China see Xiangcheng
Sang Qu r. China 86 A2
Sangre de Cristo Range mts U.S.A. 181 F5
San Gregorio de Polanco Uruguay 204 G4
Sangre Grande Trin. and Tob. 187 H5
Sangri China 89 F6
also known as Xueba
Sangro r. Italy 56 G6
Sangrur India 96 B3
Sangsang China 89 D6
Sangu r. Bangl. 97 F5
Sangue r. Brazil 201 F3
Sangüesa Spain 55 J2
San Guiliano Milanese Italy 56 B3
Sangu'īyeh Iran 100 D4
also known as Isfandaqeh
Sangyuan China see Wuqiao
Sangzhi China 87 D2
also known as Liyuan
Sanhe China see Sandu
Sanhe China 85 I2
Sanhezhen China 87 F2
San Hilario Mex. 184 C3
San Hipólito, Punta pt Mex. 184 B3
Sanhūr Egypt 121 F2
San Ignacio Belize 185 H5
San Ignacio Beni Bol. 200 D3
San Ignacio Santa Cruz Bol. 201 E4
San Ignacio Santa Cruz Bol. 201 E4
San Ignacio Baja California Sur Mex. 184 B3
San Ignacio Sonora Mex. 184 C2
San Ignacio Para. 201 F6
San Ignacio Peru 198 B6
San Ignacio, Laguna l. Mex. 184 B3
Sanikiluaq Canada 168 E1
San Ildefonso Peninsula Phil. 74 B2
Sanin-kaigan National Park Japan 91 D7
Sanipas pass S. Africa 133 N6
Sanislău Romania 49 T8
Sanitz Germany 49 J1
Sāniyat al Fawākhir well Libya 120 C3
San Jacinto Col. 198 C2
San Jacinto Phil. 74 B3
San Jacinto U.S.A. 183 H8
San Jacinto Peak U.S.A. 183 H8
Sanjai r. India 97 E5
San Jaime Arg. 204 F3
San Javier Arg. 204 F3
San Javier Beni Bol. 200 D3
San Javier Santa Cruz Bol. 201 E4
San Javier Spain 55 K7
San Javier de Loncomilla Chile 204 C4
Sanjawi Pak. 101 G4
Sanjbod Iran 100 B2
San Jerónimo Mex. 185 E5
San Jerónimo Peru 200 B1
Sanjiang China see Liannan
Sanjiang China 87 D3
also known as Guyi
Sanjiang China see Jinping
Sanjiaocheng China see Haiyan
Sanjiaoping China 87 D2
Sanjie China 87 G2
Sanjō Japan 90 F6
San Joaquín Bol. 200 D3
San Joaquín Para. 201 F6
San Joaquin U.S.A. 182 D5
San Joaquin r. U.S.A. 182 C3
San Joaquin Valley U.S.A. 182 D4
San Jon U.S.A. 178 B5
San Jorge Arg. 204 E3
San Jorge, Golfo de g. Arg. 205 D7
San Jorge, Golfo de g. Spain see Sant Jordi, Golf de
San José Col. 199 D4
▶San José Costa Rica 186 B5
Capital of Costa Rica.
San José watercourse Mex. 181 D8
San Jose Luzon Phil. 74 B3
San Jose Mindoro Phil. 74 B3
San Jose Mindoro Phil. 74 B3
San Jose CA U.S.A. 182 C4
San Jose NM U.S.A. 181 F6
San Jose watercourse U.S.A. 181 F6
San José Venez. 199 E2
San José, Cabo c. Arg. 205 D7
San José, Cuchilla de hills Uruguay 204 F3
San José, Golfo g. Arg. 205 D6
San José, Isla i. Mex. 184 C3
San José, Volcán vol. Chile 204 C4
San José de Amacuro Venez. 199 F2
San José de Bavicora Mex. 184 D2
San Jose de Buenavista Phil. 74 B4
San José de Chiquitos Bol. 201 E4
San José de Comondú Mex. 184 C3
San José de Gracia Baja California Sur Mex. 184 B3
San José de Gracia Sonora Mex. 184 C2
San José de Guaribe Venez. 187 G5
San José de Jáchal Arg. 204 C3
San José de la Brecha Mex. 184 C3
San José de la Dormida Arg. 204 E3
San José de la Mariquina Chile 204 B5
San José del Boquerón Arg. 204 E2
San José del Cabo Mex. 184 C4
San José del Guaviare Col. 198 C4
San José de Mayo Uruguay 204 F4
San José de Ocuné Col. 198 D3
San José de Primas Mex. 181 E7
San José de Raíces Mex. 185 E3
San Juan Arg. 204 C3
San Juan prov. Arg. 204 C3
San Juan Bol. 201 E4
San Juan Col. 198 B2
San Juan r. Col. 198 B3
San Juan r. Costa Rica/Nicaragua 186 C5
San Juan mt. Cuba 186 C2
San Juan Dom. Rep. 187 F3
San Juan Chihuahua Mex. 184 D3
San Juan Coahuila Mex. 185 E3
San Juan Peru 200 B3
San Juan Phil. 74 C4
▶San Juan Puerto Rico 187 G3
Capital of Puerto Rico.
San Juan r. CA U.S.A. 182 D6
San Juan r. UT U.S.A. 183 N4
San Juan Venez. 199 E3
San Juan, Cabo c. Arg. 205 E9
San Juan, Cabo c. Equat. Guinea 125 H6
San Juan, Punta pt El Salvador 186 A4
San Juan Bautista Para. 201 F6
San Juan Bautista Spain 55 M5
San Juan Bautista U.S.A. 182 C5
San Juan Bautista Tuxtepec Mex. 185 F5
San Juan Capistrano U.S.A. 182 G8
San Juancito Hond. 186 B4
San Juan de César Col. 198 C2
San Juan de Guadalupe Mex. 185 E3
San Juan dela Costa Chile 204 B6
San Juan de la Peña, Sierra de mts Spain 55 K2
San Juan del Norte Nicaragua 186 C5
San Juan del Norte, Bahía de b. Nicaragua 186 C5
San Juan de los Cayos Venez. 198 D2
San Juan de los Morros Venez. 199 E2
San Juan del Río Durango Mex. 184 D3
San Juan del Río Querétaro Mex. 185 F4
San Juan del Sur Nicaragua 186 B5
San Juan de Salvamento Arg. 205 E9
San Juan Evangelista Mex. 185 G5
San Juan Islands U.S.A. 180 B2
San Juanito Mex. 184 D3
San Juanito, Isla i. Mex. 184 D4
San Juan Mountains U.S.A. 181 F5
San Juan y Martínez Cuba 186 C2
San Julián Arg. 205 D8
San Just mt. Spain 55 K4
San Justo Arg. 204 E3
Sankarani r. Côte d'Ivoire/Guinea 124 C4
Sankarankovil India 94 C4
Sankeshwar India 94 B2
Sankh r. India 97 E5
Sankosh r. Bhutan see Sunkosh
Sankra Chhattisgarh India 94 D1
Sankra Rajasthan India 96 A4
Sankt Andrä Austria 49 L9
Sankt Gallen Switz. 51 P5
Sankt Gotthard Hungary see Szentgotthárd
Sankt Johann im Pongau Austria 49 K8
Sankt Moritz Switz. 51 P6
Sankt-Peterburg Rus. Fed. see St Petersburg
Sankt Peter-Ording Germany 48 F1
Sankt Pölten Austria 49 M7
Sankt Veit an der Glan Austria 49 L9
Sankt Wendel Germany 48 E6
Sankuru r. Dem. Rep. Congo 126 D6
San Lázaro Para. 201 F5
San Lázaro, Cabo c. Mex. 184 B3
San Leandro U.S.A. 182 B4
San Leonardo in Passiria Italy 56 D2
Şanlıurfa Turkey 107 D3
formerly known as Urfa; historically known as Edessa
Şanlıurfa prov. Turkey 109 J1
San Lorenzo Corrientes Arg. 204 F3
San Lorenzo Santa Fé Arg. 204 E4
San Lorenzo Beni Bol. 200 D3
San Lorenzo Pando Bol. 200 D2
San Lorenzo Tarija Bol. 200 D5
San Lorenzo Ecuador 198 B4
San Lorenzo Hond. 186 B4
San Lorenzo Mex. 184 D2
San Lorenzo Peru 200 C2
San Lorenzo mt. Spain 55 I2
San Lorenzo, Cabo c. Ecuador 198 A5
San Lorenzo, Cerro mt. Arg./Chile 205 B7
San Lorenzo, Isla i. Mex. 184 B2
San Lorenzo, Isla i. Peru 200 A3
Sanlúcar de Barrameda Spain 54 E8
San Lucas Bol. 200 D5
San Lucas Baja California Sur Mex. 184 B3
San Lucas Baja California Sur Mex. 184 C4
San Lucas, Cabo c. Mex. 184 C4
San Lucas, Serranía de mts Col. 198 C3
San Luis Arg. 204 D4
San Luis prov. Arg. 204 D4
San Luis Brazil 200 D2
San Luis Cuba 186 E2
San Luis Guat. 185 H5
San Luis Mex. 185 E5
San Luis Peru 198 C5
San Luis AZ U.S.A. 183 J9
San Luis AZ U.S.A. 183 M9
San Luis CO U.S.A. 181 F5
San Luis Venez. 198 D2
San Luis, Isla i. Mex. 184 B2
San Luis, Sierra de mts Arg. 204 D4
San Luis de la Paz Mex. 185 E4
San Luis del Palmar Arg. 204 F2
San Luis Gonzaga Mex. 184 C3
San Luisito Mex. 184 B2
San Luis Obispo U.S.A. 182 D6
San Luis Obispo Bay U.S.A. 182 D6
San Luis Potosí Mex. 185 E4
San Luis Potosí state Mex. 185 E4
San Luis Reservoir U.S.A. 182 C4
San Luis Río Colorado Mex. 184 E1
Sanluri Sardegna Italy 57 A9
San Manuel U.S.A. 183 N9
San Marcello Pistoiese Italy 56 C4
San Marcial, Punta pt Mex. 184 C3
San Marco, Capo c. Sardegna Italy 57 A9
San Marco, Capo c. Sicilia Italy 57 F11
San Marcos Chile 204 C3
San Marcos Col. 198 C2
San Marcos Guat. 185 H6
San Marcos Hond. 186 B4
San Marcos Mex. 185 F5
San Marcos Peru 200 A1
San Marcos U.S.A. 179 C6
San Marcos r. U.S.A. 179 C6
San Marcos, Isla i. Mex. 184 B3
▶San Marino country Europe 56 E5
europe [countries] 32–35
▶San Marino San Marino 56 E5
Capital of San Marino.
San Martín research station Antarctica 222 T2
long form General San Martín
San Martín Catamarca Arg. 204 C3
San Martín Mendoza Arg. 204 C4
San Martín r. Bol. 201 E3
San Martín dept Peru 200 A1
San Martín, Lago l. Arg./Chile 205 B8
San Martín, Volcán vol. Mex. 185 G5
San Martín de los Andes Arg. 204 C6
San Martín de Valdeiglesias Spain 54 G4
San-Martino-di-Lota Corse France 51 P10
San Mateo Peru 198 D5
San Mateo U.S.A. 182 B4
San Mateo Venez. 199 E2
San Matías Bol. 201 F4
San Matías, Golfo g. Arg. 204 D6
San Mauricio Venez. 199 E2
Sanmen China 87 G2
also known as Haiyou
Sanmen Wan b. China 87 G2
Sanmenxia China 87 D1
San Miguel Arg. 204 F3
San Miguel Bol. 201 E4
San Miguel r. Bol. 201 E3
San Miguel r. Col. 198 C4
San Miguel El Salvador 185 H6
San Miguel Panama 186 D5
San Miguel Peru 200 B3
San Miguel U.S.A. 182 D6
San Miguel r. U.S.A. 181 E5
San Miguel Bay Phil. 74 B3
San Miguel de Allende Mex. 185 E4
San Miguel de Cruces Mex. 184 D3
San Miguel de Horcasitas r. Mex. 184 C2
San Miguel de Huachi Bol. 200 D3
San Miguel del Monte Arg. 204 F4
San Miguel de Tucumán Arg. 204 D2
short form Tucumán
San Miguel do Araguaia Brazil 202 B5
San Miguel el Alto Mex. 185 E4
San Miguel Island U.S.A. 182 D7
San Miguel Islands Phil. 74 A5
San Miguelito Panama 186 D5
San Miguel Sola de Vega Mex. 185 F5
Sanming China 87 F3
San Miniato Italy 56 C5
Sanna r. Poland 49 S5
San Narciso Phil. 74 B3
Sannaspos S. Africa 133 K6
Sanndatti India 94 B3
Sanndraigh i. U.K. see Sandray
Sannicandro Garganico Italy 56 H7
San Nicolás Mex. 185 F3
San Nicolas Phil. 74 B2
San Nicolás, Bahía b. Peru 200 E3
San Nicolás de los Arroyos Arg. 204 E4
San Nicolás del Presidio Mex. 184 D3
San Nicolas Island U.S.A. 182 E8
Sânnicolau Mare Romania 58 B2
formerly spelt Sînnicolau Mare
Sannieshof S. Africa 133 J3
Sanniquellie Liberia 124 C5
Sannohe Japan 90 G4
Sañogasta, Sierra de mts Arg. 204 D3
Sanok Poland 49 T6
San Onofre Col. 198 C2
San Pablo Arg. 205 D9
San Pablo Potosí Bol. 200 D5
San Pablo Santa Cruz Bol. 201 E3
San Pablo r. Bol. 201 E3
San Pablo Col. 198 D3
San Pablo Mex. 185 F4
San Pablo Phil. 74 B3
San Pablo U.S.A. 182 B4
San Pablo de Manta Ecuador see Manta
San Pedro Buenos Aires Arg. 204 F4
San Pedro Catamarca Arg. 204 D2
San Pedro Jujuy Arg. 200 D6
San Pedro Misiones Arg. 204 G2
San Pedro Belize 185 I5
San Pedro Beni Bol. 200 D3
San Pedro Santa Cruz Bol. 201 E4
San Pedro r. Bol. 200 D4
San-Pédro Côte d'Ivoire 124 D5
San Pedro r. Cuba 186 D2
San Pedro Mex. 184 C4
San Pedro r. Mex. 181 F7
San Pedro Para. 201 F5
San Pedro Peru 200 C2
San Pedro Phil. 74 B3
San Pedro watercourse U.S.A. 183 N9
San Pedro, Punta pt Costa Rica 186 C5
San Pedro, Sierra de mts Spain 54 D5
San Pedro Carchá Guat. 185 H6
San Pedro Channel U.S.A. 182 F8
San Pedro de Atacama Chile 200 C5
San Pedro de las Colonias Mex. 185 E3
San Pedro de Lloc Peru 200 A1
San Pedro del Pinatar Spain 55 K7
San Pedro de Macorís Dom. Rep. 187 F3
San Pedro de Ycuamandyyú Para. 201 F6
San Pedro el Saucito Mex. 184 C2
San Pedro Mártir, Parque Nacional nat. park Mex. 184 B2
San Pedro Sula Hond. 186 A4
San Pietro, Isola di i. Sardegna Italy 57 A9
San Pietro in Cariano Italy 56 C3
San Pitch r. U.S.A. 183 M2
Sanqaçal Azer. 107 G2
also spelt Sangachaly
Sanquhar U.K. 46 I8
Sanquianga, Parque Nacional nat. park Col. 198 B4
San Quintín, Cabo c. Mex. 184 A2
San Rafael Arg. 204 C4
San Rafael Bol. 201 E4
San Rafael U.S.A. 182 B4
San Rafael r. U.S.A. 183 N3
San Rafael Venez. 198 D2
also known as San Rafael del Moján
San Rafael del Moján Venez. see San Rafael
San Rafael del Norte Nicaragua 186 B4
San Rafael del Yuma Dom. Rep. 187 F3
San Rafael Knob mt. U.S.A. 183 N3
San Rafael Mountains U.S.A. 182 D7
San Ramón Beni Bol. 200 D3
San Ramón Santa Cruz Bol. 201 E4
San Remo Italy 51 N9
San Rodrigo watercourse Mex. 179 B6
San Román, Cabo c. Venez. 198 D1
San Roque Andalucía Spain 54 F8
San Roque Galicia Spain 54 C1
San Roque Galicia Spain 54 C2
San Roque, Punta pt Mex. 184 B3
San Saba U.S.A. 179 C6
San Saba r. U.S.A. 179 C6
Sansalé Guinea 124 B4
San Salvador Arg. 204 F3
San Salvador i. Bahamas 187 E1
formerly known as Watling Island
▶San Salvador El Salvador 185 H6
Capital of El Salvador.
San Salvador Peru 198 D5
San Salvador de Jujuy Arg. 200 D6
San Salvo Italy 56 G6
Sansané Haoussa Niger 125 F3
Sansanné-Mango Togo 125 F4
San Sebastián Arg. 205 C9
San Sebastián hill Spain 54 C2
San Sebastián, Bahía de b. Arg. 205 C9
San Sebastián de los Reyes Spain 55 H4
Sansepolcro Italy 56 E5
San Severo Marche Italy 56 F5
San Severo Italy 56 H7
Sansha China 87 G3
San Silvestre Bol. 200 C2
San Silvestre Venez. 198 D2
San Simon U.S.A. 183 O9
Sanski Most Bos.-Herz. 56 I4
Sanson N.Z. 152 J8
Sansoral Islands Palau see Sonsorol Islands
Sansui China 87 D3
also known as Bagong
Santa Peru 200 A2
Santa r. Peru 200 A2
Santa Adélia Brazil 206 E8
Santa Ana Arg. 204 D2
Santa Ana La Paz Bol. 200 D3
Santa Ana Santa Cruz Bol. 201 F4
Santa Ana El Salvador 185 H6
Santa Ana Mex. 184 C2
Santa Ana U.S.A. 182 G8
Santa Ana de Yacuma Bol. 200 D3
Santa Anita Mex. 184 C4
Santa Anna U.S.A. 179 C6
Santa Bárbara Brazil 201 F3
Santa Bárbara Cuba see La Demajagua
Santa Bárbara Hond. 186 A4
Santa Bárbara Mex. 184 D3
Santa Bárbara mt. Spain 55 I7
Santa Bárbara mt. Spain 55 J6
Santa Barbara U.S.A. 182 E7
Santa Bárbara Amazonas Venez. 199 E4
Santa Bárbara Barinas Venez. 198 D3
Santa Bárbara, Ilha i. Brazil 207 O4
Santa Barbara, Parque Nacional nat. park Hond. 186 A4
Santa Bárbara, Serra de hills Brazil 203 A7
Santa Barbara Channel U.S.A. 182 D7
Santa Bárbara d'Oeste Brazil 206 F9
Santa Bárbara do Sul Brazil 203 A9
Santa Barbara Island U.S.A. 182 E8
Santa Catalina Chile 204 C2
Santa Catalina Panama 186 C5
Santa Catalina Venez. 199 F2
Santa Catalina, Gulf of U.S.A. 182 G8
Santa Catalina, Isla i. Mex. 184 C3
Santa Catalina de Armada Spain 54 C1
Santa Catalina Island U.S.A. 182 F8
Santa Catarina state Brazil 203 B8
Santa Catarina Baja California Norte Mex. 184 B2
Santa Catarina Nuevo León Mex. 185 E3
Santa Catarina Neth. Antilles 187 F4
also spelt Santa Catharina
Santa Catarina, Ilha de i. Brazil 203 B8
Santa Catharina Neth. Antilles see Santa Catarina
Santa Clara Col. 198 D5
Santa Clara Cuba 186 D2
Santa Clara r. Mex. 181 F7
Santa Clara CA U.S.A. 182 C4
Santa Clara UT U.S.A. 183 K4
Santa Clara r. U.S.A. 182 E7
Santa Clara, Barragem de resr Port. 54 C7
Santa Clarita U.S.A. 182 F7
Santa Clotilde Peru 198 C5
Santa Coloma de Farners Spain 55 N3
Santa Coloma de Gramanet Spain 55 N3
Santa Comba Angola see Waku-Kungo
Santa Comba Dão Port. 54 C4
Santa Croce Camerina Sicilia Italy 57 G12
Santa Cruz prov. Arg. 205 C8
Santa Cruz r. Arg. 205 C8
Santa Cruz Bol. 201 E4
Santa Cruz dept Bol. 201 E4
Santa Cruz Espírito Santo Brazil 207 M6
Santa Cruz Pará Brazil 199 H5
Santa Cruz Pará Brazil 202 B2
Santa Cruz Costa Rica 186 B5
Santa Cruz Mex. 184 C2
Santa Cruz Peru 198 C6
Santa Cruz Luzon Phil. 74 A3
Santa Cruz Luzon Phil. 74 B2
Santa Cruz Luzon Phil. 74 B3
Santa Cruz mt. Spain 55 J3
Santa Cruz U.S.A. 182 B5
Santa Cruz watercourse U.S.A. 183 L8
Santa Cruz, Isla i. Mex. 184 C3
Santa Cruz, Puerto inlet Arg. 205 C8
Santa Cruz Barillas Guat. 185 H6
Santa Cruz Cabrália Brazil 202 E6
Santa Cruz das Palmeiras Brazil 206 F8
Santa Cruz de Goiás Brazil 206 E4
Santa Cruz de la Palma Canary Is 122 A3
Santa Cruz del Quiché Guat. 185 H6
Santa Cruz del Sur Cuba 186 D2
Santa Cruz de Mudela Spain 55 H6
▶Santa Cruz de Tenerife Canary Is 122 A3
Joint capital of the Canary Islands.
Santa Cruz de Yojoa Hond. 186 B4
Santa Cruz do Rio Pardo Brazil 206 D9
Santa Cruz do Sul Brazil 203 A9
Santa Cruz Island U.S.A. 182 E7
Santa Cruz Islands Solomon Is 145 F3
Santa Efigênia de Minas Brazil 207 K5
Santa Elena Buenos Aires Arg. 204 E5
Santa Elena Entre Ríos Arg. 204 F3
Santa Elena Bol. 200 D5
Santa Elena Peru 198 C6
Santa Elena Venez. 199 F3
Santa Elena, Cabo c. Costa Rica 186 B5
Santa Elena, Punta pt Ecuador 198 A5
Santa Eufemia, Golfo di g. Italy 57 I10
Santa Eugenia Spain 54 C2
Santa Eulalia del Río Spain 55 M6
Santa Fé Arg. 204 E3
Santa Fé prov. Arg. 204 E3
Santa Fé Cuba 186 C2
Santa Fé Panama 186 C5
Santa Fe Phil. 74 B3
Santa Fe Spain 54 H7
▶Santa Fe U.S.A. 181 F6
State capital of New Mexico.
Santa Fé de Bogotá Col. see Bogotá
Santafé de Bogotá municipality Col. 198 C4
Santa Fé de Minas Brazil 202 C6
Santa Fé do Sul Brazil 206 C7
Santa Filomena Brazil 202 C4
Sant'Agata di Militello Sicilia Italy 57 G10
Santa Helena Brazil 202 C2
Santa Helena de Goiás Brazil 206 C4
Santai Sichuan China 86 C2
also known as Tongchuan
Santai Xinjiang China 88 C2
Santa Inês Bahia Brazil 202 E5
Santa Inês Maranhão Brazil 202 C2
Santa Inés, Isla i. Chile 205 B9
Santa Isabel Arg. 204 D5
Santa Isabel Bol. 200 D5
Santa Isabel Brazil 201 E3
Santa Isabel Equat. Guinea see Malabo
Santa Isabel i. Solomon Is 145 E2
formerly spelt Santa Ysabel
Santa Isabel, Ilha Grande de i. Brazil 202 D2
Santa Isabel, Sierra mts Mex. 184 B2
Santa Isabel de Sihuas Peru 200 B4
Santa Isabel do Araguaia Brazil 201 H1
Santa Juliana Brazil 206 F6
Santalpur India 96 A5
Santa Lucia Chile 200 C5
Santa Lucía Ecuador 198 B5
Santa Lucia Guat. 185 H6
Santa Lucía, Cerro de mt. Spain 54 G7
Santa Lucia Range mts U.S.A. 182 C5
Santa Luzia Maranhão Brazil 202 C3
Santa Luzia Paraíba Brazil 202 E3
Santa Luzia i. Cape Verde 124 [inset]
Santa Magdalena Arg. 204 E4
Santa Margarita Arg. 204 E3
Santa Margarita Spain 55 O5
Santa Margarita U.S.A. 182 D6
Santa Margarita, Isla i. Mex. 184 C3
Santa María Arg. 204 D2
Santa María Bol. 201 E3
Santa Maria Amazonas Brazil 199 F5
Santa Maria Amazonas Brazil 199 G5
Santa Maria Pará Brazil 199 H5
Santa Maria Rio Grande do Sul Brazil 203 A9
Santa Maria r. Brazil 203 A9
Santa Maria r. Brazil 206 G1
Santa Maria Cape Verde 124 [inset]
Santa María Mex. 185 H5
Santa María r. Mex. 184 D2
Santa Maria U.S.A. 182 D7
Santa Maria r. U.S.A. 183 K7
Santa María Venez. 199 E3
Santa Maria, Cabo de c. Moz. 131 G5
Santa Maria, Cabo de c. Port. 54 D8
Santa Maria, Cape Bahamas 175 F8
Santa María, Cayo i. Cuba 186 D2
Santa Maria, Chapadão de hills Brazil 202 C5
Santa María, Isla i. Chile 204 B5
Santa María, Punta pt Peru 200 B3
Santa Maria, Serra de hills Brazil 206 G1
Santa Maria Capua Vetere Italy 56 G7
Santa Maria da Boa Vista Brazil 202 E4
Santa Maria das Barreiras Brazil 202 B4
Santa Maria da Vitória Brazil 202 C5
Santa María de Ipire Venez. 199 E2
Santa María del Oro Mex. 184 D3
Santa María del Río Mex. 185 E4
Santa Maria di Leuca, Capo c. Italy 57 K9
Santa Maria do Salto Brazil 207 M3
Santa Maria do Suaçuí Brazil 203 D6
Santa Maria Island Vanuatu 145 F3
Santa Maria Mountains U.S.A. 183 L7
Santa Marina Salina Isole Lipari Italy 57 G10
Santa Marinella Italy 56 D6
Santa Marta Col. 198 C2
Santa Marta, Cabo de c. Angola 127 B8
Santa Marta, Serra de mts Brazil see Divisões, Serra das
Santa Marta Grande, Cabo de c. Brazil 203 B9
Santa Martha, Cerro mt. Mex. 185 G5
Santa Maura i. Greece see Lefkada
Santa Monica U.S.A. 182 F7
Santa Monica Bay U.S.A. 182 F8
Santan Indon. 77 G3
Santana Amazonas Brazil 199 E4
Santana Bahia Brazil 202 D5
Santana r. Brazil 206 B6
Sântana Romania 58 C2
Santana da Boa Vista Brazil 203 A9
Santana do Acarau Brazil 202 D2
Santana do Araguaia Brazil 202 B4
Santana do Cariri Brazil 202 E3
Santana do Livramento Brazil 204 G3
Santander Col. 198 B4
Santander dept Col. 198 C3
Santander Spain 54 H1
Santa Nella U.S.A. 182 C4
Sant'Angelo in Lizzola Italy 56 E5
Sant'Angelo Lodigiano Italy 56 B3
Santanghu China 84 B2
Santanilla, Islas is Caribbean Sea see Swan Islands
Santan Mountain hill U.S.A. 183 M8
Sant'Anna, Ilha de i. Brazil 207 L9
Sant'Antioco Sardegna Italy 57 A9
historically known as Sulci or Sulcis
Sant'Antioco, Isola di i. Sardegna Italy 57 A9
Santany Spain see Santanyí
Santanyí Spain 55 O5
also spelt Santany
Santa Paula U.S.A. 182 E7
Santapilly India 95 D2
Santa Pola Spain 55 K6
Santa Pola, Cabo de c. Spain 55 K6
Santaquin U.S.A. 183 M2
Santa Quitéria Brazil 202 D3
Sant Arcangelo Italy 57 I8
Santarém Brazil 199 H5
Santarém Port. 54 C5
Santarém admin. dist. Port. 54 C5
Santa Rita Mato Grosso Brazil 201 F1
Santa Rita Paraíba Brazil 202 F3
Santa Rita Col. 198 C4
Santa Rita Mex. 185 E3
Santa Rita Guárico Venez. 199 E2
Santa Rita Zulia Venez. 198 D2
Santa Rita de Cassia Brazil 202 C4
Santa Rita do Araguaia Brazil 203 A6
Santa Rita do Pardo Brazil 206 A8
Santa Rita do Sapucaí Brazil 207 H9
Santa Rita do Weil Brazil 198 D5
Santa Rosa Corrientes Arg. 204 F3
Santa Rosa La Pampa Arg. 204 D5
Santa Rosa Río Negro Arg. 204 D6
Santa Rosa Salta Arg. 200 D6
Santa Rosa Bol. 200 D3
Santa Rosa Acre Brazil 200 C2
Santa Rosa Rio Grande do Sul Brazil 203 A8
Santa Rosa Col. 198 D4

S index

Santa Rosa Ecuador 198 B5
Santa Rosa Mex. 185 H5
Santa Rosa Para. 201 F6
Santa Rosa Loreto Peru 198 C5
Santa Rosa Puno Peru 200 C3
Santa Rosa CA U.S.A. 182 B3
Santa Rosa NM U.S.A. 181 F6
Santa Rosa Venez. 199 E4
Santa Rosa de Copán Hond. 186 A4
Santa Rosa de la Roca Bol. 201 E4
Santa Rosa del Conlara Arg. 204 D4
Santa Rosa del Palmar Bol. 201 E4
Santa Rosa de Osos Col. 198 C3
Santa Rosa de Vigo Bol. 200 D3
Santa Rosa de Viterbo Brazil 206 F8
Santa Rosa Island U.S.A. 182 D8
Santa Rosalía Mex. 184 B3
Santa Rosa Mountains U.S.A. 183 H8
Santa Rosa Range mts U.S.A. 180 C4
Santa Rosa Wash watercourse U.S.A. 183 L8
Santa Sylvina Arg. 204 E2
Santa Teresa Australia 148 B5
Santa Teresa Brazil 207 M6
Santa Teresa r. Brazil 202 B4
Santa Teresa Mex. 185 F3
Santa Teresa, Embalse de resr Spain 54 F4
Santa Teresa Aboriginal Land res. Australia see Ltyentye Apurte Aboriginal Land
Santa Teresa di Gallura Sardegna Italy 56 B7
Santa Terezinha Brazil 202 B4
Santa Vitória Brazil 206 C5
Santa Vitória do Palmar Brazil 204 G4
Santa Vittoria, Monte mt. Sardegna Italy 57 B9
Santa Ynez r. U.S.A. 182 D7
Santa Ysabel i. Solomon Is see Santa Isabel
Sant Carles de la Ràpita Spain 55 L4
also spelt San Carlos de la Rápita
Sant Celoni Spain 55 N3
also spelt San Celoni
Santee U.S.A. 183 H9
Santee r. U.S.A. 175 E5
Santeramo in Colle Italy 57 I8
Santerno r. Italy 56 D4
Sant Feliu de Guíxols Spain 55 O3
also spelt San Feliú de Guíxols
Santiago Brazil 203 A9

▶Santiago Chile 204 C4
Capital of Chile.
southamerica [countries] ▶▶ 192–193

Santiago admin. reg. Chile 204 C4
Santiago Dom. Rep. 187 F3
long form Santiago de los Caballeros
Santiago Baja California Sur Mex. 184 C4
Santiago Nuevo León Mex. 185 E3
Santiago Panama 186 C5
Santiago Para. 201 F6
Santiago Peru 200 B3
Santiago r. Peru 198 B6
Santiago Phil. 74 B2
Santiago, Cabo c. Chile 205 B8
Santiago, Cerro mt. Panama 186 C5
Santiago, Río Grande de r. Mex. 184 D4
Santiago, Sierra de hills Bol. 201 F4
Santiago Astata Mex. 185 G5
Santiago de Cao Peru 200 A1
Santiago de Compostela Spain 54 C2
Santiago de Cuba Cuba 186 E2
Santiago de la Espada Spain 55 I6
Santiago del Estero Arg. 204 D2
Santiago del Estero prov. Arg. 204 E2
Santiago de los Caballeros Dom. Rep. see Santiago
Santiago de Mendez Ecuador 198 B5
Santiago de Pacaguaras Bol. 200 C3
Santiago do Cacém Port. 54 C6
Santiago Ixcuintla Mex. 184 D4
Santiago Peak U.S.A. 182 G8
Santiago Temple Arg. 204 E3
Santiago Vazquez Uruguay 204 F4
Santiaguillo, Laguna de l. Mex. 184 D3
Santillana Spain 54 G1
San Timoteo Venez. 198 D2
Santipur India see Shantipur
Santisteban del Puerto Spain 55 H6
Sant Jordi, Golf de g. Spain 55 L4
also spelt San Jorge, Golfo de
Sant Llorenç del Munt i de la Serra de L'Obac, Parque Natural de nature res. Spain 55 M3
Santo Amaro Brazil 202 E5
Santo Amaro de Campos Brazil 207 L8
Santo Anastácio r. Brazil 206 A8
Santo André Brazil 206 G10
Santo André Port. 54 C6
Santo Angelo Brazil 203 A9

▶Santo Antão i. Cape Verde 124 [inset]
Most westerly point of Africa.

Santo Antônio Amazonas Brazil 199 F5
Santo Antônio Maranhão Brazil 202 C3
Santo Antônio Rio Grande do Norte Brazil 202 F3
Santo Antônio r. Brazil 203 D6
Santo António São Tomé and Príncipe 125 G6
Santo Antônio, Ponta pt Brazil 207 O3
Santo Antônio da Barra Brazil 206 C4
Santo Antônio da Cachoeira Brazil 199 H5
Santo Antônio da Platina Brazil 206 C10
Santo Antônio de Jesus Brazil 202 E5
Santo Antônio de Leverger Brazil 201 F3
Santo Antônio de Pádua Brazil 207 K8
Santo Antônio do Amparo Brazil 207 I7
Santo Antônio do Içá Brazil 199 E5
Santo Antônio do Jacinto Brazil 207 M3
Santo Antônio do Monte Brazil 207 H7
Santo Antônio do Rio Verde Brazil 206 F4
Santo Antônio dos Cavaleiros Port. 54 B6

Santo António do Zaire Angola see Soyo
Santo Corazón Bol. 201 F4
Santo Domingo Cuba 186 C2

▶Santo Domingo Dom. Rep. 187 F3
Capital of the Dominican Republic. Formerly known as Ciudad Trujillo.

Santo Domingo Baja California Norte Mex. 184 B2
Santo Domingo San Luis Potosí Mex. 185 E4
Santo Domingo Nicaragua 186 B4
Santo Domingo Peru 200 C3
Santo Domingo country West Indies see Dominican Republic
Santo Domingo de la Calzada Spain 55 I2
Santo Domingo Pueblo U.S.A. 181 F6
Santo Domingo Tehuantepec Mex. 185 G5
Santo Eduardo Brazil 207 L8
Santo Hipólito Brazil 207 I5
Santo Inácio Brazil 206 B9
San Tomé Venez. 199 E2
Santoña Spain 55 H1
Santong r. China 82 B4
Santo Niño i. Phil. 74 C4
Santorini i. Greece see Thira
Santos Brazil 207 G10
Santos Dumont Brazil 207 J8
Santos Mercado Bol. 200 D2
Santo Stefano di Camastra Sicilia Italy 57 G10
Santo Tirso Port. 54 C3
Santo Tomás Chihuahua Mex. 181 F7
Santo Tomás Sonora Mex. 181 D7
Santo Tomás Nicaragua 186 B4
Santo Tomás Peru 200 B3
Santo Tomé Arg. 204 F3
Santrampur India 96 B5
Sanup Plateau U.S.A. 183 K5
San Valentín, Cerro mt. Chile 205 B7
San Vicente El Salvador 185 H6
San Vicente Mex. 184 A2
San Vicente Phil. 74 B2
San Vicente de Cañete Peru 200 A3
San Vicente de la Barquera Spain 54 G1
San Vicente del Caguán Col. 198 C4
San Vicente del Raspeig Spain 55 K6
San Vincenzo Italy 56 C5
San Vito, Capo c. Sicilia Italy 57 E10
San Vito al Tagliamento Italy 56 E3
San Vito Chietino Italy 56 G6
San Vito dei Normanni Italy 57 J8
San Vito lo Capo Sicilia Italy 57 E10
Sanwer India 96 B5
Sanya China 87 D5
formerly known as Yaxian
San Yanaro Col. 198 D4
Sanyati r. Zimbabwe 131 F3
Sanyuan China 87 D1
Sanza Pombo Angola 127 C6
Sao, Phou mt. Laos 78 C4
São Bartolomeu r. Brazil 206 F3
São Benedito Brazil 202 D3
São Bento Amazonas Brazil 200 D1
São Bento Maranhão Brazil 202 C2
São Bento Roraima Brazil 199 F4
São Bento do Norte Brazil 202 F3
São Bernardo Brazil 202 D2
São Bernardo do Campo Brazil 206 G10
São Borja Brazil 204 F3
São Carlos Rondônia Brazil 201 D2
São Carlos Santa Catarina Brazil 201 E2
São Carlos São Paulo Brazil 206 F9
São Desidério Brazil 202 C5
São Domingos Brazil 202 C5
São Domingos r. Mato Grosso do Sul Brazil 203 A7
São Domingos r. Minas Gerais Brazil 206 C6
São Domingos r. Brazil 206 G2
São Domingos do Norte Brazil 207 M6
São Felipe, Serra de hills Brazil 202 C5
São Félix Bahia Brazil 202 E5
São Félix Mato Grosso Brazil 202 B4
São Félix Pará Brazil 199 I6
São Fidélis Brazil 203 D7
São Filipe Cape Verde 124 [inset]
São Francisco Acre Brazil 200 C2
São Francisco Amazonas Brazil 199 F6
São Francisco Minas Gerais Brazil 202 C5
São Francisco r. Brazil 200 D2
also known as Espalha

▶São Francisco r. Brazil 207 H4
5th longest river in South America.
southamerica [landscapes] ▶▶ 190–191

São Francisco, Ilha de i. Brazil 203 B8
São Francisco de Assis Brazil 203 A9
São Francisco de Goiás Brazil 206 D2
São Francisco de Paula Brazil 203 B9
São Francisco de Sales Brazil 206 D6
São Francisco do Sul Brazil 203 B8
São Gabriel Brazil 203 A9
São Gabriel da Palha Brazil 207 M6
São Gabriel de Goiás Brazil 206 F2
São Gonçalo Brazil 203 D7
São Gonçalo do Abaeté Brazil 203 C6
São Gotardo Brazil 207 H6
Sao Hill Tanz. 129 B7
São Jerônimo da Serra Brazil 206 C10
São João Brazil 199 E5
São João, Ilhas de is Brazil 202 C2
São João, Serra de hills Brazil 201 E2
São João da Aliança Brazil 202 C5
São João da Barra Brazil 203 D7
São João da Boa Vista Brazil 206 G8
São João da Madeira Port. 54 C4
São João da Ponte Brazil 207 I2
São João das Duas Pontes Brazil 206 C7
São João del Rei Brazil 203 C7
São João de Meriti Brazil 207 J9
São João do Araguaia Brazil 202 B3
São João do Caiuá Brazil 206 A9
São João do Cariri Brazil 202 E3
São João do Paraíso Brazil 202 D5
São João do Piauí Brazil 202 D4
São João dos Patos Brazil 202 D3
São João do Sul Angola 127 B8
São João Evangelista Brazil 207 K5
São Joaquim Amazonas Brazil 199 E4
São Joaquim Santa Catarina Brazil 203 B9
São Jorge da Mina Ghana see Elmina
São José Amazonas Brazil 199 E5
São José Santa Catarina Brazil 203 B8
São José do Anauá Brazil 199 F4
São José do Belmonte Brazil 202 E3
São José do Divino Brazil 207 L5
São José do Egito Brazil 202 E3
São José do Jacuri Brazil 207 K5
São José do Norte Brazil 204 G4
São José do Peixe Brazil 202 D3
São José do Rio Pardo Brazil 206 G8
São José do Rio Preto Brazil 206 D7
São José dos Campos Brazil 207 H10
São José dos Dourados r. Brazil 206 B7
São José dos Pinhais Brazil 203 B8
São Lourenço Brazil 207 H9
São Lourenço r. Brazil 201 F4
São Lourenço do Sul Brazil 204 H3
São Lucas Angola 127 C7
São Luís Brazil 202 C2
São Luís Brazil 199 G6
São Luís de Montes Belos Brazil 206 C3
São Luís do Paraitinga Brazil 207 H10
São Luís do Quitunde Brazil 202 F4
São Luís Gonzaga Brazil 203 A9
São Manuel Brazil 206 E9
São Marcelino Brazil 199 E4
São Marcos r. Brazil 206 F5
São Marcos, Baía de b. Brazil 202 C2
São Martinho Brazil 199 G6

São Mateus Brazil 203 E6
São Mateus r. Brazil 207 N5
São Mateus do Sul Brazil 203 B8
São Miguel i. Azores 216 M3
São Miguel r. Brazil 206 G3
São Miguel Arcanjo Brazil 206 F10
São Miguel do Tapuio Brazil 202 D3
São Miguel Jesuit Missions tourist site Brazil 203 A9
Saona, Isla i. Dom. Rep. 187 F3
Saône r. France 51 K7
São Nicolau Angola see Bentiaba
São Nicolau i. Cape Verde 124 [inset]

▶São Paulo Brazil 206 G10
Most populous city in South America and 4th in the world.
world [cities] ▶▶ 24–25

São Paulo state Brazil 206 E9
São Paulo de Olivença Brazil 198 D5
São Pedro Amazonas Brazil 199 G6
São Pedro Mato Grosso do Sul Brazil 206 B6
São Pedro Rondônia Brazil 201 E2
São Pedro São Paulo Brazil 206 F9
São Pedro da Aldeia Brazil 203 D7
São Pedro do Desterro Brazil 200 D2
São Pedro do Ivaí Brazil 206 B10
São Pedro do Sul Brazil 203 A9
São Pedro do Sul Port. 54 C4
São Pedro e São Paulo is N. Atlantic Ocean 216 M5
English form St Peter and St Paul Rocks
São Pires r. Brazil see Teles Pires
São Raimundo das Mangabeiras Brazil 202 C3
São Raimundo Nonato Brazil 202 D4
São Romão Amazonas Brazil 199 E6
São Romão Minas Gerais Brazil 202 C6
São Roque Brazil 206 F10
São Roque de Minas Brazil 206 G7
São Salvador Angola see M'banza Congo
São Salvador do Congo Angola see M'banza Congo
São Sebastião Amazonas Brazil 200 C1
São Sebastião Pará Brazil 199 H6
São Sebastião Rondônia Brazil 201 E2
São Sebastião São Paulo Brazil 203 C7
São Sebastião, Ilha do i. Brazil 203 C7
São Sebastião da Amoreira Brazil 206 C10
São Sebastião da Boa Vista Brazil 202 B2
São Sebastião do Paraíso Brazil 206 G7
São Simão Mato Grosso do Sul Brazil 201 F5
São Simão Minas Gerais Brazil 206 C5
São Simão, Barragem de resr Brazil 206 C6
São Simão, Represa de resr Brazil 206 D5
Sao-Siu Indon. 75 C2
São Tiago Brazil 207 I7
São Tiago i. Cape Verde 124 [inset]

▶São Tomé São Tomé and Príncipe 125 G6
Capital of São Tomé and Príncipe.

São Tomé i. São Tomé and Príncipe 125 G6
São Tomé, Cabo de c. Brazil 203 D7
São Tomé, Pico de mt. São Tomé and Príncipe 125 G6
▶São Tomé and Príncipe country Africa 125 G6
africa [countries] ▶▶ 114–117
Saoura, Oued watercourse Alg. 123 E3
São Vicente Brazil 206 G10
São Vicente i. Cape Verde 124 [inset]
São Vicente, Cabo de c. Port. 54 C7
English form St Vincent, Cape
São Vicente Ferrer Brazil 202 C2
Sápai Greece see Sapes
Sapallanga Peru 200 B3
Sapanca Turkey 106 B2
Sapão r. Brazil 202 C4
Saparua Indon. 75 D3
Saparua i. Indon. 75 D3
Sape, Selat sea chan. Indon. 75 A5
Sape, Teluk b. Indon. 77 G5
Sapele Nigeria 125 G5
Sapes Greece 58 G7
also known as Sápai
Saphane Turkey 59 K9
Sapientza i. Greece 59 C12
Sapo, Serranía del mts Panama 186 D6
Sa Pobla Spain 55 O5
also spelt La Puebla
Sapo National Park Liberia 124 C5
Sapotskin Belarus 42 E8
Sapouy Burkina 125 E4
Sapozhok Rus. Fed. 41 G5
Sappa Creek r. U.S.A. 178 C3
Sapporo Japan 90 G3
Saptamukhi r. India 97 F5
Sapucai r. Minas Gerais Brazil 207 H8
Sapucaí r. São Paulo Brazil 206 E7
Sapucaia Brazil 199 G5
Sapudi i. Indon. 77 F4
Sapulpa U.S.A. 179 C4
Sapulut Sabah Malaysia 77 G1
Sāq, Jabal hill Saudi Arabia 104 C2
Saqi Iran 101 D3
Saqqaq Greenland 165 N2
Saqqez Iran 100 A2
Sara Bangl. 97 F4
Sarā Iran 100 A2
Sarāb Iran 100 A2
Sarābit el Khâdim tourist site Egypt 108 E8
Sara Buri Thai. 79 C5
Saracá, Lago l. Brazil 199 G5
Saraf Doungous Chad 120 C6
Saragossa Spain see Zaragoza
Saraguro Ecuador 198 B5
Saraikela India 97 E5
Sarai Sidhu Pak. 101 H4
Säräisniemi Fin. 44 N2

▶Sarajevo Bos.-Herz. 56 K5
Capital of Bosnia-Herzegovina. Historically known as Bosna Saray.

Sarakhs Turkm. 102 E5
Sarakiniko, Akra pt Greece 59 E10
Sarakino i. Greece 59 F10
Saraktash Rus. Fed. 102 D2
Saraland U.S.A. 175 B6
Saralzhin Kazakh. 102 C2
Saramati mt. India/Myanmar 97 G4
Sarameriza Peru 198 B6
Saran France 51 H5
Saran' Kazakh. 103 H2
Saran, Gunung mt. Indon. 77 E3
Saranac r. U.S.A. 177 L1
Saranac Lake U.S.A. 177 K1
Sarandë Albania 59 B9
Sarandi Paraná Brazil 206 B10
Sarandi Rio Grande do Sul Brazil 203 A8
Sarandib country Asia see Sri Lanka
Sarandí del Yí Uruguay 204 G4
Sarandí Grande Uruguay 204 F4
Sarangani i. Phil. 74 C5
Sarangani Bay Phil. 74 C5
Sarangani Islands Phil. 74 C5
Sarangani Strait Phil. 74 C5
Sarangarh India 97 D5
Sarangpur India 96 C5
Saransk Rus. Fed. 41 H5
Sara Peak Nigeria 125 H4
Sarapul Rus. Fed. 40 J4
Sarasota U.S.A. 175 D7
Saraswati r. India 96 A5
Sărata r. Moldova 58 J2
Sărata r. Romania 58 H4
Sarata Ukr. 41 D7
Sarata r. Ukr. 58 K3

Saratoga CA U.S.A. 182 B4
Saratoga WY U.S.A. 180 F4
Saratoga Springs U.S.A. 177 L2
Saratok Sarawak Malaysia 77 E2
Saratov Rus. Fed. 41 H6
Saratov Oblast admin. div. Rus. Fed. see Saratovskaya Oblast'
Saratovskaya Oblast' admin. div. Rus. Fed. 102 A2
English form Saratov Oblast
Saratovskoye Vodokhranilishche resr Rus. Fed. 102 A1
Saravan Iran 101 E5
Saravan Laos 79 D5
Sarawa r. Myanmar 79 B5
Sarawak state Malaysia 77 E2
Saray Turkey 106 A2
Saraya Guinea 124 C4
Saraya Senegal 124 C3
Saraya, Pulau reg. Sing. 76 [inset]
Sarayçık Turkey 59 K10
Sarayköy Turkey 106 B3
Saraylar Turkey 58 I8
Sarayönü Turkey 106 C3
Sarbāz Iran 101 E5
Sarbāz r. Iran 101 E5
Sarbāz reg. Iran 101 E5
Sărbeni Romania 58 G4
Sarbhang Bhutan 97 F4
Sarbisheh Iran 101 D3
Sárbogárd Hungary 49 P9
Sarbulak China 84 A2
Sarcham Iran 100 B2
Sarco Chile 204 C3
Sarda r. India/Nepal 99 K4
Sardab Pass Afgh. 101 G2
Sardarpur India 96 B5
Sardarshahr India 96 B3
Sar Dasht Iran 100 A2
Sardasht Būshehr Iran 100 B4
Sardasht Khūzestān Iran 100 B3
Sardegna admin. reg. Italy 57 B8
Sardegna i. Italy see Sardinia
Sardica Bulg. see Sofia
Sardinata Col. 198 C2
Sardinia Costa Rica 186 B5
Sardinia i. Italy 57 A8
also spelt Sardegna
Sardis U.S.A. 174 B5
Sardis Lake resr U.S.A. 174 B5
Sardoal Port. 54 C5
Sareb, Rās-as- pt U.A.E. 105 E2
Sareks nationalpark nat. park Sweden 44 L2
Sarektjåkkå mt. Sweden 44 L2
Sarempaka, Gunung mt. Indon. 77 F3
Sar-e Pol Afgh. 101 F2
Sar-e Pol prov. Afgh. 101 F2
Sar Eskandar Iran see Hashtrud
Sare Yazd Iran 100 C4
Sarez, Kŭli l. Tajik. 101 H2
also known as Sarezskoye Ozero
Sarezskoye Ozero l. Tajik. see Sarez, Kŭli
Sargasso Sea Europe 216 J4
Sargentu Loros Peru 198 C5
Sargodha Pak. 101 H3
Sarh Chad 126 C2
formerly known as Fort Archambault
Sarhad reg. Iran 101 E4
Sarhro, Jbel mt. Morocco 122 D3
Sārī Iran 100 C2
Saria i. Greece 59 I13
Sar-i-Bum Afgh. 101 F3
Sáric Mex. 184 C2
Sarichioi Romania 58 J4
Sarigan i. N. Mariana Is 73 K3
Sarıgöl Turkey 59 J10
Sarıkamış Turkey 107 E2
Sarikei Sarawak Malaysia 77 E2
Sarıkemer Turkey 59 I11
Sarıköy Turkey 59 I8
Sarikŭl, Qatorkŭhi mts China/Tajik. see Sarykol Range
Sarila India 96 C4
Sarimbun Reservoir Sing. 76 [inset]
Sarina Australia 149 F4
Sariñena Spain 55 K3
Sarıoğlan Turkey see Belören
Sar-i Pīrān mt. Iraq 100 A2
Sar-i-Pul Afgh. 101 F3
Sārī Qamish Iran 100 C2
Sariqamish Kuli salt l. Turkm./Uzbek. see Sarykamyshkoye Ozero
Sarir Tibesti des. Libya 120 C4
Sarir Water Wells Field Libya 120 D3
Sarishabari Bangl. 97 F4
Sarita U.S.A. 179 C7
Sarıveliler Turkey 108 D1
Sariwŏn N. Korea 83 B5
Sarıyer Turkey 106 B2
Sarız Turkey 107 D3
Sark i. Channel Is 50 D3
Sarkad Hungary 49 S9
Sarkand Kazakh. 103 I3
also spelt Sarqant
Sarkari Tala India 96 A4
Şarkikaraağaç Turkey 106 B3
Särkisalo Fin. 42 D1
Şarkışla Turkey 107 D3
Sarkör watercourse Iran 101 E5
Şarköy Turkey 106 A2
Sarlath Range mts Afgh./Pak. 101 F4
Sarlat-la-Canéda France 50 H8
Sarmanovo Rus. Fed. 40 J5
Şărmăşag Romania 58 D1
Sărmașu Romania 58 F2
Sarmento r. Italy 57 I8
Sarmi Indon. 73 I7
Sarmiento Arg. 205 C7
Särna Sweden 45 K3
Sarnate Latvia 42 C4
Sarneh Iran 100 A3
Sarnen Switz. 51 O6
Sarni India see Amla
Sarnia Canada 168 D5
Sarny Ukr. 41 C6
Saroako Indon. 75 B3
Sarogozha r. Rus. Fed. 43 Q3
Sarolangun Indon. 76 C3
Saroma-ko l. Japan 90 H2
Sarona U.S.A. 172 B5
Saronikos Kolpos g. Greece 59 E11
Saros Körfezi b. Turkey 106 A2
Sárospatak Hungary 49 S7
Sarotra India 96 B4
Sarova Rus. Fed. 40 G5
Sarowbī Afgh. 101 G3
Sarpa, Ozero l. Rus. Fed. 41 H7
Sarpan i. N. Mariana Is see Rota
Šar Planina mts Macedonia/Yugo. 58 B7
Sarpsborg Norway 45 J4
Sarqant Kazakh. see Sarkand
Sarre r. France 51 N3
Sarrebourg France 51 N4
Sarreguemines France 51 N3
Sarre-Union France 51 N4
Sarria Spain 54 D2
Sarrión Spain 55 K4
Sarro Mali 124 D3
Sarròch Sardegna Italy 57 B9
Sars Rus. Fed. 40 K4
Sartana Ukr. 41 F7
formerly known as Prymors'ke
Sartène Corse France 56 A7
Sarthe r. France 50 F5
Sarti Greece 59 E8
Sartininkai Lith. 42 C6
Sartu China see Daqing
Sarud, Rūdkhāneh-ye r. Iran 100 B3
Saruhanlı Turkey 59 I10
Saruna r. Pak. 101 F5
Sarupsar India 96 B3

Şārur Azer. 107 F3
also spelt Sharur; formerly known as Il'ichevsk
Saru Tara tourist site Afgh. 101 E4
Sarvābād Iran 100 A3
Sarvani Georgia see Marneuli
Sárvár Hungary 49 N8
Sarvestān Iran 100 C4
Sărviz r. Romania 49 P9
Sarwar India 96 B4
Sarya r. India 94 B2
Saryagach Kazakh. 103 G4
Sary-Bulak Kyrg. 103 H4
Sarydhaz r. Kyrg. see Sary-Jaz
Sarydzhas Kazakh. see Saryzhaz
Sarygamysh Köli salt l. Turkm./Uzbek. see Sarykamyshkoye Ozero
Sary-Ishikotrau, Peski des. Kazakh. see Saryyesik-Atyrau, Peski
Sary-Jaz r. Kyrg. 103 I4
also spelt Sarydhaz
Sarykamys Kazakh. 102 C3
also spelt Saryqamys
Sarykamyshkoye Ozero salt l. Turkm./Uzbek. 102 D4
also known as Sariqamish Kuli or Sarygamysh Köli
Sarykemer Kazakh. 103 G4
formerly known as Mikhaylovka
Sarykiyak Kazakh. 103 H2
Sarykol Range mts China/Tajik. 88 A4
also known as Sarikŭl, Qatorkŭhi
Sarymoyyn, Ozero salt l. Kazakh. 103 F2
Saryozek Kazakh. 103 I3
Saryqamys Kazakh. see Sarykamys
Saryshagan Kazakh. 103 H3
Sarysu watercourse Kazakh. 103 F3
formerly known as Zhaksy Sarysu
Sary-Tash Kyrg. 103 H5
Saryter, Gora mt. Kyrg. 103 I4
Saryumir Kazakh. 102 B2
Sary Yazikskoye Vodokhranilishche resr Turkm. 103 E5
Saryyesik-Atyrau, Peski des. Kazakh. 103 H3
formerly known as Sary-Ishikotrau, Peski
Saryzhal Kazakh. see Sarzhal
Saryzhaz Kazakh. 103 I4
also spelt Sarydzhas
Sarzana Italy 56 B4
Sarzeau France 50 D5
Sarzhal Kazakh. 103 I2
also spelt Saryzhal
Sasak Indon. 76 B2
Sasar, Tanjung pt Indon. 75 A5
Sasaram India 97 E4
Sásd Hungary 49 P9
Sasebo Japan 91 A8
Saskatchewan prov. Canada 167 J4
Saskatchewan r. Canada 167 K4
Saskatoon Canada 167 J4
Saskylakh Rus. Fed. 39 L2
Saslaya mt. Nicaragua 186 B4
Saslaya, Parque Nacional nat. park Nicaragua 186 B4
Sasnovy Bor Belarus 43 K9
also spelt Sosnovyy Bor; formerly known as Golyashi
Sasolburg S. Africa 133 L3
Sasovo Rus. Fed. 41 G5
Sass r. Canada 167 H2
Sassandra Côte d'Ivoire 124 D5
Sassandra r. Côte d'Ivoire 124 D5
Sassari Sardegna Italy 57 A8
Sassnitz Germany 49 K1
Sassoferrato Italy 56 E5
historically known as Sentinum
Sasso Marconi Italy 56 D4
Sass Rigais mt. Italy 56 D2
Sass Town Liberia 124 C5
Sassuolo Italy 56 C4
Sastobe Kazakh. 103 G4
also spelt Saztöbe
Sastre Arg. 204 E3
Sasvad India 94 B2
Sasykkol', Ozero l. Kazakh. 103 J3
also known as Sasyqköl
Sasyqköl l. Kazakh. see Sasykkol', Ozero
Satadougou Mali 124 C3
Satahual i. Micronesia see Satawal
Sata-misaki c. Japan 91 B9
Satana India 94 B1
Satara India 94 B2
Satara S. Africa 131 F5
Satawal i. Micronesia 73 K5
also spelt Satahual
Sätbaev Kazakh. see Satpayev
Satchinez Romania 58 C3
Satéma Cent. Afr. Rep. 126 D3
Satengar i. Indon. 77 G4
Säter Sweden 45 K3
Satevó Mex. 184 D3
Saticoy U.S.A. 182 E7
Satihaure l. Sweden 44 L2
Satilla r. U.S.A. 175 D6
Satipo Peru 200 B2
Satiri Burkina 124 D4
Satırlar Turkey see Yeşilova
Satka Rus. Fed. 38 F4
Satkania Bangl. 97 G5
Satkhira Bangl. 97 F5
Satluj r. India/Pak. see Sutlej
Satmala Range hills India 94 C2
Satna India 96 D4
Sátoraljaújhely Hungary 49 S7
Satorina mt. Croatia 56 H4
Satpayev Kazakh. 103 F3
also spelt Sätbaev; formerly known as Nikol'skiy
Satpura Range mts India 96 B5
Šatrijos kalnis hill Lith. 42 D6
Satsuma-hantō pen. Japan 91 B9
Satsunai-gawa r. Japan 90 H3
Sattahip Thai. 79 C5
Sattanen Fin. 44 N2
Sattenapalle India 94 D2
Satthwa Myanmar 78 A4
Satti Jammu and Kashmir 96 C2
Satu Mare Romania 53 G2
Satun Thai. 79 C7
Satwas India 96 C5
Saubi i. Indon. 77 F4
Sauce Arg. 204 F3
Sauceda Mountains U.S.A. 183 L9
Sauce de Luna Arg. 204 F3
Saucillo Mex. 184 D2
Sauda Norway 45 I4
Saudakent Kazakh. 103 G4
formerly known as Baykadam or Bayqadam
Sauðárkrókur Iceland 44 [inset] C2
▶Saudi Arabia country Asia 104 C3
known as Al 'Arabīyah as Sa'ūdīyah in Arabic
asia [landscapes] ▶▶ 62–63
asia [countries] ▶▶ 64–67
Saue Estonia 42 F2
Sauêruiná r. Brazil 201 F3
also known as Papagaio
Saug r. Phil. 74 C5
Sauga r. Estonia 42 F3
Saugeen r. Canada 168 D4
Saugerties U.S.A. 177 L3
Saugues France 51 J8
Sāūjbolāgh Iran see Mahābād
Saujil Arg. 204 D3
Saujon France 50 F7
Saukas ezers l. Latvia 42 G5
Sauk Center U.S.A. 178 D2
Sauk City U.S.A. 172 D7
Saul Fr. Guiana 199 H4
Sauland Norway 45 J4
Sauldre r. France 51 H5
Saulgau Germany 48 G7
Saulieu France 51 K5

Saulkrasti Latvia 42 F4
Sault Sainte Marie Canada 168 C4
Sault Ste Marie U.S.A. 173 I4
Saumalkol' Kazakh. 103 G1
formerly known as Volodarskoye
Saumarez Reef Australia 149 G4
Saumlakki Indon. 73 H8
Saumur France 50 F5
Saunavaara Fin. 44 N2
Saunders, Mount hill Australia 148 A2
Saunders Coast Antarctica 222 O1
Saunders Island Falkland Is 205 E8
Saunemin U.S.A. 172 E10
Saungka Myanmar 78 B2
Sauquoit U.S.A. 177 J2
Saur, Khrebet mts China/Kazakh. 88 D2
Saurieši Latvia 42 F5
Saurimo Angola 127 D7
formerly known as Henrique de Carvalho
Sausalito U.S.A. 182 B4
Sausar India 96 C5
Sautar Angola 127 C7
Sava r. Europe 49 M9
Savá Hond. 186 B4
Sava Italy 57 J8
Savage U.S.A. 177 I6
Savage River Australia 147 E5
Savai'i i. Samoa 145 H3
historically known as Chatham Island
Savala r. Rus. Fed. 41 G6
Savalou Benin 125 F5
Savanat Iran see Eşţahbān
Savane r. Canada 169 G3
Savane Moz. 131 G3
Savanna U.S.A. 174 B3
Savannah GA U.S.A. 175 D5
Savannah MO U.S.A. 178 D4
Savannah OH U.S.A. 176 C5
Savannah TN U.S.A. 174 B5
Savannah r. U.S.A. 175 D5
Savannah Sound Bahamas 186 D1
Savannakhét Laos 78 D4
Savanna-la-Mar Jamaica 186 D3
Savanne Canada 172 C2
Savant Lake Canada 168 B3
Savantvadi India see Vadi
Savanur India 94 B3
Sävar Sweden 44 M3
Săvârșin Romania 58 D2
Sävast Sweden 44 M2
Savaştepe Turkey 106 A3
Savè Benin 125 F4
Save r. France 50 H9
Save Moz. 131 G4
Save r. Moz./Zimbabwe 131 G4
formerly spelt Sabi
Sāveh Iran 100 B3
Savelugu Ghana 125 E4
Savenay France 50 E5
Saveretik Guyana 199 G3
Saverne France 51 N4
Savigliano Italy 51 N8
Săvinești Romania 58 H2
Savinja r. Slovenia 56 H2
Savino Rus. Fed. 40 G4
Savinskiy Rus. Fed. 40 G3
Savinskoye Rus. Fed. 43 U6
Savio r. Italy 56 E4
Savitaipale Fin. 45 N3
Savitri r. India 94 B2
Sävja Sweden 45 L4
Šavnik Crna Gora Yugo. 58 A6
Savoie reg. France see Savoy
Savona Italy 56 A4
Savonlinna Fin. 45 O3
Savonranta Fin. 44 O3
Savoonga U.S.A. 164 B3
Savoy reg. France 51 M6
also spelt Savoie
Savozero, Ozero l. Rus. Fed. 43 O1
Şavşat Turkey 107 E2
Sävsjö Sweden 45 K4
Savu i. Indon. 75 B5
also spelt Sawu
Savudrija, Rt pt Croatia 56 F3
Savukoski Fin. 44 O2
Savur Turkey 107 E3
Savute r. Botswana 130 E3
Savuti Botswana 131 E3
Saw Myanmar 78 A3
Şawab, Wādī aş watercourse Iraq 109 K4
Şawāb, Wādī aş watercourse Syria 109 L3
Sawahlunto Indon. 76 C3
Sawai, Teluk b. Indon. 75 D3
Sawai Madhopur India 96 C4
Sawan Indon. 77 F3
Sawan Myanmar 78 B2
Sawankhalok Thai. 78 B4
also known as Wang Mai Khon
Sawar India 96 B4
Sawara Japan 91 G7
Sawasaki-bana pt Japan 90 F6
Sawata Japan 90 F5
Sawatch Range mts U.S.A. 180 F5
Sawdā', Jabal as hills Libya 120 B2
Sawi, Ao b. Thai. 79 B6
Şawl Egypt 108 C8
Sawla Ghana 124 E4
Sawmills Zimbabwe 131 F3
Sawn China 86 A4
Şawqirah, Dawhat b. Oman 105 G4
English form Şawqirah Bay
Şawqirah, Ra's c. Oman 105 G4
Şawqirah Bay Oman see Şawqirah, Dawhat
Sawtell Australia 147 G2
Sawtooth Mountains hills U.S.A. 174 B2
Sawtooth Range mts ID U.S.A. 180 D3
Sawtooth Range mts WA U.S.A. 180 B2
Sawu Indon. 75 B5
Sawu i. Indon. see Savu
Sawu Sea Indon. 75 B5
Saxby r. Australia 149 D3
Saxnäs Sweden 44 K2
Saxony land Germany see Sachsen
Saxony-Anhalt land Germany see Sachsen-Anhalt
Saxton KY U.S.A. 176 A9
Saxton PA U.S.A. 176 G5
Say Mali 124 D3
Say Niger 125 F3
Sayabouri Laos see Muang Xaignabouri
Sayafi i. Indon. 75 D2
Sayak Kazakh. 103 I3
also spelt Sayaq
Sayalkudi India 94 C4
Sayam well Niger 125 I3
Sayán Peru 200 A2
Sayang i. Indon. 75 D2
Sayano-Shushenskoye Vodokhranilishche resr Rus. Fed. 80 E2
Sayaq Kazakh. see Sayak
Sayat Turkm. 103 E5
also spelt Sayot; formerly spelt Sayyod
Sayda Lebanon see Sidon
Sāyen Iran 100 C4
Sayer Island Thai. 79 B6
Sayghān Afgh. 101 F3
Şayh well Yemen 104 D4
Şayh al Aḥmar reg. Oman 105 G3
Sayhūt Yemen 105 E5
Sayingpan China 86 B3
Saykhin Kazakh. 102 A2
also spelt Sayqyn
Saylac Somalia 128 D2
Saylan country Asia see Sri Lanka
Saynshand Mongolia 85 F2
Sayn-Ust Mongolia 84 B2
Sayot Turkm. see Sayat
Sayot-Ötesh Kazakh. see Say-Utes
Şayqal, Baḥr imp. l. Syria 109 I4
Sayqyn Kazakh. see Saykhin
Sayram Hu salt l. China 88 C2

Sayramskiy, Pik mt. Uzbek. 103 G4
Sayre OK U.S.A. 179 C5
Sayre PA U.S.A. 177 I4
Sayreville U.S.A. 177 K5
Sayula Jalisco Mex. 184 E5
Sayula Veracruz Mex. 185 G5
Say'ūn Yemen 105 E4
Say-Utes Kazakh. 102 C3
also spelt Say-Ötesh
Sayward Canada 166 E5
Sayy well Oman 105 G4
Sayyod Turkm. see Sayat
Sazan i. Albania 58 A8
Sázava r. Czech Rep. 49 L6
Sazonovo Rus. Fed. 43 Q2
Saztöbe Kazakh. see Sastobe
Sbaa Alg. 123 E3
Sbeitla Tunisia 123 H2
Sbiba Tunisia 57 B13
Scaddan Australia 151 C7
Scaër France 50 C4
Scafell Pike hill U.K. 47 I9
Scalea Italy 57 H9
Scaletta Zanclea Sicilia Italy 57 H10
Scalloway U.K. 46 K3
Scalpaigh, Eilean i. U.K. see Scalpay
Scalpay i. U.K. 46 F6
also known as Scalpaigh, Eilean
Scandicci Italy 56 D5
Scansano Italy 56 D6
Scânteia Romania 58 I4
Scanzano Jonico Italy 57 I8
Scapa Flow inlet U.K. 46 I5
Scarba i. U.K. 46 G7
Scarborough Canada 168 E5
Scarborough Trin. and Tob. 187 H5
Scarborough U.K. 47 L9
Scarborough Shoal sea feature S. China Sea 73 E3
Scargill N.Z. 153 G10
Scarinish U.K. 46 F7
Scarp i. U.K. 46 E5
Scarpanto i. Greece see Karpathos
Scaterie Island Canada 169 J4
Scawfell Shoal sea feature S. China Sea 77 D1
Sceale Bay Australia 146 B3
Šćedro i. Croatia 56 I5
Schaale r. Germany 48 H2
Schaalsee l. Germany 48 H2
Schaalsee park Germany 48 H2
Schaffhausen Switz. 51 O5
Schagen Neth. 48 B3
Schakalskuppe Namibia 130 C5
Schao watercourse Afgh./Iran 101 E4
Scharbeutz Germany 48 H1
Schärding Austria 49 K7
Scharhörn sea feature Germany 48 F2
Schaumburg U.S.A. 172 E8
Scheeßel Germany 48 G2
Schefferville Canada 169 H2
formerly known as Knob Lake
Scheibbs Austria 49 M7
Schell Creek Range mts U.S.A. 183 J3
Schellsburg U.S.A. 176 G5
Schellville U.S.A. 182 B3
Schenectady U.S.A. 177 L3
Schenefeld Germany 48 G2
Schertz U.S.A. 179 C6
Schesaplana mt. Austria/Switz. 51 P5
Scheßlitz Germany 48 I6
Schierling Germany 48 J7
Schiermonnikoog i. Neth. 48 D2
Schiermonnikoog Nationaal Park nat. park Neth. 48 D2
Schiers Switz. 51 P6
Schimatari Greece 59 E10
also known as Skhimatárion
Schio Italy 56 D3
Schirmeck France 51 N4
Schitu Duca Romania 58 I1
Schiza i. Greece 59 C12
also spelt Skhíza
Schkeuditz Germany 49 J4
Schladen Germany 48 H3
Schladming Austria 49 K8
Schlei r. Germany 48 H1
Schleiz Germany 48 I5
Schleswig Germany 48 G1
Schleswig-Holstein land Germany 48 G1
Schleswig-Holsteinisches Wattenmeer, Nationalpark nat. park Germany 48 F1
Schlosshof tourist site Austria 49 N7
Schloß Holte-Stukenbrock Germany 48 F4
Schluchsee Germany 48 F8
Schlüchtern Germany 48 G5
Schlüsselburg Rus. Fed. see Shlissel'burg
Schmallenberg Germany 48 F4
Schmidt Island Rus. Fed. see Shmidta, Ostrov
Schmidt Peninsula Rus. Fed. see Shmidta, Poluostrov
Schmidtsdrif S. Africa 132 I5
Schneidemühl Poland see Piła
Schneverdingen Germany 48 G2
Schoemanskloof pass S. Africa 133 O2
Schoharie U.S.A. 177 K3
Schokland tourist site Neth. 48 C3
Schombee S. Africa 133 J8
Schönebeck (Elbe) Germany 48 I3
Schönefeld airport Germany 49 K3
Schöningen Germany 48 H3
Schoodic Point U.S.A. 177 R1
Schoolcraft U.S.A. 172 H8
Schoonhoven Neth. 48 B4
Schöpfl hill Austria 49 M7
Schorfheide reg. Germany 49 K3
Schouten Island Australia 147 F5
Schouten Islands P.N.G. 73 J7
Schrankogel mt. Austria 48 I8
Schreiber Canada 168 C3
Schrems Austria 49 M7
Schrobenhausen Germany 48 I7
Schroon Lake U.S.A. 177 L2
Schröttersburg Poland see Płock
Schulenburg U.S.A. 179 C6
Schull Rep. of Ireland 47 C12
Schultz Lake Canada 167 L1
Schuyler U.S.A. 178 C3
Schuyler Lake U.S.A. 177 J3
Schuylerville U.S.A. 177 L2
Schuylkill Haven U.S.A. 177 I5
Schwaan Germany 49 J2
Schwabach Germany 48 I6
Schwäbische Alb mts Germany 48 F8
Schwäbisch-Fränkischer Wald, Naturpark nature res. Germany 48 G7
Schwäbisch Hall Germany 48 G6
Schwabmünchen Germany 48 H7
Schwalm r. Germany 51 P1
Schwanden Switz. 51 P5
Schwandorf Germany 48 J6
Schwaner, Pegunungan mts Indon. 77 F3
Schwangau Germany 48 H8
Schwartz Range mts Antarctica 223 D2
Schwarzenbek Germany 48 H2
Schwarzenberg Germany 49 J5
Schwarzer Mann hill Germany 48 D5
Schwarzrand mts Namibia 130 C5
Schwarzwald mts Germany see Black Forest
Schwaz Austria 48 I8
Schwedeneck Germany 48 H1
Schwedt an der Oder Germany 49 L2
Schweinfurt Germany 48 H5
Schweiz country Europe see Switzerland
Schweizer-Reneke S. Africa 133 J4
Schwerin Germany 48 I2
Schweriner See l. Germany 48 I2
Schweriner Seenlandschaft park Germany 48 I2
Schwyz Switz. 51 O5
Sciacca Sicilia Italy 57 F11
Scicli Sicilia Italy 57 G12
Science Hill U.S.A. 176 A8
Scilla Italy 57 H10
Scilly, Île atoll Fr. Polynesia see Manuae
Scilly, Isles of U.K. 47 F14
Scio U.S.A. 176 D5
Scioto r. U.S.A. 176 C7
Scipio U.S.A. 183 L2
Scobey U.S.A. 180 F2
Scodra Albania see Shkodër
Scofield Reservoir U.S.A. 183 M2
Scone Australia 147 F3
Scordia Sicilia Italy 57 G11
Scoresby Land reg. Greenland 165 Q2
Scoresbysund Greenland see Ittoqqortoormiit
Scoresby Sund sea chan. Greenland see Kangertittivaq
Scornicești Romania 58 F4
Scorpion Bight b. Australia 151 D7
Scorzè Italy 56 E3
Scotia Sea S. Atlantic Ocean 217 K9
▶Scotland admin. div. U.K. 46 I6
historically known as Caledonia
europe [environments] 36–37
Scotland U.S.A. 177 I7
Scotstown Canada 169 G4
Scott, Cape Australia 148 A2
Scott, Cape Canada 166 D5
Scott, Mount hill U.S.A. 179 C5
Scott Base research station Antarctica 223 L1
Scottburgh S. Africa 133 O7
Scott City U.S.A. 178 B4
Scott Coast Antarctica 223 K1
Scott Glacier Antarctica 223 G2
Scott Glacier Antarctica 223 N1
Scott Inlet Canada 165 L2
Scott Island Antarctica 223 L2
Scott Islands Canada 166 D5
Scott Mountains Antarctica 223 D2
Scott Reef Australia 150 C2
Scottsbluff U.S.A. 178 B3
Scottsboro U.S.A. 174 C5
Scottsburg U.S.A. 174 C4
Scottsdale Australia 147 E5
Scotts Head Dominica 187 H4
Scottsville KY U.S.A. 174 C4
Scottsville VA U.S.A. 176 G8
Scottville U.S.A. 172 G7
Scourie U.K. 46 G5
Scranton U.S.A. 177 J4
Scugog, Lake Canada 168 E4
Scunthorpe U.K. 47 L10
Scuol Switz. 51 Q6
Scupi Macedonia see Skopje
Scutari Albania see Shkodër
Scutari, Lake Albania/Yugo. 58 A6
also known as Shkodrës, Liqeni i or Skardarsko Jezero
Seaboard U.S.A. 176 H9
Seabrook, Lake salt flat Australia 151 B6
Seaca Romania 58 F4
Seaford U.K. 47 M13
Seaford U.S.A. 177 J7
Seaforth Canada 173 L7
Seahorse Bank sea feature Phil. 74 A4
also known as Routh Bank
Seal r. Canada 167 M3
Seal, Cape S. Africa 132 H11
Sea Lake Australia 147 D3
Seal Bay Antarctica 223 X2
Seal Cove Canada 169 J3
Seal Island U.S.A. 177 Q2
Seal Lake Canada 169 I2
Sealy U.S.A. 179 C6
Seaman U.S.A. 176 B7
Seaman Range mts U.S.A. 183 I4
Searcy U.S.A. 174 B5
Searles Lake U.S.A. 183 G6
Searsport U.S.A. 177 Q1
Seascale U.K. 47 I9
Seaside CA U.S.A. 182 C5
Seaside OR U.S.A. 180 B3
Seaside Park U.S.A. 177 K6
Seaton Glacier Antarctica 223 D2
Seattle U.S.A. 180 B3
Sea View S. Africa 133 J11
Seaview Range mts Australia 149 E3
Seaville U.S.A. 177 K6
Seaward Kaikoura Range mts N.Z. 153 H10
Seba Indon. 75 B5
Sebaco Nicaragua 186 B4
Sebago Lake U.S.A. 177 O2
Sebakwe Recreational Park Zimbabwe 127 F9
Sebangan, Teluk b. Indon. 77 F3
Sebangka i. Indon. 76 D2
Sebastea Turkey see Sivas
Sebastian U.S.A. 175 D7
Sebastián Vizcaíno, Bahía b. Mex. 184 B2
Sebasticook r. U.S.A. 177 P1
Sebastopol Ukr. see Sevastopol'
Sebastopol U.S.A. 182 B3
Sebatik i. Indon. 77 G1
Sebauh Sarawak Malaysia 77 F2
Sebayan, Bukit mt. Indon. 77 E3
Sebba Burkina 125 F3
Sebderat Eritrea 121 H6
Sebdou Alg. 123 E2
Sébékoro Mali 124 C3
Seben Turkey 106 B2
Sebenico Croatia see Šibenik
Sebennytos Egypt see Samannûd
Sebeș Romania 58 E3
Sebeș r. Romania 58 E2
Sebewaing U.S.A. 173 J7
Sebezh Rus. Fed. 43 J5
Șebinkarahisar Turkey 107 D2
Șebiș Romania 58 D2
Sebisseb, Oued r. Alg. 55 O9
Sebla r. Rus. Fed. 43 S3
Seblat, Gunung mt. Indon. 76 C3
Sebrell U.S.A. 177 H9
Sebring U.S.A. 175 D7
Sebuku i. Indon. 77 G3
Sebuku r. Indon. 77 G1
Sebuku, Teluk b. Indon. 77 G2
Sečanj Vojvodina, Srbija Yugo. 58 B3
Secaș r. Romania 58 E2
Secas, Islas is Panama 186 C6
Secchia r. Italy 56 D3
Seccia Mountains Eth. 128 C3
Sechelt Canada 166 F5
Sechenovo Rus. Fed. 40 H5
Sechura Peru 198 A6
Sechura, Bahía de b. Peru 198 A6
Second Cataract rapids Sudan see 2nd Cataract
Second Mesa U.S.A. 183 N6
Second Three Mile Opening sea chan. Australia 149 D2
Secos, Ilhéus is Cape Verde 124 [inset]
also known as Rombo, Ilhéus do
Sečovce Slovakia 49 S7
Secretary Island N.Z. 153 A13
Secunda S. Africa 133 N4
Secunderabad India 94 C2
Sécure r. Bol. 200 D3
Seda Latvia 42 G4
Seda r. Lith. 42 C4
Seda Lith. 42 D5
Seda r. Port. 54 C6
Sedalia U.S.A. 178 D4
Sedam India 94 C2
Sedan France 51 K3
Sedan U.S.A. 178 C4
Seddon N.Z. 153 I9
Seddonville N.Z. 153 F9
Sedeh Fārs Iran 100 C4
Sedeh Khorāsan Iran 101 D3
Sedgefield U.S.A. 176 F9
Sedgewick Canada 167 I4
Sedgwick U.S.A. 177 Q1
Sédhiou Senegal 124 B3
Sedico Italy 56 E2
Sedlčany Czech Rep. 49 L6
Sedlets Poland see Siedlce
Sedom Israel 108 G6
Sedona U.S.A. 183 M7
Sédrata Alg. 123 G1
Šeduva Lith. 42 E6
Sędziszów Poland 49 R5
Seebad Heringsdorf Germany 49 L2
Seeberg pass Austria/Slovenia 49 L9
Seehausen (Altmark) Germany 48 I3
Seeheim Namibia 130 C5
Seeheim-Jugenheim Germany 48 F6
Seekoegat S. Africa 132 G10
Seekoei r. S. Africa 133 I7
Seekoevlei Nature Reserve S. Africa 133 N4
Seela Pass Canada 166 B1
Seeley U.S.A. 183 I9
Seelig, Mount Antarctica 222 R1
Seelow Germany 49 L3
Seenu Atoll Maldives see Addu Atoll
Sées France 50 G4
Seesen Germany 48 H4
Seevetal Germany 48 H2
Sefadu Sierra Leone 124 C4
also known as Koidu
Seferihisar Turkey 59 H10
Sefīd, Kūh-e mt. Iran 100 B3
Sefid, Kūh-e mts Iran 100 B4
Sefophe Botswana 131 E4
Ségala Mali 124 C3
Segalstad Norway 45 J3
Segama r. Sabah Malaysia 77 G1
Segamat Malaysia 76 C2
Segangane Morocco 55 H9
Șegarcea Romania 58 E4
Ségbana Benin 125 F4
Segen Wenz watercourse Eth. 128 C3
Segera Tanz. 129 C6
Segezha Rus. Fed. 40 E3
Seggeur, Oued watercourse Alg. 123 F2
Seghnān Afgh. 101 G2
Seghouane Alg. 55 N8
Segiz, Ozero salt l. Kazakh. 103 F3
Segontia U.K. see Caernarfon
Segontium U.K. see Caernarfon
Segonzac France 50 F7
Segorbe Spain 55 K5
Ségou Mali 124 D3
Ségou admin. reg. Mali 124 D3
Segovia Col. 198 C3
Segovia r. Hond./Nicaragua see Coco
Segovia Spain 54 G4
Segozerskoye, Ozero resr Rus. Fed. 40 E3
Segré France 50 F5
Segre r. Spain 55 L3
Séguédine Niger 125 I1
Séguéla Côte d'Ivoire 124 D5
Séguéla Mali 124 D3
formerly spelt Sagala
Séguénéga Burkina 125 E3
Seguin U.S.A. 179 C6
Segura r. Spain 55 K6
Segura, Sierra de mts Spain 55 I7
Sehithwa Botswana 130 D4
Sehlabathebe Lesotho 133 N6
Sehlabathebe National Park Lesotho 133 N6
Seho i. Indon. 75 C3
Sehore India 96 C5
Sehwan Pak. 101 F5
Seiche r. France 50 E5
Seignelay r. Canada 169 G3
Seikpyu Myanmar 78 A3
Seiland i. Norway 44 M1
Seiling U.S.A. 179 C4
Seille r. France 51 K6
Seille r. France 51 M3
Šeimena r. Lith. 42 D7
Sein, Île de i. France 50 B4
Seinäjoki Fin. 44 M3
Seine r. Canada 168 B3
Seine r. France 51 G3
Seine, Baie de b. France 50 F3
Seine, Sources de la tourist site France 51 K5
Seine, Val de valley France 51 J4
Seipinang Indon. 77 F3
Seistan reg. Iran see Sīstān
Seitsemisen kansallispuisto nat. park Fin. 45 M3
Seival Brazil 204 G3
Sejny Poland 49 U1
Sekadau Indon. 77 E2
Sekanak, Teluk b. Indon. 76 D3
Sekatak Bengara Indon. 77 G2
Sekayu Indon. 76 C3
Sekčov r. Slovakia 49 S7
Seke China see Sêrtar
Seke-Banza Dem. Rep. Congo 127 B6
Sekhukhune S. Africa 133 O1
Seki Japan 91 E7
Seki Turkey 108 A1
Seki r. Turkey 108 A1
Sekicau, Gunung vol. Indon. 76 D4
Sekoma Botswana 131 D5
Sekondi Ghana 125 E5
Sek'ot'a Eth. 128 C1
Sekseūil Kazakh. see Saksaul'skiy
Sekūheh Iran 101 E4
Șela Rus. Fed. see Shali
Šelagan r. Indon. 76 C3
Selah U.S.A. 180 B3
Selangor state Malaysia 76 C2
Selargius Sardegna Italy 57 B9
Selaru i. Indon. 73 H8
Selatan, Tanjung pt Indon. 77 F4
Selatpanjang Indon. 76 C2
Selawik U.S.A. 164 C3
Selbjørnsfjorden sea chan. Norway 46 Q4
Selbu Norway 44 J3
Selby U.K. 47 K10
Selby U.S.A. 178 B2
Selbyville U.S.A. 177 J7
Selçuk Turkey 59 I11
also known as Akıncılar
Sele r. Italy 57 G8
Selebi-Phikwe Botswana 131 E4
formerly spelt Selebi-Pikwe
Selebi-Pikwe Botswana see Selebi-Phikwe
Selečka Planina mts Macedonia 58 C7
Selemdzha r. Rus. Fed. 82 C1
Selemdzhinskiy Khrebet mts Rus. Fed. 82 D1
Selendi Turkey 59 J10
Selenduma Rus. Fed. 85 E1
▶Selenga r. Rus. Fed. 85 E1
Part of the Yenisey-Angara-Selenga, 3rd longest river in Asia.
asia [landscapes] 62–63
Selenge Dem. Rep. Congo 126 C5
Selenge Mongolia 84 D1
Selenge prov. Mongolia 85 E1
Selenge Mörön r. Mongolia 85 E1
Selenginsk Rus. Fed. 85 E1
Selenicë Albania 58 A8
Sélestat France 51 N4
Seletar Sing. 76 [inset]
Seletar, Pulau i. Sing. 76 [inset]
Seletar Reservoir Sing. 76 [inset]
Seletinskoye Kazakh. 103 H1
also known as Sileti
Selety r. Kazakh. see Sileti
Seletyteniz, Ozero salt l. Kazakh. see Siletiteniz, Ozero
Seleucia Turkey see Silifke
Seleucia Pieria Turkey see Samandağı
Seleznevo Rus. Fed. 43 J1
Selezni Rus. Fed. 43 M6
Selfoss Iceland 44 [inset] B3
Sel'gon Stantsiya Rus. Fed. 82 D2
Selib Rus. Fed. 40 I3
Sélibabi Mauritania 124 B3
Seligenstadt Germany 48 F5
Seliger, Ozero l. Rus. Fed. 43 O4
Seligman U.S.A. 183 L6
Selikhino Rus. Fed. 82 E2
Selîma Oasis Sudan 121 F4
Selimiye Turkey 59 I11
Sélingué, Lac de l. Mali 124 C4
Selinnkegni Mali 124 C3
Selinous r. Greece 59 D10
Selinsgrove U.S.A. 177 I5
Selinunte tourist site Sicilia Italy 57 E11
Selishche Rus. Fed. 43 O5
Selishchi Rus. Fed. 41 G5
Selitrennoye Rus. Fed. 102 A3
Seliu i. Indon. 77 D3
Selizharovo Rus. Fed. 43 O5
Selje Norway 44 I3
Seljord Norway 45 J4
Selkirk Canada 167 L5
Selkirk U.K. 46 J8
Selkirk Mountains Canada 167 G4
Selkopp Norway 44 N1
Sellia Marina Italy 57 I10
Sellore Island Myanmar see Saganthit Kyun
Selma AL U.S.A. 175 C5
Selma CA U.S.A. 182 E5
Selmer U.S.A. 174 B5
Selmęt Wielki, Jezioro l. Poland 49 T2
Selong Indon. 77 G5
Selongey France 51 L5
Selonsrivier S. Africa 133 N2
Sélouma Guinea 124 C4
Selous, Mount Canada 166 C2
Selous Game Reserve nature res. Tanz. 129 C7
Selseleh-ye Pīr Shūrān mts Iran 101 E4
Selsey Bill hd U.K. 47 L13
Sel'tso Bryanskaya Oblast' Rus. Fed. 43 P8
Sel'tso Bryanskaya Oblast' Rus. Fed. 43 P8
Selty Rus. Fed. 40 J4
Seluan i. Indon. 77 D1
Selukwe Zimbabwe see Shurugwi
Selvagens, Ilhas is Madeira 122 B3
Selvānā Iran 100 A2
Selvas reg. Brazil 199 D6
Selviria Brazil 206 B7
Selway r. U.S.A. 180 D3
Selwyn Lake Canada 167 J2
Selwyn Mountains Canada 166 D1
Selwyn Range hills Australia 149 C4
Seman r. Albania 58 A8
Semangka, Teluk b. Indon. 76 D4
Semarang Indon. 77 E4
Sematan Sarawak Malaysia 77 E2
Semau i. Indon. 75 B5
Semayang, Danau l. Indon. 77 G3
Sembakung r. Indon. 77 G2
Sembawang Sing. 76 [inset]
Sembawang, Sungai r. Sing. 76 [inset]
Sembé Congo 126 B4
Șemdinli Turkey 107 F3
also known as Navşar
Semendire Srbija Yugo. see Smederevo
Semendua Dem. Rep. Congo 126 C5
Semendyayevo Rus. Fed. 43 T4
Semenic, Vârful mt. Romania 58 D3
Semenivka Ukr. 41 E5
also spelt Semenovka
Semenov Rus. Fed. 40 H4
Semenovka Ukr. see Semenivka
Semenovskoye Rus. Fed. 43 U3
Semeru, Gunung vol. Indon. 77 F5
Semey Kazakh. see Semipalatinsk
Semhar prov. Eritrea 104 B5
Semibratovo Rus. Fed. 43 U4
Semidi Islands U.S.A. 164 D4
Semigorodnyaya Rus. Fed. 43 V2
Semikarakorsk Rus. Fed. 41 G7
Semiluki Rus. Fed. 41 F6
Semily Czech Rep. 49 M5
Seminoe Reservoir U.S.A. 180 F4
Seminole U.S.A. 179 B5
Seminole, Lake U.S.A. 175 C6
Semiozernoye Kazakh. 103 F1
Semipalatinsk Kazakh. 103 J2
also known as Semey
Semirara i. Phil. 74 B3
Semirara Islands Phil. 74 B4
Semīrom Iran 100 B4
Semitau Indon. 77 E2
Semiyarka Kazakh. 103 I2
Semizbuga Kazakh. 103 H2
also known as Semizbughy
Semizbughy Kazakh. see Semizbuga
Semkhoz Rus. Fed. 43 T5
Sem Kolodezey Ukr. see Lenine
Semlac Romania 58 B2
Semlevo Smolenskaya Oblast' Rus. Fed. 43 O6
Semlevo Smolenskaya Oblast' Rus. Fed. 43 O6
Semnān Iran 100 C3
Semnān prov. Iran 100 B3
Sêmnyi China 84 D4
Semois r. Belgium 51 K3
Semonkong Lesotho 133 M6
Sempach Switz. 51 O5
Semporna Sabah Malaysia 77 G1
Sempu i. Indon. 77 F5
Sem Tripa Brazil 199 H6
Semtsy Rus. Fed. 43 O9
Semyonovskoye Rus. Fed. see Bereznik
Semyonovskoye Rus. Fed. see Ostrovskoye
Sên, Stœng r. Cambodia 79 D5
Sena Bol. 200 D2
Senador Canedo Brazil 206 D3
Senador Pompeu Brazil 202 E3
Senafe Eritrea 104 B5
Senaki Georgia 107 E2
formerly known as Mikha Tskhakaia or Tskhakaia
Sena Madureira Brazil 200 C2
Senanayake Samudra l. Sri Lanka 94 D5
Senanga Zambia 127 D9
Sénas France 51 L9
Senatobia U.S.A. 174 B5
Sendai Kagoshima Japan 91 B9
Sendai Miyagi Japan 90 G5
Sendai-wan b. Japan 90 G5
Sendelingsfontein S. Africa 133 K3
Senden Germany 48 H7
Șendreni Romania 58 I3
Şene r. Ghana 125 E5
Senebui, Tanjung pt Indon. 76 C2
Seneca IL U.S.A. 172 E9
Seneca KS U.S.A. 178 C4
Seneca OR U.S.A. 180 C3
Seneca PA U.S.A. 176 F4
Seneca Lake U.S.A. 177 I3
Seneca Rocks U.S.A. 176 F7
Senecaville Lake U.S.A. 176 D6
▶Senegal country Africa 124 B3
world [countries] 10–11
africa [countries] 114–117
Sénégal r. Mauritania/Senegal 124 A2
Seneka, Mys hd Rus. Fed. 82 E1
Senekal S. Africa 133 L5
Seney National Wildlife Refuge nature res. U.S.A. 172 G4
Senftenberg Germany 49 L4
Senga Malawi 129 B8
Senga Hill Zambia 127 F7
Sengar r. India 96 C4
Sengata Indon. 77 G2
Sengerema Tanz. 128 B5
Sengés Brazil 206 D11
Sengeyskiy, Ostrov i. Rus. Fed. 40 I1
Sengiley Rus. Fed. 41 I5
Sengirli, Mys pt Kazakh. see Syngyrli, Mys
Sengirli, Mys pt Kazakh. 102 C4
also spelt Syngyrli, Mys
Sêngli Co l. China 89 D6
Senguerr r. Arg. 205 C7
Sengwa r. Zimbabwe 131 F3
Senhit prov. Eritrea 104 B5
Senhor do Bonfim Brazil 202 D4
Senica Slovakia 49 O7
Senigallia Italy 56 F5
Senj Croatia 56 G4
Senja i. Norway 44 L1
Senjehopen Norway 44 L1
Șenkaya Turkey 107 E2
also known as Örtülü
Senko Guinea 124 C4
Senkobo Zambia 127 E9
Sen'kove Ukr. 41 F6
Sen'kovo Rus. Fed. 43 L6
Șenköy Turkey 108 H1
Senku Jammu and Kashmir 96 C2
Senlac S. Africa 132 H2
Senlin Shan mt. China 82 C4
Senlis France 51 I3
Senmonorom Cambodia 79 D5
Sennar Sudan 121 G6
Sennar state Sudan 121 G6
Senneterre Canada 168 E3
Senno Belarus see Syanno
Senonches France 50 H4
Senorbì Sardegna Italy 57 B9
Senqu r. Lesotho 133 L7
Sens France 51 J4
Sensuntepeque El Salvador 185 H6
Senta Vojvodina, Srbija Yugo. 58 B3
also spelt Zenta
Sentinel Peak Canada 166 F4
Sentinel Range mts Antarctica 222 S1
Sentinum Italy see Sassoferrato
Sentosa i. Sing. 76 [inset]
formerly known as Blakang Mati, Pulau
Șenyurt Turkey 107 E3
also known as Derbesiye
Seo de Urgell Spain see Le Seu d'Urgell
Seonath r. India 97 D5
Seondha India 96 C4
Seoni India 96 C5
Seoni Chhapara India 96 C5
Seoni-Malwa India 96 C5
▶Seoul S. Korea 83 B5
Capital of South Korea. Also spelt Sŏul.
world [cities] 24–25
Séoune r. France 50 G8
Sepanjang i. Indon. 77 F4
Separation Point N.Z. 152 G8
Separation Well Australia 150 C4
Separ Shāhābād Iran 100 A3
Sepasu Indon. 77 G2
Sepatini r. Brazil 200 D1
Sepetiba, Baía de b. Brazil 207 I10
Sepik r. P.N.G. 73 J7
Sepinang Indon. 77 G2
Sepino Italy 56 G7
Sep'o N. Korea 83 B5
Sępólno Krajeńskie Poland 49 O2
Sepotuba r. Brazil 201 F3
Seppa India 97 G4
Șepreuș Romania 58 C2
Septèmes-les-Vallons France 51 L9
Sept-Îles Canada 169 H3
also known as Seven Islands
Sept-Îles-Port-Cartier, Réserve Faunique de nature res. Canada 169 H3
Sepupa Botswana 130 D3
Seputih r. Indon. 77 D4
Sequillo r. Spain 54 F3
Sequoia National Park U.S.A. 182 F5
Serae prov. Eritrea 104 B5
Serafimovich Rus. Fed. 41 G6
Sêraitang China see Baima
Seram i. Indon. 75 D3
English form Ceram
Seram Sea Indon. 75 D3
English form Ceram Sea
Serang Indon. 77 D4
Serangoon, Pulau i. Sing. 76 [inset]
also known as Coney Island
Serangoon, Sungai r. Sing. 76 [inset]
Serangoon Harbour b. Sing. 76 [inset]
Serapeum Egypt 108 D7
Serapong, Mount hill Sing. 76 [inset]
Serasan i. Indon. 77 E2
Serasan, Selat sea chan. Indon. 77 E2
Seraya i. Indon. 77 E2
Serbâl, Gebel mt. Egypt 108 E9
Serbia aut. rep. Yugo. see Srbija
Sêrbug Co l. China 89 E5
Sêrca China 97 G3
Serdica Bulg. see Sofia
Serdo Eth. 128 D2
Serdoba r. Rus. Fed. 41 H5
Serdobsk Rus. Fed. 41 H5
Serebryanka Rus. Fed. 40 J3
Serebryansk Kazakh. 88 C1
Serebryanyye Prudy Rus. Fed. 43 T7
Sered' Slovakia 49 O7
Sereda Moskovskaya Oblast' Rus. Fed. 43 Q6
Sereda Yaroslavskaya Oblast' Rus. Fed. 43 V4
Seredeyskiy Rus. Fed. 43 Q7
Seredka Rus. Fed. 43 J3
Serednikovo Rus. Fed. 43 U6
Seredniy Kuyal'nyk r. Ukr. 58 L2
Seredyna-Buda Rus. Fed. 43 P9
Seredyne Ukr. 49 T7
Șereflikoçhisar Turkey 106 C3
Serein r. France 51 J5
Seremban Malaysia 76 C2
Serengeti National Park Tanz. 128 B5
Serengeti Plain Tanz. 128 B5
Serenje Zambia 127 F8
Serere Uganda 128 B4
Serezha r. Rus. Fed. 40 G5
Serezha r. Rus. Fed. 43 L5
Sergach Rus. Fed. 40 H5
Sergeikha Rus. Fed. 43 V5
Sergelen Dornod Mongolia 85 G1
Sergelen Sühbaatar Mongolia 85 F2
Sergen Turkey 58 I7
Sergeyavka Rus. Fed. 90 C3
Sergeyevka Akmolinskaya Oblast' Kazakh. 103 G2
Sergeyevka Severnyy Kazakhstan Kazakh. 103 F1
Sergino Rus. Fed. 38 G3
Sergipe state Brazil 202 E4
Sergiyev Posad Rus. Fed. 43 T5
formerly known as Zagorsk
Sergiyevskiy Rus. Fed. see Fakel
Sergiyevskoye Rus. Fed. 43 S9
Sergo Ukr. see Stakhanov
Serhiyivka Ukr. 58 L2
Seria Brunei 77 F1
Serian Sarawak Malaysia 77 E2
Seribu, Kepulauan is Indon. 77 D4
Seribudolok Indon. 76 B2
Serifos Greece 59 F11
Serifos i. Greece 59 F11
Serifou, Steno sea chan. Greece 59 F11
Sérignan France 51 J9
Sérigny r. Canada 169 G2
Sérigny, Lac l. Canada 169 G2
Serik Turkey 106 B3
Serikbuya China 88 B4
Serikkembelo Indon. 75 C3
Sèrinama Madag. 131 [inset] J3
Seringa, Serra da hills Brazil 199 I6
Seringapatam Reef Australia 150 C2
Serinhisar Turkey 59 K11
Serio r. Italy 56 B3
Serio, Parco del park Italy 56 B3
Sêrkang China see Nyainrong
Sermata i. Indon. 75 D5
Sermata, Kepulauan is Indon. 75 D5
Sermersuaq glacier Greenland 165 M2
also known as Humboldt Gletscher
Sermersuaq glacier Greenland 165 N2
also known as Steenstrup Gletscher
Sērmūkši Latvia 42 G4
Sernovodsk Rus. Fed. 41 I5
Sernur Rus. Fed. 40 I4
Sernyy Zavod Turkm. see Kukurtli
Serón Spain 55 I7
Seronga Botswana 130 D3
Serouenout well Alg. 123 G4
Serov Rus. Fed. 38 G4
Serowe Botswana 131 E4
Serpa Port. 54 D7
Serpa Pinto Angola see Menongue
Serpent r. Canada 169 G3
Serpent, Vallée du watercourse Mali 124 C3
Serpentine r. Australia 151 A7
Serpentine Lakes salt flat Australia 146 A2
Serpent's Mouth sea chan. Trin. and Tob./Venez. 187 H5
Serpeysk Rus. Fed. 43 Q7
Serpis r. Spain 55 K6
Serpneve Ukr. 58 K2
Serpukhov Rus. Fed. 43 S7
Serra Brazil 203 D7
Serra Bonita Brazil 206 G2
Serra da Bocaina, Parque Nacional da nat. park Brazil 203 C7
Serra da Canastra, Parque Nacional da nat. park Brazil 206 G7
Serra da Capivara, Parque Nacional da nat. park Brazil 202 D4
Serra da Estrela, Parque Natural da nature res. Port. 54 D4
Serra da Mesa, Represa resr Brazil 202 B5
Serra das Araras Brazil 207 H2
Serra de Outes Spain 54 C2
Serradilla Spain 54 E5
Serra do Divisor, Parque Nacional da nat. park Brazil 200 B2
Serra do Navio Brazil 199 H4
Serra dos Aimorés Brazil 207 M4
Serra do Salitre Brazil 206 G6
Sérrai Greece see Serres
Serramanna Sardegna Italy 57 A9
Serrana Brazil 206 F8
Serrana Bank sea feature Caribbean Sea 186 C4
Serranía de la Neblina, Parque Nacional nat. park Venez. 199 E4
Serranilla Bank sea feature Caribbean Sea 186 D4
Serrano i. Chile 205 B8
Serranópolis Brazil 206 A5
Serraria, Ilha i. Brazil see Queimada, Ilha
Serra San Bruno Italy 57 I10
Serras de Aire e Candeeiros, Parque Natural das nature res. Port. 54 C5
Serra Talhada Brazil 202 E3
Serravalle Scrivia Italy 56 A4
Serre r. France 51 J3
Serres Greece 58 E7
also known as Sérrai
Serrezuela Arg. 204 D3
Serrinha Brazil 202 E4
Serrita Brazil 202 E3
Sêrro Brazil 203 D6
Serrota mt. Spain 54 F4
Sers Tunisia 57 A12
Sersou, Plateau du Alg. 55 M9
Sertã Port. 54 C5
Sertânia Brazil 202 E4
Sertanópolis Brazil 206 B10
Sertão de Camapuã reg. Brazil 206 A6
Sertãozinho Brazil 206 F8
Sêrtar China 86 B1
also known as Seke
Sertavul Geçidi pass Turkey 108 E1
Sertolovo Rus. Fed. 43 L1
Serua vol. Indon. 75 D4
Serui Indon. 73 I7
Serule Botswana 131 E4
Serutu i. Indon. 77 E3
Seruyan r. Indon. 77 F3
Servach r. Belarus 42 I7
Servia Greece 59 D8
Servol r. Spain 55 L4
also spelt Cerbol
Serwaru Indon. 75 C5
Sêrxu China 86 A1
also known as Nixia
Sesayap Indon. 77 G2
Sesayap r. Indon. 77 G2
Sese Dem. Rep. Congo 126 E4
Sesekinika Canada 173 M2
Sesel country Indian Ocean see Seychelles
Sesepe Indon. 75 C3
Sesfontein Namibia 130 B3
Seshachalam Hills India 94 C3
Seshcha Rus. Fed. 43 O8
Sesheke Zambia 127 E9
Sesia r. Italy 56 A3
Seskar Furö i. Sweden 44 M2
Sesklio i. Greece 59 I12
Sesostris Bank sea feature India 94 A3
S'Espalmador i. Spain 55 M6
also known as Espalmador, Isla
Sessa Angola 127 D8
Ses Salines, Cap de c. Spain 55 O5
also spelt Salinas, Cabo de
Sestra r. Rus. Fed. 43 S5
Sestri Levante Italy 56 B4
Sestroretsk Rus. Fed. 43 K1
Sestrunj i. Croatia 56 G4
Sestu Sardegna Italy 57 B9
Šešupė r. Lith./Rus. Fed. 42 D6
Sesvete Croatia 56 I3
Set r. Spain 55 L3
Set, Phou mt. Laos 79 D5
Sète France 51 J9
Sete Barras Brazil 206 F11
Šetekšna r. Lith. 42 G6
Sete Lagoas Brazil 203 C6
Setermoen Norway 44 L1
Setesdal valley Norway 45 I4
Seti r. Nepal 97 D3
Seti r. Nepal 97 E4
Setia Italy see Sezze
Sétif Alg. 123 G1
also spelt Stif
Setit r. Africa 121 H6
Seto Japan 91 E7
Seto-naikai sea Japan 91 C8
English form Inland Sea
Seto-naikai National Park Japan 91 C7
Setsan Myanmar 78 A4
Settat Morocco 122 D2
Setté Cama Gabon 126 A5
Settepani, Monte mt. Italy 56 A4
Settimo Torinese Italy 51 N7
Settle U.K. 47 J9
Settlement Creek r. Australia 148 C3
Settlers S. Africa 133 M1
Setúbal Port. 54 C6
Setúbal r. Brazil 207 K3
Setúbal admin. dist. Port. 54 C6
Setúbal, Baía de b. Port. 54 B6
Setubinha Brazil 207 K4
Seul, Lac l. Canada 168 A3
Seurre France 51 L5
Sev r. Rus. Fed. 43 P9

index

S

Sevan Armenia **107** F2
Sevan, Lake Armenia **107** F2
also known as Sevan, Ozero or Sevana Lich
Sevan, Ozero *l.* Armenia *see* Sevan, Lake
Sevana Lich *l.* Armenia *see* Sevan, Lake
Sevaruyo Bol. **200** D3
Sevastopol' Ukr. **41** E7
English form Sebastopol
Seven Islands Canada *see* Sept-Îles
Sevenoaks S. Africa **133** O6
Sevenoaks U.K. **47** M12
Seventeen Seventy Australia **149** F5
Seventy Mile House Canada *see*
70 Mile House
Sévérac-le-Château France **51** J8
Severino Ribeiro Brazil **204** G3
Severka r. Rus. Fed. **43** T6
Severn r. Australia **147** F2
Severn r. Canada **168** C2
Severn est. N.Z. **153** H10
Severn S. Africa **132** G4
Severn r. U.K. **47** J12
Severn U.S.A. **177** H9
Severnaya Dvina r. Rus. Fed. **40** G2
English form Northern Dvina
Severnaya Mylva r. Rus. Fed. **40** K3
Severnaya Osetiya-Alaniya, Respublika
aut. rep. Rus. Fed. *see*
North Ossetia; *formerly known
as Severo-Osetinskaya A.S.S.R.*
Severnaya Zemlya *is* Rus. Fed. **39** K1
English form North Land
Severnoye Rus. Fed. **40** J5
formerly known as Sol-Karmala
Severnyy Moskovskaya Oblast' Rus. Fed.
43 S5
Severnyy Nenetskiy Avtonomnyy Okrug
Rus. Fed. **40** I1
Severnyy Respublika Komi Rus. Fed. **40** J2
Severnyy Anyuyskiy Khrebet *mts* Rus. Fed.
39 R3
Severnyy Berezovyy, Ostrov *i.* Rus. Fed.
43 J1
Severnyy Chink Ustyurta esc. Kazakh.
102 D3
Severnyy Kazakhstan *admin. div.* Kazakh.
103 G1
*English form North-Kazakhstan Oblast; also
known as Soltüstik Qazaqstan Oblysy; long
form Severo-Kazakhstanskaya Oblast'*
Severnyy Kommunar Rus. Fed. **40** J4
Severnyy Suchan Rus. Fed. *see*
Uglekamensk
Severnyy Ural *mts* Rus. Fed. **40** K3
Severo-Baykal'skoye Nagor'ye *mts*
Rus. Fed. **81** H1
Severobaykal'sk Rus. Fed. **81** H1
Severodonetsk Ukr. *see* Syeverodonets'k
Severodvinsk Rus. Fed. **40** G2
formerly known as Molotovsk
Severo-Kazakhstanskaya Oblast'
admin. div. Kazakh. *see* Severnyy Kazakhstan
Severo-Kuril'sk Rus. Fed. **39** Q4
Severomorsk Rus. Fed. **44** P1
formerly known as Vayenga
Severoonezhsk Rus. Fed. **40** G3
Severo-Osetinskaya A.S.S.R. *aut. rep.*
Rus. Fed. *see*
Severnaya Osetiya-Alaniya, Respublika
Severo-Sibirskaya Nizmennost' *lowland*
Rus. Fed. *see* North Siberian Lowland
Severoural'sk Rus. Fed. **40** K3
Severo-Yeniseyskiy Rus. Fed. **39** J3
Severo-Zadonsk Rus. Fed. **43** T7
Severskaya Rus. Fed. **107** D1
Severskiy Donets r. Rus. Fed./Ukr. **41** G7
*English form Northern Donets; also spelt
Sivers'kyy Donets'*
Seveso Italy **56** B3
Sevettijärvi Fin. **44** O1
also spelt Čevetjävri
Sevier U.S.A. **183** L3
Sevier r. U.S.A. **183** L2
Sevier Bridge Reservoir U.S.A. **183** M2
Sevier Desert U.S.A. **183** L2
Sevier Lake U.S.A. **183** K3
Sevierville U.S.A. **174** C4
Sevilla Col. **198** C3
Sevilla Spain *see* Seville
Seville Spain **54** F7
*also spelt Sevilla; historically known as
Hispalis*
Sevlievo Bulg. **58** G5
Sevnica Slovenia **56** H2
Sevojno Srbija Yugo. **58** A5
Sèvre Nantaise r. France **50** E5
Sevsk Rus. Fed. **43** P9
Sewani r. India **94** B2
Sewani India **96** B3
Seward AK U.S.A. **164** E3
Seward IL U.S.A. **172** D8
Seward NE U.S.A. **178** C3
Seward PA U.S.A. **176** F5
Seward Mountains Antarctica **222** T2
Seward Peninsula U.S.A. **164** C3
Sewell Chile **204** C4
Sewell Inlet Canada **166** C4
Sexi Spain *see* Almuñécar
Sexsmith Canada **166** G4
Sextín Mex. **184** D3
Sextín r. Mex. **184** D3
Seyah Band Koh *mts* Afgh. **101** E3
Seyakha Rus. Fed. **38** H2
Seybaplaya Mex. **185** H5
▶Seychelles *country* Indian Ocean **218** K6
also spelt Sesel
africa [countries] ▶▶ 114–117
Seydi Turkm. **103** E5
formerly known as Neftezavodsk
Seydişehir Turkey **106** B3
Seyðisfjörður Iceland **44** [inset] D2
Seyfe Gölü *salt flat* Turkey **106** C3
Seyhan Turkey *see* Adana

Seyhan r. Turkey **106** C3
Seyitgazi Turkey **106** B3
Seyitömer Turkey **59** K9
Seym r. Rus. Fed. **41** E6
Seymchan Rus. Fed. **39** P3
Seymour Australia **147** E4
Seymour S. Africa **133** K9
Seymour IN U.S.A. **174** C4
Seymour TX U.S.A. **179** C5
Seymour Inlet Canada **166** E5
Seymour Range *mts* Australia **148** B5
Seynod France **51** M7
Seypan *i.* N. Mariana Is *see* Saipan
Seytan r. Turkey **58** I7
Seyyedābād Afgh. **101** G3
Sežana Slovenia **56** F3
Sézanne France **51** J4
Sezela S. Africa **133** O7
Sezha r. Rus. Fed. **43** P6
Sezze Italy **56** F7
historically known as Setia
Sfakia Greece **59** F13
Sfântu Gheorghe Romania **58** G3
formerly spelt Sfîntu Gheorghe
Sfântu Gheorghe Romania **58** K4
Sfântu Gheorghe, Braţul *watercourse*
Romania **58** K3
Sfântu Gheorghe-Palade-Perişor
nature res. Romania **58** K4
Sfax Tunisia **123** H2
also spelt Aş Şafāqis
Sfendami Greece **59** D8
Sfîntu Gheorghe Romania *see*
Sfântu Gheorghe
Sfizef Alg. **55** L8
Sgiersch Poland *see* Zgierz
's-Gravenhage Neth. *see* The Hague
Sgurr Alasdair *hill* U.K. **46** F6
Sgurr Mor *mt.* U.K. **46** G5
Sgurr na Ciche *mt.* U.K. **46** G6
Sha r. China **85** G4
Shaanxi *prov.* China **87** D1
English form Shensi
Shaba *prov.* Dem. Rep. Congo *see* Katanga
Shāba Egypt **108** B6
Shabani Zimbabwe *see* Zvishavane
Shabbaz Uzbek. *see* Beruni
Shabeellaha Dhexe *admin. reg.* Somalia
128 E4
Shabeellaha Hoose *admin. reg.* Somalia
128 D5
Shabestar Iran **100** A2
Shabla Bulg. **58** J5
Shabla, Nos *pt* Bulg. **58** J5
Shablykino Rus. Fed. **43** Q9
Shabogamo Lake Canada **169** H2
Shabunda Dem. Rep. Congo **126** E5
Shabwah Yemen **105** D5
Shabwah *governorate* Yemen **105** D5
Shacha r. Rus. Fed. **41** H8
Shache China **88** B4
formerly known as Yarkand or Yarkant
Shacheng China *see* Huailai
Shackleton Coast Antarctica **223** L1
Shackleton Glacier Antarctica **223** M1
Shackleton Ice Shelf Antarctica **223** G2
Shackleton Range *mts* Antarctica **223** V1
Shadād Saudi Arabia **104** C4
Shadadkot Pak. **101** F5
Shadaogou China **87** D2
Shade U.S.A. **176** C6
Shādegān Iran **100** A4
Shādkam *watercourse* Iran **100** C4
Shadrinsk Rus. Fed. **38** G4
Shadwān Island Egypt *see* Shākir, Gezîret
Shadwell U.S.A. **176** G7
Shady Grove U.S.A. **180** B4
Shady Spring U.S.A. **176** D8
Sha'fāt al Bashir *hill* Syria **109** K2
Shafer, Lake U.S.A. **172** G10
Shafi'abad Iran **100** D3
Shafranovo Rus. Fed. **40** J5
Shafirkan Uzbek. **103** F4
also known as Shofirkon; formerly spelt Shafirkan
Shafranovo Rus. Fed. **40** J5
Shafter U.S.A. **182** E6
Shaftesbury U.K. **47** J12
Shag r. N.Z. **153** E13
Shagamu r. Canada **168** C2
Shagamu Nigeria *see* Sagamu
Shagan *watercourse* Kazakh. **102** D3
Shagan *watercourse* Kazakh. **103** I2
Shagedu China **85** F4
also known as Jungar Qi
Shaghab *oasis* Saudi Arabia **104** B2
Shaghan Kazakh. *see* Chagan
Shaghray Üstirti *plat.* Kazakh. *see*
Shagyray, Plato
Shagonar Respublika Tyva Rus. Fed. **84** B1
Shagonar Respublika Tyva Rus. Fed. **84** B1
Shag Point N.Z. **153** E13
Shag Rocks *is* S. Georgia **217** L9
Shagyray, Plato *plat.* Kazakh. **102** D3
*also known as Shaghray Üstirti; formerly
known as Chagrayskoye Plato*
Shagyrlyk Uzbek. **102** D3
Shahabad Andhra Pradesh India **94** C2
Shahabad *Haryana* India **96** C3
Shahabad *Karnataka* India **94** C2
Shahabad *Rajasthan* India **96** C4
Shāhābād *Uttar Pradesh* India **96** D4
Shāhābād *i. see* Eslāmābād-e Gharb
Shahada India **96** B5
Shah Alam Malaysia **76** C2
Shahana Pak. **101** E5
Shahapur *Karnataka* India **94** B3
Shahapur *Maharashtra* India **94** B2
Shahbâ' Syria **109** H5
Shahbazpur *sea chan.* Bangl. **97** F5
Shahdād Iran **100** D4
Shahdadpur Pak. **101** G5
Shahdol India **97** D5
Shahe *Chongqing* China **87** D2
Shahe *Shandong* China **85** H4
Shahe *Shanxi* China **85** G4
Shahejie China *see* Jiujiang
Shahepu China *see* Linze
Shahezhen China *see* Linze
Shahezhen China *see* Jiujiang
Shah Fuladi *mt.* Afgh. **101** F3
Shaganj India **97** D4
Shahgarh *Madhya Pradesh* India **96** C4
Shahgarh *Rajasthan* India **96** A4
Shahhât Libya **120** D1
Shāhîn Dezh Iran **100** A2
Shah Ismail Afgh. **101** F4
Shahjahanpur *Uttar Pradesh* India **96** C4
Shahjui Afgh. **101** F3
Shāh Kūh *mt.* Iran **101** D3
Shahpur *Karnataka* India **94** C2
Shahpur *Madhya Pradesh* India **96** C5
Shahpur *Madhya Pradesh* India **96** C5
Shahpur *Madhya Pradesh* India **96** C5
Shāhpur *Iran see* Salmās
Shahpur *Balochistan* Pak. **101** G4
Shahpur *Punjab* Pak. **101** H3
Shahpur *Sindh* Pak. **101** G4
Shahpur *Madhya Pradesh* India **96** C5
Shahpur *Madhya Pradesh* India **96** D5
Shahpura *Madhya Pradesh* India **96** C5
Shahpura *Rajasthan* India **96** B4
Shahr *oasis* Saudi Arabia **105** E4
Shahrak Afgh. **101** F3
Shāhrakht Iran **101** E3
Shahran *reg.* Saudi Arabia **104** C4
Shahrezā Iran *see* Qomishēh

Shahrisabz Uzbek. *see* Shakhrisabz
Shahriston Tajik. **101** G2
also spelt Shakhristan
Shahr Rey Iran **100** B3
Shahr Sultan Pak. **101** G4
Shahtuz Tajik. **101** G2
also spelt Shaartuz
Shāhrūd Iran *see* Emāmrūd
Shāhrūd, Rūdkhāneh-ye r. Iran **100** B2
Shahrud Bustam *reg.* Iran **100** C3
Shāh Savārān, Kūh-e *mts* Iran **100** D4
Shāh Taqī Iran *see* Emām Taqī
Sha'ibān al Jiraniyat *watercourse*
Saudi Arabia **109** J6
Shaidara, Step' *plain* Kazakh. **103** F4
Shaikh Husain *mt.* Pak. **101** F4
Shā'ir, Jabal *mts* Syria **109** I3
Sha'ira, Gebel *mt.* Egypt **108** F8
Shaj'ah, Jabal *hill* Saudi Arabia **105** E2
Shajapur India **96** C5
Shakar Bolāghī Iran **100** A2
Shakaskraal S. Africa **133** P6
Shakaville S. Africa **133** P6
Shakawe Botswana **130** D3
Shakespeare Island Canada **168** B3
Shakh Tajik. **101** G2
Shakhbuz Azer. *see* Şahbuz
Shakhovskaya Rus. Fed. **43** Q5
Shakhrikhan Uzbek. **103** H4
formerly known as Moskovskiy or Stalino
Shakhrisabz Uzbek. **103** F5
also spelt Shahrisabz
Shakhristan Tajik. *see* Shahriston
Shakhtars'k Ukr. **41** F6
*also spelt Shakhtërsk or Shakhtyorsk;
formerly known as Katyk*
Shakhtinsk Kazakh. **103** H2
Shakhtty Rus. Fed. **41** G7
Shakhtërsk Ukr. *see* Shakhtars'k
Shakhun'ya Rus. Fed. **40** H4
Shaki Nigeria *see* Saki
Shākir, Gezîret *i.* Egypt **121** G3
English form Shadwān Island
Shakopee U.S.A. **178** D2
Shakotan-hantō *pen.* Japan **90** G3
Shakotan-misaki *c.* Japan **90** G3
Shakou China **87** E3
Sha Hâyk' *l.* Eth. **128** C3
Shalakusha Rus. Fed. **40** G3
Shalamzar Iran **100** B3
Shalday Kazakh. **103** I2
Shalginskiy Kazakh. **103** G3
*also known as Shalqīya; formerly known as
Shalgiya*
Shalgiya Kazakh. *see* Shalginskiy
Shali Rus. Fed. **41** H8
*also known as Şela; formerly known as
Mezhdurechnye*
Shalim Oman **105** F4
Shaliuhe China *see* Gangca
Shalkar, Ozero *salt l.* Kazakh. **102** B2
*also known as Shalqar Köli; formerly spelt
Chalkar, Ozero*
Shalkar Karashatau *salt l.* Kazakh. **103** E2
Shalkar-Yega-Kara, Ozero *l.* Rus. Fed.
103 E2
Shālma Egypt **108** B6
Shalqar Kazakh. *see* Chelkar
Shalqar Köli *salt l.* Kazakh. *see*
Shalkar, Ozero
Shalqīya Kazakh. *see* Shalginskiy
Shaluli Shan *mts* China **86** A2
Shaluni *mt.* India **97** H3
Shama r. Tanz. **129** D6
Shamāl Sînâ' *governorate* Egypt **108** D7
*English form North Sinai; also known as
Sinai ash Shamālīya*
Shamalzā'ī Afgh. **101** F4
Shamary Rus. Fed. **40** K4
Shāmat al Akbād *des.* Saudi Arabia **104** C1
Shambar Iran **100** B3
Shambe Sudan **128** A3
Shambu Eth. **128** C2
Shambuanda Dem. Rep. Congo **127** D6
Sham Chun r. China **87** [inset]
Shamgarh India **96** B4
Shamgong Bhutan *see* Zhemgang
Shamis U.A.E. **105** F3
Shamkhal Rus. Fed. **102** A4
Shamkhor Azer. *see* Şämkir
Shāmkūh *mt.* Iran **100** D2
Shamokha Rus. Fed. **43** O1
Shamrock U.S.A. **179** B5
Shamva Zimbabwe **131** F3
Shan *state* Myanmar **78** B3
Shancheng China *see* Nanjing
Shancheng China *see* Shanxian
Shand Afgh. **101** E4
Shandan China **84** D4
Shandian r. China **85** H3
Shandiz Iran **101** D2
Shandong *prov.* China **85** H4
English form Shantung
Shandong Bandao *pen.* China **85** I4
Shandrūkh Iraq **107** F4
Shandur Pass Pak. **101** H2
Shanganj *i.* Zimbabwe **131** E3
Shangcai China *see* Caidu
Shangcheng China **87** E2
Shang Chu r. China **89** E6
Shangchuan Dao *i.* China **87** E4
Shangchuankou China *see* Minhe
Shangdu China **85** G3
Shangganling China **82** C3
Shanggao China **87** E2
Shanghai China **87** G2
4th most populous city in Asia and 9th in
the world.
world [cities] ▶▶ 24–25
Shanghai *municipality* China **87** G2
Shanghang China **87** F3
also known as Linjiang
Shanghe China **85** H4
Shanghekou China **83** B4
Shangjie China *see* Xichuan
Shangjie China *see* Yangbi
Shangjin China **87** D1
Shangkuli China **85** I1
Shangnan China **87** D1
Shangombo Zambia **127** D9
Shangpai China *see* Feixi
Shangpaihe China *see* Feixi
Shangqiu *Henan* China **85** H5
Shangqiu *Henan* China **87** E1
Shangrao China **87** F2
Shangshui China **87** E1
Shangsi China **87** D4
Shangtang China *see* Yongjia
Shangyou China **87** E3
also known as Dongshan
Shangyou Shuiku *salt flat* China **88** C3
Shangyu China **87** G2
also known as Baiguan
Shangzhi China **82** B3
Shangzhou China **87** D1
Shani Nigeria **125** I4

Shankou China **84** B3
Shannon N.Z. **152** J8
Shannon *airport* Rep. of Ireland **47** D11
Shannon est. Rep. of Ireland **47** D11
Shannon r. Rep. of Ireland **47** D11
Shannon S. Africa **133** K6
Shannon U.S.A. **172** D8
Shannon, Mouth of the Rep. of Ireland
47 C11
Shannon National Park Australia **151** B7
Shannon Ø *i.* Greenland **165** R2
Shanshan China **88** E3
also known as Piqan
Shanshanzhan China **88** E3
Shansi *prov.* China *see* Shanxi
Shantarskiye Ostrova *is* Rus. Fed. **39** N4
Shan Tei Tong *hill* Hong Kong China *see*
Stenhouse, Mount
Shan Teng *hill* Hong Kong China *see*
Victoria Peak
Shantipur India **97** F5
Shantou China **87** F4
formerly known as Swatow
Shantung *prov.* China *see* Shandong
Shanwei China **87** E4
Shanxi *prov.* China **85** F4
English form Shansi
Shanxian China **85** H5
also known as Shancheng
Shanya r. Rus. Fed. **43** Q7
Shanyang China **87** D1
Shanyin China **85** G4
Shaodong China **87** D3
Shaoguan China **87** E3
Shaoshan China **87** E3
Shaowu China **87** F3
Shaoxing China **87** G2
Shaoyang China **87** D3
Shapa China **87** D4
Shapembe Dem. Rep. Congo **126** D6
Shaping China *see* Ebian
Shapinsay *i.* U.K. **46** J4
Shapki r. Rus. Fed. **43** M2
Shapkina r. Rus. Fed. **43** P1
Shapyalyevichy Belarus **43** K7
Shaqlāwa Iraq **109** P1
Shaqq el Giefer, Wadi *watercourse* Sudan
121 E6
Shaqq el Khadir Sudan **121** E6
Shaqra' Saudi Arabia **105** D2
Shar Kazakh. **103** J2
Shār, Jabal *mt.* Saudi Arabia **104** A2
Sharaf Iraq **107** F4
Sharafa Sudan **121** E6
Sharald ay r. Rus. Fed. **85** E1
Sharanga Rus. Fed. **40** H4
Sharan Jogizai Pak. **101** G4
Sharashova Belarus **42** F9
Sharātib, Rās *pt* Egypt **108** E9
Sharawrā, Jabal *hills* Saudi Arabia **109** H9
Sharawrā', Qa' *salt pan* Saudi Arabia
109 H9
Sharbaqty Kazakh. *see* Shcherbakty
Sharbithāt, Ra's *c.* Oman **105** F4
Sharbulag Mongolia **84** B1
Sharchino Rus. Fed. **103** J1
Shardara Kazakh. **103** G4
formerly spelt Chardara
Shardara Bögeni *resr* Kazakh./Uzbek. *see*
Chardarinskoye Vodokhranilishche
Shardi Pak. **101** H3
Sharga *Govĭ-Altay* Mongolia **84** A2
Sharga *Hövsgöl* Mongolia **84** C1
formerly known as Tsagaan-Uul
Shargun' Uzbek. **103** F5
also spelt Shorghun
Sharhorod Ukr. **41** D6
also spelt Shargorod
Sharhulsan Mongolia **84** E2
Shari r. Cameroon/Chad *see* Chari
Shari Japan **90** I3
Shāri, Buḩayrat *imp. l.* Iraq **107** F4
Shari-dake *vol.* Japan **90** I3
Sharira Pass Egypt **108** F9
Sharjah U.A.E. **105** F2
also known as Ash Shāriqah
Sharka-leb La *pass* China **89** E6
Sharkawshchyna Belarus **42** I6
Shark Bay Australia **151** A5
Shark Fin Bay Phil. **74** A4
Sharkh *Oman* **105** F3
Shark Reef Australia **149** E2
Sharlawuk Turkm. *see* Sharlouk
Sharlouk Turkm. **102** C5
Sharlyk Rus. Fed. **102** C1
Sharm ash Shaykh Saudi Arabia **104** A1
Sharm el Sheikh Egypt **121** G3
Sharon PA U.S.A. **176** E4
Sharon WI U.S.A. **172** E8
Sharon Springs U.S.A. **178** B4
Sharonville U.S.A. **176** A6
Sharpe, Lake *salt flat* Australia **151** C7
Sharpe Lake Canada **167** M4
Sharp Peak *hill* Hong Kong China **87** [inset]
also known as Nam She Tsim
Sharpsburg U.S.A. **176** D6
Sharqat Iraq *see* Ash Sharqāt
Sharqi, Jabal ash *mts* Lebanon/Syria **108** G4
English form Anti Lebanon
Sharqiya *governorate* Egypt **108** C7
Sharqpur Pak. **101** H4
Shar Us Gol r. Mongolia **84** C2
Shary *well* Saudi Arabia **104** C2
Shar'ya Turkm. *see* Şähur
Shar'ya r. Rus. Fed. **40** H4
Shar'ya r. Rus. Fed. **43** N2
Sharyn Kazakh. *see* Charyn
Shashe r. Botswana/Zimbabwe **131** F4
Shashemenë Eth. **128** C3
Shashi China *see* Jingzhou
Shashi *prov.* China *see* Shanxi
Shashubay Kazakh. **103** H3
Shasta, Mount *vol.* U.S.A. **180** B4
Shasta Dam U.S.A. **182** B1
Shasta Lake U.S.A. **182** B1
Shatalovo Rus. Fed. **43** N7
Sha Tau Kok Hoi *inlet* Hong Kong China *see*
Starling Inlet
Shāti', Wādī ash *watercourse* Libya **120** B2
Shatilki Belarus *see* Svyetlahorsk
Sha Tin Hong Kong China **87** [inset]
Shatki Rus. Fed. **40** H5
Shaṭnat as Salmás, Wādī *watercourse*
Syria **109** J2
Sha Tong Hau Shan *i.* Hong Kong China *see*
Bluff Island
Shatoy Rus. Fed. **41** H8
Shatsk Rus. Fed. **41** G5
formerly known as Sovetskoye
Shatsk Ukr. **41** J6
Shatt al 'Arab r. Iran/Iraq **107** G5
Shaṭṭ al Gharrāf r. Iraq **107** F5
Shattuck U.S.A. **179** C4
Shatura Rus. Fed. **43** U5
Shaubak Jordan *see* Ash Shawbak
Shāūildir Kazakh. *see* Shaul'der
Shaul'der Kazakh. **103** G4
also spelt Shāūildir

Shaunavon Canada **167** I5
Shaverki Rus. Fed. **43** U5
Shaver Lake U.S.A. **182** E4
Shavers Fork r. U.S.A. **176** F7
Shaw r. Australia **150** B4
also known as Sandaohezi
Shawano U.S.A. **172** E6
Shawano Lake U.S.A. **172** E6
Shawāq *well* Saudi Arabia **104** B2
Shawnee U.S.A. **179** C5
Shawsville U.S.A. **176** E8
Sha Xi r. China **87** F3
Shaxian China **87** F3
also known as Fenggang
Shayang China **87** E2
formerly spelt Chayan
Shaybārā *i.* Saudi Arabia **104** B2
Shayboveyem r. Rus. Fed. **39** Q3
Shay Gap Australia **150** C4
Shaykh, Shā'ib ash *watercourse* Iraq
109 N5
Shaykh Jūwī Iraq **107** F4
Shaykh Sa'd Iraq **107** F4
Shaykovka r. Rus. Fed. **43** P7
Shāzand Iran **100** B3
Shazaoyuan China **84** B4
English form Shanzheng
Shazāz, Jabal *mt.* Saudi Arabia **104** C2
Shāzi Ḩāmir, Wādī *watercourse*
Saudi Arabia **109** M6
Shazud Tajik. **101** H2
Shchara r. Belarus **42** F8
Shchekino Rus. Fed. **43** S7
Shchelkanovo Rus. Fed. **43** Q7
Shchelkovo Rus. Fed. **43** T6
Shchel'yayur Rus. Fed. **40** J2
Shcherbakov Rus. Fed. *see* Rybinsk
Shcherbakty Kazakh. **103** I1
also spelt Sharbaqty
Shchetinskoye Rus. Fed. **43** T3
Shchigry Rus. Fed. **41** E6
Shcholkine Ukr. **41** E7
Shchomyslitsa Belarus **42** I8
Shchors Ukr. **41** D6
formerly known as Snovsk
Shchuchin Belarus *see* Shchuchyn
Shchuchinsk Kazakh. **103** G1
Shchuchye Rus. Fed. **42** I8
also spelt Shchuchin
Shchuger r. Rus. Fed. **40** K2
Shchytkavichy Belarus **42** J8
Shea Guyana **199** G4
Shebalino Rus. Fed. **88** D1
Shebandowan Lakes Canada **172** C2
Shebekino Rus. Fed. **41** F6
Sheberghān Afgh. **101** F2
Sheboygan U.S.A. **172** F7
Shebshi Mountains Nigeria **125** H4
Shebunino Rus. Fed. **82** F3
Shecheng China *see* Shexian
Shediac Canada **169** H4
Shedin Peak Canada **166** E4
Shedok Rus. Fed. **107** E1
Sheelin, Lough *l.* Rep. of Ireland **47** E10
Sheepmoor S. Africa **133** O3
Sheep Peak U.S.A. **183** I5
Sheerness U.K. **47** M12
Sheet Harbour Canada **169** I4
Shefar'am Israel **108** G5
Sheffield N.Z. **153** G11
Sheffield U.K. **47** K10
Sheffield AL U.S.A. **174** C5
Sheffield IL U.S.A. **172** D9
Sheffield PA U.S.A. **176** F4
Sheffield TX U.S.A. **179** B6
Sheffield Lake Canada **169** J3
Shegaon India **94** C1
Sheguiandah Canada **173** L5
Shehong China **86** C2
*also known as Taihe; formerly known as
Taihezhen*
Sheikh, Jebel esh *mt.* Lebanon/Syria *see*
Hermon, Mount
Sheikh, Wâdi es *watercourse* Egypt **108** E9
Sheikh Othman Yemen *see*
Ash Shaykh 'Uthman
Shekak r. Canada **168** C3
Shekhawati *reg.* India **96** B4
Shekhem West Bank *see* Näblus
Shekhupura Pak. **101** H4
Sheki Azer. *see* Şäki
Shekka Ch'ün-Tao *is* Hong Kong China *see*
Soko Islands
Shek Kwu Chau *i.* Hong Kong China **87** [inset]
Shekou China **87** [inset]
Shek Pik Reservoir *resr* Hong Kong China *see*
Shek Pik Reservoir
Shek Pik Reservoir Hong Kong China
87 [inset]
also known as Shek Pik
Sheksna Rus. Fed. **43** T2
formerly known as Nikol'skoye
Sheksna r. Rus. Fed. **43** T2
Sheksninskoye Vodokhranilishche *resr*
Rus. Fed. **43** T2
Shek Uk Shan *mt.* Hong Kong China
87 [inset]
Shela China **89** F6
Shelag *watercourse* Afgh./Iran **101** E4
Shelagskiy, Mys *pt* Rus. Fed. **39** R2
Shelbiana U.S.A. **176** C8
Shelbina U.S.A. **178** D4
Shelburn U.S.A. **174** C4
Shelburne N.S. Canada **169** H5
Shelburne Ont. Canada **173** M6
Shelburne Bay Australia **149** D1
Shelburne Falls U.S.A. **177** M3
Shelby MS U.S.A. **174** B5
Shelby MT U.S.A. **180** E2
Shelby NC U.S.A. **174** D5
Shelby OH U.S.A. **176** C5
Shelbyville IL U.S.A. **174** B4
Shelbyville IN U.S.A. **174** C4
Shelbyville MO U.S.A. **178** D4
Shelbyville TN U.S.A. **174** C5
Shelbyville, Lake U.S.A. **174** B4
Sheldon IA U.S.A. **178** D3
Sheldon IL U.S.A. **172** F10
Sheldon WI U.S.A. **172** C5
Sheldon National Wildlife Refuge
nature res. U.S.A. **180** C4
Sheldon Springs U.S.A. **177** M1
Sheldrake Canada **169** H3
Shelek Kazakh. *see* Chilik
Shelekhov Rus. Fed. **84** D1
Shelikhova, Zaliv *g.* Rus. Fed. **39** Q3
Shelikof Strait U.S.A. **164** D4
Shellbrook Canada **167** J4
Shelley U.S.A. **180** E4
Shell Lake Canada **167** J4
Shell Lake U.S.A. **172** B5
Shell Lakes *salt flat* Australia **151** D6
Shell Mountain U.S.A. **182** A1
Shellsburg U.S.A. **172** B8
Shelon' r. Rus. Fed. **43** L3
Shelopugino Rus. Fed. **85** H1
Shelter Bay Canada *see* Port-Cartier
Shelter Island U.S.A. **177** M4
Shelter Point N.Z. **153** C15
Shelton CT U.S.A. **177** L4
Shelton U.S.A. **180** B3
Sheltozero Rus. Fed. **40** F3
Shemakha Azer. *see* Şamaxi
Shemankar r. Nigeria **125** H4
Shemgang Bhutan *see* Zhemgang
Shemonaikha Kazakh. **88** C1
Shemordan Rus. Fed. **40** I4
Shemursha Rus. Fed. **40** H5
Shenandoah IA U.S.A. **178** D3
Shenandoah PA U.S.A. **177** I5
Shenandoah VA U.S.A. **176** G7
Shenandoah r. U.S.A. **176** H6
Shenandoah Mountains U.S.A. **176** F7
Shenandoah National Park U.S.A. **176** G7
Shenbertal Kazakh. **103** E2
Shenchi China **85** F3
Shendam Nigeria **125** H4
Shendi Sudan **121** G5
Shending Shan *hill* China **82** D3
Shenge Sierra Leone **124** B5
Shengel'di Kazakh. **103** G4
Shengel'dy Kazakh. **103** E3
formerly spelt Chengel'dy
Shëngjin Albania **58** A7
Shengji China **87** E2
Shengli Daban *pass* China **88** D3
Shengli Feng *mt.* China/Kyrg. *see*
Pobeda Peak
Shengrenjian China *see* Pinglu
Shengsi China **87** G2
also known as Caiyuanzhen
Shengsi Liedao *is* China **87** G2
Shengzhou China *see* Shengxian
Shengzhou China **87** G2
also known as Shengxian
Shënkoli Albania **58** A7
Shenkursk Rus. Fed. **40** G3
Shenmu China **85** F4
Shennongjia China **87** D2
also known as Songbai
Shenqiu China **87** E1
also known as Huaidian
Shenshu China **82** C3
Shensi *prov.* China *see* Shaanxi
Shentala Rus. Fed. **40** I5
Shenton, Mount *hill* Australia **151** C6
Shenxian China *see* Shenzhou
Shenxian China **85** G4
Shenyang China **85** I3
formerly spelt Chengel'dy
Shenyang China **85** I3
▶Shenzhen China **87** [inset]
also known as Bao'an
world [changes] ▶▶ 20–21
Shenzhen Wan *b.* Hong Kong China *see*
Deep Bay
Shenzhou China **85** G4
formerly known as Shenxian
Sheogani India **96** C4
Sheopur India **96** C4
Shepard Island Antarctica **222** P2
Shepetivka Ukr. **41** C6
also spelt Shepetovka
Shepetovka Ukr. *see* Shepetivka
Shepherd Islands Vanuatu **145** F3
Shepparton Australia **147** E4
Sheptaky Ukr. **43** O9
Sheqi China **87** E1
Sherabad Uzbek. **103** F5
also spelt Sherobod
Sherard, Cape Canada **165** K2
Sherborne S. Africa **133** I8
Sherborne U.K. **47** J13
Sherbro Island Sierra Leone **124** B5
Sherbrooke N.S. Canada **169** I4
Sherbrooke Que. Canada **169** G4
Sherburne U.S.A. **177** J3
Shercock Rep. of Ireland **47** F10
Sherda *well* Chad **120** C4
Sherdoyak Kazakh. **88** C1
Shereiq Sudan **121** G5
Shergarh India **96** B4
Sherghati India **97** E4
Sheridan AR U.S.A. **179** D5
Sheridan WY U.S.A. **180** F3
Sherkaly Rus. Fed. **38** H3
Sherlock r. Australia **150** B4
Sherlovaya Gora Rus. Fed. **85** H1
Sherman NY U.S.A. **176** F3
Sherman TX U.S.A. **179** C5
Sherman Mountain U.S.A. **183** I1
Sherobod Uzbek. *see* Sherabad
Sherovichi Rus. Fed. **43** M7
Sherpur *Dhaka* Bangl. **97** F4
Sherpur *Rajshahi* Bangl. **97** F4
Sherridon Canada **167** K4
Shertally India **94** C4
also known as Cherthala
's-Hertogenbosch Neth. **48** C4
also known as Den Bosch
Sherwood U.S.A. **176** A4
Sherwood Downs N.Z. **153** E11
Sherwood Lake Canada **167** K2
Sheryshevo Rus. Fed. **82** C2
Sheshegwaning Canada **173** K5
Sheshtamad Iran **100** D2
Shesley Canada **166** D3
Shesley r. Canada **166** C3
Shestikhino Rus. Fed. **43** T4
Shetanei Lake Canada **167** L3
Shetland *admin. div.* U.K. **46** L3
Shetpe Kazakh. **102** B4
Sheung Shui Hong Kong China **87** [inset]
Sheung Sze Mun *sea chan.* Hong Kong
China **87** [inset]
Shevaroy Hills India **94** C4
Shevchenko Kazakh. *see* Aktau
Shevchenko, Zaliv *l.* Kazakh. **102** C3
formerly known as Paskevicha, Zaliv
Shevgaon India **94** B2
Shevli r. Rus. Fed. **82** D1
Shexian *Anhui* China **87** F2
also known as Huicheng
Shexian *Hebei* China **85** G4
also known as Shecheng
Sheya Rus. Fed. **39** L3
Sheyang China **87** G1
also known as Hede
Sheybukhta Rus. Fed. **43** V2
Sheyenne r. U.S.A. **178** C2
Sheykh Sho'eyb *i.* Iran **100** C5
Sheykino Rus. Fed. **43** M5
Shey Phoksundo National Park Nepal
97 D3
Shiant Islands U.K. **46** F6
Shiashkotan, Ostrov *i.* Rus. Fed. **81** Q3
Shiawassee r. U.S.A. **173** J7
Shibām Yemen **105** D5
Shibar Pass Afgh. **101** G3
Shibata Japan **90** F6
Shibazhan China **82** B1
Shibetsu *Hokkaidō* Japan **90** H2
Shibetsu *Hokkaidō* Japan **90** I3
Shibīn el Kôm Egypt **121** F2
Shibing China **87** D3
Shibogama Lake Canada **168** B2
Shibotsu-jima *i.* Rus. Fed. *see*
Zelenyy, Ostrov
Shibukawa Japan **91** F6
Shibushi Japan **91** B9
Shibushi-wan *b.* Japan **91** B9
Shicheng China **87** F3
Shibata Japan **90** F6
Shichinohe Japan **90** G4
Shickshinny U.S.A. **177** I4
Shicun China *see* Xiangfen
Shidad al Mismā' *hill* Saudi Arabia **109** J6
Shidao China **85** I4
Shideri r. Kazakh. **103** H1
Shidongsi China *see* Gaolan
Shiel, Loch *l.* U.K. **46** G7
Shield, Cape Australia **148** C2
Shifa, Jabal ash *mts* Saudi Arabia **104** A2
Shifang China **86** C2
Shiga *pref.* Japan **91** D7
Shigatse China *see* Xigazê

Shiggaon India 94 B3
Shigong China 88 F3
Shigony Rus. Fed. 41 I5
Shiguai China 85 F3 formerly known as Shiguaigou
Shiguaigou China see Shiguai
Shihan Yemen 105 F4
Shihan, Wādī r. Oman 105 F4
Shihezi China 88 D2
Shihkiachwang China see Shijiazhuang
Shiikh Somalia 128 E2
Shijak Albania 58 A7
Shijiao China see Fogang
Shijiazhuang China 85 G4 formerly spelt Shihkiachwang
Shiju Hu l. China 87 F2
Shijiusuo China see Rizhao
Shikabe Japan 90 G3
Shikag Lake Canada 168 B3
Shikar r. Pak. 101 E4
Shikarpur India 94 B3
Shikarpur Pak. 101 G5
Shikengkong mt. China 87 E3
Shikhany Rus. Fed. 102 A1
Shikohabad India 96 C4
Shikoku i. Japan 91 C8
Shikoku-sanchi mts Japan 91 C8
Shikotan, Ostrov i. Rus. Fed. 82 G4 also known as Shikotan-tō
Shikotan-tō i. Rus. Fed. see Shikotan, Ostrov
Shikotsu vol. Japan 90 G3 also known as Tarumae-san
Shikotsu-Tōya National Park Japan 90 G3
Shil'da Rus. Fed. 102 D2
Shilega Rus. Fed. 40 H2
Shiliguri India 97 F4 also spelt Siliguri
Shilipu China 87 E2
Shiliu China see Changjiang
Shilka Rus. Fed. 85 H1
Shilla mt. Jammu and Kashmir 96 C2
Shillelagh Rep. of Ireland 47 F11
Shillington Canada 173 M2
Shillo r. Israel 108 F5
Shillong India 97 F4
Shilou China 85 F4
Shilovo Ryazanskaya Oblast' Rus. Fed. 41 G5
Shilovo Tul'skaya Oblast' Rus. Fed. 43 T8
Shilüüstey Mongolia see Balgatay
Shimabara Japan 91 B8
Shimabara-wan b. Japan 91 B8
Shimada Japan 91 F7
Shimamaki Japan 90 G3
Shimane pref. Japan 91 C7
Shimane-hantō pen. Japan 91 C7
Shimanovsk Rus. Fed. 82 B1
Shimbiris mt. Somalia 128 E2 also known as Surud Ad
Shimbirre waterhole Kenya 128 D4
Shimen China 87 D2
Shimian China 86 B2 also known as Xinmian
Shimizu Hokkaidō Japan 90 H3
Shimizu Shizuoka Japan 91 F7
Shimla India 96 C3 formerly spelt Simla
Shimminato Japan see Shinminato
Shimoda Japan 91 F7
Shimodate Japan 91 F6
Shimoga India 94 B3
Shimokawa Japan 90 H2
Shimokita-hantō pen. Japan 90 G4
Shimoni Kenya 129 C6
Shimonoseki Japan 91 B8 formerly known as Akamagaseki
Shimotsuma Japan 91 F6
Shimsha r. India 94 C3
Shimshal Jammu and Kashmir 96 B1
Shimsk Rus. Fed. 43 L3
Shin, Loch l. U.K. 46 H5
Shināfiyah Iraq see Ash Shanāfiyah
Shinan China 87 D4
Shindand Afgh. 101 E3 also known as Sabzawar
Shingbwiyang Myanmar 78 B2
Shinghshal Pass Pak. 101 H2
Shinglehouse U.S.A. 176 G4
Shingleton U.S.A. 172 G4
Shingletown U.S.A. 182 C1
Shing Mun Reservoir Hong Kong China 87 [inset] also known as Ngan Hei Shui Tong
Shingozha Kazakh. 103 J3 also spelt Shyngqozha
Shingū Japan 91 E8
Shingwedzi S. Africa 131 F4
Shining Tree Canada 173 L3
Shinjō Japan 90 G5
Shinkai Hills Afgh. 101 G3
Shinkāy Afgh. 101 F4
Shinminato Japan 91 E6 also spelt Shimminato
Shinnan-yō Japan 91 B7
Shinnston U.S.A. 176 E6
Shinshiro Japan 91 E7
Shintoku Japan 90 H3
Shinyanga Tanz. 128 B5
Shinyanga admin. reg. Tanz. 129 B5
Shiogama Japan 90 G5
Shiojiri Japan 91 E6
Shiono-misaki c. Japan 91 D8
Shioya-zaki pt Japan 90 G6
Shipai China see Huaining
Ship Chan Cay i. Bahamas 175 E7
Shipchenski Prokhod pass Bulg. 58 G6
Shipilovo Rus. Fed. 43 T4
Shiping China 86 B4 also known as Yilong
Shipki Pass China/India 89 B6
Shipman U.S.A. 176 G8
Shippegan Canada 169 H4
Shippegan Island Canada 169 H4
Shippensburg U.S.A. 176 H5
Shippenville U.S.A. 176 F4
Shiprock U.S.A. 183 P5
Shiprock Peak U.S.A. 183 P5
Shipu China see Huanglong
Shipu China 87 G2
Shipunskiy, Mys hd Rus. Fed. 39 Q4
Shiqian China 87 D3
Shiqiao China see Panyu
Shiqizhen China see Zhongshan
Shiqqat al Kharītah des. Saudi Arabia 105 D4
Shiquan China 87 D1
Shiquanhe China see Ali
Shiquanhe China see Gar
Shiquanh He r. China see Indus
Shi'r, Jabal hill Saudi Arabia 104 C2
Shirā'awh i. Qatar 105 F2
Shīrābād Iran 100 B2
Shirakami-misaki pt Japan 90 G4
Shirakawa Fukushima Japan 90 G6
Shirakawa Gifu Japan 91 E6
Shirane-san mt. Japan 91 F7
Shirane-san vol. Japan 90 F6
Shiranuka Japan 90 I3
Shiraoi Japan 90 G3
Shirase Coast Antarctica 223 O1
Shirase Glacier Antarctica 223 C2
Shirataki Japan 90 H3
Shirati Tanz. 128 B5
Shīrāz Iran 100 C4
Shirbīn Egypt 108 C6
Shire r. Malawi 129 B9
Shireet Mongolia 85 G2
Shirega Rus. Fed. 43 V1
Shiretoko-hantō pen. Japan 90 I3
Shiretoko-misaki c. Japan 90 I2
Shiretoko National Park Japan 90 I2
Shirin Uzbek. 103 G4
Shirinab r. Pak. 101 F4
Shīrīn Tagāb Afgh. 101 F2
Shiriya-zaki c. Japan 90 G4
Shirkala reg. Kazakh. 102 D3
Shīr Kūh mt. Iran 100 C4
Shiroishi Japan 90 G6
Shirone Japan 90 F6
Shiroro Reservoir Nigeria 125 G4
Shirotori Japan 91 E7
Shirpur India 96 B5
Shirten Höloy Gobi des. China 84 C3
Shirvān Iran 100 D2
Shisanjianfang China 88 E3
Shisanzhan China 82 B2
Shiselweni admin. dist. Swaziland 133 P4
Shishaldin Volcano U.S.A. 164 C4
Shisha Pangma mt. China see Xixabangma Feng
Shishou China 87 E2
Shishovka Rus. Fed. 43 T3
Shitai China 87 F2 also known as Qili
Shitan China 87 E3
Shitang China 87 G2
Shitanjing China 85 E4
Shithāthah Iraq 109 O5
Shiv India 96 A4
Shiveluch, Sopka vol. Rus. Fed. 39 Q4
Shivpuri India 96 C4
Shivta tourist site Israel 108 F7 also known as Subeita
Shivwits U.S.A. 183 K4
Shivwits Plateau U.S.A. 183 K5
Shiwan Dashan mts China 87 C4
Shiwa Ngandu Zambia 127 F7
Shixing China 87 E3 also known as Taiping
Shiyan China 87 D1
Shizhu China 87 D2 also known as Nanbin
Shizilu China see Junan
Shizipu China 87 F2
Shizong China 86 B3 also known as Danfeng
Shizugawa Japan 90 G5
Shizuishan China 85 E4 also known as Dawukou
Shizukuishi Japan 90 G5
Shizuoka Japan 91 F7 historically known as Sumpu
Shizuoka pref. Japan 91 F7
▶Shkhara mt. Georgia/Rus. Fed. 107 E2 3rd highest mountain in Europe. europe [landscapes] ▶ 30–31
Shklov Belarus see Shklow
Shklow Belarus 43 L7 also spelt Shklov
Shkodër Albania 58 A6 formerly known as Scutari; historically known as Scodra
Shkodrës, Liqeni i l. Albania/Yugo. see Scutari, Lake
Shkotovo Rus. Fed. 90 C3
Shkumbin r. Albania 58 A7
Shlina r. Rus. Fed. 43 P4
Shlino, Ozero l. Rus. Fed. 43 O4
Shlissel'burg Rus. Fed. 43 M2 also spelt Schlüsselburg; formerly known as Petrokrepost'
Shmidta, Ostrov i. Rus. Fed. 39 J1 English form Schmidt Island
Shmidta, Poluostrov pen. Rus. Fed. 82 F1 English form Schmidt Peninsula
Shmoylovo Rus. Fed. 43 J4
Shoalhaven r. Australia 147 F3
Shoal Lake Man. Canada 167 K5
Shoal Lake Sask. Canada 167 K4
Shoals U.S.A. 174 C4
Shoalwater Bay Australia 149 F4
Shōbara Japan 91 C7
Shōdo-shima i. Japan 91 D7
Shoemakersville U.S.A. 177 J5
Shofirkon Uzbek. see Shafirkan
Shoghlābād Iran 100 D2
Shoh Tajik. see Shakh
Shohi Pass Pak. see Tal Pass
Shokanbetsu-dake mt. Japan 90 G3
Shokotsu-gawa r. Japan 90 H2
Shokpar Kazakh. see Chokpar
Shola r. Rus. Fed. 43 S1
Sholaksay Kazakh. 103 F2 also spelt Sholaqsay
Sholapur India see Solapur
Sholaqorghan Kazakh. see Shollakorgan
Sholaqsay Kazakh. see Sholaksay
Shollakorgan Kazakh. 103 G4 also spelt Sholaqorghan; formerly spelt Chulakkurgan
Shomba r. Rus. Fed. 40 E2
Shongar Bhutan 97 F4
Shonzha Kazakh. see Chundzha
Shopsha Rus. Fed. 43 U4
Shoptykol' Kazakh. 103 H2
Shoqpar Kazakh. see Chokpar
Shoranur India 94 C4
Shorap Pak. 101 F5
Shorapur India 94 C2
Shorawak reg. Afgh. 101 F4
Shor Barsa-Kel'mes salt marsh Uzbek. 102 D4
Shorghun Uzbek. see Shargun'
Shorkot Pak. 101 H4
Shorkozakhly, Solonchak depr. Turkm. 102 D4
Shornaq Kazakh. see Chernak
Shorobe Botswana 130 D3
Shortandy Kazakh. 103 G2
Shortsville U.S.A. 177 H3
Shosambetsu Japan see Shosanbetsu
Shosanbetsu Japan 90 G2 also spelt Shosambetsu
Shosha r. Rus. Fed. 43 R5
Shoshone CA U.S.A. 183 H6
Shoshone ID U.S.A. 180 D4
Shoshone r. U.S.A. 180 E3
Shoshone Mountains U.S.A. 183 G2
Shoshone Peak U.S.A. 183 H5
Shoshong Botswana 131 E4
Shoshoni U.S.A. 180 E4
Shostka Ukr. 41 E6
Shouguang China 85 H4
Shouxian China 87 F1
Shouyang China 85 G4
Shouyang Shan mt. China 87 D1
Showak Sudan 121 G6
Show Low U.S.A. 183 N7
Shoyna Rus. Fed. 40 H2
Shpakovskoye Rus. Fed. 41 G7 formerly known as Mikhaylovskoye
Shpola Ukr. 41 D6
Shqipërisë, Republika e country Europe see Albania
Shreve U.S.A. 176 C5
Shreveport U.S.A. 179 D5
Shrewsbury U.K. 47 J11
Shrigonda India 94 B2
Shri Lanka country Asia see Sri Lanka
Shri Mohangarh India 96 A4
Shrirampur India 97 F5
Shrirangapattana India 94 C3
Shtefan-Vode Moldova see Ştefan Vodă
Shtërmen Albania 58 B8
Shtiqën Albania 58 B6
Shu r. China 87 F1
Shu Kazakh. 103 H4 formerly spelt Chu
Shu'ab, Ghubbat b. Yemen 105 F5
Shu'ab, Ra's pt Yemen 105 F5
Shu'aiba Iraq 107 F5
Shuajingsi China 86 B1
Shuangbai China 86 B3 also known as Tuodian
Shuangcheng China see Zherong
Shuangcheng China 82 B3
Shuanghe China 87 E2
Shuanghechang China 87 C2
Shuanghedagang China 82 C2
Shuanghuyu China see Zizhou
Shuangjiang China see Jiangkou
Shuangjiang China see Tongdao
Shuangjiang China 86 A4 also known as Mengmeng
Shuangjiang China see Eshan
Shuangliao China 85 I3 formerly known as Zhengjiatun
Shuangpai China 87 D3
Shuangshipu China see Fengxian
Shuangyang China 82 B4
Shuangyashan China 82 C3
Shuangzhong China see Hukou
Shu'ayt, Wādī r. Yemen 105 E4
Shubarkuduk Kazakh. 102 D2
Shubarshi Kazakh. 102 D2
Shubayh well Saudi Arabia 109 J7
Shubrā el Kheima Egypt 121 F2
Shubrāmiyah well Saudi Arabia 104 C3
Shucheng China 87 F2
Shucushuyacu Peru 198 C6
Shufu China 88 A4
Shuganu India 97 G4
Shughnon, Qatorkŭhi mts Tajik. 101 G2 also known as Shugnanskiy Khrebet
Shugnanskiy Khrebet mts Tajik. see Shughnon, Qatorkŭhi
Shugozero Rus. Fed. 43 P2
Shugur Rus. Fed. 38 G3
Shuicheng China see Lupanshui
Shuiding China see Huocheng
Shuidong China see Dianbai
Shuihu China see Changfeng
Shuiji China 87 F3
Shuiji China see Laixi
Shuijing China 86 C1
Shuikou Guangdong China 87 E4
Shuikou Hunan China 87 D3 also known as Tuojiang
Shuikouguan China 86 C4
Shuikoushan China 87 E3
Shuiluocheng China see Zhuanglang
Shuiquanzi China 84 D4
Shuituo He r. China 86 B3
Shuizhai China see Wuhua
Shujaabad Pak. 101 G4
Shulan China 82 B3
Shule China 88 B4
Shule He r. China 84 B3
Shule Nanshan mts China 84 C4
Shulinzhao China 85 F3 also known as Dalad Qi
Shul'mak Tajik. see Novobod
Shulu China see Xinji
Shum Rus. Fed. 43 M2
Shumagin Islands U.S.A. 164 C4
Shumanay Uzbek. 102 D4 formerly known as Taza-Bazar
Shumarinai-ko l. Japan 90 H2
Shumen Bulg. 58 H5 formerly known as Kolarovgrad
Shumensko Plato nat. park Bulg. 58 H5
Shumerlya Rus. Fed. 40 H5
Shumikha Rus. Fed. 38 G4
Shumilina Belarus 43 K6
Shumshu, Ostrov i. Rus. Fed. 39 P4
Shumyachi Rus. Fed. 43 N8
Shunak, Gora mt. Kazakh. 103 H3
Shūnat Nimrīn Jordan 108 G6
Shunde China 87 E4 also known as Daliang
Shunga Rus. Fed. 43 V4
Shunyi China 85 H3
Shuolong China 86 C4
Shuoxian China see Shuozhou
Shuozhou China 85 G4 formerly known as Shuoxian
Shupiyan Jammu and Kashmir 89 A5
Shuqqat Najrān depr. Saudi Arabia 105 D4
Shuqrah Yemen 105 D5
Shūr r. Iran 100 C4
Shūr r. Iran 100 C4
Shūr r. Iran 100 D3
Shūr r. Iran 101 E3
Shūr r. Iran 101 E4
Shūr watercourse Iran 100 C4
Shūr watercourse Iran 100 C4
Shūr watercourse Iran 100 C5
Shūr watercourse Iran 100 D3
Shūrāb Chahār Maḥāll va Bakhtīārī Iran 100 B3
Shūr Āb r. Iran 100 B3
Shūrāb Khorāsan Iran 100 D3
Shūrāb Yazd Iran 100 C3
Shūr Āb watercourse Iran 100 C4
Shurab Tajik. see Shūrob
Shurchi Uzbek. 103 F5
Shureghestan Iran 100 C3
Shūr Gaz Iran 101 D4
Shūrjestān Iran 100 C4
Shurma Rus. Fed. 40 I4
Shūrob Tajik. 101 G1 also spelt Shurab
Shūrū Iran 101 E4
Shurugwi Zimbabwe 131 F3 formerly spelt Selukwe
Shuruppak tourist site Iraq 107 F5
Shusf Iran 101 E4
Shūsh Iran 100 B3
Shusha Azer. see Şuşa
Shushicë r. Albania 59 A8
Shushkodom Rus. Fed. 43 V3
Shushtar Iran 100 B3
Shuswap Lake Canada 166 G5
Shutar Khun Pass Afgh. 101 F3
Shuwaysh, Tall ash hill Jordan 109 I6
Shuya Ivanovskaya Oblast' Rus. Fed. 40 G4
Shuya Respublika Kareliya Rus. Fed. 40 E3
Shuyak Island U.S.A. 164 D4
Shuyang China 87 F1
Shuyskoye Rus. Fed. 43 V2
Shvartsevskiy Rus. Fed. 43 S7
Shwebandaw Myanmar 78 A4
Shwebo Myanmar 78 A3
Shwedaung Myanmar 78 A4
Shwedwin Myanmar 78 A3
Shwegun Myanmar 78 B4
Shwegyin Myanmar 78 B4
Shwelaung r. Myanmar 78 A4
Shweli r. Myanmar 78 B3 also known as Mao, Nam
Shwenyaung Myanmar 78 B3
Shweudaung mt. Myanmar 78 B3
Shyghanaq Kazakh. see Chiganak
Shyghys Qazaqstan Oblysy admin. div. Kazakh. see Vostochnyy Kazakhstan
Shyghys-Qongyrat Kazakh. see Shygys Konyrat
Shygys Konyrat Kazakh. 103 H3 also spelt Shyghys-Qongyrat; formerly known as Vostochno-Kounradskiy
Shymkent Kazakh. 103 G4 formerly spelt Chimkent
Shyngghyrlau Kazakh. see Chingirlau
Shyngqozha Kazakh. see Shingozha
Shyok r. India 96 B2
Shyok Jammu and Kashmir 96 C2
Shypuvate Ukr. 41 F6
Shyshchytsy Belarus 42 I8
Si, Laem pt Thai. 79 B6
Sia Indon. 73 H8
Siabu Indon. 76 B2
Siachen Glacier Jammu and Kashmir 96 C2
Siahan Range mts Pak. 101 E5
Siah Chashmeh Iran 100 A2
Siahgird Afgh. 101 F2
Siah Koh mts Afgh. 101 F3
Siāh Kūh mts Iran 100 C3
Siak r. Indon. 76 C2
Siak Sri Inderapura Indon. 76 C2
Sialkot Pak. 101 H3
Siam country Asia see Thailand
Sian China see Xi'an
Sianów Poland 49 N1
Siantan i. Indon. 77 D2
Siapa r. Venez. 199 E4
Siargao i. Phil. 74 C4
Siasconset U.S.A. 177 P4
Siasi Phil. 74 B5
Siasi i. Phil. 74 B5
Siatista Greece 59 C8
Siaton Phil. 74 B4
Siau i. Indon. 75 C2
Šiauliai Lith. 42 E6
Siavonga Zambia 127 F9
Siayan i. Phil. 74 B1
Siazan' Azer. see Siyäzän
Sīb Iran 101 E5
Sīb Oman 105 G3
Sibanicú Cuba 186 D2
Sibati China see Xibet
Sibay i. Phil. 74 B4
Sibay Rus. Fed. 102 D1
Sibayi, Lake S. Africa 133 Q4
Sibbald, Cape Antarctica 223 L2
Sibbo Fin. 45 N3
Sibbofjärden b. Fin. 42 G1
Šibenik Croatia 56 H5 formerly spelt Sebenico
Siberia Rus. Fed. see Central Siberian Plateau
Siberut i. Indon. 76 B3
Siberut, Selat sea chan. Indon. 76 B3
Siberut National Park Indon. 76 B3
Sibi Pak. 101 F4
Sibidiri P.N.G. 73 J8
Sibigo Indon. 76 A2
Sibiloi National Park Kenya 128 C4
Sibirtsevo Rus. Fed. 82 D3 formerly known as Manzovka
Sibiryakova, Ostrov i. Rus. Fed. 39 H2
Sibiti Congo 126 B5
Sibiu Romania 58 F3
Sibley U.S.A. 178 D3
Siboa Indon. 75 B2
Sibolga Indon. 76 B2
Siborongborong Indon. 76 B2
Sibowe r. Swaziland 133 P3
Sibsagar India 97 G4
Sibu Sarawak Malaysia 77 E2
Sibuco Phil. 74 B5
Sibuco Bay Phil. 74 B5
Sibuguey r. Phil. 74 B5
Sibuguey Bay Phil. 74 B5
Sibut Cent. Afr. Rep. 126 C3
Sibutu i. Phil. 74 A5
Sibutu Passage Phil. 74 A5
Sibuyan i. Phil. 74 B3
Sibuyan Sea Phil. 74 B3
Sic Romania 58 E2
Sicamous Canada 166 G5
Sicapoo mt. Phil. 74 B2
Sicca Veneria Tunisia see Le Kef
Siccus watercourse Australia 146 C2
Sicheng China see Lingyun
Sichon Thai. 79 B6
Sichuan prov. China 86 B2 English form Szechwan
Sichuan Pendi basin China 86 C2 English form Red Basin
Sicié, Cap c. France 51 L9
Sicilia admin. reg. Italy 57 G11
Sicilia i. Italy see Sicily
Sicilian Channel Italy/Tunisia 57 E11
Sicily i. Italy 57 G10 also known as Sicilia
Sicuani Peru 200 C3
Šid Vojvodina, Srbija Yugo. 58 A3
Sidangoli Indon. 75 C2
Siddhapur India 96 B5 also spelt Sidhpur
Siddharthanagar Nepal see Bhairawa
Siddipet India 94 C2
Sideby Fin. 45 M3 also known as Siipyy
Sideia Island P.N.G. 149 F1
Sid el Na'âm, Gebel hill Egypt 108 C8
Sidenreng, Danau l. Indon. 75 A3
Sidensjö Sweden 44 L3
Sidéradougou Burkina 124 D4
Sideros, Akra pt Greece 59 H13
Sidesaviwa S. Africa 132 G9
Sidhauli India 96 D4
Sidhi India 97 D4
Sidhirókastron Greece see Sidirokastro
Sidhpur India see Siddhapur
Sidi Aïssa Alg. 55 O9
Sidi Ali Alg. 55 L8
Sidi Ameur Alg. 55 O9
Sidi Barrani Egypt 121 E2
Sidi Bel Abbès Alg. 123 E2
Sidi Bennour Morocco 122 C2
Sidi Bou Sa'id Tunisia see Sidi Bouzid
Sidi Bouzid Tunisia 123 H2 also known as Sidi Bou Sa'id
Sidi El Hani, Sebkhet de salt pan Tunisia 123 H2
Sidi el Mokhtâr well Mali 124 E2
Sidi Ifni Morocco 122 C3
Sidi Kacem Morocco 122 D2 formerly known as Petitjean
Sidikalang Indon. 76 B2
Sidi Khaled Alg. 123 G2
Sidi Ladjel Alg. 55 N9
Sidi Mannsour well Alg. 123 E3
Sidi Mhamed well W. Sahara 122 B5
Sidi Okba Alg. 123 G2
Sidirokastro Greece 58 E7 also known as Sidhirókastron
Sidi Saâd, Barrage dam Tunisia 57 B13
Sidi Sâlim Egypt 108 B6
Sidi-Smaïl Morocco 122 C2
Sid Lake Canada 167 J2
Sidlaw Hills U.K. 46 I7
Sidley, Mount Antarctica 222 P1
Sidmouth U.K. 47 I13
Sidmouth, Cape Australia 149 D2
Sidnaw U.S.A. 172 E4
Sidney Canada 166 F5
Sidney IA U.S.A. 178 D3
Sidney MT U.S.A. 180 F3
Sidney NE U.S.A. 178 B3
Sidney NY U.S.A. 177 J3
Sidney OH U.S.A. 176 A5
Sidney Lanier, Lake U.S.A. 174 D5
Sido Mali 124 D4
Sidoan Indon. 75 B2
Sidoarjo Indon. 77 F4
Sidoktaya Myanmar 78 A3
Sidon Lebanon 108 G4 also spelt Saïda or Sayda
Sidorovo Rus. Fed. 43 V3
Sidra r. Poland 49 U2
Sidri, Wâdi watercourse Egypt 108 E9
Sidrolândia Brazil 203 A7
Sidvokodvo Swaziland 133 P3
Sidwadweni S. Africa 133 M8
Sidzhak Uzbek. 103 G4 also spelt Sijjak; formerly spelt Sydzhak
Siebe Norway 44 M1
Siedlce Poland 49 T3 historically known as Sedlets
Sieg r. Germany 48 E5
Siegen Germany 48 F5
Siemianówka, Jezioro l. Poland 49 U3
Siemiatycze Poland 49 T3
Siĕmréab Cambodia 79 C5 also spelt Siem Reap
Siem Reap Cambodia see Siĕmréab
Si'en China see Huanjiang
Siena Italy 56 D5 historically known as Saena Julia
Sieniawa Poland 49 T5
Sieppijärvi Fin. 44 M2
Sieradz Poland 49 P4
Sieraków Poland 49 N3
Sierpc Poland 49 Q3
Sierpienica r. Poland 49 Q3
Sierra Bahoruco nat. park Dom. Rep. 187 F3
Sierra Blanca U.S.A. 181 F7
Sierra Chica Arg. 204 E5
Sierra Colorada Arg. 204 D6
Sierra de Cazorla Segurla y las Villas park Spain 55 I6
Sierra del Gistral mts Spain see Xistral, Serra do
Sierra Grande Arg. 205 D6
▶Sierra Leone country Africa 124 B4 africa [countries] ▶ 114–117
Sierra Madre Mountains U.S.A. 182 D6
Sierra Mojada Mex. 184 E3
Sierra Nevada, Parque Nacional nat. park Venez. 198 D2
Sierra Nevada de Santa Marta, Parque Nacional nat. park Col. 198 C2
Sierraville U.S.A. 182 D2
Sierra Vista U.S.A. 181 E7
Sierre Switz. 51 N6
Siesartis r. Lith. 42 D7
Siesartis r. Lith. 42 F6
Şieu Romania 58 F1
Şieu r. Romania 58 F1
Sieve r. Italy 56 D5
Sievi Fin. 44 N3
Sifang Ling mts China 87 C4
Sifeni Eth. 128 D1
Sifié Côte d'Ivoire 124 D5
Sifnos i. Greece 59 F11
Sifnou, Steno sea chan. Greece 59 F11
Sig Alg. 123 E2 formerly known as St-Denis-du-Sig
Sig, Ozero l. Rus. Fed. 43 O4
Sigani well Saudi Arabia 105 F4
Sigatoka Fiji 145 G3 also spelt Singatoka
Sigave Wallis and Futuna Is 145 H3 also known as Leava; also spelt Singave
Sigean France 51 I9
Sigep, Tanjung pt Indon. 76 B3
Sigguup Nunaa pen. Greenland 165 N2 also known as Svartenhuk Halvø
Sighişoara Romania 58 F2
Sigiriya Sri Lanka 94 D5
Siglap Sing. 76 [inset]
Sigli Indon. 76 A1
Siglufjörður Iceland 44 [inset] C2
Sigma Phil. 74 B4
Sigmaringen Germany 48 G7
Signal de Mailhebiau mt. France 51 J8
Signal de Randon mt. France 51 J8
Signal du Pic hill France 50 H7
Signal Peak U.S.A. 183 J8
Signy-l'Abbaye France 51 K3
Sigoga S. Africa 133 M7
Sigoisooinan Indon. 76 B3
Sigourney U.S.A. 174 A3
Sigri, Akra pt Greece 59 G9
Siguatepeque Hond. 186 B4
Sigüeiro Spain 54 C2
Sigüenza Spain 55 I3
Siguiri Guinea 124 C4
Sigulda Latvia 42 F4
Sigurd U.S.A. 183 M3
Sihanoukville Cambodia 79 C6 formerly known as Kâmpóng Saôm or Kompong Som
Sihanoukville, Chhâk b. Cambodia 79 C6 formerly known as Kompong Som Bay
Sihaung Myauk Myanmar 78 A3
Sihawa India 94 D1
Sihhoya Swaziland 133 P2
Sihong China 87 F1 also known as Qingyang
Sihora Madhya Pradesh India 96 D5
Sihora Maharashtra India 96 C5
Sihou China see Changdao
Sihuas Peru 200 A2
Sihui China 87 E4
Siikainen Fin. 45 M3
Siikajoki Fin. 44 N2
Siikajoki r. Fin. 44 N2
Siilinjärvi Fin. 44 N3
Siipyy Fin. see Sideby
Siirt Turkey 107 E3 historically known as Tigranocerta
Sijjak Uzbek. see Sidzhak
Sijunjung Indon. 76 C3
Sika India 96 A5
Sikakap Indon. 76 C3
Sikandra Rao India 96 C4
Sikanni Chief Canada 166 F3
Sikanni Chief r. Canada 166 F3
Sikar India 96 B4
Sikaram mt. Afgh. 101 G3
Sikasso Mali 124 D4
Sikasso admin. reg. Mali 124 D4
Sikaw Myanmar 78 B3
Sikea Greece 59 E8
Sikeli Indon. 75 B4
Sikeston U.S.A. 174 B4
Sikhote-Alin' mts Rus. Fed. 82 D4
Sikhote-Alinskiy Zapovednik nature res. Rus. Fed. 82 E3
Sikinos Greece 59 G12
Sikinos i. Greece 59 G12
Sikirevci Croatia 56 K3
Sikkim state India 97 F4
Siklós Hungary 56 K3
Sikongo Zambia 127 D8
Siksjö Sweden 44 L2
Sikta India 97 E4
Sikuaishi China see Changhai
Sikuati Sabah Malaysia 77 G1
Sila' i. Saudi Arabia 104 A2
Silago Phil. 74 C4
Šilalė Lith. 42 D6
Silandro Italy 56 C2
Si Lanna National Park Thai. 78 B4
Silao Mex. 185 E4
Sila Point Phil. 74 C3
Silawaih Agam vol. Indon. 76 A1
Silay Phil. 74 B4
Silba i. Croatia 56 G4
Silchar India 97 G4
Şile Turkey 58 K7
Silene Latvia 42 H6
Siler City U.S.A. 174 E5
Sileru r. India 94 D2
Silesia reg. Czech Rep./Poland 49 N5
Silet Alg. 123 G5
Sileti Kazakh. see Seletinskoye
Sileti r. Kazakh. 103 H1 formerly spelt Selety
Siletiteniz, Ozero salt l. Kazakh. 103 H1 formerly spelt Seletyteniz, Ozero
Silgadi Nepal see Silgarhi
Silgarhi Nepal 96 D3 also spelt Silgadi
Silghat India 97 G4
Siliana Tunisia 123 H1
Silifke Turkey 106 C3 historically known as Seleucia
Siliguri India see Shiliguri
Sililo Zambia 127 E9
Siling Co salt l. China 89 E6
Silipur India 96 C4
Silisili, Mount Samoa 145 H3
Silistat Turkey see Bozkır
Siliştea Romania 58 G4
Siliştea Nouă Romania 58 F4
Silistra Bulg. 58 I4 historically known as Dorostol or Durostorum or Silistria
Silistria Bulg. see Silistra
Silivri Turkey 106 B2
Siljan Norway 45 J4
Siljan l. Sweden 45 K3
Silkaatskop S. Africa 133 K2
Silkeborg Denmark 45 J4
Silla Spain 55 K5
Sillamäe Estonia 42 I2
Sillaro r. Italy 56 D4
Sille Turkey 106 C3
Silleda Spain 54 C2
Silleiro, Cabo c. Spain 54 C2
Sillé-le-Guillaume France 50 F4
Silli India 97 E5
Sillod India 94 B1
Sillon de Talbert pen. France 50 C4
Siloam Springs U.S.A. 179 D4
Silobela S. Africa 133 O3
Silovayakha r. Rus. Fed. 40 L2
Silsbee U.S.A. 179 D6
Silsby Lake Canada 167 M4
Siltaharju Fin. 44 N2
Siltakylä Fin. 42 H1
Siltou well Chad 120 B5
Siluas Indon. 77 E2
Silūp r. Iran 101 E5
Šilutė Lith. 42 C6
Silutshana S. Africa 133 O5
Šiluva Lith. 42 E6
Silva Jardim Brazil 207 K9
Silvan Turkey 107 E3
Silvânia Brazil 206 E3
Silvassa India 94 B1
Silver Bank sea feature Turks and Caicos Is 187 F2
Silver Bank Passage Turks and Caicos Is 187 F2
Silver Bay U.S.A. 174 B2
Silver City Canada 166 B2
Silver City U.S.A. 181 E6
Silver Creek U.S.A. 176 F3
Silver Creek r. U.S.A. 183 N7
Silverdale N.Z. 152 I4
Silver Islet Canada 172 E2
Silver Lake U.S.A. 172 D6
Silver Lake l. CA U.S.A. 183 H6
Silver Lake l. MI U.S.A. 172 F4
Silvermine Mountains hills Rep. of Ireland 47 D11
Silver Peak Range mts U.S.A. 182 G4
Silver Spring U.S.A. 177 I7
Silver Springs U.S.A. 182 E2
Silverthrone Mountain Canada 166 E5
Silvertip Mountain Canada 180 B2
Silverton Australia 146 D2
Silverton Canada 166 G5
Silverton CO U.S.A. 181 F5
Silverton TX U.S.A. 179 B5
Silver Water Canada 173 K5
Silves Brazil 199 G5
Silves Port. 54 C7
Silvia Col. 198 B4
Silvies r. U.S.A. 180 C4
Silvituc Mex. 185 H5
Silvretta Gruppe mts Switz. 51 Q6
Sim r. Rus. Fed. 40 K5
Sima Comoros 129 E8
Sima Rus. Fed. 43 U5
Simao China 86 B4
Simão Dias Brazil 202 E4
Simaraña Venez. 199 F3
Simārd, Lac l. Canada 173 O3
Simaria Jharkhand India 97 E4
Simaria Madhya Pradesh India 96 D4
Simatang i. Indon. 75 B2
Simav Turkey 106 B3
Simav Dağları mts Turkey 106 B3
Simayr i. Saudi Arabia 104 C4
Simba Dem. Rep. Congo 126 D4
Simbirsk Rus. Fed. see Ul'yanovsk
Simbruini, Monti mts Italy 56 F7
Simbukhovo Rus. Fed. 43 R6
Simcoe Canada 168 D5
Simcoe, Lake Canada 168 E4
Simdega India 97 E5
Simeå Sweden 45 L3
Simēn Mountain National Park Eth. 128 C1
Simēn Mountains Eth. 128 C1
Simeonovgrad Bulg. 58 G6 formerly known as Maritsa
Simeria Romania 58 E3
Simeto r. Sicilia Italy 57 H11
Simeulue i. Indon. 76 B2
Simferopol' Ukr. 41 E7
Simi i. Greece see Symi
Simikot Nepal 97 D3
Simindou Cent. Afr. Rep. 126 D3
Siminy mt. Slovakia 49 R6
Simitli Bulg. 58 E7
Simi Valley U.S.A. 182 F7
Simla India see Shimla
Şimleu Silvaniei Romania 58 D1
Simmern (Hunsrück) Germany 48 E6
Simmesport U.S.A. 175 B6
Simm's Bahamas 187 E2
Simnas Lith. 42 E7
Simo Fin. 44 N2
Simojärvi l. Fin. 44 N2
Simonette r. Canada 166 G4
Simonhouse Canada 167 K4
Šimonka mt. Slovakia 49 S7
Simons U.S.A. 176 E4
Simon's Town S. Africa 132 C11
Simontornya Hungary 49 P9
Simon Wash watercourse U.S.A. 183 O9
Simpang Indon. 76 D3
Simpang Mangayau, Tanjong pt Sabah Malaysia 77 G1
Simplicio Mendes Brazil 202 D3
Simplon Pass Switz. 51 O6
Simpson Canada 167 J5
Simpson Desert Australia 148 C5
Simpson Desert Conservation Park nature res. Australia 148 C5
Simpson Desert National Park Australia 148 C5
Simpson Desert Regional Reserve nature res. Australia 146 C1
Simpson Hill hill Australia 151 D5
Simpson Island Canada 172 F2
Simpson Islands Canada 167 H2
Simpson Park Mountains U.S.A. 183 H2
Simpson Peninsula Canada 165 K3
Simpsonville U.S.A. 174 D5
Simra Nepal 97 E4
Simrishamn Sweden 45 K5
Simuk i. Indon. 76 B3
Simulubek Indon. 76 B3
Simunjan Sarawak Malaysia 77 E2
Simunul i. Phil. 74 C5
Simushir, Ostrov i. Rus. Fed. 81 Q3
Sina r. India 94 B2
Sinā', Shibh Jazīrat pen. Egypt see Sinai
Sinabang Indon. 76 B2
Sinabung vol. Indon. 76 B2
Sina Dhaqa Somalia 128 E3
▶Sinai pen. Egypt 121 G2 also known as Sīnā', Shibh Jazīrat world [physical features] ▶ 8–9
Sinai, Mont hill France 51 K3
Sinai, Mount Egypt 108 E9 also known as Mûsa, Gebel
Sinaia Romania 58 G3
Sinai al Janūbîya governorate Egypt see Janūb Sīnā'
Sinai ash Shamālîya governorate Egypt see Shamāl Sīnā'
Si Nakarin Reservoir Thai. 79 B5

Sinaloa state Mex. **184** C3
Sinamaica Venez. **198** D2
Sinan China **87** D3
Sinancha Rus. Fed. see Cheremshany
Sinarades Greece **59** A9
Sināwin Libya **120** A2
Sinazongwe Zambia **127** E9
Sinbaungwe Myanmar **78** A4
Sinbo Myanmar **78** B3
Sinbyugyun Myanmar **78** A3
Sincan Turkey **107** D3
Sincé Col. **198** C2
Sincelejo Col. **198** C2
Sinchu Taiwan see T'aoyüan
Sinclair, Lake U.S.A. **175** D5
Sinclair Mills Canada **166** F4
Sincora, Serra do hills Brazil **202** D5
Sind r. India **96** C4
Sind prov. Pak. see Sindh
Sinda Rus. Fed. **82** E2
Sinda Zambia **127** F8
Sindal Denmark **45** J4
Sindangan Phil. **74** B4
Sindangbarang Indon. **77** D4
Sindara Gabon **126** A5
Sindari India **96** A4
Sindeh, Teluk b. Indon. **75** B5
Sindelfingen Germany **48** F7
Sindgi India **94** C3
Sindh prov. Pak. **101** G5
formerly spelt Sind
Sindhnur India **94** C3
Sindhuli Garhi Nepal **97** E4
also known as Sindhulimadi
Sindhulimadi Nepal see Sindhuli Garhi
Sindi Estonia **42** F3
Sindi India **94** C1
Sındırgı Turkey **106** B3
Sindkhed India **94** C2
Sindkheda India **96** B5
Sindominic Romania see Sândominic
Sindor Rus. Fed. **40** I3
Sindou Burkina **124** D4
Sindphana r. India **94** C2
Sindri India **97** E5
Sind Sagar Doab lowland Pak. **101** G4
Sinegor'ye Rus. Fed. **40** I4
Sinekçi Turkey **59** I8
Sinel'nikovo Ukr. see Synel'nykove
Sinendé Benin. **124** E4
Sines Port. **54** C7
Sines, Cabo de c. Port. **54** C7
Sinettä Fin. **44** N2
Sinezerki Rus. Fed. **43** P8
Sinfra Côte d'Ivoire **124** D5
Sing Myanmar **78** B3
Singa Sudan **121** G6
Singahi India **96** D3
Singaingmyo Myanmar **78** B3
► Singapore country Asia **76** C2
known as Hsin-chia-p'o in Chinese; spelt
Singapura in Malay
asia [countries] — 64–67
► Singapore Sing. **76** C2
Capital of Singapore. Also known as Hsin-
chia-p'o; also spelt Singapura; historically
known as Tumasik.
Singapore r. Sing. **76** [inset]
Singapore, Strait of Indon./Sing. **76** C2
Singapura country Asia see Singapore
Singapura Sing. see Singapore
Singaraja Indon. **77** F5
Singareni India **94** D2
Singatoka Fiji see Sigatoka
Singave Wallis and Futuna Is see Sigave
Sing Buri Thai. **79** C5
Singen (Hohentwiel) Germany **48** F8
Singeorgiu de Pădure Romania see
Sângeorgiu de Pădure
Singeorz-Băi Romania see Sângeorz-Băi
Singera Moldova **58** K3
formerly spelt Sângera
Singgimtay China **88** E3
formerly known as Singim
Singh India **89** B4
Singhampton Canada **173** M6
Singida Tanz. **129** B6
Singida admin. reg. Tanz. **129** B6
Singidunum Srbija Yugo. see Belgrade
Singim China see Singgimtay
Singkaling Hkamti Myanmar **78** A2
Singkang Indon. **75** B4
Singkawang Indon. **77** E2
Singkep i. Indon. **76** D3
Singkil Indon. **76** B2
Singkuang Indon. **76** B2
Singleton Australia **147** F3
Singleton, Mount hill N.T. Australia **148** A4
Singleton, Mount hill W.A. Australia **151** B6
Singoli India **96** B4
Singon Myanmar **78** A3
Singora Thai. see Songkhla
Sin'gosan N. Korea see Kosan
Singou, Réserve Totale du nature res.
Burkina **125** F4
Singra India **95** F4
Singu Myanmar **78** A3
Singureni Romania **58** G4
Sin'gye N. Korea **83** B5
Sinhala country Asia see Sri Lanka
Sinharaja Forest Reserve nature res.
Sri Lanka **94** D5
Sinhüng N. Korea **83** B4
Siniloan Phil. **74** B3
Sining China see Xining
Sinio, Gunung mt. Indon. **75** A3
Siniscola Sardegna Italy **57** B8
Sini Vrükh mt. Bulg. **58** D7
Sinj Croatia **56** I5
Sinjai Indon. **75** B4
Sinjär Iraq **107** E3
Sinjär, Jabal mt. Iraq **107** E3
Sinkat Sudan **121** H5
Sinkiang aut. reg. China see
Xinjiang Uygur Zizhiqu
Sinkiang Uighur Autonomous Region
aut. reg. China see Xinjiang Uygur Zizhiqu
Sinking Spring U.S.A. **176** B6
Sinkyevichy Belarus **42** I9
Sinmamary Fr. Guiana **199** H3
Sinmi-do i. N. Korea **83** B5
Sinnamahoning U.S.A. **176** G4
Sinnar India **94** B2
Şinnār, Khashm hill Saudi Arabia **109** O8
Sinneh Iran see Sanandaj
Sinn el Kaddāb esc. Egypt **121** F4
Sinnemahoning U.S.A. **176** G4
Sinni r. Italy **57** I8
Sinnicolau Mare Romania see
Sânnicolau Mare
Sinnūris Egypt **108** B8
Sinoia Zimbabwe see Chinhoyi
Sinoie, Lacul lag. Romania **58** J4
Sinole Latvia **42** H4
Sinop Brazil **201** G2
Sinop Turkey **106** C2
historically known as Sinope
Sinope Turkey see Sinop
Sinoquipe Mex. **184** C2
Sinp'a N. Korea **82** E4
Sinp'a N. Korea **83** C4
Sinp'yông N. Korea **83** B5
Sinsang N. Korea **83** B5
Sinsheim Germany **48** F6
Sintang Indon. **77** F2
Sint-Laureins Belgium **51** J1

► Sint Maarten i. Neth. Antilles **187** H3
Part of the Netherlands Antilles. The
northern part of the island is the French
territory of St Martin.

Sint Nicolaas Aruba **187** F4
Sint-Niklaas Belgium **51** K1
also known as St Nicolas
Sinton U.S.A. **179** C6
Sintsovo Rus. Fed. **43** R5
Sint-Vith Belgium **51** M2
Sinú r. Col. **198** C2
Sinüiju N. Korea **82** I9
Sinujiif Somalia **128** F2
Sinyaya r. Rus. Fed. **43** J4
Siocon Phil. **74** B5
Siófok Hungary **49** P9
Sioma Zambia **127** D9
Sioma Ngwezi National Park Zambia
127 D9
Sion Switz. **51** N6
Siorapaluk Greenland **165** L2
Sioule r. France **51** J6
Sioux Center U.S.A. **178** C3
Sioux City U.S.A. **178** C3
Sioux Falls U.S.A. **178** C3
Sioux Lookout Canada **168** B3
Sipacate Guat. **185** H6
Sipalay Phil. **74** B4
Sipang, Tanjong pt Sarawak Malaysia **77** E2
Siphageni S. Africa see Flagstaff
Siping China **82** B4
Sipiwesk Canada **167** L4
Sipiwesk Lake Canada **167** L4
Siple, Mount Antarctica **222** P2
Siple Coast Antarctica **223** N1
Siple Island Antarctica **222** P2
Sipolilo Zimbabwe see Guruve
Sipora i. Indon. **76** B3
Siq, Wādī al watercourse Egypt **108** D8
Siqirah Yemen **105** F5
Siqueira Campos Brazil **206** D10
Siquijor Phil. **74** B4
Siquijor i. Phil. **74** B4
Siquisique Venez. **198** D2
Sir r. Pak. **101** G6
Sira India **94** C3
Sira Norway **45** I4
Şïr Abū Nu'āyr i. U.A.E. **105** F2
Si Racha Thai. **79** C5
Siracusa Sicilia Italy see Syracuse
Siraha Nepal see Sirha
Sirajganj Bangl. **97** F4
Sir Alexander, Mount Canada **166** F4
Siran Turkey **107** D2
Sirathu India **97** D4
Sir Bani Yās i. U.A.E. **105** F2
Sircilla India see Sirsilla
Sirdaryo r. Asia see Syrdar'ya
Sirdaryo Uzbek. see Syrdar'ya
Sirdaryo Wiloyati admin. div. Uzbek. see
Syrdar'inskaya Oblast'
Sirdingka China see Lhari
Sire Tanz. **129** A6
Sir Edward Pellew Group is Australia
148 C2
Siren U.S.A. **172** A5
Siret r. Romania **58** J3
Sir Graham Moore Islands Australia
150 D2
Sirha Nepal **97** E4
formerly spelt Siraha
Sirhān, Wādī as watercourse
Jordan/Saudi Arabia **109** I6
Sirhind India **96** C3
Siri, Cape P.N.G. **149** G1
Siri Romania **58** C2
Şîrîk Iran **100** D5
Sirik, Tanjong pt Sarawak Malaysia **77** E2
Sirikit Reservoir Thai. **78** C4
Sirina r. Greece see Syrna
Siritoi r. Pak. **101** G4
Sirjā Iran **101** E5
Sir James MacBrien, Mount Canada
166 F2
Sîrjän Iran **100** C4
Sîrjän salt flat Iran **100** C4
Sir Joseph Banks Group Conservation
Park nature res. Australia **146** C3
Sirkka Fin. **44** N2
Sirmaur India **96** D4
formerly spelt Sirmur
Sirmium Vojvodina, Srbija Yugo. see
Sremska Mitrovica
Sirmour India see Sirmaur
Sirmur India see Sirmaur
Şırnak Turkey **107** F3
Sirohi India **96** B4
Sironcha India **94** D2
Sironj India **96** C4
Síros i. Greece see Syros
Sirotsina Belarus **43** K6
Siroua, Jbel mt. Morocco **122** D3
Sirpur India **94** C2
Sirrayn Island Saudi Arabia **104** C4
Sirrei Eth. **128** D3
Sirretta Peak U.S.A. **182** F6
Sirri, Jazireh-ye i. Iran **100** C4
Sirsa India **96** C3
Sir Sandford, Mount Canada **166** G5
Sirs el Laiyāna Egypt **108** B7
Sirsi Karnataka India **94** B3
Sirsi Uttar Pradesh India **96** C3
Sirsilla India **94** C2
formerly spelt Sircilla
Sirte Libya **120** C2
also spelt Surt
Sirte, Gulf of Libya **120** C2
also known as Surt, Khalij

Sir Thomas, Mount hill Australia **146** A1
Siruguppa India **94** C3
Sirupa r. Mex. **181** E7
Sirur Karnataka India **94** B2
Sirur Maharashtra India **94** B2
Sirutiškis Lith. **42** E6
Širvan Turkey **107** E3
Širvel India **94** C3
Širvintos Lith. **42** F6
Şirwāh Yemen **104** D5
Şirwān r. Iraq **107** F4
Sir Wilfrid Laurier, Mount Canada **166** G4
Sir William Thompson Range hills Australia
149 D2
Siryan Iran **100** D3
Sis Turkey see Kozan
Sisak Croatia **56** I3
historically known as Siscia
Sisaket Thai. **79** D5
Sisal Mex. **185** H4
Sisante Spain **55** I5
Siscia Croatia see Sisak
Sishen S. Africa **132** H4
Sishilipu China **85** E5
Sisian Armenia **107** F3
Sisimiut Greenland **165** N3
also known as Holsteinsborg
Sisipuk Lake Canada **167** K4
Sisikwit Bay U.S.A. **172** E3
Sisogüichic Mex. **184** D3
Sisophon Cambodia **79** C5
Sisquoc r. U.S.A. **182** D7
Sissach Switz. **51** N5
Sisseton U.S.A. **178** C2
Sissili r. Burkina **125** E4
Sissonville U.S.A. **176** D7
Sîstân reg. Iran **101** F4
also spelt Seistan
Sistan, Daryācheh-ye marsh Afgh. **101** E4
Sister Bay U.S.A. **172** F5
Sisteron France **51** L8
Sisters U.S.A. **180** B3
Sistersville U.S.A. **176** E6
Sisto r. Italy **56** F7
Sit' r. Rus. Fed. **43** S3
Sitalike Tanz. **129** A7
Sitamarhi India **97** E4
Sitamau India **96** B5
Sitampiky Madag. **131** [inset] J3
Sitapur India **96** D4
Siteia Greece **59** H13
formerly spelt Sitía
Sithonia pen. Greece **59** E8
Sitía Greece see Siteia
Sitian China **84** B3
Sitila Moz. **131** G4
Siting China **87** C3
Sitio da Abadia Brazil **202** C5
Sitio do Mato Brazil **202** D5
Sitka India **89** D7
Sitka U.S.A. **164** F4
Sitnica r. Yugo. **58** B6
Sitno mt. Slovakia **49** P7
Sitnya r. Rus. Fed. **43** K4
Sitra oasis Egypt **121** E2
Sitsyenyets Belarus **43** K6
Sittang r. Myanmar **78** B4
also spelt Sittaung or Sittoung
Sittard Neth. **48** C5
Sittaung Myanmar **78** A2
Sittaung r. Myanmar see Sittang
Sittoung r. Myanmar see Sittang
Sittwe Myanmar **78** A3
formerly known as Akyab
Situbondo Indon. **77** F4
Siu A Chau i. Hong Kong China **87** [inset]
Siumpang, Rubha an t- hd U.K. see
Tiumpan Head
Siumpu i. Indon. **75** B4
Siuna Nicaragua **186** B4
Siuntio Fin. **42** F1
Siuri India **97** E5
formerly spelt Suri
Siva Rus. Fed. **40** J4
Sivaganga India **94** C4
Sivakasi India **94** C4
Sivaki Rus. Fed. **82** B1
Sivand Iran **100** C4
Sivas Turkey **107** D3
historically known as Sebasteia
Sivaslı Turkey **106** B3
Siverek Turkey **107** D3
Sivers l. Latvia **42** H5
Siverskiy Rus. Fed. **43** L2
Sivers'kyy Donets' r. Rus. Fed./Ukr. see
Severskiy Donets
Sivomaskinskiy Rus. Fed. **40** L2
Sivrice Turkey **107** D3
Sivrihisar Turkey **106** B3
Sivukile S. Africa **133** N3
Siwa Egypt **121** E2
Siwa Indon. **75** B3
Siwalik Range mts India/Nepal **96** C3
Siwan India **97** E4
Siwana India **96** B4
Siwa Oasis Egypt **121** E2
Six Cross Roads Barbados **187** I4
Six-Fours-les-Plages France **51** L9
Sixian China **87** F1
Six Lakes U.S.A. **173** H7
Sixtymile Canada **166** A1
Siyabuswa S. Africa **133** N2
Siyang China **87** F1
also known as Zhongxing
Siyathemba S. Africa **133** M3
Siyathuthuka S. Africa **133** O2
Siyäzän Azer. **107** G2
also spelt Siazan'; formerly known as
Kyzyl-Burun
Siyitang China **85** F3
Siyom r. India **78** A1
Siyuni Iran **100** C3
Siziwang Qi China see Ulan Hua
Sizyabsk Rus. Fed. **40** J2
Sjælland i. Denmark see Zealand
Sjaunja naturreservat nature res. Sweden
44 L2
Sjenica Srbija Yugo. **58** B5
Sjoa Norway **45** J3
Sjöbo Sweden **45** K5
Sjøholt Norway **44** I3
Sjona sea chan. Norway **44** K2
Sjøvegan Norway **44** L1
Sjulsmark Sweden **44** M2
Sjuoyane i. Svalbard **38** C1
Skäckerfjällen mts Sweden **44** K3
Skadarsko Jezero l. nat. park Yugo. **58** A6
Skadovs'k Ukr. **41** E7
Skælsør Denmark **45** J5
Skærbæk Denmark **45** I5
Skærfjorden inlet Greenland **165** R2
Skaftafell nat. park Iceland **44** [inset] C2
Skaftáros r. mouth Iceland **44** [inset] C2
Skagafjörður inlet Iceland **44** [inset] B2
Skagaheiði reg. Iceland **44** [inset] B2
Skagen Denmark **45** J4
Skagern l. Sweden **45** K4
Skagerrak strait Denmark/Norway **45** J4
Skagit r. U.S.A. **180** B2
Skagit Mountain Canada **166** F5
Skagway U.S.A. **164** E3
Skaidi Norway **44** N1
Skaidiškės Lith. **42** G7
Skala Notio Aigaio Greece **59** H11
Skala Peloponnisos Greece **59** D12
Skala Kallonis Greece **59** H9
Skaland Norway **44** L1
Skalino Rus. Fed. **43** V3

Skallelv Norway **44** O1
Skalmodal Sweden **44** K2
Skanderborg Denmark **45** J4
Skåne county Sweden **45** K5
Skaneateles U.S.A. **177** I3
Skaneateles Lake U.S.A. **177** I3
Skånevik Norway **45** I4
Skansholm Sweden **44** L2
Skara Sweden **45** K4
Skara Brae tourist site U.K. **46** I4
Skarberget Norway **44** L1
Skärblacka Sweden **45** K4
Skärgårdshavets Nationalpark nat. park
Fin. **45** M4
also known as Saaristomeren Kansallispuisto
Skarnes Norway **45** J3
Skärplinge Sweden **45** L3
Skärsjövålen Sweden **45** K3
Skarstind mt. Norway **45** J3
Skarszewy Poland **49** N1
Skarvedalsseggen mt. Norway **45** J3
Skarvsjöby Sweden **44** L2
Skaryszew Poland **49** S4
Skaudvilė Lith. **42** D6
Skaulo Sweden **44** M2
Skaune Belarus **45** N4
Skaupsjøen-Hardangerjøkulen park
Norway **45** I3
Skawa r. Poland **49** Q5
Skawina Poland **49** Q6
Skaymat W. Sahara **122** B4
Skeena r. Canada **166** D4
Skeena Mountains Canada **166** D3
Skegness U.K. **47** M10
Skeiðarársandur sand area Iceland
44 [inset] C2
Skeleton Coast Game Park nature res.
Namibia **130** B3
Skellefteå Sweden **44** M2
Skellefteälven r. Sweden **44** M2
Skellefteebukten b. Sweden **44** M2
Skelleftehamn Sweden **44** M2
Skeppshamn Sweden **44** L3
Skerries Rep. of Ireland **47** F10
Skhimatárion Greece see Schimatari
Skhira Tunisia **123** H2
Škilbheni Latvia **42** I4
formerly known as Philippeville
Škinari, Akra pt Greece **59** B11
Skinnskatteberg Sweden **45** K4
Skio Jammu and Kashmir **96** C2
Skipskog S. Africa **132** E11
Skipton Australia **147** D4
Skipton U.K. **47** J10
Skiropoúla i. Greece see Skyropoula
Skíros i. Greece see Skyros
Skive Denmark **45** J4
Skjálfandafljót r. Iceland **44** [inset] C2
Skjálfandi b. Iceland **44** [inset] C2
Skjelatinden mt. Norway **44** K2
Skjellbreid Norway **44** K2
Skjellinhovde hill Norway **45** J3
Skjerkeknuten hill Norway **45** I4
Skjern Denmark **45** J5
Skjern r. Denmark **45** J5
Skjerstadfjorden inlet Norway **44** K2
Skjervøy Norway **44** M1
Skjolden Norway **45** I3
Sknyatino Rus. Fed. **43** S4
Skobelev Uzbek. see Fergana
Skobeleva, Pik mt. Kyrg. **103** H5
Skocjanske Jame tourist site Slovenia
56 F3
Skoenmakerskop S. Africa **133** J11
Škofja Loka Slovenia **56** F2
Skog Sweden **45** L3
Skoganvarre Norway **44** N1
Skogfoss Norway **44** O1
Skoki Poland **49** O3
Skokie U.S.A. **172** F8
Skol' Kazakh. **103** I2
Sköllersta Sweden **45** K4
Skomvær i. Norway **44** J2
Skopelos Greece **59** E9
Skopelos i. Greece **59** E9
Skopia hill Greece **59** D9
Skopin Rus. Fed. **43** U8

► Skopje Macedonia **58** C7
Capital of Macedonia. Also spelt Skoplje;
historically known as Scupi.

Skoplje Macedonia see Skopje
Skopunarfjørður sea chan. Faroe Is **46** F1
Skórcz Poland **49** P2
Skorodnoye Rus. Fed. **41** F6
Skørping Denmark **45** J4
Skotoussa Greece **58** E7
Skotterud Norway **45** K4
Skoutari Greece **58** E7
Skoutaros Greece **59** H9
Skövde Sweden **45** K4
Skovorodino Rus. Fed. **82** A1
Skowhegan U.S.A. **177** P1
Skriveri Latvia **42** G5
Škrlatica mt. Slovenia **56** F2
Skröven Sweden **44** M2
Skrunda Latvia **42** D5
Skrwa r. Poland **49** Q3
Skrydlyeva Belarus **43** L6
Skúgvoy i. Faroe Is **46** F2
Skukum, Mount Canada **166** C2
Skukuza S. Africa **133** P1
Skuleskogens nationalpark nat. park
Sweden **44** L3
Skull Peak U.S.A. **183** H5
Skull Valley U.S.A. **183** L7
Skultuna Sweden **45** L4
Skunk r. U.S.A. **174** B3
Skuodas Lith. **42** C5
Skuratovskiy Rus. Fed. **43** S7
Skurup Sweden **45** K5
Skūt r. Bulg. **58** E5
Skutskär Sweden **45** L3
Skwentna r. U.S.A. **164** E3
Skwierzyna Poland **49** M3
Skye i. U.K. **46** F6
Skykula hill Norway **45** I4
Skyring, Seno b. Chile **205** B9
Skyropoula i. Greece **59** F10
also spelt Skiropoúla
Skyros i. Greece **59** F10
Skytrain Ice Rise Antarctica **222** S1
Slabodka Belarus **42** I6
Slættaratindur hill Faroe Is **46** F1
Slagelse Denmark **45** J5
Slagnäs Sweden **44** L2
Slamet, Gunung vol. Indon. **77** E4
Slaná r. Slovakia **49** R7

Slaney r. Rep. of Ireland **47** F11
Slănic Romania **58** G3
Slănic r. Romania **58** H3
Slănic Moldova Romania **58** H2
Slantsy Rus. Fed. **43** J2
Slaný Czech Rep. **49** L5
Šlapaberžė Lith. **42** E6
Slapovi Krke nat. park Croatia **56** H5
Slashers Reefs Australia **149** E3
Slate Islands Canada **168** C4
Slatina Croatia **56** J3
Slatina Romania **58** F4
Slatina r. Slovakia **49** Q7
Slatina-Timiş Romania **58** D3
Slaty Fork U.S.A. **176** E7
Slautnoye Rus. Fed. **39** Q3
Slave r. Canada **167** H2
Slave Coast Africa **125** F5
Slave Lake Canada **167** H4
Slave Point Canada **167** G2
Slavgorod Belarus see Slawharad
Slavgorod Rus. Fed. **43** R5
Slavonia reg. Croatia **56** J3
also spelt Slavonija
Slavonija reg. Croatia see Slavonia
Slavonska Požega Croatia see Požega
Slavonski Brod Croatia **56** K3
Slavsk Rus. Fed. **42** C7
historically known as Heinrichswalde
Slavuta Ukr. **41** C6
Slavutych Ukr. **41** D6
Slavyanka Kazakh. see Myrzakent
Slavyanka Rus. Fed. **82** C4
Slavyanovo Bulg. **58** F5
Slavyansk Ukr. see Slov"yans'k
Slavyanskaya Rus. Fed. see
Slavyansk-na-Kubani
Slavyansk-na-Kubani Rus. Fed. **41** F7
formerly known as Slavyanskaya
Sława Poland **49** N4
Slawharad Belarus **43** M8
also spelt Slavgorod
Sławno Poland **49** N1
Slayton U.S.A. **178** D3
Sleaford U.K. **47** L10
Sleaford Bay Australia **146** B3
Slea Head Rep. of Ireland **47** B11
Sleat, Sound of sea chan. U.K. **46** G6
Sled Lake Canada **167** J4
Sleeper Islands Canada **168** E1
Sleeping Bear Dunes National Lakeshore
nature res. U.S.A. **172** G6
Sleeping Bear Point U.S.A. **172** G6
Sleep Island Hong Kong China **87** [inset]
Sleman Indon. **77** F4
Sleptsovskaya Rus. Fed. **41** H8
formerly known as Ordzhonikidzevskaya
Slessor Glacier Antarctica **223** W1
Śleza hill Poland **49** N5
Slick Rock U.S.A. **183** P3
Sliddell U.S.A. **175** B6
Slide Mountain U.S.A. **177** K4
Slidre Norway **45** J3
Slieve Car hill Rep. of Ireland **47** C9
Slieve Donard hill U.K. **47** G9
Slieve Gamph hills Rep. of Ireland **47** C10
also known as Ox Mountains
Slieve Mish Mountains hills Rep. of Ireland
47 B11
Sligachan U.K. **46** F6
Sligeach Rep. of Ireland see Sligo
Sligo Rep. of Ireland **47** D9
also spelt Sligeach
Sligo U.S.A. **176** F4
Sligo Bay Rep. of Ireland **47** D9
Slipper Island N.Z. **152** J5
Slippery Rock U.S.A. **176** E4
Slīteres rezervāts nature res. Latvia **42** D4
Sliven Bulg. **58** H6
Slivo Pole Bulg. **58** H5
Slijeme mt. Croatia **56** H3
Sloan r. Canada **167** G1
Sloan U.S.A. **183** I6
Sloat U.S.A. **182** D2
Sloboda Rus. Fed. see Ezhva
Sloboda Rus. Fed. **41** G6
Slobodchikovo Rus. Fed. **40** I3
Slobodka Rus. Fed. **43** R9
Slobodskoy Rus. Fed. **40** I4
Slobodzeya Moldova see Slobozia
Slobozia Moldova **58** K2
formerly spelt Slobodzeya
Slobozia Romania **58** I4
Slobozia Bradului Romania **58** I3
Słomniki Poland **49** R5
Slonim Belarus **42** G8
Slough U.K. **47** L12
► Slovakia country Europe **49** P7
known as Slovensko in Slovakian
europe [countries] — 32–35
► Slovenia country Europe **56** G2
spelt Slovenija in Slovenian
europe [countries] — 32–35
Slovenia country Europe see Slovenia
Slovenj Gradec Slovenia **56** F1
Slovenska Bistrica Slovenia **56** G1
Slovenske Gorice hills Slovenia **56** H1
Slovenské Rudohorie mts Slovakia **49** Q7
Slovensko country Europe see Slovakia
Slovenský kras mts Slovakia **49** R7
Slovenský raj nat. park Slovakia **49** R7
Slov"yans'k Ukr. **41** F6
formerly known as Slavyansk
Słubice Poland **49** L3
Sluch r. Belarus **42** I9
Sluch r. Ukr. **53** H1
Sludka Rus. Fed. **40** I4
Slunj Croatia **56** H3
Słupca Poland **49** O3
Słupia r. Poland **49** N1
Słupsk Poland **49** O1
historically known as Stolp
Slussfors Sweden **44** L2
Slutsk Belarus **42** I8
Slyne Head Rep. of Ireland **47** B10
Slyudyanka Rus. Fed. **84** D1
Smackover U.S.A. **179** D5
Småländsstenar Sweden **45** K4
Small Point U.S.A. **177** P2
Smallwood Reservoir Canada **169** H2
Smalowka Belarus **42** J8
Smalyavichy Belarus **42** J7
also spelt Smolevichi
Smarhon' Belarus **42** H7
also spelt Smorgon'
Smartt Syndicate Dam resr S. Africa
132 H7
Smeaton Canada **167** J4
Smederevo Srbija Yugo. **58** B4
historically known as Semendrie
Smederevska Palanka Srbija Yugo. **58** B4
Smeeni Romania **58** H3
Smela Ukr. see Smila
Smelror Norway **44** O1
Smethport U.S.A. **176** G4
Smigiel Poland **49** N3
Smila Ukr. **41** D6
formerly known as Smela
Smilavichy Belarus **42** J8
Smiltene Latvia **42** G4
Smiltiņu kalns hill Latvia **42** D5
Smines Norway **44** K1
Smirnykh Rus. Fed. **82** F2

Smith Canada **167** H4
Smith r. MT U.S.A. **180** E3
Smith r. VA U.S.A. **176** F9
Smith Arm b. Canada **166** F1
Smith Bay U.S.A. **164** D2
Smith Center U.S.A. **178** C4
Smithers Canada **166** E4
Smithers Landing Canada **166** E4
Smithfield S. Africa **133** K7
Smithfield NC U.S.A. **174** E5
Smithfield UT U.S.A. **180** E4
Smithfield VA U.S.A. **177** I9
Smith Glacier Antarctica **222** Q1
Smith Island Antarctica **222** T2
Smith Island U.S.A. **95** G3
Smith Island MD U.S.A. **177** I7
Smith Island VA U.S.A. **177** J8
Smithland U.S.A. **174** B4
Smith Mountain Lake U.S.A. **176** F8
Smith River Canada **166** E3
Smithsburg U.S.A. **176** H6
Smiths Falls Canada **168** F4
Smith Sound sea chan. Canada/Greenland
165 L2
Smithton Australia **147** E5
Smithville TN U.S.A. **174** C5
Smithville WV U.S.A. **176** D6
Smitskraal S. Africa **133** I10
Smjörfjöll mts Iceland **44** [inset] D2
Smoke Creek Desert U.S.A. **182** E1
Smoky r. Canada **166** G3
Smoky Bay Australia **146** B3
Smoky Cape Australia **147** G2
Smoky Falls Canada **168** D3
Smoky Hill r. U.S.A. **178** B4
Smoky Hill, North Fork r. U.S.A. **178** B4
Smoky Hills KS U.S.A. **178** C4
Smoky Lake Canada **167** H4
Smoky Mountains U.S.A. **180** D4
Smøla i. Norway **44** I3
Smolenka Rus. Fed. **102** B2
Smolensk Rus. Fed. **43** N7
Smolenskaya Oblast' admin. div. Rus. Fed.
43 O7
English form Smolensk Oblast
Smolensk Oblast admin. div. Rus. Fed. see
Smolenskaya Oblast'
Smolensko-Moskovskaya Vozvyshennost'
hills Rus. Fed. **43** N7
Smolevichi Belarus see Smalyavichy
Smolikas mt. Greece **59** B8
Smolyan Bulg. **58** F7
Smolyoninovo Rus. Fed. **82** D4
Smooth Rock Falls Canada **168** D3
Smoothrock Lake Canada **168** B3
Smoothstone Lake Canada **167** J4
Smørfjord Norway **44** N1
Smorgon' Belarus see Smarhon'
Smotrova Buda Rus. Fed. **43** N9
Smyadovo Bulg. **58** I5
Smyley Island Antarctica **222** S2
Smyrna Turkey see İzmir
Smyrna DE U.S.A. **177** J6
Smyrna GA U.S.A. **175** C5
Smyrna TN U.S.A. **174** C5
Smyth, Canal sea chan. Chile **205** B8
Snæfell mt. Iceland **44** [inset] D2
Snaefell hill Isle of Man **47** H9
Snæfellsjökull ice cap Iceland **44** [inset] B2
Snæfellsnes pen. Iceland **44** [inset] B2
Snake r. Canada **166** C1
Snake r. NE U.S.A. **178** B3
Snake r. U.S.A. **180** C3
Snake Range mts U.S.A. **183** J2
Snake River Canada **166** F3
Snake River Plain U.S.A. **180** D4
Snare r. Canada **167** G2
Snare Lake Canada **167** J3
Snare Lakes Canada see Wekweti
Snares Islands N.Z. **145** F6
also known as Tini Heke
Snåsa Norway **44** K3
Snåsvatn l. Norway **44** K2
Sneedville U.S.A. **176** B9
Sneek Neth. **48** C2
Sneem Rep. of Ireland **47** C12
Sneeuberg mt. S. Africa **132** I7
Sneeuberge mts S. Africa **133** I8
Snegamook Lake Canada **169** I2
Snegurovka Ukr. see Tetiyiv
Snelling U.S.A. **182** D4
Snèpele Latvia **42** C5
Snezhed' r. Rus. Fed. **43** R8
Snezhnogorsk Rus. Fed. **39** J3
Snēžka mt. Czech Rep. **49** M5
Snēžnik mt. Slovenia **56** G3
Śniardwy, Jezioro l. Poland **49** S2
Sniečkus Lith. see Visaginas
Sniežka mt. Czech Rep. see Snēžka
Śnieżnik mt. Poland **49** N5
Snihurivka Ukr. **41** E7
Snina Slovakia **49** T7
Snohetta mt. Norway **44** J3
Snohomish U.S.A. **180** B3
Snønuten mt. Norway **45** I4
Snøpoti' r. Rus. Fed. **43** O9
Snov r. Ukr. **43** N9
Snova r. Rus. Fed. **43** R9
Snova r. Rus. Fed. **43** T9
Snovsk Ukr. see Shchors
Snow Belarus **42** I7
Snowbird Lake Canada **167** K2
Snowcrest Mountain Canada **167** G5
Snowdon mt. U.K. **47** H10
also known as Yr Wyddfa
Snowdonia National Park U.K. **47** I11
Snowdrift Canada see Łutselk'e
Snowdrift r. Canada **167** I2
Snowflake U.S.A. **183** N7
Snow Hill MD U.S.A. **177** J7
Snow Hill NC U.S.A. **174** E5
Snow Lake Canada **167** K4
Snowtown Australia **146** C3
Snow Water Lake U.S.A. **183** J1
Snowy r. Australia **147** F4
Snowy Mountain U.S.A. **177** K2
Snowy Mountains Australia **147** F4
Snudy, Vozyera l. Belarus **42** I6
Snug Corner Bahamas **187** F2
Snug Harbour Nfld. Canada **169** K2
Snug Harbour Ont. Canada **173** M5
Snyder OK U.S.A. **179** C5
Snyder TX U.S.A. **179** B5
Snyderspoort pass S. Africa **132** E8
Snykhovo Rus. Fed. **43** R8
Soahany Madag. **131** [inset] J3
Soaigh i. U.K. see Soay
Soalala Madag. **131** [inset] J3
Soamanonga Madag. **131** [inset] J4
Soanierana-Ivongo Madag. **131** [inset] K3
Soan-kundo is S. Korea **83** B6
Soata Col. **198** C3
Soavinandriana Madag. **131** [inset] J3
Soay i. U.K. **46** D6
also spelt Soaigh
Sobaek-sanmaek mts S. Korea **83** B6
Sobaek-san National Park S. Korea **83** C5
Sobat r. Sudan **128** A2
Sobēslav Czech Rep. **49** L6
Sobger r. Indon. **73** J7
Sobinka Rus. Fed. **43** V6
Sobolevo Rus. Fed. **43** T6
Sobo-san mt. Japan **91** B8
Sobradinho Brazil **206** F2
Sobradinho, Barragem de resr Brazil
202 D4
Sobrado Bahia Brazil **202** D4
Sobrado Pará Brazil **199** H5
Sobral Brazil **202** D2
Sobrance Slovakia **49** T7
Soča r. Italy see Isonzo

Soča r. Slovenia 56 F3
Sochaczew Poland 49 R3
Sochi Rus. Fed. 41 F8
Sŏch'ŏn S. Korea 83 B5
Sochos Greece 58 E8
also spelt Sokhós
Société, Archipel de la is Fr. Polynesia see Society Islands
▶Society Islands Fr. Polynesia 221 H7
also known as Société, Archipel de la
oceania [issues] ▶ 140–141
Socol Romania 58 C4
Socompa Chile 200 C6
Soconusco, Sierra de mts Mex. see Madre, Sierra
Socorro Brazil 206 G9
Socorro Col. 198 C3
Socorro U.S.A. 181 F6
Socorro, Isla i. Mex. 184 C5
Socota Peru 198 B6
Socotra i. Yemen 105 F5
also spelt Suquṭrā
Socovos Spain 55 J6
Soc Trăng Vietnam 79 D6
formerly known as Khan Hung
Socuéllamos Spain 55 I5
Soda Lake CA U.S.A. 182 E6
Soda Lake CA U.S.A. 183 H6
Sodankylä Fin. 44 N2
Soda Plains Aksai Chin 89 B5
Soda Springs U.S.A. 180 E4
Söderhamn Sweden 45 L3
Söderköping Sweden 45 L4
Södermanland county Sweden 45 L4
Södertälje Sweden 45 L4
Sodiri Sudan 121 F6
Sodium S. Africa 132 H7
Sodo Eth. 128 C3
Södra Kvarken strait Fin./Sweden 45 L3
Sodus U.S.A. 177 H2
Sodwana Bay National Park S. Africa 133 Q4
Soë Indon. 75 C5
Soekmekaar S. Africa 131 F4
Soela väin sea chan. Estonia 42 D3
Soerabaia Indon. see Surabaya
Soest Germany 48 F4
Soetdoring Nature Reserve S. Africa 133 K5
Soetendalsvlei l. S. Africa 132 D11
Sofades Greece 59 D9
Sofala Moz. 131 G4
Sofala prov. Moz. 131 G3
formerly known as Beira
Sofala, Baía de b. Moz. 131 G4

▶Sofia Bulg. 58 E6
Capital of Bulgaria. Also spelt Sofiya; historically known as Sardica or Serdica or Sredets.

Sofia r. Madag. 131 [inset] J2
Sofiko Greece 59 E11
Sofiya Bulg. see Sofia
Sofiyevka Ukr. see Vil'nyans'k
Sofiysk Khabarovskiy Kray Rus. Fed. 82 D1
Sofiysk Khabarovskiy Kray Rus. Fed. 82 E2
Soforog Rus. Fed. 44 O2
Sofrino Rus. Fed. 43 S5
Softa Kalesi tourist site Turkey 108 D1
Sōfu-gan i. Japan 81 O7
English form Lot's Wife
Sog China 89 F6
also known as Garqêntang
Sogamoso Col. 198 C3
Sogat China 88 D3
formerly spelt Süget
Sogda Rus. Fed. 82 D2
Sogma China 89 C5
Søgne Norway 45 I4
Sognefjorden inlet Norway 45 I3
Sogn og Fjordane county Norway 45 I3
Sogo Rus. Fed. 39 M2
Sogod Phil. 74 C4
Sogod Bay Phil. 74 C4
Sogo Hills Kenya 128 C4
Sogolle well Chad 120 B6
Sogo Nur l. China 84 D3
Sogozha r. Rus. Fed. 43 U3
Söğüt Turkey 106 B2
Söğüt Dağı mts Turkey 106 B3
Sŏgwip'o S. Korea 83 B6
Sohâg Egypt 121 F3
also spelt Sūhāj
Sohagpur India 96 C5
Sohalinskiy Kazakh. 103 G2
Sohan r. Pak. 101 G3
Sohano P.N.G. 145 E2
Sohar Oman see Şuḩār
Sohela India 97 D5
Sohna India 96 C3
Sohng Gwe, Khao hill Myanmar/Thai. 79 B5
Soignies Belgium 51 K2
Soila China 86 A2
Soini Fin. 44 N3
Soissons France 51 J3
Sōja Japan 91 C7
Sojat India 96 B4
Sojat Road India 96 B4
Sojoton Point Phil. 74 B4
Sok r. Rus. Fed. 41 I5
Sokch'o S. Korea 83 C5
Söke Turkey 106 A3
Sokele Dem. Rep. Congo 127 E7
Sokhondo, Gora mt. Rus. Fed. 85 F1
Sokhor, Gora mt. Rus. Fed. 85 E1
Sokhós Greece see Sochos
Sokhumi Georgia 107 E2
also known as Aq"a; also spelt Sukhumi; historically known as Dioscurias or Sukhum-Kale
Sokiryany Ukr. see Sokyryany
Sokkuram Grotto tourist site S. Korea 90 A7
Soknedal Norway 44 J3
Sokobanja Srbija Yugo. 58 C5
Sokodé Togo 125 F4
Soko Islands Hong Kong China 87 [inset]
also known as Shekka Ch'ün-Tao
Sokol Rus. Fed. 82 F3
Sokol Rus. Fed. 43 V2
Sokolac Bos.-Herz. 56 K5
Sokółka Poland 49 U2
Sokol'niki Tul'skaya Oblast' Rus. Fed. 43 T7
Sokol'niki Tverskaya Oblast' Rus. Fed. 43 P5
Sokolo Mali 124 D3
Sokolov Czech Rep. 49 J5
Sokolovka Rus. Fed. 90 C3
Sokołów Małopolski Poland 49 T5
Sokołów Podlaski Poland 49 T3
Sokolozero, Ozero l. Rus. Fed. 44 O2
Sokone Senegal 124 A3
Sokosti hill Fin. 44 O1
Sokoto Nigeria 125 G3
Sokoto r. Nigeria 125 G4
Sokoto state Nigeria 125 G3
Sokourala Guinea 124 C4
Sokyryany Ukr. 41 C6
also spelt Sokiryany
Sola Cuba 186 D2
Sola r. Poland 49 Q6
Sola i. Tonga see Ata
Solan India 96 C3
Solana Beach U.S.A. 183 G9
Solander Island N.Z. 153 A14
Solanet Arg. 204 F5
Solano Phil. 74 B2
Solano Venez. 199 E4
Solapur India 94 B2
formerly spelt Sholapur
Soldado Bartra Peru 198 C5
Soldotna U.S.A. 164 D3
Solec Kujawski Poland 49 P2
Soledad Arg. 204 E3
Soledad U.S.A. 182 C5
Soledad Venez. 199 F2
Soledad de Doblado Mex. 185 F5
Soledade Brazil 198 D6
Solen mt. Norway 45 J3
Solenoye Rus. Fed. 41 G7
Solenzo Burkina 124 D3
Solfjellsjøen Norway 44 K2
Solginskiy Rus. Fed. 40 G3
Solhan Turkey 107 E3
Soligalich Rus. Fed. 40 G4
Soligorsk Belarus see Salihorsk
Solihull U.K. 47 K11
Solikamsk Rus. Fed. 40 K4
Sol'-Iletsk Rus. Fed. 102 C2
Soliman Tunisia 57 C12
Solimón, Punta pt Mex. 185 I5
Solingen Germany 48 E4
Solita Col. 198 C4
Solita Venez. 187 F5
Sol-Karmala Rus. Fed. see Severnoye
Sölktäler nature res. Austria 49 K8
Sollefteå Sweden 44 L3
Sollentuna Sweden 45 L4
Sóller Spain 55 N5
Sollerön Sweden 45 K3
Solling hills Germany 48 G4
Solnechnogorsk Rus. Fed. 43 R5
Solnechnyy Rus. Fed. 82 E2
Solnechnyy Rus. Fed. see Gornyy
Solo r. Java Indon. 77 F4
Solo r. Sulawesi Indon. 75 B3
Solofra Italy 57 G8
Solok Indon. 76 C3
Sololá Guat. 185 H6
Solomon U.S.A. 183 O9
Solomon r. U.S.A. 178 C4
Solomon, North Fork r. U.S.A. 178 C4
Solomon, South Fork r. U.S.A. 178 C4

▶Solomon Islands country S. Pacific Ocean 145 F2
4th largest and 5th most populous country in Oceania. Formerly known as British Solomon Islands.
oceania [countries] ▶ 138–139

Solomon Sea P.N.G./Solomon Is 145 E2
Solon China 85 I2
Solon U.S.A. 172 B9
Solor i. Indon. 75 B5
Solor, Kepulauan is Indon. 75 B5
Solotcha Rus. Fed. 43 U7
Solothurn Switz. 51 N5
Solovetskiy Rus. Fed. 40 E2
formerly known as Kreml'
Solovetskiye Ostrova is Rus. Fed. 40 E2
Solovetskoye Rus. Fed. 40 H4
Solov'yevo Rus. Fed. 43 N7
Solov'yevsk Mongolia 85 G1
Solov'yevsk Rus. Fed. 82 B1
Solsona Spain 55 M3
Solt Hungary 49 Q9
Šolta i. Croatia 56 I5
Solṭānābād Khorāsan Iran 100 D2
Solṭānābād Iran 101 D3
Solṭānābād Tehrān Iran 100 B3
Soltān-e Bakva Afgh. 101 E3
Soltānī, Khowr-e b. Iran 100 B4
Solṭanqolī Iran 100 A3
Soltau Germany 48 G3
Sol'tsy Rus. Fed. 43 L3
Soltüstik Qazaqstan Oblysy admin. div. Kazakh. see Severnyy Kazakhstan
Soltvadkert Hungary 49 Q9
Solunska Glava mt. Macedonia 58 C7
Solvang U.S.A. 182 D7
Solvay U.S.A. 177 I2
Sölvesborg Sweden 45 K4
Sol'vychegodsk Rus. Fed. 40 H3
Solway Firth est. U.K. 47 I9
Solwezi Zambia 127 E8
Sōma Japan 90 G6
Soma Turkey 106 A3
Somabhula Zimbabwe 131 F3
formerly spelt Somabula
Somabula Zimbabwe see Somabhula
Somali admin. reg. Eth. 128 D3
▶Somalia country Africa 128 E4
spelt Soomaaliya in Somali; long form Somali Republic
africa [countries] ▶ 114–117
Somali Republic country Africa see Somalia
Somanga Tanz. 129 C7
Somanya Ghana 125 E5
Sombang, Gunung mt. Indon. 77 G2
Sombo Angola 127 D7
Sombor Vojvodina, Srbija Yugo. 58 A3
also spelt Zombor
Sombrerete Mex. 184 E4
Sombrero i. Anguilla 187 H3
Sombrero Chile 205 C9
Sombrero Channel India 95 G5
Somdari India 96 B4
Somero Fin. 45 M3
Somerset KY U.S.A. 176 A8
Somerset MA U.S.A. 177 N4
Somerset MI U.S.A. 173 I8
Somerset OH U.S.A. 176 C6
Somerset PA U.S.A. 176 F6
Somerset East S. Africa 133 J9
Somerset Island Canada 165 J2
Somerset West S. Africa 132 C11
Somersworth U.S.A. 177 O2
Somerton U.S.A. 183 J9
Someru Estonia 42 H2
Somerville NJ U.S.A. 177 K5
Somerville TN U.S.A. 174 B5
Somerville Reservoir U.S.A. 179 C6
Someșan, Podișul plat. Romania 58 E2
Someșu Cald r. Romania 58 E2
Someșul Mare r. Romania 58 E1
Someșu Mic r. Romania 58 E1
Somesville U.S.A. 177 Q1
Someydeh Iran 100 A3
also spelt Samaida
Somino Rus. Fed. 43 P2
Somkele S. Africa 133 Q5
Sommarøy Norway 44 L1
Somme r. France 50 H2
Sommen l. Sweden 45 K4
Sömmerda Germany 48 I4
Somnath India 94 A1
also known as Patan
Somogyszob Hungary 49 O9
Somosomo Fiji 145 H3
Somotillo Nicaragua 186 B4
Somoto Nicaragua 186 B4
Somovo Orlovskaya Oblast' Rus. Fed. 43 Q9
Somovo Tul'skaya Oblast' Rus. Fed. 43 R8
Sompeta India 95 E2
Sompolno Poland 49 P3
Somport, Col du pass France/Spain 55 K2
Šomrda hill Yugo. 58 C4
Somuncurá, Mesa Volcánica de plat. Arg. 204 D6
Somvarpet India 94 B3
Son r. India 96 E4
Soná Panama 186 C6
Sonag China see Zêkog
Sonai r. India 97 G4
Sonai r. India 97 G4
Sonakhan India 97 D5
Sonala India 94 C1
Sonaly Kazakh. 103 G2
Sonamukhi India 97 E5
Sonapur India 95 D1
Sonari India 97 G4
Sŏnch'ŏn N. Korea 83 B5
Sondalo Italy 56 C2
Sønderå r. Denmark 48 F1
Sønderborg Denmark 45 J5
Sondershausen Germany 48 H4
Sønderup Denmark 45 J4
Søndre Strømfjord Greenland see Kangerlussuaq
Søndre Strømfjord inlet Greenland see Kangerlussuaq
Søndre Upernavik Greenland see Upernavik Kujalleq
Sondrio Italy 56 B2
Sonepet India 94 C2
Song Nigeria 125 I4
Songa Indon. 75 C3
Songad India 96 A5
Songbai China see Shennongjia
Songbu China 87 E2
Sông Cau Vietnam 79 E5
Songcheng China see Xiapu
Sông Đa, Hô resr Vietnam 78 D3
Songea Tanz. 129 B7
Sŏnggan N. Korea 83 B4
Songhua Hu resr China 82 B4
Songhua Jiang r. China 82 D3
English form Sungari
Songjiachuan China see Wubu
Songjiang Jilin China 82 C4
formerly known as Antu
Songjiang Shanghai China 87 G2
formerly known as Sungkiang
Songjianghe China 82 B4
Sŏngjin N. Korea see Kimch'aek
Sŏngju S. Korea 91 A7
Songkan China 86 C2
Songkhla Thai. 79 C7
also known as Singora
Song Khram, Mae Nam r. Thai. 78 D4
Songköl l. Kyrg. 103 H4
also known as Sonkël', Ozero
Songling China 85 I2
Song Ling mts China 85 H3
Songmai China see Dêrong
Songming China 86 B3
also known as Songyang
Sŏngnam S. Korea 83 B5
Songnim N. Korea 83 B5
Songni-san National Park S. Korea 83 B5
Songo Angola 127 B6
Songo Moz. 131 G2
Songololo Dem. Rep. Congo 127 B6
Songololo Dem. Rep. Congo see Mbanza-Ngungu
Songpan China 86 B1
also known as Jin'an or Sungqu
Songsak India 97 F4
Sŏngsan S. Korea 83 B6
Songshan China see Ziyun
Song Shan mt. China 87 E1
Songtao China 87 D2
Songxi China 87 F3
also known as Songyuan
Songxian China 87 E1
Songyang China see Songming
Songyuan China see Songxi
Songyuan China 82 B3
also known as Ningjiang; formerly known as Fuyu
Songzi China 87 D2
formerly known as Xinjiangkou
Sonhat India 97 D5
Sonid Youqi China see Saihan Tal
Sonid Zuoqi China see Mandalt
Sonipat India 96 C3
Sonkach India 96 C5
Sonkajärvi Fin. 44 N3
Sonkël', Ozero l. Kyrg. see Songköl
Sonkovo Rus. Fed. 43 S4
Son La Vietnam 78 C3
Sonmiani Bay Pak. 101 F5
Sonneberg Germany 48 I5
Sonnenjoch mt. Austria 48 J8
Sono r. Minas Gerais Brazil 203 C6
Sono r. Tocantins Brazil 202 B4
Sonoita watercourse Mex. 181 D7
Sonoma U.S.A. 182 B3
Sonoma Peak U.S.A. 182 G1
Sonora r. Mex. 184 C2
Sonora state Mex. 184 C2
Sonora CA U.S.A. 182 D4
Sonora TX U.S.A. 179 B6
Sonora Peak U.S.A. 182 E3
Sonqor Iran 100 A3
Sonseca Spain 54 H5
Son Servera Spain 55 O5
Sonsón Col. 198 C3
Sonsonate El Salvador 185 H6
Sonsorol Islands Palau 73 H5
also spelt Sansoral Islands
Sonstraal S. Africa 132 G4
Son Tây Vietnam 78 D3
Sonthofen Germany 48 H8
Sonwabile S. Africa 133 M8
Soochow China see Suzhou
Soodla r. Estonia 42 G2
Soomaaliya country Africa see Somalia
Soperton U.S.A. 175 D5
Sopi, Tanjung pt Indon. 75 D2
Sopo watercourse Sudan 126 E2
Sopot Bulg. 58 F6
Sopot Poland 49 P1
Sopot Srbija Yugo. 58 B4
Sopron Hungary 49 N8
historically known as Ödenburg
Sopu-Korgon Kyrg. 88 A3
also known as Sufi-Kurgan
Sopur Jammu and Kashmir 96 B2
Soputan, Gunung vol. Indon. 75 C2
Sor r. France 51 I9
Sor r. Port. 54 C6
Sor r. Spain 54 D1
Sora Italy 56 F7
Sorab India 94 B3
Söråker Sweden 44 L3
Sŏrak-san mt. S. Korea 83 C5
Sŏrak-san National Park S. Korea 83 C5
Sorata Bol. 200 C3
Sorau Poland see Żary
Sør-Audnedal Norway 45 I4
Sorbas Spain 55 I7
Sorbe r. Spain 55 H4
Sor Donyztau dry lake Kazakh. 102 D3
Sorel Canada 169 F4
Sorell Australia 147 E5
Soreq r. Israel 108 F6
Sørfjorden inlet Norway 45 I3
Sorgono Sardegna Italy 57 B8
Sorgues France 51 K8
Sorgues r. France 51 I9
Sorgun Yozgat Turkey 106 C3
also known as Yesilova
Sorgun r. Turkey 108 F1
Soria Spain 55 I3
Sorikmarapi vol. Indon. 76 B2
Sørkappøya i. Svalbard 38 B2
Sor Kaydak dry lake Kazakh. 102 C3
Sorkh, Kūh-e mts Iran 100 C3
Sorkheh Iran 100 C3
Sørland Norway 44 K2
Sørli Norway 44 K2
Sor Mertvyy Kultuk dry lake Kazakh. 102 C3
also known as Öli Qoltyq Sory
Sörmjöle Sweden 44 M3
Sorø Denmark 45 J5
Soro India 97 E5
Soro, Monte mt. Sicilia Italy 57 G11
Soroca Moldova 41 D6
formerly spelt Soroki
Sorocaba Brazil 206 F10
Sorochinsk Rus. Fed. 102 C1
Soroki Moldova see Soroca
Sorokino Rus. Fed. 43 K4
Sorol atoll Micronesia 73 J5
formerly known as Philip Atoll
Sorong Indon. 73 H7
Sororó r. Brazil 202 B3
Sororoca Brazil 199 F4
Sorot' r. Rus. Fed. 43 J4
Soroti Uganda 128 B4
Sørøya i. Norway 44 M1
Sørøysundet sea chan. Norway 44 M1
Sorp Turkey see Reşadiye
Sorraia r. Port. 54 C5
Sørreisa Norway 44 L1
Sorrento Italy 57 G8
Sorsakoski Fin. 44 N3
Sorsatunturi hill Fin. 44 O2
Sorsele Sweden 44 L2
Sorso Sardegna Italy 57 A8
Sorsogon Phil. 74 C3
Sortavala Rus. Fed. 45 O3
Sortland Norway 44 K1
Sortot Sudan 121 F5
Sør-Trøndelag county Norway 44 J3
Sørvær Norway 44 M1
Sørvågen Norway 44 K2
Sõrve väin sea chan. Estonia/Latvia see Irbe Strait
Sŏsan S. Korea 83 B5
Sosedno Rus. Fed. 43 J3
Sosenskiy Rus. Fed. 43 Q7
Soshanguve S. Africa 133 M2
Soskovo Rus. Fed. 43 Q9
Sosna r. Rus. Fed. 43 T9
Sosnogorsk Rus. Fed. 40 J3
formerly known as Izhma
Sosnovka Kazakh. 103 I2
Sosnovka Arkhangel'skaya Oblast' Rus. Fed. 40 H3
Sosnovka Murmanskaya Oblast' Rus. Fed. 40 G2
Sosnovka Tambovskaya Oblast' Rus. Fed. 41 G5
Sosnovka Vologod. Obl. Rus. Fed. 43 S3
Sosnovka Vologod. Obl. Rus. Fed. 43 U2
Sosnovo Rus. Fed. 43 L1
Sosnovoborsk Rus. Fed. 41 H5
Sosnovo-Ozerskoye Rus. Fed. 81 I2
Sosnovyy Rus. Fed. 44 P2
Sosnovyy Bor Belarus see Sasnovy Bor
Sosnovyy Bor Rus. Fed. 43 K2
Sosnowiec Poland 49 Q5
historically known as Sosnowitz
Sosnowitz Poland see Sosnowiec
Sosny Belarus 42 I9
Sosso Cent. Afr. Rep. 126 B4
Sos'va Rus. Fed. 38 G4
Sot' r. Rus. Fed. 43 V4
Sota r. Benin 125 F4
Sotang China 97 G3
Sotério r. Brazil 201 D2
Sotillo r. Spain 54 G4
Sotkamo Fin. 44 O2
Soto Arg. 204 D3
Soto la Marina Mex. 185 F4
Sotouboua Togo 125 F4
Sotteville-lès-Rouen France 50 H3
Sottunga Fin. 45 M3
Sotuta Mex. 185 H4
Souanké Congo 126 B4
Soubré Côte d'Ivoire 124 D5
Soucis, Cape N.Z. 152 H9
Souda Greece 59 F13
also spelt Soúdha
Soudan Australia 148 C4
Soudas, Ormos b. Greece 59 F13
Soúdha Greece see Souda
Soufli Greece 58 H7
Soufrière vol. Guadeloupe 187 H3
Soufrière St Lucia 187 H4
Soufrière vol. St Vincent 199 F1
Soufrière Hills Montserrat 187 H3
Souguéta Guinea 124 B4
Sougueur Alg. 55 M9
Souillac France 50 H8
Souk Ahras Alg. 123 G1
Souk el Arbaâ du Rharb Morocco 122 D2
Souk el Had el Rharbia Morocco 54 F9
Souk el Kella Morocco 54 F9
Souk Khemis du Sahel Morocco 54 E9
Soukoukoutane Niger 125 F3
Souk Tleta Taghramet Morocco 54 F9
Souk-Tnine-de-Sidi-el-Yamani Morocco 54 F9
Sŏul S. Korea see Seoul
Soulac-sur-Mer France 50 E7
Sounding Creek r. Canada 167 I4
Sounfat well Mali see Tessoûnfat
Sounio nat. park Greece 59 F11
Soûr Lebanon see Tyre
Sourdeval France 50 F4
Soure Brazil 202 B2
Sour el Ghozlane Alg. 55 O8
Souris Man. Canada 167 K5
Souris P.E.I. Canada 169 I4
Souris r. Canada 167 L5
Souriya country Asia see Syria
Souroumelli well Mauritania 124 C2
Sous, Oued watercourse Morocco 122 C3
Sousa Brazil 202 E3
Sousa Lara Angola see Bocoio
Sousel Port. 54 D6
Sousse Tunisia 123 H2
also spelt Susah; historically known as Hadrumetum
Soussellem, Oued watercourse Alg. 55 N9
Soustons France 50 E9
Sout r. S. Africa 132 C8
Sout watercourse S. Africa 132 E5
South Africa country Africa see South Africa, Republic of
▶South Africa, Republic of country Africa 130 D6
known as Suid-Afrika in Afrikaans; short form South Africa
africa [countries] ▶ 114–117
South Alligator r. Australia 148 B2
Southampton Canada 168 D4
Southampton U.K. 47 K13
historically known as Hamwic
Southampton U.S.A. 177 M5
Southampton Island Canada 167 O1
South Andaman i. India 95 G4
South Anna r. U.S.A. 176 H8
South Aulatsivik Island Canada 169 I1
South Australia state Australia 146 B2
Southaven U.S.A. 174 B5
South Baldy mt. U.S.A. 181 F6
South Bay U.S.A. 175 D7
South Bend IN U.S.A. 174 C3
South Bend WA U.S.A. 180 B3
South Bluff pt Bahamas 187 E2
South Boston U.S.A. 176 G9
Southbridge N.Z. 153 G11
Southbridge U.S.A. 177 M3
South Brook Canada 169 J3
South Burlington U.S.A. 177 L1
Southburn N.Z. 153 F12
South Carolina state U.S.A. 175 D5
South Charleston OH U.S.A. 176 B6
South Charleston WV U.S.A. 176 D7
South China Sea N. Pacific Ocean 72 E4
South Coast Town Australia see Gold Coast
South Dakota state U.S.A. 178 B2
South Deerfield U.S.A. 177 M3
South Downs hills U.K. 47 L13
South East admin. dist. Botswana 133 J2
South East Cape Australia 147 E5
South East Isles Australia 151 C7
Southend Canada 167 K3
Southend-on-Sea U.K. 47 M12
Southern admin. reg. Eth. 128 C3
Southern admin. reg. Malawi 129 B8
Southern prov. Sierra Leone 124 B5
Southern prov. Zambia 127 E9
Southern Aegean admin. reg. Greece see Notio Aigaio
Southern Alps mts N.Z. 153 E11
also known as Kā Tiritiri o te Moana
Southern Central Aboriginal Reserve Australia 151 D5
Southern Cross Australia 151 B6
Southern Darfur state Sudan 126 E2
Southern Indian Lake Canada 167 L3
Southern Kordofan state Sudan 128 A2
Southern Lau Group is Fiji 145 H3
Southern National Park Sudan 126 F3
Southern Ocean 222 F3
Southern Pines U.S.A. 174 E5
Southern Rhodesia country Africa see Zimbabwe
Southern Uplands hills U.K. 46 H8
Southern Urals mts Rus. Fed. see Yuzhnyy Ural
Southern Ute Indian Reservation res. U.S.A. 181 F5
South Esk Tableland reg. Australia 150 D3
Southey Canada 167 J5
Southeyville S. Africa 133 L8
South Fabius r. U.S.A. 178 E4
Southfield U.S.A. 173 J8
Southfields U.S.A. 177 K4
South Fork CA U.S.A. 182 A1
South Fork CO U.S.A. 181 F5
South Fork PA U.S.A. 176 G5
South Fox Island U.S.A. 172 H5
Southgate r. Canada 166 E5
South Geomagnetic Pole (2000) Antarctica 223 H1

▶South Georgia and South Sandwich Islands terr. S. Atlantic Ocean 217 L9
United Kingdom Overseas Territory.
southamerica [countries] ▶ 192–193

South Gillies Canada 172 D2
South Grand r. U.S.A. 178 D4
South Hatia Island Bangl. 97 F5
South Haven U.S.A. 172 G8
South Head N.Z. 152 I4
South Head N.Z. 152 I4
South Henik Lake Canada 167 L2
South Hero U.S.A. 177 L1
South Hill U.S.A. 176 G9
South Horr Kenya 128 C4
South Indian Lake Canada 167 L3
South Island India 94 B4

▶South Island N.Z. 153 G12
2nd largest island in Oceania. Also known as Te Waipounamu.
oceania [landscapes] ▶ 136–137

South Islet reef Phil. 74 A4
South Junction Canada 167 M5
South Kazakhstan Oblast admin. div. Kazakh. see Yuzhnyy Kazakhstan
South Kitui National Reserve nature res. Kenya 128 C5
South Koel r. India 97 E5
▶South Korea country Asia 83 B5
asia [countries] ▶ 64–67
South Lake Tahoe U.S.A. 182 D3
Southland admin. reg. N.Z. 153 B13
South Loup r. U.S.A. 178 C3
South Luangwa National Park Zambia 127 F8
South Macmillan r. Canada 166 C2
South Magnetic Pole (2000) Antarctica 223 J2
South Manitou Island U.S.A. 173 G5
South Mills U.S.A. 177 I9
Southminster U.K. 47 M12
South Moose Lake Canada 167 K4
South Mountains hills U.S.A. 177 H6
South Muiron Island Australia 150 A4
South Nahanni r. Canada 166 D1
South Negril Point Jamaica 186 D3
South New Berlin U.S.A. 177 J3
South Orkney Islands S. Atlantic Ocean 222 V2
South Paris U.S.A. 177 O1
South Passage Australia 151 A5
South Patrick Shores U.S.A. 175 D6
South Platte r. U.S.A. 178 B3
South Point pt U.S.A. 181 [inset] Z2
South Pole Antarctica 223 T1
South Porcupine Canada 173 L2
Southport Australia 147 E5
Southport U.K. 47 I10
Southport NC U.S.A. 175 E5
Southport NY U.S.A. 177 I3
South Portland U.S.A. 177 O2
South River Canada 173 N5
South Ronaldsay i. U.K. 46 J5
South Royalton U.S.A. 177 M2
South Salt Lake U.S.A. 183 M1
South San Francisco U.S.A. 182 B4
South Saskatchewan r. Canada 167 J4
South Seal r. Canada 167 L3
South Shetland Islands Antarctica 222 U2
South Shields U.K. 47 K8
South Sinai governorate Egypt see Janūb Sīnā'
South Skunk r. U.S.A. 174 A3
South Taranaki Bight b. N.Z. 152 I7
South Tent mt. U.S.A. 183 M2
South Tons r. India 97 D4
South Tucson U.S.A. 183 N9
South Turkana Nature Reserve Kenya 128 B4
South Twin Island Canada 168 E2
South Twin Lake Canada 169 K3
South Uist i. U.K. 46 E6
also known as Uibhist a' Deas
South Umpqua r. U.S.A. 180 B4
South Wellesley Islands Australia 148 C3
South-West Africa country Africa see Namibia
South West Cape Australia 147 E5
South West Cape N.Z. 153 B15
also known as Puhiwaero
South West Cay reef Australia 149 G4
Southwest Conservation Area nature res. Australia 147 E5
South West Entrance sea chan. P.N.G. 149 F1
Southwest Harbor U.S.A. 177 Q1
South West Island Australia 149 F3
South West National Park Australia 147 E5
South West Rocks Australia 147 G2
South Whitley U.S.A. 172 H9
South Williamson U.S.A. 176 C8
South Williamsport U.S.A. 177 I4
South Windham U.S.A. 177 O2
Southwold U.K. 47 N11
Southwood National Park Australia 147 F1
South Zanesville U.S.A. 176 C6
Soutpansberg mts S. Africa 131 F4
Souttouf, Adrar mts W. Sahara 122 B5
Souvigny France 51 J6
Sovata Romania 58 G2
Soveja Romania 58 H2
Soverato Italy 57 I10
Sovet Tajik. 101 G2
also known as Sovetskiy
Sovetabad Uzbek. see Khanabad
Sovetsk Kaliningradskaya Oblast' Rus. Fed. 42 C6
historically known as Tilsit
Sovetsk Kirovskaya Oblast' Rus. Fed. 40 I4
Sovetsk Tul'skaya Oblast' Rus. Fed. 43 S8
Sovetskaya Rus. Fed. 107 F1
Sovetskaya Gavan' Rus. Fed. 82 F2
Sovetskiy Khanty-Mansiyskiy Avtonomnyy Okrug Rus. Fed. 38 G3
Sovetskiy Leningradskaya Oblast' Rus. Fed. 43 J1
Sovetskiy Respublika Mariy El Rus. Fed. 40 I4
Sovetskiy Tajik. see Sovet
Sovetskoye Rus. Fed. see Shatoy
Sovetskoye Rus. Fed. 102 A2
Sovetskoye Rus. Fed. see Zelenokumsk
Sovići Bos.-Herz. 56 J5
Sowa Botswana 131 E4
Sowa China 86 A2
formerly known as Dagxoi
Sowa Pan salt pan Botswana 131 E4
Soweto S. Africa 133 L3
Sōya-kaikyō strait Japan/Rus. Fed. see La Pérouse Strait
Soyaló Mex. 185 G5
Sōya-misaki c. Japan 90 G2
Soyana r. Rus. Fed. 40 G2
Soyang-ho l. S. Korea 83 B5
Soyaux France 50 G7
Sōya-wan b. Japan 90 G2
Soylan Armenia see Vayk'
Soyma r. Rus. Fed. 40 I2
Soyo Angola 127 B6
formerly known as Santo António do Zaire
Sozaq Kazakh. see Suzak
Sozh r. Europe 43 L9
Sozimskiy Rus. Fed. 40 J4
Sozopol Bulg. 58 I6
historically known as Apollonia
Spaatz Island Antarctica 222 T2
Spadafora Sicilia Italy 57 H10

▶Spain country Europe 54 F4
4th largest country in Europe. Known as España in Spanish; historically known as Hispania.
europe [countries] ▶ 32–35

Spalato Croatia see Split
Spalatum Croatia see Split
Spalding Australia 146 C3
Spalding U.K. 47 L11
Spaniard's Bay Canada 169 K4
Spanish Canada 168 D4
Spanish r. Canada 168 D4
Spanish Fork U.S.A. 183 M1
Spanish Guinea country Africa see Equatorial Guinea
Spanish Netherlands country Europe see Belgium
Spanish Point Rep. of Ireland 47 C11
Spanish Sahara terr. Africa see Western Sahara
Spanish Town Jamaica 186 D3
Spanish Wells Bahamas 175 E7
Sparagio, Monte mt. Sicilia Italy 57 E10
Sparks U.S.A. 182 E2
Sparta Greece see Sparti
Sparta GA U.S.A. 175 D5
Sparta MI U.S.A. 172 H7
Sparta NC U.S.A. 176 D9
Sparta TN U.S.A. 174 C5
Sparta WI U.S.A. 172 C7
Spartanburg U.S.A. 174 D5
Spartansburg U.S.A. 176 F4
Spartel, Cap c. Morocco 54 F9
Sparti Greece 59 D11
historically known as Lacedaemon or Sparta
Spartivento, Capo c. Sardegna Italy 57 A10
Spartivento, Capo c. Italy 57 I11
Sparwood Canada 167 H5
Spas-Demensk Rus. Fed. 43 P7
Spas-Klepiki Rus. Fed. 43 V6
Spass Rus. Fed. 43 Q6
Spasskaya Polist' Rus. Fed. 43 M3
Spassk-Dal'niy Rus. Fed. 82 D3
Spasskoye Kazakh. 103 G1
Spasskoye-Lutovinovo Rus. Fed. 43 R8
Spas-Ugol Rus. Fed. 43 S5
Spatha, Akra pt Greece 59 E13
Spatsizi Plateau Wilderness Provincial Park Canada 166 D3
Spean Bridge U.K. 46 H7
Spearfish U.S.A. 178 B2
Spearman U.S.A. 179 B4
Speers Canada 167 J4
Speightstown Barbados 187 I4
Speikkogel mt. Austria 49 M8
Speke Gulf Tanz. 128 B5
Spence Bay Canada see Taloyoak
Spencer IA U.S.A. 178 D3
Spencer ID U.S.A. 180 D3
Spencer IN U.S.A. 174 C4
Spencer MA U.S.A. 177 N3
Spencer NY U.S.A. 177 I3
Spencer VA U.S.A. 176 E9
Spencer, Cape Australia 146 C3
Spencer, Cape U.S.A. 166 B3
Spencer, Point U.S.A. 39 T3
Spencer Gulf est. Australia 146 C3
Spencer Range hills N.T. Australia 148 A2
Spencer Range hills N.T. Australia 148 B2
Spences Bridge Canada 166 F5
Spenser Mountains N.Z. 153 G10
Spercheios r. Greece 59 D10
also spelt Sperkhiós
Sperkhiós r. Greece see Spercheios
Spermezeu Romania 58 F1
Sperrin Mountains hills U.K. 47 E9
Sperryville U.S.A. 176 G7
Spētsai i. Greece see Spetses
Spetses Greece 59 E11
Spetses i. Greece 59 E11
also known as Spétsai
Spey r. U.K. 46 I6
Speyer Germany 48 F6
Spezand Pak. 101 F4
Spice Islands Indon. see Moluccas
Spiekeroog i. Germany 48 E2
Spiez Switz. 51 N6
Spijkenisse Neth. 48 B4
Spil Dağı Milli Parkı nat. park Turkey 59 I10
Spilimbergo Italy 56 E2
Spīn Būldak Afgh. 101 F4
Spioenkop Dam Nature Reserve S. Africa 133 N5
Spirit Lake U.S.A. 178 D3
Spiritwood Canada 167 J4
Spirovo Rus. Fed. 43 P4
Spišská Nová Ves Slovakia 49 R7
Spitak Armenia 107 F2
Spiti r. India 96 C3
Spit Point Australia 150 B4

▶Spitsbergen i. Svalbard 38 B2
5th largest island in Europe. Also spelt Spitzbergen.
europe [landscapes] ▶ 30–31

Spitskop mt. S. Africa 132 G10
Spitskopvlei S. Africa 133 J8
Spitsyno Rus. Fed. 42 I3
Spittal an der Drau Austria 49 K9
Spitzbergen i. Svalbard see Spitsbergen
Split Croatia 56 I5
formerly known as Spalato; historically known as Spalatum
Split Lake Canada 167 L3
Split Lake l. Canada 167 L3
Spokane U.S.A. 180 C3
Spokane r. U.S.A. 180 C3
Spokane Indian Reservation res. U.S.A. 180 C3
Spoon r. U.S.A. 174 B3
Spooner U.S.A. 172 B5
Spot Bay Cayman Is 186 D3
Spotsylvania U.S.A. 176 H7
Spragge Canada 173 K4
Sprague r. U.S.A. 180 B4
Spranger, Mount Canada 166 F4
Spratly Island S. China Sea 72 D5
Spratly Islands S. China Sea 72 D5
also known as Nansha Qundao or Quan Dao Truong Sa or Truong Sa

index

S

Spread Eagle U.S.A. **172** E5
Spreča r. Bos.-Herz. **56** K4
Spree r. Germany **49** K5
Spreewald park Germany **49** L4
Spremberg Germany **49** L4
Spring r. U.S.A. **178** D4
Spring Bay Canada **173** K5
Springbok S. Africa **132** B6
Spring City U.S.A. **183** M1
Spring Creek r. Australia **148** C3
Spring Creek U.S.A. **183** I1
Springdale Canada **169** K3
Springdale U.S.A. **179** D4
Springe Germany **48** G3
Springer U.S.A. **181** F5
Springerville U.S.A. **183** O7
Springfield N.Z. **153** F11
Springfield CO U.S.A. **178** B4
Springfield GA U.S.A. **175** D5
▶ **Springfield** IL U.S.A. **174** B4
State capital of Illinois.

Springfield KY U.S.A. **174** C4
Springfield MA U.S.A. **177** M3
Springfield MN U.S.A. **178** D2
Springfield OH U.S.A. **176** B6
Springfield OR U.S.A. **180** B3
Springfield TN U.S.A. **174** C4
Springfield VT U.S.A. **177** M2
Springfield WV U.S.A. **176** C7
Springfontein S. Africa **133** J7
Spring Garden Guyana **199** G3
Spring Glen U.S.A. **183** M2
Spring Green U.S.A. **172** C7
Spring Grove MN U.S.A. **172** B7
Spring Grove VA U.S.A. **177** I8
Springhill Canada **169** H4
Spring Hill U.S.A. **175** D6
Springhouse Canada **166** F5
Spring Mountains U.S.A. **183** I5
Springport U.S.A. **173** I8
Springs S. Africa **133** M3
Springs Junction N.Z. **153** G10
Springsure Australia **149** F5
Spring Valley S. Africa **133** K9
Spring Valley U.S.A. **183** H9
Springview U.S.A. **178** C3
Springville CA U.S.A. **182** F5
Springville NY U.S.A. **176** F3
Springville PA U.S.A. **177** J4
Springville UT U.S.A. **183** M1
Springwater U.S.A. **176** H3
Spruce Grove Canada **167** H4
Spruce Knob mt. U.S.A. **176** F7
Spruce Mountain CO U.S.A. **183** P3
Spruce Mountain NV U.S.A. **183** I5
Spulico, Capo c. Italy **57** H10
Spurn Head U.K. **47** M10
Spurr, Mount vol. U.S.A. **164** C3
Spuzzum Canada **166** F5
Squamish Canada **166** F5
Squamish r. Canada **166** F5
Squam Lake U.S.A. **177** M2
Square Lake U.S.A. **174** G2
Squillace Italy **57** I10
Squillace, Golfo di g. Italy **57** I10
Squinzano Italy **57** K8
Squire U.S.A. **176** D8
Squires, Mount hill Australia **151** D5
Sragen Indon. **77** E4
Srbica aut. rep. Yugo. **58** B5
English form Serbia
Srbinje Bos.-Herz. see Foča
Srbobran Bos.-Herz. see Donji Vakuf
Srbobran Vojvodina, Srbija Yugo. **58** A3
Srebarna tourist site Bulg. **58** I4
Srebrenica Bos.-Herz. **56** L4
Sredets Bulg. **58** I6
formerly known as Grudovo
Sredets Bulg. see Sofia
Sredetska Reka r. Bulg. **58** I6
formerly known as Mandrenska
Sredinnyy Khrebet mts Rus. Fed. **39** P4
Sredishte Bulg. **58** I6
Sredna Gora mts Bulg. **58** E6
Srednebelaya Rus. Fed. **82** B2
Srednekolymsk Rus. Fed. **39** P3
Sredne-Russkaya Vozvyshennost' hills
Rus. Fed. see Central Russian Upland
Sredne-Sibirskoye Ploskogor'ye plat.
Rus. Fed. see Central Siberian Plateau
Sredneye Kuyto, Ozero r. Rus. Fed. **44** O2
Srednogorie Bulg. **58** F6
Srednyaya Akhtuba Rus. Fed. **41** H6
Srem Poland **49** O3
Srem reg. Yugo. **58** A3
Sremska Mitrovica Vojvodina, Srbija Yugo.
58 A4
historically known as Sirmium
Srépok, Tônlé r. Cambodia **79** D5
Sretensk Rus. Fed. **81** J2
Sri Aman Sarawak Malaysia **77** E2
formerly known as Simanggang
Sriharikota Island India **94** D3
▶ **Sri Jayewardenepura Kotte** Sri Lanka
94 C5
Capital of Sri Lanka. Short form Kotte.

Srikakulam India **95** E2
formerly known as Chicacole
Sri Kalahasti India **94** C3
▶ **Sri Lanka** country Asia **94** D5
also known as Sarandib or Saylan; also spelt
Shri Lanka; formerly known as Ceylon;
historically known as Lanka or Sinhala or
Taprobane
asia [countries] ▶▶▶ 64–67
Sri Madhopur India **96** B4
Srimangal Bangl. **97** F4
Srinagar India **96** B3
Srinagar Jammu and Kashmir **96** B2

Sringeri India **94** B3
Sri Pada mt. Sri Lanka see Adam's Peak
Srirangam India **94** C4
Srisailam India **94** C2
Srivaikuntam India **94** C4
Srivardhan India **94** B2
Srivilliputtur India **94** C4
Srnetica mts Bos.-Herz. **56** I4
Srnice Bos.-Herz. **56** K4
Środa Śląska Poland see Hasić
Środa Wielkopolska Poland **49** O3
Srpska Crnja Vojvodina, Srbija Yugo. **58** B3
Srpska Kostajnica Bos.-Herz. see
Bosanska Kostajnica
Srpski Brod Bos.-Herz. see Bosanski Brod
Srpski Itebej Vojvodina, Srbija Yugo. **58** B3
Srungavarapukota India **95** D2
Sselki Rus. Fed. **43** U9
Staansaam S. Africa **132** E4
Staaten r. Australia **149** D3
Staaten River National Park Australia
149 D3
Stabbursdalen Nasjonalpark nat. park
Norway **44** N1
Staberhuk c. Germany **48** I1
Stabroek Guyana see Georgetown
Stade Germany **48** G2
Städjan-Nipfjällets naturreservat
nature res. Sweden **45** I3
Stadskanaal Neth. **48** D3
Stadtallendorf Germany **48** G5
Stadthagen Germany **48** G3
Staffa i. U.K. **46** F7
Staffelstein Germany **48** H5
Stafford U.K. **47** J11
Stafford Creek Bahamas **186** D1
Stafford's Post S. Africa **133** N7
Stafford Springs U.S.A. **177** M4
Stagen Indon. **77** G3
Stagg Lake Canada **167** H2
Stahlstown U.S.A. **176** F5
Staicele Latvia **42** F4
Stakhanov Ukr. **41** F6
formerly known as Kadiyevka or Sergo
Stakhanovo Rus. Fed. see Zhukovskiy
Stalin Bulg. see Varna
Stalin, Mount Canada **166** E3
Stalinabad Tajik. see Dushanbe
Stalingrad Rus. Fed. see Volgograd
Stalingradskaya Oblast' admin. div.
Rus. Fed. see Volgogradskaya Oblast'
Staliniri Georgia see Ts'khinvali
Stalino Ukr. see Donets'k
Stalino Uzbek. see Shakhrikhan
Stalinogorsk Rus. Fed. see Novomoskovsk
Stalinogród Poland see Katowice
Stalinsk Rus. Fed. see Novokuznetsk
Stalowa Wola Poland **49** T5
Stâlpu Romania **58** H3
Stalwart Point S. Africa **133** L10
Stamboliyski Bulg. **58** F6
Stamford Australia **149** D4
Stamford U.K. **47** L11
Stamford CT U.S.A. **177** L4
Stamford NY U.S.A. **177** K3
Stamford TX U.S.A. **179** C5
Stampalia i. Greece see Astypalaia
Stampriet Namibia **130** C5
Stamsund Norway **44** K1
Stanardsville U.S.A. **176** G7
Stancomb-Wills Glacier Antarctica **223** W1
Standerton S. Africa **133** N3
Standing Rock Indian Reservation res.
U.S.A. **178** B2
Standish U.S.A. **173** J7
Stănești Romania **58** F4
Stanfield U.S.A. **183** M9
Stanford S. Africa **132** D11
Stanford KY U.S.A. **176** A8
Stanford MT U.S.A. **180** E3
Stangentestind hill Norway **44** O1
Stanger S. Africa **133** P6
Stănilești Romania **58** J2
Stanisic Vojvodina, Srbija Yugo. **58** A3
Stanislav Ukr. see Ivano-Frankivs'k
Stânișoarei, Munții mts Romania **58** G1
Stanke Dimitrov Bulg. see Dupnitsa
Stanley Australia **147** E5
Stanley Hong Kong China **87** [inset]
also known as Chek Chue
▶ **Stanley** Falkland Is **205** F8
Capital of the Falkland Islands. Long form
Port Stanley.

Stanley ID U.S.A. **180** D3
Stanley ND U.S.A. **178** B1
Stanley NY U.S.A. **176** G7
Stanley WI U.S.A. **172** C6
Stanley, Chutes waterfall Dem. Rep. Congo
see Boyoma Falls
Stanley, Mount hill N.T. Australia **148** A4
Stanley, Mount hill Tas. Australia **147** E5
Stanley, Mount Dem. Rep. Congo/Uganda
see Margherita Peak
Stanley Reservoir India **94** C4
Stanleyville Dem. Rep. Congo see
Kisangani
Stanmore Zimbabwe **131** F4
Stann Creek Belize see Dangriga
Stanos Greece **59** C10
Stanovaya Rus. Fed. **43** T9
Stanovoye Rus. Fed. **43** T9
formerly known as Ploskoye
Stanovoye Nagor'ye mts Rus. Fed. **81** J1
Stanovoy Khrebet mts Rus. Fed. **39** N3
Stanovoy Kolodez' Rus. Fed. **43** R9
Stans Switz. **51** O6
Stansmore Range hills Australia **150** D4
Stansted airport U.K. **47** M12
Stanton KY U.S.A. **176** B8
Stanton MI U.S.A. **173** H7
Stanton ND U.S.A. **178** B2
Stanton NE U.S.A. **178** C3
Stanton TX U.S.A. **179** B5
Stantsiya Babarykino Rus. Fed. **43** T9
Stantsiya Skuratovo Rus. Fed. **43** S8
Stantsiya-Yakkabag Uzbek. see Yakkabag
Staples U.S.A. **178** D2
Stapleton U.S.A. **178** C3
Staporków Poland **49** R4
Star' Rus. Fed. **43** P8
Starachowice Poland **49** S4
Stara Huta Ukr. **43** O8
Stará Ľubovňa Slovakia **49** R6
Stara Pazova Vojvodina, Srbija Yugo. **58** B4
Stara Planina mts Bulg./Yugo. see
Balkan Mountains
Staraya Kulatka Rus. Fed. **102** A1
Staraya Poltavka Rus. Fed. **102** A2
Staraya Russa Rus. Fed. **43** N4
Staraya Toropa Rus. Fed. **43** M5
Stara Zagora Bulg. **58** G6
Starbuck Island Kiribati **221** H6
formerly known as Barren Island or Low
Island or Starve Island
Starchiojd Romania **58** H3
Star City AR U.S.A. **174** B5
Star City IN U.S.A. **172** G10
Star City WV U.S.A. **176** F6
Stargard in Pommern Poland see
Stargard Szczeciński
Stargard Szczeciński Poland **49** M2
historically known as Stargard in
Pommern
Stari Ras and Sopoćani tourist site Yugo.
58 B5
Staritsa Rus. Fed. **43** P5
Starke U.S.A. **175** D6
Starkey U.S.A. **176** F8

Starkovo Rus. Fed. **43** V6
Starkville U.S.A. **43** O9
Star Lake U.S.A. **177** J1
Starling Inlet Hong Kong China **87** [inset]
also known as Sha Tau Kok Hoi
Starnberg Germany **48** I8
Starnberger See l. Germany **48** I8
Staroaleyskoye Rus. Fed. **88** C1
Starobel'sk Ukr. see Starobil's'k
Starobil's'k Ukr. **41** F6
also spelt Starobel'sk
Starobyn Belarus **42** I9
Starodub Rus. Fed. **43** N9
Starogard Gdański Poland **49** P2
historically known as Preußisch Stargard
Starokonstantinov Ukr. see
Starokostyantyniv
Starokostyantyniv Ukr. **41** C6
also spelt Starokonstantinov
Starokozache Ukr. **58** K2
Starokotovo Rus. Fed. **43** U7
Starominskaya Rus. Fed. **41** F7
Staro Oryakhovo Bulg. **58** I6
Starosel Bulg. **58** F6
Staro Selo Bulg. **58** H5
Staroshcherbinovskaya Rus. Fed. **41** F7
Starosubkhangulovo Rus. Fed. **102** D1
Staroye Rus. Fed. **43** V2
Staroye Istomino Rus. Fed. **43** O6
Staroye Melkovo Rus. Fed. **43** R5
Staroye Sandovo Rus. Fed. **43** R3
Staroye Syalo Belarus **43** K6
Staroyur'yevo Rus. Fed. **43** U5
Starozhilovo Rus. Fed. **43** U7
Star Peak U.S.A. **182** F1
Start Point U.K. **47** I13
Starve Island Kiribati see Starbuck Island
Starynki Belarus **42** I7
Staryya Darohi Belarus **43** J8
also spelt Staryye Dorogi
Staryy Dvor Rus. Fed. **43** V5
Staryye Dorogi Belarus see Staryya Darohi
Staryye Yurkovichi Rus. Fed. **43** M9
Staryy Kayak Rus. Fed. **39** J2
Staryy Nadym Rus. Fed. **38** H3
Staryy Oskol Rus. Fed. **41** F6
Staryy Sambir Ukr. **49** T6
also spelt Staryy Sambor
Staryy Sambor Ukr. see Staryy Sambir
Staßfurt Germany **48** I4
Staszów Poland **49** S5
State College U.S.A. **176** H5
Staten Island Arg. see Los Estados, Isla de
Statenville U.S.A. **175** D6
State Road U.S.A. **176** D5
Statesboro U.S.A. **175** D5
Statesville U.S.A. **174** D5
Stathelle Norway **45** J4
Station U.S.A. **174** B5
Station No. 6 Sudan **121** G4
Station No. 10 Sudan **121** E5
Station Nord Greenland **165** R1
also known as Nord
Statzberg hill Austria **49** M7
Stăuceni Moldova **58** J1
Staunton U.S.A. **176** F7
Stavanger Norway **45** I4
Stavertsi Bulg. **58** F5
Stavropol' Rus. Fed. **41** G7
formerly known as Voroshilovsk
Stavropol Kray admin. div. Rus. Fed. see
Stavropol'skiy Kray
Stavropol'-na-Volge Rus. Fed. see Tol'yatti
Stavropol'skaya Vozvyshennost' hills
Rus. Fed. **41** G7
Stavropol'skiy Kray admin. div. Rus. Fed.
41 G7
English form Stavropol Kray
Stavros Greece **58** E8
Stavros, Akra pt Kriti Greece **59** F13
Stavros, Akra pt Naxos Greece **59** G11
Stawbun Belarus **43** M9
Stawell Australia **147** D4
Stawell r. Australia **149** D4
Stawiski Poland **49** T2
Stawiszyn Poland **49** P4
Stawki, Park Krajobrazowy Poland **49** Q5
Stayki Rus. Fed. **43** J8
Stayner Canada **173** M6
Stayton U.S.A. **180** B3
Steamboat U.S.A. **182** E2
Steamboat Springs U.S.A. **180** F4
Stearns U.S.A. **176** A9
Stebbins U.S.A. **164** C3
Steckdorings S. Africa **133** I4
Steel r. Canada **168** C3
Steele U.S.A. **178** C2
Steele Island Antarctica **222** T2
Steelpoort S. Africa **133** O1
Steelton U.S.A. **177** I5
Steelville U.S.A. **174** B4
Steen r. Canada **167** G3
Steenkampsberg mts S. Africa **133** O2
Steen River Canada **167** G3
Steens Mountain U.S.A. **180** C4
Steenstrup Gletscher glacier Greenland
see Sermersuaq
Steenvoorde France **51** I2
Steenwijk Neth. **48** D3
Steep Point Australia **151** A5
Stefanoviki Greece **59** D9
Stefansson Bay Antarctica **223** D2
Stefansson Island Canada **165** I2
Ștefan Vodă Moldova **58** K2
formerly known as Biruința or Kyzyl or
Suvorovo; formerly spelt Shtefan-Vode
Ștefan Vodă Romania **58** I4
also known as Doctor Petru Groza
Steigerwald hills Germany **48** H6
Steigerwald park Germany **48** H6
Steilrand S. Africa **133** P4
Steinar Iceland **44** [inset] C2
Steinbach Canada **167** L5
Steinfurt Germany **48** E3
Steingaden Germany **48** H8
Steinhausen Namibia **130** C4
Steinhuder Meer, Naturpark nature res.
Germany **48** G3
Steinkjer Norway **44** J2
Steinkopf S. Africa **132** B6
Steinsland Norway **46** H3
Stekaar S. Africa **132** H6
Stella S. Africa **133** I3
Stella Maris Bahamas **187** E2
Stellenbosch S. Africa **132** C10
Stello, Monte mt. Corse France **51** P10
Stelvio, Parco Nazionale dello nat. park
Italy **56** C2
Stelvio, Passo dello pass Italy **56** C2
Stenay France **51** L3
Stendal Germany **48** I3
Stende Latvia **42** D4
Stenlose, Mount hill Hong Kong China **87** [inset]
also known as Shan Tei Tong
Stenudden Sweden **44** L2
Stenungsund Sweden **45** J4
Steornabhagh U.K. see Stornoway
Stepanakert Azer. see Xankändi
Stepanovka Kazakh. **102** D2
Stephens watercourse Australia **146** C3
Stephens, Cape N.Z. **152** H8
Stephens City U.S.A. **176** G6
Stephens Lake Canada **167** M3
Stephenson, Mount Antarctica **222** T2
Stephenville Canada **169** J3

Stephenville U.S.A. **179** C5
Stonehenge Australia **149** D5
Stonehenge tourist site U.K. **47** K12
Stone Lake U.S.A. **172** B5
Stone Mountain Provincial Park Canada
166 E3
Stone Ridge U.S.A. **177** K4
Stoneville U.S.A. **176** H9
Stonewall Canada **167** L5
Stoney Creek Canada **173** N7
Stoney Point U.S.A. **173** K8
Stongfjorden Norway **46** R2
Stonington U.S.A. **177** Q1
Stony Creek U.S.A. **176** H9
Stony Gorge Reservoir U.S.A. **182** B2
Stony Lake Canada **167** L3
Stony Point U.S.A. **177** L2
Stony Rapids Canada **167** J3
Stooping r. Canada **168** D2
Stör r. Germany **48** G2
Stora Le l. Sweden **45** J4
Stora Lulevatten l. Sweden **44** L2
Stora Sjöfallets nationalpark nat. park
Sweden **44** L2
Storavan l. Sweden **44** L3
Storbäcken Sweden **45** K3
Storbekkfjellet mt. Norway **45** J3
Stord i. Norway **45** I4
Stordal Norway **44** J3
Store mt. Norway **45** J3
Store Bælt sea chan. Denmark see
Great Belt
Storebø Norway **46** R3
Store Heddinge Denmark **45** K5
Store Jukleeggi mt. Norway **45** J3
Store Koldewey i. Greenland **165** R2
Store Lenangstind mt. Norway **44** M1
Store Moss nationalpark nat. park Sweden
45 K4
Storen Norway **44** J3
Store Sotra i. Norway **45** I3
Storfjorden l. Sweden **45** L3
Storfjorden sea chan. Svalbard **38** B2
Storforshei Norway **44** K2
Storjola Sweden **44** K3
Storjord Norway **44** K2
Storjuktan l. Sweden **44** L3
Storkerson Peninsula Canada **165** I2
Storm Bay Australia **147** E5
Stormberg S. Africa **133** K7
Stormberg r. S. Africa **133** K7
Stormberge mts S. Africa **133** K8
Storm Lake U.S.A. **178** D3
Stormsrivier S. Africa **132** H10
Stornoway U.K. **46** F6
also spelt Steornabhagh
Storo Italy **56** C3
Storøya i. Svalbard **38** C2
Storozhenskiy, Mys pt Rus. Fed. **43** N1
Storozhevsk Rus. Fed. **40** J3
Storozhynets' Ukr. **41** C6
Storseleby Sweden **44** L2
Storsjoen l. Norway **45** J3
Storsjön l. Sweden **44** K3
Storsjön l. Sweden **45** L3
Storskarhe mt. Norway **44** J3
Storskog Sweden **44** L2
Storslett Norway **44** M1
Storstrømmen sea chan. Denmark **45** J5
Stortemelk sea chan. Neth. **48** C2
Storuman Sweden **44** L2
Storuman l. Sweden **44** L2
Storvigelen mt. Norway **44** K3
Storvik Sweden **45** L3
Storvorde Denmark **45** J4
Storvreta Sweden **45** L3
Stosch, Isla i. Chile **205** B8
Stoughton Canada **167** K5
Stoughton U.S.A. **172** C7
Stour r. Dorset, England U.K. **47** J13
Stour r. Essex/Suffolk, England U.K. **47** N12
Stour r. Kent, England U.K. **47** N12
Stout Lake Canada **168** B3
Stovall U.S.A. **176** D2
Stowbtsy Belarus **42** H8
also known as Stolbtsy
Stowmarket U.K. **47** N11
Stoyba Rus. Fed. **82** C1
Straatsdrif S. Africa **133** K2
Strabane U.K. **47** E9
Stradella Italy **56** B3
Strahan Australia **147** E5
Straight Cliffs ridge U.S.A. **183** M4
Strakonice Czech Rep. **49** K6
Straldzha Bulg. **58** H6
Stralsund Germany **49** K1
Strand S. Africa **132** C11
Stranda Norway **44** I3
Strandfjord Lough inlet U.K. **47** G9
Strangnäs Sweden **45** L4
Strangways r. Australia **148** B3
Strangways Range mts Australia **148** B4
Stranraer U.K. **47** G9
Strasbourg France **51** N4
historically known as Argentoratum, or
Strassburg
Strasburg Germany **49** K2
Strasburg OH U.S.A. **176** D5
Strasburg PA U.S.A. **177** I5
Strasburg VA U.S.A. **176** G7
Strășeni Moldova **58** J1
formerly spelt Strasheny
Strasheny Moldova see Strășeni
Strassburg France see Strasbourg
Straßwalchen Austria **49** K8
Stratford Canada **168** C3
Stratford CA U.S.A. **182** E5
Stratford CT U.S.A. **177** L4
Stratford TX U.S.A. **178** B4
Stratford WI U.S.A. **172** C6
Stratford-upon-Avon U.K. **47** K11
Strathalbyn Australia **146** C3
Strathcona, Mount Antarctica **223** G2
Strathcona Provincial Park Canada **166** E5
Strathgordon Australia **147** E5
Strathmore Canada **167** H5
Strathmore r. U.K. **46** H5
Strathmore U.S.A. **182** E5
Strathnaver Canada **166** F4
Strathroy Island P.N.G. **149** F1
Strathpeffer U.K. **46** H6
Strathroy Canada **168** D5
Strathspey valley U.K. **46** I6
Stratton Mountain U.S.A. **177** M2
Straubing Germany **49** J7
Straume Norway **44** K1
Straumen Nordland Norway **44** K2
Straumen Nordland Norway **44** K2
Straumnes pt Iceland **44** [inset] B2
Strausberg Germany **49** K3
Strawberry U.S.A. **183** M7
Strawberry Mountain U.S.A. **180** C3
Strawberry Point U.S.A. **172** B8
Strawberry Reservoir U.S.A. **183** M1
Strawn U.S.A. **172** E10
Straža mt. Macedonia **58** D6
Strážа r. Macedonia **58** D6
Streaky Bay Australia **146** A3
Streaky Bay b. Australia **146** A3
Streator U.S.A. **174** B3
Strehaia Romania **58** E4
Strei r. Romania **58** E3
Strei r. Romania **49** E6
Strelcha Bulg. **58** F6
Strel'na Rus. Fed. **39** F3
Strelkovo Rus. Fed. **43** P1
Strelley Australia **150** B4
Strelley r. Australia **150** B4

Strelley Aboriginal Reserve Australia **150** B4
Strel'na r. Rus. Fed. **40** F2
Strenči Latvia **42** G4
Stretta di Messina strait Italy see
Messina, Strait of
Streymoy i. Faroe Is **46** E1
Strezhevoy Rus. Fed. **38** H3
Stříbro Czech Rep. **49** J6
Strickland r. P.N.G. **73** J8
Strimonas r. Greece **58** E8
Strimonikos Kolpos b. Greece **58** E8
Strizivojna Croatia **56** L3
Stroeder Arg. **204** E6
Strofades i. Greece **59** C11
Ströhen Germany **48** F3
Stromboli, Isola i. Isole Lipari Italy **57** H10
Stromeferry U.K. **46** G6
Stromness S. Georgia **205** [inset]
Stromness U.K. **46** I5
Stromsburg U.S.A. **178** C3
Strømsmo Norway **44** L1
Strömstad Sweden **45** J4
Strömsund Sweden **44** K3
Strongoli Italy **57** I9
Strongsville U.S.A. **176** D4
Stronsay i. U.K. **46** J5
Stropkov Slovakia **49** S6
Stroud U.K. **47** J12
Strücklingen (Saterland) Germany **48** E2
Struer Denmark **45** J4
Struga Macedonia **58** B7
Strugi-Krasnyye Rus. Fed. **43** K3
Struis Bay S. Africa **132** E11
Struis Bay b. S. Africa **132** E11
Struma r. Bulg. **58** E7
Strumica Macedonia **58** D7
Strumica r. Macedonia **58** D7
Strunino Rus. Fed. **43** T5
Struthers U.S.A. **176** E4
Stryama r. Bulg. **58** F6
Strydenburg S. Africa **132** H6
Stryn Norway **45** I3
Stryy Ukr. **53** G2
Strzegomka r. Poland **49** N5
Strzelce Krajeńskie Poland **49** M3
Strzelce Opolskie Poland **49** P5
Strzelecki, Mount hill Australia **148** B4
Strzelecki Creek watercourse Australia
146 C2
Strzelecki Regional Reserve nature res.
Australia **146** C2
Strzelin Poland **49** O5
Strzelno Poland **49** P3
Strzyżów Poland **49** S6
Stuart r. Australia **149** E3
Stuart FL U.S.A. **175** D7
Stuart IA U.S.A. **178** D3
Stuart VA U.S.A. **176** E8
Stuart Bluff Range mts Australia **148** B4
Stuart Lake Canada **166** E4
Stuart Mountains N.Z. **153** B13
Stuart Range hills Australia **146** B2
Stuarts Draft U.S.A. **176** F7
Stubaier Alpen mts Austria **48** I8
Stubbenkammer hd Germany **49** K1
Stubica Srbija Yugo. **58** C5
Stubline Srbija Yugo. **58** B4
Stuchka Latvia see Aizkraukle
Stučka Latvia see Aizkraukle
Studenica tourist site Yugo. **58** B5
Studen Kladenets, Yazovir resr Bulg. **58** G7
Studenoye Rus. Fed. **43** S9
Studholme Junction N.Z. **153** F12
Studis S. Africa **132** I10
Stugun Sweden **44** K3
Stupicani Romania **58** G1
Stupart r. Canada **167** M4
Stupino Rus. Fed. **43** T7
Stura di Demonte r. Italy **51** N8
Sturgeon r. Ont. Canada **168** D2
Sturgeon r. Sask. Canada **167** J4
Sturgeon r. U.S.A. **172** G5
Sturgeon Bay b. Canada **167** L4
Sturgeon Bay U.S.A. **172** F6
Sturgeon Bay b. U.S.A. **172** F6
Sturgeon Bay Canal lake channel U.S.A.
172 F6
Sturgeon Falls Canada **168** E3
Sturgeon Lake Canada **173** O6
Sturgis KY U.S.A. **174** C4
Sturgis MI U.S.A. **172** H9
Sturgis SD U.S.A. **178** B2
Šturlić Bos.-Herz. **56** H3
Sturt, Mount hill Australia **146** D2
Sturt Bay Australia **146** C3
Sturt Creek Australia **150** C3
Sturt Creek watercourse Australia **150** B3
Sturtevant U.S.A. **172** F8
Sturt National Park Australia **146** D2
Sturt Plain Australia **148** B3
Sturt Stony Desert Australia **146** D2
Stutterheim S. Africa **133** L8
Stuttgart Germany **48** G7
Stuttgart U.S.A. **174** B5
Stykkishólmur Iceland **44** [inset] B2
Stylida Greece **59** D10
Styr r. Belarus/Ukr. **58** L1
Suaçuí Grande r. Brazil **203** D6
Suai East Timor **75** C5
Suaita Col. **198** C3
Suakin Sudan **121** H5
Suakin Archipelago is Sudan **121** H5
Suana Dem. Rep. Congo **127** D6
Suao Taiwan **87** G3
Suaqui Grande Mex. **184** C2
Suara, Mount Eritrea **121** H6
Surdi Arg. **204** E3
Suárez Col. **198** B4
Suata Venez. **199** E2
Suau P.N.G. **149** F1
Subačius Lith. **42** F6
Subang Indon. **77** D4
Subansiri r. India **78** A2
Subarnarekha r. India **97** E5
Subāshi Iran **100** A3
Subaşı Turkey **58** J7
Subate Latvia **42** G5
Subay reg. Saudi Arabia **105** D3
Subaybah Saudi Arabia **104** D1
Subayhī reg. Yemen **104** D5
Subcetate Romania **58** G2
Subei China **84** B4
also known as Dangchengwan
Subeita tourist site Israel see Shivta
Subiaco Italy **56** F7
Subi Besar i. Indon. **77** E2
Subi Kecil i. Indon. **77** E2
Sublette U.S.A. **178** B4
Subotica Vojvodina, Srbija Yugo. **58** A2
also known as Szabadka
Subucle mt. Chile U.S.A. **182** F5
Success, Lake U.S.A. **182** F5
Suceava Romania **53** H2
formerly spelt Suczawa
Sucha Beskidzka Poland **49** Q6
Suchan Rus. Fed. see Partizansk
Suchan r. Rus. Fed. **82** C4
Suchedniów Poland **49** R4
Suchitepec Mex. **185** F5
Sucio r. Col. **198** B3
Suciu de Sus Romania **58** F1
Suck r. Rep. of Ireland **47** D10
Sucker Creek Landing Canada **173** M4
▶ **Sucre** Bol. **200** D4
Legislative capital of Bolivia.
world [countries] ▶▶▶ 10–11

Sucre dept Col. **198** C2

Sucre state Venez. 199 F2
Sucuaro Col. 198 D3
Sucumbíos prov. Ecuador 198 B5
Sucunduri r. Brazil 199 G6
Sucuriú r. Brazil 206 B7
Suczawa Romania see Suceava
Sud prov. Cameroon 125 H6
Sud, Rivière du r. Canada 177 L1
Suda Rus. Fed. 43 S2
Suda r. Rus. Fed. 43 S2
Sudak Ukr. 41 E7

▶Sudan country Africa 121 E5
Largest country in Africa and 10th largest in the world. Historically known as Anglo-Egyptian Sudan.
world [countries] ▶ 10–11
africa [countries] ▶ 114–117

Suday Rus. Fed. 40 G4
Sudayr reg. Saudi Arabia 105 D2
Sudayr, Sha'ib watercourse Iraq 107 F5
Sudbishchi Rus. Fed. 43 S9
Sud'bodarovka Rus. Fed. 102 C1
Sudbury Canada 168 D4
Sudbury U.K. 47 M11
Sudd swamp Sudan 126 F3
Suddie Guyana 199 G3
Sude r. Germany 48 H2
Sudest Island P.N.G. see Tagula Island
Sudetenland mts Czech Rep./Poland see Sudety
Sudety mts Czech Rep./Poland 49 M5
historically known as Sudetenland
Sudimir Rus. Fed. 43 P8
Sudislavl' Rus. Fed. 40 G4
Sud-Kivu prov. Dem. Rep. Congo 126 F5
Sudlersville U.S.A. 177 J6
Sudogda Rus. Fed. 40 G5
Sudomskiye Vysoty hills Rus. Fed. 43 K4
Sudost' r. Rus. Fed. 43 O9
Sud-Ouest prov. Cameroon 125 H5
Sudr Egypt 121 G2
Sudr, Râs el pt Egypt 108 D8
Suðurland constituency Iceland 44 [inset] B2
Suðuroy i. Faroe Is 46 F2
Suðuroyarfjørður sea chan. Faroe Is 46 F2
Sue watercourse Sudan 126 F3
Sueca Spain 55 K5
Süedinenie Bulg. 58 F6
Suez Egypt 121 G2
also spelt El Suweis or As Suways
Suez, Gulf of Egypt 121 G2
also known as Suweis, Khalîg el or Suways, Khalij as
Suez Bay Egypt 108 D8
also known as Qulzum, Baḥr el
Suez Canal Egypt 121 G2
also known as Suweis, Qanâ el
Şufaynah Saudi Arabia 104 C3
Suffolk U.S.A. 177 I9
Sūfiān Iran 100 A2
Sufi-Kurgan Kyrg. see Sopu-Korgon
Sug-Aksy Rus. Fed. 88 E1
Sugar r. U.S.A. 172 D8
Sugarbush Hill hill U.S.A. 172 E5
Sugar Grove NC U.S.A. 176 D9
Sugar Grove OH U.S.A. 176 C6
Sugarloaf Mountain U.S.A. 174 G2
Sugarloaf Point Australia 147 G3
Sugar Notch U.S.A. 173 R9
Sugbuhan Point Phil. 74 C4
Süget China see Sogat
Sugi i. Indon. 76 C2
Sugun China 88 B4
Sugut r. Sabah Malaysia 77 G1
Sugut, Tanjong pt Sabah Malaysia 77 G1
Suhaia Romania 58 G5
Suhai Hu l. China 84 B4
Suhait China 84 E4
Sūhāj Egypt see Sohâg
Şuḥār Oman 105 G2
English form Sohar
Sühbaatar Mongolia 85 E1
Sühbaatar prov. Mongolia 85 G2
Suheli Par i. India 94 B4
Suhl Germany 48 H5
Suhopolje Croatia 56 J3
Suhul reg. Saudi Arabia 105 D3
Suhūl al Kidan plain Saudi Arabia 105 F3
Suhum Ghana 125 E5
Şuhut Turkey 106 B3
Suiá Missur r. Brazil 202 A4
Sui'an China see Zhangpu
Suibin China 82 C3
Suichang China 87 F2
also known as Miaogao
Suicheng China see Jianning
Suicheng China see Suixi
Suichuan China 87 E3
also known as Quanjiang
Suid-Afrika country Africa see South Africa, Republic of
Suide China 85 F4
also known as Mingzhou
Suidzhikurmsy Turkm. see Madau
Suifen r. China 82 C4
Suifenhe China 82 C3
Suigam India 96 A4
Suihua China 82 B3
Suijiang China 86 B2
also known as Zhongcheng
Suileng China 82 B3
Suining Hunan China 87 D3
also known as Changpu
Suining Jiangsu China 87 F1
Suining Sichuan China 86 C2
Suiping China 87 E1
also known as Zhuoyang
Suippes France 51 K3
Suir r. Rep. of Ireland 47 E11
Suisse country Europe see Switzerland
Suixi Anhui China 87 F1
Suixi Guangdong China 87 D4
also known as Suicheng
Suixian China 87 E1
Suixian China see Suizhou
Suiyang China 87 C3
also known as Yangchuan
Suizhai China see Xiancheng
Suizhong China 85 I3
Suizhou China 87 E2
formerly known as Suixian
Sujangarh India 96 B4
Sujawal Pak. 101 G5
Sukabumi Indon. 77 D4
Sukadana Kalimantan Barat Indon. 77 E3
Sukadana Sumatra Indon. 77 D4
Sukadana, Teluk b. Indon. 77 E3
Sukagawa Japan 90 G6
Sukaramai Indon. 77 E3
Sukarnapura Indon. see Jayapura
Sukarno, Puntjak mt. Indon. see Jaya, Puncak
Suket India 96 C4
Sukeva Fin. 44 N3
Sukhanovka Rus. Fed. 90 C1
Sukhary Belarus 43 L8
Sukhinichi Rus. Fed. 43 Q7
Sukhodol'skoye, Ozero l. Rus. Fed. 43 L1
Sukhodrev r. Rus. Fed. 43 Q7
Sukhona r. Rus. Fed. 43 V2
Sukhothai Thai. 78 B4
Sukhoverkovo Rus. Fed. 43 Q5
Sukhumi Georgia see Sokhumi
Sukhum-Kale Georgia see Sokhumi
Sukkertoppen Greenland see Maniitsoq
Sukkozero Rus. Fed. 40 E3
Sukkur Pak. 101 G5
Sukkur Barrage Pak. 101 G5
Sukma India 94 D2
Sukpay Rus. Fed. 82 E3
Sukpay r. Rus. Fed. 82 E3
Sukri r. India 96 B4
Sukromlya Rus. Fed. 43 P5
Sukromny Rus. Fed. 43 R4
Sukses Namibia 130 C4
Suktel r. India 95 D1
Sukumo Japan 91 C8
Sukun i. Indon. 75 B5
Sul, Canal do sea chan. Brazil 202 B2
Sul, Pico do mt. Brazil 207 J7
Sula i. Norway 46 Q2
Sula r. Rus. Fed. 40 I2
Sula, Kepulauan is Indon. 75 C3
Sula, Ozero l. Rus. Fed. 44 O3
Sulabesi i. Indon. 75 C3
Sulaiman Ranges mts Pak. 101 G4
Sulak Rus. Fed. 102 A4
Sulak r. Rus. Fed. 102 A4
Sūlār Iran 100 B4
Sula Sgeir i. U.K. 46 F4
Sulasih, Gunung vol. Indon. 76 C3
Sulat Phil. 74 C4
Sulawesi i. Indon. see Celebes
Sulawesi Selatan prov. Indon. 75 A3
Sulawesi Tengah prov. Indon. 75 B3
Sulawesi Tenggara prov. Indon. 75 B4
Sulawesi Utara prov. Indon. 75 C2
Sulaymān Beg Iraq 107 F4
Sulayyimah Saudi Arabia 105 D3
Sulci Sardegna Italy see Sant'Antioco
Sulcis Sardegna Italy see Sant'Antioco
Sulechów Poland 49 M3
Sulęcin Poland 49 M3
Suledeh Iran 100 B2
Sulejów Poland 49 Q4
Sulejowskie, Jezioro l. Poland 49 Q4
Suleman, Teluk b. Indon. 75 A2
Sule Skerry i. U.K. 46 H4
Sule Stack i. U.K. 46 H4
Süleymanlı Turkey 107 D3
Suliki Indon. 76 C3
Sulima Sierra Leone 124 C5
Sulina Romania 58 K3
Sulina, Braţul watercourse Romania 58 K3
Suliskongen mt. Norway 44 L2
Sulitjelma Norway 44 L2
Sulkava Fin. 45 O3
Sullana Peru 198 A6
Süller Turkey 59 K10
Sullivan IL U.S.A. 174 B4
Sullivan IN U.S.A. 174 C4
Sullivan Bay Canada 166 E5
Sullivan Island Myanmar see Lanbi Kyun
Sullivan Lake Canada 167 I5
Sully-sur-Loire France 51 I5
Sulmo Italy see Sulmona
Sulmona Italy 56 F6
historically known as Sulmo
Süloğlu Turkey 58 H7
Sulphur LA U.S.A. 179 D6
Sulphur OK U.S.A. 179 C5
Sulphur r. U.S.A. 179 D5
Sulphur Draw watercourse U.S.A. 179 B5
Sulphur Springs U.S.A. 179 D5
Sulphur Springs Draw watercourse U.S.A. 179 B5
Sultan Canada 168 D4
Sultan Libya 120 D2
Sultan, Koh-i- mts Pak. 101 E4
Sultanabad India see Osmannagar
Sultanabad Iran see Arāk
Sultanbeyli Turkey 58 K8
Sultanhanı Turkey 106 C3
Sultanhisar Turkey 59 J11
Sultaniça Turkey 58 H8
Sultanıye Turkey see Karapınar
Sultanpur India 97 D4
Sultansandzharskoye Vodokhranilische resr Turkm. 103 E4
Sulu Dem. Rep. Congo 126 E6
Suluan i. Phil. 74 C4
Sulu Archipelago is Phil. 74 B5
Sülüklü Turkey 106 C3
Sülüktü Kyrg. 103 G5
also spelt Sulyukta
Suluntah Libya 120 D1
Sulūq Libya 120 D2
Suluru India 94 D3
Sulu Sea N. Pacific Ocean 74 A4
Sulyukta Kyrg. see Sülüktü
Sulzbach-Rosenberg Germany 48 I6
Sulzberger Bay Antarctica 222 N1
Sumaco, Volcán vol. Ecuador 198 B5
Šumadija reg. Yugo. 58 B4
Sumāil Oman 105 G3
Sumalata Indon. 75 B2
Sumampa Arg. 204 E3
Sumangat, Tanjong pt Sabah Malaysia 74 A5
Sumapaz, Parque Nacional nat. park Col. 198 C4
Sumatera i. Indon. see Sumatra
Sumatera Barat prov. Indon. 76 C3
Sumatera Selatan prov. Indon. 76 C3
Sumatera Utara prov. Indon. 76 B2

▶Sumatra i. Indon. 76 B2
2nd largest island in Asia and 6th in the world. Also spelt Sumatera.
asia [landscapes] ▶ 62–63

Sumaúma Brazil 201 E1
Šumava mts Czech Rep. 49 K6
Šumava nat. park Czech Rep. 49 K6
Sumba i. Indon. 75 B5
Sumba, Île i. Dem. Rep. Congo 126 C4
Sumba, Selat sea chan. Indon. 75 A5
Sumbar r. Turkm. 102 C5
Sumbawa i. Indon. 77 G5
Sumbawabesar Indon. 77 G5
Sumbawanga Tanz. 129 A6
Sumbay Peru 200 C3
Sumbe Angola 127 B7
formerly known as Ngunza or Ngunza-Kabolu or Novo Redondo
Sumbing, Gunung vol. Indon. 76 C3
Sumbu Zambia 127 F7
Sumbu National Park Zambia 127 F7
also spelt Nsumbu National Park
Sumburgh U.K. 46 K4
Sumburgh Head U.K. 46 K4
Sumbuya Sierra Leone 124 C5
Sumdo Aksai Chin 89 B5
Sumdo China 86 B2
Sumdum, Mount U.S.A. 166 C3
Sumé Brazil 202 E3
Sumedang Indon. 77 D4
Sume'eh Sarā Iran 100 B2
Sümeg Hungary 49 O9
Sumeih Sudan 126 E2
Sumenep Indon. 77 F4
Sumerpur India 96 B4
Sumgait Azer. see Sumqayıt
Sumisu-jima i. Japan 91 G9
Sümiyn Bulag Mongolia 85 G1
Summēl Iraq 107 E3
Summer Beaver Canada 168 B2
Summerdown Namibia 130 C4
Summerford Canada 169 K3
Summer Island U.S.A. 172 G5
Summerland Canada 166 G5
Summerside Canada 169 I4
Summersville U.S.A. 176 E7
Summersville Lake U.S.A. 176 E7
Summerville GA U.S.A. 174 C5
Summerville SC U.S.A. 175 D5
Summit Lake B.C. Canada 166 E3
Summit Lake B.C. Canada 166 F4
Summit Mountain U.S.A. 183 H2
Summit Peak U.S.A. 181 F5
Sumnal Aksai Chin 89 B5
Sumner U.S.A. 174 B5
Sumner, Lake N.Z. 153 G10
Sumner Strait U.S.A. 166 C3
Sumon-dake mt. Japan 90 F6
Sumoto Japan 91 D7
Sumpangbinangae Indon. 75 A4
Šumperk Czech Rep. 49 N6
Sumprabum Myanmar 78 B2
Sumpu Japan see Shizuoka
Sumqayıt Azer. 107 G2
also spelt Sumgait
Sumqayıt r. Azer. 107 G2
Sumsar Kyrg. 103 G4
Sumskiy Posad Rus. Fed. 40 E2
Sumter U.S.A. 175 D5
Sumy Ukr. 41 E6
Sun r. U.S.A. 180 E3
Suna Rus. Fed. 40 I4
Sunagawa Japan 90 G3
Sunam India 96 B3
Sunamganj Bangl. 97 F4
Sunan China 84 C4
also known as Hongwansi
Sunan N. Korea 83 B5
Sunaynah Oman 105 F3
Sunaysilah salt l. Iraq 109 M2
Sunbright U.S.A. 176 A9
Sunbula Kuh mts Iran 100 A3
Sunbury Australia 147 E4
Sunbury NC U.S.A. 177 I9
Sunbury OH U.S.A. 176 C5
Sunbury PA U.S.A. 177 I5
Sunchales Arg. 204 E3
Suncho Corral Arg. 204 E2
Sunch'ŏn N. Korea 83 B5
Sunch'ŏn S. Korea 83 B6
Sun City S. Africa 133 L2
Sun City U.S.A. 183 L8
Suncook U.S.A. 177 N2
Sund Fin. 42 B1
Sunda, Selat strait Indon. 77 D4
English form Sunda Strait
Sunda Kalapa Indon. see Jakarta
Sundance U.S.A. 180 F3
Sundarbans reg. Bangl./India 97 F5
Sundarbans National Park Bangl./India 97 F5
Sundargarh India 97 E5
Sundarnagar India 96 C3
Sunda Strait Indon. see Sunda, Selat
Sundays r. E. Cape S. Africa 133 J10
Sundays r. Kwazulu-Natal S. Africa 133 O5
Sunday Strait Australia 150 C3
Sunderland U.K. 47 K9
Sündiken Dağları mts Turkey 106 B3
Sundre Canada 167 H5
Sundridge Canada 168 E4
Sundsvall Sweden 45 L3
Sundukli, Peski des. Turkm. 103 E5
also known as Sandykly Gumy
Sundumbili S. Africa 133 P6
Sunel India 96 C4
Sunga Tanz. 129 C6
Sungaiapit Indon. 76 C2
Sungaiguntung Indon. 76 C2
Sungailiat Indon. 77 D3
Sungaipenuh Indon. 76 C3
Sungaipinyuh Indon. 77 E2
Sungai Tuas Basin dock Sing. 76 [inset]
Sungari r. China see Songhua Jiang
Sungei Petani Malaysia 76 C1
Sungei Seletar Reservoir Sing. 76 [inset]
Sungguminasa Indon. 75 A4
Sungikai Sudan 121 F6
Sungkiang China see Songjiang
Sung Kong i. Hong Kong China 87 [inset]
Sungo Moz. 131 G3
Sungqu China see Songpan
Sungurlare Bulg. 58 H6
Sungurlu Turkey 106 C2
Sunja Croatia 56 I3
Sunkar, Gora mt. Kazakh. 103 H3
Sunkosh r. Bhutan 97 F4
also spelt Sankosh
Sun Kosi r. Nepal 97 E4
Sunndal Norway 45 I3
Sunndalsøra Norway 44 J3
Sunne Sweden 45 K4
Sunnyside UT U.S.A. 183 N2
Sunnyside WA U.S.A. 180 C3
Sunnyvale U.S.A. 182 B4
Sun Prairie U.S.A. 172 D7
Sunsas, Sierra de hills Bol. 201 F4
Sunset House Canada 167 G4
Sunset Peak hill Hong Kong China 87 [inset]
also known as Tai Tung Shan
Sunshine Island Hong Kong China 87 [inset]
also known as Chau Kung To
Suntar Rus. Fed. 39 L3
Suntsar Pak. 101 E5
Suntu Eth. 128 C2
Sunwi-do i. N. Korea 83 B5
Sunwu China 82 B2
Sunyani Ghana 124 E5
Suojanperä Fin. 44 O1
Suolahti Fin. 44 N3
Suoljärvet l. Fin. 40 D2
Suoločielgi Fin. see Saariselkä
Suoluvuobmi Norway 44 M1
Suomenniemi Fin. 45 N3
Suomi Canada 172 D2
Suomi country Europe see Finland
Suomusjärvi Fin. 42 E1
Suomussalmi Fin. 44 O2
Suō-nada b. Japan 91 B8
Suonenjoki Fin. 44 N3
Suŏng Cambodia 79 D6
Suong r. Laos 78 C4
Suontee Fin. 44 N3
Suontienselkä l. Fin. 44 N3
Suoyarvi Rus. Fed. 40 E3
Suozhen China see Huantai
Supa India 94 B3
Supai U.S.A. 183 L5
Supaul India 97 E4
Superfosfatnyy Uzbek. 103 F5
Superior AZ U.S.A. 183 M8
Superior MT U.S.A. 180 D3
Superior NE U.S.A. 178 C3
Superior WI U.S.A. 172 A4
Superior, Laguna lag. Mex. 185 G5

▶Superior, Lake Canada/U.S.A. 172 F3
Largest lake in North America and 2nd in the world.
northamerica [landscapes] ▶ 156–157

Supetar Croatia 56 I5
Suphan Buri Thai. 79 C5
Süphan Dağı mt. Turkey 107 E3
Supiori i. Indon. 73 I7
Suponevo Rus. Fed. 43 P8
Support Force Glacier Antarctica 223 V1
Supraśl Poland 49 U2
Supraśl r. Poland 49 U2
Sup'sa r. Georgia 107 E2
Supung N. Korea 83 B4
Sūq al Inān Yemen 104 D4
Sūq ar Rubū' Saudi Arabia 104 C3
Sūq ash Shuyūkh Iraq 107 F5
Suqian China 87 F1
Sūq Suwayq Saudi Arabia 104 B2
Suquṭrā i. Yemen see Socotra
Sur r. Ghana 125 E4
Súr Hungary 49 P3
Şūr Oman 105 G3
Sur, Point U.S.A. 182 C5
Sur, Punta pt Arg. 204 F5
Sura Rus. Fed. 41 H5
Sura r. Rus. Fed. 41 H4
Şuraabad Azer. 107 G2
Surab Pak. 101 F4
Surabaya Indon. 77 F4
formerly spelt Soerabaia
Surajpur India 97 D5
Sūrak Iran 100 D5
Surakarta Indon. 77 E4
Suramana Indon. 75 A3
Şura Mare Romania 58 F3
Sūrān Iran 101 E5
Şūrān Syria 109 H2
Surára Brazil 199 F6
Surat Australia 147 F1
Surat India 96 B5
Suratgarh India 96 B3
Surat Thani Thai. 79 B6
also known as Ban Don
Suraż Poland 49 T3
Surazh Belarus 43 L6
Surazh Rus. Fed. 43 N8
Surbiton Australia 149 E4
Sūrdāsh Iraq 107 F4
Surdila-Greci Romania 58 I3
Surduc Romania 58 E1
Surdulica Srbija Yugo. 58 D6
Sûre r. Germany/Lux. 51 M3
Surendranagar India 96 A5
formerly known as Wadhwan
Suretka Costa Rica 186 C5
Surf U.S.A. 182 D7
Surgana India 94 B1
Surgères France 50 F6
Surgidero de Batabanó Cuba 186 C2
Surgut Rus. Fed. 38 H3
Suri India see Siuri
Suriapet India 94 C2
also spelt Suryapet
Surigao Phil. 74 C4
Surigao Strait Phil. 74 C4
Surimena Col. 198 C4
Surin Thai. 79 C5
Surinam country S. America see Suriname
▶Suriname country S. America 199 G3
also spelt Surinam; formerly known as Dutch Guiana
southamerica [countries] ▶ 192–193
Suriname r. Suriname 199 H3
Suripá Venez. 198 D3
Suriyān Iran 100 C4
Surkhābād Iran 100 C3
Surkhandar'inskaya Oblast' admin. div. Uzbek. 103 F5
English form Surkhandarya Oblast; also known as Surkhondaryo Wiloyati
Surkhandar'ya r. Uzbek. 103 F5
Surkhandarya Oblast admin. div. Uzbek. see Surkhandar'inskaya Oblast'
Surkhet Nepal 97 D3
also known as Birendranagar
Surkhob r. Tajik. 101 G2
Surkhondaryo r. Uzbek. see Surkhandar'ya
Surkhondaryo Wiloyati admin. div. Uzbek. see Surkhandar'inskaya Oblast'
Surmaq Iran 100 C4
Sürmene Turkey 107 E2
Surnadalsøra Norway 44 J3
Surnevo Bulg. 58 G6
Surovikino Rus. Fed. 41 G6
Surprise Canada 166 C3
Surprise Lake Canada 166 C3
Surrey Canada 166 F5
Surskoye Rus. Fed. 41 H5
Surt Libya see Sirte
Surt, Khalīj g. Libya see Sirte, Gulf of
Surtsey i. Iceland 44 [inset] B3
Sürü Iran 100 D5
Suru, Vârful mt. Romania 58 F3
Surubiú r. Brazil 202 B2
Suruç Turkey 107 D3
Surud, Raas pt Somalia 128 E2
Surud Ad mt. Somalia see Shimbiris
Suruga-wan b. Japan 91 F7
Surulangun Indon. 76 C3
Surumú r. Brazil 199 F4
Surup Phil. 74 C5
Suryapet India see Suriapet
Şuşa Azer. 107 F3
also spelt Shusha
Susa Italy 51 N7
Susa Japan 91 B7
Sušac i. Croatia 56 I6
Susah Tunisia see Sousse
Susak i. Croatia 56 G4
Susaki Japan 91 C8
Susami Japan 91 D8
Susan U.S.A. 177 I8
Sūsangerd Iran 100 B4
Susanville U.S.A. 182 D1
Suşehri Turkey 107 D2
Sushitsa Bulg. 58 G5
Sushui r. China 87 D1
Sušice Czech Rep. 49 K6
Suškova Latvia 43 J5
Susner India 96 C5
Susong China 87 F2
Susquehanna U.S.A. 177 J4
Susquehanna r. U.S.A. 177 I6
Susquehanna, West Branch r. U.S.A. 176 I5
Susques Arg. 200 D5
Sussex Canada 169 H4
Sussex U.S.A. 177 K4
Susua Indon. 75 B3
Susuman Rus. Fed. 39 O3
Susupu Indon. 75 C2
Susurluk Turkey 106 B3
Sušvė r. Lith. 42 E6
Suswa, Mount Kenya 128 B5
Susz Poland 49 Q2
Sutak Jammu and Kashmir 96 C2
Sutaşı Turkey 108 G1
Sutay Uul mt. Mongolia 84 B2
Sutherland Australia 147 F3
Sutherland S. Africa 132 E9
Sutherland NE U.S.A. 178 B3
Sutherland VA U.S.A. 176 H8
Sutherland Range hills Australia 151 D5
Sutjeska nat. park Bos.-Herz. 56 K5
Sutlej r. India/Pak. 96 A3
also spelt Satluj
Sutlepa meri l. Estonia 42 E2
Sütlüce Turkey 108 E1
Sütlüce Turkey 58 I7
Sutter U.S.A. 182 C2
Sutter Creek U.S.A. 182 D3
Sutton r. Canada 168 D2
Sutton U.K. 47 M11
Sutton NE U.S.A. 178 C3
Sutton WV U.S.A. 176 E7
Sutton Coldfield U.K. 47 K11
Sutton Lake Canada 168 C2
Sutton Lake U.S.A. 176 E7
Suttor r. Australia 149 E4
Suttsu Japan 90 G3
Sutwik Island U.S.A. 164 D4
Sutyr' r. Rus. Fed. 82 D2
Suugant Mongolia 85 E2
Suurberg mt. S. Africa 133 J8
Suurberg mts S. Africa 133 J10
Suurbraak S. Africa 132 E11
Suure-Jaani Estonia 42 G3
Suuremõisa Estonia 42 D3
Suur katel b. Estonia 42 D3
Suur-Pakri i. Estonia 42 E2
Suurpea Estonia 42 G2
Suur väin sea chan. Estonia 42 E3

▶Suva Fiji 145 G3
Capital of Fiji.

Suvalki Poland see Suwałki
Suva Reka Kosovo, Srbija Yugo. 58 B6
Suvarov atoll Cook Is see Suwarrow
Suvorov Rus. Fed. 43 R7
Suvorove Ukr. 58 J3
Suvorovo Bulg. 58 I5
formerly known as Novgradets
Suvorovo Moldova see Ştefan Vodă
Suwa Japan 91 F6
Suwakong Indon. 77 F3
Suwałki Poland 49 T1
formerly spelt Suvalki
Suwannaphum Thai. 79 C5
Suwannee r. U.S.A. 175 D6
Suwanose-jima i. Japan 83 C7
Suwaran, Gunung mt. Indon. 77 G2
Suwarrow atoll Cook Is 221 H6
also known as Anchorage Island; also spelt Suvorov
Suwaylih Jordan 108 G5
also spelt Suweilih
Suwayqiyah, Hawr as imp. l. Iraq 107 F4
Suwayr well Saudi Arabia 107 E5
Suways, Khalij as g. Egypt see Suez, Gulf of
Suweilih Jordan see Suwaylih
Suweis, Khalig el g. Egypt see Suez, Gulf of
Suweis, Qanâ el canal Egypt see Suez Canal
Suwŏn S. Korea 83 B5
Suxu China 87 D4
Suykbulak Kazakh. 103 J2
Suyo Peru 198 A6
Süyqbulaq Kazakh. see Suykbulak
Suz, Mys pt Kazakh. 102 C4
Sūzā Iran 100 D5
Suzak Kazakh. 103 G3
also spelt Sozaq
Suzaka Japan 91 F6
Suzdal' Rus. Fed. 43 V5
Suzemka Rus. Fed. 43 P9
Suzhou Anhui China 87 F1
Suzhou China see Jiuquan
Suzhou Jiangsu China 87 G2
formerly spelt Soochow
Suzi r. China 82 B4
Suzu Japan 90 E6
Suzuka Japan 91 E7
Suzu-misaki pt Japan 83 E5
Suzzara Italy 56 C4
Sværholthalvøya pen. Norway 44 N1

▶Svalbard terr. Arctic Ocean 38 A2
Part of Norway.

Svalenik Bulg. 58 H5
Svanstein Sweden 44 M2
Svapa r. Rus. Fed. 43 Q9
Svappavaara Sweden 44 M2
also known as Veaikevárri
Svapushcha Rus. Fed. 43 N4
Svärdsjö Sweden 45 K3
Svarta r. Fin. 42 G1
Svartälven r. Sweden 45 K4
Svartbyn Sweden 44 M2
Svartenhuk Halvø pen. Greenland see Sigguup Nunaa
Svartlå Sweden 44 M2
Svatove Ukr. 41 F6
Svay Riĕng Cambodia 79 D6
Svecha Rus. Fed. 40 H4
Svėdasai Lith. 42 G6
Sveg Sweden 45 K3
Svegsjön l. Sweden 45 K3
Sveio Norway 45 I4
Sveki Latvia 42 H4
Švėkšna Lith. 42 C6
Svelgen Norway 45 I3
Svellingen Norway 44 J3
Švenčionėliai Lith. 42 G6
Švenčionys Lith. 42 H6
Svendborg Denmark 45 J5
Svenljunga Sweden 45 K4
Svenstavik Sweden 44 K3
Šventoji r. Lith. 42 F6
Sverchkovo Rus. Fed. 43 Q6
Sverdlovsk Rus. Fed. see Yekaterinburg
Sverdlovs'k Ukr. 41 F6
Sverdlovsk Uzbek. 103 F5
Sverdlovskaya Oblast' admin. div. Rus. Fed. 40 L4
English form Sverdlovsk Oblast
Sverdlovsk Oblast admin. div. Rus. Fed. see Sverdlovskaya Oblast'
Sverdrup Channel Canada 165 J2
Sverdrup Islands Canada 165 J2
Sverige country Europe see Sweden
Sveta Andrija i. Croatia 56 H5
Švėtė r. Lith. 42 E5
Sveti Ivan Zelina Croatia see Zelina
Sveti Jure mt. Croatia 56 J5
Sveti Nikole Macedonia 58 C7
Svetlaya Rus. Fed. 82 E3
Svetlodarskoye Rus. Fed. 82 F2
Svetlogorsk Belarus see Svyetlahorsk
Svetlogorsk Kaliningradskaya Oblast' Rus. Fed. 42 B7
historically known as Rauschen
Svetlogorsk Krasnoyarskiy Kray Rus. Fed. 39 I3
Svetlograd Rus. Fed. 41 G7
formerly known as Petrovskoye
Svetlopolyansk Rus. Fed. 40 J4
Svetlovodsk Ukr. see Svitlovods'k
Svetlyy Rus. Fed. 42 B7
historically known as Zimmerbude
Svetlyy Rus. Fed. 103 E2
Svetlyy Yar Rus. Fed. 41 H6
Svetogorsk Rus. Fed. 43 J1
Svetozarevo Srbija Yugo. see Jagodina
Švētupe r. Latvia 42 F4
Sviahnúkar vol. Iceland 44 [inset] C2
Svidnik Slovakia 49 S6
Sviibi Estonia 42 E3
Svilaja mts Croatia 56 I5
Svilajnac Srbija Yugo. 58 C4
Svilengrad Bulg. 58 H7
Svinecea Mare, Vârful mt. Romania 58 D4
Svino i. Faroe Is see Svínoy
Svínoy i. Faroe Is 46 F1
also spelt Svinø
Svintsovyy Rudnik Turkm. 103 F5
Svir Belarus 42 H7
Svir' r. Rus. Fed. 43 P1
Svir, Vozyera l. Belarus 42 H7
Sviritsa Rus. Fed. 43 N1
Svirskaya Guba b. Rus. Fed. 43 N1
Svir'stroy Rus. Fed. 43 O1
Svishtov Bulg. 58 G5
Svislach Hrodzyenskaya Voblasts' Belarus 42 F8
Svislach Minskaya Voblasts' Belarus 42 I8
Svislach r. Belarus/Poland 42 F8
also spelt Svisloch or Świslocz
Svislach r. Belarus 42 J8
also spelt Svisloch
Svisloch r. Belarus see Svislach
Svisloch r. Belarus see Svislach
Svit Slovakia 49 R6
Svitava r. Czech Rep. 49 N7
Svitavy Czech Rep. 49 N6
Svitlovods'k Ukr. 41 E6
also spelt Svetlovodsk; formerly known as Khrushchev or Kremges
Svizzera country Europe see Switzerland
Svoboda Rus. Fed. 42 C7
Svobodnyy Rus. Fed. 82 C2
Svoge Bulg. 58 E6
Svol'nya r. Belarus 43 J6
Svolvær Norway 44 K1
Svratka r. Czech Rep. 49 N6
Svrljig Srbija Yugo. 58 D5
Svrljiške Planine mts Yugo. 58 D5
Svyantsyanskiya Hrady hills Belarus 42 H7
Svyatoy Nos, Mys c. Rus. Fed. 40 I2
Svyatsk Rus. Fed. 43 M9
Svyetlahorsk Belarus 43 K9
also spelt Svetlogorsk; formerly known as Shatilki
Svyha r. Ukr. 43 O9
Swabi Pak. 101 H3
Swaershoek S. Africa 133 J9
Swaershoekpas pass S. Africa 133 J9
Swain Reefs Australia 149 G4
Swainsboro U.S.A. 175 D5
Swains Island American Samoa 145 H3
also known as Olosenga
Swakop watercourse Namibia 130 B4
Swakopmund Namibia 130 B4
Swale r. U.K. 47 K9
Swallow Islands Solomon Is 145 F3
Swampy r. Canada 169 G1
Swan r. Australia 151 A6
Swan r. Man./Sask. Canada 167 K4
Swan r. Ont. Canada 168 D2
Swanage U.K. 47 K13
Swana-Mume Dem. Rep. Congo 127 E7
Swandale U.S.A. 176 E7
Swanepoelspoort mt. S. Africa 132 H10
Swan Hill Australia 147 D3
Swan Hills Canada 167 H4
Swan Islands is Caribbean Sea 186 C3
also known as Santanilla, Islas
Swan Lake B.C. Canada 166 D4
Swan Lake Man. Canada 167 K4
Swan Lake U.S.A. 172 B8
Swanlinbar Rep. of Ireland 47 E9
Swanquarter U.S.A. 174 E5
Swanquarter National Wildlife Refuge nature res. U.S.A. 174 E5
Swan Reach Australia 146 C3
Swan River Canada 167 K4
Swansea Australia 147 F5
Swansea U.K. 47 I12
also known as Abertawe
Swansea Bay U.K. 47 I12
Swans Island U.S.A. 177 Q1
Swanton CA U.S.A. 182 B4
Swanton VT U.S.A. 177 L1
Swartberg S. Africa 133 N7
Swartberg mt. S. Africa 132 D11
Swartbergpas pass S. Africa 132 F10
Swartdoorn r. S. Africa 132 B7
Swart Kei r. S. Africa 133 L9
Swartkolkvloer salt pan S. Africa 132 E7
Swartkops r. S. Africa 133 J10
Swart Nossob watercourse Namibia see Black Nossob
Swartplaas S. Africa 133 K3
Swartputs S. Africa 132 H5
Swartput se Pan salt pan Namibia 132 D3
Swartruggens S. Africa 133 K2
Swartruggens mts S. Africa 133 K2
Swartz Creek U.S.A. 173 J8
Swarzędz Poland 49 O3
Swasey Peak U.S.A. 183 K2
Swastika Canada 173 M2
Swat r. Pak. 101 G3
Swat Kohistan reg. Pak. 101 H3
Swatow China see Shantou
▶Swaziland country Africa 133 P3
known as Ngwane in Swazi
africa [countries] ▶ 114–117

▶Sweden country Europe 45 K4
5th largest country in Europe. Known as Sverige in Swedish.
europe [countries] ▶ 32–35

Swedesburg U.S.A. 172 B9
Sweet Briar U.S.A. 176 F8
Sweet Home U.S.A. 180 B3
Sweet Springs U.S.A. 176 E8
Sweetwater U.S.A. 179 B5
Sweetwater r. U.S.A. 180 F4
Swellendam S. Africa 132 E11
Swempoort S. Africa 133 L8
Świder r. Poland 49 S3
Świdnica Poland 49 N5
Świdnik Poland 49 T4
Świdwin Poland 49 M2
Świebodzice Poland 49 N5
Świebodzin Poland 49 M3
Świecie Poland 49 P2
Świętokrzyskie, Góry hills Poland 49 R5
Świętokrzyski Park Narodowy nat. park Poland 49 R5
Swift r. U.S.A. 177 O1
Swift Current Canada 167 J5
Swiftcurrent Creek r. Canada 167 J5
Swilly, Lough inlet Rep. of Ireland 47 E8
Swindon U.K. 47 K12
Swinkpan imp. l. S. Africa 133 J5
Świnoujście Poland 49 L2
Swiss Confederation country Europe see Switzerland
Swiss National Park Switz. 51 Q6
Świstocz r. Belarus see Svislach
▶Switzerland country Europe 51 N6
known as Schweiz in German or Suisse in French or Svizzera in Italian; also known as Swiss Confederation; long form Confoederatio Helvetica
europe [countries] ▶ 32–35
Swords Rep. of Ireland 47 F10
Swords Range hills Australia 149 D4
Syalyets Belarus 43 L8
Syalyets Vodaskhovishcha resr Belarus 42 F9
Syamozero, Ozero l. Rus. Fed. 40 E3
Syamzha Rus. Fed. 43 V2
Syang Nepal 97 D3
Syanno Belarus 43 K7
also spelt Senno
Syarednenemanskaya Nizina lowland Belarus/Lith. 42 F8
Syas' r. Rus. Fed. 43 N1
Syas'troy Rus. Fed. 43 N1
Sybrandskraal S. Africa 133 M2
Sycamore U.S.A. 172 E9
Sychevka Rus. Fed. 43 P6
Sychevo Rus. Fed. 43 R6
Syców Poland 49 O4
Sydenham atoll Kiribati see Nonouti

▶Sydney Australia 147 F3
State capital of New South Wales. Most populous city in Oceania. Historically known as Port Jackson.
world [cities] ▶ 24–25
oceania [features] ▶ 142–143

Sydney Canada 169 I4
Sydney Island Kiribati see Manra
Sydney Lake Canada 167 M5
Sydney Mines Canada 169 I4
Sydzhak Uzbek. see Sidzhak
Syedra tourist site Turkey 108 D1
Syeverodonets'k Ukr. 41 F6
also spelt Severodonetsk; formerly known as Leskhimstroy
Sykesville U.S.A. 176 G4
Sykkylven Norway 44 I3
Syktyvkar Rus. Fed. 40 I3
Sylacauga U.S.A. 175 C5
Sylhet Bangl. 97 F4
Sylhet admin. div. Bangl. 97 F4
Sylt i. Germany 48 F1
Sylva r. Rus. Fed. 40 K4
Sylva U.S.A. 174 D5
Sylvania GA U.S.A. 175 D5
Sylvania OH U.S.A. 176 B4
Sylvan Lake Canada 167 H4
Sylvester U.S.A. 175 D6
Sylvester, Lake salt flat Australia 148 B3
Sylvia, Mount Canada 166 E3

index

S T

Symi Greece 59 I12
Symi *i.* Greece 59 I12
  also spelt Simi
Syndicate Phil. 74 B3
Synel'nykove Ukr. 41 E6
  also spelt Sinel'nikovo
Syngagyn, Mys Kazakh. 41 J8
  also spelt Sengirli, Mys
Syngyrli, Mys *pt* Kazakh. *see* Sengirli, Mys
Synnagyn, Khrebet *mts* Rus. Fed. 39 M4
Synnfjell *mt.* Norway 45 J3
Synnott Range *hills* Australia 150 D3
Synya Rus. Fed. 40 K2
Synya *r.* Rus. Fed. 40 M2
Syowa *research station* Antarctica 223 C2
Syracusae Sicilia Italy *see* Syracuse
Syracuse Sicilia Italy 57 H11
  also spelt Siracusa; historically known as Syracusae
Syracuse KS U.S.A. 178 B4
Syracuse NY U.S.A. 177 I2
Syrdar'inskaya Oblast' *admin. div.* Uzbek. 103 G4
  English form Syr Darya Oblast; also known as Sirdaryo Wiloyati
Syr Darya *r.* Asia *see* Syrdar'ya
Syrdar'ya *r.* Asia 99 H1
  English form Syr Darya; also known as Dar'yoi Sir; also known as Sirdaryo
Syrdar'ya Uzbek. 103 G4
  also spelt Sirdaryo; formerly known as Syrdaryinskiy
Syrdarya Oblast *admin. div.* Uzbek. *see* Syrdar'inskaya Oblast'
Syrdaryinskiy Uzbek. *see* Syrdar'ya
Syria *country* Asia 109 I2
  spelt As Sūriyah or Souriya in Arabic
  asia [countries] ▶▶ 64–67
Syriam Myanmar 78 B4
Syrian Desert Asia 107 D4
  also known as Bādiyat ash Shām
Syrna *i.* Greece 59 H12
  also spelt Sirína
Syrokvashino Rus. Fed. 43 L5
Syros *i.* Greece 59 F11
  also spelt Síros
Syrskiy Rus. Fed. 43 U9
Sysmä Fin. 45 N3
Sysola *r.* Rus. Fed. 40 I3
Sysoyevo Rus. Fed. 43 R2
Syumsi Rus. Fed. 40 I4
Syun *r.* Rus. Fed. 40 J5
Syurkum Rus. Fed. 82 C2
Syurkum, Mys *pt* Rus. Fed. 82 C2
Syzran' Rus. Fed. 41 I5
Szabadka Vojvodina, Srbija Yugo. *see* Subotica
Szabadszállás Hungary 49 Q9
Szamocin Poland 49 P4
Szamocin Poland 49 N3
Szamos *r.* Hungary 49 T7
Szamotuły Poland 49 N3
Szany Hungary 49 O8
Szarvas Hungary 49 R9
Szatmár-Beregi *park* Hungary 49 T7
Szczebrzeszyn Poland 49 T5
Szczecin Poland 49 L2
  historically known as Stettin
Szczecinek Poland 49 N2
Szczekociny Poland 49 Q5
Szczuczyn Poland 49 S2
Szczytno Poland 49 R2
Szechwan *prov.* China *see* Sichuan
Szeged Hungary 49 R9
Szeghalom Hungary 49 S8
Székesfehérvár Hungary 49 P8
Szekszárd Hungary 49 P9
Szentes Hungary 49 R9
Szentgotthárd Hungary 49 N9
  historically known as Sankt Gotthard
Szentőrinc Hungary 49 O9
Szerencs Hungary 49 S7
Szestra Góra Poland 49 T1
Szigetszentmiklós Hungary 49 Q8
Szigetvár Hungary 49 O9
Szkwa *r.* Poland 49 S3
Szlichtyngowa Poland 49 N4
Szolnok Hungary 49 R8
Szombathely Hungary 49 N8
Szprotawa Poland 49 M4
Sztálinváros Hungary *see* Dunaújváros
Sztum Poland 49 Q2
Szubin Poland 49 O3
Szúcsi Hungary 49 R8
Szydłowiec Poland 49 R4
Szypliszki Poland 49 T1

↓ **T**

Taabo, Lac de *l.* Côte d'Ivoire 124 D5
Taagga Duudka *reg.* Somalia 128 D2
Taal, Lake Phil. 74 B3
Tab Hungary 49 P9
Tabaco Phil. 74 B3
Tābah Saudi Arabia 104 C2
Tabajara Brazil 201 E3
Tabakat *well* Mali 125 E3
Tabanan Indon. 77 F5
Tabang Indon. 77 G2

Tabang *r.* Indon. 77 F2
Tabankulu S. Africa 133 N7
Tabaqah Syria 109 J2
Tabaqah Syria *see* Madīnat ath Thawrah
Tabar Islands P.N.G. 145 E2
Tabarka Tunisia 57 A12
Tabas Khorāsān Iran 100 D3
Tabas Khorāsān Iran 101 E3
Tabasalu Estonia 42 F2
Tabāsīn Iran 100 D4
Tabasco *state* Mex. 185 G5
Tābask, Kūh-e *mt.* Iran 100 B4
Tabatinga Brazil 199 D6
Tabatinga, Serra da *hills* Brazil 202 C4
Tabayoo, Mount Phil. 74 B2
Tabēdē *well* Chad 120 B6
Tabelbala Alg. 123 E3
Taber Canada 167 H5
Taberdga Alg. 123 G2
Tabernas Spain 55 I11
Tabernes de Valldigna Spain *see* Tavernes de la Valldigna
Tabet, Nam *r.* Myanmar 78 B2
Tabia Tsaka *salt l.* China 89 D6
Tabin Wildlife Reserve *nature res.* Sabah Malaysia 77 G1
Tabir *r.* Indon. 76 C3
Tabiteuea *atoll* Kiribati 145 G2
  also known as Taputeouea; formerly known as Drummond
Tabivere Estonia 42 H3
Tablas *i.* Phil. 74 B3
Tablas Strait Phil. 74 B3
Table Bay S. Africa 132 C10
Table Cape N.Z. 152 L7
Table Islands India 79 A5
Table Mountain *hill* S. Africa 132 C10
Table Point Phil. 74 A4
Table Rock Reservoir U.S.A. 178 D4
Tabligbo Togo 125 F5
Taboca Brazil 199 F5
Tabocal *r.* Brazil 199 F6
Taboco *r.* Brazil 201 G4
Tabong Myanmar 78 B2
Tábor Czech Rep. 49 L6
Tabora Tanz. 129 B6
Tabora *admin. reg.* Tanz. 129 B6
Taboshar Tajik. 101 G1
Tabou Côte d'Ivoire 124 D5
Tabriz Iran 100 A2
Tabuaeran *i.* Kiribati 221 H5
Tabūk Saudi Arabia 104 B1
Tabūk *prov.* Saudi Arabia 104 B1
Tabulam Indon. 75 B3
Tabuny Rus. Fed. 103 I1
Tabuyung Indon. 76 B2
Täby Sweden 45 L4
Tacaipu, Serra *hills* Brazil 199 H5
Tacalé Brazil 199 I4
Tacámbaro Mex. 185 E5
Tacaná, Volcán de *vol.* Mex. 185 G6
Tacaruna, Cerro *mt.* Panama 186 D5
Tachdaït *well* Mali 125 F2
Tacheng China 88 C2
  also known as Qoqek; formerly known as Chuguchak
Tachibana-wan *b.* Japan 91 A8
Tachie Canada 166 E4
Tachikawa Tōkyō Japan 91 F7
Tachikawa Yamagata Japan 90 F5
Táchira *state* Venez. 198 C2
Tachiumet *well* Libya 120 A3
Tachov Czech Rep. 49 J6
Tacina *r.* Italy 57 I10
Taciuã, Lago *l.* Brazil 199 F6
Tacloban Phil. 74 C4
Tacna Col. 198 D5
Tacna Peru 200 C4
Tacna *dept* Peru 200 C4
Tacoma U.S.A. 180 B3
Taconite Harbor U.S.A. 172 C3
Taco Pozo Arg. 204 E2
Tacuarembó Uruguay 204 G3
Tacupeto Mex. 184 C2
Tadami Japan 90 F6
Tadami-gawa *r.* Japan 90 F6
Tadêlaka *well* Niger 125 G3
Tademaït, Plateau du Alg. 123 F3
  English form Tademaït Plateau
Tademaït Plateau du Alg. *see* Tademaït, Plateau du
Tadine New Caledonia 145 F4
Tadjentourt *hill* Alg. 123 H4
Tadjeraout, Oued *watercourse* Alg. 123 F5
Tadjikistan *country* Asia *see* Tajikistan
Tadjoura Djibouti 128 D2
Tadjoura, Golfe de *g.* Djibouti 128 D2
Tadjrouna Alg. 123 F2
Tadmur Syria 109 J3
  also known as Tamar; historically known as Palmyra
Tadó Col. 198 B3
Tadohae Haesang National Park S. Korea 83 B6
Tadoule Lake Canada 167 L3
Tadoussac Canada 169 G3
Tadpatri India 94 C3
Tadrart Acacus *tourist site* Libya 120 A3
Tadwale India 94 C2
Tadzhikabad Tajik. 101 H2
Tadzhikskaya S.S.R. *country* Asia *see* Tajikistan
T'aean Haean National Park S. Korea 83 B5
T'aebaek-sanmaek *mts* N. Korea/S. Korea 83 B5
Taebla Estonia 42 E3
Taech'ŏn S. Korea 83 B5
Taech'ŏng-do *i.* S. Korea 83 B5
Taedong-gang *r.* N. Korea 83 B5
  formerly known as Daido
Taedong-man *b.* N. Korea 83 B5
Taegu S. Korea 83 C5
Taehüksan-kundo *is* S. Korea 83 B6
Taejŏn S. Korea 83 B5
Taejŏng S. Korea 83 B6
T'aepaek S. Korea 83 C5
Taevaskoja Estonia 42 I3
Tafahi *i.* Tonga 145 H3
  formerly known as Keppel Island
Tafalla Spain 55 J2
Tafassasset, Oued *watercourse* Alg./Niger 123 H5
Tafelberg S. Africa 133 J8
Tafelberg *mt.* S. Africa 132 F3
Tafelberg *mt.* Suriname 199 G4
Tafelberg, Natuurreservaat *nature res.* Suriname 199 G4
Tafila Jordan *see* At Tafilah
Tafiré Côte d'Ivoire 124 D4
Tafí Viejo Arg. 204 D2
Tafjord Norway 44 I3
Tafraoute Morocco 122 C3
Tafresh Iran 100 B3
Taft Iran 100 C4
Taft U.S.A. 182 E6
Taftān, Kūh-e *mt.* Iran 101 E4
Taftanāz Syria 109 H2
Tagab Sudan 121 F5
Tagajō Japan 90 G5
Tagânet Keyna *well* Mali 124 C2
Taganrog Rus. Fed. 41 F6
Taganrog, Gulf of Rus. Fed./Ukr. 41 F7
  also known as Taganrogskiy Zaliv or Taganroz'ka Zatoka
Taganrogskiy Zaliv *b.* Rus. Fed./Ukr. *see* Taganrog, Gulf of
Tagant *admin. reg.* Mauritania 124 C2
Tagarev, Gora *mt.* Iran/Turkm. 100 D2
Tagawa Japan 91 B8
Tagay Rus. Fed. 41 H5

Tagaza *well* Niger 125 G2
Tagbilaran Phil. 74 B4
Tagchagpu Ri *mt.* China 89 C5
Tagdempt Alg. *see* Tiaret
Taggia Italy 51 N9
Taghmanant *well* Mali 122 D4
  also spelt Tarhmanant
Tagish Canada 166 C3
Tagish Lake Canada 166 C3
Tagliacozzo Italy 56 F6
Tagliamento *r.* Italy 56 F3
Tagloan *r.* Phil. 74 C4
Tagnout Chaggueret *well* Mali 123 E4
Tagolo Point Phil. 74 C4
Tagomago *i.* Spain 55 M5
Tagourāret *well* Mauritania 124 D2
Tagta Turkm. 102 D4
  formerly spelt Takhta
Tagtabazar Turkm. 101 E3
  formerly spelt Takhta-Bazar
Taguatinga Minas Gerais Brazil 206 D2
Taguatinga Tocantins Brazil 202 C5
Tagudin Phil. 74 B2
Taguenout Haggueret *well* Mali 123 E4
  also spelt Tagnout Chaggueret
Tagula P.N.G. 149 G1
Tagula Island P.N.G. 149 G1
  also known as Sudest Island
Tagum Phil. 74 C5
Tagus *r.* Port./Spain 54 D5
  also known as Tajo (Spain) or Tejo (Portugal)
Tah, Sabkhat *salt pan* Morocco 122 B4
Taha China 85 J2
Tahaetkun Mountain Canada 166 G5
Tahalra *reg.* Alg. 123 G5
Tahan, Gunung *mt.* Malaysia 76 C1
Tahanroz'ka Zatoka *b.* Rus. Fed./Ukr. *see* Taganrog, Gulf of
Tahat, Mont *mt.* Alg. 123 G5
Tahaurawe *i.* U.S.A. *see* Kahoolawe
Tahe China 82 B1
Taheke N.Z. 152 H3
Tāhemaa Estonia 42 I3
Tahifet Alg. 123 G5
Tahiti *i.* Mongolia 84 C2
Tahiti *i.* Fr. Polynesia 221 I7
  also spelt Otahiti
Tahkuna nina *pt* Estonia 42 D2
Tahlab *r.* Iran/Pak. 101 E4
Tahlab, Dasht-i *plain* Pak. 101 E4
Tahlequah U.S.A. 179 D5
Tahltan Canada 166 D3
Tahoe, Lake U.S.A. 182 D2
Tahoe City U.S.A. 182 D2
Tahoe Vista U.S.A. 182 D2
Tahoka U.S.A. 179 B5
Tahora N.Z. 152 I7
Tahorakuri N.Z. 152 K6
Tahoua Niger 125 G3
Tahoua *dept* Niger 125 G3
Tahrūd Iran 100 D4
Tahrūd *r.* Iran 100 D4
Taht, Oued El *watercourse* Alg. 55 L9
Tahta Egypt 121 F3
Tahtali Dağ *mt.* Turkey 108 B1
Tahtsa Peak Canada 166 E4
Tahua Bol. 200 D4
Tahuamanú *r.* Bol. 200 D2
Tahuamanú Peru 200 C2
Tahulandang *i.* Indon. 75 C2
Tahuna Indon. 75 C2
Taï, Parc National de *nat. park* Côte d'Ivoire 124 D5
Tai A Chau *i.* Hong Kong China 87 [inset]
Tai'an Liaoning China 85 I3
Tai'an Shandong China 85 H4
Taibai China 87 C1
  also known as Zuitou
Taibai Shan *mt.* China 87 C1
Taibei Taiwan *see* T'aipei
Taïbet Alg. 123 G2
Taibilla *r.* Spain 55 I6
Taibilla, Sierra de *mts* Spain 55 I6
Taibus Qi China *see* Baochang
T'aichung Taiwan 87 G3
  also spelt Taizhong
Taidong Taiwan *see* T'aitung
Taieri *r.* N.Z. 153 E14
Taigu China 85 G4
Taihang Shan *mts* China 85 G4
Taihang Shan *mts* China 85 G4
Taihape N.Z. 152 I7
Taihe Anhui China 87 E1
Taihe Jiangxi China 87 E3
  also known as Chengjiang
Taihe China *see* Shehong
Taihezhen China *see* Shehong
Tai Ho Wan Hong Kong China 87 [inset]
Taihu China 87 F2
Tai Hu *l.* China 87 G2
Taikang Heilong. China 85 J2
  formerly known as Dorbod
Taikang Henan China 87 E1
Tailai China 85 J2
Tailako East Timor 75 C5
Tai Lam Chung Reservoir Hong Kong China 87 [inset]
Taileleo Indon. 76 B3
Tai Long Wan *b.* Hong Kong China 87 [inset]
Tailuge Taiwan *see* T'ailuko
T'ailuko Taiwan 87 G3
  also spelt Tailuge
Tailem Bend Australia 146 C3
Taimani *reg.* Afgh. 101 E3
Tai Mo Shan *hill* Hong Kong China 87 [inset]
Tain U.K. 46 H6
T'ainan Taiwan 87 G4
  also spelt Tainan
Tainaro, Akra *pt* Greece 59 D12
Tai O Hong Kong China 87 [inset]
Taiobeiras Brazil 202 D5
Taipa Indon. 75 B3
Taipa N.Z. 152 H3
Tai Pak Wan *b.* Hong Kong China *see* Discovery Bay
Taipalsaari Fin. 45 O3
Tai Pang Wan *b.* Hong Kong China *see* Mirs Bay
Taipei Taiwan *see* T'aipei

Taishun China 87 F3
  also known as Luoyang
Tai Siu Mo To *is* Hong Kong China *see* The Brothers
Taitaitanopo *i.* Indon. 76 C3
Taitanu N.Z. 153 G11
Taitao, Península de *pen.* Chile 205 B7
Taitao, Punta *pt* Chile 205 B7
Taiti *mt.* Kenya 128 B5
Tai To Yan *mt.* Hong Kong China 87 [inset]
T'aitung Taiwan 87 G4
  also spelt Taidong
Tai Tung Shan *hill* Hong Kong China *see* Sunset Peak
T'aitung Shan *mts* Taiwan 87 G4
Taivalkoski Fin. 44 O2
Taivaskero *hill* Fin. 44 N1
Taivassalo Fin. 45 M3
▶ **Taiwan** *country* Asia 87 G3
  also known as China, Republic of or Chung-hua Min-kuo; formerly known as Formosa
  asia [countries] ▶▶ 64–67
Taiwan Haixia *strait* China/Taiwan *see* Taiwan Strait
Taiwan Shan *mts* Taiwan *see* Chungyang Shanmo
Taiwan Strait China/Taiwan 87 F4
  also known as Taiwan Haixia; formerly known as Formosa Strait
Taixian China *see* Jiangyan
Taixing China 87 G1
Taïyetos Óros *mts* Greece *see* Tavgetos
Tai Yue Shan *i.* Hong Kong China *see* Lantau Island
Taiyue Shan *mts* China 85 F4
Taizhao China 89 F6
Taizhong Taiwan *see* T'aichung
Taizhou Jiangsu China 87 F1
Taizhou Zhejiang China 87 F2
Taizhou Liedao *i.* China 87 G2
Taizhou Wan *b.* China 87 G2
Taizi *r.* China 83 B4
Ta'izz Yemen 104 C5
Ta'izz *governorate* Yemen 104 C5
Tajam, Tanjong *pt* Sing. 76 [inset]
Tajamulco, Volcán de *vol.* Guat. 185 H6
Tajarhī Libya 120 B3
Tajik, Gunung *mt.* Indon. 77 D3
▶ **Tajikistan** *country* Asia 101 G2
  spelt Tojikiston or Tochikiston; formerly known as Tadzhikskaya S.S.R.; formerly spelt Tadjikistan
  asia [countries] ▶▶ 64–67
Tajima Japan 90 F6
Tajitos Mex. 184 B2
Taj Mahal *tourist site* India 96 C4
Tajo *r.* Spain 54 D5 *see* Tagus
Tajobim India 86 A2
Tajrish Iran *see* Hashtpar
Tajsara, Cordillera de *mts* Bol. 200 D5
Tajuña *r.* Spain 55 H4
Tak Thai. 78 B4
Takāb Iran 100 A2
Takabba Kenya 128 D4
Taka'Bonerate, Kepulauan *atolls* Indon. 75 B4
  also known as Macan, Kepulauan
Takada Cent. Afr. Rep. 126 D2
Takahagi Japan 90 G6
Takahashi Japan 91 C7
Takahe, Mount Antarctica 222 Q1
Takaka N.Z. 152 G8
Takal India 96 C4
Takalaou Chad 126 C2
Takalous, Oued *watercourse* Alg. 123 G5
Takama Guyana 199 G3
Takamatsu Japan 91 D7
Takamori Japan 91 B8
Takanabe Japan 91 B8
Takanosu Japan 90 G4
Takaoka Japan 91 E6
Takapau N.Z. 152 J7
Takapuna N.Z. 152 I5
Takara-jima *i.* Japan 83 C7
Takasaki Japan 91 F6
Takatokwane Botswana 131 E5
Takatshwaane Botswana 130 D4
Takatsuki Japan 91 D7
Takatsuki-yama *mt.* Japan 91 C8
Ta-Kaw Myanmar 78 B3
Takayama Japan 91 E6
Tak Bai Thai. 79 C7
Takefu Japan 91 E7
Takengon Indon. 76 B1
Takeo Cambodia *see* Takêv
Takeo Japan 91 B8
Takêv Cambodia 79 D6
  also spelt Takeo
Take-shima *i.* N. Pacific Ocean *see* Liancourt Rocks
Taketa Japan 91 B8
Takfon Tajik. 101 G2
Takhādīd *well* Iraq 107 F5
Takhar *prov.* Afgh. 101 G2
Takhatpur India 96 D5
Takhemaret Alg. 55 L9
Takhiatash Uzbek. *see* Gulabie
Takhini *r.* Canada 166 C2
Takhini Hotspring Canada 166 C2
Ta Khli Thai. 79 B5
Ta Khmau Cambodia 79 D6
Takhta Turkm. *see* Tagta
Takhta-Bazar Turkm. *see* Tagtabazar
Takhtabrod Kazakh. 103 F1
Takhtakupyr Uzbek. 102 E4
Takht Apān, Kūh-e *mt.* Iran 100 B3
Takht-i-Sulaiman *mt.* Pak. 101 G4
Takht-i-Suleiman *mt.* Iran 100 B2
Takiéta Niger 125 H3
Takijuq Lake Canada *see* Napaktulik Lake
Takikawa Japan 90 G3
Takinoue Japan 90 H2
Takisset, Oued *watercourse* Alg./Libya 123 H4
Takisung Indon. 77 F3
Takitimu Mountains N.Z. 153 B13
Takla Lake Canada 166 E4
Takla Landing Canada 166 E4
Takla Makan *des.* China *see* Taklimakan Desert
▶ **Taklimakan Desert** China 88 C3
  also known as Takla Makan or Taklimakan Shamo
  world [land images] ▶▶ 12–13
Taklimakan Shamo *des.* China *see* Taklimakan Desert
Takob Tajik. 101 H2
Takoradi Ghana 125 E5
Takpa Shiri *mt.* China 89 F6
Taku Canada 166 C3
Taku *r.* Canada/U.S.A. 164 F4
Taku Japan 91 B8
Takua Pa Thai. 79 B6
Takua Thung Thai. 79 B6
Takum Nigeria 125 H5
Takundi Dem. Rep. Congo 126 C6
Tal India 96 B5
Tala Egypt 108 B7
Tala Uruguay 204 G4
Talachyn Belarus 43 K7
  also spelt Tolochin
Talagang Pak. 101 H3

Talaiassa, Serra *hill* Spain 55 M6
Talaja India 96 B5
Talakan Amurskaya Oblast' Rus. Fed. 82 C2
Talakan Khabarovskiy Kray Rus. Fed. 82 C2
Talala India 94 A1
Talandzha Rus. Fed. 82 C2
Talang, Gunung *vol.* Indon. 76 C3
Talangbatu Indon. 77 D3
Talangbetutu Indon. 76 C3
Talara Peru 198 A6
Talas Kazakh./Kyrg. 103 G3
Talas Kyrg. 103 H4
Talas *admin. div.* Kyrg. 103 G4
  English form Talas Oblast; also known as Talasskaya Oblast'
Talas Ala-Too *mts* Kyrg. 103 G4
  English form Talas Range; also known as Talasskiy Alatau, Khrebet
Talas Oblast *admin. div.* Kyrg. *see* Talas
Talas Range Kyrg. *see* Talas Ala-Too
Talasskaya Oblast' *admin. div.* Kyrg. *see* Talas
Talasskiy Alatau, Khrebet *mts* Kyrg. *see* Talas Ala-Too
Tal'at al Jamā'ah, Rujm *mt.* Jordan 108 G7
Talata-Mafara Nigeria 125 G3
Ţal 'at Mūsá *mt.* Lebanon/Syria 109 H3
Talaud, Kepulauan *is* Indon. 75 C1
Talavera de la Reina Spain 54 G5
Talawanta Australia 149 D3
Talawgyi Myanmar 78 B2
Talaya Rus. Fed. 39 P3
Talayan Phil. 74 C5
Talayuela Spain 54 F5
Talayuelo *mt.* Spain 55 I5
Talbehat India 96 C4
Talbot, Mount *hill* Australia 151 D5
Talbot Inlet Canada 165 L2
Talbot Lake Canada 167 L4
Talbotton U.S.A. 175 F5
Talbragar *r.* Australia 147 F3
Talca Chile 204 C4
Talca, Punta *pt* Chile 204 C4
Talcahuano Chile 204 B5
Talcher India 95 E1
Taldan Rus. Fed. 82 B1
Taldom Rus. Fed. 43 S5
Taldyk, Pereval *pass* Kyrg. 103 H5
Taldykorgan Kazakh. 103 I3
  also spelt Taldyqorghan; formerly spelt Taldy-Kurgan
Taldy-Kurgan Kazakh. *see* Taldykorgan
Taldyqorghan Kazakh. *see* Taldykorgan
Taldysu Kyrg. *see* Taldy-Suu
Taldy-Suu Kyrg. 103 I4
  also spelt Taldysu
Talegaon Maharashtra India 94 B2
Talegaon Maharashtra India 94 C1
Talen India 96 C5
Taleni S. Africa 133 M9
Talēsh Iran *see* Hashtpar
Talets, Ozero *l.* Rus. Fed. 43 R2
Talga *r.* Australia 150 B4
Talgar Kazakh. 103 I4
Talgar, Pik *mt.* Kazakh. 103 I4
Talguharai Sudan 121 G5
Ţalḩah Saudi Arabia 104 C3
Taliabu *i.* Indon. 75 C3
Talibon Phil. 74 C4
Talikota India 94 C2
Talikud *i.* Phil. 74 C5
Talimardzhan Uzbek. 103 F5
  also spelt Tallymerjen or Tollimarjon
Taliouine Morocco 122 D3
Taliparamba India 94 B3
  also spelt Thaliparamba
Tali Post Sudan 128 A3
Talisay Phil. 74 B4
Talisayan Indon. 77 G2
Talisayan Phil. 74 C4
Ţāliş Dāğları *mts* Azer./Iran 107 G3
  also known as Talyshskiye Gory
Talisei *i.* Indon. 75 B2
Talitsa Kostromskaya Oblast' Rus. Fed. 40 H4
Talitsa Lipetskaya Oblast' Rus. Fed. 43 T9
Taliwang Indon. 77 G5
Tal'ka Belarus 43 K7
Tallacootra, Lake *salt flat* Australia 146 B2
Talladega U.S.A. 175 C5
Tall 'Afar Iraq 107 E3
▶ **Tallahassee** U.S.A. 175 C6
  State capital of Florida.
Tallangatta Australia 147 E4
Tallapoosa *r.* U.S.A. 175 C5
Tallaringa Conservation Park *nature res.* Australia 146 B2
Talla Talla Seghir Island Sudan 104 B4
Tall Baydar Syria 109 L1
▶ **Tallinn** Estonia 42 F2
  Capital of Estonia. Historically known as Reval or Revel.
Tallinna laht *b.* Estonia 42 F2
Tall Kalakh Syria 108 H3
Tall Kayf Iraq 107 E3
Tallmadge U.S.A. 176 D4
Tall Tamr Syria 109 L1
Tallulah U.S.A. 175 B5
Tall 'Uwaynāt Iraq 107 E3
Tallymerjen Uzbek. *see* Talimardzhan
Tălmaciu Romania 58 F3
Talmiã Brazil 199 H4
Talmont-St-Hilaire France 50 E6
Tal'ne Ukr. 41 D6
  also spelt Tal'noye
Tal'noye Ukr. *see* Tal'ne
Talod India 96 B5
Taloda India 96 B5
Talodi Sudan 128 A2
Taloga U.S.A. 179 C4
Taloi Range *mts* Pak. 101 F5
Talon, Lac *l.* Canada 169 H2
Tāloqān Afgh. 101 G2
Talos Dome *ice feature* Antarctica 223 K2
Ta Loung San *mt.* Laos 78 C3
Taloyoak Canada 165 J2
  formerly known as Spence Bay
Talpa Mex. 184 D4
Tal Pass Pak. 101 H3
  also known as Shohi Pass
Talras *well* Niger 125 H3
Talshand Mongolia 84 C2
Talsi Latvia 42 D4
Tal Siyāh Iran 101 E4
Taltal Chile 204 C2
Taltson *r.* Canada 167 H2
Talu China 89 F6
Talu Indon. 76 B2
Taludaa Indon. 75 B2
Taluti, Teluk *b.* Indon. 75 D3
Talvik Norway 44 M1
Talwood Australia 147 F2
Taly Rus. Fed. 41 G6
Talyawalka *r.* Australia 147 D3
Talyshskiye Gory *mts* Azer./Iran *see* Ţāliş Dāğları
Tama, Nam *r.* Myanmar 78 B2

Tamaki Strait N.Z. 152 I4
Tamala Australia 151 A5
Tamala Rus. Fed. 41 G5
Tamalameque Col. 187 E5
Tamale Ghana 125 E4
Tamalung Indon. 77 F3
Tamana Japan 91 B8
Tamana *i.* Kiribati 145 G2
  formerly known as Rotch Island
Tamanar Morocco 122 C3
Tamanco Peru 198 C6
Tamanhint Libya 120 B3
Tamani Mali 124 D3
Taman Negara National Park Malaysia 76 C1
Tamano Japan 91 C7
Tamanrasset Alg. 123 G5
  also known as Tamenghest; formerly known as Fort Laperrine
Tamanrasset, Oued *watercourse* Alg. 123 F5
Tamanthi Myanmar 78 A2
Tamaqua U.S.A. 177 J5
Tamar India 97 E5
Tamar Syria *see* Tadmur
Tamar *r.* U.K. 47 H13
Tamaradant *well* Mali 125 F3
Tamarai Japan 91 B8
Tamarugal, Pampa de *plain* Chile 200 C4
Tamasane Botswana 131 E4
Tamási Hungary 49 P9
Tamaşi Romania 58 I2
Tamatave Madag. *see* Toamasina
Tamaulipas *state* Mex. 185 F4
Tamaulipas, Sierra de *mts* Mex. 185 F4
Tama Wildlife Reserve *nature res.* Eth. 128 C3
Tamayama Japan 90 G5
Tamazula Durango Mex. 184 D3
Tamazula Jalisco Mex. 185 E5
Tamazulápam Mex. 185 F5
Tamazunchale Mex. 185 F4
Tambach Kenya 128 B4
Tambacounda Senegal 124 B3
Tambangsawah Indon. 76 C3
Tambankulu Swaziland 133 P3
Tamboura, Falaise de *esc.* Mali 124 C3
Tambaqui Brazil 199 F6
Tambara Moz. 131 G3
Tambau Brazil 206 F9
Tambawel Nigeria 125 G3
Tambelan, Kepulauan *is* Indon. 77 D2
Tambelan Besar *i.* Indon. 77 D2
Tambellup Australia 151 B7
Tamberu Indon. 77 F4
Tambisan Sabah Malaysia 77 G1
Tambo *r.* Australia 147 E4
Tambo *r.* Peru 200 C3
Tambobamba Peru 200 B3
Tambo Grande Peru 198 A6
Tambohorano Madag. 131 [inset] I3
Tambopata *r.* Peru 200 C3
Tambor Angola 127 B9
Tambora, Gunung *vol.* Indon. 77 G5
Tamboril Brazil 202 D3
Tamboryacu *r.* Peru 198 C5
Tamboura Cent. Afr. Rep. 126 E3
Tambov Rus. Fed. 41 G5
Tambovka Rus. Fed. 82 C2
Tambov Oblast *admin. div.* Rus. Fed. *see* Tambovskaya Oblast'
Tambovskaya Oblast' *admin. div.* Rus. Fed. 41 G5
  English form Tambov Oblast
Tambre *r.* Spain 54 C2
Tambu, Teluk *b.* Indon. 75 A2
Tambunan Sabah Malaysia 77 G1
  formerly known as Tibabar
Tambura Sudan 126 E3
Tambuyukon, Gunung *mt.* Sabah Malaysia 77 G1
Tâmchekkeţ Mauritania 124 C2
Tamdy Kazakh. 102 D2
Tamdybulak Uzbek. 103 F3
  also spelt Tomdibuloq
Tamdytau, Gory *hills* Uzbek. 103 F4
  also known as Tomditow Toghi
Tame Col. 198 D3
Tamega *r.* Port. 54 C3
Tamel Aike Arg. 205 C8
Tamelos, Akra *pt* Greece 59 F11
Tamenghest Alg. *see* Tamanrasset
Tamenglong India 97 G4
Tamerlanovka Kazakh. *see* Temirlanovka
Tamesna *reg.* Niger 125 G3
Tamgak, Adrar *mt.* Niger 125 H2
Tamgout de Lalla Khedidja *mt.* Alg. 55 P8
Tamgué, Massif du *mt.* Guinea 124 B3
Tamia India 96 C5
Tamiahua Mex. 185 F4
Tamiahua, Laguna de *lag.* Mex. 185 F4
Tamiami Canal U.S.A. 175 D7
Tamiang *r.* Indon. 76 B1
Tamiang, Ujung *pt* Indon. 76 B1
Tamil Nadu *state* India 94 C4
  formerly known as Madras
Tamirin Gol *r.* Mongolia 84 C2
Tamiš *r.* Yugo. 58 B4
Tamita Rus. Fed. 40 F2
Tāmiya Egypt 121 F2
Tamiyah, Jabal *hill* Saudi Arabia 104 C3
Tamjit *well* Niger 125 H1
Tamlelt, Plaine de *plain* Morocco 123 E2
Tamluk India 97 E5
Tammaro *r.* Italy 56 G7
Tammarvi *r.* Canada 167 K1
Tammela Etelä-Suomi Fin. 42 F1
Tammela Oulu Fin. 44 O2
Tammerfors Fin. *see* Tampere
Tammio *i.* Fin. 42 I1
Tammisaaren Saariston Kansallispuisto *nat. park* Fin. *see* Ekenäs skärgårds Nationalpark
Tammisaari Fin. *see* Ekenäs
Tammispää Estonia 42 I3
Tamnava *r.* Yugo. 58 B4
Tamou Niger 125 F3
Tamou, Réserve Totale de Faune de *nature res.* Niger 125 F3
Tampa U.S.A. 175 D7
Tampa Bay U.S.A. 175 D7
Tampang Indon. 76 D4
Tampere Fin. 45 M3
  also known as Tammerfors
Tampico Mex. 185 F4
Tampines Sing. 76 [inset]
Tampin Malaysia 76 C2
Tampo Indon. 75 B4
Tamsag Bulag Mongolia 85 H2
Tamsalu Estonia 42 H2
Tamshiyacu Peru 198 C6
Tamsweg Austria 49 K8
Tamu Myanmar 78 A2
Tamuin Mex. 185 F4
Tamur *r.* Nepal 97 E4
Tamworth Australia 147 F2
Tamworth U.K. 47 K11
Tan Kazakh. 103 I2
Tana *r.* Kenya 128 D5
Tana Madag. *see* Antananarivo
Tana *i.* Vanuatu *see* Tanna
Tana, Lake Eth. 128 C2
  also known as T'ana Hāyk'
Tanabe Japan 91 D8
Tanabi Brazil 206 C9
Tana Bru Norway 44 O1

Tanafjorden *inlet* Norway **44** O1
also known as Deanuvuotna
Tanagro *r.* Italy **57** H8
Tanah, Tanjung *pt* Indon. **77** E4
also known as Tana, Lake
T'ana Häyk' *l.* Eth. *see* Tana, Lake
Tanahbala *i.* Indon. **76** B3
Tanahgrogot Indon. **77** F3
Tanahjampea *i.* Indon. **75** B4
Tanahmasa *i.* Indon. **76** B3
Tanahmerah Indon. **77** G2
Tanahputih Indon. **76** C2
Tanakeke *i.* Indon. **75** A4
Tanambung Indon. **96** D3
Tanami Australia **148** A3
Tanami Desert Australia **148** A3
Tanami Downs Aboriginal Land *res.* Australia **148** A3
Tân An Vietnam **79** D6
Tananarive Madag. *see* Antananarivo
Tanandava Madag. **131** [inset] I4
Tanāqīb, Ra's *pt* Saudi Arabia **105** G3
Tanaro *r.* Italy **56** D2
Tanauan Phil. **74** B3
Tanda Côte d'Ivoire **124** E5
Tanda *Uttar Pradesh* India **96** C3
Tanda *Uttar Pradesh* India **97** D4
Tandag Phil. **74** C4
Ţăndărei Romania **58** I4
Tandaué Angola **127** C2
Tandek *Sabah* Malaysia **77** G1
formerly known as Taritipan
Tandi India **96** C2
Tandil Arg. **204** F5
Tandjilé *pref.* Chad **126** C2
Tando Adam Pak. **101** G5
Tando Alahyar Pak. **101** G5
Tando Bago Pak. **101** G5
Tando Muhammmad Khan Pak. **101** G5
Tandou Lake *imp. l.* Australia **147** D3
Tandubatu *i.* Phil. **74** B5
Tandula *r.* India **96** C5
Tandur *Andhra Pradesh* India **94** C2
Tandur *Andhra Pradesh* India **94** C2
Taneatua N.Z. **152** K6
Tanega-shima *i.* Japan **91** B9
Taneichi Japan **90** G4
Tanen Range *mts* Thai. **78** B4
Taneti *i.* Indon. **75** C3
Tanew *r.* Poland **49** T5
Taneytown U.S.A. **177** H6
Tanezrouft *reg.* Alg./Mali **123** E5
Tanezrouft Tan-Ahenet *reg.* Alg. **123** G5
Ţanf, Jabal aţ *hill* Syria **109** J4
Tang, Ra's-e *pt* Iran **101** D5
Tanga Tanz. **85** F1
Tanga Tanz. **85** F1
Tanga *admin. reg.* Tanz. **129** C6
Tangaehe N.Z. **152** I4
Tangail Bangl. **97** F4
Tanga Islands P.N.G. **145** E2
Tangalla Sri Lanka **94** D5
Tanganyika *country* Africa *see* Tanzania
▶ Tanganyika, Lake Africa **127** F6
Deepest and 2nd largest lake in Africa and 7th largest in the world.
africa [landscapes] ▶▶▶ 112–113
Tangar Iran **100** C2
Tangasseri India **94** C4
Tangdan China **86** B3
formerly known as Dongshuan
Tangeli Iran **100** D2
Tange Promontory *hd* Antarctica **223** D2
Tanger Morocco *see* Tangier
Tangerang Indon. **77** D4
Tangermünde Germany **48** I3
Tanggor China **86** B1
Tanggu China **85** H4
Tanggulashan China *see* Tuotuoheyan
Tanggula Shan *mt.* China **89** E5
Tanggula Shan *mts* China **89** E5
also known as Dangla Shan
Tanggula Shankou *pass* China **89** E5
Tangguo China **89** E4
Tanghe China **87** E1
Tang He *r.* China **87** E1
Tangi Pak. **101** G3
Tangimoana N.Z. **152** J8
Tangkittebak, Gunung *mt.* Indon. **76** D4
Tang La *pass* China **89** E7
Tanglag China **86** A1
Tanglin Sing. **76** [inset]
Tangmai China **97** G3
Tango Japan **91** D7
Tangorin Australia **149** E4
Tangra Yumco *salt l.* China **89** D6
Tangse Indon. **76** A1
Tangshan China **85** H4
Tangsyq Kazakh. *see* Tansyk
Tangte *mt.* Myanmar **78** B3
Tangub *Mindanao* Phil. **74** B4
Tangub *Negros* Phil. **74** B4
Tanguieta Benin **125** F4
Tangwan China **87** E2
Tangwang *r.* China **82** C3
Tangwanghe China **82** C2
Tangxian China **85** G4
also known as Renhou
Tangxianzhen China **87** E2
Tang-yan Myanmar **78** B3
Tangyin China **85** G5
Tangyuan China **82** C3
Tanhaçu Brazil **202** D5
Tanhua Fin. **44** N2
Taniantaweng Shan *mts* China **86** A2
Tanimbar, Kepulauan *is* Indon. **73** H8
Taninthari Myanmar *see* Tenasserim
Taninthari *admin. div.* Myanmar *see* Tenasserim
Taninthayi Myanmar *see* Tenasserim
Taniwel Indon. **75** D3
Tanjah Morocco *see* Tangier
Tanjay Phil. **74** B4
Tanjore India *see* Thanjavur
Tanjung *Kalimantan Selatan* Indon. **77** F3
Tanjung *Sumatra* Indon. **76** D3
Tanjungbalai *Sumatra* Indon. **76** B2
Tanjungbalai *Sumatra* Indon. **76** C2
Tanjungbalaiha Indon. **75** D3
Tanjungbatu *Kalimantan Timur* Indon. **77** G2
Tanjungbuayabuaya, Pulau *i.* Indon. **77** G2
Tanjunggaru Indon. **77** D3
Tanjungkarang-Telukbetung Indon. **76** D4
also known as Telukbetung; formerly known as Bandar Lampung
Tanjungpandan Indon. **77** D3
Tanjungpinang Indon. **76** D2
Tanjungpura Indon. **76** B2
Tanjung Puting National Park Indon. **77** E3
Tanjungraja Indon. **76** D3
Tanjungredeb Indon. **77** G2
Tanjungsaleh *i.* Indon. **77** E3
Tanjungsari Indon. **77** E3
Tanjungselor Indon. **77** G2
Tank Pak. **101** G3
Tankara India **96** A5
Tankavaara Fin. **44** N1
Tankhala India **96** B5

Tankhoy Rus. Fed. **85** E1
Tankse *Jammu and Kashmir* **96** C2
Tankuhi India **97** E4
Tankwa *r.* S. Africa **132** D9
Tankwa-Karoo National Park S. Africa **132** D9
Tanlwe *r.* Myanmar **78** A4
Tanna *i.* Vanuatu **145** F3
also known as Tana
Tännäs Sweden **44** K3
Tanner, Mount Canada **166** G5
Tannila Fin. **44** N2
Tannu-Ola, Khrebet *mts* Rus. Fed. **84** A1
Tannu Tuva *aut. rep.* Rus. Fed. *see* Tyva, Respublika
Tano *r.* Ghana **124** E5
Tañon Strait Phil. **74** B4
Tanot India **96** A4
Tanquian Mex. **185** F4
Tansen Nepal **97** D3
Tanshui Taiwan **87** G3
also spelt Danshui
Tansilla Burkina **124** D3
Tansyk Kazakh. **103** I3
also spelt Tangsyq
Tanta Egypt **121** F2
Tantabin *Pegu* Myanmar **78** B4
Tantabin *Sagaing* Myanmar **78** A3
Tan-Tan Morocco **122** C3
Tantoyuca Mex. **185** F4
Tantpur India **96** C4
Tantu China **85** I2
Tantura Israel **108** F5
Tanuku India **94** D2
Tanumshede Sweden **45** J4
Tanwakka, Sabkhat *well* W. Sahara **122** B5
▶ Tanzania *country* Africa **129** B6
formerly known as Tanganyika
africa [countries] ▶▶▶ 114–117
Tanzilla *r.* Canada **166** D3
Tao, Ko *i.* Thai. **79** B6
Tao'an China *see* Taonan
Taocheng China *see* Yongchun
Taocheng China *see* Daxin
Taodeni Mali *see* Taoudenni
Tao'er *r.* China **85** I2
Tao He *r.* China **84** D5
also known as Lu Qu
Taohong China *see* Longhui
Taohuaping China *see* Longhui
Taojiang China **87** E2
Taolanaro Madag. *see* Tôlañaro
Taole China **85** E4
also known as Mataigou
Taonan China **85** I2
formerly known as Tao'an
Taongi *atoll* Marshall Is **220** F5
Taormina *Sicilia* Italy **57** H11
Taos U.S.A. **181** F5
Taouârdeï *well* Mali **125** F2
Taoudenni Mali **122** E5
also spelt Taodeni
Taounate Morocco **122** D2
Taoudannt *well* Mali **123** F3
Taourirt Morocco **123** E2
Taoxi China **87** F3
Taoyang China *see* Lintao
Taoyuan China **87** G3
Tapa Estonia **42** G2
Tapaan Passage Phil. **74** B5
Tapachula Mex. **185** G6
Tapaktuan Indon. **76** B2
Tapalqué Arg. **204** E5
Tapan Indon. **76** C3
Tapan Turkey *see* Mansurlu
Tapanahoni *r.* Suriname **199** H3
Tapanatepec Mex. **185** G5
Tapanuli, Teluk *b.* Indon. **76** B2
Tapará, Ilha Grande do *i.* Brazil **199** H5
Tapara, Serra do *hills* Brazil **199** H5
Tapati *i.* Indon. **75** C3
Tapauá Brazil **199** F6
Tapauá *r.* Brazil **199** E6
Tapawera N.Z. **152** G9
Tapera *Rio Grande do Sul* Brazil **203** A9
Tapera *Roraima* Brazil **199** F5
Tapera Chile **205** C7
Taperoá Brazil **202** E5
Tapes Brazil **203** B9
Tapeta Liberia **124** C3
Tapi *r.* India **96** B5
Tapia, Sierra de *hills* Bol. **201** E4
Tapi Aike Arg. **205** C8
Tapiau Rus. Fed. *see* Gvardeysk
Tapiche *r.* Peru **198** C6
Tápió *r.* Hungary **49** R8
Tapiocanga, Chapada do *hills* Brazil **206** C3
Tápiószecső Hungary **49** Q8
Tapira Brazil **206** D5
Tapiracanga Brazil **202** C5
Tapirai Brazil **206** F10
Tapira *r.* Brazil **202** B4
Tapirapecó, Sierra *mts* Brazil/Venez. **199** E4
Tapirapuã Brazil **201** F3
Tapis *mt.* Malaysia **76** C1
Tapisuelas Mex. **184** C3
Taplejung Nepal **97** E4
Tap Mun Chau *i.* Hong Kong China **87** [inset]
Tapoa *watercourse* Burkina **125** F3
Tapol Chad **126** C2
Tapolca Hungary **49** O9
Ta-pom Myanmar **78** B3
Tappahannock U.S.A. **177** I8
Tappal India **96** C3
Tappeh, Kûh-e *hill* Iran **100** B3
Tappi-zaki *pt* Japan **90** F4
Tapul Phil. **74** B5
Tapul Group *is* Phil. **74** B5
Tapulonanjing *mt.* Indon. **76** B2
Tapung *r.* Indon. **76** C2
Tapurú Brazil **199** F5
Tapurucuara Brazil **199** E5
Taqah Oman **105** F4
Taqatu'Hasa *watercourse* Jordan **108** G7
Taqiau Rus. Fed. **39** J3
Taqīq Iraq **107** F4
Taquara Brazil **203** B9
Taquaral Brazil **203** A6
Taquari Brazil **203** A6
Taquari *r.* mark Yugo. **58** A2
Taquaritinga Brazil **206** E8
Taquarituba Brazil **206** D10
Taquaruçu *r.* Brazil **206** A8
Tara *r.* Bos.-Herz./Yugo. **56** K5
Tara *nat. park* Yugo. **58** A5
Taraba *r.* Nigeria **125** H4
Taraba *state* Nigeria **125** H4
Tarabuco Bol. **200** D4
Ţarābulus Libya *see* Tripoli
Taraclia Moldova **58** J4
formerly known as Tarakl'ya
Taraco Peru **200** C3
Taracua Brazil **199** E4
Taradale N.Z. **152** K7
Tarāghin Libya **120** B3
Tarai *reg.* India **97** F4
Traira *r.* Brazil *see* Traíra
Tarairí Bol. **201** E5
Tarakan Indon. **77** G2
Tarakan *i.* Indon. **77** G2
Tarakki *reg.* Afgh. **101** F3
Taraklı Turkey **106** B2

Tarakliya Moldova *see* Taraclia
Tarakua Fiji **145** H3
Taran, Mys *pt* Rus. Fed. **42** A7
Tarana India **96** C5
Taranagar India **96** B3
Taranaki *admin. reg.* N.Z. **152** H7
Taranaki, Mount *vol.* N.Z. **152** I7
also known as Egmont, Mount
Tarancón Spain **55** H4
Tarangambadi India **94** C4
Tarangara Chad **126** C2
Tarangire National Park Tanz. **129** C6
Tarapaca *r.* Kazakh. *see* Tarankol', Ozero
Tarankol', Ozero *l.* Kazakh. **103** G1
formerly known as Tarangul
Taranovskoye Kazakh. **103** F1
formerly known as Viktorovka
Taranto Italy **57** J8
historically known as Tarentum
Taranto, Golfo di *g.* Italy **57** J8
Tarapacá *admin. reg.* Chile **200** D3
Tarapacá Col. **198** D5
also known as Terrassa
Tarrasa Spain *see* Terrassa
Tàrrega Spain **55** M3
Tarrong China *see* Nyêmo
Tarso Ahon *mt.* Chad **120** C4
Tarso Emissi *mt.* Chad **120** C4
Tarso Kobour *mt.* Chad **120** C4
Tarsus Turkey **106** C3
Tarta Turkm. *see* Darta
Tartagal *Salta* Arg. **201** E5
Tartagal *Santa Fé* Arg. **204** F3
Tärtär Azer. **107** F2
also spelt Terter; formerly known as Mir-Bashir
Tartas France **50** F9
Tartu Estonia **42** H3
formerly known as Yuryev; historically known as Dorpat
Ţarţūs Syria **108** G3
Ţarţūs *governorate* Syria **108** H2
Tarumae-san *vol.* Japan **90** G3 Shikotsu
Tarumirim Brazil **207** L6
Tarumizu Japan **91** B9
Tarung Hka *r.* Myanmar **78** B2
Tarusa Rus. Fed. **43** S7
Tarusa *r.* Rus. Fed. **43** S7
Ţārūt Saudi Arabia **105** E2
Tarutung Indon. **76** B2
Tarutyne Ukr. **58** K2
Tarvisio Italy **56** F2
Tarvo *r.* Bol. **201** E3
Tarz Iran **100** D4
Tasaral Kazakh. **88** A2
Tasbuget Kazakh. **103** F3
Taschereau Canada **173** O2
Taseko Mountain Canada **166** F5
Tasendjanet, Oued *watercourse* Alg. **123** F4
Tasgaon India **94** B2
Tashauz Turkm. *see* Dashkhovuz
Tashauzskaya Oblast' *admin. div.* Turkm. *see* Dashkhovuzskaya Oblast'
Tashbunar *r.* Ukr. **47** I12
Tashi Chho Bhutan *see* Thimphu
Tashigang Bhutan *see* Trashigang
Tashino Rus. Fed. *see* Pervomaysk
Tashir Armenia **107** F2
formerly known as Kalinino
Tashk, Daryācheh-ye *l.* Iran **100** C4
▶ Tashkent Uzbek. **103** G4
Capital of Uzbekistan. Also spelt Toshkent.
Tashkent Oblast' *admin. div.* Uzbek. *see* Tashkentskaya Oblast'
Tashkentskaya Cb'ast' *admin. div.* Uzbek. **103** G4
English form Tashkent Oblast; also known as Toshkent Wiloyati
Tashkepri Turkm. **103** E5
also spelt Dashtopri
Tash-Kömür Kyrg. **103** H4
also spelt Tash-Kumyr
Tash-Kumyr Kyrg. *see* Tash-Kömür
Tashla Rus. Fed. **102** C2
Tāshqurghān Afgh. *see* Kholm
Tasialujuaq, Lac *l.* Canada **169** F1
Tasiat, Lac *l.* Canada **169** F1
Tasiilap Karra *c.* Greenland **165** P3
also known as Gustav Holm, Kap
Tasiilaq Greenland *see* Ammassalik
Tasikmalaya Indon. **77** D4
Tasiujaq Canada **169** G1
formerly known as Baie-aux-Feuilles or Leaf Bay
Tasiusaq Greenland **165** N2
Task *well* Niger **125** H3
Tasker Niger **125** H3
Taşköprü Turkey **106** C2
Taşlıçay Turkey **107** E3
Tasman *admin. reg.* N.Z. **152** G9
Tasman *r.* N.Z. **153** E12
Tasman, Mount N.Z. **153** E11
Tasman Bay N.Z. **152** H9
▶ Tasmania *state* Australia **147** E5
4th largest island in Oceania. Historically known as Van Diemen's Land.
oceania [landscapes] ▶▶▶ 136–137
Tasman Peninsula Australia **147** F5
Tasman Sea S. Pacific Ocean **145** G4
Tāşnac Romania **58** D7
Taşova Turkey **107** D2
also known as Yemişenbükü
Tassara Niger **125** G3
Tassel'c, Mont *hill* France **51** K5
Tassi Gabon **126** B5
Tassialuec, Lac *l.* Canada **169** F1
Tassi i'du Hoggar *plat.* Alg. **123** G5
Tassili n'Ajjer *plat.* Alg. **123** G4
Tass'n-la-Demi-Lune France **51** K7
Tâst'up Denmark **45** K5
Tas-Tumus Rus. Fed. **39** M3
Tasty Kazakh. **103** G3
Tasty-Taldy Kazakh. **103** F2
Tasu Canada **166** D4
Taşucu Turkey **108** E1
Tas-Yuryakh Rus. Fed. **39** L3
Tata Hungary **49** P8
Tata Morocco **122** D3
Tataba Indon. **75** B3
Tatabánya Hungary **49** P8
Tatamailau, Mount *mt.* East Timor **75** C5
Tataouine Tunisia **123** H2
Tatarbunary Ukr. **41** D7
Tatarka Belarus **43** J8
Tatarpur India **96** C4
Tatarsk Rus. Fed. **80** B1
Tatarsk Rus. Fed. **43** M7
Tatarskaya A.S.S.R. *aut. rep.* Rus. Fed. *see* Tatarstan, Respublika
Tatarskiy Proliv *strait* Rus. Fed. **82** F2
English form Tatar Strait
Tatarstan, Respublika *aut. rep.* Rus. Fed. **40** I5
formerly known as Tatarskaya A.S.S.R.
Tatar Strait Rus. Fed. *see* Tatarskiy Proliv
Tatárújfalu Romania **58** H1
Tătăruşi Romania **58** H2
Tatarów Poland **49** R5
Tarnowskie Góry Poland **49** P5
historically known as Tarnowitz
Taro *r.* Italy **56** C4
Tarō Japan **90** G4

Taro Co *salt l.* China **89** C6
Ţārom Iran **100** C4
Taroom Australia **149** E5
Taroudant Morocco **122** C3
Tarpasa Bangl. **97** F5
Tarpaulin Swamp Australia **148** C2
Tarpon Springs U.S.A. **175** D6
Tarpum Bay Bahamas **175** E7
Tarq Iran **100** B3
Tarquinia Italy **56** D6
historically known as Corneto or Tarquinii
Tarquinii Italy *see* Tarquinia
Tarrabool *salt flat* Australia **148** B3
Tarracina Italy *see* Terracina
Tarraco Spain *see* Tarragona
Tarragona Spain **55** M3
historically known as Tarraco
Tarraleah Australia **147** E5
Tarrant Point Australia **148** C3
Tarras N.Z. **153** D12
Tarrasa Spain *see* Terrassa
Tàrrega Spain **55** M3
Tarrong China *see* Nyêmo
Tarso Ahon *mt.* Chad **120** C4
Tarsus Turkey **106** C3
Tartu Estonia **42** H3
Tathlina Lake Canada **167** G2
Tathlith Saudi Arabia **104** C4
Tathlīth, Wādī *watercourse* Saudi Arabia **104** D3
Tathra Australia **147** F4
Tati Botswana **131** E4
Tatitek *well* Mauritania **124** B2
Tatkon Myanmar **78** B3
Tatla Lake Canada **166** E5
Tatlatui Provincial Park Canada **166** E3
Tatlayoko Lake Canada **166** E5
Tatlisu Cyprus *see* Akanthou
Tatnam, Cape Canada **167** N3
Tatra Mountains Poland/Slovakia **49** Q6
also known as High Tatras or Tatry
Tatrang China **88** D3
Tatranský *nat. park* Slovakia **49** R6
Tatry *mts* Poland/Slovakia **49**
see Tatra Mountains
Tatrzański Park Narodowy *nat. park* Poland **49** Q6
Tatsuno Japan **91** D7
Tatta Pak. **101** F5
Tatti Kazakh. **103** H4
formerly known as Krasnoarmeysk
Tatty Kazakh. *see* Tatti
Tatuk Mountain Canada **166** E4
Tatui Brazil **206** F10
Tatum *NM* U.S.A. **178** B5
Tatum *TX* U.S.A. **179** D5
Tatvan Turkey **107** E3
Tau Brazil **202** D3
Taubaté Brazil **203** C7
Tauber *r.* Germany **48** G6
Tauberbischofsheim Germany **48** G6
Tauchik Kazakh. **102** B3
also known: Taushyq
Taufkirchen (Vils) Germany **48** J7
Tauhara *r.* N.Z. **152** K6
Tauhoa N.Z. **152** I4
Tauini *r.* Brazil **199** G4
Taukum, Peski *des.* Kazakh. **103** H3
Taumarunui N.Z. **152** J6
Taumaturgo Brazil **200** B2
Taung S. Africa **133** I4
Taungbon Myanmar **78** B5
Taungdwingyi Myanmar **78** B3
Taunggyi Myanmar **78** B3
Taunglau Myanmar **78** B3
Taungnyo Range *mts* Myanmar **78** B5
Taunqup Pak. **101** G4
Taunsa Pak. **101** G4
Taunton U.K. **47** I12
Taunton U.S.A. **177** N4
Taunus *hills* Germany **48** E5
Taupiri N.Z. **152** J5
Taupo N.Z. **152** K6
Taupo, Lake N.Z. **152** K6
Tauragé Lith. **42** D6
Tauralaukis Lith. **42** C6
Tauramena Col. **198** C3
Tauranga N.Z. **152** K5
Taureau, Réservoir Canada **169** F3
Taurianova Italy **57** I10
Taurion *r.* France **51** I7
Taurion *r.* France **50** H7
Tauroa Point N.Z. **152** H3
Taurus Mountains Turkey **106** C3
also known as Toros Dağları
Taūshyq Kazakh. *see* Tauchik
Tauste Spain **55** J3
Tauu Islands P.N.G. **145** F2
formerly known as Mortlock Islands
Tauwharaparae N.Z. **152** M6
Tauz Azer. *see* Tovuz
Tavaco *r.* Italy **56** F2
Tavaputs Plateau U.S.A. **183** M3
Tavares U.S.A. **175** D6
Tavas Turkey **106** B3
Tavda Rus. Fed. **38** G4
Tavda *r.* Rus. Fed. **38** G4
Taveiro Portugal **54** C4
Tavşanlı Turkey **106** B3
Tavernes de la Valldigna Spain **55** K5
also spelt Tabernes de Valldigna
Taveuni *i.* Fiji **145** H3
Tavignano *r.* Corse France **56** B6
Tavil'dara Tajik. **101** G2
also spelt Tovil'-Dora
Tavira Portugal **54** D7
Tavistock Canada **173** M7
Tavistock U.K. **47** H13
Tavodzhi Kazakh. **103** I1
Tavolara, Isola *i.* Sardegna Italy **56** B8
Tavolzhan Kazakh. **103** I1
Tavoy Myanmar **79** B5
Tavoy *b.* Myanmar **79** B5
also known as Dawei
Tavoy Island Myanmar *see* Mali Kyun
Tavoy Point Myanmar **79** B5
Tavrichanka Rus. Fed. **90** B3
Tavricheskoye Kazakh. **103** J2
formerly known as Tavril
Tavril Kazakh. *see* Tavricheskoye
Taw *r.* U.K. **47** H12
Tawakoni, Lake U.S.A. **179** D5
Tawallah Range *hills* Australia **148** B2
Tawang India **97** F4
Tawas Bay U.S.A. **173** J6
Tawas City U.S.A. **173** J6
Tawau *Sabah* Malaysia **77** G1
Tawau, Telukan *b. Sabah* Malaysia **77** G1
Tawê Myanmar *see* Tavoy
Tawi-Tawi *i.* Phil. **74** B5
Tawi Hafir *well* U.A.E. **105** F2
Tawila Sudan **120** E6
Tawitawi *i.* Phil. **74** B5
Tawi Murra *well* U.A.E. **105** F2
Tawkar Sudan *see* Tokar
Tawtawa Myanmar **78** B2
Tawu Taiwan **87** G4
Taxco Mex. **185** F5
Taxkorgan China **88** D4
Tay *r.* Canada **166** C2
Tay *r.* U.K. **46** I7
Tay, Firth of *est.* U.K. **46** I7
Tay, Loch *l.* U.K. **46** H7
Tayabamba Peru **200** A1
Tayabas Bay Phil. **74** B3
Tayan Indon. **77** E2
Tayeeglow Somalia **128** E3
Tayga Rus. Fed. **80** C1
Taygan Mongolia **84** C2
Tayinloan U.K. **46** F7
Taylor Canada **166** F3
Taylor *AZ* U.S.A. **183** N7
Taylor *NE* U.S.A. **178** C3
Taylor *TX* U.S.A. **179** C6

Taylor, Mount N.Z. **153** F11
Taylor, Mount U.S.A. **181** F6
Taylorsville U.S.A. **174** C4
Taylorville U.S.A. **174** B4
Taymā' Saudi Arabia **104** C2
Taymura *r.* Rus. Fed. **39** J3
Taymyr, Ozero *l.* Rus. Fed. **39** K2
Taymyr, Poluostrov *pen.* Rus. Fed. *see* Taymyr Peninsula
Taymyr Peninsula Rus. Fed. **39** I2
also known as Taymyr, Poluostrov
Tây Ninh Vietnam **79** D6
Taypak Kazakh. **102** B2
also spelt Taypaq; formerly known as Taypak
Taypaq Kazakh. *see* Taypak
Tayport U.K. **46** J7
Tayshet Rus. Fed. **80** F1
Taysoygan, Peski *des.* Kazakh. **102** C2
Tayspun *tourist site* Iraq *see* Ctesiphon
Taytan Turkey **59** J10
Taytay *Luzon* Phil. **74** B3
Taytay *Palawan* Phil. **74** A4
Taytay Bay Phil. **74** A4
Tayu Indon. **77** E4
Tayuan China **82** B2
Tayyebād Iran **101** E3
Tayynsha Kazakh. **103** G1
Taz *r.* Rus. Fed. **39** H3
Taza Morocco **122** D2
Taza-Bazar Uzbek. *see* Shumanay
Tâza Khurmātū Iraq **107** F4
Taze Myanmar **78** A3
Tazeh Kand Azer. **107** F3
Tazenakht Morocco **122** D3
Tazewell *TN* U.S.A. **176** B9
Tazewell *VA* U.S.A. **176** D9
Tazin *r.* Canada **167** I2
Tazirbū Libya **120** D3
Tazirbū Water Wells Field Libya **120** D3
Tazizilet *well* Niger **125** I2
Tazlău Romania **58** H2
Tazlău *r.* Romania **58** H2
Tazmalt Alg. **55** P8
Tazoghrane Tunisia **57** C12
Tazouikert *hill* Mali **123** F4
Tazovskaya Guba *sea chan.* Rus. Fed. **39** H3
Tazovskiy Rus. Fed. **39** H3
Tazrouk Alg. **123** G5
Tazzarine Morocco **122** D3
Tazzouguert Morocco **122** D3
Tbessa Alg. *see* Tébessa
▶ T'bilisi Georgia **107** F2
Capital of Georgia. English form Tbilisi; historically known as Tiflis
Tbilisi Georgia *see* T'bilisi
Tchabal Mbabo *mt.* Cameroon **125** I5
Tchad *country* Africa *see* Chad
Tchamba Togo **125** F4
Tchaourou Benin **125** F4
Tchetti Benin **125** F5
Tchibanga Gabon **126** A5
Tchidoutene *watercourse* Niger **125** G2
Tchié *well* Chad **120** B5
Tchigaï, Plateau du Niger **123** I5
Tchikala-Tcholohanga Angola **127** C8
formerly known as Vila Nova
Tchin-Tabaradene Niger **125** G3
Tchollié Cameroon **125** I4
Tczew Poland **49** P1
historically known as Dirschau
Te, Prêk *r.* Cambodia **79** D5
Tea *r.* Brazil **199** E5
Teacapán Mex. **184** D4
Teague, Lake *salt flat* Australia **151** C5
Te Anau N.Z. **153** B13
Te Anau, Lake N.Z. **153** B13
Te Anga N.Z. **152** I6
Teano Italy **56** G7
historically known as Teanum Sidicinum
Teano Range *mts* Australia **150** B5
Te Araroa N.Z. **152** M5
Te Aroha N.Z. **152** J5
Te Aroha, Mount *hill* N.Z. **152** J5
Teate Italy *see* Chieti
Te Awamutu N.Z. **152** J6
Tébarat Niger **125** G3
Tebedu *Sarawak* Malaysia **77** E2
Teberda Rus. Fed. **41** G8
Teberdinskiy Zapovednik *nature res.* Rus. Fed. **107** E2
Tébessa Alg. **123** H2
also spelt Tbessa; historically known as Theveste
Tébessa, Monts de *mts* Alg. **123** H2
Tebicuary Para. **201** F6
Tebicuary *r.* Para. **201** F6
Tebingtinggi *Sumatra* Indon. **76** C3
Tebingtinggi *Sumatra* Indon. **76** C3
Tebo *r.* Indon. **76** C3
Téboursouk Tunisia **57** B12
Tébourba Tunisia **57** B12
Tecalitlán Mex. **185** E5
Tecate Mex. **184** E5
Tece Turkey **108** E1
Tech *r.* France **51** J10
Techiman Ghana **125** E5
Techirghiol Romania **58** J4
Tecka Arg. **205** C6
Tecka *r.* Arg. **205** C6
Tecolotlán Mex. **184** E5
Tecomán Mex. **184** E5
Tecoripa Mex. **184** C2
Técpan Mex. **185** E5
Tecuala Mex. **184** D4
Tecuci Romania **58** I3
Tecumseh *MI* U.S.A. **173** J9
Tecumseh *NE* U.S.A. **178** D3
Ted Somalia **128** D3
Tedzhen Turkm. **102** E5
also spelt Tejen
Tedzhen *r.* Turkm. **102** E5
Tedzhenstroy Turkm. **102** E5
Teec Nos Pos U.S.A. **183** O5
Teeklof Pass S. Africa **132** D9
Teel Mongolia **84** D1
Teeli Rus. Fed. **84** A1
Teeswater Canada **173** L6
Tefé Brazil **199** E5
Tefé *r.* Brazil **199** E5
Tefedest *mts* Alg. **123** G4
Téfoûlest *well* Mali **125** H2
Tegal Indon. **77** D4
Tegal *airport* Germany **49** K3
Tegina Nigeria **125** G4
▶ Tegucigalpa Hond. **186** A4
Capital of Honduras.
Teguidda-n-Tessoumt Niger **125** G2
Tehachapi U.S.A. **182** F6
Tehachapi Mountains U.S.A. **182** E7
Te Hana N.Z. **152** I4
Te Hauke N.Z. **152** K7
Tehek Lake Canada **167** M1
Tehery Lake Canada **167** M1
Tehran Iran *see* Tehrān
▶ Tehran Iran **100** B3
Capital of Iran. Also spelt Tehrān

index

T

▶ Tehrān Iran 100 B3
Capital of Iran. Also spelt Teheran.

Tehrān prov. Iran 100 B3
Tehri India see Tikamgarh
Tehri India 96 C3
Tehuacán Mex. 185 F5
Tehuantepec, Gulf of Mex. 185 G6
also known as Tehuantepec, Golfo de
Tehuantepec, Istmo de isthmus Mex. 185 G5
Tehuitzingo Mex. 185 F5
Teičiu rezervāts nature res. Latvia 42 H5
Teide, Pico del vol. Canary Is 122 A3
Teifi r. U.K. 47 H11
Teignmouth U.K. 47 I13
Teiškot well Mali 125 F2
Teita Hills Kenya 128 C5
Teiu Romania 58 E2
Teiuş Romania 58 E2
Teixeira Brazil 202 E3
Teixeira da Silva Angola see Bailundo
Teixeira de Freitas Brazil 207 N4
Teixeira de Sousa Angola see Luau
Teixeiras Brazil 207 K7
Tejakula Indon. 77 F5
Tejeda y Almijara, Sierra de nature res. Spain 54 H8
Tejen Turkm. see Tedzhen
Tejgaon Bangl. 97 F5
Tejira well Niger 125 H3
Tejo r. Port. 54 C5 see Tagus
Tejupan, Punta pt Mex. 184 E5
Te Kaha N.Z. 152 L5
Te Kao N.Z. 152 G2
Tekapo r. N.Z. 153 E12
Tekapo, Lake N.Z. 153 E11
Tekari India 97 E4
Te Kauwhata N.Z. 152 J5
Tekax Mex. 185 H4
Teke Kazakh. 103 G4
Teke r. Turkey 58 H7
Teke, Ozero salt l. Kazakh. 103 H1
Tekeli Aktyubinskaya Oblast' Kazakh. 102 C3
Tekeli Almatinskaya Oblast' Kazakh. 103 I3
Tekes China 88 C3
Tekes Kazakh. 103 I3
Tekes He r. China 88 C3
Tekezē Wenz r. Eritrea/Eth. 121 H6
Tekiliktag mt. China 89 C4
Tekin Rus. Fed. 82 D2
Tekirdağ Turkey 106 A2
formerly known as Rodosto
Tekirdağ prov. Turkey 58 I7
Tekirova Turkey 108 B3
Tekkali India 95 E2
Tekman Turkey 107 E3
Teknaf Bangl. 97 G5
Tekoa, Mount N.Z. 153 G10
Tekong Kechil, Pulau i. Sing. 76 [inset]
Te Kopuru N.Z. 152 H4
Tekoulat, Oued watercourse Alg. 123 F5
Te Kowhai N.Z. 152 J5
Tékro well Chad 120 D5
Tektek Dağları hills Turkey 109 K1
Teku Indon. 75 B3
Te Kuiti N.Z. 152 J6
Tel r. India 95 D1
Tela Dem. Rep. Congo 127 F8
Tela Hond. 186 B4
Telanaipura Indon. see Jambi
Télataï Mali 125 F2
T'elavi Georgia 107 F2
Tel Aviv-Yafo Israel 108 F5
English form Jaffa; also known as Yafa; historically known as Joppa
Telč Czech Rep. 49 M6
Teichac Puerto Mex. 185 H4
Tel'ch'ye Rus. Fed. 43 R8
Telciu Romania 58 E1
Tele, Lac l. Mali 124 E2
Telegjen r. Romania 58 E3
Telegapulang Indon. 77 F3
Telegraph Creek Canada 166 D3
Telekhany Belarus see Tsyelyakhany
Telêmaco Borba Brazil 206 B4
Telemark county Norway 45 J4
Telén Arg. 204 D5
Telen r. Indon. 77 G2
Te'eorman r. Romania 58 G5
Teiertheba, Djebel mt. Alg. 123 G4
Telescope Peak U.S.A. 183 G5
Teles Pires r. Brazil 201 I3
also known as São Pires
Teletskoye, Ozero l. Rus. Fed. 88 D1
Telfer Mining Centre Australia 150 C4
Telford U.K. 47 J11
Telfs Austria 48 I8
Telig well Mali 122 E5
Télimélé Guinea 124 B4
Télissour well Chad 120 D5
Teljo, Jebel mt. Sudan 121 E6
Telkwa Canada 166 E4
Tellaro r. Sicilia Italy 57 H12
Tell Atlas mts U.K. see Atlas Tellien
Teller U.S.A. 164 C2
Tell es-Sultan West Bank see Jericho
Tellicherry India 94 B4
also known as Thalassery
Telloar U.K. 58 L2
Telloh Iraq 107 F5
Tell Rāk Syria 109 L2
Telluride U.S.A. 181 F5
Tel'mansk Turkm. see Gubadag
Tel Megiddo tourist site Israel 108 G5
historically known as Armageddon
Telmen Nuur salt l. Mongolia 84 D1
Telo Indon. 76 B3
Teloloapan Mex. 185 F5
Telo Mart'us France see Toulon
Tel'pos-Iz, Gora mt. Rus. Fed. 40 K3
Telsen Arg. 205 D6
Telšiai Lith. 42 D6

Teluk Anson Malaysia 76 C1
also known as Teluk Intan
Telukbajur Indon. see Telukbayur
Telukbatang Indon. 77 E3
Telukbayur Indon. 76 C3
formerly known as Emmahaven; formerly spelt Telukbajur
Telukbetung Indon. see Tanjungkarang-Telukbetung
Telukdalam Indon. 76 B2
Teluk Intan Malaysia see Teluk Anson
Telukkuantan Indon. 76 C3
Teluknaga Indon. 77 D4
Telukpakedai Indon. 77 E3
Telyazh'ye Rus. Fed. 43 S9
Tema Ghana 125 F5
Temagami Canada 173 N3
Temagami Lake Canada 168 E4
Temaju i. Indon. 77 E2
Temanggung Indon. 77 E4
Temapache Mex. 185 F4
Te Mapou hill N.Z. 152 I7
Temax Mex. 185 H4
Temba S. Africa 133 M2
Tembagapura Indon. 73 I7
Tembe r. Moz. 133 Q3
Tembe Elephant Park nature res. S. Africa 133 Q3
Tembenchi r. Rus. Fed. 39 J3
Tembesi r. Indon. 76 C3
Tembilahan Indon. 76 C3
Tembisa S. Africa 133 M3
Tembo Aluma Angola 127 C6
Tembué Moz. see Chifunde
Tembuland reg. S. Africa 133 M8
Tembwe Zambia 129 B7
Teme r. U.K. 47 J11
Temecula U.S.A. 183 G8
Temelli Turkey 106 C3
also known as Samutlu
Temenchula, Gora mt. Rus. Fed. 84 C1
Temengor, Tasik resr Malaysia 76 C1
Téméra Mali 125 E2
Temerin Vojvodina, Srbija Yugo. 58 A3
Temerloh Malaysia 76 C2
Teminabuan Indon. 73 H7
Temir Kazakh. 102 C2
Temir Kazakh. see Tumur
Temirlan Kazakh. see Temirlanovka
Temirlanovka Kazakh. 103 G4
also known as Temirlan; also spelt Tamerlanovka
Temirtau Kazakh. 103 H2
Témiscamie r. Canada 169 F3
Temiscaming Canada 168 E4
Témiscamingue, Lac l. Canada 173 N3
also known as Timiskaming, Lake
Témiscouata, Lac l. Canada 169 G4
Temiyang i. Indon. 76 D2
Temkino Rus. Fed. 43 P6
Temmes Fin. 44 N2
Temnikov Rus. Fed. 41 G5
Temora Australia 147 E3
Temósachic Mex. 184 D2
Tempe U.S.A. 183 M8
Tempe, Danau l. Indon. 75 A4
Tempe Downs Australia 148 B5
Tempio Pausania Sardegna Italy 56 B8
Temple MI U.S.A. 173 H6
Temple TX U.S.A. 179 C6
Temple Bay Australia 149 D2
Templemore Rep. of Ireland 47 E11
Templer Bank sea feature Phil. 74 A4
Templeton watercourse Australia 148 C4
Templeton N.Z. 153 G11
Templeton U.S.A. 182 D6
Templin Germany 49 K2
Tempoal Mex. 185 F4
Tempoal r. Mex. 185 F4
Tempué Angola 127 C8
Têmpung China 84 C4
Temryuk Rus. Fed. 43 S5
Temryukskiy Zaliv b. Rus. Fed. 41 F7
Temuco Chile 204 B5
Temuka N.Z. 153 F12
Temuli China see Butuo
Temyasovo Rus. Fed. 102 D1
Tena Ecuador 198 B5
Tenabo Mex. 185 H4
Tenabo, Mount U.S.A. 183 H1
Tenala Fin. 42 E1
Tenali India 94 D2
Tenango Mex. 185 F5
Tenasserim Myanmar 79 B5
also known as Tanintharyi or Tanintharyi
Tenasserim admin. div. Myanmar 79 B5
also known as Tanintharyi
Tenasserim r. Myanmar 79 B5
Tenby U.K. 47 H12
Tenby Bay Canada 173 J4
Tence France 51 K7
Tendaho Eth. 128 D2
Tende France 51 N8
Tende, Col de pass France/Italy 51 N8
Ten Degree Channel India 95 G4
Tendelti Sudan 121 F6
Te-n-Dghâmcha, Sebkhet salt marsh Mauritania 124 A2
Tendô Japan 90 G5
Tendrara Morocco 123 E2
Tendre, Mont mt. Switz. 51 M6
Tendukheda India 96 C5
Téné r. Guinea 124 C4
Tenedos i. Turkey see Bozcaada
Ténenkou Mali 124 D3
Tenenys r. Lith. 42 C6
Ténéré du Tafassâsset des. Niger 125 H1
Tenerife i. Canary Is 122 A3
Ténès Alg. 123 F1
Ténès, Cap c. Alg. 55 M8
Tenevo Bulg. 58 H6
Teng, Nam r. Myanmar 78 B3
Tengah, Kepulauan is Indon. 77 G4
Tengah, Sungai r. Sing. 76 [inset]
Tengchong China see Tengxian
Tengchong China 86 A3
Tenge Kazakh. 102 C4
Tengeh Reservoir Sing. 76 [inset]
Tenggarong Indon. 77 G3
Tengger Shamo des. China 84 E4
Tengiz, Ozero salt l. Kazakh. 103 G2
Tengréla Côte d'Ivoire 124 D4
also known as Tingrela
Ten'gushevo Rus. Fed. 40 G5
Tengxian China 87 D4
also known as Tengcheng
Tengxian China see Tengzhou
Tengzhou China 85 H5
formerly known as Tengxian

Tenniöjoki r. Fin./Rus. Fed. 44 O2
Tennyson U.S.A. 172 C8
Teno Chile 204 C4
Tenojoki r. Fin./Norway 44 O1
also known as Tana
Tenom Sabah Malaysia 77 F1
Tenosique Mex. 185 H5
Tenryū Japan 91 E7
Tenryū-gawa r. Japan 91 E7
Tenteno Indon. 75 B3
Tenterfield Australia 147 G2
Ten Thousand Islands U.S.A. 175 D7
Tentolomatinan, Gunung mt. Indon. 75 B2
Tentudia mt. Spain 54 E6
Tenu r. France 50 E5
Teocaltiche Mex. 185 E4
Teocelo Mex. 185 F5
Teodoro Sampaio Brazil 206 A9
Teófilo Otôni Brazil 203 D6
Teomabal i. Phil. 74 B5
Teopisca Mex. 185 G5
Teotihuacán tourist site Mex. 185 F5
Tepa Ghana 125 E5
Tepa Indon. 75 D4
Tepache Mex. 184 C2
Te Paki N.Z. 152 G2
Tepasto Fin. 44 N2
Tepatitlán Mex. 185 E4
Tepehuanes Mex. 184 D3
Tepeji Mex. 185 F5
Tepeköy Turkey see Karakoçan
Tepelmeme de Morelos Mex. 185 F5
Tepelenë Albania 59 B8
Tepequem, Serra mts Brazil 199 F4
Tepianlangsat Indon. 77 G2
Tepic Mex. 184 D4
Teploplaya Gora Rus. Fed. 40 K4
Teplice Czech Rep. 49 K5
Teploye Lipetskaya Oblast' Rus. Fed. 43 T8
Teploye Tul'skaya Oblast' Rus. Fed. 43 S8
Tepopa, Punta pt Mex. 184 B2
Te Puke N.Z. 152 K5
Te Puna N.Z. 152 K5
Tequila Mex. 184 E4
Tequisistlán Mex. 185 G5
Tequisquiapán Mex. 185 F4
Ter r. Spain 55 O2
Tera r. Niger 125 F3
Tera r. Port. 54 C6
Tera r. Spain 54 F3
Terakeka Sudan 128 A3
Teram Kangri mt. China/Jammu and Kashmir 89 B5
Teramo Italy 56 F6
historically known as Interamna
Terang Australia 147 D4
Teratani r. Pak. 101 G4
Terbuny Rus. Fed. 43 T9
Tereben' Rus. Fed. 43 Q8
Terebovlya Ukr. 41 C6
Terebush Rus. Fed. 43 T7
Teregova Romania 58 D3
Terek r. Rus. Fed. 107 F2
Tere-Khol' Rus. Fed. 84 B1
Tere-Khol', Ozero l. Rus. Fed. 84 C1
Terek-Say Kyrg. 103 G4
Terektinskiy Khrebet mts Rus. Fed. 88 D1
Terekty Karagandinskaya Oblast' Kazakh. 103 G2
Terekty Vostochnyy Kazakhstan Kazakh. 88 D1
formerly known as Alekseyevka
Teren'ga Rus. Fed. 41 I5
Terengganu state Malaysia 76 C1
formerly known as Trengganu
Terengözek Kazakh. see Terenozek
Terenos Brazil 203 A7
Terenozek Kazakh. 103 F3
also spelt Terengözek or Teren-Uzyak
Terensay Rus. Fed. 102 D2
Terentang, Pulau i. Indon. 77 G3
Tereshka r. Rus. Fed. 102 A2
Teresina Brazil 202 D3
Teresina de Goias Brazil 202 C5
Teresita Col. 198 D4
Teresópolis Brazil 207 K9
Terespol Poland 42 I9
Teressa Island India 95 G4
Terezinha Brazil 199 H4
Terges r. Port. 54 D7
Tergeste Italy see Trieste
Tergnier France 51 J3
Terhiyn Tsagaan Nuur l. Mongolia 84 D1
Teriberka Rus. Fed. 44 P1
Teriberka r. Rus. Fed. 44 P1
Teriberskiy, Mys pt Rus. Fed. 44 P1
Terisakkan r. Kazakh. 103 F2
formerly known as Tersakkan
Terjît well Mauritania 122 B5
Terka Reba Eth. 128 D3
Terkezi well Chad 120 D5
Terlingua Creek r. U.S.A. 179 B6
Terma, Ras pt Eritrea 104 C5
Termas de Socos Chile 204 C3
Terme Turkey 107 D2
Termessos Milli Parkı nat. park Turkey 108 B1
Termez Uzbek. 103 F5
also spelt Termiz
Termination Island Australia 151 C7
Termini Imerese Sicilia Italy 57 F11
Termini Imerese, Golfo di b. Sicilia Italy 57 F10
Términos, Laguna de lag. Mex. 185 H5
Termit well Niger 120 A5
Termit, Massif de mt Niger 125 H2
Termit-Kaoboul Niger 125 H2
Termiz Uzbek. see Termez
Termo U.S.A. 182 D1
Termoli Italy 56 G7
Termonde Belgium see Dendermonde
Tern r. U.K. 47 J11
Ternate Indon. 75 C2
Ternate i. Indon. 75 C2
Terneuzen Neth. 48 A4
Terney Rus. Fed. 82 E3
Terni Italy 56 E6
Ternitz Austria 49 N8
Ternopil' Ukr. 41 C6
also spelt Ternopol'; formerly spelt Tarnopol'
Ternopol' Ukr. see Ternopil'
Terowie Australia 146 C3
Terpeniya, Mys c. Rus. Fed. 82 G2
Terpeniya, Zaliv g. Rus. Fed. 82 F2
Terra Alta U.S.A. 176 F7
Terra Bella U.S.A. 182 E6
Terra Boa Brazil 206 B10
Terra Branca Brazil 207 J4
Terrace Canada 166 D4
Terrace Bay Canada 168 C3
Terracina Italy 56 F7
formerly spelt Tarracina; historically known as Anxur
Terra Firma S. Africa 132 H2
Terra Nova Bay Antarctica 223 K1
Terranuova Bracciolini Italy 56 D5
Terra Preta Brazil 199 G6
Terra Rica Brazil 206 B10
Terrasini Sicilia Italy 57 F10
Terrassa Spain 55 N3
also spelt Tarrasa
Terrasson-la-Villedieu France 50 H7

Terrazas Mex. 184 D2
Terre Adélie reg. Antarctica see Adélie Land
Terrebonne Bay U.S.A. 175 B6
Terre Haute U.S.A. 174 C4
Terrell U.S.A. 179 C5
Terre Plaine plain France 51 K5
Terrero Mex. 184 D2
Terres Australes et Antarctiques Françaises terr. Indian Ocean see French Southern and Antarctic Lands
Terril mt. Spain 54 F8
Terry U.S.A. 180 F3
Tersakkan r. Kazakh. see Terisakkan
Terschelling i. Neth. 48 C2
Terskey Alatau, Khrebet mts Kyrg. see Terskey Ala-Too
Terskey Ala-Too mts Kyrg. 103 I4
also known as Terskey Alatau, Khrebet
Terskiy Bereg coastal area Rus. Fed. 40 F2
Tersko-Kumskiy Kanal canal Rus. Fed. 107 F1
Tertenia Sardegna Italy 57 B9
Terter Azer. see Tärtär
Teruel Spain 55 J4
Terutao i. Thai. 79 B7
Terutao National Park Thai. 79 B7
Tervakoski Fin. 42 H1
Tervel Bulg. 58 I5
Tervo Fin. 44 N3
Tervola Fin. 44 N2
Teryayevo Rus. Fed. 43 R5
Tešanj Bos.-Herz. 56 J4
Teseney Eritrea 121 H6
Tesha r. Rus. Fed. 40 G5
Teshekpuk Lake U.S.A. 164 D2
Teshikaga Japan 90 I3
Teshio Japan 90 G2
Teshio-dake mt. Japan 90 H3
Teshio-gawa r. Japan 90 G2
Teshio-sanchi mts Japan 90 G2
Tešica Srbija Yugo. 58 C5
Tesiyn Gol r. Mongolia 84 B1
Teslić Bos.-Herz. 56 J4
Teslin Canada 166 C2
Teslin r. Canada 166 C2
Teslin Lake Canada 166 C2
Teslui r. Romania 58 F4
Teso Santo hill Spain 54 F3
Tesouras r. Brazil 206 C1
Tesouro Brazil 202 A6
Tesovo-Netyl'skiy Rus. Fed. 43 M3
Tesovskiy Rus. Fed. 43 L3
Tessala, Monts du mts Alg. 55 K9
Tessalit Mali 123 F5
Tessaoua Niger 125 G3
Tesséroukane well Niger 125 G3
Tessolo Moz. 131 G4
Tessöunfat well Mali 123 F5
formerly spelt Sounfat
Test r. U.K. 47 K13
Testour Tunisia 123 H1
Têt r. France 51 J10
Tetachouck Lake Canada 166 E4
Tetagouche r. Canada 169 H4
Tetas, Punta pt Chile 200 C5
Tete Moz. 131 G2
Tete prov. Moz. 131 G2
Tetehosi Indon. 76 B2
Tête Jaune Cache Canada 166 G4
Te Teko N.Z. 152 K6
Teterev r. Ukr. 41 D6
Teterow Germany 49 J2
Teteven Bulg. 58 F6
Tetiyiv Ukr. see Tetiyev
Tetiyev Ukr. 41 D6
also spelt Tetiyiv; formerly known as Snegurovka
Teton r. U.S.A. 180 E3
Teton Range mts U.S.A. 180 E4
Tétouan Morocco 122 D2
also known as Tetuán; historically known as Titawin
Tetovo Macedonia 58 B6
Tetpur India 96 A5
Tetuán Morocco see Tétouan
Tetulia sea chan. Bangl. 97 F5
Tetyukhe Rus. Fed. see Dal'negorsk
Tetyukhe-Pristan' Rus. Fed. see Rudnaya Pristan'
Tetyushi Rus. Fed. 40 I5
Teuchezhsk Rus. Fed. see Adygeysk
Teuchi Japan 91 A9
Teuco r. Arg. 204 E2
Teulada Sardegna Italy 57 A10
Teulada, Capo c. Sardegna Italy 57 A10
Teul de González Ortega Mex. 184 E4
Teun vol. Indon. 75 D4
Teunom Indon. 76 A1
Teupitz-Köriser Seengebiet park Germany 49 K3
Teustepe Nicaragua 186 B4
Teutoburger Wald hills Germany 48 F3
Teuri-tô i. Japan 90 G2
Teuva Fin. 44 M3
Tevere r. Italy see Tiber
Teverya Israel see Tiberias
Teviot N.Z. 153 B13
Teviot r. U.K. 46 J8
Teviothead U.K. 46 J8
Te Waewae N.Z. 153 B14
Te Waewae Bay N.Z. 153 B14
Te Waiponamu i. N.Z. see South Island
Tewane Botswana 131 E4
Tewantin Australia 149 G5
Tewara r. Indon. 77 F3
Te Wera North I. N.Z. 152 I7
Te Wera North I. N.Z. 152 L6
Te Wharau N.Z. 152 J9
Tewli Belarus 42 F9
Têwo China 86 B1
also known as Dêngka; formerly known as Dêngkagoin
Texarkana AR U.S.A. 179 D5
Texarkana TX U.S.A. 179 D5
Texas Australia 147 F2
Texas state U.S.A. 179 C5
Texas City U.S.A. 179 D6
Texcoco Mex. 185 F5
Texel i. Neth. 48 B2
Texoma, Lake U.S.A. 179 C5
Teyateyaneng Lesotho 133 L5
Teykovo Rus. Fed. 43 V5
Teyvareh Afgh. 101 F3
Teza r. Rus. Fed. 40 G4
Teziutlán Mex. 185 F5
Tezpur India 97 G4
Tezu India 97 H4
Tha r. Laos 78 C3
Tha, Nam r. Laos 78 C3
Tha-anne r. Canada 167 M2
Thabana-Ntlenyana mt. Lesotho 133 N6
Thaba Nchu S. Africa 133 K6
Thabankulu mt. S. Africa 133 O4
Thaba Putsoa mt. Lesotho 131 E6
Thaba Putsoa mts Lesotho 133 M6
Thaba-Tseka Lesotho 133 M6
Thabazimbi S. Africa 133 L2
Thabeikkyin Myanmar 78 B3
Thabo Lan National Park Thai. 79 C5
Thabong S. Africa 133 K4
Thabt, Gebel el mt. Egypt 108 F9
Thabyedaung Myanmar 78 B3
Thac Ba, Hô l. Vietnam 78 C3
Thade r. Myanmar 78 A4
Thädiq Saudi Arabia 105 D2
Thagyettaw Myanmar 79 B5
Tha Hin Thai. see Lop Buri

Thai Binh Vietnam 78 D3
▶ Thailand country Asia 78 C4
known in Thai as Muang Thai or Prathes Thai; formerly known as Siam
asia [countries] ▶▶ 64–67
Thailand, Gulf of Asia 79 C6
Thai Muang Thai. 79 B6
Thai Nguyên Vietnam 78 D3
Thaj Saudi Arabia 105 E2
Thakurgaon Bangl. 97 F4
Thakurtola India 96 D5
Thal Pak. 101 G3
Thala Tunisia 123 H2
Thalang Thai. 79 B6
Thalassery India see Tellicherry
Thal Desert Pak. 101 G4
Thale (Harz) Germany 48 I4
Thale Luang lag. Thai. 79 C7
Thalgau Austria 49 K8
Tha Li Thai. 78 C4
Thaliparamba India see Taliparamba
Thallon Australia 147 F2
Thamad Bù Hashishah well Libya 120 C3
Thamaga Botswana 131 E5
Thamar, Jabal mt. Yemen 105 D5
Thamarit Oman 105 F4
English form Midway
Thames r. Canada 173 K8
Thames N.Z. 152 J5
Thames est. U.K. 47 M12
Thames r. U.K. 47 M12
Thames, Firth of b. N.Z. 152 J4
Thamesford Canada 173 M7
Thamesville Canada 173 L8
Thamûd Yemen 105 E4
Thamugadi tourist site Alg. see Timgad
Thana India see Thane
Thana Ghazi India 96 C4
Thanatpin Myanmar 78 B4
Thanbyuzayat Myanmar 78 B5
Thandla India 96 B5
Thandwê Myanmar see Sandoway
Thane India 94 B2
formerly spelt Thana
Thangadh India 96 A5
Thangool Australia 150 C5
Thanh Hoa Vietnam 78 D4
Thanjavur India 94 C4
also known as Tanjore
Than Kyun i. Myanmar 79 B6
Thanlwin r. Myanmar see Salween
Thano Bula Khan Pak. 101 F5
Than Uyen Vietnam 86 B4
Thaoge r. Botswana 131 D4
Thaolintoa Lake Canada 167 L2
Thap Put Thai. 79 B6
Thap Sakae Thai. 79 B6
Thara India 96 A5
Tharad India 96 A5
Thar Desert India/Pak. 96 A4
also known as Indian Desert
Thargomindah Australia 147 D1
Tharrawaddy Myanmar 78 A4
Tharrawaw Myanmar 78 A4
Tharthār, Buhayrat ath l. Iraq 107 E4
Tharthār Canal Iraq see Dijlah - Ath Tharthār, Qanāt
Tharwāniyah U.A.E. 105 F3
Thasos Greece 58 F8
Thasos i. Greece 58 F8
Thatcher U.S.A. 183 O9
Thất Khê Vietnam 78 D3
Thaton Myanmar 78 B4
Thau, Bassin de lag. France 51 J9
Thaungdut Myanmar 78 A2
Thaungyin r. Myanmar/Thai. 78 B4
Tha Uthen Thai. 78 D4
Thawr, Jabal mt. Jordan 108 G8
Thayawthadangyi Kyun i. Myanmar 79 B5
Thayetmyo Myanmar 78 A4
Thazi Myanmar 78 B3
The Aldermen Islands N.Z. 152 K4
Theba U.S.A. 183 L9
Thebae tourist site Egypt see Thebes
▶ The Bahamas country West Indies 186 D1
northamerica [countries] ▶▶ 158–159
Thebes tourist site Egypt 121 G3
historically known as Diospolis Magna or Thebae
Thebes Greece see Thiva
The Bluff Bahamas 186 D1
The Broads nat. park U.K. 47 N11
The Brothers is Hong Kong China 87 [inset]
also known as Tai Siu Mo To
The Brothers is Yemen see Al Ikhwān
The Calvados Chain is P.N.G. 149 G1
The Cheviot hill U.K. 46 J8
The Coorong inlet Australia 146 C4
The Dalles U.S.A. 180 B3
also known as Dalles City
Thedford U.S.A. 178 B3
The English Company's Islands Australia 148 C1
The Entrance Australia 147 F3
Theewaterskloof Dam resr S. Africa 132 D11
The Fens reg. U.K. 47 L11
▶ The Gambia country Africa 124 A3
africa [countries] ▶▶ 114–117
The Great Oasis Egypt see Kharga Oasis
The Grenadines is St Vincent 187 H4
The Gulf Asia 105 C1
also known as Persian Gulf or Arabian Gulf
▶ The Hague Neth. 48 B3
Seat of government of the Netherlands. Also known as Den Haag or 's-Gravenhage.
world [countries] ▶▶ 10–11
The Haven S. Africa 133 M9
The Horseshoe mt. S. Africa 132 H8
The Hunters Hills N.Z. 153 E12
Theinkun Myanmar 79 B6
Theinzeik Myanmar 78 B4
The Key N.Z. 153 B13
Thekulthili Lake Canada 167 I2
The Lakes National Park Australia 147 E4
Thelon r. Canada 167 J2
Thelon Game Sanctuary nature res. Canada 167 K1
The Lynd Junction Australia 149 E3
Themar Germany 48 H5
Thembalesizwe S. Africa 133 I9
Thembalihle S. Africa 133 N4
The Minch sea chan. U.K. 46 F5
The Mullet b. Rep. of Ireland 47 B9
The Needles stack U.K. 47 K13
Theni India 96 C5
Thenia Alg. 55 O8
Theniet El Had Alg. 55 N9
Thenon France 50 H7
Theodore Australia 149 F5
Theodore Canada 167 K5
Theodore Roosevelt r. Brazil 201 E1
Theodore Roosevelt Lake U.S.A. 183 M8
Theodore Roosevelt National Park U.S.A. 178 B2
Theodosia Ukr. see Feodosiya
The Officer Creek watercourse Australia 146 B1
The Paps hill Rep. of Ireland 47 C11
The Pas Canada 167 K4
Thera i. Greece see Thira
Thérain r. France 51 I3
The Remarkables mts N.Z. 153 C13
Theresa U.S.A. 177 J1
Theresa Creek r. Australia 149 E4
Therma Greece 58 G8

Thermaïkos Kolpos g. Greece 59 D8
Thermo Greece 59 C10
also known as Thérmon
Thérmon Greece see Thermo
Thermopolis U.S.A. 180 E4
The Salt Lake salt flat Australia 147 D2
▶ The Settlement Christmas I. 220 B6
Capital of Christmas Island.
Thesiger Bay Canada 164 G2
The Skaw spit Denmark see Grenen
The Slot sea chan. Solomon Is see New Georgia Sound
The Solent strait U.K. 47 K13
Thesprotiko Greece 59 B9
Thessalia admin. reg. Greece 59 C9
English form Thessaly
Thessalon Canada 168 D4
Thessalonica Greece see Thessaloniki
Thessaloniki Greece 58 D8
also known as Salonika or Thessalonica; formerly known as Salonica
Thessaly admin. reg. Greece see Thessalia
The Storr hill U.K. 46 F6
The Teeth mt. Phil. 74 A4
The Terraces hills Australia 151 C6
Thetford U.K. 47 M11
Thetford Mines Canada 169 G4
The Thumbs mt. N.Z. 153 E11
Thetkethaung r. Myanmar 78 A5
The Triangle mts Myanmar 78 B2
The Twins Australia 146 B2
Theun r. Laos 78 D4
Theunissen S. Africa 133 K5
Theva-i-Ra reef Fiji see Ceva-i-Ra
▶ The Valley Anguilla 187 H3
Capital of Anguilla.
Thevenard Australia 146 B3
Thevenard Island Australia 150 A4
Thévenet, Lac l. Canada 169 G1
Theveste Alg. see Tébessa
The Wash b. U.K. 47 M11
The Weald reg. U.K. 47 M12
The Woodlands U.S.A. 179 D6
Thiamis r. Greece see Thyamis
Thiboudaux U.S.A. 179 E6
Thief River Falls U.S.A. 178 C1
Thiel Neth. see Tiel
Thiel Mountains Antarctica 223 R1
Thielsen, Mount U.S.A. 180 B4
Thielt Belgium see Tielt
Thiers France 51 J7
Thiès Senegal 124 A3
Thika Kenya 128 C5
Thikombia i. Fiji see Cikobia
Thiladhunmathee Atoll Maldives 94 B5
Thilogne Senegal 124 B3
Thimbu Bhutan see Thimphu
▶ Thimphu Bhutan 97 F4
Capital of Bhutan. Also known as Tashi Chho; also spelt Thimbu.
Thingvallavatn (Pingvallavatn) l. Iceland 44 [inset] B2
Thingvellir (Pingvellir) Iceland 44 [inset] B2
formerly known as Diedenhofen
Thionville France 51 M3
Thira Greece 59 G12
Thira i. Greece 59 G12
also known as Santorini; historically known as Thera
Thirasia i. Greece 59 G12
Third Cataract rapids Sudan see 3rd Cataract
Thirsk U.K. 47 K9
Thirty Mile Lake Canada 167 L2
Thiruvananthapuram India see Trivandrum
Thiruvarur India 94 C4
Thiruvattiyur India see Tiruvottiyur
Thissavros, Techniti Limni resr Greece 58 F7
Thisted Denmark 45 J4
Thistilfjörður (Pistilfjörður) b. Iceland 44 [inset]
Thistle Creek Canada 166 B2
Thistle Island Australia 146 C3
Thistle Lake Canada 167 I1
Thityabin Myanmar 78 A3
Thiva Greece 59 E10
also known as Thívai; historically known as Thebes
Thívai Greece see Thiva
Thiviers France 50 G7
Thjórsá (Pjórsá) r. Iceland 44 [inset] B3
Thlewiaza r. Canada 167 M2
Thoa r. Canada 167 I2
Thô Chu, Đao i. Vietnam 79 C6
Thoen Thai. 78 B4
Thoeng Thai. 78 C4
Thohoyandou S. Africa 131 F4
Tholen i. Neth. 48 B4
Thomas r. Australia 151 B5
Thomas, Lake salt flat Australia 148 C5
Thomas Hill Reservoir U.S.A. 178 D4
Thomas Hubbard, Cape Canada 165 J1
Thomas Mountain U.S.A. 183 H8
Thomaston CT U.S.A. 177 L4
Thomaston GA U.S.A. 175 C5
Thomaston ME U.S.A. 177 P1
Thomastown Rep. of Ireland 47 E11
Thomasville AL U.S.A. 175 C6
Thomasville GA U.S.A. 175 D6
Thomasville NC U.S.A. 174 D5
Thomonde Haiti 187 F3
Thompson Canada 167 L4
Thompson r. Canada 166 F5
Thompson MI U.S.A. 172 G5
Thompson UT U.S.A. 183 O3
Thompson r. U.S.A. 174 A4
Thompson Falls U.S.A. 180 D3
Thompson Peak U.S.A. 181 F6
Thompson's Falls Kenya see Nyahururu
Thompson Sound Canada 166 E5
Thompson Sound inlet N.Z. 153 A13
Thompsonville U.S.A. 172 G6
Thomson watercourse Australia 149 D5
Thomson GA U.S.A. 175 D5
Thomson IL U.S.A. 172 C9
Thon Buri Thai. 79 C5
Thongwa Myanmar 78 B4
Thonon-les-Bains France 51 M6
Thoreau U.S.A. 181 I6
Thorhild Canada 167 H4
Thórisvatn (Pórisvatn) l. Iceland 44 [inset] C2
Thorn Poland see Toruń
Thornapple r. U.S.A. 173 H8
Thornbury N.Z. 153 C14
Thorne Canada 173 N4
Thorne U.K. 47 L10
Thornhill U.K. 47 I8
Thornton r. Australia 149 D3
Thornton U.S.A. 172 E6
Thorp U.S.A. 172 C6
Thorsby Canada 167 H4
Thorshavn Faroe Is see Tórshavn
Thorshavnfjella reg. Antarctica see Thorshavnheia
Thorshavnheia reg. Antarctica 223 B2
also known as Thorshavnfjella
Thota-ea-Moli Lesotho 133 L6
Thouars France 50 F6
Thoubal India 97 G4
Thouet r. France 50 F5

Thouin, Cape pt Australia 150 B4
Thourout Belgium see Torhout
Thousand Islands Canada/U.S.A. 173 Q6
Thousand Lake Mountain U.S.A. 183 M3
Thousand Oaks U.S.A. 182 F7
Thousand Palms U.S.A. 183 H8
Thousandsticks U.S.A. 176 B8
Thrace reg. Turkey 106 A2
also spelt Thraki or Trakiya or Trakya
Thraki reg. Turkey see Thrace
Thrakiko Pelagos sea Greece 58 F8
Thredbo Australia 147 F4
Three Fathoms Cove b. Hong Kong China 87 [inset]
also known as Kei Ling Ha Hoi
Three Forks U.S.A. 180 E3
▶Three Gorges Project resr China 87 D2
asia [changes] ▶ 68–69
Three Hummock Island Australia 147 E5
Three Kings Islands N.Z. 152 G2
Three Oaks U.S.A. 172 G9
Three Pagodas Pass Myanmar/Thai. 79 B5
Three Points U.S.A. 183 M9
Three Points, Cape Ghana 125 E5
Three Rivers CA U.S.A. 182 F5
Three Rivers MI U.S.A. 172 H9
Three Rivers TX U.S.A. 179 C6
Three Sisters S. Africa 132 H8
Three Sisters mt. U.S.A. 180 B3
Three Springs Australia 151 A6
Thrissur India see Trichur
Throckmorton U.S.A. 179 C5
Throssell, Lake salt flat Australia 151 D5
Throssel Range hills Australia 150 C4
Thrushton National Park Australia 147 E1
Thubun Lakes Canada 167 I2
Thu Dâu Môt Vietnam 79 D6
formerly known as Phu Cuong
Thuin Belgium 51 K2
Thul Sudan 128 A2
Thul watercourse Sudan 128 A2
Thulaythawāt Gharbī, Jabal hill Syria 109 K2
Thule Greenland 165 M2
also known as Qaanaaq
Thuli Zimbabwe 131 F4
Thuli r. Zimbabwe 131 F4
Thumayl, Wādī watercourse Iraq 109 O4
Thun Switz. 51 N6
Thunda Australia 149 D5
Thundelarra Australia 151 B6
Thunder Bay Canada 168 B3
Thunder Bay b. Canada 168 B3
Thunder Bay b. U.S.A. 173 J5
Thunder Creek r. Canada 167 J5
Thunder Knoll sea feature Caribbean Sea 186 C3
Thuner See l. Switz. 51 N6
Thung Salaeng Luang National Park Thai. 78 C4
Thung Song Thai. 79 B6
Thung Wa Thai. 79 B7
Thung-yai-naresuan Wildlife Reserve nature res. Thai. 79 B5
Thur r. Switz. 51 O5
Thüringen land Germany 48 H4
English form Thuringia
Thüringer Becken reg. Germany 48 I4
Thüringer Wald mts Germany 48 H5
English form Thuringian Forest
Thüringer Wald park Germany 48 H5
Thuringia land Germany see Thüringen
Thuringian Forest mts Germany see Thüringer Wald
Thurles Rep. of Ireland 47 E11
also spelt Durlas
Thurmont U.S.A. 176 H6
Thursby U.K. 47 I9
Thursday Island Australia 149 D1
Thurso U.K. 46 I5
Thurso r. U.K. 46 I5
Thurston Island Antarctica 222 R2
formerly known as Thurston Peninsula
Thurston Peninsula i. Antarctica see Thurston Island
Thusis Switz. 51 P6
Thwaites Glacier Tongue Antarctica 222 Q1
Thy reg. Denmark 45 J4
Thyamis r. Greece 59 B9
also spelt Thíamis
Thyatira Turkey see Akhisar
Thyborøn Denmark 45 J4
Thylungra Australia 149 D5
Thymaina i. Greece 59 H11
Thyolo Malawi 129 B9
Thyou Burkina 125 E4
Thyou Burkina see Tiou
Thysville Dem. Rep. Congo see Mbanza-Ngungu
Tīāb Iran 100 D5
Tiahuanaco Bol. 200 C4
Tiancang China 84 C3
Tianchang China 87 F1
Tiancheng China see Chongyang
Tianchi China see Lezhi
Tiandeng China 87 C4
Tiandiba China see Jinyang
Tiandong China 86 C4
also known as Pingma
Tian'e China 87 C3
also known as Liupai
Tianfanjie China 87 F2
Tiângol Lougguéré watercourse Senegal 124 B3
Tianguá Brazil 202 D2
Tianjin China 85 H4
English form Tientsin
Tianjin municipality China 85 H4
English form Tientsin
Tianjun China 84 C4
also known as Xinyuan
Tiankoye Senegal 124 B3
Tianlin China 86 C3
also known as Leli
Tianmen China 87 E2
Tianmu Shan mts China 87 F2
Tianqiaoling China 82 C4
Tianquan China 86 B2
also known as Chengxiang
Tianshan China 85 I3
also known as Ar Horqin Qi
Tian Shan mts China/Kyrg. see Tien Shan
Tianshifu China 82 B4
Tianshui China 86 C1
Tianshuihai Aksai Chin 89 B5
Tianshuijing China 84 B3
Tiantai China 87 G2
Tiantaiyong China 85 H3
Tiantang China see Yuexi
Tianyang China 86 C4
also known as Tianzhou
Tianyi China see Ningcheng
Tianzhen China see Gaoqing
Tianzhen China 85 G3
Tianzhou China see Tianyang
Tianzhu Gansu China 84 D4
also known as Huazangsi
Tianzhu Guizhou China 87 D3
Tiaret Alg. 123 F2
also known as Tagdempt
Tiaret well Tunisia 123 H3
Tiassalé Côte d'Ivoire 124 D5
Tibabar Sabah Malaysia see Tambunan
Tibagi Brazil 203 B8
Tibagi r. Brazil 206 C10
also spelt Tibaji
Tibaji r. Brazil see Tibagi
Tibal, Wādī watercourse Iraq 107 E4
Tibaná Col. 198 C3
Tibati Cameroon 125 I5
Tibba Pak. 101 G4
Tibé, Pic de mt. Guinea 124 C4
Tiber r. Italy 56 E7
also spelt Tevere
Tiberghamine Alg. 123 F3
Tiberias Israel 108 G5
also spelt Teverya
Tiberias, Lake Israel see Galilee, Sea of
Tiber Reservoir U.S.A. 180 E2
Tibesti mts Chad 120 C4
Tibet aut. reg. China see Xizang Zizhiqu
Tibet, Plateau of China 89 D5
also known as Qingzang Gaoyuan or Xizang Gaoyuan
Tibet Autonomous Region aut. reg. China see Xizang Zizhiqu
Tibiri Niger 125 G3
Tibleş, Vârful mt. Romania 58 F2
Tiboku Falls Guyana 199 G3
Tibooburra Australia 147 D2
Tibrikot Nepal 97 D3
Tibuga, Ensenada b. Col. 198 B3
Tibur Italy see Tivoli
Tiburón, Isla i. Mex. 184 B2
Ticao i. Phil. 74 B3
Ticha r. Bulg. 58 H5
Tichak mt. Bulg. 58 D6
Tichau Poland see Tychy
Tichborne Canada 173 Q6
Tichégami r. Canada 169 F3
Tichet well Mali 125 F2
Tichit Mauritania 124 C2
Tichla W. Sahara 122 B5
Ticino r. Italy/Switz. 56 B3
Ticinum Italy see Pavia
Ţicleni Romania 58 E4
Ticonderoga U.S.A. 177 L2
historically known as Fort Carillon
Ticul Mex. 185 H4
Ticumbia i. Fiji see Cikobia
Tiddim Myanmar 78 A3
Tiderìdjaouine, Adrar mts Alg. 123 F5
Tidikelt, Plaine du plain Alg. 123 F4
Tidioute U.S.A. 176 F4
Tidjerouene well Mali 125 F2
Tidjikja Mauritania 124 C2
Tidore i. Indon. 75 C2
Tiébissou Côte d'Ivoire 124 D5
Tiéboro Chad 120 C4
Tiefa China 85 I3
also known as Diaobingshan
Tiel Neth. 48 C4
formerly spelt Thiel
Tiel Senegal 124 B3
Tieli China 82 B3
Tieling China 82 A4
Tielongtan Aksai Chin 89 B5
Tielt Belgium 51 J2
also spelt Thielt
Tiémé Côte d'Ivoire 124 D4
Tienen Belgium 51 K2
also known as Tirlemont
Tien Shan mts China/Kyrg. 88 B3
also spelt Tian Shan or Tyan' Shan'
Tien Shan Oblast admin. div. Kyrg. see Naryn
Tientsin China see Tianjin
Tientsin municipality China see Tianjin
Tiên Yên Vietnam 78 D3
Tierfontein S. Africa 133 K5
Tierp Sweden 45 L3
Tierra Amarilla U.S.A. 181 F5
Tierra Blanca Mex. 185 F5
Tierra Blanca Peru 198 C6
Tierra Colorada Mex. 185 F5
Tierra del Fuego prov. Arg. 205 D9

▶Tierra del Fuego, Isla Grande de i. Arg./Chile 205 C9
Largest island in South America.
southamerica [landscapes] ▶ 190–191

Tierra del Fuego, Parque Nacional nat. park Arg. 205 D9
Tierra Llana de Huelva plain Spain 54 D7
Tierralta Col. 198 B2
Tiétar r. Spain 54 F5
Tiétar, Valle de valley Spain 54 F4
Tietê Brazil 206 F10
Tietê r. Brazil 206 B7
Tieyon Australia 148 B5
Tiffin U.S.A. 176 B4
Tiflis Georgia see T'bilisi
Tifore i. Indon. 75 C2
Tifton U.S.A. 175 D6
Tifu Indon. 75 C3
Tiga i. Sabah Malaysia 77 F1
Tigane S. Africa 133 K3
Ţigăneşti Romania 58 G5
Tigapuluh, Pegunungan mts Indon. 76 C3
Tigen Kazakh. 102 B3
Tigh Āb Iran 101 E5
Tigheciului, Dealurile hills Moldova 58 J3
Tighina Moldova 58 K2
formerly known as Bender or Bendery
Tigiretskiy Khrebet mts Kazakh./Rus. Fed. 88 C1
Tigiria India 95 E1
Tignère Cameroon 125 I5
Tignish Canada 169 H4
Tigoda r. Rus. Fed. 43 M2
Tigranocerta Turkey see Siirt
Tigray admin. reg. Eth. 128 C1
Tigre r. Ecuador/Peru 198 C6
Tigre, Cerro del mt. Mex. 185 F4
Tigris r. Asia 107 F4
also known as Dicle (Turkey) or Dijlah, Nahr (Iraq/Syria)
Tigrovaya Balka Zapovednik nature res. Tajik. 101 G2
Tiguent Mauritania 124 B2
Tiguesmat hills Mauritania 122 C4
Tiguidit, Falaise de esc. Niger 125 G2
Tiguir well Niger 125 H2
Tih, Gebel el plat. Egypt 121 G2
Tihāmah reg. Saudi Arabia 104 C4
Tihuatlán Mex. 185 F4
Tijamuchi r. Bol. 200 D3
Tijara India 96 C4
Tijī Libya 120 A1
Tijirīt reg. Mauritania 122 B5
Tijuana Mex. 184 A1
Tijucas Brazil 203 B8
Tijucas, Bahia de b. Brazil 203 B8
Tijuco r. Brazil 206 C5
Tikal tourist site Guat. 185 H5
Tikal, Parque Nacional nat. park Guat. 185 H5
Tikamgarh India 96 C4
also known as Tehri
Tikanlik China 88 D3
Tikchik Lake U.S.A. 164 D4
Tikhereo Greece see Tykhero
Tikhmenevo Rus. Fed. 43 T3
Tikhonova Pustyn' Rus. Fed. 43 R7
Tikhoretsk Rus. Fed. 41 G7
Tikhtozero Rus. Fed. 44 O2
Tikhvin Rus. Fed. 43 O2
Tikhvinka r. Rus. Fed. 43 O2
Tikhvinskaya Gryada ridge Rus. Fed. 43 O2
Tikiktene well Niger 125 G2
Tikitiki N.Z. 152 M5
Tikkakoski Fin. 44 N3
Tikkurila Fin. 42 G1
Tikokino N.Z. 152 K7
Tikrīt Iraq 107 E4
Tikshozero, Ozero l. Rus. Fed. 44 P2
Tiksi Rus. Fed. 39 M2
Tikumbia i. Fiji see Cikobia
Tikveš Ezero l. Macedonia 58 C7
Tikwana S. Africa 133 J4
Tila r. Nepal 97 D3
Tilaiya Reservoir India 97 E4
Tilavar Iran 100 C2
Tilbeşar Ovasi plain Turkey 109 I1
Tilbooroo Australia 147 E1
Tilburg Neth. 48 C4
Tilbury Canada 173 K8
Tilbury U.K. 47 M12
Tilcara Arg. 200 D5
Tilcha Australia 146 D2
Tilden U.S.A. 179 C6
Tileagd Romania 58 D1
Tilemsès Niger 125 G3
Tilemsi, Vallée du watercourse Mali 125 F2
Tilghman U.S.A. 177 I7
Tilhar India 96 C4
Tilia, Oued watercourse Alg. 123 F4
Tilimsen Alg. see Tlemcen
Tilin Myanmar 78 A3
Tillabéri Niger 125 F3
Tillabéri dept Niger 125 F3
Tillamook U.S.A. 180 B3
Tillanchong Island India 95 G4
Tille r. France 51 L5
Tilley Canada 167 I5
Tillia Niger 125 G2
Tillsonburg Canada 168 D5
Tiloa Niger 125 F3
Tilogne Senegal see Thilogne
Tilomonte Chile 200 C5
Tilos i. Greece 59 I12
Tilpa Australia 147 E2
Tilsa r. Latvia 42 I5
Tilsit Rus. Fed. see Sovetsk
Tilton U.S.A. 177 N2
Tiltža Latvia 42 I5
Tim Rus. Fed. 41 F6
Tim r. Rus. Fed. 43 S9
Tima Egypt 121 F3
Timakara i. India 94 B4
Timane r. Para. 201 F5
Timanskiy Kryazh ridge Rus. Fed. 40 I2
Timar Turkey 107 E3
Timaru N.Z. 153 F12
Timashevsk Rus. Fed. 41 F7
formerly known as Timashevskaya
Timashevskaya Rus. Fed. see Timashevsk
Timbákion Greece see Tympaki
Timbalier Bay U.S.A. 175 B6
Timbaúba Brazil 202 F3
Timbedgha Mauritania 124 C2
Timber Creek Australia 148 A2
Timber Lake U.S.A. 178 B2
Timber Mountain U.S.A. 183 H4
Timberville U.S.A. 176 G7
Timbiquí Col. 198 B4
Timbué, Ponta pt Moz. 131 H3
Timbuktu Mali 124 E2
also spelt Tombouctou
Timbun Mata i. Sabah Malaysia 77 G1
Timelkam Austria 49 K7
Timétrine Mali 125 E2
Timétrine reg. Mali 125 E2
Timgad tourist site Alg. 123 G2
also known as Thamugadi
Timia Niger 125 H2
Timiaouine Alg. 123 F5
Timimoun Alg. 123 F3
Timirist, Râs pt Mauritania 124 A2
Timiryazev Kazakh. 103 F1
Timiryazevo Kazakh. 103 F1
Timiş r. Romania 58 B3
Timiskaming, Lake Canada see Témiscamingue, Lac
Timişoara Romania 58 C3
Timişului, Câmpia plain Romania 58 B3
Timkovichi Belarus see Tsimkavichy
Ti-m-Meghsoi watercourse Niger 125 G2
Timmelsjoch pass Austria/Italy 48 I9
Timmins Canada 168 D3
Timms Hill hill U.S.A. 172 C5
Timok r. Yugo. 58 D4
Timokhino Rus. Fed. 43 R2
Timon Brazil 202 D3
Timor i. Asia 75 C5
Timor Sea Australia/Indon. 144 B3
Timor Timur terr. Asia see East Timor
Timoshino Rus. Fed. 43 R1
Timóteo Brazil 207 K6
Timoudi Alg. 123 E3
Timperley Range hills Australia 151 C5
Timrå Sweden 44 L3
Timsâh, Bahra el l. Egypt 108 D7
Tims Ford Lake U.S.A. 174 C5
Timshor r. Rus. Fed. 40 J3
Timur Kazakh. see Tumur
Timurni Muafi India 96 C5
Tīn, Jabal hill Saudi Arabia 104 C2
Tin r. S. Africa 133 N8
Tîna, Khalîg el b. Egypt 108 D6
English form Pelusium, Bay of
Ti-n-Aba well Mali 125 E2
Tin Alkoum Libya 120 A3
Tin Amzi, Oued watercourse Alg. 123 G5
Ti-n-Azabo well Mali 125 F2
Ti-n-Bessaïs well Mauritania 122 C5
Tin Can Bay Australia 149 G5
Tinchebray France 50 F4
Ti-n-Didine well Mali 123 E5
Tindivanam India 94 C3
Tindouf Alg. 122 C4
Tiné Chad 120 D6
Ti-n-Echeri well Mali 125 E2
Tinée r. France 51 N9
Tineo Spain 54 E1
Tinerhir Morocco 122 D3
Ti-n-Etissane well Mali 125 E2
Tinfouchy Alg. 122 D3
Tinggi i. Malaysia 76 D2
Tingi Mountains Sierra Leone 124 C4
Tingis Morocco see Tangier
Ting Jiang r. China 87 F3
Tingkawk Sakan Myanmar 78 B2
Tinglev Denmark 45 J5
Tingo Maria Peru 200 B2
Tingréla Côte d'Ivoire see Tengréla
Tingri China 89 D6
Tingsryd Sweden 45 K4
Tingstäde Sweden 45 L4
Tingvatn Norway 45 I4
Tingvoll Norway 44 J3
Tingzhou China see Changting
Tinharé, Ilha de i. Brazil 202 E5
Tinian i. N. Mariana Is 73 K4
formerly known as Buena Vista
Tiniéré well Mauritania 124 B2
Tinigua, Parque Nacional nat. park Col. 198 C4
Tini Heke is N.Z. see Snares Islands
Tiniroto N.Z. 152 L6
Tinja r. Bos.-Herz. 56 K4
Tinjar r. Sarawak Malaysia 77 F1
Tinkisso r. Guinea 124 C4
Tinline, Mount N.Z. 153 H10
Tinn Norway 45 J4
Tinnelvelly India see Tirunelveli
Tinnsjo l. Norway 45 J4
Tinogasta Arg. 204 D3
Tinompo Indon. 75 B2
Tinos Greece 59 G11
Tinos i. Greece 59 G11
Tiñosa mt. Spain 54 G7
Tinrhert, Plateau du Alg. 123 G3
Ti-n-Srir well Mali 125 F2
Tinsukia India 97 G4
Tintagel Canada 166 E4
Tinţâne Mauritania 124 C2
Ti-n-Tarabine well Alg. 123 G5
Ti-n-Tarabine, Oued watercourse Alg. 123 G5
Ti-n-Tehoun well Mali 124 E2
Tintejert, Adrar mt. Alg. 123 F4
Ti-n-Tersi well Mali 125 F2
Tintina Arg. 204 E2
Tintinara Australia 146 D3
Tinto r. Spain 54 E7
Tin Tounnant well Mali see Taounnant
Tinui N.Z. 152 K8
Ti-n-Zaouâtene Mali 125 F2
Tioga ND U.S.A. 178 B1
Tioga PA U.S.A. 177 H4
Tioga r. U.S.A. 177 H3
Tioman i. Malaysia 76 D2
Tionaga Canada 173 K2
Tioribougou Mali 124 C3
Tiou Burkina 124 E3
formerly spelt Thyou
Tioughnioga r. U.S.A. 177 J3
Tipasa Alg. 123 F1
Tipitapa Nicaragua 186 B4
Tipler U.S.A. 172 E5
Tippecanoe r. U.S.A. 174 C3
Tipperary Rep. of Ireland 47 D11
Tiptala Bhanjyang pass Nepal 97 E4
Tipton CA U.S.A. 182 E5
Tipton IA U.S.A. 174 B3
Tipton MO U.S.A. 178 D4
Tipton, Mount U.S.A. 183 J6
Tiptonville U.S.A. 174 B4
Tiptop U.S.A. 176 D8
Tip Top Hill hill Canada 168 C3
Tiptur India 94 C3
Tipuani Bol. 200 C3
Tiquié r. Brazil 198 D4
Tiquisate Guat. 185 H6
Tiracambu, Serra do hills Brazil 202 C3
Tirahart, Oued watercourse Alg. 123 F5
Tīrān Iran 100 B3
Tīrān i. Saudi Arabia 104 A2

▶Tirana Albania 58 A7
Capital of Albania. Also spelt Tiranë.

Tiranë Albania see Tirana
Tirano Italy 56 C2
Tiraouene well Niger 125 G2
Tirap India 97 G4
Tiraraouine well Mali 125 E2
Tirari Desert Australia 146 C1
Tiraspol Moldova 58 K2
Tirau N.Z. 152 J5
Tiraumea N.Z. 152 K8
Tiraz Mountains Namibia 130 C5
Tire Turkey 59 I10
Tiree i. U.K. 46 F7
Tirek well Alg. 123 F5
Tirest well Mali 123 F5
Tîrgovişte Romania see Târgovişte
Tîrgu Bujor Romania see Târgu Bujor
Tîrgu Cărbuneşti Romania see Târgu Cărbuneşti
Tîrgu Frumos Romania see Târgu Frumos
Tîrgu Jiu Romania see Târgu Jiu
Tîrgu Lăpuş Romania see Târgu Lăpuş
Tîrgu Mureş Romania see Târgu Mureş
Tîrgu Neamţ Romania see Târgu Neamţ
Tîrgu Ocna Romania see Târgu Ocna
Tîrgu Secuiesc Romania see Târgu Secuiesc
Tirich Mir mt. Pak. 101 G2
Tirinie, Oued watercourse Alg 123 H5
Tiris Zemmour admin. reg. Mauritania 122 C5
Tirkšliai Lith. 42 D5
Tirlemont Belgium see Tienen
Tirna r. India 94 C2
Tîrnăveni Romania see Târnăveni
Tírnavos Greece see Tyrnavos
Tiro hill Spain 54 F6
Tirodi India 96 C5
Tiros Brazil 203 C6
Tiroungoulou Cent. Afr. Rep. 126 D2
Tirourda, Col de pass Alg. 55 P8
Tirreno, Mare sea France/Italy see Tyrrhenian Sea
Tirso r. Sardegna Italy 57 A9
Tirthahalli India 94 B3
Tiruchchendur India 94 C4
Tiruchchirappalli India 94 C4
formerly known as Trichinopoly
Tiruchengodu India 94 C4
Tirukkoyilur India 94 C3
Tirumangalam India 94 C4
Tirunelveli India 94 C4
formerly known as Tinnelvelly
Tiruntán Peru 200 B1
Tirupati India 94 C3
Tiruppattur Tamil Nadu India 94 C3
Tiruppattur Tamil Nadu India 94 C4
Tiruppur India 94 C4
Tiruttani India 94 C3
Tirutturaippundi India 94 C4
Tiruvallur India 94 C3
Tiruvannamalai India 94 C3
Tiruvettipuram India 94 C3
Tiruvottiyur India 94 D3
also spelt Thiruvattiyur
Tiryns tourist site Greece 59 D11
Tirza r. Latvia 42 H4
Tisa r. Yugo. 58 B3
also known as Tisza
Tisa r. Yugo. 58 C5
Tisaiyanvilai India 94 C4
Tisău Romania 58 H3
Tisdale Canada 167 J4
Tishomingo U.S.A. 179 C5
Tiska, Mont mt. Alg. 123 H5
Tissemsilt Alg. 123 F2
formerly known as Vialar
Tista r. India 97 F4
Tisza r. Hungary see Tisa
Tiszabezdéd Hungary 49 T7
Tiszaföldvár Hungary 49 R9
Tiszafüred Hungary 49 R8
Tiszakécske Hungary 49 R9
Tiszaújváros Hungary 49 S8
Tiszavasvári Hungary 49 S8
formerly known as Büdszentmihály
Tit Alg. 123 F4
Tit Alg. 123 G5
Titabar India 97 G4
Titan Dome ice feature Antarctica 223 K1
Titao Burkina 125 E3
Titarisios r. Greece 59 D9
Tit-Ary Rus. Fed. 39 M2
Titawin Morocco see Tétouan
Titel Vojvodina, Srbija Yugo. 58 B3
Tithwal Pak. 101 H3
Titicaca, Lago l. Bol./Peru see Titicaca, Lake

▶Titicaca, Lake Bol./Peru 200 C3
Largest lake in South America. Also known as Titicaca, Lago.
southamerica [landscapes] ▶ 190–191
southamerica [countries] ▶ 192–193

Titirea mt. N.Z. see Aspiring, Mount
Titlagarh India 95 D1
Titlis mt. Switz. 51 O6
Titograd Crna Gora Yugo. see Podgorica
Titova Mitrovica Kosovo, Srbija Yugo. see Kosovska Mitrovica
Titov Drvar Bos.-Herz. 56 I4
Titovka r. Rus. Fed. 44 O1
Titovo Užice Srbija Yugo. see Užice
Titovo Velenje Slovenia see Velenje
Titov Veles Macedonia see Veles
Titov Vrbas Vojvodina, Srbija Yugo. see Vrbas
Ti Tree Australia 148 B4
Tittabawassee r. U.S.A. 173 J7
Titteri mts Alg. 55 O8
Tittmoning Germany 49 J7
Titu Romania 58 G4
Titule Dem. Rep. Congo 126 E4
Titusville FL U.S.A. 175 D6
Titusville PA U.S.A. 176 F4
Tiu Chung Chau i. Hong Kong China 87 [inset]
Tiumpan Head U.K. 46 F5
also known as Siumpain, Rubha an t-
Tiva watercourse Kenya 128 C5
Tivari India 96 B4
Tivat Crna Gora Yugo. 56 K6
Tiveden nationalpark nat. park Sweden 45 K4
Tiverton Canada 173 L6
Tiverton U.K. 47 I13
Tivoli Italy 56 E7
historically known as Tibur
Tiwal, Wadi watercourse Sudan 126 D2
Ţiwāl al 'Abā reg. Syria 109 K1
Tiwi Oman 105 G3
Tiwi Aboriginal Land res. Australia 148 A1
Tiworo, Selat sea chan. Indon. 75 B4
Tixkokob Mex. 185 H4
Tixtla Mex. 185 F5
Tiya tourist site Eth. 128 C2
Tizi El Arba hill Alg. 55 O8
Tizi Mighert pass Morocco 122 C3
Tizimín Mex. 185 H4
Tizi-n-Test pass Morocco 122 C3
Tizi-n-Tichka pass Morocco 122 D3
Tizi Ouzou Alg. 123 G1
Tiznap He r. China 88 B4
Tiznit Morocco 122 C3
Tizoc Mex. 185 E3
Tjaktjajaure l. Sweden 44 L2
Tjåmotis Sweden 44 L2
Tjaneni Swaziland 133 P2
Tjappsåive Sweden 44 L2
Tjautas Sweden 44 M2
Tjeggelvas l. Sweden 44 L2
Tjirebon Indon. see Cirebon
Tjirrkarli Aboriginal Reserve Australia 151 D5
Tjolotjo Zimbabwe see Tsholotsho
Tjörn i. Sweden 45 J4
Tjörnes pen. Iceland 44 [inset] C2
Tjøtta Norway 44 K2
Tkibuli Georgia see Tqibuli
Tkvarcheli Georgia see Tqvarch'eli
Tlacolula Mex. 185 F5
Tlacotalpán Mex. 185 G5
Tlacotepec, Cerro mt. Mex. 185 E5
Tlalnepantla Mex. 185 F5
Tlancualpican Mex. 185 F5
Tlapa Mex. 185 F5
Tlapacoyan Mex. 185 F5
Tlaxcala Mex. 185 F5
Tlaxcala state Mex. 185 F5
Tlaxco Mex. 185 F5
Tlaxcoapan Mex. 185 F4
Tlaxiaco Mex. 185 F5
Tlell Canada 166 D4
Tlemcen Alg. 123 E2
formerly spelt Tilimsen
Tleta Rissana Morocco 54 F9
Tlhabologang S. Africa 133 K3
Tlhakalatlou S. Africa 132 G5
Tlhakgameng S. Africa 133 I3
Tlholong S. Africa 133 M5
Tlokweng Botswana 131 E5
Tluszcz Poland 49 S3
Tlyarata Rus. Fed. 107 F2
T'ma r. Rus. Fed. 43 Q5
Tmeïmichât Mauritania 122 B5
Tnaôt, Prêk r. Cambodia 79 D6
To r. Myanmar 78 B4
also known as China Bakir
Toad r. Canada 166 E3
Toad River Canada 166 E3
Toamasina Madag. 131 [inset] K3
formerly known as Tamatave
Toamasina prov. Madag. 131 [inset] K3
Toana mts U.S.A. 183 J1
Toano U.S.A. 177 I8
Toa Payoh Sing. 76 [inset]
Toast U.S.A. 176 E9
Toatoa N.Z. 152 L6
To Awai well Sudan 121 G4
Toay Arg. 204 D5
Toba China 86 A2
Toba Japan 91 E7
Toba, Danau l. Indon. 76 B2
English form Toba, Lake
Toba, Lake Indon. see Toba, Danau
Toba and Kakar Ranges mts Pak. 101 F4
Tobago i. Trin. and Tob. 187 H5
Toba Inlet Canada 166 E5
Tobarra Spain 55 J6
Tobas Arg. 204 E3
Toba Tek Singh Pak. 101 H4
Tobelo Indon. 75 C2
Tobermorey Australia 148 C4
Tobermory Australia 147 D1
Tobermory Canada 168 D4
Tobermory U.K. 46 F7
Tōbetsu Japan 90 G3
Tobi i. Palau 73 H6
Tobias Barreto Brazil 202 E4
Tobin, Lake salt flat Australia 150 D4
Tobin, Mount U.S.A. 183 G1
Tobin Lake Canada 180 G1
Tobique r. Canada 169 H4
Tobi-shima i. Japan 90 F5
Toboali Indon. 77 D3
Tobol Kazakh. 103 E1
also spelt Tobyl
Tobol r. Kazakh./Rus. Fed. 103 E1
also spelt Tobyl
Tobol'sk Rus. Fed. 38 G4
Toboso Phil. 74 B4
Tobruk Libya see Tubruq
Tobyhanna U.S.A. 177 J4
Tobyl Kazakh. see Tobol
Tobyl r. Kazakh./Rus. Fed. see Tobol
Tobylzhan Kazakh. see Tavolzhan
Tobysh r. Rus. Fed. 40 I2
Tocache Nuevo Peru 200 A2
Tocantinópolis Brazil 202 C3
Tocantins r. Pará Brazil 199 G6
Tocantins r. Brazil 202 B2
Tocantins state Brazil 202 B4
Toccoa U.S.A. 174 D5
Toce r. Italy 56 A3
Tochi r. Pak. 101 G3
Tochigi Japan 91 F6
Tochigi pref. Japan 91 F6
Tochio Japan 90 F6
Töcksfors Sweden 45 J4
Tocoa Hond. 186 B4
Tocopilla Chile 200 C5
Tocorpuri, Cerros de mts Bol./Chile 200 D5
Tocumwal Australia 147 E3
Tod, Mount Canada 166 G5
Toda Bhim India 96 C4
Toda Rai Singh India 96 B4
Todd watercourse Australia 148 B5
Todd Range hills Australia 151 D5
Todi Italy 56 E6
historically known as Tuder
Todi mt. Switz. 51 O6
Todog China 88 C2
formerly spelt Todok
Todohokke Japan 90 G4
Todok China see Todog
Todos os Santos r. Brazil 207 M4
Todos Santos Bol. 200 D4
Todos Santos Mex. 184 C4
Todtmoos Germany 48 E8
Toe Jaga, Khao hill Thai. 79 B5
Toekomstig Stuwmeer resr Suriname 199 G4
Toéni Burkina 124 E3
Tofield Canada 167 H4
Tofino Canada 166 E5
Toft U.K. 46 K3
Tofte U.S.A. 172 C3
Toftlund Denmark 45 J5
Tofua i. Tonga 145 H3
Toga U.S.A. 176 G8
Tōgane Japan 91 G7
Togdheer admin. reg. Somalia 128 E2
Togi Japan 91 E6
Togiak U.S.A. 164 C4
Togian i. Indon. 75 B3
Togian, Kepulauan is Indon. 75 B3
Togliatti Rus. Fed. see Tol'yatti
▶Togo country Africa 125 F4
africa [countries] ▶ 114–117
Tograsay He r. China 88 E4
Tögrög Mongolia 84 B2
formerly known as Manhan
Togrog Ul China 85 G3
also known as Qahar Youyi Qianqi
Togtoh China 85 F3
Toguchin Rus. Fed. 80 C1
Toguz Kazakh. 103 E3
Tog Wajaale Somalia 128 D2
Tohamiyam Sudan 121 H5
Tohana India 96 B3
Tohenbatu mt. Sarawak Malaysia 77 F2
Tohmajärvi Fin. 44 O3
Tohmajärvi l. Fin. 44 O3
Toholampi Fin. 44 N3
Tohom China 85 E3
Töhöm Mongolia 85 F2
Tohono O'Odham (Papago) Indian Reservation res. U.S.A. 183 L9
Tohoun Togo 125 F5
Toi Hokkaidō Japan 90 G4
Toi Shizuoka Japan 91 F7
Toiba China 89 E6
also spelt Doba
Toijala Fin. 45 M3
Toili Indon. 75 B3
Toi-misaki pt Japan 91 B9
Toineke Indon. 75 C5
Toiyabe Range mts U.S.A. 183 G2
Tojikiston country Asia see Tajikistan
Tojikobod Tajik. 101 G2
also spelt Tadzhikabad
Tōjō Japan 91 C7
Tok r. Rus. Fed. 102 C1
Tok U.S.A. 164 E3
Tokachi-gawa r. Japan 90 H3
Tōkai Japan 91 E7
Tokaj Hungary 49 S7
Tokala, Gunung mt. Indon. 75 B3
Tōkamachi Japan 90 F6
Tokanui N.Z. 153 C14
Tokar Sudan 121 H5
Tokarahi N.Z. 153 E12
Tokara-rettō is Japan 81 L7
Tokarevka Kazakh. 103 H2
Tokat Turkey 107 D2
Tokatoka N.Z. 152 H4
Tŏkch'ŏk-to i. S. Korea 83 B5
Tŏkch'ŏn N. Korea 83 B5
Tokdo i. N. Pacific Ocean see Liancourt Rocks

▶Tokelau terr. S. Pacific Ocean 221 G6
New Zealand Overseas Territory.
oceania [countries] ▶ 138–139

Tokhtamysh Tajik. see Tŭkhtamish
Toki Japan 91 E7
Tokkuztara China see Gongliu
Tokmak Kyrg. 103 H4
also spelt Tokmok; formerly known as Bol'shoy Tokmak
Tokmak Ukr. 41 E7
formerly known as Bol'shoy Tokmak or Velykyy Tokmak
Tokmok Kyrg. see Tokmak
Tokomaru Bay N.Z. 152 M6
Tokoroa N.Z. 152 J6
Tokoro-gawa r. Japan 90 I2
Tokounou Guinea 124 C4
Tokoza S. Africa 133 M3
Tokrau watercourse Kazakh. see Tokyrau
Toksu China see Xinhe
Toksun China 88 E3
Tok-tō i. N. Pacific Ocean see Liancourt Rocks
Toktogul Kyrg. 103 H4
formerly known as Muztor
Toktogul'skoye Vodokhranilishche resr Kyrg. see Toktogul Suu Saktagychy
Toktogul Suu Saktagychy resr Kyrg. 103 H4
also known as Toktogul'skoye Vodokhranilishche
Tokto-ri i. N. Pacific Ocean see Liancourt Rocks
Tokty Kazakh. 88 C2
Toku i. Tonga 145 H3
Tokur Rus. Fed. 82 D1
Tokushima Japan 91 D7
Tokushima pref. Japan 91 D8
Tokuyama Japan 91 B7
Tokwe r. Zimbabwe see Tugwi
Tokyo Japan see Tōkyō

▶Tōkyō Japan 91 F7
Capital of Japan. Most populous city in the world and in Asia. English form Tokyo; historically known as Edo.
world [population] ▶ 22–23
world [cities] ▶ 24–25

Tōkyō municipality Japan 90 F7
Tōkyō-wan b. Japan 91 F7
Tokyrau watercourse Kazakh. 103 H3
also spelt Toqyraū; formerly spelt Tokrau
Tokyu-san National Park S. Korea 83 B6
Tokzār Afgh. 101 F3
Tolaga Bay N.Z. 152 M6

largest cities

	city	population	location	page#
1	Tōkyō	26 444 000	Japan Asia	91 F7
2	Mexico City	18 131 000	Mexico North America	185 F5
3	Mumbai (Bombay)	18 066 000	India Asia	94 B2
4	São Paulo	17 755 000	Brazil South America	206 G10
5	New York	16 640 000	USA North America	177 L5
6	Lagos	13 427 000	Nigeria Africa	125 F5
7	Los Angeles	13 140 000	USA North America	182 F7
8	Kolkata (Calcutta)	12 918 000	India Asia	97 F5
9	Shanghai	12 887 000	China Asia	87 G2
10	Buenos Aires	12 560 000	Argentina South America	204 F4

index T

Tōlañaro Madag. **131** [inset] J5
also known as Faradofay; formerly known as Fort-Dauphin; formerly spelt Taolanaro
Tolar, Cerro *mt.* Arg. **204** D2
Tolbazy Rus. Fed. **40** J5
Tolbo Mongolia **84** A1
Tolbukhin Bulg. *see* **Dobrich**
Tolbukhino Rus. Fed. **43** V4
formerly known as Davydkovo
Tolchin, Mount Antarctica **223** T1
Tolé Panama **186** C5
Tole Bi Kazakh. **103** H4
formerly known as Novotroitskoye
Toledo *Amazonas* Brazil **198** C6
Toledo *Paraná* Brazil **203** A8
Toledo Chile **204** C2
Toledo Spain **54** G5
historically known as Toletum
Toledo *IA* U.S.A. **174** A3
Toledo *OH* U.S.A. **176** B4
Toledo *OR* U.S.A. **180** B3
Toledo, Montes de *mts* Spain **54** G5
formerly known as Oretana, Cordillera
Toledo Bend Reservoir U.S.A. **179** D6
Tolentino Italy **56** F5
Toletum Spain *see* **Toledo**
Tolga Norway **44** J3
Toli China **88** C2
Toliara Madag. **131** [inset] I4
formerly spelt Tuléar
Toliara *prov.* Madag. **131** [inset] J4
Tolima *dept* Col. **198** C4
Toling China *see* **Zanda**
Tolitoli Indon. **75** B2
Tol'ka Rus. Fed. **39** I3
Tolkmicko Poland **49** Q1
Tollense *r.* Germany **49** K2
Tollensesee-Becken *park* Germany **49** K2
Tolleson U.S.A. **183** L8
Tollimarjon Uzbek. *see* **Talimardzhan**
Tolmachevo Rus. Fed. **43** K3
Tolmezzo Italy **56** F2
Tolmin Slovenia **56** F2
Tolna Hungary **49** P9
Tolo Dem. Rep. Congo **126** C5
Tolo Channel *Hong Kong* China **87** [inset]
also known as Chek Mun Hoi Hap
Tolochin Belarus *see* **Talachyn**
Tolo Harbour *b. Hong Kong* China **87** [inset]
also known as Tai Po Hoi
Tolonen Fin. **44** N1
Tolosa France *see* **Toulouse**
Tolosa Spain **55** I1
Tolsan-do *i.* S. Korea **83** B6
Tolsmaville Canada **173** J5
Tolstoy, Mys *c.* Rus. Fed. **39** P4
Toltén Chile **204** B5
Tolú Col. **198** C2
Toluca Mex. **185** F5
Tolvand, Ozero *l.* Rus. Fed. **44** O2
Tol'yatti Rus. Fed. **41** I5
English form Togliatti; formerly known as Stavropol'-na-Volge
Tolybay Kazakh. **103** E2
Tom' *r.* Rus. Fed. **82** B2
Toma Burkina **124** E3
Tomah U.S.A. **172** C7
Tomahawk U.S.A. **172** D5
Tomakomai Japan **90** G3
Tomales U.S.A. **182** B3
Tomamae Japan **90** G2
Tomani *Sabah* Malaysia **77** F1
Tomar Brazil **199** F5
Tomar Port. **54** C5
Tomari Japan **90** G3
Tomari Rus. Fed. **82** F3
Tomaros *mt.* Greece **59** B9
Tomarza Turkey **106** C3
Tomaszów Mazowiecki Poland **49** R4
Tomatlán Mex. **184** D5
Tomave Bol. **200** D5
Tomazina Brazil **206** D10
Tombador, Serra do *hills Bahia* Brazil **202** D4
Tombador, Serra do *hills Mato Grosso* Brazil **201** F3
Tombigbee *r.* U.S.A. **175** C6
Tombo S. Africa **133** N8
Tomboco Angola **127** B6
Tombos Brazil **207** K7
Tombouctou Mali *see* **Timbuktu**
Tombouctou *admin. reg.* Mali **124** E2
Tombstone U.S.A. **181** E7
Tombua Angola **127** A8
formerly known as Porto Alexandre
Tom Burke S. Africa **131** E4
Tomdibuloq Uzbek. *see* **Tamdybulak**
Tomditow Toghi *hills* Uzbek. *see* **Tamdytau, Gory**
Tomé Chile **204** B5
Tome Moz. **131** G4
Tomea *i.* Indon. **75** B4
Tomelilla Sweden **45** K5
Tomelloso Spain **55** H5
Temenaryk Kazakh. **103** F4
formerly spelt Tyumen'-Aryk
Tomi Romania *see* **Constanța**
Tomiko Canada **173** N4
Tomina Bol. **201** D4
Tominé *r.* Guinea **124** B3
Tomingley Australia **147** F3
Tomini, Teluk *g.* Indon. **75** B3
Tominian Mali **124** D3
Tomioka *Fukushima* Japan **90** G6
Tomioka *Gumma* Japan **91** F6
Tomislavgrad Bos.-Herz. **56** J5
formerly known as Duvno
Tomkinson Ranges *mts* Australia **146** A1
Tømmerneset Norway **44** K2
Tommot Rus. Fed. **39** M4
Tomo Col. **199** E4
Tomo *r.* Col. **198** E3
Tomóchic Mex. **184** D2
Tomorit, Maja e *mt.* Albania **58** B8
Tomorlog China **88** E4
Tomortei China **85** G3
Tompa Hungary **49** Q9
Tompira Indon. **75** B3
Tompi Seleka S. Africa **133** N1
Tompo Indon. **75** A3
Tompo Rus. Fed. **39** N3
Tom Price Australia **150** B4
Tomra China **89** D6
Tomsk Rus. Fed. **80** D1
Toms River U.S.A. **177** K6
Tomtor Rus. Fed. **39** O3
Tömük Turkey **108** F1
also known as Elvanlı
Tomuraushi-yama *mt.* Japan **90** H3
Tomur Feng *mt.* China/Kyrg. *see* **Pobeda Peak**
Tomuzlovka *r.* Rus. Fed. **41** H7
Tom White, Mount U.S.A. **164** E3
Tonalá *Chiapas* Mex. **185** G5
Tonalá *Veracruz* Mex. **185** G5
Tonami Japan **91** E6
Tonantins Brazil **199** E5
Tonate Fr. Guiana **199** H3
Tonawanda U.S.A. **176** G2
Tonb-e Bozorg, Jazīreh-ye *i.* The Gulf *see* **Greater Tunb**
Tonb-e Küchek, Jazīreh-ye *i.* The Gulf *see* **Lesser Tunb**
Tonbridge U.K. **47** M12
Tondano Indon. **75** C2
Tondela Port. **54** C4
Tønder Denmark **45** J5
Tondi India **94** C4
Toney Mount Antarctica **222** Q1
Tonga Cameroon **125** H5
▶**Tonga** *country* S. Pacific Ocean **145** H3
historically known as Friendly Islands
oceania [countries] ▶▶ 138–139
Tonga Sudan **128** A2
Tongaat S. Africa **133** P6
Tong'an China **87** F3
also known as Datong
Tonga Plateau Zambia **127** E9
Tongaporutu N.Z. **152** I6
Tongareva *atoll* Cook Is *see* **Penrhyn**
Tongariro *vol.* N.Z. **152** J7
Tongariro National Park N.Z. **152** J7
Tongatapu *i.* Tonga **145** H4
Tongatapu Group *is* Tonga **145** H4

▶**Tonga Trench** *sea feature* S. Pacific Ocean **220** G7
2nd deepest trench in the world.

Tongbai China **87** E1
Tongbai Shan *mts* China **87** E1
Tongcheng *Anhui* China **87** F2
Tongcheng *Hubei* China **87** E2
also known as Juanshui
Tongcheng China *see* **Dong'e**
T'ongch'ŏn N. Korea **83** B5
Tongchuan China **85** F5
Tongchuan China *see* **Santai**
Tongdao China **87** D3
also known as Shuangjiang
Tongde China **84** D5
also known as Gabasumdo
Tongduch'ŏn S. Korea **83** B5
Tongeren Belgium **51** L2
also spelt Tongres
Tonggu China **87** E2
also known as Yongning
Tongguan China **87** D1
Tonggu Jiao *pt* China **87** D5
Tonghae S. Korea **83** C5
Tonghai China **86** B3
also known as Xiushan
Tonghe China **82** C3
Tonghua *Jilin* China **82** B4
also known as Kuaidamao
Tonghua *Jilin* China **82** B4
Tongi Bangl. *see* **Tungi**
Tongjiang *Heilong.* China **82** D3
Tongjiang *Sichuan* China **87** C2
also known as Nuojiang
Tongken *r.* China **82** B3
Tongking, Gulf of China/Vietnam **78** E3
Tongle China *see* **Leye**
Tongliao China **85** I3
Tongling *Anhui* China **87** F2
Tongling *Anhui* China **87** F2
Tonglu China **87** F2
Tongnae S. Korea **91** A7
Tongo Australia **147** D2
Tongobory Madag. **131** [inset] J4
Tongo Lake *salt flat* Australia **147** D2
Tongquan China *see* **Malong**
Tongquil *i.* Phil. **74** B5
Tongren *Guizhou* China **87** D3
Tongren *Qinghai* China **84** D5
also known as Rongwo
Tongres Belgium *see* **Tongeren**
Tongsa Bhutan *see* **Trongsa**
Tongshan China **87** F1
also known as Xuzhou
Tongshi China **87** D5
formerly known as Hongqizhen
Tongta Myanmar **78** B3
Tongtian He *r.* China *see* **Yangtze**
Tongue U.K. **46** H5
Tongue *r.* U.S.A. **180** F3
Tongue of the Ocean *sea chan.* Bahamas **186** D1
Tongwei China **84** E5
also known as Pingxiang
Tongxian China *see* **Tongzhou**
Tongxiang China **87** G2
Tongxin China **85** E4
T'ongyŏng S. Korea **83** C6
formerly known as Ch'ungmu
Tongyu China **85** I2
also known as Kaitong
Tongzhou China **85** H4
formerly known as Tongxian
Tongzi China **86** C2
Tonhil Mongolia *see* **Dzüyl**
Tonica U.S.A. **172** D9
Tónichi Mex. **184** C2
Tonila Mex. **184** E5
Tonj Sudan **126** F3
Tonj *watercourse* Sudan **126** F3
Tonk India **96** B4
Tonkābon Iran **100** B2
Tonkawa U.S.A. **178** C4
Tonkin *reg.* Vietnam **78** D3
Tônle Repou *r.* Laos **79** D5
Tônlé Sab *l.* Cambodia *see* **Tonle Sap**

▶**Tonle Sap** *l.* Cambodia **79** C5
Largest lake in Southeast Asia. Also spelt Tônlé Sab.

Tonnay-Charente France **50** F7
Tonneins France **50** G8
Tonnerre France **51** J5
Tönning Germany **48** F1
Tōno Japan **90** G5
Tonopah *AZ* U.S.A. **183** L8
Tonopah *NV* U.S.A. **183** G3
Tonosí Panama **186** C6
Tons *r.* India **89** B6
Tønsberg Norway **45** J4
Tonshalovo Rus. Fed. **43** S2
Tonstad Norway **45** I4
Tontelbos S. Africa **132** E7
Tonto Basin U.S.A. **183** M8
Tonto Creek *watercourse* U.S.A. **183** M8
Tonzang Myanmar **78** A3
Toobeah Australia **147** F2
Toobli Liberia **124** C5
Tooele U.S.A. **183** L1
Toolonga Nature Reserve Australia **151** A5
Toompine Australia **147** E1
Toorberg *mt.* S. Africa **132** I9
Toowoomba Australia **147** F1
Tooxin Somalia **128** F2
Top Afgh. **101** G3
Topalki Rus. Fed. **43** R3
Topana Romania **58** F4
Topaz Lake U.S.A. **182** E3

▶**Topeka** U.S.A. **178** D4
State capital of Kansas.

Topia Mex. **184** D3
Topkanovo Rus. Fed. **43** T7
Topki Rus. Fed. **80** D1
Topla *reg.* India **96** D5
Topľa *r.* Slovakia **49** S7
Toplana, Gunung *mt.* Indon. **75** D3
Topley Canada **166** E4
Topley Landing Canada **166** E4
Toplica *r.* Yugo. **58** C5
Toplița Romania **58** G2
Topocalma, Punta *pt* Chile **204** B4
Topock U.S.A. **183** J7
Topoľčany Slovakia **49** P7
Topolnitsa *r.* Bulg. **58** F6
Topolobampo Mex. **184** C3
Topolog Romania **58** J4
Topolog *r.* Romania **58** F3
Topoloveni Romania **58** G4
Topolovgrad Bulg. **58** H6
Topozero, Ozero *l.* Rus. Fed. **44** P2
Toppenish U.S.A. **180** B3
Topraisar Romania **58** J4
Topterek China *see* **Jeminay**
Topuni N.Z. **152** I4
Toqyraū *watercourse* Kazakh. *see* **Tokyrau**
Tor Eth. **128** B3
Tora Dem. Rep. Congo **126** F4
Torata Peru **200** C4
Tor Baldak *mt.* Afgh. **101** F4
Torbalı Turkey **106** A3
Torbat-e Heydarīyeh Iran **101** D3
Torbat-e Jām Iran **101** E3
Torbay Bay Australia **151** B7
Torbeyevo *Respublika Mordoviya* Rus. Fed. **41** G5
Torbeyevo *Smolenskaya Oblast'* Rus. Fed. **43** P6
Torch *r.* Canada **167** K4
Torchino Rus. Fed. **43** V5
Tordesillas Spain **54** G3
Tórdiga, Puerto de *pass* Spain **55** I5
Tordino *r.* Italy **56** F6
Töre Sweden **44** M2
Töreboda Sweden **45** K4
Torelló Spain **55** N2
Toreno Spain **54** E2
Toreo Indon. **75** B3
Torere N.Z. **152** L5
Toretam Kazakh. *see* **Baykonur**
Torey Rus. Fed. **84** E1
Torgau Germany **49** J4
Torgelow Germany **49** L2
Torghay Kazakh. *see* **Turgay**
Torgun *r.* Rus. Fed. **102** A2
Torhamn Sweden **45** K4
Torhout Belgium **51** J1
also spelt Thourout
Tori Estonia **42** F3
Tori India **97** E5
Tori *r.* Sudan **128** A3
Torigni-sur-Vire France **50** F3
Torine *pass* Bos.-Herz. **56** K5
Torino Italy *see* **Turin**
Tori-shima *i.* Japan **91** G9
Torit Sudan **128** B3
Torixoreu Brazil **206** A3
Torkamān Iran **100** A2
Torkovichi Rus. Fed. **43** L3
Torma Estonia **42** H3
Törmänen Fin. **44** N1
Torment, Point Australia **150** C3
Tormes *r.* Spain **54** E3
Tornado Mountain Canada **167** H5
Tornaľa Slovakia **49** R7
formerly known as Šafárikovo
Tornavacas, Puerto de *pass* Spain **54** F4
Torneå Fin. *see* **Tornio**
Torneälven *r.* Sweden **44** N2
Torneträsk Sweden **44** L1
Torneträsk *l.* Sweden **44** L1
Torngat, Monts *mts* Canada *see* **Torngat Mountains**
Torngat Mountains Canada **169** H1
also known as Torngat, Monts
Tornik *mt.* Yugo. **58** A5
Tornio Fin. **44** N2
also spelt Torneå
Tornquist Arg. **204** E5
Toro Nigeria **125** H4
Toro Spain **54** F3
Toro, Lago del *l.* Chile **205** B8
Toro, Pico del *mt.* Mex. **185** E3
Torobuku Indon. **75** B4
Torodi Niger **125** F3
Törökszentmiklós Hungary **49** R8

▶**Toronto** Canada **168** E5
Provincial capital of Ontario and 5th most populous city in North America.
world [cities] ▶▶ 24–25

Toronto U.S.A. **176** E5
Toropatsa Rus. Fed. **43** M5
Toro Peak U.S.A. **183** H8
Toropets Rus. Fed. **43** M5
Tororo Chad **120** C6
Tororo Uganda **128** B4
Toros Dağları *mts* Turkey *see* **Taurus Mountains**
Toroshino Rus. Fed. **43** J4
Torquato Severo Brazil **204** G3
Torquay Australia **147** E4
Torquay U.K. **47** I13
Torrance U.S.A. **182** F8
Torre *mt.* Port. **54** D4
Torre Annunziata Italy **57** G8
Torreblanca Spain **55** L4
Torre Blanco, Cerro *mt.* Mex. **184** B1
Torrecerredo *mt.* Spain **54** G1
Torrecilla *mt.* Spain **54** G8
Torre del Greco Italy **57** G8
Torre de Moncorvo Port. **54** D3
Torredonjimeno Spain **54** H7
Torrejón de Ardoz Spain **55** H4
Torrejón-Tajo, Embalse de *resr* Spain **54** F5
Torrelaguna Spain **55** H4
Torrelavega Spain **54** G1
Torremaggiore Italy **56** H7
Torremolinos Spain **54** G8

▶**Torrens, Lake** *salt flat* Australia **146** C2
2nd largest lake in Oceania.
oceania [landscapes] ▶▶ 136–137

Torrens Creek Australia **149** E4
Torrent Arg. **204** F3
Torrent Spain **55** K5
also spelt Torrente
Torrente Spain *see* **Torrent**
Torreón Mex. **185** E3
Torre Orsaia Italy **57** H8
Torre-Pacheco Spain **55** K7
Torreperedones *hill* Spain **54** G7
Torres Brazil **203** B9
Torres del Paine, Parque Nacional *nat. park* Chile **205** B8
Torres Islands Vanuatu **145** F3
Torres Novas Port. **54** C5
Torres Strait Australia **144** D2
Torres Vedras Port. **54** B5
Torrevieja Spain **55** K7
Torrey U.S.A. **183** M3
Torridge *r.* U.K. **47** H13
Torriglia Italy **56** B4
Torrijos Spain **54** G5
Torrington U.S.A. **180** F4
Torroella de Montgrí Spain **55** O2
Torrön *l.* Sweden **44** K3
Torronsuon kansallispuisto *nat. park* Fin. **42** E1
Torrox Spain **54** H8
Torsa Chhu *r.* Bhutan **97** F4
Torsby Sweden **45** K3

▶**Tórshavn** Faroe Is **46** F1
Capital of the Faroe Islands. Also spelt Thorshavn.

Torsvåg Norway **44** L1
Tortilla Flat U.S.A. **183** M8
Törtköl Uzbek. *see* **Turtkul'**
Tortkuduk Kazakh. **103** H2
Tortola *i.* Virgin Is (U.K.) **187** G3
Tortolì *Sardegna* Italy **57** B9
Tortomanu Romania **58** J4
Tortona Italy **56** A4
Tortorici *Sicilia* Italy **57** G10
Tortosa Spain **55** L4
Tortuga, Laguna *l.* Mex. **185** F4
Tortuguero, Parque Nacional *nat. park* Costa Rica **186** C5
Tortum Turkey **107** E2
Torūd Iran **100** C3
Torugart, Pereval *pass* China/Kyrg. *see* **Turugart Pass**
Torul Turkey **107** D2
Toruń Poland **49** P2
historically known as Thorn
Tõrva Estonia **42** G3
Torvløysa *mt.* Norway **44** I3
Tory Island Rep. of Ireland **47** D8
Torysa *r.* Slovakia **49** S7
Tory Sound *sea chan.* Rep. of Ireland **47** D8
Torzhkovskaya Gryada *hills* Rus. Fed. **43** P5
Torzhok Rus. Fed. **43** P4
Tosa Japan **91** C8
Tosashimizu Japan **91** C8
Tosa-wan *b.* Japan **91** C8
Tosa-yamada Japan **91** C8
Tosbotn Norway **44** K2
Tosca S. Africa **132** H2
Tosca, Punta *pt* Mex. **184** C3
Toscana *admin. reg.* Italy **56** D5
English form Tuscany
Toscana *reg.* Italy *see* **Tuscany**
Toscano, Arcipelago *is* Italy **56** B5
Tosenfjorden *inlet* Norway **44** K2
To-shima *i.* Japan **91** F7
Tōshima-yama *mt.* Japan **90** G4
Toshkent Uzbek. *see* **Tashkent**
Toshkent Wiloyati *admin. div.* Uzbek. *see* **Tashkentskaya Oblast'**
Toshnya *r.* Rus. Fed. **43** U2
Tosno Rus. Fed. **43** L2
Toson Hu *l.* China **84** C4
Tosontsengel Mongolia **84** C1
Tossal de la Baltasana *mt.* Spain **55** M3
Tossal de l'Orri *mt.* Spain **55** M2
also spelt Tozal del Orri
Tostado Arg. **204** E3
Tõstamaa Estonia **42** E3
Tostedt Germany **48** G2
Tosu Japan **91** B8
Tosya Turkey **106** C2
Toszek Poland **49** P5
Totana Spain **55** J7
Totapola *mt.* Sri Lanka **94** D5
Totaranui N.Z. **152** G8
Toteng Botswana **130** D4
Tôtes France **50** H3
Tot'ma Rus. Fed. **40** G4
Totness Suriname **199** G3
Totolapan Mex. **185** F5
Totonicapán Guat. **185** H6
Totora Bol. **200** D4
Totoral Chile **204** C2
Totoralejos Arg. **204** D3
Totoya *i.* Fiji **145** H3
Totskoye Rus. Fed. **102** C1
Tottori Japan **91** D7
Tottori *pref.* Japan **91** C7
Touâret *well* Niger **125** G1
Touba Côte d'Ivoire **124** D4
Touba Senegal **124** B3
Toubkal, Parc National *nat. park* Morocco **122** D3
Touboro Cameroon **125** I5
Touchet *r.* U.S.A. **180** C3
Toucy France **51** J5
Toudaohu China **84** E4
Toueïrma *well* Mauritania **122** B5
Touérât *well* Mali **124** E2
Toufourine *well* Mali **122** D4
Tougan Burkina **124** E3
Touggourt Alg. **123** G2
Tougouri Burkina **125** E3
Touil Mauritania **124** C3
Toukoto Mali **124** C3
Toul France **51** L4
Toulépleu Côte d'Ivoire **124** C5
Toulfé Burkina **125** E3
Touliu Taiwan **87** G4
also spelt Douliu
Toulnustouc *r.* Canada **169** G3
Toulon France **51** L9
historically known as Telo Martius
Toulon U.S.A. **174** B3
Touloukwell Niger **125** G2
Toulouse France **50** H9
historically known as Tolosa
Toumbélaga *well* Niger **125** G3
Toummo *well* Niger **123** I5
Toumodi Côte d'Ivoire **124** D5
Toungo Nigeria **125** I4
Toungoo Myanmar **78** B4
Toupai China **87** D3
Touraine *reg.* France **50** G5
Tourane Vietnam *see* **Đa Năng**
Tourassine *well* Mauritania **122** C4
Tourba Chad **120** B6
Tourgis Lake Canada **167** J1
Touriñán, Cabo *c.* Spain **54** B1
Tourlaville France **50** E3
Tour Matagrin *hill* France **51** K7
Tournai Belgium **51** J2
Tournavista Peru **200** B2
Tourndo, Oued *watercourse* Alg./Niger **123** H5
Tournon-sur-Rhône France **51** K7
Tournus France **51** K6
Touros Brazil **202** F3
Touroua Cameroon **125** I4
Tours France **50** G5
historically known as Caesarodunum or Turones
Tous, Embalse de *resr* Spain **55** K5
Toussiana Burkina **124** D4
Toussidé, Pic *mt.* Chad **120** C4
Toussoro, Mont *mt.* Cent. Afr. Rep. **126** D2
Toutai China **82** B3
Touws *r.* S. Africa **132** E10
Touwsrivier S. Africa **132** E10
Tõv *prov.* Mongolia **85** E2
Tovar Venez. **198** D2
Tovarkovo Rus. Fed. **43** Q7
Tovarkovskiy Rus. Fed. **43** T8
formerly known as Kaganovich
Tovarnik Croatia **56** L3
Tovil'-Dora Tajik. *see* **Tavil'dara**
Tovu Fiji **145** H3
Tovuz Azer. **107** F2
also spelt Tauz
Towada Japan **90** G4
Towada-Hachimantai National Park Japan **90** G5
Towada-ko *l.* Japan **90** G4
Towai N.Z. **152** I3
Towakaima Guyana **199** G3
Towak Mountain *hill* U.S.A. **164** C3
Towanda U.S.A. **177** I4
Towaoc U.S.A. **183** P4
Towari Indon. **75** B4
Tower U.S.A. **172** A3
Tower City U.S.A. **177** I5
Towerhill Creek *watercourse* Australia **149** E4
Towner U.S.A. **178** B1
Towns *r.* Australia **148** B2
Townsend *MA* U.S.A. **177** N3
Townsend *MT* U.S.A. **180** E3
Townshend Island Australia **149** F4
Townsville Australia **149** E3
Towori, Teluk *b.* Indon. **75** B3
Towot Sudan **128** B3
Towr Kham Afgh. **101** G3
Towson U.S.A. **177** I6
Towuti, Danau *l.* Indon. **75** B3
Toxkan He *r.* China **88** C3
Toy U.S.A. **182** F1
Toyah U.S.A. **179** B6
Tōya-ko *l.* Japan **90** G3
Toyama Japan **91** E6
Toyama *pref.* Japan **91** E6
Toyama-wan *b.* Japan **90** E6
Tōyo Japan **91** C8
Toyohashi Japan **91** E7
Toyokawa Japan **91** E7
Toyonaka Japan **83** D6
Toyooka Japan **91** D7
Toyosaka Japan **90** F6
Toyota Japan **91** E7
Toyotomi Japan **90** G2
Toysa Fin. **44** M3
Toytepa Uzbek. **103** G4
also spelt Tŭytepa
Tozal del Orri *mt.* Spain *see* **Tossal de l'Orri**
Tozanlı Turkey *see* **Almus**
Tozê Kangri *mt.* China **89** C5
Tozeur Tunisia **123** H2
Tqibuli Georgia **107** E2
also spelt Tkibuli
Tqvarch'eli Georgia **107** E2
also spelt Tkvarcheli
Trâblous Lebanon *see* **Tripoli**
Trabotivište Macedonia **58** D7
Trabzon Turkey **107** D2
English form Trebizond; historically known as Trapezus
Tracy *CA* U.S.A. **182** C4
Tracy *MN* U.S.A. **178** D2
Trade Lake U.S.A. **172** A5
Trading *r.* Canada **168** B3
Træna *i.* Norway **44** K2
Trænfjorden *sea chan.* Norway **44** K2
Traer U.S.A. **174** A3
Trafalgar, Cabo *c.* Spain **54** E8
Traffic Mountain Canada **166** D2
Traian Romania **58** G5
Traiguén Chile **204** B5
Trail Canada **166** G5
Traill Island Greenland *see* **Traill Ø**
Traill Ø *i.* Greenland **165** Q2
English form Traill Island
Traipu Brazil **202** E4
Traira *r.* Brazil **198** D5
also spelt Taraíra
Trairas *r.* Brazil **206** G4
Trairi Brazil **202** E2
Traisen *r.* Austria **49** M7
Trajano de Morais Brazil **207** K9
Trajectum Neth. *see* **Utrecht**
Traka *r.* S. Africa **132** H10
Trakai Lith. **42** F7
Trakai *nat. park* Lith. **42** F7
Trakiya *reg.* Turkey *see* **Thrace**
Trakt Rus. Fed. **40** I3
Trakya *reg.* Turkey *see* **Thrace**
Tralee Rep. of Ireland **47** C11
also spelt Trá Lí
Trá Lí Rep. of Ireland *see* **Tralee**
Trá Mhór Rep. of Ireland *see* **Tramore**
Trammel U.S.A. **176** C8
Tramore Rep. of Ireland **47** E11
also spelt Trá Mhór
Tramuntana, Serra de *mts* Spain **55** N5
Tranås Sweden **45** K4
Trancas Arg. **204** D2
Trancoso Port. **54** D4
Tranebjerg Denmark **45** J5
Tranemo Sweden **45** K4
Trang Thai. **79** B7
Trangan *i.* Indon. **73** H8
Trangie Australia **147** E3
Trani Italy **56** I7
Tranoroa Madag. **131** [inset] J5
Tranqueras Uruguay **204** G3
Transantarctic Mountains Antarctica **223** K2
Trans Canada Highway Canada **167** H5
Transcona Canada **167** L5
Transtrand Sweden **45** K3
Transylvanian Alps *mts* Romania **58** D3
also known as Carpații Meridionali
Transylvanian Basin *plat.* Romania **58** F2
also known as Podișul Transilvaniei
Tra Ôn Vietnam **79** D6
Trapani *Sicilia* Italy **57** E10
Trapezus Turkey *see* **Trabzon**
Trapper Peak U.S.A. **180** D3
Trappes France **51** I4
Trapua *r.* Brazil **203** A9
Traralgon Australia **147** E4
Traras, Monts des *mts* Alg. **55** J9
Trarza *admin. reg.* Mauritania **124** B2
Trascăului, Munții *mts* Romania **58** E2
Trashigang Bhutan **97** F4
also spelt Tashigang
Trasimeno, Lago *l.* Italy **56** E5
Trás-os-Montes *reg.* Port. **54** D3
Trasvase, Canal de Spain **55** I5
Trasvase Tajo-Segura, Canal de Spain **55** I5
Trat Thai. **79** C5
Traun Austria **49** L7
Traun *r.* Austria **49** L7
Traunreut Germany **49** J8
Traunsee *l.* Austria **49** K8
Traunstein Germany **49** J8
Traupis Lith. **42** F6
Trave *r.* Germany **48** H2
Travellers Lake *imp. l.* Australia **147** D3
Traverse City U.S.A. **172** H6
Travesía Puntana *des.* Arg. **204** D4
Travesía Tunuyán *des.* Arg. **204** D4
Travessão Brazil **207** L8
Tra Vinh Vietnam **79** D6
formerly known as Phu Vinh
Travis, Lake U.S.A. **179** C6
Travnik Bos.-Herz. **56** J4
Trbovlje Slovenia **56** H2
Trebebvić *nat. park* Bos.-Herz. **56** K5
Trebel *r.* Germany **49** K2
Trèbes France **51** I9
Třebíč Czech Rep. **49** M6
Trebinje Bos.-Herz. **56** K6
Trebisacce Italy **57** I9
Trebišnjica *r.* Bos.-Herz. **56** J6
Trebišov Slovakia **49** S7
Trebižat *r.* Bos.-Herz. **56** J5
Trebizond Turkey *see* **Trabzon**
Trebnje Slovenia **56** H3
Třeboň Czech Rep. **49** L6
Tree *r.* Canada **167** I1
Tree Island India **94** B4
Treene *r.* Germany **48** G1
Trefaldwyn U.K. *see* **Montgomery**
Trefynwy U.K. *see* **Monmouth**
Tregosse Islets and Reefs Australia **149** F3
Treignac France **50** H7
Treinta y Tres Uruguay **204** G4
Trelew Arg. **205** D6
Trelleborg Sweden **45** K5
Trélon France **51** K2
Trem *mt.* Yugo. **58** D5
Tremblant, Mont *hill* Canada **169** F4
Trembleur Lake Canada **166** E4
Tremiti, Isole *is* Italy **56** H6
Tremlya *r.* Belarus **43** K9
Tremont U.S.A. **177** I5
Tremonton U.S.A. **180** D4
Tremp Spain **55** L2
Trempealeau *r.* U.S.A. **172** B6
Trenche *r.* Canada **169** F4
Trenčín Slovakia **49** P7
Trenggalek Indon. **77** E5
Trengganu *state* Malaysia *see* **Terengganu**
Trenque Lauquén Arg. **204** E4
Trent Italy *see* **Trento**
Trent *r.* U.K. **47** L10
Trentino - Alto Adige *admin. reg.* Italy **56** D2
Trento Italy **56** D2
English form Trent; historically known as Tridentum
Trenton Canada **168** E4
Trenton *FL* U.S.A. **175** D6
Trenton *GA* U.S.A. **174** C5
Trenton *MO* U.S.A. **174** A3
Trenton *NC* U.S.A. **174** E5
Trenton *NE* U.S.A. **178** B3

▶**Trenton** *NJ* U.S.A. **177** K5
State capital of New Jersey.

Trenton *TN* U.S.A. **174** B5
Trepang Bay Australia **148** A1
Trepassey Canada **169** K4
Tres Arboles Uruguay **204** F4
Tres Arroyos Arg. **204** E5
Tres Cerros Arg. **205** D8
Três Corações Brazil **203** C7
Tres Cruces Arg. **200** D5
Tres Cruces Chile **204** C3
Tres Esquinas Col. **198** C4
Tres Forcas, Cabo *c.* Morocco *see* **Trois Fourches, Cap des**
Três Irmãos, Represa *resr* Brazil **206** C7
Tres Isletas Arg. **204** E2
Treska *r.* Macedonia **58** C6
Treski Estonia **42** I4
Três Lagoas Brazil **206** B7
Tres Lagos Arg. **205** C8
Tres Lomas Arg. **204** E5
Três Marias Brazil **207** H5
Três Marias, Represa *resr* Brazil **203** C6
Tres Matas Venez. **199** E2
Tres Montes, Península *pen.* Chile **205** B7
Tres Picachos, Sierra *mts* Mex. **181** F7
Tres Picos Arg. **205** C6
Tres Picos Mex. **185** G6
Tres Picos, Cerro *mt.* Arg. **204** E5
Tres Picos, Cerro *mt.* Mex. **185** G5
Tres Piedras U.S.A. **181** F5
Tres Pinos U.S.A. **182** C5
Três Pontas Brazil **203** C7
Tres Puentes Chile **204** C2
Tres Puntas, Cabo *c.* Arg. **205** D7
Três Ranchos Brazil **206** F5
Três Rios Brazil **203** D7
Třešť Czech Rep. **49** M6
Trestino Rus. Fed. **43** O4
Trestna Rus. Fed. **43** Q4
Três Unidos Brazil **198** D6
Tres Zapotes *tourist site* Mex. **185** G5
Tretten Norway **45** J3
Treuchtlingen Germany **48** H7
Treuenbrietzen Germany **49** J3
Treungen Norway **45** J4
Trevelín Arg. **205** C6
Treves Germany *see* **Trier**
Trevi Italy **56** E6
Treviglio Italy **56** B3
Treviso Italy **56** E3
historically known as Tarvisium
Trevose Head U.K. **47** G13
Trgovište *Srbija* Yugo. **58** D6
Triabunna Australia **147** E5
Tri An, Hồ *resr* Vietnam **79** D6
Triánda Greece *see* **Trianta**
Triangle U.S.A. **177** H7
Tria Nisia *i.* Greece **59** H12
Trianta Greece **59** J12
also spelt Triánda
Tribal Areas *admin. div.* Pak. **101** G3
Tribeč *mts* Slovakia **49** P7
Tri Brata, Gora *hill* Rus. Fed. **82** F1
Tribune U.S.A. **178** B4
Tricarico Italy **57** I8
Tricase Italy **57** K9
Trichinopoly India *see* **Tiruchchirappalli**
Trichonida, Limni *l.* Greece **59** C10
Trichur India **94** C4
also known as Thrissur
Trida Australia **147** E3
Tridentum Italy *see* **Trento**
Trier Germany **48** D6
historically known as Augusta Treverorum or Treves
Trieste Italy **56** F3
historically known as Tergeste
Trieste, Golfo di *g.* Europe *see* **Trieste, Gulf of**
Trieste, Gulf of Europe **56** F3
also known as Trieste, Golfo di
Trie-sur-Baïse France **50** G9
Trieux *r.* France **50** C4
Triggiano Italy **56** I7
Triglavski Narodni Park *nat. park* Slovenia **56** F2
Trigno *r.* Italy **56** G6
Trikala Greece **59** C9
also spelt Tríkkala
Tríkkala Greece *see* **Trikala**
Trikomo Cyprus *see* **Trikomon**
Trikomon Cyprus **108** E2
also known as Trikomo or İskele

▶**Trikora, Puncak** *mt.* Indon. **73** I7
2nd highest mountain in Oceania.
oceania [landscapes] ▶▶ 136–137

Trikorfa *mt.* Greece **59** D10
Trilj Croatia **56** I5
Trim Rep. of Ireland **47** F10
Trincheras Mex. **184** C2
Trincomalee Sri Lanka **94** D4
Trindade Brazil **206** D3
Trindade, Ilha da *i.* S. Atlantic Ocean **217** L7
Tringia *mt.* Greece **59** C9
Trinidad Bol. **200** D3
Trinidad Cuba **186** D2
Trinidad *i.* Trin. and Tob. **187** H5
Trinidad Uruguay **204** F4
Trinidad U.S.A. **181** F5
Trinidad, Golfo *b.* Chile **205** B8
▶**Trinidad and Tobago** *country* West Indies **187** H5
northamerica [countries] ▶▶ 158–159
Trinitapoli Italy **56** I7
Trinity U.S.A. **179** D6
Trinity *r. CA* U.S.A. **182** A1
Trinity *r. TX* U.S.A. **179** D6
Trinity, West Fork *r.* U.S.A. **179** C5

Trinity Bay Australia 149 E3
Trinity Bay Canada 169 K4
Trinity Dam U.S.A. 182 B1
Trinity Islands U.S.A. 164 D4
Trinity Range *mts* U.S.A. 182 E1
Trinkat Island India 95 G4
Trinkitat Sudan 104 B4
Trino Italy 56 A3
Trinway U.S.A. 176 C5
Trionto, Capo *c.* Italy 57 I9
Tripa *r.* Indon. 76 B2
Tripoli Greece 59 D11
also known as Trípolis
Tripoli Lebanon 108 G3
also known as Trâblous; *historically known as* Tripolis

▶**Tripoli** Libya 120 B1
Capital of Libya. Also known as Ţarābulus; historically known as Oea.

Trípolis Greece *see* **Tripoli**
Tripolis Lebanon *see* **Tripoli**
Tripolitania *reg.* Libya 120 B2
Tripunittura India 94 C4
Tripura *state* India 97 F5
Trischen *i.* Germany 48 F1

▶**Tristan da Cunha** *i.* S. Atlantic Ocean 217 N8
Dependency of St Helena.

Tristao, Îles *is* Guinea 124 B4
Trisul *mt.* India 96 C3
Triton Canada 169 K3
Triton Island *atoll* Paracel Is 72 D3
Triunfo *Pernambuco* Brazil 202 E3
Triunfo *Rondônia* Brazil 200 D2
Triunfo Hond. 186 B4
Trivandrum India 94 C4
also spelt Thiruvananthapuram
Trivento Italy 56 G7
Trizina Greece 59 E11
Trnava Slovakia 49 O7
Trobriand Islands P.N.G. 145 E2
also known as Kiriwina Islands
Trofa Port. 54 C3
Trofaiach Austria 49 M8
Trofors Norway 44 K2
Trogir Croatia 56 I5
Troglav *mt.* Croatia 56 I5
Troina *Sicilia* Italy 57 G11
Troisdorf Germany 48 E5
Trois Fourches, Cap des *c.* Morocco 123 E2
also known as Tres Forcas, Cabo *or* Uarc, Ras
Trois-Pistoles Canada 169 G3
Trois-Rivières Canada 169 F4
Troitsa Rus. Fed. 38 G3
Troitsk *Chelyabinskaya Oblast'* Rus. Fed. 38 G4
Troitsk *Moskovskaya Oblast'* Rus. Fed. 43 S6
formerly known as Troitskiy
Troitskiy Rus. Fed. *see* **Troitsk**
Troitsko-Pechorsk Rus. Fed. 40 K3
Troitskoye *Khabarovskiy Kray* Rus. Fed. 82 E2
Troitskoye *Orenburgskaya Oblast'* Rus. Fed. 102 C1
Troitskoye *Respublika Bashkortostan* Rus. Fed. 102 D1
Troitskoye *Respublika Kalmykiya - Khalm'g-Tangch* Rus. Fed. 41 H7
Trolla *well* Chad 120 B6
Trollhättan Sweden 45 K4
Trollheimen *park* Norway 44 J3
Trombetas *r.* Brazil 199 G5
Tromelin, Île *i.* Indian Ocean 218 K7
English form Tromelin Island
Tromelin Island Indian Ocean *see* **Tromelin, Île**
Tromelin Island Micronesia *see* **Fais**
Tromen, Volcán *vol.* Arg. 204 C5
Trompsburg S. Africa 133 J7
Troms *county* Norway 44 L1
Tromsø Norway 44 L1
Trona U.S.A. 183 G6
Tronador, Monte *mt.* Arg. 204 C6
Tronçais, Forêt de *for.* France 51 I6
Trondheim Norway 44 J3
Trondheimsfjorden *sea chan.* Norway 44 J3
Trondheimsleia *sea chan.* Norway 44 J3
Trongsa Bhutan 97 F4
also spelt Tongsa
Trongsa Chhu *r.* Bhutan 97 F4
also known as Mangde Chhu
Tronto *r.* Italy 56 F6
Troödos, Mount Cyprus 108 D3
Troödos Mountains Cyprus 108 D3
Troon U.K. 46 H8
Tropaia Greece 59 C11
Troparevo Rus. Fed. 43 Q6
Tropas *r.* Brazil 199 G6
Tropea Italy 57 H10
Tropeiros, Serra dos *hills* Brazil 202 C5
Tropic U.S.A. 183 L4
Trosh Rus. Fed. 40 J2
Trosna Rus. Fed. 43 Q9
Trostan' Rus. Fed. 43 N9
Trostan *hill* U.K. 47 F8
Trostberg Germany 49 J7
Trotuş *r.* Romania 58 H2
Trout *r. B.C.* Canada 166 E3
Trout *r. N.W.T.* Canada 166 G2
Trout Creek Canada 173 N5
Trout Creek U.S.A. 172 D4
Trout Dale U.S.A. 176 D9
Trout Lake *Alta* Canada 167 H3
Trout Lake *N.W.T.* Canada 166 F2
Trout Lake *l. N.W.T.* Canada 166 F2
Trout Lake *l. Ont.* Canada 167 M5
Trout Lake *l.* U.S.A. 172 D4
Trout Run U.S.A. 177 H4
Troutville U.S.A. 176 F8
Trowbridge U.K. 47 J12
Trowutta Australia 147 E5
Troy *tourist site* Turkey 106 A3
also known as Truva; *historically known as* Ilium
Troy *AL* U.S.A. 175 C6
Troy *KS* U.S.A. 178 D4
Troy *MI* U.S.A. 173 J8
Troy *MO* U.S.A. 174 B4
Troy *NC* U.S.A. 174 E5
Troy *NH* U.S.A. 177 M3
Troy *NY* U.S.A. 177 L3
Troy *OH* U.S.A. 176 A5
Troy *PA* U.S.A. 177 I4
Troyan Bulg. 58 F6
Troyekurovo *Lipetskaya Oblast'* Rus. Fed. 43 T9
Troyekurovo *Lipetskaya Oblast'* Rus. Fed. 43 U8
Troyes France 51 K4
Troy Lake U.S.A. 183 H7
Troy Peak U.S.A. 183 I3
Trstenik *Srbija* Yugo. 58 C5
Trubchevsk Rus. Fed. 43 O9
Trubetchino Rus. Fed. 43 U9
Trubia *r.* Spain 54 F1
Truc Giang Vietnam *see* **Bên Tre**
Trucial Coast *country* Asia *see* **United Arab Emirates**
Trucial States *country* Asia *see* **United Arab Emirates**
Truckee U.S.A. 182 D2
Trud Rus. Fed. 43 O4
Trudovoy Kazakh. *see* **Kuybyshevskiy**
Trudovoy Rus. Fed. *see* **Yusta**
Trudovoye Rus. Fed. 82 D4
Trudy *r.* Rus. Fed. 43 S9
Truer Range *hills* Australia 148 A4
Trufanovo Rus. Fed. 40 H2
Trujillo Hond. 186 B4
Trujillo Peru 200 A2
Trujillo Spain 54 F5
Trujillo Venez. 198 D2
Trujillo *state* Venez. 198 D2
Trujillo, Monte *mt.* Dom. Rep. *see* **Duarte, Pico**
Trumann U.S.A. 174 B5
Trumansburg U.S.A. 177 I3
Trumbull U.S.A. 177 L4
Trumbull, Mount U.S.A. 183 K5
Trumon Indon. 76 B2
Trŭn Bulg. 58 D6
Trun France 50 G4
Trŭna *mt.* Bulg. 58 E6
Trung Khanh Vietnam 78 D3
Truong Sa *is* S. China Sea *see* **Spratly Islands**
Truro Canada 169 I4
Truro U.K. 47 G13
Trusan *Sarawak* Malaysia 77 F1
Trusan *r. Sarawak* Malaysia 77 F1
Truskmore *hill* Rep. of Ireland 47 D9
Trus Madi, Gunung *mt. Sabah* Malaysia 77 G1
Trŭstenik Bulg. 58 F5
Trutch Canada 166 F3
Trutch Creek *r.* Canada 166 F3
Truth or Consequences U.S.A. 181 F6
formerly known as Hot Springs
Trutnov Czech Rep. 49 M5
Truva *tourist site* Turkey *see* **Troy**
Truyère *r.* France 51 I8
Truzhenik Rus. Fed. 43 Q3
Tryavna Bulg. 58 G6
Tryon U.S.A. 178 B3
Trypiti, Akra *pt Kriti* Greece 59 F13
Trypiti, Akra *pt* Greece 59 F9
Trysil Norway 45 K3
Trysilelva *r.* Norway 45 K3
Trysilfjellet *mt.* Norway 45 K3
Tryškiai Lith. 42 D5
Tržac Bos.-Herz. 56 H4
Trzcianka Poland 49 N2
Trzebiatów Poland 49 M1
Trzebinia Poland 49 Q5
Trzebnica Poland 49 O4
Trzemeszno Poland 49 O3
Tržič Slovenia 56 G2
Trzrcińsko-Zdrój Poland 49 L3
Tsagaannuur *Bayan-Ölgiy* Mongolia 84 A1
Tsagaannuur *Dornod* Mongolia 85 H2
Tsagaan Nuur *salt l.* Mongolia 84 B2
Tsagaan-Olom Mongolia 84 C2
Tsagaan Ovoo Mongolia 85 G1
Tsagaan-Ovoo Mongolia 84 D2
Tsagaan-Uul Mongolia *see* **Sharga**
Tsagan Aman Rus. Fed. 102 A3
formerly known as Burunniy
Tsagan Khurtey, Khrebet *mts* Rus. Fed. 85 F1
Tsagan-Nur Rus. Fed. 41 H7
Tsaidam Basin China *see* **Qaidam Pendi**
Tsåktso *mt.* Sweden 44 M1
Tsalenjikha Georgia 107 E2
Tsama I Congo 126 B5
Tsangatjåkkå *mt.* Sweden 44 K2
Tsao Botswana 130 D4
Tsaratanana, Massif du *mts* Madag. 131 [inset] K2
Tsarevo Bulg. 58 I6
formerly known as Michurin
Tsarevo-Zaymishche Rus. Fed. 43 P6
Tsaribrod *Srbija* Yugo. *see* **Dimitrovgrad**
Tsarimir Bulg. 58 F6
Tsaritsyn Rus. Fed. *see* **Volgograd**
Tsatsana *mt.* S. Africa 133 M7
Tsat Tsze Mui *pt Hong Kong* China *see* **North Point**
Tsaukaib Namibia 130 B5
Tsavo East National Park Kenya 128 C5
Tsavo West National Park Kenya 129 C5
Tsazo S. Africa 133 L8
Tsebanana Botswana 131 E3
Tseel Mongolia 84 B2
Tsefat Israel *see* **Ẕefat**
Tselina Rus. Fed. 41 G7
Tselinnyy Rus. Fed. 103 E2
Tselinograd Kazakh. *see* **Astana**
Tselinogradskaya Oblast' *admin. div.* Kazakh. *see* **Akmolinskaya Oblast'**
Tsementnyy Rus. Fed. *see* **Fokino**
Tsengel Mongolia 84 D1
Tsenogora Rus. Fed. 40 H2
Tsentralen Balkan *nat. park* Bulg. 58 F6
Tsentral'nyy *Kirovskaya Oblast'* Rus. Fed. 40 I4
Tsentral'nyy Rus. Fed. *see* **Radovitskiy**
Tsentral'nyy *Ryazanskaya Oblast'* Rus. Fed. 43 U8
Tserkovishche Rus. Fed. 43 L6
Tserovo Bulg. 58 E5
Tses Namibia 130 C5
Tsetsegnuur Mongolia 84 B2
Tsetseng Botswana 130 D4
Tsetserleg Mongolia 84 D2
Tsetserleg Mongolia *see* **Halban**
Tsévié Togo 125 F5
Tshabong Botswana 130 D5
Tshad *country* Africa *see* **Chad**
Tshchikskoye Vodokhranilishche *resr* Rus. Fed. 41 F7
Tshela Dem. Rep. Congo 126 B6
Tshene Dem. Rep. Congo 126 C6
Tshibala Dem. Rep. Congo 127 D6
Tshibuka Dem. Rep. Congo 127 D6
Tshibwika Dem. Rep. Congo 127 D7
Tshidilamolomo Botswana 133 I2
Tshikapa Dem. Rep. Congo 127 D6
Tshikapa *r.* Dem. Rep. Congo 127 D6
Tshilenge Dem. Rep. Congo 127 D6
Tshimbulu Dem. Rep. Congo 127 D6
Tshing S. Africa 133 K3
Tshipise S. Africa 131 F4
Tshiumbe *r.* Angola/Dem. Rep. Congo 127 D6
Tshofa Dem. Rep. Congo 127 E6
Tshokwane S. Africa 133 P1
Tsholotsho Zimbabwe 131 E3
formerly spelt Tjolotjo
Tshootsha Botswana 130 D4
Tshuapa *r.* Dem. Rep. Congo 126 D5
Tshumbiri Dem. Rep. Congo 126 C5
Tsiazonano *mt.* Madag. 131 [inset] J3
Tsibritsa *r.* Bulg. 58 E5
Tsiigehtchic Canada 164 F3
formerly known as Arctic Red River
Tsil'ma *r.* Rus. Fed. 40 I2
Tsimkavichy Belarus 42 H8
also spelt Timkovichi
Tsimlyansk Rus. Fed. 41 G7
Tsimlyanskoye Vodokhranilishche *resr* Rus. Fed. 41 G7
Tsinan China *see* **Jinan**
Tsineng S. Africa 132 H4
Tsinghai *prov.* China *see* **Qinghai**
Tsing Shan *hill Hong Kong* China *see* **Castle Peak**
Tsing Shan Wan *b. Hong Kong* China *see* **Castle Peak Bay**
Tsing Shui Wan *b. Hong Kong* China *see* **Clear Water Bay**
Tsingtao China *see* **Qingdao**
Tsingy de Bemaraha, Réserve *nature res.* Madag. 131 [inset] J3
Tsing Yi *i. Hong Kong* China 87 [inset]
Tsining China *see* **Jining**
Tsinjomay *mt.* Madag. 131 [inset] J3
Tsintsabis Namibia 130 C3
Tsiombe Madag. 131 [inset] J5
Tsiroanomandidy Madag. 131 [inset] J3
Tsiteli Tskaro Georgia *see* **Dedop'listsqaro**
Tsitondroina Madag. 131 [inset] J4
Tsitsihar China *see* **Qiqihar**
Tsitsikamma Forest and Coastal National Park S. Africa 132 H11
Tsitsutl Peak Canada 166 E4
Tsivil'sk Rus. Fed. 40 H5
Tskhakaia Georgia *see* **Senaki**
Tskhaltubo Georgia *see* **Tsqaltubo**
Ts'khinvali Georgia 107 E2
formerly known as Staliniri
Tsna *r.* Belarus 42 I9
Tsna *r.* Rus. Fed. 41 G5
Tsna *r.* Rus. Fed. 43 P4
Tsna *r.* Rus. Fed. 43 U6
Tsnori Georgia 107 F2
Tsodilo Hills Botswana 130 D3
Tsolo S. Africa 133 M8
Tsomo S. Africa 133 L9
Tsomo *r.* S. Africa 133 L9
Tso Morari Lake Jammu and Kashmir 96 C2
Tson *r.* Rus. Fed. 43 R9
Tsona China *see* **Cona**
Tsopan *hill* Greece 58 G8
Tsqaltubo Georgia 107 E2
also spelt Tskhaltubo
Tsu Japan 91 E7
Tsubame Japan 90 F6
Tsubata Japan 91 E6
Tsubetsu Japan 90 I3
Tsuchiura Japan 91 G6
Tsuen Wan *Hong Kong* China 87 [inset]
also known as Quanwan
Tsugarū-kaikyō *strait* Japan 90 G4
English form Tsugaru Strait
Tsugaru Strait Japan *see* **Tsugarū-kaikyō**
Tsukigata Japan 90 G3
Tsukuba Japan 91 G6
Tsukumi Japan 91 B8
Tsul-Ulaan Mongolia 84 E2
Tsumeb Namibia 130 C3
Tsumis Park Namibia 130 C4
Tsumkwe Namibia 130 D3
Tsuno-shima *i.* Japan 91 B7
Tsuru Japan 91 F7
Tsuruga Japan 91 E7
Tsurugi-san *mt.* Japan 91 D8
Tsurukhaytuy Rus. Fed. *see* **Priargunsk**
Tsuruoka Japan 90 F5
Tsushima Japan 91 E7
Tsushima *is* Japan 91 A7
Tsushima-kaikyō *strait* Japan/S. Korea *see* **Korea Strait**
Tsuyama Japan 91 D7
Tsvetino Bulg. 58 E7
Tswaane Botswana 130 D4
Tswaraganang S. Africa 133 J5
Tswelelang S. Africa 133 J4
Tsyelyakhany Belarus 42 G9
also spelt Telekhany
Tsyerakhowka Belarus 43 M9
Ts'yl-os Provincial Park Canada 166 E5
Tsyomny Lyes Belarus 43 M7
Tsyp-Navolok Rus. Fed. 44 P1
Tsyurupyns'k Ukr. 41 E7
formerly known as Aleshki *or* Oleshky
Tthenaagoo Canada *see* **Nahanni Butte**
Tua *r.* Port. 54 C3
Tua, Tanjung *pt* Indon. 77 D4
Tuakau N.Z. 152 I5
Tual Indon. 73 H8
Tuam Rep. of Ireland 47 D10
Tuamarina N.Z. 152 H9
Tuamotu, Archipel des *is* Fr. Polynesia *see* **Tuamotu Islands**
Tuamotu Archipelago *is* Fr. Polynesia *see* **Tuamotu Islands**
Tuamotu Islands Fr. Polynesia 221 I6
English form Tuamotu Archipelago; *also known as* Tuamotu, Archipel des; *formerly known as* Paumotu, Îles
Tuân Giao Vietnam 78 C3
Tuangku *i.* Indon. 76 B2
Tuapeka Mouth N.Z. 153 D14
Tuapse Rus. Fed. 41 F7
Tuaran *Sabah* Malaysia 77 G1
Tuas Sing. 76 [inset]
Tuatapere N.Z. 153 B14
Tuath, Loch a' *b.* U.K. *see* **Broad Bay**
Tuba City U.S.A. 183 M5
Tubalai *i.* Indon. 75 D3
Tuban Indon. 77 F4
Tubarão Brazil 203 B9
Ţūbās West Bank 108 G5
Tubau *Sarawak* Malaysia 77 F2
Tubbataha Reefs Phil. 74 A4
Tubeya Dem. Rep. Congo 127 D6
Tubigan *i.* Phil. 74 B5
Tübingen Germany 48 G7
Tubinskiy Rus. Fed. 102 D1
Tubmanburg Liberia 124 C5
Tubo *r.* Nigeria 125 G4
Tubod Phil. 74 B4
Tubou Fiji 145 H3
also spelt Tumbou
Tubruq Libya 120 D1
English form Tobruk
Tubu *r.* Indon. 77 G2
Tubuai *i.* Fr. Polynesia 221 I7
Tubuai Islands Fr. Polynesia 221 H7
also known as Australes, Îles
Tubutama Mex. 184 C2
Tucandera Brazil 199 F5
Tucannon *r.* U.S.A. 180 C3
Tucano Brazil 202 E4
Tucavaca Bol. 201 F4
Tucavaca *r.* Bol. 201 F4
Tuchitua Canada 166 D2
Tuchkovo Rus. Fed. 43 R6
Tuchodi *r.* Canada 166 F3
Tuchola Poland 49 O2
Tuchów Poland 49 S6
Tuckanarra Australia 151 B5
Tucker Glacier Antarctica 223 L2
Tuckerton U.S.A. 177 K6
Tucson U.S.A. 183 N9
Tucson Mountains U.S.A. 183 M9
Tuctuc *r.* Canada 169 H1
Tucumán Arg. *see* **San Miguel de Tucumán**
Tucumán *prov.* Arg. 204 D2
Tucumcari U.S.A. 179 B5
Tucunuco Arg. 204 C3
Tucuparé Brazil 199 H6
Tucupita Venez. 199 F2
Tucuracas Col. 198 C2
Tucuruí Brazil 202 B2
Tucuruí, Represa *resr* Brazil 202 B3
Tuczno Poland 49 N2
Tudela Spain 55 J2
also spelt Tutera
Tudela de Duero Spain 54 G3
Tuder Italy *see* **Todi**
Tudor Vladimirescu Romania 58 I3
Tudovka *r.* Rus. Fed. 43 O5
Tudu Estonia 42 H2
Tudulinna Estonia 42 I2
Tuen Mun *Hong Kong* China 87 [inset]
Tuensang India 97 G4
Tueré *r.* Brazil 199 I5
Tuerto *r.* Spain 50 A10
Tufanovo Rus. Fed. 43 V3
Ţufayḩ Saudi Arabia 105 E2
Tufi P.N.G. 145 D2
Tugela *r.* S. Africa 133 P6
Tugela Ferry S. Africa 133 O5
Tūghyl Kazakh. *see* **Tugyl**
Tuglung China 89 F6
Tugnug Point Phil. 74 C4
Tuguancun China 86 B3
Tuguegarao Phil. 74 B2
Tugur Rus. Fed. 82 E1
Tugurskiy Zaliv *b.* Rus. Fed. 82 E1
Tugwi *r.* Zimbabwe 131 F4
formerly spelt Tokwe
Tugyl Kazakh. 88 D2
also spelt Tūghyl; *formerly known as* Priozernyy
Tuhai *r.* China 85 H4
Tuhemberua Indon. 76 B2
Tui Spain 54 C2
also spelt Túy
Tuichi *r.* Bol. 200 D3
Tuilianpui *r.* Bangl./India 97 G5
Tuinplaas S. Africa 133 M1
Tuins *watercourse* S. Africa 132 E6
Tūja Latvia 42 F4
Tujiabu China *see* **Yongxiu**
Tujuh, Kepulauan *is* Indon. 77 D3
Tukan Rus. Fed. 102 D1
Tukangbesi, Kepulauan *is* Indon. 75 B4
Tukangbesi Marine Reserve *nature res.* Indon. 75 B4
Tukarak Island Canada 168 E1
Tukayel Eth. 128 E2
Tûkh Egypt 108 C7
Tukhavichy Belarus 42 G9
Tŭkhtamish Tajik. 101 H2
also spelt Tokhtamysh
Tukituki *r.* N.Z. 152 K7
Tūkrah Libya 120 D1
Tuktoyaktuk Canada 164 F3
formerly known as Fort Brabant
Tuktut Nogait National Park Canada 164 G3
Tukums Latvia 42 E5
Tukung, Bukit *mt.* Indon. 77 E3
Tukuringra, Khrebet *mts* Rus. Fed. 82 B1
Tukuyu Tanz. 129 B7
Tula *watercourse* Kenya 128 C5
Tula Mex. 185 F4
Tula Rus. Fed. 43 S7
Tulach Mhór Rep. of Ireland *see* **Tullamore**
Tulagt Ar Gol *r.* China 89 F4
Tulai China 84 C4
Tulai Nanshan *mts* China 84 C4
Tulai Shan *mts* China 84 C4
Tulak Afgh. 101 E3
Tula Mountains Antarctica 223 D2
Tulancingo Mex. 185 F4
Tulangbawang *r.* Indon. 76 D4
Tula Oblast *admin. div.* Rus. Fed. *see* **Tul'skaya Oblast'**
Tulare U.S.A. 182 E5
Tulare Lake Bed U.S.A. 182 E6
Tularosa U.S.A. 181 F6
Tulasi *mt.* India 94 D2
Tulcán Ecuador 198 B4
Tulcea Romania 58 J3
Tul'chin Ukr. *see* **Tul'chyn**
Tul'chyn Ukr. 41 D6
also spelt Tul'chin
Tule *r.* U.S.A. 182 E5
Tulé Venez. 187 E5
Tuléar Madag. *see* **Toliara**
Tulehu Indon. 75 D3
Tulelake U.S.A. 180 B4
Tule Mod China 85 I2
Tulgheş Romania 58 G2
Tulia U.S.A. 179 B5
Tulihe China 85 I1
Tuliszków Poland 49 P3
Tulít'a Canada 166 E1
formerly known as Fort Norman
Tuljapur India 94 C2
Tulkarm West Bank *see* **Ţūlkarm**
Ţūlkarm West Bank 108 G5
English form Tulkarm
Tullahoma U.S.A. 174 C5
Tullamore Australia 147 E3
Tullamore Rep. of Ireland 47 E10
also spelt Tulach Mhór
Tulle France 50 H7
Tullibigeal Australia 147 E3
Tulln Austria 49 N7
Tullow Rep. of Ireland 47 F11
Tully Australia 149 E3
Tully Falls Australia 149 E3
Tulnici Romania 58 H3
Tuloma *r.* Rus. Fed. 44 P1
Tulos Rus. Fed. 44 O3
Tulppio Fin. 44 O2
Tulsa U.S.A. 179 D4
Tulsequah Canada 166 C3
Tulsipur Nepal 97 D3
Tul'skaya Oblast' *admin. div.* Rus. Fed. 43 S8
English form Tula Oblast
Tul'skoye Kazakh. 103 H1
Tuluá Col. 198 B3
Tuluceşti Romania 58 J3
Tuluksak U.S.A. 164 C3
Tulūl al Ashāqif *hills* Jordan 109 I5
Tulūl al Bissah *hills* Saudi Arabia 109 K6
Tulum *tourist site* Mex. 185 I4
Tulun Rus. Fed. 80 G2
Tulungagung Indon. 77 E5
Tulu-Tuloi, Serra *hills* Brazil 199 F4
Tulu Welel *mt.* Eth. 128 B2
Tulva *r.* Rus. Fed. 40 J4
Tuma Rus. Fed. 40 G5
Tumaco Col. 198 B4
Tumahole S. Africa 133 L3
Tumain China 89 E5
Tumak Rus. Fed. 102 B3
Tūmān Āqā Iran 101 E3
Tuman-gang *r.* Asia *see* **Tumen Jiang**
Tumannaya *r.* Asia *see* **Tumen Jiang**
Tumannyy Rus. Fed. 40 E1
Tumanovo Rus. Fed. 43 F6
Tumanskiy Rus. Fed. 39 R3
Tumasik Sing. *see* **Singapore**
Tumatumari Guyana 199 G3
Tumazy Rus. Fed. 43 P1
Tumba Sweden 45 L4
Tumbangmiri Indon. 77 F3
Tumbangsamba Indon. 77 F3
Tumbangtiti Indon. 77 E3
Tumbao Phil. 74 C5
Tumbarumba Australia 147 F3
Tumbes Peru 198 A5
Tumbes *dept* Peru 198 A5
Tumbiscatio Mex. 185 E5
Tumbler Ridge Canada 166 F4
Tumbou Fiji *see* **Tubou**
Tumby Bay Australia 146 C3
Tumcha *r.* Fin./Rus. Fed. 44 O2
Tumd Youqi China *see* **Salaqi**
Tumd Zuoqi China *see* **Qasq**
Tumen *Jilin* China 82 C4
Tumen *Shaanxi* China 87 D1
Tumen Jiang *r.* Asia 82 C4
also known as Tuman-gang *or* Tumannaya
Tumeremo Venez. 199 F3
Tumereng Guyana 199 F3
Tumindao *i.* Phil. 74 A5
Tumiritinga Brazil 203 D6
Tumkur India 94 C3
Tumlingtar Nepal 97 E4
Tummo, Mountains of Libya/Niger 120 B4
Tumnin *r.* Rus. Fed. 82 F2
Tump Pak. 101 E5
Tumpah Indon. 77 F3
Tumpôr, Phnum *mt.* Cambodia 79 C5
Tumpu, Gunung *mt.* Indon. 75 B3
Tumputiga, Gunung *mt.* Indon. 75 B3
Tumsar India 96 C5
Tumshuk Uzbek. 103 F5
Tumu Ghana 125 E4
Tumucumaque, Serra *hills* Brazil 199 G4
Tumudibandh India 95 D2
Tumupasa Bol. 200 D3
Tumur Kazakh. 103 G4
also spelt Temir; *formerly spelt* Timur
Tumusla Bol. 200 D5
Tumut Australia 147 F3
Tumutuk Rus. Fed. 40 J5
Tumxuk China 88 C3
Tuna Ghana 124 E4
Tunapuna Trin. and Tob. 187 H5
Tunas de Zaza Cuba 186 D2
Ţunb al Kubrá *i.* The Gulf *see* **Greater Tunb**
Ţunb aş Şughrá *i.* The Gulf *see* **Lesser Tunb**
Tunbridge Wells, Royal U.K. 47 M12
Tunçbilek Turkey 59 K9
Tunceli Turkey 107 D3
Tuncurry Australia 147 G3
Tundla India 89 B7
Tundubai *well* Sudan 121 F5
Tunduma Tanz. 129 B7
Tundun-Wada Nigeria 125 H4
Tunduru Tanz. 129 C7
Tundzha *r.* Bulg. 58 H7
Tunes Tunisia *see* **Tunis**
Tunga Nigeria 125 H4
Tungabhadra *r.* India 94 C3
Tungabhadra Reservoir India 94 C3
Tungawan Phil. 74 B5
Tungdor China *see* **Mainling**
Tungi Bangl. 97 F5
also spelt Tongi
Tungku *Sabah* Malaysia 77 G1
Tungla Nicaragua 186 B4
Tung Lung Chau *i. Hong Kong* China *see* **Tung Lung Island**
Tung Lung Island *Hong Kong* China 87 [inset]
also known as Tung Lung Chau
Tungnaá *r.* Iceland 44 [inset] C2
Tungor Rus. Fed. 82 F1
Tungozero Rus. Fed. 44 O2
Tung Pok Liu Hoi Hap *sea chan. Hong Kong* China *see* **East Lamma Channel**
Tungsten Canada 166 D2
Tungun, Bukit *mt.* Indon. 77 F2
Tungurahua *prov.* Ecuador 198 B5
Tung Wan *b. Hong Kong* China 87 [inset]
Tuni India 95 D2
Tunica U.S.A. 174 B5
Tunis Canada 173 M2

▶**Tunis** Tunisia 123 H1
Capital of Tunisia. Historically known as Tunes.

Tunis, Golfe de *g.* Tunisia 123 H1
▶**Tunisia** *country* Africa 123 H2
spelt At Tūnisīyah in Arabic; *historically known as* Africa Nova
africa [countries] ▶ 114–117
Tunja Col. 198 C3
Tunkhannock U.S.A. 177 J4
Tunki Nicaragua 186 B4
Tunkinskiye Gol'tsy *mts* Rus. Fed. 84 D1
Tunliu China 85 G4
Tunnel City U.S.A. 172 C6
Tunnelton U.S.A. 176 F6
Tunnsjøen *l.* Norway 44 K2
Tunoshna Rus. Fed. 43 V4
Tuntsa Fin. 44 O2
Tunulic *r.* Canada 169 H1
Tununak U.S.A. 164 C3
Tunungayualok Island Canada 169 I1
Tunuyán Arg. 204 C4
Tunuyán *r.* Arg. 204 D4
Tunxi China *see* **Huangshan**
Tuodian China *see* **Shuangbai**
Tuo He *r.* China 87 F1
Tuojiang China *see* **Fenghuang**
Tuojiang China *see* **Shuikou**
Tuo Jiang *r.* China 86 C2
Tuolumne U.S.A. 182 D4
Tuolumne *r.* U.S.A. 182 C4
Tuolumne Meadows U.S.A. 182 E4
Tuoniang Jiang *r.* China 86 C3
Tuotuo He *r.* China 97 G2
Tuotuoheyan China 84 B5
also known as Tanggulashan
Tüp Kyrg. 103 I4
also spelt Tyup
Tupã Brazil 206 C8
Tupaciguara Brazil 206 E5
Tupanaóca Brazil 199 F5
Tupanciretã Brazil 203 A9
Tupelo U.S.A. 174 B5
Tupinambarama, Ilha *i.* Brazil 199 G5
Tupi Paulista Brazil 206 B8
Tupiza Bol. 200 D5
Tupper Canada 166 F4
Tupper Lake U.S.A. 177 K1
Tupper Lake *l.* U.S.A. 177 K1
Tüpqaraghan Tübegi *pen.* Kazakh. *see* **Mangyshlak, Poluostrov**
Tupungato Arg. 204 C4

▶**Tupungato, Cerro** *mt.* Arg./Chile 204 C4
5th highest mountain in South America.
southamerica [landscapes] ▶ 190–191

Tuqayyid *well* Iraq 107 F5
Tuquan China 85 I2
Túquerres Col. 198 B4
Tuqu Wan *b.* China 87 D5
Tura China 89 D4
Tura India 97 F4
Tura Rus. Fed. 39 K3
Turabah *Hā'il* Saudi Arabia 104 C1
Turabah *Makkah* Saudi Arabia 104 C3
Turabah, Wādī *watercourse* Saudi Arabia 104 C3
Turagua, Serranía *mt.* Venez. 199 E3
Turakina N.Z. 152 J8
Turakina *r.* N.Z. 152 J8
Turana, Khrebet *mts* Rus. Fed. 82 C2
Turangi N.Z. 152 J6
Turan Lowland Asia 101 D2
also known as Turanskaya Nizmennost'
Turanskaya Nizmennost' *lowland* Asia *see* **Turan Lowland**
Ţurāq al 'Ilab *hills* Syria 109 J4
Tura-Ryskulova Kazakh. 103 G4
formerly known as Vannovka
Turaw Belarus 42 I9
Turayf Saudi Arabia 107 D5
Turayf *well* Saudi Arabia 105 E2
Ţurayf, Wādī *watercourse* Iraq 109 N4
Turba Estonia 42 F2
Turbaco Col. 198 C2
Turbacz *mt.* Poland 49 R6
Turbat Pak. 101 E5
Turbo Col. 198 B2
Turčianske Teplice Slovakia 49 P7
Turco Bol. 200 C4
Turda Romania 58 E2
Tūreh Iran 100 B3
Turek Poland 49 P3
Turfan China *see* **Turpan**
Turfan Depression China *see* **Turpan Pendi**
Turgay *Akmolinskaya Oblast'* Kazakh. 103 H2
Turgay *Kustanayskaya Oblast'* Kazakh. 103 E2
also spelt Torghay
Turgay *r.* Kazakh. 103 E3
Turgayskaya Dolina *valley* Kazakh. 103 E2
Turgayskaya Stolovaya Strana *reg.* Kazakh. 103 E2
Türgen Uul *mt.* Mongolia 84 A1
Türgen Uul *mts* Mongolia 84 A1
Turgeon *r.* Canada 168 E3
Tŭrgovishte Bulg. 58 H5
Turgut Turkey 106 B3
Turgut Turkey 59 J11
Turgutalp Turkey 59 I9
Turgutlu Turkey 106 A3
also known as Kasaba
Turgutreis Turkey 59 I12
Turhal Turkey 106 D2
Türi Estonia 42 G3
Turi Italy 56 J8
Turia *r.* Spain 55 K5
Turiaçu Brazil 202 C2
Turiaçu *r.* Brazil 202 C2
Turiaçu, Baía de *b.* Brazil 202 C2
Turiamo Venez. 199 E2
Turiec *r.* Slovakia 49 P6
Turin Canada 167 H5
Turin Italy 51 N7
also spelt Torino; *historically known as* Augusta Taurinorum *or* Taurasia
Turinsk Rus. Fed. 38 G4
Turiy Rog Rus. Fed. 82 C3
Türje Hungary 49 O9
Turka Rus. Fed. 81 H2
Turkana, Lake *salt l.* Eth./Kenya 128 B4
formerly known as Rudolf, Lake
Türkeli Turkey 58 I8
Türkeli Adası *i.* Turkey 58 I8
Turkestan Kazakh. 103 G4
also spelt Türkistan
Turkestan Range *mts* Asia 99 H2
Túrkeve Hungary 49 R8
▶**Turkey** *country* Asia 106 B3
asia [countries] ▶ 64–67
Turkey U.S.A. 176 B8
Turkey *r.* U.S.A. 174 B3
Turki Rus. Fed. 41 G6
Türkistan Kazakh. *see* **Turkestan**
Turkmenabat Turkm. *see* **Chardzhev**
Turkmen Adasy *i.* Turkm. *see* **Ogurchinskiy, Ostrov**
Türkmen Aylagy *b.* Turkm. *see* **Turkmenskiy Zaliv**
Turkmenbashi Turkm. 102 C4
formerly known as Krasnovodsk
Türkmen Dağı *mt.* Turkey 106 B3
Turkmengala Turkm. 103 E5
formerly spelt Turkmen-Kala
▶**Turkmenistan** *country* Asia 102 D5
spelt Türkmenostan in Turkmen; *formerly known as* Turkmeniya *or* Turkmenskaya S.S.R.
asia [countries] ▶ 64–67
Turkmeniya *country* Asia *see* **Turkmenistan**
Turkmen-Kala Turkm. *see* **Turkmengala**
Turkmenkarakul' Turkm. 101 E3
Türkmenostan *country* Asia *see* **Turkmenistan**
Turkmenskaya S.S.R. *country* Asia *see* **Turkmenistan**
Turkmenskiy Zaliv *b.* Turkm. 102 C5
also known as Türkmen Aylagy
Türkoğlu Turkey 107 D3
Turkova Belarus 42 J6

▶**Turks and Caicos Islands** *terr.* West Indies 187 F2
United Kingdom Overseas Territory.
oceania [countries] ▶ 138–139

Turks Island Passage Turks and Caicos Is 187 F2
Turks Islands Turks and Caicos Is 187 F2
Turku Fin. 45 M3
also known as Åbo
Turkwel *watercourse* Kenya 128 C4
Turlock U.S.A. 182 D4
Turlock Lake U.S.A. 182 D4
Turmalina Brazil 203 D6
Turmus, Wādī at *watercourse* Saudi Arabia 104 C2
Turnagain *r.* Canada 166 E3
Turnagain, Cape N.Z. 152 K8
Turnbull, Mount U.S.A. 183 N8
Turneffe Islands Belize 185 I5
Turner *r.* Australia 150 B4
Turner *watercourse* Australia 151 B5
Turner U.S.A. 173 J6
Turner River Australia 150 E3
Turner's Peninsula Sierra Leone 124 B5
Turner Valley Canada 167 H5
Turnhout Belgium 51 K1
Turnor Lake Canada 167 I3
Turnor Lake *l.* Canada 167 I3
Turnov Czech Rep. 49 M5
Tŭrnovo Bulg. *see* **Veliko Tŭrnovo**
Turnu Măgurele Romania 58 F5
Turnu Severin Romania *see* **Drobeta - Turnu Severin**
Turon *r.* Australia 147 F3
Turones France *see* **Tours**
Turopolje *plain* Croatia 56 H3
Turovets Rus. Fed. 40 G4
Turovo Rus. Fed. 43 S7
Turpan China 88 E3
also spelt Turfan

▶**Turpan Pendi** *depr.* China 88 E3
Lowest point in northern Asia. English form Turfan Depression.

Turpan Zhan China 88 E3
also known as Daheyan
Turrialba Costa Rica 186 C5
Turriff U.K. 46 J6
Turris Libisonis *Sardegna* Italy *see* **Porto Torres**
Tursāq Iraq 107 F4
Turtkul' Uzbek. 103 E4
also spelt Törtköl; *formerly known as* Petroaleksandrovsk
Turtle Flambeau Flowage *resr* U.S.A. 172 C4
Turtleford Canada 167 I4
Turtle Island Australia 149 F3
Turtle Island Fiji *see* **Vatoa**
Turtle Islands Phil. 74 A5
Turtle Lake *l.* Canada 167 I4
Turtle Lake U.S.A. 172 A5
Turugart Pass China/Kyrg. 88 A3
also known as Torugart, Pereval *or* Turugart Shankou
Turugart Shankou *pass* China/Kyrg. *see* **Turugart Pass**
Turukhansk Rus. Fed. 39 I3
Turuna *r.* Brazil 199 G4
Turunçova Turkey 108 B1
Turush Kazakh. 102 D3
Turuvanur India 94 C3
Turvelândia Brazil 206 C4
Turvo Brazil 203 B9
Turvo *r. Goiás* Brazil 206 C4
Turvo *r. São Paulo* Brazil 206 D6
Turvo *r. São Paulo* Brazil 206 D9
Ţūs Iran 101 D2
Tusayan U.S.A. 183 L6
Tuscaloosa U.S.A. 175 C5
Tuscania Italy 56 D6
Tuscany *admin. reg.* Italy *see* **Toscana**
Tuscany *reg.* Italy 56 C5
also known as Toscana
Tuscarawas *r.* U.S.A. 176 D5
Tuscarora Mountains *hills* U.S.A. 176 H5
Tuscola U.S.A. 174 B4
Tuscumbia *AL* U.S.A. 174 C5
Tuscumbia *MO* U.S.A. 178 D4
Tuskegee U.S.A. 175 C5
Tussey Mountains *hills* U.S.A. 176 G5
Tustin U.S.A. 172 H6
Tuszyn Poland 49 Q4
Tutak Turkey 107 E3
Tutaul Rus. Fed. 82 B1
Tutayev Rus. Fed. 43 U4
Tutera Spain *see* **Tudela**
Tuticorin India 94 C4
Tutoh *r. Sarawak* Malaysia 77 F2
Tutong Brunei 77 F1
Tutova *r.* Romania 58 I2
Tutrakan Bulg. 58 H4
Tuttle Creek Reservoir U.S.A. 178 C4
Tuttlingen Germany 48 F8

Tuttut Nunaat reg. Greenland 165 Q2
also known as Renland
Tutuala East Timor 75 C5
Tutubu Tanz. 129 B6
Tutuila i. American Samoa 145 H3
formerly known as Masuna
Tutukaka N.Z. 152 I3
Tutume Botswana 131 E4
Tutún Egypt 108 B8
Tutunendo Col. 198 B3
Tutupaca, Volcán vol. Peru 200 C4
Tuturumuri N.Z. 152 J9
Tututepec Mex. 185 F5
Tuul Gol r. Mongolia 85 E1
Tuun-bong mt. N. Korea 83 B4
Tuupovaara Fin. 44 O3
Tuusniemi Fin. 44 O3
Tuusula Fin. 45 N3
Tuva aut. rep. Rus. Fed. see Tyva, Respublika
▶**Tuvalu** country S. Pacific Ocean 145 G2
formerly known as Ellice Islands
oceania [countries] ➡ 138–139
Tuvana-i-Colo i. Fiji 145 H4
also spelt Tuvana-i-Tholo
Tuvana-i-Tholo i. Fiji see Tuvana-i-Colo
Tuve Sweden 45 J4
Tuve, Mount Antarctica 222 S2
Tuvinskaya A.S.S.R. aut. rep. Rus. Fed. see
Tyva, Respublika
Tuuk Indon. 77 G2
Tuwau r. Indon. 77 G2
Tuwayq, Jabal hills Saudi Arabia 105 D2
Tuwayq, Jabal mts Saudi Arabia 105 D2
Ţuwayyil al Ḩajj mt. Jordan 108 G8
Ţuwayyil ash Shiḩāq mt. Jordan 108 H7
Tuwwal Saudi Arabia 104 B3
Tuxer Gebirge mts Austria 48 I8
Tuxpan Jalisco Mex. 185 E5
Tuxpan Nayarit Mex. 184 D4
Tuxpan Veracruz Mex. 185 F4
Tuxtla Gutiérrez Mex. 185 G5
Túy Spain see Tui
Tuya Lake Canada 166 D3
Tuy Duc Vietnam 79 D5
Tuyên Quang Vietnam 78 D3
Tuy Hoa Vietnam 79 E5
Tuymazy Rus. Fed. 40 J5
Tüysarkān Iran 100 B3
Tüytepa Uzbek. see Toytepa
Tuz, Lake salt l. Turkey 106 C3
also known as Tuz Gölü
Tuz Gölü salt l. Turkey see Tuz, Lake
Tůzha Bulg. 58 G6
Tuzha Rus. Fed. 40 H4
Tuz Khurmātū Iraq 107 F4
Tuzla Bos.-Herz. 56 K4
Tuzla Romania 58 J4
Tuzla Turkey 107 E3
Tuzla r. Turkey 107 E3
Tuzu r. Myanmar 78 A2
Tuzlov r. Rus. Fed. 41 G7
Tuzu r. Myanmar 78 A2
Tuzugu well Libya 120 C4
Tvååker Sweden 45 K4
Tväärälund Sweden 44 K4
Tvedestrand Norway 45 J4
Tver' Rus. Fed. 43 Q5
formerly known as Kalinin
Tver Oblast admin. div. Rus. Fed. see
Tverskaya Oblast'
Tverskaya Oblast' admin. div. Rus. Fed.
43 Q4
English form Tver Oblast; formerly known
as Kalininskaya Oblast'
Tvertsa r. Rus. Fed. 43 Q5
Tverøyri Faroe 46 F2
Tvorozhkovo Rus. Fed. 43 J5
Tvürditsa Bulg. 58 G6
Twain Harte U.S.A. 182 D3
Twardogóra Poland 49 O4
Tweed r. U.K. 46 J8
Tweed Heads Australia 147 G2
Tweedie Canada 167 I4
Tweedsmuir Provincial Park Canada
166 E4
Twefontein S. Africa 132 D9
Tweeling S. Africa 133 M4
Twee River Namibia 130 C5
Twee Rivieren Botswana 132 E3
Tweespruit S. Africa 133 L6
Twentynine Palms U.S.A. 183 H7
Twillingate Canada 169 K3
Twin Bridges U.S.A. 182 D3
Twin Buttes Reservoir U.S.A. 179 B6
Twin Falls Canada 169 H2
Twin Falls U.S.A. 180 D4
Twingi Zambia 127 F7
Twin Heads hill Australia 150 D4
Twin Mountain U.S.A. 177 N1
Twin Peak U.S.A. 182 D2
Twin Peaks hill Australia 151 B7

Twinsburg U.S.A. 176 D4
Twins Creek watercourse Australia 146 C2
Twisp U.S.A. 180 B2
Twitchen Reservoir U.S.A. 182 D6
Twitya r. Canada 166 D1
Twizel N.Z. 153 E12
Two Butte Creek r. U.S.A. 178 B4
Two Harbors U.S.A. 174 B2
Two Hills Canada 167 I4
Two Rivers U.S.A. 172 F6
Tyan' Shan' mts China/Kyrg. see Tien Shan
Tyanshanskaya Oblast' admin. div. Kyrg.
see Naryn
Tyao r. India/Myanmar 97 G5
Tyatya, Vulkan vol. Rus. Fed. 82 G3
Tychy Poland 49 P5
historically known as Tichau
Tyczyn Poland 49 T6
Tydal Norway 44 J3
Tyddewi U.K. see St David's
Tygart Valley U.S.A. 176 F7
Tygda Rus. Fed. 82 B1
Tygda r. Rus. Fed. 82 B1
Tyinkrysset Norway 45 J3
Tykhero Greece 58 H7
also known as Tikherón
Tykocin Poland 49 T2
Tyler U.S.A. 179 D5
Tylertown U.S.A. 175 B6
Tylihul r. Ukr. 58 L1
Tyl'skiy Khrebet mts Rus. Fed. 82 D1
Tym' r. Rus. Fed. 82 F2
Tymovychi Ukr. 43 N9
Tymovskoye Rus. Fed. 82 F2
Tympaki Greece 59 F13
also known as Timbákion
Tynda Rus. Fed. 81 K1
formerly known as Tyndinskiy
Tyndall U.S.A. 178 C3
Tyndinskiy Rus. Fed. see Tynda
Tyndrum U.K. 46 H7
Tyne r. U.K. 47 J7
Tyngsboro U.S.A. 177 N3
Tyngsjö Sweden 45 K3
Tyn nad Vltavou Czech Rep. 49 L6
Tynset Norway 45 J3
Tyr Lebanon see Tyre
Tyras Ukr. see Bilhorod-Dnistrovs'kyy
Tyre Lebanon 108 G4
also known as Ţūr; also spelt Tyr;
historically known as Tyrus
Tyree, Mount Antarctica 222 S1
Tyrifjorden l. Norway 45 J3
Tyrma Rus. Fed. 82 D2
Tyrma r. Rus. Fed. 82 C2
Tyrnävä Fin. 44 N2
Tyrnavos Greece 59 D9
also spelt Tírnavos
Tyrnyauz Rus. Fed. 107 E2
Tyrone U.S.A. 176 G5
Tyrrell r. Australia 147 D3
Tyrrell, Lake dry lake Australia 147 D3
Tyrrell Lake Canada 167 J2
Tyrrhenian Sea France/Italy 57 C8
also known as Tirreno, Mare
Tyrus Lebanon see Tyre
Tysnesøy i. Norway 45 I4
Tyson Wash watercourse U.S.A. 183 J8
Tysse Norway 45 I4
Tytuvėnai Lith. 42 E6
Tyubelyakh Rus. Fed. 39 O3
Tyub-Karagan, Mys pt Kazakh. 102 B3
Tyukalinsk Rus. Fed. 38 H4
Tyulen'i, Ostrova is Kazakh. 102 B3
Tyul'gan Rus. Fed. 102 D1
Tyul'kino Rus. Fed. 40 K4
Tyumen' Rus. Fed. 38 G4
Tyumen'-Aryk Kazakh. see Tomenaryk
Tyung r. Rus. Fed. 39 M3
Tyup Kyrg. see Tüp
Tyuratam Kazakh. see Baykonur
Tyuva-Guba Rus. Fed. 44 P1
Tyuyamuyunskoye Vodokhranilische resr
Turkm./Uzbek. 103 E4
Tyva, Respublika aut. rep. Rus. Fed. 84 C1
formerly known as Tuva or Tuvinskaya
A.S.S.R.; historically known as Tannu Tuva
Tywi r. U.K. 47 H12
Tzaneen S. Africa 131 F4
Tzucacab Mex. 185 H4

↓ U

Uacauyén Venez. 199 F3
Uaco Congo Angola see Waku-Kungo
Uainambi Brazil 198 D4
Uainambi Brazil 198 D4
Ualan atoll Micronesia see Kosrae
Uamanda Angola 127 D9
Uape Moz. 131 H3
Uara Brazil 199 E5
Uarc, Ras r. Morocco see
Trois Fourches, Cap des
Ugar r. Bos.-Herz. 56 J4
Uarini Brazil 199 E5
Uaroo Australia 150 A4
Uaruma Brazil 198 D4
Uasadi-jidi, Sierra mts Venez. 199 E3
Uatatás r. Brazil 199 F4
also known as Parima
Uatumã r. Brazil 199 G5
Uauá Brazil 202 E4
Uaupés Brazil 199 E5
Uaupés r. Brazil 199 E5
Uaxactún Guat. 185 H5
U'ayfirah well Saudi Arabia 104 D3
U'aylī, Wādī r. watercourse Saudi Arabia
109 J7
U'aywij well Saudi Arabia 104 D1
U'aywij, Sha'ib al watercourse Saudi Arabia
109 H8
U'aywij, Wādī al watercourse Saudi Arabia
107 F5
Ub Srbija Yugo. 58 B4
Ubá Brazil 203 D7
Uba r. Kazakh. 103 J2
Ubagan r. Kazakh. 103 F1
also spelt Obaghan
Ubaí Brazil 202 D6
Ubaid well Sudan 121 E6
Ubaitaba Brazil 202 E5
Ubal Yemen 105 G4
also known as Ubalá
Ubaí Brazil 202 C5
Ubal Karabaur hills Uzbek. 102 C3
Ubal Muzbel' hills Uzbek. 102 C3
Ubangi r. Cent. Afr. Rep./Dem. Rep. Congo
126 C5
also spelt Oubangui
Ubangi-Shari country Africa see
Central African Republic
Ubaporanga Brazil 207 K6
Ubate Col. 198 C3
Ubatuba Brazil 207 H10
Ubauro Pak. 101 G4
'Ubaydah, Wādī al watercourse Iraq
109 N6
Ubayyid, Wādī al watercourse
Iraq/Saudi Arabia 107 E4
Ube Japan 91 B8
Úbeda Spain 55 H6
Ubenazomozi Tanz. 129 C6
Uberaba Brazil 206 E7
Uberaba r. Brazil 206 E7
Uberlândia Brazil 206 E5
Überlingen Germany 48 G8
Ubin, Pulau i. Sing. 76 [inset]
Ubinskoye, Ozero l. Rus. Fed. 80 C1
Ubly U.S.A. 173 K7

Ubombo S. Africa 133 Q4
Ubon Ratchathani Thai. 79 D5
Ubori Sudan 126 F2
Ubrique Spain 54 F8
Ubundu Dem. Rep. Congo 126 E5
also known as Ponthierville
Ucar Azer. 107 F2
also spelt Udzhary
Ucayali dept Peru 200 B2
Ucayali r. Peru 198 C6
Ucero r. Spain 55 I3
Uch Pak. 101 G4
Uch-Adzhi Turkm. 103 E5
also spelt Üchajy
Üchajy Turkm. see Uch-Adzhi
Üchän Iran 100 B2
Ucharal Kazakh. 103 J3
also spelt Usharal
Uchinoura Japan 91 B9
Uchiura Japan 90 F5
Uchiura-wan b. Japan 90 G3
English form Volcano Bay
Uchiza Peru 200 A2
Uchkuduk Uzbek. 103 E4
also spelt Uchquduq
Uchkyay Uzbek. 103 F5
Uchquduq Uzbek. see Uchkuduk
Uchsay Uzbek. 102 D4
also spelt Uchsoy
Uchsoy Uzbek. see Uchsay
Uchte r. Germany 48 I3
Uchto r. Pak. 101 F5
Uchur r. Rus. Fed. 39 N4
Uckermark reg. Germany 49 K2
Uckfield U.K. 47 M13
Ucluelet Canada 166 F5
Uda r. Rus. Fed. 82 C2
Uda r. Rus. Fed. 85 E1
Udachnoye Rus. Fed. 102 A3
Udachnyy Rus. Fed. 39 L3
Udagamandalam India 94 C4
also known as Udhagamandalam; formerly
known as Ootacamund
Udaipur Rajasthan India 96 B4
Udaipur Tripura India 97 F5
Udaipura India 96 C5
Udaipur Garhi Nepal 97 E4
Udalguri India 97 G4
Udanti r. India/Myanmar 95 D1
Uda Walawe Reservoir Sri Lanka 94 D5
Udayagiri India 94 D2
'Udaynān well Saudi Arabia 105 E3
Uddeholm Sweden 45 K3
Uddevalla Sweden 45 J4
Uddjaure l. Sweden 44 L2
'Udeid, Khōr al inlet Qatar 105 E2
Uden Neth. 48 L4
Udgir India 94 C2
Udhagamandalam India see
Udagamandalam
Udhampur Jammu and Kashmir 96 B2
Udimskiy Rus. Fed. 40 H3
Udine Italy 56 F2
Udjuktok Bay Canada 169 I2
Udmalaippettai India see Udumalaippettai
Udmurtia aut. rep. Rus. Fed. see
Udmurtskaya Respublika
Udmurtskaya A.S.S.R. aut. rep. Rus. Fed.
see Udmurtskaya Respublika
Udmurtskaya Respublika aut. rep.
Rus. Fed. 40 J4
English form Udmurtia; formerly known as
Udmurtskaya A.S.S.R.
Udokan, Khrebet mts Rus. Fed. 81 J1
Udomlya Rus. Fed. 43 Q4
Udon Thani Thai. 78 C4
Udskoye Rus. Fed. 82 D1
Udumalaippettai India 94 C4
also known as Udmalaippettai
Udupi India 94 B3
Udyl', Ozero l. Rus. Fed. 82 E1
Udzhary Azer. see Ucar
Uéa i. New Caledonia see Ouvéa
Uébonti Indon. 75 B3
Uecker r. Germany 49 L2
Ueckermünde Germany 49 L2
Ueda Japan 91 H7
Uekuli Indon. 75 B3
Uele r. Dem. Rep. Congo 126 D3
Uelen Rus. Fed. 39 T3
Uel'kal' Rus. Fed. 39 S3
Uelzen Germany 48 H3
Ueno Japan 91 E7
Uere r. Dem. Rep. Congo 126 E4
Ufa Rus. Fed. 40 J5
Ufa r. Rus. Fed. 40 K5
Uffing am Staffelsee Germany 48 I8
Uftyuga r. Rus. Fed. 40 H3
Uftyuga r. Rus. Fed. 43 U2
Ugab watercourse Namibia 130 B4
Ugâle Latvia 42 D4
Ugalla r. Tanz. 129 A6
Ugalla River Game Reserve nature res.
Tanz. 129 A6
▶**Uganda** country Africa 128 A4
africa [countries] ➡ 114–117
Ugar, Ras r. Bos.-Herz. 56 J4
Ugento Italy 57 K9
Uggdal Norway 45 I3
Ughelli Nigeria 125 G5
Ugie S. Africa 133 M8
Uginak Iran 101 E5
Ugine France 51 M7
Uglegorsk Rus. Fed. 82 F2
Uglekamensk Rus. Fed. 82 D4
formerly known as Severnyy Suchan
Ugleural'skiy Rus. Fed. 40 K4
formerly known as Polovinka
Uglich Rus. Fed. 43 T4
Ugljan i. Croatia 56 H4
Uglovka Rus. Fed. 43 O3
also spelt Ölkeyok
Uglovoye Amurskaya Oblast' Rus. Fed. 82 C2
Uglovoye Primorskiy Kray Rus. Fed. 82 D4
Ugly r. Rus. Fed. 43 U2
Ugodskiy Zavod Rus. Fed. see Zhukovo
Ugol'noye Rus. Fed. 39 O3
Ugol'nyy Rus. Fed. see Beringovskiy
Ugol'nyye Kopi Rus. Fed. 39 R3
Ugra Rus. Fed. 43 P7
Ugra r. Rus. Fed. 43 P7
Ugürchin Bulg. 58 F5
Ugut Rus. Fed. 38 H3
Uher Hudag China 85 F3
Uherské Hradiště Czech Rep. 49 O6
Uhlava r. Czech Rep. 49 K6
Uhniv Ukr. 49 U6
Uíge Angola 127 B6
formerly known as Carmona or Vila
Marechal Carmona
Uíge prov. Angola 127 B6
Uíjin N. Korea 83 B6
Uíju N. Korea 83 B4
Uil r. Kazakh. 102 C2
Uimaharju Fin. 44 O3
Uinkaret Plateau U.S.A. 183 K5
Uinskoye Rus. Fed. 40 K4
Uinta r. U.S.A. 183 O1
Uintah and Ouray Indian Reservation res.
U.S.A. 183 O1
Uinta Mountains U.S.A. 183 N1
Üiryŏng S. Korea 91 A7
Uis Mine Namibia 130 B4
Uitenhage S. Africa 133 J10
Uithuizen Neth. 48 D2
Uitkyk S. Africa 132 C6
Uitsakpan salt pan S. Africa 132 E4
Uitspankraal S. Africa 132 D9

Újfehértó Hungary 49 S8
Ujhani India 96 C4
Uji Japan 91 D7
Uji-guntō is Japan 91 A9
Ujiyamada Japan see Ise
Ujjain India 96 B5
Újkígyós Hungary 49 S9
Ujohbilang Indon. 77 F2
Újszász Poland 49 K2
Ujung Kulon National Park Indon. 76 D4
Ujung Pandang Indon. 75 A4
formerly known as Macassar or Makassar
Újvidék Vojvodina, Srbija Yugo. see Novi Sad
Ukal Sagar l. India 96 B5
Ukata Nigeria 125 G4
'Ukayrishah well Saudi Arabia 104 D2
Ukerewe Island Tanz. 128 B5
Ukhaydir tourist site Iraq 107 E4
Ukhḍūd tourist site Saudi Arabia 104 D4
Ukholovo Rus. Fed. 41 G5
Ukhra r. Rus. Fed. 43 U4
Ukhrul India 97 G4
Ukhta Rus. Fed. see Kalevala
Ukhta Rus. Fed. 40 J3
Ukhtoma r. Rus. Fed. 43 U3
Ukhvala Belarus 43 K7
Ukiah U.S.A. 182 A2
Ukimbo Tanz. 129 A6
Ukkusissat Greenland 165 N2
Ukmergé Lith. 42 F6
▶**Ukraine** country Europe 41 D6
2nd largest country in Europe. Spelt
Ukrayina in Ukrainian; formerly known as
Ukrainskaya S.S.R.
europe [countries] ➡ 32–35
Ukrainka Kazakh. 88 C1
Ukrainskaya S.S.R. country Europe see
Ukraine
Ukrayina country Europe see Ukraine
Ukrina r. Bos.-Herz. 56 J4
Uku Angola 127 B7
formerly known as Vila Nova do Seles
Uku-jima i. Japan 91 A8
Ukuma Angola 127 B8
Ukwi Botswana 130 D4
Ul r. India 89 B6
Ula Belarus 43 K6
Ula r. Belarus 43 K6
Ula Turkey 59 J11
also known as Gökova
Ulaanbaatar Mongolia see Ulan Bator
Ulaanbaatar municipality Mongolia 85 E2
Ulaan-Ereg Mongolia 85 F2
Ulaangom Mongolia 84 B1
Ulaanhudag Mongolia 84 E2
Ulaan Nuur salt l. Mongolia 84 D2
Ulaan-Uul Bayanhongor Mongolia 84 D2
Ulaan-Uul Dornogovi Mongolia 85 F2
Ulan Nei Mongol China 85 F4
formerly known as Otog Qi
Ulan Qinghai China 84 C4
also known as Xiligou
▶**Ulan Bator** Mongolia 85 E2
Capital of Mongolia. Also spelt Ulaanbaatar;
historically known as Urga.
Ulanbel' Kazakh. 103 G3
Ulan Buh Shamo des. China 85 E3
Ulan Erge Rus. Fed. 41 H7
formerly known as Kalmytskoye
Ulanhad China see Chifeng
Ulanhot China 85 I2
also known as Horqin Youyi Qianqi
Ulan Hua China 85 F3
also known as Dorbod Qi or Siziwang Qi
Ulan-Khol Rus. Fed. 102 A3
Ulansuhai Nur l. China 85 F3
Ulan Tohoi China 84 D3
Ulan-Ude Rus. Fed. 85 E1
Ulan Ul Hu l. China 89 F5
Ulapes Arg. 204 D3
Ulaş Turkey 107 D3
Ulaş Turkey 58 I7
Ulastai China 88 D3
Ulaya Tanz. 129 C6
'Ulayam aẓ Ẓama' hill Saudi Arabia 109 L9
Ulayyah well Saudi Arabia 105 D3
Ul'ba Kazakh. 88 C1
also spelt Ülbi
Ulbroka Latvia 42 H5
Ulchin S. Korea 83 C5
Ulcinj Crna Gora Yugo. 58 A7
Ulco S. Africa 133 I5
Uldz Mongolia 85 F1
Uldz r. Mongolia 85 F1
Uleåborg Fin. see Oulu
Ulefoss Norway 45 J4
Ulei Vanuatu 145 F3
Ulety Rus. Fed. 85 G1
Ülfborg Denmark 45 J4
Ulgain Gol r. China 85 H2
Ul'gili Turkey 107 F2
Ulhasnagar India 94 B2
Uliastai China 85 H2
also known as Dong Ujimqin Qi
Uliastay Mongolia 84 C2
Uliatea i. Fr. Polynesia see Raiatea
Ulie atoll Micronesia see Woleai
Ulindi r. Dem. Rep. Congo 126 E5
Ulithi atoll Micronesia 73 I4
also known as Mackenzie
Ul'kayak r. Kazakh. 103 E2
Ul'ken-Karoy, Ozero salt l. Kazakh. 103 G1
Ülkenözen r. Kazakh./Rus. Fed. see
Bol'shoy Uzen'
Ul'ken Sulutor Kazakh. 103 H4
also spelt Ölkeyok
Ülken Vladimirovka Kazakh. see
Bol'shaya Vladimirovka
Ulla r. Spain 54 C2
Ulladulla Australia 147 F3
Ullapool U.K. 46 G6
Ullatti Sweden 44 M2
Ullawarra Aboriginal Reserve Australia
150 B4
Ulldecona Spain 55 L4
Ullmer, Mount Antarctica 222 S1
Ulloma Bol. 200 C4
Ullsfjorden sea chan. Norway 44 L1
Üllung-do i. S. Korea 83 C5
Ul'ma r. Rus. Fed. 82 C1
Ulmeni Romania 58 H4
Ulmeni Romania 58 H1
Ullongue Moz. 131 G2
Umm Silah, Sha'ib watercourse Iraq 109 O5
Ulooranie, Lake salt flat Australia 148 C5
Ulricehamn Sweden 45 K4
Ulsan S. Korea 83 C6
Ulsberg Norway 44 J3
Ulsta U.K. 46 K3
Ulsteinvik Norway 44 I3
Ulster reg. Rep. of Ireland/U.K. 47 E9
Ulster U.S.A. 177 I4
Ultima Australia 147 D3
Ultima tourist site Iraq 107 F5
Ultraoriental, Cordillera mts Peru 200 B1
also known as Divisor, Sierra de
Ulu Indon. 75 C2
Ulu Sudan 128 B2
Ulua r. Hond. 185 I6
Ulubat Gölü l. Turkey 106 B2
Ulubey Turkey 106 B3

Uluborlu Turkey 106 B3
Uluçay r. Turkey 107 E3
Uludağ mt. Turkey 106 B2
Uludağ Milli Parkı nat. park Turkey 59 K8
Uluggat China see Wuqia
Ulu Kali, Gunung mt. Malaysia 76 C2
Ulukışla Turkey 106 C3
Ulundi S. Africa 133 P5
Ulungur He r. China 84 A2
Ulungur Hu l. China 88 D2
Ulupalakua U.S.A. 181 [inset] Z1
Ulu Pandan Sing. 76 [inset]
Uluqsaqtuuq Canada see Holman
▶**Uluru** hill Australia 148 A5
also known as Ayers Rock
world [land cover] ➡ 18–19
oceania [features] ➡ 142–143
Uluru National Park Australia 148 A5
Ulus Dağı mt. Turkey 59 J9
Ulutau Kazakh. see Ulytau
Ulutau, Gory mts Kazakh. 103 F3
Ulverston U.K. 47 I9
Ulverstone Australia 147 E5
Ulvsjön Sweden 45 L3
Ul'yanikha Rus. Fed. 43 S3
Ul'yanovo Rus. Fed. 43 T6
Ul'yanov Kazakh. see Ul'yanovskiy
Ul'yanovka Rus. Fed. 43 L2
Ul'yanovo Kaliningradskaya Oblast' Rus. Fed.
42 D7
Ul'yanovo Kaluzhskaya Oblast' Rus. Fed.
43 Q8
Ul'yanovo Uzbek. 103 G4
Ul'yanovsk Rus. Fed. 41 I5
also known as Simbirsk; also spelt Uljanovsk
Ul'yanovskaya Oblast' admin. div. Rus. Fed.
41 H5
English form Ulyanovsk Oblast
Ul'yanovskiy Kazakh. 103 H2
formerly known as Ul'yanov; formerly known as
Ul'yanovskoye
Ulyanovsk Oblast admin. div. Rus. Fed. see
Ul'yanovskaya Oblast'
Ul'yanovskoye Kazakh. see Ul'yanovskiy
Ulyatuy Rus. Fed. 85 H1
Ulysses KS U.S.A. 178 B4
Ulysses KY U.S.A. 176 C8
Ulytau Kazakh. 103 F2
formerly spelt Ulutau
Uly-Zhylanshyk r. Kazakh. 103 E2
Umag Croatia 56 F3
Umala Bol. 200 C4
Umán Mex. 185 H4
Uman' Ukr. 41 D6
Umango, Cerro mt. Arg. 204 C3
'Umari, Qa' al salt pan Jordan 109 H6
Umaria India 96 D5
Umarkhed India 94 C2
Umarkot India 95 D2
Umarkot Pak. 101 G5
Umaroona, Lake salt flat Australia 146 C3
Umarpada India 96 B5
Umatilla U.S.A. 180 C3
Umayan r. Phil. 74 C4
'Umayrī, Wādī watercourse Oman 105 G3
Umba r. Rus. Fed. 40 E2
formerly known as Lesnoy
Umba r. Tanz. 128 D5
Umbagog Lake U.S.A. 177 N1
Umbakumba Australia 148 C2
Umbeara Australia 148 B5
Umbelasha watercourse Sudan 126 E2
Umbertide Italy 56 E6
Umboi i. P.N.G. 73 K8
formerly known as Rooke Island
Umbozero Rus. Fed. 44 P2
Umbrella Mountains N.Z. 153 D13
Umbria admin. reg. Italy 56 E6
Umeå Sweden 44 M3
Umeälven r. Sweden 44 M3
Umet Rus. Fed. 41 G5
Umfolozi r. S. Africa 133 Q5
Umfolozi Game Reserve nature res.
S. Africa 133 P5
Umfreville Lake Canada 167 M5
Umfuli r. Zimbabwe see Mupfure
Umgeni r. S. Africa 133 P6
Umhlanga S. Africa 133 Q5
Umhlatuzi Lagoon S. Africa 133 Q5
Umiiviip Kangertiva inlet Greenland 165 O3
also known as Gyldenløve Fjord
Umingmaktok Canada 165 I3
Umirzak Kazakh. 102 B4
Umiujaq Canada 168 E1
Umkomaas S. Africa 133 O7
Umkomaas r. S. Africa 133 O7
Umlazi S. Africa 133 O6
Umm ad Daraj, Jabal mt. Jordan 108 G5
Umm al Birak Saudi Arabia 104 C2
Umm al Ghār, Khabrat waterhole Iraq
109 N5
Umm al Hashīm, Jabal mt. Jordan 108 D5
Umm al Jamājim well Saudi Arabia 105 D2
Umm al Qaiwain U.A.E. see
Umm al Qaywayn
Umm al Qaywayn U.A.E. 105 F2
English form Umm al Qaiwain
Umm ar Raghbah watercourse Iraq 109 N3
Umm ar Raqabah, Khabrat imp. l.
Saudi Arabia 109 N3
Umm as Samīm salt flat Oman 105 F3
Umm at Qalbān Saudi Arabia 104 C2
Umm az Zumūl well Oman 105 F3
Umm Bāb Qatar 105 E2
Umm Badr Sudan 121 E6
Umm Dam Sudan 121 F6
Umm Ḩarb Saudi Arabia 104 C3
Umm Jumayyil waterhole Saudi Arabia
109 N9
Umm Keddada Sudan 121 E6
Umm Lajj Saudi Arabia 104 B2
Umm Mafrūd, Gebel mt. Egypt 108 F8
Umm Mukhbār, Jabal hill Saudi Arabia
104 B3
Umm Nukhaylah hill Saudi Arabia 109 J8
Umm Nukhaylah Saudi Arabia 108 G9
Umm Qaṣr Iraq 107 F5
Umm Qurein well Sudan 121 F5
Umm Quşur i. Saudi Arabia 104 A2
Umm Raqm, Gebel hill Egypt 108 C7
Umm Rumeila well Sudan 121 G5
Umm Ruwaba Sudan 121 F6
Umm Sa'ad Libya 120 E2
Umm Saiyala Sudan 121 F6
Umm Saṭūr Qatar 105 E2
also known as Musay'id
Umm Sayala Saudi Arabia 104 B3
Umm Samā Saudi Arabia 104 B3
Umm Saysabān, Jabal mt. Jordan 108 D5
Umm Shaitiya well Sudan 121 F6
Umm Shomar, Gebel mt. Egypt 108 E9
Umm Shugeira Sudan 121 F6
Umm Sināh, Sha'ib watercourse Iraq 109 O5
Umm Tināşşib, Gebel mt. Egypt 108 D9
Umm Urūmah i. Saudi Arabia 104 B2
Umm Wa'āl hill Saudi Arabia 109 J6
Umm Wazir well Saudi Arabia 105 D3
Umm Zanatīr mt. Egypt 108 D9
Umnak Island U.S.A. 164 C4
Umpqua r. U.S.A. 180 B4
Umred India 94 C1
Umtali Zimbabwe see Mutare
Umtamvuna r. S. Africa 133 O8
Umtata S. Africa 133 N8
Umtata r. S. Africa 133 N8
Umtata Dam resr S. Africa 133 M8

Umtentweni S. Africa 133 O7
Umuahia Nigeria 125 G5
Umuarama Brazil 203 A7
Umurbey Turkey 59 H8
Umurlar Turkey 59 J9
Umutoi N.Z. 152 J8
Umvoti r. S. Africa 133 P6
Umzimhlava r. S. Africa 133 N8
Umzimkulu r. S. Africa 133 O7
Umzimkulu r. S. Africa 133 N7
Umzimvubu r. S. Africa 133 N8
Umzingwani r. Zimbabwe see Mzingwani
Umzinto S. Africa 133 O7
Una Belarus 43 L6
Una r. Bos.-Herz./Croatia 56 I3
Una Brazil 202 E5
Una r. Brazil 202 E4
Una India 96 C3
Una, Mount N.Z. 153 G10
'Unāb, Jabal al hill Jordan 109 H8
English form Black Rock
'Unāb, Wādī al watercourse Jordan 109 H7
Unac r. Bos.-Herz. 56 I4
Unadilla U.S.A. 177 I3
Unadilla r. U.S.A. 177 J3
Unaí Brazil 206 G3
Unai Pass Afgh. 101 G3
Unalaska U.S.A. 164 C4
Unalaska Island U.S.A. 164 C4
Unango Moz. 129 B8
Unari Fin. 44 N2
Unauna i. Indon. 75 B3
'Unayzah Saudi Arabia 104 C2
'Unayzah, Jabal hill Iraq 107 D4
also spelt 'Aneiza, Jabal
Unchahra India 96 D4
Unda r. Rus. Fed. 85 H1
Undara National Park Australia 149 E3
Undeni i. Sweden 45 K4
Underberg S. Africa 133 N6
Underbool Australia 146 D3
Undersåker Sweden 44 K3
Undersåker Sweden 44 K3
Undva Estonia 42 C3
Unecha Rus. Fed. 43 N9
Unecha r. Rus. Fed. 43 M9
Uneiuxi r. Brazil 199 E5
Unga Island U.S.A. 164 C4
Ungarie Australia 147 E3
Ungava, Baie d' b. Canada see Ungava Bay
Ungava, Péninsule d' pen. Canada 165 L2
also known as Ungava Peninsula
Ungava Bay Canada 169 H1
also known as Ungava, Baie d'
Ungava Peninsula Canada see
Ungava, Péninsule d'
Ungeny Moldova see Ungheni
Unggi N. Korea 82 C4
Ungheni Moldova 58 I1
formerly spelt Ungeny
Ungheni Romania 58 F2
Ungusa Moz. 131 G4
Unguja North admin. reg. Tanz. see
Zanzibar North
Unguja South admin. reg. Tanz. see
Zanzibar South
Unguja West admin. reg. Tanz. see
Zanzibar West
Unguraşi Romania 58 F1
Unguz, Solonchakovyye Vpadiny salt flat
Turkm. 102 D5
Üngüz Angyrsyndaky Garagum des. Turkm.
see Zaunguzskiye Karakumy
Ungvár Ukr. see Uzhhorod
Ungwana Bay Kenya 128 D5
Uni Rus. Fed. 40 I4
União Acre Brazil 200 C2
União Minas Gerais Brazil 206 C6
União da Vitória Brazil 203 B8
União do Mararã Brazil 199 F5
União dos Palmares Brazil 202 F4
Uniara India 96 C4
Unicoí U.S.A. 176 C9
Uniejów Poland 49 P4
Unije i. Croatia 56 G4
Unimak Island U.S.A. 164 C4
Unini r. Brazil 199 F5
Unini Peru 200 A2
Unión Arg. 204 D4
Unión Para. 201 F6
Union ME U.S.A. 177 P1
Union MO U.S.A. 174 B4
Union OR U.S.A. 180 C3
Union WV U.S.A. 176 E8
Unión, Bahía b. Arg. 204 E5
Unión, Mount U.S.A. 183 L7
Union City OH U.S.A. 176 A5
Union City PA U.S.A. 176 F4
Union City TN U.S.A. 174 B4
Uniondale S. Africa 132 H10
Unión de Reyes Cuba 186 C2
▶**Union of Soviet Socialist Republics**
Divided in 1991 into 15 independent
nations: Armenia, Azerbaijan, Belarus,
Estonia, Georgia, Kazakhstan, Kyrgyzstan,
Latvia, Lithuania, Moldova, the Russian
Federation, Tajikistan, Turkmenistan,
Ukraine and Uzbekistan.

Union Springs AL U.S.A. 175 C5
Union Springs NY U.S.A. 177 I3
Uniontown U.S.A. 176 F6
Union Valley Reservoir U.S.A. 182 D3
Unionville MI U.S.A. 173 J7
Unionville MO U.S.A. 174 A3
Unionville NV U.S.A. 182 F1
Unionville VA U.S.A. 176 H7
▶**United Arab Emirates** country Asia 105 F3
also known as Al Imārāt al 'Arabīyah at
Muttaḥidah, in Arabic; formerly known as
Trucial Coast or Trucial States
asia [countries] ➡ 64–67
United Arab Republic country Africa see
Egypt

▶**United Kingdom** country Europe 47 L8
3rd most populous country in Europe.
europe [countries] ➡ 32–35

United Provinces state India see
Uttar Pradesh

▶**United States of America** country
N. America 170 E3
Most populous country in North America
and 3rd in the world. 2nd largest country in
North America and 3rd in the world.
world [countries] ➡ 10–11
world [changes] ➡ 20–23
world [population] ➡ 22–23
northamerica [countries] ➡ 158–159

United States Range mts Canada 165 M1
Unity Canada 167 I4
Unjab watercourse Namibia 130 B4
Unjha India 96 B5
Unnao India 96 D4
Ŭnp'a N. Korea 83 B5
Unsan N. Korea 83 B5
Ŭnsan N. Korea 83 B5
Unst i. U.K. 46 L2
Unstrut r. Germany 48 I4
Unstrut-Trias-Land park Germany 48 I4
Untere Havel park Germany 48 J3
Unteres Oderbal nat. park Germany 49 L3
Unterschleißheim Germany 48 I7
Unturán, Sierra de mts Venez. 199 E4
Unuk r. Canada/U.S.A. 166 D3
Unuli Horog China 97 F2

Un'ya r. Rus. Fed. 40 K3
Unzen-Amakusa National Park Japan 91 B8
Unzen-dake vol. Japan 91 B8
Unzha Rus. Fed. 40 H4
Uozu Japan 91 E6
Úpa r. Czech Rep. 49 M5
Upa r. Rus. Fed. 43 R7
Upalco U.S.A. 183 N1
Upar Ghat reg. India 97 E5
Upata Venez. 199 F2
Upemba, Lac l. Dem. Rep. Congo 127 E7
Upernavik Greenland 165 N2
Upernavik Kujalleq Greenland 165 N2
also known as Søndre Upernavik
Upi Phil. 74 C5
Upía r. Col. 198 C3
Upington S. Africa 132 F5
Upinniemi Fin. 45 N3
Upland U.S.A. 182 G7
Upleta India 96 A5
Upokongaro N.Z. 152 J7
Upoloksha Rus. Fed. 44 O2
Upolu i. Samoa 145 H3
formerly known as Ojalava
Upolu Point U.S.A. 181 [inset] Z1
Upper Alkali Lake U.S.A. 180 B4
Upper Arlington U.S.A. 176 B5
Upper Arrow Lake Canada 166 G5
Upper Chindwin Myanmar see Mawlaik
Upper East admin. reg. Ghana 125 E4
Upper Fraser Canada 166 F4
Upper Garry Lake Canada 167 K1
Upper Hutt N.Z. 152 J9
Upper Iowa r. U.S.A. 174 B3
Upper Klamath Lake U.S.A. 180 B4
Upper Liard Canada 166 D2
Upper Lough Erne l. U.K. 47 E9
Upper Marlboro U.S.A. 177 I7
Upper Mazinaw Lake Canada 173 P6
Upper Nile state Sudan 128 B2
Upper Peirce Reservoir Sing. 76 [inset]
Upper Preoria Lake U.S.A. 172 D10
Upper Red Lake U.S.A. 178 D1
Upper Sandusky U.S.A. 176 B5
Upper Saranac Lake U.S.A. 177 K1
Upper Seal Lake Canada see Iberville, Lac d'
Upper Takaka N.Z. 152 G9
Upper Tunguska r. Rus. Fed. see Angara
Upper Volta country Africa see Burkina
Upper West admin. reg. Ghana 125 E4
Uppinangadi India 94 B3
Upplands-Väsby Sweden 45 L4
Uppsala Sweden 45 L4
Uppsala county Sweden 45 L3
Upsala Canada 168 B3
Upshi Jammu and Kashmir 96 C2
Upson U.S.A. 172 C4
Upstart, Cape Australia 149 E3
Upstart Bay Australia 149 E3
Upton U.S.A. 177 N3
'Uqayqah, Wādī watercourse Jordan 108 G7
'Uqayribāt Syria 109 I2
Uqlat al 'Udhaybah well Iraq 107 F5
'Uqlat aş Şuqūr Saudi Arabia 104 C2
Uqturpan China see Wushi
Urabá, Golfo de b. Col. 198 B2
Urad Qianqi China see Xishanzui
Urad Zhongqi China 85 F3
also known as Haliut
Ūrāf Iran 100 D4
Uraga-suidō sea chan. Japan 91 F7
Uragawara Japan 90 F6
Ura-Guba Rus. Fed. 44 P1
Urahoro Japan 90 H3
Urakam India 94 C4
Urakawa Japan 90 H3
Ural hill Australia 147 E3
Ural r. Kazakh./Rus. Fed. 102 B3
also known as Zhayyq
Uralla Australia 147 F2
Ural Mountains Rus. Fed. 40 K2
also known as Ural'skiye Gory or Ural'skiy Khrebet
Uralovka Rus. Fed. 82 C1
Ural'sk Kazakh. 102 B2
also known as Oral
Ural'skaya Oblast' admin. div. Kazakh. see Zapadnyy Kazakhstan
Ural'skiye Gory mts Rus. Fed. see Ural Mountains
Ural'skiy Khrebet mts Rus. Fed. see Ural Mountains
Urambo Tanz. 129 B6
Uran India 94 B2
Urana Australia 147 E3
Urana, Lake Australia 147 E3
Urandangi Australia 148 C4
Urandi Brazil 202 D5
Uranium City Canada 167 I3
Urapunga Australia 148 B2
Urapuntja Australia 148 B4
Uraricoera Brazil 199 F4
Uraricoera r. Brazil 199 F4
Urartu country Asia see Armenia
Uras Sardegna Italy 57 A9
Ura-Tyube Tajik. see Üroteppa
Uravakonda India 94 C3
Uravan U.S.A. 183 P3
Urawa Japan 91 F7
Uray Rus. Fed. 38 G3
Uray'irah Saudi Arabia 105 E2
'Urayq ad Duḩūl des. Saudi Arabia 105 D2
'Urayq Sāqān des. Saudi Arabia 105 D2
Urazovka Rus. Fed. 40 H5
Urazovo Rus. Fed. 41 F6
Urbana IA U.S.A. 172 B8
Urbana IL U.S.A. 174 B3
Urbana IN U.S.A. 172 H10
Urbana OH U.S.A. 176 B5
Urbania Italy 56 E5
Urbano Santos Brazil 202 D2
Urbel r. Spain 54 H2
Urbino Italy 56 E5
historically known as Urbinum
Urbinum Italy see Urbino
Urbión mt. Spain 55 I2
Urbs Vetus Italy see Orvieto
Urcos Peru 200 C3
Urda Spain 54 H5
Ur'devarri hill Fin./Norway see Urtivaara
Urdoma Rus. Fed. 40 I3
Urd Tamir Gol r. Mongolia 84 D2
Urdyuzhskoye, Ozero l. Rus. Fed. 40 I2
Urdzhar Kazakh. 88 C2
also spelt Ürzhar
Ure r. U.K. 47 K9
Urechcha Belarus 42 I9
Urechești Romania 58 I2
Urein Egypt 108 B7
Uren' Rus. Fed. 40 H4
Urengoy Rus. Fed. 39 H3
Urenosi mt. Norway 45 I4
Urenui N.Z. 152 I6
Uréparapara i. Vanuatu 145 F3
Urewera National Park N.Z. 152 L6
Urfa Turkey see Şanlıurfa
Urga Mongolia see Ulan Bator
Urgal r. Rus. Fed. 82 D2
Urganch Uzbek. see Urgench
Urganlı Turkey 59 I10
Urgench Uzbek. 102 E4
also spelt Urganch
Ürgüp Turkey 106 C3
Urgut Uzbek. 103 F5
Urho China 88 D2
Urho Kekkosen kansallispuisto nat. park Fin. 44 N1
Uri Jammu and Kashmir 96 B2
Uribia Col. 198 C2
Uripitijuata, Cerro mt. Mex. 185 E5
Urique r. Mex. 181 F8
Urisino Australia 147 D2
Uritskiy Kazakh. 103 F1
Uritskoye Rus. Fed. 43 T9
Urī Wenz r. Eth. 104 B5
Urjala Fin. 45 M3
Urk Neth. 48 C3
Urkan Rus. Fed. 82 B1
Urkan r. Rus. Fed. 82 B1
Urkut Somalia 128 D4
Urla Turkey 106 A3
Urlaţi Romania 58 H4
Urlui r. Romania 58 G5
Urluk Rus. Fed. 85 E1
Urmai China 89 D6
Urmary Rus. Fed. 40 H5
Urmetan Tajik. 101 G2
Urmi r. Rus. Fed. 82 D2
Urmia Iran 100 A2
also spelt Orūmīyeh; formerly known as Reẕā'īyeh
Urmia, Lake salt l. Iran 100 A2
also known as Orūmīyeh, Daryācheh-ye; formerly known as Reẕā'īyeh, Daryācheh-ye
Urmston Road sea chan. Hong Kong China 87 [inset]
Uromi Nigeria 125 G5
Uroševac Kosovo, Srbija Yugo. 58 C6
Urosozero Rus. Fed. 40 E3
Üroteppa Tajik. 101 G2
also spelt Ura-Tyube
Urru Co salt l. China 89 D6
also known as Jagok Tso
Ursat'yevskaya Uzbek. see Khavast
Urshel'skiy Rus. Fed. 43 V6
Urt Mongolia 84 D3
Urtivaara hill Fin./Norway 44 M1
also spelt Ur'devarri
Urt Moron China 84 B4
Uru r. Brazil 206 D2
Uruáchic Mex. 184 C3
Uruaçu Brazil 202 B5
Uruana Brazil 206 D2
Uruapan Baja California Norte Mex. 184 A2
Uruapan Michoacán Mex. 185 E5
Urubamba Peru 200 B3
Urubaxi r. Brazil 199 E5
Urubu r. Brazil 199 G5
Urubupungá, Salto do waterfall Brazil 206 B7
Urucara Brazil 199 G5
Uruch'ye Rus. Fed. 43 O9
Urucu r. Brazil 199 F6
Uruçuí Brazil 202 C3
Uruçuí, Serra do hills Brazil 202 C4
Urucuia Brazil 202 C6
Urucuia r. Brazil 202 C6
Uruçui Preto r. Brazil 202 C3
Urucum Brazil 201 F4
Urucurituba Brazil 199 G5
Uruguai r. Brazil 203 A8
also spelt Uruguay
Uruguaiana Brazil 204 F3
Uruguay r. Arg./Uruguay 204 F4
also spelt Uruguai
▶Uruguay country S. America 204 F4
southamerica [countries] ▶▶ 192–193
Uruk tourist site Iraq see Erech
Urukthapel i. Palau 73 H5
Urumchi China see Ürümqi
Ürümqi China 88 D3
English form Urumchi
Urundi country Africa see Burundi
Urunga Australia 147 G2
Urup r. Rus. Fed. 41 G7
Urup, Ostrov i. Rus. Fed. 81 Q3
Urup, Proliv strait Rus. Fed. 81 Q3
Urupá r. Brazil 201 E2
Uru Pass China/Kyrg. 88 B3
'Urūq al Awārik des. Saudi Arabia 105 D4
'Urūq ash Shaybah des. Saudi Arabia 105 F3
Urusha Rus. Fed. 82 A1
Urusha r. Rus. Fed. 82 A1
Urussu Rus. Fed. 40 J5
Uruti N.Z. 152 I6
Uruwira Tanz. 129 A6
Uryl' Kazakh. 88 D1
Uryū Japan 90 G3
Uryupinsk Rus. Fed. 41 G6
Ürzhar Kazakh. see Urdzhar
Urzhum Rus. Fed. 40 I4
Urziceni Romania 58 H4
Usa r. Belarus 43 J8
Usa Japan 91 B8
Usa r. Rus. Fed. 40 K2
Usada i. Phil. 74 B5
Uşak Turkey 106 B3
Uşak prov. Turkey 59 K10
Usakos Namibia 130 B4
Usambara Mountains Tanz. 129 C6
Usangu Flats plain Tanz. 129 B7
Usarp Mountains Antarctica 223 K2
'Usaylān Yemen 105 D5
Usborne, Mount hill Falkland Is 205 F8
Usedom Germany 49 K2
Usedom i. Germany 49 L2
Useless Loop Australia 151 A5
Usengi Kenya 128 B5
Usfān Saudi Arabia 104 B3
Usha r. Belarus 42 G8
Usha r. Belarus 43 J8
Ushachi Belarus see Ushachy
Ushachy Belarus 43 J6
also spelt Ushachi
Ushakova, Ostrov i. Rus. Fed. 39 H1
Ushanovo Kazakh. 88 C1
Ushant i. France see Ouessant, Île d'
Üsharal Kazakh. see Ucharal
Usharal Kazakh. 103 G4
Ushayqir Saudi Arabia 105 D2
'Ushayrah Saudi Arabia 104 C3
Ushcha r. Rus. Fed. 43 K6
Ushcherp'ye Rus. Fed. 43 M9
Ushibuka Japan 91 B8
Ushirombo Tanz. 128 A5
Ushtobe Kazakh. 103 I3
formerly spelt Ush-Tyube
Ush-Tyube Kazakh. see Ushtobe
Ushuaia Arg. 205 C9
Uši Latvia 42 D4
Usina Brazil 202 A3
Usinsk Rus. Fed. 40 K2
Usk r. U.K. 47 J12
Uska India 97 D4
Uskhodni Belarus 42 I8
Uskoplje Bos.-Herz. see Gornji Vakuf
Üsküdar Turkey 106 B2
Üsküp Turkey 58 I7
Usma Latvia 42 D4
Usman' Rus. Fed. 41 F5
Usmas ezers l. Latvia 42 D4
Usmat Uzbek. 103 F5
formerly spelt Usmet
Usmet Uzbek. see Usmat
Usmyn' Rus. Fed. 43 M6
Uso r. Spain 54 F5
Usogorsk Rus. Fed. 40 I3
Usoke Tanz. 129 B6
Usol'ye Rus. Fed. 40 K4
Usol'ye-Sibirskoye Rus. Fed. 80 G2
Usora r. Bos.-Herz. 56 K4
Usozha r. Rus. Fed. 43 P9
Usozha r. Rus. Fed. 43 Q9
Uspallata Arg. 204 C4
Uspenka Kazakh. 103 I1
Uspenskiy Kazakh. 103 H2
Uspenskoye Rus. Fed. 43 L5
Uspen'ye Rus. Fed. 40 G4
Ussel France 51 I7
Ussuri r. Rus. Fed. 82 D2
also known as Wusuli Jiang
Ussuriysk Rus. Fed. 82 C4
formerly known as Voroshilov
Ust'-Abakanskoye Rus. Fed. see Abakan
Ust'-Alekseyevo Rus. Fed. 40 H3
Usta Muhammad Pak. 101 G4
Ust'-Balyk Rus. Fed. see Nefteyugansk
Ust'-Barguzin Rus. Fed. 81 H2
Ust'-Dolyssy Rus. Fed. 43 K5
Ust'-Donetskiy Rus. Fed. 41 G7
Ust'-Dzheguta Rus. Fed. 41 G7
formerly known as Ust'-Dzhegutinskaya
Ust'-Dzhegutinskaya Rus. Fed. see Ust'-Dzheguta
Uster Switz. 51 O5
Ustica, Isola di i. Sicilia Italy 57 F10
Ust'-Ilimsk Rus. Fed. 39 K4
Ust'-Ilimskiy Vodokhrinilishche resr Rus. Fed. 80 G1
Ust'-Ilya Rus. Fed. 85 G1
Ust'-Ilych Rus. Fed. 40 K3
Ústí nad Labem Czech Rep. 49 L5
Ústí nad Orlicí Czech Rep. 49 N6
Ustinov Rus. Fed. see Izhevsk
Ustirt plat. Kazakh./Uzbek. see Ustyurt Plateau
Ustka Poland 49 N1
Ust'-Kamchatsk Rus. Fed. 39 Q4
Ust'-Kamenogorsk Kazakh. 88 C1
also known as Öskemen
Ust'-Kan Rus. Fed. 88 D1
Ust'-Kara Rus. Fed. 40 M1
Ust'-Koksa Rus. Fed. 88 D1
Ust'-Kulom Rus. Fed. 40 J3
Ust'-Kut Rus. Fed. 80 H1
Ust'-Kuyga Rus. Fed. 39 N2
Ust'-Labinsk Rus. Fed. 41 F7
formerly known as Ust'-Labinskaya
Ust'-Labinskaya Rus. Fed. see Ust'-Labinsk
Ust'-Luga Rus. Fed. 43 J2
Ust'-Lyzha Rus. Fed. 40 K2
Ust'-Maya Rus. Fed. 39 N3
Ust'-Mongunay Rus. Fed. see Primorskiy
Ust'-Munduyka Rus. Fed. 39 I3
Ust'-Nem Rus. Fed. 40 J3
Ust'-Nera Rus. Fed. 39 O3
Ust'-Olenek Rus. Fed. 39 L2
Ust'-Omchug Rus. Fed. 39 O3
Ust-Orda Buryat Autonomous Okrug admin. div. Rus. Fed. see Ust'-Ordynskiy Buryatskiy Avtonomnyy Okrug
Ust'-Ordynskiy Rus. Fed. 80 G2
Ust'-Ordynskiy Buryatskiy Avtonomnyy Okrug admin. div. Rus. Fed. 80 G2
English form Ust-Orda Buryat Autonomous Okrug
Ust'-Port Rus. Fed. 39 I3
Ustrem Bulg. 58 H6
Ustrzyki Dolne Poland 49 T6
formerly known as Nizhniye Ustriki
Ust'-Sara Rus. Fed. 43 O1
Ust'-Shonosha Rus. Fed. 40 G3
Ust'-Tsil'ma Rus. Fed. 40 J2
Ust'-Ulagan Rus. Fed. 88 D1
Ust'-Umalta Rus. Fed. 82 D2
Ust'-Ura Rus. Fed. 40 H3
Ust'-Usa Rus. Fed. 40 K2
Ust'-Vayen'ga Rus. Fed. 40 G3
Ust'-Voya Rus. Fed. 40 K2
Ust'ya r. Rus. Fed. 40 G3
Ust'-Yansk Rus. Fed. 39 N2
Ust'ye Tverskaya Oblast' Rus. Fed. 43 M5
Ust'ye Vologod. Obl. Rus. Fed. 40 G4
Ust'ye Vologod. Obl. Rus. Fed. 43 U2
Ust'ye Yaroslavskaya Oblast' Rus. Fed. 43 U4
Ust'ye r. Rus. Fed. 43 U4
Ust'ye-Kirovskoye Rus. Fed. 43 Q3
Ustyurt, Plato plat. Kazakh./Uzbek. see Ustyurt Plateau
Ustyurt Plateau Kazakh./Uzbek. 102 D4
also known as Ustirt or Ustyurt, Plato or Ustyurt Platosi
Ustyurt Platosi plat. Kazakh./Uzbek. see Ustyurt Plateau
Ustyutskoye Rus. Fed. 43 Q3
Ustyuzhna Rus. Fed. 43 R3
Usu China 88 D2
Usuki Japan 91 B8
Usulután El Salvador 185 H6
Usumacinta r. Guat./Mex. 185 G5
Usumbura Burundi see Bujumbura
Usun Apau, Dataran Tinggi plat. Sarawak Malaysia 77 F2
Usutu r. Africa 133 Q3
also known as Great Usutu or Lusutufu
Usvyaty Rus. Fed. 43 L6
Usvyeyka r. Belarus 43 K7
Uta Indon. 73 I7
Utah state U.S.A. 183 M2
Utah Lake U.S.A. 183 M1
Utajärvi Fin. 44 N2
Utan Indon. 77 G5
Utashinai Rus. Fed. see Yuzhno-Kuril'sk
'Utaybah reg. Saudi Arabia 104 C3
'Utaybah, Buḩayrat al imp. l. Syria 109 H4
Utayyiq Saudi Arabia 105 E2
Utbjoa Norway 45 I4
Utebo Spain 55 K3
Ute Creek r. U.S.A. 179 B5
Utembo r. Angola 127 D9
Ute Mountain Indian Reservation res. U.S.A. 183 P4
Utena Lith. 42 G6
Utete Tanz. 129 C7
Uthai Thani Thai. 79 C5
Uthal Pak. 101 F5
Utiariti Brazil 201 F3
Utica NY U.S.A. 177 J2
Utica OH U.S.A. 176 C5
Utiel Spain 55 J5
Utikuma Lake Canada 167 H4
Utila Hond. 186 B3
Utinga r. Brazil 202 D5
Utladalen park Norway 45 I3
Utlwanang S. Africa 133 J4
Uto Japan 91 B8
Utrata r. Poland 49 R3
Utraula India 97 D4
Utrecht Neth. 48 C3
historically known as Trajectum
Utrecht S. Africa 133 O4
Utrera Spain 54 F7
Utroya r. Rus. Fed. 42 J4
Utsira Norway 46 Q4
Utsjoki Fin. 44 N1
also spelt Ohcejohka
Utsunomiya Japan 91 F6
Utta Rus. Fed. 102 A3
Uttaradit Thai. 78 C4
Uttaranchal state India 96 C3
Uttarkashi India 96 C3
Uttar Pradesh state India 96 C4
formerly known as United Provinces
Utu China see Miao'ergou
Utubulak China 88 D2
Utupua i. Solomon Is 145 F3
formerly known as Edgecumbe Island
Utva r. Kazakh. 102 C2
Uulu Estonia 42 F3
Uummannaq Greenland see Dundas
Uummannaq Greenland 165 N2
Uummannaq Fjord inlet Greenland 165 N2
Uummannarsuaq c. Greenland see Farewell, Cape
Uurainen Fin. 44 N3
Üüreg Nuur salt l. Mongolia 84 A1
Üür Gol r. Mongolia 84 D1
Uusikaarlepyy Fin. see Nykarleby
Uusikaupunki Fin. 45 M3
also known as Nystad
Uutapi Namibia 130 B3
also known as Ombalantu
Uva r. Col. 198 D4
Uva Rus. Fed. 40 J4
Uvac r. Bos.-Herz./Yugo. 58 A5
Uvalde U.S.A. 179 C6
Uvaravichy Belarus 43 L9
Uvarovka Rus. Fed. 43 Q6
Uvarovo Rus. Fed. 41 G6
Uvéa i. New Caledonia see Ouvéa
Uver' r. Rus. Fed. 43 P3
Uvinza Tanz. 129 A6
Uvira Dem. Rep. Congo 126 F5
Uvod' r. Rus. Fed. 43 V4
Uvongo S. Africa 133 O7
Uvs prov. Mongolia 84 B1
Uvs Nuur salt l. Mongolia 84 B1
Uwa Japan 91 C8
Uwainid, Wādī al watercourse Saudi Arabia 109 H9
Uwajima Japan 91 C8
Uwa-kai b. Japan 91 C8
'Uwayfī Oman 105 G3
'Uwayja well Saudi Arabia 104 C2
'Uwaynāt Wannīn Libya 120 B2
'Uwayriḑ, Ḩarrat al lava field Saudi Arabia 104 B2
Uwaysiţ well Saudi Arabia 109 J7
Uweinat, Jebel mt. Sudan 120 E4
Uwemba Tanz. 129 B7
Uwi i. Indon. 77 D2
Uxin Ju China 85 F4
Uxin Qi China see Dabqig
Uxmal tourist site Mex. 185 H4
Uxxaktal China 88 D3
Uyaly Kazakh. 103 E3
Uyaly, Ozero l. Kazakh. see Koshkarkol', Ozero
Uyar Rus. Fed. 80 E1
Üydzin Mongolia 85 E2
Uyo Nigeria 125 G5
Üyönch Mongolia 84 B2
Üyönch Gol r. China 84 A2
Uyu Chaung r. Myanmar 78 A2
Uyuk Kazakh. 103 G4
also spelt Oyyq; formerly spelt Oik
Uyun Saudi Arabia 105 E2
Uyuni Bol. 200 D5
Uyuni, Salar de salt flat Bol. 200 D5
Uza r. Rus. Fed. 41 H5
'Uzaym, Nahr al r. Iraq 107 F4
▶Uzbekistan country Asia 102 D4
spelt O'zbekiston or Ŭzbekiston in Uzbek; formerly known as Uzbekskaya S.S.R. or Uzbek S.S.R.
asia [countries] ▶▶ 64–67
Ŭzbekiston country Asia see Uzbekistan
Uzbekskaya S.S.R. country Asia see Uzbekistan
Uzbek S.S.R. country Asia see Uzbekistan
Uzda Belarus 42 I8
Uzen' Kazakh. see Kyzylsay
Uzengyu-Kuush, Gora mt. China/Kyrg. 88 B3
Uzerche France 50 H7
Uzès France 51 K8
Uzgen Kyrg. see Özgön
Uzh r. Ukr. 49 T7
Uzha r. Rus. Fed. 43 O7
Uzhgorod Ukr. see Uzhhorod
Uzhhorod Ukr. 49 T7
also spelt Uzhgorod; formerly spelt Užhorod; historically known as Ungvár
Uzhok Ukr. 49 T7
Užhorod Ukr. see Uzhhorod
Užice Srbija Yugo. 58 A5
formerly known as Titovo Užice
Uzlovaya Rus. Fed. 43 T8
Uzola r. Rus. Fed. 40 G4
Üzümlü Turkey 59 K12
Uzun Uzbek. 103 G5
Uzun Ada i. Turkey 59 H10
Uzunagach Almatinskaya Oblast' Kazakh. 103 I4
also spelt Uzynaghash
Uzunagach Almatinskaya Oblast' Kazakh. 103 I4
Uzunbulak China 88 D2
Uzuncaburç Turkey 108 E1
Uzunköprü Turkey 106 A2
Užventis Lith. 42 D6
Uzvoz Rus. Fed. 43 M6
Uzyn Ukr. 41 D6
Uzynaghash Kazakh. see Uzunagach
Uzynkair Kazakh. 103 E3

↓ V

Vaajakoski Fin. 44 N3
Vaal r. S. Africa 132 H6
Vaala Fin. 44 N2
Vaalbos National Park S. Africa 133 I5
Vaal Dam S. Africa 133 M4
Vaal Dam Nature Reserve S. Africa 133 M3
Vaalplass S. Africa 133 M2
Vaalwater S. Africa 131 F5
Vaartsi Estonia 42 I4
Vaasa Fin. 44 M3
also spelt Vasa
Vabalninkas Lith. 42 F6
Vabich r. Belarus 43 K8
Vabkent Uzbek. 103 F4
also spelt Wobkent
Vablya r. Rus. Fed. 43 O9
Vác Hungary 49 Q8
Vacaré r. Brazil 207 H8
Vacaria Brazil 203 B9
Vacaria r. Mato Grosso do Sul Brazil 203 A7
Vacaria r. Minas Gerais Brazil 202 D6
Vacaria, Campo da plain Brazil 203 B9
Vacaria, Serra hills Brazil 203 A7
Vacaville U.S.A. 182 C3
Vache, Île-à- i. Haiti 187 E3
Väckelsång Sweden 45 K4
Vad Rus. Fed. 40 H5
Vad r. Rus. Fed. 41 G5
Vada India 94 B2
Vadakste r. Latvia/Lith. 42 D5
Vădăstriţa Romania 58 F5
Vadehavet nature res. Denmark 45 J5
Văđeni Romania 58 I3
Vadi India 94 B3
also known as Savantvadi
Vadodara India 96 B5
formerly known as Baroda
Vadsø Norway 44 O1
Vadstena Sweden 45 K4
Vadu Crişului Romania 58 D2

▶Vaduz Liechtenstein 48 G8
Capital of Liechtenstein.

Værøy i. Norway 44 K2
Vaga r. Rus. Fed. 43 V1
Vågåmo Norway 45 J3
Vaganski Vrh mt. Croatia 56 H4
Vágar i. Faroe Is 46 E1
Vagavaram India 94 D2
Vagnhärad Sweden 45 L4
Vagos Port. 54 C4
Vägsele Sweden 44 L2
Vågsfjorden sea chan. Norway 44 L1
Váh r. Slovakia 49 P8
Vahhābī Iran 100 D4
Vahsel, Cape S. Georgia 205 [inset]
Vahto Fin. 45 M3

▶Vaiaku Tuvalu 145 G2
Capital of Tuvalu, on Funafuti atoll.
world [countries] ▶▶ 10–11

Vaida Estonia 42 F2
Vaiden U.S.A. 175 B5
Vaigai r. India 94 C4
Vaijapur India 94 B2
Vaikam India 94 C4
Väike Emajõgi r. Estonia 42 H3
Väike-Maarja Estonia 42 H2
Väike-Pakri i. Estonia 42 E2
Vaikijaur Sweden 44 L2
Väimela Estonia 42 I4
Vaiņode Latvia 42 C5
Vaippar r. India 94 C4
Vair r. France 51 L4
Vairowal India 96 B3
Vaison-la-Romaine France 51 L8
Vaitupu i. Tuvalu 145 G2
also spelt Oaitupu
Vajrakarur India see Kanur
Vajszló Hungary 56 J3
Vakaga pref. Cent. Afr. Rep. 126 D2
Vakaga r. Cent. Afr. Rep. 126 D2
Vakhan Tajik. 96 B1
Vakhsh Tajik. 101 G2
formerly known as Vakhstroy
Vakhsh r. Tajik. 101 G2
Vakhstroy Tajik. see Vakhsh
Vakīlābād Iran 100 D4
Vaksdal Norway 45 I3
Vålådalen naturreservat nature res. Sweden 44 K3
Valamaz Rus. Fed. 40 J4
Valandovo Macedonia 58 D7
Valašské Klobouky Czech Rep. 49 P6
Valašské Meziříčí Czech Rep. 49 O6
Valaxa i. Greece 59 F10
Val-Barrette Canada 173 R4
Vâlcăneşti Romania 58 G3
Vâlcanului, Munţii mts Romania 58 D3
Valcheta Arg. 204 D6
Valdai Hills Rus. Fed. see Valdayskaya Vozvyshennost'
Valday Rus. Fed. 43 O4
Valdayskaya Vozvyshennost' hills Rus. Fed. 43 N5
English form Valdai Hills
Valdayskoye, Ozero l. Rus. Fed. 43 O3
Valdecañas, Embalse de resr Spain 54 F5
Val del Ticino, Parco della park Italy 56 A3
Valdemārpils Latvia 42 D4
Valdemarsvik Sweden 45 L4
Val-de-Meuse France 51 L4
Valdemoro Spain 54 H4
Valdepeñas Spain 55 H6
Valderaduey r. Spain 54 F3
Valderas Spain 54 F2
Val-de-Reuil France 50 H3
Valders U.S.A. 172 F6

▶Valdés, Península pen. Arg. 205 E6
Lowest point in South America.
southamerica [landscapes] ▶▶ 190–191

Val-des-Bois Canada 173 R5
Valdez U.S.A. 164 E3
Valdivia Chile 204 B5
Valdivia Col. 198 C3
Valdobbiadene Italy 56 D3
Val-d'Or Canada 168 E3
Valdosa mt. Spain 55 H3
Valdosta U.S.A. 175 D6
Valdres valley Norway 45 J3
Vale Georgia 107 E2
Vale U.S.A. 180 C3
Valea lui Mihai Romania 49 T8
Valea Lungă Romania 58 F2
Valea Lungă Romania 58 G3
Valemount Canada 166 G4
Valença Brazil 202 E5
Valença do Piauí Brazil 202 D3
Valençay France 50 H5
Valence Midi-Pyrénées France 50 G8
Valence Rhône-Alpes France 51 K8
Valencia Spain 55 K5
historically known as Valentia
Valencia aut. comm. Spain 55 K5
also known as Valenciana, Comunidad
Valencia Venez. 199 E2
Valencia, Golfo de g. Spain 55 L5
Valencia de Alcántara Spain 54 D5
Valencia de Don Juan Spain 54 F2
Valencia Island Rep. of Ireland 47 B12
Valenciana, Comunidad aut. comm. Spain see Valencia
Valenciennes France 51 J2
Vălenii de Munte Romania 58 H3
Valensole, Plateau de France 51 M9
Valentia Spain see Valencia
Valentin Rus. Fed. 82 D4
Valentine U.S.A. 178 B3
Valentine National Wildlife Refuge nature res. U.S.A. 178 B3
Valenza Italy 56 A3
Valenzuela Phil. 74 B3
Våler Norway 45 J3
Valera Venez. 198 D2
Vale Verde Brazil 207 N3
Valga Estonia 42 H4
Valgejõgi r. Estonia 42 G2
Valhalla Provincial Park Canada 166 G5
Valikhanovo Kazakh. 103 G1
also known as Ūālīkhanov
Valinco, Golfe de b. Corse France 56 A7
Valinhos Brazil 206 G9
Valjevo Srbija Yugo. 58 A4
Valka Latvia 42 H4
Valkeakoski Fin. 45 N3
Valkenswaard Neth. 48 C4
Valkla Estonia 42 G2
Valko Fin. 42 H1
also spelt Valkoni
Valkoni Fin. see Valko
Valky Ukr. 41 E6
Valkyrie Dome ice feature Antarctica 223 C1
Vallabhipur India 96 A5
Valladolid Mex. 185 H4
Valladolid Spain 54 G3
Vallard, Lac l. Canada 169 G2
Valldal Norway 44 I3
Vall de Uxó Spain 55 K5
Valle dept Col. 198 B4
Valle Norway 45 I4
Vallecito Arg. 204 D3
Valle d'Aosta admin. reg. Italy 51 N7
Valle de la Pascua Venez. 199 E2
Valle de Rosario Mex. 181 F8
Valle de Santiago Mex. 185 E4
Valle de Zaragoza Mex. 184 D3
Valledupar Col. 198 C2
Vallée-Jonction Canada 169 G4
Valle Fértil, Sierra de mts Arg. 204 C3
Valle Grande Bol. 201 D4
Valle Hermoso Mex. 185 F3
Vallejo U.S.A. 182 B3
Vallelunga Pratameno Sicilia Italy 57 F11
Valle Nacional Mex. 185 F5
Vallenar Chile 204 C3
Vallentuna Sweden 45 L4

▶Valletta Malta 57 G13
Capital of Malta.

Valley r. Canada 167 L5
Valley Center U.S.A. 183 G8
Valley City U.S.A. 178 C2
Valley Falls U.S.A. 180 B4
Valley Head Phil. 74 B2
Valley Head U.S.A. 176 E7
Valley of The Kings tourist site Egypt 121 G3
Valley Springs U.S.A. 182 D3
Valley Station U.S.A. 174 C4
Valley Stream U.S.A. 177 L5
Valleyview Canada 167 G4
Valley View U.S.A. 176 A8
Vallo della Lucania Italy 57 H8
Valls Spain 55 M3
Vallsta Sweden 45 L3
Val Marie Canada 167 J5
Valmaseda Spain see Balmaseda
Valmiera Latvia 42 G4
Valmy U.S.A. 183 G1
Valnera mt. Spain 55 H1
Valognes France 50 E3
Valona Albania see Vlorë
Valozhyn Belarus 42 H7
also spelt Volozhin
Valpaços Port. 54 D3
Val-Paradis Canada 168 E3
Valparai India 94 C4
Valparaíso Brazil 206 C8
Valparaíso Chile 204 C4
Valparaíso admin. reg. Chile 204 C4
Valparaíso Mex. 184 E4
Valparaiso FL U.S.A. 185 I2
Valparaiso IN U.S.A. 174 C3
Valpelline valley Italy 51 N7
Valpoi India 94 B3
Valpovo Croatia 56 K3
Valronquillo hill Spain 54 G5
Vals r. S. Africa 133 K4
Vals, Tanjung c. Indon. 73 I8
Valsad India 94 B1
Valshui Wash watercourse U.S.A. 181 D7
Valspan S. Africa 131 E5
Valsrivier S. Africa 133 M5
Valtimo Fin. 44 O3
Valtou mts Greece 59 C9
Valua i. Vanuatu see Mota Lava
Valuyets Rus. Fed. 43 O9
Valuyevka Rus. Fed. 41 G7
Valuyki Rus. Fed. 41 F6
Valverde Dom. Rep. see Mao
Valverde del Camino Spain 54 E7
Valverde del Fresno Spain 54 E4
Vam Co Dông r. Vietnam 79 D6
Vam Co Tay r. Vietnam 79 D6
Vamizi, Ilha i. Moz. 129 D7
Vammala Fin. 45 M3
Vampula Fin. 45 M3
Vamsadhara r. India 95 E2
Vamvakas, Akra pt Greece 59 H10
Van Turkey 107 E3
Van, Lake salt l. Turkey 107 E3
also known as Van Gölü
Vanadzor Armenia 107 F2
formerly known as Karaklis or Kirovakan
Vanajavesi l. Fin. 45 N3
Vana-Koiola Estonia 42 I4
Vanån r. Sweden 45 K3
Vânători Romania 58 J3
Vânători Romania 58 F2
Vanavara Rus. Fed. 39 K3
Van Buren AR U.S.A. 179 D5
Van Buren IN U.S.A. 172 H10
Van Buren MO U.S.A. 174 B4
Van Buren U.S.A. see Kettering
Vanceburg U.S.A. 176 B7
Vanch Tajik. see Vanj
Vanchskiy Khrebet mts Tajik. see Vanj, Qatorkŭhi
Vancleve U.S.A. 176 B8
Vancouver Canada 166 F5
Vancouver U.S.A. 180 B3
Vancouver, Mount Canada/U.S.A. 166 B2
Vancouver Island Canada 166 E5
Vanda Fin. see Vantaa
Vandalia IL U.S.A. 174 B4
Vandalia OH U.S.A. 176 A6
Vandavasi India 94 C3
formerly spelt Wandiwash
Vandekerckhove Lake Canada 167 K3
Vandellós Spain 55 L3
Vanderbijlpark S. Africa 133 L3
Vanderbilt U.S.A. 173 I5
Vandergrift U.S.A. 176 F5
Vanderhoof Canada 166 E4
Vanderkloof Dam resr S. Africa 133 I7
Vanderlin Island Australia 148 C2
Van Diemen, Cape N.T. Australia 148 A1
Van Diemen, Cape Qld Australia 148 C3
Van Diemen Gulf Australia 148 B1
Van Diemen's Land state Australia see Tasmania
Vändra Estonia 42 G3
Vandyksdrif S. Africa 133 N3
Vandžiogala Lith. 42 E6
Vāne Latvia 42 D5
Väner, Lake Sweden see Vänern

▶Vänern l. Sweden 45 K4
4th largest lake in Europe. English form Väner, Lake.
europe [landscapes] ▶▶ 30–31

Vänersborg Sweden 45 K4
Vaneteze r. Moz. 133 Q2
Vang, Mount Antarctica 222 T2
Vanga Kenya 129 C6
Vangaindrano Madag. 131 [inset] J4
Vangaži Latvia 42 F4
Van Gölü salt l. Turkey see Van, Lake
Vangsvik Norway 44 L1
Vanguard Canada 167 J5
Van Horn U.S.A. 181 F7
Vanier Canada 168 F4
formerly known as Eastview
Vanikoro Islands Solomon Is 145 F3
also known as Mannicolo Islands; formerly known as Pitt Islands
Vanil Noir mt. Switz. 51 N6
Vanimo P.N.G. 73 J7
Vanino Rus. Fed. 82 F2
Vanivilasa Sagara resr India 94 C3
Vaniyambadi India 94 C3
Vanj Tajik. 101 G2
also spelt Vanch
Vanj, Qatorkŭhi mts Tajik. 101 G2
also known as Vanchskiy Khrebet
Vänjaurträsk Sweden 44 L2
Vânju Mare Romania 58 D4
formerly spelt Vînju Mare
Vankarem Rus. Fed. 39 S3
Vankavesi l. Fin. 45 M3
Vanna i. Norway 44 L1
Vännäs Sweden 44 L3
Vanne r. France 51 J4
Vannes France 50 D5
Vannes, Lac l. Canada 169 H2
Vannovka Kazakh. see Tura-Ryskulova
Vanntindan mt. Norway 44 L1
Van Reenen S. Africa 133 N5
Van Rees, Pegunungan mts Indon. 73 I7
Vanrhynsdorp S. Africa 132 C8
Van Riebeeck Nature Reserve S. Africa 133 M2
Vanrook Australia 149 D3
Vanrook Creek r. Australia 149 D3
Vansada India 94 B1
Vansant U.S.A. 176 C8
Vansbro Sweden 45 K3
Vanse Norway 45 I4
Vansittart Bay Australia 150 D2
Vansittart Island Canada 165 K3
Vanstadensrus S. Africa 133 L6
Vantaa Fin. 45 N3
also spelt Vanda
Vantaa r. Fin. 42 F1
Van Truer Tableland reg. Australia 151 C5
Vant's Drift S. Africa 133 O5
Vanua Balavu i. Fiji 145 H3
also spelt Vanua Mbalavu or Vanua Valavo
Vanua Lava i. Vanuatu 145 F3
Vanua Levu i. Fiji 145 G3
Vanua Mbalavu i. Fiji see Vanua Balavu

index V

▶**Vanuatu** *country* S. Pacific Ocean **145** F3
formerly known as New Hebrides *or* Nouvelles Hébrides
oceania [countries] ▶ 138–139
oceania [features] ▶ 142–143
Vanua Valavo *i.* Fiji *see* **Vanua Balavu**
Van Wert U.S.A. **176** A5
Van Wyksdorp S. Africa **132** F10
Vanwyksvlei S. Africa **132** F7
Vanwyksvlei *l.* S. Africa **132** F7
Van Zylsrus S. Africa **132** G3
Vao, Embalse de *resr* Spain **54** D2
also spelt Bao, Embalse del
Var *r.* France **51** N9
Vara Estonia **42** H3
Vara Sweden **45** K4
Varada *r.* India **94** C3
Varadero Cuba **186** C2
Varahi India **96** A5
Varaita *r.* Italy **51** N8
Varakļāni Latvia **42** H5
Varalé Côte d'Ivoire **124** E4
Varallo Italy **56** A3
Varāmin Iran **100** B3
Varanasi India **97** D4
formerly known as Benares; *historically known as* Kasi
Varandey Rus. Fed. **40** K1
Varangerfjorden *sea chan.* Norway **44** O1
Varangerhalvøya *pen.* Norway **44** O1
also known as Várnjárg
Varano, Lago di *lag.* Italy **56** H7
Varapayeva Belarus **42** I6
Varaždin Croatia **56** I2
Varazze Italy **56** A4
Varberg Sweden **45** K4
Varbla Estonia **42** E3
Varda Greece **59** C10
Vardak *prov.* Afgh. **101** G3
Vardannapet India **94** C2
Vardar *r.* Macedonia **58** D7
Varde Denmark **45** J5
Vardenis Armenia **107** F2
formerly known as Basargechar
Vårdö Fin. **42** B1
Vardø Norway **44** O1
Varduva *r.* Lith. **42** D5
Varegovo Rus. Fed. **43** U4
Varel Germany **48** F2
Varela Arg. **204** D4
Varėna Lith. **42** F7
Vareš Bos.-Herz. **56** K4
Varese Italy **56** A3
Varfolomeyevka Rus. Fed. **82** D3
Vårgårda Sweden **45** K4
Vargas Arg. **204** C4
Vargem *r.* Brazil **202** E4
Vargem Alta Brazil **207** L7
Vargem Grande Brazil **202** D2
Vargem Grande do Sul Brazil **206** G8
Varginha Brazil **203** C7
Varhaug Norway **45** I4
Varkana Iran *see* **Gorgān**
Varkaus Fin. **44** N3
Varkhi Belarus **43** K6
Varmahlíð Iceland **44** [inset] C2
Varmeln *l.* Sweden **45** K4
Värmland *county* Sweden **45** K4
Värmlandsnäs *i.* Sweden **45** K4
Varna Bulg. **58** I5
formerly known as Stalin; *historically known as* Odessus
Varna *r.* India **94** B2
Varna Rus. Fed. **103** E1
Värnamo Sweden **45** K4
Värnäs Sweden **45** K3
Varnavino Rus. Fed. **40** H4
Varnek Rus. Fed. **40** L1
Varniai Lith. **42** D6
Varnja Estonia **42** I3
Várnjárg *pen.* Norway *see* **Varangerhalvøya**
Varnyany Belarus **42** H7
Varosha Cyprus *see* **Varosia**
Varosia Cyprus **108** E2
also known as Maraş; *also spelt* Varosha
Varoška Rijeka Bos.-Herz. **56** I3
Varpaisjärvi Fin. **44** N3
Várpalota Hungary **49** P8
Värriön luonnonpuisto *nature res.* Fin. **44** O2
Vârşag Romania **58** G2
Varsaj Afgh. **101** G2
Vârşand Romania **58** C2
Varsh, Ozero *l.* Rus. Fed. **40** H2
Varsinais-Suomi *reg.* Fin. **45** M3
also known as Egentliga Finland
Värska Estonia **42** I4
Vartashen Azer. *see* **Oğuz**
Vartdalsfjorden *inlet* Norway **44** I3
Vartholomio Greece **59** C11
Varto Turkey **107** E3
also known as Gümgüm
Vârtop Romania **58** E4
Vârtop, Pasul *pass* Romania **58** D2
Värtsilä Fin. **44** O3
Var'yegan Rus. Fed. **38** H3
Varzaneh Iran **100** C3
Várzea Alegre Brazil **202** E3
Várzea da Palma Brazil **203** C6
Várzea Grande Brazil **202** D3
Varzelândia Brazil **207** I2
Varzo Italy **56** A2
Varzob Tajik. **101** G2
Varzuga Rus. Fed. **40** F2
Vasa Fin. *see* **Vaasa**
Vasa Barris *r.* Brazil **202** E4
Vasai India **94** B2
Vasalemma Estonia **42** F2
Vasalemma *r.* Estonia **42** F2
Vásárosnamény Hungary **49** T7
Vascão *r.* Port. **54** D7
Vaşcău Romania **58** D2
Vashka *r.* Rus. Fed. **40** H2
Vasht Iran *see* **Khāsh**
Vasilika Greece **58** E8
Vasilkov Ukr. *see* **Vasyl'kiv**
Vasilyevichy Belarus **43** K9
Vasil'yevo Rus. Fed. **42** I4
Vasil'yevskiy Mokh Rus. Fed. **43** Q4
Vas'kavichy Belarus **43** L8
Vaskivesi Fin. **45** M3
Vasknarva Estonia **42** I2
Vaslui Romania **58** I2
Vassar U.S.A. **173** J7
Vassenden Norway **45** I3
Vassfaret og Vidalen *park* Norway **45** J3
Vas-Soproni-síkság *hills* Hungary **49** N8
Vassouras Brazil **207** J9
Vastan Turkey *see* **Gevaş**
Västana Sweden **44** L3
Västanfjärd Fin. **42** D1
Västansjö Sweden **44** L2
Vastemõisa Estonia **42** G3
Vastenjaure *l.* Sweden **44** L2
Västerås Sweden **45** L4
Västerbotten *county* Sweden **44** K2
Västerdalälven *r.* Sweden **45** K3
Västerhaninge Sweden **45** L4
Västernorrland *county* Sweden **44** L3
Västervik Sweden **45** L4
Västmanland *county* Sweden **45** K4
Vasto Italy **56** G6
Västra Götaland *county* Sweden **45** K4
Västra Ormsjö Sweden **44** L2
Vastse-Kuuste Estonia **42** H3
Vasvár Hungary **49** N8
Vasyl'kiv Ukr. **41** D6
also spelt Vasilkov
Vatan France **50** H5
Väte Sweden **45** L4
Vaté *i.* Vanuatu *see* **Éfaté**
Vatersay *i.* U.K. **46** E7
Vathi Greece *see* **Ithaki**
Vathí Greece *see* **Vathy**
Vathia Greece **59** D12
Vathy *Notio Aigaio* Greece **59** H12
Vathy *Voreio Aigaio* Greece **59** H11
also spelt Vathí
▶**Vatican City** Europe **56** E7
Independent papal state, the smallest country in the world. English form Holy See; known as Città del Vaticano in Italian
world [countries] ▶ 10–11
europe [countries] ▶ 32–35
Vaticano, Capo *c.* Italy **57** H10
Vaticano, Città del Europe *see* **Vatican City**
Vatio Greece **59** I12
Vatnajökull *ice cap* Iceland **44** [inset] C2
Vatne Norway **44** I3
Vatoa *i.* Fiji **145** H3
also known as Turtle Island
Vatomandry Madag. **131** [inset] K3
Vatoussa Greece **59** H9
Vatra Dornei Romania **58** G1
Vätter, Lake Sweden *see* **Vättern**
Vättern *l.* Sweden **45** K4
English form Vätter, Lake
Vattrång Sweden **45** L3
Vatulele *i.* Fiji **145** G3
Vaucluse, Monts de *mts* France **51** L9
Vaucouleurs France **51** L4
Vaughan Springs Australia **148** A4
Vaughn U.S.A. **181** F6
Vaulx-en-Velin France **51** K7
Vaupés *dept* Col. **198** D4
Vaupés *r.* Col. **198** D4
Vauquelin *r.* Canada **168** E2
Vauvert France **51** K9
Vauxhall Canada **167** H5
Vav India **96** A4
Vavatenina Madag. **131** [inset] K3
Vava'u *i.* Tonga **145** H3
Vava'u Group *is* Tonga **145** H3
Vavitao *i.* Fr. Polynesia *see* **Raivavae**
Vavoua Côte d'Ivoire **124** D5
Vavozh Rus. Fed. **40** I4
Vavuniya Sri Lanka **94** D4
Vawkalata Belarus **42** I7
Vawkavichy Belarus **43** L8
also known as Volkovichi
Vawkavysk Belarus **42** F8
also known as Volkovysk
Vawkavyskaye Wzvyshsha *hills* Belarus **42** F8
also known as Volkovyskiye Vysoty
Växjö Sweden **45** K4
Vây, Đao *i.* Vietnam **79** C6
Vayalpad India **94** C3
Vayenga Rus. Fed. *see* **Severomorsk**
Vaygach, Ostrov *i.* Rus. Fed. **40** K1
Vayittiri India **94** C4
Vayk' Armenia **107** F3
formerly known as Azizbekov *or* Soylan
Vazante Brazil **206** G4
Vazáš Sweden *see* **Vittangi**
Vazobe *mt.* Madag. **131** [inset] J3
Vazuza *r.* Rus. Fed. **43** P6
Vazuzskoye Vodokhranilishche *resr* Rus. Fed. **43** P6
Veaikevárri Sweden *see* **Svappavaara**
Vecht *r.* Neth. **48** D3
also known as Vechte (Germany)
Vechta Germany **48** F3
Vechte *r.* Germany **48** D3
also known as Vecht (Neth.)
Vecmikeļi Latvia **42** E5
Vecumnieki Latvia **42** F5
Vedana Rus. Fed. *see* **Vedeno**
Vedaranniyam India **94** C4
Vedasandur India **94** C4
Veddige Sweden **45** K4
Vedea Romania **58** F4
Vedea Romania **58** G5
Vedea *r.* Romania **58** G5
Vedeno Rus. Fed. **107** F2
also known as Vedana
Vedi Armenia **107** F3
Vedia Arg. **204** E4
Vedlozero Rus. Fed. **40** E3
Vedrych *r.* Belarus **43** L9
Veendam Neth. **48** D2
Veenendaal Neth. **48** C3
Vega *i.* Norway **44** J2
Vega U.S.A. **179** B5
Vegadeo Spain **54** D1
Vegarshei Norway **45** J4
Vegoritis, Limni *l.* Greece **58** C8
Vegreville Canada **167** H4
Vegueta Peru **200** A2
Vehkalahti Fin. **42** I1
Vehmaa Fin. **45** M3
Vehoa *r.* Pak. **101** G4
Veidnes Norway **44** N1
Veinticinco de Mayo Arg. *see* **25 de Mayo**
Veinticinco de Mayo Arg. *see* **25 de Mayo**
Veinticinco de Mayo Arg. *see* **25 de Mayo**
Veiros Brazil **199** H5
Veisiejis Lith. **42** E7
Veitsiluoto Fin. **44** N2
Vejer de la Frontera Spain **54** F8
Vejle Denmark **45** J5
Velachha India **96** B5
Vela Luka Croatia **56** I6
Velardena Mex. **184** E3
Vèlas, Cabo *c.* Costa Rica **186** B5
Velasco, Sierra de *mts* Arg. **204** D3
Vela Vrata, Kanal *sea chan.* Croatia **56** G3
Velázquez Uruguay **204** G4
Velbŭzhdki Prokhod *pass* Macedonia **58** D6
also known as Deve Bair
Velddrif S. Africa **132** C9
Velden am Wörther See Austria **49** L9
Veldhoven Neth. **48** C4
Veldurti India **94** C3
Velebit *mts* Croatia **56** G4
Velebitski Kanal *sea chan.* Croatia **56** G3
Veleka *r.* Bulg. **58** I6
Velen Germany **48** D4
Velenje Slovenia **56** H2
formerly known as Titovo Velenje
Veles Macedonia **58** C7
formerly known as Titov Veles
Velës, Mali i *mt.* Albania **58** A7
Velež *mts* Bos.-Herz. **56** J5
Vélez Col. **198** C3
Vélez-Málaga Spain **54** G8
Vélez-Rubio Spain **55** I7
Velhas *r. Minas Gerais* Brazil **203** C6
Velhas *r. Minas Gerais* Brazil **206** F6
Velia *tourist site* Italy **57** H8
Velibaba Turkey *see* **Aras**
Velichayevskoye Rus. Fed. **41** H7
Velika Drenova *Srbija* Yugo. **58** C5
Velika Gorica Croatia **56** I3
Velika Kapela *mts* Croatia **56** G3
Velika Kladuša Bos.-Herz. **56** H3
Velika Mlaka Croatia **56** I3
Velika Morava *canal* Yugo. **58** C4
Velika Plana *Srbija* Yugo. **58** C4
Velikaya Rus. Fed. **40** I4
Velikaya *r.* Rus. Fed. **39** R3
Velikaya *r.* Rus. Fed. **40** I4
Velikaya *r.* Rus. Fed. **43** J4
Velikaya Guba Rus. Fed. **40** E3
Velikaya Kema Rus. Fed. **82** E3
Veliki Drvenik *i.* Croatia **56** I5
Veliki Jastrebac *mts* Yugo. **58** C5
Veliki Preslav Bulg. **58** H5
formerly known as Preslav
Veliki Risnjak *mt.* Croatia **56** G3
Veliki Šiljegovac *Srbija* Yugo. **58** C5
Veliki Šturac *mt.* Yugo. **58** B4
Velikiye Luki Rus. Fed. **43** L5
Velikiy Novgorod Rus. Fed. **43** M3
formerly known as Novgorod; *historically known as* Holmgard
Velikiy Ustyug Rus. Fed. **40** H3
Velikonda Range *hills* India **94** C3
Velikooktyabr'skiy Rus. Fed. **43** O4
Veliko Tŭrnovo Bulg. **58** G5
formerly known as Tŭrnovo
Velikoye *Vologod. Obl.* Rus. Fed. **43** R2
Velikoye *Yaroslavskaya Oblast'* Rus. Fed. **43** U4
Velikoye, Ozero *l.* Rus. Fed. **43** R4
Velikoye, Ozero *l.* Rus. Fed. **43** V6
Vélingara Senegal **124** B3
Vélingara Senegal **124** B3
Velingrad Bulg. **58** F6
Velino *r.* Italy **56** E6
Velino, Monte *mt.* Italy **56** F6
Veliuona Lith. **42** E6
Velizh Rus. Fed. **43** M6
Velká Bíteš Czech Rep. **49** N6
Veľká Domaša, Vodná nádrž *resr* Slovakia **49** S6
Veľká Fatra *mts* Slovakia **49** P7
Velká Javořina *hill* Czech Rep./Slovakia **49** O7
Veľké Kapušany Slovakia **49** T7
Velké Meziříčí Czech Rep. **49** N6
Velkua Fin. **42** C1
Veľký Krtíš Slovakia **49** Q7
Veľký Meder Slovakia **49** O8
formerly known as Čalovo
Vella Lavella *i.* Solomon Is **145** E2
Vellar *r.* India **94** C4
Velletri Italy **56** E7
Vellinge Sweden **45** K5
Vellore India **94** C3
Vel'mo *r.* Rus. Fed. **39** J3
Velopoula *i.* Greece **59** E12
Vel'sk Rus. Fed. **40** G3
Velsuna Italy *see* **Orvieto**
Vel't Rus. Fed. **40** I1
Velten Germany **49** K3
Veluwezoom, Nationaal Park *nat. park* Neth. **48** C3
Velvendos Greece **59** D8
Vel'ye, Ozero *l.* Rus. Fed. **43** N4
Velyka Mykhaylivka Ukr. **58** K1
Velykodolyns'ke Ukr. **58** L2
Velykyy Tokmak Ukr. *see* **Tokmak**
Vel'yu *r.* Rus. Fed. **40** J3
Vemalwada India **94** C2
Vembanad Lake India **94** C4
Vemor'ye Rus. Fed. **82** F3
Vempalle India **94** C3
Venado Tuerto Arg. **204** E4
Venafro Italy **56** G7
Venamo *r.* Guyana/Venez. **199** F3
Venamo, Cerro *mt.* Venez. **199** F3
Venarey-les-Laumes France **51** K5
Venaria Italy **51** N7
Vencedor Brazil **199** F6
Venceslau Bráz Brazil **206** D10
Venčiūnai Lith. **42** F7
Venda Nova Brazil **207** L7
Vendenheim France **51** N4
Vendeuvre-sur-Barse France **51** K4
Vendinga Rus. Fed. **40** H3
Vendôme France **50** H5
Vendrell Spain *see* **El Vendrell**
Venecia Col. **198** C4
Venegas Mex. **185** E4
Veneta, Laguna *lag.* Italy **56** E3
Venetia Italy *see* **Venice**
Veneto *admin. reg.* Italy **56** D3
Venev Rus. Fed. **43** T7
Venezia Italy *see* **Venice**
Venezia, Golfo di *g.* Europe *see* **Venice, Gulf of**
▶**Venezuela** *country* S. America **199** E3
5th most populous country in South America.
southamerica [countries] ▶ 192–193
Venezuela, Golfo de *g.* Venez. **198** D2
Vengurla India **94** B3
Veniaminof Volcano U.S.A. **164** D4
Venice Italy **56** E3
also known as Venezia; *historically known as* Venetia
Venice *FL* U.S.A. **175** D7
Venice *LA* U.S.A. **179** E6
Venice, Gulf of Europe **56** E3
also known as Venezia, Golfo di
Vénissieux France **51** K7
Venjan Sweden **45** K3
Venkatagiri India **94** C3
Venkatapuram India **94** D2
Venlo Neth. **48** D4
Vennesla Norway **45** I4
Venosa Italy **56** H8
historically known as Venusia
Venosta, Val *valley* Italy **56** C2
Venray Neth. **48** C4
Venta *r.* Latvia/Lith. **42** D5
Venta Lith. **42** D5
Venta de Baños Spain **54** G3
Ventania Brazil **206** C11
Ventersburg S. Africa **133** K5
Ventersdorp S. Africa **133** K3
Venterstad S. Africa **133** J7
Ventimiglia Italy **51** N9
Ventisquero *mt.* Arg. **205** C6
Ventnor U.K. **47** K13
Ventotene, Isola *i.* Italy **57** F8
Ventoux, Mont *mt.* France **51** L8
Ventspils Latvia **42** C4
historically known as Windau
Ventuari *r.* Venez. **199** E3
Ventura U.S.A. **182** E7
Venus Bay Australia **147** E4
Venusia Italy *see* **Venosa**
Venustiano Carranza, Presa *resr* Mex. **185** E3
Venzone Italy **56** F2
Vepsovskaya Vozvyshennost' *hills* Rus. Fed. **43** P1
Vera Arg. **204** E3
Vera Spain **55** J7
Verá, Lago *l.* Para. **201** F6
Vera Cruz *Amazonas* Brazil **200** D2
Vera Cruz *São Paulo* Brazil **206** D9
Vera Cruz Mex. *see* **Veracruz**
Veracruz Mex. **185** F5
also spelt Vera Cruz
Veracruz *state* Mex. **185** F4
Vera de Bidasoa Spain **55** J1
Veranópolis Brazil **203** B9
Veraval India **94** A1
Verbania Italy **56** A3
Verbilki Rus. Fed. **43** S5
Verbovskiy Rus. Fed. **40** G5
Vercelli Italy **56** A3
Vercors *reg.* France **51** L8
Vercors, Parc Naturel Régional du *nature res.* France **51** L8
Vercovicium *tourist site* U.K. *see* **Housesteads**
Verda *r.* Rus. Fed. **43** V8
Verdalsøra Norway **44** J3
Verde *r.* Arg. **205** D6
Verde *r. Bahia* Brazil **202** D4
Verde *r. Goiás* Brazil **206** C5
Verde *r. Goiás/Minas Gerais* Brazil **206** F5
Verde *r. Mato Grosso* Brazil **201** G2
Verde *r. Mato Grosso do Sul* Brazil **206** B8
Verde *r. Minas Gerais* Brazil **206** C6
Verde *r. Minas Gerais* Brazil **206** D6
Verde *r. Minas Gerais* Brazil **207** H8
Verde *r.* Brazil **206** E2
Verde *r.* Mex. **184** D3
Verde *r.* Para. **201** F5
Verde *r.* U.S.A. **183** M8
Verde, Cabo *c.* Senegal *see* **Vert, Cap**
Verde, Península *pen.* Arg. **204** E5
Verde Grande *r.* Brazil **202** D5
Verde Island Passage Phil. **74** B3
Verden (Aller) Germany **48** G3
Verde Pequeno *r.* Brazil **202** D5
Verdi U.S.A. **182** E2
Verdigris *r.* U.S.A. **178** D5
Verdikoussa Greece **59** C9
Verdinho *r.* Brazil **206** C4
Verdinho, Serra do *mts* Brazil **206** B5
Verdon *r.* France **51** L9
Verdun France **51** L3
Verdun-sur-Garonne France **50** H9
Vereeniging S. Africa **133** L3
Verena S. Africa **133** N2
Vereshchagino Rus. Fed. **40** J4
Verestovo, Ozero *l.* Rus. Fed. **43** R4
Vereya Rus. Fed. **43** R6
Verfeil France **50** H9
Verga, Cap *c.* Guinea **124** B4
Vergara Uruguay **204** G4
Vergeleë S. Africa **133** I2
Vergennes U.S.A. **177** L1
Vergina Greece **58** D8
also spelt Veryina
Véria Greece *see* **Veroia**
Verigino Rus. Fed. **43** T5
Verín Spain **54** D3
Veriora Estonia **42** I3
Veríssimo Brazil **206** E6
Veríssimo Sarmento Angola *see* **Camissombo**
Verkeerdevlei S. Africa **133** K5
Verkhne-Avzyan Rus. Fed. **102** D1
Verkhne-berezovskiy Kazakh. **88** C1
Verkhnedneprovsk Ukr. *see* **Verkhn'odniprovs'k**
Verkhnedneprovskiy Rus. Fed. **43** O7
Verkhneimbatsk Rus. Fed. **39** I3
Verkhnekolvinsk Rus. Fed. **40** K2
Verkhneruzskoye Vodokhranilishche *resr* Rus. Fed. **43** Q6
Verkhnespasskoye Rus. Fed. **40** H4
Verkhnetulomskiy Rus. Fed. **44** O1
Verkhnetulomskoye Vodokhranilishche *resr* Rus. Fed. **44** O1
Verkhneural'sk Rus. Fed. **102** D1
Verkhnevilyuysk Rus. Fed. **39** M3
Verkhnevolzhskoye Vodokhranilishche *resr* Rus. Fed. **43** N4
Verkhneyarkeyevo Rus. Fed. **40** J5
Verkhneye Kuyto, Ozero *l.* Rus. Fed. **44** O2
Verkhnezeysk Rus. Fed. **82** C1
Verkhniy At-Uryakh Rus. Fed. **39** P3
Verkhniy Baskunchak Rus. Fed. **102** A2
Verkhniye Koshevichi Rus. Fed. **43** M6
Verkhniye Mokhovichi Rus. Fed. **43** M6
Verkhniy Lomovets Rus. Fed. **43** T9
Verkhniy Mamon Rus. Fed. **41** G6
Verkhniy Shergol'dzhin Rus. Fed. **85** F1
Verkhniy Tatyshly Rus. Fed. **40** J4
Verkhniy Vyalozerskiy Rus. Fed. **40** E2
Verkhn'odniprovs'k Ukr. **41** E6
also spelt Verkhnedneprovsk
Verkhnyaya Inta Rus. Fed. **40** L2
Verkhnyaya Pakhachi Rus. Fed. **39** Q3
Verkhnyaya Taymyra *r.* Rus. Fed. **39** J2
Verkhnyaya Toyma Rus. Fed. **40** H3
Verkhnyaya Troitsa Rus. Fed. **43** S4
Verkhnyaya Tunguska *r.* Rus. Fed. *see* **Angara**
Verkhnyaya Yelovka Kazakh. **88** D1
Verkhoshizhem'ye Rus. Fed. **40** I4
Verkhovazh'ye Rus. Fed. **40** G3
Verkhov'ye Rus. Fed. **43** S9
Verkhoyanskiy Khrebet *mts* Rus. Fed. **39** M2
Verkhuba Kazakh. **88** C1
Verkné *r.* Lith. **42** F7
Verkola Rus. Fed. **40** H3
Verkykerskop S. Africa **133** N4
Verlatekloof *pass* S. Africa **132** E9
Verma Norway **44** J3
Vermaaklikheid S. Africa **132** F11
Vermelha, Serra *hills* Brazil **206** C10
Vermelho *r. Mato Grosso* Brazil **206** B1
Vermelho *r. Pará* Brazil **202** B3
Vermelho *r. Tocantins* Brazil **202** C3
Vermenton France **51** J5
Vermeş Romania **58** C3
Vermilion Canada **167** I4
Vermilion *r.* U.S.A. **174** B3
Vermilion Bay U.S.A. **179** E6
Vermilion Cliffs *esc. AZ* U.S.A. **183** L5
Vermilion Cliffs *esc. UT* U.S.A. **183** L4
Vermilion Lake U.S.A. **174** A2
Vermilion Range *hills* U.S.A. **172** A3
Vermillion U.S.A. **178** C3
Vermillion *r.* U.S.A. **178** C3
Vermillion Bay Canada **168** A3
Vermillon *r.* Canada **174** F2
Vermont *state* U.S.A. **177** M1
Vernadskiy *research station* Antarctica **222** T2
long form Academician Vernadskiy
Vernal U.S.A. **183** O1
Verner Canada **168** D4
Verneuil-sur-Avre France **50** G4
Verneuk Pan *salt pan* S. Africa **132** F6
Vernier Switz. **51** M6
Vernio Italy **56** D4
Vernon Canada **166** G5
Vernon France **50** H3
Vernon *AL* U.S.A. **175** B5
Vernon *TX* U.S.A. **179** C5
Vernon, Mount *hill* Australia **150** B5
Vernon Islands Australia **148** A2
Vernoye Rus. Fed. **82** C2
Vernyy Kazakh. *see* **Almaty**
Vero Beach U.S.A. **175** D7
Veroia Greece **58** D8
also spelt Véria; *historically known as* Beroea
Verona Italy **56** C3
Verona *VA* U.S.A. **176** F7
Verona *WI* U.S.A. **172** D8
Verres Italy **51** N7
Versailles France **51** I4
Versailles *IN* U.S.A. **174** C4
Versailles *KY* U.S.A. **176** A7
Versailles *MO* U.S.A. **178** D4
Versailles *OH* U.S.A. **176** A5
Versalles Bol. **201** E3
Versec *Vojvodina, Srbija* Yugo. *see* **Vršac**
Verseka *r.* Lith. **42** F7
Versmold Germany **48** F3
Versoix Switz. **51** M6
Vert, Cap *c.* Senegal **124** A3
also known as Verde, Cabo
Vert, Île *i.* Canada **169** G3
Vertentes *r.* Brazil **202** B4
Vertesi *park* Hungary **49** P8
Vertientes Cuba **186** D2
Vertou France **50** E5
Vertus France **51** K4
Verulam S. Africa **133** P6
Verulamium U.K. *see* **St Albans**
Verviers Belgium **51** L2
Vervins France **51** J3
Verwoerdburg S. Africa *see* **Centurion**
Verwood Canada **167** J5
Veryina Greece *see* **Vergina**
Vesanto Fin. **44** N3
Vescovato *Corse* France **51** P10
Vesele Ukr. **41** E7
Veselevo Rus. Fed. **43** R6
Veselina *r.* Bulg. **58** G5
Veselí nad Lužnicí Czech Rep. **49** L6
Veselí nad Moravou Czech Rep. **49** O7
Veselovskoye Vodokhranilishche *resr* Rus. Fed. **41** G7
Veseloyarsk Rus. Fed. **88** C1
Veselyy Rus. Fed. **41** G7
Veselyy Podol Kazakh. **103** F1
Veshenskaya Rus. Fed. **41** G6
Vesijärvi *l.* Fin. **45** N3
Vesle *r.* France **51** J3
Veslyana *r.* Rus. Fed. **40** J3
Vesontio France *see* **Besançon**
Vesoul France **51** M5
Vesselyy Yar Rus. Fed. **90** D3
Vest-Agder *county* Norway **45** I4
Vesterålen *is* Norway **44** K1
Vesterålsfjorden *sea chan.* Norway **44** K1
Vestfirðir *constituency* Iceland **44** [inset] B2
Vestfjorddalen *valley* Norway **45** J4
Vestfjorden *sea chan.* Norway **44** K2
Vestfold *county* Norway **45** J4
Vestfold Hills Antarctica **223** F2
Vestmanna Faroe Is **46** E1
Vestmannaeyjar *is* Iceland **44** [inset] B3
English form Westman Islands
Vestnes Norway **44** I3
Vestre Jakobselv Norway **44** O1
Veststraumen Glacier Antarctica **223** X2
Vesturland *constituency* Iceland **44** [inset] B2
Vestvågøy *i.* Norway **44** K1
Vesuvio *vol.* Italy *see* **Vesuvius**
Vesuvio, Parco Nazionale del *nat. park* Italy **57** G8
Vesuvius *vol.* Italy **57** G8
also spelt Vesuvio
Ves'yegonsk Rus. Fed. **43** S3
Veszprém Hungary **49** O8
Vésztő Hungary **49** S9
Vet *r.* S. Africa **133** J4
Vetauua *i.* Fiji **145** H3
Veteli Fin. **44** M3
Veteran Canada **167** I4
Veternik *Vojvodina, Srbija* Yugo. **58** A3
Vetlanda Sweden **45** K4
Vetlefjorden Norway **45** I3
Vetluga Rus. Fed. **40** H4
Vetluga *r.* Rus. Fed. **40** H4
Vetluzhskiy *Kostromskaya Oblast'* Rus. Fed. **38** E4
formerly known as Golyshi
Vetluzhskiy *Nizhegorodskaya Oblast'* Rus. Fed. **40** H4
Vet'ma *r.* Rus. Fed. **43** O8
Vetovo Bulg. **58** H5
Vetralla Italy **56** E6
Vetren Bulg. **58** I6
formerly known as Zhitarovo
Vetrişoaia Romania **58** J2
Vetsikko Fin. **44** N1
Vettasjärvi Sweden **44** M2
Vettore, Monte *mt.* Italy **56** F6
Veurne Belgium **51** I1
also known as Furnes
Vevay U.S.A. **174** C4
Veveno *r.* Sudan **128** B3
Vevey Switz. **51** M6
Veydelevka Rus. Fed. **41** F6
Veyle *r.* France **51** K6
Veynes France **51** L8
Veyo U.S.A. **183** K4
Veys Iran **100** B4
Vėžaičiai Lith. **42** C6
Vézère *r.* France **50** G8
Vezhen *mt.* Bulg. **58** F6
Vezirköprü Turkey **106** C2
Via *r.* Liberia **124** C5
Viacha Bol. **200** C4
Viadana Italy **56** C4
Vialar Alg. *see* **Tissemsilt**
Viamao Brazil **203** B9
Viamonte Arg. **205** D9
Viana Angola **127** B7
Viana *Espírito Santo* Brazil **207** M7
Viana *Maranhão* Brazil **202** C2
Viana del Bollo Spain *see* **Viana do Bolo**
Viana do Alentejo Port. **54** D6
Viana do Bolo Spain **54** D2
also spelt Viana del Bollo
Viana do Castelo Port. **54** C3
Viana do Castelo *admin. dist.* Port. **54** C3
Vianden Lux. **51** M3
Viangchan Laos *see* **Vientiane**
Viangphoukha Laos **78** C3
Viaño Pequeno Spain **54** C1
Vianópolis Brazil **206** E3
Viar *r.* Spain **54** F7
Viareggio Italy **56** C5
Viaur *r.* France **51** H8
Viborg Denmark **45** J4
Viborg Rus. Fed. *see* **Vyborg**
Vibo Valentia Italy **57** I10
historically known as Hipponium
Vic Spain **55** N3
also spelt Vich
Vicam Mex. **184** C3
Vicdessos *r.* France **50** H10
Vicecomodoro Marambio *research station* Antarctica *see* **Marambio**
Vic-en-Bigorre France **50** G9
Vicente, Point U.S.A. **182** F8
Vicente Guerrero Mex. **184** A2
Vicenza Italy **56** D3
Vic-Fezensac France **50** G9
Vich Spain *see* **Vic**
Vichada *dept* Col. **198** D3
Vichada *r.* Col. **198** E3
Vichadero Uruguay **204** G3
Vichuga Rus. Fed. **40** G4
Vichy France **51** J6
Vicksburg *AZ* U.S.A. **183** K8
Vicksburg *MI* U.S.A. **172** H8
Vicksburg *MS* U.S.A. **175** B5
Vic-le-Comte France **51** J7
Vico, Lago di *l.* Italy **56** E6
Viçosa *Alagoas* Brazil **202** E4
Viçosa *Minas Gerais* Brazil **203** D7
Vic-sur-Cère France **51** I8
Victor, Mount Antarctica **223** C2
Victor Harbor Australia **146** C3
Victoria Arg. **204** E4
Victoria *r.* Australia **148** A2
Victoria *state* Australia **147** E4
Victoria Cameroon *see* **Limbe**
▶**Victoria** Canada **166** F5
Provincial capital of British Columbia.
Victoria *La Araucania* Chile **204** B5
Victoria *Magallanes* Chile **205** C9
Victoria Hond. **186** B4
Victoria Malaysia *see* **Labuan**
Victoria Malta **57** G12
also known as Rabat
Victoria Phil. **74** B3
Victoria Romania **58** I4
Victoria Romania **58** F3
▶**Victoria** Seychelles **218** K6
Capital of the Seychelles.
Victoria *TX* U.S.A. **179** C6
Victoria *VA* U.S.A. **176** G9
Victoria, Isla *i.* Chile **205** B7
▶**Victoria, Lake** Africa **128** B5
Largest lake in Africa and 3rd in the world.
africa [landscapes] ▶ 112–113
Victoria, Lake Australia **146** D3
Victoria, Mount Myanmar **78** A3
Victoria, Mount N.Z. **153** G10
Victoria, Mount P.N.G. **73** K8
Victoria and Albert Mountains Canada **165** L2
▶**Victoria Falls** *waterfall* Zambia/Zimbabwe **127** E9
africa [locations] ▶ 118–119
Victoria Falls Zimbabwe **131** E3
Victoria Falls National Park Zimbabwe **131** E3
also known as Mosi-oa-Tunya National Park
Victoria Fjord *inlet* Greenland **165** O1
Victoria Forest Park *nature res.* N.Z. **153** G9
Victoria Harbour *sea chan. Hong Kong* China *see* **Hong Kong Harbour**
▶**Victoria Island** Canada **165** H2
3rd largest island in North America and 9th in the world.
northamerica [landscapes] ▶ 156–157
Victoria Lake Canada **169** J3
Victoria Land *coastal area* Antarctica **223** K2
Victoria Peak *hill Hong Kong* China **87** [inset]
also known as Shan Teng
Victoria Range *mts* N.Z. **153** G10
Victoria River Australia **148** A2
Victoria River Downs Australia **148** A3
Victoria Valley N.Z. **152** H3
Victoriaville Canada **169** G4
Victoria West S. Africa **132** H8
Victorica Arg. **204** D5
Victorino Venez. **199** E4
Victor Rosales Mex. **185** E4
Victorville U.S.A. **183** G7
Victory U.S.A. **177** I2
Victory Downs Australia **148** B5
Vicuña Chile **204** C3
Vicuña Mackenna Arg. **204** D4
Vidal, Isla *i.* Chile **205** B8
Vidalia U.S.A. **175** B6
Vidal Junction U.S.A. **183** J7
Vidamlya Belarus **42** E9
Videle Romania **58** G4
Viden *mt.* Bulg. **58** D6
Vidigueira Port. **54** D6
Vidima *r.* Bulg. **58** G6
Vidin Bulg. **58** D5
Vidisha India **96** C5
Vidlitsa Rus. Fed. **40** E3
Vidnoye Rus. Fed. **43** S6
formerly known as Rastorguyevo
Vidourle *r.* France **51** K9
Vidova Gora *hill* Croatia **56** I5
Vidsel Sweden **44** M2
Vidukle Lith. **42** D6
Viduša *mts* Bos.-Herz. **56** K6
Vidzemes Centrālā Augstiene *hills* Latvia **42** G5
Vidzy Belarus **42** H6
Viechtach Germany **49** J6
Viedgesville S. Africa **133** M8
Viedma Arg. **204** E6
▶**Viedma, Lago** *l.* Arg. **205** B8
southamerica [landscapes] ▶ 190–191
Viehberg *mt.* Austria **49** L7
Viejo, Cerro *mt.* Mex. **184** B2
Viekšniai Lith. **42** D5
Vielha Spain **55** L2
also spelt Viella
Viella Spain *see* **Vielha**
Vielsalm Belgium **51** L2
Vienenburg Germany **48** H4
▶**Vienna** Austria **49** N7
Capital of Austria. Also known as Wien; historically known as Vindobona.
Vienna *GA* U.S.A. **175** D5
Vienna *IL* U.S.A. **174** B4
Vienna *MD* U.S.A. **177** J7
Vienna *MO* U.S.A. **174** B4
Vienna *WV* U.S.A. **176** D6
Vienne France **51** K7
Vienne *r.* France **50** G5
▶**Vientiane** Laos **78** C4
Capital of Laos. Also spelt Viangchan.
Vieques *i.* Puerto Rico **187** G3
Vieremä Fin. **44** N3
Viersen Germany **48** D4
Vierwaldstätter See *l.* Switz. **51** O5
Vierzon France **51** I5
Viesca Mex. **185** E3
Viesīte Latvia **42** G5
Vieste Italy **56** I7
Viešvilės rezervatas *nature res.* Lith. **42** D6
Vietas Sweden **44** L2
▶**Vietnam** *country* Asia **78** D4
also spelt Viet Nam
asia [countries] ▶ 64–67
Viet Nam *country* Asia *see* **Vietnam**
Việt Tri Vietnam **78** D3
Vieux Comptoir, Lac du *l.* Canada **168** E2
Vieux-Fort Canada **169** J3
Vieux Fort St Lucia **187** H4
Vieux Poste, Pointe du *pt* Canada **169** I3
Vievis Lith. **42** F7
Vigala *r.* Estonia **42** F3
Vigan Phil. **74** B2
Vigeois France **50** H7
Vigevano Italy **56** A3
Vigia Brazil **202** B2
Vigia *hill* Port. **54** C7
Vigía Chico Mex. **185** I5
Viglio, Monte *mt.* Italy **56** F7
Vignemale *mt.* France **50** F10
Vignola Italy **56** D4
Vigny France **51** H3
Vigo Spain **54** C2
Vigo, Ría de *est.* Spain **54** C2
Vigors, Mount Australia **150** B4
Vihanti Fin. **44** N2
Vihari Pak. **101** H4
Vihiers France **50** F5
Vihorlat *mt.* Slovakia **49** T7
Vihterpalu *r.* Estonia **42** E2
Vihti Fin. **45** N3
Viiala Fin. **45** M3
Viipuri Rus. Fed. *see* **Vyborg**

Viirinkylä Fin. 44 N2
Viitasaari Fin. 44 N3
Viitka Estonia 42 I4
Vijainagar India 96 B3
Vijapur India 96 B5
Vijayadurg India 94 B2
Vijayanagar India see Hampi
Vijayapati India 94 C4
Vijayawada India 94 D2
also known as Bezwada
Vík Iceland 44 [inset] C3
Vik Norway 44 K2
Vikajärvi Fin. 44 N2
Vikarabad India 94 C2
Vikedal Norway 45 I4
Vikeke East Timor 75 C5
also known as Viqueque
Vikersund Norway 45 J4
Vikhra r. Rus. Fed. 43 M7
Vikhren mt. Bulg. 58 E7
Viking Canada 167 I4
Vikna i. Norway 44 J2
Vikos-Aoos nat. park Greece 59 B9
Vikøyri Norway 45 I3
Vikran Norway 44 L1
Viktorovka Kazakh. see Taranovskoye
Vila Spain 54 C3
Vila Vanuatu see Port Vila
Vila Alferes Chamusca Moz. see Guija
Vila Arriaga Angola see Bibala
Vila Bittencourt Brazil 198 D5
Vila Braga Brazil 199 G6
Vila Bugaço Angola see Camanongue
Vila Cabral Moz. see Lichinga
Vila Caldas Xavier Moz. see Muende
Vilacaya Bol. 200 D4
Vila Coutinho Moz. see Ulongue
Vila da Ponte Angola see Kuvango
Vila da Ribeira Brava Cape Verde 124 [inset]
Vila de Aljustrel Angola see Cangamba
Vila de Almoster Angola see Chiange
Vila de João Belo Moz. see Xai-Xai
Vila de Junqueiro Moz. see Gurué
Vila de Sal Rei Cape Verde 124 [inset]
Vila de Sena Moz. 131 G3
Vila de Trego Morais Moz. see Chókwé
Vila do Conde Port. 54 C3
Vila do Tarrafal Cape Verde 124 [inset]
Vila Flor Port. 54 D3
Vila Fontes Moz. see Caia
Vilafranca del Penedès Spain 55 M3
also spelt Vilafranca del Penedès
Vila Franca de Xira Port. 54 C6
Vilagarcía de Arousa Spain 54 C2
also spelt Villagarcía de Arosa
Vila Gomes da Costa Moz. 131 G5
Vila Gouveia Moz. see Catandica
Vilaine r. France 50 D5
Vilaka Latvia 42 I4
Vilalba Spain 54 D1
Vila Luísa Moz. see Marracuene
Vila Marechal Carmona Angola see Uíge
Vila Miranda Moz. see Macaloge
Vila Murtinho Brazil 200 D2
Vilanandro, Tanjona pt Madag. 131 [inset] J3
formerly known as St-André, Cap
Vilanculos Moz. 131 G4
Viļāni Latvia 42 H5
Vila Nova Angola see Tchikala-Tcholohanga
Vila Nova da Fronteira Moz. 131 G3
Vilanova de Arousa Spain 54 C2
also spelt Villanueva de Arosa
Vila Nova de Foz Coa Port. 54 D3
Vila Nova de Gaia Port. 54 C3
Vila Nova de Ourém Port. 54 C5
Vila Nova de Paiva Port. 54 D4
Vila Nova de Seles Angola see Uku
Vilanova i la Geltrú Spain 55 M3
also spelt Villanueva-y-Geltrú
Vila Nova Sintra Cape Verde 124 [inset]
Vila Paiva de Andrada Moz. see Gorongosa
Vila Pery Moz. see Chimoio
Vila Pouca de Aguiar Port. 54 D3
Vila Real Port. 54 D3
Vila Real admin. dist. Port. 54 D3
Vila-real de los Infantes Spain 55 K5
also spelt Villareal de los Infantes; formerly known as Villareal
Vilar Formoso Port. 54 E4
Vila Salazar Angola see N'dalatando
Vila Salazar Zimbabwe see Sango
Vila Teixeira de Sousa Angola see Luau
Vilavankod India 94 C4
Vila Velha Amapá Brazil 199 I4
Vila Velha Espírito Santo Brazil 203 D7
formerly known as Espírito Santo
Vila Velha de Ródão Port. 54 D5
Vila Verde Port. 54 C3
Vilcabamba, Cordillera mts Peru 200 B3
Vilcanota, Cordillera de mts Peru 200 C3
Vil'cheka, Zemlya i. Rus. Fed. 38 G1
English form Wilczek Land
Viled' r. Rus. Fed. 40 H3
Vileyka Belarus see Vilyeyka
Vil'gort Permskaya Oblast' Rus. Fed. 40 K3
Vil'gort Respublika Komi Rus. Fed. 40 I3
Vilhelmina Sweden 44 L2
Vilhena Brazil 201 E3
Viliya r. Belarus/Lith. 42 G7
Viljandi Estonia 42 G3
Viljoenskroon S. Africa 133 K4
Vilkaviškis Lith. 42 F7
Vilkija Lith. 42 E6
Vil'kitskogo, Ostrov i. Rus. Fed. 39 H2
Vil'kitskogo, Proliv strait Rus. Fed. 39 J2
Villa Abecia Bol. 200 D5
Villa Adriana tourist site Italy 56 E7
Villa Ahumada Mex. 184 D2
Villa Alba Arg. 204 E5
Villa Altagracia Dom. Rep. 187 F3
Villa Ana Arg. 204 F3
Villa Angela Arg. 204 E2
Villa Bella Bol. 200 D2
Villa Bens Morocco see Tarfaya
Villablino Spain 54 E2
Villacañas Spain 55 H5
Villacarrillo Spain 55 H6
Villach Austria 49 K9
also known as Beljak
Villacidro Sardegna Italy 57 A9
Villa Cisneros W. Sahara see Ad Dakhla
Villa Constitución Arg. 204 E4
Villa Constitución Mex. see Ciudad Constitución
Villa de Álvarez Mex. 184 E5
Villa de Cos Mex. 185 E4
Villa de Cura Venez. 199 E2
Villa de Guadalupe Mex. 185 H5
Villa del Rosario Arg. 204 E3
Villa del Totoral Arg. 204 D3
Villa Diego Arg. 204 E4
Villadiego Spain 54 G2
Villa Dolores Arg. 204 D3
Villadossola Italy 56 A2
Villa Flores Mex. 185 G5
Villafranca Spain 55 J2
Villafranca del Bierzo Spain 54 E2
Villafranca del Cid Spain 55 K4
Villafranca de los Barros Spain 54 E6
Villafranca del Penedès Spain see Vilafranca del Penedès
Villafranca di Verona Italy 56 C3
Villagarcía de Arosa Spain see Vilagarcía de Arousa
Villa Gesell Arg. 204 F5
Villagrán Mex. 185 F3
Villaguay Arg. 204 F3
Villa Guillermina Arg. 204 F3
Villa Hayes Para. 201 F6
Villahermosa Mex. 185 G5
Villa Hidalgo Mex. 181 E7
Villa Huidobro Arg. 204 D4
Villaines-la-Juhel France 50 F4
Villa Insurgentes Mex. 184 C3
Villa Iris Arg. 204 E5
Villajoyosa Spain 55 K6
Villa Juárez Mex. 181 E8
Villaldama Mex. 185 E3
Villalonga Arg. 204 E5
Villa María Arg. 204 E4
Villa María Grande Arg. 204 F3
Villa Martín Bol. 200 D5
Villamartín Spain 54 F8
Villa Matoque Arg. 204 E2
Villa Montes Bol. 201 E5
Villanova Monteleone Sardegna Italy 57 A8
Villa Nueva Arg. 204 E4
Villanueva Col. 198 C2
Villanueva Mex. 185 E4
Villanueva de Arosa Spain see Vilanova de Arousa
Villanueva de Córdoba Spain 54 G6
Villanueva de la Serena Spain 54 F6
Villanueva de los Castillejos Spain 54 D7
Villanueva de los Infantes Spain 55 I6
formerly known as Infantes
Villanueva-y-Geltrú Spain see Vilanova i la Geltrú
Villa Ocampo Arg. 204 F3
Villa Ocampo Mex. 184 D3
Villa Ojo de Agua Arg. 204 E3
Villa O. Pereyra Mex. see Villa Orestes Pereyra
Villa Orestes Pereyra Mex. 184 D3
short form Villa O. Pereyra
Villa Oropeza Bol. 200 D4
Villa Pesqueira Mex. 181 E7
Villaputzu Sardegna Italy 57 B9
Villar del Rey Spain 54 E5
Villareal Spain see Vila-real de los Infantes
Villareal de los Infantes Spain see Vila-real de los Infantes
Villa Regina Arg. 204 D5
Villarrica Chile 204 B5
Villarrica Para. 201 F6
Villarrica, Lago l. Chile 204 B5
Villarrica, Parque Nacional nat. park Chile 204 C5
Villarrobledo Spain 55 I5
Villarrubia de los Ojos Spain 55 H5
Villas U.S.A. 177 K6
Villasalazar Zimbabwe see Sango
Villasana de Mena Spain 55 H1
Villa San Giovanni Italy 57 H10
Villa Sanjurjo Morocco see Al Hoceima
Villa San Martín Arg. 204 D3
Villasboas Uruguay 204 F4
Villa Serrano Bol. 201 D4
Villasimius Sardegna Italy 57 B9
Villa Unión Arg. 204 C3
Villa Unión Coahuila Mex. 185 E2
Villa Unión Durango Mex. 184 D4
Villa Unión Sinaloa Mex. 184 D4
Villa Valeria Arg. 204 D4
Villa Vásquez Dom. Rep. 187 F3
Villavicencio Col. 198 C3
Villaviciosa Spain 54 F1
Villaviciosa de Córdoba Spain 54 F6
Villa Viscarra Bol. 200 D4
Villazon Bol. 200 D5
Villedieu-les-Poêles France 50 E4
Villefranche-de-Lauragais France 50 H9
Villefranche-de-Rouergue France 51 I8
Villefranche-sur-Saône France 51 K7
Ville-Marie Canada see Montréal
Ville-Marie Canada 173 N3
Villemontel Canada 173 O2
Villemur-sur-Tarn France 50 H9
Villena Spain 55 K6
Villenauxe-la-Grande France 51 J4
Villeneuve-de-Marsan France 50 F9
Villeneuve-sur-Lot France 50 G8
Villeneuve-sur-Yonne France 51 J4
Ville Platte U.S.A. 179 D6
Villers-Bocage France 50 F3
Villers-Cotterêts France 51 J3
Villeta Para. 201 F6
Villeurbanne France 51 K7
Villicun, Sierra mts Arg. 204 C3
Villiers S. Africa 133 M4
Villingen Germany 48 F7
Villupuram India see Viluppuram
Vilna Canada 167 I4
Vilna Lith. see Vilnius

Vilnius Lith. 42 G7
Capital of Lithuania. Formerly known as Wilno; historically known as Vilna.

Vil'nyans'k Ukr. 41 E7
also spelt Vol'nyansk; formerly known as Chervonoarmeyskoye or Sofiyevka
Vilppula Fin. 45 N3
Vils r. Germany 48 I6
Vils r. Germany 49 K7
Vilsandi i. Estonia 42 C3
Vilsandi nature res. Estonia 42 C3
Vilsbiburg Germany 49 J7
Vilshofen Germany 49 K7
Viluppuram India 94 C4
also spelt Villupuram
Vilvoorde Belgium 51 K2
Vilyeyka Belarus 42 H7
also spelt Vileyka
Vilyeyskaye, Vozyera l. Belarus 42 I7
Vilyuy r. Rus. Fed. 39 M3
Vilyuyskoye Vodokhranilishche resr Rus. Fed. 39 L3
Vimbe mt. Zambia 127 F8
Vimercate Italy 56 B3
Vimianzo Spain 54 B1
Vimioso Port. 54 E3
Vimmerby Sweden 45 K4
Vimoutiers France 50 G4
Vimpeli Fin. 44 M3
Vimperk Czech Rep. 49 K6
Vina r. Cameroon 125 I5
also spelt Wina
Vina U.S.A. 182 B2
Viña del Mar Chile 204 C4
Vinalhaven U.S.A. 177 Q1
Vinalopó r. Spain 55 K6
Vinanivao Madag. 131 [inset] K2
Vinaròs Spain 55 L4
also spelt Vinaroz
Vinaroz Spain see Vinaròs
Vincelotte, Lac l. Canada 169 F2
Vincennes U.S.A. 174 C4
Vincennes Bay Antarctica 223 H2
Vinces r. Ecuador 198 B5
Vinchina Arg. 204 C3
Vinchos Peru 200 B3
Vindelälven r. Sweden 44 L3
Vindelfjällens naturreservat nature res. Sweden 44 K2
Vindeln Sweden 44 L2
Vindhya Range hills India 96 B5
Vindobona Austria see Vienna
Vineland U.S.A. 177 J6
Vinga Romania 58 C2
Vingăi, Câmpia plain Romania 58 C2
Vingåker Sweden 45 K4
Vinh Vietnam 78 D4
Vinhais Port. 54 E3
Vinh Long Vietnam 79 D6
Vinh Thuc, Đao i. Vietnam 78 D3
Vinh Yên Vietnam 78 D3
Vinica Macedonia 58 D7
Vinita U.S.A. 178 D4
Vinjhan India 96 A5
Vînju Mare Romania see Vânju Mare
Vinkovci Croatia 56 K3
Vinland i. Canada see Newfoundland
Vinni Estonia 42 H2
Vinnitsa Ukr. see Vinnytsya
Vinnitsy Rus. Fed. 43 P1
Vinnytsya Ukr. 41 D6
also spelt Vinnitsa
Vinogradovo Rus. Fed. 43 T6

Vinson Massif mt. Antarctica 222 S1
Highest mountain in Antarctica.
antarctica [features] 212–213

Vinstra Norway 45 J3
Vintar Phil. 74 B2
Vinton U.S.A. 174 A3
Vinukonda India 94 C2
Vinza Congo 126 B5
Viola CA U.S.A. 182 C1
Viola IL U.S.A. 172 C9
Violeta Cuba see Primero de Enero
Violet Valley Aboriginal Reserve Australia 150 D3
Vioolsdrif S. Africa 132 B5
Viphya Mountains Malawi 129 B8
Vipiteno Italy 56 D2
Viqueque East Timor see Vikeke
Vir i. Croatia 56 H4
Virac Phil. 74 C3
Virac Point Phil. 74 C3
Viramgam India 96 B5
Viranşehir Turkey 107 D3
Virarajendrapet India 94 B3
Virawah Pak. 101 G5
Virawlya Belarus 43 K6
Vircava r. Latvia/Lith. 42 E5
Virchow, Mount hill Australia 150 B4
Virdáánjarga Fin. see Virtaniemi
Virden Canada 167 K5
Vire France 50 F4
Virei Angola 127 B8
Virful Highiş hill Romania 58 C2
Virgenes, Cabo c. Arg. 205 C9
Virgilina U.S.A. 176 G9
Virgin r. U.S.A. 183 J5
Virginatown Canada 173 N2
Virgin Gorda i. Virgin Is (U.K.) 187 G3
Virginia S. Africa 133 K5
Virginia U.S.A. 174 A2
Virginia state U.S.A. 176 G8
Virginia Beach U.S.A. 177 J9
Virginia City MT U.S.A. 180 E3
Virginia City NV U.S.A. 182 E2
Virginia Falls Canada 166 E2

Virgin Islands (U.K.) terr. West Indies 187 G3
United Kingdom Overseas Territory.
oceania [countries] 138–139

Virgin Islands (U.S.A.) terr. West Indies 187 G3
United States Unincorporated Territory.
oceania [countries] 138–139

Virgin Mountains U.S.A. 183 J5
Virginópolis Brazil 203 D6
Virje Croatia 56 J2
Virkkala Fin. 45 N3
Virmasvesi l. Fin. 44 N3
Virôchey Cambodia 79 D5
Virolahti Fin. 45 N3
Viroqua U.S.A. 172 C7
Virovitica Croatia 56 J3
Virpe Latvia 42 D4
Virrat Fin. 44 M3
Virserum Sweden 45 K4
Virtaniemi Fin. 44 O1
also known as Virdáánjarga
Virton Belgium 51 L3
Virtsu Estonia 42 E3
Virú Peru 200 A2
Virudunagar India 94 C4
Virunga, Parc National des nat. park Dem. Rep. Congo 126 F5
formerly known as Albert, Parc National
Virvytė r. Lith. 42 D5
Vis Croatia 56 I5
also known as Issa or Lissa
Vis i. Croatia 56 I5
Visaginas Lith. 42 H6
formerly known as Sniečkus
Visakhapatnam India see Vishakhapatnam
Visalia U.S.A. 182 E5
Vişani Romania 58 I3
Visapur India 94 B2
Visavadar India 96 A5
Visayan Sea Phil. 74 B4
Visby Sweden 45 L4
Visconde do Rio Branco Brazil 207 K8
Viscount Melville Sound sea chan. Canada 165 H2
Visé, Ostrov i. Rus. Fed. 39 H2
Višegrad Bos.-Herz. 56 L5
Viseu Brazil 202 C2
Viseu Port. 54 D4
Viseu admin. dist. Port. 54 D4
Vishakhapatnam India 95 D2
also spelt Visakhapatnam; formerly spelt Vizagapatam
Vishegrad hill Bulg. 58 H7
Vishera r. Rus. Fed. 40 J3
Vishera r. Rus. Fed. 40 K4
Vishera r. Rus. Fed. 43 M3
Vishnevka Kazakh. 103 H2
Vishnyeva Belarus 42 H7
Visikums Latvia 42 I4
Vişina Romania 58 G4
Višķi Latvia 42 H5
Viški Kanal sea chan. Croatia 56 I5
Visnagar India 96 B5
Viso, Monte mt. Italy 51 N8
Viso del Marqués Spain 55 H6
Visoko Bos.-Herz. 56 K5
Visp Switz. 51 N6
Visrivier S. Africa 133 J8
Vissannapeta India 94 D2
Vista U.S.A. 183 G8
Vista Alegre Amazonas Brazil 199 D4
Vista Alegre Amazonas Brazil 199 D6
Vista Alegre Amazonas Brazil 199 F6
Vista Alegre Mato Grosso do Sul Brazil 201 F4
Vista Alegre Roraima Brazil 199 F4
Vista Lake U.S.A. 182 E6
Vistonida, Limni lag. Greece 58 G7
Vistula r. Poland 49 P1
also spelt Wisła
Vištytis Lith. 42 D7
Vit r. Bulg. 58 F5
Vita r. Col. 198 D3
Vitao mt. Yugo. 56 K5
Vitebsk Belarus see Vitsyebsk
Vitebskaya Oblast' admin. div. Belarus see Vitsyebskaya Voblasts'
Vitebsk Oblast admin. div. Belarus see Vitsyebskaya Voblasts'
Viterbo Italy 56 E6
Vitez Bos.-Herz. 56 J4
Vitez pass Bos.-Herz. 56 K5
Vitigudino Spain 54 E3
Viti Levu i. Fiji 145 G3
Vitim r. Rus. Fed. 81 I1
Vitimskoye Ploskogor'ye plat. Rus. Fed. 81 I2
Vitina Kosovo, Srbija Yugo. 58 C6
Vitomirica Kosovo, Srbija Yugo. 58 B6
Vitor Peru 200 C4
Vitor r. Peru 200 C4
Vitória Espírito Santo Brazil 203 D7
Vitória Pará Brazil 199 H5
Vitoria Spain see Vitoria-Gasteiz
Vitória da Conquista Brazil 202 D5
Vitoria-Gasteiz Spain 55 I2
also known as Gasteiz or Vitoria
Vitosha nat. park Bulg. 58 E6
Vitré France 50 E4
Vitrolles France 51 L9
Vitry-en-Artois France 51 I2
Vitry-le-François France 51 K4
Vitsyebsk Belarus 43 L6
English form Vitebsk
Vitsyebskaya Voblasts' admin. div. Belarus 43 J6
English form Vitebsk Oblast; also known as Vitebskaya Oblast'
Vittangi Sweden 44 M2
Vitteaux France 51 K5
Vittel France 51 L4
Vittoria Sicilia Italy 57 G12
Vittorio Veneto Italy 56 E3
Vivarais, Monts du mts France 51 K8
Viveiro Spain 54 D1
also spelt Vivero
Vivero Spain see Viveiro
Vivian U.S.A. 179 D5
Vivo S. Africa 131 F4
Vivorata Arg. 204 F5
Vivorillo, Cayos is Hond. 186 C4
Vizagapatam India see Vishakhapatnam
Vizcaíno Mex. 181 D8
Vizcaíno, Desierto de des. Mex. 184 B3
Vizcaíno, Sierra mts Mex. 184 B3
Vize Turkey 106 A2
Vizhas r. Rus. Fed. 40 H2
Vizianagaram India 95 D2
Vizinga Rus. Fed. 40 I3
Viziru Romania 58 I3
Vizzini Sicilia Italy 57 G11
V. J. José Perez Bol. 200 C3
Vjosë r. Albania 59 A8
Vlaardingen Neth. 48 B4
Vlădeasa, Vârful mt. Romania 58 D2
Vladičin Han Srbija Yugo. 58 D6
Vladikavkaz Rus. Fed. 41 H8
also known as Dzaudzhikau; formerly known as Ordzhonikidze
Vladimir Rus. Fed. 90 D3
Vladimir Rus. Fed. 43 V5
historically known as Lodomeria
Vladimiro-Aleksandrovskoye Rus. Fed. 82 D4
Vladimir Oblast admin. div. Rus. Fed. see Vladimirskaya Oblast'
Vladimirovka Kazakh. 103 F1
formerly known as Vladimirovskiy
Vladimirovo Bulg. 58 E5
Vladimirovskiy Kazakh. see Vladimirovka
Vladimirskaya Oblast' admin. div. Rus. Fed. 43 V6
English form Vladimir Oblast
Vladimirskiy Tupik Rus. Fed. 43 O6
Vladimir-Volynskiy Ukr. see Volodymyr-Volyns'kyy
Vladivostok Rus. Fed. 82 C4
Vladychnoye Rus. Fed. 43 U3
Vlahiţa Romania 58 G2
Vlajna mt. Yugo. 58 C6
Vlasenica Bos.-Herz. 56 K4
Vlašić Planina mts Yugo. 58 A4
Vlašim Czech Rep. 49 L6
Vlasotince Srbija Yugo. 58 D6
Vlasovo Rus. Fed. 43 U6
Vlas'yevo Rus. Fed. 82 F1
Vlazovichi Rus. Fed. 43 N8
Vleesbaai b. S. Africa 132 F11
Vlieland i. Neth. 48 B2
Vlissingen Neth. 48 A4
historically known as Flushing
Vlorë Albania 58 A8
also known as Aulon or Valona; historically known as Avlona
Vlorës, Gjiri i b. Albania 58 A8
Vlotslavsk Poland see Włocławek
Vltava r. Czech Rep. 49 L5
Vnina r. Rus. Fed. 43 R2
Vöcklabruck Austria 49 K7
Vodice Croatia 56 H5
Vodlozero, Ozero l. Rus. Fed. 40 F3
Vodňany Czech Rep. 49 L6
Vodnjan Croatia 56 F4
Vodopyanovo Rus. Fed. see Donskoye
Voël r. S. Africa 133 J10
Vogan Togo 125 F5
Vogelkop Peninsula Indon. see Doberai, Jazirah
Vogelsberg hills Germany 48 F5
Voghera Italy 56 B4
Vognill Norway 44 J3
Vogošća Bos.-Herz. 56 K5
Vohburg an der Donau Germany 48 I7
Vohémar Madag. see Iharaña
Vohibinany Madag. see Ampasimanolotra
Vohilava Fianarantsoa Madag. 131 [inset] J4
Vohilava Fianarantsoa Madag. 131 [inset] K4
Vohimarina Madag. see Iharaña
Vohimena, Tanjona c. Madag. 131 [inset] J5
formerly known as Ste-Marie, Cap
Vohipeno Madag. 131 [inset] J4
Võhma Estonia 42 G3
Voi Kenya 128 C5
Voikoski Fin. 45 N3
Voineasa Romania 58 E3
Voinești Romania 58 I1
Voinjama Liberia 124 C4
Voin Pervyy Rus. Fed. 43 R8
Voiron France 51 L7
Voitsberg Austria 49 M8
Vojvodina prov. Yugo. 58 A3
Voka Estonia 42 I2
Vokhma Rus. Fed. 40 H4
Vokhtoga Rus. Fed. 43 V3
Voknavolok Rus. Fed. 44 O2
Voko Cameroon 125 I4
Vol' r. Rus. Fed. 40 J3
Volaterrae Italy see Volterra
Volcán Arg. 200 D5
Volcán, Cerro vol. Bol. 200 D5
Volcán Barú, Parque Nacional nat. park Panama 186 C5
Volcano Bay Japan see Uchiura-wan

Volcano Islands N. Pacific Ocean 220 D4
Part of Japan. Also known as Kazan-rettō.

Volcans d'Auvergne, Parc Naturel Régional des nature res. France 51 I7
Volchas r. Belarus 43 M8
Volchikha Rus. Fed. 103 J1
Volchina r. Rus. Fed. 43 Q4
Volchiy Nos, Mys pt Rus. Fed. 43 N1
Volda Norway 44 I3
Vol'dino Rus. Fed. 40 J3
Volens U.S.A. 176 F9
Volga Rus. Fed. 43 T4

Volga r. Rus. Fed. 43 Q5
Longest river in Europe.
europe [landscapes] 30–31

Volga r. U.S.A. 172 B8
Volga Upland hills Rus. Fed. see Privolzhskaya Vozvyshennost'
Volgodonsk Rus. Fed. 41 G7
Volgograd Rus. Fed. 41 H6
formerly known as Stalingrad; historically known as Tsaritsyn
Volgograd Oblast admin. div. Rus. Fed. see Volgogradskaya Oblast'
Volgogradskaya Oblast' admin. div. Rus. Fed. 41 H6
English form Volgograd Oblast; formerly known as Stalingradskaya Oblast'
Volgogradskoye Vodokhranilishche resr Rus. Fed. 41 H6
Volissos Greece 59 G10
Völkermarkt Austria 49 L9
Volkhov Rus. Fed. 43 N2
Volkhov r. Rus. Fed. 43 N1
Volkhovskaya Guba b. Rus. Fed. 43 N1
Volkhovskiy Rus. Fed. 43 M3
Völklingen Germany 48 D6
Volkovichi Belarus see Vawkavichy
Volkovo Rus. Fed. 43 L7
Volkovysk Belarus see Vawkavysk
Volkovyskiye Vysoty hills Belarus see Vawkavyskaye Wzvyshsha
Volksrust S. Africa 133 N4
Vol'no-Nadezhdinskoye Rus. Fed. 82 C4
Volnovakha Ukr. 41 F7
Vol'nyansk Ukr. see Vil'nyans'k
Volochanka Rus. Fed. 39 J2
Volochayevka-Vtoraya Rus. Fed. 82 D2
Volochisk Ukr. see Volochys'k
Volochys'k Ukr. 41 C6
also spelt Volochisk
Volodars'ke Ukr. 41 F7
Volodarskiy Rus. Fed. 102 B3
Volodarskoye Kazakh. see Saumalkol'
Volodymyr-Volyns'kyy Ukr. 41 C6
also spelt Vladimir-Volynskiy
Vologda Rus. Fed. 43 U2
Vologda r. Rus. Fed. 43 U2
Vologda Oblast admin. div. Rus. Fed. see Vologodskaya Oblast'
Vologodskaya Oblast' admin. div. Rus. Fed. 43 T1
English form Vologda Oblast
Volokolamsk Rus. Fed. 43 Q5
Volokonovka Rus. Fed. 41 F6
Volokoslavinskoye Rus. Fed. 43 T2
Volop S. Africa 132 G5
Volos Greece 59 D9
Voloshka Rus. Fed. 40 G3
Volosovo Rus. Fed. 43 K2
Volot Rus. Fed. 43 L4
Volovo Lipetskaya Oblast' Rus. Fed. 43 S9
Volovo Tul'skaya Oblast' Rus. Fed. 43 T8
Voloye Rus. Fed. 43 P7
Volozhin Belarus see Valozhyn
Volsini, Monti mts Italy 56 D6
Volsinii Italy see Orvieto
Vol'sk Rus. Fed. 102 A1
Volstruisleegte S. Africa 132 H10
Volstruispoort pass S. Africa 132 G7
Volta admin. reg. Ghana 125 F5
Volta r. Ghana 125 F5
Volta Blanche watercourse Burkina/Ghana see White Volta

Volta, Lake resr Ghana 125 F5
5th largest lake in Africa.
africa [landscapes] 112–113

Voltaire, Cape Australia 150 D2
Volta Noire r. Africa see Black Volta
Volta Redonda Brazil 203 C7
Volterra Italy 56 C5
historically known as Volaterrae
Voltoya r. Spain 54 G3
Volturino, Monte mt. Italy 57 H8
Volturno r. Italy 56 F7
Volubilis tourist site Morocco 122 D2
Voluntari Romania 58 H4
Volunteer Point Falkland Is 205 F8
Volvi, Limni l. Greece 58 E8
Vol'ya r. Rus. Fed. 40 L3
Volzhsk Rus. Fed. 40 I5
Volzhskiy Samarskaya Oblast' Rus. Fed. 41 I5
formerly known as Bol'shaya Tsarevshchina
Volzhskiy Volgogradskaya Oblast' Rus. Fed. 41 H6
Vomano r. Italy 56 G6
Vondanka Rus. Fed. 40 H4
Vondrozo Madag. 131 [inset] J4
Vonga Rus. Fed. 40 G2
Vonitsa Greece 59 B10
Võnnu Estonia 42 I3
Vonozero Rus. Fed. 43 P1
Vontimitta India 94 C3
Voorheesville U.S.A. 177 L3
Voosi kurk sea chan. Estonia 42 E2
Vop' r. Rus. Fed. 43 N7
Vopnafjörður Iceland 44 [inset] D2
Vopnafjörður b. Iceland 44 [inset] D2
Vörå Fin. 44 M3
also spelt Vöyri
Voran' Belarus 43 J6
Voranava Belarus 42 G7
Vordingborg Denmark 45 J5
Vordorf Germany 48 H3
Vorë Albania 58 A7
Voreio Aigaio admin. reg. Greece 59 G9
English form Northern Aegean
Voreioi Sporades is Greece 59 E9
English form Northern Sporades; also spelt Vórioi Sporádhes
Voreios Evvoïkos Kolpos sea chan. Greece 59 E10
Vorga Rus. Fed. 43 N8
Vorgashor Rus. Fed. 40 M2
Vórioi Sporádhes is Greece see Voreioi Sporades
Vorjing mt. India 97 G3
Vorkuta Rus. Fed. 40 M2
Vormsi i. Estonia 42 E2
Vorob'yevka Lipetskaya Oblast' Rus. Fed. 43 U9
Vorob'yevka Voronezhskaya Oblast' Rus. Fed. 41 G6
Vorob"yivka Ukr. 43 O9
Vorogovo Rus. Fed. 39 I3
Vorona r. Rus. Fed. 41 G6
Voronezh Rus. Fed. 41 F6
Voronezh r. Rus. Fed. 43 U9
Voronezh Oblast admin. div. Rus. Fed. see Voronezhskaya Oblast'
Voronezhskaya Oblast' admin. div. Rus. Fed. 41 G6
English form Voronezh Oblast
Voronov, Mys pt Rus. Fed. 40 G2
Voronov, Mys pt Rus. Fed. 43 N1
Voronovo Rus. Fed. 43 S6
Vorontsovka Kazakh. 103 J2
Vorontsovo Rus. Fed. 43 J4
Vorontsovo-Aleksandrovskoye Rus. Fed. see Zelenokumsk
Voron'ye Rus. Fed. 40 G4
Voroshilov Rus. Fed. see Ussuriysk
Voroshilovgrad Ukr. see Luhans'k
Voroshilovsk Rus. Fed. see Stavropol'
Voroshilovsk Ukr. see Alchevs'k
Vorot'kovo Rus. Fed. 43 O6
Vorotynets Rus. Fed. 40 H4
Vorotynsk Rus. Fed. 43 R7
Vorozhba Ukr. 41 E6
Vorpommersche Boddenlandschaft, Nationalpark nat. park Germany 49 J1
Vorposten Peak Antarctica 223 B2
Vorskla r. Rus. Fed. 41 E6
Vorstershoop S. Africa 132 H2
Vørterkaka Nunatak mt. Antarctica 223 B2
Võrtsjärv l. Estonia 42 G3
Võru Estonia 42 I4
Voruh Tajik. 101 G2
Vorya r. Rus. Fed. 43 P7
Vosburg S. Africa 132 G7
Vose Tajik. 101 G2
formerly known as Aral
Vosges mts France 51 M5
Vosges du Nord, Parc Naturel Régional des nature res. France 51 N4
Voshchazhnikovo Rus. Fed. 43 U4
Voskresensk Rus. Fed. 43 T6
Voskresenskoye Lipetskaya Oblast' Rus. Fed. 43 T8
Voskresenskoye Respublika Bashkortostan Rus. Fed. 102 D1
Voskresenskoye Tul'skaya Oblast' Rus. Fed. 43 S7
Voskresenskoye Vologod. Obl. Rus. Fed. 43 S2
Voskresenskoye Yaroslavskaya Oblast' Rus. Fed. 43 S4
Voss Norway 45 I3
Vostochnaya Litsa Rus. Fed. 40 F1
Vostochno-Kazakhstanskaya Oblast' admin. div. Kazakh. see Vostochnyy Kazakhstan
Vostochno-Kounradskiy Kazakh. see Shygys Konyrat
Vostochno-Sakhalinskiy Gory mts Rus. Fed. 82 F2
Vostochno-Sibirskoye More sea Rus. Fed. see East Siberian Sea
Vostochnyy Rus. Fed. 40 J4
Vostochnyy Chink Ustyurta esc. Uzbek. 102 D4
Vostochnyy Kazakhstan admin. div. Kazakh. 103 I2
English form East Kazakhstan Oblast; also known as Shyghys Qazaqstan Oblysy; long form Vostochno-Kazakhstanskaya Oblast'
Vostochnyy Sayan mts Rus. Fed. 80 E2
English form Eastern Sayan Mountains

Vostok research station Antarctica
Lowest recorded screen temperature in the world.
world [climate and weather] 16–17

Vostok Rus. Fed. 82 D3
Vostok Rus. Fed. see Neftegorsk
Vostok Island Kiribati 221 H6
Vostretsovo Rus. Fed. 82 D3
Vostroye Rus. Fed. 40 H3
Võsu Estonia 42 G2
Votkinsk Rus. Fed. 40 J4
Votkinskoye Vodokhranilishche resr Rus. Fed. 40 J4
Votorantim Brazil 206 F10
Votrya r. Rus. Fed. 43 N6
Votuporanga Brazil 206 D7
Voudi, Akra pt Greece 59 J12
Vouga Angola see Cunhinga
Vouga r. Port. 54 C4
Vouillé France 50 G6
Voula Greece 59 E11
Vourinos mt. Greece 59 C8
Vouziers France 51 K3
Voves France 50 H4
Vovodo r. Cent. Afr. Rep. 126 E3
Voxna Sweden 45 K3
Voxnan r. Sweden 45 L3
Voya r. Rus. Fed. 40 I4
Voyageurs National Park U.S.A. 174 A1
Voykar r. Rus. Fed. 40 M2
Voynitsa Rus. Fed. 44 O2
Vöyri Fin. see Vörå
Voyvozh Respublika Komi Rus. Fed. 40 J2
Voyvozh Respublika Komi Rus. Fed. 40 J3
Vozdvizhenskoye Moskovskaya Oblast' Rus. Fed. 43 R5
Vozdvizhenskoye Moskovskaya Oblast' Rus. Fed. 43 T5
Vozha r. Rus. Fed. 43 U7
Vozhayel' Rus. Fed. 40 I3
Vozhd' Proletariata Rus. Fed. 43 U6
Vozhe, Ozero l. Rus. Fed. 43 T1
Vozhega Rus. Fed. 43 V1
Vozhega r. Rus. Fed. 43 U1
Vozhgora Rus. Fed. 40 I2
Voznesenka Kazakh. 103 G1
Voznesens'k Ukr. 41 D7
Voznesen'ye Rus. Fed. 43 Q1
Vozrovdenye Uzbek. 102 D3
Vozrozhdeniya, Ostrov i. Uzbek. 102 D3
also known as Wozrojdeniye Oroli
Vozzhayevka Rus. Fed. 82 C2
Vrå Denmark 45 J4
Vrabevo Bulg. 58 F5
Vrachionas hill Greece 59 B11
also known as Vrakhiónas Óros
Vrachnaiika Greece 59 C10
also spelt Vrakhnaiika
Vrådal Norway 45 J4
Vrakhiónas Óros hill Greece see Vrachionas
Vrakhnaiika Greece see Vrachnaiika
Vran mt. Bos.-Herz. 56 J5
Vrana r. Bulg. 58 H5
Vrangel' Rus. Fed. 82 D4
Vrangelya, Mys pt Rus. Fed. 82 E1
Vrangelya, Ostrov i. Rus. Fed. see Wrangel Island
Vranjak Bos.-Herz. 56 K4
Vranje Srbija Yugo. 58 C6
Vranjska Banja Srbija Yugo. 58 D6
Vranov, Vodní nádrž resr Czech Rep. 49 M7
Vranov nad Topľou Slovakia 49 S7
Vrapčište Macedonia 58 B7
Vrasidas, Akra pt Greece 58 F8
Vratnik pass Bulg. 58 H6
Vratsa Bulg. 58 E5
Vrbanja r. Bos.-Herz. 56 J4
Vrbas r. Bos.-Herz. 56 J4
Vrbas Vojvodina, Srbija Yugo. 58 A3
formerly known as Titov Vrbas
Vrbno pod Pradědem Czech Rep. 49 O5
Vrbovec Croatia 56 I3
Vrbovsko Croatia 56 H3
Vrchlabí Czech Rep. 49 M5
Vrede S. Africa 133 N4
Vredefort S. Africa 133 L3
Vredenburg S. Africa 132 B9
Vredendal S. Africa 132 C8
Vredeshoop Namibia 132 D4
Vreed-en-Hoop Guyana 199 G3
Vrela Kosovo, Srbija Yugo. 58 B6
Vrhnika Slovenia 56 G3
Vriddhachalam India 94 C4
Vrigstad Sweden 45 K4
Vrindavan India 89 B7
Vrnjačka Banja Srbija Yugo. 58 B5
Vrolijkheid Nature Reserve S. Africa 132 D10
Vrrin Albania 58 A7
Vršac Vojvodina, Srbija Yugo. 58 C3
also known as Versec
Vryburg S. Africa 133 I3
Vryheid S. Africa 133 O4
Vsetín Czech Rep. 49 O6
Vsevolozhsk Rus. Fed. 43 L1
Vskhody Rus. Fed. 43 P7
Vtáčnik mt. Slovakia 49 P7
Vtáčnik mts Slovakia 49 P7
Vŭcha r. Bulg. 58 F7
Vučica r. Croatia 56 K3
Vučitrn Kosovo, Srbija Yugo. 58 B6
Vučje Srbija Yugo. 58 C6
Vuka r. Croatia 56 L3
Vukovar Croatia 56 L3
Vuktyl' Rus. Fed. 40 K3
Vukuzakhe S. Africa 133 N4
Vulcan Canada 167 H5
Vulcan Romania 58 E3
Vulcănești Moldova 58 J3
formerly spelt Vulkaneshty
Vulcan Island P.N.G. see Manam Island
Vulcano, Isola i. Isole Lipari Italy 57 G10
Vŭlchedrŭm Bulg. 58 E5
Vŭlchidol Bulg. 58 I5
Vulkaneshty Moldova see Vulcănești
Vulture Mountains U.S.A. 183 K8
Vung Dung Quat b. Vietnam 79 E5

index

V
W

Vung Tau Vietnam 79 D6
  formerly known as St Jacques, Cap
Vuohijärvi Fin. 42 H1
Vuohijärvi r. Fin. 45 N3
Vuokatti Fin. 44 O2
Vuoksa r. Rus. Fed. 43 L1
Vuolijoki Fin. 44 N2
Vuolvojaure r. Sweden 44 L2
Vuostimo Fin. 44 N2
Vuotso Fin. 44 N2
Vūrbitsa Bulg. 58 H6
Vurpăr Romania 58 F3
Vürshets Bulg. 58 E5
Vustye Belarus 42 I6
Vutcani Romania 58 I2
Vuyyuru India 94 D2
Vuzlove Ukr. 49 T7
Vvedenka Kazakh. 103 E1
Vwaza Game Reserve nature res. Malawi 129 B7
Vyalikiya Bortniki Belarus 43 K8
Vyal'ye, Ozero I. Rus. Fed. 43 L2
Vyara India 96 B5
Vyarechcha Belarus 43 L6
Vyarkhovichy Belarus 42 E9
Vyarkhowye Belarus see Ruba
Vyatchyn Belarus 42 J9
Vyatka Rus. Fed. see Kirov
Vyatka r. Rus. Fed. 40 I5
Vyatskiye Polyany Rus. Fed. 40 I4
Vyatskoye Rus. Fed. 43 V4
Vyaz Rus. Fed. 43 K5
Vyazemskiy Rus. Fed. 82 D3
Vyaz'ma Rus. Fed. 43 P6
Vyaz'ma r. Rus. Fed. 43 O6
Vyazniki Rus. Fed. 40 G4
Vyazovka Rus. Fed. 102 A1
Vyazovka Rus. Fed. 41 G6
Vyazovo Rus. Fed. 43 U8
Vyborg Rus. Fed. 43 J1
  formerly known as Viipuri; formerly spelt Viborg
Vyborgskiy Zaliv b. Rus. Fed. 43 J1
Vychegda r. Rus. Fed. 40 H3
Vychegodskiy Rus. Fed. 40 H3
Vydrino Rus. Fed. 85 C1
Vyeramyeyki Belarus 43 M8
Vyerkhnyadzvinsk Belarus 42 I6
  formerly known as Drissa
Vyetka Belarus 43 M9
Vyetryna Belarus 43 J6
Vygozero, Ozero I. Rus. Fed. 40 E3
Vyksa Rus. Fed. 40 G5
Vylkove Ukr. 41 D7
Vym' r. Rus. Fed. 40 I3
Vypolzovo Rus. Fed. 43 O4
Vyritsa Rus. Fed. 43 L2
Vyselki Rus. Fed. 41 F7
Vyshgorod Rus. Fed. 43 V7
Vyshhorod Ukr. 41 E6
Vyshkov Rus. Fed. 43 M9
Vyshkov Rus. Fed. 43 P8
Vyshnevolotskaya Gryada ridge Rus. Fed. 43 P5
Vyshnevolotskoye Vodokhranilishche resr Rus. Fed. 43 P4
Vyshneye-Ol'shanoye Rus. Fed. 43 S9
Vyshniy-Volochek Rus. Fed. 43 P4
Vyškov Czech Rep. 49 O6
Vyskod' Rus. Fed. 43 L1
Vyškov Czech Rep. 49 O7
Vysoká hill Slovakia 49 P7
Vysokaye Belarus 42 E9
  also spelt Vysokoye
Vysokaye Belarus 43 L7
Vysoké Mýto Czech Rep. 49 N6
Vysokinichi Rus. Fed. 43 R7
Vysokogorniy Rus. Fed. 82 E2
  formerly known as Muli
Vysokov-Rus. Fed. 43 T4
Vysokovsk Rus. Fed. 43 R5
Vysokoye Belarus see Vysokaye
Vysokoye Rus. Fed. 43 J3
Vysotsk Rus. Fed. 43 J1
Vystupovychi Ukr. 41 D6
Vytebet' r. Rus. Fed. 43 Q8
Vytegra Rus. Fed. 40 F3
Vyyenka Rus. Fed. 39 Q3
Vyya r. Rus. Fed. 40 H3
Vyžuona r. Lith. 42 G6

W

→ ↓ W

Wa Ghana 124 E4
Waajid Somalia 128 D4
Waal r. Neth. 48 B4
Waalwijk Neth. 48 C4
Waanyi/Garawa Aboriginal Land res. Australia 148 C2
Waat Sudan 128 B2
Wabag P.N.G. 73 J8
Wabakimi Lake Canada 168 B3
Wabal well Oman 105 G3
Wabamun Lake Canada 167 H4
Wabasca r. Canada 167 H3
Wabasca-Desmarais Canada 167 H4

Wabash IN U.S.A. 174 C3
Wabash OH U.S.A. 173 I10
Wabash r. U.S.A. 174 B4
Wabasha U.S.A. 174 A2
Wabassi r. Canada 168 C3
Wabatongushi Lake Canada 173 I2
Wabē Gestro r. Eth. 128 D3
Wabē Mena r. Eth. 128 D3
Wabeno U.S.A. 172 E5
Wabē Shebelē Wenz r. Eth. 128 E3
Wabigoon Lake Canada 168 A3
Wabowden Canada 167 L4
Wabrah well Saudi Arabia 105 D2
Wąbrzeźno Poland 49 P2
Wabu China 87 F1
Wabuk Point Canada 168 C2
Wabush Canada 169 H2
Wabush Lake Canada 169 H2
Waccamaw r. U.S.A. 175 E5
Waccamaw, Lake U.S.A. 174 E5
Waccasassa Bay U.S.A. 175 D6
Wachapreague U.S.A. 177 J8
Wächtersbach Germany 48 G5
Wachusett Reservoir U.S.A. 177 N3
Waco Canada 169 H3
Waco U.S.A. 179 C6
Waconda Lake U.S.A. 178 C4
Wad Pak. 101 F5
Wada'a Sudan 121 E6
Wada Wadalla Aboriginal Land res. Australia 148 C2
Wadayama Japan 91 D7
Wad Banda Sudan 121 F6
Wadbilliga National Park Australia 147 F4
Waddān Libya 120 C2
Waddān, Jabal hills Libya 120 B2
Waddell Dam U.S.A. 183 L8
Waddeneilanden is Neth. see West Frisian Islands
Wadden Islands Neth. see West Frisian Islands
Waddenzee sea chan. Neth. 48 B3
Waddikee Australia 146 C3
Waddington Canada 166 E4
Waddinxveen Neth. 48 B3
Wadena Canada 167 K5
Wadena U.S.A. 178 D2
Wad en Nail Sudan 121 G6
Wadesboro U.S.A. 174 D5
Wadeye Australia 148 A2
  formerly known as Port Keats
Wadgaon Maharashtra India 94 B2
Wadgaon Maharashtra India 94 C1
Wad Hamid Sudan 121 G5
Wadhwan India 96 A5
Wadhwan India see Surendranagar
Wadi India 94 C2
Wadian China 87 E1
Wādī as Sīr Jordan 108 G6
Wādī Gimāl, Gezīret i. Egypt 104 A2
  English form Wādī Gimāl Island
Wādī Gimāl Island Egypt see Wādī Gimāl, Gezīret
Wadi Halfa Sudan 121 F4
Wādī Ḥammān Saudi Arabia 104 C3
Wādī Mūsā Jordan 108 G7
Wad Medani Sudan 121 G6
Wadsworth NV U.S.A. 182 E2
Wadsworth OH U.S.A. 176 D4
Waegwan S. Korea 91 A7
Waenhuiskrans S. Africa 132 E11
Waesche, Mount Antarctica 222 P1
Wafangdian China 85 I4
  formerly known as Fuxian
Wafra Kuwait see Al Wafrah
Wagah India 96 B3
Wagait Aboriginal Land res. Australia 148 A2
Wageningen Neth. 48 C4
Wageningen Suriname 199 G3
Wager Bay Canada 167 N1
Wagga Wagga Australia 147 E3
Wagin Australia 151 B7
Wagluia Canada 166 D4
Wagner Brazil 202 D5
Wagner U.S.A. 178 C3
Wagoner U.S.A. 179 D4
Wagon Mound U.S.A. 181 F5
Wągrowiec Poland 49 O3
Wah Pak. 101 H3
Wahai Indon. 75 D3
Wahda state Sudan 126 F2
Wahemen, Lac I. Canada 169 G2
Wahiawa U.S.A. 181 [inset] Y1
Wahoo U.S.A. 178 C3
Wahpeton U.S.A. 178 C2
Wahran Alg. see Oran
Wah Wah Mountains U.S.A. 183 K3
Wai India 94 B2
Waiapu r. N.Z. 152 M5
Waiau N.Z. 153 H10
Waiau r. North I. N.Z. 152 L6
Waiau r. South I. N.Z. 153 H10
Waiau r. South I. N.Z. 153 H10
Waidhofen an der Thaya Austria 49 M7
Waidhofen an der Ybbs Austria 49 L8
Waigama Indon. 75 D3
Waigeo i. Indon. 73 H7
Waihao Downs N.Z. 153 E12
Waiharara N.Z. 152 H2
Waiharoa N.Z. 152 J5
Waiheke Island N.Z. 152 J4
Waihi N.Z. 152 J5
Waihi Beach N.Z. 152 J5
Waihou r. N.Z. 152 J5
Waihua N.Z. 152 L6
Waikabubak Indon. 75 A5
Waikaia N.Z. 153 C13
Waikaka r. N.Z. 153 C13
Waikaka N.Z. 153 D13
Waikanae N.Z. 152 I8
Waikare, Lake N.Z. 152 J5
Waikaremoana, Lake N.Z. 152 K6
Waikaretu N.Z. 152 I5
Waikari N.Z. 153 G10
Waikato admin. reg. N.Z. 152 I5
Waikato r. N.Z. 152 I5
Waikawa N.Z. 153 D14
Waikeria N.Z. 152 J6
Waikerie Australia 146 C3
Waikiki U.S.A. 181 [inset] Z2
Waikirikiri r. N.Z. 152 K6
Waiklibang Indon. 75 B5
Waikoikoi N.Z. 153 D14
Waikokopa N.Z. 152 L7
Waikouaiti N.Z. 153 E13
Wailuku U.S.A. 181 [inset] Z1
Waimahake N.Z. 153 C14
Waimakariri r. N.Z. 153 G11
Waimangaroa N.Z. 153 F9
Waimana N.Z. 152 K7
Waimarie N.Z. 152 M5
Waimate N.Z. 153 F12
Waimatenui N.Z. 152 H3
Waimauku N.Z. 152 I4
Waimea U.S.A. 181 [inset] Z1
Wainganga r. India 94 C2
Waingapu Indon. 75 B5
Waini Point Guyana 199 G2
Wainwright Canada 167 I4
Wainwright U.S.A. 164 D2
Waiotira N.Z. 152 I3
Waiouru N.Z. 152 J7
Waipahi N.Z. 153 D14
Waipahu U.S.A. 181 [inset] Y1
Waipaoa r. N.Z. 152 L6
Waipapa Point N.Z. 153 C14
Waipara N.Z. 153 G11

Waipawa N.Z. 152 K7
Waipipi N.Z. 152 I5
Waipu N.Z. 152 I3
Waipukurau N.Z. 152 K7
Wairakei N.Z. 152 K6
Wairarapa, Lake N.Z. 152 J9
Wairau r. N.Z. 153 I9
Wairau Valley N.Z. 152 H9
Wairoa N.Z. 152 I7
Wairoa r. North I. N.Z. 152 I4
Wairoa r. North I. N.Z. 152 L7
Waishe China 87 F2
Waitahanui N.Z. 152 K6
Waitahuna N.Z. 153 D13
Waitakaruru N.Z. 152 J5
Waitaki r. N.Z. 153 F12
Waitara N.Z. 152 I6
Waitati N.Z. 153 E13
Waitangi S. Pacific Ocean 145 H6
Waitangitaona r. N.Z. 153 E11
Waitara N.Z. 152 I6
Waitati N.Z. 153 E13
Waite River Australia 148 B4
Waitomo Caves N.Z. 152 J6
Waitotara N.Z. 152 I7
Waitotari r. N.Z. 152 I7
Waitsburg U.S.A. 180 C3
Waiuku N.Z. 152 I5
Waiwera South N.Z. 153 D14
Waiya Indon. 75 D3
Waiyang China 87 F3
Waiyevu Fiji 145 H3
Wajid, Jabal al hills Saudi Arabia 104 C3
Wajiki Japan 91 D8
Wajima Japan 90 E6
Wajir Kenya 128 D4
Waka Dem. Rep. Congo 126 D5
Waka, Tanjung pt Indon. 75 C3
Wakami Lake Canada 173 K3
Wakapuaka N.Z. 152 H9
Wakasa Japan 91 D7
Wakasa-wan b. Japan 91 D7
Wakatipu, Lake N.Z. 153 C13
Wakatoma Lake Canada 173 J4
Wakaw Canada 167 J4
Wakayama Japan 91 D7
Wakayama pref. Japan 91 D8
► Wake Atoll terr. N. Pacific Ocean 220 F4
  United States Unincorporated Territory. Also known as Aneen-Kio or EnenKio; formerly known as Wake Island.
  oceania [countries] ►► 138-139
WaKeeney U.S.A. 178 C4
Wakefield Canada 173 R5
Wakefield N.Z. 152 H9
Wakefield U.K. 47 K10
Wakefield MI U.S.A. 172 D4
Wakefield OH U.S.A. 176 B7
Wakefield RI U.S.A. 177 N4
Wakefield VA U.S.A. 177 I9
Wakeham Canada see Kangiqsujuaq
Wake Island terr. N. Pacific Ocean see Wake Atoll
Wakema Myanmar 78 A4
Wakhan reg. Afgh. 101 H2
Waki Japan 91 D8
Wakinosawa Japan 90 G4
Wakiro watercourse Eritrea 104 B5
Wakkanai Japan 90 G2
Wakkerstroom S. Africa 133 O4
Wakool Australia 147 E3
Wakool r. Australia 147 D3
Wakuach, Lac I. Canada 169 H2
Waku-Kungo Angola 127 B7
  formerly known as Santa Comba; formerly spelt Uaco Congo
Wakuya Japan 90 G5
Wakwayowkastic r. Canada 168 D3
Walagunya Aboriginal Reserve Australia 150 C4
Walajapet India 94 C3
Wałbrzych Poland 49 N5
  historically known as Waldenburg
Walcha Australia 147 F2
Walcott U.S.A. 180 F4
Wałcz Poland 49 N2
Waldaist r. Austria 49 L7
Waldburg Range mts Australia 151 B5
Walden U.S.A. 177 K4
Waldenburg Poland see Wałbrzych
Waldkraiburg Germany 49 J7
Waldo U.S.A. 177 J2
Waldorf U.S.A. 177 I7
Waldport U.S.A. 180 A3
Waldron U.S.A. 179 D5
Waldron, Cape Antarctica 223 H2
Waldshut Germany 48 F8
Walea, Selat sea chan. Indon. 75 B3
Waleabahi i. Indon. 75 B3
Walēg China 86 B2
  formerly known as Warli
Walej, Sha'ib al watercourse Iraq 109 K5
Wales admin. div. U.K. 47 I11
  also known as Cymru; historically known as Cambria
Walewale Ghana 125 E4
Walford U.S.A. 172 B9
Walgett Australia 147 E2
Walgreen Coast Antarctica 222 Q1
Walhalla U.S.A. 178 C1
Walhalla ND U.S.A. 178 C1
Walhalla SC U.S.A. 175 D5
Walikale Dem. Rep. Congo 126 F5
Walker r. Australia 148 B2
Walker watercourse Australia 148 B5
Walker IA U.S.A. 172 B8
Walker MI U.S.A. 172 H7
Walker MN U.S.A. 178 D2
Walker r. U.S.A. 182 F3
Walker Bay S. Africa 132 D11
Walker Cay i. Bahamas 186 D1
Walker Creek r. Australia 149 D3
Walker Lake r. Canada 167 L4
Walker Lake U.S.A. 182 F3
Walker Lake I. U.S.A. 182 F3
Walker Mountains Antarctica 222 R2
Walker River Indian Reservation res. U.S.A. 182 F3
Walkersville MD U.S.A. 176 H6
Walkersville WV U.S.A. 176 E7
Walkill U.S.A. 181 [inset] Z2
Wall, Mount hill Australia 150 B4
Wallabi Group is Australia 151 A6
Wallaby Island Australia 149 D2
Wallace ID U.S.A. 180 C3
Wallace VA U.S.A. 176 C9
Wallaceburg Canada 168 D5
Wallal Downs Australia 150 C3
Wallambin, Lake salt flat Australia 151 B6
Wallangarra Australia 147 F2
Wallaroo Australia 146 C3
Walla Walla U.S.A. 180 C3
Walldürn Germany 48 G6
Wallekraal S. Africa 132 B7
Wallenpaupack, Lake U.S.A. 177 J4
Wallingford CT U.S.A. 177 M4
Wallingford VT U.S.A. 177 M2
Wallis, Îles is Wallis and Futuna Is see Wallis Islands

Wallis Islands Wallis and Futuna Is 145 H3
  also known as Wallis, Îles
Wallis Lake inlet Australia 147 G3
Wallops Island U.S.A. 177 J8
Wallowa Mountains U.S.A. 180 C3
Walls U.K. 46 K3
Walls of Jerusalem National Park Australia 147 E5
Wallumbilla Australia 149 F5
Walmsley Lake Canada 167 I2
Walney, Isle of i. U.K. 47 I9
Walnut Bottom U.S.A. 176 H5
Walnut Cove U.S.A. 176 E5
Walnut Creek U.S.A. 182 B4
Walnut Creek r. U.S.A. 178 C4
Walnut Grove U.S.A. 182 C3
Walnut Ridge U.S.A. 174 B4
Walong China 97 H3
Walpole U.S.A. 177 M2
Walpole, Île i. New Caledonia 145 F4
Walsall U.K. 47 K11
Walsenburg U.S.A. 181 F5
Walsh r. Australia 149 D3
Walsrode Germany 48 G3
Waltair India 95 D2
Walterboro U.S.A. 175 D5
Walter F. George Reservoir U.S.A. 175 C6
Walters U.S.A. 179 C5
Walter's Range hills Australia 147 E2
Walthall U.S.A. 175 B5
Waltham Canada 173 Q5
Waltham MA U.S.A. 177 N3
Waltham ME U.S.A. 177 Q1
Walton IN U.S.A. 172 G10
Walton KY U.S.A. 176 A7
Walton NY U.S.A. 177 J3
Walton WV U.S.A. 176 D7
Walton-on-the-Naze U.K. 47 N12
Walvisbaai Namibia see Walvis Bay
Walvis Bay Namibia 130 B4
Walvis Bay Namibia 130 B4
  also spelt Walvisbaai
Wamala, Lake Uganda 128 A4
Wamba Dem. Rep. Congo 126 E4
Wamba Dem. Rep. Congo 126 C5
Wamba Nigeria 125 H4
Wambardi Aboriginal Land res. Australia 148 A2
Wamena Indon. 73 I7
Wami r. Tanz. 129 C6
Wamlana Indon. 75 C3
Wampaya Aboriginal Land res. Australia 148 B3
Wampsville U.S.A. 173 R7
Wampusirpi Hond. 186 B4
Wanaaring Australia 147 E2
Wanaka N.Z. 153 D12
Wanaka, Lake N.Z. 153 D12
Wan'an China 87 E3
  also known as Furong
Wanapitei Lake Canada 173 M4
Wanaque Reservoir U.S.A. 177 K4
Wanasabari Indon. 75 B4
Wanbi Australia 146 D3
Wanbi China 86 B3
Wanci Indon. 75 B4
Wanda Arg. 204 G2
Wandana Nature Reserve Australia 151 A6
Wandering River Canada 167 H4
Wanding China 86 A3
  formerly known as Wandingzhen
Wandingzhen China see Wanding
Wandiwash India see Vandavasi
Wandle Downs N.Z. 153 H10
Wandlitz Germany 49 K3
Wandoan Australia 149 F5
Wang, Mae Nam r. Thai. 78 B4
Wanganui N.Z. 152 I7
Wanganui r. North I. N.Z. 152 I7
Wanganui r. South I. N.Z. 153 E11
Wangaratta Australia 147 E4
Wangary Australia 146 C3
Wangcang China 86 C1
  also known as Hongjiang; formerly known as Fengjiaba
Wangcheng China 87 E2
  formerly known as Gaotangling
Wangda China see Zogang
Wangdu China 85 G4
Wangdue Phodrang Bhutan 97 F4
Wangerooge i. Germany 48 E2
Wanggamet, Gunung mt. Indon. 75 B5
Wang Gaxun China 84 C4
Wanggezhuang China see Jiaonan
Wangiwangi i. Indon. 75 B4
Wangjiang China 87 F2
Wangkibila Hond. 186 B4
Wangkui China 82 B3
Wang Mai Khon Thai. see Sawankhalok
Wangmo China 87 D4
Wangmo China 86 C3
  also known as Fuxing
Wangolodougou Côte d'Ivoire see Ouangolodougou
Wangqing China 82 C4
Wangying China see Huaiyin
Wangziguan China 86 C1
Wanham Canada 166 G4
Wanhatti Suriname 199 H3
Wan Hsa-la Myanmar 78 B4
Wanie-Rukula Dem. Rep. Congo 126 E4
Wanimiyn Aboriginal Reserve Australia 148 A2
Waniyang China 84 M4
Wankaner India 96 A5
Wankie Zimbabwe see Hwange
Wanlaweyn Somalia 128 E4
Wanna Lakes salt flat Australia 151 E6
Wanning China 87 D5
Wanrong China 85 F5
Wanshan China 87 D2
Wanshan Qundao is China 87 E4
  English form Lima Islands
Wanstead N.Z. 152 K8
Wantage U.K. 47 K12
Wanup Canada 173 M4
Wanxian China 87 D2
Wanyuan China 87 D1
Wanzai China 87 E2
  also known as Kangle
Wanzhi China see Wuhu
Wapakoneta U.S.A. 176 A5
Wapawekka Lake Canada 167 J4
Wapello U.S.A. 172 B9
Wapikopa Lake Canada 168 B2
Wapiti r. Canada 166 G4
Wapotih Indon. 75 C3
Wappingers Falls U.S.A. 177 L4
Wapsipinicon r. U.S.A. 172 B8
Waqēn China 86 B1
Waq aş Şawwān, Jibāl hills Jordan 109 H6
Wāqişah well Iraq 107 F4
Waqr well Saudi Arabia 105 E3
Wāqr Maryamah well Yemen 105 D4
War U.S.A. 176 D8
Wa'r, Wādī al watercourse Syria 109 L3
Warab Sudan 126 F2
Warab state Sudan 126 F2
Waradi waterhole Kenya 128 D4
Warah Pak. 101 F5
Warakurna-Wingellina-Irrunytju Aboriginal Reserve Australia 151 D5
Warandab Eth. 128 E3
Warangal India 94 C2
Waraseoni India 94 D5
Waratah Australia 147 E5
Warbreccan Australia 149 D5
Warburg Germany 48 G4
Warburton Vic. Australia 147 E4

Warburton W.A. Australia 151 D5
Warburton watercourse Australia 146 C1
Warburton S. Australia 133 C3
Warburton Aboriginal Reserve Australia 151 D5
Warburton Bay Canada 167 I2
Warburton Range hills Australia 151 D5
Warche r. Belgium 51 L2
Ward watercourse Australia 149 E5
Ward N.Z. 153 I9
Ward, Mount Antarctica 222 T2
Ward, Mount South I. N.Z. 153 B13
Ward, Mount South I. N.Z. 153 D11
Wardang Island Australia 146 C3
Wardegole waterhole Kenya 128 D4
Warden S. Africa 133 M4
Wardha India 94 C1
Wardha r. India 94 C2
Ward Hill hill U.K. 46 I5
Ware Canada 166 E3
  also known as Fort Ware
Ware U.S.A. 177 M3
Wareham U.K. 47 J13
Waremme Belgium 51 L2
Waren Germany 49 J2
Warendorf Germany 48 E4
Warginburra Peninsula Australia 149 F4
Wargla Alg. see Ouargla
War Gunbi waterhole Somalia 128 E2
Warialda Australia 147 F2
Wari India P.N.G. 149 F1
Warin Chamrap Thai. 79 D5
Warka Poland 49 S4
Warkworth N.Z. 152 I4
War Island Somalia 128 E2
Warli China see Walēg
Warmbad Namibia 130 C6
Warmbad S. Africa 133 M1
Warmfontein Namibia 132 D4
Warmia reg. Poland 49 R1
Warminster U.K. 47 J12
Warm Springs NV U.S.A. 183 H3
Warm Springs VA U.S.A. 176 F7
Warm Springs Indian Reservation res. U.S.A. 180 B3
Warmwaterberg S. Africa 132 E10
Warmwaterberg mts S. Africa 132 E10
Warner Canada 167 I5
Warner Lakes U.S.A. 180 C4
Warner Mountains U.S.A. 180 B4
Warner Robins U.S.A. 175 D5
Warner Springs U.S.A. 183 H8
Warnes Bol. 201 E4
Warnow r. Germany 49 J1
Waronda India 94 C2
Waroona Australia 151 A7
Warora India 94 C1
Warra Australia 149 F5
Warrabri Aboriginal Land res. Australia 148 B4
Warrackabeal Australia 147 D4
Warragamba Reservoir Australia 147 F3
Warragul Australia 147 E4
Warrakalanna, Lake salt flat Australia 146 C2
Warramboo hill Australia 151 B6
Warrambool r. Australia 147 E2
Warrandirrnna, Lake salt flat Australia 146 C1
Warrâq el-'Arab Egypt 108 C7
Warrawagine Australia 150 C4
Warrego r. Australia 147 E2
Warrego Range hills Australia 149 E5
Warren Australia 147 E2
Warren r. Australia 151 A7
Warren Canada 173 M4
Warren AR U.S.A. 179 D5
Warren IL U.S.A. 172 D8
Warren IN U.S.A. 172 H10
Warren MI U.S.A. 173 J8
Warren MN U.S.A. 178 C1
Warren OH U.S.A. 176 E4
Warren PA U.S.A. 176 F4
Warren Hastings Island Palau see Merir
Warren Island U.S.A. 166 C4
Warrenpoint U.K. 47 F9
Warrens U.S.A. 172 C6
Warrensburg MO U.S.A. 178 D4
Warrensburg NY U.S.A. 177 L2
Warrenton S. Africa 133 I5
Warrenton GA U.S.A. 175 D5
Warrenton MO U.S.A. 178 B4
Warrenton NC U.S.A. 176 G9
Warrenton VA U.S.A. 176 H7
Warri Nigeria 125 G5
Warrie Australia 151 B6
Warrina Australia 146 C1
Warrnambool Australia 147 D4
Warrnambool r. Australia 151 C6
Warroad U.S.A. 178 D1
Warrumbungle National Park Australia 147 F2
Warrumbungle Range mts Australia 147 F2
Warruwi Australia 148 B1
Warry Warry watercourse Australia 146 D2
► Warsaw Poland 49 S3
  Capital of Poland. Also spelt Warszawa.
Warsaw IN U.S.A. 174 C3
Warsaw KY U.S.A. 176 A7
Warsaw MO U.S.A. 178 D4
Warsaw NY U.S.A. 177 I8
Warsingsfehn Germany 48 E2
Warszawa Poland see Warsaw
Warta Poland 49 P4
Warta r. Poland 49 L3
  also known as Chenying
Wanning China 87 D5
Wanrong China 85 F5
Wartburg U.S.A. 176 A9
Wartburg, Schloß tourist site Germany 48 H4
Waru Indon. 77 G3
Warud India 96 C5
Warumungu Aboriginal Land res. Australia 148 B3
Warwick Australia 147 G2
Warwick U.K. 47 K11
Warwick NY U.S.A. 177 K4
Warwick RI U.S.A. 177 N4
Warwick Channel Australia 148 C2
Warzhong China 86 B2
Wasa Canada 167 H5
Wasaga Nigeria 125 G4
Wasaga Beach Canada 173 M6
Wasatch Range mts U.S.A. 183 M2
Wasbank S. Africa 133 O5
Wascana Creek r. Canada 167 J5
Wasco U.S.A. 182 E6
Waseca U.S.A. 174 A2
Washademoak Lake Canada 167 I3
Washap Pak. 101 E5
Washburn ND U.S.A. 178 B2
Washburn WI U.S.A. 172 C4
Washim India 94 C1
Washimeska r. Canada 169 F3
► Washington DC U.S.A. 177 H7
  Capital of the United States of America.
  world [countries] ►► 10-11
Washington GA U.S.A. 175 D5
Washington IL U.S.A. 172 D9
Washington IN U.S.A. 174 C4
Washington KS U.S.A. 178 C4

Washington KY U.S.A. 176 B7
Washington NC U.S.A. 174 E5
Washington NH U.S.A. 177 M2
Washington NJ U.S.A. 177 K5
Washington PA U.S.A. 176 E5
Washington UT U.S.A. 183 K4
► Washington state U.S.A. 180 B3
  world [changes] ►► 20-21
Washington, Cape Antarctica 223 L2
Washington, Mount U.S.A. 177 N1
Washington Court House U.S.A. 176 B6
Washington Island U.S.A. 172 G5
Washington Land reg. Greenland 165 M2
Washir Afgh. 101 E3
Washita r. U.S.A. 179 C5
Washpool National Park Australia 147 G2
Washtucna U.S.A. 180 C3
Wasi' Saudi Arabia 105 D2
Wasi' well Saudi Arabia 105 E3
Wasilków Poland 49 U2
Wasilla U.S.A. 164 E3
Wāsiţ governorate Iraq 107 F4
Wasit tourist site Iraq 107 F4
Wāsiţah Saudi Arabia 104 B3
Waskaganish Canada 168 E3
  also known as Fort Rupert
Waskaiowaka Lake Canada 167 L3
Waskatenau Canada 167 H4
Wąsosz Poland 49 N4
Waspán Nicaragua 186 B4
Wassadou Senegal 124 B3
Wassamu Japan 90 H2
Wassenaar Neth. 48 B3
Wasser Namibia 130 C5
Wasserkuppe hill Germany 48 G5
Wassou Guinea 124 B4
Wassuk Range mts U.S.A. 182 F3
Wassy France 51 K4
Waswanipi, Lac I. Canada 168 E3
Watabeag Lake Canada 173 M2
Watambayoli Indon. 75 B3
Watampone Indon. 75 B4
Watapi Lake Canada 167 I4
Watarrka National Park Australia 148 A5
Watauga r. U.S.A. 176 C9
Watauga Lake U.S.A. 176 C9
Watenstedt-Salzgitter Germany see Salzgitter
Waterberg Namibia 130 C4
Waterberg Plateau Game Park nature res. Namibia 130 C4
Waterbury CT U.S.A. 177 L4
Waterbury VT U.S.A. 177 M1
Water Cays i. Bahamas 186 D2
Waterdown Canada 173 N7
Wateree r. U.S.A. 175 D5
Waterford Rep. of Ireland 47 E11
  also known as Port Láirge
Waterford S. Africa 133 J10
Waterford CA U.S.A. 182 D4
Waterford PA U.S.A. 176 F4
Waterford Harbour Rep. of Ireland 47 F11
Waterhen r. Canada 167 J4
Waterhen Lake Canada 167 L4
Waterhouse r. Australia 148 B2
Waterhouse Range mts Australia 148 B5
Waterloo Canada 168 D5
Waterloo Sierra Leone 124 B4
Waterloo IA U.S.A. 174 A3
Waterloo IL U.S.A. 174 B4
Waterloo NY U.S.A. 177 I3
Waterloo WI U.S.A. 172 E7
Waterlooville U.K. 47 K13
Waterman U.S.A. 172 E9
Waterpoort S. Africa 131 F4
Waterton Lakes National Park Canada 167 H5
Waterton Park Canada 167 H5
Watertown NY U.S.A. 177 J2
Watertown SD U.S.A. 178 C2
Watertown WI U.S.A. 172 E7
Waterval r. S. Africa 133 M3
Waterval-Boven S. Africa 133 O2
Water Valley U.S.A. 174 B5
Waterville Rep. of Ireland 47 B12
Waterville ME U.S.A. 177 P1
Waterville WA U.S.A. 180 B3
Watervliet U.S.A. 177 L3
Wates Indon. 77 E4
Watford Canada 173 L8
Watford U.K. 47 L12
Watford City U.S.A. 178 B2
Wathaman r. Canada 167 K3
Wathaman Lake Canada 167 K3
Watheroo Australia 151 B6
Watheroo National Park Australia 151 A6
Watino Canada 167 G4
Watīr, Wādī watercourse Egypt 108 F8
Watkins Glen U.S.A. 177 I3
Watkinsville U.S.A. 175 D5
Watling Island Bahamas see San Salvador
Watonga U.S.A. 179 C5
Watowato, Bukit mt. Indon. 75 D2
Watrous Canada 167 J4
Watseka U.S.A. 181 F6
Watsi Dem. Rep. Congo 126 D4
Watseka U.S.A. 174 C3
Watson r. Australia 149 D2
Watson Canada 167 J4
Watson Escarpment Antarctica 223 P1
Watson Lake Canada 166 D2
Watsonville U.S.A. 182 C4
Watt, Mount hill Australia 151 D5
Watterson Lake Canada 167 L2
Wattiwarriganna watercourse Australia 146 C2
Watts Bar Lake resr U.S.A. 174 C5
Watubela, Kepulauan is Indon. 73 H7
Wau P.N.G. 73 K8
Wau Sudan 126 E3
Wau watercourse Sudan 126 E3
Waubay Lake U.S.A. 178 C2
Wauchope N.S.W. Australia 147 G2
Wauchope r. Australia 148 B4
Wauchula U.S.A. 175 D7
Waukara, Gunung mt. Indon. 75 A3
Waukarlycarly, Lake salt flat Australia 150 C4
Waukee U.S.A. 172 E7
Waukegan U.S.A. 174 C3
Waukesha U.S.A. 172 E7
Waukon U.S.A. 174 B3
Waunakee U.S.A. 172 D7
Waupaca U.S.A. 172 D6
Waupun U.S.A. 172 E7
Waurika U.S.A. 179 C5
Wausau U.S.A. 172 D6
Wauseon U.S.A. 176 A4
Wautoma U.S.A. 172 D6
Wave Hill Australia 148 B3
Waverley N.Z. 152 I7
Waverly IA U.S.A. 174 A3
Waverly NY U.S.A. 177 I3
Waverly OH U.S.A. 176 C6
Waverly TN U.S.A. 174 C4
Waverly VA U.S.A. 177 H8
Wavre Belgium 51 K2
Waw Myanmar 78 B4
Wawa Canada 168 C4
  formerly known as Jamestown
Wawa Nigeria 125 F4
Wawagosic r. Canada 168 E3
Wawalalindu Indon. 75 B3
Wāw al Kabīr Libya 120 C3
Wāw an Nāmūs waterhole Libya 120 C3
Wawasee, Lake U.S.A. 172 H9
Wawo Indon. 75 B3
Wawoi r. P.N.G. 73 J8
Wawotebi Indon. 75 B3
Waxahachie U.S.A. 179 C5

Waxü China 86 B1
Waxxari China 88 D4
Way, Lake salt flat Australia 151 C5
Wayabula Indon. 75 D2
Wayag i. Indon. 75 D2
Wayamli Indon. 75 D2
Wayaobu China see Zichang
Waycross U.S.A. 175 D6
Way Kambas National Park Indon. 77 D4
Waykilo Indon. 75 C3
Wayland KY U.S.A. 176 C8
Wayland MI U.S.A. 172 H8
Wayland NY U.S.A. 176 H3
Wayne MI U.S.A. 173 J8
Wayne NE U.S.A. 178 C3
Wayne WV U.S.A. 176 C7
Waynesboro GA U.S.A. 175 D5
Waynesboro MS U.S.A. 175 B6
Waynesboro PA U.S.A. 176 H6
Waynesboro TN U.S.A. 174 C5
Waynesboro VA U.S.A. 176 G7
Waynesburg U.S.A. 176 E6
Waynesville MO U.S.A. 178 D4
Waynesville NC U.S.A. 174 D5
Waza Myanmar 78 B2
Waza, Parc National de nat. park Cameroon 125 I4
Wazi Khwa Afgh. 101 G3
also known as Marjan
Wazirabad Pak. 101 H3
Wda r. Poland 49 P2
W du Niger, Parcs Nationaux du nat. park Niger 125 F4
We New Caledonia 145 F4
We, Pulau i. Indon. 76 A1
Weagamow Lake Canada 168 B2
Wear r. U.K. 47 K9
Weare U.S.A. 177 N2
Wearyan r. Australia 148 C3
Weatherford OK U.S.A. 179 C5
Weatherford TX U.S.A. 179 C5
Weatherly U.S.A. 177 J5
Weaver Lake Canada 167 L4
Weaverville U.S.A. 182 B1
Webequie Canada 168 C2
Weber N.Z. 152 K8
Weber r. U.S.A. 183 M1
Weber, Mount Canada 166 D4
Weber Basin sea feature Indon. 218 P6
Weber Inlet Antarctica 222 T2

▶ Webi Shabeelle r. Somalia 128 D4
5th longest river in Africa.
africa [landscapes] 112–113

Webster MA U.S.A. 177 N3
Webster SD U.S.A. 178 C2
Webster WI U.S.A. 172 A5
Webster City U.S.A. 174 A3
Webster Springs U.S.A. 176 E7
Webuye Kenya 128 B4
formerly known as Broderick Falls
Wecho r. Canada 167 H2
Wecho Lake Canada 167 H2
Weda Indon. 75 C2
Weda, Teluk b. Indon. 75 D2
Weddell Island Falkland Is 205 E8
Weddell Sea Antarctica 222 V2
Wedderburn N.Z. 153 E13
Wedge Mountain Canada 166 F5
Weed U.S.A. 180 B4
Weedville U.S.A. 176 G4
Weenen S. Africa 133 O5
Weenen Nature Reserve S. Africa 133 O5
Weener Germany 48 E2
Weert Neth. 48 C4
Wee Waa Australia 147 F2
Wegberg Germany 48 D4
Węgliniec Poland 49 M4
Węgorzewo Poland 49 S1
Węgorzyno Poland 49 M2
Węgrów Poland 49 T3
Wehni Eth. 104 B5
Wei r. Henan China 85 G4
Wei r. Shaanxi China 86 D1
Wei r. Shandong China 85 H4
Weichang China 85 H3
Weiden in der Oberpfalz Germany 48 J6
Weidongmen China see Qianjin
Weifang China 85 H4
Weihai China 85 I4
Weihui China 85 G5
formerly known as Jixian
Weihu Ling mts China 82 B4
Weilburg Germany 51 O2
Weilheim in Oberbayern Germany 48 I8
Weimar Germany 48 I5
Weinan China 87 D1
Weingarten Germany 48 G8
Weinheim Germany 48 F6
Weining China 86 C3
Weipa Australia 149 D2
Weipa Aboriginal Reserve Australia 149 D2
Weipa South Aboriginal Reserve Australia 149 D2
Weiqu China see Chang'an
Weir r. Australia 147 F2
Weiragoo Range hills Australia 151 B5
Weir River Canada 167 M3
Weiser U.S.A. 180 C3
Weiser r. U.S.A. 180 C3
Weishan Shandong China 87 F1
also known as Xiazhen
Weishan Yunnan China 86 B3
also known as Wenhua
Weishan Hu l. China 87 F1
Weishi China 87 E1
Weiße Elster r. Germany 51 R1
Weißenburg in Bayern Germany 48 H6
Weißenfels Germany 48 I4
Weisshorn mt. Switz. 51 N6
Weiss Lake U.S.A. 179 F5
Weissmies mt. Switz. 51 O6
Weissrand Mountains Namibia 130 C5
Weißwasser Germany 49 L4
Weixian China 85 G4
also known as Mingzhou
Weixin China 86 C3
also known as Zhaxi
Weiya China 84 B3
Weiyuan China 84 E5
also known as Qingyuan
Weiyuan China see Huzhu
Weiyuan China see Jinggu
Weiyuan Jiang r. China 86 B4
Weiz Austria 49 M8
Weizhou China see Wenchuan
Weizhou Dao i. China 87 D4
Weizi China 85 I3
Wejherowo Poland 49 P1
Wekusko Canada 167 L4
Wekusko Lake Canada 167 L4
Wekweti Canada 167 H1
formerly known as Snare Lakes
Wel r. Poland 49 Q2
Welatam Myanmar 78 B2
Welbedacht Dam S. Africa 133 K6
Welbourn Hill Australia 146 B1
Welch U.S.A. 176 D8
Weld U.S.A. 177 O1
Weld, Mount hill Australia 151 C6
Weldiya Eth. 128 C2
Weldon U.S.A. 176 H9
Weld Range hills Australia 151 B5
Welford National Park Australia 149 D5
formerly known as Barcoo National Park
Welk'īt'ē Eth. 128 C2
Welkom S. Africa 133 K4
Welland Canada 173 N8
Welland r. U.K. 47 L11
Welland Canal Canada 173 N7
Wellesley Canada 173 M7

Wellesley Islands Australia 148 C3
Wellesley Islands Aboriginal Reserve Australia 148 C3
Wellesley Lake Canada 166 B2
Wellfleet U.S.A. 177 O4
Wellingborough U.K. 47 L11
Wellington Australia 147 F3
Wellington Canada 173 P7

▶ Wellington N.Z. 152 I9
Capital of New Zealand.
world [countries] 10–11

Wellington admin. reg. N.Z. 152 J9
Wellington S. Africa 132 C10
Wellington CO U.S.A. 180 F4
Wellington KS U.S.A. 178 C4
Wellington NV U.S.A. 182 E3
Wellington OH U.S.A. 176 C4
Wellington TX U.S.A. 179 B5
Wellington UT U.S.A. 183 N2
Wellington, Isla i. Chile 205 B8
Wellington Range hills N.T. Australia 148 B2
Wellington Range hills W.A. Australia 151 C5
Wells Canada 166 F4
Wells U.K. 47 J12
Wells U.S.A. 180 D4
Wells, Lake salt flat Australia 151 C5
Wellsboro U.S.A. 177 H4
Wellsford N.Z. 152 I4
Wells Gray Provincial Park Canada 166 F4
Wells-next-the-Sea U.K. 47 M11
Wellston U.S.A. 172 H6
Wellsville NY U.S.A. 176 H3
Wellsville OH U.S.A. 176 E5
Wellton U.S.A. 183 J9
Wełna r. Poland 49 N3
Weloka U.S.A. 181 [inset] Z2
Wels Austria 49 L7
Welshpool U.K. 47 I11
also known as Y Trallwng
Welton U.S.A. 172 C9
Welwel Eth. 128 E3
Welwitschia Namibia see Khorixas
Wema Dem. Rep. Congo 126 D5
Wembere r. Tanz. 129 B6
Wembesi S. Africa 133 N6
Wembley Canada 166 G4
Wemindji Canada 168 E2
formerly known as Nouveau-Comptoir or Paint Hills
Wemyss Bight Bahamas 186 D1
Wen r. China 85 H5
Wenamu r. Guyana/Venez. 199 F3
Wenatchee U.S.A. 180 B3
Wenatchee Mountains U.S.A. 180 B3
Wenchang China 87 D5
Wenchang China see Zitong
Wencheng China 87 G3
also known as Daxue
Wenchi Ghana 125 E5
Wench'īt Shet' r. Eth. 128 C2
Wenchow China see Wenzhou
Wenchuan China 86 B2
also known as Weizhou
Wendelstein mt. Germany 48 J8
Wenden Latvia see Cēsis
Wenden U.S.A. 183 K8
Wendeng China 85 I4
Wendo Eth. 128 C3
Wéndou Mbôrou Guinea 124 B4
Wendover U.S.A. 183 J1
Wenebegon Lake Canada 173 J3
Wenfeng China see Yongfeng
Wengshui China 86 A2
Wengyuan China 87 E3
also known as Longxian
Wenhua China see Weishan
Wenjiang China see Gaoxian
Wenjiashi China 87 E3
Wenlan China see Mengzi
Wenlin China see Renshou
Wenling China 87 G2
Wenlock r. Australia 149 D2
Wenona IL U.S.A. 172 D9
Wenona MD U.S.A. 177 J7
Wenping China see Ludian
Wenquan Chongqing China 87 D2
Wenquan Guizhou China 87 C2
Wenquan China see Yingshan
Wenquan Qinghai China 84 C5

▶ Wenquan Qinghai China 89 E5
Highest settlement in the world.

Wenquan Xinjiang China 88 C2
also known as Arixang
Wenquanzhen China 87 E2
Wenshan China 86 C4
also known as Kaihua
Wenshui China 86 C2
Wensu China 88 C3
Wensum r. U.K. 47 N11
Wentworth Australia 146 D3
Wentworth NC U.S.A. 176 F9
Wentworth NH U.S.A. 177 N2
Wenxi China 85 F5
Wenxian China 86 C1
Wenyu r. China 85 F4
Wenzhou China 87 G3
formerly spelt Wenchow
Wer India 96 C4
Werda Botswana 130 D5
Werdau Germany 49 J5
Werdēr Eth. 128 E3
Werder Germany 49 J3
Wêreldend S. Africa 132 E1
Werinama Indon. 75 D3
Werl Germany 48 E4
Wermsdorfer Forst park Germany 49 J4
Wernberg-Köblitz Germany 49 J6
Wernecke Mountains Canada 166 B1
Wernigerode Germany 48 H4
Werota Eth. 128 C2
Werra r. Germany 48 G4
Werrimull Australia 146 D3
Werris Creek Australia 147 F2
Wertheim Germany 48 G6
Werwaru Indon. 75 D5
Wesel Germany 48 D4
Wesendorf Germany 48 H3
Weser r. Germany 48 F2
Weser sea chan. Germany 48 F2
Wesergebirge hills Germany 48 F3
Weska Weka Eth. 128 B3
Weslemkoon Lake Canada 173 P5
Wesley S. Africa 133 L10
Wesleyville Canada 169 K3
Wessel, Cape Australia 148 C1
Wessel Islands Australia 148 C1
Wesselsbron S. Africa 133 K4
Wesselsvlei S. Africa 132 H4
Wesselton S. Africa 133 N3
Wessington Springs U.S.A. 178 C2
West Alligator r. Australia 148 B2
West Allis U.S.A. 172 E7
West Antarctica reg. Antarctica 222 P1
West Baines r. Australia 148 A2
West Banas r. India 96 A5

▶ West Bank terr. Asia 108 G6
Territory occupied by Israel.
asia [countries] 64–67

West Bay Canada 169 J2
West Bay Cayman Is 186 C3
West Bay b. U.S.A. 175 B6
West Bend U.S.A. 172 E7
West Bengal state India 97 E5
also known as Bangla
West Branch U.S.A. 173 I6
Westbrook U.S.A. 177 O2
West Burke U.S.A. 177 N1

Westby U.S.A. 172 C7
West Caicos i. Turks and Caicos Is 187 E2
West Cape N.Z. 153 A13
West Cape Howe Australia 151 B7
West Chester U.S.A. 177 J6
Westcliffe U.S.A. 181 F5
West Coast admin. reg. N.Z. 153 E10
West Coast National Park S. Africa 132 C10
West Dome mt. N.Z. 153 C13
West End Bahamas 175 E7
West End U.S.A. 177 J3
Westerburg Germany 48 E5
Westerholt Germany 48 E2
Westerland Germany 48 F1
Western watercourse Australia 149 D4
Western r. Canada 167 J1
Western admin. reg. Ghana 124 E5
Western prov. Kenya 128 B4
Western prov. Zambia 127 D8
Western Area admin. div. Sierra Leone 124 B4
Western Australia state Australia 146 A2
Western Bahr el Ghazal state Sudan 126 E3
Western Cape prov. S. Africa 132 E10
Western Darfur state Sudan 120 D6
Western Desert Egypt 121 F3
also known as Şahara el Gharbîya
Western Desert Aboriginal Land res. Australia 148 A3
Western Dvina r. Europe see Zapadnaya Dvina
Western Equatoria state Sudan 126 F3
Western Ghats mts India 94 B3
also known as Sahyadri
Western Kordofan state Sudan 126 F2
Western Lesser Sunda Islands prov. Indon. see Nusa Tenggara Barat
Western Port b. Australia 147 E4
Western Province prov. Zambia see Copperbelt

▶ Western Sahara terr. Africa 122 B4
Disputed territory (Morocco). Formerly known as Spanish Sahara.
africa [countries] 114–117

Western Samoa country S. Pacific Ocean see Samoa
Western Sayan Mountains reg. Rus. Fed. see Zapadnyy Sayan
Westerschelde est. Neth. 48 A4
Westerstede Germany 48 E2
Westerville U.S.A. 176 C5
Westerwald hills Germany 48 E5
West Falkland i. Falkland Is 205 E8
West Fargo U.S.A. 178 C2
West Fayu atoll Micronesia 73 K5
Westfield MA U.S.A. 177 M3
Westfield NY U.S.A. 176 F3
Westfield PA U.S.A. 176 H4
Westfield WI U.S.A. 172 D7
West Frisian Islands Neth. 48 B2
also known as Wadden Islands or Waddeneilanden
Westgate Australia 149 E5
West Grand Lake U.S.A. 169 H4
West Hamlin U.S.A. 176 C7
West Hartford U.S.A. 177 M4
West Haven U.S.A. 177 M4
West Ice Shelf Antarctica 223 F2
West Indies N. America 171 L7
West Irian prov. Indon. see Irian Jaya
West Island India 95 G3
West Jordan U.S.A. 183 M1
West Kazakhstan Oblast admin. div. Kazakh. see Zapadnyy Kazakhstan
West Lafayette U.S.A. 174 C3
West Lamma Channel Hong Kong China 87 [inset]
Westland Australia 149 D4
Westland National Park N.Z. 153 E11
also known as Tai Poutini National Park
West Liberty IA U.S.A. 172 B9
West Liberty KY U.S.A. 176 B8
West Liberty OH U.S.A. 176 B5
Westlock Canada 167 H4
West Lorne Canada 168 D5
West Lunga r. Zambia 127 E8
West Lunga National Park Zambia 127 E8
West MacDonnell National Park Australia 148 B4
West Malaysia pen. Malaysia see Peninsular Malaysia
Westmalle Belgium 51 K1
Westman Islands Iceland see Vestmannaeyjar
Westmar Australia 147 F1
West Memphis U.S.A. 174 B5
West Milton U.S.A. 176 A6
Westminster U.S.A. 177 I6
West Monroe U.S.A. 179 D5
Westmoreland Australia 148 C3
Westmoreland U.S.A. 178 C4
Westmorland U.S.A. 183 I8
West Nicholson Zimbabwe 131 F4
West Nueces r. U.S.A. 179 C6
Westoe Dam S. Africa 133 O3
Weston OH U.S.A. 176 B4
Weston WV U.S.A. 176 E6
Westonaria S. Africa 133 L3
Weston-super-Mare U.K. 47 J12
Westover U.S.A. 177 J7
West Palm Beach U.S.A. 175 D7
West Papua prov. Indon. see Irian Jaya
West Plains U.S.A. 178 E4
West Point pt Australia 147 E5
West Point CA U.S.A. 182 D3
West Point IA U.S.A. 172 B10
West Point MS U.S.A. 175 B5
West Point NE U.S.A. 178 C3
West Point NY U.S.A. 177 L4
West Point OH U.S.A. 176 E5
West Point VA U.S.A. 177 I8
West Point Lake resr U.S.A. 175 C5
Westport Canada 173 Q6
Westport N.Z. 153 F9
Westport Rep. of Ireland 47 C10
Westport CA U.S.A. 182 A2
Westport NY U.S.A. 177 L1
Westray Canada 167 K4
Westray i. U.K. 46 I4
Westray Firth sea chan. U.K. 46 I4
Westree Canada 168 D4
West Road r. Canada 166 F4
West Rutland U.S.A. 177 L2
West Sacramento U.S.A. 182 C3
West Salem U.S.A. 176 C5
West Seneca U.S.A. 176 G3
West Siberian Plain Rus. Fed. 38 I3
also known as Zapadno-Sibirskaya Nizmennost' or Zapadno-Sibirskaya Ravnina
West Stewartstown U.S.A. 177 N1
West Topsham U.S.A. 177 M1
West Union IA U.S.A. 174 B3
West Union OH U.S.A. 176 B7
West Union WV U.S.A. 176 E6
West Valley City U.S.A. 183 M1
Westville IN U.S.A. 172 G9
Westville OK U.S.A. 179 D5
West Virginia state U.S.A. 176 E7
West Walker r. U.S.A. 182 E3
Westwood Australia 149 F4
Westwood U.S.A. 182 D1
West Wyalong Australia 147 E3
West York U.S.A. 177 I6
Wetan i. Indon. 75 D4
Wetar i. Indon. 75 C4
Wetar, Selat sea chan. Indon. 75 C5
Wetaskiwin Canada 167 H4
Wete Dem. Rep. Congo 126 E6

Wete Tanz. 129 C6
Wethersfield U.S.A. 177 M4
Wetmore U.S.A. 172 G4
Wetmore Glacier Antarctica 222 T2
Wetumpka U.S.A. 175 C5
Wetzlar Germany 48 F5
Wever U.S.A. 172 B10
Wewahitchka U.S.A. 175 C6
Wewak P.N.G. 73 J7
Wewoka U.S.A. 179 C5
Wexford Rep. of Ireland 47 F11
also known as Loch Garman
Wexford Harbour b. Rep. of Ireland 47 F11
Weyakwin Canada 167 J4
Weyauwega U.S.A. 172 E6
Weyburn Canada 167 K5
Weyer Markt Austria 49 L8
Weyhausen Germany 48 H3
Weyhe Germany 48 F3
Weymouth Canada 169 H4
Weymouth U.K. 47 J13
Weymouth U.S.A. 177 O3
Weymouth, Cape Australia 149 D2
Whakaari i. N.Z. 152 L5
also known as White Island
Whaka a Te Wera inlet N.Z. see Paterson Inlet
Whakaki N.Z. 152 L7
Whakamaru N.Z. 152 J6
Whakapunake hill N.Z. 152 L6
Whakarewarewa Forest Park nature res. N.Z. 152 K6
Whakatane N.Z. 152 K5
Whalan Creek r. Australia 147 F2
Whale r. Canada see La Baleine, Rivière à
Whale Bay U.S.A. 166 C3
Whale Cay i. Bahamas 186 D1
Whale Cove Canada 167 M2
Whale Island N.Z. see Motuhora Island
Whaleyville U.S.A. 177 I9
Whalsay i. U.K. 46 L3
Whampoa, Sungai r. Sing. 76 [inset]
Whangaehu r. N.Z. 152 J8
Whangamata N.Z. 152 J5
Whangamoa N.Z. 152 H9
Whangamomona N.Z. 152 I7
Whanganui Inlet N.Z. 152 G8
Whanganui National Park N.Z. 152 I7
Whangaparaoa N.Z. 152 I4
Whangara N.Z. 152 M6
Whangarei N.Z. 152 I3
Whangaroa Bay N.Z. 152 H3
Whapmagoostui Canada 168 E2
Wharanui N.Z. 153 I9
Whareama N.Z. 152 K8
Wharfe r. U.K. 47 K10
Wharncliffe Canada 173 J4
Wharncliffe U.S.A. 176 D8
Wharton U.S.A. 179 C6
Wharton Lake Canada 167 L1
Whataroa N.Z. 153 E11
Wha Ti Canada 167 G2
formerly known as Lac la Martre
Wheatland CA U.S.A. 182 C2
Wheatland IA U.S.A. 172 C9
Wheatland WY U.S.A. 180 F4
Wheatley Canada 173 K8
Wheatley U.S.A. 176 A7
Wheaton IL U.S.A. 174 B3
Wheaton MN U.S.A. 178 C2
Wheaton-Glenmont U.S.A. 177 H6
Wheeler TX U.S.A. 179 B5
Wheeler WI U.S.A. 172 B5
Wheeler Lake Canada 167 H2
Wheeler Lake resr U.S.A. 174 C5
Wheeler Peak NM U.S.A. 181 F5
Wheeler Peak NV U.S.A. 183 J3
Wheelersburg U.S.A. 176 C7
Wheeler Springs U.S.A. 182 E7
Wheeling U.S.A. 176 E5
Wheelwright Arg. 204 E4
Whernside hill U.K. 47 J9
Whim Creek Australia 150 B4
Whinham, Mount Australia 148 A5
Whirinaki Forest Park nature res. N.Z. 152 K6
Whiskey Jack Lake Canada 167 K3
Whiskeytown Lake U.S.A. 182 B1
Whispering Pines U.S.A. 182 B3
Whistler Canada 166 F5
Whitbourne Canada 169 K4
Whitby Canada 173 O7
Whitby U.K. 47 L9
Whitchurch U.K. 47 J11
Whitchurch-Stouffville Canada 173 N7
Whitcombe, Mount N.Z. 153 E11
White r. Canada 168 C3
White r. Canada/U.S.A. 166 B2
White r. AR U.S.A. 174 B5
White r. CO U.S.A. 183 O1
White r. IN U.S.A. 174 C4
White r. MI U.S.A. 172 G7
White r. NV U.S.A. 183 J5
White r. SD U.S.A. 178 C3
White r. VT U.S.A. 177 M2
White r. WI U.S.A. 172 C4
White watercourse AZ U.S.A. 183 N8
White watercourse TX U.S.A. 179 B5
White, East Fork r. U.S.A. 174 C4
White, Lake salt flat Australia 148 A4
White, North Fork r. U.S.A. 178 D4
White Bay Canada 169 J3
White Butte mt. U.S.A. 178 B2
White Canyon U.S.A. 183 N4
White Cliffs Australia 147 D2
White Cloud U.S.A. 172 H7
Whitecourt Canada 167 H4
White Earth Indian Reservation res. U.S.A. 178 D2
Whiteface Lake U.S.A. 172 A3
Whiteface Mountain U.S.A. 177 L1
Whitefield U.S.A. 177 N1
Whitefish Canada 173 L4
Whitefish r. Canada 166 E1
Whitefish U.S.A. 180 D2
Whitefish r. U.S.A. 172 G5
Whitefish Bay U.S.A. 172 F6
Whitefish Lake N.W.T. Canada 167 J2
Whitefish Lake Ont. Canada 172 D2
Whitefish Point U.S.A. 173 I4
White Hall U.S.A. 174 B4
Whitehall MI U.S.A. 172 G7
Whitehall MT U.S.A. 180 D3
Whitehall NY U.S.A. 177 L2
Whitehall OH U.S.A. 176 C6
Whitehall WI U.S.A. 172 B6
Whitehaven U.K. 47 I9
White Haven U.S.A. 177 J4
White Hill hill Canada 169 I4

▶ Whitehorse Canada 166 C2
Territorial capital of Yukon.

White Horse, Vale of valley U.K. 47 K12
White Island Antarctica 223 D2
White Island N.Z. see Whakaari
White Kei r. S. Africa 133 L9
White Lake salt flat Australia 151 C5
White Lake Ont. Canada 168 C3
White Lake Ont. Canada 168 E4
White Lake LA U.S.A. 179 D6
White Lake MI U.S.A. 172 G7
Whitemark Australia 147 F5
White Mountain Peak U.S.A. 182 F4
White Mountains U.S.A. 177 N1
White Mountains National Park Australia 149 E4
Whitemouth r. Canada 171 G1
Whitemouth Lake Canada 167 M5
White Nile r. Sudan/Uganda 126 G1
also known as Abiad, Bahr el or Jebel, Bahr el
White Nile Dam Sudan 121 G6

White Nossob watercourse Namibia 130 C4
White Oak U.S.A. 176 B8
White Otter Lake Canada 168 B3
White Pass Canada/U.S.A. 166 C3
White Pine MI U.S.A. 172 D4
White Pine TN U.S.A. 176 B9
White Pine Range mts U.S.A. 183 I3
White River Canada 168 C3
Whiteriver U.S.A. 183 O8
White River U.S.A. 178 B3
White River Junction U.S.A. 177 M2
White River National Wildlife Refuge nature res. U.S.A. 174 B5
White River Valley U.S.A. 183 I3
White Rock Peak U.S.A. 183 J3
White Russia country Europe see Belarus
Whitesail Lake Canada 166 E4
White Salmon U.S.A. 180 B3
Whitesand r. Alta/N.W.T. Canada 167 H2
Whitesand r. Sask. Canada 167 K5
White Sands National Monument nat. park U.S.A. 181 F6
Whitesboro U.S.A. 177 J2
Whitesburg U.S.A. 176 C8
White Sea Rus. Fed. 40 F2
also known as Beloe More or Beloye More
White Stone U.S.A. 177 I8
White Sulphur Springs MT U.S.A. 180 E3
White Sulphur Springs WV U.S.A. 176 E8
Whitesville U.S.A. 176 D8
White Umfolozi r. S. Africa 133 P5
Whiteville U.S.A. 174 E5
White Volta watercourse Burkina/Ghana 125 E3
also known as Nakambé or Nakanbe or Volta Blanche
White Water U.S.A. 183 H8
Whitewater CO U.S.A. 183 P3
Whitewater WI U.S.A. 172 E8
Whitewater Baldy mt. U.S.A. 181 E6
White Well Australia 146 A2
White Woman Creek r. U.S.A. 178 B4
Whitewood Australia 149 D4
Whitewood Canada 167 K5
Whithorn U.K. 47 H9
Whitianga N.Z. 152 J4
Whitley City U.S.A. 176 A9
Whitmire U.S.A. 174 D5
Whitmore S. Africa 133 M8
Whitmore Mountains Antarctica 222 Q1
Whitney Canada 173 O5
Whitney, Lake U.S.A. 179 C5
Whitney, Mount U.S.A. 182 F5
Whitstable U.K. 47 N12
Whitsunday Group is Australia 149 F4
Whitsunday Island Australia 149 F4
Whitsunday Island National Park Australia 149 F4
Whitsunday Passage Australia 149 F4
Whitsun Island Vanuatu see Pentecost Island
Whittemore U.S.A. 173 J6
Whittier U.S.A. 182 F8
Whittington Range hills Australia 148 B3
Whittlesea S. Africa 133 K9
Whittlesey U.K. 47 L11
Whittlesey U.S.A. 172 C5
Whittlesey, Mount hill U.S.A. 172 C4
Whitton Australia 147 E3
Whitula watercourse Australia 149 D5
Wholdaia Lake Canada 167 J2
Why U.S.A. 183 L9
Whyalla Australia 146 C3
Whydah Benin see Ouidah
Wiang Kosai National Park Thai. 78 B4
Wiang Pa Pao Thai. 78 B4
Wiang Phran Thai. 78 B3
Wiang Sa Thai. 78 C4
Wiarton Canada 168 D4
Wiasi Ghana 125 E4
Wibaux U.S.A. 180 F3
Wichelen Belgium 48 A4
Wichita U.S.A. 178 C4
Wichita r. U.S.A. 179 C5
Wichita Falls U.S.A. 179 C5
Wichita Mountains U.S.A. 179 C5
Wichita Mountains National Wildlife Refuge nature res. U.S.A. 179 C5
Wick U.K. 46 I5
Wickenburg U.S.A. 183 L8
Wickepin Australia 151 B7
Wickham Australia 150 B4
Wickham r. Australia 148 A3
Wickham, Cape Australia 147 D4
Wicklow Rep. of Ireland 47 F11
also known as Cill Mhantáin
Wicklow Head Rep. of Ireland 47 G11
Wicklow Mountains Rep. of Ireland 47 F11
Wicklow Mountains National Park Rep. of Ireland 47 F10
Wicko, Jezioro lag. Poland 49 N1
Widawa r. Poland 49 O4
Widawka r. Poland 49 P4
Wide Bay Australia 149 G5
Wideröe, Mount Antarctica 223 B2
Widgeegoara watercourse Australia 147 E1
Widgiemooltha Australia 151 C6
Widi, Kepulauan is Indon. 75 D3
Wi-do i. S. Korea 83 B6
Więcbork Poland 49 O2
Wied r. Germany 48 E5
Wiehengebirge hills Germany 48 F3
Wiehl Germany 48 E5
Wielen Poland 49 N3
Wielka Sowa mt. Poland 49 N5
Wielkopolskie, Pojezierze reg. Poland 49 O3
Wielkopolski Park Narodowy nat. park Poland 49 N3
Wieluń Poland 49 P4
Wien Austria see Vienna
Wiener Neustadt Austria 49 N8
Wiensberg mt. Austria 49 M7
Wieprz r. Poland 49 S4
Wieprza r. Poland 49 N1
Wieprz-Krzna, Kanał canal Poland 49 U4
Wieringerwerf Neth. 48 C3
Wieruszów Poland 49 P4
Wierzyca r. Poland 49 P2
Wiesbaden Germany 48 F5
Wiesloch Germany 48 F6
Wiesmoor Germany 48 E2
Wieżyca hill Poland 49 P1
Wigan U.K. 47 J10
Wiggins U.S.A. 175 B6
Wight, Isle of i. U.K. 47 K13
Wigierski Park Narodowy nat. park Poland 49 U1
Wignes Lake Canada 167 J2
Wigry, Jezioro l. Poland 49 U1
Wigtown U.K. 47 H9
Wigtown Bay U.K. 47 H9
Wijchen Neth. 48 C4
Wikieup U.S.A. 183 K7
Wik'ro Eth. 128 C1
Wikwemikong Canada 173 L5
Wil Switz. 51 P5
Wilber U.S.A. 178 C3
Wilberforce r. N.Z. 153 F11
Wilberforce, Cape Australia 148 C1
Wilbur U.S.A. 180 C3
Wilburton U.S.A. 179 D5
Wilcannia Australia 147 D2
Wilcox U.S.A. 176 G4
Wilczek Land i. Rus. Fed. see Vil'cheka, Zemlya
Wildalpener Salzatal nature res. Austria 49 M8
Wildcat Hill Wilderness Area nature res. Canada 167 K4
Wildcat Peak U.S.A. 183 H3
Wild Coast S. Africa 133 N8

Wilderness S. Africa 132 G10
Wilderness U.S.A. 176 H7
Wilderness National Park S. Africa 132 G11
Wildeshausen Germany 48 F3
Wild Goose Canada 172 D2
Wildhay r. Canada 167 G4
Wildhorn mt. Switz. 51 N6
Wild Horse Draw r. U.S.A. 181 F7
Wild Horse Hill mt. U.S.A. 178 B3
Wildon Austria 49 M9
Wild Rice r. MN U.S.A. 178 C2
Wild Rice r. ND U.S.A. 178 C2
Wild Rice Lake U.S.A. 172 A4
Wildwood Canada 167 H4
Wildwood FL U.S.A. 175 D6
Wildwood NJ U.S.A. 177 K7
Wiley Ford U.S.A. 176 G6
Wilga r. Poland 49 S4
Wilge r. Free State S. Africa 133 M4
Wilge r. Gauteng/Mpumalanga S. Africa 133 N2
Wilgena Australia 146 B2

▶ Wilhelm, Mount P.N.G. 73 J8
5th highest mountain in Oceania.
oceania [landscapes] 136–137

Wilhelmina Gebergte mts Suriname 199 G4
Wilhelm-Pieck-Stadt Germany see Guben
Wilhelmsburg Austria 49 M7
Wilhelmshaven Germany 48 F2
Wilhelmstal Namibia 130 C4
Wilkes-Barre U.S.A. 177 J4
Wilkesboro U.S.A. 176 D9
Wilkes Coast Antarctica 223 I2
Wilkes Land reg. Antarctica 223 I2
Wilkie Canada 167 I4
Wilkinsburg U.S.A. 176 F5
Wilkins Coast Antarctica 222 T2
Wilkins Ice Shelf Antarctica 222 T2
Wilkinson Lakes salt flat Australia 146 B2
Will, Mount Canada 166 D3
Willamette r. U.S.A. 180 B3
Willandra Billabong watercourse Australia 147 E3
Willandra National Park Australia 147 E3
Willapa Bay U.S.A. 180 A3
Willard Mex. 184 C2
Willard NM U.S.A. 181 F6
Willard OH U.S.A. 176 C4
Willards U.S.A. 177 J7
Willcox U.S.A. 183 O9
Willcox Playa salt flat U.S.A. 183 O9
Willebroek Belgium 51 K1
Willem Pretorius Game Reserve nature res. S. Africa 133 L5

▶ Willemstad Neth. Antilles 187 F4
Capital of the Netherlands Antilles.

Willeroo Australia 148 A2
William r. Canada 167 I3
William, Mount Australia 147 D4
William Creek Australia 146 C2
William Lake Canada 167 L4
Williams Australia 151 B7
Williams r. Qld Australia 149 D4
Williams r. W.A. Australia 151 B7
Williams AZ U.S.A. 183 L6
Williams CA U.S.A. 182 B2
Williamsburg IA U.S.A. 174 A3
Williamsburg KY U.S.A. 176 A9
Williamsburg MI U.S.A. 172 H6
Williamsburg OH U.S.A. 176 A6
Williamsburg PA U.S.A. 176 G5
Williamsburg VA U.S.A. 177 I8
Williams Lake Canada 166 F4
Williamson NY U.S.A. 177 H2
Williamson WV U.S.A. 176 C8
Williamsport IN U.S.A. 174 C3
Williamsport OH U.S.A. 176 B6
Williamsport PA U.S.A. 177 H4
Williamston MI U.S.A. 173 I8
Williamston NC U.S.A. 174 E5
Williamstown KY U.S.A. 176 A7
Williamstown MA U.S.A. 177 L3
Williamstown NY U.S.A. 177 J2
Willimantic U.S.A. 177 M4
Willis Group atolls Australia 149 F3
Willis Islands S. Georgia 205 [inset]
Williston S. Africa 132 E8
Williston FL U.S.A. 175 D6
Williston ND U.S.A. 178 B1
Williston SC U.S.A. 175 D5
Williston Lake Canada 166 F4
Willits U.S.A. 182 A2
Willmar U.S.A. 178 D2
Willmore Wilderness Provincial Park Canada 166 G4
Willochra watercourse Australia 146 C2
Willoughby U.S.A. 176 D4
Willow r. Canada 166 F4
Willow Beach U.S.A. 183 J6
Willow Bunch Canada 167 J5
Willow Creek r. Canada 167 H5
Willow Creek U.S.A. 180 B4
Willow Creek r. OR U.S.A. 180 B3
Willow Creek r. UT U.S.A. 183 O1
Willow Hill U.S.A. 176 H5
Willow Lake Canada 167 G2
Willowlake r. Canada 166 F2
Willowmore S. Africa 132 H10
Willowra Australia 148 B4
Willowra Aboriginal Land Trust res. Australia see Wirliyajarrayi Aboriginal Land Trust
Willow Reservoir U.S.A. 172 D5
Willows U.S.A. 182 B2
Willow Springs U.S.A. 178 E4
Willowvale S. Africa 133 M9
Wills, Lake salt flat Australia 150 E4
Wills Creek watercourse Australia 148 D4
Willunga Australia 146 C3
Wilmington Australia 146 C3
Wilmington DE U.S.A. 177 J6
Wilmington NC U.S.A. 175 E5
Wilmington OH U.S.A. 176 B6
Wilmington VT U.S.A. 177 M3
Wilmington Island U.S.A. 175 D5
Wilmore U.S.A. 176 A8
Wilno Lith. see Vilnius
Wilnsdorf Germany 48 F5
Wilpattu National Park Sri Lanka 94 D4
Wilpena watercourse Australia 146 C2
Wilson r. Australia 150 E3
Wilson watercourse Australia 147 D1
Wilson atoll Micronesia see Ifalik
Wilson MN U.S.A. 172 B7
Wilson NC U.S.A. 174 E5
Wilson NY U.S.A. 176 G2
Wilson, Mount CO U.S.A. 181 F5
Wilson, Mount NV U.S.A. 183 J3
Wilson, Mount OR U.S.A. 180 B3
Wilsons Hills Antarctica 223 K2
Wilsonia U.S.A. 182 F5
Wilson Lake resr U.S.A. 174 C5
Wilsons U.S.A. 176 H8
Wilson's Promontory pen. Australia 147 E4
Wilson's Promontory National Park Australia 147 E4
Wilton r. Australia 148 B2
Wilton ME U.S.A. 177 O1
Wilton NH U.S.A. 177 N3
Wiltz Lux. 51 L3
Wiluna Australia 151 C5
Wimbledon N.Z. 152 K8
Wimereux France 50 H2
Wimmera r. Australia 147 D4
Wina r. Cameroon see Vina
Winamac U.S.A. 174 C3
Winam Gulf Kenya 128 B5
formerly known as Kavirondo Gulf
Winbin watercourse Australia 149 E5

Winburg S. Africa 133 L5
Wincanton S. Africa 132 G4
Wincanton U.K. 47 J12
Winchendon U.S.A. 177 M3
Winchester N.Z. 153 F12
Winchester U.K. 47 K12
Winchester IL U.S.A. 174 B4
Winchester IN U.S.A. 176 A5
Winchester KY U.S.A. 176 A8
Winchester NH U.S.A. 177 M3
Winchester TN U.S.A. 175 I8
Winchester VA U.S.A. 176 G6
Wind r. Canada 166 C1
Wind r. U.S.A. 180 E4
Windabout, Lake salt flat Australia 146 C2
Windau Latvia see Ventspils
Windber U.S.A. 176 G5
Wind Cave National Park U.S.A. 178 B3
Winder U.S.A. 175 D6
Windermere U.K. 47 J9
Windham U.S.A. 176 D4

▶ Windhoek Namibia 130 C4
Capital of Namibia.

Windidda Aboriginal Reserve Australia 151 C5
Windigo r. Canada 168 C2
Windigo Lake Canada 168 B2
Windischgarsten Austria 49 L8
Wind Mountain U.S.A. 181 F6
Windom U.S.A. 178 D3
Windorah Australia 149 D5
Window Rock U.S.A. 183 O6
Wind Point U.S.A. 172 F8
Wind Ridge U.S.A. 176 E6
Wind River Range mts U.S.A. 180 E4
Winds, Bay of Antarctica 223 G2
Windsor Australia 147 F3
Windsor Nfld. Canada 169 K3
Windsor N.S. Canada 169 H4
Windsor Ont. Canada 168 D5
Windsor Que. Canada 169 F4
Windsor U.K. 47 L12
Windsor NC U.S.A. 174 E5
Windsor NY U.S.A. 177 J3
Windsor VA U.S.A. 177 I9
Windsor VT U.S.A. 177 M2
Windsor Dam U.S.A. 177 M3
Windsor Locks U.S.A. 177 M4
Windsorton S. Africa 133 I5
Windula watercourse Australia 149 D5
Windward Islands Caribbean Sea 187 L6
Windward Passage Cuba/Haiti 187 E3
Windy Harbour Australia 151 A7
Winefred Lake Canada 167 I4
Winfield AL U.S.A. 175 C5
Winfield IA U.S.A. 172 B5
Winfield KS U.S.A. 178 C4
Winfield WV U.S.A. 176 E4
Wingate Mountains hills Australia 148 A2
Wingene Belgium 51 J1
Wingham Canada 168 D5
Wini East Timor 75 C5
Winifred, Lake salt flat Australia 150 C4
Winifreda Arg. 204 D5
Winisk Canada 168 C2
Winisk r. Canada 168 C2
Winisk Lake Canada 168 C2
Winisk River Provincial Park Canada 168 C2
Winkana Myanmar 79 B5
Winkelhaaks r. S. Africa 133 I3
Winkelman U.S.A. 183 N9
Winkelpos S. Africa 133 K4
Winkler Canada 167 L5
Winlock U.S.A. 180 B3
Winnalls Ridge Australia 148 A5
Winneba Ghana 125 E5
Winnebago U.S.A. 178 D3
Winnebago, Lake U.S.A. 172 E6
Winnebago Indian Reservation res. U.S.A. 178 C3
Winneconne U.S.A. 172 E6
Winnemucca U.S.A. 182 G1
Winnemucca Lake U.S.A. 182 E1
Winner U.S.A. 178 B3
Winnett U.S.A. 180 E3
Winnfield U.S.A. 179 D6
Winnibigoshish, Lake U.S.A. 178 D2
Winning Australia 150 A4

▶ Winnipeg Canada 167 L5
Provincial capital of Manitoba.

Winnipeg r. Canada 167 L5
Winnipeg, Lake Canada 167 L5

Winnipegosis Canada 167 L5
Winnipegosis, Lake Canada 167 K4
Winnipesaukee, Lake U.S.A. 177 N2
Winnsboro SC U.S.A. 174 D5
Winnsboro TX U.S.A. 179 D5
Winona AZ U.S.A. 183 M6
Winona MI U.S.A. 172 B1
Winona MN U.S.A. 174 B2
Winona MO U.S.A. 174 B4
Winona MS U.S.A. 175 B5
Winooski U.S.A. 177 L1
Winooski r. U.S.A. 177 L1
Winschoten Neth. 48 E2
Winsen (Aller) Germany 48 G3
Winsen (Luhe) Germany 48 H2
Winslow AZ U.S.A. 183 N6
Winslow ME U.S.A. 177 P1
Winsted U.S.A. 177 L4
Winston-Salem U.S.A. 176 E9
Winter U.S.A. 172 B5
Winterberg Germany 48 F4
Winterberg mts S. Africa 133 K9
Winter Harbor U.S.A. 177 Q1
Winter Haven U.S.A. 175 D6
Winterport U.S.A. 177 Q1
Winters CA U.S.A. 182 C3
Winters TX U.S.A. 179 C6
Winterset U.S.A. 178 D3
Winterswijk Neth. 48 E4
Winterthur Switz. 51 O5
Winterton S. Africa 133 N5
Winterveld S. Africa 133 M2
Winthrop U.S.A. 177 P1
Winton Australia 149 D4
Winton N.Z. 153 C14
Winton U.S.A. 177 I9
Wirliyajarrayi Aboriginal Land Trust res. Australia 148 B4
formerly known as Willowra Aboriginal Land Trust
Wirrabara Australia 146 C3
Wirraminna Australia 146 C2
Wirrida, Lake salt flat Australia 146 B2
Wirrulla Australia 146 B3
Wisbech U.K. 47 M11
Wiscasset U.S.A. 177 P1
Wisconsin r. U.S.A. 172 B7
Wisconsin state U.S.A. 174 B2
Wisconsin, Lake U.S.A. 172 D7
Wisconsin Dells U.S.A. 172 D7
Wisconsin Rapids U.S.A. 172 D6
Wise U.S.A. 174 C9
Wisil Dabarow Somalia 128 F3
Wisła r. Poland see Vistula
Wisłok r. Poland 49 T5
Wisłoka r. Poland 49 S5
Wismar Germany 48 I2
Wisner U.S.A. 175 B6
Wissota Lake U.S.A. 172 B6
Wistaria Canada 166 E4
Witbank S. Africa 133 N2
Witbooisvlei Namibia 130 C5
Witdraai S. Africa 132 E3
Witham r. U.K. 47 M11
Witherbee U.S.A. 177 L1
Withernsea U.K. 47 M10
Withlacoochee r. FL U.S.A. 175 D6
Withlacoochee r. FL U.S.A. 175 D6
Witjira National Park Australia 146 B1
Witkoppies mt. S. Africa 133 N4
Witkowo Poland 49 Q3
Witkransnek pass S. Africa 133 J8
Witmos S. Africa 133 J9
Witnek S. Africa 133 M2
Witney U.K. 47 K12
Witnica Poland 49 L3
Witput S. Africa 133 I6
Witrivier S. Africa 133 P2
Wittberg mt. E. Cape S. Africa 132 G10
Wittberg mt. Free State S. Africa 133 M5
Wittberg mts S. Africa 133 L7
Wittdeberg mts S. Africa 132 E10
Wittenberg Germany see Lutherstadt Wittenberg
Wittenberg U.S.A. 172 D6
Wittenberge Germany 48 I3
Wittenburg Germany 48 H2
Wittenheim France 51 N5
Wittenoom Australia 150 B4
also known as Wittenoom Gorge
Wittenoom Gorge Australia see Wittenoom
Witti, Banjaran mts Sabah Malaysia 77 G1
Wittingen Germany 48 H3
Wittlich Germany 48 D6
Wittmund Germany 48 D2
Wittstock Germany 49 K1
Witu Kenya 128 D5
Witu Islands P.N.G. 145 D2
Witvlei Namibia 130 C4
Witwatersberg mts S. Africa 133 L3
Witwatersrand mts S. Africa 133 K3
Witzenhausen Germany 48 G4
Wivenhoe, Lake Australia 147 G1
Wkra r. Poland 49 R3
Władysławowo Poland 49 Q1
Włocławek Poland 49 Q3
historically known as Vlotslavsk
Włoszczowa Poland 49 Q5
Wobkent Uzbek. see Vabkent
Wodonga Australia 147 E3
Wodzisław Śląski Poland 49 P5
historically known as Loslau
Wohko watercourse Sudan 126 F3
Wohlthat Mountains Antarctica 223 A2
Wōjjā atoll Marshall Is see Wotje
Wokam i. Indon. 73 H8
Woken r. China 82 C3
Wokha India 97 G4
Woking U.K. 47 L12
Wokingham watercourse Australia 149 D4
Woko National Park Australia 147 F2
Wolcott IN U.S.A. 172 F10
Wolcott NY U.S.A. 177 I6
Wolcott VT U.S.A. 177 M1
Wolcottville U.S.A. 172 H9
Wołczyn Poland 49 P4
Woldegk Germany 49 K2
Wolea atoll Micronesia see Woleai
Woleai atoll Micronesia 73 J5
also known as Ulie; also spelt Wolea
Woleu-Ntem prov. Gabon 126 A4
Wolf r. Canada 166 C2
Wolf r. U.S.A. 172 E6
Wolf Creek MT U.S.A. 180 D3
Wolf Creek OR U.S.A. 180 B4
Wolf Creek U.S.A. 179 C4
Wolf Creek Pass U.S.A. 181 F5
Wolfen Germany 49 J4
Wolfenbüttel Germany 48 H3
Wolfhagen Germany 48 G4
Wolf Lake Canada 166 D2
Wolf Point U.S.A. 180 F2
Wolfsberg Austria 49 L9
Wolfsburg Germany 48 H3
Wolfstein Germany 48 E6
Wolfville Canada 169 H4
Wolgast Germany 49 K1
Wolhusen Switz. 51 O5
Wolin Poland 49 L2
Wolin i. Poland 49 L2
Woliński Park Narodowy nat. park Poland 49 L2
Wolkersdorf Austria 49 N7
Wollaston, Islas is Chile 205 D9
Wollaston Lake Canada 167 K3
Wollaston Lake l. Canada 167 K3
Wollaston Peninsula Canada 165 H3
Wollemi National Park Australia 147 F3
Wollerau Switz. 51 O5

Wollongong Australia 147 F3
Wolmaransstad S. Africa 133 J4
Wolmirstedt Germany 48 I3
Wołomin Poland 49 S3
Wolong Reserve nature res. China 86 B2
Wołów Poland 49 N4
Wolowaru Indon. 75 B5
Wolseley Australia 146 D4
Wolseley S. Africa 132 D10
Wolsztyn Poland 49 N3
Wolvega Neth. 48 D3
Wolverhampton U.K. 47 J11
Wolverine U.S.A. 172 H5
Wolwefontein S. Africa 133 I10
Wolwespruit S. Africa 133 J5
Wolya r. Indon. 76 A1
Wonarah Australia 148 C3
Wondai Australia 149 F5
Wonderfontein S. Africa 133 N2
Wonderkop mt. S. Africa 133 L5
Wondermere S. Africa 133 K2
Wongalarroo Lake salt l. Australia 147 E2
Wonga Wongué, Réserve de nature res. Gabon 126 A5
Wong Chhu r. Bhutan 97 F4
Wong Chuk Hang Hong Kong China 87 [inset]
Wong Wan Chau i. Hong Kong China see Double Island
Wŏnju S. Korea 83 B5
Wonogiri Indon. 77 E4
Wonosari Indon. 77 E4
Wonosobo Indon. 77 E4
Wonowon Canada 166 F3
Wonreli Indon. 75 D5
Wŏnsan N. Korea 83 B5
Wonthaggi Australia 147 E4
Wonyulgunna, Mount hill Australia 151 B5
Woocalla Australia 146 C2
Wood, Mount Canada 166 A2
Woodbine U.S.A. 177 K6
Woodboro U.S.A. 172 D5
Woodbourne U.S.A. 177 K4
Woodbridge NJ U.S.A. 177 K5
Woodbridge U.K. 47 N11
Woodbridge NJ U.S.A. 177 H7
Wood Buffalo National Park Canada 167 H3
Woodburn IN U.S.A. 176 A4
Woodburn OR U.S.A. 180 B3
Woodbury CT U.S.A. 177 L4
Woodbury MI U.S.A. 173 H8
Woodbury NJ U.S.A. 177 J6
Woodend Australia 147 E4
Woodfords U.S.A. 182 C3
Woodhall Spa U.K. 47 L10
Woodhull U.S.A. 172 C9
Wood Lake Canada 167 K4
Woodlake U.S.A. 182 E5
Woodland CA U.S.A. 182 C3
Woodland NC U.S.A. 177 H9
Woodland WA U.S.A. 180 B3
Woodland Park U.S.A. 180 F5
Woodlands Sing. 76 [inset]
Woodlark Island P.N.G. 145 E2
also known as Murua
Woodmurra Creek watercourse Australia 146 C1
Woodridge Canada 167 L5
Woodroffe watercourse Australia 148 C4
Woodroffe, Mount Australia 146 A1
Woodruff U.S.A. 172 D5
Woods, Lake salt flat Australia 148 B3
Woods, Lake of the Canada/U.S.A. 165 J5
Woodsfield U.S.A. 176 D6
Wood's Hole U.S.A. 177 O4
Woodstock N.B. Canada 169 H4
Woodstock Ont. Canada 168 D5
Woodstock IL U.S.A. 174 B3
Woodstock VA U.S.A. 176 G7
Woodstock VT U.S.A. 177 M2
Woodstock Dam resr S. Africa 133 N5
Woodstown U.S.A. 177 J6
Woodsville U.S.A. 177 M1
Woodville N.Z. 152 J8
Woodville MS U.S.A. 175 B6
Woodville OH U.S.A. 176 B4
Woodville TX U.S.A. 179 D6
Woodward U.S.A. 179 C4
Woody U.S.A. 182 F6
Wooler U.K. 46 J8
Woolgar r. Australia 149 D4
Woolgoolga Australia 147 G2
Woolla Downs Australia 148 B4
Woollard, Mount Antarctica 222 R1
Wooltana Australia 146 C2
Woomera Australia 146 C2
Woomera Prohibited Area Australia 146 B2
Woonsocket U.S.A. 178 C2
Woorabinda Australia 149 F5
Wooramel r. Australia 151 A5
Wooster U.S.A. 176 D5
Woqooyi Galbeed admin. reg. Somalia 128 D2
Worak-san National Park S. Korea 83 C5
Worb Switz. 51 N6
Worbody Point Australia 149 D2
Worcester S. Africa 132 D10
Worcester U.K. 47 J11
Worcester MA U.S.A. 177 N3
Worcester NY U.S.A. 177 K3
Wörgl Austria 48 J8
Workai i. Indon. 73 H8
Workington U.K. 47 I9
Worland U.S.A. 180 F3
Worms Germany 48 F6
Worms Head U.K. 47 H12
Worofla Côte d'Ivoire 124 D4
Woronora watercourse Australia 149 D4
Wörth am Rhein Germany 48 F6
Worthing U.K. 47 L13
Worthington IN U.S.A. 178 D3
Worthington OH U.S.A. 176 B5
Wosi Indon. 75 D3
Wotjalum Aboriginal Reserve Australia 150 C3
Wotje atoll Marshall Is 220 F6
also known as Wōjjā; formerly known as Otdia
Wotu Indon. 75 B3
Wour Chad 120 B4
Wouri r. Cameroon 125 H5
Wowoni, Selat sea chan. Indon. 75 B3
Wowoni i. Indon. 75 B3
Wozrojdeniye Oroli i. Uzbek. see Vozrozhdeniya, Ostrov
Wrangel Island Rus. Fed. 39 S2
also known as Vrangelya, Ostrov
Wrangell U.S.A. 166 C3
Wrangell, Mount U.S.A. 164 D3
Wrangell Mountains U.S.A. 164 D4
Wrangell-St Elias National Park and Preserve U.S.A. 164 E3
Wrath, Cape U.K. 46 G5
Wray U.S.A. 178 B3
Wreck Reef Australia 149 G4
Wrecsam U.K. see Wrexham
Wrens U.S.A. 175 D5
Wrexham U.K. 47 J10
also spelt Wrecsam
Wriezen Germany 49 L3
Wright Phil. 74 C4
Wrightmyo India 95 G4
Wright Patman Lake U.S.A. 179 D5
Wrightson, Mount U.S.A. 181 E7
Wrightsville U.S.A. 175 D5
Wrightwood U.S.A. 182 G7
Wrigley Canada 166 F2
Wrigley U.S.A. 176 B7

Wrigley Gulf Antarctica 222 P2
Wrocław Poland 49 O4
historically known as Breslau
Wronki Poland 49 N3
Września Poland 49 O3
Września r. Poland 49 N4
Wschowa Poland 49 N4
Wu'an China see Changtai
Wu'an China 85 G4
Wubalawun res. Australia see Larrimah Aboriginal Land
Wubin Australia 151 B6
Wubu China 85 F4
also known as Songjiachuan
Wuchagou China 85 I2
Wuchang Heilong. China 82 B3
Wuchang Hubei China 87 E2
formerly known as Jiangxia
Wucheng China 87 F2
Wuchow China see Wuzhou
Wuchuan Guangdong China 87 D4
also known as Meilu
Wuchuan Guizhou China 87 C2
Wuchuan Nei Mongol China 85 F3
Wuda China 85 H3
also known as Ongniud Qi
Wudang Shan mts China 87 D1
Wudao China 85 I4
also known as Puji
Wuding China 86 B3
Wuding r. China 85 F4
Wudinna Australia 146 B3
Wudu China 86 C1
Wufeng China 87 D2
Wufeng China see Zhenxiong
Wugang China 87 D3
Wugong China 87 D1
Wuhai China 85 E4
also known as Haibowan
Wuhan China 87 E2
Wuhe China 87 F1
Wuhu Anhui China 87 F2
also known as Wanzhi
Wuhu Anhui China 87 F2
Wuhua China 87 E4
also known as Shuizhai
Wújiang China 89 B5
Wujiang China 87 G2
Wu Jiang r. China 87 C2
Wujin China see Changzhou
Wujin China see Xinjin
Wukari Nigeria 125 H5
Wuleidao Wan l. China 85 I4
Wulian Feng mts China 86 B2
Wuliang Shan mts China 86 B3
Wuliaru i. Indon. 73 H8
Wuling Shan mts China 87 D2
Wulong China 87 C2
also known as Xiangkou
Wulong r. China 83 B5
Wulongji China see Huaibin
Wulur Indon. 75 D4
Wum Cameroon 125 H5
Wumeng Shan mts China 86 B3
Wuming China 87 D4
Wümme r. Germany 48 F2
Wungda China 84 B2
Wuning China 87 E2
Wunnummin Lake Canada 168 B2
Wun Rog Sudan 126 F2
Wun Shwai Sudan 126 F2
Wunsiedel Germany 49 J5
Wunstorf Germany 48 G3
Wuntau Sudan 126 F2
Wuntho Myanmar 78 A3
Wupatki National Monument nat. park U.S.A. 183 M6
Wuping China 87 F3
Wuppertal Germany 48 E4
formerly known as Barmen-Elberfeld
Wuppertal S. Africa 132 D9
Wuqi China 85 F4
Wuqia Xinjiang China 88 A4
also known as Ulugqat
Wuqia Xinjiang China 88 A4
Wuqiang China 85 G4
also known as Xiaofan
Wuqiao China see Sangyuan
Wuqing China 85 H4
also known as Yangcun
Wuquan China see Wuyang
Wuqub, Wādī watercourse Saudi Arabia 108 F9
Wuranga Australia 151 B6
Würm r. Germany 48 I7
Wurno Nigeria 125 G3
Wurralibbi Aboriginal Land res. Australia 148 C2
Würzbach Germany 48 I5
Würzburg Germany 48 G6
Wurzen Germany 49 J4
Wushan Chongqing China 87 D2
also known as Wuxia
Wushan China see Chong'an
Wushan China 87 C1
Wu Shan mts China 87 D2
Wusheng Sichuan China 86 C2
Wusheng Zhejiang China 87 F2
Wushi China 88 B3
also known as Uqturpan
Wüstegarten hill Germany 48 G4
Wusuli Jiang r. Rus. Fed. see Ussuri
Wutai China 85 G4
Wutai Shan mts China 85 G4
Wutong China 87 D3
Wutongqiao China 88 E3
Wutunwu Quan well China 84 B3
Wuvulu Island P.N.G. 73 J7
Wuwei Anhui China 87 F2
Wuwei Gansu China 84 D4
formerly known as Liangzhou
Wuxi Chongqing China 87 D2
also known as Chengxiang
Wuxi China see Luxi
Wuxi Jiangsu China 87 G2
Wuxia China see Wushan
Wuxing China see Huzhou
Wuxu China 87 D4
Wuxuan China 87 D4
Wuxue China 87 E2
Wuyang China see Zhenyuan
Wuyang China 87 E1
also known as Wuquan
Wuyi China 87 F2
also known as Hushan
Wuyiling China 82 C2
Wuyishan China 87 F3
Wuyi Shan mts China 87 F3
Wuyi Shan tourist site China 87 F3
Wuyuan Jiangxi China 87 F2
also known as Ziyang
Wuyuan Nei Mongol China 85 F3
also known as Haiyan
Wuyun China see Jinyun
Wuzhai China 85 F4
Wuzhi China 85 G5
Wuzhi Shan mts China 87 D5
Wuzhong China 85 E4

Wuzhou China 87 D4
formerly spelt Wuchow
Wyaaba Creek r. Australia 149 D3
Wyalkatchem Australia 151 B6
Wyalusing PA U.S.A. 177 I4
Wyalusing WI U.S.A. 172 B8
Wyandra Australia 147 E1
Wyanet U.S.A. 172 D9
Wyangala Reservoir Australia 147 F3
Wyara, Lake salt flat Australia 147 E2
Wye r. U.K. 47 J12
Wyemandoo hill Australia 151 B6
Wye Mills U.S.A. 177 I7
Wyeville U.S.A. 172 C6
Wyk auf Föhr Germany 48 F1
Wylliesburg U.S.A. 176 G9
Wyloo Australia 150 A4
Wymondham U.K. 47 N11
Wymore U.S.A. 178 C3
Wynbring Australia 146 B2
Wyndham Australia 150 E2
Wyndham N.Z. 153 C14
Wyndham-Werribee Australia 147 E4
Wynne U.S.A. 174 B5
Wynniatt Bay Canada 165 H2
Wynyard Australia 147 E5
Wynyard Canada 167 J5
Wyocena U.S.A. 172 D7
Wyola Lake salt flat Australia 146 A2
Wyoming DE U.S.A. 177 J6
Wyoming IA U.S.A. 172 B8
Wyoming IL U.S.A. 172 D9
Wyoming MI U.S.A. 172 H8
▶ Wyoming state U.S.A. 180 F4
northamerica [environments] ▶ 162–163
Wyoming Peak U.S.A. 180 F4
Wyoming Range mts U.S.A. 180 E4
Wyong Australia 147 F3
Wyperfeld National Park Australia 146 D3
Wysoka Poland 49 O2
Wysokie Mazowieckie Poland 49 T3
Wysox U.S.A. 177 I4
Wyszków Poland 49 S3
Wytheville U.S.A. 176 D9
Wyżnica r. Poland 49 S4

↓ X

▶ Xaafun, Raas pt Somalia 128 F2
Most easterly point of Africa.

Xaafuun Somalia 128 F2
Xaçmaz Azer. 107 G2
also spelt Khachmas
Xade Botswana 130 D4
Xagnay China 89 C5
Xago China 89 E6
Xagquka China 89 F5
Xaidulla China 89 B4
Xainza China 89 E6
also known as Kangsangdobdê
Xaitongmoin China 89 E6
also known as Qabka
Xai-Xai Moz. 131 G5
formerly known as João Belo or Vila de João Belo
Xal, Cerro de hill Mex. 185 H4
Xalapa Mex. see Jalapa Enríquez
Xalin Somalia 128 F2
Xaltianguis Mex. 185 F5
Xamavera Angola 127 C8
Xamba China 85 E3
Xam Hua Laos 78 C3
formerly known as Sam Neua
Xá-Muteba Angola 127 C7
formerly known as Cinco de Outubro
Xan r. Laos 78 C4
Xan, Xé r. Vietnam 79 D5
Xangda China see Nangqên
Xangdin Hural China 85 F3
Xangdoring China see Xungba
Xangongo Angola 127 B9
formerly known as Roçadas
Xankändi Azer. 107 F3
also known as Stepanakert; also spelt Khankendi
Xanlar Azer. 107 F2
Xanthi Greece 58 F7
Xanxerê Brazil 203 A8
Xapuri Brazil 200 C2
Xarardheere Somalia 128 E3
Xarba La pass China 89 D6
Xar Burd China see Bayan Nuru
Xar Moron r. China 85 I3
Xar Moron r. China 85 I3
Xarrama r. Port. 54 C6
Xarsingma China see Yadong
Xassengue Angola 127 C7
Xátiva Spain 55 K6
also spelt Játiva
Xau, Lake Botswana 131 E4
also known as Dow, Lake
Xaudum watercourse Botswana/Namibia 130 D3
Xavantes, Represa de resr Brazil 206 D10
Xavantes, Serra dos hills Brazil 202 B5
Xa Vo Đat Vietnam 79 D6
Xayar China 88 C3
Xcalak Mex. 185 I5
X-Can Mex. 185 I4
Xekar China 88 B4
Xenia U.S.A. 176 B6
Xeriuini r. Brazil 199 F5
Xero Potamos r. Cyprus see Xeros
Xeros r. Cyprus 108 D3
also known as Xero Potamos
Xhora S. Africa see Elliotdale
Xhorodomo Pan salt pan Botswana 131 E4
Xi r. China 85 I3
Xiabancheng China 85 H3
Xiabole Shan mt. China 82 B2
Xiachengzi China 82 C3
Xiachuan Dao i. China 87 E4
Xiacun China see Rushan
Xiadong China 84 B3
Xiaguan China see Dali
Xiahe China 84 D5
also known as Labrang
Xiajiang China 87 F3
also known as Baqiu
Xiajiang China see Qusum
Xiajin China 85 H4
Xiamen China 87 F4
also known as Amoy
Xi'an China 87 D1
formerly known as Sian
Xiancheng China see Suizhai
Xianfeng China 87 D2
Xiangcheng Henan China 87 E1
Xiangcheng Sichuan China 86 A2
also known as Qagchêng or Sangpi
Xiangcheng China see Xiangyang
Xiangfan China 87 E1
also known as Xiangyang
Xiangfeng China see Laifeng
Xianggang China see Hong Kong
Xianggang Hong Kong China see Hong Kong
Xianggang Tebie Xingzhengqu special admin. reg. China see Hong Kong
Xianghuang Qi China see Xin Bulag
Xiangjiang China see Huichang

Xiang Jiang r. China 87 E2
Xiangkhoang Laos 78 C4
also known as Xieng Khouang
Xiangkhoang Plateau Laos 78 C4
Xiangkou China see Wulong
Xiangning China 85 F5
Xiangquan He r. China 89 B6
Xiangride China 84 C5
Xiangshan China see Menghai
Xiangshan Gang b. China 87 G2
Xiangshui China 87 F1
Xiangshuiba China 87 D3
Xiangtan China 87 E3
Xiangxiang China 87 E3
Xiangyang Hu l. China 89 E5
Xiangyin China 87 E3
Xiangyun China 86 B3
also known as Xiangcheng
Xianju China 87 G2
Xianning China 87 E3
Xiannümiao China see Jiangdu
Xianshui China 87 F2
Xianshui He r. China 86 B2
Xiantao China 87 E2
formerly known as Mianyang
Xianxia Ling mts China 87 F3
Xianxian China 85 H4
also known as Leshou
Xianyang China 87 D1
Xianyou China 87 F3
Xiaoba China see Qingtongxia
Xiaochang China 87 E2
also known as Huayuan
Xiaodong China 87 D4
Xiao'ergou China 85 I1
Xiaofan China see Wuqiang
Xiaogan China 87 E2
Xiaoguai China 88 D2
Xiao Hinggan Ling mts China 82 B2
English form Lesser Khingan Mountains
Xiaojin China 86 B2
also known as Meixing or Zainlha
Xiaomei China 87 F3
Xiaonan China 84 D5
Xiaonanchuan China 84 B5
Xiao Qaidam China 84 B4
Xiaoqing r. China 85 H4
Xiaosanjiang China 87 E3
Xiaoshan China 87 G2
Xiao Surmang China 86 A1
Xiaotao China 87 F3
Xiaowutai Shan mt. China 85 G4
Xiaoxi China see Pinghe
Xiaoxian China see Longcheng
Xiaoxiang Ling mts China 86 B2
Xiaoyi China see Gongyi
Xiaoyi China 85 F4
Xiapu China 87 G3
also known as Songcheng
Xiaqiong China see Batang
Xiatil Mex. 185 H5
Xiaxian China 85 F5
Xiayanjing China see Yanjing
Xiayingpan China see Luzhi
Xiayingpan China see Lupanshui
Xiazhen China see Weishan
Xibdê China 86 A2
Xibet China 84 A2
formerly known as Sibati
Xibing China 87 F3
Xibu China see Dongshan
Xichang China see Yangyuan
Xichou China 86 B2
also known as Xisa
Xichuan China see Shangji
Xide China 86 B2
Xidu China see Hengyang
Xié r. Brazil 199 E4
Xiejiaji China see Qingyun
Xiemahe' China 87 D2
Xieng Khouang Laos see Xiangkhoang
Xieyang Dao i. China 87 D4
Xifei He r. China 87 F1
Xifeng Gansu China 85 E5
formerly known as Xifengzhen
Xifeng Guizhou China 86 C3
also known as Yongjing
Xifeng Liaoning China 82 B4
also known as Yongjing
Xifengzhen China see Xifeng
Xigazê China 89 E6
formerly spelt Shigatse
Xihan Shui r. China 86 C1
Xihe China 86 C1
also known as Hanyuan
Xihu China 84 A3
Xihua China 87 E1
Xihuachi China see Heshui
Xiji China 85 E5
Xi Jiang r. China 87 E4
Xijian Quan well China 84 C3
Xijir Ulan Hu salt l. China 97 F2
Xil China 85 G3
Xilaganí Greece see Xylagani
Xilaotou Shan mt. China 85 I2
Xiligou China see Ulan
Xilin China 86 C3
also known as Bada
Xilinhot China 85 H3
formerly known as Abagnar Qi
Xilinji China see Mohe
Xilókastron Greece see Xylokastro
Xilópolis Greece see Xylopoli
Ximiao China 84 D3
Xin China 85 F4
Xin'an China see Lai'an
Xin'an China see Anxin
Xin'an China 87 E1
Xin'anjiang Shuiku resr China 87 F2
Xinavane Moz. 133 Q2
Xin Barag Youqi China see Altan Emel
Xin Barag Zuoqi China see Amgalang
Xinbin China 82 B4
Xin Bulag China 85 G3
also known as Hobot Xar Qi or Xianghuang Qi
Xincai China 87 E1
also known as Gulu
Xinchang China see Yifeng
Xinchang China 87 G2
also known as Gutian
Xincheng China see Xinxing
Xincheng Guangxi China 87 D3
also known as Yuanqu
Xincheng China see Zhaojue
Xinchengbu China 85 F4
Xincun China see Dongchuan
Xindi China 87 D4
Xindi China see Honghu
Xindu Guangxi China 87 D4
Xindu China see Luhuo
Xindu Sichuan China 86 C2
Xinduqiao China 86 B2
Xinfeng Guangdong China 87 E3
Xinfeng China see Fengcheng
Xinfeng Jiangxi China 87 E3
Xinfengjiang Shuiku resr China 87 E4
Xing'an China 87 D3

Xingan China 87 E3
also known as Jinchuan
Xingba China see Lhünzê
Xingcheng China see Qianxi
Xingcheng China 85 I3
Xingdi China 88 D3
Xinge Angola 127 C7
Xingguo China see Qin'an
Xingguo China 87 E3
also known as Lianjiang
Xinghai China 84 C5
also known as Ziketan
Xinghua China 87 F1
Xinghua Wan b. China 87 F3
Xingkai China 82 D3
Xingkai Hu l. China/Rus.Fed. see Khanka, Lake
Xinglong Hebei China 85 H3
Xinglong Heilong. China 82 B2
Xinglongzhen China 82 B3
Xingning China 87 E3
Xingou China 87 E2
Xingping China 87 D1
Xingren China 86 C3
Xingrenbu China 84 E4
Xingsagoinba China 86 B1
Xingshan China see Majiang
Xingshan China 87 D2
also known as Gufu
Xingtai China 85 G4
Xingtang China 85 G4
Xingu r. Brazil 199 H5
Xingu, Parque Indígena do res. Brazil 202 A4
Xinguara Brazil 202 B3
Xingxian China 85 F4
Xingxingxia China 84 B3
Xingyang China 87 E1
Xingyi China 86 C3
also known as Huangcaoba
Xingzi China 87 F2
also known as Nankang
Xinhe Hebei China 85 G4
Xinhe Xinjiang China 88 C3
also known as Toksu
Xin Hot China 85 G3
also known as Abag Qi
Xinhua China see Huadu
Xinhua China 87 D3
Xinhua China see Qiaojia
Xinhua China see Funing
Xinhuacun China 84 D4
Xinhuang China 87 D3
Xinhui China 85 H3
also known as Aohan Qi
Xining China 84 D4
formerly spelt Sining
Xinji China 85 G4
formerly known as Shulu
Xinji China see Xinxian
Xinjian China 87 E2
also known as Changleng
Xinjiang China 85 F5
Xinjiang aut. reg. China see Xinjiang Uygur Zizhiqu
Xin Jiang r. China 87 F2
Xinjiangkou China see Songzi
Xinjiang Uygur Autonomous Region aut. reg. China see Xinjiang Uygur Zizhiqu
Xinjiang Uygur Zizhiqu aut. reg. China 84 B3
English form Sinkiang Uighur Autonomous Region or Xinjiang Uygur Autonomous Region; short form Sinkiang or Xinjiang; formerly known as Chinese Turkestan
Xinjie China 85 F4
Xinjie China see Yuanyang
Xinjin China see Pulandian
Xinjin China 86 B2
also known as Wujin
Xinjing China see Jingxi
Xinkai r. China 85 I3
Xinling China see Badong
Xinlong China 86 B2
also known as Nyagrong or Rulong
Xinmi China 87 E1
formerly known as Mixian
Xinmian China see Shimian
Xinmin China 85 I3
Xinning China see Ningxian
Xinning China see Fusui
Xinning China 87 D3
also known as Jinshi
Xinning China see Wuning
Xinning China see Kaijiang
Xinping China 86 B3
also known as Guishan
Xinqing China 82 C2
Xinquan China 87 F3
Xinshan China see Anyuan
Xinshao China 87 D3
also known as Niangxi
Xinshi China see Jingshan
Xinshiba China see Ganluo
Xintai China 85 H5
Xintanpu China 87 E2
Xintian China 87 E3
Xinxian China 87 E2
also known as Xinji
Xinxiang China 85 G5
Xinxing China 87 E4
also known as Xincheng
Xinyang China 87 E1
Xinyang Gang r. China 87 G1
Xinye China 87 E1
Xinye r. China 87 F1
Xinyi Guangdong China 87 D4
Xinyi Jiangsu China 87 F1
Xinying China 87 D5
Xinying Taiwan see Hsinying
Xinyu China 87 E3
Xinyuan China see Tianjun
Xinyuan China 88 C3
also known as Künes
Xinzhangfang China 85 I1
Xinzheng China 87 E1
Xinzhou China see Longlin
Xinzhou China see Huangping
Xinzhou Hubei China 87 E2
Xinzhou Shanxi China 85 G4
Xinzhu Taiwan see Hsinchu
Xinzo de Limia Spain 54 D2
also spelt Ginzo de Limia
Xiongshan China see Zhenghe
Xiongzhou China see Nanxiong
Xipamanu r. Bol./Brazil 200 D2
Xiping Henan China 87 D1
also known as Baicheng
Xiping Henan China 87 E1
Xiqing Shan mts China 86 B1
Xique Xique Brazil 202 D4
Xiro hill Greece 59 E10
Xirokampo Greece 59 H11
Xiruá r. Brazil 198 E6
Xisa China see Xichou
Xishanzui China 85 F3
also known as Urad Qianqi
Xisha Qundao is S. China Sea see Paracel Islands
Xishuangbanna reg. China 86 B4
Xishui Guizhou China 86 C2
Xishui Hubei China 87 E2
also known as Qingquan
Xistral, Serra do mts Spain 54 D1
also spelt Sierra del Gistral
Xi Taijnar Hu l. China 84 B4
Xitole Guinea-Bissau 124 B4
Xiucaiwan China see Fengdu
Xiugu China see Jinxi
Xi Ujimqin Qi China see Bayan Ul Hot
Xiuning China 87 F2
also known as Haiyang
Xiushan China 87 D2
also known as Zhonghe
Xiushan China see Tonghai
Xiushui China 87 E2
also known as Yining
Xiu Shui r. China 87 E2
Xiuwen China 86 C3
Xiuwu China 85 G5
Xiuyan China 85 I3
Xiuyan China see Qingjian
Xiuying China 87 D4
Xiwanzi China see Chongli
Xiwu China 86 A1
Xixabangma Feng mt. China 89 D6
also known as Shisha Pangma; formerly known as Gosainthan
Xixia China 87 D1
Xixian Henan China 87 E1
Xixian Shanxi China 85 F4
Xixiang China 87 C1
Xixón Spain see Gijón
Xiyang China 85 G4
Xiyang Dao i. China 87 G3
Xiyang Jiang r. China 86 C3
Xizang aut. reg. China see Xizang Zizhiqu
Xizang Gaoyuan plat. China see Tibet, Plateau of
Xizang Zizhiqu aut. reg. China 86 A2
English form Tibet or Tibet Autonomous Region; short form Xizang
Xizhong Dao i. China 85 I4
Xocavänd Azer. 107 F3
also spelt Khodzhavend
Xodoto, Akra pt Greece 59 H12
Xoi China see Qüxü
Xolobe S. Africa 133 L9
Xom An Lôc Vietnam 79 D6
Xom Dưc Hanh Vietnam 79 D6
Xonxa Dam S. Africa 133 L8
Xorkol China 88 E4
Xuancheng China see Xuanzhou
Xuan'en China 87 D2
also known as Zhushan
Xuanhan China 87 C2
also known as Dongxiang
Xuanhua China 85 G3
Xuân Lôc Vietnam 79 D6
Xuanwei China 86 C3
Xuanzhou China 87 F2
formerly known as Xuancheng
Xuchang Henan China 87 E1
Xucheng China see Xuwen
Xudat Azer. 107 G2
also spelt Khudat
Xuddur Somalia 128 D3
Xudun Somalia 128 E2
Xueba China see Sangri
Xuefeng China see Mingxi
Xuefeng Shan mts China 87 D3
Xuehua Shan hill China 87 D1
Xue Shan mts China 86 A3
Xugou China 87 F1
Xugui China 84 B5
Xuguit Qi China see Yakeshi
Xujiang China see Guangchang
Xulun Hobot Qagan Qi China see Qagan Nur
Xulun Hoh Qi China see Dund Hot
Xümatang China 86 A1
Xun r. China 82 C2
Xundian China 86 B3
also known as Rende
Xungba China 89 C5
also known as Xangdoring
Xungmai China 89 E6
Xung Qu r. China 89 F6
Xungru China 89 D6
Xunhe China 82 B2
Xun He r. China 87 D1
Xunhua China 84 D5
also known as Jishi
Xun Jiang r. China 87 D4
Xunke China 82 C2
Xunwu China 87 E3
also known as Changning
Xunxian China 85 G5
Xunyang China 87 D1
Xunyi China 85 F5
Xupu China 87 D3
also known as Lufeng
Xuru Co salt l. China 89 D6
Xushui China 85 G4
also known as Ansu
Xuwen China 87 D4
also known as Xucheng
Xuyang China see Rongxian
Xuyi China 87 F1
Xuyong China 86 C2
also known as Yongning
Xuzhou China see Tongshan
Xylagani Greece 58 G8
also spelt Xilaganí
Xylokastro Greece 59 D10
also known as Xilókastron
Xylopoli Greece 58 E8
also known as Xilópolis

↓ Y

Ya'an China 86 B2
Yaapeet Australia 147 D3
Yabanabat Turkey see Kızılcahamam
Yabassi Cameroon 125 H5
Yabēlo Eth. 128 C3
Yabēlo Wildlife Sanctuary nature res. Eth. 128 C3
Yablanitsa Bulg. 58 F5
Yablanovo Bulg. 58 H6
Yablonovyy Khrebet mts Rus. Fed. 85 F1
Yabo Nigeria 125 G3
Yabrai Shan mts China 84 D4
Yabrai Yanchang China 84 D4
Yabrīn reg. Saudi Arabia 105 E3
Yabrūd Syria 109 H4
Yabuli China 82 C3
Yabuyanos Peru 198 C5
Yacha China see Baisha
Yacheng China 87 D5
Yachi He r. China 86 C3
Yaciretá, Isla i. Para. 201 F6
Yaciretá Apipé, Embalse resr Para. 201 F6
Yacuiba Bol. 201 E5
Yacurai Venez. 199 E3
Yadé, Massif du mts Cent. Afr. Rep. 126 B3
Yadgir India 94 C2
Yadiki India 94 C3
Yadkin r. U.S.A. 174 D5
Yadkinville U.S.A. 176 E9
Yadong China 89 E7
also known as Xarsingma; formerly known as Chomo
Yadrin Rus. Fed. 40 H5
Yaeyama-rettō is Japan 81 K8
Yafa Israel see Tel Aviv-Yafo
Yafran Libya 120 B1
Yagaba Ghana 125 E4
Yagaing state Myanmar see Arakan
Yağcılı Turkey 59 I9
Yağda Turkey see Erdemli
Yagman Turkm. 102 C5
Yagmo China 89 D6
Yagnitsa Rus. Fed. 43 S3
Yago Mex. 184 D4
Yagoda Bulg. 58 G6
Yagodnaya Polyana Rus. Fed. 41 H6
Yagodnoye Kaluzhskaya Oblast' Rus. Fed. 43 Q8
Yagodnoye Magadanskaya Oblast' Rus. Fed. 39 O3
Yagodnyy Rus. Fed. 82 E2
Yagoua Cameroon 125 I4
Yagra China 89 C6
Yagradagzê Shan mt. China 84 B5
Yaguajay Cuba 186 D2
Yaguarón r. Brazil/Uruguay see Jaguarão
Yaguas r. Peru 198 D5
Yaha Thai. 79 C7
Yahk Canada 167 G5
Yahualica Mex. 185 E4
Yahyalı Turkey 98 B2
also known as Gazibenli
Yahya Wana Afgh. 96 A3
Yai, Khao hill Thai. 79 B5
Yaita Japan 90 F6
Yaizu Japan 91 F7
Yajiang China 86 B2
also known as Hekou or Nyagquka
Yakacık Turkey 108 H1
Yakapınar Turkey 108 G1
Yakeshi China 85 I1
formerly known as Xuguit Qi
Yakhab waterhole Iran 100 D3
Yakhehal Afgh. 101 F4
Yakhroma Rus. Fed. 43 S5
Yakima U.S.A. 180 B3
Yakima r. U.S.A. 180 C3
Yakima Indian Reservation res. U.S.A. 180 B3
Yakinish Iran 100 C3
Yakkabag Uzbek. 103 F5
formerly known as Stantsiya-Yakkabag
Yakmach Pak. 101 E4
Yako Burkina 125 E3
Yakobi Island U.S.A. 166 B3
Yakoma Dem. Rep. Congo 126 D3
Yakoruda Bulg. 58 E6
Yakovlevka Rus. Fed. 82 D3
Yakumo Japan 90 G3
Yaku-shima i. Japan 91 B9
Yakutat U.S.A. 166 B3
Yakutat Bay U.S.A. 164 E4
Yakutsk Rus. Fed. 39 M3
Yakymivka Ukr. 41 E7
Yala Ghana 125 E4
Yala Thai. 79 C7
Yalai China 89 D6
Yalakdere Turkey 58 K8
Yala National Park Sri Lanka see Ruhuna National Park
Yalan Dünya Mağarası tourist site Turkey 108 D1
Yalata Aboriginal Lands res. Australia 146 A2
Yale Canada 166 F5
Yale U.S.A. 173 K7
Yalgoo Australia 151 B6
Yalıkavak Turkey 59 I11
Yalıköy Turkey 58 J7
Yalinga Cent. Afr. Rep. 126 D3
Yalizava Belarus 43 K8
Yalkubul, Punta pt Mex. 185 H4
Yalleroi Australia 149 E5
Yallo Burkina 124 E3
Yallourn Australia 147 E4
Yaloké Cent. Afr. Rep. 126 C3
Yalong Jiang r. China 86 B3
Yalova Turkey 106 B2
Yalova prov. Turkey 58 K8
Yaloven' Moldova see Ialoveni
Yalpirakinu Aboriginal Land res. Australia 148 B4
Yalpuh, Ozero l. Ukr. 58 J3
Yalpukh r. Moldova see Ialpug
Yalta Ukr. 41 E7
Yaltins'kyy Zapovidnyk nature res. Ukr. 106 C1
Yalu Jiang r. China 85 I2
Yalu Jiang r. China/N. Korea 83 B4
also known as Amnok-kang
Yalutorovsk Rus. Fed. 38 G4
Yalvaç Turkey 106 B3
Yām reg. Saudi Arabia 105 D4
Yamada Japan 90 G5
Yamaga Japan 91 B8
Yamagata Iwate Japan 90 G4
Yamagata Yamagata Japan 90 G5
Yamagata pref. Japan 90 F5
Yamaguchi Japan 91 B7
Yamaguchi pref. Japan 91 B7
Yamal, Poluostrov pen. Rus. Fed. see Yamal Peninsula
Yam Alin', Khrebet mts Rus. Fed. 82 D1
Yamal Peninsula Rus. Fed. 38 G2
also known as Yamal, Poluostrov
Yamanashi pref. Japan 90 F7
Yamanie Falls National Park Australia 149 E3
Yamankhalinka Kazakh. see Makhambet
Yamarovka Rus. Fed. 85 F1
Yamasaki Japan 91 D7
Yamatsuri Japan 90 G6
Yamba Australia 147 G2
Yambacoona Australia 147 D4
Yambarran Range hills Australia 148 A2
Yambéring Guinea 124 B4
Yambi, Mesa de hills Col. 198 D4
Yambio Sudan 126 F3
Yambol Bulg. 58 H6
Yambrasbamba Peru 198 B6
Yamdena i. Indon. 73 H8
Yame Japan 91 B8
Yamethin Myanmar 78 B3
Y'ami i. Phil. 74 B1

▶Yamin, Puncak mt. Indon. 73 I7
4th highest mountain in Oceania.
oceania [landscapes] ▶ 136–137

Yamizo-san mt. Japan 90 G6
Yamkanmardi India 94 B2
Yamkhad Syria see Aleppo
Yamkino Rus. Fed. 43 K4
Yamm Rus. Fed. 43 J3
Yamma Yamma, Lake salt flat Australia 149 D5
also known as Mackillop, Lake

▶Yamoussoukro Côte d'Ivoire 124 D5
Capital of Côte d'Ivoire.

Yampil' Ukr. 41 D6
also spelt Yampol'
Yampol' Ukr. see Yampil'
Yamuna r. India 96 D4
English form Jumna
Yamunanagar India 96 C3
Yamzho Yumco l. China 89 E6
Yan r. China 85 F4
Yana r. Rus. Fed. 39 N2
Yanac Australia 146 D4
Yanachaga-Chemillen, Parque Nacional nat. park Peru 200 B2
Yanadani Japan 91 C8
Yanai Japan 91 C8
Yanam India 95 D2
formerly known as Yanaon
Yan'an China 85 F4
Yanaoca Peru 200 C3
Yanaon India see Yanam
Yanaul Rus. Fed. 40 J4
Yanavichy Belarus 43 L6
Yanayacu Peru 198 C5
Yanbian China 86 B3
also known as Dapingdi
Yanbu' al Baḩr Saudi Arabia 104 B2
Yanbu' an Nakhl reg. Saudi Arabia 104 B2
Yanceyville U.S.A. 176 F9
Yanchang China 85 F4
Yancheng China 87 G1
Yancheng China see Qihe
Yancheng China see Jingyan
Yanchep Australia 151 A6
Yanchi Ningxia China 85 E4
Yanchi Xinjiang China 84 B3
Yanchuan China 85 F4
Yanco Creek r. Australia 147 E3
Yanco Glen Australia 146 D2
Yanda watercourse Australia 147 E2
Yandama Creek watercourse Australia 146 D2
Yandang Shan mts China 87 G3
Yandao China see Yingjing
Yandaxkak China 88 E4
Yandeyarra Aboriginal Reserve Australia 150 B4
Yandil Australia 151 B5
Yandina Solomon Is 145 E2
Yandja Dem. Rep. Congo 126 C5
Yandoon Myanmar 78 A4
Yandun China 84 B3
Yanega Rus. Fed. 43 O1
Yanfolila Mali 124 C4
Yang r. China 85 G3
Yangalia Cent. Afr. Rep. 126 D3
Yangambi Dem. Rep. Congo 126 E4
Ya'ngamdo Xizang China 89 F6
Ya'ngamdo Xizang China 89 F6
Yangasso Mali 124 D3
Yangbajain China 89 E6
Yangbi China 86 A3
also known as Shangjie
Yangcheng China see Yangshan
Yangcheng China 85 G5
Yangchuan China see Suiyang
Yangchun China 87 D4
Yangcun China 87 E4
Yangcun China see Wuqing
Yangdok N. Korea 83 B5
Yanggao China 85 G3
Yanggu China 85 G4
Yanghe China see Yongning
Yang Hu l. China 89 D5
Yangiaryk Uzbek. 102 E4
Yangi Davan pass Aksai Chin/China 89 B5
Yangi-Nishan Uzbek. 103 F5
Yangi Qal'eh Afgh. 101 G2
Yangirabad Uzbek. 103 F4
Yangiyul' Uzbek. 103 G4
Yangjialing China 85 F4
Yangjiang China 87 D4
Yangjiaogou China 85 H4
Yangôn Myanmar see Rangoon
Yangôn admin. div. Myanmar 78 B4
English form Rangoon; also spelt Rangôn
Yangping China 87 D2
Yangquan China 85 G4
Yangshan China 87 E3
also known as Yangcheng
Yangshuo China 87 D3
Yang Talat Thai. 78 C4
Yangtouyan China 86 B3

▶Yangtze r. China 87 G2
Longest river in Asia and 3rd in the world. Also known as Yangtze Kiang or Chang Jiang or Jinsha Jiang or Tongtian He or Zhi Qu.
asia [landscapes] ▶ 62–63

Yangtze Kiang r. China 87 F2
also known as Yangtze
Yangtze, Mouth of the China 87 G2
also known as Changjiang Kou
Yangudi Rassa National Park Eth. 128 D2
Yangweigang China 87 F1
Yangxian China 87 C1
Yangyang S. Korea 83 C5
Yangyuan China 85 G3
also known as Xicheng
Yangzhou China see Hanjiang
Yanhe China 87 D2
also known as Heping
Yanhu China 88 E3
Yaninee, Lake salt flat Australia 146 B3
Yanishpole Rus. Fed. 40 E3
Yanis"yarvi, Ozero l. Rus. Fed. 44 O3
Yanji China 82 C4
Yanjin Henan China 85 G5
Yanjin Yunnan China 86 C2
also known as Yanjing
Yanjing China see Yanyuan
Yanjing China 86 A2
also known as Xiayanjing; formerly known as Caka'lho
Yanjing China see Yanjin
Yankara National Park Nigeria 125 H4
Yankavichy Belarus 43 J6
Yankou China see Wusheng
Yankton U.S.A. 178 C3
Yankton Indian Reservation res. U.S.A. 178 C3
Yanling Henan China 87 E1
also known as Anling
Yanling Hunan China 87 E3
formerly known as Lingxian
Yannina Greece see Ioannina
Yano-Indigirskaya Nizmennost' lowland Rus. Fed. 39 O2
Yanovo Rus. Fed. 43 N7
Yanov-Stan Rus. Fed. 39 I3
Yan Oya r. Sri Lanka 94 D4
Yanqi China 88 D3
Yanqing China 85 G3
Yanqul Oman 105 G3
Yanrey r. Australia 150 A4
Yanshan Hebei China 85 H4
Yanshan Jiangxi China 87 F2
also known as Hekou
Yanshan Yunnan China 86 C4
also known as Jiangna
Yan Shan mts China 85 H3
Yanshi China 87 E1
Yanshiping China 97 G2
Yanshou China 82 C3
Yanskiy Zaliv g. Rus. Fed. 39 N2
Yantabulla Australia 147 E2
Yantai China 85 I4
formerly known as Chefoo
Yántales, Cerro mt. Chile 205 B6
Yantarnyy Rus. Fed. 42 A7
historically known as Palmnicken
Yanting China 86 C2
also known as Yunxi
Yantongshan China 82 B4
Yantou China 87 G2
Yantra r. Bulg. 58 G5
Yanūfī, Jabal al hill Saudi Arabia 104 C3
Yany-Kurgan Kazakh. see Zhanakorgan
Yanyuan China 86 B3
also known as Yanjing
Yanzhou China 85 H5
Yao'an China 86 B3
also known as Dongchuan
Yaodu China see Dongzhi
Yaojie China see Honggu
Yaoli China 87 F2

▶Yaoundé Cameroon 125 H6
Capital of Cameroon.

Yaoxian China 87 D1
Yao Yai, Ko i. Thai. 79 B6
Yaozhen China 85 F4
Yap i. Micronesia 73 I5
formerly spelt Eap
Yapacana, Parque Nacional nat. park Venez. 199 E4
Yapacani r. Bol. 201 D3
Yapen i. Indon. 73 I7
Yapen, Selat sea chan. Indon. 73 I7
Yappar r. Australia 149 D3
Yapukarri Guyana 199 G4
Yapuparra Aboriginal Reserve Australia 151 D5
Yaqui r. Mex. 184 C3
Yar Rus. Fed. 40 J4
Yara Cuba 186 D2
Yaracal Venez. 198 D2
Yaracuy state Venez. 198 D2
Yaradzha Turkm. see Yaradzhi
Yaradzhi Turkm. 102 D5
formerly spelt Yaradzha
Yaraka Australia 149 E5
Yarangüme Turkey see Tavas
Yaransk Rus. Fed. 40 H4
Yardan Uzbek. see Iordan
Yardea Australia 146 B3
Yardımcı Burnu pt Turkey 106 B3
also known as Gelidonya Burnu
Yardımlı Azer. 107 G3
also spelt Yardymly
Yardley U.S.A. 177 K5
Yardoi China 89 E6
Yardymly Azer. see Yardımlı
Yare r. U.K. 47 N11
Yarega Rus. Fed. 40 J3

▶Yaren Nauru 145 F2
Capital of Nauru.
world [countries] ▶ 10–11

Yarenga r. Rus. Fed. 40 I3
Yarensk Rus. Fed. 40 I3
Yargara Moldova see Iargara
Yari r. Col. 198 C5
also known as Engaños, Río de los
Yariga-take mt. Japan 91 E6
Yarīm Yemen 104 D5
Yarımca Turkey see Körfez
Yaringa watercourse Australia 148 C4
Yaripo Brazil 199 H4
Yaris well Niger 125 G3
Yaritagua Venez. 187 F5
Yarkand China see Shache
Yarkant China see Shache
Yarkant He r. China 88 B4
Yarker Canada 173 Q6
Yarkhun r. Pak. 101 H2
Yarlovo Bulg. 58 E6
Yarlung Zangbo r. China 89 D6 see Brahmaputra
Yarmouth Canada 169 H5
Yarmouth U.K. see Great Yarmouth
Yarmouth U.S.A. 177 O2
Yarmūk r. Asia 108 G5
Yarnell U.S.A. 183 L7
Yaroslavichi Rus. Fed. 43 P1
Yaroslavl' Rus. Fed. 43 U4
Yaroslavl Oblast admin. div. Rus. Fed. see Yaroslavskaya Oblast'
Yaroslavskaya Oblast' admin. div. Rus. Fed. 43 U4
English form Yaroslavl Oblast
Yaroslavskiy Rus. Fed. 82 D3
Yarqon r. Israel 108 F5
Yarrabah Aboriginal Reserve Australia 149 E3
Yarra Junction Australia 147 E4
Yarralin Aboriginal Land res. Australia 148 A3
Yarram Australia 147 E4
Yarraman Australia 149 F5
Yarrawonga Australia 147 E4
Yarra Yarra Lakes salt flat Australia 151 A6
Yarrie Australia 150 C4
Yarronvale Australia 149 E5
Yarrowmere Australia 149 E4
Yartsevo Krasnoyarskiy Kray Rus. Fed. 39 I3
Yartsevo Smolenskaya Oblast' Rus. Fed. 43 N6
Yaru r. China 89 D6
Yarumal Col. 198 C3
Yarwa China 86 A2
Yary Rus. Fed. 40 M1
Yarzhong China 86 A2
Yaş Romania see Iaşi
Yasa Dem. Rep. Congo 126 D5
Yasai r. India 95 E1
Yasawa Group is Fiji 145 G3
Yasenkovo Bulg. 58 H5
Yashi Nigeria 125 G3
Yashikera Nigeria 125 F4
Yashilkŭl l. Tajik. 101 H2
Yashkino Rus. Fed. 41 J5
Yashkul' Rus. Fed. 41 H7
formerly known as Peschanoye
Yasin Jammu and Kashmir 96 B1
Yaskavichy Belarus 42 I9
Yasna Polyana Bulg. 58 I6
Yasnogorsk Rus. Fed. 43 S7
formerly known as Laptevo
Yasnyy Amurskaya Oblast' Rus. Fed. 82 C1
Yasnyy Orenburgskaya Oblast' Rus. Fed. 102 D2
Yasothon Thai. 78 D5
Yass Australia 147 F3
Yass r. Australia 147 F3
Yassı Burnu c. Cyprus see Plakoti, Cape
Yasski Rus. Fed. 43 L4
Yasugi Japan 91 C7
Yāsūj Iran 100 B4
Yasuni nat. park Ecuador 198 C5
Yasur vol. Vanuatu 145 F3
Yat well Niger 125 I1
Yata r. Bol. 200 D2
Yata r. Cent. Afr. Rep. 126 D2
Yatağan Turkey 106 B3
Yatakala Niger 125 F3
Yata Plateau Kenya 128 C5
Yaté New Caledonia 145 F4
Yates r. Canada 167 H2
Yates Center U.S.A. 178 D4
Yathkyed Lake Canada 167 L2
Yathong Nature Reserve Australia 147 E3
Yatolema Dem. Rep. Congo 126 E4
Yatou China see Rongcheng
Yatsuga-take vol. Japan 91 F7
Yatsushiro Japan 91 B8
Yatsushiro-kai b. Japan 91 B8
Yaţţa West Bank 108 G6
also spelt Yuta
Yauca Peru 200 B3
Yauca r. Peru 200 B3
Yauco Puerto Rico 187 G3
Yauli Peru 200 A2
Yauna Maloca Col. 198 D5
Yauri Peru 200 C3
Yauricocha Peru 200 B3
Yau Tong b. Hong Kong China 87 [inset]
Yauyos Peru 200 B3
Yavan Tajik. see Yovon
Yavari r. Peru 198 D6
also spelt Javari
Yávaros Mex. 184 C3
Yavatmal India 94 C1
formerly spelt Yeotmal
Yavero r. Peru 200 B3
also known as Paucartambo
Yaví, Cerro mt. Venez. 199 E3
Yavr r. Fin./Rus. Fed. 44 O1
Yavuzlu Turkey 109 I1
Yawatahama Japan 91 C8
Yawatongguz He r. China 89 C4
Yawatongguzlangar China 89 C4
Yaw Chaung r. Myanmar 78 A3
Yawng-hwe Shan Myanmar 78 B3
Yaxchilan tourist site Guat. 185 H5
Yaxian China see Sanya
Yayladağı Turkey 108 H2
also known as Ordu
Yayva Rus. Fed. 40 K4
Yazagyo Myanmar 78 A3
Yazd Iran 100 C4
Yazd prov. Iran 100 C4
Yazdān Iran 101 E3
Yazd-e Khvāst Iran 100 C4
also known as Samirum
Yazgulemskiy Khrebet mts Tajik. see Yazgulom, Qatorkŭhi
Yazgulom, Qatorkŭhi mts Tajik. 101 G2
also known as Yazgulemskiy Khrebet
Yazhelbitsy Rus. Fed. 43 N3
Yazıhan Turkey 107 D3
also known as Fethiye
Yazıkent Turkey 59 J11
Yazoo r. U.S.A. 175 B5
Yazoo City U.S.A. 175 B5
Yaz'va r. Rus. Fed. 40 K3
Ybakoura well Chad 120 B4
Y Bala U.K. see Bala
Ybbs r. Austria 49 M7
Ybbs an der Donau Austria 49 M7
Ybycui Para. 201 F6
Yding Skovhøj hill Denmark 45 J5
Ydra Greece 59 E11
Ydra i. Greece 59 E11
English form Hydra; also spelt Idhra or Idra
Ydras, Kolpos sea chan. Greece 59 E11
also spelt Ídhras, Kólpos
Y Drenewydd U.K. see Newtown
Ye Myanmar 79 B5
Ye r. Myanmar 79 B5
Yebaishou China see Jianping
Yebawmi Myanmar 78 A2
Yebbi-Bou Chad 120 C4
Yebekshi Kazakh. 103 G4
Yecheng China 88 B4
formerly known as Karghalik or Kargilik
Yecla Spain 55 J6
Yécora Mex. 184 C2
Yedashe Myanmar 78 B4
Yedatore India 94 C3
Yedi Burun Başı pt Turkey 59 K12
Yedoma Rus. Fed. 40 H3
Yedri well Chad 120 C4
Yedrovo Rus. Fed. 43 O4
Yedy Belarus 42 I6
Yeed Eth. 128 D3
Yeeda River Australia 150 C3
Yeelanna Australia 146 B3
Yefimovskiy Rus. Fed. 43 P2
Yefremov Rus. Fed. 43 T8
Yêgainnyin China see Henan
Yeggueba well Niger 125 I2
Yeghegnadzor Armenia 107 F3
formerly known as Mikoyan; formerly spelt Yekhegnadzor
Yegindybulak Kazakh. 103 I2
also spelt Egindibulaq
Yegorlyk r. Rus. Fed. 41 G7
Yegorlykskaya Rus. Fed. 41 G7
Yegorova, Mys pt Rus. Fed. 82 E3
Yegor'ye Rus. Fed. 43 O6
Yegor'yevsk Rus. Fed. 43 U6
Yégué Togo 125 F4
Yei Sudan 128 A3
Yei r. Sudan 128 A3
Yeina Island P.N.G. 149 G1
Yeji China 87 E2
formerly known as Yejiaji
Yeji Ghana 125 E4
Yejiaji China see Yeji
Yekaterinburg Rus. Fed. 38 G4
formerly known as Sverdlovsk
Yekaterinodar Rus. Fed. see Krasnodar
Yekaterinoslav Ukr. see Dnipropetrovs'k
Yekaterinoslavka Rus. Fed. 82 C2
Yekaterinovka Lipetskaya Oblast' Rus. Fed. 43 T9
Yekaterinovka Saratovskaya Oblast' Rus. Fed. 41 H5
Yekhegnadzor Armenia see Yeghegnadzor
Yekimovichi Rus. Fed. 43 O7
Yekokora r. Dem. Rep. Congo 126 D4
Yelabuga Rus. Fed. 82 D2
Yelabuga Rus. Fed. 40 I5
Yelan' Rus. Fed. 41 G6
Yelbarsli Turkm. 102 E5
Yeleğen Turkey 59 J10
Yelenovskiye Kar'yery Ukr. see Dokuchayevs'k
Yelenskiy Rus. Fed. 43 Q8
Yelets Rus. Fed. 43 T9
Yeletskiy Rus. Fed. 40 M2
Yeligovo Rus. Fed. 43 O3
Yélimané Mali 124 C3
Yelino Rus. Fed. 43 U7
Yelizavetgrad Ukr. see Kirovohrad
Yelizovo Rus. Fed. 39 P4
Yelkhovka Rus. Fed. 41 I5
Yell i. U.K. 46 K3
Yellabina Regional Reserve nature res. Australia 146 B2
Yellandu India 94 D2
Yellapur India 94 B3
Yellareddi India 94 C2

▶Yellow r. China 85 H4
4th longest river in Asia and 7th in the world. Also known as Huang He or Ma Qu; formerly spelt Hwang Ho.
asia [landscapes] ▶ 62–63

Yellow r. U.S.A. 172 C7
Yellow Bluff hd Canada 167 O1
Yellowdine Australia 151 B6
Yellowhead Pass Canada 166 G4

▶Yellowknife Canada 167 H2
Capital of Northwest Territories.

Yellowknife r. Canada 167 H2
Yellow Mountain hill Australia 147 E3
Yellow Sea N. Pacific Ocean 83 B6
Yellow Springs U.S.A. 176 B6
Yellowstone r. U.S.A. 178 B2
Yellowstone Lake U.S.A. 180 E3
▶Yellowstone National Park U.S.A. 180 E3
northamerica [environments] ▶ 162–163
Yell Sound strait U.K. 46 K3
Yellville U.S.A. 179 D4
Yelm U.S.A. 180 B3
Yel'nya Rus. Fed. 43 O7
Yeloten Turkm. 103 E5
also spelt Yolöten; formerly spelt Iolotan'
Yelovo Rus. Fed. 40 J4
Yel'sk Belarus 41 D6
Yel'tsy Rus. Fed. 43 O5
Yelva r. Rus. Fed. 40 I3
Yelverton Bay Canada 165 K1
Yelwa Nigeria 125 H4
Yema Nanshan mts China 84 B4
Yema Shan mts China 84 B4
Yematan China 84 C4
Yembo Eth. 128 C2
▶Yemen country Asia 104 D5
asia [countries] ▶ 64–67
Yemetsk Rus. Fed. 40 G3
Yemişenbükü Turkey see Taşova
Yemmiganur India see Emmiganuru
Yemtsa Rus. Fed. 40 G3
Yemva Rus. Fed. 40 I3
formerly known as Zheleznodorozhnyy
Yena Rus. Fed. 44 O2
Yenagoa Nigeria 125 G5
Yenakiyeve Ukr. 41 F6
also spelt Yenakiyevo; formerly known as Rykovo
Yenakiyevo Ukr. see Yenakiyeve
Yenangyat Myanmar 78 A3
Yenangyaung Myanmar 78 A3
Yenanma Myanmar 78 A4
Yên Bai Vietnam 78 D3
Yendi Ghana 125 E4
Yêndum China see Zhag'yab
Yénéganou Congo 126 B5
Yenge r. Dem. Rep. Congo 126 D5
Yengejeh Iran 100 A2
Yengema Sierra Leone 124 C4

index

Y
Z

Yexian China 87 E1
also known as Kunyang
Yexian China see Laizhou
Yeygen'yevka Kazakh. 103 I4
Yeyik China 89 C4
Yeysk Rus. Fed. 41 F7
Yeyungou China 88 D3
Yezerishche, Ozero l. Belarus/Rus. Fed. 43 L6
Yezhou China see Jianshi
Yezhuga r. Rus. Fed. 40 H2
Yezo i. Japan see Hokkaidō
Yezyaryshcha Belarus 43 K6
Y Fenni U.K. see Abergavenny
Y Fflint U.K. see Flint
Yi r. Henan China 87 D1
Yi r. Shandong China 87 F1
Yi r. Uruguay 204 F4
Yiali i. Greece see Gyali
Yi'allaq, Gebel mt. Egypt 108 E7
Yialousa Cyprus see Aigialousa
Yi'an China 82 B3
Yianisádha i. Greece see Gianysada
Yiannitsá Greece see Giannitsa
Yibā, Wādī watercourse Saudi Arabia 104 C4
Yibin Sichuan China 86 C2
also known as Baixi
Yibin Sichuan China 86 C2
Yibug Caka salt l. China 89 D5
Yicheng China 87 D2
Yicheng Hubei China 87 D1
Yicheng Shanxi China 85 F5
Yichuan Henan China 87 E1
Yichuan Shaanxi China 85 F5
also known as Danzhou
Yichun Heilong. China 82 C3
Yichun Jiangxi China 87 E3
Yidu China 86 A2
Yidun China 86 A2
Yifeng China 87 E2
also known as Xinchang
Yiggêlong China see Qumarlêb
Yihuang China 87 E3
also known as Fenggang
Yijiang China see Yiyang
Yijun China 87 F5
Yilaha China 85 J1
Yilan China 82 C3
Yilan Taiwan see Ilan
Yıldız Dağları mts Turkey 106 A2
Yıldızeli Turkey 107 D3
Yilehuli Shan mts China 85 I1
Yiliang Yunnan China 86 A3
also known as Kuangyuan
Yiliang Yunnan China 86 C3
also known as Jiaokui
Yiliping China 84 B4
Yilliminning Australia 151 B7
Yilong Heilong. China 82 B3
Yilong Sichuan China 86 C2
also known as Jincheng
Yilong China see Shiping
Yilong Hu l. China 86 B4
Yimatu r. China 85 H3
Yimianpo China 82 C3
Yimin r. China 85 H1
Yinan China 85 H5
also known as Jiehu
Yincheng China see Dexing
Yinchuan China 85 E4
Yindarlgooda, Lake salt flat Australia 151 C6
Yingawunarri Aboriginal Land res. Australia 148 A3
Yingcheng China 87 E2
Yingde China 87 E3
Ying He r. China 87 F1
Yingjing China 86 C2
also known as Yandao
Yingkou China 85 I3
historically known as Newchwang
also known as Dashiqiao
Yingpanshui China 84 E4
Yingshan Hubei China 87 E2
also known as Wenquan
Yingshan Sichuan China 86 C2
also known as Chengzhou
Yingshang China 87 F1
Yingtan China 87 F2
Yingtaoyuan China see Fanxian
Yingxian China 85 G4
Yining China see Xiushui
Yining China 88 C3
also known as Gulja; formerly known as Kuldja
Yiningarra Aboriginal Land res. Australia 148 A3
Yinjiang China 87 D3
Yinkeng China 87 E3
Yinma r. China 82 B4
Yinmabin Myanmar 78 A3
Yinnyein Myanmar 78 A4
Yin Shan mts China 85 F3
Yinxian China China see Ningbo
Yi'ong Zangbo r. China 89 F6
Yioúra i. Greece see Gioura
Yipinglang China see Meitan
Yiquan China see Meitan
Yirga Alem Eth. 128 C3
Yirol Sudan 128 A3
Yirrkala Australia 148 C2
Yirshi China see Yirxie
Yirxie China 85 H2
formerly known as Yirshi
Yisa China see Honghe
Yishan China see Yizhou
Yishan China see Guanyun
Yi Shan mt. China 85 H4
Yi Shan mts China 85 H4
Yishui China 85 H5
Yishun Sing. 76 [inset]
Yi Tchoume well Niger 125 I1
Yithion Greece see Gytheio
Yitiaoshan China see Jingtai
Yitong China 82 B4
Yitong r. China 82 B3
Yi Tu, Nam r. Myanmar 78 B3
Yitulihe China 85 I1
Yiwanquan China 84 B3
Yiwu China 84 B3
also known as Aratürük
Yiwulü Shan mts China 85 I3
Yixian Anhui China 87 F2
also known as Biyang
Yixian Hebei China 85 G4
also known as Yizhou
Yixian Liaoning China 85 I3
Yixing China 87 F2
Yixun r. China 85 H3
Yiyang Hunan China 87 E2
Yiyang Jiangxi China 87 F2
also known as Yijiang
Yiyang Yunnan China 86 B3
also known as Nanma
Yizhang China 87 E3
Yizheng China 87 F1
Yizhou China 87 D3
formerly known as Qingyuan or Yishan
Yizhou China see Yixian
Yizra'el country Asia see Israel
Yläne Fin. 45 M3
Ylihärmä Fin. 44 N3
Yli-Ii Fin. 44 N2
Yli-Kärppä Fin. 44 N2

Ylikiiminki Fin. 44 N2
Yli-Kitka l. Fin. 44 O2
Ylistaro Fin. 44 M3
Ylitornio Fin. 44 M2
Ylivieska Fin. 44 N2
Ylläs hill Fin. 44 N2
Ylöjärvi Fin. 45 M3
Ymer Ø i. Greenland 165 Q2
Ymer Nunatak Greenland 165 Q2
Ynykchanskiy Rus. Fed. 39 N3
Ynys Môn i. U.K. see Anglesey
Yoakum U.S.A. 179 C6
Yobe state Nigeria 125 H4
Yobetsu-dake vol. Japan 90 G3
Yoboki Djibouti 128 D2
Yogan, Cerro mt. Chile 205 C9
Yogoum well Chad 120 C5
Yogyakarta Indon. 77 E4
formerly spelt Jogjakarta
Yogyakarta admin. dist. Indon. 77 E5
Yoho National Park Canada 167 G5
Yoichi Japan 90 G3
Yoichi-dake mt. Japan 90 G3
Yojoa, Lago de l. Hond. 186 B4
Yōka Japan 91 D7
Yokadouma Cameroon 125 I6
Yōkaichi Japan 91 E7
Yokaichiba Japan 91 G7
Yoko Cameroon 125 I5
Yokohama Aomori Japan 90 G4
Yokohama Kanagawa Japan 91 F7
Yokosuka Japan 91 F7
Yokote Japan 90 G5
Yokotsu-dake mt. Japan 90 G4
Yola Nigeria 125 I4
Yolo U.S.A. 182 C3
Yolombo Dem. Rep. Congo 126 D5
Yolöten Turkm. see Yeloten
Yoluk Mex. 185 I5
Yom, Mae Nam r. Thai. 78 C5
Yomou Guinea 124 C5
Yonago Japan 91 C7
Yŏnan N. Korea 83 B5
Yoneshiro-gawa r. Japan 90 G4
Yonezawa Japan 90 G6
Yŏng-am S. Korea 83 B6
Yong'an China see Fengjie
Yong'an China 87 F3
Yongbei China see Yongsheng
Yongchang China 84 D4
Yongcheng China 87 F1
Yŏngch'ŏn S. Korea 83 C6
Yongchuan China 86 C2
Yongchun China 87 F3
also known as Taocheng
Yongdeng China 84 D4
Yongding China 87 F3
also known as Fengcheng
Yongding China see Yongren
Yongding China see Fumin
Yongding r. China 85 H4
Yongfeng China 87 E3
also known as Wenfeng; formerly known as Jishui
Yongfeng China see Guangfeng
Yongfengqu China see Fumin
Yongfu China 87 D3
Yŏnggwang S. Korea 83 B6
Yŏnghŭng N. Korea 83 B5
Yŏnghŭng-man b. N. Korea 83 B5
Yongji China 87 D2
also known as Kouqian
Yongjia China see Shangtang
Yongjing China 84 D5
Yongjing China see Liujiaxia
Yongjing China see Xifeng
Yongjing China see Xifeng
Yŏngju S. Korea 83 C5
Yongkang China 87 G2
Yongle China see Zhen'an
Yongle China see Nanping
Yongling China 82 B4
Yongnian China 85 G4
also known as Linmingguan
Yongning Guangxi China 87 D4
also known as Pumiao
Yongning China see Tonggu
Yongning Ningxia China 85 E4
also known as Yanghe
Yongning China see Xuyong
Yongqing China see Qingshui
Yongren China 86 B3
also known as Yongding
Yŏngsan-gang r. S. Korea 83 B6
Yongshan China 86 B3
also known as Jingxin
Yongsheng China 86 B3
also known as Yongbei
Yongshou China 87 D1
Yongshun China 87 D2
also known as Lingxi
Yongtai China 87 F3
also known as Zhangcheng
Yongxin China 87 E3
Yongxing Hunan China 87 E3
Yongxing Jiangxi China 87 E3
also known as Hechuan
Yongxiu China 87 E2
Yongzhou China 87 D3
Yonkers U.S.A. 177 L5
Yonne r. France 51 I4
Yoo Baba well Niger 125 I2
Yopal Col. 198 C3
Yopurga China 88 B4
Yordon Uzbek. see Iordan
Yordu Jammu and Kashmir 96 B2
York Australia 151 B6
York r. Canada 167 M4
York U.K. 47 K10
historically known as Eburacum
York AL U.S.A. 175 B5
York NE U.S.A. 178 C3
York PA U.S.A. 177 I6
York, Cape Australia 149 D1
York, Kap c. Greenland see Innaanganeq
York Downs Australia 149 D2
Yorke Peninsula Australia 146 C3
Yorkshire Dales National Park U.K. 47 J9
Yorkshire Wolds hills U.K. 47 L10
York Springs U.S.A. 177 H5
Yorkton Canada 167 K5
Yorktown U.S.A. 177 I8
Yoro Hond. 186 B4
Yoronga i. Indon. 75 D3
Yöröö Gol r. Mongolia 85 F1
Yosemite U.S.A. 176 A8
Yosemite National Park U.S.A. 182 D4
Yosemite Village U.S.A. 182 D4
Yoshino-gawa r. Japan 91 D7
Yoshino-Kumano National Park Japan 91 E8
Yoshkar-Ola Rus. Fed. 40 H4
Yos Sudarso i. Indon. see Dolak, Pulau
Yōsu S. Korea 83 B6
Yotau Bol. 201 E4
Yōtei-zan mt. Japan 90 G3
Yotvata Israel 108 G8
Youbou Canada 166 E5
Youdunzi China 88 D3
You Jiang r. China 87 D4
Youlin China 85 H4
Youngal Rep. of Ireland 47 E12
also spelt Eochaill
Ylämäa Fin. 45 O3
Yläne Fin. 45 M3
Ylihärmä Fin. 44 N3
Yli-Ii Fin. 44 N2
Yli-Kärppä Fin. 44 N2

Young Uruguay 204 F4
Young U.S.A. 183 N7
Younghusband, Lake salt flat Australia 146 C2
Younghusband Peninsula Australia 146 C3
Young Island Antarctica 223 K2
Young Nicks Head N.Z. 152 L6
Young Range mts N.Z. 153 D12
Youngstown Canada 167 I5
Youngstown U.S.A. 176 E4
Youngsville NC U.S.A. 176 G9
Youngsville PA U.S.A. 176 F4
Yountville U.S.A. 182 B3
Youshashan China 88 B4
You Shui r. China 87 D2
Youssoufia Morocco 122 C2
formerly known as Louis-Gentil
Youvarou Mali 124 D3
Youxi China 87 F3
Youxian China 87 E3
also known as Zhongduo
Youyi China 82 C3
Youyi Feng mt. China/Rus. Fed. 88 D1
Youyu China 85 G4
also known as Liangjiayoufang
Yovon Tajik. 101 G2
also spelt Yavan
Yowah watercourse Australia 147 E2
Yowereena Hill hill Australia 151 B5
Yozgat Turkey 106 C3
Ypé-Jhú Para. 201 G5
Yppäri Fin. 44 N3
Ypres Belgium see Ieper
Ypsilanti U.S.A. 173 J8
Yreka U.S.A. 180 B4
Yrghyz Kazakh. see Irgiz
Yr Wyddfa mt. U.K. see Snowdon
Yser r. France 51 I2
also known as IJzer (Belgium)
Yssingeaux France 51 K7
Ystad Sweden 45 K5
Ysyk-Köl Kyrg. see Balykchy
Ysyk-Köl admin. div. Kyrg. 103 I4
English form Issyk-Kul Oblast; also known as Issyk-Kul'skaya Oblast'
▶ Ysyk-Köl salt l. Kyrg. 103 I4
5th largest lake in Asia. Also known as Issyk-Kul', Ozero.
asia [landscapes] ▶▶ 62–63
Y Trallwng U.K. see Welshpool
Ytre Vinje Norway see Åmot
Ytyk-Kyuyel' Rus. Fed. 39 N3
Yu r. China 85 G4
Yu i. Indon. 75 D3
Yuan'an China 87 D3
also known as Mingfeng
Yuanbao Shan mt. China 87 D3
Yuanjiang Hunan China 87 E2
Yuanjiang Yunnan China 86 B4
also known as Lijiang
Yuan Jiang r. Hunan China 87 D2
Yuan Jiang r. Yunnan China 86 B4
Yuanjiazhuang China see Foping
Yüanli Taiwan 87 G3
Yuanling China 87 D2
Yuanma China see Yuanmou
Yuanmou China 86 B3
also known as Yuanma
Yuanping China 85 G4
Yuanquan China see Anxi
Yuanshan China see Lianping
Yuanshanzi China 84 C4
Yuanyang China 86 B4
also known as Xinjie
Yuba r. U.S.A. 182 C2
Yuba City U.S.A. 182 C2
Yūbari Japan 90 G3
Yūbari-dake mt. Japan 90 H3
Yūbari-sanchi mts Japan 90 H3
Yubei China 86 C2
formerly known as Jiangbei
Yūbetsu Japan 90 H2
Yūbetsu-gawa r. Japan 90 H2
Yubileynyy Kazakh. 103 J2
Yubu Sudan 126 E3
Yucaipa U.S.A. 183 G7
Yucatán pen. Mex. 185 H4
Yucatán state Mex. 185 H4
Yucatan Channel Cuba/Mex. 171 I7
Yucca U.S.A. 183 J7
Yucca Lake U.S.A. 183 H5
Yucca Valley U.S.A. 183 H7
Yucheng China see Yunan
Yucheng Henan China 87 E1
Yucheng Shandong China 85 I4
Yuci China see Yuexi
Yuci China 85 G4
Yuchi China 86 C2
also known as Jiulong
Yuelai China see Huachuan
Yueliang Pao l. China 85 I2
Yuendumu Australia 148 A4
Yuendumu Aboriginal Land res. Australia 148 A4
Yuen Long Hong Kong China 87 [inset]
Yueqing China 87 G2
Yuexi Anhui China 87 F2
Yuexi Sichuan China 86 B2
also known as Yuecheng
Yueyang Hunan China 87 E2
also known as Rongjiawan
Yueyang China see Anyue
Yug Rus. Fed. 40 K4
Yug r. Rus. Fed. 40 H3
Yugan China 87 F2
Yug-Kamskiy Rus. Fed. 40 J4
Yugo-Kamskiy Rus. Fed. 40 J4
Yugorsk Rus. Fed. 38 G3
formerly known as Komsomol'skiy
Yugorsky Poluostrov pen. Rus. Fed. 40 L1
Yugorskiy Shar Rus. Fed. 40 L1
▶ Yugoslavia country Europe 58 B5
spelt Jugoslavija in Serbian
europe [countries] ▶▶ 32–35
▶ Yugoslavia
Up to 1993 included Bosnia-Herzegovina, Croatia, Macedonia and Slovenia.
Yuhang China 87 G2
Yuhu China see Eryuan
Yuhuan China 87 G2
also known as Huanshan
Yuhuang Ding mt. China 85 H4
Yuin Australia 151 B5
Yujiang China 87 F2
also known as Dengjiabu
Yu Jiang r. China 87 D4
Yujin China see Qianwei
Yukagirskoye Ploskogor'ye plat. Rus. Fed. 39 P3
Yukamenskoye Rus. Fed. 40 J4
Yukarı Saray Ovaları plain Turkey 106 D3
Yukarısarıkaya Turkey 106 C3
Yukhavichy Belarus 43 J5
Yukhmachi Rus. Fed. 40 I5
Yukhnov Rus. Fed. 43 Q5
Yukhovo Rus. Fed. 43 L5

Yuki Dem. Rep. Congo 126 C5
Yuki Japan 91 C7
▶ Yukon r. Canada/U.S.A. 164 C3
5th longest river in North America.
northamerica [landscapes] ▶▶ 156–157
Yukon-Charley Rivers National Preserve nature res. U.S.A. 164 C3
Yukon Crossing Canada 166 B2
Yukon Territory admin. div. Canada 166 C2
Yüksekova Turkey 107 F3
also known as Dize
Yukuhashi Japan 91 B8
Yulara Australia 148 A5
Yule r. Australia 150 B4
Yuleba Australia 149 F5
Yule Australia 146 C3
Yuli China 88 D3
also known as Lopnur
Yüli Taiwan 87 G4
Yulin Guangxi China 87 D4
Yulin Shaanxi China 85 F4
Yulongxue Shan mt. China 86 B3
Yuma AZ U.S.A. 183 J9
Yuma CO U.S.A. 178 B3
Yuma Desert U.S.A. 183 J9
Yumaguzino Rus. Fed. 102 D1
Yumbarra Conservation Park nature res. Australia 146 B2
Yumbi Bandundu Dem. Rep. Congo 126 C5
Yumbi Maniema Dem. Rep. Congo 126 E5
Yumbo Col. 198 B4
Yumen China 84 C4
also known as Laojunmiao
Yumendongzhan China 84 C4
Yumenguan China 84 B3
Yumenzhen China 84 C4
Yumin China 88 C2
also known as Karabura
Yumt Uul mt. Mongolia 84 C2
Yumurtalık Turkey 108 G1
Yuna Australia 151 A6
Yuna r. Dom. Rep. 187 F3
Yunak Turkey 106 B3
Yunan China 87 D4
also known as Yucheng
Yunchara Bol. 200 D5
Yuncheng Shandong China 85 G5
Yuncheng Shanxi China 87 D1
Yunfu China 87 E4
Yungas reg. Bol. 200 D4
Yungay Chile 200 D5
Yungay Peru 200 C4
Yun Gui Gaoyuan plat. China 86 B3
Yunhe China see Pizhou
Yunhe China see Heqing
Yunhe China 87 G2
Yunjinghong China see Jinghong
Yunkai Dashan mts China 87 D4
Yunkanjini Aboriginal Land res. Australia 148 A4
Yunling China see Yunxiao
Yun Ling mts China 86 A3
Yunmeng China 87 E2
Yunmenling China 87 E3
Yunnan prov. China 86 B3
Yun Shui r. China 87 E2
Yunta Australia 146 C3
Yuntai Shan mt. China 87 D1
Yuntut National Park Canada 164 F3
Yunwu Shan mts China 87 D4
Yunxi China 87 D1
Yunxi China see Yanting
Yunxian Hubei China 87 D1
Yunxian Yunnan China 86 B3
also known as Aihua
Yunxiao China 87 F4
also known as Yunling
Yun'yakha r. Rus. Fed. 40 L2
Yunyang Chongqing China 87 D2
Yunyang Henan China 87 E1
Yunyang China see Pingbian
Yuping China see Libo
Yuping China 87 D3
Yuqing China 87 D3
also known as Baini
Yura r. Bol. 200 D5
Yura Peru 200 C4
Yura-gawa r. Japan 91 D7
Yurappu-dake mt. Japan 90 G3
Yuratishki Belarus 42 H7
Yurba Co l. China 89 D5
Yurga Rus. Fed. 80 C1
Yurimaguas Peru 198 B6
Yurino Rus. Fed. 40 H4
Yurla Rus. Fed. 40 J4
Yurungkax He r. China 89 C4
Yur'ya Rus. Fed. 40 I4
Yur'yevets Ivanovskaya Oblast' Rus. Fed. 40 G4
Yur'yevets Vladimirskaya Oblast' Rus. Fed. 43 V5
Yur'yev-Pol'skiy Rus. Fed. 43 U5
Yuscarán Hond. 186 B4
Yushan Fujian China 87 F3
Yushan Jiangxi China 87 F2
also known as Bingxi
Yü Shan mt. Taiwan 87 G4
Yushan Liedao is China 87 G2
Yushe China 85 G4
Yushino Rus. Fed. 40 J1
Yushkozero Rus. Fed. 44 Q4
Yushu Jilin China 82 B3
Yushu Qinghai China 86 A1
also known as Gyêgu
Yushugou China 88 D3
Yushut r. Rus. Fed. 40 I4
Yushuwan China see Huaihua
Yusta Rus. Fed. 102 A3
formerly known as Trudovoy
Yusufeli Turkey 107 E2
Yusuhara Japan 91 C8
Yus'va Rus. Fed. 40 J4
Yuta West Bank see Yaṭṭa
Yutai China 87 F1
also known as Guting
Yutian Hebei China 85 H4
Yutian Xinjiang China 89 C4
also known as Keriya or Muhala
Yutpundji Djindiniwirritj res. Australia 148 A2
Roper Bar Aboriginal Land
Yuty Para. 201 F6
Yuva U.S.A. 173 J5
Yuwang China 85 E4
Yuxi China see Daozhen
Yuxi Hubei China 87 D2
Yuxi Yunnan China 86 B3
Yuxian Hebei China 85 G4
also known as Yuzhou
Yuxian Shanxi China 85 G4
Yuxikou China 87 F2
Yuyangguan China 87 D2
Yuyao China 87 G2
Yuyue China see Jiangshan
Yuza Japan 90 F5
Yuzawa Japan 90 G5
Yuzha Rus. Fed. 40 H4
Yuzhno-Alichurskiy, Khrebet mts Tajik. see Alichuri Janubí, Qatorkŭhi
Yuzhno-Kamyshovyy Khrebet ridge Rus. Fed. 82 F3

Yuzhno-Kazakhstanskaya Oblast' admin. div. Kazakh. see Yuzhnyy Kazakhstan
Yuzhno-Kuril'sk Rus. Fed. 82 G3
also known as Utashinai
Yuzhno-Muyskiy Khrebet mts Rus. Fed. 81 I1
Yuzhno-Sakhalinsk Rus. Fed. 82 F3
Yuzhno-Sukhokumsk Rus. Fed. 41 H7
Yuzhnoukrayinsk Ukr. 41 D7
also spelt Adyk
Yuzhnyy Rus. Fed. 41 G7
Yuzhnyy, Mys rd Rus. Fed. 39 P4
Yuzhnyy Altay, Khrebet mts Kazakh. 88 D1
Yuzhnyy Kazakhstan admin. div. Kazakh. 103 G4
English form South Kazakhstan Oblast; also known as Ongtüstik Qazaqstan Oblysy; formerly known as Chimkentskaya Oblast'; long form Yuzhno-Kazakhstanskaya Oblast'
Yuzhnyy Ural mts Rus. Fed. 102 D1
English form Southern Urals
Yuzhong China 84 E5
also known as Yuxian
Yuzhou China 87 E1
Yuzkuduk Uzbek. 103 E4
also spelt Yuzqudug
Yuzovka Ukr. see Donets'k
Yuzuduq Uzbek. see Yuzkuduk
Yverdon Switz. 51 M6
Yvetot France 50 G3
Ywamun Myanmar 78 A3
Ywathit Myanmar 78 B4
Yylanly Turkm. 102 D4
formerly spelt Il'yaly
Yzerfonteinpunt pt S. Africa 132 C10
Yzeure France 51 J6

Z

Za, Oued r. Morocco 123 E2
Zaaimansdal S. Africa 132 H10
Zaamin Uzbek. 103 G5
also spelt Zomin
Zaandam Neth. 48 B3
Zăbala r. Romania 58 H3
Žabalj Vojvodina, Srbija Yugo. 58 B3
Zāb al Kabir, Nahr az r. Iraq 107 E3
English form Great Zab
Zabalova Latvia 42 I4
Zāb aş Şaghīr, Nahr az r. Iraq 107 E3
English form Little Zab
Zabaykal'sk Rus. Fed. 85 H1
formerly known as Otpor
Zab-e Kuchek r. Iran 100 A3
Zabia Dem. Rep. Congo 126 E4
Zabīd Yemen 104 C5
Zabīd, Wādī watercourse Yemen 104 C5
Ząbkowice Śląskie Poland 49 N5
Zabłudów Poland 49 U2
Zabni China 87 D4
also known as Yunxiao
Żabno Poland 49 R5
Zabok Croatia 56 H2
Zábol prov. Afgh. 101 F3
Zābol Iran 101 E4
also known as Nasratabad
Zāboli Iran 101 E5
also known as Magas
Zabor'ye Rus. Fed. 43 Q2
Zabqung China see Gyêwa
Zăbrani Romania 58 C2
Zabré Burkina 125 F4
Zabrze Poland 49 P5
historically known as Hindenburg
Zaburun'ye Kazakh. 102 B3
Zacapa Guat. 185 H6
Zacapoaxtla Mex. 185 F5
Zacapu Mex. 185 E5
Zacatecas state Mex. 185 E4
Zacatecoluca El Salvador 185 H6
Zacatepec Morelos Mex. 185 F5
Zacatepec Oaxaca Mex. 185 F5
Zacatlán Mex. 185 F5
Zachagansk Kazakh. 102 B2
Zacharo Greece 59 C11
also spelt Zakháro
Zacoalco Mex. 184 E4
Zacualtipán Mex. 185 F4
Zacynthus i. Greece see Zakynthos
Zad, Col du pass Morocco 122 D2
Zadar Croatia 56 H4
formerly known as Zara; historically known as Iadera
Zadarski Kanal sea chan. Croatia 56 H4
Zadetkale Kyun i. Myanmar 79 B6
also known as St Luke's Island
Zadetkyi Kyun i. Myanmar 79 B6
also known as St Matthew's Island
Zadi Myanmar 79 B5
Zadoi China 97 G2
Zadonsk Rus. Fed. 43 T9
Zadran reg. Afgh. 101 G3
Za'farāna Egypt 121 G2
Za'farāna, Rā's pt Egypt 108 D8
Zafarwal Pak. 101 H3
Zafer Adaları is Cyprus see Kleides Islands
Zafer Burnu c. Cyprus see Apostolos Andreas, Cape
Zafora i. Greece 59 H12
Zafra Spain 54 E6
Zag Morocco 122 C3
Żagań Poland 49 M4
Zagare Lith. 42 E5
Zagazig Egypt 121 F2
also spelt Az Zaqāzīq
Zaghdeh well Iran 100 D3
Zāgheh Iran 100 A3
Zāgheh-ye Bālā Iran 100 A3
Zaghouan Tunisia 123 H1
Zagon Romania 58 H3
Zagora Greece 59 E9
Zagora Morocco 122 D3
Zagorje ob Savi Slovenia 56 G2
Zagorsk Rus. Fed. see Sergiyev Posad
Zagórz Poland 49 T6
Zagrazhden Bulg. 58 F5
▶ Zagreb Croatia 56 H3
Capital of Croatia. Historically known as Agram.
Zagros, Kūhhā-ye mts Iran see Zagros Mountains
Zagros Mountains Iran 100 A3
also known as Zagros, Kūhhā-ye
Zagros China see Lixian
Za'gya Zangbo r. China 89 E5
Zahamena, Réserve de nature res. Madag. 131 [K3]
Zaḥawn, Wādī r. Yemen 105 E4
Zāhedān Balūchestān va Sīstān Iran 101 E4
Zāhedān Fārs Iran 100 C4
Zahlé Lebanon 108 G4
Zaḥmet Turkm. see Zakhmet
Zaḥrān Saudi Arabia 104 C4
Zahrat al Baṭn plain Iraq 109 N6
Zahrez Chergui salt pan Alg. 55 O9
Zaïcevs Latvia 42 I5
Zaïginys Lith. 42 E6
Zaigrayevo Rus. Fed. 85 F1
Zaindeh r. Iran 100 C3
Zaĩnlha China see Xiaojin
Zair Uzbek. 102 D4
also spelt Zayyr or Zoir

Zaire country Africa see **Congo, Democratic Republic of**
Zaire prov. Angola 127 B6
Zaïre r. Congo/Dem. Rep. Congo see **Congo**
Zaječar Srbija Yugo. 58 D5
Zaka Zimbabwe 131 F4
Zakamensk Rus. Fed. 84 D1
formerly known as Gorodok
Zakataly Azer. see **Zaqatala**
Zakháro Greece see **Zacharo**
Zakharovka Kazakh. 103 G2
Zakharovo Rus. Fed. 43 U7
Zakhmet Turkm. 103 E5
also spelt Zähmet
Zākhō Iraq 107 E3
Zakhodnyaya Dzvina r. Europe see **Zapadnaya Dvina**
Zakhrebetnoye Rus. Fed. 40 F1
Zákinthos i. Greece see **Zakynthos**
Zakopane Poland 49 Q6
Zakouma Chad 126 C2
Zakouma, Parc National de nat. park Chad 126 C2
Zakros Greece 59 H13
Zakwaski, Mount Canada 166 F5
Zakynthos Greece 59 B11
Zakynthos i. Greece 59 B11
also spelt Zákinthos; historically known as Zacynthus
Zala Angola 127 B6
Zala r. Romania 49 O9
Zalābīyah tourist site Syria 109 K2
Zalaegerszeg Hungary 49 N9
Zalai-domsag hills Hungary 49 N9
Zalakomár Hungary 49 O9
Zalamea de la Serena Spain 54 F6
Zalanga Nigeria 125 H4
Zalantun China 85 I2
also known as Butha Qi
Zalaszentgrót Hungary 49 O9
Zalău Romania 58 E1
Zalavas Lith. 42 H7
Žalec Slovenia 56 H2
Zalegoshch' Rus. Fed. 43 R9
Zaleski U.S.A. 176 C6
Zales'ye Rus. Fed. 43 R3
Zalewo Poland 49 Q2
Zalew Szczeciński b. Poland 49 L2
Zalew Wiślany b. Poland 49 Q1
Zalim Saudi Arabia 104 C3
Zalingei Sudan 120 D6
Zalmā, Jabal az mt. Saudi Arabia 104 B2
Zaltan, Jabal hills Libya 120 C2
Zaluch'ye Rus. Fed. 43 M4
Zama Japan 91 F7
Zama Niger 125 F3
Zama City Canada 166 G3
Zamakh Saudi Arabia 105 D4
Zamani S. Africa 133 N4
Zamanti r. Turkey 106 C3
Zambales Mountains Phil. 74 B3
Zambeze r. Africa 131 G2 see **Zambezi**

▶**Zambezi** r. Africa 131 G2
4th longest river in Africa. Also spelt Zambeze.
africa [landscapes] ➤ 112–113

Zambezi Zambia 127 D8
Zambézia prov. Moz. 131 H3
Zambezi Escarpment Zambia/Zimbabwe 127 E9
Zambezi National Park Zimbabwe 131 E3
▶**Zambia** country Africa 127 E8
formerly known as Northern Rhodesia
africa [countries] ➤ 114–117
Zamboanga Phil. 74 B5
Zamboanga Peninsula Phil. 74 B5
Zamboanguita Phil. 74 B4
Zambrów Poland 49 T3
Zambue Moz. 131 F2
Zamfara state Nigeria 125 G3
Zamfara watercourse Nigeria 125 G3
Zamlat Amagraj hills W. Sahara 122 B4
Zamogil'ye Rus. Fed. 42 I3
Zamora Ecuador 198 B6
Zamora r. Ecuador 198 B5
Zamora Spain 54 F3
Zamora-Chinchipe prov. Ecuador 198 B5
Zamora de Hidalgo Mex. 185 E5
Zamość Poland 53 G1
formerly known as Zamost'ye
Zamost'ye Poland see **Zamość**
Zamtang China 86 B1
also known as Rangke; formerly known as Gamda
Zamuro, Punta pt Venez. 187 F5
Zamuro, Sierra del mts Venez. 199 F3
Zamzam, Wādī watercourse Libya 120 B2
Zanaga Congo 126 B5
Zanatepec Mex. 185 G5
Záncara r. Spain 55 H5
Zancle Sicilia Italy see **Messina**
Zanda China 89 B6
also known as Toling
Zandamela Moz. 131 G5
Zanderij Suriname 199 H3
Zandvliet Belgium 51 K1
Zanesville U.S.A. 176 C6
Zangasso Mali 124 D3
formerly spelt Sangasso
Zangelan Azer. see **Zängilan**
Zängilan Azer. 107 F3
also spelt Zangelan; formerly known as Pirchevan
Zangla Jammu and Kashmir 96 C2
Zangsêr Kangri mt. China 89 D5
Zanhuang China 85 G4
Zanjān Iran 100 B2
Zanjān prov. Iran 100 B2
Zanjān Rūd r. Iran 107 F3
Zannah, Jabal az hill U.A.E. 105 F2
Zanskar reg. Jammu and Kashmir see **Zaskar**
Zanthus Australia 151 C6
Zantiébougou Mali 124 D4
Zanzibar Tanz. 129 C6
Zanzibar Channel Tanz. 129 C6
Zanzibar Island Tanz. 129 C6
Zanzibar North admin. reg. Tanz. 129 C6
also known as Unguja North
Zanzibar South admin. reg. Tanz. 129 C6
also known as Unguja South
Zanzibar West admin. reg. Tanz. 129 C6
also known as Unguja West
Zaokskiy Rus. Fed. 43 S7
Zaonia Mornag Tunisia 57 C12
Zaoro-Songou Cent. Afr. Rep. 126 C3
Zaoshi Hubei China 87 E2
Zaoshi Hunan China 87 E3
Zaouatallaz Alg. 123 H4
formerly known as Fort Gardel
Zaouet el Kahla Alg. see **Bordj Omer Driss**
Zaouiet Kounta Alg. 123 E4
Zaoyang China 87 E1
Zaoyangzhan China 87 E1
Zaō-zan vol. Japan 90 G5
Zaozernyy Kazakh. 103 G1
formerly known as Aysarinskoye or Aysary
Zaozernyy Rus. Fed. 80 E1
Zaozer'ye Rus. Fed. 43 T4
Zaozhuang China 87 F1
Zap r. Turkey 107 E3
Zapadna Morava r. Yugo. 58 C5
Zapadnaya Dvina r. Europe 43 L6
English form Western Dvina; also spelt Zakhodnyaya Dzvina
Zapadnaya Dvina Rus. Fed. 43 N5
Zapadno-Kazakhstanskaya Oblast' admin. div. Kazakh. see **Zapadnyy Kazakhstan**
Zapadno-Sakhalinskiy Khrebet mts Rus. Fed. 82 F2
Zapadno-Sibirskaya Nizmennost' plain Rus. Fed. see **West Siberian Plain**
Zapadno-Sibirskaya Ravnina plain Rus. Fed. see **West Siberian Plain**
Zapadnyy Alamedin, Pik mt. Kyrg. 103 H4
Zapadnyy Berezovyy, Ostrov i. Rus. Fed. 43 J1
Zapadnyy Chink Ustyurta esc. Kazakh. 102 C4
Zapadnyy Kazakhstan admin. div. Kazakh. 102 B2
English form West Kazakhstan Oblast; also known as Batys Qazaqstan Oblysy; formerly known as Ural'skaya Oblast'; long form Zapadno-Kazakhstanskaya Oblast'
Zapadnyy Sayan reg. Rus. Fed. 80 D2
English form Western Sayan Mountains
Zapala Arg. 204 C5
Zapardiel r. Spain 54 F3
Zapata U.S.A. 179 C7
Zapata, Península de pen. Cuba 186 C2
Zapatoca Col. 198 C3
Zapatón r. Spain 54 E6
Zapatoza, Ciénaga de l. Col. 198 C2
Zapiga Chile 200 C4
Zaplyus'ye Rus. Fed. 43 K3
Zăpodeni Romania 58 I2
Zapolyarnyy Murmanskaya Oblast' Rus. Fed. 44 O1
Zapolyarnyy Respublika Komi Rus. Fed. 40 L2
Zapol'ye Pskovskaya Oblast' Rus. Fed. 43 K3
Zapol'ye Vologod. Obl. Rus. Fed. 43 R2
Zaporizhzhya Ukr. 41 E7
also spelt Zaporozh'ye; formerly known as Aleksandrovsk or Oleksandrivs'k
Zaporozhskoye Rus. Fed. 43 L1
Zaporozh'ye Ukr. see **Zaporizhzhya**
Zapponeta Italy 56 H7
Zaprešić Croatia 56 H3
Zaprudnya Rus. Fed. 43 S5
Zaprudy Belarus 42 F9
Zapug China 89 C5
Zaqatala Azer. 107 F2
also spelt Zakataly
Zaqên China 97 G2
Zaqqui Libya 120 C2
Za Qu r. China 86 A2
Zaqungngomar mt. China 89 E5
Zara China see **Moinda**
Zara Croatia see **Zadar**
Zara Turkey 107 D3
Zarafshan Uzbek. 103 F4
also spelt Zarafshon
Zarafshon Tajik. 101 G2
also spelt Zeravshan
Zarafshon r. Tajik. 101 G2
also spelt Zeravshan
Zarafshon Uzbek. see **Zarafshan**
Zarafshon r. Uzbek. see **Zeravshan**
Zarafshon, Qatorkŭhi mts Tajik. 101 F2
also known as Zeravshanskiy Khrebet
Zaragoza Col. 198 C3
Zaragoza Mex. 185 E2
Zaragoza Spain 55 K3
English form Saragossa; historically known as Caesaraugusta
Zarand Kermān Iran 100 D4
Zarand Markazī Iran 100 B3
Zarandului, Munții hills Romania 58 D2
Zarang China 89 B6
Zaranj Afgh. 101 E4
Zarasai Lith. 42 H6
Zárate Arg. 204 F4
Zarautz Spain 55 I1
Zaraysk Rus. Fed. 43 T7
Zaraza Venez. 199 E2
Zarbdar Uzbek. 103 G4
Zärdab Azer. 107 F2
Zardak Iran 100 D3
Zard Kuh mts Iran 100 B3
Zarechensk Rus. Fed. 40 D2
Zarechka Belarus 42 G9
Zarechnyy Rus. Fed. 85 E1
Zarechnyy Rus. Fed. 43 U8
formerly known as Pobedinskiy
Zāreh Iran 100 B3
Zarembo Island U.S.A. 166 C3
Žarėnai Lith. 42 D6
Zarghat Saudi Arabia 104 C2
Zarghūn Shahr Afgh. 101 G3
Zargun mt. Pak. 101 F4
Zari Afgh. 101 F3
Zaria Nigeria 125 G4
Zariaspa Afgh. see **Balkh**
Zarichne Ukr. 41 C6
Zarīneh Rūd r. Iran 100 A2
Zaring China 89 E6
Zarmardan Afgh. 101 E3
Zărnești Romania 58 G3
Żarnowieckie, Jezioro l. Poland 49 P1
Zarqā' Jordan see **Az Zarqā'**
Zarqā', Nahr az r. Jordan 108 G5
Zarqān Iran 100 C4
Zarubino Rus. Fed. 43 O3
Zarubino Rus. Fed. 82 C4
Żary Poland 49 M4
Zarzaïtine Alg. 123 H3
Zarzal Col. 198 B3
Zarzis Tunisia 123 H2
Zasa Latvia 42 G5
Zashchita Kazakh. 88 C1
Zasheyek Rus. Fed. 44 O2
Zaskar r. India 96 C2
Zaskar reg. Jammu and Kashmir 96 C2
also spelt Zanskar
Zaskarki Belarus 43 J6
▶**Zaskar Mountains** India 96 C2
world [land images] ➤ 12–13
Zaslawkaye Vodaskhovishcha resr Belarus 42 I8
Zaslawye Belarus 42 I7
Zastron S. Africa 133 L7
Za'tarī, Wādī az watercourse Jordan 109 H5
Žatec Czech Rep. 49 K5
Zaterechnyy Rus. Fed. 107 F1
Zatobol'sk Kazakh. 103 E1
Zatoka Ukr. 58 L2
formerly known as Bugaz
Zatyshshya Ukr. 58 K1
Zaunguzskiye Karakumy des. Turkm. 102 D4
also known as Üngüz Angyrsyndaky Garagum
Zautla Mex. 185 F5
Zavadovskiy Island Antarctica 223 F2
Zavareh Iran 100 C3
Zavety Il'icha Rus. Fed. 82 F2
Zavidoviči Bos.-Herz. 56 K4
Zavidovskiy Zapovednik nature res. Rus. Fed. 43 R5
Zavitaya Rus. Fed. see **Zavitinsk**
Zavitinsk Rus. Fed. 82 C2
formerly known as Zavitaya
Zavodskoy Rus. Fed. see **Komsomol'skiy**
Zavolzhsk Rus. Fed. 40 G4
formerly known as Zavolzh'ye
Zavolzh'ye Rus. Fed. see **Zavolzhsk**
Závora, Ponta pt Moz. 131 G5
Zavutstsye Belarus 42 J6
Zavyachellye Belarus 43 J6
Zav'yalova, Ostrov i. Rus. Fed. 39 P4
Zav'yalovo Rus. Fed. 103 J1
Zawa Qinghai China 84 D4
Zawa Xinjiang China 96 C1
Zawadzkie Poland 49 P5
Zawgyi r. Myanmar 78 B3
Zawiercie Poland 49 Q5
Zawīlah Libya 120 B3
Zāwīyah, Jabal az hills Syria 109 H2
Zāwiyat Masūs Libya 120 D2
Zawlīyah, Jiddat az plain Oman 105 F3
Zawr, Ra's az pt Saudi Arabia 105 E2
Zâwyet Shammâs pt Egypt 106 A5
Zâwyet Sîdi Ghâzi Egypt 108 B6
Zay r. Rus. Fed. 40 I5
Zaydī, Wādī az watercourse Syria 109 H5
Zaysan Kazakh. 88 D2
Zaysan, Lake Kazakh. 88 C1
also known as Zaysan, Ozero
Zaysan, Ozero l. Kazakh. see **Zaysan, Lake**
Zaytsevo Rus. Fed. 43 J4
Zayü Xizang China 86 A2
Zayü Xizang China 86 A2
also known as Gyigang
Zayü Qu r. China/India 86 A2
also known as Lohil or Luhit
Zayyr Uzbek. see **Zair**
Zazafotsy Madag. 131 [inset] J4
Zazir, Oued watercourse Alg. 123 G6
Zbąszynek Poland 49 M3
Zborište mt. Yugo. 58 A5
Žďar nad Sázavou Czech Rep. 49 M6
Žďárské Vrchy hills Czech Rep. 49 M6
Zdolbuniv Ukr. 41 C6
also spelt Zdolbunov
Zdolbunov Ukr. see **Zdolbuniv**
Zduńska Wola Poland 49 P4
Zealand i. Denmark 45 J5
also spelt Sjælland
Zēbāk Afgh. 101 G2
Zeballos mt. Arg. 205 C7
Zeballos Canada 166 E5
Zēbār Iraq 107 F3
Zebargad, Gezîret i. Egypt 104 B3
English form Zebirget Island
Zebirget Island Egypt see **Zebargad, Gezîret**
Žebrák Czech Rep. 49 K6
Zebulon GA U.S.A. 175 C5
Zebulon KY U.S.A. 176 C8
Zebulon NC U.S.A. 174 E5
Zeebrugge Belgium 51 J1
Zeehan Australia 147 E5
Zeeland U.S.A. 172 G8
Zeerust S. Africa 133 K2
Zefat Israel 108 G5
also known as Safad; also spelt Tsefat
Zegrzyńskie, Jezioro l. Poland 49 S3
Zehdenick Germany 49 K3
Zeil, Mount Australia 148 B4
formerly spelt Ziel, Mount
Žeimelis Lith. 42 F5
Zeitz Germany 48 J4
Zêkog China 86 B1
also known as Sonag
Zela Turkey see **Zile**
Żelechów Poland 49 S4
Zelena Gora mt. Bos.-Herz. 56 J5
Zelenaya Roshcha Kazakh. 103 H1
Zelengora mts Bos.-Herz. 56 K5
Zelennik Rus. Fed. 40 H3
Zelenoborskiy Rus. Fed. 44 P2
Zelenodol'sk Rus. Fed. 40 I5
Zelenogorsk Rus. Fed. 43 K1
Zelenograd Rus. Fed. 43 S5
Zelenogradsk Rus. Fed. 42 B7
historically known as Cranz
Zelenokumsk Rus. Fed. 41 G7
formerly known as Sovetskoye or Vorontsovo-Aleksandrovskoye
Zelentsovo Rus. Fed. 40 H4
Zelenyy, Ostrov i. Rus. Fed. 82 G4
also known as Shibotsu-jima
Zelenyy Gay Kazakh. 103 G2
Železné Hory hills Czech Rep. 49 M6
Zelienople U.S.A. 176 E5
Želiezovce Slovakia 49 P7
Zelina Croatia 56 I3
formerly known as Sveti Ivan Zelina
Zelinggou China 84 C4
Želivka, Vodní nádrž resr Czech Rep. 49 L6
Željin mt. Yugo. 58 B5
Zell am See Austria 49 J8
Zellerrain pass Austria 49 M8
Zelów Poland 49 Q4
Zeltiņi Latvia 42 H4
Zel'va Belarus 42 F8
Žemaičių Naumiestis Lith. 42 C6
Žemaitijos nacionalinis parkas nat. park Lith. 42 C5
Zêmdasam China 86 B1
Zemen Bulg. 58 D6
Zemeș Romania 58 H2
Zemetchino Rus. Fed. 41 G5
Zémio Cent. Afr. Rep. 126 E3
Zemmora Alg. 55 L9
Zémongo, Réserve de Faune de nature res. Cent. Afr. Rep. 126 E3
Zempleni park Hungary 49 S7
Zemplínska šírava l. Slovakia 49 T7
Zempoaltépetl, Nudo de mt. Mex. 185 G5
Zemtsy Rus. Fed. 43 N5
Zemun Srbija Yugo. 58 B4
Zênda China 86 A1
Zengcheng China 87 E4
Zengfeng Shan mt. China 82 C4
Zenica Bos.-Herz. 56 J4
Zenifim watercourse Israel 108 F7
Zenta Vojvodina, Srbija Yugo. see **Senta**
Zentsūji Japan 91 C7
Zenyeh Afgh. 101 G3
Zenzach Alg. 55 O9
Žepče Bos.-Herz. 56 K4
Zephyr Cove U.S.A. 182 E2
Zepu China 88 B4
formerly known as Poskam
Zeraf, Bahr el r. Sudan 128 A2
Zeravshan Tajik. see **Zarafshon**
Zeravshan r. Tajik. see **Zarafshon**
Zeravshan r. Uzbek. 103 E5
also spelt Zarafshon
Zeravshanskiy Khrebet mts Tajik. see **Zarafshon, Qatorkŭhi**
Zerenda Kazakh. 103 G1
Zeribet el Oued Alg. 123 G2
Żerków Poland 49 O3
Zermatt Switz. 51 N6
Zernograd Rus. Fed. 41 G7
formerly known as Zernovoy
Zernovoy Rus. Fed. see **Zernograd**
Zestafoni Georgia see **Zestap'oni**
Zestap'oni Georgia 107 E2
also spelt Zestafoni
Zeta r. Yugo. 58 A6
Zêtang China 89 E6
Zetea Romania 58 G2
Zeulenroda Germany 48 I5
Zeven Germany 48 G2
Zevenaar Neth. 48 D4
Zevgolatio Greece 59 D11
Zeya Rus. Fed. 82 B1
Zeya r. Rus. Fed. 82 B2
Zeydābād Iran 100 C4
Zēydar Iran 100 D2
Zeynalābād Iran 100 D4
Zeyskiy Zapovednik nature res. Rus. Fed. 82 B1
Zeysko-Bureinskaya Vpadina depr. Rus. Fed. 82 C2
Zeyskoye Vodokhranilishche resr Rus. Fed. 82 B1
Zeytin Burnu c. Cyprus see **Elaia, Cape**
Zeytindağ Turkey 59 I10
Zêzere r. Port. 54 C5
Zgharta Lebanon 108 G3
Zgierz Poland 49 Q4
historically known as Sgiersch
Zhabdün China 89 D6
Zhabinka Belarus 42 F9
Zhadove Ukr. 43 N9
Zhaggo China see **Luhuo**
Zhaglag China 86 A1
Zhag'yab China 86 A2
also known as Yêndum
Zhailma Kazakh. 103 E2
also spelt Zhayylma
Zhaksy Kazakh. 103 F2
also spelt Zhaqsy; formerly spelt Dzhaksy
Zhaksy-Kon watercourse Kazakh. 103 G2
Zhaksykylysh, Ozero salt l. Kazakh. 103 E3
Zhaksy Sarysu watercourse Kazakh. see **Sarysu**
Zhalaghash Kazakh. see **Dzhalagash**
Zhalanash Kazakh. 103 I4
Zhalanash Kazakh. see **Damdy**
Zhalgyztöbe Kazakh. see **Zhangiztobe**
Zhalpaktal Kazakh. 102 B2
also spelt Zhalpaqtal; formerly known as Furmanovo
Zhalpaqtal Kazakh. see **Zhalpaktal**
Zhaltyr Kazakh. 103 G2
formerly spelt Dzhaltyr
Zhaltyr, Ozero l. Kazakh. 102 B3
Zhaludok Belarus 42 F8
Zhamanakkol', Ozero salt l. Kazakh. 103 E2
Zhamansor Kazakh. 102 C3
Zhambyl Kazakh. 103 G3
Zhambyl Kazakh. see **Taraz**
Zhambyl Oblast admin. div. Kazakh. see **Zhambylskaya Oblast'**
Zhambylskaya Oblast' admin. div. Kazakh. 103 H3
English form Zhambyl Oblast; formerly known as Dzhambulskaya Oblast'
Zhameuka Kazakh. 103 J3
Zhamo China see **Bomi**
Zhan r. China 82 C2
Zhanakorgan Kazakh. 103 F4
also spelt Zhangaqorghan; formerly known as Yany-Kurgan
Zhanakurylys Kazakh. 103 E3
Zhanang China 89 E6
also known as Chatang
Zhanaortalyk Kazakh. 103 H3
Zhanaozen Kazakh. 102 C4
also spelt Zhangaözen; formerly known as Novyy Uzen'
Zhanatala Kazakh. 103 I4
Zhanatas Kazakh. 103 G4
also spelt Zhangatas
Zhanbay Kazakh. 102 B3
Zhanbei China 82 B2
formerly known as Zhanhe
Zhang r. China 85 G4
Zhangaözen Kazakh. see **Zhanaozen**
Zhangaqazaly Kazakh. see **Ayteke Bi**
Zhanga Qazan Kazakh. see **Novaya Kazanka**
Zhangaqorghan Kazakh. see **Zhanakorgan**
Zhangatas Kazakh. see **Zhanatas**
Zhangbei China 85 G3
Zhangcheng China see **Yongtai**
Zhangcunpu China 87 F1
Zhangde China see **Anyang**
Zhangdian China see **Zibo**
Zhanggu China see **Danba**
Zhangguangcai Ling mts China 82 C3
Zhanghua Taiwan see **Changhua**
Zhangiztobe Kazakh. 103 J2
also known as Zhalgyztöbe
Zhangjiajie China see **Dayong**
Zhangjiakou China 85 G3
also known as Kalgan
Zhangjiapan China see **Jingbian**
Zhangla China 86 B1
Zhanglou China 87 F1
Zhangping China 87 F3
Zhangpu China 87 F3
also known as Sui'an
Zhangqiu China 85 H4
Zhangshu China 87 E2
formerly known as Qingjiang
Zhangwei Xinhe r. China 85 H4
Zhangwu China 85 I3
Zhangxian China 86 C1
Zhangye China 84 D4
Zhangzhou China 87 F3
formerly spelt Changchow
Zhangzi China 85 G4
Zhanhe China see **Zhanbei**
Zhanhua China 85 H4
also known as Fuguo
Zhänibek Kazakh. see **Dzhanybek**
Zhanjiang China 87 D4
formerly spelt Changkiang
Zhansügirov Kazakh. see **Dzhansugurov**
Zhanterek Kazakh. 102 C3
Zhanyi China 86 B3
Zhao'an China 87 F4
also known as Nanzhao
Zhaodong China 82 B3
Zhaoge China see **Qixian**
Zhaojue China 86 B2
also known as Xincheng
Zhaoliqiao China 87 E2
Zhaoping China 87 D3
Zhaoqing China 87 E4
Zhaoren China see **Changwu**
Zhaosu China 88 C3
also known as Mongolküre
Zhaosutai r. China 85 I3
Zhaotong China 86 B3
Zhaoxian China 85 G4
also known as Zhaozhou
Zhaoyuan Heilong. China 82 B3
Zhaoyuan Shandong China 85 I4
Zhaozhen China see **Jintang**
Zhaozhou China see **Zhaoxian**
Zhaozhou China 82 B3
Zhapo China 87 D4
Zhaqsy Kazakh. see **Zhaksy**
Zharbulak Kazakh. see **Kabanbay**
Zharbulak Kazakh. 88 C2
Zhardzyazhzha Belarus 42 I7
Zhari Namco salt l. China 89 D6
Zharkamys Kazakh. 102 D3
Zharkent Kazakh. 103 J3
formerly known as Panfilov; formerly spelt Dzharkent
Zharkovskiy Rus. Fed. 43 N6
Zharma Kazakh. 103 J2
Zharmysh Kazakh. 102 C3
Zharsuat Kazakh. 103 J3
Zharyk Kazakh. see **Saken Seyfullin**
Zhashkiv Ukr. 41 D6
also spelt Zhashkov
Zhashkov Ukr. see **Zhashkiv**
Zhashui China 87 D1
also known as Qianyou
Zhaslyk Uzbek. 102 D4
also spelt Jasliq
Zhastkovo Rus. Fed. 43 N8
Zhaxi China see **Weixin**
Zhaxi Co salt l. China 89 D5
Zhaxigang China 89 B5
Zhaxizê China 86 A2
Zhayrem Kazakh. 103 G2
Zhayü China 86 A2
Zhayylma Kazakh. see **Zhailma**
Zhayyq r. Kazakh./Rus. Fed. see **Ural**
Zhdanov Ukr. see **Mariupol'**
Zhdanovo Kazakh. 103 G4
Zhdanovo Rus. Fed. 43 O4
Zhdanovsk Azer. see **Beyläqan**
Zhecheng China 87 E1
Zhedao China see **Lianghe**
Zhêhor China 86 B2
Zhejiang prov. China 87 G2
English form Chekiang
Zhelang China 87 E4
Zhelaniya, Mys c. Rus. Fed. 39 G2
Zhelcha r. Rus. Fed. 42 I3
Zhelezinka Kazakh. 103 H1
Zheleznodorozhnyy Rus. Fed. 42 C7
historically known as Gerdauen
Zheleznodorozhnyy Rus. Fed. see **Yemva**
Zheleznodorozhnyy Uzbek. see **Kungrad**
Zheleznogorsk Rus. Fed. 43 Q9
Zheleznya Rus. Fed. 43 S7
Zhelou China see **Ceheng**
Zheltorangy Kazakh. 103 H3
Zheltyye Vody Ukr. see **Zhovti Vody**
Zhelyu Voyvoda Bulg. 58 H6
Zhem Kazakh. see **Emba**
Zhemgang Bhutan 97 F4
also spelt Shamgong
Zhen'an China 87 D1
also known as Yongle
Zhenba China 87 C1
Zheng'an China 87 C2
also known as Fengyi
Zhengding China 85 G4
Zhenghe China 87 F3
also known as Xiongshan
Zhengjiakou China see **Gucheng**
Zhengjiatun China see **Shuangliao**
Zhengkou China see **Gucheng**
Zhenglan Qi China see **Dund Hot**
Zhengning China 85 F5
also known as Shanhe
Zhengxiangbai Qi China see **Qagan Nur**
Zhengyang China 87 E1
also known as Zhenyang
Zhengzhou China 87 E1
formerly spelt Chengchow
Zhenhai China 87 G2
Zhenjiang China see **Dantu**
Zhenjiangguan China 86 B1
Zhenlai China 85 I2
Zhenning China 86 C3
Zhenping China 87 D2
Zhenwudong China see **Ansai**
Zhenxi China 85 I2
Zhenxiong China 86 C3
also known as Wufeng
Zhenyang China see **Zhengyang**
Zhenyuan Gansu China 85 E5
Zhenyuan Guizhou China 87 D3
also known as Wuyang
Zhenyuan Yunnan China 86 B4
also known as Enle
Zhenziling China 87 D2
Zherdevka Rus. Fed. 41 G6
formerly known as Chibizovka
Zherdevo Rus. Fed. 43 R8
Zherong China 87 F3
also known as Shuangcheng
Zheshart Rus. Fed. 40 I3
Zhestylevo Rus. Fed. 43 S5
Zhetibay Kazakh. see **Zhetybay**
Zhetikara Kazakh. see **Zhitikara**
Zhetisay Kazakh. see **Zhetysay**
Zhetybay Kazakh. 102 C4
also spelt Zhetibay
Zhety-Kol', Ozero l. Rus. Fed. 103 E2
Zhetysay Kazakh. 103 G4
also spelt Zhetisay; formerly spelt Dzhetysay
Zhêxam China 89 D6
Zhexi Shuiku resr China 87 D2
Zhezdy Kazakh. 103 F2
formerly known as Marganets; formerly spelt Dzhezdy
Zhezkazgan Kazakh. 103 F3
also spelt Zhezqazghan; formerly spelt Dzhezkazgan
Zhezqazghan Kazakh. see **Zhezkazgan**
Zhicheng China see **Changxing**
Zhichitsy Rus. Fed. 43 M6
Zhidan China 85 F4
also known as Bao'an
Zhidoi China 97 G2
also known as Gyaijêpozhanggê
Zhigansk Rus. Fed. 39 M3
Zhigung China 89 E6
Zhijiang China 87 D3
Zhijin China 86 C3
Zhilevo Rus. Fed. 43 T7
Zhilino Rus. Fed. 43 R8
Zhilyanka Kazakh. see **Kargalinskoye**
Zhi Qu r. China see **Yangtze**
Zhirnovsk Rus. Fed. 41 H6
formerly known as Zhirnovskiy or Zhirnoye
Zhirnovskiy Rus. Fed. see **Zhirnovsk**
Zhirnoye Rus. Fed. see **Zhirnovsk**
Zhiryatino Rus. Fed. 43 O8
Zhitarovo Bulg. see **Vetren**
Zhitikara Kazakh. 103 E1
also spelt Zhetikara; formerly known as Dzhetygara
Zhitkovichi Belarus see **Zhytkavichy**
Zhitkovo Rus. Fed. 43 K1
Zhitkur Rus. Fed. 102 A2
Zhitomir Ukr. see **Zhytomyr**
Zhizdra Rus. Fed. 43 P8
Zhizdra r. Rus. Fed. 43 R7
Zhizhitsa Rus. Fed. 43 M5
Zhizhitskoye, Ozero l. Rus. Fed. 43 M5
Zhlobin Belarus 43 L9
Zhmerinka Ukr. see **Zhmerynka**
Zhmerynka Ukr. 41 D6
also spelt Zhmerinka
Zhob Pak. 101 G4
formerly known as Fort Sandeman
Zhob r. Pak. 101 G3
Zhodzina Belarus 43 J7
Zhokhova, Ostrov i. Rus. Fed. 39 P2
Zholnuskay Kazakh. 88 C1
Zholymbet Kazakh. 103 G2
Zhong'an China see **Fuyuan**
Zhongba China 87 E4
Zhongba China see **Jiangyou**
Zhongcheng China see **Suijiang**
Zhongdian China 86 A3
also known as Zhongxin
Zhongduo China see **Youyang**
Zhongguo country Asia see **China**
Zhongguo Renmin Gongheguo country Asia see **China**
Zhonghe China see **Xiushan**
Zhongmou China 87 E1
Zhongning China 85 E4
Zhongping China see **Huize**
Zhongshan research station Antarctica 223 F2
Zhongshan Guangdong China 87 E4
formerly known as Shiqizhen
Zhongshan Guangxi China 87 D3
Zhongshan China see **Lupanshui**
Zhongsha Qundao sea feature S. China Sea see **Macclesfield Bank**
Zhongshu China see **Luxi**
Zhongshu China see **Luliang**
Zhongtai China see **Lingtai**
Zhongtiao Shan mts China 87 D1
Zhongwei China 84 E4
Zhongxian China 87 D2
also known as Zhongzhou
Zhongxin China 87 E3
Zhongxin China see **Zhongdian**
Zhongxin China see **Huaping**
Zhongxing China see **Siyang**
Zhongxingji China 87 F2
Zhongyang China 85 F4
Zhongyicun China 86 B3
Zhongze China 87 G2
Zhongzhai China 86 C1
Zhongzhou China see **Zhongxian**
Zhosaly Kazakh. see **Dzhusaly**
Zhosaly Kazakh. 103 I2
Zhoujiajing China 84 D4
Zhoujiaping China see **Nanzheng**
Zhoukou China 87 E1
Zhoukou China see **Peng'an**
Zhouning China 87 F3
also known as Shicheng
Zhoushan China 87 G2
Zhoushan Dao i. China 87 G2
Zhoushan Qundao is China 87 G2
Zhouzhi China 87 D1
also known as Erqu
Zhovten' Ukr. 58 L1
Zhovti Vody Ukr. 41 E6
formerly known as Zheltyye Vody
Zhualy Kazakh. 103 E2
Zhuanghe China 85 I4
Zhuanglang China 85 E5
also known as Shuiluocheng
Zhuantobe Kazakh. 103 G3
Zhubgyügoin China 86 A1
Zhucheng China 85 H5
Zhudong Taiwan see **Chutung**
Zhugqu China 86 C1
Zhuhai China 87 E4
formerly known as Chuhai
Zhuji China see **Shangqiu**
Zhuji China 87 G2
Zhujia Chuan r. China 85 F4
Zhujing China see **Jinshan**
Zhukeng China 87 E4
Zhukopa r. Rus. Fed. 43 N5
Zhukovka Rus. Fed. 43 O8
Zhukovo Rus. Fed. 43 R6
formerly known as Ugodskiy Zavod
Zhukovskiy Rus. Fed. 43 T6
formerly known as Stakhanovo
Zhulong r. China 85 G4
Zhumadian China 87 E1
Zhumysker Kazakh. 102 B3
Zhuolu China 85 G3
Zhuoyang China see **Suiping**
Zhuozang r. China 85 G4
Zhuozhou China 85 H4
Zhuozi China 85 G3
also known as Zhuozishan
Zhuozishan China see **Zhuozi**
Zhuravlevka Kazakh. 103 G2
Zhurki Belarus 42 I6
Zhuryn Kazakh. 102 D2
formerly spelt Dzhurun
Zhusandala, Step' plain Kazakh. 103 H3
Zhushan China 87 D1
Zhushan China see **Xuan'en**
Zhuxi China 87 D1
Zhuyang China see **Dazhu**
Zhuzhou Hunan China 87 E3
also known as Lukou
Zhuzhou Hunan China 87 E3
Zhydachiv Ukr. 41 C6
Zhympity Kazakh. 102 C2
formerly known as Dzhambeyty
Zhyngyldy Kazakh. 102 B3
formerly known as Kuybyshevo
Zhytkavichy Belarus 42 I9
also spelt Zhitkovichi
Zhytomyr Ukr. 41 D6
also spelt Zhitomir
Zi r. China 85 H4
Ziama mt. Guinea 124 C4
Ziarat Iran 100 D2
Žiar nad Hronom Slovakia 49 P7
Zibā salt pan Saudi Arabia 109 J7
Zībār Iraq 107 E3
Zibo China 85 H4
formerly known as Zhangdian
Zichang China 85 F4
also known as Wayaobu
Zicheng China see **Zijin**
Zichtauer Berge und Klötzer Forst park Germany 48 I3
Ziddí Tajik. 101 G2
Zidi Pak. 101 F5
Ziębice Poland 49 O5
Ziel, Mount Australia see **Zeil, Mount**
Zielona Góra Poland 49 M4
historically known as Grünberg
Ziemelkursas Augstiene hills Latvia 42 D4
Ziemeris Latvia 42 I4
Ziemupe Latvia 42 C5
Ziesar Germany 49 J3
Zifta Egypt 121 F2
Zigaing Myanmar 78 A3
Zigê Tangco l. China 89 E5
Ziggurat of Ur tourist site Iraq 107 F5
Zīghan Libya 120 D3
Zigon Myanmar 78 A4
Zigong China 86 C2
Ziguey Chad 120 B6
Zigui China 87 D2
also known as Jiandaoyu
Ziguinchor Senegal 124 A3
Žīguri Latvia 42 I4
Zihuatanejo Mex. 185 E5
Zijin China 87 E4
also known as Zicheng
Ziketan China see **Xinghai**
Zikeyevo Rus. Fed. 43 P8
Zikhron Ya'aqov Israel 108 F5
Zilair Rus. Fed. 102 D1
Zilaiskalns Latvia 42 G4
Zile Turkey 106 C2
historically known as Zela
Zilim r. Rus. Fed. 40 K5
Žilina Slovakia 49 P6
Zillah Libya 120 C2
Zillertaler Alpen mts Austria 48 I8
Zilupe Latvia 42 J5
Zima Rus. Fed. 80 G2
Zimapán Mex. 185 F4
Zimatlán Mex. 185 F5
Zimba Zambia 127 E9
▶**Zimbabwe** country Africa 131 F3
formerly known as Rhodesia or Southern Rhodesia
africa [countries] ➤ 114–117
Zimbabwe tourist site Zimbabwe see **Great Zimbabwe National Monument**
Zīmkān, Rūdkhāneh-ye r. Iran 100 A3
Zimmerbude Rus. Fed. see **Svetlyy**
Zimmi Sierra Leone 124 C5
Zimnicea Romania 58 G5
Zimniy Bereg coastal area Rus. Fed. 40 F2
Zimovniki Rus. Fed. 41 G7
Zin watercourse Israel 108 G6
Zinave, Parque Nacional de nat. park Moz. 131 G4
Zinder Niger 125 H3
Zinder dept Niger 125 H3
Zindo China 86 B2
formerly known as Jimda
Zing Nigeria 125 H4
Zinga Mulike Tanz. 129 C7
Ziniaré Burkina 125 E3
Zinihu China 85 E4
Zinjibār Yemen 105 D5
Zinkwazi Beach S. Africa 133 P6
Zinovo Rus. Fed. 43 V5
Zinoyevsk Ukr. see **Kirovohrad**
Zinzana Mali 124 D3
Zion U.S.A. 172 F8
Zion National Park U.S.A. 183 K4
Ziqudukou China 97 G2
Zīrab Iran 100 C2
Zirbitzkogel mt. Austria 49 L8
Zirc Hungary 49 O8
Žirje i. Croatia 56 H5
Zirkel, Mount U.S.A. 180 F4
Zirkūh i. U.A.E. 105 F2
Ziro India 97 G4
Zi Shui r. China 87 E2
Zistersdorf Austria 49 N7
Zitácuaro Mex. 185 E5
Zitava r. Slovakia 49 P8
Žitište Vojvodina, Srbija Yugo. 58 B3
Zitiua r. Brazil 202 C2
Zito China see **Lhorong**
Zitong China 86 C2
also known as Wenchang

Ziyang China *see* Wuyuan
Ziyang *Shaanxi* China **87** D1
Ziyang *Sichuan* China **86** C2
Ziyaret Dağı *hill* Turkey **108** F1
Ziyuan China **87** D3
  also known as Dahe
Ziyun China **86** C3
  also known as Songshan
Zizhong China **86** C2
  also known as Chonglong
Zizhou China **85** F4
  also known as Shuanghuyu
Zlatar *mts* Yugo. **58** A5
Zlaté Moravce Slovakia **49** P7
Zlaten Rog Bulg. **58** D4
Zlatibor *mts* Yugo. **58** A5
Zlatica *r.* Yugo. **58** B3
Zlatna Romania **58** E2
Zlatni Pyasŭtsi *nat. park* Bulg. **58** J5
Zlatograd Bulg. **58** G7
Zlatoust Rus. Fed. **38** F4
Zlatoustovsk Rus. Fed. **82** D1
Zlatý Stôl *mt.* Slovakia **49** R7
Zlín Czech Rep. **49** O6
  formerly known as Gottwaldow
Zlīţan Libya **120** B1
Złocieniec Poland **49** N2
Złoczew Poland **49** P4
Złotoryja Poland **49** M4
Złotów Poland **49** O2
Zlynka Rus. Fed. **43** M9
Zmeinogorsk Rus. Fed. **88** C1
Żmigród Poland **49** N4
Zmiyev Ukr. *see* Zmiyiv
Zmiyevka Rus. Fed. **43** R9
Zmiyiv Ukr. **41** F6
  also spelt Zmiyev; *formerly known as*
  Gotval'd
Znamenka Kazakh. **103** I2
Znamenka *Altayskiy Kray* Rus. Fed.
  103 I1
Znamenka *Orlovskaya Oblast'* Rus. Fed.
  43 Q9
Znamenka *Smolenskaya Oblast'* Rus. Fed.
  43 P7

Znamenka Ukr. *see* Znam"yanka
Znamenskoye *Lipetskaya Oblast'* Rus. Fed.
  43 U8
Znamenskoye *Orlovskaya Oblast'* Rus. Fed.
  43 Q8
Znam"yanka Ukr. **41** E6
  also spelt Znamenka
Žnin Poland **49** O3
Znobivka *r.* Ukr. **43** O9
Znob Novhorods'ke Ukr. **43** O9
Znojmo Czech Rep. **49** N7
Zoar S. Africa **132** F10
Zóbuè Moz. **131** G2
Zogainrawar China *see* Huashixia
Zogang China **86** A2
  also known as Wangda
Zogqên China **86** A1
Zografos Greece **59** E11
Zohreh *r.* Iran **100** B4
Zoigê China **86** B1
Zoir Uzbek. *see* Zair
Zoissa Tanz. **129** C6
Zoji La *pass* Jammu and Kashmir **96** C1
Zola S. Africa **133** K9
Zolochev Ukr. *see* Zolochiv
Zolochev Ukr. *see* Zolochiv
Zolochiv *Kharkivs'ka Oblast'* Ukr. **41** E6
  also spelt Zolochev
Zolochiv *L'vivs'ka Oblast'* Ukr. **41** C6
  also spelt Zolochev
Zolotaya Gora Rus. Fed. **82** B1
Zolotinka Rus. Fed. **81** K1
Zolotonosha Ukr. **41** E6
Zolotukhino Rus. Fed. **43** R9
Zomandao *r.* Madag. **131** [inset] J4

▶**Zomba** Malawi **129** B8
Former capital of Malawi.

Zombor *Vojvodina, Srbija* Yugo. *see*
  Sombor
Zomin Uzbek. *see* Zaamin
Zongga China *see* Gyirong
Zongo Dem. Rep. Congo **126** C3
Zonguldak Turkey **106** B2
Zongyang China **87** F2

Zonūž Iran **100** A2
Zoo Baba *well* Niger **125** I2
Zoppo, Portella dello *pass Sicilia* Italy
  57 G11
Zorgho Burkina **125** E3
  also spelt Zorgo
Zorgo Burkina *see* Zorgho
Zorita Spain **54** F5
Zorleni Romania **58** I2
Zorlenţu Mare Romania **58** C3
Zorn *r.* France **51** O4
Zornitsa Bulg. **58** H6
Zorritos Peru **198** A5
Żory Poland **49** P5
Zorzor Liberia **124** C5
Zossen Germany **49** K3
Zouan-Hounien Côte d'Ivoire **124** C5
Zouar Chad **120** C4
Zoucheng China **85** H5
  formerly known as Zouxian
Zouina *well* Mauritania **124** D2
Zoulang Nanshan *mts* China **84** C4
Zouping China **85** H4
Zourvas, Akra *pt* Greece **59** E11
Zoushi China **87** D2
Zouxian China *see* Zoucheng
Zovka Rus. Fed. **43** J3
Zrenjanin *Vojvodina, Srbija* Yugo. **58** B3
  also known as Nagybecskerek
Zrmanja *r.* Croatia **56** H4
Zu Afgh. **101** G2
Zuata *r.* Venez. **199** E3
Zubālah, Wādī *watercourse* Saudi Arabia
  109 O8
Zubayr, Jazā'ir az *i.* Yemen **104** C5
Zubia Spain **55** H7
Zubkovo Rus. Fed. **43** R8
Zubova Polyana Rus. Fed. **41** G5
Zubovo Rus. Fed. **43** R1
Zubtsov Rus. Fed. **43** P5
Zuckerhütl *mt.* Austria **48** I9
Zuénoula Côte d'Ivoire **124** D5
Zuera Spain **55** K3
Żufār *admin. reg.* Oman **105** F4
  also spelt Dhofar

Zug Switz. **51** O5
Zugdidi Georgia **107** E2
Zuger See *l.* Switz. **51** O5
Zughaytūn *r.* Iraq **109** P3
Zugm, Birket el *salt l.* Egypt **108** B7
Zugu Nigeria **125** G4
Zuider Zee *l.* Neth. *see* IJsselmeer
Zuid-Willemsvaart *canal* Neth. **51** L1
Zuitai China *see* Kangxian
Zuitaizi China *see* Kangxian
Zuitou China *see* Taibai
Zújar *r.* Spain **54** F5
Żukowo Poland **49** P1
Zulia *state* Venez. **198** D2
Zülpich Germany **48** D5
Zumarraga Spain **55** I1
Zumba Ecuador **198** B6
Zumbo Moz. **131** F2
Zumbro *r.* U.S.A. **174** A2
Zumbrota U.S.A. **174** A2
Zummār Iraq **109** N1
Zumpango Mex. **185** F5
Zumpango del Río Mex. **185** F5
Zungeru Nigeria **125** G4
Zunhua China **85** H3
Zuni U.S.A. **181** E6
Zuni *watercourse* U.S.A. **183** O7
Zuni Mountains U.S.A. **181** E6
Zun-Torey, Ozero *l.* Rus. Fed. **85** G1
Zunyi *Guizhou* China **86** C3
  also known as Nanbai
Zunyi *Guizhou* China **86** C3
Zuo Jiang *r.* China/Vietnam **87** D4
Zuoquan China **85** G4
Zuoyun China **85** G4
Županja Croatia **56** K3
Zuqāq *i.* Saudi Arabia **104** C4
Żur *Kosovo, Srbija* Yugo. **58** B6
Zūrābād *Khorāsan* Iran **101** E3
Zürich Switz. **51** O5
Zürichsee *l.* Switz. **51** O5
Zurmat *reg.* Afgh. **101** G3
Zürnevo Bulg. **58** I5
Żuromin Poland **49** Q2
Zuru Nigeria **125** G4
Zurzuna Turkey *see* Çıldır

Zusha *r.* Rus. Fed. **43** R8
Zusmarshausen Germany **48** H7
Zutphen Neth. **48** D3
Zuurberg National Park S. Africa
  133 J10
Žuvinto rezervatas *nature res.* Lith.
  42 E7
Zuwārah Libya **120** B1
Zuyevka Rus. Fed. **40** I4
Zuytdorp Nature Reserve Australia
  151 A5
Zvečan *Kosovo, Srbija* Yugo. **58** B6
Zvejniekciems Latvia **42** F4
Zvenigorod Rus. Fed. **43** R6
Zvenigorodka Ukr. *see* Zvenyhorodka
Zvenyhorodka Ukr. **41** D6
  also spelt Zvenigorodka
Zverino Bulg. **58** E5
Zvezdë Albania **58** B8
Zvijezda *mts* Bos.-Herz. **56** K4
Zvishavane Zimbabwe **131** F4
  formerly spelt Shabani
Zvolen Slovakia **49** Q7
Zvornik Bos.-Herz. **56** L4
Zwarkop S. Africa **132** F4
Zwedru Liberia **124** C5
Zweibrücken Germany **48** E6
Zweletemba S. Africa **132** D10
Zwelitsha S. Africa **133** L9
Zwettl Austria **49** M7
Zwickau Germany **49** J5
Zwierzyniec Poland **49** T5
Zwiesel Germany **49** K6
Zwingli S. Africa **133** K1
Zwoleń Poland **49** S4
Zwolle Neth. **48** D3
Zyal'ki Belarus **43** J6
Żychlin Poland **49** Q3
Zyembin Belarus **43** J7
Żyrardów Poland **49** R3
Zyryan Kazakh. *see* Zyryanovsk
Zyryanka Rus. Fed. **39** P3
Zyryanovo Rus. Fed. **39** I3
Zyryanovsk Kazakh. **88** D1
  also known as Zyryan
Żywiec Poland **49** Q6

Žitorsđa *Srbija* Yugo. **58** C5
Zittau Germany **49** L5
Živinice Bos.-Herz. **56** K4
Ziway Häyk' *l.* Eth. **128** C2
Zixi China **87** F3
  also known as Hecheng
Zixing China **87** E3
Ziya *r.* China **85** H4
Ziyanchurino Rus. Fed. **102** D2

index Z

acknowledgements

MAPS AND DATA

General

Maps designed and created by HarperCollins Cartographic, Glasgow, UK

Design: One O'Clock Gun Design Consultants Ltd, Edinburgh, UK

Continental perspective views (pp30–31, 62–63, 112–113, 136–137, 156–157, 190–191) and globes (pp 14–15, 26–27, 214): Alan Collinson Design, Llandudno, UK

The publishers would like to thank all national survey departments, road, rail and national park authorities, statistical offices and national place name committees throughout the world for their valuable assistance, and in particular the following:

British Antarctic Survey, Cambridge, UK

Bureau of Rural Sciences, Barton, ACT, Australia, a scientific agency of the Department of Agriculture, Fisheries and Forestry, Australia

Tony Champion, Professor of Population Geography, University of Newcastle upon Tyne, UK

Mr P J M Geelan, London, UK

International Boundary Research Unit, University of Durham, UK

The Meteorological Office, Bracknell, Berkshire, UK

Permanent Committee on Geographical Names, London, UK

Data

Antarctica (pp222–223): Antarctic Digital Database (versions 1 and 2), © Scientific Committee on Antarctic Research (SCAR), Cambridge, UK (1993, 1998)

Bathymetric data: The GEBCO Digital Atlas published by the British Oceanographic Data Centre on behalf of IOC and IHO, 1994

Earthquakes data (pp14–15, 71): United States Geological Survey (USGS) National Earthquakes Information Center, Denver, USA

Coral reefs data (p141): UNEP World Conservation Monitoring Centre (UNEP-WCMC), Cambridge, UK. 'Reefs at Risk', 1998 Washington, DC, USA from World Resources Institute (WRI), the International Center for Living Aquatic Resources Management (ICLARM) and UNEP-WCMC

PHOTOGRAPHS AND IMAGES

page	image number	credit
3		NASA/Science Photo Library
6		NASA/Science Photo Library
7		NASA
8–9	1	NASA
	2	NASA/Science Photo Library
10–11	1	CNES, 1996 Distribution Spot Image/Science Photo Library
	2	US Geological Survey/Science Photo Library
	3	CNES, 1991 Distribution Spot Image/Science Photo Library
	4	CNES, 1986 Distribution Spot Image/Science Photo Library
12–13	1	NASA
	2	NASA/Science Photo Library
	3	NASA
	4	ImageState
	5	Bernhard Edmaier/Science Photo Library
	6	Earth Science Corporation/Science Photo Library
	7	CNES, 1996 Distribution Spot Image/Science Photo Library
	8	Digital image © 1996 CORBIS; Original image courtesy of NASA/CORBIS
14–15	1	Axiom Photographic Agency Ltd
	2	David Parker/Science Photo Library
	3	Chris Johns/NGS Image Collection
16–17	Fig. 1	Courtesy of NASA/JPL/Caltech
	Fig. 2	Courtesy of NASA/JPL/Caltech
	Fig. 3	Courtesy of NASA/JPL/Caltech
	Fig. 4	NRSC Ltd/Science Photo Library
	Fig. 9	NASA/Goddard Space Flight Center
	Fig. 10	Reproduced by permission of The Met Office, Bracknell, Berkshire
	Fig. 11	Reproduced by permission of The Met Office, Bracknell, Berkshire
18–19	1	Francois Suchel/Still Pictures
	2	Earth Satellite Corporation/Science Photo Library
	3	NRSC/Still Pictures
	4	M & C Denis-Huot/Still Pictures
	5	Pictor International - London
	6	Dick Ross/Still Pictures
	7	ImageState
	8	Klaus Andrews/Still Pictures
20–21	1	NASA/Science Photo Library
	2	Earth Satellite Corporation/Science Photo Library
	3	Daniel Dancer/Still Pictures
	4 left	NASA - Goddard Space Flight Center Scientific Visualization Studio
	4 right	NASA - Goddard Space Flight Center Scientific Visualization Studio
	5 left	NPA Group www.satmaps.com
	5 right	NPA Group www.satmaps.com
22–23	1	David Reed/Panos pictures
	2	Cities Revealed ® aerial photography © The GeoInformation ® Group, 1998
24–25	1	Earth Satellite Corporation/Science Photo Library
	2	Spaceimaging.com
	3	NRSC/Still Pictures
	4	NASA
26–27		NRSC/Still Pictures
	Fig. 1	TeleGeography, Inc, Washington D.C., USA www.telegeography.com
	Fig. 2	TeleGeography, Inc, Washington D.C., USA www.telegeography.com
28		© Marc Garanger/CORBIS
29		NASA
30–31	1	Digital image © 1996 CORBIS; Original image courtesy of NASA/CORBIS
	2	NASA
	3	NASA
32–33	1	P. Tatlow/Panos Pictures
	2	CNES, 1993 Distribution Spot Image/Science Photo Library
	3	CNES, 1991 Distribution Spot Image/Science Photo Library
34–35	1	Wim Van Cappellen/Still Pictures
	2	NASA
	3	Andrew Tatlow/Panos Pictures

page	image number	credit
36–37	1	Geoslides Photography
	2	Pictor International - London
	3	CNES, 1992 Distribution Spot Image/Science Photo Library
	4	ESA, Eurimage/Science Photo Library
	5	Dick Ross/Still Pictures
	6	NRSC/Science Photo Library
	7	Cities Revealed ® aerial photography © The GeoInformation ® Group, 1999
60		Pictures Colour Library Ltd
61		NASA
62–63	1	ImageState
	2	CNES, 1992 Distribution Spot Image/Science Photo Library
	3	CNES, 1987 Distribution Spot Image/Science Photo Library
64–65	1	Digital image © 1996 CORBIS; Original image courtesy of NASA/CORBIS
	2	Marc Schlossman/Panos pictures
	3	Georg Gerster/NGS Image Collection
66–67	1	NASA
	2	© Hanan Isachar/CORBIS
	3	Pictor International - London
68–69	1 top	© Wolfgang Kaehler/CORBIS
	1 middle	© Keren Su/CORBIS
	1 bottom	DERA/Still Pictures
	2 top	NASA
	2 bottom	NASA
	3 top	Science Photo Library
	3 bottom	CNES, 1987 Distribution Spot Image/Science Photo Library
70–71	1	NOAA
	2	NASA
	3	Shehzad Nooran/Still Pictures
	4	Digital image © 1996 CORBIS; Original image courtesy of NASA/CORBIS
	5	NASA
110		Pictures Colour Library Ltd
111		NASA
112–113	1	CNES, 1988 Distribution Spot Image/Science Photo Library
	2	© CORBIS
	3	NASA/JPL/Caltech
114–115	1	Peter Hering
	2	Libe Taylor/Panos pictures
116–117	1	NASA
	2	NASA
	3	Christian Aid/Glynn Griffiths/Still Pictures
	4	Mark Edwards/Still Pictures
	5 left	CNES, 1998 Distribution Spot Image/Science Photo Library
	5 right	CNES, 2001 Distribution Spot Image/Science Photo Library
118–119	1	Paul Springett/Still Pictures
	2	CNES, 1994 Distribution Spot Image/Science Photo Library
	3	Alan Collinson Design
	4	Pierre Gleizes/Still Pictures
	5	Voltchev-Unep/Still Pictures
	6	Spaceimaging.com
134		Pictures Colour Library Ltd
135		NASA
136–137	1	Pictor International - London
	2	CNES, 1986 Distribution Spot Image/Science Photo Library
	3	Mike Schroder/Still Pictures
138–139	1	The aerial photograph on page 138 is Copyright © Commonwealth of Australia, AUSLIG, Australia's national mapping Agency. All rights reserved. Reproduced by permission of the General Manager, Autralian Surveying and Land Information Group, Department of Industry, Science and Resources, Canberra, ACT.
	2	eMAP Ltd
	3	eMAP Ltd
140–141	1 left	Pictor International - London
	1 right	NASA/Science Photo Library
	2	Bill van Aken © CSIRO Land and Water
	3 left	CNES, Distribution Spot Image/Science Photo Library
	3 right	Gerard & Margi Moss/Still Pictures
	Fig. 1	Bureau of Rural Sciences, Australia

page	image number	credit
142–143	1	NASA
	2	NASA
	3	ImageState
	4	Institute of Geological & Nuclear Sciences, New Zealand
	5	Spaceimaging.com
	6	NASA
	7	Image provided by ORBIMAGE © Orbital Imaging Corporation and processing by NASA Goddard Space Flight Center.
154		Pictures Colour Library Ltd
155		NASA
156–157	1	© Owen Franken/CORBIS
	2	© Lowell Georgia/CORBIS
	3	NASA
158–159	1	Gregor Turk
	2	NASA/Marshall Space Flight Center
	3	NASA
160–161	1	Infoterra Ltd
	2	© Roger Ressmeyer/CORBIS
	3	CNES, 1996 Distribution Spot Image/Science Photo Library
	4	NASA/Goddard Space Flight Center/Science Photo Library
	4 inset	NASA
162–163	1	NRSC/Still Pictures
	2	NASA
	3	Alex S. Maclean/Still Pictures
	4	NASA
	5	© David Muench/CORBIS
	6	Bernhard Edmaier/Science Photo Library
188		Pictures Colour Library Ltd
189		NASA
190–191	1	NASA
	2	© Yann Arthus-Bertrand/CORBIS
	3	NASA
192–193	1	Earth Satellite Corporation/Science Photo Library
	2	CNES, 1995 Distribution Spot Image/Science Photo Library
	3	NASA
194–195	1	Ron Giling/Still Pictures
	2	Jeremy Horner/Panos pictures
	3	NASA
	4	CNES, 1988 Distribution Spot Image/Science Photo Library
	5	Alan Collinson Design
	6	CNES, 1986 Distribution Spot Image/Science Photo Library
	7	Jacques Jangoux/Science Photo Library
	8	Digital image © 1996 CORBIS; Original image courtesy of NASA/CORBIS
	9	NASA
196–197	1	NASA/Science Photo Library
	2	Mark Edwards/Still Pictures
	3 top right	NASA/Goddard Space Flight Center/Science Photo Library
	3 left	Michael Nichols/NGS Image Collection
	3 bottom right	NASA/Goddard Space Flight Center/Science Photo Library
208		Pictures Colour Library Ltd
209		NASA
210–211	1	Alan Collinson Design
	2	WHF Smith, US National Oceanic and Atmospheric Administration (NOAA), USA
	Fig. 2	NASA/JPL
212–213	1	NASA
	2	Data provided by the EOS Distributed Active Archive Center (DAAC) procesed at the National Snow and Ice Data Center, University of Colorado, Boulder, CO.
	3	NASA
	4	Courtesy of the David Vaughan/BEDMAP Consortium
	5	RADARSAT data Canadian Space Agency/Agence Spatiale Canadienne 1997. Received by the Canada Centre for Remote Sensing. Processed and distributed by RADARSAT International.
214–215	1	B&C Alexander
	2	Data provided by the EOS Distributed Active Archive Center (DAAC) procesed at the National Snow and Ice Data Center, University of Colorado, Boulder, CO.
	3	Alan Collinson Design
	4 and 5	B&C Alexander
	6	NASA